T0135316

IFIP Advances in Information and Communication Technology

627

Editor-in-Chief

Kai Rannenberg, Goethe University Frankfurt, Germany

Editorial Board Members

IFIP – The International Federation for Information Processing

IFIP was founded in 1960 under the auspices of UNESCO, following the first World Computer Congress held in Paris the previous year. A federation for societies working in information processing, IFIP's aim is two-fold: to support information processing in the countries of its members and to encourage technology transfer to developing nations. As its mission statement clearly states:

> IFIP is the global non-profit federation of societies of ICT professionals that aims at achieving a worldwide professional and socially responsible development and application of information and communication technologies.

IFIP is a non-profit-making organization, run almost solely by 2500 volunteers. It operates through a number of technical committees and working groups, which organize events and publications. IFIP's events range from large international open conferences to working conferences and local seminars.

The flagship event is the IFIP World Computer Congress, at which both invited and contributed papers are presented. Contributed papers are rigorously refereed and the rejection rate is high.

As with the Congress, participation in the open conferences is open to all and papers may be invited or submitted. Again, submitted papers are stringently refereed.

The working conferences are structured differently. They are usually run by a working group and attendance is generally smaller and occasionally by invitation only. Their purpose is to create an atmosphere conducive to innovation and development. Refereeing is also rigorous and papers are subjected to extensive group discussion.

Publications arising from IFIP events vary. The papers presented at the IFIP World Computer Congress and at open conferences are published as conference proceedings, while the results of the working conferences are often published as collections of selected and edited papers.

IFIP distinguishes three types of institutional membership: Country Representative Members, Members at Large, and Associate Members. The type of organization that can apply for membership is a wide variety and includes national or international societies of individual computer scientists/ICT professionals, associations or federations of such societies, government institutions/government related organizations, national or international research institutes or consortia, universities, academies of sciences, companies, national or international associations or federations of companies.

More information about this series at http://www.springer.com/series/6102

Ilias Maglogiannis · John Macintyre ·
Lazaros Iliadis (Eds.)

Artificial Intelligence Applications and Innovations

17th IFIP WG 12.5 International Conference, AIAI 2021
Hersonissos, Crete, Greece, June 25–27, 2021
Proceedings

 Springer

Editors
Ilias Maglogiannis (iD)
University of Piraeus
Piraeus, Greece

John Macintyre
University of Sunderland
Sunderland, UK

Lazaros Iliadis (iD)
Democritus University of Thrace
Xanthi, Greece

ISSN 1868-4238   ISSN 1868-422X (electronic)
IFIP Advances in Information and Communication Technology
ISBN 978-3-030-79152-0   ISBN 978-3-030-79150-6   (eBook)
https://doi.org/10.1007/978-3-030-79150-6

Preface

Artificial Intelligence (AI) continues to advance, following extreme development rhythms in the new era of the 21st century. It has already made its way into our daily lives in various forms. It is estimated that more than 80 billion USD have been invested by car industries for the design and development of autonomous self-driving vehicles. AI technologies like *Google Duplex* are accomplishing real-world conversations and arrangements with humans, using *Deep Neural Networks* (e.g., Google voice search, Wavenet). It is estimated by the International Data Corporation, a global provider of market intelligence, that investments in AI business globally will reach up to 110 billion USD by 2024.

AI is a major part of the Fourth Industrial Revolution, together with other technologies like the *Internet of Things*, *Genetic Engineering*, *Quantum Computing*, and its impact in the evolution of our post-modern societies in various domains is huge and growing. On the other hand, there are major areas of ethical concern for our societies, namely privacy, surveillance, bias-discrimination, and elimination of entire job categories. Moreover, serious questions arise on the superiority and indispensability of human judgment on important aspect of life. In other words, "Can smart machines outthink our human judgment?".

The *17th International Conference on Artificial Intelligence Applications and Innovations* (AIAI 2021) offered insight into all timely challenges related to technical, legal, and ethical aspects of intelligent systems and their applications. New algorithms and potential prototypes employed in diverse domains were introduced.

AIAI is a mature international scientific conference series that has been held all over the world and it is well established in the scientific area of AI. Its history is long and very successful, following and propagating the evolution of intelligent systems.

The first event was organized in Toulouse, France, in 2004. Since then, it has had a continuous and dynamic presence as a major global, but mainly European, scientific event. It has been organized in China, Greece, Cyprus, Australia, and France. It has always been technically supported by the International Federation for Information Processing (IFIP) and more specifically by Working Group 12.5, which is interested in AI applications.

Following a long-standing tradition, this Springer volume belongs to the IFIP AICT series and it contains the papers that were accepted to be presented orally at the AIAI 2021 conference. An additional volume comprises the papers that were accepted and presented at the workshops and were held as parallel events. The event was held during June 25–27, 2021, in Greece (virtually). The diverse nature of papers presented demonstrates the vitality of AI algorithms and approaches. It certainly proves the very wide range of AI applications as well.

The response of the international scientific community to the AIAI 2021 call for papers was more than satisfactory, with 113 papers initially submitted by authors in 21 different countries from all over the globe, namely Australia, Austria, Belgium, Czech

Republic, Egypt, France, Germany, Greece, Lebanon, Netherlands, India, Italy, China, Poland, Portugal, Romania, Sweden, Taiwan, Turkey, UK, and USA.

All papers were peer reviewed by at least two independent academic referees. Where needed, a third referee was consulted to resolve any potential conflicts. A total of 54 papers (47.79% of the submitted manuscripts) were accepted to be published as full papers (12 pages long) in the proceedings. Owing to the high quality of the submissions, the Program Committee decided that it should accept 7 more papers to be published as short papers (10 pages long).

The accepted papers cover the following thematic topics:

Activity Recognition
Adaptive Learning
Adversarial Neural Networks
AI for Media
AI for Music Composition
Anomaly Detection and AI
Anxiety Recognition and AI
Autoencoders
Autonomous Driving
Bioinformatics and AI
Classification in Pattern Recognition
Clustering
Computer Vision
Convolutional and Recurrent ANN
Cybersecurity and AI
Cyber Supply-Chain and AI
Data Mining
Deep Learning ANN
Dialogue Act Recognition
Embedded Machine Learning
Fake News Detection and AI
Feature Selection
Financial Applications of AI
Fuzzy Modeling
Genetic Algorithms and Optimization
Hybrid Intelligent Models
Interoperability and AI
Image Analysis for Face Recognition
Machine Learning
Meta-Learning and AutoML
Multi Agent Systems
Natural Language
Recommendation Systems
Robotics
Social Media Intelligent Modeling
SOM

Swarm Intelligence
Text Mining and Machine Translation
Time Series
Emotion recognition

Eight keynote speakers were invited to give lectures on timely aspects of AI. We wish to thank all keynote speakers for enlightening our conference with their state-of-the-art lectures.

In addition to the main conference, the following eight scientific workshops on timely AI subjects were organized under the framework of AIAI 2021:

- The *6th Workshop on 5G-Putting Intelligence to the Network Edge* (5G-PINE 2021)
- The *1st Workshop on Artificial Intelligence in Biomedical Engineering and Informatics* (AI-BIO 2021)
- The *1st Workshop on Defense Applications of AI* (DAAI 2021)
- The *1st Workshop on Distributed AI for REsource-Constrained Platforms* (DARE 2021)
- The *1st Workshop on Energy Efficiency and Artificial Intelligence* (EEAI 2021)
- The *10th Mining Humanistic Data Workshop* (MHDW 2021)
- The *1st Workshop on AI and Ethics* (AIETH 2021)
- Designing a Novel Adaptive Cybersecurity Solution for Internet-of-Vehicle Workshop (nIoVe)

We are grateful to everyone who made AIAI 2021 such a success, and we hope that we can meet again in person at the next event.

June 2021   Ilias Maglogiannis
                                                                 Lazaros Iliadis
                                                                 John MacIntyre

Organization

Executive Committee

General Chairs

Ilias Maglogiannis	University of Piraeus, Greece
John Macintyre	University of Sunderland, UK

Program Co-chairs

Lazaros Iliadis	Democritus University of Thrace, Greece
Xiao-Jun Wu	Jiangnan University, China
Petia Koprinkova	Bulgarian Academy of Sciences, Bulgaria

Honorary Co-chairs

Plamen Angelov	Lancaster University, UK
Vera Kurkova	Czech Academy of Sciences, Czech Republic

Advisory Chairs

Pietro Lio	University of Cambridge, UK
Barbara Hammer	University of Bielfeld, Germany
Costas Iliopoulos	King's College London, UK

Publication and Publicity Chair

Antonis Papaleonidas	Democritus University of Thrace, Greece

Liaison Co-chairs

Ioannis Chochliouros	Hellenic Telecommunication Organization (OTE), Greece
Panagiotis Kikiras	European Defence Agency, Belgium

Special Sessions/Tutorials Co-chairs

Dimitrios Kalles	Hellenic Open University, Greece
Dimitrios Kosmopoulos	University of Patras, Greece
Kostantinos Delibasis	University of Thessaly, Greece

Steering Committee

Ilias Maglogiannis	University of Piraeus, Greece
Plamen Angelov	Lancaster University, UK
Lazaros Iliadis	Democritus University of Thrace, Greece

Workshops Co-chairs

Christos Makris	University of Patras, Greece
Katia Kermanidis	Ionian University, Greece
Phivos Mylonas	Ionian University, Greece
Spyros Sioutas	University of Patras, Greece

Program Committee

Georgios Alexandridis	University of the Aegean, Greece
Serafín Alonso Castro	University of Leon, Spain
Ioannis Anagnostopoulos	University of Thessaly, Greece
Costin Badica	University of Craiova, Romania
Giacomo Boracchi	Politecnico di Milano, Italy
Francisco Carvalho	Polytechnic Institute of Tomar, Portugal
Diego Casado-Mansilla	Polytechnic School of the University of Alcalá, Spain
Ioannis Chamodrakas	National and Kapodistrian University of Athens, Greece
Kostantinos Delibasis	University of Thessaly, Greece
Konstantinos Demertzis	Democritus University of Thrace, Greece
Georgios Drakopoulos	Ionian University, Greece
Mauro Gaggero	National Research Council of Italy, Italy
Eleonora Giunchiglia	University of Oxford, UK
Peter Hajek	University of Pardubice, Czech Republic
Giannis Haralabopoulos	University of Nottingham, UK
Lazaros Iliadis Democritus	University of Thrace, Greece
Andreas Kanavos	Ionian University, Greece
Nikos Karacapilidis	University of Patras, Greece
Petros Kefalas	CITY College, International Faculty of the University of Sheffield, Greece
Katia Kermanidis	Ionian University, Greece
Petia Koprinkova-Hristova	Bulgarian Academy of Sciences, Bulgaria
Stelios Krinidis	Centre for Research and Technology Hellas, Greece
Florin Leon	Technical University of Iasi, Romania
Aristidis Likas	University of Ioannina, Greece
Pietro Liò	University of Cambridge, UK
Ioannis Livieris	University of Patras, Greece
Doina Logofătu	Frankfurt University of Applied Sciences, Germany
Ilias Maglogiannis	University of Piraeus, Greece
Goerge Magoulas	Birkbeck, University of London, UK
Christos Makris	University of Patras, Greece
Mario Malcangi	University of Milan, Italy
Andreas Menychtas	University of Piraeus, Greece
Vangelis Metsis	Texas State University, USA
Nikolaos Mitianoudis	Democritus University of Thrace, Greece
Antonio Moran	University of Leon, Spain

Konstantinos Moutselos	University of Piraeus, Greece
Phivos Mylonas	Ionian University, Greece
Stefanos Nikiforos	Ionian University, Greece
Stavros Ntalampiras	University of Milan, Italy
Vladimir Olej	University of Pardubice, Czech Republic
Mihaela Oprea	University Petroleum-Gas of Ploiesti, Romania
Ioannis P. Chochliouros	Hellenic Telecommunications Organization (OTE), Greece
Basil Papadopoulos	Democritus University of Thrace, Greece
Antonis Papaleonidas	Democritus University of Thrace, Greece
Pavlidis George	Centre for Research and Technology Hellas, Greece
Isidoros Perikos	University of Patras, Greece
Elias Pimenidis	University of the West of England, UK
Panagiotis Pintelas	University of Patras, Greece
Bernardete Ribeiro	University of Coimbra, Portugal
Antonio Staiano	University of Naples Parthenope, Italy
Christos Timplalexis	Centre for Research and Technology Hellas, Greece
Nicolas Tsapatsoulis	Cyprus University of Technology, Cyprus
Tsolakis Apostolos	Centre for Research and Technology Hellas, Greece
Petra Vidnerová	Czech Academy of Sciences, Czech Republic
Paulo Vitor de Campos Souza	CEFET-MG, Brazil
Gerasimos Vonitsanos	University of Patras, Greece

Abstracts of Keynotes

Is "Big Tech" Becoming the "Big Tobacco" of Artificial Intelligence?

John Macintyre

Pro Vice Chancellor at the University of Sunderland, UK gave a Keynote Lecture on a very hot topic related to AI and Ethics.

Abstract. Recent developments in research, development, implementation and use of AI include worrying trends which ask big questions about the future direction of the whole field. As part of this, the role of "Big Tech" – the huge corporate entities who now dominate the development of AI technologies and products – is crucial, both in terms of the technology they develop, and the researchers they employ. Their dominance places them at the apex of the R&D and product development activity in AI, which in turn means they have a great responsibility to ensure that this activity leads to fair, transparent, accountable, and ethical AI systems and products. They also have a great responsibility to support and nurture their staff. This talk will examine recent developments in AI and the role of Big Tech, and ask whether they are stepping up to these responsibilities.

Machine Learning: A Key Ubiquitous Technology in the 21st Century

Hojjat Adeli

Ohio State University, Columbus, USA, Fellow of the Institute of Electrical and Electronics Engineers (IEEE), Honorary Professor, Southeast University, Nanjing, China, Member, Polish and Lithuanian Academy of Sciences, Elected corresponding member of the Spanish Royal Academy of Engineering.

Abstract. Machine learning (ML) is a key and increasingly pervasive technology in the 21st century. It is going to impact the way people live and work in a significant way. In general, machine learning algorithms simulate the way brain learns and solves an estimation/recognition problem. They usually require a learning phase to discover the patterns among the available data, similar to the humans. An expanded definition of ML is advanced as algorithms that can learn from examples and data and solve seemingly interactable learning and unteachable problems, referred to as ingenious artificial intelligence (AI). Recent and innovative applications of ML in various fields and projects currently being pursued by leading high-tech and industrial companies such as Boeing, Google, IBM, Uber, Baidu, Facebook, and Tesla are reviewed. Then, machine learning algorithms developed by the author and his associates are briefly described. Finally, examples are presented in different areas from health monitoring of smart highrise building structures to automated EEG-based diagnosis of various neurological and psychiatric disorders such as epilepsy, the Alzheimer's disease, Parkinson's disease, and autism spectrum disorder.

Human-Centered Computer Vision: Core Components and Applications

Antonis Argyros[1,2]

[1] Computer Science Department, University of Crete, Greece
[2] Researcher, Foundation for Research and Technology – Hellas (FORTH)

Abstract. Computer vision is an area of artificial intelligence aimed at developing technical systems capable of perceiving the environment through image and video processing and analysis. In this talk, we mainly focus on human-centered computer vision, that is, computer vision for capturing aspects of human presence such as the geometry and motion of the human body, as well as for recognizing human actions, behavior, intentions and emotional states. Such technologies may constitute a fundamental building block for the development of a variety of applications in almost all aspects of human life (health, security, work, education, transportation, entertainment, etc.). In this special area, we give specific examples of our research activity and highlight the significant boost achieved due to the exploitation of state-of-the-art machine learning techniques and deep neural networks. We also give examples of applications developed based on these technologies in the field of robotics and ambient intelligence environments.

Unveiling Recurrent Neural Networks - What Do They Actually Learn and How?

Peter Tino

School of Computer Science, University of Birmingham, UK

Abstract. When learning from "dynamic" data where the order in which the data is presented does matter, the key issue is how such temporal structures get represented within the learning machine. In the case of artificial neural networks, an often-adopted strategy is to introduce feedback-connections with time delays. This enables the neurons to form their activation patterns based on the past, as well as the current neural activations. Neural networks of this kind became known as Recurrent Neural Networks (RNN). Many diverse architectures fall under this umbrella, with a wide variety of application domains. We will briefly review past attempts to understand the way RNNs learn to represent the past in order to perform the tasks they are trained on.

To that end, we will adopt the general view of RNNs as parameterized state space models and input driven non-autonomous dynamical systems. We will then present some new results connecting RNNs to a widely known class of models in machine learning - kernel machines. In particular, we will show that RNNs can be viewed as "temporal feature spaces". This framework will enable us to understand how high-dimensional RNNs constructed with very few degrees of freedom in their parameterization can still achieve competitive performances. Such observations can be viewed as "dynamical analogs" to classical "static" kernel machines that often achieve excellent performance using rich feature spaces constructed with very few degrees of freedom (e.g. single scale parameter in Gaussian kernels).

Deep Learning and Kernel Machines

Johan Suykens

KU Leuven, ESAT-Stadius and Leuven AI Institute, Belgium

Abstract. Over the last decades, with neural networks and deep learning, several powerful architectures have been proposed, including e.g., convolutional neural networks (CNN), stacked autoencoders, deep Boltzmann machines (DBM), deep generative models and generative adversarial networks (GAN). On the other hand, with support vector machines (SVM) and kernel machines, solid foundations in learning theory and optimization have been achieved. Within this talk, we outline a unifying picture and show several new synergies, for which model representations and duality principles play an important role. A recent example is restricted kernel machines (RKM), which connects least squares support vector machines (LS-SVM) to restricted Boltzmann machines (RBM). New developments on this will be shown for deep learning, generative models, multi-view and tensor-based models, latent space exploration, robustness and explainability.

How Can Artificial Intelligence Efficiently Support Sustainable Development?

Eunika Mercier-Laurent

Université de Reims Champagne-Ardenne, CReSTIC/MODECO, France

Abstract. This talk considers the multiple role AI may play in sustainability. Actually, sustainable development is among the greatest challenges for humanity. Sustainability and development are apparently opposite. The current efforts to face the Planet Crisis by separate actions generate less impact than expected. Artificial Intelligence approaches and capacity of available technologies are underexplored. Eco-innovation actions focus mainly on smart transportation, smart use of energy and water and waste recycling but do not consider the necessary evolution of behaviors and focus. The trendy Digital transformation follows mostly traditional approaches. The concepts such as Smart, Intelligent, Innovative, Green or Wise City invented to promote existing technology transform the IT market. Most of offers consist in data processing with statistical/optimization methods. But AI can do better – the AI approaches and techniques combined with adequate thinking may help innovating the way of facing Planet Crisis.

Backpropagation Free Deep Learning

Jose C. Principe

University of Florida, USA

Abstract. This talk presents recent results that show the feasibility of training deep networks classifiers without backpropagation. We will prove that it is possible to substitute error propagation in general conditions and practically achieve the same performance as conventional algorithms. This methodology allows modularization of the algorithmic pipeline and improves explainability. We will then address some of the benefits of this technology for applications.

Brain-Inspired Data Analytics for Incremental and Transfer Learning of Cognitive Spatio-Temporal Data and for Knowledge Transfer

Nikola Kasabov

Fellow IEEE, Fellow RSNZ, Fellow INNS College of Fellows
Professor of Knowledge Engineering and Founding Director KEDRI
Auckland University of Technology, Auckland, New Zealand
George Moore Chair/Professor, University of Ulster, UK
Honorary Professor Teesside University UK and the University of Auckland, NZ

Abstract. The talk argues and demonstrates that brain-inspired spiking neural network (SNN) architectures can be used for incremental and transfer learning, i.e. to learn new data and new classes/tasks/categories incrementally utilising some previously learned knowledge. Similarly to how the brain manifests transfer learning, these SNN models do not need to be restricted in number of layers, neurons in each layer, etc. as they adopt self-organising learning principles. The new learned knowledge can be extracted in forms of graphs and symbolic fuzzy rules and its evolution traced over time. The presented approach is illustrated on an exemplar brain-inspired SNN architecture NeuCube (free software and open source available from www.kedri.aut.ac.nz/neucube and from www.neucube.io). The extraction of symbolic rules from NeuCube at each learning tasks and each subject allows for knowledge transfer between humans and machines in an adaptive, evolving, interactive way. This opens the field to build new types of open and transparent BCI and AI systems.

More details can be found in: N.Kasabov, Time-Space, Spiking Neural Networks and Brain-Inspired Artificial Intelligence, Springer, 2019, https://www.springer.com/gp/book/9783662577134.

Abstracts of Tutorials

Modern Methods and Tools for Human Biosignal Analysis

Vangelis Metsis

Texas State University, USA

Abstract. The term biosignal refers to any signal that can be measured from living organisms. Biosignals have been used in medicine, sports science, and psychology for diagnoses, and there have been impressive advancements in these areas. Recently, the fields of human-computer interaction and affective computing have found an interest in using biosignals as a means of understanding the human state and intention. This interest has been reinforced by the fact that acquiring information with sensors and interfacing electrically with the human body has become much easier in the past few years. Moving from large analog technologies to digital ones has led to the miniaturization of sensing devices. Wireless transmission technologies (e.g., Bluetooth low energy), which can be easily integrated with the acquisition hardware, have removed the need for bulky wiring. This tutorial will present an overview of modern applications of human biosignals and will provide practical examples of machine learning-based methods and tools for biosignal analysis. Traditional machine learning algorithms for feature extraction and classification will be compared with recent developments in deep learning and its applications to biosignal and time-series data processing in general.

Anomaly Detection in Images

Giacomo Boracchi

Politecnico di Milano, Italy

Anomaly detection problems are ubiquitous in engineering: the prompt detection of anomalies is often a primary concern, since these might provide precious information for understanding the dynamics of a monitored process and for activating suitable countermeasures. In fact, anomalies are typically the most informative regions in an image (e.g., defects in images used for quality control). Not surprisingly, anomaly detection problems have been widely investigated in the image processing and pattern recognition communities and are key in application scenarios ranging from quality inspection to health monitoring. The tutorial presents a rigorous formulation of the anomaly-detection problem that fits with many imaging scenarios and applications. The tutorial describes, by means of illustrative examples, the most important anomaly-detection approaches in the literature, and their connection with the machine-learning perspective of semi-supervised and unsupervised learning/monitoring. Special emphasis will be given to anomaly-detection methods based on learned models, which are often adopted to handle images and signals. In particular, these will be divided into traditional models (including dictionaries yielding sparse representations) and deep learning models. The tutorial is accompanied by various examples from our research projects where we applied anomaly-detection algorithms to solve real world problems: visual quality inspection for monitoring chip and nanofiber production.

Contents

Automated Machine Learning

Autonomous Agents

Clustering

Convolutional NN

Machine Learning

Multi Agent Systems

Natural Language

Recommendation Systems

Adaptive Modeling/Neuroscience

'If Only I Would Have Done that…': A Controlled Adaptive Network Model for Learning by Counterfactual Thinking

Raj Bhalwankar and Jan Treur[✉]

Social AI Group, Vrije Universiteit Amsterdam, Amsterdam, The Netherlands
r.p.bhalwankar@student.vu.nl, j.treur@vu.nl

Abstract. In this paper counterfactual thinking is addressed based on literature mainly from Neuroscience and Psychology. A detailed literature review was conducted in identifying processes, neural correlates and theories related to counterfactual thinking from different disciplines. A familiar scenario with respect to counterfactual thinking was identified. Based on the literature, an adaptive self-modeling network model was designed. This model captures the complex process of counterfactual thinking and the learning and control involved.

Keywords: Counterfactual thinking · Adaptive network model · Mental model · Learning · Control

1 Introduction

Human beings have a great ability to think and infer how a current situation (especially goal failure) could have turned out differently given a set of alternative actions or decisions they could have chosen from [4]. This process of deconstructing the current reality to imagine (a) new one(s) is called Counterfactual Thinking [17]. Such a type of thinking is important as in the first place it helps in making sense of the past, in planning actions, in making emotional & social judgements. Not less important, in the second place it plays an important functional role to guide adaptive behavior and learning [22] for the own benefit for the future. Such learning is a form of learning from mistakes, which involves the notion of regret which arises from comparing the alternative realities. This type of learning helps to generate new courses of actions which, after the failure experience, are believed to be more successful when similar situations occur in future. Various parts of the brain have been implicated to play a role in counterfactual thinking.

Yet also many questions about counterfactual thinking still have no full answers. How does the process of counterfactual thinking actually work in day-to-day life? What is its role in mental health, learning and decision-making? How does it affect our emotional health and how does it update our beliefs or perceptions? How can counterfactual thinking prove useful in AI applications like reinforcement learning?

Thus, the present study is meant to contribute some answers to these questions by providing a Neuroscience-inspired controlled adaptive network model that is able to

© IFIP International Federation for Information Processing 2021
Published by Springer Nature Switzerland AG 2021
I. Maglogiannis et al. (Eds.): AIAI 2021, IFIP AICT 627, pp. 3–16, 2021.
https://doi.org/10.1007/978-3-030-79150-6_1

simulate processes of counterfactual thinking, including the learning effects of it and control over it. Computational modeling plays a important role here in making sense of behavioral and neurological data. Computational models represent different 'algorithmic hypotheses' about how behavior is generated [24]. Such simulations involve running the model with specific parameter settings to generate 'fake' behavioral data. These simulated data can then be analyzed in much the same way as one would analyze real data, to make precise, falsifiable predictions about qualitative and quantitative patterns in the data. These simulations contribute to theory building by making theoretical predictions more precise and testable [24].

Mental models are essential for construction of knowledge and play a crucial role in learning, retrieving and problem solving. Van Hoeck et al. [22] proposed that counterfactuals depend upon the mental models of alternative possibilities in form of mental simulations, which suggests that these previous modeling approaches to mental model development can be used to study counterfactual thinking. In the present study, a network-oriented modeling approach was utilized to study the process of counterfactual thinking based on literature and neuro-scientific evidence. Network-Oriented Modeling is a useful method to represent the complex real-world processes concerning human beings and has proven to be able to address adaptivity and control that play an important role in counterfactual thinking.

The paper begins in Sect. 2 with a brief literature overview of the existing state of research related to counterfactual thinking. Then, after a brief introduction of the modeling approach used in Sect. 3, in Sect. 4 the design of the developed controlled adaptive network model with its various parts is discussed. Simulations of some example scenarios are discussed in Sect. 5; here it is shown that the model generates patterns as expected from the empirical literature. In Sect. 6, correctness of the implemented model against its conceptual design specifications is verified by analysis of stationary points. Section 7 addresses discussion and conclusions.

2   Literature Review

As stated earlier, counterfactual thinking can be helpful in learning from past mistakes and in developing more promising intentions for the future [12, 13, 15]. Mental models of imagined past events or future outcomes that have not yet occurred support *counterfactual thinking* [4, 11]. Norm Theory proposed by Kahneman and Miller [11] provides a theoretical basis to describe the rationale for counterfactual thoughts. According to them, counterfactual thinking is driven by simulations of previously encoded exemplars and they emphasize the role of counterfactual thinking in reframing such scenarios—generating alternative possibilities that change the norms (and expectations) used to interpret a situation [22]. The theory suggests that the counterfactual alternatives created depend on the ease of imagining different outcomes. The norms involve a pairwise comparison between a cognitive standard and an experiential outcome. A discrepancy that is created by such a comparison elicits an affective response which is influenced by the magnitude and direction of the difference.

Rational Imagination Theory proposed by Byrne [5] says that the counterfactual imagination is rational and it depends on three assumptions: (1) humans are capable of rational thought; (2) they make inferences by thinking about possibilities; and (3) their counterfactual thoughts rely on thinking about possibilities, just as rational thoughts do. Byrne [6] proposed a set of cognitive directives that guide these possibilities when people imagine alternatives. The theory states that individuals' ability to entertain multiple parallel models corresponding to alternative possibilities suggests that counterfactual thought is engaged to search the space of possible alternatives.

According to Byrne [7], an algorithm to specify the mental representations and cognitive processes that create counterfactuals takes as input the relevant facts of the actual event and produces as output a counterfactual alternative. The intervening processes change aspects of the mental representation of the facts to create a second mental representation, the counterfactual alternative. According to [8], the dynamic nature of memory reconstruction allows to mentally modify aspects of autobiographical memory when simulating on retrieval, leading to counterfactual thinking. Computational mechanisms underlying counterfactual thinking maintain and update two representations, the imagined alternative and the known or presupposed reality.

The neural representations of counterfactual inference that are implicated in the neural systems for constructing mental models of the past and future, involve prefrontal and medial temporal lobe structures of the brain [10, 21]. A functional perspective on counterfactual thinking views it as a useful, and essential component of behavior regulation. It considers counterfactual thoughts closely connected to goal cognitions where counterfactual thinking is activated usually by goal-failure [9]. It suggests that at its root counterfactual thinking is a regulatory loop–governing behavior which operates through a negative feedback model. This model operates by preserving homeostasis by correcting behavior when a discrepancy is detected between the current state and an ideal reference state for example goal-progress. In the theory of core affect [14], affective experiences function as indicators of a discrepancy between current and an ideal state, thus affect often mediates behavior change. Also, once the discrepancy reduces between the current state and the reference state, corrective activity is terminated. In a review on counterfactual thinking [9], it was mentioned that cognitive experiments indicated counterfactual thinking influencing behavior by either of two routes: (1) a content-specific pathway where specific informational events affect behavioral intentions which then influence the behavior itself and (2) a content neutral pathway which has indirect effects by affect, mindsets and motivations.

The structured event complex theory proposed by Barbey et al. [1], state that counterfactual thinking engages a network of regions within prefrontal cortex (PFC) that represent alternative goals, behavioral intentions, mindsets, motivations, and self-inferences that enable behavioral change and adaptation [22]. They also stated that counterfactual thought depends on mental models of alternative possibilities that are represented in the form of structured event complexes (SEC). SEC is a goal-oriented set of events that is structured in sequence and represents event features (like agents, objects, actions, mental states and background settings), social norms of behavior, ethical and moral rules and temporal event boundaries.

Building upon these frameworks, Van Hoeck et al. [22] proposed that counterfactual thinking depends upon the co-ordination of multiple information processing systems that involve three neural networks: (1) the mental simulation network, (2) the cognitive control network, (3) the reward network. Thus, they proposed three stages of processing in counterfactual thinking: Activation, Inference and Adaptation; see Fig. 1.

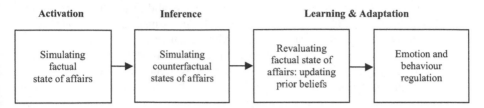

Fig. 1. Schematic overview of the stages in counterfactual thinking [22]

Activation. Counterfactual thoughts are triggered automatically in response to real world experiences, especially negative emotions triggered by violations of expectations and motivations (e.g., an unsuccessful application for a university), implicit/explicit goal failure (e.g., failing an exam), or close calls (e.g., missing the train by few seconds). As mentioned earlier, they proposed that counterfactuals depend upon the mental models of alternative possibilities in form of mental simulations. Such simulations provide the foundation for constructing and evaluating mental models of reality and of imagined alternative possibilities. Van Hoeck et al. [22] state that counterfactuals activate areas of the medial prefrontal cortex which are related to conflict detection.

Counterfactual Inference. Counterfactual inference adheres to the 'nearest possible world' constraint. Thus a counterfactual must closely model one's own experience of the real state of the world which helps in setting the constraint to specific situational features and prior knowledge of the situation. The alternatives suggested from such a constraint deviates only marginally from the reality, thus is probable. This also separates counterfactual thinking from less constrained forms of imagination or fantasy. For example, the chosen counterfactuals often are around factors like: (1) factor that played the strongest role (2) most deviation from expectation, or (3) is mostly under participant's own control. Apart from being influenced by meaning and relevance of specific events, counterfactuals are influenced by a specific individual perspective where implicit belief of attainability or self-efficacy plays an important role. The counterfactual outcome value plays an important role and impacts how an individual perceives the factual, as well as the experienced outcome and its relative value. Such evaluations of how a counterfactual could have been better lead to emotional and social reactions.

Learning and Adaptation. The information inferred from counterfactual state of affairs will then in incorporated in the representation of the current state of affairs leading to re-evaluation and updating of prior beliefs and action-values. This leads to behavioral and affective modifications that last for the future. Counterfactual thinking provides an opportunity to improve performance for the future and elicits behavioral motivations to pursue the counterfactual outcome. This regulates one's perception of control and preparedness, boosting persistence and performance [22].

3   The Modeling Approach for Controlled Adaptive Networks

Temporal-causal network models as addressed in [18, 19] can be represented by a conceptual representation and by a numerical representation. A conceptual representation involves representing in a declarative manner states and connections between them that represent the causal impacts of states on each other. The states are assumed to have activation levels that vary over time. Causal relations have weights. Furthermore, when more than one causal relation affects a state, some way to aggregate multiple causal impacts on a state is used. This aggregation is indicated by some combination function from a library. For the timing of the state dynamics, a speed factor is used, so that no synchronous processing is required. The notions for connectivity (connection weights $\omega_{X,Y}$), aggregation (combination functions $c_Y(..)$)) and timing (speed factors η_Y) are the network characteristics that define a conceptual representation of a temporal-causal network model; they are summarized in Table 1, first four rows.

Table 1. Conceptual and numerical representation of a temporal-causal network [19, 20].

Concepts	Notation	Explanation
States and connections	$X, Y, X{\to}Y$	Describes the nodes and links of a network structure
Connection weight	$\omega_{X,Y}$	The connection weight $\omega_{X,Y}$ represents the strength of the causal impact of state X on state Y with $X{\to}Y$
Aggregating multiple causal impacts	$c_Y(..)$	For each state Y a combination function $c_Y(..)$ is chosen to combine the causal impacts of other states on state Y
Timing of the causal effect	η_Y	For each state Y a speed factor $\eta_Y \geq 0$ is used to represent how fast a state is changing upon causal impact
Concepts	Numerical representation	Explanation
State values over time t	$Y(t)$	At each time point t each state Y in the model has a real number value
Single causal impact	$\mathbf{impact}_{X,Y}(t)$ $= \omega_{X,Y}X(t)$	At t state X with a connection to state Y has an impact $\omega_{X,Y}X(t)$ on Y, using weight $\omega_{X,Y}$
Aggregating multiple causal impacts	$\mathbf{aggimpact}_Y(t)$ $= c_Y(\mathbf{impact}_{X_1,Y}(t),..., \mathbf{impact}_{X_k,Y}(t))$ $= c_Y(\omega_{X_1,Y}X_1(t), ..., \omega_{X_k,Y}X_k(t))$	The aggregated impact of X_i on Y at t, is determined by applying combination function $c_Y(..)$ on $\mathbf{impact}_{X_i,Y}(t)$.
Timing of the causal effect per state	$Y(t+\Delta t)$ $= Y(t) + \eta_Y\,[\mathbf{aggimpact}_Y(t) - Y(t)]\,\Delta t$ $= Y(t) + \eta_Y[c_Y(\omega_{X_1,Y}X_1(t), ..., \omega_{X_k,Y}X_k(t)) - Y(t)]\Delta t$	The causal impact on Y is exerted over time gradually, using speed factor η_Y

Combination functions can be selected from an available combination function library provided by the dedicated software environment that has been developed. For each state Y one or more basic combination functions $c_j(..), j = 1, .., m$ can be selected by indicating *weights* $\gamma_{j,Y}$ (real numbers) which makes that within the software environment a weighted average of these functions $c_j(..), j = 1, .., m$, from the library is used as combination function $c_Y(..)$ for state Y; these basic combination functions $c_j(..)$ have combination function *parameters* $\pi_{i,j,Y}$. Currently there are more than 40 combination functions in the library. New combination functions can be added easily and the library has also facilities to apply function composition to define new functions by composing any number of functions from the library. In the model presented here, for the states, the two basic combination functions shown in Table 2 were used.

Table 2. The basic combination functions from the library used in the presented model

	Notation	Formula	Parameters
Advanced logistic sum	$\mathbf{alogistic}_{\sigma,\tau}(V_1, \ldots, V_k)$	$[\frac{1}{1+e^{-\sigma(V_1+\cdots+V_k-\tau)}} - \frac{1}{1+e^{\sigma\tau}}](1+e^{-\sigma\tau})$	Steepness $\sigma>0$ Threshold τ
Stepmod	$\mathbf{stepmod}_{\rho,\delta}(V_1, \ldots, V_k)$	0 if t mod $\rho < \delta$, else 1	Repetition ρ Duration δ

Note that 'network characteristics' and 'network states' are two distinct concepts for a network. Self-modeling is a way to relate these concepts to each other in an interesting and useful way. A *self-model* is making the implicit network characteristics (such as connection weights or excitability thresholds) explicit by adding states to the network representing these characteristics. Thus,he network gets an internal self-model of part of the network structure; this can be used to obtain an *adaptive network*; see [19]. In this way, multiple self-modeling levels can be created where network characteristics from one level relate to states at a next level. This can be used to design *second-order* or *higher-order adaptive networks*; see, for example, [19]. More specifically, adding a self-model for a temporal-causal network is done in the way that for some of the states Y of the base network and some of its related network structure characteristics for connectivity, aggregation and timing (i.e., some from $\omega_{X,Y}$, $\gamma_{i,Y}$, $\pi_{i,j,Y}$, η_Y), additional network states $\mathbf{W}_{X,Y}$, $\mathbf{C}_{i,Y}$, $\mathbf{P}_{i,j,Y}$, $\mathbf{H}_Y$ (self-model states) are introduced:

Connectivity self-model
Self-model states $\mathbf{W}_{X,Y}$ are added representing connection weights $\omega_{X,Y}$
Aggregation self-model
Self-model states $\mathbf{C}_{j,Y}$ are added representing combination function weights $\gamma_{i,Y}$ and/or self-model states $\mathbf{P}_{i,j,Y}$ representing combination function parameters $\pi_{i,j,Y}$
Timing self-model
Self-model states $\mathbf{H}_Y$ are added representing speed factors η_Y. The notations $\mathbf{W}_{X,Y}$, $\mathbf{C}_{i,Y}$, $\mathbf{P}_{i,j,Y}$, $\mathbf{H}_Y$ for the self-model states indicate the referencing relation with respect to the characteristics $\omega_{X,Y}$, $\gamma_{i,Y}$, $\pi_{i,j,Y}$, η_Y: here $\mathbf{W}$ refers to ω, $\mathbf{C}$ refers to γ, $\mathbf{P}$ refers to π, and $\mathbf{H}$ refers to η, respectively. For the processing, these self-model states define the dynamics of state Y in a canonical manner according to equations in Table 2, bottom row, whereby $\omega_{X,Y}$, $\gamma_{i,Y}$, $\pi_{i,j,Y}$, η_Y are replaced by the state values of $\mathbf{W}_{X,Y}$, $\mathbf{C}_{i,Y}$, $\mathbf{P}_{i,j,Y}$, $\mathbf{H}_Y$ at time t, respectively.

As the outcome of the addition of a self-model to a temporal-causal network is also a temporal-causal network model itself, as has been shown in [19], Ch 10, this construction can easily be applied iteratively to obtain multiple levels of self-models. Therefore second-order adaptation as, for example, plays an important role to control adaptive processes, can easily be modelled as well. This also has been applied here for the control of the processes in counterfactual thinking.

4 A Controlled Adaptive Network Model for Counterfactual Thinking

To explain the introduced network model (see Fig. 2), the following scenario is used.

Scenario: Jimmy believes he can do an internship & study at the same time (Belief). He fails an exam (goal failure), this created an unpleasant situation for him (Feeling).

Activation Process: Initially this evokes a mental simulation of the entire event (simulating factual state of affairs) and previous memories are triggered. Activation spreads leading to recall of memories in similar situations from the past (Search Space). He Focuses on the most relevant memories (Nearness); for example: (1) Recalls time he joined private tuitions, (2) Time he studied with friends/study group, (3) Spent extra time on weekends.

Inference Process: Jimmy mentally simulates based on the most relevant memories (nearest), alternatives to the situation and makes inferences and evaluations on them.

Learning and Adaptation Process: Once the counterfactuals are inferred, the present situation is re-evaluated by incorporating them in the present situation. This leads to changes in beliefs, as well as action-values (learning). Jimmy's behavior changes, he joins private tuitions and studies more effectively for next exams.

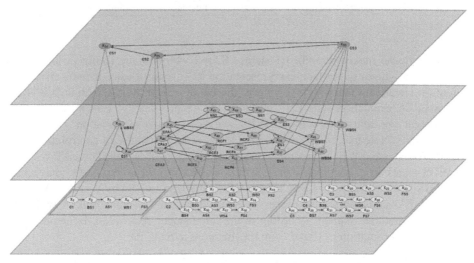

Fig. 2. Connectivity of the controlled adaptive network model for counterfactual thinking.

The lower base (pink) plane contains the base network where the different colored outlined sections are just added for reasons of presentation to make a clear visual distinction between current states, counterfactuals, future states (C-states, BS-states, AS-states, WS-States, FS-states) involved in the three stages. These colored outlines are not part of the network specification as such. The (blue) plane above the base plane represents the first-order self-model (WBS-states, ES-states, CFA-states, RCF-states, N-states). The upper (purple) plane above the first-order self-model plane represents the second-order self-model for the control (CS-states). These states at the different levels are explained in more detail in Tables 3, 4, and 5. In the network model introduced here, the states about the current situation are represented in the red outlined section of the base plane. As mentioned in the scenario, the current situation leads to unpleasant feeling (FS1) which leads to re-evaluation and then to updating the beliefs. This update of beliefs is modelled by ES-states and WBS-states in the first-order self-model. The NS-states allow to only focus on the counterfactuals which have small deviations from reality and then choose the best among them (within the orange outlined area in the base plane).

Table 3. Description of abbreviations used in the model

C	Context States
BS	Belief States
AS	Action States
WS	World States
FS	Feeling States
ES	Evaluation States
WBS	Belief weight representation states for connections from C-states to BS-States
NS	Nearness Indication States
CFA	Counterfactual Activation states
RCF	Representation states for active Counterfactuals
CS	Control States for the three stages Activation, Inference, and Learning and Adaptation

These choices make use of the ES-states ES2 to ES4 for counterfactuals which have links from the active counterfactual representation RCF-states. Based on the (persistent) evaluation states, the learning takes place: the belief weight representation WBS1 is suppressed by evaluation state ES1, and evaluation states ES2 to ES4 make that the belief weight representations WBS5 to WBS7 will become activated as soon as a relevant context occurs. Note that, in addition to the second-order CS-states for control, the first-order CFA-states and WBS-states play a crucial role in control as well. These CFA-states and WBS-states are controlled by the CS-states and in turn they themselves control the related BS-states: BS2 to BS4 by CFA1 to CFA3 and BS5 to BS7 by WBS5 to WBS7. Through this overall control, the processes involved in counterfactual thinking will take place in a structured manner according to the three stages Activation, Inference, and Learning and Adaptation as found from the literature in Sect. 2.

5 Simulation Results

The computational network model was simulated using a dedicated software environment implemented in MatLab described in [19], Ch 9. For an example simulation, see Figs. 3, 4 and 5 which all display one and the same simulation but just for the sake of presentation are displayed in parts for the overall processes according to the three stages found in Sect. 2. For the simulation $\Delta t = 0.5$ was chosen, the total time 100. The context

Table 4. Overview of the base states

Base States		Explanation
X_1	C1	Context State 1
X_2	BS1	Belief State 1: 'I can do internship and studies at the same time'
X_3	AS1	Action State 1 for taking up the internship, not studying enough
X_4	WS1	World state 1 for Failing the Exam
X_5	FS1	Feeling state 1: unpleasant
X_6	C2	Context State 2
X_7	BS2	Belief State 2 for Counterfactual thinking: 'Taking private tuitions helps to study well' so 'If I would have taken up private tuitions to prepare, as I had done in the past'
X_8	AS2	Action State 2 for Counterfactual thinking: 'Taking up private tuitions and studying effectively with help from a tutor'
X_9	WS2	World state 2 for BS2: 'Passing the Exam'
X_{10}	FS2	Feeling state 2: 'Feeling pleasant after passing'
X_{11}	BS3	Belief State 3 for Counterfactual thinking: 'one must work extra on the weekends to pass the exam ' so If I would have studied extra on the weekends as well'
X_{12}	AS3	Action State 3 for Counterfactual thinking: 'Studying extra time on weekends as done in the past'
X_{13}	WS3	World state 3 for BS3: 'Passing the Exam'
X_{14}	FS3	Feeling state 3: 'Feeling pleasant after passing'
X_{15}	BS4	Belief State 4 for Counterfactual thinking: 'Studying with friends help to study effectively ' so 'If I would have studied with my friends'
X_{16}	AS4	Action State 4 for Counterfactual thinking: 'studying with friends, learning effectively'
X_{17}	WS4	World state 4 for BS4: 'Passing the Exam'
X_{18}	FS4	Feeling state 4: 'Feeling plesant after passing'
X_{19}	C3	Context State 3 (Future context)
X_{20}	BS5	Belief State 5: 'I can will have to study harder and study more on the weekends'
X_{21}	AS5	Action State 5 for studying more on the weekends,
X_{22}	WS5	World state 5 for passing the Exam
X_{23}	FS5	Feeling State 5: pleasant
X_{24}	C4	Context State 4 (Future context)
X_{25}	BS6	Belief State 6: 'I can join tuitions, it will help me to study as in the past'
X_{26}	AS6	Action State 6 for joining private tuitions
X_{27}	WS6	World state 6 for Passing the Exam
X_{28}	FS6	Feeling state 6: pleasant
X_{29}	C5	Context state 5 (Future context)
X_{30}	BS7	Belief state 7: 'I Should take help from friends, study with them'
X_{31}	AS7	Action state 7 for taking help from friends
X_{32}	WS7	World state 7 for passing the Exam
X_{33}	FS7	Feeling state 7: pleasant

states are considered external factors and use the **stepmod** function to let them occur at some time. The speed factor for the context states C1 and C2 was set at 0 so that they always are there, whereas for C3 to C5 it was set at 2, and by setting appropriate values for the **stepmod** function's parameters they occur at time 60. For all other states (BS-, AS-, WS-, FS-states) the speed factor was set 0.5. The connection weights between the states and the other characteristics of the network model and the initial values are shown in the Appendix; see the Linked Data at https://www.researchgate.net/publication/348 324898. All states in the model have initial value 0 except C1, C2 which all have it as 1, and the NS-states (1 to 3) which have it as specific values depending on the considered variant of the scenario.

Table 5. Overview of the first-order and second-order self-model states

Self-Model States		Explanation
X_{34}	ES1	Evaluation state 1 for BS1 & FS1
X_{35}	ES2	Evaluation state 2 for BS2 & FS2 via RCF1 & RCF2
X_{36}	ES3	Evaluation state 3 for BS3 & FS3 via RCF3 & RCF4
X_{37}	ES4	Evaluation state 4 for BS4 & FS4 via RCF5 & RCF6
X_{38}	WBS1	Belief weight representation state for the connection from C1 to BS1
X_{39}	WBS2	Belief weight representation state for the connection from C3 to BS5
X_{40}	WBS3	Belief weight representation state for the connection from C4 to BS6
X_{41}	WBS4	Belief weight representation state for the connection from C5 to BS7
X_{42}	NS1	Nearness Indication State for BS2
X_{43}	NS2	Nearness Indication State for BS3
X_{44}	NS3	Nearness Indication State for BS4
X_{45}	CFA1	Counterfactual Activation State 1 for BS2
X_{46}	CFA2	Counterfactual Activation State 2 for BS3
X_{47}	CFA3	Counterfactual Activation State 3 for BS4
X_{48}	RCF1	Counterfactual Representation State 1 for BS2
X_{49}	RCF2	Counterfactual Representation State 2 for FS2
X_{50}	RCF3	Counterfactual Representation State 3 for BS3
X_{51}	RCF4	Counterfactual Representation State 4 for FS3
X_{52}	RCF5	Counterfactual Representation State 5 for BS4
X_{53}	RCF6	Counterfactual Representation State 6 for FS4
X_{54}	CS1	Control State 1 for stage 1: via activation of WBS1 to BS1
X_{55}	CS2	Control State 2 for stage 2: via activation of CFA2, CFA3, CFA4 to BS2, BS3, BS4
X_{56}	CS3	Control State 3 for stage 3: via activation of WB5, WB6, WB7 to BS5, BS6, BS7

In the first stage shown in Fig. 3, due to evaluation state ES1, via WBS1 the initial belief state BS1 is suppressed and only BS5 and states that follow it go up representing that an appropriate counterfactual was chosen based on the outcome of the first stage.

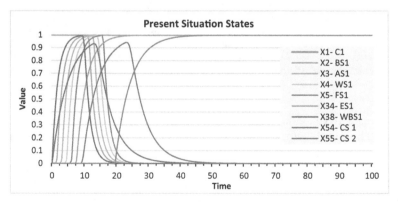

Fig. 3. Present Situation States representing the impact of ES-1, WBS-1 and CS-1 on initial belief state BS-1.

The second stage is shown in Fig. 4. The NS-states are set in such a way that only one of the future states (within the green outline in the base plane) goes for value 1. A typical pattern is that first initial context state and belief state trigger a chain of events leading to activation of ES1. This leads to the activation of different counterfactuals based on their nearness and to their evaluation via evaluation states ES2 to ES4.

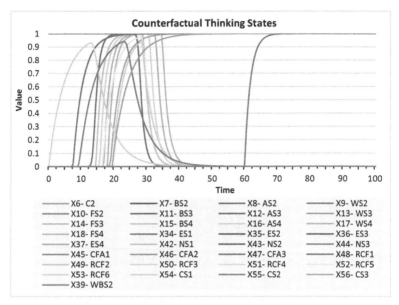

Fig. 4. Counterfactual thinking leading to evaluation states, nearness states and updating of beliefs represented by WBS2 going up to 1.

For the third stage shown in Fig. 5, the evaluation states ES2 to ES4 use their links to the CS3 state which controls the base-level BS5 to BS7 states through WBS5 to WBS7 states in order to make better future choices than in the past.

6   Verification of the Model by Analysis of Stationary Points

To verify whether the implemented network model behaves as expected from its conceptual specification, a number of stationary points were analyzed for a simulation example. As a stationary point for a state Y is a point where $dY(t)/dt = 0$, from the equation in Table 2, bottom row, the following general criterion for it can be derived: $\eta_Y = 0$ or

$$c_Y(x_1, _Y X_1(t), \ldots, x_k, _Y X_k(t)) = Y(t) \tag{2}$$

where X_1 to X_k are the states from which Y gets its incoming connections. It has been verified that the aggregated impact $\mathbf{aggimpact}_{X_i}(t)$ defined by the left hand side of (2) matches the state value for some stationary points observed in the example simulation. The results are shown in Table 6. The model generated correct values as there were no serious deviations for the stationary points as can be seen from the table: the maximal deviation was 0.001.

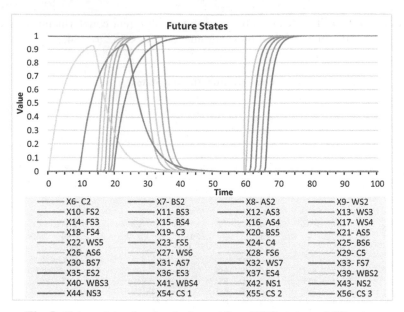

Fig. 5. Future states showing the impact from WBS-states and CS-states.

Table 6. Analysis of stationary points of the model

State X_i	X_{38}-WBS1	X_2-BS1	X_3-AS1	X_4-WS1	X_5-FS1	X_{54}-CF1	X_{52}-RCF5
Time point t	8.48	10.21	11.62	13.02	14.42	12.41	27.29
$X_i(t)$	0.984526	0.98714	0.987113	0.986998	0.986879	0.910897	0.964102
aggimpact$_{X_i}(t)$	0.983823	0.986161	0.98606	0.986017	0.985946	0.909804	0.963555
Deviation	-0.0007	-0.00098	-0.00105	-0.00098	-0.00093	-0.00109	-0.00055

7 Discussion

In the presented paper, counterfactual thinking was studied based on empirical literature from Neuroscience and Psychology. First, a detailed literature review was conducted in identifying processes, neural correlates and theories related to counterfactual thinking from different disciplines. Especially, the dynamic, adaptive and control aspects of counterfactual thinking were given the attention they deserve, as they are important but often neglected as soon as formalization or computational modeling of counterfactual thinking is addressed. A realistic scenario with respect to counterfactual thinking processes was identified. Based on the literature, a self-modeling temporal-causal network model was designed. This model captures the process of counterfactual thinking, including the dynamics, learning and control involved. Counterfactual thinking has been studied from various perspectives. But, as far as the authors know, a formalized computational model for it from a neuroscientific perspective including dynamics, adaptation and control of the thoughts and learning was never proposed.

By the implemented adaptive network model, the process of counterfactual thinking was simulated and shown to work as expected from the literature. For the model also some parameter tuning experiments have been performed which produced appropriate parameters as was expected from the literature, with a Root Mean Square Error RMSE < 0.08. Further mathematical analysis was conducted that has shown that the implemented model generated correct values compared to the model's design with maximal deviation of 0.001.

The network-oriented modeling approach used here makes it easy to integrate different theories and findings about a phenomenon into a more complex whole. It helps to understand the interactions within the processes. For the current focus, the present study contributes to theory building in understanding the processes of counterfactual thinking from a human-like modeling perspective, thereby taking into account adaptation and control for these processes. This goes much further than what is found in logical approaches to counterfactual reasoning that often abstract most of the dynamic, adaptive and control aspects involved in realistic counterfactual thinking away; e.g., [16].

The development of mental models for other types of learning processes has recently been addressed for the case of how mental models for operating a device are formed and how certain learning processes at the primary school take place [2, 3, 20].

The notion of counterfactual thinking can also be a useful source of inspiration for (not necessarily human-like) AI applications. Counterfactual thinking has already been used as a source of inspiration to refine and optimize well-known Q-learning approaches to reinforcement learning to let agents in a multi-agent setting improve their competitive abilities. A study done by Wang et al. [23], showed that counterfactual thinking can make the agents obtain more accumulative rewards from the environments with fair information in comparison to their opponents.

Further research detailing the selection of the features and evaluation process of counterfactuals can build more accurate human-like or more useful non-human-like models. Also, further validation of the network model against empirical data or other types of empirical information is one of the next steps to be undertaken; the process of model building is an iterative one and always ends with an invitation to make a next iteration.

References

1. Barbey, A.K., Krueger, F., Grafman, J.: Structured event complexes in the medial prefrontal cortex support counterfactual representations for future planning. Philos. Trans. R. Soc. B: Biol. Sci. **364**(1521), 1291–1300 (2009)
2. Bhalwankar, R., Treur, J.: Modeling the development of internal mental models by an adaptive network model. In: Proceedings of the 11th Annual International Conference on Brain-Inspired Cognitive Architectures for AI, BICA*AI'20. Procedia Computer Science, Elsevier (2021)
3. Bhalwankar, R., Treur, J.: A second-order adaptive network model for learner-controlled mental model learning processes. In: Benito, R.M., Cherifi, C., Cherifi, H., Moro, E., Rocha, L.M., Sales-Pardo, M. (eds.) COMPLEX NETWORKS 2020 2020. SCI, vol. 944, pp. 245–259. Springer, Cham (2021). https://doi.org/10.1007/978-3-030-65351-4_20
4. Byrne, R.M.J.: Mental models and counterfactual thoughts about what might have been. Trends Cognit. Sci. **6**(10), 426–431 (2002)

5. Byrne, R.M.J.: The Rational Imagination: How People Create Alternatives to Reality. MIT Press, Cambridge (2005)
6. Byrne, R.M.J.: Precis of 'the rational imagination: how people create alternatives to reality'. Behav. Brain Sci. **30**(5–6), 439–453 (2007)
7. Byrne, R.M.J.: Counterfactual thought. Annu. Rev. Psychol. **67**, 135–157 (2016)
8. De Brigard, F., Hanna, E., St Jacques, P.L., Schacter, D.L.: How thinking about what could have been affects how we feel about what was. Cognit. Emot. **33**, 646–659 (2019)
9. Epstude, K., Roese, N.J.: The functional theory of counterfactual thinking. Pers. Soc. Psychol. Rev. **12**(2), 168–192 (2008)
10. Fortin, N.J., Agster, K.L., Eichenbaum, H.B.: Critical role of the hippocampus in memory for sequences of events. Nat. Neurosci. **5**(5), 458–462 (2002)
11. Kahneman, D., Miller, D.T.: Norm theory: comparing reality to its alternatives. Psychol. Rev. **93**(2), 136 (1986)
12. Markman, K.D., Gavanski, I., Sherman, S.J., McMullen, M.N.: The mental simulation of better and worse possible worlds. J. Exp. Soc. Psychol. **29**(1), 87–109 (1993)
13. Roese, N.J.: The functional basis of counterfactual thinking. J. Pers. Soc. Psychol. **66**(5), 805 (1994)
14. Russell, J.A.: Core affect and the psychological construction of emotion. Psychol. Rev. **110**(1), 145 (2003)
15. Sanna, L.J., Schwarz, N., Small, E.M.: Accessibility experiences and the hindsight bias: I knew it all along versus it could never have happened. Mem. Cognit. **30**(8), 1288–1296 (2002)
16. Starr, W.B.: Conditional and counterfactual logic. In: Knauff, M., Spohn, W. (eds.) The Handbook of Rationality. MIT Press, Cambridge (2020)
17. Timberlake, B.: The effects of counterfactual comparison on learning and reasoning (Doctoral dissertation, University of Trento) (2019)
18. Treur, J.: Network-Oriented Modeling: Addressing Complexity of Cognitive, Affective and Social Interactions. Springer, Cham (2016). https://doi.org/10.1007/978-3-319-45213-5
19. Treur, J.: Network-Oriented Modeling for Adaptive Networks: Designing Higher-Order Adaptive Biological, Mental and Social Network Models. Springer, Cham (2020). https://doi.org/10.1007/978-3-030-31445-3
20. Treur, J.: An Adaptive Network Model Covering Metacognition to Control Adaptation for Multiple Mental Models. Cognit. Syst. Res. **67**, 18–27 (2021)
21. Tulving, E., Markowitsch, H.J.: Episodic and declarative memory: role of the hippocampus. Hippocampus **8**(3), 198–204 (1998)
22. Van Hoeck, N., Watson, P.D., Barbey, A.K.: Cognitive neuroscience of human counterfactual reasoning. Front. Hum. Neurosci. **9**, 420 (2015)
23. Wang, Y., Wan, Y., Zhang, C., Bai, L., Cui, L., Yu, P.: Competitive multi-agent deep reinforcement learning with counterfactual thinking. In: 2019 IEEE International Conference on Data Mining (ICDM), pp. 1366–1371. IEEE (2019)
24. Wilson, R.C., Collins, A.G.: Ten simple rules for the computational modeling of behavioral data. Elife **8**, (2019)

A Computational Model for the Second-Order Adaptive Causal Relationships Between Anxiety, Stress and Physical Exercise

Lars Rass and Jan Treur[✉]

Social AI Group, Department of Computer Science,
Vrije Universiteit Amsterdam, Amsterdam, The Netherlands
l.f.science@b-rass.de, j.treur@vu.nl

Abstract. Mental disorders are more and more seen as based on complex networks of symptoms and predispositions that create the disorder as an emergent behaviour of the network's dynamics. This paper aims to provide a computational model reflecting the adaptive causal relations between anxiety, stress and physical exercise based on a network-oriented modelling approach. The model was evaluated by executing several simulations and validated through an examination of its emergent properties and their cross-reference to the available literature. The created model offers the possibility of simulating different treatments, and offers a basis to develop a virtual patient model.

Keywords: Anxiety · Stress · Physical exercise · Adaptive network · Temporal-causal

1 Introduction

Everyone likely experiences stress and anxiety from time to time in their life. While the majority will only experience mild non-clinical symptoms, one should still be cautious. Although mild symptoms might not impact one's life substantially, mild symptoms can still have adverse effects on the affected individuals [14]. Furthermore, leaving mild symptoms untreated increases the individual's risk of their anxiety progressing to a clinical state [14]. It is estimated that the prevalence of anxiety symptoms in the general population is around 32% [17], and around 25% of the American population had at least one episode of anxiety [25]. Also, urgency arises from the current stressful situation created through the COVID-19 pandemic and its related effects, as the prevalence of anxiety and related psychological disorders seem to increase [17]. Therefore, to reduce the risk of onsetting severe anxiety, a range of treatment approaches should always be considered. One of such approaches could be physical activity. Not only does this bring general health benefits with it, but it is also something easy and accessible to reduce one's symptoms without extra medication [9, 14, 25].

In the classical psychopathological model, it is assumed that the disorder causes the combination of symptoms to appear, as it requires both a categorical and dimensional

© IFIP International Federation for Information Processing 2021
Published by Springer Nature Switzerland AG 2021
I. Maglogiannis et al. (Eds.): AIAI 2021, IFIP AICT 627, pp. 17–29, 2021.
https://doi.org/10.1007/978-3-030-79150-6_2

latent classification for symptoms of psychological disorders and does not take causal relations between the symptoms into account. Lately, however, a network-oriented approach towards psychological disorders was proposed. This approach offers another view, stating that a mental disorder is not the reason for its underlying symptoms to co-appear, but a mental disorder is based on a network of distinct symptoms, dynamically interacting with each other ultimately causing the emergent behaviour classified as, e.g., Anxiety [4, 6, 10, 15]. In this effort, given the complexity of the underlying neurobiological mechanisms [25] and the necessity of further research in the domain, an integrated approach showing changes in anxiety in response to physical activity is of great value enabling to simulate the effects of different exercise frequencies.

2 Literature Overview

Many meta-studies have observed a significant but modest anxiety-reducing effect of physical exercise [13, 14, 25] and an overall increase in one's mood [25]. However, there still is a debate if clinical or non-clinical populations benefit more from the effects of physical exercising [14, 25]. Physical exercise however should still be promoted given its preventative and rehabilitative qualities, through direct and indirect effects [13, 14, 25], concerning brain-related psychiatric disorders. Although exercise always has a positive effect on one's emotions [8], its anxiety-reducing effects depend on the intensity of the exercise. Research has shown that the anxiolytic effect of exercise is highest when it is performed under the ventilatory threshold, the threshold at which the breathing rate increases disproportionally regarding the oxygen uptake. Training above this threshold reduces the mood-increasing effects of the exercising [8]. The literature here suggests that aerobic training of around 20 to 35 min is most beneficial [8, 13, 25], with first positive effects on an individual's mood already showing after 15 to 20 min [8]. Therefore, a timescale of 30 min is considered to induce exercises' anxiolytic effect, considering the above-mentioned factors.

Research additionally has shown that physical exercise leads to a positive effect on an individual's stress response [9, 25]. Due to a positive correlation between anxiety and stress [11, 12], this also effects one's anxiousness. This correlation already begins to show with only mild stress symptoms [11]. Further studies have also shown a reduction of the activation of the general stress response in physically active individuals [9]. A reduction in amplitude of the stress response and the time needed to recover to baseline levels, could also be observed in physically active individuals [25]. This is important given a stress response is mostly defined by the individuals' ability to quickly recover to the baseline following a stressful event [3]. Furthermore, the interconnection of stress and anxiety urges one to also address indirect effects on anxiety.

In a typical stress response, when a stressor is apparent, the threat recognising brain regions (amygdala, prefrontal cortex, and hippocampus) will initiate the release of Corticotrophin-releasing factors (CRFs). This release triggers the production of glucocorticoid in the HPA Axis leading to the release of cortisol and the production of epinephrine. Usually this is described as the "Fight or Flight response" of the body [20]. The ways in which exercise influences this stress response are multifold [9], and seem to be of both psychological and neurophysical nature [14]. Part of the neurophysical changes can be united under their effects on the biological stress response. One of these effects can be seen in a reduction of anxiety through effects on the hypothalamic-pituitary adrenal axis (HPA axis) [25] Another can be observed in an increase of the threshold that needs to be surpassed by stressful events to induce biological stress response, due to a reduction in the likelihood of the sympathetic nervous system's activation [9]. This is mostly based on changing baseline cortisol levels [13, 25] and a reduction of the level of cortisol in an active stress response [13]. Other long-term changes of the HPA Axis through exercise also include inhibition of cortisol synthesis and a higher functioning of mineralocorticoid receptors [13]. This suggests an decreased sensitivity of the HPA axis due to an increased activation threshold following physical exercise.

Other effects of neurological nature indirectly influence the psychological responses and emotion regulation abilities [19]. Physical exercise does not only increase blood flow and the oxygenation and metabolism of the brain, it also induces the release of opioids and endocannabinoids, which were shown to have a direct anxiolytic effect [13]. Furthermore, it induces the release of neurotrophic factors [13, 25] and the synthesis of several neurotransmitters (BDNF, IGF-1, WEGF, NT3, FGF-2, GDNF, EGF and NGF) [13]. The release of these neurotransmitters and neurotrophic factors has several effects. First the neurotransmitter release contributes to a less suppressed cortical activity [13]. Second, neurogenesis-reducing effects of stress and neurodegenerative diseases are counteracted by an increased neurogenesis, attributable to a higher neurotrophin availability. Third, the ability to adapt to stress is increased due to an increased neuroplasticity induced by the neurotrophic factors [13]. The improved neuroplasticity also strengthens the adaptivity of the ventromedial prefrontal cortex, a brain region significantly involved in the emotional and behavioural control network [19]. Furthermore, the release of brain-derived neurotrophic factors (BDNF) due to exercise also leads to a better responsivity to environmental stress, given BDNF's enhancing effect on the synaptic connectivity and signal transduction [21]. Therefore, this research indicates that one's emotion regulation ability is indirectly influenced by exercise induced release of neurotransmitters and neurotrophic factors.

Drawing on the above-mentioned correlations and underlying mechanisms, this paper aims to contribute to the research effort by providing a computational model. Surprisingly, until today the above-mentioned factors have not yet been incorporated into an computational model, despite the growing interest in an network-oriented approach of modelling neurophysical diseases [4, 6, 10, 15]. While the created model should offer the possibility of simulating different treatment procedures, it could later also be used as a possible basis or extension of a virtual agent model representing and simulating a patient.

3   The Adaptive Computational Network Model

3.1   The Modelling Approach Used

The adaptive computational network model introduced here was developed using the adaptive network-oriented modeling approach described in Treur [23, 24], which is based on self-modeling network models and a dedicated software environment. The adaptive computational network model's dynamics can be defined by a number of network characteristics: its connections and their weights, its timing via speed factors, and the aggregation characteristics as follows.

Connections
The connections between nodes in this type of network represent a translation of real-world causal relations into a network structure. They are defined by the nodes X and Y they connect and by their weight $\omega_{X,Y}$ demonstrating the strength of that connection. In adaptive networks, this weight is represented by another (self-model) node (see below).

Timing
The model's timing is determined by the speed factors η_Y of each node Y, which can be understood as indication of the node's rate of change.

Aggregation
The type of aggregation chosen determines how multiple incoming inputs are combined into one effect on the destination node. For this, various combination functions $c_Y(..)$ are provided by a dedicated library.

Standard Difference Equation
All network nodes Y (also called states) have time-dependent values $Y(t)$ where t indicates time. Based on the network characteristics for connectivity, aggregation and timing defined above, the following difference equation defines the network's dynamics for any state Y:

$$Y(t + \Delta t) = Y(t) + \eta_Y \left[c_Y(\omega_{X_1,Y} X_1(t), \ldots, \omega_{X_k,Y} X_k(t)) - Y(t) \right] \Delta t \qquad (1)$$

Here, $X_1, \ldots, X_k$ are the network states from which Y has incoming connections.

Higher-Order Self-models
Self-models can represent adaptive characteristics of the network. These usually consist of self-model states, also called reification states [24]. Typically, the weight $\omega_{X,Y}$ of a connection or a node's speed factor η_Y can be made adaptive through including a self-model state named $\mathbf{W}_{X,Y}$ (for connection weight) or $\mathbf{H}_Y$ (for speed factor) for it. However, self-model states can also represent other network characteristics like the parameters of combination functions.

Combination Functions
The dedicated software environment comes with a pre-selection of many (more than 45) commonly used combination functions with differing parameters and use cases. A selection of combination functions used in the introduced model is given here.

The *identity combination function* **id**(..) is mostly used to directly transfer the activation of the source node to the receiving node or in a circular manner of a node to itself to model persistence of activation by keeping the already reached numerical value. It has no parameters, and its formal definition is as follows:

$$\mathbf{id}(V) = V \qquad (2)$$

The *Hebbian learning combination function* $\mathbf{hebb}_\mu(..)$ is used to model the Hebbian learning principle. It has one parameter μ, which describes the persistence factor. Its formal definition is as follows:

$$\mathbf{hebb}_\mu(V_1, V_2, W) = V_1 V_2(1 - W) + \mu W \tag{3}$$

The *advanced logistic sum combination function* $\mathbf{alogistic}_{\sigma,\tau}(V_1, \ldots, V_k)$ is an often-used function to combine inputs when a node has multiple incoming connections. It has two parameters σ, which describes the steepness of the logistic function, and τ, which describes the threshold. Its formal definition is as follows:

$$\mathbf{alogistic}_{\sigma,\tau}(V_1, \ldots, V_k) = [\frac{1}{1 + e^{-\sigma(V_1 + \cdots + V_k - \tau)}} - \frac{1}{1 + e^{\sigma\tau}}](1 + e^{-\sigma\tau}) \tag{4}$$

Additionally, two custom *step mod functions* will be used to create cyclically recurring inputs; see the Appendix [2].

Software Environment Used
Designed network models are usually specified in a standard table format, called the role matrices format, for which examples and explanations can be found in [24], Ch. 9. Given these specifications and each state's initial values, the simulation can be performed using the provided dedicated software environment, implemented in the form of MatLab scripts and functions; for more details, see [24], Ch. 9. The script for simulation of adaptive (self-modeling) network models used here will then calculate the state values over time based on the dynamics for the states described by Eq. (1), thereby picking the values for the adaptive characteristics from the self-model states representing them, and gives the possibility to export the generated data for further investigation and visualization.

3.2 The Designed Adaptive Self-modeling Network Model

Following the approach to Network-Oriented Modelling described in [22, 24], a network model was created based on the literature review. The graphical representation of the connectivity of this model is depicted in Fig. 1, while Table 1 describes the states shown in Fig. 1 in more detail. The model consists of 19 states, of whom twelve represent base level states, three portray first-order self-model states and four display second-order self-model states. The states in the first reification level (or first-order self-model level) represent the principle of Hebbian learning for two connections at the base level, while the states in the second reification level (or second-order self-model level) express metaplasticity, namely persistence of what is learned and the speed of learning.

The base-level causal relations can be described according to two groups, one concerning the general stress and anxiety response, the other regarding the effects of physical exercise on the general stress and anxiety response. The general stress and anxiety response is mostly defined by the biological stress response and psychological emotion regulation. Like Fig. 1 shows, a stressor (**ws**) will lead to the preparation of the stress response (**pssr**), which will then have two effects. On one side, it will trigger the biological stress response (**bsr**) through activation of the HPA axis and the release of cortisol. On the other side is the psychological stress response, depicted in the stress regulation

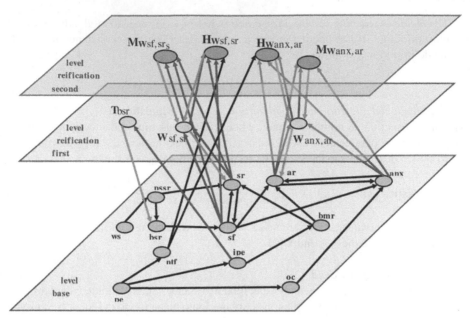

Fig. 1. Connectivity of the second-order adaptive network model concerning anxiety and stress emotion regulation covering plasticity and metaplasticity. Interlevel relations are depicted by upward connections (blue) and downward connections (pink-red). With a base level (pink plane) depicting the basic causal relations (black arrows), a first reification level (blue plane) depicting neuroplasticity and a second reification level (purple plane) depicting metaplasticity. (Color figure online)

control state (**sr**). The biological and psychological stress response together will then cause the stress feeling (**sf**) in the individual, which through further causal relations will cause the feeling of anxiety (**anx**), which is controlled by the anxiety regulation control state (**ar**).

Both the causal relation between the stress feeling and the stress regulation, as well as the connection between the anxiety feeling and the anxiety regulation, are, however, influenced by the first-order self-model states. In this model, they are used to represent the Hebbian learning principle '*what fires together, wires together*' ([18], p. 64). Therefore, the weight of the connection from the feeling towards its respective control state was made adaptive by introducing the self-model states **W**. The **W**-states, representing the plasticity that is described by Hebbian learning, furthermore are influenced by a second-order self-model state representing the concept of metaplasticity. The respective **H**-states represent the speed factor η of **W**, while the **M**-states represent the persistence factors μ of **W**. The **H**-states intend to represent the principle of an increased adaptation speed and therefore learning speed. Research has shown that the adaptation speed itself shows adaptive characteristics, most notably an acceleration of the adaptation process if stimulus exposure increases [16], also known as meta-adaptation [1]. In this model, the **H**-states' activation should increase in value relative to its exposed stimuli. Therefore, such an increased level of stimulus exposure should relate to an increase in the learning speed over time. In this model, the **H**-state values are further influenced by neurotrophic factors (**ntf**). These lead to an increased adaptation speed, which will translate into improved neuroplasticity.

Table 1. Description of the states of the second-order adaptive network model

State nr	State name	Explanation	Level
X_1	ws	World state for stressor	
X_2	pssr	Preparation state of stress response	
X_3	bsr	Biological Stress Response (HPA Axis)	
X_4	sf	Feeling of Stress	
X_5	sr	Stress Regulation control state	
X_6	anx	Feeling of Anxiety	Base
X_7	ar	Anxiety Regulation control state	level
X_8	bmr	Behavioural and Mood Responses	
X_9	ipe	Indirect Effects of Physical Exercise	
X_{10}	pe	Physical Exercise	
X_{11}	ntf	Neurotrophic Factors	
X_{12}	oc	Opioids and Cannabinoids	
X_{13}	$\mathbf{T}_{bsr}$	First-order self-model state for the Biological Stress Responses activation treshold	First-order
X_{14}	$\mathbf{W}_{anx,ar}$	First-order self-model state for connection weight $\omega_{anx,ar}$	self-model level
X_{15}	$\mathbf{W}_{sf,sr}$	First-order self-model state for connection weight $\omega_{sf,sr}$	
X_{16}	$\mathbf{HW}_{anx,ar}$	Second-order self-model state for speed factor $\eta\mathbf{W}_{anx,ar}$ first-order self-model self-model state $\mathbf{W}_{anx,ar}$	
X_{17}	$\mathbf{MW}_{anx,ar}$	Second-order self-model state for persistence factor parameter $\mu\mathbf{W}_{anx,ar}$ first-order self-model self-model state $\mathbf{W}_{anx,ar}$	Second-order self-model level
X_{18}	$\mathbf{HW}_{sf,sr}$	Second-order self-model state for speed factor $\eta\mathbf{W}_{sf,sr}$ first-order self-model self-model state $\mathbf{W}_{sf,sr}$	
X_{19}	$\mathbf{MW}_{sf,sr}$	Second-order self-model state for persistence factor parameter $\mu\mathbf{W}_{sf,sr}$ first-order self-model self-model state $\mathbf{W}_{sf,sr}$	

The above-described network, however, can be influenced by the effects of physical exercise. Physical exercise affects the stress and anxiety response of an individual in both a direct and an indirect manner.

The indirect effect of physical exercise is represented by the ipe state, which influences both the HPA axis sensitivity through its threshold (represented by self-model state $\mathbf{T_{bsr}}$) and the behavioural and mood responses (**bmr**). The indirect effect of physical exercise on the HPA axis is based on an increase of the biological stress responses threshold, while the behavioural and mood responses elevate the emotion regulation ability. The **T**-state in this network models influences the excitability of the Biological Stress Response related neurons. These influences result in a modification of the neuron's response to the triggering synaptic activity [5, 7]. Therefore, an increase in the value of the self-model state $\mathbf{T_{bsr}}$ would result in lessened excitability of the HPA axis activating neurons. This should result in a changed reaction of the Biological Stress Response state (**bsr**) to input it receives from the stress response preparation state (**pssr**).

The direct effects of physical exercise on stress and anxiety, comprise the release of Opioids and Cannabinoids (**oc**), which directly reduce the feeling of anxiety and the release of neurotrophic factors (**ntf**), which increase the brains' neuroplasticity. In the model, this causal relation is realized through a direct increasing influence of the neurotrophic factors on the **H**-states, representing the learning speed.

4 Simulations

To obtain a full detailed design description of all characteristics of the model, it was specified in a standardized form in role-matrices format. This format describes all characteristics that define the model: the connections and their weights, the speed factors and the combination functions used with their parameters. Moreover, the available dedicated software environment can use these matrices as input and run simulations for the model from it. Table 2, 3, 4, 5 in the Appendix [2] show the role-matrices for the first run scenario.

To explore the claim of a reductive effect of physical exercise on anxiety, three different scenarios depicting different levels of physical activity integration into the individual's life are performed. The simulation will represent the time of 8:00 until 22:00 over three days. Each time point in the simulation corresponds to a timeframe of five minutes, resulting in a total of 504 Steps in our simulation. In each scenario, the individual will be presented with a stressor from 12:30 until 13:30 to observe its effect on the model's different states. In Scenario 2 (below) and 3 [2], one or more physical exercises of 30 min will be added to each day.

Scenario 1: No Exercising
In the first scenario, the individual will be confronted with a stressor, lasting one hour, each of the three days, with the initial values chosen to depict an individual that already has a higher base level of stress. While the simulation's full result can be seen in Fig. 9 in Appendix [2], an examination of the results based on different parts of the model will take place. For this, the general model will be divided into three sections, one for the stress response, one for the anxiety response and one for the effects of physical exercise. For the first scenario however, given no physical exercise is present, only the stress and anxiety response will be inspected. In Fig. 2 (upper graph), the stress response and its related states are shown. As expected, the preparation state for the stress response gets triggered when a stressor is present, which subsequently also relates to an activated biological stress response and feeling of stress. With a slight delay, this results in activation of the Stress Regulation Control State, increases the adaptive connection weight (**W**-stress) and speed factor (**H**-stress).

These increases are triggered as part of the Hebbian learning process, given the simultaneous firing of the feeling and control state. Moreover, the Activation Threshold of the Biological Stress Response (**T**-bsr) stays unaffected and constant, given no physical exercise is performed. As expected, the stress response is of similar nature each day and the level of stress persists over time. Furthermore, the constant high-stress level results in a constant decrease in the persistence factor (**M**-stress) virtually blocking learning. The process only shows plateauing while the Hebbian learning process is triggered.

Contrary to the stress response, the anxiety response (lower graph in Fig. 2) is only slightly affected by the periodic occurrence of the stressor. Due to the direct correlation between stress and anxiety, this is expected behaviour. The stress feeling state does

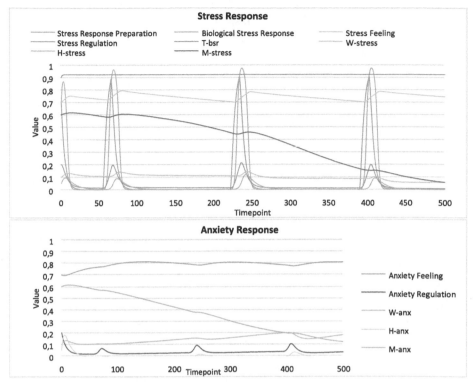

Fig. 2. Graphical representation of the stress response (upper graph) and anxiety response (lower graph) in scenario 1

not show much volatility over time which is reflected in the correlated anxiety state. Therefore, effects shown by the Hebbian learning states of the anxiety response occur in a significantly lower amplitude when compared with the stress responses Hebbian Learning states.

Scenario 2: Occasional Workout
In the second scenario (see Fig. 3), the individual will again be confronted with a one-hour lasting stressor each of the three days.

The initial values will again be chosen to reflect an individual with a higher baselevel of stress. Contrary to the first scenario, however, a physical exercise of 30 min at 10:00 in the morning will be added. This corresponds to the physical exercise state being activated during the timepoints 24–30, 192–198, 360–366. For this we will need to change the function parameter specifications according to Table 6 in (Appendix, [2]). The other specifications stay the same. To better understand the model's dynamics, the behaviour of the different subsystems will again be examined separately. However, the simulation's full result can also be seen in Fig. 10 of (Appendix, [2]). As can be seen in Fig. 3, similar responses to the stressor as in Scenario 1 take place. However, these processes are influenced and disrupted to an extend by the effects of physical exercise. As expected better behavioural and mood responses and the decreased sensitivity of the

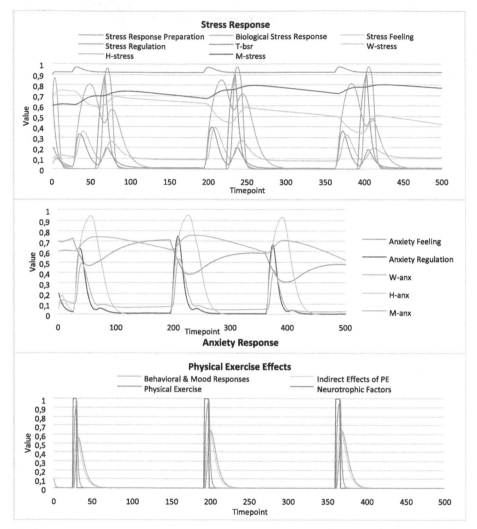

Fig. 3. Graphical representation of the stress response (upper graph) and anxiety response (middle graph) and physical exercising (lower graph) in scenario 2

HPA axis result in a decreasing base level of the feeling of stress after physical exercise. This process is likely aided by strengthened Hebbian learning principles.

Another drastic change compared to Scenario 1 can be seen in the processes connected to Hebbian learning. As the release of neurotrophic factors increases the neurogenesis, the learning speed (**H**-stress) increases significantly, which as a result also keeps the persistence factor (**M**-stress) on an stable but slightly increasing level. Interestingly, however, the connection weight (**W**-stress) between the stress feeling and its emotion regulation control state, returns to a stable base level once outside influences subside. This suggests that there are not yet long-term persisting learning effects, at this level of exercise integration in one's life. Further, an increase in the HPA axis activation threshold (**T-bsr**) can be seen following physical activity. However, given the threshold returns to its baselevel at the time the stressor activates the biological stress response, no reduction in the response can be observed.

Contrary to the first scenario, the feeling of stress in this scenario was more volatile, resulting in higher volatility of the states connected to the anxiety response. As expected, the periodically decreased feeling of stress and the increased behavioural and mood responses after physical activity led to a decreased feeling of anxiety after exercises. This is aided by the anxiolytic effects of opioids and cannabinoids that are released as a result of physical exercise. Moreover, the decrease of the stress feeling over time translates to a decrease of anxiety over time.

Furthermore, the increased metaplasticity induced by the neurotrophic factors leads to a periodically increased learning speed (**H-anx**) and connection weight (**W-anx**) of the anxiety feeling and regulation connection. This causes the persistence factor to rebound to higher levels in these times of increased activation of the Hebbian learning processes, leading to an overall fluctuating but only minimally decreasing persistence factor over time. As expected, these influences lead to a reduction of the anxiety base level.

As Fig. 3, lower graph shows, physical exercise induces the acute release of neurotrophic factors as well as opioids and cannabinoids. Through its indirect effects, physical exercise increases behavioural and mood responses for a short timeframe after the physical exercise ended.

5   Discussion

This paper aimed to describe the creation of a adaptive computational temporal-causal network model for the effects of physical exercise on stress and anxiety based on real-world causal relations. According to the proposed paradigm shift in the view of psychological disorders as dynamic networks [4, 6, 10, 15]. The model was built to recreate the known patterns as indirectly emerging from adaptive causal relations. The network model incorporates three types of adaptation principles to recreate Hebbian learning, excitability adaptation and adaptive adaptation speed.

By the use of the network model and a dedicated software environment implemented as a MatLab script, three different scenarios were simulated, depicting different levels of integration of physical exercise into the individual's life. The first scenario portrayed three days of an individual being confronted with a stressor each day with no physical exercise and showed that the stress and anxiety level will always return to the same base level. In the second scenario, a workout of 30 min in the morning was added to the individual's routine, which, through direct and indirect effects, lead to a visible reduction of the stress and anxiety base levels over time. In the third scenario, in addition to the morning exercise, another workout in the evening was added. This resulted in a further extended reduction of the anxiety and stress base levels throughout the simulation.

Overall, the model successfully showed emergent behaviour reflecting the empirical findings in the discussed literature, confirming its validity. Further this research contribution enables a visualisation of the underlying effects of physical exercise on stress and anxiety. While this model, by the generated simulation graphs, confirms that physical exercise could positively influence the treatment of anxiety and should be promoted, it could also act as a basis or extension of future virtual agent models to display these outcomes in a more relatable manner. Nevertheless, the presented model is not without limitations. While it reflects the causal relations on a macroscopic level, a more advanced model could incorporate the underlying mechanisms of the biological stress response and the emotion regulation in greater detail. Additionally, to create a holistic representation of the complex biological and neurological interdependencies of psychological disorders, a combination with additional computational models in this domain could be added as well.

Taking into consideration the numerous imbricating symptoms of anxiety and other psychological disorders like depression, further research may focus on the creation of a generalized model representing typical neurological and biological symptoms of serotonin and dopamine availability impacting disorders. This would enable broader possibilities in simulations and increase the comparability amid different models.

References

1. Adorjan, P., Schwabe, L., Wenning, G., Obermayer, K.: Rapid adaptation to internal states as a coding strategy in visual cortex? NeuroReport 13(3), 337–342 (2002)
2. Appendix: Linked Data (2021). https://www.researchgate.net/publication/350049733
3. Barlow, D.H., Ellard, K.K., Sauer-Zavala, S., Bullis, J.R., Carl, J.R.: The origins of neuroticism. Perspect. Psychol. Sci. 9(5), 481–496 (2014)
4. Borsboom, D.: A network theory of mental disorders. World Psychiatry 16(1), 5–13 (2017)
5. Chandra, N., Barkai, E.: A non-synaptic mechanism of complex learning: modulation of intrinsic neuronal excitability. Neurobiol. Learn. Mem. 154, 30–36 (2018)
6. Cramer, A.O., Borsboom, D.: Problems attract problems: a network perspective on mental disorders. Emerg. Trends Soc. Behav. Sci. Interdiscip. Searchable Linkable Resour., 1–15 (2015)
7. Debanne, D., Inglebert, Y., Russier, M.: Plasticity of intrinsic neuronal excitability. Curr. Opin. Neurobiol. 54, 73–82 (2019)
8. Ekkekakis, P., Hall, E., Petruzzello, S.: The relationship between exercise intensity and affective responses demystified: to crack the 40-year-old nut, replace the 40-year-old nutcracker! Ann. Behav. Med. 35(2), 136–149 (2008)
9. Greenwood, B.N., Fleshner, M.: Exercise, stress resistance, and central serotonergic systems. Exerc. Sport Sci. Rev. 39(3), 140–149 (2011). https://doi.org/10.1097/jes.0b013e31821f7e45
10. Hofmann, S.G., Curtiss, J., McNally, R.J.: A complex network perspective on clinical science. Perspect. Psychol. Sci. J. Assoc. Psychol. Sci. 11(5), 597–605 (2016)
11. Konstantopoulou, G., Iliou, T., Karaivazoglou, K., Iconomou, G., Assimakopoulos, K., Alexopoulos, P.: Associations between (sub) clinical stress- and anxiety symptoms in mentally healthy individuals and in major depression: a cross-sectional clinical study. BMC Psychiatry 20(1) (2020)
12. Kurebayashi, L.F.S., Do Prado, J.M., Da Silva, M.J.P.: Correlations between stress and anxiety levels in nursing students. J. Nurs. Educ. Pract. 2(3), 128 (2012)
13. Matta Mello Portugal, E., et al.: Neuroscience of exercise: from neurobiology mechanisms to mental health. Neuropsychobiology 68(1), 1–14 (2013). https://doi.org/10.1159/000350946
14. Rebar, A.L., Stanton, R., Geard, D., Short, C., Duncan, M.J., Vandelanotte, C.: A metameta-analysis of the effect of physical activity on depression and anxiety in non-clinical adult populations. Health Psychol. Rev. 9(3), 366–378 (2015). https://doi.org/10.1080/17437199.2015.1022901

15. Robinaugh, D.J., Hoekstra, R.H., Toner, E.R., Borsboom, D.: The network approach to psychopathology: a review of the literature 2008–2018 and an agenda for future research. Psychol. Med. **50**(3), 353 (2020)
16. Robinson, B.L., Harper, N.S., McAlpine, D.: Meta-adaptation in the auditory midbrain under cortical influence. Nat. Commun. **7**(1), 1–8 (2016)
17. Salari, N., et al.: Prevalence of stress, anxiety, depression among the general population during the COVID-19 pandemic: a systematic review and meta-analysis. Glob. Health **16**(1), 1–11 (2020)
18. Shatz, C.J.: The developing brain. Sci. Am. **267**(3), 60–67 (1992)
19. Sinha, R., Lacadie, C.M., Constable, R.T., Seo, D.: Dynamic neural activity during stress signals resilient coping. Proc. Natl Acad. Sci. U. S. Am. **113**(31), 8837–8842 (2016). https://doi.org/10.1073/pnas.1600965113
20. Stranahan, A.M., Lee, K., Mattson, M.P.: Central mechanisms of HPA axis regulation by voluntary exercise. NeuroMol. Med. **10**(2), 118–127 (2008). https://doi.org/10.1007/s12017-008-8027-0
21. Sylvia, L.G., Ametrano, R.M., Nierenberg, A.A.: Exercise treatment for bipolar disorder: potential mechanisms of action mediated through increased neurogenesis and decreased allostatic load. Psychother. Psychosom. **79**(2), 87–96 (2010). https://doi.org/10.1159/000270916
22. Treur, J.: Dynamic modeling based on a temporal–causal network modeling approach. Biol. Inspir. Cognit. Archit. **16**, 131–168 (2016)
23. Treur, J.: Adaptive networks at the crossroad of AI and formal, biological, medical and social sciences. In: Rezaei, N. (ed.) Integrated Science - Science without Borders, vol. 1. Springer, Cham (2021)
24. Treur, J.: Network-Oriented Modeling for Adaptive Networks: Designing Higher-Order Adaptive Biological, Mental and Social Network Models. SSDC, vol. 251. Springer, Cham (2020). https://doi.org/10.1007/978-3-030-31445-3
25. Wegner, M., Helmich, I., Machado, S., Nardi, A., Arias-Carrion, O., Budde, H.: Effects of exercise on anxiety and depression disorders: review of meta-analyses and neurobiological mechanisms. CNS Neurol. Disord. Drug Targets (Former. Curr. Drug Targets-CNS Neurol. Disord.) **13**(6), 1002–1014 (2014)

AI in Biomedical Applications

ebioMelDB: Multi-modal Database for Melanoma and Its Application on Estimating Patient Prognosis

Aigli Korfiati[1]([envelope]), Giorgos Livanos[1], Christos Konstantinou[1], Sophia Georgiou[2], and George Sakellaropoulos[1]

[1] Department of Medical Physics, School of Medicine, University of Patras, Patras, Greece
livanosg@upnet.gr, {chrikon,gsak}@upatras.gr
[2] Department of Dermatology, School of Medicine, University of Patras, Patras, Greece
sgeo@upatras.gr

Abstract. Data availability is important when researchers want to apply artificial intelligence algorithms to extract biomarkers and generate predictive models for disease diagnosis, response to treatment and prognosis. For cutaneous melanoma clinical, biological and imaging data are scattered through the web. ebioMelDB is the first database to integrate the widest collections of RNA-Seq gene expression and clinical data with clinical and dermoscopy images, all manually curated and organized in categories. ebioMelDB aspires also to host our under development predictive models in cutaneous melanoma diagnosis, response to treatment and prognosis based on combinations of the different data types hosted. As a first step towards this direction, we apply an ensemble dimensionality reduction technique employing a multi-objective optimization heuristic algorithm that finds the best feature subset, the best classifier among linear SVM, Radial Basis Function Kernel SVM and random forest and their optimal parameters to predict the vital status of patients in different time windows based on a large cohort of patients' gene expression data. The results are very encouraging in performance metrics compared with state-of-the-art algorithms. The database is available at http://www.med.upatras.gr/ebioMelDB.

Keywords: Cutaneous melanoma · Database · Prognosis · Machine learning

1 Introduction

Cutaneous melanoma (CM), commonly developed from malignant transformation of melanocytes cells that produce melanin in the skin, constitutes ~5% of all skin cancers [1]. However, >75% of skin cancer deaths originate from melanoma, which has a 5-year survival rate of 23% in patients with late stage of the disease [1]. Early detection is the most important determinant of the associated mortality reduction and towards this direction, in 1985, the ABCD rule [2] was devised by Kopf et al. as a simple framework that physicians, novice dermatologists and non-physicians can use to detect melanocytic

© IFIP International Federation for Information Processing 2021
Published by Springer Nature Switzerland AG 2021
I. Maglogiannis et al. (Eds.): AIAI 2021, IFIP AICT 627, pp. 33–44, 2021.
https://doi.org/10.1007/978-3-030-79150-6_3

lesions with atypical features. Based on the above rule, atypical melanocytic nevi are characterized by A (Asymmetry), B (Border irregularities), C (Colors variety) and D (Diameter >6 mm) [2].

The introduction and application of dermoscopy in clinical practice has provided a new dimension in the evaluation of pigmented skin lesions. With this non-invasive technique and the pattern analysis method, melanocytic lesions are distinguished from non-melanocytic lesions. However, dermoscopy as a method has its limitations, as it depends on the examiner's experience. Traditional radiomics practice uses machine learning methods towards the development of computer-aided diagnosis (CAD) tools that can be used by dermatologists to overcome the aforementioned issues [3]. These systems follow a pipeline: i) image preprocessing, ii) lesion segmentation, iii) feature extraction, iv) feature selection (optional), and v) classification. Recently, a vast number of deep learning methods have been employed in CM research, but these as well have challenges and limitations [4].

CM is considered a multifactorial disease, the result of genetic predisposition and environmental factors [5] and survival outcomes and response to treatment can vary widely among patients due to the biological heterogeneity of melanoma [6]. Thus, in the effort to better understand the disease mechanisms and apply individualized treatment protocols to CM patients, omics data have been explored for the identification of diagnostic and prognostic biomarkers. Four subtypes of cancer, which include mutant BRAF, mutant RAS, mutant NF1, triple WT (wild-type) based on mutant genes have been widely reported [7] and a recent review on the genomic features characterizing the development of CM can be found in [8]. Apart from genomics, studies have demonstrated that CM arises from the anomalies in transcriptomic and epigenetic factors such as expression of mRNAs, miRNAs, the aberration in methylation patterns of CpG islands of genes and histone modifications [9]. In an attempt to find melanoma subtypes based on transcriptomics data, four major signatures have been found: immune, keratin, melanocyte inducing transcription factor (MITF)-low and MITF-high [10]. In the last decade, an extraordinary leap forward in the treatment of melanoma occurred, taking advantage of the advent of targeted therapies and immunotherapies [11]. At present, the methods commonly used in the treatment of melanoma include surgical resection, chemotherapy and immunotherapy. Interestingly, 13 FDA-approved treatments are presented in a review by Donelly et al. [12] for different molecular subtypes of the disease, most originating from CM omics biomarkers. But again, because of the molecular heterogeneity, not all patients respond well to treatments and some present drug resistance. Therefore, it is imperative to develop prognostic biomarkers for risk stratification and treatment optimization [13].

However, analyzing only a single type of omics measurement poses limitations, because it cannot comprehensively and accurately describe the biological processes underlying the disease and may lead to partial and uninformative biomarkers. Thus, multidimensional studies which profile multiple types of omics changes on the same subjects have emerged [14]. A representative example is TCGA (The Cancer Genome Atlas) which is organized by NIH. TCGA is one of the most prominent and inclusive repositories containing genomic, transcriptomic, epigenetic, proteomics and clinical information of 33 types of cancer [15], among which CM with its TCGA-SKCM project [7].

Several studies have been conducted to identify prognostic biomarkers based on various TCGA-SKCM omics data with most of them including expression data. Jiang et al. [14] focused on a multi-omics analysis by integration of mutation, copy number variation, methylation, and messenger RNA expression data to achieve this objective, while the authors in [16] identified molecular subtypes associated with differences in CM prognosis by integrating epigenomic and genomic data. The authors in [17] support that integrating gene expression regulators when analyzing gene expression data can more accurately identify biomarkers. A number of studies have generated immune related prognostic gene signatures (a 239-gene signature in [18], a 33-gene signature in [19], a 25-gene signature in [20], a 7-gene signature in [21] and a 6-gene signature in [22]). In [23] the authors generated a 121 metastasis-associated prognostic signature and the authors in [9] are trying to distinguish metastatic melanoma from primary tumors based on the mRNA, miRNA and methylation data of TCGA providing their prediction models through the webserver, CancerSPP. The STATegra framework is presented in [24] as a multi-omics integrative pipeline used on mRNA and miRNA expression and methylation data. Several studies present web-servers which provide survival analysis based on gene expression [13]. However, these tools analyze statistically the association between single genes and survival prognosis in TCGA cancers.

Integrating omics and clinical data with imaging data is promising [25]. In melanoma, there is limited relevant research. In [26], the authors studied melanoma prognosis in terms of recurrence-free survival, based on clinical data, gene expression, and whole slide image features. Their best performing model included 20 automatically generated whole slide image features, 3 clinicopathologic variables, and mutation status of 2 genes. Maglogiannis et al. [27] propose a platform able to integrate omics, histological images and clinical data for skin cancer patients and construct a synthetic dataset with mutated genes and images in order to discriminate melanoma from dysplastic nevi.

In the present paper we introduce ebioMelDB, a multi-modal database for cutaneous melanoma aspiring to enable researchers perform studies for extraction of biomarkers combining different types of data, including clinical, biological and imaging data. In its current version, ebioMelDB incorporates publicly available RNA-Seq gene expression data from GEO and TCGA, manually curated and organized in categories. It also includes the widest collection of clinical and dermoscopy images organized in 3 benign and 2 malignant categories, including Nevus, Benign Non-Nevus, Benign but Suspicious for malignancy, Melanoma and Non-Melanocytic Carcinomas, respectively. In its future versions, ebioMelDB will host our predictive models in CM diagnosis, response to treatment and prognosis based on combinations of the different data types hosted. As a first step towards this vision, we apply a machine learning classifier to predict the vital status of CM patients in different time windows based on gene expression data from TCGA.

2 Database

2.1 Image Data Collection

The image data is a collection of diverse public datasets and include:

- The dataset provided from Kawara et al. [28] (referred herein as 7-PT), which has been used for 7-point melanoma checklist criteria classification and skin lesion diagnosis, including 2022 dermoscopic and clinical images of the lesions.
- 27962 images from ISIC 2019 [29–31] Challenge dataset for dermoscopic image classification among nine different diagnostic categories.
- 33126 images from ISIC 2020 [32] Challenge for dermoscopic image classification tasks of benign and malignant skin lesions.
- 170 non-dermoscopic image dataset from Giotis et al. [33] on the computer-assisted diagnostic system MED-NODE.
- The PH^2 [34] dermoscopic image dataset which contains 200 images for common/atypical nevi and melanoma.

The different datasets include different naming conventions and different skin disease categories. Due to this high diversity, it was necessary to merge the diagnostic classes under broader categories. The broader categories we selected are 3 benign categories including Nevus (NV), Benign Non-Nevus (NNV), Benign but Suspicious for malignancy (SUS) and 2 malignant categories including Melanoma (MEL) and Non-Melanocytic Carcinomas (NMC). The grouping of the naming conventions of the different datasets is presented in Table 1.

Table 1. Naming conventions as presented in the original datasets and the respective grouping in ebioMelDB categories: Nevus (NV), Benign Non-Nevus (NNV), Benign but Suspicious for malignancy (SUS), Melanoma (MEL) and Non-Melanocytic Carcinomas (NMC)

Categories	NV	NNV	SUS	MEL	NMC
7-PT	Blue, clark, combined, congenital, dermal, recurrent, reed or spitz nevus	Dermatofibroma, lentigo, melanosis, miscellaneous, seborrheic keratosis, vascular lesion,	–	Melanoma, melanoma metastasis	Basal cell carcinoma
ISIC2019	NV	BKL, DF, VASC	AK	MEL	BCC, SCC
ISIC2020	Nevus, unknown	Cafe-au-lait macule, lentigo NOS, lichenoid keratosis	Atypical melanocytic proliferation	Melanoma	–
MED-NODE	Naevus	–	–	Melanoma	–
PH^2	Common nevus	–	Atypical nevus	Melanoma	–

Figure 1 presents the counts of images originating from each dataset when assigned to ebioMelDB categories.

Information like image, image type and diagnosis exist for images of all datasets. The next most frequent fields are the anatomical site (88.6%), sex (96.7%) and

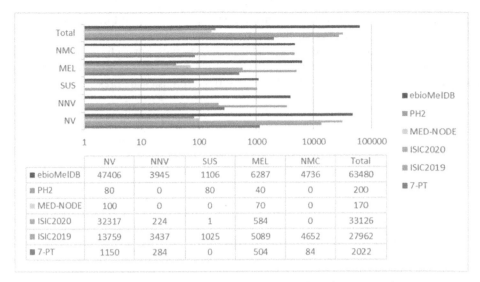

Fig. 1. Image distribution along datasets and ebioMelDB categories.

age (93.5%). The counts of dermoscopic and clinical images are 62308 and 1172, respectively.

2.2 Biological Data Collection

Biological data were collected from the NCBI Gene Expression Omnibus (GEO) [35]. GEO (http://www.ncbi.nlm.nih.gov/geo/) is a public repository for high-throughput microarray and next-generation sequencing functional genomic data sets submitted by the research community including raw data, processed data and metadata and organized in series (GSE) of datasets. To download the data and their related metadata, the R package GEOmetadb [36] was used. The keyword "melanoma" was searched against all the GSE titles, summaries and overall designs, selecting only Expression profiling by high throughput sequencing as experiment type and Homo sapiens as organism. This resulted in 291 series, which were subsequently manually curated to keep only series that actually included melanoma datasets, ending up with 178 series that consist of 4490 samples.

In order to better organize the data, we characterized them as belonging or not to a number of categories. The first group of categories is related to the origin of the biological samples and includes patients' specimens, cell lines, xenograft models and other cells. Another category is the presence or not of healthy control, non-melanoma samples to facilitate users aspiring to perform diagnostic studies. For the same reason, the category other disease indicates whether samples of another disease exist in a series. The category treatment shows that some samples of the series were treated with a specific drug or other kind of treatment to facilitate users interested in treatment studies. The category variation includes various types of perturbations in the samples, such as the overexpression or knockdown of a gene (which could be used as drug targets or help us better understand the disease mechanism), or resistance to a therapy. Finally, the category clinical information indicates whether accompanying clinical information, such as age, sex, disease state, vital status, etc. is available for the samples. For each category assigned to a series, there is also a respective field with a brief description of why the category is assigned. Summary statistics of the database series of datasets are presented in Fig. 2.

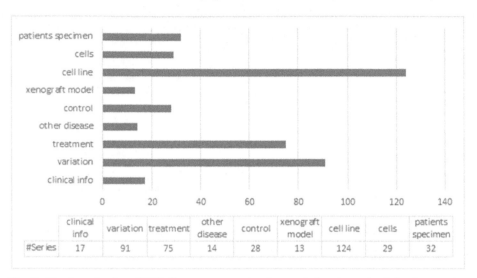

	clinical info	variation	treatment	other disease	control	xenograft model	cell line	cells	patients specimen
#Series	17	91	75	14	28	13	124	29	32

Fig. 2. Number of series of RNA-Seq gene expression datasets belonging to the defined categories.

2.3 Database Infrastructure

All the collected images and biological data are organized in a web accessible database at http://www.med.upatras.gr/ebioMelDB. One page presents the images and another one the biological data. Both are organized in datatables which are searchable and sortable. Moreover, filtering based on user defined criteria on the data categories and characteristics is available enabling the user to access in a more targeted way data of interest. For example, for the biological data, if a user is interested in series with a) patients' specimen, that also have b) clinical info, c) control samples and d) the samples count of each series is 20 or more, he applies the relevant filters and only 3 out of the 178 series are presented. Each biological series or image can be viewed in more detail in a dedicated view page. The database is developed based on the Django Web Framework, with the usage of python3.8, html5, JavaScript and SQLite and is running on a Linux server.

3 Estimating Melanoma Prognosis

3.1 Data Collection and Preprocessing

Gene expression quantification data were downloaded from the GDC Data Portal [37] of NIH. GDC hosts among others TCGA (https://www.cancer.gov/tcga) data, that has molecularly characterized over 20,000 primary cancer and matched normal samples spanning 33 cancer types. For each cancer type, a combination of molecular biology (mRNA, protein and miRNA expression, copy number, DNA, DNA methylation), clinical and whole slide images data for the same patients are provided. The TCGA-SKCM [7] project has 470 cases of patients and data ranging the following categories: simple nucleotide variation, copy number variation, transcriptome profiling, biospecimen, sequencing reads, DNA methylation and clinical. For the estimation of melanoma prognosis, we downloaded the RNA-Seq gene expression quantification files (HTSeq-Counts) with a total of 472 files for 468 cases. The respective clinical data were also downloaded. 247 of them had vital status alive, 224 dead and 1 case with not reported vital status was excluded from the analysis. Custom python scripts were created to process the single count files and merge them in one file with 471 samples (expression files) and 60488 features (genes). The vital status was also mined from the clinical data and matched to the samples as labels with python scripts.

Genes with count less than 5 reads per sample were excluded from further analysis narrowing the number of genes down to 11339. Count data normalization and statistical analysis was performed with InSyBio Biomarkers tool (https://www.insybio.com/bio markers.html). For the statistical analysis, the wilcoxon ranked sum test was employed and correction of p-values for multiple testing was performed using the Benjamini-Hochberg FDR adjustment method. Setting the adjusted p value threshold to 0.01, we identified 611 statistically significant differentially expressed genes.

3.2 Machine Learning Algorithm Description

In order to predict the patients' vital status from the gene expression data, we applied the machine learning method incorporated in the InSyBio Biomarkers tool. This method is an extension of the one presented in [38, 39] and is an ensemble dimensionality reduction technique employing a multi-objective optimization heuristic algorithm that finds the best feature subset, the best classifier among linear SVM, Radial Basis Function Kernel SVM and random forest and their optimal parameters. In this extended version, multiple models performing equally well on the user-defined goals are the final outcome. And the final prediction is the one made by the majority of the classifiers. The weights used for the goals were Selected Features Number Minimization 1, Accuracy 10, F1 score 10, F2 score 1, Precision 1, Recall 1, ROC_AUC 1, Number of SVs or Trees Minimization 1.

3.3 Results

The experiments for the prediction of the patients' vital status were performed with 5-fold cross validation and for 100 generations. The cross-validation accuracy achieved was 68.84% with specificity 70.61% and sensitivity 67.22%. The selected features were 414 and the predictions were based on 25 Random Forest models, each with different number of trees ranging from 10 to 471.

The vital status is defined by TCGA as the survival state of the person and can have values dead or alive. The time period it refers to is up to almost 30 years after the diagnosis (10863 days). Thus, we wanted to examine the vital status of the patients in a 5-year, 3-year and 1-year period. From the clinical TCGA data and the Days to death field we computed the respective labels treating again each problem as a two-class classification problem. The respective 5-fold cross validation metrics (accuracy, specificity and sensitivity), the number of selected features, the number of classification models and their characteristics are presented in Table 2. The performance metrics get better as the examined time slot gets shorter.

Table 2. 5-fold cross validation metrics (accuracy -ACC, specificity-SP and sensitivity-SEN), number of selected features, number of classification models and their characteristics in the prediction of total, 5-,3- and 1-year vital status.

	Vital status (in a ~30-year follow-up)	5-year vital status	3-year vital status	1-year vital status
Cross validation ACC	68.84%	92.46%	97.80%	100.00%
Cross validation SP	70.61%	99.69%	99.73%	100.00%
Cross validation SEN	67.22%	85.23%	95.88%	100.00%
# Selected features	414	13	163	7
# Classification models	25	11	16	4
# RF models	25 with 10–471 trees	1 with 38 trees	7 with 333–352 trees	–
# SVM models	–	10 rbf SVM with 435–471 SVs	9 rbf SVM with 471 SVs	4 rbf SVM with 282–459 SVs

Next, we wanted to compare with other methods, so we employed the SVM and Random Forest implementations of WEKA with default parameters and with 5-fold cross validation and the results are shown in Table 3. The proposed method clearly outperforms the other two methods in all cases, and the fact that the proposed method handles better imbalanced datasets is even more clear in the 5-, 3- and 1-year prediction problems where the samples of the minority class are 148, 110 and 27, respectively.

4 Discussion

CM is a skin cancer with high mortality and although diagnosis and treatment methods have made progress, its survival rate is still poor. Many studies, taking advantage of multi-omics data available in repositories like TCGA, have identified several prognostic biomarkers for CM. Identifying prognostic omics markers leads to a better understanding of the biological mechanisms underlying prognosis and also assists patient stratification, treatment selection, and prediction of prognosis paths.

Table 3. Comparison of the proposed method in terms of accuracy -ACC, specificity-SP and sensitivity-SEN in the prediction of total, 5-,3- and 1-year vital status.

Metrics	Vital status (in a ~30-year follow-up)			5-year vital status		
	ACC	SP	SEN	ACC	SP	SEN
WEKA SVM	54.14%	59.50%	48.20%	60.08%	72.10%	33.80%
WEKA RF	59.45%	63.20%	55.40%	67.94%	98.50%	1.40%
Proposed method	**68.84%**	**70.61%**	**67.22%**	**92.46%**	**99.69%**	**85.23%**
Metrics	3-year vital status			1-year vital status		
	ACC	SP	SEN	ACC	SP	SEN
WEKA SVM	65.45%	79.20%	24.50%	91.08%	96.20%	4.80%
WEKA RF	76.43%	99.70%	0.00%	94.48%	100.00%	0.00%
Proposed method	**97.80%**	**99.73%**	**95.88%**	**100.00%**	**100.00%**	**100.00%**

In the present paper, we applied a machine learning method, that has been previously shown to perform better than other state-of-the-art algorithms, on CM patients' vital status prediction based on RNA-Seq gene expression data. The accuracy achieved was 68.84% for the whole follow up period, significantly increasing with smaller time windows: 92.46% for 5-year vital status, 97.80% for 3-year and 100.00% for 1-year and significantly outperforming in all cases other implementation of Support Vector Machines and Random Forests.

Jiang et al. [14] in their effort to predict survival time, thus treating the problem as a regression problem and not a classification one, achieved a C-statistic of 0.665 using the same data and 5-fold cross validation and similarly Sheng et al. [22] achieved an AUC of 0.70, 0.69 and 0.68 for predicting 2, 3 and 5-year survival in their training set and Zeng et al. [21] an AUC of 0.701 for 1 year, 0.726 for 3 years, and 0.745 for 5 years. We also plan to apply the regression version of the proposed method to get comparative results with these studies.

Another limitation of the proposed analysis is that for the calculation of the performance metrics, we have only relied on cross validation and have not used an external test set. Testing the generated prediction models in independent RNA-Seq gene expression data is also one of our immediate plans and the data collected in ebioMelDB will be useful for this task. Additionally, the gene signatures identified include 414, 13, 163 and 7 genes for the four prediction problems, respectively. We strongly believe that by experimenting with the goals (i.e. increasing the significance of selected features minimization) of the employed machine learning method, we will manage to generate smaller gene signatures without having a classification performance drop.

Single omics may not be enough for estimating CM patient prognosis and an analysis based on multi-omics data or even better multi-modal data is necessary. This was essentially the vision before conceptualizing ebioMelDB. However, gene expression is the downstream product of other omics changes and "closest" to clinical outcomes as suggested in a number of studies and this is why it was chosen as our starting point. Ultimately, integrating omics and clinical data with imaging data is promising and we aspire that ebioMelDB will assist the research community to make the limited relevant research wider.

Data availability is important when researchers want to apply machine learning methods for disease diagnosis, response to treatment and prognosis and for CM, clinical, biological and imaging data are scattered through the web. ebioMelDB is the first database to integrate the widest collections of RNA-Seq gene expression and clinical data with clinical and dermoscopy images, all manually curated and labelled with categories. In its future versions, ebioMelDB will host our under development predictive models in CM diagnosis, response to treatment and prognosis based on combinations of the different data types hosted.

Acknowledgements. This research is co-financed by Greece and the European Union (European Social Fund- ESF) through the Operational Programme «Human Resources Development, Education and Lifelong Learning 2014-2020» in the context of the project "Biomarkers extraction from imaging and molecular biology data using computational models to assist malignant melanoma diagnosis, prognosis and treatment" (MIS 5047174).

**Operational Programme
Human Resources Development,
Education and Lifelong Learning**

European Union
European Social Fund

Co-financed by Greece and the European Union

References

1. Rebecca, V.W., Somasundaram, R., Herlyn, M.: Pre-clinical modeling of cutaneous melanoma. Nat. Commun. **11**(1), 1–9 (2020)
2. Ali, A.R.H., Li, J., Yang, G.: Automating the ABCD rule for melanoma detection: a survey. IEEE Access **8**, 83333–83346 (2020)
3. Barata, C., Celebi, M.E., Marques, J.S.: A survey of feature extraction in dermoscopy image analysis of skin cancer. IEEE J. Biomed. Health Inf. **23**(3), 1096–1109 (2018)
4. Adegun, A., Viriri, S.: Deep learning techniques for skin lesion analysis and melanoma cancer detection: a survey of state-of-the-art. Artif. Intell. Rev., 1–31 (2020)
5. Dimitriou, F., et al.: The world of melanoma: epidemiologic, genetic, and anatomic differences of melanoma across the globe. Curr. Oncol. Rep. **20**(11), 1–9 (2018)
6. Xiong, J., Bing, Z., Guo, S.: Observed survival interval: a supplement to TCGA pan-cancer clinical data resource. Cancers **11**(3), 280 (2019)
7. Akbani, R., et al.: Genomic classification of cutaneous melanoma. Cell **161**(7), 1681–1696 (2015)
8. Papadodima, O., Kontogianni, G., Piroti, G., Maglogiannis, I., Chatziioannou, A.: Genomics of cutaneous melanoma: focus on next-generation sequencing approaches and bioinformatics. J. Transl. Genet. Genomics **3** (2019)
9. Bhalla, S., Kaur, H., Dhall, A., Raghava, G.P.: Prediction and analysis of skin cancer progression using genomics profiles of patients. Sci. Rep. **9**(1), 1–16 (2019)
10. Lauss, M., Nsengimana, J., Staaf, J., Newton-Bishop, J., Jonsson, G.: Consensus of melanoma gene expression subtypes converges on biological entities. J. Invest. Dermatol. **136**(12), 2502–2505 (2016)

11. Pilla, L., et al.: Molecular and immune biomarkers for cutaneous melanoma: current status and future prospects. Cancers **12**(11), 3456 (2020)

12. Donnelly III, D., Aung, P.P., Jour, G.: The "-OMICS" facet of melanoma: heterogeneity of genomic, proteomic and metabolomic biomarkers. In: Seminars in Cancer Biology, vol. 59, pp. 165–174. Academic Press, December 2019

13. Zhang, L., et al.: OSskcm: an online survival analysis webserver for skin cutaneous melanoma based on 1085 transcriptomic profiles. Cancer Cell Int. **20**, 1–8 (2020)

14. Jiang, Y., Shi, X., Zhao, Q., Krauthammer, M., Rothberg, B.E.G., Ma, S.: Integrated analysis of multidimensional omics data on cutaneous melanoma prognosis. Genomics **107**(6), 223–230 (2016)

15. Tomczak, K., Czerwińska, P., Wiznerowicz, M.: The Cancer Genome Atlas (TCGA): An immeasurable source of knowledge. Wspolczesna Onkol. **2015**(1A), A68–A77 (2014)

16. Chen, W., Cheng, P., Jiang, J., Ren, Y., Wu, D., Xue, D.: Epigenomic and genomic analysis of transcriptome modulation in skin cutaneous melanoma. Aging (Albany NY) **12**(13), 12703 (2020)

17. Chai, H., Shi, X., Zhang, Q., Zhao, Q., Huang, Y., Ma, S.: Analysis of cancer gene expression data with an assisted robust marker identification approach. Genet. Epidemiol. **41**(8), 779–789 (2017)

18. Han, W., Huang, B., Zhao, X.Y., Shen, G.L.: Data mining of immune-related prognostic genes in metastatic melanoma microenvironment. Biosci. Rep. **40**(11) (2020)

19. Meng, L., et al.: Predicting the clinical outcome of melanoma using an immune-related gene pairs signature. PLoS ONE **15**(10), e0240331 (2020)

20. Zhao, Y., et al.: A leukocyte infiltration score defined by a gene signature predicts melanoma patient prognosis. Mol. Cancer Res. **17**(1), 109–119 (2019)

21. Zeng, Y., et al.: Exploration of the immune cell infiltration-related gene signature in the prognosis of melanoma. Aging (Albany NY) **13**(3), 3459 (2021)

22. Sheng, Y., Tong, L., Geyu, L.: An immune risk score with potential implications in prognosis and immunotherapy of metastatic melanoma. Int. Immunopharmacol. **88**, (2020)

23. Garg, M., et al.: Tumour gene expression signature in primary melanoma predicts long-term outcomes. Nat. Commun. **12**(1), 1–14 (2021)

24. Planell, N., et al.: STATegra: multi-omics data integration–a conceptual scheme with a bioinformatics pipeline. Front. Genet. **12**, 143 (2021)

25. Antonelli, L., Guarracino, M.R., Maddalena, L., Sangiovanni, M.: Integrating imaging and omics data: a review. Biomed. Signal Process. Control **52**, 264–280 (2019)

26. Peng, Y., et al.: Combining texture features of whole slide images improves prognostic prediction of recurrence-free survival for cutaneous melanoma patients. World J. Surg. Oncol **18**(1), 1–8 (2020)

27. Maglogiannis, I., Kontogianni, G., Papadodima, O., Karanikas, H., Billiris, A., Chatziioannou, A.: An integrated platform for skin cancer heterogenous and multilayered data management. J. Med. Syst. **45**(1), 1–13 (2021)

28. Kawahara, J., Daneshvar, S., Argenziano, G., Hamarneh, G.: Seven-point checklist and skin lesion classification using multitask multimodal neural nets. IEEE J. Biomed. Health Inf. **23**(2), 538–546 (2018)

29. Tschandl, P., Rosendahl, C., Kittler, H.: The HAM10000 dataset, a large collection of multi-source dermatoscopic images of common pigmented skin lesions. Sci. Data **5**, 180161 (2018)

30. Codella, N.C., et al.: Skin lesion analysis toward melanoma detection: a challenge at the 2017 international symposium on biomedical imaging (ISBI), hosted by the international skin imaging collaboration (ISIC). In: 2018 IEEE 15th International Symposium on Biomedical Imaging (ISBI 2018), pp. 168–172. IEEE, April 2018

31. Combalia, M., et al.: BCN20000: dermoscopic lesions in the wild. arXiv preprint arXiv:1908. 02288 (2019)

32. Rotemberg, V., et al.: A patient-centric dataset of images and metadata for identifying melanomas using clinical context. Sci. Data **8**(1), 1–8 (2021)
33. Giotis, I., Molders, N., Land, S., Biehl, M., Jonkman, M.F., Petkov, N.: MED-NODE: a computer-assisted melanoma diagnosis system using non-dermoscopic images. Expert Syst. Appl. **42**(19), 6578–6585 (2015)
34. Mendonça, T., Ferreira, P.M., Marques, J.S., Marcal, A.R., Rozeira, J.: PH 2-A dermoscopic image database for research and benchmarking. In: 2013 35th Annual International Conference of the IEEE Engineering in Medicine and Biology Society (EMBC), pp. 5437–5440. IEEE, July 2013
35. Barrett, T., et al.: NCBI GEO: archive for functional genomics data sets—update. Nucleic Acids Res. **41**(D1), D991–D995 (2012)
36. Zhu, Y., Davis, S., Stephens, R., Meltzer, P.S., Chen, Y.: GEOmetadb: powerful alternative search engine for the Gene Expression Omnibus. Bioinformatics **24**(23), 2798–2800 (2008)
37. Gao, G.F., et al.: Before and after: comparison of legacy and harmonized TCGA genomic data commons' data. Cell Syst. **9**(1), 24–34 (2019)
38. Corthésy, J., et al.: An adaptive pipeline to maximize isobaric tagging data in large-scale MS-based proteomics. J. Proteome Res. **17**(6), 2165–2173 (2018)
39. Gudin, J., Mavroudi, S., Korfiati, A., Theofilatos, K., Dietze, D., Hurwitz, P.: Reducing opioid prescriptions by identifying responders on topical analgesic treatment using an individualized medicine and predictive analytics approach. J. Pain Res. **13**, 1255 (2020)

Improved Biomedical Entity Recognition via Longer Context Modeling

Nikolaos Stylianou[1(✉)], Panagiotis Kosmoliaptsis[1,2], and Ioannis Vlahavas[1]

[1] Aristotle University of Thessaloniki, 54124 Thessaloniki, Greece
{nstylia,kosmoliap,vlahavas}@csd.auth.gr
[2] General Hospital of Thessaloniki "George Papanikolaou",
57010 Thessaloniki, Greece

Abstract. Biomedical Named Entity Recognition is a difficult task, aimed to identify all named entities in medical literature. The importance of the task becomes apparent as these entities are used to identify key features, enable better search results and can accelerate the process of reviewing related evidence to a medical case. This practice is known as Evidence-Based Medicine (EBM) and is globally used by medical practitioners who do not have the time to read all the latest developments in their respective fields. In this paper we propose a methodology which achieves state-of-the-art results in a plethora of Biomedical Named Entity Recognition datasets, with a lightweight approach that requires minimal training. Our model is end-to-end and capable of efficiently modeling significantly longer sequences than previous models, benefiting from inter-sentence dependencies.

Keywords: Natural Language Processing · Deep Learning ·
Biomedical Named Entity Recognition · Evidence Based Medicine

1 Introduction

Named Entity Recognition (NER) refers to the Natural Language Processing (NLP) task of identifying all the Named Entities in a span of text. It can be used as an Information Extraction (IE) tool, to identify important entities in texts, but also finds uses in many downstream tasks such as question answering, summarization, information retrieval and knowledge graph construction [20]. When the source information is from documents in the clinical domain, this task is separately identified as Biomedical Named Entity Recognition (BioNER) and the focal point is to identify entities of interest in that domain.

The entities that are recognized by BioNER systems are focused on either Disease, Chemicals, Genes, Molecules of Cells and Drugs, or a combination of the above. As a result, BioNER's domain of application extends that of classic NER systems to domain specific tasks such as, adverse drug event extraction [10], drug-drug interactions [35] and protein-protein interactions [27].

© IFIP International Federation for Information Processing 2021
Published by Springer Nature Switzerland AG 2021
I. Maglogiannis et al. (Eds.): AIAI 2021, IFIP AICT 627, pp. 45–56, 2021.
https://doi.org/10.1007/978-3-030-79150-6_4

Daily, a staggering number of new research is published in the plethora of biomedical fields, with the number of articles of interest to a medical practitioner increasing exponentially. Evidence-Based Medicine (EBM) is the practice with which medical practitioners identify all the relevant previous research, usually in the form of Clinical Trials (CTs) or Randomized Control Trials (RCTs), to create informed treatment plans. The most dominant method to achieve this is through the PICO Framework, named after its elements Population, Intervention, Comparator and Outcome [21].

A combination of advancements in both Deep Learning (DL) and Natural Language Processing (NLP) techniques has contributed significantly in the increased performance of modern BioNER systems [5,11,33]. In comparison to general purpose Named Entity Recognition (NER), BioNER systems suffer in performance due to the high variance and complexity of terms found in medical literature [3]. This complexity is worsened in the case of EBM, in which a term, e.g. "high blood sugar", can be identified in multiple classes, i.e. Population or Outcome in this case, depending on the context of the study.

Current state-of-the-art approaches across all entity domains, attempt to identify the entities described in a sequence, in a sentence by sentence manner. With such an approach, inter-sentence dependencies are never considered. Consequently, in cases such as EBM, in which entities can change their class depending on the document's context, considering such dependencies can be the determining factor between for example identifying "high blood sugar" as a Population rather than an Outcome or vice-versa.

In this work, we propose a state-of-the-art, transformer based, BioNER model. Our approach is based on Transformers, requires minimal training as it makes use of transfer learning techniques and can effectively model significantly longer sequences than traditional models. Effectively, we are able to model abstracts instead of sentences in one pass, utilizing long term dependencies during both training and inference. We evaluate our model in both Disease, Chemicals, Molecules of Cells (cell lines, genes and proteins) and EBM data, where we showcase an overall performance increase compared to the previous state-of-the-art.

2   Related Work

Biomedical Named Entity Recognition has been of significant research interest due to its distinctive applications in a plethora of scientific fields [20]. For that reason, there is an abundance of research works and datasets that refer to different field of bio-medicine [12]. Two major categories of interest have been identified in BioNER, for the task of Named Entity Recognition, identifying a specific entity type [5,11], and identifying all specified entity types using multiple datasets [13,33].

The first category is more limited in scope, with their contributions mainly focused on architectural changes that improve the performance when identifying a specific entity category. A significant number of research has been completed in such models [12], with the most recent models attempting to tackle the distinct issue in BioNER of longer entity sequences. In [11], they propose a model architecture to create a combination of unary and pairwise hidden states to increase the models expressiveness over longer entity sequences. A different approach introduces a combinatorial embedding [5], making use of two character level architectures and a word level architecture to create token representations. The expressiveness of Recurrent Neural Networks (RNNs), and more specifically Bidirectional Long Short-term Memory (BiLSTM) networks for the main model architecture has been the key component to both studies.

The focus of the second category has been on developing a more general BioNER system which is not bound to one entity type. Due to the plurality of entities and their different scopes, these entities are only identified to their highest level, i.e. Disease, Drugs, Chemical Compounds. In order to effective identify all entities, an ensemble of entity specific models based on BiLSTMs is introduced in [32]. The model is later extended with the use of Flair embeddings [33], to further increase its performance. Levering the pre-trained BioBERT model to extract more informed word representations, a multi-task learning approach is introduced in [13], with entity specific layers to handle multiple entity predictions. A significant flaw to such approaches is that while the test set is a union of the respective single entity dataset test sets, each sequence still only identifies one entity, making it easier for the respective models to build dependencies.

Evidence-Based Medicine approaches, much like the second category attempt to identify more than one entity type in each sequence. However, instead of generic bio-medicine terms, the entities are identified using the PICO Framework, and as such approached with a variety of ways. The best performing NER EBM system [26], is introducing a deep BiLSTM-based model with residual connections to model the intersequence dependencies. The current state-of-the-art model [25] is solving EBM as a Question-Answering task, using the whole documents as context to extract the PICO entities.

3   LongSeq: Our Proposed Approach

LongSeq is an end-to-end Transformer-based model that enables the effective modeling of longer sequences in each step, resulting in better overall performance. In comparison to traditional RNN based approaches, LongSeq does not suffer from vanishing gradient when modeling very long sequences [23], due to the Transformer-based architecture.

Furthermore, our approach is faster to train overall, requiring both less time per iteration as well as less training epochs than traditional approaches. This is achieved with a combination of a pre-trained language model for word representations as well as computationally efficient transformer architectures that can model such long sequences. As a result, it can model dependencies past the sentence scope of previous approaches, which can be efficiently used by Conditional Random Fields (CRF) during prediction [18].

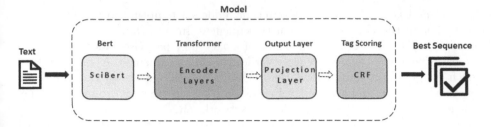

Fig. 1. LongSeq model architecture

3.1 Our Model

Our proposed model, is an end-to-end Transformer-based model consisting of a pre-trained BERT model to create contextualized word representations, stacked Transformer encoders and a CRF layer to handle predictions. Figure 1 illustrates the architecture of LongSeq.

Our model takes as input a sequence of tokens $W = (w_1, \ldots, w_l)$, where l is the max number of tokens in each input. This sequence is transformed into an embeddings sequence $X = (x_1, \ldots, x_n)$ after being passed through a BERT model, such that $x_i \in \mathbb{R}^{n \times d_{BERT}}$, where n is the number of vectors in the final sequence after preprocessing and padding and d_{BERT} is the BERT embeddings size. Each vector in X is forwarded through N stacked Transformer encoder layers, each with h number of attention heads, in order to create better representations of the input sequence. The resulting vector is of size $X \in \mathbb{R}^{n \times d_{Enc}}$, with d_{Enc} being the encoder's hidden size, which will be passed through a projection layer for dimensionality reduction to $X \in \mathbb{R}^{n \times d_{Proj}}$, followed by a CRF layer that handles predictions. The CRF uses the Viterbi algorithm to efficiently predict the most likely sequence of labels [18].

3.2 Transformer Encoders

LongSeq is modularly designed to use a number of different Transformer architectures. In our approach, we experiment with four different Transformer encoder architectures designed for computational efficiency via changes to their attention mechanisms (Fig. 2).

A Transformer can represent both an Encoder and a Decoder layer, with some architectural differences. However, in our approach we are only interested in the Encoder component. Each Transformer encoder has two sub-layers blocks, each wrapped with a normalization layer and a residual connection around them. The first block consists of a multi-headed self attention mechanism and the second consists of a position-wise fully connected feed-forward layer. Each layer takes as input a vector $X \in \mathbb{R}^{n \times d_{Enc}}$, where n is the sequence length and the d_{Enc} is the model specific hidden size, and outputs a similar sized vector. Formalized, the Transformer encoder can be expressed as:

$$E_A = \texttt{LayerNorm}(\texttt{MultiHeadSelfAttention}(X)) + X \qquad (1)$$

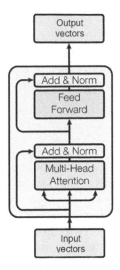

Fig. 2. Transformer encoder layer [29]

$$E_B = \texttt{LayerNorm}(\texttt{PositionFFN}(E_A)) + E_A \tag{2}$$

where X is the input vector and E_B will become the input (X) in the following Transformer layer. Detailed architectural information are provided in [29].

However, the Multi-headed self attention mechanism proposed in [29] is inefficient, leading to quadratic computational complexity – $O(n^2)$. This is attributed to the dense operation in each attention head in which each element in the sequence learns to gather from the other tokens in the sequence. As a result, the bigger the input sequence, the more computationally demanding is the model.

In our model, except from Vanilla Transformers, we consider three alternative Transformer architectures, which change the attention mechanism to introduce different forms of sparsity in order to reduce the computational complexity.

Reformer [15] is based on locality sensitive hashing (LSH). Consequently, the query-keys are hashed into buckets using a random projection. The intuition behind the LSH is that nearby vectors should maintain similar hash, and hence require less computations leading to a computational complexity of $O(n \ log(n))$. In a different approach, Longformer [2] introduces a combination of local sliding windowed attention and task-specific global attention. The introduced sparsity in the attention mechanism lowers the original quadratic computation complexity to $O(n \times w))$, where w is the window size. The last architecture we experimented with, is Linformer [30], which uses a low rank projection technique on the length dimension to project the dimensional keys and values in the Query, Key, Value attention scheme to a lower dimension (k). As a result, the computational complexity of Linformer is $O(n)$ due to k being sufficiently small and stable. A detailed survey on the efficiency of different Transformer architectures, including the aforementioned, has been conducted in [28].

4   Experiments

To evaluate the effectiveness of our approach, we compare the performance of our model on four datasets, with four different scopes (EBM, Diseases, Molecules of Cells, Chemicals). The models are tested while modeling sentence-level input as well as whole abstracts.

4.1   Data and Processing

In using four benchmark datasets, we attempt to cover the majority of biomedical fields. As shown in Table 1, in this study we use EBM-NLP [22], NCBI-Disease [8], JNLPBA [14] and SCAI-Chemicals [17], covering four different biomedical entity categories. All of the aforementioned datasets are from abstracts of publications from PubMed/MEDLINE. With the exception of EBM-NLP, which poses the restriction that the abstracts must come from CTs or RCTs type studies, the other datasets are collected using MeSH terms to limit the search results.

Table 1. Dataset characteristics

Dataset	Entities	# of Sents	# of Absts	Max words per Sent	Max words per Abst	% over 512 tokens
EBM-NLP	PICO	53397	4982	241	838	1.69%
NCBI-Disease	Disease	7421	793	124	501	0%
JNLPBA	Gene & Proteins	24716	2404	208	645	0.41%
SCAI-Chemicals	Chemicals	965	100	169	666	8.08%

Sent(s) is used to identify Sentence(s) and Abst(s) is used to identify Abstract(s).

EBM-NLP is annotated under the PICO scheme, identifying *Population, Intervention/Comparator* and *Outcome* as the three main classes. Its inherited difficulty stems from the possible change in entity class of a span of text, depending on the context. Similarly, NCBI-Disease is used to evaluate the performance of our approach on identifying *Disease* class entities in medical documents. Both of these datasets annotate entities on a higher level, which contain specific subclasses for their entity types. SCAI-Chemical identifies eight classes of Chemicals (*IUPAC, PART, TRIVIAL, ABB, SUM, FAMILY, MODIFIER* and *TRIVIAL-VAR*). Finally JNLPBA is consisted of five classes of Molecules of Cells (*DNA, RNA, CellLine, CellType, Protein*).

In all datasets we use, Inside-Outside (IO) annotations scheme, as we are not dealing with nested entities. Furthermore, we tokenize all documents using BERT's Byte-Pair Encoding (BPE) tokenizer, and adding the special CLS and SEP tokens appropriately. Lastly, we apply padding to 512 tokens when necessary.

4.2 Experimental Setup

We train LongSeq on all datasets previously described, taking as input either sentences ($LongSeq_{sent}$) or whole abstracts ($LongSeq_{abst}$). We are also using different transformer encoders, each with its own set of parameters, depending on the dataset.

In all models we experimented with different batch sizes {6,8,16,32}, learning rates {3e–3,3e–4,3e–5} and training epochs {2,4,6,8,10}. SciBERT [1] was used for word embeddings, with $d_{BERT} = 768$. Our final models are trained for 6 epochs with a learning rate of 3e–5. Having two input scopes, we used different batch sizes to consider the same amount of context per training step, with $LongSeq_{sent}$ having a batch size of 32 and $LongSeq_{abst}$ having a batch size of 4.

For all transformer encoders we considered combinations of {2,4,6,8} number of layers (N) and {2,4,6,8} number of heads (h), regardless of input scope. In our final models, Vanilla Transformer and Reformer both have $N = 6$ and $h = 6$. Longformer [2] has $N = 4$, $h = 4$ and uses the sliding chunks attention approach with a window size $w = 256$. Finally, Linformer [30] is defined with $N = 4$, $h = 4$ and $k = 512$ where k is a special parameter to define the projection length inside the sparse attention mechanism. In all models we define a maximum sequence length of 512 tokens, $d_{Enc} = 768$ and d_{Proj} to the number of entity classes.

All experiments were run using Google Colab, with a P100 GPU (16 GB vRAM). The code to reproduce our experiments is available on GitHub[1].

4.3 Results

We compare the performance of our best LongSeq model, with the state-of-the-art approaches in all four datasets in terms of macro-averaged overall Precision, Recall and F1-score, following past approaches to enable direct comparisons.

In all cases we use the reported scores from the respective publications without reproducing the experiments. We opt to use the reported scores as we are comparing LongSeq to a total of 15 models, the majority of which are only tested on one of the datasets and designed for that specific use-case.

Table 2. Results on EBM-NLP dataset

Models	Precision	Recall	F1
LongSeq	**79%**	**81%**	**79%**
EBM+ [26]	70%	70%	71%
BERT [7]	69%	66%	68%
EBM-PICO [22]	71%	64%	67%
QA-PICO [25]	–	–	75%

Table 3. Results on NCBI-Disease dataset

Models	Precision	Recall	F1
LongSeq	**96%**	**96%**	**96%**
BioBert [19]	89%	89%	89%
MT-BioNER [13]	86%	89%	88%
CNN-BiLSTM [5]	86%	87%	86%
Gramm-Cnn [4]	84%	84%	84%
CollaboNet [34]	83%	85%	84%
Spark [16]	–	–	89%

---

[1] https://github.com/AUTH-MINT/LongSeq/.

In Table 2 we present the comparative performance of our best model with recent research on EBM-NLP dataset. We achieve a 4% overall increase when identifying Population, Intervention/Comparator and Outcomes, with a 10% increase from the second best approach.

When compared to other models on NCBI-Disease (Table 3), LongSeq achieves a 7% macro-average F1 increase, compared to Spark [16] and 7% increase in all measures compared to BioBERT [19].

We follow a similar trend with a 20% overall increase when comparing the performance of LongSeq on identifying Chemical entities in Table 5. Most notably, other approaches that test on SCAI-Chemicals dataset have big variance in both Precision and Recall, leading to lackluster F1 scores. Our approach is consistent across all metrics.

Unavailingly, LongSeq performs worse from the compared models on JNLPBA dataset (Table 4). While we manage to get a high average Recall, our model struggles in terms of Precision leading to an insignificant outcome. Compared to the other approaches which use character level features to increase their Precision, LongSeq considers inputs at a token level, as per SciBERT.

We separate the scores of QA-PICO and Spark from the other implementations, in Tables 2 and 3 and 4 respectively, as the original publications do not report detailed results. We use **bold** to identify the best performance per metric and we also underline the scores of the second-best model.

Table 4. Results on JNLPBA dataset

Models	Precision	Recall	F1
CollaboNet [34]	**72%**	**82%**	**77%**
Gridach [9]	74%	77%	76%
MTM-CW [31]	70%	76%	73%
MO-MTM [6]	–	–	69%
LongSeq	67%	80%	65%
Spark [16]	–	–	81%

Table 5. Results on SCAI-Chemicals dataset

Models	Precision	Recall	F1
LongSeq	**91%**	**87%**	**88%**
ChemSpot [24]	67%	69%	68%
OSCAR3 [17]	52%	72%	60%
ChemSpot + CRF [24]	88%	28%	42%

4.4 Ablation Study

LongSeq's performance depends on both the input scope and the Transformer architecture. We performed a comparative study, in both scopes with all Transformer architectures to discover the best setup per biomedical domain. We repeated each experiment five times to account for any fluctuation in the results. In Tables 6, 7, 8 and 9 we use **bold** for the best performing architecture in abstract level and underline for the best model in sentence level.

At sentence level, there is no clear better architecture, as all approaches tend to have at least one best performance for one biomedical domain. At abstract level, Longformer performs best in all datasets, with the exception of JNLPBA, which is also our worst performing one.

Table 6. Architecture and scope results on EBM-NLP dataset

Transformer architectures	Sentences			Abstracts		
	P	R	F1	P	R	F1
Vanilla	76%	77%	75%	79%	80%	78%
Linformer	75%	79%	76%	81%	78%	78%
Reformer	78%	79%	78%	79%	80%	78%
Longformer	75%	77%	75%	**79%**	**81%**	**79%**

Table 7. Architecture and scope results on NCBI-Disease dataset

Transformer architectures	Sentences			Abstracts		
	P	R	F1	P	R	F1
Vanilla	95%	96%	95%	96%	95%	96%
Linformer	96%	95%	95%	95%	96%	96%
Reformer	45%	50%	47%	45%	50%	47%
Longformer	95%	95%	95%	**96%**	**96%**	**96%**

It is noteworthy to mention that the best performing architecture per dataset is usually different when changing the input scope from sentences to abstracts. This is on par with our initial expectations based on the different attention mechanisms used in the selected architectures.

Table 8. Architecture and scope results on JLNBPA Dataset

Transformer architectures	Sentences			Abstracts		
	P	R	F1	P	R	F1
Vanilla	63%	74%	57%	**67%**	**80%**	**65%**
Linformer	63%	77%	59%	64%	79%	63%
Reformer	62%	76%	58%	**67%**	**80%**	**65%**
Longformer	62%	75%	57%	66%	79%	63%

Table 9. Architecture and scope results on SCAI-chemical dataset

Transformer architectures	Sentences			Abstracts		
	P	R	F1	P	R	F1
Vanilla	83%	78%	75%	94%	78%	84%
Linformer	1%	11%	0%	90%	86%	87%
Reformer	85%	72%	76%	91%	87%	88%
Longformer	85%	72%	76%	91%	87%	88%

Finally, we compare the overall training times of Longformer, our best performing architecture overall, in all datasets and in both scopes in Table 10.

Table 10. Longformer training time comparison

Dataset	Sentences	Abstracts
EBM-NLP	722 m 38 s	93 m 19 s
NCBI	111 m 40 s	15 m 52 s
JNLPBA	455 m 13 s	49 m 47 s
SCAI-Chemical	24 m 47 s	3 m 2 s

From Table 10, it becomes obvious that models that use abstracts need much less time for training due to smaller number of instances (Table 1 – 3rd & 4th columns) in otherwise using sentences and due to less required backward optimization steps.

5   Discussion

In this study we presented a novel NER architecture, with stacked Transformers, for BioNER. Our approach can be trained on longer sequences that previous approaches due to the novel Transformer architecture and does not suffer from vanishing gradient. We showcased state-of-the-art performance in three of the four biomedical domains that we tested our approach, boasting an average 10% overall increase for Disease, EBM and Chemicals.

Our model makes used of SciBERT, a pre-trained BERT language model on scientific documents. This leads to word representations and requires less training time. We also compare our architecture with four different Transformer architectures, the Vanilla Transformer and three other approaches designed for computational efficiency by introducing attention sparsity.

We experimentally prove that Longformer is more suitable for the majority of cases, while Reformer and Vanilla, are better suited when predicting Molecules of Cells. Furthermore, we show a degrade performance in Molecules of Cells compared to other architectures which is attributed to lacking word representations for this task and absence of character level features.

LongSeq utilizes the whole abstract instead of each individual sentence as an input, leading to better performance and faster training times. This is due to the fact that in sentence level the number of predictions required is increased due to sentence padding at batch level. This increased number of predictions and error propagation cycles is computationally expensive and time consuming. Moreover, our approach instills more context to each sequence leading to better predictions.

6   Conclusions

In this paper we introduced LongSeq, a long context BioNER model. LongSeq leverages the contextual information of the whole abstract, which along with a combination of stacked Transformers results in state-of-the-art performance in EBM, Disease and Chemical identification. We also experimentally evaluate the performance of different Transformer architectures in the task, emerging Longformer as the best option concerning overall performance.

In the future, we aim to expand our current work to consider both word and character level features to increase generalizability and cover more medical domains of applications, creating a holistic approach to medical information extraction.

References

1. Beltagy, I., Lo, K., Cohan, A.: Scibert: A pretrained language model for scientific text. arXiv preprint arXiv:1903.10676 (2019)
2. Beltagy, I., Peters, M.E., Cohan, A.: Longformer: The long-document transformer. arXiv preprint arXiv:2004.05150 (2020)

3. Campos, D., Matos, S., Oliveira, J.L.: Biomedical named entity recognition: a survey of machine-learning tools. Theory Appl. Adv. Text Mining **11**, 175–195 (2012)
4. Cho, H., Lee, H.: Biomedical named entity recognition using deep neural networks with contextual information. BMC Bioinf **20**(1), 1–11 (2019)
5. Cho, M., Ha, J., Park, C., Park, S.: Combinatorial feature embedding based on CNN and LSTM for biomedical named entity recognition. J. Biomed. Inf. **103**, 103381 (2020)
6. Crichton, G., Pyysalo, S., Chiu, B., Korhonen, A.: A neural network multi-task learning approach to biomedical named entity recognition. BMC Bioinf **18**(1), 1–14 (2017)
7. Devlin, J., Chang, M.W., Lee, K., Toutanova, K.: Bert: Pre-training of deep bidirectional transformers for language understanding. arXiv preprint arXiv:1810.04805 (2018)
8. Doğan, R.I., Leaman, R., Lu, Z.: Ncbi disease corpus: a resource for disease name recognition and concept normalization. J. Biomed. Inf. **47**, 1–10 (2014)
9. Gridach, M.: Character-level neural network for biomedical named entity recognition. J. Biomed. Inf. **70**, 85–91 (2017)
10. Gurulingappa, H., Mateen-Rajpu, A., Toldo, L.: Extraction of potential adverse drug events from medical case reports. J. Biomed. Inf. **3**(1), 1–10 (2012)
11. Hong, S., Lee, J.G.: Dtranner: biomedical named entity recognition with deep learning-based label-label transition model. BMC Bioinf **21**(1), 53 (2020)
12. Huang, M.S., Lai, P.T., Lin, P.Y., You, Y.T., Tsai, R.T.H., Hsu, W.L.: Biomedical named entity recognition and linking datasets: survey and our recent development. Brief. Bioinf. **21**(6), 2219–2238 (2020)
13. Khan, M.R., Ziyadi, M., AbdelHady, M.: Mt-bioner: Multi-task learning for biomedical named entity recognition using deep bidirectional transformers. arXiv preprint arXiv:2001.08904 (2020)
14. Kim, J.D., Ohta, T., Tsuruoka, Y., Tateisi, Y., Collier, N.: Introduction to the bio-entity recognition task at jnlpba. In: Proceedings of the International Joint Workshop on Natural Language Processing in Biomedicine and its Applications, pp. 70–75. Citeseer (2004)
15. Kitaev, N., Kaiser, Ł., Levskaya, A.: Reformer: The efficient transformer. arXiv preprint arXiv:2001.04451 (2020)
16. Kocaman, V., Talby, D.: Biomedical named entity recognition at scale. arXiv preprint arXiv:2011.06315 (2020)
17. Kolárik, C., Klinger, R., Friedrich, C.M., Hofmann-Apitius, M., Fluck, J.: Chemical names: terminological resources and corpora annotation. In: Workshop on Building and Evaluating Resources for Biomedical Text Mining (6th edition of the Language Resources and Evaluation Conference) (2008)
18. Lafferty, J.D., McCallum, A., Pereira, F.C.N.: Conditional random fields: probabilistic models for segmenting and labeling sequence data. In: Proceedings of the Eighteenth International Conference on Machine Learning, ICML 2001, pp. 282–289. Morgan Kaufmann Publishers Inc., San Francisco (2001)
19. Lee, J., et al.: Biobert: a pre-trained biomedical language representation model for biomedical text mining. Bioinformatics **36**(4), 1234–1240 (2020)
20. Li, J., Sun, A., Han, J., Li, C.: A survey on deep learning for named entity recognition. IEEE Trans. Knowl. Data Eng. (2020)

21. Methley, A.M., Campbell, S., Chew-Graham, C., McNally, R., Cheraghi-Sohi, S.: Pico, picos and spider: a comparison study of specificity and sensitivity in three search tools for qualitative systematic reviews. BMC Health Serv. Res. **14**(1), 1–10 (2014)

22. Nye, B., et al.: A corpus with multi-level annotations of patients, interventions and outcomes to support language processing for medical literature. In: Proceedings of the Conference. Association for Computational Linguistics, Meeting, vol. 2018, p. 197. NIH Public Access (2018)

23. Pascanu, R., Mikolov, T., Bengio, Y.: Understanding the exploding gradient problem. CoRR abs/1211.5063 (2012). http://arxiv.org/abs/1211.5063

24. Rocktäschel, T., Weidlich, M., Leser, U.: Chemspot: a hybrid system for chemical named entity recognition. Bioinformatics **28**(12), 1633–1640 (2012)

25. Schmidt, L., Weeds, J., Higgins, J.: Data mining in clinical trial text: Transformers for classification and question answering tasks. arXiv preprint arXiv:2001.11268 (2020)

26. Stylianou, N., Razis, G., Goulis, D.G., Vlahavas, I.: Ebm+: advancing evidence-based medicine via two level automatic identification of populations, interventions, outcomes in medical literature. Artif. Intell. Med. **108**, 101949 (2020)

27. Szklarczyk, D., et al.: String v10: protein-protein interaction networks, integrated over the tree of life. Nucl. Acids Res. **43**(D1), D447–D452 (2015)

28. Tay, Y., Dehghani, M., Bahri, D., Metzler, D.: Efficient transformers: A survey. arXiv preprint arXiv:2009.06732 (2020)

29. Vaswani, A., et al.: Attention is all you need. In: Guyon, I., et al. (eds.) Advances in Neural Information Processing Systems, vol. 30, pp. 5998–6008. Curran Associates, Inc. (2017)

30. Wang, S., Li, B., Khabsa, M., Fang, H., Ma, H.: Linformer: Self-attention with linear complexity. arXiv preprint arXiv:2006.04768 (2020)

31. Wang, X., et al.: Cross-type biomedical named entity recognition with deep multi-task learning. Bioinformatics **35**(10), 1745–1752 (2019)

32. Weber, L., Münchmeyer, J., Rocktäschel, T., Habibi, M., Leser, U.: Huner: improving biomedical ner with pretraining. Bioinformatics **36**(1), 295–302 (2020)

33. Weber, L., Sänger, M., Münchmeyer, J., Habibi, M., Leser, U., Akbik, A.: Hun-Flair: an easy-to-use tool for state-of-the-art biomedical named entity recognition. Bioinformatics (2021). https://doi.org/10.1093/bioinformatics/btab042

34. Yoon, W., So, C.H., Lee, J., Kang, J.: Collabonet: collaboration of deep neural networks for biomedical named entity recognition. BMC Bioinf. **20**(10), 55–65 (2019)

35. Zhang, W., Chen, Y., Liu, F., Luo, F., Tian, G., Li, X.: Predicting potential drug-drug interactions by integrating chemical, biological, phenotypic and network data. BMC Bioinf **18**(1), 1–12 (2017)

Scalable NPairLoss-Based Deep-ECG for ECG Verification

Yu-Shan Tai[1]($\boxtimes$), Yi-Ta Chen[2]($\boxtimes$), and (Andy) An-Yeu Wu[2]($\boxtimes$)

[1] Department of Electrical Engineering, National Taiwan University, Taipei, Taiwan
`clover@access.ee.ntu.edu.tw`
[2] Graduate Institute of Electronics Engineering, National Taiwan University, Taipei, Taiwan
`edan@access.ee.ntu.edu.tw, andywu@ntu.edu.tw`

Abstract. In recent years, Electrocardiogram (ECG) applications are blooming, such as cardiovascular disease detection and mental condition assessment. To protect the sensitive ECG data from data breach, ECG biometrics system are proposed. Compared to the traditional biometric systems, ECG biometric is known to be ubiquitous, difficult to counterfeit and more suitable in cleanroom or IC fabs. ECG biometric system mainly contains identification task and verification task, and Deep-ECG is the state-of-the-art work in both tasks. However, Deep-ECG only trained on one specific dataset, which ignored the intra-variability of different ECG signals across different situations. Moreover, Deep-ECG used cross-entropy loss to train the deep convolutional neural networks (CNN) model, which is not the most appropriate loss function for such embedding-based problem. In this paper, to solve the above problems, we proposed a scalable NPairLoss-based Deep-ECG (SNL-Deep-ECG) system for ECG verification on a hybrid dataset, mixed with four public ECG datasets. We modify the preprocessing method and trained the deep CNN model with NPairLoss. Compared with Deep-ECG, SNL-Deep-ECG can reduce 90% of the signal collection time during inference with only 0.9% AUC dropped. Moreover, SNL-Deep-ECG outperforms Deep-ECG for approximately 3.5% Area Under ROC Curve (AUC) score in the hybrid dataset. Moreover, SNL-Deep-ECG can maintain its verification performance over the increasing number of the subjects, and thus to be scalable in terms of subject number. The final performance of the proposed SNL-Deep-ECG is 0.975/0.970 AUC score on the seen/unseen-subject task.

Keywords: Biometrics · ECG · Deep learning

1 Introduction

The ECG is the most commonly used non-invasive tool to collect bio-signals from the heart over a period of time. Therefore, by analyzing ECG signals, we can diagnose several cardiovascular diseases, such as atrioventricular block, ventricular tachycardia and atrial fibrillation [1]. On the other hand, we can also assess the subject's mental condition, such as emotion, mental workload, and sustained attention from ECG signals, too. Thus, by

© IFIP International Federation for Information Processing 2021
Published by Springer Nature Switzerland AG 2021
I. Maglogiannis et al. (Eds.): AIAI 2021, IFIP AICT 627, pp. 57–68, 2021.
https://doi.org/10.1007/978-3-030-79150-6_5

getting a specific subject's ECG, we can obtain lots of personal information from it. To protect the subject's ECG signals from data breach, biometric system is required. The definition of a biometric system is to check the identity of the collected signal. Although the traditional biometric system using fingerprint and face is popular, it still has several disadvantages [2]:

- Traditional biometrics can be easily imitated or artificially cracked, which may make users' security exposed in high risk.
- In several scenarios such as in cleanroom or IC fabs, where workers need to wear gloves, masks, or goggles, traditional biometrics, such as fingerprint, face, iris, would hardly be measured without taking off the equipment.

Therefore, researches on ECG biometrics have gained more and more attention. There are some advantages of the ECG biometrics system:

- ECG signals can only be measured from living people. Therefore, ECG signals are more difficult to counterfeit and can also be used to detect the liveness of the subject.
- ECG signals contain clinical information. Therefore, they can not only be used for recognition but also for other applications, such as disease detection, at the same time.
- Users don't need extra operations to get long time periods ECG signals. Hence, ECG signals are also suitable for long-term periodic re-authentication.

However, since ECG performs high interclass variability due to sensor placement or users' motion, there still exist some challenges to design a highly accurate ECG biometric system.

When it comes to ECG biometrics, two of the most popular tasks are identification and verification. The goal of identification is to classify who the person is in a priorly known subject pool, while verification is to check whether who someone claims to be is the same with his/her real identity. So far, most studies about ECG biometrics put emphasis on identification, but fewer researchers take attention to using ECG for verification. Thus, our work would focus on how to improve the existed ECG verification system. Deep-ECG [3] is the state-of-the-art to tackle the above two tasks until now. The authors of [3] designed a model composed of deep CNN to extract high-level features from the preprocessed ECG signal. During the training phase, Deep-ECG applied cross-entropy loss on output of the model and user id pairs to train the whole network. During inferencing, if the task is identification, then the output neuron with the largest value would be the predicted user id. During verification, they calculate the distance between two output vectors before the fully connected layer of the model from two different input data and determine whether they are from the same user or not. The training and inferencing flows of Deep-ECG [3] are shown in Fig. 1a.

Although Deep-ECG outperformed the other works in both identification and verification task, there exist several issues to be discussed. First, their model is trained on a single dataset, which ignores the intra-variability of different ECG signals across different situations, such as collection methods, kind of sensors and sensor placement. Second, the loss function used in Deep-ECG [3] is the cross-entropy loss, which is computed using the model output probability and the ground truth. Therefore, it outperforms

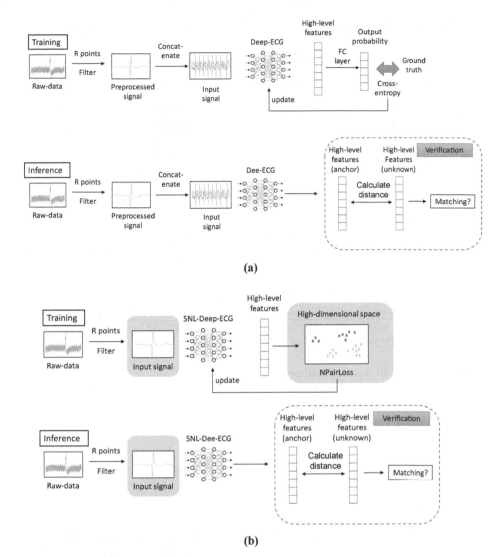

Fig. 1. (a) The flowchart of Deep-ECG; (b) the flowchart of proposed SNL-Deep-ECG, and the contributions are marked in red. (Color figure online)

other works in identification tasks, which is classification-based problems, as expected. Whereas, verification is an embedding-based problem, the performance of the cross-entropy loss might drop when the verification task becomes harder. In order to enhance deep learning-based method in ECG verification, we propose scalable NPairLoss-based deep-ECG (SNL-Deep-ECG) verification system as shown in Fig. 1b.

The three main contributions are as follows and shown in Table 1:

(1) Applying NPairLoss to train the SNL-Deep-ECG: This is the first work to apply embedding loss in the ECG verification task. We select NPairLoss as the loss function of

Table 1. Comparison between original Deep-ECG and proposed SNL-Deep-ECG.

	Deep-ECG	SNL-Deep-ECG	Description
Loss function	Cross-entropy	NPairLoss	Proposed method is scalable to larger # subjects in ECG verification task.
Signal period	8 heartbeats	1 heartbeat	Proposed method saves signal collection time.
Dataset	Single	Mixed	There is higher variability and larger amount of data in the proposed mixed dataset.

the model, which is computed by the relation of output embeddings instead of labels and output probabilities to perform better in the ECG verification task. From the experiment results, SNL-Deep-ECG outperforms Deep-ECG approximately 2.5% AUC and scores 0.969 AUC in the hybrid dataset.

(2) Reduce the signal collection time during verification: We modify the preprocessing method of the Deep-ECG framework, from concatenating 8 QRS segmentations to only using one ECG pulse. Our method reduces 90% of the signal collection time with only 0.9% AUC degradation.

(3) Generate hybrid dataset settings: This is the first study to mix four different datasets together to test the capability of the verification system, and therefore the variety and the amount of data are much higher than all of the existed datasets, and is more similar to the real-world scenario.

2   Related Works

2.1   ECG Biometrics

ECG biometric systems can be classified into three ways according to the features used for recognition, which are fiducial, non-fiducial, and hybrid methods [4]. In a healthy ECG signal, there exists 6 fiducial points: P, Q, R, S, T and U. Since R point is the highest peak in one heartbeat, it is the easiest to be searched and is usually used for segmentation. Fiducial methods extract features from the fiducial points, such as amplitude, angle, or some dynamic features. For example, the authors of [5] converted the raw ECG signals into latency and amplitude features, which are obtained from the fiducial points; the authors of [6] took QRS signals with maximum cross-correlation and the average pattern as the template, afterwards, calculating the similarity score between input signals and each template. As for non-fiducial methods, discriminative information directly extracted from the ECG waveform is used instead of considering fiducial points. Take [5] as an instance, the authors applied non-uniform quantization to the ECG signals, and then applied string matching for classification. Another example is [7]. They utilized a sliding window to obtain signal segments with fixed length, and then generated a codebook by k-means. Afterwards, they calculated the appearance of specific codewords and received the bag-of-words (BOW) representation of each signal. Finally, they fed the vectors into a SVM classifier and obtained the final prediction. Lastly, hybrid methods combined the above two different ways to classify the target signal.

2.2 Deep-ECG

Different from the above methods, which required predefined feature sets from domain experts, Deep-ECG [3] used a deep CNN to extract discriminative features in a data-dependent manner and received state-of-the-art results in ECG biometrics. Deep-ECG [3] got 100% identification accuracy for Physikalisch-Technische Bundesanstalt (PTB) Diagnostic ECG Database [8] and outperformed the correlation-based method in the verification task. In Deep-ECG, the ECG signals are segmented by R points and fed into a deep CNN to extract their high-level features. Finally, these features are used in both identification and verification tasks. The flow chart of Deep-ECG [3] is shown in Fig. 1a, which includes signal preprocessing, CNN feature extraction, and recognition.

In the signal preprocessing, noise was striped by a notch infinite impulse response (IIR) filter and a third order high-pass Butterworth filter with cutoff frequency of 0.5 Hz. After that, they applied a time window of 0.125 s for each R point and concatenated the most discriminative windows with cross-correlation. Finally, they subtracted the signals by their mean value and multiplied by 256.

The CNN in Deep-ECG is composed of six convolution layers followed by Rectified Linear Unit (ReLU) layers, three Local Response Normalization (LRN) layers, one dropout layer, and a fully connected layer as well as a Soft-max layer used for identification. The model is trained with Stochastic gradient descent (SGD) and updated by the cross-entropy loss. The above-mentioned architecture is optimized empirically.

After extracting features, the output vectors can be used for identification or verification. For identification, the output dimension will be reduced to be the same as the number of class by a fully-connected layer, and a soft-max layer transforms the output to [0, 1], representing the probability of belonging to each class. The system will further output the class with maximum corresponding probability as the predicted identity. As for verification, fully-connected layer and soft-max layer are not included. The output vectors will directly be used to compute Euclidean distance with another output vector from different source. If the distance is smaller than a predetermined threshold, they will be considered from the same user, and vice versa.

3   The Proposed Scalable NPairLoss-Based Deep-ECG System

Since embedding-based NPairLoss [9] is calculated by the distance between different embeddings, it has a competitive edge over the cross-entropy loss in the verification tasks, which is also an embedding-based problem. Therefore, we propose another framework—Scalable NPairLoss-based Deep-ECG (SNL-Deep-ECG) comparing to Deep-ECG, replacing the original loss function from cross-entropy to NPairLoss. On the other hand, we removed the concatenation step from the original signal preprocessing, which reduce the required length of input signals with slight degradation of AUC.

3.1 Signal Preprocessing

First, we use a butterworth band pass filter with $f_{low} = 1$ Hz and $f_{high} = 40$ Hz to remove noise and then normalize signals to [0, 1]. Second, we use a 1-second window to select the surrounding 200 points for each R point as shown in Fig. 2. In general, a normal heart rate for adults ranges from 60 to 100 beats/min, so there are 1 to 2 heartbeats contained in the window in most cases. Compared to the original settings of Deep-ECG, they concatenated eight heartbeats together as one input signal. In other words, the system of Deep-ECG required to wait until collecting enough signals, while proposed SNL-Deep-ECG can train and recognize with only one heartbeat.

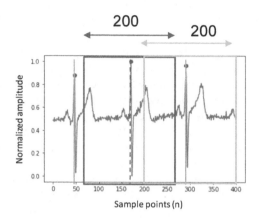

Fig. 2. The main difference between the proposed preprocessing methods and Deep-ECG.

3.2 Training Phase

In the training phase, we extract hard data by MultiSimilarityMiner [10], which selects hard samples according to the following equations:

$$S(anchor, positive) < \max(S(anchor, k) + \in) \forall \, y_{anchor} \neq y_k, \tag{1}$$

$$S(anchor, negative) > \min(S(anchor, k) - \in) \forall \, y_{anchor} = y_k. \tag{2}$$

Positive samples and negative samples stand for signals from the user of anchor and signals from different users respectively. $S(x, y)$ stands for the cosine similarity between the two input embeddings, y_x is the corresponding label of sample x, and $\in$ is the determined margin term.

Since verification is an embedding-based task, we apply NPairLoss to train our model. The goal of the embedding-based loss functions [11] are utilizing the relationships among sample points to make the model capable of projecting raw data to a high dimensional space, where similar data are close together and dissimilar ones are far apart. NPairLoss [9] is known for its stability and high convergence rate during training. For each anchor in a training batch, a positive sample and N-1 negative samples will

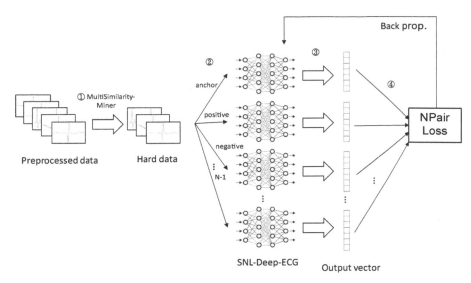

Fig. 3. The training flowchart of SNL-Deep-ECG. 1) Use MultiSimilarityMiner to select hard data. 2) Select a positive sample and N-1 negative samples corresponding to the anchor. 3) Feed selected samples to SNL-Deep-ECG and get their embeddings. 4) Calculate NPairLoss by embedding distances between anchor and other samples, and then update the model by iterative back propagation.

be selected. After that, we feed these samples to our model and get their corresponding embeddings. Eventually, we calculate NPairLoss by their embedding distances with anchor, and the anchor will gradually approach the positive sample and keep away from negative samples after updating the model by iterative back propagation. Intuitively, there are batch_size × (N + 1) data needed to calculate their embeddings in each training batch, which leads to huge computational overhead. However, an efficient way is proposed to solve this problem. In each training phase, two data will be selected from each class to serve as its anchor and positive sample, which can be displayed as: $\{f(x_1), f(x'_1), f(x_2), f(x'_2), \ldots, f(x_N), f(x'_N)\}$. As for negative samples, they directly use the positive samples from other classes except the class of anchor. For example, $\{f(x'_2), f(x'_3) \ldots, f(x'_N)\}$ are treated as the negative samples of anchor x_1, and $\{f(x'_1), f(x'_3) \ldots, f(x'_N)\}$ are for x_2. By NPairLoss proposed method, only 2N embeddings are calculated in each training batch, reducing the overall computations and making this algorithm feasible. NPairLoss [9] is formulated as follows:

$$L_{NPair} = \frac{1}{N} \sum_{i=1}^{N} \log\left(1 + \sum_{j \neq i} \exp(dist(f(x_i), f(x'_i)) - dist(f(x_i), f(x'_j)))\right). \tag{3}$$

3.3 Inference Phase

During the inference phase, two signals will be sent into the system at the same time, which are anchor and unknown, representing the claimed identity and the real input

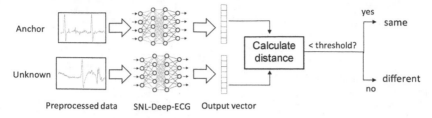

Fig. 4. The inference flow chart of proposed SNL-Deep-ECG.

identity respectively. The system will calculate the embeddings of these two signals first, and then output the Euclidean distance between them. If the distance is smaller than the threshold, the two signals are considered from the same person, and vice versa. The flow chart of inference is shown in Fig. 4. The evaluation metric we used to judge performance is the AUC.

4 Experiments

In this section, we will introduce how we design our hybrid dataset, as well as the settings and results of three experiments, which include comparing the preprocessing methods between Deep-ECG and SNL-Deep-ECG, and comparing the performance between Deep-ECG and SNL-Deep-ECG while the subject number included in the training process increased.

4.1 Dataset Design and Experimental Settings

Since most available datasets have the limitation of user number, using only one dataset to train and evaluate the model performance can hardly show the generalizability on the real-world scenario. Therefore, we mixed four datasets from different source together, making a hybrid dataset with higher variety and larger amount of data than all the other datasets. To keep consistency, we resampled all these data into the same frequency, which is 200 Hz.

The aforementioned four datasets are: ECG-ID, You Snooze You Win, Telemetric and Holter ECG Warehouse (THEW), and MIT-BIH Normal Sinus Rhythm Database.

a. **ECG-ID** [8] contains 310 ECG recordings from 90 individuals of 20 s. The users are composed of 44 men and 46 women aged from 13 to 75 years old, who were the author's student, colleagues, and friends. The number of records of each person ranges from 2 to 20.

b. **You Snooze You Win** [8] is The PhysioNet Computing in Cardiology Challenge 2018, which aims to detect arousal during sleeping. The dataset includes 994 users in training set and 989 users in testing set, which is the largest publicly available ECG dataset. All the signals are recorded during these users slept, and this dataset also contains other signals such as electroencephalography (EEG), electromyography (EMG), and electrooculography (EOG) to be further investigated.

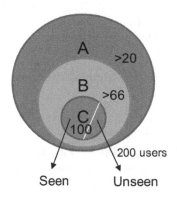

Fig. 5. The schematic diagram of the hybrid dataset design according to different number of data for each subject. The entire hybrid dataset is separated into A, B, and C categories. In category C, several subjects are preserved to be the testing data of the unseen-subject dataset.

c. **Telemetric and Holter ECG Warehouse (THEW)** [12] contains three-lead 24 h' recordings from 202 healthy subjects from the Intercity Digital Electrocardiogram Alliance (IDEAL) database. Among these users, 100 of them are male, another 100 are female, and 2 are undefined.

d. **MIT-BIH Normal Sinus Rhythm Database** [8] includes long-term ECG signals from 18 individuals without significant arrhythmias referred to Beth Israel Deaconess Medical Center. There are 5 men, aged from 26 to 45, and 13 women, aged from 20 to 50, contained in this dataset.

After mixing the aforementioned four datasets, we divided the subjects into 3 sets according to their number of data, which is shown in Fig. 5:

A. *Subjects with number of data larger or equal to 20 but less than 66* would be used for training, while those who contain fewer valid data are abandoned due to data insufficiency.

B. *Subjects with number of data larger or equal to 66 but less than 100* would divide their data into two parts evenly, and put them in training set and validation set respectively.

C. *Subjects with number of data larger or equal to 100* would just select 100 of their data, and put them in training, validation, and testing set evenly while testing data are those late in chronological order. Then, we randomly select 200 subjects from C set to serve as the unseen testing set, which is only used for testing the generalization performance.

To evaluate the performance of verification tasks, area under ROC curve (AUC) and equal error rate (EER) are the two most popularly used metrics [3, 5–7]. In fact, EER is a point of ROC curve where the false acceptance rate and the false rejection rate are equal. On the other hand, AUC score measures the area under the ROC curve which is meant to be the overall performance of a verification system. Therefore, we select AUC score as our evaluation metric for the following experiment. The proposed SNL-Deep-ECG and its experiment are implemented using pytorch 1.6.0 based on python 3.9.1.

4.2 Comparison of the Preprocess Methods Between Deep-ECG and SNL-Deep-ECG

As mentioned in Sect. 3.1, Deep-ECG and proposed SNL-Deep-ECG used different period of signals as input data. In Deep-ECG, one preprocessed data containing eight concatenated heartbeats, while SNL-Deep-ECG just used signals of one second period. As a consequence, Deep-ECG requires to wait until collecting enough heartbeats before inferencing, which are time consuming. In Table 2, we show the average required signal period of Deep-ECG and SNL-Deep-ECG and their corresponding AUC for unseen-subject test. Comparing to Deep-ECG, SNL-Deep-ECG can reduce 90% of the waiting time during verification with only 0.009 AUC dropped. This experiment result shows that our preprocessing method is located at a better trade-off between the signal collection time and verification performance.

Table 2. The average required signal period for each input data of different methods and their corresponding AUC with number of class is 1500.

Method	Signal period (s)	AUC Score
Deep-ECG	9.47	0.984
SNL-Deep-ECG	1(-89.45%)	0.975(-0.009)

4.3 Comparison Verification Performance Between Deep-ECG and SNL-Deep-ECG in Terms of Number of Class

In this section, we use different number of class which ranges from 100 to 1500, and observe how this affect the performance of both Deep-ECG and SNL-Deep-ECG. Number of class means the amount of users selected from total training set to train the two models respectively. For example, number of class is 100 means the model is just trained with the data of 100 subjects, and it would be tested by the same 100 subjects during seen test and tested by the 200 subjects during the unseen test.

First, we test the performance of Deep-ECG on the task. We trained the model for 500 epochs with learning rate of 1e−5, batch size of 125 samples, early stop with patience of 5, number of trials is 5, and used Adam as our optimizer. The results are shown in Fig. 6, and the blue and orange lines stand for AUC of Deep-ECG for seen-subject test and unseen-subject test respectively. In Fig. 6, we can observe that the performance of unseen-subject test is lower than seen-subject test, since the model was trained with data from the same subjects from the seen-subject test.

On the other hand, the left part of the two curves in Fig. 6, where number of class ranges from 100 to 500, is ascending roughly. However, on the right part where number

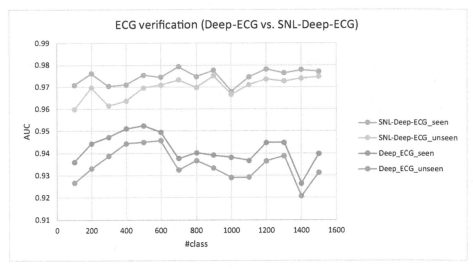

Fig. 6. AUC of Deep-ECG and proposed SNL-Deep-ECG for ECG verification with different number of class

of class becomes larger and larger, the performance seems to drop. In the beginning, the number of class is small, which also implies training data is scarce. As a consequence, increasing the number of classes improves the data sufficiency and makes the model trained better. Nevertheless, when the performance reaches the peak, keeping adding more classes would enhance the difficulty of the task since classifying from thousands of subjects is of course harder than the same task for hundreds of subjects. By the result, we can come to the conclusion that verification performance of cross entropy drops when number of class becomes larger and larger.

In the next step, we operate the same experiment but instead using our proposed SNL-Deep-ECG. The results are shown in the grey and yellow curves of Fig. 6. We trained the model for 500 epochs with learning rate of 1e−4, weight decay of 5e−4, batch size of 500 samples, number of trials is 5, and early stop with patience of 5. We use Adam as our optimizer, and utilize Cosine Similarity to calculate distance as well as LpRegularizer to regularize embedding for NPairLoss [9].

We can observe that SNL-Deep-ECG works well at both small and large class number, and outperforms original Deep-ECG in most cases. The average seen/unseen AUC among different number of class of Deep-ECG are 0.942/0.935, while these of SNL-Deep-ECG are 0.975/0.970, which improves 0.032/0.035. Moreover, the tendency of AUC is ascending with the number of class. How makes SNL-Deep-ECG capable of solving more difficult problem is due to its higher computational complexity comparing to Deep-ECG. We found that SNL-Deep-ECG took 1.5 longer time to train than Deep-ECG per epoch.

5 Conclusions

In this work, we propose SNL-Deep-ECG for the ECG verification task. To test the model with high-variability ECG data, we propose a hybrid dataset by mixing four open ECG datasets. Moreover, to improve the usability of the ECG verification system, we simplified the preprocessing procedure, which saves 90% of the collection time. In addition, we propose to apply NPairLoss to train the model and SNL-Deep-ECG outperforms Deep-ECG by 3.5% AUC score on the hybrid dataset. The final performance of SNL-Deep-ECG is 0.975/0.970 AUC score on the seen/unseen-subject task.

References

1. Hong, S., Zhou, Y., Shang, J., Xiao, C., Sun, J.: Opportunities and challenges of deep learning methods for electrocardiogram data: a systematic review (2020)
2. Chou, C.-Y., Pua, Y.-W., Sun, T.-W., Wu, A.-Y.: Compressed-domain ECG-Based biometric user identification using compressive analysis. Sensors **20**, 3279 (2020)
3. Donida Labati, R., Muñoz, E., Piuri, V., Sassi, R., Scotti, F.: Deep-ECG: convolutional neural networks for ECG biometric recognition. Pattern Recognit. Lett. **126**, 78–85 (2019)
4. Odinaka, I., Lai, P., Kaplan, A.D., O'Sullivan, J.A., Sirevaag, E.J., Rohrbaugh, J.W.: ECG biometric recognition: a comparative analysis. IEEE Trans. Inf. Forensi. Secur. **7**, 1812–1824 (2012)
5. Pereira Coutinho, D., Silva, H., Gamboa, H., Fred, A., Figueiredo, M.: Novel fiducial and non-fiducial approaches to electrocardiogram-based biometric systems. IET Biom. **2**, 64–75 (2013)
6. Labati, R.D., Sassi, R., Scotti, F.: ECG biometric recognition: permanence analysis of QRS signals for 24 hours continuous authentication. In: 2013 IEEE International Workshop on Information Forensics and Security (WIFS) (2013)
7. Ciocoiu, I.B.: Comparative analysis of bag-of-words models for ECG-based biometrics. IET Biom. **6**, 495–502 (2017)
8. Goldberger Ary, L., et al.: PhysioBank, PhysioToolkit, and PhysioNet. Circulation **101**, e215–e220 (2000)
9. Sohn, K.: Improved deep metric learning with multi-class N-pair loss objective. In: Advances in Neural Information Processing Systems (2016)
10. Wang, X., Han, X., Huang, W., Dong, D., Scott, M.R.: Multi-similarity loss with general pair weighting for deep metric learning (2020)
11. Musgrave, K., Belongie, S., Lim, S.-N.: A metric learning reality check. In: Vedaldi, A., Bischof, H., Brox, T., Frahm, J.-M. (eds.) ECCV 2020. LNCS, vol. 12370, pp. 681–699. Springer, Cham (2020). https://doi.org/10.1007/978-3-030-58595-2_41
12. Couderc, J.-P., Xiaojuan, X., Zareba, W., Moss, A.J.: Assessment of the stability of the individual-based correction of QT interval for heart rate. Ann. Noninvasive Electrocardiol. **10**, 25–34 (2005)

Comparative Study of Embedded Feature Selection Methods on Microarray Data

Hind Hamla[1]® and Khadoudja Ghanem[2](✉)

[1] University of Abdelhamid Mehri Constantine2, Constantine, Algeria
`hind.hamla@univ-constantine2.dz`
[2] Laboratory of Modelling and Implementation of Complex Systems,
Constantine, Algeria

Abstract. Microarray data collects information from tissues that could be used in early diagnosis such as cancer. However, the classification of microarray data is a challenging task due to the high number of features and a small number of samples leading to poor classification accuracy. Feature selection is very effective in reducing dimensionality; it eliminates redundant and irrelevant features to enhance the classifier's performance. In order to shed light on the strengths and weaknesses of the existing techniques, we compare the performances of five embedded feature selection methods namely decision tree, random forest, lasso, ridge, and SVM-RFE. Ten well-known microarray datasets are tested. Obtained results show the outperformance of SVM-RFE in term of accuracy, and comes in the second position after decision tree in terms of number of selected features and execution time.

Keywords: Feature selection · Machine learning · Embedded methods · Microarray data · SVM-RFE

1 Introduction

Artificial intelligence AI based learning is able to substantially "automate discovery" across many domains where classification and prediction tasks play an important role. It hold out the prospect of dramatically lower costs and improve performance especially with DNA microarray data. Within this specific field, AI based learning can learn to read the genome in ways that human cognition and perception cannot as it was argued by Leung et al. 2016 [13].

DNA Microarray technology collects information from tissues and cell samples, analyze this type of data allows research to early diagnose diseases such as cancer [10]. Artificial intelligence techniques have made it possible to analyze this data for classification using statistical methods. However, there are often a few samples (often fewer than 100 samples) and a huge number of features in the raw data up to 60,000 which causes the curse of dimensionality [2].

According to [23] only a small number of features are used in classification, hence, feature selection plays an important role in removing irrelevant features

ⓒ IFIP International Federation for Information Processing 2021
Published by Springer Nature Switzerland AG 2021
I. Maglogiannis et al. (Eds.): AIAI 2021, IFIP AICT 627, pp. 69–77, 2021.
https://doi.org/10.1007/978-3-030-79150-6_6

from microarray data. Feature selection is used for dimensionality reduction, it eliminates irrelevant and redundant features and preserves all or most informative features [22]. As mentioned in [20], feature selection improves the performance of machine learning algorithms either by increasing the classification accuracy or by decreasing the learning speed.

Feature selection methods are categorized into three categories namely: filter, wrapper, and embedded [4]. Wrapper methods use the classification model to measure the goodness of features [14], these methods are slower than filter methods but they have better performance. Filter methods, however, select features independently from classification models and use statistical proprieties of data to select features. These methods are more time-saving compared to wrapper methods, but they show poorer performance [14]. Embedded methods are a combination of filters and wrapper methods. They integrate the process of selection features in the model training phase. With these methods, the search for the best features subset is guided by the learning model. Embedded methods perform better than filter methods and have less computational time compared to wrapper methods. This is way we explore in this paper this category of feature selection methods.

In order to shed light on the strengths and weaknesses of the existing techniques, we compare the performances of five embedded feature selection methods namely: decision tree, random forest, lasso, ridge, and SVM-RFE. This work tests ten well-known microarray datasets that suffer from the high dimensional problem. The remainder of the paper is organized as follows: Sect. 2 presents the related works and Sect. 3 describes the five embedded methods used in this study. Experimental results are given and discussed in Sect. 4. Finally, Sect. 5 concludes the paper.

2   Related Works

Wrapper methods suffer from high computational cost while filter methods do not interact with classifiers [12]. Embedded methods can solve these two problems by including the feature selection method in the learning process. In [20], some of the popular feature selection methods were reviewed, and the performance of some of these methods was evaluated in medical domain. Authors in [23], presented a comprehensive state of the art of many existing feature selection methods. Below we present an overview of several recent embedded methods.

In [9], the authors proposed an embedded feature selection method named Recursive Feature Addition (RFA), RFA worked in a forward fashion and based on SVM. The authors used five datasets to test the performance of the proposed method, the results showed superior performance of the proposed method over filter, wrapper, and other embedded methods.

A stable feature selection method based on the L1-norm support vector machine (SVM) was proposed in [19], the proposed method combined L1-norm with SVM classifier for the classification of renal clear cell carcinoma stage classification using backward feature elimination. RNA-seq gene expression dataset was used to evaluate the performance of the proposed method. The results showed the outperformance of the proposed method.

The authors of [5] propose an embedded feature selection method named MAGS for gene selection and classification of microarray data. This method uses SVM not only to evaluate the quality of the subsets but also to provide valuable information about gene relevancy to design specialized crossover and local search operators. The performance of the proposed method was evaluated over eight microarray datasets, the results illustrate that the proposed method improves the classification accuracy.

In [16] the authors proposed an embedded feature selection method to solve the class imbalance problem called GI-FSw. In this approach, the weighted Gini index was used as splitting criteria of the CART decision tree classifier. The proposed method was tested over two datasets and it has achieved high levels of ROC and f-measure.

Markov blanket-embedded genetic algorithm (MBEGA) for gene selection problem was proposed in [24], in this approach, Markov blanket-based deleted or added features from a solution of genetic algorithm in order to improve the final solution, the performance of this approach was evaluated over four synthetic datasets and eleven microarray datasets, the results proved the effectiveness of the proposed method in eliminating redundant and irrelevant features and it outperforms existing methods in terms of accuracy, number of selected features and computational cost.

In [15], the authors proposed an improved version of RFE that used variable step size named (VSSRFE) in which the step size was decreased as the number of features is eliminated. This method was combined with a more efficient implementation of SVM called (LLSVM). Six well-known microarray datasets were used in the experiments, the results showed that the proposed methods have obtained a comparable classification performance and reduced the computational time.

From this overview, we found that most of the embedded methods presented in the literature to solve feature selection problem are: Decision tree, Rondom Forest, SVM associated with different techniques like L1, L2, RFE... Like it has been mentioned. SVM-RFE was compared in [15] with new variants of SVM-RFE and it has been shown that these variants outperform SVM-RFE. In this paper, we compare DT, RF, L1, and L2 with SVM-RFE on specific data which are microarray data.

3   Methods and Materials

As stated before, in embedded methods the selection of features and the learning are dependent. In the following section, the principles of the used embedded methods are introduced.

3.1   Decision Tree

Decision tree [21] is a well-known machine learning classifier in form of a tree structure that consists of decision nodes and leaves, whereas each leaf represents a class. Decision tree selects features. This classifier is known by its ability to select features that are important in classification. There are several algorithms for constructing a decision tree using different splitting criteria for example ID3 uses impurity measure, C4.5 uses the concept of information entropy, and CART uses Gini index [16]. Decision tree is able of selecting informative features required for classification because the selection of features is inherent in the decision tree classifier [7].

3.2   Random Forest

Random Forest was proposed by [3], it is an embedded feature selection method that uses variable importance to select features. Random forest constructs a large number of classification trees using bootstrapped samples and determines the predictive class using majority voting. This method is well suited for microarray data because it shows excellent performance when the number of samples is much less than the number of features [4].

3.3   Lasso

Least Absolute Shrinkage and Selection Operator (LASSO) is an embedded feature selection method proposed by Robert Tibshirani in 1996, it applies a regularization process that penalizes the coefficients of the regression variables (features) shrinking some of them to zero [6] and preserves features that still have non-zero coefficient after the regularization process. Lasso is an effective feature selection method considering high-dimensional data due to its ability to produce sparse models in a reasonable time [17].

3.4   Ridge

Ridge is another shrinkage-based embedded method proposed by (Hoerl and Kennard, 1988) [11], it penalizes the square root of the sum of the squared weights (L2 norm). This method applies the regularization process by penalizing the feature coefficients toward zero but never attempt exactly zero [18]. Ridge does not reduce the number of variables since it never leads to a zero coefficient.

3.5   SVM-RFE

SVM-RFE was introduced by [8], it is an iteration backward elimination method that trains SVM with the current set of features and removes the least performing features indicated with SVM recursively until finding the optimal subset [20]. SVM-RFE steps for feature set selection are shown as follows.

- Train the classifier (SVM) with the current dataset.
- Calculates the ranking criterion for all features.
- Delete the least important features (has the smallest ranking criterion).

More than one feature can be removed in one iteration [1].

4   Experimental Results and Discussion

4.1   Datasets

To analyze and test the embedded feature selection performance, ten well-known microarray datasets [24] for various cancer diagnoses were used. Table 1 shows datasets details.

Table 1. Microarray datasets details.

Datasets	Number of features	Number of instances	Number of classes
Colon tumor	2000	60	2
Central Nervous System	7129	60	2
Leukemia	7129	72	2
Breast cancer	24481	97	2
Lung_cancer	12533	181	2
Ovarian cancer	15154	253	2
Leukemia 3 classes	7129	72	3
Luekemia 4 classes	7129	72	4
Lymphoma	4026	62	3
MLL	12582	72	3

The above datasets are partitioned into training and testing sets, eight parts were used to train the classifiers and the remaining two were used to test the classifiers. We replace missing values with the mean of the observed values for the corresponding feature. The 10-fold cross-validation method was used in this study.

4.2   Experimental Setup

The five methods used in this study were implemented in python using scikit-learn library. All experiments are performed on a Personal Computer (PC) with an Intel Core i7 processor, 2.9 GHz, and 8 GB of RAM. The parameters values selected to perform the experiments are recorded in Tables 2 and 3 . It worth to mention that we perform several runs to select the suited parameters.

Table 2. List of classification algorithms with parameter tuning details.

Classifiers name	Parameter tuning
Decision tree (DT)	Criterion = 'gini', splitter = 'best', min_samples_split = 2 min_samples_leaf = 1, presort = 'deprecated'
Random Forest (RF)	n_estimators = 100, criterion = 'gini', min_samples_split = 2 min_samples_leaf = 1, bootstrap = True
Lasso	dual = false, tol = 1e−4 C = 1.0, fit_intercept = True
Ridge	Alpha = 1.0, fit_intercept = True normalize = False, tol = 1e−3
SVM-RFE	C = 1.0, Kernal = 'linear', degree = 3, gamma = 'scale' shrinking = True, tol = 1e−3, step = 1

In addition, we set the max-depth parameter of decision tree classifier max-depth = 10 for all the data sets except for colon and leukemia-4C max-depth = 20 and breast max-depth = 100.

Table 3 presents the classification accuracy and execution time in milliseconds without using any feature selection methods, whereas, Table 4 presents classification accuracy and execution time (in millisecond) and the number of selected features using embedded methods. The results are the average of five runs.

4.3 Discussion

From the tables above it is evident that using embedded methods significantly improves classification accuracy and reduces execution time. SVM-RFE outperforms all methods on the ten used datasets in term of accuracy using less than twenty features, it is worth to mention that SVM-RFE reaches 100% accuracy in the case of seven datasets, and it comes in the second place after decision tree in term of execution time and the number of selected features. Decision tree selects the least number of features and has the best execution time on nine of the ten datasets, it also has the best performance in term of accuracy after SVM-RFE in the case of five datasets (colon, CNS, leukemia 4-C, breast, and lung), with regard to the other datasets, the accuracy remains quite important.

Random forest has the lowest classification accuracy and requires high execution time, however, the number of selected features is reasonable. Thus, when considering these three parameters (accuracy, Execution time and number of selected features), it is suggested to avoid this method in the presence of this type of datasets. But, lasso has average results when compared to the other methods and ridge provides sufficient classification accuracy however it requires the longest execution time on almost all the datasets and it selects the largest

Table 3. Classification accuracy and execution time using all features.

Datasets		DT	RF	Lasso	Ridge	RFE-SVM
Colon	Time ACC	16.18 75.46%	10.60 75.63%	10.20 85.76%	7.32 78.16%	8414.06 75.16%
CNS	Time ACC	71.03 44.66%	13.86 62.83%	49.57 70.83%	8.82 72.5%	181601.87 72.0%
Leukemia	Time ACC	73.31 87.44%	41.11 91.10%	88.24 97.71%	82.25 96.33%	169159.77 93.14%
Leukemia 3-C	Time ACC	85.84 84.25%	39.79 84.62%	168.67 96.57%	77.07 94.57%	159072.89 96.0%
Leukemia 4-C	Time ACC	131.84 69.90%	93.22 77.33%	326.56 92.92%	95.02 91.21%	255629.21 94.64%
Breast	Time ACC	443.38 52.49%	34.45 61.05%	182.76 72.43%	35.85 66.58%	4758377.28 64.44%
Lung cancer	Time ACC	673.86 85.40%	63.49 88.55%	965.80 92.63%	49.48 93.28%	2016552.5 90.42
Ovarian	Time ACC	639.34 96.27%	225.18 97.09%	352.96 100.0%	435.79 100.0%	2099057.88 100.0%
Lymphoma	Time ACC	62.29 85.1%	50.37 93.32%	79.70 94.16%	107.13 100.0%	37563.19 96.66%
MLL	Time ACC	147.90 80.54%	51.48 90.95%	291.64 98.57%	115.85 96.07%	444714.36 90.23%

Table 4. Classification accuracy and execution time and the number of selected features.

Datasets		DT	RF	L1	L2	SVM-RFE
ColonTumor	Time ACC Nb FS	0.55 91.9% 4	12.74 80.56% * 42	4.85 84.16% 204.6	3.45 89.49% 590	1.33 96.0% 10
CNS	Time ACC Nb FS	0.34 89.89% 4	9.43 76.09% 44.2	2.07 79.33% 290.6	2.77 81.0% 1822	1.09 98.00% 15
Leukemia	Time ACC Nb FS	0.79 96.33% 2	9.72 96.40% 28.8	3.08 97.8% 167.8	12.96 98.00% 1741	1.31 100.0% 10
Leukemia 3-C	Time ACC Nb FS	0.50 93.24% 3	9.51 90.96% 46.6	8.68 97.77% 349.2	15.96 94.57% 1748	1.26 100.0% 10
Leukemia 4-C	Time ACC Nb FS	0.50 94.54% 5	9.32 88.26% 57.2	12.92 93.63% 449.6	13.98 91.21% 1771	0.94 100.0% 8
Breastcancer	ACC Time Nb FS	0.66 96.58% 5	10.41 65.5% 61.6	2.67 76.19% 75.8	13.79 82.81% 9255	1.44 98.57% 15
Lung cancer	Time ACC Nb FS	0.98 95.17% 8	14.13 91.46% 101.6	62.08 92.58% 665.6	15.46 95.17% 3437	3.86 100.0% 20
Ovarian	Time ACC Nb FS	0.59 98.81% 3	10.90 97.53% 71.8	4.05 100.0% 42.6	62.09 100.0% 5003	1.58 100.0% 3
Lymphoma	Time ACC Nb FS	0.49 95.03% 2	7.51 96.66% 25.4	1.68 97.5% 41.2	24.99 100.0% 1574	0.54 100.0% 2
MLL	Time ACC Nb FS	0.97 95.99% 3	8.81 94.85% 44.4	8.92 98.92% 512.6	20.56 96.07% 3303	0.59 100.0% 4

number of features (over one thousand features for nine datasets). Finally, we think that it remains preferable to leave the choice to the user, who will use the method that suits his needs in terms of precision (very Sensitive applications), time (Reel time applications) or number of features (Mobile applications) . . .

4.4 Comparison with Other Works

In this section, we give a comparison of the results obtained by SVM-RFE and some other works presented in the literature. The results are presented in Table 5.

From Table 5, we can see that the method proposed in [15] has achieved better classification accuracy with colon dataset and has selected less number of features. With leukemia, lung, ovarian, and lymphoma, both SVM-RFE and the method in [15] achieved 100% accuracy. With CNS and breast, SVM-RFE outperforms the method proposed in [15] in terms of classification accuracy and the number of selected features. SVM-RFE has better performance than the proposed method in [18] considering the only tested dataset (colon). SVM-RFE produced better performances than the method in [20] in terms of classification accuracy and the number of selected features for the ten datasets.

Table 5. Comparison with other works.

Datasets		DT	RF	Lasso	Ridge	RFE-SVM
Colon	Time ACC	16.18 75.46%	10.60 75.63%	10.20 85.76%	7.32 78.16%	8414.06 75.16%
CNS	Time ACC	71.03 44.66%	13.86 62.83%	49.57 70.83%	8.82 72.5% '	181601.87 72.0%
Leukemia	Time ACC	73.31 87.44%	41.11 91.10%	88.24 97.71%	82.25 96.33%	169159.77 93.14%
Leukemia 3-C	Time ACC	85.84 84.25%	39.79 84.62%	168.67 96.57%	77.07 94.57%	159072.89 96.0%
Leukemia 4-C	Time ACC	131.84 69.90%	93.22 77.33%	326.56 92.92%	95.02 91.21%	255629.21 94.64%
Breast	Time ACC	443.38 52.49%	34.45 61.05%	182.76 72.43%	35.85 66.58%	4758377.28 64.44%
Lung cancer	Time ACC	673.86 85.40%	63.49 88.55%	965.80 92.63%	49.48 93.28%	2016552.5 90.42
Ovarian	Time ACC	639.34 96.27%	225.18 97.09%	352.96 100.0%	435.79 100.0%	2099057.88 100.0%
Lymphoma	Time ACC	62.29 85.1%	50.37 93.32%	79.70 94.16%	107.13 100.0%	37563.19 96.66%
MLL	Time ACC	147.90 80.54%	51.48 90.95%	291.64 98.57%	115.85 96.07%	444714.36 90.23%

5   Conclusion and Future Work

In this paper we evaluate the performances of five embedded feature selection methods namely decision Tree, random forest, lasso, ridge, and SVM-RFE on ten cancer microarray gene expression datasets which are (Colon, CNS, Leukemia, Leukemia 3-C, Leukemia 4-C, breast, lung, ovarian, lymphoma, and MLL). The experiments show that SVM-RFE gives the highest accuracy among the five tested methods, using a reduced number of features. Decision tree provides high classification accuracy and selects the smallest number of features, it is the fastest method among the other methods discussed in this work and random forest produces the lowest classification accuracy. These are mathematical and algorithmic results, we believe that an expert opinion about the pertinence and the relevance of a specific feature in the final decision making is crucial especially in this domain because he is the only one who can ensure the stability criterion. This is the limitation of this study. As future work, we aim to consider more feature selection methods as well as use other evaluation metrics such as ROC. A main drawback of SVM-RFE is that the calculation time is very high. Therefore, we aim to develop a faster version of SVM-RFE in the future.

References

1. Adorada, A., Permatasari, R., Wirawan, P.W., Wibowo, A., Sujiwo, A.: Support vector machine-recursive feature elimination (svm-rfe) for selection of microrna expression features of breast cancer. In: 2018 2nd International Conference on Informatics and Computational Sciences (ICICoS), pp. 1–4. IEEE (2018)
2. Larriba, Y., Rueda, C., Fernández, M.A., Peddada, S.D.: Microarray data normalization and robust detection of rhythmic features. In: Bolón-Canedo, V., Alonso-Betanzos, A. (eds.) Microarray Bioinformatics. MMB, vol. 1986, pp. 207–225. Springer, New York (2019). https://doi.org/10.1007/978-1-4939-9442-7_9
3. Breiman, L.: Bagging predictors. Mach. Learn. **24**(2), 123–140 (1996)
4. Díaz-Uriarte, R., De. Andres, S.A.: Gene selection and classification of microarray data using random forest. BMC Bioinf. **7**(1), 3 (2006)

5. Duval, B., Hao, J.K., Hernandez Hernandez, J.C.: A memetic algorithm for gene selection and molecular classification of cancer. In: Proceedings of the 11th Annual Conference on Genetic and Evolutionary Computation, pp. 201–208 (2009)
6. Fonti, V., Belitser, E.: Feature selection using lasso. VU Amsterdam Res. Paper Bus. Anal. **30**, 1–25 (2017)
7. Grabczewski, K., Jankowski, N.: Feature selection with decision tree criterion. In: Null (2005)
8. Guyon, I., Weston, J., Barnhill, S., Vapnik, V.: Gene selection for cancer classification using support vector machines. Mach. Learn. **46**(1–3), 389–422 (2002)
9. Hamed, T., Dara, R., Kremer, S.C.: An accurate, fast embedded feature selection for SVMs. In: 2014 13th International Conference on Machine Learning and Applications, pp. 135–140. IEEE (2014)
10. Hameed, S.S., Muhammad, F.F., Hassan, R., Saeed, F.: Gene selection and classification in microarray datasets using a hybrid approach of pcc-bpso/ga with multi classifiers. J. Comput. Sci. **14**(6), 868–880 (2018)
11. Hoerl, A.E., Kennard, R.W.: Ridge regression: biased estimation for nonorthogonal problems. Technometrics **12**(1), 55–67 (1970)
12. Kumar, C.A., Sooraj, M., Ramakrishnan, S.: A comparative performance evaluation of supervised feature selection algorithms on microarray datasets. Procedia Comput. Sci. **115**, 209–217 (2017)
13. Leung, M.K., Delong, A., Alipanahi, B., Frey, B.J.: Machine learning in genomic medicine: a review of computational problems and data sets. Proc. IEEE **104**(1), 176–197 (2015)
14. Li, H., Guo, W., Wu, G., Li, Y.: A rf-pso based hybrid feature selection model in intrusion detection system. In: 2018 IEEE Third International Conference on Data Science in Cyberspace (DSC), pp. 795–802. IEEE (2018)
15. Li, Z., Xie, W., Liu, T.: Efficient feature selection and classification for microarray data. PLoS ONE **13**(8), e0202167 (2018)
16. Liu, H., Zhou, M., Liu, Q.: An embedded feature selection method for imbalanced data classification. IEEE/CAA J. Automatica Sinica **6**(3), 703–715 (2019)
17. Ma, S., Song, X., Huang, J.: Supervised group lasso with applications to microarray data analysis. BMC Bioinf. **8**(1), 60 (2007)
18. Marafino, B.J., Boscardin, W.J., Dudley, R.A.: Efficient and sparse feature selection for biomedical text classification via the elastic net: application to ICU risk stratification from nursing notes. J. Biomed. Inf. **54**, 114–120 (2015)
19. Moon, M., Nakai, K.: Stable feature selection based on the ensemble l 1-norm support vector machine for biomarker discovery. BMC Genom **17**(13), 1026 (2016)
20. Remeseiro, B., Bolon-Canedo, V.: A review of feature selection methods in medical applications. Comput. Biol. Med. **112**, 103375 (2019)
21. Tahir, N.M., Hussain, A., Samad, S.A., Ishak, K.A., Halim, R.A.: Feature selection for classification using decision tree. In: 2006 4th Student Conference on Research and Development, pp. 99–102. IEEE (2006)
22. Zhang, X., Shi, Z., Liu, X., Li, X.: A hybrid feature selection algorithm for classification unbalanced data processsing. In: 2018 IEEE International Conference on Smart Internet of Things (SmartIoT), pp. 269–275. IEEE (2018)
23. Zheng, Y., et al.: Retracted: a hybrid feature selection algorithm for microarray data. Concurr. Comput. Pract. Exp. **31**(12), e4716 (2019)
24. Zhu, Z., Ong, Y.S., Dash, M.: Markov blanket-embedded genetic algorithm for gene selection. Pattern Recogn. **40**(11), 3236–3248 (2007)

AI Impacts/Big Data

The AI4Media Project: Use of Next-Generation Artificial Intelligence Technologies for Media Sector Applications

Filareti Tsalakanidou[1] , Symeon Papadopoulos[1] , Vasileios Mezaris[1] ,
Ioannis Kompatsiaris[1]([✉]) , Birgit Gray[2], Danae Tsabouraki[3], Maritini Kalogerini[3],
Fulvio Negro[4] , Maurizio Montagnuolo[4] , Jesse de Vos[5], Philo van Kemenade[5],
Daniele Gravina[6], Rémi Mignot[7], Alexey Ozerov[8], Francois Schnitzler[8],
Artur Garcia-Saez[9], Georgios N. Yannakakis[10], Antonios Liapis[10],
and Georgi Kostadinov[11]

[1] Information Technologies Institute, Centre for Research and Technology Hellas,
6th km Charilaou-Thermi Road, 57001 Thermi, Thessaloniki, Greece
ikom@iti.gr
[2] Deutsche Welle, Kurt-Schumacher-Straße 3, 53113 Bonn, Germany
[3] Athens Technology Center (ATC), Rizariou 10, 15233 Chalandri, Athens, Greece
[4] RAI - Radiotelevisione Italiana, Via G.C. Cavalli 6, 10138 Turin, Italy
[5] Netherlands Institute for Sound and Vision, Mediaparkboulevard 1, Hilversum,
The Netherlands
[6] modl.ai, Nørrebrogade 184, 1, 2200 Copenhagen, Denmark
[7] IRCAM, 1 pl. Stravinsky, 75004 Paris, France
[8] InterDigital, 975 av. de Champs Blancs, 35510 Cesson-Sévigné, France
[9] Barcelona Supercomputing Center (BSC), c/Jordi Girona 31, 08034 Barcelona, Spain
[10] University of Malta, Msida MSD 2080, Malta
[11] Imagga Technologies Ltd., 47A Cherni Vrah blvd., 1407 Sofia, Bulgaria

Abstract. Artificial Intelligence brings exciting innovations in all aspects of life
and creates new opportunities across industry sectors. At the same time, it raises
significant questions in terms of trust, ethics, and accountability. This paper offers
an introduction to the AI4Media project, which aims to build on recent advances of
AI in order to offer innovative tools to the media sector. AI4Media unifies the fragmented landscape of media-related AI technologies by investigating new learning
paradigms and distributed AI, exploring issues of AI explainability, robustness
and privacy, examining AI techniques for content analysis, and exploiting AI to
address major societal challenges. In this paper, we focus on our vision of how
such AI technologies can reshape the media sector, by discussing seven industrial
use cases that range from combating disinformation in social media and supporting journalists for news story creation, to high quality video production, game
design, and artistic co-creation. For each of these use cases, we highlight the
present challenges and needs, and explain how they can be efficiently addressed
by using innovative AI-driven solutions.

Keywords: Artificial Intelligence · Media · Democracy · Society · Use cases ·
Social media · Content automation · Vision · Journalism · Co-creation · Gaming

© IFIP International Federation for Information Processing 2021
Published by Springer Nature Switzerland AG 2021
I. Maglogiannis et al. (Eds.): AIAI 2021, IFIP AICT 627, pp. 81–93, 2021.
https://doi.org/10.1007/978-3-030-79150-6_7

1 Artificial Intelligence in the Service of Media, Society and Democracy: Current Challenges and Opportunities

Following a series of breakthroughs in the field of Artificial Intelligence (AI), new technologies are emerging which are ushering a wave of innovations in all aspects of business and society, across industry sectors such as transportation, health or finance, for global goals such as fighting climate change, also impacting the media industry, journalism and politics [1]. In all these facets of economic and social life, AI is disrupting existing practices and creates opportunities. The exploitation of these opportunities brings significant socio-economic changes that necessitate a focus on issues of trust, ethics and accountability, besides the pursuit of technological excellence and financial profit.

This human-centric and trustworthy ethical brand of AI is particularly relevant to the media sector. Digital media permeates most aspects of human and social activity and is intertwined with information exchange and knowledge transfer. Machine vision and visual content understanding were some of the first fields to exhibit significant breakthroughs in the evolution of AI, including advances in audio/music analysis and generation, text and language analysis, and modeling of social trends. The media market is already benefiting from AI-based support across the value chain: for media newsgathering, production, distribution, and delivery as well as audience analysis. This includes a range of tools and services for processes such as information analysis, content creation, media editing, content optimisation, audience preference analysis, and recommender systems [2].

Furthermore, it has become apparent that society and politics are increasingly affected by AI developments. There is strong concern that the combination of the power held by the major, globally operating social media platforms and the large-scale automation capabilities associated with these platforms offered by AI technology could prove detrimental to individuals, society and democracy [3]. For instance, AI-powered bot collectives were found to have played an important role in shaping the results of US Elections in 2016 and the Brexit referendum [4] while the recent advent of synthetic media technology is posing new risks to citizens' trust in online content.

AI technologies are expected to disrupt the media industry through advances in content synthesis, analysis, and distribution, but also by offering new deeper insights into the complex and rapidly evolving social processes that unfold online and offline by sensing citizen activities, interests and opinions [2]. AI technology could help shape the democratic role of the media by enabling new ways of being informed, of deliberation, political participation, and decision making. In addition, AI technologies could support the relationship between media providers and their audiences, helping to align with the needs of media users and citizens. The use of AI can also cut down operating costs and ultimately free up resources for more in-depth and quality journalism. In addition, the use of AI can also create opportunities for the better realization of public values, such as media diversity, freedom of expression, and inclusiveness.

Motivated by the challenges, risks and opportunities that a wider use of AI brings to the media sector and society, the EU-funded AI4Media project [5] aspires to i) deliver the next generation of core AI technologies, ii) ensure the embedding of ethical and trustworthy AI into future AI deployments, and iii) reimagine AI as a human-centered, trusted and beneficial enabling technology for media and society.

AI4Media aims to advance the AI state-of-the-art in four key technology areas, with a view to unify a currently fragmented landscape of media related AI and offer solutions for the ever-growing needs and challenges of media organizations:

- *New learning paradigms and distributed AI*: AI models that adapt and learn on-the-fly, models that teach each other, algorithms that learn from limited data; Distributed AI and AI systems operating on the Edge.
- *Explainability, robustness and privacy in AI*: Federated learning and privacy-enhancing technologies ensuring data privacy; Technologies that protect information systems from malicious attacks and increase robustness; Approaches for evaluation, systematization, and explainability of AI.
- *Content-centered AI*: Multimedia metadata extraction, summarization, and clustering; Automatic audiovisual content generation and enhancement; Linguistic analysis; Learning with sparse data and transfer learning.
- *Human- and Society-centered AI*: Technologies for multimedia manipulation detection; Political opinion mining, disinformation detection, and local news detection; User perception measurement algorithms for personalization and bias detection; Privacy-preserving content recommendation.

The developed technologies will be tested in the context of seven industrial use cases that focus on the media sector, with relevance for both society and the economy. They cover different forms of media, such as digital content, broadcast video, film, audio, music, games, and virtual environments. Content areas include news stories, social media, media archives, and user-generated content. The use cases also address a variety of societal and democracy related topics such as disinformation, public discourse, media moderation, consumer privacy, creativity, and human-machine interaction. The seven use cases will be realized through close collaboration between AI researchers and European media organizations or content related companies.

The rest of the paper is organized as follows: Sect. 2 discusses the AI technologies explored in AI4Media that focus on the media sector. Section 3 presents the seven AI4Media use cases. Finally, Sect. 4 draws the conclusions.

2   AI Technologies for the Media Sector

AI4Media will conduct research in cutting-edge AI areas, focusing on tools and applications for the Media Industry. In the following, we briefly discuss the spectrum of AI technologies that will be examined in the context of the project and the use cases.

New Learning Paradigms. The AI explosion was initially spearheaded by Convolutional Neural Networks (CNNs) and Recurrent Neural Networks (RNNs) applied to well-known classification tasks. Building on this, we focus on developing faster and more accurate learning models by examining: techniques for lifelong learning to allow updating system capabilities without forgetting past knowledge [6]; new spaces and operators for unsupervised manifold learning to exploit non-annotated data; transfer learning to allow reusing models trained for different tasks [7]; transfer neural architecture search to find suitable DNN architectures fast by leveraging past experience in different datasets [8]; and deep Quality Diversity methods for DNNs to improve quality and diversity of generated outcomes in gaming [9]. We leverage Quantum architectures and test the efficiency of Quantum-inspired ML algorithms dealing with large datasets. We also move AI from centralized cloud architectures to networks of heterogeneous devices, to allow lightweight devices sitting on the Cloud Edge to run their own DNN models [10]. In this direction, we explore distributed learning and decentralized graph mining.

Trustworthy AI. To ensure trustworthy AI for media applications, AI robustness, explainability, privacy and fairness are explored. We focus on enhancing system resilience towards adversarial attacks like poisoning or evasion [11]; improving AI interpretability [12] with regard to the use of DNNs for tasks like deepfake detection; improving the privacy aspect of recommendation systems by combining de-centralized methods for federated learning [13], differential privacy and encryption; and improving fairness through detection and mitigation of bias in recommendation systems [14]. These contributions will be supplemented by a new benchmarking framework aiming to evaluate effectiveness and reproducibility of AI systems.

Multimedia Content Analysis and Creation. The aim is to provide improvements on the state of the art, such as development of better automatic video summarization algorithms for news agencies based on Generative Adversarial Networks (GANs) [15] and on combination of knowledge representation and deep learning; and to design better audio generation algorithms for games, exploiting DNNs and domain-specific knowledge for music annotation and audio analysis [16]. In addition, we explore vision-based DNNs for automatic online cinematography based on UAV footage [17], while also developing image enhancement techniques for 360 videos, thermal imagery, depth, etc. We also improve visual detection tasks by using GANs and 3D virtual world simulators to tackle data scarcity [18]. Finally, we improve Word Embeddings for NLP algorithms [19] to provide efficient multi-language models.

Human-Centered AI. Online platforms have become a central source of information, shaping the democratic debate and society [3]. To support journalists in providing trustworthy information and citizens in being adequately informed outside of filter bubbles, AI4Media: tackles multimedia content manipulation (deepfakes) by combining text verification based on graph mining [20], audio analysis, and video analysis based on extended GANs [21] and novel video pre-processing approaches [22]; promotes healthy political debate by including diversity and novelty in recommender systems to avoid over-personalisation [23], and by modeling disinformation and political polarization in national and local scale; and finally, analyzes user perception of social media through a combination of user studies and content analysis [24].

3   The AI4Media Use Cases

AI4Media has designed seven use cases that demonstrate the use of AI in the media industry, including aspects of human-centric, ethical and trustworthy AI (see Fig. 1).

The AI4Media use cases (UC) are inspired by market needs, emerging opportunities, and a range of industry challenges, and they highlight how AI applies throughout the media and content value chain and how different types of media players aim to address user and business needs with novel AI solutions.

Fig. 1. The AI4Media use cases.

The use cases deal with a broad range of media processes that will be optimized and enhanced by the application of state-of-the-art AI technologies. The industry partners gather a set of user requirements for new AI functionalities with a view to upgrade available tools already used by the media sector with AI features developed by the project (see Sect. 2). In the following, we present the seven use cases.

3.1 UC1: AI for Social Media and Against Disinformation

While disinformation activities and the volume of related verification work increase, the workflow for verifying digital content items and detecting disinformation remains complex, time-consuming and often requires specialists. The current generation of support tools lack functions for identifying the most recent forms of manipulated content and easily understanding disinformation patterns in social media. In addition, technologies used for content manipulation and disinformation have become more advanced, also involving synthetic media. There is a need for upgraded, easy-to-use tools with trusted AI functions, as more journalists and other researchers will be involved in content verification and disinformation detection tasks. In order to ensure acceptance of AI-based tools and the feasibility of their implementation, users need to judge aspects of trustworthiness with regard to machine-generated results and predictions, such as *Explainability*, *Bias Mitigation*, *Robustness* or *Ethical Compliance*.

This use case from Deutsche Welle and ATC leverages AI technologies to improve support tools used by journalists and fact-checking experts for digital content verification and disinformation detection. New AI-based features will be made available within two existing journalism tools: *Truly Media* [25] (web-based platform for collaborative verification) and *TruthNest* [26] (Twitter analytics and bot detection tool).

Two topics are covered: i) verification of content from social media with a focus on *synthetic media detection*, and ii) detection of communication narratives and patterns that are related to *disinformation*. Another aspect is the exploration of *Trustworthy AI* in relation to these topics and the specific needs of media organisations.

The detection and verification of synthetic media refers to both synthetically generated media items and synthetic elements within media items. This provides contextual information for the verification process, helping journalists and researchers to understand specific manipulation activities. The more advanced synthetic media becomes, the more difficult and time-consuming it will be to detect it. While there are useful and entertaining applications for synthetic media, it is also used for targeted, malicious disinformation. Synthetic media items misused for disinformation purposes are colloquially known as *Deepfakes* [27]. All types of content can be synthetically generated (or manipulated): text, images, audio, video and elements within AR/VR experiences. *Synthetic Characters* can be either fictional or with high levels of likeness to a person, its voice and personality.

Another goal is to provide AI-based tools for better understanding communication patterns in social media that are related to disinformation. This includes the detection of topical disinformation campaigns or stories, which may entail false or distorted information. The latter can emerge dynamically, or be steered by certain social media actors and networked communities in order to achieve a specific objective.

We address these challenges by collecting specific user needs in the area of content verification and disinformation detection that might be solved by advanced AI functionalities, including needs for associated Trustworthy AI features. Once respective AI tools have been developed in AI4Media, they will be tested against end user and business needs within Truly Media and TruthNest (see Fig. 2).

Fig. 2. AI technologies for content verification and disinformation detection developed in AI4Media will be integrated in existing journalism tools like Truly Media.

3.2   UC2: AI for News - the Smart News Assistant

Journalists face a challenging environment where the amount of incoming content is ever increasing while the need to publish news as fast as possible is extremely pressing. On top of that, journalists need to ensure that published content is trustworthy and relevant for its audience. The use case focuses on the concept of a Smart News Assistant, i.e. a tool that will support journalists in the creation of news stories by providing a variety of AI-enabled functionalities for story production and development, story curation and publication, and audience engagement.

Story development will be facilitated by providing automatic story suggestions based on analytics of past audience engagement and trend detection in social media, as well as by providing real-time suggestions during article preparation, e.g. suggesting relevant articles or video content from news archives and warning about fake news. Functionalities for automated news articles summaries, automated article indexing and annotation for easier search, automated content curation and adaptation to different audience needs, and personalised news experiences based on past behaviour of news consumers will be supported to enhance story curation. Finally, semi-automated moderation of online discussions about news articles, including polarisation detection and classification of disagreements, and automatic management of audience feedback will be supported to facilitate audience interaction and engagement.

3.3   UC3: AI for High Quality Video Production and Content Automation

This use case aims at supporting broadcasters' newsrooms (and in general information and entertainment production) in reporting unexpected events like natural disasters (e.g., floods, earthquakes). Generally, whenever similar events occur, newsrooms need to readily publish and update fresh news in a very short timeframe. It is evident that the "time" variable plays a crucial role: providing and getting news on time can make all the difference and the entire production process is stressed. Together, content quality and reliability must always be properly and readily verified before flowing into the production chain. AI4Media aims to broaden the horizons along three perspectives involved in such just-in-time, high-quality production process (Fig. 3).

| Autonomous Video Shooting | Multi-source news topic analysis | 4K/HDR/HFR end to end chain |

Fig. 3. AI4Media aims to empower the whole news production process: from news analysis to high-quality and impactful content creation.

First, *timely coverage* of unexpected events must be ensured. Several tools for professional news search and filtering are available, but they lack in providing new and engaging information as soon as an event occurs. However, auxiliary sources (e.g., social media and video sharing platforms) provide a plethora of information such as the nature of the disaster, affected people's emotions and relief efforts. Unfortunately, that content cannot be used indiscriminately due to e.g., quality, privacy and reliability issues. AI tools for content quality enhancement (e.g., denoising, dehazing, inpainting), privacy protection (e.g., identity obfuscation) and manipulation detection are the key to overcome such obstacles. Furthermore, AI computer vision technologies can speed up the creation of metadata, e.g., descriptive information about actions, places and things identifiable within the content, making it easier to be searched.

Second, *broadcaster's archives* are a valuable source of information about how the landscape was in the past. However, archive material might be impaired and inadequately documented. Thus, appropriate AI-based technologies are needed for video restoration (e.g., artifacts reduction, colourisation) and metadata extraction (e.g., image and video captioning). Furthermore, drone technology can provide unprecedented viewing experiences, e.g., by gathering data from inaccessible or arduous areas. Archives and drones might work in synergy and even amplify each other's results. Archive material might help in pre-setting operational drone's parameters (e.g., flight paths, altitude, speed) while drone camera footage might be used to assist the video restoration process, e.g., by providing chroma information for video colourisation.

At last, *open data, professional newsgathering services and broadcast archives* are the main data sources that could be used to enrich the storytelling with e.g., graphics, statistics and reports about past events related to the present one. AI may help the editorial staff analyse data and identify patterns and insights from these sources, thus reducing the effort for data scraping, aggregation, mining and transformation.

Results of AI4Media are expected to bring benefit along the whole value chain, including journalists, editorial staff, TV production, rights and privacy management departments, as well as media researchers. Finally, to the audience, who will enjoy always new, modern, original and high-quality content.

3.4   UC4: AI for Social Sciences and Humanities

Scholars from the humanities and social sciences have been adopting digital methods into their respective fields. Large, publicly accessible datasets allow researchers to distill trends beyond individual occurrences of media phenomena. This use case provides researchers (and by extension investigative journalists) with practical methods to sift, connect and analyze various data and media collections in search of factual responses to broad societal research questions. Our aim is to provide the AI-based tools that facilitate identification of patterns or new research questions in aggregated, multi-modal collections. Based on the AI tools, we envision an infrastructure that will facilitate gathering and preparation of data to support *macro-level analysis*, e.g. the role of political and gender bias in media programs, and *micro-level analysis*, e.g. close reading of specific programs, bias effects of speaker selection, and topic presentation. This includes the use of Computer Vision analysis and Natural Language Processing, but goes beyond detection of individual features, to equip researchers with reliable and explainable analyses and visualisations at aggregated levels.

This use case focuses on issues of framing, representation and bias: topics of great interest to social sciences and humanities. However, the definition and operationalization of such complex societal issues is itself subject to debate. Scholars will develop their own understanding and identify more specific instances of these broad phenomena, e.g. the degree to which talk show hosts interrupt female versus male speakers, or the representation of violence in news channels covering a conflict. To facilitate such research with AI-based tools requires a great degree of flexibility and configurability. At the core, the tools should enable researchers to perform basic operations: detect entities in various modalities within large multi-modal datasets. But for example, what exactly the tools detect, which confidence scores for results are to be used and in which combinations entities should occur should be configurable by the researchers.

Finally, academic research has the highest standards when it comes to transparency of methodologies, fairness of representation in training sets and research reproducibility. Therefore, this use case will also evaluate the pre-conditional requirements for trustworthy AI-based tooling, which allows scholars to confidently deploy the tooling.

3.5 UC5: AI for Games

Over the past decade, the game industry has undergone drastic changes. There has been an increase of online games, digital distribution platforms, mobile and social games. Digital games are now services that rely on continuously developing and adding new content over the lifetime of the product in a winner-takes-all market. Before launch, optimizing a game for the market is crucial for its success.

AI can provide a radically new approach for testing and optimizing games by letting developers test thousands of different configurations and cases instead of a few hundred or less. It can replace or augment existing practices by providing product evaluations faster than current methods. Additionally, AI may even provide methods for generating content automatically. The game industry is seeing an increased need for automation and improved efficiency. Finally, AI has the capacity to provide new gaming interactions. For the past decade, new control devices have been appearing with the aim to replace the traditional gamepad and provide more natural interaction.

To address these issues, this use case aims to advance the game testing, design and interaction through AI algorithmic innovations. It focuses on three topics:

"*Automated testing for Games*": AI agents can be used to automatically detect bugs and glitches in video games by autonomously playing them and compiling test reports as human testers would do. Video game testing is a time-consuming process that traditionally has been entrusted to human testers. However, the future of the game market sees an increasing adoption of the game-as-a-service model, where new content has to be provided to players on a monthly basis. Therefore, quality assurance becomes a vital part of the game development cycle, as the new content produced has to be continuously tested.

"*Improved music analysis and synthesis for Games*": This aims to help developers to choose or conceive background music or sounds. In video games, the audio track has the role to strengthen the atmosphere of the present scene, and it has an impact on the emotion felt by the user. Developers can either choose music from a catalog or delegate this task to music composers or sound designers; but automatic AI tools may help, especially in the case of dynamic changes and procedural content generation.

"*Natural game interaction through edge analysis of camera stream*": With cloud gaming, end users can play games without dedicated hardware and directly interact with games running on the cloud and streamed to their home. A Smart TV equipped with a standard RGB camera coupled with AI on the edge will replace the gamepad for natural game interactions. The camera stream will be analyzed with AI models that dynamically adapt to the available resources and offloaded to the edge. The output of the analysis (e.g. human body detection, gestures) will be interpreted into game commands within stringent latency requirements and ensure the privacy of end users.

3.6 UC6: AI for Human Co-creation

Content generation is an exhaustive project often developed by a single or a reduced group of people. Many of the tasks involved require a high level of craftsmanship, and as such are available to a reduced number of experts after extensive training. In an era where content is consumed in a greedy manner by a gigantic audience, content creators face the necessity of novel tools to assist them in their creative process.

Music creation uses novel technologies in many ways, and a wide range of techniques are employed by composers routinely. These technologies have been evolving dramatically in recent years, with the introduction of AI into music generation. While this is a great opportunity for creators, it requires an increasing level of technical proficiency, out of reach of non-experts. A novel industry may emerge from this set of possibilities and requirements, giving each user a new personal experience of media addressed particularly to each taste. Authors need novel tools to develop their work and expand their creativity beyond the constraint of potentially automatized tasks.

Our goal is to reduce the gap between novel content creation techniques, in particular raw audio music, and artists/creators. The content may be also created and manipulated in real time according to external inputs. Tasks related to content creation are of different complexity, some of which are already performed in an automated way. In this context, novel tools may contribute to an efficient creation task, where efforts of the artist or creator are focused on deeply creative tasks, relying on less critical parts to be performed by an AI assistant.

The elaboration of creative assistants has a wide application to many different fields of creation. While visual arts are suited to the application of AI tools based on CNNs, recent developments on RNNs or similar techniques allow the efficient processing of music, speech, or video. In this context, the scope of interest of these techniques will soon cover the complete spectrum of content production.

This approach has potential impact in a broad range of disciplines, where the combination of data sources could add value. Beyond visual arts, we find many areas of human creation where language, image, sound, and other information are combined in complex ways, such as games. Tools to generate, modify and synchronise all these data sources are in need to automatically ensure quality and consistency of novel digital content. In this use case, we collaborate with *music composers* with previous experience with the use of AI to help us define new work methodologies and new ways of using AI in their creation. In particular, we focus on coupling raw audio CNNs with GANs trained with mood and emotional labels, lyrics, and other data extracted from music knowledge. Also, general purpose RNNs used in speech synthesis will be explored to process RAW audio from music tracks. The aim is to produce a novel way of content co-creation based on AI tools that reach a wide range of content.

3.7 UC7: AI for (Re-)Organisation and Content Moderation

Media companies have accumulated vast digital archives and collections of images and videos over the years. Since these collections have been gradually and iteratively built over time, often by different departments and units of media companies, they usually have little or no metadata such as tags, categories, and other types of annotations. This lack of coherent media asset organisation tailored to the media company business and services precludes the successful monetisation of these media assets and the creation and offering of new services. In addition, both big traditional media companies and more so digital media platforms combine in their collections both media content, created by these companies, but increasingly also User-Generated Content (UGC). Such hybrid media archives need advanced Content Moderation (CM) solutions, often working in real time to safeguard viewers and meet laws and regulations.

To address these challenges, this use case utilizes several AI-enabled tools such as visual tagging, categorization, and content moderation to facilitate:

a) *Automated (re)organisation of large media collections of photos and video*: Techniques for mapping existing taxonomies and ontologies used by media companies, to restructure them to more optimal ones, and training of specialized models for such companies using state-of-the-art CNNs for media asset categorisation will be used. The know-how of consortium partners with personal and enterprise photo collection organisation will be extended to mixed collections of photos and video.

b) *Automated and human-in-the-loop moderation of user-generated media content*: We will also use existing CM solutions that combine automated detection of diverse and customizable types of inappropriate content, such as weapons, drugs, nudity, pornography, etc. with a CM platform and option to add internal or external data teams to verify inappropriate content flagged by AI algorithms. As part of this use case, Imagga's CM platform [28] (Fig. 4) will be tested and further optimised with mixed and hybrid media collections and platforms where UGC can come both as standalone new visual content (photos, video) or as comments to existing media assets, such as films, news, etc. Additional focus will be on implementing a live-stream optimization module for optimizing costs and precision of automated real-time moderation. This will meet the growing demand of media companies to have scalable real-time content moderation to safeguard users and meet various regulations.

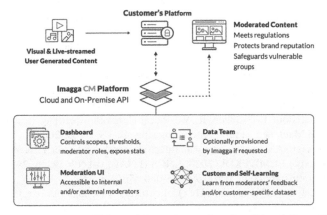

Fig. 4. Imagga's CM platform will be enriched with AI functionalities delivered by AI4Media.

Additionally, the two demonstrators presented in this use case will be tested by target groups of real users from media companies in Living Lab trials, in order to validate their performance and help tailor them further to meet user requirements.

4 Conclusions

This paper offers an introduction to the AI4Media H2020 project. AI4Media aims to deliver the next generation of core AI technologies, including new AI learning paradigms and distributed AI; ensure the embedding of ethical and trustworthy AI into future AI deployments by exploring technologies for AI explainability, robustness and privacy; and reimagine AI as a human-centered, trusted and beneficial enabling technology for media and society. To this end, AI4Media introduces use cases focusing on the media sector that cover different forms of media and digital content while examining various societal and democracy related topics, such as disinformation, public discourse, media moderation, consumer privacy, creativity, and human-machine interaction. AI4Media is expected to build on the rich and diverse European media culture and its role in advancing public values, such as democracy, inclusiveness, political participation, diversity, and self-expression and thus contribute into strengthening Europe's position in the global AI research landscape.

Acknowledgment. This work was supported by European Union's Horizon 2020 research and innovation programme under grant agreement No 951911 - AI4Media.

References

1. Russel, S., Norvig, P.: Artificial Intelligence: A Modern Approach. Pearson, London (2020)
2. AI and the Media: Too Hot, Too Cold, Just Right? A Mapping of Artificial Intelligence Applications. https://tinyurl.com/7erhbyky. Accessed 09 Mar 2021
3. Sunstein, C.R.: # Republic: Divided Democracy in the Age of Social Media. Princeton University Press, Princeton (2018)
4. Smialek, J.: Twitter Bots Helped Trump and Brexit Win, Economic Study Says, Bloomberg article. https://doi.org/https://tinyurl.com/3p4x38uu. Accessed 09 Mar 2021
5. AI4Media Website. https://ai4media.eu/. Accessed 09 Mar 2021
6. Parisi, G.I., Kemker, R., Part, J.L., Kanan, C., Wermter, S.: Continual lifelong learning with neural networks: a review. Neural Netw. **113**, 54–71 (2019)
7. Bengio, Y., Louradour, J., Collobert, R., Weston, J.: Curriculum learning. In: 26th International Conference on Machine Learning Proceedings, pp. 41–48. ACM (2009)
8. Wistuba, M.: XferNAS: transfer neural architecture search. In: Hutter, F., Kersting, K., Lijffijt, J., Valera, I. (eds.) ECML PKDD 2020. LNCS (LNAI), vol. 12459, pp. 247–262. Springer, Cham (2021). https://doi.org/10.1007/978-3-030-67664-3_15
9. Gravina, D., Liapis, A., Yannakakis, G.: Quality diversity through surprise. IEEE Trans. Evol. Comput. **23**(4), 603–616 (2019)
10. Szegedy, C., Liu, W., Jia, Y., Sermanet, P., Reed, S., Anguelov, D.: Going deeper with convolutions. In: Conference on Computer Vision and Pattern Recognition Proceedings. IEEE (2015)

11. Yuan, X., He, P., Zhu, Q., Li, X.: Adversarial examples: attacks and defenses for deep learning. IEEE Trans. Neural Netw. Learn. Syst. **30**(9), 2805–2824 (2019)
12. AI Explainability 360 Website. http://aix360.mybluemix.net/. Accessed 09 Mar 2021
13. Jalalirad, A., Scavuzzo, M., Capota, C., Sprague, M.: A simple and efficient federated recommender system. In: 6th IEEE/ACM International Conference on Big Data Computing, Applications and Technologies Proceedings, pp. 53–58. ACM (2019)
14. Ntoutsi, E., et al.: Bias in data-driven artificial intelligence systems - an introductory survey. WIREs Data Min. Knowl. Discov. **10**(3) (2020)
15. Apostolidis, E., Metsai, A., Adamantidou, E., Mezaris, V., Patras, I.: A stepwise, label-based approach for improving the adversarial training in unsupervised video summarization. In: 1st International Workshop on AI for Smart TV Content Production, Access and Delivery Proceedings, pp. 17–25. ACM (2019)
16. Pons, J., Nieto, O., Prockup, M., Schmidt, E.M., Ehmann, A.F., Serra, X.: End-to-end learning for music audio tagging at scale. In: 19th International Society for Music Information Retrieval Conference Proceedings, pp. 637–44 (2018)
17. Nägeli, T., Meier, L., Domahidi, A., Alonso-Mora, X., Hilliges, O.: Real-time planning for automated multi-view drone cinematography. ACM Trans. Graph. **36**(4) (2017)
18. Reed, S., Akata, Z., Mohan, S., Tenka, S., Schiele, B., Lee, H.: Learning what and where to draw. In: 30th International Conference on Neural Information Processing Systems Proceedings, pp. 217–225. ACM (2016)
19. Mikolov, T., Sutskever, I., Chen, K., Corrado, G., Dean, J.: Distributed representations of words and phrases and their compositionality. In: 26th International Conference on Neural Information Processing Systems Proceedings, pp. 3111–3119. ACM (2013)
20. Zellers, R., et al.: Defending against neural fake news. In: Annual Conference on Neural Information Processing Systems Proceedings, pp. 9051–9062 (2019)
21. Mercier, G., et al.: Detecting manipulations in video. In: Mezaris, V., Nixon, L., Papadopoulos, S., Teyssou, D. (eds.) Video Verification in the Fake News Era, pp. 161–189. Springer, Cham (2019). https://doi.org/10.1007/978-3-030-26752-0_6
22. Charitidis, P., Kordopatis-Zilos, G., Papadopoulos, S., Kompatsiaris, I.: Investigating the impact of pre-processing and prediction aggregation on the DeepFake detection task. arXiv preprint: https://arxiv.org/abs/2006.07084 (2020)
23. Kaminskas, M., Bridge, D.: Diversity, serendipity, novelty, and coverage: a survey and empirical analysis of beyond-accuracy objectives in recommender systems. ACM Trans. Interact. Intell. Syst. **7**(1) (2016)
24. Koelstra, S., Patras, I.: Fusion of facial expressions and EEG for implicit affective tagging. Image Vis. Comput. **31**(2), 164–174 (2013)
25. Truly Media homepage. https://www.truly.media/. Accessed 09 Mar 2021
26. TruthNest homepage. https://www.truthnest.com/. Accessed 09 Mar 2021
27. Mirsky, Y., Lee, W.: The creation and detection of deepfakes: a survey. ACM Comput. Surv. **54**(1), 1–41 (2021)
28. Imagga Content Moderation Platform. https://imagga.com/content-moderation-platform. Accessed 09 Mar 2021

Regression Predictive Model to Analyze Big Data Analytics in Supply Chain Management

Elena Puica(✉)

Economic Informatics Doctoral School, The Bucharest University of Economic Studies,
Bucharest, Romania

Abstract. The research problem that is the interest in this thesis is to understand the Big Data Analytics (BDA) potential in achieving a much better Supply Chain Management (SCM). Based on this premise, it was conducted a Regression Predictive Model to comprehend the usage of Big Data Analytics in SCM and to have insights of the requirements for the potential applications of BDA. In this study were analyzed the main sources of BDA utilized in present by Supply Chain professionals and it was provided future suggestions. The findings of the study suggest that BDA may bring operational and strategic benefit to SCM, and the application of BDA may have positive implication for industry sector.

Keywords: Big Data Analytics · Supply chain · Supply Chain Management · Regression predictive model · Big data in supply chain management

1 Introduction

The present study aims to identify the expectations, the requirements, and implications from the application of Big Data Analytics (BDA) in Supply Chain Management (SCM). Growing network complexity, global competition, and increasing product diversity, while customer expectation remains as high as ever [1] has directed the SCM in the direction of development. The research contributes to the existing literature by a regression predictive model to discover the most common used sources of BDA in SCM. This way, the research adds to the literature the implication of BDA in SCM by applying a regression predictive model to discover what is the principal usage of BDA and to understand what are the less ways that BDA is used in SCM. The research can lead to inspire the SCM professionals to take proactive actions and to discover opportunities in bettering their processes, which can lead to a high positive impact in the industry sector.

The remainder of this paper is organized as follows: Section two, reviews relevant BDA literature and the studies related to the practices and techniques of BDA used. Section three is concentrated to provide a better understanding of the implication of BDA in SCM. Section four presents the model applied to analyze the use of BDA in SCM and presents the results of regression predictive model analyses. The last section is composed of the conclusion of the study and provides direction for future research.

© IFIP International Federation for Information Processing 2021
Published by Springer Nature Switzerland AG 2021
I. Maglogiannis et al. (Eds.): AIAI 2021, IFIP AICT 627, pp. 94–101, 2021.
https://doi.org/10.1007/978-3-030-79150-6_8

2 Big Data Analytics

Data is expressed in different types and formats, and the access to data is also different, these facts all point the issue in one direction: the ability to search, aggregate, visualize and cross-reference large data sets in a reasonable time and when BDA is linked to SCM, new challenges arise. BDA, generally, supports SCM in innovation, productivity, and competition [2] and has been defined as the technique that is deployed to uncover hidden patterns and bring insight into interesting relations in understanding contexts by examining, processing, discovering, and exhibiting the result [3]. The four main types of analytics techniques will be discussed: descriptive analytics, diagnostic analytics, predictive analytics, and prescriptive analytics.

Predictive and prescriptive analytics play a vital role in helping SCM to make effective decisions about the strategic direction. BDA is driving the SCM for development, and it uses models, technologies, and tools to help SCM make performance analysis that is fast, efficient, and effective (see Fig. 1).

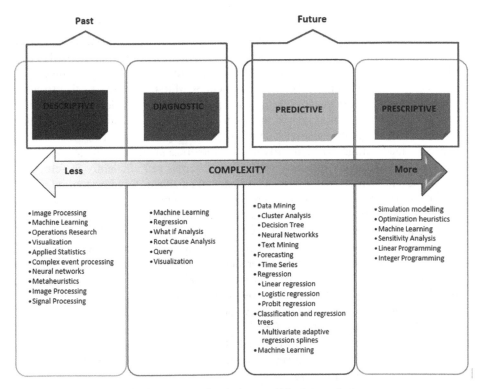

Fig. 1. Types and techniques of big data analytics

Descriptive analytics summarize the raw data and is a data analysis used to describe past situations to make trends, patterns, and anomalies visible [4]. While descriptive analytics describes what has happened, diagnostic analytics attempts to get at the root cause of some anomaly or occurrence. Predictive analysis examines real-time and historical data, using mathematical algorithms and programming to discover interpretation and prediction patterns within the data, in other words, it makes predictions in the form of probabilities for the future events [5]. Predictive analytics uses advanced statistics, machine learning techniques and data-driven algorithms to generate models and fall into two major categories: regression techniques and machine learning techniques. Prescriptive analysis mainly is determining and evaluating many complex objectives and alternative decisions. It mainly uses data and mathematical algorithms to achieve the purpose of improving business performance and includes multi-criteria decision making, optimization, and simulation. BDA will make the organization's system generates a large amount of information [6] and identifying problems and opportunities in existing processes and functions, can be achieved by using BDA, which generates competitive advantage for the SCM [7].

3   Big Data Analytics in Supply Chain Management

Digital technologies can lead to a better understand for a more complex SCM, which can continuously monitor the physical environment and generate large amounts of data at an unprecedented rate. These technologies are generating large amounts of data, called Big Data [8], which gradually becomes an important information technology regarding SCM decisions [9]. BDA should not only be used to help SCM to make strategic decisions in procurement, supply chain network design, and product design and development, but it should also be applied to all stages of the entire SCM [10], in order to industry sector to benefit from it. Predictive analytics can have the ability to predict consumer behaviors, prevent fraud, mitigate risk, identify new customers, and improve operations, being able to identify customer's spending behaviors and cross-sell efficiently or sell additional products to their customers, enhance customer satisfaction and customer loyalty, identify the most effective marketing campaign and communication channels, identify fraudulent payment transactions, flag potential fraudulent claims and pay legitimate insurance claims immediately and predict when machinery will fail. SCM professionals are overwhelmed by massive amounts of data, on one side, opens new ways to generate, organize, and analyze data, and on the other side, is pushing SCM to adopt and improve BDA functions to enhance SCM processes and ultimately improve performance [12].

Predictive analytics can help SCM mitigate their risk, maximize their profits, optimize their operations, and gain a competitive advantage. SCM use predictive analytics to solve complex business problems for different sectors (construction, manufaturing, retail, transportation, telecommunication and utilities), in order to discover new opportunities, and to gain competitive advantages. The data utilized in SCM is extracted from different sources, these sources are:

a.   Analyse big data from geolocation of portable devices;
b.   Analyse big data from smart devices or sensors;
c.   Analyse big data generated from social media;
d.   Analyse big data internally from any data source.

Applications of BDA captures customer demand, micro-segmentation and predicts consumers' behavior, is minimizing transportation costs, in the process of helping the products to be transported through the supply chain. In operations applications BDA can optimize labour, track attendance, and reduce costs while ensuring service. Sourcing applications, use BDA to optimize procurement channel selection and integrate suppliers into their operations, these data sources include expenses, supplier performance assessments, and internal or external negotiations [13].

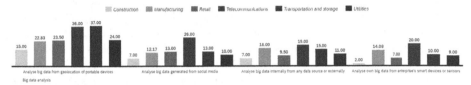

Fig. 2. Percentage of enterprises that use big data Source: own processing based on https://ec.eur opa.eu/eurostat

BDA technology in the industry sectors was used by 15% of enterprises in the construction industry, 22.83% in manufacturing, 23.5% in retail, 36% in the telecommunications industry, 37% in the transport industry and 24% in the utilities industry for the cathegory that analyse Big Data from the geolocation of portable devices. For cathegory that used Big Data from social media, 7% was in the construction, 12.17% in manufacturing, 13% in retail, 26% in telecommunications, 13% in the transportation and 10% in utilities. The enterprises that used Big Data internally from their own or external data sources had a percentage of 7% in construction, 16% in manufacturing, 9.5% in retail, 19% in telecommunications, 15% in transportation and 11% in utilities. The companies that used Big Data from their own smart devices or sensors had a percentage of 2% in construction, 14.08% in manufacturing, 7% in retail, 20% in telecommunications, 10% in transportation and 9% in utilities (see Fig. 2).

4 Implementation of Regression Predictive Model with SAP Analytics Cloud

Regression analysis examines the degree of relationship that exists between a set of input variables and a target variable. The relationships between the target variable and the input variables are associative only and any cause-effect is merely subjective. To analyze the usage of BDA in SCM for different industry sectors (construction, manufaturing, retail, transportation, telecommunication, and utilities) it was used the application of SAP Analytic Cloud (SAC), which is an analytic software provided by SAP. SAC is a platform independent and allows to discover, analyze, plan, and predict data. SAC offers connection to a variety of data sources to create models and develop reports with charts, including Geo Maps, and tables.

4.1 Identification of the Business Problem

The regression predictive model it is applied in this study to discover what is exactly the usage of BDA among SCM for different industry sectors (construction, manufaturing, retail, transportation, telecommunication, and utilities).

4.2 Definition of the Hypotheses

The purpose of the hypotheses is to narrow down the business problem and make predictions about the relationships between two or more data variables. By applying the regression predictive model, the following objectives are intended to be met, the first one is to find out what is the principal usage of BDA in SCM, the second is to understand what are the less applied sources of usage of BDA in SCM, the third, is to know from where to start, in order to take action to discover opportunities for those sources where BDA is used less and the last one is to encourage SCM professionals to take proactive actions to use BDA in SCM. The target variable is the "percentage of Big Data usage", which represents the event to be predicted.

The following hypotheses where analyzed:

- H1 - Analyze big data from geolocation of portable devices.
- H2 - Analyze big data from smart devices or sensors.
- H3 - Analyze big data generated from social media.
- H4 - Analyze big data internally from any data source.

4.3 Collecting the Data

Data collected is classified as structured (spreadsheets) and it was extracted from the Eurostat database. Eurostat is the statistical office of the European Union, is a world-leading database, widely known for its extensive, reliable content and high-quality statistics and data on Europe [14].

4.4 Data Analysis, Development of the Predictive Model and the Determination of the Best-Fit Model

The analyze the quality of the model more indicators were considered. The Prediction Confidence, which measures the robustness of the predictive model or its ability to reproduce the same detection on new data and has the role to measure if the predictive model can do the predictions with the same reliability when new cases arrive. The Prediction Confidence should be as close as possible to 100%. The quality of the regression model is measured by The Root Mean Square Error (RMSE). It is a statistical indicator which measures the average of the square difference between values predicted by the predictive model and actual values of the target for all cases of the validation dataset. The smaller is this difference, the better the quality of the predictive model is.

The model that was trained for this study has the result of RMSE equal with 3.83 and the prediction confidence indicator is 94,91% (see Fig. 3).

Fig. 3. Performance indicators

The mean of the target is around 5,2 for the estimation results and 4,75 for the validation dataset. The standard deviation is around 4,95 for the estimated results and 3,85 for the validated results (see Fig. 4). The predictive model has a good quality, its robustness is around 95%, and thus is also very good.

Data Partition	Minimum	Maximum	Mean	Standard Deviation
Training	0	23	5.2	4.95
Validation	0	22	4.75	3.85

Fig. 4. Target statistics

In Fig. 5 is described the predicted versus actual data, the green curve represents the perfect model, which shows no error and predicts exactly the correct opportunity value. The blue curve is the predictive model determined by SAC Smart Predict. The dotted-blue curves are the error min and error max on the validation dataset. If the green and blue curves do not match at all, this mean that the quality and the robustness of the predictive model are quite poor. If these two curves match closely, the predictive model is good and can be trusted to predict the value of the unknown target. Last case is when the two curves match a lot except on few segments. This means that the predictive model is good but can be improved.

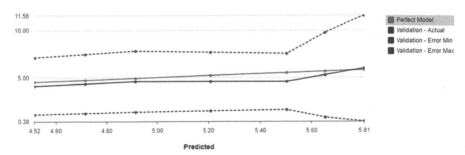

Fig. 5. Predicted vs. actuals data. (Color figure online)

4.5 Utilize the Model, Referred to as Scoring

Following the choice of the best variables to build a qualitative and robust model, a predictive regression model was determined.

In Fig. 6 is the representation of the validated data, the category that has the lowest value of the target mean is represented in the graphic by orange dot, the variable "Analyze Big Data from social media". The lowest values of frequency are represented by the blue dot, the variable "Analyze Big Data from geolocation of portable devices". The highest value of target mean is for the "Analyze Big Data from devices or sensors" and "Analyze Big Data internally" which are the most frequent variables determined in the model (see Fig. 6).

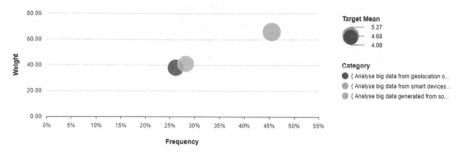

Fig. 6. Usage of big data analysis in SCM

In Fig. 7. is the representation of statistics explanation of variable validated. For example, the category that contains the variables "Analyze Big Data from devices or sensors" and "Analyze Big Data internally from any data sources" have the value 45,52%, which indicates that these are the most common ways BDA is used in SCM. The second used is the variable "Analyze Big Data generated from social media", which represents 28,28% and last source of BDA used in SCM is the variable "Analyze Big Data from geolocation of portable devices", which is 26,21% (see Fig. 7).

Influencer	Category	Frequency		Target Mean	Target Standard Deviation
Big Data Usage	{ Analyse big data from geolocation of portable devices }		26.21%	4.58	3.22
Big Data Usage	{ Analyse big data from smart devices or sensors, Analyse big data internally from any data source }		45.52%	5.27	4.53
Big Data Usage	{ Analyse big data generated from social media }		28.28%	4.09	3

Fig. 7. Explanation of category validated statistics.

5 Conclusion

The advancements in the sphere of artificial intelligence and machine learning have revolutionized the world of computation. This article initiates a possibility of development of new models of regression predictive analytics and add additional highlights to literature review of the existing models. The Regression predictive model applied in this study is providing insights for the objective proposed, which is to find out what is the principal usage of BDA in SCM for different industry sectors (construction, manufaturing, retail, transportation, telecommunication, and utilities), to understand what are the less used sources of BDA in SCM, to know from where to start, in order to act and to discover opportunities for the less used BDA ways of usage and lastly, to encourage the SCM professionals to take proactive actions to use BDA in SCM. According to the results of this study, the most popular ways or used sources of BDA in SCM is to analyze Big Data from devices or sensors and to analyze Big Data internally from any data sources. Analysis of Big Data from geolocation of portable devices is the least used source in SCM.

For SCM to have o positive impact and change is to invest in portable and geolocation devices, because the data that is generated from these devices is valuable and voluminous, which could help the SCM to make improved decisions and have better control over their process. In this paper, it is presented ongoing research work about BDA solutions for increasing the SCM visibility. The future prospect is that several SCM enterprises from different industries will develop Big Data ecosystems for achieving new business models and offering new services to customers and will lead to even a more increased complexity of SCM.

References

1. Dawe, P., Pittman, A., von Koeller,E.: Segmentation in the Consumer Supply Chain: One Size Does Not Fit All, Technical Report. The Boston Consulting Group (2015)
2. Dong, J., Yang, C.: Business value of big data analytics: a systems-theoretic approach and empirical test. Inf. Manage. (2018). https://doi.org/10.1016/j.im.2018.11.001
3. Wang, H., et al.: Randomly attracted firefly algorithm with neighborhood search and dynamic parameter adjustment mechanism. J. Soft Comput. **21**(18), 5325–5339 (2017)
4. Ansari, Z., Kant, R.: A State-Of-Art literature review reflecting 15 years of focus on sustainable supply chain management. J. Cleaner Prod. (e-journal), 2524–2543. (2016). 10.1016/j.jclepro.2016.11.023
5. Arunachalam, D., Kumar, N., Kawalek, J.: Understanding big data analytics capabilities in supply chain management: unravelling the issues, challenges and implications for practice. Transp. Res. Part E (e-journal), 416–436 (2017). 10.1016/j.tre.2017.04.001
6. Barbosa, M., Vicente, A., Ladeira, M., Oliveira, M.: Managing supply chain resources with big data analytics: a systematic review. Int. J. Logistics Res. Appl. (e-journal) **21**(3), 177–200 (2018). https://doi.org/10.1080/13675567.2017.1369501
7. Smart Village Technology. Modeling and Optimization in Science and Technologies. Cham: Springer. vol 17, (2020)
8. Ahearn, M., Armbruster, W., Young, R.: Big Data's potential to improve food supply environment sustainability and food safety. Int. Food Agribus. Manage. Rev. (e-journal) **19**, 177–172 (2016). http://dx.doi.org/10.22004/ag.econ.240704
9. Bronson, K., Knezevic, I.: Big data in food and agriculture. Big Data Soc. (e-journal) **3**(1) (2016). https://doi.org/10.1177/2053951716648174
10. Hazen, B.T., Skipper, J.B., Ezell, J.D., Boone, C.A.: Big data and predictive analytics for supply chain sustainability: A theory-driven research agenda. Comput. Ind. Eng. **101**, 592–598 (2016)
11. Hazen, B.T., Boone, C.A., Ezell, J.D., Jones-Farmer, L.A.: Data quality for data science, predictive analytics, and big data in supply chain management: an introduction to the problem and suggestions for research and applications. Int. J. Prod. Econ. (e-journal) **154**, 72–80 (2014). 10.1016/j.ijpe.2014.04.018
12. Addo-Tenkorang, R., Helo, P.: Big data applications in operations/supply-chain management: a literature review. Comput. Ind. Eng. (e-journal), 528–543 (2016). 10.1016/j.cie.2016.09.023
13. Eurostat. Accessed at 24 Apr 2021. https://ec.europa.eu/eurostat

Automated Machine Learning

An Automated Machine Learning Approach for Predicting Chemical Laboratory Material Consumption

António João Silva[ID] and Paulo Cortez[✉][ID]

ALGORITMI Center, Department of Information Systems, University of Minho,
4804-533 Guimarães, Portugal
id7322@alunos.uminho.pt, pcortez@dsi.uminho.pt

Abstract. This paper address a relevant business analytics need of a chemical company, which is adopting an Industry 4.0 transformation. In this company, quality tests are executed at the Analytical Laboratories (AL), which receive production samples and execute several instrumental analyses. In order to improve the AL stock warehouse management, a Machine Learning (ML) project was developed, aiming to estimate the AL materials consumption based on week plans of sample analyses. Following the CRoss-Industry Standard Process for Data Mining (CRISP-DM) methodology, several iterations were executed, in which three input variable selection strategies and two sets of AL materials (top 10 and all consumed materials) were tested. To reduce the modeling effort, an Automated Machine Learning (AutoML) was adopted, allowing to automatically set the best ML model among six distinct regression algorithms. Using real data from the chemical company and a realistic rolling window evaluation, several ML train and test iterations were executed. The AutoML results were compared with two time series forecasting methods, the ARIMA methodology and a deep learning Long Short-Term Memory (LSTM) model. Overall, competitive results were achieved by the best AutoML models, particularly for the top 10 set of materials.

Keywords: Industry 4.0 · Automated machine learning · Regression · Time series forecasting · Deep learning

1 Introduction

With the emergence of the Industry 4.0 concept, there is an increase of digital transformation, where industrial physical processes generate data that can be analyzed by Machine Learning (ML) algorithms to provide valuable Business Analytics (BA) [19]. These analyses can impact several production aspects, including stock management. However, in the Chemical industry the usage of ML and BA is still scarce.

© IFIP International Federation for Information Processing 2021
Published by Springer Nature Switzerland AG 2021
I. Maglogiannis et al. (Eds.): AIAI 2021, IFIP AICT 627, pp. 105–116, 2021.
https://doi.org/10.1007/978-3-030-79150-6_9

In this work, we address a BA need of a chemical organization that is adopting an Industry 4.0 transformation in their Analytical Laboratories (AL). During the production process, selected samples are sent to be tested at the AL, which is responsible for assuring that the products are compliant with quality standards. The analysis of a sample at the AL requires diverse instrumental analyses, each consuming one or more materials (e.g., Acetone, Dichloromethane, Ethanol, Methanol). Under this context, predicting the amount of materials needed for the quality tests is crucial to support a AL stock management, preventing quality inspection delays which would prejudice production. In previous work [20], we have adopted a ML approach to successfully predict the arrival times of samples at the AL. By using this predictive approach, the chemical organization can now perform weekly plans of the expected instrumental AL usage. Under this context, this paper describes a ML approach to predict the weekly consumption of AL materials based on the expected instrument usage. The approach was developed using the CRoss-Industry Standard Process for Data Mining (CRISP-DM) methodology [26]. Similarly to the work conducted in [20], to better focus on feature engineering (data preparation phase of CRISP-DM), we adopt an Automated Machine Learning (AutoML) [8], which is executed during the modeling CRISP-DM phase and that allows to automatically select and tune the hyperparameters of the predictive ML models. Using real-word data, collected from a chemical company, we executed several CRISP-DM iterations, exploring three main input variable selection strategies and two sets of AL materials (top 10 and all consumed materials). The experimentation adopts a realistic rolling window evaluation scheme, which simulates several train and test modeling updates through time. For benchmark purposes, the proposed ML approach is compared with two time series forecasting methods: the known ARIMA methodology [1] and a deep learning Long Short-Term Memory (LSTM) [17].

The paper is structured as follows. Section 2 describes the related work. The problem contextualization is presented in Sect. 3. Next, the analyzed data and prediction methods are presented in Sect. 4. Then, the obtained results are shown and discussed in Sect. 5. Finally, Sect. 6 concludes the paper.

2   Related Work

The Industry 4.0 concept [19] is impacting diverse industrial sectors. With the increased usage of interconnected sensors (e.g., Internet-of-Things), factories generate more digital data that reflect their production processes. All these data can be analyzed by AI and ML algorithms, providing valuable BA. In some cases, real-world ML project fail due to to a misalignment between business needs and ML analyses [7]. The CRISP-DM methodology was precisely developed to solve this issue, increasing the success of ML projects [26]. The methodology involves both business and ML experts and includes six main phases: business understanding, data understanding, data preparation, modeling, evaluation and deployment. In previous works, we have employed CRISP-DM to successfully model the business needs of textile [18] and chemical [20] companies.

Turning to the specific chemical sector, in several organizations the Industry 4.0 concept is not yet fully embraced. For instance, while quality tests are rigorously stored in digital databases, the same does not occur with the AL processes [13,21]. Also, it is common to have information silos (e.g., production, AL) and thus this lack of database interoperability diminishes the full potential to use ML to extract valuable BA from the data [20]. Thus, most predictive analytics studies for the chemical sector involve the production processes, rather than AL (such as executed in this paper). For instance, Roe et al. [25] used a Fuzzy Neural Network model to perform a predictive control on a solar-thermal chemical processing. Moreover, Longone et al. [14] used a Logistic Regression to predict production anomalies in a chemical plant that adopted the Industry 4.0 concept. It should be highlighted that most predictive ML studies in industry are focused on non chemical sectors and target the predictive maintenance task. Examples of ML algorithms that were proposed for such task include: Random Forest (RF) [3], Neural Networks (NN) [22], Gradient Boosting Machines (GBM) [15] and Support Vector Machines (SVM) [23]. In all these ML predictive studies, expert knowledge and trial-error experiments were used to select and tune the predictive ML algorithms, which is a common ML practice. However, there is a recent ML trend that assumes the usage of AutoML [8]. The main advantage of AutoML is that it alleviates the ML analyst effort, allowing to focus on other aspects of the ML pipeline process (e.g., data engineering). In [20], we have adopted an AutoML approach to predict the arrival of production samples at the AL, allowing to support the allocation of human resources and analytical equipment. In this paper, we adopt a similar AutoML approach but focusing on a different business need from the same chemical company: to predict the week AL material consumption based on quality instrumental usage estimates.

3   Problem Formulation

Figure 1 presents the flow of main transactions that occur between three main sections of the analyzed chemical company: Warehouse, Production and Analytical Laboratories (AL). The Warehouse is responsible for storing and managing the different materials that are provided by the suppliers and that are needed by the company. (e.g., raw production materials). In this work, we focus on analytical materials, which are used in the AL. The Production line is where the production process is performed. A production of a certain product starts when there is a production order for that product on that specific date. A production order contains the several informational elements: the product to be produced, the quantity in batches to be produced, the raw materials to be used and the start and end dates. The dates are added to the database when the production ordered ends. During the production period, several production samples, called In Production (IP), are sent to the AL for quality assessment. If quality is below the client requirements, then the production line will have to perform adjustments, in order improve the expected quality of the product. Thus, the AL are a critical element of the production process, with delays in AL testing resulting in production stops and delays in the execution of new production orders.

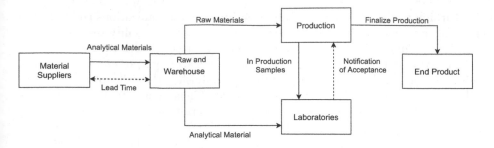

Fig. 1. Workflow of materials and production transactions.

At the AL, the quality tests use several instrumental analyses that require analytical materials, in order to guarantee the feasibility of the tests. When there is an AL shortage of materials, they are ordered from the Warehouse, using the Enterprise Resource Planning (ERP) production system. In some cases, there is a low stock of the analytical materials in the Warehouse, which needs to produce supplier orders that take time, thus producing AL quality testing delays. In previous work [20], we have adopted an AutoML approach to predict the arrival of IP production samples at the AL. Using such predictions, the company information system is capable of producing accurate week plans of AL instrumental needs. In this paper, the ML goal is to use the AL tests (or plans) as the inputs of a regression model, aiming to predict a particular analytical material consumption. Let $\mathbf{X}$ denote a data matrix $N \times Q$ with the elements $x_{i,j}$, each representing the number of quality tests of type j that were executed (or are planned) for a particular week i, where N is the total number of weeks and Q is the total number of distinct quality tests. Let $\mathbf{Y}$ denote a matrix $N \times M$ with the elements $y_{i,m}$, each representing the quantity of consumed material of type $m \in \mathcal{M}$ for the week i, where $\mathcal{M} = \{1, 2, ..., M\}$ denotes a selection set with M distinct analytical materials. Another relevant business concept is the AL total weekly consumption quantity $(T_{\mathcal{M}})$, computed as $T_{\mathcal{M}} = \sum_{m=1}^{M} y_{i,m}$. The total consumption quantity is useful for resizing the AL warehouse.

The business goal is to estimate the w weekly quantity $\hat{y}_{w,m}$ based on the quality tests that use the m material:

$$\hat{y}_{w,m} = f(x_{w,k_1}, ..., x_{w,k_K}) \tag{1}$$

where $\{k_1, ..., k_K\}$ denotes the set of laboratory tests that are used as inputs and f is the data-driven function that will be learned using the AutoML approach. In this work, each m material consumption prediction requires the training of a different ML model. Moreover, the $\{k_1, ..., k_K\}$ input tests are dependent of the adopted feature selection strategy (Sect. 4.2). Once the distinct ML predictive models are built, the AL total weekly consumption quantity for selection $\mathcal{M}$ can be computed as: $\hat{T}_{\mathcal{M}} = \sum_{m=1}^{M} \hat{y}_{w,m}$.

4   Materials and Methods

4.1   Data

The data used in this study was retrieved by executing an Extract, Transform & Load (ETL) process, which extracted data records from two main databases related with the production and AL units. The resulting dataset includes a total of $N = 177$ weeks of data, from January 2016 to May 2019. In total, the input X matrix includes a total of $Q = 30$ distinct quality tests, thus with 177×30 elements. Some of the analyzed input tests have a strong correlation, while other variables often include a large portion of zero values. In Sect. 4.2, we will use these properties to design feature selection strategies. As for the target Y matrix, it includes a total of $M = 26$ analytical materials (e.g., Acetone, Ethanol, Methanol) After consulting the company experts, we explore two main sets of prediction targets: top 10 - with the $M = 10$ highest consumed materials ($\mathcal{M} = \{1, ..., 10\}$); and all – with all $M = 26$ materials ($\mathcal{M} = \{1, ..., 26\}$). Due to commercial privacy concerns, we do not disclose further details about the specific analyzed variables.

4.2   Prediction Methods

We adopted the R computational tool and its rminer package [6] for data manipulation and computation of the ML regression metrics. The AutoML is based on the H2O open-source tool (https://www.h2o.ai/products/h2o-automl/) [5]. The auto.arima from the forecast R package was used to automate and fit the ARIMA models [1,11,12]. Finally, the LSTM model was implemented using the PyTorch Python module [17].

The AutoML models were configured to select the best regression model and its hyperparameters for each targeted m material. The selection is based on the best Root Mean Squared Error (RMSE) computed using a validation set that is obtained by applying an internal 10-fold cross-validation method over the training data. All computational experiments were executed on the same personal computer and each individual ML model was trained up to a maximum running time of 3,600 s. Once a ML model is selected, the model was retrained with all training data. As in [8], the AutoML was configured to include a total of 6 distinct regression algorithms: RF, Extremely Randomized Trees (XRT), Generalized Linear Model (GLM), GBM, XGBoost (XG) and a Stacked Ensemble (SE). The RF is a popular ensemble method that combines a large number of decision trees based on bagging and random selection of input features [10]. The XRT algorithm extends the RF approach by randomly selecting the decision thresholds of the tree nodes [9]. GLM estimates regression models for exponential distributions (e.g., Gaussian, Poisson, gamma) [10]. The GBM algorithm is a based on a generalization of tree boosting, sequentially building regression trees for all data features [10]. XG is another ensemble tree method that uses boosting to enhance the prediction results [4]. The SE method, also known as stacked regression [2], combines the predictions of different base learners by using a second-level ML algorithm. The H2O implementation [5] uses the following AutoML setup: RF and XRT – set with the default hyperparameters; GLM - grid search used to set one hyperparameter (*alpha*, a regularization parameter); GBM and XG – grid search used to tune nine and ten hyperparameters (e.g., number of trees, maximum depth, minimum rows); SE – all five algorithms (RF, XRT, GLM, GBM, XG) are used as base learners and the individual predictions are weighted by using a second-level GLM learner.

The input matrix $\mathbf{X}$ includes several variables that are either correlated with other variables or contain a large number of zero values. In order to improve the AutoML results, we explore three main input Feature Selection (FS) strategies, that were applied to the training data: ALL - with all $Q = 30$ inputs, executed during the first CRISP-DM iteration; FS1 – all variables with a correlation higher than 60% or with more than 90% of zeros are removed (resulting in $Q = 15$), executed during the second CRISP-DM iteration; and FS2 - all variables with a correlation higher than 90% or with more than 90% of zeros are removed (leading to $Q = 19$), executed during the first CRISP-DM iteration.

For comparison purposes, we also consider two main time series forecasting methods, each using only the $y_{i,m}$ past observations ($i \in \{1, ..., m-1\}$) to predict $\hat{y}_{w,m}$ at week w: ARIMA and LSTM. The ARIMA is automatically build using the `forecast` R package, while the LSTM assumes a default parametrization with one input node (first time lag, y_{t-1}, where t is the current time), one hidden layer with 100 hidden nodes and hyperbolic tangent activation function, one output node (current observation, y_t), the Adam optimizer, Mean Squared Error (MSE) loss function and 150 training epochs.

4.3   Evaluation

We adopted a Rolling Window (RW) evaluation scheme [16,24], which simulates a realistic execution of the AutoML models by performing several training and test updates through time (Fig. 2). With this scheme, the initial training set with a fixed size of W time periods is used to generate the training models and execute a one week ahead prediction ($T = 1$). Then, the W data is updated by discarding the oldest week observations and adding one subsequent week of data. A new prediction model is built, allowing to issue a new prediction, and so on. In total, the RW results in $U = N - W$ training and testing updates. In this work, we have set $W = 147$, which allows to obtain $U = 30$ RW iterations. In order to reduce the computational effort, since we conduct a large number of ML experiments (e.g., we target $M = 26$ distinct outputs), the AutoML model and hyperparameter selection is only executed once for each m material, using the training data from the first RW iteration. Once the ML is selected, it is retrained for each RW iteration.

As for the regression metrics, using the $U = 30$ test predictions, we compute five measures [10,16]: Mean Absolute Error (MAE), Normalized MAE (NMAE), RMSE, Relative Squared Error (RSE), and the coefficient of determination (R^2). The lower the MAE, NMAE and RMSE values the better are the predictions. The NMAE measure is computed as $\frac{MAE}{\max(y_{i,m}) - \min(y_{i,m})}$, where $y_{i,m}$ denotes the target

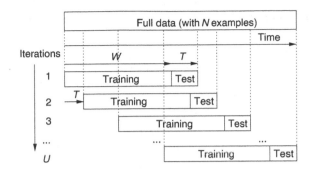

Fig. 2. Schematic of the Rolling Window (RW) evaluation.

variable for material m. When compared with MAE, the NMAE metric presents two main advantages [16]: it is more easy to interpret, since it expresses the error as a percentage of the full target scale (y); it is scale independent, which is useful for the analytical consumption data given that we handle different materials and thus distinct consumption scales. The RMSE measure is particularly important in this domain, since it is more sensitive to extreme values when compared with MAE. Thus, a lower RMSE should be aligned with a better upper or lower peak prediction, which is more useful to assist the stock management of the consumed AL materials. The RSE is computed as $\frac{SSE_{\hat{y}_{i,m}}}{SSE_{\overline{y}_{i,m}}}$, where SSE denotes the sum of squared errors and $\overline{y}_{i,m}$ the average of the target variable on the test data. The RSE is similar to the RMSE measure in the sense that it is also more sensitive to extreme errors. The advantage is that RSE is scale independent. While the RSE values can be also presented as percentages (such as NMAE), the RSE values are more difficult to interpret by end users, since it only expresses how good are the predictions when compared with the average target values. As for R^2, it measures the goodness of fit. The higher value, the better is the alignment between consecutive changes in the predicted and real values, with the perfect regression model producing a maximum of $R^2 = 1$.

Since we target a large number of individual models (up to $M = 26$), the value of each forecasting approach is globally measured by considering the predictive measures applied to total quantity consumption target for a particular $\mathcal{M}$ selection. For instance, the RW MAE is computed as $MAE = \sum_{u_1}^{U} |T_\mathcal{M} - \hat{T}_\mathcal{M}|/U$, where u is a RW iteration and $\hat{T}_\mathcal{M}$ is the predicted total quantity consumption.

5   Results and Discussion

Table 1 summarizes the obtained RW predictive results for the total quantity consumption and $\mathcal{M}$ selection of materials. For instance, the upper left value of 193.0 corresponds to the MAE average when considering all $m \in \mathcal{M}, \mathcal{M} = \{1, 2, ..., 10\}$ highest consumed analytical materials of the top 10 selection set. The results from Table 1 confirm that different CRISP-DM iterations produced improved predictions, with the FS2 feature selection strategy obtaining the best AutoML results for all regression metrics. As for the time series forecasting baselines, the ARIMA methodology outperformed the LSTM neural network approach. Overall, the AutoML FS2 method produces the best predictions for the top 10 selection (for all regression measures) and the best RMSE, RSE and R^2 values for the all selection ($M = 26$). As explained in Sect. 4.3, for the improving stock management of the analytical materials, the squared error measures (RMSE and RSE) are more important than absolute error ones (MAE and NMAE). Regarding the optimized ML models, the AutoML procedure selected only three of the six considered regression algorithms: GLM, GBM and RF.

Table 1. Summary of the RW predictive results (best values in **bold**).

Method	Top 10 ($M = 10$)					All ($M = 26$)				
	MAE	NMAE	RMSE	RSE	R^2	MAE	NMAE	RMSE	RSE	R^2
AutoML ALL	193.0	6.30	338.0	51.9	0.49	80.58	2.63	205.6	42.4	0.58
AutoML FS1	203.7	6.66	347.4	54.9	0.46	83.86	2.74	209.6	44.1	0.56
AutoML FS2	**187.7**	**6.13**	**330.2**	**49.5**	**0.51**	78.89	2.58	**200.8**	**40.5**	**0.60**
ARIMA	189.1	6.18	349.0	55.3	0.47	**76.92**	**2.51**	210.4	44.5	0.57
LSTM	230.0	7.52	367.7	61.4	0.41	90.67	2.96	219.1	48.2	0.53

For demonstration purposes, Fig. 3 shows the RW predictions for the selected AutoML FS2 method, which provided the lowest squared errors and highest coefficient of determination values. Due to business privacy issues, the scale values of the y-axis are omitted from the plots. In the plots, we also present in brackets the NMAE errors, since these are more easy to be interpreted by the chemical experts. The top two graphs show the results when predicting the total consumption (top 10 or all), while the middle and bottom graphs denote the prediction results for four individual materials ($m \in \{2, 10, 13, 17\}$). Overall, the real and predictive curves are very close and the prediction models are capable of correctly identifying several high and low consumption peaks, thus confirming that high quality predictions were obtained by the AutoML FS2 method.

The obtained results were shown to the chemical company experts, which highlighted the total quantity results, which can be used to resize the AL warehouse. Moreover, the chemical experts considered that individual material predictions are interesting, such as for $m = 2$ and $m = 17$ from Fig. 3, which have a strong potential to improve the stock management of these materials.

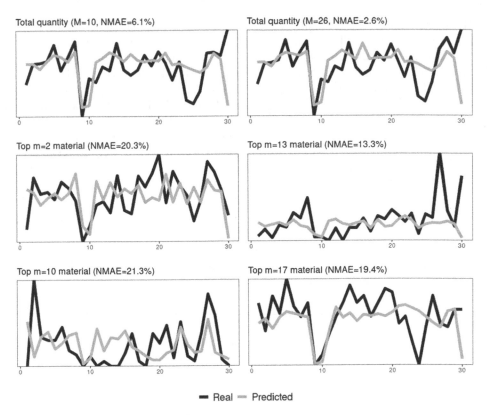

Fig. 3. RW predictive results for AutoML FS2 method (x-axis denotes the considered week, from March 2019 to May 2019; y-axis shows the analytical material consumption).

6   Conclusions

This study addresses a relevant business goal of a chemical company that is being transformed under the Industry 4.0. In particular, a Machine Learning (ML) approach was conducted, aiming to predict the needs of materials (e.g., Acetone, Ethanol) used in their Analytical Laboratories (AL). The ML project was conducted using the CRoss-Industry Standard Process for Data Mining (CRISP-DM) methodology. At the data understanding CRISP-DM stage, we collected 177 weeks of data, from January 2016 to May 2019, involving a total of 30 quality tests and up to 26 consumed AL materials. It should be noted that the chemical company is currently capable of producing weekly quality test usage plans with a good accuracy. Thus, the regression goal is to model AL material consumption as a function of the conducted quality tests. Using the collected data, we have developed large set of regression models (total of $M = 26$ models), which were analyzed in terms of two major sets of material selections: top 10 most consumed materials ($M = 10$) and all materials ($M = 26$). To reduce the

ML analyst effort, we have employed an Automated Machine Learning (AutoML) procedure during the CRISP-DM modeling stage, which allows to automatically select the best among six different regression algorithms. A total of three CRISP-DM iterations were executed, each exploring a different Feature Selection (FS) method. For comparison purposes, we also considered two time series forecasting methods: ARIMA and a Long Short-Term Memory (LSTM) neural network.

Several computational experiments were executed, by considering a realistic Rolling Window (RW) procedure that simulated 30 training and testing iterations through time. The best overall results were achieved by the AutoML FS2 method (corresponding to the third CRISP-DM iteration), which obtained a total quantity Normalized Mean Absolute Error (NMAE) of 6.1% (top 10 selection) and 2.6% (all materials). The predictive results were shown to the AL managers, which provided a positive feedback. Indeed, in future work, we intend to focus on the development stage of CRISP-DM, deploying the studied prediction models in the chemical company information system. This will allow to measure the business value of using these predictions to improve the warehouse stock management of analytical materials.

Acknowledgments. This work has been supported by FCT – Fundação para a Ciência e Tecnologia within the R&D Units Project Scope: UIDB/00319/2020. The authors also wish to thank the chemical company staff involved with this project for providing the data and also the valuable domain feedback.

References

1. Box, G.E.P., Pierce, D.A.: Distribution of residual autocorrelations in autoregressive-integrated moving average time series models. J. Am. Stat. Assoc. **65**(332), 1509–1526 (1970). http://www.jstor.org/stable/2284333
2. Breiman, L.: Stacked regressions. Mach. Learn. **24**(1), 49–64 (1996). https://doi.org/10.1007/BF00117832
3. Canizo, M., Onieva, E., Conde, A., Charramendieta, S., Trujillo, S.: Real-time predictive maintenance for wind turbines using big data frameworks. In: 2017 IEEE International Conference on Prognostics and Health Management, ICPHM 2017, Dallas, TX, USA, 19–21 June 2017, pp. 70–77. IEEE (2017). https://doi.org/10.1109/ICPHM.2017.7998308
4. Chen, T., Guestrin, C.: Xgboost: a scalable tree boosting system. In: Krishnapuram, B., Shah, M., Smola, A.J., Aggarwal, C.C., Shen, D., Rastogi, R. (eds.) Proceedings of the 22nd ACM SIGKDD International Conference on Knowledge Discovery and Data Mining, San Francisco, CA, USA, 13–17 August 2016, pp. 785–794. ACM (2016). https://doi.org/10.1145/2939672.2939785
5. Cook, D.: Practical Machine Learning with H2O: Powerful, Scalable Techniques for Deep Learning and AI. O'Reilly Media Inc., Newton (2016)
6. Cortez, P.: Modern Optimization with R. Springer, Heidelberg (2014). https://doi.org/10.1007/978-3-319-08263-9
7. Deal, J.: The ten most common data mining business mistakes (2013). https://www.elderresearch.com/most-common-data-science-business-mistakes

8. Ferreira, L., Pilastri, A., Martins, C., Santos, P., Cortez, P.: An automated and distributed machine learning framework for telecommunications risk management. In: Rocha, A.P., Steels, L., van den Herik, H.J. (eds.) Proceedings of the 12th International Conference on Agents and Artificial Intelligence, ICAART 2020, Valletta, Malta, 22–24 February 2020, vol. 4, pp. 99–107. SCITEPRESS (2020). https://doi.org/10.5220/0008952800990107
9. Geurts, P., Ernst, D., Wehenkel, L.: Extremely randomized trees. Mach. Learn. **63**(1), 3–42 (2006). https://doi.org/10.1007/s10994-006-6226-1
10. Hastie, T., Tibshirani, R., Friedman, J.: The Elements of Statistical Learning: Data Mining, Inference, and Prediction. Springer, Heidelberg (2009)
11. Hyndman, R., et al.: forecast: Forecasting functions for time series and linear models (2020). https://pkg.robjhyndman.com/forecast/, r package version 8.13
12. Hyndman, R.J., Khandakar, Y.: Automatic time series forecasting: the forecast package for R. J. Stat. Softw. **26**(3), 1–22 (2008). https://www.jstatsoft.org/article/view/v027i03
13. Kammergruber, R., Robold, S., Karliç, J., Durner, J.: The future of the laboratory information system-what are the requirements for a powerful system for a laboratory data management? Clin. Chem. Lab. Med. (CCLM) **52**(11), 225–230 (2014)
14. Langone, R., Cuzzocrea, A., Skantzos, N.: Interpretable anomaly prediction: Predicting anomalous behavior in industry 4.0 settings via regularized logistic regression tools. Data Knowl. Eng. **130**, 101850 (2020). https://doi.org/10.1016/j.datak.2020.101850
15. Liulys, K.: Machine learning application in predictive maintenance. In: 2019 Open Conference of Electrical, Electronic and Information Sciences (eStream), pp. 1–4. IEEE (2019)
16. Oliveira, N., Cortez, P., Areal, N.: The impact of microblogging data for stock market prediction: using twitter to predict returns, volatility, trading volume and survey sentiment indices. Expert Syst. Appl. **73**, 125–144 (2017). https://doi.org/10.1016/j.eswa.2016.12.036
17. Paszke, A., et al.: Pytorch: an imperative style, high-performance deep learning library. In: Wallach, H., Larochelle, H., Beygelzimer, A., d'Alché Buc, F., Fox, E., Garnett, R. (eds.) Advances in Neural Information Processing Systems, vol. 32, pp. 8024–8035. Curran Associates, Inc. (2019). http://papers.neurips.cc/paper/9015-pytorch-an-imperative-style-high-performance-deep-learning-library.pdf
18. Ribeiro, R., et al.: Predicting physical properties of woven fabrics via automated machine learning and textile design and finishing features. In: Maglogiannis, I., Iliadis, L., Pimenidis, E. (eds.) AIAI 2020. IAICT, vol. 584, pp. 244–255. Springer, Cham (2020). https://doi.org/10.1007/978-3-030-49186-4_21
19. Shrouf, F., Ordieres, J., Miragliotta, G.: Smart factories in industry 4.0: a review of the concept and of energy management approached in production based on the internet of things paradigm. In: 2014 IEEE International Conference on Industrial Engineering and Engineering Management, pp. 697–701 (2014). https://doi.org/10.1109/IEEM.2014.7058728
20. Silva, A.J., Cortez, P., Pilastri, A.: Chemical laboratories 4.0: a two-stage machine learning system for predicting the arrival of samples. In: Maglogiannis, I., Iliadis, L., Pimenidis, E. (eds.) AIAI 2020. IAICT, vol. 584, pp. 232–243. Springer, Cham (2020). https://doi.org/10.1007/978-3-030-49186-4_20
21. Skobelev, D., Zaytseva, T., Kozlov, A., Perepelitsa, V., Makarova, A.: Laboratory information management systems in the work of the analytic laboratory. Meas. Techn. **53**(10), 1182–1189 (2011)

22. Spendla, L., Kebisek, M., Tanuska, P., Hrcka, L.: Concept of predictive maintenance of production systems in accordance with industry 4.0. In: 2017 IEEE 15th International Symposium on Applied Machine Intelligence and Informatics (SAMI), pp. 000405–000410. IEEE (2017)
23. Straus, P., Schmitz, M., Wostmann, R., Deuse, J.: Enabling of predictive maintenance in the brownfield through low-cost sensors, an iiot-architecture and machine learning. In: 2018 IEEE International Conference on Big Data (Big Data), pp. 1474–1483 (2018).https://doi.org/10.1109/BigData.2018.8622076
24. Tashman, L.J.: Out-of-sample tests of forecasting accuracy: an analysis and review. Int. J. Forecast. **16**(4), 437–450 (2000). https://doi.org/10.1016/S0169-2070(00)00065-0
25. Wen, Z., Xie, L., Fan, Q., Feng, H.: Long term electric load forecasting based on ts-type recurrent fuzzy neural network model. Electric Power Syst. Res. **179** (2020). https://doi.org/10.1016/j.epsr.2019.106106
26. Wirth, R., Hipp, J.: Crisp-dm: towards a standard process model for data mining. In: Proceedings of the 4th International Conference on the Practical Applications of Knowledge Discovery and Data Mining, pp. 29–39 (2000)

An Ontology-Based Concept for Meta AutoML

Bernhard G. Humm⬭ and Alexander Zender⬭(✉)⬭

Hochschule Darmstadt - University of Applied Sciences,
Haardtring 100, 64295 Darmstadt, Germany
{bernhard.humm,alexander.zender}@h-da.de

Abstract. Automated machine learning (AutoML) supports ML engineers and data scientists by automating tasks like model selection and hyperparameter optimization. A number of AutoML solutions have been developed, open-source and commercial. We propose a concept called *OMA-ML* (Ontology-based Meta AutoML) that combines the strengths of existing AutoML solutions by integrating them (meta AutoML).

OMA-ML is based on a ML ontology that guides the meta AutoML process. It supports multiple user groups, with and without programming skills. By combining the strengths of AutoML solutions, it supports any number of ML tasks and ML libraries.

1 Introduction

Machine learning (ML) is an important sub-domain of artificial intelligence (AI), allowing to make predictions using models based on previous observations [22]. Engineering ML applications for practical use requires sound experience of ML engineers respectively data scientists. Tasks to be performed include data analysis, data preparation, feature engineering, model selection, validation, learning curve analysis and hyperparameter optimization. To support data scientists and also enable domain experts to create ML pipelines, the field of *automated ML (AutoML)* [28] has emerged. AutoML aims at automating model selection and hyperparameter optimization, leading to higher efficiency and, potentially, better results. More progressive AutoML solutions also perform data preparation, feature engineering, and validation, allowing to create entire ML pipelines automatically [15].

Currently, AutoML is focused on supervised ML [28]. There is a growing number of AutoML solutions available, both academic as well as commercial. Current state-of-the-art AutoML solutions target one concrete ML library and compute a ML pipeline for this library only, e.g., Autosklearn [5] for Scikit-learn [21], Auto-Keras [12] for Keras [3], and Google AutoML [8] for Tensorflow [1].

To the best of our knowledge, no existing AutoML solution combines multiple ML libraries.

The targeted user groups of AutoML solutions differ. Commercial solutions like RapidMiner Auto Model [14] or Google AutoML [8] offer a graphical user

© IFIP International Federation for Information Processing 2021
Published by Springer Nature Switzerland AG 2021
I. Maglogiannis et al. (Eds.): AIAI 2021, IFIP AICT 627, pp. 117–128, 2021.
https://doi.org/10.1007/978-3-030-79150-6_10

interface (GUI) usable for domain experts without programming skills (e.g., biologists), providing a workflow and deployment inside their ecosystem. Auto-WEKA [13] is an open source solution which also provides a GUI. Other open source solutions like Autosklearn [5], Auto-Keras [12], Auto-PyTorch [18], or TPOT [15] offer libraries that require programming skills.

This paper presents a concept for meta AutoML which supports multiple ML libraries by combining the strengths of several AutoML solutions. This concept is based on a ML ontology which guides meta AutoML. We call this method *OMA-ML* (Ontology-based Meta AutoML); the implementation is ongoing work in progress.

This paper is structured as follows. Section 2 presents related work. In Sect. 3, we introduce the basics of AutoML. Section 4 is the core of the paper, introducing meta AutoML and OMA-ML. Section 5 concludes the paper and indicates future work.

2   Related Work

The concept of meta AutoML is novel. We are only aware of one article [27] which presents a similar concept called *Ensemble Squared*, but this preprint is not a peer-reviewed publication. Like OMA-ML, Ensemble Squared uses third-party AutoML solutions which are invoked in parallel. Insofar, both OMA-ML and Ensemble Squared are meta AutoML approaches. A difference of our approach is the use of the ML ontology to guide various components of OMA-ML: the GUI for entering the AutoML configuration, dataset analysis and pre-processing, and the controller component of OMA-ML. We see considerable benefits in this approach regarding extensibility. Adding new AutoML solutions to OMA-ML can largely be accomplished by extending the ML ontology and implementing new adapters.

3   Basics of AutoML

3.1   Input and Output

Figure 1 shows the inputs and outputs of AutoML as a BPMN diagram (Business Process Model and Notation [11]).

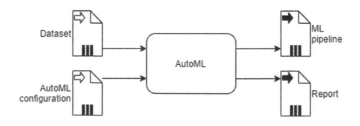

Fig. 1. AutoML input and output

AutoML requires the following input:

1. **Dataset**: the dataset for the ML task, e.g., a CSV file for classification on tabular data;
2. **AutoML configuration**:
   (a) ML task, e.g.,
       i. Classification or regression on tabular data;
       ii. Classification or regression on image and video data;
       iii. Classification or regression on text data;
   (b) ML target: e.g., label column in classification or regression tasks;
   (c) Additional configuration parameters (optional): e.g. maximum run-time, model performance or hardware restrictions.

AutoML produces the following output:

1. **ML pipeline**: The ML pipeline generated by AutoML is a piece of source code which can be executed to perform the ML task specified.
2. **Report**: A textual or graphical explanation of the AutoML result, including a listing of ML configurations and their respective performance measures.

AutoML solutions generate ML pipelines. A ML pipeline implements data preparation (e.g., feature selection, encoding or missing values imputation) the selected ML approach and its hyperparameter configuration [28].

AutoML solves the *Combined Algorithm Selection and Hyperparameter optimization (CASH) problem* [26]. Algorithms that solve the CASH problem search for the best ML approach and hyperparameter setting for a given ML task [28].

Different AutoML solutions use different algorithms to solve the CASH problem, e.g.:

1. Auto-Sklearn: SMAC [6,10];
2. TPOT: Evolutionary algorithm [15];
3. H2O AutoML: Grid Search [16];
4. ATM: A combination of multi-armed bandit learning with Gaussian processes [24].

3.2 Example: Auto-Sklearn

One of the more popular AutoML solutions by citations is Auto-sklearn [6]. It offers pipeline generation for classification and regression of tabular data.

Listing 1.1 displays a simple Auto-sklearn implementation. In Auto-sklearn, the ML tasks is specified by the class used, e.g., `AutoSklearnClassifier` for classification of tabular datasets. The AutoML process is triggered by executing the `fit` function.

Code Listing 1.1. Auto-sklearn example

```
import autosklearn.classification
cls = autosklearn.classification.AutoSklearnClassifier()
cls.fit(X_train, y_train)
predictions = cls.predict(X_test)
```

Without custom parameterization, Auto-sklearn will use its default config-uration. Advanced users may customize the Auto-sklearn process [17] with a multitude of parameters, e.g.

1. Hardware usage, e.g., `memory_limit`;
2. Pipeline size or generation constrains, e.g., `ensemble_size`;
3. Pipeline scoring/metrics, e.g., `metric`;
4. Pre-processing constrains, e.g., `exclude_preprocessors`;
5. Runtime constraints, e.g., `time_left_for_this_task`;
6. Meta configuration (logging, save folder location, etc.), e.g., `output_folder`;

The Auto-sklearn result is a pipeline that can be used to make predictions using the `predict` function (see Listing 1.1). The `sprint_statistics` function display statistics about the found ML pipelines [17]:

1. Dataset name;
2. Metric used;
3. Best validation score;
4. Number of target algorithm runs;
5. Number of successful target algorithm runs;
6. Number of crashed target algorithm runs;
7. Number of target algorithm runs that exceeded the memory limit;
8. Number of target algorithm runs that exceeded the time limit.

3.3   Discussion of Existing AutoML Solutions

AutoML solutions are implemented on top of a specific ML library. They produce pipelines using software from this ML library that can be exported and imported into this ML library. Deciding on an AutoML solution results in a technology lock-in for the corresponding ML library. Comparing the performance between different ML libraries is not possible.

ONNX [25] is an open format for artificial neural networks (ANN) to enable interoperability between ML libraries. However, not every ML library supports ONNX. Furthermore ONNX does not support other ML model types besides ANN.

AutoML solutions target specific user groups. Most open source AutoML solutions target users with programming skills, e.g. in Python. Commercial AutoML solutions provide a GUI which also address users without program-ming skills, e.g., domain experts.

All existing AutoML solutions have their individual strengths. They all solve the CASH problem, support specific ML tasks, target specific user groups and generate ML pipelines for specific ML libraries. Meta AutoML allows combining the strengths of individual AutoML solutions, while alleviating their limitations: it may support various ML tasks, support various user groups and is technology-independent.

In the next section, we introduce OMA-ML, our concept for a meta AutoML. First, we present the goals we aspire for OMA-ML.

4   OMA-ML: An Ontology-Based Concept for Meta AutoML

4.1   Goals for OMA-ML

By combining the strengths of individual AutoML solutions, we pursue the following goals for OMA-ML:

1. **AutoML**: OMA-ML shall perform AutoML, i.e., generate an executable ML pipeline and a report based on a configuration and a dataset.
2. **User Groups**: OMA-ML shall target user groups with and without programming skills. It shall provide a GUI which allows intuitive configuration of AutoML and interactive reporting. Additionally, it shall provide an API.
3. **Technology-independent**: OMA-ML shall support any number of ML libraries.
4. **ML tasks**: A wide range of ML tasks shall be supported.

4.2   Meta AutoML

Figure 2 shows the concept of meta AutoML as a BPMN diagram.

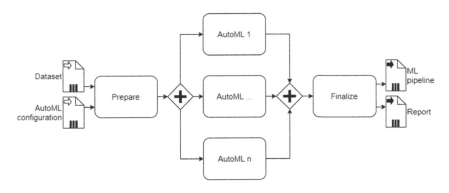

Fig. 2. Meta AutoML workflow

Similar to other AutoML solutions, the user enters the required input (dataset and AutoML configuration). The meta AutoML prepares various AutoML solutions to be executed in parallel. The results of the AutoML solutions are collected and the results of meta AutoML (ML pipeline and report) are finalized.

4.3   ML Ontology

An ontology is a formal, explicit specification of a shared conceptualization of a problem domain [23]. We are in the process of developing an ontology for the domain of ML [9]. One of the use cases of this ML ontology is to guide the meta AutoML process. The ML ontology is modelled in RDF [4] using SKOS [20]. It currently consists of about 500 RDF triples, specifying 63 ML approaches, 15 ML tasks, 22 prediction performance measures, 9 AutoML solutions, 7 ML libraries, their characteristics and interrelationships, and more.

Figure 3 shows some exemplary concepts of the ML ontology and their relationships.

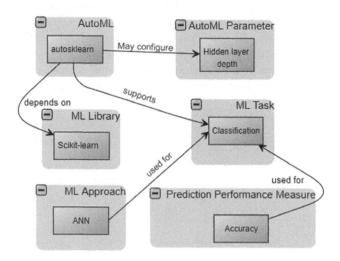

Fig. 3. Exemplary concepts the ML ontology

In this exemplary subset of the ML ontology it is expressed that the ML approach *ANN* can be used for *classification* tasks. *autosklearn* is an AutoML solution performing classification tasks. Autosklearn depends on the ML library *Sikit-learn* and allows to configure the *Hidden layer depth*. *Accuracy* can be used as a prediction performance measure for classification tasks.

The ML ontology is the information backbone of OMA-ML and is used in several components of OMA-ML, as shown in the next section.

4.4   OMA-ML Software Architecture

Figure 4 shows the software architecture of OMA-ML as a UML (Unified Modeling Language) component diagram.

OMA-ML is designed as a 3-layer-architecture.

1. **Presentation layer**: This is the user interface of OMA-ML. A GUI allows interaction and visualization. An ontology-guided wizard supports configuring OMA-ML. Additionally, an API provides batch access to OMA-ML.

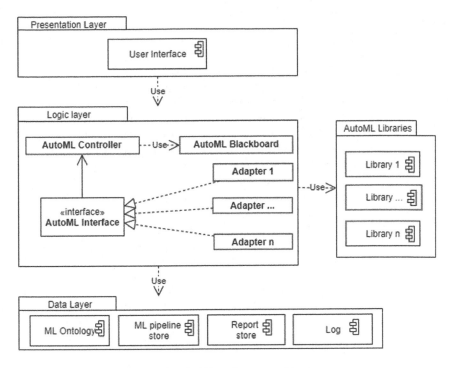

Fig. 4. OMA-ML software architecture

2. **Logic Layer**: This implements the control logic of OMA-ML, designed as a blackboard architecture [2]. The OMA-ML controller invokes individual AutoML libraries via the adapter pattern [7], thus providing a plug-in architecture for multiple AutoML solutions.
3. **Data Layer**: This layer provides access to the ML ontology (read access), the ML model store and AutoML logs (write access).

4.5   User Interface

In the GUI, a wizard guides the user to enter mandatory and optional AutoML configuration parameters. The wizard is based on the ML ontology, providing plausible configuration options only. For example, if the user selects AutoML solutions that produce ANN pipelines only, the wizard will only display configuration options for ANN.

Configuration parameters are as follows:

1. **Mandatory**:
   (a) **Dataset**: The dataset with labeled training data;
   (b) **ML Task**: The task the user wants to perform on the dataset, e.g., classification on tabular data (options from the ML ontology);
   (c) **ML target**: The name of the label column in the dataset.

2. **Optional**:
   (a) **Dataset schema**: Schema information on dataset columns including data types (e.g., int, float, string, date) and categories (e.g., numerical, categorical, textual) (options from the ML ontology);
   (b) **Scoring**: The prediction performance measure to be used as optimization target, e.g., accuracy (options from the ML ontology);
   (c) **AutoML solutions**: Usage restriction on particular AutoML solutions or ML libraries, e.g., autosklearn (options from the ML ontology);
   (d) **ML Model constraints**: Restrictions on ML approaches and custom configuration of ML approaches, e.g., ANN with maximum 10 hidden layers (options from the ML ontology);
   (e) **AutoML runtime constraints**: General meta AutoML constraints (monetary, time, hardware restriction) to influence the execution time, e.g., runtime limit 1 h (options from the ML ontology);
   (f) **Training Type**: Training strategy for meta AutoML, e.g. use a subset of the dataset (options from the ML ontology);

After starting the OMA-ML process, the user interface is updated regularly with the current status of the AutoML processes which are executed in parallel. After termination of the OMA-ML process, the following output is provided:

1. **ML pipeline**: The user can download the successfully generated ML pipelines as a Python script and files specifying the pipeline structure. The Python scripts provide the following functionality:
   (a) Import the file specifying the pipeline structure;
   (b) Make predictions for a new, unlabeled dataset;
   (c) Save the prediction result.
2. **Report**:
   (a) Description of the used AutoML solutions, their produced ML pipelines and respective performance evaluations;
   (b) ML Pipeline leader board with scores.

When using OMA-ML in batch mode, the configuration file, including a link to the dataset can be passed to an API. The runtime state and output can be pulled from the API. Like in the online mode, the output consists of ML pipelines and reports.

4.6 OMA-ML Control Logic

The OMA-ML control logic is designed using the Blackboard pattern. Figure 5 shows an overview of the OMA-ML control logic as a BPMN diagram.

When a new run of OMA-ML is triggered, the dataset is first analyzed, extracting the following metadata:

1. Number of rows and columns;
2. Data types of columns;
3. Missing values.

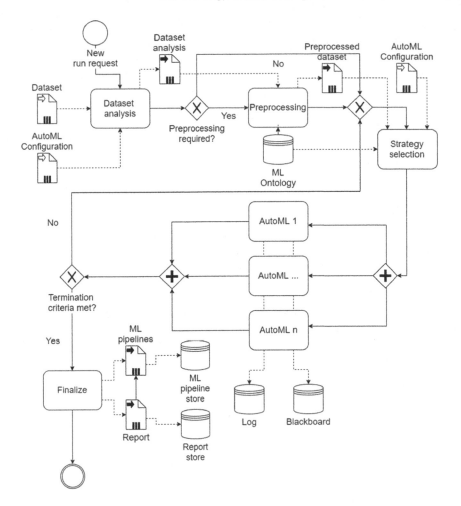

Fig. 5. OMA-ML control logic

Those metadata are needed for deciding whether pre-processing the dataset is necessary for individual AutoML solutions. The OMA-ML strategy selection is based on the ML ontology, taking into account the configuration and the dataset analysis result. It selects AutoML solutions which perform the ML tasks specified in the configuration. The dataset is pre-processed if needed. For example, if an AutoML solution requires numeric features only, but the dataset contains textual features, then the textual features are encoded. If the dataset is very large (e.g., 100 Mio. rows) and a small runtime limit is specified (e.g., 1 h), then approaches with fast training times are selected or the dataset is downsized.

The selected AutoML solutions are triggered via their adapters in parallel by the OMA-ML controller. While executing AutoML, they continuously report their progress to the blackboard. The OMA-ML controller monitors the blackboard. After reaching the termination criteria (e.g., required accuracy is met, or run time limit is reached), the OMA-ML controller finalizes the OMA-ML run, saving the best performing executable ML pipelines to the ML pipeline store, generating a report, and storing it in the report store. Otherwise, the strategy may be altered, or alternative AutoML solutions may be triggered.

4.7 Logging

All OMA-ML runs are logged in a structured format, including the following data:

1. AutoML configuration;
2. Dataset analysis result;
3. OMA-ML strategy;
4. Hardware configuration (kernels, memory, processor, etc.);
5. AutoML actual run time (time spent);
6. Generated ML pipelines characteristics (accuracy, size, etc.).

With many OMA-ML runs, we expect the log data to be a valuable source of information. Data mining techniques may be used to gain insights to improve the OMA-ML controller's strategy selection. Using this log data additionally for supervised ML in the OMA-ML controller is subject to future work.

5 Conclusions and Future Work

In this paper, we have presented OMA-ML, a novel ontology-based concept for meta AutoML. OMA-ML combines the strengths of different AutoML solutions. It supports multiple ML libraries by employing multiple AutoML solutions via a plug-in architecture. This supports the extensibility of OMA-ML regarding future third-party AutoML developments. It supports multiple user groups, with and without programming skills. By combining the strengths of several AutoML solutions, it supports a wide range of ML tasks and ML libraries.

The implementation of OMA-ML is ongoing work in progress. OMA-ML is being implemented open-source as a micro-service architecture. It will be usable as a cloud service without installation. The GUI is implemented using the Blazor Framework [19]. The OMA-ML controller is implemented in Python. The OMA-ML batch access will be available via web services. Additionally, OMA-ML can be installed locally. The batch access is additionally available via a REST API. Individual AutoML libraries are installed in Docker containers and can be invoked in parallel.

As soon as the first OMA-ML release is available, we plan to thoroughly analyze it regarding usability and generated ML pipelines quality.

Future work includes the use of supervised ML on OMA-ML log data to improve the strategy selection in the OMA-ML controller. Furthermore, we plan to use learning curve analysis in the OMA-ML controller.

Acknowledgement. This work is funded by the German federal ministry of education and research (BMBF) in the program Zukunft der Wertschöpfung (funding code 02L19C157), and supported by Projektträger Karlsruhe (PTKA). The responsibility for the content of this publication lies with the authors.

References

1. Abadi, M., et al.: Tensorflow: Large-scale machine learning on heterogeneous distributed systems. https://arxiv.org/pdf/1603.04467
2. Buschmann, F., Meunier, R., Rohnert, H., Sommerlad, P., Stal, M.: Pattern-Oriented Software Architecture, A System of Patterns. Wiley Software Patterns Series, Wiley, s.l., 1. aufl. edn. (2013)
3. Chollet, F.: Keras (2021). https://keras.io
4. Cyganiak, R., Wood, D., Lanthaler, M.: Rdf 1.1 concepts and abstract syntax (2021). https://www.w3.org/TR/rdf11-concepts/
5. Feurer, M., Eggensperger, K., Falkner, S., Lindauer, M., Hutter, F.: Auto-sklearn 2.0: The next generation. https://arxiv.org/pdf/2007.04074
6. Feurer, M., Klein, A., Eggensperger, K., Springenberg, J.T., Blum, M., Hutter, F. (eds.): Efficient and Robust Automated Machine Learning. MIT Press, Cambridge (2015). https://doi.org/10.5555/2969442.2969547
7. Gamma, E.: Design Patterns: Elements of Reusable Object-Oriented Software. Addison-Wesley Professional Computing Series, 39th edn. Addison-Wesley, Boston (2011)
8. Google Cloud: Cloud automl (2021). https://cloud.google.com/automl?hl=de
9. Humm, B.G., et al.: Machine intelligence today: applications, methodology, and technology. Informatik Spektrum, 1–11 (2021). https://doi.org/10.1007/s00287-021-01343-1
10. Hutter, F., Hoos, H.H., Leyton-Brown, K.: Sequential model-based optimization for general algorithm configuration. In: Coello, C.A.C. (ed.) LION 2011. LNCS, vol. 6683, pp. 507–523. Springer, Heidelberg (2011). https://doi.org/10.1007/978-3-642-25566-3_40
11. Information technology – Object Management Group Business Process Model and Notation (2013). www.iso.org/standard/62652.html
12. Jin, H., Song, Q., Hu, X.: Auto-keras: an efficient neural architecture search system. In: Teredesai, A. (ed.) Proceedings of the 25th ACM SIGKDD International Conference on Knowledge Discovery & Data Mining, pp. 1946–1956. ACM Digital Library, Association for Computing Machinery (2019). https://doi.org/10.1145/3292500.3330648
13. Kotthoff, L., Thornton, C., Hoos, H.H., Hutter, F., Leyton-Brown, K.: Auto-WEKA: automatic model selection and hyperparameter optimization in WEKA. In: Hutter, F., Kotthoff, L., Vanschoren, J. (eds.) Automated Machine Learning. TSSCML, pp. 81–95. Springer, Cham (2019). https://doi.org/10.1007/978-3-030-05318-5_4
14. Lanio, K.: Rapidminer auto model (2018). https://rapidminer.com/products/auto-model/
15. Le, T.T., Fu, W., Moore, J.H.: Scaling tree-based automated machine learning to biomedical big data with a feature set selector. Bioinf. (Oxford, England) **36**(1), 250–256 (2020). https://doi.org/10.1093/bioinformatics/btz470

16. LeDell, E., Poirier, S.: H2o automl: scalable automatic machine learning. In: 7th ICML Workshop on Automated Machine Learning (AutoML) (2020). https://www.automl.org/wp-content/uploads/2020/07/AutoML_2020_paper_61.pdf

17. Machine Learning Professorship Freiburg: Autosklearn documentation (2021). https://automl.github.io/auto-sklearn/master/api.html

18. Mendoza, H., et al.: Towards automatically-tuned deep neural networks. In: Hutter, F., Kotthoff, L., Vanschoren, J. (eds.) Automated Machine Learning. TSSCML, pp. 135–149. Springer, Cham (2019). https://doi.org/10.1007/978-3-030-05318-5_7

19. Microsoft: Blazor (2021). https://dotnet.microsoft.com/apps/aspnet/web-apps/blazor

20. Miles, A., Bechhofer Sean: Skos simple knowledge organization system namespace document (2011). https://www.w3.org/2009/08/skos-reference/skos.html

21. Pedregosa, F., et al.: Scikit-learn: machine learning in python. J. Mach. Learn. Res. 12, 2825–2830 (2011). https://dl.acm.org/doi/10.5555/1953048.2078195

22. Russell, S.J., Norvig, P.: Artificial intelligence: A modern approach. Prentice Hall Series in Artificial Intelligence, Pearson, Upper Saddle River, 3. edition. global edition edn. (2016)

23. Studer, R., Benjamins, V., Fensel, D.: Knowledge engineering: Principles and methods. Data Knowl. Eng. 25(1–2), 161–197 (1998). https://doi.org/10.1016/S0169-023X(97)00056-6

24. Swearingen, T., Drevo, W., Cyphers, B., Cuesta-Infante, A., Ross, A., Veeramachaneni, K.: Atm: a distributed, collaborative, scalable system for automated machine learning. In: 2017 IEEE International Conference on Big Data (Big Data), pp. 151–162. IEEE (2017). https://doi.org/10.1109/BigData.2017.8257923

25. The Linux Foundation: Onnx (2021). https://onnx.ai/

26. Thornton, C., Hutter, F., Hoos, H.H., Leyton-Brown, K.: Auto-weka. In: Dhillon, I.S. (ed.) KDD '13 : the 19th ACM SIGKDD International Conference on Knowledge Discovery and Data Mining : August 11–14, 2013, Chicago, Illinois, USA, pp. 847–855. ACM (2013). https://doi.org/10.1145/2487575.2487629

27. Yoo, J., Joseph, T., Yung, D., Nasseri, S.A., Wood, F.: Ensemble squared: A meta automl system. https://arxiv.org/pdf/2012.05390

28. Zöller, M.A., Huber, M.F.: Benchmark and survey of automated machine learning frameworks. J. Artif. Intell. Res. 70, 409–472 (2021). https://doi.org/10.1613/jair.1.11854

Object Migration Automata
for Non-equal Partitioning Problems
with Known Partition Sizes

Rebekka Olsson Omslandseter[1(✉)], Lei Jiao[1], and B. John Oommen[1,2]

[1] University of Agder, Grimstad, Norway
{rebekka.o.omslandseter,lei.jiao}@uia.no
[2] Carleton University, Ottawa, Canada
oommen@scs.carleton.ca

Abstract. Solving partitioning problems in random environments is a classic and challenging task, and has numerous applications. The existing Object Migration Automaton (OMA) and its proposed enhancements, which include the Pursuit and Transitivity phenomena, can solve problems with equi-sized partitions. Currently, these solutions also include one where the partition sizes possess a Greatest Common Divisor (GCD). In this paper, we propose an OMA-based solution that can solve problems with both equally and non-equally-sized groups, without restrictions on their sizes. More specifically, our proposed approach, referred to as the Partition Size Required OMA (PSR-OMA), can solve *general* partitioning problems, with the only additional requirement being that the unconstrained partitions' sizes are known *a priori*. The scheme is a fundamental contribution in the field of partitioning algorithms, and the numerical results presented demonstrate that PSR-OMA can solve both equi-partitioning and non-equi-partitioning problems efficiently, and is the only known solution that resolves this problem.

Keywords: Learning Automata · Object Migration Automata · Object partitioning with non-equal sizes

1 Introduction

What is Object Partitioning: In the Object Partitioning Problem (OPP), we aim to divide a set of "objects" into groups in an optimal manner based on some hidden or unknown criterion. The "object" itself can be the "abstract" representation of a true, real-life data entity. The grouping criterion is always unknown, and only known to an Oracle, which provides information to the system that processes interactions with the real world. A sub-problem and constrained version of the OPP is the Equi-Partitioning Problem (EPP) [5], where all the partitioned groups have an equal size. The family of Object Migration Automata (OMA) algorithms, which are Learning Automata (LA)-based solutions, were first presented in [5,6]. They could solve EPPs two orders of magnitudes faster than the

© IFIP International Federation for Information Processing 2021
Published by Springer Nature Switzerland AG 2021
I. Maglogiannis et al. (Eds.): AIAI 2021, IFIP AICT 627, pp. 129–142, 2021.
https://doi.org/10.1007/978-3-030-79150-6_11

previously-reported solutions. Over the decades, enhancements have emerged, and include the Enhanced OMA (EOMA) [3], the Pursuit EOMA (PEOMA) [13], and the Transitivity PEOMA (TPEOMA) [12]. In [11], we introduced a solution to the Non-Equal-Partitioning Problem (NEPP) where the sizes of the partitions have a non-unity Greatest Common Divisor (GCD), namely the GCD-OMA.

Although partitioning problems are akin to the related field of clustering, which involves Machine Learning (ML) algorithms like, e.g., K-Means, spectral clustering, and Gaussian mixtures, it is crucial to understand the distinct aspects of OPPs, and the way by which OMA solve them. While clustering problems, often, have a relation between the objects that can be represented through distance metrics, which in, turn, are required "up-front", OMA algorithms are based on their ability to process *queries* (consisting, for example, of object pairs) presented along time. Consequently, OMA algorithms do not require complete information of the "up-front" inter-relationships between the objects themselves. Thus, OMA algorithms can follow even the stochastic nature of the relations, over time. We emphasize that the true nature of such a partitioning problem is always unknown. However, the presented queries consist of objects that *stochastically* belong together, or should be considered to be together, for some underlying and unknown reasons. The OMA uses this information to infer the groupings.

Applications of Partitioning: One of the numerous applications (extensively given in [9]) for the OMA is cryptanalysis. In [7] and [8], the OMA was employed to solve a cipher using only plaintext and its corresponding ciphertext. This solution achieved a 90% cost reduction compared to its competitors. The authors of [4] proposed an OMA-based scheme to create an image database using conceptually similar images. Recently, the authors of [10] proposed an OMA-based algorithm for mobile radio communications, by partitioning users in a Non-Orthogonal Multiple Access (NOMA) system.

Advancement from the State-of-the-Art: The GCD-OMA represents the state-of-the-art. It rendered the OMA capable of solving NEPPs with *specially-constrained* group cardinalities. However, *this* solution cannot handle general partitioning, due to the GCD requirement on the partition sizes. This paper presents a novel solution, namely the so-called Partition Size Required OMA (PSR-OMA), to EPPs and NEPPs, which does not require a non-unity GCD between the partition sizes. The PSR-OMA can solve partitioning problems with partitions of arbitrary equal or non-equal sizes. The change between the existing OMA solutions and the PSR-OMA is that the latter can adaptively swap the partition sizes. The algorithm still requires us to provide information about the partition sizes, and hence its name, the PSR-OMA. We emphasize that one can use the PSR-OMA with any of the already-existing OMA's "incarnations" and that the PSR-OMA stands apart from the GCD-OMA. The reader should also note that proposing a solution to both EPPs and NEPPs is the same as offering a solution to OPPs, but that we use the EPP and NEPP terminologies to differentiate between the two.

Contributions of this Paper: The contributions of this paper are as follows:

1. We present the novel PSR-OMA scheme applicable for both EPPs and NEPPs, which can be employed with all the existing versions of the OMA algorithms.
2. We demonstrate the convergence and efficiency properties of the PSR-OMAs, showing that it can be used for further applications.

The remainder of the paper is organized as follows. In Sect. 2, we formulate the nature of the partitioning problems considered in this paper and analyze their complexity. In Sect. 3, we present the PSR-OMA algorithm in detail. The performance of the proposed algorithm is presented in Sect. 4, and conclude the paper in Sect. 5.

2 Problem Formulation

We now formalize the partitioning problem as follows: Our problem consists of O objects, where the set of objects is denoted by $\mathcal{O} = \{o_1, o_2, ..., o_O\}$. We want to divide the O objects into K disjoint partitions. The set of partitions is indicated by $\mathcal{K}$, where $\mathcal{K} = \{\varrho_1, \varrho_2 ..., \varrho_K\}$. For example, partition ϱ_3 might consist of o_4, o_5 and o_6, denoted by $\varrho_3 - \{o_4, o_5, o_6\}$. The problem, however, is that the identities of the objects that should be grouped together are unknown, but are based on a specific but hidden criterion, known only to an "Oracle", referred to as the "State of Nature". The Oracle *noisily* presents the objects that should be together in pairs, where the degree of noise specifies the difficulty of the problem. Thus, we assume that there is an true partitioning of the objects, Δ^*, and the solution algorithm determines a partitioning, say Δ^+. The solution is optimal if $\Delta^+ = \Delta^*$. The initialization of the objects is indicated by Δ^0.

The Combinatorics of the OPP: The combinatorial nature of partitioning leads to the complexity of the issues related to the existing OMA and the PSR-OMA algorithms. In OPPs, queries are encountered as time proceeds, and we do not have a performance parameter that directly indicates a particular partitioning's fitness. Thus, we cannot perform an exhaustive search to determine the optimal partitioning of an OPP.

Bell Numbers: An unordered Bell number gives the number of possible partitions of a set of objects. In OPPs, we assume that the ordering of the objects does not matter. Consequently, the Bell number is of an unordered type, and we only consider whether the correct objects are together. Here, we want to partition O objects into K non-empty sets, where each object can only be inside a single group. Accordingly, we have B_O partitioning options, where B_O is the O-th Bell number, and the O-th Bell number is given by $B_O = \sum_{k=1}^{O} \{^O_k\}$, with $\{^O_k\}$ being the Stirling numbers of the second kind [1], and $k \in \{1, ..., O\}$. The O-th Bell number obeys: $\left(\frac{O}{e \ln O}\right)^O < B_O < \left(\frac{O}{e^{1-\lambda} \ln O}\right)^O$, which has an exponential behavior for O and $\lambda > 0$. However, in our case, the partitioning is pre-defined, independent of whether we have an EPP or an NEPP. Consequently, we need to consider the different combinations of objects in the various partitions. For the partitions, where each of the groups has the possibility to consist of a different number of objects, the number of possible combinations, W, can be expressed as $W = \frac{O!}{\rho_1!\rho_2!\rho_3!...\rho_K!}$, where ρ_k, $k \in \{1, ..., K\}$, is the number of objects in each partition [2]. Further, ρ_1 is the number of objects in ϱ_1, ρ_2 the number of objects in ϱ_2 and so on. Note that in the given expression for W, none of the numbers of objects are equal, and thus, $\rho_1 \neq \rho_2 \neq \rho_3 \neq ... \neq \rho_K$ and $\rho_1 + \rho_2 + \rho_3 + ... + \rho_K = O$. For partitions in which some of the partition sizes are equal, we have $W = \frac{O!}{(u!)^x x!(v!)^y y!...(w!)^z z!}$, where we have x groups of size u, y groups of size v, and so on for all groups and sizes, implying that, in this case, $ux + vy + ... + wz = O$. Furthermore, when all the groups are of equal size, we can express W as: $W = \frac{O!}{\left(\frac{O}{K}!\right)^K K!}$, where $\frac{O}{K}$ is an integer. As a result of the above, we observe that the solution space for an EPP or an NEPP has a combinatorial complexity.

Complexity of EPPs/NEPPs: EPPs and NEPPs have fewer possible combinations than a Bell number because the partition sizes are specified and known. However, the interactions between the Environment and the algorithm may be contaminated by noise. This means that the queries may include misleading messages. Thus, due to the system's stochastic nature, the problem is more complicated than just finding an optimal partitioning for a given time instant. The optimal partitioning is defined *stochastically*.

Evaluation Criteria: As in [11], γ will be the accuracy of the partitioning determined by the algorithm. We calculate γ by dividing the number of object pairs in Δ^+ that exist in Δ^* with the total number of possible correct object pairs in Δ^*. Clearly, when $\Delta^+ = \Delta^*$, the scheme will have 100% accuracy, which implies an optimal solution. We denote the number of queries generated from the Environment by Ψ_Q, and let Ψ be the number of queries that the LA has considered. We also use symbol Ψ_T to denote the number of transitivity pairs made in the TPEOMA variant. Note that $\Psi = \Psi_Q$ for the OMA and the EOMA variants.

3   The Proposed PSR-OMA Scheme

The newly-proposed PSR-OMA can handle partitioning problems with partitions of arbitrary non-equal or equal sizes. The primary difference between PSR-OMA and the existing OMA solutions is that PSR-OMA can adaptively swap the partition sizes throughout its operation. In designing it, we encounter some obstacles that are not present for the EPP and the GCD-OMA solution of [11]. Specifically, when we have partitions of pre-specified cardinalities, the objects can become stuck in situations that we refer to as a *Standstill Situations*[1]. Such

---

[1] The *Standstill Situation* must not be confused by the *Deadlock Situation* previously considered by the authors of [3].

a "Standstill Situation" is one in which the objects become "stuck" in a loop that might not even be resolved after an infinite time-frame.

Standstill Situation: In this situation, the LA cannot reach convergence due to the constraints imposed by the pre-specified cardinalities. Also, once the partitions have been initialized with their respective number of objects, these allocations will, without modification, be the same. Thus, the objects of a smaller partition, that randomly happen to be within a larger partition, prevent the excess objects in *that* partition from being grouped with the objects that they, in reality, should be together with, and traps them. Because the traditional OMA algorithms need to have the same number of objects in each partition, our initial belief was that a new initialization process was the only component needed to solve the NEPP. However, as discussed above, the Standstill Situation is a serious issue, and the difficulty associated with solving NEPPs is more intricate.

We can explain this with an example where we have a partitioning problem with three partitions. We have room for three objects in one partition, three objects in the second, and two objects in the third. Consequently, we have eight objects and three partitions. Let us assume that there are four states associated with each partition, and that the true partitioning is given by $\Delta^* = \{\{o_1, o_2, o_3\}, \{o_4, o_5, o_6\}, \{o_7, o_8\}\}$. Consider the case in which we use the existing EOMA, and we randomly initialize the objects into the different boundary states. After considering an arbitrary number of queries, the EOMA might be stuck in a Standstill Situation, as visualized in Fig. 1.

We observe that in Fig. 1, o_4 is stuck in ϱ_1. o_4 will, most likely, depending on the level of noise in the system, be queried together with o_5 or o_6. Consequently, o_4 will be swapped with o_5 or o_6 according to the policy schemes of the EOMA, since our starting premise is that we specify the cardinalities a *priori*, and make no additional modifications to the algorithm. The swapping process will then continue until the objects are randomly moved out of ϱ_1 and made accessible by the whole *group* of o_4, which makes convergence unlikely to occur within a reasonable time-frame.

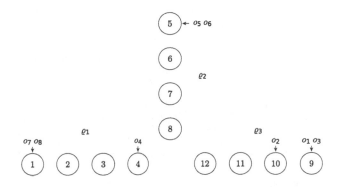

Fig. 1. Example of objects stuck in a standstill situation.

The reader should note that the scenario depicted in Fig. 1 is not merely included for explanatory purposes. Rather, this represents an actual Standstill Situation which can occur for many different distributions of objects, and for other courses of action. Thus, sometimes the OMA might be able to converge due to the randomness in the initialization process and the levels of noise in the system. However, without changing the policy schemes according to the constraints imposed by NEPPs, we can have OMA algorithms that perform poorly by yielding slow convergence, or by not even attaining to convergence at all. Specifically, if the queries provided by the Environment are noise-free, upon entering a Standstill Situation, an OMA will not be able to converge at all. On the contrary, if some queries are noisy, the OMA algorithm could resolve the issue, and be able to ultimately converge. However, the convergence rate would be very slow.

Understandably, the Standstill Situation becomes more critical as more partitions are introduced to the OMA algorithm, and its effect increases with the difference in the number of objects in each partition. Thus, when we have more possibilities for a smaller partition to be stuck in a larger partition, the complexity for solving the problem with pre-specified cardinalities increases, and the probability of the OMA algorithm having a slow convergence rate, or not converging at all, correspondingly increases. To mitigate this, the PSR-OMA (which deviates from the OMA) is designed in detail below. In the interest of brevity, the algorithms for the OMA Reward, the OMA Penalty and the EOMA Penalty are not given here. They can be found in [9] and [11], respectively.

Proposed Functionality: The PSR-OMA can be seen to be an extension of the existing OMA algorithms. Its first phase concerns the initialization of the objects. Because the fundamental operation of the OMA and the EOMA algorithms are different, these two methods will be considered separately. To achieve this, we first remember that for the OMA, the objects are distributed randomly across the KS states of the LA, while the objects in the EOMA are distributed randomly across the LA's K *boundary* states. For both the algorithms, the difference due to the pre-specification of cardinalities is that we need to distribute the objects among the partitions of the automaton according to the pre-specified number of objects in each partition. The new functionality is similar, independent of whether the group sizes are equal or unequal.

In the second phase of the PSR-OMA, we try to mitigate the Standstill Situation by introducing a new policy when the system receives a Penalty. This occurs when an object in a query is in a boundary state, and at the same time, the other object is in the innermost state of *another* partition. When such a situation occurs, we check the number of objects in the partition of the object in the innermost state. We, thereafter, move the boundary object to the innermost object's partition if such a transition fulfills the size requirements for all the partitions. If such a transition requires more objects to fulfill the size requirements, and if there are more objects in the boundary or in the second nearest state to the boundary of the boundary object's partition, we check the partition sizes and move the required number of objects from these states (chosen randomly) together with the boundary object, to the innermost object's partition. This solution to the Standstill Situation is depicted in Fig. 2, where o_4 is allowed to move to the partition of o_5 and o_6, without requiring any replacement.

Algorithm 1. PSR Process for Standstill Situation

Input:
  - The states of all objects θ_l, where $l \in \{1, 2, ..., O\}$.
  - The query $Q = \langle o_i, o_j \rangle$.
  - ρ_k for all $k \in \{1, 2, ..., K\}$.
  - The boundary states, B_k of all $k \in \{1, 2, ..., K\}$.

Output:
  - The next states of o_i, o_j and other affected objects.

For ease of explanation, let us assume that o_i is in the innermost state of ϱ_i and o_j is in the boundary state of ϱ_j.

1: **if** moving o_j to ϱ_i will let our system keep the specified sizes **then**
2:     $\theta_j = \theta_i$ // Move o_j to ϱ_i
3: **else**   // If more than one object is required to fulfill all ρ_k
4:     **for** all objects o_x in $\varrho_j \setminus o_j$ **do**   // All objects in ϱ_j except o_j
5:         **if** $\theta_x = \theta_j$ or $\theta_x = \theta_j - 1$ **then**   // If o_x is in (or nearest to) the boundary state
6:             $I \leftarrow o_x$ // I is the set of possible objects to move
7:         **end if**
8:     **end for**
9:     **if** $|\varrho_i| > |\varrho_j|$ **then**   // There are more objects in ϱ_i than in ϱ_j
10:         $\nu = |\varrho_i| - |\varrho_j|$ // $|\varrho_i|$ is the number of objects in ϱ_i
11:     **else if** $|\varrho_i| < |\varrho_j|$ **then**   // There are more objects in ϱ_j than in ϱ_i
12:         $\nu = |\varrho_j| - |\varrho_i|$
13:     **else**   // This means $|\varrho_i| = |\varrho_j|$
14:         Continue Process Penalty   // Continue with the remaining statements in
            Alg. 2/3
15:     **end if**
16:     **if** $|I| + 1 \geq \nu$ **then** // The number of objects in I are bigger than (or equal to) ν
17:         Randomly select $\nu - 1$ objects from I and put them in a new set J.
18:         **if** $|\varrho_i| + \nu$ and $|\varrho_j| - \nu$ fulfills all ρ_k **then**   // If the size requirement is fulfilled
19:             $\theta_j = B_i$ // Move o_j to boundary of ϱ_i
20:             **for** all objects o_z in J **do**
21:                 $\theta_z = B_i$ // Move objects in J to boundary state of ϱ_i
22:             **end for**
23:         **end if**
24:     **else**   // It was not possible to make a legal swapping of objects
25:         Continue Process Penalty   // Continue with the remaining statements in
            Alg. 2/3
26:     **end if**
27: **end if**

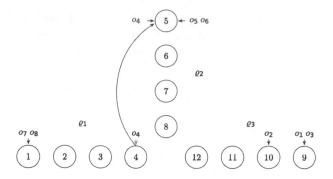

Fig. 2. Example of the Penalty functionality for the Standstill Situation.

Migration of Objects: We emphasize that when we move a single object according to the new policy, we move it to the same state as the queried object in the innermost state. If we move more than a single object, we might choose some objects in the process that, in reality, should not be changing its partition. Thus, when moving more than a single object in this process, we will move them to the boundary state of the innermost object's partition. In this way, we compromise between the scheme's convergence rate and accuracy. The new Penalty function is presented in Algorithm 1. Observe that for Algorithm 1, we introduce the parameter θ_{B_k}, which indicates the boundary state of partition k, $k \in \{1, 2, ..., K\}$. Additionally, we assume that the distribution of the randomly-chosen objects in the scheme is uniform. If we are not able to move any objects in the new Penalty, we check the rest of the Penalty statements. Thus when, for example, an object is in an innermost state, the other is in a boundary state, and we are not able to swap partition sizes, we handle them as if one object is in the boundary and the other object not being in the boundary according to the EOMA's existing rules.

By introducing the new functionality, the LA can actively swap the cardinalities and partition relations while it is executing its operation. An example of this functionality, where one object changes its partition without replacement, and thus, changes the partition size of the partition it moves to, is depicted in Fig. 2.

Implementation Details: The PSR-OMA includes a new initialization of objects. Thus, the objects need to initialized into the partitions according to their pre-specified sizes. This should be done randomly. The second part of the new functionality is invoked as the machine encounters a certain placement of the objects and receives a Penalty. More specifically, the new functionality comes into play when the LA receives a Penalty and one queried object is in the innermost state, and the other queried object is in the boundary state. Consequently, if moving the boundary object, or more objects from the partition of the boundary object, fulfills the size requirements for the partitions, a legal swapping of object(s) from the boundary object's partition to the innermost object's partition

---

Algorithm 2. PSR-OMA Process Penalty

Input:
- The query $Q = \langle o_i, o_j \rangle$, and ρ_k for all $k \in \{1, 2, ..., K\}$.
- The states of the objects in Q ($\{\theta_i, \theta_j\}$).

Output:
- The next states of o_i, o_j and other affected objects.

1: **if** θ_i mod $S \neq 0$ and θ_j mod $S \neq 0$ **then**　　　// Neither are in boundary states
2:　　$\theta_i = \theta_i + 1$
3:　　$\theta_j = \theta_j + 1$
4: **else if** θ_i mod $S = 1$ and θ_j mod $S = 0$ **then**　　　// o_i is in innermost state
5:　　PSR Process for Standstill Situation (Algorithm 1)
6: **else if** θ_i mod $S = 0$ and θ_j mod $S = 1$ **then**　　　// o_j is in innermost state
7:　　PSR Process for Standstill Situation (Algorithm 1)
8: **else if** θ_i mod $S \neq 0$ and θ_j mod $S = 0$ **then**　　　// o_j is in boundary state
9:　　$\theta_i = \theta_i + 1$
10: **else if** θ_i mod $S = 0$ and θ_j mod $S \neq 0$ **then**　　　// o_i is in boundary state
11:　　$\theta_j = \theta_j + 1$
12: **else**　　　// Both are in boundary states
13:　　$temp = \theta_i$ or θ_j　　　// Store the state of *Moving* Object, o_i or o_j
14:　　$\theta_i = \theta_j$ or $\theta_j = \theta_i$　　　// Put *Moving* Object and *Staying* Object together
15:　　o_l =*unaccessed* object in group of *Staying* Object closest to boundary
16:　　$\theta_l = temp$　　　// Move o_l to the old state of *Moving* Object
17: **end if**

---

is executed. Consequently, the LA is able to change the partition sizes throughout its operation, as long as we, in total, always maintain the pre-specified sizes. By way of example, consider the scenario that we have a problem with the pre-specified sizes of 5, 6 and 7. If ϱ_1 changes from being the size of 5 to 6, the earlier partition with size 6 needs to become the 5-sized one. By operating in this manner, we will always maintain the partition sizes as being 5, 6 and 7.

The reader should observe that the proposed functionality can be directly implemented into the currently-existing algorithms by merely changing some of their already-established behaviors. To crystallize matters for the new Penalty functionality, the proposed Penalty operations for the OMA and the EOMA are given in Algorithms 2 and 3 respectively.

To summarize, for the PSR-OMA its Penalty functionality is given by Algorithm 2, while the rest of the established method remains the same. For the PSR-EOMA, the Penalty scheme is given by Algorithm 3. Again, the other functionalities of the PSR-EOMA behavior are similar to that of the existing EOMA. Additionally, the functionality of "PSR"-based functionalities can be easily extended to the PEOMA and the TPEOMA, yielding what we will refer to as the PSR-PEOMA and PSR-TPEOMA respectively. The details of these LA is trivial and not included to avoid repetition.

Algorithm 3. PSR-EOMA Process Penalty

Input:
   – The query $Q = \langle o_i, o_j \rangle$, and ρ_k for all $k \in \{1, 2, ..., K\}$.
   – The states of the objects in Q ($\{\theta_i, \theta_j\}$).
Output:
   – The next states of o_i, o_j and other affected objects.
1: **if** θ_i mod $S \neq 0$ and θ_j mod $S \neq 0$ **then**   // Neither are in boundary states
2:     $\theta_i = \theta_i + 1$
3:     $\theta_j = \theta_j + 1$
4: **else if** θ_i mod $S = 1$ and θ_j mod $S = 0$ **then**   // o_i is in innermost state
5:     PSR Process for Standstill Situation (Algorithm 1)
6: **else if** θ_i mod $S = 0$ and θ_j mod $S = 1$ **then**   // o_j is in innermost state
7:     PSR Process for Standstill Situation (Algorithm 1)
8: **else if** θ_i mod $S \neq 0$ and θ_j mod $S = 0$ **then**   // o_j is in boundary state
9:     $\theta_i = \theta_i + 1$
10:     $temp = \theta_j$ // Store the state of o_j
11:     l = index of an *unaccessed* object in group of o_i closest to the boundary
12:     $\theta_j = \theta_i$
13:     $\theta_l = temp$
14: **else if** θ_i mod $S = 0$ and θ_j mod $S \neq 0$ **then**   // o_i is in boundary state
15:     $\theta_j = \theta_j + 1$
16:     $temp = \theta_i$ // Store the state of o_i
17:     l = index of an *unaccessed* object in group of o_j closest to the boundary
18:     $\theta_i = \theta_j$
19:     $\theta_l = temp$
20: **else**   // Both are in boundary states
21:     $temp = \theta_i$ or θ_j // Store the state of *Moving* Object, o_i or o_j
22:     $\theta_i = \theta_j$ or $\theta_j = \theta_i$ // Put *Moving* Object and *Staying* Object together
23:     o_l =unaccessed object in group of *Staying* Object closest to boundary
24:     $\theta_l = temp$ // Move o_l to the old state of *Moving* Object
25: **end if**

4   Numerical Results

In this section, we demonstrate the performance of the PSR-OMA, both for an EPP and two NEPPs. Section 4.1 demonstrates results for an EPP, and it is compared with other existing OMA algorithms. Section 4.2 displays the PSR's performance for NEPPs, which cannot be compared with any of the existing OMA algorithms due to their limitation of requiring equally-sized partitions. Our simulations included "Noise", which represents the proportion of queries with objects that did not belong together in Δ^*. Such queries present disinformation to the LA, and indeed, the hardness of the problem (the *Environment*) increases with the level of noise. Therefore, we use:

$$Noise = 1 - Pr\{o_i, o_j \text{ accessed together}\} = 1 - \Pi_{o_i, o_j}, \quad \text{for } o_i, o_j \in \Delta^*, \forall i, j,$$

as the probability measurement for the LA being presented with a noisy query in the simulations [11], to demonstrate its performance in harder Environments.

Consequently, Π_{o_i,o_j} is the probability of o_i and o_j being accessed together and being together in Δ^*.

4.1 Existing OMA and PSR-OMA for an EPP

Let us first consider the simulations for an EPP where we simulated a partitioning problem with 30 objects to be grouped into three partitions, implying that $\frac{O}{K} = 10$. Table 1 shows the simulation results for different existing OMA types, and Table 2 presents results obtained for the PSR-OMA types.

One of the main differences between the PSR-EOMA and the existing EOMA is that it considers the scenario when a single object in the query is in the boundary, and the other is in the innermost state of another partition. However, because in problems with equally-sized partitions, no legal swapping of objects is possible without replacement, the new policy does not apply to these problems. We thus expect the PSR-OMA to yield results similar to those of the existing OMA types. The results obtained in Tables 1 and 2 verify this hypothesis, as the existing OMA types and the PSR-OMA types have similar performance for the different noise levels.

Note that for the PEOMA and TPEOMA, we have the κ value indicating the number of queries that have to be processed before we start filtering the queries before letting the LA process them (i.e., deploying the Pursuit concept)

Table 1. Statistics of existing OMA types for a case involving 30 objects, 3 partitions and 10 states averaged over 1,000 experiments.

Type	Noise	γ	$\Delta^+ = \Delta^*$	Not Conv.	Ψ	Ψ_Q	Ψ_T	κ	τ
EOMA	0%	100%	100%	0%	305.36	305.36	-	-	-
EOMA	10%	100%	100%	0%	425.08	425.08	-	-	-
PEOMA	0%	100%	100%	0%	307.42	309.71	-	270	$\frac{0.1}{O}$
PEOMA	10%	100%	100%	0%	398.11	417.58	-	270	$\frac{0.1}{O}$
TPEOMA	0%	100%	100%	0%	369.55	275.46	96.28	270	$\frac{0.2}{O}$
TPEOMA	10%	100%	100%	0%	555.63	316.91	253.81	270	$\frac{0.2}{O}$

Table 2. Statistics of PSR-OMA types for a case involving 30 objects, 3 partitions and 10 states averaged over 1,000 experiments.

Type	Noise	γ	$\Delta^+ = \Delta^*$	Not Conv.	Ψ	Ψ_Q	Ψ_T	κ	τ
PSR-EOMA	0%	100%	100%	0%	304.44	-	-	-	-
PSR-EOMA	10%	100%	100%	0%	417.89	-	-	-	-
PSR-PEOMA	0%	100%	100%	0%	308.65	310.91	-	270	$\frac{0.1}{O}$
PSR-PEOMA	10%	100%	100%	0%	393.14	411.80	-	270	$\frac{0.1}{O}$
PSR-TPEOMA	0%	100%	100%	0%	362.26	274.16	90.08	270	$\frac{0.2}{O}$
PSR-TPEOMA	10%	100%	100%	0%	551.48	315.43	250.13	270	$\frac{0.2}{O}$

and making transitivity pairs. Additionally, we have τ, indicating the threshold for whether a query should be considered or not [12,13].

4.2 PSR-OMA for NEPPs

We now demonstrate the performance of the PSR-EOMA for general NEPPs. Clearly, the existing OMA types cannot solve these problems because they do not have equally-sized partitions. Further, the reader should observe that unlike the problems presented for the GCD-OMA in [11], these do not possess a non-unity GCD requirement. We configured 10^6 as the maximum number of queries.

We considered two partitioning problems in our simulations. The first problem had "many partitions", and the second problem had "big partition size differences". These problems are referred to as NEPP 1 and NEPP 2, respectively. The first problem, NEPP 1, has $\rho_1 = 4$, $\rho_1 = 5$, $\rho_2 = 6$, $\rho_3 = 7$, and $\rho_4 = 8$. The second problem, NEPP 2, has $\rho_1 = 4$, $\rho_2 = 9$, and $\rho_3 = 13$. Note that only results for PSR-EOMA are presented here due to space limitations.

Results for the PSR-EOMA for NEPP 1: Let us first consider PSR-EOMA's performance for NEPP 1. In Table 3, the percentage of experiments that discovered the optimal partitioning increases from 91% to 98% and 99% for 10%, 20% and 30% noise, respectively. The PSR-OMA was able to find accurate solutions that were not far from the optimal ones. The accuracy level increased together with the noise level. With increased noise levels, the objects were forced to move in "unexpected ways", which could have contributed to discovering the optimal partitioning with a higher probability. Nevertheless, independent of the noise level, we observed that the average accuracy (γ) was at the same level. Combining the results for the accuracy and the percentage of finding the optimal partitioning, we understand that for the non-optimal solutions, there were only one or two objects in the incorrect partitioning as the LA converged.

Table 3. Statistics of PSR-EOMA for NEPP 1, with different noise levels and 6 states, averaged over 100 experiments.

Noise	γ	$\Delta^+ = \Delta^*$	Not Conv.	Conv. Rate ($\Psi = \Psi_Q$)
10%	99.25%	91.0%	0%	1,704.01
20%	99.83%	98.0%	0%	3,379.18
30%	99.95%	99.00%	0%	22,631.58

Results with PSR-EOMA for NEPP 2: In Table 4, we present the statistics for simulations for NEPP 2 with PSR-EOMA. From these results, we see that the method again had better performance in terms of accuracy and convergence as the noise increased. For 30% noise compared with 20% noise, the required number of queries was less than halved. Ironically, the noise seemed to increase the algorithm's ability to reach convergence for NEPP 2.

Table 4. Statistics of PSR-EOMA for NEPP 2, with different noise levels and 6 states, averaged over 100 experiments.

Noise	γ	$\Delta^+ = \Delta^*$	Not Conv.	Conv. Rate ($\Psi = \Psi_Q$)
10%	97.11%	90.62%	36%	134,405.40
20%	100%	100%	0%	44,974.36
30%	100%	100%	0%	4,764.84

As the results above indicate, the PSR-EOMA struggled for partitioning problems with lower noise levels as the difference between the partition sizes increased, as for NEPP 1. For such cases, the noise helps the algorithm continue "exploring" by keeping objects in the outer states. This happens when all the objects, except some, are correctly placed. In that case, they might be introduced to a noisy query that could help them get "un-stuck". For more manageable problems, like for NEPP 1, the noise has the opposite effect by increasing its number of required queries. Indeed, for problems with smaller differences between the partition sizes, the noise complicated the LA's convergence by misleading it. For both issues, in general, we attained relatively high accuracy levels.

5   Conclusion

Existing algorithms within the OMA paradigm can only solve partitioning problems with partitions of equal sizes or problems with a GCD between the partition sizes. In this paper, we have proposed a solution that can solve NEPPs in general with known partition sizes. Our experimental results show that the proposed algorithm has comparable performance to the existing algorithms regarding solving EPPs and that it can also solve NEPPs accurately. As far as we know, this is the only known solution that resolves this problem.

References

1. Berend, D., Tassa, T.: Improved bounds on bell numbers and on moments of sums of random variables. Probab. Math. Stat. **30**(2), 185–205 (2010)
2. Brualdi, R.A.: Introductory Combinatorics, 5th edn. Pearson, London (2009)
3. Gale, W., Das, S., Yu, C.T.: Improvements to an algorithm for equipartitioning. IEEE Trans. Comput. **39**(5), 706–710 (1990). https://doi.org/10.1109/12.53585
4. Oommen, B.J., Fothergill, C.: Fast learning automaton-based image examination and retrieval. Comput. J. **36**(6), 542–553 (1993)
5. Oommen, B.J., Ma, D.C.Y.: Deterministic learning automata solutions to the equipartitioning problem. IEEE Trans. Comput. **37**(1), 2–13 (1988)
6. Oommen, B.J., Ma, D.C.Y.: Stochastic automata solutions to the object partitioning problem. Comput. J. **35**, A105–A120 (1992)
7. Oommen, B.J., Zgierski, J.R.: A learning automaton solution to breaking substitution ciphers. IEEE Trans. Pattern Anal. Mach. Intell. **15**(2), 185–192 (1993). https://doi.org/10.1109/34.192492

8. Oommen, B.J., Zgierski, J.R.: Breaking substitution cyphers using stochastic automata. IEEE Trans. Pattern Anal. Mach. Intell. **15**(2), 185–192 (1993). https://doi.org/10.1109/34.192492

9. Omslandseter, R.O.: Learning Automata-Based Object Partitioning with Pre-Specified Cardinalities. 178 (2020), University of Agder

10. Omslandseter, R.O., Jiao, L., Liu, Y., Oommen, B.J.: User grouping and power allocation in NOMA systems: a reinforcement learning-based solution. In: IEA/AIE 2020

11. Omslandseter, R.O., Jiao, L., Oommen, B.J.: A learning-automata based solution for non-equal partitioning: partitions with common GCD sizes. In: IEA/AIE 2021

12. Shirvani, A., Oommen, B.J.: On invoking transitivity to enhance the pursuit-oriented object migration automata. IEEE Access **6**, 21668–21681 (2018). https://doi.org/10.1109/ACCESS.2018.2827305

13. Shirvani, A., Oommen, B.J.: On enhancing the deadlock-preventing object migration automaton using the *pursuit* paradigm. Pattern Anal. Appl. **23**(2), 509–526 (2019). https://doi.org/10.1007/s10044-019-00817-z

Autonomous Agents

Enhanced Security Framework for Enabling Facial Recognition in Autonomous Shuttles Public Transportation During COVID-19

Dimitris Tsiktsiris[1,2]([envelope]) [iD], Antonios Lalas[1,2] [iD], Minas Dasygenis[2] [iD], Konstantinos Votis[1] [iD], and Dimitrios Tzovaras[1] [iD]

[1] Information Technologies Institute, Center for Research and Technology Hellas, 6th Km Xarilaou - Thermi, 57001 Thessaloniki, Greece
{tsiktsiris,lalas,kvotis,dimitrios.tzovaras}@iti.gr
[2] Department of Electrical and Computer Engineering, University of Western Macedonia, 50100 Kozani, Greece
mdasyg@ieee.org

Abstract. Autonomous Vehicles (AVs) can potentially reduce the accident risk while a human is driving. They can also improve the public transportation by connecting city centers with main mass transit systems. The development of technologies that can provide a sense of security to the passenger when the driver is missing remains a challenging task. Moreover, such technologies are forced to adopt to the new reality formed by the COVID-19 pandemic, as it has created significant restrictions to passenger mobility through public transportation. In this work, an image-based approach, supported by novel AI algorithms, is proposed as a service to increase autonomy of non-fully autonomous people such as kids, grandparents and disabled people. The proposed real-time service, can identify family members via facial characteristics and efficiently ignore face masks, while providing notifications for their condition to their supervisor relatives. The envisioned AI-supported security framework, apart from enhancing the trust to autonomous mobility, could be advantageous in other applications also related to domestic security and defense.

Keywords: Autonomous vehicles · Public transportation · Neural networks · Image processing · Security

1 Introduction

The concept of autonomous mobility as a service (MaaS) [5] is progressively adopted by public transportation systems. However, transitioning to fully

Supported by the European Union's Horizon 2020 Research and Innovation Programme Autonomous Vehicles to Evolve to a New Urban Experience (AVENUE) under Grant Agreement No 769033.

© IFIP International Federation for Information Processing 2021
Published by Springer Nature Switzerland AG 2021
I. Maglogiannis et al. (Eds.): AIAI 2021, IFIP AICT 627, pp. 145–154, 2021.
https://doi.org/10.1007/978-3-030-79150-6_12

autonomous public vehicles in the real world is not a seamless process and has several obstacles that derive mainly from the safety concerns of the passengers [2,14]. These perceptions of traffic safety and in-vehicle security have a significant impact on the acceptance of the overall concept of autonomous public transportation. The prospective passengers fear several possible instances that could arise in case there is no driver or staff in the shuttle. More indicatively:

- Passengers feeling discomfort traveling alone during night-time.
- Parents not being able to know if their kids have reached their destination safely.
- Caregivers not being able to track passengers with dementia or other health issues.

To address the aforementioned concerns on social and personal safety and security into the vehicle, certain measures need to be implemented. For example, third parties monitoring the route of minors or passengers with health issues could make their route much easier and less frightening. This may be followed by appropriate notifications and/or instructions to the third party, while the vehicle may also implement respective actions. We propose a service to increase autonomy of non-fully autonomous people such as kids, grandparents and disabled individuals. This service will both ensure carers or family members that their beloved ones are safe while commuting around the city and increase confidence to the non-fully autonomous people to use public transport knowing that their family can "be with them". To achieve such functionality, we rely on one-shot (or single-shot) facial recognition techniques capable of identifying or verifying a person from a video frame [4,17]. In general, facial recognition, uses computing techniques for the identification of human faces in an image or a video, and then proceeds to measure specific facial characteristics. This information is later combined to create a facial signature, or profile. On the other hand, when used for facial verification, a frame from the camera footage is compared to the recorded facial signature. However, as these profiles are based on mathematical models as a result of the relative positions of their facial features, anything that can lead to reduced visibility of key characteristics, such as the nose, mouth and chin, intervenes with facial recognition [6]. Since the beginning of COVID-19 pandemic, people began to increasingly wear masks as they prevent people from getting and spreading the virus [15] and it seems obvious that algorithms designed to analyze faces and facial features will be less accurate if part of the face is concealed.

In this paper, we present an image-based approach, supported by novel AI algorithms, as an end-to-end service to increase the COVID-19 safety rules adherence of the passengers inside an autonomous shuttle. The proposed real-time service can identify family members via facial characteristics and effectively ignore face masks. The main contributions of this work can be summarized as follows:

- We propose a service to increase confidence of non-fully autonomous people such as kids, grandparents and disabled individuals in order to use autonomous public transportation.

- We present an end-to-end service based on deep learning, for automated facial recognition in autonomous shuttles.
- We introduce techniques based on attention to mitigate the occlusion issues introduced by face masks during the COVID-19 pandemic.

2   Related Work

There are multiple methods in which facial recognition systems work, but in general, they work by comparing selected facial features from a given image with faces within a database. It is also described as a Biometric Artificial Intelligence based application that can uniquely identify a person by analyzing patterns based on the person's facial textures and shape. Many face recognition techniques require multiple data of the subject in the training dataset, in order to correctly identify the face of a person. From our perspective this is not possible as we rely in one single input image of the subject. In order to be able to overcome this problem, we are using one shot (or single shot) facial recognition algorithms.

Over the last years, Deep Learning algorithms have achieved great success in the field of facial recognition, as deep features are quite common in occlusion conditions, showing better performance over shallow features. In [10], the authors proposed a Dynamic Feature Matching approach, combining a Fully Convolutional Network (FCN) with a Sparse Representation-based Classification (SRC) to recognize face parts of random size. Finally, after the last pooling layer, the deep features were linearly presented using gallery feature maps. In another approach of [16], the authors established a mask dictionary by computing the difference between the top convolution features with or without occlusion. After that, the damaged features were discarded by querying the mask dictionary. However, this method cannot be easily adopted, as it requires paired images. On the other hand, Duan et al. [8] proposed an end-to-end BoostGAN model for profile facial recognition with occlusion. In this approach, firstly, a non-occluded image was developed by the occluded image and, then, it was used for refined facial recognition. Nonetheless, this is also a hard method to reproduce, especially in cases of large area occlusions, like face masks.

Based on the reviewed literature, we have concluded that, even though the aforementioned approaches show the latest progress of Deep Learning technology in facial recognition with occlusion, most of the work done is not suitable for mask facial recognition in real life, when the key discriminating features of the nose, mouth and chin are completely damaged.

3   Methodology

A high-level overview of the service is depicted in Fig. 1. The first layer of sensors connects to the Hardware Abstraction Layer (HAL). The HAL implements the IP and the USB protocol supporting IP and USB cameras respectively but also can request raw data by the API endpoints in order to perform face recognition. The input data is converted and transformed in a compatible format and passed into the analytics algorithms. The result is then transferred via the API endpoints into the cloud. The user has access to the data and acts accordingly. A new passenger can be enrolled to the service using a single image of his face which will be stored in a database. Using this as the reference image, the network will calculate the similarity for any new instances presented to it.

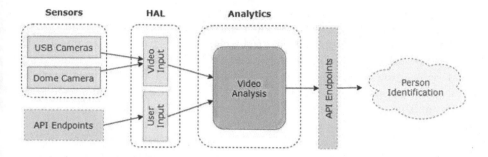

Fig. 1. High-level overview of the proposed service

As for the video analysis, facial recognition techniques identify human faces in images or videos by measuring specific facial characteristics. The extracted information is later combined to create a facial signature, or profile. On the other hand, when used for facial verification, a frame from the camera footage is compared to the recorded profile. In our architecture, a Multi-task Cascaded Convolutional Network (MTCNN) [18] receives the input frame in order to extract and align facial images. The facial images are then pre-processed and passed into a feature extractor (CNN backbone) linked with the explainable cosine (xCos) module [13] that features an explainable cosine metric.

3.1   Data Collection and Preprocessing

We used the MS1M-ArcFace [9] dataset for training our network and the LFW [11] for the testing. The two datasets were augmented via pre-processing in order to include face masks using the MaskTheFace tool [3]. The data were artificially generated due to the limited available datasets that include face masks and are suitable for the face verification task. For the sake of simplicity, we name the synthetic datasets MS1M-ArcFace+M and LFW+M, respectively.

3.2   Network Pipeline

As current face verification models use fully connected layers, spatial information is lost along with the ability to understand the convolution features in a human sense. To address this obstacle, the plug-in xCos module is integrated as described below.

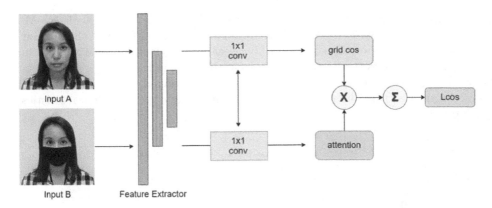

Fig. 2. Network Pipeline: The two input images are preprocessed and passed into the backbone CNN for feature extraction along with the plug-in xCos module.

Input. The two input images are preprocessed and passed into the feature extractor. The Input A is the database image while the Input B is the image cropped from the video stream.

Backbone. We implement the same CNN feature extractor as in ArcFace [7]. However, in order to employ the xCos module, the last fully connected layer and the previous flatten layer are replaced with an 1×1 convolutional layer.

Lcos Calculation (xCos). Patch-wise cosine similarity is multiplied by the attention maps and then summed to calculate the Lcos.

3.3 Results

Table 1 shows the testing accuracy on the original MS1M-ArcFace, LFW and the artificially created MS1M-ArcFace+M and LFW+M, which contain additional masked samples. As we can see, despite the minimal loss caused by the explainability module on the original datasets, a significant improvement of about 6.2% has been accomplished in our augmented datasets which contain face masks.

Table 1. Accuracy comparison between methods and different datasets indicate a significant improvement of about 6.2% in our augmented datasets which contain face masks.

Method	Training dataset	Testing dataset	Masks	Accuracy
ArcFace	MS1M-ArcFace	LFW	No	99.83%
ArcFace-xCos	MS1M-ArcFace	LFW	No	99.35%
ArcFace+M	MS1M-ArcFace+M	LFW+M	Yes	68.33%
ours, ArcFace-xCos+M	MS1M-ArcFace+M	LFW+M	Yes	74.52%

Figure 3 also highlights the improvements made over the original ArcFace+M. The maps are generated (a) by the original ArcFace+M while (b) by our improved model. The cosine similarity between the two faces is negative both in (a) and (b) on the bottom half of the faces as the mask portrays different characteristics such as shape and color. However, the attention map in our improved (b) model indicated that the network focuses more on the upper half characteristics around the eyes and the nose.

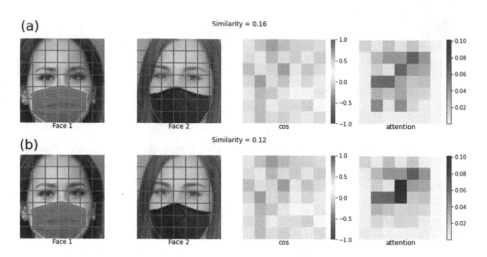

Fig. 3. Input and maps generated by (a) the original ArcFace+M and (b) our improved model. Although, the cosine (cos) similarity is negative both in (a) and (b) on the bottom half of the faces, the attention map in our improved (b) model indicated that the network focuses more on the upper half characteristics around the eyes and the nose, ignoring the region covered by the mask.

Figure 4 showcases an experimental real-world scenario on a autonomous shuttle, running on the NVIDIA Jetson AGX Xavier [1]. The proposed system is able to correctly identify the two passengers among a database of 20 people.

Figure 5 shows additional results of our improved model. The attention maps verify that the bottom parts of the face are efficiently ignored while the upper face characteristics have the most significant impact on calculating the similarity score.

Fig. 4. An experimental real-world demonstration running on the NVIDIA Jetson AGX Xavier. The proposed system is able to correctly identify the two passengers of the autonomous shuttle, among a database of 20 people.

The system was designed as a flexible and end-to-end service accessible by an Android mobile application. In Fig. 6, the architecture of the proposed system is depicted. A new passenger can be enrolled to the service via the mobile application, using a single image of his face. The image will be processed and stored temporarily in a database on the cloud platform. By using this as the reference image, the network calculates the similarity for any new instance presented to it from the shuttle. The network can predict a similarity score in one shot and inform the client via an API call and relevant notification through the mobile phone. The proposed approach can be further extended to support homeland security surveillance infrastructures in order to mitigate domestic security risks. In this context, it is envisioned to establish a highly adaptable security framework capable of leveraging the capabilities of autonomous public transport operators as well as law enforcement agencies.

The solution was build upon several power consumption constraints as we target an autonomous platform. The system operates on the edge and draws power from the vehicle batteries; therefore, it needs to be efficient and conserve energy. Several optimizations were applied in order to reduce the energy footprint on the vehicle's battery life. We optimized the network using TensorRT but also offloaded some convolutional layers to the more energy efficient Deep Learning Accelerator (DLA) engines provided by the Nvidia Jetson. Moreover, the integration with other vehicle services that are able to report the passengers on board helped us to selectively perform inference and further reduce the power consumption to a total average of 6.43 W.

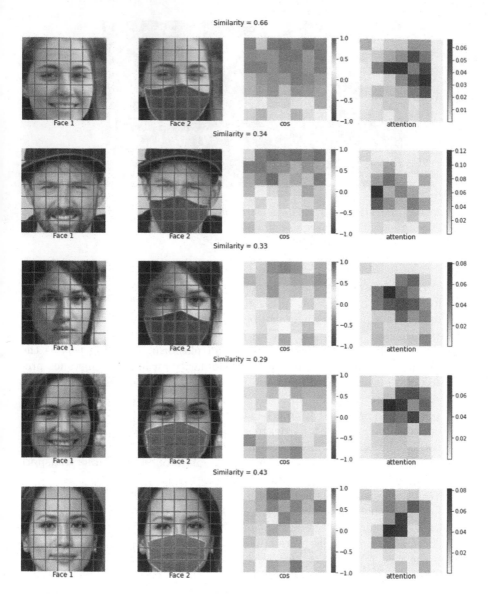

Fig. 5. Additional results of our improved model. Facial images are artificially generated using StyleGAN [12] and post-processed to include masks using MaskTheFace [3]

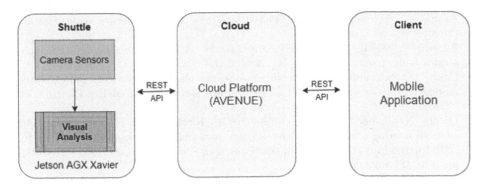

Fig. 6. The architecture of the proposed system. A new passenger is enrolled by the client. A single image of his face will be processed and stored temporarily in a database and the network will calculate similarities with current passengers. The client is informed via an API call and relevant notification through the mobile phone.

4 Conclusions

In this paper, we present a deep learning approach deployed as a real-time service in order to increase autonomy of non-fully autonomous people such as kids, grandparents and disabled individuals. The service can identify the passengers of an autonomous vehicle via facial characteristics to provide a sense of safety to the passenger and his family relatives via appropriate notifications. Legal issues related to GDPR and privacy concerns could be solved using dedicated consent forms of the passengers. To address the occlusion issues introduced by face masks during COVID-19, we propose a model based on ArcFace-xCos trained and evaluated on artificially generated datasets that include face masks. Experimental results indicated that the network yields better accuracy versus the original ArcFace due to the attention on the upper face characteristics such as eyes, eyebrows and nose. The system was deployed as a real-time service on the Jetson AGX Xavier. Future work will support real-time notifications to inform the relatives about the density of the passengers and the number of the people near their relative. We believe that our research will be a stepping stone towards increased AI-based safety and security in the autonomous public transport and other application domains as well, i.e. homeland security and defense. It will also significantly contribute in advancing the trust of the passengers to a human driverless transport system during the pandemic and beyond.

References

1. NVIDIA Jetson AGX Xavier. https://developer.nvidia.com/embedded/jetson-agx-xavier-developer-kit. Accessed 28 Mar 2021
2. Anania, E.C., Rice, S., Walters, N.W., Pierce, M., Winter, S.R., Milner, M.N.: The effects of positive and negative information on consumers' willingness to ride in a driverless vehicle. Transp. Policy **72**, 218–224 (2018)

3. Anwar, A., Raychowdhury, A.: Masked face recognition for secure authentication (2020)
4. Azeem, A., Sharif, M., Raza, M., Murtaza, M.: A survey: face recognition techniques under partial occlusion. Int. Arab J. Inf. Technol. **11**(1), 1–10 (2014)
5. Cruz, C.O., Sarmento, J.M.: Mobility as a service platforms: a critical path towards increasing the sustainability of transportation systems. Sustainability **12**(16), 6368 (2020)
6. Damer, N., Grebe, J.H., Chen, C., Boutros, F., Kirchbuchner, F., Kuijper, A.: The effect of wearing a mask on face recognition performance: an exploratory study. In: 2020 International Conference of the Biometrics Special Interest Group (BIOSIG), pp. 1–6. IEEE (2020)
7. Deng, J., Guo, J., Xue, N., Zafeiriou, S.: Arcface: Additive angular margin loss for deep face recognition. In: Proceedings of the IEEE/CVF Conference on Computer Vision and Pattern Recognition, pp. 4690–4699 (2019)
8. Duan, Q., Zhang, L.: Look more into occlusion: realistic face frontalization and recognition with boostgan. IEEE Trans. Neural Netw. Learn. Syst. **32**(1), 214 – 228 (2020)
9. Guo, Y., Zhang, L., Hu, Y., He, X., Gao, J.: MS-Celeb-1M: a dataset and benchmark for large-scale face recognition. In: Leibe, B., Matas, J., Sebe, N., Welling, M. (eds.) ECCV 2016. LNCS, vol. 9907, pp. 87–102. Springer, Cham (2016). https://doi.org/10.1007/978-3-319-46487-9_6
10. He, L., Li, H., Zhang, Q., Sun, Z.: Dynamic feature learning for partial face recognition. In: Proceedings of the IEEE Conference on Computer Vision and Pattern Recognition, pp. 7054–7063 (2018)
11. Huang, G.B., Mattar, M., Berg, T., Learned-Miller, E.: Labeled faces in the wild: a database forstudying face recognition in unconstrained environments. In: Workshop on faces in'Real-Life'Images: detection, alignment, and recognition (2008)
12. Karras, T., Laine, S., Aittala, M., Hellsten, J., Lehtinen, J., Aila, T.: Analyzing and improving the image quality of StyleGAN. In: Proceedings of CVPR (2020)
13. Lin, Y.S., et al.: xcos: An explainable cosine metric for face verification task. arXiv preprint arXiv:2003.05383 (2020)
14. Ngan, M.L., Grother, P.J., Hanaoka, K.K.: Ongoing face recognition vendor test (frvt) part 6a: Face recognition accuracy with masks using pre-covid-19 algorithms (2020)
15. Organization, W.H., et al.: Advice on the use of masks in the context of covid-19: interim guidance, 6 April 2020. World Health Organization, Tehnical Report (2020)
16. Song, L., Gong, D., Li, Z., Liu, C., Liu, W.: Occlusion robust face recognition based on mask learning with pairwise differential siamese network. In: Proceedings of the IEEE/CVF International Conference on Computer Vision, pp. 773–782 (2019)
17. Wang, L., Li, Y., Wang, S.: Feature learning for one-shot face recognition. In: 2018 25th IEEE International Conference on Image Processing (ICIP), pp. 2386–2390. IEEE (2018)
18. Zhang, K., Zhang, Z., Li, Z., Qiao, Y.: Joint face detection and alignment using multitask cascaded convolutional networks. IEEE Signal Process. Lett. **23**(10), 1499–1503 (2016)

Evaluating Task-General Resilience Mechanisms in a Multi-robot Team Task

James Staley and Matthias Scheutz[(✉)] [iD]

Tufts University, Medford, MA 02155, USA
{James.Staley625703,Matthias.Scheutz}@tufts.edu

Abstract. Real-word intelligent agents must be able to detect sudden and unexpected changes to their task environment and effectively respond to those changes in order to function properly in the long term. We thus isolate a set of perturbations that agents ought to address and demonstrate how task-agnostic perturbation detection and mitigation mechanisms can be integrated into a cognitive robotic architecture. We present results from experimental evaluations of perturbation mitigation strategies in a multi-robot system that show how intelligent systems can achieve higher levels of autonomy by explicitly handling perturbations.

Keywords: Resilience · Intelligent autonomous agents · Long-term autonomy

1 Introduction

Resilience allows intelligent agents to accomplish their goals despite unexpected degradation of their task environment, including their own operational platform. When perturbations are possible or expected in a particular task setting, agents are typically already designed with mechanisms to cope with them (e.g., the wheels on the Mars Rovers were designed to work even when they had holes in them as it was expected that holes would eventually emerge as a result of driving over pointy rocks). While there is a large amount of literature on fault detection and recovery through software in cases where the system has a model of its operation, there are few proposals for task-general mechanisms for detecting, classifying, and mitigating perturbations.

In this paper, we discuss six dimensions of perturbations and demonstrate with a particular implementation of detection and mitigation mechanisms for a class of perturbations (those of actuation failures) how changing roles within its team allows an agent to adapt to a perturbation that cannot otherwise be mitigated. Using experimental evaluations in a simulated space-station environment of the implemented mechanisms in a multi-robot repair team, we should how detecting perturbations to a single agent's effectors and mitigating them by adapting the team member roles can enable significantly higher performance than failing to address the perturbation.

This work was in part supported by ONR grant #N00014-18-1-2831.

I. Maglogiannis et al. (Eds.): AIAI 2021, IFIP AICT 627, pp. 155–166, 2021.
https://doi.org/10.1007/978-3-030-79150-6_13

2   Motivation

Perturbations happen in the real world as real task environments are not always well-behaved. A robot tasked with searching a building might be plunged into darkness when the building's power fails, for example, making it impossible to continue searching with its regular camera. The same robot's camera might fail half-way through the task, resulting in task failure. Perturbations are not limited to the environment or the robot's body, they can also occur inside the robot's computational system (e.g., an object detection algorithm could run out of memory, or have a bug that causes a crash). Some perturbations are permanent (e.g., the broken camera), while others are transient (e.g., short power outage). Some perturbations might be harmless (a door closed that was supposed to be open, that can be opened) and have no impact on the robot's task performance, or might be prohibitive (the door locked). Some could be anticipated by the robot (a storm outside might make power outages likely), while others remain unpredictable (the camera failing all of a sudden). Some perturbations can be detected by the robot (i.e., sensed or inferred such as noticing a camera must be broken because the image is frozen despite the robot's motion), while others remain undetectable (e.g., radiation that eventually destroys the computational platform). Some perturbations are avoidable (e.g., running out of battery power by charging the battery in time), while others cannot be avoided (e.g., eventually running out of memory due to increasing log files). And some perturbations can be mitigated by the robot (e.g., unlocking the locked door), while others cannot (e.g., no more memory can be added). We thus get the following six dimensions characterizing perturbations: (1) transient/permanent, (2) impactless/impactful, (3) predictable/unpredictable, (4) detectable/undetectable, (5) avoidable/unavoidable, and (6) mitigable/unmitigable.

Overall, which type of perturbation a robot encounters as part of its task performance will depend on the environment, the task, the robot's body and computational capabilities (e.g., for detecting perturbations). We would like the robot to be resilient to as many perturbations as possible, which requires it to watch out for and ideally predict perturbations in an effort to avoid them. If they are not predictable, the robot should at least detect and attempt to mitigate them, leading to the following task-independent resilience policy:

1. predict a perturbation or detect its presence
2. classify the perturbation to determine the best response
3. enact the mitigation strategy (if available)

Different refinements of this policy are possible based on the exact nature of the perturbation. For example, for a transient perturbation (e.g., light out for a short time) the best policy might be to ignore the perturbation, whereas for a permanent perturbation (e.g., camera sensor broken) the mitigation strategy might involve finding alternative ways to perform the task (e.g., tactile investigation of objects).

In the context of a multi-robot system, a perturbation must be handled with an escalating response based on the impact is has on the whole system, not just the individual agent. In simple cases, an agent might be able to cope with the effects of the perturbation in a way that at most has a negligible impact on task performance. However, in more complex cases, a perturbation affecting a single agent might have major ramifications for the team and its organization, preventing the agent from fulfilling a critical role in the team. In such a case, the mitigation strategy cannot stop at the single agent, but must involve other agents as well, e.g., redistributing the amount and type of work each agent does.

3   Related Work

Much work on introspection and behavior modeling has focused on fault detection, diagnosis and recovery [13,19,23] and system reconfiguration to accomplish a high-level goal [5,7]. Prerequisite to fault recovery is the ability to isolate a fault and determine its severity [3]. Fault detection and diagnosis methods are either analytic or data-driven (although this division becomes blurred by techniques that automate the process of traditionally analytic methods [6]). Analytic methods have a long successful history in the various engineering disciplines (e.g., the Livingstone system developed by NASA for use on Deep Space One [24]), but they are limited to tasks in constrained environments with a small number of well-understood states. Data-driven approaches employ various classification algorithms (e.g., neural networks, Bayesian networks) to learn fault models from past performance data, but this presumes the data is available (e.g., applications in aerospace can build on decades of telemetry data [14]). Golombek et al. [10,11] attempt to find structure in temporal patterns of communications among architectural components and learn a model of normal and faulty operation by clustering those patterns. This approach is similar to our own [2] except that they can also utilize knowledge-based, top-down constraints for recovery policies.

For fault recovery (the "self-adjustment" phase in [1]), it is necessary to develop policies for how to react to faults once they have been detected. The policy can either be pre-defined or it can be learned. For example, in the Livingstone system, a recovery mechanism based on conflict resolution in a feedback controller was developed, where the control command was based on the analytic model [24]. While (possibly optimal) policies can be pre-defined or learned from existing labeled data for known faults, recovery policies for unknown faults will have to be learned dynamically, especially for systems where fault models can change during their operation.

The system employed here is able to detect anomalies faster and with less required initialization by describing an agent's actions in terms of logical primitive pre- and post-conditions. When an action systematically fails to produce its expected post-conditions it is considered to be under the effect of a perturbation. In addition, these fault detection systems typically focus on single-agent systems and so ignore the possible mitigation techniques that may be available to multi-agent systems. As a consequence, role-switching, which our experiment focuses on, has not been studied in the context of fault detection and recovery.

Multi-agent systems that are robust to perturbations have been proposed in the past. The ALLIANCE architecture designed for multi-agent fault tolerance, for example, used internal motivations and assessments to determine when an agent was underperforming at a task (potentially due to a perturbation) and should switch tasks [12,20]. Other approaches, like Christensen et al. [4], implement an exogenous approach to fault detection, whereby member of the multi-agent group that are not perturbed can recognize reduced capabilities in their collaborators. These approaches find success in replacing a poorly performing agent, but do not investigate whether that agent may still contribute to the overall performance of the system by reassigning its role.

As we will show, role re-allocation can offer additional boosts in system performance when the agent's role explicitly depends on its dynamic capability. By first detecting that an agent's capability has changed and then assigning the compromised agent to a role where it can still contribute to the system's performance allows the multi-agent system to achieve higher performance.

4   Resilience Mechanisms and Experimental Evaluation

We are interested in evaluating architectural mechanisms for increasing an agent's resilience that are task-general and can be integrated into different agent architectures, based on the three aspects – perturbation detection, classification, and mitigation, which form a task- and hardware-independent resilience framework that cannot be found in other robotic architectures. Briefly, using introspection, an agent should monitor its task performance and compare it to expected outcomes, which allows it to recognize that action or task is systematically failing (e.g., based prior expectations of action outcomes, inferred post conditions, or other unexpected changes in the system). Specifically, through repeated monitoring and comparison of outcomes and other system states, the agent will then be able detect whether unexpected outcomes or events are simply sporadic or random, or are systematic and due to some kind of perturbation that can potentially be addressed by the agent. The overall sequence of agent actions then is: (1) model body, architectural and environmental states, as well as task performance, (2) determine whether unexpected outcomes, states or behavior, internal or external to the agent are likely noise or systematic, and in the latter case, (3) attempt to classify the kind of perturbation in terms of whether it has an impact on task performance, and if so, whether it can be mitigated. In the former case, the agent might be able to ignore it, in the latter, based on the type of perturbation, it needs to attempt to mitigate it using a number of strategies. The agents might redirect cognitive resources, change its bodily configuration, otherwise adapt to the new environment or elicit help from other agents in the context of the team.

We leverage the existing multi-agent simulation infrastructure in [8] together with a multi-agent cognitive robotic architecture (described below) to implement and evaluate a first set of perturbation detection, classification, and mitigation mechanisms and to demonstrate the utility of automatic role switching as a possible mitigation policy in multi-robot team settings (as opposed to solely individual-based mitigation mechanisms that in some cases will fail because individual mitigation of the perturbation is not possible).

4.1 Resilience Mechanisms in the DIARC Architecture

We used the *Distributed Integrated Affect Reflection Cognition* (DIARC) architecture [22] as the basis for all algorithm developments and integration. DIARC is a component-based architecture scheme that can be instantiated for different tasks and settings with different components present in the system. It is implemented in the "Agent Development Environment" ADE [16,21], which, different from other robotic infrastructures such as the Robot Operating System (ROS) [?], was from the very beginning *designed to be as secure and fault-tolerant as possible*.[1] Hence, ADE provides the extensive architectural multi-level introspection and notification mechanisms (e.g., see [17,18]) that can be utilized to detect and classify perturbation. System models for DIARC can either be learned offline from logged information about system states (e.g., [2]) or online as part of *anomaly detection* (e.g., [9]). DIARC's fault detection and recovery mechanisms have also been empirically evaluated in HRI studies (e.g., [15]). In the context of multi-robot teams, DIARC can be configured to run with shared architectural components that allow multiple agents to easily share information and implement distributed multi-agent architectures such as the blackboard architecture or shared mental models (e.g., [8]). We utilize this component-sharing capability to allow robots to write status and role updates to the share workspace called "Belief component" in DIARC (as it stores the agents' beliefs about themselves and the world) which allows any team member to determine what role another team member assumes and thus react to any role changes that might be necessitated by perturbations. If agents keep track of all possible roles they can assume in a team, then the Belief component could run a role assignment algorithm every time a change to the set of possible roles for a team member occurs to optimize role assignment and team performance.

In order to evaluate the effects of role-switching in response to perturbations we developed a task using the components described in this section.

We examined the beneficial effects of perturbation detection and tested the effectiveness of a multi-agent role switching mitigation strategy by performing a repair task in a simulated environment with two Willow Garage PR2 robots. The robots are simulated in ROS's Gazebo simulator, their behavior and knowledge states are governed by the DIARC architecture, and all visuals and environmental logic are controlled through Unity3D.

4.2 The Space Station Environment

We utilize an existing space station simulation environment [8] (see Fig. 1) which was designed and implemented in Unity3D. The environment consisted of three

---

[1] A detailed conceptual and empirical comparison of robotic infrastructures up to 2006 can be found in [16].

wings extending away from a central hub. In each wing there are two rows of 12 fuel tubes. The wings are identical but for their name designations of Alpha, Beta or Gamma. The two robots were responsible for the maintenance of fuel-tubes in an orbiting space station. Fuel-tube failures occurs regularly due to unpredictable and undetectable circumstances and all non-failing tubes have an equal chance to fail at each interval. A failed fuel-tube's condition will decay until it breaks. Once a fuel-tube has broken it cannot be repaired or fixed in any way. If enough fuel tubes break (15 for these experiments) the space station can no longer operate and must perform an emergency landing.

Fig. 1. Space station layout. One central hub with three marked wings.

4.3   The Robots

The simulated robots are responsible for maintaining the space station. All of the robots' planning and motion dynamics are simulated in the ROS Gazebo simulator to incorporate as realistic timing and dynamics effects on the task as possible. Robots can repair failed fuel-tubes and can perform scans that determine the condition for every fuel-tube within the wing they currently occupy.

Robots may assume one of two roles: *Repair agent* or *Sensor agent*. Repair agents move around the environment sensing and fixing failing fuel-tubes. Sensor agents cannot repair tubes, but can continue to scan wings of the space station and report their findings to the multi-agent system. The algorithms that govern these roles are described in Sect. 4.5.

4.4   The Search-and-Repair Task

Within this environment, two agents perform a search-and-repair task in order to keep the space installation running. Each agent initially assumes both roles of Repair and Sensor which leads to the highest task performance. We then introduce a perturbation in the form of a broken repair tool in one robot, but give the robot no way to directly sense that this perturbation has occurred. While the robot cannot determine exactly what happened, after a few failed repair attempts the goal monitoring system within DIARC architecture can infer that the error is systematic and determine that the robot can no longer repair fuel tubes. Within the DIARC action execution subsystem this means that the *repair(tube)* action no longer produces the expected post-condition of a tube in perfect (repaired) condition.

Without the ability to repair tubes, the agent's ability set has changed and it can no longer fulfill the role of Repair agent. It checks whether there is a role its ability set can still satisfy and switches to that role, in this case becoming a sole Sensor agent. The Sensor agent communicates this role change to DIARC's knowledge base and the functioning Repair agent may now use the Sensor agent's information to make better decisions for which tubes to repair (where "better decisions" in this context are heuristically implemented to keep the space station operational for longer).

4.5   Experimental Design and Procedure

Right room the beginning both robots patrol the space station and under normal operating conditions (i.e., both robots hold both Repair and Sensor roles) follow a basic algorithm:

1. Move to an unoccupied wing
2. Scan the wing for damaged tubes
3. Repair all damaged tubes in the currently occupied wing
4. Update the Knowledge Base

The task ends once fifteen fuel tubes have been destroyed or eighteen fuel tubes have been repaired. A maximum of eighteen is to give a hard stopping point for the case with two fully functional agents, which under ideal conditions can keep the space station operational indefinitely.

Conditions. Our base condition includes two fully functioning agents who remain in perfect condition over the course of the trial. They work independently with minimal communication[2] They follow the simple algorithm described above without modification, and are expected to maintain the space station the longest.

Our two experimental conditions include one fully functioning agent and one agent with a broken welding implement, rendering the agent unable to repair

---

[2] Agents avoid occupying the same area of the space station.

tubes. The broken implement is a permanent, unpredictable, unavoidable, but detectable perturbation that impacts the performance of the multi-agent team. Our first experimental condition, *silent-failure*, uses an agent that is unable to detect this perturbation and continues following the simple algorithm above.

Algorithm 1: Introspective Repair Agent Role

Move to unoccupied wing;
Get list of damaged tubes within wing;
otherAgentIsDamaged = Check Knowledge Base for state of other agent;
if *otherAgentIsDamaged and heuristic()* **then**
  | Move to damaged Sensor agent wing;
while *damagedTubesInWing()* **do**
  Go to nearest damaged tube in wing;
  Repair nearest damaged tube;
  if *fixed(tube)* **then**
    | Update Knowledge Base about tube status;
  else if *amDamaged()* **then**
    Change role to Sensor agent role;
    Update Knowledge Base about own status;
    break;
end

Our second experimental condition, *role-switching*, uses an agent that can detect the existence of perturbation through its own reduced performance. Once this detection occurs the multi-agent team can adopt a new operating regime wherein the damaged agent drops its repair role and maintains only its role as a mobile sensor. The functioning robot, when deciding which wing of the station it should care about, can use the non-functioning robot to increase its understanding of the context and make a better decision about which action to take next. The *role-switching* team follows a new algorithm.

Algorithm 2: Introspective Sensor Agent Role

Move to unoccupied wing;
roles = Check Knowledge Base for own roles;
Scan wing for damaged tubes;
Update Knowledge Base about state of wing;
if *!role.contains(Repair)* **then**
  while *absent(Repair Robot)* **do**
    wait;
    Scan wing for damaged tubes;
    Update Knowledge Base about state of wing;
  end

The base condition and *role-switching* conditions can be described by role Algorithms 1 and 2.

The agents in the base case successfully perform the Repair and Sensor roles for the duration of the task. They can scan the wing they're in and repair every damaged tube in that wing before moving on. They never enter the perturbation mitigating blocks of code because in the Repair case (1) their partner is not damaged and (2) they are not damaged, and in the Sensor case they can always hold the Repair role.

Algorithm 3: Basic Repair Agent Role

Move to unoccupied wing;
Get list of damaged tubes within wing;
while *damagedTubesInWing()* **do**
    | Go to nearest damaged tube in wing;
    | Repair nearest damaged tube;
    | Update Knowledge Base about tube status;
end

The agents in *silent-failure* behave exactly like the base-condition agents, but to worse effect. In their case, the damaged agent has no mechanism to check whether its performance is impacted by a perturbation. Their less introspective roles can be described by Algorithms 3 and 4.

Algorithm 4: Basic Sensor Agent Role

Move to unoccupied wing;
Scan wing for damaged tubes;
Update Knowledge Base about state of wing;

These basic roles perform well in the absence of perturbations, but have no ability to handle problems. We expect the multi-agent team that can *role-switch* to perform worse than the fully functioning team, because only one robot can repair tubes, but better than the *silent-failure* team, because it will cause the agent with the perturbation to attempt to repair the same tube over and over again.

4.6   Results

We ran the two robots with their respective role algorithms for $n = 17$ trials in Search-and-Repair Task. As expected, the robots in the baseline condition with no perturbation are able to keep the space station operational indefinitely as indicated by their exact average of 18 with zero standard deviation (recall, the simulation was terminated when 18 tubes were repaired). Robots in the two perturbation conditions never made it to 18 repaired tubes (rather, 12 repaired tubes was the maximum in the role-switching condition). A two-sided Welch t-test (adjusting of unequal variances) shows a significant difference ($t(31.32) = 3.245, p = .0027$) between the silent-failure condition ($\mu = 7.58$ repaired tubes on average, $SD = 1.46$) and the resilience condition ($\mu = 9.35$ repaired tubes on average, $SD = 1.69$), as hypothesized, demonstrating that the team with perturbation detection and mitigation is able to last longer. The results thus demonstrate the utility of the introspective failure detection mechanisms that causes the agent encountering repeated action failures to give up on roles that require it to perform the failed action successfully.

5   Discussion

The multi-agent team that is able to detect the presence of a perturbation and switch roles in response outperforms the multi-agent team that can not. *Role-switching* sees numeric improvement over *silent-failure*. In certain cases the two conditions have comparable performances because the nature of this task makes the gains from a Sensor agent highly dependent on the order that the fuel-tubes break. The Sensor agent is most useful when the information it provides leads the Repair agent to a wing of the space station that it would otherwise not give immediate attention to. If this situation doesn't arise, and the Repair agent is already going to the wing most in need, then the damaged multi-agent team performs equally well with and without the *role-switching* mitigation strategy. However, we see from the data that this situation does arise often enough to justify the additional computational load required for the mitigation strategy.

Note that while both conditions perform significantly worse that the baseline condition where no perturbation occurs – as mentioned above we set the frequency of tubes breaking in such a way that two fully functional robots could about keep up with the repairs – there are cases where the resilient robots will be able to maintain an operational station while the silent failure condition will not (as a single robot will not be able to keep up with the repairs). And while this proof-of-concept evaluation is only a first indication of the utility of resilience mechanisms that adapt the agent policies in teams (to compensate for unavoidable, unrecoverable perturbations), there are many more architectural reasoning mechanisms and mitigation policies to be explored that will significantly improve the resilience of multi-agent teams.

6   Conclusion

In this paper we showed the downstream benefits of a system that can perform task-agnostic detection of perturbations and task-specific mitigation strategies to address the loss of performance associated with a given perturbation. We use a cognitive architecture, DIARC, to determine when an agent is experiencing a systematic perturbation by detecting when an action is systematically failing to produce its expected post-conditions. Detecting the perturbation is itself extremely significant because it enables the system to respond.

We experimentally demonstrate how a multi-agent system can respond to the detected perturbation of one agent. Once an agent is damaged and cannot fulfill the repair role, the system responds by reassigning the agent to the role in which it can still contribute. The system performs better when it can perform task-specific adaptation, which it can only do because of its ability to perform task-independent perturbations detection. The ability to detect and mitigate perturbations is a requirement for an intelligent system to achieve higher levels of autonomy than what is currently possible.

References

1. Anderson, M.L., Perlis, D.R.: Logic, self-awareness and self-improvement: the metacognitive loop and the problem of brittleness. J. Logic Comput. **15**(1), 21–40 (2005). http://cogprints.org/3950/
2. Berzan, C., Scheutz, M.: What am i doing? automatic construction of an agent's state-transition diagram through introspection. In: Proceedings of AAMAS 2012 (2012)
3. Blanke, M., Kinnaert, M., Lunze, J., Staroswiecki, M.: Diagnosis of I/O automata networks. Diagnosis and Fault-Tolerant Control, pp. 607–639. Springer, Heidelberg (2016). https://doi.org/10.1007/978-3-662-47943-8_12
4. Christensen, A.L., OGrady, R., Dorigo, M.: From fireflies to fault-tolerant swarms of robots. IEEE Trans. Evol. Comput. **13**(4), 754–766 (2009). https://doi.org/10.1109/TEVC.2009.2017516
5. Edwards, G., et al.: Architecture-driven self-adaptation and self-management in robotics systems. In: Proceedings of the 2009 ICSE Workshop on Software Engineering for Adaptive and Self-Managing Systems, pp. 142–151. IEEE Computer Society (2009)
6. Ernits, J., Dearden, R., Pebody, M.: Automatic fault detection and execution monitoring for AUV missions. In: Autonomous Underwater Vehicles (AUV), 2010 IEEE/OES, pp. 1–10. IEEE (2010)
7. Georgas, J.C., Taylor, R.N.: Policy-based self-adaptive architectures: a feasibility study in the robotics domain. In: Proceedings of the 2008 International Workshop on Software Engineering for Adaptive and Self-Managing Systems, pp. 105–112. SEAMS 2008, ACM (2008)
8. Gervits, F., Thurston, D., Thielstrom, R., Fong, T., Pham, Q., Scheutz, M.: Toward genuine robot teammates: Improving human-robot team performance using robot shared mental models. In: Proceedings of AAMAS (2020)
9. Gizzi, E., Vie, L.L., Scheutz, M., Sarathy, V., Sinapov, J.: A generalized framework for detecting anomalies in real-time using contextual information. In: Proceedings of the 2018 IJCAI Workshop on Modeling and Reasoning in Context (MRC) (2018)
10. Golombek, R., Wrede, S., Marc, H., Martin, H.: On-line data-driven fault detection for robotic systems. In: IEEE/RSJ International Conference on Intelligent Robots and Systems, San Francisco, CA (2011)
11. Golombek, R., Wrede, S., Hanheide, M., Heckmann, M.: Learning a probabilistic self-awareness model for robotic systems. In: IEEE/RSJ International Conference on Intelligent Robots and Systems (2010)

12. Guo, Z., Yang, W., Li, M., Yi, X., Cai, Z., Wang, Y.: ALLIANCE-ROS: a software framework on ROS for fault-tolerant and cooperative mobile robots. Chin. J. Electron. **27**(3), 467–475 (2018). https://doi.org/10.1049/cje.2018.03.001

13. Haidarian, H., et al.: The metacognitive loop: an architecture for building robust intelligent systems. In: PAAAI Fall Symposium on Commonsense Knowledge (AAAI/CSK2010), Arlington, VA, USA (Nov 2010)

14. Iverson, D.L.: Inductive system health monitoring. In: International Conference on Artificial Intelligence. CSREA Press (2004)

15. Kramer, J., Scheutz, M.: Reflection and reasoning mechanisms for failure detection and recovery in a distributed robotic architecture for complex robots. In: Proceedings of the 2007 IEEE International Conference on Robotics and Automation, pp. 3699–3704, Rome, Italy (Apr 2007)

16. Kramer, J., Scheutz, M.: Robotic development environments for autonomous mobile robots: a survey. Auton. Rob. **22**(2), 101–132 (2007)

17. Kramer, J., Scheutz, M., Schermerhorn, P.: 'Talk to me!': enabling communication between robotic architectures and their implementing infrastructures. In: Proceedings of the 2007 IEEE/RSJ International Conference on Intelligent Robots and Systems, pp. 3044–3049, San Diego, CA (Oct/Nov 2007)

18. Krause, E., Schermerhorn, P., Scheutz, M.: Crossing boundaries: multi-level introspection in a complex robotic architecture for automatic performance improvements. In: Proceedings of the Twenty-Sixth AAAI Conference on Artificial Intelligence (2012)

19. Morris, A.C.: Robotic Introspection for Exploration and Mapping of Subterranean Environments. Ph.D. thesis, Robotics Institute, Carnegie Mellon University (Dec 2007)

20. Parker, L.E.: ALLIANCE: an architecture for fault tolerant multirobot cooperation. IEEE Trans. Robot. Autom. **14**(2), 220–240 (1998). https://doi.org/10.1109/70.681242

21. Scheutz, M.: ADE - steps towards a distributed development and runtime environment for complex robotic agent architectures. Appl. Artif. Intell. **20**(4–5), 275–304 (2006)

22. Scheutz, M., Williams, T., Krause, E., Oosterveld, B., Sarathy, V., Frasca, T.: An overview of the distributed integrated cognition affect and reflection DIARC architecture. In: Aldinhas Ferreira, M.I., Silva Sequeira, J., Ventura, R. (eds.) Cognitive Architectures. ISCASE, vol. 94, pp. 165–193. Springer, Cham (2019). https://doi.org/10.1007/978-3-319-97550-4_11

23. Sykes, D., Heaven, W., Magee, J., Kramer, J.: From goals to components: a combined approach to self-management. In: Proceedings of the 2008 International Workshop on Software Engineering for Adaptive and Self-Managing Systems, pp. 1–8. SEAMS 2008, ACM, New York, NY, USA (2008)

24. Williams, B., Nayak, P., et al.: A model-based approach to reactive self-configuring systems. In: Proceedings of the National Conference on Artificial Intelligence, pp. 971–978 (1996)

Clustering

A Multi-view Clustering Approach for Analysis of Streaming Data

Vishnu Manasa Devagiri$^{(\boxtimes)}$, Veselka Boeva, and Shahrooz Abghari

Blekinge Institute of Technology, Karlskrona, Sweden
{vmd,vbx,sab}@bth.se

Abstract. Data available today in smart monitoring applications such as smart buildings, machine health monitoring, smart healthcare, etc., is not centralized and usually supplied by a number of different devices (sensors, mobile devices and edge nodes). Due to which the data has a heterogeneous nature and provides different perspectives (views) about the studied phenomenon. This makes the monitoring task very challenging, requiring machine learning and data mining models that are not only able to continuously integrate and analyze multi-view streaming data, but also are capable of adapting to concept drift scenarios of newly arriving data. This study presents a multi-view clustering approach that can be applied for monitoring and analysis of streaming data scenarios. The approach allows for parallel monitoring of the individual view clustering models and mining view correlations in the integrated (global) clustering models. The global model built at each data chunk is a formal concept lattice generated by a formal context consisting of closed patterns representing the most typical correlations among the views. The proposed approach is evaluated on two different data sets. The obtained results demonstrate that it is suitable for modelling and monitoring multi-view streaming phenomena by providing means for continuous analysis and pattern mining.

Keywords: Multi-view clustering · Multi-instance learning · Closed patterns · Streaming data · Formal concept analysis

1   Introduction

In recent years, the amount of data being generated in areas such as web, social media, IoT, and smart monitoring applications is increasing rapidly. Data generated in most of these areas is usually heterogeneous as the data is generally collected at different locations using variety of devices (e.g., mobile devices, edge nodes, sensors in IoT networks) and/or streaming in nature as new data is continuously produced. Another common factor of the data generated in streaming

This work is funded in part of the research project "Scalable resource efficient systems for big data analytics" funded by the Knowledge Foundation (grant: 20140032) in Sweden.

I. Maglogiannis et al. (Eds.): AIAI 2021, IFIP AICT 627, pp. 169–183, 2021.
https://doi.org/10.1007/978-3-030-79150-6_14

scenarios is its evolving nature. Change of data characteristics over a period of time, known as concept drift, is an important challenge to be addressed when dealing with streaming data.

Clustering techniques are well-known tools and broadly used for analysis and extraction of interesting patterns from unlabeled data sets. Traditional clustering algorithms however, are not suitable and cannot deal with the data generated in today's smart monitoring applications due to characteristics already mentioned above like heterogeneity, streaming nature, concept drift [7]. There is a need for new clustering algorithms that are able to address these challenges. Data stream mining is an area dealing with the challenges concerning analysis and understanding of streaming data scenarios. Multi-view clustering, a distributed clustering technique, is capable of analysing heterogeneous data that are generated by different sources and represents different views or perspectives about the studied phenomenon. In multi-view clustering scenarios different views, contexts or interpretations of the data bringing complementary information (e.g., numerical reports of a patient and reports like ECG), are analysed in order to extract meaningful correlations among the different views. Although many research studies have been conducted and published in both data stream mining and multi-view clustering fields, the area of multi-view stream clustering is still in its infancy and there is a need for clustering techniques addressing and analysing streaming data in a multi-view fashion [13,18]. Some of the major challenges of multi-view stream clustering techniques are data heterogeneity [22], incomplete views [16,18,23] and evolving nature of the data [13].

In this work, we propose a multi-view clustering algorithm, entitled MV Multi-Instance Clustering, that can be used for monitoring and continuous analysis of streaming data scenarios. The proposed algorithm allows for parallel monitoring of the individual view clustering models and analyzing the views' correlations revealed by the integrated (global) clustering model. The individual view clustering models at each data chunk are initially updated when new data arrives by applying multi-instance clustering. Then, a global model can be built at each data chunk as a formal concept lattice generated by a formal context. The latter consists of selected closed patterns presenting the most typical correlations among the different views. Such a hierarchical global model allows to analyse and compare the views' correlations derived by two consecutive data chunks. Note that the local models' data values are not needed in order to build the global model which supports data privacy and lowers the required memory for data processing. In addition, if there are missing data in some of the views the previously extracted correlations among the views could be used to reconstruct the missing values.

2   Related Work

Distributed clustering techniques can deal with large, unlabelled and heterogeneous data sets which cannot be gathered centrally [2,9,12,19]. Characteristics of distributed data like heterogeneity, scalability, security, etc., demand novel robust clustering algorithms to address these challenges [9]. While some researchers [2] have tried to tackle various challenges in the field, others [9,12,19] have proposed an overview of the research being done. Gan et al. [9] discuss various challenges and provide a summary on the state-of-the-art distributed clustering techniques. The authors cover various important concepts in the field of data mining like frequent itemset mining, frequent sequence mining, frequent graph mining, clustering and privacy for distributed context. In [12,19], a comparative study on the various state-of-the-art distributed clustering techniques has been done. Bendechache and Kechadi [2] propose an algorithm, entitled Distributed Dynamic Clustering algorithm, which is based on k-means for spatial data that is distributed and heterogeneous.

Multi-view clustering deals with clustering techniques in which same data is available in different perspectives or views complementing each other [18]. Studies published in [7,22], provide an overview and analysis of different multi-view clustering techniques proposed. Fu et al. [7] evaluate the selected multi-view algorithms on seven real-world data sets using cluster validation metrics like accuracy, purity, and normalized mutual information. In [22], the authors have reviewed available multi-view clustering algorithms by grouping them into five categories. In series of papers [16,18,23], the authors address the challenges of incomplete views, where data in some views maybe missing. Shao et al. [18] develop an algorithm, entitled Online Multi-View clustering, based on non-negative matrix factorization for large scale incomplete distributed data sets.

It is interesting to note that in [14], the authors treat multi-view clustering as a multi-objective optimization problem. In [15], a multi-view clustering approach based on non-negative matrix factorization and probabilistic latent semantic analysis is proposed to obtain common consensus clustering across views. Research in [13,18] deals with streaming data in multi-view scenarios. Huang et al. [13] propose a novel multi-view clustering approach for streaming data.

In the current state-of-the-art algorithms for multi-view clustering there are not many solutions dealing with monitoring and analysis of streaming data and the challenges that come along with it. The proposed MV Multi-Instance Clustering algorithm address these challenges.

3   Background

3.1   Multi-Instance Clustering and Hausdorff Distance

Multi-Instance (MI) clustering is an unsupervised learning process, where the data objects are bags of instances and there is no information about the labels of bags [24]. This is a typical setting for many real world application scenarios in which, it is costly and even in many cases impossible to obtain labeled data.

Multi-Instance clustering algorithms are supposed to partition a set of unlabeled bags into a number of groups on the basis of a similarity measure. However, the task of distributing objects into clusters is more difficult in the multi-instance context, since the ambiguity due to the fact that the objects are bags of unlabeled often related instances. In this sense, the similarity measures used in single-instance clustering may not be appropriate for multi-instance clustering scenarios. *Maximal Hausdorff distance* has been proposed in [5] to measure the distance between two bags and later successfully applied to the standard multi-instance learning problem [21]. However, in [24] the maximal Hausdorff distance has been found to not work well in the generalized multi-instance learning problems due to its sensitivity to outliers. Therefore, the authors have proposed another distance called *average Hausdorff distance*.

In this paper, we use average Hausdorff distance to measure the distance between two bags A and B, since the preliminary experiments with this distance have generated better results than the ones produced by the maximal Hausdorff distance. Formally, given two bags of data instances A and B, the *average Hausdorff distance* is defined by Eq. 1, where $dist(a, b)$ is the distance between instances $a \in A$ and $b \in B$, which usually takes the form of Euclidean distance, and $| \, . \, |$, represents the set cardinality.

$$H(A, B) = \frac{\sum_{a \in A} \min_{b \in B} dist(a, b) + \sum_{b \in B} \min_{a \in A} dist(a, b)}{|A| + |B|}. \tag{1}$$

3.2 Formal Concept Analysis

Formal Concept Analysis (FCA) [10] is a mathematical apparatus for deriving a concept hierarchy from a collection of objects and their properties. FCA allows to generate and visualize the concept hierarchies. FCA is used for data analysis, information retrieval, and knowledge discovery. In addition, it can be understood as conceptual clustering method, which clusters simultaneously objects and their descriptions.

FCA derives a concept lattice from a formal context constituted of a set of objects O, a set of attributes A, and a binary relation defined on the Cartesian product $O \times A$. The context is described as a table, the rows correspond to objects and the columns to attributes or properties and a cross in a table cell means that "an object possesses a property". The *concept lattice* is composed of formal concepts organized into a hierarchy by a partial ordering (a subsumption relation allowing to compare concepts). Intuitively, a concept is a pair (X, Y) where $X \subseteq O$, $Y \subseteq A$, and X is the maximal set of objects sharing the whole set of attributes in Y and vice-versa. Relying on the subsumption relation, the set of all concepts extracted from a context is organized within a complete lattice, which means that for any set of concepts there is a smallest super-concept and a largest sub-concept, called the *concept lattice*.

3.3 Closed Patterns

Sequential pattern mining is the problem of finding interesting frequent ordered patterns from a sequence database [1]. Given a sequence database $\mathcal{T}$ and a pattern α the support for α is the number of sequences in $\mathcal{T}$ that contain α as a sub-sequence. The pattern α is called frequent if its support is equal or greater than a user-specified support threshold. Mining frequent patterns in big databases can lead to generating a large number of patterns. In order to mitigate this problem, one can only extract frequent closed sequential patterns. A pattern α is closed when none of its super patterns has the same support as α.

In this study, we apply BIDE [20], which is a famous frequent closed sequential pattern mining algorithm, to extract patterns. The Python implementation of BIDE is adopted from prefixspan library.

4   MV Multi-Instance Clustering Using Closed Patterns

In [4], an extension of the Split-Merge Evolutionary Clustering algorithm (abbreviated Split-Merge Clustering) [3] for multi-view data streaming scenarios has been introduced. The introduced algorithm, MV Split-Merge Clustering, has been demonstrated to be able to integrate data from multiple views in a streaming manner. The algorithm can be applied for grouping distinct chunks of multi-view streaming data so that a global clustering model is built on each data chunk. Initially, an updated clustering solution (local model) is produced on each view of the current data chunk by applying the Split-Merge Clustering. In that way updated local models reflecting the information presented in the current and previous data chunks are obtained. FCA is then used in order to integrate information from the local clustering models and generate a global model that reveals the relationships among the local models.

We have recognized two main limitations of the MV Split-Merge Clustering [4]. First, the Split-Merge Clustering algorithm [3], used for updating the local clustering models, needs to find the cluster centroids in order to integrate the local models of two consecutive data chunks. Our proposed MV Multi-Instance Clustering algorithm overcomes this by interpreting the integration of two local models as a Multi-Instance clustering problem, i.e. each cluster (bag) is regarded as an atomic object. Evidently, by exploiting Multi-Instance clustering analysis, we enable to improve the performance of the algorithm and also handle the ambiguity which is typical for real-world streaming data. For example, we would be able to model semi-supervised learning scenarios where some bags may be labeled. Second, the MV Split-Merge Clustering [4] builds a global model by using all the identified correlation patterns among the views. This leads to the generation of a large and complex concept lattice that is not easy to be interpreted and analysed. In comparison, our MV Multi-Instance clustering algorithm uses closed patterns, which considers the most typical correlations among the views, to create a global clustering model. In this way, unimportant concepts are excluded and do not complicate the understanding and analysis of the built global model. In addition, there is an opportunity to obtain even a smaller set of the most frequent (top-ranked) patterns based on the frequency or support score associated with each closed pattern.

Let us formally describe our MV Multi-Instance Clustering algorithm. We consider a streaming scenario where a particular phenomenon (physical object, biological process, machine asset, patient etc.) is monitored under n different circumstances (views). We further assume that the data arrives over time in chunks. Each chunk t can contain different number of data points and can be represented by a list of n different data matrices $D_t = \{D_{t1}, D_{t2}, \ldots, D_{tn}\}$, one per view. Each matrix D_{ti} $(i = 1, 2, \ldots, n)$ contains the information about the data points in the current chunk t with respect to the corresponding view i. Assume that chunk t contains N_t data points. In addition, n clustering models, one per view, can be built on each data chunk. Let $C_t = \{C_{t1}, C_{t2}, \ldots, C_{tn}\}$ be a set of clustering solutions (local models), such that C_{ti} $(i = 1, 2, \ldots, n)$ represents the grouping of the data points in tth chunk with respect to ith view, i.e. a local model built on data set D_{ti}.

On each data chunk, the proposed algorithm conducts two main operations. They are described in Algorithms 2 and 3. The local models built on the current chunk C_t are first updated by analysing the newly arrived data D_{t+1}. Clustering solutions C_{t+1} are initially built on the new data chunk $t + 1$ and correlated with ones of chunk t in order to generate updated clustering models C_t' with respect to $t + 1$. Then, these local models C_t' are used to build a global model that consists of three parts providing information about different aspects of the studied phenomenon. Namely, the model includes the formal context, closed patterns and concept lattice. The latter two are generated based on the built formal context. The formal context F_t consists of the set of $(N_t + N_{t+1})$ data points, the set of K $(K = k_1 + k_2 + \ldots + k_n)$ clustering labels of C_t' and an indication of which data points are associated with which clusters. Thus the context is described as a matrix, with the data points corresponding to the rows and the cluster labels corresponding to the columns of the matrix, and a value 1 in cell (i, j) whenever data point i belongs to cluster C_j' $(j = 1, 2, \ldots, K)$. Evidently, the formal context F_t contains all view correlation patterns supported by the local clustering models. The set of closed patterns, denoted by F_t^c, contains the most typical correlations that exist among the views. Finally, the concept lattice provides description of the hierarchical organisation of the concepts it produces.

The operations for updating the local clustering models on data chunk t are given in Algorithm 1.

Algorithm 1: Use Bi-Correlation MI-Clustering to update the local clustering models on data chunk t

---

Input: local clustering models C_t and newly arrived data D_{t+1}

for *each view i $(i = 1, 2, \ldots, n)$* **do**

    Build a clustering model $C_{(t+1)i}$

    Bi-Correlation MI-Clustering $(C_{ti}, C_{(t+1)i})$ (Algorithm 2)

end

Algorithm 2 describes Bi-Correlation MI-Clustering that is applied for updating the local clustering models on data chunk t. Average Hausdorff distance (see Sect. 3.1) is used to find the correlations between the two clustering solutions C_{ti} and $C_{(t+1)i}$ for each view i $(i = 1, 2, \ldots, n)$. Global threshold T_i (see Eq. 2) is calculated for each $| C_{ti} | \times | C_{(t+1)i} |$ adjacency matrix as follows:

$$T_i = \frac{\sum_{p \in C_{ti}} \min_{q \in C_{(t+1)i}} H(p,q) + \sum_{q \in C_{(t+1)i}} \min_{p \in C_{ti}} H(p,q)}{|C_{ti}| + |C_{(t+1)i}|}, \tag{2}$$

where $H(p,q)$ is the average Hausdorff distance (see Eq. 1) between a cluster $p \in C_{ti}$ and a cluster $q \in C_{(t+1)i}$. T_i averages the Hausdorff distances between each cluster in C_{ti} and its nearest cluster in $C_{(t+1)i}$ and vice-versa. Evidently, T_i measures the average Hausdorff distance between two clustering solutions.

Algorithm 2: Bi-Correlation MI-Clustering of C_{ti} and $C_{(t+1)i}$

Input: local clustering models C_{ti} and $C_{(t+1)i}$

Build a $|C_{ti}| \times |C_{(t+1)i}|$ adjacency matrix based on Hausdorff distance (Eq. 1)

Calculate global threshold T_i (Eq. 2)

Remove edges in the adjacency matrix for which $H(p,q) > T_i$

for *each uniformly random cluster p in C_{ti}* **do**

> Find average distance of adjacent nodes, denoted by T_i^p
>
> Remove edges in adjacency matrix for which $H(p,q) > T_i^p$
>
> Find neighbours of p in $C_{(t+1)i}$, denoted by $N_{(t+1)i}^p$
>
> Find neighbours of each $q \in N_{(t+1)i}^p$ in C_{ti}, denoted by N_{ti}^q
>
> Create cluster $C_p' = \{p\} \cup N_{(t+1)i}^p \cup_{q \in N_{(t+1)i}^p} N_{ti}^q$
>
> $C_{ti} = C_{ti} \setminus \{p\}$

end

The adjacency matrix can also be visualized as a bipartite graph to illustrate how the clusters are correlated. The nodes on the left side of the graph represent clustering solution of chunk t, i.e. C_{ti}, and those on the right hand side represents new clustering solution i.e. $C_{(t+1)i}$. T_i is used to filter out the edges between clusters which are far apart and thus avoiding considering too many clusters to decide which ones to merge. The average local distance T_i^p could be considered as the local threshold for each cluster p in C_{ti} and it is used to find its closest clusters in $C_{(t+1)i}$. The motivation of using T_i^p is that, it facilitates identifying new trends in the scenarios of concept drift, where a group of data points can form a new cluster by slowly moving away from their current cluster at each data chunk. By considering the average local distance as a merging condition, we avoid early merging which allows such new clusters to naturally form.

Algorithm 3: Use FCA and closed patterns to build a global model on data chunk t

---

Input: updated local clustering models C_t'

Build a formal context, denoted by F_t. F_t is a $(N_t + N_{t+1}) \times K$ binary matrix that indicates for each data point belonging to $D_t \cup D_{t+1}$ which clusters of C_t' it is associated with

Derive closed patterns, denoted by F_t^c ($F_t^c \subset F_t$), from the set of all built patterns of F_t

Produce a formal concept lattice from F_t^c

5   Evaluation

5.1   Data Sets and Experimental Setup

Anthropometric Data: Initial analysis is done on a comparatively small public data set [11] that describes the medical conditions of 399 undergraduate students based on their anthropometric data. Each student is described by the following features: age, obesity, body mass index (BMI), waist circumference (WC), hip circumference (HC), and waist hip ratio (WHR), Systolic Blood Pressure (SBP), Diastolic Blood Pressure (DBP), *preh* for women and *hyper* for men, where the *preh* and *hyper* are classification labels that show what kind of blood pressure the individual has (e.g., regular or hyper). In order to mimic the streaming data scenario required for the proposed algorithm, the data set is divided into historical and newly arriving data. The historical data set is composed of the 70% of total data and the remaining 30% is treated as the newly arriving data. The features of the data set are divided into three views, where view 1 (v_1) contains details about age and gender, view 2 (v_2) contains details about BMI, WC, HC, WHR, and view 3 (v_3) presents information about blood pressure (SBP, DBP). Initial grouping of data points in each view is given in Table 1.

Table 1. Cluster categories in the views of Anthropometric data set

Label	Cluster description	Size
v_{10}	Adolescence, male (age < 20)	44
v_{11}	Adolescence, female (age < 20)	63
v_{12}	Early adulthood, male ($20 \leq$ age ≤ 39)	124
v_{13}	Early adulthood, female ($20 \leq$ age ≤ 39)	157
v_{14}	Adulthood, male (age > 39)	7
v_{15}	Adulthood, female (age > 39)	4
v_{20}	underweight (BMI ≤ 18.49)	21
v_{21}	normal weight ($18.50 \leq$ BMI ≤ 24.99)	234
v_{22}	overweight ($25.00 \leq$ BMI ≤ 29.99)	113
v_{23}	obese (BMI ≥ 30.00)	31
v_{30}	Level 1 (SBP < 120 and DBP < 80)	141
v_{31}	Level 2 ($120 \leq$ SBP ≤ 129 and/or $80 \leq$ DBP ≤ 84)	83
v_{32}	Level 3 ($130 \leq$ SBP ≤ 139 and/or $85 \leq$ DBP ≤ 89)	67
v_{33}	Level 4 ($140 \leq$ SBP ≤ 159 and/or $90 \leq$ DBP ≤ 99)	80
v_{34}	Level 5 ($160 \leq$ SBP ≤ 179 and/or $100 \leq$ DBP ≤ 109)	23
v_{35}	Level 6 (SBP ≥ 180 and/or DBP ≥ 110)	5

Our objective is to use this data set to build controlled and easy to interpret experimental multi-view streaming scenarios for studying and comparing the two multi-view clustering algorithms described in Sect. 4. In this setup two experiments are conducted to evaluate the algorithms. Bi-Correlation MI-Clustering step of the proposed algorithm is initially compared with Split-Merge Clustering [4] for updating the local models. We also analyse how different views are related to each other using the closed patterns derived from the global model.

Real-World Sensor Data: The potential of the proposed approach is also demonstrated on a real-world data set from a company in the smart building domain. The data has been used in [6] for analysing and monitoring the control valve system behaviour. In smart building domain different types of metrics are collected from a wide range of sensors available for systems such as heating, ventilation, air conditioning, and refrigeration. Data covering a year period (Jan 1st 2019 till Dec 27th 2019) is used in the current study. The eight features listed in Table 2, seven of which also considered in [6], are used in our experiments.

Table 2. Features included in the real-world sensor data set

View	Id	Acronyms	Feature name	Units
Operation	1	SST	Secondary Supply Temperature	°C
	2	SRT	Secondary Return Temperature	°C
	3	PHL	Primary Heat Load	kW
Performance	4	VOM	Valve Openness Mean	%
	5	VOS	Valve Openness Standard Deviation	%
	6	SE	Sub-station Efficiency	%
Context	7	OTM	Outdoor Temperature Mean	°C
	8	OTS	Outdoor Temperature Standard Deviation	°C

The available data features are analysed and partitioned in three distinctive views: system operational behaviour parameters, performance indicators and contextual factors. The features SST, SRT, and PHL are selected to model the system typical operational behaviour. The system performance can be evaluated by these three indicators: VOM, VOS, and SE. Finally, the contextual factors are represented by the features: OTM and OTS.

5.2 Results and Discussion

Anthropometric Data: This data can be used to study and associate different age categories with the patients' anthropometric measurements to identify patients with increased risk for cardiovascular disease, e.g., hypertension. The data set is used to generate 10 test data set couples by randomly separating the individual profiles into two sets, as it was explained in Sect. 5.1. Thus the first set (279 patients) of each couple presents the current data chunk of individual profiles, and the other one (120 individuals) is the new chunk of patients' profiles. In that way, we have created 10 test data set couples.

MV Split-Merge Clustering and MV Multi-Instance Clustering are applied and compared on the built 10 test data sets. For MV Multi-Instance Clustering, we have additionally studied and conducted the experiments with two different (maximal Hausdorff versus average Hausdorff) distance measures in order to select the better one, i.e. we have done 20 experiments in total. The average Hausdorff distance has outperformed the maximal Hausdorff distance on all the 10 test data sets. This confirms the discovery in [24], hence we have chosen to use this distance measure in the definition of Algorithm 2 and discuss its experimental results further in this section.

Out of the ten experimental iterations of the proposed approach, we have selected the results of one of the iterations (same as the one in [4]) to be presented and discussed in detail further in this section. The lattice produced in this iteration by MV Split-Merge Clustering has a total of 160 non-empty concepts. Out of these, 82 concepts link clusters from all the three views. The lattice size generated by MV Multi-Instance Clustering on the built formal context is very similar, namely it has 165 non-empty concepts, out of which 83 concepts link clusters from all three views. In the considered iteration, the local models generated in the three views have 6, 5 and 7 clusters, respectively. In view 1, the clusters presented in Table 1 are retained, i.e. the same six age categories. In view 2, the cluster presenting all individuals with obese weight (v_{23}) has been split into two different clusters and similarly with the individuals having blood pressure Level 5 (v_{34}) in view 3. It can be observed that most of the original clustering structure is retained with the proposed MV Multi-Instance Clustering.

Table 3. Closed patterns showing correlations between all three views (support 10)

Blood pressure level	S/N	Concept	Size	Blood pressure
Level 1	1	v_{13}, v_{21}	53	Regular
(v_{30})	2	v_{11}, v_{21}	26	Regular
	3	v_{13}, v_{22}	15	Regular
	4	v_{12}, v_{21}	12	Regular
Level 2	5	v_{13}, v_{21}	22	Regular, Pre
(v_{31})	6	v_{12}, v_{21}	15	Regular
Level 3	7	v_{12}, v_{21}	18	Regular
(v_{32})	8	v_{12}, v_{22}	12	Regular
	9	v_{13}, v_{21}	10	Pre, 1 Regular
Level 4	10	v_{12}, v_{22}	18	Regular, Hyper
(v_{33})	11	v_{13}, v_{21}	15	Pre
	12	v_{12}, v_{21}	14	Regular, Hyper

We compare MV Split-Merge Clustering [4] and MV Multi-Instance Clustering algorithms with respect to the purity of the produced clustering solutions. For this purpose, we first consider how the four main classes (Regular male, Regular female, Hyper and Pre) are distributed among the clusters. The average value calculated on the ten conducted iterations of MV Split-Merge Clustering algorithm is 0.76. While the corresponding value generated by the proposed MV Multi-Instance Clustering is 0.895. We have also evaluated the two algorithms with the six blood pressure levels (Levels 1 to 6) as main classes, where the score generated by the MV Multi-Instance Clustering is 1.0 versus 0.65 for the MV Split-Merge Clustering algorithm. The MV Multi-Instance Clustering has demonstrated a better performance in the both evaluation scenarios, i.e. it is able to detect more efficiently the correlations between the current and new incoming data chunks. We have further used the adjusted Rand Index [17] to determine the similarity between the partitions generated by MV Multi-Instance clustering algorithm and benchmark clustering (used in [4]) as a function of positive and negative agreements in pairwise cluster assignments. The average score produced by the proposed algorithm is 0.99 versus 0.44 for the MV Split-Merge Clustering.

We are interested in discovering the relationships among the views. Hence we have specially studied patterns with length 2 or 3 in order to reveal correlations that exist between two or three views. Closed patterns (see Sect. 3.3) have been used for this purpose. We have generated closed patterns with support 10 (patterns that cover ≈2.5% of the data set) which resulted in 43 concepts of which 12 patterns show the relationship between all the three views. Table 3 lists all 12 derived concepts from the retrieved closed patterns as examples to study the relations among the views. The generated closed patterns do not contain concepts where the blood pressure levels are either 5 or 6. This could be due to the less number of instances in these clusters which are 23 and 5, respectively (see Table 1).

It is interesting to notice that the first three top frequent patterns among the three views (see rows 1, 2 and 5 in Table 3) represent typical categories in female population: females of age between 20 and 39 (early adulthood) with Level 1 blood pressure and normal weight; females in the same blood pressure and weight group, but in adolescent age category (age less than 20); and females again in early adulthood and normal weight category, but Level 2 blood pressure. In comparison with these categories, the three least frequent concepts (see rows 4, 8 and 9 in Table 3) can also be considered. For example, rows 8 and 9 represent respectively, overweight males and normal weight females in early adulthood age category with Level 3 blood pressure. One can get further insight into the discussed concepts by analyzing frequent concepts that connect two views (not included in Table 3). For example, it can be observed that females in their early adulthood typically have normal weight. This is demonstrated by a concept with support 104. Females in this age group are less likely to be overweight (31 individuals) or underweight (11 individuals) since only small size concepts supports this. In addition, the individuals in this female age category are less likely to be obese as there is no concept with size above 10 to support this.

Real-World Sensor Data: This data can be used for modelling, understanding and monitoring the control valve system behaviour. For example, it would be useful if one can link or trace back certain performance to specific operational modes by taking into account the influence of contextual factors (e.g., outdoor temperature). Initially, the available data features are partitioned in three distinctive views as it is explained in Sect. 5.1. For each view averaged daily values of the corresponding features are calculated to build daily profiles. The created daily profiles (361 in total) are then split into two parts in order to simulate two data chunks: the initial one with 243 daily profiles (January - August) used to build the system behaviour model and the new data chunk used for the model update contains 118 daily profiles (September - December).

Table 4. Closed patterns correlating all three views after the new data chunk is added

S/N	PHL	SST	SRT	VOM	VOS	SE	OTM	OTS	Month	Size
1	2.42	26.24	26.01	0.03	±0.06	58	21.34	±0.48	6, 7, 8	36
2	4.39	27.41	26.61	3.25	±1.13	68	17.77	±0.46	6, 7, 8	55
3	5.54	28.13	26.93	4.76	±1.16	76	16.13	±0.35	9	12
4	7.45	29.70	28.15	6.34	±0.99	77	15.45	±0.50	5	14
5	**3.00**	31.35	29.30	7.05	±1.09	86	13.48	±0.56	4	9
6	13.26	35.90	32.36	11.87	±0.65	87	10.65	±0.44	9	11
7	15.65	37.01	33.58	12.18	±0.41	92	9.48	±0.30	10, 11	13
8	16.74	37.81	33.61	12.85	±0.60	91	9.17	±0.49	5	12
9	**3.36**	41.61	35.33	14.99	±0.63	95	6.19	±0.44	3, 4	40
10	20.93	43.13	37.86	13.26	±0.45	95	5.30	±0.34	10, 11	32
11	20.75	43.68	38.36	13.23	±0.45	95	4.81	±0.30	12	16
12	37.45	47.36	38.29	17.37	±0.42	96	1.17	±0.40	3	11
13	42.54	48.20	38.49	18.04	±0.54	96	0.46	±0.33	1,2	54
Total										315

Note. The unit for PHL is kW and for SST, SRT, OTM, and OTS is °C. VOM, VOS, and SE are expressed in %. For the full form of each feature see Table 2. Row enumerations in bold italic represent patterns repeated from the initial chunk. The bold in PHL column represents deviating behavior.

Initial clustering in views 1 and 2 is done by applying k-means. Silhouette index and elbow method are used to find the optimal number of initial clusters. In the initial data chunk, the optimal number of clusters in these two views are 3 and 4, respectively. In the second data chunk, the optimal number of clusters for view 1 is 4 while for view 2 is the same as in the initial chunk, i.e. 4. In view 3, the data points are grouped into 4 clusters according to the yearly seasons based on [8], i.e. the context view has the following four clusters: December to February (winter); March, April, October and November (early spring, late autumn); May and September (late spring, early autumn); June to August (summer). After applying MV Multi-Instance clustering algorithm to update local models the number of clusters in the three views are 5, 5 and 6, respectively.

In order to analyse how the correlations among the views are updated, the global model built on the initial data chunk is compared with the one produced on the updated clustering solutions when the new data chunk is added. The lattice built on the initial local models generated 32 non-empty concepts and 14 concepts connecting all the three views. The new global model produced on the updated local models, after the new data chunk has arrived, contains 59 non-empty concepts from which 26 concepts connect all three views. We further compare the sets of closed patterns produced by the corresponding formal contexts using one and the same support ($\approx$2.5% of the data set). The latter gives 18 concepts (support 6) connecting two or three views for initial data chunk and 32 concepts (support of 9), respectively on the second formal context. Table 4 lists all 13 concepts linking three views extracted after adding the new data chunk. Each concept is presented by its mean vector and additionally, the concepts are grouped into two groups with respect to the contextual view, i.e. average outdoor temperature above and below 10°C. It is interesting to notice that 8 (rows 1, 2, 4, 5, 8, 9, 12 and 13) of these 13 concepts have been discovered by analysing the initial data chunk and they are the only discovered concepts with the same support linking the three views. By considering the concepts linking two views we observe that they are retained in the global model built on the new data chunk and are further expanded with data points from it. Evidently, the integration procedure of our algorithm demonstrates to have a stable behaviour with respect to discovered patterns. Five new patterns presented in the new data chunk have also been extracted, i.e. the proposed algorithm can be used as a continuous data mining technique. The newly discovered patterns may be labelled with the expected performance under a particular context. In addition, our results are comparable to the ones reported in [6], where 49 days in March and April have been marked as having deviating behaviour. Our algorithm presents those with two different concepts (5 and 9 in Table 4), both of which show sudden drop in PHL with respect to the other concepts in the same contextual group.

6 Conclusion and Future Work

In this study, we have proposed a novel multi-view clustering approach, entitled MV Multi-Instance Clustering, that uses average Hausdorff distance, closed patterns and Formal Concept Analysis for analysis of streaming data. The MV Multi-Instance Clustering allows for parallel monitoring of the individual view clustering models and analysing view correlations in the global model generated at each data chunk.

The proposed algorithm has been evaluated on two different data sets. In addition, its performance has been benchmarked to MV Split-Merge Clustering. The MV Multi-Instance Clustering has outperformed the latter algorithm in the studied evaluation scenarios. In general, the obtained results have demonstrated that the proposed algorithm is a robust technique for modelling and continuous analysis and mining of streaming data.

The potential of the MV Multi-Instance Clustering has been demonstrated on real-world data from smart building domain. Our future aim is to pursue further evaluation and study whether the proposed approach is fit for other real-world distributed streaming scenarios.

References

1. Agrawal, R., Srikant, R.: Mining sequential patterns. In: Proceedings of the 11th International Conference on Data Engineering, pp. 3–14. IEEE (1995)
2. Bendechache, M., Kechadi, M.T.: Distributed clustering algorithm for spatial data mining. In: 2015 2nd IEEE ICSDM (2015)
3. Boeva, V., Angelova, M., Devagiri, V.M., Tsiporkova, E.: Bipartite split-merge evolutionary clustering. In: van den Herik, J., Rocha, A.P., Steels, L. (eds.) ICAART 2019. LNCS (LNAI), vol. 11978, pp. 204–223. Springer, Cham (2019). https://doi.org/10.1007/978-3-030-37494-5_11
4. Devagiri, V.M., Boeva, V., Tsiporkova, E.: Split-merge evolutionary clustering for multi-view streaming data. Procedia Comput. Sci. **176**, 460–469 (2020)
5. Edgar, G.: Measure, Topology, and Fractal Geometry, 3rd edn. Springer, Berlin (1995)
6. Eghbalian, A., et al.: Multi-view data mining approach for behaviour analysis of smart control valve. In: Proceedings of 19th IEEE ICMLA, pp. 1238–1245 (2020)
7. Fu, L., Lin, P., Vasilakos, A.V., Wang, S.: An overview of recent multi-view clustering. Neurocomputing **402**, 148–161 (2020)
8. Gadd, H., Werner, S.: Heat load patterns in district heating substations. Appl. Energy **108**, 176–183 (2013)
9. Gan, W., et al.: Data mining in distributed environment: a survey. Wiley Interdisc. Rev. Data Min. Knowl. Discov. **7**(6), e1216 (2017)
10. Ganter, B., Stumme, G., Wille, R. (eds.): Formal Concept Analysis. LNCS (LNAI), vol. 3626. Springer, Heidelberg (2005). https://doi.org/10.1007/978-3-540-31881-1
11. Golino, H.F., et al.: Predicting increased blood pressure using machine learning. J. Obes. **2014**(5), 637635 (2014)
12. Hai, M., et al.: A survey of distributed clustering algorithms. In: 2012 International Conference on Industrial Control and Electronics Engineering, pp. 1142–1145 (2012)
13. Huang, L., et al.: MVStream: multiview data stream clustering. IEEE Trans. Neural Netw. Learn. Syst. **31**(9), 3482–3496 (2020)
14. Jiang, B., et al.: Evolutionary multi-objective optimization for multi-view clustering. In: 2016 IEEE CEC 2016, pp. 3308–3315 (2016)
15. Liu, J., et al.: Multi-view clustering via joint non-negative matrix factorization. In: Proceedings of the 2013 SIAM International Conference on Data Mining, SDM 2013, pp. 252–260 (2013)
16. Liu, X., et al.: Late fusion incomplete multi-view clustering. IEEE Trans. Pattern Anal. Mach. Intell. **41**(10), 2410–2423 (2019)
17. Rand, W.M.: Objective criteria for the evaluation of clustering methods. J. Am. Stat. Assoc. **66**(336), 846–850 (1971)
18. Shao, W., et al.: Online multi-view clustering with incomplete views. In: 2016 IEEE International Conference on Big Data (Big Data), pp. 1012–1017 (2016)
19. Singh, D., Gosain, A.: A comparative analysis of distributed clustering algorithms: a survey. In: 2013 International Symposium on Computational and Business Intelligence, pp. 165–169 (2013)
20. Wang, J., Han, J.: BIDE: efficient mining of frequent closed sequences. In: Proceedings of the 20th International Conference on Data Engineering, pp. 79–90 (2004)

21. Wang, J., Zucker, J.D.: Solving the multiple-instance problem: a lazy learning approach. In: Proceedings of the 17th ICML, pp. 1119–1125 (2000)
22. Yang, Y., Wang, H.: Multi-view clustering: a survey. Big Data Min. Anal. **1**(2), 83–107 (2018)
23. Ye, Y., et al.: Incomplete multiview clustering via late fusion. Comput. Intell. Neurosci. **2018**, 1–11 (2018)
24. Zhang, M., Zhou, Z.: Multi-instance clustering with applications to multi-instance prediction. Appl. Intell. **31**, 47–68 (2009)

Efficient Approaches for Density-Based Spatial Clustering of Applications with Noise

Pretom Kumar Saha and Doina Logofatu[✉]

Frankfurt University of Applied Sciences, Nibelungenplatz 1,
60318 Frankfurt am Main, Germany
saha@stud.fra-uas.de, logofatu@fb2.fra-uas.de

Abstract. A significant challenge for the growing world of data is to analyze, classify and manipulate spatial data. The challenge starts with the clustering process, which can be defined to characterize the spatial data with their relative properties in different groups or classes. This process can be performed using many different methods like grids, density, hierarchical and others. Among all these methods, the use of density for grouping leads to a lower noise data in result, which is called Density-Based Spatial Clustering of Applications with Noise (DBSCAN). The DBSCAN algorithm defines a data set in a group and separates the group from the other groups based on the density of the data surrounding the selection of data points. These data points and the density of the data are calculated depending on two parameters. One parameter is used as the radius of the data point to find the neighborhood data points. Another parameter is used to identify the noise in the collected data by keeping the minimum number of data points for the data density. Like other popular method k-means, DBSCAN does not require any input of the cluster number. It can sort the data set with the number of clusters according to data density. The purpose of this article is to explain the Efficient Density-based Spatial Clustering of Applications with Noise (DBSCAN) using a sample of data set, compare the results, identify the constraints, and suggest some possible solutions.

Keywords: Clustering · DBSCAN · Density-based algorithms

1 Introduction

An approach through which we can draw references from data sets consisting of input records without a specified classification is called the unsupervised learning method. Generally, this unsupervised learning method is used for creating a set of data in a meaningful structure, explanatory underlying processes, generative features, and groupings.

The technique for uniting related items in one group is clustering which is a crucial task in the field of data mining. Clustering can be utilized as an initial

© IFIP International Federation for Information Processing 2021
Published by Springer Nature Switzerland AG 2021
I. Maglogiannis et al. (Eds.): AIAI 2021, IFIP AICT 627, pp. 184–195, 2021.
https://doi.org/10.1007/978-3-030-79150-6_15

process for overall data mining or an independent technique. In the field of unsupervised learning methods, clustering can be used in several ways, e.g., outlier detection, data reduction, and identification of natural data types and classes.

Clustering is the endeavor to assemble info in a hasty manner that meets with human instinct. Tragically, our self-generated thoughts of what makes a 'cluster' are inefficaciously characterized and passing settings delicate [1]. This comes concerning in an exceedingly lots of cluster calculations each of that match a somewhat distinctive natural plan of what a typical gathering is [2]. In spite of the vulnerability basic, the cluster prepares its takings to be used in a very immense range of logical areas. The fundamental issue of finding groupings is inevitable and comes concerning, in any case impoverished, are still imperative and enlightening [2]. It's used in several areas like atomic flow [14], plane flight manner investigation [15], natural philosophy [16], and social analytics [17], among varied others. Whereas cluster has varied activities to different people, our specific point is on clump for the explanation of investigating data analysis [2].

In the field of Data analysis, numerous conventional clustering calculations are ineffectively suited. In specific, most clustering calculations endure from the issues of troublesome parameter determination, inadequately strength to commotion within the information, and distributional presumptions approximately the clusters themselves [2]. Numerous calculations require the choice of the number of clusters, either expressly, or implicitly through intermediary parameters. Within the larger part of utilizing cases we have experienced, selecting the number of clusters is exceptionally troublesome a priori [2]. Strategies to decide the number of clusters such as the elbow strategy and outline strategy are frequently subjective and can be difficult to apply in the hone. Eventually, these strategies all pivot on the clustering quality degree chosen; these are different and frequently profoundly related with specific clustering calculations [1].

There are six techniques that can be actualized for clustering namely partitioning, hierarchical, density, grid, model, and constraint-based models [9]. Since the density-based strategy bunch data objects based on comparative density locale, it is exceptionally viable and more reasonable for spatial databases [9]. It considers a cluster as a high-density region when compared to its enveloping locale. In huge spatial database applications, the clustering calculations require to take following necessities [18]:

1. Less space information to choose input parameters
2. Recognizing subjective formed clusters
3. Great adequacy on huge databases [9].

Depending on six vital variables such as time complexity, input parameters, taking care of shifted thickness, dealing with of self-assertive shape, vigor to clamor, and insensitiveness to information input arrange, there exist fifteen algorithms like DBSCAN, DBCLASD, GDBSCAN, DENCLUE, OPTICS, DBRS, IDBSCAN, VDBSCAN, LDBSCAN, ST-DBSCAN, DDSC, DVBSCAN, DBSC, DMDBSCAN, and DCURS [9].

2   General Description of DBSCAN Algorithm

Density Based Spatial Clustering of Application with Noise (DBSCAN) is a concept that uses density to cluster data [17]. That means the minimum density of data depending on a certain feature is used as a cluster. The main advantage of this method is that it can identify clusters without entering the required cluster number. DBSCAN algorithm depend on to variable the radius (eps) and the minimum number of data nodes in a certain place (min_{pts}) [3]. The following conditions are used concerning these two variables:

Neighborhood Points: All the nodes, which presents in the range of radios eps neighborhood from center node p is the definition as neighborhood node of p. These neighborhood nodes are classified into core node and border node.

Core node $= neighbour_{pts} > min_{pts}$.
Border Node $= neighbour_{pts} < min_{pts}$.

Here, $neighbour_{pts}$ is the number of neighborhood node respect of center node p [2].

Direct Density Reachable: If there is a connection between two nodes p and q, through which direct travel is possible from p to q. if p=p1 and q= pn then the direct travel path p1, p2, p3...... and pn. Then, this p and q node are called direct density reachable [4].

Density Connected: If two-node p and q are individually density reachable from a common node o within the same min_{pts} and eps value, then this p and q node are density connected [3].

Cluster: Node p and q are in the same cluster C of a dataset define by min_{pts} and eps. if $p \epsilon C$ and q is density connected or density reachable from p then $q \epsilon C$ [13].

Noise: If p is a node of the dataset but does not belong in any cluster of that dataset concerning min_{pts} and eps, Then, this p node is called Noise [13].

3   DBSCAN Algorithm Details

K-means is one of the foremost well-known clustering algorithms. However, the biggest problem with K-means clustering is that it cannot determine the number of clusters. Based on this problem, DBSCAN has the advantage that it can identify the number of clusters in the data set.

Algorithm 1: Configuring Parameters for DBSCAN

Result: Return A dictionary with eps, min_{pts}, dim

1 initialization read config file ;
2 **for** *line* **to** *lines* **do**
3 | **if** *line* $! = \#$ **then**
4 | | $eps, min_{pts}, dim \leftarrow line$;
5 | **else**
6 | | continue;
7 | **end**
8 **end**

The proposed clustering is implemented in PYTHON on a 2-dimensional data set. The implementation starts with the configuration of the DBSCAN algorithm, which includes the maximum allowable distance for neighboring points (eps), the minimum number of neighbors surrounding a point (min_{pts}), and the dimension of the data set [8] in Algorithm 1.

The next step is processing the data set and refine them so that the algorithm can be established and find out the cluster from the data set in Algorithm 2.

Algorithm 2: Check Data Set

Result: Return A List of *data* in dimension *dim*

1 initialization read csv data file ;
2 initialization number of data *rows* ;
3 **for** *row* **to** *rows* **do**
4 | **if** *isinstance*(*row, str*) **then**
5 | | continue;
6 | **else**
7 | | *data* $\leftarrow$ *row* ;
8 | **end**
9 **end**

The algorithm shows in the Algorithm ?? bellow is the DBSCAN written in Python. At the begging of the algorithm, it selects one fresh point randomly that is not used to calculate the density of data yet depending surrounding that point in the radius of eps neighborhood. By finding out the actual center point of the density, DBSCAN defines the center point of the density with a cluster number and also defines the other direct reachable points in that density with a similar cluster number. The points will be defined as noise if it is not directly reachable from the core point. The whole process will be continuing until all the points of the data set are not defined with at least one cluster. All the points do not belong in any cluster that points will be classified as noise. The DBSCAN iterate all the points of the data set, so if the data set has n number of data points then the computational complexity of the whole algorithm is $O(n)^2$ [10] .

Algorithm 3: DBSCAN

   Result: Plot Data Clusters with different Colors

1 initialization *data,params*;

2 initialization *noise*;

3 **for** *point* **to** *data* **do**

4 | **if** *not visited* **then**

5 | | *point* ← *visited*;

6 | | $neighbour_{pts}$ ← distance between two points in *eps*;

7 | | **if** $len(neighbour_{pts}) < min_{pts}$ **then**

8 | | | *noise* ← *point*;

9 | | **else**

10 | | | *cluster* ← *point*;

11 | | **end**

12 | **end**

13 **end**

---

4   Performance and Evaluation

Source of data collection is https://www.kaggle.com/ and for this project I select a numeric data set with 2 dimensions. The information is collected within the shape of .csv. The flowchart of DBSCAN and execution results are appeared in the Figs. 1, 2, 3 and 4 .

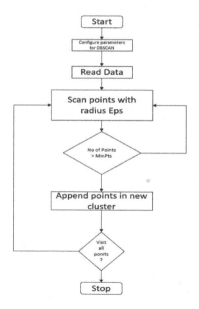

Fig. 1. Flowchart of the DBSCAN algorithm

At the beginning, 1000 data is applied on this DBSCAN and the Fig. 2 represents the output for this 1000 data.

Figure 3 represents the output of 10000 data. Different colors are used here to make it easier to the identification of noise and clusters. The blue color represents the noise and other colors for clusters.

If we try to explain the result in mathematical way then it can say that *eps* with 10 and min_{pts} with 5 the DBSCAN gives 143 clusters. Where the total data points are 10000 including 634 noise points.

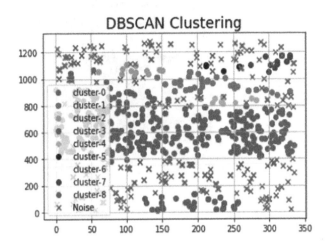

Fig. 2. DBSCAN Cluster using 1000 data

First, The algorithm was overviewed as a flowchart Fig. 1, then with some sequence of pseudocode 3 and finally with python scripts [15]. Here one example is presented to understand the process of DBSCAN with input and output forms:

---

1 $(0, 10)(0, 20)(0, 27)(10, 15)(20, 10)(25, 20)(0, 30), (10, 20)(60, 70)(65, 70)$
   $(67, 71)(67, 72), (5, 40).$;
2 $eps = 10.0$;
3 $min_{pts} = 3$;
4 Output Cluster points;
5 $Cluster1 - (0, 10)(0, 20)(0, 27)(10, 15)(0, 30)(10, 20)$;
6 $Cluster2 - (60, 70)(65, 70)(67, 70)(67, 71)(67, 72)$;
7 Noise points $- - (20, 10)(25, 20)(5, 10)$;

From the above discussion, for the actual data it does not looks the same but anyhow the overall procedure of density-based concept is the same. DBSCAN is appropriate for any numeric data. It has been taken note that, for huge information measure, the era of comes about corrupted within the shape logarithmic nature. Two screenshots are given here which represent the output of DBSCAN using the actual data set. First One is for the 1000 data Fig. 2 and the 2nd is for the 10000 Fig. 3.

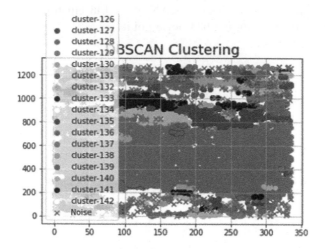

Fig. 3. DBSCAN Cluster using 10000 data

As shown in Fig. 4 the DBSCAN is better in terms of small numbers of data and run time is also small. DBSCAN makes a direct increment in computing time related to the number of data in the data set. Figure 4 is produced on different measure of information units and comes about are computed at common computer machine. Confinement and future perspectives are said within the another stage.

DBSCAN may be summarized as follows:

- DBSCAN is more exact in the density reachability approach.
- DBSCAN can discover self-assertive formed clusters. It gives way better execution for near focuses having different properties and exceptionally near clusters at the boundary, that's, border points.
- Do not require the number of clusters (k) in advance.
- DBSCAN requires 2 parameters.
- Outlier discovery is much superior in DBSCAN.

5   Drawbacks of DBSCAN

We are at the center of discussion on the DBSCAN, which is proposed by Ester [18]. DBSCAN is one of the foremost broadly utilized calculations in numerous

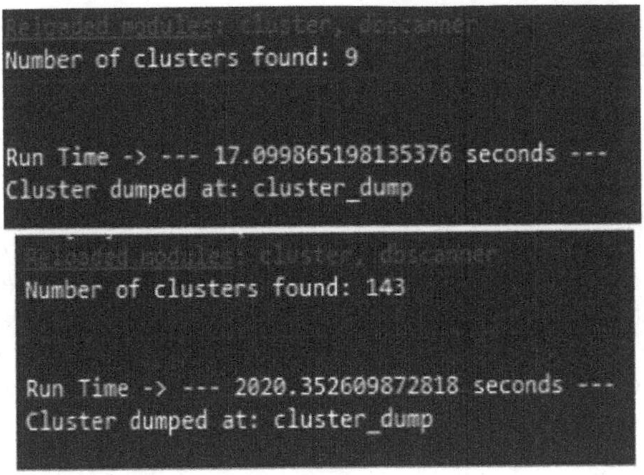

Fig. 4. Run time representation for data 1000 and 10000

applications, such as chemistry, spectroscopy, social science, gracious designing, peculiarity location, therapeutic and biomedical picture examination [13]. As a pioneer of density-based clustering calculations, it has the same nonignorable confinements as the conventional density-based calculations which have been specified here.

– The execution of clustering depends on two indicated parameters. It is troublesome to assess fitting values of these two parameters for different datasets without any sufficient earlier information [13].
– The computational complexity is high when managing with a high dimensional dataset [11].
– This algorithm prefers proper arranging dataset, distinctive orderings of data in the same dataset distort the result [6].
– Due to the use of global density parameter, adjoining clusters of diverse densities cannot be appropriately distinguished [13].

6   Analogous Evolution of DBSCAN

In this segment, the related development of density-based algorithms is introduced. Here the focus on the DBSCAN calculation beneath the density-based clustering calculations [18]. To facilitate understanding of the content of this article, some approaches already proposed to extend and improve the DBSCAN calculation are examined in detail here. The density around a protest is accomplished by checking the number of objects in a locale of indicated parameter radius, say *eps*, around the object [18]. An object is treated as dense if it is having *eps* neighborhood of that object more noteworthy than or break even with to an indicated edge least objects (u), something else scanty (non-core). Non-core objects that indicated radius are known as DBSCAN may have wide variety [18]. Such clusters may be spoken to by a few smaller clusters so that each cluster may have a sensibly uniform density. DBSCAN does not characterize the upper constrain of a center object i.e. how much objects may display in $neighbour_{pts}$. So due to this if there's a wide variety in local thickness. It'll consolidate into the same have a center protest inside the noise.

OPTICS [19]: In full form Ordering Points To Identify the Clustering Structure algorithm for the reason of cluster examination which does not deliver a clustering of a data set unequivocally, but instep makes an increased ordering of the database speaking to density-based clustering structure. This cluster-ordering contains data that is proportionate to the density-based clustering comparing to a wide run of parameter settings. Be that as it may, OPTICS needs another algorithm beside it to deliver unequivocal clusters.

DENCLUE [20]: This algorithm follows the process of DBSCAN with some improvements. It clusters the dataset independently with Eps and Minpts, then blends joined and comparative clusters together agreeing to the given edge. The other difference is that this algorithm uses a very efficient grid method. The main difficulty is that it depends on a large number of input parameters.

VDBSCAN [21]: The essential approach of this algorithm is the use of k-dist to decide the parameters Eps and MinPts is to see at the behavior of the separate from a point to its kth closest neighbor. The k-dists are computed for all the information focuses for a few k, sorted in climbing arrange, and after that plotted to utilize the sorted values, as a result, a sharp alter is anticipated to see. The sharp alter at the esteem of k-dist compares to the appropriate esteem of Eps.

DD DBSCAN [22]: One of the updated forms of DBSCAN which apply the upper restrain amid the development of a cluster. The clusters are created in distinctive shapes, sizes and vary in neighborhood density [22]. But this calculation is having a downside that still it cannot handle the density variety inside the cluster. On the off chance that we watch the cluster arrangement at that point, it too implies the wide density variety inside the cluster.

WaveCluster [10]: This Density base algorithm mostly works on low dimensional data. It's one kind of grid-based algorithm and applies wavelet transform to the feature space. To find clusters in different scales of shape the required complexity is O(n) for the WaveCluster algorithm.

CLIQUE [11]: The CLIQUE algorithm is used the partitional or hierarchical clustering techniques. It can be implemented for distance-based or connectivity-based. Some special improvements are developed for the case of high-dimensional data such as Irrelevance of distances, Sparsity of the data, and different features or a different correlation of features that may be relevant for varying clusters.

DDSC [23]: Once more an expansion of the DBSCAN to distinguish clusters of diverse shapes, sizes, and vary in neighborhood density. Clusters recognized by it are having non-overlapped spatial district regions with sensible homogeneous thickness varieties inside them. Adjoining locales are isolated into diverse clusters in case there's a critical alter in densities. The clusters may be touching i.e. not isolated by any meager locale as required by DBSCAN. In this way, characteristic clusters in a dataset can be extricated. An included advantage is that the affectability of the input parameter X which is a vital impediment of DBSCAN is diminished essentially.

CHAMELEON [24]: Algorithm finds clusters of datasets by the two-phase algorithm. Firstly, it produces a k-nearest neighbor graph. Finally, it blends comparative sub-clusters.

DENCLUE [6]: Another upgrade of the DBSCAN calculation is DENCLUE [5], it calculates an impact work that portrays the effect of a question upon its neighborhood. The calculation presents the scientific establishment and scales well since it can prepare exceedingly inadequate datasets with the slightest work.

CURD [10]: CURD captures the shape and degree of a cluster by references, and after that analyzes the data based on the references. It can discover clusters with subjective shapes and is uncaring to noise information. Mining exceptionally huge databases are its goal; however, the adequacy could be an issue.

ST-DBSCAN [10]: ST-DBSCAN is an expansion of DBSCAN to handle spatial-temporal datasets. It reclassifies border points to find adjoining clusters and commotion centers among abutting clusters. ST-DBSCAN does not handle moved densities well.

There are many other density-based algorithms, all developed to solve the limitations of DBSCAN. However, each algorithm also has some limitations. In this paper, an overview of DBSCAN is given with the differences between the other updated algorithms.

7   Conclusion

In this literature, we presented a density-based clustering algorithm. The following issues are unraveled by DBSCAN:

- Does not require a-priori determination of number of clusters
- Able to recognize noise information whereas clustering
- DBSCAN calculation is able to discover subjectively measure and subjectively molded clusters [12].

DBSCAN is proposed to handle specified clustering issues. Other algorithms attempted to fathom these issues sometime recently like DBSCAN, but still have concerns with different-densities databases and adjoining clusters as well because it includes unused parameters other *eps* and min_{pts}. DBSCAN works with two parameters only and demonstrated its capacity to overcome clustering issues-particularly densities clusters. There are a few openings for future inquire. For illustration on the off chance that DBSCAN is begun with distinctive center focuses, there will be a few borders focuses that will be created into diverse clusters. Presently, these border focuses areas were relegated to the cluster found to begin with. These border focuses don't fundamentally have a place in the certain cluster and they can be allotted to a few clusters at the same time. In expansion, the current satisfactory density extend is calculated agreeing to the density of the current point. It might abdicate a more sensible result on the off chance that weights are allotted to the focuses as that allotted to the same cluster of the current point.

References

1. Hennig, C.: What are the true clusters? In: Pattern Recognition Letters, vol. 64, pp. 53–62, 2015, philosophical Aspects of Pattern Recognition. http://www.sciencedirect.com/science/proc/pii/S0167865515001269

2. McInnes, L., Healy, J.: Accelerated hierarchical density based clustering. In: International Conference on Data Mining Workshops. IEEE (2017)

3. Wang, W.T., Wu, Y.L., Tang, C.Y., Hor, M.K.: Adaptive density-based spatial clustering of applications with noise (DBSCAN) according to data. In: Conference on Machine Learning and Cybernetics (ICMLC). IEEE (2015)

4. Rahmanz, M.F., Liuy, M., Suhaimy, S.B., Zhangy, N., Thirumuruganathanz, S., Das, G.: HDBSCAN: density based clustering over location based service. arXiv:1602.03730v2 (2016)

5. Hassanin, M.F., Hassan, M., Shoeb, A.: DDBSCAN: different densities-based spatial clustering of applications with noise. In: International Conference on Control, Instrumentation, Communication and Computational Technologies (lCCICCT). IEEE (2015)

6. Uncu, O., Gruver, W.A., Kotak, W.B., Sabaz, D., Alibhai, Z., Ng, C.: GRIDB-SCAN: GRId density-based spatial clustering of applications with noise. In: International Conference on Systems, Man, and Cybernetics, Oct 2006, Taipei, Taiwan. IEEE (2016)

7. Ram, A., Sharma, A., Jalall, A.S., Singh, R., Agrawal, A.: An enhanced density based spatial clustering of applications with noise. In: International Advance Computing Conference (IACC 2009) Patiala, India. IEEE (2016)

8. Nanda, J., Panda, G.: Design of computationally efficient density-based clustering algorithms. In: Data and Knowledge Engineering (2014)

9. Nafees Ahmed, K., Abdul Razak, T.: A comparative study of different density based spatial clustering algorithms. Int. J. Comput. Appl. **99**(8), 18–25 (2014)

10. Duan, L., Xu, L., Guo, F., Lee, J., Yan, B.: A local-density based spatial clustering algorithm with noise. Inf. Syst. **32**, 978–986 (2006). Elsevier B.V

11. Liu, P., Zhou, D., Wu, N.: VDBSCAN: varied density based spatial clustering of applications with noise. In: School of Information Management and Engineering, Shanghai University of Finance and Economics, Shanghai, 200433, China. IEEE (2007)

12. Sharma, A., Gupta, R.K., Tiwari, A.: Improved density based spatial clustering of applications of noise clustering algorithm for knowledge discovery in spatial data. Math. Prob. Eng. **2016**, 9 (2016). proc ID 1564516. Hindawi Publishing Corporation

13. Lv, Y., et al.: An efficient and scalable density-based clustering algorithm for datasets with complex structures. Neurocomputing **171**, 9–22 (2015). Elsevier B.V

14. Melvin, R.L., Godwin, R.C., Xiao, J., Thompson, W.G., Berenhaut, K.S., Salsbury Jr., F.R.: Uncovering large-scale conformational change in molecular dynamics without prior knowledge. J. Chem. Theor. Comput. **12**(12), 6130–6146 (2016)

15. Wilson, A.T., Rintoul, M.D., Valicka, C.G.: Exploratory trajectory clustering with distance geometry. In: Schmorrow, D.D.D., Fidopiastis, C.M.M. (eds.) AC 2016, Part II. LNCS (LNAI), vol. 9744, pp. 263–274. Springer, Cham (2016). https://doi.org/10.1007/978-3-319-39952-2_26

16. Spackman, P.R., Thomas, S.P., Jayatilaka, D.: High throughput profiling of molecular shapes in crystals. Sci. Rep. **6**, 1–9 (2016)

17. Korakakis, M., Mylonas, P., Spyrou, E.: Xenia: a context aware tour recommendation system based on social network metadata information. In: Semantic and Social Media Adaptation and Personalization (SMAP), 2016 11th International Workshop on, pp. 59–64. IEEE (2016)

18. Ester, M., Kriegel, H.-P., Sander, J., Xu, X.: A density-based algorithm for discovering clusters in large spatial databases with noise. In: Proceedings of 2nd International Conference on Knowledge Discovery and Data Mining (KDD-96) (1996)

19. Ankerst, M., Breunig, M., Kriegel, H.P., Sander, J.: OPTICS: ordering objects to identify the clustering structure. In: Proceedings of ACM SIGMOD, in International Conference on Management of Data, pp. 49–60 (1999)

20. Hinneburg, A., Keim, D.: DENCLUE: an efficient approach to clustering in large multimedia data sets with noise. In: 4th International Conference on Knowledge Discovery and Data Mining, pp. 58–65 (1998)

21. Liu, P., Zhou, D., Wu, N.: VDBSCAN: varied density based spatial clustering of applications with noise. In: Proceedings of IEEE ICSSSM2007, pp. 528–531 (2007)

22. Borach, B., Bhattacharya, D.K.: A clustering technique using density difference. In: ICSCN, pp. 585–588, India (Feb 2007)

23. Borah, B., Bhattacharyya, D.K.: DDSC, "a density differentiated spatial clustering technique. J. Comput. **3**(2) 72–79 (2008)

24. Karypis, G., Han, E.H., Kumar, V.: CHAMELEON: a hierarchical clustering algorithm using dynamic modeling. Computer **32**(8), 68–75 (1999)

Self-organizing Maps for Optimized Robotic Trajectory Planning Applied to Surface Coating

Maria Tzinava[1], Konstantinos Delibasis[1(✉)], and Spyros Kamnis[2]

[1] Department of Computer Science and Biomedical Informatics, University of Thessaly,
35131 Lamia, Greece
{mtzinava,kdelimpasis}@uth.gr
[2] Monitor Coatings, 2 Elm Road, Tyne and Wear NE29 8SE, UK
spyros@monitorcoatings.com

Abstract. The process of surface coating is widely applied in the manufacturing industry. The accuracy of coating strongly affects the mechanical properties of the coated components. This work suggests the use of Self-Organizing Maps (Kohonen neural networks) for an optimal robotic beam trajectory planning for surface coating applications. The trajectory is defined by the one-dimensional sequence of neurons around a triangulated substrate and the neuron weights are defined as the position, beam vector and node velocity. During the training phase, random triangles are selected according to local curvature and the weights of the neurons whose beam coats the selected triangles are gradually adapted. This is achieved using a complicated coating thickness model as a function of stand-off distance, spray impact angle and beam surface spot speed. Initial results are presented from three objects widely used in manufacturing. The accuracy of this method is validated by comparing the simulated coating resulting from the SOM-planned trajectory to the coating performed for the same objects by an expert.

Keywords: Surface coating · Self-Organizing Maps · Robotic beam trajectory · Triangulated substrate · Coating thickness

1 Introduction

High value manufacturing sectors are continually seeking new ways to improve the performance and durability of critical components such as those used in aerospace, defense and automotive sectors. Great variations in the application method of coating materials, the deposition kinematic effects, the new complex substrate (component to be coated) designs adopted by the original equipment manufacturers (OEM) and the lack of information related to the mode of operation of the coated components are common problems in the coating sector. As a result, multiple design iterations of thermal or cold spray are required in an effort to converge to a coating plan for any given substrate, which come at high cost for both the OEM's and the supply chain.

Given the industry's transition away from hard chromium plating to more environmentally friendly alternatives, such as spray processes, the need for accurate and flexible

© IFIP International Federation for Information Processing 2021
Published by Springer Nature Switzerland AG 2021
I. Maglogiannis et al. (Eds.): AIAI 2021, IFIP AICT 627, pp. 196–206, 2021.
https://doi.org/10.1007/978-3-030-79150-6_16

coating planning tools comes at an opportune time. Within the context of thermal and cold spraying, a pre-spray optimization strategy has to satisfy several requirements. The central requirement is minimizing the coating thickness variation, achieve uniform or tailored coating properties using a model which cannot be expected to be analytically available. The ability to predict, evaluate and visualize the coating properties on difficult to reach areas of intricate components is of paramount importance and an issue that industrialists come across regularly at the qualification stage of a coating application. A further important requirement is the optimization of the kinematic quality of the robotic spray path, with respect for example to the surface curvature, shadowing and velocity.

Among numerous neural network architectures that could be used to address the robotic gun trajectory planning challenges, one is of particular interest and was introduced by Teuvo Kohonen in the 1980s [1]. Self-organizing map (SOM), sometimes also called Kohonen map, is a single layer neural network with units arranged along an n-dimensional grid. Most applications use two-dimensional, rectangular or hexagonal grids. SOMs use unsupervised, competitive learning to produce low-dimensional projections of high-dimensional data, preserving the similarity and topology relations between the data items. These characteristics are very desirable for our application, since smooth trajectories that follow the object's local curvature without sharp changes of consecutive positions and beam vectors are required, without the need for generating training datasets. SOMs have been used in various applications, despite their simplicity, including visualizations, generation of feature maps, pattern recognition and classification. Some applications focus on control of robotic arm, learning motion maps, collision avoidance for multi-vehicle systems including navigation and robotics [2–4]. Other applications can be found in chemistry [5], disease recognition in medical images, psycholinguistic studies [6], similarity of music recordings [7], maritime applications for the analysis of passive sonar recordings and for planning ship trajectories [8], classification of satellite images [9] and many other.

In this work, we propose the use of a SOM, arranged in 1D with appropriate weight vectors, in order to derive a smooth robotic gun trajectory that performs surface coating within required specifications. The training algorithm has been redesigned to generate optimized coating thickness along the substrate's surface. Results are presented for three different objects, typical in manufacturing, which compare favorably with the ones achieved by an expert.

2 Methodology

2.1 An Overview of the Proposed Algorithm

The proposed SOM is defined as an ordered sequence of 256 nodes (or neurons). The nodes represent the consecutive positions of the spraying gun as it moves along its trajectory with variable speed, pointing at a coating beam direction at each position. Thus, each node i contains its position p_i, the speed magnitude s_i with direction from the current node to the next one and the beam direction $\mathbf{g}_i$. A triangle is considered visible by a node if it lies within a cylindrical beam of a predetermined radius (r_0) and it is not shadowed by another triangle.

For each repetition up to a total number N_{rep}, a nested loop of b_s iterations (referred to as batch size) is performed, in a manner similar to batch stochastic optimization of feedforward neural networks. The triangles visible from at least one node are stored in table **A**. This calculation takes place once for each repetition, in order to reduce the computational complexity.

For each iteration, a random triangle is selected from **A** and the winner node and its neighbors are determined. The correction of the weights δp, δs and $\delta \mathbf{g}$ (position, speed and direction of the beam) of these nodes are appropriately calculated, according to the learning algorithm. During the iterations of the same batch, the corrections δp, δs and $\delta \mathbf{g}$ are accumulated into Δp, Δs and $\Delta \mathbf{g}$ respectively and the node weights $(p,s,\mathbf{g})$ are updated at the end of the batch. These steps are encoded in the pseudocode below:

```
Initialize neuron weights, calculate barycenter and
normal vector for each triangle of the substrate
For rep=1: Nrep       // Repetition Loop
  Calculate table A
  Initialize Δp =0, Δs=0 and Δg=0
  For t=1: bs          // Iteration Loop
    Select random triangle r from A
    Find winner node w and its neighbors Γw
    Calculate δgw, δgi, δsw, δsi, δpw, δpi where i ∈ Γw
    Δgw= Δgw+ δgw, Δgi= Δgi+ δgi
    Δsw= Δsw+ δsw, Δsi= Δsi+ δsi
    Δpw= Δpw+ δpw, Δpi= Δpi+ δpi
    Update direction gw= gw+ Δgw, gi= gi+ Δgi
    Update speed sw= sw+ Δsw, si= si+ Δsi
    Update position pw= pw+ Δpw, pi= pi+ Δpi
```

2.2 SOM Initialization

A substrate with arbitrary geometry in a triangulated form is inserted in the algorithm, in STL format. The object is placed with its center of mass at the origin of the frame of reference (0,0,0). The normal vectors **n** and the position of the barycenter **B** for each triangle of the object is calculated.

For a given substrate, the SOM is initialized with the position of the nodes equally spaced in a full circle, clockwise, around the center of mass of the object on a plane vertical to z axis. For each node, the beam's direction is initialized towards the center of the axis system. The initial value of the speed is set to 0.05 m/s for all nodes. The ideal stand-off distance (SoD) and coating thickness are set.

Substrate Curvature Pre-processing. During the training phase, triangles of the substrate are randomly selected and presented to the SOM. Substrate areas of high curvature require more precise neuron weight adaptation, thus they should be sampled more densely. To this end a quantity c that represents the local curvature of the object at each triangle is calculated.

First, a matrix **T** is created, whose i^{th} row **T**$_i$, contains the neighbor triangles of triangle i. Two triangles are considered to be neighbors if they have at least one common edge. For each triangle i the dot product of its normal vector and the normal vectors of all neighbor triangles are calculated and the one with the smallest value is selected for the calculation of the local curvature (see Fig. 1a).

$$c_i^0 = 1 - \min(\mathbf{n}_i \cdot \mathbf{n}_j),\ j \in \mathrm{T}_i \tag{1}$$

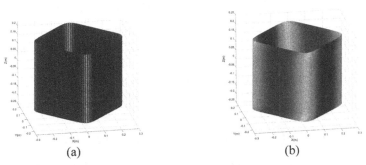

(a)   (b)

Fig. 1. a) Initial object curvature in color scale. b) Object curvature in color after the diffusion.

Then an iterative diffusion method is applied to those curvature values (see algorithm below) to achieve a smoother curvature distribution over the substrate (see Fig. 1b). This process takes place once for every new substrate and is not to be confused with the iterative training of the SOM:

```
For each iteration m
    For each triangle i
```

$$k_i = c_i^{m-1} + b\left(\left(\sum\nolimits_{j=1}^{\beta_i} c_j^{m-1}\right) - \beta_i \cdot c_i^{m-1}\right)$$

$$\mathbf{c}' = \mathbf{k}$$

where b is a constant in [0,1], β is the number of neighbors for each triangle.

2.3   Learning Algorithm

In the beginning of each repetition, matrix **A** is constructed. The barycenter of the triangle that is closest to the beam of node (p) and the speed of the beam's projection on this triangle v_{spot} are also calculated [10].

Random Triangle Selection - Winner Determination. For each iteration, a random triangle r from matrix **A** is selected, with probability proportional to substrate's diffused curvature (c), as follows. Triangles with curvature $c_k = 0$ will have zero probability to be randomly selected in the aforementioned method. To alleviate this problem the curvature of each triangle is increased by a constant quantity empirically set equal to 0.1. The curvature value of each triangle is converted to probability by dividing it by the sum of all curvatures and the cumulative curvature is computed.

$$C_i = \frac{1}{\sum\limits_{m=1}^{N} c_m} \sum_{k=1}^{i} c_k \qquad (2)$$

A random number ξ is selected according to the uniform distribution between 0 and 1. The triangle r satisfies the following condition:

$$C_r \le \xi < C_{r+1} \qquad (3)$$

The triangles that belong to a part of the object with larger curvature are more likely to be selected than the ones that are on a flatter surface. This results in greater object sampling and thus enhanced accuracy in areas with more complex shape.

Subsequently, using the matrix $\mathbf{A}$, a winner node is selected, as following. For every node i for which the particular triangle r with barycenter B_r is visible, the parameter b_i is calculated as shown below:

$$b_i = c_r(d_{i,r} - d_0)/d_0 + (1 - c_r)\sin(|\pi/2 - \theta_{i,r}|), \qquad (4)$$

where $d_{i,r} = |B_r - p_i|$ is the Euclidean distance between p_i and B_r, referred to as Stand-of-Distance (SoD). Thus, quantity b_i is dominated by the percentage difference of the current and the ideal SoD d_o at object areas with high curvature, whereas at areas with low curvature, the second term that quantifies the deviation of the impact angle from the ideal value of $\pi/2$ becomes dominant. The node with the smallest value of b is declared as the winner node w.

$$w = \arg\min(b_i) \qquad (5)$$

Definition of Neighborhood. After the determination of winner node w, a set of neighbor nodes $i \in \Gamma_w$ is defined, with $|w - i| \le n_b$. Thus, n_b nodes before and after the current winner are considered to be winner's neighbors. In case the geometric setup of nodes is not a closed loop the number of neighbors affected is smaller, if the winner node is on the edges. The learning rate of each node in the neighborhood is adjusted by a weight calculated using a Gaussian function of node index with respect to the winner node and standard deviation that decreases linearly from σ_0 to σ_1 with the number of epochs n_{ep}:

$$a_w(i) = a_{w,i} = \begin{cases} \exp\left(-(w-i)^2 / \left(2\sigma_n^2\right)\right), & |i - w| \le n_b \\ 0, & \text{otherwise} \end{cases} \qquad (6)$$

The standard deviation is obtained as following:

$$\sigma_n = n_b\left(\frac{\sigma_1 - \sigma_0}{n_{ep}}k + \sigma_0\right) \qquad (7)$$

The variables of these nodes are affected in the same way to the winner node, but to a lesser degree, depending on their distance from the winner (see Fig. 2).

Fig. 2. Change of weight factors with repetitions

Coating Thickness Calculation. The coating thickness h for a random triangle r that is being coated by neuron i, is calculated as a function of the following variables: stand-off distance (SoD) d, impact angle θ and the speed of beam's spot on the triangle r (spot speed) v_{spot}. For node i positioned at p_i with beam vector $\mathbf{g_i}$, that coats triangle r with normal vector n_r, (visible by node i), the v_{spot} is calculated according to [10] and the SoD and the impact angle θ_i, r are calculated as follows:

$$d_{i,r} = \|p_i - B_r\| \tag{8}$$

$$\theta_{i,r} = \cos^{-1}(\mathbf{g_i} \cdot \mathbf{n_r}) \tag{9}$$

For the calculation of coating thickness h, we derive the thickness h_o for the given SoD and impact angle θ_i, r using bilinear interpolation, according to [10] as follows:

$$h_o = a_1 d_{i,r} + a_2 \theta_{i,r} + a_3 d_{i,r} \theta_{i,r} \tag{10}$$

where a_1, a_2 and a_3 are parameters calculated from experimental results [10, 11].

The calculated thickness h_0 corresponds to spot speed of 502 m/s. In order to convert the thickness to the current spot speed we apply the following:

$$h = h_o \frac{f_h(v_{spot})}{f_h(v_{spot} = 502)} \tag{11}$$

where f_h is the hyperbolic interpolation of thickness versus spot speed is performed according to

$$f_h(v_{spot}) = \frac{1}{b v_{spot} + c} \tag{12}$$

The parameters b, c are calculated using experimental results [11].

Updating the Neuron Weights. The first variable that is updated during SOM learning is the direction of the beam. Aiming at an impact angle between the winner node and triangle close to $\pi/2$, the beam direction of the winner w and the neighbor nodes i, is updated as shown below:

$$\delta\mathbf{g}_i^t = sign(\mathbf{n}_r \cdot \mathbf{g}_w)\lambda_v a_{w,i}\mathbf{n}_r \tag{13}$$

where $\delta\mathbf{g}_i^t$ is the change of the beam node vector during iteration t, $\mathbf{g}_w$ is the beam vector of the winner node, $\mathbf{n}_r$ is the normal vector of random triangle r and $\lambda_v = 0.1$. It follows that the update for the winner becomes $\delta\mathbf{g}_w^t = sign(\mathbf{n}_r \cdot \mathbf{g}_w)\lambda_v\mathbf{n}_r$, since $a_{w,w} = 1$ according to Eq. (6), whereas for neurons outside the winner's neighborhood ($|w - n| \le n_b$), $a_{w,i} = 0$.

Subsequently, the node speed s, which represents the speed of the gun as it passes through the positions of the nodes in reference, is updated. The initial value of the speed is set to 0.05 m/s with direction from the current node to next one clockwisely. The speed changes in order for an ideal thickness to be achieved in the spraying process. The formula for the node speed update δs_i^t during iteration t is:

$$\delta s_i^t = \begin{cases} (h_i - \hat{h})\lambda_s a_{w,i}s_w^2, & i = w \\ (s_w - s_i)\lambda_s a_{w,i}, & i \ne w \end{cases}, \tag{14}$$

where h is the calculated thickness for triangles visible by the winner node beam, if the spraying gun was placed in the position of the winner node, h_i is an ideal thickness, $\lambda_s = 0.1$, s_w is the speed of the winner node and s_i the neighbor's speed. The value of speed for neighbor nodes is updated differently. The change is defined in reference to the speed difference between the winner's and each neighbor's speed.

Then, the position of the nodes is updated. The vector δp_i that defines this change is calculated using the following formula:

$$\delta p_i^t = \frac{D_i - d_o}{\max(D, d_o)}\lambda_p a_{w,i}\mathbf{g}_i, \tag{15}$$

where $D = |B_r - (p_i + \Delta p_i^{t-1})|$ and $\lambda_p = 0.2$. Figure 3 below depicts schematically the update of the position and beam direction of a winner node and a neighbor node for a randomly selected triangle r of the object during one iteration:

As mentioned in the overview of the proposed system, the evolution of the proposed SOM is performed in N_{rep} repetitions of batches with b_s iterations. Thus, the updates for each neuron are accumulated during each batch:

$$\Delta\mathbf{g}_i = \sum_{t=1}^{b_s}\delta\mathbf{g}_i^t, \quad \Delta s_i = \sum_{t=1}^{b_s}\delta s_i^t, \quad \Delta p_i = \sum_{t=1}^{b_s}\delta p_i^t \tag{16}$$

and are used to update the neuron weights at the end of each batch:

$$\mathbf{g}_i^{rep} = \mathbf{g}_i^{rep-1} + \Delta\mathbf{g}_i^t, \quad s_i^{rep} = s_i^{rep-1} + \Delta s_i^t, \quad p_i^{rep} = p_i^{rep-1} + \Delta p_i^t \tag{17}$$

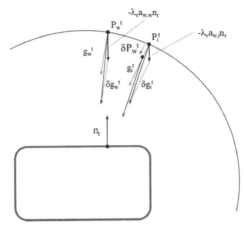

Fig. 3. Position and beam direction correction of a winner and a neighbor node for one iteration

3   Results

A billet mold, a component with epitrochoid cross section and a mud-rotor are typical objects used as substrates for coating, thus they were selected for our test objects. Figure 4 summarizes the training of the SOM for 500 repetitions and batch size equal to 10 (thus 5000 iterations in total), for the three test objects. The node position, beam vector and speed are depicted for the initial repetition, every 100 intermediate repetitions and the final one (blue, green and red color respectively). The length of the vectors is analogous to the gun speed.

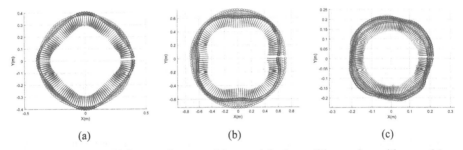

(a)   (b)   (c)

Fig. 4. Initial, every 100 intermediate repetitions and final repetition node positions and beam vectors (blue, green and red color respectively) for a) the billet mold, b) epitrochoid and c) the mud-rotor. SOM evolution was performed for 500 repetitions and batch size equal to 10 for all three objects. The length of the vectors is analogous to the gun speed. (Color figure online)

The coating achieved by the proposed algorithm is shown in Fig. 5 in comparison to the manual, expert-based coating for the billet mold (left column) and the epitrochoid (right column). The triangulated substrates are shown in the 1st row, with the coating plane indicated in yellow color. The coating thickness at the indicated plane achieved by the SOM-based method and by the expert is shown in the 2nd and 3rd raw respectively.

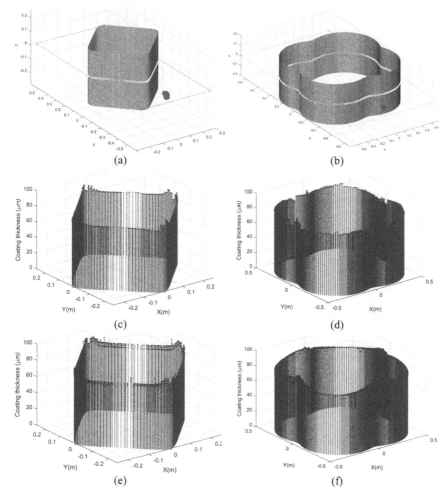

Fig. 5. Coating plane of the triangulated substrates: a) billet mold and b) epitrochoid. Coating thickness of the billet mold using c) proposed method and e) manual method and of the epitrochoid substrate using d) proposed method and f) manual method. (Color figure online)

The coating achieved by the proposed algorithm for the mud rotor is shown in Fig. 6 at the plane indicated in Fig. 6a. The coating thickness along the object intersection marked in yellow is plotted for the SOM based method and for the expert in Fig. 6b and c respectively. It can be visually observed that the thickness achieved by the SOM method is more uniform than the one achieved by the expert.

The coating thickness distribution is summarized using boxplots for the three test objects, for the proposed SOM-based and the expert-based coating. It can be observed in Fig. 7 that the thickness achieved by the SOM-based coating is better distributed round the required value, with both the 1st, 3rd quartile and the minimum and maximum thickness being closer to the ideal value, compared to the expert-based result.

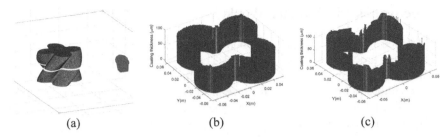

(a)   (b)   (c)

Fig. 6. a) Coating plane of the triangulated mud rotor. Coating thickness of the mud rotor at the selected plane using the b) proposed method and c) manual method. (Color figure online)

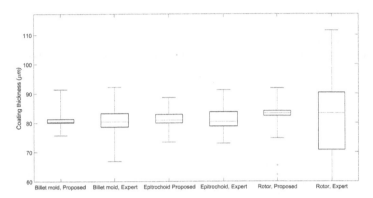

Fig. 7. Distribution of thickness values of proposed method for triangles of the coating plane of the object in comparison with the ones derived from a manual process for the three test objects.

The convergence of the SOM is assessed by calculating the following quantities:

$$C_1(rep) = N - \sum_{i=1}^{N} \left(\mathbf{g}_i^{rep-1} \cdot \overline{\Delta \mathbf{g}_i^{rep}} \right), \quad C_2(rep) = \sum_{i-1}^{N} \left| \Delta s_i^{rep} \right|, \quad C_3(rep) = \sum_{i=1}^{N} \left\| \Delta p_i^{rep} \right\|$$

(18)

Typical results of the evolution of the quantities C_1, C_2 and C_3 for the coating of the billet mold object are shown in Fig. 8.

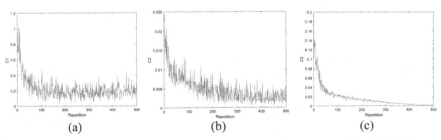

(a)   (b)   (c)

Fig. 8. The evolution of quantities C_1, C_2 and C_3 for the SOM-based coating of the billet mold.

4 Conclusions and Further Work

A SOM-based method for planning robotic arm trajectories for the optimization of surface coating processes has been presented. The proposed approach adapts the robotic gun kinematics utilizing a complicated coating thickness model to generate coating thickness within strict specifications for several surfaces. Three different objects, typical in the manufacturing industry have been tested, in comparison to an expert. Results show that the distribution of SOM-coating thickness is superior to the one achieved by an expert. The coating planning is performed within few minutes for an object with 10^5 triangles, using Matlab in a MW-Windows laptop (Intel i7@2.6 GHz, 16 GB RAM).

Further work incudes the extension of SOM on a 2D mesh of neurons that will cover arbitrarily complicated object geometries.

Acknowledgment. This work was partially financially supported by the Interdepartmental Postgraduate Programme "Informatics and Computational Biomedicine", School of Science, University of Thessaly, Greece.

References

1. Kohonen, T.: Self-organized formation of topologically correct feature maps. Biol. Cybern. **43**, 59–69 (1982)
2. Kubota, N., Nojima, Y., Kojima, F., Fukuda, T., Shibata, S.: Intelligent control of self-organizing manufacturing system with local learning mechanism. In: IECON Proceedings (Industrial Electronics Conference) (1999)
3. Razavian, A.A., Sun, J.: Cognitive based adaptive path-planning algorithm for autonomous robotic vehicles. In: Proceedings of the IEEE SoutheastCon, Ft. Lauderdale, FL, USA, 8–10 Apr 2005
4. Miljković, D.: Brief review of self-organizing maps. In: 40th International Convention on Information and Communication Technology, Electronics and Microelectronics (MIPRO), Opatija, pp. 1061–1066 (2017)
5. Maltarollo, V.G., Honório, K.M., da Silva, A.B.F.: Applications of artificial neural networks in chemical problems. In: Artificial Neural Networks-Architectures and Applications, pp. 203–223, InTech (2013)
6. Kohonen, T.: MATLAB Implementations and Applications of the Self-Organizing Map. Unigrafia, Helsinki, Finland (2014)
7. Pampalk, E., Dixon, S., Widmer, G.: Exploring music collections by browsing different views. Comput. Musical J. **28**(2), 49–62 (2004)
8. Lobo, V.J.: Application of self-organizing maps to the maritime environment. In: Popovich, V.V., Claramunt, C., Schrenk, M., Korolenko, K.V. (eds.) Information Fusion and Geographic Information Systems, pp. 19–36. Springer, Berlin, Heidelberg (2009)
9. Richardson, A.J., Risien, C., Shillington, F.A.: Using self-organizing maps to identify patterns in satellite imagery. Prog. Oceanogr. **59**(2–3), 223–239 (2003)
10. Tzinava, M., Delibasis, K., Allcock, B., Kamnis, S.: A general-purpose spray coating deposition software simulator. Surf. Coat. Technol. **399**, (2020)
11. Katranidis, V., Gu, S., Allcock, B., Kamnis, S.: Experimental study of high velocity oxy-fuel sprayed WC-17Co coatings applied on complex geometries. Part A: influence of kinematic spray parameters on thickness, porosity, residual stresses and microhardness, Surf. Coat. Technol. **311**, 206–215 (2017)

Convolutional NN

An Autoencoder Convolutional Neural Network Framework for Sarcopenia Detection Based on Multi-frame Ultrasound Image Slices

Emmanuel Pintelas[1], Ioannis E. Livieris[1(✉)], Nikolaos Barotsis[2],
George Panayiotakis[2], and Panagiotis Pintelas[1]

[1] Department of Mathematics, University of Patras, Patras, Greece
`{e.pintelas,livieris}@upatras.gr`
[2] Department of Medicine, University of Patras, Patras, Greece
`nbarotsis@icloud.com, panayiot@upatras.gr`

Abstract. Multi-Frame classification applications are constituted by instances composed by a package of image frames, such as videos, which frequently require very high computational re-sources. Furthermore, when the input instances contain a large proportion of noise, then the incorporation of noise filtering pre-processing techniques are considered essential. In this work, we propose an AutoEncoder Convolutional Neural Network model for Multi-Frame input applications. The AutoEncoder model aims to reduce the huge dimensional size of the initial instances, compress useful information while simultaneously remove the noise from each frame. Finally, a Convolutional Neural Network classification model is applied on the new transformed and compressed data instances. As a case study scenario for the proposed framework, we utilize Ultrasound images (image slices/frames extracted from every patient via a portable ultrasound device) for Sarcopenia detection. Based on our experimental re-sults the proposed framework outperforms traditional approaches.

Keywords: AutoEncoders · Deep learning · Transfer learning · Computer vision · Image classification · Sarcopenia detection · Ultrasound

1 Introduction

Multi-Frame (MF) input data mining applications require a significant amount of computational resources. A MF instance can be considered as a package of images arranged in time or space, such as videos or image slices extracted from 3D objects. One fast and light approach solution for solving such MF problems could be via the utilization of a CNN model applied only on one image slice/frame per MF instance. Nevertheless, by such an approach it is obvious

© IFIP International Federation for Information Processing 2021
Published by Springer Nature Switzerland AG 2021
I. Maglogiannis et al. (Eds.): AIAI 2021, IFIP AICT 627, pp. 209–219, 2021.
https://doi.org/10.1007/978-3-030-79150-6_17

that significant information from the initial MF instance is lost. Another common and efficient approach in terms of computation speed and accuracy lies on utilizing a CNN, which takes as input every image frame via a Multi-Channel (MC) input layer [19]. Nevertheless, when the initial dataset contains a large ratio of noisy instances, the incorporation of pre-processing noise filtering techniques is considered essential [18].

In order to reduce the high dimensional input size of such applications and create an efficient prediction framework in terms of accuracy, robustness, and computation cost, the incorporation of dimensionality reductions algorithms becomes imperative. AutoEncoders (AE) constitute a popular dimensional reduction algorithm proved to filter out noise from an initial feature space; thus, create more robust final feature representations [18].

In this work, we propose an AutoEncoder Convolutional Neural Network framework (AE-CNN) for noisy MF input applications. More specifically, an AutoEncoder model will transform every input image frame into a new compressed image representation. Then, a concatenation layer will create a new composite image constituted by all the encoded image frames. As a result, the initial MF input instance is transformed into a compressed 2D flattened image. Finally, this flattened image is used as input into a common CNN prediction model. As a case study scenario, we utilize MF Ultrasound images (image slices/frames extracted from every patient via an ultrasound device) for Sarcopenia detection.

Ultrasound scanning for sarcopenia diagnosis is an emerging imaging tool which recently has attracted a lot of interest [1,2,8,10,12,17]. Compared to traditional Computed Tomography (CT) scans and Magnetic Resonance Imaging (MRI), which are considered the gold standards in the detection of low muscle mass in sarcopenia, the low cost and the portability characteristic of ultrasound device are two of the greatest advantages of this diagnostic method. Full-body Dual Energy X-ray Absorptiometry (DXA) is widely used for the diagnosis of sarcopenia. However, DXA machines are not portable, limiting their use in the community, the measurements might be influenced by hydration status and the full-body scan exposes the subject to ionizing radiation. Contrarywise, ultrasound is a widely available, non-ionizing, low-cost and portable imaging modality, which could allow the large-scale screening of the population. A common disadvantage of MRI, CT and DXA is the training requirements for the staff, whereas the acquisition of ultra-sound images for muscle measurements can be done by minimally qualified staff and eventually be augmented by computer aided systems. Recently in [2], the authors developed a non-automatic sarcopenia detection system with 4 degrees of freedom to scan the human thigh with ultrasound probe and determine if he/she has sarcopenia by inspecting the length of muscle thickness in the thigh by ultrasound image.

Nevertheless, in the literature there is a great lack of research works, which actually managed to efficiently incorporate artificial intelligence methodologies, in order to make the ultrasound diagnosis for sarcopenia fully automatic. This is probably due to the fact that there is lack of medical data instances for efficiently training a DL model (such over of 100 instances) and because such images have a high proportion of noise comparing to CT scans, which is in general a more powerful but with a high cost diagnostic tool.

The main contributions of this work are summarized as follows: First, we managed to develop a fully automatic Ultrasound scanning detection system for sarcopenia detection based on DL algorithms. Second, we propose the idea of combining an AutoEncoder and a CNN prediction model as a general tool for removing noise from instances and compressing the huge dimensional size of the initial MF input instances, without degrading the final prediction performance. As a result, the proposed prediction model will be an efficient way for addressing noisy MF applications which require also high computational resources.

The remainder of this paper is organized as follows: Sect. 2 describes the proposed framework and Sect. 3 presents the utilized dataset. Section 4 presents our experimental results and Sect. 5 summarizes our conclusive remarks.

2 Proposed Framework

A high-level description of the proposed framework is presented in Fig. 1. For every input case, the ultrasound device extracts high frequency spatial multiple image frames. In order to build a fast and computationally efficient total prediction framework, we subsampled the initial high frequency MF input and created a lower frequency MF input composed by 9 frames per instance. It is worth mentioning that a lower number of frames (1 and 4) was leading to performance degradation while a higher number $(16, 25, 36, \dots)$ was leading to a rapid increase in terms of computational costs.

More specifically, an AutoEncoder (AE) model is trained via the whole set of single-frame images. When AE training procedure finishes, the proposed framework is composed by three main phases as presented in Fig. 1.

In first phase, the trained AE model is applied on every instance's frame ($\mathbf{Fr_i}$) (nine frames in total per input case) in order to compress useful information and also remove the noise from each frame, creating $H \times W$ image representations $\mathbf{F_i}$ (where H and W is the height and the width size of every image). In second phase, the output images of the AE model are concatenated together via a Concatenation Layer (CL) building a 2D Flattened Image (FI) $3H \times 3W$. Finally, in the third phase, the flattened images are utilized for training a common CNN classification model.

Figure 2 presents three additional different approaches in which our proposed model (AE-FI-CNN) will be compared with and are described in brief as follows: By removing the AE from the AE-FI-CNN model, then the FI is created via the raw unprocessed ultrasound frames. This means that the CNN model will be trained with the raw FI (FI-CNN) as presented in Fig. 2(a). Furthermore, by removing the AE and CL and replacing them with a Multi-Channel (MC) layer (MC-CNN), then the CNN model can be trained via the whole set of raw MF instances at once (each channel will take as input each frame) as presented in Fig. 2(c). It is worth mentioning that the utilization of a MC-CNN model is the main baseline approach for solving such MF applications [19]. Finally, by

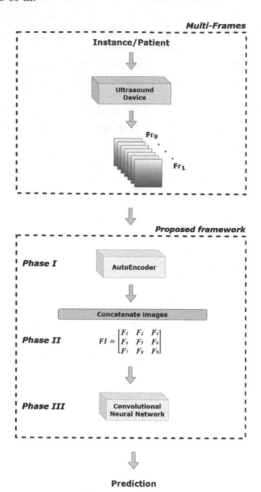

Fig. 1. Main pipeline of proposed Multi-Frame AutoEncoder Convolutional Neural Network model applied on the Ultrasound Sarcopenia detection problem.

interjecting the AE into the MC-CNN topology then the MC-CNN will be trained via the AE's pre-processed frames (AE-MC-CNN) as presented in Fig. 2(b).

2.1 AutoEncoders

AutoEncoders (AE) are unsupervised dimensionality reduction techniques constituted by artificial neural networks able to create a compressed knowledge representation of the original input. They can be used for reducing and compressing the dimension size of an initial feature space removing also noise and thus extracting and composing robust features [18].

More specifically, AE are composed by two main neural networks subcomponents, called *Encoder* and *Decoder*. The Encoder component is responsible

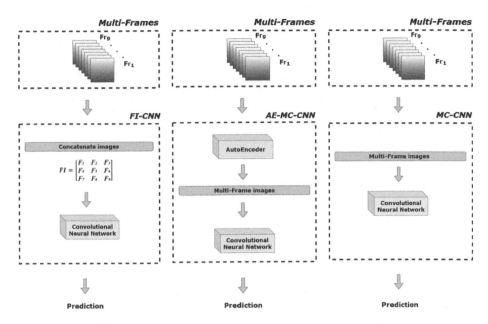

Fig. 2. Baseline approaches: (a) FI-CNN, (b) AE-MC-CNN and (c) MC-CNN multi-frame frameworks

for encoding an initial input feature space into a lower dimension one, while the Decoder component is responsible for reconstructing the compressed feature space into the initial one. Finally, the Encoder's output can be used as a robust and compressed feature representation for feeding a new classification model.

Figure 3 presents the architecture of the utilized AE topology of the proposed prediction framework. The Encoder component (left symmetric part of the whole topology) is constituted by three batches of blocks. The first block is composed by a 2D convolutional layer of 32 filters with 3×3 kernel size, a batch normalization layer, a ReLU activation layer, and a 2D max pooling layer with 2×2 kernel size. The second block is composed by a 2D convolutional layer of 8 filters with 3×3 kernel size, a batch normalization layer, a ReLU activation layer, and a 2D max pooling layer with 2×2 kernel size. The third block is composed by a 2D convolutional layer of 1 filter with 3×3 kernel size, a batch normalization layer and a Sigmoid activation layer. In the Decoder (right symmetric part of the topology), the main difference is that the max pooling layer is replaced by a 2×2 upsampling layer.

We recall that the output of the Encoder is the compressed image representation $\mathbf{F_i}$, which is used as input into the CNN classification model. The Decoder was only utilized during the initial AE training procedure. During inference mode, the Decoder is totally discarded since in our proposed framework we utilized only the Encoder component, in order to compress the initial multi-frame images and filter out the noise.

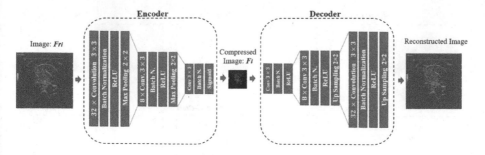

Fig. 3. The utilized AutoEncoder's architecture

2.2 Convolutional Neural Networks and Transfer Learning

Convolutional Neural Networks (CNNs) are a type of artificial neural networks mainly constituted by convolutional layers which are responsible for extracting and creating features from raw data matrices (such as images). They have proved to be very efficient feature extractors achieving remarkable performance especially in image classification problems [6,9,11].

Nowadays, the state of the art approach for solving automatic image recognition tasks is mainly based on utilizing pre-trained CNNs models [16]. These models can be used for inheriting their feature extraction knowledge into a small neural network without the need of training a new CNN model from scratch. This procedure is also known as Transfer Learning. Some widely used and efficient pre-trained CNN topologies are ResNet [5], Xception [4], and DenseNet [7].

ResNet (also called Residual Network), is a pretrained CNN model composed by residual blocks of 3×3 and 1×1 convolution filters and identity connections which transfer their input directly to the end of each residual block. This type of connections is well known for addressing the degradation problem, which is mainly caused by exceedingly large network depths.

Xception is another pretrained CNN model, which relies solely on depth-wise separable convolution layers. Xception architecture is based on the hypothesis that the mapping of cross-channels and spatial correlations in the feature maps of convolutional neural networks can been entirely decoupled [4].

DenseNet is a modified version of ResNet and is implemented by dense blocks connecting each layer to every other layer in a feedforward way. This leads to plenty of advantages such as parameter efficiency, feature reuse and implicit deep supervision. DenseNets have proved to be superior comparing to most state-of-the-art CNNs [7].

3 Dataset

The utilized dataset was taken from the Rehabilitation Department of Patras University Hospital. It has exams for Sarcopenia detection based on multi-frame image slices taken for every patient/subject using the GE Logiq P9 ultrasound system equipped with the ML6-15 linear array transducer (GE Healthcare

GmbH, Freiburg, Germany). More specifically, the dataset is composed by 1100 cases, from various muscle groups, of which 17% were detected with sarcopenia. The ultrasound images were acquired according to the protocol described by Barotsis et al. [3].

4 Experimental Results

In this section, we present our experimental results regarding the proposed framework for sarcopenia detection based on ultrasound multi-frame image slices. In order to provide a higher visibility of the utilized shortcuts in this work, we summarized them in Table 1.

Table 1. List of acronyms and abbreviations for the utilized prediction models

Model	Acronyms
Auto Encoder	AE
Flattened Image	FI
Multi-Frame	MF
Multi-Channel	MC
Concatenation Layer	CL
Convolutional Neural Network	CNN

We utilized as CNN models a custom architecture, ResNet, Xception, and Dense-Net. Table 2 presents our experimental results for every utilized model. The Multi-Channel CNN (MC-CNN) models refer to the CNN models applied on the raw multi-frame inputs, the AutoEncoder Multi-Channel CNN (AE-MC-CNN) models refer to the CNN models applied on the transformed multi-frame inputs via the AE model, the FI-CNN models refer to the CNN models applied on the Flattened Images (FI), while finally the AE-FI-CNN (it is the proposed prediction frame-work) refer to the CNN models applied on the transformed flattened images via the AE model. Finally, Figs. 4 and 5 present two examples with the original image with dimension 1024×1024 and the corresponding output of the encoder (encoded) with dimension 256×256.

The validation of our experimental simulations was based on the following performance metrics: Accuracy (Acc), Area Under the Curve (AUC) Geometric Mean (GM), F_1-score (F_1), Sensitivity (Sen), and Specificity (Spe) [15]. Additionally, we splitted the initial dataset into a 75% and 25% ratio for creating a training and a test set respectively maintaining also the same balance ratio of the corresponding classes.

Based on our experimental results, we are able to conclude that the proposed AE-FI-CNN framework significantly outperforms every other approach for every utilized CNN topology (Custom CNN, ResNet, Xception, and DenseNet). More

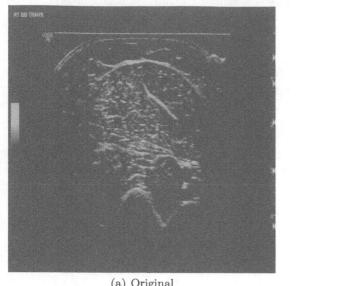

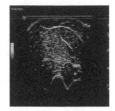

(a) Original   (b) Encoded

Fig. 4. Example of the application of encoder (a) original image with dimension 1024×1024 and (b) encoded image with dimension 256×256

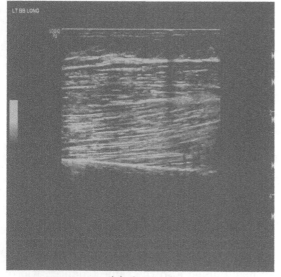

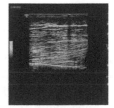

(a) Original   (b) Encoded

Fig. 5. Example of the application of encoder (a) original image with dimension 1024×1024 and (b) encoded image with dimension 256×256

specifically, the AE-FI-DenseNet model managed to achieve the higher overall performance.

It is also revealed that the incorporation of the AE model managed to drastically improve the overall performance of every CNN model for both approaches (MC and FI) especially for the Sensitivity score. However, it leaded to a slight performance degradation for the Specificity score. The Sensitivity score, for this specific application case study scenario measures the accuracy for the sarcopenia cases. At this point, it is essential to mention that since this case study is based on a medical application, the Sensitivity score is considered as the most important metric; this is because it is vital for the patients that the model will correctly classify the sarcopenia instances. On the other hand, the Specificity score, for this specific application case study scenario measures the accuracy for classifying correctly the healthy subjects, which is in general a much less significant matter. It is obvious that the misclassification of the healthy subjects is not as vital as the misclassification of the sarcopenia ones.

Table 2. Performance results of utilized models

Model	Acc	AUC	GM	F_1	Sen	Spe
MC-CUSTOM CNN	83.71%	0.662	33.24	0.185	0.109	0.987
FI-CUSTOM CNN	84.85%	0.739	33.47	0.196	0.109	1.000
AE-MC-CUSTOM CNN	46.75%	0.252	28.86	0.089	0.152	0.531
AE-FI-CUSTOM CNN	87.09%	0.675	67.04	0.545	0.457	0.955
MC-RESNET	80.04%	0.639	32.48	0.156	0.109	0.942
FI-RESNET	77.03%	0.667	56.98	0.354	0.370	0.853
AE-MC-RESNET	80.04%	0.766	73.64	0.518	0.620	0.835
AE-FI-RESNET	81.16%	0.816	74.23	0.532	0.630	0.848
MC-XCEPTION	75.67%	0.546	49.83	0.283	0.283	0.853
FI-XCEPTION	65.20%	0.490	51.99	0.266	0.370	0.710
AE-MC-XCEPTION	79.67%	0.682	45.28	0.267	0.217	0.915
AE-FI-XCEPTION	84.40%	0.784	71.24	0.543	0.543	0.906
MC-DENSENET	83.03%	0.709	43.99	0.281	0.196	0.960
FI-DENSENET	77.47%	0.655	44.61	0.247	0.217	0.888
AE-MC-DENSENET	84.14%	0.612	29.87	0.157	0.087	0.996
AE-FI-DENSENET	90.70%	0.802	76.72	0.684	0.587	0.973

At this point, it is worth mentioning that the performance metrics AUC and GM as well as the balance between Sen and Spe present the information provided by a confusion matrix in compact form; hence, they constitute the proper metrics to evaluate the ability of model of not overfitting the training data.

5   Conclusions and Future Work

In this work, we proposed an AutoEncoder Convolutional Neural Network framework (AE-CNN) for Sarcopenia detection based on multi-frame ultrasound image slices. An AutoEncoder model was used for transforming every initial input image frame into a new compressed image representation, filtering out the noise. Next, a new composite flattened image was constructed via the concatenation of every AE transformed image frame and finally it was fed into a CNN final classification model. The experimental results revealed the efficiency of the proposed framework since it managed to significantly outperform every other approach for every utilized CNN architecture and thus establish it as a very promising tool for automatically detecting Sarcopenia from Ultrasound scans. Such technique might allow a fast and large-scale screening of the population for the early detection in sarcopenia. Additionally, it might lead to a fast, easy and user-independent method for the follow-up of patients suffering from sarcopenia and the assessment of the efficacy of therapeutic interventions.

It is also revealed that the incorporation of the AE component for removing the noise and compressing every image frame managed to drastically increase the performance results of the final CNN model, comparing to the common approach which utilize the image frames in their raw form. Finally, the proposed FI construction from the multi-frame input instance led also to a performance increase comparing to the MC approach [19] (feeding of every image frame into a different CNNs input channel).

Nevertheless, one minor limitation of our approach is that the AE initial training requires a significant amount of computational resources. However, from our perspective, the main limitation is that the proposed framework is inherently Black Box model meaning that no explanation and interpretation of the model's final prediction mechanism can be given. Explainability and Interpretability are two exceedingly significant issues, especially in medical applications [13,14].

In future work, we intent to include other information such as gender, age and also incorporate ensemble learning philosophy, such as averaging and stacking [20] into the proposed AutoEncoder CNN model in order to further improve the performance results. Finally, we also aim to incorporate transfer learning into an intrinsic interpretable machine learning model, such as a linear Logistic Regression model, in order to provide a significant degree of explainability [13,14] into the whole proposed framework.

References

1. Albano, D., Messina, C., Vitale, J., Sconfienza, L.M.: Imaging of sarcopenia: old evidence and new insights. Eur. Radiol. **30**(4), 2199–2208 (2020)
2. Barotsis, N., Galata, A., Hadjiconstanti, A., Panayiotakis, G.: The ultrasonographic measurement of muscle thickness in sarcopenia. a prediction study. Eur. J. Phys. Rehabil. Med. **56**(4), 427–437 (2020)
3. Barotsis, N., Tsiganos, P., Kokkalis, Z., Panayiotakis, G., Panagiotopoulos, E.: Reliability of muscle thickness measurements in ultrasonography. Int. J. Rehabil. Res. **43**(2), 123–128 (2020)

4. Chollet, F.: Xception: deep learning with depthwise separable convolutions. In: Proceedings of the IEEE Conference on Computer Vision and Pattern Recognition, pp. 1251–1258 (2017)
5. He, K., Zhang, X., Ren, S., Sun, J.: Deep residual learning for image recognition. In: Proceedings of the IEEE Conference on Computer Vision and Pattern Recognition, pp. 770–778 (2016)
6. Hemanth, D.J., Estrela, V.V.: Deep Learning for Image Processing Applications, vol. 31. IOS Press, Amsterdam (2017)
7. Huang, G., Liu, Z., Van Der Maaten, L., Weinberger, K.Q.: Densely connected convolutional networks. In: Proceedings of the IEEE Conference on Computer Vision and Pattern Recognition, pp. 4700–4708 (2017)
8. Katakis, S., et al.: Muscle type and gender recognition utilising high-level textural representation in musculoskeletal ultrasonography. Ultrasound Med. Biol. **45**(7), 1562–1573 (2019)
9. Kim, J., Nguyen, A.D., Lee, S.: Deep CNN-based blind image quality predictor. IEEE Trans. Neural Netw. Learn. Syst. **30**(1), 11–24 (2018)
10. Kim, Y.J., Kim, S., Choi, J.: Sarcopenia detection system using RGB-D camera and ultrasound probe: system development and preclinical in-vitro test. Sensors **20**(16), 4447 (2020)
11. Lu, L., Wang, X., Carneiro, G., Yang, L. (eds.): Deep Learning and Convolutional Neural Networks for Medical Imaging and Clinical Informatics. ACVPR, Springer, Cham (2019). https://doi.org/10.1007/978-3-030-13969-8
12. Mombiela, R.M., Vucetic, J., Rossi, F., Tagliafico, A.S.: Ultrasound biomarkers for sarcopenia: what can we tell so far? In: Seminars in Musculoskeletal Radiology, vol. 24, pp. 181–193. Thieme Medical Publishers (2020)
13. Pintelas, E., Liaskos, M., Livieris, I.E., Kotsiantis, S., Pintelas, P.: Explainable machine learning framework for image classification problems: case study on glioma cancer prediction. J. Imaging **6**(6), 37 (2020)
14. Pintelas, E., Livieris, I.E., Pintelas, P.: A grey-box ensemble model exploiting black-box accuracy and white-box intrinsic interpretability. Algorithms **13**(1), 17 (2020)
15. Raschka, S.: An overview of general performance metrics of binary classifier systems. arXiv preprint arXiv:1410.5330 (2014)
16. Shao, L., Zhu, F., Li, X.: Transfer learning for visual categorization: a survey. IEEE Trans. Neural Netw. Learn. Syst. **26**(5), 1019–1034 (2014)
17. Stringer, H.J., Wilson, D.: The role of ultrasound as a diagnostic tool for sarcopenia. J. Frailty Aging **7**(4), 258–261 (2018)
18. Vincent, P., Larochelle, H., Bengio, Y., Manzagol, P.A.: Extracting and composing robust features with denoising autoencoders. In: Proceedings of the 25th International Conference on Machine Learning, pp. 1096–1103 (2008)
19. Zhao, M., Chang, C.H., Xie, W., Xie, Z., Hu, J.: Cloud shape classification system based on multi-channel CNN and improved FDM. IEEE Access **8**, 44111–44124 (2020)
20. Zhou, Z.H.: Ensemble Methods: Foundations and Algorithms. CRC Press, Boca Raton (2012)

Automatic Classification of XCT Images in Manufacturing

Bertram Sabrowsky-Hirsch[1][(✉)] [iD], Roxana-Maria Holom[1] [iD],
Christian Gusenbauer[2], Michael Reiter[2] [iD], Florian Reiterer[2] [iD],
Ricardo Fernández Gutiérrez[2] [iD], and Josef Scharinger[3] [iD]

[1] RISC Software GmbH, Softwarepark 35, 4232 Hagenberg, Austria
`office@risc-software.at`
[2] Nemak Linz GmbH, Zeppelinstraße 24, 4030 Linz, Austria
[3] Johannes Kepler University, Altenbergerstraße 69, 4040 Linz, Austria
`https://risc-software.at/`, `https://www.nemak.com/`, `https://www.jku.at/`

Abstract. X-ray computed tomography (XCT) is an established non-destructive testing (NDT) method that, in combination with automatic evaluation routines, can be successfully used to establish a reliable 100% inline inspection system for defect detection of cast parts. While these systems are robust in automatically localizing suspected defects, human know-how in a secondary assessment and decision-making step remains indispensable to avoid an excess of rejected parts. Rather than changing the existing defect detection system and risking difficult to anticipate changes to a solid evaluation process, we propose the integration of human know-how in a subsequent support system through end-to-end learning. Using XCT data and the corresponding decisions performed by the XCT operator, we aim to support and possibly automate the secondary quality assessment process. In our paper we present a Convolutional Neural Network (CNN) architecture to predict both, the final decision of the XCT operator and a defect class indication, for cast parts rejected by the defect detection system based on XCT slice images. On a dataset of 19,459 defect records categorized in 7 classes, we achieved an accuracy of 92% for the decision and 93% for the defect class indication on the testing split. We further show that, by binding decisions to the reliability of the predicted defect class, our model has the potential to enhance also a production process with a near-faultless condition. Based on production-line data, we estimate that our model can reliably relabel 11% of defects reported during production and provide a defect class indication for another 57%.

Keywords: Machine learning · Deep learning · X-ray computed tomography · Quality control · Casting · Manufacturing

---

Supported by EU H2020 and "Innovatives OÖ 2020" programs.

I. Maglogiannis et al. (Eds.): AIAI 2021, IFIP AICT 627, pp. 220–231, 2021.
https://doi.org/10.1007/978-3-030-79150-6_18

1   Introduction

Manufacturing, similar to other areas, is going through a transformation period. This is mainly because of the digitalization activities that manufacturing companies are experiencing. Therefore, terms like smart industry and zero defect manufacturing are very popular nowadays because of the cutting edge technologies involved, such as Internet of Things (IoT), big data, data analytics and machine learning (ML).

In the context of the European project called Big Data Value Spaces for COmpetitiveness of European COnnected Smart FacTories 4.0 (BOOST 4.0) [2] Nemak Linz GmbH and RISC Software GmbH, together with other partners, tried to achieve a better understanding of the data recorded along the production process and implement different data analytics applications to optimize the light metal casting processes. Nemak Linz GmbH focusses on the production of high-quality cylinder heads for engines by using the Nemak-owned Rotacast® [15] technology. One of the use cases identified in the project was empowering the quality assessment of cast parts through data analytics. For quality control, Nemak Linz GmbH provides extensive equipment for the assessment of the cast parts, including automatic X-ray computed tomography (XCT) inspection systems, as well as equipment for conventional X-ray imaging, leakage testing, etc.

In this paper, we are making use of ML to automatically reassess cast parts based on XCT images, which have been previously identified as faulty by an XCT inspection system. Hence, the expected impact is an optimization of the casting process at Nemak Linz GmbH and, consequentially, making more human resources available, since the XCT slice images are typically assessed by XCT and casting experts. However, this is not a straightforward solution. The XCT data is counter-balanced as some defects only occur at specific casting situations and at substantially different rates. In addition, XCT data is only collected for faulty parts, whereas the vast majority of defect-free parts is not recorded. Therefore, the imbalanced XCT data represents a challenge for the success of the ML algorithm [4]. In combination with strict requirements for quality assurance, it is important to identify conditions that allow for optimization without the possibility of disregarding actual defects.

The paper is structured as follows: Sect. 2 summarizes the background information and the related work, Sect. 3 details the challenges and enumerates the objectives, Sect. 4 describes the core aspects of the proposed solution and Sect. 5 concludes the paper by presenting the outcomes of the research and some observations related to future work.

2   Background

2.1   Quality Assessment Using X-Ray Computed Tomography (XCT)

Serial inline XCT inspection is used to optimise cast parts by automatically identifying defects that determine their quality. In the context of the use case

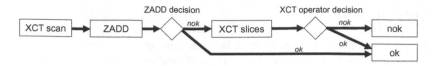

Fig. 1. The decision process used for XCT inspection outlined: Scanned production parts are analysed by the ZADD, which rates each part either as *ok* or *nok*. For every *nok* part, the system generates XCT slice images for the XCT operator, who will yield a final manual decision.

presented in this paper, the ZEISS VoluMax 1500 G2 XCT system is used to generate *ok* and *nok* (not OK) part decisions in combination with the ZEISS Automated Defect Detection (ZADD) software [17]. The ZADD software automatically detects, localizes and classifies manufacturing defects based on the original CAD data and on a reference model to detect deviations in the actual part to be analyzed. This reference model is the combined result of XCT data acquired from several exceptionally flawless parts [15]. For each inspected cast part, deviations are localized and based on their properties predefined defect types assigned. Finally, the system makes a binary decision - *ok* or *nok* - by comparing the determined properties with the specified limit values. In case of a *nok* decision, a manual decision is requested from the XCT operator, who is presented with the defect information including orthogonal slices of the XCT images at the defect locations. If the XCT operator declares the defect as tolerable, the part is relabelled as *ok* and is returned to the next manufacturing step. Figure 1 summarizes the previously described XCT inspection and quality control steps. The goal of the work presented in this paper is to extend the current system with a machine learning algorithm to support and possibly automate the manual decision process using end-to-end learning.

2.2   Related Work

The scenario described in Sect. 2.1 is an instance of Non-destructive Inspection (NDI), where XCT imaging has been established as a tool for the image-based defect detection of casting defects [19]. While existing solutions still often rely on traditional computer vision methods, deep learning and especially Convolutional Neural Networks (CNNs) have been used for defect detection throughout many industrial fields [3,5,10]. In combination with methods like transfer learning [6] and data augmentation [14] to overcome training data limitations, CNNs typically outperform traditional methods, with the benefit of end-to-end learning. However, most works in the context of defect detection rather revolve around the extension of CNNs to segmentation or detection architectures, such as U-net [1] and Mask R-CNN [6]. In our scenario, the detection of defects is already handled by the upstream ZADD software that we do not seek to replace or change, but rather implement a secondary assessment based on its output. For this reason traditional classification (in disregard of detection and/or segmentation) much closer reflects the reality of our use case, with few comparable works in the field of XCT defect detection. However, Masci et al. [12] showed that CNNs can be effective in a similar setup, reporting a 7% error rate on their data. In another work by Park et al. [13], the authors show that even strong class imbalances can be overcome with the use of sampling strategies and data augmentation. One aspect that we did not find discussed in related literature, is the evaluation of a proposed model towards its practical use for industrial quality assurance, which usually mandates a near-faultless requirement. We account for this by identifying reliably predicted defect classes and by assessing the rate at which the model can automate decisions as well as provide indications without the risk of disregarding actual defects.

3   Motivation

The quality assessment process of cast parts involves many assessment steps. As an example, 100% inline XCT inspection relies on visual inspection and manual decisions and re-evaluation of *nok* parts detected by XCT and casting experts that may consume a lot of working hours. Therefore, the quality assessment process is expensive (time- and resource-intensive), i.e. can contribute very significantly to the overall costs of an cast part. Hence, there is a significant potential for cost savings in this area by automatizing those tasks at least partially.

3.1   Challenges

XCT inspection in smart manufacturing is dealing with the challenges imposed by the complexity of cast parts. Gradual changes to the cast parts induced by tolerable casting variations during the lifetime of a product can be handled by periodically examining and updating the reference model. Although ZADD is reliable and efficient in creating binary decisions, its scope of identifying different defect classes is limited as its decisions are rule-based and rely on configured examinations for defined regions of interest and local limits. Therefore, the XCT operator has to inspect all *nok* parts to review the ZADD decision and determine a specific defect class (e.g.: core fracture, core defect, metal shavings, etc.). Aiming at a fully automated quality assessment process, a strategy for extending ZADD with a ML-based classification is essential.

The success of ML is massively influenced by the data quantity and quality. Automatically predicting the *ok/nok* decision and defect classes assessment of the XCT experts is challenging. As in many other real industry cases, faulty cast parts are outweighed by samples of good performance. This effect is further amplified, as the data for our use case can inherently only be collected for reported defects, which creates another division (definite *nok* and relabelled *ok*) for an already under-represented class. Further discrimination of different defect classes, some of which have an especially rare rate of occurrence, creates a major hindrance for the acquisition of sufficient samples, which leads to greatly imbalanced data. In this paper, we approach the data imbalances with a combination of resampling and data augmentation methods. While these methods can be very effective, they are only able to compensate for imbalances up to a certain degree. This is why we focus on classes reasonably well represented in the data and reserve the omitted classes for future extensions subsequent to further focussed data acquisition towards these under-represented classes. One other distinctive challenge is the strong bias towards avoiding False Positives (FP, i.e., parts incorrectly relabelled as *ok*) over False Negatives (FN, i.e., parts incorrectly confirmed as *nok*) as the former case undermines quality control, while the latter "merely" translates to added costs. We adapted our model architecture in order to reflect this bias in the models decisions.

3.2 Objectives

In order to achieve the goal of supporting and minimizing the manual decision process by end-to-end learning, the following objectives have been defined:

(i) Automatic classification of XCT slice images via CNNs.
(ii) Support the domain experts in identifying the quality of the classification for each defect image and understanding the decisions of the algorithm.
(iii) The machine learning algorithm should be optimized to minimize the FP.

4   Solution

4.1   Data

Our dataset consists of real XCT and reference data exported by the ZADD software in use at the Nemak production site. The data has been collected over a time of eight months and consists of a series of ZADD detection records for each production part. Each record is comprised of three slices that correspond to the principal axes and intersect at the center of the identified defect region. Three channels are provided for each slice: The channels *mean* and *std* correspond to the mean and standard deviation values of the reference part, and the channel *xct* to the real production part. All channels have been registered to CAD data by the ZADD software and thus extend over the same region. Figure 2 visualizes the *xct* channels of the three slices of a detection record in 3D space and compares the three different channels of a single slice. In addition to the slices, each record is associated with two annotation labels:

> **defect:** the defect class assigned by the XCT operator
> **decision:** the final assessment of the XCT operator, either *ok* or *nok*

Figure 3 outlines the number of detection records for each of the 13 defect classes and the respective share of parts finally labelled as *ok* and *nok*. There is clearly a strong imbalance in the distribution of defect classes corresponding partially to the frequency of occurrence of the respective type of defect in the production process. For the total of 20,378 records reported as *nok* 42% have been relabelled to *ok* by the XCT operator.

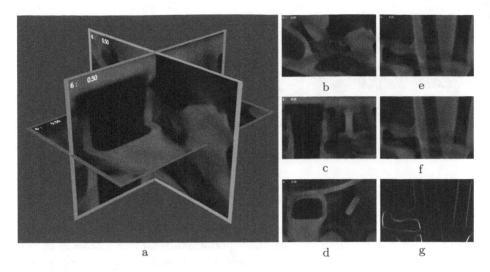

Fig. 2. Left: The channel *xct* for the slices of one detection record aligned in 3D space (a). Middle: for (a) the respective slices in 2D (b, c, d). Images of the channel *xct* do contain minimal annotations from the ZADD in form of text in the top left corner, which will be omitted through cropping during training and prediction. Right: the channels *xct* (e), *mean* (f) and *std* (g) of a single slice of another detection record. We applied strong contrast adjustments to the last channel *std* in order to make the contents visible and printable.

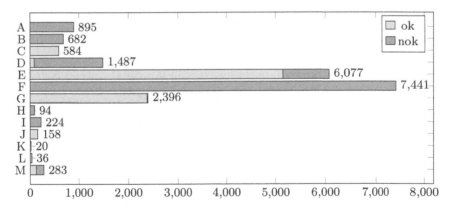

Fig. 3. Overview of the number of records for each of the 13 defect classes in our dataset, corresponding to the label *defect*. Each defect class is further split into records manually labelled as *ok* and *nok* by the XCT operator, corresponding to the label *decision*. Note, that we will later select a subset of 7 defect classes due to the strong imbalance in the dataset.

4.2   Model Architecture

Based on the dataset of annotated detection records, we train a CNN to automatically classify both annotation labels, *defect* and *decision*. By combining these

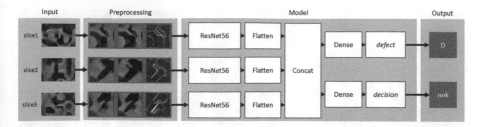

Fig. 4. The model architecture with exemplary input slice images and output values.

labels in one model, we hope to exploit label dependencies through multi-label learning as suggested by [2]. We empirically evaluated different configurations of the models *VGG* [18], *EfficientNet* [20] and *ResNet* [8], and found a combination of multiple ResNets to yield the best performance for our dataset. Figure 4 illustrates the final model architecture. For a given defect, we process the corresponding three slices in separate input paths that are combined within the model to connect to the two output labels. Following the input path of one slice, first the related intensity images for its three channels xct, *mean* and *std* are processed separately using z-score normalization (based on the channel's deviation over the entire dataset). The preprocessed channels are then merged to a single vector image of size $1150 \times 790(x3)$, which is rotated and flipped randomly for augmentation before extracting a central region of $448 \times 448(x3)$. As the image is centered at the defect and spans a large extent, the extracted image still retains most of the relevant information. Finally, the resulting image is downscaled to an input size of $224 \times 224(x3)$ using a local mean filter. This size is commonly used and standard for models pretrained on the well-known dataset *ImageNet* [11]. A standard ResNet56 is employed, excluding its top layer and instead connecting to a concatenation layer that aggregates all three input paths. Finally, each label is implemented through a dense layer using a softmax activation function that connects to the concatenation via an intermediate dense layer. An exemplary output of D/nok would indicate defect class D and a final decision: *nok*.

4.3   Training and Inference

We created stratified splits of the dataset for training, validation and testing in a 7:1:2 ratio. For stratification we used both labels, *defect* and *decision*. Groups of less than 500 records were discarded for our experiment to avoid excessive oversampling. This excluded the defect classes H-M as well as the combinations D/ok and G/nok, leaving a total of 19,459 records for 7 final defect classes (A-G). We used an Adam optimizer [6] with categorical cross-entropy loss to train the model in epochs of 2,000 batches of 10 records each. To counter the unbalanced nature of the dataset we used a combination of oversampling and augmentation during training. Samples were again grouped by both labels with minority groups being oversampled. Random rotations and flipping were used for augmentation as described in Sect. 4.2.

Table 1. Evaluation for the *decision* label grouped by the 7 selected defect classes using the optimized threshold and class rules.

Actual-defect	A	B	C	D	E	F	G	Total
Accuracy	100%	99%	99%	96%	79%	99%	95%	92%
FPs	0%	1.5%	0%	4.3%	2.9%	0.8%	0%	1.6%

Training converged within 100 epochs, an observation affirmed by the lack of further improvements of the validation score up to the termination of training at epoch 250. The accuracy scores of the model on the training, validation and testing splits were 97%, 93% and 94% respectively for the *decision* label and 98%, 92% and 93% respectively for the *defect* label. This indicates minor signs of overfitting to the training data, especially for the *defect* label and less so for the *decision* label, which could be mitigated by further augmentation methods or more preferably the extension of the dataset.

To bias the model towards the avoidance of FPs, we empirically evaluated the use of weighted outputs during training with no notable improvements. However, adjusting the probability threshold of the label *decision*, a technique described by Li et al. [9], yielded the desired effect. Based the model's softmax predictions on the training data, we optimized the threshold to balance a minimal ratio of FPs and high accuracy, changing the threshold from the default value of 0.5 to 0.79 (i.e., predictions with a softmax value below 0.79 for *ok* count as *nok*). We were able to lower the ratio of FPs for the *decision* label from 2.9% to 1.8% for a decreased accuracy of 92% on the testing split (or from 0.8% to 0.4% at 97% accuracy on the training split), which we deemed an acceptable compromise.

We achieved a final improvement with the use of class rules, which overrule the decision based on the predicted *decision* label, specifically for the defect classes without any *ok* representation in the dataset (e.g., A, B and F) to *nok*. This also reflects the production-line reality as these defects are without exception labelled *nok*. Introducing these class rules further decreased the rate of FPs to 1.6% (or 0.2% on the training split) for a insignificant 0.18% increase in FNs.

Table 1 outlines the final results on the testing split for each defect class. We evaluate the metrics Accuracy and FPs for the *decision* label using the optimized probability threshold and class rules over the testing split specified for each defect class. We further evaluated the confusion between defect classes as outlined in Table 2. The model struggles significantly with the class D, which can be difficult to distinguish even for experts as it is visually very similar to E and F. For class C on the other hand the model performs quite robust classifications. Similarly, the two related classes A and B, despite mutual confusion, can be predicted with high confidence.

4.4 Production-Line Evaluation

For the evaluation on actual production-line data we first continued to train the model for another 200 epochs on the detection records of all three splits to

Table 2. The confusion between defect classes for the testing split. The values are normalized by rows with the respective absolute number of Records for the actual defect class in the rightmost column.

		Predicted							
		A	B	C	D	E	F	G	Records
	A	0.89	0.06	-	0.02	0.01	0.02	-	179
	B	0.05	0.90	-	0.01	0.04	-	-	136
	C	-	-	0.97	-	0.02	0.01	0.01	117
Actual	D	-	-	-	0.77	0.11	0.09	0.03	280
	E	-	-	-	0.02	0.93	0.01	0.03	1216
	F	-	-	-	0.02	0.01	0.96	-	1488
	G	-	-	-	0.01	0.06	-	0.93	476

incorporate all available data into the model. The final accuracy values on the full dataset were 96% for the *decision* and 98% for the *defect* label. The evaluation was then conducted on an independent dataset of 1,299 detection records, of which 37% have been labelled *ok* by the XCT operator. The records have been collected over eight weeks from the production-line. The accuracy values for the production-line dataset were 92% for the *decision* and 87% for the *defect* label.

Table 3 illustrates evaluation metrics for the *part-ok* label over the production-line dataset for each *predicted* defect class. Grouping by the predicted instead of the true defect class allows us to assess the reliability of the model for each distinct defect class during real-time operation, when the true defect class is not known without further manual inspection. Other than standard metrics also used for the training evaluation, we evaluated the ratio of *Critical False Positives* (CFP). For the CFP metric, a domain expert reassessed all FPs manually, excluding those that are ambiguous, i.e., close to the decision limit. This makes the combination of FPs and CFPs the most important metrics to assess the potential use of the model in the production-line.

For the defect classes A, B, D and F the model does default to a *nok* decision, which can be explained by the omission of *ok* instances for these classes during training. Defects associated with these defect classes will have to be checked manually, with the benefit of a defect class indication by the model.

Class C only relates to *ok* instances, which is reliably predicted by the model. As the class does not show any FPs, defects can be automatically relabelled without further inspection. The case of Class D is curious as it does not yield any FPs in the production-line evaluation, a stark contrast to the 4.3% FPs in the previous evaluation. This can be explained by the FP cases being confused with the classes E-G and thus no longer contribute to the predicted class D.

Class E, which is arguably the most difficult class to correctly assess, shows a high 24.3% of FNs, but a relatively low 3.2% of FPs resp. 1.6% of CFPs. The class could become viable in the future with more training data to improve the model. Class G was problematic due to the high number of FPs (which

Table 3. The production-line evaluation for the *decision* label grouped by the predicted defect classes.

Predicted-defect	A	B	C	D	E	F	G	Total
Accuracy	98.6%	97.3%	100.0%	93.7%	72.5%	99.0%	85.6%	92.0%
FPs	0%	0%	0%	0%	3.2%	0%	14.4%	2.2%
CFPs	0%	0%	0%	0%	1.6%	0%	13.7%	1.8%
Overall rate	6%	6%	11%	10%	17%	41%	9%	100%
Rate of TPs	0%	0%	**11%**	0%	11%	0%	9%	31%
Rate of TNs	**5%**	**5%**	0%	**8%**	3%	**39%**	0%	61%

exclusively relate to confusions with other defect classes) rendering the class unsuitable for automatic decision making.

To assess the potential for optimization in the production-line process, the table also outlines the *Overall Rate* for each defect class, i.e., the rate at which a specific defect occurs during production based on its proportion in the production-line dataset. *Rate of TPs* (i.e., *True Positives*) relates to the ratio of defects that the model correctly classified as *ok*. Although a total of 31% of defects were correctly relabelled, only class C can be deemed reliable, leaving effectively 11% of defects that can be automatically relabelled and thus require no further manual inspection. *Rate of TNs* (i.e., *True Negatives*) relates to the ratio of defects the model correctly confirmed as *nok*. In total 61% of the defects were correctly confirmed, counting the classes deemed reliable the model could give a defect indication to guide manual inspection for 57% of all defects.

5   Conclusion and Future Work

With regards to the objectives formulated in Sect. 3.2, we have shown that it is possible to perform automatic classification of XCT slice images using our CNN model architecture. Using the XCT slice images provided by the defect detection system the model is able to predict a defect class with an accuracy of 93% for our dataset of seven selected defect classes. This assessment could traditionally only be determined through manual inspection at a considerable cost of time. Other than predicting the defect class, the model is also able to reproduce the expert decision and predict whether to keep or discard a production part with an accuracy of 92%. On actual data from the production-line, featuring a different distribution of defect classes, the model still yields an accuracy of 87% for the defect class. The model may not be reliable enough to fully replace manual inspections for all defects, it can however be used to decide for certain reliably predicted defect classes and to obtain defect class indications to guide the XCT operator. The model performs the expert decision reliably for 5 defect classes, which account for 74% of reported defects based on the production-line dataset. We further assessed the rate at which the model can be utilized given those five selected classes. We estimate that the model is able to correctly relabel

11% of reported defects to *ok* and thus significantly relieve the XCT operator. For another 57% of reported defects, the model confirms the *nok* decision and provide a defect class indication to guide the manual inspection.

The greatest challenge lay in the large imbalances between the defect classes in our training dataset, which is due to the rare occurrence of many of these types of defects during production. In combination with the strict quality requirements that do not tolerate any oversight of actual defects, we were still able to show that our model has the potential to optimize the inspection process. For near-term application, we suggest the use of the model as a support tool for the XCT operator to guide the manual decision and produce defect class indications. As more detection records are collected, especially for the under-represented defect classes, the model can be further trained to improve its reliability and extended to predict all of the original 13 defect classes. Fully automatic relabelling in lieu of manual inspections should be delayed to the point, when all defect classes have been integrated into the model. In order to reach a reasonable threshold for the integration of under-represented classes sooner, Generative Adversarial Networks (GANs) [7] might be an important concept to explore on our model. In the meantime, the addition of model-agnostic explanations [16] may further extend the supportive aspect of the model by providing context to the classification, i.e., outlining the supposed defect region in the XCT slice images.

Acknowledgements. This work was supported by the BOOST 4.0 project, which has received funding from the European Union's Horizon 2020 research and innovation program under grant agreement No. 780732 and by the strategic economic and research programme "Innovatives OÖ 2020" of the province of Upper Austria. RISC Software GmbH is a Member of UAR (Upper Austrian Research) Innovation Network.

References

1. Bellens, S., Vandewalle, P., Dewulf, W.: Deep learning based porosity segmentation in X-ray CT measurements of polymer additive manufacturing parts. Procedia CIRP **96**, 336–341 (2021). https://doi.org/10.1016/j.procir.2021.01.157
2. BOOST 4.0 Project Partners: Boost 4.0 - big data for factories. https://boost40.eu/
3. Du, W., Shen, H., Fu, J., Zhang, G., He, Q.: Approaches for improvement of the X-ray image defect detection of automobile casting aluminum parts based on deep learning. NDT E Int. **107** (2019). https://doi.org/10.1016/j.ndteint.2019.102144
4. Fathy, Y., Jaber, M., Brintrup, A.: Learning with imbalanced data in smart manufacturing: a comparative analysis. IEEE Access **9**, 2734–2757 (2021). https://doi.org/10.1109/ACCESS.2020.3047838
5. Ferguson, M., Ak, R., Lee, Y.T., Law, K.H.: Automatic localization of casting defects with convolutional neural networks. In: 2017 IEEE International Conference on Big Data, Boston, MA, USA, 11–14 December 2017, pp. 1726–1735. https://doi.org/10.1109/BigData.2017.8258115
6. Ferguson, M.K., Ronay, A., Lee, Y.T.T., Law, K.H.: Detection and segmentation of manufacturing defects with convolutional neural networks and transfer learning. Smart Sustain. Manuf. Syst **2** (2018). https://doi.org/10.1520/ssms20180033

7. Goodfellow, I.J., et al.: Generative adversarial nets. In: Proceedings of the 27th International Conference on Neural Information Processing Systems - Volume 2, NIPS 2014, pp. 2672–2680. MIT Press (2014)

8. He, K., Zhang, X., Ren, S., Sun, J.: Deep residual learning for image recognition. In: IEEE Conference on Computer Vision and Pattern Recognition, pp. 770–778 (2016). https://doi.org/10.1109/CVPR.2016.90

9. Li, X., Liu, Z., Luo, P., Loy, C.C., Tang, X.: Not all pixels are equal: difficulty-aware semantic segmentation via deep layer cascade. In: IEEE Conference on Computer Vision and Pattern Recognition, pp. 6459–6468 (2017). https://doi.org/10.1109/CVPR.2017.684

10. Lin, J., Yao, Y., Ma, L., Wang, Y.: Detection of a casting defect tracked by deep convolution neural network. Int. J. Adv. Manuf. Technol. **97**, 573–581 (2018). https://doi.org/10.1007/s00170-018-1894-0

11. Marmanis, D., Datcu, M., Esch, T., Stilla, U.: Deep learning earth observation classification using imagenet pretrained networks. IEEE Geosci. Remote Sens. Lett. **13**(1), 105 (2016)

12. Masci, J., Meier, U., Ciresan, D., Schmidhuber, J., Fricout, G.: Steel defect classification with max-pooling convolutional neural networks. In: The 2012 International Joint Conference on Neural Networks (IJCNN), pp. 1–6 (2012). https://doi.org/10.1109/IJCNN.2012.6252468

13. Park, J.K., An, W.H., Kang, D.J.: Convolutional neural network based surface inspection system for non-patterned welding defects. Int. J. Precis. Eng. Manuf. **20**(3), 363–374 (2019)

14. Perez, L., Wang, J.: The effectiveness of data augmentation in image classification using deep learning. CoRR abs/1712.04621 (2017). http://arxiv.org/abs/1712.04621

15. Reiter, M., Gusenbauer, C., Huemer, R., Kastner, J.: At-line X-ray computed tomography of serial parts optimized by numerical simulations. In: International Symposium on Digital Industrial Radiology and Computed Tomography - DIR 2019 (2019). https://www.ndt.net/article/dir2019/papers/Th.2.A.1.pdf

16. Ribeiro, M.T., Singh, S., Guestrin, C.: "Why should I trust you?": explaining the predictions of any classifier. In: Proceedings of the 22nd ACM SIGKDD International Conference on Knowledge Discovery and Data Mining, KDD 2016, pp. 1135–1144. Association for Computing Machinery (2016). https://doi.org/10.1145/2939672.2939778

17. Schlotterbeck, M., et al.: Automated defect detection for fast evaluation of real inline CT scans. Nondestr. Test. Eval. **35**(3), 266–275 (2020). https://doi.org/10.1080/10589759.2020.1785446

18. Simonyan, K., Zisserman, A.: Very deep convolutional networks for large-scale image recognition. arXiv 1409.1556 (2015). http://arxiv.org/abs/1409.1556

19. Staude, A., et al.: Quantification of the capability of micro-CT to detect defects in castings using a new test piece and a voxel-based comparison method. NDT E Int. **44**, 531–536 (2011). https://doi.org/10.1016/j.ndteint.2011.05.006

20. Tan, M., Le, Q.V.: EfficientNet: rethinking model scaling for convolutional neural networks. In: Proceedings of the 36th International Conference on Machine Learning. Proceedings of Machine Learning Research, vol. 97, pp. 6105–6114 (2019)

Cross-Lingual Approaches for Task-Specific Dialogue Act Recognition

Jiří Martínek[1,2]([✉]), Christophe Cerisara[3], Pavel Král[1,2], and Ladislav Lenc[1,2]

[1] Department of Computer Science and Engineering, Faculty of Applied Sciences,
University of West Bohemia, Plzeň, Czech Republic
{jimar,pkral,llenc}@kiv.zcu.cz
[2] NTIS - New Technologies for the Information Society, Faculty of Applied Sciences,
University of West Bohemia, Plzeň, Czech Republic
[3] Université de Lorraine, CNRS, LORIA, 54000 Nancy, France
cerisara@loria.fr

Abstract. In this paper we exploit cross-lingual models to enable dialogue act recognition for specific tasks with a small number of annotations. We design a transfer learning approach for dialogue act recognition and validate it on two different target languages and domains. We compute dialogue turn embeddings with both a CNN and multi-head self-attention model and show that the best results are obtained by combining all sources of transferred information. We further demonstrate that the proposed methods significantly outperform related cross-lingual DA recognition approaches.

Keywords: Dialogue act recognition · Cross-lingual · Transfer learning · BERT · Multi-head self-attention

1 Introduction

Automatic dialogue act (DA) recognition has reached near-human performance on standard corpora, such as the Switchboard Dialogue Act corpus. However, various application domains lead to different types of dialogues: this variability, which is illustrated in the French corpus described in Sect. 5.2, severely impacts the direct application of a model trained on a standard corpus to many other types of application tasks, as shown next. Furthermore, developing DA-recognition models in other languages than English requires the costly annotation of large-enough corpora. We propose investigating cross-lingual transfer learning methods to reduce the amount of annotation required for each new domain and language.

Transfer learning aims to reuse knowledge gained from a large corpus to improve the models trained on a related task with few annotations. We investigate in this work two sources of information from which we transfer knowledge:

© IFIP International Federation for Information Processing 2021
Published by Springer Nature Switzerland AG 2021
I. Maglogiannis et al. (Eds.): AIAI 2021, IFIP AICT 627, pp. 232–242, 2021.
https://doi.org/10.1007/978-3-030-79150-6_19

pre-trained English BERT sentence embeddings and an English corpus annotated with dialogue acts. Two dialogue act recognition tasks are considered: appointment scheduling in German and casual conversations in French. The amount of French annotated dialogue acts is limited to a few hundred samples that may be annotated by one application developer within a few hours. The definition of the dialogue acts are the same in English and German but different in French.

In addition to the relatively large resources available in English, we further assume the availability of an automatic translation system; we will use for this purpose Google's translation. Section 3 describes our transfer learning strategy.

2   Related Work

New approaches in the dialogue act recognition field are mainly evaluated on English datasets. Some methods have also been tested on other languages, such as Spanish (DIHANA corpus [3]), Czech [12], French [2] and German (Verbmobil [11] corpus).

A nice review of the state-of-the-art of the domain is summarised in [17], where the models typically reach 80% of accuracy on standard DA datasets. Nevertheless, the variety of DA labels in datasets is an obstacle for effective multi-lingual and multi-dataset research. Several interesting research efforts have thus emerged to define and exploit generic dialogue acts [14]. However, in practice, the specific requirements of most target tasks prevent a widespread usage of such standards. We rather focus next on specific types of dialogues and task-related dialogue acts.

Transfer learning has been quite a popular approach in deep learning in recent years. Such approaches have proven particularly useful in the computer vision and Natural Language Processing (NLP) domains. For instance, for automated pavement distress detection and classification [10] or for face verification [5]. A well-known transfer learning approach consists in using pre-trained word embeddings, such as Word2vec (W2V) [15], ELMO [16] and BERT [9].

In standard transfer learning, information flows from the source to the target domain (one direction only). A related approach is multi-task learning [6] where information flow across all tasks (usually more than two): information learned in each task may improve other tasks learning.

In the dialogue act recognition domain, Dai et al. [8] fine-tune BERT to classify a single utterance with quite good results, while Wu et al. [19] propose task-oriented dialogue BERT (ToD BERT).

3   Models

3.1   English DA Classifier

Our initial English dialogue act recognition model trained on the English dataset annotated with dialogue acts is a multi-layer perceptron (MLP) with BERT embeddings as inputs. We have tested various topologies for this initial model and chosen this one because of its good performances and fast training times.

Each speaker turn, composed of a variable number of words, is first encoded into a single pre-trained 1024-dimensional sentence embedding vector with BERT Large[1].

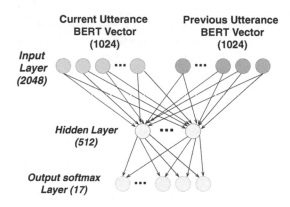

Fig. 1. English MLP model

As shown in Fig. 1, two such vectors are computed, respectively, for the previous, and the current speaker turns and concatenated as an input to the MLP. The MLP outputs 17 tags, which correspond to the dialogue act labels of the Verbmobil-EN corpus. This MLP has been trained on the training part of the Verbmobil-EN corpus.

3.2   Speaker Turn Embeddings

In our MLP model described previously, variable-length sentences are encoded into a unique speaker turn embedding vector with a pre-trained BERT model. We have further used two other models to compute the speaker turn embeddings: a convolutional neural network (CNN) and a multi-head self-attention (MH-SAtt) model.

The CNN model, shown in Fig. 2, is derived from the model of Martinek et al. [13]. It takes as an input a word sequence truncated/padded to 15 words that always include the last two words of the sequence, following [7]. These 15 words are encoded into either random embeddings or W2V vectors. The CNN outputs a 256-dimensional vector for the current speaker turn.

The MH-SAtt model transforms each input random word embedding with the standard scaled dot-product multi-head self-attention module [18][2]. A global

---

[1] from https://github.com/google-research/bert#pre-trained-models – BERT-Large, Uncased (Whole Word Masking): 24-layer, 1024-hidden, 16-heads, 340M parameters.
[2] https://github.com/CyberZHG/keras-multi-head.

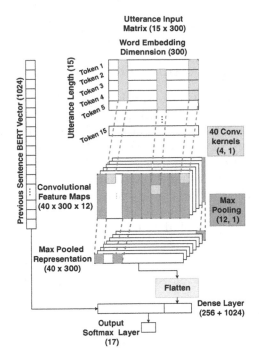

Fig. 2. CNN model for DA recognition

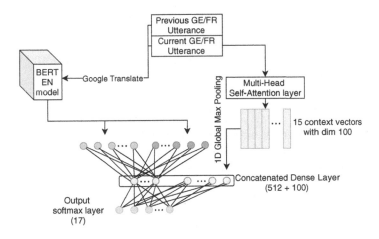

Fig. 3. Multi-head self-attention model

max pooling operation is then applied to compute the speaker turn embedding. Figure 3 shows how this model is used in our experiments.

In all our models, the previous speaker turn is also encoded into a 1024-dimensional vector with BERT and injected into the classification step: this is an easy way to take into account the previous dialogue act without requiring a costly RNN, CRF and/or beam search process.

4   Transfer Learning Approach

Pre-trained BERT is famous for transferring general English lexical information into a large variety of downstream NLP tasks. We exploit them for cross-lingual dialogue act recognition through automatic language translation. Similarly, we evaluate pre-trained word2vec English vectors in this context. We further investigate the option to stack the translated inputs with the original foreign representations in the MH-SAtt model to increase the robustness of the model to translation errors. Then, given a target non-English task with a few hundred annotated samples only, we evaluate the benefit from fine-tuning the English DA classifier on this target small dataset. Our global transfer learning approach thus consists of two phases:

1. **Initial phase**
   The original English model in Fig. 1 is trained on a large corpus annotated with dialogue acts.
2. **Fine-tuning phase**
   - The foreign sentences of the task-specific corpus annotated with dialogues acts are automatically translated into English with Google Translate[3];
   - The final classification layer (in Figs. 1, 2, 3) is replaced by a random layer with the same number of outputs than DAs in the target task;
   - The model parameters are trained for a few epochs on the small target training corpus translated into English, as well as on the original foreign corpus for the MH-Satt model.

The diagram shown in Fig. 4 summarises the two phases for both target tasks and languages that we have used in our experiments.

5   Experiments

In the following experiments, we use two target tasks, one in German and another one in French. Every experiment is run ten times and the results are averaged. The standard deviation is also computed.

5.1   German Task

Our first dialogue task consists in scheduling an appointment in German. Our target corpus is built by randomly sampling 100 utterances from the Verbmobil-GE training corpus with the same dialogue acts distribution as in the complete training corpus, see Table 1. We could have used the full Verbmobil corpus for training, but this would not have represented a realistic situation, where annotated training data for a specific task is usually scarce. However, to better evaluate the quality of our approach, the model trained on this small corpus is tested on the complete (1460 utterances), standard Verbmobil-GE test corpus.

---

[3] Any other translation system may also be used.

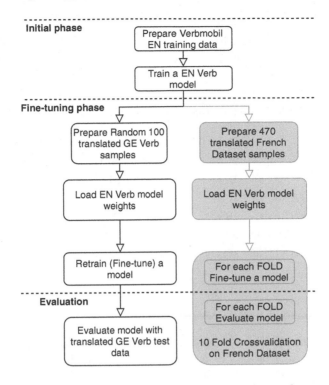

Fig. 4. Transfer learning process for both our experimental target tasks

Table 1. Distribution of DAs in Verbmobil-GE corpus

Label	Occurrence	Label	Occurrence
FEEDBACK	28%	DELIBERATE	3%
SUGGEST	19%	INTRODUCE	2%
INFORM	18%	COMMIT	1%
REQUEST	9%	CLOSE	1%
GREET	4%	POLIT. FORM	1%
BYE	4%	THANK	1%
INIT	4%	DEFER	1%
BACKCHANNEL	3%	OFFER	1%

5.2   French Task

The French tasks consist in manual transcriptions of spoken dialogues recorded by linguists in real-life situations involving volunteer citizens. We manually anno- tate 470 turns from the TCOF corpus [1] with dialogue acts. The types of dia- logue in our 470 turns are very different from the ones found in standard DA corpora. They involve two friends trying to find a suitable gift, three students talking about their courses while chatting with someone else on their smart-phone, and an adult talking with a young girl who is drawing. The dialogue acts distribution is shown in Table 2. This French corpus is freely distributed with a CC BY-NC-SA license[4].

Table 2. Distribution of DAs in the French corpus

Label	Occurrence	Label	Occurrence
INFORM	26%	OPEN ANSWER	7%
AGREE	13%	DISAGREE	5%
BACKCHANNEL	10%	YES ANSWER	5%
Y/N QUESTION	10%	NO ANSWER	5%
OPEN QUESTION	9%	OTHER ANSWERS	1%
PERFORMATIVE	8%	GREETINGS	<1%

5.3   Initial Phase: English Model

The initial English MLP model is trained on the full Verbmobil-EN corpus. The hyper-parameters of this model are tuned on the English corpus: this model is thus trained for 200 epochs with a learning rate of 0.002. Table 3 compares its accuracy when trained either from BERT embeddings or from speaker turn embeddings obtained with the CNN model. The CNN may use either initial random or pre-trained W2V word embeddings. Every experiment is run ten times and the results are averaged.

Table 3. Initial phase – English MLP Model trained on Verbmobil-EN (9599 turns) and tested on Verbmobil-EN (1460 turns). The **Embeddings** column indicates how the word embeddings are initialised.

Model	Embeddings	Epochs	Test Acc	Std. Dev.
MLP	BERT	200	0.734	0.010
CNN	W2V	200	0.704	0.009
CNN	Random	200	0.702	0.008

5.4   Fine-Tuning Phase

Fine-tuning consists in training the last classification layers of the models pre-sented in Sect. 3 on the small foreign corpus. This fine-tuning process thus involves some additional hyper-parameters, such as the learning rate and the

---

[4] https://github.com/cerisara/TCOFDA.

fixed number of epochs, which are tuned on a German development corpus composed of 10,000 utterances randomly sampled from the Verbmobil-GE training corpus. The same hyperparameter values found on this German corpus are also used for the French model[5].

5.5   Baseline Approaches

Three baseline classifiers are shown in the first part of Table 4:

1. **Majority Class Classifier (MC)**: it always predicts the most common DA in the training dataset.
2. **Training from Scratch**: Instead of transferring the model parameters from the initial English MLP model, the parameters (without the embeddings) are randomly initialised in this baseline.
3. **No-Fine-Tuning**: The model parameters are simply transferred from the initial English MLP model, and no further training is done.

5.6   Fine-Tuning Experiments

German Results. Table 4 shows the results of our models on the Verbmobil-GE test set. All these models process only translated English sentences, except for the last MH-SAtt model that further includes the original German words, as shown in Fig. 3.

Table 4. Accuracy on the Test Verbmobil-GE corpus

Model	Embeddings	Epochs	Test Acc	Std. Dev.
Baseline MC		–	0.279	–
From scratch				
CNN	W2V	15	0.410	0.012
MLP	BERT	25	0.468	0.008
No-Fine-tuning				
CNN	W2V	–	0.380	
MLP	BERT	–	0.479	
Fine-tuning				
CNN	W2V	15	0.463	0.008
MLP	BERT	25	0.484	0.025
MH-SAtt	BERT + GE	50	0.502	0.012

With regard to transfer from pre-trained models, BERT is consistently better than W2V. Simply reusing the English models without fine-tuning gives the

---

[5] All hyperparameter values along with the source code are distributed with an open-source license in https://github.com/cerisara/TCOFDA.

worst results, while fine-tuning the English models on the small target corpus systematically improves the results. The best performances are obtained with the MH-SAtt model that combines both BERT pre-trained vectors and fine-tuning transfer learning with the original and translated words sequences.

French Results. We carried out 10-fold cross-validation on the 470 speaker turns of the French corpus. As we do not have enough data to create a development corpus in French, we share the same hyper-parameters as found on the German corpus. Table 5 shows the results of this experiment.

Table 5. French cross-validation experiments

Model	Embeddings	Epochs	Acc	Std. Dev.
Baseline MC		–	0.210	–
From scratch				
CNN	W2V	15	0.403	0.006
MLP	BERT	25	0.421	0.005
Fine-Tuning				
CNN	W2V	15	0.400	0.009
MLP	BERT	25	0.430	0.008
MH-SAtt	BERT + FR	50	0.436	0.007

The relative contributions of the various sources of information and models are similar to the German experiments. However, the differences between the results are much smaller, which is likely due to the fact that the hyper-parameters have not been tuned on French but on German.

5.7   Comparison with Related Work

We compare in Table 6 our proposal with other cross-lingual methods for dialogue act recognition that we are aware of. This related work projects German word embeddings into the English word embeddings space with the canonical correlation analysis method (CCA) [4]. The comparison is done on the German Verbmobil test corpus. Table 6 clearly shows that the proposed methods are significantly better than the previous work. To the best of our knowledge, no other study dealing with cross-lingual dialogue act recognition has been published.

Table 6. Comparison with previous cross-lingual DA recognition on the German Verbmobil test corpus

Methods	Acc
CNN + CCA [13]	0.315
BiLSTM + CCA [13]	0.340
MLP + BERT	0.484
MH-SAtt + BERT + GE	0.502

6 Conclusions

We explore two types of transfer learning for cross-lingual DA recognition: pretrained word embeddings and classifier fine-tuning. Three types of dialogue turn embeddings are computed, based respectively on BERT, CNN and multi-head self-attention. The objective is to leverage large available English resources annotated in dialogue acts to enable DA recognition on a specific target task and language with a limited amount of annotations.

We have validated these approaches on two tasks and languages, German and French, and released a dedicated French DA corpus with real-life dialogues recorded in quite different conditions than the existing standard DA corpora. The best results are obtained when all available sources of information are included, with both the BERT and multi-head self-attention dialogue turn embeddings.

We further demonstrated that the proposed methods significantly outperform cross-lingual DA recognition approaches developed previously.

Acknowledgements. This work has been partly supported by Cross-border Cooperation Program Czech Republic - Free State of Bavaria ETS Objective 2014–2020 (project no. 211), by Grant No. SGS-2019-018 Processing of heterogeneous data and its specialized applications and by GENCI-IDRIS (Grant 2021-AD011011668R1).

References

1. ATILF: Tcof : Traitement de corpus oraux en français (2018). https://hdl.handle.net/11403/tcof/v2, ORTOLANG (Open Resources and TOols for LANGuage) - www.ortolang.fr
2. Barahona, L.M.R., Lorenzo, A., Gardent, C.: Building and exploiting a corpus of dialog interactions between French speaking virtual and human agents. In: The Eighth International Conference on Language Resources and Evaluation (LREC), pp. 1428–1435 (2012)
3. Benedí, J.M., et al.: Design and acquisition of a telephone spontaneous speech dialogue corpus in Spanish: Dihana. In: Fifth International Conference on Language Resources and Evaluation (LREC), pp. 1636–1639 (2006)
4. Brychcín, T.: Linear transformations for cross-lingual semantic textual similarity. Knowl.-Based Syst. **187**, 104819 (2020)

5. Cao, X., Wipf, D., Wen, F., Duan, G., Sun, J.: A practical transfer learning algorithm for face verification. In: Proceedings of the IEEE International Conference on Computer Vision, pp. 3208–3215 (2013)
6. Caruana, R.: Multitask learning. Mach. Learn. **28**(1), 41–75 (1997)
7. Cerisara, C., Král, P., Lenc, L.: On the effects of using word2vec representations in neural networks for dialogue act recognition. Comput. Speech Lang. **47**, 175–193 (2018). https://doi.org/10.1016/j.csl.2017.07.009
8. Dai, Z., Fu, J., Zhu, Q., Cui, H., Qi, Y., et al.: Local contextual attention with hierarchical structure for dialogue act recognition. arXiv preprint arXiv:2003.06044 (2020)
9. Devlin, J., Chang, M.W., Lee, K., Toutanova, K.: BERT: pre-training of deep bidirectional transformers for language understanding. arXiv preprint arXiv:1810.04805 (2018)
10. Gopalakrishnan, K., Khaitan, S.K., Choudhary, A., Agrawal, A.: Deep convolutional neural networks with transfer learning for computer vision-based data-driven pavement distress detection. Constr. Build. Mater. **157**, 322–330 (2017)
11. Jekat, S., Klein, A., Maier, E., Maleck, I., Mast, M., Quantz, J.J.: Dialogue acts in verbmobil. Technical report VM-Report 65, UniversitätHamburg, DFKI GmbH, UniversitätErlangen, and TU Berlin (1995)
12. Král, P., Cerisara, C., Klečková, J.: Combination of classifiers for automatic recognition of dialog acts. In: Interspeech 2005, ISCA, Lisboa, Portugal, pp. 825–828, September 2005
13. Martínek, J., Král, P., Lenc, L., Cerisara, C.: Multi-lingual dialogue act recognition with deep learning methods. In: Interspeech 2019, Graz, Austria, pp. 1463–1467, 15–19 September 2019. https://doi.org/10.21437/Interspeech. 2019-1691
14. Mezza, S., Cervone, A., Stepanov, E., Tortoreto, G., Riccardi, G.: ISO-standard domain-independent dialogue act tagging for conversational agents. In: Proceedings of the 27th International Conference on Computational Linguistics, Santa Fe, New Mexico, USA, pp. 3539–3551. Association for Computational Linguistics, August 2018. https://www.aclweb.org/anthology/C18-1300
15. Mikolov, T., Chen, K., Corrado, G., Dean, J.: Efficient estimation of word representations in vector space. arXiv preprint arXiv:1301.3781 (2013)
16. Peters, M.E., et al.: Deep contextualized word representations. arXiv preprint arXiv:1802.05365 (2018)
17. Ribeiro, E., Ribeiro, R., de Matos, D.M.: A multilingual and multidomain study on dialog act recognition using character-level tokenization. Information **10**(3), 94 (2019)
18. Vaswani, A., et al.: Attention is all you need. In: Advances in Neural Information Processing Systems, pp. 5998–6008 (2017)
19. Wu, C.S., Hoi, S., Socher, R., Xiong, C.: TOD-BERT: pre-trained natural language understanding for task-oriented dialogues. arXiv preprint arXiv:2004.06871 (2020)

Just-in-Time Biomass Yield Estimation with Multi-modal Data and Variable Patch Training Size

Patricia O'Byrne[1]([⊠]) (iD), Patrick Jackman[1] (iD), Damon Berry[1] (iD), Thomas Lee[1], Michael French[2], and Robert J. Ross[1] (iD)

[1] Technological University Dublin, Dublin D07 ADY7, Ireland
patricia.obyrne@tudublin.ie
[2] Tanco Autowrap, Carlow R21 E278, Ireland

Abstract. The just-in-time estimation of farmland traits such as biomass yield can aid considerably in the optimisation of agricultural processes. Data in domains such as precision farming is however notoriously expensive to collect and deep learning driven modelling approaches need to maximise performance but also acknowledge this reality. In this paper we present a study in which a platform was deployed to collect data from a heterogeneous collection of sensor types including visual, NIR, and LiDAR sources to estimate key pastureland traits. In addition to introducing the study itself we address two key research questions. The first of these was the trade off of multi-modal modelling against a more basic image driven methodology, while the second was the investigation of patch size variability in the image processing backbone. This second question relates to the fact that individual images of vegetation and in particular grassland are texturally rich, but can be uniform, enabling subdivision into patches. However, there may be a trade-off between patch-size and number of patches generated. Our modelling used a number of CNN architectural variations built on top of Inception Resnet V2, MobileNet, and shallower custom networks. Using minimum Mean Absolute Percentage Error (MAPE) on the validation set as our metric, we demonstrate strongest performance of 28.23% MAPE on a hybrid model. A deeper dive into our analysis demonstrated that working with fewer but larger patches of data performs as well or better for true deep models – hence requiring the consumption of less resources during training.

Keywords: Deep learning · CNN · Multimodal processing · LiDAR · Patch-size · Biomass · Precision agriculture

1 Introduction

Optimised silage production is a key enabler in allowing milk and beef production levels to continue to grow in the face of the joint challenges of population

© IFIP International Federation for Information Processing 2021
Published by Springer Nature Switzerland AG 2021
I. Maglogiannis et al. (Eds.): AIAI 2021, IFIP AICT 627, pp. 243–255, 2021.
https://doi.org/10.1007/978-3-030-79150-6_20

growth [29] and diminishing resources [19]. While feeding trends vary from nation to nation, grass silage should ideally provide 20% to 30% of an animal's feed in a grass-fed environment[1]. When harvesting for silage, farmers benefit from knowing many different traits in the grassland being harvested. One of these is the biomass yield of their pasture [26]. Any systematic approach that can provide such information accurately and in a just-in-time manner can provide benefit to the silage optimisation process.

Beyond grassland management, food production and agriculture have embraced a wide variety of technological advances in recent years. Both proximal and remote sensing methods are now well recognised as important enablers for precision agriculture [10]. We are now at the point of developing sensor networks that can be applied to day-to-day farming activities. However, leveraging these technologies is not always straightforward, due to the costs involved in collecting datasets for training and the high levels of variability in environmental conditions. Even if we consider the simple application of so-called vegetation indices to biomass [30], we see that correlations between electromagnetic signatures and biomass vary according to plant phenology, ecology and sensing environment [23], rendering simple indices unreliable under diverse real world conditions.

In recent years there has been a trend towards methods that take a wider range of signals into account to overcome the limitations of vegetation indices. Image-based systems for example typically apply deep learning methods from the field of artificial intelligence to take advantage, not only of electromagnetic signatures, but also the true appearance of vegetation [6]. The challenge with Deep Learning driven methods tend to centre on the need to source large volumes of data to minimise bias in modelling. The application of transfer learning [16] to bootstrap model construction can be applied to help reduce training data requirements, but as always, a suitable source dataset is needed and when working beyond raw visible images, suitable source data sets are not always available [9].

Given the technical requirements of developing just-in-time pastureland assessment systems, in this paper we present a new study that has aimed to provide just-in-time robust estimation of biomass for silage production while considering a number of questions related to model optimisation under limited data constraint situations. In particular we explore a number of transfer learning and custom model designs that integrate data from a number of sensor types to estimate biomass yield. We specifically consider the relative impact of adding both LiDAR and NIR (near infrared) data to baseline image data, given that transfer learning from ImageNet driven models is straightforwardly available for RGB image data, but not for multispectral data. Alongside this, as grassland data is heterogeneous by nature, samples can be subdivided into patches to augment the dataset. We consider the impact that subdividing into different patch sizes has on model performance.

---

[1] https://www.teagasc.ie/media/website/publications/2016/Teagasc-Quality-Grass-Silage-Guide.pdf.

In light of more recent worries about the environmental impact of deep learning methods, we also ask what, if anything, we can learn regarding the costs of training and systems optimisation.

2   Related Work

We proceed by first setting out some key background concepts relevant to our study; including the sensor-based estimation of biomass, the application of machine learning based methods to vegetation trait estimation, and issues related to the application of transfer learning in CNNs in overcoming limited training data constraints.

2.1   Remote Sensing of Vegetation

Traditionally, remote methods for estimating vegetation biomass have taken advantage of the relative absorption of different wavelengths of light through simple functions called vegetation indices (VIs). For example, for many decades the Normalized Difference Vegetation Index (NDVI) [18] has been applied to true remote sensing such as satellite data [28], but also hand-held sensing devices [2] and farm machinery mounted equipment [22]. Unfortunately, estimations from VIs such as NDVI are known to be highly subject to a range of conditions. NDVI correlates well to biomass early in the growing season, but saturates as vegetation becomes denser [27] and is influenced by soil exposure, topography, senescent vegetation and atmospheric contaminants [5]. Various modifications of basic vegetation indices have been proposed to overcome limitations; for example, canopy height has been used in conjunction with NDVI to extend its usefulness in dense vegetation [22].

Rather than focusing only on electromagnetic reflectance, more recent state-of-the-art remote sensing systems take advantage of the full visual analysis of vegetation. Such analysis is based on the principle that the texture and shape of a pasture canopy can help identify target characteristics [1]. Images may show droplets of water on the leaves, or evidence of drought, seed heads or leaf size, while canopy height is a strong indicator of biomass, as well as other vegetation traits. One such automated system that was developed to estimate vegetation cover and type, applied Local Binary Patterns (LBPs) to $1\,\mathrm{m} \times 1\,\mathrm{m}$ photos of vegetation [15]. Deep learning has also been used to estimate NDVI from Sentinel satellites, even on a cloudy day [21], while the performance of a deep convolutional neural network (DCNN) was compared to that of conventional models built on feature extraction such as image segmentation, colour comparison of R/G, B/G and 2G-R-B without segmenting images [14]. This reflects a more general trend of applying state-of-the-art data processing methods, such as deep learning, in agriculture [11].

2.2   Deep Learning Architectures for Remote Sensing

In applying deep learning to image-centric precision agriculture data, there are a number of considerations to take into account in architectural choice. Although we might assume the application of CNNs as a backbone for image data channels, the range of CNN architectural variations is vast, as is the range of methods that can be applied to try to mitigate low volumes of training data. Two notable architectures that we build upon here are the Inception Networks [24,25] and MobileNet [7]. The Inception Networks are some of the most widely applied in computer vision at this time. The inception networks aim to overcome issues in scale invariance, through the application of heterogeneous kernel architectures and factorisation of large networks to produce predictors that give accurate estimations, while also incorporating skip-connections to increase network depth.

One challenge with the most sophisticated deep learning based image processing models such as Inception ResNet is that they are typically very large and subsequently require significant computational resources. This can be a challenge for deployment in fields such as agricultural machinery, where we may wish to limit the applied computational resources. Given such challenges, MobileNet, as its name would suggest, was designed for use on mobile devices, specifically for embedded computer vision applications using RGB data [7]. It uses a combination of multiple depth-wise and point-wise convolution layers to replace fewer, more resource-hungry convolutional layers. MobileNet V2 introduced residual connections to reinforce feature maps, and bottleneck layers to compress the data [20].

For problems targeting vegetation, where the cost of image labelling is high, in principle we can apply transfer learning to benefit from training on more generic image training datasets. ImageNet [3] has provided fertile ground for the production of pre-trained architectures for many years. Early examples in the agriculture domain include the use of AlexNet [12] and GoogLeNet [25] to detect plant diseases from a repository of plant health images [8,16]. More recently, another interesting work has shown how a more accurate classification of hyperspectral images for vegetation analysis has been developed using ResNet and transfer learning [9].

As indicated, transfer learning is frequently applied successfully in situations where there is a lack of training samples [4]. One caveat however on the use of transfer learning is that the data needs to be somewhat similar to the data on which the model has been trained; generally, this is straightforward for visual images, though differences of scale between images focused on vegetation and more generic training images such as people, places, and everyday objects can potentially cause challenges. Moreover, for many vegetation analysis tasks, such as our own, where multi-spectral data is to be used, there is a lack of pre-trained weights across different spectral bands. The result of this is that transfer learning cannot be applied straightforwardly in such cases without information loss.

3   Data Collection

Our analysis, presented later, has been constructed around a study we conducted to estimate grassland traits for a just-in-time estimation task. This study required a series of field and lab measurements, in order to build a dataset for pastureland traits and sensor data prior to silage production. This study built on an earlier pilot study presented previously [17], but was considerably more varied in terms of source data collections and the range and resolution of sensors deployed.

Data was collected using proximal sensors on a bespoke data collection trolley. Sensors included a four-channel JAI AD-130 GE camera to take RGB and NIR images, and a LiDAR-Lite v3HP device to record canopy height. Full details of the procedure used to perform data collection were presented in our previous study – including the procedure for data collection and labelling. In short however, a $50\,\mathrm{cm^2}$ area was harvested and later weighted in lab conditions to determine biomass yield (Kg/Ha). Over 300 samples were collected from multiple locations around Ireland over 25 collection events during the growing season of 2019.

To prepare for modelling, a series of pre-processing steps were applied to our data to account for the relatively low data volumes for deep learning. The method we apply is similar to that used by Kubach et al. [13] in the field of histopathology. Firstly, a variant of 5-fold cross validation was applied. Specifically, the set of images was subdivided into five sets, labelled 1 to 5. These sets were recombined into five $4 + 1$ datasets, in each case holding out one of the sets for validation and using the remaining four for training. Each sample had been recorded with image size of 964×1296 pixels for the RGB image and 966×1296 pixels for the NIR image. As the images are of grass, they are reasonably uniform in presentation. Because of this, we opted to subdivide the image data to augment the dataset, copying height and biomass values from the full image. Two approaches were taken. The first approach split each sample image into 156×156 pixel patches, giving a dataset of almost 10,000 patches. We named this dataset Small Patch, or SP. The second approach split the samples into 240×240 pixels, giving around 5,000 patches. This dataset is named Large Patch or LP. There are a lot more patches in SP than there are in LP, but there is not as much information in a given patch.

Every patch had an RGB image, an NIR image, a height scalar (cm) and a biomass scalar (Kg/Ha). As we see in the modelling later, whilst biomass was always the target, and RGB data was always used, the NIR data and height data were used in specific model variants to explore the relative advantage provided by these data channels to augment the central image information.

4   Modelling

In order to systematically investigate the relative merits of different architectural variations under our limited data constraint, we investigated a number of different models that varied in terms of backbone architecture, use of pre-training, data source modalities and patch sizes. In the following we summarise our model choices and their rationale.

4.1   Image Processing Backbone

Each of our models assume an image processing backbone for RGB image data. For this image processing backbone we have applied three variants which also differed in terms of whether transfer learning was applied. Our first variant is a shallow custom CNN (*Shallow*) which feeds the RGB image data into two 2D consecutive convolution layers using a 3×3 kernel, generating 24 feature maps, each with a relu activation function. 2×2 max pooling is then applied. This pattern is repeated, this time using 48 feature maps for both convolutional layers, before a final pooling layer. The output is flattened and fed into fully connected layers before a final target layer.

For the image processing backbone we also made use of both the Inception Renset V2 and MobileNet architectures. Inception Resnet V2 is well regarded for high performance. One factor of note here is the Inception Network's ability to mitigate scale variance in input images. However Inception Networks are expensive to train and smaller networks can be useful in domains such as our own. Therefore we also make use of the MobileNet architecture as a third candidate. Our overall network architecture based on both these backbones is similar to that used in the shallow network. An input is passed through the backbone before being flattened and fed through fully connected layers and finally to an output layer.

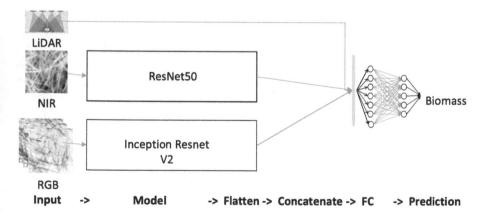

Fig. 1. Hybrid NIR I L model. RGB and NIR image data are fed through CNN variants with outputs concatenated along with the scalar LiDAR information. The concatenated output is then fed through fully connected layers.

Inception ResNet and MobileNet can of course be trained from scratch, but can also be used within a transfer learning methodology where pre-trained weights are loaded and then fine-tuned within the target application. For our image processing backbone we applied both transfer learning and 'from scratch' training methodologies. Models using ImageNet pre-trained weights are indexed with an 'I' for ImageNet. To facilitate the use of pre-trained weights, our input image, specifically input patches, were re-scaled to the required input image dimensions for both Inception Resnet and MobileNet, namely 299×299 and 224×224 pixels respectively.

4.2 Multi-spectral and Multi-sensor Analysis

Our second batches of analyses use a similar structure to the processing of visual data, but also introduce elements to incorporate NIR information into the processing backbone. For the shallow model we directly add a fourth channel to the visual input pipeline and 32 and 64 resultant image maps; this model is known as *Shallow NIR*. This four channel input was also used in one of the Inception ResNet models that trained from scratch *IncResNet NIR*. As ImageNet weights are trained for RGB data, we devised a further model design, using IncResNet with ImageNet weights on the RGB data and a parallel CNN architecture which focused on processing the NIR image before concatenating the results of that analysis to the output of the backbone image architecture. The NIR component was based on a ResNet-50 architecture. We refer to this integrated model as a 'Hybrid' model since it is neither strictly ResNet nor Inception ResNet.

Finally, we also introduce model variants that made use of LiDAR scalar data. Within an architecture the LiDAR distance estimates to the canopy were concatenated with the outputs of flattened CNN outputs before the concatenated vector was fed through fully connected layers. Models which made use of the LiDAR data have the suffix 'L' affixed. To illustrate this approach, Fig. 1 depicts the *Hybrid NIR I L* model. Here RGB data is fed into the pre-trained Inception ResNet V2 and NIR data is fed into ResNet50. The output of both is flattened and concatenated with LiDAR data, before going through the fully connected layers. Both Inception ResNet and ResNet50 use pre-trained ImageNet weights.

4.3 Influence of Patch Size

As described earlier, our data was pre-processed into two different size variants. One set, small patches (SP) was a dataset of ~10,000 patches; each of size 156×156 pixels. The other set, large patches (LP), was a dataset of of ~5,000 patches each of 240×240 pixels. Each of our models above were trained and tested against both the SP and LP data.

4.4 Training

In summary, ten models, cross-validated using 5-fold validation were trained and tested for each dataset. Two models used a shallow CNN, one with and one without NIR data. Four included Inception Resnet, three included MobileNet and the final one is a hybrid model that included both ResNet 50 and Inception ResNet. A full list is provided in Table 1. Where NIR data was used, the suffix NIR is shown. Where height data was used, the suffix L (for LiDAR) is shown. Where ImageNet weights were used to pre-train the model, the suffix I is shown.

Table 1. Model architecture

Model	Includes	NIR	LiDAR	Weights
Shallow				
IncResNet	Inception ResNet			
IncResNet I	Inception ResNet			Y
MobileNet	MobileNet			
MobileNet I	MobileNet			Y
Shallow NIR		Y		
IncResNet NIR	Inception ResNet	Y		
IncResNet I L	Inception ResNet		Y	Y
MobileNet I L	MobileNet		Y	Y
Hybrid NIR I L	Inception ResNet and ResNet50	Y	Y	Y

All models were trained with a mean square error loss function and the Adam optimizer. Our metric for analysis is the Mean Absolute Percentage Error (MAPE). All models were trained for 300 epochs; early stopping was not applied in this case. All models were implemented using the Keras wrapper to Tensorflow. Training runs were carried out across two hardware platforms, one with a single Nvidia K40 GPU (A PowerEdge R730 with two 4-core Intel Xeon Processors

Table 2. Minimum mean absolute percentage error values on validation data for each model variant for both large and small patch datasets. 'NIR' : NIR channel, 'I' : ImageNet pretraining, 'L': LiDAR scalars.

Model	Small	Large
Shallow	60.70%	62.84%
IncResNet	39.57%	39.42%
IncResNet I	37.55%	35.84%
MobileNet	41.26%	44.64%
MobileNet I	36.71%	33.31%
Shallow NIR	51.84%	57.02%
IncResNet NIR	41.44%	48.30%
IncResNet I L	29.60%	28.56%
MobileNet I L	30.93%	30.24%
Hybrid NIR I L	28.23%	31.11%

@ 2.8 GHz, 512 GB RAM) and a higher-powered machine (Dell Dimension T5810 Tower with two 4-core Intel Xeon Processor @ 2.8 GHz, 4 GB RAM, a single RTX 2080 GPU).

5   Results and Discussion

Table 2 presents minimum Mean Absolute Percentage Error values for each model on a given patch size averaged over five runs. Referring to these results, the improvement between the shallow CNNs and the deeper Inception and MobileNet based networks is very evident. This in itself should not be surprising, but it does emphasise the need for relatively deep network architectures in IOT domains such as precision farming, despite the relative cost of needing more sophisticated hardware devices. In terms of the use of the deeper baseline models, the use of pre-trained ImageNet weights (i.e. those with a suffix 'I') is notable.

With respect to the incorporation of NIR and LiDAR data, the results are more mixed. The use of NIR data on the Shallow CNN improved performance in both patch size cases, but it proved to be an inhibitor when used with IncResNet. The additional use of NIR data with the IncResNet model did not improve performance and in fact, this poor performance was the impetus for developing the hybrid model, as with the hybrid model, both NIR and RGB images could be supplemented by pre-trained weights. Anywhere that LiDAR data was used, performance improved substantially.

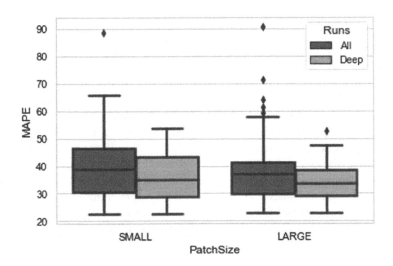

Fig. 2. Distribution of minimum MAPE over all runs and deep runs

As mentioned, in addition to enhancing model performance, we also wished to minimize resources. Therefore we also need to look at trade-offs between model performance and efficiency. As can be seen, the best performing model, with a minimum MAPE of 28.23% was the *Hybrid NIR I L* on the small patch data. This is not surprising, as this model was the largest and most resource intensive. It made full use of all of the data provided. However, the five folds ran for an average of almost 23 h on our higher spec machine. The next best performer was *IncResNet I L* on the large patch data with an average minimum MAPE of 28.58%. The average runtime over the five runs of this model, on the same machine, was 8 h. Whilst the difference in performance is very small, it is worth noting that the deeper model using extra NIR data and with double the number of patches does not seem to perform significantly better than the more economical one. Another question we wish to ask is whether there was a significant difference in outcome between a large number of small patches or a smaller number of large patches given that such variation is possible with our dataset type. To test this we applied a t-test across all runs, split into SP and LP groups. In all, there were 50 runs, 5 for each model on the small patch (SP) data and 5 for each model on the large patch (LP) data. The t-test on minimum MAPE over all runs showed 0.78, with a p-value of 0.439, suggesting that there was in fact no difference between the use of the SP and LP datasets. The distribution of MAPE values is shown in Fig. 2 as All Runs. Note that both small and large patch results have outliers at around 90%. However, the shallow CNN results gave averages between 51.84% and 62.84% and can be thought of as more greedy for samples as they have no prior knowledge to build upon. If we repeat our analysis with *Shallow* and *Shallow NIR* models omitted, the results change considerably. The distribution of values for the deep runs are also shown in Fig. 2, this time as Deep Runs. On just the 40 deeper runs, the mean is 35.66 for SP and 33.71 for LP, with a t-test of 2.55 and p-value = 0.016.

Our interpretation overall is that choice of patch size matters, but in complex ways. For networks trained from scratch there is advantage in having a large number of patches available to progress training quickly, given that there is no pre-trained knowledge to build upon. However, when using pre-trained networks, this advantage disappears. In fact in many cases larger samples, though fewer in number, perform as well as, if not better than a larger number of small samples. This suggests the pre-trained networks are better able to take advantage of the information present in the larger images. From an environmental perspective we point out that there is a training cycle advantage here to be noted. Training with fewer larger inputs will naturally result in fewer training batches and hence an energy/cost saving relative to training with a larger number of small batches. In both cases the potential for over-fitting the data remains, but here the focus on the validation rather than training metrics on a suitably split dataset help to minimise this potential.

6 Conclusion

In this paper we have presented an overview of a data collection platform for the assessment of biomass in a precision farming context. Our modelling approach has built on previous findings based on the use of vegetation indices and image processing. Whilst traditionally, NIR data has been considered an essential ingredient in predicting biomass, in our analyses with deeper models it has been eclipsed by the use of RGB data using pre-trained ImageNet weights, supplemented by LiDAR data. When augmenting the dataset by subsetting image samples, we found that running a model on large patch data using just RGB data and LiDAR took fewer resources with negligible performance loss.

Acknowledgements. The authors wish to thank Enterprise Ireland and Tanco Autowrap Ltd. for the their support for this paper under Innovation Partnership Project IP2018-0728 which is co-funded by the European Regional Development Fund.

References

1. Abadi, M., Capelle-Laizé, A.-S., Khoudeir, M., Combes, D., Carré, S.: Grassland species characterization for plant family discrimination by image processing. In: Elmoataz, A., Lezoray, O., Nouboud, F., Mammass, D., Meunier, J. (eds.) ICISP 2010. LNCS, vol. 6134, pp. 173–181. Springer, Heidelberg (2010). https://doi.org/10.1007/978-3-642-13681-8_21

2. Abičić, I., Lalić, A., Galić, V., Mlinarić, S., Begović, L.: Application of biomass sensor in the winter barley selection. Zbornik radova 54. Hrvatskog i 14. međnarodnog simpozija agronoma, p. 179 (Feb 2019). https://doi.org/10.1007/978-3-642-13681-8-21. https://www.bib.irb.hr/987036?rad=987036

3. Deng, J., Dong, W., Socher, R., Li, L.J., Li, K., Fei-Fei, L.: ImageNet: a large-scale hierarchical image database. In: 2009 IEEE Conference on Computer Vision and Pattern Recognition, pp. 248–255. IEEE, Miami (2009). https://doi.org/10.1109/CVPR.2009.5206848. https://ieeexplore.ieee.org/document/5206848/

4. Ferreira, C., et al.: Classification of breast cancer histology images through transfer learning using a pre-trained inception Resnet V2. Lecture Notes in Computer Science (including subseries Lecture Notes in Artificial Intelligence and Lecture Notes in Bioinformatics) 10882 LNCS, pp. 763–770 (2018). https://doi.org/10.1007/978-3-319-93000-8-86

5. Garroutte, E.L., Hansen, A.J., Lawrence, R.L.: Using NDVI and EVI to map spatiotemporal variation in the biomass and quality of forage for migratory Elk in the greater yellowstone ecosystem. Remote Sens. 8(5), 404 (2016). https://doi.org/10.3390/rs8050404. http://www.mdpi.com/2072-4292/8/5/404

6. Halstead, M., McCool, C., Denman, S., Perez, T., Fookes, C.: Fruit quantity and ripeness estimation using a robotic vision system. IEEE Robot. Autom. Lett. 3(4), 2995–3002 (2018). https://doi.org/10.1109/LRA.2018.2849514. Conference Name: IEEE Robotics and Automation Letters

7. Howard, A.G., et al.: MobileNets efficient convolutional neural networks for mobile vision applications. arXiv:1704.04861 [cs] (2017). http://arxiv.org/abs/1704.04861. arXiv: 1704.04861

8. Hughes, D.P., Salathe, M.: An open access repository of images on plant health to enable the development of mobile disease diagnostics. arXiv:1511.08060 [cs] (2015). http://arxiv.org/abs/1511.08060. arXiv: 1511.08060

9. Jiang, Y., Li, Y., Zhang, H.: Hyperspectral image classification based on 3-D separable ResNet and transfer learning. In: IEEE Geoscience and Remote Sensing Letters, pp. 1–5 (2019). https://doi.org/10.1109/LGRS.2019.2913011

10. Jiménez, J.d.l.C., Leiva, L., Cardoso, J.A., French, A.N., Thorp, K.R.: Proximal sensing of Urochloa grasses increases selection accuracy. Crop Pasture Sci. **71**(4), 401–409. CSIRO PUBLISHING (2020). https://doi.org/10.1071/CP19324. https://www.publish.csiro.au/cp/CP19324
11. Kamilaris, A., Prenafeta-Boldú, F.X.: Deep learning in agriculture: a survey. Comput. Electron. Agric. **147**, 70–90 (2018). https://doi.org/10.1016/j.compag.2018.02.016. https://linkinghub.elsevier.com/retrieve/pii/S0168169917308803
12. Krizhevsky, A., Sutskever, I., Hinton, G.E.: ImageNet classification with deep convolutional neural networks. Commun. ACM. **60**(6), 84–90 (2017). https://doi.org/10.1145/3065386. http://dl.acm.org/citation.cfm?doid=3098997.3065386
13. Kubach, J., et al.: Same same but different: a Web-based deep learning application revealed classifying features for the histopathologic distinction of cortical malformations. Epilepsia **61**(3), 421–432 (2020). https://doi.org/10.1111/epi.16447.
14. Ma, L., Liu, Y., Zhang, X., Ye, Y., Yin, G., Johnson, B.A.: Deep learning in remote sensing applications: a meta-analysis and review. ISPRS J. Photogrammetry Remote Sens. **152**, 166–177 (2019). https://doi.org/10.1016/j.isprsjprs.2019.04.015. http://www.sciencedirect.com/science/article/pii/S0924271619301108
15. McCool, C., Beattie, J., Milford, M., Bakker, J.D., Moore, J.L., Firn, J.: Automating analysis of vegetation with computer vision: cover estimates and classification. Ecol. Evol. **8**(12), 6005–6015 (2018). https://doi.org/10.1002/ece3.4135.
16. Mohanty, S.P., Hughes, D.P., Salathé, M.: Using deep learning for image-based plant disease detection. Front. Plant Sci. **7**, 1419 (2016). https://doi.org/10.3389/fpls.2016.01419.
17. O'Byrne, P., Jackman, P., Berry, D., Lee, T., French, M., Ross, R.J.: Transfer learning performance for remote pastureland trait estimation in real-time farm monitoring. In: IGARSS IEEE International Geoscience and Remote Sensing Symposium. Brussels, Belgium (2021)
18. Rouse, Jr., J.W., Haas, R.H., Schell, J.A., Deering, D.W.: Monitoring vegetation systems in the great plains with ERTS. NASA Special Publication **351**, 309 (1974). https://ntrs.nasa.gov/archive/nasa/casi.ntrs.nasa.gov/19740022614.pdf
19. Sadhukhan, J., et al.: Perspectives on "game changer" global challenges for sustainable 21st century: plant-based diet, unavoidable food waste biorefining, and circular economy. Sustain. **12**(5), 1976 (2020). https://doi.org/10.3390/su12051976. https://www.mdpi.com/2071-1050/12/5/1976
20. Sandler, M., Howard, A., Zhu, M., Zhmoginov, A., Chen, L.C.: Mobilenetv2 inverted residuals and linear bottlenecks. In: Proceedings of the IEEE Conference on Computer Vision and Pattern Recognition, pp. 4510–4520. IEEE (2018)
21. Scarpa, G., Gargiulo, M., Mazza, A., Gaetano, R.: A CNN-based fusion method for feature extraction from sentinel data. Remote Sens. **10**(2), 236 (2018)
22. Schaefer, M.T., Lamb, D.W.: A combination of plant NDVI and LiDAR measurements improve the estimation of pasture biomass in tall fescue (Festuca arundinacea var. Fletcher). Remote Sens. **8**(2), 109 (2016). https://doi.org/10.3390/rs8020109. http://www.mdpi.com/2072-4292/8/2/109
23. Sims, D.A., Gamon, J.A.: Relationships between leaf pigment content and spectral reflectance across a wide range of species, leaf structures and developmental stages. Remote Sens. Environ. **81**(2–3), 337–354 (2002). https://doi.org/10.1016/S0034-4257(02)00010-X. http://linkinghub.elsevier.com/retrieve/pii/S003442570200010X
24. Szegedy, C., Ioffe, S., Vanhoucke, V., Alemi, A.A.: Inception-v4, inception-resnet and the impact of residual connections on learning. In: Thirty-First AAAI Conference on Artificial Intelligence (2017)

25. Szegedy, C., et al.: Going deeper with convolutions. In: 2015 IEEE Conference on Computer Vision and Pattern Recognition (CVPR), pp. 1–9. IEEE, Boston (2015). https://doi.org/10.1109/CVPR.2015.7298594. http://ieeexplore.ieee.org/document/7298594/

26. Tan, A.E., Richards, S., Sarrabezolles, L., Platt, I., Woodhead, I.: Proximal soil moisture sensing of dairy pasture. In: 2014 IEEE Conference on Antenna Measurements Applications (CAMA), pp. 1–4 (2014). https://doi.org/10.1109/CAMA.2014.7003402

27. Tanaka, S., Kawamura, K., Maki, M., Muramoto, Y., Yoshida, K., Akiyama, T.: Spectral index for quantifying leaf area index of winter wheat by field hyperspectral measurements: a case study in Gifu Prefecture. Central Japan. Remote Sens. 7(5), 5329–5346 (2015). https://doi.org/10.3390/rs70505329. https://www.mdpi.com/2072-4292/7/5/5329

28. Townshend, J.R.G., Justice, C.O.: Selecting the spatial resolution of satellite sensors required for global monitoring of land transformations. Int. J. Remote Sens. 9(2), 187–236 (1988). https://doi.org/10.1080/01431168808954847

29. UN: World Population Prospects The 2015 revision key findings and advance tables. Technical Report ESA/P/WP.241, United Nations, Department of Economic and Social Affairs, Population Division, New York City (2015). https://esa.un.org/unpd/wpp/publications/files/key_findings_wpp_2015.pdf

30. Xue, J., Su, B.: Significant remote sensing vegetation indices: a review of developments and applications. J. Sens. (2017). https://doi.org/10.1155/2017/1353691

Robustness Testing of AI Systems: A Case Study for Traffic Sign Recognition

Christian Berghoff[1]([✉]), Pavol Bielik[2], Matthias Neu[1], Petar Tsankov[2],
and Arndt von Twickel[1]

[1] Federal Office for Information Security, Bonn, Germany
christian.berghoff@bsi.bund.de
[2] LatticeFlow, Zurich, Switzerland

Abstract. In the last years, AI systems, in particular neural networks, have seen a tremendous increase in performance, and they are now used in a broad range of applications. Unlike classical symbolic AI systems, neural networks are trained using large data sets and their inner structure containing possibly billions of parameters does not lend itself to human interpretation. As a consequence, it is so far not feasible to provide broad guarantees for the correct behaviour of neural networks during operation if they process input data that significantly differ from those seen during training. However, many applications of AI systems are security- or safety-critical, and hence require obtaining statements on the robustness of the systems when facing unexpected events, whether they occur naturally or are induced by an attacker in a targeted way. As a step towards developing robust AI systems for such applications, this paper presents how the robustness of AI systems can be practically examined and which methods and metrics can be used to do so. The robustness testing methodology is described and analysed for the example use case of traffic sign recognition in autonomous driving.

Keywords: Neural networks · Robustness · Autonomous driving

1 Introduction

AI systems based on neural networks have tremendously increased their performance over the course of the last years and are now used in a plethora of very diverse areas. The improved performance is in particular based on a strong increase in available computing power and data, but also on theoretic advances in the area of AI in general and in the design of the networks in particular. Current applications of neural networks range from predictions based on structured data to natural language processing and computer vision tasks. In the latter domain, AI systems are for instance used in biometrics for identifying people, and as an important building block of (partially) autonomous driving for processing and analysing sensor data.

© IFIP International Federation for Information Processing 2021
Published by Springer Nature Switzerland AG 2021
I. Maglogiannis et al. (Eds.): AIAI 2021, IFIP AICT 627, pp. 256–267, 2021.
https://doi.org/10.1007/978-3-030-79150-6_21

However, unlike the classical systems of symbolic AI, neural networks can, in most cases, not be manually developed by experts, but are instead trained on the basis of large data sets so as to provide the desired functionality. As a result of this training procedure, several problems arise when evaluating the behaviour of AI systems after they have been deployed to live operation. On the one hand, the systems are strongly dependent on the quality and representativeness of training data, whose amount is necessarily limited and which, in most realistic application scenarios, cannot cover all possible inputs [2]. Furthermore, it is becoming increasingly evident that even if we could easily obtain much larger data sets, this alone will not be sufficient to ensure the safe operation of these models [7,12].

As a result, significant effort has been recently devoted to developing techniques capable of providing formal robustness guarantees [11,14,15,19]. Such guarantees are of paramount importance, especially when considering use cases where severe damages may potentially arise. As an example, malfunction of an AI system used in autonomous driving can lead to significant material loss and in extreme cases to fatalities. Unfortunately, such techniques are currently not applicable to state-of-the-art computer vision models due to their limited scalability and the limited type of robustness properties they support.

This article focuses on the complementary approach of developing a methodology for testing the robustness of AI systems. This allows the developers of the AI systems to assess the robustness of any state-of-the-art system in a principled way and to identify failure modes that need to be explored in more detail and remedied before the system can be deployed. While this empirical approach cannot provide absolute guarantees, the amount of robustness testing carried out can be adjusted to achieve the required confidence level about the model correctness. It allows systematically taking into account prior human knowledge by defining task-specific robustness properties, and thus aids in making the development of robust neural networks more efficient. In what follows, we will briefly describe the main components of our work and instantiate the approach to the concrete use case of traffic sign recognition.

2   Related Work

The robustness of AI systems has been extensively studied in the literature, but the large majority of research has focused on their robustness to attacks specially designed to break the system, an area commonly referred to as adversarial machine learning (AML). Starting with the first publication [21] applying adversarial attacks (more generally known as evasion attacks years in advance [6]) to neural networks, many approaches to mitigating the vulnerability of neural networks to these attacks have been developed and many of them have been broken subsequently [4]. Another similar, albeit somewhat less popular subject of research are poisoning attacks [4]. One common feature of research in AML is the lack of a standardised and agreed-upon framework for evaluating robustness, although some progress has been made towards this end [5].

When considering research on the robustness of AI systems to perturbations that may occur naturally during operation and should thus be much easier to cope with than malicious attacks, results are much more scarce. Some publications deal with the robustness to natural perturbations and propose measures for increasing it [16–18], but they do not set out to perform a fine-grained and systematic assessment of the phenomenon. Probably the work most closely related to ours is [22,23]. Similar to our work, the authors define a set of robustness properties and assess the model robustness against them. However, while the main goal of their work is to introduce a new benchmark, the goal of our work is a thorough assessment of state-of-the-art models. As a result, (i) we assess the robustness of significantly better models that achieve 99% standard accuracy (compared to models with at most 90% accuracy used in [23]), (ii) we show the need of considering robustness properties jointly, rather than in isolation, and (iii) we focus on an iterative methodology to assess and improve model robustness (which includes eliciting new properties and discovering model failure modes), rather than proposing a fixed data set.

One line of work that can yield results for this research question is that of formal verification [11,14,15,19]. The main limitations of formal verification are that the methods developed so far do not scale to large neural networks used in practice and that the type of robustness properties that can be efficiently encoded is limited. For example, the majority of the current works consider only norm-constrained pixel perturbations, and verifying even simple geometric transformations such as rotations is highly non-trivial [1]. Further, formal verification approaches suffer from the issue of incomplete specification, since the number of robustness properties they can encode is limited (mostly pixel perturbations). As a result, one has to be careful when interpreting their results and make sure not to incur a false sense of security by performing a thorough assessment of a wide range of the robustness properties, not only a subset of those for which formal verification can provide strong guarantees.

3   Approach

This section presents details about our case study on the robustness testing of traffic sign classifiers. Figure 1 provides an overview of the approach. Robustness testing is performed on a neural network based on a test data set and a specification of certain properties. A metric is used to compute the robustness scores. Apart from identifying common failure modes of the model, the results can be used to understand how to enhance the data set and to define additional custom properties, which improve both the neural network and the testing process. More detailed information on the individual components for the case study on traffic sign classifiers is described in Sect. 3.2–3.4. The general methodology depicted in provides an overview of the Fig. 1 can be applied to other use cases by exchanging and adjusting the components in a suitable way.

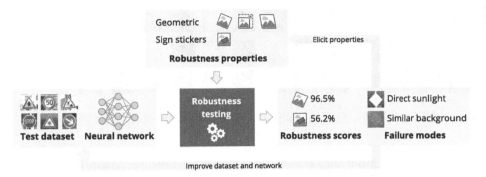

Fig. 1. Robustness assessment of neural networks. The testing approach takes as input a neural network and its test data set, along with robustness properties that capture important environmental conditions (e.g., camera position, sign stickers), and assesses the neural network against these together with its common failure modes.

3.1 Models

The following models, which were trained by the authors, were used for the robustness testing:

- The first neural network, called pre-trained, has 99.0% accuracy. It uses the pre-trained Inception-v3 model [20], which is trained on the ImageNet data set [8] and fine-tuned for the GTSRB data set [13].
- The second one, called self-trained, has 97.4% accuracy. It uses an architecture based on Inception-v3 but with reduced size and without pre-training.

Both networks were trained on the GTSRB data set with a data augmentation policy that applies the following random transformations: random cropping of a portion of the original image with a side length between 0.6 and 1.0 of its original length, rotation by an angle within −15 and +15°, colour changes – brightness, contrast, saturation, and hue – by a factor of up to 0.1, and random change to a gray-scale format with a probability of 0.1. The transformed images are then scaled to the neural networks' expected resolution – 32 × 32 pixels for the self-trained network and 299 × 299 pixels for the pre-trained network.

3.2 Data Set

We use the German Traffic Sign Recognition Benchmark data set (GTSRB) [13], as illustrated in Fig. 2. This data set consists of 39,209 colour images used for training and 12,630 images for testing, each assigned to one of 43 classes. The data set images have different resolutions, with height and width ranging between 25–266 and 25–232 pixels, respectively.

3.3 Robustness Properties

The robustness properties used were chosen according to the ambient conditions of the use case. Traffic sign recognition, and autonomous driving in particular, is

Fig. 2. Example traffic signs drawn from the GTSRB data set [13], one for each class.

a very challenging but also relevant use case in this respect. Since autonomous driving technologies are deployed in the real world and on the roads, ambient conditions can change dramatically depending on the time of day, season or weather. Traffic signs may also to some extent be rotated, occluded and damaged. The sensors used to capture images of the traffic signs may themselves be degraded from long use, damaged or soiled, and the quality of the images captured can strongly vary depending on the specific lighting conditions. This situation is in (stark) contrast to other sensitive use cases such as medical image classification or biometrics used in border control, where ambient conditions can be standardised to a (much) larger extent, and the conditions after deployment can be made reasonably close to the ones considered during training.

The following list provides a brief overview of the robustness properties used. For the complete list of properties along with the used robustness bounds, we refer the reader to our detailed technical report [3].

- **Image noise** includes Gaussian noise, uniform noise and impulse noise, each of them modelling different deviations from optimal conditions in image capture or pre-processing.
- **Pixel perturbations** define the robustness over individual pixels, each of which is allowed to change independently from other pixels subject to a total perturbation budget measured in the L_0 or L_∞ norm. The L_0 norm allows modifying a limited amount of pixels to any extent, while the L_∞ norm allows changing all pixels by less than a certain threshold.
- **Geometric transformations** model different orientations or positions of the traffic signs as well as faults in image acquisition and pre-processing. The perturbations considered are rotation, translation, scaling, shearing, blurring, sharpening and flipping (flipping was only considered on images whose class was not changed by applying it).
- **Colour transformations** model changes in lighting conditions or colour post-processing performed on the images. The colour transformations considered are brightness, contrast, saturation, hue, gray-scale and colour-depth.

3.4   Metric

The metric used to assess the robustness of a model to a specified property is the robustness score, defined as the fraction of robust samples in the data set. A sample is called robust to a given property if the network produces the correct

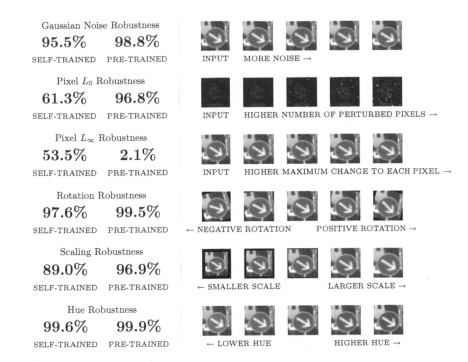

Fig. 3. Overview of the models' robustness to different transformations.

label for all transformations captured by the property. For example, suppose the model achieves 86.5% robustness to rotations up to 15°. This indicates that for 13.5% of the input samples, a rotation of the original image within 15° was found which causes the model to predict the wrong label. Robustness is defined only over input images for which the model already predicts the correct label as all incorrect inputs are trivially non-robust.

4   Results

This section provides a summary of the results obtained using the data set, models, robustness properties and metric from Sect. 3. For comprehensive results, as well as exact definitions of the tested properties, the reader is referred to [3].

4.1   Basic Robustness Tests

Figure 3 shows the robustness of the models with respect to the robustness properties as outlined in Sect. 3.3. Each part of Fig. 3 is organised as follows: The robustness score of both the self-trained and pre-trained model to the respective property is given, and the result of applying different intensities of the property on the original image is provided to show the visual impact for easy

Fig. 4. Robustness comparison of the basic (top) and adaptive brightness (bottom). Basic brightness applies the same transformation to the whole image, whereas adaptive brightness allows different transformations for different parts of the image.

Fig. 5. Task-specific property that inserts a single sticker of varying position, size and orientation on the traffic sign.

human inspection. Figure 3 shows that the robustness scores significantly differ, both between models and properties. Whereas both models are relatively robust (score $\geq 93.9\%$) to Gaussian noise, rotations and colour transformations such as changes in brightness (Fig. 4) and hue, the robustness of the self-trained model to rescaling the input is lower and its robustness to pixel L_0 perturbations even much lower, with more than one-third of the inputs being non-robust. Of the properties selected for Fig. 3, the robustness to pixel L_∞ perturbations exhibits by far the lowest scores, with only about half the inputs being robust for the self-trained model and virtually none for the pre-trained one.

4.2   Stronger and Task-Specific Properties

In addition to the generic and basic computer vision properties considered in Sect. 4.1, many of which naturally transfer to other use cases and application domains, the robustness of the models for traffic sign recognition was assessed with respect to more-task specific and stronger properties. Generally speaking, these properties better reflect specific ambient conditions that may occur in this use case. Figures 4 and 5 show the results for two task-specific properties. On the one hand, the adaptive brightness property is defined as a generalisation of the basic brightness transformation. While the basic brightness transformation applies brightness changes uniformly to the whole image, the adaptive brightness transformation makes fine-grained changes, allowing some parts of the image to become brighter, and others darker. This better reproduces situations that can occur in practice, as a result of the material properties of object surfaces with respect to absorption and reflection of light. On the other hand, the robustness to generic stickers placed on the traffic signs is assessed. Especially in metropolitan areas, it is not uncommon for such stickers to be placed on traffic signs. As can be

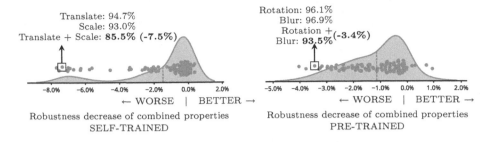

Fig. 6. Effect of assessing model against combinations of robustness properties. Each point corresponds to the relative change in robustness of a selected properties combination compared to considering the properties independently. For most properties, their combination decreases the robustness (shown as negative change).

seen from Figs. 4 and 5, the models become much more brittle when generalising the basic brightness transformation to its adaptive version, and their robustness to stickers is very low indeed.

4.3   Testing Combinations

So far, the robustness properties were analysed independently from each other. However, a combination of all of the properties with different strengths reflects real-world conditions more realistically. As a first step towards evaluating these situations, the properties can be composed together (e.g., combining brightness with rotation), effectively creating a new set of properties with additional degrees of freedom that should be assessed for robustness. Figure 6 provides an overview of robustness scores of the models when tested against combinations of two properties. In most cases, the robustness scores for combinations decrease. For instance, combining translation and scaling yields a robustness score of 85.5%, whereas the robustness to translation and scaling only is 94.7% and 93.0%, respectively. The combination thus decreases robustness by an additional 7.5% as compared to the lower of the two individual robustness scores.

5   Discussion

The results in Sect. 4 show that significant differences in robustness exist both between models and properties. Variations in robustness scores can be partly ascribed to differences in the structure of the models and in the resolution of their input images (which were taken into account in testing in order not to distort the results). The different levels of brittleness the models exhibit to different properties at least partly correlate with the degree of representation of these properties in the training data set or the data augmentation process. It is assumed that, hereby, the models are actively endowed with a certain baseline robustness against such properties. It is concerning to see that the models'

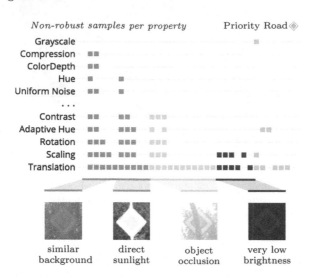

Fig. 7. Example of failure modes for the self-trained model. For a given property, each square denotes a non-robust sample (or a set of samples). Analysis of the robust (not shown) and non-robust samples identifies failure modes such as direct sunlight.

robustness to some properties is very low indeed, and using such brittle models in safety- and security-relevant use cases seems audacious.

The more detailed analyses of stronger and task-specific properties as well as of combinations of properties outlined in Sect. 4.2 and 4.3 show that performing a standard set of basic robustness tests provides a good baseline, but more comprehensive tests can yield higher levels of confidence and better insights as to under what conditions the models are robust.

As an additional refinement, the aggregate robustness scores can be replaced with more precise plots of model robustness across the perturbation parameter space (e.g., [9,10]). This can provide detailed insights into the specific regions where models may fail, which is especially beneficial in safety- and security-critical applications. Beyond that, a careful, fine-grained inspection of the robustness results can help pinpoint failure modes, i.e. specific conditions where model robustness is lower than in others (e.g., direct sunlight or very low brightness, as shown in Fig. 7). Improving the training data sets based on the results obtained in the robustness tests, e.g. by using specially selected, augmented or synthesised data, seems a promising direction for alleviating their shortcomings.

The results presented in Sect. 4 are those obtained using the specific use case of traffic sign recognition, a specific data set and two specific models trained with very limited resources. It is to be expected that models deployed in the real-world by car vendors will have been trained using much larger resources and will, therefore, exhibit higher robustness on average. Nevertheless, a principled procedure for testing their robustness is necessary and the approach discussed in this article yields one possible solution.

6   Conclusion and Outlook

The tests that were performed in the scope of this work mainly focus on the robustness of models against naturally occurring, random properties. They only address to a limited extent the stability of the models with respect to perturbations crafted by an attacker in a targeted way. On the one hand, it is to be expected that the models' robustness can be further decreased by using specialised attacks and that remedying this problem is much harder than improving robustness to certain naturally occurring failure modes as identified by the tests. On the other hand, the effort required for performing different kinds of attacks strongly varies and, therefore, not all attacks are realistic depending on the use case, the motivation and the capabilities of possible attackers.

The testing methodology was applied to the special use case of traffic sign recognition. The results show that performing such tests in a principled way is feasible, and they yield valuable insights into the existing limitations of the models. As a next step, such tests should also be applied to other use cases, in order to obtain the respective results. In doing so, the questions to what extent the testing methodology from traffic sign recognition can be transferred to other use cases and where it needs to be adapted should be addressed. Whereas the basic tests do not have any specific connection to the example use case considered and can probably be transferred easily to check models solving different computer vision problems, the task-specific properties may well need to be adjusted to reflect the specific ambient conditions that may arise in such new use cases. More generally, the abstract testing methodology might also be generalised to AI models solving problems not based on image data, but on data from other input domains, e.g. acoustic signals or even structured tabular data, and to other model architectures beyond neural networks.

For AI models to be used in safety- and security-critical areas such as (partly) autonomous driving in the years to come, a standardised methodology and concrete test criteria will be required in order to assess and evaluate the robustness of these models with respect to random as well as targeted perturbations. For ensuring an adequate level of safety and security, such criteria must be developed, and checking compliance with them must be made compulsory.

Another question that should be further studied is under what conditions and to what extent it is feasible not only to test the robustness of the models in an empirical, though principled, way but also to obtain formally verified statements, which could guarantee the required level of safety and security. Intense research should be devoted to this question, while aiming at practical applicability of solutions at least as a mid-term goal. Combining robustified models with a reject option for specific, non-verifiable regions of the input space might be a first step in this direction. In addition to that, further research effort should be devoted to investigating defensive measures that are able to ensure a high security level even when facing strong attackers, i.e. adaptive attackers with knowledge of the security measures in place (e.g., [24]), and to developing fundamental approaches for increasing the robustness of AI models.

Acknowledgements. The authors would like to thank the reviewers for their helpful suggestions.

References

1. Balunovic, M., Baader, M., Singh, G., Gehr, T., Vechev, M.: Certifying geometric robustness of neural networks. In: Wallach, H., Larochelle, H., Beygelzimer, A., d'Alché Buc, F., Fox, E., Garnett, R. (eds.) Advances in Neural Information Processing Systems, vol. 32. Curran Associates, Inc. (2019)
2. Berghoff, C., Neu, M., von Twickel, A.: Vulnerabilities of connectionist AI applications: evaluation and defense. Front. Big Data **3**, 23 (2020). https://doi.org/10.3389/fdata.2020.00023
3. Bielik, P., Tsankov, P., Krause, A., Vechev, M.: Reliability assessment of traffic sign classifiers. Technica report, Bundesamt für Sicherheit in der Informationstechnik (2020). https://www.bsi.bund.de/ki
4. Biggio, B., Roli, F.: Wild patterns: ten years after the rise of adversarial machine learning. Pattern Recognit. **84**, 317–331 (2018). https://doi.org/10.1016/j.patcog.2018.07.023
5. Carlini, N., et al.: On evaluating adversarial robustness. CoRR abs/1902.06705 (2019)
6. Dalvi, N.N., Domingos, P.M., Sanghai, S.K., Verma, D.: Adversarial classification. In: Kim, W., Kohavi, R., Gehrke, J., DuMouchel, W. (eds.) Proceedings of the Tenth ACM SIGKDD International Conference on Knowledge Discovery and Data Mining, pp. 99–108. ACM (2004). https://doi.org/10.1145/1014052.1014066
7. D'Amour, A., et al.: Under specification presents challenges for credibility in modern machine learning. CoRR abs/2011.03395 (2020)
8. Deng, J., Dong, W., Socher, R., Li, L., Li, K., Li, F.: ImageNet: a large-scale hierarchical image database. In: 2009 IEEE Computer Society Conference on Computer Vision and Pattern Recognition, pp. 248–255. IEEE Computer Society (2009). https://doi.org/10.1109/CVPR.2009.5206848
9. Engstrom, L., Tran, B., Tsipras, D., Schmidt, L., Madry, A.: Exploring the landscape of spatial robustness. In: Proceedings of the 36th International Conference on Machine Learning, vol. 97, pp. 1802–1811. PMLR (2019)
10. Fawzi, A., Moosavi-Dezfooli, S.M., Frossard, P., Soatto, S.: Empirical study of the topology and geometry of deep networks. In: 2018 IEEE/CVF Conference on Computer Vision and Pattern Recognition, pp. 3762–3770 (2018). https://doi.org/10.1109/CVPR.2018.00396
11. Gehr, T., Mirman, M., Drachsler-Cohen, D., Tsankov, P., Chaudhuri, S., Vechev, M.T.: AI2: safety and robustness certification of neural networks with abstract interpretation. In: 2018 IEEE Symposium on Security and Privacy, pp. 3–18. IEEE Computer Society (2018). https://doi.org/10.1109/SP.2018.00058
12. Geirhos, R., et al.: Shortcut learning in deep neural networks. Nature Mach. Intell. **2**, 665–673 (2020)
13. Houben, S., Stallkamp, J., Salmen, J., Schlipsing, M., Igel, C.: Detection of traffic signs in real-world images: the German traffic sign detection benchmark. In: The 2013 International Joint Conference on Neural Networks, pp. 1–8. IEEE (2013). https://doi.org/10.1109/IJCNN.2013.6706807
14. Huang, X., Kwiatkowska, M., Wang, S., Wu, M.: Safety verification of deep neural networks. In: Majumdar, R., Kunčak, V. (eds.) CAV 2017. LNCS, vol. 10426, pp. 3–29. Springer, Cham (2017). https://doi.org/10.1007/978-3-319-63387-9_1

15. Katz, G., Barrett, C., Dill, D.L., Julian, K., Kochenderfer, M.J.: Reluplex: an efficient SMT solver for verifying deep neural networks. In: Majumdar, R., Kunčak, V. (eds.) CAV 2017. LNCS, vol. 10426, pp. 97–117. Springer, Cham (2017). https://doi.org/10.1007/978-3-319-63387-9_5

16. Kim, Y., Hwang, H., Shin, J.: Robust object detection under harsh autonomous-driving environments. IET Image Process. (2021). https://doi.org/10.1049/ipr2.12159

17. Michaelis, C., et al.: Benchmarking robustness in object detection: autonomous driving when winter is coming. CoRR abs/1907.07484 (2019)

18. Ponn, T., Kröger, T., Diermeyer, F.: Identification and explanation of challenging conditions for camera-based object detection of automated vehicles. Sensors **20**(13), 3699 (2020). https://doi.org/10.3390/s20133699

19. Singh, G., Gehr, T., Püschel, M., Vechev, M.T.: An abstract domain for certifying neural networks. In: Proceedings of ACM Program Language, 3(POPL), pp. 1–30 (2019). https://doi.org/10.1145/3290354

20. Szegedy, C., Vanhoucke, V., Ioffe, S., Shlens, J., Wojna, Z.: Rethinking the inception architecture for computer vision. In: 2016 IEEE Conference on Computer Vision and Pattern Recognition, pp. 2818–2826. IEEE Computer Society (2016). https://doi.org/10.1109/CVPR.2016.308

21. Szegedy, C., et al.: Intriguing properties of neural networks. In: Bengio, Y., LeCun, Y. (eds.) 2nd International Conference on Learning Representations (2014). http://arxiv.org/abs/1312.6199

22. Temel, D., Chen, M., AlRegib, G.: Traffic sign detection under challenging conditions: a deeper look into performance variations and spectral characteristics. IEEE Transactions on Intelligent Transportation Systems, pp. 1–11 (2019). https://doi.org/10.1109/TITS.2019.2931429

23. Temel, D., Kwon, G., Prabhushankar, M., AlRegib, G.: CURE-TSR: challenging unreal and real environments for traffic sign recognition. In: Neural Information Processing Systems (NeurIPS) Workshop on Machine Learning for Intelligent Transportation Systems (2017)

24. Tramer, F., Carlini, N., Brendel, W., Madry, A.: On adaptive attacks to adversarial example defenses. In: Advances in Neural Information Processing Systems, vol. 33, pp. 1633–1645. Curran Associates, Inc. (2020)

Data Mining/Word Counts

BIBLIOBICLUSTER: A Bicluster Algorithm for Bibliometrics

Gloria Gheno[✉]

Ronin Institute, Montclair, NJ 07043, USA
gloria.gheno@ronininstitute.org

Abstract. Bibliographic coupling and co-citation analysis methodologies were proposed in the early 60's and 70's to study the structure and production of scientific communities. Bibliographic coupling is fundamental to understand the current state of a particular research area and its possible and potential future direction. Co-citation analysis, instead, is used to map the roots of academic works, fundamental to the development of a specific research field. With the first method, papers which have a common reference are grouped and the strength of their link results from the number of references in common. The second, instead, groups together the papers co-cited by one or more documents. Both methodologies assume that the papers citing the same articles or cited from the same article have similar aspects. Since until now these two methodologies have been considered separately, a new algorithm, based on bicluster analysis, which applies them together, is proposed. The importance of this new methodology is therefore to group together the paired bibliographic papers and the co-cited references but keeping them divided. In the resulting bicluster, the references grouped together represent the roots from which was born the trend to which the citing papers, grouped together, adhere.

Keywords: Bibliographic coupling · Co-citation analysis · Direct citation · Text mining

1 Introduction

Given the significant increase in academic and scientific production, its analysis becomes essential to understand the state of the art and the evolution of new currents in different scientific fields. To carry out this analysis, Bibliometrics mainly uses two procedures: performance analysis and science mapping [7]. Performance analysis analyzes the performance of groups of scientific actors, for example universities, departments, researchers [7]. Science mapping, instead, analyzes the structural and dynamic aspects of scientific research [7]. It is mainly based on the principle of information co-occurance, i.e., if two or more elements are present together in one or more documents, they are closely linked [17]. Both performance analysis and science mapping are based on the analysis of the citation [23].

The analysis of the citation to study performance, in its basic form, counts the number of citations of specific papers [23]. There are two measures to calculate performance:

© IFIP International Federation for Information Processing 2021
Published by Springer Nature Switzerland AG 2021
I. Maglogiannis et al. (Eds.): AIAI 2021, IFIP AICT 627, pp. 271–282, 2021.
https://doi.org/10.1007/978-3-030-79150-6_22

popularity and prestige. Popularity is measured considering the number of citations [9]. For example, in a network analysis, it is represented by the in-degree measure, which counts the number of head endpoints adjacent to a node [6]. The prestige, instead, is measured considering the number of citations obtained from the most cited papers [8, 11].

To study science mapping, the scholar proceeds to the analysis of the citations dividing the main network into two secondary networks, defined as co-citation and bibliographic coupling, and grouping their elements in clusters using the strength of the link among the elements of the secondary networks [4]. Co-citation analysis groups the papers co-cited by one or more documents and the strength of their link is given by the number of citing papers in common [20]. Bibliographic coupling, instead, groups the papers which have a common reference, and the strength of their link is given by the number of references in common [14]. To illustrate this distinction, a network composed of four papers (see Fig. 1) is used. Paper A cites paper C, while paper B cites papers C and D. Then papers A and B are the citing papers, while papers C and D are the cited papers or references. For bibliographic coupling, papers A and B are linked, having both cited C. For co-citation analysis, papers C and D are linked because both are cited by paper B. Vogel and Güttel [24] consider the differences between these two methodologies. Bibliographic coupling is useful for understanding the state of the art and the possible and eventual developments of a particular research area, while co-citation analysis is used to map its roots. Bibliographic coupling is a static approach, while co-citation analysis is dynamic. Bibliographic coupling is an indicator of publication activity, while co-citation analysis is an indicator of the impact of the publications on research.

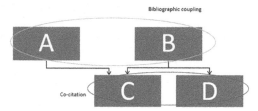

Fig. 1. Subdivision of a network into elements connected according to bibliographic coupling and those connected according to co-citation analysis

Until now, these two methodologies have never been considered together, but it would be interesting to be able to do it so to understand the roots from which the state of the art and its future developments are developed. For this reason, this work proposes a new bicluster (abbreviation BCL) method which considers together bibliographic analysis, co-citation analysis and text analysis, which is generally applied to the results of the first two. Liu and Hsu [12] tried to link bibliographic coupling, co-citation analysis and text mining, proposing a method of bibliographic coupling with a grouping rule based on co-citation analysis and text analysis. Unlike Liu and Hsu [12], which have only the citing papers as result of their methodology, the analysis proposed in this work, using BCL methodology to link the three methods together, becomes more complete because its results contain both the citing papers and the cited papers. This new proposed method can be considered as a co-citation analysis and a bibliographic coupling done together, while the method proposed by Liu and Hsu [12] is a bibliographic coupling with only the addition of the information obtained from co-citation analysis. The advantage of the proposed method is given by the use of the bicluster technique.

BCL analysis was developed to study biological data [5] and has subsequently been applied to many fields, but until now never to Bibliometrics. A bicluster algorithm groups both rows and columns simultaneously. There are many types of BCL depending on the similarity which is considered: bicluster with constant values, with constant values in the rows or columns, BCL with consistent values on the rows and columns and bicluster with consistent correlation on the rows and columns [16]. This paper proposes a BCL method which produces biclusters with constant values, and which is based on the BCL methodology for binary data proposed by Prelić et al. [18] and its modified version [10, 25]. The difference between the method proposed by Prelić et al. [18] and the modified version [10, 25] consists in the possibility of the biclusters to be overlapping. In Prelić's method the BCLs can have both columns and rows in common, while in the modified version only the columns can be in common. The bicluster algorithm, which is proposed in this work, finds BCLs with only columns in common. The difference between the method proposed in this paper and that proposed by Dolničar et al. [10] and by Wang et al. [25] consists in the training and selection procedure of the biclusters.

2 Methodology

Linking co-citation analysis, which determines the roots, to bibliographic coupling, which determines the current state of the art and its future direction, it is possible to better study the evolution of a particular research area. This paper introduces a modified version of the bicluster methodology for binary data, in order to link the two approaches. This new algorithm, which is called BIBLIOBICLUSTER (abbreviation BIBICL), simultaneously groups the references and the citing papers. The references grouped together represent the roots from which the trend of the citing papers, grouped together, is developed. The simplified example in Fig. 2 explains the result of the algorithm. To study a specific research area, the scholar considers only papers A and B, which cite papers C, D and E. Co-citation analysis finds the link only among the three references and therefore finds only the roots of this specific field of research. Applying to the titles a textual analysis, based on the frequency of the words, it is found that this field of research is mainly based on the study of dogs and cats. Bibliographic coupling links the two citing papers and, applying again textual analysis based on the frequencies, finds three main trends: food, health, and environment. By combining the two analyses, the algorithm obtains that, from a generic study of dogs and cats, scholars have moved on to focus on their food, their health, and the environment in which they live.

The algorithm analyses a matrix (see Fig. 3) in which the columns represent the references and the rows the citing papers. If paper 1 cites reference 1, a_{11} is equal to 1, if it does not cite it, a_{11} is equal to 0, so the input of the algorithm is a matrix of 0 and 1. If a citing paper is also a cited paper, it compares in the dataset both as reference and as citing paper. For example, if paper A is both citing and cited paper, it is called both Paper 1 and Reference 1. The relative a_{11} is equal to 0, so in each bicluster the argument of paper A is only root or trend.

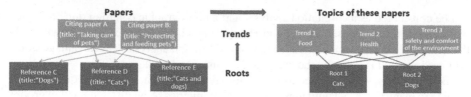

Fig. 2. Example of data interpretation

	Reference 1	Reference 2	...	Reference k	...	Reference K
Paper 1	a_{11}	a_{12}	...	a_{1k}	...	a_{1K}
Paper 2	a_{21}	a_{22}	...	a_{2k}	...	a_{2K}
⋮	⋮	⋮	⋱	⋮	⋱	⋮
Paper j	a_{j1}	a_{j2}	...	a_{jk}	...	a_{jK}
⋮	⋮	⋮	⋱	⋮	⋱	⋮
Paper J	a_{J1}	a_{J2}	...	a_{Jk}	...	a_{JK}

Fig. 3. Example of analysed dataset

From this matrix, the algorithm derives all possible BCLs using the method proposed by Prelić et al. [18]. Among these found biclusters, the algorithm selects the one that maximizes the function

$$C_m * R_m + \lambda \max \mathit{freq\ of}\ B_m \tag{1}$$

where C_m and R_m respectively represent the number of the columns and that of the rows of the generic BCL B_m, "max $\mathit{freq\ of}\ B_m$" represents the frequency of the word mostly present in the titles of the papers in B_m and λ is a parameter whose value is included in the interval $[0,1]$, measuring the importance of text analysis. If the parameter λ is equal to 0, text analysis is not considered. The introduction of λ can eliminate one of the weaknesses of bibliographic coupling. Bibliographic coupling, indeed, can group two unrelated articles just because they cited the same reference [12]. The introduction of the study of the titles of the references seeks to reduce this problem trying to favor biclusters in which the references have titles with similar words and therefore more connected.

There are cases in which two or more BCLs maximize formula (1) and then among them the algorithm chooses the one that maximizes the following function

$$Index = \sum_k \left(\frac{\left(\sum_j a_{jk} - 1 \right)_+}{R_m} + I \left(\sum_j a_{jk} \right)_{\sum_j a_{jk} = 0} \right) \tag{2}$$

where a_{jk} is the value of dataset relative to the row j and the column k (j is selected among the rows included and k among the columns excluded from the bicluster B_m) and R_m is the number of rows of the BCL B_m. This index analyzes the goodness of the bicluster considering the ungrouped columns. They represent the references and therefore the more a reference is cited by the members of a BCL, the more similar are the elements of the bicluster. Indeed, it is sufficient that only one of the members of the bicluster does not mention this reference and this column is excluded. The same consideration is valid if no member of the BCL mentions a reference. The more the number of references which are not cited by any member of a bicluster increases, the more the goodness of the BCL increases because there are no other arguments.

To explain how this mechanism works, the matrix of Fig. 4 is used and λ equal to 0 is chosen. The blue and pink biclusters have the same size ($C_{blue} * R_{blue} = C_{pink} * R_{pink} = 2 * 4 = 8$) and then the algorithm applies formula (2) to choose the best.

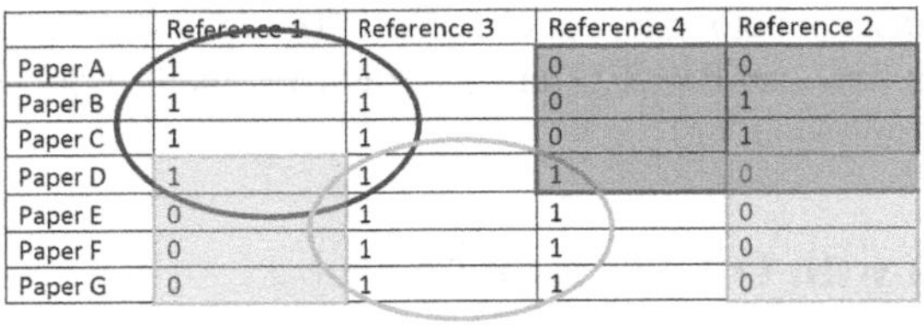

	Reference 1	Reference 3	Reference 4	Reference 2
Paper A	1	1	0	0
Paper B	1	1	0	1
Paper C	1	1	0	1
Paper D	1	1	1	0
Paper E	0	1	1	0
Paper F	0	1	1	0
Paper G	0	1	1	0

Fig. 4. Choice between two biclusters with the same size. (Color figure online)

The analysed columns are those in blue for the blue BCL and the pink ones for the pink bicluster. For simplicity, the rows are denoted as A, B, C, D, E, F, G and the columns as 1,3,4,2. Using formula (2), the algorithm selects the pink BCL. Reference 2 represents a sub-topic of the blue bicluster and therefore confirms an even closer link among some papers of the BCL. Reference 2 is never cited by the pink bicluster papers, thus confirming a close link among them.

$$Index_{blue} = \sum_{k=4,2} \left(\frac{\left(\sum_{j=A,B,C,D} a_{j,k} - 1\right)_+}{R_{blue}} + I\left(\sum_{j=A,B,C,D} a_{jk}\right)_{\sum_{j=A,B,C,D} a_{jk}=0} \right)$$

$$= \frac{(1-1)_+}{4} + I(1)_{\sum_{j=A,B,C,D} a_{j4}=0} + \frac{(2-1)_+}{4} + I(2)_{\sum_{j=A,B,C,D} a_{j2}=0}$$

$$= 0 + 0 + 0.25 + 0 = 0.25 \tag{3}$$

$$Index_{pink} = \sum_{k=1,2} \left(\frac{\left(\sum_{j=D,E,F,G} a_{j,k} - 1\right)_+}{R_{pink}} + I\left(\sum_{j=D,E,F,G} a_{jk}\right)_{\sum_{j=D,E,F,G} a_{jk}=0} \right)$$

$$= \frac{(1-1)_+}{4} + I(1)_{\sum_{j=D,E,F,G} a_{j1}=0} + \frac{(0-1)_+}{4} + I(0)_{\sum_{j=D,E,F,G} a_{j2}=0}$$

$$= 0 + 0 + 0 + 1 = 1 \tag{4}$$

The concept expressed by this index is summarized in Fig. 5. Therefore, formula (2) tries to eliminate the second and final weakness noted by Liu and Hsu [12] of bibliographic coupling. Liu and Hsu [12] noted that two related articles may cite different references. The study of non-grouped references, therefore, determines the goodness of the BCL, preferring biclusters whose non-grouped references are similar or those which group all the references.

Once the BCL has been chosen, the algorithm eliminates the rows which belong to the selected bicluster from the data matrix. Then the algorithm keeps repeating as long as it continues to find BCLs with a size greater than or equal to two. The elimination of the rows and not of the columns is to emphasize that the same roots can lead to more

Number of excluded References	Concept	Similarity
Number of references >1	Subgroup topic	similarity (↑ number => ↑ similarity)
Number of references =1	Different topic	dissimilarity
Number of references =0	No excluded topics	maximum similarity

Fig. 5. Concepts expressed by the goodness index

trends. This last step determines that the obtained biclusters have exclusive rows, i.e. that only the columns can belong to more BCLs. Formula (1) and formula (2) highlight the main difference between BIBICL and the bicluster method proposed by Dolničar et al. [10] and by Wang et al. [25].

3   Comparison with Other Methods

To better explain the functioning of BIBICL algorithm and to compare it with the methods already present in the literature, some simplified datasets are used. The methods of comparison are direct citation, also called intercitations [3, 15, 19], co-citation analysis [20] and bibliographic coupling [14]. Small [21, 22] grouped the three methods together, considering all the papers, cited and citing, and, using the three methodologies, he calculates the strength of the relationships. The difference between the proposed method and Small's method is substantial. The approach introduced in this paper distinguishes between the citing papers and the cited ones, while he considers them together without distinguishing them. To implement these analyses, Gephi software [1] is used with the modularity algorithm [2] implemented in the software itself. In order to highlight the main difference between BIBICL and the three methodologies, the substantial difference between a bicluster and a cluster must be well understood. BIBICL produces BCLs, while the three methodologies present in the literature produce clusters. Bicluster method groups a set of objects considering two variables, the cluster method, instead, considers only one variable. For this reason, direct citation has the limitation of not being able to distinguish between the citing papers and the cited papers, co-citation analysis that of considering only the cited papers and the bibliographic coupling that of considering only the citing papers. BIBICL, instead, manages to group both the cited papers and the citing papers considering them together, but distinguishing them. The first example shows how the solution of the algorithm varies using $\lambda = 0$ and $\lambda = 2$. The dataset used is shown in Fig. 6 and it is created with titles without any underlying scientific theory, just to show the functioning of the algorithm. In the dataset the first row is represented by the titles of the references and therefore, for example, reference 1 has the title "Animals: white cat". Since it assumes that the citing papers are selected using the word Animals, this vocable is deleted from text analysis, assuming that even the references often have the word animals in the title.

When $\lambda = 0$, the algorithm finds only a bicluster (rows: Paper A, Paper B, Paper C, Paper D; columns: "Animals: white cat", "Animals: dog"). When $\lambda = 2$ is set, the algorithm finds 2 BCLs (see Fig. 7). Without text analysis the algorithm selects only the bicluster with the maximum size (green BCL in Fig. 7), with text analysis the algorithm, when it applies formula (1), finds 2 biclusters (green BCL and blue bicluster in Fig. 7) which have the same value. To choose, therefore, the best of them, the algorithm applies

	Animals: white cats	Animals: European cat	Animals: dog	Animals: pets
Paper A	1	0	1	0
Paper B	1	1	1	0
Paper C	1	1	1	0
Paper D	1	0	1	1

Fig. 6. Dataset of the example 1

formula (2). From the algorithm without text analysis, the papers on the white cat and on the dog are the roots of all of the four citing papers, while from the algorithm with text analysis, the papers on the white cat and on the dog are the roots of the trend of papers A and D, while the same papers, together with the one on the European cat, represent the basis of the trend of papers B and C. In citation analysis, co-citation analysis and bibliographic coupling, text analysis is carried out subsequently and then the two results obtained by BIBICL are compared with a single result for each method. Direct citation finds three clusters, while the other methodologies find only one cluster (see Fig. 8). The thickness of the lines, which join the various elements, represents the strength of the link between the two documents. BIBICL, without text analysis, groups the two references, which are more closely linked by co-citation analysis, and the four citing papers grouped together by bibliographic coupling. BIBICL, therefore, considers the groups of bibliographic coupling and the strong relationships of co-citation analysis. The results of BIBICL with text analysis, adding information which the other three methods do not consider, find new and unprecedented links. BIBICL is also useful as a method of data reduction, indeed, both with text analysis and without text analysis, the algorithm eliminates the references which are less cited, while the three methods proposed in the literature continue to consider all the data.

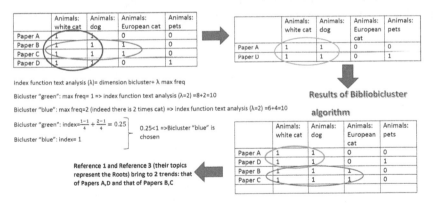

Fig. 7. BIBLIOBICLUSTER applied to the first example with $\lambda = 2$. (Color figure online)

To further show the functioning of BIBICL and compare it with the 3 methods proposed in the literature, a second example is used, whose dataset is shown in Fig. 4. With this example it is possible to better understand the problem of the different references of related articles. To analyse this problem, it is better not to consider text analysis and therefore to set λ equal to 0. In the first step, the algorithm finds two biclusters with

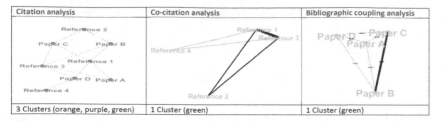

Fig. 8. Results of the methodologies present in the literature relating to example 1

the same size (see Fig. 9), the pink one and the blue one and, applying formula (2), the pink BCL is chosen. The blue bicluster has, indeed, as residual columns reference 4 and reference 2, which are cited respectively 1 and 2 times. The pink BCL, instead, has reference 1 and reference 2 as residual columns, which are cited 1 and 0 times respectively. Since it is more likely that the linked papers of the pink bicluster did not mention different references, having a column equal to 0 and one with only 1, the pink BCL is preferred to the blue bicluster. Now the rows relative to the citing papers of the pink BCL are removed and the biclusters are looked for again. As in the previous step, also in this case there are two BCLs with the same size (the green one and the red one) and, always applying formula (2), the green one is chosen. The green bicluster has, indeed, as residual columns reference 2 and reference 4, which are cited 2 and 0 times respectively. The red BCL, instead, has reference 4 as its residual column, which is cited 0 times. Since reference 2 is cited 2 times out of 3 by the green bicluster papers, it is very likely that paper A is linked to B and C even if they have cited different articles, being reference 4 not cited by anyone. The red BCL cannot be chosen because it excludes only one column of all zeros. In this case, the exclusion of a single column of all zeros is insufficient to determine the goodness of the bicluster.

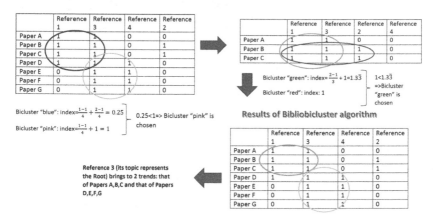

Fig. 9. BIBLIOBICLUSTER applied to the second example with $\lambda = 0$. (Color figure online)

In conclusion, BIBICL finds two BCLs and excludes reference 2 from the analysis. If, instead, direct citation, co-citation analysis and bibliographic coupling are applied to the same dataset, the results are shown in Fig. 10. Therefore, the three methods do not delete the reference 2, as BIBICL does. Direct citation produces two clusters, co-citation analysis one cluster and bibliographic coupling two clusters. As in example 1, also in this case BIBICL considers the strong relationships of co-citation analysis and the clusters of bibliographic coupling.

Direct citation analysis	Co-citation analysis	Bibliographic coupling analysis
2 Clusters (pink,green)	1 Cluster (green)	2 Clusters (pink,green)

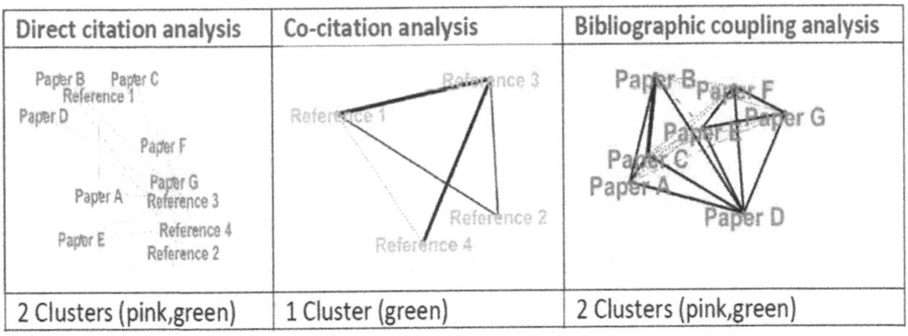

Fig. 10. Results of the three methodologies present in the literature relating to example 2

Now an example, where the papers A and B are both citing and cited, is presented. Paper A cites Paper B, Reference C and Reference D, while Paper B cites Paper A, Reference C and Reference D. BIBICL finds 1 bicluster (rows: Paper A, Paper B; columns: Reference C, Reference D). Co-citation analysis finds 1 cluster with elements Paper B, Paper A, Reference C and Reference D, while bibliographic coupling finds 1 cluster with elements Paper A and Paper B. Direct citation finds 1 cluster with elements Paper B, Paper A, Reference C and Reference D. As in the previous examples, BIBICL considers the strong relation of co-citation analysis (Reference C and Reference D) and the cluster of bibliographic coupling.

4 Application to a Real Case

The new proposed algorithm is applied to the analysis of economic papers relative to accounting published between 2011 and the first quarter of 2020, which have big data among the keywords. As it can be seen from Fig. 11, the papers on big data tend to increase in number, demonstrating the increase in importance of this topic. From the keywords cloud graph, in which the increase in font size of the word demonstrates the highest frequency, it can be seen that big data is the word with the greatest frequency actually. Precisely this term is the discriminating factor in order that a paper is included in the dataset. The initial dataset is made up of 160 documents extracted from Scopus. These documents are articles, books, book chapters, conference articles, editorials and short questionnaires. The dataset is composed of only 91 articles, eliminating, however, three of them because they have no references.

The algorithm without text analysis ($\lambda = 0$) is applied to the dataset, to show how this can be done later, as in the methods already present in the literature. BIBICL finds sixteen biclusters, but text analysis is applied only to the BCLs that are larger than 8, believing that the smallest ones represent niche topics. Of course, all biclusters could

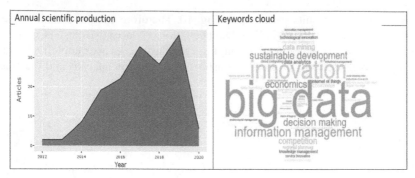

Fig. 11. Graph of the number of articles per year of production and keywords cloud

also be analyzed. In this case both the titles of the references and those of the citing papers are examined. This analysis considers both the frequency with which a word is found in titles and the one with which it is found next to another word [13]. Of course, this analysis, or other similar ones, can also be applied to the results of the algorithm with λ greater than 0. The results of the text analysis are shown in Table 1. For example, if BCL 1 is considered, it is found that the study of the ability to learning about the business and its performance led to three main analyses: the innovation, the role of intuition and the impact of data on businesses.

Table 1. Results of the text analysis applied to the ten biclusters

	trends	roots
Bicluster 1	1)Innovation and enhance of the firm 2)Role of insight in the firms 3)The impact of the data on the firms	The capacities of learning of firm and its performance
Bicluster 2	Resilient enterprise and sustainability	The sustainability: innovation, the keys and the drivers, ecologic and social aspects (for example psychology and work)
Bicluster 3	Understanding the determinants of the use of the big data	Adoption of different technologies (cloud and data, e-commerce and its process, communication and electronic interchange)
Bicluster 4	Innovation and big data analysis	Competition and management
Bicluster 5	Green innovation management	New data and environmental
Bicluster 6	Business model (initiative and process, impacts and success)	Business model (innovation, strategy, design)
Bicluster 7	Innovation service and incubators	Services (innovation, research, learning)
Bicluster 8	Empirical analysis	Business and technological performance
Bicluster 9	Technology systems and emergent technology	Emergent technologies and innovation: information and competition
Bicluster 10	Relation among supply chain, performance and innovation	Supply chain prediction

5   Conclusions

Until now, co-citation analysis, bibliographic coupling and text analysis have been applied separately with consequent limitations. This work proposes a new algorithm, called BIBICL, to solve these limitations. This algorithm produces biclusters, in which the references, grouped together, represent the roots from which is born the trend to which the citing papers, grouped together, belong. BIBICL can be used both considering only the citations and considering together the citations and text analysis. Obtaining a mixed method is fundamental and, indeed, some authors [12] are trying to link bibliographic coupling, co-citation analysis and text mining using the theory of clusters. Liu and Hsu [12], indeed, propose a method of bibliographic coupling with a selection rule based on co-citation analysis and text analysis. Indeed, linking them together using the BCLs, the proposed algorithm obtains a more complete analysis and with cited papers and citing papers present in the results, unlike them which group only the citing papers.

References

1. Bastian, M., Heymann, S., Jacomy, M.: Gephi: an open source software for exploring and manipulating networks. In: ICWSM, vol. 8, pp. 361–362 (2009)
2. Blondel, V.D., Guillaume, J.L., Lambiotte, R., Lefebvre, E.: Fast unfolding of communities in large networks. J. Stat. Mech. Theor. Exp. **2008**, P10008 (2008). 10.1088/1742-5468/2008/10/P10008/meta
3. Boyack, K.W., Klavans, R.: Co-citation analysis, bibliographic coupling, and direct citation: which citation approach represents the research front most accurately? J. Am. Soc. Inform. Sci. Technol. **61**, 2389–2404 (2010)
4. Chen, C., Morris, S.: Visualizing evolving networks: minimum spanning trees versus pathfinder networks. In: IEEE Symposium on Information Visualization 2003 (IEEE Cat. No. 03TH8714), pp. 67–74. IEEE (2003)
5. Cheng, Y., Church, G.M.: Biclustering of expression data. In: ISMB, vol. 8, pp. 93–103 (2000)
6. Cherven, K.: Network Graph Analysis and Visualization with Gephi. Packt Publishing Ltd. (2013)
7. Cobo, M.J., López-Herrera, A.G., Herrera-Viedma, E., Herrera, F.: An approach for detecting, quantifying, and visualizing the evolution of a research field: a practical application to the fuzzy sets theory field. J. Inform. **5**, 146–166 (2011)
8. Ding, Y., Yan, E., Frazho, A., Caverlee, J.: PageRank for ranking authors in co-citation networks. J. Am. Soc. Inform. Sci. Technol. **60**, 2229–2243 (2009)
9. Ding, Y., Cronin, B.: Popular and/or prestigious? Measures of scholarly esteem. Inf. Process. Manage. **47**, 80–96 (2011)
10. Dolnicar, S., Kaiser, S., Lazarevski, K., Leisch, F.: Biclustering: overcoming data dimensionality problems in market segmentation. J. Travel Res. **51**, 41–49 (2012)
11. Fahimnia, B., Bell, M.G.H., Hensher, D.A., Sarkis, J.: Green Logistics & Transportation: A Sustainable Supply Chain Perspective. Greening of Industry Networks Studies. Springer, New York City, USA (2015)
12. Liu, R.L., Hsu, C.K.: Improving bibliographic coupling with category-based cocitation. Appl. Sci. **9**(23), 1576 (2019). https://doi.org/10.3390/app9235176
13. Hornik, K., Grün, B.: Topicmodels: an R package for fitting topic models. J. Stat. Softw. **40**, 1–30 (2011)
14. Kessler, M.M.: Bibliographic coupling between scientific papers. Am. Doc. **14**, 10–25 (1963)
15. Klavans, R., Boyack, K.W.: Identifying a better measure of relatedness for mapping science. J. Am. Soc. Inform. Sci. Technol. **57**, 251–263 (2006)
16. Madeira, S.C., Oliveira, A.L.: Biclustering algorithms for biological data analysis: a survey. IEEE/ACM Trans. Comput. Biol. Bioinf. **1**, 24–45 (2004)
17. Noyons, C.M.: Science maps within a science policy context. In: Moed, H.F., Glänzel, W., Schmoch, U. (eds.) Handbook of Quantitative Science and Technology Research, pp. 237–255. Springer, Dordrecht (2004). 10.1007/1-4020-2755-9_11
18. Prelić, A., et al.: A systematic comparison and evaluation of biclustering methods for gene expression data. Bioinformatics **22**, 1122–1129 (2006)

19. Shibata, N., Kajikawa, Y., Takeda, Y., Matsushima, K.: Detecting emerging research fronts based on topological measures in citation networks of scientific publications. Technovation **28**, 758–775 (2008)
20. Small, H.: Co-citation in the scientific literature: a new measure of the relationship between two documents. J. Am. Soc. Inf. Sci. **24**, 265–269 (1973)
21. Small, H.: Update on science mapping: Creating large document spaces. Scientometrics **38**, 275–293 (1997)
22. Small, H.: Visualizing science by citation mapping. J. Am. Soc. Inf. Sci. **50**, 799–813 (1999)
23. Van Raan, A.F.: Advances in bibliometric analysis: research performance assessment and science mapping. In: Blockmans, W., Engwall, L., Wcairem, D. (eds.) Bibliometrics Use and Abuse in the Review of Research Performance, vol. 87, pp. 17–28. Portland Press Ltd., London (2014)
24. Vogel, R., Güttel, W.H.: The dynamic capability view in strategic management: a bibliometric review. Int. J. Manage. Rev. **15**, 426–446 (2013)
25. Wang, B., Miao, Y., Zhao, H., Jin, J., Chen, Y.: A biclustering-based method for market segmentation using customer pain points. Eng. Appl. Artif. Intell. **47**, 101–109 (2016)

Topic Identification via Human Interpretation of Word Clouds: The Case of Instagram Hashtags

Stamatios Giannoulakis[✉][iD] and Nicolas Tsapatsoulis

Department of Communication and Internet Studies, Cyprus University
of Technology, 30, Arch. Kyprianos Street, 3036 Limassol, Cyprus
{s.giannoulakis,nicolas.tsapatsoulis}@cut.ac.cy

Abstract. Word clouds are a very useful tool for summarizing textual
information. They can be used to illustrate the most frequent and important words of text documents or a set of text documents. In that respect
they can also be used for topic visualisation. In this paper we present
an experiment investigating how the crowd understands topics visualised
via word clouds. In the experiment we use the topics mined from Instagram hashtags of a set of Instagram images corresponding to 30 different
subjects. By subject we mean the research hashtag we use to gather pairs
of Instagram images and hashtags. With the aid of an innovative topic
modelling method, developed in a previous work, we constructed word
clouds for the visualisation of each topic. Then we used a popular crowd-
sourcing platform (*Appen*) to let users identify the topic they believe
each word cloud represents. The results show some interesting variations
across subjects which are analysed and discussed in detail throughout
the paper. Given that the topics were mined from Instagram hashtags,
the current study provides useful insights regarding the appropriateness
of hashstags as image annotation tags.

Keywords: Wordclouds · Topic modelling · Instagram hashtags ·
Image annotation · Visualisation

1 Introduction

Word clouds are used to depict word frequencies derived from a text or a set
of text documents. The size of each depicted word in the cloud depends on
its frequency: words that occur often are shown larger than words with rare
appearance while stopwords are removed. Thus, a Word cloud can be seen as a
synopsis of the main themes contained in textual information [2, 11]. Word clouds
became popular in practical situations and are commonly used for summarizing
a set of reviews presented as free texts (i.e., "open questions").

In order to construct a classic word cloud it is necessary to calculate the word
frequencies in a text or set of texts. However, word frequencies can be replaced by

© IFIP International Federation for Information Processing 2021
Published by Springer Nature Switzerland AG 2021
I. Maglogiannis et al. (Eds.): AIAI 2021, IFIP AICT 627, pp. 283–294, 2021.
https://doi.org/10.1007/978-3-030-79150-6_23

any other measure that reflects the importance of a word in a text document. In that respect word clouds can be used for the visualisation of topics derived from a collection of texts. Topic models infer probability distributions from frequency statistics, which can reflect co-occurrence relationships of words [4]. Through topic modeling we can reveal the subject of a document or a set of documents and present in a summarized fashion what the document(a) is/are about. This is why topic modeling is, nowadays, a state-of-the-art technique to organize, understand and summarize large collections of textual information [1].

Let us now assume a set of Instagram photos grouped together via a common property such as the queried hashtag that was used to collect them. In the context of the current word we name the query hashtag as *subject*. Instagram photos are frequently accompanied by hashtags [3] that the photo owner and other Instagram users use to describe photos' content and, in several cases, their feelings, moments and reactions related with those photos. We can see, therefore, the hashtags of an Instagram image as a textual representation of it and in this way Instagram collections of images can be seen as textual documents and can be analysed via topic modelling techniques once textual preprocessing, such as word splitting is applied first. Since with topic modelling we can measure the most relevant terms of a topic we can assume that by applying topic modelling on the hashtags sets [19] we can derive a set of terms best describing the set of Instagram photos grouped together within a subject.

In this paper we investigate how the crowd understands the topics derived from the hashtag sets of Instagram photos that were grouped together by a common query hashtag which we call subject. The topics are illustrated as word clouds with the queried hashtags (subjects) hidden and the crowd is asked to guess the hidden hashtag providing their best four guesses. The aim of the current work is first to assess whether a word cloud presentation is appropriate for visualising hashtags sets and, second, to investigate any variations in interpreting word clouds corresponding to different subjects. We believe that through this meta-analysis we gain useful insights on whether words mined form Instagram hashtags [6] can be used for image tagging in a collective manner allowing for quick development training sets for Automatic Image Annotation [15,17,18].

2   Related Work

Word clouds is an informative data visualisation tool [16] primarily used to summarize textual information but it has been also applied for the analysis of social media data.

Jin [10] used Twitter data about Hurricane Maria to identify and understand the main communication patterns of the related thread. She approached that problem in quantitative manner by topic modeling and word clouds to capture topics related to Hurricane Maria, and then, to qualitatively explain the results.

Nogra analysed Instagram comments in order to locate words that are mentioned more frequently according to the media photo and visualised the results with word clouds [14]. The overall aim was to identify appropriate words to be associated with online product advertisements to better target possible customers.

In a study on how the Instagram is used to depict and portray breastfeeding, and how users share perspectives and information about that topic. Marcon *et al.* analysed 4089 images and 8331 corresponding comments posted with popular breastfeeding-related hashtags such as *#breastfeeding, #breastmilk, #breastisbest*, and *#normalizebreastfeeding*. They used word clouds to visualize the comment discussions in order to quickly identify the main discussion trends [12].

Vitale *et al.* [20] investigated how Igers ('instagrammers' which allow people who do not follow them to find their photos) represent themselves and their experience at museums in a textualised fashion. They analyzed the captions and hashtags of Igers' Instagram photos and presented the most frequent words used in word clouds for quick interpretation.

Mittal *et al.* [13] study some user interaction properties, such as hashtags and post time, along with photo properties such as photo features or applied image filters to understand users' engagements with Instagram posts. As a part of their analysis, they apply the Latent Dirichlet Allocation (LDA) algorithm in order to locate the most commonly used hashtags at a specific location. The most common hashtags per location are depicted as word clouds.

Kamil *et al.* [9] collected 1017 Instagram posts, tracked with the hashtag *#prayfornepal*, related to the Nepal earthquake in April 2015 to investigate how the people respond and express themselves emotionally for a disaster of such massive scale. By using posts' date, time, geolocation, image, post ID, username and ID, caption, and associated hashtags they categorized the posts into seven categories and they created the word clouds for each one of those categories using the captions and the hashtags to visually illustrate the main topic facets related with the disaster.

In order to study the reactions of Instagram users on an Indonesian action entitled GERMAS, aiming to promote healthy living community movement, Habibi *et al.* [8] collected posts related to hashtag *#germas*. They applied topic modeling on the captions of those posts and used word clouds to illustrate the resulting topics. For topic modelling the authors used the Latent Dirichlet Allocation (LDA) algorithm.

The previous discussion shows that while presentation of Instagram related textual data, such as captions, comments and hashtags, via word clouds is quite common, no meta analysis of the word clouds themselves has been conducted in anyone of those works. Word clouds have been mainly used for visualisation purposes but the appropriateness of this visualisation format was never assessed. Thus, in addition to the application perspective of our work, which emphasizes on mining terms from Instagram hashtags for image tagging, the crowd-based meta analysis of word clouds provides also useful insights about their appropriateness for topic visualisation. Some of the reported works applied topic modelling to summarize textual information using the classic LDA approach. Our topic modeling algorithm [19] is quite different and tailored to the specific case of Instagram posts. Photos and associated hashtags are modelled as a bipartite network and the importance of each hashtags is computed via its authority score obtained by applying the HITS algorithm [7].

3   Word Clouds Creation

As already mentioned the main purpose of the current work is to investigate and discuss the crowd-based interpretation of word clouds created from Instagram hashtags. A dataset of 1680 Instagram posts (photos along with their associated hashtags) was created by querying with 30 different hashtags (see Table 1) which in the context of the current work are called *subjects*.

All collected hashtags were undergone preprocessing so as to derive meaningful tokens (words in English). Instragram hashtags, are unstructured and ungrammatical, and it is important to use linguistic processing to (a) remove stophashtags [5], that is hashtags that are used to fool the search results of the Instagram platform, (b) split a composite hashtag to its consisting words (e.g. the hashtag '#spoilyourselfthisseason' should be split into four words: 'spoil', 'yourself', 'this', 'season'), (c) remove stopwords that are produced in the previous stage (e.g. the word 'this' in the previous example), (d) perform spelling checks to account for (usually intentionally) misspelled hashtags (e.g. '#headaband', '#headabandss' should be changed to '#headband'), and (e) perform lemmatization to merge words that share the same or similar meaning. Preprocessing was conducted with the help of Natural Language ToolKit (NLTK - https://www.nltk.org/.), Wordnet[1] and personally developed code in Python.

Fig. 1. Two different word clouds for the subject (queried hashtag) parrot

By finishing all preprocessing steps we ended up with a token set for each one of the 1680 Instagram photos. Instagram photos and the associated hashtag sets belonging to a common subject were grouped together and modeled as a bipartite network. Then, topic models were created for each one of the subjects following the approach described in [19]. A total of 46 different topic models were developed since for some subjects we had two or more topics. The importance of each token within a topic model was assessed by applying the HITS algorithm as described in [7]. For each one of the topics a word cloud was created. The

---

[1] https://wordnet.princeton.edu/.

token corresponding to the associated subject (query hashtag) was excluded in order to examine whether the crowd would guess it correctly (see Sect. 4 for the details). Word clouds visualization (see an example in Fig. 1) was done with the help of WordCloud[2] Python library.

Fig. 2. The way the wordclouds were presented to the crowd through the Appen crowd-sourcing platform

4   Crowd-Based Interpretation of Word Clouds

Crowd-based interpretation of word clouds was conducted with the aid of the *Appen* (https://appen.com/.) crowdsourcing platform. The word clouds were presented to the participants as shown in Fig. 2 and the participants were asked to select one to four of the subjects that best match the shown word cloud according to their interpretation. The participants were clearly informed that the token corresponding to the correct subject was not shown in the cloud.

Every word cloud was judged by at least 30 annotators (contributors in Appen's terminology) while eight word clouds were also used as 'gold questions' for quality assurance, i.e., identification of dishonest annotators and task

---

[2] https://amueller.github.io/word_cloud/.

difficulty assessment. The correct answer(s) for the gold clouds were provided to the crowdsourcing platform and all participants had to judge those clouds. However, gold clouds were presented to the contributors in random order and they could not know which of the clouds were the gold ones. A total of 165 contributors from more than 25 different countries participated in the experiment. The cost per judgement was set to $0.01 and the task was completed in less than six hours.

(a) Word cloud for the subject 'fish'

(b) Crowd based interpretation of the 'fish' word cloud

(c) Word cloud for subject 'laptop'

(d) Crowd based interpretation of the 'laptop' word cloud

Fig. 3. Word clouds and crowd-based interpretation for the subjects 'fish' and 'laptop'

The crowd interpretations of each one of the word clouds were also transformed as word clouds, i.e., meta word clouds, for illustration purposes. The importance of each token in a meta word cloud was based on the frequency of its selection by the contributors. Meta word clouds are presented in Figs. 3b, 3d, 4b, 4d, 5b, 6b, 7b. The tokens in a meta word cloud can be seen as the topic model suggested by the crowd for the Instagram photos grouped under the corresponding subject. For instance we could say that the topic model for the images grouped under the subject 'microphone' includes also the words 'guitar' and 'piano' and thus all three words can be used for tagging the corresponding photos even for creating training datasets for AIAI purposes [19].

Not all word clouds present the same difficulty in interpretation. Thus, in order to quantitatively estimate that difficulty per subject we used the typical accuracy metric, that is the percentage of correct subject identifications by the crowd. By correct identification we mean that a contributor had selected the right subject within her/his one to four choices (see Fig. 2). We see for instance in Table 1 that the accuracy of the first guitar word cloud is 93%. This means that 93% of the contributors included the word 'guitar' in their interpretation for that word cloud, regardless the number (1 to 4) of contributor choices.

Table 1. Crowd-based topic identification accuracy.

Subject	Acc. (%)	Subject	Acc. (%)	Subject	Acc. (%)	Subject	Acc. (%)
Guitar	93	Dress	80	Cat	90	Chair	47
Guitar	87	Dress	60	Dog	87	Chair	43
Microphone	67	Shirt	53	Fish	100	Laptop	100
Microphone	57	Shirt	33	Fish	93	Laptop	80
Piano	70	Earrings	90	Hamster	7	Table	77
Piano	47	Handbag	93	Hamster	3	Table	73
		Hat	7	Parrot	90		
Bear	43	Hat	3	Parrot	87	Hedgehog	0
Elephant	37	Headband	30	Rabbit	77	Hedgehog	0
Giraffe	63	Headband	17	Turtle	21	Horse	87
Lion	60	Sunglasses	67	Turtle	20	Rose	63
Lion	67	Watch	87				
Monkey	33						
Zebra	57						

5   Results and Discussion

The accuracy of interpretation for all word clouds is presented in Table 1. In order to better facilitate the discussion that follows the subjects (query hash-tags) were divided into six categories: (a) **Music**: Guitar, Piano, Microphone (b) **Wild animals**: Bear, Elephant, Giraffe, Lion, Monkey, Zebra (c) **Fashion**: Dress, Earrings, Handbag, Hat, Headband, Shirt, Sunglasses (d) **Office**: Chair, Laptop, Table, (e) **Pets**: Cat, Dog, Fish, Hamster, Parrot, Rabbit, Turtle (f) **Miscellaneous**: Hedgehog, Horse, Rose.

We see in Table 1 that the interpretation accuracy varies within and across categories. As we explain later through specific examples, there are three main parameters which affect the difficulty of interpretation. The first one is the conceptual context for a specific term. It is very easy, for instance, to define a clear conceptual context for the term fish but very difficult to define clear conceptual contexts for terms such as hat and hedgehog. This difficulty is, obviously, reflected in the use of hashtags that accompany photos presenting those terms. As a result the corresponding word clouds do not provide the textual context and hints that allow the correct interpretation of word clouds. Thus, textual context and key tokens in the word clouds is the second parameter affecting the difficulty of interpretation. This is, obviously, a data related factor and its effect can be minimized by creating word clouds from a larger number of Instagram posts per subject (note that in our case we have used on average 56 Instagram posts per subject). The third parameter that affects interpretation, is the familiarity of people with the concepts. Concepts such as dog, cat and horse are far more familiar to everyday people than concepts such as hedgehog and hamster.

Overall, the word clouds corresponding to the subjects 'Laptop' and 'Fish' had the highest interpretation accuracy both reaching the absolute 100%. In the case of fish word cloud (see Fig. 3a) the prominent presence of the tokens fisherman, aquarium created as strong and clear context and led the annotators to select the concept fish as their single selection. That resulted in a meta word cloud (see Fig. 3b) consisting of a single word, the word fish. A similar case is seen in the case of the laptop word cloud (see Fig. 3c). The prominent presence of tokens apple, macbook, computer and portable make it clear to the annotators that the right concept choice is laptop. We see in the corresponding meta word cloud that the a significant number of contributors chose the concept 'table' as well triggered mainly by the strong presence in the cloud of the token coffee (see Fig. 3d).

In the following we present and discuss some representative/interesting examples for each one of the six categories mentioned above.

The word clouds in the Music category have very high scores of interpretation accuracy. Music related terms share a strong conceptual context which results in clear textual contexts in the Instagram hashtags. In Fig. 4 we see two different word clouds for the subject 'microphone'. While the word clouds are quite different (see Figs. 4b and 4c) the music-singing conceptual context is prominent. Tokens like band, singer, music, hop, hip and stage create a strong and clear textual content. Thus, the annotators chose all music-singing related terms, namely guitar, piano and microphone, as it can be seen in the corresponding meta word clouds (see Figs. 4b, 4d).

The monkey word cloud (see Fig. 5a) was in fact a confusing one. The most prominent tokens were art, animal and nature while some other terms such as artist, artwork, and work could also confuse the contributors (annotators). We see in the meta word cloud (Fig. 5b), however, that the key tokens animal and nature combined with the term gorilla in the upper right corner of the word cloud led the contributors to make selections from the wild animal category including the correct subject (accuracy 33%).

In the case of subject 'hat' (see word cloud in Fig. 6) we have a situation where there are many different conceptual contexts. As a result, the hashtags appeared in different Instagram photos differ significantly and the resulting word cloud is

(a) The first word cloud for 'microphone'

(b) Crowd based interpretation of the first 'microphone' word cloud

(c) The second word cloud for 'microphone'

(d) Crowd based interpretation of the second 'microphone' word cloud

Fig. 4. Two different word clouds and the corresponding crowd-based interpretations for the subject 'microphone'

(a) Word cloud for the 'monkey' subject

(b) Crowd based interpretation of the 'monkey' word cloud

Fig. 5. Word cloud and crowd-based interpretation for the subject 'monkey'

confusing. We see that the most prominent tokens in the cloud are blogger, style, sun, and beach (obviously these are concepts shown in some of the Instagram photos grouped under the subject 'hat'). There is no doubt that the subject 'hat' fits well with those terms. However, the same terms fit well or even better to other subjects such as 'sunglasses' and dress which were the primary choices of the annotators (see Fig. 6b).

(a) Word cloud for the 'hat' subject

(b) Crowd based interpretation of the 'hat' word cloud

Fig. 6. Word cloud and crowd-based interpretation for the subject 'hat'

The case of hedgehog is a classic example showing that the familiarity with a concept affects the difficulty in interpretation of the word cloud derived from Instagram hashtags. While in the word cloud (see Fig. 7a) the words pygmy, pet and animal are by far the most important ones none of the participants selected the right subject. It appears that the contributors were non-familiar with the word pygmy. The African pygmy hedgehog is the species often used as pet. By

(a) Word cloud for the 'hedgehog' subject

(b) Crowd based interpretation of the 'hedgehog' word cloud

Fig. 7. Word cloud and crowd-based interpretation for the subject 'hedgehog'

examining the meta word cloud (see Fig. 7b) we see that the contributors mixed up concepts related to pets with concepts related to wild animals.

6 Conclusion

Presentation of Instagram related textual data (or social media data in general), such as captions, comments and hashtags through word clouds for quick interpretation is quite common both in real-world applications and in the scientific community. In the current work we have presented a crowd-based meta analysis of word clouds created from Instagram hashtags. The main purpose was to identify appropriate tags for Instagram photos that share (and grouped together) a common hashtag (called subject in the current work). Through this meta analysis we concluded that there is significant variation in the difficulty of interpretation of word clouds corresponding to different terms and we named three parameters affecting this interpretation: conceptual context, textual context and familiarity with concept. Terms having a clear conceptual context, for instance the terms 'fish', 'guitar', 'laptop', have an easily interpreted word cloud of Instagram hashtags as a clear conceptual context is reflected on a clear textual context. On the contrary, terms whose conceptual context can vary a lot, such as the term 'hat', result on a confusing word cloud of Instagram hashtags. The familiarity with a term is also an important reason affecting the ease of interpretation of its word cloud. For instance the word clouds corresponding to the concept 'hedgehog' were far more difficult to interpret than their counterparts for the concepts 'dog' and 'cat'.

The main conclusion is that we can mine information from Instagram hashtags for image tagging, and subsequently for developing training sets for Automatic Image Annotation (AIA) purposes, but not for every single concept/term. We are currently in the process to assess deep learning models, trained on Instagram photos corresponding to the 30 subjects included in the current study, in terms of image classification. The aim is to examine whether the difficulty in crowd-based word cloud interpretation is correlated with the effectiveness of the trained models.

References

1. Alami, N., Meknassi, M., En-nahnahi, N., El Adlouni, Y., Ammor, O.: Unsupervised neural networks for automatic Arabic text summarization using document clustering and topic modeling. Expert Syst. Appl. **172**, 114652 (2021)
2. Atenstaedt, R.: Word cloud analysis of the BJGP: 5 years on. Br. J. Gen. Pract. **67**(658), 231–232 (2017)
3. Daer, A., Hoffman, R., Goodman, S.: Rhetorical functions of hashtag forms across social media applications. Commun. Des. Q. **3**, 12–16 (2015)
4. Fu, X., Wang, T., Li, J., Yu, C., Liu, W.: Improving distributed word representation and topic model by word-topic mixture model. In: Durrant R.J., Kim K.-E.b (eds.) Proceedings of the Asian Conference on Machine Learning, vol. 63, pp. 190–205 (2016)

5. Giannoulakis, S., Tsapatsoulis, N.: Defining and identifying stophashtags in Instagram. In: Angelov, P., Manolopoulos, Y., Iliadis, L., Roy, A., Vellasco, M. (eds.) INNS 2016. AISC, vol. 529, pp. 304–313. Springer, Cham (2017). https://doi.org/10.1007/978-3-319-47898-2_31

6. Giannoulakis, S., Tspatsoulis, N.: Evaluating the descriptive power of Instagram hashtags. J. Innov. Digital Ecosyst. **3**(2), 114–129 (2016)

7. Giannoulakis, S., Tspatsoulis, N.: Filtering Instagram hashtags through crowd-tagging and the HITS algorithm. IEEE Trans. Comput. Soc. Syst. **6**(3), 592–603 (2019)

8. Habibi, M., Priadana, A., Saputra, A., Cahyo, P.: Topic modelling of germas related content on Instagram using Latent Dirichlet Allocation (LDA). In: 2nd International Conference of Health, pp. 260–264. Atlantis Press (2020)

9. Kamil, P., Pratama, A., Hidayatulloh, A.: Did we really #prayfornepal? Instagram posts as a massive digital funeral in Nepal earthquake aftermath. In: AIP Conference Proceedings, 1730, 090002-1-090002-10 (2016)

10. Jin, X.: Understanding social-mediated disaster and risk communication with topic model. In: Djalante, R., Bisri, M.B.F., Shaw, R. (eds.) Integrated Research on Disaster Risks. DRR, pp. 159–174. Springer, Cham (2021). https://doi.org/10.1007/978-3-030-55563-4_19

11. Lohmann, S., Heimerl, F., Bopp, F., Burch, M., Ertl, T.: ConcentriCloud: word cloud visualization for multiple text documents. In: Banissi, E., et al. (eds.) Proceedings of the 19th International Conference on Information Visualisation, pp. 114–120. IEEE, Piscataway (2015)

12. Marcon, A., Bieber, M., Azad, M.: Protecting, promoting, and supporting breast-feeding on Instagram. Maternal and Child Nutrition **15**(1), e12658 (2019)

13. Mittal, V., Kaul, A., Gupta, S., Arora, A.: Multivariate features based Instagram post analysis to enrich user experience. Procedia Comput. Sci. **122**, 138–145 (2017)

14. Nogra, J.A.E.: Text analysis on Instagram comments to better target users with product advertisements. Int. J. Adv. Trends Comput. Sci. Eng. **9**, 175–181 (2020)

15. Ntalianis, K., Tsapatsoulis, N., Doulamis, A., Matsatsinis, N.: Automatic annotation of image databases based on implicit crowdsourcing, visual concept modeling and evolution. Multimedia Tools Appl. **69**(2), 397–421 (2012). https://doi.org/10.1007/s11042-012-0995-2

16. Shahid, N., Ilyas, M., Alowibdi, J., Aljohani, N.: Word cloud segmentation for simplified exploration of trending topics on Twitter. IET Softw. **11**, 214–220 (2017)

17. Theodosiou, Z., Tsapatsoulis, N.: image retrieval using keywords: the machine learning perspective. In: Spyrou, E., Iakovides, D., Mylonas, P. (eds.) Semantic Multimedia Analysis and Processing, pp. 3–30. CRC Press (2014)

18. Tsapatsoulis, N.: Web image indexing using WICE and a learning-free language model. In: Iliadis, L., Maglogiannis, I. (eds.) AIAI 2016. IAICT, vol. 475, pp. 131–140. Springer, Cham (2016). https://doi.org/10.1007/978-3-319-44944-9_12

19. Tsapatsoulis, N.: Image retrieval via topic modelling of Instagram hashtags. In: 15th International Workshop on Semantic and Social Media Adaptation and Personalization, pp. 1–6. IEEE, Piscataway (2020)

20. Vitale, P., Mancuso, A., Falco, M.: Museums' tales: visualizing Instagram users' experience. In: Barolli, L., Hellinckx, P., Natwichai, J. (eds.) 3PGCIC 2019. LNNS, vol. 96, pp. 234–245. Springer, Cham (2020). https://doi.org/10.1007/978-3-030-33509-0_21

Deep Learning

A Comparative Study of Deep Learning Techniques for Financial Indices Prediction

Argyrios P. Ketsetsis[1], Konstantinos M. Giannoutakis[1(✉)], Georgios Spanos[1],
Nikolaos Samaras[2], Dimitrios Hristu-Varsakelis[2], Dimitrios Thomas[3],
and Dimitrios Tzovaras[1]

[1] Information Technologies Institute, Centre for Research and Technology Hellas,
Thessaloniki, Greece
{argykets,kgiannou,gspanos,Dimitrios.Tzovaras}@iti.gr
[2] Department of Applied Informatics, University of Macedonia, Thessaloniki, Greece
{samaras,dcv}@uom.edu.gr
[3] Effect Computer Applications S.A., Athens, Greece
thomasd@effect.gr

Abstract. Automated trading is an approach to investing whereby market predictions are combined with algorithmic decision-making strategies for the purpose of generating high returns while minimizing downsides and risk. Recent advancements in Machine and Deep learning algorithms has led to new and sophisticated models to improve this functionality. In this paper, a comparative analysis is conducted concerning eight studies which focus on the American and the European stock markets. The simple method of Golden Cross trading strategy is being utilized for the assessment of models in real-world trading scenarios. Backtesting was performed in two indices, the S&P 500 and the EUROSTOXX 50, resulting in relative good performance, aside from the significant downfall in global markets due to COVID-19 outbreak, which appeared to affect all models.

Keywords: Stock market prediction · Deep learning · Portfolio backtesting · Comparative analysis

1 Introduction

Stock market analysis and automated trading have gained significant attention, due to the inherent complexity of trading markets and to the potential financial profit. Recent advancements in Machine and Deep Learning techniques and the increasing access to high-performance computational hardware have fueled research efforts, oftentimes with results which are much better compared to more traditional statistical time series approaches.

Stock prices are modelled as discrete time series, where financial data are represented as continuous data points indexed in temporal order. Historically,

© IFIP International Federation for Information Processing 2021
Published by Springer Nature Switzerland AG 2021
I. Maglogiannis et al. (Eds.): AIAI 2021, IFIP AICT 627, pp. 297–308, 2021.
https://doi.org/10.1007/978-3-030-79150-6_24

statistical methods, like ARIMA and ARMA were extensively utilized for modeling and forecasting future stock prices. The gradual emergence of machine learning techniques, led to the advent of more sophisticated predictive time series models. Decision Trees (DT), Support Vector Machines (SVM) and Multilayer Perceptrons (MLP) are some of the most prominent techniques [19]. Deep learning techniques and more specifically the recurrent networks, which added a memory-like feature, enhanced the modelling and predictive capabilities of the proposed algorithms. These include Long Short Term Memories (LSTM) [8] and Gated Recurrent Units (GRU) [4] to name a few.

In [12], research studies that incorporated machine/deep learning techniques to predict European stock market securities were collected and reviewed. For the purpose of this study, the methods proposed in these papers were implemented and tested in order to compare them in common datasets and extract more insights. The models were trained and tested on the S&P 500 index and the EUROSTOXX 50 index. The evaluation metrics include the Mean Squared Error (MSE) and the Mean Absolute Percentage Error (MAPE). Moreover, a trading strategy was implemented, the Moving Crossing Average (Golden Cross) [2], in order to test the predictive ability of the selected methods in real-world trading scenarios. While state-of-the-art models come with a thorough comparison to previous models, there are insufficient studies that try to perform a unified comparative analysis of various machine learning and deep learning methods in American and European stock markets.

The remainder of this paper is as follows. In Sect. 2, some background and related studies are presented, while in Sect. 3, the evaluation setup implemented for the comparison of the selected studies is analytically described. In Sect. 4, the results of the predictions and the back-testing outcomes are illustrated, where in Sect. 5, a summarization of the findings are given.

2   Background

In this section, studies that either are dealing with the application/comparison of machine/deep learning techniques and traditional techniques or are related to the moving average technical indicator are presented.

Regarding the application of the moving averages as a trading strategy, Metghalchi et al. [15] examined the efficiency of this technical indicator (among others) in the stock market of 16 European countries over a period spanning from 1990 to 2006. The results highlighted the fact that the moving average can outperform the buy-and-hold strategy for most of the European stock markets.

In [17], the authors compared nine machine and two deep learning models in the prediction task of four stock market groups from the Tehran Stock Exchange. The methods reviewed were: Decision Trees, Random Forest, Boosting algorithms, Support Vector Classifier (SVC), Naive Bayes, K-nearest neighbors (KNN), Logistic Regression, Artificial Neural Networks (ANN), Recurrent Neural Networks (RNNs) and Long-Short-Term-Memories (LSTMs). Their analysis indicated the superiority of RNNs and LSTMs in predicting continuous data.

The authors of [1], implemented different deep neural network topologies, a Support Vector Regressor (SVR) model and the Random Forest (RF) algorithm to predict one month ahead stock returns in the Japanese stock market. Additionally, they examined the performance of a simple long-short portfolio strategy, noting that the best returns are achieved by Deep Neural Networks.

In [12], a systematic literature review has been conducted including primary studies that deal with the prediction of stock prices in the European Union, using machine learning and deep learning techniques. This work motivated this proposed comparative study. Although the survey of [12] included twelve papers, four papers were excluded in this work from the comparative analysis. In two of them, natural language features were utilized [3,13], one incorporated a Hybrid Fuzzy-Neural model [7], while in [5] there was no model testing in a real-world dataset, rather than a theoretical analysis of LSTM topologies.

The works [11,16], both suggest a MLP model with Back Propagation learning rule, while [9] proposes a similar MLP topology, whereas the learning phase is achieved with the Widrow-Hoff learning rule. In [6], a hybrid ARMA-MLP method is incorporated. [10,14,20] propose LSTM topologies for the prediction of closing prices, while [18] proposes a Gated Recurrent Unit (GRU). The characteristics of each work of this analysis are summarized in Table 1.

Table 1. Research works characteristics, [12]

Research work	Features	Methodologies used
Janeski et al. [11]	Time series (OHLCVM)	ANN
Dunis et al. [6]	Time series (Close)	ARMA-MLP
Kyoung-Sook et al. [14]	Time series (OHLCV), Financial indicators	LSTM
Stoean et al. [20]	Time series (Close)	LSTM
Magnus et al. [10]	Time series (Close)	LSTM
Shen et al. [18]	Time series (Close)	GRU
Mourelatos et al. [16]	Financial indicators, Gold prices	MLP
Hanias et al. [9]	Time series (Close)	ANN

3 Evaluation Setup

The purpose of this work is the evaluation of the methodologies depicted in Table 1 in a common setting, in order to make a robust comparative analysis. The evaluation was performed on two stock indices, the Standard and Poor's 500 (S&P 500) and the EUROSTOXX 50, spanning from January 2, 2013 to December 31, 2020. S&P 500 is a market-capitalization-weighted index of the 500 largest publicly-traded companies in the United States, while EUROSTOXX 50 is a market-capitalization weighted index of 50 large, blue-chip European companies that operate within the Eurozone nations. All the approaches to be compared were adapted so as to predict closing prices during the last 650 d of the selected time range, not taking into consideration the binary problem of predicting the direction of price movement. In the case of missing information regarding topology properties and training configuration, the parameter settings were fine-tuned in order to utilize the full potential of each method.

The evaluation procedure was comprised of two distinct scenarios. First, predictive metrics were calculated, in order to gauge the models' forecasting ability. Mean Squared Error (MSE) and Mean Absolute Percentage Error (MAPE) are two common evaluation metrics utilized in the bibliography and used in this study. In addition, a portfolio back-testing scenario was implemented so as to provide a more tangible insight into each model's potential. For this, the crossing moving average strategy was implemented, where two moving averages were applied, one shorter and one longer in time span. When the shorter-term moving average crosses above the longer-term moving average, a buy signal (buy 100 shares) is triggered, as it indicates that the asset's price trend is shifting upwards. On the other hand, when the shorter-term moving average crosses below the long-term moving average, that indicates a sell signal (sell 100 shares), as it is taken to mean that the price trend is shifting downwards. The short-term window was set to 40 d ahead while the long-term to 100 d. Every portfolio was given a starting capital of 100,000\$ and it is assumed that it only contains shares of a stock index. The portfolio evaluation includes the Sharpe Ratio (SR) and the overall return [21]. The overall return refers to the gain or loss realized by a portfolio and depends on the price of the portfolio's components. The Sharpe Ratio is given as $SR = \frac{R_p - R_f}{\sigma_p}$, where R_p denotes the return of portfolio, R_f the risk-free rate and σ_p the standard deviation of the portfolio's return.

4 Numerical Results

In this section, the comparative analysis findings are presented. The methods proposed in the selected studies were tested on their forecasting accuracy, and their predictions were used to construct a moving crossing average strategy for back-testing in two real-world trading scenarios. The testing phase used data from June 2018 through December 2020. It is worth mentioning that during this time period, significant disturbances in the global market took place, due to COVID-19 outbreak, thus resulting in global market instability.

Two stock indices were used to train and test the proposed algorithms. S&P500 is one of the most commonly studied indices in bibliography, and the EUROSTOXX 50 index, which was used in order to provide an insight in European markets, which are relatively less popular in bibliography. The closing price of both indices in the selected time range are presented in Fig. 1.

In Table 2 and Table 3, the MSE, MAPE, SR and Overall Returns are presented for S&P 500 and EUROSTOXX 50 respectively. In both test sets, the method proposed in [18] achieves the smallest MSE and MAPE. The satisfactory forecasting results of [10, 14], which implement LSTM models, confirm the common tendency in the bibliography, that is the superiority of recurrent models in modeling and predicting stock market securities. Taking into consideration both MSE and MAPE metrics, GRU-based method in [18] is the most predictive accurate model in both datasets. It is clear that the MLP-based models achieve greater MSE. One exception is the ARMA-MLP model proposed in [6], which scores 0.00051 MSE and 1.5477 MAPE. This result suggests that hybrid or ensemble models are greatly improved.

As SR is an indicator of risk with respect to the returns, it is clear that the more stable nature of S&P 500 index, results in less risky portfolios. This fact can be deducted by the positive SRs in Table 2. However, this fact comes with mediocre returns, both positive and negative, as seen in the Overall Returns column in Table 2 and in Fig. 2. On the other hand, the volatile EUROSTOXX 50 index, is more risky and presents significant losses, like in [10,14]. In general, one can notice from Fig. 3 and Fig. 5 that the trading strategy was able to detect the downward movement of indices during the COVID-19 outbreak and sell the shares. However, the amount of downfall was not accurately measured in order to add a buy signal at the time when the price was in the lowest possible level in order to achieve maximal return.

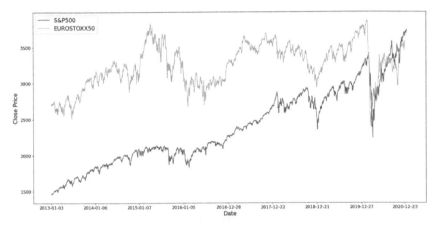

Fig. 1. S&P 500 and EUROSTOXX 50 closing prices from 02/01/2013 to 31/12/2020

Table 2. Evaluation metrics in S&P 500 dataset

Research work	MSE	MAPE	Sharpe ratio	Overall return
Janeski et al. (MLP) [11]	0.00159	0.02999	0.498	0.2102
Dunis et al. (ARMA-MLP) [6]	0.00051	1.54770	−1.163	−17.8186
Kyoung-Sook et al. (LSTM) [14]	0.01105	0.02201	0.974	0.3555
Stoean et al. (LSTM) [20]	0.03362	0.19827	0.964	0.3311
Magnus et al. (LSTM) [10]	0.00064	0.02545	0.871	0.3179
Shen et al. (GRU) [18]	0.00036	0.01904	0.894	0.3283
Mourelatos et al. (MLP-HONN) [16]	0.01162	73.56474	0.867	0.3323
Hanias et al. (MLP) [9]	0.26503	0.49547	0.997	−0.2107
S& P 500 Ground Truth	–	–	0.498	0.8916

Table 3. Evaluation metrics in EUROSTOXX 50 dataset

Research work	MSE	MAPE	Sharpe ratio	Overall return
Janeski et al. (MLP) [11]	0.00762	0.06506	0.231	0.1113
Dunis et al. (ARMA-MLP) [6]	2.04E+05	0.13184	−0.029	−0.1536
Kyoung-Sook et al. (LSTM) [14]	0.00017	0.01125	−0.897	−4.4256
Stoean et al. (LSTM) [20]	0.02545	0.14148	−0.724	−3.422
Magnus et al. (LSTM) [10]	0.00038	0.01803	−0.925	−4.5571
Shen et al. (GRU) [18]	0.00017	0.01158	−0.896	−4.3709
Mourelatos et al. (MLP-HONN) [16]	0.00088	0.02527	−0.92	−4.3901
Hanias et al. (MLP) [9]	0.5623	8.44117	−0.821	−4.075
EUROSTOXX 50 Ground Truth	–	–	−0.03	−0.0471

In the S&P 500 index almost all methods achieve positive overall returns, 33% in approximate. On the other hand, in EUROSTOXX 50, almost all methods achieve negative returns, reflecting the fact that EUROSTOXX 50 is highly volatile. The highest returns in S&P 500 are achieved by [14,16,20]. The first two methods, incorporate LSTM topologies, which confirms the fact that recurrent networks present robust forecasting ability. The latter method, includes additional input features, like gold price, thus providing a more elaborate insight in stock market mechanisms. On EUROSTOXX 50, only [11] was able to provide positive return, while all other methods result in severe losses, 400% approximately. As it is illustrated in Table 3, the overall ground truth return of EUROSTOXX 50 is negative. These losses are due to the inability of the models to predict the striking downfall during COVID-19 outbreak.

In Fig. 2 the frequency of returns of each portfolio is illustrated based on the forecasts of each model for the S&P 500 index. In Fig. 3 the predictions of each model is presented along with the short moving averages (SMA) and the long moving averages (LMA). Based on SMA and LMA, the buy and sell signals are defined, that are illustrated with the triangles. In Fig. 4, the returns of each portfolio based on the predictions of each models for the EUROSTOXX 50 index are indicated, while in Fig. 5, the trading signals for this index are presented.

An additional analysis was carried out regarding the Spearman's rank correlation between MAPE and Overall Returns. For the S&P 500 index, the correlation was slightly positive (0.129) and a slightly negative correlation (−0.176) was observed in the EUROSTOXX 50 index. These two weak correlations for both indices state the fact that a better model with regard to the forecasting ability does not guarantee better results with respect to the profit.

Finally, it is prominent to note that the profitability of each method is dependent to the dataset, since methods that have high profits in the S&P do not perform well in the EUROSTOXX 50 (for instance [10,14]) in comparison with methods that do not perform so well in S&P 500 ([11]). The aforementioned is validated statistically by the negative and medium correlation between the returns of the methods in each dataset provided from the result of spearman's correlation rank test (−0.57).

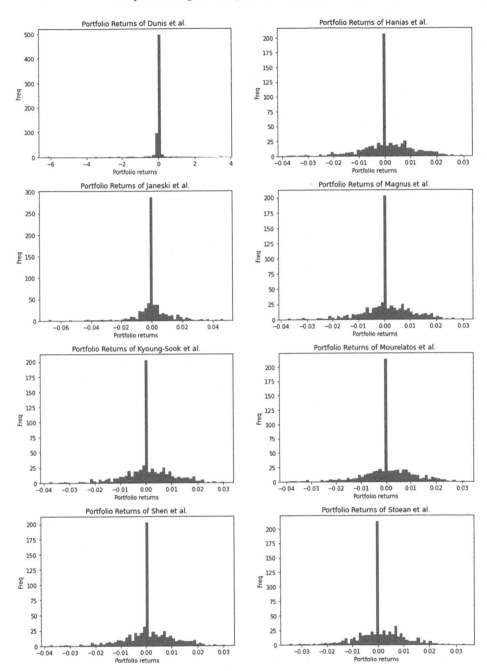

Fig. 2. S&P 500 returns

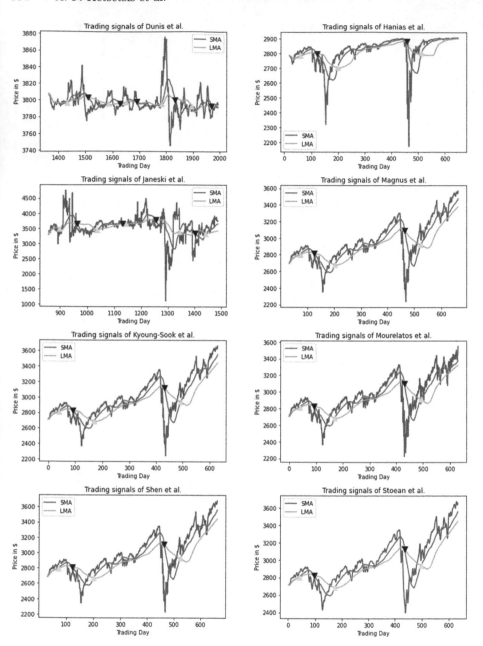

Fig. 3. S&P 500 trading signals

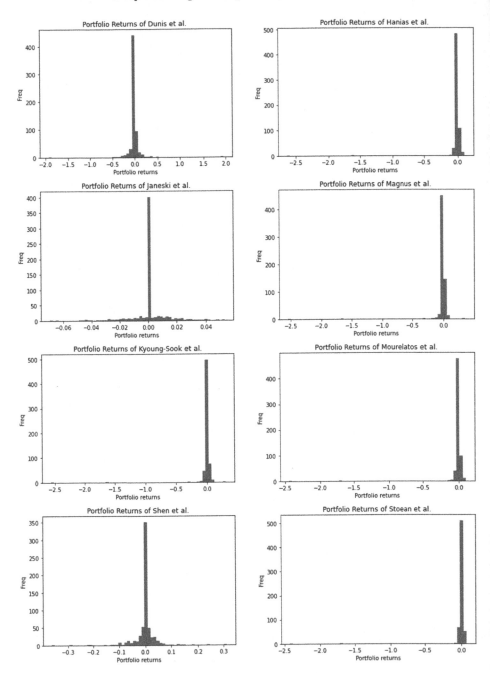

Fig. 4. EUROSTOXX 50 returns

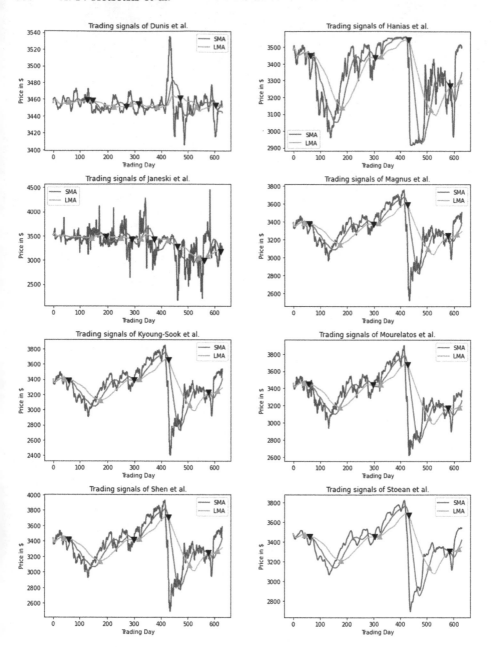

Fig. 5. EUROSTOXX 50 trading signals

5   Conclusions

In this paper, a comparative analysis of 8 studies concerning stock market prediction using a common trading strategy and time span was carried out.

These studies were implemented and tested on two common datasets, the closing prices of the S&P 500 and the EUROSTOXX 50 indices. The evaluation metrics included the MSE and MAPE for the assessment of the price predictions. In order to come closer to a real world evaluation, the Moving Average Crossing Strategy was implemented to evaluate the performance of the studies in the two stock markets. The trading strategy evaluation metrics were the overall portfolio return and the Sharpe Ratio.

The superiority of the recurrent algorithms, and the difference in Moving Average Crossing strategy results between the two datasets were observed. This, likely indicates the difference in the stock market reaction to COVID-19 outbreak between American and European markets. Following the comparative analysis, it appears that none method proved to be universally superior on both datasets. Finally, it is worth noting that an accurate prediction model does not guarantee positive returns in the backtesting scenario as proved by the correlation analysis between MAPE and Overall Returns. Further analysis should be carried out regarding portfolio optimization, as Moving Crossing Average is just one of a multitude of possible trading strategies and also because the portfolio's components were only stock indices for the purposes of this study.

Co-financed by Greece and the European Union

Acknowledgments. The authors would like to thank Mr. Christos Kourounis for his support on the implementation of the research works [6,11,16]. This research has been co-financed by the European Regional Development Fund of the European Union and Greek national funds through the Operational Program Competitiveness, Entrepreneurship and Innovation, under the call RESEARCH – CREATE – INNO-VATE (project code:T2EDK-03743).

References

1. Abe, M., Nakayama, H.: Deep learning for forecasting stock returns in the cross-section. In: Phung, D., Tseng, V.S., Webb, G.I., Ho, B., Ganji, M., Rashidi, L. (eds.) PAKDD 2018. LNCS (LNAI), vol. 10937, pp. 273–284. Springer, Cham (2018). https://doi.org/10.1007/978-3-319-93034-3_22
2. Bailey, D.H., Borwein, J., Lopez de Prado, M., Zhu, Q.J.: Pseudo-mathematics and financial charlatanism: the effects of backtest overfitting on out-of-sample performance. Not. Am. Math. Soc. **61**(5), 458–471 (2014)
3. Borovkova, S., Dijkstra, M.: Deep learning prediction of the eurostoxx 50 with news sentiment. Available at SSRN 3253043 (2018)
4. Chung, J., Gulcehre, C., Cho, K., Bengio, Y.: Empirical evaluation of gated recurrent neural networks on sequence modeling. In: NIPS 2014 Workshop on Deep Learning, December 2014 (2014)
5. Dezsi, E., Nistor, I.A.: Can deep machine learning outsmart the market? a comparison between econometric modelling and long- short term memory. Rom. Econ. Bus. Rev. **11**(4.1), 54–73 (2016)

6. Dunis, C.L., Laws, J., Karathanassopoulos, A.: Modelling and trading the Greek stock market with mixed neural network models. Appl. Financ. Econ. **21**(23), 1793–1808 (2011)
7. García, F., Guijarro, F., Oliver, J., Tamošiūnienė, R.: Hybrid fuzzy neural network to predict price direction in the German dax-30 index. Technol. Econ. Dev. Econ. **24**(6), 2161–2178 (2018)
8. Gers, F.A., Schmidhuber, J., Cummins, F.: Learning to forget: continual prediction with LSTM. In: 1999 Ninth International Conference on Artificial Neural Networks ICANN 99. (Conf. Publ. No. 470), vol. 2, pp. 850–855 vol. 2 (1999)
9. Hanias, M.P., Curtis, P.G., Thalassinos, E.: Time series prediction with neural networks for the athens stock exchange indicator (2012)
10. Hansson, M.: On stock return prediction with LSTM networks (2017)
11. Janeski, M., Kalajdziski, S.: Neural network model for forecasting Balkan stock exchanges. In: Huang, D.-S., Gan, Y., Bevilacqua, V., Figueroa, J.C. (eds.) ICIC 2011. LNCS, vol. 6838, pp. 17–24. Springer, Heidelberg (2011). https://doi.org/10.1007/978-3-642-24728-6_3
12. Ketsetsis, A.P., et al.: Deep learning techniques for stock market prediction in the European union: a systematic review. In: 2020 International Conference on Computational Science and Computational Intelligence, to appear (2021)
13. Kraus, M., Feuerriegel, S.: Decision support from financial disclosures with deep neural networks and transfer learning. Decis. Support Syst. **104**, 38–48 (2017)
14. Kyoung-Sook, M., Hongjoong, K.: Performance of deep learning in prediction of stock market volatility. Econ. Comput. Econ. Cybern. Studies Res. **53**(2), 77–92 (2019)
15. Metghalchi, M., Marcucci, J., Chang, Y.H.: Are moving average trading rules profitable? evidence from the European stock markets. Appl. Econ. **44**(12), 1539–1559 (2012)
16. Mourelatos, M., Alexakos, C., Amorgianiotis, T., Likothanassis, S.: Financial indices modelling and trading utilizing deep learning techniques: The Athens se ftse/ase large cap use case. In: 2018 Innovations in Intelligent Systems and Applications (INISTA), pp. 1–7 (2018)
17. Nabipour, M., Nayyeri, P., Jabani, H., Shahab, S., Mosavi, A.: Predicting stock market trends using machine learning and deep learning algorithms via continuous and binary data; a comparative analysis. IEEE Access **8**, 150199–150212 (2020)
18. Shen, G., Tan, Q., Zhang, H., Zeng, P., Xu, J.: Deep learning with gated recurrent unit networks for financial sequence predictions. Procedia Comput. Sci. **131**, 895–903 (2018)
19. Shen, S., Jiang, H., Zhang, T.: Stock market forecasting using machine learning algorithms. Department of Electrical Engineering, Stanford University, Stanford, CA, pp. 1–5. (2012)
20. Stoean, C., Paja, W., Stoean, R., Sandita, A.: Deep architectures for long-term stock price prediction with a heuristic-based strategy for trading simulations. PLOS ONE **14**(10), 1–19 (2019)
21. Zhang, Z., Khushi, M.: Ga-MSSR: Genetic algorithm maximizing sharpe and sterling ratio method for robotrading. In: 2020 International Joint Conference on Neural Networks, pp. 1–8. IEEE (2020)

An Effective Loss Function for Generating 3D Models from Single 2D Image Without Rendering

Nikola Zubić$^{1(\boxtimes)}$ (iD) and Pietro Liò$^{2(\boxtimes)}$ (iD)

^{1} Faculty of Technical Sciences, 21125 Novi Sad, Serbia
`nikola.zubic@uns.ac.rs`
^{2} University of Cambridge, Cambridge CB3 0FD, UK
`pietro.lio@cst.cam.ac.uk`

Abstract. Differentiable rendering is a very successful technique that applies to a Single-View 3D Reconstruction. Current renderers use losses based on pixels between a rendered image of some 3D reconstructed object and ground-truth images from given matched viewpoints to optimise parameters of the 3D shape.

These models require a rendering step, along with visibility handling and evaluation of the shading model. The main goal of this paper is to demonstrate that we can avoid these steps and still get reconstruction results as other state-of-the-art models that are equal or even better than existing category-specific reconstruction methods. First, we use the same CNN architecture for the prediction of a point cloud shape and pose prediction like the one used by Insafutdinov & Dosovitskiy. Secondly, we propose the novel effective loss function that evaluates how well the projections of reconstructed 3D point clouds cover the ground-truth object's silhouette. Then we use Poisson Surface Reconstruction to transform the reconstructed point cloud into a 3D mesh. Finally, we perform a GAN-based texture mapping on a particular 3D mesh and produce a textured 3D mesh from a single 2D image. We evaluate our method on different datasets (including ShapeNet, CUB-200-2011, and Pascal3D+) and achieve state-of-the-art results, outperforming all the other supervised and unsupervised methods and 3D representations, all in terms of performance, accuracy, and training time.

Keywords: 3D reconstruction · Single-view 3D reconstruction

1 Introduction

One of the main problems in 3D Computer Graphics and Vision is the ability of a model to learn 3D structure representation and reconstruction [9]. Supervised 3D

N. Zubić–Work performed while the author was Research Intern Apprentice under the supervision of professor Pietro Liò.

I. Maglogiannis et al. (Eds.): AIAI 2021, IFIP AICT 627, pp. 309–322, 2021.
https://doi.org/10.1007/978-3-030-79150-6_25

Deep Learning is highly efficient in direct learning from 3D data representations [1], such as meshes, voxels, and point clouds. They require a large amount of 3D data for the training process, and also, their representation is sometimes complex for the task of direct learning. These factors lead to the abandonment of this approach because of its inefficient performance and time consumption. Unsupervised 3D structural learning learns 3D structure without 3D supervision and represents a promising approach.

Differentiable rendering is a novel field that allows the gradients of 3D objects to be calculated and propagated through images [11]. It also reduces the requirement of 3D data collection and annotation, while enabling a higher success rate in various applications. Their ability to create a bond between 3D and 2D representations, by computing gradients of 2D loss functions with the respect to 3D structure, makes them a key component in unsupervised 3D structure learning. These loss functions are based on differences between RGB pixel values [13]. By rendering the predicted 3D structure from a specific viewpoint and then evaluating the loss function based on pixel-wise loss between rendered and ground-truth image, model parameters are optimised to reconstruct the desired 3D structure.

However, these evaluation techniques are very time-consuming. They don't contribute at all to an accurate 3D structure reconstruction. Here, we propose a novel idea for fast 3D structure reconstruction (in the form of a point cloud silhouette) and then we convert it to a 3D mesh and transfer the object's texture from a 2D image onto the reconstructed 3D object. Hence, unlike in loss functions that are based on pixels, our approach has an effective loss function that arises exclusively from the 2D projections of 3D points, without interpolation based on pixels, shading and visibility handling.

2 Related Work

2.1 3D Representations

Previous works [23,29] have concentrated on mesh reconstruction by using the full 3D supervision approach. The main problem with these approaches, besides inefficiency, is the usage of ground-truth 3D meshes, and they are mostly available in a limited number of datasets. Some approaches [24,25] solved this problem by using 2D supervision from multiple-scene images based on voxels.

2.2 Differentiable Rendering

Prediction of 3D models from single images while achieving high-quality visual results is possible by using the differentiable renderer. A differentiable rendering framework allows gradients to be analytically (or approximately) computed for all pixels in an image. Famous frameworks include: RenderNet [19] and OpenDR [17].

2.3 Unsupervised Learning of Shape and Pose with Differentiable Point Clouds

The work that inspired us addresses the learning of an accurate 3D shape and camera pose from a collection of unlabeled category-specific images [8]. It uses a specific convolutional neural network architecture to predict both model's shape and the pose from a single image. However, it is still time-consuming since it uses differentiable point cloud projection.

3 Proposed Method

3.1 Intuitive Overview

In order to overcome the problems of structural 3D learning, unsupervised methods introduced different differentiable renderers [3,8,9,11,16,17,19] to first render the reconstructed 3D shape into 2D images from different view-angles and then portray them as what got obtained through complete supervision. After this, we can calculate the pixel-wise losses between those 2D images from different view-angles and real (ground-truth) images from the dataset. Since the renderer is differentiable, the loss between these images back-propagates through the network to train it.   To evaluate the pixel-wise loss, previous differentiable

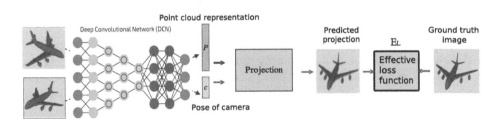

Fig. 1. Our method removes the rendering process and requires only 2D projections of 3D point clouds. During the generation of 3D shapes using multiple silhouette images (from different viewing angles), 2D projections of all points on the shape should uniformly cover the silhouette from each viewing angle. We implement this using two key ideas (that together form effective loss function). (1) For 3D shapes formed by 3D points, their projections for each view should locate within the silhouette. (2) All projections for each silhouette should distribute uniformly. We achieve this by maximising the loss between each of the pairs of these 2D projections. **P** - Point cloud representation, **c** - Pose of camera.

renderers rendered the images by taking into account some form of interpolation [3] of the reconstructed 3D structure over each pixel, such as rasterisation and visibility handling.

We train a network that learns to generate a 3D point cloud based on a single image using the images from a dataset (from different view-angles) as supervision which is opposed to those that use ground-truth point clouds as supervision.

Current methods render based on differentiable renderers that render images of the reconstructed 3D shape and actual images and then minimise the pixel-wise loss to optimise the reconstructed 3D shape.

Total effective loss informs us how well the projected points cover the objective silhouette. The process includes two terms, one that forces all the projections into the silhouette where the projections initialise randomly, and the other term moves the projections such that the distance between every two of them is the maximum possible, which allows the projections to cover the silhouette uniformly. Starting from some point cloud (randomly initialised), we can force all the projections in the silhouette using the first term, and then using the second term, we can uniformly distribute projections to cover the whole silhouette.

Fig. 2. Generated 3D point cloud is transformed into 3D mesh and then textured.

After completing the process shown in Fig. 1, we generate 3D point cloud for a desired image. After this, we apply Poisson Surface Reconstruction [12] to generate 3D mesh from given 3D point cloud and then we use GAN for texture mapping on a particular 3D mesh and produce a textured 3D mesh based on the input image texture, which is shown in the Fig. 2. Main paper deals with implementation details of an Effective Loss Function E_L which is our novelty, and compares the results with other approaches. More details and case study is available in Appendix A.

3.2   Implementation Details

Our goal is to learn the structure of 3D point clouds (P) formed by N points n_j only from G_t ground-truth images of the silhouette S_i, where $j \in [1, N]$ and $i \in [1, G_t]$. Current differentiable renderers rely on point clouds (P) rendering into raster images S_i' from i-th viewing angle, which are used to produce a loss by comparing S_i' and S_i pixel by pixel. These steps are not necessary to get a precise solution.

Let the projection of the point n_j in view i be p_j^i. The error evaluates how well the sets of projected points $\{p_j^i \mid j \in [1, N]\}$ cover the silhouette of the object. So, the loss is composed of two parts.

If we have a predicted 3D point cloud and a binary image of the silhouette, the loss calculates as follows: First, we project the points n_j and get projections

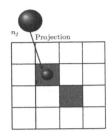 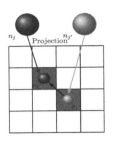

Fig. 3. The left and right grids represent two ground-truth silhouette images S_i. n_j point projects onto an image, and its projection is p_j. **Left:** For 3D shapes formed by 3D points, their projections for each view should locate within the silhouette, where the whole white grid is a silhouette, and its pixel values are 1 (red square). So, we are minimising differences between pixel values of projections and 1 for every projection. **Right:** Besides that, we must not only minimise the first term loss but also the second term loss which maximises the distance between two different point projections from a 3D point cloud: p_j and $p_{j'}$. (Color figure online)

p_j (we write abbreviated without i, this is $\boldsymbol{p}_j^i$) on the images of the silhouette S_i, where the pixel value of the projection p_j is denoted by $\boldsymbol{\pi}_i$. The first term penalises points outside of the foreground by calculating the difference $1 - \boldsymbol{\pi}_i$, assuming that the foreground in the binary silhouette image has a value of 1. Minimising this loss will force all projections into the foreground. Additionally, the second term adjusts the spatial distribution of the projected points. It forces the pairs of projections in the foreground to be as far apart from each other as possible (right grid shown in the Fig. 3). Thus, such a system arranges the 3D locations of the points n_j through their projections p_j by simultaneously optimising these two losses.

The first term is calculated as the difference between 1 and the pixel value π_i of each projection p_j^i on the silhouette image S_i. We make use of bilinear interpolation to calculate the value π_i using the binary pixel values of the nearest pixels around p_j^i. All projections are forced to the foreground for all silhouette images by minimising the following L_1 norm:

$$L_1(\pi_i) = \|1 - \pi_i\|_1 \tag{1}$$

However, it is impossible to force all projections into the foreground by minimising this $L1$ norm. If we optimise point cloud according to some silhouette image (a) and start from some randomly initialised points (b), then we will get inadequate point projections if we use $L1$ norm, as shown in the Fig. 4.

There are two reasons why this problem occurs. One reason is the fact that $L1$ norm is non-differentiable. Even if we only look at the difference, the second reason is that we only examine the pixel intensity based on the difference between 1 and the interpolated pixel value π_i based on the four closest binary pixel values. This prevents training if the projections p_j^i are too far from the foreground.

Our goal is to produce non-zero gradients anywhere in the background part, while the pixel values in the foreground part do not require a modification. We

(a)   (b)   (c)

Fig. 4. We are given a silhouette image **(a)** and randomly initialized projections **(b)**. Then we cannot force projections into the foreground **(c)** because standard first term loss has a local minimum problem, which results in a non-uniform disposition of projections (blue dots). This problem is solved by smoothing the original silhouette to obtain pixel values of projections and calculate the difference. (Color figure online)

will denote these processed silhouette images as S_i^G, to distinguish between the original silhouette image S_i and the processed image. For each pixel x on the background of the silhouette image S_i, we write:

$$S_i^G(x) = \begin{cases} 1, & x \in \mathcal{F} \\ 1 - d(x, \partial\mathcal{F}), & x \in \bar{\mathcal{F}} \end{cases} \quad (2)$$

where $\mathcal{F} = \{x \mid \pi_i(x) = 1\}$ is the foreground, while $\bar{\mathcal{F}} = \{x \mid \pi_i(x) = 0\}$ is a background, and $\partial\mathcal{F}$ is the foreground's boundary. $d(x, \partial\mathcal{F})$ represents the L_2 distance between x and his closest $\partial\mathcal{F}$, which is normalised by the resolution of the S_i.

Normalisation is also performed on the processed pixel values in the background for them to lie in the interval $(0, 1)$. Min-max normalisation is used for this sub-task: $S_i^G(\bar{\mathcal{F}}) = \text{minmax}\left(S_i^G(\bar{\mathcal{F}})\right)$. Finally, the modified first term loss function is:

$$\mathcal{M}_1(\pi_i) = \left\|1 - \pi_i^G\right\|_1 \quad (3)$$

According to Fig. 5, using only the first term loss leads to non-uniform point projections in the foreground. To accurately represent the 3D shape and cover the silhouette, we will use a second term loss. Through this loss, we will model the spatial relationship between every two pairs of projections. That loss should force projections inside the foreground. They should be as far away from each other as possible.

To solve this problem, we propose a second-term loss function that increases the distance between projection pairs that are deeper within the foreground and reduces it for projection pairs around the foreground's boundary. It skips projections within the background.

Fig. 5. With modified first term loss function, it is possible to force all projections of randomly initialised points **(b)** from a smoothed silhouette image **(a)** into the foreground **(c)** by minimising the (3). Blue dots represent the projections. (Color figure online)

For every projection pair p_j^i and $p_{j'}^i$, the $L2$ distance is calculated by the formula:

$$d\left(p_j^i, p_{j'}^i\right) = \left\|p_j^i - p_{j'}^i\right\|_2, \tag{4}$$

which we then normalise according to the resolution of the silhouette image.

This approach tends to maximise the distance $d\left(p_j^i, p_{j'}^i\right)$. We use the Gaussian function [14] to obtain a loss based on the invariance of the structure which decreases with increasing the distance. So, we can essentially minimise the loss of invariance along with the modified first term loss $\mathcal{M}_1$.

For each projection p_j^i, loss based on the invariance of the structure models its spatial relationship with all other projections $p_{j'}^i$:

$$\mathcal{L}_2\left(p_j^i, \{p_{j'}^i\}\right) = w_j^i \sum_{j'=1}^{N} \left[w_{j'}^i \cdot \exp\left(\frac{-d\left(p_j^i, p_{j'}^i\right)}{\theta} + \mu_j^i\right)\right], \tag{5}$$

where w_j^i and $w_{j'}^i$ are weights corresponding to the projections p_j^i and $p_{j'}^i$ respectively, $\theta > 0$ is the decay parameter, $\mu_j^i > 0$ is the boundary bias for the projection p_j^i.

w_j^i expresses to what level the projection p_j^i merges with the background. If that weight is set to zero, the projection p_j^i is such that the invariance of the structure is completely removed so that the modified first term loss $\mathcal{M}_1$ immediately forces p_j^i within the foreground. The decay (merge) parameter controls the merge interval (invariance of the structure intensity) of a given background 3D model. The projection boundary bias μ_j^i for projection p_j^i controls the distance to the foreground's boundary where the invariance over that projection reduces.

Weight w_j^i is calculated using bilinear interpolation based on the closest binary pixel values in the silhouette image S_i, as shown in the Fig. 3. We use multi-scale gradients [21] to compute μ_j^i. Binary pixel values are extracted from adjacent points located at the vertices of the squares in the grid (around the projection p_j^i) - Fig. 3. We perform interpolations over them, and we take the mean value of all of these interpolations to calculate μ_j^i. This approach progressively reduces invariance of the structure as p_j^i approaches the foreground's boundary.

Finally, the effective loss function E_L is calculated through simultaneous minimisation of the modified first term loss function $\mathcal{M}_1$ and the second term loss function $\mathcal{L}_2$ based on the invariance of the structure. The total error E_L is obtained by the following formula (α and β are used for balancing the losses, we average over points N and views G_t):

$$E_L = \frac{\sum_{i=1}^{G_t} \sum_{j=1}^{N} \left(\alpha \mathcal{M}_1 \left(\pi_i \right) + \beta \mathcal{L}_2 \left(p_j^i, \{ p_{j'}^i \} \right) \right)}{G_t \cdot N} \tag{6}$$

After this process, we have a 3D point cloud which is then transformed to a 3D mesh using Poisson Surface Reconstruction [12]. We use GAN [30] for texture mapping on a particular 3D mesh and produce a textured 3D mesh based on the input image texture, which is shown in Fig. 2. The generator generates displacement maps and textures, and the discriminator discriminates between real/fake displacement maps and textures.

4   Results

In this section, we succinctly report the results, primarily through comparison with other approaches. More details and case study is available in Appendix A.

The quantitative results using Chamfer's distance [22] are shown in Table 1. Our point cloud output (Ours) outperforms its voxel equivalent (Ours-V) in all cases. Chamfer's distance improves with the increase of resolution. We also outperform the previous best method that used rendering [8] and DRC method [24].

Table 1. Quantitative results on shape prediction with known camera pose (on ShapeNet dataset). We report the Chamfer's distance between normalised point clouds, multiplied by 100 and use three categories: Airplanes, Cars and Chairs. Our point cloud output outperforms all other methods in terms of Chamfer's distance. Lower value is better; bold = best.

	Resolution 32				Resolution 64		Resolution 128	
	DRC [25]	DPC [8]	Ours-V	Ours	DPC [8]	Ours	DPC [8]	Ours
Airplane	8.35	4.52	4.49	**3.99**	3.50	**3.15**	2.84	**2.63**
Car	4.35	4.22	3.75	**3.79**	2.98	**2.86**	2.42	**2.37**
Chair	8.01	5.10	5.34	**4.64**	4.15	**3.99**	3.62	**3.46**
Mean	6.90	4.61	4.53	**4.14**	3.55	**3.33**	2.96	**2.82**

Our results outperform state-of-the-art differentiable renderers in the Volumetric IoU metric [20] while simultaneously being less time-consuming during the training phase, as shown in Table 2. For cars, our outcome is better than renderers

Table 2. Quantitative volumetric IoU [20] comparison with differentiable renderers for different 3D representations and supervised methods (on ShapeNet dataset). We use three categories: Airplanes, Cars and Chairs. Bigger value is better; bold = best.

| | Unsupervised learning | | | Supervised learning | | | | | | | |
	SoftRas [16]	DIB-R [3]	Ours	P2M [27]	IN [15]	RN [4]	AN [6]	DSN [32]	3DN [28]	ON [18]	Ours
Airplane	58.4	57.0	62.4	51.5	55.4	42.6	39.2	57.5	54.3	57.1	**75.3**
Car	77.1	**78.8**	75.6	50.1	74.5	66.1	22.0	74.3	59.4	73.7	**75.1**
Chair	49.7	52.7	**58.3**	40.2	52.2	43.9	25.7	54.3	34.4	50.1	**57.8**
Mean	61.7	62.8	**65.43**	47.3	60.7	50.9	29.0	62.0	49.4	60.3	**64.97**

Table 3. Training time efficiency in hours.

	3D representations	Rendering	32^2 image 2000 points/ 32^3 voxels	64^2 image 8000 points/ 64^3 voxels	128^2 image 16000 points/ 128^3 voxels
DRC [25]	Voxels	Yes	$\approx$14 h	$\approx$60 h	$\approx$216 h
DPC [8]	Point clouds	Yes	$\approx$14 h	$\approx$24 h	$\approx$72 h
Ours	Point clouds	No	$\approx$**6.5** h	$\approx$**11** h	$\approx$**34.5** h

based on voxels but very similar to renderers based on meshes because meshes represent a superior initial 3D representation for large areas of flat surfaces [10] (such as cars).

Also, FID scores on Mesh (produced from 3D point cloud), Texture (extracted by a GAN) and Both (final output - textured 3D mesh) produced state-of-the art results, which can be seen in Fig. 6.

5 Datasets, Metrics and Code

Datasets. We used the following datasets: ShapeNet [2] (train/test split from [8]), CUB-200-2011 [26] (train/test split from [10]), and Pascal3D+ dataset [31] (train/test split from [10]).

Metrics. Numerical evaluation for point clouds is performed by using Chamfer's distance [22] between predicted and real (ground-truth) point clouds.

Volumetric IoU [20] comparison is used by comparing the 3D grid voxelised from the predicted point cloud with the one voxelised from the ground-truth point cloud.

Fréchet Inception Distance (FID) is widely used as an evaluation metric [7] (not only for 2D GANs but also for our task). FID scores will evaluate 2D projections of generated point clouds to meshes. 3D mesh and textures are evaluated separately in this process.

Code. Implementation, data and trained models are available at: https://github.com/NikolaZubic/2dimageto3dmodel

6   Possible Extensions and Limitations

Our work can be used as part of more complex software that deals with video games, animation, or any aspect where it is necessary to have base 3D models which can be additionally polished with more sculpting. The work can be extended by taking even more account of the smooth characteristics of the functions. Our work is the first one to tackle the challenging problem of Single-View 3D Reconstruction without Rendering. Results are impressive, but this task is far from being fully solved. Our model struggles to predict camera poses that are rare in the training dataset. Also, it captures the major shape characteristics of each instance but ignores some details. For example, legs of zebras, cows and horses are not separated (Figs. 5 and 6).

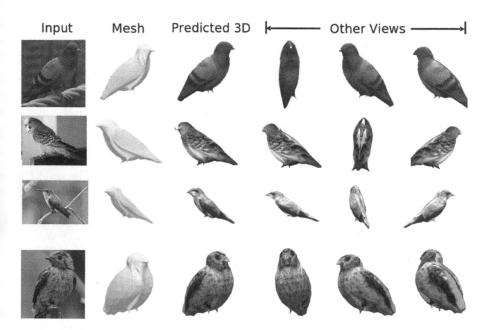

Fig. 6. We use real-world 2D bird images as input for generating a 3D model. In the first column is the input where we have images of the real birds, in the second column, there is a generated 3D mesh (obtained from 3D point cloud after Poisson Surface Reconstruction [12]), and in the next four columns, there is a predicted 3D model visible in 4 poses.

7   Conclusion

In this paper, we proposed a 3D reconstruction based on a single image, a method for learning the pose and shape of 3D objects given only their 2D projections, using the initial point cloud representation and then converting that representation to a 3D mesh. Mesh is textured using GANs to produce the final output. Extensive experiments have shown that point clouds compare well with the voxel-based representation, such as performance and accuracy. The proposed framework learns to predict shape, texture, and pose from single images, without rendering step, based solely on 2D projections of 3D point clouds and their coverage of the ground-truth silhouette. While rendering requires exhaustive computation, our key finding is that it does not endow accuracy in 3D structure learning.

Acknowledgements. We would like to thank the anonymous reviewers for reviewing the paper before final submission and providing helpful and detailed comments.

A   Appendix - Network architecture details

The network we used for the $3D$ reconstruction (in a point cloud representation) based on a single image is composed of a $2D$ encoder and a $3D$ point cloud decoder. The $2D$ encoder represents a 7-layer CNN. The first layer consists of a 5×5 kernel with 16 channels and a stride of 2. Each of the remaining layers has three kernels and comes in pairs, where the given layer in pairs has a stride of 2, while the second one has a stride of 1. The number of channels increases by a factor of 2 after each layer with a stride. These convolutional layers are followed by two fully connected layers whose dimensions are 1024. The $3D$ point cloud decoder has one fully connected layer whose dimensions are 1024, and it then predicts the point cloud representation. The point cloud that is consisted of N points gets predicted as a vector whose dimensions are $3N$ (point coordinates).

We have chosen this architecture because it achieved state-of-the-art results for the problem of Single-View 3D Reconstruction, but the process of differentiable rendering was unnecessary, and we obtained a more precise solution without it. This architecture represents an optimal solution because it can firmly reconstruct real-world data, despite the absence of accurate ground-truth camera poses. Also, it can be used as a basis to learn colors and textures, but that would require explicit reasoning about lighting and shading.

B   Appendix - More results and discussion

Figure 7 shows a few generated, textured meshes rendered from the multiple views in Blender [5], and also their corresponding textures. Results on the CUB-200-2011 dataset have high resolution, but the back of the cars in the Pascal3D+ dataset has some irregularities. After further analysis, we found that the dataset is very imbalanced, with only 20% of the images showing the back of the car and the majority of them showed the frontal part. So, this issue could be solved by using more training data.

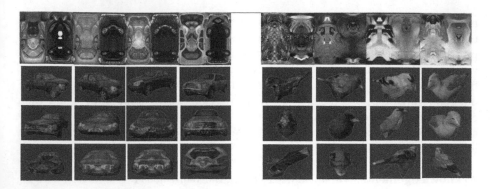

Fig. 7. Qualitative results on Pascal3D+ (**left**) and CUB-200-2011 (**right**) dataset. Each object has been rendered from three views (in Blender [5]), and the top row represents the texture learned by GAN.

C   Appendix - Ablation study and efficiency

We carried out ablation studies to justify our claims in terms of the effectiveness of each element of our method under airplanes at a resolution of 2000 points in Table 1. In Table 4, we report results with only some losses, fewer views (like $G_t = 3$ and $G_t = 2$), and without weights and biases.

Table 4. Ablation studies in terms of Chamfer's distance (CD).

	$\mathcal{M}_1$	$\mathcal{L}_2$	Pixel+$\mathcal{L}_2$	$\mathcal{M}_1$ + no w_j^i	$\mathcal{M}_1$ + no μ_j^i	$G_t = 2$	$G_t = 3$	$G_t = 4$
CD	19.50	139.10	24.59	4.58	4.41	4.79	4.54	**4.01**

This study shows that our loss E_L cannot learn the structure of shapes using only $\mathcal{M}_1$ or $\mathcal{L}_2$ loss, also not with standard L_1 loss because of the local minimum issue and non-differentiability. The second term loss and its hyperparameters (indicator weights and boundary bias) contribute to the reconstruction accuracy and efficiency of optimization. Parameters α and β contribute to the conflict and trade-off between modified first term loss and second term loss based on structure invariance. Using fewer views than our $G_t = 4$ views in training degenerates the structure learning performance.

As for efficiency, we compared our model's training time with state-of-the-art differentiable renderers for 3D shapes, as shown in Table 3. The voxel-based method (DRC) has a weakness in terms of a vast computational burden due to the cubic complexity of voxel grids, which limits it to work only in low resolutions such as 32^3 and 64^3 with a slow convergence rate. Although the point cloud-based method by Insafutdinov & Dosovitskiy [8] does not require 3D convolutional layers as DRC, the rendering procedure still requires intensive computation with discrete 3D grids. So, this method requires more time (6×10^5 mini-batch iterations) during training than our method (1×10^5 mini-batch iterations).

We used parameters learned in different steps during training to reconstruct a shape from a corresponding image in a test set. Additionally, by using an image from test rather than the training set we demonstrated the generalization ability learned in optimization, which strongly justifies our effectiveness. Also, it is shown that our model adapts well to real-world images.

References

1. Ahmed, E., et al.: A survey on deep learning advances on different 3D data representations (2019)
2. Chang, A.X., et al.: Shapenet: an information-rich 3D model repository (2015)
3. Chen, W., et al.: Learning to predict 3D objects with an interpolation-based differentiable renderer. In: Wallach, H., Larochelle, H., Beygelzimer, A., d'Alché-Buc, F., Fox, E., Garnett, R. (eds.) Advances in Neural Information Processing Systems, vol. 32, pp. 9609–9619. Curran Associates, Inc. (2019). https://proceedings.neurips.cc/paper/2019/file/f5ac21cd0ef1b88e9848571aeb53551a-Paper.pdf
4. Choy, Christopher B., Xu, Danfei, Gwak, JunYoung, Chen, Kevin, Savarese, Silvio: 3D-R2N2: a unified approach for single and multi-view 3D object reconstruction. In: Leibe, Bastian, Matas, Jiri, Sebe, Nicu, Welling, Max (eds.) ECCV 2016. LNCS, vol. 9912, pp. 628–644. Springer, Cham (2016). https://doi.org/10.1007/978-3-319-46484-8_38
5. Community, B.O.: Blender - a 3D modelling and rendering package. Blender Foundation, Stichting Blender Foundation, Amsterdam (2018). http://www.blender.org
6. Groueix, T., Fisher, M., Kim, V.G., Russell, B.C., Aubry, M.: Atlasnet: a papier-mâché approach to learning 3D surface generation (2018)
7. Heusel, M., Ramsauer, H., Unterthiner, T., Nessler, B., Hochreiter, S.: GANs trained by a two time-scale update rule converge to a local nash equilibrium (2018)
8. Insafutdinov, E., Dosovitskiy, A.: Unsupervised learning of shape and pose with differentiable point clouds. CoRR abs/1810.09381 (2018). http://arxiv.org/abs/1810.09381
9. Rezende, D.J., Eslami, S.M.A., Mohamed, S., Battaglia, P., Jaderberg, M., Heess, N.: Unsupervised learning of 3D structure from images. In: Lee, D., Sugiyama, M., Luxburg, U., Guyon, I., Garnett, R. (eds.) Advances in Neural Information Processing Systems, vol. 29, pp. 4996–5004. Curran Associates, Inc. (2016). https://proceedings.neurips.cc/paper/2016/file/1d94108e907bb8311d8802b48fd54b4a-Paper.pdf
10. Kanazawa, A., Tulsiani, S., Efros, A.A., Malik, J.: Learning category-specific mesh reconstruction from image collections (2018)
11. Kato, H., et al.: Differentiable rendering: a survey (2020)
12. Kazhdan, M., Bolitho, M., Hoppe, H.: Poisson surface reconstruction. In: Proceedings of the Fourth Eurographics Symposium on Geometry Processing, SGP 2006, p. 61–70. Eurographics Association, Goslar (2006)
13. Kumar, T., Verma, K.: A theory based on conversion of RGB image to gray image. Int. J. Comput. Appl. **7**(2), 7–10 (2010)
14. Li, Z., Shafiei, M., Ramamoorthi, R., Sunkavalli, K., Chandraker, M.: Inverse rendering for complex indoor scenes: shape, spatially-varying lighting and svbrdf from a single image (2019)

15. Liu, J., Lu, H.: IMNet: a learning based detector for index modulation aided MIMO-OFDM systems (2019)
16. Liu, S., Chen, W., Li, T., Li, H.: Soft rasterizer: differentiable rendering for unsupervised single-view mesh reconstruction (2019)
17. Loper, Matthew M., Black, Michael J.: OpenDR: an approximate differentiable renderer. In: Fleet, David, Pajdla, Tomas, Schiele, Bernt, Tuytelaars, Tinne (eds.) ECCV 2014. LNCS, vol. 8695, pp. 154–169. Springer, Cham (2014). https://doi.org/10.1007/978-3-319-10584-0_11
18. Mescheder, L., Oechsle, M., Niemeyer, M., Nowozin, S., Geiger, A.: Occupancy networks: learning 3D reconstruction in function space (2019)
19. Nguyen-Phuoc, T., Li, C., Balaban, S., Yang, Y.L.: RenderNet: a deep convolutional network for differentiable rendering from 3D shapes (2019)
20. Niemeyer, M., Mescheder, L., Oechsle, M., Geiger, A.: Differentiable volumetric rendering: learning implicit 3D representations without 3D supervision (2020)
21. Sreegadha, G.: Image interpolation based on multi scale gradients. Procedia Comput. Sci. **85**, 713–724 (2016). https://doi.org/10.1016/j.procs.2016.05.258. https://www.sciencedirect.com/science/article/pii/S1877050916306081. In: International Conference on Computational Modelling and Security (CMS 2016)
22. Sun, X., et al.: Pix3D: dataset and methods for single-image 3D shape modeling (2018)
23. Tatarchenko, M., Dosovitskiy, A., Brox, T.: Octree generating networks: efficient convolutional architectures for high-resolution 3D outputs (2017)
24. Tulsiani, S., Efros, A.A., Malik, J.: Multi-view consistency as supervisory signal for learning shape and pose prediction (2018)
25. Tulsiani, S., Zhou, T., Efros, A.A., Malik, J.: Multi-view supervision for single-view reconstruction via differentiable ray consistency (2017)
26. Wah, C., Branson, S., Welinder, P., Perona, P., Belongie, S.J.: The caltech-UCSD birds-200-2011 dataset (2011)
27. Wang, N., Zhang, Y., Li, Z., Fu, Y., Liu, W., Jiang, Y.G.: Pixel2mesh: generating 3D mesh models from single RGB images (2018)
28. Wang, W., Ceylan, D., Mech, R., Neumann, U.: 3DN: 3D deformation network (2019)
29. Wu, J., Wang, Y., Xue, T., Sun, X., Freeman, W.T., Tenenbaum, J.B.: Marrnet: 3D shape reconstruction via 2.5D sketches (2017)
30. Xian, W., et al.: TextureGAN: controlling deep image synthesis with texture patches (2018)
31. Xiang, Y., Mottaghi, R., Savarese, S.: Beyond pascal: a benchmark for 3D object detection in the wild. In: IEEE Winter Conference on Applications of Computer Vision (WACV) (2014)
32. Xu, Q., Wang, W., Ceylan, D., Mech, R., Neumann, U.: DISN: Deep implicit surface network for high-quality single-view 3D reconstruction (2019)

Collaborative Edge-Cloud Computing for Personalized Fall Detection

Anne H. Ngu, Shaun Coyne, Priyanka Srinivas, and Vangelis Metsis[(⊠)]

Texas State University, San Marcos, TX 78666, USA
{angu,spc51,p_s231,vmetsis}@txstate.edu

Abstract. The use of smartwatches as devices for tracking one's health and well-being is becoming a common practice. This paper demonstrates the feasibility of running a real-time personalized deep learning-based fall detection system on a smartwatch device using a collaborative edge-cloud framework. In particular, we demonstrate how we automate the fall detection pipeline, design an appropriate UI on the small screen of the watch, and implement strategies for the continuous data collection and automation of the personalization process with the limited computational and storage resources of a smartwatch.

Keywords: Fall detection · Smart health · Model personalization · Deep learning · Edge computing · Wearables

1 Introduction

Wearable smartwatches paired with smartphones have brought health monitoring applications, such as fall detection, closer to reality. However, a one size fits all algorithm such as Apple's "hard fall" detection [1] or even more advanced deep learning models [12] have proven to be ineffective at covering all patterns of falls and ADL (Activity of Daily Living) data. Our previous work [5], using simulated data from fourteen young and healthy adults, demonstrated that we can detect most falls as well as ADLs by utilizing a personalization strategy. This strategy involved a deep learning model trained offline on simulated falls, plus labeled ADL data collected from the user (feedback data) while wearing the watch for a specified period. The feedback data from each user was used to create a personalized fall detection model that had over 90% recall with very few false alarms. However, there are two main issues with this personalized fall detection system.

First, our previous fall detection application, called SmartFall, runs the full user interface (UI) on the phone, with the watch used mainly for sensing of accelerometer data. This is problematic because elderly people have difficulties

This work is supported by the National Science Foundation under the awards CNS-1358939, CCF-1659807, CNS-1757893, at Texas State University, and the infrastructure was provided by the NSF-CRI 1305302 award.

I. Maglogiannis et al. (Eds.): AIAI 2021, IFIP AICT 627, pp. 323–336, 2021.
https://doi.org/10.1007/978-3-030-79150-6_26

keeping up with devices that are not directly attached to them and may find phones difficult to retrieve from their pockets/purses after a fall. A watch's UI, on the other hand, would allow interaction with the SmartFall App at any time and anywhere.

The second issue is that creating a personalized model in the previous system was done manually as a proof of concept. The SmartFall App is designed to save the collected data on the phone using a CSV file format. After data have been collected for a period of time, a programmer has to manually organize the data in a file to prepare it for re-training. This is not scalable and leaves room for human error.

We aim to solve the above problems by automating the entire personalization process using a collaborative edge-cloud framework, from the user initially wearing the device/watch, to getting feedback or labeled ADL data from the user, re-training a new fall detection model tailored to the user, validating the new model on the cloud, and finally, pushing the new model to the watch automatically. Some of the challenges for automating the personalization process on the watch include continuous collection and robust archiving of labeled data on a limited watch's storage, keeping track of personalized training dataset, and the validation and selection of the new model.

In this paper, we propose a solution that involves migrating the SmartFall App (UI and the prediction logic) to a single device (smartwatch) and using a robust and efficient Couchbase [6] storage system on both the watch and the cloud for data collection and archiving. The Couchbase on the watch and on the cloud can be synchronized periodically and allows the data on the watch to be purged automatically after synchronization. Couchbase on the cloud provides a central place to store all user's feedback data reliability including tracking the best personalized fall detection model for each user, the personalized training dataset for each user, and the fast retrieval of user's feedback data for re-training on the cloud.

We demonstrate the feasibility of automated real-time personalized fall detection on a commodity-based smartwatch. We describe how we can robustly collect labeled feedback data from the user in real-time, the automation of the pipeline, and the intuitiveness of the App's user interface on the watch. The main contribution of the paper is a prototype data engineering architecture consisting of the following components:

- A simplified UI on the watch interface tailored to the small screen space.
- An automated personalization pipeline including strategies used for re-training, and accurate offline validation of new models.
- Robust archiving of feedback data using Couchbase, a NoSQL database.
- The edge-cloud collaborative framework that enables optimization of limited resources of the watch, while achieving a robust fall detection performance.

2   Background and Related Work

A recent survey on fall detection systems shows much progress in using machine learning to detect falls given accelerometer data [4]. The datasets used to train models are all synthetically created by utilizing simulated falls and ADLs collected in controlled experiments with young, healthy adult participants.

There has been a wide range of success levels, however, the most success has been achieved using custom hardware mounted on the chest or waist. Unfortunately, chest or waist-mounted fall detection systems can be invasive, uncomfortable, or self-conscious for users to wear in public. Other systems that range from infrared monitoring [9] to location monitoring [11] all require wearable custom hardware [4]. It is not reasonable to set up a custom array of cameras and sensors throughout a home to detect falls; not only is it invasive, but also it does not help seniors who need to venture outside of the detection area. This is one of the main motivations for creating a fall detection system on a single wearable device such as smartwatch which has unrestricted mobility. Thus, we propose a smartwatch-based fall detection system as a familiar device that an elder person would be more inclined to use.

Another challenge of the fall detection system is the high rate of false positives generated. A survey paper in [3], described the various strategies used to help combat false positives. However, this remains a challenging issue. This is partially due to difficulties in obtaining a large amount of quality labeled data for model training. Not only are the datasets synthetic and not representative of the elderly population, but also they are relatively small with limited variation in types of falls and ADLs. When taken to the real world, any activity not represented in the training set can lead to a false positive. This could lead to hundreds, if not thousands of incorrect alarms when scaled to a single nursing home [3]. There have been some proposed strategies to reduce false positives by detecting relevant context to a fall. Specifically, it has been proposed that if you can detect a fall and someone lying still, then they have truly fallen [2,8]. This strategy greatly reduced the false positives. However, this assumes expert knowledge on a dataset that does not exist. Currently, there is no dataset of elderly people falling or performing ADLs while wearing a watch-based accelerometer sensor. There are various instances in which a fall occurs but movement continues to occur. These cases could be things such as Parkinson's, seizures, injury, or any instance in which the user is conscious but unable to get up or dial for help. We do not know to what proportions of elderly falling resulted in total stillness vs continued movement. While false positives are annoying, false negatives can be deadly. Therefore, any proposed system will need to rely solely on its ability to learn patterns of falls and ignore patterns in ADLs without expert knowledge.

Most recently, personalization has been used to reduce false positives. Solutions utilized some form of a generic model that was trained on a synthetic fall dataset from wrist-worn devices. The system in [14], utilized a bag-of-words strategy to collect labeled FP (False Positive) data from the user. Each ADL was added to the bag and future detected falls were compared against these previous ADLs. If the data were similar, then it was an ADL. Otherwise, it was a fall. After each detected fall, the user could confirm if this was a fall or another ADL. This personalized bag of words strategy was able to reduce some of the false positives without affecting recall. This system also attempted to use common ADLs for transfer learning, such that new users could benefit from this labeled data. However, it was found that most of the labeled data in the bag were never encountered again. Meaning the bag kept growing as new ADLs kept being received. This does not scale well for mobile devices. There was a severe lack of commonly occurring ADLs and this prevented transfer learning from being a practical solution. The authors in [13] also studied personalization of fall detection models using a traditional K-Nearest Neighbor (KNN) machine learning algorithm. To incorporate personalization, the authors added the misclassified ADLs (i.e., false positives) back into the training dataset one sample at a time and concluded that seven samples could reduce false positives by 10%. Their data was collected using a smartphone while ours was via a smartwatch, which poses extra computational and user interaction challenges.

The personalization process in our prior work is manual and the fall detection App only runs on a smartphone with the watch being a data sensing device. In this paper, we will show how to automate the personalization process using an edge to cloud collaborative framework so that fall detection can be adapted to a particular person in real-time and run on a single wearable device.

3   SmartFall with Edge-Cloud Collaboration

Our main goal is to demonstrate the feasibility of implementing a practical and robust automated personalized fall detection system on a single personal device (i.e., smartwatch) within an edge-cloud collaborative framework. People can wear the watch and use it as a fall detection device without worrying about their mobility and privacy.

3.1   Overview of the Personalization Process

The personalization strategy enables us to create models that are highly tuned to the user's personal ADL patterns. The personalization process starts when a user is asked to wear the watch for the first time for half an hour of prescribed list of ADL activities. This is referred to as the calibration phase or the first round of personalization. During this phase, whenever the system generates a prediction, the user will provide feedback through the watch's UI, see Fig. 1b.

The labeled feedback data is stored locally on the watch and is uploaded periodically to the cloud storage if consent to upload is available from the user. If the user did not give consent, only the generic model trained with the combination of aggregated ADL data from multiple users is used on the watch. On the cloud, during the night or when a certain number of false alarms have been generated, re-training of the model is initiated, and a new model is created. This model is validated and automatically pushed onto the watch if it is deemed to be a better model. An overview of the SmartFall system with personalization is shown in Fig. 2. Our system is structured such that all user-identifying data are only stored locally on the watch to preserve privacy. The real-time fall prediction is performed on the watch. The training and personalization of the prediction

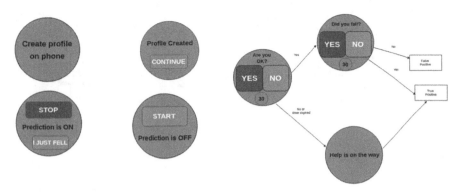

(a) Various UI smartwatch screens.   (b) User interface display when a fall is detected.

Fig. 1. Smartwatch screens displayed at different states of the fall detection App.

model is done offline in the cloud server. All archived data are de-identified and indexed by a randomly generated key which is only known to the watch wearer and the caregiver. Archived data are configured to expire periodically to manage the finite cloud storage space.

3.2 Watch-Based Fall Detection App (SmartFall)

Figure 1 shows a few of the screens displayed on the smartwatch fall detection application. As part of the activation process of the SmartFall App, the user needs to create a profile on the phone. After the watch and the phone are paired, by opening the SmartFall App on the phone and then opening the corresponding App on the watch, the watch will display "Create profile on phone" as shown in Fig. 1a. After the profile is created, it is pushed to the watch and the watch will respond with "Profile Created". When the user presses the "continue" button on this UI, the SmartFall App is activated. At any time, if the user pressed the "stop" button in Fig. 1a, the SmartFall App will be deactivated.

When a fall is detected, the top left watch's UI screen in Fig. 1b is displayed. It is designed to start with just two "yes" and "no" buttons, asking the user if they are okay. If the user pressed "yes", the next screen will ask the user to confirm whether it is a fall or not. If the user did not press either "yes" or "no" on this screen, after a specified period of time (e.g., 30 s), an alert message will be sent automatically to the designated caregiver. If the user responded with "yes" on the second screen, the sensed data will be labeled and saved as true positive data. If the user responded with "no", the data will be saved as false positive. The "I just fell", button on Fig. 1a should be pressed if the system missed the fall. This data sample will be saved as a false negative. We followed the best practices advocated in [10] for the design of the UI for the elderly.

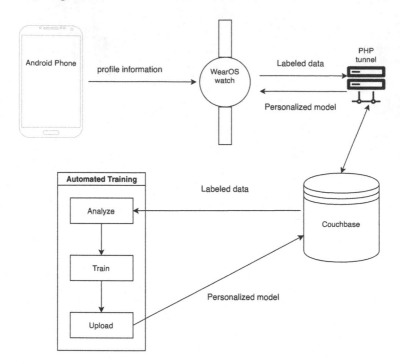

Fig. 2. Overview of the system and data flow between different components.

3.3   Real-Time Fall Detection

The fall detection is made using a pre-trained recurrent deep learning model created in TensorFlow 2.0 as described in [7]. The fall prediction is made on a sliding window of data that is 35 samples (time steps) in length. This window size corresponds to a little over one second of accelerometer data which aligns with the duration of a typical fall. Each window is classified as positive (fall) or negative (not fall). The sliding window shifts by one time step at each prediction. That means consecutive windows have a $K - 1$ time step overlap, where K is the size of the window.

Each prediction will output a probability of a fall and we average the last 20 probabilities of prediction together to infer fall or not fall. If the averaged probability reaches a threshold, we determine that a fall has occurred. The threshold of 0.3 was determined via grid search to give the best results in our dataset and it is adjusted for different users via personalization. We use a nested queue data structure to store the sensed data in memory during prediction and mark them for archiving as labeled feedback data after getting confirmation from the user.

If the system infers that a fall has occurred (threshold is >0.3), we empty the queue by saving the data to the database on the watch with unknown label at this point because we do not yet know whether it is TP or FP. However, these data is saved immediately as it could contain true positive fall data which is rare and valuable and thus must be archived robustly. This eager archiving of data also ensures that our system is robust in collecting user's feedback data which is very important for personalization. When the user provides the correct feedback on the UI, these data will be labeled and can be used for re-training as discussed in the next section.

3.4 Data Archiving

Couchbase [6] is chosen as the storage system in both the watch and the cloud. Couchbase is an open-source NoSQL document-oriented database. Couchbase was chosen for its ability to scale up easily, fast I/O, and compact JSON format. All data are stored using Couchbase's document structure.

There are 4 document types used to store the sensed accelerometer data. These correlate to true positive ("TP"), false positive ("FP"), true negative ("TN"), false negative ("FN") data. These four types of data are tracked for each user for personalization. When a fall is detected, the entire queue's data in the memory is saved to the database. Since data is processed in windows with $K - 1$ time steps overlap, to save only unique data samples, we have to remove the overlapping data such that the samples are in temporal order, and each sample is unique. After obtaining the actual feedback from the user from the UI's prompt, the saved data is updated with the correct label.

The final type of accelerometer data that needs to be archived is the FN (False Negative) data. These data are generated when a fall has occurred but was not detected by the application. We designed a button on one of the UI screens of the watch labeled "I JUST FELL" to allow for the recording of a timestamp marking the moment when a conscious user indicated that a fall occurred but was missed by the fall detection system. This is used by the system to re-label sections of the data as fall. False negative information is thus saved to the database in a simple meta record consists of only timestamp and user-id to facilitate the re-labeling process later.

Other important database structures that are needed for automatic personalization are the *Tracker*, the *Model* and the *Dataset*. The Tracker document is first created by the SmartFall App on the watch. It associates a specific deep learning fall detection model the App was using when it was activated. As better models are downloaded to the watch, newer tracker documents are created to track which set of feedback data was recorded with which model. Tracker document contains the *ID* of the first and last data sample recorded when using the model. It also contains the *model* and the *UUID*, the id of the user, which tells us which user this tracker document belongs to.

The Model document is used to store different personalized fall detection models that have been generated for a user. The *fpaths* field is an array that stores the filenames and locations of all the models. The *scores* field is a map of all the statistics generated during offline validation (including the precision and recall curve) when the best model was tested on the test dataset. The training time is the number of seconds it took to generate this model. The *threshold* stores the best threshold value to use for the best model.

The Dataset document is used to store the *training dataset* used for each user. With personalization, each model is trained using data specific to a user. This document contains a *training type* parameter that identifies which re-training strategy was used.

3.5 Database Synchronization

Synchronizing data collected on the watch to the cloud database is a core part of achieving automation in the personalization of fall detection. We upload 20 saved documents in batches periodically to avoid continuous usage of the watch's Wifi connection which can drain the battery. There is also a limit on the size of a file that can be uploaded over HTTP Post. Uploading in chunks of 20 documents avoids the data file being too large to be posted.

Once data are confirmed to be uploaded successfully, we delete them from the watch's database to free up storage. A Tracker document is designed to synchronize the fall detection model used on the watch and the cloud's database. The Tracker details are also uploaded to the cloud database periodically, but never deleted from the watch. User's profile information is never uploaded to the cloud database to preserve the user's privacy.

All archived data is associated with a user-id (UUID) which is a 32-character string that is generated at random during profile creation. Each time the user starts the SmartFall App, the App queries the cloud's database for the best model using the UUID of the user. If the watch does not already have the best model, it is then downloaded to the watch. Fall detection then proceeds to start with the best model.

3.6 Automation of Model Validation and Selection

The automation is divided into two parts; both parts are run and co-dependent on each other. The first part is run to evaluate the user's feedback data stored in the database, it determines if the current model is generating too many false positives or false negatives and if the system needs to train a new model. The second part of the system handles re-training of the model in the cloud using GPU, offline validation of the trained model, and saving of the new model to the cloud database for eventual transfer to the watch.

Part One

Criteria for Re-training. We analyze the archived data of a user in the database within a specific time interval to see if we need to train a better model. Since each user's fall detection model and the archived data is tracked using the Tracker documents, we simply need to grab the latest tracker document for each user. This tracker document contains the first and last document ID that contains data relevant to the model the user is currently using. With the relevant data retrieved, we need a way to evaluate how the current model is performing. If the model is performing well, there is no need to retrain. Our evaluation metrics put emphasis on retaining high recall performance, i.e., our model should not miss a true fall and still have reasonable precision.

It is expected that activities that produce high acceleration values on the wrist will generate more false positives than sedentary activities. To evaluate the number of false positives that occur for each user while controlling for different activity levels and lifestyles (e.g., active subjects vs. less active ones), we leverage a new custom metric for measuring false positives for evaluation in our prior work [7]. This metric takes into consideration the number of acceleration "spikes" that occurred during a time period and uses those as a normalization factor for the false positive count.

The total number of false positives (FP) a particular model detects will be compared against the total number of spikes a user emitted to give our *Spike Score* value:

$$SpikeScore = \frac{\#\_of\_spikes - FP}{\#\_of\_spikes} \tag{1}$$

We choose .98 to be the threshold for which if the spike score achieves, we do not need to re-train. This means that 2% or less of all high acceleration activities result in a false alarm. If the spike score does not reach the threshold, the retrieved FP data is prepared for re-training.

Data Trimming and Dataset Creation. In analyzing when re-training should happen, we use all the captured data in a specific interval to calculate the spikes. Note that majority of data collected from a user is TN (True Negative) data which can contain a large amount of low acceleration data if the user is not active. Adding too much low acceleration data to the training dataset will result in a highly unbalanced fall training data set.

This trimming process removes some low accelerometer data such that the percentage and diversity of each type of data should remain the same as the original generic dataset. We found that removing data points that is not within 750 data points from a spike (roughly 24 s) and keeping a buffer of around 250 data points on each spike (roughly 6 s) will achieve the right diversity of data. The data remains in chronological order after being trimmed; however, now all long periods of low acceleration data are removed.

After data is trimmed, a new training dataset is created and appended to the original dataset (generic set), then written to a CSV file with a new version number. The file path of this CSV file is uploaded to the database as the latest training set for this user. Finally, the file path of the new training set is passed to the second part of the system that is responsible for model creation and validation.

Part Two
Model Generation. Creating models in TensorFlow 2.0 using the TFS (Training From Scratch) method has been described in our previous work [5]. To recap, the TFS method discards the previous model and trains a new model from a random initialized state using the new dataset. This new dataset is a combination

of the original dataset with new data appended to it. The re-training takes place in the cloud/server. To manage multiple users using this personalized SmartFall system, we implemented a FIFO queue to schedule re-training automatically. An array consisting of the UUID, version number of model, training dataset path, and testing dataset path is used to store the detail of each job. The training thread periodically checks the queue every few minutes. If there is a job in the queue, it schedules the job to run using a GPU server in the cloud/server. Each job in the queue is run one by one sequentially until the queue is empty.

Model Validation. Once training is complete, the new model must be validated offline. A high performing personalized fall detection model is a model that has high sensitivity and specificity. A missed fall is represented as a False Negative (FN) and a "false alarm" is represented as a False Positive (FP).

Since we are dealing with time-series data, validation of the model needs to account for the sequential nature of the data. We evaluate the model on the test set using a simulation program that replicates how predictions are made in real time as mentioned earlier in Sect. 3.3.

In our system, the final inference of fall or not fall is based on a threshold that is set at 0.3 in the generic model. With personalization, this threshold will vary between users and play a critical role in selecting the best model. Therefore, for a newly generated model, we first validate that model against test data with various thresholds until we can find a threshold that will give the precision better than the existing model with a pre-determined recall of 95%. If we cannot find a threshold that gives a better precision at 95% recall, this means the newly generated model is not better than the generic model or the prior one. Otherwise, the new model with the specified threshold is set as the best model for this particular user.

Figure 3a shows a red box highlighting the best precision for the personalized and the generic model when the recall is fixed above .95. Here, the new personalized model is better and will be selected as the user's new model.

4   Evaluation

Performance of Personal Model. We first want to confirm that the personalized model from the automated pipeline is indeed better than the generic model. We used the SmartFall dataset[1] collected from 14 volunteers to train and test the generic model. This dataset is divided into 2/3 for training and 1/3 for testing. For personalization, we recruited two volunteers to wear the watch running our SmartFall for a period of time (45 mins to an hour) and performed a scripted set of ADLs. Whenever a fall is predicted, if it is false positive, the volunteer will label that. All the labeled data will be used to train the personalized model at the end of this personalization period. We tested the two personalized models using the test dataset. Figure 3a shows that at 0.95 recall, both the two

---

[1] This dataset is available from http://www.cs.txstate.edu/~hn12/data/Smart FallDataSet under the smartwatch folder.

personalized models have above 0.9 precision versus the generic model whose precision is below 0.9 with the same recall.

Personalization Pipeline. Next, we want to confirm that the automated personalization pipeline as a whole can repeat the results of the previous manual method for personalizing fall detection models described in [5]. The manually generated model did not use a database to archive the collected data or store the personal test dataset for each user and data must be prepared manually for each user for re-training which is labor-intensive. Moreover, the manual system cannot handle multiple users' personalization at the same time. We validated both personalized models using the simulated fall prediction program on the test data set. Figure 3b shows the comparable Precision-Recall (PR) curves of both models.

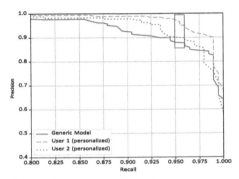

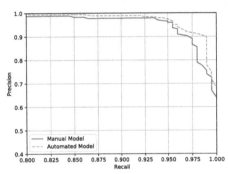

(a) Performance of Generic vs Personalized model created using the automated pipeline.

(b) Automated model vs Manual model.

Fig. 3. Precision-Recall curves comparing the performance of different models at different thresholds. (Color figure online)

As stated in Sect. 3.6, we used an additional metric called "spike score" to further validate the model generated via the automated pipeline. The spike score takes into consideration the number of acceleration "spikes" that occurred during a time period and uses those as a normalization factor for the false positive rate. Different users can have varying levels of activities and counting the absolute number of false positives generated is not accurate in deriving the accuracy of the model. We computed the spike score for the personalized model generated automatically. The spike score is 0.97 which is close to the personalized model generated manually that achieved a spike score of 0.98.

To ensure recall is still as good as the manually generated model, We asked the same two volunteers to perform 20 simulated falls on a mattress (five of each: back, front, left, and right) and recorded the correctly detected (TP) and missed falls (FN), as well as possible false alarms (FP). The confirmed recall is around 90% for both models.

How Long Does It Take to Personalize? We want to evaluate how many rounds of personalization are needed to derive a satisfactory model for a user. The following protocol is used for the initial round of personalization:

1. The user is first told to wear the watch running SmartFall App with the generic model on their left arm wrist.
2. The user performs a set of prescribed activities for half an hour. This is like a calibration phase.
3. The user provides feedback when prompted during the calibration phase.
4. The user performs the simulated fall test to record the recall of the generic model at the end of the calibration phase.
5. The user will press the "STOP" button to deactivate the SmartFall App at the end of the calibration phase. The recorded feedback data will be uploaded to the cloud's database automatically at this point.

In the cloud, the system analyzes the feedback data and computes the spike score. If the spike score is high (above .98), no new model is generated. This means no personalization is needed. Otherwise, a new model is generated and validated as described in Sect. 3.6.

After this initial round, we ask the same user to wear the watch for a few hours each day for five days and label the false positive, true positive, or false negative predictions if they pop up using the newly created personalized model. At the end of each night, the system will analyze the feedback data and create a new personalized model if the spike score is below .98. If the newly created model validated to be better than the existing model, the watch will automatically download the new model and the associated threshold value the next time when the SmartFall App is activated. This process repeats for five days.

Table 1 shows the result of personalization for three different users over a period of five days. At the end of the five day testing period, we found that User3 only requires one round, User1 requires two rounds, and User2 required four rounds to achieve a spike score of ≥ 0.97. All users performed simulated test falls at the start and end of the personalization process to verify that the recall is retained. Table 2 shows the recall of the model before and after the personalization. For User1, the recall is 0.95 before personalization and it decreased to 0.85 on the fifth round of personalization. For User2, the recall is 0.85 before personalization and it is 0.7 after the personalization. For User3, the recall is 0.85 and decreased to 0.75. This shows that there is a definite trade off between recall and precision. The falls that are missed are mostly the right falls when the users are wearing the watch on their left wrists.

This experiment suggested that there is no fixed number of personalization rounds for every user. It is highly dependent on how the current model performs in relation to the kind of ADL activities performed. Our personalization is a continuous process and the goal is to always have the best model for each user.

Table 1. Performance of the model with continuous personalization.

		R1	R2	R3	R4	R5
User1	Hours worn	0.87	2.99	2.83	2.72	3.65
	# of FP	27	20	5	9	12
	# of spikes	314	922	1099	953	1863
	Spike Score	0.91	0.97	0.99	0.99	0.99
User2	Hours worn	1.15	0.72	2.95	2.06	2.08
	# of FP	109	16	14	36	8
	# of Spikes	779	343	2753	1295	581
	Spike score	0.86	0.95	0.97	0.97	0.98
User3	Hours worn	0.65	2.3	1.9	2.2	2.1
	# of FP	50	5	9	14	18
	# of spikes	674	693	1607	2718	2667
	Spike score	0.92	0.99	0.99	0.99	0.99

Table 2. Comparison of recall before and after personalization, when the required spike score is set to 0.98.

	User1	User2	User3	Average
Recall with generic model	0.95	0.85	0.85	0.88
Recall with personalization	0.85	0.7	0.75	0.76

5 Conclusion

Our work demonstrates the feasibility of running a personalized real-time fall detection application on a commodity-based wearable device. This work paves the way for creating a fall detection system that can be tailored to each person. The infrastructure for collecting and labeling data is reliable and secure, while preserving patient privacy. The personalization process requires no intervention from any programmer and only requires a brief period of calibration and willingness to wear the watch and activate the SmartFall App.

A robust automatic personalization process can be achieved using an edge-cloud collaborative framework where the computational intensive re-training of a new model can be done in the cloud and the real-time detection can be performed on the edge without loss in prediction accuracy and delay. Management of each user's model, feedback data and personal test data is achieved by using a NoSQL database which is scalable for many users and where data can be versioned.

The complete automation of the personalization process demonstrates the feasibility of collecting a dataset of accelerometer data from the users (e.g., elderly people) by just asking them to wear the watch for a period of time in hope of being able to generate real datasets for future fall detection algorithms.

References

1. Apple watch series 4. http://www.apple.com/apple-watch-series-4/activity/. Accessed 18 Apr 2019
2. Chandra, I., Sivakumar, N., Gokulnath, C.B., Parthasarathy, P.: IoT based fall detection and ambient assisted system for the elderly. Cluster Comput. **22**(1), 2517–2525 (2018). https://doi.org/10.1007/s10586-018-2329-2
3. Fanca, A., Puscasiu, A., Gota, D.I., Valean, H.: Methods to minimize false detection in accidental fall warning systems. In: 2019 23rd International Conference on System Theory, Control and Computing (ICSTCC), pp. 851–855 (2019)
4. Gigantesco, A., Ramachandran, A., Karuppiah, A.: A survey on recent advances in wearable fall detection systems. Biomed. Res. Int. **2020**, 1–17 (2020)
5. Ngu, A.H., Metsis, V., Coyne, S., Chung, B., Pai, R., Chang, J.: Personalized fall detection system. In: The proceedings of the 5th IEEE PerCom Workshop on Pervasive Health Technologies, Austin, TX (March 2020)
6. Hubail, M.A., et al.: Couchbase analytics: NoETL for scalable NoSQL data analysis. Proc. VLDB Endow. **12**(12), 2275–2286 (2019)
7. Mauldin, T., Ngu, A.H., Metsis, V., Canby, M.E.: Ensemble deep learning on wearables using small datasets. ACM Trans. Comput. Healthcare 2(1) (2021). https://doi.org/10.1145/3428666. https://doi-org.libproxy.txstate.edu/10.1145/3428666
8. Mirchevska, V., Luštrek, M., Gams, M.: Combining domain knowledge and machine learning for robust fall detection. Exp. Syst. **31**(2), 163–175 (2014)
9. Riquelme, F., Espinoza, C., Rodenas, T., Minonzio, J.G., Taramasco, C.: ehome-seniors dataset: an infrared thermal sensor dataset for automatic fall detection research. Sensors (Basel, Switz.) **19**(20), 4565 (2019)
10. Salman, H.M., Ahmad, W.F.W., Sulaiman, S.: Usability evaluation of the smartphone user interface in supporting elderly users from experts' perspective. IEEE Access **6**, 22578–22591 (2018)
11. Shastry, M.C., et al.: Context-aware fall detection using inertial sensors and time-of-flight transceivers. In: 2016 38th Annual International Conference of the IEEE Engineering in Medicine and Biology Society (EMBC), pp. 570–573. IEEE (2016)
12. Theodoridis, T., Solachidis, V., Vretos, N., Daras, P.: Human fall detection from acceleration measurements using a recurrent neural network. In: Maglaveras, N., Chouvarda, I., de Carvalho, P. (eds.) Precision Medicine Powered by pHealth and Connected Health. IP, vol. 66, pp. 145–149. Springer, Singapore (2018). https://doi.org/10.1007/978-981-10-7419-6_25
13. Tsinganos, P., Skodras, A.: A smartphone-based fall detection system for the elderly. In: Proceedings of the 10th International Symposium on Image and Signal Processing and Analysis, pp. 53–58 (September 2017)
14. Villar, J.R., de la Cal, E., Fañez, M., González, V.M., Sedano, J.: User-centered fall detection using supervised, on-line learning and transfer learning. Prog. Artif. Intell. **8**(4), 453–474 (2019). https://doi.org/10.1007/s13748-019-00190-2

Deep Dense and Convolutional Autoencoders for Machine Acoustic Anomaly Detection

Gabriel Coelho[1], Pedro Pereira[1], Luis Matos[1], Alexandrine Ribeiro[3],
Eduardo C. Nunes[1], André Ferreira[2], Paulo Cortez[1(✉)],
and André Pilastri[3]

[1] ALGORITMI Centre, Department of Information Systems, University of Minho,
Guimarães, Portugal
{a82137,id6927,id6929}@alunos.uminho.pt, pcortez@dsi.uminho.pt
[2] Bosch Car Multimedia, Braga, Portugal
andre.ferreira2@pt.bosch.com
[3] EPMQ - IT Engineering Maturity and Quality Lab, CCG ZGDV Institute,
Guimarães, Portugal
andre.pilastri@ccg.pt

Abstract. Recently, there have been advances in using unsupervised learning methods for Acoustic Anomaly Detection (AAD). In this paper, we propose an improved version of two deep AutoEncoders (AE) for unsupervised AAD for six types of working machines, namely Dense and Convolutional AEs. A large set of computational experiments was held, showing that the two proposed deep autoencoders, when combined with a mel-spectrogram sound preprocessing, are quite competitive and outperform a recently proposed AE baseline. Overall, a high-quality class discrimination level was achieved, ranging from 72% to 92%.

Keywords: Acoustic Anomaly Detection · Unsupervised learning ·
Autoencoders · Convolutional Neural Network

1 Introduction

With the advent of the Industry 4.0 phenomenon, the amount of digital data is growing exponentially. In effect, currently there is a widespread usage of interconnected sensors that can capture diverse physical aspects of the productive process (e.g., images, sound, temperatures, torque, energy consumption values). All this data can be used by Artificial Intelligence (AI) and Machine Learning (ML) to extract valuable productive analytics. A particularly relevant ML task is anomaly detection, which intends to distinguish abnormal events from normal ones [18,34]. In industrial processes, the early detection of operating machines with a defects by using ML can potentially [25,31]: reduce maintenance time and costs; prevent or reduce production stops, and increase the

I. Maglogiannis et al. (Eds.): AIAI 2021, IFIP AICT 627, pp. 337–348, 2021.
https://doi.org/10.1007/978-3-030-79150-6_27

safety of human operators that operate the machines. In this work, we focus on ML methods for Acoustic Anomaly Detection (AAD) [8], which aims to detect abnormal behaviours using audio data. In particular, we aim to automatically detect, beforehand, if a given industrial machine is not working correctly, by using only the sound produced by it. Several studies addressed this issue as an unsupervised ML task, since data labeling is highly costly and time consuming, requiring great manual human work subject to errors [4].

Over the years, several algorithms were applied to unsupervised AAD problems, including Isolation Forest (IF) [9,10] and One-Class Support Vector Machines (OCSVM) [4,29]. Following the success of Deep Learning, there has been a growing usage of neural network architectures for AAD. In particular, AutoEncoders (AE) are becoming popular for unsupervised AAD [15,24]. When compared with other ML approaches (e.g., IF and OCSVM), AE present the advantage of requiring a lower computational effort [19].

AEs compressed the input features into a lower dimensional space, named latent space, learning their most relevant relationships, and are composed by two main components [5,22]: an encoder that maps the input vector (features) into the latent space, via a nonlinear transformation; and a decoder that attempts to reconstruct the reverse transformation to the original input signal. The difference between the original input vector and the AE output is called reconstruction error [3]. This error can be used to detect anomalies. AEs assume that normal and anomalous events follow different distributions and it is trained to learn the normal multi-dimensional space of the data, by using only normal event records, aiming to minimize the reconstruction error on such data. When an AE tries to reconstruct new unseen data containing anomalies, the reconstruction errors are higher and by using a predefined threshold, the samples can be signaled as anomalous [5,22].

Following on good results obtained in previous studies [14,18,26,32], in this work we address unsupervised AAD task in industrial machines using two different AE architectures: deep Dense and Convolutional. In order to use audio as input, it is often necessary to preprocess the raw data by extracting features from the signal. In this work, we use Mel Frequency Energy Coefficients (MFECs), which are a popular sound preprocessing method [7,28]. Moreover, we use two public datasets [17,27] to test the proposed AEs that are fed with MFECs. For benchmark purposes, we compare the Dense and Convolutional AEs with a baseline AE architecture that was recently proposed [16].

The paper is organized as follows: Sect. 2 describes the used datasets, the audio features used and its extraction process, the proposed AE architectures, and the evaluation process. Section 3 presents the experimentation developed and obtained results. Lastly, final conclusions are discussed in Sect. 4.

2   Materials and Methods

2.1   Dataset

The data used for this task comprises parts of the ToyADMOS [17] and the MIMII [27] datasets, consisting of the normal and anomalous operating sounds of six types of toy/real machines, as obtained from the DCASE 2020 challenge [16]. The data is divided into two datasets (development and evaluation) for 6 different machine types: ToyCar, ToyConveyor, Slider, Pump, Fan, and Valve.

The ToyCar and ToyConveyor data belong to ToyADMOS dataset. This dataset involved miniature machines (toys) that were damaged deliberately to record anomalous behavior. As for the MIMII Dataset, the sounds were recorded from different industrial machines, aiming to resemble a real-life scenario. In the development datasets, each machine type has 4 different specific machines, except for ToyConveyor, which has only 3. Each machine sound was recorded using only one microphone and sampled at 16 kHz.

The machine sound datasets include normal and anomaly labels that are available for the test data, allowing to estimate the AAD performance of the ML models. Regarding the evaluation data, it contains audio for new machines (new IDs) in each machine type, both for model training and testing. Table 1

Table 1. Summary of the machine AAD datasets.

	Development			Evaluation		
	Machine ID	Audio files		Machine ID	Audio files	
		Train	Test		Train	Test
ToyCar	01	1000	614	05	1000	515
	02	1000	615	06	1000	515
	03	1000	615	07	100	515
	04	1000	615			
ToyConveyor	01	1000	1200	04	1000	555
	02	1000	1155	05	1000	555
	03	1000	1154	06	1000	555
Fan	00	911	507	01	911	426
	02	916	549	03	916	458
	04	933	448	05	1000	458
	06	915	461			
Pump	00	906	243	01	903	2016
	02	905	211	03	606	213
	04	602	200	05	908	348
	06	936	202			
Slider	00	968	456	01	968	278
	02	968	367	03	968	278
	04	434	278	05	434	278
	06	434	189			
Valve	00	891	219	01	679	220
	02	608	220	03	863	220
	04	900	220	05	899	500
	06	892	220			

summarizes the analyzed datasets. A different number of approximately 10 s Waveform Audio File (WAV) files is used for each machine.

2.2   Feature Extraction

MFCCs, which are derived from the mel-cepstrum representation of the audio, is one of the best known and most popular audio processing features [30]. However, when computing MFCCs, a Discrete Cosine Transform (DCT) is applied to the logarithm of the filter bank outputs, resulting in decorrelated MFCC features. Therefore, they have the drawback of having non-local features, which makes them unsuitable for Convolutional AE (CAE) processing.

In this paper, we address a feature for audio signal processing named MFECs, which are log-energies derived directly from the filter-banks energies. These are similar to MFCCs, yet they do not include the DCT operation. This feature provided good results in detecting different audio sounds and classification of sounds in previous studies [2,13,33].

To prepare the features for the first proposed deep learning architecture, the Dense AE, some operations were made. Audio data are buffered in fixed-length 1 s intervals with 50% overlap. For each audio buffer obtained, the segment is then divided into 64 ms analysis frames, with 50% overlap and 128 MFECs are extracted from the magnitude spectrum of each frame. In this way, 5 time-frames are concatenated to form a 640-dimensional input vector as shown in Fig. 1.

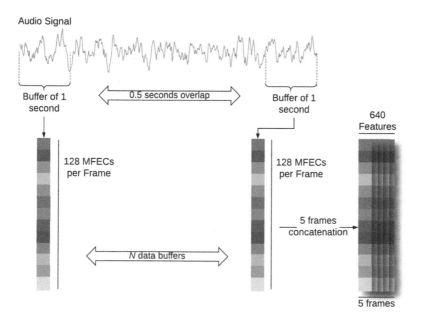

Fig. 1. Feature extraction procedure for the Dense AE.

The second deep learning architecture, the Convolution Neural Network (CNN) AE, requires a different feature extraction method. For each audio, 128 log mel-band energy features were extracted from the magnitude spectrum, considering 64 ms analysis frames with 50% overlap. Then, each feature was normalized to zero mean and unit standard deviation by using statistics from the training data. Finally, the mel spectrogram was segmented every second into 32 column data, with approximately 100 ms of hop size. This procedure is shown in Fig. 2.

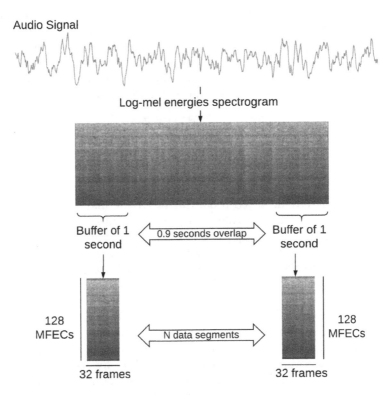

Fig. 2. Feature extraction procedure for the CNN AE.

2.3   Autoencoder Architectures

The two proposed AEs contain a large number of hyperparameters. In order to select the best architectures, we have first conducted several preliminary experiments, in which we only used development data, selecting the best configuration (in terms of the reconstruction error) when varying element such as the number of hidden layers and units per layer. Once the neural architecture was selected, it was fixed and applied to all datasets. For both AEs, the training only uses normal machine sounds.

The first proposed architecture consists of a deep fully-connected AE (top of Fig. 3), which was adopted in the baseline AE proposed in [16]. The best preliminary results were achieved by a Dense AE that includes encoder and decoder components with four fully-connected layers with 512 hidden units, followed by Batch Normalization, with all neural nodes using the popular ReLU as activation function. The Batch Normalization layer allows reduce the internal covariate shift, discarding the need of dropout, and normalizes the inputs for each batch of data [12]. As for ReLU, it presents the advantage of non-saturation of its gradient, which greatly accelerates the convergence of stochastic gradient descent compared to other activation functions, including logistic or hyperbolic tangent [20]. The bottleneck layer is set as one fully-connected layer with 8 hidden units, resulting in an 8-dimensional latent space. To train the AE only normal event audio was used, aiming to learn the data normal event distribution. Turning to the loss function, we adopted the popular Mean Squared Error (MSE), which is more sensitive to extreme errors and that is computed as:

$$MSE_i = \frac{\sum_{k=1}^{I}(x_{i,k} - \hat{x}_{i,k})^2}{I} \tag{1}$$

where i denotes a data instance, $x_{i,k}$ the k-th input value for instance i, $\hat{x}_{i,k}$ the AE predicted output response for the same input and I the total number of inputs of the AE.

Recently, CNNs have achieved promising results on many AAD benchmarks [6,11,21]. By integrating 2D convolutional operations in an AE structure, CNN AEs are capable of learning the spatial structure of the input features and reconstruct them while taking into account their spatial structural patterns. Based on this property, the second proposed deep learning architecture for the unsupervised AAD task consists of a deep CNN AE (shown in the bottom of Fig. 3). With such an architecture, the AAD task is handled as a computer vision problem by exploring image-like time-frequency representations of audio. The encoder and decoder networks are comprised of convolutional blocks, each consisting of 2D Convolution and Batch Normalization layers, using ReLU as the activation function. The encoder network is composed by a stack of five convolutional layers with 32, 64, 128, 256, and 512 convolutional filters, kernel sizes of 5, 5, 5, 3, and 3 to capture local patterns, and strides of $(1,2)$, $(1,2)$, $(2,2)$, $(2,2)$, and $(2,2)$, respectively. The feature size map is reduced throughout the encoder by the convolution operation stride. The bottleneck consists of a layer with 40 convolutional filters, reducing the encoder feature maps to a 40-dimensional compressed input representation. Concerning the decoder network, it starts with a fully-connected layer that increases the latent space dimensionality, equalizing encoder last layer's shape, followed by five 2D transposed convolutional layers that mirror the encoder layers.

Regarding the training algorithm used to train both Dense AE and CNN AE architectures, we employed the Adam optimizer, which also was used in [16], using a learning rate of 0.001. Both AE were trained to minimize MSE between input and its reconstruction (the loss function). The training procedure was iterated up to a maximum of 100 epochs. In each epoch, 10% of training

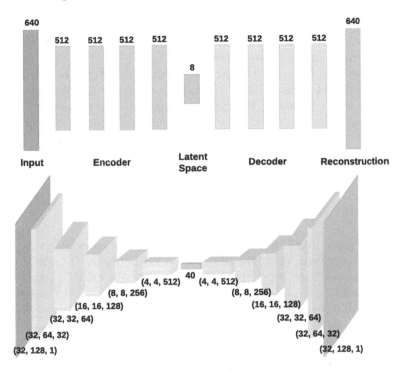

Fig. 3. Proposed AE Network architectures: Dense AE (top) and CNN AE (bottom).

data is randomly divided for validation, which is used for evaluating training process evolution, by computing the reconstruction error on such data. If MSE does not improve on validation data after 10 epochs, an early stopping callback is activated, ending the training process and storing the weights of the model that achieved a lower reconstruction error on validation data. The batch size for both Dense AE and CNN AE architectures was set as 512 and 64, respectively.

Once the AE is trained, the reconstruction error for an unseen sound sample j is used as the decision score (d_j), where $d_j = MSE_j$. A anomaly class label is considered true if $d_j > Th$, where Th is a decision threshold.

2.4 Evaluation

We evaluated our methods, we used two popular metrics on AAD that are based on the Receiver Operating Characteristic (ROC) analysis [17,27]: Area Under the ROC Curve (AUC) and partial-AUC (pAUC). The ROC curve shows the False Positive Rate (FPR) versus the True Positive Rate (TPR) for different threshold values (Th). In this study, the positive class is the anomaly.

AUC represents the overall ML discrimination performance, while pAUC focuses on a particular range of interest from the ROC curve, defined in this work as the FPR values from 0 to 0.1, which reflects in a model with fewer false alarms. Both metrics are not influenced by unbalanced data, which in occurs in our datasets. The AUC and pAUC values can be interpreted as follows: 50% – performance of a random classifier; 60% - reasonable; 70% - good; 80% - very good; 90% - excellent; and 100% - perfect.

As mentioned in Sect. 2.1, the datasets used in this work contain a total of 6 types of machines, most of them containing 4 specific machine data, except ToyConveyor that contains 3. We used development data to select two first fix AE architectures and then train the models for each specific machine. As for the predictive results, they are measured on the test sets from the evaluation datasets. A single model was created for each machine type and evaluated over each specific machine, using both AUC and pAUC.

3   Results

The proposed dense and CNN AE architectures were implemented in the Python programming language, using the TensorFlow-GPU library [1]. The computational experiments were conducted using two different GPUs (Titan Xp and 1080Ti). To evaluate the model performance, both AUC and pAUC metrics were used, as defined in Sect. 2.4. Table 2 presents the obtained predictive results for each specific machine, also showing the average value for each machine type. For comparison purposes, the Baseline system results from [16] are also provided in the table.

In terms of the average AUC and pAUC values for each machine type, the Dense AE outperforms the Baseline system in all machine types. Furthermore, the Baseline system only achieved better results in 5 of the 23 analyzed specific machines, namely ToyCar ID 3, pump (IDs of 0, 2, and 4) and slider ID 0. Regarding the CNN AE overall performance, it outperformed the Baseline system, although the latter achieved a higher average AUC values for 2 of 6 machine types (ToyCar and pump).

The two proposed AE architectures[1] are quite competitive in terms of mean AUC and pAUC values, outperforming the Baseline system for all machine types. The Dense AE obtains the best average AUC and pAUC results for ToyCar, ToyConveyor and fan, while the CNN AE achieves the best AAD measures for the slider and valve tasks. Turning to the pump machine, the best AUC value is provided by the Dense AE and the best pAUC is returned by the CNN AE. In particular, when considering the AUC measure, a high quality anomaly class discrimination was achieved by the proposed AEs, since most AUC values are above 70%. Furthermore, the CNN AE architecture obtained excellent results for slider machine type, presenting the highest AUC value (91.77%).

---

[1] https://github.com/APILASTRI/DCASE_Task2_UMINHO.

Table 2. Comparison of AUC and pAUC results for all AE architectures for each machine (best average values are denoted in **bold**)

Machine type	Machine ID	Baseline		Dense AE		CNN AE	
		AUC (%)	pAUC (%)	AUC (%)	pAUC (%)	AUC (%)	pAUC (%)
ToyCar	1	81.36	68.40	83.87	72.64	81.59	71.88
	2	85.97	77.72	87.56	80.35	85.46	79.92
	3	63.30	55.21	63.12	55.02	62.73	55.08
	4	84.45	68.97	88.60	76.68	82.38	69.60
	Average	78.77	67.58	**80.79**	**71.17**	78.04	69.12
ToyConveyor	1	78.07	64.25	81.67	69.41	79.90	62.71
	2	64.16	56.01	68.04	58.31	67.78	54.85
	3	75.35	61.03	79.59	63.64	80.11	62.53
	Average	72.53	60.43	**76.43**	**63.79**	75.93	60.03
Fan	0	54.41	49.37	56.73	49.72	51.77	49.05
	2	73.40	54.81	79.60	54.00	72.71	55.51
	4	61.61	53.26	70.11	54.11	62.60	52.80
	6	73.92	52.35	81.69	55.15	80.05	53.19
	Average	65.83	52.45	**72.03**	**53.25**	66.78	52.63
Pump	0	67.15	56.74	66.94	56.83	66.37	54.95
	2	61.53	58.10	60.77	60.31	54.31	53.58
	4	88.33	67.10	87.00	66.32	94.64	77.26
	6	74.55	58.02	77.53	60.32	76.97	58.05
	Average	72.89	59.99	**73.06**	60.94	72.07	**60.96**
Slider	0	96.19	81.44	96.12	82.30	98.86	94.47
	2	78.97	63.68	79.55	64.42	84.06	69.33
	4	94.30	71.98	95.44	76.14	97.69	87.82
	6	69.59	49.02	77.22	49.56	86.46	53.16
	Average	84.76	66.53	87.08	68.10	**91.77**	**76.20**
Valve	0	68.76	51.70	74.61	52.28	78.69	52.59
	2	68.18	51.83	76.68	52.72	85.02	55.92
	4	74.30	51.97	79.58	50.96	82.59	53.68
	6	53.90	48.43	57.78	48.73	69.03	50.22
	Average	66.28	50.98	72.16	51.17	**78.83**	**53.10**

4 Conclusions

In this paper, we proposed two AutoEncoder (AE) deep learning architectures for an unsupervised Acoustic Anomaly Detection (AAD) task: a Dense AE and a Convolutional Neural Network (CNN) AE. The two AE architectures were applied to six different real-world industrial machine sound datasets. Using development records from the datasets and sound energy features from mel-spectrograms to preprocess the raw sounds, several preliminary experiments were conducted in order to tune the AE hyperparameters, namely in terms of hidden layers and nodes and activation functions. Then, the selected AE architectures were trained and tested using the evaluation instances from the public domain datasets.

Overall, competitive results were obtained by the Dense and CNN AEs when compared with a recently proposed baseline AE architecture [16]. For two machine types (slider and valve), the best results were achieved by the CNN AE, while the Dense AE provided the best results for the remaining machines

(ToyCar, ToyConveyor, fan, and pump). In general, a high anomaly class discrimination was achieved by both proposed AEs, ranging from 72% (good) to 92% (excellent discrimination level).

As future work, we aim to explore different deep learning architectures for AAD, such as Variational AEs [23]. Furthermore, we intend to study the effect of using audio data augmentation techniques (e.g., pitching, time-shifting, Generative Adversarial Networks) or signal frequency filtering tools, aiming to further improve the AAD results.

Acknowledgments. This work is supported by the European Structural and Investment Funds in the FEDER component, through the Operational Competitiveness and Internationalization Programme (COMPETE 2020) - Project n° 039334; Funding Reference: POCI-01-0247-FEDER-039334.

References

1. Abadi, M., et al.: TensorFlow: large-scale machine learning on heterogeneous distributed systems (2016)
2. Afrillia, Y., Mawengkang, H., Ramli, M., Fadlisyah, Fhonna, R.P.: Performance measurement of mel frequency ceptral coefficient (MFCC) method in learning system of Al-Qur'an based in Nagham Pattern recognition. J. Phys. Conf. Ser. **930**, 012036 (2017). https://doi.org/10.1088/1742-6596/930/1/012036
3. An, J., Cho, S.: Variational autoencoder based anomaly detection using reconstruction probability. Special Lecture on IE, vol. 2, no. 1, pp. 1–18 (2015)
4. Aurino, F., Folla, M., Gargiulo, F., Moscato, V., Picariello, A., Sansone, C.: One-class SVM based approach for detecting anomalous audio events. In: 2014 International Conference on Intelligent Networking and Collaborative Systems, pp. 145–151. IEEE (2014)
5. Charte, D., Charte, F., García, S., del Jesus, M.J., Herrera, F.: A practical tutorial on autoencoders for nonlinear feature fusion: taxonomy, models, software and guidelines. Inf. Fus. **44**, 78–96 (2018). https://doi.org/10.1016/j.inffus.2017.12.007
6. Chen, C., et al..: Novelty detection via non-adversarial generative network. arXiv preprint arXiv:2002.00522 (2020)
7. Chu, S., Narayanan, S., Kuo, C.C.J.: Environmental sound recognition with time-frequency audio features. IEEE Transa. Audio Speech Lang. Process. **17**, 1142–1158 (2009). https://doi.org/10.1109/TASL.2009.2017438
8. Duman, T.B., Bayram, B., İnce, G.: Acoustic anomaly detection using convolutional autoencoders in industrial processes. In: Martínez Álvarez, F., Troncoso Lora, A., Sáez Muñoz, J.A., Quintián, H., Corchado, E. (eds.) SOCO 2019. AISC, vol. 950, pp. 432–442. Springer, Cham (2020). https://doi.org/10.1007/978-3-030-20055-8_41
9. Farzad, A., Gulliver, T.A.: Unsupervised log message anomaly detection. ICT Exp. **6**(3), 229–237 (2020)
10. Harar, P., Galaz, Z., Alonso-Hernandez, J.B., Mekyska, J., Burget, R., Smekal,Z.: Towards robust voice pathology detection. Neural Comput. Appl., 1–11 (2018). https://doi.org/10.1007/s00521-018-3464-7
11. Hershey, S., et al.: CNN architectures for large-scale audio classification. In: 2017 IEEE International Conference on Acoustics, Speech and Signal Processing (ICASSP), pp. 131–135. IEEE (2017)

12. Ioffe, S., Szegedy, C.: Batch normalization: accelerating deep network training by reducing internal covariate shift. In: International Conference on Machine Learning, pp. 448–456. PMLR (2015)
13. Jam, M.M., Sadjedi, H.: Identification of hearing disorder by multi-band entropy cepstrum extraction from infant's cry. In: 2009 International Conference on Biomedical and Pharmaceutical Engineering, pp. 1–5 (2009)
14. Kawaguchi, Y., Endo, T.: How can we detect anomalies from subsampled audio signals? In: 2017 IEEE 27th International Workshop on Machine Learning for Signal Processing (MLSP), pp. 1–6. IEEE (2017)
15. Kohlsdorf, D., Herzing, D., Starner, T.: An auto encoder for audio dolphin communication. In: 2020 International Joint Conference on Neural Networks (IJCNN), pp. 1–7. IEEE (2020)
16. Koizumi, Y., et al.: Description and discussion on DCASE2020 challenge task2: unsupervised anomalous sound detection for machine condition monitoring. CoRR abs/2006.05822 (2020)
17. Koizumi, Y., Saito, S., Uematsu, H., Harada, N., Imoto, K.: ToyADMOS: a dataset of miniature-machine operating sounds for anomalous sound detection. In: 2019 IEEE Workshop on Applications of Signal Processing to Audio and Acoustics (WASPAA), pp. 313–317. IEEE (2019). https://ieeexplore.ieee.org/document/8937164
18. Koizumi, Y., Saito, S., Uematsu, H., Kawachi, Y., Harada, N.: Unsupervised detection of anomalous sound based on deep learning and the Neyman-Pearson Lemma. IEEE/ACM Trans. Audio Speech Lang. Process. **27**(1), 212–224 (2018)
19. Koizumi, Y., Saito, S., Yamaguchi, M., Murata, S., Harada, N.: Batch uniformization for minimizing maximum anomaly score of DNN-based anomaly detection in sounds (2019)
20. Krizhevsky, A., Sutskever, I., Hinton, G.E.: ImageNet classification with deep convolutional neural networks. Adv. Neural. Inf. Process. Syst. **25**, 1097–1105 (2012)
21. Li, J., Dai, W., Metze, F., Qu, S., Das, S.: A comparison of deep learning methods for environmental sound detection. In: 2017 IEEE International Conference on Acoustics, Speech and Signal Processing (ICASSP), pp. 126–130. IEEE (2017)
22. Liu, Y., Zhuang, C., Lu, F.: Unsupervised two-stage anomaly detection (2021)
23. Ntalampiras, S., Potamitis, I.: Acoustic detection of unknown bird species and individuals. CAAI Trans. Intell. Technol. (2021). https://doi.org/10.1049/cit2.12007
24. Oh, D.Y., Yun, I.D.: Residual error based anomaly detection using auto-encoder in SMD machine sound. Sensors **18**(5), 1308 (2018)
25. Panfilenko, D., Poller, P., Sonntag, D., Zillner, S., Schneider, M.: BPMN for knowledge acquisition and anomaly handling in CPS for smart factories. In: 2016 IEEE 21st International Conference on Emerging Technologies and Factory Automation (ETFA), pp. 1–4. IEEE (2016)
26. Provotar, O.I., Linder, Y.M., Veres, M.M.: Unsupervised anomaly detection in time series using LSTM-based autoencoders. In: 2019 IEEE International Conference on Advanced Trends in Information Theory (ATIT), pp. 513–517. IEEE (2019)
27. Purohit, H., et al.: MIMII dataset: sound dataset for malfunctioning industrial machine investigation and inspection. In: Proceedings of the Detection and Classification of Acoustic Scenes and Events 2019 Workshop, DCASE 2019, pp. 209–213 (November 2019)
28. Purwins, H., Li, B., Virtanen, T., Schlüter, J., Chang, S., Sainath, T.N.: Deep learning for audio signal processing. IEEE J. Sel. Top. Sig. Process. **13**(2), 206–219 (2019). https://doi.org/10.1109/JSTSP.2019.2908700

29. Rovetta, S., Mnasri, Z., Masulli, F.: Detection of hazardous road events from audio streams: an ensemble outlier detection approach. In: 2020 IEEE Conference on Evolving and Adaptive Intelligent Systems (EAIS), pp. 1–6. IEEE (2020)
30. Sharma, G., Umapathy, K., Krishnan, S.: Trends in audio signal feature extraction methods. Appl. Acoust. **158**, 107020 (2020)
31. Sonntag, D., Zillner, S., van der Smagt, P., Lörincz, A.: Overview of the CPS for smart factories project: deep learning, knowledge acquisition, anomaly detection and intelligent user interfaces. In: Jeschke, S., Brecher, C., Song, H., Rawat, D.B. (eds.) Industrial Internet of Things. SSWT, pp. 487–504. Springer, Cham (2017). https://doi.org/10.1007/978-3-319-42559-7_19
32. Tagawa, T., Tadokoro, Y., Yairi, T.: Structured denoising autoencoder for fault detection and analysis. In: Asian Conference on Machine Learning, pp. 96–111 (2015)
33. Torfi, A., Iranmanesh, S.M., Nasrabadi, N.M., Dawson, J.M.: 3D convolutional neural networks for cross audio-visual matching recognition. IEEE Access **5**, 22081–22091 (2017)
34. Zhu, T., Wang, J., Cheng, S., Li, Y., Li, J.: Retrieving the relative kernel dataset from big sensory data for continuous queries in IoT systems. EURASIP J. Wirel. Commun. Netw. **2019**(1), 1–14 (2019). https://doi.org/10.1186/s13638-019-1467-4

Neural Network Compression Through Shunt Connections and Knowledge Distillation for Semantic Segmentation Problems

Bernhard Haas[ID], Alexander Wendt$^{(\boxtimes)}$[ID], Axel Jantsch[ID],
and Matthias Wess[ID]

Christian Doppler Laboratory for Embedded Machine Learning,
Institute of Computer Technology, TU Wien, Vienna, Austria
e1525110@student.tuwien.ac.at,
{alexander.wendt,axel.jantsch,matthias.wess}@tuwien.ac.at

Abstract. Employing convolutional neural network models for large scale datasets represents a big challenge. Especially embedded devices with limited resources cannot run most state-of-the-art model architectures in real-time, necessary for many applications. This paper proves the applicability of shunt connections on large scale datasets and narrows this computational gap. Shunt connections is a proposed method for MobileNet compression. We are the first to provide results of shunt connections for the MobileNetV3 model and for segmentation tasks on the Cityscapes dataset, using the DeeplabV3 architecture, on which we achieve compression by 28%, while observing a 3.52 drop in mIoU. The training of shunt-inserted models are optimized through knowledge distillation. The full code used for this work will be available online.

Keywords: Shunt connections · Knowledge distillation ·
Optimization · Latency · Accuracy · CIFAR · Cityscapes · DeepLab ·
MobileNet · Machine learning · Embedded machine learning

1 Introduction

Compression of deep neural networks is an active field of research. Many state-of-the-art neural network architectures [1,6,15] are too computationally expensive to run within set latency requirements on modern embedded hardware. In particular semantic segmentation tasks represent a challenge, since a high image resolution is required to extract high level features, which is computationally expensive. Modern embedded devices like the Nvidia Jetson series and their on-board GPUs have advanced significantly over the last years but real time applications are still challenging.

Neural network compression helps to close this computational gap while still achieving satisfactory accuracy. One proposed method, called shunt connections

© IFIP International Federation for Information Processing 2021
Published by Springer Nature Switzerland AG 2021
I. Maglogiannis et al. (Eds.): AIAI 2021, IFIP AICT 627, pp. 349–361, 2021.
https://doi.org/10.1007/978-3-030-79150-6_28

[14], shows high potential as big parts of a model are replaced by a significantly smaller convolutional model, yielding a considerable speed-up. While in [14] shunt connections were only applied on simple datasets for classification networks, this work aims to enhance shunt connections for deep neural networks and test them on large scale datasets. In this work, we analyze the number of saved multiply-accumulations and the resulting latency reduction, when applying shunt connections to the MobileNetV3Small-DeeplabV3 model [2,3,8] trained on the Cityscapes dataset [4].

We use the following methodology: First, we show that shunt insertion is also applicable to the newer MobileNetV3 model by replicating the original authors' results on the CIFAR datasets [10]. Next, the final fine-tuning step is improved by applying knowledge distillation. Finally, to test for applicability on large scale datasets, we apply shunt connections to compress the MobileNetV3 backbone of the DeeplabV3 architecture trained on the Cityscapes dataset and compare the results against compressing MobileNetV3 using the built-in depth multiplier. Our work contributes to research in the following ways:

- Full information about how to apply shunt connections for easy reproduction
- Improved training of shunt connections through knowledge distillation
- Shunt connections applied to MobileNetV3 trained on the Cityscapes dataset

The full code for inserting shunt connections in residual CNNs will soon be available online[1].

This work does not claim to present the best possible solution regarding shunt connections for a given model and dataset. Instead, it should prove that good results can be achieved for various tasks, including large scale datasets. Hence, we limit ourselves to placing only a single shunt connection into the models and reduce the design space for shunts to two different architectures.

2 Related Work

Shunt connections describe the convolutional neural network compression method of replacing contiguous blocks with a simpler, smaller neural network block. The idea was originally proposed for residual CNNs and motivated by the insight that short paths inside a residual CNN are much more important than long paths [16]. It means that single blocks can be deleted without large accuracy losses. The original paper [14] defines the relative accuracy drop of the block-deleted model as knowledge quotient. By looking at the quotient, one can determine which blocks are easily replaceable by shunt connection.

Shunt architectures are inspired by encoder-decoder models and get trained on extracted feature maps from the original model. The following workflow was proposed by [14]: (1) Train baseline, unmodified model; (2) Calculate knowledge quotients for residual blocks and choose shunt locations; (3) Extract input and output feature maps for shunt training from original model; (4) Choose

---

[1] https://github.com/embedded-machine-learning/ShuntConnector.

shunt architecture and train shunt connection; and (5) Place shunt inside original model and fine-tune model.

In [14], this workflow was applied to the CIFAR [10] and CALTECH[2] datasets. For both datasets the trained networks heavily tend to overfit. Therefore, it is not surprising, that parts of the model can easily be replaced by a simpler model with fewer parameters. More complicated datasets where networks do not tend to overfit, consequently do not contain as much redundancy. Hence, the question appears whether shunt connections also work in those circumstances. Our approach is to apply this concept on a wider scope.

Five different shunt architectures were proposed in the original paper, which consist of blocks similar to the blocks used in the MobileNetV2 model without residual connections. In this work, two of those architectures are used for shunt connections: arch1 and arch4. Arch1 represents a big shunt, consisting of two blocks with a high number of channels, while arch4 consists of a single block with a lower amount of channels. Arch1 is visualized in Fig. 1, while for the exact architecture of arch4, it is referred to the original paper [14].

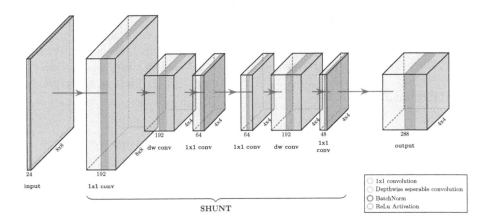

Fig. 1. Shunt architecture used for the CIFAR experiments. Called 'arch1' in [14]. (Modified from https://github.com/HarisIqbal88/PlotNeuralNet).

A method that can be used to fine-tune the shunt inserted model is knowledge distillation [7]. It describes the method through which knowledge can be transferred from a big *teacher* model to a smaller *student* model. This way, the student model can achieve better results than without using knowledge distillation.

One possible variant of knowledge distillation is called dark knowledge, which was first proposed in [7] and uses softened targets to transfer information about how similar two classes are. It helps to extract additional information about the dataset from the teacher (t) model, which can be used to train the student

---

[2] CALTECH: http://www.vision.caltech.edu/Image_Datasets/CaltechPedestrians.

(s) model. Let $\mathcal{L}_{CE}(x, y)$ denote the cross-entropy loss between two probability vectors and sm the softmax activation function which gets applied to the output feature map (out) of a model, then the default loss for our tasks can be defined as

$$\mathcal{L}_D = \mathcal{L}_{CE}(y, \mathrm{sm}(\mathrm{out})). \tag{1}$$

By dividing the output feature map before the softmax by the constant hyperparameter, called temperature, the produced probability distribution is softened up, and similarities between classes become visible. The total loss is then given by:

$$\mathcal{L}_{Total} = \mathcal{L}_D + \lambda \cdot \mathcal{L}_{CE}\left(\mathrm{sm}\left(\frac{\mathrm{out}_t}{T}\right), \mathrm{sm}\left(\frac{\mathrm{out}_s}{T}\right)\right), \tag{2}$$

with λ being a hyperparameter controlling the strength of the distillation loss.

We choose adaptive cross-entropy (ACE) [12] as the distillation method for semantic segmentation tasks since it works similarly to dark knowledge and is simple to implement compared to other approaches [9,11]. Like other methods, it also takes the produced output from the teacher model and compares them to the student's output. However, this time, the target probability map P will be formed by adding ground truth values p_{gt} and teacher predictions p_t. Since the teacher model most probably will produce some wrong pixel labels, the teacher's prediction will only be added to pixels, correctly labeled by the teacher model (*). Using the hyperparameter κ to control the strength of distillation, the expanded probability map is given by:

$$P(x, y) = \begin{cases} \kappa \cdot p_t(x, y) + (1 - \kappa) \cdot p_{gt}(x, y), & \text{if } (*) \\ p_{gt}(x, y), & \text{otherwise} \end{cases} \tag{3}$$

As we are interested in minimizing latency in embedded systems, MobileNet architectures provide a good base. MobileNetV3 [8] uses a similar architecture as MobileNetV2 [13] with small changes. This architecture was obtained through a network architecture search on the ImageNet dataset [5]. The main addition to its previous version is its use of squeeze-and-excite modules in most residual blocks and hard-swish activation functions instead of standard ReLu. So the standard blocks of the MobileNetV3 consist of a 1×1 expand convolution followed by a 3×3 depthwise-separable convolution with a squeeze-and-excitation module attached and a 1×1 project convolution. Two different model variants: *Small* and *Large*, are defined for MobileNetV3. Additionally, the model can be modified by the depth multiplier parameter, which controls the network's channel numbers.

A custom, lightweight segmentation head for MobileNetV3 was introduced, which architecture is similar to the DeeplabV3+ [3] segmentation head. Low-level features are fed to the Lite Reduced Atrous Spatial Pyramid Pooling (LR-ASPP) module on top of the feature extractor. In contrast, high-level features are extracted by a simple connection followed by a 1×1 convolutional layer. This simple setup allows fast computations with competitive results, especially when combined with the MobileNetV3 as a feature extractor.

3   Generation of Shunt Models

We use the shunt architectures arch1, and arch4 from [14], while small modifications like different channel numbers are made for experiments.

3.1   Shunt Training

The first step of training shunt connections is straight forward. We extract feature maps from the input and the output layer of the shunt connection. Then, we train the shunt as an encoder-decoder to match those outputs for a given input afterward. If feature maps are extracted before training, they must be stored either in memory or on disk. If data augmentation also is applied during feature map extraction, it is much more applicable to do the extraction and training within one step. It means a model gets built, which takes an image as input and calculates the original model's output feature maps and the shunt's output simultaneously. Computing the mean squared loss between those outputs gives us the gradients for updating the shunt's weights.

[14] already showed that a final round of training of the shunt-inserted model is essential to achieve good accuracy. This step is not further explained in that paper, but the name fine-tuning indicates that the model gets partly trained for a small number of epochs and small learning rates. We apply three different setups to analyze the effect of fine-tuning: (1) Train the whole model; (2) Freeze all layers before the shunt connection, and the shunt itself; (3) Apply knowledge distillation while not freezing any layers. Regarding the third option, we use dark knowledge for classification tasks and ACE for segmentation tasks.

For these two training steps, two different learning rate policies are used. The first one is called *poly* and was proposed for the DeeplabV3 architecture in [2]. Poly is used for training baseline models as well as fine-tuning shunt inserted models. Learning rate is reduced by a small amount after every epoch according to Eq. 4:

$$
\mathrm{lr_{epoch}} = \mathrm{lr_{base}} \cdot \left(1 - \frac{\mathrm{epoch}}{\mathrm{max\_epochs}}\right)^{\mathrm{power}}, \tag{4}
$$

with 'power' being a hyperparameter, which is usually set close to 1. In our case, we use a power $= 0.9$ for all experiments.

We use another learning strategy for training shunt connections on the feature maps called *plateau*. In our experience, the best way to train shunts is to start with a base learning rate of 0.1 and reduce the learning rate by a factor of 0.1 once the loss of the model reaches a plateau, meaning no improvement for 4 consecutive epochs. We observed that this procedure yields good results independent of shunt architecture and location without any hyperparameter optimization.

3.2   Measuring Performance

Counting multiply-accumulations (MAdds) as a metric of a model is usually used to compare the computational cost of a CNN since they represent the main contribution to a network's latency. They represent the basic operation in CNNs since MAdds are performed to compute convolutional kernels. Additional to absolute MAdds, we also measure the relative reduction of MAdds for a shunt-inserted model to get a compressed model's theoretical speed-up.

However, as latency is the essential metric for speed on embedded systems and statements through MAdds are limited, we try to measure achieved speed-ups on devices too. Getting meaningful results on embedded devices is not easy, since platform optimizers like NVIDIA TensorRT[3] or Intel OpenVino[4] may not cover all layer types of your model or other problems may occur. Therefore, setting up customized networks on embedded hardware often demands high engineering effort.

Latency estimators like ANNETTE [17] for the Intel NCS2 are handy, since they enable fast testing of compressing techniques. We used this estimator during development of our method and will also report results for the estimated inference speed for DeeplabV3 models.

4   Shunt Architectures on Classification Tasks

We conduct experiments on classification tasks on the small dataset CIFAR10, and CIFAR100 similar to [14]. However, we apply those experiments on the newer MobileNetV3Small and extend them by applying dark knowledge distillation to the fine-tuning step. We use the shunt model and the methodology presented in the previous chapter.

4.1   Datasets

The CIFAR10 [10] dataset consists of 60000 images categorized into 10 classes with 50000 train and 10000 validation images. With an image size of 32×32, it can be trained relatively fast and therefore is used for the first test of our method. The CIFAR100 [10] dataset has the same properties as the other version, expect images are grouped into 100 classes containing 600 images each.

Regarding preprocessing for both datasets, each channel gets standardized independently. Data augmentation for training images is applied through a rotation of images by up to $45°$, a maximum shift by up to 6 pixels, and a random horizontal flip.

4.2   Model Setup and Baseline Generation

As a baseline for our experiments, we choose the MobileNetV3Small model with a depth multiplier of 0.5. Original MobileNet architectures are designed with an output stride of 32. Feeding exactly this network with images of CIFAR datasets with an input size of 32×32 would result in feature maps with 1×1

---

[3] TensorRT: https://developer.nvidia.com/Tensorrt.
[4] OpenVino: https://01.org/openvinotoolkit.

spatial resolution. Better results are achieved by changing the first two stages of the network not to downsample the image. As a result, we get an output stride of 8, resulting in 4×4 feature maps for the last stage. We run the CIFAR experiments on a single PC using a GTX970, with the software CUDA 10.1 and Tensorflow 2.3 with Keras API is used for all experiments.

The resulting model needs around 6.8 million MAdds. To produce the baseline for all other experiments, the model gets trained for 350 epochs with a batch size of 64 and the poly learning policy with a base learning rate of $1e-2$. We use stochastic gradient descent (SGD) with a momentum of 0.9 as the optimizer. A weight decay of $4e-5$ is also applied to all layers. The accuracy of the model yields 91.93% for CIFAR10 and 67.10% for CIFAR100.

4.3 Shunt Architecture, Locations and Training

As heuristic to select the location of the shunt connection we calculate the knowledge quotients of blocks with skip connections. Table 1 shows the knowledge quotients of the model for both CIFAR datasets. For blocks without skip connections, the knowledge quotient can not be defined. In the MobileNetV3Small model, these are blocks with stride $= 2$ or a changing number of input and output channels.

Knowledge quotients for the CIFAR10 datasets are low for every block, which means we can freely choose the shunt location. For the CIFAR100 dataset, knowledge quotients are generally slightly higher, which is expected for a more complex dataset. If possible, block 4 should not be replaced due to its high knowledge quotient.

For maximum effect, we replace blocks 4–10 for CIFAR10 and blocks 5–10 in the case of CIFAR100. It means that the shunt connects two different network stages; hence, it must have a stride 2 layer. It is executed at the start of the shunt, at the first depthwise separable convolution to reduce floating-point operations. Its whole architecture is taken from [14], where it is called architecture 1. The exact setup including channel sizes can be seen in Fig. 1.

The final step of the procedure is training the shunt-inserted model on the dataset. We found this step crucial to achieving accuracy close to the accuracy of the original model. In [14], this step is called fine-tuning, indicating a low amount of training epochs with very small learning rates. In our experience, higher learning rates may achieve better results. However, we do not want to completely override the learned weights from the original model. The term 'fine-tuning' does not correctly describe this training setup. In the CIFAR datasets, the shunt-inserted model is trained with a batch size of 64 for 300 epochs using the poly learning rate policy with a base learning rate of $1e-3$. This setup is used whether or not knowledge distillation is applied.

4.4 Results

Results for both shunt-inserted models and fine-tuned models are summarized in Table 2. Without knowledge distillation, accuracy of the fine-tuned model does

Table 1. Knowledge quotients (KQ) of blocks of the MobileNetV3Small model trained on the CIFAR datasets. Yellow coloured blocks are replaced by the shunt connection.

Block ID	MAdds	KQ CIFAR10	KQ CIFAR100
0	918k	-	-
1	584k	-	-
2	588k	0.12	0.25
3	465k	-	-
4	683k	0.13	0.54
5	683k	0.06	0.16
6	339k	0.02	0.09
7	339k	0.01	0.10
8	400k	-	-
9	599k	0.03	0.24
10	599k	0.03	0.15
Head	567k	-	-
	$\sum$ 6.8M		

		FLOPS REDUCTION	
		~42%	~31%

not reach the one achieved by the original model. Actually, freezing a part of the network to avoid overfitting worsens results. In contrast, dark knowledge helps us achieve almost the original accuracy for CIFAR10 and even better than original accuracy for CIFAR100. This matches the results obtained by [14] for MobileNetV2 on CIFAR, but would not be possible without the addition of knowledge distillation.

5   Shunt Architectures on Segmentation Tasks

Applying shunt connections on fairly large benchmark datasets resembles another challenge, which is investigated in the next section. We show that shunt connections provide competitive results when applied to MobileNetV3 trained on Cityscapes [4] and beats compression using depth multipliers to all metrics.

5.1   Dataset

The Cityscapes [4] contains 19 different classes for semantic segmentation of urban scenes, including cars, pedestrians, vegetation, and cyclists. This dataset is well established for measuring the performance of semantic segmentation models [8], which is why it is chosen for shunt experiments.

Table 2. Results for CIFAR datasets.

	Acc. CIFAR10 [%]	Acc. CIFAR100 [%]
Original model	91.93	67.10
Shunt-inserted models		
	79.78	53.56
Fine-tuned models with standard shunt		
Standard	88.09	64.63
Freeze	85.66 (-2.43)	60.04 (-4.59)
DK $(T = 5, \lambda = 2)$	**91.36 $(+3.27)$**	**67.54 $(+2.91)$**

It also represents a real-world problem and a much more difficult task than classification on CIFAR datasets. Fine and coarse annotation is available, but only fine annotations are used for training. 2975 images are used for training and 500 for validation, normalized between $[-1, 1]$ as preprocessing. Data augmentation is applied through scaling train images with factors between 0.5 and 2.0 and random cropping to 513×1025.

5.2 Model Setup and Baseline Generation

We use our own Keras implementation[5] of the MobileNetV3Small segmentation architecture, proposed in [8]. We verified the model by achieving the same accuracy as the original model from Tensorflow[6] with their pre-trained weights. We tried to replicate the training protocol from [3], which is also referenced by [8]. Due to incomplete details given we achieved only an mIoU of around 10 points lower than in [8].

The best result were achieved by training the model for 700 epochs with batch size 24 and the `poly` learning rate with a base learning rate of 5e−2. We use an output stride (OS) of 8 during training and 32 during evaluation and weight decay of 4e−5 for all layers. The images are validated in full size: 1025×2049, and the ASPP module has not been changed while switching from training to evaluation using 13×13 pooling size with stride 4,5.

All semantic segmentation tasks run on a cluster of eight GTX1080 to have enough graphical memory available. With this setup, we achieve 59.50 mIoU for the Cityscapes dataset.

The knowledge quotients for this baseline model can be seen in Table 3. Note that no result can be reported for the third block since features are extracted from it and fed into the segmentation head. We can see, that no block is particularly hard to replace, which would restrict the decision of possible shunt locations.

---

[5] https://github.com/embedded-machine-learning/MobileNetV3-Segmentation-Keras.

[6] Tensorflow: https://github.com/tensorflow/models/tree/master/research/deeplab.

Table 3. Knowledge quotients (KQ) of blocks of the MobileNetV3Small-DeeplabV3 model trained on the Cityscapes datasets.

Block ID	0	1	2	3	4	5	6	7	8	9	10	Head	
MAdds	227 M	53 M	230 M	166 M	128 M	211 M	211 M	114 M	146 M	160 M	75 M	247 M	$\sum$ 2.0 B
KQ	-	-	-	-	0.13	0.15	-	0.20	-	0.20	0.19	-	

5.3 Shunt Architecture, Locations, and Training

Since this section aims to compare shunt connections with the built-in compression technique of MobileNetV3 in the form of depth multipliers, we have to make sure that we achieve similar MAdds reduction. See Table 4 for more information. To do this, we use arch1 and arch4, both proposed by [14]. We also choose two different shunt locations: 4–10 and 5–10. We observed that shunt training is more effective in OS = 32 mode. Therefore, we use it along with the same training procedure as in Sect. 4.3.

Table 4. Results of the MobileNetV3 segmentation model trained on the Cityscapes dataset for different depth multipliers (DM). Percentages in brackets indicate the relative reduction of MAdds and speed-up compared to the baseline model. HS indicates inference on half sized images.

DM	1.0	0.8	0.6
MAdds	196 M	166 M (-15%)	121 M (-38%)
ANNETTE (NCS2)	463 ms	437 ms (-5.6%)	400 ms (-13.6%)
NCS2 (HS)	127 ms	121 ms (-4.7%)	111 ms (-12.6%)
mIoU	59.50	52.73	44.59

Regarding fine-tuning the shunt-inserted model, we observed that training is more effective using OS = 32. Again, we do want to train with quite high learning rates, while not destroying all learned knowledge. Hence we use a base learning rate of 1e−2 for the poly learning policy. We are training for 500 epochs and a batch size of 12. We reduce the batch size here since we need extra memory computing the original model for knowledge distillation, and we want a fair comparison between fine-tuning methods.

5.4 Measuring Latency on Embedded Hardware

Optimization on Intel platforms is done by OpenVINO. We use version 2021.2 and measure inference for half sized images (513×1025) with a single request size on the NCS2. Inference for the full image size gives us an error, which is not further debuggable without big efforts.

Table 5. Results for the Cityscapes datasets. The header describes shunt locations as well as used architectures. The relative reduction of MAdds and speed-up compared to the baseline are written in parentheses. HS indicates inference on half sized images.

	7–10-Arch4	5–10-Arch1	4–10-Arch1
MAdds	166 M (−15%)	141 M (−28%)	120 M (−39%)
ANNETTE (NCS2)	417 ms (−9.9%)	375 ms (−19%)	342 ms (−26.1%)
NCS2 (HS)	111 ms (−12.6%)	98 ms (−22.8%)	92 ms (−27.6%)
Shunt-inserted models - mIoU			
	34.84	37.97	35.13
Fine-tuned models with standard shunt - mIoU			
Standard	**56.52**	54.91	**51.83**
ACE ($\kappa = 0.3$)	56.03 (−0.49)	**55.98 (+1.07)**	51.14 (−0.69)

5.5 Results

The results of the experiments are summarized in Table 5. First of all, one can see that higher MAdd-reduction does not linearly correspond to faster inference. Using shunt connections, around 2/3 of relative MAdd-reduction translates into inference speed-up.

Regarding fine-tuned models, we consider all shunt-connections as successful since the compressed model can achieve relatively high mIoU. Applying knowledge distillation through ACE leads to mixed results. 7–10-arch4 and 4–10-arch1 result in worse results, while 5–10-arch1 gains a boost of one whole point. Knowledge distillation may work well for CIFAR it also acts as strong regularization. Hence, for problems, which tend to overfit, knowledge distillation may have a strong positive effect, while for other problems, like Cityscapes, distillation is less beneficial.

Using the same training procedure as in Sect. 5.2, we achieve the following result for using different depth multipliers for the MobileNetV3 model. See Table 4 for results. Note that we make sure, that the channel number of each layer is dividable by 8. Therefore, we cannot observe a smooth curve for model size when lowering the depth multiplier, but rather encounter large steps.

The achieved accuracies and estimated inference speed-ups can be seen in Table 4. One can see that for the depth multiplayer method, only around 1/3 of relative MAdd-reduction translates into speed-up inference.

Figure 2 shows the quantitative comparison between the two methods. This comparison is valid since very similar compression factors are used for both methods: 16% and 38%. We also compare runtimes for half sized images, since the reduction factors only vary slightly with input size. It is visible that shunt-inserted models provide higher mIoU while estimated and measured to running faster on the NCS2 than the models slimmed through depth multipliers. In conclusion, shunt connections provide faster models, which perform better on

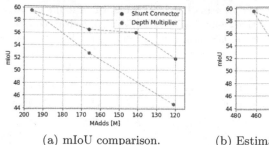
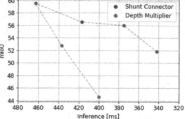

(a) mIoU comparison.   (b) Estimated inference comparison.

Fig. 2. Comparison between shunt connected models and models obtained through smaller depth multipliers.

Cityscapes, compared to compressed models using low depth multipliers. Hence, shunt-inserted models should always be preferred.

6   Conclusion

It was shown that shunt connections can successfully be applied to various tasks, including classification on CIFAR and semantic segmentation on Cityscapes.

Knowledge distillation in the form of dark knowledge is highly effective for overfitting classification tasks. Applying ACE distillation to large scale segmentation tasks do not provide the same benefit. The increase in performance depends on the exact scenario so that no general statement can be made. Analyzing additional knowledge distillation methods for such problems to get a clearer picture is left as future work.

It is shown that shunt insertion is a competitive method applicable for different tasks and large datasets. Shunt connections should always be preferred over compression using depth multipliers. Especially the actual speedup of the compressed model is convincing.

The problem of finding the optimal shunt location and architecture is still an open problem. Ideally, a systematic, automatable method could be developed. Another open task is also comparing shunt connections with other compression techniques. Especially the comparison between compression rate and translated speed-up seems interesting.

Acknowledgements. The financial support by the Austrian Federal Ministry for Digital and Economic Affairs, the National Foundation for Research, Technology and Development and the Christian Doppler Research Association is gratefully acknowledged. The computational results presented have been achieved [in part] using the Vienna Scientific Cluster (VSC).

References

1. Bochkovskiy, A., Wang, C.Y., Liao, H.Y.M.: Yolov4: optimal speed and accuracy of object detection (2020)

2. Chen, L., Papandreou, G., Schroff, F., Adam, H.: Rethinking atrous convolution for semantic image segmentation. CoRR abs/1706.05587 (2017). http://arxiv.org/abs/1706.05587
3. Chen, L.-C., Zhu, Y., Papandreou, G., Schroff, F., Adam, H.: Encoder-decoder with atrous separable convolution for semantic image segmentation. In: Ferrari, V., Hebert, M., Sminchisescu, C., Weiss, Y. (eds.) ECCV 2018. LNCS, vol. 11211, pp. 833–851. Springer, Cham (2018). https://doi.org/10.1007/978-3-030-01234-2_49
4. Cordts, M., et al.: The cityscapes dataset for semantic urban scene understanding (2016)
5. Deng, J., Dong, W., Socher, R., Li, L.J., Li, K., Fei-Fei, L.: ImageNet: a large-scale hierarchical image database. In: CVPR 2009 (2009)
6. He, K., Zhang, X., Ren, S., Sun, J.: Deep residual learning for image recognition. CoRR abs/1512.03385 (2015). http://arxiv.org/abs/1512.03385
7. Hinton, G., Vinyals, O., Dean, J.: Distilling the knowledge in a neural network (2015)
8. Howard, A., et al.: Searching for mobilenetv3 (2019)
9. Kothandaraman, D., Nambiar, A., Mittal, A.: Domain adaptive knowledge distillation for driving scene semantic segmentation (2020)
10. Krizhevsky, A.: Learning multiple layers of features from tiny images (2009)
11. Liu, Y., Chen, K., Liu, C., Qin, Z., Luo, Z., Wang, J.: Structured knowledge distillation for semantic segmentation. CoRR abs/1903.04197 (2019). http://arxiv.org/abs/1903.04197
12. Park, S., Heo, Y.: Knowledge distillation for semantic segmentation using channel and spatial correlations and adaptive cross entropy. Sensors 20, 4616 (2020). https://doi.org/10.3390/s20164616
13. Sandler, M., Howard, A.G., Zhu, M., Zhmoginov, A., Chen, L.: Inverted residuals and linear bottlenecks: mobile networks for classification, detection and segmentation. CoRR abs/1801.04381 (2018). http://arxiv.org/abs/1801.04381
14. Singh, B., Toshniwal, D., Allur, S.K.: Shunt connection: an intelligent skipping of contiguous blocks for optimizing MobileNet-V2. Neural Networks 118, 192–203 (2019). https://doi.org/10.1016/j.neunet.2019.06.006. http://www.sciencedirect.com/science/article/pii/S0893608019301790
15. Tao, A., Sapra, K., Catanzaro, B.: Hierarchical multi-scale attention for semantic segmentation (2020)
16. Veit, A., Wilber, M., Belongie, S.: Residual networks behave like ensembles of relatively shallow networks (2016)
17. Wess, M., Ivanov, M., Unger, C., Nookala, A., Wendt, A., Jantsch, A.: ANNETTE: accurate neural network execution time estimation with stacked models. IEEE Access 9, 3545–3556 (2021). https://doi.org/10.1109/ACCESS.2020.3047259

System-Wide Anomaly Detection of Industrial Control Systems via Deep Learning and Correlation Analysis

Gordon Haylett, Zahra Jadidi$^{(\boxtimes)}$, and Kien Nguyen Thanh

Cyber Security Cooperative Research Centre, Queensland University of Technology (QUT),
Brisbane, Australia
zahra.jadidi@qut.edu.au

Abstract. In the last few decades, as industrial control systems (ICSs) became more interconnected via modern networking techniques, there has been a growing need for new security and monitoring techniques to protect these systems. Advanced cyber-attacks on industrial systems take multiple steps to reach ICS end devices. However, current anomaly detection systems can only detect attacks on individual local devices, and they do not consider the impact or consequences of an individual attack on the rest of the ICS devices. In this paper, we aim to explore how deep learning recurrent neural networks and correlation analysis techniques can be used collaboratively for anomaly detection in an ICS network on the scale of the entire systems. For each detected attack, our presented system-wide anomaly detection method will predict the next step of the attack. We use iTrust SWaT dataset and Power System Attack datasets from MSU national Labs to explore how the addition of correlation analysis to recurrent networks can expand anomaly detection methods to the system-wide scale.

Keywords: Anomaly detection · Correlation analysis · Deep learning · Industrial control system

1 Introduction

Traditional industrial control systems (ICSs) were not designed for security as they were isolated networks running proprietary control protocols. However, due to the connection of current ICS networks to the Internet, the cybersecurity of ICSs becomes a growing concern. A cyber-attack in an ICS network can be caused by an attack spreading maliciously from information technology (IT) networks to operational technology (OT) networks [1].

Many anomaly detection methods have been proposed to detect anomalies against ICS devices. Existing work on anomaly detection in ICSs can be divided into two broad categories, network traffic-based and physical process-based [2]. Network traffic-based anomaly detection systems are based on the analysis of communication patterns between different devices in an ICS network [3], while physical process-based anomaly detection

© IFIP International Federation for Information Processing 2021
Published by Springer Nature Switzerland AG 2021
I. Maglogiannis et al. (Eds.): AIAI 2021, IFIP AICT 627, pp. 362–373, 2021.
https://doi.org/10.1007/978-3-030-79150-6_29

methods are built on the analysis of ICS device logs that record the state of physical devices such as sensors and actuators [4]. These anomaly detection methods only focus on monitoring a single source of data without considering the consequence of attacks on other devices. Analysis of correlation among various data sources is required to provide comprehensive and system-wide anomaly detection [5]. This enables security experts to predict and prevent future steps of an attack. Correlation analysis was employed in some papers [6] to improve the security of enterprise networks. However, the novelty of our paper is presenting a combination of anomaly detection and correlation analysis to provide a system-wide anomaly detection in ICS networks. Recurrent networks will be coupled with correlation analysis to detect when and where an anomaly occurs and subsequently search correlated devices for signs of further attack or influence. The results will be evaluated using real-world ICS datasets to show the efficiency of the presented method.

The rest of this paper is organised as follows. Section 2 explains background and related works. Section 3 describes the system-wide anomaly detection method proposed in this paper. Evaluation datasets are explained in Sect. 4. Section 5 discusses the evaluation results of our method in ICS datasets. Section 6 analyses the results. Section 7 concludes the paper.

2 Background and Related Works

Historically ICSs were immune to cyber-attacks because they were "Air-Gapped" [7]. This is a term used to describe a physical disconnect between the ICS and the organization's cyber network. Meaning there is no connection an attacker could use to get from the corporate network onto the ICS network. This changed near the end of the 1990s with the development of new IT systems and technologies that improved the ICS workflow but also made it less secure to outside threats [7]. This increasing trend of legacy industrial devices being connected to normal IT networks and the internet means these ICS networks are now vulnerable to new types of attacks. Zero-day attacks are almost inevitable in these ICS networks and are a serious concern. This is where anomaly detection and machine learning are used to detect anomalous events [8]. Different machine learning methods have been used for anomaly detection. However, research shows that deep learning methods outperform traditional methods as the scale of data increases, shown in Fig. 1 [9, 17].

There are many papers that performed deep learning-based anomaly detection for ICSs [11, 17], and their results showed the high accuracy of deep learning-based analysis. Motivated by the above discussions, a deep learning-based anomaly detection method is deployed in our paper to analyse ICS data.

Advanced ICS attacks have multiple steps to gain access to their target device. Therefore, detecting a single anomaly cannot identify the future steps of an advanced attack. Using correlation analysis, we can assess correlated features and identify if an anomaly is isolated or potentially part of a larger complex multi-part attack [5, 6, 18]. In this paper, we use correlation analysis to expand the anomaly detection system-wide.

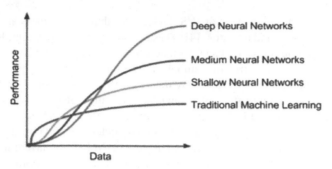

Fig. 1. Performance comparison of deep learning Vs traditional anomaly detection methods [9]

When working with high dimensional data with low-value density, it is crucial to select correct features for analysis as a large amount of sensor data streams can lead to serious performance impacts [5, 6, 18]. Paper [10] used sensor data correlation changes to improve the performance of IoT equipment anomaly detection by correlating duplicate deployed sensors and clustering them. The IoT devices used in the paper are sensors measuring things much like those in ICS networks. The paper states "dynamic data correlations among industrial equipment sensors prevalently exist" is a key component of correlation analysis as if there is a change in a device then it is likely there will be impacts to correlated devices. Figure 2 that is an example from paper [10], shows a clear correlation when the coal flow dips power dips after a small delay.

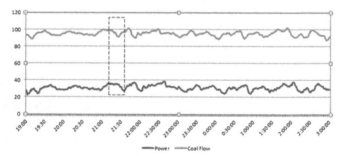

Fig. 2. Correlated power and coal flow of coal mil [10].

The methods used in the paper [10] would be an effective way to perform correlation analysis, however; on low dimensionality systems with few weakly correlated nodes or features, such as a limited number of sensors that only monitor isolated features, this method has the potential to be ineffective. If the features are not correlated strongly enough to impact each other when there is a change, the analysis method would need to be highly tuned or sensitive to changes. This can lead to false positives and misleading correlations. The paper on correlation-change anomaly detection [10] provides important information and methods for effectively correlating data.

Inspired by the paper [10], we present our correlation-based solution to explore a method of system-wide anomaly detection in ICS networks. Using anomaly detection on a selection of key features, we will then use correlation analysis to explore other potentially anomalous features which may be related to a detected anomaly.

3   System-Wide Anomaly Detection

In this section, we will be discussing the methods and processes used to perform correlation analysis, anomaly detection and the experimental process.

3.1   Process

The process involves identifying correlated features from a map of all features as nodes. Firstly, features that have the greatest impact on other features and features which are likely to change in clusters are identified using correlation analysis. This is done so that our single feature anomaly detection method can become system-wide. This means that it can comprehensively track anomalies throughout an entire system. This is advantageous as many detection systems focus on monitoring individual devices and features but here, we incorporate correlation analysis on top of that to create a broader system-wide detection system. Once several nodes are correlated then if an anomaly is detected in one the correlated nodes are checked for anomalies to see if the anomaly is isolated, spreading or a part of a larger chain of anomalies.

When dealing with multidimensional datasets, it is important to filter out non-correlated features. This can lead to difficulties with automated model-building methods struggling to select the important features from among thousands of candidates. As it is better to use fewer correlated features to train a model [12], the network map of correlated nodes can be used to identify nodes that are most correlated to other nodes, and it provides a good starting point for identifying high priority nodes for monitoring. Figure 3 provides an example of a correlation map.

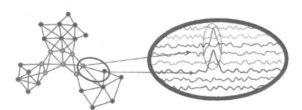

Fig. 3. Example of two correlated features

3.2   Methodology

Different phases of this paper were as follows (Fig. 4):

1. First feature reduction is performed to remove duplicate sensors or isolate key features.

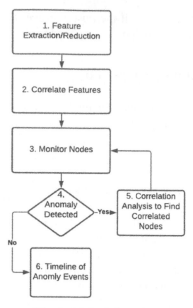

Fig. 4. Methodology flow

2. Correlation analysis is performed on the system or dataset in question. This helps to identify correlated nodes and which features share the strongest relations to other features.
3. We identify the key features/nodes for anomaly detection. Then, we monitor the nodes for anomalies using Long Short-Term Memory (LSTM) models to detect changes in the expected behaviour of the nodes.
4. If an anomaly is detected in a node, then we perform correlation analysis and examine each of its correlated nodes in turn. If an anomaly is identified or detected in a correlated node, its correlated nodes are checked as well. This process continues until no further anomalies are found or until every unique node is checked.
5. Using the detected anomalies and their timestamps, it is then possible to show when the detected anomalies occurred in the system.

Our model is a combination of deep learning for anomaly detection and correlation analysis to expand it to be system-wide. This combination allows for the anomaly detection segment to focus on detection and the correlation analysis to provide the next target. This process allows us to follow the path an anomaly or attacker may have taken through a system and which devices may have been impacted and in what order. This can also be used to help identify attack insertion points and which nodes need hardening or further examination.

Anomaly Detection. For anomaly detection, an LSTM recurrent neural network was used as it is well suited for processing and making predictions based on time series data [9]. After correlation analysis is performed, nodes (aka features) are monitored by LSTM models of the features. If an anomaly is detected, then the correlated and adjacent nodes are also checked to see if the anomaly is isolated or if the anomaly is potentially part of greater concern. The LSTM used here is relatively simple and consists of an input and output layer and 4 LSTM layers using 'relu' activation method separated by an attention layer.

Correlation Analysis. When dealing with multidimensional datasets, it is important to filter out non-correlated features. This is done because two devices might monitor the same sensor or device and would end up appearing highly correlated if there were a change in whatever device they were monitoring. This would create the impression these two sensors are linked or in some way impact each other when they do not. In this case, it may be better to use fewer highly correlated features to train a model [13]. For this paper, we use the Pearson correlation coefficient [16] as it indicates whether a statistically significant relationship exists between two continuous variables and whether a change in one variable may be associated with a proportional change in another variable.

When correlation analysis is performed, we can create a correlation matrix or correlation map to display the data in a more human-readable way as shown in Fig. 5. The map on the right of Fig. 5 shows the more highly correlated features from the matrix on the left in a more concise easy to read format. This map is beneficial when dealing with datasets which require some significant feature reduction or when it is unclear which parts of the system are the most interconnected. In highly connected systems, this may also be beneficial to reduce noise and prevent correlations being shown between every node and confusing the model with extraneous data. The size of the node in Fig. 5 is indicative of how many edges (correlations) it has and the darker the edge the more highly correlated the nodes are. This map can also give a visual representation of clustering if there is any.

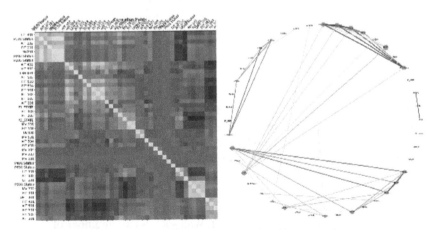

Fig. 5. SWaT matrix and map side by side comparison

4 Datasets

Our proposed model was evaluated using two ICS datasets, the Tommy Morris Power Systems dataset and the iTrust Secure Water Treatment (SWaT) dataset. These datasets were divided into training (70%), validation (10%) and testing sets (20%) for the evaluation of our model.

Power Systems. The ICS Cyber Attack Power System Datasets was developed in [14]. It contains 37 scenarios divided into 8 cases of Natural Events, 1 case of No Events and 28 Attack Events. The power system testbed used in generating the test scenarios contains power generators, breakers, and Intelligent Electronic Devices (IEDs) that can switch the breakers on or off.

iTrust SWaT. The Secure Water Treatment (SWaT) dataset is a water treatment testbed for cybersecurity research [15]. The dataset consists of a modern six-stage process. There are 6 attacks performed on the dataset: Attack on FIT401 (Spoof value from 0.8 to 0.5), Attack on LIT301 (Spoof value from 835 to 1024), Attack on P601 (Switch from OFF to ON), Multi-point Attack (Switch from CLOSE to OPEN (MV201) and OFF to ON (P101)), Attack on MV501 (Switch from OPEN to CLOSE), and Attack on P301 (Switch from ON to OFF). FIT 401 sensor is a Flow Transmitter which controls the UV dechlorinator. LIT301 sensor is a Level Transmitter. P601 actuator pumps water from RO permeate tank to raw water tank. MV201 actuator is a motorized valve. P101 actuator pumps water from the raw water tank to the second stage. P301 actuator is a UF feed Pump.

5 Results

The experimental results are separated into two sections. The first section is for the Tommy Morris Power System Dataset, which is a simple case where the anomaly is fast and affects multiple devices in the same way. The second section is for the SWaT dataset.

5.1 Power Systems

The data in this section is from the line maintenance scenario where one or more relays are disabled on a specific line to do maintenance for that line [14]. Figure 6 shows the correlation matrix for the line maintenance scenario in this system. The correlation matrix uses Pearson correlation and shows which features have a correlation between each other, with highly correlated features being shown in yellow-green. This matrix has been sorted to show some clustering.

This matrix can be converted to a correlation map to show the correlations in a more readable format as shown in Fig. 7. However, with such a large number of features so many correlations would make the map almost solid and impossible to read so the map is split into the strongest positive (>0.5, left) and negative (<-0.5, right) correlations. The first node monitored was R1-PA4:IH. Figure 7 shows the nodes readings in blue and the time periods where attacks were performed in red.

In Fig. 8, the anomaly graph shows that several anomalies were detected in node R1-PA4:IH. These were determined to be anomalies by training a model of the data and taking the Mean Absolute Error (MAE) and lowering it by a small percentage to get a threshold for anomalies. As anomalies were detected in the initial node, as shown in Fig. 8, all correlated nodes were also checked for anomalies. This process continues until no further anomalies were detected. This resulted in checking the following nodes:

R1-PA1:VH	R1-PA7:VH	R1-PA10:IH	R2-PA1:VH
R2-PA7:VH	R3-PA1:VH	R3-PA7:VH	R4-PA1:VH
R4-PA4:IH	R4-PA7:VH	R4-PA10:IH	R1-PA4:IH

All of which also had detected anomalies. This shows that if an anomaly is detected in any one node whether that be from a directed attack or other reasons the algorithm will spread out fro that node and search all adjacent and correlated nodes to find other anomalous behaviour. The accuracy of our LSTM in anomaly detection in the Power System dataset was 95%, and the precision was 95%.

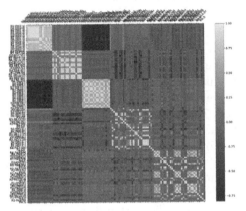

Fig. 6. Power systems line maintenance correlation analysis matrix

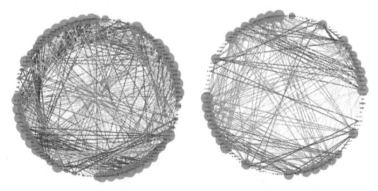

Fig. 7. Power systems line maintenance positive and negative correlation network map

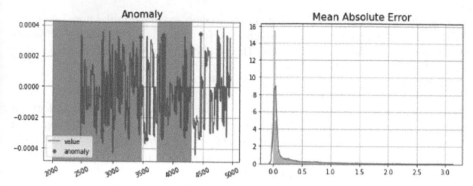

Fig. 8. R1-PA4:IH detected anomalies

5.2 iTrust SWaT

In the SWAT dataset, there are 6 different attacks performed. The first attack is on FIT401 trying to spoof value from 0.8 to 0.5 with the intent to stop de-chlorination by switching off UV401. Correlation analysis is performed to identify which nodes should be monitored most closely. The matrix in Fig. 9 shows the correlations.

Using Fig. 9 correlation Matrix, we construct the two maps in Fig. 10 based on all the strongest positive (>0.5) and negative (<-0.5) correlations. Where a positive correlation represents a 'perfect' increasing relationship and negative correlations represent a 'perfect' decreasing relationship.

Using these maps, we can identify key nodes of interest with many strong positive correlations such as AIT402 and LIT401 as well as many strong negative correlations such as FIT401, AIT501 and LIT101. Any change in these nodes will likely have an impact on the network at large thus they are ideal for monitoring. The first node monitored for this dataset is FIT 401. This node is the first one attacked in the dataset. The anomaly graph in Fig. 11 shows the anomalies detected in the node. The attacks are also highlighted in red. An anomaly that is detected within one of the red areas can be

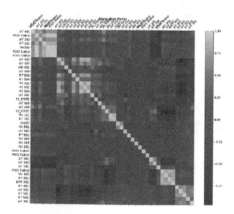

Fig. 9. SWaT correlation matrix

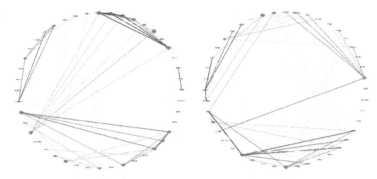

Fig. 10. SWaT positive and negative correlations

considered to be a true positive detection representing an anomaly that was detected as a part of an attack. An anomaly found outside of one of the red zones can be considered a false positive. The accuracy of our LSTM in detecting anomalies in the SWaT dataset was 97%, and the precision was 96%.

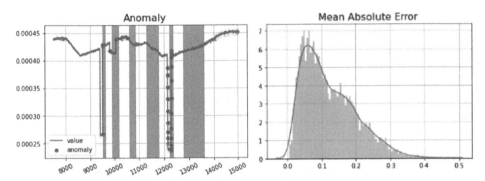

Fig. 11. FIT 401 detected anomalies

6 Analysis

The Power Systems dataset contains many different types of events which makes it challenging to perform anomaly detection. For R1-PA4:IH, there were 10 detected anomalies. An LSTM is used to predict the expected behaviour of each node (Fig. 13), and a threshold value (Fig. 12) helps to identify the anomaly area. The anomaly threshold is 10% in this paper to ensure as many anomalies are detected as possible. The area above this threshold shows anomalies, Fig. 12. The LSTM models effectively predicted values closely aligned with the testing data (Fig. 13).

The similar threshold value was used for the SWaT dataset. The testing and predicted data for FIT401 sensor in the SWaT dataset is shown in Fig. 14. The accuracies of our LSTM in detecting anomalies in Power System and SWaT datasets were 95% and 97% respectively.

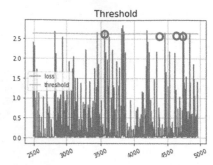

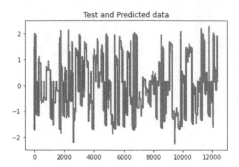

Fig. 12. Anomaly detection threshold (Power System Dataset)

Fig. 13. LSTM prediction of normal behaviour in R1-PA4:IH (Predicted values (red) and the actual values (green)) (Color figure online)

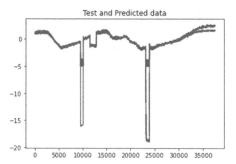

Fig. 14. FIT401 testing and predicted data (predicted (red) and the actual values (green)) (Color figure online)

Existing anomaly detection methods can detect anomalies happening in each ICS device. However, advanced ICS attacks are mostly multi-step, and existing methods are not able to detect the correlation between different steps of an anomaly. In both Power System and SWaT datasets, our system-wide anomaly detection method provided high accuracy in anomaly detection, and it could detect the events correlated with each anomaly.

7   Conclusion

Using deep learning-based anomaly detection in conjunction with correlation analysis, we could effectively expand single feature anomaly detection to be system-wide anomaly detection. This method of system-wide anomaly detection had the potential to accurately detect anomalies and then immediately check adjacent and correlated nodes for other anomalies. In this paper, our focus was on identifying other correlated nodes to the node with anomalous behaviour, and we wanted to identify the future steps of the ICS attacks. Our presented solution was evaluated using two real-world ICS datasets and it showed high accuracy in both datasets. In our future work, we will improve our method to include the time lag of anomalies during correlation analysis.

Acknowledgements. The authors acknowledge the support of the Commonwealth of Australia and Cybersecurity Research Centre Limited.

References

1. Maglaras, L., et al.: Cyber security of critical infrastructures. ICT Express **4**, 42–45 (2018). https://doi.org/10.1016/j.icte.2018.02.001
2. Hu, Y., Yang, A., Li, H., Sun, Y., Sun, L.: A survey of intrusion detection on industrial control systems. Int. J. Distrib. Sens. Netw. **14**(8), 1–14 (2018). https://doi.org/10.1177/155014771 8794615
3. Dong, R., Wu, D., Zhang, Q., Zhang, T.: Traffic characteristic map-based intrusion detection model for industrial internet. Int. J. Netw. Secur. **20**(2), 359–370 (2018). https://doi.org/10. 6633/IJNS.201803.20(2).17
4. Hussain, M., Foo, E., Suriadi, S.: An improved industrial control system device logs processing method for process-based anomaly detection. In: International Conference on Frontiers of Information Technology (FIT), pp. 150–1505. IEEE (2019)
5. Tian, Z., et al.: A real-time correlation of host-level events in cyber range service for smart campus. IEEE Access **6**, 35355–35364 (2018)
6. Gottwalt, F., Chang, E., Dillon, T.: CorrCorr: a feature selection method for multivariate correlation network anomaly detection techniques. Comput. Secur. **83**, 234–245 (2019)
7. Sommestad, T., Ericsson, G.N., Nordlander, J.: SCADA system cyber security - a comparison of standards. In: IEEE PES General Meeting, Providence, RI, pp. 1–8 (2010)
8. Parrend, P., Navarro, J., Guigou, F., Deruyver, A., Collet, P.: Foundations and applications of artificial Intelligence for zero-day and multi-step attack detection. EURASIP J. Inf. Secur. **2018**, 4 (2018)
9. Chalapathy, R., Chawla, S.: Deep learning for anomaly detection: a survey, arXiv:1901.03407 (2019)
10. Su, S., Sun, Y., Gao, X., Qiu, J., Tian, Z.: A correlation-change based feature selection method for IoT equipment anomaly detection. Appl. Sci. **9**(3), 437 (2019). https://doi.org/10.3390/ app9030437
11. Bhamare, D., Zolanvari, M., Erbad, A., Jain, R., Khan, K., Meskin, N.: Cybersecurity for industrial control systems: a survey. Comput. Secur. **89**, (2020). https://doi.org/10.1016/j. cose.2019.101677
12. Tološi, T., Legauer, T.: Classification with correlated features: unreliability of feature ranking and solutions. Bioinformatics **27**(14), 1986–1994 (2011)
13. Ayinde, B., Inanc, T., Zurada, J.: On correlation of features extracted by deep neural. In: International Joint Conference on Neural Networks (IJCNN) (2019)
14. Adhikari, U., Pan, S., Morris, T.: Industrial Control System (ICS) Cyber Attack Datasets. https://sites.google.com/a/uah.edu/tommy-morris-uah/ics-data-sets
15. iTrust: Secure Water treatment – iTrust (2020). https://itrust.sutd.edu.sg/testbeds/secure-water-treatment-swat/
16. Wang, L., Jones, R.: Big data analytics in cyber security: network traffic and attacks. J. Comput. Inf. Syst. 1–8 (2020)
17. Jadidi, Z., Dorri, A., Jurdak, R., Fidge, C.: Securing manufacturing using blockchain. In: 2020 IEEE 19th International Conference on Trust, Security and Privacy in Computing and Communications (TrustCom), Guangzhou, China, pp. 1920–1925 (2020)
18. Kushal, T.R.B., Illindala, M.S.: Correlation-based feature selection for resilience analysis of MVDC shipboard power system. Int. J. Electr. Power Energy Syst. **117**, (2020)

Verification of Size Invariance in DNN Activations Using Concept Embeddings

Gesina Schwalbe[1,2]([envelope]) [iD]

[1] Continental AG, Regensburg, Germany
gesina.schwalbe@continental-corporation.com
[2] Cognitive Systems, University of Bamberg, Bamberg, Germany

Abstract. The benefits of deep neural networks (DNNs) have become of interest for safety critical applications like medical ones or automated driving. Here, however, quantitative insights into the DNN inner representations are mandatory [10]. One approach to this is *concept analysis*, which aims to establish a mapping between the internal representation of a DNN and intuitive semantic concepts. Such can be sub-objects like human body parts that are valuable for validation of pedestrian detection. To our knowledge, concept analysis has not yet been applied to large object detectors, specifically not for sub-parts. Therefore, this work first suggests a substantially improved version of the Net2Vec approach [5] for post-hoc segmentation of sub-objects. Its practical applicability is then demonstrated on a new concept dataset by two exemplary assessments of three standard networks, including the larger Mask R-CNN model [9]: (1) the consistency of body part similarity, and (2) the invariance of internal representations of body parts with respect to the size in pixels of the depicted person. The findings show that the representation of body parts is mostly size invariant, which may suggest an early intelligent fusion of information in different size categories.

Keywords: Concept embedding analysis · MS COCO · Explainable AI

1 Introduction

The high performance and flexibility of deep neural networks (DNNs) makes them interesting for many complex computer vision applications. This includes ethically involved or safety critical fields where silent biases can become a matter of unfairness, or even life-threatening decisions. Hence, responsible artificial intelligence is required, allowing for thorough assessments of trained DNNs [1]. For example in the area of automated driving, quantitative insights into the inner representation of trained DNNs are mandatory [10].

The research leading to these results was partly funded by the German Federal Ministry for Economic Affairs and Energy within the project "KI-Absicherung".

I. Maglogiannis et al. (Eds.): AIAI 2021, IFIP AICT 627, pp. 374–386, 2021.
https://doi.org/10.1007/978-3-030-79150-6_30

One step towards this direction is the research area of *concept (embedding) analysis* [5,11], that started with the work in [2] in 2017. Supervised concept analysis aims to answer the question how (well) information on a visual semantic concept is embedded in the intermediate output of one layer of a trained DNN. A concept can be, e.g., a texture, material, scene, object, or object part [2], and should be given as samples with binary annotations. The question is answered by training a simple model to predict the concept from the layer output, with simplicity ensuring interpretability [2,11]. Once these *concept models* are obtained, several means for verification open up: The embedding quality can be measured as the prediction quality of the concept model; if a similarity measure for concept models is available, semantic relations between concepts can be validated (e.g., legs are similar to arms) [5]; and lastly, if the information embedding can be represented as a vector in the latent space, one can use sensitivity analysis to investigate dependencies of outputs on certain concepts [11]. The vector can be the normal vector of a linear model, or the center of a cluster, and is called the embedding of the concept [5].

While concept analysis opens up a wide variety of verification options, existing methods suffer from some limitations. For one, the methods are either restricted to image-level concepts, or, like Net2Vec [5], report poor results for part objects. But part objects, such as human body parts, are substantial to verify logical plausibility of pedestrian detectors needed for automated driving. This brings up the second issue: To our knowledge, existing proposals have not been evaluated on large networks like standard object detectors. Concretely, we uncovered some severe performance limitations of Net2Vec that impede application to state-of-the-art sized DNNs or larger concept datasets than the original Broden dataset proposed in [2].

In order to overcome the practical issues, this paper suggests some substantial improvements to the Net2Vec method, demonstrated on a new large MS COCO [15] based concept dataset for human body parts. The applicability of concept analysis for simple verification is demonstrated by exemplary assessment of three networks with different sizes, tasks, and training data (AlexNet, VGG16, and Mask R-CNN [9]). Concretely, the semantic similarity of different concepts is validated, and it is checked whether the internal representation of the networks is biased towards one size category (i.e., distance to the camera). Interestingly, our findings suggest that convolutional DNNs are not biased towards one size. Instead, from early layers onwards, they use an efficient common representation for instances of the same part object but different sizes. The main contributions of this paper are:

- A Net2Vec-based concept analysis approach that can deal with large models and large concept datasets is presented and demonstrated. It is found to considerably surpass the state-of-the-art for object part concepts.
- The first evaluation of size invariance of the internal representations of convolutional DNNs is conducted.
- For this, an approach is presented to estimate the pixel size of persons in 2D images from skeletal annotations, which can be used for concept mask generation.

After a revision of concept analysis methods in Sect. 2, our approach is introduced in Sect. 3. Finally, in Sect. 4 it is validated and used for the exemplary assessment.

2 Related Work

An early approach to supervised concept analysis was NetDissect by Bau et al. [2]. They associated single convolutional filters with semantic concepts, and provided the Broden dataset, a combined dataset featuring a wide variety of concepts. Building upon NetDissect, Net2Vec [5] expanded from single filters to combinations of filters and trains a 1 × 1 convolution to predict concept masks from latent space outputs. Intuitively, the weight vector of the convolution, the concept embedding vector, encodes the direction within the layer output space that adds the concept. The authors investigate the similarity of different concepts via cosine similarity of their concept vectors. Similarly, TCAV by Kim et al. [11] trains linear models but using a support vector machine on the complete latent space output for binary classification instead of segmentation. The authors suggest to use partial directional derivatives along the concept vectors to assess how outputs depend on concepts in intermediate layers. Future work may investigate how this can be applied to concept segmentation instead of concept classification. Other than the previous linear model approaches, SeVec [8] uses a k-means clustering approach, demonstrated on a dataset other than Broden, but again only on image-level concepts and with a manual step in the process. The Net2Vec-based proof of concept in [19] uses a small concept dataset for traffic sign letters. This work also details the value of concept analysis for safety assessment, and suggests that a mismatch of concept size and receptive field of concept models can cause a texture bias, that is, predictions purely based on texture. This is investigated for larger nets in this paper.

More relevant for inspection than requirements verification purposes, unsupervised concept analysis approaches aim to find and visualize repetitive concepts in the intermediate output of a DNN. A simple example is feature visualization [16], where noise is optimized to maximally activate a convolutional filter. ACE [7] instead uses super-pixels as concept candidates, which are then clustered by their latent space proximity. In the direction of representation disentanglement, [21] introduced a measure for the completeness of a set of concept vectors with respect a given task. Their idea is that post-hoc adding a semantic bottleneck with unit vectors aligned to the concepts should not decrease the model performance. Similarly, but with invertible DNNs instead of linear maps, the recent work in [4] tries to find a bijection of a latent space to a product of semantically aligned sub-spaces (and a residual space).

Experiments so far have been conducted on small resolution image datasets like the 224 × 224 pixels of the Broden [2,5,11] and ImageNet [8] data or less [19], and have not yet been applied to large models or object detectors.

3   Approach

This section introduces our concept analysis approach with its modifications to the Net2Vec concept analysis method, and an approach to estimate the body size in pixels for persons in 2D images from skeletal annotations. Size estimation is later used to generate ground truth segmentation masks for body part concepts, and to categorize them by size.

3.1   Concept Embedding Analysis

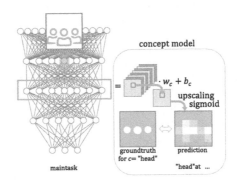

Fig. 1. Illustration of the used concept analysis approach. For a concept c, here "head", it predicts binary segmentation masks from convolutional activation maps via (1) a 1-filter convolution with kernel w_c and bias b_c, (2) bilinear upscaling (here depicted using nearest pixel upscaling), and finally (3) normalization.

Our method is illustrated in Fig. 1. As a foundation, the Net2Vec [5] approach was chosen. It allows to localize non-image-level concepts like object parts in convolutional activation maps by predicting binary segmentation masks. For this the spatial resolution of the convolutional layers is used: The mask predictor is a 1×1 convolution followed by bilinear upscaling, then sigmoid normalization (and, for binarizing, thresholding at 0.5). For comparability, the quality measure set intersection over union (set IoU) is adopted which divides the total area of intersections by the total area of unions between the binary ground truth masks M_i and the predicted segmentation masks M_i^{pr} (binarized at 0.5):

$$\text{set IoU}\left((M_i)_i, (M_i^{\mathrm{pr}})_i\right) = \frac{\sum_i \sum M_i \cap (M_i^{\mathrm{pr}} > 0.5)}{\sum_i \sum M_i \cup (M_i^{\mathrm{pr}} > 0.5)} .$$

We here took the mean of batch-wise set IoU values. It must be noted that the set IoU measure penalizes errors on small objects more than on large ones, and it suffers under low resolution of activation maps. Below, four further limitations of Net2Vec are collected and our countermeasures explained.

Most notably, Net2Vec uses denoising of activation maps with a ReLU suggested in [2]. The threshold is calculated to keep the 0.5% highest activations. This requires to load activations of the complete dataset into memory at once, which is infeasible both for large models and large datasets. Experiments showed that denoising makes no noticeable difference, hence it is skipped.

Next, to push the decision boundary of the model towards a value of 0.5, Net2Vec uses a binary cross-entropy (BCE) loss with per-class-weights where each weight is the mean proportion of pixels of the opposite class. Obtaining the weight is an expensive pre-processing step. Here we found that global weighting could be replaced either by calculating weights batch-wise, or using an unweighted Tversky loss [18]—also called Dice or F1 loss—that directly optimizes the F1 score of the segmentation per $h \times w$ image ("$\cdot$" pixel-wise):

$$\text{Dice loss}\,(M, M^{\text{pr}}) = 1 - \frac{2 \sum M \cdot M^{\text{pr}}}{\sum M + \sum M^{\text{pr}}} \quad \text{for } M, M^{\text{pr}} \in [0, 1]^{h \times w}.$$

Further, the original method reports average set IoU values lower than 0.05 for part objects, which we could confirm. This can be achieved by constantly predicting white masks (1 for all pixels). In a series of experiments we found settings fixing this: We use a Tversky loss, Adam optimizer [12] instead of stochastic gradient descent (SGD), with a batch size of 8 instead of 64, and learning rate of 10^{-3} rather than 10^{-4}.

Another modification used in some experiments is *adaptive kernel size*. The original Net2Vec method uses a 1×1 kernel, so each prediction only has a spatial context of one pixel. As found in [19], this may be too small for larger concepts and layers with higher resolution, and possibly leads to a texture bias [6]. Following [19], this can be mitigated using a kernel size that covers an area of the expected size of the concept, assuming low size variance. Note that this may improve performance of a concept model, but destroys comparability amongst models of differently sized concepts due to incompatible kernel shapes.

3.2 Distance Category Estimation

Assume an image dataset is given that provides 2D skeletal information of persons (cf. Fig. 2), possibly bounding boxes, but no depth information. The goal of this approach is to estimate and categorize the body size of a person depicted in a 2D image in pixels, given only lengths between keypoints. The challenges are that keypoint information may be incomplete due to occlusion or cropping, and that 2D projected lengths may be inaccurately short. Thus, redundant calculation of body size from as many link types as possible is needed. One major drawback of this method is that assumptions on "standard" proportions must be made. This cannot be overcome without additional information. Despite that, it was found that the approach yields surprisingly good and intuitive results, with errors not infringing the quality of body size categorization.

The following sources were used to relate the true length l of (combinations of) keypoint links to the true body height h: arts for facial and head-to-body

Formulas for total height		Formulas for derived lengths
$1 \cdot$ bbox_width/_height	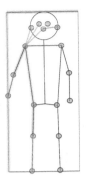	body_height $\approx$ leg* + hip_to_shoulder* + shoulder_to_eye*/_ear*/_nose $\approx$ arm + shoulder_width
$1.1 \cdot$ body_height		
$2.4 \cdot$ hip_to_shoulder		leg $\approx$ lower_leg + upper_leg
$7 \cdot$ head_height		arm $\approx$ lower_arm + upper_arm
$1.485 \cdot$ leg $\cdot \frac{h}{h-0.433}$		head_height $\approx 1.1 \cdot$ head_width $\approx \frac{8}{7}$ head_depth
$2.77 \cdot$ upper_leg $\cdot \frac{h}{h-0.405}$		
$3.075 \cdot$ lower_leg $\cdot \frac{h}{h-0.501}$		head_width $\approx$ ear_to_opposite_ear $\approx 2.5 \cdot$ eye_to_eye
$3.72 \cdot$ upper_arm $\cdot \frac{h}{h-0.449}$		head_depth $\approx 2 \cdot$ ear_to_eye* $\approx \frac{7}{4}$ ear_to_nose
$4.46 \cdot$ lower_arm $\cdot \frac{h}{h-0.569}$		

* involved keypoints must be on the same side

Fig. 2. Used keypoints and links with formulas to estimate the total body height of a person from link lengths and assumed "standard" height h in meters.

proportions [14]; standard educational material relating the wrist-to-wrist span [3]; and linear models used in archeology to estimate the body size from single long bones [14]. For long bone relations, the mean model parameters were taken between genders. Relations involving approximate body_height and bounding box (bbox) dimensions were estimated manually. The resulting relation models are all of the linear nature $h = s \cdot l + c$ for some slope s, and offset c in meters. Given the downscaled length $l' = f \cdot l$ in pixels, the formula for the downscaled body size is $f \cdot h = l' \cdot \frac{h}{h-c}$. If c is non-zero, a "standard" real person size h must be assumed, which was set to 1.7 m following [14]. The final formulas are shown in Fig. 2. Whenever one value has several estimation results, the maximum was used to cope with possible length shortenings due to 2D projection.

The formulas were now leveraged to sort annotations into four size categories. These were chosen such that in each the minimum and maximum estimated size do not differ by more than a factor of two. Very small and very large persons were discarded. The resulting size categories with their range of relative sizes arc: *far* in $[0.2, 0.38]$, *middle* in $[0.38, 0.71]$, *close* in $[0.71, 1.33]$, and *very close* in $[1.33, 2.5]$. Categories are depicted in Fig. 3.

4   Experiments

After detailing our experiment settings, this section will validate the used approach including hyperparameters (Sect. 4.1), then conduct exemplary assessments of embedding quality and semantics (Sect. 4.2), as well as size bias (Sect. 4.3).

For the experiments, we chose three networks of different size, training objective, and training dataset, with pretrained weights from the torchvision model zoo[1]: ImageNet-trained classifiers VGG16 [20] and AlexNet [13], and the object detector Mask R-CNN [9] trained on MS COCO.

---

[1]   https://pytorch.org/vision/stable/models.html.

As layers we chose the activated convolutional output before each downsampling step except the first. In case of Mask R-CNN we considered the output of each residual grouping in the backbone and the feature pyramid. For concepts we selected a set of five large and small concepts that are common to the Broden and MS COCO datasets: leg, arm, foot and hand (for COCO approximated via ankle and wrist keypoints), and eye. Images were zero-padded to square size then resized to 400 × 400 respectively 224 × 224 (VGG16, AlexNet) pixels to avoid feature distortion. Ground truth masks on concepts for MS COCO images were generated by drawing links (leg, arm) respectively points (foot, hand, eye) of width 0.025 times the image height or times the body size if this can be estimated (see Fig. 5). Intermediate outputs of the DNNs were cached with bi-float 16 precision to speed up experiments, except for the very large Mask R-CNN feature pyramid blocks 0 and 1, and backbone layer 1. On cached layers, concept model training was done with 5-fold cross-validation. The original train-test splits were used.

4.1 Validation of the Proposed Methods

Size Distribution in MS COCO To validate the size estimation approach, an analysis of the size distribution on the popular MS COCO dataset was conducted. The size of an annotation cannot be estimated if it provides no keypoints (very small persons and crowds) or only disconnected keypoints. Nevertheless, size estimations could be made for a decent proportion of the annotations in both training and test set (ca. 46%), see Fig. 3. Also, for each chosen body part, a sufficient amount of annotations is available in size categories *far*, *middle*, and *close*: more than 10,000 in the train, and 300 in the test set. These categories were thus used for experiments. Training and test set were found to be similarly distributed, with significantly more keypoint annotations estimated far than close. This suggests, that the total amount of positive pixels for masks of small far body parts is similar to that of large close ones.

Improvement of Net2Vec. Settings for the concept analysis approach were needed that (1) work for large models and datasets (no expensive thresholds and weights), and (2) work for part objects. First, the necessity to threshold the activation maps was disproved: Skipping it had no effect on the test performance. Then, without thresholding, a series of experiments was conducted comparing different optimizers (SGD, Adam), batch sizes (bs), learning rates (lr), and losses (globally weighted BCE, batch-wise weighted BCE, and Tversky). Each setting was evaluated on AlexNet and VGG16, on all selected layers and concepts, using the original Broden dataset [2]. Firstly, the better optimizer was chosen, then the better batch-size and learning rate combination, and lastly losses were compared. The consistently best and stable setting proved to be Adam optimizer with lr 10^{-3}, bs 8, with maximum five epochs due to fast convergence. Find a comparison to the baseline for AlexNet in Fig. 3 (VGG16 similar).

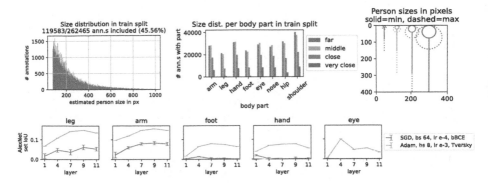

Fig. 3. *Top:* Distribution by estimated person size of all annotations (*left*) and per body part (*center*) for COCO train images (padded to square size and resized to 400 × 400 px); used person size categories are illustrated on the *right*. *Bottom:* Performance comparison of used settings with Net2Vec baseline (cf. [5, Fig. 2]). Best viewed in color. (Color figure online)

4.2   Embedding Quality and Similarity Validation

Two applications of concept analysis are to verify sufficient embedding qualities, and to use the similarity measure on the concept models for validation of semantic relations. For this, concept models for all chosen concepts, networks, and layers were trained on the complete MS COCO concept dataset. Performance results are depicted in Fig. 6 (size category *all*). As before, the variance was very low, evidencing good convergence of the linear concept models. Convincing embedding qualities were found except for the small concepts hand and foot in small networks. This may origin from the approximate and noisy ground truth, and the higher set IoU penalties for low resolution. In general, later layers with low resolution showed the best embedding results, indicating that body parts are relatively complex concepts. These may require larger network structures, since Mask R-CNN significantly surpassed AlexNet and VGG16. Some exemplary output for Mask R-CNN is shown in Fig. 6.

Next, the concept model similarities were measured as the mean cosine similarity between the normal vectors of the models, shown in Fig. 4. Cosine similarity $\frac{a \cdot b}{\|a\| \cdot \|b\|}$ of vectors $a, b \in \mathbb{R}^n$ is the cosine of the angle between the vectors, with 1 meaning $0°$ angle, and -1 meaning $180°$. The results show intuitive relations between the concepts: No similarity values were below zero, so no body part concepts are mutually exclusive. And eye is most different from the other parts, while hand and arm are more closely related, similarly leg and foot. Interestingly, in the later low-resolution layers concepts were more dissimilar, so better distinguishable, explaining the better performance here.

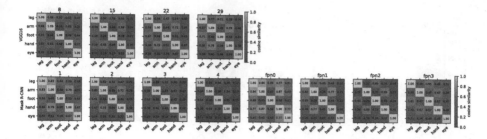

Fig. 4. Mean cosine similarities between normal vectors of concept models for different body parts, by layer. AlexNet results were similar to VGG16 (*top*).

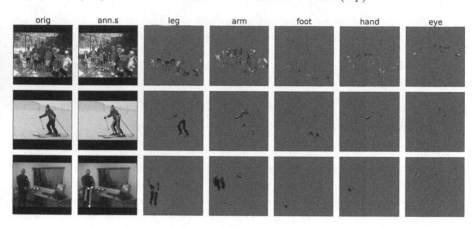

Fig. 5. Overlay (green) of segmentation masks predicted by the mean concept model of Mask R-CNN backbone layer block 3. Original images are shown in first column, generated ground truth annotations in second column in different colors. Mean is taken over normalized concept vectors, cf. [17]. Masks are upsampled using nearest rule to demonstrate resolution. Note how predicted masks clearly correlate with the ground truth instead of being purely white. Images are taken from test set (MS COCO `val2017`). For the used images thanks to: top: Oleg Klementiev http://farm5.staticflickr.com/4115/4906536419_6113bd7de4_z.jpg © CC BY 2.0; middle: Nick Webb http://farm8.staticflickr.com/7015/6795644157_f019453ae7_z.jpg © CC BY 2.0; bottom: Yandle http://farm4.staticflickr.com/3179/2986591710_d76622fdf0_z.jpg © CC BY 2.0 (Color figure online)

4.3 Correlations of Person Size and Segmentation Quality

The last series of experiments means to investigate the following questions: 1) Does the internal representation of a concept differ for different sizes of the concept? And is there a safety critical bias towards one size (i.e., distance from the camera)? 2) Is adaptive kernel size needed to avoid texture bias? A yes to 1) would suggest that different and better embeddings can be found if concept information is assessed separately for each size category. Then, especially for larger size categories, adaptive kernel sizes might be necessary. To answer the

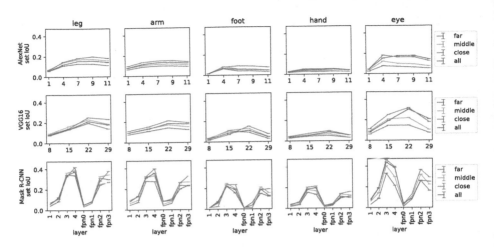

Fig. 6. Test set IoU results of concept models trained on the complete dataset, by layer, annotation size category, model (top to bottom), and concept (left to right). Note that standard deviations are marked but negligible. Best viewed in color. (Color figure online)

questions, results on a test set restricted to one size category were collected on the MS COCO concept data. This was done and compared for concept models trained on the complete dataset (all nets), and models trained on the respective size category either with 1 × 1 or adaptive kernel size (AlexNet, VGG16). Adaptive kernel sizes were chosen to cover the following areas relative to the mean person size of the size category (in height × width): 0.3 × 0.1 for leg, 0.2 × 0.15 for arm, 0.1 × 0.1 for foot and hand, and 0.04 × 0.04 for eye. The two main results were: The internal representation of body parts seems to be mostly size invariant, and adaptive kernel sizes are not necessary.

Results. In Fig. 6 the performance of concept models trained on *all* data was compared for different test subsets. The differences between size categories did not exceed what was expected from the different set IoU penalties, so no bias could be found here. Since a concept model trained on all data may not be the optimal one for a size, we also compared the *all* models to models solely trained on the respective size category, see Fig. 7. This showed that a restricted training set may even decrease test results, indicating that at least parts of the internal representation used for the different sizes must be shared. To substantiate that, the normal vectors of the linear models for the different size categories were compared. In the best performing layers the restricted size categories had high cosine similarity (over 0.7) to *all*, with *far* deviating the most. However, *all* could not be represented as a linear combination of the sub-sizes, and cosine similarities of least squares solutions did not top 0.95. So, some information even seems to get lost when training only on single size categories. Lastly, results on single size categories were also compared to adaptive kernel size results in Fig. 7. Adaptive kernel size would show some improvements but the best layer rarely changed.

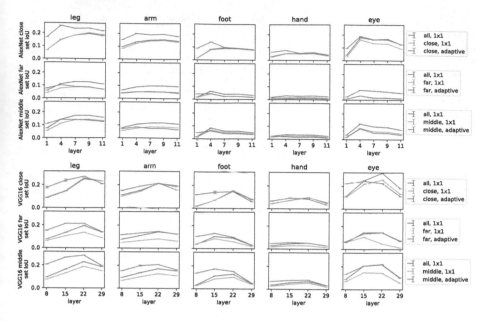

Fig. 7. Test set IoU results of concept models trained on a size subset by layer and kernel setting. Results were obtained on the test set restricted to the respective training size category. Results for the models trained on all data are added for comparison, cf. Fig. 6. Best viewed in color. (Color figure online)

5   Conclusion

This paper proposed an efficient concept analysis approach that is fit for practical application to large networks and datasets, and to object part concepts. It was demonstrated how this method can be used to assess consistency and size bias in the internal representations of a DNN. For this, a size estimation method from 2D skeletal data is proposed together with a new concept dataset based on MS COCO keypoint annotations. Our assessment results suggest that the representations within standard models AlexNet, VGG16, and Mask R-CNN are mostly invariant to different sizes respectively camera distances. Despite drawbacks of the used set IoU metric, concept analysis is shown to be a promising approach for verification and validation of deep neural networks. Future work will investigate further assessment possibilities arising from post-hoc explainable access to DNN intermediate output. This can, e.g., be used to test or formally verify logical properties that are formulated on the enriched DNN output.

References

1. Arrieta, A.B., et al.: Explainable artificial intelligence (XAI): concepts, taxonomies, opportunities and challenges toward responsible AI. Inf. Fusion **58**, 82–115 (2020)

2. Bau, D., Zhou, B., Khosla, A., Oliva, A., Torralba, A.: Network dissection: quantifying interpretability of deep visual representations. In: Proceedings of the 2017 IEEE Conference on Computer Vision and Pattern Recognition, pp. 3319–3327. IEEE Computer Society (2017). https://doi.org/10.1109/CVPR.2017.354

3. De Brabandere, S.: Human Body Ratios. Scientific American (Bring Science Home) (March 2017). https://www.scientificamerican.com/article/human-body-ratios/

4. Esser, P., Rombach, R., Ommer, B.: A disentangling invertible interpretation network for explaining latent representations. In: Proceedings of the 2020 IEEE Conference on Computer Vision and Pattern Recognition, pp. 9220–9229 (June 2020)

5. Fong, R., Vedaldi, A.: Net2Vec: quantifying and explaining how concepts are encoded by filters in deep neural networks. In: Proceedings of the 2018 IEEE Conference on Computer Vision and Pattern Recognition, pp. 8730–8738. IEEE Computer Society (2018)

6. Geirhos, R., Rubisch, P., Michaelis, C., Bethge, M., Wichmann, F.A., Brendel, W.: ImageNet-trained CNNs are biased towards texture; increasing shape bias improves accuracy and robustness. In: Proceedings of the 7th International Conference on Learning Representations. OpenReview.net (2019)

7. Ghorbani, A., Wexler, J., Zou, J.Y., Kim, B.: Towards automatic concept-based explanations. Adv. Neural. Inf. Process. Syst. **32**, 9273–9282 (2019)

8. Gu, J., Tresp, V.: Semantics for global and local interpretation of deep neural networks. CoRR abs/1910.09085 (October 2019). http://arxiv.org/abs/1910.09085

9. He, K., Gkioxari, G., Dollár, P., Girshick, R.: Mask R-CNN. In: 2017 IEEE International Conference on Computer Vision (ICCV), pp. 2980–2988 (October 2017)

10. ISO/TC 22/SC 32: ISO 26262–6:2018(En): Road Vehicles—Functional Safety—Part 6: Product Development at the Software Level, ISO 26262:2018(En), 2nd edn., vol. 6. International Organization for Standardization (December 2018)

11. Kim, B., et al.: Interpretability beyond feature attribution: quantitative testing with concept activation vectors (TCAV). In: Proceedings of the 35th International Conference on Machine Learning. Proceedings of Machine Learning Research, vol. 80, pp. 2668–2677. PMLR (July 2018)

12. Kingma, D.P., Ba, J.: Adam: a method for stochastic optimization. In: Proceedings of the 3rd International Conference on Learning Representations (2015)

13. Krizhevsky, A.: One weird trick for parallelizing convolutional neural networks. CoRR abs/1404.5997 (2014). http://arxiv.org/abs/1404.5997

14. Larson, D.: Standard proportions of the human body (January 2014). https://www.makingcomics.com/2014/01/19/standard-proportions-human-body/

15. Lin, T.-Y., et al.: Microsoft COCO: common objects in context. In: Fleet, D., Pajdla, T., Schiele, B., Tuytelaars, T. (eds.) ECCV 2014. LNCS, vol. 8693, pp. 740–755. Springer, Cham (2014). https://doi.org/10.1007/978-3-319-10602-1_48

16. Olah, C., Mordvintsev, A., Schubert, L.: Feature visualization. Distill, vol. 2, no. 11 (November 2017). https://doi.org/10.23915/distill.00007

17. Rabold, J., Schwalbe, G., Schmid, U.: Expressive explanations of DNNs by combining concept analysis with ILP. In: Schmid, U., Klügl, F., Wolter, D. (eds.) KI 2020. LNCS (LNAI), vol. 12325, pp. 148–162. Springer, Cham (2020). https://doi.org/10.1007/978-3-030-58285-2_11

18. Salehi, S.S.M., Erdogmus, D., Gholipour, A.: Tversky loss function for image segmentation using 3D fully convolutional deep networks. In: Wang, Q., Shi, Y., Suk, H.-I., Suzuki, K. (eds.) MLMI 2017. LNCS, vol. 10541, pp. 379–387. Springer, Cham (2017). https://doi.org/10.1007/978-3-319-67389-9_44

19. Schwalbe, G., Schels, M.: Concept enforcement and modularization as methods for the ISO 26262 safety argumentation of neural networks. In: Proceedings of the 10th European Congress Embedded Real Time Software and Systems (January 2020). https://hal.archives-ouvertes.fr/hal-02442796
20. Simonyan, K., Zisserman, A.: Very deep convolutional networks for large-scale image recognition. In: Proceedings of the 3rd International Conference on Learning Representations (2015)
21. Yeh, C.K., Kim, B., Arik, S., Li, C.L., Pfister, T., Ravikumar, P.: On completeness-aware concept-based explanations in deep neural networks. In: Advances in Neural Information Processing Systems, vol. 33, pp. 20554–20565 (2020)

Artificial Intelligence in Music Composition

Mincer Alaeddine[✉][iD] and Anthony Tannoury[✉][iD]

Antonine University, Baabda, Beirut, Lebanon
anthony.tannoury@ua.edu.lb
https://ua.edu.lb/

Abstract. Technology has had a remarkable influence on music. As society advances technologically, the music industry does as well. An example that illustrates the use of technology in music is the use of artificial intelligence (AI) as a creative and inspiring tool. Music helps shape emotional responses, creates a rhythm, and comments on the action. It is often a very crucial element to any experience. However, music, like any form of art, is an extremely challenging field to tackle using AI. The amount of information in a musical structure can be overwhelmingly large. If we factor in the different and unpredictable nuances invoked by human imperfection and emotion, it becomes clear why, even though AI excels at handling large amounts of data, generating good music can be very challenging, especially when it comes to Jazz and similarly complex genres.

Keywords: Technology · Advancement · Music · Artificial intelligence · Generation · Emotion · Imperfection · Genre · Training · Challenge · Prediction · Rhythm · Tempo · MIDI · Instruments · Patterns · Harmony · Melody · Caching

1 Introduction

In the past few years, AI has proven to be useful in the technical aspect of music. However, AI still lacks in the creative process, like music composition. The reason behind that becomes more evident as we start experimenting. The most common course of action for building AI applications is to train a model using a large dataset with enough data. That is known as batch training. That might be a good idea if music consisted of only a couple of genres, but that is not the case. Out of every genre, hundreds of subgenres emerge, and some pieces do not belong to any genre at all. Another challenge that music composition presents is the long-term interdependent structures [1]. Naturally, a music composition consists of repetition, and every note is somehow related to one or multiple musical notes in the same sequence. That makes it much harder for neural networks to learn without short-term memory [2]. The added value of this project is combining

I. Maglogiannis et al. (Eds.): AIAI 2021, IFIP AICT 627, pp. 387–397, 2021.
https://doi.org/10.1007/978-3-030-79150-6_31

both online training and batch training to provide cross-genre predictions while maintaining accuracy. The focus will be on the online training as it will have the most impact on the output. While online training is very useful when working with flexible predictions and learning over time, it also comes at the cost of speed and responsiveness, especially when it has to be done on the spot. Training models on the spot can be very resource-demanding, and this quickly becomes a problem the richer the input is, and from a UX perspective, for an application to be useable, it has to be highly responsive [3]. In the first chapter of this paper, we will go through the state of the art, shedding the light on other great projects in the field of AI for music composition, especially MIDI. Chapter 2 explains the added value of this project in detail by going over all the challenges imposed by music composition one by one, how we managed to solve those challenges, which challenges are still unsolved, and why.

2   Literature Review

2.1   Introduction

Music is, more often than not, classified by genres, which refers to the overall structure and character of particular musical composition. To create a track of a specific genre, we must meet some requirements like rhythm, tempo, key, and structure, to name a few. For example, when we hear an electronic dance music track or a disco track, we notice the kick on every beat [4]. While this might be an easy task to accomplish for humans, it is considered fairly complicated for AI. The purpose of this project is to provide an AI tool that takes a MIDI file from a user and generate multiple structurally similar pieces of music based on the data learned from said file.

2.2   Related Works

Google Magenta. [5] The Google Magenta team has been working on blending AI with Music for a long time. Their projects Magenta and NSynth are great examples of how powerful AI can be when mixed with human creativity. The Magenta library contributed considerably to the execution of this project. Magenta Studio Allows:

– Generating drum beats for an existing melody
– Generating melodies from scratch
– Complete an already existing melody
– Interpolate between two samples

NSynth is still in beta. However, the main idea behind it is to synthesize a new sound using the acoustic properties of another sound, which tackles a different field in the world of music.

MuseNet. [6] MuseNet is a general-purpose deep neural network (DNN) that can generate musical compositions with up to 10 instruments, combining styles from different epochs, artists, or bands. MuseNet, unlike other projects, was not trained through music knowledge, but instead discovered patterns of harmony, rhythm, and style by learning from hundreds of thousands of MIDI files.

Captain Plugins by Mixed in Key. Mixed in Key is a digital music software company that has developed multiple products aiming to make the life of musicians easier. They are most recognized for creating Mixed in Key, a software that detects the key, BPM, and the energy of given songs. The company recently created a plugin suite called Captain Plugins. The suite focuses on generating melodies, and basslines, and drum patterns to a given chord progression.

This Time with Feeling: Learning Expressive Musical Performance. [7] The authors of this journal discuss training a machine to generate music, focusing on the time and feel of the generated pieces. In simpler terms, the goal of their model is to produce human-like performances. Said model demonstrates generating music in the form of MIDI that successfully recreates the timing and velocity of a professional pianist. The music felt like an authentic performance by a musician. While this is great, it comes at the cost of the long-term structure, one of the problems tackled in this paper.

3 Problem Definition and Proposed Solutions

3.1 Introduction

Music composition, as we mentioned before, is a very complex field to tackle through AI because of the numerous challenges and problems that it presents. This chapter will go over the contribution of this paper to AI music composition, the challenges that we faced and how we tackled them.

3.2 Challenges and Solutions

Human Imperfection. While computers excel at being perfect, humans tend to make mistakes sometimes. These unintentional mistakes are the soul of music and art in general. Without human imperfection, music will sound too generic and will lack emotion. In electronic music, artists tend to deliberately reproduce those imperfections to give the otherwise perfect song a bit of a human feel. For example, after drawing notes on a computer, artists tend to nudge the notes of the perfect tempo grid intentionally to reproduce the groovy feel of a real musician playing. The same goes for how hard musicians play the notes. Human imperfection remains one of the complex challenges of artificially generating music and is yet to be solved because imperfections are not the result of specific patterns and rules, but rather invoked through human emotion.

Cross-Genre Compatibility and Future Proofing. Music is made of count-less genres, and each genre of countless sub-genres, and every day, new genres and sub-genres are being created. When it comes to AI, this means one thing: Learning to generate music by associating an input with a specific genre is not the optimal solution as it requires thousands of hours of batch learning using structured datasets, and all that training is rendered useless when the model encounters a new genre. Our model has been trained with an unstructured dataset of more than 13000 melodies from various genres. That, however, does not make our model future-proof, so in addition to that, we must integrate online training that will be done on-the-spot to learn the essence of the user's sample. That frees us of the genre issue and guarantees that the generated samples are always in the same style, tempo, and rhythm as the presented sample, nevertheless, this solution creates another problem, which is the amount of time and resources it takes to perform an online training on-the-spot.

Training On-The-Spot. Training on the spot is both resource-dependent and time-consuming, thus, there is only so much that can be done to improve the responsiveness of such a resource-dependent process. The solution adopted in this project consists of using the cloud to perform all the heavy lifting, then rendering the result to the user using Server-Side Rendering or SSR for short. That helps us run our heavy processing on a platform that can adapt and scale accordingly, thus ridding us of the user's limited resources barrier. After multiple tests, I discovered that with the ability to retraining the model using the generated samples, the user will most likely try to retrain using a very similar sample, therefore, using very similar training data to generate new samples, thus, caching has been introduced to temporarily store the trained data, reducing the time it takes to perform a follow-up training by more than 50%.

Long-Term Structure in Music. One of the core elements of a musical piece is structure. Songs are built of short sections, and every section includes patterns. For humans, it is natural to pick up on these patterns, thanks to our memory, and this is one of the main factors that make a song catchy and delightful to hear. However, when it comes to AI, this poses a challenge that requires a hierarchical decoder to solve. A hierarchical decoder is based on Long Short Term Memory networks or LSTM for short. LSTM is a type of RNN (recurrent neural network) that can learn order dependence in a given sequence [9], making it the perfect solution to the long-term structural problem.

Polyphonic Samples. In most cases, creators will stumble upon a song that they like, search for the midi file for that song on the internet, and use it for online training. MIDI files on the internet often contain multiple instruments at once. This is called polyphonic music. However, generating a monophonic melody (a melody that consists of a single instrument) will not produce an accurate result if the data that is was processed is polyphonic especially if the notation of the instruments overlap. Therefore, it is necessary to extract the melody from the sample before proceeding with the training phase. This topic is still being researched and big music companies like Ableton are to this day struggling to get an accurate result by automatically extracting a monophonic melody from a polyphonic sample. For the sake of not re-inventing the wheel, we have used the Google Melody Extraction algorithm in this project.

4 Implementation[1]

4.1 Choice of Technology

For the front-end, the technology of choice was Nuxt.js. Nuxt is built on top of Vue.js, a JavaScript framework. Nuxt supports Server-Side Rendering out of the box and helps organize the project allowing it to scale as big as needed while keeping everything structured. These features combined with Vue's ease of use, make the process of creating extremely complex applications easier to manage and make sure everything is well organized. Additionally, Nuxt allows developing custom plugins that can be attached to any application seamlessly which helped us integrate Google's plugins and algorithms into our application. Furthermore, Nuxt integrates seamlessly with Google Cloud Services, which will be discussed in the Hosting section.

The batch learning process was done over Ubuntu using Anaconda and Python with the help of TensorFlow and the Magenta library. Anaconda makes it easier to manage long term projects by separating dependencies of every project in a virtual environment.

Google's Cloud Computing services were the hosting services of choice. The reason behind that choice is to benefit from the full potential of Server-Side-Rendering. Cloud hosting means that our project will not be limited to the user's resources, and it will scale with ease. Furthermore, this allows us to benefit from Google Cloud tools to optimize and improve in the future.

As for the final exported type, we chose to export MIDI files. Exporting as MP3 or any other codec adds unnecessary load to the server because it will force us to pre-load high-quality samples, which will then need to be rendered as audio, taking more time. Additionally, creators may often need to fine-tune the generated melody to fit their liking.

4.2 Implementation Process

Training the main model requires Magenta's development environment. Magenta was developed for Linux. In our case, we had to work with a Windows machine, therefore, we had to use WSL 2 (Windows Subsystem for Linux) to get started with the training without having to install a new OS. After downloading Magenta, it is recommended to create a new virtual python environment using

---

[1] The project source code is available in the following GitHub repository: https://github.com/minceralaeddine/ai-music-producer.

Anaconda to avoid any unwanted conflicts and library issues with other projects. After finishing with the environment setup, we have to start building our dataset.

Curating a proper dataset is the most laborious and time-consuming part of every AI project. In our case, we had to collect thousands of midi files and sanitize them so we can train our AI model and avoid as much noise as possible. There were no specific requirements or features that decided whether a MIDI file is fit for the learning process or not. The reason behind that is that if we narrow all our MIDI files into 1 genre, style or tempo, we will be overfitting our model making it biased towards a specific genre, and it will no longer serve as a good base for other genres and styles. Therefore, any midi file could work as long as we balance out the genres. To accelerate the process of building the dataset, we used datasets with diverse genres from https://archive.org/, https://bitmidi.com/ and the MAESTRO Dataset. Additionally, we used Mincer's own library of midi files to cover the electronic music genre, since he is an electronic music producer and already has a clean collection. We ended up with a dataset that consisted of more than 13000 midi files of diverse styles, bpm, and scales.

Once the dataset is ready, we can begin the training process. The Magenta library makes it easy to train models using midi data. Magenta offers basic pre-trained models out of the box that we could have used, however, for our case, we had to train a custom model. Magenta's models are relatively basic and offer no flexibility, therefore, if the predictions were inaccurate we will need to revert to creating our custom model. We ended up creating four separate models using the magenta development environment: Two big models that require short on-the-spot training and two small models that require long on-the-spot training. One model of every batch is capable of generating a 16 bars melody, and the other is capable of generating a 4 bars melody. To start the training, we first need to convert our midi dataset to a TensorFlow-friendly type. Fortunately, the Magenta library makes that easy by providing a midi to note sequence converter, ready to be fed to our TensorFlow model. [8] To begin the training, we first need to convert our MIDI dataset into a format that we can work with using TensorFlow. We picked Magenta's NoteSequence [10] because it offers flexibility when it comes to exporting and manipulating MIDI files. Furthermore, note sequences contain information on how every note is played and where it is laid out in the song. All of this information will serve as input data. We could have easily parsed the MIDI file ourselves and optimized the attributes (like velocity and note length etc.) to create our own TensorFlow Record but that would be an unnecessary extra step since the conversion script is already there. Once the conversion is done, we can then initiate the training of our model using the generated sequences. The RNN used for this training is Magenta's Melody_RNN [12]. Melody_RNN is a neural network that generates monophonic melody predictions no matter how many voices it receives [13]. We could have used a polyphony RNN to generate polyphonic samples, but that would have taken a lot of time to get a decent accuracy as it involves harmony and chords [14]. That being said, the amount of time required to get an accurate polyphonic prediction will be directly dependent on the number of voices present in a chord. For example, training the model using a melody and strictly triads will take a lot less time than using a melody on top of 9th, 11th, or 13th chords that are most commonly found in dominant chords in Jazz music.

Once everything is set up, we can use the trained model's checkpoint for the online training. The user will be asked to provide a MIDI sample of their choice. Once the sample is uploaded, we need to convert it to a NoteSequence just like we previously did to train our model. Online training relies heavily on detecting MIDI attributes from the provided file. To avoid unexpected errors, we must predefine some default settings as constants to fall back to in case the MIDI analysis fails, like the default velocity and note length. After the conversion is completed, we then need to quantize the sequence to match the BPM grid and then proceed to split our note sequence into bars of the size that the model is going to generate (4 or 16). Quantizing helps detect the tempo accurately, however, this will cause pieces played by real musicians to lose their original groove and might drastically change the rhythm [15]. Since we already trained a base model, re-analyze the entire input sample will cause the training to take much longer than it should. We can use the base model as a checkpoint instead, and then analyze small parts of the sample, which is why we split it into 4 or 16 bar samples. To proceed, we encode our chunks using a variational autoencoder to ensure that there is enough variation to create a new sample and not just replicate the user's input, and then initiate the training. Variational Autoencoders (VAEs) are encoders that use complex mathematical encoders that can be applied to all sorts of data types [11]. Once the training is done, we generate 5 samples by calling the model.sample(1) command. Then we use the VAE again to decode that sample and using Tone.js, the user can listen to the results inside the browser. If the user was happy with one of the results and would like more of that sample, they could ask for new samples based on that result. The same algorithm will run again using the chosen sample as input data.

5   Experiments and Performance Analysis

5.1   Testing Multiple Genres and Analysing the Results

The model performs very well when the sample input is of a generic genre, like electronic music with an accuracy of 70% to 80% since human imperfection (see "Human Imperfection") does not dictate the structure of such genres. However, when exposed to more complex genres, Middle Eastern music or Jazz, for example, we notice a drop in accuracy. The reason behind the confusion when it comes to Middle Eastern music is rather simple to understand but harder to incorporate into the network. Middle Eastern music, unlike western music, contains quarter tones, meanwhile, western music only consists of semi-tones and whole tones [16]. This causes confusion once our model runs into a quarter-tone because the way this is portrayed in MIDI is using microtones, which adds another layer of complexity to the network. For example, if the note that is being played is B semi-flat, it will be recorded as a B flat with 50 cents microtones in the MIDI sequence. Jazz, on the other hand, does not follow the same theory as other music genres and features unpredictable off-beat notes and complex chord progressions. Quantizing Jazz pieces will drastically alter the rhythm of the song so the predictions will be inaccurate. Leaving the piece unquantized, however, will lead to a failure in tempo detection therefore the predicted results will not respect the tempo of the original piece. To perform an in-depth analysis of our samples we loaded them into Ableton Live, a digital audio workstation. If we compare the predicted sample from Avicii's Levels (see Fig. 1) with the original (see Fig. 2), we can see that the generated sample is in the same key and respects the rhythm of the original sample.

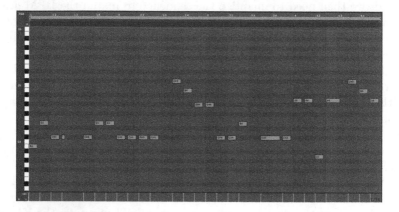

Fig. 1. Predicted sample from Avicii-Levels. The vertical axis is the pitch, the horizontal axis is time, the green rectangles are notes, and the red bars at the bottom represent velocity. (Color figure online)

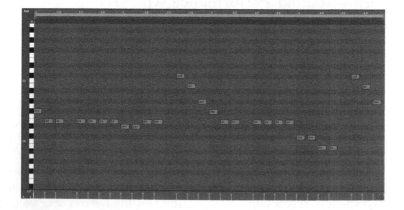

Fig. 2. Original sample of Avicii-Levels

Dealing with an acoustic Jazz Guitar, however, produces a much less accurate result. If we compare the generated sample (see Fig. 3) with the original (see Fig. 4), we can see that even though the AI managed to detect the key and scale of the sample and extract the melody, the rhythm and feel is still off.

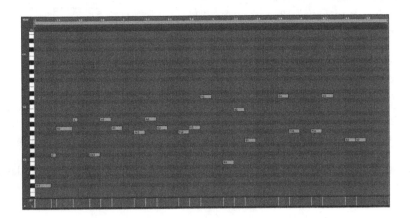

Fig. 3. Predicted sample from a Jazz piano

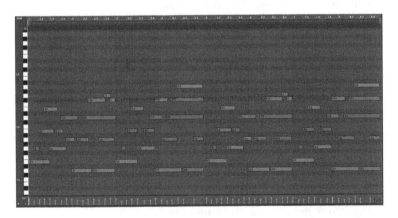

Fig. 4. Original sample of a Jazz piano

We performed the analyses on five different genres, each using five samples (Table 1). The results were as follows:

Table 1. Analysis of 25 predicted samples from 5 different genres.

GENRE	Rhythm accuracy	Key accuracy	Tempo accuracy	Samples
Electronic music	100%	80%	100%	5
Jazz	40%	80%	40%	5
Classical music	80%	80%	100%	5
Middle eastern music	80%	20%	60%	5
Game music	100%	80%	100%	5

5.2 Conclusion

The analysis and experimentation above showcase this model's capability of generating very accurate structures quickly until a certain level of structural complexity, then the accuracy starts to fall off. While it is true that we only used 25 samples in our analysis, it was more than enough to reveal the strong and weak points of this model. The weak points being complex genres like Jazz and Oriental Music, and the strong points being genres that follow strict music theory rules like classical music, electronic music, and game music.

6 Future Work

There is still a lot to improve on this approach of music generation through a combination of both online and batch training:

- Improving the accuracy for non-generic music played by instrumentalists
- Improving the accuracy of Jazz music generation by exposing the base model to more Jazz pieces so it can learn the theoretical exceptions
- Supporting middle eastern music by exposing the base model to more sequences with quarter tones and pitch bends
- Improving velocity detection for non-generic music genres

In the long, this approach can support a lot more complex features, to list a few:

- Using polyphony and harmony to create chords to complement the generated melody
- Generating drum beats for a given melody
- Using AI to identify weaknesses in a musical piece and suggesting improvements
- Providing high-level controls to the user allowing him to customize the predictions to his taste

7 Conclusion

AI will, without a doubt, have a major impact on the music industry and should not be looked at as a technology that will replace the creative process but as one that will develop it and open up more opportunities for creativity. Even though AI music composition faces some tough challenges, especially when it comes to making the result more humane, it's already doing a great job. Generating music using AI can help musicians overcome their creative barriers, it can automate the repetitive technical process that is inevitable in every music composition session, and it can expand the toolset of musicians allowing them to express themselves better by focusing on the creative process. To conclude, while humans excel at composing music and art, AI can still help humanity understand music even better and shed light on unexplored bits of the world of music composition.

References

1. Jones, M.R.: Dynamic pattern structure in music: recent theory and research. Percept. Psychophys. **41**, 621–634 (1987)
2. Analytics Vidhya. https://www.analyticsvidhya.com/blog/2020/01/how-to-perform-automatic-music-generation/. Accessed 9 Mar 2021
3. UX Planet. https://uxplanet.org/why-fast-matters-a-lot-14c202e352f8. Accessed 9 Mar 2021
4. Musical U. https://www.musical-u.com/learn/rhythm-tips-for-identifying-music-genres-by-ear/. Accessed 7 Mar 2021
5. Tensorflow. https://magenta.tensorflow.org/studio. Accessed 7 Mar 2021
6. MuseNet. https://openai.com/blog/musenet/. Accessed 9 Mar 2021
7. Oore, S., Simon, I., Dieleman, S., Eck, D., Simonyan, K.: *This time with feeling: learning expressive musical performance.* Neural Comput. Appl. **32**(4), 955–967 (2018). https://doi.org/10.1007/s00521-018-3758-9
8. Twilio. https://www.twilio.com/blog/training-a-neural-network-on-midi-music-data-with-magenta-and-python/. Accessed 7 Mar 2021
9. Machine Learning Mastery. https://machinelearningmastery.com/gentle-introduction-long-short-term-memory-networks-experts/. Accessed 7 Mar 2021
10. GitHub Magenta. https://github.com/magenta/note-seq. Accessed 9 Mar 2021
11. Jeremy Jordan. https://www.jeremyjordan.me/variational-autoencoders/. Accessed 7 Mar 2021
12. GitHub Magenta. https://github.com/magenta/magenta/tree/master/magenta/models/melody_rnn. Accessed 11 Mar 2021
13. Britannica Art. https://www.britannica.com/art/monophony. Accessed 11 Mar 2021
14. Britannica Art. https://www.britannica.com/art/polyphony-music. Accessed 11 Mar 2021
15. Midi.org Midi Quantization. https://www.midi.org/midi-articles/5-midi-quantization-tips-1. Accessed 11 Mar 2021
16. Ghrab, A.: The western study of intervals in "Arabic Music," from the eighteenth century to the cairo congress. World Music **47**(3), 55–79 (2005)

Deep Learning and AI for 5G Technology: Paradigms

Mahnaz Olfati[1]($\boxtimes$) and Kiran Parmar[2]

[1] Faculty of Engineering, University of Regina, Regina, SK, Canada
[2] Adani Institute of Infrastructure Engineering, Ahmedabad, India

Abstract. Nowadays Internet of Things (IoT) is a major paradigm shift that will mark an epoch in communication technology such that every physical object can be connected to the Internet. 5G makes a significant breakthrough in the traditional mobile communication system and support the applications of IoT in various fields including business, manufacturing, health care and transportation.

5G is increasing the service capability of future IoT and operates and connects the whole society. 5G is facing enormous challenges when it supports differentiated applications with a uniform technical framework. In recent years, Artificial Intelligence (AI) is rising to these challenges with the rapid development. It is a potential solution to the problems in the 5G era and will lead to a revolution in the capabilities and concepts of the communication systems. Many researches have already been done for applying AI in 5G. In this paper, we focus on clarifying the promising research directions with the greatest potential rather than trying to review all the existing literatures. In this research, 5G can be anticipated to achieve significantly better performance and more convenient implementations compared to the traditional communication systems. With the inspiring research paradigms introduced in this paper, we are looking forward to the remarkable achievements of AI in 5G in the near future.

Keywords: Artificial intelligence · IT convergence · Machine learning · Deep learning · 5G networks

1 Introduction

Artificial Intelligence is great for problems in which existing solutions require a lot of hand-tuning or long lists of rules, for complex problems for which there is no good solution at all using traditional approaches, for adaptation to fluctuating environments, to get insights about complex problems that use large amounts of data, and in general to notice the patterns that a human can miss [1]. Hard-coded software can go from a long list of complex rules that can be hard to maintain to a system that automatically learn from previous data, detect anomalies, predict future scenarios, etc. These problems can be tackled adopting the capability of learn offered by AI along with the dense amount of transmitted data or wireless configuration datasets.

© IFIP International Federation for Information Processing 2021
Published by Springer Nature Switzerland AG 2021
I. Maglogiannis et al. (Eds.): AIAI 2021, IFIP AICT 627, pp. 398–407, 2021.
https://doi.org/10.1007/978-3-030-79150-6_32

We have witnessed explosive growth in AI, mobile and computing systems becoming an essential social infrastructure, mobilizing our daily life and facilitating the digital economy in multiple shapes [2]. Certain applications available in this intersection of fields have been addressed within specific topics of AI and next- generation wireless communication systems. Li et al. [3], highlighted the potentiality of AI as an enabler for cellular networks to cope with the 5G standardization requirements. Authors in [4, 33], discussed the Machine Learning (ML) techniques in the context of fog (edge) computing architecture, aiming to distribute computing power, storage, control and networking functions closer to the users. Jiang et al. [5], focused on the challenges of AI in assisting the radio communications in intelligent adaptive learning, and decision-making. The next generation of cellular communication technologies also requires the use of optimization to minimize or maximize certain objective functions like spectrum utilization, data rates or energy consumption. Many of the problems in cellular communications are not linear or polynomial, in consequence, they demand to be approximated. Artificial Neural Networks (ANN) are an AI technique that has been suggested to model the objective function of the non- linear problem that requires optimization [6]. 5G networks will offer various applications and services compared to 4G and hence is more challenging with the complicated compatibility issues and evolving service requirements. Before 5G, researches of communication systems mainly aim at enhancing data transmission rate and efficient mobility management. In the 5G era, the communication systems will have the abilities to interact with the environment, and the optimizations of ever-increasing numbers of Key Performance Indicators (KPIs) like latency, reliability, connection density, user experience, etc. would be very important [7]. The field of AI research was born in 1950 s, which went through varied interests and is revived in recent years due to the rapid development of modern computing and data storage technologies. The general problem of simulating intelligence contains sub-problems like reasoning, inference, data fitting, clustering and optimization, which involves approaches including genetic algorithms [8] and ANN [9–11]. Specially, AI learning techniques are universally applicable for various problems and are increasingly used in different fields. In the work [35] AI learning tasks are typically classified into two broad categories, supervised and unsupervised learning, depending on whether labels of the training data are available to the learning system. And another learning approach, reinforcement learning, is not exactly supervised neither unsupervised, hence can be listed in a new category. In this paper, we introduce the potential of AI algorithms into the next generation i.e 5G wireless networks to solve the requirements of the 5G standards so that they operate in a fully automated fashion, they provide increased capacity demand and they serve the users with superior Quality of Experience (QoE). This paper is divided according to the level of supervision the AI technique. The major categories discussed in the following sections are in supervised learning, unsupervised learning, and reinforcement learning. Reinforcement Learning interacts with the environment, getting feedback loops between the learning system and its experiences, in terms of rewards and penalties [5, 13, 22].

2 Supervised Learning in 5G Mobile and Wireless Communications Technology

In this approach, the goal is to learn a general function that related the inputs to the outputs and then detects the unknown outputs of the future inputs. sample data of inputs and desired outputs are fed into the computer. According to works [10], the typical well-known example of supervise learning is illustrated in Fig. 1. In supervised learning, each training example has to be fed along with their respective label. In this example the labeled data pairs are fed in a multi-layer Deep Neural Network (DNN) to train the weights between the nodes in the DNN. The training is carried out offline, and after convergence, the trained DNN will be ready for recognition and inference of new inputs. A typical task on supervised learning is to predict a target numeric value, given a set of features, called predictors. This description of the task is called regression. The notion is that training a learning model on a sample of the problem instances with known optimal and then use the model to recognize optimal solutions to new instances.

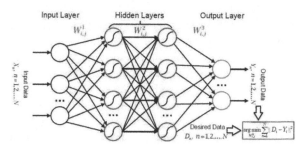

Fig. 1. Example of supervised learning: learning in deep neural networks [10].

Transfer Learning is a popular technique often used to classify vectors. Essentially, one would train a Convolutional Neural Network (CNN) on a very large dataset, for example ImageNet [9, 10], and then fine-tune the CNN on a different vector dataset. The advantage of this approach is that the training on the large dataset is already done by some researchers who offer the learned weights for future research use. Another typical task of Supervised Learning is regression or prediction. The key difference between classification is that with ML algorithms like Logistic Regression, the model can output the probability of that certain value belongs to a given class. This type of system is trained with multiple examples of a class, along with their label, and the model must learn how to classify new instances [28–32]. Long Term Evolution (LTE) small cells are nowadays deployed in 5G networks to meet the ever-increasing high traffic demands. These small size cells are characterized by its unpredictable and dynamic interference patterns leading to different S/I ratios, expanding the demand for self-optimized solutions that can lead to lower call drops, higher data rates, and lower cost for the cellular operators. An extensive interest in path-loss prediction has raised since researchers noticed the power of AI to model more efficient and accurate path-loss models based on publicly available datasets [11]. Timoteo et al. [12], proposed a path loss prediction model for urban environments using support vector regression to ensure an acceptable level of Quality of Service

(QoS) for wireless network users. They employed different kernels and parameters over the Okumura-Hata model and Ericsson 9999 model, and obtained similar results as a complex neural network, but with a lower computational complexity thereby saving time and memory.

Wireless communications depend heavily on wireless Channel State Information (CSI) to make an accurate decision in the operations of the network and employ digital signal processing. Liu et al. [13], investigated the unobservable CSI for wireless communications and proposed a neural-network-based approximation for channel learning, to infer this unobservable information, from an observable channel. Their framework was built upon the dependence between channel responses and location information. To build the supervised learning framework, they train the network with channel samples, where the unobservable metrics can be calculated from traditional pilot-aided channel estimation. The applications of their work can be extended to cell selection in multi-tier networks, device discovery for Device-to-Device (D2D) communications, or end-to-end user association for load balancing, among others. Sarigiannidis et al. [14], used a machine-learning framework based on supervised learning on a Software-Defined-Radio (SDR)- enabled hybrid optical wireless network. The machine-learning framework receives the traffic-aware knowledge from the SDN controllers and adjusts the uplink-downlink configuration in the LTE radio communication. The authors argue that their mechanism is capable of determining the best configuration based on the traffic dynamics from the hybrid network, offering significant network improvements in terms of jitter and latency.

An AI architecture which is used to model or approximate objective functions for existing models or to create accurate models that were impossible to represent in the past without the intervention of learning machines, is ANN. ANNs have been proposed to solve propagation loss estimation in dynamic environments, where the input parameters can be selected from the information of the transmitter, receiver, obstacles like buildings, frequency, and so on, and the learning network will train on that data to learn to estimate the function that best approximates the propagation loss for next-generation wireless networks [15–18]. In the same context, Ayadi et al. [19], proposed a Multi-Layer Perceptron (MLP) architecture to predict coverage for either short or long distance, in multiple frequencies, and in all environmental situations. The MLP presented uses feedforward training with back propagation to update the weights of the ANN. They used the inputs of the ITU-R P.1812-4 model [20], to feed their network composed by an input layer, a hidden layer, and one output layer. They showed that the ANN model is more accurate to predict coverage in outdoor environments than the ITU model, using the standard deviation and correlation factor as a comparison measure. Among other AI techniques with potential for wireless communications, there are K-Nearest Neighbors, Logistic Regression, Decision Trees and Random Forests.

3 Unsupervised Learning in 5G Mobile and Wireless Communications Technology

According to work [21], in unsupervised learning, no labels are given to the learning algorithm and structure in its input should be found on its own. Self-Organizing Map

(SOM) is an example that is trained using unsupervised learning. In SOM, unlabeled data are fed in to a neural network to produce a low-dimensional (usually two-dimensional), discretized representation of the input space of the training samples, called a map (as illustrated in Fig. 2), and is therefore a method to do dimensionality reduction.

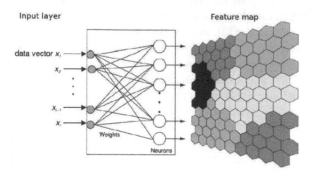

Fig. 2. Example of unsupervised learning: self-organizing Network [21].

In unsupervised learning, the system attempts to learn without any guidance. This technique is particularly useful when we want to detect groups of similar characteristics. At no point, we tell the algorithm to try to detect groups of related attributes; the algorithm solves this connection without intervention. However, in some cases, we can select the number of clusters we want the algorithm to create. Balevi et al. [21], incorporated fog networking into heterogeneous cellular networks and used an unsupervised soft-clustering algorithm to locate the fog nodes that are upgraded from Low Power Nodes (LPNs) to High Power Nodes (HPNs). The authors showed that by applying machine learning clustering to a priori known data like the number of fog nodes and location of all LPNs within a cell, they were able to determine a clustering configuration that reduced latency in the network. A typical unsupervised learning technique is K-means clustering; numerous authors have investigated the applications of this particular clustering technique in the next generation wireless network system.

AI for SON: Automatic root cause analysis. Self-Organizing Networks (SONs) establish a new concept of network management which provide intelligence in the operation and maintenance of the network. It has been introduced by 3GPP as a key component of LTE network. In the 5G era, network densification and dynamic resource allocation will result in new problems for coordination, configuration and management of the network, hence bringing increased demand for the improvements of the SON functions. SON modules in mobile networks can be divided into three main categories: self-configuration, self-optimization and self-healing. The main objectives of SON are to automatically perform network planning, configuration and optimization without human intervention, in order to reduce the overall complexity, Operational Expenditure (OPEX), Capital Expenditure (CAPEX) and man-made faults. Various researches of AI in SON have been summarized in [32, 34] which includes AI applied in automatic base station configuration, new cell and spectrum deployment, coverage and capacity optimization, cell outage detection and compensation, etc., using approaches including ANN, ant colony optimization, genetic algorithm, etc.

In this section, we introduce the automatic root cause analysis framework proposed in [35] as an example for AI in SON. The design of the fault identification system in LTE networks faces two main challenges: (1) A huge number of alarms, KPIs and configuration parameters can be taken as fault indicators in the system. Meanwhile, most of the symptoms of these indicators are not labeled with fault causes, hence are difficult to identify; (2) The system is not automatic and experts are involved to analyze each fault cause. With the huge amount of high-dimensional data, human intervention is not efficient while expensive. Authors of [35] proposes an AI-based automatic root cause analysis system which combines supervised and unsupervised learning techniques as summarized in the following steps:

1. Unsupervised SOM training. SOM is applied for an initial classification of the high-dimensional KPIs. An SOM is a type of unsupervised neural network capable of acquiring knowledge and learning from a set of unlabeled data. It will process high-dimensional data and reducing it to a two-dimensional map of neurons that preserves the topological properties of the input data. Hence, inputs close to each other will be mapped to adjacent neurons.
2. Unsupervised clustering. After SOM training, all the neurons in the SOM system will be clustered into a certain number of groups using an unsupervised algorithm. Since the SOM neurons are already ordered and the difference between the original inputs can be represented by Euclidean distance between the corresponding neurons.

Labeling by Experts. After the above two steps, the original high-dimensional data are clustered into several classes. We will finally have the experts to analyze and identify the fault causes of each obtained cluster to have all the clusters labeled. With the training, clustering and labeling, an automatic system for network diagnosis is constructed by the workflow shown in Fig. 3. For a new input of KPIs, it will firstly be mapped to a neuron in SOM. Then by the label of the cluster this neuron belongs to, we can identify the fault and the causes. After obtaining a certain amount of new fault data, we can verify whether the system is right or not and update it by re-training with the above three steps.

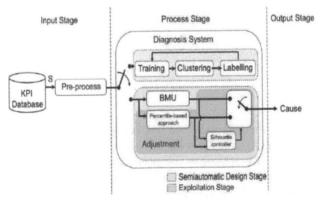

Fig. 3. Automatic root cause analysis workflow [23]

In [23], the authors discussed how K-means clustering algorithm and its classification capabilities can aid in selecting an efficient relay selection among urban vehicular networks. The authors investigated the methods for multi-hop wireless broadcast and how K-means is a key factor in the decision-making and learning steps of the base stations, that learn from the distribution of the devices and chooses automatically which are the most suitable devices to use as a relay.

4 Reinforcement Learning in 5G Mobile and Wireless Communications Technology

This technique is based on alternative interaction between Agent and Environment and the process is illustrated in Fig. 4. The Agent will perform certain action and as a result of this action his state will change which leads to either a reward or a penalty. The Agent will then decide the next action based on this result. By iterating through action and reward/penalty process, Agent learns the Environment.

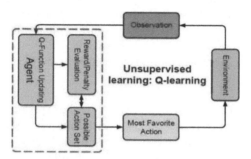

Fig. 4. Reinforcement learning: Q-learning [5].

The philosophy of Reinforcement Learning scheme is based on a learning system often called agent, that reacts to the environment. The agent performs actions and gets rewards or penalties (negative rewards) in return for its actions. That means that the agent has to learn by itself creating a policy that defines the action that the agent should choose in a certain situation. The aim of the reinforcement-learning task is to maximize the aforementioned reward over time [5, 13].

5 Conclusion

The advent of 5G is introducing new challenges for mobile communications service providers, and integrating AI techniques into networks is one way the industry is addressing these complexities. AI is already being incorporated into networks, with a primary focus on reducing capital expenditure, optimizing network performance and building new revenue streams. AI will be vital for improving customer service and enhancing customer experience. The 5th wireless communication (5G) techniques not only fulfil the requirement of increasing the internet traffic in the next decade, but also offer the underlying technologies to the entire industry and ecology for internet of everything. The resurgence of artificial intelligence techniques which is possibly superior over traditional ideas and performance, offers as an alternative option. Compared to the existing mobile communication techniques, 5G techniques are more-widely applicable and the corresponding system design is more complicated. Potential research directions to which AI can make promising contributions need to be identified and evaluated. This overview paper first combs through promising research directions of AI for 5G, based on the understanding of the 5G key techniques. This work also devotes itself in providing design paradigms including optimal resource allocation, 5G network optimization, end-to-end physical layer joint optimization, 5G physical layer unified acceleration, and so on.

References

1. Geron, A.: Hands-on machine learning with Scikit-Learn and TensorFlow: concepts, tools, and techniques to build intelligent systems, p. 543 (2017)
2. Osseiran, A., Monserrat, J.F., Marsch, P.: 5G Mobile and Wireless Communications Technology, 1st ed. Cambridge University Press, United Kingdom (2017). www.cambridge.org/9781107130098
3. Bojović, B., Meshkova, E., Baldo, N., Riihijärvi, J., Petrova, M.: Machine learning-based dynamic frequency and bandwidth allocation in self-organized LTE dense small cell deployments. EURASIP J. Wirel. Commun. Netw. **2016**(1), 183 (2016). https://doi.org/10.1186/s13638-016-0679-0
4. Jiang, C., Zhang, H., Ren, Y., Han, Z., Chen, K.C., Hanzo, L.: Machine learning paradigms for next-generation wireless networks. IEEE Wirel. Commun. **24**, 98–105 (2017). https://doi.org/10.1109/MWC.2016.1500356WC
5. Nguyen, D.D., Nguyen, H.X., White, L.B.: Reinforcement learning with network-assisted feedback for heterogeneous RAT selection. IEEE Trans. Wirel. Commun. **16**(9), 6062–6076 (2017). https://doi.org/10.1109/TWC.2017.2718526
6. Balevi, E., Gitlin, R.D.: Unsupervised machine learning in 5G networks for low latency communications. In: 2017 IEEE 36th International Performance Computing and Communications Conference, IPCCC 2017, vol. 2018, pp. 1–2 (2018)
7. Fossorier, M.P.C., Mihaljevic, M., Imai, H.: Reduced complexity iterative decoding of low-density parity check codes based on belief propagation. IEEE T Commun. **47**(5), 673–680 (1999)
8. Alnwaimi, G., Vahid, S., Moessner, K.: Dynamic heterogeneous learning games for opportunistic access in LTE-based macro/femtocell deployments. IEEE Trans. Wirel. Commun. **14**(4), 2294–2308 (2015)
9. G_omez-Andrades, A., Munoz, P., Serrano, I., et al.: Automatic root cause analysis for LTE networks based on unsupervised techniques. IEEE T. Veh. Technol. **65**(4), 2369–2386 (2016)
10. Sobabe, G., Song, Y., Bai, X., Guo, B.: A cooperative spectrum sensing algorithm based on unsupervised learning. In: 10th International Congress on Image and Signal Processing, BioMedical Engineering and Informatics (CISP-BMEI 2017), vol. 1, pp. 198–201 (2017)
11. Villarrubia, G., De Paz, J.F., Chamoso, P., la Prieta, F.D.: Artificial neural networks used in optimization problems. Neurocomputing **272**, 10–16 (2018)
12. Goodfellow, I., Bengio, Y., Courville, A.: Deep Learning, 1st edn., edited by Dietterich, T. (ed.). The MIT Press, London, England (2016). www.deeplearningbook.org
13. Kaelbling, L.P., Littman, M.L., Moore, A.W.: Reinforcement learning: a survey. J. Artif. Intell. Res. **4**, 237–285 (1996)

14. International Telecommunication Union: A path-specific propagation prediction method for point-to-area terrestrial services in the VHF and UHF bands. ITU P-Series Radiowave propagation, no. P.1812-4, pp. 1–35 (2015). https://www.itu.int/dms_pubrec/itu-r/rec/p/R-REC-P.1812-4-201507-I!!PDF-E.pdf

15. Liu, J., Deng, R., Zhou, S., Niu, Z.: Seeing the unobservable: channel learning for wireless communication networks. In: 2015 IEEE Global Communications Conference, GLOBECOM 2015 (2015)

16. Mom, J.M., Mgbe, C.O., Igwue, G.A.: Application of artificial neural network for path loss prediction in urban macrocellular environment. Am. J. Eng. Res. (AJER) **03**(02), 270–275 (2014)

17. Klaine, P.V., Imran, M.A., Onireti, O., et al.: A survey of machine learning techniques applied to self-organizing cellular networks. IEEE Commun. Surv. Tut. **19**(4), 2392–243134 (2017)

18. Wang, L.-C., Cheng, S.H.: Data-driven resource management for ultra-dense small cells: an affinity propagation clustering approach. IEEE Trans. Netw. Sci. Eng. **4697**(c), 1 (2018). https://ieeexplore.ieee.org/document/8369148/

19. Liu, L., Yuen, C., Guan, Y.L., et al.: Gaussian message passing iterative detection for MIMO-NOMA systems with massive access. In: Proceedings of IEEE Global Communications Conference (GLOBECOM), pp. 1–6 (2016)

20. Ayadi, M., Ben Zineb, A., Tabbane, S.: A UHF path loss model using learning machine for heterogeneous networks. IEEE Trans. Antennas Propag. **65**(7), 3675–3683 (2017)

21. Parwez, M.S., Rawat, D.B., Garuba, M.: Big data analytics for user-activity analysis and user-anomaly detection in mobile wireless network. IEEE Trans. Ind. Inf. **13**(4), 2058–2065 (2017)

22. P_erez-Romero, J., Sallent, O., Ferrs, R., et al.: Knowledge-based 5G radio access network planning and optimization. In: Proceedings of IEEE International Symposium on Wireless Communication Systems (ISWCS), pp. 359–365 (2016)

23. Sarigiannidis, P., Sarigiannidis, A., Moscholios, I., Zwierzykowski, P.: DIANA: a machine learning mechanism for adjusting the TDD uplink-downlink configuration in XG-PON-LTE systems. Mob. Inf. Syst. **2017**, 8198017 (2017)

24. P.U. Stanford Vision Lab, Stanford University, "ImageNet. http://image-net.org/about-overview

25. Le, Q.V., Jaitly, N., Hinton Google, G.E.: A simple way to initialize recurrent networks of rectified linear units, Technical report (2015). https://arxiv.org/pdf/1504.00941v2.pdf

26. Timoteo, R.D.A., Cunha, D.C., Cavalcanti, G.D.C.: A proposal for path loss prediction in urban environments using support vector regression. In: Advanced International Conference on Telecommunications, vol. 10, no. c, pp. 119–124 (2014)

27. Li, R., et al.: Intelligent 5G: when cellular networks meet artificial intelligence. IEEE Wirel. Commun. **24**(5), 175–183 (2017). http://www.rongpeng.info/files/Paper_wcm2016.pdf

28. Pascanu, R., Mikolov, T., Bengio, Y.: On the difficulty of training recurrent neural networks, Technical report (2013). http://proceedings.mlr.press/v28/pascanu13.pdf?spm=5176.100239.blogcont292826.13.57KVN0&file=pascanu13.pdf

29. Ren, Y.R., Zhang, C., Liu, X., et al.: Efficient early termination schemes for belief-propagation decoding of polar codes. In: Proceedings of IEEE International Conference on ASIC (ASICON), pp. 1–4 (2015)

30. Sotiroudis, S.P., Siakavara, K., Sahalos, J.N.: A neural network approach to the prediction of the propagation path-loss for mobile communications systems in urban environments. PIERS Online **3**(8), 1175–1179 (2007)

31. Sotiroudis, S.P., Goudos, S.K., Gotsis, K.A., Siakavara, K., Sahalos, J.N., Fellow, L.: Application of a composite differential evolution algorithm in optimal neural network design for propagation path-loss prediction in mobile communication systems. IEEE Antennas Wirel. Propag. Lett. **12**, 364–367 (2013)

32. Han, S.Y., Abu-ghazaleh, N.B., Member, S.: Efficient and Consistent Path loss Model for Mobile Network Simulation," IEEE/ACM Trans. Netw. vol. PP, no. 99, pp. 1–1 (2015)
33. Bogale, T.E., Wang, X., Le, L.B.: Machine intelligence techniques for next-generation context-aware wireless networks. In: ITU Special Issue: The impact of Artificial Intelligence (AI) on communication networks and services., vol. 1 (2018). https://arxiv.org/pdf/1801.04223.pdf
34. Mitchell, T.M.: Machine Learning, 1st edn. McGraw-Hill Science/Engineering/Math (1997). https://www.cs.ubbcluj.ro/~gabis/ml/ml-books/McGrawHill-MachineLearning-Tom Mitchell.pdf
35. Challita, U., Dong, L., Saad, W.: Deep learning for proactive resource allocation in LTE-U networks. In: 23rd European Wireless Conference on European Wireless 2017 (2017). http://ieeexplore.ieee.org/stamp/stamp.jsp?tp=&arnumber=8011311

Fuzzy Modeling

Intuitionistic Fuzzy Neural Network for Time Series Forecasting - The Case of Metal Prices

Petr Hajek[1]([✉])[iD], Vladimir Olej[1][iD], Wojciech Froelich[2][iD], and Josef Novotny[3][iD]

[1] Science and Research Centre, Faculty of Economics and Administration, University of Pardubice, Studentska 84, Pardubice, Czech Republic
{petr.hajek,vladimir.olej}@upce.cz
[2] Institute of Computer Science, University of Silesia, ul. Bedzinska 39, Sosnowiec, Poland
wojciech.froelich@us.edu.pl
[3] Institute of Business Economics and Management, Faculty of Economics and Administration, University of Pardubice, Studentska 84, Pardubice, Czech Republic
josef.novotny@upce.cz

Abstract. Forecasting time series is an important problem addressed for years. Despite that, it still raises an active interest of researchers. The main issue related to that problem is the inherent uncertainty in data which is hard to be represented in the form of a forecasting model. To solve that issue, a fuzzy model of time series was proposed. Recent developments of that model extend the level of uncertainty involved in data using intuitionistic fuzzy sets. It is, however, worth noting that additional fuzziness exhibits nonlinear behavior. To cope with that issue, we propose a time series model that represents both high uncertainty and non-linearity involved in the data. Specifically, we propose a forecasting model integrating intuitionistic fuzzy sets with neural networks for predicting metal prices. We validate our approach using five financial multivariate time series. The results are compared with those produced by state-of-the-art fuzzy time series models. Thus, we provide solid evidence of high effectiveness of our approach for both one- and five-day-ahead forecasting horizons.

Keywords: Fuzzy time series · Fuzzy neural network · Intuitionistic fuzzy sets

1 Introduction

Despite spectacular achievements in the field, forecasting time series still raises an active interest among researchers. Their efforts' main goal is to design a

Supported by the scientific research project of the Czech Sciences Foundation Grant No: 19-15498S.

I. Maglogiannis et al. (Eds.): AIAI 2021, IFIP AICT 627, pp. 411–422, 2021.
https://doi.org/10.1007/978-3-030-79150-6_33

forecasting model that would be able to capture the uncertainty involved in data and, thanks to that, produce more accurate forecasts.

One of the most essential approaches models time series using fuzzy sets. The method consists of three main stages. First, time series are partitioned and fuzzified. Then, the prediction model is created using fuzzy logic relations (fuzzy if-then rules). The model is used to predict future values of the fuzzified time series (fuzzy time series). Finally, if the knowledge of their crisp values is required for the considered application, the predictions are defuzzified.

In the literature, for data partitioning, equal-sized intervals were typically used [2–4]. However, if the data distribution were not uniform over the universe of discourse, the equally distributed fuzzy sets did not represent the underlying data effectively. This in turn led to higher forecasting errors [1]. To address this issue, the parameters of fuzzy time series were determined using different methods, including mathematical optimization and clustering-based methods. Due to their robustness and capacity to solve global optimization problems, evolutionary algorithms were frequently used to optimize the parameters of fuzzy sets. In this case, the limitation is the susceptibility to over-fitting. Clustering-based methods, in turn, usually provided a good trade-off between computational demand and forecasting accuracy [5,6]. It is, however, worth noting that the existing fuzzification methods are not capable of modeling the dynamic behavior of time series. To overcome this problem, we propose in this paper a fuzzification method that assigns membership and non-membership values of fuzzy sets by incorporating variance in the time series.

To perform forecasts, fuzzy logic relations between previous and forecasted values were traditionally produced from the historical time series. The relations were generated and selected using the fuzzy sets with the highest membership values. The weighted and polynomial constructions were introduced for each fuzzy logic relationship to assign larger weights to recent time series observations (compared with the latter) [7] or to those with higher empirical probabilities [8]. The fuzzy trend of the forecasted value was also incorporated into the final forecasts [9,10]. The main problem with the construction of traditional fuzzy logic relationships is their poor generalization capacity, this is poor out-of-sample forecasts. Moreover, for many observations, no matched fuzzy logic relations are available and, hence, no reliable forecast can be performed [11]. To address these issues, neural networks were employed to learn the relationships using different strategies.

Several studies used neural networks to predict the consequences of the relationships based on the index numbers of input fuzzy sets (antecedents) [12,13]. Central values of fuzzy sets were used for the same purpose [14]. Alternatively, input and output membership degrees were used to represent the fuzzy sets [2,15]. Multilayer perceptron neural networks were employed in the above studies. Pi-Sigma neural network used by [16] represents an a higher-order alternative with a fewer number of units, leading to enhancement in convergence speed. However, this neural network model is more susceptible to over-fitting. Support vector regression was applied to produce predictions for unrecognized multivariate fuzzy logic relationships [17]. In an adaptive neuro-fuzzy inference system (ANFIS) [18,19], hidden units of neural network represent the if-then rules given in advance, and neural network is used to learn the consequent parameters of the rules. Another layer can be used to represent the parameters of fuzzy sets. Interval type-2 (intuitionistic) fuzzy sets were used in ANFIS to represent the additional uncertainty in financial time series [20–23].

Hesitant fuzzy sets and probabilistic fuzzy sets represent other extensions of fuzzy sets used for fuzzy time series forecasting [4,24,25]. To avoid the overfitting problem of single prediction models, several studies introduced combinations of fuzzy neural networks utilizing both interval type-2 fuzzy sets [26] and intuitionistic fuzzy sets [27]. The main drawback of the presented interval type-2 (intuitionistic) fuzzy neural networks is their use of static membership functions (lower, upper, or non-membership functions). This is, the degree of hesitancy does not consider volatility in the time series data.

We propose an intuitionistic fuzzy neural network that incorporates this concept. In addition, it utilizes intuitionistic fuzzy operators to calculate the firing weights of if-then rules and a defuzzification method designed for intuitionistic fuzzy sets to aggregate the outcomes of the rules. Gradient descent is used as a training algorithm for the intuitionistic fuzzy neural network. The proposed model is also highly computationally efficient because only consequent parameters of the rules are adapted while the parameters of fuzzy sets and rule antecedents are generated using a clustering algorithm.

As far as we know, this is the first extension of a fuzzy neural network that considers the volatility in the time series to assign the degree of hesitancy to observations in the data partitioning stage. For the first time, a generalization of a neuro-fuzzy system is used for predicting metal prices.

The rest of this paper is organized in the following way. Section 2 outlines the proposed intuitionistic fuzzy neural network for time series forecasting. Section 3 presents the metal price datasets. Section 3 shows the results of the experiments and comparisons with existing time series methods. Section 4 concludes this paper and discusses future research.

2 Intuitionistic Fuzzy Neural Network for Time Series Forecasting

Let us remind at first the definition of an intuitionistic fuzzy set A which is [28]:

$$A = \{\langle x, \mu_A(x), \nu_A(x)\rangle \,|\, x \in X\},\tag{1}$$

where $\mu_A(x)$ and $\nu_A(x)$ respectively is the membership and a non-membership degree of element x to the set A, X is the universe of discourse. It holds that $0 \le \mu_A(x) \le 1$, $0 \le \nu_A(x) \le 1$ and $0 \le \mu_A(x) + \nu_A(x) \le 1$. The hesitation degree $\pi_A(x)$ denotes an additional degree of uncertainty, $\pi_A(x) = 1 - \mu_A(x) - \nu_A(x)$.

Here we propose an intuitionistic fuzzy neural network which is based on that outlined in [29] and consists of six layers (Fig. 1).

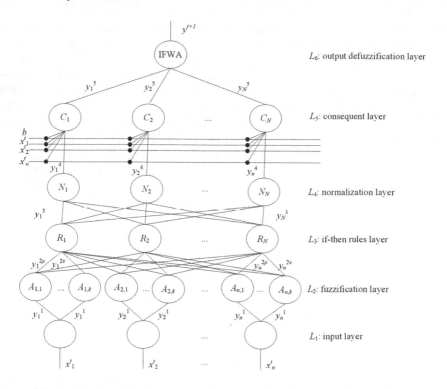

Fig. 1. Intuitionistic fuzzy neural network for time series forecasting.

Input layer: The first layer is used to forward the crisp inputs $x_1^t, x_2^t, \ldots, x_n^t$ to the next layer.

Fuzzification layer: Neurons in this layer represent antecedent intuitionistic fuzzy sets for the i-th input attribute x_i^t. To fuzzify the crisp values, the input attributes are first compared with the membership functions. Here, we use the Gaussian membership function defined as follows:

$$\mu(x_i^t) = e^{-\frac{(x_i^t - c)^2}{2\sigma^2}}, \tag{2}$$

where c is the center and σ is the width of the membership function. The values of these parameters are obtained automatically using the subtractive clustering algorithm [30]. To obtain the intuitionistic fuzzy sets, the following fuzzification method is used [31]:

$$\mu_A(x_i^t) = \mu(x_i^t) \times (1 - \delta D), \tag{3}$$

$$\nu_A(x_i^t) = 1 - \mu(x_i^t) \times (1 - \delta D) - \delta D, \text{where} \tag{4}$$

$$D = (max(\mu(x_i^t), \mu(x_i^{t-1}), \ldots, \mu(x_i^{t-4})) - min(\mu(x_i^t), \mu(x_i^{t-1}), \ldots, \mu(x_i^{t-4}))) \tag{5}$$

and δ is set to 1 in agreement with [31]. Hence, intuitionistic fuzzy sets are given as $A = \{\langle x_i^t, \mu_A(x_i^t), \nu_A(x_i^t)\rangle \,|\, x_i^t \in X_i \}$, where X_i is the universe of discourse for the i-th input attribute. Note that the fuzzification parameter D considers the volatility of the last five observations in the time series. Still, this number can be adapted to the needs of the specific forecasting problem.

If-then rules layer: Neurons in this layer represent the if-then rules of the first-order Takagi-Sugeno-Kang type. The j-th rule R_j, $j = 1, 2, \ldots, N$, can be defined as follows:

$$R_j : \text{if } x_1^t \text{ is } A_{1,j} \text{ and } x_2^t \text{ is } A_{2,j} \text{ and } \ldots \text{ and } x_i^t \text{ is } A_{i,j} \text{ and } \ldots \text{ and}$$
$$x_n^t \text{ is } A_{n,j} \text{then } y_j^{t+h} = a_{0,j} + a_{1,j}x_1^t + \cdots + a_{i,j}x_i^t + \cdots + a_{n,j}x_n^t, \tag{6}$$

where $A_{i,j}$ is antecedent intuitionistic fuzzy set for the i-th input attribute x_i^t and j-th rule R_j, y_j^{t+h} is the predicted output for the j-th rule, h is the forecasting horizon, and $a_{0,j}, a_{1,j}, \ldots, a_{i,j}, \ldots, a_{n,j}$ are the consequent parameters.

To calculate the firing weight w_j of the j-th rule R_j, Gödel t-norm operators are used as follows:

$$w_j^\mu = \min_{j=1,2,\ldots,N}(\mu_A(x_1^t), \mu_A(x_2^t), \ldots, \mu_A(x_n^t)), \tag{7}$$

$$w_j^\nu = \max_{j=1,2,\ldots,N}(\nu_A(x_1^t), \nu_A(x_2^t), \ldots, \nu_A(x_n^t)), \tag{8}$$

$$w_j = w_j^\mu - w_j^\nu, \tag{9}$$

where w_j^μ and w_j^ν denote the membership and non-membership degrees of the firing weight W_j, respectively. Note that only positive firing weights are considered (with acceptance degree higher than non-acceptance degree) in agreement with [32].

Normalization layer: Neurons in this layer calculate the normalized values of the firing weights w_j^{norm}.

Consequent layer: Consequent parameters $a_{0,j}, a_{1,j}, \ldots, a_{n,j}$ are represented by neurons in this layer by calculating the outputs of the rules as $y_j^{t+h} = a_{0,j} + a_{1,j}x_1^t + \cdots + a_{i,j}x_i^t + \cdots + a_{n,j}x_n^t$.

Defuzzification layer: One output neuron in this layer calculates the weighted average of outputs from the preceding layer to obtain the defuzzified forecast as follows:

$$y_{IFWA}^{t+h} = \frac{\sum_{j=1}^N y_j^{t+h}w_j^{norm}}{\sum_{j=1}^N w_j^{norm}}. \tag{10}$$

To train the synapse weights of the intuitionistic fuzzy neural network, the gradient descent algorithm was used due to its stable convergence reported in earlier studies [23, 29]. The algorithm can be defined as follows:

$$w_{i+1} = w_i - \eta \nabla_\theta J\left(w_i; x^{(t)}; y^{(t+h)}\right), \tag{11}$$

where w is synapse weight, η is learning rate, i denotes the iteration index, J is the objective function (root mean square error (RMSE)), $x^{(t)}$ and $y^{(t+h)}$ represent the input and output for the t-th observation in the time series.

3   Model Validation

In this section, we validate the proposed intuitionistic fuzzy neural network for time series forecasting (IFNN-TS).

3.1   Experimental Setup

The data used in this study are the closing prices of five major metals, namely gold, silver, palladium, platinum, and rhodium. The dataset covers the period from 2007 to 2017, including 3,949 trading days. Specifically, daily spot prices in USD per ounce were collected from the Kitco database. The prices are depicted in Fig. 2. To evaluate the proposed forecasting model's robustness, two datasets were generated for each metal price, the one-day-ahead (daily) and five-day-ahead (weekly) forecasting. Sequential validation was used by partitioning data into the training set immediately followed by the testing set in ratio 9:1 following earlier relevant studies [33]. This is, the first 3,554 samples represented training data, and the following 395 samples were used as testing data.

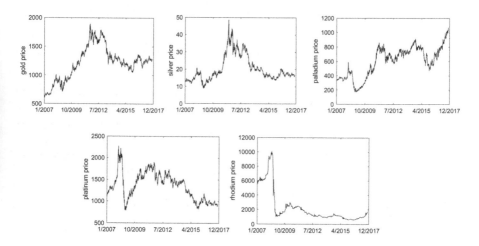

Fig. 2. Metal price data.

We followed earlier research [34–36] and consider the technical indicators of respective metal prices, previous oil price (Brent crude oil price, BRN), exchange rate (US\$ to Chinese Yuan, USDCNY), and news sentiment indicators as input attributes. More precisely, 20-day technical indicators were calculated, including exponential moving average (EMA, trend-type indicator), relative strength index (RSI, oscillator-type indicator), and rate of change (ROC, volatility-type indicator):

$$EMA_t = \frac{2}{21}(SMA_t - EMA_{t-1}) + EMA_{t-1}, \tag{12}$$

$$RSI_t = 100 - \frac{100}{1 + RS}, ROC_t = \frac{P_t - P_{t-20}}{P_{t-20}} \times 100, \tag{13}$$

where SMA_t is 20-day simple moving average, RS is the ratio of smoothed average of 20-day upward / downward ROC, and P_t is the metal price at day t.

The previous day's closing prices were used for BRN and USDCNY, and the data for these inputs were obtained from the MarketWatch database. To consider the information effects on metal prices, we calculated the intensity of positive and negative news sentiment using SentiWordNet publicly available at https://github.com/aesuli/SentiWordNet. The Thomson Reuters newswire service was used to obtain the news related to metals for the respective period. In total, 266,165 news articles were collected, and the mean values of SentiWordNet sentiment indicators were calculated for each day.

The following state-of-the-art models were considered for comparison:

- ANFIS-GA [37], initialized using the subtractive clustering algorithm with the same settings as in IFNN-TS and trained using the genetic algorithm with the parameters adopted from [37].
- INFN-PSO [29], an intuitionistic neuro-fuzzy network trained using particle swarm optimization. Again, we used the subtractive clustering algorithm to initialize the parameters of the model and trained it in agreement with the settings recommended in [29].
- IT2FLS-EKM [38], the interval type-2 fuzzy logic system with the enhanced Karnik-Mendel algorithm, generated in fuzzy logic toolbox as the interval type-2 Sugeno FIS and tuned using the gradient descent algorithm.
- ES (exponential smoothing) [39], represented by triple ES (Holt-Winters) model with smoothing factors of 0.2.
- ARIMA [40], adopting the ARIMA(1,1,0) model found by [40] using the Hyndman and Khandakar algorithm.
- RF [41], random forest trained using 100 random trees.
- MLP [40], multilayer perceptron NN with the settings adopted from [40] as follows: one hidden layer of 24 sigmoidal neurons, the momentum of 0.5, and the learning rate of 0.001.
- LSTM [42], long short-term memory NN with an LSTM layer of 200 neurons followed by a dense layer of 32 neurons (the structure was adopted from [42]) trained using stochastic gradient descent.

Forecasting performance was evaluated using RMSE and mean absolute error (MAE) on the testing data separately for the 1-day-ahead and 5-day-ahead forecasting horizon. In addition, we present the mean directional accuracy (MDA) to evaluate the proposed system's capacity to predict the correct forecast direction (upward or downward) and investigate the financial performance of the constructed precious metals portfolio in terms of its return and risk. All the experiments were carried out in the Matlab Fuzzy Logic Toolbox in Matlab R2020a.

3.2   Experimental Results

First, we used the subtractive clustering algorithm to generate the antecedent intuitionistic fuzzy sets and the rule base. Note that the use of the subtractive clustering algorithm to generate the if-then rules enabled us to substantially reduce the complexity of the rule base. Experiments were performed for different values of the radius of influence (resulting in different numbers of antecedent intuitionistic fuzzy sets and rules) to prevent under-fitting and over-fitting. More precisely, we examined three settings with $N = \{3, 5, 7\}$ rules and antecedent intuitionistic fuzzy sets. Due to space limitations, we only show the performance of IFNN-TS for $N=3$ and $N=5$ rules (Table 1) because the performance for $N=7$ deteriorated substantially. Obviously, $N=3$ was a preferable setting in terms of both forecasting accuracy and interpretability at the rule base/fuzzy partition level. In all experiments, we used the gradient descent algorithm (with 100 iterations and the learning rate $\eta = 0.01$) to train the IFNN-TS. For the example of the gold price, the obtained rule base is as follows:

R_1 : if EMA_t is *medium* and RSI_t is *medium* and ROC_t is *high* and BRN_t is *low* and $USDCNY_t$ is *medium* and POS_t is *low* and NEG_t is *high* then
$y_1^{t+1} = 0.11 + 0.97 \times EMA_t - 0.09 \times RSI_t + 6.18 \times ROC_t - 0.17 \times BRN_t$
$+6.82 \times USDCNY_t + 0.0006 \times POS_t - 0.04 \times NEG_t,$

R_2 : if EMA_t is *high* and RSI_t is *low* and ROC_t is *low* and BRN_t is *high* and $USDCNY_t$ is *low* and POS_t is *high* and NEG_t is *low* then
$y_1^{t+1} = 0.06 + 1.06 \times EMA_t - 0.002 \times RSI_t + 11.72 \times ROC_t - 1.18 \times BRN_t$
$+1.08 \times USDCNY_t + 0.003 \times POS_t + 0.04 \times NEG_t,$

R_3 : if EMA_t is *low* and RSI_t is *high* and ROC_t is *medium* and BRN_t is *medium* and $USDCNY_t$ is *high* and POS_t is *medium* and NEG_t is *medium* then $y_1^{t+1} = -0.14 + 0.92 \times EMA_t + 0.12 \times RSI_t - 6.83 \times ROC_t$
$+1.38 \times BRN_t - 8.02 \times USDCNY_t - 0.03 \times POS_t + 0.04 \times NEG_t.$

Experimental results in Table 1 show the effectiveness of the proposed IFNN-TS by comparison with three models of fuzzy neural networks and five other benchmark forecasting models used previously for metal price prediction. The results of the comparisons show that IFNN-TS was highly competitive regarding all metal prices in terms of both forecasting horizons. Best performance in terms of RMSE was achieved for one-day-ahead forecasting of gold, silver and platinum prices. A non-parametric Friedman test was used to compare the results of the models statistically. The average ranks of the IFNN-TS models were as follows: 2.2 for MAE and one-day-ahead forecast, 2.0 for RMSE and one-day-ahead forecast, 2.0 for MAE and five-day-ahead forecast, and 2.4 for RMSE and five-day-ahead forecast. Significant differences were observed for the average ranks of the compared methods at $p < 0.05$, indicating significantly different performance across the error measures and forecasting horizons. In the next step, the Holm–Bonferroni posthoc procedure was used to compare the performance between the best forecasting model and the other models. For the one-day-ahead forecasting, IFNN-TS significantly outperformed ARIMA, ES, RF, MLP, and LSTM at $p < 0.05$. For the five-day-ahead forecasting, IFNN-TS performed significantly better than RF, MLP, LSTM, and ANFIS-GA at $p < 0.05$. These results were consistent for MAE and RMSE.

Table 1. Results of metal price forecasting (the best result is in bold).

| | | IFNN-TS | | IFNN-TS | | ANFIS-GA | | INFN-PSO | | IT2FLS-EKM | |
| | | $N = 3$ rules | | $N = 5$ rules | | $N = 3$ rules | | $N = 3$ rules | | $N = 3$ rules | |
Metal	Forecast	MAE	RMSE	MAE	RMSE	MAE	RMSE	MAE	RMSE	MAE	RMSE
Gold	1-day	6.687	**9.689**	10.248	13.426	7.045	9.994	**6.684**	9.764	9.731	13.067
Gold	5-day	15.408	19.680	18.022	22.962	16.980	21.335	16.058	20.497	18.011	22.820
Silver	1-day	**0.155**	**0.223**	0.268	0.340	0.175	0.243	0.177	0.246	0.194	0.257
Silver	5-day	**0.364**	0.474	0.435	1.453	0.461	0.602	0.369	0.483	0.379	0.502
Palladium	1-day	7.843	10.978	11.617	15.291	7.976	10.997	**7.792**	**10.811**	7.993	10.917
Palladium	5-day	16.873	21.681	19.973	25.187	19.306	24.697	17.611	22.643	17.365	22.480
Platinum	1-day	8.658	**11.550**	11.830	14.973	**8.635**	11.579	9.670	12.536	9.698	12.800
Platinum	5-day	**18.968**	25.000	19.973	25.187	21.537	27.881	19.340	25.186	19.468	25.430
Rhodium	1-day	16.766	23.574	10.814	21.852	**12.605**	**18.007**	13.460	21.996	15.723	22.537
Rhodium	5-day	24.100	38.365	22.623	42.414	33.144	47.137	22.204	36.562	24.543	39.459

| | | ES | | ARIMA | | RF | | MLP | | LSTM | |
Metal	Forecast	MAE	RMSE	MAE	RMSE	MAE	RMSE	MAE	RMSE	MAE	RMSE
Gold	1-day	16.092	20.665	9.949	12.538	11.434	14.933	10.936	13.697	23.845	26.618
Gold	5-day	17.066	21.485	**10.747**	**13.431**	18.630	23.104	11.851	14.659	40.757	44.271
Silver	1-day	0.376	0.471	0.305	0.377	0.239	0.311	0.422	0.484	0.331	0.386
Silver	5-day	0.389	0.499	0.567	0.683	0.369	**0.471**	0.607	0.674	0.514	0.581
Palladium	1-day	19.008	24.491	8.117	10.997	28.084	44.407	13.240	16.733	23.173	28.449
Palladium	5-day	18.628	23.833	**11.789**	**15.408**	39.000	52.530	19.293	23.892	32.040	40.103
Platinum	1-day	19.954	25.342	15.398	18.626	15.986	21.408	18.385	21.249	19.900	25.642
Platinum	5-day	20.185	26.426	19.387	**23.135**	23.957	31.448	24.599	27.542	27.569	35.163
Rhodium	1-day	19.948	32.646	35.700	46.425	100.64	126.57	56.930	67.615	65.726	87.358
Rhodium	5-day	**19.532**	**35.204**	125.17	178.98	104.28	127.36	103.62	120.43	95.874	130.39

In addition to the error measures, we evaluated the performance of the model in predicting MDA. Figure 3 shows that IFNN-TS consistently exceeded 55% across metal prices. Correct forecast of upward/downward direction is important for generating 'buy', 'hold' and 'sell' signals. Therefore, we further investigated the financial performance (return and risk) of the precious metals portfolio constructed based on signals generated using the IFNN-TS-based trading strategy ('buy' ('hold') signal for upward price forecast, and 'sell' signal for downward price forecast). The closing metal prices were used for trading, and the weights of the five metals in the portfolio were equal. We obtained an average return of 54.63% (for one-day-ahead forecasting) and 87.91% (for five-day-ahead forecasting) for the testing period. The forecasting-based trading strategy was more profitable than the traditional buy-and-hold strategy (with an average daily return of 41.29% and weekly return 41.17%). However, it should be noted that our trading strategy was associated with a higher portfolio risk. The standard deviation of returns was used to calculate the risk, obtaining $\sigma = 6.32\%$ and $\sigma = 7.22\%$ for the one-day-ahead and five-day-ahead IFNN-TS forecasting strategies, hence exceeding those for the buy-and-hold strategy ($\sigma = 4.36\%$ and $\sigma = 6.44\%$).

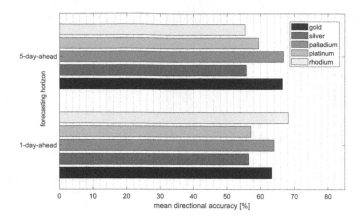

Fig. 3. Mean directional accuracy of IFNN-TS.

4 Conclusion

In this study, we proposed an efficient forecasting model that incorporates intuitionistic fuzzy sets to consider uncertainty present in the time series volatility in the fuzzification process. To defuzzify the forecast, an intuitionistic fuzzy weighted averaging operator was proposed. In the learning process, the model utilizes the capability of neural networks to minimize forecasting error. Good interpretability at the fuzzy partition and rule base level is ensured using a clustering algorithm in the initialization process.

We validated the proposed model using five time series of major metal prices. The proposed model outperformed existing fuzzy neural networks, but it was also competitive compared to existing models used for forecasting metal prices. In addition to low forecasting errors, the model provides investors with an interpretable set of trading rules. Compared with the buy-and-hold strategy, the trading strategy based on our model directional forecasts achieved a higher average return (and risk) of the metals portfolio.

A limitation of the proposed model is that a high degree of hesitancy (caused by high volatility in the time series data) may negatively affect the rules' firing weights. Consequently, no matched if-then rules are available in the rule base. Future research should investigate alternative approaches to generate the rule base to overcome this limitation, such as evolutionary rule selection. The parameters of membership functions and fuzzification could also be adapted in further investigation. Further research might also explore comparisons with recent time series forecasting methods such as Bi-LSTM.

References

1. Bose, M., Mali, K.: Designing fuzzy time series forecasting models: a survey. Int. J. Approximate Reasoning **111**, 78–99 (2019)
2. Yu, T.H-K., Huarng, K.: A neural network-based fuzzy time series model to improve forecasting. Expert Syst. Appl. **37**, 3366–3372 (2010)

3. Chen, S.M., Tanuwijaya, K.: Multivariate fuzzy forecasting based on fuzzy time series and automatic clustering techniques. Expert Syst. Appl. **38**(8), 10594–10605 (2011)
4. Bisht, K., Kumar, S.: Fuzzy time series forecasting method based on hesitant fuzzy sets. Expert Syst. Appl. **64**, 557–568 (2016)
5. Bose, M., Mali, K.: A novel data partitioning and rule selection technique for modeling high-order fuzzy time series. Appl. Soft Comput. **63**, 87–96 (2018)
6. Roy, A.: A novel multivariate fuzzy time series based forecasting algorithm incorporating the effect of clustering on prediction. Soft Comput. **20**(5), 1991–2019 (2015). https://doi.org/10.1007/s00500-015-1619-3
7. Talarposhti, F.M., Sadaei, H.J., Enayatifar, R., Guimarães, F.G., Mahmud, M., Eslami, T.: Stock market forecasting by using a hybrid model of exponential fuzzy time series. Int. J. Approximate Reasoning **70**, 79–98 (2016)
8. de Lima Silva, P.C., Sadaei, H.J., Ballini, R., Guimarães, F.G.: Probabilistic forecasting with fuzzy time series. IEEE Trans. Fuzzy Syst. **28**(8), 1771–1784 (2020)
9. Wang, W., Liu, X.: Fuzzy forecasting based on automatic clustering and axiomatic fuzzy set classification. Inf. Sci. **294**, 78–94 (2015)
10. Abhishekh, Kumar, S.: A modified weighted fuzzy time series model for forecasting based on two-factors logical relationship. Int. J. Fuzzy Syst. **21**(5), 1403–1417 (2019)
11. Li, F., Yu, F.: Multi-factor one-order cross-association fuzzy logical relationships based forecasting models of time series. Inf. Sci. **508**, 309–328 (2020)
12. Chen, M.Y.: A high-order fuzzy time series forecasting model for internet stock trading. Future Gener. Comput. Syst. **37**, 461–467 (2014)
13. Egrioglu, E., Aladag, C.H., Yolcu, U., Uslu, V.R., Basaran, M.A.: A new approach based on artificial neural networks for high order multivariate fuzzy time series. Expert Syst. Appl. **36**(7), 10589–10594 (2009)
14. Singh, P., Borah, B.: High-order fuzzy-neuro expert system for daily temperature forecasting. Knowl.-Based Syst. **46**, 12–21 (2013)
15. Yolcu, O.C., Yolcu, U., Egrioglu, E., Aladag, C.H.: High order fuzzy timeseries forecasting method based on an intersection operation. Appl. Math. Model. **40**, 8750–8765 (2016)
16. Bas, E., Grosan, C., Egrioglu, E., Yolcu, U.: High order fuzzy time series method based on pi-sigma neural network. Eng. Appl. Artif. Intell. **72**, 350–356 (2018)
17. Wu, H., Long, H., Wang, Y., Wang, Y.: Stock index forecasting: a new fuzzy time series forecasting method. J. Forecast. (2020). https://doi.org/10.1002/for.2734
18. Peng, H.W., Wu, S.F., Wei, C.C., Lee, S.J.: Time series forecasting with a neuro-fuzzy modeling scheme. Appl. Soft Comput. **32**, 481–493 (2015)
19. Su, C.H., Cheng, C.H.: A hybrid fuzzy time series model based on ANFIS and integrated nonlinear feature selection method for forecasting stock. Neurocomputing **205**, 264–273 (2016)
20. Yihong, F., Weimin, L., Xiaoguang, Z., Xin, X.: Threat assessment based on adaptive intuitionistic fuzzy neural network. In: 2011 Fourth International Symposium on Computational Intelligence and Design, vol. 1, pp. 262–265 (2011)
21. Gaxiola, F., Melin, P., Valdez, F., Castillo, O.: Interval type-2 fuzzy weight adjustment for backpropagation neural networks with application in time series prediction. Inf. Sci. **260**, 1–14 (2014)
22. Luo, C., Tan, C., Wang, X., Zheng, Y.: An evolving recurrent interval type-2 intuitionistic fuzzy neural network for online learning and time series prediction. Appl. Soft Comput. **78**, 150–163 (2019)

23. Eyoh, I., John, R., De Maere, G., Kayacan, E.: Hybrid learning for interval type-2 intuitionistic fuzzy logic systems as applied to identification and prediction problems. IEEE Trans. Fuzzy Syst. **26**(5), 2672–2685 (2018)

24. Bisht, K., Kumar, S.: Hesitant fuzzy set based computational method for financial time series forecasting. Granular Comput. **4**(4), 655–669 (2018). https://doi.org/10.1007/s41066-018-00144-4

25. Gupta, K.K., Kumar, S.: A novel high-order fuzzy time series forecasting method based on probabilistic fuzzy sets. Granular Comput. **4**(4), 699–713 (2019). https://doi.org/10.1007/s41066-019-00168-4

26. Soto, J., Melin, P., Castillo, O.: A new approach for time series prediction using ensembles of IT2FNN models with optimization of fuzzy integrators. Int. J. Fuzzy Syst. **20**(3), 701–728 (2018)

27. Bas, E., Yolcu, U., Egrioglu, E.: Intuitionistic fuzzy time series functions approach for time series forecasting. Granular Computing, pp. 1–11 (2020) https://doi.org/10.1007/s41066-020-00220-8

28. Atanassov, K.T.: Intuitionistic fuzzy sets. Fuzzy Sets Syst. **20**, 87–96 (1986)

29. Hájek, P., Olej, V.: Intuitionistic neuro-fuzzy network with evolutionary adaptation. Evolving Syst. **8**(1), 35–47 (2016). https://doi.org/10.1007/s12530-016-9157-5

30. Chiu, S.L.: Fuzzy model identification based on cluster estimation. J. Intell. Fuzzy Syst. **2**(3), 267–278 (1994)

31. Hajek, P., Froelich, W., Prochazka, O.: Intuitionistic fuzzy grey cognitive maps for forecasting interval-valued time series. Neurocomputing **400**, 173–185 (2020)

32. Angelov, P.: Crispification: defuzzification over intuitionistic fuzzy sets. BUSEFAL **64**, 51–55 (1995)

33. Wang, C., Zhang, X., Wang, M., Lim, M.K., Ghadimi, P.: Predictive analytics of the copper spot price by utilizing complex network and artificial neural network techniques. Resour. Policy **63**, 101414 (2019)

34. Ergen, I., Rizvanoghlu, I.: Asymmetric impacts of fundamentals on the natural gas futures volatility: an augmented GARCH approach. Energy Econ. **56**, 64–74 (2016)

35. Kristjanpoller, W., Hernández, E.: Volatility of main metals forecasted by a hybrid ANN-GARCH model with regressors. Expert Syst. Appl. **84**, 290–300 (2017)

36. Shen, J., Najand, M., Dong, F., He, W.: News and social media emotions in the commodity market. Rev. Behav. Finance **9**(2), 148–168 (2017)

37. Alameer, Z., Abd Elaziz, M., Ewees, A.A., Ye, H., Jianhua, Z.: Forecasting copper prices using hybrid adaptive neuro-fuzzy inference system and genetic algorithms. Natural Res. Res. **28**(4), 1385–1401 (2019)

38. Wu, D., Mendel, J.M.: Enhanced Karnik-Mendel algorithms. IEEE Trans. Fuzzy Syst. **17**, 923–934 (2009)

39. Hassani, H., Silva, E.S., Gupta, R., Segnon, M.K.: Forecasting the price of gold. Appl. Econ. **47**(39), 4141–4152 (2015)

40. Lasheras, F.S., de Cos Juez, F.J., Sanchez, A.S., Krzemien, A., Fernandez, P.R.: Forecasting the COMEX copper spot price by means of neural networks and ARIMA models. Res. Policy **45**, 37–43 (2015)

41. Liu, D., Li, Z.: Gold price forecasting and related influence factors analysis based on random forest. Adv. Intell. Syst. Comput. **502**, 711–723 (2017)

42. Livieris, I.E., Pintelas, E., Pintelas, P.: A CNN-LSTM model for gold price time-series forecasting. Neural Comput. Appl. **32**(23), 17351–17360 (2020)

Hyperdimensional Computing

PQ-HDC: Projection-Based Quantization Scheme for Flexible and Efficient Hyperdimensional Computing

Chi-Tse Huang[✉], Cheng-Yang Chang, Yu-Chuan Chuang, and An-Yeu (Andy) Wu

Graduate Institute of Electronics Engineering, National Taiwan University, Taipei, Taiwan
{rickhuang,kevin,frankchuang}@access.ee.ntu.edu.tw,
andywu@ntu.edu.tw

Abstract. Brain-inspired Hyperdimensional (HD) computing is an emerging technique for low-power/energy designs in many machine learning tasks. Recent works further exploit the low-cost quantized (bipolarized or ternarized) HD model and report dramatic improvements in energy efficiency. However, the quantization loss of HD models leads to a severe drop in classification accuracy. This paper proposes a projection-based quantization framework for HD computing (PQ-HDC) to achieve a flexible and efficient trade-off between accuracy and efficiency. While previous works exploit thresholding-quantization schemes, the proposed PQ-HDC progressively reduces quantization loss using a linear combination of bipolarized HD models. Furthermore, PQ-HDC allows quantization with flexible bit-width while preserving the computational efficiency of the Hamming distance computation. Experimental results on the benchmark dataset demonstrate that PQ-HDC achieves a 2.82% improvement in accuracy over the state-of-the-art method.

Keywords: Brain-inspired computing · Hyperdimensional Computing · Dynamic model · Energy efficiency

1 Introduction

In the era of the Internet of Things (IoT), a huge amount of data is generated daily. Machine learning (ML) models on edge devices spring up to collect and analyze these data. Nowadays, deep neural network (DNN) is the most prevalent ML models. However, DNN requires considerable computational resources with iterative gradient decent and a huge number of parameters, which are not available on resource-constrained edge devices. Therefore, a lightweight alternative is more desirable for efficient model deployment. Brain-inspired Hyperdimensional Computing (HDC) [1] has been proposed as a lightweight classifier with the low training cost, which emulates the patterns of neural activities by computing with high-dimensional (HD) vectors, called hypervectors (HVs).

The original version of this chapter was revised: the acknowledgement has been updated. The correction to this chapter is available at https://doi.org/10.1007/978-3-030-79150-6_62

I. Maglogiannis et al. (Eds.): AIAI 2021, IFIP AICT 627, pp. 425–435, 2021.
https://doi.org/10.1007/978-3-030-79150-6_34

HDC exhibits many remarkable characteristics, including high energy efficiency [2] and few-shot learning ability [3]. Moreover, HDC achieves the great success in various real-world applications, such as text classification [4], speech recognition [5], genome sequencing [6], and emotion recognition [7]. These properties make HDC suitable for efficient deployment on edge devices and realistic applications.

However, to provide acceptable accuracy on realistic classification problems, most works calculate computation-intensive cosine similarity between HVs with integer representation. On the contrary, the quantized HD model trades classification accuracy for drastically improved computational efficiency. As the work of [8] pointed out, the integer HD model consumes much more energy than the bipolarized one. To illustrate this idea, Fig. 1 compares the classification accuracy of full-precision (integer) and quantized (bipolarized) HD models with different HD dimensions. Figure 1 shows that the bipolarized HD model suffers from a significant accuracy drop. While QuantHD [9] introduces a retraining mechanism which iteratively adjusts the model on data with wrong predictions to close the accuracy gap, there are still some open issues:

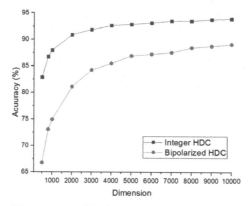

Fig. 1. The accuracy of the integer and bipolarized HD models.

(1) There is still a large gap between the classification accuracy of the bipolarized HD model and that of the integer one. Therefore, quantizing HD models with less information loss is worth investigating.
(2) The ultra-low complexity of the Hamming distance computation is only applicable to one-bit bipolarized HD models. For HD models quantized to multiple bits, computation-intensive cosine similarity is required. Thus, the lack of flexibility in bit-width for representing HD models should be addressed.

In this paper, we propose a Projection-based Quantization framework for HDC (PQ-HDC) to improve the flexibility and the accuracy of quantized HD models. QuantHD [9] utilizes a single bit to quantize the integer HVs into bipolarized ones, leading to large quantization loss. Instead, PQ-HDC uses multiple bits to shrink the quantization loss progressively while preserving the computational efficiency of the Hamming distance computation. The main contributions of this paper are summarized as follows:

(1) **Multi-bit quantized HD model using Hamming distance metric:** PQ-HDC acts as an intermediate between the integer and bipolarized HD models. Compared to traditional methods which quantize the integer HD model into a single bipolarized one, PQ-HDC utilizes a linear combination of bipolarized AMs to reduce the quantization loss progressively. Additionally, by normalizing the combination of bipolarized HVs in each class, PQ-HDC can quantize HD models with arbitrary bit-width while preserving the computational efficiency of the Hamming distance computation.

(2) **Improve the computation-efficient:** Compared to the state-of-the-art [9] quantized HDC scheme based on the Hamming distance computation, PQ-HDC improves 2.82% and 0.79% in accuracy on MNIST and ISOLET datasets, respectively. To show that PQ-HDC achieves a scalable accuracy–complexity trade-off, we also discuss the memory and the computational complexity at the end of this article.

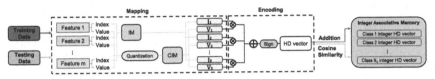

Fig. 2. The processing flow of HDC.

2 Review of Hyperdimensional Computing

HDC is based on the high-dimensional and dense bipolarized HVs. In the training phase, HDC transforms training data into bipolarized HVs and aggregates those bipolarized HVs of the same class to construct the class HVs. In the inference phase, testing data forms query HVs through the same transformation procedures. Then, HDC checks similarities between the query HV and the class HVs. Finally, the class with the highest similarity is the prediction.

Mapping

In HDC, the goal of mapping is to project the information of a feature vector $X = [x_1, x_2, \ldots, x_m]^T$ with m features into D-dimensional HD space. Each feature identifier (ID) and its value are mapped to a pair of bipolarized HVs through an Item Memory (IM) and a Continuous Item Memory (CiM), respectively. IM identifies the feature information of every element in the feature vector X. $IM = \{I_1, I_2, \ldots, I_m\}$, *where* $I_i \in \{-1, +1\}^D$ *for* $i = 1 \sim m$. I_i is the item HV that represents the ID of x_i in X. To isolate the feature information, the bipolarized HVs in IM are approximately orthogonal with each other. In other words, $\frac{Hamming(I_i, I_j)}{D} \cong 0.5$, $i \neq j$, where $Hamming(\cdot, \cdot)$ denotes the Hamming distance between two HVs. To achieve this purpose, HDC assigns $\{I_1, I_2, \ldots, I_m\}$ as m independently and randomly generated bipolarized HVs.

Meanwhile, CiM preserves the magnitude information of every element in the feature vector X. CiM quantizes the numerical range of feature values into l levels, each of which corresponds to a quantization level. In other words, $CiM = \{CI_1, CI_2, \ldots, CI_l\}$

and $\frac{Hamming(CI_i, CI_j)}{D} = \frac{\|i-j\|}{l-1}$, $i \neq j$. This design maintains the spatial relationship of quantization levels. To achieve this purpose, HDC assigns CI_1 as one randomly generated bipolarized HV. Then, HDC flips $\frac{D}{l-1}$ bits which were not flipped to generate the continuous item HV of the next level. The same bit-flipping mechanism applies to other HVs in CiM.

Based on IM and CiM, HDC maps the feature vector X into the HD space. Specifically, x_i is mapped to a pair of HVs, consisting of the HV from IM I_i and the HV from CiM V_i. Note that V_i is selected from $\{CI_1, CI_2, \ldots, CI_l\}$ according to the actual value of x_i. After the HDC mapping stage, the feature vector X will be mapped to m pairs of bipolarized HVs (I_i, V_i).

Encoding

The encoding stage of HDC combines m pairs of HVs into one bipolarized HV that represents the original feature vector X. Specifically, for each pair of HVs, HDC binds the feature information and magnitude information together by multiplying I_i with V_i. $I_i * V_i$ results in a single HV that represents x_i in the feature vector X.

Next, HDC bundles these resulting encoded HVs (i.e. $I_i * V_i$) by summarizing them into an integer HV. This integer HV $T^{int} \in R^D$ is the representation of X in the HD space. Finally, HDC bipolarizes this integer HV T^{int} into bipolarized HV T^{bip} by the *sign* function.

$$T^{bip} = sign\left[T^{int}\right] = sign[I_1 * V_1 + I_2 * V_2 + \ldots + I_m * V_m]. \qquad (1)$$

Training

In the training phase, all training data go through the same mapping and encoding stages mentioned above. Then, the resulting HVs are sent to the associative memory (AM) for aggregation. In detail, the set of HVs that correspond to training data belonging to the same class are summed up to form a class HV. For a N_c-class classification task, HDC stores N_c class HVs in the AM, as shown in Fig. 2. For the jth class, the corresponding integer class HV $\left(AM_j^{int}\right)$ is computed as:

$$AM_j^{int} = \sum T^{bip}, T^{bip} \text{ which belongs to class } j,$$
$$\text{and } j \leq N_c \text{ (number of class).} \qquad (2)$$

Besides, HDC often bipolarizes AM^{int}, resulting in AM^{bip} for both storage-efficiency and computational-efficiency. Bipolarized AM only consumes a single bit to represent each element in a class HV. Moreover, bipolarization reduces inference computation from cosine similarity to Hamming distance.

Inference

In the inference phase, the testing data is transformed to a bipolarized query HV $Q \in \{-1, 1\}^D$ by the same processing flow of mapping and encoding in the training phase. As shown in Fig. 2, since AM stores the most representative class HV of each class, HDC makes predictions by checking similarities (S^{int}) between Q and all integer class

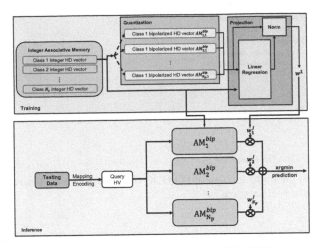

Fig. 3. System flow of the proposed PQ-HDC.

HVs. Then, the class with the highest similarity is the prediction of this data. On the other hand, bipolarized HD model has significantly lower computational complexity and energy cost [10]; however, bipolarization leads to a drop in the accuracy due to the quantization loss.

$$prediction^{int} = \underset{class}{\mathrm{argmax}}\ S_{class}^{int}. \tag{3}$$

3 Proposed Projection-Based Quantization for Hyperdimensional Computing (PQ-HDC)

PQ-HDC quantizes the integer class HV AM_j^{int} into multiple bipolarized class HVs and weights. Specifically, the linear combination of these bipolarized class HVs approximates the values in the integer class HV. In the training phase, PQ-HDC sequentially finds N_p, the number of bipolarized class HVs used to recover a single integer class HV, bipolarized class HVs to progressively reduce the quantization loss. Note that N_p also denotes the bit-width of the quantized HDC model. The weights for each bipolarized class HV are derived through linear regression and normalization techniques. In the inference phase, PQ-HDC checks the pseudo-hamming distances (PHD), which is defined as the weighted Hamming distance between the query HV and each set of bipolarized class HVs. The class with the lowest PHD value is the prediction.

3.1 Off-line Training Phase

Given an integer AM, PQ-HDC transforms the integer class HV of each class into N_p bipolarized class HVs. The procedure of PQ-HDC off-line training phase is summarized in Algorithm 1 and depicted in Fig. 4, respectively. Since each class is processed independently and separately, we take the jth class as an example in the following description.

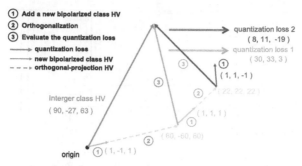

Fig. 4. Procedure in the training phase of PQ-HDC that generates a bipolarized class HV and updates HV^{loss} for the next iteration.

First, PQ-HDC defines HV_j^{loss}, which is an HV that records the quantization loss in each HD dimension, as the target that the bipolarized HVs aim to approximate. The initialization procedure of PQ-HDC includes setting HV_j^{loss} as AM_j^{int}. Next, as shown in Fig. 4, we define a procedure that contains three steps. PQ-HDC iterates over this procedure N_p times, each of which generates a pair of HVs, denoted as $AM_{i,j}^{bip}$, and quantization loss HV (HV_j^{loss}) for the next iteration. The three steps in the procedure are described as follows:

Step 1. Add a new bipolarized class HV: PQ-HDC acquires $AM_{i,j}^{bip}$, which represents the bipolarized class HV of the jth class in the ith iteration, by bipolarizing HV_j^{loss}. This step is depicted in row 5 of Algorithm 1.

$$AM_{i,j}^{bip} = sign\left[HV_j^{loss}\right]. \tag{4}$$

Step 2. Orthogonalization: Since $AM_{i,j}^{bip}$ and HV_j^{loss} are not parallel to each other, PQ-HDC decomposes HV_j^{loss} into two components. The first component is parallel to $AM_{i,j}^{bip}$ while the second one is orthogonal to $AM_{i,j}^{bip}$. Note that the decomposition can be simply done by orthogonal projection. Specifically, PQ-HDC calculates the orthogonal-projection HV (HV_j^{op}) of HV_j^{loss} on $AM_{i,j}^{bip}$. This step is depicted in row 6 of Algorithm 1. The resulting HV_j^{op} is the parallel component of HV_j^{loss} on $AM_{i,j}^{bip}$.

$$HV_j^{op} = AM_{i,j}^{bip}\left[\left(HV_j^{loss} \cdot AM_{i,j}^{bip}\right)/\left\|AM_{i,j}^{bip}\right\|^2\right]. \tag{5}$$

Step 3. Evaluate the quantization loss: To ensure that the updated HV_j^{loss} for the next iteration is orthogonal to $AM_{i,j}^{bip}$, PQ-HDC subtracts HV_j^{loss} with HV_j^{op}. This step is depicted in row 7 of Algorithm 1.

After iterating the above procedure N_p times, a set of bipolarized class HVs $S = \left\{AM_{i,j}^{bip} \text{ for } i = 1, 2, \ldots, N_p\right\}$ is generated. Note that the HVs in S are not mutually orthogonal. To approximate the integer class HV AM_j^{int} based on the linear combination of HVs in S, PQ-HDC uses linear regression to project AM_j^{int} onto the span of S. Therefore, the weights for the linear combination of S, denoted $\left\{w_i^j \; for \; i = 1, 2, \ldots, N_p\right\}$, minimize the quantization loss, as shown in Eq. (6). This step is depicted in rows 8–11 of Algorithm 1.

$$Recover\left(AM_j^{int}\right) = \sum_{i=1}^{N_p} w_i^j AM_{i,j}^{bip}. \tag{6}$$

$$Norm\left(Recover\left(AM_{c1}^{int}\right)\right) \neq Norm\left(Recover\left(AM_{c2}^{int}\right)\right), \; if \; c1 \neq c2. \tag{7}$$

However, the sets of weights for different classes vary. Consequently, the approximated integer class HVs have different norms. This phenomenon is in favor of the class HV with the larger norm for prediction. To unify the norms, PQ-HDC normalizes the weights, depicted in rows 12 in Algorithm 1. Based on the normalization technique, PQ-HDC can perform Hamming distance computation without considering the norm of each class HV.

Algorithm 1 Off-line Training Phase of PQ-HDC

Input:	AM^{int} – integer AM with N_c classes
	N_p – number of PQ AMs
Output:	$AM^{bip} = \{AM_1^{bip}, AM_2^{bip}, \ldots, AM_{N_p}^{bip}\}$ – PQ AMs
	$w = \{w^1, w^2, \ldots, w^{N_c}\}$ – weights of classes

1:   **for** (*class* in 1: N_c) **do**

2:      $X \leftarrow R^{[N_p, D]}$

3:      $HV_{class}^{loss} \leftarrow AM_{class}^{int}$

4:      **for** (*index* in 1: N_p) **do**

5:        $AM_{index,class}^{bip} = sign[\, HV_{class}^{loss}\,]$

6:        $HV_{class}^{op} \leftarrow AM_{index,class}^{bip}[HV_{class}^{loss} \cdot AM_{index,class}^{bip} \, / \, \left\| AM_{index,class}^{bip} \right\|^2\,]$

7:        $HV_{class}^{loss} \leftarrow HV_{class}^{loss} - HV_{class}^{op}$

8:        $X[index-1] \leftarrow AM_{index,class}^{bip}$

9:      $Y \leftarrow AM_{class}^{int}$

10:     $P \leftarrow X^T (XX^T)^{-1}$

11:     $w^{class} \leftarrow YP$

12:     $w^{class} \leftarrow \sqrt{D}\, w^{class} \, / \, \|w^{class} * AM_{class}^{bip}\|$

3.2 On-line Inference Phase

The Inference flow of PQ-HDC is depicted in Fig. 3. In the inference phase, testing data undergoes the same processing flow in the training phase to become a query HV Q, as shown in Eq. (1).

Based on the normalization, PQ-HDC can reduce the cosine similarity between Q and the recovering integer class HV to the weighted Hamming distance PHD between Q and the set of bipolarized class HVs like Eq. 8, where $COS(\cdot, \cdot)$ denotes the cosine similarity between two HVs.

$$
\begin{aligned}
S_j^{int} \cong \widetilde{S_j^{int}} &= COS\left(Q, Recover\left(AM_j^{int}\right)\right) \\
&= 1 - 2\frac{PHD\left(Q, Recover\left(AM_j^{int}\right)\right)}{D}.
\end{aligned}
\tag{8}
$$

$$
PHD\left(Q, Recover\left(AM_j^{int}\right)\right) = \frac{D}{2} + \sum_{i=1}^{N_p} w_i^j\left(Hamming\left(Q, AM_{i,j}^{bip}\right) - \frac{D}{2}\right).
\tag{9}
$$

Taking the class j as an example, PQ-HDC evaluates the Hamming distance between Q and all bipolarized class HVs of the class j separately. Namely, $H_j = \left\{Hamming\left(Q, AM_{i,j}^{bip}\right) for\ i = 1, 2, \ldots, N_p\right\}$ is generated. Then, PQ-HDC multiplies these Hamming distances in H_j with their corresponding weights to calculate the PHD between Q and the recovering integer class HV by (9). The same PHD computation mechanism applies to other classes. Finally, the class with the lowest PHD value is the prediction. The algorithm of the PQ-HDC on-line inference phase is summarized in Algorithm 2.

Algorithm 2 On-line Inference Phase of PQ-HDC

    Input: D_{test} – testing data

                N_p – number of PQ AMs

                $AM^{bip} = \{AM_1^{bip}, AM_2^{bip}, \ldots, AM_{N_p}^{bip}\}$ – PQ AMs

                $w = \{w^1, w^2, \ldots, w^{Nc}\}$ – weights of classes

    Output: Prediction Pre_{test}

1:    Transform D_{test} to Q by (1)

2:    $PHD \leftarrow R^{[Nc]}$

3:    **for** ($class$ in $1: N_c$) **do**

4:        **for** (i in $1: N_p$) **do**

5:                $H_{class,i} = Hamming(Q, AM_{i,class}^{bip})$

6:                $PHD_{class} = \frac{D}{2} + \Sigma_{k=1}^{N_p}\left(w_k^{class}\left(H_{class,k} - \frac{D}{2}\right)\right)$

7:    $Pre_{test} = \underset{class}{\arg\min}(PHD_{class})$

---

4 Experimental Settings and Simulation Results

4.1 Dataset and Simulation Settings

We conducted experiments on MNIST [11] and ISOLET [12] datasets, which are both common benchmarks for HDC. Our proposed PQ-HDC is implemented in Python running on AMD Core TR-2950X processor with 128 GB memory. To evaluate the effectiveness of PQ-HDC, we compare our framework with HD models with full-precision (integer) and quantized representations based on QuantHD [9]. Classification accuracy, storage requirement, and computational complexity of each method are summarized in Table 1. All experiments are conducted over 10 independent runs to obtain the averaged simulation results.

Table 1. Summary of storage and computational complexity between different models

Model	Averaged accuracy	Normalized storage	Computational complexity
Integer HD model	93.36%	1	$O(D * N_c)$ times multiplications + $O(D * N_c)$ times additions
Bipolarized HD model [9]	90.15%	0.03125	$O(D * N_c)$ times additions
Ternarized HD model [9]	91.68%	0.0625	$O(D * N_c)$ times multiplications + $O(D * N_c)$ times additions
PQ2 HD model $(N_p = 2)$	**91.95%**	**0.0627**	$O(N_p * N_c)$ **times multiplications +** $O(N_p * D * N_c)$ **times additions**
PQ3 HD model $(N_p = 3)$	92.75%	0.09405	$O(N_p * N_c)$ times multiplications + $O(N_p * D * N_c)$ times additions

4.2 Comparisons of Classification Accuracy

Figure 5 shows the averaged retrained accuracy of the HD models with different quantization schemes and HD dimensions. The integer HD model has the highest accuracy among all models; however, its memory and computational overhead are not affordable on resource-constrained edge devices. On the contrary, bipolarized HD shows the highest computational efficiency, since it does not require any multiplication operation. Nevertheless, the drop in the accuracy is not acceptable.

As intermediate solutions, the ternarized HDC model can close the accuracy gap between the integer and bipolarized HD models with computation-intensive cosine similarity. Meanwhile, as shown in Fig. 5, the PQ2($N_p = 2$) HDC model can improve 2.82% and 0.79% in accuracy against the bipolarized HD model on the MNIST and ISOLET dataset, respectively ($D = 10000$). Note that the storage overhead of PQ2 HDC model is comparable to the ternarized HD model.

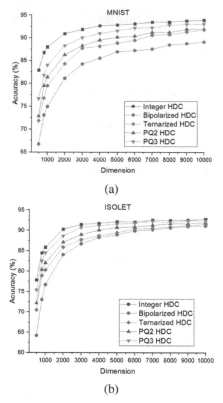

(a)

(b)

Fig. 5. Comparisons of the averaged accuracy among different frameworks. The line PQi HDC denotes PQ-HDC model with N_p set as i.

4.3 Performance Analysis

For PQ-HDC, since the extra storage space for weights ($32 * N_p$ bits for a class) is negligible compared to high-dimension HVs, the storage complexity is $O(N_p * D)$. Namely, the storage complexity of the PQ2 HDC model is equal to that of the ternarized HD model with higher classification accuracy.

Next, we evaluate the computational complexity for inferencing on testing data in terms of operation counts. The inference procedures of integer and ternarized HD models include computing N_c times cosine similarities, where $O(D)$ times multiplications and $O(D)$ times additions are required. Meanwhile, bipolarized HD model computes N_c Hamming distance, where only $O(D)$ times additions are required. Finally, the PHD computation of PQ-HDC includes the calculation of $N_p \times N_c$ times Hamming distances along with $N_p \times N_c$ times multiplications. Therefore, PQ-HDC is more computational-efficient than the ternarized HD model of the state-of-the-art.

5 Conclusions

In this paper, we propose a Projection-based Quantization HD computing (PQ-HDC) framework to effectively improve the accuracy-complexity trade-off. PQ-HDC also shows scalability by utilizing a linear combination of bipolarized AMs to achieve quantization with arbitrary bit-width while preserving the computational efficiency of the Hamming distance computation. The experimental results demonstrate that PQ-HDC with N_p set as 2 and 3 can save 93.7% and 90.6% memory overhead, respectively, compared to the HDC model with full precision. Furthermore, PQ-HDC also has higher accuracy against ternary HDC with the same storage and lower computation complexity.

Acknowledgments. This work was supported by the Ministry of Science and Technology of Taiwan under Grants MOST 109-2221-E-002-175 and MOST 110-2218-E-002-034 -MBK.

References

1. Kanerva, P.: Hyperdimensional computing: an introduction to computing in distributed representation with high-dimensional random vectors. Cogn. Comput. **1**(2), 139–159 (2009)
2. Rahimi, A., et al.: Efficient biosignal processing using hyperdimensional computing: network templates for combined learning and classification of ExG signals. Proc. IEEE **107**(1), 123–143 (2019)
3. Rahimi, A., et al.: Hyperdimensional computing for noninvasive brain–computer interfaces: blind and one-shot classification of EEG error-related potentials. In: Proceedings of the 10th ACM/EAI International Conference on Bio-Inspired Information and Communications Technologies (BICT), pp. 19–26 (2017)
4. Najafabadi, F.R., Rahimi, A., Kanerva, P., Rabaey, J.M.: Hyperdimensional computing for text classification. In: Design, Automation Test in Europe Conference Exhibition (DATE). University Booth (2016)
5. Imani, M., et al.: VoiceHD: hyperdimensional computing for efficient speech recognition. In: ICRC, pp. 1–6. IEEE (2017)
6. Imani, M., et al.: HDNA: energy-efficient dna sequencing using hyperdimensional computing. In: BHI, pp. 271–274. IEEE (2018)
7. Chang, E., et al.: Hyperdimensional computing-based multimodality emotion recognition with physiological signals. In: Proceedings of the IEEE International Symposium on AI for Circuits and Systems (AICAS), March 2019, pp. 137–141 (2019)
8. Horowitz, M.: Computing's energy problem (and what we can do about it). In: IEEE International Solid-State Circuits Conference on Digest of Technical Papers (ISSCC), February 2014, pp. 10–14 (2014)
9. Imani, M., et al.: QuantHD: a quantization framework for hyperdimensional computing. In: IEEE Transactions on Computer-Aided Design of Integrated Circuits and Systems (TCAD) (2019)
10. Chuang, Y.-C., Chang, C.-Y., Wu, A.-Y.A.: Dynamic hyperdimensional computing for improving accuracy-energy efficiency trade-offs. In: IEEE Workshop on Signal Processing Systems (SiPS). IEEE (2020)
11. LeCun, Y., Bottou, L., Bengio, Y., Haffner, P.: Gradient-based learning applied to document recognition. Proc. IEEE **86**(11), 2278–2324 (1998). http://yann.lecun.com/exdb/mnist/
12. UCI ML repository. http://archive.ics.uci.edu/ml/datasets/ISOLET

Hyperdimensional Computing with Learnable Projection for User Adaptation Framework

Yu-Ren Hsiao[✉], Yu-Chuan Chuang, Cheng-Yang Chang, and An-Yeu (Andy) Wu

Graduate Institute of Electronics Engineering, National Taiwan University, Taipei, Taiwan
{max,frankchuang,kevin}@access.ee.ntu.edu.tw, andywu@ntu.edu.tw

Abstract. Brain-inspired Hyperdimensional Computing (HDC), a machine learning (ML) model featuring high energy efficiency and fast adaptability, provides a promising solution to many real-world tasks on resource-limited devices. This paper introduces an HDC-based user adaptation framework, which requires efficient fine-tuning of HDC models to boost accuracy. Specifically, we propose two techniques for HDC, including the learnable projection and the fusion mechanism for the Associative Memory (AM). Compared with the user adaptation framework based on the original HDC, our proposed framework shows 4.8% and 3.5% of accuracy improvements on two benchmark datasets, including the ISOLET dataset and the UCIHAR dataset, respectively.

Keywords: Brain-inspired computing · Hyperdimensional computing · User adaptation

1 Introduction

With the emergence of Internet of Things (IoT), much data is generated by embedded devices [1]. Many IoT applications collect and analyze those data to train machine learning (ML) models in cloud servers and deploy the trained models back to devices for inference. However, performance of deployed models is sensitive to misaligned data distribution caused by subject difference [2] and time-varying properties [3, 4], as depicted in Fig. 1(a). To compensate for the potential performance degradation, a user adaptation framework is required to boost model performance by dynamically adapting models to user data [5–7]. The authors of [2] proposed a cloud-based model adaptation framework that requires edge clients to upload data for retraining. However, the wirelessly transmitted data poses a threat to user's privacy [8] and introduces extra energy consumption. Therefore, an on-device adaptation framework is preferable [9, 10]. However, an ML model with high energy efficiency and fast adaptability is necessary due to limited resources on embedded devices.

Recently, brain-inspired Hyperdimensional Computing (HDC) is emerging as a lightweight alternative to high-complexity ML models. HDC emulates patterns of neural

---

The original version of this chapter was revised: the acknowledgement has been updated. The correction to this chapter is available at https://doi.org/10.1007/978-3-030-79150-6_62

© IFIP International Federation for Information Processing 2021, corrected publication 2021
Published by Springer Nature Switzerland AG 2021
I. Maglogiannis et al. (Eds.): AIAI 2021, IFIP AICT 627, pp. 436–447, 2021.
https://doi.org/10.1007/978-3-030-79150-6_35

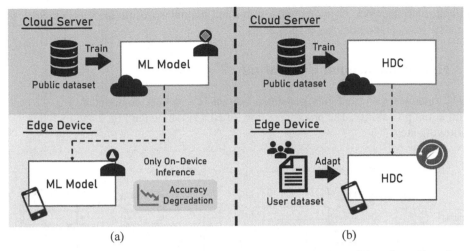

Fig. 1. (a) Without user adaptation, the accuracy of the deployed model easily suffers from misaligned data distribution and time-varying properties. (b) The characteristics of high energy efficiency and fast adaptability make HDC suitable for the user adaptation framework.

activities in human brains by projecting data into high-dimensional (HD) vectors, called Hypervectors (HVs) [11]. Through exploiting the mathematical properties of HVs in the HD space, HDC has shown the characteristics of high energy efficiency and fast adaptability in a wide variety of real-world applications, such as image classification [12, 13], speech recognition [14], and bio-signal processing [15]. These advantages make HDC suitable for on-device user adaptation framework, as depicted in Fig. 1(b). However, we argue that the original HDC algorithm ignores significant correlation between features during projection, leading to suboptimal accuracy.

To close the knowledge gap, we enable HDC to learn the feature correlation of input data to improve its overall performance. In the cloud, we first transform the original processing flow of HDC into a learnable network, called learnable HDC (L-HDC). L-HDC explicitly emulates the fundamental operations of HDC and learns the feature correlation of input data by backpropagation. After training, we transform L-HDC back to the original HDC, while the weights of L-HDC are kept in the original HDC to perform feature-aware projection. Given the characteristics of high energy efficiency and fast adaptability, HDC models on resource-limited devices can efficiently adapt to the user data. We evaluate the effectiveness of our proposed framework on two benchmark datasets, including the speech recognition dataset ISOLET [16] and the human activity recognition dataset UCIHAR [17]. Based on our simulation results under the settings of a user adaptation framework, our proposed HDC with learnable projection outperforms that with the original projection by 4.8% and 3.5% in ISOLET and UCIHAR, respectively. To the best of our knowledge, this paper first applies HDC with learnable projection to a user adaptation framework to improve classification accuracy.

The rest of the paper is organized as follows. Section 2 describes the algorithm of HDC. Section 3 illustrates our proposed HDC with learnable projection for the user adaptation framework. Experimental settings and simulation results are shown in Sect. 4. Finally, we conclude this paper in Sect. 5.

2 Hyperdimensional Computing

HDC operates with randomly generated bipolar HVs whose components are -1 or 1 with equal probability. The processing flow of HDC is shown in Fig. 2 and includes the following steps.

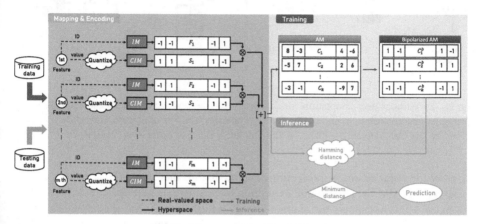

Fig. 2. The processing flow of HDC.

Projection into HD Space. The first step of HDC is to project features into HVs. A feature comprises two parts, i.e., its feature identifier (ID) and its actual value, which are projected into d-dimensional HVs through an Item Memory (IM) and a Continuous Item Memory (CIM), respectively. Assume there are m features in one data sample, $IM = \{F_1, F_2, \ldots F_m\} \in \{+1, -1\}^d$, where F_k is the projected HV for the kth feature ID. When d is large enough, every two HVs in IM are nearly orthogonal [18], which means $Hamming(F_i, F_j) \cong 0.5$, if $i \neq j$ and $Hamming(\cdot)$ is the normalized Hamming distance between two vectors. In other words, the projection of the original HDC assumes that there is approximately no correlation among each feature.

CIM is used as a look-up table to project the actual value into an HV. HDC generates the CIM by the following procedures. First, HDC finds the maximum value V_{max} and minimum value V_{min} for each feature. The range between V_{max} and V_{min} is then equally quantized to Q levels, denoted by $\{l_1, l_2, \ldots l_Q\} \in \mathbb{Z}$ with l_1 and l_Q corresponding to V_{max} and V_{min}. Each scalar in $\{l_1, l_2, \ldots l_Q\}$ is associated with an HV in $CIM = \{L_1, L_2, \ldots L_Q\} \in \{+1, -1\}^d$. Namely, L_k is the projected HV for l_k. Moreover, to preserve the spatial correlation of neighboring levels, if l_i and l_j are relatively close, L_i and L_j have relatively small Hamming distance. To achieve this, two randomly generated HVs L_1 and L_Q are first assigned to V_{max} and V_{min}, respectively. Then, d/Q randomly selected bits are flipped to generate an HV for the next level. This process repeats until

Q HVs in *CIM* are generated. The bit-flipping approach ensures a high correlation between adjacent levels, while L_1 and L_Q are orthogonal. For each feature, by looking up the nearest quantized level to its actual value, the HV for its value is selected and denoted as S_k, where $S_k \in CIM, k = 1, 2, \ldots, m$. After projecting each feature into HVs, a set of two-vector pairs $P = \{(F_1, S_1), (F_2, S_2), \ldots, (F_m, S_m)\}$ is generated for the following step.

Encoding. In this stage, HDC encodes the set P into one representative HV. First, HDC performs the binding operation, an element-wise XOR operation ($\otimes$) between two HVs, to each two-vector pair in the set P and generates m HVs. Then, HDC bundles those m HVs into an encoded HV $T \in \{+1, -1\}^d$ by performing element-wise addition (+) followed by a sign function [·], which is expressed as

$$T = [F_1 \otimes S_1 + F_2 \otimes S_2 + \ldots + F_m \otimes S_m]. \tag{1}$$

Training. After encoding, we denote T_i^j as the encoded HV of the jth data sample corresponding to the ith class. Then, HVs belonging to the ith class are accumulated to form a class HV $C_i \in \mathbb{Z}^d$, which is computed as:

$$C_i = T_i^1 + T_i^2 + \cdots + T_i^{(n_i)}. \tag{2}$$

n_i is the number of data samples in the ith class. For a k-class classification task, there are k class HVs stored in an Associative Memory $AM = \{C_1, C_2, \ldots C_k\} \in \mathbb{Z}^d$. To perform efficient inference on devices, HDC bipolarizes each class HV in AM into a bipolarized one and generate a corresponding bipolarized AM $AM^b = \left\{C_1^b, C_2^b, \ldots C_{(k)}^b\right\} \in \{+1, -1\}^d$, where $C_i^b = [C_i]$.

Inference. In the inference phase, a testing data is first transformed by (1) and is encoded as a query HV. Then, HDC computes the Hamming distance between the query HV and the class HVs in the bipolarized AM. The class with the minimum distance is outputted as a prediction.

Adaptation. To enhance the classification accuracy, HDC performs adaptation by iteratively validating the training data. If the training sample is correctly classified, no change happens. However, if the query HV H of the training sample is misclassified, then H is added to the correct class HV $C_{correct}$ in AM and subtracted from the incorrectly predicted class HV C_{miss}, which can be computed as:

$$C_{correct} = C_{correct} + H, C_{miss} = C_{miss} - H. \tag{3}$$

Note that we compute the Hamming distance with the AM^b but update the AM. After several iterations, the new AM^b is obtained by bipolarizing the updated AM.

3 Proposed Hyperdimensional Computing with Learnable Projection for User Adaptation Framework

In this section, we introduce two proposed techniques used in HDC for the user adaptation framework, as illustrated in Fig. 3. The first one is the learnable projection, which transforms the original HDC into a learnable network L-HDC. The architecture of L-HDC is similar to a binarized neural network (BNN) [19] since both models compute with bipolar weights. When training on cloud, L-HDC learns a better feature-aware projection by backpropagation compared with the original one described in Sect. 2. Then, the weights of learnable projection in L-HDC are transformed back to the learned *IM* and learned *CIM* to utilize the efficient and fast adaptability of HDC on resource-limited devices. The second one is the AM fusion mechanism to exploit the information learned from L-HDC and further improve the performance when we deploy HDC on devices. The details of these two techniques are elaborated as follows.

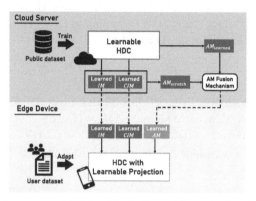

Fig. 3. Overview of the proposed HDC with the learnable projection for the user adaptation framework.

3.1 Learnable Projection

Model Architecture and Parameters. Assume that HDC is with d dimensions, m feature components, Q quantized levels, and k classes. Then, the components of IM, CIM, and AM of HDC are represented in Fig. 4(a). To transform HDC into a learnable network, L-HDC comprises two layers, as shown in Fig. 4(b). The first layer is tailored to emulate the projection and encoding parts of the original HDC. The parameters of the first layer contain two sets of weights denoted as $W^{IM} \in \{+1, -1\}^{m \times d}$ and $W^{CIM} \in \{+1, -1\}^{Q \times d}$ corresponding to the IM and CIM in the original HDC. The second layer is a fully connected (FC) layer whose weights represent the AM in the original HDC and are denoted as $W^{AM} \in \{+1, -1\}^{k \times d}$. In this paper, $W^{IM}[i][j]$, $W^{CIM}[i][j]$, and $W^{AM}[i][j]$ symbolize the entry of the ith row and the jth column of the W^{IM}, W^{CIM}, and W^{AM}, respectively.

Index of Feature Values. To facilitate the subsequent training, we find the index of each feature value by looking up its nearest quantized level and record the index in

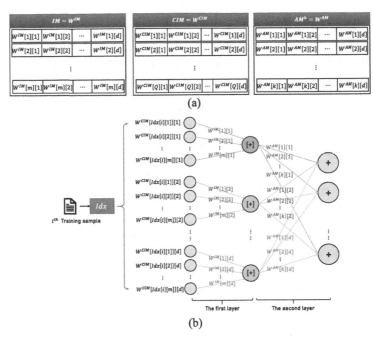

Fig. 4. (a) Demonstration of weights in L-HDC corresponding to memory tables in the original HDC. (b) The overall architecture of L-HDC.

a matrix $Idx \in \mathbb{Z}^{n \times m}$, where n is the number of the training samples with m feature components. $Idx[i][j]$ symbolizes the entry of the ith row and the jth column of Idx.

Training with Bipolar Weights. In L-HDC, the training method used in the second layer (FC layer) is similar to that in BNN [19], which uses bipolar weights to compute gradients and accumulates the gradients on real-valued weights. However, the connection of the first layer tailored for HDC is not FC so that we cannot directly apply the training method in BNN. To solve this problem, we illustrate how to update and compute the gradients of W^{IM} and W^{CIM} as follows.

Suppose the gradient of the output of the first layer computed by the ith training sample is $g \in R^d$, the gradient of W^{IM}, denoted as $g^{IM} \in R^{m \times d}$, is computed as

$$g^{IM}[j] = g \cdot W^{CIM}[Idx[i][j]], for\, j = 1, 2, \ldots, m, \qquad (4)$$

where $\cdot$ is the dot product of two vectors. And the gradient of W^{CIM}, denoted as $g^{CIM} \in R^{Q \times d}$, is computed as

$$g^{CIM}[Idx[i][j]] = \sum \left(g \cdot W^{IM}[j] \right), for\, j = 1, 2, \ldots, m. \qquad (5)$$

Finally, we update W^{IM} and W^{CIM} by the gradients obtained from (4) and (5) with the updating techniques mentioned in [19].

3.2 AM Fusion Mechanism

In the training and adaptation process, L-HDC needs to iteratively compute gradients of weights and update weights by the gradient descent, which cause huge computational burdens on edge devices. Therefore, after completing training L-HDC in the cloud, we transform the architecture of L-HDC back to that of the original HDC to efficiently adapt to user's data by using (3). Note that the W^{IM} and W^{CIM} of L-HDC become the corresponding HVs in the learned *IM* and the learned *CIM* of HDC, which preserves the information of the feature correlations. However, since W^{AM} is in the bipolar representation and the adaptation of HDC relies on updating *AM*, whose components are integers, we cannot directly apply W^{AM} to the original HDC.

Intuitively, based on the learned *IM* and the learned *CIM*, we can obtain a new AM, denoted as $AM_{scratch}$, by training HDC from scratch. Nevertheless, the information learned in W^{AM} of L-HDC can be further exploited to improve the performance. To inherit the information in W^{AM}, we first transform W^{AM} into an AM, whose HVs corresponds to the weights of W^{AM}. Then, we multiply the AM by a scaling factor γ to generate $AM_{learned}$ with integer HVs and add $AM_{scratch}$ to $AM_{learned}$ followed by division by 2. Lastly, the combined AM is deployed to edge devices for further user adaptation. In Sect. 4, we demonstrate that the AM fusion mechanism which combines two types of AMs achieves higher accuracy than directly using one $AM_{scratch}$.

4   Experimental Settings and Simulation Results

4.1   Datasets and Experimental Setup

To evaluate the effectiveness of our proposed techniques for the user adaptation framework, we conduct experiments on two benchmark datasets, including the speech recognition ISOLET dataset [16] and the human activity recognition UCIHAR dataset [17]. In ISOLET, 150 subjects speak the name of 26 letters of the alphabets, and 617 features of voice signals are extracted. Each subject contains 52 data samples. As for UCIHAR, it recognizes 6 human activities based on 3-axial linear acceleration and angular velocity at a constant rate of 50 Hz. There are 30 subjects in UCIHAR and each is with 343 data samples on average.

To simulate the scenario of user adaptation, we refer to the experimental settings in [5, 7]. For both datasets, we first divide them by subjects into two parts, representing the public dataset on cloud and the user dataset on edge. In practice, we randomly divide the ISOLET dataset into 100 subjects and 50 subjects as the public dataset and the user dataset, respectively. Likewise, we randomly divide UCIHAR dataset into 25 subjects and 5 subjects as the public dataset and the user dataset. Then, we further separate the public dataset into the public training dataset and the public validation dataset set with the ratio of 3:1. And the user dataset is also divided into the user adaptation dataset and the user testing dataset with the ratio of 1:1.

In the experiments, we first train L-HDC by the public training data with a learning rate of 0.001 and evaluate it with the public validation data to obtain the best model. After training, we generate the learned *IM*, *CIM*, and the new *AM* by the AM fusion mechanism for the HDC model on edge. Then, the user adaptation data is used to adapt the HDC model. Finally, we utilize the user testing data to evaluate the accuracy of the HDC model. All experiments are conducted over 10 independent trials to obtain the averaged simulation results. The experimental setups are summarized in Table 1.

Table 1. Experimental setups for the user adaptation framework in (a) the ISOLET dataset and (b) the UCIHAR dataset.

Dataset	(a) ISOLET	(b) UCIHAR
# of subjects	150	30
# of classes	26	6
# of data in public training dataset	3,900	6,435
# of data in public validation dataset	1,300	2,140
# of data in user adaptation dataset	1,300	865
# of data in user testing dataset	1,300	850

4.2 Comparisons

We compare our proposed framework with the other two for user adaptation, including the original HDC framework, and the L-HDC framework without the AM fusion mechanism. All the frameworks train the model with 100 iterations on cloud and adapt the model with 50 iterations to ensure performance saturation. The details of these two compared frameworks are described as follows.

Original HDC Framework. Compared with our proposed framework, the original HDC framework trains the original HDC model on cloud and directly deploys the trained HDC model on devices for user adaptation. As shown in the simulation results, our proposed framework with the learnable projection achieves higher accuracy than the original HDC framework which ignores the feature correlations.

Our Proposed Framework without AM Fusion Mechanism. After training L-HDC on cloud, the learned IM and the learn CIM are deployed to the HDC model on edge. But in this comparison, we only transfer $AM_{scratch}$ to edge devices for user adaptation rather than that obtained by the AM fusion mechanism. The simulation results demonstrate that the AM fusion mechanism performs better than that with $AM_{scratch}$ after adaptation.

4.3 Analysis of Accuracy

Figure 5 illustrates the accuracy curves on the user testing data of different frameworks in ISOLET and UCIHAR. Compared with the original HDC framework with $d = 3,000$, our proposed framework with the same dimensionality improves 4.9% and 11.3% of accuracy in ISOLET and UCIHAR, respectively, before adaptation (training iterations $= 100$). On the other hand, our proposed framework still provides 1.1% and 3.5%

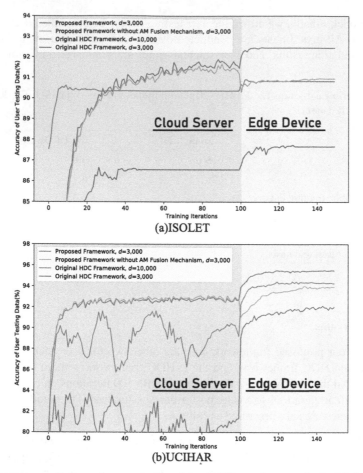

Fig. 5. Accuracy analysis on the user testing data of different frameworks in (a) the ISOLET dataset and (b) the UCIHAR dataset.

accuracy improvement compared to the original HDC framework with higher dimension $d = 10{,}000$. Both simulation results demonstrate L-HDC with the learnable projection achieves better performance than HDC with the original projection method since the feature correlations are considered. Compared with our proposed framework without the AM fusion mechanism, that with the AM fusion mechanism achieves 1.5% and 1.6% higher accuracy in ISOLET and UCIHAR, respectively, after adaptation (training iterations $= 150$). The results show that the AM fusion mechanism can effectively preserve the knowledge learned from L-HDC and thus improve the performance. Overall, the proposed framework outperforms the original HDC framework by 4.8% and 3.5% in ISOLET and UCIHAR, respectively. All simulation results are summarized in Table 2.

Table 2. Averaged accuracy of different frameworks on the user testing data in (a) the ISOLET dataset and (b) the UCIHAR dataset

	Accuracy on User Testing Data (%)			
	(a) ISOLET		(b) UCIHAR	
Training iterations	100	150	100	150
Proposed framework, $d = 3,000$	91.46	**92.44**	92.72	**95.54**
Proposed framework without AM fusion mechanism, $d = 3,000$	91.46	90.93	92.72	93.95
Original HDC framework, $d = 10,000$	90.34	90.81	89.26	94.3
Original HDC framework, $d = 3,000$	86.54	87.65	81.38	92.04

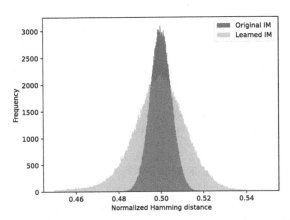

Fig. 6. Histogram of the normalized Hamming distance between each two HVs in the learned IM (orange) and the original IM (blue) (Color figure online)

4.4 Analysis of Learnable Projection

Figure 6 illustrates the histogram of the normalized Hamming distance between each HV in the *IM* of the original HDC and the learned *IM* obtained from L-HDC, respectively. As mentioned in Sect. 2, HVs in *IM* of the original HDC are nearly orthogonal to each other. This indicates that features are uncorrelated to each other, and thus most of their mutual normalized Hamming distance is around 0.5. For the learned *IM*, L-HDC can learn the feature correlations during the training process. Therefore, the histogram of the learned *IM* is more diverse and provides HDC with a better projection for higher performance, as shown in Sect. 4.3.

5   Conclusions

In this paper, we propose two techniques, learnable projection and AM fusion mechanism, to improve the performance of HDC in the user adaptation framework. We transform the architecture of the original HDC into L-HDC to learn the feature correlations of data. Moreover, the AM fusion mechanism exploits the AM obtained from L-HDC to further improve HDC model's performance.

Based on the simulation results, L-HDC gives each deployed model a better initial point than the original HDC in terms of accuracy for 4.9% and 11.3% improvement in ISOLET and UCIHAR, respectively. Moreover, AM fusion mechanism avoids the accuracy degradation and enhances the accuracy progress on edge devices. Overall, our proposed framework compared with the original HDC framework improves 4.8% and 3.5% of accuracy in ISOLET and UCIHAR, respectively.

Acknowledgments.. This work was supported by the Ministry of Science and Technology of Taiwan under Grants MOST 109-2221-E-002-175 and MOST 110-2218-E-002-034 -MBK.

References

1. Gubbi, J., Buyya, R., Marusic, S., Palaniswami, M.: Internet of Things (IoT): a vision, architectural elements, and future directions. Future Gener. Comput. Syst. **29**(7), 1645–1660 (2013)
2. Song, M., et al.: In-Situ AI: towards autonomous and incremental deep learning for iot systems. In: IEEE International Symposium on High Performance Computer Architecture (HPCA), Vienna, Austria, pp. 92–103. IEEE (2018)
3. Rahimi, A., Kanerva, P., Benini, L., Rabaey, J.M.: Efficient biosignal processing using hyperdimensional computing: Network templates for combined learning and classification of ExG signals. Proc. IEEE **107**(1), 123–143 (2019)
4. He, J., Zhang, D., Jiang, N., Sheng, X., Farina, D., Zhu, X.: User adaptation in long-term, open-loop myoelectric training: implications for EMG pattern recognition in prosthesis control. J. Neural Eng. **12**(4), (2015)
5. Choi, S., Sim, J., Kang, M., Choi, Y., Kim, H., Kim, L.S.: An energy-efficient deep convolutional neural network training accelerator for in situ personalization on smart devices. IEEE J. Solid-State Circuits **55**(10), 2691–2702 (2020)
6. Lange, M.D., Jia, X., Parisot, S., Leonardis, A., Slabaugh, G., Tuytelaars, T.: Unsupervised model personalization while preserving privacy and scalability: an open problem. In: Proceedings of the IEEE/CVF Conference on Computer Vision and Pattern Recognition, pp. 14463–14472 (2020)
7. Matsui, S., Inoue, N., Akagi, Y., Nagino, G., Shinoda, K.: User adaptation of convolutional neural network for human activity recognition. In: 25th European Signal Processing Conference (EUSIPCO), Kos, pp. 753–757. IEEE (2017)
8. Satyanarayanan, M.: The emergence of edge computing. Computer **50**(1), 30–39 (2017)
9. Huang, S.A., Chang, K.C., Liou, H.H., Yang, C.H.: A 1.9-MW SVM processor with on-chip active learning for epileptic seizure control. IEEE J. Solid-State Circuits **55**(2), 452–464 (2019)
10. Choi, S., Shin, J., Choi, Y., Kim, L.S.: An optimized design technique of low-bit neural network training for personalization on IoT devices. In: Proceedings of the 56th Annual Design Automation Conference, pp. 1–6 (2019)
11. Kanerva, P.: Hyperdimensional computing: an introduction to computing in distributed representation with high-dimensional random vectors. Cognit. Comput. **1**(2), 139–159 (2009)
12. Chang, C.-Y., Chuang, Y.-C., Wu, A.-Y.A.: Task-projected hyperdimensional computing for multi-task learning. In: Maglogiannis, I., Iliadis, L., Pimenidis, E. (eds.) AIAI 2020. IAICT, vol. 583, pp. 241–251. Springer, Cham (2020). https://doi.org/10.1007/978-3-030-49161-1_21

13. Chuang, Y.-C., Chang, C.-Y., Wu, A.-Y.A.: Dynamic hyperdimensional computing for improving accuracy-energy efficiency trade-offs. In: IEEE Workshop on Signal Processing Systems (SiPS), Coimbra, Portugal, pp. 1–5. IEEE (2020)
14. Chang, C.-Y., Chuang, Y.-C., Wu, A.-Y.A.: IP-HDC: information-preserved hyperdimensional computing for multi-task learning. In: IEEE Workshop on Signal Processing Systems (SiPS), Coimbra, Portugal, pp. 1–6. IEEE (2020)
15. Chang, E.J., Rahimi, A., Benini, L., Wu, A.Y.: Hyperdimensional computing-based multimodality emotion recognition with physiological signals. In: IEEE International Conference on Artificial Intelligence Circuits and Systems (AICAS), Hsinchu, Taiwan, pp. 137–141. IEEE (2019)
16. Uci machine learning repository. http://archive.ics.uci.edu/ml/datasets/ISOLET. Accessed 01 Mar 2021
17. Anguita, D., Ghio, A., Oneto, L., Parra, X., Reyes-Ortiz, J.L.: A public domain dataset for human activity recognition using smartphones. In: European Symposium on Artificial Neural Networks, pp. 1–3 (2013)
18. Plate, T.A.: Holographic reduced representations. IEEE Trans. Neural Netw. $6(3)$, 623–641 (1995)
19. Courbariaux, M., Hubara, I., Soudry, D., El-Yaniv, R., Bengio, Y.: Binarized neural networks: training deep neural networks with weights and activations constrained to $+1$ or -1. arXiv preprint arXiv:1602.02830 (2016)

Internet of Things/Internet of Energy

"SAVE" – An Integrated Approach of Personal and Home Safety for Active Assisted Living

Sorin-Aurel Moraru[1]([✉]), Adrian Alexandru Moşoi[2], Dominic Mircea Kristaly[1],
Florin Sandu[3], Dan Floroian[1], Delia Elisabeta Ungureanu[1], and Liviu Marian Perniu[1]

[1] Department of Automatics and Information Technology,
Transilvania University of Braşov, Braşov, Romania
`smoraru@unitbv.ro`
[2] Department of Psychology, Education and Teacher Training, Faculty of Psychology
and Education Sciences, Transilvania University of Braşov, Braşov, Romania
[3] Department of Electronics and Computers,
Transilvania University of Braşov, Braşov, Romania

Abstract. The paper presents the concept and demonstrator of "SAVE – SAfety of elderly people and Vicinity Ensuring", an integrated approach of personal and residential security. This AAL (Active Assisted Living) system aims to support elderly end-users staying in their familiar home and surroundings for as long as possible, being safely and permanently in contact with their caregivers. The top-down Universal Modeling Language (UML) service orientation enabled a unified co-design of both human and machine communications. Furthermore, the present concept includes an integrated subscription mechanism for people and devices, in a multi-tier user structure and a central-local distributed processing (Cloud-Edge). There are presented the end-user perspective, selection and involvement (in pilot prototyping of the SAVE demonstrator), considering cognitive age-related issues, oriented on usability and on the functional specifications of interfacing via web-apps (independent of the mobile platforms operating system). Location Based Services (LBS) manage data from the Geographical Information Systems (GIS) in a unified modern way, based on LISP – Location - (from) Identity Separation Protocol. These services of "orientation" – localization, real-time tracking – are integrated with another aspect of "restoring the referential" (both personal and communitarian): (re-) planning service, improving alert information in case of emergency, bilateral push-pull of security notifications. Restoring the end-users well-being takes benefit of eHealth and actigraphy services. The other approach, bottom-up, is based on micro-services software/netware implementation, modern smartwatches/smartphones and wearable devices, leveraging their programmability and multi-modal and multi-range (near-field or cellular) communications.

Keywords: Active Assisted Living · Micro-services · Internet of Things · Wearable devices

I. Maglogiannis et al. (Eds.): AIAI 2021, IFIP AICT 627, pp. 451–464, 2021.
https://doi.org/10.1007/978-3-030-79150-6_36

1 Introduction

Maintaining the health of the elderly is a continuing concern in communities. The use of technologies becomes an important resource in achieving this goal and an opportunity in using them. The purpose of these technologies is to provide an active lifestyle mode to the elderly [1] by involving them in various activities. The technologies aimed to the elderly are limited in usability as they are not familiar about of their own coordinates, security, alerts, use of a smart-phones or a e-Health system [2]. Developing non-intrusive technologies is becoming a challenge nowadays [3]. Moreover, not only technologies can make a significant contribution, but also the physical exercise [4]. Elderly people feel to be more inactive, start to be at risk on a sedentary behavior. A possible solution is Internet of Thinks (IoT) integrated in an e-Health system that could be adaptable to the elderly and caregivers needs. Furthermore, another concern is about creating an infrastructure capable of collecting data in an independent and continuous manner [5].

This paper proposes a concept and a demonstrator that is intended to be a possible response for the integrated approach of security of the elderly. Furthermore, this system should be also used like a product for an intelligent home. This concept is called SAVE ("SAfety of elderly people and Vicinity Ensuring").

2 Sensor Networking

The SAVE solution (see Fig. 1) uses several types of sensors (wearable and ambient/domotic) to obtain information about the well-being of the elderly in his/her habitat (home, neighborhood, etc.) and to ensure safety. The solution also has several features that older people can use in case of danger (SOS button fall detection). In Fig. 1 are presented the users and the technologies that work together in order to obtain the goals. The elderly habitat is the host for ambient sensors, eHealth device and also for the user that has many sensors grouped in the smartwatch and smartphone. The systems collect the info from all the sensors but will only activate the needed ones. Data collected by the sensors refers to biological signals, GPS data, humidity of the environment, light of the environment, human presence in the habitat. They are secured by coding them, and are separated from personal details in order to prevent data leakage. After that, they are sent by GSM or Wi-Fi network in the SAVE Cloud. Here after some basic processing steps, they are used to alert or inform the caregivers on their smartphones, and also are collected to be analyzed by SAVE experts and also if needed by the 3rd part services.

The sensors are installed in the end-user's habitat. The smartwatch can connect to the Internet directly, using the GSM network (if eSIM is supported), through a smartphone to which is connected (by Bluetooth or Wi-Fi) or through other Wi-Fi connections. In the scenario considered by the SAVE project, the smartwatch supports eSIM, to be able to send - without delays - the location data.

All the sensing devices connect through the Internet to the SAVE cloud application. This application is built on the micro-services architecture. The data collector service manages the access to the sensor data, the sensors adapters shape the raw sensor data to match the data collector's input and the security center provides the cryptographic-based security layer (based on HTTPS – Hypertext Transfer Protocol/Secure, API keys and JWT – JSON Web Tokens). The data is collected in a partitioned relational database.

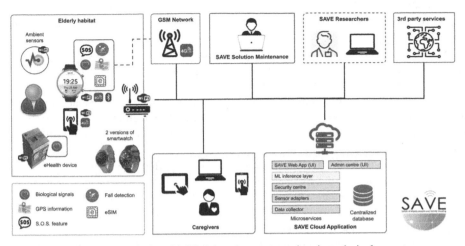

Fig. 1. SAVE solution, highlighting the actors and main technical aspects

There are 2 use interfaces: one for the elderly and the caregivers (SAVE Web App) and one for the SAVE solution maintainers and SAVE researchers (AdminCentre). Both user interfaces are developed as responsive web applications.

3   Involvement of the Elderly and Their Caregivers

The SAVE solution offers seniors a set of sensors that contain, at a minimum, an e-Health device and a smartwatch (e.g. Samsung Galaxy Watch 3) with SAVE software pre-installed. The kit may include other environmental sensors (e.g. presence, magnetic contact, flood sensor), which will connect to the SAVE Cloud application in the classical "Edge/Cloud" local/centralized allocation of resources – from embedded systems to high-capacity data-centers. Elderly people also receive rights to access the SAVE web application, also can request additional accreditation for their caregivers.

For the pilot sites, the support will be provided, when necessary, by maintaining the SAVE solution for caregivers in order to configure the SAVE software on the smartwatch and to make other necessary configurations (WiFi connection, eSim installation, sensor configuration, etc.).

4   An Integrated Solution – The e-Health System

The e-Health equipment is actually "a complex sensor", consisting of several individual devices for measuring (e.g. blood biological parameters pressure, pulse, temperature) and activities (e.g. body position) of the elderly. This equipment connects to the Internet through the local WiFi network. The smartwatch acts as a portable sensor and connects to the Internet via the GSM network (if the LTE function is used and an eSIM is present) – this is the scenario recommended in SAVE – or via WiFi, by connecting to the local WiFi network or to a hotspot opened by the elderly smartphone (which has mobile data enabled). In the current phase of the SAVE demonstrator, they are included also some extra safety features (SOS and fall detection) associated with a Bluetooth tethering connection.

Samsung Galaxy Smartwatch 3 includes a wide range of sensors that can be used to assess physical activity (steps, frequency of steps, speed of movement) and to read some basic biological signals (e.g. pulse) that will be used in the analysis of user data regarding his/her wellness. The GPS sensor, together with the gyroscope and accelerometer [6] are used to ensure the safety of the elderly (location, fall detector). This smartwatch is a leading edge for smartwatch world and its own specification grows with each release [7].

The smartwatch selected for the SAVE demonstrator offers LTE communication and includes in its firmware the SOS and fall detection features. The elderly can call for emergency help and assistance by quickly pressing the power button 3 times. The smartwatch sends a SMS containing a standard message and the location of the smartwatch owner and then calls the designated caregiver.

If a fall is detected [8], the smartwatch will display a 60-s warning to the elderly; if the warning is not manually rejected, the smartwatch will send SMS messages and automatically call a designated contact (a caregiver).

5   Use of Technological Resources in SAVE

The SAVE minimal kit can be complemented by commercially available sensor sets (for example, the Xiaomi Mi Smart Home kit). However, these kits have their own user interfaces, but once configured they do not require any additional human intervention [9]. These kits usually include devices that can generate audible warnings when certain situations are detected (the door left open too much, the unexpected presence in a certain perimeter, etc.).

The work is underway to include more physiological wearable sensors in the SAVE minimal kit. Some cheaper alternatives to the smartwatch (for example, the LilyGo "TTGO" [10] programmable watch) are also being investigated.

All sensors included in the minimum kit communicate with the SAVE Cloud application via the Internet, supplying it with sensor data and receiving commands when needed. The preferred mode of communication in the SAVE sensor network is WiFi – in the WSAN [11] (Wireless Sensors & Actuators Network) paradigm.

6   SAVE - Online Health Service

The service is implemented as an online health service (OnHS) and/or an offline health service (OffHS), both involving eHealth sensors used at home. As established in the technology choice phase, in order to meet one of the main requirements of the European AAL initiative in terms of interoperability and open interfaces – to access the European market – the eHealth system concept is oriented towards Open-Source Hardware (OSHW) and COTS (Commercial OF The Shelf) platforms (eHealth, includes COTS biosensors [12]).

The SAVE eHealth system is based on the low-cost platform from Libelium, namely the "MySignals" Hardware Development Platform – an eHealth and Medical IoT Development Platform for Arduino. The demonstrator of eHealth system is based on short and long-range communication protocols, as a scalable base station that offers two services:

- A built-in C++ application provides connection and reading of biometric sensors; it shares data with the Cloud through a web service.
- A web application that allows the management and configuration of the base station; this option was considered better than an application for a smartphone dependent on the operating system (iOS/Android); it allows the configuration of the specific sensor, the trigger of a specific measurement, the display of the measurement result, and sets the connection parameters used for Cloud interaction, from any device connected to the same network as the base station (PC/laptop/smartphone).

The overall architecture of the SAVE system, described in Fig. 2, is composed of several independent components that communicate with each other, in order to serve certain functionalities. The architecture is based on a central server that offers the micro-services to all subsystems. Also here it is located the database and the gateway module for accessing data through the 3$^\text{rd}$ party monitoring and safety systems for user interface. All the micro-services are used to send and receive data to and from all the equipment used: sensors, smart sensors, mobile devices and also web-based user interface.

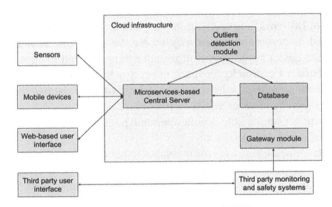

Fig. 2. General architecture of the SAVE system

7   UI Design and Development Requirements

Possible implication in software design according to cognitive decline in the elders:

- **Vision:** one of the most appropriate texts for information display is *sans-serif fonts* with the *size between 12 and 14 points* [13] - the width of the visual field of elderly people reduce;

- **Color:** older people have *less sensitivity to color contrast* especially in the *blue green range*; designers *should not use colors to communicate meaning*, but should use for supporting information presentation;
- **Memory:** the average of the related items to be shown in the display panel used for the older people should be around **5.5 items** for older people, use of long term memory is much more effective than short term memory;
- **Sound:** the devices that require sound as alarm, instruction or any activity that require attention from the elderly users should use the *lower range of frequency* (between 500 and 1000 Hz) - high pitched sounds with peaks over 2500 Hz are mostly missed by the elderly;
- **Attention and Simplicity:** the use of *relevant graphics and pictures* are more significant than the use of detailed decorations; *multitasking* operations *should not be applied* as well - older adults have problems maintaining attention over long periods of time;
- **Motor decline:** small screen on mobile devices may limit usage of elderly users, but a tablet device still has mobility and is still not compromised with screen size - physical decline is one of the general problems for the elderly;
- **Reduction of complexity:** the design of the interaction should *avoid complexities*, for example using short and long press, using combination keys, using multi-fingers, using multi-touch, etc. - *simpler is more usable for elderly users*;
- **Clear structure of tasks:** clearly separated task is the factor that may increase usage performance for elderly [14] - single task per page reduce attention load for older users;
- **Consistency of information:** navigation bars, labelling or any interface components should be used *to communicate exactly where the users are in the application* - elderly users are easier to recognize information than to recall memory [15];
- **Rapid and distinct Feedback:** feedback of every action should be provided within a certain time and it should indicate result or response of each action – due to limitation of short-term memory of older adults;
- **On screen help:** on screen help within operation page should be used - older people have anxiety of using new products;
- **User support:** reduce usage of error messages to become as low as possible; in case that error messages have to be shown, error messages should be simple, precise, polite and understandable - elderly users are sensitive to errors from their actions.

Interface optimization (according to the limitation of motor skills and cognitive abilities of the elderly people):

- Make use of proper size interface components:

  - Touch sensitive area/Size of button should be 16.5 mm to 19.05 mm;
  - Spacing size between button/touch sensitive 3.15 mm to 12.7 mm;

- Avoid using scroll bar;
- Keep operation area in the center of the working page;
- Make use of multi model communication;

- Make use of real object-liked interface;
- Present text the simplest way:

  – Size 14 (~5 mm on 72 dpi screen) or higher

  Make use of sans-serif fonts;
  Make use of black font on white background;
  Avoid using fancy text (moving, non-horizontal orientation, splash).

8   Smartwatch Interface – The SAVE Development

For the smartwatch, a specific SAVE interface has been developed in the form of a clock frame, which fulfills a dual role: portable user interface for the elderly, regardless of its location (inside or outside the house) and portable sensor (for basic biological signals – e.g. pulse, activity monitor - and location) [16].

The dial of the watch is customized according to the SAVE visual identity (as shown in Fig. 3) and has a minimal set of information. To set up the connection to the SAVE Cloud application (performed only once), a separate application has been developed.

Fig. 3. SAVE watch-face

The watch face has been designed to display in an aesthetic and efficient way the necessary information and to collect data provided by the sensors, the location and to display the notifications defined by the user (end-user and/or caregiver) in the web application interface (developed for this purpose), all with minimum energy consumption. The configuration application aims to ensure security and identify the user's profile. Once the application is opened, a text box will appear where a 6-digit PIN must be entered (which is associated with the end-user). After pressing the validation button, the authentication will be confirmed or denied by a corresponding message on the screen, along with the instructions needed to continue the process (see Fig. 4).

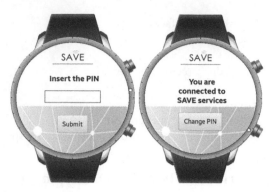

Fig. 4. Registering the smartwatch in the SAVE cloud application

9 SAVE Web Application

The web application has been developed so that end-users (elderly and caregivers) can efficiently and securely access the SAVE solution's features, using a coherent and uniform user interface. This application will be further developed and will offer an even simpler and more intuitive interface for both elderly and their caregivers [17].

The interface now offers two main features:

- management of scheduled notifications;
- real-time tracking service.

The data that is collected from the Cloud server is displayed in a graphical manner, in dedicated pages that are currently under post-prototype development. According to the results of co-design and co-creation with potential SAVE users, these pages are able to present data differently for the elderly and caregivers.

10 Scheduled Notifications

The home page of the web application displays active scheduled notifications (Fig. 5) and also allows the user, who may be elderly and/or caregiver, to define new ones.

The users can customize the notifications according to their needs by typing their own messages, choosing an icon and by setting notification display frequency: every day, on certain days of the week, on a specific date. For each of the previous options, the user will also choose the time when the notification will be displayed. The application also offers the users the possibility to delete notifications.

10.1 Real-Time Tracking Service

The app offers a user location function [18] that can be accessed from the menu bar. A person's current location is marked on a map in real-time, along with the location of his/her home and his/her 10 previous locations (see Fig. 6).

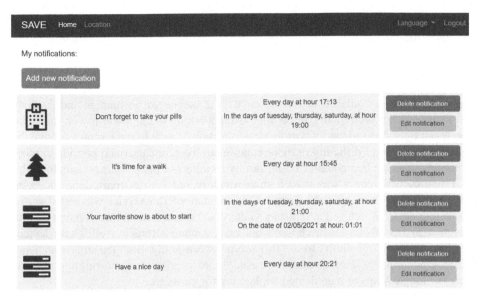

Fig. 5. Active notifications on the dashboard page

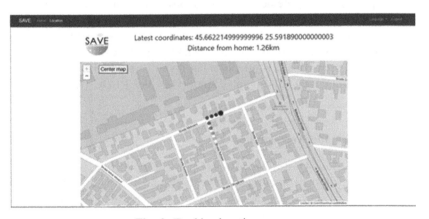

Fig. 6. Tracking location screen

This helps caregivers to check if the end user is in a location, away from home, that they would not normally go to, suggesting that he/she might be disoriented. The distance from home is calculated and can be used to trigger alarms in the case of end users known to have cognitive problems.

Tracking information is kept for a limited period of time and will be used to detect possible disorientation of older people wearing smartwatches (e.g. walking in circles, going back and forth repeatedly, getting lost far away from home etc.).

Users can customize notifications according to their needs, editing their own messages, choosing an icon, and setting how often notifications are displayed: every day, on certain days of the week or at a certain date. For each of the above options, the user can also choose when to display the notification. The app also gives users the ability to delete notifications.

10.2 Localization

The application is available, at this moment, in 2 languages: Romanian and English, and switching between them can be done using a button in the menu bar on the right. The service can be used via a smartphone application: it aims to track routes outside the home and, in case of difficulty or disorientation, to locate the user and provide him/her directions to return home and/or notify family members or personal assistants for help.

For these services it was used a smartwatch paired with a smartphone to get an exact location and to use a public service for orientation. This service was tested with a Samsung Galaxy Watch and a Samsung Galaxy S20 smartphone for demonstration, but the watch and the phone can be chosen from another manufacturer as well. These devices have demonstrated the ability to use this service successfully. Both the smartwatch and the smartphone have GPS sensors and we used "share location" for reporting applications such as Google Maps or a dedicated application for guidance.

In order to take benefit from the new Location (from) Identity Separation Protocols, we used "The LISP Beta Network" [19] that stopped providing services in May 2020 and we are in the process to migrate our SAVE solutions to an own server. To enable easier identification of an end-user in need LISP separates the ID of the wearable devices from their location – thus, direct connection to the device(s) is used and, in the case of multi-homing, reliability is improved by providing multiple paths for this data connection. LISP is commonly used with IPv4 or IPv6, but it can be used with any other type of addressing for the dual EID (End-point IDentifier) and/or RLOC (Routing LOCator) addresses.

10.3 Compatibility and Accessibility

The SAVE web application is developed as a responsive application, using the Bootstrap library, so the user interface is compatible with all major browsers and with mobile devices (smartphones/tablets) with a wide range of screen resolutions [20].

10.4 Admin Centre Web Application

Admin Centre is a web application developed to manage data efficiently and securely within the SAVE system. The Admin Centre application is on its 3rd major version; there were several major and minor versions, as a result of multiple design iterations.

The data collecting process is organized in a hierarchical structure; the SAVE solution recognizes several *device types*, that are registered in the SAVE database. The *devices* are also registered in the database and it is mandatory to associate existing device types to them, so the user interfaces will know how to interpret the data (*values*) coming from them. A set of devices form a SAVE *kit*, which is associated with one elderly end-user.

10.5 Security

The service is uniquely able to perform alerts, technological training, bilateral services (push-pull, alert and "ping"), thus giving both the end-user and the supervisor the opportunity to track the patient's health history, automatically storing the results. It can be launched either by the person, but in some cases (for example, loss of consciousness) it should be launched automatically. In case of emergency, it is important to allow the urgent request for help and assistance in the simplest way.

10.6 Improving Alert Information - Personal Alerting/Home Automation Service

This service aims to contribute to the future of "Emergency Calls" which should assist people on "both sides of the line" - not just end users who need (who cannot open applications) such as Google Maps, not only because of cognitive impairment or lack of technical knowledge, but even because of extreme momentary pain), but even volunteers or operators of organizations that cannot interpret complex GIS (Geographic Information Systems) data. For prototyping, it was used a smartwatch that can operate both with a smartphone and stand-alone. It can be customized for any emergency application that will connect to the Cloud.

10.7 Adaptation of Physical Exercise and Social Activities for the Elderly

These activities are led by voluntary organizations, in terms of stress/cognitive assessment services, services based on actigraphy and virtual coach.

Facing health conditions that limit their mobility, they should try to be active daily – examples of activities that require moderate effort for most people include: walking, ballroom dance, pushing various objects, playing table tennis (simple or double). Muscle strength is required for: (a) all daily movements; (b) building and maintaining strong bones (improving balance and daily matching activities); (c) maintaining a healthy weight).

The smartwatch we test will provide alerts and notifications from time to time to keep you active throughout the day. Follow the exercises and can give small indications for simple movements. The Choice Reaction Time (CRT) methodology is based on a visual CRT based on several visual stimuli and two response buttons.

10.8 Personal (Re) Planning Service - "TO DO" List

The purpose of this service is to increase security, prevent social isolation, participate in various programs or occasional activities and maintain the multifunctional network around the person. This tool will help you in planning and conducting daily activities in a safer and more efficient way; care also involves social motivation and involvement. Through the "To Do" section of the application, the elderly user will be helped to remember/update the planned activities, will be informed about the following activities, synchronized in the "personal cloud" of relatives, friends and their formal caregivers).

11   The Co-creation of SAVE Services

In order to know the expectations of end-users, we created cartoon Cards that contained the initial proposals for the possible services. The purpose of these Cards was to stimulate a discussion with potential end-users and caregivers about their real needs in the areas covered by SAVE services. The answers to the questions were left in the mailboxes, so one of the SAVE researchers collected them from each user. Our argument was that the share of the Internet on the Romanian elderly population is low, by 13%, compared to the European elderly population, by 45% [21].

Following the responses, each of the users was called to have a feedback and to understand their needs and most importantly their expectation on our part, in accordance with the SAVE objectives.

For example, many older Romanians have mobile phones, but fewer also have home sensors in their homes. Only 44% of the Romanian population between 55 and 74 years old use the internet [22], only 30% of them use it several times in four days (on average). A 2013 statistics report showed that only 16% of the Romanian population over the age of 65 had internet at home. Therefore, the human-computer interaction was new for almost all elderly Romanians targeted by SAVE.

12   Conclusions

The "SAVE" proof-of-concept is a system integration solution, based on top-down universal modeling – service-oriented and state-driven.

The service co-creation involved end-users and caregivers, with a multi-criteria selection and prioritization, an "Agile" interface design considering not only usability but also carefully documented age-related cognitive limitations.

The services are centered on security and (re-)orientation, not only as location but also as restoring a personal and communitarian referential through (re-)planning, notifications, alerts, enhanced information in case of emergency. End-users are enabled to restore also their well-being and to use frequently the eHealth services.

The unified safety approach of the person in the intelligent house is made possible by the recent progress in H2H, H2M, and M2M (Human-to-...-Machine) communications, using same Internet-based protocols. These are ranging from IoT to LISP. SAVE data structures are flexible, for both Edge & Cloud processing and storage, adapted to microservices and RE presentational State Transfer (REST) based web-services.

COTS (Commercial Of The Shelf) devices – both "domotic" and wearable – have built-in radio interfaces and can interact with WSAN (Wireless and Actuators Networks) via a smartphone data concentrator or even stand-alone. SAVE demonstrator integrates smartwatches with own programmability that have improved battery life.

Last but not least, the SAVE tele-services were re-considered and improved in the dramatic context of the corona virus pandemic.

References

1. Tornero-Quiñones, I., Sáez-Padilla, J., Espina Díaz, A., Abad Robles, M.T., Sierra Robles, Á.: Functional ability, frailty and risk of falls in the elderly: relations with autonomy in daily living. Int. J. Environ. Res. Public Health **17**, 1006 (2020). https://doi.org/10.3390/ijerph170 31006
2. Ben Hassen, H., Dghais, W., Hamdi, B.: An E-health system for monitoring elderly health based on Internet of Things and Fog computing. Health Inf. Sci. Syst. **7**, 24 (2019). https://doi.org/10.1007/s13755-019-0087-z
3. Ihianle, I-K., Naeem, U., Tawil, A-R., Azam, M-A.: Recognizing activities of daily living from patterns and extraction of web knowledge. In: Proceedings of the 2016 ACM International Joint Conference on Pervasive and Ubiquitous Computing, pp. 1255–1262 (2016). https://doi.org/10.1145/2968219.2968440
4. Chen, F.-T., et al.: The effect of exercise training on brain structure and function in older adults: a systematic review based on evidence from randomized control trials. J. Clin. Med. **9**, 914 (2020)
5. Almeida, A., Mulero, R., Rametta, P., Urošević, V., Andrić, M., Patrono, L.: A critical analysis of an IoT—Aware AAL system for elderly monitoring. Future Gener. Comput. Syst. **97**, 598–619 (2019). https://doi.org/10.1016/j.future.2019.03.019
6. Koene, I., Klar, V., Viitala, R.: IoT connected device for vibration analysis and measurement. Hardw. X **7**, 1–15 (2020)
7. https://www.samsung.com/ro/watches/galaxy-watch/galaxy-watch3-45mm-mystic-black-lte-sm-r845fzkaeue/
8. Majumder, S., et al.: Smart homes for elderly healthcare—Recent advances and research challenges. Sensors **17**, 2496 (2017). https://doi.org/10.3390/s17112496
9. https://www.mi.com/global/mi-smart-sensor-set/
10. Lousado, J.P., Antunes, S.: Monitoring and support for elderly people using LoRa communication technologies: IoT concepts and applications. Future Internet **12**, 206 (2020)
11. Cheng, N., Lu, N., Zhang, N., Xuemin, S., Jon, W.: MarkVehicular WiFi offloading: challenges and solutions. Veh. Commun. **1**(1), 13–21 (2014). https://doi.org/10.1016/j.vehcom.2013.11.002
12. Boumpa, E., Kakarountas, A.: Home supporting smart systems for elderly people. In: Paiva, S., Paul, S. (eds.) Convergence of ICT and Smart Devices for Emerging Applications. EICC, pp. 81–98. Springer, Cham (2020). https://doi.org/10.1007/978-3-030-41368-2_4
13. Charness, N., Schaie, W.-K.: Impact of Technology on Successful Aging. Springer, Heidelberg (2003)
14. Moraru, S.-A., et al.: Home assisted living of elderly people using wireless sensors networks in a cloud system. In: International Symposium in Sensing and Instrumentation in IoT Era (ISSI). IEEE, Shanghai, China (2018). ISBN 978-1-5386-5638-9
15. Dey, P., Sinha, B.R., Amin, M., Badkoobehi, H.: Best practices for improving user interface design. Int. J. Softw. Eng. Appl. (IJSEA) **10**, 5 (2019). https://doi.org/10.5121/ijsea.2019.10505
16. Dodd, C., Adam, M.T.P., Athauda, R.: Designing user interfaces for the elderly: a systematic literature review. In: Australasian Conference on Information Systems, Hobart, Australia (2017)
17. Wong, C.Y.: Mobile user interface for seniors: an impact of ageing population on mobile design. Des. Principles Pract. **4**(4), 231–248 (2010)
18. Alsswey, A., Al-Samarraie, H.: Elderly users' acceptance of mHealth user interface (UI) design-based culture: the moderator role of age. J. Multimodal User Interfaces **14**, 49–59 (2019)

19. Balan, T., Robu, D., Sandu, F.: LISP optimisation of mobile data streaming in connected societies. Mob. Inf. Syst. (2016)
20. Baharum, A., Zain, N.H.M., Taharudin, A., Hanapi, R.: Guidelines of user interface design for elderly mobile applications: a preliminary study. Asian J. Inf. Technol. **16**(1), 38–44 (2017)
21. https://ec.europa.eu/eurostat/cache/infographs/elderly/index.html
22. https://insse.ro/cms/en/content/official-statistics-romania

BEMS in the Era of Internet of Energy: A Review

Asimina Dimara[1,2(✉)], Christos-Nikolaos Anagnostopoulos[2],
Konstantinos Kotis[2], Stelios Krinidis[1], and Dimitrios Tzovaras[1]

[1] Centre for Research and Technology Hellas, Information Technologies Institute,
Thessaloniki, Greece
{adimara,krinidis,Dimitrios.Tzovaras}@iti.gr
[2] Department of Cultural Technology and Communication, Intelligent, Systems Lab,
University of the Aegean, Mytilene, Greece
{canag,kotis}@aegean.gr

Abstract. A Building Energy Management System (BEMS) is a fundamental computer-based system aiming at optimizing management of building assets towards energy savings without compromising occupants' comfort, while developing a potential to apply demand response strategies. Building energy management systems nowadays have evolved and comprise of heterogeneous components and complex architectures. Building management systems monitor indoor building conditions while controlling building assets like lights, security systems, and heating and air ventilation's systems. Furthermore, to facilitate the specification of the building's attributes for building energy management systems the use of semantic technologies is needed within building energy tools. This paper undertakes a comprehensive review of Building Energy systems in the context of Internet of Energy.

Keywords: Building management systems · Building energy
management systems · Building automation · IoT · IoE · SIM

1 Introduction

Presently, one of the most important topics is sustainable development and the preservation of energy levels. The global energy demand is estimated to increase by almost 2/3 until the year 2035 [31]. Moreover, the increased energy demand leads to increased emissions and green house effect, which makes the problem of energy usage even more challenging. Therefore, the concept of energy management and smart grids has been exploited to manage energy demand and energy savings while preserving comfort for the residents.

Particularly, Building Management Systems (BMS) intend to increase energy awareness, control RES distribution, and storage aiming to mitigate the total world energy demand. Nowadays, the BMS have focused more on energy BMS (Building Energy Management Systems (BEMS) and their main purpose is to

Published by Springer Nature Switzerland AG 2021
I. Maglogiannis et al. (Eds.): AIAI 2021, IFIP AICT 627, pp. 465–476, 2021.
https://doi.org/10.1007/978-3-030-79150-6_37

distribute the energy efficiently. Hence, the Internet of Energy (IoE) [21] has been developed for these systems as an extension of the Internet of Things (IoT) to manage Energy in Buildings [30]. This is different from IoE representing the Internet of Everything, and shall be used carefully. In this paper, the IoE will be used with the meaning of Internet of Energy.

IoE is a fusion of smart grid and IoT, combining the basic features of smart grid and IoT, providing a more powerful and tailored-to-energy technology [24]. IoT facilitates the exchange of big data and information retrieved by sensors and smart objects while producing useful services. The IoT is an Internet-based architecture widely used in various sectors like safety systems, military applications, energy monitoring, smart grid management and many others.

The BEMS intend to follow a pattern that will create the Zero Energy Buildings (ZEB) or the modern net zero Energy Buildings (nZEB) [15] (Fig. 1). Based on the European Energy Performance of Buildings Directive Recast 2010 legislation all types of buildings that are going to be built after 31st December 2020 must meet this standard [4]. The nZEB comprises of many parameters like the energy consumed, the renewable supply facilities, the connection to the Distribution System Operators (DSO) and the energy requirements of the building [29]. In view of this, BEMS use building information and data for real-time energy optimization, carbon reduction and also the production of more cost benefit models. Many of the techniques of the IoE-based BEMS are in an early development stage and their performance is under research.

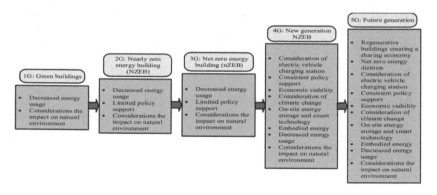

Fig. 1. ZEB history [15]

This paper aims to highlight the different applications of the IoE-based BEMS and Semantics for smart energy management. This review is organized as follows: in Sect. 2 the BEMS are presented. Moreover, in Sect. 3 the semantics for integrating smart control and data management are presented, Finally, conclusions are drawn in the final Sect. 4.

2 Building Energy Management Systems (BEMSs)

A BEMS is a highly developed multi-objective technique aiming to monitor and control the energy balance of a building [29]. Subsequently, the objective of a BEMS is to gain access and maintain the proper energy profile for each building without the need to be fed in detailed parameters for all electric equipment and building's structural information. In addition, a BEMS is supposed to reduce the amount of energy consumed without compromising the residents comfort levels (thermal and visual) through an optimization process that integrates a passive heating and cooling system.

2.1 Energy Consumption Monitoring and Management

To manage the energy consumed in a building there must be a system installed that monitors the power consumption of the facilities. The load monitoring system is one of the main aspects of the energy management of BEMS. There are two approaches used to monitor the energy load, the Intrusive Load Monitoring (ILM) and the Non-Intrusive Load Monitoring (NILM). Another widely disseminated approach for energy consumption monitoring is by exploiting measuring devices.

Intrusive Load Monitoring (ILM). The term intrusive, refers to a metering device installed in the habitation, usually close or inside to the appliance that needs to be monitored. This device is commonly a low-end metering device [37]. ILM is used in many applications like local energy consumption understanding, global energy consumption understanding, appliance monitoring, evaluation of NILM environments, simulation of NILM environments, human activity recognition and appliance localization. The ILM framework comprises of three basic layers. In the first layer, a sensor technology is used to detect the load of an appliance. In the second layer (middleware), there is the software needed to interpret the load of the device. The final layer represents the operational status of the device and is used to monitor and control the device.

Non-Intrusive Load Monitoring (NILM). The NILM approach does not require an installation to each device for the load monitoring. The NILM approach is based on a single device installation at the central electric panel [23]. NILM commonly exploits the disaggregation process to estimate the individual device's consumption [23]. Disaggregation receives an aggregated signal and decomposes it into its individual devices' consumption. Energy disaggregation is a thorny task as each building has many and different appliances, operating at a different power level (nominal power). The load wave forms are decomposed based on the load signatures of each appliance.

Measuring Devices. Measuring devices are all devices used in measuring the energy load of the selected building. There are many types of load monitoring devices like current sensors, voltage sensors, smart meters, smart plugs, fluke meters, energy detectives, and power quality transducers [22]. Moreover, smart plugs can measure and monitor the distinct device load. There are many commercially used smart plugs [22]. The most common device used for load measurement is a smart meter. A smart meter is a device that is used to collect data from the end-users' home appliances and monitors the energy consumption [22]. The handling of an Advanced Metering Infrastructure (AMI) service can support real-time data regarding electricity power [22]. Energy monitoring is essential as energy savings is the fundamental goal of an IoE-based BEMS. The energy management refers to balancing the buildings energy by using multi-attribute decision making methods like the ones proposed in [20].

2.2   IoE-Based Management Applications

Hernández et al. [25] introduced a novel version of an IoE enabled system which is separated into layers and modules comprising of functional components. This layered structure facilitates the interoperability and common operation of the BEMS. Specifically, the model includes three layers: the sensing, delivery and management layer, the data processing and modeling layer, and the smart building services buildings layer as depicetd in Fig. 2.

Sensing, Delivery and Management Layer. This layer is responsible for the sensing, delivery, and management enriched with the important functions of data collection and translation. Initially, all the sensors and actuators retrieving real-time data are installed in the building's specific location. The raw input data is retrieved by an IoT based framework including the sensors, the actuators and databases. Afterwards, this raw data is preprocessed, encoded, and translated in a standard data type that is compatible with all various sub-systems while simplifying the data processing of the next stages.

Data Processing and Modeling Layer. This layer processes and models data based on the key functions. Data processing is used to create the knowledge base for the final stage. This knowledge is user-oriented and customized based on the specific situations and services provision of this stage. Specific forms of provisions are generated like the control actions of household devices, energy consumption monitoring, energy savings etc. Finally, this layer includes the third-party operation modes and encodes the rules and output sources to the specified information platform.

Smart Building Services Buildings Layer. In this layer, the output services like thermal comfort, energy efficiency, security, management, and visual comfort are provided and analyzed. The results reflect the processing of all data which was retrieved in the previous layers. Moreover, this layer includes all applications that may be provided to the end-user, such as graphics, notifications, functions, alarms, and sections of the graphical user interface.

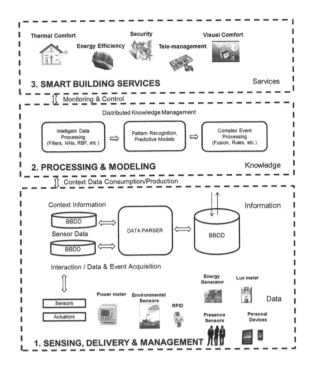

Fig. 2. Conceptual architecture for smart buildings [25]

2.3   Integration of Several Systems to One Overall System

Existing BEMS are comprised by sub-systems where each sub-system monitors and controls its own system separately from the other systems. Specifically, each sub-system is a unique system that could be autonomous. The same procedure is followed by the sensors. Under those circumstances, the same sensors cannot operate and be used in parallel by the sub-systems as there is no inter communication and connection.

To reduce the cost and increase the BEMS efficiency, new technologies are suggested by using a single IP backbone (Fig. 3) for the communication with all the sub-systems needed for the integration of BEMS [33]. As a consequence, all systems may exchange data and information and interact with each other deployed as a unified system. A standard proposed architecture of a BEMS includes of a centralized system which interacts with all the sub-systems and retrieves and sends real-time data while exploiting open communication protocols for buildings.

Using the various protocols, a BEMS is capable to communicate with all sub-systems. The most common supported communication protocols (wired and wireless) of a centralized BEMS are:

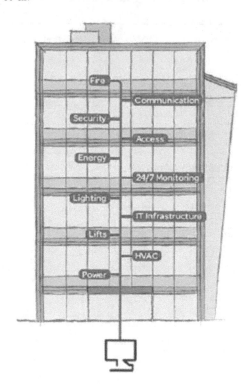

Fig. 3. Single IP backbone [33]

- Modbus is a method mainly used for transmitting over serial lines between devices. The simplest setup is a single serial cable connecting the serial ports on two devices, a Master and a Slave [8].
- BacNet is a standard, open protocol specifically for the building automation industry. BacNet offers an open architecture and the ability to control and monitor any building automation process [1].
- LonWorks is a networking solution for Building Automation. The novelty of LonWorks is that it can use twisted pair, Ethernet or even a power line as its communication channel [6].
- Zigbee standard operates on the IEEE 802.15.4 physical radio specification and operates in unlicensed bands including 2.4 GHz, 900 MHz and 868 MHz [12].
- Z-wave is a wireless, radio frequency (RF) based communications technology designed particularly for control, monitoring and status reading of household applications [11].
- Mbus is a communication standard. It is determined for applications of the data collection from consumption meters of various types [7].
- KNX is a uniform, manufacturer-independent communication protocol for intelligently networking state-of-the-art home and building system technologies [5].

- "Digital Addressable Lighting Interface" (DALI) is a communication protocol for building lighting applications and is used for communication between lighting control devices, such as electronic ballasts, brightness sensors, or motion detectors [2].
- Structure of Management Information (SMI) defines the rules for describing management information. The SMI is defined using ASN.1 [10].
- EnOcean protocol is defined by the new ISO/IEC 14543-3-10 standard, is the first energy harvesting wireless protocol [3].

3   Semantics for Smart Control and Data Management

In order to satisfy the specific requirements of BEMS and enable communication between disparate and heterogeneous technologies of both IoE and IoT devices, technological mappings must be introduced to cover all levels of IoT interoperability [35]. The mapping is usually used between the management level and the automation level. This type of technique is used at the gateways to integrate isolated Building Automation Systems (BAS). This type of integration facilitates syntactic and semantic interoperability. Ontologies have been already exploited for semantic modeling and reasoning [16]. Nowadays, many semantic frameworks are utilizing ontologies for semantically describing heterogeneous systems related to building automation and energy management for a complete IoT/IoE-based BEMS.

3.1   Conceptual BEMS Architecture

The modern BEMS are based on the efficiency and effectiveness of high-quality data and information. The key objective of this data and information transportation is to retain the interoperability of different Building Automation technologies and sub-systems that compose the overall system while providing compatibility to the data and information transportation in a perpetual basis. Furthermore, interoperability must be provided on top of the protocol stacks at the information level [39]. Exclusively, integration of resources, context information, raw data, systems functionality must be enriched with semantics to ensure a dynamic control of the BAS. Considering this, the most suitable technology is to use ontological models for representing the related knowledge, as well as to use reasoning mechanisms to infer new one [39].

The traditional BMS propose a hierarchical integration [40] where the BAS is directly linked to the top-level BMS. On the contrary, new BEMS using ontologies propose a system where a semantic layer exists between the BAS and the BMS [39] (Fig. 4). This intermediate layer is the central layer of the overall architecture. This central layer leads to high-level abstraction between the connected technologies and data while concentrating a point for information and knowledge sharing and exchange. As a result, the inferred knowledge based on ontologies and links over various technologies and their generated data may be deployed [39].

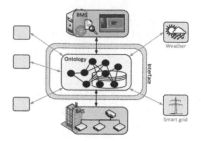

Fig. 4. Conceptual BEMS architecture

A prevailing consistent interface may be used to gain access to the semantic layer. The semantic layer is facilitating the interconnection and communication with the knowledge base. A technology connector aware to the ontology must be exploited [38] to map the formentioned interface. Based on the protocols that the BAS uses, the automation level can be also directly linked to the semantic layer. All the control actions are implemented in the semantic layer and the BMS and BAS do not communicate directly, but they are informed about the changes in the semantic layer. Specifically, all actions like turn off the lights, reduce indoor temperature are made through the BAS control layer, and the ontology retains this historical information.

Several components and sub-systems may be connected to the central semantic layer, like a smart grid, APIs, agents etc. As a result, the communication between different components and sub-systems is handled by the semantic layer interface. To sum up, this setup aims to promote interoperability and integrate semantically enriched and interlinked data while providing access to the knowledge base from various technologies and systems.

3.2 Ontologies

The purpose of the ontology is to interlink the building's information, the building's automation components, and the control actions, at a semantically-enriched level of abstraction. Several ontology engineering (OE) methodologies have been proposed and used so far for the engineering of domain ontologies. A recent and detailed review on the use of modern collaborative OE methodologies and their impact to developed ontologies is presented in Kotis et al., 2020 [28]. Furthermore, there are already developed ontologies for both the BA and the building components. Some of the most well-known and widely-used are described in the following paragraphs.

– DogOnt [17] was initially presented in 2008 and was used to address interoperability mainly for home automation devices. During the years, DogOnt was extended and now includes almost all devices and technologies that comprise an indoor IoT network. DogOnt is implemented through five hierarchical trees [17]: Building Thing, which models available thing, Building Environment, which models where things are located. State, which models the stable configurations of controllable things. Functionality, which models what controllable things can do. Domotic Network Component, which models the features peculiar to each domotic plant (or network)

- BASont [27]. The BASont undertakes different use cases over the life cycle of a building automation system for design, operation, and refurbishment [27]. The BASont is divided into several parts. The central element of the ontology describes the device instances. Around this, there are other ontologies like the location of instances in the building structure, the instances' device types and their semantics, the used abstract and detailed design templates, the topology of the BAS as well as the network addresses of the devices.

- The ThinkHome ontology [36] formalizes all relevant concepts needed to realize energy analysis in residential buildings and was addressed in 2010. The ThinkHome system consists of two main parts, a comprehensive knowledgebase (KB) and a multi-agent system (MAS).

- Smart Appliances REFerence (SAREF) ontology [19]. This ontology facilitates the communication of existing standards and protocols mainly for smart appliances using the ETSI TS 103 267 [13]. SAREF is widely used in energy realted aplications but is easily adopted for many different sectors like transportation, health, smart grid, and others.

The above is not an in-depth list of BEMS and energy-related ontologies as there are other ontologies that due to space limitations, were not presented here.

3.3   Building Energy Performance Simulation Tools

Moreover, there exist many building energy performance simulation tools. The main objective of energy simulation tools is to simulate the buildings energy performance and the comfort levels of the building while predicting the energy demand. Such simulation tools are EnergyPlus [18] and DOE-2 [41], which use custom schema definitions like IDD [26] and BDL [26]. A Simulation Domain Model (SimModel) [32] was proposed for a new interoperable XML-based data model for building simulation domain. Its ontology moves away from tool-specific, non-standard nomenclature by implementing an industry-validated terminology aligned with the Industry Foundation Classes (IFC) [32] (Fig. 5).

SimModel was introduced [9] as an internal data model by the Simergy software developed at LBNL [9], the successor of the Mojito platform presented by [14]. Data flow was possible to all existing tools like DOE-2, EnergyPlus and all tools that used gbXML export. Data from any of these environments can be mapped to and from the SimModel data model using the Simergy software [9]. The underlying SimModel is an object-oriented data model which defines all object/attribute/relationship sets used for Building Energy Performance (BEP) simulation [34]. The primary aim of the SimModel is to exploit the existing infrastructure and data input of EnergyPlus, while facilitating mapping towards and from other data models and establishement of additional definitions [14].

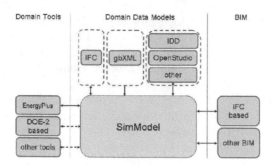

Fig. 5. Conceptual SIM architecture [32]

SimModel is represented using the XML markup language. The SimModel can be converted easily into an OWL ontology.

4   Conclusions

In the course of the past decades, BEMS have become quite popular mainly due to the information technology development in the field of automation in buildings and is mostly deployed in the commercial sector. As a consequence, exploiting the appropriate technologies, it is feasible to ensure both comfort conditions and energy savings for the residents. Furthermore, unlike to the conventional electrical installations, these systems are characterized by the application of structured cabling and wireless systems, through which the maintenance of the installation becomes a simple process. Furthermore, the diversity of various technologies and protocols used for BEMS demand the exploitation of existing protocols and energy ontologies. To sum up, BEMS's data models enriched with semantic information can manage all the data that is retrieved, created, and saved in the overall system.

Acknowledgements. This work is partially supported by the PLUG-N-HARVEST project funded by the EU H2020 under Grant Agreement No. 768735.

References

1. Bacnet. http://www.bacnet.org/Bibliography/EC-9-97/EC-9-97.html. Accessed 03 Feb 2021
2. Digital addressable lighting interface. https://www.infineon.com/dgdl/tp4-9.pdf? fileId=5546d462533600a401535748acdd3fe7. Accessed 03 Feb 2021
3. Enocean. https://www.enocean.com/en/technology/. Accessed 03 Feb 2021
4. Europeean union law. https://eur-lex.europa.eu/homepage.html?locale=en. Accessed 03 Feb 2021
5. Knx. https://www.csanyigroup.com/knx-architecture. Accessed 03 Feb 2021
6. Lonworks. https://www.ecmweb.com/content/article/20892561/the-basics-of-lonworks. Accessed 03 Feb 2021

7. M-bus. http://www.metro-fr.com/en/. Accessed 03 Feb 2021
8. Modbus, url: https://radiflow.com/blog/hack-the-modbus/ Accessed 03 Feb 2021
9. Simergy homepage. https://simergy-beta.lbl.gov/. Accessed 03 Feb 2021
10. Structure of management information. http://osr507doc.sco.com/%E2%80%A6n/ NetAdminG/snmpC.smi.html. Accessed 03 Feb 2021
11. Z-wave. https://z-wavealliance.org/. Accessed 03 Feb 2021
12. Zigbee. https://zigbeealliance.org/. Accessed 03 Feb 2021
13. Appliances, S.: Smartm2m; smart appliances; reference ontology and onem2m mapping (2017)
14. Bazjanac, V.: Acquisition of building geometry in the simulation of energy performance (2001)
15. Berardi, U.: Zeb and nzeb (definitions, design methodologies, good practices, and case studies). Handbook of Energy Efficiency in Buildings: A Life Cycle Approach, vol. 88, Butterworth-Heinemann, Oxford (2018)
16. Bonatti, P.A., Decker, S., Polleres, A., Presutti, V.: Knowledge graphs: New directions for knowledge representation on the semantic web (dagstuhl seminar 18371). In: Dagstuhl Reports. vol. 8. Schloss Dagstuhl-Leibniz-Zentrum fuer Informatik (2019)
17. Bonino, D., Corno, F.: DogOnt - ontology modeling for intelligent Domotic environments. In: Sheth, A., et al. (eds.) ISWC 2008. LNCS, vol. 5318, pp. 790–803. Springer, Heidelberg (2008). https://doi.org/10.1007/978-3-540-88564-1_51
18. Crawley, D.B., et al.: Energyplus: creating a new-generation building energy simulation program. Energy Buildings **33**(4), 319–331 (2001)
19. Degha, H.E., Laallam, F.Z., Said, B.: Intelligent context-awareness system for energy efficiency in smart building based on ontology. Sustainable Comput. Inf. Syst. **21**, 212–233 (2019)
20. Dimara, A., Timplalexis, C., Krinidis, S., Arvanitis, K., Tzovaras, D.: Energy consumption in public buildings-a survey in Greece. In: 2020 5th International Conference on Smart and Sustainable Technologies (SpliTech), pp. 1–6. IEEE (2020)
21. Doost, H.: Internet of energy: A solution for improving the efficiency of reversible energy. In: 2018 IEEE Global Engineering Education Conference (EDUCON), pp. 1890–1895. IEEE (2018)
22. Giaconi, G., Gündüz, D., Poor, H.V.: Smart meter privacy with renewable energy and an energy storage device. IEEE Trans. Inf. Forensics Secur. **13**(1), 129–142 (2017)
23. Gopinath, R., Kumar, M., Joshua, C.P.C., Srinivas, K.: Energy management using non-intrusive load monitoring techniques-state-of-the-art and future research directions. Sustainable Cities Soc. **62**, 102411 (2020). https://www.sciencedirect.com/science/article/pii/S2210670720306326?via%3Dihub
24. Hannan, M.A., et al.: A review of internet of energy based building energy management systems: issues and recommendations. IEEE Access **6**, 38997–39014 (2018)
25. Hernández-Ramos, J.L., Moreno, M.V., Bernabé, J.B., Carrillo, D.G., Skarmeta, A.F.: Safir: secure access framework for IoT-enabled services on smart buildings. J. Comput. Syst. Sci. **81**(8), 1452–1463 (2015)
26. Horrocks, I., Patel-Schneider, P.F., Van Harmelen, F.: From SHIQ and RDF to owl: the making of a web ontology language. J. Web Semant. **1**(1), 7–26 (2003)
27. Kofler, M.J., Reinisch, C., Kastner, W.: A semantic representation of energy-related information in future smart homes. Energy Buildings **47**, 169–179 (2012)
28. Kotis, K.I., Vouros, G.A., Spiliotopoulos, D.: Ontology engineering methodologies for the evolution of living and reused ontologies: status, trends, findings and recommendations. Knowl. Eng. Rev. **35**, 1–34 (2020). https://doi.org/10.1017/S0269888920000065

29. Marszal, A.J., et al.: Zero energy building-a review of definitions and calculation methodologies. Energy Buildings **43**(4), 971–979 (2011)
30. Moghaddam, M.H.Y., Leon-Garcia, A.: A fog-based internet of energy architecture for transactive energy management systems. IEEE Internet Things J. **5**(2), 1055–1069 (2018)
31. Newell, R.G., Qian, Y., Raimi, D.: Global energy outlook 2015. Technical Report, National Bureau of Economic Research (2016)
32. O'Donnell, J.: Simmodel: A domain data model for whole building energy simulation (2012)
33. Papantoniou, S., Mangili, S., Mangialenti, I.: Using intelligent building energy management system for the integration of several systems to one overall monitoring and management system. Energy Procedia **111**, 639–647 (2017)
34. Pauwels, P., Corry, E., O'Donnell, J.: Representing simmodel in the web ontology language. Comput. Civil Building Eng. **2014**, 2271–2278 (2014)
35. Pliatsios, A., Goumopoulos, C., Kotis, K.: A review on IoT frameworks supporting multi-level interoperability-the semantic social network of things framework. Int. J. Adv. Internet Technol. **13**, 46–64 (2020)
36. Ploennigs, J., Hensel, B., Dibowski, H., Kabitzsch, K.: Basont-a modular, adaptive building automation system ontology. In: IECON 2012–38th Annual Conference on IEEE Industrial Electronics Society, pp. 4827–4833. IEEE (2012)
37. Ridi, A., Gisler, C., Hennebert, J.: A survey on intrusive load monitoring for appliance recognition. In: 2014 22nd International Conference on Pattern Recognition, pp. 3702–3707. IEEE (2014)
38. Roldan-Molina, G.R., Mendez, J.R., Yevseyeva, I., Basto-Fernandes, V.: Ontology fixing by using software engineering technology. Appl. Sci. **10**(18), 6328 (2020)
39. Schachinger, D., Kastner, W.: Semantics for smart control of building automation. In: 2016 IEEE 25th International Symposium on Industrial Electronics (ISIE), pp. 1073–1078. IEEE (2016)
40. Schustek, P., Hyafil, A., Moreno-Bote, R.: Human confidence judgments reflect reliability-based hierarchical integration of contextual information. Nature Commun. **10**(1), 1–15 (2019)
41. Sousa, J.: Energy simulation software for buildings: review and comparison. In: International Workshop on Information Technology for Energy Applicatons-IT4Energy, Lisabon (2012)

Machine Learning

A Survey of Methods for Detection and Correction of Noisy Labels in Time Series Data

Gentry Atkinson[✉] and Vangelis Metsis[✉]

Texas State University, San Marcos, TX 78666, USA
{gma23,vmetsis}@txstate.edu

Abstract. Mislabeled data in large datasets can quickly degrade the performance of machine learning models. There is a substantial base of work on how to identify and correct instances in data with incorrect annotations. However, time series data pose unique challenges that often are not accounted for in label noise detecting platforms. This paper reviews the body of literature concerning label noise and methods of dealing with it, with a focus on applicability to time series data. Time series data visualization and feature extraction techniques used in the denoising process are also discussed.

Keywords: Label noise · Machine learning · Data quality

1 Introduction

Machine learning is well established as a useful field in artificial intelligence. But poor quality training data can quickly degrade the performance of a machine learning model in terms of accuracy, time to train, and the size of the classifier [69]. Noise has been defined as any disruption in the observed relationship between the features of an instance in a dataset and its class [25]. When this disruption occurs in the features it can be called attribute noise and in the labels, label noise [26]. The focus of this work will be on label noise, which is common in real-world datasets [69], but less widely addressed by denoising approaches.

Label noise is only one of the names used to refer to degraded quality in the assigned labels of datasets. Other names include: class noise, mislabeled data, poorly annotated data, and the borderline accusatory sloppily labeled data [52]. This work has chosen to use the name label noise because it is common and because it conforms with the taxonomy presented in [25]. Following that taxonomy, every instance of data has an abstract and true identification known as its class (Y). Its label (Ỹ) is an assigned annotation which should, but does not always, identify the instance's correct class.

Frenay's taxonomy[26] divides label noise into three categories: noise completely at random, noise at random, and noise not at random based on the

I. Maglogiannis et al. (Eds.): AIAI 2021, IFIP AICT 627, pp. 479–493, 2021.
https://doi.org/10.1007/978-3-030-79150-6_38

dependencies between Y, Ỹ, the feature space X, and an error rate E. When noise is completely at random (NCAR), every class is equally likely to be mislabeled. Noise at random (NAR) has an error rate that is affected by the class. Noise not at random (NNAR) mislabels data at a rate that depends on both the class and the feature space. The dependencies are shown in Fig. 1. These categories were inspired by early work on missing data [46].

Time series data offer challenges to researchers which are not present in other classes of data, such as images or text. The phrase time series refers to "[a] set of observations arranged chronologically", or in more charming terms from the same author a "wiggly record" [42]. Time series can be modeled as the output of a continuous function on some set of time steps. This continuity makes time series different from other ordered, sequential data. A feature extractor working on time series data must preserve the temporal relationships between nearby samples in the data.

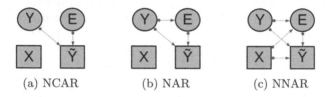

(a) NCAR   (b) NAR   (c) NNAR

Fig. 1. A visual taxonomy of label noise adapted from [25]. (a) shows noise completely at random (NCAR), (b) shows noise at random (NAR), and (c) shows noise not at random. Y represents true classes of instances, E the error (or mislabeling) rate, X the features, and Ỹ the assigned label. Arrows indicate a dependency between elements.

Label noise is an old and long-standing problem discussed since the early days of digital data analysis [19]. Section 2 of this paper will summarize recent works in noise detection. Section 2 is subdivided following a taxonomy of detection techniques defined in [30]. This work distinguished detection techniques based on the type of learning as: local learning, ensemble learning, or single model learning.

Section 3 will document recent approaches to feature extraction and visualization for time series data. Human review of labels is an effective technique for cleaning noisy labels [69]. But, the ability of human annotators to clean labels in time series data is largely dependent on their ability to visualize that data meaningfully.

Section 4 will explore techniques for mitigating the effect of classifier performance with noisy labels. Broadly the approaches to improve a model are: data cleansing, robust learning algorithms, and model hardening [25]. Section 5 concludes with a discussion of the material presented and our main observations.

2   Detection of Label Noise

Following the work presented in [30], label noise detection platforms can be divided into local learning methods, ensemble learning methods, and single classifier learning methods. This division is based on the method used to distinguish one instance as being mislabeled. Local learning methods compare instances to their nearest neighbors using methods such as K-Nearest Neighbors (KNN). Ensemble learning methods train multiple classifiers and identify mislabeled points based on a vote of those classifiers on the correct label for each instance. Single model learning methods train a single classifier (often a neural network) on some data and use the labels predicted by that classifier to distinguish mislabeled instances in the data. These three methods are summarized in Fig. 2.

2.1   Local Learning

Local learning methods assume that instances that are close in the feature space should share a label [30]. They frequently employ K-Nearest Neighbors which has the advantage of not needing to be trained. KNN is identified in [20,40] as being exceptionally robust to label noise. This particular property of that model will be discussed more in Sect. 4 but it should be sufficient for now to say that this observation makes it a reliable choice for a noise detection system. A demonstration of the use of KNN for identifying label noise is shown in Fig. 2a.

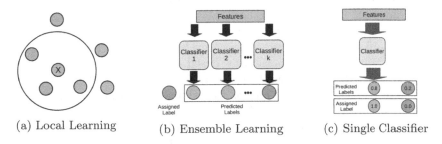

(a) Local Learning   (b) Ensemble Learning   (c) Single Classifier

Fig. 2. A summary of the three noise detection approaches defined in [30]

Several adaptations have been made to the basic KNN algorithm (identified in some older source as Instance-based Learning [2]) to make it suited to the task of identifying mislabeled instances. Edited nearest neighbor (ENN) automatically removes all instances misclassified by KNN from a training set [58] while its cousin Repeated-ENN iteratively applies ENN until all instances share a label with their nearest neighbors [58]. An advancement on Repeated-ENN, called All-KNN, was presented in [55] that used increasing values for K across iterations.

Later work applied Gabriel Graphs [56] and Relative Neighbourhood Graphs [34] to improve on the ability of KNN to recognize mislabeled instances in overlapping class regions of a dataset. The technique used a proximity graph to refine the set of neighbors used in order to mitigate occurrences of label noise in the set of neighbors used by a KNN classifier [45].

Biclusters, selections of features and instances that demonstrate high coherence of values across attributes and labels [21], have also been applied to the problem of identifying label noise. These selections are learned in an unsupervised manner. BicNoise [24] computed a mean square residue value (a measure of error between real and calculated values) of sets of instances as instances were experimentally inserted into highly coherent subsets from the training data. Instances that caused the MSRV to rise over some threshold were removed as noise.

Cluster validation measures provide a quantitative metric for the fit of a data partitioning. These measures have also been employed as a label noise filter [13]. This approach treated the dataset labels as clusters and calculated several cluster validity measures for each instance, following the intuition that poorly clustered points would be more likely to be mislabeled [13]. The measures employed were: the Silhouette Index, Connectivity, and the Average Intracluster gap.

2.2   Ensemble Learning

Ensemble learning can improve the performance of machine learning techniques [30]. Comparing the outputs of several classifiers can also be a useful approach for identifying mislabeled data [30]. This can either be several classifiers of different types (e.g., a decision tree, KNN, and a neural network) or several classifiers of the same type trained on different manipulations of the training data [30].

Employing sets of classifiers as a noise detection platform was shown to improve classification accuracy for noise levels up to 30% [18]. The technique presented in [18] developed a noise filter based on the residual error of classifiers trained on noisy data. This work was able to demonstrate the residual noise from ensemble classifiers was superior to residual noise from a single classifier and majority voting by ensemble classifiers.

Data partitioning is one strategy for ensemble learning approaches. The Partitioning Filter [70] was one technique that used data partitioning by dividing large datasets into several subsets, developing a good rule set to classify each partition, merging the rule sets into a single set for the full dataset, and filtering instances that are misclassified by the new ruleset. Partition Filtering was showed to be effective on datasets with up to 40% label noise [70]. Another application of data partitioning separated a full dataset into several overlapping partitions, trained several classifiers of each partition, and then tested combinations of majority voting and consensus voting on the label predictions from the classifiers [31]. Mislabeling rates of up to 40% were also tested in this paper but in some datasets, the accuracy of the noise detector fell below 50% when the mislabeling rate was higher than 30% [31].

Repeated labeling was applied in [48] to improve the label quality of chosen sets of low-quality instances. This work focused on cheap and crowd-sourced human labelers and developed analytical measures of label quality to determine instances that should be relabeled. The output of a model trained on the labeled instances was used to compute uncertainty of labeled datasets, and that measure was used to inform the relabeling process [48].

An adaptation of 10-fold Cross Validation is presented in [38] that used an ensemble of machine learning classifiers to filter mislabeled instances. Although the ML models employed in this approach were comparatively simple, this team reported classification accuracies in datasets with up to a 20% mislabeling rate can be increased to the same rate of accuracy as a classifier trained on data with no mislabeled instances using their filter [38].

2.3 Single Classifier Learning

Single classifier learning detection methods are more suitable for highly dynamic noisy data [30]. This approach can also be more efficient than ensemble learning approaches [30] but newer single classifier learning approaches tend to utilize deep learning models with powerful feature extraction techniques, which can easily require more time and computing power to train than an ensemble of simpler models.

It has been observed that mislabeled points do not necessarily behave like outliers in datasets [57]. Support vector machines (SVM) have been employed in a single classifier learning approach using a form of data partitioning to address this issue [57]. In this approach, a subspace of the full feature space was selected using domain expertise to train a classifier that would better identify the true class of the classified instances.

Label noise identification can also be incorporated as a portion of a classification model. The authors in [17] designed and implemented a model which included a sparse Bayesian Logistic Regression algorithm that was used to identify mislabeled instances. This training algorithm alternated between training the classifier and estimating label noise probabilities. The output of this approach is both a robust classifier and a list of suspect instances that could be addressed later.

Selecting an appropriate feature extractor can have a substantial effect on the efficacy of a classifier (a point that will be discussed further in Sect. 3). Labelfix [39] is a platform that automatically selected a deep feature extractor and trained a classifier using the learned features. Instances were then sorted based on the distance between the assigned one-hot label vector and the predicted label vector. This detection technique can also be built into a model training pipeline [44].

Our previous work has also expanded on the approach of sorting instances based on the distance between assigned and predicted labels [6,7]. A convolutional neural network (CNN) is applied as a feature extractor that is well-suited to time series data and the extracted features are used to produce interpretable visualizations for human reviewers. Human review is an effective technique for noise removal but is generally too expensive to be applied to a full dataset [69].

3   Feature Extraction and Visualization

Time series are a class of data that covers many different applications: financial, medical, engineering, scientific, social, and military [49]. Many of these fields can produce attribute vectors that can be very large [4]. Consider 10 s sound clips recorded at 44,100 Hz, or a minute of a 64-channel electroencephalogram (EEG) collected 1000 Hz. Either example would be untenable as an input layer for a neural network, or as an input vector for another model (e.g., an SVM or decision tree).

The human brain is a very powerful tool for recognizing and finding connections between time series but this ability depends on the visual appearance of the data [33]. Like the classifiers mentioned earlier, the human mind can benefit greatly from techniques of data abstraction that preserve the temporal properties of the original signal. The size of contemporary data is a significant challenge for time series visualization and analysis [49].

A good feature extractor is often enough by itself to help reduce the impact that label noise can have on a classifier [43]. What's more, extracted features that have captured the temporal relationships of samples in a time series can be processed as numerical data using many of the techniques presented in Sects. 2 and 4 that were not specifically crafted for temporal data.

Dimensionality reduction techniques can reduce the size of attributes without sacrificing the information they have captured. Principal component analysis (PCA) [35] is one approach to reduce the size of an attribute vector by selecting the most impactful channels from the full attribute set. PCA has been successfully applied to time series data [11,61]. PCA can be used to aid a task of visualization by selecting the two or three most meaningful features to plot in a flat figure [23].

Autoencoders were introduced as a method for dimensionality reduction [37] but have also been used effectively as feature extractors for signal visualization [62,63]. By mapping attributes into lower dimension embedding spaces, autoencoders can produce features that capture the relationship between instances in a way that is learn-able. This set of features can be further projected into 2 or 3 dimensions using a technique such as tSNE [32] to make the full dataset visually interpretable [7,12,63].

Convolutional neural networks have been used as part of label noise detection platforms [6,39] and have also been shown to be particularly effective as feature learners for time series data [23]. CNNs train nodes on small clusters of samples in the original attribute set. This process effectively captures the temporal relationship between samples in time series data. CNN layers can be incorporated smoothly feature learners in single model learning noise detection platforms [39] or built into autoencoders. Features extracted from signal data in [23] showed reliable separation of classes in 2-dimensional visualizations of data collected from audio sources and inertial measurement units (IMUs).

Segmentation divides time series instances into contiguous runs of samples that share some trend. A good technique for segmentation is one of the fundamental approaches to time series analyses [27]. A method for segmenting signals based on binary tree representations was presented in [27] and a similar technique followed in [67]. Both approaches build binary trees of samples whose root is a Perceptually Important Point (PIP) [22]. A simplified demonstration of signal segmentation based on PIP is presented in Fig. 3.

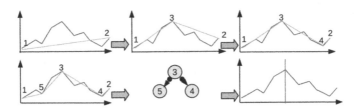

Fig. 3. A simplified demonstration of SB-Tree segmentation as outlined in [27]. PIPs are identified, built into a tree (the first and last point are generally excluded), and the roots of each tree are considered first to be a cut point for segmentation.

Prarzen notes that any time series data can be thought of as some function or sum of functions whose domain is a set of time steps [42]. Several feature extractors have been constructed around approaches that approximate the fundamental functions of time series. Fourier transforms represent arbitrary signals in the frequency domain, and [1] demonstrated that only a few fundamental frequencies can effectively abstract time series data while reducing the size of the representation. [60] presented a method for online approximation of a time series using polynomials.

Clustering has been applied to the problem of feature extraction. VAFLE, an approach based on spectral clustering, was able to reduce the dimensionality of data while identifying points of interest [28]. Another work has used Haar wavelet transformation to inform the dimensionality of a feature vector which was then clustered using hierarchical K-means [66].

A good visualization should be easily interpretable by a user. Even with a simple graph like a line plot (or waveform, or "wiggly record" [42]) there are choices that need to be made with interpretability in mind. Bertin Indexing has been shown to produce line plots from time series financial data that is easier to use than line plots prepared using linear scale juxtaposition and log scale juxtaposition [3]. Bertin Indexing scales heterogenous time series to make comparisons easier [10].

One consideration of time series datasets is that the data are not always exclusively time datasets. An example would be geo-referenced sensor data being collected from a sensor network. One system to address this example focuses on giving the user a "big picture" understanding of the sensor network over time [51]. This system allowed the user to view a 2D map of signals which was clustered by similarity with each region have a representative waveform overlayed on it.

There are many standard techniques for visualizing time series data. A collection of these techniques are presented in the early works of [4] and [50]. VisInfo is a more recent product whose goal is to provide visual access to time series data [9]. Some common and accepted methods for presenting time-oriented data are presented in Fig. 4.

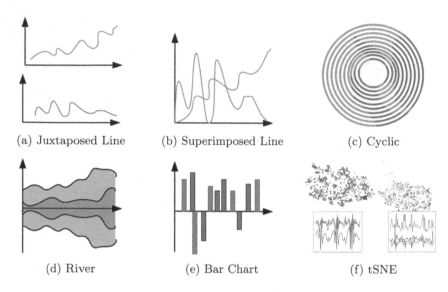

(a) Juxtaposed Line   (b) Superimposed Line   (c) Cyclic

(d) River   (e) Bar Chart   (f) tSNE

Fig. 4. A selection of plotting techniques suited to time series data. The juxtaposed and superimposed line plots are useful for comparing linear signals, as is the bar chart. The cyclic plot is best used for finding periodicities in cyclic series. River plots can be used for percentage estimation. tSNE allows full dataset exploration. (f) shows a tSNE plot of two classes of data juxtaposed with line plots of an instance from each class.

4 Label Correction

Detecting label noise is only the first step in improving the performance of supervised classifiers when working with noisy data. Some method also needs to be adopted for dealing with that noise. Three main approaches exist for dealing with label noise: training noise-tolerant models, cleansing data sets, and crafting noise-tolerant learning algorithms [25]. Techniques do not always fit neatly into only one of the three categories so each body of work will be discussed in the section that best fits it, but might overlap with work discussed in other sections.

4.1 Data Cleansing

Having identified some of the mislabeled instances in a dataset, data cleansing techniques will either remove or relabel those instances. The first approach is easier to implement, but re-labeling has the advantage of not removing training data that could improve the performance of a classifier.

TimeCleanser [29], an approach based on visual analytics, capitalized on the documented efficacy of the human eye [49] to analyze large datasets. As the name suggests, this platform focuses on temporal data, which the authors note has very specific challenges which make it distinct from other classes of data [29]. Users of this product can select from several good graphics to visually interpret datasets. Instances which the user identifies as noise are removed from the data.

Another approach that relied on human analysis for data cleansing is presented in [68]. This platform used crowd-sourced reviewers to re-annotate samples of IMU data that had been selected from a human activity recognition dataset. This approach used video recorded of the instances to allow human reviewers to correct the label of instances in the dataset which an active learner had trouble labeling correctly.

A pair of techniques that did not rely on human reviewers were introduced in [41]. The first of the two was named Self-Training Correction, which uses a classification model with an integrated noise filtering algorithm. The second technique employs K-Means clustering repeatedly using weights based on the assigned label for each instance. The labels in datasets are updated using a technique which these authors have named Polishing Labels in tribute to the data polishing algorithm described by Cho-Man Teng [53].

Similar to the Self-Training Correction described above was the earlier work Automated Data Enhancement (ADE) [64]. This approach used a neural network that was repeatedly re-trained on a noisy dataset, each time assigning or updating a probability vector representing each class to each instance. As the model was re-trained the probability vector gradually drifts away from the mislabelled class and towards the true class.

Probabilistic labeling can be used as part of a label cleaning platform. By assuming that there is some hidden probability of each point having a true class distinct from the assigned label Bootkrajang and Kaban developed an analysis which they called robust Normal Discriminant Analysis (rDNA) [15]. Labels in the dataset are flipped based on a function that calculates the probability of the instance being in each class of the dataset.

4.2 Robust Learning

Boosting is a machine learning method that gives greater weight to instances that a classifier struggles with during training [47]. The method, including the popular AdaBoost optimizer, greatly improves the training rate of machine learning models but can be particularly susceptible to the presence of label noise in training data [36]. Bagging, by contrast, partitions the dataset into subsets and trains a classifier on each [8] outperforms boosting on data that have noisy labels [36]. Boosting can be modified to make it more robust to label noise by adding probabilistic factors representing uncertainty in the assigned labels [16]. The process of label flipping has been expanded by the same author in later work [14].

Ensemble classifiers can be trained with resilience to label noise in mind. One approach is to use a principle of minimum-variance during the combined training of the several classifiers [71]. This approach minimizes the error rate of the ensemble by minimizing the sum of the variances of the collected classifiers. This technique was demonstrated to be effective in tasks of active learning from noisy, stream data [71].

Skeptical Supervised Machine Learning introduces a confidence measure that is used to represent the reliability of annotations made by human labelers [65]. Labels are generated both by human input and by the predictions of an ensemble of machine learning classifiers. The models are trained iteratively on the human input and conflict resolution is applied to decide the correct label for each instance.

Rather than removing mislabeled instances from datasets, we can omit them while training a classifier. A loss function has been proposed that skips confusing samples from training in order to improve the performance of deep neural networks on noisy data [54]. Instances with high cross-entropy error are driven into the abstention category in this platform, which the authors call a deep abstaining classifier.

Rather than completely abstaining from training on uncertain points, a model can weigh down the high uncertainty points and weight up low uncertainty points. This approach was demonstrated as reducing both the bias and variance when added as part of the loss function in neural networks [5]. The measure of certainty is calculated by means of comparison to k nearest neighbors (with $k = 5$ in the presented experiment).

4.3 Model Hardening

Some machine learning models inherently more robust to certain classes of noise. One study identified Naive Bayes and KNN as being more robust to label noise than support vector machines and decision trees [40]. More recent work has reached the conclusion that KNN and SVM were comparatively robust to label noise [20]. When considering these two results it is important to remember that there are many varieties of SVM and that the earlier result is experimentally derived while the later work is based on asymptotic analysis. Researchers working with data that are known to have some rate of mislabeling might be best served by sticking to models that are less sensitive to label noise.

As mentioned in Sect. 3, CNNs are an excellent tool for working with time series data. Expectation-Maximization has been applied to CNNs to increase their robustness to label noise and to integrate a model of noise distribution in the training of a CNN [59]. The noise model is learned as the CNN trains.

5 Conclusion

This work summarized the most common label noise detection and correction approaches. Many of these approaches are not exclusively used with time series data, but are general platforms for use with arbitrary, numeric data. A good feature extractor is often sufficient to process time series for use with these general approaches.

Without a standardized testing procedure or data set, it is difficult to say which of the many approaches discussed here are the "best" way to process data with noisy labels. Single classifier learning can incorporate deep feature extractors which makes them a good approach for time series data. For the time it also appears that human review is going to remain an important component of data cleansing.

Analysts who are going to employ human reviewers as part of a label cleaning method should take care to use visualizations that are suited to the data. The type of data and target application should inform the choice of visualization. Segmentation and dimensionality reduction can reveal relationships in data and help produce more interpretable abstractions for reviewers.

Data cleaning comes with some risks. Removing instances from a dataset can increase classifier bias and degrade its accuracy, especially when instances near the borders between classes are removed. Cleaning a training dataset can also harm a classifier when label noise will still be present in the test data. A model that is going to be tested on noisy data will perform better with a robust learning algorithm. But this comes at the risk of knowingly leaving incorrect instances in a dataset.

Intelligent problem-solving methods with pre-collected data are impressive but truly responsive systems require some ability to process online, streaming data. Such data will always have temporal properties, and so intelligent systems (artificial or otherwise) will always have to wrestle with the problems of time series data. Data collected in the real world will always have some noise, label, or otherwise. But with attention and good practices, machine learning with noisy labels is possible and reliable.

References

1. Agrawal, R., Faloutsos, C., Swami, A.: Efficient similarity search in sequence databases. In: Lomet, D.B. (ed.) FODO 1993. LNCS, vol. 730, pp. 69–84. Springer, Heidelberg (1993). https://doi.org/10.1007/3-540-57301-1_5
2. Aha, D.W., Kibler, D., Albert, M.K.: Instance-based learning algorithms. Mach. Learn. **6**(1), 37–66 (1991)
3. Aigner, W., Kainz, C., Ma, R., Miksch, S.: Bertin was right: an empirical evaluation of indexing to compare multivariate time-series data using line plots. In: Computer Graphics Forum, vol. 30, pp. 215–228. Wiley Online Library (2011)
4. Aigner, W., Miksch, S., Müller, W., Schumann, H., Tominski, C.: Visual methods for analyzing time-oriented data. IEEE Trans. Vis. Comput. Graph. **14**(1), 47–60 (2007)
5. Almeida, M., Zhuang, Y., Ding, W., Crouter, S.E., Chen, P.: Mitigating class-boundary label uncertainty to reduce both model bias and variance. ACM Trans. Knowl. Disc. Data (TKDD) **15**(2), 1–18 (2021)
6. Atkinson, G., Metsis, V.: Identifying label noise in time-series datasets. In: Adjunct Proceedings of the 2020 ACM International Joint Conference on Pervasive and Ubiquitous Computing and Proceedings of the 2020 ACM International Symposium on Wearable Computers, pp. 238–243 (2020)

7. Atkinson, G., Metsis, V.: TSAR: a time series assisted relabeling tool for reducing label noise. In: 14th PErvasive Technologies Related to Assistive Environments Conference (2021)
8. Bauer, E., Kohavi, R.: An empirical comparison of voting classification algorithms: bagging, boosting, and variants. Mach. Learn. **36**(1), 105–139 (1999)
9. Bernard, J., et al.: VisInfo: a digital library system for time series research data based on exploratory search—a user-centered design approach. Int. J. Digit. Libr. **16**(1), 37–59 (2014). https://doi.org/10.1007/s00799-014-0134-y
10. Bertin, J.: Semiology of graphics; diagrams networks maps. Technical report (1983)
11. Bingham, E., Gionis, A., Haiminen, N., Hiisilä, H., Mannila, H., Terzi, E.: Segmentation and dimensionality reduction. In: Proceedings of the 2006 SIAM International Conference on Data Mining, pp. 372–383. SIAM (2006)
12. Birjandtalab, J., Pouyan, M.B., Nourani, M.: Nonlinear dimension reduction for EEG-based epileptic seizure detection. In: 2016 IEEE-EMBS International Conference on Biomedical and Health Informatics (BHI), pp. 595–598. IEEE (2016)
13. Boeva, V., Lundberg, L., Angelova, M., Kohstall, J.: Cluster validation measures for label noise filtering. In: 2018 International Conference on Intelligent Systems (IS), pp. 109–116. IEEE (2018)
14. Bootkrajang, J., Chaijaruwanich, J.: Towards instance-dependent label noise-tolerant classification: a probabilistic approach. Pattern Anal. Appl. **23**(1), 95–111 (2020)
15. Bootkrajang, J., Kabán, A.: Multi-class classification in the presence of labelling errors. In: ESANN, pp. 345–350. Citeseer (2011)
16. Bootkrajang, J., Kabán, A.: Boosting in the presence of label noise. arXiv preprint arXiv:1309.6818 (2013)
17. Bootkrajang, J., Kabán, A.: Classification of mislabelled microarrays using robust sparse logistic regression. Bioinformatics **29**(7), 870–877 (2013)
18. Brodley, C.E., Friedl, M.A.: Identifying mislabeled training data. J. Artif. intell. Res. **11**, 131–167 (1999)
19. Bross, I.: Misclassification in 2 × 2 tables. Biometrics **10**(4), 478–486 (1954)
20. Cannings, T.I., Fan, Y., Samworth, R.J.: Classification with imperfect training labels. Biometrika **107**(2), 311–330 (2020)
21. Cheng, Y., Church, G.M.: Biclustering of expression data. In: ISMB, vol. 8, pp. 93–103 (2000)
22. Chung, F.L., Fu, T.C., Luk, R., Ng, V., et al.: Flexible time series pattern matching based on perceptually important points (2001)
23. Cruciani, F., et al.: Feature learning for human activity recognition using convolutional neural networks. CCF Trans. Pervasive Comput. Interact. **2**(1), 18–32 (2020). https://doi.org/10.1007/s42486-020-00026-2
24. de França, F.O., Coelho, A.L.: A biclustering approach for classification with mislabeled data. Exp. Syst. Appl. **42**(12), 5065–5075 (2015)
25. Frénay, B., Kabán, A., et al.: A comprehensive introduction to label noise. In: ESANN. Citeseer (2014)
26. Frénay, B., Verleysen, M.: Classification in the presence of label noise: a survey. IEEE Trans. Neural Netw. Learn. Syst. **25**(5), 845–869 (2013)
27. Fu, T., Chung, F., Ng, C.: Financial time series segmentation based on specialized binary tree representation. In: DMIN 2006, pp. 26–29 (2006)
28. Ghoniem, M., Shurkhovetskyy, G., Bahey, A., Otjacques, B.: VAFLE: visual analytics of firewall log events. In: Visualization and Data Analysis 2014, vol. 9017, p. 901704. International Society for Optics and Photonics (2014)

29. Gschwandtner, T., et al..: Timecleanser: a visual analytics approach for data cleansing of time-oriented data. In: Proceedings of the 14th International Conference on Knowledge Technologies and Data-Driven Business, pp. 1–8 (2014)
30. Guan, D., Yuan, W.: A survey of mislabeled training data detection techniques for pattern classification. IETE Tech. Rev. **30**(6), 524–530 (2013)
31. Guan, D., Yuan, W., Ma, T., Lee, S.: Detecting potential labeling errors for bioinformatics by multiple voting. Knowl. Based Syst. **66**, 28–35 (2014)
32. Hinton, G., Roweis, S.T.: Stochastic neighbor embedding. In: NIPS, vol. 15, pp. 833–840. Citeseer (2002)
33. Höppner, F.: Time series abstraction methods-a survey. Informatik bewegt: Informatik 2002–32. Jahrestagung der Gesellschaft für Informatik ev (GI) (2002)
34. Jaromczyk, J.W., Toussaint, G.T.: Relative neighborhood graphs and their relatives. Proc. IEEE **80**(9), 1502–1517 (1992)
35. Jolliffe, I.: Principal component analysis. Technometrics **45**(3), 276 (2003)
36. Khoshgoftaar, T.M., Van Hulse, J., Napolitano, A.: Comparing boosting and bagging techniques with noisy and imbalanced data. IEEE Trans. Syst. Man Cybern. Part A Syst. Hum. **41**(3), 552–568 (2010)
37. Kramer, M.A.: Nonlinear principal component analysis using autoassociative neural networks. AIChE J. **37**(2), 233–243 (1991)
38. Li, Y., Cui, W.: Identifying the mislabeled training samples of ECG signals using machine learning. Biomed. Signal Process. Control **47**, 168–176 (2019)
39. Müller, N.M., Markert, K.: Identifying mislabeled instances in classification datasets. In: 2019 International Joint Conference on Neural Networks (IJCNN), pp. 1–8. IEEE (2019)
40. Nettleton, D.F., Orriols-Puig, A., Fornells, A.: A study of the effect of different types of noise on the precision of supervised learning techniques. Artif. Intell. Rev. **33**(4), 275–306 (2010)
41. Nicholson, B., Zhang, J., Sheng, V.S., Wang, Z.: Label noise correction methods. In: 2015 IEEE International Conference on Data Science and Advanced Analytics (DSAA), pp. 1–9. IEEE (2015)
42. Parzen, E., et al.: An approach to time series analysis. Annals of Math. Stat. **32**(4), 951–989 (1961)
43. Pechenizkiy, M., Tsymbal, A., Puuronen, S., Pechenizkiy, O.: Class noise and supervised learning in medical domains: the effect of feature extraction. In: 19th IEEE Symposium on Computer-Based Medical Systems, CBMS 2006, pp. 708–713. IEEE (2006)
44. Rädsch, T., Eckhardt, S., Leiser, F., Pandl, K.D., Thiebes, S., Sunyaev, A.: What your radiologist might be missing: using machine learning to identify mislabeled instances of x-ray images. In: Proceedings of the 54th Hawaii International Conference on System Sciences (HICSS)
45. Sánchez, J.S., Pla, F., Ferri, F.J.: Prototype selection for the nearest neighbour rule through proximity graphs. Pattern Recogn. Lett. **18**(6), 507–513 (1997)
46. Schafer, J.L., Graham, J.W.: Missing data: our view of the state of the art. Psychol. Meth. **7**(2), 147 (2002)
47. Schapire, R.E., Freund, Y., Bartlett, P., Lee, W.S., et al.: Boosting the margin: a new explanation for the effectiveness of voting methods. Ann. Stat. **26**(5), 1651–1686 (1998)
48. Sheng, V.S., Provost, F., Ipeirotis, P.G.: Get another label? Improving data quality and data mining using multiple, noisy labelers. In: Proceedings of the 14th ACM SIGKDD International Conference on Knowledge Discovery and Data Mining, pp. 614–622 (2008)

49. Shurkhovetskyy, G., Andrienko, N., Andrienko, G., Fuchs, G.: Data abstraction for visualizing large time series. In: Computer Graphics Forum, vol. 37, pp. 125–144. Wiley Online Library (2018)

50. Silva, S.F., Catarci, T.: Visualization of linear time-oriented data: a survey. In: Proceedings of the 1st International Conference on Web Information Systems Engineering, vol. 1, pp. 310–319. IEEE (2000)

51. Steiger, M., et al.: Visual analysis of time-series similarities for anomaly detection in sensor networks. In: Computer Graphics Forum, vol. 33, pp. 401–410. Wiley Online Library (2014)

52. Stempfel, G., Ralaivola, L.: Learning SVMs from sloppily labeled data. In: Alippi, C., Polycarpou, M., Panayiotou, C., Ellinas, G. (eds.) ICANN 2009. LNCS, vol. 5768, pp. 884–893. Springer, Heidelberg (2009). https://doi.org/10.1007/978-3-642-04274-4_91

53. Teng, C.M.: Correcting noisy data. In: ICML, pp. 239–248. Citeseer (1999)

54. Thulasidasan, S., Bhattacharya, T., Bilmes, J., Chennupati, G., Mohd-Yusof, J.: Combating label noise in deep learning using abstention. arXiv preprint arXiv:1905.10964 (2019)

55. Tomek, I., et al.: An experiment with the edited nearest-nieghbor rule (1976)

56. Tüceryan, M., Chorzempa, T.: Relative sensitivity of a family of closest-point graphs in computer vision applications. Pattern Recogn. 24(5), 361–373 (1991)

57. Venkataraman, S., Metaxas, D., Fradkin, D., Kulikowski, C., Muchnik, I.: Distinguishing mislabeled data from correctly labeled data in classifier design. In: 16th IEEE International Conference on Tools with Artificial Intelligence, pp. 668–672. IEEE (2004)

58. Wilson, D.L.: Asymptotic properties of nearest neighbor rules using edited data. IEEE Trans. Syst. Man Cybern. 3, 408–421 (1972)

59. Xiao, T., Xia, T., Yang, Y., Huang, C., Wang, X.: Learning from massive noisy labeled data for image classification. In: Proceedings of the IEEE Conference on Computer Vision and Pattern Recognition, pp. 2691–2699 (2015)

60. Xu, Z., Zhang, R., Kotagiri, R., Parampalli, U.: An adaptive algorithm for online time series segmentation with error bound guarantee. In: Proceedings of the 15th International Conference on Extending Database Technology, pp. 192–203 (2012)

61. Yang, K., Shahabi, C.: A PCA-based similarity measure for multivariate time series. In: Proceedings of the 2nd ACM International Workshop on Multimedia Databases, pp. 65–74 (2004)

62. Yuan, Y., Xun, G., Suo, Q., Jia, K., Zhang, A.: Wave2Vec: learning deep representations for biosignals. In: 2017 IEEE International Conference on Data Mining (ICDM), pp. 1159–1164. IEEE (2017)

63. Yuan, Y., Xun, G., Suo, Q., Jia, K., Zhang, A.: Wave2Vec: deep representation learning for clinical temporal data. Neurocomputing 324, 31–42 (2019)

64. Zeng, X., Martinez, T.R.: An algorithm for correcting mislabeled data. Intell. Data Anal. 5(6), 491–502 (2001)

65. Zeni, M., Zhang, W., Bignotti, E., Passerini, A., Giunchiglia, F.: Fixing mislabeling by human annotators leveraging conflict resolution and prior knowledge. In: Proceedings of the ACM on Interactive, Mobile, Wearable and Ubiquitous Technologies, vol. 3, no. 1, pp. 1–23 (2019)

66. Zhang, H., Ho, T.B., Zhang, Y., Lin, M.S.: Unsupervised feature extraction for time series clustering using orthogonal wavelet transform. Informatica 30(3), 305–319 (2006)

67. Zhang, Z., Jiang, J., Wang, H.: A new segmentation algorithm to stock time series based on pip approach. In: 2007 International Conference on Wireless Communications, Networking and Mobile Computing, pp. 5609–5612. IEEE (2007)
68. Zhao, L., Sukthankar, G., Sukthankar, R.: Incremental relabeling for active learning with noisy crowdsourced annotations. In: 2011 IEEE 3rd International Conference on Privacy, Security, Risk and Trust and 2011 IEEE 3rd International Conference on Social Computing, pp. 728–733. IEEE (2011)
69. Zhu, X., Wu, X.: Class noise vs. attribute noise: a quantitative study. Artif. Intell. Rev. **22**(3), 177–210 (2004)
70. Zhu, X., Wu, X., Chen, Q.: Eliminating class noise in large datasets. In: Proceedings of the 20th International Conference on Machine Learning, ICML 2003, pp. 920–927 (2003)
71. Zhu, X., Zhang, P., Lin, X., Shi, Y.: Active learning from stream data using optimal weight classifier ensemble. IEEE Trans. Syst. Man Cybern. Part B (Cybern.) **40**(6), 1607–1621 (2010)

An Automated Tool to Support an Intelligence Learner Management System Using Learning Analytics and Machine Learning

Shareeful Islam[1]([⊠]), Haralambos Mouratidis[2,3], and Hasan Mahmud[4]

[1] School of ACE, University of East London, London E16 2RD, UK
shareeful@uel.ac.uk
[2] Centre for Secure, Intelligent and Usable Systems, University of Brighton, Brighton, UK
h.mouratidis@brighton.ac.uk
[3] Department of Computer and System Science, University of Stockholm, Stockholm, Sweden
[4] Mediprospects, Hawley House, London E13 0AD, UK

Abstract. Learner Management Systems (LMSs) are widely deployed across the industry as they provide a cost-saving approach that can support flexible learning opportunities. Despite their benefits, LMSs fail to cater for individual learning behavior and needs and support individualised prediction and progression. Learning Analytics (LAs) support these gaps by correlating existing learner data to provide meaningful predictive and prescriptive analysis. The industry and research community have already recognised the necessity of LAs to support modern learning needs. But a little effort has been directed towards the integration of LA into LMSs. This paper presents a novel automated Intelligence Learner Management System (iLMS) that integrates learner management and learning analytics into a single platform. The presented iLMS considers Machine Learning techniques to support learning analytics including descriptive, predictive and perspective analytics.

Keywords: Machine learning · Learning analytics · Predictive analytics · Perspective analytics

1 Introduction

The demand for using technology to effectively support teaching and learning is constantly increasing. Technology enhanced Learning emerges quickly and many institutions rapidly adopted the eLearning where web-based Learner Management Systems (LMSs) have been embedded [1]. LMSs are rapidly deployed across the industry with any provider size and the market is expected to reach a value of $25.7 billion by 2025 [2]. Despite of the wider adoption, the traditional LMS cannot support the modern learning trends in terms of understanding individual learning behavior and needs, engagement, and prediction of assessment outcomes. Learning Analytics (LAs) can effectively support for a better learning experience by analyzing and correlating learner data to predicate

© IFIP International Federation for Information Processing 2021
Published by Springer Nature Switzerland AG 2021
I. Maglogiannis et al. (Eds.): AIAI 2021, IFIP AICT 627, pp. 494–504, 2021.
https://doi.org/10.1007/978-3-030-79150-6_39

future needs [11, 12]. LA is an emerging field of research based on ideas from other domains such as technology-enhanced learning, data visualisation and integration [3]. There are works that consider various techniques to support LAs, mainly descriptive and limited predicated analytics [3, 4, 6, 7, 9, 11]. However, there is a lack of focus on how LA can be integrated into the LMS based on the existing learner data generated from the LMS.

This paper presents a novel automated Intelligence Learner Management System (iLMS) that integrates learner enrolment, learner content management and learning analytics into a single platform. Initial work for ILMS started through a Knowledge Transfer Partnership (KTP) project between the University of East London and Mediprospects [11]. This paper extends our previous work by providing an automation of iLMS and its unique features [11, 12]. iLMS uses various indicators such as learner highest education, assessment data and engagement logs and considers Machine Learning (ML) algorithms, i.e., Logistic Regression (LR), KNN, and decision tree for the Learning Analytics (LA). The LA part of iLMS initially focuses on the descriptive and predictive analysis based on the learner data generated by LMS and finally provides various actions decisions as a part of perspective analytics to support overall teaching and learning support.

2 Related Work

Technology-enhanced learning plays an important role for quality teaching and learning. The LMS and eLearning platform market is among the busiest in the technology industry nowadays [1, 2]. Several contributions focus on developing various techniques for learning analytics and underlying issues. A literature review performed regarding relevant data sources for LA by [6] emphasizes that the choice of data sources depends on the purpose of the learning analytics and data integration is one of the main challenges for the LA. Students' data are stored in different platforms in different formats as they leave tracks while using different systems [7]. Educational Data Mining (EDM) is considered to discover knowledge from data originating from educational environments [5, 6]. Educational Data Mining uses many techniques such as Decision Trees, Neural Networks, Naïve Bayes, K-Nearest neighbor, and many others. EDM is used to analyse data produced during the learning process to predict students' behavior to take an actionable decision. For improving the students' learning progress using huge education data, modern intelligent learning analytics depends on appropriate machine learning models [8]. However, the integration of a single ML model to different sources is challenging and depends on excessive computing power. ML models are strongly data-driven and require systems that have the capacity of collecting data and proposing actionable decision for the stakeholders [8]. A study by Wong reviews how LA has been used by 43 higher education institutions and results show the benefits of using LA in terms of Improving student retention, supporting informed decision making, cost effectiveness and learning behavior [13]. The same study summarizes various predicate models relating to students' academic performance, engagement and early alert. Avella et al. review the literature for methods, benefits, and challenges of LA in Higher Education sector [14]. The LA process focuses on the tracking the analytical information from the students to the stakeholders, specifically data related to learners' interactions with course content, other students, and instructors. Despite of benefits, several challenges relating to tracking, collection, evaluation and analysis of data and learning environment optimization, and issues concerning ethics and privacy are mentioned. Recently a study by Chen et al. assesses the impact of AI on the administration, instruction, and learning areas of the education sector [15]. The study highlights that AI learning system playing an important role for improving independent learning capabilities based on intelligence education technologies using machine learning, learning analytics and data mining. Busch et al. develop a predictive model to identify students at risk using apache web server log data of student engagement from a large cohort [16]. The work identifies influential predicate attribute such as grade prediction based on various machine learning algorithms such as decision tree, random forest and support vector machines. The result shows that support vector machines provides the highest accuracy among the three chosen algorithm. Akçapınar et al. also use learning analytics to predicate student at risk using ML algorithm using 76 student records [17]. The result shows that the KNN algorithm provides highest accuracy for measuring end-of-term academic performance. The work investigates whether end-of-term performance of students could be predicted in earlier weeks using the selected algorithm, features, and data transformation techniques.

To summarise, the current literature propose a number of techniques to support Learning Analytics and reviews the suitability of AI based approached for technology enhanced learning. However, little effort has taken place related to how LA can be integrated into LMS. Additionally, there is lack of guidelines and approaches for considering descriptive, predicative and prescriptive analytics for an effective LA. Our work contributes to address these limitations and presents an automated intelligence Learner Management System.

3 Machine Learning for Learning Analytics

Learning Analytics (LA) is defined as the measurement, collection, analysis, and reporting of data about learners for purposes of understanding and optimizing learning and the environments in which it occurs [9]. The purpose of LA is to collect data from various sources and analyse it to support different institutional needs related to potential learner engagement and progression and other issues. Machine Learning (ML) can effective support to analyse the learners data in order to discover pattern and correlating among the data for the prediction and future actions. LA requires extracting useful information from the large sets of educational data sets and correlate the data for various purposes. A common characteristic of all ML algorithms is that they run on and learn from data, to find rules, hidden patterns and to predict future behaviors [10]. ML models are trained with learners' data for predictive analysis which institution can use for making actionable decisions.

LA requires analysing existing learners to understand patterns and predication for the overall teaching and learning support. Traditional LMS is not capable of answering what will happen from the existing learner data despite managing a vast amount of learner data relating to learner enrolment, progression, engagement and other relevant areas. Additionally, it is difficult to provide a personal learning experience through traditional LMS. The goal of individualizing learning to each student's needs is not wholly new

[11], yet education is still a long way from achieving this goal. ML models are trained with learners' data for predictive analysis which institution can use for making actionable decisions. But with the help of ML, LMS will be able to drip feed content to the students according to their understanding and performance. The iLMS uses three ML algorithms for the LA purpose. An overview of the algorithms is given below:

- LR: Logistic Regression is a statistical analysis technique which is used for predictive analysis. It uses binary classification to reach specific outcomes and models the probabilities of default classes. We have used LR for predicting student's course outcome either as pass or fail and given us important insight into learner's success rate.
- KNN: KNN algorithm is used in industrial applications in tasks such as when a user wants to look for similar items in comparison to others. It is a supervised machine learning algorithm can be used for both classification and regression. We have compared our results obtained from the logistic regression for performance tuning.
- Decision tree: The decision tree algorithm creates a tree-like structure for the data feed and process outcome at the leaf. For our case, we used the categorical variable decision tree to predict students result either as pass or fail.

4   An Overview of Intelligence Learner Management System

This section provides an overview of iLMS and its key features.

4.1   Conceptual View of iLMS

Figure 1 shows the conceptual view of the iLMS which consists of two main components, i.e., learner data management and analytics. The data management part mainly feds the data from both internal and external sources. The internal sources include enrolment system, learner management including assessment and engagement and external includes mainly data from awarding body and funding agency. Data can be in various formats; therefore, data integration plays an important role in the learning analytics. The LA consider three types of analytics in our case, i.e., descriptive, predicative, and perspective analytics using multiple set of indicators such as engagement, age, gender, and location. The upper part of Fig. 1 shows the traditional LMS system, which is also used by the project industry partner, i.e., Mediprospects. It includes learner enrolment, management, and reporting. The data integration from various sources certainly is a challenging task for the existing system. The bottom part of the Fig. 1 shows the proposed iLMS. It integrates the data from various sources including the learner enrolment data and external sources into learner record system and performs Exploratory Data Analysis (EDA) to clean the data for the analytics. Finally, the Machine Learning algorithms are used to analyse and correlated the data to discover various patterns depending on the stakeholder needs. The outcome from the predicative analytics supports undertaking various actionable decision as a part of perspective analytics to improve overall teaching and learning support. Therefore, iLMS uses various indicators explain in the later sub sections for both predicative and perspective analytics.

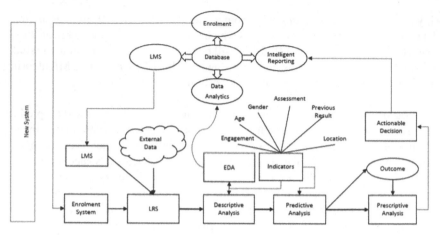

Fig. 1. Conceptual view of iLMS

4.2 Integration of Learning Analytics into iLMS

Learning Analytics (LA) provide measurement, analysis and reporting of the gathered data and their context to understand the patterns and suitable measurement. LA is one of the key features of iLMS that supports descriptive, predictive and perspective analytics.

- Descriptive analytics Descriptive analytics provides an overall view of existing learner status. Past data is analysed to provide insight into what has happened. Existing works that consider LA mainly focuses on descriptive analytics [1]. Traditional business intelligence system uses previous data to visualize them for better understanding of previous results. This stage is also the preparation stage for the predictive analysis. Existing data is explored using Exploratory Data Analysis (EDA). EDA aims to understand the data sets by summarizing their main characteristics often plotting them visually. Through the EDA process, we can understand the data and its domain or definition on our very important data set. During EDA we try to discover a pattern and try to detect anomalies in the data set. EDA will help to choose our feature(s) by knowing the data set, this will improve the accuracy of the predictive models.

- Predictive analytics: Predictive analysis is mainly based on the descriptive analysis report. It forecasts various institutional needs by following three ML algorithms i.e., LR, KNN and Decision Tree. The ML algorithms are applied at this stage to predicate any outcome relating to teaching and learning outcomes. ML algorithms are mainly used for the predication. For instance, the models can predict learner performance for a specific course and identified learners at risks. We have considered the outcome and the accuracies of the different algorithms. iLMS considers various indicators for the predictive analytics such as:

  - Engagement log: Students' engagement with system leave behind huge activity logs. This log is helpful to create a relationship between engagement and outcome. As stated previously we have considered various general indicators for the prediction of engagement. The log data containing student's login information, online duration, resource access logs, assignment upload logs, quiz and other online assessment tools using logs. These logs correlate with student's performance data.

- Assessment data: Students' on course assessment is very important indicators of their outcome. Based on their results throughout the academic, trainers will have an idea on their risk of failing or passing. Apart from these results from the previous academic year is also an important factor, at the same time results of different groups can predict a trend based on learner's demographic and historical data.

- Drop out: Students' drop out is another important indicator to take an actionable decision. Drop out data can be tagged with students on course behavior to identify students at risk. On the other hand, predicting dropout rate for a future cohort based on the current trend can also be achieved.

- Career progression: Predictive analysis can also help to gauge students' career progression. Based on the historical record predictive model can suggest possible future progression.

- Demographic Distribution: The system will predict student success rate based on the demographic background of the existing learner.

- Highest Education: We have considered student's previous academic achievement, during the enrolment students provide this information.

- Prescriptive analytics: Prescriptive analytics suggests a possible measure to take to intervene in the outcome. iLMS considers several actionable decisions for prescriptive analytics such as awareness, personalized support, new course offering, target marketing, performance evaluation. Awareness helps both the learners and instructors to identify the current status of the learners and identifies any unnoticed issue. Such awareness for learners supports to reflect changing their learning behavior. The instructors can also aware of the learners' interest, activity, and additional learner needs. Awareness can also support the personalized learning facility for the learner. It is one of the key requirements from learning analytics by providing support achieving personal learning goals, additional flexible online learning materials, virtual one to one learning session, summative feedback and encouragement. Instructors may also require additional support specifically when a large number of the learner is enrolled for a course or adjustment of learning and assessment content. Prescriptive analytics also support taking business decision in terms of future course offering and target marketing for the potential learners.

4.3 System Architecture

The iLMS is fully deployed and managed through the Platform as a Service (PaaS) cloud-based infrastructure and accessible through https://ilms.mediprospects.ac.uk. Note that only authorised users are allowed to access the platform. It combines learner enrolment, management and analytics through a single platform. The overall iLMS architecture is presented in Fig. 2. It consists of five different levels of abstraction, i.e., user interface, security, application, learning record store, and analytics engine. The first layer of abstraction is the user interface to allow legitimate users to access the system using pre-created authentication details. There are different categories of users such as learner, admin, instructor and management with different access rights. The second layer authenticates the users based on their roles and directs them to specific dashboards. iLMS uses security features for identity and access management and data encryption in transit and rest. The enrolment layer is responsible for managing learner enrolment and holds detailed information related to learners. Learners are assigned to different groups based on their enrolment data and cohort and they are managed through this group structure. In the learning management system, each group has a group leader as an instructor responsible for delivering the course. The LMS has different types of functionality like content management, communication, course delivery, notification, assignment, feedback, forum and resource sharing. Learner activity logs are recorded in the Learning Record Store (LRS). The Learning Analytic Engine (LAE) processes all the logs and performs data analytics using the chosen ML algorithms. The outcomes of the analytics are a number of detailed reports and data visualization of the various analytics report. LAE includes three main components, i.e., Exploratory Data Analytics (EDA), Machine Learning Classifiers and Data Visualization. EDA cleans the data and extracts the features and feds into the ML algorithms for descriptive, perspective and predicative analytics. To improve the accuracy feature engineering is done through EDA (refer to Fig. 1). Data Visualization modules produce visualization of the past and future possible outcome.

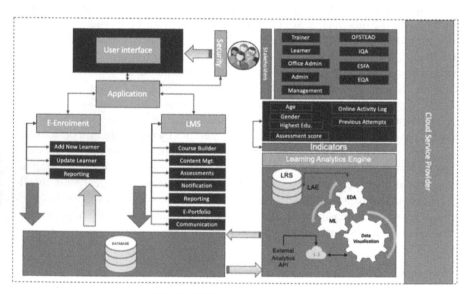

Fig. 2. iLMS system architecture

4.4 Key Features

There are several features of the iLMS which are managed through users dashboard. Each functionality contains important components of learner management and learning analytics. This section presents the key iLMS features.

User Interface and Security: iLMS allows users to interact with the system based on the roles, i.e., management, instructors, admins and learners. The user interfaces have some standard functionalities which are irrespective of user role i.e., user profile, messaging system, course navigation, and shared course contents. Additional functionalities are added based on the specific role, for instance, management interface includes audit logs, instructors' performance against courses, retention rate, withdrawal rate, new enrolment rate, and so on. iLMS supports system access to the external stakeholder such as funding agency and awarding body, with limited capabilities, they will able to view learners progress, performance and course work. The application is hosted on a SSL enabled cloud platform. User will be given access details after their enrolment. The system authenticates users based on multiple factors. The system will support single sign-on and two factors authentication to enhance security measures. The system provides real-time traffic monitoring which offers regular backup and audit trails. Figure 3 shows the snapshot of the e-enrolment dashboard. The left-hand side of the interface is the navigation for the system and the content is in the middle of the web page. The enrolment dashboard provides a quick snapshot of the enrolment activities. By clicking on the icon, the top right corner, the user can access their profile and message related the users.

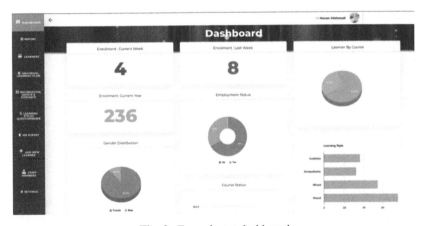

Fig. 3. E-enrolment dashboard

Learning Support Session: The system supports one to one and group session as required by the quality framework. The instructor can assign the task to individual learners where the learner will be able to upload/submit his/her work. This will support the company to adhere to quality assurance guidelines. An instructor will be able to produce a review report, observation report of individual learners. In traditional LMS courses are offered in group settings, our system also supports that. We have added TODO, FILES and COMMENTS. Comments support one to one or specific group communication. A trainer will able to share additional materials with the learner according to his/her needs and trainer will be able to assign additional tasks to the learner. The learner will be able to upload his/her work. This feature will improve engagement and decrease the risk of dropping out.

Report Dashboard: iLMS provides customised report generation facility depending on the various stakeholders' needs. In particular, reports that are necessary for the teaching and learning team are different from the report that needs for the management and external stakeholder. iLMS generates several reports such as the course progress, individual learner progression, learner's activity, learner success rate, learner's engagement, and learner's assessment. Figure 4 shows a snapshot of course reports and we have masked for two-column which contains identifiable information about learners. From this report, an instructor can view course activities. He/she can send individual email right from the report page by clicking the E-mail button on the right column. The button on the bottom left corner enables easy to export data in CSV format.

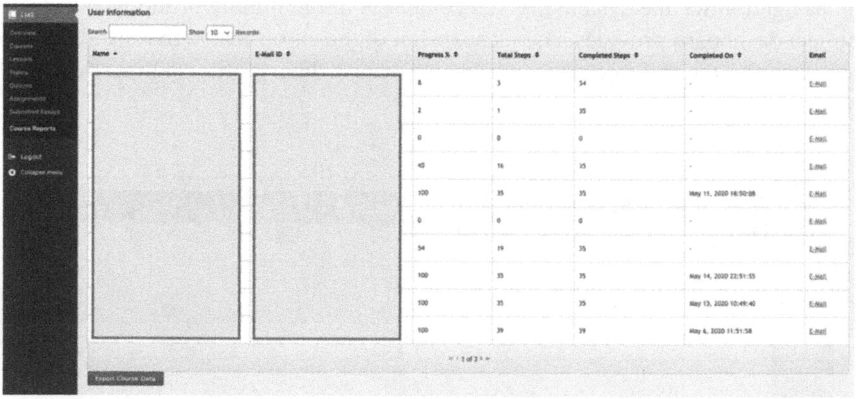

Fig. 4. Course report

Learning Analytics: Learning analytics, important features of the iLMS, allows the user to get important information regarding the overall system and the user's activities. As the system support released access control, the analytics are shown based on user role. An instructor will be able to see the group-wise progress report, individual learners performance and corresponding activity logs. An instructor will be able to flag the students early based on their performance and who is on the risk of dropping out. Based on this analytics instructor will be to intervene in the learner early with additional and personalized learning support. The management will be able to redesign their course offerings and course contents, they will also able to offer student with an additional course based on their performance in the current course. The analytics features will also be available for the learners as they will be able to see their performance data act based on those.

Figure 5 shows the prediction engine in the test environment as a part of predicative analytics. The prediction engine is developed based on the data cleaned by EDA and the ML algorithms. As mentioned earlier, we have used LR, KNN and Decision Tree algorithm. The decision tree provides the highest accuracy among the three classifiers. It takes three inputs as based on the three selected features i.e. assessment score, highest qualification and engagement score. With the information provided the system predict the outcome. In the screenshot, we have entered student qualification of A-Level, average score of 82 (the average score is calculated based on the marks obtained in different assessments) and engagement score 18615 (this score is near our threshold value of 2000). The system accurately predicts the learner will pass which establishes our finding in the descriptive analysis.

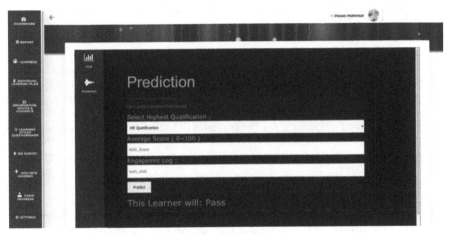

Fig. 5. Prediction engine interface

5   Conclusion

Technology-enhanced learning has already become one of the key elements for teaching and learning support. LMS is now widely adopted across the industry to support the teaching and learning needs. The steep market growth and the post-COVID-19 will change the LMS landscape. This paper presents an automated intelligence learner management system (iLMS) and its key features. iLMS integrates learner enrolment, management and learning analytics through a single platform. The learning analytics correlates the learners data generated from the LMS and provides descriptive, predictive and perspective analytics. We believe iLMS can effectively supports the institutions to understand the learners' needs and undertakes the necessary actions to improve the overall learning support. The iLMS development and testing phase is recently completed. We are planning to deploy the iLMS into the project context based on the chosen Cohort. Upon completion of the deployment and users feedback, iLMS will be fully operational into the project industrial partner context. Therefore, an empirical investigation of the iLMS and its finding to demonstrate its applicability are next step of this work.

References

1. Bezovski, Z., Poorani, S.: The evolution of e-learning and new trends. In: Information and Knowledge Management, vol. 6, no. 3, pp. 50–57. IISTE (2016)
2. LMS Market by Component (Solution and Services), Delivery Mode (Distance Learning, Instructor-Led Training and Blended Learning), Deployment Type, User Type (Academic and Corporate), and Region - Global Forecast to 2025. https://www.marketsandmarkets.com/PressReleases/learning-management-systems.asp
3. Kumar, K., Vivekanandan, V.: Advancing learning through smart learning analytics: a review of case studies. Asian Assoc. Open Univ. J. (2018)
4. Herodotou, C., Rienties, B., Boroowa, A., Zdrahal, Z., Hlosta, M.: Large-scale implementation of predictive learning analytics in higher education: the teachers' role and perspective. Educ. Tech. Res. Dev. 67(5), 1273–1306 (2019)
5. Viberg, O., Hatakka, M., Bälter, O., Mavroudi, A.: The current landscape of learning analytics in higher education. Comput. Hum. Behav. 89, 98–110 (2018)
6. Papamitsiou, Z., Economides, A.: Learning analytics and educational data mining in practice: a systematic literature review of empirical evidence. Educ. Technol. Soc. 17(4), 49–64 (2014)
7. Rosé, C.P., McLaughlin, E.A., Liu, R., Koedinger, K.R.: Explanatory learner models: why machine learning (alone) is not the answer. Br. J. Edu. Technol. 50(6), 2943–2958 (2019)
8. Carmen, C., Davis, B., Wagner, E.D.: The Evolution of LMS: From Management to Learning. The eLearning Guild, Santa Rosa (2009)
9. Siemens, G., Long, P.: Penetrating the fog: analytics in learning and education. EDUCAUSE Rev. 46(5), 30 (2011)
10. Andriotis, N.: Will Artificial Intelligence Bring Real Smarts To Elearning?. https://www.efrontlearning.com/blog/2017/06/artificial-intelligence-elearning.html. Accessed 17 May 2020
11. Islam, S., Mahmud, H.: Integration of learning analytics into learner management system using machine learning. In: 2020 the 2nd International Conference on Modern Educational Technology ICMET. ACM (2020)
12. Islam, S., Mahmud, H.: An intelligence learner management system using learning analytics and machine learning. In: 12th International Conference on Education Technology and Computers, ICETC 2020. ACM (2020)
13. Wong, B.T.M.: Learning analytics in higher education: an analysis of case studies. Asian Assoc. Open Univ. J. 12, 21–40 (2017)
14. Avella, J.T., Kebritchi, M., Nunn, S.G., Kanai, T.: Learning analytics methods, benefits, and challenges in higher education: a systematic literature review. Online Learn. 20, 13–29 (2016)
15. Chen, L., Chen, P., Lin, Z.: Artificial intelligence in education: a review. IEEE Access 8, 75264–75278 (2020)
16. Busch, J., Hanna, P., O'Neill, I., McGowan, A., Collins M.: Can machine learning on learner analytics produce a predictive model on student performance?. In: Innovative and Creative Education and Technology International Conference (ICETIC) (2017)
17. Akçapınar, G., Altun, A., Aşkar, P.: Using learning analytics to develop early warning system for at-risk students. Int. J. Educ. Technol. High. Educ. 16, 1–20 (2019)

Classification of Point Clouds with Neural Networks and Continuum-Type Memories

Stefan Reitmann[1]([✉]) [ID], Elena V. Kudryashova[2], Bernhard Jung[1],
and Volker Reitmann[2]

[1] Institute of Computer Science, Chair of Virtual Reality and Multimedia,
Freiberg University of Mining and Technology, Freiberg, Germany
`stefan.reitmann@informatik.tu-freiberg.de`
[2] Department of Mathematics and Mechanics, Chair of Applied Cybernetics,
St. Petersburg State University, Saint Petersburg, Russia
`e.kudryashova@spbu.ru`

Abstract. This paper deals with the issue of evaluating and analyzing geometric point sets in three-dimensional space. Point sets or point clouds are often the product of 3D scanners and depth sensors, which are used in the field of autonomous movement for robots and vehicles. Therefore, for the classification of point sets within an active motion, not fully generated point clouds can be used, but knowledge can be extracted from the raw impulses of the respective time points. Attractors consisting of a continuum of stationary states and hysteretic memories can be used to couple multiple inputs over time given non-independent output quantities of a classifier and applied to suitable neural networks. In this paper, we show a way to assign input point clouds to sets of classes using hysteretic memories, which are transferable to neural networks.

Keywords: Point clouds · Classification · Neural network · Hysteretic memory

1 Introduction

Depth sensors have become ubiquitous in many application areas, e.g. robotics, driver assistance systems, geo modeling, and 3D scanning using smartphones. Depth sensing is achieved by means of waves or rays that are sent out by a transmitter, reflected at surfaces and detected again by an receiver. The time difference between emitting and receiving gives information about the distance covered. Various physical principles are used, such as electromagnetic waves (radar), acoustic waves (sonar) or laser beams (LiDAR). In our research, we aim at developing an autonomous robotic platform that serves as a carrier for various LiDAR and sonar sensors for 3D mapping and environmental data acquisition in inland waters [2]. 3D point clouds obtained from ultrasonic and LiDAR mapping need to get semantically segmented and classified through machine learning analysis to extract knowledge for object detection and autonomous movement. In order to train such classifiers, however, large amounts of training data are required that provide labeled examples of correct classifications. Therefore we developed an approach where virtual worlds with virtual depth sensors are used to generate

© IFIP International Federation for Information Processing 2021
Published by Springer Nature Switzerland AG 2021
I. Maglogiannis et al. (Eds.): AIAI 2021, IFIP AICT 627, pp. 505–517, 2021.
https://doi.org/10.1007/978-3-030-79150-6_40

labeled point clouds (Fig. 1 [16]). To prepare an application in certain use cases, AI algorithms (e.g. neural networks) are trained with synthetic data obtained in virtual environments under various conditions and signal qualities [16].

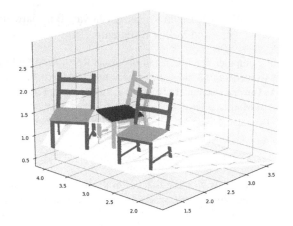

Fig. 1. Exemplary synthetic labeled point cloud of virtual LiDAR sensor with ground truth data for part segmentation of 3D chair meshes. The axes represent independent units of measurement of the virtual environment (Blender 3D software suite).

However, a distinction must be made here between a completely registered point cloud (as depicted in Fig. 1) and raw temporal impulses from the sensors. For active use in robotic movement and automization, the raw temporal impulses must be evaluated, while the completely registered point cloud is created in postprocessing, but initially offers no added value for the motion behavior. Therefore, ways have to be found to extract knowledge for object recognition and classification from the raw temporal impulses, as these are the data the robot gets at a certain point of time.

This approach differs from a variety of considerations on how machine learning can be used to classify point clouds (see Sect. 2.2). In order to use temporal impulses for classification in a meaningful way, it must be possible to link several impulses of different points of time with each other. Accordingly, it must be possible to link historical output variables with each other via a memory. The classifier is thus not solely dependent on the input variables (sensor pulses), but also on the previous state of the output variable. The system can thus - depending on the previous history - assume one of several possible states for the same input variable. These considerations lead us to the assumption that hysteresis memories and neural network applications can be coupled with each other.

2   Background

This section details the fundamental concepts of light and sound propagation and reflection under ideal and perturbed conditions.

2.1 Depth Sensing

LiDAR & Time-of-Flight (ToF). LiDAR is a common method for optical distance measurement. Generally, passive and active sensor systems can be distinguished. In this article we focus on active distance measurement, where radiation is introduced into the environment by the measuring device. An example are cameras that can determine distances by means of ToF or the active triangulation [11].

Sonar/Ultrasonic. Sonar is a distance measurement method based on sound waves. Like LiDAR, measurements devices can be divided into active and passive[1] Sonar. Again, only the more common active type is considered in this paper. Here, the transmitter emits a signal in the form of a sound wave. The sound wave is reflected at the target object and registered at the receiver. The time difference between signal transmission and reception provides information about the distance. The type can be one of the options rotating, static, or side-scan. Depending on the sensor, different configuration options are available for the sensor's field of view. The first two sensors have a field of view in horizontal and vertical direction, while the side-scan sensor only has a downward opening angle. Active sonars are used, for example, to locate schools of fish in waters or to map underwater stuctures (see Fig. 2).

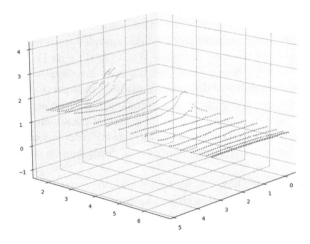

Fig. 2. Temporal pulses of side scan sonar in virtual underwater environment. Red points are grouped to the underground, blue points to irregularities, e.g. certain underwater objects. Each segment compries one sonar pulse at one certain point of time. Again the axes represent independent units of measurement of the virtual environment (Blender). (Color figure online)

The task is now to be able to correctly assign the points to object classes with an arbitrary classification function f. However, since there is no complete point cloud, but

---

[1] In passive Sonar, the target object itself rather than the sensing device emits a sound signal. This signal can be identified by its characteristic signal profile.

only individual pulses, the object classes must be detected via the connection of several time steps. This approach has different requirements than those found, for example, in [13]. In the following section, we therefore discuss previous approaches and work out the requirements for the model.

2.2 Classification and Semantic Segmentation

Following the assumptions of [14], we can summarize the main properties of the input point clouds or a subset of them:

- Unordered: points in a point cloud are typically not assumed to have any particular structure
- Density variability: non-constant density within the point clouds due to perspective effects, movements or measurement errors
- Invariance under transformation: as a set, such data must be invariant to mutations of its members

One option for automated processing of point clouds with machine learning, e.g. for segmentation, is unsupervised learning. For example, a cluster analysis can be used to segment a point cloud into certain parts. Such a procedure is described in [4] and [3]. The classification of data points into groups (also: *clusters*) is done by grouping elements that are as similar as possible to each other. More detailed information on this can be found in [1].

Supervised learning is usually used for classification tasks and, in contrast to unsupervised learning, requires semantically labeled examples for training. For 2D image data, the learning of classifies from examples is described e.g. or [15]. Learning of classifiers for the case of three-dimensional data has been investigated e.g. in [13,14] and [24]. Regardless of the number of dimensions, methods of supervised learning are often used to automatically recognize patterns and relationships. Such an approach, however, requires a large amount of training data with the correct classification for each pixel or point in a scene (pixel-wise or point-wise segmentation). Alternatively, smallest circumscribing rectangles or bounding boxes may be used depending on the needed amount of precision.

So various applications have shown that the use of neural networks in the analysis of LiDAR and sonar data yields promising results for classification and semantic segmentation. However, for most of the methods a pre-processing of the pulse signals derived from LiDAR sensors is necessary, which results in high computational overhead and considerable latency. Spiking Neural Networks (SNN), referred as third generation neural networks, showed promising results in modeling time dependent data as depth sensing signals (see 2.1) are. SNN are capable to compute the raw temporal impulses of LiDAR and sonar and are so meaningful in the real-time automization of robotic movements. Using the synthetic raw pulse data of simulated depth sensors derived in the virtual environments (like in Fig. 2), we want to address the object recognition problem with SNN on raw temporal pulses.

However, both conventional Deep Learning structures and SNN suffer from a non-transparent representation from an input set to an output class. To extend these capabilities, hysteresis memories can be used, which can address the described classification problem through convergence behavior.

3 Continuum Stationary Sets in an Acoustic-ODE Problem

3.1 Stability Investigations by Abstract Volterra Integral Equations

In this section we consider a boundary control problem for the interactions of acoustic waves with some control processes on the boundary described by an ODE. Note that on the level of time-series this coupling problem can arise as temporal coding in SNN [6]. Our aim is to provide frequency-domain conditions for the convergence of trajectories of the process to the stationary set (attractor) which consists of a continuum of functions. In order to show this we introduce some function spaces needed in the sequel and consider a general Volterra integral equation. The problem of convergence of solutions of the PDE/ODE problem will be reduced to the investigation of such an integral equation.

The interaction of acoustic and laser signals with a structure (control or heating part) can be described as hybrid system consisting of different types of PDE's and ODE's connected by special boundary conditions. In the case of a microwave heating problem the incoming signal is given by Maxwell's equations, the heating process is defined by parabolic equations. Under certain assumptions in this situation a multivalued dynamical system having a global attractor is generated [19].

For a Hilbert space Y with scalar product $(\cdot,\cdot)$ and norm $|\cdot|$ the space $L^2_{\mathrm{loc}}(\mathbb{R};Y)$ consists of locally L^2-functions on $\mathbb{R}$ with values in Y and with a topology defined by the family of seminorms $|y|_n := \left(\int_{-n}^{n} |y(t)|^2 dt \right)^{1/2}$, $n = 1,2,\dots$. Thus the space $L^2_{\mathrm{loc}}(\mathbb{R};Y)$ is considered as a *Fréchet space*, i.e. as a complete metrizable linear topological space. For any interval $\mathscr{J} \subset \mathbb{R}$ we regard $L^2_{\mathrm{loc}}(\mathscr{J};\mathscr{Y})$ as a subspace of $L^2_{\mathrm{loc}}(\mathbb{R};Y)$ identifying $L^2_{\mathrm{loc}}(\mathscr{J};Y)$ with the set of functions in $L^2_{\mathrm{loc}}(\mathbb{R};Y)$ which vanish outside of $\mathscr{J}$. For any interval $\mathscr{J} \subset \mathbb{R}$, a Hilbert space Y and a parameter $\rho \in \mathbb{R}$ we introduce the *weighted spaces* $L^2_\rho(\mathscr{J};Y)$ and $W^{1,2}_\rho(\mathscr{J};Y)$ by

$$L^2_\rho(\mathscr{J};Y) := \left\{ f \in L^2_{\mathrm{loc}}(\mathscr{J};Y) \,\Big|\, \int_{\mathscr{J}} e^{-2\rho t} |f(t)|^2_Y \, dt < \infty \right\}$$

$$\text{and} \quad W^{1,2}_\rho(\mathscr{J};Y) := \{ f \in L^2_\rho(\mathscr{J};Y) \,|\, \dot{f} \in L^2_\rho(\mathscr{J};Y) \}.$$

($\dot{f}$ denotes the distribution derivative.)

Assume that the map $t \in \mathbb{R}_+ \mapsto \mathscr{L}(U,Z)$ is twice piecewise-differentiable and satisfies the following condition: There exists a $\rho_0 > 0$ and a constant $\gamma > 0$ such that

$$\| K(t) \|_{\mathscr{L}(U,Z)} \leq \gamma e^{-\rho_0 t}, \quad \forall t > 0, \tag{3.1}$$

$$\text{and} \quad \int_0^\infty \left[\| \dot{K}(t) \|^2_{\mathscr{L}(U,Z)} + \| \ddot{K}(t) \|^2_{\mathscr{L}(U,Z)} \right] e^{2\rho_0 t} dt < \infty. \tag{3.2}$$

Consider the *Volterra integral equation*

$$z(t) = h(t) + \int_0^t K(t-\tau)\phi(z(\tau),\tau)d\tau, \tag{3.3}$$

where $K(t) \in \mathscr{L}(U,Z)$ (U,Z Hilbert spaces) is twice piecewise-differentiable satisfies (3.1) and (3.2), and has therefore a state-space realization. Suppose that $\phi: Z \times \mathbb{R}_+ \to U$ is a continuous function.

Instead of one fixed nonlinearity ϕ we consider a family $\mathcal{N}$ of continuous maps, such that for any $\phi \in \mathcal{N}$ and any $h \in \mathcal{D}(A)$ with $\mathcal{D}(A)$ from the nonlinear integral Eq. (3.3) has a unique solution $z(\cdot, h, \phi)$ and this solution is continuous.

In order to describe the absolute stability or instability behavior of (3.3) in the following theorem we need an additional assumption on the class $\mathcal{N}$. Let us assume that there is a linear bounded operator $R : Z \to U$ such that the "nonlinearity" $\varphi(z) = Rz$ belongs to $\mathcal{N}$.

Theorem 3.1. *([17]) Suppose that $\chi(\cdot)$ is the Laplace transform of K and the operator function $(I - \chi(\lambda)R)^{-1}$ has poles in the right half-plane and the frequency-domain condition from [18] is satisfied. Then there exists a bounded linear self-adjoint operator*

$$P : W^{1,2}_{-\rho}(0, +\infty; Z) \to W^{1,2}_{-\rho}(0, +\infty; Z) \qquad \text{such that}$$
$$\mathcal{C} := \{h \in W^{1,2}_{-\rho}(0, +\infty; Z) \,|\, (Ph, h)_{W^{1,2}_{-\rho}(0, +\infty; Z)} < 0\}$$

is a quadratic cone $\mathcal{C} \neq \emptyset$ in $W^{1,2}_{-\rho}(0, +\infty; Z)$ with the following properties:

a) *There exists a constant $\beta > 0$ such that for any $h \in \mathcal{C}$ and any $\phi \in \mathcal{N}$*

$$\lim_{t \to \infty} e^{-\beta t} \int_0^t \| \phi(z(s, h, \phi), s) \|_U^2 \, ds = \infty. \tag{3.4}$$

b) *Any solution $z(\cdot, h, \phi)$ of (3.3) which does not satisfy (3.4) has the property $\int_0^\infty \| \phi(z(s, h, \phi), s) \|_U^2 \, ds < \infty$ and, consequently,*

$$\phi(z(\cdot, h, \phi), \cdot) \in L^2(0, \infty; U) \quad \text{and} \quad z(\cdot, h, \phi) \in L^2(0, \infty; Z). \tag{3.5}$$

In the next subsection we show an application of this theorem.

3.2 Hyperbolic PDE's with Boundary Control as Realizations of Volterra Equations

Let us investigate the question how to suppress vibrations in a fluid conveying tube via control on the boundary. We consider for this a system of equations which is described in [12,21].

The motion of an incompressible fluid is given for $t > 0$ in the acoustic approximation by the hyperbolic PDE's

$$\frac{\partial v}{\partial t} = a_1 \frac{\partial w}{\partial x}, \qquad \frac{\partial w}{\partial t} = a_2 \frac{\partial v}{\partial x}, \; x \in (0, 1), \tag{3.6}$$

where a_1 and a_2 are positive parameters, v denotes the relative velocity of the fluid and w denotes the pressure. The boundary conditions are given for $t > 0$ by

$$w(t, 1) = 0, \qquad \frac{1}{2} w(t, 0) - v(t, 0) = -u(t), \tag{3.7}$$

where $u(\cdot)$ is a function ("boundary control") which describes the relative displacement of the piston of a servomotor. The equation of the turbine for $t > 0$ is

$$T_a \frac{dq}{dt} + q(t) = u(t) + \frac{3}{2} w(0,t). \tag{3.8}$$

Here q denotes the relative angular speed of the turbine, T_a is a positive parameter. The regulator is described by the equation

$$T_r^2 \frac{d^2 \zeta}{dt^2} + T_k \frac{d\zeta}{dt} + c_0 \zeta + k\phi(\dot\zeta) + q(t) = 0, \tag{3.9}$$

where ζ represents the displacement of the clutch of the regulator and T_r, T_k, c_0 and k are positive parameters. The friction term is given by a continuous function $\phi : \mathbb{R} \to \mathbb{R}$ defined through a parameter $\kappa > 0$ by

$$\phi(z) = \begin{cases} 1 & \text{if } z \geq \kappa, \\ \frac{1}{\kappa} z & \text{if } z \in (-\kappa, \kappa), \\ -1 & \text{if } z \leq -\kappa, \end{cases} \text{ and thus satisfying the property } \phi(z) z \geq 0, \ \forall z \in \mathbb{R}.$$

The equation of the servomotor is

$$T_s \frac{du}{dt} = \eta(t), \tag{3.10}$$

where T_s is a positive parameter and η denotes the displacement of the slide value. The last condition is for $t > 0$ and with a positive parameter β

$$\eta(t) - \zeta(t) + \beta u(t) = 0. \tag{3.11}$$

A direct computation shows that the transfer function of the linear part of (3.6) – (3.11) which connects the (formal) Laplace transforms of $-\phi$ and ζ is given by

$$\chi(\lambda) = k \frac{\lambda \, (T_a \lambda + 1)(T_s \lambda + \beta)(\sinh \lambda \tau + \alpha \cosh \lambda \tau)}{(T_r^2 \lambda^2 + T_k \lambda + c_0) Q(\lambda) + R(\lambda)}, \tag{3.12}$$

where

$$\alpha = 2\sqrt{\frac{a_1}{a_2}}, \quad \tau = 1/\sqrt{a_1 a_2}, \tag{3.12.a}$$

$$Q(\lambda) = (T_s \lambda + \beta)(T_a \lambda + 1)(\alpha \cosh \lambda \tau + \sinh \lambda \tau), R(\lambda) = 2\cosh \lambda \tau - 2\sinh \lambda \tau.$$

Note that $\chi(\lambda)$ can be written with some $c > 0$ as

$$\chi(\lambda) = \frac{k}{T_r^2 \lambda + c} + \chi_1(\lambda). \tag{3.13}$$

The representation (3.13) shows that $\chi_1(\lambda)$ is analytic in some halfplane $\{\text{Re}\,\lambda > -\varepsilon\}$ with $\varepsilon > 0$. From this it follows that $\chi_1(\lambda)$ has the Laplace original $K_1(t)$ which is absolute continuous, satisfies the inequalities

$$|K_1(t)| \leq \text{const}\, e^{-\varepsilon_0 t} \tag{3.14}$$

with some $\varepsilon_0 > 0$ and such that K_1 and $\dot{K}_1$ belong to $L^2(0,\infty;\mathbb{R})$. Since the first part of (3.13) has the Laplace original $\frac{k}{T_r^2}e^{-ct/T_r^2}$ the whole original of $\chi(\lambda)$ can be represented as $K(t) = K_1(t) + \frac{k}{T_r^2}e^{-ct/T_r}$. It is shown in [21] that any solution component $z(t) := \dot{\zeta}(t)$ from (3.9) can be written as

$$z(t) = h(t) + \int_0^t K(t - \tau)\phi(z(\tau))\,d\tau, \tag{3.15}$$

where again h is absolute continuous, satisfies an inequality of type (3.14) and $h, \dot{h}$ belong to $L^2(0,\infty;\mathbb{R})$. The quadratic constraints can be described in $Z = U = \mathbb{R}$ by the inequality

$$\phi(z)(z - \kappa\phi(z)) \geq 0, \quad \forall z \in \mathbb{R}. \tag{3.16}$$

Using the transfer function (3.13) and the constraints (3.16) we can verify the frequency-domain condition from [18]. A direct computation shows (see [21]) that if

$$T_k(\alpha^2 - 1)\beta^2 \leq \left(\frac{55}{32} + \alpha^2\right)(\beta\,T_a + T_s) \tag{3.17}$$

is satisfied, the condition

$$\alpha(T_k\beta^2 - (\beta\,T_a + T_s)) \geq 3\,\tau\beta. \tag{3.18}$$

is necessary and sufficient for the frequency-domain condition. The stability and instability domains of the denominator of $\chi(\lambda)$ where investigated in [12] and characterized in the (T_k, T_r^2)-plane by domains Ω_{st} and Ω_{unst}, respectively. It follows now that under the conditions (3.16)–(3.18) for parameters from Ω_{st} or Ω_{unst} the solutions of the integral Eq. (3.15) (and the solutions of the PDE problem (3.6)–(3.11)) have the properties described by Theorem 3.1.

Particularly one can derive frequency-domain conditions for the point-wise strong (in the sense of L^p) convergence of solutions of the above fluid control system to the stationary set (attractor) consisting of a continuum of functions ([21]).

4   Convergence to the Stationary Set in Systems with Hysteresis

4.1   Evolutionary Variational Inequalities

It is widely recognized that the Dirac delta function δ plays an important role in neural network theory, e.g., for the description of integrate and fire neurons. We now show one way of introducting δ into the framework of nonlinear systems with hysteresis nonlinearity, which can be used for constructing continuum-type memories. Some applications of hysteretic memories are demonstrated in [8,23]. The multivalued properties of hysteresis operators are described by variational inequalities or differential inclusions ([22]) which are defined in some abstract setup.

Suppose that Y_0 is a real Hilbert space with $(\cdot,\cdot)_0$ and $\|\cdot\|_0$ as scalar product resp. norm. Suppose also that $A : \mathscr{D}(A) \subset Y_0$ is a closed (unbounded) densely defined linear operator. The Hilbert space Y_1 is defined as $\mathscr{D}(A)$ equipped with the scalar product

$$(y,\eta)_1 := ((\beta I - A)y, (\beta I - A)\eta)_0, \quad y,\eta \in \mathscr{D}(A),$$

where $\beta \in \rho(A)$ ($\rho(A)$ is the resolvent set of A) is an arbitrary but fixed number the existence of which we assume.

The Hilbert space Y_{-1} is by definition the completion of Y_0 with respect to the norm $\|z\|_{-1} = \|(\beta I - A)^{-1}z\|_0$. Thus we have the dense and continuous embedding $Y_1 \subset Y_0 \subset Y_{-1}$ which is called *Hilbert space rigging structure*. The duality pairing $(\cdot,\cdot)_{-1,1}$ on $Y_1 \times Y_{-1}$ is the unique extension by continuity of the functionals $(\cdot,y)_0$ with $y \in Y_1$ onto Y_{-1}.

If $-\infty \leq T_1 < T_2 \leq +\infty$ are arbitrary numbers, we define the norm for Bochner measurable functions in $L^2(T_1,T_2;Y_j)$, $j = 1,0,-1$, through $\|y\|_{2,j} := (\int_{T_1}^{T_2} \|y(t)\|_j^2 \, dt)^{1/2}$. For an arbitrary interval $\mathscr{J}$ in $\mathbb{R}$ denote by $\mathscr{W}(\mathscr{J})$ the space of functions $y(\cdot) \in L^2_{loc}(\mathscr{J};Y_1)$ for which $\dot{y}(\cdot) \in L^2_{loc}(\mathscr{J};Y_{-1})$ equipped with the norm defined for any compact interval $[T_1,T_2]$ by $\|y(\cdot)\|_{\mathscr{W}(T_1,T_2)} := (\|y(\cdot)\|_{2,1}^2 + \|\dot{y}(\cdot)\|_{2,-1}^2)^{1/2}$. Suppose that U,Z are real Hilbert spaces with scalar products $(\cdot,\cdot)_U, (\cdot,\cdot)_Z$ and norms $\|\cdot\|_U, \|\cdot\|_Z$ and $A \in \mathscr{L}(Y_1,Y_{-1})$, $B \in \mathscr{L}(U,Y_{-1})$, $C \in \mathscr{L}(Y_0,U)$ are linear operators. Assume that $\phi : \mathscr{D}(\phi) \subset W^{1,2}(0,T;Z) \times U \to W^{1,2}(0,T;U)$ is a strongly continuous hysteresis operator with $\mathscr{E} : Z \to 2^U$, $\mathscr{D}(\phi) = \{(z,u_0) \in W^{1,2}(0,T;Z) \times U \mid u_0 \in \mathscr{E}(z(0))\}$ and $\psi : Y_1 \to \mathbb{R} \cup \{+\infty\}, \psi \not\equiv +\infty$, is a convex, lower semi-continuous map. Consider the *variational inequality*

$$(\dot{y}(t) - Ay(t) - Bu(t), \eta - y(t))_{-1,1} + \psi(\eta) - \psi(y(t)) \geq 0, \quad \forall \eta \in Y_1 \text{ a.e. } t \in (0,T) \tag{4.1}$$

$$u(t) = \phi(z,u_0)(t), \ z(t) = Cy(t), \quad y(0) = y_0 \in Y_0, \quad u_0 \in \mathscr{E}(z(0)). \tag{4.2}$$

A pair of functions $\{y,u\} \in \mathscr{W}(0,T) \cap (C(0,T);Y_0) \times L^2(0,T;U)$ which satisfies (4.1), (4.2), is called *solution* of (4.1), (4.2) on $(0,T)$ with initial conditions $y(0) = y_0$ and $u(0) = u_0$; $y(\cdot)$ is the *state trajectory*, $u(\cdot)$ is the *control*.

A solution $\{y,u\}$ of (4.1), (4.2) with $y(t) \equiv \hat{y} \in Y_1$ and $u(t) \equiv \hat{u} \in U$ is called *stationary*. The set of all stationary solutions of (4.1), (4.2) is the *stationary set S*.

Any stationary solution $\{\hat{y},\hat{u}\}$ satisfies the *stationary variational inequality*

$$(-A\hat{y} - B\hat{u}, \eta - \hat{y})_{-1,1} + \psi(\eta) - \psi(\hat{y}) \geq 0, \quad \forall \eta \in Y_1 \tag{4.3}$$

$$\hat{u} = \phi(\hat{z},\hat{u}), \ \hat{z} = C\hat{y}, \quad \hat{u} \in \mathscr{E}(\hat{z}). \tag{4.4}$$

4.2   Convergence to the Stationary Set

Let us introduce the following assumptions using additional properties of a control system with hysteresis operator ([22]).

(A0) *Existence of Solutions.*
The inequality (4.1), (4.2) has for arbitrary $y_0 \in Y_0$ and $u_0 \in \mathscr{E}(Cy_0(0))$ at least one solution $\{y,u\}$. The stationary set S, given by (4.3), (4.4), is non-empty.

(A1) *Generalized Clausius - Duhem Inequality.*
$$\exists F_1 \in \mathscr{L}(Z,U)\ \exists F_2 \in \mathscr{L}(U,U)\quad \forall T \geq 0 \quad \forall z \in W^{1,2}(0,T;Z)\quad \forall u_0 \in \mathscr{E}(z(0)):$$
$$\int_0^T (\dot{\phi}(z,u_0)(t), F_1\dot{z}(t))_U - (\dot{\phi}(z,u_0)(t), F_2\dot{\phi}(z,u_0)(t))_U\, dt \geq 0.$$

(A2) *Counter Clockwise Circulation.*
$$\exists\varkappa \in \{-1,1\}\quad \exists G_1 \in \mathscr{L}(U,Z)\quad \forall T \geq 0\quad \forall z \in W^{1,2}(0,T;Z)\quad \forall u_0 \in \mathscr{E}(z(0))$$
$$\exists\gamma(z(0)) \geq 0:\quad \varkappa\int_0^T (G_1\dot{\phi}(z,u_0)(\tau), \dot{z}(\tau))_Z\, d\tau \geq -\gamma(z(0)).$$

(A3) *Controllability of the Linear Part.*
The pair (A,B) is L^2-controllable, i.e. $\forall y_0 \in Y_0$ $\exists u(\cdot) \in L^2(0,+\infty;U)$ such that $\dot{y} = Ay + Bu$, $y(0) = y_0$, is well-posed in the variational sense on $(0,+\infty)$.

(A4) *Exponential Stability of the System Operator.*
Any solution of $\dot{y} = Ay$, $y(0) \in Y_0$, is exponentially decreasing for $t \to +\infty$.

(A5) *Regularity of the System Operator.*
The operator $A \in \mathscr{L}(Y_1, Y_{-1})$ is regular, i.e. $\forall T > 0, y_0 \in Y_1, w_T \in Y_1$ and $\forall f \in L^2(0,T;Y_{-1})$ the solutions of $\dot{y} = Ay + f(t)$, $y(0) = y_0$, and of $\dot{w} = -A^+w + f(t)$, $w(T) = w_T$, are strongly continuous in the norm of Y_1. A^+ is the adjoint operator. Define the quadratic form

$$\mathscr{F}(\zeta, \vartheta; \tau) := (\vartheta, F_1Cw)_U - (\vartheta, F_2\vartheta)_U - \tau(G_1Cw, u)_U,$$
$$\zeta = (w,u) \in Y_0 \times U, \quad \vartheta \in U\ (F_1, F_2\ \text{from (A1)}, \tau \in \mathbb{R}\ \text{a parameter}).$$

(A6) *Frequency Domain Condition.*

$$\exists\tau \in \mathbb{R}, \quad \varkappa\tau \leq 0, \quad \exists\delta > 0 \qquad \mathscr{F}^c(\tilde{\zeta},\tilde{\vartheta};\tau) \leq -\delta|\tilde{\zeta}|^2$$
$$\forall\tilde{\zeta} \in U^c\quad \forall\omega \in \mathbb{R}, \quad \tilde{\zeta} = (i\omega(i\omega I - A)^{-1}B\tilde{u}, \tilde{u}), \quad \tilde{\vartheta} = i\omega\tilde{u}.$$

Here U^c is the complexification of U and $\mathscr{F}^c$ is the Hermitian extension of $\mathscr{F}$.

(A7) *Convexity and Lower Semi-Continuity of the Transformed Hysteresis Operator.*
For any operator $P = P^* \in \mathscr{L}(Y_0, Y_0)$ such that

$$P \in \mathscr{L}(Y_{-1}, Y_0) \cap \mathscr{L}(Y_0, Y_1)\quad \text{we have}\quad \psi(y_1) - \psi(y_1 - P(y_1 - y_2))$$
$$+ \psi(y_2) - \psi(y_2 + P(y_1 - y_2)) \geq 0, \quad \forall y_1, y_2 \in Y_1.$$

On Y_1 the function $\psi_p(y) := \psi(y - Py) - \psi(y)$ is convex and lower semi-continuous.

Theorem 4.1. *([18]) Under the above assumptions any solution $\{y,u\}$ of (4.1), (4.2) converges strongly in $Y_0 \times U$ to the stationary set S as $t \to \infty$.*

Example 4.1. We consider the boundary problem for the temperature $\theta(x,t)$ on the string $(0,1)$ with hysteresis control on the boundary given by

$$\theta_t = \theta_{xx} - b\theta, \quad x \in (0,1), \quad \theta(x,0) = \theta_0(x), \quad \theta_x(0,t) = 0,$$

$$\theta_x(1,t) = \rho\,\phi(z,u_0)(t), \quad z(t) = \int_0^1 \theta(x,t)\,dx. \tag{4.5}$$

Here $z(t)$ is the mean temperature at t, $b > 0$ and $\rho \in \mathbb{R}\backslash\{0\}$ are parameters, $\theta_0(x)$ is an initial function, $\phi : \mathscr{D}(\phi) \subset W^{1,1}(0,T) \times \mathbb{R} \to W^{1,1}(0,T)$, $(z,u_0) \in \mathscr{D}(\phi) \mapsto \phi(z,u_0)(\cdot).\mathscr{E} : \mathbb{R} \to 2^{\mathbb{R}}$ s. th. $\mathscr{D}(\phi) = \left\{(z,u_0) \in W^{1,1}(0,T) \times \mathbb{R} \mid u_0 \in \mathscr{E}(z(0))\right\}$ is a continuous hysteresis operator.

Quadratic Constraints:
(A1) $: 0 \le \dot{\phi}(z,u_0)(t)\dot{z}(t) \le (\dot{z}(t))^2 \quad \forall z \in W^{1,1}(0,T)$

(A2) $: \varkappa = -1, \quad \varkappa \int_{t_1}^{t_2} \phi(z,u_0)(t)\dot{z}(t)dt \ge -\gamma(z(0)) \,\forall z \in W^{1,1}(0,T), \, \gamma(z(0)) \ge 0$

Interpretation as variational inequality:

$$Y_0 := L^2(0,1), \quad (v,w)_0 := \int_0^1 v(x)w(x)dx, \quad \forall v,w \in L^2(0,1).$$

$$Y_1 := W^{1,2}(0,1) \quad (v,w)_1 := \int_0^1 (v(x)w(x) + v'(x)w'(x))dx, \quad \forall v,w \in W^{1,2}(0,1)$$

$$Y_{-1} := Y_1' \text{ dual. } A \in \mathscr{L}(Y_1, Y_{-1}) \text{ is given by } (Av,w)_{-1,1} := \int_0^1 (Av)(x)w(x)dx$$

$$= -\int_0^1 (v'(x)w'(x) + bv(x)w(x))dx, \quad \forall v,w \in W^{1,2}(0,1).$$
$U := \mathbb{R}$, $B \in \mathscr{L}(\mathbb{R}, Y_{-1})$ is defined by

$$(Bu,w(x))_{-1,1} = \rho\,uw(1), \, \forall v \in \mathbb{R}, \, \forall v \in W^{1,2}(0,1),$$
$$\text{i.e.} \quad B = [\rho\,\delta(x-1)], \delta \text{ is the Dirac's distribution.}$$

$Z := \mathbb{R}$, $C \in \mathscr{L}(Y_0, Z)$ is given by $Cv := \int_0^1 v(x)dx, \quad \forall v \in L^2(0,1)$.

It follows that assumptions **(A0)**–**(A5)** are satisfied. The verification of **(A6)** and **(A7)** is shown in [17]. It follows from Theorem 4.1 that any solution of (4.5) converges to the stationary set for $t \to \infty$, see Fig. 3 and 4 for the case of a play operator.

Note that parabolic equations with Dirac's delta function at the right-hand side arise also as Fokker-Planck-Kolmogorov equation for the probability density of neurons in nonlinear noisy leaky integrate and fire models of neural networks [5]. Convergence to the stationary set is connected with the construction of global attractors as working memory [7,9,20]. General Hausdorff dimension and stability properties of such attractors for smooth and non-smooth dynamical systems and cocycles (non-autonomous dynamical systems) are considered in [10].

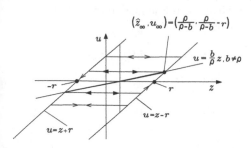

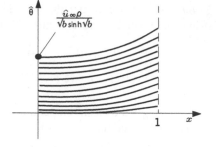

Fig. 3. Intersection of $u = \frac{b}{\rho}z$ with the graph of the hysteresis

Fig. 4. Continuum of stationary temperature fields

5   Conclusion

With this paper, we could present an approach to bring continuum-type memories and neural networks together. The convergence behavior of continuum-type memories in the representation of a trajectory from input data set to an output class can be used to improve the understanding and further analysis for neural networks. For distance measurement methods, which are mainly represented by temporally offset pulses that can be better recognized by specific neural networks (e.g., spiking neural networks), this is a subject for further research to be verified in experiments.

Acknowledgement. Part 3 and 4 of the work are supported by the 2020–2021 program Leading Scientific Schools of the Russian Federation (project NSh-2624.2020.1) and Saint Petersburg State University (ID 75206671).

References

1. Aggarwal, C.C., Reddy, C.K.: Data Clustering - Algorithms and Applications. CRC Press, Boca Raton (2013)
2. AI and Robotics for GeoEnvironmental Modeling and Monitoring (AIRGEMM). https://tu-freiberg.de/airgemm Accessed 12 Mar 2021
3. Kisner., H., Thomas., U.: Segmentation of 3d point clouds using a new spectral clustering algorithm without a-priori knowledge. In: Proceedings of the 13th International Joint Conference on Computer Vision, Imaging and Computer Graphics Theory and Applications, vol. 4m VISAPP, pp. 315–322. INSTICC, SciTePress (2018). https://doi.org/10.5220/0006549303150322
4. Nakagawa, M.: Point cloud clustering using panoramic layered range image. IntechOpen (2018). https://doi.org/10.5772/intechopen.76407
5. Carrillo, J., Perthame, B., Salort, D., Smets, D.: Qualitative properties of solutions for the noisy integrate and fire model in computational neuroscience. Comput. Neurosci. Nonlinearity 28(9), 3365–3388 (2015)
6. Comsa, I. M., Potempa, K., Versari, L., Fischbacher, T., Gesmundo, A., Alakuijala, J.: Temporal Coding in Spiking Neural Networks with Alpha Synaptic Function: Learning with Backpropagation (2020). https://arxiv.org/pdf/1907.13223.pdf

7. Eliasmith, C.: A unified approach to building and controlling spiking attractor networks. Neural Comput. **17**(6), 1276–1314 (2005)
8. Farrokh, M., Dizaji, M., Dizaji, F., Moradinasab, N.: Universal hysteresis identification using extended Preisach Neural Network (2019). https://arxiv.org/pdf/2001.01559.pdf
9. Fusi, S.: Hebbian spike-driven synaptic plasticity for learning patterns of mean firing rates. Biol. Cybern. **87**(5–6), 459–470 (2002)
10. Kuznetsov, N., Reitmann, V.: Attractor Dimension Estimates for Dynamical Systems: Theory and Computation. ECC, vol. 38. Springer, Cham (2021). https://doi.org/10.1007/978-3-030-50987-3
11. Mutto, C.D., Zanuttigh, P., Cortelazzo, G.M.: Time-of-Flight Cameras and Microsoft Kinect^{TM}; Springer, Boston (2012) https://doi.org/10.1007/978-1-4614-3807-6_2
12. Neimark, Yu. I.: On Lyapunov stability of systems with distributed wave units. Uchenye Zapiski Gor'kovskogo Gos. Universiteta, Ser. Fiz., XVI (1950) (Russian)
13. Qi, C.R., Su, H., Mo, K., Guibas, L.J.: Pointnet: Deep learning on point sets for 3d classification and segmentation. abs/1612.00593 (2016). http://arxiv.org/abs/1612.00593
14. Qi, C.R., Yi, L., Su, H., Guibas, L.J.: Pointnet++: Deep hierarchical feature learning on point sets in a metric space. abs/1706.02413 (2017). http://arxiv.org/abs/1706.02413
15. Rajpura, P.S., Goyal, M., Bojinov, H., Hegde, R.S.: Dataset augmentation with synthetic images improves semantic segmentation. CoRR abs/1709.00849 (2017). http://arxiv.org/abs/1709.00849
16. Reitmann, S., Neumann, L., Jung, B.: BLAINDER—a blender AI add-on for generation of semantically labeled depth-sensing data. Sensors **21**, 2144 (2021). https://doi.org/10.3390/s21062144
17. Reitmann, V.: Convergence in evolutionary variational inequalities with hysteresis nonlinearities. In: Proceedings of Equadiff 11, Bratislava, pp. 395–404 (2005)
18. Reitmann, V.: Realization theory methods for the stability investigation of nonlinear infinite-dimensional input-output systems. Mathematica BOHEMICA **136**(2), 185–194 (2011)
19. Reitmann, V., Zyryanov, D.: The global attractor of a multivalued dynamical system generated by a two-phase heating problem. Differ. Eqn. Control Processes **4**, 118–138 (2017). (Russian)
20. Seeholzer, A., Deger, M., Gerstner, W.: Stability of working memory in continuous attractor networks under the control of short-term plasticity. PLoS Comput. Biol. **15**(4), e1006928 (2019)
21. Smirnova, V.B.: On the asymptotic behavior of a class of control systems with distributed parameters. Avtomatika i Telemekhanika **10**, 5–12 (1973). (Russian)
22. Visintin, A.: Differential Models of Hysteresis. Springer, Berlin (1994). https://doi.org/10.1007/978-3-662-11557-2
23. Jyh-Da, W., Chuen-Tsai, S.: Constructing hysteretic memory in neural networks. IEEE Trans. Syst. Man Cybern. Part B **30**(4), 601–609 (2000) Journal **2**(5), 99–110 (2016)
24. Yi, L., et al.: A scalable active framework for region annotation in 3d shape collections. ACM Trans. Graph. **35**(6) (2016). https://doi.org/10.1145/2980179.2980238

Cyber Supply Chain Threat Analysis and Prediction Using Machine Learning and Ontology

Abel Yeboah-Ofori[1]([⊠]), Haralambos Mouratidis[2,3], Umar Ismai[1], Shareeful Islam[1], and Spyridon Papastergiou[4]

[1] School of Computer Science, The University of West London, Ealing, W5 5RF London, UK
Abel.yeboah-ofori@uwl.ac.uk, {u.ismail,shareeful}@uel.ac.uk
[2] Centre for Secure, Intelligent and Usable Systems, University of Brighton, Brighton, UK
[3] Department of Computer and System Science, University of Stockholm, Stockholm, Sweden
haralambos@dsv.su.se
[4] Department of Informatics, University of Piraeus, Piraeus, Greece
paps@unipi.gr

Abstract. Cyber Supply Chain (CSC) security requires a secure integrated network among the sub-systems of the inbound and outbound chains. Adversaries are deploying various penetration and manipulation attacks on an CSC integrated network's node. The different levels of integrations and inherent system complexities pose potential vulnerabilities and attacks that may cascade to other parts of the supply chain system. Thus, it has become imperative to implement systematic threats analyses and predication within the CSC domain to improve the overall security posture. This paper presents a unique approach that advances the current state of the art on CSC threat analysis and prediction by combining work from three areas: Cyber Threat Intelligence (CTI), Ontologies, and Machine Learning (ML). The outcome of our work shows that the conceptualization of cybersecurity using ontological theory provides clear mechanisms for understanding the correlation between the CSC security domain and enables the mapping of the ML prediction with 80% accuracy of potential cyberattacks and possible countermeasures.

Keywords: Cyber security · Ontology · Cyber supply chain · Machine learning · Threat prediction · Cyber threat intelligence

1 Introduction

Cyber Supply Chain (CSC) security nowadays is more challenging due to the inherent system complexity and vulnerabilities among various system components and their cascading effect. Cybersecurity risks in CSC have increased exponentially leading to major security breaches in most organizations [1, 2]. The recent high profile cyberattacks such as Ukraine 2015 and Saudi Aramco 2017 smart grid attacks have brought diverse challenges, different threat landscape and unexpected challenges with unpredictable consequences [3]. Therefore, it has become imperative to have a comprehensive understanding

© IFIP International Federation for Information Processing 2021
Published by Springer Nature Switzerland AG 2021
I. Maglogiannis et al. (Eds.): AIAI 2021, IFIP AICT 627, pp. 518–530, 2021.
https://doi.org/10.1007/978-3-030-79150-6_41

of the CSC threat landscape. However, threat analysis in CSC is challenging due to a lack of understanding of the evolving threat landscape which often hinders the ability of organizations to analyze and effectively predict threats [1, 2].

This paper presents a novel threat analysis and prediction approach that uniquely combines work from Cyber Threat Intelligence (CTI), Ontology, and Machine Learning. In particular, this paper provides three main contributions. Firstly, we analyze CSC threats using CTI and ontological theory. Ontologies provide semantic mapping and explicit knowledge necessary for threat analysis. Secondly, we present a systematic process to analyse and predicate cyber threats. The process includes activities related to cyber threat intelligence and machine learning techniques such as Random Forest (RF) and GBoost algorithms for threat analysis and prediction. ML is considered for mapping the relationships between cyberattack, cyber threat propagations and their cascading impact on the various supplier chain nodes. Thirdly, we integrate knowledge from datasets from the Microsoft Malware Prediction to support threat prediction [5]. The results show that the ontological approach provides mechanisms for understanding the correlation between the CSC security domain. Both RF and GBoost algorithms provide accuracy around 80%.

2 Related Work

2.1 Cyber Supply Chain and Threat Intelligence

Cyber supply chain (CSC) security provides secure integrated networks for various organizations. CSC attacks have increased exponentially, and its cascading impact is unquantifiable, causing collateral damage to organizations. Threat actors are using sophisticated attacks including advanced persistent threats (ATP) and command and control (C&C) methods to penetrate, manipulate and obfuscate in the supply inbound and outbound chains [7–9]. Cyber Threat Intelligence (CTI) provides technical indicators, context, and actionable advice relating to existing and emerging threat [9]. Pokorny 2018 proposed a CTI lifecycle approach required to identify intelligence goals [10]. Friedman & Buchanan, proposed a CTI approach based on organizational requirements, gathering information, analysis and dissemination to protect assets and documents [11]. Miller proposed a cyber supplier chain framework and attack pattern that provides a comprehensive view of supply chain attacks of malicious insertions across a full question life cycle [12]. The protection of the CSC is critical as it incorporates various embedded networks, software and computational algorithms for information flows and data structures in the live and mission-critical system [13].

2.2 Ontology and Machine Learning for Cyber Security

Security ontology from the CSC perspective describes organizational security concepts, properties relationships and their interdependencies in a formal and structured manner [14]. The goal of security ontology is to extract relevant attack instances and information from data to ensure consistency and accuracy in the CSC security concepts and for knowledge reuse in the threat intelligence domain. Mozzaquatro et al. proposed a model driven ontology-based cybersecurity framework for the internet of things that considers design time and run time concepts for knowledge reasoning [4]. Gao et al., proposed an ontology-based model of network and computer attacks for security assessment and standards classifications that establishes relationships among network security services, threats, vulnerabilities and causes of failures [15]. Gyrard et al. proposed an ontology for attacks and countermeasures for capturing and presenting concepts of security requirements [16]. Machine Learning (ML) in cybersecurity uses various algorithms to learn and train datasets to determine their classifications and for threat predictions. ML algorithm is initially trained to allow the system to learn the data [17]. The purpose of using ML is to get the system to use past events to make an informed decision that can be used to predict future attacks [18].

3 Approach

This section provides an overview of the proposed approach and the underlying process for threat analysis and predication.

3.1 Integration of CTI, Ontology, and Machine Learning

The cyber threat intelligence is based on the threat actor profile, Tactic, Technique and Procedure (TTP), attack context and Indicator of Compromise (IoC) to provide an intelligence analysis about the threat. The proposed approach includes additional concepts related to CSC such as supply chain actor and controls. The ontology uses these concepts for a common understanding of the threat domain of CSC. Note that, due to the space limitations the details related to the concepts are not included in the paper. The ML techniques can effectively be used to analyse large data and discover the hidden patterns specifically relating to current and future threats. Such approach significantly assists organizations to gain situational awareness and understanding of the threat landscape.

Figure 1 shows the proposed approach that integrates CTI, ontology, and ML. The threat intelligence concepts are formalized using ontological theory and further used by the ML for the prediction. The CTI concepts provide information regarding threat actor intention, underlying techniques and indicators of the attack. The ontology concepts are then considered for the knowledge representation, semantic visualization and reusability of the knowledge which are useful for the CSC threat analysis [9]. Finally, the ML considers two classification models to determine the best performance and accuracy for the threat predication. We have considered Random Forest (RF) and GBoost classification algorithms for this purpose. RF is widely used for large and diverse datasets as it uses randomly selected subsets of samples to construct models to form a forest. Similarly, GBoost can also be used for large and diverse datasets and can train large datasets by gradually sequentially adding each subset in the optimization algorithms. A pipeline was used in an ensemble to link the RF and Gboost algorithms in a voting machine (VM) and ROC-AUC to plot the classifiers.

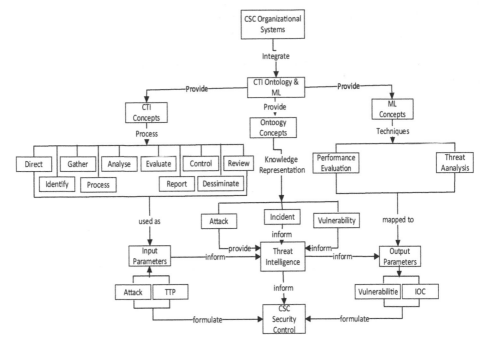

Fig. 1. Proposed approach

3.2 Ontological View for Threat Analysis

An Ontology provides a formal language that enables the explicit specification and conceptualization of ideas that represent an abstract model of a phenomenon [12]. An Ontology enables the construction of knowledge and provides the advantage of knowledge representation in organized metadata of complex information resources. Ontology concepts are applied to address the challenges of hierarchical relationship, taxonomy and structured set of rules by facilitating, formalizing, decomposition and specification of the general categories of concepts in the CSC security domain. The ontology allows the provision of relationships and concepts representing the invariant conditions of CSC security. By using semantic rules and logical representation of the concepts, we modelled a graphical visualization of the concepts to aid the automated assessment, analysis, and data processing.

The ontological view of concepts presented in the previous section provides a taxonomy of the CSC concepts. However, it is imperative to use a knowledge representation technique to provide a general overview of the CSC concepts, including a detailed vocabulary that shows conditional obligations and logical reasoning that support ML reasoning. Hence, the ontological view of the concepts is explicitly transformed into their corresponding semantic rules to express the valid conditions that exist between the concepts. Such rules are vital for expressing any complex CSC domain knowledge, relationships and statements, as well as the reuse, extensibility, and sharing of the CSC concepts. Also, without such a precise formalization, the CSC knowledge representation may appear vague and ambiguous. Thus, the rules are vital for supporting machine reasoning. Figure 2 explains the rules defining the ontological view of the CSC security concepts and provides an overview of the ontological presentation and the underlying concepts. Figure 3 shows the rule set relevant for the threat and asset which are relevant for the threat analysis [20] and note that only a part of rules is added due to the space restriction.

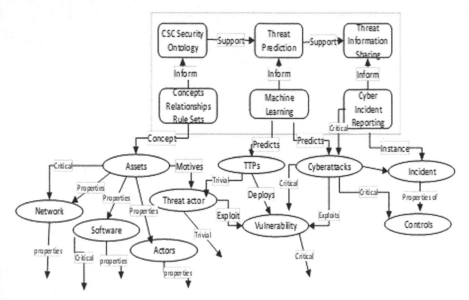

Fig. 2. Ontology concepts and properties

[∀x(actor(x) → cambe(y) → internalActor(r) ∧ externalActor(x) ∧ threatActor(z)¬ canBe(r,x,z))]

[∀x(threatActor(x) → employs(y) → TTP(r) → toExploit(e) ∧ vulnerabilities(v)¬ canBe(r,x,z))]

[∀x(asset(x) → has(x) → assetType(q) →   data(d) ∧ software(s) ∧ hardware(q) ↔ canBe (q,d,s,q,)]

[∀x(attack(x) → has(q) ∧ attackSeverity(s) ∧ attackVector(v) ∧ attackType(y) → for(f) → hardwareAsset(h)

∧ softwareAsset(w) ∧ dataAsset(d) ↔ canBe (s,v,y,h,w,d))]

[∀x(attackSeverity(x) → camBe(q) → lowSeverity(r) ∧ highSeverity(s) ∧ mediumSeverity(x) ¬ canBe(r.s.x))]

[∀x(attackVector(v) → camBe(q) → designFlaws(f) ∧ incorrectPermission(p) ∧ insufficientValidation(v)

∧ minsconfiguration(z) ↔ canBe (f,p,v,z,))]

[∀x(attackType(v) → camBe(q) → manipulationAttack(x) ∧ penetrationAttack(z) ↔ canBe (x,z,))]

Fig. 3. Ontology rule set for threat analysis

3.3 Process

This section presents the overall process of threat analysis and prediction. It consists of two phases for the CSC threat analysis and predication.

Phase 1: Threat Analysis
The threat analysis phase considers the underlying CTI gathering process and ontology concepts for analyzing the CSC security domain. It considers a number of steps, i.e., CTI gathering, CSC ontology and ML. CTI provides information required for actionable decision makings to preventing cyber-attacks. CTI gathering follows steps to identify, gather and analyze the threat information for evaluate and controls. CTI provides evidence-based knowledge of threat actor's motives, intents, TTPs, and indicators of compromise (IoC) and control mechanisms relating to the existing and emerging threat. Once the threat data is consolidated then ontology is used to present the underlying concepts for the threat. This phase follows cybersecurity ontology learning to describe CSC security concepts, properties and the relationships required to model CSC security goals. Thi step considers all the relationships required to ensure control mechanisms are in place on the supply chain environment and their implementation standards.

Phase 2: Threat Prediction
The final phase of the process is to predicate the threat using ML techniques. It includes, data representation, feature selection, choosing and classification algorithm for the ML techniques to learn a dataset, input and output features for the prediction purpose.

- **Data Presentation:** the dataset was collected from the chosen data sets [5].
- **Feature Selection:** the feature selection process assists in normalizing the dataset. The feature selection identifies irrelevant column, removes duplicate columns, reduces dimensions, and prepares the dataset for training and testing.
- **Classification for Prediction:** RF and GBoost algorithms are run in MV to learn classification for accurate responses. The AUC-ROC distinguishes between probabilities and determines the right performance metrics to evaluate the algorithms.
- **Performance Evaluation:** The performance of the models is evaluated based on the TP, TN, FP and FN values and the elements of the confusion matrix [19].

The evaluation criteria considers precision and recall in determining actual or predictive values in the feature extraction. The F-Score determine the harmonic mean for precision and recall [18].

4 Implementation

The objective of the implementation phase is to explore the applicability of our approach by using ML classification algorithms for threat predictions.

4.1 Cyber Threat Intelligence Gathering

The CTI gathering and process lifecycle steps include Direct, Identify, Gather, Process, Analyze, Evaluate, Report, Controls, Disseminate and Review.

- Direct: CTI goals are put together by strategic management to identify security goals and inform proper CSC security controls.
- Identify: Identify organizational goals, CSC requirements, assets, CSC network nodes, IP address, technical threats, and user threats actors.
- Gather: Data gather indicators of compromise from various endpoint's nodes, including firewalls logs, IDS/IPS reports, signatures, antimalware reports
- Analyze: Analyze IDS/IPS logs, firewall logs, and Antimalware intrusions to predict attacks that could be fed into the CTI.
- Evaluate: Evaluate threats, levels of risks, impacts on the CSC system and the effects on organizational goal.
- Report: Analysis and evaluations of Known and Unknown attacks for strategic management decision-making on threats levels.
- Disseminate: Designates cyber threat information sharing to all stakeholders on the CSC system.
- Review: Requires ad-hoc, periodical and annual reviews and updates to monitor current trends and alerts.

The application of ontology for the CSC security concepts enables the exchange, sharing and reuse of cyber threat information automatically, thereby providing a semantically stable structure of the underlying knowledge of CSC systems security. We use ontology to identify and map CSC concepts such as actors, assets, threats, attacks, vulnerability, TTPs and incident reporting that provide conceptual reasoning, relational knowledge and understanding of cyber threat intelligence required.

4.2 ML Threat Prediction

This section follows ML techniques to learn the dataset as discussed in Sect. 3 for threat predictions. That include data preparation, description, feature extraction, choosing an optimization algorithm and determining the performance accuracies as follows.

Data Description: The dataset used is from a publicly available data source from a Microsoft Malware Prediction data website [5]. The data was collected by Microsoft Windows Defender with over 40,000 entries with 62 columns and each row represents different telemetry data entries. Each row in the dataset corresponds to a machine uniquely identified by a machine Identifier. The dataset integrates systems using other operating systems that do not represent Microsoft customer's machine only as it has been sampled to include a much larger proportion of malware machines.

Data Preparation: The format of the data is mainly csv files. We used the Kaggle API to downloaded the dataset. A NaN dictionary was created to handle all the unwanted duplicates and removed 8 duplicates leaving 54 columns as relevant from the 62 columns.

Feature Extraction: There are total 64 features in the data set. However, 32 features extracted which are relevant to understand the attack profile. The rest are features with duplicate samples and those with zero variances. Thus, we reduce the features by setting the selection criteria and the variance threshold in the code to remove all zeros to ensure dimensionality reduction during the training. Further, we derived the secondary data from the primary data by identifying features considered as probable threat in [2] for the ML.

Choosing an Optimization Algorithm for the Classifiers: The ML algorithms used for the work are RF and GBoost. A multiclass classifications approach was used in a AUC_ROC to model the selection metric for the multiclass classification problem. We used each classifier against all to distinguish between the probabilities of the classes to obtain the performance indices for Precision, Recall and F-Score. A pipeline was used to connect the algorithms in the loop to determine the best optimization algorithm. A 10-Fold cross-validation was used to determine the parameter estimation and validation for consistent and accurate result. We combine the algorithms using Majority Voting (MV) in the classifiers to determine the mean score of the results. Finally, the ROC-AUC distinguished between the accuracies of the binary classifiers for the predictions.

Determining the Performance Evaluation and Accuracies: Figure 4 depicts the results of the accuracies and combines 2 classification algorithms, RF and GB in a pipeline and run in a ROC curve to determine the true positive and false positive rates using the 10-Fold cross-validation. RF produces a performance result of 73% compared to GB 79% with a majority voting of 78%. The highest classifier from the performance model was GB as it can predict better performance in predicting attack. However, the results show a slight reduction in the overall score with the MV score of 78%. Further, it shows higher accuracy for the TPRs and FPRs as compared to Fig. 2 where the performance went down when we included the RF algorithm.

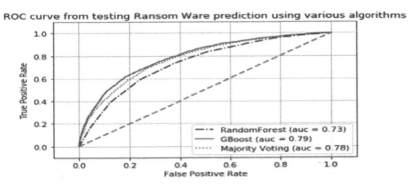

Fig. 4. Roc curve for prediction the RM and GBoost algorithms in VM

10-Fold Cross-Validation:

ROC AUC: 0.73 (+/- 0.01) [RandomForest]
ROC AUC: 0.79 (± 0.02) [GBoost]
ROC AUC: 0.78 (± 0.01) [Majority Voting]

5 Results

This section presents the results of using ML algorithms and presents the accuracies of the threats predication using ML evaluation using Precision, Recall, and F-Score.

Predicting the Different Types of Responses Based on the Type of Cyberattack:
To predicting the different types of responses based on the type of cyberattack, we refer to the probabilities of cyberattacks in our previous work [6], for the various accuracies of the attacks. Table 1 presents the performance of the classifications of RF and GBoost algorithms in identifying the various responses of cyberattacks based on the given malicious attack. From the table, RF achieved an accuracy of 80% and GBoost 78%. Comparing the performance of the classifiers, RF performed better for the Precision (P), Recall (R) and F-Score (F), whilst GBoost received a low precision, recall and F-score. Comparing that to the attack's categories signifies that Malware, Ransomware and spyware attacks provided different types of responses with 80% accuracy.

Table 1. Threat predication on endpoint nodes using RF and GBoost classifiers

Accuracy	RF 80%	GBoost 78%
Attacks	P R F	P R F
XSS/session Hijacking	0.74 0.66 0.72	0.72 0.70 0.71
Ransomware	0.80 0.76 0.78	0.79 0.76 0.77
Spear phishing	0.73 0.69 0.71	0.74 0.70 0.72
RAT/Island hopping	0.76 0.74 0.75	0.72 0.70 0.71
Malware	0.79 0.76 0.77	0.79 0.76 0.77
Spyware	0.77 0.74 0.76	0.78 0.75 0.76
DDoS	0.71 0.69 0.70	0.78 0.75 0.76

Predicting TTPs Deployed Based on the Response of the Cyberattacks: To predicting the different types of responses based on the type of TTPs deployed, we determine the various accuracies of the attacks. Table 2 presents the performance of the classification algorithms in identifying the various TTPs deployed and the responses based on the given attack vectors. Comparing the TTPs deployed against the cyberattack such as XSS, session hijacking and RAT attack, RF achieved a low accuracy of

79% whereas GBoost achieved a higher accuracy of 82% for the precision, recall and F-score. Furthermore, ransomware, malware and spyware attacks identified different types of responses for the TTPs with 82% accuracy for the harmonic mean in identifying the attack vectors spear Phishing, email attachments, RAT and rootkit attacks.

Table 2. Identify the different TTP deployed based on the response of the cyberattacks

Accuracy	RF 79%	GBoost 82%
Attacks	P R F	P R F
XSS/session Hijacking	0.75 0.71 0.72	0.76 0.72 0.74
Ransomware	0.79 0.75 0.78	0.81 0.76 0.79
Spear phishing	0.76 0.73 0.75	0.76 0.73 0.75
RAT/Island hopping	0.77 0.74 0.76	0.77 0.75 0.76
Malware	0.79 0.75 0.77	0.82 0.77 0.81
Malware/Spyware	0.78 0.74 0.77	0.79 0.76 0.78
DDoS	0.72 0.70 0.71	0.73 0.72 0.71

6 Discussion

This section discusses the observations made from the evaluation of the accuracies and results of the CSC threat predictions. The study revealed several challenges facing organizations in securing the CSC systems as threat actors are executing arbitrary commands on the supply chain systems remotely and manipulating systems. For us to predict the accuracies of the threats, that identified vulnerable spots on the CSC network system that could be exploited, the percentage score of manipulation and the probability levels [2]. The vulnerable spots include network, vendor, website, firewall, IDS/IPS, software, IP, and the database system.

Comparing the features descriptions listed in Table 1 with the cyber-attack prediction Table 1 and TTP Table 2, we predict various cyberattacks that could be initiated on the vulnerable spots in Table 3. CSC systems integrate with other network systems using public-facing IPs. Threat actors could exploit the default browsers, websites and initiate attacks to penetrate the system and cause various manipulations as in Table 3.

6.1 Comparison with Existing Works

A number of works focus on using CTI, ML, and ontology for the threat analysis. For instances, [10] considered CTI approach for gathering intelligence goals, [11] considered CTI approach that protect assets, and [12] proposed a comprehensive CSC framework for attack pattern. Further, [4] proposed cybersecurity ontology framework for IoT and knowledge reasoning, [15] considered an ontology model that establishes relationships

Table 3. Predicting threat indicators on vulnerable spots

Attacks	Vulnerable spots	Penetration	Manipulation%	Probability
Remote access Trojan	Firewall	Y	80%	High
Island hopping	IDS/IPS	Y	75%	High
Ransomware	Vendor	Y	90%	High
Session Hijacking	Network	Y	70%	Medium
DDoS	IP	Y	80%	Medium
Malware	Database	Y	75%	High
Malware	Software	Y	95%	High
XSS	Website	Y	90%	High

among networks, and [16] proposed a security ontology for capturing requirements. Furthermore, [17–19] used ML techniques on various algorithms to learn datasets for performance accuracies and predictions. All the works are relevant and contributes to cyber security improvement, however none of the works considered integrating CTI, ontology and ML to extract relevant attack instances for knowledge representation and threat predictions in CSC security domain.

6.2 CSC Controls

This section discusses controls that support CSC security threats and predictions in line with the control ontology. The challenge of developing security controls, configuration settings with the best security properties is a complex task and goes beyond the ability of individual users as it requires analysis of potential threats and risks on the CSC system. It is therefore required to have an inventory of current control mechanism including audit trails of the other organizations and third-party vendors. This certainly supports to determine the existing security capabilities, prediction of TTP and indicators in order to determine the necessity of additional controls for the overall cyber security improvement. Establish, implement, and actively managing, tracking, reporting on, and correcting the security configuration using configuration management tools and change control process could prevent external penetration and manipulations that could lead to malware and ransomware attacks. There are different types of controls such as directive, preventive, and preventive need to select based on the nature of threat.

7 Conclusions

Predicting cyber supply chain threats has proved daunting due to the various network integrations and the complexities involved in the different configurations. Further, the sophisticated and stealthy nature of cyberattacks on CSC systems has made a threat analysis of CSC security threat analysis very challenging. In this work, we have used CTI and CSC security ontology concepts to analyse the threat and ML techniques to predict threats. CSC ontology concepts provided us with knowledge reuse in the CTI domain and an understanding of the attack instances. The ML predictions indicate the precision of 80% accuracy for cyberattacks such as malware and ransomware on systems without regular antivirus updated. The ontology provided knowledge of security controls that systematize all security phenomenon. Future works include data sets from other sources to generalize and improve our prediction results. Further, it is also required to automate the process so that CSC organizations can feed the data into the tools and obtain the prediction results.

Acknowledgments This research has received funding from the European Union's Horizon 2020 research and innovation programme under grant agreement No 952690. The results of this paper reflect only the author's view and the Commission is not responsible for any use that may be made of the information it contains.

References

1. Woods, B., Bochman, A.: Supply Chain in the Software Era. Atlantic Council, Washington, DC (2018). https://doi.org/10.1109/5254.920602
2. Yeboah-Ofori, A., Islam, S.: Cyber security threat modeling for supply chain organizational environments. Future Internet **11**, 63 (2019). https://doi.org/10.3390/fi11030063
3. Department for Business Innovation and Skill. Information Security Breaches Survey. Technical report. PWC and InfoSecurity (2013)
4. Mozzaquatro, B.A., Agostinho, C., Goncalves, D., Martins, J., Jardim-Goncalves, R.: An ontology-based cybersecurity framework for the Internet of Things. MDPI. Sens. **18**, 3053 (2018). https://doi.org/10.3390/s18093053
5. Microsoft malware prediction. Research prediction. Kaggle dataset (2019). https://www.kaggle.com/c/microsoft-malware-prediction/data. Accessed 28 Jan 2021
6. Maedche, A., Staab, S.: Ontology learning for the semantic web. IEEE Intell. Syst. **16**, 72–79 (2001)
7. CERT-UK.: Cyber-security risks in the supply chain. TLP Whitepaper (2020)
8. US-Cert. Building security in software & supply chain assurance. https://www.us-cert.gov/bsi/articles/knowledge/attack-patterns. Accessed 24 Nov 2020
9. ENISA. Exploring the opportunities and limitations of current threat intelligence platforms Version 1 (2017)
10. Porkorny, Z.: What Are the Phases of The Threat Intelligence Lifecycle? The Threat Intelligence Handbook (2018)
11. Freidman, J., Bouchard. M.: Cyber threat intelligence guide: using knowledge about adversary to win the war against targeted attacks. iSightPartners (2018)
12. Miller, J. F.: Supply chain attack framework and attack pattern. Mitre (2013)
13. Boyens. J.: Integrating Cybersecurity into Supply Chain Risk Management. RSA. Moscone Center, San Francisco (2016)
14. Arbanas, K., Cubrilo, M.: Ontology in formation security. JIOS **39**(2), 107–136 (2015)
15. Gao, J., Zhang, B., Chen, X., Luo, Z.: Ontology-based model of network and computer attacks for security assessment. **18**(5), 554–562 (2013). https://doi.org/10.1007/s12204-013-1439-5
16. Gyrard, A., Bonnet, C., Boudaoud, K.: The STAC (Security Toolbox: Attacks & Countermeasures) Ontology. Conference, pp. 165–166, Rio de Janeiro, Brazil (2013)
17. Villano. E.G.V.: Classification of Logs Using Machine Learning. Norwegian University of Science and Technology (2018)

18. Boschetti, A., Massaron. L: Python Data Science Essentials. 2nd edn. (2016). ISBN 978-1-78646-213-8
19. Mohasseb, B., Aziz, J.J., Lee, J.: predicting cyber security incidents using machine learning algorithms: a case study of Korean SMEs. University of Portsmouth (2019)
20. Martimiano, L.A.F., Moreira, E.S.: An OWL-based security incident ontology Protégé. Conference, pp. 1–4, Madrid, Spain. (2005). Semantic Scholar

Intelligent Techniques and Hybrid Systems Experiments Using the Acumen Modeling and Simulation Environment

Sotirios Tzamaras[1](✉), Stavros Adam[1](✉), and Walid Taha[2]

[1] Autonomous Systems Laboratory, Department of Informatics and
Telecommunications, University of Ioannina, Ioannina, Greece
sotiris@tzamaras.com, adamsp@uoi.gr
[2] School of Information Technology, Halmstad University, Halmstad, Sweden
walid.taha@hh.se

Abstract. Hybrid systems are dynamical systems of both continuous and discrete nature and constitute an important field of control systems theory and engineering. On the other hand, intelligent data processing has become one of the most critical devices of modern computer based systems as these systems operate in environments featuring increasing uncertainty and unpredictability. While these two approaches set completely different objectives, modern cyber-physical systems, taken as variants of hybrid systems, seem to constitute a field of increasing interest for applying intelligent techniques. Moreover, the examples of, not so recent, intelligent control systems are suggestive for considering a study on getting intelligent techniques close to hybrid systems. In this paper we present the experimental investigation we undertook in this direction. More specifically, we present and discuss the experiments carried out using Acumen a hybrid systems modeling and simulation environment. Without urging towards setting and solving questions of conceptual order we tried to figure out whether it is possible to represent intelligent behavior using a tool for modeling dynamical systems focusing on the study of its ability to permit the representation of both continuous and discrete intelligent techniques, namely, Reinforcement Learning and Hopfield neural networks. The results obtained are indicative of the problems related to the specific computational context and are useful in deriving conclusions concerning the functionality that needs to be provided by such modeling and simulation environments, in order to allow for the coexistence of hybrid systems and intelligent techniques.

1 Introduction

The increasing demand on systems theory and applications, especially regarding control, has caused a significant interest in the study of processes exhibiting both

Part of this work was conducted by Sotirios Tzamaras, during his internship at the University of Halmstad, funded by the Erasmus+ program.

© IFIP International Federation for Information Processing 2021
Published by Springer Nature Switzerland AG 2021
I. Maglogiannis et al. (Eds.): AIAI 2021, IFIP AICT 627, pp. 531–542, 2021.
https://doi.org/10.1007/978-3-030-79150-6_42

continuous and discrete dynamic behavior. These processes are studied by means of complex systems known as hybrid systems [1] which comprise two constituent elements, namely, the continuous-time models and the discrete-time components. Continuous-time models are governed by differential or difference equations while discrete-time components are driven by logic rules and are discrete-event systems using models, such as, automata, finite state machines, etc. In practical applications, it is commonplace to obtain a hybrid system whenever some continuous physical process is controlled by some embedded software system implementing a finite number of states, such as, on/off switches. Modern hybrid systems have received extensive interest due to a number of advances and developments in nonlinear control theory, intelligent control, adaptive control, computer science etc. Last but not least one should mention the increasing use of hybrid systems known as Cyber-Physical Systems (CPS). Typically, a CPS controls some physical process interacting with it through specialized computer and network interfaces. From the point of view of networked computer systems CPS's constitute entities residing in ecosystems commonly known as Internet of Things.

It is well known that modern systems operate in highly unpredictable and uncertain environments affecting the complexity of the physical processes and thereof the control systems. To a considerable extent, dealing with uncertainty has become possible thanks to a class of data driven techniques either of statistical nature originating from machine learning or based on nature inspired approaches from the field of computational intelligence. While the former seem to be more suitable for parameter or system identification tasks the latter have mostly been applied to control function design tasks. The ensemble of these data driven techniques and approaches constitute intelligent approaches and techniques which, recently, are considered to form a new field called machine learning control [5].

As a result, bringing together hybrid systems and intelligent approaches seems to be unavoidable towards designing efficient CPS's which undertake more and more demanding tasks. In a broader sense this perspective does not seem to be new as the control systems community posed the question of the very nature of intelligent control systems since the early '90s [2]. Modern intelligent techniques are based on a wide range of approaches elaborated on a variety of concepts of either statistical or heuristic nature. This implies that bringing close hybrid systems and intelligent behavior is a task which needs important conceptual work to be done in order to bridge the gap between analytical techniques on one hand and statistical and/or heuristic on the other. Moreover, at a more practical level it is important to consider the problem of having suitable tools for designing and simulating hybrid systems together with intelligent behavior in the same operational context.

1.1 Contributions

The work presented in this paper deals with this latter point of view. By means of an experimental study of an environment used for designing hybrid systems this study intends to contribute on the following issues:

1. Investigate the ability of such environments to support implementation of discrete structures and events.
2. Study the possibility to implement control structures governed by intelligent agents.
3. Draw conclusions on the possible level of interaction between intelligent modules and hybrid systems.

Note that, the exact role of the intelligent function, as well as, its detailed study of interaction and/or integration with the control function of a hybrid system are important matters that need careful and exhaustive study and are beyond the scope of this paper.

The rest of the paper is organized as follows. In Sect. 2, we present the work related to the problem described in the beginning of this Sect. 1 together with a literature review which highlights specific points of the problem set. Section 3 is devoted to a presentation of the Acumen environment pointing out the most interesting concepts and constructs allowing for this study. In Sect. 4 we give examples of implementing intelligent agents in Acumen and we discuss advantages and pitfalls detected in this work. Finally, Sect. 5 closes the paper with some concluding remarks.

2   Related Work

Though the hybrid systems community has not adopted intelligent techniques, recently, some interest on these techniques has been manifested by a number of researchers in the area of control systems. A number of recent publications on this topic can be found in the literature. In [12] Moe et al. give an overview and describe the state of the art concerning the use of machine learning techniques in control systems. Javadi-Moghaddam and Bagheri in [6] present an adaptive neuro-fuzzy genetic algorithm based on sliding-mode control system for a remotely operated vehicle with four degrees of freedom. A survey of Evolutionary Algorithms in Control Systems Engineering is presented by Fleming and Purshouse in [5]. Some older research includes the work of Lemmon and Anstaklis [10] on hybrid systems and their relation to intelligent control and the work of Lee and Kim in [9] describing the use of a neural network for designing an adaptive controller applied to turbulent channel flow for drag reduction.

However, the most significant part of this research deals with use of Reinforcement Learning (RL) a concept in Artificial Intelligence which corresponds to Neuro-Dynamic Programming. In Koch et al. [8] the authors study the use of RL for the control of UAV. More specifically, they investigate the performance and accuracy of the inner control loop providing attitude control when using intelligent flight control systems trained with state-of-the-art RL algorithms, Deep Deterministic Policy Gradient, Trust Region Policy Optimization, and Proximal Policy Optimization. In [20] Wang et al. present a novel approach to feedback control with deep RL. In a review paper [3] Bosoniu et al. present important advances in RL for control concerning performance, stability analysis, and deep approximators. Recently, Quade et al. [15] archived their research on explainable machine learning on control issues such as robust control and stability analysis.

Moreover, intelligent approaches are more and more used in various applications of CPS's. For instance, one may cite the review paper [16] of Radanliev et al. on artificial intelligence in cyber physical systems and references therein. We may, also, cite the archived review paper [14] of Olowononi et al. on security issues of machine learning for networked CPSs. In addition to these, one may cite the most recent special issues by journals such as Computer Communication: Special Issue on AI-Driven Sensing and Computing for Cyber-Physical Systems and the special issue on Artificial Intelligence and Cyber-Physical Systems by the ACM Transactions on Cyber Physical Systems. This literature review highlights the potential interest in studying ways of bridging the gap between hybrid systems and intelligent techniques. Starting from the simple interaction, between these two approaches, one may envisage the implementation of intelligent techniques using hybrid systems in a unique environment. Hence, studying the infrastructure necessary to support both approaches is an important issue.

In the context of this paper considering intelligent behavior and hybrid systems implies taking into account the environments and/or languages available for designing hybrid systems and how it is possible to implement intelligent behavior on these environments. In these terms it seems that the MATLAB© computing environment together with its Toolboxes such as Simulink, Control System, Neural Networks, etc. stand above other available tools as it disposes numerous libraries both for designing hybrid systems as well as for implementing machine learning techniques. Probably, besides cost restrictions, the most serious inconvenience is that all these tools are proprietary and they are not open to user-made modifications.

Another well known environment for hybrid systems is Modelica; an equational modeling language implemented with different front-ends as a simulation computing engine which can be interfaced with other external libraries. As an example, Modelica has been used by Schaub et al. [17] in order to simulate autonomous vehicles using intelligent agents. Moreover, Lukianykhin et al. [11] proposed an approach which allows connecting models using a Functional Mock-up Interface to the OpenAI Gym toolkit. The objective is to exploit Modelica equation-based modeling and co-simulation together with RL algorithms. While such interface capabilities are not available in Acumen, to the best of our knowledge, Modelica constitutes a modeling environment displaying similar functionality as Acumen.

Finally, creating a modeling environment from scratch, in any of the well known programming languages (Python, Scala, etc.), constitutes an alternative possibility which proves to be an extremely time consuming option. Typically, programming environments offer the possibility to develop tools for simulating intelligent behavior which can be used in conjunction with integrated environments. This underlines the fact that integrated environments incorporating intelligent functionality are not commonplace.

3 Acumen: A Hybrid Systems Modeling and Simulation Environment

3.1 Description of the Environment

Acumen [4] is an experimental Domain-Specific Language (DSL) written in Scala [13], a programming language that runs on top of the Java Virtual Machine (JVM). It is distributed as an Integrated Developing Environment (IDE) and provides a wide range of tools to the user, some of which include a code editor, error reporting and visualization of 3D animations.

The purpose of the language is to model and simulate hybrid systems, which are dynamical systems that can exhibit discrete, continuous or hybrid (discrete and continuous) behavior. Although small in size, the language provides a variety of expressions to the user allowing for simulation of larger systems, as well as the ability to model systems that contain multiple variables dynamically changing over time. Originally, Acumen was motivated by the absence of robust developing tools for modeling CPS. There is an obscure gap between verification tools and running simulators [21], and Acumen was built as an experimental bridge between the two. At the highest level, the leading goal of the language is to explore ways of designing a "rigorous-but-practical" tool for hybrid systems developers, as long as it encapsulates mathematical correctness, practicality and scalability [18] (Fig. 1).

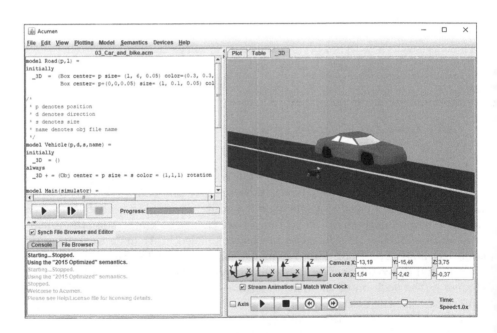

Fig. 1. Layout of the Acumen environment.

3.2   Conceptual Approach

Acumen uses the notion of *models* as its core data structure. Hereafter, we will denote an Acumen model by A-model. Each A-model may consist of two sections, which are the *initially* and the *always* section. The *initially* section takes care of the initialization of all the variables used by the A-model. On the other hand, the *always* section describes the dynamic behavior of the model over time by means of simple or conditional statements. We need to note, here, that statements in Acumen are executed in parallel, i.e. at the same time, and so *the order of such statements is irrelevant.* In this sense Acumen statements do not follow the semantics of statements met in classical programming languages and other computing environments. In order to depict the conceptual structure of Acumen, highlighting the constructs which permit to model and simulate hybrid systems, let us consider a concrete example of modeling and simulating a bouncing ball.

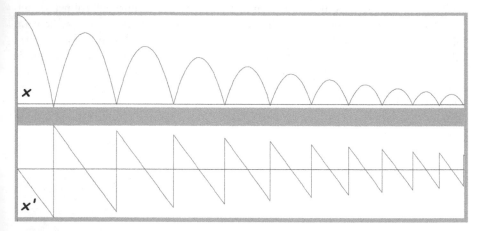

Fig. 2. Bouncing ball model. Evolution of the position and its derivative.

In Fig. 2, we see the Acumen result while executing the A-model configuration for a bouncing ball. This A-model is rather simple and can be described by an Acumen 3-D object, such as a sphere, and a position variable x with its respective first and second derivatives, $\dot{x}$ for the rate of change of x and $\ddot{x}$ for the gravity acceleration. Such expressions can be easily modeled in Acumen by writing the code as shown in Fig. 3. This Acumen example highlights the way one may model a hybrid system such as a bouncing ball. Continuous behavior concerning change in the position of the ball over time is described by the two differential equations while the discrete event corresponding to the ball touching the ground is formulated by the *if* statement.

Another notable example is a hybrid dynamical system in intelligent control [10], that is a system consisting of a continuous-state plant interfaced to a discrete event supervisor. The supervisor of the hybrid system is the component deriving

```
model Main(simulator) =
initially
  x = 3 , x' = 0 , x'' = -9.8,
  _3D = ()
always
  x''=-9.8,
  if x<0 && x'<0 then
    x' += -0.9*x'
  noelse,
  _3D =(Sphere center=(0,0,x) size=0.2 color=(1,0,0) rotation=(0,0,0))
```

Fig. 3. Acumen algorithm for the bouncing ball model.

and setting provably correct goals for the control function. These goals are the result of decisions taken by a subsystem or a function implementing some form of intelligent decision support. Studying the feasibility to represent such intelligent behavior in a modeling and simulation environment for hybrid systems such as Acumen [18] results in investigating a) the expressive power of the environment and the type of intelligent behavior that it is possible to represent, b) the level of interaction that is possible to achieve between continuous and discrete time components and c) the changes and upgrades needed for the language constructs in order to fully support the previous points.

4 Experiments and Results

In order to achieve the goals set by the previous items we choose to implement two specific intelligent techniques, namely, RL and Hopfield neural networks. The reason for these choices is that these techniques have both a continuous and a discrete time version. Moreover, the problem chosen for RL is the exploration of a 2-dimensional maze which requires its representation by means of discrete constructs. It is thus possible to investigate the performance of Acumen in both continuous and discrete time together with some framework triggering some discrete time events.

4.1 Q-Learning Intelligent Agent

Let us recall that RL is a machine learning technique used to solve complex optimization problems in uncertain/unknown environments. The approach uses agents to explore the unknown environment by taking actions [7] and giving them rewards based on the progress of the optimization task. So, during this process agents are able to adjust and optimize their behavior through a feedback mechanism based on the rewards strategy [19]. The Q-learning algorithm used in this experiment is described by Eq. (1).

$$Q^{new}(s_t, a_t) \leftarrow Q^{old}(s_t, a_t) + \alpha * (r_t + \gamma * maxQ(s_{t+1}, \alpha) - Q^{old}(s_t, a_t)). \quad (1)$$

In our implementation an intelligent agent traverses and learns its way to a goal position. This agent is an abstract entity implemented using two A-models. The first A-model, which is called the "Main Model", simulates the maze environment and runs the Q-learning algorithm, while being in charge of reacting to the different actions and providing the appropriate rewards. The second A-model is the "Moving Model" which navigates in the maze environment. By default operation of the agent for these two functions is continuous in time but this specific implementation uses discrete time steps. The reason for this choice is justified by the fact that in a continuous time setup for Q-learning we would have to compute the terms of Eq. (1) in continuous time. Yet, it is known that typical implementations of this strategy use a neural network. The following Fig. 4 outlines the maze used for this experiment.

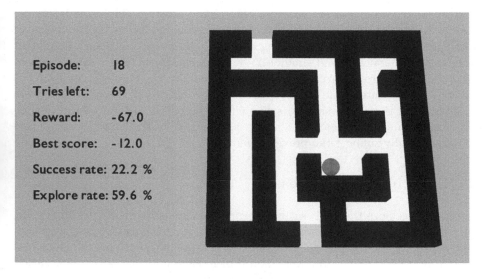

Fig. 4. Simulation of a maze environment in Acumen.

In addition to the above an A-Model is needed for setting up and updating the 2-dimensional maze, represented in Acumen using 3-dimensional objects. This is done by initializing an A-model called the Environment. This is a static A-model responsible for creating all the 3-dimensional objects needed to visualize the maze layout for the simulation. The A-model configuration corresponding to the Moving Agent instantiates parameters tied to the agent's behavior such as the current and the reset positions, the moves executed and the accumulated reward. It also creates a 3D object, i.e. the red sphere, in order to visualize the agent. On the other hand the A-model related to the Main Model comprises the Acumen code for executing the Q-learning algorithm while communicating with the Environment and the Moving Model for retrieving its position and moving behavior.

In conclusion, this set up comprises two concurrent A-Models responsible for carrying out two different functions of the intelligent agent, as well as a static A-model for the objects forming the maze. The Moving Model handles the motion of the red sphere while the Main Model is responsible for updating the Q-table with the appropriate values guiding the motion of the Moving Agent. This experiment permits to exploit Acumen language constructs mainly for implementing intelligent agents by investigating alternatives on how to implement the Q-learning algorithm. Another option would be to define two different agents one represented by the Main Model and a second one represented by the Moving Model. This architecture assigns a specific task to each agent thus breaking the intelligent agent into two communicating agents. Despite the fact that interaction between A-Models is supported by Acumen by means of shared memory access and concurrent execution of the A-Models, we believe that a supplementary level of abstraction in the definition of agents would add to the complexity of the representation without, essentially, solving any problem.

Finally, implementation of Q-learning requires the creation of a Q-Table which describes the quality of the different actions of the agent in any state. Hence, implementation of Q-Table in Acumen requires a suitable data structure while the actions described in Q-Table need to be implemented by a set of discrete states, e.g. a form of a matrix of states. So, Acumen should be able to allow for the creation of discrete structures, such as matrices, while permitting direct or indexed access to the elements of these structures. However, it was found that such constructs were not part of the specifications of Acumen and so we had to undertake a number of significant modifications to endow Acumen with this functionality.

4.2 Simple Hopfield Networks

In this experiment we studied the simulation of two Hopfield network models in order to obtain hands-on experience with the implementation of intelligent models with dynamic behavior. It is well known that Hopfield networks are recurrent artificial neural networks which are able to simulate associative memory systems with binary output neurons. The dynamics of the Hopfield network can be studied either in discrete time steps or in continuous time flow.

For this case study we implemented both discrete and continuous time models pre-trained as it was not within our goals to verify how the Hebbian update rule modifies the networks' weights. Simulation of both models gave the expected results with the continuous model exhibiting for each neuron smooth transition between the extreme values of the bipolar function *tanh* used for the activation function of the neurons. Figure 5 displays the output of each model after convergence.

$$C_t \frac{dx_i(t)}{dt} = -\frac{x_i(t)}{R_i} + \sum_{j=1}^{N} w_{ij}\phi_j(x_j(t)) + I_i. \tag{2}$$

The differential equation for the continuous model is given by Eq. (2) and the corresponding Acumen code is shown in Fig. 6. This model configuration displays

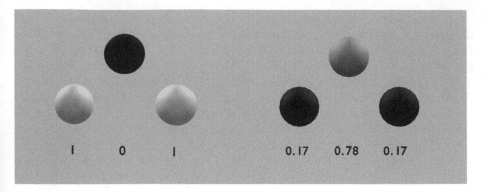

Fig. 5. Hopfield models in Acumen (left: discrete, right: continuous)

how Acumen handles randomness and the reaction based on the different random numbers which leads to the appropriate use of differential equation for the
specific neuron. In this experiment we investigated the possibility to implement
both a continuous and a discrete time intelligent model such as the Hopfield network. In both cases Acumen provided the necessary constructs to successfully
model and simulate both models thus providing the expressive power suitable
for implementing both discrete and continuous behavior. However, we need to
note that Acumen is not a computational environment giving the possibility to
define and execute vector equations of any form. This constitutes a minor disadvantage which, again, is related to the lack of suitable data structures with
direct or indexed access in Acumen.

```
always
  n0.output = N(0),
  n1.output = N(1),
  n2.output = N(2),
  match rnd with [
    0 -> N'(0) = (-(N(0)/R) * (W(0,1)*tanh(N(1)) + W(0,2)*tanh(N(2))) + theta)/C,
         N'(1) = N'(1),
         N'(2) = N'(2)
  | 1 -> N'(1) = (-(N(1)/R) * (W(1,0)*tanh(N(0)) + W(1,2)*tanh(N(2))) + theta)/C,
         N'(0) = N'(0),
         N'(2) = N'(2)
  | 2 -> N'(2) = (-(N(2)/R) * (W(2,0)*tanh(N(0)) + W(2,1)*tanh(N(1))) + theta)/C,
         N'(0) = N'(0),
         N'(1) = N'(1)
  ],
  rnd += argrand((0,1,2))
```

Fig. 6. Acumen algorithm for the continuous Hopfield model.

The main result of the experiments performed is that Acumen proves to have the constructs necessary to implement intelligent behavior both for continuous and discrete time models. This is achieved using the *model* construct which encapsulates both the dynamics of an agent and the static elements related to its outlook or the environment. *Models* in Acumen are executed concurrently thus simulating parallelism. Information is exchanged between *models* by means of accessing shared memory and so there is no need of some specific communication or message passing mechanism. Different behaviors of the same agent can be implemented using specific Acumen *models* which co-exist and act as whole for simulating the agent as a single entity.

5   Concluding Remarks

In this paper we, experimentally, evaluated the potential of a hybrid systems design and simulation environment such as Acumen, to support implementation of intelligent behavior by means of independent interacting models. However, while Acumen has the necessary expressive power for such implementations it lacks some elementary but necessary data structures of direct or indexed access to their elements. This was the main obstacle we faced. The add-ons built to remedy this disadvantage proved to be insufficient as these constructs were not within the requirements set for Acumen. We need to note that either Acumen or any other similar environment should offer such data structures in order to permit building more complex intelligent behavior such as fully interacting agents. The level of interaction between intelligent modules and hybrid systems is defined by the interaction set by Acumen for its models.

The experiments carried out permit to draw conclusions on the possibility to represent intelligent techniques using hybrid systems modeling tools, thus bringing closer these two different concepts. Though these partial conclusions are hopeful we consider that effective cooperation of intelligent techniques and hybrid systems is feasible for specific tasks and problems under the essential requirement that intelligent approaches do not set serious problems on issues such as stability, convergence and optimality of the control systems. Finally, in general terms we may conclude that this study can be applied to draw conclusion for a wider spectrum of modeling and simulation applications such as intelligent robotic systems, intelligent drones etc.

Acknowledgments. The authors would like to thank the anonymous reviewers for their suggestions and comments on earlier version of the manuscript, that helped to improve the paper at hand.

References

1. Alur, R., et al.: The algorithmic analysis of hybrid systems. Theoret. Comput. Sci. **138**(1), 3–34 (1995)
2. Antsaklis, P.J.: On Intelligent Control: Report of the IEEE CSS Task Force on Intelligent Control. Technical report, University of Notre Dame (January 1994)

3. Busoniu, L., de Bruin, T., Tolić, D., Kober, J., Palunko, I.: Reinforcement learning for control: performance, stability, and deep approximators. Ann. Rev. Control **46**, 8–28 (2018)
4. Effective Modeling Group: Acumen modeling language. http://acumen-language. org
5. Fleming, P., Purshouse, R.: Evolutionary algorithms in control systems engineering: a survey. Control Eng. Pract. **10**(11), 1223–1241 (2002)
6. Javadi-Moghaddam, J., Bagheri, A.: An adaptive neuro-fuzzy sliding mode based genetic algorithm control system for under water remotely operated vehicle. Expert Syst. Appl. **37**(1), 647–660 (2010)
7. Kaelbling, L.P., Littman, M.L., Moore, A.W.: Reinforcement learning: a survey. J. Artif. intell. Res. **4**, 237–285 (1996)
8. Koch, W., Mancuso, R., West, R., Bestavros, A.: Reinforcement learning for UAV attitude control. ACM Trans. Cyber-Phys. Syst. **3**(2), 1–21 (2019)
9. Lee, C., Kim, J., Babcock, D., Goodman, R.: Application of neural networks to turbulence control for drag reduction. Phys. Fluids **9**(6), 1740–1747 (1997)
10. Lemmon, M., Antsaklis, P.: Hybrid systems and intelligent control. In: Proceedings of 8th IEEE International Symposium on Intelligent Control, pp. 174–179 (1993)
11. Lukianykhin, O., Bogodorova, T.: ModelicaGym: applying reinforcement learning to Modelica models. In: Proceedings of the 9th International Workshop on Equation-based Object-oriented Modeling Languages and Tools, pp. 27–36 (2019)
12. Moe, S., Rustad, A.M., Hanssen, K.G.: Machine learning in control systems: an overview of the state of the art. In: Bramer, M., Petridis, M. (eds.) SGAI 2018. LNCS (LNAI), vol. 11311, pp. 250–265. Springer, Cham (2018). https://doi.org/ 10.1007/978-3-030-04191-5_23
13. Odersky, M., Spoon, L., Venners, B.: Programming in Scala. Artima Inc, Mountain View (2008)
14. Olowononi, F.O., Rawat, D.B., Liu, C.: Resilient machine learning for networked cyber physical systems: a survey for machine learning security to securing machine learning for CPS. IEEE Commun. Surv. Tutorials **23**(1), 524–552 (2021)
15. Quade, M., Isele, T., Abel, M.: Explainable Machine Learning Control - robust control and stability analysis (2020)
16. Radanliev, P., De Roure, D., Van Kleek, M., Santos, O., Ani, U.: Artificial intelligence in cyber physical systems. AI Soc. 1–14 (2020) https://doi.org/10.1007/ s00146-020-01049-0
17. Schaub, A., Hellerer, M., Bodenmüller, T.: Simulation of artificial intelligence agents using modelica and the DLR visualization library. In: Proceedings of the 9th International MODELICA Conference, pp. 339–346 (2012)
18. Taha, W., et al.: Acumen: an open-source testbed for cyber-physical systems research. In: Mandler, B., et al. (eds.) IoT360 2015. LNICST, vol. 169, pp. 118–130. Springer, Cham (2016). https://doi.org/10.1007/978-3-319-47063-4_11
19. van Otterlo, M., Wiering, M.: Reinforcement learning and Markov decision processes. In: Wiering, M., van Otterlo, M. (eds.) Reinforcement Learning. Adaptation, Learning, and Optimization, vol. 12, pp. 3–42. Springer, Berlin (2012). https://doi.org/10.1007/978-3-642-27645-3_1
20. Wang, Y., Velswamy, K., Huang, B.: A novel approach to feedback control with deep reinforcement learning. IFAC-PapersOnLine **51**(18), 31–36 (2018). 10th IFAC Symposium on Advanced Control of Chemical Processes ADCHEM 2018
21. Zhu, Y., R., et al.: Mathematical equations as executable models of mechanical systems. In: Proceedings of the 1st ACM/IEEE International Conference on Cyber-Physical Systems, pp. 1–11 (2010)

Predicting CO_2 Emissions for Buildings Using Regression and Classification

Alexia Avramidou and Christos Tjortjis[✉] (iD)

The Data Mining and Analytics Research Group, School of Science and Technology,
International Hellenic University, Thessaloniki, Greece
{aavramidou,c.tjortjis}@ihu.edu.gr

Abstract. This paper presents the development of regression and classification algorithms to predict greenhouse gas emissions caused by the building sector, and identify key building characteristics, which lead to excessive emissions. More specifically, two problems are addressed: the prediction of metric tons of CO_2 emitted annually by a building, and building compliance to environmental laws according to its physical characteristics, such as energy, fuel, and water consumption. The experimental results show that energy use intensity and natural gas use are significant factors for decarbonizing the building sector.

Keywords: Greenhouse gas (GHG) emissions prediction · Machine learning (ML) · Data mining · Buildings · Energy consumption · Regression · Classification

1 Introduction

It is widely known that climate change is a global threat; immediate actions need to be taken to limit its most important side effects. The operation of buildings accounts for approximately 40% of primary energy consumption globally, drawing the attention of governments to act instantly by adopting energy policies and carbon emission measures [1]. Given this reality, countries and cities have already set strict long-term energy efficiency and carbon reduction goals for existing and new buildings. To support global and city-scale decarbonization goals, energy disclosure directives are a significant policy tool to accelerate the transition towards climate neutrality [2].

This work evaluates several regression and classification algorithms, for predicting the annual greenhouse gas (GHG) emissions using properties reported at energy disclosure records. It proposes a methodology for emissions prediction utilizing feature engineering on energy and fuel consumption data, collected from large residential and public buildings in New York. The feature selection and engineering phase includes grouping buildings into 9 main categories according to their type and applying a logarithmic transformation to the Total GHG emissions to eliminate outliers. Also, high correlated features are removed from the analysis. In addition, this work analyzes various classification algorithms for predicting compliance to environmental laws. For this

© IFIP International Federation for Information Processing 2021
Published by Springer Nature Switzerland AG 2021
I. Maglogiannis et al. (Eds.): AIAI 2021, IFIP AICT 627, pp. 543–554, 2021.
https://doi.org/10.1007/978-3-030-79150-6_43

problem, the same data source is used, combined with emissions limits provided by the Local Law 97 (LL97), for two compliance periods.

This work differs from standard data-driven predictive models for the building sector in several ways. Although there are numerous studies discussing energy waste and performance predictive models for buildings, there is limited research focusing on forecasting emissions. Also, emissions prediction at a building-scale level has not been used so far, as most of the relevant studies mainly present their results at a city-scale or country-scale level [21, 22]. So, this work tries to fill this gap in the literature by predicting GHG emissions caused by the building sector at a building-scale level, analyzing their spatial characteristics and behavior. Additionally, our contribution could help governments and building owners understand the environmental footprint of buildings and take actions for energy efficiency and decarbonization.

The paper is structured as follows: Sect. 2 presents background information and reviews the literature, Sect. 3 provides the problem definition along with a brief description of the datasets, the pre-processing steps and the methods used. Section 4 presents exploratory data analysis results along with predictions. In Sect. 5 results are discussed and evaluated and Sect. 6 concludes the paper with future directions.

2   Literature Review

Building performance and energy consumption has been the subject of abundant academic research, driven by the need for a "greener" building sector. Unsupervised data analytics and clustering techniques are considered more practical and promising in discovering knowledge given limited prior information, concerning building operational and consumption data [3].

K-means clustering has been used to identify buildings with similar temporal energy performance patterns [4, 5]. Also, clustering tenants' behavior has proven that there is a strong relationship between the number of bedrooms and energy consumption, as well as home working [6]. In addition, K-means has been applied to group educational buildings according to their energy performance for space heating and evaluate energy savings in the building sector [7]. Another study used K-means to cluster school buildings to create a priority list for retrofit measures [8].

Furthermore, Artificial Neural Networks (ANNs) are commonly used in such problems because of their high predictive power [9]. However, their implementation is challenging because several hyperparameters need to be adjusted for accurate results [10]. ANNs are often compared with ensemble methods like Random Forest. In [11] it is mentioned that ANNs performed marginally better than Random Forest in predicting hourly HVAC energy consumption, but ensemble methods tend to deal with multidimensional data better. Also, fuzzy systems and ANNs using occupancy data are used to describe how energy is consumed within a building [12].

Another study compares ANNs with Support Vector Machines (SVM) for predicting building energy consumption in four office buildings [13]. The results have shown that SVM performs better than ANNs and the reason could be the small data pool used in this study, thus abnormal data were not so frequent. Also, when applying SVM for prediction someone needs less hyperparameters to optimize compared to ANNs. Additionally,

Support Vector Regression (SVR) has been used to develop sensor-based forecasting models for residential buildings [14] and to improve energy efficiency of HVAC systems analyzing historical data for buildings [15].

A common practice in predicting electricity consumption is to transform a regression model to a binary classification problem with 'high' and 'low' target labels [16]. It is stated that turning the regression problem to a binary one, achieves better results when the point of separation is the mean of all instances [17, 18].

Another work focuses on generalizing self-reported energy data from a small sample of buildings to a city-scale level [19]. Three different Machine Learning (ML) algorithms are used, namely Linear Regression, Random Forest, and SVR, along with feature selection techniques to make predictions from the Local Law 84 (LL84) self-reported energy disclosure data for large buildings. The results showed that Linear Regression performs better when predicting total building energy consumption at the zip code-level for the entire city, while SVR performs better in terms of accuracy when estimating energy use within the sample of LL84 buildings. Also, building size, use and morphology seem to be significant attributes for energy use prediction at the building and zip code levels. Larger buildings are found to have smaller Energy Use Intensity (EUI), while taller ones are more intensive.

Energy benchmarking is often used to evaluate the energy performance of buildings and is a crucial step towards reducing emissions. Comparability is a vital element to the success of a benchmarking system and has been the subject of many studies. In order to improve the comparability of benchmarking the energy performance of English schools was examined, assessing the impact of various features, such as built form or occupancy [20]. By analyzing the dataset using ANNs, the floor area and the number of pupils seemed to be very important determinants of school energy use.

Another work presented a method for energy classification and rating of school based on fuzzy clustering techniques compared with frequency rating techniques [21]. The fuzzy clustering method forms more robust classes avoiding imbalanced classes and classifies the buildings more precisely according to their common characteristics and similarities. The results indicated that school buildings should improve considerably their energy consumption and environmental quality.

In another study a new methodology for buildings energy benchmarking is discussed [22]. It comprises feature selection, clustering algorithm adaptation, result validation and interpretation. In comparison with the energy star approach, the proposed methodology was able to provide a more comprehensive benchmarking approach. This is because the clustering approach incorporates various building characteristics which affect energy usage, while the Energy Star approach classifies the buildings according to their use type.

Several studies observed factors affecting CO$_2$ emissions in the building sector and proposed methods for predicting building environmental footprint. More specifically, a Back Propagation (BP) ANN has been utilized for predicting CO$_2$ emissions caused by the Chinese commercial sector [23]. The most affecting indicators for emissions associated with the building sector were energy intensity, coal consumption, second industry GDP, education level, total population, business sector GDP and imports.

Other works focused on estimating indirect building carbon emissions within the boundaries of various types of Local Climate Zones (LCZs) [24]. The aim was to discover interesting patterns and help improving energy management in specific regions. The authors conclude that it is necessary to include not only morphological parameters, which are used in this study, but also information about occupancy, HVAC systems, building use, materials and more.

3   Approach

Several studies have been conducted to predict energy consumption patterns and evaluate the factors that affect energy waste, both in existing buildings and new constructions. Despite the significance of the afore mentioned studies, there is limited research focusing on forecasting carbon emissions caused by the building sector and which factors contribute most to the environmental footprint of a building.

3.1   Problem Definition

This work analyzes an energy disclosure dataset with the primary purpose of predicting the total GHG emissions of a building and focused on discovering any useful information about factors causing excessive emissions. Also, this work can give insights to building owners and decision makers on whether a building complies or not to the specific requirements of decarbonization legislations.

3.2   Data Description

Two data sources were used for this study. LL84, or the NYC Benchmarking Law requires annual benchmarking and disclosure of energy and water usage information. LL84 covers properties with a single building with a gross floor area greater than 50000 square feet and lots having more than one building with a gross floor area greater than 100000 square feet. This dataset includes information about energy use by fuel type, physical descriptors, as well as information concerning occupancy, water use and GHG emissions. We chose data for 2017, which is the latest version publicly available.

The second data source is LL97. LL97 sets detailed requirements for two initial compliance periods: 2024–29 and 2030–34. Buildings over 25000 square feet are required to meet annual carbon intensity limits during each compliance period based on building type. To comply, building owners must submit an emissions intensity report every year or pay substantial fines. In this work, we aim to predict whether a building complies or not for a compliance period, using the LL84 dataset, combined with the carbon emissions intensity limits provided by LL97. The emissions intensity limits are listed in Table 1.

3.3   Data Processing

LL84 data are self-reported, therefore many data fields suffer from missing values and outliers. Several cleaning and filtering steps were conducted prior to analysis. First, entries with duplicate or missing Borough, Block and Lot (BBL) number were removed,

Table 1. Carbon emissions intensity limits by property type and period.

Space use	Carbon limit 2024–29 (kgCO2e/sf)	Carbon limit 2030–34 (kgCO2e/sf)
Medical office	23.81	11.93
Retail	11.81	4.3
Assembly	10.74	4.2
Hotel	9.87	5.26
Office	8.46	4.53
School	7.58	3.44
Multifamily Housing	6.75	4.07
Factory	5.74	4.67
Storage/Warehouse	4.26	1.1

because BBL is a unique spatial identifier for properties in NYC. Then observations with zero or missing values either in their reported weather normalized source EUI or in their total GHG emissions were dropped, which consisted almost 19% of the total number of observations. Also, some features were removed because they either suffered from a high percentage of missing values, reaching almost 95% for some features or were not relevant to our predictions, like street name and number or the date of submission of the report.

Then, for the remaining features, missing entries have been replaced with the mean value of the respective column. Additionally, some features were excluded from the analysis, as they were highly correlated with other features, like energy consumption fields with different units. Finally, one hot encoding has been performed for the Primary Property Type feature to fit our data to several algorithms. Figure 1 shows the feature selection process.

The final dataset kept for analysis consists of 15 features listed below:

Weather Normalized Site EUI (kBtu/ft^2)	Weather Normalized Site Electricity Intensity (kWh/ft^2)
Self-Reported Gross Floor Area (ft^2)	Weather Normalized Site Natural Gas Intensity (kWh/ft^2)
Primary Property Type Self-Selected	Water Use Intensity (All Water Sources) (gal/ft^2)
Year Built	Total GHG Emissions (Metric Tons CO$_2$e)
Number of Buildings	Weather Normalized Source EUI (kBtu/ft^2)
ENERGY STAR Score	Weather Normalizer Site Natural Gas Use (therms)
Occupancy	Electricity Use- Grid Purchase (kWh)
Borough	

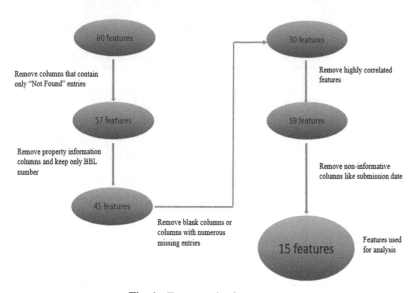

Fig. 1. Feature selection process.

The next step was to group building type values to be compatible with the building types listed in LL97. More specifically, the building types were grouped into 9 main categories: Office, Educational, Hotel, Residential, Warehouse, Public Building, Retail, Hospital, and Other. Most of the buildings were residential, only 30% being non-residential properties. To filter our data from misreported or anomalous entries, a logarithmic transformation to the Total GHG values was applied for each building type. The aim was to approximate the normal distribution given that a log-normal distribution was observed in the raw data, as shown in Fig. 2. Observations were excluded from the analysis if they outside the threshold of two standard deviations from the logged mean. The percentage of outliers eliminated from the analysis was 30.5%.

4   Experimental Results

This section presents prediction results for the two problems; predicting the annual CO_2 emissions (in metric tons emitted) using regression and the second determines which buildings comply to emissions limits via classification.

4.1   Predictions for Total GHG Emissions

Using regression, the following results were achieved (Table 2). Before applying any regression algorithm, a train test split was performed, keeping 25% of the data for testing. The algorithms examined were Linear Regression, SVR, Random Forest, XGBoost, CatBoost and ANNs. Also, a hyperparameter tuning was conducted to improve model

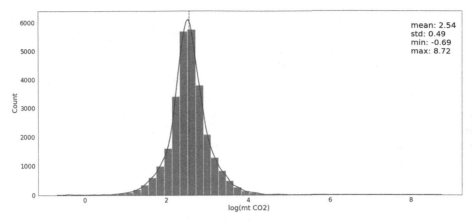

Fig. 2. Histogram of log transformed GHG emissions. The red line shows the log sample mean.

performance. The hyperparameter grid was selected by exploring the documentation for each algorithm and also by taking into consideration the values suggested in a relevant study [19]. Three evaluation metrics were used, Mean Absolute Error (MAE), Root Mean Squared Error (RMSE) and R^2. The ANN model used in the study is a feed forward MLP with 3 hidden layers and a Rectified Linear Unit (ReLu) activation function. The scores achieved are shown in Table 2. The best performing algorithm was ANNs achieving the lowest RMSE and highest R^2. Also, CatBoost performed very well, resulting in the lowest MAE among all algorithms.

Table 2. Regression results after the selection of the optimal hyperparameters

	MAE	RMSE	R^2
Linear regression	33.59	63.67	0.8563
SVR	13.6	32.62	0.9622
Random forest	9.37	19.68	0.9862
XGBoost	11.09	19.3	0.9868
CatBoost	8.81	17.26	0.9894
ANN	9.15	16.75	0.9900

4.2 Predicting Compliance for 2024–29

The goal of the experiments in this section was to predict compliance for properties contained in the LL84 dataset, using the LL97 carbon limits for each building type. This problem is a binary classification one, determining whether a certain building complies or not to the LL97 regulation.

For this binary classification problem, the feature "self-reported gross floor area" was excluded, as it was used to calculate the limits for compliance and thus it would affect predictions. We kept the same features for prediction as these used for the regression problem. A train/test split was conducted keeping 25% of the data to evaluate the predictions. The algorithms used were Random Forest, XGBoost, CatBoost and ANNs. For this problem, a feed forward MLP was developed, with 1 hidden layer. The metrics used for evaluation were accuracy and F-score. A grid search was conducted to determine if there are any hyperparameters which could enhance model accuracy. Table 3 illustrates the models' prediction performance tested on unknown data. Random Forest is the most powerful predictor with 98,7% accuracy and 0.9918 F-score. All algorithms performed well with insignificant differences between them.

Table 3. Classification results for the period 2024–29

	Accuracy	F-score
Random forest	0.987	0.9918
XGBoost	0.983	0.9896
CatBoost	0.985	0.9911
ANN	0.984	0.9902

Table 4 shows the confusion matrix using the best performing algorithm for this period which is Random Forest. Rows represent the actual target values and columns the predicted labels.

Table 4. Confusion matrix for the period 2024–29

	Predicted 0	Predicted 1
Actual **0**	947	33
Actual **1**	30	3845

4.3 Predicting Compliance for 2030–34

The acceptable CO_2 limits emitted from buildings for the period 2030–34 are much lower than the limits of the previous period examined, but the procedure is almost identical. The results are shown in Table 5. In this case, CatBoost appears to be the best predictor, but again the scores are very similar for all algorithms.

Table 6 shows the confusion matrix using the best performing algorithm for this period, which is CatBoost. Now most of the buildings do not comply with the regulations and thus belong to class 0.

Table 5. Classification results for the period 2030–34

	Accuracy	F-score
Random forest	0.981	0.9538
XGBoost	0.981	0.9548
CatBoost	0.982	0.9561
ANN	0.978	0.9472

Table 6. Confusion matrix for the period 2030–34

		Predicted 0	Predicted 1
Actual	0	3808	60
Actual	1	28	987

5 Discussion

Results on the regression problem indicate that tree-based algorithms perform very well, with CatBoost appearing to be the best among them for all metrics. However, the differences are insignificant observing the R^2 score, which is almost 0.99 for all tree-based algorithms. Thus, ensemble methods seem to be more promising for this kind of problem, compared with traditional regression algorithms like Linear Regression or SVR which resulted in less accurate predictions. Indeed, for Linear Regression MAE and RMSE scores were 3 times bigger compared with ANNs and the ensemble models. However, SVR overall performance was good reaching an R^2 score of 0.96. It is worth mentioning, that increasing the number of trees for Random Forest, XGB and CatBoost from 100 to 1000 during hypertuning led to lower errors in all metrics. In addition, ANNs gave the best results in terms of RMSE and R^2, but it was more difficult to find the best hyperparameters and their execution time is longer compared with tree-based algorithms.

Concerning the pre-processing phase, the outlier detection process, which was proposed in previous studies [5, 17], significantly improved model performance. Observations that fell out of the threshold of two standard deviations of their logged mean were excluded from the analysis. Also, missing values have been replaced with the mean value of the respective column. This procedure limited the number of data entries which were drastically misreported and narrowed the range of the target value between 123 and 805 metric tons of CO$_2$ emitted.

Another interesting finding is that the most important predictors are the gross floor area, source and site energy use intensity, electricity, and natural gas use. That means that these characteristics could be the key for decarbonizing buildings. On the contrary, building type does not seem to play a significant role for carbon emissions. This could be explained by highlighting that almost 70% of the buildings reported in the dataset were residential, so it was difficult to draw conclusions for other building types, which appeared only about 5% of times. Therefore, a more balanced dataset regarding the property type may have been more informative about the environmental footprint of different types.

Also, site energy use intensity tends to be more influencing for building emissions than source intensity. An explanation for that could be the fact that site EUI is the amount of heat and electricity consumed by a building as reflected in utility bills. On the contrary, source EUI represents the total amount of raw fuel that is required to operate the building and it incorporates all transmission, delivery, and production losses. Consequently, it is more likely that building owners are more aware of their site energy use by looking at their bills, but more unlikely to have calculated their source energy use properly. So, site EUI tends to be more reliable for our predictions because it has a lower possibility to be misreported in the LL84 dataset. However, the Environmental Protection Agency (EPA) suggested that source energy is the most equitable unit of evaluation and provides a complete assessment of energy efficiency in a building [25].

Comparing our findings for the classification problems, for the first period (2024–29) examined almost 80% of the buildings comply with LL97 regulations, while for the second period (2030–34) only 20% of the buildings fulfill the requirements. This indicates the need to make a transition towards greener technologies and energy efficiency refurbishments in the next few years. Additionally, there is a slight difference for model performance between the two periods, with the first period achieving higher F scores than the second, for all algorithms. Indeed, false positives for the second period experiments increased significantly compared with the first period. However, the overall performance for all algorithms was good, achieving almost $R^2 = 0.96$.

6 Conclusions

Understanding building environmental footprint is a crucial component of improving urban sustainability plans, reach carbon reduction goals, as well as achieve higher levels of energy efficiency and comfort. The analysis presented here aims to predict the total GHG emissions of buildings using the LL84 self-reported energy disclosure data from properties in New York.

Using the acceptable limits of carbon by building category, which are provided by a carbon reduction legislation applied in NYC, we tried to predict whether a building complies to the carbon law for two periods. Using six ML algorithms for the regression problem and three for the classification problems, the results suggest that the data from LL84 sample can produce reasonably accurate predictions of carbon emissions across the city at a building scale.

Overall, we found that tree-based algorithms and ANNs perform better than traditional algorithms like Logistic Regression and SVR, achieving impressively higher scores. Additionally, the preprocessing procedure seems to be very important in filtering self-reported datasets, which suffer from numerous missing and misreported values. It is also observed that building size and energy use intensity play a major role in buildings' environmental footprint.

However, some assumptions or personal estimations may affect the validity of the results. Although a preprocessing and data cleaning procedure has been followed, still it was difficult to understand if all entries are correct or detect all anomalous ones, since LL84 is self-reported. Also, most of the buildings examined were residential and the commercial buildings were very limited. This imbalance does not favor the results and makes it harder to draw conclusions about specific property types and their environmental footprint.

Future work should collect more energy disclosure data from previous years and incorporate new data, publicly available by the end of the year. Also, data from different regions or cities along with weather information would provide a more comprehensive view of carbon emissions caused by the urban building stock.

In addition, more ML algorithms, as well as feature selection techniques, could improve performance. Regarding ANNs implementation, a more detailed selection of hyperparameters is desirable to explore their dynamic in these types of problems. Finally, the importance of focusing on forecasting emissions is worth mentioning, as there is little research on this specific field. Combining building with transportation data could also be an idea for future research, as the transportation sector accounts for a significant amount of urban carbon emissions and could be beneficial for city-scale level sustainability plans.

Acknowledgments. The authors would like to thank the Hellenic Artificial Intelligence Society (EETN) for covering part of their expenses to participate in AIAI 2021.

References

1. Zhao, H.-X., Magoulès, F.: A review on the prediction of building energy consumption. Renew. Sustain. Energy Rev. **16**(6), 3586–3592 (2012)
2. Kontokosta, C.E.: Energy disclosure, market behavior, and the building data ecosystem. Ann. New York Acad. Sci. **1295**(1), 34–43 (2013)
3. Fan, C., Xiao, F., Li, Z., Wang, J.: Unsupervised data analytics in mining big building operational data for energy efficiency enhancement: a review. Energy Build. **159**, 296–308 (2018)
4. Yang, J., et al.: k-Shape clustering algorithm for building energy usage patterns analysis and forecasting model accuracy improvement. Energy Build. **146**, 27–37 (2017)
5. Papadopoulos, S., Bonczak, B., Kontokosta, C.E.: Pattern recognition in building energy performance over time using energy benchmarking data. Appl. Energy **221**, 576–586 (2018)
6. Baker, K.J., Rylatt, R.M.: Improving the prediction of UK domestic energy-demand using annual consumption-data. Appl. Energy **85**(6), 475–482 (2008)
7. Gaitani, N., Lehmann, C., Santamouris, M., Mihalakakou, G., Patargias, P.: Using principal component and cluster analysis in the heating evaluation of the school building sector. Appl. Energy **87**(6), 2079–2086 (2010)
8. Lara, R.A., Pernigotto, G., Cappelletti, F., Romagnoni, P., Gasparella, A.: Energy audit of schools by means of cluster analysis. Energy Build. **95**, 160–171 (2015)
9. Mena, R., Rodríguez, F., Castilla, M., Arahal, M.R.: A prediction model based on neural networks for the energy consumption of a bioclimatic building. Energy Build. **82**, 142–155 (2014)
10. Seyedzadeh, S., Rahimian, F., Glesk, I.Roper, Roper, M.: Machine learning for estimation of building energy consumption and performance: a review. Vis. Eng. **6**(1), 5 (2018)

11. Waseem, A.M., Mourshed, M., Rezgui, Y.: Trees vs neurons: comparison between random forest and ANN for high-resolution prediction of building energy consumption. Energy Build. **147**, 77–89 (2017)

12. Pombeiro, H., Santos, R., Carreira, P., Silva, C., Sousa, J.M.C.: Comparative assessment of low-complexity models to predict electricity consumption in an institutional building: Linear regression vs. fuzzy modeling vs. neural networks. Energy Build. **146**, 141–151 (2017)

13. Dong, B., Cao, C., Lee, S.E.: Applying support vector machines to predict building energy consumption in tropical region. Energy Build. **37**(5), 545–553 (2005)

14. Jain, R.K., Smith, K.M., Culligan, P.J., Taylor, J.E.: Forecasting energy consumption of multi-family residential buildings using support vector regression: Investigating the impact of temporal and spatial monitoring granularity on performance accuracy. Appl. Energy **123**, 168–178 (2014)

15. Solomon, D., Winter, R., Boulanger, A., Anderson, R., Wu, L.: Forecasting energy demand in large commercial buildings using support vector machine regression (2011)

16. Christantonis, K., Tjortjis, C., Manos, A., Filippidou, D.E., Christelis, E.: Smart cities data classification for electricity consumption & traffic prediction. Autom. Softw. Eng. **31**(1) (2020)

17. Mystakidis, A., Tjortjis, C.: Big data mining for smart cities: predicting traffic congestion using classification. In: Proceedings of 11th IEEE International Conference on Information, Intelligence, Systems and Applications (IISA 20) (2020)

18. Christantonis, K., Tjortjis, C., Manos, A., Filippidou, D.E., Mougiakou, E., Christelis, E.: Using classification for traffic prediction in smart cities. In: 16th International Conference on Artificial Intelligence Applications and Innovations (AIAI 20) (2020)

19. Kontokosta, C.E., Tull, C.: A data-driven predictive model of city-scale energy use in buildings. Appl. Energy **197**, 303–317 (2017)

20. Hong, S.-M., Paterson, G., Mumovic, D., Steadman, P.: Improved benchmarking comparability for energy consumption in schools. Build. Res. Inf. **42**(1), 47–61 (2014)

21. Santamouris, M., et al.: Using intelligent clustering techniques to classify the energy performance of school buildings. Energy Build. **39**(1), 45–51 (2007)

22. Gao, X., Malkawi, A.: A new methodology for building energy performance benchmarking: an approach based on intelligent clustering algorithm. Energy Build. **84**, 607–616 (2014)

23. Wen, L., Yuan, X.: Forecasting CO_2 emissions in Chinas commercial department, through BP neural network based on random forest and PSO. Sci. Total Env. **718**, (2020)

24. Wu, Y., Sharifi, A., Yang, P., Borjigin, H., Murakami, D., Yamagata, Y.: Mapping building carbon emissions within local climate zones in Shanghai. Energy Procedia **152**, 815–822 (2018)

25. Energystar.gov. https://www.energystar.gov/buildings/facility-owners-and managers/existing -buildings/use-portfolio-manager/understand-metrics/difference

Robust Pose Estimation Based on Maximum Correntropy Criterion

Qian Zhang and Badong Chen[✉] [ID]

Institute of Artificial Intelligence and Robotics, Xi'an Jiaotong University, Xi'an, Shaanxi, People's Republic of China
zhangqian2018@stu.xjtu.edu.cn, chenbd@mail.xjtu.edu.cn

Abstract. Pose estimation is a key problem in computer vision, which is commonly used in augmented reality, robotics and navigation. The classical orthogonal iterative (OI) pose estimation algorithm builds its cost function based on the minimum mean square error (MMSE), which performs well when data disturbed by Gaussian noise. But even a small number of outliers will make OI unstable. In order to deal with outliers problem, in this paper, we establish a new cost function based on maximum correntropy criterion (MCC) and propose an accurate and robust correntropy-based OI (COI) pose estimation method. The proposed COI utilizes the advantages of correntropy to eliminate the bad effects of outliers, which can enhance the performance in the pose estimation problems with noise and outliers. In addition, our method does not need an extra outliers detection stage. Finally, we verify the effectiveness of our method in synthetic and real data experiments. Experimental results show that the COI can effectively combat outliers and achieve better performance than state-of-the-art algorithms, especially in the environments with a small number of outliers.

Keywords: Pose estimation · Orthogonal Iterative (OI) algorithm · Maximum Correntropy Criterion (MCC)

1 Introduction

Pose estimation is widely used in augmented reality, robotics and navigation. It determines the orientation and position of the perspective camera through n known 3D reference points in the object coordinates and their imaging 2D points. Pose estimation is also known as the perspective-n-point (PnP) problem in computer vision, which has been studied for several decades.

In the past few years, there have been many methods to solve the PnP problem. One of the typical PnP methods is the orthogonal iterative (OI, also referred to as LHM) algorithm that calculates the orthogonal rotation matrix directly by minimizing the collinearity error in object space and has been proven to be globally convergent [21]. Later works apply the OI algorithm to different scenarios, such as augmented reality [22] and unmanned aerial vehicle systems

© IFIP International Federation for Information Processing 2021
Published by Springer Nature Switzerland AG 2021
I. Maglogiannis et al. (Eds.): AIAI 2021, IFIP AICT 627, pp. 555–566, 2021.
https://doi.org/10.1007/978-3-030-79150-6_44

[8,28], mainly studying how to provide a closer initial guess to obtain accurate pose estimation. In addition, other works improve this algorithm to adapt to complex noise environments. GOI [14] uses the inverse covariance matrix to describe the uncertainty of the feature points. SoftOI [9] introduces the Assign algorithm to determine the correspondences. Although these methods have a certain ability to suppress the influence of outliers, they are time-consuming.

Almost all of the above methods build their cost function based on the minimum mean square error (MMSE). MMSE can provide optimal solution under Gaussian noise, but it is sensitive to outliers. Recently, the maximum correntropy criterion (MCC) is shown to perform well in dealing with outliers [19]. MCC uses the characteristics of a kernel function to weaken the bad influence of outliers and non-Gaussian noise, ensuring the performance of the algorithm. In the present paper, we propose a correntropy-based OI (COI) method. The new method is robust to outliers without requiring the additional outliers detection stage. In particular, COI can achieve desirable performance for the case of small number of outliers, which is a very common situation in practical applications.

2 Related Works

For PnP problems with a small set of correspondences ($n \leq 5$), we can obtain a closed-form solution through P3P [15], P4P [3] or P5P [27] problems. These methods have higher calculation speed, but they are more sensitive to image noise and outliers. Generally, we roughly divide PnP methods into two categories: non-iterative and iterative.

For non-iterative methods, EPnP [23] is an efficient solution that controls the computational complexity to $O(n)$ for the first time, and then Lepetit et al. [16] combined it with the Gauss-Newton algorithm to further improve accuracy. In addition, many non-iterative methods utilize polynomial solving techniques. For example, the direct least squares (DLS) [13] method analytically determines the roots of the polynomial system with the multiplication matrix. However, DLS applies Cayley-Gibbs-Rodriguez (CGR) to parameterize rotation, which would cause its degradation at 180° [29]. In order to remove this limitation, ASPnP [30] and OPnP [29] use quaternion representation to parameterize the rotation and retrieve all stationary points through Gröbner basis technique.

Compared with non-iterative methods, iterative methods are usually more robust to noise. The classic iterative method is based on optimizing the image space collinearity error. In addition, Dementhon [7] proposed an iterative method (POSIT) based on proportional orthographic projection, but did not prove the convergence. Moreover, SoftPOSIT [6] improves POSIT to the unknown correspondences situations. SoftPOSIT can deal with a variety of noise data, but it is time-consuming because all matches need to be tried during the computing process. Later, Lu [21] developed a globally convergent OI algorithm that minimizes the object space collinearity error, which is the most accurate iterative method currently.

So far, most PnP methods suppose that image points are disturbed by Gaussian noise, which means 3D-2D correspondences do not contain outliers. However, image feature detection and matching methods, such as SITF [20], SURF [2] and ORB [25], would be affected by illumination, scaling and occlusion, so that feature points may be mismatched in practical applications. These mismatches would seriously reduce the accuracy of pose estimation. The traditional solution combines the P3P algorithm with the RANSAC [12] scheme to reject outliers in a preliminary stage, and then executes another PnP method on the remaining inliers. However, the RANSAC scheme requires many trials to obtain the best results. Later, Ferraz et al. [11] proposed a very fast solution (REPPnP) to integrate outliers rejection schemes into the linear formula of the PnP solution. However, REPPnP is not suitable for small sets of correspondences [17]. Zhou et al. [31] proposed a robust 1-point RANSAC-based (R1PPnP) method, which introduces a soft weighting mechanism to distinguish between inliers and outliers by setting the inliers threshold. In addition, Li et al. [17] proposed a new cost function based on the l_q-norm for the PnP problem. This method can handle a high percentage of outliers, but it needs to provide a good initial value, which is difficult to achieve in practical applications. In recent years, many studies have shown that the correntropy can effectively deal with outliers, so we introduce MCC into the pose estimation algorithm. Compared with the above methods, our method can automatically suppress the effects of outliers and especially perform better in environments with a small number of outliers.

3   MCC-Based Pose Estimation

In this section, we briefly review the OI algorithm and MCC and propose a pose estimation algorithm based on correntropy and the OI algorithm.

3.1   Problem Formulation and OI Algorithm

Assume that the camera internal calibration is known, and then we give n non-collinear 3D points $\mathbf{p}_i = (x_i, y_i, z_i)^t, i = 1, \ldots, n, n \geq 3$ in an object coordinate system and their corresponding camera coordinates $\mathbf{q}_i = (x_i, y_i, z_i)^t$. The relation between them can be written as:

$$\mathbf{q}_i = \mathbf{R}\mathbf{p}_i + \mathbf{t}, \tag{1}$$

where $\mathbf{R} = (\mathbf{r}_1^t, \mathbf{r}_2^t, \mathbf{r}_3^t)^t$ and $\mathbf{t} = (t_x, t_y, t_z)^t$ are the rotation matrix and the translation vector, respectively. The image point $\mathbf{v}_i = (u_i, v_i, 1)^t$ is the projection of $\mathbf{p}_i$ on the normalized image plane. Under an ideal perspective camera model, the imaging relation can be expressed as:

$$\begin{cases} u_i = \frac{\mathbf{r}_1^t \mathbf{p}_i + t_x}{\mathbf{r}_3^t \mathbf{p}_i + t_z} \\ v_i = \frac{\mathbf{r}_2^t \mathbf{p}_i + t_y}{\mathbf{r}_3^t \mathbf{p}_i + t_z}, \end{cases} \tag{2}$$

or

$$\mathbf{v}_i = \frac{1}{\mathbf{r}_3^t \mathbf{p}_i + t_z} (\mathbf{R}\mathbf{p}_i + \mathbf{t}), \tag{3}$$

which is called the collinearity equation. Moreover, collinearity can be considered as the orthogonal projection of the camera coordinate point $\mathbf{q}_i$ on $\mathbf{v}_i$ should coincide with $\mathbf{q}_i$ itself, which is expressed as follows:

$$\mathbf{R}\mathbf{p}_i + \mathbf{t} = \mathbf{V}_i (\mathbf{R}\mathbf{p}_i + \mathbf{t}), \tag{4}$$

where $\mathbf{V}_i = \mathbf{v}_i \mathbf{v}_i^t / (\mathbf{v}_i^t \mathbf{v}_i)$ is the line-of-sight projection matrix. Based on collinearity in object space, the OI algorithm formulates the pose estimation problem as minimizing the following sum of squared object-space collinearity error:

$$E(\mathbf{R}, \mathbf{t}) = \sum_{i=1}^{n} \|e_i\|^2 = \sum_{i=1}^{n} \|(\mathbf{I} - \mathbf{V}_i)(\mathbf{R}\mathbf{p}_i + \mathbf{t})\|^2. \tag{5}$$

Since the above objective function is quadratic in $\mathbf{t}$, we can assume that the rotation matrix $\mathbf{R}$ is fixed, then the optimal value of $\mathbf{t}$ can be obtained by:

$$\mathbf{t}(\mathbf{R}) = \frac{1}{n} \left(\mathbf{I} - \frac{1}{n} \sum_{i=1}^{n} \mathbf{V}_i \right)^{-1} \sum_{i=1}^{n} (\mathbf{V}_i - \mathbf{I}) \mathbf{R}\mathbf{p}_i. \tag{6}$$

We can compute the optimal $\mathbf{R}^*$ iteratively through the following steps: First, suppose that $\mathbf{R}^{(k)}$ is the estimated value for the k-th iteration, so $\mathbf{t}^{(k)} = \mathbf{t}(\mathbf{R}^{(k)})$, $\mathbf{q}_i^{(k)} = \mathbf{R}^{(k)}\mathbf{p}_i + \mathbf{t}^{(k)}$. Then $\mathbf{R}^{(k+1)}$ is determined by solving the following absolute orientation problem [21]:

$$\mathbf{R}^{(k+1)} = \arg \min_{\mathbf{R}} \sum_{i=1}^{n} \left\| \mathbf{R}\mathbf{p}_i + \mathbf{t} - \mathbf{V}_i \mathbf{q}_i^{(k)} \right\|^2, \tag{7}$$

The translation is $\mathbf{t}^{(k+1)} = \mathbf{t}(\mathbf{R}^{(k+1)})$. This process is repeated until the termination condition is reached.

3.2   Maximum Correntropy Criterion

In previous studies, MCC has been successfully used in the field of signal processing, machine learning and point set registration [4,5,10]. Unlike MMSE, which is sensitive to complex noise, MCC has been proven to be robust to outliers [19]. In information theoretic learning, correntropy [24] is a nonlinear measure of similarity between two random variables X and Y:

$$V_\sigma(X, Y) = E[\kappa_\sigma(X, Y)], \tag{8}$$

where $\kappa_\sigma(.)$ is a positive kernel function and σ is the kernel width. We take Gaussian kernel, which is the most widely used, as the kernel function in this paper:

$$\kappa_\sigma(x, y) = \frac{1}{\sqrt{2\pi}\sigma} \exp(-\frac{\|x - y\|^2}{2\sigma^2}). \tag{9}$$

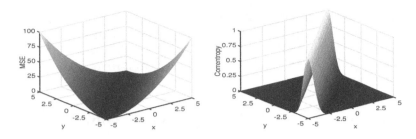

Fig. 1. Mean square error (MSE) (left) and correntopy (right) in the joint space

In practice, only a finite number of samples $(x_i, y_i)_{i=1}^N$ can be obtained, then correntropy can be estimated as:

$$\hat{V}_{N,\sigma}(X, Y) = \frac{1}{N} \sum_{i=1}^N \kappa_\sigma(x_i, y_i). \tag{10}$$

Usually, we hope that the estimated $\hat{X}$ is as close to the desired X as possible. Therefore, it is necessary to maximize the correntropy between X and $\hat{X}$, as follows:

$$\arg\max_\omega \hat{V}_\sigma(X, \hat{X}), \tag{11}$$

which is called MCC, where ω is the unknown parameter. As shown in Fig. 1, MSE is a quadratic function in the joint space. For MSE, the value increases quadratically for the points away from the $x = y$ line, so it amplifies the influence of non-Gaussian noise and outliers on the mean value. However, correntropy has its maximum value along the $x = y$ line, and the value decreases exponentially away from this line. In other words, MCC considers more about the data near $x = y$ and has advantages in dealing with outliers.

3.3 Orthogonal Iterative Algorithm Based on MCC

It is well konwn that OI pose estimation algorithm is one of the most accurate PnP iterative methods. However, OI is based on MMSE, so it is not satisfactory in the situations with outliers. In order to solve this problem, we introduce MCC to improve the ability to deal with outliers. First, the correntropy-based cost function can be formulated as:

$$(\mathbf{R}^*, \mathbf{t}^*) = \arg\max_{\mathbf{R}, \mathbf{t}} \sum_{i=1}^n \exp(-\frac{\|(\mathbf{I} - \mathbf{V}_i)(\mathbf{R}\mathbf{p}_i + \mathbf{t})\|^2}{2\sigma^2}). \tag{12}$$

Notice that (12) is very similar to the form of (5). Inspired by the iterative process of OI algorithm [21], we assume that a fixed rotation matrix $\mathbf{R}$ is given and take the partial derivative of (12) with respect to $\mathbf{t}$. We have:

$$\frac{\partial \sum_{i=1}^n \exp(-\|e_i\|^2/2\sigma^2)}{\partial \mathbf{t}} = \sum_{i=1}^n g(e_i) \frac{(\mathbf{V}_i - \mathbf{I})(\mathbf{R}\mathbf{p}_i + \mathbf{t})(\mathbf{I} - \mathbf{V}_i)}{\sigma^2}, \tag{13}$$

where $g(e_i) = \exp(-\|(\mathbf{I} - \mathbf{V}_i)(\mathbf{Rp_i} + \mathbf{t})\|^2/2\sigma^2)$ and $e_i = (\mathbf{I} - \mathbf{V}_i)(\mathbf{Rp_i} + \mathbf{t})$.

Considering that $g(e_i)$ is the exponential term and changes little in the iteration process, we replace $\mathbf{R}^{(k-1)}$ with $\mathbf{R}$ and $\mathbf{t}^{(k-1)}$ with $\mathbf{t}$, so the k-th iteration kernel term is $g(e_i) = g(\mathbf{R}^{k-1}, \mathbf{t}^{k-1})$. Setting (13) to zero, one can get a closed form solution of $\mathbf{t}$ as follows:

$$\mathbf{t} = \left[\sum_{i=1}^{n} g(e_i)(\mathbf{I} - \mathbf{V}_i) \right]^{-1} \sum_{i=1}^{n} g(e_i)(\mathbf{V}_i - \mathbf{I})\mathbf{Rp}_i, \tag{14}$$

then (14) can be rewritten as:

$$\mathbf{t} = \left(\sum_{i=1}^{n} g(e_i)(\mathbf{V}_i - \mathbf{I})\mathbf{Rp}_i + \sum_{1}^{n} g(e_i)\mathbf{V}_i\mathbf{t} \right) \Big/ \sum_{i=1}^{n} g(e_i). \tag{15}$$

We substitute $\mathbf{t}$ in the cost function (12) with (15) and define :

$$\begin{cases} \mathbf{q}_i(\mathbf{R}) = \mathbf{V}_i(\mathbf{Rp}_i + \mathbf{t}) \\ \mathbf{p}'_i = \mathbf{p}_i - \left(\sum_{i=1}^{n} g(e_i)\mathbf{p}_i \right) \Big/ \sum_{i=1}^{n} g(e_i) \\ \mathbf{q}'_i(\mathbf{R}) = \mathbf{q}_i(\mathbf{R}) - \left(\sum_{i=1}^{n} g(e_i)\mathbf{q}_i(\mathbf{R}) \right) \Big/ \sum_{i=1}^{n} g(e_i), \end{cases} \tag{16}$$

then we get the following simplified objective function:

$$(\mathbf{R}^*, \mathbf{t}^*) = \arg\max_{\mathbf{R}, \mathbf{t}} \sum_{i=1}^{n} \exp\left(-(\|\mathbf{Rp}'_i - \mathbf{q}'_i(\mathbf{R})\|^2)/2\sigma^2 \right). \tag{17}$$

Inspired by the singular value decomposition (SVD) method [1], we first construct a matrix $\mathbf{M}$:

$$\mathbf{M} = \sum_{i=1}^{n} \mathbf{q}'_i(\mathbf{R})g(e_i)\mathbf{p}'^t_i, \tag{18}$$

which can be decomposed into $\mathbf{M} = \mathbf{U\Sigma V}^t$. We calculate the estimation of $\mathbf{R}^{(k)}$ as follows:

$$\mathbf{R}^{(k)} = \mathbf{V\tilde{I}U}^t, \tag{19}$$

and determine $\mathbf{\tilde{I}}$ according to the value of $\det(\mathbf{VU}^t)$. If $\det(\mathbf{VU}^t) = 1$, we need $\mathbf{\tilde{I}} = \mathbf{I}_3$; and if $\det(\mathbf{VU}^t) = -1$, we need $\mathbf{\tilde{I}} = \mathrm{diag}(1, 1, -1)$. It can be seen from mathematics that when $\sigma \to \infty$, COI degenerates to the OI algorithm.

Here we make a summary of the method flow.

1. For a given set of 3D-2D points, the initial estimate of $\mathbf{R}^{(0)}$ can be computed using EPnP, then we can calculate $\mathbf{t}^{(0)}$ by (6).
2. We use the initial $\mathbf{R}^{(0)}$ and $\mathbf{t}^{(0)}$ to start the first iteration. $\mathbf{R}$ and $\mathbf{t}$ can be calculated iteratively from (19) and (14), respectively.
3. The second step needs to be repeated until the reprojection error converges or reaches the maximum number of iterations.

4   Experimental Results

In this section, we show the accuracy and stability of COI in both synthetic and real data situations. Our method is implemented in MATLAB.

4.1   Synthetic Experiments

In synthetic experiments, we compare our method against recent PnP solutions, including EPnP+GN [16], LHM [21], EPnP+LHM, RPnP [18], DLS [13], OPnP [29], ASPnP [30], SDP [26], EPPnP [11], REPPnP [11] and R1PPnP [31].

We assume a virtual well-calibrated camera with a resolution of 2048×1152 pixels, focal length of 1500 and principal point in the image center. Then 3D-2D correspondences are generated randomly. For the ordinary-3D case, the reference 3D points are uniformly distributed into the interval $[-2, 2] \times [-2, 2] \times [4, 8]$. For the quasi-singular case, the interval is $[1, 2] \times [1, 2] \times [4, 8]$. Finally, the ground-truth translation $\mathbf{t}_{true}$ is set as the mean value of the reference 3D points. The ground-truth rotation matrix $\mathbf{R}_{true}$ is generated randomly. For our method, the kernel width σ experimentally select from 0.1 to 2 with a step 0.5, besides, we use 10^5 to represent $\sigma \to \infty$. For the metric errors, the rotation error between $\mathbf{R}_{true}$ and the estimated $\mathbf{R}$ in degree is measured as (20), and then the translation error is defined as (21).

$$e_{rot}(\deg) = \max{}_{k=1}^{3} \arccos\left(\mathbf{r}_{k,true} \cdot \mathbf{r}_k\right) \times 180/\pi \tag{20}$$

$$e_{trans}(\%) = \|\mathbf{t}_{ture} - \mathbf{t}\|/\|\mathbf{t}\| \times 100, \tag{21}$$

where $r_{k,true}$ and r_k are the k-th column of $\mathbf{R}_{true}$ and $\mathbf{R}$, respectively.

All results of experiments are the average of 500 independent experiments.

Outlier-Free Synthetic Situations. Most PnP methods can only deal with outlier-free situations. Their performance are significantly reduced with a small number of outliers. Although our method is mainly aimed at outliers, in order to verify the universality of COI, it is compared with other methods in outlier-free situations.

The first and second columns in Fig. 2 show the results of varying the number of correspondences n from 10 to 100. The Gaussian noise with a standard deviation of $\delta = 5$ pixels is added to image points. Then, in the second set of experiments, the number of correspondences is fixed as $n = 30$. We vary the level of Gaussian noise from 2 to 20 pixels, as shown in the third and fourth columns in Fig. 2. The ordinary case and quasi-singular case results indicate that some methods can accurately estimate the rotation matrix, and so does COI. However, the translation estimation of our method is not so accurate in quasi-singular case. LHM cannot handle quasi-singular case, while LHM+EPnP is still stable in the same situations. Furthermore, when using LHM to optimize the EPnP solution, the results have better accuracy than that of Gauss-Newton optimization. The accuracy of RPnP and ASPnP decreases significantly when the Gaussian noise is large.

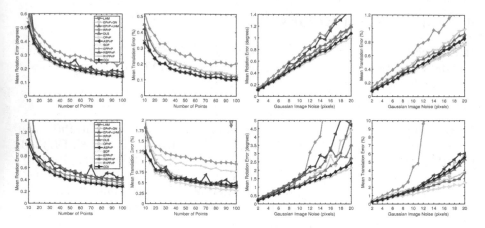

Fig. 2. Synthetic experiments without outliers, varying the number of corresponding points and the level of Gaussian noise, ordinary case (first row) and quasi-singular case (second row)

Robustness to Outliers. In this experiments, the number of correct matches between image points and object points is fixed as $n_{in} = 30$, then a Gaussian noise with standard deviation of $\delta = 10$ pixels is added to image points. In addition, we randomly generate corresponding points $n_{out} = n \times p_{out}$ as outliers, where p_{out} is the true percentage of outliers and $n = n_{in} + n_{out}$. For outliers, their image points are randomly distributed across the entire image plane. Figure 3 shows the experimental results of varying the p_{out} from 5 to 50. The inliers threshold of R1PPnP is set as $h = 10$. Most PnP algorithms cannot correctly estimate the pose when there are outliers in the correspondences, only COI, REPPnP and R1PPnP maintain good accuracy.

In order to further demonstrate the robustness of our method to outliers and noise, we compare COI with REPPnP and R1PPnP. In addition, COI is also compared with some traditional methods, such as RANSAC+P3P+OPnP, RANSAC+P3P+ASPnP, RANSAC+P3P and RANSAC+RP4P+RPnP methods. For COI, the kernel width σ experimentally select from 0.1 to 1 with a step 0.1 and 1.2 to 3.5 with a step 0.2, besides, we use 10^5 to represent $\sigma \to \infty$.

Figure 4 (a) shows the mean errors for increasing the percentage of outliers from 5 to 50. Then, the percentage of outliers p_{out} is fixed at $p_{out} = 20$. We add different levels of Gaussian image noise from 1 to 15, as shown in Fig. 4 (b). The performance of REPPnP is not as good as expected. This may be because in our experimental setting, the number of inliers is small, but REPPnP is more suitable in situations with a large number of correspondences. The RANSAC-based methods perform well, but they need to combine with another PnP method or set suitable inliers threshold to distinguish inliers and outliers, which is more complicated to use. However, COI can automatically suppress the impact of outliers and perform better than other methods when the percentage of outliers is less than 30%. Moreover, Fig. 4 (b) indicates that COI can achieve stronger robustness to Gaussian noise under the same outliers percentage.

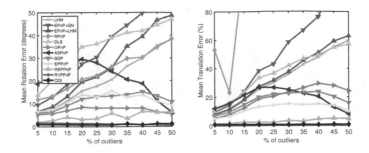

Fig. 3. Synthetic experiments without outliers, varying the percentage of outliers

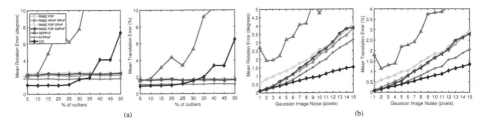

Fig. 4. Synthetic experiments with outliers, the number of inlier points was fixed as $n_{in} = 30$. (a) varying the percentage of outliers (b) varying the level of Gaussian noise

4.2 Real Data Experiments

In real data experiments, we use PnP methods to determine the rotation and translation of the mixed reality device relative to the RGBD camera at a certain moment, and obtain the transformation between these two device coordinate systems. First, the RGBD data is obtained by an Intel RealSense D435 depth camera with an image resolution of 640 × 480. Then we use a mixed reality device, the Microsoft HoloLens, to capture current scene image with a resolution of 2048 × 1152. SIFT algorithm is used to compute image features and inital matches. Finally, the correspondences are obtained by brute force method. Cause the correspondences are affected by many external factors, there may be some mismatches in the results.

Figure 5 shows a set of sample images, with 23 pairs of corresponding points and about 3 pairs of outliers. Outliers are basically due to missing depth data or mismatches. For R1PPnP, the inliers threshold is set as $h = 5$. The reprojection results show that the result of COI is closest to the original matches, which means that COI well overcomes the effects of outliers. However, REPPnP has a rather messy result after reprojection. Moreover, due to the effects of outliers, the results of R1PPnP have a tendency of collective translation.

(a) COI   (b) R1PPnP   (c) REPPnP

Fig. 5. Real image experiments, we use the estimated rotation and translation to reproject these correspondences. The pose estimation methods from left to right are COI, R1PPnP and REPPnP. (The red lines and green lines represent the original matches and reprojected matches, respectively.) (Color figure online)

5   Conclusion

The OI algorithm is one of the most accurate iterative pose estimation algorithms, but it is not robust enough to combat outliers. In this paper, we propose a robust pose estimation algorithm based on MCC to complement the shortcomings of the OI algorithm. The proposed COI utilizes its non-linear similarity measure and performs well when dealing with outliers and noise. Synthetic and real data experiments indicate that this method has ability to combat noise and performs better in the situations with a small number of outliers. These advantages are at the cost of introducing a free parameter σ. We will further study how to select this parameter in future work.

Acknowledgment. This work was supported by the National Natural Science Foundation of China (No. 61976175, 91648208) and Fundamental Research Funds for the Central Universities (No. xzy022020045).

References

1. Arun, K.S., Huang, T.S., Blostein, S.D.: Least-squares fitting of two 3D point sets. IEEE Trans. Pattern Anal. Mach. Intell. **9**(5), 698–700 (1987)
2. Bay, H., Tuytelaars, T., Van Gool, L.: SURF: speeded up robust features. In: Leonardis, A., Bischof, H., Pinz, A. (eds.) ECCV 2006. LNCS, vol. 3951, pp. 404–417. Springer, Heidelberg (2006). https://doi.org/10.1007/11744023_32
3. Bujnak, M., Kukelova, Z., Pajdla, T.: A general solution to the P4P problem for camera with unknown focal length. In: 2008 IEEE Conference on Computer Vision and Pattern Recognition, pp. 1–8 (2008). https://doi.org/10.1109/CVPR.2008.4587793
4. Chen, B., Xing, L., Liang, J., Zheng, N., Príncipe, J.C.: Steady-state mean-square error analysis for adaptive filtering under the maximum correntropy criterion. IEEE Signal Process. Lett. **21**(7), 880–884 (2014)
5. Chen, B., Xing, L., Zhao, H., Zheng, N., Príncipe, J.C.: Generalized correntropy for robust adaptive filtering. IEEE Trans. Signal Process. **64**(13), 3376–3387 (2016)
6. David, P., Dementhon, D., Duraiswami, R., Samet, H.: SoftPOSIT: simultaneous pose and correspondence determination. Int. J. Comput. Vis. **59**(3), 259–284 (2004)

7. Dementhon, D.F., Davis, L.S.: Model-based object pose in 25 lines of code. Int. J. Comput. Vis. **15**(1), 123–141 (1995)
8. Ding, M., Wei, L., Wang, B.: Vision-based estimation of relative pose in autonomous aerial refueling. Chinese J. Aeronaut. **24**(6), 807–815 (2011)
9. Dong, H., Sun, C., Zhang, B., Wang, P.: Simultaneous pose and correspondence determination combining softassign and orthogonal iteration. IEEE Access **7**, 137720–137730 (2019)
10. Du, S., Xu, G., Zhang, S., Zhang, X., Gao, Y., Chen, B.: Robust rigid registration algorithm based on pointwise correspondence and correntropy. Recognit. Lett. **132**, 91–98 (2020)
11. Ferraz, L., Binefa, X., Moreno-Noguer, F.: Very fast solution to the PnP problem with algebraic outlier rejection. In: 2014 IEEE Conference on Computer Vision and Pattern Recognition, pp. 501–508. IEEE Computer Society (2014). https://doi.org/10.1109/CVPR.2014.71
12. Fischler, M.A., Bolles, R.C.: Random sample consensus: a paradigm for model fitting with applications to image analysis and automated cartography. Commun. ACM **24**(6), 381–395 (1981)
13. Hesch, J.A., Roumeliotis, S.I.: A direct least-squares (DLS) method for PnP. In: 2011 International Conference on Computer Vision, pp. 383–390. IEEE (2011). https://doi.org/10.1109/ICCV.2011.6126266
14. Huo, J., Zhang, G., Cui, J., Yang, M.: A novel algorithm for pose estimation based on generalized orthogonal iteration with uncertainty-weighted measuring error of feature points. J. Mod. Opt. **65**(3), 331–341 (2018)
15. Kneip, L., Siegwart, R., Scaramuzza, D.: A novel parametrization of the perspective-three-point problem for a direct computation of absolute camera position and orientation. In: 2013 IEEE Conference on Computer Vision and Pattern Recognition, pp. 2969–2976. IEEE Computer Society (2011). https://doi.org/10.1109/CVPR.2011.5995464
16. Lepetit, V., Moreno-Noguer, F., Fua, P.: EPnP: an accurate o(n) solution to the PnP problem. Int. J. Comput. Vis. **81**(2), 155–166 (2009)
17. Li, J., Hu, Q., Zhong, R., Ai, M.: Exterior orientation revisited: a robust method based on lq-norm. Amer. Soc. Photogrammetry **83**(1), 47–56 (2017)
18. Li, S., Xu, C., Xie, M.: A robust o(n) solution to the perspective-n-point problem. IEEE Trans. Pattern Anal. Mach. Intell. **34**(7), 1444–1450 (2012)
19. Liu, W., Pokharel, P.P., Principe, J.C.: Correntropy: properties and applications in non-gaussian signal processing. IEEE Trans. Signal Process. **55**(11), 5286–5298 (2007)
20. Lowe, D.G.: Distinctive image features from scale-invariant keypoints. Int. J. Comput. Vis. **60**(2), 91–110 (2004)
21. Lu, C.P., Hager, G.D., Mjolsness, E.: Fast and globally convergent pose estimation from video images. IEEE Trans. Pattern Anal. Mach. Intell. **22**(6), 610–622 (2000)
22. Ma, J., Zhou, Y., Liu, W., Hao, Q.: More improved robust orthogonal iterative algorithm for pose estimation in AR. In: Zhou, L. (ed.) International Symposium on Photoelectronic Detection and Imaging 2007: Image Processing, vol. 6623, pp. 642–652. International Society for Optics and Photonics, SPIE (2008). https://doi.org/10.1117/12.791589
23. Moreno-Noguer, F., Lepetit, V., Fua, P.: Accurate non-iterative o(n) solution to the PnP problem. In: 2007 IEEE 11th International Conference on Computer Vision, pp. 1–8. IEEE (2007). https://doi.org/10.1109/ICCV.2007.4409116
24. Principe, J.C.: Information Theoretic Learning. ISS, Springer, New York (2010). https://doi.org/10.1007/978-1-4419-1570-2

25. Rublee, E., Rabaud, V., Konolige, K., Bradski, G.: ORB: an efficient alternative to sift or surf. In: 2011 International Conference on Computer Vision, pp. 2564–2571 (2011). https://doi.org/10.1109/ICCV.2011.6126544
26. Schweighofer, G., Pinz, A.: Globally optimal o(n) solution to the PnP problem for general camera models. In: Proceedings of the British Machine Vision Conference, pp. 1–10. BMVA Press (2008). https://doi.org/10.5244/C.22.55
27. Triggs, B.: Camera pose and calibration from 4 or 5 known 3d points. In: Proceedings of the Seventh IEEE International Conference on Computer Vision, vol. 1, pp. 278–284 (1999). https://doi.org/10.1109/ICCV.1999.791231
28. Zhang, W., Xu, G., Cheng, Y., Liu, T.: Research on orthogonal iteration algorithm of visual pose estimation for UAV landing. In: 2018 IEEE CSAA Guidance, Navigation and Control Conference (CGNCC), pp. 1–6. IEEE (2018). https://doi.org/10.1109/GNCC42960.2018.9019144
29. Zheng, Y., Kuang, Y., Sugimoto, S., Åström, K., Okutomi, M.: Revisiting the PnP problem: a fast, general and optimal solution. In: 2013 IEEE International Conference on Computer Vision, pp. 2344–2351. IEEE (2013). https://doi.org/10.1109/ICCV.2013.291
30. Zheng, Y., Sugimoto, S., Okutomi, M.: ASPnP: an accurate and scalable solution to the perspective-n-point problem. IEICE Trans. Inf. Syst. **96**(7), 1525–1535 (2013)
31. Zhou, H., Zhang, T., Jagadeesan, J.: Re-weighting and 1-point ransac-based PnP solution to handle outliers. IEEE Trans. Pattern Anal. Mach. Intell. **41**(12), 3022–3033 (2019)

The Generative Adversarial Random Neural Network

Will Serrano[✉]

The Bartlett University College London, London, UK
w.serrano@ucl.ac.uk

Abstract. Generative Adversarial Networks (GANs) have been proposed as a method to generate multiple replicas from an original version combining a Discriminator and a Generator. The main applications of GANs have been the casual generation of audio and video content. GANs, as a neural method that generates populations of individuals, have emulated genetic algorithms based on biologically inspired operators such as mutation, crossover and selection. This paper presents the Generative Adversarial Random Neural Network (RNN) with the same features and functionality as a GAN: an RNN Generator produces individuals mapped from a latent space while the RNN Discriminator evaluates them based on the true data distribution. The Generative Adversarial RNN has been evaluated against several input vectors with different dimensions. The presented results are successful: the learning objective of the RNN Generator creates replicas at low error whereas the RNN Discriminator learning target identifies unfit individuals.

Keywords: Generative Adversarial Networks · Random Neural Network

1 Introduction

Generative Adversarial Networks [1] were proposed as a machine learning generative model for unsupervised learning. GANs consist basically of two neural networks which learning algorithms compete against each other: Discriminator (D) and Generator (G). The Discriminator (D) objective is to learn the properties of the individual based on true data in order to identify the replicas created by the Generator. On the other side, the Generator (G) learning objective is to create data replicas by learning to map from a latent space to a data distribution of interest that deceive the Discriminator. The better an algorithm performs, the worse the other achieves and both learnings will reciprocally and dynamically try to improve their current performance. Generally, GANs suffer from four key drawbacks: 1) failure to converge between the discriminator and the generator. In addition, the difference in the dimensionality space between the source and the target may lead to unstable training. 2) model collapse where the generator only creates a reduced set of replicas. 3) diminished gradient due to an optimal discriminator feedbacks to the generator a vanished gradient that inhibits its learning. 4) overfitting when the generator does not create enough random replicas reducing its creating capabilities to an error limit.

© IFIP International Federation for Information Processing 2021
Published by Springer Nature Switzerland AG 2021
I. Maglogiannis et al. (Eds.): AIAI 2021, IFIP AICT 627, pp. 567–580, 2021.
https://doi.org/10.1007/978-3-030-79150-6_45

Following this learning structure, GAN applications have been purely the generation of image [2] and video [3] content with ramifications to video games [4], art [5], fashion [6], advertising [7], and science [8]. GANs have also been used as variational autoencoders by learning a data distribution from a latent space [9]. Due to the random generation of replicas, quantum computing has also been applied to GANs [10, 11]. Due to this generation of random examples from a common truth or set of rules, GANs have the potential to inspire or replace designers and artists in creative industries. GANs, as a neural method to generate populations of individuals, have emulated genetic algorithms based on biologically inspired operator such as mutation, crossover and selection.

1.1 Research Proposal

This paper presents the Generative Adversarial Random Neural Network (RNN) with the same features and use cases as a GAN: an RNN Generator produces individuals mapped from a latent space while the RNN Discriminator evaluates them based on the true data distribution. The RNN [12–14] is a recurrent stochastic mathematical model of an interconnected neural network of neurons that exchange information via spiking signals. Excitatory spikes increase the potential of the receiving neuron whereas inhibitory spikes decrease it. Neurons fire spikes at random only when their potential is positive. The Random Neural Network represents more closely how signals are transmitted in many biological neural networks where they travel as spikes or impulses, rather than analogue signal levels. The RNN has already been applied as a process that gradually finds the ground truth (Generator) based on the direct user feedback (Discriminator) although not in direct adversarial learning. The iterative search and adaptation between dynamic user interests and results within a universe of entities or ideas [15–17] apply an RNN where each neuron represents a dimension. The RNN with Deep Learning algorithm emulates the human brain within a management decision structure where generated judgements are taken in a structured way as a discriminative process based on a hierarchical process [18, 19].

1.2 Research Structure

Section 2 of this paper presents the generative adversarial network research background, GANs have been applied in different applications that require random samples from a common source of truth. In addition, there are several algorithms and mathematical models that generate a GAN. Section 3 defines the General Adversarial Random Neural Network mathematical model: Discriminator, Generator and learning algorithm. The Generative Adversarial RNN is validated for several neural configurations and vector dimensions for the Generator and Discriminator respectively. Section 4 presents the experimental results of two Discriminators: single output neuron and the same number of output neurons as the Generator. Conclusions and future work are shared in Sect. 5. The learning objective of the RNN Generator meets the RNN Discriminator expectations whereas the RNN Discriminator learning target identifies unfit individuals.

2   Research Background

Generative Adversarial Networks (GANs) estimate Generative models via an adversarial process in which two models are simultaneously trained. A Generative model "G" captures the data distribution and a Discriminative model "D" estimates the probability that a sample is from training data rather than G [1]. The training method for G is to maximize the probability of D making a mistake. New architectural features and training procedures improve the semi-supervised learning performance and improved sample generation of the GANs [20]; several techniques based on a heuristic understanding of the non-convergence problem are introduced to optimize the convergence of the GAN. An adversarial autoencoder is based on the variational inference between the aggregated of the hidden code vector of the autoencoder with an arbitrary prior distribution [21]; the adversarial autoencoder learns a deep generative model that maps the imposed prior to the data distribution.

Conditional adversarial networks are proposed as a general purpose solution to the image to image translation problems [22]; the networks learn the mapping from the input image to output image and a loss function to train this mapping. Stacked GANs generate high-resolution images [23]. The first GAN sketches the original shape and colours of a scene based on a given text description producing low-resolution images, the second GAN generates high-resolution images with photo-realistic details based on the outputs of the first GAN. GANs improve noise robustness of automatic speech recognition systems [24] when operating in GANs on log-Mel filterbank spectra instead of waveforms. GANs can effectively suppress additive noise in raw waveform speech signals, improving perceptual quality metrics.

An evolutionary GANs framework offers stable GAN training and improved generative performance [25]. The model evolves a population of generators to play the adversarial game with the discriminator where different adversarial training objectives are applied as mutation operations and each individual generator. GANs are also applied as unsupervised learning in clustering tasks. The cluster structure is not retained in the GAN latent space using traditional methods [26]. By sampling latent variables from a mixture of encoded variables and continuous latent variables, coupled with an inverse network trained jointly with a clustering specific loss achieve clustering in the latent space. Triangle Generative Adversarial Networks GAN consists of two generators and two discriminators for cross-domain joint distribution matching [27]. The generators learn the two-way conditional distributions between two domains, while the discriminators distinguish real data pairs and two kinds of fake data pairs. GAN mode collapse is the production of replicas with reduced diversity. To solve this issue, a discriminator is modified to make decisions based on multiple samples from the same class, either real or artificially generated [28]. A generative model for time-series data preserves temporal dynamics where new sequences include the original relationships between variables across time. A framework for generating realistic time series combines the flexibility of the unsupervised paradigm with the control afforded by supervised training [29].

3 The Generative Adversarial Random Neural Network

The Random Neural Network (RNN) [12–14] is a spiking recurrent stochastic model for neural networks that represents more closely how signals are transmitted in many biological neural networks where they travel as spikes or impulses, rather than as analogue signal levels (Fig. 1).

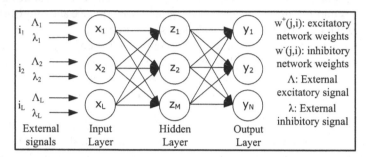

Fig. 1. The Random Neural Network structure

3.1 The Random Neural Network

The RNN is composed of P neurons where each neuron receives excitatory (positive) and inhibitory (negative) spike signals from external sources which may be L sensory impulses or P internal neurons:

- $X_L = (x_1, x_2, ..., x_L)$, a variable L-dimensional vector $X \in [0,1]^L$ represents the input state q_L for the neuron L; where scalar L values range $1 < L < \infty$;
- $Z_M = (z_1, z_2, ..., z_M)$, a M-dimensional vector $Z \in [0,1]^M$ that represents the hidden neuron state q_M for the neuron M; where scalar M values range $1 < M < \infty$;
- $Y_N = (y_1, y_2, ..., y_N)$, an N-dimensional vector $Y \in [0,1]^N$ that represents the neuron output state q_N for the neuron N; where scalar N values range $1 < N < \infty$.

These spike signals occur following independent Poisson processes of rates $\lambda^+(m)$ for the excitatory spike signal and $\lambda^-(m)$ for the inhibitory spike signal respectively, to neuron $m \in \{1,...P\}$ (Fig. 2).

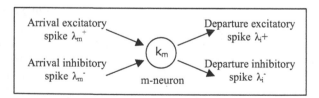

Fig. 2. The random neural network

3.1.1 Principles

The state of the m neuron network at time t is represented by the vector of non-negative integers $k(t) = [k_1(t), \ldots k_m(t)]$ where $k_m(t)$ is the potential of neuron m at time t. Neurons interact with each other by interchanging signals in the form of spikes of unit amplitude:

- A positive spike is interpreted as an excitation signal because it increases by one unit the potential of the receiving neuron m, $k_m(t^+) = k_m(t) + 1$;
- A negative spike is interpreted as an inhibition signal decreasing by one unit the potential of the receiving neuron m, $k_m(t^+) = k_m(t) - 1$, or does not affect if the potential is already zero, $k_m(t) = 0$.

Each neuron i accumulates signals and it will fire if its potential is positive. Firing will occur at random and spikes will be sent out at rate r(i) with independent, identically and exponentially distributed inter-spike intervals:

- Positive spikes will go out to neuron j with probability $p^+(i,j)$ as excitatory signals;
- Negative spikes with probability $p^-(i,j)$ as inhibitory signals.

3.1.2 Model

Neuron i may send spikes out of the network with probability d(i). We have:

$$d(i) + \sum_{j=1}^{n} \left[p^+(i,j) + p^-(i,j) \right] = 1 \quad \text{for} 1 \leq i \leq n \tag{1}$$

Neuron potential decreases by one unit when the neuron fires either an excitatory spike or an inhibitory spike (Fig. 3). External (or exogenous) excitatory or inhibitory signals to neuron i will arrive at rates $\Lambda(i)$, $\lambda(i)$ respectively by stationary Poisson processes. The RNN weight parameters $w^+(j,i)$ and $w^-(j,i)$ are the non-negative rate of excitatory and inhibitory spike emission respectively from neuron i to neuron j:

$$w^+(j,i) = r(i)p^+(i,j) \geq 0$$

$$w^-(j,i) = r(i)p^-(i,j) \geq 0 \tag{2}$$

Information in this model is transmitted by the rate or frequency at which spikes travel. Each neuron i, if it is excited, behaves as a frequency modulator emitting spikes at rate $w(i,j) = w^+(i,j) + w^-(i,j)$ to neuron j. Spikes will be emitted at exponentially distributed random intervals. Each neuron acts as a non-linear frequency demodulator transforming the incoming excitatory and inhibitory spikes into potential.

This network model has a product form solution; the network's stationary probability distribution can be represented as the product of the marginal probabilities of the state of each neuron where q_i is the probability neuron i is excited.

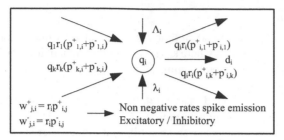

Fig. 3. The random neural network model

3.1.3 Theorem

The probability distribution of the network state is defined as $p(k,t) = \text{Prob}[k(t) = k)]$ and the marginal probability a neuron i is excited at time t as $q_i(t) = \text{Prob}[k_i(t) > 0]$. The stationary probability distribution $p(k) = \lim_{t \to \infty} p(k,t)$ and $q_i = \lim_{t \to \infty} q_i(t)$ where $k(t)$ is a continuous time Markov chain that satisfies Chapman-Kolmogorov equations [12–14].

$$q_i = \frac{\lambda^+(i)}{r(i) + \lambda^-(i)} \tag{3}$$

$$r(i) = \sum_{j=1}^{n} \left[w^+(i,j) + w^-(i,j) \right] \quad \text{for } 1 \le i \le n \tag{4}$$

where the $\lambda^+(i)$, $\lambda^-(i)$ for $i = 1,\ldots,n$ satisfy the system of nonlinear equations:

$$\lambda^+(i) = \sum_{j=1}^{n} \left[q_j r(j) p^+(j,i) \right] + \Lambda(i) \tag{5}$$

$$\lambda^-(i) = \sum_{j=1}^{n} \left[q_j r(j) p^-(j,i) \right] + \lambda(i) \tag{6}$$

3.1.4 Learning Algorithm

The RNN learning algorithm is based on the gradient descent of a quadratic error function. The backpropagation model requires the solution of n linear and n nonlinear equations each time the n neuron network learns a new input and output pair. Gradient Descent learning algorithm optimizes the network weight parameters W in order to learn a set of k input-output pairs (i,y) where successive inputs are denoted $i = \{i_1,\ldots,i_k\}$ and the successive desired outputs are represented $y = \{y_1,\ldots,y_k\}$. Each input vector $i_k = (\Lambda_k, \lambda_k)$ is the pair of the excitatory and inhibitory signals entering each neuron: $\Lambda_k = [\Lambda_k(1),\ldots, \Lambda_k(n)]$, $\lambda_k = [\lambda_k(1),\ldots, \lambda_k(n)]$. Each output vector $y_k = (y_{1k},\ldots, y_{nk})$, $y_{ik} \in [0,1]$ is composed of the desired values of each neuron. The desired output vectors are approximated by minimizing the cost function E_k:

$$E_k = \frac{1}{2} \sum_{i=1}^{n} a_i (q_i - y_{ik})^2 \quad a_i \geq 0 \tag{7}$$

Each of the n neurons of the network is considered an output neuron. The function of the variable a_i is to remove neurons from the network output. The network learns both n x n weight matrices $W_k^+ = \{w_k^+(i,j)\}$ and $W_k^- = \{w_k^-(i,j)\}$ by calculating new values of the network parameters for each input $i_k = (\Lambda_k, \lambda_k)$.

3.2 The Generative Adversarial Random Neural Network

The Generative Adversarial Random Neural Network (RNN) is composed of two Random Neural Networks (Fig. 4) with different learning algorithms where l^k defines the latent space and d^k represents the true distribution respectively.

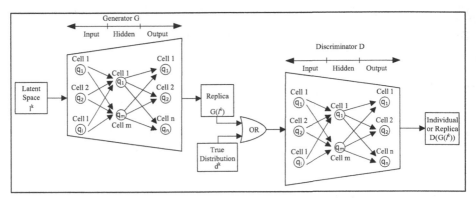

Fig. 4. Generative Adversarial Random Neural Network

3.2.1 Discriminator

The Discriminator D is defined as an RNN that consists of L input neurons, M hidden neurons and N output neurons as:

- $X_{DIS} = (x_{Dis-1}, x_{Dis-2}, \ldots, x_{Dis-L})$, a variable L-dimensional vector $X \in [0,1]^L$ represents the input state q_L for the neuron L; where scalar L values range $1 < L < \infty$;
- $Z_{DIS} = (z_{Dis-1}, z_{Dis-2}, \ldots, z_{Dis-M})$, a M-dimensional vector $Z \in [0,1]^M$ that represents the hidden neuron state q_M for the neuron M; where scalar M values range $1 < M < \infty$;
- $Y_{DIS} = (y_{Dis-1}, y_{Dis-2}, \ldots, y_{Dis-N})$, a N-dimensional vector $Y \in [0,1]^N$ that represents the neuron output state q_N for the neuron N; where scalar N values range $1 < N < \infty$. The output neuron potential codify the probability that input is from true data distribution rather than the latent space;

- $W_{DIS}(j,i)$ is the $(L+M+N)x(L+M+N)$ matrix of network weights that represents the connection from neuron j to neuron i; where $i \in [x_L, z_M, y_N]$ and $j \in [x_L, z_M, y_N]$.

The learning objective of the Discriminator is to maximize the probability of assigning the correct label to both real individuals and replicas from the Generator, therefore, is trained to minimize the error of the real data distribution. The learning equation of the Discriminator and the rule for weight update takes the generic form:

$$W_{DIS}^k(i,j)=W_{DIS}^{k-1}(i,j)-\eta \sum_{i=1}^n \left(d_i^k-y_{DIS-i}^k\right)\left[\frac{\partial q_{DIS-i}}{\partial W_{DIS}(i,j)}\right]_k \qquad (8)$$

where η is the learning rate, the term $W_{DIS}(i,j)$ denotes either $w^+(i,j)$ or $w^-(i,j)$, d_i^k is the true distribution and q_{DIS-i} represents the output state of the discriminator neuron i respectively.

3.2.2 Generator

The Generator G is defined as an RNN that consists of L input neurons, M hidden neurons and N output neurons as:

- $X_{GEN} = (x_{Gen-1}, x_{Gen-2}, ..., x_{Gen-L})$, a variable L-dimensional vector $X \in [0,1]^L$ represents the input state q_L for the neuron L; where scalar L values range $1 < L < \infty$. The input neuron potential represents the latent space or noise;
- $Z_{GEN} = (z_{Gen-1}, z_{Gen-2}, ..., z_{Gen-M})$, a M-dimensional vector $Z \in [0,1]^M$ that represents the hidden neuron state q_M for the neuron M; where scalar M values range $1 < M < \infty$;
- $Y_{GEN} = (y_{Gen-1}, y_{Gen-2}, ..., y_{Gen-N})$, an N-dimensional vector $Y \in [0,1]^N$ that represents the neuron output state q_N for the neuron N; where scalar N values range $1 < N < \infty$. The output of the generator represents the individual replica;
- $W_{GEN}(j,i)$ is the $(L+M+N)x(L+M+N)$ matrix of network weights that represents the connection from neuron j to neuron i; where $i \in [i_L, z_M, y_N]$ and $j \in [i_L, z_M, y_N]$.

The learning objective of the Generator is to minimize the error of the Discriminator, therefore, is trained based on the Discriminator output or probability of the true data. The number of output neurons of the Generator y_{Gen-N} is the same as the number of input neurons in the Discriminator x_{Dis-L}. The learning equation of the Generator and the rule for weight update take the generic form:

$$W_{GEN}^k(i,j)=W_{GEN}^{k-1}(i,j)-\eta \sum_{i=1}^n \left(y_{DIS-i}^k\right)\left[\frac{\partial q_{GEN-i}}{\partial W_{GEN}(i,j)}\right]_k \qquad (9)$$

where η is the learning rate, the term $W_{GEN}(i,j)$ denotes either $w^+(i,j)$ or $w^-(i,j)$ and q_{GEN-i} represents the output state of the generator neuron i respectively.

3.2.3 Learning Algorithm

The proposed learning algorithm is based on data from the latent space, l^k, and data from the true distribution, d^k:

1) the Discriminator D learns $W_{DIS}^k(i, j)$ where $Y_{DIS} = D(d^k)$ represents the probability d^k is an individual data from the true distribution;
2) the Generator G creates a replica from the latent space $G(l^k)$;
3) the Discriminator D assesses the replica $Y_{DIS} = D(G(l^k))$;
4) the Generator G learns $W_{GEN}^k(i, j)$ based on Y_{DIS};
5) the method iterates on step 2) until either the Generator can not further learn to reduce the Discriminator probability of detection or the Discriminator can not distinguish between the replica and the real individual.

4 Experimental Results

This section evaluates the Generative Adversarial RNN against two neural configurations:

- Generator: Learning rate of 0.1 with input and output vectors of five, ten and twenty dimensions;
- Discriminator: Learning rate of 1.0 with output vector of one and same as the Generator dimensions.

Experimental results are obtained based on 1,000 independent experiments with random inputs to the Generator and Discriminator rather than a prescribed dataset. The time series consists of 10,000 data points per experiment. Other GAN algorithms prosed in the literature review evaluate GANs as a classification method or image generator rather than as an autoencoder as proposed in this paper therefore there is not a direct comparison between algorithms.

Statistical information includes Standard Deviation and 95% Confidence Range. The variables represented cover the average error of the Discriminator after learning the individual with the required number of iterations and time. In addition, the average error of the Generator creating the replica is also shown with its validation time and the detection of the Discriminator. This detection corresponds to the output neurons of the Discriminator y_{Dis-N}.

4.1 Discriminator Output Neurons: One

The Discriminator learns at a very reduced error after very few iterations and detects replicas from the Generator with only one neuron on its output layer. The larger the number of generator neurons, the lesser learning iterations required; however its learning time also increases. A Generator with larger neurons has a greater error in the replica and requires a longer learning time, this is due to the replica becomes more complex too.

Table 1. Generative Adversarial RNN Validation – Discriminator: 1 neuron

Stage	Variable	Generator Neurons	Value	σ	95% CR
Discriminator	Error	5	4.78E−31	2.61E−31	1.62E−32
		10	4.12E−31	2.92E−31	1.81E−32
		20	3.34E−31	2.90E−31	1.80E−32
	Iteration	5	37.39	3.82	0.24
		10	28.01	3.87	0.24
		20	23.49	3.96	0.25
	Time (ns)	5	4.77E+06	2.45E+07	1.52E+06
		10	4.69E+06	1.53E+07	9.46E+05
		20	9.54E+06	1.82E+07	1.13E+06
Generator	Error Discriminator	5	1.64E−09	9.39E−07	4.48E−08
		10	5.62E−08	1.49E−05	7.49E−07
		20	5.07E−08	8.96E−05	5.26E−06
	Error Generator	5	1.09E−02	1.30E−02	6.21E−04
		10	1.83E−02	7.30E−03	3.66E−04
		20	2.18E−02	4.08E−02	2.39E−03
	Time (ns)	5	5.63E+09	1.18E+11	5.64E+09
		10	9.87E+09	1.25E+11	6.25E+09
		20	1.51E+10	4.91E+09	2.88E+08

The error that the Discriminator feedbacks to the Generator is very reduced and almost constant to the Generator size (Table 1).

The Discriminator with only one output neuron does not provide enough resolution for the Generator to learn suffering diminished gradient (Fig. 5). The Discriminator error converges to a constant value, independent of the Generator neurons.

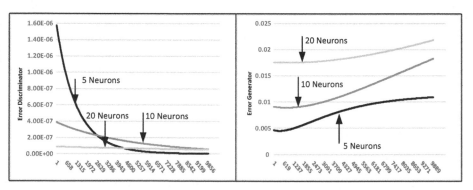

Fig. 5. Discriminator and Generator Replica error – Discriminator: 1 neuron

4.2   Discriminator Output Neurons: Same as Generator

The Discriminator with the same neurons as the Generator on its output layer detects replicas from the Generator although it requires more learning iterations than the previous validation due to the increase of the output neurons (Table 2). The number of learning iterations of the Discriminator is nearly constant against the Generator neurons, however, its learning time increases with the number of Generator neurons. The error of the Discriminator is still lower than the Generator, therefore outperforming its detection capabilities.

Table 2. Generative Adversarial RNN Validation – Discriminator: Generator neurons

Stage	Variable	Generator Neurons	Value	σ	95% CR
Discriminator	Error	5	8.29E−31	1.62E−31	1.01E−32
		10	8.38E−31	1.61E−31	9.97E−33
		20	8.22E−31	1.70E−31	1.06E−32
	Iteration	5	124.41	3.68	0.23
		10	124.22	2.71	0.17
		20	124.37	1.84	0.11
	Time (ns)	5	2.12E+07	3.59E+07	2.23E+06
		10	4.76E+07	5.62E+07	3.48E+06
		20	1.59E+08	5.79E+07	3.59E+06
Generator	Error Discriminator	5	3.29E−05	3.39E−05	2.10E−06
		10	3.33E−05	1.11E−05	6.90E−07
		20	3.27E−05	8.21E−06	4.65E−07
	Error Generator	5	1.67E−03	2.04E−03	1.26E−04
		10	3.40E−03	2.50E−03	1.55E−04
		20	6.68E−03	3.57E−03	2.02E−04
	Time (ns)	5	1.10E+09	4.82E+08	2.99E+07
		10	3.64E+09	2.15E+09	1.33E+08
		20	1.68E+10	6.13E+09	3.47E+08

The Discriminator provides a greater resolution to the Generator enabling its stable learning to converge to a non-optimum value suffering overfitting (Fig. 6). The error of the Discriminator reduces following the Generator learning where the more complex (larger dimensions) the Generator is, the greater the error.

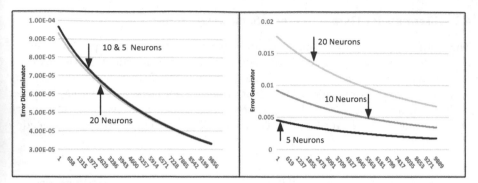

Fig. 6. Generative Adversarial RNN Validation – Discriminator: 5 neurons

5   Conclusions

This paper has presented the Generative Adversarial Random Neural Network (RNN) with the same features and use cases as a Generative Adversarial Network: an RNN Generator produces individuals mapped from a latent space while the RNN Discriminator evaluates them based on the true data distribution. The validation results are successful although not optimum: the learning objective of the RNN Generator creates replicas at low error whereas the RNN Discriminator learning target identifies unfit individuals. The number of output neurons in the Discriminator has a clear effect on the Generator learning capabilities.

The error that the discriminator feedbacks to the Generator (diminished gradient) may not be large enough for the Generator to learn (overfitting), although a large error may cause the Generator not to converge (instability). In addition, experimental results show that the larger the dimensions of the Generator, the worse the replica becomes, although this is due to its greater complexity.

Future work will include additional experiments to increase the dimensions of the input vector. The modifications within the Generator cost function obtained from the Discriminator feedback to enhancement its learning capabilities will be analysed. Finally, the addition of Deep Learning clusters will be assessed in terms of learning performance and quality for both the Generator and the Discriminator.

References

1. Goodfellow, I., et al.: Generative adversarial nets. Adv. Neural. Inf. Process. Syst. **27**, 1–9 (2014)
2. Wang, X., Gupta, A.: Generative image modeling using style and structure adversarial networks. In: Leibe, B., Matas, J., Sebe, N., Welling, M. (eds.) ECCV 2016. LNCS, vol. 9908, pp. 318–335. Springer, Cham (2016). https://doi.org/10.1007/978-3-319-46493-0_20
3. Wang, L., Mostafavi, S., Ho, Y.-S., Yoon, K.-J.: Event-based high dynamic range image and very high frame rate video generation using conditional generative adversarial networks. In: Proceedings of the IEEE/Computer Vision Foundation. Conference on Computer Vision and Pattern Recognition, pp. 10081–10090 (2019)

4. Fadaeddini, A., Majidi, B., Eshghi, M.: A case study of generative adversarial networks for procedural synthesis of original textures in video games. In: International Digital Games Research Conference: Trends, Technologies, and Applications, pp. 118–122 (2018). https://doi.org/10.1109/DGRC.2018.8712070

5. Matsumura, N., Tokura, H., Kuroda, Y., Ito, Y., Nakano, K.: Tile art image generation using conditional generative adversarial networks. In: International Symposium on Computing and Networking Workshops, pp. 209–215 (2018). https://doi.org/10.1109/CANDARW.2018.00047

6. Ak, K., Lim, J., Tham, J., Kassim, A.: Attribute manipulation generative adversarial networks for fashion images. In: Proceedings of the IEEE Computer Vision Foundation. Conference on Computer Vision, pp. 10541–10550 (2019)

7. Lee, M-C., Gao, B., Zhang, R.: Rare query expansion through generative adversarial networks in search advertising. In: ACM International Conference on Special Interest Group on Knowledge Discovery and Data Mining, 500–508 (2018)

8. Emami, H., Dong, M., Nejad, C.G.: Generating synthetic CTs from magnetic resonance images using generative adversarial networks. Med. Phys. **45**(8), 3627–3636 (2018)

9. Husain, H., Nock, R., Williamson, R.: A primal-dual link between GANs and autoencoders. In: Advances in Neural Information Processing Systems, p. 32, pp. 1–10 (2019)

10. Dallaire, P., Killoran, N.: Quantum generative adversarial networks. Phys. Rev. A **98**(012324), 1–8 (2018)

11. Lloyd, S., Weedbrook, C.: Quantum generative adversarial learning. Phys. Rev. Lett. **121**(040502), 1–5 (2018)

12. Gelenbe, E.: Random neural networks with negative and positive signals and product form solution. Neural Comput. **1**, 502–510 (1989)

13. Gelenbe, E.: Stability of the random neural network model. Neural Comput. **2**(2), 239–247 (1990)

14. Gelenbe, E.: Learning in the recurrent random neural network. Neural Comput. **5**, 154–164 (1993)

15. Serrano, W., Gelenbe, E.: Intelligent search with deep learning clusters. In: Intelligent Systems Conference, pp. 632–637 (2017)

16. Serrano, W.: Neural networks in big data and web search. Data **4**(7), 1–41 (2019)

17. Serrano, W., Gelenbe, E., Yin, Y.: The random neural network with deep learning clusters in smart search. Neurocomputing **396**, 394–405 (2020)

18. Serrano, W.: Fintech model: the random neural network with genetic algorithm. Procedia Comput. Sci. **126**, 537–546 (2018)

19. Serrano, W.: Genetic and deep learning clusters based on neural networks for management decision structures. Neural Comput. Appl. **32**(9), 4187–4211 (2019). https://doi.org/10.1007/s00521-019-04231-8

20. Salimans, T., Goodfellow, I., Zaremba, W., Cheung, V., Radford, A., Chen, X.: Improved techniques for training GANs. In: International Conference on Neural Information Processing Systems, pp. 2234–2242 (2016)

21. Makhzani, A., Shlens, J., Jaitly, N., Goodfellow, I., Frey, B.: Adversarial autoencoders. In: International Conference on Learning Representations, pp. 1–16 (2016)

22. Isola, P., Zhu, J., Zhou, T., Efros, A.: Image-to-image translation with conditional adversarial networks. In: IEEE Conference on Computer Vision and Pattern Recognition, pp. 5967–5976 (2017)

23. Zhang, H., et al.: StackGAN++: realistic image synthesis with stacked generative adversarial networks. IEEE Trans. Pattern Anal. Mach. Intell. **41**(8), 1947–1962 (2019)

24. Donahue, C., Li, B., Prabhavalkar, R.: Exploring speech enhancement with generative adversarial networks for robust speech recognition. In: IEEE International Conference on Acoustics, Speech and Signal Processing, pp. 5024–5028 (2018)

25. Wang, C., Xu, C., Yao, X., Tao, D.: Evolutionary generative adversarial networks. IEEE Trans. Evol. Comput. **23**(6), 921–934 (2019)
26. Mukherjee, S., Asnani, H., Lin, E., Kannan, S.: ClusterGAN: latent space clustering in generative adversarial networks. In: Association for the Advancement of Artificial Intelligence, 4610- 4617 (2019)
27. Gan, Z., et al.: Triangle generative adversarial networks. Adv. Neural. Inf. Process. Syst. **30**, 1–10 (2017)
28. Lin, Z., Khetan, A., Fanti, G., PacGAN, S.: The power of two samples in generative adversarial networks. IEEE J. Sel. Areas Inf. Theory. **1**(1), 324–335 (2020)
29. Yoon, J., Jarrett, D., Schaar, M.: Time-series generative adversarial networks. In: Conference on Neural Information Processing Systems, pp. 1–11 (2019)

Using Machine Learning Methods to Predict Subscriber Churn of a Web-Based Drug Information Platform

Georgios Theodoridis[✉] and Athanasios Tsadiras

Aristotle University of Thessaloniki, Thessaloniki, Greece
ttgeorgio@csd.auth.gr, tsadiras@econ.auth.gr

Abstract. Nowadays, businesses are highly competitive as most markets are extremely saturated. As a result, customer management is of critical importance to avoid dissatisfaction that leads to customer loss. Thus, predicting customer loss is crucial to efficiently target potential churners and attempt to retain them. By classifying customers as churners and non-churners, customer loss is equated to a binary classification problem. In this paper, a new real-world dataset is used, originating from a popular web-based drug information platform, in order to predict subscriber churn. A number of methods that belong to different machine learning categories (linear, nonlinear, ensemble, neural networks) are constructed, optimized and trained on the subscription data and the results are presented and compared. This study provides a guide for solving churn prediction problems as well as a comparison of various models within the churn prediction context. The findings co-align with the notion that ensemble methods are, in principle, superior whilst every model maintains satisfying results.

Keywords: Machine learning · Data mining · Customer churn · Ensemble methods · Neural networks

1 Introduction to Customer Churn Prediction

Due to saturated markets and intense competition, many companies realize that their existing database is their most valuable asset [1, 12, 22]. This trend is particularly prevalent in subscription services where companies are beginning to move away from traditional, mass marketing strategies in favor of targeted marketing techniques [4]. The idea of identifying churners, meaning customers who are more prone to change and eventually cancel their subscription, has a high strategic priority.

Van Den Poel and Larivière [6] have suggested that in the current environment, in which potential customers have a huge selection of offers from numerous service providers, attracting new customers is a costly and difficult process. Therefore, more effort to retain existing customers has become necessary for service-oriented companies.

In order to effectively manage customer churn, it is vital to build an effective and accurate customer churn prediction model via multiple predictive modeling techniques.

© IFIP International Federation for Information Processing 2021
Published by Springer Nature Switzerland AG 2021
I. Maglogiannis et al. (Eds.): AIAI 2021, IFIP AICT 627, pp. 581–593, 2021.
https://doi.org/10.1007/978-3-030-79150-6_46

The machine learning models that apply these techniques belong to different categories (linear, nonlinear, ensemble, neural networks) and they vary in theoretical background, statistical technique, input parameters, number of features selected and included, execution time, and required processing power. Therefore, it is particularly interesting to build, implement and evaluate multiple models with the goal of enriching their bibliographic background within the context of predicting Web-based subscriber churn. In doing so, a methodology guide is presented to assist any Web-based platform in creating and streamlining subscriber retention systems from data collection to model selection and feature analysis. Programmatically, Python 3 was used as it provides excellent modules for data processing (mainly Pandas and NumPy) and method modeling (mainly Sklearn and TensorFlow).

2 Dataset

The dataset used within this paper is a new real-world dataset that was extracted from the usage data of a popular Greek Web-based platform that offers information relating to pharmaceutical products and substances. The platform has 55,000 unique visitors per day and 4,200,000 page views per month. It is a professional tool used by doctors, pharmacists, nurses as well as medical students that aims to support pharmacotherapy decision making. Surface-level information is provided for free whilst users have the option to subscribe in order to access premium analytics and features. In more detail, the dataset reflects 10 years of website usage (July 2010–December 2020) containing information about the actions/activities that every subscriber performed, accompanied by the general demographic information of each subscriber as well as their subscription history. The original dataset consists of 878,788 activities performed by 779 subscribers throughout 2,270 different subscriptions.

3 Defining the Problem and Preprocessing the Dataset

In our study, a subscriber is considered churned after not renewing his/her latest subscription within 3 months, as a 3-month plan is the shortest subscription plan offered by the service, hence postponing a renewal for more than 3 months is a direct loss of profit. As a result, the problem of predicting subscriber churn is equated to predicting the non-renewal of subscriptions in the near future. Subsequently, the focus of the problem is moved, from the general subscriber, towards each individual subscription.

At this point, it is important to note the potential differences between classic customer churn and Web-based subscriber churn. After analyzing the renewal delays within the dataset, meaning the time (in days) in between each consecutive subscription, the mean renewal delay is 66 days whilst the median is 6 days, indicating the existence of numerous outliers with large renewal delays (15% are detected as outliers via boxplot analysis). Another crucial observation is that 40% of the subscriptions are 3-month plans (shortest plan provided). Therefore, many users subscribe for the shortest amount of time possible, as they want to use some of the premium features provided by the website, and then do not renew their subscription until they want to use said premium features again. Hence, subscribers oftentimes churn, based on the 3-month churning condition explained in the previous paragraph, but eventually return. This contrasts the classic customer churn profile observed in mobile telecommunications [8] and insurances [13] where customers sign years-long contracts and, once churned, tend to not return. As such, Web-based subscriber churn should be differentiated from general customer churn for the current dataset as well as any other Web-based subscriber dataset with similar properties.

In order to preprocess the data, we extracted the dependent variable (binary variable containing 0 for retention and 1 for churning) as well as a number of features to be used by the prediction models. In order to extract the dependent variable, every renewal point within the last 5 years is inspected (January 2015–September 2020) ensuring that the data is up-to-date. The features, described in Table 1, are collected by inspecting the entire dataset in relation to each individual renewal point detected by the aforementioned dependent variable extraction. The features are categorized in two levels; the subscription level (Sn) and the subscriber level (Sr). The subscription level includes information about the latest, at that time, subscription that was about to be renewed or not whilst the subscriber level includes data from every subscription of the related subscriber. For example, when predicting subscriber churn, the number of activities the subscriber made during their latest subscription should be included as a feature (subscription level) but it is also important to include the number of activities the subscriber has historically made throughout their entire subscription history as a separate feature (subscriber level). Using this collection method, an individual timeline per subscriber is formed for every renewal point within the last 5 years, as presented in Fig. 1. The total number of subscription renewal points, which by extension is the sample set to be used for training/testing, is 1238 with the retained-churned ratio being 64.6%–35.4%

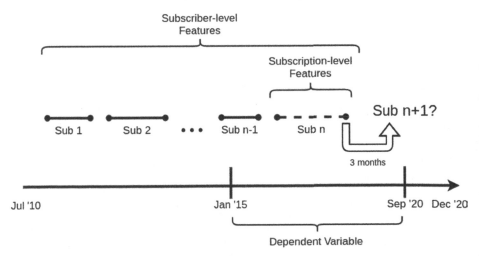

Fig. 1. Presentation of the problem regarding a single potential renewal point (Sub n – Sub n + 1) of a subscriber's subscription history, displaying the feature extraction method.

To construct the training and test sets, the sample set is split so that 20% belongs to the test set (248 samples) and the retained-churned ratio within it represents the original ratio. The training set is sampled (from the remaining 80%) so that the retained-churned ratio is 50%–50% for better results [14] (700 samples). It is also important to note that every continuous feature is normalized within the closed interval (0, 1) while the categorial features are one-hot encoded with each category becoming a new binary feature. In practice, feature selection was performed to construct the final list of features presented in Table 1 by estimating feature importance (as presented in Sect. 5.2) as well as feature correlation (using Pearson correlation coefficient [2]) in order to discard potential features that do not correlate with the dependent variable or highly correlate with another feature.

Table 1. List of features and statistics (Mean – Std for normalized continuous features and Yes - No percentages for binary categorial features) of dependent variable.

Feature	Level	Churned	Retained
The subscriber's gender (Are they male or not)	Sr	42% (M)–45%(F)	58% (M)–55% (F)
The subscriber's age	Sr	0.49–0.13	0.49–0.12
The subscriber's city as defined in his profile	Sr	Varies among 19 categories	Varies among 19 categories
The subscriber's group, found via clustering, performed by the website's developers	Sr	Varies among 27 categories	Varies among 27 categories
The number of offences the subscriber performed as detected by an internal anti-spam/bot system	Sr	0.003–0.05	0.003–0.04
The number of activities the subscriber performed during morning hours	Sr & Sn	Sr: 0.02–0.05 Sn: 0.02–0.04	Sr: 0.07–0.12 Sn: 0.04–0.09
The number of activities the subscriber performed during evening hours	Sr & Sn	Sr: 0.04–0.07 Sn: 0.02–0.05	Sr: 0.1–0.12 Sn: 0.04–0.08
The number of activities the subscriber performed during night hours	Sr & Sn	Sr: 0.01–0.05 Sn: 0.01–0.03	Sr: 0.03–0.06 Sn: 0.02–0.06
The number of drugs the subscriber viewed	Sr & Sn	Sr: 0.06–0.1 Sn: 0.05–0.09	Sr: 0.15–0.17 Sn: 0.1–0.13
The number of drug substances the subscriber viewed	Sr & Sn	Sr: 0.06–0.1 Sn: 0.04–0.09	Sr: 0.15–0.17 Sn: 0.07–0.1

(continued)

Table 1. (*continued*)

Feature	Level	Churned	Retained
The number of drug packages the subscriber viewed	Sr & Sn	Sr: 0.05–0.09 Sn: 0.05–0.1	Sr: 0.13–0.16 Sn: 0.11–0.14
The number of subscriptions the subscriber made	Sr	0.03–0.06	0.09–0.15
This is the first subscription of the subscriber	Sn	64%–33%	36%–67%
The duration (in days) between the start of the latest subscription and the end of the previous one (last renewal delay)	Sn	0.05–0.14	0.02–0.08
The average of all the last renewal delays.	Sr	0.05–0.14	0.02–0.06
The last renewal was instant	Sn	14%–47%	86%–53%
The duration (in days) the subscriber is subscribed for. (Cumulatively for Sr level)	Sr & Sn	Sr: 0.13–0.15 Sn: 0.09–0.11	Sr: 0.25–0.21 Sn: 0.10–0.12
The duration (in days) of the subscriber's account	Sr	0.25–0.21	0.33–0.22
The month the subscription is ending	Sn	Varies among 12 categories	Varies among 12 categories

4   Categories of Machine Learning Customer Churn Predictive Methods

Predicting customer churn is a binary classification problem outputting two possible classes – churn as the positive class and retention as the negative class. Thus, any machine learning model that is able to handle classification problems is suitable for churn prediction. In the present work, multiple models covering various categories of machine learning methods (linear, nonlinear, ensemble, neural networks) are utilized to compare their suitability and effectiveness. In the following paragraphs a general overview of each model used in this study is presented, summarizing their predictive methods, accompanied by a description of their parameters and their optimized values. Optimization is performed via grid search and 5-fold Cross Validation (CV) so that the Matthews Correlation Coefficient (MCC) metric, which tends to be preferred in binary classification problems over other metrics such as the accuracy, f-score or ROC AUC [7], is maximized.

4.1 Linear Category - Logistic Regression

Regarding the linear category, the popular logistic regression method is studied. Logistic methods expect that the target value is a linear combination of the features [19]. In mathematical notation, if $\hat{y}$ is the predicted value then:

$$\hat{y}(w, x) = w_0 + w_1 x_1 + \ldots + w_n x_n$$

In order to optimize the coefficient values w, logistic regression uses a designated solver that attempts to minimize a cost function. For the current problem, the "lbfgs" solver was chosen, alongside with the l_2 cost function, as it is recommended for relatively small datasets and generally considered robust [19].

The method's parameters to optimize, accompanied by the searched values, follow (optimal value in bold):

- C - the regularization term of l_2, Values: 0.1, 0.5, 1, 10, **50**, 100
- The tolerance for stopping criteria, Values: 0.001, **0.00001**, 0.000001

4.2 Nonlinear Category - Support Vector Machines

Support vector machines (SVMs) are a set of supervised learning methods used for classification, regression and outlier detection. In a binary classification context, SVMs try to find a linear optimal hyperplane so that the margin of separation between the positive and the negative samples is maximized [14]. However, in practice, the data is often not linearly separable which necessitates the usage of a kernel function to transform the input space into a higher dimensional feature space. Two kernels will be tested in this paper; the Polynomial kernel and the Radial Basis Function (RBF) kernel that allow nonlinear hyperplanes [23].

Several experiments are performed with various parameters to optimize. The parameters and the searched values are the following (optimal value in bold):

SVM (Polynomial)

- C - the regularization term, Values: 0.1, **0.5**, 1, 10, 50, 100, 250, 500, 750, 1000
- The degree of the polynomial, Values: **2**, 3, 4

SVM (RBF)

- C - the regularization term. Values: 0.1, 0.5, 1, 10, 50, 100, 250, 500, **750**, 1000
- γ - the kernel coefficient. Values: 0.1, 0.01, 0.001, **0.0001**, 0.00001

4.3 Ensemble Methods Category

Random Forest. Random Forests [3] are an ensemble learning method that uses a subset of randomly chosen features to grow decision trees on a bootstrap sample of the training data. After a large number of trees are generated, each tree separately classifies the input. The final class is decided on majority vote amongst the decision trees.

The implementation involves the optimization of a number of parameters. The parameters involved are presented below, followed by the examined values (optimal in bold):

- Function to measure the quality of a split of the decision trees. Values: Information gain or **Gini impurity.**
- The minimum number of samples needed to perform a split. Values: 2, **3**, 4.
- The maximum depth of every decision tree (pre-pruning). Values: 7, 8, 9, 10, **None.**
- The number of randomly chosen features. Values: 9, 10, 11, **12**, 13, 14.
- The number of decision trees to be created. Values: 100, 150, 200, **250**, 300.

XGBoost. XGBoost (eXtreme Gradient Boosting) is an optimized distributed gradient boosting library designed to be highly efficient, flexible and portable [5]. It implements parallel tree boosting (also known as GBDT, GBM) under the Gradient Boosting ensemble learning framework. Vinayak and Gilad-Bachrach [20] proposed a new boosting method, the DART booster, to add dropout techniques to boosted trees and reported better results, hence the DART booster will be used for parallel tree boosting.

The parameters to consider optimizing in XGBoost are numerous and a subset of them is chosen for optimization, while the default values will be used [24] for the rest. The searched values follow, having the optimal value in bold:

- The normalization type of the DART booster algorithm. Values: **Decision Tree** or Random Forest.
- The dropout rate of the DART booster algorithm. Values: 0.05, **0.1**, 0.3.
- The learning rate of the booster. Values: 0.01, 0.1, **0.4**, 0.5, 0.7.
- The minimum sum of instance weight (hessian) needed in a child node. Values: 0.5, **1**, 2.
- The minimum loss reduction required to make a further partition on a leaf node of the tree (gamma). Values: **0.005**, 0.001, 0.0005.
- The maximum depth of every decision tree (pre-pruning). Values: 7, 8, **9**, 10, None.
- The number of boosted trees to be created. Values: 100, **150**, 200, 250, 300.

LightGBM. LightGBM is yet another gradient boosting framework that uses tree-based learning algorithms. It is a predecessor to the XGBoost framework and achieves faster training speed and higher efficiency [17]. LightGBM uses histogram-based algorithms [15] which bucket continuous feature values into discrete bins and grows trees leaf-wise (best-first) [21]. Similar to XGBoost, the DART booster will be used.

To optimize LightGBM, the following parameters are examined (the optimal value in bold) while the default values are used for the other parameters [17]:

- The dropout rate of the DART booster algorithm. Values: 0.05, **0.1**, 0.3.
- The learning rate of the booster. Values: 0.01, **0.1**, 0.4, 0.5, 0.7.
- The minimum sum of instance weight (hessian) needed in a child node. Values: 0.5, 1, **2.**

- The maximum depth of every decision tree (pre-pruning). Values: 7, 8, 9, **10**, None.
- The number of leaves in a full tree. Values: 100, 150, **200**, 250, 300.
- The number of boosted trees to be created. Values: 100, 150, 200, **250**, 300.

4.4 Neural Networks

Artificial neural networks are mathematical models inspired by biological neural networks [11]. A neural network is trained by adjusting the weights of each feature, throughout multiple rounds of training called epochs, so that a cost function is minimized or a specific metric is maximized.

The neural network used in this paper is a feed-forward network having the following architecture:

- Batch size is set to 0.25 times the size of the input sample set
- 4 layers
- The rectifier function (ReLU) is used as the activation function of every neuron
- 4 dropout layers, one for each layer
- Optimization via the "Adam" optimizer [9]
- 5000 maximum epochs that are controlled by an Early Stopping function every 250 epochs (terminates the training if the chosen metric, MCC, is not further optimized within 250 epochs and restores the optimal feature weights)

To optimize the parameters of the neural network, a 50 trial Bayesian Optimization [10] is used, instead of grid search, to fasten the process as the number of all possible combinations is extremely high. The parameters that are optimized are (optimal value in bold):

- The number of neurons per layer. Values: 50–1000, step 50. **Optimal:** layer 1 set to 600 neurons, 2 to 50, 3 to 250 and 4 to 250.
- The dropout rate of every dropout layer. Values: 0, 0.3, 0.5. **Optimal:** layer 1 set to 0.3, 2 to 0.5, 3 to 0.3 and 4 to 0.
- The learning rate of the optimizer. Values: 0.1, **0.01**, 0.001.

5 Results

5.1 Training and Testing

Having optimized the parameters, the models can now be trained and tested. In reality, using 5-fold Cross Validation (CV) is, in and of itself, a training and testing procedure performed five times within the training set. Therefore, tracking metrics while performing cross validation can measure the effectiveness of a model. In Table 2, the average MCC as well as the average ROC AUC of the optimal parameters is tracked, accompanied by the results (tp-true positives, tn-true negatives, fp-false positives, fn-false negatives) of the trained models classifying the test set as well as the training set itself. The Cohen's Kappa [18] of the test set is also presented to measure the accuracy of each model in

Table 2. Model metrics and results.

Method (rank)/metrics	LR (7)	SVM Pol (6)	SVM RBF (5)	RF (2)	XGB (1)	LGBM (3)	NN (4)
CV MCC	0.34	0.33	0.35	0.42	**0.44**	0.38	0.40
CV ROC AUC	0.72	0.72	0.73	**0.78**	0.77	0.76	0.77
Training set tp	264	242	231	**350**	**350**	**350**	261
Training set tn	246	251	255	**350**	**350**	**350**	264
Training set fp	104	99	95	**0**	**0**	**0**	86
Training set fn	86	108	119	**0**	**0**	**0**	89
Test set tp	63	59	58	65	**68**	64	64
Test set tn	96	113	115	112	114	**116**	110
Test set fp	64	47	45	48	46	**44**	50
Test set fn	25	29	30	23	**20**	24	24
Test set precision	0.5	0.56	0.56	0.58	**0.6**	0.59	0.56
Test set recall	0.72	0.67	0.66	0.74	**0.77**	0.73	0.73
Test set Kappa	0.29	0.36	0.36	0.41	**0.45**	0.43	0.39

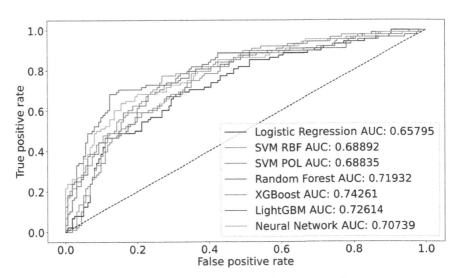

Fig. 2. ROC curves and AUC scores of every model on the test set.

relation to the random classifier (based on class frequency) to better understand the usefulness of every model on imbalanced data. The ROC Curves of every model on the test set are also depicted in Fig. 2.

The results, both in Table 2 and Fig. 2, rank logistic regression as the weakest of competitors and the ensemble methods as the better choices. LightGBM seems to fall behind XGBoost by a slim margin and the Neural Network is outperforming the SVM models whilst its CV metrics manage to reach those of LightGBM. Detecting churners seems to be challenging but the results are satisfactory. Relatively high recall reassures the prediction of most churners but low precision indicates the existence of numerous false alarms (non-churners classified as churners) amongst them. Nonetheless, Kappa values greater than 0.4 suggest moderate agreement with the truth deeming all ensemble methods practically useful.

Furthermore, the predictive models output not only the predicted class but also the probability of churning. Using said probability, a cumulative gain chart is created by sorting every prediction from highest to lowest. Cumulative gain charts display the accumulated percentage of positive and negative classes on the percentage of sorted samples. Such analysis is highly important as approaching every single potential churner, in an attempt to retain them, is oftentimes impossible due to time restrains or financial limitations. For example, in Fig. 3 and by using the Random Forest classifier, if the top 20% of possible churners are targeted for retention, 45% of the overall churners will successfully be approached but, simultaneously, 25% of the overall non-churners will be pointlessly targeted. The chart indicates that Random Forest is the superior model in this type of analysis thus deeming it more practical in real life scenarios. It also indicates that numerous non-churners are strongly classified as churners, suggesting that some subscribers seemingly act like churners but ultimately renew their subscriptions. This observation is not necessarily negative; subscribers that use the service less (most important indicator of churning as suggested by the Feature Importance analysis in the next section) will renew their subscription nonetheless, potentially proposing that they are loyal and they depend on the service even if they rarely take advantage of it.

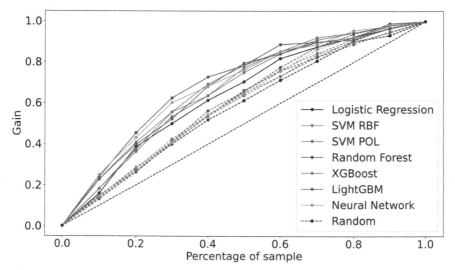

Fig. 3. Cumulative gain chart of every model (Solid lines - Positive Class, Dashed lines - Negative Class)

5.2 Feature Importance

In this section, an overview is given regarding the features that play the most important role on the prediction. The outcome of the Random Forest importance measures shall be used for two reasons: (i) Neural Networks are "black box" models and, consequently, extremely tedious to analyze for feature importance, (ii) compared to other ensemble methods, Random Forest is the only one that samples random features which makes it really effective against multicollinear features [16].

In Table 3 the top 10 most impactful features are presented. It becomes clear that the website usage is, almost singlehandedly, the prime indicator of churning or retention. The subscriber level features also seem to outweigh their subscription counterparts. The only features amongst the top 10 that are not related to usage are a) the cumulative time subscribed, indicating to having loyal customers that choose long lasting subscription plans, and b) the average renewal time, hinting to the conclusion that "if a subscriber is, on average, skeptical or forgetful about renewing their subscription then they will continue being skeptical or forgetful about it (the same applies for loyal subscribers but on the opposite way)". It should be noted that one-hot encoded features might show low impact count in isolation but the original categorial feature might be of relative greater importance necessitating further analysis on that regard to extract a better estimate.

Table 3. Top 10 important features.

Feature	Level	Average importance per prediction
Number of evening activities	Sr	8%
Number of drug packages viewed	Sr	8%
Number of morning activities	Sr	7%
Number of drugs viewed	Sr	6%
Number of drug substances viewed	Sr	6%
Number of nighttime activities	Sr	5%
Average renewal time	Sr	5%
Cumulative time subscribed	Sr	5%
Number of drugs viewed	Sn	4%
Number of morning activities	Sn	4%

6 Conclusions and Future Research

In this study, various methods of different machine learning categories are presented to predict customer churn and assist a web-based drug information platform to sustain preexisting customers in a saturated market. Every model is overviewed, optimized via 5-fold Cross Validation and compared to one another. The results indicate that, even though every model delivers respectable results, the ensemble methods are the strongest choice.

Moreover, the results point to unpredictable non-churners that hinder the accuracy of every model, but subscriber loyalty is also existent and prevalent.

Future research will focus on introducing new methods as well as further optimizing the neural network, mainly its architecture, which can vastly change by removing static parts and introducing them as parameters, as well as escaping from the monotonic feed-forward design. Data-wise, upscaling methods could be applied so that the training set can remain within class balance without wasting samples. Lastly, we anticipate the practical usage of this work by the development team that trustingly provided us the dataset and the potential metadata we can collect from it to further optimize all models.

Acknowledgements. The authors would like to thank Ergobyte Informatics S.A. for providing the dataset and for their valuable comments and suggestions on the preparation of this study.

References

1. Athanassopoulos, A.D.: Customer satisfaction cues to support market segmentation and explain switching behavior. J. Bus. Res. **47**(3), 191–207 (2000)
2. Benesty, J., et al.: Pearson correlation coefficient. In: Benesty, J., et al. (eds.) Noise Reduction in Speech Processing, pp. 1–4. Springer, Berlin, Heidelberg (2009)
3. Breiman, L.: Random forests. Mach. Learn. **45**(1), 5–32 (2001)
4. Burez, J., Van den Poel, D.: CRM at Canal+ Belgique: reducing customer attrition through targeted marketing. Expert Syst. Appl. **32**, 277–288 (2007)
5. Chen, T., Guestrin, C.: XGBoost: a scalable tree boosting system. In: Proceedings of the 22nd ACM SIGKDD International Conference on Knowledge Discovery and Data Mining, pp. 785–794 (2016)
6. Van den Poel, D., Larivière, B.: Customer attrition analysis for financial services using proportional hazard models. Eur. J. Oper. Res. **157**(1), 196–217 (2004)
7. Chicco, D., Jurman, G.: The advantages of the Matthews correlation coefficient (MCC) over F1 score and accuracy in binary classification evaluation. BMC Genomics **21**, Article no. 6 (2020)
8. Mozer, D.G.M., Wolniewicz, R., Kaushansky, H.: Predicting subscriber dissatisfaction and improving retention in the wireless telecommunications industry. IEEE Trans. Neural Netw. **11**, 690–696 (2000)
9. Diederik, P.K., Ba, J.L.: ADAM: a method for stochastic optimization. In: Published as a Conference Paper at ICLR 2015 (2015)
10. Sterling, D., Sterling, T., Zhang, Y., Chen, H.: Welding parameter optimization based on Gaussian process regression Bayesian optimization algorithm. In: IEEE International Conference on Automation Science and Engineering (CASE), 24–28 August 2015, Gothenburg, Sweden (2015)
11. Gupta, N.: Artificial neural network. Netw. Complex Syst. **3**(1), 24–28 (2013)
12. Jones, M.A., Mothersbaugh, D.L., Beatty, S.E.: Switching barriers and repurchase intentions in services. J. Retail. **76**(2), 259–374 (2000)
13. Morik, K., Kopcke, H.: Analysing customer churn in insurance data a case study. In: Proceedings of the 8th European Conference on Principles and Practice of Knowledge Discovery in Databases, pp. 325–336, New York, USA (2004)
14. Coussement, K., Van den Poel, D.: Churn prediction in subscription services: an application of support vector machines while comparing two parameter-selection techniques. Expert Syst. Appl. **34**, 313–327 (2008)

15. Li, P., Wu, Q., Burges, C.J.: Mcrank: learning to rank using multiple classification and gradient boosting. Adv. Neural Inf. Process. Syst. **20**, 897–904 (2008)
16. Auret, L., Aldrich, C.: Empirical comparison of tree ensemble variable importance measures. Chemometr. Intell. Lab. Syst. **105**(2), 157–170 (2011)
17. LightGBM's documentation. https://lightgbm.readthedocs.io/. Accessed 10 Mar 2021
18. McHugh, M.L.: Interrater reliability: the kappa statistic. Biochemia Medica **22**(3), 276–282 (2012). https://hrcak.srce.hr/89395. Accessed 1 May 2021
19. Pedregosa, F., et al.: Scikit-learn: machine learning in python. JMLR **12**, 2825–2830 (2011)
20. Rashmi, K.V., Gilad-Bachrach, R.: DART: dropouts meet multiple additive regression trees (2015). http://arxiv.org/abs/1505.01866
21. Shi, H.: Best-first decision tree learning. The University of Waikato (2007)
22. Thomas, J.S.: A methodology for linking customer acquisition to customer retention. J. Mark. Res. **38**(2), 262–268 (2001)
23. Vert, J.P., Tsuda, K., Schölkopf, B.: A primer on kernel methods. In: Kernel Methods in Computational Biology, pp. 35–70 (2004)
24. XGBoost's documentation. https://xgboost.readthedocs.io/. Accessed 10 Mar 2021

Analysis and Prediction for House Sales Prices by Using Hybrid Machine Learning Approaches

S. M. Soliman Hossain, Jyoti Rawat, and Doina Logofatu[(✉)]

Frankfurt University of Applied Sciences, Frankfurt Am Main, Germany
logofatu@fb2.fra-uas.de

Abstract. Over the past few years, machine learning has played an increasingly vital role in every aspect of our society. There are countless applications of machine learning, from tradition topic such as image recognition or spam detection, to advanced areas like automatic customer service or secure automobile systems. This paper analyzes a popular machine learning application, namely housing price prediction, by applying a full machine learning process: feature extraction, data preparation, model selection, model training and optimization, and last, but not least, prediction and evaluation. We experiment with different algorithms: linear regression, random forest, and gradient boosting. This paper demonstrates the comparison of effectiveness of these algorithms that may help sellers and buyers to have a fair deal of their respective businesses.

Keywords: Housing price · Linear model · Random forest · Gradient boosting

1 Introduction

As the world population is increasing, the demand for affordable housing has soared like never before. Housing becomes a major concern of the society. The mismanagement in housing prices can have a negative impact on the economy of a country. That is why a scientific and deterministic approach should be considered to determine a fair price and ensure the benefits and fairness for both sellers and buyers. A good housing price predictive software can assist real estate developers in figuring out the selling price of the house and can guide the customer to decide the right time to make a purchase. A lot of research work has been conducted to untangle the secret of housing price prediction. For example, numerous researchers believe that the geographical position, cultural and socioeconomic situation of an area will decide the future increase or decrease in the demand of a house. In practice, those are just a small portion of the numerous relevant factors. The goal of this paper is to identify the deciding factors and generate a model that provides a good estimation of the market price of a given house.

© IFIP International Federation for Information Processing 2021
Published by Springer Nature Switzerland AG 2021
I. Maglogiannis et al. (Eds.): AIAI 2021, IFIP AICT 627, pp. 594–604, 2021.
https://doi.org/10.1007/978-3-030-79150-6_47

In this study, our dataset is provided by a Kaggle competition, namely *House Price Prediction* [9]. The data is collected based on information from the city of Ames, USA. Each residential property is characterized by a set of up to 79 explanatory variables. The task is to train a model that can make predictions as close to the given prices as possible.

2 Related Work

In 2017, Wu [8] applies Support Vector Regression (SVR) on an open-source dataset which consists of 20 explanatory features and 21,613 housing entries. In his research, various methods for feature extract were used such as Recursive Feature Elimination (RFE), Lasso, Ridge, and Random Forest Selector and Principal Component Analysis (PCA). The test results showed that there was no significant distinction in performance among feature selection methods.

Towne (2016) [7] suggested a visualization process for estimating price for single-family properties. He analyzes a total of 5,142 online property listings between 2012 and 2015 in different areas. The selected features consist of mostly listed specifications, including interior square footage, lot size, number of bedrooms, number of bathrooms, the year the house was built, and date of sale. Various regression models such as multiple linear regression, k-nearest-neighbors, tree-based methods, and nonlinear regression techniques like splines are explored and compared to find an appropriate fit. His results showed that generalized additive models would perform best.

Pow, Emil and Liu (2014) [3] analyzed the real estate property prices in Montreal with respect to geological area, living region, and several rooms, and even geographical features such as the nearest police station and fire station. They apply and compared regression methods such as linear regression, Support Vector Regression (SVR), k-Nearest Neighbours (kNN), and Regression Tree/Random Forest Regression. In their paper, they predicted the asking price with an error of 0.0985 using an ensemble of kNN and Random Forest algorithms. Moreover, where applicable, the final price sold was also prophesy with an error of 0.023 using the Random Forest Regression. They presented the details of the analysis of the real estate listings, and the testing and validation results for the different algorithms in this paper. Besides, they were also discussing the significance of their approach and methodology.

3 Machine Learning Methodology

3.1 Data Collection

The process of data collection relies on the type of project. The dataset can be gathered from different sources such as a file, database, sensor, and many other sources. We can also use different datasets present on the internet like Kaggle and UCI Machine learning Repository. Kaggle is one of the most popular websites used for evaluating ML algorithms, and they also arrange competitions in which different people can participate and get the opportunity to test their knowledge of ML. In this paper, we use a dataset from Kaggle [9].

3.2   Data Pre-processing

Data pre-processing is a technique of cleaning the raw data. When we collect the data from different sources in a raw format, and this data is not feasible for the analysis. Then some steps are executed to convert the data into a clean dataset, this part of the process is called as data pre-processing [5]. Messy data can be categorized as missing or noisy/inconsistent data. Some pre-processing methods can be applied to cleaning raw data such as:

- **Data conversion.** In this process, categorical and ordinal data must be somehow converted into numeric features while the missing values can be temporarily ignored. This process is sufficient if the data were missing in a row or column more than 70%.
- **Filling the missing values.** We can fill the lost data automatically, like by using the mean, median, or highest frequency value in the dataset.

3.3   Data Analysis

Data analysis is the technique of analyzing raw data in order to extract meaningful information. Any type of information can be used to optimize the overall efficiency of a system or human activity. Some steps like grouping, collecting and cleaning data can be helpful for the effective data analysis process [2]. A few basic types of data analysis can be mentioned as follows:

- **Descriptive analysis** describes what has happened in a given period.
- **Diagnostic analysis** focuses more on why something happened.
- **Predictive analysis** predicts what is likely going to happen in the near term.

3.4   Data Modelling

For data modelling, we summarize the shape of the dataset, then visualize it with summary statistics to get the mean, standard deviation, min, max, cardinality, quantile, and a preview of the dataset. Then we build unique views with window functions, filtering, binning, and derived columns. Finally, we design a random or stratified sampling plan to generate datasets for model training and scoring [4].

- **Model Selection** process where we can configure and train the model as a model selection. In each iteration, we deal with a new model we could choose to use or to modify, and the choice of a machine learning algorithm is part of that model selection process. All the possible existing models for a problem, a given algorithm and algorithm configuration on the chosen training dataset will provide a finally selected model.
- **Train Models** is a process depending on the dataset. For training a model, we initially divided the model into three sections, which are Training data, Validation data, and Testing data. For training, the classifier use the training dataset, tune the parameters using the validation set and finally test the

performance of the classifier on an unseen test dataset. The important point is that during training, the classifier is available only for the training and for the validation set. The informational test index may be accessible during testing the classifier.

3.5 Analysing Model Performance

The model performance is an integral part of the model development process in a ML approach. It helps to find the best model representing the perfect result of our dataset and help us to choose a model working properly in the future.

4 Implementation Details

4.1 Analyze of the Dataset

We can analyze the data in a couple of ways. We need to know the dimensions that mean how many instances(rows) and how many attributes (columns) contain a data file. In our train.csv file, we have 1259 rows and 81 columns. In our test.cvs file, we have 201 rows and 80 columns. As the goal is to predict the House Price we consider "Sales Price" as our independent variable and remove it from the dataset. The intended ML algorithm will predict the price and will compare it against this independent column.

Different variables can be analyzed using different visual means. Categorical variables like 'Neighbourhood' and 'Yearsold' are best visualized with a bar graph. However, numerical variables should be plotted in a line graph against Sales Price, which, in this case, shows that our data set is right-skewed.

4.2 Feature Engineering

Real-world data can be messy and disorganized. A processed called feature engineering can reveal extra attributes or features from raw data by using data mining techniques.

- **Data Correlation** Correlation is a statistical process where we can see how strongly dependent variables are independent related in the dataset. That means how our features correspond with our output [1]. Now the following figure shows the Correlation variable with our target variable (sale price).
- **Scatter Matrix Plot** shows the correlation between pairs of variables. It can be helpful to find a predictable relationship between them.
- **Handling Outliers** As shown from the scatter plot, there are various outliers. For example, there is a two-house size more than 12000 sq with unusually low sale price. We have to remove all such abnormal data points [6] (Figs. 1 and 2).

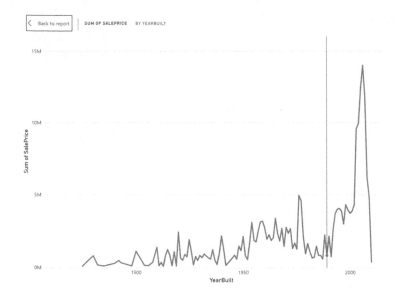

Fig. 1. Distribution of sales price as per year built

Fig. 2. Bar graph distribution of neighbourhood and Yearsold columns

4.3   Handling Missing Values

As can be seen, this dataset contains a lot of missing values. Columns like 'PoolQC', 'Alley' and 'MiscFeature' where more than 99.5% values are missing can be dropped as they do not have any significant information. Column 'ID' contains the sequence number of each row and is also not useful. After that we can group the data by neighborhood and fill in the missing values of a certain attribute with its median per neighborhood.

4.4   Preparing Data for Prediction

Here we separate the features and the target variable for modeling. We will assign the features to X and the target variable (Sales Price) to y and take the target variable into Y. Next, we split data into train and test sets, accounting for 70% and 30% of the total data, respectively (Figs. 3, 4, 5, 6 and 7).

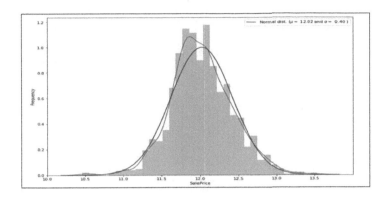

Fig. 3. Show the distribution plot after log transformation.

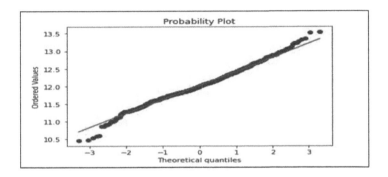

Fig. 4. Show the probability plot after log transformation.

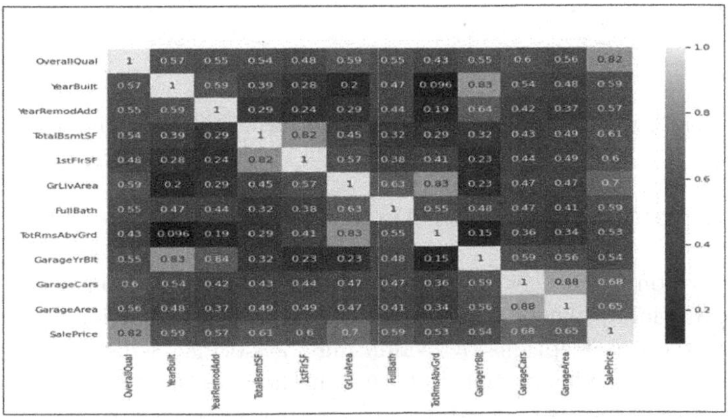

Fig. 5. Showing correlation where variable are correlated more than 50% with a target variable.

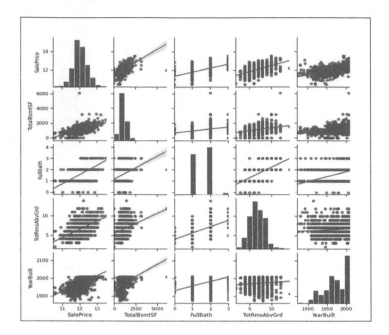

Fig. 6. Scatter matrix plot for some input variable.

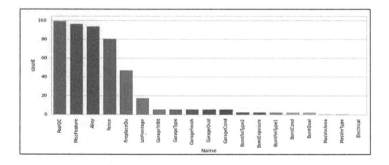

Fig. 7. Show bar plot for every column which have missing value.

5   Experimental Results and Statically Analysis

Experimentation frequently produces various estimations of something very similar, for example, duplicate estimations. Statistical investigation can be utilized to sum up, those perceptions by evaluating the normal, which gives a gauge of the genuine mean. This section is based on the experimental data results and some statistical analysis (Fig. 8).

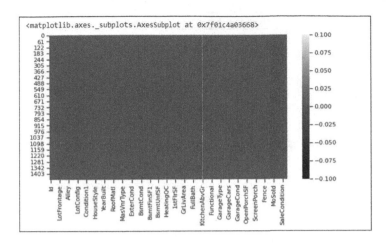

Fig. 8. Heatmap shows we have no missing value in dataset after handling.

5.1 Test of Goodness of Fit via Predicted vs. Actual Plot

The scatter plot is one of the more reliable forms of data visualization. Here it shows how accurate our model prediction is for the predicted price vs. the actual price and how the model is a good fit. As can be seen from all plots, the results are excellent, and most predicted values are close to actual ones. Hence, it can be concluded that = the model is a good fit and Gradient Boosting Regression is a slightly better than from Linear Regression and Random Forest Regression (Figs. 9, 10, 11).

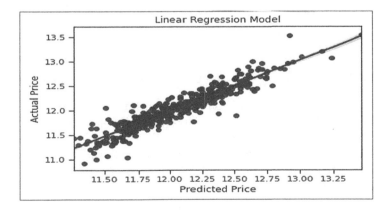

Fig. 9. Predicted vs. Actual plot for linear regression.

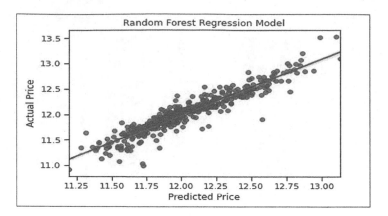

Fig. 10. Predicted vs. Actual plot for random forest regression.

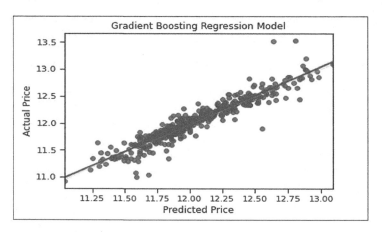

Fig. 11. Predicted vs. Actual plot for gradient boosting regression.

5.2   Experimental Score and Result Based on the Evaluation

The table below summarizes and compares our results based on the Accuracy score, R^2 score, MAE score, MSE score, and RMSE Score in demand forecasting using the Linear Regression, Random Forest Regression and Gradient Boosting regression algorithms. The results clearly show that Gradient Boosting outperform all others (Table 1).

Table 1. Experimental result based on the evaluation

	Linear regression	Random forest	Gradient boosting
Accuracy	87.56281245499873	88.09710339228504	89.71355497536405
R^2	0.8756281245499874	0.8809710339228504	0.8971355497536404
MAE	0.10410390943855012	0.0957662809858385	0.08787608733016163
MSE	0.02037090699516133	0.019495790257359046	0.016848199333612097
RMSE	0.14272668634548105	0.13962732632747446	0.12980061376438903

6   Conclusion and Future Work

In this paper, we have completed the goal of predicting house prices by using different machine approaches, including Linear Regression, Random Forest, and Gradient Boosting. We have provided a detailed process, starting with analyzing the dataset to generating the regression model. In addition, we visualize each model's performance using different performance metrics and compared them based on these metrics. We found that Gradient Boosting regression gives in our case the highest accuracy of 89.53% with an excellent performance.

For future work, we can try to deal with a considerably larger dataset. This would yield a better and genuine picture of the model and to identify a set of optimal hyperparameters for a learning approach. We have embraced just a few Machine Learning approaches regarding classifiers; however, we have to enhance various classifiers and comprehend their anticipating conduct for nonstop qualities as well. By improving the error esteems, this exploration work can be valuable for enhancing the utilization of different individual urban communities.

References

1. Bock, T.: What is correlation. In: Archived by online at https://www.displayr.com/what-is-correlation/. Displayr Blog (2019)
2. Frankenfield, J.: Data analytics. In: Archived by online at https://www.investopedia.com/terms/d/data-analytics.asp. Investopedia (2019)
3. Liu, Emil Janulewicz, N.P.: Applied ml project for a forecast of real estate property prices in the city montreal. In: Archived by online at http://rl.cs.mcgill.ca/comp598/fall2014/comp598_submission_99.pdf. Semantic Scholar (2014)
4. McLaurin, J.: Data modeling machine learning data sets. In: Archived by online at https://dzone.com/articles/data-modeling-machine-learning-datasets. AI Zone (2017)
5. Pant, A.: Workflow of a machine learning project. In: Archived by online at https://towardsdatascience.com/workflow-of-a-machine-learning-project-ec1dba419b94. Towards Data Science (2019)
6. Santoyo, S.: A brief overview of outlier detection techniques. In: Archived by online at https://towardsdatascience.com/a-brief-overview-of-outlier-detection-techniques-1e0b2c19e561. Towards Data Science (September 2017)

7. Towne, A.K.: Modles and visualizations for housing price prediction. In: Archived by online at https://broncoscholar.library.cpp.edu/bitstream/handle/10211.3/185729/KomagometowneAnh_Thesis2016.pdf?sequence=4 (2016)
8. Wu, J.Y.: Housing price prediction using support vector regression. In: Archived by online at https://scholarworks.sjsu.edu/cgi/viewcontent.cgi?referer=www.google.com/&httpsredir=1&article=1540&context=etd_projects (May 2017)
9. 2020KaggleInc: House prices: Advanced regression techniques. In: Archived by online at https://www.kaggle.com/c/house-prices-advanced-regression-techniques/data (August 2016)

Multi Agent Systems

Dynamic Plume Tracking Utilizing Symbiotic Heterogeneous Remote Sensing Platforms

Iakovos T. Michailidis$^{(\boxtimes)}$ (iD), Athanasios Ch. Kapoutsis (iD),
Elias B. Kosmatopoulos (iD), and Yiannis Boutalis (iD)

Electrical and Computer Engineering Department (ECE) of the Democritus
University of Thrace (D.U.TH.), Kimmeria Campus, 67100 Xanthi, Greece
{imichai,akapouts,kosmatop,ybout}@ee.duth.gr

Abstract. The current study focuses on the problem of continuously tracking a dynamically evolving CH_4 plume utilizing a mutually built consensus by heterogeneous sensing platforms: mobile and static sensors. Identifying the major complexities and emergent dynamics (leakage source, intensity, time) of such problem, a distributed, multi-agent, optimization algorithm was developed and evaluated in an indoor continuous plume-tracking application (where reaction time is critical due to the limited volume available for air saturation by the CH_4 dispersion). The high-fidelity ANSYS Fluent suite realistic simulation environment was used to acquire the gas diffusion evolution through time. The analysis of the simulation results indicated that the proposed algorithm was capable of continuously readapting the mobile sensing platforms formation according to the density and the dispersed volume plume; combining additive information from the static sensors. Moreover, a scalability analysis with respect to the number of mobile platforms revealed the flexibility of the proposed algorithm to different numbers of available assets.

Keywords: Swarm intelligence · Symbiotic remote sensing ·
Multi-agent system · Dynamic plume tracking · ANSYS fluent testbed

1 Introduction

Recent research results related to robotized applications have been introduced in literature [4,21]. Low production costs, high agility, high parts-reliability, low operational costs, lightness and deployment ease, long range operation, large variety of sensory add-ons and chassis customization; have rendered unmanned tele-operated platforms into a quite appealing solution for even more complicated missions.

Severely hazardous accidents or terrorist attacks; caused by unnoticed flammable toxic or epidemiological contagious plume dispersion are more than

© IFIP International Federation for Information Processing 2021
Published by Springer Nature Switzerland AG 2021
I. Maglogiannis et al. (Eds.): AIAI 2021, IFIP AICT 627, pp. 607–618, 2021.
https://doi.org/10.1007/978-3-030-79150-6_48

often reported in industry [6,27] where mid-, or even short-, term exposure may cause permanent respiratory or cardio-vascular issues. More specifically, on the 6th of January 2005, a 54,915 kg chlorine release was caused after a rail-accident in Graniteville, South Carolina, USA where 500 workers cohort revealed significant reductions in lung function immediately after the incident while 9 fatalities were also reported [9]. On the 28th of June 2004, a pre-dawn train collision and derailment just outside of San Antonio, TX, USA released 60 tons of chlorine in less than three minutes. Due to poor situation overview, all of the first responding units arrived were almost entirely killed, the Union Pacific train engineer, 23 civilians, and 6 emergency responders were treated for respiratory distress as well. The environmental cleanup costs were estimated at 150,000$ [7].

Things become way more dangerous when indoor leaks are dispersed; usually in industrial hangars, warehouses or production plants. In an indoor plant, a gas plume is limited to consume the fixed volume of the building, thus the concentration of the leaked gas may rapidly increase where, given sufficient time, even the smallest of leaks can exceed the LEL (explosive) or TLV (toxic) levels; leading to nonrecoverable fatalities [16].

Reaction time is the most critical indicator for a successful emergency situation management. Unmanned Vehicles (UxVs) can offer emergent reaction capabilities with minimal on-site human interception; properties which are considered critical especially during highly-unlikely events when effective situation management and reaction time can significantly minimize human lives risk [28,35].

However, UxVs may not always be appropriate to constantly maintain a highly-elaborate situation overview and awareness. As the remote sensory platform increases its complexity and operational diversity, the demand for more computational power and energy reserves increases as well, rendering autonomous UxVs still inappropriate for patrolling and long-term missions in general [8,29]. Lightness is still an issue for multipurpose remote sensing platforms intended for long-range/long-term missions, significantly limiting their extensibility and operational effectiveness.

For this reason, significant work has been undertaken recently towards the development of low-power, high-performance sensor networks, developed for long-term, uninterrupted and reliable operation. Hyperspectral analysis of mobile visual sensors or satellite images have been proposed in literature; suffering from low point accuracy during early dispersion stages and high computational costs (usually adopting highly elaborate methodologies such as deep CNNs) [5,19].

Existing static networked sensory elements - which may be limited to cover the same specified area/range of interest - are considered ideal for constant long term low-cost monitoring [11,33]. Therefore, specific dispersion monitoring cases are addressed with static UV sensors [30], mounted IR sensors [25] or low-cost customized sensor networks [1]. UxVs are usually utilized complementary and synthetically to static area sensors; when needed. Since both monolithic approaches have advantages and disadvantages, several studies focus on the symbiosis of the two heterogeneous types of remote sensing (mobile and static) [10, 34]. On the same matter, the current study focuses on a gas plume tracking simulative application where static and remote sensing platforms are called to form a symbiotic network of heterogeneous yet collaborative elements where both are exploited according to their particular operational advantages.

2   Contribution and Literature Analysis

As the reaction time is the most critical aspect in emergency cases, the objective of the current study is to test and analyze the behavior of symbiotic static and mobile (autonomous ground and/or aerial or even handheld) sensing platforms to quickly detect, locate and track leaking incidents. The static sensors are responsible for collecting concentration measurements from their area-of-interest (AoI). The chemical sensors are strategically positioned so as to detect as soon as possible any potential leak. Moreover, mobile platforms are called to effectively deploy in order to mutually locate its source and levels of spread at the minimum possible time.

Several literature studies have already been proposed that consider centralized optimization and coordination topologies [13, 31]. Centralization allows for a more elaborate situation consensus exploiting every observable state variable at one single node. However, as the scale of the problem (number of sensing elements) increases, centralized approaches severely suffer from communication and computational intensity. This translates to significantly higher communication (for transmitting of sensory readings from every corner of the network to a central node) and computational (for processing larger amounts of aggregated data) demand. Multi-agent studies have been also proposed in literature, mimicking biologically-inspired algorithms employing open-loop control and proprietary mission planning [20, 32]. Proven efficient enough, this kind of solutions is based on random search principles which may lead to poor convergence rates and sub-optimal solutions [2, 26]. This study proposes a systematic approach for the time-efficient coordination of autonomous mobile sensory platforms when measurements from static sensors are also available as well. Ultimately the swarm is responsible to self-deploy its assets in order to mutually build an extended situation consensus with minimum intra-communication requirements. Initially, the problem of dynamically tracking a continuous evolving plume is transformed to an optimization setup. To appropriately tackle the transformed optimization problem, a distributed approach tailored to the problem at hand is developed. The developed approach is based on a recently proposed optimization methodology for multi-agent system with a priori non-computable objective functions [14, 18]. The approach belongs to the family of Local4Global Cognitive Adaptive Optimization (L4GCAO) algorithms [17] which has already been successfully evaluated in several simulative [22, 24] and real-life tests [12, 23].

3   Simulative Environment

The test case focuses on an emulated indoor gas leak where static gas sensors are already strategically positioned and are constantly monitoring a large indoor industrial plant, consisted by large indoor obstacles, while aerial mobile sensory platforms are called to complement the gas plume tracking task as well as to locate the leakage source as quickly as possible.

More specifically, the high fidelity ANSYS Fluent CFD suite [3] was used to emulate the dispersion of methane CH_4 inside a cluttered environment. The interior space was designed to be a rectangle area of $92 \times 42\,\mathrm{m}^2$ with both convex and non-convex, non-traversable obstacles as depicted in Fig. 1(a). For the space discretization, a standard linear model, specialized for computational fluid dynamics, with a default element size of 5.1 m is employed (green grid). A constant airflow with a velocity 1 m/s, turbulent intensity of 10% and hydraylic diameter of 0.44 m was also applied on the left side of the environment (blue arrows). The environment's outlet was on the right-hand side and is depicted with red arrows. The methane was dispersed inside the environment from two sources, as indicated by the blue arrows inside the grid.

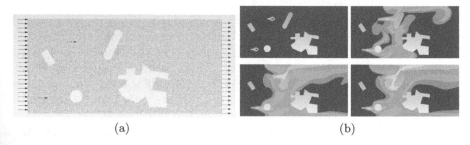

(a)   (b)

Fig. 1. CH_4 simulative instance. (a) Space geometry along with inlets and outlets, blue and red arrows respectively; (b) Evolution of CH_4 dispersion over time. (Color figure online)

4   Problem Formulation and Proposed Methodology

4.1   Problem Constraints

Based on the aforementioned description of the modeled problem, we consider that both static and mobile sensing assets are fully operational and seamlessly interconnected i.e., all assets are within communication range with a central station which is only responsible to collect the local performance observations and calculate the overall consensus at each cycle. In order to render the evaluation more realistic, specific operational constraints were imposed in the behavior of the system, as follows:

- The formulation of the problem considers a continuous state space which reflects the position of every movable sensing asset. The state transition (position change) is limited only by the imposed operational constraints of the UxVs i.e., each mobile asset has a maximum movement step in every cycle. This limitation imposes linear constraints on the control variables.

- As already discussed in Sect. 3 above, the environment involves large obstacles that do not allow UxVs to pass through (or over for AUVs) that represent industrial machines and infrastructure (see Fig. 1(a)). To this matter, all UxVs are simulated with safety mechanisms based on sonar proximity sensors and are able to avoid collision with the obstacles as well as with each other during the execution of the mission. This dynamic will impose strongly non-linear constraints on the positioning decisions (state variables).
- Moreover, the sensing radius and profile of both static and mobile assets is modeled to sense a sub-part of the environment; more specifically, a circular area of interest (AoI) centered by the current position of each UxV's location. The sensing profile represents the decaying measurement reliability as the distance from the sensor increases by considering a truncated 3-D Gaussian distribution centered at the sensor location. The non-linear measurements-reliability profile emulates the behavior of "electronic-noses" i.e., relates the sensitivity/accuracy of the measurement with the distance from that sensing point. Note that the proposed algorithm is agnostic to the analytic sensor models. As shown in Subsect. 4.3, the sensor models are considered as unknown implicit dynamics of the system.
- At this point it must be highlighted that the specified operational constraints were directly implemented in the simulation dynamics of the system instead of the distributed optimization algorithm performance index as penalty functions. Therefore, feasible solutions were directly generated complying a priori with the default system dynamics and imposed limitations without requiring feasibility check.

Finally, as already discussed the objective of the current application is to detect and track the diffused gas volume emphasizing on the convergence rate and the overall plume-volume coverage maintained as the incident evolves. Equivalently, based on the available observations of the system, the accumulated concentration of gas that is measured by all sensing assets at every timestep is considered as the optimization goal to maximize. Note that when the concentration of a single point in the environment is within the AoI by more than one sensing assets, only the most reliable (the measurement from the closest sensor) is considered for the calculation of the total accumulated one. Conceptually, at each simulation timestep, by maximizing this objective, the swarm is "forced" to utilize wisely its overall sensors' capabilities, spreading the team members over the whole mass of gas, while aggregating in areas of high intensity.

4.2 Problem Formulation

Based on the aforementioned rationale, the problem of dynamically choosing the values for a set of decision variables $u(k) = \Delta x(k)$, where $u(k)$ represents the UxVs' augmented positions $x(k)$ change, where k represents the simulation timestep, can be equivalently formulated as follows:

$$\begin{aligned} max &: \Pi(y(x(k))) \\ s.t. &: C(u(k), x(k)) \leq 0 \end{aligned} \tag{1}$$

where $y(k)$ is the augmented vector of the gas concentration measurements both from static and mobile assets; $\Pi()$ is the performance criterion function value at the $k-th$ timestep i.e., the observed accumulated concentration of dispersed gas at the current timestep; $C()$ represents the appropriately reformulated set of operational constraints as described above.

Evidently, as the dispersion phenomenon evolves the optimal formation that maximizes the monitored gas plume volume varies through time. As a result, the maximum of $\Pi(y(x(k)))$ is also evolving according to the dispersion model and the stochastic/unknown environment characteristics (e.g. wind direction, source intensity, type of gas, environment shape/structure). Therefore traditional gradient-based optimization is not appropriate for the aforementioned problem since the performance criterion function is not analytically available.

4.3   Proposed Intelligence Methodology

The proposed methodology attempts to effectively address the distribution of the optimization problem allowing seamless scaling up with minimized communication requirements. The problem is being mutually solved by equivalent locally-driven problems through a paralleled operation of a virtual network of cooperative agents which are self-orchestrated based on the accumulated performance results by a single common overarching central node. The swarm intelligence of agent is linked to each remote sensing (AUV) platform based, however; on a mutually built consensus of the external environment by all sensing elements (both remote and static).

The distributed algorithm has been theoretically established in [14] based on a thoroughly evaluated approach [17] and has already been successfully tested in a relevant simulative, comparative case study in [15] where the environmental situation awareness is driven solely by the mobile remote sensing platforms' observations. However, this is the first study that the proposed algorithm is being considered for coordinated dynamic plume tracking applications that utilize information originated both by static and mobile sensory platforms.

The proposed distributed plume detecting, locating and tracking algorithm capable of coordinating the positioning of $N \in \mathbb{N}$ UxVs on-the-fly, aiming at optimizing the objective function Eq. (1) based on a mutually built consensus from $M > N \in \mathbb{N}$ assets, can be described as follows:

- Initialize — Choose a positive time-smoothly-decaying function $\alpha(k)$ and initialize $0 < \alpha(0) \leq 1$.
- Step 1 — At the end of every timestep k, collect the corresponding measurements $y(x(k))$ from every sensing asset, referring to their AoI.
- Step 2 — A central node responsible accumulates the performance index $\Pi(y(x(k))$ based on each (static and mobile) of the M sensing platform's visibility / measurements and calculates $\Delta_i(k) = \Pi(y(x(k))) - \Pi(y(\Delta x_i(k)))$ only for the moveable mobile $i-th$ assets; where $\Delta x_i(k) = [x_1(k), \ldots, x_i(k-1), \ldots, x_N(k)]$

- Step 3 — The contribution $\Delta_i(k)$ from each robot to the overall performance is sent back to each agent to construct a linear-in-the-parameters (LIP) estimator to approximate $\tilde{J}_i(k) \approx J_i(k) = J_i(k-1) + \Delta_i(k)$
- Step 4 — Generate $R \in \mathbb{N}$ random feasible (within feasible displacement normalized radius $\alpha(k)$ from the current position $x_i(k)$) control decisions $u_i^r(k)$ for every moveable asset.
- Step 5 — The next position for every moveable sensing asset is determined by proactively validating the randomly generated corresponding control decisions $u_i^r(k)$ (see Step 4) on the constructed distributed LIP estimators (see Step 3); selecting the one that is expected to maximize the overall performance $u_i^*(k) = argmax \left\{ \tilde{J}_i(k) \right\}$.
- Step 6 — If overall $J_i(k)$ performance convergence is achieved then STOP otherwise GO TO Step 1.

Due to space limitations, the interested reader is referred to [14,17] for more background details.

5   Evaluation of Results

5.1   Performance Analysis

To examine the effectiveness and efficiency of the plume tracking algorithm, as described in the previous section, a team of $N = 8$ UAVs is deployed in the simulation set-up of Sect. 3. Along with the team of UAVs, 3 stationary sensors have been placed on the perimeter of the obstacle volumes. As long as the static sensor readings contribute to the mutual perception of the region; consequently the algorithm is responsible to readapt the formation of the UAV swarm to unmonitored areas, accordingly.

Figure 2 depicts the swarm configurations for such a simulation instance. The intensity of CH_4 is illustrated with a contour representation, the values of which are denoted in the colorbar on the left-hand side of the figure. Figure 2(a) illustrates the initial deployment of the UAVs (cyan rhombuses) along with their sensing capabilities (fading cyan region around each UAV). Also, the position of the static sensors along with their field of coverage is illustrated in red tones. For this first timestamp, almost the whole terrain is considered CH_4-free. Sub-figures 2(b),(c) and (d) demonstrate the changes in swarm formation with respect to the evolution of the CH_4 dispersion for 33%, 66% and 100% of the experiment's progress, respectively. Figure 2(e) depicts the evolution of the objective function (1) during the experiment.

Figures 2(b)–(d) demonstrate that the formation of the UAVs is deployed to critical positions that maximize the cumulative coverage (consensus) of the CH_4 plume density. In addition, the deployed formation (i.e., position) of the mobile assets achieved to constantly adapt to the static sensors coverage; reasonably leading to tracking positions over unmonitored AoI that did not additively overlap with others. Thus, although the intensity of CH_4 around the static sensor,

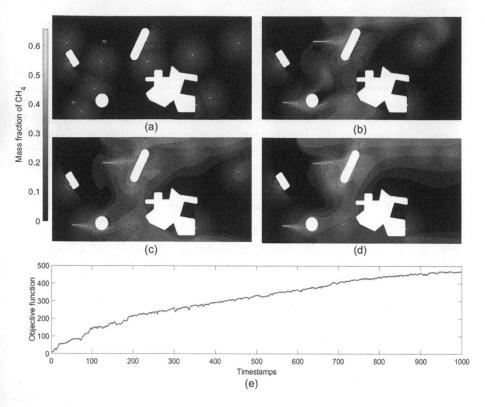

Fig. 2. Experiment with 8 UAVs (cyan areas) and 3 static sensors (red areas). (a) Initial random deployment the UAVs and static sensors locations. (b),(c) and (d) denote to the formation of the UAVs with respect to the CH_4 dispersion at 33.3%, 66.7% and 100% of the experiment, respectively. (e) Evolution of the objective function over the experiment's horizon (Color figure online)

in the north of the terrain, is relatively high, no UAV is assigned to be close to that region, as there is a constant flow of information regarding this sub-area. Another important feature is revealed by the study of the objective function (see Fig. 2(e)) where despite the fact that the nature of the problem at hand is time-variant (1), having a different optimal configuration per timestamp, the proposed plume tracking algorithm is capable of following these changes without any significant peaks and valleys in the objective function value.

5.2   Scalability Analysis

The experimental analysis is concluded by performing a series of experiments for swarms with different team members. More specifically, 6 different swarm configurations were deployed with 4, 6, 8, 10, 12, and 14 UAVs. 100 experimental instances with randomly chosen initial UAVs' positions were generated for each different size of UAV-team. For all investigated setups the number (3) and location of static sensors remained the same, as depicted in Fig. 2. Table 1 reports the average objective function score along with the corresponding standard deviation. Apart from the final value of (1), $\sum_{k=1}^{T_{max}} \Pi(y(x(k)))$ is also reported to evaluate the overall performance during the experiment. The results indicate that the proposed, plume-tracking algorithm is capable of exploiting the additional UAVs. This can be extracted from the substantial increases in the perception scores, as the number of UAVs is growing. The last remark is devoted to the evolution of the deviation around the average scores. Although an increase in the number of UAVs leads to higher average values for both scores, the deviation around these values is shrinking. The causality behind this trend is that the effect of the initial deployment of UAVs is reduced with the increase in the number of (randomly initiated) UAVs. This can be better understood by focusing on the average final values for 4 and 6 UAVs, respectively. Although the average value for 6 UAVs is increased by 91.34 ($\approx$ 30% increase), the deviation is reduced from 10.6% of the average value for 4 UAVs to 3.4% of the average value for 6 UAVs.

Table 1. System's performance for varying number of UAVs

# UAVs	Final $\Pi(\cdot)$	Cumulative $\Pi(\cdot)$
4	305.53 ± 16.18	202028.08 ± 8814.86
6	396.87 ± 6.75	259214.70 ± 9513.94
8	464.02 ± 5.27	307607.19 ± 8495.18
10	526.59 ± 5.77	348339.71 ± 8150.65
12	583.71 ± 6.36	387004.46 ± 7530.05
14	632.56 ± 5.27	419231.78 ± 5396.50

6   Conclusions

The current study focuses on the evaluation of a novel approach that tackles the problem of continuously tracking a dynamically evolving CH_4 plume, utilizing a symbiotic team of heterogeneous sensing platforms: mobile (i.e., UAVs) and static sensors. The proposed approach is responsible for the continuous adaptation of the mobile platforms formation in order to maximize the plume volume and density that is being monitored by all sensing assets, at a constant basis.

Initially, 8 mobile and 3 static sensory platforms were considered. Figures 2(b)–(d) demonstrate that the proposed approach was capable of defining the formation of the moveable assets (i.e., UAVs) in a real-time manner as the plume volume was increasing and diffusing dynamically in order to constantly maximize the cumulative coverage (consensus) of the monitored CH_4 plume density. The position of the static sensors is also adopted inside the overall design of the UAVs formation.

Finally, the results of the scalability analysis indicate that the proposed, plume-tracking algorithm is capable of effectively exploiting the additional UAVs. Table 1 quantifies the increasing trend of the cumulative performance function which also reflects to the plume-monitoring accuracy as well as the reaction time of the overall tracking system.

Acknowledgments. This research is carried out/funded in the context of the project "Development and evaluation of an optimal decision-making algorithm for cooperative autonomous vehicles" (MIS 5050057) under the call for proposals "Researchers' support with an emphasis on young researchers- 2nd Cycle" (EDULLL 103). The project is co-financed by Greece and the European Union (European Social Fund- ESF) by the Operational Programme Human Resources Development, Education and Lifelong Learning 2014–2020.

References

1. Abraham, S., Li, X.: A cost-effective wireless sensor network system for indoor air quality monitoring applications. Procedia Comput. Sci. **34**, 165–171 (2014). https://doi.org/10.1016/j.procs.2014.07.090. In: The 9th International Conference on Future Networks and Communications (FNC 2014)/The 11th International Conference on Mobile Systems and Pervasive Computing (MobiSPC 2014)/Affiliated Workshops
2. Albani, D., Nardi, D., Trianni, V.: Field coverage and weed mapping by UAV swarms. In: 2017 IEEE/RSJ International Conference on Intelligent Robots and Systems (IROS), pp. 4319–4325 (2017). https://doi.org/10.1109/IROS.2017.8206296
3. ANSYS, I.: Ansys fluent user's guide, release 19.0. Equation (6.68) (2018)
4. Ben-Ari, M., Mondada, F.: Elements of Robotics. Springer, Cham (2018). https://doi.org/10.1007/978-3-319-62533-1
5. Ayasse, A.K., et al.: Evaluating the effects of surface properties on methane retrievals using a synthetic airborne visible/infrared imaging spectrometer next generation (AVIRIS-NG) image. Remote Sens. Environ. **215**, 386–397 (2018). https://doi.org/10.1016/j.rse.2018.06.018
6. Bhaganagar, K., Bhimireddy, S.R.: Assessment of the plume dispersion due to chemical attack on April 4, 2017, in Syria. Natural Hazards **88**(3), 1893–1901 (2017). https://doi.org/10.1007/s11069-017-2936-x
7. Board, N.T.S.: Railroad accident report ntsb/rar-06/03 pb2006-916303 notation 7675d. https://www.ntsb.gov/investigations/AccidentReports/Reports/RAR0603.pdf
8. Chen, X., Tang, J., Lao, S.: Review of unmanned aerial vehicle swarm communication architectures and routing protocols. Appl. Sci. **10**(10), 3661 (2020)
9. Clark, K., et al.: Lung function before and after a large chlorine gas release in Graniteville, South Carolina. Ann. Am. Thorac. Soc. **13**(3), 356–363 (2016). https://doi.org/10.1513/AnnalsATS.201508-525OC
10. Hackner, A., Oberpriller, H., Ohnesorge, A., Hechtenberg, V., Müller, G.: Heterogeneous sensor arrays: merging cameras and gas sensors into innovative fire detection systems. Sens. Actuators B **231**, 497–505 (2016). https://doi.org/10.1016/j.snb.2016.02.081

11. Ishida, H., Wada, Y., Matsukura, H.: Chemical sensing in robotic applications: a review. IEEE Sens. J. **12**(11), 3163–3173 (2012). https://doi.org/10.1109/JSEN. 2012.2208740
12. Kapoutsis, A.C., et al.: Real-time adaptive multi-robot exploration with application to underwater map construction. Auton. Robots **40**(6), 987–1015 (2016)
13. Kapoutsis, A.C., Chatzichristofis, S.A., Kosmatopoulos, E.B.: DARP: divide areas algorithm for optimal multi-robot coverage path planning. J. Intell. Robot. Syst. **86**(3–4), 663–680 (2017)
14. Kapoutsis, A.C., Chatzichristofis, S.A., Kosmatopoulos, E.B.: A distributed, plug-n-play algorithm for multi-robot applications with a priori non-computable objective functions. Int. J. Robot. Res. **38**(7), 813–832 (2019)
15. Kapoutsis, A.C., Michailidis, I.T., Boutalis, Y., Kosmatopoulos, E.B.: Building synergetic consensus for dynamic gas-plume tracking applications using UAV platforms. Comput. Electr. Eng. **91**, 107029 (2021). https://doi.org/10.1016/j. compeleceng.2021.107029
16. KGaA, H.D.S.A.C.: Gas dispersion. https://www.draeger.com/library/content/ gas_dispersion_br_9046434_en.pdf
17. Kosmatopoulos, E.B., Michailidis, I.T., Korkas, C.D., Ravanis, C.: Local4global adaptive optimization and control for system-of-systems. In: 2015 European Control Conference (ECC), pp. 3536–3541 (2015). https://doi.org/10.1109/ECC.2015. 7331081
18. Koutras, D.I., Kapoutsis, A.C., Kosmatopoulos, E.B.: Autonomous and cooperative design of the monitor positions for a team of UAVS to maximize the quantity and quality of detected objects. IEEE Robot. Autom. Lett. **5**(3), 4986–4993 (2020)
19. Kumar, S., Torres, C., Ulutan, O., Ayasse, A., Roberts, D., Manjunath, B.S.: Deep remote sensing methods for methane detection in overhead hyperspectral imagery. In: 2020 IEEE Winter Conference on Applications of Computer Vision (WACV), pp. 1765–1774 (2020). https://doi.org/10.1109/WACV45572.2020.9093600
20. Mathews, E., Graf, T., Kulathunga, K.S.S.B.: Biologically inspired swarm robotic network ensuring coverage and connectivity. In: 2012 IEEE International Conference on Systems, Man, and Cybernetics (SMC), pp. 84–90 (2012). https://doi.org/ 10.1109/ICSMC.2012.6377681
21. McIlvaine Parsons, H.: Chapter 34 - robot programming/handbook of human-computer interaction, pp. 737–754 (1988). https://doi.org/10.1016/B978-0-444-70536-5.50039-7
22. Michailidis, I.T., Manolis, D., Michailidis, P., Diakaki, C., Kosmatopoulos, E.B.: A decentralized optimization approach employing cooperative cycle-regulation in an intersection-centric manner: a complex urban simulative case study. Transp. Res. Interdisc. Perspect. **8**, 100232 (2020). https://doi.org/10.1016/j.trip.2020.100232
23. Michailidis, I.T., et al.: Energy-efficient HVAC management using cooperative, self-trained, control agents: a real-life German building case study. Appl. Energy **211**, 113–125 (2018). https://doi.org/10.1016/j.apenergy.2017.11.046
24. Michailidis, I., et al.: Balancing energy efficiency with indoor comfort using smart control agents: a simulative case study. Energies **13**(23), 6228 (2020)
25. Peng, X., Qin, H., Hu, Z., Cai, B., Liang, J., Ou, H.: Gas plume detection in infrared image using mask R-CNN with attention mechanism. In: AOPC 2019: AI in Optics and Photonics, vol. 11342, pp. 204–209 (2019). https://doi.org/10.1117/ 12.2548179
26. Saska, M., Langr, J., Preucil, L.: Plume tracking by a self-stabilized group of micro aerial vehicles. In: Modelling and Simulation for Autonomous Systems, pp. 44–55 (2014). https://doi.org/10.1007/978-3-319-13823-7

27. Services, C.C.C.H.: Major accidents at chemical/refinery plants. https://cchealth. org/hazmat/accident-history.php
28. Sheu, J.B.: An emergency logistics distribution approach for quick response to urgent relief demand in disasters. Transp. Res. Part E Logistics Transp. Rev. **43**, 687–709 (2007). https://doi.org/10.1016/j.tre.2006.04.004
29. Tahir, A., Böling, J., Haghbayan, M.H., Toivonen, H.T., Plosila, J.: Swarms of unmanned aerial vehicles – a survey. J. Ind. Inf. Integr. **16**, 100106 (2019). https:// doi.org/10.1016/j.jii.2019.100106
30. Thomas, H., Watson, I., Kearney, C., Carn, S., Murray, S.: A multi-sensor comparison of sulphur dioxide emissions from the 2005 eruption of Sierra Negra volcano, Galapagos Islands. Remote Sens. Environ. **113**(6), 1331–1342 (2009). https://doi. org/10.1016/j.rse.2009.02.019
31. Tosato, P., Facinelli, D., Prada, M., Gemma, L., Rossi, M., Brunelli, D.: An autonomous swarm of drones for industrial gas sensing applications. In: 2019 IEEE 20th International Symposium on A World of Wireless, Mobile and Multimedia Networks (WoWMoM), pp. 1–6 (2019). https://doi.org/10.1109/WoWMoM.2019. 8793043
32. Viseras, A., Wiedemann, T., Manss, C., Karolj, V., Shutin, D., Marchal, J.: Beehive-inspired information gathering with a swarm of autonomous drones. Sensors **19**(19), 4349 (2019). https://doi.org/10.3390/s19194349
33. Visvanathan, R., et al.: Gas sensing mobile robot: a review. J. Telecommun. Electron. Comput. Eng. (JTEC). **10**(1–15), 101–105 (2018)
34. Xing, Y., Vincent, T., Cole, M., Gardner, J.: Real-time thermal modulation of high bandwidth MOX gas sensors for mobile robot applications. Sensors **19**(5), 1180 (2019). https://doi.org/10.3390/s19051180
35. Zhang, Y., Zou, D., Zheng, J., Fang, X., Luo, H.: Formation mechanism of quick emergency response capability for urban rail transit: inter-organizational collaboration perspective. Adv. Mech. Eng. **8**(6), 1–14 (2016). https://doi.org/10.1177/ 1687814016647881

Improving the Flexibility of Production Scheduling in Flat Steel Production Through Standard and AI-Based Approaches: Challenges and Perspectives

Vincenzo Iannino[1]([✉])(iD), Valentina Colla[1]([✉])(iD), Alessandro Maddaloni[2],
Jens Brandenburger[3], Ahmad Rajabi[3], Andreas Wolff[3], Joaquin Ordieres[4](iD),
Miguel Gutierrez[4](iD), Erwin Sirovnik[5], Dirk Mueller[5], and Christoph Schirm[5]

[1] Scuola Superiore Sant'Anna, TeCIP Institute, Via Moruzzi 1, 56124 Pisa, Italy
{v.iannino,v.colla}@santannapisa.it
[2] Télécom SudParis, Institut Polytechnique de Paris, 19 Place Marguerite Perey, 91120
Palaiseau, France
alessandro.maddaloni@telecom-sudparis.eu
[3] VDEh- Betriebsforschungsinstitut, Sohnstraße 65, 40237 Düsseldorf, Germany
{jens.brandenburger,ahmad.rajabi,andreas.wolff}@BFI.de
[4] Universidad Politécnica de Madrid, Escuela Técnica Superior de Ingenieros Industriales, Calle
de José Gutiérrez Abascal 2, 28006 Madrid, Spain
{j.ordieres,miguel.gutierrez}@upm.es
[5] Thyssenkrupp Rasselstein GmbH, Koblenzer Str. 141, 56626 Andernach, Germany
{erwin.sirovnik,dirk.mueller2,christoph.schirm}@thyssenkrupp.com

Abstract. In recent years, the European Steel Industry, in particular flat steel production, is facing an increasingly competitive market situation. The product price is determined by competition, and the only way to increase profit is to reduce production and commercial costs. One method to increase production yield is to create proper scheduling for the components on the available machines, so that an order is timely completed, optimizing resource exploitation and minimizing delays. The optimization of production using efficient scheduling strategies has received ever increasing attention over time and is one of the most investigated optimization problems. The paper presents three approaches for improving flexibility of production scheduling in flat steel facilities. Each method has different scopes and modelling aspects: an auction-based multi-agent system is used to deal with production uncertainties, a multi-objective mixed-integer linear programming-based approach is applied for global optimal scheduling of resources under steady conditions, and a continuous flow model approach provides long-term production scheduling. Simulation results show the goodness of each method and their suitability to different production conditions, by highlighting their advantages and limitations.

Keywords: Flat steel industry · Dynamic production scheduling · Hybrid approach · Mixed-integer linear programming · Agent-based · Continuous flow model

© The Author(s) 2021
I. Maglogiannis et al. (Eds.): AIAI 2021, IFIP AICT 627, pp. 619–632, 2021.
https://doi.org/10.1007/978-3-030-79150-6_49

1   Introduction

Today in the steel sector there are very few monopoly companies and most of them must compete in the national and international global market. The product price is, therefore, determined by competition, and the only way to increase the profit is to reduce production and commercial costs. Companies that are not capable to update their strategies and their organizational processes, face the risk to lose competitiveness. On the other hand, the steel sector is facing the challenge of digitalization [1], which opens new possibilities for implementing advanced approaches, including the ones based on Artificial Intelligence (AI) in any aspects of production management and control and offers new opportunities and tools to increase productivity.

A way to increase company productivity is to create proper scheduling for components on available machines so that each order is completed on time, maximizing resources use and minimizing the average due date.

Most scheduling problems are considered to be Non-deterministic Polynomial-Time Hard (NP-hard) [4], i.e. the computational times of all known solving algorithms exponentially increase with problem size. Thus, affordable procedures to find an optimal solution are not available. Production scheduling in the steel industry is recognized as one of the most difficult and complex industrial scheduling problems [6]. It involves several production steps, each of which needs multiple resources, such as materials, machineries, transport systems (e.g. cranes, forklifts), and needs to fulfil critical production constraints. Furthermore, the production process can be affected by unpredicted events, such as breakdowns, orders cancellations. Such events can compromise the initial scheduling plan. Two main approaches are usually adopted to deal with production scheduling problems: deterministic scheduling and dynamic scheduling.

Classical deterministic approaches dominated the manufacturing scene since long time and are still used. In these approaches all the parameters of the systems, such as number of jobs, machines processing time, and many others parameters are known in advance. However, deterministic approaches are not suitable to face unforeseen events, such as breakdowns, special maintenance operations or delays in the arrival of raw materials, that can affect the schedule, by preventing fulfilment of the desired goals. In this context, the problem of scheduling in the presence of unforeseen events is called dynamic scheduling [19], and three main approaches are generally applied [2, 13], namely proactive scheduling, reactive scheduling and hybrid scheduling.

This paper presents three complementary approaches for improving flexibility of production scheduling in flat steel production highlighting strengths and limitations of each method to face the different challenges of the scheduling in steel production processes. The proposed methods have different scopes and modelling aspects: an auction-based Multi-Agent System (MAS) is used to deal with uncertainties of the production, a Multi-Objective Mixed-Integer Linear Programming (MOMILP)-based approach supports global optimal resources scheduling under steady conditions, a Continuous Flow Model (CFM) approach faces long-term production scheduling.

The paper is organized as follows. Section 2 presents a survey on production scheduling in flat steel industries. Section 3 briefly describes the real industrial use case. In Sect. 4

the proposed methods for flexible production scheduling are presented. Numerical simulation results are presented and discussed in Sect. 5. Finally, Sect. 6 proposes some concluding remarks and hints for future work.

2   Background on Production Scheduling in Flat Steel Industry

The optimization of production using efficient scheduling strategies has received ever increasing attention over time in the steel sector and is one of the most investigated optimization problems. Concerning flat production, literature presents some studies regarding production scheduling. For instance, in [14] the Hot Strip Mill (HSM) production scheduling problem is formulated as a Prize Collecting Traveling Salesman Problem (PCTSP) model and solved through a Tabu Search (TS) approach. In [26] the production scheduling problem in a Cold Rolling Mill (CRM) is formulated in two parts, a coil-merging optimization and batch planning model. The former problem is solved through a discrete differential evolution approach, while the latter one is faced through a hybrid heuristic approach. A scheduling approach for continuous galvanizing lines based on TS is presented in [24], while [22] presents two hybrid strategies based on heuristic and metaheuristic facing the HSM scheduling. All these approaches concern deterministic scheduling and thus they neglect practical problems ranging from unexpected machine faults and breakdowns, job cancellations, lack of quality for a coil along the process, date and priority changings among other common events. Therefore, dynamic scheduling approaches are necessary.

A comprehensive literature review about scheduling in the steel industries under uncertainties is proposed in [13]. According to this study, major contributions are related to the primary steelmaking process and only few papers focused on forming processes, especially the cold rolling of strip. In this context, [3] and [20] propose a reactive scheduling approach based on Multi-Agent Systems (MAS) to solve the problem of the integrated dynamic scheduling of continuous caster and HSM. A reactive scheduling approach based on brokers in MAS for the dynamic resource allocation of a cold rolling process is presented in [11]. Other examples of reactive scheduling approaches can be found in [8, 23, 25] which exploit different heuristics and metaheuristics techniques. In [9] a proactive scheduling of coils at the CRM is presented, which optimizes the rolling forces through a robust optimization problem solved by Particle Swarm Optimization (PSO). In [18] a proactive planning system optimizing the routing of steel coils among different processing lines applying a multi-objective evolutionary algorithm is proposed, the Strength Pareto Evolutionary Algorithm 2 (SPEA2), in order to satisfy as set of Key Performance Indices (KPIs) defined on the basis of customer orders and on production constraints. A proactive scheduling for steel plates production is presented in [17], where Bayesian network models forecast the probability distributions of production loads and production times, while [5] presents a reactive approach covering the whole production chain from primary steelmaking to CRM. The rescheduling problem is formulated as a mixed-integer programming model considering the original objective, the deviation from the initial scheduling and the equilibrium of production capacity, which is solved through a discrete differential evolution algorithm.

3   Use Case Description

Steel is cold rolled to produce flat products such as deep-drawing sheet, packaging steel and stainless-steel flats. The most widespread process is the Cold Rolling (CR) of strip, which exploits hot rolled strips as raw material and outputs flat products in different shapes. In particular, the industrial process addressed in this work is the CR process of Rasselstein (RAS), a company located in Andernach, Germany, which is schematically depicted in Fig. 1.

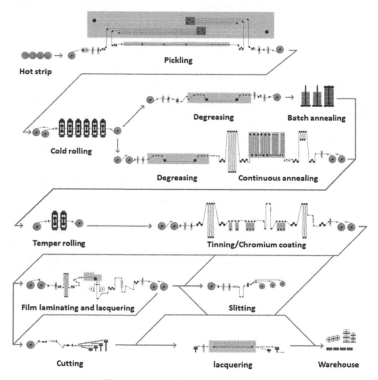

Fig. 1. Cold rolling process scheme.

The first step of the production chain is the pickling process, where the scale that has formed on the surface of the hot rolled strips is removed using chemicals. After-wards, semi-finished products are cold rolled. Being metal at room temperature, it is less malleable than metal above its recrystallization temperature. Therefore, CR is more labor-intensive and expensive than Hot Rolling (HR). CR produces a smoother surface with higher dimensional accuracy and, due to the work hardening effect, greater strength as well. In order to eliminate work hardening after CR, heat treatment by annealing, e.g. batch-based or continuous-based, is frequently applied. A degreasing process is usually carried out before annealing, to remove substances from the surface of cold rolled strips such as mineral or vegetable oils that come from mechanical processing and cleaning. After annealing, two types of coating processes are carried out, i.e. tinning and chromium plating, which provide corrosion resistance, or increase strip surface hardness. This production step is then followed by other typical treatments, such as tension levelling, side trimming, cutting, welding, recoiling, etc.

In the present work, the scheduling problem from pickling to coating stages is covered. Each process step is composed by the following facilities: first stage holds 1 pickling line (P1), the second stage holds 2 CR lines (CR1 and CR2), the third stage holds 2 degreasing lines (D1 and D2), the fourth stage holds 2 Batch Annealing lines (BA1 and BA2) and 3 Continuous Annealing lines (CA1, CA2 and CA3), the fifth stage holds 3 Temper Rolling lines (TR1, TR2 and TR3), and the sixth stage holds 5 coating lines (C1, C2, C3, C4 and C5). The lines are characterized by different speed and functionality, processing quantity and quality and setup times. Intermediate buffers are used for supporting continuous production, where output products of the previous process stage are stored, and serve as inputs for the next processing step. The stocks of semi-finished products have different capacities.

The target is to produce a flexible scheduling maximizing the overall plant utilization, meeting the monthly planned production volume by considering order priorities as well as quality, production constraints and machines breakdowns.

4 Approaches to Flexible Production Scheduling

4.1 Multi-objective Mixed-Integer Linear Programming-Based Approach

The first approach combines Multi-Objective Optimization (MOO) techniques with Mixed-Integer Linear Programming (MILP) formulation to provide a preliminary global optimal resources scheduling under static conditions, i.e. based on production orders and not considering unexpected events. MILP techniques are used to solve different types of industrial problems, including energy and by-products management [15, 16], production planning [7] and scheduling. Their importance lies in both their wide application and the availability of effective general-purpose techniques for finding optimal solutions.

The proposed approach is based on the lexicographic method [10], which is an a priori method, used when a preference exists among the objective functions, and a Pareto front is not needed because trade-off information is not required. Let $f_1(x) = c_1^T x$, ..., $f_M(x) = c_M^T x$ be the objective functions expressed in order of importance, i.e. $f_1(x)$, is the most important and $f_M(x)$ is the least important. The method solves a sequence of Single-Objective Optimisation (SOO) problems in the following form:

$$
\begin{cases}
min f_\omega(x) = c_\omega^T x \\
A_{eq} x = 0, Ax \le 0 \\
x_i^{(L_i)} \le x_i \le x_i^{(U_i)} \ i = 1, \ldots, N', x_j \in Z \text{ for some } j \\
f_k(x) \le f_k^* \ k = 1, \ldots, \omega - 1
\end{cases}
\tag{1}
$$

where $c_\omega^T x$ is the cost function of a N-component vector argument $x = (x_1, \ldots, x_N)$, $A_{eq} x = 0$ are the equality constraints, $Ax \le 0$ are the inequality constraints, $x_i^{(L)}$ and $x_i^{(U)}$ are lower and upper bounds of the i-th component x_i, x_j are integer variables, and f_k^* is the optimal value of the problem with $\omega = k$.

Furthermore, an iterative strategy that allows producing a scheduling of a selected number of jobs over a specific timeframe has been implemented. In this way, the algorithm is iteratively run with updated plant information. At each iteration a number of jobs is selected in order to be processed. A job is considered as a group of coils belonging to the same order, and this group is processed as a unique block from start to end of its production. Modelling jobs instead of single semi-finished products allows the mathematical optimization solver managing problem variables in an easier way, by avoiding computational overloading and long optimization times. Several aspects of the production plant are taken into account as reported in Table 1.

Table 1. Description of MILP objective functions and constraints.

Objective 1:	Production volume (i.e. total weight of jobs that finish each production stage)
Objective 2:	Completion time (i.e. the sum of the finishing times of all the products in all the stages)
Constraint set 1:	Jobs must not overlap in time over the same machine
Constraint set 2:	Jobs must wait process-related idle times before undergoing the next stage
Constraint set 3:	Jobs must follow their routing path on continuous or batch annealing
Constraint set 4:	Priorities can be set for a set of jobs in order to complete a given stage
Constraint set 5:	Finishing times of jobs must not exceed a specified timeframe
Constraint set 6:	The weight of stocked jobs in any storage must never exceed the given bounds

The variables used to model the problem, describe starting and finishing times of each job, assignments of jobs to machines and storages, and it is possible to define the scheduling in a precise way. The method is original and aims at improving common simplified centralized methods that are usually adopted in the steel sector [12].

4.2 Auction-Based Multi-agent Approach

Auction-based multi-agent scheduling system was selected as a convenient alternative to the problem providing enough feasibility and flexibility when uncertainty regarding resource availability is relevant. In this way a negotiation platform is setup using the Extensible Messaging and Presence Protocol (XMPP) protocol where different agents representing both the relevant production plants and the coils being produced, as well as some auxiliary agents (logger, launcher and browser agents) exchange information in real time. The adopted architecture enables distributing negotiations where the platform can be operated inside one container, virtual system or computer while agents can operate at different systems connected through TCP protocol. Indeed, to avoid inter-lock mechanisms an asynchronous dialog was implemented.

Figure 2 presents the implemented sequence diagram for an agent representing a Continuous Annealing plant, where some of the innovative components have been introduced. First of all, multi-optimization objectives are allowed, where an equilibrium between benefits for plants and for coils need to be find incrementally. Coils belonging to different production orders become equipped with the recommended routing as well as with operating characteristics and a virtual budget, allowing them to bid to the different auction processes at the different resources, according to their status. The auction is a multistep system including counterbidding was implemented. The bidding also includes intelligence as the coil agent ask for context costs to the browser agent and it is sensitive to the urgency depending on the deadline and the number of failed auctions already experienced, using a rule-based approach. Additional complexity is implemented by integrating inner logistics rules in the scoring process of coils bidding for available pro-duction slots throughout a subagent mechanism, where the plant agent is in charge of recruiting transport and warehouse resources for the operation before launching the auc-tion itself (pre-auction phase), where different costs for inner logistics are considered, such effect was highlighted in blue in Fig. 2.

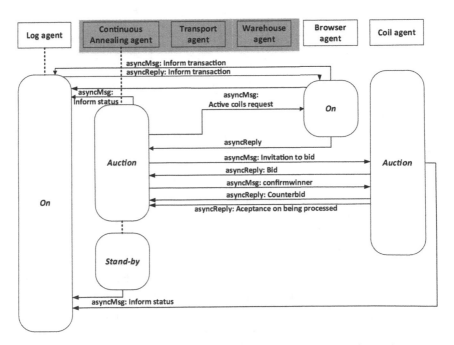

Fig. 2. Sequence diagram adopted by the continuous annealing agent in auction state.

The maximization of the benefit at each resource agent is balanced with the objec-tive of the coil agent to find appropriate slot at the lowest virtual cost. As far as such negotiation can be easily parallelized, it becomes robust against scalability requirements.

4.3 Decomposition Approach Based on Continuous Flow Model

For long-term planning it is reasonable to simplify the formulation of the planning problem. Therefore, a manufacturing system can be represented approximately by a time continuous or time discrete dynamic model. Let us for instance consider an M stages process as shown in Fig. 3.

The following model applies to the first storage:

$$y_{ij,k+1} = y_{ij,k} + d_{i,k} - r_{i,1,k}u_{i,1,k} \tag{2}$$

and to all others:

$$y_{ij,k+1} = y_{ij,k} + r_{ij,k}u_{ij,,k} - r_{ij+1,k}u_{ij+1,k} \tag{3}$$

where $y_{ij,k}$ is the amount of product i stored in the storage j at the time step k and $r_{ij,k}$ is the processing rate of product i on machines j and u is the proportion of product i in the total production on machines j. For the upper and lower limit of production on the machine j applies: $0 \leq \sum_i u_{ij,k} \leq \overline{u}_{j,k}$ and $u_{ij,k} \geq 0$ and for the storage the following limits apply $\underline{y}_{j,k} \leq \sum_i y_{ij,k} \leq \overline{y}_{j,k}$.

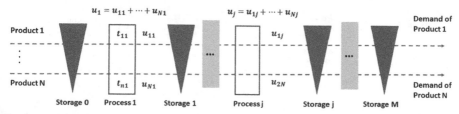

Fig. 3. M Stages manufacturing system for N products consisting of M machines and $M + 1$ storages.

The continuous scheduling problem as formulated above is an optimal control problem with state constraints, and this can then be calculated in a rendering horizontal scheme [21]. The performance of the optimization problem is as:

$$\min_{u_{ij,k}} \sum_{k=0}^{n} J_{demand}(u_{ij,k}) + J_{maschine,cost}(u_{ij,k}) + J_{use}(u_{ij,k}) + J_{store}(u_{ij,k}) + J_{change}(u_{ij,k}) \tag{4}$$

where $J_{demand}(u_{ij,k}) = \sum_{i=1}^{N} c_{demand,i}\|d_{i,k} - u_{ij,k}\|_2$ ensure that at the end of the process the prescribed production rate per product or production quantity $J_{demand}(y_{ij,k}) = \sum_{i=1}^{N} c_{demand,i}\|d_{i,k} - y_{ij,k}\|_2$ is achieved. The production costs and other quality parameters per product i on the machine j can be taken into account as $J_{maschine,cost}(u_{ij,k}) = \sum_{ij=} c_{maschine,ij,k}u_{ij,k}$. If more than one production route for a product is possible or if the full capacity of the machines is not necessary for the production, the use of a machine $J_{use}(u_{ij,k}) = \sum_{ij=} c_{use,ij,k}|u_{ij,k}|$ can be penalized over the 1 norm to achieve a sparse solution, i.e. the machines that are not in use are stopped. The deviation from the preset storage level can be considered as $J_{store}(u_{ij,k}) = \sum_j c_{ij,+} \max\left(\sum_i^N y_{ij,k} - \overline{y}_{j,k}, 0\right) + c_{ij,-}\max\left(\underline{y}_{j,k} - \sum_i y_{ij,k}\right)$ The variation in storage level is proportional to tardiness or earliness. If the storage level is above a soft limit, the product arrives later (tardiness); if it is below a soft limit the product arrives earlier (earliness). Furthermore, a frequent change between the products can be dampened or prevented by the following $J_{change}(u_{ij,k}) = \sum_{ij} c_{ij,k}|u_{ij,k} - u_{ij,k-1}|$.

5   Results and Discussions

5.1   Multi-objective Mixed-Integer Linear Programming-Based Approach

The designed MOMILP-based approach is implemented through the PuLP library of Python objective-oriented programming language. The library allows modelling linear programming problems and is supported by different optimization solvers. In particular, the solver used for the simulations is GUROBI, as it shows the best performances among the tested ones. Furthermore, Gantt charts are used for the graphical representations of the scheduling, which are built through Plotly (a library for Python based on Dash framework).

In the simulation experiment, the global scheduling of 704 jobs each of which composed of 3 coils with a weight of 10 tons has to be accomplished in a daily timeframe. Jobs are selected according to their due date and are equally distributed among the production stages. Since a job can be batch or continuous annealed, its routing path is randomly selected. Furthermore, machines average processing times are considered for the simulation, machines setup times between subsequent jobs are assumed to be negligible, the minimum process-related idle time for each job is about 24 h, and stocks weight limits are taken into account.

The scheduling problem is solved in 5 iterations so that the solver can handle more jobs in the selected timeframe. For each iteration, 141 jobs are handled by the MILP algorithm. The time limit for the solver has been set to 5 min for each sub-problem.

The Gantt chart of the simulation results is shown in Fig. 4 (the legend shows only few jobs due to the high number). At the end of the simulation, 120 jobs are completed at the Coating stage in less than 18 h with an improvement of about 33% and 25%, respectively, on the daily production volume rate and completion time observed in the real use case respectively. The solution found by the optimizer is not far from being optimal (an average gap of 7.55% from the best bound for the first sub-problem and of 35.25% of average gap from the best bound for the second sub-problem at each iteration, the gap can be reduced by increasing the solver time).

5.2   Agent-Based Approach

The interest for this approach is to carry out the best solution depending on status and availability of individual resources by considering local demand and specific conditions and constraints imposed by the process and the inner logistics. The results are presented in a Gantt oriented dashboard, including the performance as shown in Fig. 5. In this way operators are able to realize how the proposed sequencing is distributed through time. The information is processed from the log agent as it collects all the evidences, making it possible post mortem analysis to check how the rules and strategies worked, in order to learn short term and long term logic. As far as scheduling is carried out in real time, the system is intrinsically flexible to any issue happening either at plant level or coil level due to quality losses, where relocation of coils inside orders is handled smoothly, avoiding the full rescheduling.

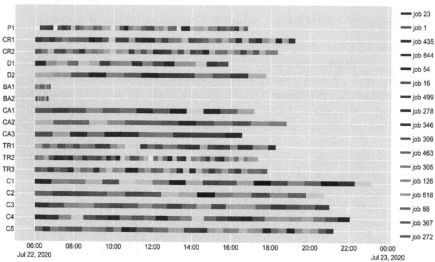

Fig. 4. Gantt chart of the simulation results.

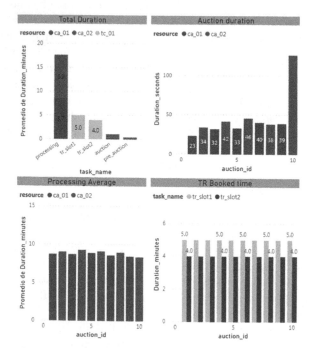

Fig. 5. Agent based system showing several auction processes and their performance.

5.3 Continuous Flow Model-Based Approach

For simulation of the CFM approach, let us consider a 2 steps process as shown in Fig. 6, in which two different products, Product 1 and Product 2, are to be manufactured.

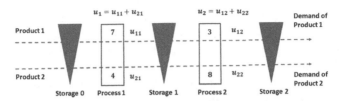

Fig. 6. A two-stage process for two products.

The process chain consists of a raw material storage unit Storage 0, a first machine 1, followed by a storage unit and then a second machine 2 and a finished product storage unit Storage 2. The processing time for product 1 on machine 1 is 7 min and for product 2 it is 4 min. Machine 2 needs 3 min for product 1 and 8 min for product 2. The production time is inversely proportional to the production rate. Furthermore, it is assumed that each product weights 20 tons per item. The aim is to produce 1200 tons, i.e., 60 items per product as quickly as possible. The next step is to investigate how a production stop for product 1 on machine 1 and 2 affects production. In this case it is assumed that the production of product 1 on machine 2 will be stopped in intervals of 1 to 3 h and on machine 1 in intervals of 5 to 7 h. The results are shown in Fig. 7. As soon as the production of product 1 on machine 2 fails, the quantity produced on machine 1 is temporarily stored in the storage 1. If the production of product 1 in machine 2 fails, the full production capacity of machine 1 is used for product 2 and the surplus production

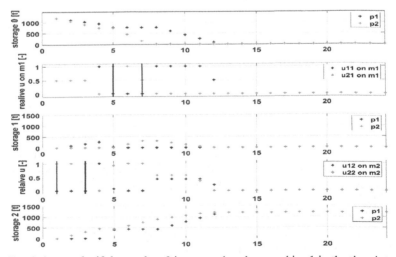

Fig. 7. Simulation results if the product 2 is not produced on machine 1 in the time interval 1 to 3 h and on machine 1 in the time interval 5 to 7 h.

of machine 2 cannot yet be processed in the storage 1 between storage and later. Thus, the model shows the expected behavior.

6 Conclusions

In the present work, three different approaches have been presented in order to deal with the production scheduling problem of an industrial cold rolling use case with the aim of improving the flexibility of production scheduling. Comparing different approaches, it is not possible to strictly compare each method as each one is suited for a specific scope. Nevertheless, it can be realized that each method and algorithm has its own specific strengths and limitations as shown in Table 2.

Table 2. Summary of methods characteristics (Rankings 1 = poor to 5 = very good)

		MOMILP	MAS	CFM
Scope/granularity		Orders	Coils	Material flow
Modelling precision	Modelled aspects	5	5	1
	Considered constraints	4	5	3
Reliability	Solution quality	4	5	4
	Solvability	5	4	5
Forecasting ability		4	2	5
Efficiency	Computing time	3	4	4
	Resourced used	5	4	5
Usability	Acceptance	4	2	5
	Interpretability	3	2	5
Maintainability	Number of parameters	3	3	5
Transferability	Setup time	4	3	5
	Application requirements	3	5	4

The MOMILP is very useful and reliable in situations where the normal production flow is not affected by disturbances. It allows maximizing the capacity utilization providing nearly optimal solution of the scheduling problem. Nevertheless, it presents difficulties in handling dynamic situations as well as the complexity and the size of the problem may affect its solution time. The MAS enables short term local optimal decision-making process granting consideration for detailed production rules as per resource. It shows its flexibility in dynamic contexts, however it can provide suboptimal decisions from the global perspective. It requires close connection to the production resources, to be aware of unavailability of resources as well as process end-ups for coils. The CFM approach has the lowest modelling precision referring to the planning granularity and cannot handle individual coils and/or orders, but it is robust and fast providing results with the highest forecasting ability (e.g. 1 month).

To sum up, the proposed approaches are more complementary than competing. Therefore, a hybrid approach seems feasible and very promising, as it can combine the benefits of the single approaches while overcoming their drawbacks. So doing, the robustness and the flexibility of the production scheduling can be improved. On the other hand, the maintainability of the final solution needs to be carefully considered for its real industrial deployment. Future work will be focused both on development and testing of the hybrid approach and on addressing practical aspects related to make the system usable in a real industrial context.

Acknowledgment. The research described in the present paper has been developed within the project entitled *"Refinement of production scheduling through dynamic product routing, considering real-time plant monitoring and optimal reaction strategies (DynReAct)"* (G.A. No 847203), which was funded by Research Fund for Coal and Steel (RFCS) of the European Union (EU). The sole responsibility of the issues treated in the present paper lies with the authors; the Commission is not responsible for any use that may be made of the information contained therein. The authors wish to acknowledge with thanks the EU for the opportunity granted that has made possible the development of the present work. The authors also wish to thank all partners of the project for their support and the fruitful discussion that led to successful completion of the present work.

References

1. Branca, T.A., Fornai, B., Colla, V., Murri, M.M., Streppa, E., Schröder, A.J.: The challenge of digitalization in the steel sector. Metals **10**(2), 1–23 (2020)
2. Chaari, T., Chaabane, S., Aissani, N., Trentesaux, D.: Scheduling under uncertainty: survey and research directions. In: 2014 International Conference on Advanced Logistics and Transport (ICALT), pp. 229–234. IEEE (2014).
3. Cowling, P.I., Ouelhadj, D., Petrovic, S.: Dynamic scheduling of steel casting and milling using multi-agents. Prod. Plan. Control **15**(2), 178–188 (2004)
4. Garey, M.R., Johnson, D.S.: Computers and Intractability: A Guide to the Theory of NP-Completeness, 1st edn. W. H. Freeman and Co., New York (1979)
5. Guo, Q., Tang, L.: Modelling and discrete differential evolution algorithm for order rescheduling problem in steel industry. Comput. Ind. Eng. **130**, 586–596 (2019)
6. Harjunkoski, I., Grossmann, I.E.: A decomposition approach for the scheduling of a steel plant production. Comput. Chem. Eng. **25**(11–12), 1647–1660 (2001)
7. Heydarabadi, H., Doniavi, A., Babazadeh, R., Azar, H.S.: Optimal production-distribution planning in electromotor manufacturing industries: a case study. Int. J. Adv. Oper. Manage. **12**(1), 1–27 (2020)
8. Hou, D.L., Li, T.K.: Analysis of random disturbances on shop floor in modern steel production dynamic environment. Procedia Eng. **29**, 663–667 (2012)
9. Hong, Y., Wang, X.: Robust operation optimization in cold rolling production process. In: 26th Chinese Control and Decision Conference (2014 CCDC), pp. 1365–1370. IEEE (2014)
10. Hwang, C.-L., Yoon, K.: Multiple Attribute Decision Making, 1st edn. Springer, Berlin (1981). https://doi.org/10.1007/978-3-642-48318-9
11. Iannino, V., Mocci, C., Colla, V.: A brokering-based interaction protocol for dynamic resource allocation in steel production processes. In: Rocha, Á., Adeli, H., Dzemyda, G., Moreira, F., Ramalho Correia, A.M. (eds.) Trends and Applications in Information Systems and Technologies. AISC, vol. 1368, pp. 119–129. Springer, Cham (2021). https://doi.org/10.1007/978-3-030-72654-6_12

12. Iannino, V., Vannocci, M., Vannucci, M., Colla, V., Neuer, M.: A multi-agent approach for the self-optimization of steel production. Int. J. Simul. Syst. Sci. Technol. **19**(5), 1–20 (2018)
13. Iglesias-Escudero, M., Villanueva-Balsera, J., Ortega-Fernandez, F., Rodriguez-Montequín, V.: Planning and scheduling with uncertainty in the steel sector: a review. Appl. Sci. **9**(13), 1–15 (2019)
14. Lopez, L., Carter, M.W., Gendreau, M.: The hot strip mill production scheduling problem: a tabu search approach. Eur. J. Oper. Res. **106**(2–3), 317–335 (1998)
15. Maddaloni, A., Porzio, G.F., Nastasi, G., Colla, V., Branca, T.A.: Multi-objective optimization applied to retrofit analysis: a case study for the iron and steel industry. Appl. Therm. Eng. **91**, 638–646 (2015)
16. Matino, I., Colla, V., Branca, T.A., Romaniello, L.: Optimization of by-products reuse in the steel industry: valorization of secondary resources with a particular attention on their pellettization. Waste Biomass Valor **8**, 2569–2581 (2017)
17. Mori, J., Mahalec, V.: Planning and scheduling of steel plates production. Part I: estimation of production times via hybrid Bayesian networks for large domain of discrete variables. Comput. Chem. Eng. **79**, 113–134 (2015)
18. Nastasi, G., Colla, V., Del Seppia, M.: A multi-objective coil route planning system for the steelmaking industry based on evolutionary algorithms. Int. J. Simul. Syst. Sci. Technol. **16**(1), 1–8 (2015)
19. Ouelhadj, D., Petrovic, S.: A survey of dynamic scheduling in manufacturing systems. J. Sched. **12**, 417–431 (2009)
20. Ouelhadj, D., Petrovic, S., Cowling, P.I., Meisels, A.: Inter-agent cooperation and communication for agent-based robust dynamic scheduling in steel production. Adv. Eng. Inform. **18**(3), 161–172 (2004)
21. Suri, R., Fu, B.R.: On using continuous flow lines to model discrete production lines. Discret. Event Dyn. Syst. **4**, 129–169 (1994)
22. Tang, L., Zhang, X., Guo, Q.: Two hybrid metaheuristic algorithms for hot rolling scheduling. ISIJ Int. **49**(4), 529–538 (2009)
23. Tang, L., Wang, X.: A predictive reactive scheduling method for color-coating production in steel industry. Int. J. Adv. Manuf. Technol. **35**, 633–645 (2008)
24. Valls Verdejo, V., Alarcó, M.A.P., Sorlí, M.P.L.: Scheduling in a continuous galvanizing line. Comput. Oper. Res. **36**(1), 280–296 (2009)
25. Wang, L., Zhao, J., Wang, W., Cong, L.: Dynamic scheduling with production process reconfiguration for cold rolling line. IFAC Proc. Volumes **44**(1), 12114–12119 (2011)
26. Zhao, J., Liu, Q.L., Wang, W.: Models and algorithms of production scheduling in tandem cold rolling. Acta Autom. Sin. **34**(5), 565–573 (2008)

Natural Language

A Comparative Assessment of State-Of-The-Art Methods for Multilingual Unsupervised Keyphrase Extraction

Nikolaos Giarelis[✉] (iD), Nikos Kanakaris[✉] (iD), and Nikos Karacapilidis (iD)

Industrial Management and Information Systems Lab, MEAD, University of Patras, 26504 Rio Patras, Greece

giarelis@ceid.upatras.gr, nkanakaris@upnet.gr, karacap@upatras.gr

Abstract. Keyphrase extraction is a fundamental task in information management, which is often used as a preliminary step in various information retrieval and natural language processing tasks. The main contribution of this paper lies in providing a comparative assessment of prominent multilingual unsupervised keyphrase extraction methods that build on statistical (RAKE, YAKE), graph-based (TextRank, SingleRank) and deep learning (KeyBERT) methods. For the experimentations reported in this paper, we employ well-known datasets designed for keyphrase extraction from five different natural languages (English, French, Spanish, Portuguese and Polish). We use the F1 score and a partial match evaluation framework, aiming to investigate whether the number of terms of the documents and the language of each dataset affect the accuracy of the selected methods. Our experimental results reveal a set of insights about the suitability of the selected methods in texts of different sizes, as well as the performance of these methods in datasets of different languages.

Keywords: Natural language processing · Keyphrase extraction · Unsupervised learning · Deep learning · Graph-based models · Empirical research

1 Introduction

Keyphrase (or keyword) extraction (KE) is a fundamental task in information management systems; it has been defined as the process of extracting keyphrases from a document, i.e. a set of phrases consisting of one or more words that are considered to be meaningful and representative for a document (Hasan and Ng 2010). Various Information Retrieval (IR) and Natural Language Processing (NLP) tasks - such as text classification, text categorization, text summarization and generation of recommendations based on textual descriptions - greatly benefit from the use of KE methods (Wan and Xiao 2008). A variety of supervised and unsupervised KE methods have been proposed so far in the literature, with both categories demonstrating certain advantages and drawbacks. Supervised KE methods demonstrate higher F1 scores than their unsupervised counterparts, but fail to operate on large document collections with no predefined keyphrases, mainly due to the sheer size of manual work needed by human annotators.

© IFIP International Federation for Information Processing 2021
Published by Springer Nature Switzerland AG 2021
I. Maglogiannis et al. (Eds.): AIAI 2021, IFIP AICT 627, pp. 635–645, 2021.
https://doi.org/10.1007/978-3-030-79150-6_50

In this paper, we focus on a selected set of prominent unsupervised KE methods. This selection takes into account recent literature reviews (Papagiannopoulou and Tsoumakas 2020; Campos et al. 2020) and a promising deep learning method. These methods are classified into three categories, upon the approach they build on, namely statistical, graph-based, or deep learning. Statistical methods considered include TF-IDF (Term Frequency - Inverse Document Frequency) (Hasan and Ng 2010), RAKE (Rapid Automatic Keyword Extraction) (Rose et al. 2010), and YAKE (Yet Another Keyword Extractor) (Campos et al. 2020). Graph-based methods include TextRank (Mihalcea and Tarau 2004) and SingleRank (Wan and Xiao 2008). Finally, the deep learning approach elaborated is KeyBERT (Grootendorst 2020).

We assess the selected KE methods through a partial match evaluation framework proposed by Rousseau and Vazirgiannis (2015), which calculates the partial F1 score for each document and the final mean F1 score for each dataset. For our experimentations, we use a set of datasets consisting of multiple documents of different length, from five natural languages, namely English, French, Spanish, Portuguese and Polish.

The contribution of this paper lies in: (i) the assessment of prominent unsupervised KE methods based on three different approaches; (ii) the assessment of the selected methods on datasets of different size of documents, topics, and language; (iii) the investigation of whether the language of each dataset affects the accuracy of the selected methods. The remainder of the paper is organized as follows: Sect. 2 describes the unsupervised KE methods assessed. Section 3 presents the proposed partial match evaluation framework and the outcome of the comparative assessment of the selected methods. Concluding remarks and future work directions are outlined in Sect. 4.

2   Related Work: Unsupervised Keyphrase Extraction

According to Papagiannopoulou and Tsoumakas (2020), unsupervised KE methods follow a common three-step methodology. Firstly, they select the candidate lexical units by applying a set of heuristics, mostly to filter out unnecessary units from the input text. Secondly, they rank the aforementioned units by utilizing certain syntactic/semantic relationships with other candidate units. Finally, keyphrases are extracted based on the ranked list of candidate words. This section describes the most prominent KE methods that build on statistical, graph-based and deep learning methods. For all mathematical formulations given below, $|x|$ denotes the number of elements found in a set x.

2.1   Statistical Methods

TF-IDF is one of the most common baseline methods in the literature. This method computes a TF-IDF score for each term of a document, based on its frequency in this document and the number of other documents that include it. It is:

$$TF-IDFt = TFt \times \log\left(\frac{|D|}{|d \in D : t \in d|}\right) \tag{1}$$

where $TF\text{-}IDF_t$ is the homonym score for term t, TF_t is its term frequency, $|D|$ the number of documents, and $|d \in D: t \in d|$ the number of documents where t is included.

Due to the increased runtime in large datasets, since for each term every document in the collection must be traversed and iterated upon its terms, we have slightly altered this method by employing the *TfidfVectorizer* class of *scikit-learn*; instead of |D|, we consider the total number of sentences in a document and the total number of sentences where *t* appears in.

RAKE is a prominent statistics-based method (Rose et al. 2010), which uses a list of stopwords and a set of phrase/word delimiters that are used in a combined manner in order to divide the text into candidate keyphrases, while maintaining the sequence of terms as they occur in text. By using these candidate keyphrases, the method builds a term co-occurrence matrix, which is used to calculate the significance of keyphrase as the sum of three metric scores, namely *keyphrase frequency*, *keyphrase degree* (the number of other candidate keyphrases that appear alongside the considered keyphrase), and *ratio of degree to frequency*.

A third method of this category is *YAKE* (Campos et al. 2020), which apart from term frequency utilizes new statistical metrics that consider context and terms spread throughout the document. YAKE first splits the text into individual terms and then calculates a score $S(t)$ for each individual term t. This score relies on five metrics: T_{case} (casing aspect of a term, which considers uppercase terms and terms with their first letter capitalized, excluding those at the beginning of a sentence, to be more significant than others), T_{pos} (the positional of a term, which favors words found near the start of the document), TF_{norm} (term frequency normalization), T_{rel} (term relatedness to context, which computes the number of different terms that occur on the left and right side of the term), and $T_{difsent}$ (which measures how often a term appears in different sentences). $S(t)$ is computed using the formula:

$$S(t) = \frac{T_{rel} * T_{pos}}{T_{case} + \frac{TF_{norm}}{T_{rel}} + \frac{T_{difsent}}{T_{rel}}} \tag{2}$$

As soon as this equation is calculated for each term, a sequence of 1, 2 … *n-gram* candidate keyphrases is produced by utilizing a sliding window of n-grams. For each candidate keyphrase (*ck*), a score $S(ck)$ is calculated. It is noted that for smaller values of $S(ck)$, the quality of the *ck* is increased.

$$S(ck) = \frac{\prod_{t \in ck} S(t)}{TF(ck) * \left(1 + \sum_{t \in ck} S(t)\right)} \tag{3}$$

2.2 Graph-Based Methods

Graph-based unsupervised KE methods represent a document as a graph, where candidate keyphrases are represented as nodes and the connections between them as edges. After the construction of the document graph, these methods rely on graph measures that consider various graph structural properties to rank the candidate phrases and select the *top-N* among them.

TextRank (Mihalcea and Tarau 2004) is one of the most well-known KE methods. It starts by assigning part-of-speech (POS) tags for each term in the text, then the nouns and adjectives are selected for the candidate list. Each candidate keyphrase is added to the graph as a node. Edges are added between terms that are present in a sliding window of N terms. In the case of undirected and unweighted edges, the TextRank score ($S(v_i)$) for each node (v_i) is described by the following recursive formula:

$$S(v_i) = (1-d) + d \times \sum_{v_j \in \Gamma(v_i)} \frac{1}{|\Gamma(v_j)|} S(v_j) \tag{4}$$

where d is the damping factor, set to 0.85 as proposed in (Hasan and Ng 2010) and $\Gamma(v_j)$ denotes the set of neighboring nodes of v_j. When Eq. (4) converges, the nodes are sorted in descending order by their calculated scores.

SingleRank (Wan and Xiao 2008) is similar to TextRank, with three key differences (Hasan and Ng 2010). Firstly, TextRank supports weighted graphs with a slightly different formula than the one stated above (each weighted edge has the same pre-defined weight); on the contrary, in SingleRank each edge has a weight equal to the number of times the connected terms co-occurred in the same sliding window. Secondly, while in TextRank only the highest ranking terms are considered in the candidate keyphrase forming process, low ranked terms can also participate in SingleRank. This causes candidate keyphrases to not be ranked up by individual terms, rather by the sum of all terms forming a keyphrase. The resulting score is then used in descending order to obtain the *top-N* highest scored candidate keyphrases. Thirdly, SingleRank employs a larger window size (usually 10), instead of smaller window sizes used by TextRank (with 2 as minimum). The mathematical formulation of the SingleRank weighted score ($WS(v_i)$) is nearly identical to the weighted version of TextRank, the major difference being that the weight of an edge between two nodes v_i and v_j is replaced by the number of co-occurrences (c_{ij}) between these nodes.

$$WS(v_i) = (1-d) + d \times \sum_{v_j \in \Gamma(v_i)} \frac{c_{ij}}{\sum_{v_k \in \Gamma(v_j)} c_{jk}} WS(v_j) \tag{5}$$

2.3   Deep Learning Methods

Recent advances in deep learning enabled researchers to augment classical KE methods, which utilize only graph and statistical measures, by employing word embeddings as a means to capture the semantic relationships between terms in the text, and thus improve the quality of the extracted keyphrases.

KeyBERT (Grootendorst 2020) relies on BERT-based pre-trained models of word embeddings to augment the quality of the extracted keyphrases. BERT, which stands for Bidirectional Encoder Representations from Transformers, is the original model developed by Google researchers (Devlin et al. 2019). It was made to improve state-of-the-art NLP tasks. In the scope of this paper, we utilize a similar multilingual pre-trained model for unsupervised KE, as described below.

Firstly, for each document the model creates a list of candidate keyphrases, by using the `CountVectorizer` class of scikit-learn. This class implements a simple bag-of-words implementation, which measures the frequency of these keyphrases.

Secondly, a document embedding vector based on the words of the document and an embedding vector for each candidate keyphrase are produced. These embeddings are produced by utilizing the *sentence-transformer* package, introduced in (Reimers and Gurevych 2019), which is built by using the popular `pytorch` deep learning python library (`pytorch.org`). The aforementioned package comes with many pre-trained BERT-based models; in this paper, we opt for the pretrained model called `distiluse-base-multilingual-cased-v2`, which is based on Distilbert (Sanh et al. 2019). Distilbert is a multilingual knowledge distilled model made after the original multilingual Universal Sentence Encoder (MUSE) (Yang et al. 2020). While the original MUSE model supports only 16 languages, this distilled model supports more than 50 languages.

Thirdly, after the production of the required embedding vectors, for each candidate keyphrase, a pairwise cosine similarity score is calculated between the former and the embedding vector of the document. Afterwards the keyphrases are sorted based on their similarity score, in descending order, as a way of ranking them. The basic idea is that keyphrases, which have a vector representation highly similar to the one of the document, are the most representative of the document. In contrast with other methods, KeyBERT includes an extra diversification step of the results. This diversification step of the results is applied using either the Maximal Marginal Relevance or Max Sum Similarity measure. Both of these measures require certain parameters to balance out the number of similar keyphrases without reducing the overall accuracy of the model.

Maximal Marginal Relevance. As mentioned in the previous section, to remedy the shortcomings of highly similar results, a diversification step is applied using the Maximal Marginal Relevance (MMR) measure described in (Bennani-smires et al. 2018). This measure, which is also leveraged by KeyBERT, is:

$$MMR = argmax_{c_i \in C \backslash k} \left[\lambda * \widetilde{cos}_{sim}(c_i, doc) - (1 - \lambda) max_{c_j \in K} \widetilde{cos}_{sim}(c_i, c_j) \right] \quad (6)$$

where C is the set of candidate phrases, K is the set of extracted keyphrases, doc is the document embedding vector, C_i, C_j are the embedding vectors of candidate keyphrases i, j respectively, $\widetilde{cos}_{sim}$ the normalized cosine similarity function, applied between two vectors, and λ is a parameter that controls the relevance and the diversity of the candidate keyphrases. A value of $\lambda = 0.5$, ensures balance among them. Grootendorst (2020), suggests a value of $\lambda = 0.7$ to ensure more diversification in the final list of extracted keywords.

Max Sum Similarity. The second measure for applying diversification to the candidate keyphrases is Max Sum Similarity (Grootendorst 2020). This measure selects similar keyphrases to the document, which when considered in pairs are mostly dissimilar to one another. This measure gains its name from the summing of the vector cosine similarities for each pair of terms found in every pair of candidate phrases. The most dissimilar pairs with the maximum sum of distance between their vector representations are considered. To control the number of dissimilar pairs found in the final list of extracted keywords, the author uses a parameter for his method called nr_candidates, which selects the number of unique candidate phrases.

3 Experiments

For the implementation and evaluation of the selected KE methods, we used the Python programming language. The full code, datasets, and evaluation results of our experiments are freely available at https://github.com/NC0DER/KeyphraseExtraction.

3.1 Datasets

To test how well multilingual unsupervised KE methods work, we chose five datasets from five different natural languages, which can be found online at https://github.com/NC0DER/KeyphraseExtraction/tree/main/Datasets. Specifically:

- For English, we opted for the validation subset (500 documents) out of the entire *Hulth* dataset (Hulth 2003), which contains 2000 abstracts of computer science papers. Specifically, we used the uncontrolled keyphrases, since they appear more often in the text.
- For French, we opted for *WikiNews* (Bougouin et al. 2013), which contains 100 documents from French news articles published from May to December 2012.
- For Portuguese, we opted for *110-PT-BN-KP* (Marujo et al. 2012), which contains 110 transcripted text documents from 8 broadcast news programs talking about various subjects such as politics, sports, finance and other.
- For Polish, we opted for *pak2018* (Campos et al. 2020) which contains 50 abstracts from scientific articles.
- For Spanish, we opted for a small subset of *Cacic* and *Wicc* (Aquino and Lanzarini, Aquino and Lanzarini 2015) datasets. Wicc is composed of 1640 computer science scientific articles published between 1999 and 2012, while Cacic contains 888 scientific papers between 2005 and 2013. When we manually inspected all those datasets, we noticed that both Cacic and Wicc had a low number of keyphrases found as-is in the text; for this reason, we selected a small subset out of both datasets (57 and 78 documents, respectively); these documents were selected because their associated keyphrase files had at least one keyphrase present in each document.

3.2 Experimental Setup

For our experiments, we start by calculating TfidfVectorizer (see Sect. 2.1). For the other two statistical methods, we employ a popular implementation of RAKE (https://github.com/fabianvf/python-rake) and the official implementation of YAKE (https://github.com/LIAAD/yake). For graph-based methods, we use the implementations of TextRank and SingleRank available at https://github.com/DerwenAI/pytextrank and https://github.com/boudinfl/pke (Boudin 2016). For the deep learning method, we use the official implementation of KeyBERT (Grootendorst 2020) available at https://github.com/MaartenGr/KeyBERT.

Regarding their parametric setup, all methods are set to produce n-grams of size ranging from 1 to 3. For each method, the *top-10* keyphrases are extracted and then compared with the manually assigned keyphrases, as analytically described in Sect. 3.3. A list of parameters, which are set for each KE method, can be seen below:

Table 1. Parameter configurations for each of the unsupervised KE methods.

Method	Parameters	Approach
TfidfVectorizer	ngram_range = (1, 3), top_n = 10	Statistical
RAKE	top_n = 10	Statistical
YAKE (seqm)	n = 3, top_n = 10, dedupLim = 0.9, dedupFunc = 'seqm', windowsSize = 1	Statistical
TextRank	top_n = 10	Graph-based
SingleRank	top_n = 10	Graph-based
KeyBERT (mmr)	ngram_range = (1, 3), top_n = 10, method = 'mmr', diversity = 0.7	Deep learning
KeyBERT (maxsum)	ngram_range = (1, 3), top_n = 10, method = 'maxsum', diversity = 0.7	Deep learning

On a sidenote, the parameters (method, diversity) of KeyBERT refer to the diversification measures explained in Sect. 2.3. YAKE uses the term deduplication function (dedupFunc) for its diversification measure. In their work, Campos et al. (2020) consider various such functions, with the best being the sequence matcher (seqm), after extensive evaluation. For both methods, we use the recommended parameters of their respective authors for optimal use.

3.3 Evaluation

To evaluate the selected methods, we adopt the partial match framework pro-posed by Rousseau and Vazirgiannis (2015). The rationale behind this framework is that while KE methods often form the correct keyphrase, when tested under exact matching the tests often yield low results. According to this framework, the following metrics are defined:

$$Partial\ Precision\ =\ \frac{number\ of\ partially\ matched\ keyphrases}{total\ amount\ of\ extracted\ keyphrases} \qquad (7)$$

$$Partial\ Recall\ =\ \frac{number\ of\ partially\ matched\ keyphrases}{total\ amount\ of\ assigned\ keyphrases} \qquad (8)$$

We also note that the partial F1 score ($pF1$), which is the harmonic mean be-tween the partial precision and recall, is defined as:

$$pF1\ =\ \frac{2*PartialPrecision*PartialRecall}{PartialPrecision + PartialRecall} \qquad (9)$$

The number of partially matched keyphrases corresponds to the number of extracted keyphrases that partially match with those assigned by human authors. The total number of extracted keyphrases is equal to the number of *top-N* extracted keyphrases, which is set to 10 in our experiments. The total number of assigned keyphrases correspond to the number of keyphrases manually assigned by human annotators of the specific dataset.

Table 2. Statistics of each dataset; Words per Document (W/D), Text Category based on W/D (Mean) and Number of Documents.

Dataset	W/D (Mean)	W/D (Max)	W/D (Min)	Text category	Number of documents
Cacic (57)	3894	6301	1713	Long (Full texts)	57
Wicc (78)	1863	4347	10	Long (Full texts)	78
110-PT-BN-KP (110)	301	955	13	Medium (News Articles)	110
WikiNews (100)	282	1026	126	Medium (News Articles)	100
Hulth Validation (500)	119	285	16	Short (Abstracts)	500
pak2018 (50)	97	170	55	Short (Abstracts)	50

Before we compare the keyphrases between the human annotators and those extracted from the KE methods, we lowercase all keyphrases, remove punctuation marks and apply stemming. For stemming, we use the *Snowball Stemmer* found in the *NLTK toolkit* (https://www.nltk.org/), due to its ability to stem texts from different languages, such as English, French, Spanish, Portuguese and others. Since this stemmer does not support the Polish language, we use the *pystempel* stemmer for the Polish dataset (https://pypi.org/project/pystempel/). The parameter configurations are summarized in Table 1. Statistics of each dataset are presented in Table 2, while the experimental results are shown in Table 3. The code of all experimentations reported in this paper can be found on the following GitHub repository: https://github.com/NC0DER/KeyphraseExtraction.

As shown in Table 3, KeyBERT achieves the highest F1 score for the Spanish (Cacic, Wicc) and Portuguese (110-PT-BN-KP) datasets. For the English (Hulth Validation) and Polish (pak2018) datasets, the graph-based methods achieve the best results. For the French (WikiNews) dataset, YAKE has the best performance. YAKE also achieves the best results among all statistical methods. It is also noted that, throughout all datasets, SingleRank outperforms TextRank.

Moreover, our experimentations indicate that the best method for long texts is Key-BERT (MaxSum) and for short texts is SingleRank. We also conclude that SingleRank is able to model the correlations between the words more accurately than other methods for short texts. However, in long texts, significant keyphrases that do not appear as often as others are not extracted. This is due to the fact that graph-based methods rely on co-occurrence of terms, thus a suboptimal ranking of non-frequent keyphrases is produced.

Table 3. Partial F1 score at 10 extracted keywords (pF1@10), per KE method, for each diversification measure. Bold font indicates the best combination of method (and measure if it uses any) in brackets.

Dataset (pF1@10)	TfidfVectorizer	Rake	Yake (Seqm)	KeyBERT (MMR)	KeyBERT (MaxSum)	TextRank	SingleRank
Cacic (57)	0.077	0.212	0.213	0.206	**0.316**	0.244	0.266
Wicc (78)	0.043	0.201	0.231	0.233	**0.270**	0.256	0.266
110-PT-BN-KP (110)	0.187	0.252	0.333	0.248	**0.380**	0.297	0.336
WikiNews (100)	0.242	0.387	**0.578**	0.373	0.567	0.490	0.522
Hulth Validation (500)	0.378	0.593	0.541	0.493	0.580	0.618	**0.629**
pak2018 (50)	0.085	0.177	0.173	0.158	0.159	0.202	**0.205**

Furthermore, we conclude that KeyBERT increases the quality of extracted keyphrases on long texts for two reasons: (i) it utilizes word embeddings, which are able to capture contextual similarity between terms; (ii) it employs a selected diversification method, which leads to a richer set of keyphrases.

Finally, we observe that the language of a dataset does not affect the accuracy of any of the selected methods. As seen in Tables 2 and 3, for datasets belonging to the same text category, even for different natural languages, the selected methods are ranked similarly.

4 Conclusions

We have comparatively assessed a set of unsupervised multilingual KE methods across different datasets. Our experimental results reveal that the deep learning method (KeyBERT) employed is more suitable for long sized texts, whereas the graph-based methods are more suitable for short sized texts. A known technical limitation of KeyBERT is that it does not work for extremely short texts, i.e. texts with less than $2 * top\text{-}N$ unique terms.

A limitation of this work is certainly the limited number of employed datasets. Additional datasets will be considered in future work, aiming to further validate the outcomes of this paper. Future work directions also include: (i) the use of larger pre-trained BERT models, aiming to improve the contextual similarity between terms; (ii) the fine-tuning of these models for domain-specific applications; (iii) the comparative evaluation of additional unsupervised deep learning KE methods, including. EmbedRank (Bennani-Smires et al. 2018), Key2Vec (Mahata et al. 2018) and Reference Vector Algorithm (Papagiannopoulou and Tsoumakas 2018).

Acknowledgments. The work presented in this paper is supported by the inPOINT project (https://inpoint-project.eu/), which is co-financed by the European Union and Greek national funds through the Operational Program Competitiveness, Entrepreneurship and Innovation, under the call RESEARCH – CREATE – INNOVATE (Project id: T2EDK- 04389).

References

Aquino, G.O., Lanzarini, L.C.: Keyword identification in Spanish documents using neural networks. J. Comput. Sci. Technol. **15**(2), 55–60 (2015)

Bennani-Smires, K., Musat, C., Hossmann, A., Baeriswyl, M., Jaggi, M.: Simple unsupervised keyphrase extraction using sentence embeddings. In: Proceedings of the 22nd Conference on Computational Natural Language Learning, pp. 221–229. Association for Computational Linguistics, Brussels (2018)

Boudin, F.: pke: an open source python-based keyphrase extraction toolkit. In: Proceedings of the 26th International Conference on Computational Linguistics: System Demonstrations, pp. 69–73. The COLING 2016 Organizing Committee, Osaka (2016)

Bougouin, A., Boudin, F., Daille, B.: TopicRank: graph-based topic ranking for keyphrase extraction. In: Proceedings of the Sixth International Joint Conference on Natural Language Processing, pp. 543–551. Asian Federation of Natural Language Processing, Nagoya (2013)

Campos, R., Mangaravite, V., Pasquali, A., Jorge, A., Nunes, C., Jatowt, A.: YAKE! Keyword extraction from single documents using multiple local features. Inf. Sci. **509**, 257–289 (2020)

Devlin, J., Chang, M. W., Lee, K., Toutanova, K.: BERT: pre-training of deep bidirectional transformers for language understanding. In: Proceedings of the 2019 Conference of the North American Chapter of the Association for Computational Linguistics: Human Language Technologies, vol. 1 (Long and Short Papers), pp. 4171–4186 (2019)

Grootendorst, M.: KeyBERT: minimal keyword extraction with BERT, v0.1.3. Zenodo (2020)

Hasan, K., Ng, V.: Conundrums in unsupervised keyphrase extraction: making sense of the state-of-the-art. In: Coling 2010: Posters, pp. 365–373. Coling 2010 Organizing Committee, Beijing (2010)

Hulth, A.: Improved automatic keyword extraction given more linguistic knowledge. In: Proceedings of the 2003 conference on Empirical Methods in Natural Language Processing, pp. 216–223. Association for Computational Linguistics (2003)

Mahata, D., Kuriakose, J., Shah, R. R., Zimmermann, R.: Key2Vec: automatic ranked keyphrase extraction from scientific articles using phrase embeddings. In: Proceedings of the 2018 Conference of the North American Chapter of the Association for Computational Linguistics: Human Language Technologies, vol. 2 (Short Papers), pp. 634–639. Association for Computational Linguistics, New Orleans (2018)

Marujo, L., Gershman, A., Carbonell, J., Frederking, R., Neto, J. P.: Supervised topical key phrase extraction of news stories using crowdsourcing, light filtering and co-reference normalization. In: Proceedings of the Eighth International Conference on Language Resources and Evaluation (LREC 2012), pp. 399–403. European Language Resources Association (ELRA), Istanbul (2012)

Mihalcea, R., Tarau, P., TextRank: bringing order into texts. In: Proceedings of the 2004 Conference on Empirical Methods in Natural Language Processing, pp. 404–411. Association for Computational Linguistics, Barcelona (2004)

Papagiannopoulou, E., Tsoumakas, G.: Local word vectors guiding keyphrase extraction. Inf. Process. Manage. **54**(6), 888–902 (2018)

Papagiannopoulou, E., Tsoumakas, G.: A review of keyphrase extraction. Wires Data Min. Knowl. Disc. **10**(2), e1339 (2020)

Reimers, N., Gurevych, I.: Sentence-BERT: sentence embeddings using siamese BERT-networks. In: Proceedings of the 2019 Conference on Empirical Methods in Natural Language Processing and the 9th International Joint Conference on Natural Language Processing, pp. 3982–3992. Association for Computational Linguistics (2019)

Rose, S., Engel, D., Cramer, N., Cowley, W.: Automatic keyword extraction from individual documents. In: Berry, M.W., Kogan, J. (eds.) Text Mining: Applications and Theory. John Wiley & Sons, Ltd (2010)

Rousseau, F., Vazirgiannis, M.: Main core retention on graph-of-words for single-document keyword extraction. In: Hanbury, A., Kazai, G., Rauber, A., Fuhr, N. (eds.) Advances in Information Retrieval. LNCS, vol. 9022, pp. 382–393. Springer, Cham (2015). https://doi.org/10.1007/978-3-319-16354-3_42

Sanh, V., Debut, L., Chaumond, J., Wolf, T.: DistilBERT, a distilled version of BERT: smaller, faster, cheaper and lighter. In: Proceedings of the 5th Workshop on Energy Efficient Machine Learning and Cognitive Computing (NeurIPS) (2019)

Yang, Y., et al.: Multilingual universal sentence encoder for semantic retrieval. In: Proceedings of the 58th Annual Meeting of the Association for Computational Linguistics: System Demonstrations, pp. 87–94. Association for Computational Linguistics (2020)

Wan, X., Xiao, J.: CollabRank: towards a collaborative approach to single-document keyphrase extraction. In: Proceedings of the 22nd International Conference on Computational Linguistics (Coling), pp. 969–976. Coling 2008 Organizing Committee, Manchester (2008a)

Wan, X., Xiao, J.: Single document keyphrase extraction using neighborhood knowledge. In: Proceedings of the 23rd National Conference on Artificial intelligence (AAAI), pp. 855–860, Chicago, Illinois, USA (2008b)

An Approach Utilizing Linguistic Features
for Fake News Detection

Dimitrios Panagiotis Kasseropoulos and Christos Tjortjis$^{(\boxtimes)}$ ⓘ

The Data Mining and Analytics Research Group, School of Science and Technology,
International Hellenic University, Thessaloniki, Greece
{dkasseropoulos,c.tjortjis}@ihu.edu.gr

Abstract. Easy propagation and access to information on the web has the potential to become a serious issue when it comes to disinformation. The term "fake news" describes the intentional propagation of news with the intention to mislead and harm the public and has gained more attention recently. This paper proposes a style-based Machine Learning (ML) approach, which relies on the textual information from news, such as manually extracted lexical features e.g. part of speech counts, and evaluates the performance of several ML algorithms. We identified a subset of the best performing linguistic features, using information-based metrics, which tend to agree with the literature. We also, combined Named Entity Recognition (NER) functionality with the Frequent Pattern (FP) Growth association rule algorithm to gain a deeper perspective of the named entities used in the two classes. Both methods reinforce the claim that fake and real news have limited differences in content, setting limitations to style-based methods. Results showed that convolutional neural networks resulted in the best accuracy, outperforming the rest of the algorithms.

Keywords: Fake news · Social media · Machine Learning (ML) · Natural Language Processing (NLP) · Association Rule (AR) Mining · Data mining

1 Introduction

Social media are an important part of our everyday lives, changing the way we interact with other people [8, 15]. One of the aspects that could be affected is the way we receive and publish information. Easy access to high-speed internet, tools that made website deployment easier, and the growing popularity of many microblog websites made publishing and receiving news information accessible to everyone, anytime. Although the large number of informative online sources increased the variety of aspects available, many of them have low quality, making filtering a necessity [21]. These conditions have also created a trend/danger called fake news.

Social media gave the opportunity to news to have an alternative way of reaching the public rapidly, but at the same time, they also benefit disinformation propagation. Studies have shown that fake, extremely one-side (hyperpartisan) and emotional news tend to spread far more rapidly than traditional news [13, 24].

© IFIP International Federation for Information Processing 2021
Published by Springer Nature Switzerland AG 2021
I. Maglogiannis et al. (Eds.): AIAI 2021, IFIP AICT 627, pp. 646–658, 2021.
https://doi.org/10.1007/978-3-030-79150-6_51

Some factors that benefit disinformation on the web are the difficulty of accessing trustworthy information and the lack of trust in the traditional informative means. A fake story can have serious impacts on society if a significant volume of people believes it. Finally, during the COVID-19 era, fake news is on the rise, making the work of health professionals more difficult in an already critical situation, endangering this way the public [10].

The rapid propagation of information on the web makes quick detection of fake news crucial. That is why the new technologies of Machine Learning (ML) and artificial intelligence have been utilized widely in the last years to tackle this problem and it is also the topic focus of this paper [27].

The remainder of this paper is structured as follows: Sect. 2 reviews the literature and provides background information. Section 3 presents the dataset used and the experimental approach including feature extraction and selection. Section 4 presents results which are further discussed in Sect. 5. Section 5 presents conclusions and the directions for future work.

2 Background

2.1 Fake News Characteristics

In their research, Petty, R. E. & Cacioppo J. T., presented the Elaboration Likelihood model of Persuasion (ELP) theorem, arguing that people are persuaded either by a central route, meaning that all the arguments are examined, or by the peripheral route, which focuses only on the validity of the key concepts of a claim [12]. The peripheral route is frequent in social media, since studies have shown that most of the articles shared are never read [23].

Based on the ELP theorem and Cacioppo's and Petty's findings, Khan, J. Y., et al. argue that fake news targets the peripheral route and therefore their titles contain the most important claims about people and events [6]. The titles' role in fake news mostly serves as the main mechanism of information propagation, where the body just repeats the title's claims [5].

Regarding content characteristics, fake articles are a lot smaller in length using fewer technical words, smaller words, fewer punctuation, fewer quotes, and more lexical redundancy. Also, at the linguistic level, they use simpler language resulting in fewer analytic words, more personal pronouns, fewer nouns, and more adverbs [5]. Finally, a good indicator is the emotional response the article tries to achieve. Strong emotional words and phrases draw more attention and propagate faster [17].

2.2 Fake News Categories

Most research split fake news into categories, based on the two basic characteristics: intention and quality of information. On a first level, the author's motive to mislead or not separates fake news to misinformation and disinformation [19]. In the next section we further describe some common fake news categories.

Rumors. A rumor can be defined as "a piece of circulating information whose veracity status is yet to be verified at the time of spreading" [28]. Today rumors flourish in social media and their detection becomes more difficult [9]. Studies have focused on supervised, unsupervised and hybrid methods to separate rumors from real news [1]. Other studies confirmed that the propagation style differs significantly from real news' and is used to classify rumors on the web [9].

Conspiracy Theories. This genre of fake news provides explanations for stories of the news referring to entities that exist in the center of attention, but most of the time, these explanations are based in pseudo-scientific results [18]. Conspiracy theories create a way of thinking opposite to the scientific method of explanation, making groups of people with predisposition to them more open to sharing and stand up for misinformation [13].

Click Bait. In order for an article to be considered clickbait it needs to have some basic characteristics, including: i) short text, ii) a media attachment, such as image or video and iii) the link to the publisher's article [7]. Most of the publishers in social media use click bait articles, to a greater or lesser extent, to attract more readers. However, journalistic codes of ethics are opposed to these techniques, as they use unethical means to misdirect the readers [13].

Satire. According to B.D Horne, and S. Adali, fake news has more similarities in content with satire than with real news. A basic common characteristic of the two genres is that they use similar persuasion methods based on heuristics and not arguments [5]. Although, most satirical news' primary goal is to entertain rather to mislead the reader the term "satire" has also been used by many webpages that do not have any intent to entertain, but to create fake content without being accused of deception [3, 16].

2.3   Fake News Detection Methods

According to Potthast, M., et al. the detection methods of fake news can be divided in three categories which are: 1) knowledge-based 2) style-based and 3) content-based [13].

Knowledge-Based. Knowledge-based detection method is about identifying the basic claims and statements of the article and comparing them with known facts. This procedure could become either manually or automatic. In manual evaluation a person or a group of people are responsible to judge the validity of the article's main statements [27]. Automatic denotation classifies an article in two stages: Fact extraction and fact checking [13]. For fact extraction the algorithm constructs a knowledge base by mining raw "facts" from the web, and during the fact checking stage, it extracts the basic statements of the article and compares them with the knowledge base facts [27].

Style-Based. The most common approach for fake news detection, relying on the research findings from studying the linguistic characteristics of deception [26]. Even though deceptive writers try to mimic the writing style of journalists, there are still some characteristics that could reveal the authenticity of an article, also known as Undeutsch hypothesis [22]. Those characteristics can be split in the following categories:

Lexical features: Describe character and word level signals, such as total words, characters per word, number of unique words etc. [14, 20].

Language features: Syntax in sentence-level describing number of words, syllables per sentence, number of characters per sentence, word types, and number of paragraphs [14]. Also, they calculate several readability metrics that approximate the appropriate knowledge level that a reader should have to understand the text [11].

Syntactic features: Include frequencies of function words, phrases, and punctuations, and Parts-Of-Speech (POS) tagging [20].

Domain-specific linguistic features: Specifically aligned to news domains, such as quoted words, external links, number of graphs, and average length of graphs [20].

Psycholinguistic features: Category of features based on the linguistics that have to do with the psychological aspect of words. This approach tries to identify the psychological reaction that the article tries to achieve [6].

Content-Based. Regarding fake news published in social media, information from the social network can be used, such as user-based information (number of followers of the publisher), post-based information (number of likes, shares etc.) and network-based information (propagation of the news) to effectively tackle the problem [20].

3   Approach

Our experimental approach consists of three parts, shown in Fig. 1: 1) Text Preprocessing, which includes cleaning techniques, 2) Feature Extraction, which includes the extraction and testing of different combinations of feature sets, and 3) Model Testing which tests various ML algorithms. In the following sections we detail these steps.

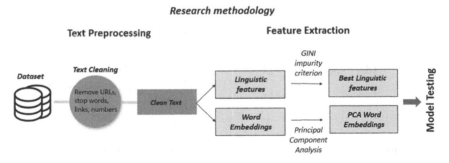

Fig. 1. Flowchart for the experimental approach

3.1   Selected Data

The dataset we used was the one provided for the "2nd Int'l TrueFact Workshop: Making a Credible Web for Tomorrow in conjunction with SIGKDD 2020", created by Kai Shu and contained news related to famous people of the timelines (https://www.kaggle.com/c/fakenewskdd2020/data). The dataset consists of 2972 real and 2014 fake news.

3.2   Data Engineering/Feature Selection

Lexical Features. We extracted 84 lexical features using either manually defined functions or pre-existing ones to be used by the classification task. Regarding text preprocessing at the sentence level, we removed stop words, numbers, and links which are entities that do not contribute significantly to the information of the text. At the word level, we tested three different text representations: i) removing stop words and links only, ii) applying stemming and iii) applying lemmatization. The raw text was used to count Part Of Speech (POS) frequencies and for Named Entities features.

To end up with an optimal feature set we used Decision Tree's feature importance method based on i) mutual information, ii) gini impurity and iii) information entropy, and kept the set for which a baseline model scored the best results. As baseline model we chose a linear Support Vector Machine (SVM), as it was also used in previous studies [4, 5].

More specifically the steps followed were:

i.   Use the full feature set.
ii. Sort features based on the selected information-based metric score.
iii. Measure the performance of the linear Support Vector Classifier.
iv. Drop the bottom two features.
v.   Repeat 2–4 until one or no features are left.

The results are shown in Table 1. The best lexical feature consists of 23 variables, shown in Table 2, corresponding to 67.02% accuracy.

Table 1. Results of the different information-based criteria

Information metric	Number of best features	Accuracy score
Mutual information	10	65.7%
Gini impurity	**23**	**67.02%**
Entropy	12	66.4%

Word Embeddings. Three different word embedding representations were tested: i) Google's pre-trained vectors, trained on part of Google News dataset (about 100 billion words), a model that contains 300-dimensional word vectors for 3 million words and phrases (available at: https://code.google.com/archive/p/word2vec/) ii) spacy's word embeddings that includes 1 million different 300-dimensional word vectors designed by using the GloVe algorithm, and iii) our own vectors trained using the word2vec algorithm in the given dataset/corpus.

By testing all three, using 10-fold cross validation to a linear SVM classifier, we ended up with spacy's representations that had the best accuracy results. After that, we chose the best preprocessing method for text which returns the best accuracy results.

Table 2. The best performing features according to gini impurity

%mverbs_freq	%punctuations	%gerund_participle
%first_person_singular	%clauses	noun_diversity
%present_verbs	semantic_redundancy	verb_diversity
%possesive_prn	%modifiers	Subjectivity
%adverbs	%third_person_singular	big_words_ratio
Redundancy	%art	function_words_diversity
%stopwords	%third_person_plural	avg_len_noun_phrase
weighted_sentiment	avg_punct_per_sentence	

The base algorithm used for testing was a linear SVM and the Clean text representation provide the best results.

The next step was to use Principal Component Analysis (PCA) to reduce the dimensions of the 300-dimensional embeddings to improve performance. The best results were achieved for 180 dimensions, using the clean text representation. Again, the utilization of linear SVM as benchmark model for comparison was chosen to keep consistency within the feature selection steps (Fig. 2).

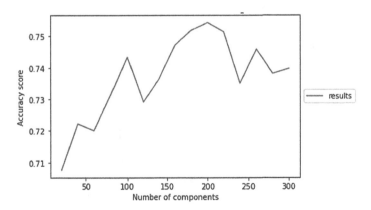

Fig. 2. Accuracy vs. feature set dimensions

Extracting Association Rules (AR) from Named Entities. Another experiment that provided better understanding of the lexical structure at the sentence level was the utilization of Frequent Pattern (FP) Growth algorithm on the set of Named Entities used in the articles. In a first step, spacy library was used to extract the named entities from each article's sentence and then FP Growth was applied to extract rules [2]. Results are presented in Sect. 4.3.

4 Results and Evaluation

4.1 Performance Results for the ML Algorithms

The first experimental results have been produced by using all the lexical features extracted from the texts. As SVMs use distances to classify their samples, scaling provided a significant performance boost. Tree based algorithms, on the other hand, are not affected by scaling dissimilarities, so we skipped the scaling step for their testing. Results are shown in Table 3.

Table 3. Accuracy scores for different feature sets and models

	SVM	Decision Tree	Random Forest	Gradient Boosting
All lexical features	59.8%	61.5%	71.9%	70.8%
All lexical features - scaled	**72.1%**	–	–	–
Best lexical features	58.9%	62.0%	**72.3%**	70.4%
Best lexical features –scaled	71.7%	–	–	
Word embeddings	74.7%	63.8%	75.3%	75.3%
Word embeddings - reduced dimensions	**77.2%**	65.5%	73.5%	74.1%
Best lexical features with word embeddings	**76.2%**	65.8%	75.8%	**76.2%**
Best lexical features with reduced word embeddings	75.8%	65.2%	75.5%	75.9%

4.2 Performance Results for Artificial Neural Networks

The Artificial Neural Networks (ANN) we tested were Convolutional Neural Network (CNN) and Long-Short Term Memory (LSTM), deployed using the Keras library. For the initial embedding layer, we used the pre-trained word embeddings of spacy's library.

Convolutional Neural Network (CNN). In order to find the best combinations of activation functions we used a simple shallow CNN constructed by four layers. First, there was the embedding layer, which consists of 300 neurons, then the Convolutional layer with 128 neurons, a max pooling layer with 128 neurons and finally, a dense layer with the activation function.

For choosing the best combination of activation functions (Relu, Sigmoid, Softmax, Softsign, Exponential, Tanh) for CNN and Dense layers, and optimizers (Adam, Adadelta, Adamx, SGD) we performed a nested "for" loop testing all the combinations.

Fifteen epochs were used for each of the combinations and the best performance was given with relu as the activation function of the CNN layer, sigmoid activation function for the dense layer, and Adam optimizer, with performance 75.6%. After testing several architectures, the best performance was achieved by the one shown in Table 4, with accuracy performance **79.2%**

Table 4. Best performing architecture for CNN

Layer	Embedding layer	Convolutional layer	Convolutional layer	Max pooling	Dense layer	Dense layer
# of neurons	300	300	128	128	28	1

Long-Short Term Memory (LSTM). Similarly, with CNN, for LSTM we tested different combinations of activation functions (Relu, Sigmoid, Softmax, Softsign, Exponential, Tanh) and optimizers (Adam, Adadelta, Adamx, SGD) in a simple network structure using a nested "for" loop.

The architecture of this baseline model consisted of an embedding layer with 300 neurons, a LSTM layer with 300 neurons, a Dropout layer with 300 neurons, a Flatten layer with 300 neurons and finally a Dense layer with one neuron. The best combination was the sigmoid activation function and the adamax optimizer. After testing several different architectures for LSTM, the maximum performance was achieved with the one shown in Table 5, with accuracy performance **75.2%**.

Table 5. Best performing architecture for LSTM.

Layer	Embedding layer	LSTM layer	Dropout	Flatten	Dense layer	Dense layer
# of neurons	300	300	300	300	30	1

4.3 AR Extracted from Named Entities of the Articles

We used FP-Growth to extract AR from the Named Entities of the articles. The results, show in Table 6, indicate that, fake and real news do not significantly differ with regards to the entities they use, confirming that fake news tend to use similar terms with real ones, limiting the scope of linguistic approaches. The only different entity in real news was the "work of art" item referring to titles of books, songs, etc.

Table 6. Items in rules extracted from named entities

Real news AR	Fake news AR
'PERSON'	'PERSON'
'DATE'	'DATE'
'ORG'	'ORG'
'CARDINAL'	'GPE'
'GPE'	'CARDINAL'
'WORK_OF_ART'	'DATE', 'PERSON'
'DATE', 'PERSON'	'ORG', 'PERSON'
'ORG', 'PERSON'	'DATE', 'ORG'
'DATE', 'ORG'	'DATE', 'ORG', 'PERSON'
'DATE', 'ORG', 'PERSON'	'GPE', 'PERSON'

5 Discussion

We extracted 84 style-based features. By using the Gini impurity metric, we ended up with an optimal subset of 23 linguistic features, which improved accuracy, providing at the same time explainable results. We further discuss some of the best performing features, information captured from the text and whether results were expected.

Third person singular/Third person plural/First Person Singular: The use of first-person singular is more frequent in real articles. This is because writers who try to deceive readers tend to separate themselves from the information they propagate [26]. Our findings, shown in Table 7, agree with the expected results, showing higher usage of the first person in real news and higher usage of the third person, plural and singular, in fake news.

Table 7. Feature statistics for two classes

Statistic	3rd person singular		3rd person plural		1st Person Singular	
	Real news	Fake news	Real news	Fake news	Real news	Fake news
Mean	1.96%	2.32%	0.32%	0.47%	0.88%	0.67%
Std. deviation	1.43%	1.52%	0.52%	0.61%	1.86%	1.47%

Percentage of modal verbs: Modal verbs indicate uncertainty (would, could, might etc.) and are most often used by deceivers. This happens because deceivers are not sure about the information they propagate, so they tend to hypothesize and imply correlations about events that do not have clear connection between them [26]. Again, our findings, shown in Table 8, were expected, showing higher usage of modal verbs in fake news.

Table 8. Statistics of "% modal verbs" for two classes

Statistic	Real news	Fake news
Mean	3.93%	4.54%
Standard deviation	1.85%	1.85%

By observing the probability distributions of the two most important lexical features (% modal verbs frequency – Fig. 3, and % first person singular – Fig. 4) we observe that there is a high amount of overlap making them difficult to be separated.

Although, style-based features provide explainable results, their performance was overpassed by the vector representations of texts. More specifically, SVM achieved 72.1% accuracy using only the lexical features, but 77.2% accuracy using the embeddings with 180 dimensions, and 76.2% by combining the full 300-dimensional embeddings with the 23 best lexical features (Table 3).

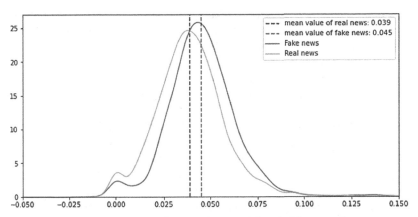

Fig. 3. Probability distribution of "% modal verbs" for two classes.

The combination of spacy's Named Entity Recognition functionality with FP-Growth for the extraction of AR between name entities, in real and fake news, produced results which, once again, support the claim that fake and real news have quite similar structure, limiting linguistic approaches. The only entity that differentiates the two classes is the "work of art" item, referring to titles of books, songs, movies etc., for which we assume it is a characteristic of the specific dataset and not a general characteristic.

Finally, the best performance was achieved by CNN, agreeing with the state-of-the-art trend to utilize ANNs in text classification tasks [25].

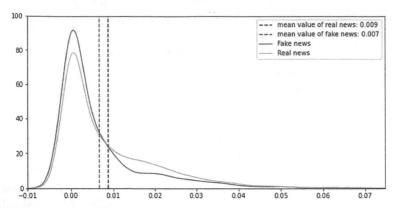

Fig. 4. Probability distribution of "% first person singular" for two classes.

6 Conclusions and Future Work

The scope of this paper was to review the state of the art on fake news detection methods and find an efficient way to perform text classification by utilizing the linguistic information of the content. We used a variety of ML algorithms with the ANNs outperforming. Since ANNs brought promising results, for future work, we could focus our research on text classification methods using ANNs. Also, the ANNs that we utilized are not considered deep, leaving space for additional searching and experimentations with deep ANNs.

On the part of style-based features, most of the psychological studies in which those features are based are contacted in real time communication, where fake articles belong to a different category. Although they bring quite satisfying explainable results, there are a lot of differences in the process of writing a fake text and telling lies in real time and first person.

Also, additional statistical analysis could be applied, like t-statistic test to normalized data, to check if the means of two sample/classes distributions for the most important features are significantly different from each other. Finally, it would be very interesting to test the style-based method in some of the most common fake news datasets and compare our results and findings.

Acknowledgments. The authors would like to thank the Hellenic Artificial Intelligence Society (EETN) for covering part of their expenses to participate in AIAI 2021.

References

1. Alzanin, S.M., Azmi, A.M.: Detecting rumors in social media: a survey. Procedia Comp. Sci. **142**, 294–300 (2018)
2. Ghafari, S.M., Tjortjis, C.: A survey on association rules mining using heuristics. WIREs Data Min. Knowl. Disc. **9**(4), e1307 (2019)
3. Golbeck, J., et al.: Fake news vs satire: a dataset and analysis. In Proceedings of 10th ACM Conference on Web Science, pp. 17–21 (2018)

4. Gravanis, G., Vakali, A., Diamantaras, K., Karadais, P.: Behind the cues: a benchmarking study for fake news detection. Expert Syst. Appl. **128**, 201–213 (2019)
5. Horne, B. D., Adali, S., Sikdar, S.: Identifying the social signals that drive online discussions: a case study of reddit communities. In 26th IEEE International Conference on Computer Communication and Networks (ICCCN), pp. 1–9 (2017)
6. Khan, J.Y., Khondaker, M., Islam, T., Iqbal, A., Afroz, S.: A benchmark study on machine learning methods for fake news detection. arXiv preprint arXiv:1905.04749 (2019)
7. Kiesel, J., et al.: Semeval-2019 task 4: hyperpartisan news detection. In: Proceedings of 13th International Workshop on Semantic Evaluation, pp. 829–839 (2019)
8. Koukaras, P., Tjortjis, C., Rousidis, D.: Social media types: introducing a data driven taxonomy. Computing **102**(1), 295–340 (2020). https://doi.org/10.1007/s00607-019-00739-y
9. Liu, Y., Xu, S.: Detecting rumors through modeling information propagation networks in a social media environment. IEEE Trans. Comput. Soc. Syst. **3**(2), 46–62 (2016)
10. Orso, D., Federici, N., Copetti, R., Vetrugno, L., Bove, T.: Infodemic and the spread of fake news in the COVID-19-era. Eur. J. Emerg. Med. (2020)
11. Pérez-Rosas, V., Kleinberg, B., Lefevre, A., Mihalcea, R.: Automatic detection of fake news. arXiv preprint arXiv:1708.07104 (2017)
12. Petty, R.E., Cacioppo, J.T.: The elaboration likelihood model of persuasion. In: Communication and Persuasion, pp. 1–24. Springer, New York (1986). https://doi.org/10.1007/978-1-4612-4964-1_1
13. Potthast, M., Kiesel, J., Reinartz, K., Bevendorff, J., Stein, B.: A stylometric inquiry into hyperpartisan and fake news. arXiv preprint arXiv:1702.05638 (2017)
14. Reis, J.C., Correia, A., Murai, F., Veloso, A., Benevenuto, F.: Supervised learning for fake news detection. IEEE Intell. Syst. **34**(2), 76–81 (2019)
15. Rousidis, D., Koukaras, P., Tjortjis, C.: Social media prediction a literature review. Multimedia Tools Appl. **79**(9–10), 6279–6311 (2020)
16. Rubin, V. L., Conroy, N., Chen, Y., Cornwell, S.: Fake news or truth? Using satirical cues to detect potentially misleading news. In: Proceedings of 2nd Workshop Computational Approaches to Deception Detection, pp. 7–17 (2016)
17. Ruchansky, N., Seo, S., Liu, Y.: CSI: a hybrid deep model for fake news detection. In: Proceedings of 2017 ACM Conference on Information and Knowledge Management, pp. 797–806 (2017)
18. Shahsavari, S., Holur, P., Tangherlini, T. R., Roychowdhury, V.: Conspiracy in the time of corona: automatic detection of covid-19 conspiracy theories in social media and the news. arXiv preprint arXiv:2004.13783 (2020)
19. Sharma, K., Qian, F., Jiang, H., Ruchansky, N., Zhang, M., Liu, Y.: Combating fake news: a survey on identification and mitigation techniques. ACM Trans. Intell. Syst. Technol. (TIST) **10**(3), 1–42 (2019)
20. Shu, K., Mahudeswaran, D., Wang, S., Lee, D., Liu, H.: FakeNewsNet: a data repository with news content, social context and dynamic information for studying fake news on social media arXiv:1809.01286 (2018)
21. Tsiara, E., Tjortjis, C.: Using Twitter to predict chart position for songs. In: Proceedings of 16th IFIP International Conference on Artificial Intelligence Applications and Innovations, pp. 62–72 (2020)
22. Tversky, A., Kahneman, D.: Judgment under uncertainty: heuristics and biases. Science **185**(4157), 1124–1131 (1974)
23. Wang, L.X., Ramachandran, A., Chaintreau, A.: Measuring click and share dynamics on social media: a reproducible and validated approach. In: 10th International AAAI Conference on Web and Social Media (2016)

24. Wu, L., Li, J., Hu, X., Liu, H.: Gleaning wisdom from the past: early detection of emerging rumors in social media. In: Proceedings 2017 SIAM International Conference on Data Mining, pp. 99–107 (2017)
25. Zhang, Y., Wallace, B.: A sensitivity analysis of (and practitioners' guide to) convolutional neural networks for sentence classification. arXiv preprint arXiv:1510.03820 (2015)
26. Zhou, L., Twitchell, D.P., Qin, T., Burgoon, J.K., Nunamaker, J.F.: An exploratory study into deception detection in text-based computer-mediated communication. In: Proceedings of 36th IEEE International Conference on System Sciences, p. 10 (2003)
27. Zhou, X., Zafarani, R., Shu, K., Liu, H.: Fake news: fundamental theories, detection strategies and challenges. In: Proceedings of 12th ACM International Conference on Web Search and Data Mining, pp. 836–837 (2019)
28. Zubiaga, A., Aker, A., Bontcheva, K., Liakata, M., Procter, R.: Detection and resolution of rumours in social media: a survey. ACM Comput. Surv. 51(2), 1–36 (2018)

CEA-TM: A Customer Experience Analysis Framework Based on Contextual-Aware Topic Modeling Approach

Ariona Shashaj[✉], Davide Stirparo, and Mohammad Kazemi

Network Contacts, Rome, Italy
{ariona.shashaj,davide.stirparo,mohammad.kazemi}@network-contacts.it

Abstract. Text mining comprises different techniques capable to perform text analysis, information retrieval and extraction, categorization and visualization, is experiencing an increase of interest. Among these techniques, topic modeling algorithms, capable of discovering topics from large documents corpora, has many applications. In particular, considering customer experience analysis, having access to topic coherent set of opinions expressed in terms of text reviews, has an important role in both customers side and business providers. Traditional topic modeling algorithms are probabilistic models words co-occurrences oriented which can mislead topics discovery in case of short-text and context-base reviews. In this paper, we propose a customer experience analysis framework which enrich a *state-of-art* topic modeling algorithm (LDA) with a semantic-base topic-tuning approach.

Keywords: NLP · Topic modeling · Text mining · Word embedding

1 Introduction

The rapid growth of digital data over the internet, experienced during this last two decades, has drew attention on tools capable to organize, understand and search them. When it comes to consider textual data, text mining field, which comprises different aspect of text analysis, information retrieval and extraction, clustering, categorization and visualization [7], is becoming a key enabling technology. In this context, topic modeling algorithms, which are able to infer latent topics from large documents corpora, have many applications such as user interest profiling [20], content classification [18], topic-driven comments rating [12], analysing and understanding customer satisfaction [19]. Traditional algorithms of topic modeling are based on probabilistic generative models, such as *probabilistic Latent Semantic Analysis* (pLSA) [8] and *Latent Dirichlet Allocation* (LDA) [3], where each topic is represented through a probability distribution over words and documents are represented through a distribution over topics.

© IFIP International Federation for Information Processing 2021
Published by Springer Nature Switzerland AG 2021
I. Maglogiannis et al. (Eds.): AIAI 2021, IFIP AICT 627, pp. 659–672, 2021.
https://doi.org/10.1007/978-3-030-79150-6_52

Even though pLSA and LDA are the *state-of-art* topic modeling algorithms and find applications in many fields, their intrinsic unpredictive nature can leads to results which are topics difficult to understand and they don't provide any tool in order to perform application-oriented topic tuning. Further, when considering short text documents like customer's reviews where the actual meaning of reviews is mostly context-base, an approach which relay on just words co-occurrence might fail discovering contextual topics. Many proposals in literature have addressed short text documents topic modeling challenges. In [1] and [11] the authors argue that techniques like word embedding [17] should be consider in order to exploit semantic relations among words. Similar to this works, in this paper we propose a customer experience analysis framework which combine LDA topic modeling approach with word embedding technique. Our contribution comprises: a *semantic topic coherence score* build on top of an word embedding model; *LDA parameter tuning*, where LDA parameters such as number of topics and the prior Dirichlet parameters, are tuned in order to maximize the overall topics semantic coherence score; a *topic tuning approach* based on clustering which split and merge topics with the final goal to maximize topics semantic coherence score. This results in a semi-automatized topic modeling framework where human evaluations is limited only to the final step of topic description. The remainder of this paper is organized as follows. In Sect. 2 we motivate our work and review related works. The proposed topic modeling it is presented in Sect. 3, while Sect. 4 shows evaluation of the approach. Finally, conclusion remarks and future works are given in Sect. 5.

2   Related Works

Topic Modeling is a promising text mining technique in the context of social science, capable to explore and gain meaning from a large set of textual corpora [15]. In literature, there are many methodologies proposed in the context of topic modeling [16]. *Non-negative Matrix Factorization* NMF [2] is a deterministic approach based on a non-negative matrix decomposition problem given the number of topics. It imposes non-negative constraints on every element of the matrix. The *probabilistic Latent Semantic Analysis* pLSA [8] derives from *Latent Semantic Analysis* [6] and it represents topics through multinomial random variables. Each word is assigned to a single topic, whereas different words in the same document can be assigned to different topics. Relaxing the assumption of assigning a document to a single topic makes this approach the first attempt towards probabilistic generative models.

Latent Dirichlet Allocation LDA [3] projects document into a vector space by considering the number of occurrences and represents topics through a probability distribution over words, whereas documents are represented through a probability distribution over topics. In the last years, in the context of social science, several variants of LDA have been proposed, such as [4,22].

On the other hand, in order to cope with sparse distribution of topics among short text corpora, such as Twitter feeds and product/offered service reviews, adaptions of LDA have been explored too. *Biterm Topic Modeling* (BTM) [5] exploits bi-terms co-occurrences, whereas in *Dirichlet Multinomial Mixture* (DMM) [21] the authors assume that there is a single latent topic per document and they introduced a collapsed Gibbs algorithm in order to sample topic for a document considering a conditional probability. GPU-DMM [11] enrich DMM with word embedding technique in order to exploit semantic relation among words. Even though the assumption of single topic per document seems to be reasonable for short text documents, in some case like caring services offered in the tourism domain, reviewers don't coherently discuss just a single topic over a comment. In this paper, similar as in [11] we enrich LDA algorithm with word embedding technique, and further, we developed a parameters and topic tuning approach based on word embedding score.

3   Topic Modeling: Contextual-Aware Approach

Latent Dirichlet Allocation is one of the most popular and most used topic modeling techniques. Despite the popularity, there are some uncertainty about the validity and reliability of the LDA results.

This study overcomes aforementioned uncertainties by defining an approach that addresses three LDA's challenges: 1-Hyper-parameters tuning. 2-Evaluation of the model's reliability. 3-Control the validly interpreting the resulting topics. We propose a methodology named Contextual-aware Topic Modeling approach, that answers these challenges and also improves the overall result.

In our approach, *text pre-processing* techniques and *vectorization* are used in order to clean, normalize and vectorized text data. Since this very step has been explained in many other papers and case studies, here we would not cover it. Then we perform *word-embedding* which is the base of semantic topic coherence score. *Semantic topic coherence score* plays an important role in the field of determination of reliability and validity interpretation of the result. The process of topic modeling is performed by, first, executing the *LDA parameter tuning* step. After finding the best parameters settings and train the LDA model, (We've considered the Sklearn [14] implementation of LDA in our work) the next step is topic tuning phase which is about cleaning topics. First, it will try to improve the topic quality by applying clustering and then find similar topics and merge them together. In both steps, the *semantic topic coherence score* will intervene in order to evaluate the result. From now on we will explain each step in detail.

3.1   LDA Tuning

Concerning the first challenges, we need to define a proper tuning process in order to find the best values for *hyper_parameters* to get the optimum result. First LDA requires an estimation of the number of topics *n_components*, for training. Second, needs to tune the LDA prior parameters α which is the distribution of topics per document and β which is the probability distribution of words per topic and finally the maximum iteration over each document max_iter is the last parameter related to the implementation of LDA which should be tune.

As we explained in the previous section, we use the semantic topic coherence score to find the best value for each hyper parameters which give us the optimum LDA result.

3.2 Coherence Score

In order to address the second LDA challenges and define a topic evaluation method, we define a coherence topic score which exploit semantic relations among words associated to the same topic. The cosine similarity it is calculated considering two scalar vectors A and B, and it returns a value from 0 to 1. Closer you get to the maximum, more similar A and B are. In our analysis, Word2Vec model, which projects words semantic meaning into a vector space embedding, was trained on custom dataset and the very first use of this score is evaluate the LDA result. Once the topics are obtained from the model, and expressed through a limited set of words, the method, first calculates the cosine similarity between all the possible pairs of Word2Vec vector projections of the words and then makes the average of all these values for a generic topic.

Algorithm 1: Coherence Score

$Top\_Topic(K, W)$: top words array according to the LDA distribution per topic
$word2vec$: The word2vec model trained on custom dataset
K: Number of Topics
W: number of words per topics semantic coherence score associated to the topics

begin
  for $t \in [0, K]$ **do**
    for $i \in [0, W]$ **do**
      | $vec[t, i] = word2vec(Top\_Topic[t, i])$
    end
  end
  $Topic\_Score \longleftarrow [\,]$**for** $t \in [0, K]$ **do**
    $Pairs \longleftarrow combination(vec[t], 2)$
    $Topic\_Score[t] = \sum_{pair \in Pairs}(cos\_sim(pair[1], pair[2])) / \|Pairs\|$
  end
end
Return $Avg\_Score = (\sum_{S \in Topic\_Scores} S) / K$

In Algorithm 1 we show how the semantic coherence score used to evaluate LDA topic. First, $vec[t, i]$, the Word2Vec projection for each word which represents a topic it is retrieved (lines 2–5). Then, the coherence score associated to single topic it is calculated as the average of the overall cosine similarity between pairs of words (lines 8–11).

Finally, the overall score is the average achieved considering all topics. Hence by using the score method we can find the optimum value of each $hyper\_parameters$ which will be used to train LDA model and obtain topics which achieve the maximum coherence score.

3.3 Topic Cleaning

In the previous step, we obtained optimal LDA parameters settings that maximize the semantic coherence score, however, high coherence score will not guarantee to have clean topics, because the score is a mathematical calculation. Unclean topics can be classified as:

- *Dirty Topics*: A topic is mixed with two or more semantic groups of topic words with different meanings. This dirty topic should be split to two or more correct topics
- *Redundant Topic*: These duplicate topics should be merged to a single topic.

To split and merge raw topics, we applied a new post–processing method based on the word embedding and unsupervised clustering techniques in which we consider Word2Vec as the word embedding model and as the unsupervised clustering method we used Density–based Spatial Clustering of Applications with Noise (DBSCAN). By using the output of tuned topic modeling, we created a list of top 25 most frequent words of each topic and we will use it in post-processing method. Below we are going to explain in details the preparation steps involved in topic cleaning.

Word2Vec Topic Projection: In our point of view, the proposed method is based on the hypothesis that one topic will form one semantic cluster in the word embedding space and a dirty topic is a mixture of multiple topics, so it contains multiple semantic clusters. Suppose that the *i-th* topic result denoted as T_i, where $T_i = \{w_j^i : j \in [0, \|T_i\|]\}$ is the array of the top words with the highest probabilities. Then, we define as f_{we} the projection of a word into Word2Vec vector space, where $\overline{w} = f_{we}(w)$ and $\overline{w}$ is the p-dimensional word embedding vector of w. In this way, the vector space corresponding to the top words of the *i-th* topic T is defined as $\overline{T_i} = \{\overline{w}_i^j = f_{we}(w_j^i) : j \in [0, \|T_i\|]\}$. In order to perform the Word2Vec projection we consider a pre-trained model on our custom target dataset.

Dimensional Reduction: When we have too many features(p-dimensional), observations become harder to cluster. In an attempt to reducing dimensional we create a mixed approach by using the *Principal Components Analysis* (PCA) [10] and *t-distributed Stochastic Neighbor Embedding* (t-SNE) [13]. PCA is a linear feature extraction technique which is focused on placing dissimilar data points far apart in a lower dimension representation, on the other hand t-SNE is a non-linear manifold and represent similar data points close together which is essential for our type analysis. We reduce initial number of dimensions linearly with PCA down to 10% latent variables, then we will apply t-SNE on the PCA result.

3.4   Topic Cleaning: DBSCAN Clustering

DBSCAN is a clustering method that is used in machine learning to separate clusters of high density from clusters of low density region. One important feature of DBSCAN is that we do not need to fix the number of clusters before executing it. The DBSCAN algorithm automatically will estimate the clusters considering two input parameters:

- *eps*: The maximum distance between two samples for one to be considered as in the neighborhood of the other.
- *min_samples*: The number of samples (or total weight) in a neighborhood for a point to be considered as a core point.

The major challenge of using DBSCAN algorithm is to find a right setting of hyper-parameters (*eps* and *min_samples* values) to fit in to the algorithm for getting accurate results. Since the DBSCAN needs to have a distance between two samples, we calculated the Euclidean distance between all the top words in each topic and then sorted them out. Then we set the calculated euclidean distance as our *eps* range and now a fix range for *min_samples* is needed.

The algorithm we've implemented, loop through these two parameter's range and returning the possible clusters scenarios. For each clusters it calculates the silhouette score, and chose the first parameters that have the top score, and consequently, the cluster labels respect that best parameters will be the final result of our analysis in this step. Nevertheless the topic cleaning phase is not completed because we have to select the best clusters for each topic.

3.5   Topic Cleaning: Clusters Evaluation

As a first step, the size of each cluster (C_i) for a generic topic T_j, will be checked. If size of $\|C_i\|$ is lower than a threshold named *min_cluster_size*, we will not consider that cluster further in the analysis. This *weak clusters*, named outliers, contribute as noise in a topic definition. Clusters, C_j, where $\|C_j\| >$ *min_cluster_size*, named as *super cluster* are candidates for topics definition. The remain part of the approach split topics which contains more than one cluster with dimension greater than *min_cluster_size* into two topics. We've also define a threshold *max_topic_size* for the maximum number of words, to use in topic definition. In case, cluster dimensions are greater than *max_topic_size*, a subset of *max_topic_size* words it is selected, which achieve the highest semantic coherence score.

Algorithm 2: Evaluate Cluster Result

C: Collection of clusters calculated for each topic where C[i,j] contains words array which characterized the j-th cluster of the i-th topic; min_size: minimum threshold for cluster dimensions; max_size: maximum threshold for final topic dimensions

T: Resulting topics list after cluster analysis

begin

    $T \longleftarrow \{\}$

    $Candidate\_C \longleftarrow \{C[i,t] : C[i,t] \in C \wedge \|C(i,t)\| > min\_size\};$

    forall the $C[i,t] \in Candidate\_C$ **do**

        if $\|C[i,t]\| < max\_size$ **then**

        | $T \longleftarrow T \cup w : w \in C[t,i]$

        end

        else

        | $C[i,t]^{max\_size}$: subset which maximize semantic coherence score

        | $T \longleftarrow T \cup w : w \in C[i,t]'$

        end

    end

    return T

end

In Algorithm 2, C refers to the calculated clusters, whereas min_size and max_size are respectively the minimum cluster dimension threshold to use for discovering *weak clusters* and the maximum topic dimension threshold. Candidate clusters are selected among those which dimension is greater than min_size (line 3), whereas output topics are selected among clusters which size is lower than max_size (line 6) or subsets of max_size elements of clusters with dimension greater than that and which achieve the maximal semantic coherence score (lines 9–10).

3.6 Topic Cleaning: Merge

Merging similar topics is the last step to be performed. The final goal of merge phase is to discover pairs of topics with at least 40% equal words, to join them as a unique topic. We use the clean topics list, obtained in the previous phases (Algorithm 2) and identifies which topic pairs have the condition to be merged. To carry out this join, the words of the two topics will be grouped into a single list then we eliminate duplicate words and subsequently we calculate the coherence maximum semantic coherence scores. In Algorithm 3 we show the implemented approach in order to automatically perform the join of similar topics. The algorithm takes as input, the list of topics T, which results after the clustering and topic splitting phase and a threshold Th_sim to be used in order to check the join condition. Topics list it is scrolled consecutively, and each topic it is compared with the next in row (lines 4–5).

If a pair of topics it is found such that they have a subset of Th_sim words the same, then considering that the join condition it is satisfied, the two topics are merged (lines 7–16). A final check it is done, in order to consider topics which didn't participate in any merge (lines 19–22). Finally, the resulting list of merged topics it is returned, as well as, the list of deleted ones (topics which participate into a merge) and the list of topics which did not take part at any merge.

We observe, that even though the previous cluster analysis clean topic from eventually noise, expressed as *dirty cluster* which have a lower size, and split into more than one represented through semantic related words, eventually in some cases it can happen than one topic participates in more than one merge (multiple merges per single topic). In that case, it is necessary to break ties between the involved merges. By setting the threshold Th_sim greater than half of the dimension of the words collection which represent a topic, it can prevent the situation of multiple merges per single topic, however this will result in a lower probability to discover semantic related topics. We show in Algorithm 4 the proposed approach capable to clean a collection of merged topics affected by multiple merges per topic. Algorithm 4 consider as input respectively,

---

Algorithm 3: Creation of a list that contains merge topics and all topics without a merge

---

$T[K, W]$: array topics results from algorithm 2 which contains K topics each represented through W words. Th_sim : a threshold which hold the merge condition. Two topics are merged if they both contains at least Th_sim words T' : the resulting list of topics after merging T^D : list of removed topics T^{NM}: list of not merged topics

begin
  $T' \longleftarrow \{\}$
  $T^D \longleftarrow \{\}$
  $T^{NM} \longleftarrow \{\}$
  for $i \in [1, K - 1]$ **do**
    for $j \in [i + 1, K]$ **do**
      counter = 0
      for $w \in T_i$ **do**
        if $w \in T_j$ **then**
          | counter = counter + 1
        end
      end
      if $counter >= Th\_sim$ **then**
        $T' \longleftarrow T' \cup (T_i \cup T_j)$
        $T^D \longleftarrow T^D \cup T_i$
        $T^D \longleftarrow T^D \cup T_j$
      end
    end
  end
  for $i \in [0, K]$ **do**
    if $T_i \notin T^D$ **then**
      | $T^{NM} \longleftarrow T^{NM} \cup T_i$
    end
  end
  Return T', T^D, T^{NM}
end

T' the collection of topics resulted after merge, T^D a collection of the original topics which participate into a merge (part of the topics list resulted from the clustering and splitting approach - Sect. 3.5) and collection T^{NM} which are topics not merged. As a first step, we define as $size\_merged$, the number of the original topics merged (line 2). Then we define a matrix $Co(size\_merged, size\_merged))$ in order to keep track of the semantic coherence score if the corresponding original are merged. So, $Co[i, j]$ will be equal to 0 if topics $T^D[i], T^D[j] \in T^D$ are not merged during the execution of Algorithm 4, otherwise it will be equal to the the coherence score calculated considering the merged topic $T^D[i] \cup T^D[j]$ (lines 4–9). Observe that Co is symmetric, and that $Co[i, j] = Co[j, i]$. To identify the merged topics which are going to be the output of the final output of the merged approach we consider to merge each topic $T^D[i]$ with the one in order to achieve the maximal semantic coherence score(lines 11–14). Finally, single original topics are added to the output (lines 13–17).

Algorithm 4: Check for the presence of topics participating in multiple merges

---

T': list of merged topics obtained in algorithm 3. T^D: list of deleted topic which were in algorithm 3. T^{NM}: list of topics which didn't participate in any merge. *word2vec*: word2vec model pre-trained on custom dataset.
T^*: list of merged topics without multiple merges per topic

begin
  $size\_merged \longleftarrow \|T^D\|$
  $Co(size\_merged, size\_merged) \longleftarrow init(0)$
  for $i \in [0, size\_merged]$ **do**
    for $j \in [0, size\_merged]$ **do**
      if $T_i^D \cup T_j^D \in T'$ **then**
        | $Co[i, j] = Co[j, i] = CoherenceScore((T_i^D \cup T_j^D), word2vec)$
      end
    end
  end
  for $i \in [0, size_merged]$ **do**
    | $j^* = \max_{j in[0, size_merged]} Co[i, j]$
    | $T^* \longleftarrow T^* \cup (T_i^D \cup T_j^D)$
  end
  for $t \in T^{NM}$ **do**
    | $T^* \longleftarrow T^* \cup t$
  end
  return T^*
end

---

4 Evaluations

For the evaluation of the proposed solution, we consider a real application scenario, in particular we refer to the scenario detailed as part of the POR PUGLIA FESR C-BAS (Customer Behavior Analysis System)[1]. The domain specific dataset was created considering three main review's sources, such as "Booking", "TripAdvisor", and "Google map"'s reviews related to tourism activities in Puglia[2]. For implementation we used python libraries such as scikit-learn for the LDA model, spacy and nltk for the preprocessing and gensim for the word2vec model.

First step is applying the pre-processing technique, which is going to consider as input the text comments and will return an output a collection of word-tokens. Table 1 shows an example of the pre-processing output pipeline. The second step consist in tuning LDA model considering the output of the pre-processing pipeline (Sect. 3.1). By using this optimal parameters setting we trained the model in order to obtain the initial topics collection, which are going be tuned in the next steps. Each topic is represented through the set of 25-top words according to the LDA weights.

---

[1] https://www.c-bas.eu/.
[2] Southern region in Italy - https://en.wikipedia.org/wiki/Apulia.

Table 1. Pre-processing pipeline output example

Original text comment	Text pre-processing output
'lovely hotel, terraces with views over the old town, tastefully furnished, clean and stylish rooms. Would definitely stay here again. It is in a great location. There is parking available near to the hotel. Reception can advise you where to park.'	['hotel', 'terrace', 'view', 'town', 'room', 'stay', 'location', 'park', 'hotel', 'reception', 'advise', 'park']

In Table 2 we show an example of the output topic obtained from LDA training.

Table 2. Sample topic with 25 keywords

Topic 0

Food	Show	Place	Service	Restaurant
Wine	Staff	Make	Recommend	Have
Order	Time	Come	Eat	Get
Dinner	Go	Price	Pasta	Menu
Cook	Take	Masseria	Seafood	Lunch

Table 3. Result of the cluster analysis on topic 0

Cluster results		Top 10 Words	
Cluster 1	Cluster 2	Cluster 1	Cluster 2
Show	Food	Show	Food
Place	Service	Place	Wine
Make	Restaurant	Make	Order
Recommend	Wine	Recommend	Eat
Have	Staff	Have	Dinner
Time	Order	Time	Pasta
Come	Eat	Come	Menu
Get	Dinner	Get	Cook
Go	Pasta	Go	Seafood
Price	Menu	Take	Lunch
Take	Cook		
Masseria	Seafood		
	Lunch		

By observing the words part of *Topic 0*, it seems clear enough that this topic is about food and restaurant, however there are some words that have nothing to do with food and restaurant, such as show, place, make and time. The third step of our approach is the cluster analysis, which the final goal is to clean topics and eventually split them in two or more clusters of semantically related words (Sect. 3.5). An example of the output of clustering analysis considering *Topic 0* it is shown in Table 3. By observing these clusters, we can say that all the words in cluster 1 have no connection with the topic (which is about food and restaurant), however we got an excellent result in cluster 2 where all words are completely related to the topic. The next step is to reduce the number of words in each cluster to top 10 words, which provides the highest semantic coherence (Table 3) and remove also impractical words. As last step of the cluster analysis is the selection of the best clusters in terms of have a clear meaning between all the others. In order to perform this, the best clusters which have the highest semantic coherence score are selected. In case of *Topic 0*, the algorithm chooses cluster 2 (discarding cluster 1), exactly as we might have expected.

As results of the cluster analysis steps, we might expect to have redundant topics with similar meaning. The final goal of the merge phase of Topic Cleaning Sect. 3.6 is to reduce this redundancy. In Fig. 1, we show the execution of the merge phase. There are two topics, *Topic 0* and *Topic 1* that have been identified for merging. This topics have exactly 4 equal words such as "hotel", "room", "staff" and "service". We've set the merging threshold equal to 40%. In Table 4 we show the final results of our work where all topics are completely clear. We show keywords for each topic which helped us to find the main aspect of every topic.

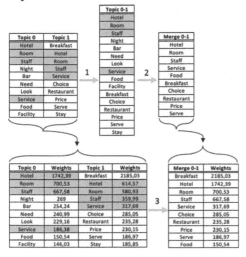

Fig. 1. Merge process

Table 4, shows us how our model has obtained two topics for the low score reviews. The first topic is about reservation, while the second one is about the location. The neutral score reviews have six topics. We have some general topics about breakfast, location, hotel services, mobility, room but, one specific topic (Topic 5) is about noise pollution, especially in the night due to a dog. It should be noted that topics 6 and 7 in neutral reviews are the result of the merge phase. The high score reviews have 4 topics which are mobility, hotel services, location, and accommodation which is the result of the merge phase. These results approve the validity of our approach otherwise we would face difficulty in interpreting topics. Since we categorise reviews score at the beginning of our process, now we can have a better picture of what are the people opinions about each places. For example we have three same Topics which is about location and we can say that the Location Topic with low review score contains negative feedback and people were not satisfied with the place location and we can go on and elaborate all topics respect to their review score.

Table 4. Final topic model result

Topic ID	Review score	Main aspect	Keywords
Topic 0	Low	Reservation	Book, Pay, Say, Check, Tell
Topic 1	Low	Location	Restaurant, Place, Location, Walk, Town, Area, Pool
Topic 2	Neutral	Mobility	Walk, Town, City, Center, Minute
Topic 3	Neutral	Location	Location, Stay, Place, Area, Recommend
Topic 4	Neutral	Breakfast	Breakfast, Food, Dinner, Well, Menu
Topic 5	Neutral	Noise pollution	Street, Night, Noisy, Noise, Dog, Neighbour
Topic 6	Neutral	Room	Room, Breakfast, Restaurant, Get, Hotel, Look, Find
Topic 7	Neutral	Hotel services	Hotel, Breakfast, Room, Staff, Restaurant
Topic 8	High	Hotel services	Hotel, Staff, Room, Service, Restaurant
Topic 9	High	Mobility	Walk, City, Town, Host, Restaurant, Owner, Minute
Topic 10	High	Location	Pool, Town, Walk, Area, Restaurant
Topic 11	High	Accommodation	Location, Room, Breakfast, Staff, Place, Stay, Hotel, Recommend, Town, Clean

5   Conclusion and Future Works

Our analysis focused on the tourism sector and in particular on tourist facilities such as hotels, B&Bs, restaurants, etc., which allows us to see the main topics of interest to customers. The division of reviews by low, neutral, and high score gave us the opportunity to have an even more clearer picture of people's opinions, for example, in low score reviews, people talked more about room problems while in the high score they talked more about the beauty of the place. Our primary goal by defining this method was to implement an automatic approach capable of carrying out these operations every time that new data is provided. The starting point of this method is based on the LDA topic model which can provides unsatisfactory topics. Subsequent operations of cleaning and merging the topics were fundamental and allowed us to obtain very clear topics, with higher coherence than the initial topics. The strengths of this method concern the ability to obtain excellent clean topics automatically and yet it can be applied to different domains of customer reviews.

Since our approach is totally automatic, in some cases the choice of clusters based on coherence can lead to the selection of not very clear topics and perhaps discarding other which are more interpretable. Still the best evaluator of topic is obviously human, however the propose parameter and topic tuning approach is important in the development of a semi-automated approach of customer experience analysis based on topic modeling. LDA is a very powerful technique for the qualitative analysis of large corpora because of its highly interpretable topics. However, LDA ignores the temporal aspect present in many document collections. The next step in our work will work on DTM (Dynamic Topic modeling) instead of LDA and try implement the DTM method inside our approach. Dynamic Topic Models (DTMs) [9] address the LDA problem which is ignorance of the temporal aspect present in many document by extending the idea of LDA to allow topic representations to evolve over fixed time intervals such as years.

Acknowledgments. Funding/Support: This work was supported by the POR PUGLIA FESR 2014–2020 project C-BAS "Customer Behaviour Analysis System".

References

1. Dieng, A.B., Ruiz, F.J., Blei, D.M.: Topic modeling in embedding spaces. Trans. Assoc. Comput. Linguist. **8**, 439–453 (2020)
2. Arora, S., Ge, R., Moitra, A.: Learning topic models-going beyond SVD. In: 2012 IEEE 53rd Annual Symposium on Foundations of Computer Science, pp. 1–10. IEEE (2012)
3. Blei, D.M., Ng, A.Y., Jordan, M.I.: Latent Dirichlet Allocation. J. Mach. Learn. Res. **3**, 993–1022 (2003)
4. Chang, J., Boyd-Graber, J., Blei, D.M.: Connections between the lines: augmenting social networks with text. In: Proceedings of the 15th ACM SIGKDD International Conference on Knowledge Discovery and Data mining, pp. 169–178 (2009)
5. Cheng, X., Yan, X., Lan, Y., Guo, J.: BTM: topic modeling over short texts. IEEE Trans. Knowl. Data Eng. **26**(12), 2928–2941 (2014)
6. Dumais, S.T., et al.: Latent semantic indexing (LSI) and trec-2. Nist Special Publication Sp, pp. 105–105 (1994)
7. Gupta, V., Lehal, G.S., et al.: A survey of text mining techniques and applications. J. Emerg. Technol. Web Intell. **1**(1), 60–76 (2009)
8. Hofmann, T.: Probabilistic latent semantic indexing. In: Proceedings of the 22nd Annual International ACM SIGIR Conference on Research and Development in Information Retrieval, pp. 50–57 (1999)
9. Iwata, T., Watanabe, S., Yamada, T., Ueda, N.: Topic tracking model for analyzing consumer purchase behavior. In: Twenty-First International Joint Conference on Artificial Intelligence. Citeseer (2009)
10. Kramer, M.A.: Nonlinear principal component analysis using auto associative neural networks. AIChE J. **37**(2), 233–243 (1991)
11. Li, C., Wang, H., Zhang, Z., Sun, A., Ma, Z.: Topic modeling for short texts with auxiliary word embeddings. In: Proceedings of the 39th International ACM SIGIR Conference on Research and Development in Information Retrieval, pp. 165–174 (2016)

12. Ma, Z., Sun, A., Yuan, Q., Cong, G.: Topic-driven reader comments summarization. In: Proceedings of the 21st ACM International Conference on Information and Knowledge Management, pp. 265–274 (2012)
13. Van der Maaten, L., Hinton, G.: Visualizing data using t-SNE. J. Mach. Learn. Res. **9**(11), 1–27 (2008)
14. Pedregosa, F., et al.: Scikit-learn: machine learning in python. J. Mach. Learn. Res. **12**, 2825–2830 (2011)
15. Ramage, D., Rosen, E., Chuang, J., Manning, C.D., McFarland, D.A.: Topic modeling for the social sciences. In: NIPS 2009 Workshop on Applications for Topic Models: Text and Beyond, vol. 5, p. 27 (2009)
16. Albalawi, R., Yeap, T.H., Benyoucef, M.: Using topic modeling methods for short-text data: a comparative analysis. Artificial Intelligence and Deep Learning for Network Management and Communication (2020)
17. Rumelhart, D.E., Hinton, G.E., Williams, R.J.: Learning representations by back-propagating errors. Nature **323**(6088), 533–536 (1986)
18. Sriram, B., Fuhry, D., Demir, E., Ferhatosmanoglu, H., Demirbas, M.: Short text classification in Twitter to improve information filtering. In: Proceedings of the 33rd International ACM SIGIR Conference on Research and Development in Information Retrieval, pp. 841–842 (2010)
19. Sutherland, I., Kiatkawsin, K.: Determinants of guest experience in Airbnb: a topic modeling approach using LDA. Sustainability **12**(8), 3402 (2020)
20. Weng, J., Lim, E.P., Jiang, J., He, Q.: Twitter rank: finding topic-sensitive influential twitterers. In: Proceedings of the Third ACM International Conference on Web Search and Data Mining, pp. 261–270 (2010)
21. Yin, J., Wang, J.: A dirichlet multinomial mixture model-based approach for short text clustering. In: Proceedings of the 20th ACM SIGKDD International Conference on Knowledge Discovery and Data Mining, pp. 233–242 (2014)
22. Zhang, H., Giles, C.L., Foley, H.C., Yen, J.: Probabilistic community discovery using hierarchical latent gaussian mixture model. AAAI **7**, 663–668 (2007)

Machine Learning Meets Natural Language Processing - The Story so Far

Nikolaos-Ioannis Galanis⬚, Panagiotis Vafiadis⬚, Kostas-Gkouram Mirzaev⬚, and George A. Papakostas⁽✉⁾⬚

HUman-MAchines INteraction Laboratory (HUMAIN-Lab),
Department of Computer Science, International Hellenic University,
Kavala, Greece
{nigaean,pavazei,gkmerza,gpapak}@cs.ihu.gr

Abstract. Natural Language Processing (NLP) has evolved significantly over the last decade. This paper highlights the most important milestones of this period, while trying to pinpoint the contribution of each individual model and algorithm to the overall progress. Furthermore, it focuses on issues still remaining to be solved, emphasizing on the groundbreaking proposals of Transformers, BERT, and all the similar attention-based models.

Keywords: Machine learning · Computational linguistics · NLP · NLU · NLG · Linguistics · Ambiguity · CNN · BERT · Transformers · GPT

1 Introduction

Records of NLP application can be found even before the early 1900s when there were attempts of using machine translation to translate text from one language to another [12]. Meanwhile, there were some conflicting views between linguistics and computer science claiming that language is generative in nature and cannot be described with mathematical concepts [41].

Alan Turing adequately answered "Can machines think?" in 1950, by introducing the research/study of "Imitation Game" [33], a simulation process of a computer acting and answering without substantially changing the outcome [20]. Thus the machine is considered to be "thinking", as long as having a conversation with it could be indistinguishable from that with a human.

The first successful attempt to achieve that was ELIZA [56], a simple program within the Project of Mathematics and Computation ("Project MAC") at MIT that managed to mislead people into believing that it's a psychologist, reflecting on questions by turning the questions back at the speaker. Another program was PARRY (Colby, 1975) mimicking a paranoid schizophrenic [47]. Over the years, programs were getting "smarter" like Eugene Goostman [3] or Cleverbot [44] that statistically analyzes huge databases of real conversations to determine the best responses.

© IFIP International Federation for Information Processing 2021
Published by Springer Nature Switzerland AG 2021
I. Maglogiannis et al. (Eds.): AIAI 2021, IFIP AICT 627, pp. 673–686, 2021.
https://doi.org/10.1007/978-3-030-79150-6_53

The downside was the inability to keep consistency and keep up with brand new subjects. There are numerous variations or alternatives to the Turing test, like when humans have to prove their non-machine nature to a computer (ex. CAPTCHA [54]) or when we use AI to create original art (Fig. 1).

1930 — Translating machines patents, Artsourni, Troyanskii propose dictionaries

1950 — Imitation Game by Alan Turing

1957 — Syntactic Structures by Noam Chomsky

1966 — ELIZA: Computer Psychotherapist by Joseph Weizenbaum

1968 — SHRDLU: NLU Computer Program by Terry Winograd (MIT)

1969 — Conceputal Dependency theory by Roger Schank

1975 — PARRY: Computer Schizophrenic person by Colby

1980 — ATN: Augmented Transition Network by William A. Woods

··· — MUBBLE,MOPTRANS,KODIAK,ABSITY,DR.SPAITSO,RACTER

2006 — AI Software (Question Answering system) from IBM by Watson

2011 — Siri : Mobile Assistant by Apple

Fig. 1. A summarized timeline of important NLP milestones.

Over the last decade, NLP grew rapidly and led to next-gen applications, such as virtual assistants like Siri or Alexa. New methodologies were developed using neural networks or unsupervised learning for acquiring vector representations of words like Word2Vec or GloVe. The latest milestone in this growth, was the introduction of the attention-based models, using a mechanism that comprehends contextual associations between words and phrases.

NLP as a sub-field of AI, examines and detects patterns in data and uses them in achieving better understanding and generating natural language. There are several applications of NLP, some of them are:

1. Search engines
2. Virtual assistangs & Chatbots
3. Sentence segmentation
4. Part of speech tagging
5. Information Extraction
6. Question Answering
7. Machine Translation
8. Deep Analysis
9. Named entity recognition
10. Spam Detection
11. Text-to-speech & Speech-to-Text
12. Sentimental analysis
13. Text Summarization

NLP converts human language from the form of raw text data, into structured data (computer-understandable), but prior, it needs to perceive the data based on grammar, context and decide on intent and entities, with a process called Natural Language Understanding(NLU). On the other hand, Natural Language Generation(NLG), is a process that converts computer-generated data into human understandable text. This system generates well structured dynamic documents using both document-planning, micro-planning and realization, by representing human-like desired sentences [24].

Though other surveys have previously presented various trends in Natural Language Processing and Machine Learning ([21,38,60]), each in a different way either with a more practical or theoretical approach. In this review, we will attempt to pinpoint and summarize the most critical and important break-throughs in the field of NLP up until today, while also focusing on the still existent and new emerging challenges.

2   Materials and Methods

2.1   The Literature Accumulation

The search begins with Google Scholar's highest cited results for the last 10 years, while also tracing references and backwards citations. The search included at least one keyword of each group: Machine Learning (Machine Learning, Trans-former, CNN, Neural Network, Recurrent, GRU, Deep Learning, Recursive, LSTM, ML) and NLP (Natural Language, NLP, NLU, NLG).

Clearly, there's a steadily increasing number of papers on the combined sub-ject, booming after the proposal of Transformers, with publications of derived models and methodologies for transfer learning (see Fig. 2).

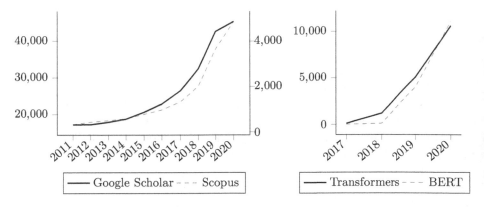

Fig. 2. Publications for NLP in general and references to popular Transformer papers.

2.2   The NLP Field Transformation

Having a strong presence within the last decade, **Word embeddings** is a term where words that have the same meaning have a similar representation. In 2013, Mikolov introduced two different techniques for text vectorization: **Skip Gram** and **Common Bag Of Words** (CBOW) [37]. Both of them were released in a library under a single name, "**Word2Vec**" and later in the same year some improvements for both of them were suggested in an attempt to remedy polysemy [35]. Not long before, in 2011, the same author had also introduced a **Recurrent Neural Net Language Model** (RNNLM) being up to 15 times more efficient compared to past approaches [36].

In 2014 Pennington proposed an unsupervised learning algorithm for retrieving vector representations for words, named **GloVe** [39]. **Recurrent/Recursive Networks and LSTMs** [22] are intriguing recent developments in ML with Sutskever suggesting the **Sequence to Sequence** (seq2seq) model [51]. Also at the same year, Kalchbrenner proposed a **Dynamic Convolutional Neural Network**(DCNN) [25] and Kim explored a variety of classification tasks [26].

Dong in 2015 introduced **multi-column convolutional neural networks** (MCCNNs) to analyze questions from multiple aspects and create their representations [19]. Yin presented a comparative study between CNN and RNN for NLP summing up the progress up until then [59]. Upadhyay in 2017 introduced a new method for managing polysemy in word embeddings [52]. Peters Suggested the Embeddings from Language Models in 2018 [40]. The Same year Chen introduced a new **LSTM** that outperformed all previous models on Natural Language Inference [15].

2.2.1   Introducing Attention: The Era of Transformers

Bahdanau, based on the previously proposed Encoder-Decoder architecture, introduced the term **"Attention"** [11]: an alignment score for each input word, based on the decoder's previous hidden state and the current input state of the sentence. Using this score, the decoder can decide which parts of the input sentence are the most important, without having to encode all of the input sentences into a fixed length vector.

Following this concept, Vaswani [53] made a rather bold proposal that leads to the **Transformers** architecture: the replacement of the costly RNNs with multi-headed self-attention layers in Encoder-Decoder models, thus increasing dramatically their performance, setting a new state-of-the-art for various tasks. Based on that idea, a whole new category of models emerged (Fig. 3). The **Transformer XL** [17] was suggested later on, attempting to resolve the limited length of the original Transformer's input.

Transfer learning and pre-training came along as another important progression. Howard and Ruder [23] proposed Universal Language Model Finetuning (**ULMFiT**) in 2018, a transfer learning method that could be applied to any task in NLP, consisting of 3 stages: training in a large amount of text to capture general features, fine tuning for the task at hand with discriminative fine tuning and slanted triangular learning rates, and finally adding and fine tuning the classifier layers. Discriminative fine tuning allows the tuning of each layer with a different learning rate, while slanted triangular learning rates linearly increases the learning rate initially, linearly reducing it then again afterwards.

By combining the idea of pre-training and separating the Encoder part of this new Transformer architecture and stacking it as many times as needed, OpenAI's team (Radford [42,43], Brown [13]) created 3 versions of the Generative Pre-Training model (a.k.a. **GPT-1/2/3**). Each version featured a larger number of parameters and pretraining in a larger corpus, achieving a new state-of-the-art for tasks like text generation and question answering with each version. The third version though is still not openly available, while a smaller model with 117 million parameters has been released for the second version.

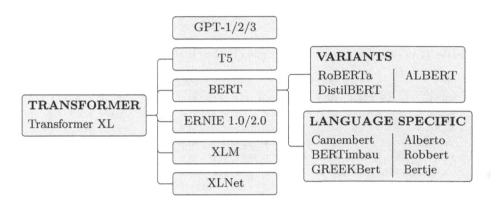

Fig. 3. The evolution of transformer based models.

Bidirectional **E**ncoder **R**epresentations from **T**ransformers (BERT) technique was introduced by Devlin [18], with an architecture similar to that of GPT. As the name suggests, one of its basic differences with GPT is the bidirectionality that helps in better understanding of the context, giving it a crucial advantage over other models. By releasing a base and an (extremely) larger model, BERT achieved state-of-the-art performance in tasks like question answering and text classification and can be used for a variety of other NLP tasks just by fine-tuning with a much smaller task-specific corpus.

Various publications branched from the initial BERT release, attempting to improve it or provide a solution to its drawbacks. **RoBERTa** [31] was proposed as a better pretraining method, while **DistilBERT** [45] and **ALBERT** [29] were smaller, faster alternatives with training speed and reduced memory consumption in mind.

Yang proposed **XLNet** [58], an autoregressive (AR) model attempting to fix a discrepancy in the MLM task of BERT where the dependency between the masked input tokens is ignored. In order to achieve that, it's using a permutation language modeling objective – meaning that all tokens are predicted instead of only the 15% of BERT's masked tokens. And though AR models can usually access the context in one direction, the permutation allows it to be bi-directional. XLNet can outperform BERT – sometimes significantly – at 20 tasks.

Sun from Baidu introduced Enhanced Representation through kNowledge IntEgration (**ERNIE**) [49] at the beginning of 2019, a character-based model antagonizing BERT for the current state-of-the-art with a slight different masking strategy - multi-stage instead of the random one BERT has. Later, in 2020, Baidu released a second version of ERNIE [50] introducing "continual pretraining" and multiple training tasks for lexical, syntactical and semantical analysis, claiming to outperform BERT and XLNet not only for the Chinese language, but for English as well (see Table 1).

Table 1. Results for various Transformers in the current GLUE Leaderboard [55].

	Score	CoLA	SST-2	MRPC	STS-B	MNLI-m	QNLI	RTE	WNLI	AX
ERNIE	**90,9**	**74,4**	**97,8**	**93,9/91,8**	**93,0/92,6**	**91,9**	**97,3**	**92,0**	**95,9**	**51,7**
ALBERT	–	69.1	97.1	93.4/91.2	92.5/92.0	91.3	91.0	89.2	89.2	50.2
XLNet	–	70.2	97.1	92.9/90.5	93.0/92.6	90.9	–	88.5	92.5	48.4
RoBERTa	88.1	67.8	96.7	92.3/89.8	92.2/91.9	90.8	95.4	88.2	89.0	48.7
XLM	83.1	62.9	95.6	90.7/87.1	88.8/88.2	89.1	94.0	76.0	71.9	44.7
BERTlarge	80.5	60.5	94.9	89.3/85.4	87.6/86.5	86.7	92.7	70.1	65.1	39.6

2.3   More Data, Please!

The General Language Understanding Evaluation (**GLUE**) benchmark is a popular tool that evaluates the ability to analyze natural language understanding systems [55] featuring its very own leaderboard. A second version of it (**SuperGLUE**) came out a year later [46], featuring more and harder tasks, to achieve an even more accurate evaluation of the ever-evolving NLP models. GLUE consists of 11 tasks and their equivalent compilation of test datasets, while SuperGLUE features 10 more.

Common Crawl [2] is a repository with a significant amount of web crawl data, used as pre-training material for many of the models. It might be vast, but since it's a web dataset it's quite possible that heavy preprocessing is required before being actually usable. Other common sources of data between pretrained models are the Wikipedia pages - the main source for many multilingual and non-English models - as well as parsed subsets of the Reddit, IMDB, or Twitter websites. **Kaggle** [5] is another great source with a wide variety of user-submitted datasets, though due to their much smaller size they might be more suitable for fine tuning, rather than actually pretraining.

2.4   The Open Toolkits

In Table 2, a summary of popular open source NLP tools is presented. Github repository stars are used as an indicator of popularity, while also making sure the projects are still active with recent/frequent releases.

Furthermore, **Huggingface** [57] maintains a carefully curated git repository since 2019, with many of the latest pretrained Transformers for PyTorch and Tensorflow, allowing the quick testing of any of these models and turning prototyping into a breeze.

As one can easily see, there's a plethora of options - each with its own advantages and drawbacks. For instance, AllenNLP is more research/education oriented, while spaCy is probably a better choice for production, and NLTK might be harder to use. In the end, it all comes down to the application's requirements, and the developing team's personal preferences.

Table 2. An overview of popular open source NLP tools & libraries.

	Stars	Description
spaCy [7]	19883	Python library with pretrained models and great multilingual support, not suggested for research and benchmarking
Flair [4]	10091	PyTorch library developed by Zalando, featuring the "Flair embeddings" for more efficient text vectorization
AllenNLP [1]	9794	Designed for quick prototyping and research with a variety of pretrained models
NLTK [6]	9711	One of the most recognizable libraries for NLP with some ML options - though not a common option for the task
Stanza [9]	5271	Stanford's Python library for "Many Human Languages". Can be used as an interface to CoreNLP for more features
SparkNLP [8]	2002	Built on top of Apache Spark and TensorFlow for speed and scalability, with generic and domain specific models available

2.5   Challenges

Although NLP has evolved a lot over the last years, there are still some challenges. All the unstructured context needs to be translated into meaningful defined data in order to perceive the intended meaning and entities, based on grammar and context.

Text-Mining is used to identify non-trivial patterns in text-data, starting with the Data Collection, by building a corpus, Data pre-Processing handles and manipulates the corpus using sub-processes of tokenization, normalization and substitution. Most of the raw data are not useful to define features, usually containing a lot of noise, so the ML model tends to become less effective and difficult to train. The initial goal is to go from chunks with text to a list of cleaned tokens, and then proceed to data exploration & visualization, having a better dataset prior to building the model. Unstructured data transformed into useful text, by splitting the text into sentences, words and converted into standard form, like expanding constructions and set them to their base style.

The semantic meaning of words, ambiguity, grammar, or even slang is something that needs to be handled. In the next figure we are quoting some of the main challenges of NLP.

2.5.1   Ambiguity

exists at every level in linguistics, as shown in Fig. 4. In natural language, it is common, words to have multiple meanings according the context of the sentence (contextual words). Contrariwise, different words can have the same meaning(synonyms). Irony, sarcasm and humor may use words with a specific state, but in fact imply the opposite. Some other main types of ambiguity are: Lexical ambiguity, where a single token can be presented as a verb, noun, or adjective, Semantic ambiguity refers to the conceptual situation described in a sentence having multiple interpretation [14] and Syntactic ambiguity is happening when there is a double meaning in a sentence and the syntax principles of the language are not followed. Additionally, errors, typos, slang and inconsistencies complicates the translation [32]. Many times in a sentence there is a discrepancy between the actual meaning and what is written. Pragmatics is the study dealing with this case [30].

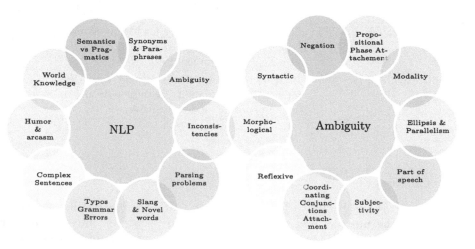

Fig. 4. NLP linguistic challenges while parsing human languages [10]

When input data is not text but speech, another ambiguity issue occurs. Phonetics and phonology refers to how tokens sound like. Phonetics deals with the vocal properties and perception, meaning how they are produced, and phonology deals with the expression in relation to each other in a language [27,34].

2.5.2   Go Big (or Maybe Not?)

With every new publication, each team enters the race for a larger number of parameters (see Fig. 5), ending up with models with billions of parameters. While that might improve the actual results, it has a huge impact on the training cost - both financially and time-wise - even if just fine tuning is required, making many of the latest architectures unusable for single GPUs, TPUs or even whole clusters of such hardware - cloud based or local - in some cases. Besides whatever environmental consequences that might have, it's also **hindering their usage in real-world scenarios**.

According to Strubell's 2019 paper [48], training a BERT base model has 1,438lbs of CO_2 emissions, about 55 times more than these of the base Transformer model. Even worse, training a Transformer model with Neural Architecture Search emits 626,155lbs of CO_2, which is roughly equal to the lifetime emissions of 5 cars. And that training has an equally large cost when cloud services are used - starting at the whopping number of $942,973 in the case of NAS Transformer training scenario. So, it would probably be more efficient if researchers focused on the hyperparameters of each model and how they affect it's performance in order to improve them, than just adding more and more parameters.

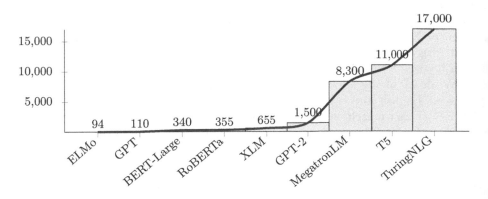

Fig. 5. Number of parameters for models over time (in millions) [45].

2.5.3   The Context Fragmentation and Text Repetition

The original Transformer architecture as well as popular deriving models has a predefined max input sequence length - in some cases defined by the model itself (e.g. 512 in BERT and GPT-1, 1024 for GPT-2) or by the overall hardware limitations (i.e. available memory). This might end up in **context loss in some marginal cases** where the input is split into segments where one's content correlates with its next or previous. Though in practice that's not usually a problem, there are some suggestions like the aforementioned Transformer XL that can help.

Furthermore, for the task of Question Answering (QA) or any other task that requires actual text generation, the output might be repetitive or even irrelevant on some occasions. Though sometimes that's due to the model itself or insufficient training, there are cases where the reason is this context fragmentation, or the lack of big/diverse enough datasets.

2.5.4   Lost in Translation

Most of today's pretrained models are focusing on the English language, with some approaches focusing on character based languages like Chinese or Arabic. Some of the very few multilingual options are sparse pretraining attempts of BERT or GPT for local languages with monolingual models as a result (see Fig. 3). The multilingual version of BERT (or **m-BERT**), trained on the Wikipedia corpora, is another such option, supporting 104 different languages. The lack of a big enough, quality, multi-lingual dataset remains though, since even in Wikipedia many languages have a significantly lower number of pages (sometimes too low to even be considered) compared to English.

The **XLM model** [28] attempts to take multilinguality one step further by adding byte pair encoding and training BERT in two languages at once, while changing the "Masked Language Modeling" objective to "Translation Language Modeling", masking tokens in either of the two languages. While that creates a multi-language model that can outperform m-BERT, it makes the data availability even harder, since now the same content is required in two languages at once. **XLM-R** [16] is an XLM successor, using a much larger dataset and improving performance at a scale that can be fine tuned for one language and then be used for cross-lingual tasks.

While all of the above do wield interesting results, there's still a huge gap between English and other languages in some tasks like QA. For instance, a F1/EM (Exact match) score of 80.6/67.8 in English becomes 68.5/53.6 in German for the MLQA question answering benchmark [16].

3   Conclusion

During the last decade there has been a tremendous progress in the field of NLP whether it's overall improvements, or task specific. It started with the vectorization revolution, with new suggestions for the most important task at the core of every NLP pipeline, ending up to the recent introduction of Transformers and transfer learning that marked the beginning of the "Golden Age".

Over this period, more and more companies started to adopt Chatbot technologies. Starting with simple pattern matching support agents, they're getting more and more sophisticated, gradually starting to adopt Machine Learning techniques and models, making them even more human-like and shifting to actual learning, away from patterns.

Machine Translation is also progressing steadily. Being one of the main tasks for the Encoder-Decoder model and their Transformer successors, automated translation applications are nowadays more accurate than ever. As the text generation models evolve, automated article generation applications start to emerge and virtual copywriters indistinguishable from humans, might soon be a reality.

But even though NLP has come this far, there are still many things to be done. Multilingual support models have still a long road ahead, and recent models will need heavy optimization and down-scaling or wider adoption of efficient hardware before they can be actually used in real-world applications. The Next Big Thing is still to be seen, and Transformers are currently leading the way.

Acknowledgements. This work was supported by the MPhil program "**Advanced Technologies in Informatics and Computers**", hosted by the Department of Computer Science, International Hellenic University, Kavala, Greece.

References

1. AllenNLP Github repository. https://github.com/allenai/allennlp. Accessed 21 Apr 2021
2. Common Crawl. https://commoncrawl.org/. Accessed 21 Apr 2021
3. Eugene goostman. http://eugenegoostman.elasticbeanstalk.com/. Accessed 21 Apr 2021
4. Flair Github repository. https://github.com/flairNLP/flair. Accessed 21 Apr 2021
5. Kaggle. https://www.kaggle.com/. Accessed 21 Apr 2021
6. NLTK Github repository. https://github.com/nltk/nltk. Accessed 21 Apr 2021
7. spaCy Github repository. https://github.com/explosion/spaCy. Accessed 21 Apr 2021
8. SparkNLP Github repository. https://github.com/JohnSnowLabs/spark-nlp. Accessed 21 Apr 2021
9. Stanza Github repository. https://github.com/stanfordnlp/stanza Accessed 21 Apr 2021
10. Baeza-Yates, R.: Challenges in the interaction of information retrieval and natural language processing. In: Gelbukh, A. (ed.) CICLing 2004. LNCS, vol. 2945, pp. 445–456. Springer, Heidelberg (2004). https://doi.org/10.1007/978-3-540-24630-5_55
11. Bahdanau, D., Cho, K., Bengio, Y.: Neural machine translation by jointly learning to align and translate. arXiv preprint arXiv:1409.0473 (2014)
12. Brown, K.: Encyclopedia of Language and Linguistics, vol. 1. Elsevier, Amsterdam (2005)
13. Brown, T.B., et al.: Language models are few-shot learners. arXiv preprint arXiv:2005.14165 (2020)
14. Bucaria, C.: Lexical and syntactic ambiguity as a source of humor: the case of newspaper headlines. Humor **17**(3), 279–309 (2004)
15. Chen, Q., Zhu, X., Ling, Z., Wei, S., Jiang, H., Inkpen, D.: Enhanced LSTM for natural language inference. arXiv preprint arXiv:1609.06038 (2016)

16. Conneau, A., et al.: Unsupervised cross-lingual representation learning at scale. arXiv preprint arXiv:1911.02116 (2019)
17. Dai, Z., Yang, Z., Yang, Y., Carbonell, J., Le, Q.V., Salakhutdinov, R.: Transformer-xl: Attentive language models beyond a fixed-length context. arXiv preprint arXiv:1901.02860 (2019)
18. Devlin, J., Chang, M.W., Lee, K., Toutanova, K.: Bert: Pre-training of deep bidirectional transformers for language understanding. arXiv preprint arXiv:1810.04805 (2018)
19. Dong, L., Wei, F., Zhou, M., Xu, K.: Question answering over freebase with multi-column convolutional neural networks. In: Proceedings of the 53rd Annual Meeting of the Association for Computational Linguistics and the 7th International Joint Conference on Natural Language Processing (Volume 1: Long Papers), pp. 260–269 (2015)
20. Epstein, R., Roberts, G., Beber, G.: Parsing the Turing test. Springer, Berlin (2009)
21. Goldberg, Y.: A primer on neural network models for natural language processing. J. Artif. Intell. Res. **57**, 345–420 (2016)
22. Hochreiter, S., Schmidhuber, J.: Long short-term memory. Neural Comput. **9**(8), 1735–1780 (1997)
23. Howard, J., Ruder, S.: Universal language model fine-tuning for text classification. arXiv preprint arXiv:1801.06146 (2018)
24. Jurafsky, D., Manning, C.: Natural language processing. Instructor **212**(998), 3482 (2012)
25. Kalchbrenner, N., Grefenstette, E., Blunsom, P.: A convolutional neural network for modelling sentences. arXiv preprint arXiv:1404.2188 (2014)
26. Kim, Y.: Convolutional neural networks for sentence classification (2014)
27. Kurdi, M.Z.: Natural language processing and computational linguistics: speech, morphology and syntax, vol. 1, Wiley, Hoboken (2016)
28. Lample, G., Conneau, A.: Cross-lingual language model pretraining. arXiv preprint arXiv:1901.07291 (2019)
29. Lan, Z., Chen, M., Goodman, S., Gimpel, K., Sharma, P., Soricut, R.: Albert: a lite bert for self-supervised learning of language representations. arXiv preprint arXiv:1909.11942 (2019)
30. Leech, G.N.: Principles of pragmatics. Routledge, London (2016)
31. Liu, Y., et al.: Roberta: A robustly optimized bert pretraining approach. arXiv preprint arXiv:1907.11692 (2019)
32. MacDonald, M.C., Pearlmutter, N.J., Seidenberg, M.S.: The lexical nature of syntactic ambiguity resolution. Psychol. Rev. **101**(4), 676 (1994)
33. Machinery, C.: Computing machinery and intelligence-am turing. Mind **59**(236), 433 (1950)
34. Mallamma, V.R., Hanumanthappa, M.: Semantical and syntactical analysis of NLP. Int. J. Comput. Sci. Inf. Technol. **5**(3), 3236–3238 (2014)
35. Mikolov, T., Chen, K., Corrado, G., Dean, J.: Efficient estimation of word representations in vector space. arXiv preprint arXiv:1301.3781 (2013)
36. Mikolov, T., Kombrink, S., Burget, L., Černockỳ, J., Khudanpur, S.: Extensions of recurrent neural network language model. In: 2011 IEEE international conference on acoustics, speech and signal processing (ICASSP), pp. 5528–5531. IEEE (2011)
37. Mikolov, T., Sutskever, I., Chen, K., Corrado, G., Dean, J.: Distributed representations of words and phrases and their compositionality. arXiv preprint arXiv:1310.4546 (2013)

38. Otter, D.W., Medina, J.R., Kalita, J.K.: A survey of the usages of deep learning for natural language processing. IEEE Trans. Neural Netw. Learn. Syst. **32**, 604–624 (2020)
39. Pennington, J., Socher, R., Manning, C.D.: Glove: Global vectors for word representation. In: Proceedings of the 2014 Conference on Empirical Methods in Natural Language Processing (EMNLP), pp. 1532–1543 (2014)
40. Peters, M.E., et al.: Deep contextualized word representations. arXiv preprint arXiv:1802.05365 (2018)
41. Pullum, G.: Philosophy of linguistics. The Cambridge Companion to History of Philosophy **2015**, (1945)
42. Radford, A., Narasimhan, K., Salimans, T., Sutskever, I.: Improving language understanding by generative pre-training (2018)
43. Radford, A., Wu, J., Child, R., Luan, D., Amodei, D., Sutskever, I.: Language models are unsupervised multitask learners. OpenAI blog **1**(8), 9 (2019)
44. Saenz, A.: Cleverbot chat engine is learning from the internet to talk like a human. Singularity Hub, Accessed 3 June 2021. https://singularityhub.com/2010/01/13/cleverbot-chat-engine-is-learning-from-the-internet-to-talk-like-a-human/
45. Sanh, V., Debut, L., Chaumond, J., Wolf, T.: Distilbert, a distilled version of bert: smaller, faster, cheaper and lighter. arXiv preprint arXiv:1910.01108 (2019)
46. Sarlin, P.E., DeTone, D., Malisiewicz, T., Rabinovich, A.: Superglue: Learning feature matching with graph neural networks. In: Proceedings of the IEEE/CVF Conference on Computer vision and Pattern Recognition, pp. 4938–4947 (2020)
47. Saygin, A.P., Cicekli, I., Akman, V.: Turing test: 50 years later. Minds Mach. **10**(4), 463–518 (2000)
48. Strubell, E., Ganesh, A., McCallum, A.: Energy and policy considerations for deep learning in nlp. arXiv preprint arXiv:1906.02243 (2019)
49. Sun, Y., et al.: Ernie: Enhanced representation through knowledge integration. arXiv preprint arXiv:1904.09223 (2019)
50. Sun, Y., et al.: Ernie 2.0: A continual pre-training framework for language understanding. In: Proceedings of the AAAI Conference on Artificial Intelligence, vol. 34, pp. 8968–8975 (2020)
51. Sutskever, I., Vinyals, O., Le, Q.V.: Sequence to sequence learning with neural networks. arXiv preprint arXiv:1409.3215 (2014)
52. Upadhyay, S., Chang, K.W., Taddy, M., Kalai, A., Zou, J.: Beyond bilingual: Multi-sense word embeddings using multilingual context. arXiv preprint arXiv:1706.08160 (2017)
53. Vaswani, A., et al.: Attention is all you need. arXiv preprint arXiv:1706.03762 (2017)
54. von Ahn, L., Blum, M., Hopper, N.J., Langford, J.: CAPTCHA: using hard AI problems for security. In: Biham, E. (ed.) EUROCRYPT 2003. LNCS, vol. 2656, pp. 294–311. Springer, Heidelberg (2003). https://doi.org/10.1007/3-540-39200-9_18
55. Wang, A., Singh, A., Michael, J., Hill, F., Levy, O., Bowman, S.R.: Glue: A multitask benchmark and analysis platform for natural language understanding. arXiv preprint arXiv:1804.07461 (2018)
56. Weizenbaum, J.: Eliza-a computer program for the study of natural language communication between man and machine. Commun. ACM **9**(1), 36–45 (1966)
57. Wolf, T., et al.: Huggingface's transformers: State-of-the-art natural language processing. arXiv preprint arXiv:1910.03771 (2019)

58. Yang, Z., Dai, Z., Yang, Y., Carbonell, J., Salakhutdinov, R., Le, Q.V.: Xlnet: Generalized autoregressive pretraining for language understanding. arXiv preprint arXiv:1906.08237 (2019)
59. Yin, W., Kann, K., Yu, M., Schütze, H.: Comparative study of CNN and RNN for natural language processing. arXiv preprint arXiv:1702.01923 (2017)
60. Young, T., Hazarika, D., Poria, S., Cambria, E.: Recent trends in deep learning based natural language processing. IEEE Comput. Intell. Mag. **13**(3), 55–75 (2018)

SemAI: A Novel Approach for Achieving Enhanced Semantic Interoperability in Public Policies

George Manias[✉], Argyro Mavrogiorgou, Athanasios Kiourtis[✉], and Dimosthenis Kyriazis

University of Piraeus, Piraeus, Greece
{gmanias,margy,kiourtis,dimos}@unipi.gr

Abstract. One of the key elements in several application domains, such as policy making, addresses the scope of achieving and dealing with the very different formats, models and languages of data. The amount of data to be processed and analyzed in modern governments, organizations and businesses is staggering, thus Big Data analysis is the mean that helps organizations to harness their data and to identify new opportunities. Big Data are characterized by divergent data coming from various and heterogeneous sources and in different types, formats, and timeframes. Data interoperability addresses the ability of modern systems and mechanisms that create, exchange and consume data to have clear, shared expectations for the context, information and value of these divergent data. To this end, interoperability appears as the mean for accomplishing the interlinking of information, systems, applications and ways of working with the wealth of data. To address this challenge, in this paper a generalized and novel Enhanced Semantic Interoperability approach is proposed, the SemAI. This approach primarily focuses on the phases of the translation, the processing, the annotation, the mapping, as well as the transformation of the collected data, which have major impact on the successful aggregation, analysis, and exploitation of data across the whole policy making lifecycle. The presented prototype and its required subcomponents associated with this approach provide an example of the proposed hybrid and holistic mechanism, verifying its possible extensive application and adoption in various policy making scenarios.

Keywords: Semantic Interoperability · Neural Machine Translation · Semantic Web · NLP · Policy Making

1 Introduction

Data have long been a critical asset for organizations, businesses, and governments and their analysis is of major importance for every stakeholder in order to be able to handle and extract value and knowledge from these data. The advances in the fields of IoT, cloud-computing, edge-computing and mobile-computing have led to the rapidly increasing volume and complexity of data, thus the concept and term of Big Data has

© IFIP International Federation for Information Processing 2021
Published by Springer Nature Switzerland AG 2021
I. Maglogiannis et al. (Eds.): AIAI 2021, IFIP AICT 627, pp. 687–699, 2021.
https://doi.org/10.1007/978-3-030-79150-6_54

experienced an enormous interest and usability over the last decade. The spectacular growth in the creation, storage, sharing and consumption of data during the last decade indicates the need for modern organizations to fuse advanced analytical techniques with Big Data in order to deal with them and to get significant value from them. Hence, Big Data and analysis of them can enable companies, organizations, and governments to increase operational efficiencies, identify business risks, predict new business opportunities, reduce costs and to provide added value and innovative strategies and mechanisms across their whole policy lifecycle and their policy making techniques. A recent survey has estimated the global market for Big Data at US$70.5 Billion in the year 2020, which is further projected to reach the size of US$86.1 Billion by 2024, growing at a CAGR of 5.25% [1].

Moreover, the term of Big Data defines a two-fold meaning in these data. In one hand it describes a change in the quality and type of data that organizations dispose of, which has potential impacts throughout the entire policy lifecycle. While, in the other hand it describes a massive volume of both structured and unstructured data that is so huge and complicated in order to be processed using traditional database and software techniques [2]. On top of this, unstructured data can be defined as data that do not comfort in predefined data models and traditional structures that can be stored in relational databases. Data generated by conversations, opinions, texts or posts on modern social networks are such type of unstructured data and their main characteristic is that they include information that is not arranged according to a predefined data model or schema. Therefore, these types of data are usually difficult to manage, and as a result analyzing, aggregating, and correlating them in order to extract valuable information and knowledge is a challenging task. Hence, deriving value and knowledge from this type of data based on the analysis of their semantics, meanings and syntactic is of major importance [3]. Data interoperability is the ability to merge data without losing meaning and is realized as a process of identifying the structural, syntactical, and semantic similarity of data and datasets and turn them into interoperable domain-agnostic ones. In practice, data are said to be interoperable when they can be easily reused and processed in different applications, allowing different information systems to work together and share data and knowledge. Hence, Semantic Interoperability is a key enabler for the policy makers in order to enhance the exploitation of Big Data and to better understand data, by extracting and taking into account parameters and information they were not aware of, thus creating efficient and effective policies in terms of good governance. The latter demonstrates the need for the modern stakeholders to implement techniques, mechanisms, and applications that focus their operations on the concept of data interoperability and more specific on Semantic Interoperability [4], for increasing their performance and enhance their entire policy making approach.

At the same time, the volume and continuous growth of the produced data, whether in the form of real-time data or stored data, in various relational and non-relational databases, has led the scientific and business communities to develop sophisticated Big Data applications based on the utilization of techniques and methods from the field of Artificial Intelligence (AI) [5]. Undoubtedly, progress in making the computer systems more human-friendly, requires the inclusion of Natural Language Processing (NLP) techniques, a subfield of the modern area of AI, as integral means of a wider communication interface. NLP leverages linguistics and computer science to make human language intelligible to machines. Therefore, NLP has been used in several applications and domains to provide enhanced approaches for generating and understanding the natural languages of humans. Speech recognition, topic detection, opinion analysis, and behavior analysis are only a few of such applications and approaches [6]. However, it can be used in concert with text mining to provide policy makers with new filtering systems and more comprehensive analysis tools [7]. In addition, NLP can be utilized as an aide to extract entities and to develop controlled vocabularies, especially enterprise schema that represent classification of a proprietary content set, which can be further utilized for creating proper ontologies [8]. To this end, an approach is being proposed in this paper which utilizes NLP and other AI techniques and tools, such as Neural Networks, and integrates them with Semantic Web technologies, such as controlled vocabularies and ontologies, for achieving Enhanced Semantic Interoperability.

The rest of the paper is organized as follows. Section 2 introduces background knowledge and information from the domain of interoperability in the policy making sector, as well as the related work that has been implemented in the fields of Semantic Interoperability, focused on the utilization of Semantic Web and NLP technologies. Moreover, Sect. 3 presents the overall methodology and the proposed holistic mechanism for achieving Enhanced Semantic Interoperability based on a hybrid mechanism which couples the utilization of advanced NLP tasks, such as Neural Machine Translation (NMT) and Named Entity Recognition (NER), along with Semantic Web technologies and approaches, such as controlled vocabularies, Resource Description Framework schemas (RDFs)[1], SPARQL[2], and ontologies. Finally, Sect. 4 concludes the paper and states the future work.

2 Related Work

2.1 Background

Nowadays, policy makers publish an increasing amount of their data on the Web in an effort with double fold meaning. In one hand, to comply with the emerging Open Data movement and in the other hand in order to optimize and improve their policy management and making lifecycle. A key to realizing Open Data and providing advanced open policies is the ability to merge divergent data and datasets coming in the majority of the cases from heterogeneous data sources and in several formats. Moreover, linking new data sources with established data sources is another one key factor for providing and improving policy making procedure. Hence, interoperability is the key "back office" element across the whole policy making lifecycle and Open Data semantics and the mean which can enable policy makers to monitor and improve their performance and trust levels [9].

On top of this, achieving true interoperability entails different representations, purposes, and syntaxes and will enable improved access to assets, records, datasets,

---

[1] https://www.w3.org/2001/sw/wiki/RDFS

[2] https://www.w3.org/TR/rdf-sparql-query/

and policies. The European Commission, through their program ISA[2] has defined the European Interoperability Framework (EIF) which defines interoperability across four layers: (i) organizational interoperability, (ii) semantic interoperability, (iii) technical interoperability and (iv) legal interoperability [10]. More specifically:

- **Organizational Interoperability**. Ensures public administrations align their processes, responsibilities and expectations to achieve commonly agreed and mutually beneficial goals. Moreover, it aims at addressing the requirements of the end-users by making services and policies available and easily identifiable.
- **Semantic Interoperability**. Ensures that the precise format and meaning of exchanged data and information is preserved and understood throughout by any other application that was not initially developed for this purpose.
- **Technical Interoperability**. Covers the technical issues of linking computer systems and services and includes key aspects such as open interfaces, interconnection services, data integration, data exchange, accessibility and security services.
- **Legal Interoperability**. Ensures that organizations operating under different legal frameworks, policies and strategies are able to work together and in compliance with different laws and regulations.

Hence, it is easily understandable that Semantic Interoperability is the aspect of interoperability which enables systems to combine received information with other information resources and to process it in a meaningful manner, therefore it is a prerequisite for the frontend multilingual delivery of services to the user. To this end, achieving meaningful Semantic Interoperability of data from heterogenous sources is a challenging issue for policy makers, as it is a complex procedure since it covers both semantic and syntactic aspects. The semantic aspect refers to the meaning of data elements and the relationship between them. It includes developing vocabularies, standards, models and schemas to describe data exchanges and ensures that data elements are understood in the same way by all communicating parties and systems. The syntactic aspect refers to describing the exact format of the information to be exchanged in terms of grammar and format. Agreements on reference data, in the form of controlled vocabularies, ontologies, and reusable data models are key prerequisites for achieving Semantic Interoperability. To this end, Semantic Interoperability can offer a way of enriching data with context and meaning and to extract semantic knowledge and good quality information from the data, in order to achieve enhanced understanding of the data, hence better data-driven policy making.

2.2 Semantic Interoperability Approaches

Currently, a wide range of data representation standards and Semantic Interoperability approaches in various domains have emerged as a means of enabling data interoperability and data exchange between different systems. In the recent years many approaches, standards, ontologies and vocabularies have been proposed as means of achieving various tasks of Semantic Interoperability between heterogeneous and independent datasets. One of the first approaches for addressing the issue of Semantic Interoperability was conducted in the scopes of a project in the archaeological domain, which highlights the use of RDFs to achieve Semantic Interoperability across datasets by extracting and exposing archaeological datasets (and thesauri) in a common RDF framework assisted by a semi-automatic custom mapping tool [11]. Moreover, a recent research focused on implementing a vocabulary (i.e. VoIDext) to formally describe virtual links in order to enable Semantic Interoperability among different datasets [12]. By defining virtual links with VoIDext RDF schema and by providing a set of SPARQL query templates to retrieve them, the research team achieved to facilitate the writing of federated queries and knowledge discovery among federated datasets. In addition, a relevant research exploited semantic similarities between datasets and proposed a method for determining Semantic Interoperability by introducing three metrics to express it between two datasets: the identifier interoperability, the relevance and the number of conflicts [13]. More recently, several approaches were introduced in the sector of IoT where the plethora of divergent datasets coming from heterogeneous sources emerges the issue of achieving high performances of Semantic Interoperability. These approaches mainly focused their operations and procedures on the modeling of a set of ontologies that describe devices and establish Semantic Interoperability between heterogeneous IoT platforms [14, 15]. Moreover, another approach in the domain of IoT introduced a Lightweight Model for Semantic annotation of Big Data using heterogeneous devices in IoT to provide data annotations. To this end, RDF and SPARQL technologies from the domain of Semantic Web were utilized in order to enhance the Semantic Interoperability of the examined datasets and to extract added value and information from them [16]. Another commonly used technology for achieving and enhancing interoperability is the JSON for Linking Data[3] (JSON-LD) format, that has been a W3C recommendation since 2014 to promote interoperability among JSON-based web services. The latter has been utilized in the scopes of a research in the biological sector, which highlights the usage of a JSON-LD system by providing a standard way to add semantic context to the existing JSON data structure, for the purpose of enhancing the interoperability between APIs and data [17]. In addition, a recent research introduced the SEMPROP approach which entails automatically discovering links between datasets through a semantic matcher which leverages Word Embeddings and other components that find links based on syntactic and semantic similarities [18]. Finally, in the healthcare domain, an advanced Semantic Interoperability technique was introduced with emphasis on the utilization of Structural and Ontology Mapping services along with Terminology Linking services in order to transform the clinical information into interoperable and processable data using eHealth standards and terminologies [19].

The above introduced approaches provide the means for common representation of domain specific datasets and the means for achieving Semantic Interoperability across diverse databases and datasets. However, these approaches are insufficient for delivering a holistic mechanism for achieving Enhanced Semantic Interoperability as they lack Semantic Interoperability across datasets from different domains. Effective policy making indicates explicit rules for communication and means for the integration of heterogeneous systems and information resources. Moreover, the above presented approaches do not consider the emerging issue of multilingualism and language-independence. In modern multicultural and multilingual environments like European Union, policy making is

---

[3] http://json-ld.org.

a complex and multilayered procedure of organizations, people, languages, information systems, information structures, rules, processes, and practices. Hence, the needs and trends in modern societies are increasingly demonstrating the need for creating multilingual and interoperable solutions and techniques that will operate in a wider and language-independent context. To this end, NMT should obtain full and effective utilization in modern interoperability systems.

3   Proposed Approach

As presented in the above section many frameworks and approaches have accomplished to provide a level of Semantic Interoperability in the data. In contrary to these introduced approaches, which focused their usability on specific domains, the proposed approach seeks to enhance Semantic Interoperability and to address the issues and lack of Semantic Interoperability across datasets from different domains and the lack of multilingualism and language-independence. Hence, SemAI seeks to address these issues based on technologies from the field of Semantic Web, such as linked data technologies (e.g. JSON-LD and RDF), standards-based ontologies and controlled vocabularies, coupled with the utilization of advanced AI and NLP tasks, such as NMT and Topic Detection. The main goal of this hybrid mechanism is to design and implement a holistic semantic layer that will address data heterogeneity. To this end, this hybrid approach aims to enhance both semantic and syntactic interoperability of data based on the aggregation, correlation, and transformation of incoming data according to the defined schemas and models. The knowledge that will be derived from these processes, shaped in a machine-readable way, can be used latter from other tools for providing Big Data analytics, i.e. Sentiment Analysis etc.

SemAI hybrid mechanism seeks to address the need for interpretable and meaningful data by providing a holistic and multi-layered mechanism from the very beginning of the data lifecycle. Most machine learning algorithms work well either with text or with structured data, but those two types of data are rarely combined to serve as a whole. Semantic web is based on machine understandable languages (RDF, OWL, JSON-LD) and related protocols (SPARQL, Linked Data, etc.), while on the other hand NLP tasks and services focuses on understanding natural languages and raw texts. To this end, the combination of Semantic Web Technologies and NLP tasks will provide a state-of-the-art approach for achieving semantic and syntactic interoperability and will enhance the ability of the SemAI mechanism to combine structured and unstructured data in multiple ways. For example, the utilization of Named Entity Recognition (NER), one of the most widely used tasks of NLP, coupled with the utilization of text mining methods based on semantic knowledge graphs will enhance the Semantic Interoperability and the final linking of divergent data and datasets. To this end, this integrated and hybrid approach will ultimately lead to a powerful and more Enhanced Semantic Interoperability. On top of this, linked data based on W3C Standards can be served as an enterprise-wide data platform and can help to provide training data for machine learning in a more cost-efficient way. The latter further enables the linking of data even across heterogeneous data sources to provide data objects as training datasets which are composed of information from structured and unstructured data at the same time. To this end, instead of generating datasets per application or use case, high-quality data can be extracted from a knowledge graph. Through this standards-based approach, also internal data and external data can be automatically linked and can be used as rich datasets for any machine learning task. Finally, the utilization of SemAI, in other words the combination of NLP and Semantic Web technologies, will provide the capability of dealing with a mixture of structured and unstructured data that is not possible using traditional, relational tools.

To this end, the hybrid SemAI mechanism incorporates and integrates three different subcomponents: the NMT component, the Semantic & Syntactic Analysis with NLP component, and the Ontology Mapping component, as presented in the below figure (see Fig. 1). One of the preliminary steps of this mechanism is to deal with the very different languages of incoming data. Hence, a NMT component is the first phase and subcomponent that is introduced and will be invoked in this hybrid mechanism, in order to translate data derived in divergent languages into a common language, e.g. English. In next phases, SemAI seeks to identify relevant, publicly available, and widely used classifications and vocabularies, such as the Core Person Vocabulary provided by DCAT Application Profile for Data Portals in Europe (DCAT-AP), that can be reused to codify and populate the content of dimensions, attributes, and measures in the given datasets [20]. Hence, this mechanism aims to adopt standard vocabularies and classifications early on, starting at the design phase of any new data collection, processing or dissemination system. Through the utilization of advanced NLP techniques and tools, such as Text Classification, NER, and Topic Detection, it is feasible to identify and classify same entities, their metadata and relationships from different datasets and sources and finally create cross-domain vocabularies in order to identify every new incoming entity. Likewise, in order to create and enhance semantic interoperability between classifications and vocabularies this component seeks to engage in structural and semantic harmonization efforts, mapping cross-domain terminology used to designate measures and dimensions to commonly used, standard vocabularies and taxonomies with final aim to provide an enhanced Ontology Mapping component. Thus, by implementing a "JSON-LD context" to add semantic annotations to SemAI mechanism's output, the system will be able to automatically integrate data from different sources by replacing the context-depended keys in the JSON output with URIs pointing to semantic vocabularies, that will be used to represent and link the data [17]. Hence, added information can be expressed by connecting data piece by piece and link by link, allows for any resource (people, policies, articles, search queries etc.) to be identified, disambiguated, and meaningfully interlinked.

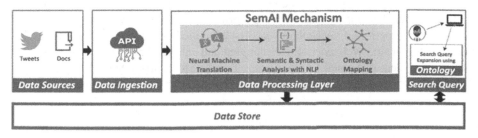

Fig. 1. SemAI Mechanism

3.1 Neural Machine Translation (NMT)

Nowadays, the overarching goal of NLP is to enable communication between humans and computers without resorting to memorable and complex processes. Modern chatbots, automatic translation engines, search engines and more are included in these applications [21]. However, the needs and trends of modern intercultural and multilingual societies are increasingly demonstrating the need for creating multilingual and language-independent solutions and techniques that will operate in a wider context. Thus, the techniques of NMT will obtain full and effective utilization in the scopes of this proposed approach. Recent advances in the field of NMT have proven to be competitive with the encoder-decoder architecture based on the utilization of Recurrent Neural Networks (RNNs), which encode the length of the variable input into unstable dimensions vector and use its encoding to then decode the desired output sequence. Hence, NMT models are often based on the seq2seq architecture [22], which is an encoder-decoder architecture and consists of two Deep Neural Networks: the encoder and the decoder [23]. The input to the encoder is the sentence in the original language, while the input to the decoder is the sentence in the translated language with a start-of-sentence token. The output is the actual target sentence with an end-of-sentence token.

Moreover, new advancements in the field of NMT introduce and propose the utilization of Transformers to solve the Machine Translation problem that relies mostly on the attention mechanism to draw the dependencies between the language models [24]. The attention mechanism enables the decoder to look backward on the whole input sequence and selectively extract the information it needs during processing. Like RNNs, the Transformer is an architecture for transforming one sequence into another using the encoder-decoder mechanism, but it differs from the previous existing seq2seq models because it does not imply any Recurrent Network (GRUs, LSTMs, etc.). Yet, unlike the RNNs the Transformer stacks several identical self-attention based layers instead of recurrent units for better parallelization, while it also handles the entire input sequence in at once and does not iterate word by word [25, 26].

Both above introduced approaches and technologies will be utilized and their performance and overall functionality will be evaluated under the scopes of SemAI hybrid mechanism.

3.2 Semantic & Syntactic Analysis with NLP

To exploit what the SemAI offers, translated data first needs to be structured and annotated. To this end, in the second subcomponent, the Semantic & Syntactic Analysis with NLP, translated data will be analyzed, transformed and annotated with appropriate URI metadata and controlled vocabularies will be identified and designed through the utilization of Semantic Web technologies coupled and enhanced by the utilization of NLP techniques, such as Named Entity Recognition (NER), Part-of-Speech Tagging etc., through the utilization of advanced and multilingual NLP tools such as spaCy[4], NLTK[5]

---

[4] https://spacy.io/
[5] https://www.nltk.org/

and CoreNLP[6]. These coupled functionalities are being utilized into three different layers/steps of the overall subcomponent as shown in the next figure (see Fig. 2). In next phases and steps, semantic and syntactic URI annotated data will be interlinked through the task of Ontology Mapping. The main objectives of this second subcomponent of SemAI mechanism is the identification and recognition of entities, which will be further used for interconnection and interlinking with widely used knowledge bases. Moreover, classifying named entities found in translated data into pre-defined categories, such as persons, places, organizations, dates etc., will make feasible the identification, design and utilization of proper widely used and controlled vocabularies and standards. In addition, the subtask of Named Entities Linking (NEL) will allow to annotate translated data with URIs pointing into corresponding widely used and known knowledge databases, such as Wikidata and DBpedia, while an automatic topic identification and dataset classification task will safeguard that datasets topic of interest are proper identified. Proper topic analysis should be facilitated in order to organize and fully understand the large collections of text data and the correlations among them.

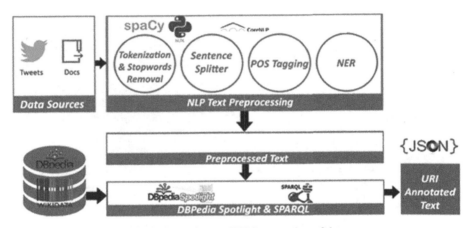

Fig. 2. Metadata and URI annotation of data

3.3 Ontology Mapping

The overall SemAI mechanism will be further enhanced and completed in the next step by the utilization of Ontology Mapping subcomponent, where an Ontology and Structuring Mapping service will be utilized in order to interlink not only URI annotated data with proper ontologies, but also to interlink and correlate datasets among them. Successful annotation, transformation and mapping of data and corresponding ontologies in terms of semantic and syntactic interoperability of data is one of the key elements of SemAI mechanism. To this end, one of the main objectives of the Ontology Mapping subcomponent is to save correlated, annotated and interoperable data in JSON-LD format

---

[6] https://stanfordnlp.github.io/CoreNLP/

and as linked ontologies. Hence, it will be feasible the storage of semantic facts and the support of the corresponding data schema models. Moreover, this subcomponent seeks to map concepts, classes, and semantics defined in different ontologies and datasets and to achieve transformation compatibility through extracted metadata. In addition, a data modelling subtask by standard metadata schemas will be defined in order to specify the metadata elements that should accompany a dataset within a domain. To this end, semantic models for physical entities/devices (i.e. sensors related to different policy sectors) and online platforms (e.g. social media) will be identified. These models will be based on a set of transversal and domain-specific ontologies and could provide a foundation for high-level Semantic Interoperability and rich semantic annotations across policy sectors, online systems and platforms. As shown in the below figure (see Fig. 3) there are several levels of structuring before reaching proper ontologies. At the beginning, the annotation and creation of metadata representations through the utilization of JSON-LD technology is a key point. Afterwards, vocabularies and taxonomies expressed by RDFs are created and in the final step they are correlated and interlinked into ontologies with high semantic expressivity through the utilization of OWL technology.

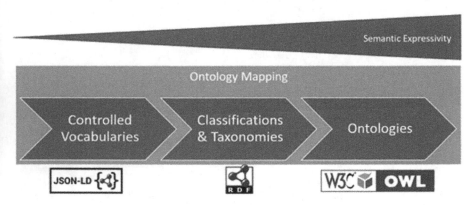

Fig. 3. Ontology mapping subcomponent in SemAI

On top of this, ontologies are central to the SemAI as they allow applications to agree on the terms that they use when communicating and they enable the correlation of divergent data and datasets from various sources. To this end, the utilization of ontologies under the scope of SemAI facilitates communication by providing precise notions that can be used to compose messages (queries, statements) about the policy making domain. In stakeholders and user level, the ontology helps to understand messages by providing the correct interpretation context. Thus, ontologies, if shared among stakeholders, may improve system interoperability across Information Systems (ISs) in different organizations and domains. The overall approach that will be followed brings together techniques in modeling, computation linguistics, information retrieval and agent communication in order to provide a semi-automatic mapping method and a prototype mapping system that support the process of Ontology Mapping for the purpose of improving and enhancing Semantic Interoperability during the whole data and policy lifecycle.

The novelty of the proposed Ontology Mapping subcomponent is not solely the use of formal application ontologies as an initial mechanism to achieve meaningful Semantic Interoperability, but moreover the utilization of divergent domain ontologies to support the formal application ontologies mapping process, integrated into an architectural framework.

4 Conclusion

In this paper, a novel approach for achieving Enhanced Semantic Interoperability in the domain of policy making was introduced, the SemAI. SemAI introduces a multi-layer and hybrid mechanism for Semantic Interoperability across diverse policy related datasets, which will facilitate Semantic Interoperability across related datasets both within a single domain and across different policy making domains. This requirement relates to local-regional public administrations and business domain, but it also goes beyond the national borders as it also seeks to invoke a language-independent hybrid mechanism. Moreover, IT systems and applications interoperability, sharing and re-use, and interlinking of information and policies, within and between domains are essential factors for the delivery of high quality, innovative, and seamless policies. Under this framework, SemAI and its required steps and subcomponents were presented to ease its adoption at data-driven policy making domain. Achieving high levels of Semantic Interoperability in the data can help organizations and businesses to turn their data into valuable information, add extra value and knowledge to them and finally achieve enhanced policy making through the combination and correlation of several data, datasets, and policies. The proposed approach in this paper is established as a service which can be adopted and integrated into different policy making scenarios and comprises an effort to deal with the Semantic Interoperability. The latter will be implemented and further evaluated in the context of a holistic environment for data-driven policy making as realized by the PolicyCLOUD project [27], where data from four different languages (Bulgarian, Italian, Spanish and English) and from various policymakers and domains of interests, such as public authorities, businesses, and organizations participate with the aim of turning raw data into valuable and actionable knowledge towards efficient policy making.

Acknowledgment. The research leading to the results presented in this paper has received funding from the European Union's funded Project PolicyCLOUD under grant agreement no 870675.

References

1. Big Data – Global Market Trajectory & Analytics, https://www.researchandmarkets.com/reports/2228010/big_data_global_market_trajectory_and_analytics. Accessed 1 March 2021
2. Chavan, V., Phursule, R.N.: Survey paper on big data. Int. J. Comput. Sci. Inf. Technol **5**(6), 7932–7939 (2014)
3. Mosley, M., Brackett, M.H., Earley, S., Henderson, D.: DAMA Guide to the Data Management Body of Knowledge. Technics Publications (2010)
4. Motta, G., Puccinelli, R., Reggiani, L., Saccone, M.: Extracting value from grey literature: processes and technologies for aggregating and analyzing the hidden «big data» treasure of organizations. Grey J. **12**(1), 15–25 (2016)

5. Yaqoob, I., et al.: Big data: from beginning to future. Int. J. Inf. Manage. **36**(6), 1231–1247 (2016)
6. Bahja, M.: Natural language processing applications in business. In: E-Business. IntechOpen (2020)
7. Kao, A., Poteet, S.R.: Natural language processing and text mining. Springer Science & Business Media (2007)
8. Zheng, S., Lu, J.J., Ghasemzadeh, N., Hayek, S.S., Quyyumi, A.A., Wang, F.: Effective information extraction framework for heterogeneous clinical reports using online machine learning and controlled vocabularies. JMIR Med. Inform. **5**(2), e12 (2017)
9. Solanas, A., Patsakis, C., Conti, M., Vlachos, I.S., Ramos, V., Falcone, F., et al.: Smart health: a context-aware health paradigm within smart cities. IEEE Commun. Mag. **52**(8), 74–81 (2014)
10. New European Interoperability Framework, https://ec.europa.eu/isa2/sites/isa/files/eif_bro chure_final.pdf. Accessed 11 March 2021
11. Binding, C., May, K., Tudhope, D.: Semantic Interoperability in Archaeological Datasets: Data Mapping and Extraction Via the CIDOC CRM. In: Christensen-Dalsgaard, B., Castelli, D., Ammitzbøll Jurik, B., Lippincott, J. (eds.) ECDL 2008. LNCS, vol. 5173, pp. 280–290. Springer, Heidelberg (2008). https://doi.org/10.1007/978-3-540-87599-4_30
12. Mendes de Farias, T., Stockinger, K., Dessimoz, C.: VoIDext: Vocabulary and Patterns for Enhancing Interoperable Datasets with Virtual Links. In: Panetto, H., Debruyne, C., Hepp, M., Lewis, D., Ardagna, C.A., Meersman, R. (eds.) OTM 2019. LNCS, vol. 11877, pp. 607–625. Springer, Cham (2019). https://doi.org/10.1007/978-3-030-33246-4_38
13. Colpaert, P., Van Compernolle, M., De. Vocht, L., Dimou, A., Vander Sande, M., Verborgh, R., et al.: Quantifying the interoperability of open government datasets. Computer **47**(10), 50–56 (2014)
14. Ganzha, M., Paprzycki, M., Pawłowski, W., Szmeja, P., Wasielewska, K.: Semantic inter-operability in the internet of things: an overview from the INTER-IoT perspective. J. Netw. Comput. Appl. **81**, 111–124 (2017)
15. Bajaj, G., Agarwal, R., Singh, P., Georgantas, N., Issarny, V. A study of existing ontologies in the IoT-domain. arXiv preprint arXiv:1707.00112 (2017)
16. Ullah, F., Habib, M.A., Farhan, M., Khalid, S., Durrani, M.Y., Jabbar, S.: Semantic interoper-ability for big-data in heterogeneous IoT infrastructure for healthcare. Sustain. Urban Areas **34**, 90–96 (2017)
17. Xin, J., et al.: Cross-linking BioThings APIs through JSON-LD to facilitate knowledge exploration. BMC Bioinform. **19**(1), 1–7 (2018)
18. Fernandez, R.C., et al: Seeping semantics: linking datasets using word embeddings for data discovery. In: 2018 IEEE 34th International Conference on Data Engineering (ICDE), pp. 989–1000. IEEE (2018)
19. Kiourtis, A., Mavrogiorgou, A., Menychtas, A., Maglogiannis, I., Kyriazis, D.: Structurally mapping healthcare data to HL7 FHIR through ontology alignment. J. Med. Syst. **43**(3), 62 (2019)
20. DCAT Application profile for data portals in Europe (DCAT-AP), https://op.europa.eu/en/web/eu-vocabularies/dcat-ap. Accessed 11 March 2021
21. Bulut, Y.E.: AI for Data Science: Artificial Intelligence Frameworks and Functionality for DEEP Learning, Optimization, and Beyond. Technics Publications (2018)
22. Tiwari, G., Sharma, A., Sahotra, A., Kapoor, R.: English-Hindi neural machine translation-LSTM Seq2Seq and ConvS2S. In: 2020 International Conference on Communication and Signal Processing (ICCSP), pp. 871–875. IEEE (2020)
23. Yang, M., Liu, S., Chen, K., Zhang, H., Zhao, E., Zhao, T.: A hierarchical clustering approach to fuzzy semantic representation of rare words in neural machine translation. IEEE Trans. Fuzzy Syst. **28**(5), 992–1002 (2020)

24. Bahar, P., Makarov, N., Ney, H.: Investigation of transformer-based latent attention models for neural machine translation. In: Proceedings of the 14th Conference of the Association for Machine Translation in the Americas (AMTA 2020), pp. 7–20 (2020)
25. Pramodya, A., Pushpananda, R., Weerasinghe, R.: a comparison of transformer, recurrent neural networks and SMT in Tamil to Sinhala MT. In: 2020 20th International Conference on Advances in ICT for Emerging Regions (ICTer), pp. 155–160. IEEE (2020)
26. Lakew, S.M., Cettolo, M., Federico, M.: A comparison of transformer and recurrent neural networks on multilingual neural machine translation. arXiv preprint arXiv:1806.06957 (2018)
27. Kyriazis, D., et al.: PolicyCLOUD: Analytics as a Service Facilitating Efficient Data-Driven Public Policy Management. In: Maglogiannis, I., Iliadis, L., Pimenidis, E. (eds.) AIAI 2020. IAICT, vol. 583, pp. 141–150. Springer, Cham (2020). https://doi.org/10.1007/978-3-030-49161-1_13

Recommendation Systems

Optimization of Multi-stakeholder Recommender Systems for Diversity and Coverage

Iordanis Koutsopoulos[1]($\boxtimes$) and Maria Halkidi[2]

[1] Department of Informatics, Athens University of Economics and Business,
Athens, Greece
jordan@aueb.gr
[2] Department of Digital Systems, University of Piraeus, Piraeus, Greece
mhalk@unipi.gr

Abstract. Multi-stakeholder recommender systems (RSs) are a major paradigm shift from current RSs because recommendations affect not only item consumers (end-users) but also item providers (owners). They also motivate the need for new performance metrics beyond recommendation quality that explicitly affect the latter. In this work, we introduce a framework for optimizing multi-stakeholder RSs under constraints on diversity and coverage. Our goal is to make recommendations to end-users while treating each item provider equally, by ensuring sufficient user base coverage and diverse profiles of users to which items are recommended. Namely, items of each provider should be recommended to a certain number of users that are also diverse enough in their preferences. The optimization objective is that the total average rating of recommended items is as close as possible to that of a baseline RS. The problem is formulated as a quadratically constrained integer program, which is NP-Hard and impractical to solve in the presence of big data and many providers. Interestingly, we show that when only the coverage constraint exists, an instance of the problem can be solved optimally in polynomial time through its Linear Programming relaxation, and this solution can be used to initialize a low-complexity heuristic algorithm. Data experiments show good performance and demonstrate the impact of these constraints on average rating of recommended items.

Keywords: Multi-stakeholder recommender systems · Optimization · Diversity · Coverage

1 Introduction

Recommender systems (RSs) provide personalized recommendations to users through web or mobile app interfaces, and they have permeated social media,

This work was supported by the CHIST-ERA grant CHIST-ERA-18-SDCDN-004, through the General Secretariat for Research and Innovation (GSRI), grant number T11EPA4-00056.

e-commerce, e-service, entertainment (e.g. music), sharing economy, and other domains. The functionality of these systems relies on data such as (*i*) explicit or implicit user feedback in the form of user records (e.g. book purchases, hotel stays, movie watches), log-on site activity (e.g. clicks, searches, item views), binary preferences (like/not like) or rating of items or services; (*ii*) items' attributes such as title, price, description; (*iii*) contextual information such as device used, location, time, and more.

These data constitute the training dataset of the RS which is provided as input to the recommendation engine to train a Machine Learning (ML) model. The model predicts preferences of users for items other than the ones that she has already experienced. A basic performance metric to optimize is the Mean Squared Error (MSE) between the predicted ratings for a specific ML model and the true ratings of the training dataset, which characterizes the quality of recommendation. A regularization term is added to the MSE error term, and the optimization of the new objective aims to avoid overfitting and increase the flexibility of the model to generalize well in unseen data.

Given the model above, a recommendation algorithm evaluates the ratings for user-item pairs that have not been rated, it selects for each user the top-L items (where $L = 5, 10, 20$) with the highest predicted ratings for that user, and it recommends them under no other constraint. Hence, items are recommended separately to each user, and the set of recommended items to one user does not affect the sets of items recommended to others.

However, more often than not, RSs are embedded in an online service platform, an online retail store or a social-media site, and there exist other entities besides end-users that are interested in recommendations. Owners, producers, providers or advertisers of recommended items may have some agreement with the recommendation engine about item promotion or about certain user outreach through recommendations, in exchange for some payment. For example, different brand chains of restaurants or hotels, editors or publishing companies of books, production and distribution companies of movies, or owners of sponsored items have paid to have the items appear in users' recommendation lists.

The terms *Two-sided markets* and *Multi-stakeholder Recommender Systems* [2] describe scenarios like the one above, where end-users (item consumers) and item providers need to be jointly taken into account when issuing recommendations. While item consumers are interested in good personalized experience through good-quality recommendations, item providers wish to receive good service by the recommendation engine as well. For example, different book publishers would like to have an adequate amount of exposure to users through recommendation. Likewise, different hosts in Airbnb would like to be represented in a fair manner in the recommendation lists of users. The consideration of the impact of the recommendation to item providers is a major paradigm shift from current RSs that focus only on rating prediction accuracy.

Our Contribution. We address the problem of *optimizing Multi-stakeholder RSs* under constraints such as diversity and coverage that are specific to such RSs. We consider the setting where each item belongs to a set (class) of items of one owner or producer. Our goal is to make the recommendation of items to end-users and treat each provider equally by ensuring sufficient user base coverage and user diversity for their recommended items. That is, each set of items must be recommended to a certain number of users that are also diverse enough in terms of user profile. For example, in the case of hotel chains, a *coverage* constraint dictates that *each* hotel chain appears in the recommendation lists of a certain minimum number (or percentage) of users. A *diversity* constraint would imply that each hotel chain should be recommended to users with sufficiently diverse profiles and tastes so as to increase hotel reach and penetration.

Our optimization objective is to recommend items to users so that the total average rating of items that are recommended to users is affected by the minimum amount, compared to the ratings of recommended items from a baseline RS, subject to maintaining sufficient diversity and coverage for each provider.

The main challenge is that these constraints on the provider side lead to a *coupling* between the sets of items to be recommended to each user, and therefore these need to be decided *jointly* for all users. For example, for multiple hotel chains and a coverage constraint, each hotel chain should appear in the recommendation lists of a certain number of users, and thus the recommendation algorithm should jointly decide on the recommendations to all users rather than separately as in conventional RSs. This makes the recommendation problem much more composite and challenging compared to state of the art, and to the best of our knowledge, this problem has not been addressed. The existence of high-dimensional data and multiple involved stakeholders further exacerbates the problem. The contributions of our work to the literature are as follows:

- We introduce the problem of optimizing Multi-stakeholder Recommender Systems subject to diversity and coverage constraints and formulate it as a quadratically constrained integer program, which is NP-Hard and impractical to solve in the presence of big data and many providers. Items to be recommended are viewed as "resources", and the framework abstracts the recommendation problem as a resource allocation one.
- We show that when only the coverage constraint exists, an instance of the problem can be solved optimally in polynomial time through its Linear Programming (LP) relaxation, and we use this solution to appropriately initialize a low-complexity heuristic algorithm.
- We perform initial experiments with the publicly available Movielens dataset, which show good performance and demonstrate the impact of coverage and diversity constraints on the achieved average rating of recommended items through our approach.

The rest of the paper is organized as follows. In Sect. 2, we present an overview of state of the art. In Sect. 3 we provide the model and some derivations and definitions that are used next in Sect. 4 to formulate and solve the problem. In Sect. 5, we present initial experimental results on publicly available datasets, and in Sect. 6 we conclude the paper. The terms "list of recommended items" and "recommendation list" refer to the set of items that are recommended to a user.

2 Related Work

Diversity, coverage and positive surprise (i.e. serendipity) are recognized as critical aspects of user Quality of Experience (QoE) in RSs, and they admit various definitions and interpretations [6]. From the point of view of the user, diversity refers to recommending diverse items to her so as to eliminate the item bubble effect. On the other hand, coverage is the number of items that appear in the lists of recommended items to all users. A broad class of techniques to address diversity and other metrics (such as coverage, serendipity) uses re-ranking [3]. In these techniques, a baseline recommendation algorithm is used to generate predicted ratings, and these are sorted in decreasing order for each user. Next, these items are re-ordered according to some further performance objective. For example, if diversity is the goal, items that are ranked lower in terms of predicted rating but differ in their profile from those in the current top-L list, are placed in that list so as to increase diversity. Likewise, if item popularity is sought in the recommendation, each item rating is re-weighted by its popularity, i.e. the number of users that have rated it, and thus the relative position of items in the recommendation list changes. The work [14] falls within that class of works and places emphasis on genre diversity and coverage for a user.

In the work [4], the authors propose system-wide diversity metrics to simultaneously achieve diversification of the categories of items that each user sees and diversification of the types of users to which each item is recommended, while maintaining high recommendation quality. In [8], diversity metrics are considered for both the items and the users, and for single-user and group recommendations. The work [5] studies the problem of identifying k products that cover maximum number of consumers so as to maximize the probability of product purchase.

Multi-stakeholder recommender systems (MSRSs) and two-sided markets have been an active research area recently, with a broad range of application areas and a promising roadmap of directions [16]. A taxonomy of multi-stakeholder RSs with respect to item providers, item consumers and their preferences as well as possible side stakeholders is given in [2]. A comprehensive survey of the area with emphasis on the recent trends of people recommendation, value-aware recommendation and fairness aspects is presented in [1]. The work in [13] formulates the problem of maximizing the rating value of recommended items subject to provider constraints as an integer programming problem that is solved using Lagrangian relaxation and subgradient methods. Coverage is studied also in [7] with the goal to find an average rating of recommended items that is as close as possible to that of a baseline RS and to balance the rating deviation from a baseline RS across users and across items.

Fairness towards item providers and consumers is an active area in MSRSs. In [11], fairness for the providers' side is addressed in the form of recommendation updates so that providers are guaranteed similar amounts of exposure to users. Fairness for both providers and consumers has also been addressed in the context of ride-hailing platforms [12], where repeated matching of providers (drivers) to consumers (ride requesters) is performed so that in the long run, similar utilities across providers and across consumers are achieved. Different notions of fairness inspired by classical economics theory are evaluated for providers and consumers of a RS in [10]. The tradeoff between providing relevant recommendations to users and guaranteeing fair representations of different music artists in users' recommendation lists is addressed in [9].

Compared to the current literature we explicitly define a novel diversity and coverage metric which give rise to non-linear and linear constraints respectively. In fact, we show that the coverage constraint helps to simplify the diversity one. Contrary to [13], we formulate the problem as a quadratically constrained integer program. We also show that if only the coverage constraint exists, an instance of the problem can be solved in polynomial time through its LP relaxation, since the constraint matrix becomes unimodular.

3   Model

We consider a set $\mathcal{I}$ of items and a set $\mathcal{U}$ of users. We assume that a baseline recommendation system (e.g. Collaborative Filtering) generates a list of recommended items $\mathcal{L}_u$ for each user u, where $|\mathcal{L}_u| = L$, with L typically taking values $1, 2, 5, 10, 20$. Denote by $\mathcal{L} = (\mathcal{L}_u : u \in \mathcal{U})$ the output of the baseline RS in terms of the list of recommended items to each user u. Let $\mathcal{U}_i$ be the subset of users to which item $i \in \mathcal{I}$ is recommended according to the baseline RS algorithm, and let $|\mathcal{U}_i|$ be its cardinality. For each user u and item i, let r_{iu} denote the predicted rating of item i for user u according to the baseline RS algorithm.

There exist C predefined item sets (classes). A set (class) stands for a different provider, for example a different book publisher if items are books, or a different production company if items are movies. Each item is assumed to belong to exactly one class. Denote by $\mathcal{C}$ the set of C classes. Let $\mathcal{I}_c$ be the set of items in class c, for $c = 1, \ldots, C$.

3.1   Deviation from Baseline Recommendations

We are interested to find a new recommendation policy with an output $\mathcal{L}' = (\mathcal{L}'_u : u \in \mathcal{U})$, where $\mathcal{L}'_u$ is the *new* list of recommended items to user u. These *new* lists of recommended items should satisfy the coverage and diversity constraints. That is, items from *each* class are recommended to a large enough number of users, and these users have diverse enough profiles. The definitions of coverage and diversity will be provided in the sequel, in Subsects. 3.2 and 3.3.

Let $\mathbf{x} = (x_{iu} : i \in \mathcal{I}, u \in \mathcal{U})$ denote this new recommendation policy, where for each item i and user u, the binary variable $x_{iu} = 1$ if item i is recommended to user u, and $x_{iu} = 0$ otherwise. Namely $x_{iu} = 1$ if $i \in \mathcal{L}'_u$, and 0 if not.

When performing the update in the list of recommended items $\mathcal{L} \to \mathcal{L}'$, we would like to minimize the cost of the impact of this change to users. For each user u, this cost is defined as the average difference between the sum of ratings of items in list $\mathcal{L}_u$ generated by the baseline RS, and the sum of ratings in the new list $\mathcal{L}'_u$. For example, consider a user u and $|\mathcal{L}_u| = 2$ so that the baseline RS recommends two items A, B with predicted ratings 4.8 and 4.6, on a scale from 1 to 5. Assume that the new recommendation list that attempts to satisfy coverage and diversity constraints comprises two items other than A, B, with predicted ratings 4.7 and 4.2 respectively. Then, the average cost incurred to the user is $\frac{1}{2}[(4.8 - 4.7) + (4.6 - 4.2)] = 0.25$.

For the entire user set $\mathcal{U}$, the total average cost is expressed as a function of policy $\mathbf{x}$ as follows:

$$\text{Cost}_{\mathcal{L} \to \mathcal{L}'}(\mathbf{x}) = \frac{1}{|\mathcal{U}|} \sum_{u \in \mathcal{U}} \frac{1}{L} \left(\sum_{i \in \mathcal{L}_u} r_{iu} - \sum_{i \in \mathcal{I}} r_{iu} x_{iu} \right) \tag{1}$$

Note that $\text{Cost}_{\mathcal{L} \to \mathcal{L}'}(\mathbf{x}) \geq 0$, for any policy $\mathbf{x}$, since the first term is always larger than the second one, because it is the result of the baseline RS which recommends to each user the L items with highest rating.

3.2   User Coverage

In an effort to treat the C providers equally, a first requirement is that the new recommendation algorithm should recommend items from each class $c \in \mathcal{C}$ to an adequate number of users i.e. make sure that items from each provider appear in the recommendation lists of enough users. This requirement is realistic and arises because of bilateral agreements between the provider and the recommendation platform.

User coverage for a class of items c can be defined in various ways, e.g. as the number of users to which items of class c are recommended, expressed as $\sum_{u \in \mathcal{U}} \min\{1, \sum_{i \in \mathcal{I}_c} x_{iu}\}$. Namely, user coverage for class c is the number of users to which at least one item of class c is recommended. If there are more than one items of class c recommended to a user u, i.e. if $\sum_{i \in \mathcal{I}_c} x_{iu} > 1$, then this user would count as one user in the coverage.

In this work, we adopt a simpler form of user coverage. For each item $i \in \mathcal{I}_c$ separately, we count the number of users to whom item i is recommended. The average per-item user coverage for items of class c is then given as

$$\overline{\text{Cov}}_c(\mathbf{x}) = \frac{1}{|\mathcal{I}_c|} \sum_{i \in \mathcal{I}_c} \sum_{u \in \mathcal{U}} x_{iu} . \tag{2}$$

Let K_c denote the constraint on the average number of times that an item of class c is assigned to a user, which is specified by the agreement between provider c and the recommendation platform. Namely, it is $\overline{\text{Cov}}_c(\mathbf{x}) = K_c$. Hence, the total number of times that an item of class c is assigned to a user is $K_c|\mathcal{I}_c|$, and K_c takes values in $[0, \dots, |\mathcal{U}|]$.

3.3   User Diversity

Another aspect of the agreement between a provider and the platform may concern user diversity. In this case, the platform should recommend the set of items $\mathcal{I}_c$ of each class (provider) c to a set of users that is as diverse as possible, in an effort to further expand item reach in the user base. For example, a book publisher may be interested in having a novel recommended to readers of diverse tastes or age groups, or an Airbnb accommodation RS may wish to recommend different accommodations owned by one host to diverse groups of users in terms of interests, and so on.

In this work, we abstract the profile similarity between a pair of users (u, v) as w_{uv}. This can be computed through *cosine similarity or the Pearson correlation coefficient* over a set of predefined features. Let d_{uv} be the *dissimilarity* between users u, v, defined as $d_{uv} = 1 - w_{uv}$, so that $0 \leq d_{uv} \leq 2$.

For items of class c, the per-item average diversity of users to which these items are recommended is

$$\text{Div}_c(\mathbf{x}) = \frac{1}{|\mathcal{I}_c|} \sum_{i \in \mathcal{I}_c} \sum_{u \in \mathcal{U}} \sum_{v \in \mathcal{U}:v \neq u} d_{uv} x_{iu} x_{iv} . \tag{3}$$

For example, consider a class with 2 items, item i_1 and i_2 and assume 3 users, u_1, u_2 and u_3. Suppose that i_1 is recommended to users u_1, u_2, and i_2 is recommended to all users u_1, u_2, u_3. Then, the average user diversity is $\frac{1}{2}(2d_{u_1 u_2} + d_{u_2 u_3} + d_{u_1 u_3})$.

We can normalize diversity by dividing with the number of pairs of users to which items of class c are assigned, which is

$$\frac{1}{2} \Big(\sum_{u \in \mathcal{U}} \sum_{i \in \mathcal{I}_c} x_{iu} \Big) \Big(\sum_{u \in \mathcal{U}} \sum_{i \in \mathcal{I}_c} x_{iu} - 1 \Big) . \tag{4}$$

E.g. in the example above, we can further divide with $\frac{1}{2} \times 5 \times 4 = 10$, where 5 is the total number of users to which an item of the class is assigned (i.e. item i_1 to users u_1, u_2, and item i_2 to users u_1, u_2, u_3).

Therefore, the average normalized diversity (per item and per-user pair) is written as

$$\overline{\text{Div}}_c(\mathbf{x}) = \frac{2}{|\mathcal{I}_c|} \frac{\sum_{i \in \mathcal{I}_c} \sum_{u \in \mathcal{U}} \sum_{v \in \mathcal{U}:v \neq u} d_{uv} x_{iu} x_{iv}}{\Big(\sum_{i \in \mathcal{I}_c} \sum_{u \in \mathcal{U}} x_{iu} \Big) \times \Big(\sum_{i \in \mathcal{I}_c} \sum_{u \in \mathcal{U}} x_{iu} - 1 \Big)} . \tag{5}$$

Because of the coverage constraint above, this is simplified to

$$\overline{\text{Div}}_c(\mathbf{x}) = 2 \times \frac{\sum_{i \in \mathcal{I}_c} \sum_{u \in \mathcal{U}} \sum_{v \in \mathcal{U}:v \neq u} d_{uv} x_{iu} x_{iv}}{K_c |\mathcal{I}_c|^2 (K_c |\mathcal{I}_c| - 1)} , \tag{6}$$

and for $K_c |\mathcal{I}_c| >> 1$, this can be approximated as

$$\overline{\text{Div}}_c(\mathbf{x}) \simeq \frac{2}{K_c^2 |\mathcal{I}_c|^3} \sum_{i \in \mathcal{I}_c} \sum_{u \in \mathcal{U}} \sum_{v \in \mathcal{U}:v \neq u} d_{uv} x_{iu} x_{iv} . \tag{7}$$

We define the constraint $\overline{\text{Div}}_c(\mathbf{x}) = D_c$, where D_c is a specified average per-item and per-user pair diversity that should be satisfied for recommendations of items of class c.

4 Problem Formulation and Solution

The objective is to generate new lists of recommended items $\{\mathcal{L}'_u\}$ for each user $u \in \mathcal{U}$ so as to minimize the cost function (1). This objective is equivalent to:

$$\max_{\mathbf{x}} \frac{1}{L|\mathcal{U}|} \sum_{u \in \mathcal{U}} \sum_{i \in \mathcal{I}} r_{iu} x_{iu} , \tag{8}$$

subject to the following constraints:

$$\sum_{c} \sum_{i \in \mathcal{I}_c} x_{iu} = L , \text{ for each user } u \tag{9}$$

$$\overline{\text{Div}}_c(\mathbf{x}) = D_c , \text{ for each provider } c , \tag{10}$$

$$\overline{\text{Cov}}_c(\mathbf{x}) = K_c , \text{ for each provider } c , \tag{11}$$

and $x_{iu} \in \{0,1\}$ for each i, u. Constraint (9) says that L items should be recommended to each user u, since $|\mathcal{L}'_u| = L$ for each u. Constraint (10) says that for each item class (provider) c, an average per-item and per-user pair user diversity D_c should be satisfied. Finally, constraint (11) says that for each provider c, the total number of times an item of class c is assigned to a user should be $K_c |\mathcal{I}_c|$, where $K_c \in [0, \ldots, |\mathcal{U}|]$. Note that $K_c/|\mathcal{U}|$ is the minimum percentage of users to which items of class c are recommended.

We refer to problem (8)–(11) as problem (**P**). This is a Quadratically constrained Integer Program (QCIP), since the objective is linear in $\mathbf{x}$ and constraints (10) are quadratic in $\mathbf{x}$. This problem is NP-Hard.

4.1 An Interesting Special Case

Consider problem (**P**) without the diversity constraints (10), and without constraints $x_{iu} \in \{0,1\}$. Call this problem (**P1**). Namely, problem (**P1**) is that of maximizing (8) subject to constraints (9), (11) and $x_{iu} \in \mathbb{Z}_+$ i.e. a positive integer for all i, u. Now, consider the Linear Program (LP) relaxation (**P1'**) of (**P1**), with the same objective and constraints, but with continuous-valued variables $x_{iu} \in \mathbb{R}_+$ for all i, u. All these constraints can be written succinctly in matrix and vector form with the following linear form:

$$\mathbf{A}\mathbf{x} = \mathbf{b} , \tag{12}$$

where $\mathbf{A}$ is a $n \times m$ matrix, with $n = |\mathcal{U}| + C$, $m = |\mathcal{U}||\mathcal{I}|$, and $\mathbf{b}$ is a vector with n elements with the first $|\mathcal{U}|$ elements equal to L, and the last C elements equal to $K_1|\mathcal{I}_1|, \ldots, K_C|\mathcal{I}_C|$.

We call a constraint matrix $\mathbf{A}$ of a LP *totally unimodular* (TU) if each square sub-matrix of $\mathbf{A}$ has determinant $+1$, -1 or 0. According to a theorem from [15, Sec. 3.2], a matrix $\mathbf{A}$ is TU if the following three conditions hold: (i) matrix elements $a_{ij} \in \{+1, -1, 0\}$ for all i, j; (ii) each matrix column contains at most two nonzero elements, and (iii) there exists a partition of the set of rows in two subsets $\mathcal{M}_1$ and $\mathcal{M}_2$, and each column j with two nonzero coefficients satisfies $\sum_{i \in \mathcal{M}_1} a_{ij} - \sum_{i \in \mathcal{M}_2} a_{ij} = 0$.

Matrix $\mathbf{A}$ satisfies all conditions above, and therefore it is TU. Next, we have the following proposition, from [15, Sec.3.2]: An LP problem with feasible set $\{\mathbf{A}\mathbf{x} = \mathbf{b}, \ \mathbf{x} \in \mathbb{R}_+\}$ has an integral optimal solution for all integer vectors $\mathbf{b}$ for which it has an optimal value, if and only if $\mathbf{A}$ is TU. In our case, vector $\mathbf{b}$ is an integer vector since L, $\{K_1, \ldots, K_C\}$ and $\{|\mathcal{I}_1|, \ldots, |\mathcal{I}_C|\}$ are positive integers by definition.

Therefore, the optimal solution of the LP problem (**P1'**) is in integer form. Thus, the optimal solution to (**P1'**) (e.g. through the Simplex algorithm) is the same as the optimal solution to (**P1**), i.e. with the coverage constraints satisfied. However, one issue is that $x_{iu} \in \mathbb{Z}_+$ in problem (**P1**), and thus in the optimal solution of (**P1**), there will exist items i and users u for which $x_{iu} > 1$. We deal with this issue in the sequel.

4.2 Heuristic Algorithm for Problem (P)

When the size of problem (**P**) is large, namely the number of items and item providers is large, the numerical evaluation of the solution becomes difficult. We consider the following low-complexity heuristic algorithm which uses the solution of the LP problem (**P1'**) as follows.

We start by finding the optimal solution to (**P1'**). This solution is feasible in terms of coverage for each provider, and it is also feasible in terms of recommending L items to each user. However, constraints $x_{iu} \in \{0, 1\}$ may not be satisfied, i.e. the algorithm may recommend the same item to the same user more than once. Furthermore, the diversity constraints may not be satisfied because they have not been taken into account in (**P1'**). If this is the case, we need to choose an item j from a provider c that has been repeatedly recommended to a user u, and substitute it with a non-recommended item k of the same provider so as to maintain coverage feasibility and the L recommended items to each user. Then, we assign item k to u.

We make the choice of j, u, c, k as follows. We choose a provider c, a user u, a recommended item j to user u to substitute, and a not yet recommended item $k \in \mathcal{I}_c$ (so as to substitute j with k) for which the rating r_{ku} is as close as possible to r_{ju}, and the diversity increase is large if it is recommended to user u. We continue the substitutions by appropriately choosing j, u, c and i in that fashion until each item is recommended at most once to the same user. Next, in order to reach feasibility in the diversity constraints, we do item substitutions across providers, by switching items from different providers between users, while keeping the coverage constraints and $|\mathcal{L}_u| = L$ satisfied for each user, by giving priority to those switches that most improve diversity.

5 Data Experiments

We experiment with the publicly available **Movielens ml-latest-small** dataset to evaluate the effect of diversity and coverage constraints on the average rating,

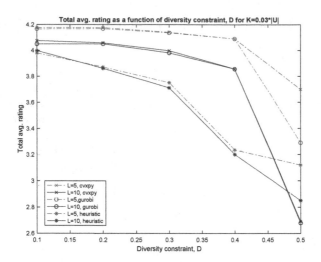

Fig. 1. Total average rating of recommendations for different solution approaches and different number of recommended items, L for $K = 0.03 \cdot |\mathcal{U}|$.

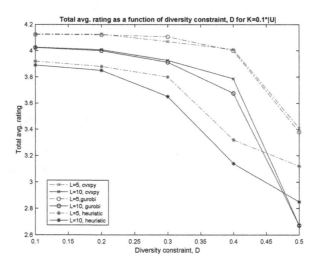

Fig. 2. Total average rating of recommendations for different solution approaches and different number of recommended items, L for $K = 0.1 \cdot |\mathcal{U}|$.

by solving problem (**P**). The dataset contains $100,000$ ratings from 671 users and $9,125$ movies, and ratings are on a 5-star scale with 0.5-star increment. We consider only those users that have rated at least two movies. We set $K_c = K$ and $D_c = D$ for all classes (providers) c. The movies in the dataset are then assigned randomly to one provider out of $C = 5$ or $C = 10$ providers.

Next, we compute the similarity w_{uv} between user pairs (u, v). For each user pair (u, v), we record which movies have been rated by both users, and we compute similarity w_{uv} as the similarity between user ratings for this common set of movies, by using Pearson correlation. We then produce the baseline RS lists for users through item-item Collaborative Filtering (CF). The output of item-item CF is a user-item ratings matrix. We take as number of recommended items to each user u, $|\mathcal{L}_u| = L = 5$ or 10.

Next, we numerically solve problem (**P**) in the following versions:

- A Non-Linear Programming problem with continuous variables $x_{iu} \in [0, 1]$, by using the Python cvxpy solver. This gives an upper bound on the total rating achieved by any algorithm that has integer variables **x**.
- A Quadratically constrained Integer Programming (QCIP) problem with discrete variables $x_{iu} \in \{0, 1\}$, by using the Gurobi solver.
- The heuristic algorithm of Subsect. 4.2 above.

Figures 1 and 2 show initial comparative results of these approaches as a function of the diversity constraint D for user coverage percentages $K = 3\%$ and $K = 10\%$, respectively. For all approaches, as both constraints become more stringent, the achieved average rating of recommended items decreases. The solver achieves an integer feasible solution with objective function value that is indeed very close to that of the LP. The heuristic algorithm achieves satisfactory rating performance for moderate values of D. From the plots above, it becomes apparent that the diversity constraint has larger impact than the coverage constraint on the reduction of average rating of recommended items.

6 Conclusion

We study the problem of optimizing multi-stakeholder recommender systems subject to user coverage and diversity constraints for different item providers that need to be treated equally in terms of guarantees for these metrics. The diversity constraint places quadratic constraints to the problem and makes it hard to solve. This study is a first step that serves as a proof-of-concept validation, and we intend to precisely quantify the various tradeoffs and impact of different parameters and constraints, through a larger dataset.

Looking ahead, the problem of equal treatment of item providers has many more angles to reveal, and we have only scratched the surface here. We viewed the problem through the lens of resource allocation where "resources" are the items to recommend. This parallelism to resource allocation may inspire different notions of fairness. For example, the average rating of recommendations for each provider should be assessed as well, and fair treatment may imply deciding on average ratings for each provider in a max-min fair sense, proportionally to the provider significance, or in an envy-free manner, whereby no provider would be willing to swap its user base and recommendations with those of another provider. A more fine-grained approach could value differently the rank (i.e. the position) of an item in the recommendation list. Other metrics could be considered for providers, such as serendipity.

References

1. Abdollahpouri, H., et al.: Beyond personalization: research directions in multistakeholder recommendation. ArXiv: abs/1905.01986 (2019)
2. Abdollahpouri, H., Burke, R.D.: Multi-stakeholder recommendation and its connection to multi-sided fairness. ArXiv: abs/1907.13158 (2019)
3. Adomavicius, G., Kwon, Y.: Improving aggregate recommendation diversity using ranking-based techniques. IEEE Trans. Knowl. Data Eng. **24**(5), 896–911 (2012)
4. Antikacioglu, A., Bajpai, T., Ravi, R.: A new system-wide diversity measure for recommendations with efficient algorithms. SIAM J. Math. Data Sci. **1**(4), 759–779 (2019)
5. Hammar, M., Karlsson, R., Nilsson, B.J.: Using maximum coverage to optimize recommendation systems in e-commerce. In: Proceedings of the 7th ACM Conference on Recommender Systems (2013)
6. Kaminskas, M., Bridge, D.: Diversity, serendipity, novelty, and coverage: a survey and empirical analysis of beyond-accuracy objectives in recommender systems. ACM Trans. Interact. Intell. Syst. **7**(1), 1–42 (2016)
7. Koutsopoulos, I., Halkidi, M.: Efficient and fair item coverage in recommender systems. In: IEEE 4th International Conference on Big Data Intelligence (DataCom) (2018)
8. Kyriakidi, M., Stefanidis, K., Ioannidis, Y.: On achieving diversity in recommender systems. In: Proceedings of the ExploreDB (2017)
9. Mehrotra, R., McInerney, J., Bouchard, H., Lalmas, M., Diaz, F.: Towards a fair marketplace: Counterfactual evaluation of the trade-off between relevance, fairness and satisfaction in recommendation systems. In: Proceedings of the ACM International Conference on Information and Knowledge Management (2018)
10. Patro, G.K., Biswas, A., Ganguly, N., Gummadi, K.P., Chakraborty, A.: Fairrec: two-sided fairness for personalized recommendations in two-sided platforms. In: Proceedings of The Web Conference (2020)
11. Patro, G.K., Chakraborty, A., Ganguly, N., Gummadi, K.P.: Incremental fairness in two-sided market platforms: on smoothly updating recommendations. ArXiv: abs/1909.10005 (2019)
12. Sühr, T., Biega, A.J., Zehlike, M., Gummadi, K.P., Chakraborty, A.: Two-sided fairness for repeated matchings in two-sided markets: a case study of a ride-hailing platform. In: Proceedings of the ACM SIGKDD International Conference on Knowledge Discovery and Data Mining (2019)
13. Sürer, O., Burke, R., Malthouse, E.C.: Multistakeholder recommendation with provider constraints. In: Proceedings of the 12th ACM Conference on Recommender Systems (2018)
14. Vargas, S., Baltrunas, L., Karatzoglou, A., Castells, P.: Coverage, redundancy and size-awareness in genre diversity for recommender systems. In: Proceedings of the ACM Conference on Recommender Systems (2014)
15. Integer Programming. GTM, vol. 271. Springer, Cham (2014). https://doi.org/10.1007/978-3-319-11008-0_9
16. Zheng, Y.: Multi-stakeholder recommendations: case studies, methods and challenges. In: Proceedings of the ACM Conference on Recommender Systems (2019)

Recommending Database Architectures for Social Queries: A Twitter Case Study

Michael Marountas[1], Georgios Drakopoulos[2]([envelope]) [ID], Phivos Mylonas[2] [ID],
and Spyros Sioutas[1]

[1] University of Patras, CEID, Patras 26504, Hellas
{marounta,sioutas}@ceid.upatras.gr
[2] Department of Informatics, Ionian University, Kerkyra 49100, Hellas
{c16drak,fmylonas}@ionio.gr

Abstract. Database deployment is a complex task depending on a multitude of operational parameters such as anticipated data scaling trends, expected type and volume of queries, uptime requirements, replication policies, available budget, and personnel training and experience. Thus, enterprise database administrators eventually rely on various performance metrics in conjunction to existing company policies in order to determine the best possible solution under these constraints. The recent advent of NoSQL databases, including graph databases such as Neo4j and document stores like MongoDB, added another degree of freedom in database selection since for a number of years relational databases such as PostgreSQL were the only available technology. In this work the scaling characteristics of a representative set of social queries executed on virtual machine installations of PostgreSQL and MongoDB are evaluated on a large volume of political tweets regarding Brexit. Moreover, Wiener filters for predicting the execution time of social query windows of fixed length over both databases are designed.

Keywords: Database administration · Database evaluation · Signal processing for databases · Information engineering · Social network analysis

1 Introduction

Database deployment is by no means a trivial engineering task since it entails the fine tuning of a plethora of high- and low-level operational parameters including hardware management, data transformations and cleansing mechanisms, integrated access policy, communication with other production-grade systems, and query optimization techniques. Additionally, the complexity as well as the performance of each database installation with respect to at least a representative set of anticipated queries should be assessed [41]. With the advent of social media, databases have been widely adopted as a reliable means for storing large volumes of (semi)structured social data in enterprise environments.

© IFIP International Federation for Information Processing 2021
Published by Springer Nature Switzerland AG 2021
I. Maglogiannis et al. (Eds.): AIAI 2021, IFIP AICT 627, pp. 715–728, 2021.
https://doi.org/10.1007/978-3-030-79150-6_56

Twitter is perhaps the most popular microblogging platform, suitable for online interplay mainly in the form of conversations [21]. The topic of the latter may well range from smart cities [34] and public health and the ongoing COVID-19 pandemic [22] to education [23] and sustainable development [31]. Nevertheless, it was the political Twitter which during the recent past years has gained considerable popularity. In part this can be attributed to the fact that Twitter was the primary media vehicle of the 45th US President [35,40], with the 2016 US presidential elections being an important milestone [10,45]. As a result, Twitter is now widely considered as a central political stage.

The primary research contribution of this conference paper is the assessment of two standalone instances of PostgreSQL and MongoDB to handle queries closely related to social analytics. First, the scaling dynamics of four representative queries forming the basis for three Twitter analytics are evaluated based on a large collection of English tweets regarding Brexit. Second, Wiener filters of various lengths are designed for the prediction of the execution time of fixed length non-overlapping query windows over these two installations. This point differentiates this work from previous approaches.

The remainder of this work is structured as follows. Section 2 summarizes the recent scientific literature regarding Twitter analytics, relational database management systems (RDBMSs), and document databases. The experimental setup and the proposed methodology are described in Sect. 3. In Sect. 4 possible future research directions are given. Random variables (r.vs) are represented with capital calligraphic letters. Technical acronyms are explained the first time they are met in the text. Table 1 summarizes notation.

Table 1. Notation of this conference paper.

Symbol	Notation	First in
$\triangleq$	Definition or equality by definition	Eq. (1)
$(t_1, \ldots, t_n)$	Tuple with elements $t_1, \ldots, t_n$	Eq. (9)
$|S|$	Set or tuple cardinality	Eq. (1)
$E[\mathcal{X}]$	Mean value of random variable $\mathcal{X}$	Eq. (11)
ρ_j	j-th autocorrelation coefficient of a random variable	Eq. (10)
$\Phi[k]$	Set of followers of the k-th account	Eq. (1)
$\Psi[k]$	Set of followees by the k-th account	Eq. (1)

2   Previous Work

Relational databases have been a productivity mainstay almost since their introduction [27]. They rely on a tabular data format as well as on a number of integrity constraints to ensure both high performance and data consistency [16].

Their performance has been evaluated in multiple ways, including query scalability [42], indexing [30], and fault tolerance [17]. From an operational complexity view normalized forms [29] and user rights assignment [24] play a central role.

Document databases typically operate on structured documents, usually in extensible markup language (XML) or JavaScript object notation (JSON) format [4]. The prospect of developing normalization and embedding operations in MongoDB is explored in [20], while the expressivity of MongoDB queries is the subject of [8]. Neural networks in keras for predicting mentions to Twitter verified accounts driven by data stored in MongoDB are described in [26]. Finally, a persistent data structure with rollback capabilities which can represent graphs but also structured documents is presented in [25].

There is a plethora of social analytics for Twitter. Digital influence as inferred through numerous attributes is paramount [36], with affective influence being also taken into consideration [7]. Also community discovery can take many forms such as spatio-linguistic [14], semantic based on hashtags [12], or hashtag similarity [44]. One-dimensional topological correlation for Twitter graphs based on structural and functional attributes is proposed in [13]. Recently data-driven approaches have been developed for examining Twitter graphs [6]. In [18] a socio-technical analysis of tweets is presented. Twitter as a vehicle for political campaigns is examined in [3]. Surveys covering the topic are [33] and [2].

3   Methodology

3.1   ACID vs BASE

During the 2010s the advent of NoSQL databases marked an addition of variation of fundamental database models. Along with the existing tabular data format of relational databases special infrastructure has been added for graphs, documents, associative arrays, and column families with the corresponding database type. Table 2 summarizes the main architectural differences between an RDBMS such as PostgreSQL and a document database like MongoDB.

Table 2. PostgreSQL vs MongoDB.

Feature	PostgresSQL	MongoDB
Data type	Table	Document collection
Data unit	Table row	JSON document
Feature	Table column	Document field
Operations	Relational model	CRUD (Create, read, update, delete)
Join	Relational joins	Embedded documents
Keys	Explicit	Implicit
Schema	Static	Dynamic

3.2 Dataset

The two databases were installed on two sepearate virtual machines (VMs) running over a public cloud. Table 3 has the technical specifications. In either case no indexing was activated. In the case of MongoDB the Python driver was used to write code for the Twitter analytics examined here.

In order to test the query dynamics of each database, a Twitter dataset containing a large number of tweets pertaining to Brexit, a term encompassing major political events since 2018, has been collected by a social crawler utilizing a topic sampling approach. Given that the actual Brexit took effect on February 1st of 2020, there was considerable interest in it during the few preceding months. Because of the paramount geopolitical importance of the event, a considerable number of English tweets was eventually collected over four months preceding it. The main properties of the dataset are shown in Table 3.

Table 3. Experimental setup.

Property	Value	Property	Value
VM operating system	Ubuntu	Number of tweets	500k
Number of processors	2	Collection interval	Nov.2019–Jan.2020
Processor type	Intel Core i7-10700	Accounts	102.3k
Level 1 cache size	16 MB	*follow* relationships	5.62 m
Available GPU	No	Hashtags	15.1k
Available memory	8 GB	Number of repetitions r_0	10000
Disk size	2TB	Number of equations N_0	10

3.3 Twitter Analytics

As stated earlier, social analytics abound for both the general case and for Twitter alone. In this work the following analytics will be used as a benchmark. More details about their respective implementations will be given later in the text.

One way to assess the impact of the k-th Twitter account is to compute the respective followers-to-followees logarithmic ratio defined as in Eq. (1):

$$J_r[k] \triangleq \log\left(1 + \frac{|\Phi[k]|}{\min\{1, \Psi[k]\}}\right) \tag{1}$$

From another perspective, the digital influence of the l-th tweet, regardless of the influence of the respective posting account, can be measured by the number of hashtags H_l it contains. This is shown in Eq. (2):

$$J_h[l] \triangleq H_l \tag{2}$$

An alternative for accounts requiring combined information is to count the total number of tweets W_k each account has posted multipied by the number of the respective followers as a visibility metric. This is shown in Eq. (3):

$$J_t[k] \triangleq W_k |\Phi[k]|$$

(3)

Observe that each of the above metrics captures a different aspect of Twitter activity, whether it is account- or tweet-oriented. In general, so far and to the best of the knowledge of the authors there is no single metric describing Twitter influence or account online behavior. From a database standpoint this translates to the need for quantifying the performance of individual queries as well as of query sequences. This can be done in terms of total execution time, system resources such as memory utilization or disk usage, or of operational complexity and personnel training costs. For the purposes of this work the total execution time has been selected as the single database performance criterion.

3.4   Response to Individual Queries

In order to execute the four queries described below, in the PostgreSQL case two tables were created, one containing information about accounts and one about tweets. After that, a set Q of reference queries, called *social queries*, was created. The wallclock time is a reliable indicator of the system execution time since these queries are strongly CPU bound [38]. Specifically, Q consists of the following queries, which are cast in SQL in addition to being verbally explained:

- q_1: This query selects rows based on the values of a given column. In social media it is frequently used to find accounts with a certain attribute and the value of the attribute in question satisfies certain numerical constraints. For instance, q_1 can be a filter for accounts having more than one follower.

  SELECT account FROM accounts WHERE followers >= 1;

- q_2: This query is similar to q_1 but the results are additionally sorted in descending order based on the values of a given column. Continuing the previous example, q_2 returns accounts as q_1 in descending order of followers. This is a popularity metric as well as a crude measure of digital influence.

  SELECT account FROM accounts WHERE followers >= 1
  ORDER BY followers DESC;

- q_3: The next step in query complexity is aggregation, in this case by the field preceding the GROUP BY clause. The following returns the total hashtags for each Twitter account.

  SELECT hastags, account FROM tweets
  GROUP BY account;

- q_4: Finally, the most time-consuming query is join. There are no such operations in the NoSQL world where each of the four primary technologies deals differently with it. The following query returns the number of tweets and followers for each account, provided the latter has more than one follower.

```
SELECT accounts.account, accounts.followers
FROM accounts INNER JOIN tweets
ON accounts.account = tweets.account
WHERE accounts.followers >= 1;
```

There is a correspondence between the above queries and the Twitter analytics presented earlier. Specifically, J_a can be implemented with two q_2 to find followers and followees respectively and one q_1, J_h with q_3 and a q_1, and J_t with q_4 and a q_1. In each case the last q_1 is used to select the top accounts or tweets.

In order to accurately determine total response times, each query for each database was run r_0 times, each time on a randomly selected subset of n tweets. The sample mean $T(n)$ was recorded as follows, where t_j is the j-th measurement:

$$T(n) \triangleq \frac{1}{r_0} \sum_{j=1}^{r_0} t_j \tag{4}$$

Equation (4) can be thought of the sample mean approximation of the true stochastic mean of the random variable counting the total execution time. Under mild conditions of ergodicity, the former converges to the latter as r_0 grows.

A metric of how much are the samples concentrated around the respective mean value is the variance. Along a similar line of reasoning, the sample variance $\sigma^2(n)$ approximates the true one and it is computed as follows:

$$\sigma^2(n) \triangleq \frac{1}{r_0 - 1} \sum_{j=1}^{r_0} (t_j - T(n))^2 \tag{5}$$

In Fig. 1 the mean times for q_1 and q_2 for both databases are displayed.

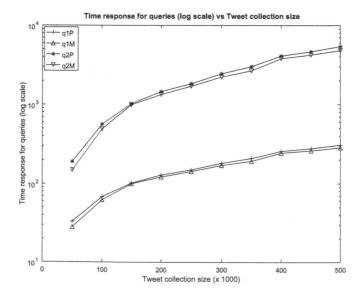

Fig. 1. Execution time for q_1 and q_2 vs query size (Source: Authors).

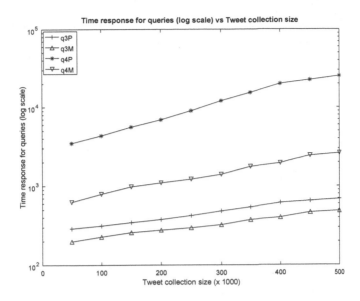

Fig. 2. Execution time for q_3 and q_4 vs query size (Source: Authors).

Likewise, in Fig. 2 the response times for queries q_3 and q_4 is shown.

The values of the sample variance are shown in Table 4. Observe that the sample variance grows very slowly compared with the growth of the respective query size. This is an indicator that the estimates obtained by the sample mean are reliable, which can be partly attributed to the selection of r_0 (for its actual value see Table 3). Note that the PostgreSQL installation tends to yield more consistent estimators, as denoted by the systematically lower sample variance.

Table 4. Sample variance vs query size and database technology (msec).

SQL	50k	100k	150k	200k	250k	300k	350k	400k	450k	500k
q_1	16.24	16.57	17.34	18.54	20.20	22.02	23.60	23.36	23.35	23.08
q_2	18.09	18.47	19.04	19.02	21.41	22.93	24.84	24.98	24.34	24.45
q_3	18.23	19.07	19.49	20.59	23.46	25.49	27.37	27.57	27.74	27.34
q_4	22.33	23.11	24.36	25.47	27.73	28.11	28.46	28.55	28.12	28.76
MDB	50k	100k	150k	200k	250k	300k	350k	400k	450k	500k
q_1	17.33	17.45	18.74	19.69	21.58	22.67	23.45	24.35	24.45	24.48
q_2	23.02	23.81	23.70	24.35	25.89	26.85	26.94	26.56	26.33	26.35
q_3	24.22	24.38	23.54	25.96	26.44	27.20	27.68	28.73	28.67	28.68
q_4	25.11	25.58	25.36	26.56	27.76	27.15	28.48	28.24	29.92	30.57

The semilogarithmic scale can reveal certain scaling patterns. In particular, the almost straight lines of time curves for both databases for q_4 suggests a power law scaling with n of the total response time $T(n)$ of the form [32]:

$$T(n; \alpha_0, \gamma_0, n_0) \triangleq \alpha_0(n + n_0)^{\gamma_0}, \qquad \alpha_0, \gamma_0, n_0 > 0 \tag{6}$$

In models like that of Eq. (6) the most important parameter is the scaling exponent γ_0 which determines the growth rate, whereas parameters α_0 and n_0 represent initial conditions and have minor effect on growth.

Taking the natural logarithm of Eq. (6) yields the equivalent (7). Notice there are N_0 equations, one for each of the possible values of n as shown in Table 4. The same value is repeated in Table 3 for convenience.

$$\ln T(n; \alpha_0, \gamma_0, n_0) = \ln \alpha_0 + \gamma_0 \ln (n + n_0) \tag{7}$$

Stacking the N_0 Eqs. (7) for the different values of n in increasing order of the latter yields the non-linear system of Eq. (8):

$$\begin{bmatrix} \ln T(n_1) \\ \vdots \\ \ln T(n_{N_0}) \end{bmatrix} = \begin{bmatrix} 1 & \ln (n_1 + n_0) \\ \vdots & \vdots \\ 1 & \ln (n_{N_0} + n_0) \end{bmatrix} \begin{bmatrix} \ln \alpha_0 \\ \gamma_0 \end{bmatrix} \tag{8}$$

Observe that (8) is non-linear and moreover the parameter n_0 is difficult to be separated from the data values n. To this end, instead of the standard least squares (LS) estimator, the following iterative scheme was used:

- The initial estimate for n_0 is used to obtain an LS solution for α_0 and γ_0.
- Using a line search with step $\mu_0 = \ln n_0$, a new estimate for n_0 is obtained.
- A new LS solution for α_0 and γ_0 is computed.
- If this solution increases residual error, then the search reverses direction.
- If two successive reverses occur, then the search terminates.
- The values of α_0, γ_0, n_0 with the least residual error are returned.

From the semilogarithmic plot of (7) these initial estimates can be deduced:

- The average arctangent of the plot of $T(\cdot)$ approximates the exponent γ_0.
- The rise of the plot of $T(\cdot)$ at the beginning of the latter is $\ln \alpha_0$.
- The shift of the plot of $T(\cdot)$ at the beginning of the latter is n_0.

From the definition of model (6) it is clear that it is the exponent γ_0 which dominates the time growth. The values obtained by the process described above for γ_0 for each query are given in Table 5. Notice that the values for q_1 are very close, but for the remaining queries MongoDB scales with a much lower rate.

Table 5. Values for the exponent γ_0.

SQL	q_1	q_2	q_3	q_4	MDB	q_1	q_2	q_3	q_4
γ_0	0.8273	1.1355	2.2148	2.8914	γ_0	0.8541	1.0534	2.0993	2.5231

3.5 Response to Query Sequences

In a typical enterprise environment even a standalone database installation is bound to serve query sequences with varying characteristics and of different sizes. The prediction of the execution time of each window allows the preemptive allocation of resources least under a certain set of normal operating conditions.

In this case the following scenario was simulated. The same batch of L_1 tweets, in the order they were created, are serially inserted to the two databases. This simulates the constant flow of tweets under normal operational conditions with no special events sparking intense activity happening. At the end of each such window the top ten accounts and tweets as determined by the three metrics of Eqs. (1), (2), and (3) are computed. The sum of the individual times of these analytics is defined as the reponse time for the respective window.

Notice that even in a simple scenario like this there is no direct correspondence between the execution time of each window and the queries it contains. This can be attributed to the following reasons:

- Although a connection between analytics and queries has been derived, the relationship between queries and response time is complicated.
- There is a non-linear connection between the time reponse of a query and its respective input size. Therefore, the reponse of an entire query sequence is more difficult to model and analyze.
- The query input size keeps growing, which translates not only to non-constant total response times but also to an increased variations thereof. Therefore, the prediction complexity is non-trivial.
- The response time depends not only on the query but also on factors such as the available memory, disk and processor utilization, disk controller performance, and the load factor which have not been modeled.

One way for predicting the execution time of a query window is a linear filter which takes as input the execution times of L_0 past windows and yields as output an estimate of the execution time of the $(L_0 + 1)$-st window. Depending on the filter as well as on the stochastic properties of the windows the coefficients of a filter may be updated periodically, updated after certain events, or remain fixed.

In this work the Wiener filter of length L_0 will be used, which has numerous applications in signal processing. It relies on approximation of input autocorrelation coefficients as computed by their respective sample counterparts. For instance, given a tuple of past window execution times as in Eq. (9):

$$X \stackrel{\triangle}{=} (x_0, \ldots, x_{L_0-1}) \tag{9}$$

Observe that tuple X essentially contains L_0 samples of the r.v $\mathcal{X}_k$ which models the response time of the k-th execution window. Since these times were generated by the same database installation under the same conditions, they can be assumed to be modeled by identically distributed r.vs. As the queries of each window do not interact with those of other windows, then $\mathcal{X}_k$ can be also assumed to be independent. This probabilistic assumption greatly facilitates the approximate computation of the autocorrelation sequence, which is necessary in order to compute the filter coefficients. Assuming a stationary distribution for the execution times, the j-th autocorrelation coefficient ρ_j be defined as in (10):

$$\rho_j \triangleq \mathrm{E}\left[\mathcal{X}_k \mathcal{X}_{k-j}\right] \tag{10}$$

For example, the first two coefficients of the autocorrelation sequence $\mathrm{E}\left[\mathcal{X}_k^2\right]$ and $\mathrm{E}\left[\mathcal{X}_k \mathcal{X}_{k-1}\right]$ are approximated as follows in Eq. (11):

$$\rho_0 \triangleq \mathrm{E}\left[\mathcal{X}_k^2\right] \approx \frac{1}{L_0} \sum_{k=0}^{L_0-1} x_k^2$$

$$\rho_1 \triangleq \mathrm{E}\left[\mathcal{X}_k \mathcal{X}_{k-1}\right] \approx \frac{1}{L_0-1} \sum_{k=0}^{L_0-2} x_k x_{k-1} \tag{11}$$

In general, the coefficients w_k of a Wiener filter of length L_0 are the solution of the following linear system (12). Observe that the coefficient matrix is diagonally dominant as determined by the properties of the autocorrelation sequence, symmetric, and Toeplitz. These lead to efficient solutions for long filters.

$$\begin{bmatrix} \rho_0 & \rho_1 & \cdots & \rho_{L_0-1} \\ \rho_{L_0-1} & \rho_0 & \cdots & \rho_{L_0-2} \\ \vdots & \vdots & \ddots & \vdots \\ \rho_{L_0-1} & \rho_{L_0-2} & \cdots & \rho_0 \end{bmatrix} \begin{bmatrix} w_0 \\ w_1 \\ \vdots \\ w_{L_0-1} \end{bmatrix} = \begin{bmatrix} \rho_1 \\ \rho_2 \\ \vdots \\ \rho_{L_0} \end{bmatrix} \tag{12}$$

Once the Wiener filter has been computed for both database architectures and for various values of the filter length L_0, the mean square error between the actual and the predicted execution times was computed. The normalized results are shown in Table 6. The latter was selected in order for the differences in errors of the various combinations to be easier to understand.

Table 6. Normalized mean square error for database architectures.

L_0	11	21	31	41	51
PostgreSQL	1.7645	1.5656	1.4456	1.3412	1.142
MongoDB	1.616	1.5671	1.4563	1.3733	1

From the values of Table 6 it follows that MongoDB achieves a lower mean square error and, thus, the time responses of its query sequences are easier to be modeled and predicted. This in turn translates to the database administrators having a better view about the scaling dynamics of incoming tweet flows. The ability for quicker responses may be vital in extraordinary events.

3.6 Remarks

The findings of this previous are consistent, to the extent where a comparison can be made, with those reported in the recent literature examining the performance of MongoDB against that of the PostgreSQL in various engineering cases. Specifically, the scaling dynamics were similar to those in [39] and in [28], although refers to spatial data. Other tests, again on spatial data, in [5] showed the strengths and weaknesses of both databases. In [19] big data considerations were examined and constraints were derived again for both databases. The perspective of queries about line intersection and spatial containment problems was given in [1] where MongoDB was better. Queries on unstructured data were run on the same pair of databases in [9] with MongoDB being the winner because of its enhanced flexibility. When it comes to queries for semistructured, high velocity sensor measurements as explored in [43], again MongoDB seems to be the choice at the cost of extensive memory use. In [11] the performance of k-nearest neighbors is explored with the relational solution offering more advantages. MongoDB was the better for handling a stock market dataset over Hadoop [37]. Finally, the potential of MongoDB for mobile applications was explored with encouraging results [15].

Based on the experiments, the following remarks can be made:

- Concerning isolated queries, MongoDB achieves lower execution times but PostgreSQL has lower variance. The latter implies that PostgreSQL performance is easier to predict. This can be attributed to the structured data format and the greater degree of automation it offers.
- Concerning query windows, the total execution time is easier to predict in the case of MongoDB with Wiener filters of lower order. Since Wiener filters are efficiently implemented in most if not all scientific computation tools and are easy to understand intuitively, database administrators can easily obtain an understanding of MongoDB scaling dynamics and, based on their experience, of the major drivers behind them.

4   Future Research Directions

This conference paper focuses on the performance comparison between MongoDB and PostgreSQL, a special case of the general BASE vs ACID question, when handling Twitter analytics. As is the case in most realistic engineering scenarios, the answer is not simple. Rather, it depends on the evaluation of the current state as well as the near-term trend of a plethora of operational variables including memory and disk utilization, system load, and input query size. In this conference paper the scaling dynamics of both individual social queries, namely queries forming the base for Twitter analytics, and query sequences were evaluated on a large number of English tweets about Brexit. Although PostgeSQL achieved consistently lower variance of query execution times, MongoDB had lower mean times. Moreover, the execution times of query sequences were easier to predict in the MongoDB case, meaning that database administrators had a much better view of the query scaling trends.

Concerning possible future research directions, the use of larger datasets with a higher variability of attributes as performance benchmarks should be examined. Moreover, the scaling dynamics of database server clusters should be investigated. Additionally, other query sequence execution time predictors, whether fixed or adaptive, can be the focus or future research.

Acknowledgments. This research has been funded by the Ionian University.

References

1. Agarwal, S., Rajan, K.: Performance analysis of MongoDB versus PostGIS/PostgreSQL databases for line intersection and point containment spatial queries. Spat. Inf. Res. **24**(6), 671–677 (2016)
2. Antonakaki, D., Fragopoulou, P., Ioannidis, S.: A survey of Twitter research: Data model, graph structure, sentiment analysis and attacks. Expert Syst. Appl. **164**, (2021)
3. Badawy, A., Ferrara, E., Lerman, K.: Analyzing the digital traces of political manipulation: The 2016 Russian interference Twitter campaign. In: ASONAM, pp. 258–265. IEEE (2018)
4. Bagga, S., Sharma, A.: A comparative study of NoSQL databases. In: Singh, P.K., Singh, Y., Kolekar, M.H., Kar, A.K., Chhabra, J.K., Sen, A. (eds.) ICRIC 2020. LNEE, vol. 701, pp. 51–61. Springer, Singapore (2021). https://doi.org/10.1007/978-981-15-8297-4_5
5. Bartoszewski, D., Piorkowski, A., Lupa, M.: The comparison of processing efficiency of spatial data for PostGIS and MongoDB databases. In: Kozielski, S., Mrozek, D., Kasprowski, P., Małysiak-Mrozek, B., Kostrzewa, D. (eds.) BDAS 2019. CCIS, vol. 1018, pp. 291–302. Springer, Cham (2019). https://doi.org/10.1007/978-3-030-19093-4_22
6. Belhadi, A., Djenouri, Y., Lin, J.C.W., Cano, A.: A data-driven approach for Twitter hashtag recommendation. IEEE Access **8**, 79182–79191 (2020)
7. Bibi, M., Aziz, W., Almaraashi, M., Khan, I.H., Nadeem, M.S.A., Habib, N.: A cooperative binary-clustering framework based on majority voting for Twitter sentiment analysis. IEEE Access **8**, 68580–68592 (2020)
8. Botoeva, E., Calvanese, D., Cogrel, B., Xiao, G.: Expressivity and complexity of MongoDB queries. In: ICDT. Schloss Dagstuhl-Leibniz-Zentrum für Informatik (2018)
9. Cheng, Y., Zhou, K., Wang, J.: Performance analysis of PostgreSQL and MongoDB databases for unstructured data. In: MBDASM. Atlantis Press (2019)
10. Clarke, I., Grieve, J.: Stylistic variation on the Donald Trump Twitter account: a linguistic analysis of tweets posted between 2009 and 2018. PLoS One **14**(9), (2019)

11. Coşkun, İ., Sertok, S., Anbaroğlu, B.: k-nearest neighbour query performance analysis on a large scale taxi dataset: PostgreSQL vs MongoDB. International archives of the photogrammetry, remote sensing, and spatial information sciences (2019)
12. Drakopoulos, D., Giotopoulos, K.C., Giannoukou, I., Sioutas, S.: Unsupervised discovery of semantically aware communities with tensor Kruskal decomposition: a case study in Twitter. SMAP. IEEE (2020). https://doi.org/10.1109/SMAP49528.2020.9248469
13. Drakopoulos, G., Kafeza, E.: One dimensional cross-correlation methods for deterministic and stochastic graph signals with a Twitter application in Julia. SEEDA-CECNSM. IEEE (2020). https://doi.org/10.1109/SEEDA-CECNSM49515.2020.9221815
14. Drakopoulos, G., et al.: A genetic algorithm for spatiosocial tensor clustering. Evol. Syst. **11**(3), 491–501 (2019). https://doi.org/10.1007/s12530-019-09274-9
15. Fotache, M., Cogean, D.: NoSQL and SQL databases for mobile applications. Case study: MongoDB versus PostgreSQL. Informatica Economica **17**(2), 41–58 (2013)
16. Freitag, M., Bandle, M., Schmidt, T., Kemper, A., Neumann, T.: Adopting worst-case optimal joins in relational database systems. PVLDB **13**(12), 1891–1904 (2020)
17. Gorbenko, A., Karpenko, A., Tarasyuk, O.: Analysis of trade-offs in fault-tolerant distributed computing and replicated databases. In: DESSERT, pp. 1–6. IEEE (2020)
18. Grover, P., Kar, A.K., Davies, G.: Technology enabled health - Insights from Twitter analytics with a socio-technical perspective. Int. J. Inf. Manage. **43**, 85–97 (2018)
19. Jung, M.G., Youn, S.A., Bae, J., Choi, Y.L.: A study on data input and output performance comparison of MongoDB and PostgreSQL in the big data environment. In: DTA. IEEE (2015)
20. Kanade, A., Gopal, A., Kanade, S.: A study of normalization and embedding in MongoDB. In: IACC. IEEE (2014)
21. Karami, A., Lundy, M., Webb, F., Dwivedi, Y.K.: Twitter and research: a systematic literature review through text mining. IEEE Access **8**, 67698–67717 (2020)
22. Kearney, M.W.: rtweet: collecting and analyzing Twitter data. J. Open Source Softw. **4**(42), 1829 (2019)
23. Khan, H.U., Nasir, S., Nasim, K., Shabbir, D., Mahmood, A.: Twitter trends: S ranking algorithm analysis on real time data. Expert Syst. Appl. **164**, 45–67 (2021)
24. Khan, M.I., O'Sullivan, B., Foley, S.N.: Towards modelling insiders behaviour as rare behaviour to detect malicious RDBMS access. In: Big Data, pp. 3094–3099. IEEE (2018)
25. Kontopoulos, S., Drakopoulos, G.: A space efficient scheme for graph representation. ICTAI. IEEE (2014). https://doi.org/10.1109/ICTAI.2014.52
26. Kyriazidou, I., Drakopoulos, G., Kanavos, A., Makris, C., Mylonas, P.: Towards predicting mentions to verified Twitter accounts: building prediction models over MongoDB with Keras. WEBIST. SCITEPRESS (2019). https://doi.org/10.5220/0007810200250033
27. Luo, S., Gao, Z.J., Gubanov, M., Perez, L.L., Jermaine, C.: Scalable linear algebra on a relational database system. TKDE **31**(7), 1224–1238 (2018)
28. Makris, A., Tserpes, K., Spiliopoulos, G., Anagnostopoulos, D.: Performance evaluation of MongoDB and PostgreSQL for spatio-temporal data. In: EDBT/ICDT Workshops (2019)

29. Masri, D.: Relational databases and normalization. Developing Data Migrations and Integrations with Salesforce, pp. 1–11. Apress, Berkeley, CA (2019). https://doi.org/10.1007/978-1-4842-4209-4_1
30. Medina, J.M., Barranco, C.D., Pons, O.: Indexing techniques to improve the performance of necessity-based fuzzy queries using classical indexing of RDBMS. Fuzzy Sets Syst. **351**, 90–107 (2018)
31. Mills, J., Reed, M., Skaalsveen, K., Ingram, J.: The use of Twitter for knowledge exchange on sustainable soil management. Soil Use Manag. **35**(1), 195–203 (2019)
32. Newman, M.E.: Network structure from rich but noisy data. Nat. Phys. **14**(6), 542–545 (2018)
33. Nugroho, R., Paris, C., Nepal, S., Yang, J., Zhao, W.: A survey of recent methods on deriving topics from Twitter: Algorithm to evaluation. Knowl. Inf. Syst. **62**(7), 2485–2519 (2020)
34. Osorio-Arjona, J., Horak, J., Svoboda, R., García-Ruíz, Y.: Social media semantic perceptions on Madrid Metro system: using Twitter data to link complaints to space. Sustainable Cities Society **64**, (2021)
35. Ott, B.L.: The age of Twitter: Donald J. Trump and the politics of debasement. Critical Studi. Media Commun. **34**(1), 59–68 (2017)
36. Rezaie, B., Zahedi, M., Mashayekhi, H.: Measuring time-sensitive user influence in Twitter. Knowl. Inf. Syst. **62**(9), 3481–3508 (2020). https://doi.org/10.1007/s10115-020-01459-y
37. Rutishauser, N., Noureldin, A.: TPC-H applied to MongoDB: How a NoSQL database performs. Department of Informatik Vertiefung, University Zurich, Technical report (2012)
38. Shanbhag, A., Madden, S., Yu, X.: A study of the fundamental performance characteristics of GPUs and CPUs for database analytics. In: SIGMOD, pp. 1617–1632 (2020)
39. Sharma, M., Sharma, V.D., Bundele, M.M.: Performance analysis of RDBMS and NoSQL databases: PostgreSQL, MongoDB, and Neo4j. In: ICRAIE, pp. 1–5. IEEE (2018)
40. Stolee, G., Caton, S.: Twitter, trump, and the base: a shift to a new form of presidential talk? Signs Soc. **6**(1), 147–165 (2018)
41. Taipalus, T.: The effects of database complexity on SQL query formulation. J. Syst. Softw. **165**, 110576 (2020)
42. Thomas, A., Kumar, A.: A comparative evaluation of systems for scalable linear algebra-based analytics. PVLDB **11**(13), 2168–2182 (2018)
43. Van der Veen, J.S., Van der Waaij, B., Meijer, R.J.: Sensor data storage performance: SQL or NoSQL, physical or virtual. In: International Conference on Cloud Computing. IEEE (2012)
44. Xu, S., Zhou, A.: Hashtag homophily in Twitter network: examining a controversial cause-related marketing campaign. Comput. Hum. Behav. **102**, 87–96 (2020)
45. Yaqub, U., Chun, S.A., Atluri, V., Vaidya, J.: Analysis of political discourse on Twitter in the context of the 2016 US presidential elections. Gov. Inf. Q. **34**(4), 613–626 (2017)

Science4Fashion: An Autonomous Recommendation System for Fashion Designers

Sotirios-Filippos Tsarouchis, Argyrios S. Vartholomaios$^{(\boxtimes)}$ (iD),
Ioannis-Panagiotis Bountouridis, Athanasios Karafyllis,
Antonios C. Chrysopoulos, and Pericles A. Mitkas

Electrical and Computer Engineering, Aristotle University of Thessaloniki,
Thessaloniki 54124, Greece

Abstract. In the clothing industry, design, development, and procurement teams have been affected more than any other industry and are constantly under pressure to present more products with fewer resources in a shorter time. The diversity of garment designs created as new products is not found in any other industry and is almost independent of the size of the business. Science4Fashion is a semi-autonomous intelligent personal assistant for fashion product designers. Our system consists of an interactive environment where a user utilizes different modules responsible for a) data collection from online sources, b) knowledge extraction, c) clustering, and d) trend/product recommendation. This paper is focusing on two core modules of the implemented system. The Clustering Module combines various clustering algorithms and offers a consensus that arranges data in clusters. At the same time, the Product Recommender and Feedback module receives the designer's input on different fashion products and recommends more relevant items based on their preferences. The experimental results highlight the usefulness and the efficiency of the proposed subsystems in aiding the creative fashion process.

Keywords: Fashion data · Mixed data · Consensus clustering · Recommendation system · Collaborative filtering

1 Introduction

The clothing industry is one of the most fast-growing sectors, with many employees around the world. Fashion brands need to adapt to the fast-fashion model to fulfill their customers' needs on time. Consequently, fashion industry designers deal with immense pressure for delivering an increasing number of products, with strict deadlines and limited resources. To this end, the creative department of a

Published by Springer Nature Switzerland AG 2021
I. Maglogiannis et al. (Eds.): AIAI 2021, IFIP AICT 627, pp. 729–742, 2021.
https://doi.org/10.1007/978-3-030-79150-6_57

fashion designing company has several tasks that need to be completed before focusing on the newest collection. These are inspiration research (from previous exhibitions, social media, photo galleries, e-shops, and many more), trend analysis of the upcoming shows, and compliance to the company's product quality standards. Thus, a designer must fulfill the creative process through a series of menial tasks.

This paper is an extension of our previous work [1], which introduced a digital assistant for fashion designers. Science4Fashion System is a combination of a clothing recommendation and a design assistant system that takes simple and easy-to-fill high-level configuration instructions and automates the aforementioned menial and time-consuming tasks. Some examples are (a) the collection of data from both internal (company databases and trend guides) and external sources (e-shops, social media, trend sites), (b) the data annotation, (c) clustering relevant fashion products to influential groups, and many more. This paper focuses on two of the core modules of the Science4Fashion system: the Clustering and the Product Recommender and Feedback Module.

For the remainder of this paper, Sect. 2 lists related work in the fields of clustering and recommendation systems, while Sect. 3 introduces the proposed methodology. Next, in Sect. 4 we present the datasets and results. Finally, in Sect. 5, we summarize our work, we offer the challenges and future work.

2 Related Work

Several research works have been presented in the domain of the clothing data analysis field, including clothing classification and clustering, feature extraction based on both images or text, and clothes recommendation.

Recent works in clustering techniques serve the fashion industry by providing insights to drive trend forecasting, new product designs, and improve recommendations. In [2] presents Rough Mean Shift Clustering, a soft clustering approach used to assist the process of product forecasting by discovering latent relationships between fashion attributes from unlabeled and ambiguous image data. Additionally, in our previous work [1], partition-based, hierarchical, and model-based algorithms were employed in the task of clustering products, according to their categorical and numerical attributes.

An extensive study on clothing recommendations systems has been made by Congying Guan et al. [3], including content-based and collaborative approaches. A hybrid system has been proposed by Xiaosong Hu et al. [4] exploiting both clothing information and user ratings while achieving better results using only the color attribute. Finally, an Advanced User-Based Collaborative Filtering algorithm has been developed by Yu Liu et al. [5], applied on the Tmall.com dataset with higher evaluation metrics than the traditional techniques.

Even though the State-of-the-Art presented above provides concrete solutions to their respective problem/field, none of them allows for a holistic approach to the real-life challenges faced by the fashion industry during the creative process. The current work proposes an AI-enabled system, facilitating the clothing products design, mainly targeting product concept development. The ultimate goal is to provide personalized suggestions to inspire designers towards fashionable products. More specifically, it is an end-to-end system that acts as a personal assistant. One great differentiator is the Product Recommender and User Feedback module. This module is implemented using a combination of (a) a hybrid algorithm for product ranking and recommendation, exploiting the benefits of different baseline algorithms, and (b) a hierarchical clustering method to improve algorithm results.

3   Methodology

This section presents an overview of the proposed methodology for clustering the fashion products included in the dataset and recommending potentially insightful products to the end-user. The Clustering module creates meaningful clusters of similar products. At the same time, it facilitates and refines the recommendation system input to provide the results in near real-time and enhance the User Experience. Furthermore, the Product Recommender is responsible for delivering personalized and relevant results by employing a feedback mechanism.

3.1   Clustering Module

Most clothing datasets used for the clustering experiments consist of numerical and categorical data that describe fashion apparel attributes such as fabric composition, genre, season, manufacturer, retail price, and more.

After data preprocessing, the features are used by a set of unsupervised clustering algorithms to create meaningful groups used as input into the Recommender module. Specifically, a) K-Means [6], b) Fuzzy C-Means (FCM) [7] and c) BIRCH [8] are employed. The generated clusters from all algorithms are encoded in a similarity matrix, used as input for an Agglomerative Hierarchical clustering model used for the consensus clustering.

The following paragraphs introduce the clustering module, starting with the data preprocessing stage and the feature extraction methodology, followed by the proposed consensus mechanism. Lastly, the metrics used for the clustering evaluation are presented.

Mixed Data Preprocessing. The first step of preprocessing is comprised of a data cleaning process that involved normalizing the numerical attributes and filling out missing values. The next step is the feature selection process.

Due to the nature of the dataset, the Factor Analysis for Mixed Data (FAMD) method [9] was used to create features out of the quantitative and qualitative attributes of the dataset. In general, Factor Analysis is a statistical method applied in data exploration and dimensionality reduction. In essence, FAMD can be described as the combination of two other Factor Analysis methodologies, the Principal Component Analysis (PCA) [10] and the Multiple Correspondence Analysis [11]. An essential feature of FAMD is that it balances the contribution of both the categorical and the numerical attributes [9], by converting to one-hot columns and then scaling the former and normalizing the latter. Similarly to PCA, the final FAMD embedding is a reduced sub-space that maps the correlation between categorical and numerical data.

In this case, the final 12 product attributes that represent the fashion dataset were transformed to 3-dimensional embeddings. Based on the explained inertia of each component, the first 2 FAMD components were selected as features by the least number of FAMD components. These embeddings are used as input to the clustering algorithms.

Consensus Clustering was a methodology initially motivated by the need to assess the "stability" of the produced clusters. A common symptom of clustering algorithms is that variations in the initialization strategy and parameterization of the algorithm can affect the resulting groups. To this end, consensus clustering was conceptualized by Monti in [12] as a method to reconcile perturbed datasets resulting from re-sampling of the data.

In this work, consensus clustering is used as an ensemble clustering algorithm [13] that combines different clustering models to unveil latent relationships between data. In other words, consensus clustering is used to formalize the agreement between different clustering algorithms.

The consensus of the different clustering results is achieved through a consensus matrix that describes the co-occurrence of data points in the same cluster. The consensus matrix is obtained as the normalized sum of the connectivity matrices produced by the different clustering outcomes. Initially, according to Monti, the consensus matrix C is a NxN matrix defined as follows:

$$C(i,j) = \left(\frac{\sum_{h=1}^{H} M^{(h)}(i,j)}{\sum_{h=1}^{H} I^h(i,j)} \right) \tag{1}$$

where M^h a list of NxN connectivity matrices resulting from the perturbed datasets obtained by re-sampling, and I^h is the indicator matrix. The value of (i,j)-th entry is equal to 1 if both i and j belong to the same cluster, or 0 otherwise. An essential property of the consensus matrix is that it acts as a similarity measure of the different data points.

In the proposed clustering module, to produce a more defined clustering result, a Radial Basis Function (RBF) kernel [14] is applied on the consensus matrix. The RBF kernel is used to exaggerate the distances captured by the consensus matrix by decreasing the Euclidean distance and is given by:

$$k(x_i, x_j) = exp(-\frac{d(x_i, x_j)^2}{2l^2}) \tag{2}$$

where d is the Euclidean distance and $l > 0$ is a kernel's scalar parameter. The resulting enhanced consensus matrix is used as an input to an Agglomerative hierarchical clustering model to produce the final clustering reconciliation using complete linkage.

3.2   Product Recommender and Feedback Module

Recommendation systems are encapsulated in the background of almost most personalization systems and aim to propose to the user options catered by the system (movies, books, services, clothes). In general recommendation strategies, can be categorized into three main types: a) content-based (CB) methods [15], which extract feature vectors describing the items and suggesting similar items according to user's preferences, b) collaborative filtering (CF) based methods [16], which make suggestions based on user preference similarities since users that have rated the same items are more likely to have similar dispositions, and c) Hybrid methods [17], which combine the two recommendation mentioned above methods, to eliminate each method's restrictions and benefit from their complementary advantages.

Collaborative Filtering - Singular Value Decomposition (SVD). Singular Value Decomposition is a table factorization technique, where a table $A(m \times n)$ is represented as follows:

$$A = U \times \Sigma \times (V)^T \tag{3}$$

where: U is a square matrix with dimensions $m \times r$, V^T is the inverse matrix of V with dimensions $n \times r$ and Σ is a diagonal matrix $r \times r$.

Matrix Σ contains the eigenvalues in descending order. The users and the clothing products can be represented in $r \times r$ dimensional space by utilizing the U and V matrices.

The Recommendation system begins by splitting the available samples into the training and testing dataset. The Singular Value Decomposition is applied to the training dataset, and the resulting recommendations are evaluated using the testing dataset. When the optimal parameter k is selected, the system creates the output data with the optimally recommended items.

Collaborative Filtering - Neural Collaborative Filtering (NCF). As mentioned earlier, the implementation with SVD recommends products based on the users' inner product and product tables. However, the inner product can only detect the latent vectors' linear combinations. To identify more complex affinities, we apply neural networks in collaborative filtering.

The architecture of NCF includes [18]:

- *Input Layer:* transforms a sparse vector for a user and item identification to binary.
- *Embedding Layer:* is a fully connected layer that projects the sparse representation to a dense vector.
- *Neural Collaborative Layers:* use multi-layered neural networks to determine the latent vectors and predict the scores.
- *Output Layer:* provides the output of the neural network.

NCF is described by the following formula:

$$\hat{y}_{ui} = f(\mathbf{P}^T \mathbf{v}_u^U, \mathbf{Q}^T \mathbf{v}_i^I | \mathbf{P}, \mathbf{Q}, \Theta_f) \tag{4}$$

where: P is the latent factor matrix for users, $\mathbf{v}$ is the binarised vector for a user and item identification, Q is the latent factor matrix for items and Θ_f are the model parameters.

The layers of the neural network created for this approach are presented in Table 1, with each layer's size decreased in half.

Table 1. Structure of the multi-layers neural network (collaborative filtering)

Layers	Neurons	Activation function	Dropout rate	Weights initialization
Layer 1	4096	ReLu	50%	he_normal
Layer 2	2048	ReLu	50%	he_normal
Layer 3	1024	ReLu	30%	he_normal
Layer 4	512	ReLu	30%	he_normal
Layer 5	256	ReLu	30%	he_normal
Layer 6	128	ReLu	30%	he_normal
Layer 7	1	Sigmoid	0%	Glorot normal

The input layer of the training dataset is transformed to a sparse matrix with the use of one hot encoding [19]. The selected activation function is the ReLu in all layers, except the last one, where the sigmoid function is used. The reason for not using sigmoid function values, which vary from 0 to 1, is that they may result in saturation, which means that the neurons don't work correctly when the value of the function is close to 0 or 1. On the other hand, ReLU function [20] is the answer to the saturation problem, and it is the proper function for a system with sparse data.

The input training dataset is entered in the embedding layer, where the dense vector is created. The embedding layer dimensions are the *totalUsers* × *factors* and accordingly *totalItems* × *factors*, where the number of factors is 70.

Next, the vector is provided as input to the multi-layer neural network. The neural network design begins with a broad layer (many neurons), and half in the number of neurons decreases every consequent layer. A small number of hidden layers enable capturing the abstract nature of the data [21]. In general, several layers and parameters were used to develop the neural network. The proposed method with the seven layers and the specific parameters was the best result of all the experiments conducted.

Content Based - Random Forest. Random Forests [22] are ideal models for analyzing dataset features, as they combine classification methods that use decision trees as classifiers. For creating a decision tree, the input data are imported in the tree's root node, and every other node contains a subset of their father node data. The father node data split into two or more subsets is based on the Gini index, entropy, or misclassification error. Every tree of the random forest can be expanded to its maximum depth or a limit depth selected before the training process.

In the proposed implementation, the Random Forest is initiated by injecting the user ratings for every cloth into every random forest. In this context, the Optuna library is used for finding the optimal values for the number of estimators and the maximum depth, which are the most critical parameters for the produced random forest models.

Content Based - Neural Networks. In this variation of the Content-Based Recommendation approach, every user rates several clothing products, and these ratings are given as input to the multi-layer neural network. The neural networks' architecture has many similarities with the neural network described in the Sect. 3.2. The parameters of the network are specified in Table 2.

Table 2. Structure of the multi-layers neural network (content based)

Layers	Neurons	Activation function	Dropout rate	Weights initialization
Layer 1	2048	ReLu	20%	he_normal
Layer 2	1024	ReLu	20%	he_normal
Layer 3	512	ReLu	10%	he_normal
Layer 4	256	ReLu	10%	he_normal
Layer 5	1	Sigmoid	0%	Glorot normal

Hybrid. The hybrid models combine two or more methods to benefit from all their advantages and eliminate their restrictions. The proposed hybrid system employs the methods mentioned above and creates a system of two recommendation packages. The first package suggests using the Regression Voting Ensemble in which the predictions are the average of contributing models. On the other hand, the second package endorses a linear regression model. The training set, given as input and used for the methods' training, is 70% of the initial dataset, and the testing set the remaining 30%.

4 Experimental Results

Having discussed the methodology behind the proposed system, we present the results of the clustering and recommendation modules separately in this section.

4.1 Fashion Data Clustering

The data collection module of the fashion trend recommendation system, provides the data to the clustering and the recommendation modules. These data consist of 22 product attributes described by both quantitative and qualitative variables (Table 3).

Table 3. Product attributes of the clothing apparels dataset

Data types	Product attributes
Numerical	Production Price, Retail Price, Sample Price, Wholesale Price
Categorical	Business Unit, Collar Design, Colors, Description, Fit, Foreign Composition, Gender, Inspiration Background, Length, LifeStage, Neck Design, Product Category, Product Subcategory, Production Manufacturer, Sample Manufacturer, Sizeset, Sleeve, Trend Theme

A preprocessing pipeline was established to clean up the noisy content collected by the social media platforms. The 12 remaining attributes and 1224 records are transformed using the FAMD method. According to the variability of each component, the first two out of the total 3 FAMD components are used as the clustering features.

Table 4. Comparison of baseline clustering algorithms and consensus clustering.

Metric	K-Means	Birch	Fuzzy C-Means	Consensus clustering
Silhouette	0.53	0.47	0.53	**0.93**
Davies-Bouldin	0.71	0.70	0.71	**0.18**
Calinski-Harabasz	1419.31	1096.08	1419.22	**18274.25**

For the clustering experiments, the employed algorithms mentioned earlier are used as baseline models and are compared against the proposed Consensus clustering model. Several iterations of each algorithm are executed to select the proper parameters. Regarding the FCM model, the fuzzifier parameter was set to 2. The ideal number of clusters was chosen using the Scaled Partition Entropy criterion, and a "hard" clustering result was produced by applying the maximum likelihood principle. The optimal number of clusters for the rest of the models was decided using (a) the Silhouette score [23], (b) Davies-Bouldin Index score [24], and (c) the Calinski-Harabasz Index score [25].

Table 4 demonstrates the superiority of the proposed clustering method, as it outperforms the rest in all of the examined metrics. Specifically, the higher Silhouette and Calinski-Harabasz scores are an indication of high density and separation. At the same time, a lower Davies-Bouldin index relates to a model with better separation between the clusters.

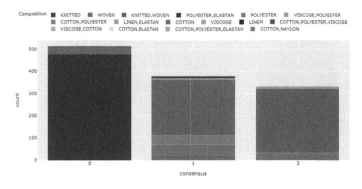

Fig. 1. Visualization of how the Consensus clusters capture the "Fabric Composition" attribute, where the first cluster consists mainly of knitted and woven products, whereas the second and third clusters contain apparels made out of polyester and cotton

Furthermore, the obtained clustering results are illustrated in Fig. 2, where the Consensus clustering, K-Means, and maximum likelihood FCM identified three clusters, whereas BIRCH revealed six groups. Also, Fig. 1 illustrates how the Consensus clusters capture the "Gender" and "Product Category" attributes of the fashion apparel dataset.

4.2 Product Recommender and Feedback Module Experiments

Dataset. Two diverse datasets were used to train and evaluate the Product Recommender and Feedback module (Table 5). The datasets were used to prepare the initial recommendation model and consist of 1700 clothing products from the ASOS website rated from 100 users. The main difference between the two datasets lies in the percentage of rated clothes per user, 30% for the first one and 60% for the second, while the clothes rating can vary from zero to ten [0,10]. The annotation for the rating of the clothing datasets was performed programmatically in a pseudo-random way.

Table 5. Dataset elements.

Dataset name	Products	Users	Ratings number	Ratings percentage	Ratings interval	Number of Categories
Asos30	1700	100	50k	30%	[0,10]	10
Asos60	1700	100	100k	60%	[0,10]	10

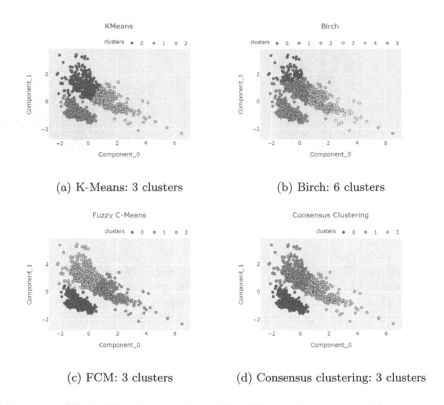

(a) K-Means: 3 clusters   (b) Birch: 6 clusters

(c) FCM: 3 clusters   (d) Consensus clustering: 3 clusters

Fig. 2. Visual comparison of the different clustering models

Table 6. Techniques results for asos datasets

(a) Asos30 dataset				(b) Asos60 dataset			
Model	Accuracy	Recall	Precision	F1 Score	Model	Accuracy	Recall	Precision	F1 Score
SVD	0.78	1.00	0.78	0.87	SVD	0.82	1.00	0.82	0.90
CF-NN	0.78	1.00	0.78	0.87	CF-NN	0.83	1.00	0.83	0.91
CB-RF	0.77	0.96	0.78	0.86	CB-RF	0.80	0.97	0.79	0.87
CB-NN	0.76	0.89	0.81	0.84	CB-NN	0.81	0.91	0.84	0.87
Hybrid	0.81	0.98	0.82	0.89	Hybrid	0.84	0.97	0.84	0.90

Results. In Table 6 we demonstrate the results of the techniques discussed in Chap. 3 for the two training datasets. Also, Table 7 contains the evaluation metrics for the evaluation of our implementation.

In the Asos30 dataset, the first three techniques have similar results; the accuracy varies from 77% to 78%, recall from 96% to 100%, and f1 score from 86% to 87%. The lower recall value is attributed to the CB-NN technique and the best overall performance to the hybrid method. More specifically, the hybrid method presents the best results for all the metrics, except for the recall value, which is close to the best value (98%).

Table 7. Evaluation metrics

(a) Asos30 dataset			(b)Asos60 dataset		
Model	RMSE	MAE	Model	RMSE	MAE
SVD	2.73	2.34	SVD	2.55	2.17
CF-NN	2.75	2.41	CF-NN	2.47	2.04
CB-RF	2.35	1.85	CB-RF	2.14	1.65
CB-NN	2.49	1.87	CB-NN	2.10	1.58
Hybrid	2.37	2.02	Hybrid	2.10	1.74

As far as the evaluation metrics are concerned, the SVD and CF-NN techniques have similarly low error values, with the RMSE varying from 2.73 to 2.75 and the MAE from 2.34 to 2.75. The CB-RF and CB-NN approaches also have similar error values. The best performance with the best evaluation metrics, 2.29 for the RMSE and 1.83 for the MAE, belongs to the hybrid method.

The results for the Asos60 dataset are similar to the Asos30, both for the accuracy, recall, precision, and evaluation metrics.

Based on the illustrated results, the hybrid method seems to be the optimal approach for the Recommendation system on the provided clothing garment dataset. It outperforms the individual techniques in most metrics utilized.

In Fig. 3, a visual representation of the hybrid method results for the query *"Coats for women"* is provided. In the first row of the figure, there are women coats already rated by the user. In contrast, there are unrated clothes with the

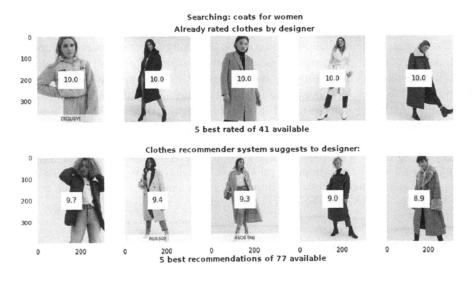

Fig. 3. Recommended clothes for the query: "Coats for women"

Recommendation system in the second row to predict their rating based on the user preferences. The coats presented by the Recommendation system as the best fits for the user are quite similar to the clothes in the first row, highlighting the accuracy and the usefulness of the proposed approach.

5   Conclusion and Future Work

Nowadays, the clothing industry has become one of the most profitable markets and moves towards fast fashion. Thus, artificial intelligence techniques have been adopted by most fashion houses. To this end, this paper has presented the clustering and the recommendation core modules of Science4Fashion, a modular digital assistant for fashion designers.

Specifically, the paper demonstrated an aggregated clustering approach, where the clustering insights produced from different algorithms are combined to a consensus clustering solution. The method was applied in a mixed dataset of categorical and numerical attributes obtained from retail websites and social media platforms. The consensus clustering approach produced more dense and segregated clusters than applying the methods individually.

Furthermore, different recommendation techniques were used as a base for the digital assistant's Product Recommender module. A hybrid approach of collaborative filtering and content-based methods outperformed the recommendations produced by applying each technique individually.

The clustering module's future extensions involve experimenting with FAMD features and various innovative clustering methods, such as spectral clustering and methods involving neural networks. Moreover, different feature encoding approaches can be explored where numerical attributes are transformed into categorical quantization techniques. In this case, K-Modes [1] algorithm, a variation of K-Means could be applied to cluster categorical data.

Extensions can also be applied to the Product Recommendation module, such as introducing pre-trained models from real-world datasets containing ratings from end-users and designers to optimize the recommendations' precision. Using user favorites, dashboards, and product sales as input would improve the Recommendation system results. Finally, the system can also include a negative vote for the clothes characterized as irrelevant by the user.

Acknowledgment. This research has been co-financed by the European Regional Development Fund of the European Union and Greek national funds through the Operational Program Competitiveness, Entrepreneurship, and Innovation, under the call RESEARCH – CREATE – INNOVATE (project code: T1EDK-03464)

References

1. Kotouza, M.T., Tsarouchis, S.F., Kyprianidis, A.-C., Chrysopoulos, A.C., Mitkas, P.A.: Towards fashion recommendation: an AI system for clothing data retrieval and analysis. In: Maglogiannis, I., Iliadis, L., Pimenidis, E. (eds.) AIAI 2020. IAICT, vol. 584, pp. 433–444. Springer, Cham (2020). https://doi.org/10.1007/978-3-030-49186-4_36
2. Wazarkar, S., Keshavamurthy, B.N.: Social image mining for fashion analysis and forecasting. Appl. Soft Comput. J. **95** (2020)
3. Guan, C., Qin, S., Ling, W., Ding, G.: Apparel recommendation system evolution: an empirical review (2016)
4. HCRS: A hybrid clothes recommender system based on user ratings and product features. In: 2013 International Conference on Management of e-Commerce and e-Government (ICMeCG) (2013)
5. Liu, Yu., Nie, J., Xu, L., Chen, Y., Xu, B.: Clothing recommendation system based on advanced user-based collaborative filtering algorithm. In: Sun, S., Chen, N., Tian, T. (eds.) ICSINC 2017. LNEE, vol. 473, pp. 436–443. Springer, Singapore (2018). https://doi.org/10.1007/978-981-10-7521-6_53
6. Bustamam, A., Tasman, H., N. Yuniarti, F., Mursidah, I.: Application of k-means clustering algorithm in grouping the DNA sequences of hepatitis B virus (HBV). In: AIP Conference Proceedings, volume 1862. American Institute of Physics Inc., July 2017
7. Bezdek, J.C., Ehrlich, R., Full, W.: FCM: the fuzzy c-means clustering algorithm. Comput. Geosci. **10**(2–3), 191–203 (1984)
8. Zhang, T., Ramakrishnan, R., Livny, M.: BIRCH: an efficient data clustering method for very large databases. SIGMOD Rec. (ACM Special Interest Group on Management of Data) **25**(2), 103–114 (1996)
9. Davidow, M., Maaeson, D.S.: Factor analysis of mixed data for anomaly detection. ACM Reference Format **9** (2016)
10. Yasuda, S.: Qualitative and quantitative data analysis. Japanese Sociol. Rev. **21**(1), 78–85, 114 (1970)
11. Murtagh, F.: Multiple correspondence analysis and related methods. Psychometrika **72**(2), 275–277 (2007)
12. Monti, S., Tamayo, P., Mesirov, J., Golub, T.: Consensus clustering: a resampling-based method for class discovery and visualization of gene expression microarray data. Mach. Learn. **52**(1–2), 91–118 (2003)
13. Alqurashi, T., Wang, W.: Clustering ensemble method. Int. J. Mach. Learn. Cybern., 1–18 (2018). https://doi.org/10.1007/s13042-017-0756-7
14. Vert, J.-P., Tsuda, K., Schölkopf, B.: A primer on kernel methods. In: Kernel Methods in Computational Biology (2019)
15. Adomavicius, G., Tuzhilin, A.: Toward the next generation of recommender systems: a survey of the state-of-the-art and possible extensions, June 2005
16. Xiaoyuan, S., Khoshgoftaar, T.M.: A survey of collaborative filtering techniques. Adv. Artif. Intell. **2009**, 1–19 (2009)
17. Çano, E., Morisio, M.: Hybrid recommender systems: a systematic literature review (2017)
18. He, X., Liao, L., Zhang, H., Nie, L., Hu, X., Chua., T.-S.: Neural collaborative filtering. CoRR, abs/1708.05031 (2017)
19. Potdar, K., Pardawala, T., Pai, C.: A comparative study of categorical variable encoding techniques for neural network classifiers. Int. J. Comput. Appl. **175**, 7–9 (2017)

20. Glorot, X., Bordes, A., Bengio, Y.: Deep sparse rectifier neural networks. In: Gordon, G., Dunson, D., Dudík, M., (eds.) Proceedings of the Fourteenth International Conference on Artificial Intelligence and Statistics, volume 15 of Proceedings of Machine Learning Research, pp. 315–323, Fort Lauderdale, FL, USA, 11–13 Apr 2011. PMLR
21. He, K., Zhang, X., Ren, S., Sun, J.: Deep residual learning for image recognition. CoRR, abs/1512.03385 (2015)
22. Zhang, H.-R., Min, F., He, X.: Aggregated recommendation through random forests. Sci. World J. **649596**(08), 2014 (2014)
23. Rousseeuw, P.J.: Silhouettes: a graphical aid to the interpretation and validation of cluster analysis. J. Comput. Appl. Math. **20**(C), 53–65 (1987
24. Davies, D.L., Bouldin, D.W.: A cluster separation measure. IEEE Trans. Pattern Anal. Mach. Intell. **PAMI-1**(2), 224–227 (1979)
25. Caliñski, T., Harabasz, J.: A dendrite method foe cluster analysis. Commun. Stat. **3**(1), 1–27 (1974)

Sentiment Analysis

A Two-Step Optimised BERT-Based NLP Algorithm for Extracting Sentiment from Financial News

Rapheal Olaniyan[✉], Daniel Stamate[✉], and Ida Pu

Data Science and Soft Computing Lab, and Computing Department,
Goldsmiths, University of London, London, UK
{D.Stamate,i.pu}@gold.ac.uk

Abstract. Sentiment analysis involving the identification of sentiment polarities from textual data is a very popular area of research. Many research works that have explored and extracted sentiments from textual data such as financial news have been able to do so by employing Bidirectional Encoder Representations from Transformers (BERT) based algorithms in applications with high computational needs, and also by manually labelling sample data with help from financial experts. We propose an approach which makes possible the development of quality Natural Language Processing (NLP) models without the need for high computing power, or for inputs from financial experts on labelling focused dataset for NLP model development. Our approach introduces a two-step optimised BERT-based NLP model for extracting sentiments from financial news. Our work shows that with little effort that involves manually labelling a small but relevant and focused sample data of financial news, one could achieve a high performing and accurate multi-class NLP model on financial news.

Keywords: Sentiment analysis · Financial news · NLP · Transfer learning · Classification · Two-step optimised BERT

1 Introduction

The internet is full of online expressions which could be in the form of social blogs, financial news, or other kinds of textual expressions - thanks to the advancement in computer systems. With this advancement comes the ease of accessing, storing and processing large amounts of textual data. And now, sentiment analysis which helps to detect the element of feelings in textual data has become popular due to its vast applicability in areas such as artificial intelligence, stock market trading, politics, psychology, among others (Qie et al. [13], Bechara [2] and Hatfield [3]). For example, the polarity of sentiment extracted from textual data can be identified using sentiment analysis. This may be categorised as factual, positive reflecting a happy state of mind, negative referring

© IFIP International Federation for Information Processing 2021
Published by Springer Nature Switzerland AG 2021
I. Maglogiannis et al. (Eds.): AIAI 2021, IFIP AICT 627, pp. 745–756, 2021.
https://doi.org/10.1007/978-3-030-79150-6_58

to sad mood, or neutral. In addition, one may also use sentiment analysis to assess the degrees of polarised sentiments by scoring the different polarities of sentiments.

Sentiment analysis in the domain of finance, especially where the sentiments obtained are used to improve the predictive power of stock market predictive models, is of utmost importance. The predictive value of sentiments is highly time-sensitive with respect to first mover advantage in the face of market imperfection (Vayanos and Wang [11]). That is, one would expect the prices of the stock market to reflect all available information. As new information becomes available, players in the market adjust their positions and this new information becomes fully incorporated into the prices. There is a gap between these two points of information arrival and the time when prices reflect the new information. This short time window is termed as market imperfection (Vayanos and Wang [11]). This aspect supports the rationale behind the time sensitivity of the statistical significance of sentiment variables. Financial news could be the source of new information, expressed as sentiment, which has proved to be useful in enhancing stock market prediction with statistical and machine learning approaches (Smales [20], Shiller [25], Olaniyan et al. [26], and Marechal et al. [12]). Advanced NLP approaches are powerful tools that can be used to reliably and effectively extract sentiment polarity information from financial news, and we propose such a novel approach here based on adapting and extending the BERT algorithm [16].

Worryingly, it appears difficult - or so it seems - applying supervised NLP methods in this domain for two obvious reasons: 1) Developing NLP classification models requires a significant amount of effort to correctly label a huge amount of the training data to be used in the model training development. 2) The model to develop depends on the domain-specific corpus for learning transfer as opposed to any general corpora which are not well-suited for supervised tasks.

As a result of these concerns NLP transfer learning methods have become a popular choice. They have been proven to be very promising and advanced the state of the art across natural language tasks. Moreover, the foundation of these models, the language model (LM) pre-training, is considered effective as the initial step required when developing natural language models (Dai and Le [4], Dolan and Brockett [28], Howard and Ruder [18], Baevski et al. [1]). The rationale for this choice of models is that they learn contextualized text representations by predicting words based on their contexts using very large corpora, and can be fine-tuned to adapt to downstream tasks (Peters et al. [21]). The challenge from the paucity of labelled data is avoided as the LM does not depend on it - rather it predicts words from contexts based on the semantic information it has learnt. And the fine-tuning of the NLP transfer learning methods on labelled data uses the semantic information learnt to predict labels. Here is where the problem lies: the fine-tuning of the NLP model on reliable labelled downstream tasks.

Manually labelling data for fine-tuning is a difficult task. First, it requires much time and effort. Second, the manually labelled data must be reliable and representative. Table 1 presents the experimental results on Financial Phrase-Bank [14] of 4845 financial news that were randomly selected from LexisNexis database and annotated by 16 financial experts. Interestingly, all the participants were able to agree on just 46% of the data's sentiment polarities. This clearly confirms the inherent challenge in manually labelling financial news data and, as a result, fine-tuning of models would suffer as a consequence.

Table 1. This table was taken from Araci [8]. Distribution of sentiment labels and agreement levels in Financial PhraseBank.

Agreement level	Positive	Negative	Neutral	Count
100%	25.2%	13.4%	61.4%	2262
75%–99%	26.6%	9.8%	63.6%	1191
66%–74%	36.7%	12.3%	50.9%	765
50%–65%	31.1%	14.4%	54.5%	627
All	28.1%	12.4%	59.4%	4845

Our framework is therefore centred on developing a reliable high-performing NLP model with no exposure to any of these aforementioned challenges.

The rest of this paper is structured as follows: Sect. 2 introduces our proposed approach. Section 3 presents the basis of the NLP model that would be used in this work. Section 4 provides information about the data sources, the various datasets, and the methodology applied. Results from the use of the primary model are presented in Sect. 5. Section 6 details the rationales behind the use of the secondary model that we propose, and presents some empirical findings about why any NLP models with very high level of accuracy may perform poorly on real life data. Finally, Sect. 7 provides the conclusion to our work.

2 Proposed Approach

Considering these challenges our research focus is centred on developing a reliable NLP model for sentence polarity identification of financial news and we aim to achieve this with very minimal effort. In fact, our proposed two-step optimised BERT-based model overcomes these challenges. The main contributions of this work are therefore highlighted below:

1. We propose a two-step approach that includes: (a) a primary model that relies on the labelled data from the experiment results on Financial PhraseBank and an optimised BERT-based NLP model called the Roberta NLP introduced by Liu et al. [30], and (b) a secondary model that combines the experimental results and a small data sample of financial news data that has been manually labelled by us and validated with the primary model. This is to ensure that the secondary model has been fine-tuned with focused data.

2. We evaluate the primary model, and compare it with other related works in terms of their respective degrees of accuracy. The aim of this comparison is to see how the model fine-tuned with just the experimental results would perform on the financial news data related to the constituents of the S&P 500 index. The data is obtained from Intrinio platform [15].

3. We evaluate the results of the secondary model and compare with the primary model with the aim of assessing if the results obtained from both models are statistically different. Findings from the results would help us to understand the relevance of the secondary model especially when it is trained on focused data. In addition, we aim to assess the quality of our proposed two-step BERT-based model that does not rely on high computing power and on inputs from financial experts on manually labelling focused data for fine-tuning.

We use the BERT model introduced by Devlin et al. [16] as the framework for developing our proposed two-step optimised NLP model. As the name implies the centre-piece of the BERT model is the transformer which was first published by Vaswani et al. [6] and which is a great breakthrough in the world of language modelling. The section that follows will detail the BERT-based NLP framework.

3   BERT NLP

The likes of convolutional neural networks (CNN) and Long-Short Term Memory (LSTM) are useful language modelling but there are some constraints around them. One of these constraints is their poor performance when it comes to processing long sentences - the probability of learning the contextual relations between words when they are far away from each other diminishes linearly (Kalchbrenner et al. [23]) or exponentially (Gehring et al. [17]) depending on the language model used. Although some transduction models -models that convert input sequence of elements into another output sequence - have been able to overcome this challenge through the coupling of neural nets with an attention learning mechanism that facilitates attention learning of specific words with the notion that these words could be embedded with contextual relevance (Bahdanau et al. [9], Kim et al. [29], Parikh et al. [5]). Another common problem with these transduction models is their inflexibility to parallel computation of tasks or their inefficient flexibility to it. This is where the transformer plays the leading role whereby it does not depend on any coupling of neural nets with attention mechanism. It uses its inherent self-attention mechanism solely to draw the contextual relations between input and output and it also allows for efficient parallel computation of input and output (Devlin et al. [16]).

In the wake of the transformer many language model pre-trainings have sprung up and results from research works support the fact that these models are effective for enhancing NLP-related undertakings (Peters et al. [21], Howard and Ruder [18]). These models are applicable in a broad range of tasks such as named entity recognition (Li et al. [19]), sentiment analysis (Sun et al. [7]), text summarisation (Miller [10]), among others.

Most of the pre-training-based models are unidirectional - from the left to the right - in learning the general language representations. Devlin et al. [16] state that such architectural constraint limits the choice of architectures in the first place and are sub-optimal for sentence-level tasks. In view of this BERT is proposed for fine-tuning because of its uniquely bidirectional approach for general language representations.

The optimised version of the pre-trained BERT model will be used in this work as originally presented by Liu et al. [30] for developing the primary model. This model will be the basis upon which our secondary model is developed.

4   Methodology

In the process of conducting sentiment analysis on financial news we source for financial news data from Intrinio platform [15]. The data collected covers the period September 2012 and July 2019 and this comprises 1.05 million records - our interest is to extract multiclass sentiment polarities from this data. The financial news data collected are related only to the constituents of the S &P 500 index. Our aim is to identify the sentiment polarities from this data by applying our proposed NLP model. Extra care is required in ensuring that false positives and false negatives are minimised. In doing this we propose a two-step optimised BERT-based NLP model where the first step is to produce the primary model that explores both the labelled data from the experimental results on Financial PhraseBank and an optimised BERT-based NLP model. The level of accuracy of the model would be examined to see if it qualifies enough to become our primary model. More specifically, we employ the Roberta NLP model which is considered the optimised version of the BERT model. We train the optimised BERT-based NLP model with the experimental results on the financial PhraseBank dataset which is the dataset used also in [24] and [8]. The dataset consists of 4,845 financial news that were randomly selected from the LexisNexis database. In the process of manually labelling the financial news data 16 financial professionals were asked to participate. 47% (2263 of the 4845) of the financial news had 100% agreements from all the participants. This implies that some sentences were assigned different labels by different participants. Clearly, this is a confirmation that manual labelling is complex and challenging to correctly assign true labels due to varyingly and subjectively contextual perspectives. It is also laborious to manually label a high volume of sentences for developing training models.

In view of these issues we resolve to using only the financial news with 100% agreement level from all the participants totalling 2263 sentences in training our primary model. The summary of the selected sample data is presented in Table 2.

The second step in our approach is to develop the secondary model that explores combined datasets from two data sources: a) the same dataset used in the primary model which is the experimental results from the Financial Phrase-Bank, and b) a small sample dataset of 2,000 records from [15] that has been manually labelled by us and also validated by the developed primary model. The aim is to see if by including focused labelled data the secondary model

Table 2. Experimental results on the Financial PhraseBank dataset containing the 2263 financial news with 100% agreement level labelled by the 16 financial professionals.

Value	Polarity	Count
0	Neutral	1390
1	Positive	570
−1	Negative	303
Grand total		**2263**

will outperform the primary model. Clearly, the primary model is a key and integral part of the secondary model. Attention would therefore be paid to the degree of accuracy of the model with the assumption that a high degree would constitute its acceptance as a basis for developing the secondary model. Recall that 16 professionals were involved in the experimental labelled results on the Financial PhraseBank. One of the possible reasons for involving many financial professionals was to ensure that the experimental results produced were reliable and of high quality in the labelling task.

Understandably, going through at least the same level of effort of involving many financial experts in the manual labelling is resource-consuming and time-taking. As a result, we are proposing the two-step NLP approach that we consider to be effective both in labelling and in model training. It is worth mentioning that the manual labelling of sentences itself is challenging not just in regard to the volume of sentences to label but also in correctly labelling sentences because sometimes there seems to be a very thin line among the classes e.g. positive and neutral for example.

Below are some examples:

1. InvestorPlace Stock Market News Stock Advice amp Trading Tips Apple NASDAQ AAPL will be reporting its third quarter earnings on July. Apple stock has performed well since the start of June posting a gain since June but on July all bets are off.
2. Why Apple Stock May Be a Case of Near-Term Pain, Long-Term Gain
3. UPDATE -Ireland invests disputed Apple taxes in low-risk bonds
4. American CEO reiterates confidence in Max return by mid-August despite unclear timetable from Boeing, FAA
5. UPDATE -Apple explores moving -% of production capacity from China - Nikkei

Manually labelling over 1 million financial news would be very laborious and we would expect a lot of disagreements in labelling some news among us, if we were to perform this task: hence, the need to manually label a small sample and use the trained model to validate the results of our labelled news. Where we have disagreements in the results between our manual labelling and the trained model, we review carefully in order to identify the true labels. We are more interested in the false positives and negatives from the model's results so that we could review the sentences that we consider to be wrongly labelled and add the reviewed sentences to the training data and finally obtain the secondary model. Eventually with help from the trained primary model, we have 2,000 labelled news - that have been randomly selected from [15] - to be added to the original training data. Our secondary model is therefore trained by combining the 2,000 labelled news that have been reviewed and the experimental results on the financial PhraseBank. The trained secondary model is then applied to over 1 million financial news data in order to obtain sentence polarities which could be positive, neutral or negative.

5   Primary NLP Model

Before the BERT NLP model could be used it has to go through two key steps. First, the BERT would have to be pre-trained like every other language model so that they could learn the contextual relations between words. Pre-training a model on a very large corpus is a very resource-consuming effort especially with the amount of time and computing architecture capacity required. For example, most of the BERT pre-training exercises were conducted on the Google cloud [16,31] and Amazon cloud [8] translating to the high dependence of the pre-training stage on high computing machines. Devlin et al. [16] pre-trained the model using the corpus that contained the combination of the BooksCorpus (800M words) (Zhu et al. [31]) and English Wikipedia (2,500M words).

The second stage would require that the pre-trained model goes through supervised learning where the training dataset contains texts and their respective labels e.g. "The US stock market is bullish" is the text and the label is "positive". The results predicted using the trained BERT-based models have been promising and this accounts for its popularity.

Araci [8] examined if by both pre-training (unsupervised learning) and training (supervised learning) the BERT on downstream tasks could improve further the BERT model. In the process, the author pre-trained the BERT model on the financial news data obtained from Reuters at first, and then trained the model using the experimental results on the financial PhraseBank dataset which was the same data used in [24]. Findings showed that such process could improve the model performance by 15% in accuracy.

Liu et al. [30] revisited the work done by [16] and concluded that the pre-trained BERT was not at its optimal level. They pre-trained the model all over and finally obtained the optimised BERT model. In view of this development we would be using the optimised BERT model to compare the results with the Araci [8]'s. Findings from this work would help us to answer the following questions:

1. Is pre-training the BERT model with targeted downstream task necessary as opposed to the huge corpus of BooksCorpus (800M words) and English Wikipedia used to pre-train the BERT?
2. Is the downstream data used by [24] and [8] for the supervised model training and evaluation representative enough of the financial news?

Table 3. Most of the information in this table was taken from Araci [8] with reference to Malo et al. [24], Krishnamoorthy [27] and Maia et al. [22] regarding the results using LPS, HSC and FinSSLX respectively. The last row added by us represents the results obtained from the optimised BERT-based model - this report was based on a 5-fold cross-validation results.

Data with 100 % agreement			
Model	Loss	Accuracy	F1 Score
LSTM	0.57	0.81	0.74
LSTM with ELMo	0.50	0.84	0.77
ULMFit	0.20	0.93	0.91
LPS	–	0.79	0.80
HSC	–	0.83	0.86
FinSSLX	–	0.91	0.88
FinBERT	0.13	0.97	0.95
ROBERTA	**0.12**	**0.97**	**0.97**

As shown in Table 3 the optimised BERT-based model appears to have achieved the same level of accuracy as the FinBERT model. The optimised BERT is only trained with the downstream tasks and the results show that it performs as highly accurate as the FinBERT's which was proposed by [8]. In view of this it would be hard to conclude that pre-training the BERT model with downstream tasks would improve the accuracy level of the BERT as [8] has claimed.

The optimised BERT model performs well with a very high level of accuracy when trained on the Financial PhraseBank dataset. Would this trained model perform well on real life data? To answer the question, we apply the trained primary model on a new financial news data in order to evaluate its reliability when applied to real life situation. This task is addressed in the next section.

6   Secondary NLP Model

We use the experimental results on the Financial PhraseBank data to train the optimised BERT model and this achieves a high accuracy level of 97% as presented in Table 3. In order to assess how representative the training data is, we evaluate the predicted results obtained from the trained model (primary model) on a new set of financial news obtained from [15]. If the results obtained show at least 90% level of accuracy on the new data, we would conclude that the training data is highly representative of the financial news and that the model is reliable without the need for the proposed secondary model.

In this process we start by manually labelling 3000 financial news randomly sourced from [15]. We understand the concern that we might not be 100% accurate in the manual labelling; hence, the need to rely on the primary model for the validation of the manual labels and the review and correction of the labels that appear as false positives and false negatives.

Table 4. This report represents the out-of-sample evaluation results from the primary model when applied to new focused data.

Class	Precision	Recall	F1-Score	Support
−1	0.93	0.93	0.93	42
0	0.86	0.59	0.70	63
1	0.77	0.93	0.84	91

Table 5. This report represents the out-of-sample confusion matrix obtained from the primary model when applied to new focused data. The confusion matrix leads to an accuracy of 82%.

		True Label			
	Label	−1	0	1	Total
	−1	39	1	2	42
Predicted label	0	2	37	24	63
	1	1	5	85	91
	Total	42	43	111	196

The results from the model are presented in Tables 4 and 5. The results show that when the trained primary model is applied to predict the sentiments from a different sample data the level of accuracy drops significantly to 82%. On this ground we conclude that the initial sample data - the experimental results on the Financial PhraseBank dataset - is short of being considered as a representative of the financial news in general. Considering this we develop the secondary model which is the second step of our proposed two-step optimised BERT-based NLP model. The secondary model clearly shows improvement judging by the performances presented in Tables 6 and 7, including an overall accuracy of 99%. We should note that in repeated test experiments we obtained accuracies of at least 97%.

Table 6. This report represents the out-of-sample evalutation results from the secondary model when applied to new focused data.

Class	Precision	Recall	F1-Score	Support
−1	0.98	1.0	0.99	42
0	1.0	1.0	1.0	63
1	1.0	0.99	0.99	91

Table 7. This table represents the confusion matrix obtained from the secondary model when applied to new focused data. The confusion matrix leads to an accuracy of 99%.

		True Label			
	Label	−1	0	1	Total
	−1	42	0	0	42
Predicted label	0	0	63	0	63
	1	1	0	90	91
	Total	43	63	90	196

7   Discussion and Conclusion

The use of BERT models in NLP modelling has gained huge popularity and we have been able to demonstrate promising results from it. Many research works have been developed using the BERT family. Some of them have attempted to improve on the BERT-related work by proposing that pre-training the BERT models on downstream tasks would provide improved results (Araci [8]). This suggested approach is clearly laboriously resource-consuming in that one would have to source for pre-training downstream tasks and that input from experts would be required on manually labelling sample data for model fine-tuning.

We acknowledge how arduous manually labelling a high volume of financial news data for training NLP models could be and the need to involve financial professional experts in the labelling effort. In view of these challenges, we have proposed a two-step optimised BERT-based approach which has the tendency of minimising the impacts of not including these two requirements. That is, with our proposed approach we would need to manually label just a small sample of focused financial news data. And noting that our manually labelled training data might contain some false labels our approach has therefore considered such occurrence by searching for false labels (otherwise known as mismatches between the results from the primary model and our manual labels) and correcting before they are fed into the secondary model which is the second step of our proposed model. This is done by establishing a primary model developed by first training the optimised BERT model using the experimental results from the Financial PhraseBank news data. The trained primary model is then applied to the small sample of 3000 manually labelled news for validation. In doing so false matches between the manual labelling and the results from the primary model are identified and reviewed. The manually labelled data - reviewed and true matches - are then added to the initial training data resulting in a combined training data which would then be used to re-train an optimised BERT model. This becomes the trained secondary model. The rationale for these two steps is that the trained primary model on its own is not sufficient due to the misrepresentation of the initial training data as shown by its low accuracy level of 82%. But with the secondary model that has been developed with more focused data and little manual input we are able to achieve a high accuracy of over 97%. This is achieved with a minimal and manageable effort. Our paper can be further extended to explore the relationship between financial sentiments and the stock markets. This can be achieved by using our model to extract the sentiment polarities from financial news.

References

1. Baevski, A., Edunov, S., Liu, Y., Zettlemoyer, L., Auli, M.: Cloze-driven pretraining of self-attention networks, arXiv preprint arXiv:1903.07785 (2019)
2. Bechara, A.: The role of emotion in decision-making: Evidence from neurological patients with orbitofrontal damage. Brain Cogn. Dev. Orbitofrontal Function **55**(1), 30–40 (2004)
3. Hatfield, A., Cacioppo, J., Rapson, R.L.: Emotional Contagion. Cambridge University Press, Cambridge (1994)
4. Dai, A.M., Le, Q.V.: Semi-supervised sequence learning. In: Advances in Neural Information Processing Systems, pp. 3079–3087 (2015)
5. Parikh, A., Täckström, O., Das, D., Uszkoreit, J.: A decomposable attention model. In: Empirical Methods in Natural Language Processing (2016)
6. Vaswani, A., et al.: Attention is all you need (2017) arXiv:1706.03762
7. Sun, C., Huang, L., Qiu, X.: Utilizing BERT for aspect-based sentiment analysis via constructing auxiliary sentence, arXiv:1903.09588 (2019)
8. Araci, D.: FinBERT: Financial sentiment analysis with pre-trained language models, arXiv:1908.10063 (2019)
9. Bahdanau, D., Cho, K., Bengio, Y.: Neural machine translation by jointly learning to align and translate, CoRR, abs/1409.0473 (2014)
10. Miller, D.: Leveraging BERT for extractive text summarization on lectures, arXiv:1906.04165 (2019)
11. Vayanos, D., Wang, J.: Market Liquidity - Theory and Empirical Evidence. In: Handbook of the Economics of Finance Volume 2, Part B, pp. 1289–1361 (2013)
12. Marechal, F., Stamate, D., Olaniyan, R., Marek, J.: On XLE index constituents'c social media based sentiment informing the index trend and volatility prediction. In: Proceedings of the 10th International Conference on Computatational Collective Intelligence (ICCCI). LNCS. Springer (2018)
13. Qiu, G., He, X., Zhang, F., Shi, Y., Bu, J., Chen, C.: DASA: dissatisfaction-oriented advertising based on sentiment analysis. Expert Syst. Appl. **37**(9), 6182–6191 (2010)
14. Malo, P., Sinha, A., Takala, P., Korhonen P.J.: FinancialPhraseBank-v1.0, July 2013. https://www.researchgate.net/publication/251231364_FinancialPhraseBank-v10
15. https://intrinio.com/
16. Devlin, J., Chang, M.W., Lee, K., Toutanova, K.: Bert: Pre-training of deep bidirectional transformers for language understanding, 2018, arXiv preprint arXiv:1810.04805
17. Gehring, J., Auli, M., Grangier, D., Yarats, D., Dauphin, Y.N.: Convolutional sequence to sequence learning, arXiv preprint arXiv:1705.03122v2 (2017)
18. Howard, J., Ruder, S.: Universal Language Model Fine-tuning for Text Classification, arXiv:1801.06146 http://arxiv.org/abs/1801.06146 (2018)
19. Li, J., Sun, A., Han, J., Li, C.: A Survey on Deep Learning for Named Entity Recognition, arXiv:1812.09449 (2018)

20. Smales, L.A.: Non-scheduled news arrival and high frequency stock market dynamics: evidence from the Australian Securities Exchange. Res. Int. Bus. Financ. **32**, 122–138 (2014)
21. Peters, M.E., et al.: Deep contextualized word representations, 2018 from https:// doi.org/10.18653/v1/N18-1202. arXiv:1802.05365
22. Maia, M., et al.: Companion of the the web conference: on the web conference 2018, WWW 2018, Lyon, France, pp. 23–27, 2018 (2018)
23. Kalchbrenner, N., Espeholt, L., Simonyan, K., Oord, A.V.D., Graves, A., Kavukcuoglu, K: Neural machine translation in linear time. arXiv preprint arXiv:1610.10099v2 (2017)
24. Malo, P., Sinha, A., Korhonen, P., Wallenius, J., Takala, P.: Good debt or bad debt: detecting semantic orientations in economic texts. J. Assoc. Inf. Sci. Technol. **65**(4), 782–796 (2014)
25. Shiller, R.J.: Irrational Exuberance. Princeton University Press, Princeton (2000)
26. Olaniyan, R., Stamate, D., Logofatu, D., Ouarbya, L.: Sentiment and stock market volatility predictive modelling - a hybrid approach. In: Proceedings of the 2nd IEEE/ACM International Conference on Data Science and Advanced Analytics (2015)
27. Krishnamoorthy, S.: Sentiment analysis of financial news articles using performance indicators. Knowledge and Information Systems **56**(2), 373–394 (2017). https://doi.org/10.1007/s10115-017-1134-1
28. Dolan, W.B., Brockett, C.: Automatically constructing a corpus of sentential paraphrases. In: Proceedings of the Third International Workshop on Paraphrasing (IWP2005) (2005)
29. Kim, Y., Denton, C., Hoang, L., Rush, A.M.: Structured attention networks. In: International Conference on Learning Representations (2017)
30. Liu, Y., et al.: RoBERTa: a robustly optimized BERT pretraining approach, arXiv:1907.11692 (2019)
31. Zhu, Y., et al.: Aligning books and movies: towards story-like visual explanations by watching movies and reading books. In: Proceedings of the IEEE International Conference on Computer Vision, pp. 19–27 (2015)

Learning Sentiment-Aware Trading Strategies for Bitcoin Leveraging Deep Learning-Based Financial News Analysis

N. Passalis[✉], S. Seficha, A. Tsantekidis, and A. Tefas

Artificial Intelligence and Information Analysis Lab, Department of Informatics,
Aristotle University of Thessaloniki,Thessaloniki, Greece
{passalis,sseficha,avraamt,tefas}@csd.auth.gr

Abstract. Even though Deep Learning (DL) models are increasingly used in recent years to develop trading agents, most of them solely rely on a restricted set of input information, e.g., price time-series. However, this is in contrast with the information that is usually available to human traders that, apart from relying on price information, also take into account their prior knowledge, sentiment that is expressed regarding various markets and assets, as well as general news and forecasts. In this paper, we examine whether the use of sentiment information, as extracted by various online sources, including news articles, is beneficial when training DL agents for trading. More specifically, we provide an extensive evaluation that includes several different configurations and models, ranging from Multi-layer Perceptrons (MLPs) to Convolutional Neural Networks (CNNs) and Recurrent Neural Networks (RNNs), examining the impact of using sentiment information when developing DL models for trading applications. Apart from demonstrating that sentiment can indeed lead to improved trading efficiency, we also provide further insight on the use of sentiment-enriched data sources for cryptocurrences, such as Bitcoin, where its seems that sentiment information might actually be a stronger predictor compared to the information provided by the actual price time-series.

Keywords: Financial trading · Sentiment analysis · Deep learning · Sentiment-aware trading

1 Introduction

Deep Learning (DL) methods are increasingly used in recent years for developing intelligent agents for financial trading [5,7,11,14,18,20], superseding, to a large extent, traditional methods, such as rule-based strategies. Indeed, powerful DL formulations led to models with enormous learning capacity, while their ability to seamlessly integrate with Reinforcement Learning (RL) methodologies allowed for directly optimizing trading policies to maximize the expected profit, even in

© IFIP International Federation for Information Processing 2021
Published by Springer Nature Switzerland AG 2021
I. Maglogiannis et al. (Eds.): AIAI 2021, IFIP AICT 627, pp. 757–766, 2021.
https://doi.org/10.1007/978-3-030-79150-6_59

the volatile and uncertain conditions that often exist in real markets [5,9,18]. Despite the encouraging results reported in the literature, current approaches operate on a restricted set of input information, i.e., they mainly rely on time-series information regarding the price of assets. This is in contrast with the information that is usually available to human traders that, apart from observing price-related information, also take into account their prior knowledge, sentiment that is expressed regarding various markets and assets, as well as general news and forecasts.

Contrary to this, trading using DL is typically tackled as a problem that can be solved solely on relying on a single modality, i.e., price time-series, without taking into account any additional external information. Indeed, the additional complexity and development cost regarding collecting the appropriate data, pre-processing them and then transforming them into a form that can be exploited by DL models, often discourage DL researchers and companies from exploiting these valuable sources of information. Recent evidence suggests that external information, mainly provided in the form of sentiment regarding various financial assets [3,4,12,19] and typically collected from social media, often has a positive effect on the accuracy of trading agents. However, little work has been done so far towards this direction, especially for exploiting large-scale datasets that contain news articles regarding financial assets.

The main contribution of this work is to examine whether the use of sentiment information, as extracted by various online sources, including news articles, is beneficial when training DL agents for trading. More specifically, in this paper, we aim to evaluate the impact of using sentiment information when training a wide variety of deep learning models, ranging from Multi-layer Percetrons (MLPs) to Convolutional Neural Networks (CNNs) and Recurrent Neural Networks (RNNs). To this end, we go beyond the existing literature that typically just evaluate a few handpicked models, with and without sentiment information, and we providing an extensive evaluation, often including more than 50 different configurations per architecture. Apart from confirming our initial hypothesis, we also provide some surprising results, demonstrating that for cryptocurrences, such as Bitcoin, sentiment information might actually be a stronger predictor compared to the information provided by price time-series.

The rest of the paper is structured as follows. First, we introduce the used notation and analytically describe the proposed method in Sect. 2. Then, we provided an extensive experimental evaluation in Sect. 3. Finally, Sect. 4 concludes the paper and discusses possible future research directions.

2   Proposed Method

In this Section we introduce the proposed data processing and fusion pipeline, as well as the employed financial forecasting setup. For the rest of this Section, we assume that both the forecasting, as well as the sampling time-step is set to one day. This is without loss of generality, since the proposed method can be trivially extended to work on longer or smaller time horizons, given that the appropriate data are collected.

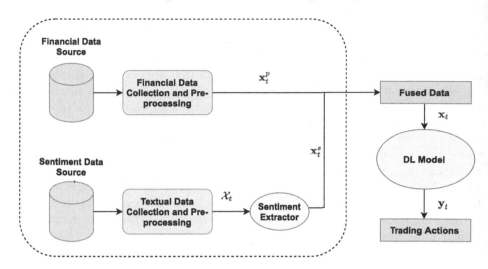

Fig. 1. Proposed trading pipeline: The trained DL models rely on two different information sources: a) financial data sources, that provide price information, as well as b) sentiment data sources, that provide sentiment information. After appropriately preprocessing both of them, the fused data are fed to a DL model that provides the trading signals.

The proposed data processing pipeline, along with the forecasting model are shown in Fig. 1. First, the DL model receives the raw price candles from a financial data source, e.g., an exchange. These data are then preprocessed in order to obtain a single scalar value for each time-step t that corresponds to the percentage change of the price of an asset as:

$$x_t^p = \frac{c_t}{c_{t-1}} - 1, \tag{1}$$

where c_t denotes the close price at time t. It is worth noting that this is among the most well-established financial data preprocessing approaches for extracting stationary features [10,17]. Then, these percentage changes are aggregated for a windows of length L to form a vector that describes the price behavior of a specific asset during the last L steps:

$$\mathbf{x}_t^p = [\frac{c_{t-L-1}}{c_{t-L-2}} - 1, \ldots, \frac{c_t}{c_{t-1}} - 1] \in \mathbb{R}^L. \tag{2}$$

Note that we use bold notation to refer to the vector that contains the *history* of the previous L percentage changes at time t, i.e., $\mathbf{x}_t^p$, while we use a regular font to refer to the scalar percentage change at time t, i.e., x_t^p .

In this work, we propose to also employ sentiment information about a financial asset, as expressed in various online sources, to extract additional information that can be useful for predicting the future behavior of the said asset. Let $\mathcal{X}_t$ denote a collection of textual documents that refer to the asset at hand

and collected at time t, i.e., after time-step $t - 1$ and until time-step t. Also, let $f_s(\mathbf{x}_d)$ denote a sentiment extractor that returns the sentiment of a document $\mathbf{x}_d$, where $\mathbf{x}_d$ is an appropriate representation of a textual document for the task of sentiment analysis, e.g., a sequence of the words that appear in the corresponding document [2]. In this work, we assume that the sentiment is represented as a scalar value that ranges from -1 (negative sentiment) to $+1$ (positive) sentiment. A sentiment extractor can be always used to extract such a scalar value as follows. For regression-based sentiment extractors we can directly use the extracted value, after appropriately normalizing it. On the other hand, for classification-based sentiment extractors, we can calculate the sentiment score simply by subtracting the confidence for the negative class from the confidence for the positive class. In this paper, we follow the latter approach, as we further explain in Sect. 3, by employing a state-of-the-art deep learning-based extractor that is fine-tuned on financial documents [2].

Therefore, for each time-step we can extract the *average polarity* regarding the asset at hand as follows:

$$x_t^s = \frac{1}{|\mathcal{X}_t|} \sum_{\mathbf{x}_d \in \mathcal{X}_t} f(\mathbf{x}_d), \tag{3}$$

where $|\mathcal{X}_t|$ denotes the number of text documents collected at time-step t. Then, we can similarly define the time-series that describes the sentiment over a horizon of L time-steps as:

$$\mathbf{x}_t^s = [x_{t-L-1}^s, \ldots, x_t^s] \in \mathbb{R}^L. \tag{4}$$

The most straightforward way to combine the price information ($\mathbf{x}_t^p$), with the sentiment information ($\mathbf{x}_t^s$) is to simply concatenate the corresponding vectors into a tensor $\mathbf{x}_t = [\mathbf{x}_t^p; \mathbf{x}_t^s] \in \mathbb{R}^{L \times 2}$. Then, this tensor is fed to the corresponding DL model, as shown in Fig. 1.

Several different approaches have been proposed in the literature for training DL models for financial trading, ranging from classification-based methods [16] to complex reinforcement learning setups which aim to simulate the trading environment [5]. In this work, we opt for following a classification-based setup, where a DL model is trained to predict the price movements that are more likely to lead to profit. More specifically, the ground labels for training the DL model are generated as:

$$l_t = \begin{cases} 1 & \text{if } \frac{c_{t+1}}{c_t} - 1 > c_{thres} \\ -1 & \text{se } \frac{c_{t+1}}{c_t} - 1 < -c_{thres} \\ 0 & \text{otherwise,} \end{cases} \tag{5}$$

where c_{thres} denotes the threshold for considering that a price movement is a potential candidate for performing a profitable trade. Therefore, the label "1" corresponds to a long position, the label "-1" to a short position, while the label "0" indicates market conditions that probably do not allow the specific agent to perform profitable trades, i.e., the agent should exit the market. Typically, c_{thres} is set to a value high enough to overcome any commission fees, as well as to account for price slippage that might occur. Please note that during back-testing, the consecutive "long" or "short" positions do not lead to multiple commissions (since the agent simply keeps the already existing position open), while the exit position ("0") closes the currently open position and materializes any gain/loss acquired.

After generating the labels, the DL model can be directly trained using the cross entropy loss, i.e.,

$$\mathcal{L} = -\frac{1}{N} \sum_{t=1}^{N} \sum_{j=1}^{3} [\mathbf{l}_t]_j \log([g_{\mathbf{W}}(\mathbf{x}_t)]_j), \tag{6}$$

where $g_{\mathbf{W}}(\cdot)$ denotes the DL model employed for 3-way classification, $\mathbf{l}_t$ is the one-hot encoding of l_t, the notation $[\mathbf{x}]_j$ is used to refer to the j-th element of a vector $\mathbf{x}$, and N is the total number of time-steps for the training time-series, assuming that the time-series is continuous. Then, the model can be readily trained using gradient descent, i.e.,

$$\mathbf{W}' = \mathbf{W} - \eta \frac{\partial \mathcal{L}}{\partial \mathbf{W}}, \tag{7}$$

where $\mathbf{W}$ denotes the parameters of the model $g_{\mathbf{W}}(\cdot)$. In this work, mini-batch gradient descent is used, while the Adam algorithm is employed for the optimization [8]. Please also note that the main aim of this work is to evaluate whether using sentiment information can have a positive impact on the trading performance of a DL agent. To this end, we used three different models, i.e., a) a Multilayer Perceptron (MLP) (after appropriately flattening the input tensor into a vector), b) a 1-D Convolutional Neural Network and c) a Long-Short-Term Memory (LSTM)-based Network. All of these network architectures are widely used for training agents that can provide trading signals [15,16,20]. As we explain in detail in Sect. 3, we performed several experiments in order to evaluate the impact of using sentiment information on trading for a wide range of different setups and architectures.

3   Experimental Evaluation

In this Section, we provide the experimental evaluation of the proposed sentiment-aware trading pipeline. First, we briefly introduce the employed setup and hyper-parameters used for the conducted experiments, while we provide some additional information regarding the dataset used as a source of financial sentiment information for the conducted experiments. Then, we present and discuss the experimental results that confirm our initial hypothesis that sentiment can be a valuable source of information for training DL agents for financial trading.

Regarding the financial data source, we use the daily close prices for Bitcoin-USD (United States Dollar) currency pair (Fig. 3). For extracting sentiment information we used a dataset published by BDC Consulting [1], which contains

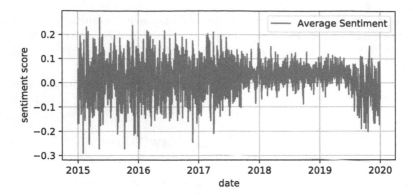

Fig. 2. Average sentiment score per day, as expressed by the documents contained in the BDC Consulting dataset. The finBERT model was used for extracting the sentiment of the titles of news articles published each day. Note that −1 corresponds to the most negative sentiment, while 1 corresponds to the most positive sentiment.

over 200,000 titles of financial articles collected from various sites that publish articles on cryptocurrencies, such as Cointelegraph and CoinDesk (Fig. 2). This dataset provides data for 5 years, from 2015 to 2020. Therefore, we used the first four years for training the DL models (2015–2020), while the last year (2019–2020) was used for performing the evaluation/back-testing of the trading agents. For both the training and testing datasets, we carefully aligned the textual data and price data, using the corresponding timestamps to ensure that no information from the future can leak into each training window.

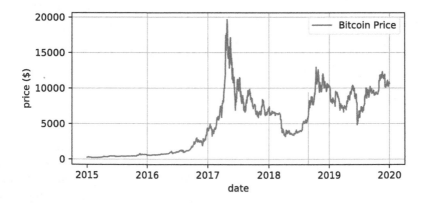

Fig. 3. BTC-USD price during the period 2015–2020

The main motivation of this work is to evaluate the impact of using sentiment information across a wide range of DL models and configurations. To this end, we did not limit the evaluation on a smaller number of handpicked

DL models. Instead, we evaluated a wide range of models for different hyper-parameters, including different number of layers, neurons per layer, learning rates and dropout rates. More specifically, for the MLP model we evaluated models with 1, 2 and 3 layers and 8, 16, 32, 64 and 128 neurons per layer. For the CNN models we evaluated models with 1, 2 and 3 convolutional layers (all followed by a final classification layer) and 4, 8 and 16 filters per layer and kernel sizes equal to 3, 4 and 5. Finally, for the LSTM models we experimented with 1, 2, 3 layers and 8, 16, 32, 64 and 128 neurons per LSTM layer. For all the configurations we used the Adam optimizer [8]. Therefore, we trained and evaluated the models with three different learning rates, i.e., 10^{-2}, 10^{-3} and 10^{-4}, as well as different dropout rates for the layers [13], i.e., 0.1, 0.2 and 0.4. All possible model configurations that were produced by the different combinations of the aforementioned parameters were trained and evaluated.

Table 1. Average Percentage (%) Profit and Loss (PnL) for the 50 top-performing configurations for each model (back-testing performed on the test set, i.e., 2019–2020). The prediction horizon was set to 1 day. The lot size used is constant for the whole duration of the backtest regardless of accumulated profits or losses.

Input modality	MLP	CNN	LSTM
Price	201%	219%	214%
Sentiment	221%	**228%**	222%
Price & sentiment	**224%**	**228%**	**224%**

First, we examined the average performance of different configurations for three different kinds of inputs: a) price alone, b) sentiment alone, and c) combined price and sentiment. The evaluation results for the test set are provided in Table 1, where we compare the average Profit and Loss (PnL) metric [17], which allows us to estimate the expected profit and/or loss of a trading agent over a specific period of time. We report the average over the top-50 performing configurations, in order to ensure a fair comparison between the different models. Using sentiment information alone provides better PnL compared to just using the price, while combining the price and sentiment together allows for slightly improving the obtained results.

These results are also confirmed in the evaluation performed for the training set for individual agents, as provided in the left column of Fig. 4, where we also examine the convergence speed of the models by evaluating three different snapshots of the agents, i.e., on epoch 100, 200 and 300. Using price alone leads to a PnL of about 7. On the other hand, the obtained results clearly demonstrate that the DL models learn significantly faster when sentiment information is available, since there are very small differences between the three model snapshots (i.e., epochs 100, 200 and 300) and the final training PnL reaches values over 30. This result demonstrates that sentiment-information for cryptocurrencies, such as Bitcoin, might actually be a stronger predictor of its future behavior

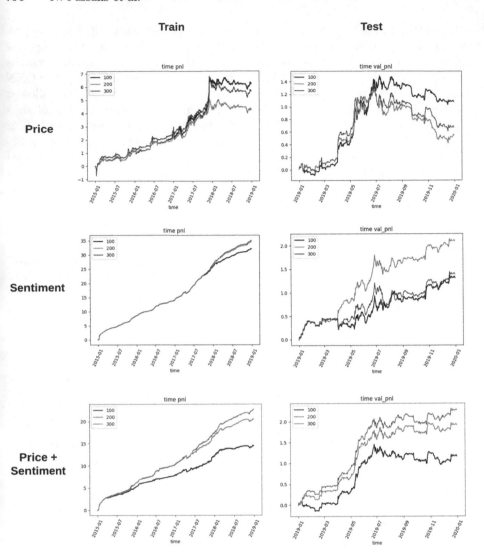

Fig. 4. Train (left column) and test (right column) PnL for MLP architectures trained on three different input sources: a) price alone, b) sentiment alone and c) combined price and sentiment.

compared to the information provided by the price time-series. Combining price and sentiment information together shows a bit mixed result, possibly limiting overfitting issues that might occur when sentiment is used, since the maximum train PnL in this case is around 20, while the models converge slower compared to only using sentiment input.

Indeed, similar results are obtained for the test evaluation, where the trained DL models are evaluated on unseen test data, as shown in right column of Fig. 4.

The models that were trained using sentiment information consistently perform better compared to the corresponding models that were trained only using price information as input. Combining price and sentiment information seems to lead to slightly better behavior. Therefore, the obtained results confirmed our initial hypothesis that taking into account sentiment information can lead to agents that perform consistently better trades, since in all the evaluated cases using sentiment information as input increased the obtained PnL.

4 Conclusion

In this work we evaluated the impact of using additional information sources, that provide sentiment information, when developing DL agents for trading cryptocurrencies. The experimental results suggest that sentiment can indeed be a strong predictor of the future behavior of cryptocurrencies and can be effectively used for a wide range of DL architectures. These results indicate that similar results might be obtained even when more advanced learning algorithms are used, e.g., Deep Reinforcement Learning algorithms [18], potentially further improving their performance. Furthermore, the impact of other information sources, e.g., sentiment from related currencies or assets, can be also evaluated, since they consist a potentially useful additional pool of information, that is typically considered by human traders. Finally, more advanced ways of combining sentiment and price information, e.g., using transformer-based architectures for data fusion [6], could further improve the obtained results, since, in some cases, combining these two sources of information only led to marginal improvements over just using sentiment information.

Acknowledgment. This work has been co-financed by the European Union and Greek national funds through the Operational Program Competitiveness, Entrepreneurship and Innovation, under the call RESEARCH - CREATE - INNOVATE (project code: T2EDK-02094).

References

1. Analyzing Crypto Headlines - BDC Consulting. https://bdcenter.digital/insights/cryptocurrency/analyzing-crypto-headlines
2. Araci, D.: Finbert: Financial sentiment analysis with pre-trained language models. arXiv preprint arXiv:1908.10063 (2019)
3. Chantona, K., Purba, R., Halim, A.: News sentiment analysis in forex trading using r-cnn on deep recurrent q-network. In: Proceedings of the Fifth International Conference on Informatics and Computing, pp. 1–7 (2020)
4. Day, M.Y., Lee, C.C.: Deep learning for financial sentiment analysis on finance news providers. In: Proceedings of the IEEE/ACM International Conference on Advances in Social Networks Analysis and Mining, pp. 1127–1134 (2016)
5. Deng, Y., Bao, F., Kong, Y., Ren, Z., Dai, Q.: Deep direct reinforcement learning for financial signal representation and trading. IEEE Trans. Neural Networks Learn. Syst. **28**(3), 653–664 (2016)

6. Devlin, J., Chang, M.W., Lee, K., Toutanova, K.: Bert: Pre-training of deep bidirectional transformers for language understanding. arXiv preprint arXiv:1810.04805 (2018)
7. Jeong, G., Kim, H.Y.: Improving financial trading decisions using deep q-learning: predicting the number of shares, action strategies, and transfer learning. Expert Syst. Appl. **117**, 125–138 (2019)
8. Kingma, D.P., Ba, J.: Adam: a method for stochastic optimization. arXiv preprint arXiv:1412.6980 (2014)
9. Lei, K., Zhang, B., Li, Y., Yang, M., Shen, Y.: Time-driven feature-aware jointly deep reinforcement learning for financial signal representation and algorithmic trading. Expert Syst. Appl. **140**, 112872 (2020)
10. Schäfer, R., Guhr, T.: Local normalization: uncovering correlations in nonstationary financial time series. Physica A **389**(18), 3856–3865 (2010)
11. Sezer, O.B., Ozbayoglu, A.M.: Algorithmic financial trading with deep convolutional neural networks: time series to image conversion approach. Appl. Soft Comput. **70**, 525–538 (2018)
12. Shi, Y., Zheng, Y., Guo, K., Ren, X.: Stock movement prediction with sentiment analysis based on deep learning networks. Concurrency Comput. Practice Exp. **33**(6), e6076 (2021)
13. Srivastava, N., Hinton, G., Krizhevsky, A., Sutskever, I., Salakhutdinov, R.: Dropout: a simple way to prevent neural networks from overfitting. J. Mach. Learn. Res. **15**(1), 1929–1958 (2014)
14. Tran, D.T., Magris, M., Kanniainen, J., Gabbouj, M., Iosifidis, A.: Tensor representation in high-frequency financial data for price change prediction. In: Proceedings of the IEEE Symposium Series on Computational Intelligence, pp. 1–7
15. Tsantekidis, A., Passalis, N., Tefas, A., Kanniainen, J., Gabbouj, M., Iosifidis, A.: Using deep learning to detect price change indications in financial markets. In: Proceedings of the European Signal Processing Conference, pp. 2511–2515
16. Tsantekidis, A., Passalis, N., Tefas, A., Kanniainen, J., Gabbouj, M., Iosifidis, A.: Forecasting stock prices from the limit order book using convolutional neural networks. Proceedings of the IEEE Conference on Business Informatics (CBI), vol. 1, pp. 7–12 (2017)
17. Tsantekidis, A., Passalis, N., Tefas, A., Kanniainen, J., Gabbouj, M., Iosifidis, A.: Using deep learning for price prediction by exploiting stationary limit order book features. Appl. Soft Comput. **93**, 106401 (2020)
18. Tsantekidis, A., Passalis, N., Toufa, A.S., Saitas-Zarkias, K., Chairistanidis, S., Tefas, A.: Price trailing for financial trading using deep reinforcement learning. IEEE Trans. Neural Networks Learn. Syst. (2020)
19. Zhang, W., Skiena, S.: Trading strategies to exploit blog and news sentiment. In: Proceedings of the International AAAI Conference on Web and Social Media, vol. 4 (2010)
20. Zhang, Z., Zohren, S., Roberts, S.: Deeplob: deep convolutional neural networks for limit order books. IEEE Trans. Signal Process. **67**(11), 3001–3012 (2019)

Smart Blockchain
Applications/Cybersecurity

Federated Blockchained Supply Chain Management: A CyberSecurity and Privacy Framework

Konstantinos Demertzis[1,2]([⊠]), Lazaros Iliadis[1], Elias Pimenidis[3], Nikolaos Tziritas[4], Maria Koziri[4], Panagiotis Kikiras[4], and Michael Tonkin[3]

[1] School of Civil Engineering, Democritus University of Thrace, Kimmeria, Xanthi, Greece
kdemertz@fmenr.duth.gr, liliadis@civil.duth.gr
[2] Department of Physics, International Hellenic University, 65404 Kavala Campus, Greece
[3] Computer Science and Creative Technologies, University of the West of England, Bristol, UK
{Elias.Pimenidis,Michael2.Tonkin}@uwe.ac.uk
[4] Department of Computer Science, University of Thessaly, 35100 Lamia, PC, Greece
{nitzirit,mkoziri,kikirasp}@uth.gr

Abstract. The complete transformation of the supply chain in a truly integrated and fully automated process, presupposes the continuous and endless collection of digital information from every stage of the production scale. The aim is not only to investigate the current situation, but also the history for every stage of the chain. Given the heterogeneity of the systems involved in the supply chain and the non-institutional interoperability in terms of hardware and software, serious objections arise as to how these systems are digitally secured. An important issue is to ensure privacy and business confidentiality. This paper presents a specialized and technologically up-to-date framework for the protection of digital security, privacy and industrial-business secrecy. At its core is Federated Learning technology, which operates over Blockchain and applies advanced encryption techniques.

Keywords: Blockchain · Meta-learning · Federated Learning · Cyber-Security · Privacy · Industry 4.0 · Supply Chain Management

1 Introduction

Digital revolution, especially big data and artificial intelligence, offers new opportunities for the full automation of the supply chain as shaped by the Industry 4.0 standard [1]. At the same time, the complexity increases exponentially, as the number of interconnected systems which participate in continuous interconnection services and uninterrupted real-time information exchange, expands. Applications that monitor security incidents and detect digital hazards, receive a continuous unlimited stream of observations from interconnected systems. In the typical case, the latest data is the most important, as there is the concept of aging based on their timing. This data is characterized by high variability,

© IFIP International Federation for Information Processing 2021
Published by Springer Nature Switzerland AG 2021
I. Maglogiannis et al. (Eds.): AIAI 2021, IFIP AICT 627, pp. 769–779, 2021.
https://doi.org/10.1007/978-3-030-79150-6_60

as their characteristics can change drastically and in an unpredictable way over time, changing their typical, normal behavior [2].

In general, the ever-increasing communication, variability and chaotic planning, exposes the supply chain and the industrial environment in general to serious digital risks.

Given the inability of traditional security systems to detect serious threats, the adoption of intelligent solutions is imperative. Intelligent systems, have the ability to transform human knowledge and experience into optimal valid and timely decisions. In the industrial environment, central storage of all historical data is not appropriate. This fact requires either the retraining of the intelligent system on a subset which contains a small percentage of the total observations, or the extraction of knowledge in real time. The prospect of comprehensive retraining creates serious technical glitches, while data-driven detection raises objections to the accuracy and reliability of the methods used. In both cases, the classifiers degrade over time and become incapable of detecting serious threats [3]. The exchange of data that could create more complete classifiers to generalize, also poses risks to the security and privacy protection of sensitive industrial data. In the context of this work, a standard intelligent digital security information system has been developed and proposed, which seeks to fully upgrade the operation of passive intelligent systems.

The target is the development of an adaptive federated auto meta-learning system through blockchain technology, which ensures privacy and industrial secrecy.

2 Proposed Framework

The proposed architecture has three main principles. The sensitive data is not transmitted through communication channels. The data is not stored in a central point of attack and the learning algorithms are constantly updating their predictive power. Specifically, this research introduces an intelligent control mechanism to detect abnormalities in the Industry 4.0 communication network [3]. This is based on the automatic analysis of digital packets of network traffic. In addition, an automated intelligent neural network was developed to monitor and detect abnormalities, to train and update the model with *federal learning*, and to communicate all involved parameters through a distributed blockchain system.

The architecture of the proposed model is the following [4]: When one device wants to communicate with another, then the proposed intelligent mechanism is activated, which implements a network traffic control to detect anomalies. In the first phase, the features of network traffic are exported. They are used as input to a neural network that is automatically developed through the *Neural Architecture Search* technique. In the beginning the model is trained on the host server, based on some initial data. Then the model is encrypted with homomorphic encryption and through blockchain and it is sent to the nodes that will use it. Then the nodes take the model and improve it using their own data at their disposal. The enhanced model encrypts and returns via blockchain to the host server. The best models are aggregated and the weighted average is selected using the *Grid Search Weighted Average Ensemble* method. The obtained final model returns a blockchain medium to the final nodes. Even if the initial data is not appropriate, there is a continuous improvement of the intelligent model so that it can categorize with great accuracy the anomalies in the network's traffic.

If the traffic is classified as normal, further communication is allowed, while otherwise, it is stopped, and an alarm is sent to the control center for further control of the transaction.

More specifically, the proposed architecture concerns the process of recording, analyzing and visualizing network traffic in the Industry 4.0 standard and the communication technologies that it integrates. The purpose is to identify abnormalities associated with digital attacks. For this reason, a hybrid technique of automated IP flow analysis was used. Its core idea of standardization and operation is based on the architecture of the open-source framework *Stream4Flow*. It uses the *IPFIXCol collector*, the *Kafka* messaging system, the *Apache Spark* and *Elastic Stack*.

The following Fig. 1, presents an overview of the proposed architecture.

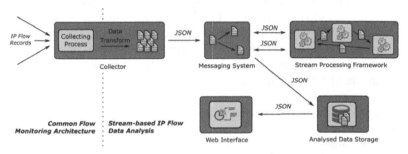

Fig. 1. Stream4Flow architecture (https://stream4flow.ics.muni.cz/)

IPFIXCol allows the conversion of incoming IP stream records in JSON format provided on the Kafka messaging system. Kafka adds serious scalability and allocation capabilities that provide adequate data performance, and Apache Spark is used as a data processing framework for fast IP data flow. The results of the analysis are stored in an *Elastic Stack* containing *Logstash, Elasticsearch and Kibana*, which allow the results

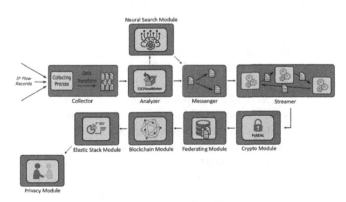

Fig. 2. The proposed architecture.

to be stored, searched and visualized. The box also contains an additional web interface to facilitate handling and to visualize the complex results of the analysis [5]. Figure 2 presents the overall architecture of the model.

3 Methodology

It is important to define a clear and consistent description of how to support the operational capabilities of the proposed architecture. Therefore, a detailed scenario will be presented in order to clearly show the use of its mode of operation and the operational requirements that it presupposes, always based on the complexity of the Industry 4.0 ecosystem [6]. This will be achieved, taking into account the basic design principles for identifying and implementing scenarios, i.e., interconnection, access to information, technical support and decentralized decision making. The usage scenario is structured on the idea that a decentralized industry consists of three smart factories each of which has separate special sections such as vertical production and quality control. There is also a decentralized management department and a decentralized department of administrative services and product promotion. To complete the project, industry shares data with a team of scientists where there is a tacit relationship of trust between them, which if violated, can affect the final result of the project and of course it can violate the industrial secrecy [7]. The digital security of the industry infrastructure is controlled by a team of engineering information systems, which uses Machine Learning techniques to protect the infrastructure.

At the same time, it is complying with the general regulation of personal data protection GDPR and seeks to ensure privacy in every phase in which personal information is involved. There is no clear way for stakeholders to work together in a safe and secure way, just as there is no historical or complete record of how they act. Consequently, the users of the IoT environment cannot receive information that may concern them, or they receive it through methods that jeopardize privacy and industrial secrecy [8]. Respectively and in a more technical context, the machine learning algorithms used have to undergo multiple cycles of training, regularization and optimization. Through this process, the teams focus on setting the hyperparameters of the model and on collecting data for its efficient training. This is done with the corresponding cost and by depending on experts on the specific process.

It is obvious that an innovative architecture is required, which standardizes the ways of transactions, while ensuring secure network communication, privacy and industrial secrecy between the traded devices. In Industry 4.0 projects, data communication becomes important as part of the value chain. An IP communication infrastructure for the internal and external parts of the dispersed modern industry is a holistic idea that facilitates operation, expansion and troubleshooting. The communication ability of the individual departments is the basis for the effective distribution and control of the project.

The usage scenario was structured according to the standards of *Industrial Communication Network* [9] IEC 61158 and *Machine to Machine* communication (M2M) OPC UA (IEC 62541), as they are implemented based on the TCP/IP standardization. IEC 61158 is the standardization of a family of industrial network protocols called *Fieldbus* used for real-time distributed control. IEC 62541 is the standardization of OPC UA which is an industrial M2M communication protocol for full interoperability. Its goal is to provide a *Service-Oriented Architecture* (SOA) for process control, while enhancing security and providing an information exchange model.

Alignment of communication between departments based on the above specifications, leads to a higher level of interoperability, stability in processes and rapid troubleshooting with end-to-end monitoring. Based on the decentralized processing of data at the edge of the network (edge computing), it is allowed to perform operations on low cost and on low computing capacity devices, as well as the collection of data in a decentralized way for their use in various systems or applications.

In a test scenario of the proposed architecture, communication (sending, receiving, and accessing data) on sensory instruments or selectors is achieved with the widely used SCADA MODBUS TCP/IP protocol. In conclusion, this model seeks to fully upgrade the mode of operation of passive intelligent systems. In conclusion, this model seeks to fully upgrade the mode of operation of passive intelligent systems, aiming at the implementation of an advanced mechanism, offering fully automatic and personalized solutions, while ensuring the privacy of participants.

The detailed steps of the described usage scenario are as follows:

Step 1 – Collector

The collection was performed using the IPFIXcol framework, in order to edit the SCADA MODBUS TCP/IP streams in the usage scenario.

Step 2 – Analyzer

The network traffic analyzer extracts the most important features that can determine the nature of the information contained in the SCADA MODBUS TCP/IP network traffic, by using the *CIC Flow Meter*.

Step 3 – Neural Search M Odule

The Neural Search Module is a holistic approach, which fully automates the creation of neural networks in a way that is not dependent on human intervention, while discovering the optimal hyperparameters, with the aim of detecting abnormalities in network traffic. It is used only once, at the beginning of the process and only for the initial development of the neural network, which is distributed to the devices that implement abnormality.

Step 4 – Messenger

The result of the export of the features performed by the analyzer is transferred to the Messenger, which, mediates the communication between the producer and the consumer using Apache Kafka. Essentially this level of architecture undertakes to route in a clear and secure way the information flows coming from the network communication.

This allows partial storage of the data flow of a large number of permanent or ad-hoc consumers and the automatic recovery in case of failure.

Step 5 – Streamer

The Streamer, which has the role of the consumer at the level of Kafka, distinguishes the flows that arise from the Messenger. After determining the time period of each batch, as well as the staging time window, the flow analysis is initiated.

Streamer prepares data batches from feeds, generates RDDs, and sends them for processing at regular intervals. Streamer also undertakes the detailed monitoring of the flow evolution that comes from the Messenger and when a batch is completed, it informs the Spark driver about the flow offsets which determine the batch to be analyzed. The Driver shares the partitions of each topic. Together with the other details that determine the parts of each batch to be processed by each subsystem, they are sending them for encryption in the Crypto Module. Practically only the information of the markers that identify each batch passes through the Streamer and not the data of the flow itself.

Step 6 – Crypto Module

Flow encryption is performed in order to create an advanced control mechanism for possible leakage of confidential data and information in the specific architecture. It is achieved with the *Crypto Module*. The idea of its operation is based on the use of an algebraic system that allows authorized third parties to perform a variety of calculations on the encrypted data. In the described scenario, fully homomorphic encryption is used to perform calculations and analysis. The proposed architecture incorporates Microsoft's opensource *Simple Encrypted Arithmetic Library* (SEAL), which uses a uniform encryption system. It is based primarily on the cryptographic schemes of Brakerski/Fan-Vercauteren (BFV) and Cheon, Kim, Kim and Song (CKKS). SEAL initially converts the flow data into polynomials and integrates them into a defined polynomial ring.

The encrypted polynomials are then calculated by applying noisy linear transformations involving the public key for each one. Numerical operations are then performed on the encrypted flow data. If the accumulated noise in the calculations does not exceed a limit, the computational output can be decrypted with a linear transformation that includes the private key. Crypto-Module in addition to the basic encryption device, includes methods that provide optimal parameters for the initial encryption setup and the budget that reflects the noise that occurs during the execution of the given procedure. Thus, the architecture fully ensures privacy and security between the trading devices.

Step 7 – Federating Module

Centralized training is intrusive, as users essentially have to exchange their privacy or sensitive industrial data by sending it to central entities for training. With the federating module, a decentralized training approach is implemented that allows devices located in different geographical locations, to benefit from the acquisition and to make use of a well-trained and continuously upgraded, learning model. It also allows all personal data and information to be kept private, as they do not need to be sent to a central entity to be used as training data. In particular, it allows remote devices to download and operate the original machine learning model, that was initially developed by the *Neural Search Module*. This model runs on the locally available data in order to improve its accuracy and then the data are sent back to the *Federating Module*. The *Dynamic Weighted Average* approach summarizes the changes, creating a new update, which again returns to the end users through the *Blockchain Module*.

End users have constant access to an ever-upgraded neural network model. The various hyperparameters of the network are shared using *Hyperledger Fabric*, where the use of smart contracts ensures unquestionable validation and control of the process between the parties involved.

Step 8 – the Blockchain Module

The proposed *Blockchain Module* is based on the *Hyperledger Fabric Project* and its architecture comprises of the following levels:

Consensus Layer – It is responsible for establishing an agreement on the order and on the verification of the correctness of all transactions that constitute a blockchain.

Smart Contract Layer – It is responsible for processing transaction requests and approving only valid ones. In the analyzed scenario, the communication of devices which is based on *Smart Contract* considers the following parameters for the contract [4]:

a. *MachineAccount.* This is the account that represents the device in the IIoT ecosystem. Each machine has its own account to sign the transactions it needs to perform.
b. *MachineAddress.* It describes the unique address of each device in the IIoT.
c. *MachineInternals.* It is related to the monitoring of the internal parameters of the device, such as operating temperature, battery status and operating time.
d. *Publisher.* The user or the application that creates the data in the network.
e. *Subscriber.* The user or the application that is using the data in the network.
f. *Sender.* The final user that sends the data that were developed by the Publisher in the network.
g. *Receiver.* The final user that receives the data produced by the Publisher in the network.
h. *MachineStatus.* Procedures to check the status of the device, such as whether it produces data (Publisher), if a procedure is required (Sender).
i. *Session.* The time period in which a transaction takes place.
j. *SessionID.* A unique number characterizing a Session.
k. *DataStream.* The data flow that one device or application wants to transfer to another.
l. *DataStreamID.* A unique number characterizing a DataStream.
m. *TrafficFlow.* A sequence of packets from one source device to a destination, which may be another device or group of devices.
n. *TrafficFlowID.* A unique number characterizing a TrafficFlow.
o. *FeaturesOfTrafficFlow.* Features exported from web traffic. In the case of the scenario under consideration, the characteristics of the network traffic extracted by the analyst (analyzer) using the CICFlowMeter.
p. *IIoT rule.* It Describes a process by which a specific action is tested to see if it can be performed (e.g., checking the necessary rights and the ones involved in the action). For example, if the specific action triggers some additional actions such as the activation of a contract.

q. *SmartContract.* The smart contract that is activated in specific cases of transactions. The SmartContract is assigned a characteristic ID (for example it can have a value equal to ID (101)).

In the performed scenario, the *IIoT_thing_thermostat* (Sender), wants to interact by sending data (DataStream) to the device.

IIoT_thing_water_tank (Receiver). The DataStreams are assigned a *StreamID* e.g., (707), while the specific action is controlled by the IIoT rule on whether the specific transaction can take place. The IIoT rule activates the *SmartContractID* (101). The specific *SmartContractID* (101), activates the *StreamID* (707), which checks if DataStream is characterized as normal or abnormal. If the traffic is declared as normal, then there is a communication with the IIoT_thing_water_tank (Receiver), while otherwise, the communication is rejected, and an alarm is sent for further control.

Communication Layer– It is responsible for the transfer of messages between peer nodes. It provides publish /subscribe functions to system resources and it is directly related to the Authorization layer. For example, a specific resource can be published to a namespace by other entities, receiving a specific URI. Subscribe permission means that a receiver_entity can receive information from the published resource, while publish permission means that this entity can publish – interact with the resource. For example, it can send a restart command, set the operating temperature of the thermostat.

The subscribe permissions are related to the "stats" of the URI, whereas the publish permissions are also related to the "cmd" permissions.

Authentication Layer– It is responsible for the validation of users' identities, the control of their rights and for the consolidation of trust in the blockchain. It Provides access levels expressing security policies in the ecosystem IIoT, by using *entities, namespaces, resources,* and Delegations of Trust (DoTs). An Entity is a standalone control unit that can grant, restore, or delete access rights.

It works as a username or a role, except that a username or a role exists in only one domain, while an entity is global. Anyone can create an entity that is characterized by a key pair (public and private). For example, the admin is an entity with $< A_{pk}, A_{vk} >$ where A_{pk} is the public key and A_{vk} the private key.

A namespace is a domain that contains a hierarchy of resources. The *Raw_Materials_Utility* is a namespace and all resources inside the namespace is reported with a unique URI.

The temperature of a thermostat in Raw_Materials_Utility is described by the URI BW://Raw_Materials_Utility/thermostat/stats/temp, where "stats" is related to data describing the operational status of the resource, whereas "cmd" includes control commands like *restart, lock.* Any other entity interacting with the resources inside a namespace must be licensed by the namespace entity, directly or indirectly. This property is known as the *Delegations of Trust* (DoT). For example, for the DoT $= <A_{pk}^{from}, A_{pk}^{to}, URI_{rsrc}, Permissions, Metadata>$ the metadata can have specific properties characterizing the resources.

Overlay layer– This is a level added to the *Hyperledger Fabric* architecture to map the communication network between IoT devices. This is responsible for providing the available services and applications, to the network. The nodes at this level, which essentially form an overlapping network over the existing physical one, can be thought of, as connected by virtual or logical links, each of which corresponds to a path in the underlying network.

Blockchain Layer– It is the level that creates and manages the blockchain. Its operation can be based on individual specifications related to the content and how to use the blockchain, while its structure can include multiple levels and architectures.

API Layer– It is the application programming interface that allows external applications or users to interface with the blockchain. One of the main purposes of the interface is to define and formulate all the functions-services that the system can provide to other programs, without allowing access to the code that implements these services.

Step 9 – Elastic Stack Module

The widely used system Elastic Stack that comprises of the Elasticsearch, Logstash and Kibana is used for the complete and effective real-time visualization of the results of the analysis carried out.

This Module enables the aggregation and visualization of log files from all systems and applications used in the proposed architecture.

Step 10 – Privacy Module

Privacy and protection of industrial confidentiality when using the *Elastic Stack* Module is ensured through the use of the Privacy Module, which implements a differential privacy system. Remote, independent observers, who want access to information or search for specific content and they want a visual output, cannot understand if this information is coming from a specific source. According to the definition of differential privacy, a randomized algorithm A with a domain defining a data set D and a value field B, presents differential privacy (ε, δ) if relation (1) is true, for all adjacent datasets D_1 and D_2 and all subsets S of the domain values $S \subseteq B$ given that $(\varepsilon, \delta) > 0$:

$$P[A(D_1) \in S] \leq e^{\varepsilon} P[A(D_2) \in S] + \delta \tag{1}$$

From the above relation it follows that the smaller the (ε, δ) the greater the security of the records in the examined data sets. For the differential privacy model (ε, δ) it is true that $\delta = 0$. The differential privacy approach (ε, δ) as a method of encryption, is achieved by adding noise to the results of queries executed in the datasets.

If q is the question and n the noise to be added to maintain data privacy, then the randomized algorithm that exhibits differential privacy (ε, δ) is described by relation (2):

$$M = f(x) + n \tag{2}$$

where f is the function of all queries q and x is the dataset. Noise is added with the Laplace mechanism.

4 Conclusion

The idea of standardizing the proposed architecture arose based on the application of a single, universal method that will cover all the industrial requirements of the new era.

It combines the most up-to-date methods, and it is able to complete specialized processes for the development of modern information systems security applications. This is achieved through an adaptable, flexible and easy-to-use operating environment. The features of the proposed architecture allow the analysis, forecasting, monitoring and management of complex situations related to information systems security. This is achieved by optimally combining and implementing a hybrid system with the most technologically advanced computing methods.

Assessing the proposed architecture as a whole, a significant advantage focuses on the ability to clearly display the information transmitted between the devices involved in the Industry 4.0 ecosystem. This leads to models of trust that are based on detailed mathematical and physical frameworks for the behavior of cyber-physical systems. Another important contribution of the proposed methodology is its contribution to the assessment of uncertainty posed by digital security problems, which is a major turning point in the adoption of new technologies. Finally, an important contribution of these methods lies in the fact that generalization is experimentally ensured by statistical validation techniques that cannot be disputed. This is true even when we are using data that contains a significant percentage of noise.

Proposals for development and future improvements of the methodology should focus on the automated optimization of the appropriate parameters of the method, so that the provision of services is achieved in a simple and categorical way.

It would be important to study the expansion of this system by implementing methods of self-improvement and redefining the parameters of the overall system, so that it can fully automate the process of engagement and disengagement in the supply chain of Industry 4.0.

References

1. Bassi, L.: Industry 4.0: Hope, hype or revolution?. In: 2017 IEEE 3rd International Forum on Research and Technologies for Society and Industry (RTSI), 2017, pp. 1–6. https://doi.org/10.1109/RTSI.2017.8065927
2. Shobol, A., Ali, M.H., Wadi, M., TüR, M.R.: Overview of big data in smart grid. In: 2019 8th International Conference on Renewable Energy Research and Applications (ICRERA), 2019, pp. 1022–1025. https://doi.org/10.1109/ICRERA47325.2019.8996527
3. Li, C.H., Lau, H.K.: A critical review of product safety in industry 4.0 applications. In: 2017 IEEE International Conference on Industrial Engineering and Engineering Management (IEEM), 2017, pp. 1661–1665. https://doi.org/10.1109/IEEM.2017.8290175
4. Demertzis, K., et al.: Anomaly detection via blockchained deep learning smart contracts in industry 4.0. Neural Comput. Appl. 32(23), 17361–17378 (2020). https://doi.org/10.1007/s00521-020-05189-8
5. Demertzis, K., Tsiknas, K., Takezis, D., Skianis, C., Iliadis, L.: Darknet traffic big-data analysis and network management for real-time automating of the malicious intent detection process by a weight agnostic neural networks framework. Electronics 10, 781 (2021). https://doi.org/10.3390/electronics10070781

6. Chen, X., Ji, J., Luo, C., Liao, W., Li, P.: When machine learning meets blockchain: a decentralized, privacy-preserving and secure design. In: 2018 IEEE International Conference on Big Data (Big Data), 2018, pp. 1178–1187. https://doi.org/10.1109/BigData.2018.8622598
7. Das, D., Sarkar, S.: Machine-to-machine learning based framework for ad-hoc IOT ecosystems. In: 2018 International Conference on Computational Techniques, Electronics and Mechanical Systems (CTEMS), 2018, pp. 431–436. https://doi.org/10.1109/CTEMS.2018.8769148
8. Tsiknas, K., Taketzis, D., Demertzis, K., Skianis, C.: Cyber threats to industrial IoT: a survey on attacks and countermeasures. IoT **2**, 163–186 (2021). https://doi.org/10.3390/iot2010009
9. Winkel, L.: Real-time ethernet in IEC 61784-2 and IEC 61158 series. In: 2006 4th IEEE International Conference on Industrial Informatics, 2006, pp. 246–250. https://doi.org/10.1109/INDIN.2006.275788

Validation and Verification of Data Marketplaces

Will Serrano[✉]

The Bartlett, University College London, London, UK
`w.serrano@ucl.co.uk`

Abstract. This paper presents a Validation and Verification (V&V) model of Data Marketplaces. Data is extracted from the sensors embedded within the Smart city, infrastructure, or building via Application Programming Interfaces (APIs) and inserted into a Data Marketplace. The technology is based on smart contracts deployed on a private ethereum blockchain. Current issues with data in Smart cities, infrastructure, buildings, or any real estate, are the difficulty of its access and retrieval, therefore integration; its quality in terms of meaningful information; its large quantity with a reduced coverage in terms of systems and finally its authenticity, as data can be manipulated for economic advantage. In order to address these issues, this paper proposes a Data Marketplace model with a hierarchical process for data validation and verification where each stage adds a layer of data abstraction, value-added services and authenticity based on Artificial Intelligence. By using a blockchain, this presented approach is based on a decentralised method where each stakeholder stores the data. The proposed model is validated in a real application with live data: Newcastle urban observatory smart city project.

Keywords: Data marketplace · Smart cities · Smart buildings · Real estate · Blockchain · Smart contracts · Artificial intelligence

1 Introduction

Smart cities, infrastructure, buildings and any real estate, as the natural outcome of a construction project, face digital challenges due to the nature of the physical environment of the design and built industry. In order to deliver a construction project or a product such as a building or an airport, the required framework comprises a large number of stakeholders (investors, insurers, designers, regulators) and a lengthy process divided into stages (planning permission, feasibility, concept and detailed design, construction, commissioning). The intrinsic properties of this particular ecosystem create fundamental digital issues: a) There is no clear data ownership or responsibility that covers the entire life cycle of the digital project from creation to decommissioning. Several independent organisations that seek economic profits may be involved in different stages with competing interests. In addition, companies organically evolve, change ownership, or even face liquidation. b) The final users are left with a product to manage, commercialise, or maintain without input on the digital design or data documentation. Normally, digital system upgrades and enhancements require re-starting again due to incompatibility

© IFIP International Federation for Information Processing 2021
Published by Springer Nature Switzerland AG 2021
I. Maglogiannis et al. (Eds.): AIAI 2021, IFIP AICT 627, pp. 780–792, 2021.
https://doi.org/10.1007/978-3-030-79150-6_61

issues. c) Due to this fragmented process, there is no efficient digital lesson learnt from the delivered projects that support the optimisation of their future integration within the design and build construction methods. Current digital platforms available such as Building Information Modelling (BIM) and Digital Twin still lack a clear delimitation of ownership, responsibility and maintenance.

In addition, Smart cities, and any Real Estate in general, also face four main key data issues: a) Difficulty to access real time-data automatically. Data can be stored within siloed servers or inconsistent nomenclature or structure. b) The quality of the data extracted is not normally very valuable with low statistical relevance due to its fragmentation where manual human intervention needs to fill the gaps or extrapolate it in order to obtain meaningful information. c) Large quantity of data with reduced coverage in terms of systems detriments the required complexity of data models for Bussiness Intelligence. d) Data users can not be guaranteed data is authentic. Cybersecurity attacks can manipulate stored data at the edge to make it look genuine. Data can be artificially manipulated to obtain an economic reward, such as an insurance premium.

1.1 Research Proposal

This paper proposes a Validation and Verification (V&V) model of a Data Marketplace based on Artificial Intelligence that manages live data streams from smart building or city systems addressing both digital and data issues. The presented model applies a hierarchical process for data verification and data validation where each layer provides a layer of data abstraction, value-added services and authenticity via Artificial Intelligence algorithms. The main three applications of AI are used in the V&V model: classification, clustering and prediction. The practical application of the proposed Data Marketplace consists of three layers of verifications:

- **Bronze verification:** selects, retrieves and classifies data inserting it into the smart contract based on a private ethereum blockchain;
- **Silver verification:** analyses, clusters the data and reports any values that do not meet a predefined threshold, range or rule as a value-added service. The silver validation has value for insurers or property managers;
- **Gold verification:** makes data predictions. The gold validation has value for city or asset managers and city or property developers.

The proposed V&V model is based on a private ethereum blockchain solution that provides a secure and decentralised approach where each party or stakeholder owns a copy of the distributed ledger removing the need for a central assessor.

1.2 Research Structure

The V&V model of data marketplaces has been applied to a real application with live data: the University of Newcastle smart city project. Data is extracted via Application Programming Interfaces (APIs) and stored in a private ethereum blockchain at University College London (UCL). Section 2 provides the research background of data marketplaces. Section 3 defines the V&V model of the proposed Data Marketplace whereas Sect. 4 describes its practical implementation. Finally, conclusions are shared in Sect. 5.

2 Research Background

2.1 Models and Algorithms

A blockchain enabled data marketplace solution is modelled as a weighted directed graph where each edge represents the transactional flow of data and each vertice represent the different sellers and buyers [1]. Distributed Big Data platforms implement a digital data marketplace based on the blockchain mechanism for data transaction integrity [2]. Data marketplaces support data providers and data requesters to retrieve the value of the data by means of combination, reconstruction, or reinterpretation through the exchange of shared data profiles [3]. An interactive platform facilitates the interactions between data providers and users where data is shared only after the match between the description items of data requests [4]. A distributed online marketplace uses an Ethereum framework to engage buyers and sellers in e-commerce transactions without the need for a central management entity [5]. Data values are efficiently guaranteed by the best possible value assigned to each data item based on the placement of data in the network, storage and processing power [6]. A real-time matching mechanism efficiently buys and sells training data for Machine Learning (ML) tasks based on prediction tasks and accuracy [7]. Open data providers and users within similar knowledge sharing activities are interconnected to increase the knowledge transfer within the ecosystem [8]. A 2D spatial data marketplace defines a data model based on a logical representation as a quadtree [9].

2.2 Economic Model

A criteria for interactive pricing in a data marketplace is based on three concepts: non-disclosure, arbitrage-free and regret-free [10]. ProDataMarket is a platform that shares and monetizes linked geospatial data based on property assets [11]. A model-based pricing framework prices ML model instances instead of pricing the data itself [12]. A transparent monetization system based on an ethereum Distributed Ledger Technology (DLT) and solidity smart contracts trades off between the overhead of tracking Internet of Things (IoT) data on a blockchain versus the accuracy of the monetization for data [13]. A broker assigns value to data owners according to their contribution to incentivize data sharing [14].

2.3 Smart Cities

Data Marketplace for smart cities can be served as several models based on the ownership and operation of the data source where sharing incentives shall not lead to concentration of monopolies that can manipulate its value [15]. IOTA technology is a blockchain developed for IoT networks that supports peer-to-peer transactions without centralised authorities collects information from different sensors in Smart cities via APIs [16].

2.4 Internet of Things

An architecture for a dynamic decentralized marketplace for the trading of IoT data is based on trust-less brokers that match and select potential data providers based on the consumer's requirements [17]. IoT data streams are traded and exchange in pairs of data providers and consumers without any prior assumption of mutual trust [18]. IoT device vendors and AI/ML solution providers interact, collaborate and create actionable insights in a blockchain-based, decentralized and trustless data marketplace that will lead to a variety of services [19]. A review system confirms the reputation of a data owner or the data traded before a transaction occurs [20]. The Intelligent IoT Integrator (I3) is a real-time data marketplace architecture platform that enables the possibility of data brokers to buy "raw" data, apply data analytics and sell back refined data streams [21]. The model uses Message Queuing Telemetry Transport (MQTT) publish-subscribe brokers integrated with an authentication and access control module [22]. An algorithm responds to data consumer's queries balancing the buyer's budget constraints and the seller's compensation for the provided IoT data services [23].

2.5 Semantics

A data marketplace based on a federation of eleven IoT deployments is applied to heterogeneous application domains to ensure the interoperability of data streams, based on the virtualisation of sensors in the cloud [24]. Meta-data and dynamic context data support the data preparation phase through a semantical approach [25]. Automatic handling of users' requests by means of Semantic Web technologies is based on a semantic model that describes the access policies [26].

2.6 Privacy and Personal Information

Sterling is a decentralised marketplace for private datasets that enables privacy-preserving distribution by using smart contracts run on a permissionless blockchain in trusted execution environments [27]. IoT generated personal data is commercialised protecting the privacy and data rights of data generators [28]. WibsonTree is a cryptographic primitive designed to preserve users' privacy by allowing them to demonstrate predicated on their personal attributes, without revealing their values [29]. A dynamic cloud-based marketplace of near real-time human sensing data is designed for environments where traditional Information Technology (IT) infrastructures are not well developed [30]. A scheme of a data marketplace in the healthcare industry negotiates data based on metadata and data properties rather than the raw data itself [31]. "Digital Me" uses an AI agent as an intermediary between buyers and sellers to anonymise personal data in accordance with the General Data Protection Regulation 2018 [32]. IoT generated personal data is traded based on a thorough analysis of personal data with a specific focus on the challenges and risks within a data licensing framework [33]. A neural network in Blockchain configuration encrypts personal information to validate the transmission channel [34].

3   Validation and Verification of Data Marketplace Model

The Data Marketplace model is defined as an M-dimensional universe of X data items where each individual entity or data within the universe is distinct from the others. We consider the universe from which the data marketplace is created as a relation U that consists of a set of X M-tuples, $U = \{v_1, v_2 \ldots v_X\}$, where $v_i = (l_{i1}, l_{i2} \ldots l_{iM})$ is data item i and l_{iM} are the M different data attribute values for $i = 1,2..X$. The important concept in the development of this proposed V&V model is that data is defined as $D_t(n(t),v)$ where:

- $n(t)$ is a variable N-dimension vector with $1 < N < M$, $n(t)$ is variable so that values can be added or removed based on the value-added services;
- t is the V&V stage represented as time t where $t > 0$;
- v is the value of the data D_t at time t.

The Data Marketplace model is based on a hierarchical process where users validate and verify data in order to add quality in terms of authentication or value-added services. The process of Validation & Verification, VV_{NM}, is defined as:

- Horizontal layer users $(1,\ldots, n,\ldots N)$ add validation to the data: this N process confirms the data stored in the smart contract is authentic;
- Vertical layer users $(1,\ldots, m,\ldots M)$ add verification to the data: this M process includes a higher layer of abstraction based on Artificial Intelligence for data analytics that provides value-added services.

Data value v of $D_t(n(t),v)$ at time or stage t is defined as:

$$v = \sum_{m=1}^{M} m^2 * \sum_{n=1}^{N} n$$

Each horizontal n layer acts as a data checker that confirms the inserted data into the marketplace whereas each vertical layer m acts as a data transfer that filters, aggregates and refines the data to meet different clients and customers' information needs based on Artificial Intelligence. In a nutshell, the more horizontal N the more genuine the data is and the more vertical M, the more valuable (Fig. 1). As a practical scenario, this paper proposes a Bronze, Silver and Gold verification service approach.

3.1   Bronze Verification

Bronze verification confirms data is real and authentic inserting it into the private ethereum blockchain via a smart contract. The purpose of this layer is to use data as a general information source such as ranking for visualisation or dashboards. Artificial Intelligence based on classification algorithms that include naive Bayes, decision trees, random forests, support vector machines, k nearest neighbours divide the input variable into different classes and then predict the class for a given input using supervised learning.

3.2 Silver Verification

Silver verification inserts a layer of value-added services analysing the value of the data. The silver validation is used for auditing purposes such as insurance, facilities management to confirm if the smart city system or asset is compliant with law or regulation such as fire alarm system monitoring within a smart building. The silver validation assembles any smart city Key Performance Indicator (KPI) as a benchmark between different smart cities. Artificial Intelligence based on clustering algorithms that include k-means, fuzzy, or hierarchical divide and organize data points into groups based on similarities within members of the group with unsupervised learning.

3.3 Gold Verification

Gold verification purpose is for Big Data models that analyse several data sources and predict future values. This layer would be used by asset managers or property developers. Artificial Intelligence and Machine Learning based on regression algorithms that include linear regression, lasso regression, logistic regression, multivariate regression, multiple regression predict the output values based on input data points via supervised machine learning algorithms.

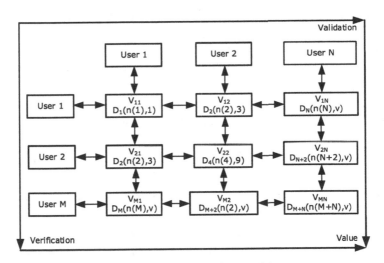

Fig. 1. Data marketplace model

4 Experimental Results

The Data Marketplace model has been validated within Newcastle urban observatory smart city project [35] where data has been extracted by open protocol RESTful (Representational State Transfer) APIs based on a JavaScript Object Notation (JSON) data structure (Fig. 2). The blockchain is implemented via Go Ethereum (Geth) and the smart

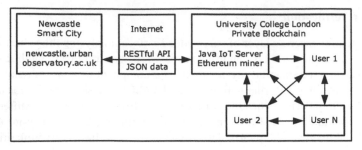

Fig. 2. Data marketplace architecture

contract via Solidity. The IoT platform has been developed on Java Maven with the embedded Blockchain and smart contract managed by web3j library. The server is a dedicated computer specifically built for Linux and optimised for mining.

Each validation or verification process generates two smart contract transactions:

- Data Insertion (DI): generated by the algorithms that create value-added services
- Data Value (DV): represents the Validation & Verification value v

Note that the purpose of the experimental results is to confirm the proof of concept of the data marketplace model rather than the V&V of the data itself. In addition, variables are considered independent although they are stored in the same Blockchain. Table 1 defines the variables used in the validation process for a month of data collection (November 2020).

Table 1. Data variables parameters

Variable	Unit	Data points	Average	Max value	Min value
Particular matter 2.5	μgm^{-3}	2974	4.37	20.32	0.19
Carbon monoxide	μgm^{-3}	1089	251.69	489.04	187.69
Sound	dB	37632	64.86	87	54
People count	Person	4230	0.01	6	0
Car count	Car	4230	0.39	7	0

Table 2 defines the blockchain addresses and gas price of the smart contract. Data inputs to the blockchain have been limited to 500 values due to software constraints.

Table 2. Smart contract parameters

Parameter	Value
Account address	0xa35b5e29e84161c9aa75d519dd8f947f7e8e9eea
Contract address	0x18b89d51cb0c30c07fbedf710ebb76fe87748e18
Gas limit	22000000000
Gas price	21000

4.1 Horizontal Validation

Different validation stages confirm that the data extracted from the different Smart City sensors is authentic. Table 3 shows the average values for the five data variables validation stages and smart contracts, Data Insertion (DI) and Data Value (DV), within the blockchain. Experimental results also include the respective transaction fees, gas price and mining time.

Table 3. Horizontal validation – smart contract and blockchain values

Validation stage	Data input	Gas price	Transaction fee (GWEI)	Mining time	V&V value v
Initialisation	N/A	2.58E+05	5.69E−03	1.09E−03	0
1-DI	500	1.49E+06	3.27E−02	1.79E−03	1
1-DV	1	4.20E+04	9.24E−04	7.68E−04	
2-DI	500	1.26E+05	2.78E−03	1.55E−03	2
2-DV	1	2.70E+04	5.94E−04	8.24E−04	
3-DI	500	1.93E+05	4.24E−03	2.31E−03	3
3-DV	1	2.70E+04	5.94E−04	7.42E−04	

The horizontal validation (Table 3) demonstrates the general blockchain equation Transaction Fee (GWEI) = Gas Limit × Gas Price where the Gas Limit is a constant value (2.20E+10). Data Insertion (DI) is more expensive to mine, from a transaction fee and mining time perspective, than Data Value (DV). This is due to DI stores a larger amount of data within the block structure, an array of doubles, rather than the single integer stored by DV (Fig. 3). The transaction fees and mining times do not fully correlate linearly to the amount of data stored in the blockchain. The main reason is Go Ethereum consensus algorithm and the random nature of the mining process.

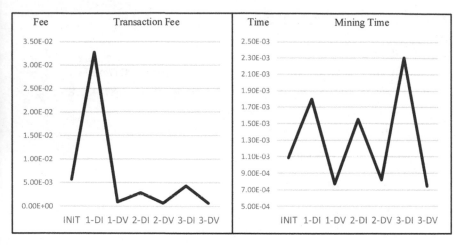

Fig. 3. Horizontal validation

4.2   Vertical Verification

Different vertical verification stages value-added services to the data. The bronze verification introduces the extracted JSON data via the API into smart contracts, classifies and finally confirms its and authenticity. The silver verification clusters the values that are above average as a simple representation or rule of uncompliant values. The gold verification predicts the next uncompliant value. As the values from the silver verification are considered as a time series, the prediction algorithm is based on a Long Short Term Memory (LSTM) network. Table 4 shows the average values for the five data variables during the different verification stages within the blockchain that includes also transaction fees, gas price and mining time.

Table 4.   Vertical verification – smart contract and blockchain values

Validation stage	Data input	Gas price	Transaction fee (GWEI)	Mining time	V&V value v
Initialisation	N/A	2.58E+05	5.69E−03	1.10E−03	0
1-DI	500	1.49E+06	3.28E−02	2.38E−03	1
1-DV	1	4.20E+04	9.24E−04	7.55E−04	
2-DI	173.4	2.01E+05	4.43E−03	2.26E−03	4
2-DV	1	2.70E+04	5.94E−04	8.03E−04	
3-DI	1	8.91E+04	1.96E−03	1.74E−03	9
3-DV	1	2.70E+04	5.94E−04	7.02E−04	

The vertical verification confirms the transaction fee (GWEI) equation with consistent results as previous the horizontal validation (Table 4).

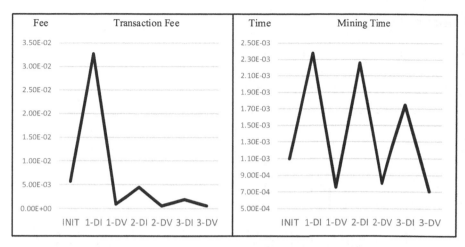

Fig. 4. Vertical verification

The transaction fees and mining time are more dependent on the block structure rather than the relative amount of information stored within the blocks themselves (Fig. 4). As DI stores a larger amount of data within the block structure than DV, the transaction fees and mining time is greater.

5 Conclusions

This paper has presented a Validation and Verification model for a Data Marketplace based on Artificial Intelligence. The proposed method is based on a hierarchical process for data verification and data validation where each stage adds a layer of data abstraction, value-added services and authenticity via Artificial Intelligence algorithms. The defined approach has been validated in a real application with live data: University of Newcastle smart city project where data is obtained via real-time APIs. Experimental results demonstrate that a private Go Ethereum blockchain and Solidity smart contracts combined with AI successfully deliver the value-added services in a decentralised network. The private blockchain performs as expected with a linear relationship between transaction fees, gas limits and gas prices. Transaction fees and mining times are more dependent on the block structure rather than the amount of information contained within the blocks themselves. Future work will include additional verification and validation stages to confirm the presented conclusions where the V&V model will be expanded with further data variables and structures. Additional AI algorithms such as Natural Language Processing (NLP) will be applied to enhance the offered services in the Bronze, Silver and Gold approach.

Acknowledgements. The author would like to express gratitude to Jeremy Barnett at UCL and Resilience Partners Ltd for participating in and funding this research. RPL are looking for methods of verification for smart data such as a traffic light or a 'bronze silver gold' approach so introduced the author to the University of Newcastle Smart City and provided other guidance and encouragement in this research project.

Appendix

Example data values (CO) in the V&V model.

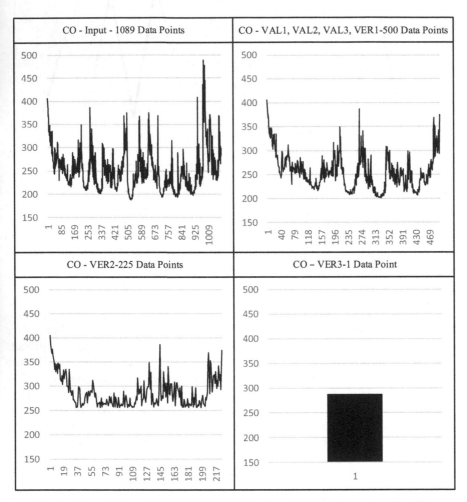

Fig. 5. CO validation (VAL1, VAL2, VAL 3) and verification (VER1,VER2,VER3)

References

1. Banerjee, P., Ruj, S.: Blockchain enabled data marketplace – design and challenges. arXiv: 1811.11462, 1–7 (2019)
2. Nasonov, D., Visheratin, A.., Boukhanovsky, A..:. Blockchain-based transaction integrity in distributed big data marketplace. International Conference on Computational Science, pp. 569–577 (2018)

3. Nakamura, J., Teramoto, M.: Concept design for creating essential hypothesis, rules, and goals: toward a data marketplace. Open J. Inform. Syst. **2**(2), 16–26 (2015)
4. Hayashi, T., Ohsawa, Y.: TEEDA: an interactive platform for matching data providers and users in the data marketplace. Information **11**(218), 1–12 (2020)
5. Kabi, O., Franqueira, V.: Blockchain-based distributed marketplace. international conference on business information systems. Business Information Systems Workshops, pp. 197–210 (2018).
6. Maruyama, H., Okanohara, D., Hido, S.: Data marketplace for efficient data placement. IEEE International Conference on Data Mining Workshops, pp. 702–705 (2013)
7. Agarwal, A., Dahleh, M., Sarkar, T.: A marketplace for data: an algorithmic solution. ACM Conference on Economics and Computation, pp. 701–726 (2019)
8. Smith, G., Ofe, H., Sandberg, J.: Digital service innovation from open data: exploring the value proposition of an open data marketplace. Hawaii International Conference on System Sciences, pp. 1277–1286 (2016)
9. Sakr, M.: A data model and algorithms for a spatial data marketplace. Int. J. Geogr. Inf. Sci. **32**(11), 2140–2168 (2018)
10. Li, C., Miklau, G.: Pricing aggregate queries in a data marketplace. WebDB, pp. 1–6 (2012)
11. Roman, D., et al.: ProDataMarket: a data marketplace for monetizing linked data. International Semantic Web Conference, pp. 1–4 (2017)
12. Chen, L., Koutris, P., Kumar, A.: Towards model-based pricing for machine learning in a data marketplace. International Conference on Management of Data, pp. 1535–1552 (2019)
13. Badreddine, W., Zhang, K., Talhi, C.: Monetization using blockchains for IoT data marketplace. International Conference on Blockchain and Cryptocurrency, pp. 1–9 (2020)
14. Liu, J:. Dealer: end-to-end data marketplace with model-based pricing. arXiv:2003.13103v1, 1–17 (2020).
15. Ramachandran, G., Radhakrishnan, R., Krishnamachari, B.: Towards a decentralized data marketplace for smart cities. IEEE International Smart Cities Conference, pp. 1–8 (2018).
16. Musso, S., Perboli, G., Rosano, M., Manfredi, A.: A decentralized marketplace for M2M economy for smart cities. IEEE International Conference on Enabling Technologies: Infrastructure for Collaborative Enterprises, pp. 27–30 (2019)
17. Gupta, P., Kanhere, S., Jurdak, R.: A decentralized iot data marketplace. arXiv:1906.01799, 1–6 (2019)
18. Bajoudah, S., Dong, C., Missier, P.: Toward a decentralized, trust-less marketplace for brokered IoT data trading using blockchain. IEEE International Conference on Blockchain, pp. 339–346 (2019)
19. Özyılmaz, K., Doğan, M., Yurdakul, A.: IDMoB: IoT data marketplace on blockchain. Crypto Valley Conference on Blockchain Technology, pp. 11–19 (2018)
20. Park, J.-S., Youn, T.-Y., Kim, H.-B., Rhee, K-H., Shin, S-U.: Smart contract-based review system for an IoT data marketplace. Sensors **18**(10), 3577 (2018)
21. Krishnamachari, B., Power, J., Kim, S.-H., Shahabi, C.: I3: an IoT marketplace for smart communities. International Conference on Mobile Systems, Applications, and Services, pp. 498–499 (2018)
22. Zhao, X., Sajan, K., Ramachandran, G., Krishnamachari, B.: Demo abstract: the intelligent IoT integrator data marketplace – version 1. International Conference on Internet-of-Things Design and Implementation, pp. 270–271 (2020).
23. Misura, K., Zagar, M.: Data marketplace for internet of things. International Conference on Smart Systems and Technologies, pp. 255–260 (2016).
24. Sánchez, L., et al.: Federation of internet of things testbeds for the realization of a semantically-enabled multi-domain data marketplace. Sensors **18**(3375), 1–32 (2018)

25. Nagorny, K., Scholze, S., Ruhl, M., Colombo, A.W.: Semantical support for a CPS data marketplace to prepare big data analytics in smart manufacturing environments. IEEE Industrial Cyber-Physical Systems, pp. 206–211 (2018).

26. Shakeri, S., et al.: Modelling and matching digital data marketplace policies. International Conference on eScience, pp. 570–577 (2019)

27. Hynes, N., Dao, D., Yan, D., Cheng, R., Song, D.: A demonstration of sterling: a privacy-preserving data marketplace. PVLDB 11(12), 2086–2089 (2018)

28. Molina, V., Kersten, M., Glatard, T.: A conceptual marketplace model for IoT generated personal data. arXiv:1907.03047, 1–17 (2019)

29. Futoransky, A., Sarraute, C., Waissbein, A., Travizano, M., Fernandez, D.: WibsonTree: efficiently preserving seller's privacy in a decentralized data marketplace. arXiv:2002.03810v1, 1–8 (2020).

30. Cao, T.-D., Pham, T.-V., Vu, Q.-H., Truong, H.-L., Le, D.-H., Dustdar, S.: MARSA: a marketplace for realtime human sensing data. ACM Trans. Internet Technol. 16, 1–21 (2016)

31. Ito, R.: ID-Link, an enabler for medical data marketplace. International Conference on Data Mining Workshops, pp. 792–797 (2016)

32. Ha, M., Kwon, S., Lee, Y., Shim, Y., Kim, J.: Where WTS meets WTB: a blockchain-based marketplace for Digital Me to trade users' private data. Pervasive Mob. Comput. 101078(59), 1–15 (2019)

33. Molina, V., Kersten, M., Glatard, T.: A conceptual marketplace model for IoT generated personal data. arXiv:1907.03047v1, 1–17 (2019)

34. Serrano, W.: The blockchain random neural network for cybersecure IoT and 5G infrastructure in smart cities. J. Netw. Comput. Appl. 175(102909), 1–16 (2021)

35. https://urbanobservatory.ac.uk/

Correction to: Artificial Intelligence Applications and Innovations

Ilias Maglogiannis ⓘ, John Macintyre, and Lazaros Iliadis ⓘ

Correction to:
I. Maglogiannis et al. (Eds.): *Artificial Intelligence Applications and Innovations*, **IFIP AICT 627,**
https://doi.org/10.1007/978-3-030-79150-6

The original versions of the chapters titled "PQ-HDC: Projection-Based Quantization Scheme for Flexible and Efficient Hyperdimensional Computing" and "Hyperdimensional Computing with Learnable Projection for User Adaptation Framework" were revised. The acknowledgement of both papers has been updated to:

This work was supported by the Ministry of Science and Technology of Taiwan under Grants MOST 109-2221-E-002-175 and MOST 110-2218-E-002-034 -MBK.

The updated version of these chapters can be found at
https://doi.org/10.1007/978-3-030-79150-6_34
https://doi.org/10.1007/978-3-030-79150-6_35

Author Index

Printed in the United States
by Baker & Taylor Publisher Services

D. Filev · J. Jabłkowski
J. Kacprzyk · M. Krawczak
I. Popchev · L. Rutkowski
V. Sgurev · E. Sotirova
P. Szynkarczyk · S. Zadrożny
Editors

Intelligent Systems'2014

Proceedings of the 7th IEEE International
Conference Intelligent Systems IS'2014,
September 24–26, 2014, Warsaw, Poland,
Volume 2: Tools, Architectures, Systems,
Applications

 Springer

Editors

D. Filev
Research and Advanced Engineering
Ford Motor Company
Dearborn, MS, USA

J. Jabłkowski
Industrial Research Institute for Automation
and Measurements (PIAP)
Warsaw, Poland

J. Kacprzyk
Polish Academy of Sciences
Systems Research Institute
Warsaw, Poland

M. Krawczak
Polish Academy of Sciences and WIT -
Warsaw School of Information
Technology
Systems Research Institute
Warsaw, Poland

I. Popchev
Bulgarian Academy of Sciences
Institute of Information and Communication
Technologies
Sofia, Bulgaria

L. Rutkowski
Department of Computer Engineering
Częstochowa University of Technology
Częstochowa, Poland

V. Sgurev
Bulgarian Academy of Sciences
Institute of Information and Communication
Technologies
Sofia, Bulgaria

E. Sotirova
Faculty of Technical Sciences
Department of Computer and Information
Technologies
"Prof. Assen Zlatarov" University
Bourgas, Bulgaria

P. Szynkarczyk
Industrial Research Institute for Automation
and Measurements (PIAP)
Warsaw, Poland

S. Zadrożny
Polish Academy of Sciences
Systems Research Institute
Warsaw, Poland

ISSN 2194-5357   ISSN 2194-5365   (electronic)
ISBN 978-3-319-11309-8   ISBN 978-3-319-11310-4   (eBook)
DOI 10.1007/978-3-319-11310-4

Library of Congress Control Number: 2014948179

Springer Cham Heidelberg New York Dordrecht London

Printed on acid-free paper

Springer is part of Springer Science+Business Media (www.springer.com)

Foreword

This two volume set of books constitutes the proceedings of the 2014 IEEE 7th International Conference Intelligent Systems (IS), or IEEE IS'2014 for short, held on September 24–26, 2014 in Warsaw, Poland. Moreover, it contains some selected papers from the collocated IWIFSGN'2014 -

Thirteenth International Workshop on Intuitionistic Fuzzy Sets and Generalized Nets held on September 25, 2014.

The conference was organized by the Systems Research Institute, Polish Academy of Sciences, Department IV of Engineering Sciences, Polish Academy of Sciences, and PIAP – Industrial Institute of Automation and Measurements. It was sponsored by the Poland Section of the IEEE (institute of Electrical and Electronics Engineers) CIS (Computational Intelligence Society), and the Polish Operational and Systems Research Society. The technical sponsors included the IEEE Systems, Man and Cybernetics Society, the IEEE Computational Intelligence Society, the Polish Neural Network Society, the Polish Association of Artificial Intelligence, and the Polish Operational and Systems Research Society.

The conference had a special session devoted to the presentation of results obtained within the "International PhD Projects in Intelligent Computing" and these two volumes contain the respective papers. The conference gathered both the Ph.D. students participating in the Project and their supervisors from Poland and abroad, as well as some foreign partners involved in the Project providing an excellent opportunity for the publication and dissemination of contributions by young researchers. This project was supported by the Foundation for Polish and financed from the European Union within the Innovative Economy Operational Programme 2007-2013 and European Regional Development Fund.

The papers included in the two proceedings volumes have been subject to a thorough review process by three highly qualified peer reviewers. Comments and suggestion from them have considerable helped improve the quality of the papers but also the division of the volumes into parts, and assignment of the papers to the best suited parts.

Thanks are due to many people and parties involved. First, in the early stage of the preparation of the conference general perspective, scope, topics and coverage, we have received an invaluable help from the members of the International Program Committee, notably the chairs responsible for various aspects of the Conference, as well as people from the IEEE, notably Mr. Kevin Uherek, who helped make formal arrangements that would be most proper for this particular Conference. In fact, an overwhelming majority of members of the International Program Committee had been the members of all our sponsors which had provided an extraordinary situation of a synergy between the International Program Committee and all the sponsoring parties. That help during the initial planning stage had resulted in a very attractive and up to date proposal of the scope and coverage that had clearly implied a considerable interest of the international research communities active in the areas covered who had submitted a large number of very interesting and high level publications. The role of many session organizers should also be greatly appreciated. Thanks to their vision and hard work, we had been able to collect many papers on focused topics which had then resulted, during the Conference, in very interesting presentations and stimulating discussions at the sessions.

The members of the International Program Committee, together with the session organizers, and a large group of other anonymous peer reviewers had undertaken a very difficult task of selecting the best papers, and they had done it excellently. They deserve many thanks for their excellent job for the entire community who is always concerned with thequality and integrity.

At the stage of the running of the Conference, many thanks are due to the members of the Organizing Committee, chaired by Ms. Krystyna Warzywoda and Ms. Agnieszka Jóźwiak, and supported by their numerous collaborators.

And last but not least, we wish to thank Dr. Tom Ditzinger, Dr. Leontina di Cecco and Mr. Holger Schaepe for their dedication and help to implement and finish this large publication project on time maintaining the highest publication standards.

July 2014

D. Filev
J. Jabłkowski
J. Kacprzyk
M. Krawczak
I. Popchev
L. Rutkowski
V. Sgurev
E. Sotirova
P. Szynkarczyk
S. Zadrożny

Contents

Part II: Issues in Distributed Knowledge Based Systems

Part III: Intelligent Decision Support Systems and Their Applications

Part IV: Applications of Intelligent Systems

Part V: Image Analysis and Pattern Recognition

Part VI: Intelligent Energy Systems

Part VII: Time Series Analysis and Frequent Pattern Mining

Part I
Intelligent Control and Robotics

An Object-Based Robot Ontology

Cezary Zieliński and Tomasz Kornuta

Warsaw University of Technology, Warsaw, Poland
{C.Zielinski,T.Kornuta}@ia.pw.edu.com
http://robotics.ia.pw.edu.pl

Abstract. An ontology encompassing objects and relations between them as well as the robot treated dually, as an object and a controlled device, is presented. Objects and relations between them are defined in terms of attributes which obtain their values through the robot's perception subsystem. Robot behaviours are defined in terms of transition functions and terminal conditions that also operate on percepts, thus tasks formulated in terms of symbolic concepts such as objects and relations can be formally transformed into control of effectors and vice versa. Thus the anchoring problem is solved. A formal approach enabling the mentioned transformations between different abstractions is presented.

Keywords: service robots, ontology, objects, relations.

1 Introduction

Humans use relations between objects, or object relations in short, to refer to abstract geometric locations of one object with respect to another, e.g. the *box* is *on* the *table* (here *on* is the relation). Description of any task involving objects always utilises such spacial relations. In the case of service robots, which are meant to closely interact with people, both physically and verbally, conveying what is wanted off them will inevitably involve the use of relations. Currently the use of full scope of any natural language for that purpose is beyond technical capabilities, thus simplified language forms have to be used. Right from the onset of creation of robot programming languages the concepts of objects and relations appeared, e.g. [1–4]. As gradually robots acquired sensors (exteroceptors) the anchoring problem had to be solved, i.e. how to associate measurements obtained by perception systems with the abstract concepts such as a particular object (e.g. *box* or *table*) or a specific relation (e.g. *on*). Currently the solution to this problem is approached through the definition of adequate ontologies and subsequently knowledge bases [5–7]. Those knowledge bases are extended to encompass also sensoric data [8, 9]. Reasoning can then be done both on the knowledge base containing abstract concepts and raw sensoric data [10]. If the description of the task that the robot is to execute is in an abstract form that does not include common sense knowledge then both the above mentioned knowledge bases and reasoning (inference) are necessary [6, 11, 12]. One of the interesting questions that this paper tries to answer is whether such ontology could be formulated that

© Springer International Publishing Switzerland 2015
D. Filev et al. (eds.), *Intelligent Systems'2014*,
Advances in Intelligent Systems and Computing 323, DOI: 10.1007/978-3-319-11310-4_1

it would not require a huge knowledge base and complex reasoning to execute the task. Obviously we still want this ontology to refer to objects and relations. Simultaneously this ontology should provide a simple solution for the anchoring problem and provide the necessary means for transforming the task defined in terms of objects and relations into the required activities of the robot. Robot systems use relations between objects being in their environment to:

1. Describe the current state of the environment (static description),
2. Enquire whether the environment has an appropriate state (query),
3. Create the required state of the environment (change of state) [4, 13].

This paper focuses on the third aspect, trying to solve the mentioned problems.

2   Ontology

This work focuses on an ontology, that is composed of objects, their classes and attributes as well as relations between objects. Relations between objects are defined in terms of mathematical relations between attributes of those objects. This ontology contains also a special object that is the robot. It should be noted that the robot is dual in its character. On the one hand, it engages in relations with other objects, thus it behaves as any other object in the environment. On the other hand, the robot exists as a system submerged in the environment, i.e. the robot and the environment are distinct. The latter role of the robot is subsumed by the term: embodied agent or an agent in short. An embodied agent is composed of several subsystems, the activities of which are described in terms of behaviours. Behaviours cause changes to the values of attributes of objects, thus bringing about the creation of relations between objects.

2.1   Embodied Agent

Any embodied agent a_j, where j is the designator of the agent, is composed of five types of subsystems [14, 15]:

- Control subsystem c_j, which is responsible for the realisation of the task allotted to the agent and coordination of its internal workings,
- Real effectors $E_{j,h}$, where h is the designator of a particular effector, i.e. the devices exerting influence on the environment,
- Real receptors $R_{j,l}$ (exteroceptors), where l is the designator of a particular receptor, i.e. the devices responsible for gathering the information about the state of the environment,
- Virtual Effectors $e_{j,n}$, where n is the designator of a particular virtual effector, i.e. subsystems responsible for the presentation of the real effectors to the control subsystem in such a form that the expression of the task is considerably simplified,
- Virtual receptors $r_{j,k}$, where k is the designator of a particular virtual receptor, i.e. subsystems responsible for aggregating data obtained from the real receptors into a form required by the control subsystem.

The control subsystem as well as the virtual effectors and receptors, are treated as subsystems s (where $s \in \{c, e, r\}$), having: internal memory ${}^s s$, input ${}_x s$ and output ${}_y s$ buffers, connecting them to some of the other subsystems. A transition function ${}^s f_{j,u}$ is responsible for computing new contents of memory and output buffers based on the contents of the memory and input buffers:

$$[{}^s s_j^{i+1}, {}_y s_j^{i+1}] := {}^s f_{j,u}({}^s s_j^i, {}_x s_j^i). \tag{1}$$

where i and $i+1$ are the consecutive instants of discrete time and u is a designator of a particular transition function. A behaviour ${}^s \mathcal{B}_{j,u}$ is defined as an iterative execution of en elementary action, that in turn is composed of the computation of the transition function and distribution of the contents of the output buffers and reading-in the new contents of the input buffers. The behaviour iterations terminate when the terminal condition ${}^s f_{j,u}^\tau({}^s s_j^i, {}_x s_j^i)$ is satisfied, i.e. becomes true. The same subsystem may exhibit many behaviours. They are invoked by a finite state machine (FSM) governing the actions of this subsystem. Thus both the control subsystem and the virtual entities are formed by their FSMs and their activities are based on the same principles. The interactions of the agent's subsystems govern the activities of the robot, however usually the control subsystem assumes the principal role in that respect.

2.2   Object and Its Attributes

The real environment $\mathcal{E}^R$ is modelled as a virtual environment $\mathcal{E}$. The embodied agent uses this model in its decision processes. The real environment $\mathcal{E}^R$ contains real objects o_ν^R, which are modelled as virtual objects o_ν. The number of objects in the real environment and the virtual one are the same, as the objects that are not modelled do not exist from the point of view of the agent. Virtual objects are divided into classes $\mathcal{O}$ depending on the attributes they posses. The set of attributes associated with a class $\mathcal{O}_\xi$ is represented by $\mathcal{D}_\xi$. The set of all attributes is $\mathcal{D}$. Attribute α of the class of objects $\mathcal{O}_\xi$ is represented by $d_{\xi,\alpha}$. Classes of objects are introduced to group objects according to their common properties, represented by the attributes of the same type. Specific objects of the same class posses attributes $d_{\xi,\alpha}$ of the same type, but their values will usually be different. Relations between objects (i.e. object relations) are defined for classes of objects, but occur between specific objects. In this paper for the sake of brevity this distinction shall not be further pursued, thus both the relation definitions and occurrence shall be expressed in terms of specific objects. Moreover, also for brevity the types of attribute values will also not be divulged.

2.3   Relation

Only unary ${}^u \mathcal{R}_\eta$ and binary ${}^b \mathcal{R}_\eta$ relations between objects are considered here (η is the relation designator). The former pertain to features of single objects, while the latter deal with mutual geometric location of two objects. The set of object relations $\mathcal{R}_\eta$ combines both unary and binary relations. Using an infix notation a relation ${}^b\mathcal{R}_\eta$ between objects o_κ and o_λ is expressed as:

$$o_\kappa \ {}^b\mathcal{R}_\eta \ o_\lambda \qquad \text{e.g.: box On table} \tag{2}$$

while unary relations will be presented in the prefix form as:

$$ {}^u\mathcal{R}_\eta \ o_\kappa \qquad \text{e.g.: Red box} \tag{3}$$

Object relations can be defined using an equality or inequality mathematical relations between the attributes of objects (other possibilities exist too). Thus a binary relation ${}^b\mathcal{R}_\eta$ assumes either of the two following forms:

$$F_{\eta,1}(d_{\kappa,\alpha}) = F_{\eta,2}(d_{\lambda,\beta}), \quad d_{\kappa,\alpha} \in \mathcal{D}_\kappa, \quad d_{\lambda,\beta} \in \mathcal{D}_\lambda \tag{4}$$

$$F_{\eta,2}(d_{\lambda,\beta}) \leqslant F_{\eta,1}(d_{\kappa,\alpha}) \leqslant F_{\eta,3}(d_{\lambda,\beta}) \tag{5}$$

where $F_{\eta,\varsigma}, \varsigma = 1, 2, 3$, are adequately defined functions of arguments.

Unary relations ${}^u\mathcal{R}_\eta$ determine the features of objects, thus their definitions relate the value of the attributes of an object to a constant, e.g.:

$$F_\eta(d_{\kappa,\alpha}) = \text{const}, \qquad d_{\kappa,\alpha} \in \mathcal{D}_\kappa \tag{6}$$

$$\text{const}_1 \leqslant F_\eta(d_{\kappa,\alpha}) \leqslant \text{const}_2 \tag{7}$$

where F_η is an adequately defined function. The definitions of relations (5) and (7) can be abbreviated when we want to define approximate equality, i.e. inequality within small regions. The symbol $\cong$ is used in that case.

When dealing with relation creation two general forms of binary relations are distinguished (e.g. [1–4]): symmetric and asymmetric (e.g. RIGID and NON-RIGID). The former assumes that the objects, being the argument of the created relation, will be bound to each other symmetrically (e.g. glued), while in the latter case the displacement of one of the objects causes the other to follow, but not vice versa, (e.g. teacup on a saucer). Skills have to form both kinds of relations. It should be noted that the relations are defined for virtual objects, however their creation is reflected in the real environment. The robot behaviours cause both changes to the state of the real environment (i.e. real objects) and the state of the model of that environment, i.e. the virtual environment, which is represented in the control system of the robot as an attribute graph. Robot behaviours must be defined in such a way that synchrony of changes in both environments is constantly maintained. Thus relations in the virtual environment will be created and destroyed to reflect what happens in real environment.

2.4   Skill

A skill $\mathcal{S}_\kappa$ is responsible for the creation of an object relation. An object relation is created by modifying the attributes of one of the objects taking part in that relation. Those attributes change their values due to the activities of the robot. Those activities can be defined as sequences of behaviours ^cB of the control subsystem of the embodied agent (robot), because this subsystem governs the activities of all subsystems of the agent. Thus a skill is expressed as an FSM invoking specific behaviours. This can be pictured as a graph of the FSM, with the behaviours associated with its nodes. The termination of each of the behaviours is due to the satisfaction of its terminal condition. The choice of a next behaviour is based on the transition table of the FSM.

A skill can be treated as a recipe for creating a relation. From the definition of the relation one can deduce the activities of the robot that will bring about the required result, i.e. occurrence of the relation. However the particular activities of the robot depend on the context in which this relation will be created, e.g. the activities will differ depending whether the robot before execution of the relation is holding an unassociated object or its gripper is free. In the former case it has to get rid of that object and in the latter it can proceed directly to execute the required relation. This context makes object relation creation difficult. Thus, as usual in such cases, the situation can be simplified by decomposition. Object relation will be decomposed into three phases. First a robot-object relation will be created, thus establishing a unique context, then the object-object relation proper will be established, and finally the post-relation-creation context will be established (leaving the robot in the required state). In this paper only an example showing this approach is presented. The goal of future research is to formulate possibly just one skill, certainly parametrised, that can create any object relation, based on the mathematical definition of the relation and the three-stage creation process. However, before such a skill can be produced many particular examples need to be studied. One of them follows.

3   Exemplary Relation Creation

The idea presented in this paper will be illustrated by a simple example of creating an On relation between a box and a table. This relation will be created by a robot having a position-force controlled manipulator equipped with a two-fingered shape gripper able to grasp the box by its corners.

3.1   Object: Robot

The robot is the cause of the exemplary object relation appearance, however before this relation occurs the robot itself must come into a robot-object relation. The latter relation establishes the required unique context for the creation of the object-object relation. Hence the robot must be first described as an object that can be an argument of the robot-object relation. As it was mentioned, relations should be defined for classes of objects, but they are created for specific objects (instants). Here, for the sake of brevity, both the definition and the execution of a relation will be presented just for the specific objects (instants rather than classes). The robot has the following attributes:

$$\mathcal{D}_{\text{robot}} = \{\, d_{\text{robot,base}}, d_{\text{robot,gripper}}, d_{\text{robot,fingerA}}, d_{\text{robot,fingerB}}, d_{\text{robot,force}}, \\ d_{\text{robot,grasp-force}}, d_{\text{robot,gripper-state}}, d_{\text{robot,workspace}}, \ldots \} \tag{8}$$

Attributes $d_{\text{robot,base}}$, $d_{\text{robot,gripper}}$, $d_{\text{robot,fingerA}}$ and $d_{\text{robot,fingerB}}$ are homogeneous matrices representing respectively: robot base coordinate frame expressed in a global reference frame, pose of the gripper (located between the fingers of the gripper) with respect to (wrt) the base coordinate frame and the location of the finger A and B frames wrt the gripper frame. Moreover the attribute $d_{\text{robot,grasp-force}}$ describes the force exerted by the fingers on the grasped object – quite often this force is being measured indirectly by measuring the current flowing in the gripper motor, but can also be measured directly by a tensometer. The attribute $d_{\text{robot,gripper-state}}$ discloses the state of the gripper, i.e. either open (no-grasp) or closed (grasp). The attribute $d_{\text{robot,force}}$ provides information about the force exerted by the manipulator on the environment – again this can be measured either by a wrist mounted force-toque sensor or by measuring the current in the joint motors. The attribute $d_{\text{robot,workspace}}$ describes the workspace of the robot, enabling the control system to check whether the objects that are to be manipulated are within reach of the robot. A more detailed description of the position-force controlled robot used in the experiments can be found in [16].

3.2   Object: Box

The box has the following set of attributes $\mathcal{D}_{\text{box}}$:

$$\mathcal{D}_{\text{box}} = \{\, d_{\text{box,base}}, d_{\text{box,bottom}}, d_{\text{box,grasp-frameA}}, d_{\text{box,grasp-frameB}}, \\ d_{\text{box,approach}}, d_{\text{box,grasp-force}}, d_{\text{box,force}}, d_{\text{box,box-state}}, \ldots \} \tag{9}$$

where $d_{\text{box,base}}$ is a homogeneous matrix representing the location of the box wrt the global coordinate frame. The base frame of the box is attached to one of its corners. The attribute $d_{\text{box,bottom}}$ represents the frame attached to the centre of the bottom of the box wrt its base frame. Moreover the box has two other attributes defining how it can be grasped, i.e. $d_{\text{box,grasp-frameA}}$ and $d_{\text{box,grasp-frameB}}$ representing frames associated with two top corners of the box located along one of the diagonals of the box top. Both frames are expressed wrt the base frame of the box. For simplicity of the example only one grasping location is permitted. The attribute $d_{\text{box,approach}}$ describes the location of the safe approach frame to the grasping location. Again this is simply for the purpose of brevity – otherwise this attribute can be substituted for a safe approach path that can be generated by a grasp planner using a virtual receptor associated with a vision perception system. The attribute $d_{\text{box,force}}$ provides the information about the allowable force with which the box may act on its environment – in the case of fragile boxes this constant will be low, while in the case of robust boxes it can be higher. The attribute $d_{\text{box,box-state}}$ discloses whether the box is to be held by the gripper after the relation has been created.

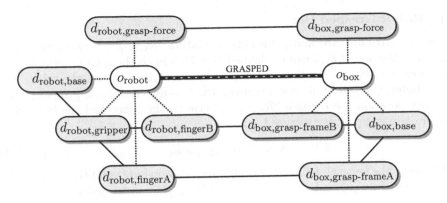

Fig. 1. Part of the attribute graph showing the Grasped relation $^b\mathcal{R}_{Grasped}$ representation

3.3   Object: Table

The table has the following set of attributes $\mathcal{D}_{\text{table}}$:

$$\mathcal{D}_{\text{table}} = \{d_{\text{table,base}}, d_{\text{table,top}}, d_{\text{table,approach}}, d_{\text{table,force}}, \dots\} \tag{10}$$

where $d_{\text{table,base}}$ is a homogeneous matrix representing the location of the table wrt the global coordinate frame, while $d_{\text{table,top}}$, $d_{\text{table,approach}}$ represent the location on which another object can be placed and the safe approach pose, both expressed wrt the base frame of the table, $d_{\text{table,force}}$ is the allowable force that can be exerted on the table while placing objects on it (this constant is used to detect contact of the placed object with the table).

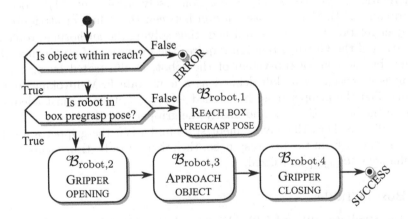

Fig. 2. Graph of the FSM defining the Grasped relation between the box and the robot, i.e. the grasped skill

3.4   Robot Grasped Box

Using the attributes (8) and (9) a binary relation ${}^{b}\mathcal{R}_{Grasped}$ between the robot o_{robot} and the object o_{box} can be defined (fig. 1). This is the relation establishing the necessary context for the *on* relation between the box and the table. The box is being grasped by its corners using the two-fingered shape gripper. Using the infix notation the relation ${}^{b}\mathcal{R}_{Grasped}$ between the robot and the box, when it is already grasped, is expressed as:

$$o_{\text{robot}} \;\; {}^{b}\mathcal{R}_{\text{Grasped}} \; o_{\text{box}} \tag{11}$$

Utilising the general definition of a binary relation expressed by: (4) and (5), supplemented by (6) and (7), the relation ${}^{b}\mathcal{R}_{Grasped}$ can be defined as:

$$\begin{aligned}
d_{\text{robot,base}} * d_{\text{robot,gripper}} * d_{\text{robot,fingerA}} &\cong d_{\text{box,base}} * d_{\text{box,grasp-frameA}} \\
d_{\text{robot,base}} * d_{\text{robot,gripper}} * d_{\text{robot,fingerB}} &\cong d_{\text{box,base}} * d_{\text{box,grasp-frameB}} \\
\mathcal{F}_{x,\text{const}} &\leqslant d_{\text{robot,grasp-force}} \leqslant d_{\text{box,grasp-force}} \\
d_{\text{robot,gripper-state}} &= \text{grasp} \\
d_{\text{box,box-state}} &= \text{grasp}
\end{aligned} \tag{12}$$

The mathematical relations contained in (12) simply state that for the object relation (11) to be created finger A of the gripper needs to be placed approximately where grasp frame A is located on the box and the same for finger B and grasp frame B. Moreover, we require the gripper to be firmly closed, i.e. the grasping force in the x direction should exceed $\mathcal{F}_{x,\text{const}}$, but be less than the allowable grasp force for the box. The last two lines of the definition tell us what should be the state of the gripper and box after the box is grasped, i.e. the gripper should remain closed (grasp state) and the box will remain held by the gripper (grasp state). In other words, if the mathematical relationships between attributes of the robot and the box satisfy (12) we can conclude that object relation expressed as (11) exists. Conversely, if we want (11) to occur we need to cause (12). Hence an association between the values of attributes and the object relation has been established, thus solving the anchoring problem.

Creation of the Grasped relation requires the execution of a sequence of behaviours by the control subsystem of the robot, as illustrated by fig. 2. This relation is executed by a skill defined as a four state FSM invoking four behaviours: first the gripper must be opened – ${}^{c}\mathcal{B}_{\text{robot,2}}$, then it must adequately approach the box – ${}^{c}\mathcal{B}_{\text{robot,3}}$, and finally the gripper must be closed – ${}^{c}\mathcal{B}_{\text{robot,4}}$. Additionally we check the environment state and when the gripper appears to located far away from the pregrasp pose, then it need to be translocated, hence the behaviour ${}^{c}\mathcal{B}_{\text{robot,1}}$ is utilized.

3.5   Box on Table

Using the attributes (9) and (10) a binary relation ${}^{b}\mathcal{R}_{On}$ between the box o_{box} and the table o_{table} can be defined. It is assumed that the box is already grasped when the *on* relation is being created.

$$o_{\text{box}} \;\; {}^{b}\mathcal{R}_{\text{On}} \; o_{\text{table}} \tag{13}$$

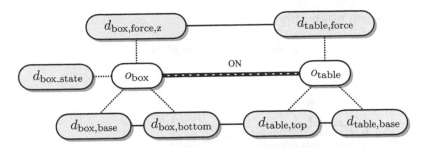

Fig. 3. Part of the attribute graph showing the On relation $^b\mathcal{R}_{On}$ representation

Utilising the general definition of a binary relation expressed by: (4) and (5), supplemented by (6) and (7), the relation $^b\mathcal{R}_{On}$ can be defined as:

$$d_{\text{box,base}} * d_{\text{box,bottom}} \cong d_{\text{table,base}} * d_{\text{table,top}}$$
$$\mathcal{F}_{z,\text{const}} \leqslant d_{\text{box,force},z} \leqslant d_{\text{table,force}} \tag{14}$$
$$d_{\text{box,box-state}} = \text{grasp}$$

The relation (14) is treated as realised when the bottom of the box is approximately where the top of the table is and the force acting on the box in the z direction is larger than $\mathcal{F}_{z,\text{const}}$ but lower than the allowable force that can be exerted on the table. Once the box is put on the table the box should remain grasped.

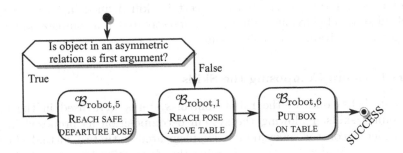

Fig. 4. Graph of the FSM defining the On relation between the box and the table

3.6   Free Box

This is a unary relation $^u\mathcal{R}_{\text{Free}}$ which changes the property of the box. After creation of this relation the box will be free, i.e. the gripper will not be holding it. The relation is represented by:

$$^u\mathcal{R}_{\text{Free}}\, o_{\text{box}} \tag{15}$$

and its definition utilises (6):

$$d_{\text{box,box-state}} = \text{no-grasp} \tag{16}$$

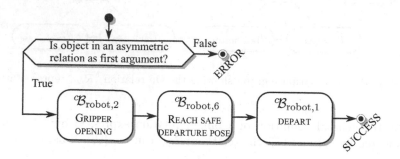

Fig. 5. Graph of the FSM defining the Free unary relation of the box

3.7 The Skill of Putting Boxes on Tables

To put a box on a table three relations must be consecutively created:

$$o_{\text{robot}}\,{}^{b}\mathcal{R}_{\text{Grasped}}\,o_{\text{box}}, \quad o_{\text{box}}\,{}^{b}\mathcal{R}_{\text{On}}\,o_{\text{table}}, \quad {}^{u}\mathcal{R}_{\text{Free}}\,o_{\text{box}}. \tag{17}$$

Each of those relations is created by a certain skill defined in terms of robot control subsystem behaviours. Thus (17) can be treated as a complex skill, hence hierarchic composition of skills is possible.

3.8 Behaviours Composing the Skills

Six unique behaviours of the robot control systems were used in the previously defined skills. Following the system decomposition as proposed in [15], the considered control subsystem is supplemented with two virtual effectors $e_{\text{robot,manipulator}}$ and $e_{\text{robot,gripper}}$, forming the abstraction layer facilitating the position-force control of the manipulator and control of the configuration of the gripper respectively. ${}^{c}\mathcal{B}_{\text{robot,1}}$ causes the robot to reach the pregrasp pose, hence the manipulator moves, while the gripper configuration remains unchanged (i.e. the distance between the fingers remains constant – $e_{\text{robot,gripper}}$ executes its idle behaviour). The behaviour ${}^{c}\mathcal{B}_{\text{robot,2}}$ of the control system is responsible for appropriate opening of the gripper. Hence c_{robot} delegates reaching of the required gripper configuration to $e_{\text{robot,gripper}}$, while the virtual effector $e_{\text{robot,manipulator}}$ runs its idle behaviour (the manipulator is supposed to stand still). ${}^{c}\mathcal{B}_{\text{robot,3}}$ commands $e_{\text{robot,manipulator}}$ to approach the box, while holding the gripper posture unchanged. ${}^{c}\mathcal{B}_{\text{robot,4}}$, while closing the gripper (grasping the box with the fingers), causes both effectors to be active: besides control of the gripper configuration the manipulator should move appropriately in order to reduce the potential tensions. For this purpose $^{c}\mathcal{B}_{robot,4}$ commands the virtual effector $e_{robot,manipulator}$ to use position-force control. The behaviour of the virtual effector is similar to the behaviour controlling the manipulator during grasping of a Rubik's cube presented in [16], with the major difference being the values of the motion parameters (such as dumping and inertia). The behaviour $^{c}\mathcal{B}_{robot,5}$ is responsible for reaching the pose, from which the departure trajectory can be started. This is realized by pure position control of the manipulator and results in lifting the box a little bit above the object on which it was placed previously (the additional effect of this action is deleting the relation between the box and the object on which it was standing from the attribute graph). $^{c}\mathcal{B}_{robot,6}$ puts the object on the table with the use of position-force control. This is realized by a guarded motion, i.e. by lowering the object until the exerted force reaches a given limit. During this maneuver $e_{robot,gripper}$ runs its idle behaviour.

4   Conclusions

As the environment state change is brought about by the robot's actions, somehow the robot must be associated with the objects it manipulates. This association is brought about by treating the robot, on the one hand, as a device having its control system and, on the other hand, as an object present in the environment. The task that the robot has to execute is preferably expressed in terms of relations between objects, describing situations in the environment that should occur for the task to be accomplished. Creation of an object relation in any environmental context is rather difficult, thus an intermediate step is proposed. The appropriate context is established by introducing robot-object relations that produce such a state of the environment and the robot that creation of the required object–object relation becomes fairly simple. Having this problem solved one has to transform the changes of state of the environment into actions of the robot. This problem is solved by treating the robot as any other object in the environment and associating adequate attributes with objects. Abstract spacial relations can be defined in terms of mathematical relations between the values of those attributes. As the robot influences the environment through its effectors and gains knowledge about the state of the environment through its receptors the allotted task, expressed in terms of relations, can be executed by the robot control system. As a side-effect the anchoring problem is solved, because attribute values can be produced by the perception subsystem. Object relations are defined in terms of relationships between the values of attributes, thus raw sensoric data is being transformed into abstract concept of object relation.

The robot control system exhibits behaviours defined in terms of transition functions. Behaviours are assembled in to skills by employing finite state machines. Skills create both the required relations and the required context enabling the creation of the relation, thus executing the required task. As each more abstract concept can be transformed formally into a less abstract one we can produce the system capable of executing abstractly described tasks.

Acknowledgement. This project was financially supported by the National Centre for Research and Development grant no. PBS1/A3/8/2012.

References

1. Mujtaba, S., Goldman, R.: AL users' manual. Stanford Artificial Intelligence Laboratory (January 1979)
2. Ambler, A.P., Corner, D.F.: RAPT1 user's manual. Department of Artificial Intelligence, University of Edinburgh (1984)
3. Blume, C., Jakob, W.: Programming languages for industrial robots (1986)
4. Zieliński, C.: TORBOL: An object level robot programming language. Mechatronics 1(4), 469–485 (1991)
5. Tenorth, M., Beetz, M.: KnowRob — knowledge processing for autonomous personal robots. In: IEEE/RSJ International Conference on Intelligent Robots and Systems, St. Louis, USA, October 10-15, pp. 4261–4266 (2009)
6. Tenorth, M., Beetz, M.: KnowRob: a knowledge processing infrastructure for cognition-enabled robots. International Journal of Robotics Research 32(5), 566–590 (2013)
7. Stenmark, M., Stolt, A.: A system for high-level task specification using complex sensor-based skills. In: Robotics: Science and Systems (RSS) 2013 Workshop on Programming with Constraints, Berlin, Germany, June 28 (2013)
8. Pangercic, D., Tenorth, M., Jain, D., Beetz, M.: Combining perception and knowledge processing for everyday manipulation. In: IEEE/RSJ International Conference on Intelligent Robots and Systems (2010)
9. Beetz, M., Mösenlechner, L., Tenorth, M.: CRAM – a cognitive robot abstract machine for everyday manipulation in human environments. In: IEEE/RSJ International Conference on Intelligent Robots and Systems, IROS, October 18-22, pp. 1012–1017. IEEE, Taipei (2010)
10. Tenorth, M., Perzylo, A.C., Lafrenz, R., Beetz, M.: Representation and exchange of knowledge about actions, objects, and environments in the RoboEarth framework. IEEE Transactions on Automation Science and Engineering 10, 643–651 (2013)
11. Tenorth, M., Beetz, M.: Knowledge processing for autonomous robot control. In: AAAI Spring Symposium on Designing Intelligent Robots: Reintegrating AI (2011)
12. Tenorth, M., Perzylo, A.C., Lafrenz, R., Beetz, M.: The RoboEarth language: Representing and exchanging knowledge about actions, objects, and environments. In: IEEE International Conference on Robotics and Automation (2012)
13. Zieliński, C.: Description of semantics of robot programming languages. Mechatronics 2(2), 171–198 (1992)
14. Zieliński, C., Kornuta, T., Boryń, M.: Specification of robotic systems on an example of visual servoing. In: 10th International IFAC Symposium on Robot Control (SYROCO 2012), vol. 10, pp. 45–50 (2012)
15. Kornuta, T., Zieliński, C.: Robot control system design exemplified by multi-camera visual servoing. Journal of Intelligent & Robotic Systems, 1–25 (2013)
16. Zieliński, C., Winiarski, T.: Motion generation in the MRROC++ robot programming framework. International Journal of Robotics Research 29(4), 386–413 (2010)

Modelling, Control and Performance Evaluation of a Combined Robotic Cell by Petri Nets

František Čapkovič*

Institute of Informatics, Slovak Academy of Sciences
Dúbravská cesta 9, 845 07 Bratislava, Slovak Republic
Frantisek.Capkovic@savba.sk
http://www.ui.sav.sk/home/capkovic/capkhome.htm

Abstract. Place/transition Petri nets (P/T PN) and timed Petri nets (TPN) are used here in order to model the attendance of industrial robot on two devices of a manufacturing system producing two different kinds of artifacts. Firstly, P/T PN are used to model the particular procedures of producing the individual artifacts by means of the robot and their joint into the single procedure without any deadlock and infeasibility. Then, the times expressing the duration of separate operation are assigned to the P/T PN transitions. In such a way the TPN model is obtained. It allows to test the performance evaluation of the system.

Keywords: Agent, cooperation, job, machine tool, place/transition Petri nets, robot, timed Petri nets, production system.

1 Introduction and Preliminaries

Petri nets (PN) represent the effective tool for modelling discrete event systems (DES). Place/transition PN (P/T PN) [5,6] are frequently used due to their simple mathematical model given in analytical terms. Their extended version containing time specifications - timed Petri nets (TPN) - are suitable for modelling the DES behaviour in time and they make possible the performance evaluation. Manufacturing systems (MS), especially the flexible MS (FMS) [10], are typical representatives of DES. Hence, the both mentioned kinds of PN are very useful for modelling, control and performance evaluation [9] of FMS. As to their structure P/T PN are bipartite directed graphs $\langle P, T, F, G \rangle$. Two kinds of nodes are represented by the places $p_i \in P$, $i = 1, \ldots, n$, and the transitions $t_j \in T$, $j = 1, \ldots, m$. Two kinds of edges, namely edges from places to transitions and the edges from transitions to places are given, respectively, in the form of the sets $F \subseteq P \times T$ and $G \subseteq T \times P$. But moreover, next to the structure, P/T PN have also their dynamics which can formally be expressed as $\langle X, U, \delta, \mathbf{x}_0 \rangle$. Here, X is the set of the state vectors $\mathbf{x}$ of the places, U is the set of the state vectors $\mathbf{u}$ of the transitions, $\delta : X \times U \to X$ is the transition function yielding

* Partially supported by the Slovak Grant Agency for Science VEGA under grant # 2/0039/13 (2013-2016) and the agency APVV under grant APVV-0261-10.

© Springer International Publishing Switzerland 2015
D. Filev et al. (eds.), *Intelligent Systems'2014*,
Advances in Intelligent Systems and Computing 323, DOI: 10.1007/978-3-319-11310-4_2

the new state (marking) vector $\mathbf{x}_{k+1} \in X$ on the basis of both the existing state $\mathbf{x}_k \in X$ and the occurrence of discrete events $\mathbf{u}_k \in U$. The dynamics, being as a matter of the fact the evolution of marking of the P/T PN places, is given by the linear discrete model $\mathbf{x}_{k+1} = \mathbf{x}_k + \mathbf{B}.\mathbf{u}_k$. Here, $\mathbf{x}_k = (\sigma_{p_1}, \ldots, \sigma_{p_n})^T$ with $\sigma_{p_i} \in \{0, 1, \ldots, c\}$ (where c is the capacity of the places - it may be either infinite or finite) is the marking vector expressing the state of the marking of the particular places (the number of tokens inside the places) and $\mathbf{u}_k = (\gamma_{t_1}, \ldots, \gamma_{t_m})^T$ with $\gamma_{t_j} \in \{0, 1\}$ is the vector of the states of transitions (either disabled or enabled). The matrix $\mathbf{B} = \mathbf{G}^T - \mathbf{F}$ expresses the structure. $\mathbf{F}$ (**Pre**) and $\mathbf{G}^T$ (**Post**) are the incidence matrices of the arcs corresponding, respectively, to the sets F and G. All of the entries of the vectors and matrices are non-negative integers. In oder to eliminate the negative integers during the marking evaluation, the condition $\mathbf{F}.\mathbf{u}_k \leq \mathbf{x}_k$ has to be met in any step k of the marking evolution. The places model activities (operations) in FMS, while the transitions model the discrete events (starting/ending the activities). P/T PN do not depend on time. Their transitions, places, arcs and tokens do not contain any time specifications.

At the model synthesis we will use the methods of the DES control theory, namely the supervisor synthesis. We will use the method of the supervisor synthesis based on the P-invariants of P/T PN [3,4] which is an extended method of the mutual exclusion. Let us start from the definition of P-invariants [1], [5] being the columns of $\mathbf{V}$

$$\mathbf{V}^T.\mathbf{B} = 0 \tag{1}$$

After imposing some restrictions on the state vector entries σ_{p_i}, $i = 1, \ldots, n$, in the vector form $\mathbf{L}.\mathbf{x} \leq \mathbf{b}$ and removing the inequality we have

$$\mathbf{L}.\mathbf{x} + \mathbf{x}_s = (\mathbf{L} \ \mathbf{I}_s).\begin{pmatrix} \mathbf{x} \\ \mathbf{x}_s \end{pmatrix} = \mathbf{b} \tag{2}$$

Here, $\mathbf{x}_s$ is the $(n_s \times 1)$ vector of slacks and $\mathbf{I}_s$ is the $(n_s \times n_s)$ identity matrix. We can force the invariants into the definition (1) as follows

$$(\mathbf{L} \ \mathbf{I}_s).\begin{pmatrix} \mathbf{B} \\ \mathbf{B}_s \end{pmatrix} = 0 \tag{3}$$

where $\mathbf{B}_s = \mathbf{G}_s^T - \mathbf{F}_s$ is the structure of supervisor (till now unknown) to be synthesized. Hence, $\mathbf{B}_s = -\mathbf{L}.\mathbf{B}$ and the initial state of the supervisor follows from (2) in the form $^s\mathbf{x}_0 = \mathbf{b} - \mathbf{L}.\mathbf{x}_0$. Imposing the extended condition

$$\mathbf{L}_p.\mathbf{x} + \mathbf{L}_t.\mathbf{u} + \mathbf{L}_v.\mathbf{v} \leq \mathbf{b} \tag{4}$$

where $\mathbf{L}_p$ (which is identical with $\mathbf{L}$ from (3)), $\mathbf{L}_t$, $\mathbf{L}_v$ are, respectively, $(n_s \times n)$, $(n_s \times m)$, $(n_s \times m)$ matrices, we can synthesized the supervisor with further properties concerning not only the entries of the state vector $\mathbf{x}$ but also the control vector $\mathbf{u}$ and the Parikh's vector $\mathbf{v}$ [2]. Namely, when $\mathbf{b} - \mathbf{L}_p.\mathbf{x} \geq \mathbf{0}$ is valid - see e.g. [3] - the supervisor with the following structure and initial state

$$\mathbf{F}_s = \max(\mathbf{0}, \mathbf{L}_p.\mathbf{B} + \mathbf{L}_v, \mathbf{L}_t) \tag{5}$$

$$\mathbf{G}_s^T = \max(\mathbf{0}, \mathbf{L}_t - \max(\mathbf{0}, \mathbf{L}_p.\mathbf{B} + \mathbf{L}_v)) - \min(\mathbf{0}, \mathbf{L}_p.\mathbf{B} + \mathbf{L}_v) \tag{6}$$

$$^s\mathbf{x}_0 = \mathbf{b} - \mathbf{L}_p.\mathbf{x}_0 - \mathbf{L}_v.\mathbf{v}_0 \tag{7}$$

guarrantees that constraints are verified for the states resulting from the initial state. Here, the max(.) is the maximum operator for matrices. However, the maximum is taken element by element.

The real devices, especially the industrial robot and machine tools can be understood to be cooperating agents.

TPN - see e.g. [7], [11] - contain time specifications. In general, the time can be assigned to TPN places, transitions, directed arcs, even to tokens. But here, in this paper, we will assign the time specifications exclusively to the TPN transitions. More precisely, putting the time specifications into the P/T PN transitions we exactly convert P/T PN into TPN. Namely, in the deterministic case the time specifications will represent time delays of the transitions while in the non-deterministic cases they will express a kind of probability distribution of timing (e.g. exponential, discrete uniformed, Poisson's, Rayleigh's, Weitbull's). In effect, the time specification assigned into a transition expresses the time which is necessary for the performance of an operation or activity modelled by the input place of the transition.

2   Case Study

Consider the manufacturing cell containing two numerically controlled machine tools $M1$, $M2$ of different kinds performing different operations on a part putting in them by the robot R. At the production of the part $P1$ only $M1$ is utilized, while at the production of another part $P2$ both $M1$ and $M2$ are exploited. Raw materials (or semi-products) are fed by the input conveyor Ci while the finished parts are taken away by the output conveyor Co. The simplified scheme of the working cell is in Fig. 1. The working cycle at producing only $P1$ is the following: the available R takes the arriving raw material from Ci (the arc $P1_1$) and loads it into $M1$ ($P1_2$) where the operation is performed and the R becomes free ($P1_3$). After finishing the operation in $M1$, R unloads the finished $P1$ ($P1_4$) from $M1$, places it on Co ($P1_5$) and becomes available ($P1_6$). Its P/T PN model is given in Fig. 2. Here, the interpretation of the places is as follows: p_1 - taking the raw material from Ci; p_2 - loading the raw material into $M1$; p_3 - performance of the operation in $M1$; p_4 - expresses the availability of $M1$; p_5 - unloading finished $P1$ from $M1$ and putting it on Co; p_6 - activity of Co; p_7 - expresses the availability of R. The particular devices can be understood as simple material agents. At the agent cooperation R is most active because it attends other agents to ensure the attachment of a global aim. The incorporation of R (i.e. p_7) into the P/T PN model of the cell to ensure the cooperation of devices means that R can be understood as a supervisor for other agents. Thus, the incorporation of p_7 can be synthesized also in analytical terms by means of DES control theory methods - in this case by the mutual exclusion principle. Namely, R can serve only one another agent, not two or several ones simultaneously. Apart from p_7 to be synthesized, $\mathbf{x_0} = (1\ 0\ 0\ 1\ 0\ 0)^T$. The condition $\sigma_{p_2} + \sigma_{p_5} \leq 1$ will guarantee the mutual exclusion concerning the loading and unloading $M1$ by R. The vector form the condition is $\mathbf{L}.\mathbf{x} \leq \mathbf{b}$, where $\mathbf{L} = (0\ 1\ 0\ 0\ 1\ 0)$ and $\mathbf{b} = (1)$. Because of

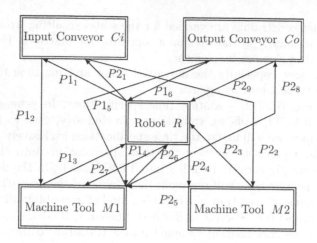

Fig. 1. The simplified scheme of the manufacturing cell. The sequence of $P1_i$, $i = 1, \ldots 6$ symbolizes the working cycle at the production of $P1$ while the sequence $P2_i$, $i = 1, \ldots 9$ symbolizes the working cycle at the production of $P2$.

[3,4], the structural matrix $\mathbf{B}_s$ expressing the addition of the supervisor p_7 (i.e. R) is given as $\mathbf{B}_s = -\mathbf{L}.\mathbf{B}$, where $\mathbf{B}$ expresses the structure before adding the p_7. The initial condition for the supervisor ${}^s\mathbf{x}_0 = \mathbf{b} - \mathbf{L}.\mathbf{x}_0 = 1 - 0 = 1$. Because

$$\mathbf{B} = \begin{pmatrix} -1 & 0 & 0 & 0 & 1 \\ 1 & -1 & 0 & 0 & 0 \\ 0 & 1 & -1 & 0 & 0 \\ 0 & -1 & 1 & 0 & 0 \\ 0 & 0 & 1 & -1 & 0 \\ 0 & 0 & 0 & 1 & -1 \end{pmatrix} ; \begin{aligned} \mathbf{B}_s &= (-1\ 1\ -1\ 1\ 0) \\ \mathbf{F}_s &= (1\ 0\ 1\ 0\ 0) \\ \mathbf{G}_s^T &= (0\ 1\ 0\ 1\ 0) \end{aligned} ; \mathbf{B}_{fin} = \begin{pmatrix} \mathbf{B} \\ \mathbf{B}_s \end{pmatrix}$$

the matrix $\mathbf{B}_{fin}$ represents the final structure given in Fig. 2 left. Likewise, we can analyze the situation when only the part $P2$ is produced. The working cycle at producing $P2$ is the following: the available R takes the arriving raw material from Ci ($P2_1$) and loads it into $M2$ ($P2_2$) where the operation is performed and the R becomes free ($P2_3$). After finishing the operation in $M2$, R unloads the finished semi-product of $P2$ from $M2$($P2_4$), loads it into $M1$ ($P2_5$) and becomes free ($P2_6$). After finishing the operation in $M1$, R unloads the finished product $P2$ from $M1$ ($P2_7$), places it on Co ($P2_8$) and becomes available ($P2_9$). Its P/T PN model is given in Fig. 3. Here, the interpretation of the places is as follows: p_1 - taking the raw material from Ci; p_2 - loading the raw material into $M2$; p_3 - performance of the operation in $M2$; p_4 - unloading semi-product of $P2$ from $M2$ and loading it into $M1$; p_5 - performance of the operation in $M1$; p_6 - unloading finished $P2$ from $M1$ and putting it on Co; p_7 - activity of Co; p_8 - expresses the availability of $M2$; p_9 - expresses the availability of $M1$; p_{10} - expresses the availability of R. Apart from p_{10} to be synthesized, $\mathbf{x}_0 = (1\ 0\ 0\ 0\ 0\ 0\ 0\ 1\ 1)^T$. The condition $\sigma_{p_2} + \sigma_{p_4} + \sigma_{p_6} \leq 1$ will guarantee the mutual exclusion concerning

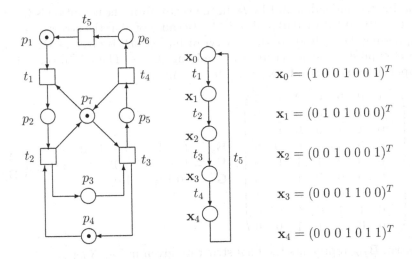

$$\mathbf{x}_0 = (1\ 0\ 0\ 1\ 0\ 0\ 1)^T$$

$$\mathbf{x}_1 = (0\ 1\ 0\ 1\ 0\ 0\ 0)^T$$

$$\mathbf{x}_2 = (0\ 0\ 1\ 0\ 0\ 0\ 1)^T$$

$$\mathbf{x}_3 = (0\ 0\ 0\ 1\ 1\ 0\ 0)^T$$

$$\mathbf{x}_4 = (0\ 0\ 0\ 1\ 0\ 1\ 1)^T$$

Fig. 2. The P/T PN-based model of the working cycle at the production of $P1$ (left), corresponding reachability graph (in the center) and meaning of its nodes (right). The entries of the vectors $\mathbf{x}_i$, $i = 0, 1, \ldots, 6$ express the marking of the corresponding P/T PN places during the working cycle.

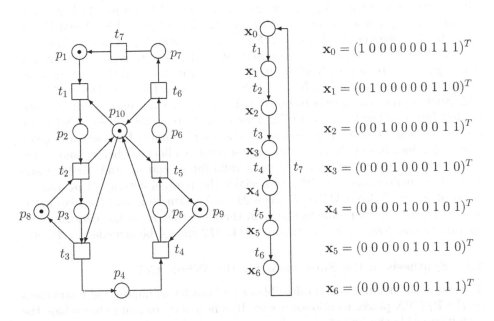

$$\mathbf{x}_0 = (1\ 0\ 0\ 0\ 0\ 0\ 0\ 1\ 1\ 1)^T$$

$$\mathbf{x}_1 = (0\ 1\ 0\ 0\ 0\ 0\ 0\ 1\ 1\ 0)^T$$

$$\mathbf{x}_2 = (0\ 0\ 1\ 0\ 0\ 0\ 0\ 0\ 1\ 1)^T$$

$$\mathbf{x}_3 = (0\ 0\ 0\ 1\ 0\ 0\ 0\ 1\ 1\ 0)^T$$

$$\mathbf{x}_4 = (0\ 0\ 0\ 0\ 1\ 0\ 0\ 1\ 0\ 1)^T$$

$$\mathbf{x}_5 = (0\ 0\ 0\ 0\ 0\ 1\ 0\ 1\ 1\ 0)^T$$

$$\mathbf{x}_6 = (0\ 0\ 0\ 0\ 0\ 0\ 1\ 1\ 1\ 1)^T$$

Fig. 3. The P/T PN-based model of the working cycle at the production of $P2$ (left), corresponding reachability graph (in the centre) and meaning of its nodes (right). The entries of the vectors $\mathbf{x}_i$, $i = 0, 1, \ldots, 9$ express the marking of the corresponding P/T PN places during the working cycle.

the loading and unloading $M1$ by R. In the vector form the condition is $\mathbf{L}.\mathbf{x} \leq \mathbf{b}$, where $\mathbf{L} = (0\ 1\ 0\ 1\ 0\ 1\ 0\ 0\ 0)$ and $\mathbf{b} = (1)$. Because of [3,4] the structural matrix $\mathbf{B}_s$ expressing the addition of the supervisor p_{10} (i.e. R) is given as $\mathbf{B}_s = -\mathbf{L}.\mathbf{B}$, where $\mathbf{B}$ expresses the structure before adding the p_7. The initial condition for the supervisor $^s\mathbf{x}_0 = \mathbf{b} - \mathbf{L}_p.\mathbf{x}_0 = 1 - 0 = 1$. As

$$
\mathbf{B} = \begin{pmatrix}
-1 & 0 & 0 & 0 & 0 & 0 & 1 \\
1 & -1 & 0 & 0 & 0 & 0 & 0 \\
0 & 1 & -1 & 0 & 0 & 0 & 0 \\
0 & 0 & 1 & -1 & 0 & 0 & 0 \\
0 & 0 & 0 & 1 & -1 & 0 & 0 \\
0 & 0 & 0 & 0 & 1 & -1 & 0 \\
0 & 0 & 0 & 0 & 0 & 1 & -1 \\
0 & -1 & 1 & 0 & 0 & 0 & 0 \\
0 & 0 & 0 & -1 & 1 & 0 & 0
\end{pmatrix}
\begin{array}{l}
\mathbf{B}_s = (-1\,1 - 1\,1 - 1\,1\,0) \\[4pt]
\mathbf{F}_s = (1\,0\,1\,0\,1\,0\,0) \\[4pt]
\mathbf{G}_s^T = (0\,1\,0\,1\,0\,1\,0)
\end{array}
\; ; \mathbf{B}_{fin} \begin{pmatrix} \mathbf{B} \\ \mathbf{B}_s \end{pmatrix}
$$

the matrix $\mathbf{B}_{fin}$ represents the final structure given in Fig. 3 left.

Up to now, we have analyzed only the autonomous production of $P1$ by $M1$ and that of $P2$ by $M1$ and $M2$. Now, let us analyze the simultaneous production of $P1$ and $P2$ when $M1$, $M2$ are served solely by the robot R. To distinguish the left parts of Fig. 2 and Fig. 3 it is necessary to rename some PN places and transitions and to join the places representing the robot into one place. In Fig. 2 left rename previous p_2 on p_8, p_3 on p_9, p_5 on p_{10} and p_4 on p_{13}. In Fig. 3 left rename p_8 on p_{11} and p_9 on p_{12}. Now join the left parts of Fig. 2 and Fig. 3 into Fig. 4. Moreover, R (denoted in Fig. 2 as p_7 and in Fig. 3 as p_{10}) in Fig. 4 is named as p_{16}. Here, also the counters of final products represented by the places p_{14}, p_{15} are added. Now, let us construct the model of the simultaneous production when only one robot, namely R, operates both machines $M1$ and $M2$. Such a procedure seems to be very simple - it is sufficient to join previous models (given in the left parts of Fig. 2 and Fig. 3) together. However, when we do this, we can be sure of the contrary. The simple joining both schemes given in Fig. 4 is insufficient. Namely, there are several deadlocks (when p_2 and p_3 are simultaneously active, when the same is valid for p_8 and p_9, and the like) and infeasible simultaneous activities (especially the parallel activity of p_4 and p_9, i.e. picking up $P1$ from $M1$ by R when $M1$ is just running, and the like) occur in such a scheme. All problems rise from the facts that R cannot perform more operations simultaneously and running $M1$, $M2$ cannot be attended by R, etc.

2.1   Synthesis of the Supervisor for the Whole Cell

To remove the deadlocks and infeasible operations let us impose the restrictions on the P/T PN places mentioned above. It is necessary to mutually exclude the activities inside the sets of places $\{p_2, p_3, p_5, p_6\}$, $\{p_4, p_9\}$, $\{p_8, p_9\}$ as follows

$$\sigma_{p_2} + \sigma_{p_3} + \sigma_{p_5} + \sigma_{p_6} \leq 1 \tag{8}$$

$$\sigma_{p_4} + \sigma_{p_9} \leq 1 \text{ being the } crucial \text{ condition between } M1 \text{ and } M2 \tag{9}$$

$$\sigma_{p_8} + \sigma_{p_9} \leq 1 \tag{10}$$

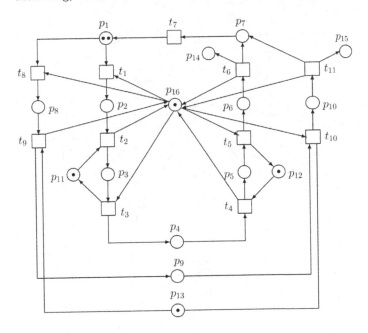

Fig. 4. The scheme arose by the simple joining of two individual ones given in Fig. 2 and Fig. 3

Thus, after expressing these conditions in the matrix form $\mathbf{L}.\mathbf{x} \leq \mathbf{b}$ we have

$$\mathbf{L} = \begin{pmatrix} 0\,1\,1\,0\,1\,1\,0\,0\,0\,0\,0\,0\,0\,0\,0\,0 \\ 0\,0\,0\,1\,0\,0\,0\,0\,1\,0\,0\,0\,0\,0\,0\,0 \\ 0\,0\,0\,0\,0\,0\,0\,1\,1\,0\,0\,0\,0\,0\,0\,0 \end{pmatrix} ; \, \mathbf{b} = \begin{pmatrix} 1 \\ 1 \\ 1 \end{pmatrix} \tag{11}$$

$$\mathbf{B}_s = -\mathbf{L}.\mathbf{B} = \begin{pmatrix} -1\,0 & 1\,-1\,0\,1\,0 & 0 & 0\,0\,0 \\ 0\,0\,-1 & 1\,0\,0\,0 & 0\,-1\,1\,0 \\ 0\,0 & 0 & 0\,0\,0\,-1 & 0\,1\,0 \end{pmatrix} = \mathbf{G}_s^T - \mathbf{F}_s \tag{12}$$

$$\mathbf{F}_s = \begin{pmatrix} 1\,0\,0\,1\,0\,0\,0\,0\,0\,0\,0 \\ 0\,0\,1\,0\,0\,0\,0\,0\,1\,0\,0 \\ 0\,0\,0\,0\,0\,0\,0\,1\,0\,0\,0 \end{pmatrix} ; \, \mathbf{G}_s^T = \begin{pmatrix} 0\,0\,1\,0\,0\,1\,0\,0\,0\,0\,0 \\ 0\,0\,0\,1\,0\,0\,0\,0\,0\,1\,0 \\ 0\,0\,0\,0\,0\,0\,0\,0\,0\,1\,0 \end{pmatrix} \tag{13}$$

$$\mathbf{x}_0 = (2\,0\,0\,0\,0\,0\,0\,0\,0\,0\,1\,1\,1\,0\,0\,1)^T \tag{14}$$

$$^s\mathbf{x}_0 = \mathbf{b} - \mathbf{L}.\mathbf{x}_0 = (1\,1\,1)^T \tag{15}$$

Finally, we have obtained the augmented system (the original system extended by means of the synthesized supervisor) in the form

$$\mathbf{F}_a = \begin{pmatrix} \mathbf{F} \\ \mathbf{F}_s \end{pmatrix} ; \, \mathbf{G}_a^T = \begin{pmatrix} \mathbf{G}^T \\ \mathbf{G}_s^T \end{pmatrix} ; \, \mathbf{x}_a = \begin{pmatrix} \mathbf{x} \\ \mathbf{x}_s \end{pmatrix} \tag{16}$$

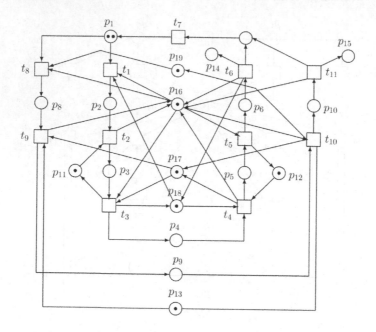

Fig. 5. The supervised joined scheme

It is given in Fig. 5. The synthesized supervisor removing the deadlocks and infeasible operations is realized by the places p_{17}, p_{18}, p_{19}. However, this is not yet everything. Namely, it is still necessary to decide the conflict between the transitions t_1 and t_8 in order to ensure the production of both parts $P1$, $P2$ in a prescribed relation. Therefore, it is necessary to define priorities [2] as follows

$$\gamma_{t_1} \leq \gamma_{t_8} \quad \text{and} \quad \gamma_{t_8} \leq \gamma_{t_1} \tag{17}$$

In our case, in the condition (4) $\mathbf{L}_p = \mathbf{0}$, $\mathbf{L}_t = \mathbf{0}$. But with respect to (17) we have

$$\mathbf{L}_v = \begin{pmatrix} 1\,0\,0\,0\,0\,0\,0\,-1\,0\,0\,0 \\ -1\,0\,0\,0\,0\,0\,0\,\,\,1\,0\,0\,0 \end{pmatrix}; \; \mathbf{v}_0 = \mathbf{0}, \, {}^s\mathbf{x}_0 = \mathbf{b} - \mathbf{L}_v.\mathbf{v}_0 = \begin{pmatrix} 1 \\ 1 \end{pmatrix} \tag{18}$$

$$\mathbf{F}_s = \max(\mathbf{0}, \mathbf{L}_v) = \begin{pmatrix} 1\,0\,0\,0\,0\,0\,0\,0\,0\,0\,0 \\ 0\,0\,0\,0\,0\,0\,0\,1\,0\,0\,0 \end{pmatrix} \tag{19}$$

$$\mathbf{G}_s^T = \max(\mathbf{0}, -\max(\mathbf{0}, \mathbf{L}_v)) - \min(\mathbf{0}, \mathbf{L}_v) = \begin{pmatrix} 0\,0\,0\,0\,0\,0\,0\,1\,0\,0\,0 \\ 1\,0\,0\,0\,0\,0\,0\,0\,0\,0\,0 \end{pmatrix} \tag{20}$$

The final structure is given in Fig. 6. The number of tokens in p_{20}, p_{21} express the mutual ratio of the repetition rates at the production of the $P1$, $P2$. In our case, the ratio is 1:1, i.e. the products $P1$ and $P2$ are produced alternately.

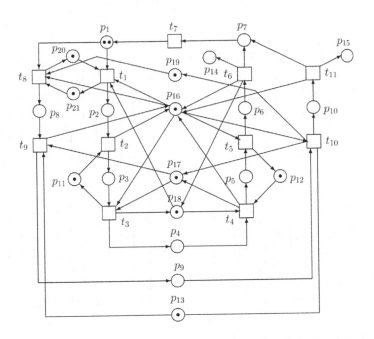

Fig. 6. The supervised joined scheme with additional supervisor solving the conflict concerning the priorities

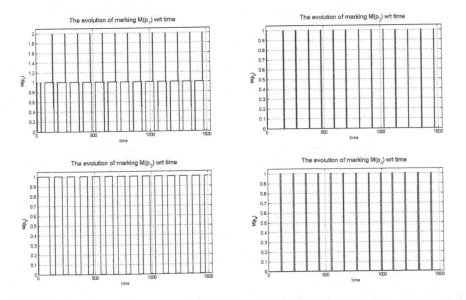

Fig. 7. TPN marking of $p_1 - p_4$ with respect to time; p_3 models machining $P2$ by $M2$

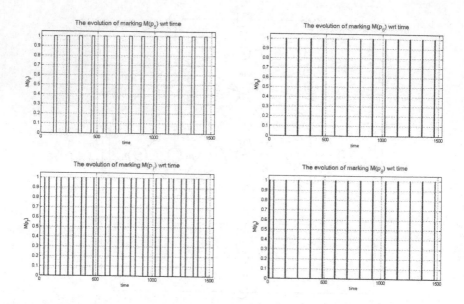

Fig. 8. TPN marking of $p_5 - p_8$ with respect to time; p_5 models machining $P2$ by $M1$

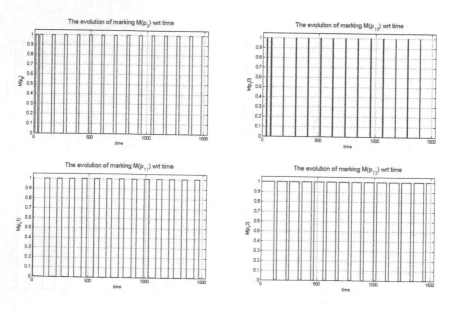

Fig. 9. TPN marking of $p_9 - p_{12}$ with respect to time; p_9 models machining $P1$ by $M1$

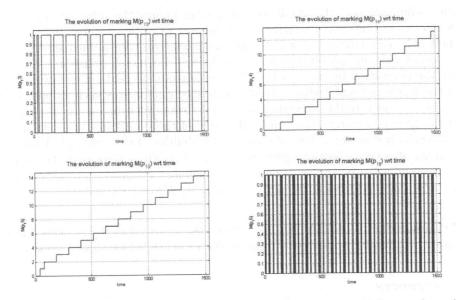

Fig. 10. TPN marking of $p_{13} - p_{16}$ with respect to time; p_{14} counts the number of finalized parts of the kind $P2$ while p_{15} counts that of the kind $P1$

2.2   Performance Evaluation of the Whole Cell

Having the complete P/T PN model of the robotic cell, free of deadlocks and conflicts, transform it into the TPN model. We can do this by means of assigning time specifications (e.g. lengths of processing the parts in particular machines, waiting times, etc.) to the corresponding transitions, namely, to the output transitions of the places modelling the devices in question. Consider the deterministic case of timing the transitions, i.e. assign ($\cong$) the time delays (corresponding to the duration of operations or activities) expressed in a time unit to the transitions as follows: $t_1 \cong 1$, $t_2 \cong 5$, $t_3 \cong 30$, $t_4 \cong 8$, $t_5 \cong 25$, $t_6 \cong 5$, $t_7 \cong 0.1$, $t_8 \cong 1$, $t_9 \cong 5$, $t_{10} \cong 25$, $t_{11} \cong 5$. To evaluate the performance of the robotic cell let us use the TPN simulation tool HYPENS [8] in Matlab. Hence, the marking evolution of the individual TPN places in time are given in Fig. 7 - Fig. 10.

3   Conclusion

The main idea of this paper is to point out the possibility of Petri net-based analytical approach to modelling, control synthesis and performance evaluation of the robotic cell, where the robot attends two machine tools (in general several) performing two (in general several) different operations. The case study was presented. Here, the cell produces two products $P1$, $P2$, where the first product needs only processing by $M1$ and the second one needs processing by both $M1$ and $M2$. First of all, the simple working cycles producing particular products were analyzed by means of P/T PN models. Then, the models were joined together into the model of manufacturing both products simultaneously.

After elimination of the problems emerging at joining the sub-models (i.e. the deadlocks and infeasible activities) and defining priorities - everything done by the PN-based analytical approach - the final model was transformed into TPN by means of assigning processing times into the P/T PN model transitions. Executing the simulation by the tool HYPENS in Matlab the performance evaluation of the whole cell was realized. To illustrate the soundness of such an approach, and to corroborate the correctness of the performance evaluation for a given set of the time parameters, the graphical results of the simulation were introduced and verbally described. They document the abilities of the approach. From the courses of marking in time given in Fig. 7 - Fig. 10 is clear that the courses corresponding to p_3 and p_5 are disjoint (machining $P2$ in $M1$ and $M2$) as well as those corresponding to p_5 and p_9 (machining $P2$ and $P1$ in $M1$).

Acknowledgement. The author thanks the Slovak Grant Agencies VEGA (grant # 2/0039/13) and APVV (grant APVV-0261-10) for their support.

References

1. Čapkovič, F.: Automatic Control Synthesis for Agents and their Cooperation in MAS. Computing and Informatics 29, 1045–1071 (2010)
2. Čapkovič, F.: Cooperation of Agents Based on Methods of DES Supervising and Control. In: Nguyen, N.T. (ed.) Transactions on CCI III. LNCS, vol. 6560, pp. 1–24. Springer, Heidelberg (2011)
3. Iordache, M.V.: Methods for the Supervisory Control of Concurrent Systems Based on Petri Nets Abstraction. Ph.D. Dissertation, University of Notre Dame, Notre Dame, Indiana, USA (2003)
4. Iordache, M.V., Antsaklis, P.J.: Supervision Based on Place Invariants: A Survey. Discrete Event Dynamic Systems 16, 451–492 (2006)
5. Murata, T.: Petri Nets: Properties, Analysis and Applications. Proceedings of the IEEE 77, 541–580 (1989)
6. Peterson, J.L.: Petri Nets Theory and the Modelling of Systems. Prentice-Hall Inc., Englewood Cliffs (1981)
7. Popova-Zeugmann, L.: Time Petri Nets: Theory, Tools and Applications, Part 1, 2 (2008), http://www2.informatik.hu-berlin.de/~popova/1-part-short.pdf, http://www2.informatik.hu-berlin.de/~popova/2-part-short.pdf
8. Sessego, F., Giua, A., Seatzu, C.: HYPENS: A Matlab Tool for Timed Discrete, Continuous and Hybrid Petri Nets. In: van Hee, K.M., Valk, R. (eds.) PETRI NETS 2008. LNCS, vol. 5062, pp. 419–428. Springer, Heidelberg (2008)
9. Sifakis, J.: Performance Evaluation of Systems Using Nets. In: Brauer, W. (ed.) Net Theory and Applications. LNCS, vol. 84, pp. 307–319. Springer, Heidelberg (1980)
10. Zhou, M.C., Venkatesh, K.: Modeling, Simulation, and Control of Flexible Manufacturing Systems. World Scientific, Singapore (2000)
11. Wang, J.: Petri Nets for Dynamic-Event Driven System Modeling. In: Fishwick, P.A. (ed.) Handbook of Dynamic System Modeling, ch. 24, pp. 24-1–24-16. Chapman & Hall/CRC, Taylor & Francis Group, Boca Raton (2007)

Intelligent Control of Flows with Risks on a Network

Vassil Sgurev and Stanislav Drangajov

Institute of Information and Communication Technologies
Bulgarian Academy of Sciences
Acad. G. Bonchev str., bl. 2, 1113 Sofia, Bulgaria
{vsgurev,sdrangajov}@gmail.com

Abstract. Methods for calculating the max network flow with min cut and a flow of min cost, considering the risk on the separate sections of the network, are proposed in this work. The capacity of each arc is so defined, that it does not exceeds 'the physical' arc constraints as well as the admissible risk of the arc network flow function. The maximal flow of minimal cost is calculated in two steps – first the max flow is calculated, and then on the base of this value the optimal arc functions of min cost are defined. Three numerical examples are described which illustrate the potentials of the proposed methods for optimization of the network flows with risks. The concepts of 'minimal cut of the network risk' and 'max flow of min cost and min cut of network risk' are introduced.

Keywords: Intelligent transportation systems, Network flows, Risk management, Max flow, Min cut, Flows of min cost.

1 Preliminary Notes

All types of transportation are carried out on a network structure, comprising of distribution points and connections between them. According to DIRECTIVE 2010/40/EU [10] Intelligent Transport Systems (ITS) are advanced applications which without embodying intelligence as such aim to provide innovative services relating to different modes of transport and traffic management and enable various users to be better informed and make safer, more coordinated and 'smarter' use of transport networks. Similar definitions are accepted in normative documents of all developed countries – USA, Japan, Canada etc. This concerns the transportation of "commodities" of any type – beginning from heavy overseas shipping, land and air transport, electronic messages over a network etc.

Transportation is of course connected with risks of losses on each section of the path. That is why it is expedient methods to be investigated for optimal intelligent control of the network flows so that the flow is maximized, the transportation cost – minimized and the risk – reduced to the minimum.

In the last two decades the "the risk society" [1] came in the focus of the social sphere although in our view this is just a modern trend and new sociologists do not bother with well-developed mathematical models – graph and probabilistic, describ-

© Springer International Publishing Switzerland 2015
D. Filev et al. (eds.), *Intelligent Systems' 2014*,
Advances in Intelligent Systems and Computing 323, DOI: 10.1007/978-3-319-11310-4_3

27

ing in an appropriate way the risk, arising by the decision maker's action which to some extent determine the probability an event to occur or not, as well as by the loss or profit in case that the event occurred. And absolutely reasonably almost all events and behaviors in social and personal life are related to risk. Here we will not consider the different personal, psychological, social, and so on interpretations of risk. We just try to use quantitative methods for risk estimation and applying proper actions for minimizing the loss. For this purpose we accept the formal definitions of risk, risk management and all others, as stated in ISO 31000 (2009) [2], i.e. the risk is the 'effect of uncertainty on objectives'.

At present, according to the same standard the risk is quantitavely defined as a complex function of the product of two measures – the amount of losses (or benefits) if the unfavorable (favorable) event occurred and the respective probability this to occur. We conditionally define four cases: both measures are of considerable value – then the risk is significant; in case that both measures converge to zero, then the risk is ignorable; the other two cases are intermediate and we try here to propose methods for quantitative evaluation of the risk to the Decision Maker who is responsible for the successful completion of the job.

The probability that a given unfavorable event arose is determined by well-developed methodologies [3, 4]. Adequate methods also exist for calculation of the possible harms caused by unfavorable events. This provides the possibility the risk to be determined by the product of these two measures.

2   The Formal Model and Related Programs of Mathematical Programming

In the present work will be considered the problems of determining the risk on an abstract network for transportation of any type of 'commodity' (natural resources, people and goods, money flows etc.), with minimum possible expenses for this activity. This network may be conveniently presented by a directed graph $G(X,U)$ [5] with a set of nodes $X = \{x_i / i \in I\}$ and a set of arcs $U = \{x_{ij} / (i, j) \in G\}$ where I is the set of indices of all vertices, and G – the set of all pairs of indices of all arcs.

In this interpretation the graph nodes correspond to the points of the network where the separate flows of the resource gather and branch, and the oriented arcs $\{x_{ij}\}$ with initial node x_i and final node x_j – to a corresponding section of the network on which only movement from x_i to x_j is possible. If we denote by f_{ij} the resource on the section (arc) x_{ij}, and by c'_{ij} – the upper bound of x_{ij} capacity, then the next inequality reflects the physical impossibility the capacity of the section (arc) to be exceeded, i.e.:

$$f_{ij} \le c'_{ij} ; (i, j) \in G \tag{1}$$

where $G = \{(i, j) / x_{ij} \in U\}$.

On the other hand the requirement for the upper bound of the admissible risk r_{ij} at transportation of the commodity along x_{ij} implies the relation

$$f_{ij}\, p_{ij} \leq r_{ij}\,;\, (i,j) \in G\,; \tag{2}$$

where p_{ij} is the probability that the unfavorable event (loss) happened on the section x_{ij}. This is of course true and for events, which provide over profit but with opposite sign. Then if we denote by c_{ij}'' – the admissible upper bound for the commodity being transported on x_{ij} considering the admissible risk r_{ij}, the following relations follows from (2):

$$f_{ij} \leq \frac{r_{ij}}{p_{ij}} = c_{ij}''\,. \tag{3}$$

Comparison between (1) and (3) shows that the admissible upper bound of the commodity being transported along x_{ij} must not simultaneously both upper bounds - c_{ij}' and c_{ij}''. This may be observed if a generalized capacity c_{ij} is introduced for the section x_{ij} through the relation

$$c_{ij} = \min[\, c_{ij}'\,, c_{ij}''\,]\,;\, (i,j) \in G\,. \tag{4}$$

Then the arc capacity guarantees the simultaneous observation of both inequalities (1) and (3). At that if for some values of c_{ij}

$$c_{ij}'' < c_{ij}'\,, \tag{5}$$

then it follows from (4) and (5) that $c_{ij} = c_{ij}''$, i.e. the generalized arc capacity is determined by the admissible risk. In the reverse inequality

$$c_{ij}' < c_{ij}''\,, \tag{6}$$

this capacity equals to the physical constraints c_{ij}' of the section x_{ij}. The case $c_{ij}' = c_{ij}''$ is trivial. In the fourth case inequality (5) will be observed for some sections and for other – (6), but as a whole the generalized capacity $\{c_{ij}\}$ is achieved with a different degree of impact of constraints $\{c_{ij}'\}$ and $\{c_{ij}''\}$.

a_{ij} will denote the value of an unit of commodity transported along x_{ij}. Mappings Γ^1 and Γ^{-1} are defined in the following way:

$$\Gamma_i^1 = \{j\,/\,(i,j) \in G\}\,;\, \Gamma_i^{-1} = \{j\,/\,(j,i) \in G\}\,. \tag{7}$$

By s will be denoted the node where the whole resource is generated and it is called *source*. In the network flow interpretation it (the flow) is denoted by v. By t is denoted the node where the whole resource is consumed and it usually called *sink*. If $f_{ij} = c_{ij}$, then the arc x_{ij} is called saturated, and otherwise – unsaturated. The network flow model thus defined provides a possibility to solve three distinct problems related to the minimal network risk, reduced to.

3   Related Network Flow Problems

3.1   Problem A

Let the value of the resource which is to be transported from s to t across the net-work be denoted by v. It is necessary to find such a realization of the resource $\{f_{ij}/(i,j) \in G\}$ at which the requirements for admissible risk are observed for the separate sections of the network $\{x_{ij}\}$ and the admissible physical capacity of the-se sections under minimum expenses for transportation, i.e. at minimization of the functional

$$\sum_{(i,j)\in G} a_{ij} f_{ij} .$$

The optimal values of the arc flow functions may be defined by solving the following problem of network flow programming:

$$L = \sum_{(i,j)\in G} a_{ij} f_{ij} \to \min \tag{8}$$

observing the relations: for each $i \in I$

$$\sum_{j\in\Gamma_i^1} f_{ij} - \sum_{j\in\Gamma_i^{-1}} f_{ji} = \begin{cases} v, \text{ if } x_i = s; \\ 0, \text{ if } x_i \neq s,t; \\ -v, \text{ if } x_i \in t; \end{cases} \tag{9}$$

$$f_{ij} \leq c_{ij} \text{ for each } (i,j) \in G\,(i,j)\,; \tag{10}$$

$$f_{ij} \geq 0 \text{ for each } (i,j) \in G\,(i,j)\,; \tag{11}$$

where L is the linear form of the objective function and $\{ f_{ij}^* / (i,j) \in G\}$ corresponds to the optimal solution of the problem from (8) to (11). [6]

3.2   Problem B

v is supposed to be variable as well as the arc network flow functions and its maxi-mum value v_{max} is sought, observing the respective constraints, including those for the capacity. Then calculating of v_{max} will be reduced to solving of the following network flow programming problem:

$$L = v \to \max \tag{12}$$

observing the requirements (9) to (11).

Let cuts $(X_0, \overline{X}_0)$ be defined between the source s and the sink t [7] as the follow-ing set of arcs:

$$(X_0, \overline{X}_0) = \{x_{ij} / x_i \in X_0; x_j \in \overline{X}_0\,; x_{ij} \in U\} \tag{13}$$

where

$$X_0 \subset X; \quad \overline{X}_0 = X \setminus \overline{X}_0; \quad X_0 \cap \overline{X}_0 = \varnothing; \tag{14}$$

and $\varnothing$ denotes the empty set.

Then according to the well-known Ford-Fulkerson's 'mincut-maxflow' theorem [7] the minimal cut $(X_0^*, \overline{X}_0^*)$ is the one for which

$$v_{max} = f(X_0^*, \overline{X}_0^*) = C(X_0^*, \overline{X}_0^*); \quad f(\overline{X}_0^*, X_0^*) = 0. \tag{15}$$

It follows from the relations above that the max flow is always equal to the min cut capacity. If the constraints (10) for each arc depend on the risk only, i.e. inequality (5) is observed for each $\{ x_{ij} / (i, j) \in G\}$ then it may be put down for the minimal cut C $(X_0^*, \overline{X}_0^*)$

$$C(X_0^*, \overline{X}_0^*) = C''(X_0^*, \overline{X}_0^*). \tag{16}$$

This result follows from the relations (2) to (5). If $G^* = \{(i, j) / x_{ij} \in (X_0^*, \overline{X}_0^*);$ $x_{ij} \in G\}$ and $k_{ij} = 1/p_{ij}$; $(i, j) \in G$, then from the same relations (2) to (5) it may be put down:

$$v_{max} = C(X_0^*, \overline{X}_0^*) = \sum_{(i,j) \in G^*} k_{ij} r_{ij}. \tag{17}$$

The result obtained in (17) proves the statement that 'the maximum flow v_{max} is equal to the minimal cut, and it depends on the risk on the arcs of this cut'. It follows from this that changes in v_{max} may be most efficiently carried out by changing the risks on the minimal cut arcs.

3.3   Problem C

If the max flow is found through Problem B and the maximal flow v_{max} is found from (12), the latter being accepted as a constant value

$$v_{max} = const; \tag{18}$$

and Problem A from (8) to (11) is solved again, then a maximum flow of min cost v_{max}^* will be achieved. The possibility for this emerges from the fact that the minimal cuts are several and realizations of the max flow of different values of the functional

$$\sum_{(i,j) \in G} a_{ij} f_{ij}$$

correspond to them. Even if the minimal cut is a single one, several realizations of the flow may correspond to it among which is the one of minimal cost. In the next section, numerical examples will be shown, illustrating the solving of the three Problems A, B, and C.

4   Numerical Examples

A network for transportation of commodities with 8 nodes, including the source s and the sink t and 15 arcs (sections) is shown in Fig.1.

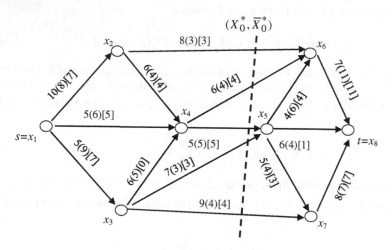

Fig. 1. Exemplary small network

Table 1 contains the source data for solving the three problems – A, B, and C, and namely arc rates a_{ij}, probability of loss p_{ij}, risks r_{ij}, constraints emerging from risks c''_{ij}, physical constraints c'_{ij}, as well as the generalized capacities c_{ij}. The corresponding arc rate a_{ij} and the generalized capacity c_{ij}, in brackets to the right, are shown on each arc in Fig. 1. Data from Table 1 show that for the four arcs – $x_{1,2}, x_{4,5}, x_{4,6},$ and $x_{5,7}$, there is equality between the arc capacities $c''_{ij} = c'_{ij} = c_{ij}$, while in all other 11 remaining arcs from U the capacities depend on the risk, i.e. $c_{ij} = c''_{ij} \neq c'_{ij}$.

Table 1.

Arcs Param	(1,2)	(1,3)	(1,4)	(2,4)	(2,6)	(3,4)	(3,5)	(3,7)	(4,5)	(4,6)	(5,6)	(5,7)	(5,8)	(6,8)	(7,8)
a_{ij}	10	5	5	6	8	6	7	9	5	6	4	5	6	7	8
p_{ij}	0,2	0,1	0,15	0,1	0,2	0,4	0,1	0,25	0,2	0,15	0,2	0,05	0,1	0,2	0,1
r_{ij}	1,6	0,9	0,9	0,4	0,6	2	0,3	1	1	0,6	1,2	0,2	0,4	0,22	0,7
c''_{ij}	8	9	6	4	3	5	3	4	5	4	6	4	4	11	7
c'_{ij}	8	10	8	6	5	6	5	7	5	4	7	4	5	13	9
c_{ij}	8	9	6	4	3	5	3	4	5	4	6	4	4	11	7

On the basis of data from Fig. 1 and Table 1 relations from (9) to (14) may be written down in the following way:

$d_1)\ f_{1,2} + f_{1,3} + f_{1,4} = v;$

$d_2)\ f_{2,4} + f_{2,6} - f_{1,2} = 0;$

$d_3)\ f_{3,4} + f_{3,5} + f_{3,7} - f_{1,2} = 0;$

$d_4)\ f_{4,5} + f_{4,6} - f_{1,4} - f_{2,4} - f_{3,4} = 0;$

$d_5)\ f_{5,6} + f_{5,7} + f_{5,8} - f_{3,5} - f_{4,5} = 0;$

$d_6)\ f_{6,8} - f_{2,6} - f_{4,6} - f_{5,6} = 0;$

$d_7)\ f_{7,8} - f_{3,7} - f_{5,7} = 0;$

$d_8)\ f_{5,8} + f_{6,8} + f_{7,8} = v;$

$d_9)\ f_{1,2} \leq 8;$

$d_{10})\ f_{1,3} \leq 9$

$d_{11})\ f_{1,4} \leq 6;$

$d_{12})\ f_{2,4} \leq 4;$

$d_{13})\ f_{2,6} \leq 3$

$d_{14})\ f_{3,4} \leq 5;$

$d_{15})\ f_{3,5} \leq 3;$

$d_{16})\ f_{3,7} \leq 4$

$d_{17})\ f_{3,5} \leq 5;$

$d_{18})\ f_{4,6} \leq 4;$

$d_{19})\ f_{5,6} \leq 6$

$d_{20})\ f_{5,7} \leq 4;$

$d_{21})\ f_{5,8} \leq 4;$

$d_{22})\ f_{6,8} \leq 11$

$d_{23})\ f_{7,8} \leq 7;$

$d_{24})\ f_{i,j} \geq 0$ for each $(i\ j) \in G.$

4.1   Problem A

Let the value of the network flow be fixed and equal to $v = 14$.

It is necessary to find an optimal plan of minimal cost (8). From the data from Table 1 we may write down:

$$L_1 = 10 f_{1,2} + 5 f_{1,3} + 5 f_{1,4} + 6 f_{2,4} + 8 f_{2,6} + 6 f_{3,4} + 7 f_{3,5} +$$

$$+ 9 f_{3,7} + 5 f_{4,5} + 6 f_{4,6} + 4 f_{5,6} + 5 f_{5,7} + 6 f_{5,8} + 7 f_{6,8} + 8 f_{7,8} \rightarrow \min \qquad (19)$$

Solving the network flow problem with the linear form from (19) under constraints from d_1 to d_{24} and considering in the equalities d_1 and d_8 the value of $v = 14$ results in optimal values $\{ f_{ij}^* \ /\ (i, j) \in G \}$ entered in the second row of Table 2 respectively. For this purpose the software product WebOptim was used [8]. The value of (19) at optimal values of $\{ f_{ij}^* \ /\ (i, j) \in G \}$ is equal to 290.

Table 2.

Problems	$f_{1,2}^*$	$f_{1,3}^*$	$f_{1,4}^*$	$f_{2,4}^*$	$f_{2,6}^*$	$f_{3,4}^*$	$f_{3,5}^*$	$f_{3,7}^*$	$f_{4,5}^*$	$f_{4,6}^*$	$f_{5,6}^*$	$f_{5,7}^*$	$f_{5,8}^*$	$f_{6,8}^*$	$f_{7,8}^*$	v	$\sum_{(i,j)\in G} a_{ij} f_{ij}$
A	4	4	6	1	3	0	1	3	3	4	0	0	4	7	3	14	290
B	7	7	5	4	3	0	3	4	5	4	4	3	1	11	7	19	469
C	7	7	5	4	3	0	3	4	5	4	4	0	4	11	4	19	433

4.2   Problem B

The flow v is supposed to be a variable value and the objective is to find its maximum value. For this purpose the following network flow programming problem: maximization of (12).under constraints d_1 to d_{24}. The optimal values received through the program product WebOptim are given in the third row of Table 2. Max flow value obtained is $max\ v = 19$.

Note: The objective is in the form:

$$\text{max: } + 1\,v + 0f_{1,2} + 0f_{1,3} + 0f_{1,4} + 0f_{2,4} + 0f_{2,6} + 0f_{3,4} + 0f_{3,5} + 0f_{3,7} + \\ + 0f_{4,5} + 0f_{4,6} + 0f_{5,6} + 0f_{5,7} + 0f_{5,8} + 0f_{6,8} + 0f_{7,8},$$

according to the syntax requirements of the software product used.

Comparison of the values of arc capacities from the last row of Table 1 to the respective arc flow functions and flow v from the last but one row of Table 2 shows that equality between them occurs on the cut

$$(X_0^*, \bar{X}_0^*) = \{x_{2,6}, x_{3,5}, x_{3,7}, x_{4,5}, x_{4,6}\}, \tag{20}$$

where

$$X_0^* = \{x_1, x_2, x_3, x_4\};$$
$$\bar{X}_0^* = \{x_5, x_6, x_7, x_8\}; \tag{21}$$
$$X_0^* \cap \bar{X}_0^* = \varnothing.$$

This cut is shown in Fig. 1 by a dotted line. If respective data from Tables 1 and 2, and Fig. 1 are compared, a conclusion may be drawn that the cut (20) is a minimal one [6] for which

$$v = f\ (X_0^*, \bar{X}_0^*)\ = C\ (X_0^*, \bar{X}_0^*)\ = 19; \tag{22}$$
$$(\bar{X}_0^*, X_0^*) = \varnothing\ ; f\ (\bar{X}_0^*, X_0^*) = 0. \tag{23}$$

In this case the value of the min cost flow is equal to

$$\sum_{(i,j)\in G} a_{ij} f_{ij} = 469. \tag{24}$$

4.3   Problem C

With a fixed flow $v = v_{max} = 19$, received from the previous Problem B, the minimal value of the linear form (19) is sought, observing constraints d_1 to d_{24}. This problem was also solved with the above mentioned software product. The optimal values received are put down in the fourth bottom row of Table 2.

Comparison of the results from Tables 1 and 2, and Fig. 1 shows than in this case also the min cut $(X_0^*, \bar{X}_0^*)$ coincides with the one from relations (20) to (24), and it is shown on Fig. 1. In Problem C. being considered the minimal value of the flow obtained through the objective (8) is equal to

$$\min \sum_{(i,j)\in G} a_{ij} f_{ij} = 433; \tag{25}$$

i.e. compared to (24) it is 36 units less, or approximately 7,6%.

Due to the specific features of Problems B and C the network risk decreases by the same percentage at the same max flow $v_{max} = 19$. This provides grounds the minimal cut $(X_0^*, \bar{X}_0^*)$ from (20) to be called '**minimal cut of the network risk**', and the network flow received in Problem C '**max flow of min cost and min cut of network risk**'.

5   Summary

In this paper, a network flow problem for the maximal flow with minimal cost is considered, when a risk exists when a unit of flow is passed along each arc of the network. The quantitative measure of risk is accepted according to the widely acknowledged definitions, mainly ISO 31000:2009.

The determination of the max flow and the max flow of min cost is according to the well-known network flow algorithms, but including the risk on the arcs when the flow passes. Although this may look like similar to flows with gains and losses the case is essentially different as a probability factor is included and as so the methods are different.

Methods are proposed for solving the problem considering the risk, so that the latter is minimized and the flow is maximized at minimum cost, minimizing at the same time the risk. These methods may be used e.g. in commodity transportation systems on arbitrary sophisticated networks where it is compulsory to evaluate the possible risks on each section of the travel network.

A numerical example is given and three problems are solved on one and the same network which demonstrate the effectiveness of the methods

References

1. Klinke, A., Renn, O.: A New Approach to Risk Evaluation and Management: Risk-Based, Precaution-Based, and Discourse-Based Strategies. Risk Analysis 22(6), 1035–1209 (2002), doi:10.1111/1539-6924.00274
2. ISO 31000:2009
3. http://www.ga.gov.au/hazards/our-techniques/modelling/how-do-we-estimate-risk-and-impact.html
4. http://www.lunduniversity.lu.se/o.o.i.s?id=12683&postid=5848 03 ISBN 951-564-393-7
5. Christofides, N.: Graph theory: An Algorithmic Approach. Academic Press, London (1986)
6. Sgurev, V.: Network Flows with General Constraints. Publishing House of the Bulgarian Academy of Sciences, Sofia (1991) (in Bulgarian)
7. Jensen, P.A., Barnes, J.W.: Network flow programming. John Wiley and Sons, Inc., New York (1980)
8. Ford, L.R., Fulkerson, D.R.: Maximal flow through a network. Canadian Journal of Mathematics 8, 399–404 (1956)
9. Genova, K., Kirilov, L., Guliashki, V., Staykov, B., Vatov, D.: A Prototype of a Web-based Decision Support, System for Building Models and Solving Optimization and Decision Making Problems. In: Rachev, B., Smrikarov, A. (eds.) Proceedings of XII International Conference on Computer Systems and Technologies, CompSysTech 2011, Wien, Austria, June 16-17, vol. 578, pp. 167–172. ACM (2011), http://weboptim.iinf.bas.bg/, ISBN 978-1-4503-0917-2
10. http://eur-lex.europa.eu/LexUriServ/LexUriServ.do?uri=OJ:L:2010:207:0001:0013:EN:PDF

Intelligent Robust Control System Based on Quantum KB-Self-organization: Quantum Soft Computing and Kansei/Affective Engineering Technologies

I.A. Barchatova[1], S.V. Ulyanov[2], and V.A. Albu[3]

[1,2] International University "Dubna", Dubna, Russia
{biriska,ulyanovsv}@mail.ru
[3] Institute of Mathematics and Computer Science, Chisinau, Republic of Moldova
vaalbu@gmail.com

Abstract. New results in robust intelligent cognitive control are introduced based on unconventional computational intelligence as quantum soft computing technology. Synergetic effect of integrated IT of Kansei / Affective and System of Systems Engineering as intelligent cognitive robust control on Benchmarks is considered. An example of designing integrated fuzzy intelligent control systems (IFICS) in unpredicted situations using Kansei / Affective Engineering is described. The background of applied unconventional computational intelligence is soft and quantum computing technology.

Keywords: Intelligent robust control, Kansei / Affective engineering, toolkit of quantum computational intelligence, quantum soft computing, quantum fuzzy inference.

1 Introduction

This report presents an example of designing integrated fuzzy intelligent control systems (IFICS) in unpredicted situations using hybrid technology of computational intelligence, cognitive processes and Kansei / Affective Engineering. The background of applied unconventional computational intelligence is soft and quantum computing technology. All researches are supported by relevant publications and patents (see http: //www.qcoptimizer.com/) [1–7].

New approach to cognitive intelligent robust fuzzy control that includes the human factor risk is considered. With the developed toolkit it can design intelligent control systems that guarantee the goal control achievement in unpredicted control situations.

2 IT Design of IFICS and Kansei / Affective Engineering Toolkit

Design processes of IFICS in unpredicted situations were constructed of two approaches [3–5]:

© Springer International Publishing Switzerland 2015
D. Filev et al. (eds.), *Intelligent Systems' 2014*,
Advances in Intelligent Systems and Computing 323, DOI: 10.1007/978-3-319-11310-4_4

- system of systems engineering technology describes the possibility of complex ill-defined (autonomous or hierarchically connected) dynamic control system's design that includes human decision making and risk factors in unpredicted (unforeseen) control situations;
- Kansei / Affective Engineering technology and its toolkit include qualitative description of human being emotion, instinct and intuition that are used effectively in design processes of smart / wise cognitive robotics and intelligent mechatronics.

Kansei process gathers the functions related to emotions, sensitivity, feelings, experience, intuition (i.e. sensory qualities related functions (Clark 1996)), including interactions between them; Kansei means are all the senses (sight, hearing, taste, smell, touch, balance, recognition...) and – probably – other internal factors (such as personality, mood, experience, and so on); Kansei result is the fruit of Kansei process (i.e. of these function processes and of their interactions) [8, 9].

Therefore, Kansei result is a synthesis of sensory brain cognitive qualities. For example, it has been argued that emotion, pain and cognitive control are functionally segregated in distinct subdivisions of the cingulate cortex of brain. However, recent observations encourage a fundamentally different view [10]. In humans and other primates, the cingulate – a thick belt of cortex encircling the corpus callosum – is one of the most prominent features on the mesial surface of the brain [11]. Early research suggested that the rostral cingulate cortex (Brodmann's "precingulate"; architectonic areas) plays a key part in affect and motivation [12].

The presence of typically quantum effects, namely superposition and interference, in what happens when human concepts are combined, and provide a quantum model in complex Hilbert space that represents faithfully experimental data measuring the situation of combining concepts [13].

We are considering the humanized technology of intelligent robotic systems design based on Kansei / Affective Engineering and System of Systems Engineering using Quantum / Soft Computing as unconventional computational intelligence toolkit. As it is well known the subject of humanized technology or human-related systems has been actively researched. With the increasing concern regarding human factors in system development Kansei Engineering and Soft Computing are the most representative research fields on this subject [10]. Soft computing toolkit is developed for emotion, instinct, and intuition recognition and expression generation [14, 15]. In particular with genetic algorithm – GA – (as effective random search of solution) an intuition process (optimization) is modeled. Fuzzy neural network (FNN) is used for description of instinct process (adaptation and learning) that modeled approximation of optimal solution in unpredicted control situation. Fuzzy logic control is used for design of an emotion according to corresponding designed look-up table [14, 16, 17]. Quantum control algorithm of self-organization is the background of wise robotic control system's design. Quantum computing toolkit is used for increasing of robustness in intelligent control systems (especially for unpredicted control situations) [4, 5, 18].

Fig. 1 demonstrates the main idea of this approach and the creation of quantum intelligent design IT.

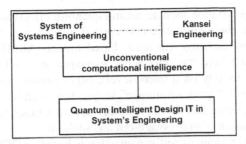

Fig. 1. Structure background of quantum intelligent design IT

The basis for the implementation of this idea is the research result that opened the new principle: *self-organization with minimization of generalized entropy production* (as the new physical measure of control quality) [3, 4]. Self-organization is a central coordination mechanism exhibited by both natural and artificial collective social-technical systems. Self-organized mechanisms are characterized by nonlinear responses to stimulus intensity, incomplete information, and randomness. Self-organization coexists with guidance from environmental templates, networks of inter-actions among individuals, and various forms of leadership or preexisting individual specialization. A general characteristic of self-organizing systems is as following: they are robust or resilient. This means that they are relatively insensitive to perturba-tions or errors, and have a strong capacity to restore themselves, unlike most human designed systems [4]. One reason for this fault-tolerance is the redundant, distributed organization: the non-damaged regions can usually make up for the damaged ones. Another reason for this intrinsic robustness is that self-organization thrives on randomness, fluctuations or "noise". A certain amount of random perturbations will facilitate rather than hinder self-organization. A third reason for resilience is the stabi-lizing effect of feedback loops. The structure of a new quantum control algorithm of self-organization is defined as [4]:

$$
\underbrace{\left| \text{Final ordered state} \right\rangle}_{\text{Self-organization of robust structure}} =
$$

$$
= \left[\underbrace{\left(\begin{array}{c} \text{Evolution of self-} \\ \text{organization process} \end{array} \right)}_{\text{Quantum random search}} \bullet \left(\begin{array}{c} Quantum \\ computing \end{array} \right) \bullet \underbrace{\overbrace{\left(\text{Type and form of correlation} \right)}^{\text{Problem orientation of control object}}}_{\text{Classical, quantum, mixed}} \right] \quad (1)
$$

$$
\left\{ \underbrace{\overbrace{\left| \text{Initial state} \right\rangle}^{\text{"Buiding" blocks}}}_{\text{Bio-inspired states}} \right\} \bullet \left(\begin{array}{c} Reproduced\ by\ given\ or \\ natural\ toolkit \end{array} \right)
$$

Quantum control algorithm of self-organization design in intelligent control sys-tems based on quantum fuzzy inference (QFI)-model below is described below.

Analysis of self-organization models gives us the following results [4].

Models of self-organization include natural quantum effects and are based on the following information-thermodynamic concepts: (i) macro- and micro-level interactions with information exchange (in agent based model (ABM) micro-level is the communication space where the inter-agent messages are exchanged and are explained by increased entropy on a micro-level); (ii) communication and information transport on micro-level ("quantum mirage" in quantum corrals); (iii) different types of quantum spin correlation that design different structure in self-organization (quantum dot); (iv) coordination control (swam-bot and snake-bot).

Quantum control algorithm of self-organization is based on QFI model [4].

QFI includes these concepts of self-organization and realizes by corresponding quantum operators, and can be considered as quantum algorithmic gate [6, 7]. Structure of QFI that realizes the self-organization process is developed on the corresponding quantum algorithmic gate [7]. QFI is one of possible realization of quantum control algorithm of self-organization that includes all of these features: (i) superposition; (ii) selection of quantum correlation types; (iii) information transport and quantum oracle; and (iv) interference.

Templating operation is realized with superposition, and is based on macro- and micro-level interactions with information exchange of active agents. Selection of quantum correlation type organize self-assembling is used the power source of communication and information transport on micro-level and based on quantum genetic algorithm toolkit [2]. In this case the type of correlation defines the level of robustness in designed KB of FC. Quantum oracle calculates "intelligent quantum state" that includes the most important (value) information transport for coordination control. Interference is used for extraction the results of coordination control and design for on-line robust knowledge base (KB) [4].

The developed QA of self-organization is applied to design robust KB of fuzzy controller (FC) in unpredicted control situations. Main goal of quantum control algorithm of self-organization is the support of optimal thermodynamic trade-off between stability, controllability and robustness of control object behavior using robust self-organized KB of intelligent control system [3]:

$$\dot{q}_i = \varphi_i\left(q,(\Psi-\Upsilon),t,u\right), \quad \underbrace{\frac{dV}{dt}}_{\text{Stability}} = \underbrace{\sum_i q_i \varphi_i\left(q,(\Psi-\Upsilon),t,u\right)}_{\text{Controllability}} + \underbrace{(\Psi-\Upsilon)(\dot{\Psi}-\dot{\Upsilon})}_{\text{Robustness}} \le 0. \quad (2)$$

The developed QA of self-organization is applied to design robust KB of FC in unpredicted control situations. Main operations of developed QA and concrete examples of QFI applications are described in [4, 5].

The information design technology of robust IFICS is presented on Fig. 2.

Information design technology includes two steps: 1) step 1 based on soft computing optimizer (SCO); and 2) step 2 based on quantum computing optimizer (QCO).

Main problem in this technology is the design of robust KB of FC that can include the self-organization of KB in unpredicted control situations. The background of this design processes is KB optimizers based on quantum / soft computing technologies [3–5].

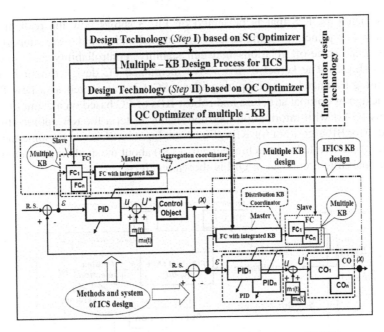

Fig. 2. Structure of information design technology of IFICS

Fig. 3 contains factors that define the control situation and shows the structure of robust intelligent control consisting of two (or more) fuzzy PID controllers (FC PID) and block QFI implementing property of KB self-organization. QFI model uses private individual KB of FC each of which is obtained by the toolbox "SCO" for fixed (standard) control situations in the external random environment.

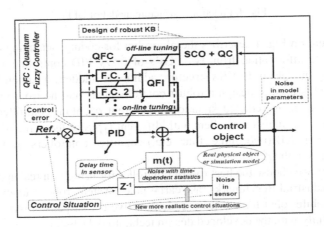

Fig. 3. Structure of robust intelligent control system (ICS) in unpredicted control situations

The structure of ICS that is presented on Fig. 3 shows how the realization the self-organization principle on the base of QFI model and includes the support of the thermodynamic trade-off relations between stability, controllability and robustness properties (Eq. 2). The kernel of the above mentioned FC design toolkit is a SCO implementing advanced soft computing ideas. SCO is considered as a new flexible tool for design of optimal structure and robust KBs of FC based on a chain of genetic algorithms (GAs) with information-thermodynamic criteria for KB optimization and advanced error BP-algorithm for KB refinement. Input to SCO can be some measured or simulated data (called as "teaching signal" (TS)) about the modeling system [3].

Functional structure model of QFI is shown on Fig. 4.

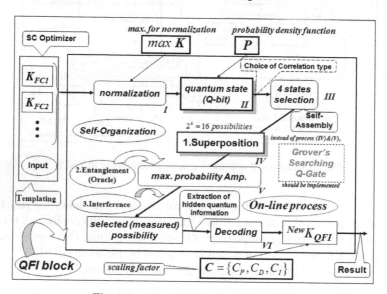

Fig. 4. Functional structure model of QFI

The structure on Fig. 4 describes the algorithm for coding, searching and extracting the valuable information from two KB's of fuzzy PID controllers designed by SCO. Applying the QFI in IFICS's structure additional (hidden) quantum information is extracted and is used to design a robust control signals on-line from responses FC that are received in unpredicted situations. Different quantum controllers based on different fuzzy controllers (controllers with different types of the correlation, controllers with different KB (two, three, four, etc.) cognitive controllers etc.) can be designed and tested with QCO.

After testing we choose the best robust controller for using it in real applications.

Concrete industrial Benchmarks (as "cart – pole" system, robotic unicycle, robotic motorcycle, mobile robot for service use, semi-active car suspension system etc.) are tested successfully with the developed design technology [19–22].

We demonstrate the efficiency of application of QFI by the Benchmark.

3 Examples

3.1 Benchmark of QFI-Application: "Cart – Pole System"

Let us consider fuzzy robust control problem of "cart-pole" system as intelligent control Benchmark. As it is well known, this system is described by the following equation of motion:

$$\ddot{\theta} = \frac{g \sin \theta + \cos \theta \left(\dfrac{(u + \xi(t)) + \{a_1 \dot{z} + a_2 z\} - ml\dot{\theta}^2 \sin \theta}{M + m} \right) - k\dot{\theta}}{l \left(\dfrac{4}{3} - \dfrac{m \cos^2 \theta}{M + m} \right)} \tag{3a}$$

$$\ddot{z} = \frac{u + \xi(t) + -\{a_1 \dot{z} + a_2 z\} + ml \left(\dot{\theta}^2 \sin \theta - \ddot{\theta} \cos \theta \right)}{M + m} \tag{3b}$$

where $\ddot{\theta}$ and z are generalized coordinates (angle of pole and position of cart, correspondingly); $u(t)$ is control force; and $\xi(t)$ is random excitation. KB of FC is designed with SCO using Gaussian and Raleigh noises, correspondingly.

Fig. 5a shows the dynamic behavior of the system (3) in unpredicted control situation. In this case a new time delay in the structure (see Fig. 5a and Fig. 3) in sensor is 0.002 sec; parametric Gaussian noise is with the amplitude 0.01; new initial state $\left[\theta_0, \dot{\theta}_0\right] = [13,1]$ (deg), $[z_0, \dot{z}_0] = [0,0]$. External noise is Raleigh noise as in the learning situation.

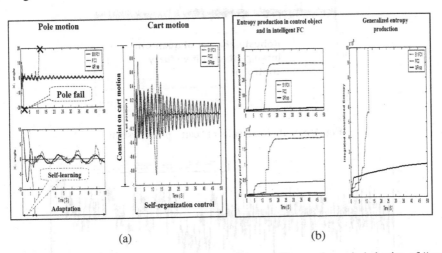

(a)   (b)

Fig. 5. Dynamic behavior of "cart - pole" system (a); and Thermodynamic behavior of "cart - pole" system (b)

Fig. 5b shows the thermodynamic behavior of the system (3) and of FC.

Fig. 5b shows that generalized entropy production of the system "control object + fuzzy PID-controller" is minimal (minimum consumption of useful source and power) and with quantum self-organization of KB required for trade-off distribution between stability, controllability and robustness is achieved.

It is a pure quantum effect and do not have a classical analogy.

Thus, results of simulation show that the winner is quantum fuzzy controller (QFC) designed from two KB controllers with minimum of generalized entropy production.

Results of simulations on Fig. 5 show also that from two unstable FC it is possible to design on-line a new robust stable FC (Parrondo paradox).

Therefore, QFI strongly supports optimal thermodynamic trade-off between stability, controllability and robustness in self-organization process (from viewpoint of physical background of global robustness in intelligent control systems).

The new result for advanced control system was also important though all other controllers (FC1, FC2) failed but QFC was designed with increasing robustness.

3.2   QFI Application in Cognitive and Intelligent FC

Figs 6 and 7 show other situation: control system includes the human factor.

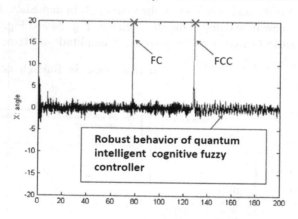

Fig. 6. Simulation results of "cart - pole" system

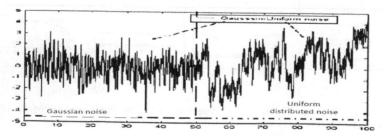

Fig. 7. Noise with time dependent probability density function

Blok QFI on Fig. 3 includes intelligent FC (FC1) and fuzzy cognitive controller (FCC2). In this case KB of FC has been designed for the surface roughness of the carriage of Gaussian type. KB of FCC was also adopted as for FC but with the ability to change production rules output proportional gain a human operator when observing the change in the type of surface displacement movement of the carriage.

Unpredicted situation of control system when roughness of surface obstacles of the carriage with a Gaussian distribution type obstacles comes to the surface with a uniform probability distribution of obstacles is shown on Fig. 7.

In this case roughness of surface obstacles of the carriage has time dependent probability density function. The simulation results show (see Figs. 6 and 7) that the robustness of FC is loss of control after 30 seconds (after the change of the type of surface). And FCC lost robustness under the same conditions after 80 sec., although time interval robustness of ICS significantly increased compared to FC.

KB quantum PID is designed on-line from the responses of no-robust FC and FCC due to quantum self-organization, and robustness ICS is increased. In this case all the properties of intelligent and cognitive control systems have been retained.

This approach was applied to other complex commercial industrial robotic systems [19–22].

3.3   Robotic Unicycle

We attempted the emulation of human riding a unicycle by a robot in the present work. It is well known that the unicycle system is an inherently unstable system and both longitudinal and lateral stability control are simultaneously needed to maintain the unicycle's postural stability. It is an unstable problem in three dimensions (3D) space [16, 17]. A new physical measure (the minimum entropy production) for the description of the intelligent dynamic behavior and thermodynamic stability condition of a biomechanical model with an AI control system for the robot unicycle is introduced. This measure is used as a fitness function in a GA for the computer simulation of the intuition mechanism as a global searching measure for the decision-making process to ensure optimal control of the global stability on the robot unicycle throughout the full space of possible solutions. The simulation of an instinct mechanism based on FNN is considered as a local active adaptation process with the minimum entropy production in the learning process of the vestibular system by teaching the control signal accordingly to the model representation results of [14].

The main idea of robotic unicycle design using Kansei / Affective and System of System Engineering approaches: with genetic algorithm the intuition of solution search is developed based on bio-inspired model of unicycle rider behavior. Instinct and emotion are introduced based on FNN and corresponding look-up tables.

Simulation and experimental results are demonstrated on Fig. 8. From the results obtained in this study by the fuzzy simulation and soft computing, based on GA and FNN it is obvious that the intelligent behavior controllability and postural stability of the robot are largely improved by two fuzzy gain schedule PD-controllers in comparison to those controlled only by a conventional PD and a fuzzy gain schedule PD-controller.

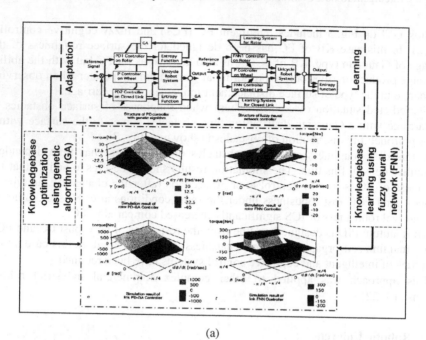

(a)

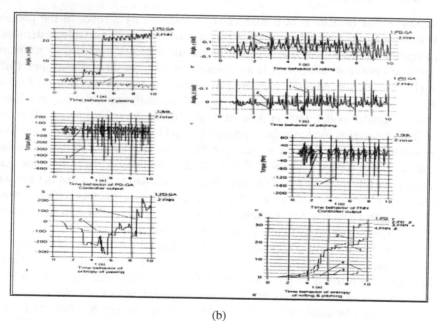

(b)

Fig. 8. System simulation (a); and simulation results of mechanics and thermodynamic behavior (b) of robotic unicycle model

As a result of this investigation the look-up tables for fuzzy robust controllers of the robotic unicycle are formed with minimum production entropy in intelligent controllers and the robotic unicycle model using this approach. The FNN controller offers a more flexible structure of controllers with a smaller torque, and the learning process produces less entropy (Fig. 8b).

FNN controller gives a more flexible structure to controllers with smaller torque and the learning process produces less entropy than GA.

Thus, an instinct mechanism produces less entropy than an intuition mechanism. However, the necessary time for achieving an optimal control with the learning process on FNN (instinct) is larger than that with the global search on GA (intuition). The general approach for forming a lookup-table with GA and the fuzzy classifier system based on FNN is described in [16]. Intuition and instinct mechanisms are considered as global and local search mechanisms of the optimal solution domains for an intelligent behavior and can be realized by GA and FNN accordingly. For the fitness function of the GA a new physical measure as the minimum entropy production for a description of the intelligent behavior in a biological model is introduced. The calculation of robustness and controllability of the robot unicycle is presented. This report provides a general measure to estimate the mechanical controllability qualitatively and quantitatively even if any control scheme is applied. Robotic unicycle is a new Benchmark [17] of non-linear mechatronics and intelligent smart control.

4 Conclusions

These examples show the possible use of new types of unconventional computational intelligence and quantum algorithm of KBs self-organization which allows on-line control to achieve the goal in unpredicted situations by improving the robustness of the IFICS in problem-oriented fields. The background of applied unconventional computational intelligence is soft and quantum computing technology. Creation and implementation of software products (using new types of intelligent computing and software and hardware support, knowledge extraction algorithms, processing and generation of knowledge in intelligent control of quantum nanotechnology, etc.) is a special kind of knowledge which can be considered as a separate item.

References

1. Ulyanov, S.V.: inventor; Yamaha Hatsudoki Kabushiki Kaisha, Shizuoka-ken (JP), assignee. System and method for control using quantum soft computing. US patent 6, 578,018 (June 10, 2003)
2. Ulyanov, S.V.: Assignee. Self-organizing quantum robust control methods and systems for situations with uncertainty and risk. Patent Application Publication US 2013/0096698. PronetLabs Ltd., Moscow (April 18, 2013)
3. Ulyanov, S., Reshetnikov, A., Nikolaeva, A.: Intelligent control systems in unpredicted situations: Soft computing optimizer of knowledge bases. LAP Lambert Academic Publishing, Saarbrücken (2013)

48   I.A. Barchatova, S.V. Ulyanov, and V.A. Albu

4. Ulyanov, S., Albu, V., Barchatova, I.: Quantum self-organization of knowledge bases: Quantum computing and quantum programming technologies. LAP Lambert Academic Publishing, Saarbrücken (2014)
5. Ulyanov, S., Albu, V., Reshetnikov, A.: Quantum optimizer of knowledge bases: Intelligent self-organizing robust embedded controllers and control systems. LAP Lambert Academic Publishing, Saarbrücken (2014)
6. Ulyanov, S., Albu, V., Barchatova, I.: Quantum Algorithmic Gates: Information Analysis & Design System in MatLab. LAP Lambert Academic Publishing, Saarbrücken (2014)
7. Ulyanov, S., Albu, V., Barchatova, I.: Design IT of quantum algorithmic gates: Quantum search algorithm simulation in MatLab. LAP Lambert Academic Publishing, Saarbrücken (2014)
8. Nagamachi, M.: Kansei / Affective engineering. CRC Press, Taylor & Francis Group (2011)
9. Cohn, R.: Kansei engineering. VSD (Omniks) (2013)
10. Ulyanov, S.V.: Intelligent self-organized robust control design based on quantum/soft computing technologies and Kansei Engineering. Computer Science J. of Moldova 21(2(62)), 242–279 (2013)
11. Sadeghieh, A., Roshanian, J., Najafari, F.: Implementation of an intelligent adaptive controller for an electrohydravlic servo system based on a brain mechanism of emotional learning. Intern. J. of Advanced Robotic Systems (INTECH) 9, 1–12 (2012)
12. Shackman, A.J., Salomons, T.V., Slagter, H.A., et al.: The integration of negative affect, pain and cognitive control in the cingulated cortex. Nature Reviews: Neuroscience 12, 154–167 (2011)
13. Aerts, D., Sozzo, S.: Quantum interference in cognition: Structural aspects of the brain. arXiv:1204.4914v1 [cs.AI] (April 22, 2012)
14. Ulyanov, S.V., Yamafuji, K.: Fuzzy intelligent emotion and instinct control of a robotic unicycle. In: Proc. of AMC 1996, Mie, Japan, pp. 127–132 (1996)
15. Dai, Y., Chakraborty, B., Shi, M.: Kansei engineering and soft computing: Theory and practice. CRC Press Taylor & Francis Group (2010)
16. Ulyanov, S.V., Watanabe, S., Litvintseva, L.V.: Soft computing for the intelligent control of a robotic unicycle with a new measure for mechanical controllability. Soft Computing 2(1), 73–88 (1998)
17. Ulyanov, S.V., Sheng, Z., Yamafuji, K.: Fuzzy intelligent control of a robotic unicycle: A new benchmark in non-linear mechanics. In: Proc. of Intern. Conf. on Recent Advances in Mechatronics (ICRAM 1995), Istanbul, Turkey, vol. 2, pp. 704–709 (1995)
18. Litvintseva, L.V., Ulyanov, S.V.: Quantum fuzzy inference for design of robust knowledge base in intelligent fuzzy controllers. Journal of Systems and Computer Sciences 49(6), 114–151 (2007)
19. Tanaka, T., Owhi, J., Ulyanov, S.V.: Soft computing algorithms for intelligent control of a mobile robot for service use. Soft Computing 1(1), 73–88 (1997)
20. Ohwi, J., Ulyanov, S.V., Yamafuji, K.: GA in continuous space and fuzzy classifier system for opening a door with a manipulator of mobile robot: New Benchmark of evolutionary intelligent computing. J. of Robotics and Mechatronics 8(3), 297–301 (1996)
21. Fujii, S., Ulyanov, S.V.: A model for motorcycle rider operation based on genetic algorithm. Yamaha Motor Technical Review (August 02, 2004)
22. Hagiwara, T., Ulyanov, S.V.: An application of a smart control suspension system for a passenger car based on soft computing. Yamaha Motor Technical Review (January 15, 2003)

Distributed Control and Navigation System for Quadrotor UAVs in GPS-Denied Environments

Konstantin Yakovlev, Vsevolod Khithov, Maxim Loginov, and Alexander Petrov

Institute for Systems Analysis of Russian Academy of Sciences, Moscow, Russia
yakovlev@isa.ru
Soloviev Rybinsk State Aviation Technical University, Rybinsk, Russia
vskhitkov@gmail.com
Soloviev Rybinsk State Aviation Technical University, Rybinsk, Russia
lunarstrainut@gmail.com
NPP SATEK plus, Rybinsk, Russia
gmdidro@gmail.com

Abstract. The problem of developing distributed control and navigation system for quadrotor UAVs operating in GPS-denied environments is addressed in the paper. Cooperative navigation, marker detection and mapping task solved by a team of multiple unmanned aerial vehicles is chosen as demo example. Developed intelligent control system complies with on 4D\RCS reference model and its implementation is based on ROS framework. Custom implementation of EKF-based map building algorithm is used to solve marker detection and map building task.

Keywords: intelligent control system, distributed architecture, 4D/RCS, visual navigation, marker detection, SLAM, map building, ROS, AR.Drone.

1 Introduction

Modern intelligent systems are characterized by increasing autonomy and distribution. From one side autonomy increases in a sense of behavior independence from operator and from other side, in case of multiagent system, its autonomy could be characterized by degree of automation in agents collaboration. Modern systems become distributed both in terms of ensuring a collective interaction of several intelligent agents (the distribution of knowledge and information between agents), and in terms of a distributed software technologies.

We present distributed control and navigation system for unmanned aerial vehicles (UAV), e.g. quadrotors, in GPS-denied environments. We demonstrate architecture and implementation of our system on map building task solved by the collaboration of UAVs. The task is following – N quadrotors (we use AR.Drones in our experiments) are operating in a GPS-denied environment, e.g. a room, and are remotely controlled (via wi-fi link) by software control system on ground station. There are several markers, that placed somewhere in the room (we use cubes with QR-codes on their sides) and AR.Drones should firstly detect markers then compute markers' position relative

© Springer International Publishing Switzerland 2015
D. Filev et al. (eds.), *Intelligent Systems'2014*,
Advances in Intelligent Systems and Computing 323, DOI: 10.1007/978-3-319-11310-4_5

to drone's start position (individual map) and after that integrate and elaborate shared map.

In this paper first we discuss conceptual framework for layered representation of intelligent system. Next we will focus on marker detection, drone and marker position estimation and map building algorithms. Next we describe control system software implementation based on ROS framework [1]. In conclusion we present experimental evaluation results and future direction of our work.

1.1   Related Works

Previous research in distributed robot control system includes: [2] which propose ALLIANCE fault-tolerant cooperative control architecture. ALLIANCE does not require any use of negotiation among robots, but rather relies upon broadcast messages from robots to announce their current activities. [3] poses solution for multiple robotic vehicles motion planning in terms of classical control theory (work is devoted to prediction of input/output reachability, structural observability, and controllability of the multiagent system). [4] describe CAMPOUT architecture for distributed control algorithms within NASA planetary surface rover systems. All sequencing in CAMPOUT is done through Finite State Machine for deterministic control. In [5] main features of cooperative grasping and transport control system for multiple quadrotors are illuminated, the main attention is paid to control signal generation for transportation of some payload simultaneous by multiple drones.

Article [6] proposes using adopted Bayesian approach for location estimation of unknown target in known, but complex environment by multiple robots. The target detection and localization is done in radio medium. Control strategy applied in [6] to solve the task is based on reduction in the uncertainty of the target estimate principle.

Previous research in cooperative map building algorithms and systems includes: [7], which considers the problem of cooperative navigation and mapping by a heterogeneous team of multiple autonomous underwater vehicles. In [7] authors address a form of cooperative Simultaneous Localization and Mapping (SLAM) in which only one vehicle is responsible for maintaining estimates of the map and poses for each robot. By combining inter-vehicle measurements with observations of the environment made by each vehicle, the result is a better knowledge of the poses of each robot in the group. In [8] describes a multi-robot map merging algorithm with the Fast-SLAM method and its evaluation on experimental map with landmarks. The article [9] proposes a novel extension to incremental smoothing and mapping (iSAM) algorithm, that facilitates multirobot mapping based on multiple pose graphs[10]. The article [11] describes a framework for cooperative 3D mapping of unstructured environments, which utilizing AR.Drone as UAV and combination of markerless and landmark SLAM algorithms.

To sum up above said, there exists numerous related works which are devoted to different aspects of distributed control system and cooperative map building exist nowadays. But in contrast with our work part of them describe 2D case, part of them lack of conceptual framework and architecture model, and others don't use ROS framework (or at least don't mention that in text). Yet another difference from most of the related work is usage of the low cost AR.Drone UAV which is turn poses some restriction on quality of income sensor data.

2   Multilevel Architecture of Distributed Control and Navigation System for Quadrotors

Different approaches to design the architecture of the UAV control system exist nowadays. Some approaches suggest the usage of flat (one-level) architecture consisting of separate interacting modules tailored to solve different tasks. An example of such architecture is described in [12] and the identified tasks (and corresponding modules) are: mission planning, collaboration, contingency management, situational awareness, communications management, air vehicle management. Other approaches (more numerous) suggest splitting the functionality not only between different modules (abstracting the functionality itself) but also between different levels or layers (abstracting the level of "deliberativeness") each of which consists of bundle of modules tied together. Examples of the most known multi-leveled architectures for intelligent agents operating in real world are 3T [13], ATLANTIS [14], Aura [15] and others. Typically in robotics (as well as in UAV design) control system consists of 3 levels: deliberative (or strategic) level (top), reactive level (bottom) and intermediate (tactical) level. Top level contains modules that deal with computational expensive (AI) reasoning and planning. Intermediate level deals with analysis of spatial data and navigation tasks (e.g. SLAM, path-planning and others). Low level controls sensors and actuators (often called subsystems) of the UAV [16]. We follow that approach and decompose our control system into 3 above mentioned levels.

In our experiments we use Parrot AR.Drone platform [17] and do not override existing modules of reactive control implemented by Parrot and described in [18]. Each AR.Drone has it's own built-in flight controller which automates the execution of basic flight maneuvers: take off, land, fly forward/backward, strafe left/right, turn clockwise/counterclockwise. Commands to execute these maneuvers are sent via the open data exchange protocol from the ground station. Also we do not implement strategic level of the control system as only one high-level task, e.g. "build-map", is addressed. As a result we mainly concentrate on the design of tactical layer capable of solving navigation tasks (e.g. identifying features and building a map of them). To do so we follow 4D/RCS reference model [19]. The main idea that lies in the basis of this model is abstract functional decomposition, e.g. each level of the architecture is composed of nodes which abstract different instances of controllable subjects and each node is composed of 4 identical functional processes (which can be viewed as bundles of modules): behavior generation, world modeling, sensory processing, value judgment (see figure 1).

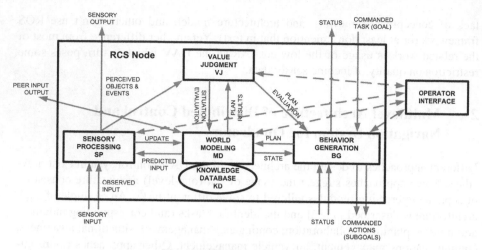

Fig. 1. 4D/RCS Node (from [19])

In our case 4D/RCS processes are interpreted as following:

SP – receiving (via wi-fi link) and transcoding videostreams from two AR.Drone's cameras (forward looking and downward looking), receiving (via wi-fi link) data regarding UAV state and orientation (AT-packets contacting measurements of the internal navigation system).

VJ – AR.Drone pose estimation, recognition and identification of visual markers, computing the distances between UAV and the markers, computing position of the markers relative to local and global coordinate systems.

WM – constructing local map, integrating multiple local maps into the global (shared) one.

BG – generating rules for choosing next flight destination.

Each 4D/RCS node is in charge of controlling a single UAV. Functional processes are implemented as a bunch of Robotic operating system [20] modules (see detailed description in section 4) executed in parallel on ground station (we use standard Linux-run laptop). Global knowledge database is maintained by the system, e.g. each AR.Drone builds it's own local map which is stored on the ground station, at the same time all the gained maps are processed and a global map consistent with the measurements of all UAVs is constructed and an access to it is granted to all drones. Details of pose estimation, markers identification, map building procedures are described further as well as the details of software implementation of the system.

3   Map Building Algorithm

Implemented map building algorithm constructs a map of markers' locations as a simplified abstraction of more general map building task, that, however, can be used for practical applications where visual marker based navigation is applicable. A map is constructed simultaneously by several drones observing different subsets of markers placed in corresponding parts of common environment and merging them into a global map. This is done in a following manner…

Each UAV performs a SLAM algorithm based on both inertial and visual data fused with Extended Kalman Filtering (EKF) while being in flight. During that, markers are observed and identified uniquely (they all are supposed to be unique) and their relative poses are calculated by each drone using vision. Any time a drone observes a marker, it checks it's existence on the global map which storage is shared appropriately. Locations of markers that appear to be already known are used to correct current UAV position state. New markers are added to the global map and their positions are fused with the next few observations to reduce inaccuracy of visual pose measuring. As subsets of markers visible by different UAV's may not overlap for a long time, these markers are stored linked to independent coordinate frames until some marker or a group is observed by two or more drones, then coordinate systems are merged, and translation of markers' poses from eliminated coordinate frame to conserved one is performed. As markers' total count is assumed to be relatively small, bundle adjustment from a set of keyposes like in [21] is used to unbias the map.

We utilize ArUco [22] marker system and library capable of detection, recognition and 6-DOF pose estimation of up to 1024 different bar-codes, distinctive reliably with the help of modified Hamming code. With the camera calibrated and known marker parameters it becomes easy to build the map in meter units.

We use Extended Kalman Filtering for drone pose estimation with state vector $h_t = (x_t, y_t, z_t, \alpha_t, \beta_t, \gamma_t)^T$, where elements correspond to 3 spatial coordinates and 3 Euler angles in global frame (totally global or one of the independent global ones) correspondingly. Odometry observation and prediction models are similar to that described in [23]. Pose observation by means of vision relies on relative pose estimation of all visible markers with known positions at some moment. Given observed marker pose, described as translation vector T_m and rotation matrix R_m in camera coordinate system, we first calculate approximate measurement noise covariance matrix (assuming measured values along 3 axes independent for simplicity). Then we use observed relative marker coordinates to calculate UAV's global pose observation; the covariance is combined with the covariance assigned to the marker on the map. The EKF state is then updated using obtained pose observation and resulting covariance. The EKF state is updated with the information obtained from each of observed already known markers.

Merging coordinate systems of drones when they observe the same markers for the first time is done in the following manner. Firstly RT matrix is calculation as 3D affine estimation based on matching markers, then this matrix is used to transform markers poses from one drone coordinate system to other drone coordinate system. After that if a new matching markers have found, RT matrix is refined and markers poses are transformed again.

4   Software Implementation of Distributed Control and Navigation System for Quadrotors Based on ROS

Software implementation of described system is based on ROS framework and 4D/RCS scheme. Structure of software is shown on figure 2.

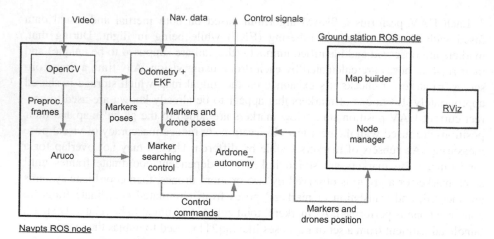

Navpts ROS node

Fig. 2. Structure of distributed control system software implementation based on ROS

ROS packages, nodes and also external libraries are shown on figure 2. There are two main ROS nodes: "Navpts" node and "Ground station" node. Several instances of Navpts node are executed simultaneously each of which controls a single AR.Drone. Ground station node implements map building and sharing algorithm and only one instance of that node is executed at a time. If we describe Navpts node following 4D/RCS we could say that OpenCV library relates to sensory processing, Aruco and EKF packages to value judgment, marker searching control package to behavior generation. 4D/RCS process of world modeling process relates to distributed between Navpts and Ground station nodes map representation.

Ground station node consists of map builder module, which implement described algorithms, and node manager, that start and remap necessary topics for Navpts nodes.

For map visualization we use Rviz package of ROS.

5   Evaluation and Conclusions

We evaluate our system implementation in laboratory environment. The result is shown in form of merged map on figure 3 (right).

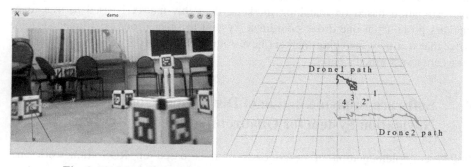

Fig. 3. Marker detection on image (left) and merged map in Rviz (right)

On figure 3 (left) experimental setup and detection of one marker is shown. On figure 3 (right) shared map is shown and trajectories of drones and position of common markers are indicated.

As a conclusion we could point out, that our implementation of map building isn't optimal solution for such task compared to related works and we use it like an illustration of chosen architecture and software implementation of distributed control and navigation system for quadrotors in GPS-denied environments. We plan to extend our system in the following direction: integrate with more powerful SLAM algorithm, which will be applicable in environment with unknown landmarks, and modify behavior generation process by introduction cooperative planning to struggle with situation in which one of drones couldn't detect any markers and to increase efficiently of the system.

Acknowledgments. This work was supported by the Ministry of Education and Science of the Russian Federation (№ 14.577.21.0030 agreement for a grant on "Conducting applied research for the development of intelligent technology and software systems, navigation and control of mobile technical equipment using machine vision techniques and high-performance distributed computing").

References

1. Robot Operation System, http://www.ros.org
2. Parker, L.E.: Distributed control of multi-robot teams: Cooperative baton-passing task. In: Proceedings of the 4th International Conference on Information Systems Analysis and Synthesis (ISAS 1998), vol. 3, pp. 89–94 (1998b)
3. Feddema, J., Lewis, C., Schoenwald, D.: Decentralized control of cooperative robotic vehicles: Theory and application. IEEE Trans. Robot. Automat. 18, 852–864 (2002)
4. Huntsberger, T.L., Trebi-Ollennu, A., Aghazarian, H., Schenker, P.S., Pirjanian, P., Nayar, H.D.: Distributed control of multi-robot systems engaged in tightly coupled tasks. Autonomous Robots 17(1), 79–92 (2004)
5. Michael, N., Fink, J., Kumar, V.: Cooperative grasping and transportation using multiple quadrotors. In: International Symposium on Distributed Autonomous Robotic Systems (DARS), Lausanne, Switzerland (2011)
6. Charrow, B., Michael, N., Kumar, V.: Cooperative multirobot estimation and control for radio source localization. In: Desai, J.P., Dudek, G., Khatib, O., Kumar, V. (eds.) Experimental Robotics. STAR, vol. 88, pp. 337–351. Springer, Heidelberg (2013)
7. Walter, M., Leonard, J.: An experimental investigation of cooperative SLAM. In: 5th International Symposium on Intelligent Autonomous Vehicles, Lisbon, July 5-7 (2004)
8. Özkucur, N.E., Akın, H.L.: Cooperative multi-robot map merging using fast-slam. In: Baltes, J., Lagoudakis, M.G., Naruse, T., Ghidary, S.S. (eds.) RoboCup 2009. LNCS (LNAI), vol. 5949, pp. 449–460. Springer, Heidelberg (2010)
9. Kim, B., et al.: Multiple Relative Pose Graphs for Robust Cooperative Mapping. In: IEEE International Conference on Robotics and Automation (ICRA), pp. 3185–3192. © Copyright 2010 IEEE (2010)
10. Kaess, M., Ranganathan, A., Dellaert, F.: iSAM: Incremental smoothing and mapping. IEEE Trans. Robotics 24, 1365–1378 (2008)

11. Nekkundi, P.S., Dulman, S.: A Framework for Cooperative 3D Mapping of Unstructured Environments. Master Thesis, Delft University of Technology (2011)
12. Jameson, S., Franke, J., Szczerba, R., Stockdale, S.: Collaborative Autonomy for Manned/Unmanned Teams. AHS International Forum 61. Grapevine, TX (2005)
13. Bonasso, R.P., Kortenkamp, D., Miller, D.P., Slack, M.: Experiences with an Architecture for Intelligent, Reactive Agents. In: Wooldridge, M., Müller, J.P., Tambe, M. (eds.) IJCAI-WS 1995 and ATAL 1995. LNCS, vol. 1037, pp. 187–202. Springer, Heidelberg (1996)
14. Gat, E.: Integrating planning and reacting in a heterogenous asynchronous architecture for controlling real-world mobile robots. In: National Conference for Artificial Intelligence (1992)
15. Arkin, R.: Motor schema based navigation for a mobile robot: An approach to programming by behavior. In: Proceedings of the IEEE International Conference on Robotics and Automation (1987)
16. Freed, M., et al.: An Architecture for Intelligent Management of Aerial Observation Missions. In: AIAA 2005, pp. 2005–6938 (2005)
17. Ar.Drone 2.0, http://ardrone2.parrot.com/
18. Bristeau, P.J., Callou, F., Vissière, D., Petit, N.: The navigation and control technology inside the AR.Drone micro UAV. In: 18th IFAC World Congress, vol. 18(1), pp. 1477–1484 (2011)
19. Albus, J., Huang, H.M., Messina, E., Murphy, K., Juberts, M., Lacaze, A., Finkelstein, R.: 4D/RCS Version 2.0: A reference model architecture for unmanned vehicle systems. National Institute of Standards and Technology, Gaithersburg (2002)
20. Quigley, M., Conley, K., Gerkey, B., Faust, J., Foote, T., Leibs, J., ... Ng, A.Y.: ROS: an open-source Robot Operating System. In: ICRA Workshop on Open Source Software, vol. 3(3.2) (2009)
21. Klein, G., Murray, D.: Parallel tracking and mapping for small AR workspaces. In: International Symposium on Mixed and Augmented Reality (2007)
22. Munoz-Salinas, R., Garrido-Jurado, S.: Aruco library, http://sourceforge.net/projects/aruco/
23. Engel, J., Sturm, J., Cremers, D.: Camera-Based Navigation of a Low-Cost Quadrocopter. In: Proc. of the International Conference on Intelligent Robot Systems (IROS) (2012)

Multi-sensory Feedback Control in Door Approaching and Opening

Tomasz Winiarski, Konrad Banachowicz, and Dawid Seredyński

Warsaw University of Technology, Warsaw, Poland
tmwiniarski@gmail.com
http://robotics.ia.pw.edu.pl

Abstract. In the article the robotic system behavior is investigated for the complex door opening task. The system consists of the 7-DOF KUKA LWR4+ manipulator, which is controlled in an impedance way and the BarrettHand gripper, which is controlled in a position way. The system utilizes multi-sensory feedback. The visual feedback is used to roughly localize door and to plan a door approach trajectory. The tactile feedback detects the contact with the door, and handle and determines an exact contact position with the handle. The system does not form a grip in a door opening stage, but the contact between the robot and the door is maintained by the gripper's fingers (with intrinsic backlash), which are pushing the handle from its one side. This concept allows to open the door when there are obstacles in the neighborhood of the handle (e.g. door jamb or frame), which make the grip impossible.

Keywords: service robot, impedance control, tactile sensing.

1 Introduction

Demographic and civilization changes are encouraging robotic community to constantly research on service robots. A number of research works regarding robotic door opening confirm, that this task will be vital for the future of service robots, which will operate in the human oriented environment. To open a door successfully, several stages have to be completed. At first, a door and its components are localized on the base of information from visual subsystem [1] to plan manipulator's end–effector approach to reach the door handle and get in contact with it [2]. When the end–effector is approaching stiff objects (e.g. door handle or Rubik's Cube [3,4]) the impact resistance is essential. This problem can be partially solved in the systems with indirect force control by applying parallel visual – force control [5]. In our article we investigate similar cooperation of visual subsystem with robot controller.

The door opening itself can be realized in various ways. For stiff connection of the manipulator's end–effector and door, there is no need to estimate door kinematics [6]. The most of the methods base on the door kinematic estimation, because for common grippers and door handles the stiff junction can not be guaranteed. The research was conducted on both cases: the velocity-controlled

© Springer International Publishing Switzerland 2015
D. Filev et al. (eds.), *Intelligent Systems'2014*,
Advances in Intelligent Systems and Computing 323, DOI: 10.1007/978-3-319-11310-4_6

manipulator with force sensing capabilities at the end-effector [7] and impedance controlled manipulator with torque controllers in its joints [8, 9]. The method of kinematic modeling of unknown 3D articulated objects was studied in the interactive robotic system [10]. In the newest papers [11] the general approach is proposed to two similar cases: a door opening and a drawer opening.

The robots, which are controlled to open a door, use the force or tactile feedback to detect and maintain contact, while the motion is in progress. In the work [12] the robot is indirectly controlled using the readings of custom force sensors located in the gripper phalanges, while typically similar systems acquire general force readings from a six-axis sensor mounted in the manipulator's wrist [13]. The robot presented in [14] is controlled in a similar way, but the force readings are aggregated from both tactile sensors in phalanges and force-torque sensor mounted in the wrist. In general the algorithms are planning and executing the motion, where the door knob or handle is grabbed from both sides to maintain the grip, while the door is moving.

In our work we specify and build the system (sec. 2), where the 7-DOF KUKA LWR4+ manipulator is controlled in impedance way (sec. 2.1) and the Barrett-Hand gripper is controlled in position way with tactile feedback (sec. 2.2). The simple visual subsystem (sec. 2.3) uses markers to roughly localize the door, then the controller plans the end–effector approach trajectory and finally robot gets in contact with door handle. As the contribution we investigate the initial manipulator approach (sec. 3.1) and subsequent door opening (sec. 3.2) with usage of information from tactile sensors of the three finger gripper. The control algorithm was especially developed to perform the task for the assumed concept of contact. The point is that the system do not form the grip in door opening stage, but the contact between the robot and the a door is maintained by the gripper fingers (with intrinsic backlash), which are pushing the handle from its one side. The fingers of typical grippers are quite thick, so this concept allows to open the door when obstacles (e.g. door jamb or frame or other handles), which are close to the handle, make the grip impossible. Several experiments (sec. 4) have been performed to verify the solution. Finally, the conclusions (sec. 5) summarize our work.

2   Control System

The general system structure is based on embodied agent approach to system development [15] and is depicted in fig. 1. Control Subsystem c with task specific door approaching and opening algorithm (sec. 3) is implemented in ROS [16] open-source, meta-operating system. The usage of ROS is adequate for fast prototyping of control algorithms and further experimental results analysis of systems equipped with grippers [17]. The Control Subsystems communicates with two Virtual Effectors e implemented in real time Orocos [18] robot programming framework through communication buffers b. The Virtual Effector e_m aims to control the Real Effector E_m of KUKA LWR4+ manipulator (sec. 2.1). The role of the Virtual Effector e_g is to control the Real Effector E_g of namely the

BarrettHand gripper (sec. 2.2). In general, Virtual Effectors were implemented to constitute universal interface or Hardware Abstraction Layer (HAL) between Control Subsystem and Real Effectors (Hardware). The aggregated data from visual subsystem (sec. 2.3) is transmitted from the Virtual Receptor r_v to the Control Subsystem c. The images originate from camera device, labeled as Real Effector R_v.

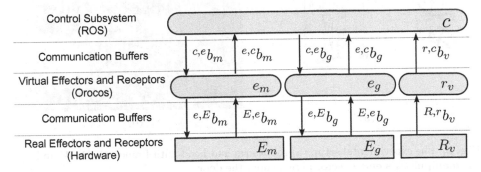

Fig. 1. General system structure

Five reference frames, which are used by the algorithm, are located in the experimental setup depicted in fig. 2:

- B – base frame of the robot,
- R – camera frame,
- W – frame of the last, seventh link of the manipulator (the wrist),
- E – gripper (end–effector) frame,
- F – finger's distal link frame,
- C – frame for contact point between handle and finger,
- M – door marker frame.

2.1   Control of Manipulator

The Control Subsystem communicates with the Virtual Effector of the manipulator using two communication buffers. The communication buffer $^{c,e}b_m$ consists of 6×6 diagonal Cartesian stiffness matrix K_t specified by the 6×1 stiffness vector k laying on the diagonal of this matrix, 6×1 normalized damping ratio vector ξ, desired equilibrium point r_t (consisting of 3×1 position vector supplemented by a unit quaterion) and trajectory segment time t. The communication buffer $^{e,c}b_m$ contains a vector $q(7 \times 1)$ of measured joint positions.

The manipulator is controlled using the Cartesian impedance [19]. The impedance control law creates the virtual spatial spring displacement Δr [20] between he pose of the wrist W measured in relation to the base B and represented by 6×1 vector r_w (consisting of the position vector supplemented by a unit

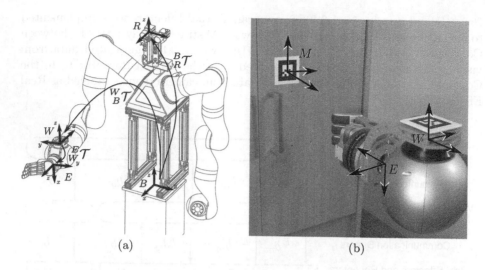

(a)   (b)

Fig. 2. The experimental setup (a) robot arm and head with frames B, R, W and E. (b) manipulator's end–effector approaching the door

quaternion) and the commanded equilibrium pose r_d represented in the same way. To ensure a stability of the system a damper is also included. The 6×1 desired force F_d at wrist frame is calculated (1) as a superposition of forces originating from the damper and the virtual spring:

$$F_d = K_c \Delta r - D_c(q, \xi) \dot{r}_w, \tag{1}$$
$$\tau = J^T(q) F_d . \tag{2}$$

In general, the pose r_w in terms of q is computed using direct kinematics. Trajectory generation provides target equilibrium points r_d for the impedance controller by interpolating between the trajectory points r_t (using linear interpolation for position and spherical interpolation for rotation). The commanded stiffness K_c is interpolated in the analogous way basing on K_t. The damping term is composed of a configuration dependent 6×6 damping matrix D_c and the velocity of the wrist frame $\dot{r}_w$. The damping matrix is calculated at every control cycle using the double-diagonalization [21] method and is parametrized by the vector ξ representing normalised damping along the main directions of the wrist frame.

Following this, the force vector is transformed from wrist frame into joint torques by the 6×7 transposed Jacobian J^T of the manipulator. The commanded 7×1 torque vector τ is then transfered to Real Effector using $^{e,E}b_m$ communication buffer. In reply Real Effector transfers measured position of joints q using $^{E,e}b_m$ communication buffer.

2.2 Control of Gripper

Control Subsystem communicates with the Virtual Effector of gripper using two communication buffers. The communication buffer $^{c,e}b_g$ consists of 4×1 desired joint position vector q_d and 4×1 maximum joint velocity vector ω. The communication buffer $^{e,c}b_g$ consists of 8×1 measured joint position vector q_m, and 4×24 measured tactile force matrix f. The difference in dimension of q_d and q_m results from the BarrettHand gripper construction. It has 4 motors propelling 8 joints, which are coupled in pairs. The Virtual Effector communicates with Real Effector with other two buffers. The communication buffer $^{e,E}b_g$ consists of 4×1 desired joint position vector q'_d and 4×1 maximum joint velocity vector ω'. The communication buffer $^{E,e}b_g$ consists of 8×1 measured joint position vector q'_m, and 4×24 measured tactile pressure matrix ψ.

The Virtual Effector has two major tasks. It initializes the Real Effector to generate the trajectory in trapezoidal mode and converts the units as follows:

$$q'_d = r_1 q_d, \tag{3}$$

$$\omega' = r_2 \omega, \tag{4}$$

$$q_m = r_3 q'_m, \tag{5}$$

$$f = r_4 \psi \circ p, \tag{6}$$

where r_1, r_2, r_3 and r_4 are constant factors obtained from the BarrettHand gripper documentation and p is a 4×24 matrix of tactile sensors' areas. The $\circ$ operator is the Hadamard product: $(A \circ B)_{ij} = A_{ij} B_{ij}$.

The Real Effector is responsible for closed loop position control (with trapezoidal velocity profile) using commanded joint position q'_d and maximum joint velocity ω'.

2.3 Image Recognition and Markers Localization

The system uses special markers attached to the door surface for rough door localization. The Virtual Receptor informs the Control Subsystem about the markers numbers and their poses in camera coordinate system R using the communication buffer $^{r,c}b_v$. The Virtual Receptor utilizes the ALVAR library to detect and track artificial markers designed for this library. The Real Receptor transmits images to the Virtual Receptor for further processing using the communication buffer $^{R,r}b_v$.

3 Task Algorithm

The task algorithm, which is implemented in the Control Subsystem of embodied agent, is subdivided into two parts: door localization and approaching is the first and actual door opening is the second one. During both motion phases a pose and a stiffness are controlled. Although the Virtual Effector e_m controls pose of W, it is possible to control pose of E or C using transformations $^E_W T$ or $^C_W T$.

Two configurations of gripper joints are employed. The first (q_{door}) is used for door approach and it is a hook with finger joint angles at $40°$, so the distal phalanges are hardly orthogonal to door surface and their artificial skin can detect contact with the door. The second configuration (q_{handle}) is proper for the door handle approach and for the door opening and it is a hook with finger joint angles at $75°$.

The task algorithm uses the following functions:

- $Trans(\boldsymbol{P})$, where $\boldsymbol{P}$ is a 3×1 vector, returns homogeneous transformation matrix with no rotation for translation from point $[0, 0, 0]^T$ to $\boldsymbol{P}$,
- $RotZ(\alpha)$ returns homogeneous transformation matrix for rotation by angle α in z axis,
- $RotY(\alpha)$ returns homogeneous transformation matrix for rotation by angle α in y axis,
- $wait(t)$ suspends the algorithm execution by time t,
- $measureEndPosition()$ returns current ${}_W^B\boldsymbol{T}$ transformation using ${}^{e,c}b_m[\boldsymbol{q}]$ and direct kinematics,
- $measureFingerPosition()$ returns current ${}_F^E\boldsymbol{T}$ transformation using ${}^{e,c}b_g[\boldsymbol{q}_m]$ and direct kinematics,
- $AddToBuffer(\boldsymbol{b}, \boldsymbol{P})$ increments size of the buffer $\boldsymbol{b}$ and writes point $\boldsymbol{P}$ at its end,
- $atan2(y, x)$ calculates the four-quadrant inverse tangent of $\frac{y}{x}$,
- $max(\boldsymbol{A})$ returns the maximum value in matrix $\boldsymbol{A}$,
- $min(\boldsymbol{v})$ returns the minimum value in vector $\boldsymbol{v}$,
- $maxIndex(\boldsymbol{A})$ returns index of the maximum element in matrix $\boldsymbol{A}$,
- $estimateCircle(\boldsymbol{b})$ returns estimated circle center and circle radius using least squares algorithm and points from buffer $\boldsymbol{b}$

3.1   Door Localization and Approaching

Door and handle approach algorithm uses the $moveRelToMarker$ function defined in alg. 1. The function controls the gripper frame $\boldsymbol{E}$ relative to marker's frame $\boldsymbol{M}$. In the line 2 the marker frame is translated to the point $\boldsymbol{P}$ and rotated so that the gripper's orientation is set to door and handle approach as shown in fig. 2(b). In the line 4 the desired transformation for wrist ${}_{W_d}^B\boldsymbol{T}$ is calculated on the basis of the following operands: marker's pose relative to robot's base ${}_M^B\boldsymbol{T}$, the desired gripper's pose relative to marker frame ${}_{E_d}^M\boldsymbol{T}$ and the constant wrist-gripper transformation ${}_{W_d}^{E_d}\boldsymbol{T} = {}_W^E\boldsymbol{T}$.

The transformation from robot's base to the camera is calculated using a visual marker on the wrist with the equation:

$$
{}_R^B\boldsymbol{T} = {}_W^B\boldsymbol{T} \, {}_{W_m}^W\boldsymbol{T} \, {}_R^{W_m}\boldsymbol{T} \tag{7}
$$

where ${}_W^B\boldsymbol{T}$ is calculated from direct kinematics of the manipulator, ${}_{W_m}^W\boldsymbol{T}$ is known as a constant transformation from robot's wrist to the wrist marker and ${}_R^{W_m}\boldsymbol{T} = {}_{W_m}^R\boldsymbol{T}^{-1}$ is wrist marker's pose taken from the Virtual Receptor. The base

---

Algorithm 1. Move relative to marker procedure

1: **procedure** MOVERELTOMARKER($\boldsymbol{P}, t$) ▷ move the gripper to P in marker frame
2:     $^M_{E_d}\boldsymbol{T} \leftarrow Trans(\boldsymbol{P}) RotY(\pi) RotZ(-\frac{\pi}{2})$ ▷ get homogenous transformation
3:         ▷ matrix for translation
4:     $^B_{W_d}\boldsymbol{T} \leftarrow {}^B_M\boldsymbol{T}\, {}^M_{E_d}\boldsymbol{T}\, {}^{E_d}_{W_d}\boldsymbol{T}$ ▷ calculate desired wrist frame
5:     $^{c,e}b_m[\boldsymbol{r_t}, t] \leftarrow [{}^B_{W_d}\boldsymbol{T}, t]$ ▷ send to Virtual Effector
6: **end procedure**

Algorithm 2. Door approach algorithm

1: $^R_M\boldsymbol{T} \leftarrow {}^{r,c}b_v[\boldsymbol{T}]$ ▷ get the marker pose from Virtual Receptor
2: $^B_M\boldsymbol{T} \leftarrow {}^B_R\boldsymbol{T}\, {}^R_M\boldsymbol{T}$ ▷ calculate marker's pose in base frame
3: $^{c,e}b_g[q] \leftarrow q_{door}$ ▷ set the gripper configuration for door approach
4: $^{c,e}b_m[\boldsymbol{K_t}, t] \leftarrow [\boldsymbol{k}_{door}, 3s]$ ▷ change the stiffness
5: $wait(3s)$
6: $moveRelToMarker(\boldsymbol{P_s}, 5s)$ ▷ move the gripper to the starting pose
7: $wait(5s)$
8: $d_{door} \leftarrow 0$
9: **repeat** ▷ move the gripper towards door
10:     $moveRelToMarker(\boldsymbol{P_s} + [0, 0, -d_{door}]^T, 0.125s)$ ▷ move the gripper
11:     $d_{door} \leftarrow d_{door} + \Delta_{door}$ ▷ decrement desired distance
12:     $wait(0.1s)$
13:     $\boldsymbol{f} = {}^{e,c}b_g[\boldsymbol{f}]$ ▷ get tactile force
14: **until** $max(\boldsymbol{f}) < f_{threshold}$ ▷ check if contact occured

---

- camera transformation $^B_R\boldsymbol{T}$ is assumed constant during the algorithm execution until door marker pose is acquired.

The initialization and the door approaching stage is shown in alg. 2. The parameter $\boldsymbol{P_s}$ is the starting point for the gripper relative to the marker pose M. At this stage there are used following other parameters: $\boldsymbol{k}_{door}$ – 6×1 vector of stiffness for the Virtual Effector e_m during the door and handle approach, δ_{door} – a small distance the gripper moves towards the door in every iteration, $f_{threshold}$ – a threshold value for tactile force to check if the contact occured.

Algorithm 3. Hand configuration change

1: $d_{door} \leftarrow d_{door} - 0.08m$ ▷ increase the distance
2: $moveRelToMarker(\boldsymbol{P_s} + [0, 0, -d_{door}]^T, 4s)$ ▷ move the gripper
3: $wait(4s)$
4: $^{c,e}b_g[q] \leftarrow q_{handle}$ ▷ set gripper configuration for handle approach
5: $wait(2s)$
6: $d_{door} \leftarrow d_{door} + 0.06m$ ▷ decrease the distance
7: $moveRelToMarker(\boldsymbol{P_s} + [0, 0, -d_{door}]^T, 3s)$ ▷ move the gripper
8: $wait(3s)$

After the first contact with door, the gripper's configuration is changed (alg. 3). At first, the gripper has to be pulled back to make the finger closing available. The distances $0.08m$ and $0.06m$ (lines 1 and 6) are chosen with respect to direct kinematics of the gripper.

Algorithm 4. Handle approach algorithm

1: $d_{handle} \leftarrow 0$ ▷ zero distance offset
2: **repeat** ▷ move the gripper towards handle
3:      $moveRelToMarker(\boldsymbol{P}_s + [-d_{handle}, 0, -d_{door}]^T, 0.125s)$ ▷ move the gripper
4:      $d_{handle} \leftarrow d_{handle} + \Delta_{handle}$ ▷ get closer
5:      $wait(0.1s)$
6:      $\boldsymbol{f} = {}^{e,c}b_g[\boldsymbol{f}]$ ▷ get tactile force
7: **until** $max(\boldsymbol{f}) < f_{threshold}$ ▷ check if contact occured
8: ${}^{c,e}b_m[\boldsymbol{K}_t, t] \leftarrow [\boldsymbol{k}_{handle}, 3s]$ ▷ change the stiffness
9: $wait(3s)$
10: $d_{handle} \leftarrow d_{handle} + r_a$ ▷ push the handle
11: $moveRelToMarker(\boldsymbol{P}_s + [-d_{handle}, 0, -d_{door}]^T, 5s)$ ▷ move the gripper
12: $wait(5s)$

After the gripper's configuration is changed, the handle approach is performed (alg.4). At this stage there are following new parameters: δ_{handle} – a small distance the gripper moves towards the handle in every iteration, $\boldsymbol{k}_{handle}$ – 6×1 stiffness vector for the Virtual Effector e_m for pushing the handle. If the contact with handle occurs, the system starts to push the handle, otherwise it finally stops due to kinematics's constraints of the manipulator.

Algorithm 5. Door opening algorithm internal procedures

1: **procedure** GetContactPointFrame ▷ get contact point position in frame $\boldsymbol{F}$
2:      $\boldsymbol{f} \leftarrow {}^{e,c}b_g[\boldsymbol{f}]$ ▷ get tactile force
3:      ${}^{F}_{C}\boldsymbol{T} \leftarrow Trans(\boldsymbol{s}_{maxIndex(\boldsymbol{f})})$ ▷ get contact point homogeneous transformation
4:      **return** ${}^{F}_{C}\boldsymbol{T}$ ▷ return contact point relative to finger frame
5: **end procedure**
6: **procedure** GetTransformations ▷ get actual transformations
7:      ${}^{B}_{W}\boldsymbol{T} \leftarrow measureEndPosition()$ ▷ get wrist pose from direct kinematics
8:      ${}^{E}_{F}\boldsymbol{T} \leftarrow measureFingerPosition()$ ▷ get finger pose from direct kinematics
9:      ${}^{F}_{C}\boldsymbol{T} \leftarrow getContactPointFrame()$ ▷ get contact point pose
10:     **return** $[{}^{B}_{W}\boldsymbol{T}, {}^{E}_{F}\boldsymbol{T}, {}^{F}_{C}\boldsymbol{T}]$ ▷ return actual transformations
11: **end procedure**

3.2   Door Opening

Door opening algorithm uses the $getContactPointFrame$ and $GetTransformations$ functions defined in alg. 5. The first one returns the homogeneous transformation matrix ${}^{F}_{C}\boldsymbol{T}$ from the contact point frame $\boldsymbol{C}$ to the finger frame $\boldsymbol{F}$.

The orientation of both frames is assumed to be identical. The 24×3 matrix s is tactile geometry and every $i - th$ element s_i is a center point of the $i - th$ tactile sensor relative to the F frame. The *GetTransformations* function returns the current transformations $^B_W T$, $^E_F T$ and $^F_C T$.

Algorithm 6. Door opening algorithm initial motion

1: $[^B_W T, ^E_F T, ^F_C T] \leftarrow GetTransformations()$ ⊳ get current transformations
2: $^E_{E_d} T \leftarrow Trans(0, r_a, -d_{init})$ ⊳ determine gripper's destination pose change
3: $^B_{C_d} T^{init}_d \leftarrow {}^B_W T \, ^W_E T \, ^E_{E_d} T \, ^{E_d}_{F_d} T \, ^{F_d}_{C_d} T$ ⊳ calculate contact point's destination pose
4: $P^{init}_d \leftarrow {}^B_C T^{init}_d [0,0,0,1]^T$ ⊳ save contact point's destination position
5: $^B_C T \leftarrow {}^B_W T \, ^W_E T \, ^E_F T \, ^F_C T$ ⊳ calculate contact point's current pose
6: $P_{contact} \leftarrow {}^B_C T [0,0,0,1]^T$ ⊳ calculate current contact point
7: $AddToBuffer(b, P_{contact})$ ⊳ add the current contact point to buffer
8: $^B_{W_d} T \leftarrow {}^B_W T \, ^W_E T \, ^E_{E_d} T \, ^{E_d}_{W_d} T$ ⊳ calculate desired wrist frame
9: $^{c,e} b_m [r_t, t] \leftarrow [^B_{W_d} T, 3s]$ ⊳ send pose and motion time to the Virtual Effector

---

The initial motion for the door opening is shown in alg. 6. The motion starts from the closed door and ends with the door handle shifted by r_a – value added to the estimated circle radius to push the handle outwards. At this stage the other parameters are: d_{init} – distance of the initial motion in the direction perpendicular to the door's surface. In the line 2, the initial motion's destination pose is calculated. It is the homogeneous transformation matrix $^E_{E_d} T$ between the current gripper's pose and the desired gripper's pose. In the line 3 the desired contact point frame is calculated and the destination for the contact point is calculated in line 4. Transformations $^{E_d}_{F_d} T$ and $^{F_d}_{C_d} T$ are constant and and respectively equal to $^E_F T$ and $^F_C T$. The actual contact point is calculated in lines 5 and 6 and it is saved to the empty buffer b in line 7. The desired wrist pose is calculated in line 8.

Algorithm 7. Door opening algorithm - the first kinematic estimation

1: **while not** $timeElapsed(3s)$ **do** ⊳ repeat this loop for 3 seconds
2: $\quad [^B_W T, ^E_F T, ^F_C T] \leftarrow GetTransformations()$ ⊳ get actual position
3: $\quad ^B_C T \leftarrow {}^B_W T \, ^W_E T \, ^E_F T \, ^F_C T$ ⊳ calculate contact point frame relative to B
4: $\quad P_{contact} \leftarrow {}^B_C T [0,0,0,1]^T$ ⊳ calculate current contact point
5: $\quad AddToBuffer(b, P_{contact})$ ⊳ add the current contact point to buffer
6: $\quad wait(0.1s)$
7: **end while**
8: $[P_c, r] \leftarrow estimateCircle(b)$ ⊳ estimate circle using least squares algorithm
9: $\alpha_{init} \leftarrow atan2(b_{first[y]} - P_{c[y]}, b_{first[x]} - P_{c[x]})$ ⊳ calculate door initial angle
10: $\alpha_{dest} \leftarrow \alpha_{init} + \alpha_{open}$ ⊳ calculate door destination angle
11: $\alpha \leftarrow atan2(P^{init}_{d[y]} - P_{c[y]}, P^{init}_{d[x]} - P_{c[x]})$ ⊳ calculate current angle

---

Acquired contact points are stored in buffer b (alg. 7). After $3s$ the initial motion ends and the points in buffer b are used to estimate a circle, which center P_c corresponds to the door axis and its radius r corresponds to the door handle – axis distance. The first element in the buffer b is b_{first} and the last one is b_{last}. The α_{init} is the angle between the door surface and xz plane of base frame B before the initial motion. Analogically, the α_{dest} angle and the α angle relate the vectors affixed to destination and current contact points to xz plane of base frame B.

The next door opening stage (alg. 8) begins with the stiffness change (line 1). In each iteration the current door angle based on the current contact point position is calculated (line 5). The desired gripper rotation β around z axis relative to the initial rotation is increased by δ_e (line 7) and limited to actual relative door angle $\alpha_{door} - \alpha_{init}$ (line 8). The desired contact point position P_d (line 9) is calculated from actual estimated circle (line 18) and destination contact point angle α which is increased in every iteration by δ (line 6), where $\delta < \delta_e$. The desired contact point pose ${}^{B}_{C_d}T$ is calculated from the contact point desired frame for the initial motion ${}^{B}_{C}T_d^{init}$ translated to the new desired contact point P_d and rotated by the desired gripper rotation β (line 10). The actual contact point $P_{contact}$ is calculated and added to buffer in lines 13, 14 and 15. The wrist destination pose is calculated in line 16, where the transformations ${}^{C_d}_{F_d}T$ and ${}^{F_d}_{W_d}T$ are constant and equal to ${}^{C}_{F}T$ and ${}^{F}_{W}T$.

Algorithm 8. Door opening algorithm - door opening

1: $\quad {}^{c,e}b_m[K_t, t] \leftarrow [k_{open}, 3s]$	▷ change the stiffness
2: $\quad wait(3s)$	
3: $\quad \beta \leftarrow 0$	
4: **repeat**	▷ open the door
5: $\quad\quad \alpha_{door} \leftarrow atan2(b_{last[y]} - P_{c[y]}, b_{last[x]} - P_{c[x]})$	▷ calculate current door angle
6: $\quad\quad \alpha \leftarrow \alpha + \delta$	▷ increase destination angle
7: $\quad\quad \beta \leftarrow \beta + \delta_e$	▷ increase destination hand rotation angle
8: $\quad\quad \beta \leftarrow min([\beta, \alpha_{door} - \alpha_{init}])$	▷ limit value to $(\alpha_{door} - \alpha_{init})$
9: $\quad\quad P_d \leftarrow P_c + (r + r_a)[cos\alpha, sin\alpha, 0]^T$	▷ calculate destination contact point
10: $\quad\quad {}^{B}_{C_d}T \leftarrow Trans(P_d - P_d^{init}) \, {}^{B}_{C}T_d^{init} RotZ(-\beta)$	▷ calculate destination
11: $\quad$	▷ contact frame
12: $\quad\quad [{}^{B}_{W}T, {}^{E}_{F}T, {}^{F}_{C}T] \leftarrow GetTransformations()$	▷ get actual position
13: $\quad\quad {}^{B}_{C}T \leftarrow {}^{B}_{W}T \, {}^{W}_{E}T \, {}^{E}_{F}T \, {}^{F}_{C}T$	▷ calculate current contact frame
14: $\quad\quad P_{contact} \leftarrow {}^{B}_{C}T[0,0,0,1]^T)$	▷ calculate current contact point
15: $\quad\quad AddToBuffer(b, P_{contact})$	▷ add the current contact point to buffer
16: $\quad\quad {}^{B}_{W_d}T \leftarrow {}^{B}_{C_d}T \, {}^{C_d}_{F_d}T \, {}^{F_d}_{W_d}T$	▷ calculate desired wrist frame
17: $\quad\quad {}^{c,e}b_m[r_t, t] \leftarrow [{}^{B}_{W_d}T, 1.0s]$	▷ send pose to the Virtual Effector
18: $\quad\quad [P_c, r] \leftarrow estimateCircle(b)$	▷ estimate circle using least squares algorithm
19: $\quad\quad wait(0.1)$	
20: **until** $\alpha < \alpha_{dest}$	▷ repeat until the door is open

4   Experiments

Experiments were performed with the presented system and a cabinet shown in fig. 2(b). The real receptor R_v was RGB camera mounted on robot's active head [22]. The experiments were performed for two different distances between door handle and hinges: $0.24m$ and $0.135m$. In the following sections the experimental results are presented for parameters, which led to the successful and robust task execution:

$$\boldsymbol{P_s} = [0, -0.1m, 0.3m]^T, \, r_a = 0.25m, \, d_{init} = 0.1m,$$
$$\alpha_{open} = 110°, \, \delta = 0.005rad, \, \delta_e = 0.04rad,$$
$$\boldsymbol{k_{door}} = [600\tfrac{N}{m}, 1000\tfrac{N}{m}, 1000\tfrac{N}{m}, 300\tfrac{Nm}{rad}, 300\tfrac{Nm}{rad}, 300\tfrac{Nm}{rad}]^T,$$
$$\boldsymbol{k_{handle}} = [500\tfrac{N}{m}, 35\tfrac{N}{m}, 1000\tfrac{N}{m}, 300\tfrac{Nm}{rad}, 300\tfrac{Nm}{rad}, 300\tfrac{Nm}{rad}]^T,$$
$$\boldsymbol{k_{open}} = [150\tfrac{N}{m}, 35\tfrac{N}{m}, 1000\tfrac{N}{m}, 300\tfrac{Nm}{rad}, 300\tfrac{Nm}{rad}, 300\tfrac{Nm}{rad}]^T,$$

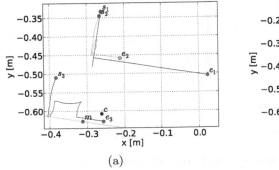
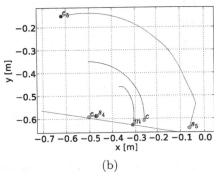

(a)   (b)

Fig. 3. Trajectories registered during the experiment: (a) for the door handle approach, (b) for the door opening, where s is the starting point and e is the end point of a trajectory. Trajectories are labeled as follows: commanded trajectory of the gripper (1), measured trajectory of the gripper (2), measured trajectory of the finger tip (3), trajectory of estimated circle center (4), commanded trajectory of contact point of the finger and the door handle (5). Point m is marker position and the straight line passing point m is a door surface. The line starting from point m is the trajectory of door marker acquired from the Virtual Receptor r_v. Point c is the first contact point of finger and door handle, and the line starting from that point is the trajectory of contact point during door opening.

4.1   Door and Handle Approach

Fig. 3(a) shows trajectories of the gripper and finger tip during door and handle approach. The force measured by tactile sensors during this stage is shown in fig. 4(a) for time $t \in (0, 15)$. The point a is a contact between door surface and finger tip. The gripper is pulled back and the measured force falls. After that, the contact between finger and door handle is measured in point b. The force rises after point b because the gripper trajectory is not canceled immediately.

4.2   Opening the Door

Fig. 3(b) shows trajectories of the gripper and finger tip during door opening. The force measured by tactile sensors during this stage is shown in fig. 4(a) for time $t \in (15, 55)$. Between points c and d the stiffness changes from k_{door} to k_{handle} and the measured force of contact falls down. Between points d and e the gripper is pushed harder towards the handle and the force rises again. After that, between points f and g, the initial door opening motion is performed. Between points h and i the stiffness changes from k_{handle} to k_{open}. From point i the door opening motion using circle estimation is performed. Fig. 4(b) shows estimated circle radius during door opening. The fluctuations in estimation are small enough to maintain stable motion.

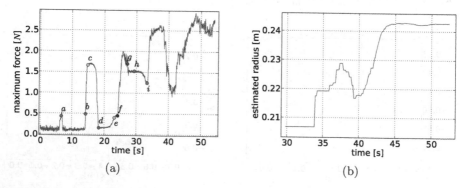

(a)   (b)

Fig. 4. The experiments: (a) maximum measured finger tip force, (b) estimated circle radius

5   Conclusions

The door approaching and opening algorithm, which has been proposed in this article, is based on the previous work of the authors and current achievements in tactile sensing and impedance control. The algorithm deals with some environment constraints, such as obstacles located in the neighborhood of the door handles or knobs, by maintaining the contact with the single side of the handle. This concept is an alternative for motion generation with force grip or closure grip. Although the controller is stable, a priori parameter determination is needed to maintain contact with handle. Otherwise, for e.g. to high stiffness, the system can fail too execute the task. The future work assumes automated impedance controller parameter learning by analysis of the task execution quality criterion (e.g. composed of contact force oscillation metrics and other statistics). The whole procedure will be verified and generalized for opening the various type of doors (the large doors will be opened with active torso and mobile base) and drawers. Finally, the manipulation system behavior will be analyzed in cooperation with the visual subsystem, which will perform door and handle detection and localization instead of markers detection.

Acknowledgment. This project was funded by the National Science Centre according to the decision number DEC-2012/05/D/ST6/03097. Tomasz Winiarski has been supported by the European Union in the framework of the European Social Fund through the Warsaw University of Technology Development Programme.

References

1. Stefańczyk, M., Walęcki, M.: Localization of essential door features for mobile manipulation. In: Szewczyk, R., Zieliński, C., Kaliczyńska, M. (eds.) Recent Advances in Automation, Robotics and Measuring Techniques. AISC, vol. 267, pp. 487–496. Springer, Heidelberg (2014)
2. Meeussen, W., Wise, M., Glaser, S., Chitta, S., McGann, C., Mihelich, P., Marder-Eppstein, E., Muja, M., Eruhimov, V., Foote, T., et al.: Autonomous door opening and plugging in with a personal robot. In: 2010 IEEE International Conference on Robotics and Automation (ICRA), pp. 729–736. IEEE (2010)
3. Zieliński, C., Winiarski, T.: Motion generation in the MRROC++ robot programming framework. International Journal of Robotics Research 29(4), 386–413 (2010)
4. Zieliński, C., Winiarski, T., Mianowski, K., Rydzewski, A., Szynkiewicz, W.: End-effector sensors' role in service robots. In: Kozłowski, K. (ed.) Robot Motion and Control 2007. LNCIS, vol. 360, pp. 401–414. Springer, Heidelberg (2007)
5. Staniak, M., Winiarski, T., Zieliński, C.: Parallel visual-force control. In: Proceedings of the IEEE/RSJ International Conference on Intelligent Robots and Systems, IROS 2008 (2008)
6. Winiarski, T., Banachowicz, K., Stefańczyk, M.: Safe strategy of door opening with impedance controlled manipulator. Journal of Automation Mobile Robotics and Intelligent Systems 7(4), 21–26 (2013)
7. Karayiannidis, Y., Smith, C., Vina, F.E., Ogren, P., Kragic, D.: "open sesame!" adaptive force/velocity control for opening unknown doors. In: 2012 IEEE/RSJ International Conference on Intelligent Robots and Systems (IROS), pp. 4040–4047. IEEE (2012)
8. Winiarski, T., Banachowicz, K.: Opening a door with a redundant impedance controlled robot. In: 9th Workshop on Robot Motion & Control (RoMoCo), pp. 221–226 (2013)
9. Ott, C., Bäuml, B., Borst, C., Hirzinger, G.: Employing cartesian impedance control for the opening of a door: A case study in mobile manipulation. In: IEEE/RSJ International Conference on Intelligent Robots and Systems Workshop on Mobile Manipulators: Basic Techniques, New Trends & Applications (2005)
10. Katz, D., Kazemi, M., Andrew Bagnell, J., Stentz, A.: Interactive segmentation, tracking, and kinematic modeling of unknown 3d articulated objects. In: 2013 IEEE International Conference on Robotics and Automation (ICRA), pp. 5003–5010. IEEE (2013)
11. Ruhr, T., Sturm, J., Pangercic, D., Beetz, M., Cremers, D.: A generalized framework for opening doors and drawers in kitchen environments. In: International Conference on Robotics and Automation (ICRA), pp. 3852–3858. IEEE (2012)
12. Chung, W., Rhee, C., Shim, Y., Lee, H., Park, S.: Door-opening control of a service robot using the multifingered robot hand. IEEE Transactions on Industrial Electronics 56(10), 3975–3984 (2009)

13. Winiarski, T., Woźniak, A.: Indirect force control development procedure. Robotica 31, 465–478 (2013)
14. Schmid, A., Gorges, N., Goger, D., Worn, H.: Opening a door with a humanoid robot using multi-sensory tactile feedback. In: International Conference on Robotics and Automation (ICRA), pp. 285–291. IEEE (2008)
15. Kornuta, T., Zieliński, C.: Robot control system design exemplified by multi-camera visual servoing. Journal of Intelligent & Robotic Systems, 1–25 (2013)
16. Quigley, M., Conley, K., Gerkey, B., Faust, J., Foote, T., Leibs, J., Wheeler, R., Ng, A.Y.: Ros: an open-source robot operating system. In: ICRA Workshop on Open Source Software, vol. 3 (2009)
17. Zubrycki, I., Granosik, G.: Test setup for multi-finger gripper control based on robot operating system (ros). In: 2013 9th Workshop on Robot Motion and Control (RoMoCo), pp. 135–140. IEEE (2013)
18. Bruyninckx, H.: Open robot control software: the orocos project. In: International Conference on Robotics and Automation (ICRA), vol. 3, pp. 2523–2528. IEEE (2001)
19. Albu-Schäffer, A., Ott, C., Hirzinger, G.: A unified passivity-based control framework for position, torque and impedance control of flexible joint robots. The International Journal of Robotics Research 26(1), 23–39 (2007)
20. Caccavale, F., Natale, C., Siciliano, B., Villani, L.: Six-dof impedance control based on angle/axis representations. IEEE Transactions on Robotics and Automation 15(2), 289–300 (1999)
21. Albu-Schaffer, A., Ott, C., Frese, U., Hirzinger, G.: Cartesian impedance control of redundant robots: Recent results with the dlr-light-weight-arms. In: International Conference on Robotics and Automation (ICRA), vol. 3, pp. 3704–3709. IEEE (2003)
22. Walęcki, M., Stefańczyk, M., Kornuta, T.: Control system of the active head of a service robot exemplified on visual servoing. In: 9th Workshop on Robot Motion and Control (RoMoCo), pp. 48–53 (2013)

Design and Multiaspect Functionality Realization of Hybrid Intelligent Control Systems via Generalized Nets

Mincho Hadjiski[1] and Krassimir Atanassov[2]

[1] University of Chemical Technology and Metalurgy,
8 Kliment Ohridski Blvd., 1756 Sofia, Bulgaria
hadjiski@uctm.bg
[2] Dept. of Bioinformatics and Mathematical Modelling,
Institute of Biophysics and Biomedical Engineering,
Bulgarian Academy of Sciences
105 Acad. G. Bonchev Str., 1113 Sofia, Bulgaria
krat@bas.bg

Abstract. A new approach for design and self-organization of complex hierarchical control systems is proposed. Using the constructive abilities of the Generalized Nets (GNs), a situation-based control is accepted in order to integrate business, operational and control functions. The main alternation is paid in organization and coordination of a big number of structured parallel procedures aiming choice of optimal, or at least rational, control strategy, current structure, algorithms and tuning parameters for each possible real life situation, covering the full range of technological, business environmental and safety conditions and requirements.

Keywords: Automatic control, Computational intelligence, Design, Generalized net, Hybridization, Integration, Reconfiguration.

1 Introduction

During the last decade, the scope of the notion "Hybrid System" (HS) has radically changed [3–5]. Now, it covers not only the continuous and discrete mode of work [12], but integrates the full spectra of functionality of the real life systems – business, operational, maintenance, dynamic control, safety, etc. [15, 16, 21]. Using well developed Building Blocks (BBs) like mathematical models, intelligent elements (Neural Networks (NNs), Fuzzy Systems (FSs), Genetic Algorithms (GAs), Knowledge Components (KC), Case-Based Reasoning (CBR), Rule-Based Reasoning (RBR), Ontologies), Autonomous Agents (AAs) and Multi Agent Systems (MASs) in combination with well established functional units as optimizers, control systems, predictors, technical condition recognizers, performance estimations, identifiers, observers, etc., a novel type of Hybrid Intelligent Systems (HISs) are under intensive consideration and studying [3, 4, 15, 16, 19, 20, 6]. It was found that

© Springer International Publishing Switzerland 2015
D. Filev et al. (eds.), *Intelligent Systems'2014*,
Advances in Intelligent Systems and Computing 323, DOI: 10.1007/978-3-319-11310-4_7

the HIS would possess considerably better performance in comparison with systems using only separate intelligent BBs [3–5, 15, 16, 20, 6]. Due to the synergic effect, the weakness and limitations inherent to each individual BB are overcome with promising success [16, 7, 9–11, 14].

Two main approaches in system hybridization have been recently established – tight integration and loose integration [5, 20, 7, 10]. Into the tight integration, a mutual penetration of functionality of BBs could be observed [6, 13]. Unfortunately, the published results show that tight integration is successful only in case of using only 2–3 intelligent BBs in relatively small systems with limited functional goals [5, 6, 9, 13]. It seems that tight integration with a real functional fusion is suitable for the HIS with small size, more compactness and limited participation of human operators.

In loose integration, particular BBs save their relative functional independence, but are strongly coordinated and optimized in order to reach the common goal. The interest in loose integration has recorded considerable growth in the last years [5, 7, 10, 18, 22]. The effors here are directed to widen the scope of the system functionality and its efficiency in all aspects – operational, technological, maintenance, safety. The loose integration could be implemented in re-engineered systems, which contain legacy components [3, 17, 8]. The existing results show that loose integration in HIS is preferable for complex dynamic systems, where intelligent and knowledge based building blocks must be used in order to utilize efficiently the domain knowledge, to overcome the large uncertainty and the unpedictability as well.

In the presented paper, the constructive abilities of the Generalized Nets (GNs, see [18, 1, 2, 23]) are considered in design and reconfiguration of complex multiface Intelligent Systems with emphasis on Hybrid Intelligent Control Systems (HICSs). The paper summarizes some new results in the theoretical development of GNs implementation as a methodology in creation of ISs, proposed earlier in [18]. The main attention is directed towards strategy and structure forming, building blocks, their algorithms and parameters choise and changing in dependance on a set of real life factors – business and economics requirements; operational, technological and safety consideration; optimization automatic control and condition based maintenance; learning, adaptation and knowledge absorbing in a common functionality.

2   Problem Formulation

This paper is focused on situation-oriented design of HICSs based mainly on loose integration of heterogeneous BBs. Taking into account the multi-aspect nature of the real life complex plant control, the below considered approach using GNs is considerably wider than the conventional design, covering mainly dynamic control tasks. The emphasis is on the following main goals:

- To extend the funtional capabilities of the control system taking into account the business requirements, operational limitations, advanced control possibilities, technical condition and faulty risk of the equipment.

- Multiface control of the complex plant to be treated as a unified procedure, where a synergic effect could be reached via incorporating some techniques from the computational intelligence, knowledge based operations and well known conventional control algorithms.
- To reach an adequate (optimal or rational) behaviour of the control system in each possible multidimensional situation, which could be fully unknown.
- Using GNs as a tool to facilitate the design of Hybrid Intelligent Control Systems (HICSs) taking into consideration the restrictions provoked by the existing legacy conventional parts.

In our approach, the behaviour of the whole system is considered as a consequence of cases $C(k)$. Each of them must be firstly recognized and after that the Control System must take decision of adequate actions, at a corresponding hierarchical level. The proposed approach aims to reach a proper initial design, flexibility by reconfiguration and ability for learning and adaptation based on current information.

In our attempt to accomplish the above scope at least in part, we accept a holistic approach with emphasis on a proper choice of the main control components – strategy, structure, BBs and their algorithms, tuning parameters and interconnections, as illustrated on Fig. 1.

Let everywhere below, k be the current time-moment.

The cases are presented in the well established "problem – solution" form [5, 6, 22]:

$$C(k) = \langle P(k), S(k) \rangle, \tag{1}$$

where $P(k)$ is the problem, $S(k)$ is the solution and k is case's index.

In the research, as problem $P(k)$ the notion of situation $H(k)$ is accepted, which could be presented as the seven-tuple

$$H(k) = P(k) = \langle ST(k), E(k), BC(k), J(k), L(k), TS(k), TC(k) \rangle, \tag{2}$$

where:

- $ST(k)$ is the system state, which could be presented in state space form as the tuple

$$ST(k) = \langle x(k), y(k) \rangle, \tag{3}$$

where

$$\begin{aligned} x(k+1) &= F(x(k), u(k), d(k), \Omega(k)) \\ y(k+1) &= G(x(k), u(k), d(k), \Omega(k)) \end{aligned} \tag{4}$$

and $x(k)$ is a dynamic state, $y(k)$ is an output, $u(k)$ is a control action, $\Omega(k)$ is a current operational area of the subsystem.
- $E(k)$ is an enviromental state, such that

$$E(k) = E(k-1) + \Delta E(k), \tag{5}$$

where $\Delta E(k)$ is the dynamic or steady state disturbance, parametric variable ($\Delta E(k) = d(k)$) into the plant model or both of them.

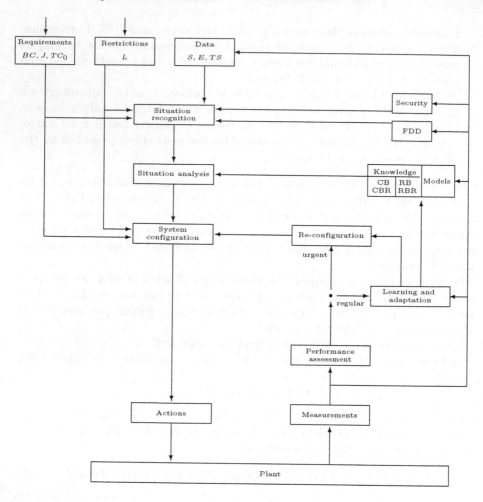

Fig. 1. Generalized situation-based design and reconfiguration scheme

- $BC(k)$ are business conditions and requirements:

$$BC(k) = BC(k-1) + \Delta BC(k). \tag{6}$$

The increment $\Delta BC(k)$ comprises settings of capacity, quality and range of production, temporal requirements, priorities, etc.

- $J(k)$ is a current scalarized objective multicomponent function

$$J(k) = \sum_i \alpha_i(k) J_i(k) \quad \text{and} \quad \sum_i \alpha_i = 1, \tag{7}$$

where the main components of J are: J_1 is the assessment of the economical efficiency in dependence on operational regimes, J_2 is the control system performance assessment, J_3 is the evaluation of availability and safety of the equipment. Weighting coefficients $\alpha_i(k)$ could vary depending on the business prioritization.

- $L(k)$ are the current limitations (technological, resourses, ecological, which could alternate as follows

$$L(k) = L(k-1) + \Delta L(k). \tag{8}$$

- $TS(k)$ are the technological settings (temperatures, flow rates, pressures, concentrations, recycles, etc.) given by the optimizing procedures, established instructions or human-operators.
- $TC(k)$ is the estimation of unit's technical conditions and

$$TC(k) = \langle \Omega(k), RUL(k), p(k), RS(k) \rangle, \tag{9}$$

where $\Omega(k)$ is the current operational area ("OK", "good", "acceptable", "dangerous", "unacceptable (damage)") of the equipment.
- $RUL(k)$ and $p(k)$ are the remaining useful life and probability of failure of the unit, respectively.
- $RS(k)$ is esimation of the current risk of damage.
- $TC(k)$ is changeable from situation to situation, and

$$TC(k) = TC(k-1) + \Delta TC(k). \tag{10}$$

In this paper, as a solution $S(k)$ in (1) is accepted the current configuration/design presented as four-tuple

$$S(k) = D(k) = \langle ST(k), HS(k), AL(k), PR(k) \rangle, \tag{11}$$

where $ST(k)$ is the current control strategy, $HS(k)$ is the Hybrid Structure (HS) of the control system, $AL(k)$ are the algorithms of BBs, $PR(k)$ are the current tuning parameters in algorithms.

HS consists of a number of BBs and InterConnections (ICs) between them:

$$HS(k) = \langle \overline{BB}(k), IC(k) \rangle. \tag{12}$$

$\overline{BB}(k)$ is the vector of BBs included into the current structure $HS(k)$:

$$\overline{BB}(k) = \langle BB_1(k), ..., BB_n(k) \rangle. \tag{13}$$

$IC(k)$ represents an incidence $(0, 1)$-matrix. Each BB is described by currently used in the k-situation particular algorithm $AL(k)$ and corresponding iterative values $PR(k, r)$ in r-reparametrization cycle

$$BB_i(k) = \langle AL(k), PR(k, r) \rangle. \tag{14}$$

Two main procedures are accepted in situation based control:

1. "Top-down". The goal of this designs stage is to derive for k-situaton an optimal design

$$D^*(k) = D^*(H(k)) = \langle ST^*(k), HS^*(k), AL^*(k), PR^*(k,0) \rangle. \qquad (15)$$

2. "Bottom up". In this stage the performance of the whole system is improved via learning and adaptation using data driven procedures.

Three basic design principles of HICS have been accepted:

1. Situation-based design.
2. Hybridization via loose integration and variety of BBs reconfiguration.
3. Improving the system performance by implementation of BBs with computational intelligence (NNS, FL), knowledge (CBR, RBR) and machine learning.

A situation-oriented design is based on the sequential discrete choice of four main functional characteristics of HICS, defined by (11): Strategy $ST(k)$, Structure $HS(k)$ (BBs, IC), Algorithms $AL(k)$ and Parameters $PR(k,r)$. No conventional control algorithms synthesis is used. The necessary cases in accordance with case-based reasoning approach (1) would be provided in different ways:

− Using historical data from Supervisory control and data aquisition system or Decentralized control system of a real plant exploration.
− Via realization of program of active experiment design [24] during the re-engineering and commissioning the control system.
− Augmentation of Situation Case Base (SCB) as a result of RE^4 CBR sycle (Retrieve, Reuse, Revise, Retain) [5, 21, 22] and learning/adaptation procedure (see Fig. 1).
− By application of simulation experiments if full collection of necessary plant, departments, units and local control loops are available.

The design is retrieval and reconfiguration oriented with systematic improvement via learning/adaptation (see Fig. 1).

In this paper we use the established hierarchical structure of days complex plant represented in four levels:

− Basic Control level,
− Ttechnological units level,
− Departements level,
− Whole plant level.

The level's functions are relatively autonomous but a strong vertical and horizontal information exchange as well as technological and operation interconnections exist. Thus common design/control task in each situation $H(k)$ must be devided into a number of parallel procedures toward two main axes − (i) operational (hierarchical levels) and (ii) functional design/reconfiguration of level's control systems (strategy, structure, BBs, their algorithms and parameters (see (14)). This complicated multiaspect design control procedure is carried out by a GN approach, modified accordingly the considered domain of the HICS creation.

3   Generalized Net Model

The GN-model (see Fig. 2) contains 9 transitions, 17 places and 7 types of tokens. The tokens from the first type (α-tokens) stay permanently in place l_5 that represent the database of the modelled process. Token α contains as a current characteristic the following information, obtained during the process functioning: sets $S(k), E(k))$ and $TS(k)$, where k be the current time-moment. The tokens from second and third types (γ- and δ-tokens) enter places l_1 and l_2, respectively, with initial characteristics

$$x_0^\gamma = \text{"requirements for the process; } BC, J, TC_0\text{"},$$

$$x_0^\delta = \text{"restrictions on the process; } L\text{"}.$$

The GN-transitions have the following forms.

$$Z_1 = \langle \{l_1, l_2, l_5, l_{13}, l_{17}\}, \{l_3, l_4, l_5\}, \begin{array}{c|ccc} & l_3 & l_4 & l_5 \\ \hline l_1 & true & true & false \\ l_2 & true & true & false \\ l_5 & true & false & true \\ l_{13} & false & false & true \\ l_{17} & false & false & true \end{array} \rangle.$$

Tokens γ, δ and α split to two tokens γ_1, γ_2; δ_1, δ_2; and α, α_1. Token α continue to stay in place l_5, while tokens $\alpha_1, \gamma_1, \delta_1$ enter place l_3, where they unite in token ε that obtains the characteristic "situation recognition".

Tokens γ_2, δ_2 enter place l_4, where they unite in token ζ that obtains the characteristic "$x_0^\gamma \cup x_0^\delta$".

Token ε from place l_{13} enters place l_5 and unites with token α.

$$Z_2 = \langle \{l_3, l_{11}\}, \{l_6\}, \begin{array}{c|c} & l_6 \\ \hline l_3 & true \\ l_{11} & true \end{array} \rangle.$$

Token ε and token ε' from place l_{11} unite in place l_6 as token ε, with the characteristic "situation analysis".

$$Z_3 = \langle \{l_4, l_6, l_{14}\}, \{l_7\}, \begin{array}{c|c} & l_7 \\ \hline l_4 & true \\ l_6 & true \\ l_{14} & true \end{array} \rangle.$$

Tokens ε, ζ and η (the latter coming from place l_{14}) unite in place l_7 as token ε, with the characteristic "system configuration".

$$Z_4 = \langle \{l_7\}, \{l_8\}, \begin{array}{c|c} & l_8 \\ \hline l_7 & true \end{array} \rangle.$$

Token ε enters place l_8 with a new characteristic "action".

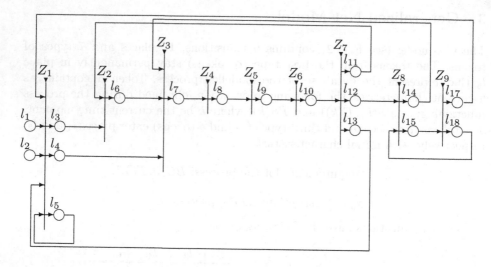

Fig. 2. The generalized net model

$$Z_5 = \langle \{l_8\}, \{l_9\}, \frac{\begin{array}{c|c} & l_9 \\ \hline l_8 & true \end{array}} \rangle.$$

Token ε enters place l_9 with a new characteristic "plant, current status".

$$Z_6 = \langle \{l_9, l_{11}\}, \{l_{10}, l_{11}\}, \frac{\begin{array}{c|cc} & l_{10} & l_{11} \\ \hline l_9 & false & true \\ l_{10} & true & false \end{array}} \rangle.$$

Token ε enters place l_{11} with a characteristic "results of the measurements".

$$Z_7 = \langle \{l_{10}\}, \{l_{11}, l_{13}, l_{13}\}, \frac{\begin{array}{c|ccc} & l_{11} & l_{13} & l_{13} \\ \hline l_{10} & true & true & true \end{array}} \rangle.$$

Token ε splits to three tokens $\varepsilon, \zeta, \varepsilon'$. Token ε enters place l_{13}, token ζ – place l_{11} and token η – place l_{12}. Tokens ε and ε' keep the last ε-characteristic, while token η obtains the characteristic "results of the performance assessment".

$$Z_8 = \langle \{l_{13}, l_{17}\}, \{l_{14}, l_{15}\}, \frac{\begin{array}{c|cc} & l_{14} & l_{15} \\ \hline l_{13} & W_{13,14} & W_{13,15} \\ l_{17} & true & false \end{array}} \rangle,$$

where

- $W_{13,14}$ = "the results of the performance assessment must be used urgently for reconfiguration";
- $W_{13,15}$ = "the results of the performance assessment must be used for regular learning".

When predicate $W_{13,14}$ is valid, token η enters place l_{14} obtaining a new characteristic "reconfiguration". In the opposite case, i.e., when predicate $W_{13,15}$ is true, token η enters place l_{15} obtaining the characteristic "learning".

If in the previous time-step, there is an η-token in place l_{17}, then it enters place l_{13} without a new characteristic.

$$Z_9 = \langle \{l_{15}\}, \{l_{16}, l_{17}\}, \frac{\begin{array}{cc} l_{16} & l_{17} \end{array}}{l_{15} \begin{array}{cc} true & true \end{array}} \rangle.$$

Token η splits to two tokens θ and η that enter places l_{16} and l_{17} without new characteristics.

4 Conclusion

GNs are suitable tool for synergy realization of multiface functionality in complex systems – hybridization of variety of BBs; relevant reconfiguration for each operational situation; improving the system performance via learning; integration of business, technological and safety aspects of plant management.

The openness and universality of GNs is a promising framework for successive creation of generalized approach for multiaspect control and management of advanced HICSs. This could contribute to a significant reduction of the design resources (cost, time, qualification), improvement the system efficiency and safety, enlargement the system functionality and operational range, thus facilitating the total plant management.

Acknowledgment. This work was supported in part from the National Science Fund of Republic of Bulgaria, Project No. DVU-10-0267/2010.

References

1. Atanassov, K.: Generalized Nets. World Scientific, Singapore (1991)
2. Atanassov, K.: On Generalized Nets Theory, "Prof. M. Drinov". Academic Publishing House, Sofia (2007)
3. Castillo, O., Melin, P., Kasprzyk, J. (eds.): Recent Advantages on Hybrid Intelligent Systems. Springer, Berlin (2013)
4. Graña Romay, M., Corchado, E., Garcia Sebastian, M.T. (eds.): HAIS 2010, Part I. LNCS, vol. 6076. Springer, Heidelberg (2010)
5. Negnevitski, M.: A Guide to Intelligent Systems. Addison Wesley (2005)
6. Ruan, D. (ed.): Intelligent Hybrid Systems: Fuzzy Logic, Neural Networks and Genetic Algorithms. Springer, London (2012)
7. Abraham, A.: Hybrid Intelligent Systems: Evolving Intelligence in Hierarchical Layers. In: Gabrys, B., Leiviskä, K., Strackeljan, J. (eds.) Hybrid Intelligent Systems: Evolving Intelligence in Hierarchical Layers. STUDFUZZ, vol. 173, pp. 159–179. Springer, Heidelberg (2005)
8. Reyes, N., Barczak, A., Susnjak, T.: A reconfigurable Hybrid Intelligent System for Robot Navigation. Res. Let. Inst. Math. Sci. 25, 21–34 (2011)

9. Man, X., Haigan, Y., Jiang, S.: New Algorithm for CBR - RBR Fusion with Robust Threshold. Chinese Journal of Mechanical Engineering 25(6), 1255–1263 (2012)
10. Prentzas, J., Hatzilygeroudis, I.: Categorizing Approaches Combining Rule-Based and Case-Based Reasoning. Expert Systems 24(2), 97–122 (2007)
11. Gao, J., Deng, G.: Semi-Automatic Construction of Ontology – Based CBR Systems for Knowledge Integration. Int. Journal of Electrical and Electronics Engineering 4(4), 620–626 (2010)
12. Bemporad, A., Morari, M.: Control of Systems, Integrating Logic, Dynamics and Constraints. Automatica 35(3), 407–427 (1999)
13. Jain, L.C., Martin, N.M.: Fusion of Neural Networks, Fuzzy Sets and genetic Algorithms: Industrial Automations. CRC Press (1998)
14. Zhang, Z., Zhang, C.: Agent Based Hybrid Intelligent Systems. Springer (2008)
15. Hadjiski, M., Boishina, V.: Hybrid Supervisory Control of Complex Systems Incorporating Case Based Reasoning. In: Proc. of the Int. Conf. on Complex Systems, COSY 2011, Ohrid, Macedonia, pp. 179–186 (2011)
16. Hadjiski, M., Sgurev, V., Boishina, V.: Intelligent Control of Uncertain Complex Systems by Adaptation of Fuzzy Ontologies. In: Sgurev, V., Hadjiski, M., Kacprzyk, J. (eds.) Intelligent Systems: From Theory to Practice. SCI, vol. 299, pp. 19–40. Springer, Heidelberg (2009)
17. Hadjiski, M., Sgurev, V., Boishina, V.: Multi Agent Intelligent Control of Centralized HVAC Systems. In: Proc. of the IFAC Workshop on Energy Saving Control in Plants and Buildings, Bansko, Bulgaria, October 3-5, pp. 195–200 (2006)
18. Atanassov, K., Hadjiski, M.: Generalized Nets and Intelligent Systems. Int. Journal of General Systems 39(5), 457–470 (2010)
19. Hadjiski, M., Sgurev, V., Boishina, V.: Adaptation of Fuzzy Ontology for Cascade Multi-Agent System. In: Proc. of 4th Int. IEEE Conference on Intelligent Systems, Varna, pp. 6-59–6-64 (2008)
20. Hadjiski, M., Boishina, V.: Functions Selection and Distribution in Hybrid Computational-Agent-Ontology Control System Ontologies. In: Hadjiski, M., Petrov, V. (eds.) Ontologies-Philosophical and Technological Problems, pp. 95–111. "Prof. Marin Drinov" Academic Publishing House, Sofia (2008)
21. Vachtsevanos, G., Lewis, F., Roemer, M., Hess, A., Wu, B.: Intelligent Fault Diagnosis and Prognosis for Engineering Systems. John Wiley (2006)
22. Pal, S., Shin, S.: Foundation of Soft Case-Based Reasoning. John Wiley (2004)
23. Melo-Pinto, P., Atanassov, K.: A generalized net model of the system "object-environment". In: Proc. of the 10th ISPE Int. Conf. on Concurrent Engineering "Advanced Design, Production and Management Systems", Madeira, July 26-30, pp. 1053–1056 (2003)
24. Keviczky, L.: Design of experiments for the identification of linear dynamic systems. Technometrics 17(3), 303–308 (1975)

Design of a Fuzzy System for the Fly the de Havilland Beaver

Leticia Cervantes and Oscar Castillo

Tijuana Institute of Technology
Lettyy2685@hotmail.com, ocastillo@tectijuana.mx

Abstract. In this paper the main idea is to control the stability in fly the de Havilland beaver, in this paper are established 2 trajectories for the airplane. In this case a fuzzy system is employ to control the flight in the 2 trajectories. Also a joystick is used to introduced disturbances to the system, this joystick is used in different ways to move the airplane and with the fuzzy system the fly of the airplane is controlled.

1   Introduction

In this paper fuzzy system and fuzzy control are employ to control an airplane specifically the de Havilland beaver [5][6][7][8][11][13]. The main idea is to maintain the stability of the plane in 2 trajectories, also a joystick is used to introduce disturbances while the plain is in flight, these movement can be simple or rough in each second in the flight. To control an airplane is important to know the movements of the plane in flight, an airplane has 3 important movements "pitch, row and yaw", and for this movements is necessary to control the elevators, the ailerons or rudder, if we want to control the pitch the elevators need to be controlled, yaw needs of the rudder to move it and roll needs the aileron to control it [14][15][16][17][18]. This paper is organized as follows, in section 2 problem description is described, section 3 presents simulation results and finally section 4 the conclusions.

2   Problem Description

In this paper the main problem is to control the stability of the airplane when a joystick is used to move the plain with disturbance and abrupt movements, in this case the control area is shown in Fig. 1.

Fig. 1. Control area

When the simulation is performed the disturbances are presented in all the simulation with different random movements.

2.1   Fuzzy System

In this case three fuzzy systems are used to control the stability of the plain, each fuzzy system has to control an axes or movements of the plane [1][2][3][4]. The first fuzzy system is used to control the elevator of the airplane, in this case the input of the fuzzy system is the wheel (push or pull) and the output is the angle of the elevators [9][10][12]. In the second fuzzy system the ailerons need to be controlled, in this part the input is the wheel (move left or right) and the output is the angle of the ailerons. The last fuzzy system is controlling the rudder, the input are the pedals(press right or press left) and the output is the angle of the rudder when it is moving right or left depending on the desire direction [19][20][21][22][23][24]. The fuzzy systems are shown in Figures 2 to 4.

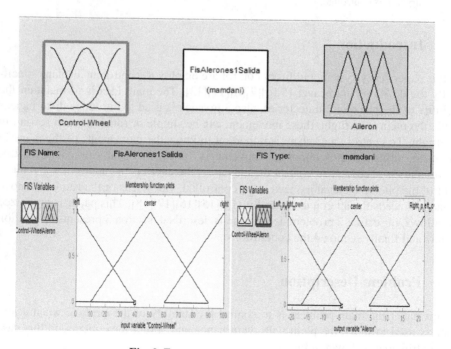

Fig. 2. Fuzzy system of aileron control

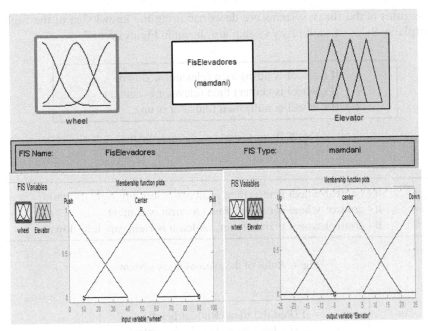

Fig. 3. Fuzzy system of elevator control

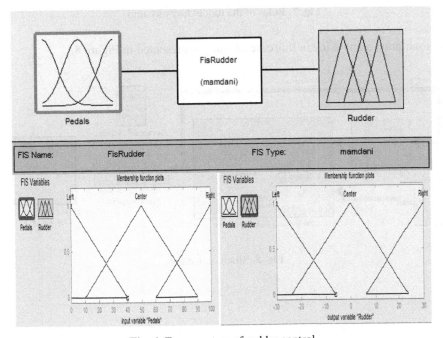

Fig. 4. Fuzzy system of rudder control

The rules of the fuzzy systems are described using the knowledge of the flight in the airplane. Rules of each fuzzy system are shown in Figures 5 to 7.

> ⭐ If (wheel is push) then (elevator is down)
> ⭐ If (wheel is center) then (elevator is center)
> ⭐ If (wheel is pull) then (elevator is up)

Fig. 5. Rules of the elevator fuzzy system

> ⭐ If (control-wheel is left) then (Aileron is left_up_right_down)
> ⭐ If (control-wheel is center) then (Aileron is center)
> ⭐ If (control-wheel is right) then (Aileron is right_up_left_down)

Fig. 6. Rules of the ailerons fuzzy system

> ⭐ If (Pedals) then (Rudder is left)
> ⭐ If (Pedals) then (Rudder is center)
> ⭐ If (Pedals) then (Rudder is right)

Fig. 7. Rules of the rudder fuzzy system

The simulation plant using in this case of study is presented in Figure 8.

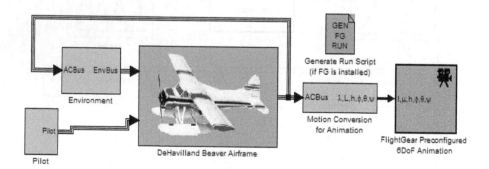

Fig. 8. Simulation plant

3   Simulation Results

In this case 2 references were established to the plain, this airplane has to follow each reference using the joystick to introduce disturbances also the simulation plant has a module that simulate some disturbances. The first reference is shown in Figure 9.

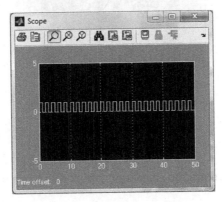

Fig. 9. Reference 1 to the plain

Using the reference before the simulation results are presented in Table 1.

Table 1. Results for the simulation plant using reference 1

Alerones	Elevadores	Rudder
0.2441	0.6142	0.398
0.3699	0.6971	0.3287
0.3583	0.6057	0.4135
0.4049	0.6809	0.3528
0.3292	0.505	0.3403
0.3717	0.6955	0.4347
0.2931	0.6649	0.3858
0.3141	0.6419	0.3713
0.3828	0.7171	0.4405
0.403	0.6527	0.4743

The second reference is presented in Figure 10.

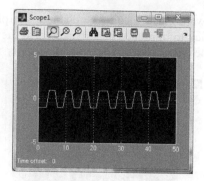

Fig. 10. Reference 2 to the plain

Using the second reference the simulation results are shown in Table 2.

Table 2. Results for the simulation plant using reference 2

Alerones	Elevadores	Rudder
0.9142	1.0481	0.8881
0.9457	1.1064	0.932
0.8901	1.1133	0.9515
0.9121	1.0851	0.9446
0.8918	1.117	0.9098
0.8598	1.0906	0.8914
0.9441	1.0878	0.9258
0.9592	1.1512	0.8962
0.9045	1.1158	0.9305
0.9033	1.0465	0.9521

Having the previous results is important to mention that when the reference is change the error is increase because the reference 2 is more complicate to follow that reference 1. The second reference has more changes in its second and is in these changes where the fuzzy systems have to control the stability of the plane.

4   Conclusions

In this paper the stability of the aircraft was performed using 2 different references to prove the fuzzy systems. The first reference was simple and more lineal and results with the reference 2 were highest because it has more changes in each second on the time. But is important to mentioned that joystick introduce some noise (disturbances) and the fuzzy systems try to control the behavior of the plain, to future work is to work with type-2 fuzzy systems that can model the noise and help when the joystick introduce disturbances.

References

1. Castillo, O.: Design of Interval Type-2 Fuzzy Logic Controllers. In: Castillo, O. (ed.) Type-2 Fuzzy Logic in Intelligent Control Applications. STUDFUZZ, vol. 272, pp. 23–47. Springer, Heidelberg (2012)
2. Castillo, O., Martinez-Marroquin, R., Melin, P., Valdez, F., Soria, J.: Comparative study of bio-inspired algorithms applied to the optimization of type-1 and type-2 fuzzy controllers for an autonomous mobile robot. Inf. Sci 192, 19–38 (2012)
3. Castillo, O., Melin, P.: New fuzzy-fractal-genetic method for automated Mathematical Modelling and Simulation of Robotic Dynamic Systems. In: IEEE International Conference on Fuzzy Systems, vol. 2, pp. 1182–1187 (1998)
4. Castillo, O., Kacprzyk, J., Pedrycz, W. (eds.): Soft Computing for Intelligent Control and Mobile Robotics. SCI, vol. 318. Springer, Heidelberg (2010)
5. Cervantes, L., Castillo, O.: Design of a Fuzzy System for the Longitudinal Control of an F-14 Airplane. In: Castillo, O., Kacprzyk, J., Pedrycz, W. (eds.) Soft Computing for Intelligent Control and Mobile Robotics. SCI, vol. 318, pp. 213–224. Springer, Heidelberg (2010)
6. Cervantes, L., Castillo, O., Melin, P.: Intelligent Control of Nonlinear Dynamic Plants Using a Hierarchical Modular Approach and Type-2 Fuzzy Logic. In: Batyrshin, I., Sidorov, G. (eds.) MICAI 2011, Part II. LNCS (LNAI), vol. 7095, pp. 1–12. Springer, Heidelberg (2011)
7. Cervantes, L., Castillo, O.: Hierarchical Genetic Algorithms for Optimal Type-2 Fuzzy System Design. In: Annual Meeting of the North American Fuzzy Information Processing Society, pp. 324–329 (2011)
8. Cervantes, L., Castillo, O.: Automatic Design of Fuzzy Systems for Control of Aircraft Dynamic Systems with Genetic Optimization. In: World Congress and AFSS International Conference, pp. OS-413-1–OS-413-7 (2011)
9. Cervantes, L., Castillo, O., Melin, P., Valdez, F.: Comparative Study of Type-1 and Type-2 Fuzzy Systems for the Three Tank Water Control Problem. In: Batyrshin, I., Mendoza, M.G. (eds.) MICAI 2012, Part II. LNCS (LNAI), vol. 7630, pp. 362–373. Springer, Heidelberg (2013)

10. Dubois, D., Prade, H.: Fuzzy sets and Systems: Theory and Applications (1980)
11. Gibbens, P., Boyle, D.: Introductory Flight Mechanics and Performance, University of Sydney, Australia. Paper (1999)
12. Melin, P., Castillo, O.: A new method for adaptive model-based control of non-linear plants using type-2 fuzzy logic and neural networks. In: IEEE International Conference on Fuzzy Systems, vol. 1, pp. 420–425 (2003)
13. Rachman, E., Jaam, J., Hasnah, A.: Non-linear simulation of controller for longitudinal control augmentation system of F-16 using numerical approach. Information Sciences Journal 164(1-4), 47–60 (2004)
14. Reiner, J., Balas, G., Garrard, W.: Flight control design using robust dynamic inversion and time- scale separation. Automatic Journal 32(11), 1493–1504 (1996)
15. Sanchez, E., Becerra, H., Velez, C.: Combining fuzzy, PID and regulation control for an autonomous mini-helicopter. Journal of Information Sciences 177(10), 1999–2022 (2007)
16. Sefer, K., Omer, C., Okyay, K.: Adaptive neuro-fuzzy inference system based autonomous flight control of unmanned air vehicles. Expert Systems with Applications Journal 37(2), 1229–1234 (2010)
17. Song, Y., Wang, H.: Design of Flight Control System for a Small Unmanned Tilt Rotor Aircraft. Chinese Journal of Aeronautics 22(3), 250–256 (2009)
18. Walker, D.J.: Multivariable control of the longitudinal and lateral dynamics of a fly by wire helicopter. Control Engineering Practice 11(7), 781–795 (2003)
19. Zadeh, L.: Fuzzy Sets and Fuzzy Information Granulation Theory. Beijing Normal University Press, Baijing (2000)
20. Zadeh, L.: Fuzzy Sets. Information and Control 8(3), 338–353 (1965)
21. Zadeh, L.: Shadows of Fuzzy Sets. Probl. Peredachi Inf. 2(1), 37–44 (1966)
22. Zadeh, L.: Fuzzy Logic, Neural Networks and Soft Computing. Commun. ACM 37(3), 77–84 (1994)
23. Zadeh, L.A.: Some reflections on soft computing, granular computing and their roles in the conception, design and utilization of information/intelligent systems. Soft Comput. 2, 23–25 (1998)
24. Zadeh, L.A.: Outline of a new approach to the analysis of complex systems and decision processes. IEEE Trans. Syst. Man Cybern. SMC-3, 28–44 (1973)

Analog PID Controller with the Digitally Controlled Parameters

R. Ugodziński[1], R. Szewczyk[2], and M. Nowicki[2]

[1] Industrial Research Institute for Automation and Measurements,
Al. Jerozolimskie 202, 02-486 Warsaw, Poland
[2] Warsaw University of Technology, Faculty of Mechatronics,
sw. A. Boboli 8, 02-525 Warsaw, Poland
rugodzinski@piap.pl

Abstract. The paper presents analog PID controller with the digitally controlled gains of individual modules. The basic analog PID circuit is modified, and the new elements matched on the basis of SPICE simulations. Prototype system was designed and built. The system was investigated for the parameters characteristics depending on controlling digital potentiometers positions. High precision of developed controller was achieved.

Keywords: analog, PID, digital, adaptative, fuzzy, controller, digital potentiometer, control system.

1   Introduction

PID controllers are widely used in industrial and precise applications as simple and effective control systems [1]. However, because of electronic progress, they are implemented as digital devices [2]. Digital PID are less precise because they use a finite number of bits of the A/D and D/A converter. Therefore a need remains to use analog controllers, when best possible accuracy and compensation of control error is necessary [3].

The problem arises, when the controlled object is characterized by strong nonlinearity. In such a case, dynamic adaptation of the control parameters, depending on the set point is imperative. In digital implementations it is easy to achieve [4][5][6], but keeping the features of analogue control is problematic. Therefore in this paper analog PID controller with the possibility of digital parameters setting is presented.

2   Topologies Overview of the Analog PID Controllers

One of the most popular implementations of analog PID controllers is topology based on three operational amplifiers, with fourth amplifier to sum the signals.

© Springer International Publishing Switzerland 2015   89
D. Filev et al. (eds.), *Intelligent Systems' 2014*,
Advances in Intelligent Systems and Computing 323, DOI: 10.1007/978-3-319-11310-4_9

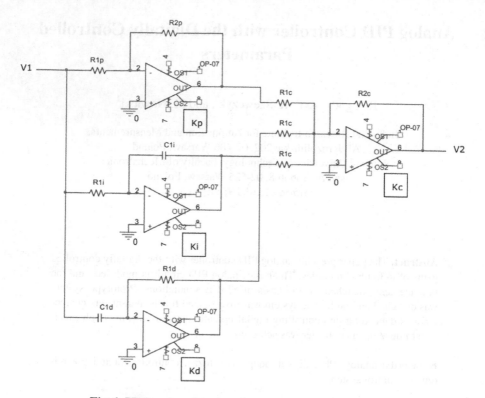

Fig. 1. PID topology based on three operational amplifiers [7]

This topology is easiest to understand and to change the controller gains. Individual controller terms are working independently and then are summed (and amplified if need be) by the last operational amplifier. There is also the possibility of gains change by setting the value of single resistor in individual modules, which is crucial for the developed solution. One can also easily weaken the output of individual modules or completely eliminate some of them.

Therefore, to implement the tuning of the PID controller the topology of independent modules of the controller is used. It allows for simple realization of parameters setting by the use of digital potentiometers. Also, because of the modules independence, setting the one potentiometer won't affect the other regulator modules.

The formulas for individual gains are as follows:

$$K_I = \frac{1}{R_{1i}C_{1i}} \tag{1}$$

$$K_D = R_{1d}C_{1d} \tag{2}$$

$$K_C = \frac{R_{2c}}{R_{1c}} \tag{3}$$

3   Modifications of the Chosen Topology to the Needs of Digital Gains Setting and Matching to the Controlled Object

In order to adapt to the target application it was necessary to modify the given topology. First of all it was necessary to use digital potentiometers in particular modules together with a resistor, which will be adequately shifting the resistance variation range. In this case Analog Device AD5290 potentiometers were used, able to work with bipolar voltages of up to +/- 15 V and 100 kΩ resistance value [8].

Next suitable decoupling capacitors were connected, matched to the operational amplifiers amplifications. They were matched experimentally on the basis of simulations done in the SPICE software.

The biggest modifications were done in the differentiator module. Due to the very unstable nature of the differentiation, the circuit in which the operational amplifier of this module works was changed from differentiating to the band-pass filter. As a result, the bandwidth of the module was effectively limited, removing the majority of the output interference.

In each module the ability to change the setpoint has been added, by supplying the external analog signal directly to the non-inverting amplifiers input. A schematic diagram of how the signal given affects the operation of the controller is as follows:

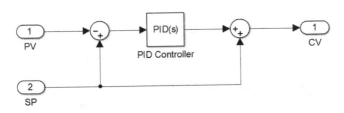

Fig. 2. Schematic of individual inputs influence on the output

It would seem that the SP signal will be repeated 3 times in the given wiring diagram. However, the summing amplifier will be, instead of summing, averaging the output of the modules, allowing the SP signal to pass directly to the CV, introducing additional regulation noise, which unfortunately cannot be avoided without increasing the number of active elements of the system.

As it was mentioned, the summing amplifier configuration will also be changed. It is required in the target configuration that the controller runs in reverse mode. Thus the last module must maintain the sign. In addition, it is required that the feedback is clear, in the sense of direct connection to the inverting input without the use of the ground the controller, so the extra power amplifier based on transistors can be used.

Final wiring diagrams of the setup are shown in figure 3.

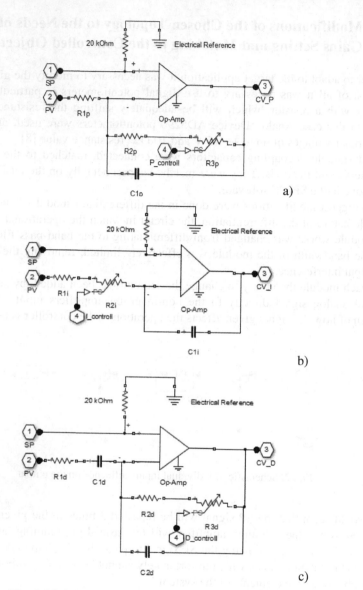

Fig. 3. Module a) proportional b) integrating c) differentiating

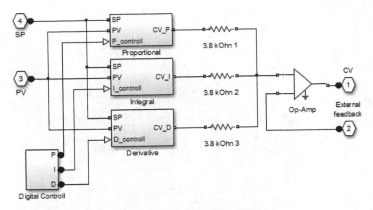

Fig. 4. Modules connections

Formulas for the gains of individual modules are without change. The only difference is with the summing amplifier. In the above mentioned configuration, where all resistors before the amplifier are equal, voltage generated on the non-inverting input will be the average of the input signals:

$$CV = \frac{CV_P + CV_I + CV_D}{3} \qquad (4)$$

By providing the external feedback we make sure that on the power amplifier built on transistors output there was voltage of value calculated from the above formula.

The operational amplifiers chosen were the Analog Device AD8639. They have low noise and the autozero function [9].

4   Test Implementation

In order to test the developed controller the prototype for a given parameters was built, assuming a + / - 20% reserve for each of the settings:

Table 1. Exemplary controller parameters

K_p	K_i	K_d
0,356	0,414-0,780	0,0099

On this basis, using the formulas 1,2 and 3 the value of main passive system components were calculated. Then on the basis of SPICE simulation software type values of decoupling elements were specified, to trim the frequency response of the system.

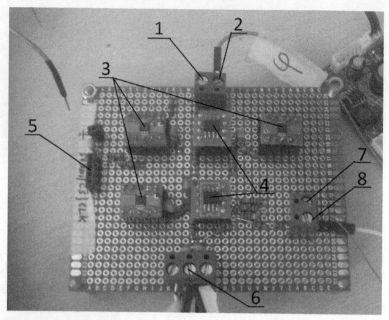

Fig. 5. Prototype adaptive regulator. 1 –SP signal input, 2 –PV signal input, 3 –AD5290 digital potentiometers, 4 –AD8639 double operational amplifiers, 5 – Connection for digital communication with the potentiometers, 6 – power supply   +/- 7,7V, 7 – regulator output, 8 – feedback to external power circuit.

5   Regulator Parameters Identification in Relations to the Potentiometers Value

Using the prototype system, it was possible to identify individual modules gains depending on the position of the potentiometer. To do this, the test signal was sent to the SP (Set Point) input of the regulator .

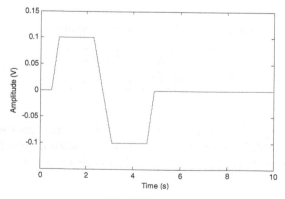

Fig. 6. SP test run

Next, for fixed set point, the input and output characteristics were gathered for different positions of the potentiometer. Then they were adjusted in accordance with second schematic, in order to obtain the dependences of control error and regulator output on time. Characteristics were collected for each of the modules by changing the position of the potentiometer, witch 5 increments step, in three different positions of the other potentiometers: 0, 127 and 250.

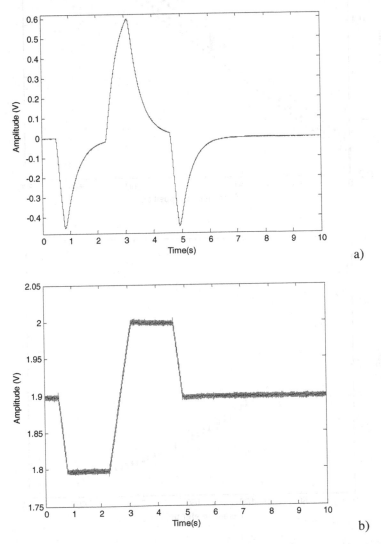

Fig. 7. Example characteristics: a) control error, b) regulator output

In this way, we obtain data which allows for optimization and identification of the controller parameters, depending on the settings of the potentiometers. The following characteristics were obtained:

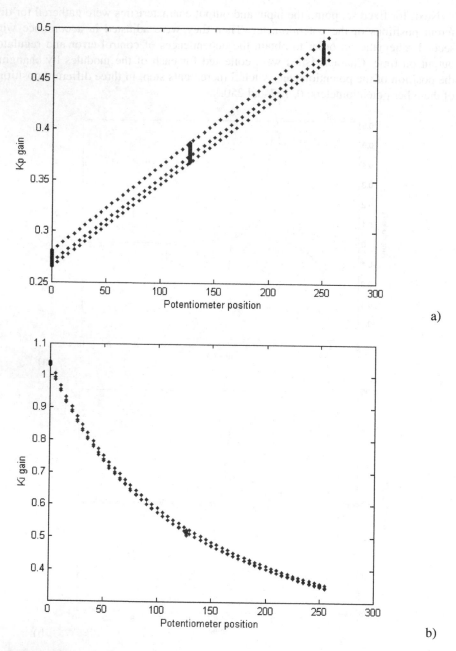

Fig. 8. Gain characteristics for individual modules of the controller depending on the module potentiometer position. Module: a) proportional b) integrating c) differentiating.

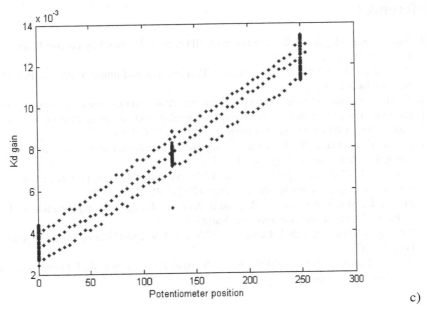

Fig. 8. (*continued*)

As you can see from the above graphs, the value of passive components was inadequate to put the requested settings in the central positions of the potentiometer. Therefore, in implementations a large uncertainty of passive components and digital potentiometers must be always assumed, and their values chosen in order to have a reserve. In this case, as mentioned before, the reserve of the required setting on the order of + / - 20% was assumed. Some interactions between individual modules can also be seen.

6   Conclusion

The analog PID controller with the possibility of digital parameters setting was designed and built. Thus, analog techniques usage do not necessarily prohibits the benefits of the digital era. The system can work as Fuzzy-PID. The possibility of rapid settings change to predictive control is planned, where in the initial phase high gain is fixed, and then the system attenuates so as not to generate too much interference at the output.

The resulting system is currently being tested in the solution where a high precision control is critical for the system functioning. First results show high efficiency of the developed controller.

References

[1] Åström, K.J., Hägglund, T.: The future of PID control. Control Engineering Practice 9(11), 1163–1175 (2001)

[2] Quevedo, J., Escobet, T.: Digital control: Past, present and future of PID control. Elsevier Science Inc. (2000)

[3] Todd, P.M.: Multipurpose analog pid controller. AOLCND University of Texas (2005)

[4] Pomerleau, A., Desbiens, A., Hodouin, D.: Development and evaluation of an auto-tuning and adaptive PID controller. Automatica 32(1), 71–82 (1996)

[5] Radke, F., Isermann, R.: A parameter-adaptive PID-controller with stepwise parameter optimization. Automatica 23(4), 449–457 (1987)

[6] Carvajal, J., Chen, G., Ogmen, H.: Fuzzy PID controller: Design, performance evaluation, and stability analysis. Information Science 123(3), 249–270 (2000)

[7] Sultan, K., Mirza, A.: Inverted Pendulum: Analysis, Design and Implementation. Institute of Industrial Electronics Engineering, Karachi

[8] Analog Devices. "AD5290: Compact +30 V / ±15 V 256-Position Digital Potentiometer Data Sheet"

[9] Analog Devices. AD8638/AD8639: 16 V Auto-Zero, Rail-to-Rail Output Operational Amplifiers Data Sheet

Dynamics Model of a Four-Wheeled Mobile Robot for Control Applications – A Three-Case Study

Maciej Trojnacki

Industrial Research Institute for Automation and Measurements PIAP, Warsaw, Poland
mtrojnacki@piap.pl

Abstract. The problem of dynamics modeling of a four-wheeled mobile robot is analyzed in this paper. All wheels of the robot are non-steered and the servomotors are used for driving the robot. Three cases of the robot drive system are considered. In the first case, two out of four wheels of the robot are independently driven, i.e., a pair of front or rear wheels. In the second case, the same wheels of the robot are driven but drive is also transmitted to the remaining wheels via toothed belts at each side of the robot. Finally, in the third case all four wheels are independently driven. Kinematic structure of the robot and its kinematics are described. The dynamics model of the robot dedicated for control applications is derived. It takes into account tire-ground contact conditions and wheel slips. The tire-ground contact conditions are characterized by coefficients of friction and rolling resistance. A simple form of the tire model, which considers only the most important effects of tire-ground interaction, is applied. The robot dynamics model also includes the presence of friction in kinematic pairs and the electromechanical model of servomotor drive unit. The presented robot dynamics model can be used for simulation-based investigations of control systems under development. Because the model was also formulated in a form linear with respect to parameters, it is possible to use it as a part of the robust or adaptive type control system.

Keywords: wheeled mobile robot, wheel slip, dynamics model, tire model, drive unit model, model of friction in kinematic pairs.

1 Introduction

Wheeled mobile robots are the vehicles whose motion is a result of interaction of wheels with the ground. An important problem associated with interaction of wheels with the ground is the slip phenomenon. Although this problem is a well-known subject of research in the automotive field (representative examples of works can be [10, 18]), in case of wheeled robots it is often neglected. Moreover, wheels of wheeled robots usually have different geometry and properties in comparison to car wheels. Robotic wheels often have non-pneumatic tires, which demands realization of dedicated investigations. This topic of research seems to be rather rare in the literature. One example of works oriented to non-pneumatic small-size robotic tires is [2].

Neglecting wheel slip in case of wheeled mobile robots is reasonable, when robot moves with small speeds and accelerations which results in longitudinal slips of

© Springer International Publishing Switzerland 2015

D. Filev et al. (eds.), *Intelligent Systems' 2014*,

Advances in Intelligent Systems and Computing 323, DOI: 10.1007/978-3-319-11310-4_10

limited magnitude. In turn, neglecting of side slips can be justified, when robot moves with small speeds, has steered or caster wheels and turning radius is large with respect to velocity of motion. However, many authors assume lack of slip a priori, that is, without any reference to conditions of robot motion and without analysis of validity of this assumption.

It is worth emphasizing that in case of wheeled robots with all non-steered wheels, which is the most popular design type in commercial solutions so far (see e.g. [6]), the phenomenon of slip is the inherent property of their motion. Robots like that are called skid-steered mobile robots and are objects of research, for example, in the works [7, 16]. In case of those robots, the side components of ground reaction forces are taken into account with aid of simple models of wheel-ground interaction, for example in [7]. As a rule, the occurrence of self-aligning moment during turning of the wheel is not considered.

With all of the above taken into account, wheeled mobile robots can be divided in two groups: (1) robots for which in typical operating conditions there is almost no wheel sliding during motion, and (2) robots for which wheel sliding is an inherent feature of motion.

Robots with steered or caster wheels belong to the first group. They are usually intended for use inside buildings (indoor robots). An example of such a design is the popular Pioneer 2-DX robot shown in Fig. 1a.

The second group is comprised of robots with all wheels non-steered. Usually robots like that are intended for use in open terrain (outdoor robots). Example of this kind of design is the IBIS robot shown in Fig. 1b [19], developed by the Industrial Institute for Automation and Measurements PIAP.

a)   b)

Fig. 1. Examples of wheeled mobile robots: a – Pioneer 2-DX, b – IBIS [19]

In case of wheeled robots from the second group, motion of robot body is not defined by a kinematic dependency on rotation of driven wheels, as it is in the case of robots from the first group. This difference is associated with occurrence of wheel sliding always during change of direction of motion. In this case, forces generated between tire tread and ground depend in a non-linear manner on various factors, e.g.: material and shape of the tread and of the ground, velocity of tire tread with respect to ground, etc.

In typical robot operating conditions, some of the factors connected with the ground may change in rather arbitrary fashion. For this reason, it is impossible to find analytical expression that would allow to associate desired motion of robot body with motion parameters of driven wheels necessary to its realization, and would be valid in any conditions.

The phenomenon of slip is connected with type of ground on which the wheel moves. It is clear that wheel moving on a ground surface made of concrete will behave in a different way than the same wheel on ice. In the latter case one will expect the occurrence of much larger wheel slips on average for the identical maneuver. Research concerning robot motion on various types of ground is the topic, for instance, of work [16].

Wheeled mobile robots are vehicles that should move along desired trajectories. As far as control of wheeled mobile robots is concerned, usually robot motion without wheel slips and on the ground with homogenous properties is assumed, which is reflected e.g. in [3, 4, 11]. The works in which the tracking control algorithms take into account wheel slips and/or diverse ground properties can be found as well. Among others there are [8, 13, 17] and [5, 7, 16] in which the authors examine the effect of diverse ground properties on the movement realized by the robot. The problem of control of the skid-steered mobile robots is in particular considered in the works [1, 7, 16] in which wheel slips are included in the control algorithm. Occurrence of the wheel slip is also taken into account, for instance, in the control algorithm of an off-road agricultural vehicle [8].

Because of the mentioned problems, in this work model of a four-wheeled skid-steered mobile robot including wheel slips will be presented. This model can be used for simulation-based investigations of control systems under development. Because the model is also formulated in the form linear with respect to parameters it may be included in the structure of robust or adaptive control systems.

2   Model of the Robot

In this paper dynamics model of the four-wheeled robot including wheel slips is derived. All wheels of the robot are non-steered and the servomotors are used for driving. Three cases of the robot drive system are taken into consideration:

- two out of four wheels of the robot are independently driven, that is, front or rear pair of wheels,
- the same wheels as in the previous case are driven, but in addition drive is transmitted to the remaining two wheels via two toothed belts (tracks), one on each side of the robot,
- all four wheels are independently driven.

2.1   Robot Kinematics

Kinematic structure of the robot and distribution of the velocity vectors are shown in Fig. 2. It is possible to distinguish the following main components of the robot: 0 – mobile platform, 1-4 – wheels, 5-6 – toothed belts.

The following designations for the ith wheel have been introduced in the robot model: A_i – geometric center, r_i – geometric (unloaded) radius, θ_i – spin angle.

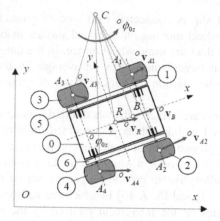

Fig. 2. Kinematic structure of the robot ($A_1A_3 = A_2A_4 = L$, $A_1A_2 = A_3A_4 = W$)

It is assumed that robot motion is realized in Oxy plane of the fixed coordinate system $\{O\}$. The moving coordinate system, considered as rigidly connected to the robot, is denoted with symbol $\{R\}$. Position and orientation of the mobile platform are described by the vector of generalized coordinates:

$$^{O}\mathbf{q} =[^{O}x_R, \,^{O}y_R, \,^{O}\varphi_{0z}]^T, \tag{1}$$

where: $^{O}x_R$, $^{O}y_R$ are coordinates of point R belonging to the mobile platform, and $^{O}\varphi_{0z}$ denotes angle of rotation of mobile platform about Oz axis with respect to the fixed coordinate system $\{O\}$.

In turn, vectors of generalized velocities respectively in $\{O\}$ and $\{R\}$ coordinate systems can be written as:

$$^{O}\dot{\mathbf{q}} = \left[^{O}\dot{x}_R, \,^{O}\dot{y}_R, \,^{O}\dot{\varphi}_{0z}\right]^T, \quad ^{R}\dot{\mathbf{q}} = \left[^{R}\dot{x}_R^O, \,^{R}\dot{y}_R^O, \,^{R}\dot{\varphi}_{0z}^O\right]^T, \tag{2}$$

where: $^{O}v_{Rx} = {}^{O}\dot{x}_R$, $^{O}v_{Ry} = {}^{O}\dot{y}_R$, $^{R}v_{Rx}^O = {}^{R}\dot{x}_R^O$, $^{R}v_{Ry}^O = {}^{R}\dot{y}_R^O$.

Those two vectors satisfy the relationship:

$$^{O}\dot{\mathbf{q}} = {}^{O}\mathbf{J}^R \, {}^{R}\dot{\mathbf{q}}, \tag{3}$$

where matrix $^{O}\mathbf{J}^R$ has the following form:

$$^{O}\mathbf{J}^R = \begin{bmatrix} \cos(^{O}\varphi_{0z}) & -\sin(^{O}\varphi_{0z}) & 0 \\ \sin(^{O}\varphi_{0z}) & \cos(^{O}\varphi_{0z}) & 0 \\ 0 & 0 & 1 \end{bmatrix}. \tag{4}$$

If one makes assumption that $^R v_{Ry}^O = 0$, then vector of generalized velocities $^O \dot{\mathbf{q}}$ can be defined on the basis of kinematic equations of motion in the form:

$$
^O \dot{\mathbf{q}} = \begin{bmatrix} ^O \dot{x}_R \\ ^O \dot{y}_R \\ ^O \dot{\varphi}_{0z} \end{bmatrix} = \begin{bmatrix} \cos(^O \varphi_{0z}) & 0 \\ \sin(^O \varphi_{0z}) & 0 \\ 0 & 1 \end{bmatrix} \begin{bmatrix} ^R v_{Rx}^O \\ ^R \dot{\varphi}_{0z}^O \end{bmatrix},
\tag{5}
$$

where vector $^R \mathbf{v} = [\,^R v_{Rx}^O, \,^R \dot{\varphi}_{0z}^O \,]^T$ contains respectively component of velocity of the point R of the robot on the Rx direction of $\{R\}$ coordinate system and the yaw rate of the mobile platform.

The above equation is valid in case when the robot moves on a horizontal ground.

Point C in Fig. 2 is the instantaneous center of rotation of the robot frame. Projection of this point on Rx axis is indicated with point B.

The analyzed robot is the nonholonomic system. From distribution of velocity vector of the point B, it follows that it is subjected to nonholonomic constraints of the form:

$$
\mathbf{a} \, ^O \dot{\mathbf{q}} = 0,
\tag{6}
$$

where $\mathbf{a} = [-\sin(^O \varphi_{0z}), \cos(^O \varphi_{0z}), \,^R x_C]$ is the vector of nonholonomic constraints.

In turn, projections of velocities of points A_i (i.e., geometric centers of wheels) on Rx and Ry axes of the $\{R\}$ coordinate system satisfy the relationships [7]:

$$
^R v_{lx}^O = {}^R v_{A1x}^O = {}^R v_{A3x}^O, \quad {}^R v_{rx}^O = {}^R v_{A2x}^O = {}^R v_{A4x}^O,
\tag{7}
$$

$$
^R v_{fy}^O = {}^R v_{A1y}^O = {}^R v_{A2y}^O, \quad {}^R v_{by}^O = {}^R v_{A3y}^O = {}^R v_{A4y}^O,
\tag{8}
$$

where: l – wheels of the left-hand side ($l = \{1,3\}$), r – wheels of the right-hand side ($r = \{2,4\}$), f – front wheels ($f = \{1,2\}$), b – back wheels ($b = \{3,4\}$).

In case of plane motion of the mobile platform, velocity vector of the point R depends on angular velocity $^R \dot{\varphi}_{0z}^O$ and radius of curvature R_z of the path according to the formula:

$$
^R v_R^O = {}^R \dot{\varphi}_{0z}^O R_z,
\tag{9}
$$

where $^R v_R^O = {}^R \dot{\varphi}_{0z}^O R_z$ is the velocity with which the point R moves with respect to the stationary coordinate system $\{O\}$.

In addition, in a general case the acceleration vector $^R \mathbf{a}_R^O$ of the point R, expressed in the robot coordinate system $\{R\}$, has both tangential and normal components, that is, the following dependencies are valid:

$$
^R \mathbf{a}_R^O = {}^R \mathbf{a}_{R\tau}^O + {}^R \mathbf{a}_{Rn}^O \quad \Rightarrow \quad {}^R \mathbf{a}_{R\tau}^O = {}^R \mathbf{a}_R^O - {}^R \mathbf{a}_{Rn}^O,
\tag{10}
$$

where $^R \mathbf{a}_{R\tau}^O$ and $^R \mathbf{a}_{Rn}^O$ denote respectively vectors of tangential and normal accelerations of the point R.

Thus, for determination of velocity components of the point R, based on the known acceleration vector ${}^R\mathbf{a}_R^O$, the following equations should be used:

$$
{}^R\dot{v}_{Rx}^O = {}^R a_{Rx}^O + {}^R v_{Ry}^O\, {}^R\dot{\varphi}_{0z}^O, \qquad {}^R\dot{v}_{Ry}^O = {}^R a_{Ry}^O - {}^R v_{Rx}^O\, {}^R\dot{\varphi}_{0z}^O. \tag{11}
$$

Those equations result from projecting acceleration vectors on axes of $\{R\}$ coordinate system.

Projections of velocities of points A_i on Rx and Ry axes of the coordinate system $\{R\}$ can be written as functions of generalized velocities in the form:

$$
\begin{bmatrix} {}^R v_{lx}^O \\ {}^R v_{rx}^O \\ {}^R v_{fy}^O \\ {}^R v_{by}^O \end{bmatrix} = \begin{bmatrix} 1 & -W/2 \\ 1 & W/2 \\ 0 & L/2 - {}^R x_C \\ 0 & -L/2 - {}^R x_C \end{bmatrix} \begin{bmatrix} {}^R v_{Rx}^O \\ {}^R \dot{\varphi}_{0z}^O \end{bmatrix} = \begin{bmatrix} 0 & -W/2 + {}^R y_C \\ 0 & W/2 + {}^R y_C \\ 1 & L/2 \\ 1 & -L/2 \end{bmatrix} \begin{bmatrix} {}^R v_{Ry}^O \\ {}^R \dot{\varphi}_{0z}^O \end{bmatrix}. \tag{12}
$$

Moreover, projections of velocity of the point A_i, which belongs to the i-th wheel, on Rx and Ry axes of $\{R\}$ coordinate system depend on angular velocity of spin of the wheel $\dot{\theta}_i$ and the velocity of slip, that is, the following equations are satisfied:

$$
{}^R v_{Aix}^O = \dot{\theta}_i\, r_i + {}^R v_{Six}^O, \qquad {}^R v_{Aiy}^O = {}^R v_{Siy}^O, \tag{13}
$$

where ${}^R v_{Six}^O$, ${}^R v_{Siy}^O$ are components of slip velocity in $\{R\}$ coordinate system, that is, velocity of motion of points of wheel which are in contact with the ground with respect to the ground.

Thus, the generalized velocities can be written in the form:

$$
{}^R v_{Rx}^O = \left({}^R v_{lx}^O + {}^R v_{rx}^O \right)/2, \quad {}^R v_{Ry}^O = -{}^R \dot{\varphi}_{0z}^O\, {}^R x_B, \quad {}^O \dot{\varphi}_{0z} = \left({}^R v_{rx}^O - {}^R v_{lx}^O \right)/W = \left({}^R v_{by}^O - {}^R v_{fy}^O \right)/L, \tag{14}
$$

Coordinates of the instantaneous center of rotation C (Fig. 2) can be calculated from dependencies:

$$
{}^R x_C = {}^R x_B = -{}^R v_{Ry}^O / {}^R \dot{\varphi}_{0z}^O, \qquad {}^R y_C = {}^R v_{Rx}^O / {}^R \dot{\varphi}_{0z}^O. \tag{15}
$$

Position of the point B has critical influence on stability of robot motion. If the origin of the coordinate system associated with the robot is situated in the middle of the distance between front and rear wheels, then one may assume that coordinates of the point B should satisfy the relationship:

$$
{}^R x_B \in (-L/2, L/2). \tag{16}
$$

2.2   Inverse Kinematics and Tracking Control

In case of tracking control of robot motion, it is necessary to solve the inverse kinematics problem, that is, to determine desired angular velocities of spin of wheels from desired motion of the robot body.

One of possible approaches to tracking control is to make assumption that robot motion is given in the form of vector of generalized velocities ${}^{R}\mathbf{v}_{d} = [{}^{R}v_{Rd}^{O}, {}^{R}\dot{\varphi}_{0zd}^{O}]^{T}$, which corresponds to desired trajectory of robot motion expressed in the form of vector of desired generalized coordinates ${}^{O}\mathbf{q}_{d} = [{}^{O}x_{Rd}, {}^{O}y_{Rd}, {}^{O}\varphi_{0zd}]^{T}$. Then, for tracking control of robot motion it is possible to apply the wheels' velocity controller. This approach is illustrated in Fig. 3.

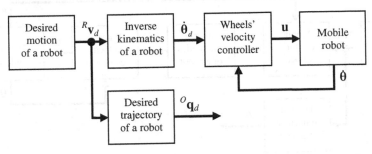

Fig. 3. Schematic diagram of robot motion control system with only controller of wheels' velocity

One should consider that motion of the analyzed robot is highly affected by the occurring wheel slips. In case of longitudinal motion of the robot, when body is in translational motion, and wheels in plane motion, if wheel slips are small, then it is possible to determine angular velocities of spin of the driven wheels required to realize the motion with desired velocity of the point R (i.e. to solve the inverse kinematics problem for the analyzed case) using the formula:

$$\dot{\theta}_{id} = {}^{R}v_{Rd}^{O} / r_{i}. \tag{17}$$

The situation becomes much more complex, when robot negotiates a curve or turns in place. Because robot wheels are non-steered, its motion depends on longitudinal forces, and also to large extent on lateral forces, that is, on robot dynamics in general.

In this case, because of action of lateral forces, the robot will rotate about the vertical axis with smaller angular velocity ${}^{R}\dot{\varphi}_{0z}^{O}$ than it follows from imposed angular velocities of wheels $\dot{\theta}_{ld}$ and $\dot{\theta}_{rd}$ as calculated based on laws of kinematics.

The difference will be the more pronounced, the smaller the number of driven wheels, because of smaller ratio of longitudinal forces which generate motion, to all forces which resist the motion (especially to the lateral forces and longitudinal forces for non-driven wheels).

Therefore, in the analyzed case of control of robot motion, it is reasonable to introduce a higher level controller of velocity of the mobile platform, which works in addition to the wheel's velocity controller. Then, the desired velocities of spin of driven wheels are given by the following relationship:

$$\dot{\boldsymbol{\theta}}_d = \begin{bmatrix} \dot{\theta}_{ld} \\ \dot{\theta}_{rd} \end{bmatrix} = \frac{1}{r}\begin{bmatrix} 1 & -W/2 \\ 1 & W/2 \end{bmatrix}\mathbf{u}_v. \tag{18}$$

where $\mathbf{u}_v$ is a control signal at the output of the wheel's velocity controller, which is at the same time the input signal for the mobile platform velocity controller. This concept is presented in Fig. 4.

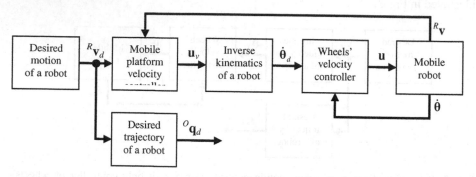

Fig. 4. Schematic diagram of robot motion control system with additional mobile platform velocity controller

Results of simulation investigations for both forms of the control system described above are presented in the work [14], whereas the results of empirical research in [15].

2.3   Dynamics of the Robot for Three Cases of the Drive System

For the needs of design and simulation of the control systems based on the object model (e.g., adaptive control), a simplified model of a four-wheeled mobile robot will be derived for the following drive system configurations:

- two out of four wheels of the robot are independently driven, that is, front or rear wheels,
- the same wheels of the robot as above are driven and drive is transmitted to the remaining two wheels via two tracks,
- all four robot wheels are independently driven.

It is assumed that robot is under action of the following external forces:

- ground reaction forces ${}^R\mathbf{F}_{Ai} = [{}^R F_{Aix}, {}^R F_{Aiy}, {}^R F_{Aiz}]^T$ acting on each wheel,
- gravity force ${}^R\mathbf{G} = m_R\,{}^R\mathbf{g}$, where m_R denotes total mass of the robot.

Reaction forces ${}^R\mathbf{F}_{Aix}$ and ${}^R\mathbf{F}_{Aiy}$, $i = \{1, 2, 3, 4\}$ acting in plane of wheel-ground contact are shown in Fig. 5. For simplicity, in further considerations the subscript A in designations of reaction forces and moments of reaction forces will be omitted.

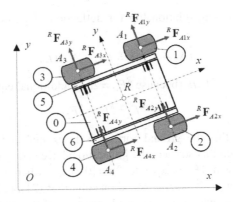

Fig. 5. Reaction forces acting on the PIAP SCOUT robot in the plane of wheel-ground contact

Force of gravity vector $^R\mathbf{G}$ is a function of gravitational acceleration vector $^R\mathbf{g} = [^Rg_x, {}^Rg_y, {}^Rg_z]^T$ and it is applied at the robot mass center, whose position is described by the vector $^R\mathbf{r}_{CM} = [^Rx_{CM}, {}^Ry_{CM}, {}^Rz_{CM}]^T$.

Under action of the mentioned forces, according to the Newton's 2nd law, the robot moves with acceleration $^R\mathbf{a}_{CM}^O = [^Ra_{CMx}^O, {}^Ra_{CMy}^O, {}^Ra_{CMz}^O]^T$.

For all configurations of the robot drive system, the following dynamic equations of motion of the robot mass centre are valid:

$$m_R \, {}^Ra_{CMx}^O = \sum_{i=1}^{4} {}^RF_{ix} + m_R \, {}^Rg_x, \tag{19}$$

$$m_R \, {}^Ra_{CMy}^O = \sum_{i=1}^{4} {}^RF_{iy} + m_R \, {}^Rg_y, \tag{20}$$

$$m_R \, {}^Ra_{CMz}^O = \sum_{i=1}^{4} {}^RF_{iz} + m_R \, {}^Rg_z. \tag{21}$$

On the assumption that the robot does not rotate about Rx and Ry axes, it is possible to write the following two equations of equilibrium of moments of force about $R'x$ and $R'y$ axes, which are situated within the wheel-ground contact plane:

$$m_R({}^Ra_{CMy}^O - {}^Rg_y)(r + {}^Rz_{CG}) + m_R \, {}^Rg_z \, {}^Ry_{CM} + ({}^RF_{1z} + {}^RF_{3z} - {}^RF_{2z} - {}^RF_{4z})W/2 = 0, \tag{22}$$

$$m_R(-{}^Ra_{CMx}^O + {}^Rg_x)(r + {}^Rz_{CG}) - m_R \, {}^Rg_z \, {}^Rx_{CM} + ({}^RF_{3z} + {}^RF_{4z} - {}^RF_{1z} - {}^RF_{2z})L/2 = 0. \tag{23}$$

Taking into account the assumptions:

- the robot mobile platform is a rigid body,
- points of wheel-ground contact lie in one plane,
- wheel tires deflect directly proportional to reaction forces acting along direction normal to the ground and inversely proportional to their stiffnesses k (tire stiffnesses are assumed the same for all wheels),

one can write the following relationship for deflection of particular flexible wheels (with rubber tires):

$$(\Delta_3 - \Delta_1)/L = (\Delta_4 - \Delta_2)/L. \tag{24}$$

After substituting $\Delta_i = {}^R F_{iz}/k$ (because ${}^R F_{iz} = \Delta_i k$) additional equation is obtained:

$${}^R F_{3z} - {}^R F_{1z} = {}^R F_{4z} - {}^R F_{2z}. \tag{25}$$

On the assumption that the ground surface is horizontal and even as well as all wheels have contact with this surface, the gravitational acceleration vector expressed in the robot coordinate system $\{R\}$ is equal to: ${}^R \mathbf{g} = [0, 0, g]^T$, where $g = 9.81$ (m/s^2).

In this case, after putting ${}^R y_{CM} = 0$, based on equations (21), (22), (23) and (25) it is possible to determine normal components of reactions of the ground (on the assumption that accelerations of the robot mass center are known ${}^R a^O_{CMx}$, ${}^R a^O_{CMy}$, ${}^R a^O_{CMz}$, and ${}^R a^O_{CMz} = 0$) in the form:

$${}^R F_{1z} = m_R \left((-{}^R a^O_{CMx}/(2L) - {}^R a^O_{CMy}/(2W))(r + {}^R z_{CM}) + g(1/4 + {}^R x_{CM}/(2L)) \right), \tag{26}$$

$${}^R F_{2z} = m_R \left((-{}^R a^O_{CMx}/(2L) + {}^R a^O_{CMy}/(2W))(r + {}^R z_{CM}) + g(1/4 + {}^R x_{CM}/(2L)) \right), \tag{27}$$

$${}^R F_{3z} = m_R \left(({}^R a^O_{CMx}/(2L) - {}^R a^O_{CMy}/(2W))(r + {}^R z_{CM}) + g(1/4 - {}^R x_{CM}/(2L)) \right), \tag{28}$$

$${}^R F_{4z} = m_R \left(({}^R a^O_{CMx}/(2L) + {}^R a^O_{CMy}/(2W))(r + {}^R z_{CM}) + g(1/4 - {}^R x_{CM}/(2L)) \right). \tag{29}$$

For calculation of values of normal components of ground reaction forces, knowledge of motion parameters of the robot mass center CM and of geometric centers of wheels, that is, characteristic points Ai, is necessary. In the calculations, values of those parameters from the previous calculation step, that is, from time instant $t - \Delta t$, where Δt is the adopted time step, are used. In the first calculation step, known initial conditions are taken into account.

Current value of longitudinal slip factor for the i-th wheel is determined from the formula:

$$\lambda_i = \begin{cases} 0 & \text{for } {}^{Ai} v^O_x = 0 \text{ and } v_{oi} = 0, \\ ({}^{Ai} v^O_x - v_{oi})/\max({}^{Ai} v^O_x, v_{oi}) & \text{for other } {}^{Ai} v^O_x \text{ and } v_{oi}, \end{cases} \tag{30}$$

where $v_{oi} = \dot{\theta}_i r_i$ and ${}^{Ai} v^O_x$ are respectively velocity at the wheel circumference and longitudinal component of velocity of wheel geometric center.

Current value of the tire adhesion coefficient on longitudinal direction for this wheel is calculated using Kiencke tire model [12] modified by the author, that is, from the formula:

$$\mu_{ix} = \begin{cases} \dfrac{2\mu_p \lambda_p \lambda_i}{\lambda_p^2 + \lambda_i^2} & \text{for } |\lambda_i| \leq \lambda_p, \\ a_{\lambda x} \lambda_i + b_{\lambda x} \operatorname{sgn}(\lambda_i) & \text{for } |\lambda_i| > \lambda_p, \end{cases} \tag{31}$$

where λ_p denotes the value of longitudinal slip corresponding to the value of maximum tire adhesion coefficient μ_p (Fig. 6).

Modification of the original Kiencke dependency is connected with calculation of the tire adhesion coefficient for $|\lambda_i| > \lambda_p$. The $\mu_{ix}(\lambda_i)$ characteristics is approximated by straight lines, so that, for longitudinal slip equal to +/–100%, the adhesion coefficient factor reaches a value corresponding to the sliding tire adhesion coefficient.

Coefficients $a_{\lambda x}$ and $b_{\lambda x}$ in (31) are described by formulas:

$$a_{\lambda x} = \frac{\mu_p - \mu_k}{\lambda_p - \lambda_{max}}, \qquad b_{\lambda x} = \mu_p - a_x \lambda_p, \tag{32}$$

where μ_k denotes sliding tire adhesion coefficient (identical to coefficient of kinetic friction), and $\lambda_{max} = 100\%$ is a maximum value of the longitudinal slip analyzed in the present work.

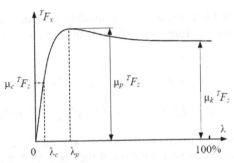

Fig. 6. Longitudinal force vs. longitudinal slip dependency for a rubber tire [18]

Longitudinal component of ground reaction force for the i-th wheel depends on current value of the adhesion coefficient on longitudinal direction, according to relationship:

$$^R F_{ix} = \mu_{ix}\,^R F_{iz}. \tag{33}$$

In turn, the current value of the lateral slip angle for i-th wheel is determined from the formula:

$$\alpha_i = \begin{cases} 0 & \text{for } ^{Ai}v_y^O = 0, \\ \arctan 2(^{Ai}v_y^O, |^{Ai}v_x^O|) & \text{for } |^{Ai}v_x^O| > 0, \end{cases} \tag{34}$$

where $^{Ai}v_x^O$ and $^{Ai}v_y^O$ are respectively longitudinal and transversal velocity of the geometric center of the i-th wheel.

Knowing the lateral slip angle it is possible to calculate current value of the adhesion coefficient on lateral direction for i-th wheel. To this end the following approximate relationship (as compared to H.B. Pacejka model [10]) is introduced:

$$\mu_{iy} = -\mu_{ymax} \sin(\alpha_i), \tag{35}$$

where μ_{ymax} denotes maximum value of adhesion coefficient on lateral direction (it is assumed that $\mu_p \geq \mu_{ymax} \geq \mu_k$).

Hence, lateral component of the ground reaction force for i-th wheel is calculated from the formula:

$$^R F_{iy} = \mu_{iy}\,^R F_{iz}. \tag{36}$$

For known components of longitudinal and lateral components of ground reaction forces for particular wheels, it is possible to calculate values of accelerations on longitudinal and lateral direction using equations (19) and (20):

$$^R a_{CMx}^O = \sum_{i=1}^{4} {^R F_{ix}} / m_R, \tag{37}$$

$$^R a_{CMy}^O = \sum_{i=1}^{4} {^R F_{iy}} / m_R. \tag{38}$$

For the robot mobile platform, it is also possible to write the following dynamic equation of motion resulting from its rotation about Rz axis with angular acceleration $^R\ddot\varphi_{0z}^O$:

$$I_{Rz}\,^R\ddot\varphi_{0z}^O = \sum_{i=1}^{4} {^R T_{iz}} - ({^R F_{1x}} + {^R F_{3x}})(W/2 - {^R y_{CM}}) + ({^R F_{2x}} + {^R F_{4x}})(W/2 + {^R y_{CM}}) +$$
$$+ ({^R F_{1y}} + {^R F_{2y}})(L/2 - {^R x_{CM}}) - ({^R F_{3y}} + {^R F_{4y}})(L/2 + {^R x_{CM}}), \tag{39}$$

where: I_{Rz} – mass moment of inertia of the robot about the Rz axis, $^R T_{iz}$ – the so-called self-aligning torque associated with rotation of the i-th wheel about Rz axis, resulting from friction forces acting in the tire-ground contact.

After making assumption that $^R T_{iz} \approx 0$, that is, the self-aligning torque is negligibly small in comparison to the remaining moments of force acting about the Rz axis, and using equation (39) it is possible to determine value of the angular acceleration associated with robot rotation about Rz axis in the form:

$$^R\ddot\varphi_{0z}^O = \left(-({^R F_{1x}} + {^R F_{3x}})(W/2 - {^R y_{CM}}) + ({^R F_{2x}} + {^R F_{4x}})(W/2 + {^R y_{CM}}) + \right.$$
$$+ ({^R F_{1y}} + {^R F_{2y}})(L/2 - {^R x_{CM}}) - ({^R F_{3y}} + {^R F_{4y}})(L/2 + {^R x_{CM}})\big)/I_{Rz}, \tag{40}$$

and then calculate, by integration, the value of angular velocity of the robot mobile platform about this axis, that is $^R\dot\varphi_{0z}^O$.

Next, based on equations (11) it is possible to calculate values of velocities $^R v_{Rx}^O$ and $^R v_{Ry}^O$. In turn, after using equation (12) one can determine values of velocities of characteristic points Ai. To do so, one may assume that $^R x_C = {^R x_B} = 0$, that is the x coordinate describing position of the instantaneous centre of rotation for the mobile platform in the robot coordinate system $\{R\}$ is equal to 0.

For each of the robot wheels it is then possible to write dynamic equation of motion associated with wheel spin:

$$I_{Wy}\,\ddot\theta_i = \tau_i + {^R T_{ti}} - {^R F_{ix}} r - {^R F_{iz}} r\, f_r\, \mathrm{sgn}(\dot\theta_i) - \tau_f\, \mathrm{sgn}(\dot\theta_i), \tag{41}$$

where: I_{Wy} – mass moment of inertia of the wheel about its spin axis, τ_i – a driving torque, τ_f – a torque of friction forces in a kinematic pair, $^RT_{ti}$ – a moment of force in the toothed belt, f_r – coefficient of rolling resistance, $\dot\theta_i$ and $\ddot\theta_i$ – angular velocity and acceleration of spin of that wheel, respectively.

In place of the signum function $\text{sgn}(\dot\theta_i)$, one may introduce a $\tanh(k_{\dot\theta}\dot\theta_i)$ function, which is better from the point of view of simulation, where the coefficient $k_{\dot\theta} > 0$ should be the larger, the more the function should be similar to $\text{sgn}(\dot\theta_i)$.

Moments of force τ_i and $^RT_{ti}$ depend on configuration of the robot drive system:

- for independent driving of rear wheels:

$$^RT_{ti} = 0, \qquad \tau_p = 0, \qquad p = \{1, 2\}, \tag{42}$$

- for the hybrid drive system (i.e., with toothed belts):

$$^RT_{tp} = \tau_a/2, \qquad ^RT_{ta} = -\tau_a/2, \qquad a = \{3, 4\}, \qquad p = \{1, 2\}, \tag{43}$$

- for independent driving of all four wheels:

$$^RT_{ti} = 0, \qquad i = a = \{1, 2, 3, 4\}, \tag{44}$$

where the subscript a is valid for driven wheels, and the subscript p for free wheels.

After taking into account the above relationships, it is possible to determine the following quantities from equation (41):

- driving torques τ_a for the driven wheels, based on desired angular parameters of their spin, i.e., $\dot\theta_a$ and $\ddot\theta_a$ (inverse dynamics problem) and angular parameters of rotation of free wheels, that is, $\dot\theta_p$ and $\ddot\theta_p$ (in case they are available);
- angular parameters of wheel spin, i.e., $\dot\theta_i$ and $\ddot\theta_i$ based on driving torques τ_a acting on the driven wheels (forward dynamics problem).

Eventually, the following solutions are obtained:

- for independent driving of either rear or front wheels:

$$\tau_a = I_{Wy}\ddot\theta_a + \tau_f\,\text{sgn}(\dot\theta_a) + {}^RF_{ax}r + {}^RF_{az}r\,f_r\,\text{sgn}(\dot\theta_a), \tag{45}$$

$$\ddot\theta_a = \left(\tau_a - {}^RF_{ax}r - {}^RF_{az}r\,f_r\,\text{sgn}(\dot\theta_a) - \tau_f\,\text{sgn}(\dot\theta_a)\right)/I_{Wy}, \tag{46}$$

$$\ddot\theta_p = \left(-{}^RF_{px}r - {}^RF_{pz}r\,f_r\,\text{sgn}(\dot\theta_p) - \tau_f\,\text{sgn}(\dot\theta_p)\right)/I_{Wy}, \tag{47}$$

- for the hybrid drive system (with toothed belts):

$$\tau_a = \tau_p = 2\left(I_{Wy}\ddot\theta_a + \tau_f\,\text{sgn}(\dot\theta_a) + {}^RF_{ax}r + {}^RF_{az}r\,f_r\,\text{sgn}(\dot\theta_a)\right), \tag{48}$$

$$\ddot\theta_a = \left(\tau_a/2 - {}^RF_{ax}r - {}^RF_{az}r\,f_r\,\text{sgn}(\dot\theta_a) - \tau_f\,\text{sgn}(\dot\theta_a)\right)/I_{Wy}, \tag{49}$$

$$\ddot{\theta}_p = \left(\tau_a/2 - {}^R F_{px} r - {}^R F_{pz} r \, f_r \, \mathrm{sgn}(\dot{\theta}_p) - \tau_f \, \mathrm{sgn}(\dot{\theta}_p)\right)/I_{Wy}, \tag{50}$$

- for independent driving of all four wheels:

$$\tau_a = I_{Wy} \ddot{\theta}_a + \tau_f \, \mathrm{sgn}(\dot{\theta}_a) + {}^R F_{ax} r + {}^R F_{az} r \, f_r \, \mathrm{sgn}(\dot{\theta}_a), \tag{51}$$

$$\ddot{\theta}_a = \left(\tau_a - {}^R F_{ax} r - {}^R F_{az} r \, f_r \, \mathrm{sgn}(\dot{\theta}_a) - \tau_f \, \mathrm{sgn}(\dot{\theta}_a)\right)/I_{Wy}. \tag{52}$$

The above equations for torques τ_a can be written for all driven wheels in the compact form, better suited for synthesis of control systems:

$$\mathbf{Y}\,\mathbf{a} = \tau, \tag{53}$$

where $\mathbf{a}$ is a vector of parameters of the dynamics model of the robot, and the matrix $\mathbf{Y}$ depends on current robot motion parameters.

In order to make the process of development of control systems easier, the model of robot dynamics should be linear with respect to the vector of robot parameters $\mathbf{a}$.

For this reason, one may assume for simplification, that the adhesion coefficient μ_{ix} for tire and ground varies according to the Kiencke model [12], that is, based on the formula:

$$\mu_{ix} = 2\mu_p \lambda_p \lambda_i /(\lambda_p^2 + \lambda_i^2). \tag{54}$$

Equation (53) can be written in expanded form for the PIAP SCOUT robot [19] with hybrid drive system, in which rear wheels are driven, in the form of two scalar equations:

$$2\Big(a_1 \ddot{\theta}_3 + a_2 \, \mathrm{tgh}(k_{\dot{\theta}} \dot{\theta}_3) + 2\lambda_p \lambda_3 /(\lambda_p^2 + \lambda_3^2)(a_3 + a_4 {}^R a_{Rx}^O - a_5 {}^R a_{Ry}^O) + \\ + (a_6 + a_7 {}^R a_{Rx}^O - a_8 {}^R a_{Ry}^O) \, \mathrm{tgh}(k_{\dot{\theta}} \dot{\theta}_3)\Big) = \tau_3, \tag{55}$$

$$2\Big(a_1 \ddot{\theta}_4 + a_2 \, \mathrm{tgh}(k_{\dot{\theta}} \dot{\theta}_4) + 2\lambda_p \lambda_4 /(\lambda_p^2 + \lambda_4^2)(a_3 + a_4 {}^R a_{Rx}^O + a_5 {}^R a_{Ry}^O) + \\ + (a_6 + a_7 {}^R a_{Rx}^O + a_8 {}^R a_{Ry}^O) \, \mathrm{tgh}(k_{\dot{\theta}} \dot{\theta}_4)\Big) = \tau_4, \tag{56}$$

where the parameters of the robot dynamics model, which occur in equations, are equal to:

$$a_1 = b_1 = I_{Wy}, \qquad a_2 = b_2 = \tau_f, \tag{57}$$

$$a_3 = b_3 b_4 = \mu_p m_R g \, r(1/4 - {}^R x_{CM} /(2L)), \qquad a_4 = b_3 b_5 = \mu_p m_R r(r + {}^R z_{CM})/(2L), \tag{58}$$

$$a_5 = b_3 b_6 = \mu_p m_R r(r + {}^R z_{CM})/(2W), \qquad a_6 = b_4 b_7 = m_R g \, r(1/4 - {}^R x_{CM} /(2L)) f_r, \tag{59}$$

$$a_7 = b_5 b_7 = m_R r(r + {}^R z_{CM})/(2L) f_r, \qquad a_8 = b_6 b_7 = m_R r(r + {}^R z_{CM})/(2W) f_r, \tag{60}$$

and:

$$b_3 = \mu_p, \quad b_4 = m_R g \, r(1/4 - {}^R x_{CM} /(2L)), \quad b_5 = m_R r(r + {}^R z_{CM})/(2L), \tag{61}$$

$$b_6 = m_R r(r + {}^R z_{CM})/(2W), \qquad b_7 = f_r. \tag{62}$$

Additionally, in place of $\mathrm{sgn}(\dot{\theta}_i)$ function one introduces the $\mathrm{tgh}(k_{\dot{\theta}}\dot{\theta}_i)$ function.

Based on the known parameters a_3–a_8, values of components of normal and longitudinal (for the driven wheels) ground reaction forces can be calculated in the form:

$${}^R F_{1z} = (a_6 - a_7\,{}^R a_{Rx}^O - a_8\,{}^R a_{Ry}^O)/(r\,f_r), \quad {}^R F_{2z} = (a_6 - a_7\,{}^R a_{Rx}^O + a_8\,{}^R a_{Ry}^O)/(r\,f_r), \tag{63}$$

$${}^R F_{3z} = (a_6 + a_7\,{}^R a_{Rx}^O - a_8\,{}^R a_{Ry}^O)/(r\,f_r), \quad {}^R F_{4z} = (a_6 + a_7\,{}^R a_{Rx}^O + a_8\,{}^R a_{Ry}^O)/(r\,f_r), \tag{64}$$

$${}^R F_{3x} = \mu_{3x}\,{}^R F_{3z} = 2\lambda_p \lambda_3 /(\lambda_p^2 + \lambda_3^2)(a_3 + a_4\,{}^R a_{Rx}^O - a_5\,{}^R a_{Ry}^O)/r, \tag{65}$$

$${}^R F_{4x} = \mu_{4x}\,{}^R F_{4z} = 2\lambda_p \lambda_3 /(\lambda_p^2 + \lambda_3^2)(a_3 + a_4\,{}^R a_{Rx}^O + a_5\,{}^R a_{Ry}^O)/r. \tag{66}$$

on condition that values of parameters r, f_r and μ_{ix} are known.

During analysis of equations (55)–(56) it can be noticed that for estimation of driving torques τ_3 and τ_4 for the configuration of the robot with the hybrid drive system, knowledge of values of the robot motion parameters like $\ddot{\theta}_3, \dot{\theta}_4, \ddot{\theta}_3, \ddot{\theta}_4, {}^R a_{Rx}^O, {}^R a_{Ry}^O$ and of wheel slips λ_3 and λ_4 (that follow from the previous quantities) are necessary. In those equations neither the angular acceleration ${}^R \ddot{\varphi}_{0z}^O$ of mobile platform rotation nor the mass moment of inertia I_{Rz} occur explicitly. Those quantities, however, affect other motion parameters of the robot.

2.4 Model of Friction in Kinematic Pairs

In research works usually the phenomenon of friction in robot kinematic pairs, e.g. in axles of wheels, is neglected, which is justified by small influence of this friction on robot motion. However, this influence becomes important for small velocities of robot motion, especially at the start and end of motion. In this case, the phenomenon of friction in kinematic pairs can lead to development of moments of values similar to the values of driving torques.

In the robot kinematic pairs the continuously differentiable friction model described in [9] may be used. According to it, the friction coefficient is assumed to have the following non-linear parameterizable form:

$$f_i = \gamma_{i.1}\left(\tanh(\gamma_{i.2}\dot{\theta}_i) - \tanh(\gamma_{i.3}\dot{\theta}_i)\right) + \gamma_{i.4}\tanh(\gamma_{i.5}\dot{\theta}_i) + \gamma_{i.6}\dot{\theta}_i, \tag{67}$$

where: $\gamma_{i.j}$ – positive constant parameters, i – kinematic pair number, $i = \{1,2,3,4\}$, j – parameter number, $j = \{1,2,...,6\}$, and the unit of $\dot{\theta}_i$ is (rad/s).

The static coefficient of friction μ_{si} is approximated by the term: $\gamma_{i.1} + \gamma_{i.4}$ whereas the kinetic one, i.e., μ_{ki} equals to $\gamma_{i.4}$. The term $\tanh(\gamma_{i.2}\dot{\theta}_i) - \tanh(\gamma_{i.3}\dot{\theta}_i)$ captures the Stribeck effect where the friction coefficient decreases from the static coefficient of friction with increasing slip velocity near the origin. A viscous dissipation term is given by $\gamma_{i.6}\dot{\theta}_i$. The Coulomb friction coefficient is modeled by the term $\gamma_{i.4}\tanh(\gamma_{i.5}\dot{\theta}_i)$. [9]

The friction torques in kinematic pairs are determined from the following relationship:

$$\tau_{fi} = -\|\mathbf{R}_i\| r_{fi} f_i, \tag{68}$$

where: $\|\mathbf{R}_i\|$ – magnitude of reaction force in the kinematic pair, r_{fi} – radius of friction in the kinematic pair.

2.5   Model of Robot Drive Units

The described simplified model of robot dynamics can be also enhanced with the model of its drive units. It is particularly important, when one wants to connect the model of robot dynamics (treated as a multi-body system) with a control system. In such case the drive unit model is an intermediate link between the control system and the robot dynamics model. The drive unit model can be used for solution of both forward and inverse dynamics problems.

It is assumed that:

- each of the robot drive units consists of identical DC motor, encoder, and transmission system,
- robot drive units are not self-locking, that is, they can freely turn under the influence of external moments of force,
- mass moments of inertia of the rotating elements of the servomechanisms (DC motor, encoder and gear unit) are small in comparison to mass moments of inertia of the driven parts of the robot (wheels), that is why they are neglected.

The DC motor model of the ith drive unit is described by the following dependences:

$$\frac{di_i}{dt} = \left(u_i - k_e n_d \dot{\theta}_i - R_d i_i\right)/L_d, \tag{69}$$

$$\tau_i = \eta_d n_d k_m i_i, \tag{70}$$

where: u_i – motor voltage input, i_i – rotor current, L_d, R_d – respectively inductance and resistance of the rotor, k_e – electromotive force constant, k_m – motor torque coefficient, n_d – gear ratio of the transmission system, η_d – efficiency factor of the transmission system.

After transforming the above equations to the form:

$$i_i = \tau_i /(\eta_d n_d k_m), \tag{71}$$

$$u_i = k_e n_d \dot{\theta}_i + L_d \frac{di_i}{dt} + R_d i_i, \tag{72}$$

one can also determine current flowing in the armature winding and the value of motor input voltage necessary for realization of motion of the wheel with desired angular velocity and with desired driving torque exerted by the wheel.

3 Conclusions and Future Works

In the present work the dynamics model of the four-wheeled robot with non-steered wheels is presented for three versions of the drive system. The most attention is devoted to the robot configuration with the hybrid drive system.

The robot model was developed based on results of empirical investigations of PIAP SCOUT robot [19] presented, for example, in works [14, 15].

As a part of this publication, author makes available the robot model implemented in the Matlab/Simulink environment, whose parameters were assumed for the version of the PIAP SCOUT robot [19] with hybrid drive system in which rear wheels are driven ([20] website).

Future works will include application of the robot dynamics model in synthesis and investigations of control systems, including those based on robot dynamics model.

Acknowledgements. The work has been realized as a part of the project entitled "Dynamics modeling of a four-wheeled mobile robot and tracking control of its motion with limitation of wheels slip". The project is financed from the means of National Science Centre of Poland granted on the basis of decision number DEC-2011/03/B/ST7/02532.

References

1. Barbosa de Oliveira Vaz, D.A., Inoue, R.S., Grassi Jr., V.: Kinodynamic Motion Planning of a Skid-Steering Mobile Robot Using RRTs. In: 2010 Latin American Robotics Symposium and Intelligent Robotics Meeting (2010)
2. Dąbek, P., Szosland, A.: Identification of rotational properties of a non-pneumatic tyre of a mobile robot. Pomiary Automatyka Robotyka 2(2011), 495–503 (2011) (in Polish: Identyfikacja parametrów skrętnych opony niepneumatycznej robota mobilnego)
3. Hendzel, Z.: An adaptive critic neural network for motion control of a wheeled mobile robot. Nonlinear Dynamics 50, 849–855 (2007)
4. Hua, J., et al.: Modeling and Control of Wheeled Mobile Robot in Constrained Environment Based on Hybrid Control Framework. In: Proceedings of the 2009 IEEE International Conference on Robotics and Biomimetics, Guilin, China (2009)
5. Iagnemma, K., Dubowsky, S.: Mobile Robots in Rough Terrain. Estimation, Motion Planning, and Control with Application to Planetary Rovers. STAR, vol. 12. Springer, Heidelberg (2004)
6. Kasprzyczak, L., Trenczek, S., Cader, M.: Robot for monitoring hazardous environments as a mechatronic product, Journal of Automation. Mobile Robotics & Intelligent Systems 6(4), 57–64 (2012)
7. Kozłowski, K., Pazderski, D.: Practical stabilization of 4WD skid-steering mobile robot – A kinematic-based Approach. In: 2006 IEEE 3rd International Conference on Mechatronics, Budapest, pp. 519–524 (2006)
8. Lenain, R., et al.: Mobile robot control in presence of sliding - Application to agricultural vehicle path tracking. In: Proceedings of the 45th IEEE Conference on Decision & Control, Manchester Grand Hyatt Hotel, San Diego, CA, USA (2006)

9. Makkar, C., Dixon, W.E., Sawyer, W.G., Hu, G.: A New Continuously Differentiable Friction Model for Control Systems Design. In: IEEE/ASME International Conference on Advanced Intelligent Mechatronics, Monterey, California, USA (2005)
10. Pacejka, H.B.: Tire and Vehicle Dynamics, 2nd edn. SAE International and Elsevier (2005)
11. Padhy, P.K., et al.: Modeling and Position Control of Mobile Robot. In: The 11th IEEE International Workshop on Advanced Motion Control, Nagaoka, Japan (2010)
12. Ping, L.Y.: Slip Modelling, Estimation and Control of Omnidirectional Wheeled Mobile Robots with Powered Caster Wheels. Doctorial Thesis, National University of Singapore, Singapore (2009)
13. Tian, Y., Sidek, N., Sarkar, N.: Modeling and control of a nonholonomic Wheeled Mobile Robot with wheel slip dynamics. In: IEEE Symposium on Computational Intelligence in Control and Automation, CICA 2009, pp. 7–14 (2009)
14. Trojnacki, M.: Dynamics modeling of wheeled mobile robots, OW PIAP, Warszawa (2013) (in Polish: Modelowanie dynamiki mobilnych robotów kołowych)
15. Trojnacki, M., Dąbek, P., Kacprzyk, J., Hendzel, Z.: Trajectory Tracking Control of a Four-Wheeled Mobile Robot with Yaw Rate Linear Controller. In: Szewczyk, R., Zieliński, C., Kaliczyńska, M. (eds.) Recent Advances in Automation, Robotics and Measuring Techniques. AISC, vol. 267, pp. 507–522. Springer, Heidelberg (2014)
16. Tu, C., et al.: Motion Control and Stabilization of a Skid-Steering Mobile Robot. In: 2nd International Conference on Adaptive Science & Technology, pp. 325–330 (2009)
17. Wang, D., Low, C.B.: Modeling and Analysis of Skidding and Slipping in Wheeled Mobile Robots - Control Design Perspective. IEEE Transactions on Robotics 24(3), 676–687 (2008)
18. Wong, J.Y.: Theory of Ground Vehicles, 3rd edn. Wiley-Interscience (2001)
19. Mobile robots for counter-terrorism (PIAP), http://www.antiterrorism.eu
20. Maciej, T.: Trojnacki: Mobile robots – models, animations and movies, http://www.mtrojnacki.republika.pl/MobileRobots/index.html

Motion Stabilization System of a Four-Wheeled Mobile Robot for Teleoperation Mode: Experimental Investigations in Indoor Environment

Maciej Trojnacki[1], Przemysław Dąbek[1], Janusz Kacprzyk[1], and Zenon Hendzel[2]

[1] Industrial Research Institute for Automation and Measurements PIAP, Warsaw, Poland
{mtrojnacki,pdabek,jkacprzyk}@piap.pl
[2] Rzeszów University of Technology, Rzeszów, Poland
zenhen@prz.edu.pl

Abstract. The paper is concerned with the problem of straight-line motion stabilization of a wheeled mobile robot with non-steered wheels. This system is dedicated for teleoperation mode of the robot and aims at improvement of control experience of a human operator. The structure of the robot motion stabilization system based on a PD regulator with feedback from actual linear velocity and yaw rate of a robot body is proposed. The motion stabilization system was implemented using a low-cost MEMS Inertial Measurement Unit and the PIAP SCOUT four-wheeled robot with non-steered wheels. In the present work the motion stabilization system is implemented in a form reduced to yaw angle stabilization only, with stabilization of linear velocity not taken into account. Reliable functioning of the linear velocity stabilization (e.g. wheel slip reduction) based on measurement signals from the low-cost IMU requires additional research. Functioning of the proposed robot motion stabilization system was verified in experimental research. Experiments were conducted for various robot velocities in indoor environment on a horizontal and even ground. Results of investigations without and with the motion stabilization system were compared. A significant improvement in accuracy of realization of desired motion was observed in the case when the motion stabilization system was active.

Keywords: wheeled mobile robot, teleoperation, motion stabilization, linear controller, INS technique, MEMS gyroscope, indoor environment, empirical research.

1 Introduction

Among commercially available mobile robots a significant group consists of robots controlled remotely by a human operator, that is, teleoperated robots. Most often the locomotion system of those robots is based on wheels [1]–[3] or tracks [4] because of simplicity of design of this type of locomotion system and simplicity of control as compared to solutions based on discrete locomotion (walking and hybrid robots). This class of robots finds its application especially in safety and security tasks associated, for instance, with neutralization of dangerous objects [5].

© Springer International Publishing Switzerland 2015
D. Filev et al. (eds.), *Intelligent Systems' 2014*,
Advances in Intelligent Systems and Computing 323, DOI: 10.1007/978-3-319-11310-4_11

Examples of this kind of design are PIAP SCOUT, INSPECTOR, EXPERT and IBIS robots shown in Fig. 1a-c [6], all designed in the Industrial Research Institute for Automation and Measurements PIAP.

a)   b)   c)

Fig. 1. Examples of mobile robots: a – PIAP SCOUT, b – INSPECTOR and EXPERT, c – IBIS

A number of problems are associated with teleoperation of robots. In particular, they are associated with difficulty of assessment of actual robot orientation and distance to an obstacle (dangerous object to be taken) in case when robot operator has feedback from camera images only. The problem becomes even more severe when robot is in motion, especially, when robot operator working in conditions of intense stress has to reach the destination as quickly as possible. During controlling the robot on the way to the assumed destination, one of the most frequently executed maneuvers is to go along a straight line. However, during realization of the straight line run, the robot may tend to pull to either side, which may be caused by a number of factors, e.g. limited resolution of drive control and of measurement of actual angular velocities of spin of wheels by wheel encoders, non-uniformities in drive transmission between robot sides, differences in wheel-ground contact properties, etc. This pull phenomenon is especially arduous for the robot operator in case of maneuvering in a limited space, and requires from the operator a constant and cautious correction of the control signal, which in case of limited possibility of observation of the environment by cameras is a difficult task that requires substantial experience.

The mentioned problems are equally relevant to wheeled and tracked robots, but in the present work we focus on solving this problem for a wheeled robot. At first let us note that because of wheel slips, robot motion stabilization cannot be realized based on regulation of angular velocities of spin of wheels only. Because robot pulling occurs for identical angular velocities of spin of wheels at both robot sides, the control system is not able to discover this phenomenon and counteract accordingly. This form of control system will not discover the occurrence of wheel slips and in consequence will not reduce them. Therefore, it is necessary to measure actual velocities of robot body (linear and angular) and introduce additional closed-loop controller for angular and linear velocities.

For measurement of those velocities it is possible to make use of inertial measurement technique based on accelerometers and gyroscopes manufactured in micro electromechanical systems (MEMS) technology [7]. With measurement of robot motion parameters of a mobile robot using inertial measurement units (IMU) is associated a number of problems including accumulation of errors caused by integration of linear acceleration to determine linear velocity or integration of angular velocity to determine Euler angles [8], [9].

However, if the aim is limited only to stabilization of the yaw angle of the robot body, then only measurement of body yaw rate is necessary. This measurement can be realized by means of a single-axis gyroscope and is not significantly influenced by roll and pitch angles of the robot body. Moreover, the task of stabilization in the described form can be realized based on the classic PID control.

It can be noticed that PID controllers are used in the context of tracking control of robots alone [10], or as a part of hybrid control structures [11], [12], but no examples of their use to robot body yaw angle stabilization in its longitudinal motion have been found. Moreover, in case of mobile robots, IMUs are in most cases used in algorithms of data fusion with other systems of motion measurement. An exception is the work [10], where the problem of tracking control using PD controller with feedback from IMU is analyzed. In turn, in the interesting work [13] authors discuss the problem of stabilization of yaw angle of the wheeled robot body, but they do not use the IMU. Article [14] covers robot body yaw rate control by means of a joystick with force feedback, but in the control structure vision sensor is used and not the IMU.

In the literature there was no example of the wheeled robot motion stabilization system, which would join the following features: yaw angle stabilization of a robot moving in teleoperation mode by means of a linear PID controller and with use of inertial measurement unit. The aim of the present work is to solve this kind of problem. The solution will be verified in empirical experiment.

2   Four-Wheeled Mobile Robot and Experimental Setup

In the present work a four-wheeled PIAP SCOUT mobile robot designed and produced in the Industrial Research Institute for Automation and Measurements PIAP, Poland [6] is analyzed. The robot has been adapted to realization of experimental research in such way that it was equipped with additional frame to allow installation of laptop and sensors (Fig. 2a).

The PIAP SCOUT robot has two rear wheels driven independently by DC servomotors with gear units and encoders. Drive is transmitted from rear to front wheels by means of toothed belts. Tires are made of viton rubber with foam filling (non-pneumatic tires).

Kinematic structure of the robot is shown in Fig. 2b. It is possible to distinguish the following main components of the robot: 0 – body with frame for installation of research equipment, 1-4 – wheels, 5-6 – toothed belts.

The most important robot parameters are ($i = \{1, ..., 4\}$):

- dimensions (see Fig. 2b for explanation of symbols): $L = 0.35$ m, $W = 0.386$ m,
- masses of the components: $m_0 = 15.02$ kg, $m_i = 0.66$ kg, $m_5 = m_6 = 0.17$ kg,
- tire unloaded radius $r_i = 0.0965$ m.

On the frame was installed laptop computer connected by means of USB-CAN adapter to robot CAN bus (Controller Area Network), which allowed to:

- impose desired velocities of spin of wheels $\dot{\boldsymbol{\theta}}_d = [\dot{\theta}_{3d}, \dot{\theta}_{4d}]^T$,
- receive actual velocities of spin of wheels $\dot{\boldsymbol{\theta}} = [\dot{\theta}_3, \dot{\theta}_4]^T$.

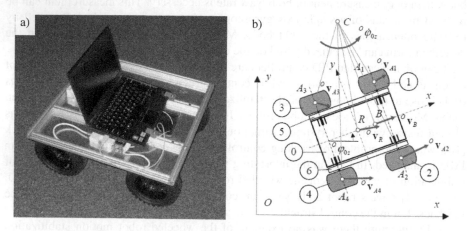

Fig. 2. PIAP SCOUT robot: a – robot adapted to experimental research, b – its kinematic structure ($A_1A_3 = A_2A_4 = L$, $A_1A_2 = A_3A_4 = W$)

The iNEMO sensors' module was mounted to the frame above the point R of the robot (see Fig. 2b) and connected to laptop via USB interface (Universal Serial Bus). Schematic diagram of the measurement and control system is shown in Fig. 3.

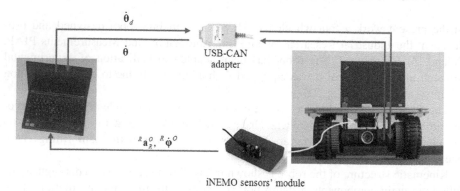

iNEMO sensors' module

Fig. 3. Schematic diagram of measurement and control system used in experimental research

The iNEMO sensors' module enabled measurement of: linear acceleration $^R\mathbf{a}_R^O = [^Ra_{Rx}^O, {}^Ra_{Ry}^O, {}^Ra_{Rz}^O]^T$ of the point R and angular velocity $^R\dot{\boldsymbol{\varphi}}^O = [^R\dot{\varphi}_x^O, {}^R\dot{\varphi}_y^O, {}^R\dot{\varphi}_z^O]^T$ of the robot body 0, both in the robot coordinate system.

The iNEMO sensors' module is based on components manufactured in the micro electromechanical systems (MEMS) technology.

The IMU installed on the robot will be used in the experimental investigations for determination of robot motion parameters. Additionally the angular velocity ${}^{R}\dot{\phi}_{z}^{O}$ obtained from the gyroscope of the iNEMO sensor's module will be used as input into the motion stabilization system.

3 Teleoperation and Motion Stabilization of the Robot

Currently, among the available commercial solutions of wheeled mobile robots prevail solutions, where robots are teleoperated and do not possess any elements of autonomy. This situation is caused mostly by intended applications of those robots. In case of the described earlier robots for safety and security tasks it is justified by the fact that for safety purposes it is human who has to be responsible for robot actions. This is associated with the fact that robot programmer is not able to foresee all threats that can occur during this kind of missions.

For this reason only the autonomy elements should be introduced to the robot motion control system. Moreover, those elements of autonomy should be optional, that is, consciously switched on/off by the robot operator.

A typical control structure for mobile robot motion used in teleoperation mode is shown in Fig. 4a. The following main elements can be distinguished in this structure:

- 'Operator' – a human involved in the teleoperation task,
- 'Control panel' – device with a human-machine interface that enables imposition of motion by the 'Operator',
- 'Wheels' velocity controller' – a system responsible for realization of the desired angular velocities of spin of driven wheels,
- 'Drive units' – assemblies typically made of a DC motor, gear unit and encoder that enable driving of robot wheels.

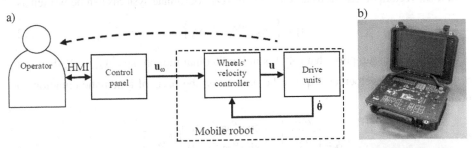

Fig. 4. Teleoperation of robot motion: a – typical structure of control of mobile robot motion used in teleoperation mode, b – example of robot control panel for IBIS robot [6]

The 'Operator' controls robot motion with aid of the 'Control panel', using dedicated human-machine interface (HMI). Elements of this interface are, for instance, buttons, joysticks and display, where views from robot cameras as well as various robot status information are displayed (Fig. 4b). Apart from the view from robot cameras, robot operator sometimes has opportunity of direct visual and audial observation of the robot, which is also marked on the diagram in Fig. 4a with a dashed line arrow.

From the 'Control panel' based on 'Operator' control activities (joystick swinging, buttons pressing) are first calculated and then sent to the robot, current control signals $\mathbf{u}_\omega = [u_{\omega 3},\ u_{\omega 4}]^T$, which are typically angular velocities of spin of driven wheels $\dot{\boldsymbol{\theta}}_d = [\dot{\theta}_{3d}, \dot{\theta}_{4d}]^T$, so $\mathbf{u}_\omega = \dot{\boldsymbol{\theta}}_d$. Based on the current values of angular velocities of spin of the driven wheels $\dot{\boldsymbol{\theta}} = [\dot{\theta}_3, \dot{\theta}_4]^T$ and the corresponding desired values $\dot{\boldsymbol{\theta}}_d = [\dot{\theta}_{3d}, \dot{\theta}_{4d}]^T$, the 'Wheels' velocity controller' determines current control signals $\mathbf{u} = [u_3, u_4]^T$ for 'Drive units'. In the present work the robot embedded 'Wheels' velocity controller' is used with its standard settings, and it is not subject of investigations.

Also a simpler structure of the control system described above is possible, that is, the one in which the 'Wheels' velocity controller' is not present and control signals sent from the 'Control panel' are at once control signals for the 'Drive units', that is $\mathbf{u}_\omega = \mathbf{u}$. This kind of solution is applied, for instance, in the INSPECTOR robot made in PIAP (Fig. 1b) [6] and is justified by the fact that the 'Operator' observes the robot movement directly or using cameras and is able to assess its velocity on their own and correct the desired motion accordingly by angle of deflection of the joystick.

For the purpose of robot motion analysis one may assume that it takes place in the Oxy plane of the fixed coordinate system $\{O\}$ and also the robot moves on horizontal ground. The moving coordinate system, considered as rigidly connected to the robot, is denoted with symbol $\{R\}$. Position and orientation of mobile platform are described by the vector of generalized coordinates:

$$^O\mathbf{q} = [^Ox_R,\ ^Oy_R,\ ^O\varphi_{0z}]^T,\tag{1}$$

where: ^Ox_R, ^Oy_R are coordinates of point R belonging to mobile platform, and $^O\varphi_{0z}$ denotes angle of spin of mobile platform about z axis (yaw angle) with respect to the fixed coordinate system $\{O\}$.

In turn, vectors of generalized velocities in $\{O\}$ coordinate systems can be written as:

$$^O\dot{\mathbf{q}} = \left[^O\dot{x}_R,\ ^O\dot{y}_R,\ ^O\dot{\varphi}_{0z}\right]^T.\tag{2}$$

If one makes assumption that robot is in longitudinal motion, i.e. $^Rv_{Ry}^O = 0$, then vector of generalized velocities $^O\dot{\mathbf{q}}$ can be defined on the basis of kinematic equations of motion in the form:

$$^O\dot{\mathbf{q}} = \begin{bmatrix} ^O\dot{x}_R \\ ^O\dot{y}_R \\ ^O\dot{\varphi}_{0z} \end{bmatrix} = \begin{bmatrix} \cos(^O\varphi_{0z}) & 0 \\ \sin(^O\varphi_{0z}) & 0 \\ 0 & 1 \end{bmatrix} \begin{bmatrix} ^Rv_{Rx}^O \\ ^R\dot{\varphi}_{0z}^O \end{bmatrix},\tag{3}$$

where vector $^R\mathbf{v} = [^Rv_{Rx}^O,\ ^R\dot{\varphi}_{0z}^O]^T$ contains respectively component of velocity of the point R of the robot on the x direction of $\{R\}$ coordinate system and the yaw rate of mobile platform 0.

In connection with the problems described earlier and associated with realization of the desired motion by the robot operator, especially for the straight-line motion, it makes sense to augment the robot control system structure shown in Fig. 4a with additional motion stabilization system. Thus, the robot control system structure can assume the form presented in Fig. 5.

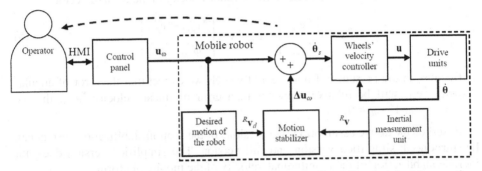

Fig. 5. Proposed structure of the motion stabilization system of mobile robot for teleoperation mode

In addition to the elements discussed earlier it contains a stabilization system, which consists of the following main blocks:

- 'Desired motion of the robot' – based on the control signals $\mathbf{u}_\omega = [u_{\omega3}, u_{\omega4}]^T$ generated at the 'Control panel' by the 'Operator' it determines desired motion of the robot, i.e. velocity vector ${}^R\mathbf{v}_d = [{}^Rv_{Rxd}^O, {}^R\dot{\phi}_{0zd}^O]^T$,
- 'Inertial measurement unit' – determines actual velocities of the robot body in the form of the vector ${}^R\mathbf{v} = [{}^Rv_{Rx}^O, {}^R\dot{\phi}_{0z}^O]^T$,
- 'Motion stabilizer' – determines the vector of control corrections $\Delta\mathbf{u}_\omega = [\Delta u_{\omega3}, \Delta u_{\omega4}]^T$ to achieve the robot motion stabilization,
- Summation block – it adds vector of control signals imposed by the 'Operator' $\mathbf{u}_\omega = [u_{\omega3}, u_{\omega4}]^T$ to the vector of control corrections $\Delta\mathbf{u}_\omega = [\Delta u_{\omega3}, \Delta u_{\omega4}]^T$, which yields vector of desired angular velocities of spin of driven wheels $\dot{\boldsymbol{\theta}}_s = [\dot{\theta}_{3s}, \dot{\theta}_{4s}]^T$, then passed to the 'Wheels' velocity controller'.

Vector of desired velocities of robot motion is determined based on solution of a forward kinematics problem. Solution of this problem in the analyzed case is possible only on the assumption of lack of wheel slips. In view of that one may use the following relationship for this purpose:

$$ {}^R\mathbf{v}_d = \begin{bmatrix} {}^Rv_{Rxd}^O \\ {}^R\dot{\phi}_{0zd}^O \end{bmatrix} = r\begin{bmatrix} 1/2 & 1/2 \\ -1/W & 1/W \end{bmatrix}\begin{bmatrix} \dot{\theta}_{3d} \\ \dot{\theta}_{4d} \end{bmatrix}, \tag{4} $$

which is justified by the fact that the straight-line robot motion is analyzed and it is assumed that angular velocities of spin of wheels imposed by the 'Operator' change in a gentle fashion, that is, only minor values of angular accelerations occur, which prevents the occurrence of large slip values.

Method of determination of motion parameters of robot motion using an inertial measurement unit is described in details in the work [8] and is not the subject of considerations of the present work.

The 'Motion stabilizer' calculates error of robot velocity in the form of vector:

$$
{}^{R}\mathbf{v}_e = \begin{bmatrix} {}^{R}e_{vRx} \\ {}^{R}e_{\omega0z} \end{bmatrix} = {}^{R}\mathbf{v}_d - {}^{R}\mathbf{v} = \begin{bmatrix} {}^{R}v_{Rxd}^{O} - {}^{R}v_{Rx}^{O} \\ {}^{R}\dot{\phi}_{0zd}^{O} - {}^{R}\dot{\phi}_{0z}^{O} \end{bmatrix}. \tag{5}
$$

Because of the presence of non-steered wheels we expect that the error of angular velocity ${}^{R}e_{\omega0z}$ will be relatively greater than error of linear velocity ${}^{R}e_{vRx}$, that is, ${}^{R}v_{Rd}^{O} = {}^{R}v_{Rxd}^{O}$ and ${}^{R}e_{vRx} \approx 0$.

Based on the above assumption two versions of the motion stabilization system can be introduced: simplified version and full version. The simplified version does not include stabilization of the longitudinal velocity of the mobile platform.

The adopted simplification is also enforced by the fact that for calculation of linear velocity error one should determine actual linear velocity of the point R, that is ${}^{R}v_{R}^{O}$, which in case of use of inertial method of measurement requires integration of accelerations. Velocity determined in this way has the worse quality the more uneven is the ground on which the robot moves, which inhibits application of full version of the stabilization system at present and requires further research.

Let us introduce the generalized error of robot yaw rate:

$$
s_{\omega0z} = {}^{R}e_{\omega0z} + \lambda_{\omega0z} \, {}^{R}e_{\phi0z}, \tag{6}
$$

where: ${}^{R}e_{\omega0z} = ({}^{R}\dot{\phi}_{0zd}^{O} - {}^{R}\dot{\phi}_{0z}^{O})$, ${}^{R}e_{\phi0z} = \int {}^{R}e_{\omega0z} \, dt$.

Then, the control law of the 'Motion stabilizer' may have the form:

$$
\Delta\mathbf{u}_{\omega} = \begin{bmatrix} \Delta u_{\omega3} \\ \Delta u_{\omega4} \end{bmatrix} = \frac{1}{r} \begin{bmatrix} 1 & -W/2 \\ 1 & W/2 \end{bmatrix} \Delta\mathbf{v}, \tag{7}
$$

where $\Delta\mathbf{v} = [0, k_{\omega0z} s_{\omega0z}]^{T}$, and the expression in front of $\Delta\mathbf{v}$ follows from robot kinematics and was derived with analogous assumptions as the relationship (4).

Hence one gets:

$$
\Delta\mathbf{u}_{\omega} = \begin{bmatrix} \Delta u_{\omega3} \\ \Delta u_{\omega4} \end{bmatrix} = \frac{W}{2r} k_{\omega0z} s_{\omega0z} \begin{bmatrix} -1 \\ 1 \end{bmatrix}, \tag{8}
$$

Finally, 'Wheels' velocity controller' receives the following signal at its input:

$$
\dot{\boldsymbol{\theta}}_s = \begin{bmatrix} \dot{\theta}_{3s} \\ \dot{\theta}_{4s} \end{bmatrix} = \mathbf{u}_{\omega} + \Delta\mathbf{u}_{\omega}. \tag{9}
$$

In the work a concept is adopted according to which subsystems 'Desired motion of the robot', 'Motion stabilizer', 'Inertial measurement unit' and summation block comprise a separate module which can be switched on by the robot operator to start sending control corrections to the 'Wheels' velocity controller'.

We assume the following settings of the 'Motion stabilizer', i.e., factors $\lambda_{\omega 0z} = 8$ and $k_{\omega 0z} = 2$, which were selected after realization of series of separate experiments. During mentioned experiments various combinations of those factors were analyzed for values of $\lambda_{\omega 0z}$ and $k_{\omega 0z}$ changing within the limits <1, 14> and <1, 8> respectively. Nearly 150 different ($\lambda_{\omega 0z}$, $k_{\omega 0z}$) pairs were examined in total.

4   Experimental Investigations

The described stabilization system was implemented in the simplified version on the PIAP SCOUT robot. Implementation included input signal from the gyroscope but not from the accelerometer. Linear velocity and position obtained from accelerometer are less reliable at the moment and require additional work to become useful as input signals for the controller in the full version. Experimental investigations were carried out for two structures of the teleoperation mode control system described earlier (see Fig. 4a and Fig. 5). The investigations were conducted in the indoor environment on a horizontal and even ground with surface made of PVC flooring. Robot motions with velocities from 0.1 m/s up to 2 m/s, close to the maximum velocity attainable by the robot, were analyzed. In the work results for only the 2 m/s case are shown.

During experiment, control signals were not imposed by the 'Operator' by means of the 'Control panel', but from the input file which contained predefined values of desired angular velocities for wheels of the left and right-hand side of the robot, which corresponded to desired motion of the robot mobile platform.

Experiment 1
The experiment was conducted on the assumption that robot has to go 20 m along a straight line with forward velocity of 2 m/s. The obtained results of experiment are shown in Fig. 6. After analysis of the plots presented in the Fig. 6a one can notice that the 'Wheels' velocity controller' realizes the control of angular velocities of spin of wheels with relatively good accuracy. In spite of this, from the graphs of robot body yaw rate and yaw angle shown in Fig. 6b it is clear that robot is slowly turning right.

The described increasing yaw angle error can be also watched on the movie, where the conduct of the analogous experiment is shown, which must have been terminated in order to prevent robot crashing into the corridor wall [15].

A conclusion follows that small inaccuracies of control of angular velocities of spin of wheels, non-uniform conditions of wheel-ground interaction, differences in properties of drive units and transmissions, etc., cause substantial errors on the distance of 20 m.

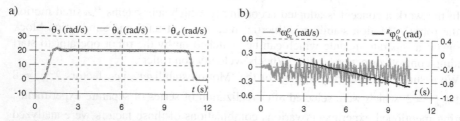

Fig. 6. Empirical results for the case of PIAP SCOUT robot straight-line motion with linear velocity of 2 m/s, without motion stabilization system: a – desired and actual angular velocities of spin of driven wheels, b – robot body yaw rate and yaw angle

Experiment 2

The second experiment was realized with the motion stabilization system described in the work turned on. Robot motion with maximum velocity of 2 m/s was imposed, and the assumed travel distance was 30 m. Results of this experiment are shown in Fig. 7. A movie presenting the robot motion is also available on the website [15].

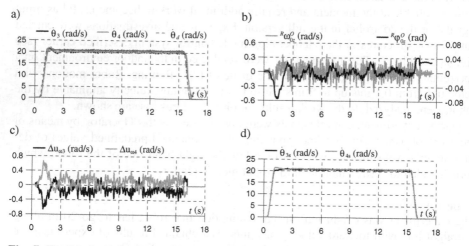

Fig. 7. Empirical results for the case of PIAP SCOUT robot straight-line motion with linear velocity of 2 m/s, with active motion stabilization system: a – desired and actual angular velocities of spin of driven wheels, b – robot body yaw rate and yaw angle, c – control corrections, d – effective control signals

After analysis of time-histories of angular velocities of spin of driven wheels (Fig. 7a,d), i.e.: desired $\dot{\theta}_d = \dot{\theta}_{3d} = \dot{\theta}_{4d}$, actual $\dot{\theta}_3, \dot{\theta}_4$ and corrected, sent to 'Wheels' velocity controller', $\dot{\theta}_{3s}, \dot{\theta}_{4s}$, one can notice only minor differences. It follows from the fact that control signals $\Delta u_{\omega 3}$ and $\Delta u_{\omega 4}$ generated by 'Motion stabilizer' (Fig. 7c) comprise at most 3% of values of the signals $\dot{\theta}_{3s}, \dot{\theta}_{4s}$. The largest deviations of the robot body from straight-line motion occur mainly during starting and stopping, which is visible from time-histories of yaw rate and yaw angle of the robot body

(Fig. 7b). Comparison of yaw rates of the robot body for both experiments (Fig. 6b and 7b respectively) shows that in both cases amplitudes of oscillations are similar. However, in case of absent stabilization system yaw rate average value has negative shift (Fig. 6b), whereas in case of present stabilization system, the average value is zero (Fig. 7b), which results in bounded yaw angle. During robot steady motion, the error associated with yaw angle does not exceed 0.04 rad = 2.3 deg, which is a negligible value from the point of view of robot operator.

5   Conclusions and Future Works

Most important conclusions of the work are summarized below:

- It is confirmed that the 'Motion stabilizer' significantly improves accuracy of realization of robot straight-line motion in comparison to the case when 'Wheels' velocity controller' is only used.
- Results of investigations indicate that the proposed solution has application potential to wheeled robots; it is likely that this solution can be applied also to other types of ground mobile robots, e.g. tracked robots.
- The proposed solution, in its full version including stabilization of linear velocity, can be used for reduction of wheels' longitudinal slip and in robots that have drive units without encoders where control occurs directly via appropriate voltages applied to the drive units.

Directions of future works will include:

- Design and implementation of more advanced structure of 'Motion stabilizer' in order to further improve accuracy of the robot motion, for instance, based on neurocontroller, like in work [16].
- Use of gyroscopes of better quality to improve resolution of the input signal to the 'Motion stabilizer' block. However, it should be considered with available resolution of drive unit control signal taken into account.
- Investigations of the stabilization system with other classes of ground robots, e.g. six-wheeled (IBIS – Fig. 1c) or tracked (EXPERT – Fig. 1b).
- Investigations of the stabilization system when robot moves on challenging ground, e.g. rough terrain, curbstones, stairs (PIAP SCOUT robot with additional front tracks – Fig. 1a).
- Implementation of complete version of the stabilization system, that includes stabilization of both yaw angle and linear velocity, to mitigate longitudinal wheel slips.

Acknowledgements. The work has been realized as a part of the project entitled "Dynamics modeling of four-wheeled mobile robot and tracking control of its motion with limitation of wheels slip". The project is financed from the means of National Science Centre of Poland granted on the basis of decision number DEC-2011/03/B/ST7/02532.

References

[1] Kasprzyczak, L., Trenczek, S., Cader, M.: Robot for monitoring hazardous environments as a mechatronic product. Journal of Automation Mobile Robotics and Intelligent Systems 6(4), 57–64 (2012)

[2] Trojnacki, M.: Modelowanie dynamiki mobilnych robotów kołowych (Dynamics modeling of wheeled mobile robots). Oficyna Wydawnicza PIAP, Warszawa (2013) (in Polish)

[3] Wołoszczuk, A., Andrzejczak, M., Szynkarczyk, P.: Architecture of Mobile Robotics Platform planned for Intelligent Robotic Porter System - IRPS project. Journal of Automation Mobile Robotics and Intelligent Systems 1(3), 59–63 (2007)

[4] Giergiel, J., Kurc, K.: Mechatronics of the inspective robot. Mechanics and Mechanical Engineering 10(1), 56–73 (2006)

[5] Trojnacki, M., Szynkarczyk, P., Andrzejuk, A.: Tendencje rozwoju mobilnych robotów lądowych (1). Przegląd robotów mobilnych do zastosowań specjalnych (Tendencies in the development of mobile ground robots (1) Review of mobile robots for special applications). Pomiary, Automatyka, Robotyka 12(6), 11–14 (2008) (in Polish)

[6] PIAP – producer of EOD equipment, EOD robots and surveillance robots, http://www.antiterrorism.eu/en/ (accessed: April 21, 2014)

[7] Dąbek, P.: Evaluation of low-cost MEMS accelerometers for measurements of velocity of unmanned vehicles. Pomiary, Automatyka, Robotyka 17(1), 102–113 (2013)

[8] Trojnacki, M., Dąbek, P.: Determination of Motion Parameters with Inertial Measurement Units. Part 1: Mathematical Formulation of the Algorithm (submitted, 2014)

[9] Trojnacki, M., Dąbek, P.: Determination of Motion Parameters with Inertial Measurement Units. Part 2: Algorithm Verification with a Four-Wheeled Mobile Robot and Low-Cost MEMS Sensors (submitted, 2014)

[10] Zhang, C.: Path tracking of a mobile robot using inertial measurement unit. Kongzhi Lilun Yu Yingyong/Control Theory and Applications 30(3), 398–403 (2013)

[11] Zuo, L., Xu, X., Liu, C., Huang, Z.: A hierarchical reinforcement learning approach for optimal path tracking of wheeled mobile robots. Neural Computing and Applications 23(7-8), 1873–1883 (2013)

[12] Hendzel, Z., Szuster, M.: Discrete Action Dependant Heuristic Dynamic Programming in Control of a Wheeled Mobile Robot. Solid State Phenomena 164, 419–424 (2010)

[13] Pazderski, D., Kozlowski, K.R.: Trajectory tracking control of skid-steering robot - Experimental validation. In: Proceedings of the 17th IFAC World Congress, vol. 17, pp. 5377–5382 (2008)

[14] Sakaino, S., Sato, T., Ohnishi, K.: Mobile-hapto with yaw rate control for traveling on rough terrain. In: IECON 2010 - 36th Annual Conference on IEEE Industrial Electronics Society, pp. 1565–1570 (2010)

[15] Trojnacki, M.T.: Mobile robots - models, animations and movies, http://www.mtrojnacki.republika.pl/MobileRobots/index.html (accessed: May 29, 2014)

[16] Hendzel, Z.: An adaptive critic neural network for motion control of a wheeled mobile robot. Nonlinear Dynamics 50(4), 849–855 (2007)

Influence of Choosing the Extending Column in Trajectory Tracking Control of SSMP Platform Using Artificial Force Method

Mateusz Cholewiński and Alicja Mazur

Chair of Cybernetics and Robotics
Electronics Faculty
Wroclaw University of Technology
ul. Janiszewskiego 11/17
50-372 Wroclaw
{mateusz.cholewinski,alicja.mazur}@pwr.edu.pl
http://www.kcir.pwr.wroc.pl

Abstract. Paper presents application of artificial force method in mathematical model of Skid Steering Mobile Platform. This method is used for controlling nonholonmic object, which is underactuated due to the lateral slippage phenomena needed for changing the orientation. Paper focuses on influence of choosing different columns in the position error and torque domain, which is important from the practical point of view. It was proved that the choose of extending column may have an influence on the quality of control.The control algorithms were tested in numerous simulations and proved to work properly under different conditions (e.g. motor torque limitations).

1 Introduction

Skid Steering Mobile Platform (SSMP) have many specific ways of use. Due to the multiple wheels or tracks based suspension, there is no problem of moving in difficult terrain e.g. sand or rubbish. Regarding this advantage, SSMP may be used for localization and rescuing people harmed by the effect of natural disasters or in counter-terrorist reconnaissance. For these purposes, the development of autonomous control system, based on the mathematical model of platform, seems to be the major issue.

On the other hand, SSMP are difficult objects to control due to slippage - during changing orientation lateral slippage occurs. Problem lies in introducing this phenomena in mathematical model of robot.

There are two solutions for the problem of uderactuating, which can be found in the literature:

- adding additional nonholonomic constraint to the system,
- adding another control output.

First way was presented in [2], where authors decided to introduce artificial nonholonomic constraint – they combined the velocity in Y direction and the

© Springer International Publishing Switzerland 2015
D. Filev et al. (eds.), *Intelligent Systems'2014*,
Advances in Intelligent Systems and Computing 323, DOI: 10.1007/978-3-319-11310-4_12

angular velocity of platform using the constant number. In other words, the ratio of these two velocities was constant during the platform movement.

Similar approach was presented in [3], however in this paper, authors assumed that this ration is not constant but only limited by some number and changes in time.

Completely different way of solving control problem of SSMP platform was proposed in [7]. In this article, the artificial force method was introduced for even more complex system: 2R manipulator mounted on the SSMP platform. This method assumes extending mathematical model on dynamic level, rather than introducing another constraint to kinematics. The more precise description is presented in the Section 3.

Several papers regarding artificial force method has already been presented and the last ones focus on the way of generation different extending columns. In this paper a comparison between results generated by the differently described model of SSMP in auxiliary coordinates is presented and investigated. It is important from the practical point of view to search for more accurate and less energy consuming algorithms.

Article is organised in the following way. In Section 2 mathematical model of SSMP platform in general coordinates is derived. Section 3 describes the artificial force method in general way. Section 4 is devoted to control problem of SSMP platform and presents the different extending columns, which are being investigated in this paper. Simulation studies are presented and discussed in Section 5. Section 6 contains concluding remarks.

2 Mathematical Model of Skid Steering Mobile Platform

Schematic of SSMP mobile platform has been presented in the Fig. 1. Motors on the same side are coupled, which means that the torques generated by those motors can be added together.

The b and a symbol denotes distances from the mass centre to, accordingly, the front and back axle. Half of platform width is c and r is the radius of wheel. m_p and m_k are, respetcively, the platform's and wheel mass. I_p is the platform's

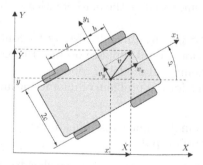

Fig. 1. SSMP platform

inertia moment along its Z axis and I_k is the wheel inertia moment along the axle to which it is fixed. SSMP, in global coordinates, can be described with the following state vector

$$q = (\, x \; y \; \phi \; \theta_1 \; \theta_2 \,)^T \in R^5. \tag{1}$$

Mathematical model of SSMP consist of two equations:

- kinematics,
- dynamics.

2.1 Kinematics

Kinematics of mobile platform can be expressed in the Pfaffian form, which describes the constraints for longitudinal slippage of SSMP platform. In the given case the kinematics has following form:

$$A(q)\dot{q} = \begin{bmatrix} \cos\phi \; \sin\phi \; -c \; -r \; 0 \\ \cos\phi \; \sin\phi \; \; c \; \; 0 \; -r \end{bmatrix} \begin{pmatrix} \dot{x} \\ \dot{y} \\ \dot{\phi} \\ \dot{\theta}_1 \\ \dot{\theta}_2 \end{pmatrix} = 0. \tag{2}$$

It describes only the lack of longitudinal slippage - no constraints on lateral slippage is needed, because this component of velocity is necessary for changing the SSMP orientation. It should be noticed, that unicycle has the same model of kinematics as SSMP platform.

2.2 Dynamics

Dynamics can be derived from the d'lembert principle for coordinates (1). Regarding the fact, that mobile platform is moving on the horizontal plane, the potential energy E_p equals to zero and the Lagrangian consists only om the kinematic energy of wheels and the cart.

General form of mobile robot dynamics is as follows:

$$\underbrace{\begin{bmatrix} m_p & 0 & 0 & 0 & 0 \\ 0 & m_p & 0 & 0 & 0 \\ 0 & 0 & I_p & 0 & 0 \\ 0 & 0 & 0 & I_k & 0 \\ 0 & 0 & 0 & 0 & I_k \end{bmatrix}}_{M(q)} \ddot{q} + \underbrace{\begin{bmatrix} F_x \cos\phi - F_y \sin\phi \\ F_x \sin\phi + F_y \cos\phi \\ M_r \\ 0 \\ 0 \end{bmatrix}}_{F(q,\dot{q})} = \underbrace{\begin{bmatrix} 0 & 0 \\ 0 & 0 \\ 0 & 0 \\ 1 & 0 \\ 0 & 1 \end{bmatrix}}_{B(q)} u + \underbrace{\begin{bmatrix} \cos\phi & \cos\phi \\ \sin\phi & \sin\phi \\ -c & c \\ -r & 0 \\ 0 & r \end{bmatrix}}_{A(q)} \lambda, \tag{3}$$

where $M(q)$ is the inertia matrix, $F(q, \dot{q})$ is the vector of ground-wheels forces and $B(q)$ is the input matrix.

2.3   Model in Auxiliary Coordinates

Equation (3) has the Lagrange multipliers component $A^T \lambda$, representing forces coming from nonholonomic constraints. Computing them is the challenging task, therefore mathematical model of SSMP can be expressed in equivalent, so-called, auxiliary coordinates [4].

Kinematics in auxiliary coordinates can be expressed in the form of a driftless control system

$$\dot{q} = G(q)\eta = \begin{bmatrix} \cos\theta & \cos\theta \\ \sin\theta & \sin\theta \\ \frac{1}{c} & -\frac{1}{c} \\ 0 & \frac{2}{r} \\ \frac{2}{r} & 0 \end{bmatrix} \begin{pmatrix} \eta_1 \\ \eta_2 \end{pmatrix}. \tag{4}$$

and dynamics have the following form

$$\underbrace{G^T M G}_{M^*} \dot{\eta} + \underbrace{G^T (M\dot{G} + CG)}_{C^*} \eta + \underbrace{G^T F}_{F^*} = \underbrace{G^T B}_{B^*} u. \tag{5}$$

Utilizing the fact that the kernel of A matrix is spanned by the columns of G matrix

$$A(q)\, G(q) = 0$$

Langrange multipliers component completely vanishes.

Equations (4) and (5) create mathematical model of SSMP in auxiliary coordinates.

3   Artificial Force Method

SSMP is equipped with two control outputs (4). Size of A matrix is $5 = m \times n = 2$ and from the control theory point of view [6], system should be equipped with $l = m - n = 3$ control outputs. It means that the SMMP is underactuated and causes that the input matrix B in auxiliary coordinates will have a rectangular form.

There are two solutions for this problem:

- first presented in [2], [3] – introducing artificial constraint, thus the n will increase and will be equal to $n = 3$,
- artificial force method – add additional control output, ensuring that the artificial control signal will equal to 0.

Using the second solution, the kinematics (4) has to be extended with additional column. However, the added column must also provide vanishing of Lagrange multiplier component.

Equations (6) and (7) present developed columns:

$$
G_e = \begin{bmatrix} \cos\phi & \cos\phi \\ \sin\phi & \sin\phi \\ \frac{1}{c} & -\frac{1}{c} \\ 0 & \frac{2}{r} \\ \frac{2}{r} & 0 \end{bmatrix} g_i \,,
\tag{6}
$$

$$
g_1 = \begin{bmatrix} -\sin\phi \\ \cos\phi \\ 0 \\ 0 \\ 0 \end{bmatrix}, \qquad
g_2 = \begin{bmatrix} \sin\phi \\ -\cos\phi \\ 1 \\ -\frac{c}{r} \\ \frac{c}{r} \end{bmatrix}, \qquad
g_3 = \begin{bmatrix} \frac{\sin\phi}{c} \\ -\frac{\cos\phi}{c} \\ \frac{r}{c} \\ -1 \\ 1 \end{bmatrix}.
\tag{7}
$$

4   Control Process of SSMP

4.1   Control Problem Statement

In the given case, control task for SSMP with applied artificial force method can be described in form of the following goals, which should be satisfied simultaneously:

1. find a control law u such, that the SSMP platform follows the desired trajectory, without longitudinal slippage,
2. value of control signal u_{3v} should be equal to zero,
3. needed motor torques should be in the specified, real ranges.

SSMP in auxiliary coordinates is a nonholonomic robot, hence the control system is divided into two sub controllers:

- kinematic controller, which generates reference velocity signals, used by the dynamic controller,
- dynamic controller, which forces the system with dynamics to follow reference velocities.

4.2   Kinematic Controler

Kinematic controler generates the reference signalls, used by the dynamic controller. As it was mentioned before, presented kinematics of SSMP is the same as for unicycle. This fact allows to use kinematic controller, especially designed for this class of mobile robots.

In the given case, Samson controler [1] was used:

$$\begin{pmatrix} v_r \\ \omega_r \end{pmatrix} = \begin{pmatrix} k_1 x_e + v_d \cos\phi_e \\ \omega_d + k_2\phi_e + v_d y_e \frac{\sin\phi_e}{\phi_e} \end{pmatrix}, \qquad k_1, k_2 > 0,$$

$$\begin{pmatrix} x_e \\ y_e \\ \phi_e \end{pmatrix} = Rot(z, -\phi) \begin{pmatrix} x_d - x \\ y_d - y \\ \phi_d - \phi \end{pmatrix},$$

$$\eta_{1ref} = \frac{v_r - c\omega_r}{2}, \qquad \eta_{2ref} = \frac{v_r + c\omega_r}{2},$$

where v_d and ω_d are, respectively, desired linear and angular velocity, taken from the trajectory generator. η_{1ref} and η_{2ref} are signals coming from the kinematic controller, guaranteeing the realization of trajectory tracking as if the SSMP dynamics was not taken into account.

4.3   Dynamic Controller

For the given system (3) numerous simulations showed that the following control law successfully realise the control task:

$$\begin{pmatrix} u_1 \\ u_2 \\ u_{3v} \end{pmatrix} = (B)^{*-1} \left\{ M^* \begin{pmatrix} \dot\eta_{r1} \\ \dot\eta_{r2} \\ \dot\eta_{r3v} \end{pmatrix} + C^* \begin{pmatrix} \eta_{r1} \\ \eta_{r2} \\ \eta_{r3v} \end{pmatrix} + F^* - K_d \begin{pmatrix} e_{\eta_1} \\ e_{\eta_2} \\ e_{\eta_{3v}} \end{pmatrix} \right\}. \qquad (8)$$

where the corresponding components are described as follows:

$$e_{\eta_i} = \eta_i - \eta_{ref_i}, \qquad K_d = K_d^T > 0.$$

4.4   Applying Artificial Force

With two previous subsections the first goal is met. However, it can be noticed that the equation (8) contains the third component of the reference velocity and acceleration vector (respectively η_{r3v} and $\dot\eta_{r3v}$) and this element is not generated by the kinematic controller. The second goal can be used as a condition for generating these signals:

$$u_{3v} = (B)^{*-1}_{3row} \{ M^* \dot\eta_r + C^* \eta_{r1} + F^* - K_d e_\eta \} = 0. \qquad (9)$$

After some transformations, the general analytic form of equation for $\dot\eta_{r3v}$ is as follows:

$$\begin{aligned}
\dot\eta_{r3v} = \{ &- B_{31}(F_1 + C_{11}\eta_{r1} + C_{12}\eta_{r2} + C_{13}\eta_{r3} - K_d e_{\eta_{r1}} + M_{11}\dot\eta_{r1} + M_{12}\dot\eta_{r2}) \\
&- B_{32}(F_2 + C_{21}\eta_{r1} + C_{22}\eta_{r2} + C_{23}\eta_{r3} - K_d e_{\eta_{r2}} + M_{21}\dot\eta_{r1} + M_{22}\dot\eta_{r2}) \\
&- B_{33}(F_3 + C_{31}\eta_{r1} + C_{32}\eta_{r2} + C_{33}\eta_{r3} - K d e_{\eta 3} + M_{31}\dot\eta_{r1} + M_{32}\dot\eta_{r2}) \} / \\
&((B_{31}M_{13}) + (B_{32}M_{23}) + (B_{33}M_{33})), \qquad (10)
\end{aligned}$$

where some elements vanish, e.g. using the chosen $G(q)$ matrices, components multiplied by η_3 are equal to 0.

It is not possible to obtain the analytic for of signal η_3 , thus the $\dot\eta_{r3v}$ has to be numerically integrated.

5   Simulation Studies

The simulations were run with MATLAB package and SIMULINK toolbox. Physical as well as the regulations parameters taken into simulations are listed in the Table 1.

Table 1. Regulation parameters

Parameter	Value	Parameter	Value
a	0.365 m	b	0.365 m
c	0.387 m		
m_p	42 kg	m_k	2.38 kg
I_p	5 kgm^2	I_k	0.15 kgm^2
r	0.127 m		
μ	0.9	f_r	0.1
v_d	1.1 $\frac{m}{s}$	ω_d	0.1 $\frac{rad}{s}$
k_1	0.2	k_2	1
K_d	100		

The simulation was organised in the way, that all three models were run parallely, in one simulation, with the same physical and regulation parameters. Together with the same method of equations solving and the same time step, it guaranteed the possibility of results comparison.

There where three scenarios running for the SSMP platform:

1. tracking the circle with radius $R = 10\ [m]$ and frequency $\omega = 1[Hz]$,
2. tracking the combined trajectory described by these conditions:
   - time interval $[0s, 10s]$ – moving the straight line with the desired linear velocity $v_d = 1\frac{m}{s}$ and desired orientation $\frac{\pi}{4}[rad]$
   - time interval $(10s, 30s]$ – the circle with radius $R = 10\ [m]$ and frequency $\omega = 1[Hz]$,
   - time interval $(30s, 50s]$ – moving the straight line with the desired linear velocity $v_d = 1\frac{m}{s}$ and desired orientation $0.5[rad]$.

   Motor torques were not limited.
3. tracking the same trajectory as above but the torques were limited to $30[Nm]$. This limitation facilitates finding such a motors - there are not so many motors generating torques more than the limit value.

For the combined trajectory scenarios, the tracking control was made even harder – at time moments $10s$ and $30s$, the desired trajectory was not continuous. This also tested if the controllers are resistant for such a disturbance.

5.1   Circle Trajectory

Figures 2(a) - 2(f) shows that there are no big differences in tracking the simple trajectory using the different models. Controllers in all model versions worked properly and converged error signals to zero after a small period of time.

5.2 Combined Trajectory

In this scenario, there are visible differences between the versions of extending column. Fig. 2(c) shows that the first version of column gives the slightly worse results than two other.

Generated torques, presented in the Fig. 2(e) and 2(f) have the similar values.

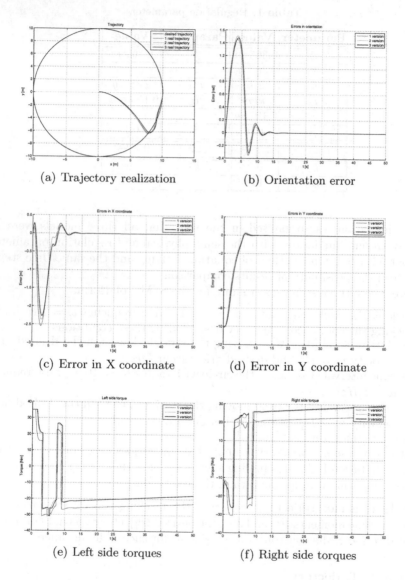

(a) Trajectory realization

(b) Orientation error

(c) Error in X coordinate

(d) Error in Y coordinate

(e) Left side torques

(f) Right side torques

Fig. 2.

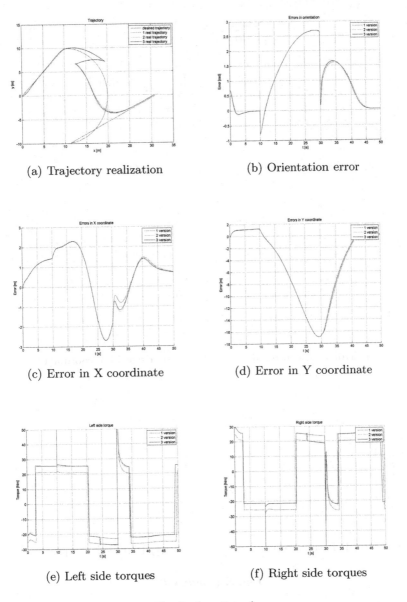

(a) Trajectory realization

(b) Orientation error

(c) Error in X coordinate

(d) Error in Y coordinate

(e) Left side torques

(f) Right side torques

Fig. 2. (*continued*)

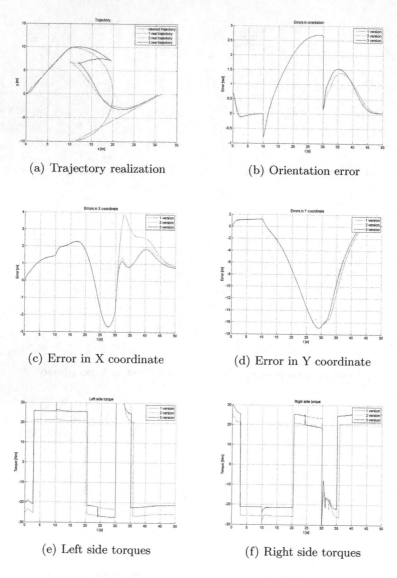

(a) Trajectory realization

(b) Orientation error

(c) Error in X coordinate

(d) Error in Y coordinate

(e) Left side torques

(f) Right side torques

Fig. 2. (*continued*)

5.3   Combined Trajectory with the Limited Torques

In this scenario the results for the first version of column are much worse that two other. This is especially visible in the Fig. 2(a), where there is a big difference between desire and realised trajectory for relevant versions.

Additionally, Fig. 2(c)-2(b) show that errors for the first versions are much bigger than for the other versions.

5.4 Numerical Data

Numerical data concerning the position errors and torques are presented in the Tables 2 - 5. For the first scenario results for all versions were very similar, which can be seen in the Fig. 2(a)-2(f).

Symbols e_x, e_y are, respectively, error in X and Y coordinate and e_ϕ denotes the orientation error. u_1 and u_2 are, respectively, the torques of left and right side of platform.

In the Tables 2 and 3 relevant data are presented. It can be noticed, that total error results for the second and third scenario are slightly smaller than for the first version. However in the same case, the torques are bigger.

Table 2. Errors for the second scenario

Column version	$\int |e_x|$	$\int |e_y|$	$\int |e_\phi|$	$\int |e_x| + \int |e_y|$
1 version	63.94 m	259.50 m	52.38 $[rad]$	323.44 m
2 version	66.08 m	252.93 m	52.33 $[rad]$	319.02 m
3 version	64.71 m	254.71 m	52.35 $[rad]$	319.43 m

Table 3. Torques for the second scenario

Column version	$\int |u_1|$	$\int |u_2|$	$\int |u_1| + \int |u_2|$
1 version	1192.48 Nm	1153.20 Nm	2345.69 Nm
2 version	1213.90 Nm	1134.03 Nm	2347.94 Nm
3 version	1226.06 Nm	1132.78 Nm	2358.85 Nm

Tables 4 and 5 present the similar data as for the second scenario. In this case, however, the errors are much smaller for the second and third version. It can be said, that the torques have the similar values.

Table 4. Errors for the third scenario

Column version	$\int |e_x|$	$\int |e_y|$	$\int |e_\phi|$	$\int |e_x| + \int |e_y|$
1 version	89.52 m	282.39 m	51.23 $[rad]$	371.91 m
2 version	72.52 m	269.65 m	51.97 $[rad]$	342.17 m
3 version	72.52 m	270.33 m	52.04 $[rad]$	340.87 m

Table 5. Torques for the third scenario

Column version	$\int |u_1|$	$\int |u_2|$	$\int |u_1| + \int |u_2|$
1 version	1193.02 Nm	1150.59 Nm	2343.61 Nm
2 version	1208.58 Nm	1136.56 Nm	2345.14 Nm
3 version	1215.60 Nm	1136.16 Nm	2351.76 Nm

6 Remarks

In this paper the method of artificial force for controlling the SSMP platform has been presented concerning the different extending columns. Influence of choosing the column has been investigated on three examples. This studies show that the results may differ in the total error of position, as well as in total generated torque. It also shows there is no only one way of solving the problem and it is worth trying to use another column in order to minimize e.g. position error. Numerous simulations have confirmed, that such an idea of controlling is working well and have the chance to be implemented in the real object.

References

[1] Samson, C., Ait-Abderrahim, K.: Feedback control of a nonholonomic wheeled cart in cartesian space. In: Proc. of the IEEE Int. Conf. on Robotics and Automation, pp. 1136–1141 (1991)

[2] Caracciolo, L., De Luca, A., Iannitti, S.: Trajectory tracking control of a four-wheel differentially driven mobile robot. In: Proc. of the IEEE Int. Conf. on Robotics and Automation, pp. 2632–2638 (1999)

[3] Kozłowski, K., Pazderski, D.: Modeling and control of a 4-wheel skid-steering mobile robot. International Journal of Applied Mathematics and Computer Science, 477–496 (2004)

[4] Mazur, A.: Model-based control for nonholonomic mobile manipulators. Oficyna Wydawnicza Politechniki Wrocławskiej (2009) (in Polish)

[5] Cholewiński, M., Arent, K., Mazur, A.: Towards practical implementation of an artificial force method for control of the mobile platform Rex. In: Szewczyk, R., Zieliński, C., Kaliczyńska, M. (eds.) Recent Advances in Automation, Robotics and Measuring Techniques. AISC, vol. 267, pp. 353–364. Springer, Heidelberg (2014)

[6] Duleba, I.: Metody i algorytmy planowania ruchu robotw mobilnych i manipulacyjnych. Akademicka Oficyna Wydawnicza EXIT, Warszawa (2001) (in Polish)

[7] Mazur, A., Cholewiński, M.: Virtual force concept in steering mobile manipulators with skid-steering platform moving in unknown environment. Journal of Intelligent and Robotic Systems, 1–11 (2013)

Low Time Complexity Collision Avoidance Method for Autonomous Mobile Robots

Piotr Bigaj and Jakub Bartoszek

Industrial Research Institute for Automation and Measurements, Warsaw, Poland
{pbigaj,jbartoszek}@piap.pl

Abstract. In this paper we present a fast and reliable method of obstacle avoidance for ground mobile robots both for outdoor and indoor navigation. The method compromises two contradictory approaches: non-complex implementation and human-like smooth steering. The method is applicable in any mobile robotic system regardless of used sensors. All calculations are done on virtual representation of surroundings, where the information about obstacles and a free space is presented in a unified way. The method results in a smooth movement, but is also equipped with a reactive calculation path that handles dangerous and damage-prone situations. The total calculation time for a desktop computer for presented method is 5[ms], resulting in real-time behavior of an algorithm.

Keywords: collision avoidance, mobile robot, autonomy.

1 Introduction

Mobile robotics still eagers for a fast, computationally inexpensive methods of obstacle avoidance that would be applicable to multisensory robotic system [1]. Those methods need to solve the problem of mobile robots' movement from the starting point to a destination point and simultaneously omitting obstacles. The key issue when solving this task is to perform a movement in a collision-free way whilst the planned path should be optimal under some criteria. Going towards a goal point fall into three consecutive phases: building environment representation, localization [2-4], movement planning and implementation. In some cases building environment representation is overlooked [5, 6]. It is justified in these situations when the dynamics of environment changes is comparable or greater than dynamics of map generation and decision-making process. In such cases generated map is not a reliable source of information since it is not up-to-date.

By multisensory we mean multiple heterogeneous sensors that work on different basis and that produce their reading different in qualitatively manner e.g. single beam ultrasonic rangefinder and 3D laser scanner. Most of the authors along the literature aim in finding methods for obstacle avoidance that are somehow related with the sensory they use and where sensors output data type is identical for all onboard sensors. In authors' opinion merging data that come from different sensor is a key issue in

© Springer International Publishing Switzerland 2015
D. Filev et al. (eds.), *Intelligent Systems'2014*,
Advances in Intelligent Systems and Computing 323, DOI: 10.1007/978-3-319-11310-4_13

building high performance, robust and fault tolerant robotics systems [7, 8]. Therefore for a full classification of detected obstacle different types of sensors are used. In laboratory conditions ultrasonic [9] or near infra-red sensors are preferred. That kind of sensors cannot be used in real outdoor conditions because they are very sensitive to variable ambient conditions. Far better results are obtained by the use of laser based sensors and recently radars and lidars [10]. Ideally a mobile robot should sense a depth map of surrounding [11-13]. This brings the necessity to equip it with stereo cameras, ToF cameras or 3D laser scanners.

On the other hand most of kinematic structures of ground mobile robots introduces holonomic constraints on robot (wheel/track) – ground junction which neglects this necessity. Concluding this one would rather place precise, fast sensors for sensing close proximity in the direction of robot's movement, whilst other directions can be either passed over or simple sensors can be used in that directions. This also mirrors how human's perception is built as most of our "obstacle omitting" senses including sight and hearing are directed towards our direction of movement. In the case of human this is possible most energy-efficient placement, which for mobile robot sensor's placement is vital due to high sensor's cost. What is more: in order to assess sensors placement and configuration one would need to run the same robot with the same obstacle avoidance techniques and an efficacy measure would have to be introduces based on which the assessment can be made. This clearly needs an algorithm that would be able to deal with different types of sensors and data type they provide.

The description of the approach falls into 6 paragraphs. Paragraph 2 describes the main outline of the algorithm. Paragraph 3 explains environment model and sensory data to model mapping. Paragraph 4 introduces constraints for calculated velocities and their role in robot's movement smoothness. Also shows details of elaborated algorithm. Paragraph 5 contains description of a software platform and experiments. Paragraph 6 is a summary, conclusion and future work.

2   An Outline of an Algorithm

The method is what is called local velocity/movement planning, or obstacle avoidance, therefore no further knowledge of the environment is given to the algorithm, apart from the one retrieved from the sensors placed on-board. The robot does not know the map, but it is fed from global path planning algorithm or human plannist with a consecutive points to visit. This means that the robot visits a path point by point to get to destination or go in the infinite loop of points.

Whole calculation is done on an environment model rather than on sensors reading directly. This is approach was shown in many elaborations concerning methods classified as Classical AI.

The main loop consist in two paths of algorithm execution: emergency path and regular path. The first path basis on completely different approach than the second one. The distinction is introduced to react on situations when damage of a robot or surrounding is highly probable i.e. when a dynamic obstacle appears suddenly on robot's trajectory. In this case the robot has to stop abruptly regardless to current velocity to avoid the damage and further a regular obstacle omitting actions are to be performed. This approach is known as a hybrid combination of the two approaches Classical AI and New AI.

The regular path is a consecutive calculating angle histogram, finding and grouping possible directions and choosing best possible movement direction. Based on this a linear and an angular velocity is being calculated. If the robot during its movement reaches current destination point the algorithm is fed with another intermediary destination and the process repeats until final destination point is reached. The path can also be of a form of infinite loop, which implements patrolling behavior.

2.1   Sensors Data Flow

Before the algorithm is run a set-up process takes place. During this process an empty environment model is created and a robot is placed in this environment. In current system version one robot is supported, but the system is not limited to use only one instance of a robot. Each robot has assigned a list of sensors that are placed on its mobile base and those sensors are also parameterized.

Each sensor instance has assigned class that describes the type of data outputted by the sensor. Such approach is vital since environment needs to present the data to an algorithm in one consistent way no matter if the installed sensor is a ultrasonic range-finder, radar true presence, 3D laser scanner or other. Such approach has been chosen so that data fusion is made in simplest possible way and sensors can be added or deleted from the system almost on the fly. This way a change in robot's sensors types or placement needs only a change of one configuration file.

Each sensor is designed as a separate service. Regardless to a sensor type within the thread the sensor is prompted for a new data frame. Since each sensor provides information about range that is expressed in the local (sensor's) coordinate system and the sensor placement and orientation is different for different sensors each data from the sensor is translated and rotated to obtain data in mobile robot's coordination system. Therefore ranges perceived by obstacle avoidance algorithm are the distances of obstacles from the robot rather that distances from the sensors. Knowing these and robot's current position and orientation we may model the environment in global coordinate system as this needs a multiplication of another translation and rotation matrices. Within the algorithm presented in this work obstacle position is converted according to robot's coordinate system that is placed in the geometrical middle point of mobile base. In current application an operation of only one robot is supported.

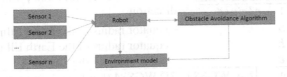

Fig. 1. The dependencies of different abstracts in the system

Table 1. Three level of processing data with the data type unionization by applied transformations

Nr	Level of data processing	Coordinate system	Data type
1	Sensor level	Sensor's coordinate system	Native for sensor. Laser Rangefinder – 1 scalar value 2D laser scanner – e.g. polar coordinate system 3D laser system – e.g. spherical coordinate system
	Applied transformation for next level: For 1D sensor (e.g. laser rangefinder). For 2D sensor (e.g. 2D scanner, polar coordinate system) and for 3D sensor (e.g. 3D scanner, spherical coordinate system), each of the measured point P in unified coordinates of the sensors origin needs to be multiplied by a matrix: $$(P \quad 1)\begin{pmatrix} R & T \\ 0 & 1 \end{pmatrix}$$ **R** – sensor placement rotation matrix 3x3 **0** – zeros matrix 1x3 **T** – translation matrix 3x1			
2	Robot level	Robot's coordinate system	3D Cartesian coordinate system
	Applied transformation for next level: $$X_{POS} = (N + h_{POS})\cos\phi_{POS}\cos\lambda_{POS} \quad (1)$$ $$Y_{POS} = (N + h_{POS})\cos\phi_{POS}\sin\lambda_{POS} \quad (2)$$ $$Z_{POS} = (N(1 - e^2) + h_{POS})\sin\phi_{POS} \quad (3)$$ ϕ_{POS} – Longitude λ_{POS} – Latitude h_{POS} – Altitude (high over earth ellipsoid) $X_{POS}, Y_{POS}, Z_{POS}$ – Coordinates of point in EFCC System (Earth Fixed Cartesian coordinates) $N(\phi_{POS}) = \dfrac{a}{\sqrt{1 - e^2 \sin^2\phi_{POS}}}$ – the radius of curvature in primary vertical direction a – equator radius of the Earth Ellipsoid b – equator radius of the Earth Ellipsoid e – eccentricity of the Earth			
3	Environment level	e.g. WGS84	3D WGS84 (Latitude, Longitude, Altitude)

2.2   Data Fusion from Different Kind of Sensors

As mentioned before, presented framework is able to capture, handle and process data from qualitatively different kind of sensors. Sensors provide the data in one, two or three dimensions, but in fact the meaning of this data is the distance to the obstacle. Therefore each data point, regardless to sensor type has assigned a point in the environment. Therefore three dimensional representation holds valid even for laser range-finder since its reading produces one single point of possible obstacle as the coordinate systems are recalculated accordingly to the description in previous chapter. Therefore on the sensor level data is presented in the sensor's native way, on Robot's level as a cloud of 3D points and on Global level of 3D coordinates. This nomenclature shows clearly that obstacle avoidance methods work on 1st of 2nd level, whilst SLAM or Global Path Planning methods on 3rd level. Referring to a sensor's data flow we also may say that 1st level data is gathered in sensors, 2nd in Robot, whilst 3rd in the environment.

2.3   Data Filtering

The raw data from the sensors needs to be filtered before it is used in the algorithm. The filtering in the presented approach done two folds: on sensor level and robot's level. The filtering on the sensor's level aims in removing data points that are impossible to be measured by a sensors. In many cases (e.g. the case of Hokuyo sensor that was used in the experiment) this step is simplified as apart from original distance data sensors provide information about illumination and data validity. If such information does not exist any data outside the measuring range provided is marked as non-valid and it is not send to robot's level. Therefore filtering on sensor's level is binary: data is either send to robot's level processing or discarded.

Apart from sensor's raw data recalculation each data point is also labeled by a timestamp and source identifier that allows identification of that point with particular sensor. Since sensors' data delivery time is not synchronized, data from particular sensors arrives on the robot's level in different time therefore capturing situation around the robot is actually capturing last data frames from sensors at that particular timespan. The history of readings that is kept for filtering purposes depends strictly on robots' velocity. It was assumed that if the robot's maximum velocity is V [m/s] one wants to have at least a time for within the robot travels from the point where it is now to the visibility boundary of the sensors B [m]. Therefore the data kept in the history has to be no older than B/V [s]. Older data is removed from representation of the robot's surroundings. Till this moment in data processing no information is lost, but in fact further processing of such amount of data could be impossible: if history length if set to 400[ms], and there are 4 2D laser scanners of 40[ms] sampling time, each producing 1024 points we end up with 40960 points to process each time new data frame arrives on the robots level. Therefore in order to build calculation efficient one needs to compress this data or present it to the robot in a different way.

3   Three Layered Angle Histogram Preparation and Filtering

For this purpose a special form of a two layered angle histogram has been prepared. An angle histogram is a method of presenting 3D Cartesian points in a polar coordinate. The one layer of a histogram H_L1 gathers the data in angle-distance to obstacle, the second layer H_L2 contains angle-max slope angle information. Therefore H_L1 contains an information of pair (X,Y) that on the azimuth X [Rad] the closest obstacle is in Y[m] whilst H_L2 contains an information of pair (X,Z) that on the azimuth X[Rad] the maximum slope angle is Z [Rad]. H_L3(X,H) inform that on the azimuth X the highest obstacle is H. Such representation in fact introduces a compression of input data - Cartesian 3D points. The level of compression depends on the granularity of both histograms: for 1 [°] granularity and quoted 40960 input points one receives compression level of ~57x. The more input points the algorithms is given (e.g. by introducing new sensors or replacing them) the more accurate the histogram is, but the compression ratio grows.

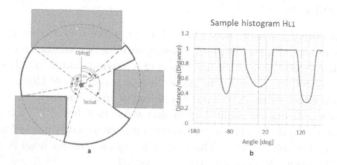

Fig. 2. a) Presentation of a sample top view of the robot b) corresponding H_{L1} histogram. $\alpha_1 = 40°$, $\alpha_1 = 40°$, $\alpha_2 = 105°$, $\alpha_3 = 160°$, $\alpha_4 = -40°$, $\alpha_5 = -110°$.

Step (0): First all three histograms are initialized H_L1 is cleared be setting an infinite distance to obstacles. Also surroundings are modeled as a flat area by setting H_L2 and H_L3 to zero. Step (1), Step (2) assigning Alpha and Dist temporary variables that mirror histogram angle index and distance to calculated obstacle. Step (3) is an update of current maximum slope angle if the one currently calculated is higher in absolute value. If this value exceeds maximum inclination then the distance in this particular dire. Step (4) is an update of maximum height on robot's way in a particular direction. Step (5) is an update of the distance to the nearest obstacle

Summarizing, H_L1 contains distance to a nearest obstacle on a particular azimuth, H_L2 refers to slope angle in that direction and H_L3 is the highest (Lowest) obstacle on the way. Next step is histogram dilation. It allows us to treat the robot as a point. Dilation consists in widening histogram by some dimension that is a function or robot's turn radius.

After this procedure each histogram is dilated and the robot can be treated as a point. At the next step the histogram is filtered out taking into an account current maximum velocity ($v_{Rmax,}$) of a robot and maximum velocity of a moving obstacle (v_{0max}). The idea behind is to remove possible misreading of sensors. The filtration is done in two steps: regarding the current maximum robots velocity and regarding maximum obstacle velocity. The current maximum robot's velocity is equal to:

$$v_{Rmax}(t_n) = v_R(t_{n-1}) + 0.5 * a_{vmax} * (t_n - t_{n-1}) \tag{4}$$

$$\omega_{Rmax}(t_n) = \omega_R(t_{n-1}) + 0.5 * a_{\omega max} * (t_n - t_{n-1}) \tag{5}$$

$v_{Rmax}(t_n)$	Maximum linear velocity of the robot in t_n moment
$\omega_{Rmax}(t_n)$	Maximum linear velocity of the robot in t_n moment
$v_R(t_{n-1})$	Linear velocity in t_{n-1} moment (during last measurement)
$\omega_R(t_{n-1})$	Angular velocity in t_{n-1} moment (during last measurement)
a_{vmax}	Maximum linear acceleration of the robot
$a_{\omega max}$	Maximum angular acceleration of the robot

These values are used in calculating boundary values for histograms, so that each histogram needs to be a shift of a histogram of previous calculation of not more that some value.

4   Algorithm Details

Once all histograms are prepared the algorithm is run to calculate linear and angular velocity. If current situation is not possible dangerous the calculation takes regular path. The first step is to calculate openings. An opening O_i is a minimum set of consecutives azimuths $\alpha_1 .. \alpha_n$ that fulfills a condition $C_1 \wedge (C_2 \vee C_3)$:

$$C_1: \forall i = 1 .. n \ |H_{L2}(\alpha_i)| < \theta_{max} \tag{6}$$

$$C_2: H_{L1}(\alpha_1) - H_{L1}(\alpha_0) > L_{safe} \wedge \sum_{i=2}^{n} H_{L1}(\alpha_i) \leq -L_{safe} \tag{7}$$

$$C_3: H_{L1}(\alpha_{n+1}) - H_{L1}(\alpha_n) < -L_{safe} \wedge \sum_{i=1}^{n-1} H_{L1}(\alpha_i) \geq L_{safe} \tag{8}$$

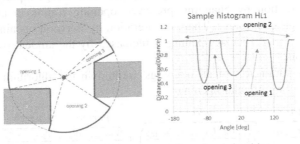

Fig. 3. A graphical representation of opening idea

The graphical illustration of an opening is presented in Fig. 4. The first condition (C_1) ensures that the robot not go in the opening that have slope angles that can be dangerous for robot's stability. C_2 and C_3 describe these opening that allow robot to get inside, since openings sites are high enough to make a turn.

$$T_k = \begin{cases} T_k \ for \ T_k < T_{kmax} - time \ for \ which \ the \ opening \ O_k \ is \ seen \\ T_{kmax} \ for \ T_k \geq T_{kmax} \end{cases} \tag{9}$$

$$W_k = \\ \sqrt{(H_{L1}(\alpha_1)\cos(\alpha_1) - H_{L1}(\alpha_n)\cos(\alpha_n))^2 + (H_{L1}(\alpha_1)\sin(\alpha_1) - H_{L1}(\alpha_n)\sin(\alpha_n))^2} \tag{10}$$

$$D_k = \max(H_{L1}(\alpha_i)) \ for \ \alpha_i \epsilon O_k \tag{11}$$

$$F_k = \begin{cases} 1 \ for \ D_k < L_{max\_vis} \\ 0 \ for \ D_k \geq L_{max\_vis} \end{cases} \tag{12}$$

$$O_{k,ctr} = \begin{cases} \frac{\alpha_{k,n} - \alpha_{k,1}}{2} \ for \ O_k : \forall i = 1..n \ H_{L1}(\alpha_{k,i}) < L_{max\_vis} \\ \frac{\alpha_{k,j_1} - \alpha_{k,j_2}}{2} \ for \ others, j_1 = i : H_{L1}(\alpha_i) \geq L_{max\_vis} \wedge \\ H_{L1}(\alpha_{k,i+1}) < L_{\max_{vis}}, j_2 = i : H_{L1}(\alpha_i) \geq L_{max\_vis} \wedge \\ H_{L1}(\alpha_{k,i-1}) < L_{\max_{vis}} \end{cases} \tag{13}$$

$$\alpha_{k,ch} = \begin{cases} \alpha_{dest} \ if \ \alpha_{k,1} \leq \alpha_{dest} \leq \alpha_{k,n} \\ O_{k,ctr} \ oterwise \end{cases} \tag{14}$$

Each opening calculated from one set of histograms (coming from one set of sensors' readings) can be either a new opening or an opening that exist in previous histograms. As sensors reading are noisy it is assumed that openings that exist for a longer period of time are more reliable and coming from correct sensor's measurements. Particular opening refers to a current obstacle placement description by histograms, but as the robot moves this obstacle placement is described by different histogram values. Therefore in order to choose possibly best opening an algorithm has to track openings for smooth movement. The smooth movement is ensured since iteration by iteration a chosen direction within the opening does not change rapidly, whilst when changing the direction by changing preferred opening results in abrupt azimuth change and non-efficient move. Therefore iteration by iteration openings are merged and T-coefficient for particular opening is increased by the amount of time it exists during calculation.

Finally as all parameters of all openings are known the algorithm calculates the cost to minimize for particular opening:

$$f(O_k) = \overbrace{\frac{|\alpha_{k,ch} - \alpha_{dest}|}{\pi}}^{part\ 1} + \overbrace{F_k \left(\frac{D_k - L_{max\_visibility}}{L_{max\_visibility}} \right)}^{part\ 2} + \overbrace{\frac{W_{kmax} - W_k}{W_{kmax}}}^{part\ 3} + \overbrace{\frac{T_{kmax} - T_k}{T_{kmax}}}^{part\ 4} \tag{15}$$

Cost is a sum of four elements (parts) each normalized to 1:

Part 1: describes what is the azimuth shift a robot needs to take from the one which the opening ($\alpha_{k,ch}$) to be guided directly towards the goal point (α_{dest})
Part 2: describes how deep the opening is. For an infinite depth opening this is equal to zero as $F_k = 0$
Part 3: describes how wide the opening is and is a measure of poor maneuverability within that opening
Part 4: describes how confident the algorithm is that the valley exists.

After the minimum cost opening is selected the algorithm calculates linear and angle velocities based on $\alpha_{k,ch}$ of selected opening:

$$v = f_{vlim}(d_{no})v_{max} \tag{16}$$

$$\omega = f_{\omega lim}(\alpha_{k,ch})\omega_{max} \tag{17}$$

v_{max} – Maximum linear velocity of the robot
ω_{max} – Maximum angular velocity of the robot
d_{no} – Distance to nearest obstacle when rotating towards $\alpha_{k,ch}$ direction.
f_{vlim} – function limiting maximum linear velocity
$f_{\omega lim}$ – function limiting maximum angular velocity.

Function limiting maximum linear velocity takes into an account the nearest obstacle when rotating to achieve desired $\alpha_{k,ch}$ direction. Therefore robot slows down when moving around obstacle and speeds up in free spaces. Typical curves of f_{vlim} and $f_{\omega lim}$ are presented below:

$$f_{vlim}(d_{no}) \propto e^{\frac{-L_{safe}}{d_{no}}} \tag{18}$$

$$f_{\omega lim}(\alpha_{k,ch}) \propto -sign(\alpha_{k,ch})e^{\frac{-C}{\alpha_{k,ch}}} \tag{19}$$

C – smoothing constant

5   The Experiment

In the experiment an IBIS robot – a commercial product of Industrial Research Institute for Automation and measurements was used together with 4 Hokuyo 2D scanners. Four scenarios have been chosen for a test purpose to check the performance of the algorithm. The results are shown below as four scenarios of trajectories when omitting obstacles.

Table 2. Experiments: a) the path taken by the robot and b) linear and c) angular velocity

Scenario 1

Scenario 2

Scenario 3

Scenario 4

Scenario 1:

In this scenario a robot need to omit three rectangular obstacles. A dashed circle shows the perception range of Hokuyo sensors mounted on the mobile robot. Until the robot gets to Point 3 no obstacle is sensed by the robot and it accelerates with a constant acceleration according to (16) and (17). After obstacle 1 is sensed robot turns on its right by decreasing its linear velocity and increasing angular velocity in point 3. The distance between obstacle 1 and obstacle 2 is too small to fit the robot, namely is smaller that L_{safe} the robot needs to turn right between point 5 and 6 and as the 3rd obstacle is sensed between points 8 and 9. This produces a change in sign of angular velocity in these points. The situation repeats in points 12 with an abrupt angular acceleration. In point 19 robot reaches the destination point and decelerates to zero linear and angular velocity. Linear velocity profile shows that the robot increases its average velocity during whole movement, whilst angular velocity profile shows oscillations around zero value that is typical for all robot's movement.

Scenario 2:

2nd scenario is a corridor like situation. The robot starts to accelerate until first obstacle is met around point 6. Until point 6 robot reaches almost full velocity of 3,3 [m/s]. Next in points 8, 9 and 10 it turns left to follow the top wall. During this movement average linear velocity is decreased as in point 9 the robot senses obstacles in half of its view. Another abrupt change in angular velocity is during the second turn in points 13, 14, 15 producing a peak of angular velocity, but as the robot finishes the turn it linearly accelerates towards the goal point and the acceleration starts in point 14. In point 21 robot reaches the destination point and decelerates to zero linear and angular velocity.

Scenario 3:
In this scenario a classic U-shape obstacle was given to a robot. It is an open U-shape obstacle, but the opening is too narrow for the robot to fit in. The robot start with a constant linear acceleration and near-zero angular velocity since the straight forward direction is a best choice at this point. The robot does not decelerate in points 2 and 3 even though the obstacle is sensed on the right hand side of the robot. This behavior is proprietorial as the obstacle and planned trajectory do not collide with each other. Passing by points 6 and 7 robot does not consider and opening in U-shape obstacle as is smaller than L_{safe} distance and therefore thanks to dilation procedure depicted in previous paragraphs.

Scenario 4:
In this scenario a robot was placed in a corridor-like environment. In the beginning stage of the movement robot accelerates with near zero angular velocity. When passing by point 9 it slows down since the opening on the left side of the robot occurs. This opening is mirrored in the opening of the histogram since width is greater thanL_{safe}, but clearly this opening is not chosen. This is because two facts: the robot passes this opening with high velocity of 3,3 [m/s] and therefore the parameter T_k of (9) in (15) is of small value as well as opening width of W_k (10) in (15). Therefore $f(O_k)$ is too large to be choosen. As the robot passes point 12 it appears that opening towards the back is of lover value of cost $f(O_k)$ and therefore the robot turns back and selects the proper opening and reaches its goal at point 21.

6   Summary, Conclusions and Future Work

In this work a time-efficient algorithm for fast obstacle avoidance has been presented. The method works regardless to used sensors thanks to a universal surroundings modeling. Computational efficiency is accomplished by compressing the cloud-of-points representation to three layer histogram that represents the environment in polar coordinates. The compression ratio for sensors set used for experiment was 11x and still the performance of the algorithm in sense of producing smooth, near human control trajectories of a mobile robot.

As for future work authors want to introduce a robot's model in velocity calculations to make the method more universal to use in any robotic platform with any set of sensors on board.

References

1. Biswas, J., Veloso, M.: Depth camera based indoor mobile robot localization and navigation. In: 2012 IEEE International Conference on Robotics and Automation (ICRA), pp. 1697–1702 (2012)
2. Emter, T., Emter, T., Saltou, A., et al.: Multi-Sensor Fusion for Localization of a Mobile Robot in Outdoor Environments. In: Robotics (ISR), 2010 41st International Symposium on and 2010 6th German Conference on Robotics (ROBOTIK), pp. 1–6 (2010)

3. Fukai, H., Mitsukura, Y., Gang, X.: The calibration between range sensor and mobile robot, and construction of a obstacle avoidance robot. In: 2012 IEEE RO-MAN, pp. 737–742 (2012)
4. Gardeazabal, D., Ponomaryov, V., Chairez, I.: Fuzzy control for obstacle avoiding in mobile robots using stereo vision algorithms. In: 2011 8th International Conference on Electrical Engineering Computing Science and Automatic Control (CCE), pp. 1–6 (2011)
5. Hashimoto, M., Ishii, T., Takahashi, K.: Sensor fault detection and isolation for mobile robots in a multi-robot team. In: 35th Annual Conference of IEEE Industrial Electronics, IECON 2009, pp. 2348–2353 (2009)
6. Hashimoto, M., Takahashi, K., Matsui, Y.: Moving-object tracking with multi-laser range sensors for mobile robot navigation. In: IEEE International Conference on Robotics and Biomimetics, ROBIO 2007, pp. 399–404 (2007)
7. Hussmann, S., Schauer, D., Macdonald, B.: Integration of a 3D-TOF camera into an autonomous, mobile robot system. In: IEEE Instrumentation and Measurement Technology Conference, I2MTC 2009, pp. 547–552. IEEE (2009)
8. Jingwen, T., Meijuan, G., Erhong, L.: Dynamic Collision Avoidance Path Planning for Mobile Robot Based on Multi-sensor Data Fusion by Support Vector Machine. In: International Conference on Mechatronics and Automation, ICMA 2007, pp. 2779–2783 (2007)
9. Kun, Q., Xudong, M., Fang, F., et al.: 3D environmental mapping of mobile robot using a low-cost depth camera. In: 2013 IEEE International Conference on Mechatronics and Automation (ICMA), pp. 507–512 (2013)
10. Luo, R.C., Chun Chi, L.: Indoor mobile robot localization using probabilistic multi-sensor fusion. In: IEEE Workshop on Advanced Robotics and Its Social Impacts, ARSO 2007, pp. 1–6 (2007)
11. Miaolei, Z., Wei, G.: Multi-sensor Data Acquisition for an Autonomous Mobile Outdoor Robot. In: 2011 Fourth International Symposium on Computational Intelligence and Design (ISCID), pp. 351–354 (2011)
12. Seong Jin, K., Byung Kook, K.: Dynamic Ultrasonic Hybrid Localization System for Indoor Mobile Robots. IEEE Transactions on Industrial Electronics 60, 4562–4573 (2013)
13. Sukumar, S.R., Bozdogan, H., Page, D.L., et al.: Sensor Selection Using Information Complexity for Multi-sensor Mobile Robot Localization. In: 2007 IEEE International Conference on Robotics and Automation, pp. 4158–4163 (2007)

Distributed Consensus Agreement of a Real Swarm Robotic System

Domenica Borra[2], Claudio Borean[1], Fabio Fagnani[2], Roberta Giannantonio[1], and Cai Tingting[1,*]

[1] SWARM Joint Open Lab, Telecom Italia, Italy
{claudio.borean,roberta.giannantonio}@telecomitalia.it
[2] Dipartimento di Scienze Matematiche,
Politecnico di Torino, Italy
{domenica.borra,fabio.fagnani}@polito.it

Abstract. This paper presents a real robotic swarm system deployed on a circuit. Each agent has constant speed and is able to detect a frontal crash, switching its direction with a given turning-back probability. Physical and logical description of the autonomous system is provided, and both a real testing and numerical experiments are presented, investigating convergence and times. Accordingly, a mathematical model assures also analytically the convergence of the swarming system to a consensus configuration, where all the robots drive with the same orientation along the closed circuit.

Keywords: Autonomous Systems, Swarm Robotics, Edge Dynamics, Distributed Randomized Algorithm.

1 Introduction

Starting from a real robotic swarm, we aim to classify our dynamical system with related randomized update rule, investigating convergence and times to reach consensus on the orientations of the robots along the cyclic circuit. In particular, we adopt the so-called gossip communication model (see e.g. [13]), i.e. only peer-to-peer asynchronous communication links are required. In this scenario, we say that the system has reached a consensus when all robots go round the circle in the same direction without bumping into each other. The aim of this work is to show with real experiments, simulations, and mathematical modeling that this system always converges to a stable solution if the system is not perturbed by external factors. It is important to notice that the adopted robots, Microbots described in Section 2, do not have any communication interface and as a consequence they cannot communicate among them or with the environment in ways other than the physical contact that can be detected thanks to a bumper put in front of the robot.

State of Art. In the last decades much interest has been devoted to consensus algorithms in the more general framework of estimates over distributed

---

* This work has been supported by Telecom Italia.

D. Filev et al. (eds.), *Intelligent Systems'2014*,
Advances in Intelligent Systems and Computing 323, DOI: 10.1007/978-3-319-11310-4_14

multiagent systems, see e.g. [1,2,3], where the system is modeled by a graph and each node has a local estimate of a global quantity and updates such estimate by means of only local communications. In literature, a wide spectrum of works propose randomized distributed algorithm in order to estimate a global quantity [4,7], with several applications to robotics, as in [6,10]. Each robot has two possible states, representing the clockwise (respectively anti-clockwise) versus orientation, therefore the system evolves in a finite state space. Related literature investigates quantized consensus over finite fields and boolean consensus, see e.g. [5,9]. The main reason of the increasing interest towards distributed and in particular consensus algorithms is due to its multiple applications to sensor networks, among them clock synchronization, and applications to social sciences, e.g. opinion dynamics [15,16]. Dealing with swarm robotic systems, the applications of consensus dynamics are several, among them coverage tasks [8], surveillance tasks [14], formation control [11,12]. In [22] there is an extensive overview from a swarm engineering perspective, and a special reference to collective intelligence behaviors emerging by simple actions from members of a swarm can be found in [23]. Swarm robotics can be a good solution for application scenarios in which human intervention could not be possible for safety reason, e.g. hazardous tasks such as gas leak detection [24], or physical constraints, e.g. water leak detection [25]: in such scenario a consensus might be reached without the need of a central coordination point that is usually unavailable.

Our Contribution. Provided a physical and logical description of the real swarm robotic system, we state the numerical results from real and simulated implementation of the algorithm, showing the emerging behavior of the system. Moreover, we provide a mathematical characterization of the system through a first abstract model, and second advanced model. For both models convergence analysis is investigated and they are proved to converge with probability 1, using tools from Markov Chains theory. The theoretical and empirical results match and convergence rates are studied in the experiments.

Paper Organization. This paper is organized as follows: the swarm robotic system is described in Section 2 with details about tests results; then Section 3 describes the simulated system and the experiment results are reported. Finally, in Section 4 the system is modeled from a mathematical point of view, and in Section 5 we draw the conclusions of this work with some insights for future research.

2   Real Swarming System

2.1   System Description

In our real swarming system we use PICAXE 20X2 Microbot, developed by Revolution Education Ltd [19], as members of the swarm. PICAXE Microbots, depicted in Fig. 2.1, might perform several tasks thanks to its sensors and computation capabilities. The main functionalities exploited in this project have been the Line Tracker and the Bumper Module. The size of each Microbot is $90 \times 100 \times 42mm$.

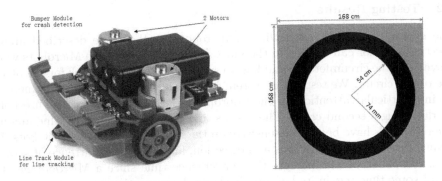

Fig. 1. (Left) Picaxe Microbot. (Right) Circuit overview

Thanks to a permanently illuminated led and a phototransistor detector, PI-CAXE Microbots are able of discriminating among different surfaces depending on the color. The Line Tracking feature has been used for letting the Microbot move over a circle (Fig. 2.1(right)) depicted as a black line on a white surface. The green area outside the circle represents the end-of-the-world for the Microbots, meaning they have to turn back and look for the black line if they get into this area. This event might occur e.g. when a robot is shoved off the circumference by other robots pushing from opposite directions.

Microbots start following the circle randomly either clockwise or anticlockwise and they might decide to change direction when they bump into another member of the swarm. A frontal crash is detected thanks to a Bumper Module placed in front of the Microbot. Our Microbots do not support additional sensors and therefore are unable to sense the direction of the Microbots they are bumping into. Therefore a Microbot might also experience a crash with another Microbot going in the same direction, and this may happen when e.g. the Microbots do not have the very same speed or when they face a Microbot that has balked at a line of bots, meaning such Microbot is not moving because of a jam caused by Microbots in a queue. At first we assumed that the Microbots maintained the same speed when programmed with the same logic, however that is unrealistic due to small hardware differences and other random factors that cause a slight drift in the velocity of the Microbots. In order to render the system more resilient to the possible different velocity of the bots and because of the formation of queues, we added a step back action working as follows. When a Microbot bumps into another bot, it will step back, wait few milliseconds, and then it will try to move forward again and only if it experiences a second crash within a very short time it will register the event as a crash. When a crash is indeed registered, the decision of inverting its direction is simply taken as a Bernoulli trial regardless of the direction of the other bot.

2.2   Testing Results

The system has been tested with 8 Microbots on the circle described above and the behavior can be seen in the video [20]. In some trial the Microbots were shoved out the circumference and had to spend some of time to seek for the black line of the circuit. We tested the system several times with different parameters, paying particular attention to the appropriate selection of the time threshold for detecting a second crash. The results, in terms of convergence time among different trials have been very sensitive on the initial deployment of the bots, in terms of their relative positions and direction, and also the occurrence of shove-outs. Shove-out events increase the convergence time since a Microbot has to spend some time regain its bearing, however the mean time to reach consensus was consistently under 2 minutes.

3   System Simulation

Different versions of the system have been simulated in Netlogo [21] to determine the best parameters for the trial, such as the turning probability, the Microbot density in the circle, and gleaming some insights into the convergence times we might experience in the real trial. The Microbots are simulated as Netlogo turtles in Fig. 2 starting with random positions and directions over a square path, without loss of generality compared to the circle. The path has a perimeter of $4 \times N \times$ Microbotsize with the same proportional scale as the real circle used in the test, with N being the number of Microbots and Microbot-size the length occupied by a single Microbot. In our simulations we assumed that Microbots had a constant a speed of 18 cm/sec, as it was measured in the demos.

Fig. 2. Microbots as Netlogo turtles

Modeling the system in a simulation environment gives more degrees of freedom with respect of the real experiments. For this reason the system has been simulated in four different scenarios even if some simulations have settings that cannot be replicated in real tests to be able of having a benchmark between theoretical and real experiments. The first simulation set, called only-frontal-crash ON, was then run with the unrealistic assumption that Microbots are able of detecting the direction of the other bots. In this scenario mean time consensus between bots is achieved in less than 1 minute. However Microbot data from a bumper-crash do not provide information about the direction of the crashing Microbot and therefore a second simulation (called only-frontal-crash OFF) has been carried out in which Microbots randomly decide to revert their direction if they detect another Microbot in front of them, regardless of direction. Results show mean time for consensus is achieved in almost 3 minutes. Working with real hardware revealed a different behavior from the simulation: due to the velocity-drift of Microbots they may detect a crash even after achieving consensus. Accordingly, the behavior explained in the previous chapter has been modeled in the simulation as follows: when a Microbot detects another Microbot on its front it first steps back and then tries to move forward again. Then and only if it detects once again the Microbot on its front it concludes it is indeed a crash and decides to revert its direction with a Bernoulli trial. In this revised version the option of having a leader, e.g. a Microbot that never changes its direction, has been introduced, resulting in 2 new simulation sets, namely Demo version no leader and Demo version with leader. With this behavior the simulated system converges in less than 2 minutes without leader, which further decreases to less than 1 minute if a leader is present.

3.1   Simulation Results

The system has been simulated in the 4 different versions described before:

1. Only-frontal-crash ON
2. Only-frontal-crash OFF
3. Demo version - no leader
4. Demo version - with leader

Table 1. Simulated Convergence Time [minutes] mean and standard deviation with 8 Microbots

	1 Demo version with leader	2 Only-frontal-crash ON	3 Demo version No leader	4 Only-frontal-crash OFF
Mean	0,8	1	1,9	2,7
STD Dev.	0,6	0,9	1,7	2,7

Table 1 reports the resulting mean and standard deviation of the convergence time for the 4 simulations sets, with decreasing performance; all simulations results are taken over 2000 runs.

It is easy to notice that solution 4 is the fastest to converge since the presence of a leader, e.g. a robot that never changes opinion, helps the system to converge faster to the same direction of the leader itself. The interesting result was that the solution 3, created for solving the practical problem of Microbots speed diversity, has produced an emerging behavior faster than solution 2. Introducing the step-back behavior makes the system more stable than the second case since, especially when queuing, they take more time to determine that a crash happen. In analogy with the decision making process we could say that Microbots take more time arguing before deciding to change opinion. Standard deviation results

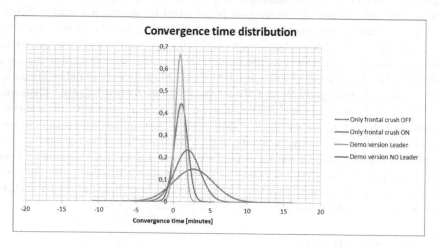

Fig. 3. Simulated Convergence Time [minutes] Distribution with 8 Microbots

confirm the ranking of the solutions proposed in Table 1, as it is easy to see looking at the convergence time distribution depicted in Fig. 3.

4   Theoretical Model

Since mathematical modeling of multi-robot systems is a complex issue due to complex interactions of the individuals and heterogeneity of the environment, often the numerical and empirical approach has been adopted by roboticists. The adopted simplifications lead to mathematical probabilistic models, with asymptotic properties that match the simulations reported in Section 3. The model of the multiagent system can be formalized with a graph $\mathcal{G} = (\mathcal{V}, \mathcal{E})$, with $\mathcal{V} = \{1, \ldots, N\}$ is the set of nodes, each of them representing a robot running through a closed circuit with constant speed, N is the total number of robots and $\mathcal{E} = \{\{i, i+1 \mod N\} \mid i \in \mathcal{V}\}$ is the set of edges and it has a ring topology. In what follows we investigate two mathematical models for our dynamical system, in Section 4.1 the abstract and simpler model where the state of the system is characterized by the only direction information; in Section 4.3

the advanced mathematical model in which the state of the system is given by both direction and relative distance data. In the first case, we assume that only frontal crashes may occur, while in the second case, also the queue phenomena are modeled and collisions may occur also when robots have coherent direction. In what follows a detailed description and related convergence analysis of both models are provided.

4.1 Abstract Model Description

The model assumes Only-frontal-crash ON, that is, each robot detects a crash if and only if two "fronts" are colliding. The initialization of the robots is randomly sampled (e.g. uniform distribution) and at any crash each the involved robots decides to switch its own direction with probability p. The state of the system is described by a vector of directions $X \in \mathcal{S} = \{-1, +1\}^N$. Suppose that the value $+1$ represents motion in the clockwise orientation and -1 in the opposite direction, and suppose that crashes do not occur simultaneously.

Dynamics is (approximately) modeled as a discrete time Markov chain $(X_n)_{n \in \mathbb{N}}$ (see [17]) on the state space $\mathcal{S}$ and with a transition matrix $P = (P_{ij}) \in [0, 1]^{2^N \times 2^N}$ defined below. Given a state $i = (i_1, \ldots i_N) \in \mathcal{S}$ we consider the set of potential crashes

$$C_i := \{s = 1, \ldots, N \mid (i_s, i_{s+1}) = (-1, +1)\}. \tag{1}$$

Denote by e_s the vector having all zeroes about a 1 in position s. We now define

$$P_{ij} := \begin{cases} \frac{p(1-p)}{|C_i|}, & \text{if } |C_i| \neq 0,\ j = i - 2i_s e_s \text{ for some } s \in C_i \\ \frac{p(1-p)}{|C_i|}, & \text{if } |C_i| \neq 0,\ j = i - 2i_{s+1}e_{s+1} \text{ for some } s \in C_i \\ \frac{p^2}{|C_i|}, & \text{if } |C_i| \neq 0,\ j = i - 2i_s e_s - 2i_{s+1}e_{s+1} \text{ for some } s \in C_i \\ \frac{(1-p)^2}{|C_i|}, & \text{if } |C_i| \neq 0,\ j = i \\ 1, & \text{if } |C_i| = 0,\ j = i \\ 0, & \text{otherwise} \end{cases} \tag{2}$$

where, we recall, $p \in (0, 1)$ is the probability of switching direction of each robot detecting a crash. Notice that $C_i = 0$ if and only if $i = \mathbf{1} = (+1, \ldots, +1)$, $i = -\mathbf{1} = (-1, \ldots, -1)$. These are (the only) two *absorbing* states for the Markov chains corresponding to a consensus motion direction of all agents.

Finally we define $\mathcal{G}(P) = (\mathcal{S}, \mathcal{E}_P)$ to be the graph associated with P where the set of edges is defined by the condition $(i, j) \in E_P$ if and only if $P_{ij} > 0$.

4.2 Convergence Analysis for Abstract Model

Our aim is to prove that P defines an *absorbing Markov Chain*, as we state in the following Lemma.

Lemma 1. (Absorbing Markov Chain property)
For any state $i \in \mathcal{S}$ there exists a directed path on $\mathcal{G}(P)$ to an absorbing state.

Proof. If i is absorbing there is nothing to prove. Suppose therefore that i is not absorbing. Then, it follows from the definition of P, that there is a directed edge from i to a state j where the number of 1's in j is one more than in i (this simply follows by transforming a crashing subvector of i of the form $(+1, -1)$ into $(+1, +1)$. This implies that, necessarily, in a finite number of steps we get to the absorbing state $\mathbf{1}$. Proof is thus complete.

Theorem 1. *(Convergence for the abstract mathematical model)*
For any initial robots configuration X_0, the Markov Chain converges to consensus w.p. 1, that is

$$\lim_{n \to +\infty} X_n = \pm 1.$$

Proof. It follows from standard results related to absorbing Markov Chains, see e.g. [17,18].

In what follows, we investigate the convergence time of the process.

Let us define the consensus agreement set as $\mathcal{A} = \{\mathbf{1}, -\mathbf{1}\}$. The convergence time is the hitting time of the consensus set $\mathcal{A}$, and it is a random variable defined as $T(\omega) = \inf \{n \geq 0 \mid X_n(\omega) \in \mathcal{A}\}$. We now define some quantities in order to characterize the convergence time of the process. In the case of absorbing Markov Chains it is called also absorption or exit time. Since we have 2 absorbing states and $2^N - 2$ transient states, the transition matrix can be written in canonical form for absorbing Markov Chain, as follows

$$P = \begin{bmatrix} Q & R \\ 0 & I_2 \end{bmatrix}$$

where $R \in (0, 1)^{(2^N - 2) \times 2}$ describes the probabilities to go from transient states to absorbing states, I_2 is the identity matrix, and $Q \in (0, 1)^{(2^N - 2) \times (2^N - 2)}$ describes the probabilities to go from transient states to transient states.

Define the *fundamental matrix* $F = (I - Q)^{-1}$, and from standard results $F = \sum_{k=0}^{\infty} Q^k$, where f_{ij} represents the expected number of times the chain is in the transient state j, given that it starts from state i. Given that the chain is in state i, the expected number of steps before the chain is absorbed is denoted by $t_i = \mathbb{E}[T_i]$, with T_i random variable. Let $t = (t_i)$ be the associated vector of expected times to absorption. The convergence time is the absorption time $T = \sum_i T_i / N$, and such random variable can be completely characterized by means of the fundamental matrix, and thus by means of Q.

Theorem 2. *(Absorption time characterization)*
The absorption time can be characterized as follows:

1. The expected time to reach consensus is finite and

$$\mathbb{E}[T] = t = F\mathbf{1}.$$

2. The variance of the absorption time is

$$Var(T) = (2F - I)t - t_h^2 = (2F - I)F\mathbf{1} - (F\mathbf{1})_h^2$$

where $t_h^2 = t * t$ is the hadamard product (i.e. element by element product).

The latter standard result on Markov Chains, gives us a hint to further investigate the convergence rates, as a function of the number of robots N, and their density in the circuit. As pointed out in Section 5, a future research direction is to characterize more explicitly the quantities $\mathbb{E}[T]$ (mean exit time) and $Var(T)$ as functions of N.

4.3 Advanced Model Description

In this framework, we aim to consider the queue phenomena, when the robots may crash even when in the same direction, considering that the sensor is placed only in the front part of each robot, moving with constant speed and switching direction with probability p. In order to include this case study, the dynamical system is described by the matrix $X = (X_s), X_s \in \{\pm 1\}^N \times D^N$. In other words, each agent s has state $X_s = (v_s, d_s)$, defined by its orientation $v_s \in \{\pm 1\}$, and its relative distance with respect to the supsequent agent $s + 1$: $d_s \in D = \{0, \delta, 2\delta, \ldots, \ell\}$, where δ is discretization step along the closed circuit that has length ℓ. The dynamical system can be described again as an absorbing Markov Chain, with transition probability matrix P and absorbing states belonging to the so-called consensus set $\mathcal{A} := \{X = (v, d) \mid v \in \{1, -1\}, d \in D^N\}$.

All the other states outside $\mathcal{A}$ are transient states: indeed a crash occurs whenever v is not a consensus vector, and there is $d_s = 0$ for some agent s, either with $v_s v_{s+1} = -1$ (i.e. the crash is frontal) or not. As in Eq. (1), we define the set of potential crashes of state $i = (v, d) \notin \mathcal{A}$, as

$$C_i := \{s = 1, \ldots, N \mid (v_s, v_{s+1}) = (-1, +1) \vee (v_s v_{s+1} = 1 \wedge d_s = 0)\}. \tag{3}$$

The possible transitions from state i to state j are as in Eq. (2) when the crash is frontal, otherwise, in queue phenomena if $v \notin \{\pm 1\}$ for each subvector $(+1, +1)$ such that $d_s = 0$, the possible evolutions are $(+1, +1)$ with probability $(1 - p)/|C_i|$ and $(+1, -1)$ with probability $p/|C_i|$. Whereas, for each subvector $(-1, -1)$ such that $d_s = 0$, the possible evolutions are $(-1, -1)$ with probability $(1 - p)/|C_i|$ and $(+1, -1)$ with probability $p/|C_i|$.

4.4 Convergence Analysis for Advanced Model

In this Section we prove that our process is an absorbing Markov Chain, similarly to Section 4.2.

Lemma 2. *(Directed path connecting transient states to absorbing ones)*
From any transient state $i = (v, d) \notin \mathcal{A}$, there exists a directed path on the associated graph going from i to an absorbing state $j = (v', d') \in \mathcal{A}$.

Proof. Given a transient state $i = (v, d) \notin \mathcal{A}$, two cases may occur.

1. If $d_s = 0$ for some s and $v_s v_{s+1} = +1$, that is, queue phenomena occur. Then, with positive probability p, the state may evolve such that $(a_s, a_{s+1}) = (+1, -1)$, thus case 2 occurs.

2. If $d_s = 0$ for some s and $v_s v_{s+1} = -1$, more precisely $(v_s, v_{s+1}) = (-1, +1)$, then a frontal crash occurs. We can proceed as in the proof of Theorem 1.

In both cases, we get a direct path with positive transition probabilities such that we reach a state in $\mathcal{A}$, from any transient state i.

Theorem 3. *(Absorbing Markov Chain property)*
The Markov Chain $(X_n)_{n \in \mathbb{N}}$ converges to the set $\mathcal{A}$ with probability 1.

Proof. As in Theorem 1, it follows from standard results concerning Absorbing Markov Chains (see e.g. [17,18]).

For the convergence time, we may refer to Section 4.2 for general results on absorbing Markov Chains.

5   Conclusions

In this paper we presented a real robotic swarm system, made of autonomous agents performing a randomized gossip algorithm: each robot follows a closed circuit with constant speed as described in Section 2, and, when bumps occur, each robot may switch orientation clock-wise or anti-clock-wise with a given turning-back probability. Such robotic system may have several applications as explained in Section 1, in a more general framework of randomized consensus algorithms. Real testing has been performed and presented in Section 2.2, and more extensive numerical experiments in Netlogo are provided in Section 3.

The two approaches lead to coherent results: the system converges to a consensus configuration where all the robots have the same orientation, and conjectures on convergence rates are provided. Finally, we formalized the robotic system from a mathematical point of view, at two different precision levels, i.e. we studied an abstract model in Section 4.1 considering only the orientations of robots, and a more advanced model in Section 4.3 able to reproduce also the queue phenomena. The system is proved to converge to consensus in both cases, using tools from standard Markov Chains theory.

Further work will be devoted to investigate analytically the convergence rates of such stochastic processes, that is, in mathematical words, the exit times of the considered absorbing Markov Chains. We aim to characterize such convergence times, as a function of the number of agents N, and the density of robots on the circuit, in order to gain scalability and robustness of the randomized algorithm.

Acknowledgments. Authors would like to thank Ennio Grasso for the prolific discussions and scientific hints on the mathematical modeling.

References

1. Moreau, L.: Stability of continuous-time distributed consensus algorithm. In: 43rd IEEE Conference on Decision and Control, Nassau, Bahamas, vol. 4, pp. 3998–4003 (2004)

2. Olfati-Saber, R., Fax, J.A., Murray, R.M.: Consensus and cooperation in networked multiagent systems. Proceedings of the IEEE 95(1), 215–233 (2007)
3. Tsitsiklis, J.N.: Problems in Decentralized Decision Making and Computation. PhD thesis, Massachusetts Institute of Technology (1984),
   http://web.mit.edu/jnt/www/Papers/PhD-84-jnt.pdf.
4. Fagnani, F., Zampieri, S.: Randomized consensus algorithms over large scale networks. IEEE Journal on Selected Areas in Communications 26(4), 634–649 (2008)
5. Carli, R., Bullo, F.: Quantized coordination algorithms for rendezvous and deployment. SIAM Journal on Control and Optimization 48(3), 1251–1274 (2009)
6. Jadbabaie, A., Lin, J., Morse, A.S.: Coordination of groups of mobile autonomous agents using nearest neighbor rules. IEEE Transactions of Automatic Control 48(6), 988–1001 (2003)
7. Aysal, T.C., Yildiz, M.E., Sarwate, A.D., Scaglione, A.: Broadcast gossip algorithms for consensus. IEEE Transactions on Signal Processing 57(7), 2748–2761 (2009)
8. Bullo, F., Carli, R., Frasca, P.: Gossip Coverage Control for Robotic Networks: Dynamical Systems on the Space of Partitions. SIAM Journal on Control and Optimization 50(1), 419–447 (2012)
9. Fagiolini, A., Visibelli, E.M., Bicchi, A.: Logical consensus for distributed network agreement. In: IEEE Conf. on Decision and Control, pp. 5250–5255, Cancun, Mexico (2008)
10. Ren, W., Beard, R.W., Atkins, E.M.: Information consensus in multivehicle cooperative control: Collective group behavior through local interaction. IEEE Control Systems Magazine 27(2), 71–82 (2007)
11. Savkin, A.V.: Coordinated collective motion of Groups of autonomous mobile robots: analysis of Vicsek's model. IEEE Transaction of Automatic Control 49(6), 981–982 (2004)
12. Bahgeci, E., Sahin, E.: Evolving aggregation behaviors for swarm Microbotic systems: a systematic case study. In: Proceedings of the 2005 Swarm Intelligence Symposium (SIS 2005), pp. 333–340 (2005)
13. Boyd, S., Ghosh, A., Prabhakar, B., Shah, D.: Randomized gossip algorithms. IEEE Transactions on Information Theory 52, 2508–2530 (2006)
14. Mullen, R.J., Monekosso, D.N., Barman, S.A., Remagnino, P.: Autonomous control laws for mobile robotic surveillance swarms. In: IEEE Symposium on Computational Intelligence for Security and Defense Applications (CISDA 2009), pp.1–6 (2009)
15. Hegselmann, R., Krause, U.: Opinion dynamics and bounded confidence: Models, analysis and simulation. Journal of Artificial Societies and Social Simulation 5, 1–24 (2002)
16. Liggett, T.M.: Stochastic Interacting Systems: Contact, Voter and Exclusion Processes. Springer (1999)
17. Kemeny, J.G., Snell, J.L.: Finite Markov Chains. University series in undergraduate mathematics. VanNostrand, New York (1969)
18. Aldous, D., Fill, J.A.: Reversible Markov Chains and Random Walks on Graphs, 2002, Unfinished monograph, recompiled (2014),
    http://www.stat.berkeley.edu/~aldous/RWG/book.html
19. PICAXE Official Website, http://www.picaxe.com/
20. Swarm MicMicrobot Demo Video,
    https://docs.google.com/file/d/0B-YBB9nYB7-gb1JXYk5FRVlQaEE/
    edit?usp=sharing&pli=1

21. NetLogo Website, http://ccl.northwestern.edu/netlogo/
22. Brambilla, M., Ferrante, E., Birattari, M., Dorigo, M.: Swarm robotics: a review from the swarm engineering perspective. Swarm Intelligence 7(1), 1–41 (2013)
23. Amé, A.J., Halloy, J., Rivault, C., Detrain, C., Deneubourg, J.L.: Collegial decision making based on social amplification leads to optimal group formation. Proceedings of the National Academy of Sciences 103(15), 5835–5840 (2006)
24. Oyekan, J.O., Hu, H.: Ant Robotic Swarm for Visualizing Invisible Hazardous Substances. Robotics 2(1), 1–18 (2013)
25. Halme, C.A., Vainio, M., Appelqvist, P., Jakubik, P., Schonberg, T., et al.: Underwater robot society doing internal inspection and leak monitoring of water systems. In: Proc. SPIE 3209, Sensor Fusion and Decentralized Control in Autonomous Robotic Systems, pp. 190–199 (1997)

A Comparative Investigation on Different Randomness Schemes in the Particle-Swarm-Based Repetitive Controller for the Sine-Wave Inverter

Bartłomiej Ufnalski and Lech M. Grzesiak

Institute of Control and Industrial Electronics,
Faculty of Electrical Engineering, Warsaw University of Technology,
75 Koszykowa Str., Warsaw 00-662, Poland
{bartlomiej.ufnalski,lech.grzesiak}@ee.pw.edu.pl
http://www.ee.pw.edu.pl

Abstract. In this paper different randomness scenarios for the recently developed direct particle swarm controller for repetitive processes are investigated and compared. The proposed controller employs the particle swarm optimizer (PSO) to solve in on-line mode the dynamic optimization problem (DOP) designed to shape the control signal in the constant-amplitude constant-frequency (CACF) voltage source inverter (VSI) with an LC output filter. The controller is of a stochastic nature. The DOP at hand is of αD dimensionality, where α denotes the number of control signal samples per each period of the reference voltage signal. Originally, the PSO requires pseudorandom number generators (PRNG) to be run throughout the iterative search to get a new set of numbers in each sample time. In DOP scenarios the swarm has to be kept alive during the operation of the inverter. This in turn implies that the pseudorandom numbers are to be generated in real-time using digital signal controller (DSC) resources. Four different randomization schemes have been tested: the dimension-and-particle-wise one, the dimension-wise one, the particle-wise one and an almost-deterministic one (also known as a list-based PSO). The last approach does not employ any PRNG in real time and as such establishes an appealing alternative in terms of its low computational burden. The effectiveness of such a scheme, when applied to the direct swarm controller, has been studied numerically in the paper.

Keywords: repetitive control, particle swarm optimization, dynamic optimization problem, voltage-source inverter, repetitive disturbance rejection, optimal control.

1 Introduction

In various applications of power electronic converters the repetitiveness of a process to be controlled is clearly apparent. The CACF VSI with an LC output filter may serve as an example. This kind of converter is a common part of systems that are designed to deliver high-quality AC voltage despite low-quality line

© Springer International Publishing Switzerland 2015   165
D. Filev et al. (eds.), *Intelligent Systems'2014*,
Advances in Intelligent Systems and Computing 323, DOI: 10.1007/978-3-319-11310-4_15

voltage and nonlinear loads. Possible applications include, but are not limited to, uninterruptible power supply (UPS) systems, power electronic transformers (PET) and off-the-grid electricity systems such as remote area power supply (RAPS) systems. There are three main approaches to control repetitive processes in CACF VSIs. Nowadays, still the most common method is to neglect the repetitiveness of a reference signal and usually constant, over many periods of the reference signal, frequency spectrum of a disturbance current. This in turn inevitably reduces quality of the output voltage waveform under nonlinear loads. The second method, by contrast, utilizes the internal model principle (IMP) and introduces oscillatory terms into the controller which makes selective harmonic rejection possible. The main limitations of multi-oscillatory controllers are related to problematic implementation of oscillatory terms near controller bandwidth and a computational burden growing with number of harmonics needed to be rejected. It has been also identified that they are sensitive to phase lags and in high-performance converters it is required to take special measures to compensate these delays [8,9]. Moreover, multi-resonant controllers are truly challenging in tuning and no optimal synthesis methods are available, except derivative-free stochastic search algorithms. The third method is also derived from the IMP, but instead of selective oscillatory terms, one universal model of any repetitive signal is being built into the feedback controller. This results in only one additional gain to be tuned and the resulting scheme can be analyzed in the uniformed framework for iterative learning control (ILC) and repetitive control (RC). However, the main obstacle in practical implementation is that most of ILCs suffer from long term stability problems and consequently a low-pass filtering with a cut-off frequency much below the Nyquist limit has to be implemented to ensure sufficient robustness [11,16,14,15]. Even the very basic P-type control law has to be modified into

$$u\,(p,k) = \boldsymbol{Q}\left(z^{-1}\right) u\,(p, k-1) + k_{\mathrm{RC}} \boldsymbol{L}\left(z^{-1}\right) e\,(p, k-1)\,, \tag{1}$$

where u denotes the control signal, e is the control error, k_{RC} is the controller gain, k is the iteration (pass, trial, cycle) index, p is the time index along the pass ($1 \leq p \leq \alpha$, where α is the pass length) with $\boldsymbol{Q}$ and $\boldsymbol{L}$ being usually non-causal low-pass zero-phase-shift filters, to stabilize the system. These filters compromise considerably the bandwidth of the controller. Moreover, there are no analytical design methods to determine $\boldsymbol{Q}$ and/or $\boldsymbol{L}$. However, probably the most serious obstacle in incorporating (1) into CACF VSIs lies in the fact that there are no formal proofs that a given pair of $\boldsymbol{Q}$ and $\boldsymbol{L}$ will stabilize the system against any repetitive load current, including disturbance currents with high absolute values of their derivative, in the infinite time horizon. The idea behind (1) is to cut-off totally the learning for higher frequencies. It should be noted that this control law constitutes integration of a control error in the k-direction. Due to a limited DC-link voltage in any VSI, the control error cannot be forced to zero for any shape of the disturbance current. If the system is then disturbed using such a "prohibited" frequency, it can have a destabilizing impact in the long run. This phenomenon has been already widely acknowledged by practitioners.

Moreover, there is a sneaking suspicion that low-pass filtering merely postpones a destructive buildup of oscillations because of the finite attenuation in the stopband of any practical digital filter. It has been tested in our laboratory that the control law of the form (1) may produce correct control signal, e.g., for hundreds of thousands of passes and then, after tens of millions of passes the system clearly manifests divergent behavior. The ILC gained some acceptance in robotics because the long-term stability issue may not be observed in many applications. Note that a robotic arm moving repeatedly at 1 Hz for one day makes less than one hundred thousand passes whereas the controller in a VSI at 50 Hz will make more than 4 million passes during the same time. That is why this scheme has not gained much (if any) acceptance among power electronics practitioners.

There is one more emerging family of solutions for repetitive process control. Their development is animated by the belief existing in the control practitioners community that performance index on-line optimization based controllers are strong candidates for future control schemes [10]. The feasibility of such solutions has already been demonstrated in the case of repetitive neurocontrollers for CACF VSIs [5,20,17]. Also the development of the proposed plug-in direct particle swarm repetitive controller (PDPSRC) [19,18] has been motivated by unsatisfactory results obtained using the classic ILC scheme.

PSO is a stochastic optimization method and it requires, in its original version, the implementation of a pseudorandom number generator (PRNG). Two such numbers would have to be generated in each controller sample time. To reduce computational burden of the developed PDPSRC several different scenarios have been tested: the dimension-and-particle-wise randomization, the dimension-wise randomization, the particle-wise randomization and two almost-deterministic ones. The term *almost-deterministic* is used to indicate that the algorithm requires only an off-line generated list of pseudorandom numbers (PRNs). The list is then used in the cyclic mode during the on-line operation of the controller. It should be noted that from the puristic point of view only PSOs with a hardware true random number generator (TRNG) can be regarded as stochastic ones. The distinction between PRNG and TRNG is crucial for cryptography whereas in stochastic evolutionary optimization algorithms such as PSO it is enough to implement a decent PRNG. The PRNGs are deterministic, i.e. a given sequence of numbers can be reproduced if the seed is known. Most (if not all) evolutionary optimizers are somewhat sensitive to a distribution of numbers but their true-randomness is of no importance. Moreover, many such optimizers, if real-time implementation is needed, are able to effectively operate even if a predefined pool of PRNs is used cyclically [3]. Nevertheless, these choices can affect the performance of the optimizer [2] and are always problem-specific. Therefore, our main goal is to verify if a list-based PDPSRC can be similarly effective as the basic one.

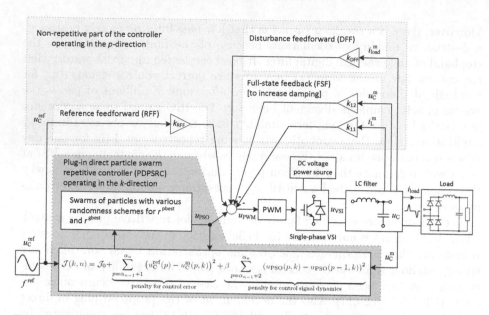

Fig. 1. Schematic diagram of the CACF VSI with the direct swarm repetitive path (*dark gray background*) and the supporting non-repetitive paths (*light gray background*) — an exemplary load in the form of a diode rectifier depicted for clarity (*the Load block*)

2   Plug-In Direct Particle Swarm Repetitive Controller

The main idea behind the PDPSRC is to store control signal samples u_{PSO} directly in particles. As the plug-in repetitive controller works only in the k-direction, it is essential to support it with a controller active in the p-direction. In this study, there are three paths that constitute the non-repetitive part of the controller as shown in Fig. 1. The full-state feedback (FSF) has been implemented to increase damping in the highly underdamped plant (compare R_{f} with R_{crit} in Tab. 1). This gives control signal

$$u_{\mathrm{FSF}} = -(k_{11}i_{\mathrm{L}}^{\mathrm{m}} + k_{12}u_{\mathrm{C}}^{\mathrm{m}}) \tag{2}$$

additive to u_{PSO}. Also, the reference feedforward (RFF) path

$$u_{\mathrm{RFF}} = (1 + k_{12})u_{\mathrm{C}}^{\mathrm{ref}} \tag{3}$$

is introduced to keep the unity gain for the zero frequency and the disturbance feedforward (DFF) path is added to compensate the resistive voltage drop

$$u_{\mathrm{DFF}} = (\hat{R}_{\mathrm{f}} + k_{11})i_{\mathrm{load}}^{\mathrm{m}} , \tag{4}$$

where $\hat{R}_{\mathrm{f}}$ is the identified resistance of the output LC filter. A significant identification error is assumed in this study ($\hat{R}_{\mathrm{f}} = 0.5R_{\mathrm{f}}$) to make control errors produced by the non-repetitive path more realistic.

Table 1. Parameters of the converter

Parameter	Symbol	Value
Filter inductance	L_f	300 µH
Filter capacitance	C_f	160 µF
Filter resistance	R_f	0.2 Ω
Filter resonant frequency	f_{res}	726 Hz
Critical damping resistance	R_{crit}	2.74 Ω
Reference frequency	f^{ref}	50 Hz
Sampling/PWM frequency	f_s	10 kHz
Pass length	α	200
DC-link voltage	–	450 V
Measurement noise (unfiltered)	–	ca. 1%
Rectifier power	–	ca. 6 kW
Rectifier current crest factor	–	ca. 2.5
Resistive load power	–	ca. 4 kW

The optimization task is 200-dimensional – the reference frequency of 50 Hz and the pulse width modulator (PWM) working at 10 kHz gives $\alpha = 200$ samples per period of the output voltage – and has been divided evenly among 5 swarms to reduce dimensionality of the optimization landscape and speed up responsiveness of the optimizer. The objective is to minimize in real-time

$$\mathcal{J}(k,n) = \mathcal{J}_0 + \underbrace{\sum_{p=\alpha_{n-1}+1}^{\alpha_n} \left(u_C^{ref}(p) - u_C^m(p,k)\right)^2}_{\text{penalty for control error}} +$$

$$+ \beta \underbrace{\sum_{p=\alpha_{n-1}+2}^{\alpha_n} \left(u_{PSO}(p,k) - u_{PSO}(p-1,k)\right)^2}_{\text{penalty for control signal dynamics}}, \tag{5}$$

where n denotes the swarm identification index, p is the sample identification index and β is the penalty factor (specific values are provided in Tab. 2). It is a model-free optimization as the plant itself serves a role of the critic (u_C^m denotes a noise corrupted measurement). Particles obey speed and position update laws

$$v_{nj}(i+1) = c_1 v_{nj}(i) + c_2 r^{pbest} \delta_p \left(q_{nj}^{pbest} - q_{nj}(i)\right) +$$

$$+ c_3 r^{gbest} \delta_p \left(q_n^{gbest} - q_{nj}(i)\right) \tag{6}$$

$$q_{nj}(i+1) = q_{nj}(i) + \min\{\max\{-v_{clmp}, v_{nj}(i+1)\}, v_{clmp}\}, \tag{7}$$

where v_{nj} and q_{nj} are speed and position of the j-th particle within the n-th subswarm, q_{nj}^{pbest} stores the best solution proposed so far by the j-th particle from the n-th subswarm, q_n^{gbest} denotes the best solution found so far by the n-th subswarm, c_1, c_2 and c_3 are the inertia, cognitive and social weights, respectively.

A velocity clamping is implemented and the speed limit is v_{clmp}. In the standard (classic) PSO, the random numbers r^{pbest} and r^{gbest} are uniformly distributed in the unit interval and are generated in each dimension for each particle in each iteration, i.e. they are dimension-and-particle-wise. In what follows, four less computationally expensive approaches will be tested:

☐ the particle-wise randomization, i.e. r^{pbest} and r^{gbest} varies from iteration to iteration and from particle to particle but are kept constant for all dimensions (also known as a linear PSO [22] because particle's velocity becomes a linear combination of the three components present in (6),

☐ the dimension-wise randomization, i.e. r^{pbest} and r^{gbest} varies from iteration to iteration and from dimension to dimension but are kept constant for all particles,

☐ the list-based PSO [3] with a memory-expensive table in which a list of random numbers is repeated every i_{cycle} swarm iterations (i_{cycle} to be specified by the designer) – these numbers have to be stored using resources of a DSC, hence i_{cycle} has to be selected with care,

☐ the list-based PSO with a memory-cheap table in which m_{cycle} (at most several hundred) of pseudorandom numbers are stored and if this pool is depleted, the list is cyclically repeated.

For the sake of compactness, the above approaches have been labeled using acronyms CPSO, LPSO, DPSO, ME-LBPSO$_{i_{cycle}}$ and MC-LBPSO$_{m_{cycle}}$, respectively. In all experiments described in this paper, the c_1, c_2 and c_3 factors have been calculated using the constricted PSO formula [6,7] and are 0.73, $0.73 \cdot 2.05$ and $0.73 \cdot 2.05$, respectively. The direction variable δ_p, having value of -1 or 1, enables to switch between attract and repel modes and is chosen to be dimension-wise (p-wise), i.e. individual control of diversity is possible in each search dimension. The Euclidean radius has been selected as the diversity measure.

Table 2. Parameters of the swarm

Parameter	Symbol	Value
Dimensionality of the problem	α	200
Number of particles	S	25
Swarms' update frequency	$f^{ref}S^{-1}$	2 Hz
Number of subswarms	N	5
Points of division (with $\alpha_0 = 0$)	α_n	$\alpha_1 = 40$, $\alpha_2 = 80$, $\alpha_3 = 120$, $\alpha_4 = 160$ and $\alpha_5 = \alpha$
Evaporation constant	ρ	1.07
Diversity threshold	D_{thold}	1.5
Penalty factor	β	0.25
Constant summand in cost function*	$\mathcal{J}_0$	0.01
Velocity clamping level	v_{clmp}	9.0

*to enable knowledge evaporation also for zero sum of squares in (5).

The optimization task at hand is dynamic due to varying load conditions. The PSO has been therefore modified to tackle the DOP (dynamic optimization problem). The first modification involves switching δ_p in (6) to -1 if the diversity of the swarm drops below a given diversity threshold D_{thold} as proposed in [13]. The second modification handles the outdated memory of q_{nj}^{pbest}-s and q_n^{gbest} by introducing gradual knowledge evaporation [4] in the following form:

$$
\begin{bmatrix} P_{nj}(i+1) \\ q_{nj}^{\text{pbest}} \end{bmatrix} = \begin{cases} \begin{bmatrix} \rho P_{nj}(i) \\ q_{nj}^{\text{pbest}} \end{bmatrix} & \text{if } \mathcal{J}(q_{nj}(i+1)) \geq \rho P_{nj}(i) \\ \begin{bmatrix} \mathcal{J}(q_{nj}(i+1)) \\ q_{nj}(i+1) \end{bmatrix} & \text{if } \mathcal{J}(q_{nj}(i+1)) < \rho P_{nj}(i) , \end{cases}
\tag{8}
$$

where P_{nj} stands for the particle's best fitness and the evaporation constant ρ has a positive value bigger than 1 for any positive-definite functional $\mathcal{J}$ and an optimization task formulated as the minimization one.

3 Numerical Experiment Results

Selected parameters of the plant are collated in Tab. 1. All randomness strategies have been tested in exactly the same load conditions to make results comparable, and the proposed scenario is as follows:
a) the swarms are initialized with near zero u_0^{PSO} control vector (no pre-tuning, e.g. for no load conditions, is assumed),
b) the resistive load of ca. 4 kW is applied for 150 s,
c) the resistive load is switched off and the diode rectifier (ca. 6 kW, current crest factor ca. 2.5) is switched on for 150 s,
d) the diode rectifier is switched off and the initial resistive load is applied once again.
It is assumed in this study that the performance of all controllers with a reduced computational burden (due to reduced number of PRNs needed to be generated in real time) is being compared to the CPSO-based controller. The CPSO requires two new random numbers to be generated each controller sample period. This means that a PRNG routine is invoked twice per controller sample time. It is also possible to use a TRNG to decrease computational complexity of the code to be run on a DSC. However, this notably increases the overall cost of the control system. Moreover, the needed entropy pool replenishment rate is challenging for off-the-shelf TRNGs [21]. For 10kHz-sampled controller and 16-bit long numbers, a constant download speed for true random bits no lower than 320kbs is expected. Consequently, it is relevant to design evolutionary algorithms in such a way that neither PRNG nor TRNG is needed in real time.

The performance of the CPSO-based PDPSRC is illustrated in Figs. 2, 3 and 4. The LPSO-based controller manifests substantially slower convergence rate (Fig. 5). It has been observed that the DPSO has the success rate lower than 100% and as such has been omitted in the comparison. The ME-LBPSO$_3$-based repetitive controller has very similar performance (Fig. 6) to the one with

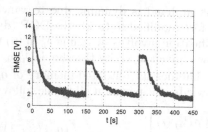

Fig. 2. The evolution of the root mean square error (RMSE) for the CPSO-based repetitive controller

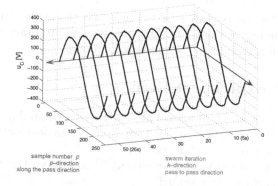

Fig. 3. The evolution of the output voltage waveform after applying the diode rectifier load in the CPSO-based repetitive controller case

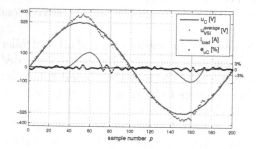

Fig. 4. Steady-state output voltage quality under the diode rectifier load in the CPSO-based repetitive controller case (*vertical lines* indicate transition points between sub-swarms)

dimension-and-particle-wise randomization scheme. The list of off-line generated PRNs is cyclically used over each 3 iterations of the swarm, i.e. the list of $3 \cdot 2 \frac{\alpha S}{N} = 6000$ PRNs is used which make the algorithm rather memory-expensive. The ME-LBPSO$_2$ with shorter list occurs to deliver significantly less satisfactory results

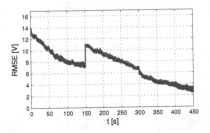

Fig. 5. The evolution of the root mean square error (RMSE) for the LPSO-based repetitive controller — much lower convergence rate as for the CPSO (to be compared with Fig. 2)

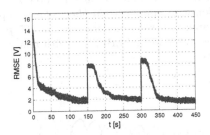

Fig. 6. The evolution of the root mean square error (RMSE) for the ME-LBPSO$_3$-based repetitive controller — similar convergence rate as for the CPSO (to be compared with Fig. 2)

than the ME-LBPSO$_3$. The less memory-expensive approach introduces a list of m_{cycle} PRNs, where m_{cycle} is smaller then the size of the pool needed for a single iteration of the swarm. This means that the PRNs, which are picked sequentially and cyclically, are repeated already before finishing a given iteration of the swarm. This has been observed to be detrimental for the search if the list has unsuitable length. For the moment, there are no sure ways to build an effective relatively small list. A hint about the minimal length in relation to the dimensionality of a problem has been given in [3], i.e. typically at most one hundred of random numbers for a 10D problem is recommended. The discussed controller operates in 200D search space subdivided into 40D subspaces. The list of $m_{\text{cycle}} = 127$ pseudorandom numbers has been used. To avoid early repetitions of pseudorandom numbers for a given particle in a given dimension, it is advised that the condition

$$\text{LCM}(m_{\text{cycle}}, 2\frac{\alpha S}{N}) = 2m_{\text{cycle}}\frac{\alpha S}{N} \; , \tag{9}$$

where LCM denotes the least common multiple, should be obeyed. The list has been generated by dividing $]0, 1[$ in m_{cycle} equally long intervals, and by choosing in each interval a number at random [3]. The performance of the MC-LBPSO$_{127}$ is illustrated in Figs. 7, 8 and 9. It can be observed that the system demonstrates very similar behavior to the CPSO-based solution. Obtained results suggest that

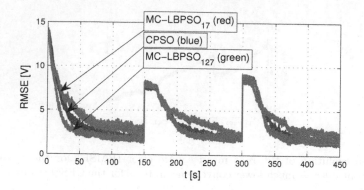

Fig. 7. The comparison of the performance of three randomization strategies: the classical particle-and-dimension-wise approach (*in blue color* – copied from Fig. 2), the memory-cheap list-based approach with moderate list of 127 pseudorandom numbers (MC-LBPSO$_{127}$ *in green color*), and MC-LBPSO$_{17}$ with relatively very(!) short list of 17 pseudorandom numbers

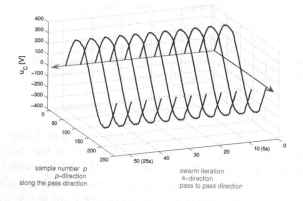

Fig. 8. The evolution of the output voltage waveform after applying the diode rectifier load in the MC-LBPSO$_{127}$-based repetitive controller case

the list-based PSO can be effectively used as a search engine in the PDPSRC. No real-time RNG is then essential, which along with distributable PSO calculations [1] makes the algorithm feasible for the implementation in an off-the-shelf industrial DSC. Shorter lists are also employable (see Fig. 7 for 17-number-long LBPSO behavior), but too short list can visibly deteriorate the performance in comparison to the original PSO algorithm. One should not generalize the above findings over plants other than the discussed CACF VSI. Nevertheless, it seems to be reasonable to assume that the strategies found to be good could be valid also for other problems of a similar or related type.

It should be noted that a list based stochastic search algorithms can adopt TRNG instead of PRNG without any additional hardware cost, because the

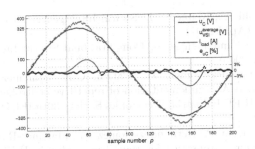

Fig. 9. Steady-state output voltage quality under the diode rectifier load in the MC-LBPSO$_{127}$-based repetitive controller case

TRNG does not have to be built into the system. The performance of the TRNG-list-based PDPSRC, with a list obtained at [12], has been also tested and the results are almost identical to the ones presented for the PRNG-list-based controller. This only reinforces the claim that a decent PRNG is sufficient for evolutionary optimizers.

4   Conclusions

The plug-in direct particle swarm repetitive controller for continuous repetitive processes has been described. Different randomization schemes for the velocity update rule have been tested. It has been verified that the list-based evolutionary search can be effectively used, instead of a pseudorandom number real-time generation, to synthesize the swarm-based repetitive controller. Therefore, the computational burden of the control algorithm has been reduced noticeably.

Acknowledgments. This research was supported by the statutory fund of Electrical Drive Division within the Institute of Control and Ind. Electron. (2014).

References

1. Biernat, P., Ufnalski, B., Grzesiak, L.M.: Direct particle swarm repetitive controller with time-distributed calculations for real time implementation. In: Proc. of the IEEE 7th International Conference on Intelligent Systems (September 2014)
2. Clerc, M.: Randomness matters. Tech. rep. (May 2012), http://hal.archives-ouvertes.fr/hal-00764990
3. Clerc, M.: List based optimisers – experiments and open questions. Tech. rep. (September 2013), http://hal.archives-ouvertes.fr/hal-00764994
4. Cui, X., Charles, J.S., Potok, T.E.: A simple distributed particle swarm optimization for dynamic and noisy environments. In: Krasnogor, N., Melián-Batista, M.B., Pérez, J.A.M., Moreno-Vega, J.M., Pelta, D.A. (eds.) NICSO 2008. SCI, vol. 236, pp. 89–102. Springer, Heidelberg (2009)
5. Deng, H., Oruganti, R., Srinivasan, D.: Neural controller for UPS inverters based on B-spline network. IEEE Transactions on Industrial Electronics 55(2), 899–909 (2008)

6. Eberhart, R.C., Shi, Y., Kennedy, J.: Swarm Intelligence, 1st edn. Morgan Kaufmann Publishers (April 2001)
7. Engelbrecht, A.P.: Fundamentals of Computational Swarm Intelligence, 1st edn. Wiley (December 2005)
8. Escobar, G., Hernandez-Gomez, M., Catzin, G.A., Martinez-Rodriguez, P.R., Valdez-Fernandez, A.A.: Implementation of repetitive controllers subject to fractional delays. In: IEEE Industrial Electronics Society 39th IECON Conference, pp. 5983–5988 (2013)
9. Escobar, G., Mattavelli, P., Hernandez-Gomez, M., Martinez-Rodriguez, P.R.: Filters with linear-phase properties for repetitive feedback. IEEE Transactions on Industrial Electronics 61(1), 405–413 (2014)
10. Kennel, R.: Predictive control – the powerful method to control power converters and drives in the future. Distinguish Lecturer IEEE Power Electronics Society Seminar, Warsaw (2012)
11. Longman, R.W.: Iterative/repetitive learning control: learning from theory, simulations, and experiments. In: Encyclopedia of the Sciences of Learning, pp. 1652–1657. Springer (2012)
12. RANDOM.ORG: True random integer generator (2014), http://www.random.org/integers/?mode=advanced (Online; accessed March 28, 2014)
13. Riget, J., Vesterstrøm, J.S.: A diversity-guided particle swarm optimizer - the ARPSO. Tech. rep., Aarhus Universitet, Denmark (2002)
14. Rogers, E., Galkowski, K., Owens, D.H.: Two decades of research on linear repetitive processes part I: Theory. In: Proc. of the 8th International Workshop on Multidimensional Systems (nDS), pp. 1–6 (2013)
15. Rogers, E., Galkowski, K., Paszke, W., Owens, D.H.: Two decades of research on linear repetitive processes part II: Applications. In: Proc. of the 8th International Workshop on Multidimensional Systems (nDS), pp. 1–6 (2013)
16. Shi, Y.: Robustification in repetitive and iterative learning control. Ph.D. thesis, Columbia University, USA (2013)
17. Ufnalski, B., Grzesiak, L.M.: Particle swarm optimization of an online trained repetitive neurocontroller for the sine-wave inverter. In: IEEE Industrial Electronics Society 39th IECON Conference, pp. 6001–6007 (2013)
18. Ufnalski, B., Grzesiak, L.M.: Feedback and feedforward repetitive control of single-phase UPS inverters – an online particle swarm optimization approach. Tech. Rep. 1/2014, Scientific Reports of the Cologne University of Applied Sciences (2014)
19. Ufnalski, B., Grzesiak, L.M.: A plug-in direct particle swarm repetitive controller for a single-phase inverter. Electrical Review (Przegląd Elektrotechniczny) 90(6), 6–11 (2014)
20. Ufnalski, B., Grzesiak, L.: Artificial neural network based voltage controller for the single phase true sine wave inverter – a repetitive control approach. Electrical Review (Przegląd Elektrotechniczny) 89(4), 14–18 (2013)
21. Wikipedia: Comparison of hardware random number generators — Wikipedia, the free encyclopedia (2014), http://en.wikipedia.org/w/index.php?title=Comparison_of_hardware_random_number_generators&oldid=600161058 (Online; accessed March 28, 2014)
22. Wilke, D.N., Kok, S., Groenwold, A.A.: Comparison of linear and classical velocity update rules in particle swarm optimization: notes on diversity. International Journal for Numerical Methods in Engineering 70(8), 962–984 (2007)

Affordances and SOA-Based Multi-robot Systems

Stanisław Ambroszkiewicz[1,2], Waldemar Bartyna[1,2],
Maciej Szymczakowski[2], and Kamil Skarżyński[2]

[1] Institute of Computer Science, Polish Academy of Science, Warsaw, Poland
[2] Institute of Computer Science, University of Podlasie, Siedlce, Poland

Abstract. A recent novel approach to ontology of mobile robot environment (common with humans) called Affordances is compared to SOA-based Multi-Robot System based on the paradigm of Service Oriented Architecture (SOA) and a generic representation of the environment. A robot, and generally a cognitive and intelligent device, is seen there as a collection of its capabilities exposed as services. The environment representation (ontology) has a form of a hierarchy of object types and relations between them defining together their structure. Possibility of adopting concepts from Affordance to enhance the object description is discussed.

1   Introduction

There is an opinion (see [15]) that the existing theories and technologies for mobile robots are insufficient for acting goal-directed in unconstrained, dynamic environments. Subject to restrictions in bandwidth, and computation time, a robot has to react to dynamic changes in such environments. There are no robust and general technologies for managing efficiently perception, action and reasoning.

A new approach to ontology of mobile robot environment (common with humans), called Affordances, is gained a lot of attention in Robotics. Generally, affordances mean opportunities for performing actions on objects. There is an interesting initiative for creating ontology called AfNet (theaffordances.net). There are several approaches to such ontology, e.g. [17].

Based on the Gibsonian principle of defining objects by their function, "affordances" have been studied extensively by psychologists and visual perception researchers, resulting in the creation of numerous cognitive models. These models are being increasingly revisited and adapted by computer vision and robotics researchers to build cognitive models of visual perception and behavioral algorithms in recent years.

This definition puts affordances into the environment as properties of objects, but states the necessary requirement of actions to be performed by a robot or generally by an agent. This makes affordances not solely dependent on an object to which the property belongs, but also on the agent, who has to complement the affordances with (at least possibility of) an action performance.

In order for the agent to be able to perform actions on objects, it needs to understand the qualitative structure of the relationships between them independent of other quantitative variation.

© Springer International Publishing Switzerland 2015
D. Filev et al. (eds.), *Intelligent Systems' 2014*,
Advances in Intelligent Systems and Computing 323, DOI: 10.1007/978-3-319-11310-4_16

The question of how to learn the (spatial, and general physical) relationships between different objects is one which has received relatively little attention in the literature, see [16] and [18].

Robots acting in complex environments need not only be aware of objects, but also of the relationships between objects. This poses an important problem to provide the basic (primitive) relations for building a new structural representation of the environment where these relations are sufficient for a robot to accomplish sophisticated tasks.

Affordances as the new approach to robot ontology is based on actions that can be performed (afforded) on objects and relations between objects. Surprisingly it has a lot of common with the Service Oriented Approach and Semantic Web Services in Information Technology. The actions are interpreted there as services whereas the relations between objects serve to express the precondition (for service invocation), and effect as the result of performing operation by the service. This very interpretation was the main reason to apply SOA to Robotics.

Our approach to SOA in multirobot systems (see [1] and [2]) requires new information technologies for developing distributed systems that allow defining tasks in a declarative way by human users and automatic task accomplishing by the system. Openness and heterogeneity of the system are essential here because they enable extensibility and scalability, that is, heterogeneous devices may be added to (or removed from) the system, in the plug and play manner. The key problem here is a representation of the environment common for people and other system components.

The interoperability presupposes a communication (defined by protocols) between heterogeneous components of the system concerning task delegation, planning, and its joint realization. The communication, in turn, presupposes a common formal language describing the environment. However, the language (understood as its syntax only) is not sufficient; it must be grounded in the environment, that is, it must have precisely defined semantics. The environment representation mentioned above serves as that semantics. In order to assure the understanding between the communication partners, the representation must be common for them, as well as for people who delegate tasks to the system to be executed. Hence, a universal representation of the environment and the corresponding description language are the basis for defining protocols needed for achieving interoperability in multirobot systems.

2   Environment Representations

The basis for providing interoperability of heterogeneous devices is universal common representation of the environment for humans and devices. Classic representations in robotics (see e.g. [3]) are based on metric and topological approaches dedicated mostly to tasks related to navigation. Another approach, Spatial Semantic Hierarchy (SSH), [4], is based on the concept of cognitive map and hierarchical representation of spatial environment structure. Recently there are object based approaches (see [5]) where the environment is represented as a map of places connected by passages. Places are probabilistic graphs encoding objects and relations between them.

The main problem here is an automation of the process of creating a map by recognition and classification of objects applying probabilistic methods. For example, object, recognized (with some probability) as a refrigerator, is supposed to belong to the class of kitchen. In the paper [6], the environment representation is composed of two object hierarchies; the first one (called spatial) related to sensor data in the form of object images or occupancy grid, and the second one (called conceptual) related to abstract notions of the representation. The recognition of places and objects consists of matching sensor data against the abstract notions. A variation of this approach is presented in [7], where the probabilistic methods are used for object recognition.

Special attention deserves the approach proposed 25 years ago by C. Zieliński, see [9], [10], and [11]. It is based on the notion of object defined by attributes, and relations between the objects. The representation was created mainly for an environment of robot manipulators, and was the semantics of robot programming language called TORBOL. Actually, the approach applied in our SOA Multirobot System is based on the general idea proposed by C. Zielinski. However, it introduces additional hierarchy between objects, and abstract objects like a space in a domestic premise. Note that this approach is the first one in Robotics (in the context of Affordances) where the qualitative relations between objects were taken as crucial element of the environment representation.

The approach represented by the AfNet project (see [12]) originates in the Gibsonian theory of qualifying objects by the functionality rendered, 'affordances' or functional descriptors afforded by objects. It has been used recently for perceptual object definitions using the principle of *form follows function*. Component or part affordances, which describe the functional (structural, material) and semantic properties along with the topological relationships between parts are used to build a generic, scalable and cognitive architecture for such object class recognition and visual perception systems. For example, structural affordance corresponds to inferred knowledge about the 2D/3D shape of the object (detection of a cylindrical or circular shape corresponding to a part of the object or as a whole, indicates a 'Roll-ability' affordance; or having a handle indicates a "Grasp-support-ability" affordance).

Information about affordances can largely improve the process of searching objects related to a given class of functionality. However, in order to obtain this knowledge, the structure of an object must be defined. Only then, the object functionality may be inferred.

3   The Concept of Object Maps

In the Computer Science related to Robotics, the term "ontology" is frequently equivalent to the "representation of an environment of multirobot system". The most popular definition of ontology was given by Tom Gruber in 1993 (see [14]) in the following way: *An ontology is a specification of a conceptualization.* Conceptualization is understood here as an abstract and simplified model (representation) of the real environment. It is a formal description of *concepts* (objects) and *relations* between them. Since the model is supposed to serve the interoperability, it must be common and formally specified, i.e., the definitions of objects and relations must be unambiguous in order to be processed automatically.

In the proposed representation, it is supposed that each object is of some predefined type. Object is determined by a collection of attributes, and optionally its internal hierarchical structure consisting of sub-objects and relations between these sub-objects (see Fig. 2.). The objects that do not have internal structure are called *elementary objects*, and their types are called *elementary types*. Object of type WALL may serve as an example of elementary object. It is determined by the attributes: width, height and color. The type ROOM may be example of a complex type; its internal structure is composed of elementary types such as walls, floor, ceiling, windows and doors, as well as the relations between these objects (see Fig. 1.).

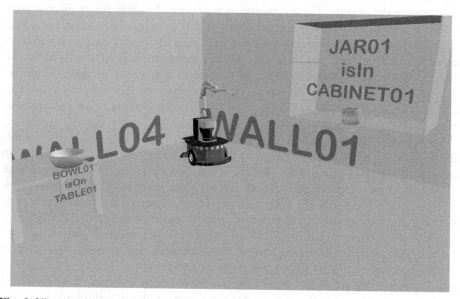

Fig. 1. Visualization of the object map of a room generated from the definitions of the objects and relations between them

A particular object (as an instance of a type) is defined by specifying concrete values of its attributes, and (if it is of complex type) also by specifying its sub-objects. Instance of the representation (called also model or a map of the environment) is defined as a specification of an object of a complex type.

The proposed approach is focused mainly on the representation of the objects and relations between objects that can be recognized by a robot. The automatic map creation by a robot (like in SLAM) without knowing at least the general structure of the environment (that is, the types) is not possible. However, a robot may measure values of attributes (for example, in an unexplored room), and, in this way, recognize specific objects specifying the map in more details, and updating it.

The hierarchical and structural definition of environment representation cannot be replaced by functional approaches (e. g. affordance), because devices need more information in order to operate on an object (not just the set of available operations).

However, the structural representation can be augmented by functional information. In the context of multirobot system abilities can be converted to object attributes or interfaces implemented by objects type (a concept from computer programing). This can largely improve overall system performance by reducing the time needed to infer whether a robot can execute a given action on a given object. Only after confirming the affordance a device may check related values of other attributes. For example, if a robot needs to hide a given object (put it in a container), it may first look for objects that support *contain-ability* and then check whether the objects have required dimensions.

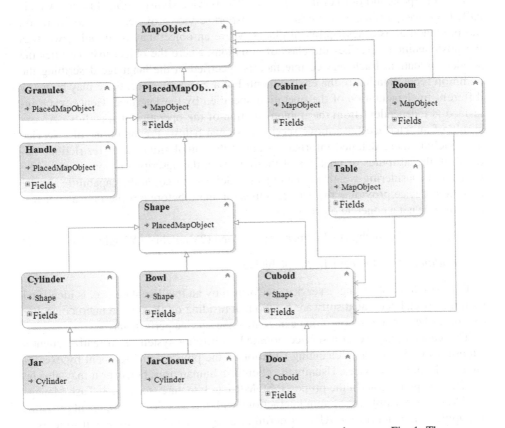

Fig. 2. The diagram of object types for the testing environment shown on Fig. 1. The arrows represent inheritance.

The representation, described roughly in the paper, is expressed in XML; that is, attributes, relations, object types, and objects are XML-structures. There is also the formal language, called Entish, see [13] for describing local situations in the environment.

4   General Architecture of Service Oriented MultiRobot System

In the proposed architecture, capabilities of devices are considered as services. Each service is able to perform an action or function, like transport service which moves an object from one place to another; or search service performed by a sensor network (or a mobile robot equipped with sensors) that can recognize and localize an object based on given set of its attributes. Another service example is a software application performing special data processing. Services should publish their ability in the form of the type of operation they perform, preconditions necessary for operation execution, and effects (postcondition) of its execution. The service ability, defined in this way, is called *service interface*. In the case of a transport service provided by a mobile robot, the precondition is a description of places where an object may be initially, whereas the postcondition describes the class of situations where the object may be after the service execution. Each service interface is specified in the language describing the common representation of the environment. For a given interface, there may be many different implementation of the operation specified by the interface. Hence, each interface is independent from the implementation of the operation it specifies. An example of an interface for a move service is shown below. Preconditions of a service may include more detailed information about the initial situation or restrictions defined on the attributes or relations of the objects in the description. For example, the restriction considering weight of the object is defined based on the capabilities of the particular device providing the service. Question mark before a name indicates that it is a variable not a concrete object name.

precondition: (?mapObject isIn ?mapObject1) and (?MapObject.Weight < 3)   (1)

postcondition: ?mapObject isIn ?mapObject2

In the multirobot setting, a service, performed by an intelligent device, is identified with the special dedicated software component residing on the device microcontroller (or somewhere in the Internet) that can control the service performance.

The general purpose of a service-oriented multirobot system is to realize client's intention by appropriately changing situation in the physical environment by executing a collection of services. Usually the client is a human user; however it may also be a software application. In the proposed SOMRS architecture, see Fig. 3, Task Manager (TM) is responsible for system interactions with the user. This component provides a graphical user interface (GUI) for defining user's intention, translates it to a common communication language, and delegates it (as a task) to an Agent to realize. In the final phase TM notifies the user on the situations emerged during the task realization. After receiving a task, the Agent discovers services (via Service Registry (SR)) that (when composed) could jointly perform the task. Then the Agent arranges (with the discovered services) conditions of their execution and composes them into a process of task realization.

For example, the client may want for the jar to be taken out of the cabinet and put on the table. Thus his intention can be described as a situation in which the jar is on the table (see formula below).

$$initial\ situation:\ \text{Jar01 isIn Cabinet01} \tag{2}$$

$$client's\ intention:\ \text{Jar01 isOn Table01}$$

In response to this request, Task Manager decomposes the task into sub-tasks that can be realized by one service (in the example there will be only one sub-task that can be realized be a *move* service). The sub-task is send to Agent that queries Service Registry about services that can realize given sub-task. After receiving information about these services, Agent arranges with them conditions of their execution, e. g. if they are able to move given object (it may be to heavy) or when the execution will be invoked. During execution of the plan Task Manager is also responsible for handling exceptional situation. For example, if invoked service will not find the object to be moved and notify Task Manager (through the Agent), the Task Manager will schedule a *search* task for a given object and then repeat the *move* task.

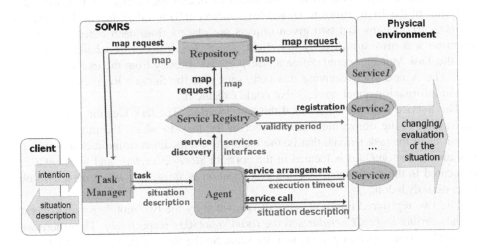

Fig. 3. General schema of the proposed multirobot system architecture, its components, and interactions between them

A new service becomes available in the system, if it publishes its interface to the Service Registry. Representation of the physical environment (in the form of object maps) is stored in the Repository. It provides the maps to the Task Manager (for intention formulation), to the Service Registry (for determining services requested by an agent for task realization), and to some services that need them for localization and navigation.

5   Experiments

The first prototype implementation of the proposed SOMRS system was realized in the Java programming language in version 1.6. The Task Manager, the Agent and the Service Registry were implemented as servlets (Java Servlet Technology) and run on the Apache Tomcat 6.0 application server. Services were provided by two mobile robots Pioneer 3 (P3-DX). The communication between the robots and work stations was based on a local wireless network. Two different test environments, consisting of a room and an adjacent corridor, were used to carry out the experiments.

Because of the available devices, two mobile robots equipped with web cameras and grippers, the possible services that they can provide include searching and moving objects. This small set of services allows, however, for realization of standard and more complex intentions like moving objects and inspecting a given set of locations. The abstract plans (used by the Task Manager) for realization of these intentions were created manually. The Service Registry can automatically decompose, if needed, the search and transport tasks into subtasks based on hierarchical routing in the object maps of the test environments.

The experiments consisted in realizations of intentions having the following description of the final situation: (*smallBox isAdjacentTo woodenCloset*). The relation *isAdjacentTo* means that two given objects are placed close each other. The initial situation was also specified by the client: (*smallBox isAdjacentTo bathroomDoor*). So, the Task Manager could define a transport task directly from the intention formulas. The Agent, after receiving this task, sent it to the Service Registry in order to obtain information about services that could execute it.

The Service Registry determined the task location. The task location is the lowest (according to the object hierarchy) object in the map to which the initial and final locations of the task belong, that is, the locations are its direct or indirect sub-objects. Because *bathroomDoor* is located in the corridor *storey2Corridor* and *woodenCloset* is located in the room *room303c* the task location is *storey2* to which these two objects directly belong.

The two registered transport services (provided by the two mobile robots) operate in the corridor *storey2Corridor* and the room *room303c* respectively. Thus there was no single service operating in the task location. So the Service Registry has to decompose the task into subtasks by determining a route between the initial and final locations. Since the two locations are placed next to each other, the route consisted of the two elements: *storey2Corridor* and *room303c* for which appropriate transport services were available. The door *door303c* was the object connecting the two elements of the route. So the final situation of the first subtask and the initial situation of the second subtask were the same: (*smallBox isAdjacentTo door303c*). An execution plan consisting of the two subtasks and the relations of succession (the subtask in the *storey2Corridor* has to be executed first) was sent to the Agent.

In the arranging phase the Agent sent the two subtasks to appropriate services (under the addresses specified in the subtasks). The Services Managers of the two robots responded positively. After the successful arrangement, the Agent sent the execution request to the service realized by the robot operating in the *storey2Corridor*.

The robot searched the region near the *bathroomDoor* (Fig. 4a) and found the *smallBox*, what verified the initial situation of its task. Then, it started the process of positioning in order to grasp the box (Fig. 4b).

Fig. 4. a) A robot searching for the box *smallBox* near the door *bathroomDoor*; b) the robot grasping the box.

In the next step, the destination location (the door *door303c*) is determined based on the object map of the test environment and the description of the final situation of the first subtask. The robot computed the route to the object in an occupancy grid, (its own low level representation of the local environment for navigation), and goes along the route (Fig. 5a). After reaching the destination the robot put away the *smallBox* (Fig. 5b) and sent to the Agent a message with a description of current situation related to the task, which in this case was identical with the final situation of the first subtask.

After receiving the response, the Agent sent the execution request to the second service provided by the robot operating in the room *room303c*. The robot executed the arranged task in the same way as the first robot and replied to the Agent. Then, the Agent sent to the Task Manager the message with the description of the current situation which was (*smallBox isAdjacentTo woodenCloset*).

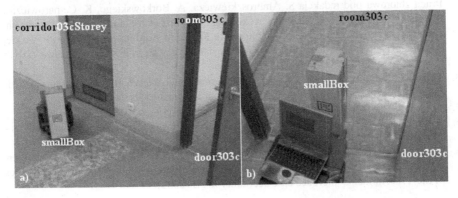

Fig. 5. a) the robot navigates in the direction of the door *door303c*; b) the robot puts away the box *smallBox*

The experiments were limited by the number of services, in this case, the number of heterogeneous robots. However, they shown that the proposed information technology can be applied to achieve interoperability in SOMRS.

6   Conclusions

A universal ontology and a system based on Service Oriented Architecture allows for building open and heterogeneous multirobot systems for accomplish sophisticated tasks delegated by human users. The general environment representation and common language based on that representation can be used to automate realization of simple and complex task including: defining tasks and service interfaces, plan generation, service arrangement and invocation, exception handling, as well as the communication between the system components.

Present work on our SOA Multirobot System focuses on implementing a simulation environment that can be automatically generated based on object maps defined in Repository. It will allow for testing the system in more complex environments and scenarios.

Coming back to Affordances it seems that the approach proposed by SOA Multirobot System is more general however the new ideas from Affordances can be implemented directly in the ontology by adding these objects affordances as the new attributes of the objects. The most important impact of Affordances is to turn attention to a new representation of the robot environment by focusing on generic qualitative relations between objects that could be sufficient for robots to accomplish sophisticated tasks. This is the real challenge in the contemporary Robotics.

References

1. Ambroszkiewicz, S., Bartyna, W., Faderewski, M., Terlikowski, G.: Multirobot system architecture: environment representation and protocols. Bulletin of the Polish Academy of Science, Technical Sciences 58 (2010)
2. Praca zbiorowa pod redakcja S. Ambroszkiewicza, A. Borkowskiego, K. Cetnarowicza i C. Zielińskiego. Tytuł: Inteligencja wokół nas: współdziałanie agentów softwareowych, robotów, inteligentnych urządzeń. Monografie Komitetu Automatyki i Robotyki Polskiej Akademii Nauk, Tom 15, Akademicka Oficyna Wydawnicza EXIT, Warszawa (2010) ISSN 1640-8969, ISBN 978-83-60434-79-6
3. Thrun, S.: Robotic mapping: a~survey. In: Lakemeyer, G., Nebel, B. (eds.) Exploring Artificial Intelligence in the New Millenium. Morgan Kaufmann (2002)
4. Kuipers, J.: The spatial semantic hierarchy. Artificial Intelligence 119, 191–233 (2000)
5. Vasudevan, S., Gächter, S., Nguyen, V., Siegwart, R.: Cognitive maps for mobile robots - an object based approach. Robotics and Autonomous Systems 55(5), 359–371 (2007)
6. Anguelov, D., Biswas, R., Koller, D., Limketkai, B., Sanner, S., Thrun, S.: Learning hierarchical object maps of non-stationary environments with mobile robots. In: Proceedings of the 17th Annual Conference on Uncertainty in AI (2002)

7. Galindo, C., Saffiotti, A., Coradeschi, S., Buschka, P., Fernández-Madrigal, J.A., Gonzá-lez, J.: Multi-Hierarchical Semantic Maps for Mobile Robotics. In: Proc. of the IEEE/RSJ Intl. Conf. on Intelligent Robots and Systems, pp. 3492–3497 (2005)
8. Zieliński, C.: Opis semantyki rozkazów języków programowania robotów". Archiwum Automatyki i Telemechaniki Politechniki Warszawskiej 35(1-2), 15–45 (1990)
9. Zieliński, C.: TORBOL: an object level robot programming language. Mechatronics 1(4), 469–485 (1991)
10. Zieliński, C.: Description of semantics of robot programming languages. Mechatronics 2(2), 171–198 (1992)
11. AfNet Project, http://affordances.alwaysdata.net
12. Ambroszkiewicz, S.: Entish: A Language for Describing Data Processing in Open Distributed Systems. Fundamenta Informaticae 60(1-4), 41–66 (2004)
13. Gruber, T.R.: A Translation Approach to Portable Ontology Specifications. Knowledge Acquisition 5(2), 99–220 (1993)
14. Rome, E., Hertzberg, J., Dorffner, G. (eds.): Towards Affordance-Based Robot Control. LNCS (LNAI), vol. 4760. Springer, Heidelberg (2008), http://link.springer.com/book/10.1007/978-3-540-77915-5
15. Rosman, B., Subramanian, R.: Learning spatial relationships between objects. The International Journal of Robotics Research 30(11), 1328–1342 (2011)
16. Hidayat, S.S., Kim, B.K., Ohba, K.: An Approach for Robots to Deal with Objects. International Journal of Computer Science & Information Technology 4(1) (2012)
17. Sjoo, K., Jensfelt, P.: Learning spatial relations from functional simulation. In: 2011 IEEE/RSJ International Conference on Intelligent Robots and Systems (IROS), pp. 1513–1519. IEEE (2011)

From High-Level Task Descriptions to Executable Robot Code

Maj Stenmark[1], Jacek Malec[1], and Andreas Stolt[2]

[1] Dept. of Computer Science, Lund University, 221 00 Lund, Sweden
{maj.stenmark,jacek.malec}@cs.lth.se
[2] Dept. of Automatic Control, Lund University, 221 00 Lund, Sweden
andreas.stolt@control.lth.se

Abstract. For robots to be productive co-workers in the manufacturing industry, it is necessary that their human colleagues can interact with them and instruct them in a simple manner. The goal of our research is to lower the threshold for humans to instruct manipulation tasks, especially sensor-controlled assembly. In our previous work we have presented tools for high-level task instruction, while in this paper we present how these symbolic descriptions of object manipulation are translated into executable code for our hybrid industrial robot controllers.

1 Introduction

Deployment of a robot-based manufacturing system involves a substantial amount of programming work, requiring background knowledge and experience about the application domain as well as advanced programming skills. To set up even a straightforward assembly system often demands many days of work of skilled system integrators.

Introducing sensor-based skills, like positioning based on visual information or force-feedback-based movements, adds yet another level of complexity to this problem. Lack of appropriate models and necessity to adapt to complexity of the real world multiplies the time needed to program a robotic task involving continuous sensor feedback. The standard robot programming environments available on the market do not normally provide sufficient sensing simulation facility together with the code development for specific industrial applications. There are some generic robot simulators used in research context that allow simulating various complex sensors like lidars, sonars or cameras, but the leap from such simulation to an executable robot code is still very long and not appropriately supported by robot programming tools.

The goal of our research is to provide an environment for robot task programming which would be easy and natural to use, even for plain users. If possible, that would allow simulation and visualization of the programmed task before the deployment phase, and that would offer code generation for a number of predefined robot control system architectures. We aim in particular at ROS-based systems and ABB industrial manipulators, but also other systems are considered.

© Springer International Publishing Switzerland 2015
D. Filev et al. (eds.), *Intelligent Systems'2014*,
Advances in Intelligent Systems and Computing 323, DOI: 10.1007/978-3-319-11310-4_17

In our work we have developed a system for translation from a high-level, task-oriented language into either the robot native code, or calls at the level of a common API like, e.g., ROS, or both, and capable to handle complex, sensor-based actions, likewise the usual movement primitives.

This paper focuses on the code generation aspect of this solution, while our earlier publications described the task-level programming process in much more detail [1–4].

Below we begin by describing the system architecture and the involved, already existing components. Then we proceed to the presentation of the actual contribution, namely the code generation process. In the next section we describe the experiments that have been performed in order to validate this approach. Finally we present a number of related works. The paper ends with conclusions and suggestions for future work.

2   System Overview

The principles of knowledge-based task synthesis developed earlier by our group [1, 9] may be considered in light of the Model-Driven Engineering principles [5]. In particular, the system described in the rest of this paper realizes the principles of separation of concerns, and separation of user roles, as spelled out recently in robotic context in [6]. It consists of the following components:

- An intuitive task-definition tool that allows the user to specify the task using graphical menys and downloading assembly skills from a knowledge base, or by using a natural-language interface [4, 7];
- An advanced graphical simulation and visualization tool for ABB robots, extended with additional capabilities taking care of other hardware used in our experiments;
- Software services transforming the task specification into a combination of a transition system (a sequential function chart) and low level code executable natively on the robot controller;
- Controllers specific for the hardware used: IRC5 and custom `ExtCtrl` [8] for the ABB industrial robots, and ROS-based (`www.ros.org`) for the Rob@Work mobile platform;
- ABB robots: a dual-arm concept robot, IRB120 and IRB140, Rob@Work platform from Fraunhofer IPA (`http://www.care-o-bot.de/en/rob-work.html`), Force/Torque sensors from ATI Industrial Automation (`http://www.ati-ia.com`) used in the experiments mentioned in this paper, as well as vision sensors (Kinect and Raspberry Pi cameras) used for localization.

The functional dependencies in the system are illustrated in Fig. 1. The knowledge base, called Knowledge Integration Framework (KIF), is a server containing robotic ontologies, data repositories and reasoning services, all three supporting the task definition functionality [2, 3, 9]. It is realized as an OpenRDF Sesame (`http://www.openrdf.org`) triple store running on an Apache Tomcat servlet

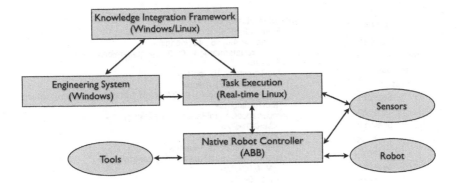

Fig. 1. The Knowledge Integration Framework provides services to the Engineering System and the Task Execution. The latter two communicate during deployment and execution of tasks. See also Fig. 5.

container (`http://tomcat.apache.org`). The Engineering System (ABB Robot-Studio [11]) is a graphical user interface for high-level robot instruction that uses the data and services provided by KIF for user support. The Engineering System uses the ontologies provided by KIF to model the workspace objects and downloads known skills and tasks from the skill libraries. Similarly, new objects and skills can be added to the knowledge base via the Engineering System. Skills that are created using classical programming tools, such as various state machine editors (like, e.g., JGrafchart [12], used both as a sequential function chart [13]—a variant of Statecharts [14]—editor, and its execution environment), can be parsed, automatically or manually annotated with semantic data, and stored in the skill libraries.

The Task Execution module is built on top of the native robot controller and sensor hardware. It compiles, with the help of KIF, a symbolic task specification (like the one shown in Fig. 2) into generic executable files and, when needed, hardware-specific code, before executing it. It is implemented on a real-time-enabled Linux machine, linking the external control coming from JGrafchart (a simple example is shown in Fig. 2(b)) or possibly other software, with the native controller of the robot. Depending on the system state (execution or teaching mode) or the action being carried out, the control is switched between the `ExtCtrl` system for sensor control and the native controller, allowing smooth integration of the low-level robot code with the high-level instructions expressed using the SFC formalism. It also runs adaption and error detection algorithms. The native robot controller is in our case an ABB IRC5 system running code written in the language RAPID, but any (accessible) robot controller might be used here. The Engineering System uses among other tools a sensor-based-motion compiler [15] translating a symbolic, constraint-based [16] motion specification into an appropriately parametrized corresponding SFC and the native controller code.

In addition to the benefit of providing modular exchangeable components, the rationale behind KIF as a separate entity is that the knowledge-providing

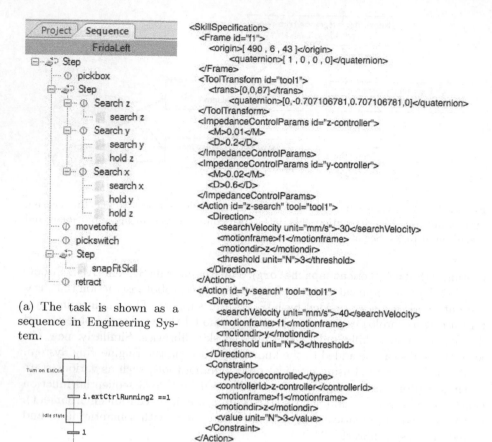

```
Project / Sequence
          FridaLeft
⊟ Step
  └ pickbox
⊟ Step
  ⊟ Search z
    └ search z
  ⊟ Search y
    ├ search y
    └ hold z
  ⊟ Search x
    ├ search x
    ├ hold y
    └ hold z
  ├ movetofixt
  ├ pickswitch
⊟ Step
    └ snapFitSkill
  └ retract
```

(a) The task is shown as a sequence in Engineering System.

```
<SkillSpecification>
  <Frame id="f1">
    <origin>[ 490 , 6 , 43 ]</origin>
      <quaternion>[ 1 , 0 , 0 , 0]</quaternion>
  </Frame>
  <ToolTransform id="tool1">
    <trans>[0,0,87]</trans>
      <quaternion>[0,-0.707106781,0.707106781,0]</quaternion>
  </ToolTransform>
  <ImpedanceControlParams id="z-controller">
    <M>0.01</M>
    <D>0.2</D>
  </ImpedanceControlParams>
  <ImpedanceControlParams id="y-controller">
    <M>0.02</M>
    <D>0.6</D>
  </ImpedanceControlParams>
  <Action id="z-search" tool="tool1">
    <Direction>
      <searchVelocity unit="mm/s">-30</searchVelocity>
      <motionframe>f1</motionframe>
      <motiondir>z</motiondir>
      <threshold unit="N">3</threshold>
    </Direction>
  </Action>
  <Action id="y-search" tool="tool1">
    <Direction>
      <searchVelocity unit="mm/s">-40</searchVelocity>
      <motionframe>f1</motionframe>
      <motiondir>y</motiondir>
      <threshold unit="N">3</threshold>
    </Direction>
    <Constraint>
      <type>forcecontrolled</type>
      <controllerId>z-controller</controllerId>
      <motionframe>f1</motionframe>
      <motiondir>z</motiondir>
      <value unit="N">3</value>
    </Constraint>
  </Action>
```

(c) A sample XML description corresponding to the guarded motion skill from Fig. 2(a) that is sent to the code generation service by Engineering System. The parameter values are either set automatically or by the user in the Engineering System. If a guarded motion is generated, e.g., from text and one of the parameters is an impedance controller, the controller is selected among the controller objects in the station. All mandatory parameters must be specified before the code generation step.

```
Turn on ExtCtrl
        ⊨ i.extCtrlRunning2 ==1
Idle state
        ⊨ 1
skill1
        ⊨ 1
Switch off ExtCtrl
        ⊨ i.extCtrlRunning2 ==0
```

(b) A small part of the state chart generated from the sequence in Fig. 2(a).

Fig. 2. A task can be created using the graphical interface of the Engineering System or by services for automatic sequence generation. The sequence shown is part of an assembly of an emergency stop button (see next section), consisting of a synthesized guarded motion, a complex *snapFitSkill* and three position-based primitives, see Fig. 2(a). In Fig. 2(b) the step named *skill1* is a macro step containing the synthesized guarded motion skill. Before and after the actual skill the steps for starting and turning off ExtCtrl are inserted. The idle state resets all reference values of the controller. Finally, Fig. 2(c) presents the corresponding input to the code generation service.

services can be treated as black boxes. Robot and system-integration vendors can offer their customers computationally expensive or data-heavy cloud-based services [10] instead of deploying them on every site and each installation.

3   Code Generation

In order to illustrate the process of code generation, we will use an example task where a switch is assembled into the bottom of an emergency stop box. Both parts are displayed in Fig. 3(a). The task is described in the Engineering System as a sequence, shown earlier in Fig. 2(a). First the box is picked and aligned to a fixture with a force sensor. Then the switch is picked and assembled with the box using a snap-fit skill. The sequence is mixing actions (`pickbox`, `movetofixt`, `pickswitch` and `retract`) that are written in native robot controller code (ordinary blind moves), guarded search motions which are actions that are force-controlled (alignment to the fixture), and it also reuses a sensor-based skill (`snapFitSkill`. In this section we present how we generate and execute code for tasks containing these three types of actions. As an example we will use the sequence shown in Fig. 2(a) that, when executed, requires switching between the native robot controller and the external, sensor-based control (`ExtCtrl`).

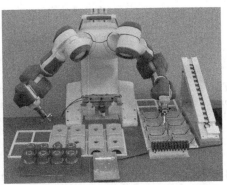

(a) The parts that are used in the process: the bottom of an emergency stop box (later "box") and a switch that will be inserted into the box.

(b) The two-armed ABB robot and the workspace setup.

Fig. 3. The example setup for the assembly experiments

The task sequence is translated into executable code in two steps. First, the native code for each primitive action is deployed on the robot controller. In this case RAPID procedures and data declarations are added to the main module and synchronized to the ABB controller from the Engineering System. In the second step a KIF service generates the task state machine (encoded as an SFC). Thus,

KIF acts both as a service provider and a database, where the service builds a complete SFC, which can include steps synthesized from skills that are stored in the KIF databases. The final SFC is executed in JGrafchart, which, when necessary, calls the RAPID procedures on the native controller. The data flow between the modules is illustrated in Fig. 4.

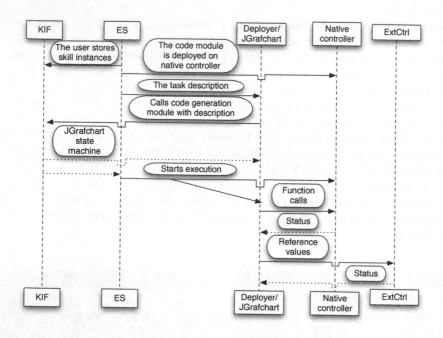

Fig. 4. The Engineering System (ES) sends the task description to a small helper program called Deployer which in turn calls the code generation service on KIF, loads the returned file and starts JGrafchart

3.1   Execution System Architecture

The execution system architecture is depicted in Fig. 5. The task is executed in JGrafchart, which in turn invokes functions on different controllers. The external controller (ExtCtrl) is implemented using Matlab/Simulink Real Time Workshop. It sends position and velocity references to the robot while measurements from the sensors are used to control the motion. Motions are specified using a symbolic framework based on iTaSC [16], by constraining variables such as positions, velocities or forces in a closed *kinematic chain* that also contains the robot.

The communication between the modules is done using a two-way protocol called LabComm (http://wiki.cs.lth.se/moin/LabComm). LabComm packages data in self-describing samples and the encoders and decoders may be

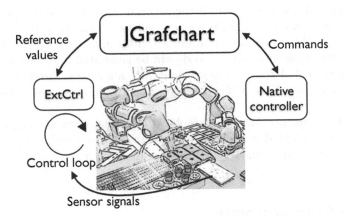

Fig. 5. A schematic image of the execution architecture. The task state machine is executed in JGrafchart, which in turn sets and reads reference values to `ExtCtrl` and sends commands to the native controller.

generated for multiple languages (C, Java, RAPID, C#). The `ExtCtrl` interface divides the samples into four categories: inputs, outputs, parameters and log signals. Hence, JGrafchart can set output signals and read inputs from the underlying controller.

LabComm is also used to send commands (strings and acknowledgements) to the native controller. In that sense, the protocol aligns well with ROS messages, and two-way LabComm-ROS bridges have also been created. This is important since a few of our robot systems are ROS-hybrids, where an ABB manipulator is mounted on top of a ROS-based mobile platform, each having a separate LabComm channel to JGrafchart.

3.2 Sequential Function Charts in JGrafchart

JGrafchart is a tool for graphical editing and execution of state charts [12]. JGrafchart is used for programming sensor-based skills and has a hierarchical structure where state machines can be nested. For each robot, the generated state machine will be a sequence. Each primitive or sensor-based skill is represented by a state (step), and transitions are triggered when the primitive action or skill has finished. Each state can either contain a few simple commands or be a nested state machine, put into a so called macro step (in Fig. 2(b) shown by a square with marked corners). The generated and reused skills are put into these macro steps while primitive actions becomes simple steps with function calls.

When alternating between sensor-based external control and the native controller, the controllers are turned on and off during the execution, so these steps need to be added as well during the generation phase. The switching between controllers is handled by the state machine in JGrafchart. When `ExtCtrl` is turned on or off, the robot has to stand still to avoid inconsistent position and velocity values. When a controller is turned on it starts by updating its position, velocity and acceleration values to the current values on the robot.

The state machine can have parallel activities and multiple communication channels at the same time. Hence, code can be generated for multiple tasks and executed in parallel. Although the state machine allows synchronization between the tasks, we do not have a high-level representation of synchronized motions yet.

Finally, the sequence IDs and graphical elements, such as positions of the blocks, have to be added in order to provide an editable view. We generate very simple layout, however, much more could be done with respect to the legibility of the generated SFCs.

3.3   Code Generation Service

The code generation is implemented as an online service which is called by the Engineering System. It takes an XML description with the sequence as input and outputs the XML-encoding of the sequential function chart understood by JGrafchart. An example of the input is shown in Fig. 2(c). Each robot has its own task, which needs to specify what LabComm port it will connect to. A primitive is specified by its procedure name and parameters to the procedure. Reusable skills are referenced by their URI, which is the unique identifier that is stored in the KIF repositories.

3.4   Reusing Skills

A skill that is created in JGrafchart as a macro step, can be uploaded to KIF and reused. During the upload, it is translated into RDF triples. The skills are annotated with types, e.g., SnapFit, and skill parameters that are exposed to the users are also annotated with types and descriptions. The RDF representation is a simple transformation, where each state in the state machine is an RDF node annotated as a *State*, together with parameters belonging to the state, the commands, a description of the state (e.g. *Search x*) and is linked to transitions (which similarly are annotated with type and values). In this way, the parameters can be retrieved and updated externally using the graphical view in the engineering system. When a skill is updated in the engineering system, the new instance is also stored in KIF with the new parameter values. The URI in the input XML file refers to the updated skill, that is retrieved during the code generation process and translated back from triples to XML describing a macro step. The macro step is then parameterized and added as a step in the task sequence XML.

3.5   Guarded Motions

One drawback of using the reusable skills is that there are implicit assumptions of the robot kinematics built into them, and thus the skill can only be used for the same (type of) robot. This limitation can be avoided by using a symbolic skill description and regenerating the code for each specific robot. This is what we do for the guarded motions. In this case, the skill specification is larger, as shown in Fig. 2(c), where three actions are described. First, a search in the negative z-direction of the force sensor frame (f1) is performed. When the surface is hit, the motion continues in negative y-direction of the same frame while holding 3 N in the z-direction, pushing the piece to the side of the sensor. The last motion is in the x-direction while both pressing down and to the side, until the piece is lodged into the corner. In order to setup the kinematic chain, the coordinate frames that are used to express the motions have to be set, as well as the tool transform, that is, the transformation from the point where the tool is attached on the robot flange to the tip of the tool. Each constraint is specified along an axis of a chosen frame. There can be one motion constraint (using the <Direction> tag) which specifies the motion direction, speed and the threshold value for stopping. The other rotational and translational axes can also be constrained. The constraint should also specify what set of impedance controller parameters to use. Knowing what robot the code is generated for, the control parameters for the kinematic chain are set to the values of the frames and each motion sets reference values on corresponding parameters. Simply put, it is a mapping, where several hundred output signals have to get a value, where most are just dependent on the robot type, while some represent the coordinates of the frames in the kinematic chain and other reference values during execution. During the code generation the right value has to be set to the corresponding reference output signal and this is calculated depending on what frame is used.

3.6   RAPID Code Generation

The actions that have native controller code are called primitives. There are several different primitives and, in fact, they do not have to be simple. The most used are simple linear motions, move primitives for translation and rotation, and actions for opening and closing the gripper. The gripper primitives are downloaded together with the tool. The simplest form of a primitive is pure native code, a RAPID primitive, which does not have any semantically described parameters but where the user can add arbitrary lines of code which will be called as a function in the program. This is an exception though, since most primitives are specified by their parameters. E.g., the properties of a linear move are shown in Fig. 6. The target positions will be calculated from the objects' CAD-models and the objects' relative frames and positions in the virtual environment. The code for each primitive type and target values are synchronized to the controller as RAPID procedures and data declarations.

Hence, JGrafchart will invoke a primitive function with a string consisting of the procedure name followed by comma-separated parameters, e.g, "MoveL target_1, v1000, z50". The string value of the procedure name can be invoked directly with late binding, however, due to the execution model of the native controller the optional parameters have to be translated into corresponding data

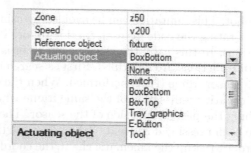

Fig. 6. The properties of a move primitive: zone data for specifying maximal allowed deviation from the target point, velocity in mm/s, the position(s) of the motion specified by a relative position of the actuated object to a (frame of a) reference object. A motion can have a list of positions added to it.

types, the target name must be mapped to a robtarget data object and, e.g., the speed data has to be parsed using native functions.

4   Experiments

In order to verify that the code generation works as expected, we tested it using the sequence from the Engineering System depicted in Fig. 2(a) which resulted in an executable state machine, the same that is partly shown in Fig. 2(b). The state machine is the nominal task execution, without any task-level error handling procedures. We have generated code for a two-armed ABB concept robot (see Fig. 3(b)) and the generation for guarded motions is working for both the left and the right arm, as well as for ABB IRB120 and IRB140 manipulators.

5   Related Work

The complexity of robot programming is a commonly discussed problem [17, 18]. By abstracting away the underlying details of the system, high-level programming can make robot instruction accessible to non-expert users. However, the workload for the experienced programmer can also be reduced by automatic generation of low-level control. Service robotics and industrial robotics have taken somewhat different but not completely orthogonal paths regarding high-level programming interfaces. In service robotics, where the users are inexperienced and the robot systems are uniform with integrated sensors and software, programming by demonstration and automatic skill extraction is popular. A survey of programming-by-demonstration models is presented by Billard [19].

Task description in industrial robotics setting comes also in the form of hierarchical representation and control, but the languages used are much more limited (and thus more amenable to effective implementation). There exist a number of standardized approaches, based e.g., on IEC 61131 standards [13] devised for programmable logic controllers, or proprietary solutions provided by robot manufacturers, however, to a large extent incompatible with each other. EU projects like RoSta [20] (www.robot-standards.org) are attempting to change this situation.

In industrial robotics, programming and demonstration techniques are used to record trajectories and target positions e.g., for painting or grinding robots. However, it is desirable to minimize downtime for the robot, therefore, much programming and simulation is done offline whereas only the fine tuning is done online [21–23]. This has resulted in a plethora of tools for robot programming, where several of them attempt to make the programming simpler, e.g., by using visual programming languages. The graphics can give meaning and overview, while still allowing a more advanced user to modify details, such as tolerances. In robotics, standardized graphical programming languages include Ladder Diagrams, Function Block Diagrams and Sequential Function Charts. Other well known languages are LabView, UML, MATLAB/Simulink and RCX. Using a touch screen as input device, icon-based programming languages such as in [24] can also lower the threshold to robot programming. There are also experimental systems using human programmer's gestures as a tool for pointing the intended robot locations [25]. However, all the systems named above offer monolithic compilation to the native code of the robot controller. Besides, all the attempts are done at the level of robot motions, focusing on determining locations. Experiences show [26] that even relatively simple sensor-based tasks, extending beyond the "drag and drop" visual programming using those tools, require a lot of time and expertise for proper implementation in mixed architecture like ours.

Reusable skill or manipulation primitives are a convenient way of hiding the detailed control structures [27]. The approach closest to ours is presented in the works of M. Beetz and his group, where high-level actions are translated, using knowledge-based techniques, into robot programs [28]. However, the resulting code is normally at the level of ROS primitives, acceptable in case of service robots, but without providing any real-time guarantees needed in industrial setting. In this context, they also present an approach to map high-level constraints to control parameters in order to flip a pancake [29].

6   Conclusions and Future Work

In this paper we have described how we generate executable code for real-time sensor-based control from symbolic task descriptions. Previous work in code generation is limited to position-based approaches. The challenge to go from high-level instructions to robust executable low-level code is an open-ended research problem, and we wanted to share our approach in high technical detail. Naturally, different levels of abstraction have different power of expression. Thus, generating code for different robots from the same symbolic description is much easier than reusing code written for one platform by extracting its semantic meaning and regenerating the skill for another platform. Hence, it is important to find suitable levels of abstraction, and in our case we have chosen to express the guarded motions using a set of symbolic constraints. The modular system simplifies the code generation, where the user interface only exposes a subset of parameters to the user, while the JGrafchart state machine contains the calculated reference values to the controllers and coordinates the high-level execution. The external controller is responsible for the real-time sensor control which is necessary for achieving the necessary performance for assembly operations.

In future work we plan to experiment using a mobile platform running ROS together with our dual-arm robot and thus evaluate how easy it is to extend the code generation to simultaneously support other platforms. The sequence can express control structures, such as loops and if-statements, ongoing work involves adding these control structures to the task state machine as well as describing and generating the synchronization between robots.

The robustness of the generated skills depends on the user input. One direction of future work is to couple the graphical user interface with haptic demonstrations and learning algorithms in order to extract e.g., force thresholds and impedance controller parameters. Another direction is to add knowledge and reasoning to the system to automatically generate error handling states to the task state machine.

Acknowledgments. The research leading to these results has received partial funding from the European Union's seventh framework program (FP7/2007-2013) under grant agreements No. 285380 (project PRACE) and No. 287787 (project SMErobotics). The third author is a member of the LCCC Linnaeus Center and the eLLIIT Excellence Center at Lund University.

The work described in this paper has been done in tight collaboration with other researchers from the project consortia. The authors are indebted for many fruitful discussions.

The authors are grateful to Anders Robertsson for careful proofreading.

References

1. Björkelund, A., Edström, L., Haage, M., Malec, J., Nilsson, K., Nugues, P., Robertz, S.G., Störkle, D., Blomdell, A., Johansson, R., Linderoth, M., Nilsson, A., Robertsson, A., Stolt, A., Bruyninckx, H.: On the integration of skilled robot motions for productivity in manufacturing. In: Proc. IEEE International Symposium on Assembly and Manufacturing, Tampere, Finland (2011), doi:10.1109/ISAM.2011.5942366
2. Malec, J., Nilsson, K., Bruyninckx, H.: Describing assembly tasks in a declarative way. In: ICRA 2013 WS on Semantics, Identification and Control of Robot-Human-Environment Interaction (2013)
3. Stenmark, M., Malec, J.: Knowledge-Based Industrial Robotics. In: Proc. of the 12th Scandinavian AI Conference, Aalborg, Denmark, November 20-22 (2013), http://dx.doi.org/10.3233/978-1-61499-330-8-265
4. Stenmark, M., Malec, J.: Describing constraint-based assembly tasks in unstructured natural language. In: Proc. IFAC 2014 World Congress, Capetown, South Africa, August 24-29 (2014)

5. Kent, S.: Model Driven Engineering. In: Butler, M., Petre, L., Sere, K. (eds.) IFM 2002. LNCS, vol. 2335, pp. 286–298. Springer, Heidelberg (2002)
6. Vanthienen, D., Klotzbuecher, M., Bruyninckx, H.: The 5C-based architectural Composition Pattern. JOSER 5(1), 17–35 (2014)
7. Stenmark, M., Nugues, P.: Natural Language Programming of Industrial Robots. In: Proc. International Symposium of Robotics 2013, Seoul, South Korea (October 2013)
8. Blomdell, A., Dressler, I., Nilsson, K., Robertsson, A.: Flexible Application Development and High-performance Motion Control Based on External Sensing and Reconfiguration of ABB Industrial Robot Controllers. In: Proc. of ICRA 2010, Anchorage, USA, pp. 62–66 (2010)
9. Björkelund, A., Malec, J., Nilsson, K., Nugues, P., Bruyninckx, H.: Knowledge for Intelligent Industrial Robots. In: Proc. AAAI 2012 Spring Symp. on Designing Intelligent Robots. Stanford Univ. (March 2012)
10. Stenmark, M., Malec, J., Nilsson, K., Robertsson, A.: On Distributed Knowledge Bases for Industrial Robotics Needs. In: Proc. Cloud Robotics Workshop at IROS 2013, Tokyo (November 3, 2013), http://www.roboearth.org/wpcontent/uploads/2013/03/final-13.pdf
11. ABB RobotStudio, http://new.abb.com/products/robotics/robotstudio (visited February 04, 2013)
12. Theorin, A.: Adapting Grafchart for Industrial Automation. Licentiate Thesis, Lund University, Department of Automatic Control (2013)
13. IEC. IEC 61131-3: Programmable controllers – part 3: Programming languages. Technical report, International Electrotechnical Commission (2003)
14. Harel, D.: Statecharts: A visual formalism for complex systems. Science of Computer Programming 8, 231–274 (1987)
15. Stenmark, M., Stolt, A.: A System for High-Level Task Specification Using Complex Sensor-based Skill. In: RSS 2013 Workshop, Programming with Constraints: Combining High-level Action Specification and Low-level Motion Execution, Berlin, Germany (2013)
16. De Schutter, J., De Laet, T., Rutgeerts, J., Decré, W., Smits, R., Aertbeliën, E., Claes, K., Bruyninckx, H.: Constraint-based task specification and estimation for sensor-based robot systems in the presence of geometric uncertainty. The International Journal of Robotics Research 26(5), 433–455 (2007)
17. Pan, Z., Polden, J., Larkin, N., van Duin, S., Norrish, J.: Recent progress on programming methods for industrial robots. In: 41st International Symposium on Robotics (ISR) and 6th German Conference on Robotics (ROBOTIK), pp. 619–626. VDE VERLAG GMBH, Berlin (2010)
18. Rossano, G., Martinez, C., Hedelind, M., Murphy, S., Fuhlbrigge, T.: Easy robot programming concepts: An industrial perspective. In: Proceedings 9th IEEE International Conference on Automation Science and Engineering, Madison, Wisconsin, USA (2013)
19. Billard, A., Calinon, S., Dillmann, R., Schaal, S.: Robot Programming by Demonstration. In: Springer Handbook of Robotics, pp. 1371–1394. Springer (2008)
20. Nilsson, A., Muradore, R., Nilsson, K., Fiorini, P.: Ontology for Robotics: a Roadmap. In: Proceedings of the Int. Conf. Advanced Robotics (ICAR 2009), Munich, Germany (2009)
21. Mitsi, S., Bouzakis, K.-D., Mansour, G., Sagris, D., Maliaris, G.: Off-line programming of an industrial robot for manufacturing. Int. J. Adv. Manuf. Technol. 26, 262–267 (2005)

22. Bottazzi, V., Fonseca, J.: Off-line Programming Industrial Robots Based in the Information Extracted From Neutral Files Generated by the Commercial CAD Tools Industrial Robotics: Programming. In: Huat, L.K. (ed.) Simulation and Application (2006) ISBN 3-86611-286-6
23. Hägele, M., Nilsson, K., Pires, J.N.: Industrial Robotics. In: Springer Handbook of Robotics, pp. 963–986. Springer (2008)
24. Bischoff, R., Kazi, A., Seyfarth, M.: The morpha style guide for icon-based programming. In: Proc. of the IEEE Int. Workshop on Robot and Human Interactive Communication (2002)
25. Neto, P., Pires, J.N., Moreira, A.P.: High-level programming and control for industrial robotics: using a hand-held accelerometer-based input device for gesture and posture recognition. Industrial Robot 37(2), 137–147 (2010)
26. Stolt, A., Linderoth, M., Robertsson, A., Johansson, R.: Force controlled assembly of emergency stop button. In: 2011 IEEE International Conference on Robotics and Automation, Shanghai, China (May 2011)
27. Kröger, T., Finkemeyer, B., Wahl, F.M.: Manipulation Primitives — A Universal Interface between Sensor-Based Motion Control and Robot Programming. In: Schütz, D., Wahl, F.M. (eds.) Robotic Systems for Handling and Assembly. STAR, vol. 67, pp. 293–313. Springer, Heidelberg (2010)
28. Beetz, M., Mösenlechner, L., Tenorth, M.: CRAM: A Cognitive Robot Abstract Machine for Everyday Manipulation in Human Environments. In: Proc. of IEEE/RSJ International Conference on Intelligent Robots and Systems, Taipei, Taiwan, October 18-22 (2010)
29. Kresse, I., Beetz, M.: Movement-Aware Action Control Integrating Symbolic and Control-Theoretic Action Execution. In: Proc. ICRA 2012, pp. 3245–3251 (2012)

Filtration and Integration System (FIS) for Navigation Data Processing Based on Kalman Filter

Mariusz Andrzejczak[1] and Martyna Ulinowicz[2]

[1] OBRUM Ltd. Mechanical Instruments R&D Centre, Gliwice, 44-117, Poland
mariusz.andrzejczak@pho.pl
[2] Department of Automation and Aeronautical Systems, Warsaw University of Technology, Warsaw, 00-665, Poland
martyna.ulinowicz@meil.pw.edu.pl

Abstract. The Filtration and Integration System (FIS) is proposed for navigation data processing. The system is based on Kalman Filter approach. FIS is implemented for ship navigation and is successfully verified exploiting the data from sea trials of passenger ship. Proposed system provide a support for navigation, especially in congested sea areas, in narrow passages and harbors, where accurate navigation information is crucial.

Keywords: signal processing, Kalman Filter, integration of navigation data.

1 Introduction

Recent years brought significant development of navigation systems, increase of their accuracy and the ability to process and display navigation information. Navigation information, which has been obtained as a result of long term calculations traditionally performed by the ship master, currently is obtained without human intervention and it is integrated with other navigation aids, which are available in electronic form. This resulted in a change of the role played by masters of vessels. Having support from navigation systems, they professional duties shifted to supervision and validation of obtained values of parameters describing the ship motion. It reduced crew workload as well and contributed to increase the safety of shipping.

Signal processing of navigation data using Filtration and Integration System provide a support for navigation, especially in congested sea areas, in narrow passages and harbors. It improve navigation accuracy using Kalman Filter based technique and integration of signals from different sources (as frequently information about the same parameter is available from few sensors).

2 Filtering Algorithm

A filter may be defined as an algorithm that aims at determination of the most accurate value of the selected physical quantity based on noisy measurement data (signals). Filtering algorithm can be exploited to perform one of three basic operations [2]:

© Springer International Publishing Switzerland 2015
D. Filev et al. (eds.), *Intelligent Systems'2014*,
Advances in Intelligent Systems and Computing 323, DOI: 10.1007/978-3-319-11310-4_18

- Filtration - determining the value of the wanted quantity at time instant t based on measurements made until time instant t (inclusive);
- Smoothing - determining the value of the wanted quantity at time instant t based on all available measurements taken both, before and after, considered   time instant ;
- Prediction - determining the value of considered quantity at time instant t+Δt (Δt>0) on the basis of measurements taken until the time instant (inclusive).

Adaptive filters are algorithms, which allow to change the filter parameters at the time of its operation, for example, depending on the difference between the filter response and the expected response for the input signal. Adaptive filters are used, between others, in signal processing and control systems and dynamical systems identification [2].

Different classification of adaptive filters may be proposed. Because the model of the system, linear and non-linear filters may be distinguished. The method of mathematical description in the time domain divide filters into discrete and continuous ones. In the paper, the discrete filters will be considered due to the possibilities of digital signal processing.

When a statistical approach is applied to solve the filtration problems, knowledge of certain statistical parameters of the signal is assumed. The signal is understood as observation data of the considered system. Such signals contain both information of searched quantity and additional noise. The purpose of the filter is to find the nearest value to the "real" one, according to the assumed statistical criterion. The most commonly used criterion   [9], [10], [11] is minimization the sum of squared errors (that is, the difference between the output value of the filter, and the searched   quantity value).

In the case when the searched quantity is stationary and the model is assumed to be linear, the algorithm that satisfies the criterion of minimizing the sum of squared errors is Wiener Filter [1]. The stationary of searched quantity significantly limits the applicability of the filter for model identification or the integration of measured signals.

Variables analyzed in the research are unsteady. In such a case, the Wiener filter does not meet the assumed statistical criterion. Filter that minimizes the sum of squared errors for the linear model of the system is the Kalman filter. A recursive form of Kalman filter, greatly facilitates its implementation. Unfortunately, recursive operation of the algorithm results in its sensitivity to the accuracy of starting value selection. The choice of starting parameters is also important for the time needed to converge to the correct solution. For the first time, the Kalman filter with its mathematical principles was described in 1960 by Richard Kalman in [2]. Since then, numerous research is conducted (for example, [1], [4], [5]), in which the properties of Kalman filter are examined and various modifications of this filter dedicated navigation applications is proposed.

In the paper, a Filtration and Integration System for navigation data processing is presented. The algorithm used for data filtration is based on Kalman Filter approach.

2.1   Kalman Filter

In Kalman Filter the linear system of followed form is considered [2]:

$$\mathbf{x}_k = \mathbf{F} \cdot \mathbf{x}_{k-1} + \mathbf{v}_{k-1},$$ (1)

$$\mathbf{z}_k = \mathbf{H} \cdot \mathbf{x}_k + \mathbf{w}_k,$$ (2)

where:

$\mathbf{x}_k$ - vector of states in (k) moment,

$\mathbf{z}_k$ - vector of measurements in (k) moment,

$\mathbf{F}$ - state matrix, the same for every step (k),

$\mathbf{H}$ -observation matrix; constant for every   step (k),

$\mathbf{v}_k, \mathbf{w}_k$ - noise vectors of white-noise with zero average and covariance matrixes $\mathbf{Q}_k, \mathbf{R}_k$.

The algorithm consist two stages: I. Prediction and II. Actualization. At the beginning, starting values are assumed (state vector $\hat{\mathbf{x}}_0$ and error covariance matrix $\mathbf{P}_0$) for time value t_0.

I. Prediction stage consists:

a)   prediction of the state vector in the next step:

$$\hat{\mathbf{x}}_{k+1}^- = \mathbf{F}\,\hat{\mathbf{x}}_k$$ (3)

b)   prediction of error covariance matrix of state vector in the next step:

$$\mathbf{P}_{k+1}^- = \mathbf{F}\,\mathbf{P}_k \mathbf{F}^T + \mathbf{Q}_k$$ (4)

II. Actualization stage consists steps:

a) Kalman gain matrix calculations:

$$\mathbf{K}_k = \mathbf{P}_k^- \mathbf{H}^T (\mathbf{H}\,\mathbf{P}_k^- \mathbf{H}^T + \mathbf{R}_k)^{-1}$$ (5)

b) actualization on the basis of current measurement data of state vector predicted in step a) of the I stage:

$$\hat{\mathbf{x}}_k = \hat{\mathbf{x}}_k^- + \mathbf{K}_k (\mathbf{z}_k - \mathbf{H}\,\hat{\mathbf{x}}_k^-)$$ (6)

c) actualization   of error covariance matrix of state vector predicted in step b) of the I stage:

$$\mathbf{P}_k = (\mathbf{I} - \mathbf{K}_k \mathbf{H})\mathbf{P}_k^-$$ (7)

KF is often considered as easy to implement. During the calculations state vector accuracy is estimated ($\mathbf{P}_k$ covariance matrix).

3   Filtration and Integration System (FIS) Implementation

International Convention for the Safety of Life at Sea (SOLAS), which defines the standards of safety at sea, includes recommendations regarding mandatory navigation equipment for ships built after 01.07.2002, depending on the displacement of the vessel [3]. The mandatory navigation equipment of vessels with a capacity of over 50,000 tons, include among others: log, DGPS, gyrocompass and angular velocity indicator .

The log is a device that allows to determine the speed of the vessel [3]. There are many types of logs, which allow to specify both the ship's speed relative to the water and relative to the ground.

Differential Global Positioning System (DGPS) [6] is a satellite receiver system for determining object GPS position, equipped with an additional module that allows the reception of transferred by radio corrections to the GPS system. Including corrections to the calculated position compensate part of the error, which increases the accuracy of determining the position.

Gyrocompass is a device used to determine changes in the course of the vessel [8]. There are many design solutions of gyrocompass varying the physical phenomena used during the measurement. Traditional mechanical gyrocompasses use for this purpose gyroscopic effect.

Turn rate indicator allows to determine speed of change of the course. The most common device which measures the angular velocity is the auxiliary device using data from gyrocompass or gyrocompass adapted to this purpose [8].

The FIS acquire data on-line from navigation sensors of the vessel, i.e. log , gyrocompass and DGPS. The information obtained from the sensors include the measurement noise, and therefore are subjected to a filtration process using Kalman filter based technique, separately for each of the sensors.

As mentioned before, data from the sensors sometimes contain " redundant " information - that is based on measurements from the various sensors the same parameter can be determined. In FIS, during the integration process, on the basis of signals from various sensors, the best estimates of the motion parameters are designated. Another Kalman filter based technique is used to achieve this aim, in which state and observation matrices are based on water vehicle kinematic relationships [1], [7].

The values of error matrices (system and measurement) are chosen on the basis of technical data and previous experience.

The state vector of use for integration purposes has six components ship forward and side velocities, rate about vertical axis, position coordinates and course:

$$\mathbf{X} = \begin{bmatrix} u & v & r & x & y & \psi \end{bmatrix}^T, \tag{8}$$

where:

u , v - forward and side velocities of the ship,

r - rate about vertical axis,

x , y - position coordinates,

ψ - heading.

The velocities and rates are represented in the ship system of coordinates and the position coordinates and course in the ground system of coordinates. The observer vector has the form:

$$\mathbf{z} = \begin{bmatrix} u^D & v^D & r^{GC} & x^{GPS} & y^{GPS} & \psi^{GC} \end{bmatrix}^T. \tag{9}$$

where:

u^D, v^D - forward and side velocities of the ship form the Doppler log ,

r^{GC} - rate about vertical axis from gyrocompass,

x^{GPS}, y^{GPS} - position coordinates form GPS,

ψ^{GC} - heading from gyrocompass .

4   Verification of FIS

Data from the sea trials of passenger ship "Golden Princess" (gathered thanks to Cetena and Fincantieri companies) are exploited for verification of proposed FIS system. Available data were gathered during four sea trials - two circulation trials and two maneuverability trials.

Accuracy of sensors (Girokompas, Log, DGPS) used for the calculation have greater value than those resulted from the technical specifications of equipment used on a cruise ship Golden Princess. Linear and angular velocities are measured in the body coordinate system associated with the ship, while the position and course are measured in the Ψ inertial system.

When checking the FIS system, all of the actual motion parameters have been modified by the additional pseudo-random disturbances generated from a normal distribution with a zero mean value and standard deviation equal to the error of indication of a considered measuring device. Subsequently, such corrupted data are used in the filtration and integration system as the simulated results of the observation.

4.1   Simulation Results

The aim of this system is to determine the best estimate of motion parameters, which then are compared with the actual data of sea trials. The results of each sea trial Table are shown in Fig. 9.1-9.4. The location and course of the vessel is visualized using segment of navy blue color (for data from sea trials) or violet color (for the values determined by filtration and integration of navigation data). The center of the segment coincides with the current position of the ship. The black dot at the end symbolizes the bow of a ship .

The calculation results in case of the circulation trials performed by the cruise ship indicates that the filtering and integration system works correctly (Fig. 1, Fig. 2). Introduced noise (green color) are eliminated. As a result, the position and course after filtration and integration (violet color) practically coincide with the measured values (dark blue color).

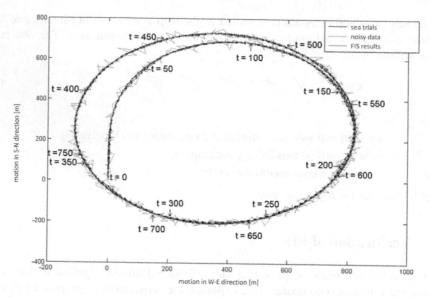

Fig. 1. The results of the filtration and integration system in case of the first circulation trial (rudder deflection from 0-15 degrees)

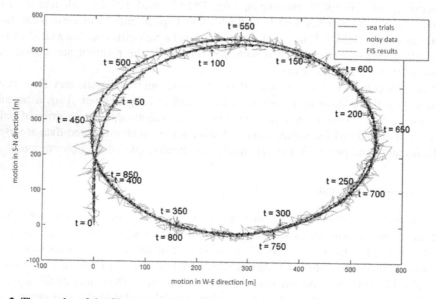

Fig. 2. The results of the filtration and integration system in case of the second circulation trial (rudder deflection from 0-35 degrees)

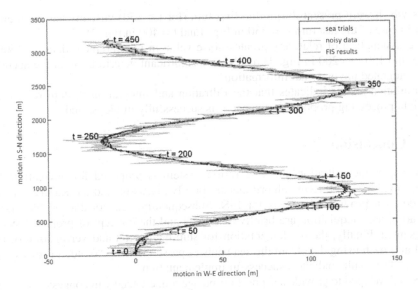

Fig. 3. The results of the filtration and integration system in case of the first maneuverability trial (rudder deflection from -10 - 10 degrees)

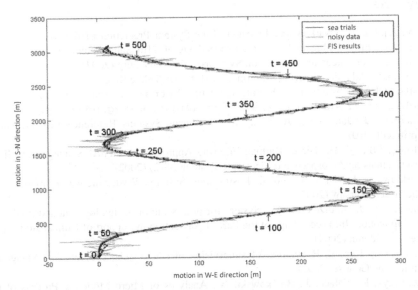

Fig. 4. The results of the filtration and integration system in case of the first maneuverability trial (rudder deflection from -20 - 20 degrees)

The results of the maneuverability trials (Fig. 3, Fig. 4) clearly shows the typical effect of the Kalman filter. At the beginning of the filter operation, the value of the gain matrix is not very accurate, resulting in significant errors in determining the position of the ship. Subsequently the filtering errors decrease. In maneuverability trials, errors which were present during the first turn (for t ≈ 150) virtually has been eliminated in case of the last turn (t = 350 in Fig. 1and t = 400 in Fig. 2).

The assumption of relatively greater noise value in measurement data (t = 500 in Fig. 3 and 150 <t <200 in Fig. 4) results in a significant deterioration in the accuracy of an integrated navigational information.

Simulation results indicates that the Filtration and Integration System for navigation data processing proposed in the paper is successfully implemented.

5   Conclusion

In the paper, the Filtration and Integration System is proposed for navigation data processing. First the filtering algorithms are briefly discussed and the Kalman Filter is recalled as it provides the basis for FIS. Subsequently, sensors that enable on-line navigation data acquisition are briefly discussed and the concept of proposed system is presented. Finally, the implementation for ship navigation and verification of proposed approach using data from the sea trials of passenger ship "Golden Princess" are recalled. The results indicates successful implementation.

FIS is developed to provide a support for navigation, especially in congested sea areas, in narrow passages and harbours, where accurate navigation information is crucial.

References

1. Andrzejczak, M., Narkiewicz, J.: An on-Line System Prediction of the Vessel Position Based on Julier-Uhlmann Filter. In: Proceedings of 11th Saint Petersburg International Conference on Integrated Navigation Systems, Saint Petersburg (2004)
2. Haykin, S.: Adaptive Filtering. Prentince-Hall, Upper Saddle River (1996)
3. IMO, SOLAS convention, ch. V, Safe navigation, https://mcanet.mcga.gov.uk/public/c4/regulations/safetyofnavigation/regindex.html
4. Kacprzyk, J., Jain, L.C., Australia, S.: Intelligent Systems Reference Library, vol. 3. Springer (2010)
5. Moore, J.B., Qi, H.: Direct Kalman Filtering Approach for GPS/INS Integration. IEEE Transactions on Aerospace and Electronic Systems 38(2) (2002)
6. Narkiewicz, J.: GPS – Global Positioning System, Wydawnictwa Komunikacji i Łączności, Warsaw (2003)
7. Narkiewicz, J., Andrzejczak, M.: System for processing of navigation data and prediction of ship motion. In: Proceedings of the Part of Navigation in Support of Human Activity on the Sea, Gdynia (2004)
8. Polish Ship Record: Regulation of supervision of sea vessels, chapter V – Navigation equipment, Gdańsk (2003)
9. Szewczyk, R., Salach, J., Bieńkowski, A.: Analyses of Micro Modeling Process of the Thermoplastic Composition with Ceramic Fillers. In: Mechatronics Recent Technological and Scientific Advances, pp. 131–138. Springer, Berlin (2011) ISBN 978-3-642-23243-5
10. Ulinowicz, M., Narkiewicz, J.: Identification of EMA dynamic model. In: Mechatronics Recent Technological and Scientific Advances, pp. 375–385. Springer, Berlin (2011) ISBN 978-3-642-23243-5
11. Ulinowicz, M., Narkiewicz, J.: Modeling and identifiaction of actuator for flap deflection. Journal of Automation, Mobile Robotics & Intelligent Systems JAMRIS (2012)

Part II
Issues in Distributed Knowledge Based Systems

AIRS: Ant-Inspired Recommendation System

Agostino Forestiero

CNR - ICAR
Institute for High Performance Computing and Networking
National Research Council of Italy
Via Pietro Bucci, 41C
87036 Rende (CS), Italy
forestiero@icar.cnr.it

Abstract. The goal of recommendation systems is to produce a set of meaningful suggestions for a group of users that can be useful for them. This paper introduces a multi-agent algorithm that builds a distributed recommendation system by exploiting nature-inspired techniques. The recommendable resources are recognized through a *metadata* represented of a bit string obtained by the application of a locality preserving hash function that maps similar resources into similar strings. Each agent works independently to replicate and wisely relocate the metadata. The agent operations are led by the application of ad-hoc probability functions. The outcome of this collective work will be a sorted logical overlay network that allows a fast recommendation service. Experimental analysis shows how the logical reorganization of metadata achieved by the agents can improve the performances of the recommendation system.

1   Introduction

A recommendation system aims to create a list of items in which a user can be interested when it has to make a choice in a given context. In other words, it uses the past opinions and/or the behaviors of the whole community to help the users of the same community to make a new choice more efficiently. These systems can be built for movies, books, communities, news, articles etc. Recommendation systems have become an important research topic and much works have been proposed both in industry and academia on developing new approaches in this field. Companies collect a large amount of transactional data that allows a careful analysis of how user interacts with the set of available choices. This can be a way to automatize the generation of recommendations based on data analysis. The way used to analyze the data and develop the concepts of affinity between users and items distinguishes the recommendation systems. Collaborative Filtering systems are based on historical interactions. Content-based Filtering systems analyze the profile attributes; and hybrid approaches try to combine both of these techniques. In the first commercial recommendation system, known as Tapestry [12], the term "collaborative filtering" was introduced. Here, a system to recommend documents obtained from newsgroups to a collection of users, was designed. A social collaboration to defend users from a flood

© Springer International Publishing Switzerland 2015
D. Filev et al. (eds.), *Intelligent Systems'2014,*
Advances in Intelligent Systems and Computing 323, DOI: 10.1007/978-3-319-11310-4_19

of streaming documents, is exploited. Conversely to the Collaborative filtering that analyzes data used by the users to find interesting relations among them is *content filtering* which comes from information retrieval. In content filtering suggestions are made to a user without explicitly utilizing information, but the user will be recommended items similar to the ones the user preferred in the past. Several efforts attempted to combine collaborative filtering with content-based methods, and to add new knowledge domains in the recommendation systems.

In this paper, a novel approach for building a recommendation system, inspired by the behavior of some species of ants [4], is proposed. The algorithm, already proposed to build a generic P2P information system [11], is able to disseminate and reorganize the metadata that describe the generic resources. To describe the resources, in peer to peer systems, bit vectors, or keys, are often exploited and with different meanings. In [10], [22], for example, the presence or absence of a given topic is represented thorough a bit. It is particularly appropriate if the metadata describe resources like documents, because it is possible to identify the different topics focussed in a document. In [6], [19], instead, a hash function was exploited to map the resource into a bit string. If the hash function is locality preserving, similar metadata are assigned to resources with similar features. The resources can be movies, books, communities, news, articles etc. So, the operations of discovery are facilitated and sped up. In particular, the algorithm at the same time achieves multiple objectives: (i) it replicates and disseminates metadata on the network; (ii) it spatially sorts metadata, so that similar metadata are placed in neighbor hosts; (iii) the process of reorganization autonomously adapts to the ever changing environment, thanks to the self-organizing features of the ant-inspired approach. In this paper, the logical reorganization of the metadata is exploited to provide a set of suggestions for the users. In fact, similar metadata are placed in the same region, thus similar and probably appreciated metadata, will be placed close to target metadata.

2   Overview and Related Works

The recommendation systems generate a list of meaningful recommendations of items or products that can be interesting for a collection of users. The usefulness of an item or product is generally represented by a rating, which indicates how a given user liked a particular item. Usually, user preferences are represented as a matrix of users and items, where each cell corresponds to the rating estimated for a given item by a given user. This matrix is typically sparse, so that the rate related to some items is not associated with a large number of users. The aim of the recommendation is to predict what rating a user assigns to an unrated item. Ratings are estimated for all items or products that have not been selected by a user. The items or products with a high value of rate are presented as recommendations for the user, called *active user*. The recommendation systems can be categorized as [1]: (i) *Collaborative Filtering* (CF) where an item or product is recommended to the user according to the past ratings of all users; (ii) *Content-based recommending* where the item or product is recommended if it is similar in content to items or products the user has chosen in the past, or matched with given attributes of the user; (iii) *Hybrid approaches* in which collaborative and content-based approaches are combined. In the collaborative filtering approach, the utility of the item i for the user u is estimated based on the utilities assigned to item i by those users v who are *similar* to user u. Practically, this kind of system tries to predict the utility of items for a given user based on the items previously rated by other similar users. For example, in a music recommendation system, to recommend music to user u, the collaborative system finds someone *similar* to user u, i.e., other users that have similar tastes in music. Then, the music that is liked by the person *similar* to user u would be recommended. Various approaches have been used to compute the similarity between two users, where, often, the similarity is based on their ratings of items that both users have rated. The most popular are correlation and cosine similarity. In the correlation-based approach, the Pearson correlation coefficient is used to compute the similarity [24], [27], as shown in formula (1):

$$similarity(u, v) = \frac{\sum_{i \in I}(r_{u,i} - \bar{r_u})(r_{v,i} - \bar{r_v})}{\sqrt{\sum_{i \in I}(r_{u,i} - \bar{r_u})^2 \sum_{i \in I}(r_{v,i} - \bar{r_v})^2}} \qquad (1)$$

where $\mathbf{I}$ is the set of all items rated by both users u and v. The value of the rating r for user u and item i is computed as an aggregate of the ratings of some other users for the same item i. The cosine-based approach [5], [25], uses two vectors in n-*dimensional* space to represent the users u and v, and n will be $|I|$. The cosine of the angle between two vectors can be computed to measure the similarity between them, as in formula(2):

$$similarity(u, v) = cos(\vec{u}, \vec{v}) = \frac{\vec{u} \cdot \vec{v}}{|\vec{u}|_2 \times |\vec{v}|_2} = \frac{\sum_{i \in I} r_{u,i} r_{v,i}}{\sqrt{\sum_{i \in I} r_{u,i}^2} \sqrt{\sum_{i \in I} r_{u,i}^2}} \qquad (2)$$

where $\vec{u} \cdot \vec{v}$ indicates the *dot-product* between the vectors $\vec{u}$ and $\vec{v}$. Different recommendation systems can use different approaches in order to provide the user similarity calculations and rating estimations as efficiently as possible. For example, one strategy is to calculate all user similarities in advance and recalculate them from time to time. Using pre-computed similarities, the ratings can be calculated on demand whenever the user asks for a recommendation. Content-based recommenders provide recommendations by comparing representations of content that interest the user with representations of content describing an item. Recommended items have associated textual content, such as books, web pages, and movies. The web pages should be associated with contents like descriptions and user reviews. Information retrieval (IR) technics address this problem, where the content associated can be handled as a query, and the unrated documents marked with a similarity value to this query [1]. The documents can be converted into TF-IDF word vectors, and then averaged to obtain a prototype vector of each category for a user, as shown in [15]. A new document is classified and compared it with each prototype vector and the rating assigned based on the cosine similarity to each category.

Collaborative and content-based approaches use the same cosine measure from information retrieval. But, content-based recommendation systems measure the similarity among vectors of TF-IDF weights, whereas, collaborative systems measures the similarity among vectors of the actual ratings specified of the users. Other approaches to recommendation consist in handling the problem as a classification task. Each pattern represents the content of an item, and a user's past ratings are used as labels for these patterns. For example, text from fields such as title, author, synopses, reviews, and subject terms are used by [18] to recommend books. Several classification algorithms have been used for content-based recommendation: decision trees, k-nearest neighbor, and neural networks [21]. Several approaches for exploiting the advantages of both collaborative and content-based systems, have been proposed. In [9] an approach to produce one ranked list with content-based method and one ranked list with collaborative filtering method, was proposed. The final list is obtained as a merger of both lists. An adaptive weighted average was used by [8] to combine the predictions performed with both methods. A sparse user ratings matrix, converted into a full ratings matrix through a content-based predictions, and then a collaborative method providing the recommendations, is the approach proposed in [17]. The documents describing the rated items for each user are used as training set for a Naive-Bayes classifier. The unrated item are predicted through this classifier. Similar neighbors are individuated by using the resulting pseudo-ratings matrix and the predictions are generated exploiting a weighted Pearson correlation.

Many hybrid approaches maintain user content-based profile, but are based on collaborative filtering guidelines. In particular, to find similar users, the content-based profiles are used. In [20], a vector of weighted words for representing each user-profile, is exploited. The vector derives from positive training examples of the Winnow algorithm. Predictions are made using collaborative filtering directly to the matrix of user-profiles. Relevance feedback is used to model an individual filter synchronously with a common "topic" filter, in [1]. Initially the documents are ranked by the common filter and subsequently with the individual filter. Both the filters, common and individual, are tuned through the relevance feedback. Personalized information filtering agents with collaborative filtering, are used in [13]. The collaborative filtering approach is applied to a set of users and active user's personalized agents to generate the predictions. Classification mechanisms were also used to achieve recommendation systems. Ripper [3] is a rule induction system to individuate a prediction function. This function can be used to predict whether a given movie will be liked or disliked by a given user. To produce a content-profile matrix in [28], a term-document matrix representing all item content is multiplied with the user-ratings matrix. A rank-k approximation of the content-profile matrix is computed, by means of latent semantic Indexing. The user's profile is produced averaging the term vectors of the user's relevant documents. Some efforts were made to combine the content and collaborative data directly in a single framework. Hofmann's model [14] to combine a three-way co-occurrence data among users, items, and item content, is extended in [23]. The model assumes that the users select the topics, and documents and their content words are generated from the selected topics. The approach on making recommendations for items that have not been rated by any user, is extended in [26].

3   Ant-Inspired Recommendation System

This section introduces the AIRS (*Ant-Inspired Recommendation System*) algorithm that exploits the work of bio-inspired agents for building a distributed recommendation system. The aim of the algorithm is to reorganize logically the metadata that describe the available and recommendable resources to allow faster recommendation operations. The algorithm cleverly disseminates the metadata on the network with the aim of spatially sorting them. Thanks to this spatial reorganization, similar metadata, representing similar resources, will be placed in neighbor hosts. A set of similar metadata representing similar resources can be detected in the neighborhood of the target resource and suggested to the user. The sorting process is progressively and continuously achieved by ant-inspired agents, which travel the network, and possibly gather metadata from host and leave them in other hosts. Probability functions steer the operations of gathering and depositing of the metadata. These simple operations are performed in local and a sort of global intelligence emerges from work of unaware agents. Two probability functions, P_1 to evaluate the probability of gathering the metadata, and P_2 to evaluate the probability of depositing the metadata, are employed. Whenever an agent gets to a new host, it evaluates a probability function: (i) when the agent does not carry any metadata, the probability function P_1, is evaluated for every metadata stored in this host, so as to decide whether or not to gather this metadata; (ii) when the agent carries some metadata, the probability function P_2 is evaluated for each of these metadata, so as to decide whether or not to deposit the metadata in the current host. The agents' decisions, i.e. probability functions, are based on a similarity function that measures the average similarity of a metadata m with all the metadata located in the local region. The similarity function can be defined based on the considered metadata. In this paper, the similarity function [16] is reported in formula (3):

$$f(\bar{m}, R) = \frac{1}{N} \sum_{m \epsilon R} N_h \cdot \left(1 - \frac{1 - cos(m, \bar{m})}{\alpha} \right) \tag{3}$$

where, N is the overall number of metadata in the region R, N_h is the number of metadata maintained in each host, while $cos(m, \bar{m})$ is the cosine distance between m and $\bar{m}$. The parameter α is the similarity scale and here it is set to 2. The value of f assumes values ranging between -1 and 1, but negative values are fixed to 0. The agent will carry the gathered metadata until it drops them into another host. When the agent is unloaded it will try to pick other metadata from another host. Based on the "mode" with which the agent operates, it can replicate the metadata, or simply move them. Whenever an unloaded agent arrives at a new host it evaluates the probability function to decide whether or not to gather one or more metadata from the current host. The agent for each single metadata in the current host evaluates the similarity with all the metadata located in the visibility region. All the hosts reachable from the current host with a given number of hops represent the visibility region. The number of hops to identify the visibility region is an algorithm parameter. The probability of gathering a metadata must be inversely proportional to the similarity of this metadata with those located in the visibility region, so that dissimilar metadata are sent away from the region. When similar metadata are accumulated the initial equilibrium is broken and a reorganization of metadata is increasingly driven. The probability function of gathering a metadata is defined in formula (4):

$$P_1 = \left(\frac{k1}{k1 + f} \right)^2 \tag{4}$$

where the parameter k1, whose value is comprised between 0 and 1, can be tuned to modulate the degree of similarity. Here k1 is set to 0.1, as in [4]. The local region accumulates similar metadata because the "dissimilar" metadata will be picked by an agent. The operation of gathering metadata can be performed with two different modes, copy and move. When an operation of gathering is executed, if the copy mode is used, the agent leaves a replica of metadata in the current host. Whereas, when the move mode is used, an agent removes the metadata from the current host when it gathers a metadata. In a decentralized fashion, to enable each agent to switch autonomously from copy to move mode, a concept of *stigmergy* [7], was considered. A pheromone-based mechanism to switch from copy to move mode, is used by the agents. Each agent maintains a pheromone base value and increases it when its activeness decreases. The agents switch to the move mode as soon as the pheromone level exceeds a predefined threshold. In detail, for each interval each agent counts the number of times that it has evaluated the probability functions and the number of times that it has actually performed the operations. The agent increases its pheromone value proportionally to the fraction of performed operations. The amount of pheromone deposited at given instant, Ph_i, is computed as in formula (5):

$$Ph_i = er * Ph_{i-1} + \left(1 - \frac{successes}{attempts} \right) \tag{5}$$

where the evaporation rate er is set to 0.9 [29]. The pheromone level can assume values comprised between 0 and 10. As soon as the pheromone level exceeds the threshold the agent switches its mode from copy to move. The value of the threshold can be used to tune the number of agents that work in the copy mode, and consequently the replication and dissemination of metadata, since these agents are able to generate new replicas. Whenever an agent gets to a new host, it must decide, if it is carrying some metadata, whether or not to drop these metadata in the current host. For each carried metadata, the agent evaluates the probability function P_2, which, as opposed to the P_1 probability function, is directly proportional to the similarity function f , i.e., to the average similarity of this metadata with the metadata maintained in the current visibility region. P_2 is reported in formula (6):

$$P_2 = \left(\frac{f}{k2 + f} \right)^2 \tag{6}$$

where the parameter k2 is set to 0.5, in order to limit the frequency of deposit operations. If the probability of leaving metadata tends to be too high, it is difficult for an agent to carry a metadata for an amount of time sufficient to move it into an appropriate region.

The traffic load generated by the process of reorganization, *traffic load*, which is the average number of agents per time units that are processed by host, does not depend either on the network size or on the churn rate. It only depends on the number of agents and the frequency of their movements across the network. *traffic load* is obtained as in formula (7):

$$traffic\ load = \frac{na}{ns \cdot t} = \frac{p}{t} \tag{7}$$

where p denotes the probability of each host of generating an agent, t denotes the time between two successive agent hops, na indicates the number of agents and ns the network size. It is possible to note that the processing load does not depend on system parameters such as the average number of resources handled by a peer or the number of hosts, which is a confirmation of the scalability properties of the algorithm.

An algorithm for exploiting the logical reorganization and then obtaining a set of metadata representing the resources that can be suggested, is very simple and immediate. A query will be issued by host (user) to search a "target metadata" representing the desired resource and it will be forwarded through the peer to peer network to collect as many target metadata as possible. Thanks to the logical reorganization arising from the bio-inspired algorithm, the queries can be forwarded towards the host with the maximum value of similarity between *representative metadata* and the target metadata. The representative metadata is a virtual metadata, for each host, built by averaging of the values of all metadata located in a current host. When a query is issued by host for a target resource, a virtual target metadata is created. The query will be forwarded towards the neighbor peer with the maximum value of similarity, based on formula 3, between the virtual target metadata of the query and the representative metadata of the host. The same operation will be done by each host that received a query and has to forward it to one of its neighbours. When the query gets to host with a representative metadata equal to the virtual target metadata, or the maximum number of query hops admissible is finished, the query will be directly forwarded to the host that has issued the request. The query going across the network collects a set of metadata similar to the virtual target metadata, which can be exploited to produce a list of suggestions/recommendations to the user. The discovery algorithm is very simple and needs very little computing and memory resources, it is very efficient as it exploits the continuous work of agents that organize the metadata.

4   Experimental Results

An event-based simulator was implemented to evaluate the performance of the bio-inspired algorithm. A P2P network with number of hosts equal to 2,500 was considered where each peer is linked to 4 hosts on average. The number of resources published by each host is equal to 15 on average and indexed with a prefixed string of bits obtained using a locality preserving hash function to guarantee that metadata give similar keys. Exploiting the algorithm of Albert and Barabasi [2]a scale-free topology network was built. In this way, the characteristics of real networks are careful considered. Since hosts, in a dynamic environment can go down and reconnect with varying frequencies, an average connection time was considered and generated according to a Gamma probability function with an average value set to 20,000 time units. The timelife of agents was correlated with the timelife of hosts in order to maintain a steady number of agents. Each host generates an agent with probability p equal to 0.5, when it joins the network for the first time. When host leaves the network, it discards the metadata previously deposited by agents, so obsolete metadata are removed. The time between two successive agent hops t is set to 10 time units, whereas an agent can perform a fixed number of hops for each single movement. According to formula 7, in a simulated scenario, each server processes about one agent every 25 time units, which can be considered an acceptable load for the host. The traffic, which is the number of agents that a host elaborates per unit time, was calculated and shown in Figure 1(a).

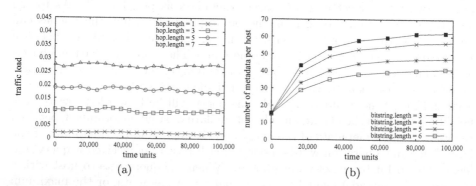

(a)   (b)

Fig. 1. (a) The traffic generated by the algorithm when the number of hops of each agent within a single movement ranges from 1 to 7; and (b) mean number of metadata handled by a host when the bitstring length ranges from 3 to 6 bits

We can see how the value of the traffic changes according to the value of maximum number of hops done within a single agent movement. It was noted that the reorganization process is accelerated if agent movements are longer, because they can scan the network more quickly. The maximum number of hops is a compromise between the traffic load tolerable and the rapidity and efficiency of the reorganization. In Figure 1(b) the mean number of metadata maintained by a host when the length of the string of bit representing the resources ranges from 3 to 6. Intuitively, for larger values of bit strings it is difficult to discriminate among metadata, so the probability functions assume lower values and the replication process is reduced. This effect of attenuation is not present for low length of bit strings.

A spatial index of *homogeneity* was defined to evaluate the goodness of the algorithm. For each peer, the homogeneity among all the local metadata within the local region, by averaging the cosine of the angle between every couple of metadata, was calculated. The values of the homogeneity was averaged for all the hosts of the network. Our aim is to increase the homogeneity value as much as possible. It would mean that similar metadata are located into neighbor hosts and an effective sorting of metadata comes about. If the agents work both copy and move operational modes, simulation results show that the value of the homogeneity function increases much more. Initially an agent works in copy mode to spread the information, but when it actualizes that the sorting process is in advanced phase, it autonomously switches from copy mode to move mode. So, its activity will be to move the metadata from one host to another. The copy mode cannot be used for a long time, since every host would collect a very large number of metadata, so weakening the efficacy of spatial reorganization. To make the algorithm effective, each agent must switch from copy to move after replicating a given number of metadata. In Figure 2(a) the homogeneity of the whole network when the length of metadata bit strings that represent the resources, is varied.

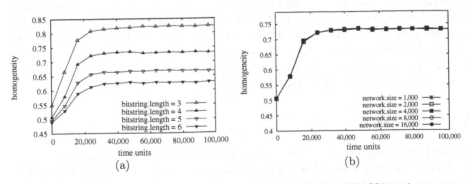

(a)   (b)

Fig. 2. (a) the homogeneity of the whole network when the length of bit strings ranges from 3 to 6; (b) the homogeneity of the whole network when the network size ranges from 1,000 to 16,000 hosts

It is possible to note how the logical reorganization is achieved independently of the length of bit strings. The scalability of the algorithm is confirmed analyzing its behavior when the network size is varied. Figure 2(b) reports the values of homogeneity when the network size ranges from 1,000 to 16,000 hosts. Notice that the number of the involved hosts in the logical reorganization, has no detectable effect on the homogeneity.

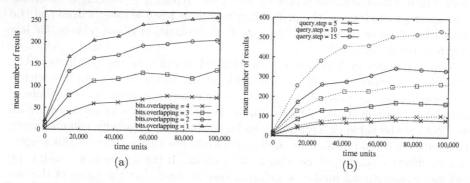

Fig. 3. (a) mean number of results collected by a query when the overlapped bit ranges from 1 to 4; (b) mean number of results with different values of query hops and (dotted line) when the number of overlapping bit is set to bitstring length -1, 4 in these experiments

To evaluate the performances of recommendation algorithm, a set of experiments was achieved and shown in Figure 3(a) and (b). Figure 3(a) shows the mean number of results collected by a query with different values of overlapping bits specified in target metadata. In this experiments the length of bit string is set to 4, and when the query is issued the number of bit that must overlap is specified. We can note as the mean number of results depends on this value. Figure 3(b) depicts the mean number of results when the query step, this is the maximum number of hops that a query performs, ranges from 5 to 15, and the length of bit strings is set to 5. Moreover, the same results are shown, with a dotted line, when the number of overlapping bits is set to bitstring - 1, 4 in these experiments, i.e. 4 bits on 5 must be equals.

5   Conclusion

A multi-agent algorithm to build a distributed recommendation system, was introduced. The available and recommendable resources in a network are described by means of metadata and logically reorganized. The metadata are arranged as bit strings obtained by the application of a locality preserving hash function that allows similar resources to be mapped into similar strings. The bio-inspired agents autonomously move metadata among hosts exploiting the peer to peer interconnections. The agents operations are guided by probability functions. The experimental results show how the algorithm achieves an effective reorganization of metadata and how the emerging logical overlay allows discovery and recommendation operations to be improved.

References

1. Balabanovic, M., Shoham, Y.: Fab: Content-Based, Collaborative Recommendation. Comm. ACM 40(3), 66–72 (1997)
2. Barabasi, A.L., Albert, R.: Emergence of scaling in random networks. Science 286(5439) (1999)
3. Basu, C., Hirsh, H., Cohen, W.: Recommendation as classification: Using social and content-based information in recommendation. In: Proceedings of the Fifteenth National Conference on Artificial Intelligence (AAAI 1998), Madison, Wisconsin, pp. 714–720 (1998)
4. Bonabeau, E., Dorigo, M., Theraulaz, G.: Swarm intelligence: from natural to artificial systems. Oxford University Press, New York (1999)
5. Breese, J.S., Heckerman, D., Kadie, C.: Empirical Analysis of Predictive Algorithms for Collaborative Filtering. In: Proc. 14th Conf. Uncertainty in Artificial Intelligence (July 1998)
6. Cai, M., Frank, M., Chen, J., Szekely, P.: Maan: A multi-attribute addressable network for grid information services. J. Grid Comput. 2(1), 3–14 (2004)
7. Camazine, S., Franks, N.R., Sneyd, J., Bonabeau, E., Deneubourg, J.L., Theraulaz, G.: Self-Organization in Biological Systems. Princeton University Press, Princeton (2001)
8. Claypool, M., Gokhale, A., Miranda, T.: Combining content-based and collaborative filters in an online newspaper. In: Proc. of the SIGIR 1999 Workshop on Recommender Systems: Algorithms and Evaluation (1999)
9. Cotter, P., Smyth, B.: PTV: Intelligent personalized TV guides. In: 12th Conference on Innovative Applications of Artificial Intelligence, Austin, Texas, pp. 957–964 (2000)
10. Crespo, A., Garcia-Molina, H.: Routing indices for peer-to-peer systems. In: Proc. 22nd Int. Conf. Distributed Computing Syst., ICDCS 2002, pp. 23–33 (July 2002)
11. Forestiero, A., Mastroianni, C.: A swarm algorithm for a selfstructured P2P information system. IEEE Transactions on Evolutionary Computation 13(4), 681–694 (2009)
12. Goldberg, D., Nichols, D., Oki, B.M., Terry, D.: Using collaborative filtering to weave an information tapestry. Communications of ACM 35(12), 61–70 (1992)
13. Good, N., Schafer, J.B., Konstan, J.A., Borchers, A., Sarwar, B., Herlocker, J., et al.: Combining collaborative filtering with personal agents for better recommendations. In: Proc. of the Sixteenth National Conference on Artificial Intelligence (AAAI 1999), Orlando, Florida, pp. 439–446 (1999)
14. Hofmann, T.: Probabilistic latent semantic analysis. In: Proc. of the Fifteenth Conference on Uncertainty in Artificial Intelligence, Stockholm, Sweden (1999)
15. Lang, K.: NewsWeeder: Learning to filter netnews. In: Proc. of the 12th International Conference on Machine Learning, Tahoe City, CA, USA, pp. 331–339. Morgan Kaufmann, San Francisco (1995)
16. Lumer, E.D., Faieta, B.: Diversity and adaptation in populations of clustering ants. In: Proc. of SAB 1994, pp. 501–508. MIT Press, Cambridge (1994)

17. Melville, P., Mooney, R.J., Nagarajan, R.: Content-boosted collaborative filtering for improved recommendations. In: Proc. of the XVIII National Conference on Artificial Intelligence (AAAI 2002), Edmonton, Alberta, pp. 187–192 (2002)
18. Mooney, R.J., Roy, L.: Content-based book recommending using learning for text categorization. In: Proc. of the 5th ACM Conference on Digital Libraries, San Antonio, Texas, pp. 195–204 (June 2000)
19. Oppenheimer, D., Albrecht, J., Patterson, D., Vahdat, A.: Design and implementation tradeoffs for wide-area resource discovery. In: Proc. 14th IEEE Int. Symp. High Performance, pp. 113–124. Research Triangle Park, Raleigh (2005)
20. Pazzani, M.J.: A framework for collaborative, content-based and demographic filtering. Artificial Intelligence Review 13(5,6), 393–408 (1999)
21. Pazzani, M.J., Billsus, D.: Learning and revising user profiles: The identification of interesting web sites. Machine Learning 27(3), 313–331 (1997)
22. Platzer, C., Dustdar, S.: A vector space search engine for web services. In: Proc. 3rd Eur. Conf. Web Services ECOWS 2005, pp. 62–71. IEEE Comput. Soc., Washington (2005)
23. Popescul, A., Ungar, L., Pennock, D.M., Lawrence, S.: Probabilistic models for unified collaborative and content-based recommendation in sparse-data environments. In: Proc. of the Seventeenth Conference on Uncertainity in Artificial Intelligence. University of Washington, Seattle (2001)
24. Resnick, P., Iakovou, N., Sushak, M., Bergstrom, P., Riedl, J.: GroupLens: An Open Architecture for Collaborative Filtering of Netnews. In: Proc. 1994 Computer Supported Cooperative Work Conf. (1994)
25. Sarwar, B., Karypis, G., Konstan, J., Riedl, J.: Item-Based Collaborative Filtering Recommendation Algorithms. In: Proc. 10th Int'l WWW Conf. (2001)
26. Schein, A.I., Popescul, A., Ungar, L.H., Pennock, D.M.: Methods and metrics for cold-start recommendations. In: Proc. of the Fith Annual International ACM SIGIR Conference on Research and Development in Information Retrieval, Tampere, Finland, pp. 253–260 (2002)
27. Shardanand, U., Maes, P.: Social Information Filtering: Algorithms for Automating Word of Mouth. In: Proc. Conf. Human Factors in Computing Systems (1995)
28. Soboroff, I., Nicholas, C.: Combining content and collaboration in text filtering. In: Proce. of IJCAI 1999 Workshop on Machine Learning in Information Filtering, pp. 86–91 (1999)
29. Van Dyke Parunak, H., Brueckner, S., Matthews, R.S., Sauter, J.A.: Pheromone learning for self-organizing agents. IEEE Transactions on Systems, Man, and Cybernetics, Part A 35(3), 316–326 (2005)

Quality of Services Method as a DDoS Protection Tool

Łukasz Apiecionek, Jacek M. Czerniak, and Wojciech T. Dobrosielski

Casimir the Great University in Bydgoszcz, Institute of Technology
ul. Chodkiewicza 30, 85-064 Bydgoszcz, Poland
{lapiecionek,jczerniak,wdobrosielski}@ukw.edu.pl

Abstract. Presently, one of the main problems of computer networks are Distributed Denial of Service attacks which can block network resources like servers. In order to prevent such situations some mechanisms are needed. This paper gives an overview of the Quality of Services methods. A DDoS attack model is described for development purposes. In conslusion some new QoS features are presented. According to presented features QoS method could be used as a protection tool against DDoS attack which is also proven in this paper. The ability to implement the proposed QoS features has already been partially tested. Presented results suggest that the method could be applied widely in practice.

Keywords: network security, IP network, DDoS.

1 Introduction

Nowadays, in IT systems' users need a fast access to information from every part of the network. Distributed Denial of Service attacks lately (DDoS in short), have become a problem as they cause network unavailability by blocking services via seizing system resources in computers inside the network until they stop working. In such situation, a user who has already started working in the system loses the connection and cannot finish his work. The user cannot even log out of the system, which has to do it for him after the connection timeout is reached or when a broken connection is detected. DDoS attacks are a big trouble for IT systems nowadays and they have to be eliminated. One of the solutions could be a new Quality of Service (QoS in short) method which could work on all routers in the network. This paper presents a possible way to protect the network resources in case of the DDoS using QoS methods. Chapter II describes how QoS methods work. There is a DDoS model proposed in chapter III. Chapter IV describes a possible QoS method for network protection. It also consists of the test results from implementation phase. Why this solution will work in global network is also proven in this cahpter. Chapter V provides a conclusion and discussion over the developed method.

© Springer International Publishing Switzerland 2015
D. Filev et al. (eds.), *Intelligent Systems'2014,*
Advances in Intelligent Systems and Computing 323, DOI: 10.1007/978-3-319-11310-4_20

2   Quality of Services Method

QoS methods are used as a network bandwidth sharing policy. Its role is to ensure a given amount of network bandwidth for special kind of traffics, for example enough bandwidth for Voice over IP calls, videoconferencing, email transfer or a special kind of user who has to be treated in special way which will not lead to unordinary network latency [1]. QoS methods are widely used by the network administrators. For the preparation of the, the administrator has to configure the whole network equipment: switches, routers and firewalls. According to special requirements the administrator has to:

- divide traffic into groups,
- set a traffic group priority,
- set a group bandwidth amount,
- describe a bandwidth sharing method for other users.

Technically, the administrator of an IP network has to prepare network equipment for the QoS method, which means, that user's IP packet have to be marked in a way which describes how this packet has to be treated. Administrators use Differentiated Services Code Point field in the IP packet header for marking packets, which has 64 traffic class level possibilities. In the older systems there was a Type of Service field which had 8 marking levels. There are two possibilities of marking a packet:

- marking by users,
- marking by first network equipment.

Marking by users means, that the users set a packet mark themselves. It can be used only in situation when the administrator can trust the user. Otherwise, the user could increase their packets QoS level. Marking by first network equipment means, that usually the first switch or router will recognize the traffic and set a mark in the IP header. In a situation, where the traffic is not recognized, the administrator uses Fair Queue method, which recognizes data streams and divides the whole bandwidth between users in a fair way.

3   Distributed Denial of Service Attack Model

There is a need to have a DDoS attack model for preparing the protection tool. To achieve this, there is a need to know how the DDoS attack works. DDoS attacks are widely described in the literature [2,3]. These attacks can be performed on various system resources: TCP/IP sockets [3,4] or Domain Name System (DNS) servers. Regardless of the method, the main principle is to simulate so many correct user connections that their number exceeds the actual system performance and drives it to abnormal operation. Papers [2,3,5,6,7] describe methods for dealing with DDoS attacks by their global detection and the necessity of cooperation between network providers. The transmission of the attackers' packets is done through the provider's network and if it cannot be blocked, it leads to data link saturation. Such saturation results in lack of connection to the server. Even applying some extra intrusion detection systems which use general purpose computing on graphics processing units [8], is not sufficient. In figure (1) authors presents how the DDoS influences the network in which there is lot of routers, computer machines and Web Servers. The DDoS attack could be described in such steps:

- at first network is stable, everything is working well,
- hacker starts to control some amount of machines (H1-H5),
- hacker starts the attack by generating traffic from the controlled machine to the Web Server,
- when the attack on the Web Server is initiated, some network connections become saturated (presented in fig.(1) with dashed lines),
- during the attack more connections are affected, and finally, all connections to the Web Servers are fully saturated and the Web Server's resources are insufficient for normal work. That is why potentially Web servers used in banks or used by universitities for e-learning [9] could stop working in the worst time.

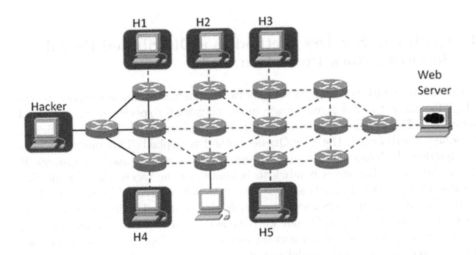

Fig. 1. Ordinary network with Hacker who blocks the Web server using DDoS attack

According to the presented steps, some DDoS attack model was developed. It should be assumed that during normal network activity n data streams are transmitted to the receiver over a router. When an attack occurs, the number of streams grows rapidly up to the maximum number supported by the network resources. Fig.(2) shows a hypothetical number of connections, which grows over time from the beginning of the attack on a particular network resource. The start of the attack was labeled in figure 2 as DDoS. When the attack stops, the number of data streams decreases to an average number in the network. The number of data streams shown on the graph is a hypothetical value, just to illustrate how this mechanism works.

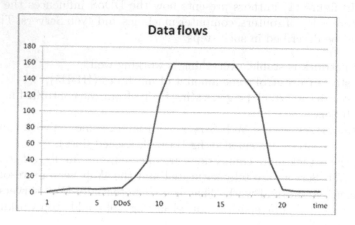

Fig. 2. Data flow IP packet

4   Quality of Services Method as a Distributed Denial of Services Attack Protection Tool

Network bandwidth is managed using network bandwidth administration methods. They allow to set a given bitrate in the network for specific users or type of network traffic. In this manner a privileged traffic is selected. For the traffic not classified as privileged, the Fair Queue method is applied. This method allows fair bandwidth division between data sources. It is widely used on routers. It should be noted that when bandwidth is limited in the receiver's network, this method divides packets fairly so that every stream can reach the receiver. Presented in [10] [11] the QoS method extends the existing traffic mechanisms. It introduces a history based "traffic activity fair queue", yet not basing on data source or category, but on connection history. According to the presented solution, some DDoS attack model was developed and described in the previous chapter. When the number of packets exceeds given limits, in order to deal with the DDoS attack, the QoS method has to remove them from the queue by using a well-known mechanism called Random Early Detection (RED) with special condition. In a standard method, the RED mechanism is executed on incoming packets with data streams categorization. In the proposed Enhanced QoS method, the RED mechanism should not be executed on the data streams that had been transmitted earlier. Key method steps are:

- keep the data streams history from the moment before the attack and this period should not be neither too long, as otherwise it will not capture the appropriate traffic, nor too short, in order to protect the device from heavy load,
- detect the moment of the attack, i.e. by monitoring the number of connections, and when this number exceeds the given limits, a potential DDoS attack signal is generated,
- after detecting the attack, set the traffic filtering rules to privilege historical packets, i.e. by selecting them with the use of filtering rules on a router module,
- block all other malicious traffic, i.e. by using RED mechanism [11] or firewall rules [12,13].

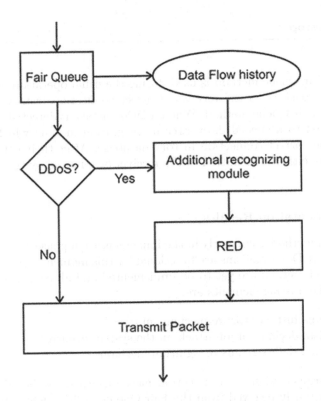

Fig. 3. IP packet flow over a router

Fig.(3) shows a general method scheme while below a pseudo code is presented:

Algorithm 1. The pseudo code of IP packet flow over a router algorithm

---

Algorithm start

for every packet arrived **to** Fair Queue **do**
  if DDoS is recognized **then**
    if packet arrived is in Additional recognizing module history **then**
      fair queue method and transmit packet;
    else
      drop packet;
    end if
  else
    do fair queue method and transmit packet;
  end if
end for

Algorithm stop

The QoS Fair Queue method is used during the usual operation of the device and transmits packets to the receiver. Correct connection history is gathered basing on the Fair Queue method. When a DDoS attack is detected, the packets are transmitted to a special data stream recognition module which compares them with the correct connection history database. After their categorization, the packets are either transmitted to the receiver or removed by the RED mechanism.

4.1 Implementation Results

The presented method is currently in the implementation phase. QoS Fair Queue methods and RED mechanisms are functional for this moment. Missing elements of the proposed method are yet to be implemented and all elements have to be integrated. The missing elements are:

- data streams history storage mechanism,
- a mechanism deciding if an attack on the system occurred,
- an additional data streams recognition mechanism.

Historical transmission data collection mechanism can be based on the information constantly received from the Fair Queue method, which monitors all the streams. Detecting the moment of the attack is another step which can be achieved using simply detecting model by monitoring the number of transmitted packets or data streams in the Fair Queue method. The third element is constructing a mechanism for filtering the privileged traffic by its identification in the network history. This mechanism can be created in the Linux system by the IPTables firewall module [13,14]. A common problem with filtering traffic is that it can reduce the device's throughput and in result, impair network operation. That is why this element was implemented in the first place. For this purpose, an IPTables module for Linux Debian system was developed, which has to detect a certain traffic based on a given signature: source IP address, sender and type of protocol. This module was prepared as an external Linux kernel module loaded on the user's demand. Then, a network performance test was made, using this module to filter packets. The bandwidth was tested with the use of IPerf software, version 2.0.5. Test environment consisted of:

- Router working on Linux Debian 2.6.32 system and IPtables 1.4.8 module, with an addtional module,
- Sender host,
- Receiver host.

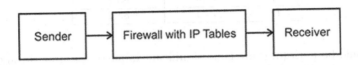

Fig. 4. Test network

The receiver host was working under Windows 7 64-bit system with Intel i3 processor. Both the router and receiver host were working in virtual VMWare environment with 512 MB of memory and 1 processor. These machines were running on test data receiver host. The objective of this test was not to achieve large network bandwidth, but to check if, and in what extent, adding another filtering rule will impact the router's bandwidth. Test conditions were as follows:

- test period: 60 seconds,
- test protocol: TCP.

The results of average transmission speed for four different conditions are listed in table table (Tab. 1). Conditions A, B, C and D define the configuration of rules in IPTables module. Whole condition was tested three times. In condition A, the module had no filtering module set. Condition B has one filtering condition:

- blocked all external traffic incoming to the firewall: INPUT deny any any.

Condition C consists of condition B with one more filtering rule implemented, executed on selected traffic while transmitting packets through a firewall:

- blocked all external traffic incoming to the firewall: INPUT deny any any,
- filtered traffic: FORWARD tcp on port 6000, with the use of the implemented module.

Condition D consists of condition C with blocking rule implemented, which was executed for other types of traffic:

- blocked all external traffic incoming to the firewall: INPUT deny any any,
- filtered traffic: FORWARD tcp on port 6000, with the use of the implemented module,
- blocked all external traffic forwarded through the firewall: FORWARD deny any any.

Table 1. Average speed test results

Test condition	Average results	
	Sender [kbit/s]	Receiver [kbit/s]
A	77.1	83.8
B	76.1	84.8
C	78.5	83.1
D	75.4	83.2

As it could be noticed, there is no significant impact on router throughput by filtering module. That is important, because it proof that this tool will have no impact on network throughput.

4.2 Proof of QoS Tool Concept as a Network Protector Against DDOS

The analysis of the results suggests that adding an additional filtering rule does not cause a drop in packet transmission speed through the router or firewall. It confirmed the thesis that the proposed method will not result in much bigger load on resources of existing devices, and thus it will not cause slowing the network performance, but can help in the fight against DDoS attacks. This method will not solve whole DDoS attack problems, but it will enable users to close their active connection when attack starts. Some tests using Web browsers were made. Over 90% of users choose Internet Explorer (12%), Mozilla Firefox (27%) and Google Chrome (55%) [15]. Using these three most popular web browsers a test was made.

Test procedure was to connect to the web server which not exist and check how browsers will send packets. Test conditions:

- operating system Windows Vista,
- Internet Explorer version 9.0.8112.16421,
- Mozilla Firefox version 16.0.2,
- Google Chrome version 23.0.1271.64 m.

Results of debug packets from Wireshark program are presented in table (Tab. 2). As it could be noticed, Mozilla Firefox browser tries to make a connection 18 times, while Google Chrome and Internet Explorer stops after 9 connection attempt.

Closing the active connection and finishing work by users will be possible because of the presented web browsers' way of working. During browsers tests,

Table 2. Wireshark Web browsers connection test results

Number of packets	Delays before the next packet is send from the browser[seconds]		
	Mozilla Firefox	Internet Explorer	Google Chrome
1	0	0	0
2	0,254	0,001	0,001
3	2,996	2,995	0,25
4	3,246	2,995	2,996
5	8,997	8,995	2,996
6	9,247	8,995	3,246
7	20,996	20,995	8,997
8	21,239	23,991	8,997
9	21,246	29,992	9,248
10	23,995		
11	24,235		
12	24,245		
13	29,998		
14	30,238		
15	30,248		
16	42,231		
17	45,23		
18	51,233		

authors recognized the fact, that web browsers made some retransmissions for the user and they try to connect to the web server more the once. Using the presented enhanced QoS method it will be possible to transmit all the packets to their destination. Depending on the choosen browser, there are nine chances to transfer appropriate data.

5   Conclusions

In this article, a QoS method concept of eliminating DDoS attacks was presented with the information which proves that using this concept is possible in the real environment. The usage of this concept should base on cooperation between all internet providers. The prepared QoS method will allow to minimize DDoS attacks. The best solution would be applying this method to all routers and firewalls in the network. When it will start dropping hackers packets in whole network routers, DDoS could be stopped. Such algorithm does not require new system resources of the network devices. Its implementation in the whole network and at all providers will result in reducing the number of attacking packets and as a result, deflect the attack. The mechanism of privileging the packets which were sent prior to the attack and come from the users operating correctly will result in their uninterrupted work in the network. Of course, it will not solve all the DDoS problems. If attack will last longer than history is stored, this method will not help fight with DDoS. The same situation will occure in situation when some new user will try to connect to network resources. But in other situation it will give some protection which means, that user will be able to close their active session that they started before the DDoS attack. Fighting with DDoS attacks is not easy, but is essential to protect the society against hackers' attacks, especially in the situations when network resources are really needed. Protection tools for this fight are on market, but they should be used in right way, as presented result showed.

References

1. Kovac, D., Vince, T., Molnar, J., Kovacova, I.: Modern internet based production technology. In: Er, M.J. (ed.) New Trends in Technologies: Devices, Computer, Communication and Industrial Systems, pp. 145–164. SCIYO (2010)
2. Rocky, K.C.C.: Defending against flooding-based distributed denial-of-service attacks: A tutorial. IEEE Communications Magazine 40(10), 42–51 (2002)
3. Moor, D., Shannon, C., Brown, D., Voelker, G.M., Savage, S.: Inferring internet denial-of-service activity. ACM Transactions on Computer Systems (TOCS) 24(2), 115–139 (2006)
4. Schuba, C.L., Krsul, I.H.M.G., Spafford, E.H., S.A.: Analysis of a Denial of Service Attack on TCP. Computer Science Technical Reports, p. 1327. Purdue University Library (1996)
5. CERT: TCP SYN Flooding and IP Spoofing Attacks. Software Engineering Institute (2000), http://www.cert.org/advisories/CA-1996-21.html
6. CERT: UDP Port Denial-of-Service Attack. Software Engineering Institute (1997), http://www.cert.org/advisories/CA-1996-01.html
7. Wrzesien, M., Olejnik, L., R.R.: Ids/ips: Detection and prevention systems of hacking the computer networks. Studies and Materials in Applied Computer Science 4(7), 16–21 (2012) (in Polish)
8. Vokorokos, L., Ennert, M., H.M., J.,R.: A survey of parallel intrusion detection on graphical processors. In: Proceedings of International Scientific Conference IN-FORMATICS 2013, pp. 50–55. Department of Computers and Informatics, FEEI TU of Košice (2013)
9. Mikoajewska, E., M.D.: E-learning in the education of people with disabilities. Advances in Clinical and Experimental Medicine 20(1), 103–109 (2011)
10. Apiecionek, L., C.J.M.: Qos solution for network resource protection. In: Proceedings of International Scientific Conference INFORMATICS 2013, pp. 73–76. Department of Computers and Informatics, FEEI TU of Košice (2013)
11. Apiecionek, Ł., Czerniak, J.M., Zarzycki, H.: Protection tool for distributed denial of services attack. In: Kozielski, S., Mrozek, D., Kasprowski, P., Małysiak-Mrozek, B. z. (eds.) BDAS 2014. CCIS, vol. 424, pp. 405–414. Springer, Heidelberg (2014)
12. Changwang, Z., Jianping, Y., Z.C., Ch., W.: Rred: Robust red algorithm to counter low-rate denial-of-service attacks. IEEE Communications Letters 14(5), 489–491 (2010)
13. Cheswick, W.R., B.S.M.: Firewalls and Internet Security: Repelling the Wily Hacker. Addison-Wesley Publishing Company (1994)
14. Chapman, B., Z.E.: Building Internet Firewalls. O'Reilly & Associates (1995)
15. w3schools team: Browser Statistics. Refsnes Data (2014), http://www.w3schools.com/browsers/browsers_stats.asp

A Proposal of the New owlANT Method for Determining the Distance between Terms in Ontology

Jacek M. Czerniak[1], Wojciech Dobrosielski[1], Hubert Zarzycki[2], and Łukasz Apiecionek[1]

[1] Casimir the Great University in Bydgoszcz, Institute of Technology
ul. Chodkiewicza 30, 85-064 Bydgoszcz, Poland
{jczerniak,wdobrosielski,lapiecionek}@ukw.edu.pl,
[2] Wroclaw School of Applied Informatics "Horyzont",
ul. Wejherowska 28, 54-239 Wroclaw, Poland
hzarzycki@horyzont.eu

Abstract. The article presents the owlANT method, which allows us to associate a collection of short text messages with ontology. The trails were conducted on the collection of communications by Reuters (the so-called second collection). As the methodological base of the method, a swarm intelligence was used, namely the ant colony optimisation. The ants, moving between the ontological nodes[1][2], left their pheromone trace. As a result, some branches of relations - after some time in evolution - were marked more strongly than the others. On the basis of the intensity of the pheromone trace, one can formulate the strength of relations between the various associations, and - indirectly - also between the associated documents. As far as the authors know, no one has so far published research on the application of ACO to the development of similarity measure of text documents with the consideration of their meaning-related embedding in ontology. The authors refer to the work [3][4], in which the ACO was used for aggregation of concepts in ontology; however, both the purpose and the method were different in that case. The research described in the report will be continued to specify the similarity measures taking into consideration the distance in ontology obtained thanks to the evolutionary processing of the meaning of terms with the use of ACO.

Keywords: ontology, ontological engineering, conceptualisation, owl, ant systems, pheromone, swarm intelligence, graph searching.

1 Introduction

The multiple information that surrounds a human being in everyday life causes commotion. Redundancy of information, lack of thematic cohesion, quality discrepancies etc. make the information unlikely to be useful. Human beings have always been trying to solve this problem with information, knowledge. The representation of knowledge has been used by the humans since time immemorial.

© Springer International Publishing Switzerland 2015   235
D. Filev et al. (eds.), *Intelligent Systems'2014*,
Advances in Intelligent Systems and Computing 323, DOI: 10.1007/978-3-319-11310-4_21

From the drawings on the walls presenting prehistoric rituals up to the contemporary electronic libraries show the evolution of recording methods, and the description of the knowledge harnessed by the humans. The term ontology is derived from Greek, meaning that, which exists, anything. This term may be interpreted as a study of everything that exists. Ancient philosophers in Greece touched upon the subjects of existence essence in their works. The first application of this term appeared in the philosophical literature thanks to Rudolf Goclenius, in the dictionary entitled: Lexicon philosophicum quo tamquam clavae philosophiae fors aperiuntur in the 17th century. Putting aside the so-far deliberations upon the concept of ontology, let us now move to the area of science related to IT studies. This term is used in research on artificial intelligence; it refers, above all, to the obtaining of knowledge formalisation methods. At the beginning of 1980s, there emerged an idea of applying the terms and concepts of ontology at the construction of information processing systems [4]. The ongoing scientific research in this area generated new terms. The resulting models and theories were referred to as engineering ontologies, while the area, from which the ontology was derived, was called ontological engineering. The arising term contains ideas from other branches of science, such as logics, linguistics, psychology and philosophy. Specificity of conceptualisation [5] within a given area is understood as a description of the extract of a given reality or way of observation [6]. The proposed definition specified in an intuitive manner the goal of applying ontology[7][8]. It is understood as a mechanism that delivers precise terms describing a given area. The precision of the used terms in a given ontology represents the use of this area by the parties concerned. The area of deliberations for ontology includes the universal issues, general terms - then we talk about upper-level ontology[9]. Examining a specific, more detailed case of a reality excerpt, ontology becomes domain ontology.

One of the aspects of knowledge formalisation is the application of descriptive logics. It makes it possible to create conceptual models, which means forming the terms of classes on the basis of general knowledge[10]. This mechanism is referred to as the conceptualisation process[11]. Using the descriptive logic, we have the opportunity to represent the relations between terms occurring in a given area. The components of descriptive logics include symbols that indicate the terms and roles as well as term constructors. Terms are divided into atomic (primitive and basic) and complex terms, defined by means of constructors. On the basis of theories from descriptive logics, languages describing ontology came into existence. The particular language is the OWL (Web Ontology Language), which was adopted as the standard W3C in the scope of ontological description. The chief idea of this language is the support of semantic network, whose all information contain the semantics understandable for machines. The ontologies written in this language are collections of axioms that determine the relations of subsumption between classes, i.e. sets of individuals[12].

2   Swarm Intelligence

Observation of living organisms is an interesting research area not only for biologists. In the last decade of the previous year, the new trend within artificial intelligence gained importance, which is currently referred to as Swarm Intelligence [13] . It derives its inspiration from the observation of animals and insects living in colonies. We have lived to finally see successful experiments and methods derived from the observations of ant or termite behaviours [14] [15] . The observations of behaviour of birds in a fight key-like arrangement inspired many researchers to create and develop the concept of Particle Swarm Optimization [16] . The inspiration for this research in the AI area was the reports of marine biologists about the group intelligence of schools of fish and plankton. Also the development of industry, in this care the automotive one in particular, generated another source of inspiration. Particle Swarm Optimization finds its application in such areas as sandblasting of car bodies and other corrosion-covered metal elements. In the general case then, it is commonly referred to as swarm intelligence [17] . The transition of these intelligence mechanisms of simple beings into computer systems generated the emergence of a trend known as Computational Swarm Intelligence. It exists simultaneously, in a manner which often overlaps the branch of science called multi-agent systems. Despite the fact that they are not based explicitly on associations with colonies of living organisms, they are similar in their nature. They make it possible to make interesting implementations in the domain of parallel computing and medicine[18].

3   Explanation of the Issue of Ant Systems

A single ant can seem to be a rather primitive organism with small causative potential. However, the ants - as a concise community - may do things which exceed the potential of a single organism belonging to species much greater than they. The concept of ant systems may be roughly defined as an IT system which analyses algorithms in a parallel manner. They operate on the principles analogous to those processes in the real world. Many of them are based on the processes which were plumbed by the zoologists or molecular physicists.

Ant systems are not the first branch of Artificial Intelligence, which is based on the observation of nature. The inspirations coming from natural phenomena also became the basis for such aspects as the Genetic Algorithms, Particle Swarm Optimization, Neuron networks, and others. The aim of the majority of implementations of Ant Systems is to find the optimum solution for the specific route. A route from the ants point of view is the path leading from the anthill to food. The most simple way to present the issue of ant systems is to represent the micro-world in the form of a nest (anthill), food, an obstacle separating the anthill from the food as well as two routes leading to the food. The aim of the ants is to reach their food as well as to return to the anthill in the shortest time possible, that means selecting the shortest route. We know, from the observation of ants in nature, that after some time they can find the shorter out of two routes available. A question must be posed: how is this possible? Ants secrete a substance which is referred to as a pheromone. Travelling from the anthill to the place of food, the ants leave the so-called pheromone trace. It is extremely important that the left pheromone trace is more intensive on the path which is more often covered. At this moment, one can notice the manner in which the ants find the shortest route. They are directed by the intensity of pheromone; the strongest it is, the more frequently a given route is chosen; the more frequently chosen a route is, the closer the food is; and being close means better and is an optimum solution. Let us see how it is presented in a figure with two available routes. As one can notice, we are presented with a route of ants from the anthill to food. There are two routes to the food. They came into existence by means of a boulder. Both routes are toured in both directions, because the ants go for the food and then return with the food to the anthill. At first sight one can notice which of the routes is shorter and which is longer, but the ants cannot see this. As I have already mentioned, the longer the distance, the less frequently it is chosen due to lesser intensity of the pheromone; the shorter the distance, the more frequently it is covered and the intensity of the pheromone is higher. Going along this path further, one should ask a question when the ants are going to reach their goal, which route to take in order to reach it and return faster. All this depends on the number of ants which have chosen the specific route as well as on the distance of the route. In the beginning, the ants choose their route randomly. It is obvious that using the shorter route, the ants will come back with the food quicker, which will result in faster accumulation of the pheromone and increase in its intensity. However, one cannot actually determine when the optimum route will be chosen. One can say for sure that sooner or later it will be chosen. The speed, to a great extent, will depend on luck. I mean a random situation; if there more ants and they choose a right path in the beginning, the finding of an optimum route will take less time; while in the case of smaller number of ants, the finding of the optimum solution in a short period of time will be highly unlikely. The concept of ant algorithms was defined by Marco Dorigo in 1992 as a multi-agent system inspired by the observations of behaviour of real ant colonies, using the issue of stigmergy (STY) (indirect communication). The area of ant algorithms derives from the observations of ants habitats. The STY concept performs an important role in ant algorithms, because thanks to the implementation of the so-called STY variables, their functioning is possible. These variables contain information used by artificial ants to execute indirect communication. For example, in the ACO algorithm, the STY variables are specifically defined and used by the ants to change the manner of constructing solutions for the problem under examination.

Ant Colony Optimisation - is one of the most famous ant algorithms in the present times. It was defined for the first time by Marco Dorego, Di Caro and Gambardella in 1999 [15] as a technique for solving the problems of discreet optimisation. ACO was presented as an algorithm which can find a good path through a graph. This is an algorithm inspired by the foraging theory [19] for ant colonies as well as the problems of discreet optimisation. The algorithm is dedicated for solving two types of optimisation problems: static and dynamic ones. The basis for the commencement of trials on the ant algorithms was the pure observation of the ant habitat. The observed curiosity was that in the majority of cases, ants communicate with one another by means of chemical substances they produce. As I have already mentioned, a crucial component in this algorithm is the indirect communication foraging, represented by the pheromone trace. Paring this pheromone has the advantage that it may prevent the convergence (confluence) for the optimum local solutions. If we assumed that there is no concept of paring, then each time, each of the paths chosen by the first artificial agents would be treated identically; would be identically attractive, which would have no application to solving the optimisation problems. In this manner, when one ant finds a good path from the colony to the source of food, the other ants show preference to this route. The idea for the ACO algorithm is the imitation of this behaviour by means of artificial agents moving within the graph in order to solve a given problem. The ACO algorithm was used for solving the TSP problem. This algorithm has an advantage over genetic algorithms and the simulated annealing algorithm. Its important feature is that for the dynamically changing graph, the ACO algorithms may work continuously and adapt to the changes in real time. The benefit of such actions is the method of network routing and the urban transportation systems. Below we can see a pseudo code of the ACO algorithm:

Pseudo Code of algorithm ACO [14]

```
procedure ACO_MetaHeuristic
   while(not_termination)
      generateSolutions()
      pheromoneUpdate()
      daemonActions()
   end while
end procedure
```

where the individual functions are responsible for:

generateSolutions() manages the colony of ants, which simultaneously and asynchronously visit the neighbouring states of a given problem under consideration, by moving through the neighbouring apexes of the described problem, a given G graph. The movement of ants is done by means of stochastically locally taken decisions, which are made on the basis of pheromone traces and other heuristic information. In this manner, the ants create a solution in an increasing manner and evaluate the partial solutions, which will be used by the pheromoneUpdate() function, to decide how much pheromone will be left.

pheromoneUpdate() this is the function used for modifying the pheromone trace. This trace may increase thanks to the work of ants which cover the individual edges (apexes), and it may decrease by naturally implemented paring. The paring of pheromone prevents the accumulation of searches on one area, and - at the same time - it encourages the searching of new places which have not been visited so far.

daemonActions() this is the function which is used for the implementation of centralised actions that cannot be conducted by a single ant. An example of this function is the activation of the local optimisation procedure or collection of global information, which may be used for making decisions, whether or not it is useful to leave additional amounts of pheromone in order to influence the process of searching from outside of the local perspective.

The two most important formulas (1, 2), which describe the concept of ant systems, include:

Path selection - the ant is going to cover a route from point i to point j with the likelihood rate equal to:

$$p_{ij} = \frac{(\tau_{i,j}^{\alpha})(\eta_{i,j}^{\beta})}{\sum(\tau_{i,j}^{\alpha})(\eta_{i,j}^{\beta})} \tag{1}$$

where:

$\tau_{i,j}$ - quantity of pheromone on the route i, j,

$\eta_{i,j}$ - defines attraction of the route i, j,

α - parameter used for effect control $\tau_{i,j}$,

β - parameter used for effect control $\eta_{i,j}$.

Pheromone update this issue is represented by the following formula

$$\tau_{i,j} = p\tau_{i,j} + \Delta\tau_{i,j} \tag{2}$$

where:

$\tau_{i,j}$ - quantity of pheromone on the route i, j,

$\Delta\tau_{i,j}$ - represents the quantity of left pheromone,

P pheromone evaporation scale.

Below one can see a more detailed pseudo code of one of the many ant algorithms, specified as ACS (from English: Ant Colony System), namely optimisation of ant colony.

The pseudocode of ACS

```
Initialize
Repeat {
 Place each ant in a randomly chosen city;
 For each ant
   Repeat {
     Choose NextCity (each ant);
     Update pheromone levels using a local rule;
   } Until (No more cities to visit);
   Return to the initial cities;
   Compute the length of the Tour found by each ant;
 End For;
 Update pheromone level using a global rule;
}
Print Best Path;
```

4   Introduction - owlANT Software

Generalising the view on ontology as a specific form of the graph, the idea that comes to our mind is the application of ant algorithms. The combination of the technique of probabilistic algorithm with the concept of ontology as a way of expressing knowledge led to the connection of these two issues. The ants behaviour is related to the search for food for their colony. The insects leave pheromone on their way, informing other insects about the possible marking of the route. The more stable and stronger a pheromone is, the more ants have toured this route. This translates into the behaviour of a colony which found an optimum route to food. The optimal character of the selected route is understood, in this case, as the shortest route [20][16].

This chapter will present the owlANT programme, which deals with the subject presented in the previous sections of the publication. The owlANT programme is a software developed and created for determining the length of a route in ontology[21]. The structure of the programme is presented in figure number 2. The first part of this software is the analysis of ontology. The deciphering of classes, relationships included in ontology is done by means of Protg-OWL API. On the basis of this information, a term graphs is constructed. It presents the possible routes that may be taken by a colony of ants. Where the classes form apexes, the relationship of the classes hierarchy forms the edges in the graph. Additionally, to fully present the occurring relations in ontology, object properties are obtained. Particularly we read the values of domain property and range property, which become additional edges for the graph. The above-described actions presented in figure 11 are grouped in the preparatory process of the graph.

The process of preparing the graph is concluded with the generation of a graph of concepts and relations, which is the source of date for the ant algorithm[22]. The generated graph can be seen in the following figure number 2.

Making use of the transition of ontology into a graph, we begin the main stage of the programme. Commencement of the ant algorithm brings into life colonies of ants. The ant is equipped with a series of features, the start, the end of route, whether it is alive. These features are used for determining the state, in which it can be found. The ant starts from a given place, the starting point being any apex in the graph. Moving about the graph, the ant leaves a trace known as a pheromone trace. The manner of selection of the apex which will be chosen by the ant for further route depends on the amount of pheromone trace. At the same time, to introduce a random element during the selection of route, a roulette mechanism was used, as presented in figure number 3 3. The concept of the roulette wheel anticipates the determination of the total amount of pheromones contained on the available edges. Calculation of the pheromone share for the given edge. The determined share becomes a proportional part of the relationship to the entire amount of pheromones. Based on the proportional distribution of the pheromone on the roulette wheel, a drawing is performed.

The figure number 3, the K1, K2, K3 and K4 are the markings of edges for which the amount of pheromone is proportional to the allocated area of the roulette wheel. The edge with higher quantity of the pheromone becomes

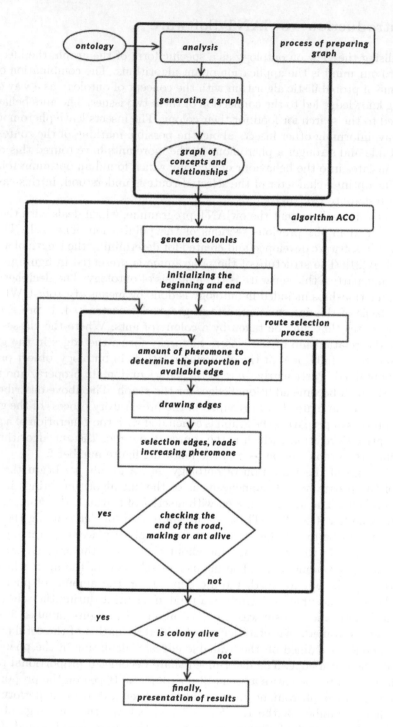

Fig. 1. Structure of the owlANT programme

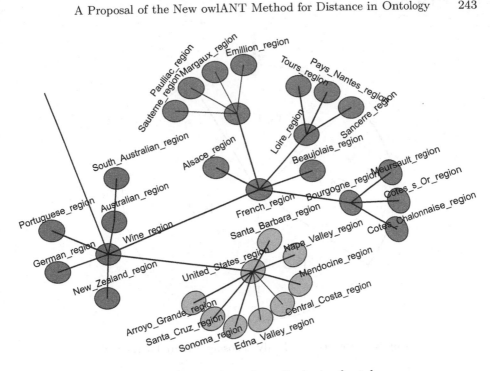

Fig. 2. The generated graph on the basis of ontology

the edge whose likelihood of selection is greater. The drawing was fulfilled on standard generator of random numbers available in Java 2. A randomly selected edge is visited by the ant, which left a trace increased by one on the edge. The process of selecting the next node is repeated until the goal is reached. The above-presented function of the programme is called the route selection process. However, there are situations in which the ant cannot reach its destination and dies. This is caused by e.g. lack of nodes to visit. The software was written in Java 2 entirely. The deciphering of classes, relationships included in ontology was done by means of Protg-OWL API. The software was tested on a PC with Pentium Dual Core processor, with an operating system of MS Windows 8.

5   Experiment – Course of the Trial

The assumption for the conduction of the experiment is the statement that by means of the probabilistic algorithm, one can determine the distance between the concepts, which are represented by the apexes in the graph. Determining the minimum distance between the two points was done each time. From the particular phase of the course of determining the distance between the apexes, the distance with minimum number of passages became the leading distance (Table 1). The other transitions, determined routes were deleted and excluded from the general rating.

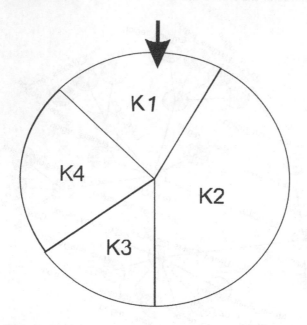

Fig. 3. A roulette randomly choosing a route for the ant

The table above presents the results of the works of the programme, namely the distances between the terms (graph apexes). The results of the calculations gathered in the table (1) show different distances on equal tracks. These differences which we can observe, come mainly from ontological relationships and the usage of the algorithm. The semantics based on description logics in this experiment reveals the problem of different distances. On the algorithm we can talk about randomization of the selection of a track other than the one with a strong pheromone. The solution of the above mentioned ambiguity of two different distances is to select the shortest one. The presented results were generated on the basis of population of twenty individuals. The low number of individuals used in the presented example was dictated by the informative nature of the research.

Table 1. The rating of term (apex) distances in a round-robin manner

	Term A	Term B	Term C	Term D	Term E	Term F	Term G
Term A	0	4	5	3	8	9	12
Term B	10	0	7	9	3	8	8
Term C	4	7	0	15	6	9	7
Term D	11	9	1	0	2	8	4
Term E	5	16	12	8	0	4	9
Term F	4	14	5	7	3	0	1
Term G	10	9	8	6	12	9	0

6 Conclusions

The course of the experiment of combining the ant algorithm and the knowledge included in ontology aimed at calculating the distance between the apexes. The distance between apex A and apex B was determined by the amount of left pheromone trace. The pheromone became an indicator determining the distance. Looking at this indicator from the nearest neighbouring position, the weights of the edges were determined. The determination of this parameter will serve as a material for further research works on the application of the accumulation algorithm for sequencing clusters of concepts from ontology. Another interesting subject for further research seems to be the relationship of similarity determined by ant colonies. They could serve as the basis for determining the measure of similarity of text documents, which was also the purpose of the above-described research.

Acknowledgments. The authors would like to express their thanks to technical staff of AIRlab - Artificial Intelligence and Robotics Laboratory at Casimir the Great University in Bydgoszcz for their commitment and help during research and tests performed within this study.

References

1. Kacprzyk, J., Zadrozny, S.: Computing with words is an implementable paradigm: fuzzy queries, linguistic data summaries, and natural-language generation. IEEE Transactions on Fuzzy Systems 18(3), 461–472 (2010)
2. Kacprzyk, J., Wilbik, A., Zadrozny, S.: Linguistic summaries of time series via an owa operator based aggregation of partial trends. In: IEEE International Fuzzy Systems Conference, FUZZ-IEEE 2007, pp. 1–6. IEEE (2007)
3. Zhang, L., Xia, S., Xia, Z., Zhou, Y.: Study on ontology partition based on ant colony algorithm software engineering. In: Ninth ACIS International Conference on Artificial Intelligence, SNPD 2008, August 6-8. Volume Networking, and Parallel/Distributed Computing, pp. 73–78 (2008)
4. Czerniak, J.M., Apiecionek, L., Zarzycki, H.: Application of ordered fuzzy numbers in a new ofnant algorithm based on ant colony optimization. In: Kozielski, S., Mrozek, D., Kasprowski, P., Małysiak-Mrozek, B.z. (eds.) BDAS 2014. CCIS, vol. 424, pp. 259–270. Springer, Heidelberg (2014)
5. Gruber, T.: Toward principles for the design of ontologies used for knowledge sharing. International Journal of Human and Computer Studies 43, 907–928 (1995)
6. Michalewicz, Z., Fogel, D.: How to Solve It: Modern Heurisics, p. 226. Springer, Heidelberg (2004)
7. Zadrożny, S., Kacprzyk, J.: Bipolar queries: An aggregation operator focused perspective. Fuzzy Sets and Systems 196, 69–81 (2012)
8. Szmidt, E., Kacprzyk, J., Bujnowski, P.: How to measure the amount of knowledge conveyed by atanassov's intuitionistic fuzzy sets. Information Sciences 257, 276–285 (2014)
9. Zadrożny, S., Kacprzyk, J., Dziedzic, M., De Tré, G.: Contextual bipolar queries. In: Jamshidi, M., Kreinovich, V., Kacprzyk, J. (eds.) Advance Trends in Soft Computing WCSC 2013. STUDFUZZ, vol. 312, pp. 421–428. Springer, Heidelberg (2014)

10. Czerniak, J.: Evolutionary approach to data discretization for rough sets theory. Fundamenta Informaticae 92(1), 43–61 (2009)
11. Czerniak, J., Dobrosielski, W., Angryk, R.: Proposed multi-criterion optimisation method of school timetabling problem. In: Atanassov, K.T., Homenda, W., Hryniewicz, O., Kacprzyk, J., Krawczak, M., Nahorski, Z., Szmidt, E., Zadrozny, S. (eds.) New Trends in Fuzzy Sets, Intuitionistic Fuzzy Sets, Generalized Nets and Related Topics, IBS PAN, pp. 39–55 (2013)
12. Czerniak, J., Dobrosielski, W.: The pipe of samples visualization method as base for evolutionary data discretisation. Metody Informatyki Stosowanej 24, 57–68 (2010)
13. Merkle, D.: Swarm Intelligence: Introduction and Application. Springer Verlag GMBH (2008)
14. Dorigo, M., Stützle, T.: Ant Colony Optimization, p. 69. The MIT Press Cambridge Massachusetts Institute of Technology, London (2004)
15. Dorigo, M., Gambardella, M.: Ant colony system: A cooperative learning approach to the traveling salesman problem. IEEE Transactions on Evolutionary Computation, 53–66 (1997)
16. Miller, P.: Swarm Theory. National Geographic Staff (2007), http://ngm.nationalgeographic.com/2007/07/swarms/miller-text
17. Engelbrecht, A.P.: Fundamentals of Computational Swarm Intelligence. Wiley (2005)
18. Mikołajewska, E., Mikołajewska, D.: Neuroprostheses for increasing disabled patients' mobility and control. Advances in Clinical and Experimental Medicine 21(2), 263–272 (2012)
19. Palmer, J.: Smart future for swarm robots. Technology Reporter, BBC News (August 2008), http://news.bbc.co.uk/2/hi/technology/7549059.stm
20. Helsgann, H., Ngassa, J.L., Kierkegaard, J.: ACO and TSP. Roskilde University (2007)
21. McCarthy, J.: Circumscription – a form of non-monotonic reasoning. Artificial Intelligence 13, 27–39 (1980)
22. Biggs, N.L., Lloyd, E.K., Wilson, R.J.: Graph Theory 1736-1936, p. 2. Oxford University Press (1998)
23. Apiecionek, Ł., Czerniak, J.M., Zarzycki, H.: Protection tool for distributed denial of services attack. In: Kozielski, S., Mrozek, D., Kasprowski, P., Małysiak-Mrozek, B. (eds.) BDAS 2014. CCIS, vol. 424, pp. 405–414. Springer, Heidelberg (2014)

KIISA: Towards a Reference Architecture for Integrated Knowledge Services

Ricardo Anderson[1] and Gunjan Mansingh[2]

[1] Department of Computing,
The University of the West Indies, Mona-Western Jamaica Campus
ricardo.anderson02@uwimona.edu.jm
[2] Department of Computing,
The University of the West Indies, Mona Campus
gunjan.mansingh@uwimona.edu.jm

Abstract. Knowledge management and knowledge-based systems can be critical to organizations and their success. Integration of knowledge resources in existing information systems can help improve decision making and possibly drive efficiency gains in business processes. We present an architecture that integrates knowledge acquired from data and experts into the current information system environment in the social welfare domain. This supports the use of knowledge in critical service administration processes to support decision making. We discuss the implications of using this architecture to support the knowledge management capability of the domain.

Keywords: Knowledge architecture, knowledge management, social welfare.

1 Introduction

Social Welfare exists in various forms across the world. Over the decade spanning 1995 to 2008, in Latin America and the Caribbean (LAC) a new type of social welfare programme was introduced and has become popular as a new paradigm in social protection. These programmes, currently existing in Jamaica (Programme for Advancement Through Health and Education -PATH), Brazil (Bolsa Familia) among other countries, require persons to qualify based on their economic / social status and to maintain conditionalities related to healthcare and education [16,28]. Generally, the poor can apply for benefits and provide economic data to support their claim. The programme management agency will assess the application and determine if the applicant meets the threshold of poverty set by the programme. Once approved, cash and non-cash benefits are disbursed to households provided they continue to maintain their educational and healthcare obligations.

Anderson and Mansingh [2] demonstrated the use of Knowledge Discovery and Data Mining (KDDM) to develop a knowledge-based decision support system (DSS) to reduce resource usage and provide for process improvement for greater

© Springer International Publishing Switzerland 2015
D. Filev et al. (eds.), *Intelligent Systems'2014*,
Advances in Intelligent Systems and Computing 323, DOI: 10.1007/978-3-319-11310-4_22

efficiency in administrating the programme towards meeting their objective of improving human capital and reducing poverty.

The integration and continued utilization of such knowledge based systems require integration into the existing environment. Such integration must also provide for continued update of the knowledge to ensure that it remain relevant to the programme administration. The typical infrastructure to facilitate such integration of KDDM based knowledge requires a data warehousing setup. In general, the data warehousing infrastructure required to support KDDM activities requires significant outlay of expenditure and expertise; these are both restricted and lacking in the developing country context of social welfare. Also, budgets are usually very limited, and spending is sometimes restricted by donor agencies. These factors impair their ability to acquire and retain expertise and the infrastructure for such outlay. Further, other knowledge integrated architectures proposed, [24,11] asserts the need for extensive infrastructure to support the knowledge initiatives within the organization.

We propose an architecture that provides for the integration of the knowledge based system into the information systems environment with continued update of knowledge through KDDM and other sources. The architecture extends the existing information system to facilitate knowledge integration for decision support without the need for such elaborate infrastructure. Given the nature of information systems in LAC based conditional cash transfer programmes, real-time availability and seamless integration is essential as these environments are in the early stages of automation. Our architecture meets these requirements.

In section 2 we give a background and context to our proposed solution followed by a description of our development methodology and a discussion of the components of the architecture. We then discuss the application of the architecture and conclude.

2   Background

Data is a collection of facts and figures, while information is organized data that provides meaning. Context, experiences, expert insights can then be added to information to produce knowledge. The concept of knowledge has long been discussed with early researchers focusing on definitions and setting frameworks for understanding knowledge construct and taxonomy.

Knowledge has been defined in different ways throughout the literature, we adopt for this study that knowledge is a fluid mix of framed experience, values, contextual information and expert insight that provide a framework for evaluation and incorporating new experiences and information [8]. Knowledge differs significantly from information and data which are lower down on the Data-Information-Knowledge (DIK) hierarchy [30].

Polyani [27] specified two types of knowledge: tacit and explicit. Tacit knowledge is said to reside in one's subconscious and is not easily codified while explicit knowledge is easily codified and can be stored on machines. This has given rise to extensive research on how to create and manage knowledge within organizational contexts. Nonaka [25] adds to this discussion and further proposes four modes of knowledge creation: Socialization, Externalization, Combination and Internalization. This provides a framework for understanding the important types of knowledge, how they can be created in different contexts and how best to develop the knowledge architecture of an organization.

Several researchers have underscored the importance of knowledge management to today's firms to the extent that it cannot be ignored as a possible source of significant competitive advantage [31,15]. Other research focus on categorizing different types of knowledge and enlisting frameworks for organizing and establishing knowledge organizations, best practices and tangible outcomes from utilizing knowledge and how this improves decision making and process improvement in firms [3,19]. Bowman argues that knowledge can be critical to an organizations success as it can leverage their abilities and lead to business success [4].Today, with the proliferation of computer based information systems, knowledge management undoubtedly must be considered within the context of how these technologies can help and or facilitate the knowledge management initiatives in the firm.

Knowledge management systems are primarily designed to provide supporting knowledge to decision makers. These extend beyond the traditional information systems as it should provide a context within which that information is coded and presented for use [10]. Knowledge management systems within this context must therefore be comprised of a tool-set that facilitates the proper organization of resources with emphasis on information technologies that will drive the knowledge processes in the organization. Therefore, knowledge management systems must provide components that will support the acquisition, modeling, representation and use of knowledge [1,32]. This is essential as knowledge must be constantly updated, suitably modeled so that it integrates into the organization and suitably represented for application. Alavi and Leidner [1] contend that information and communication technologies (ICTs) can actualize and strengthen the knowledge processes through scope enhancement, timing and overall strategy. The concern is also noted that knowledge can be applied continuously after it may be outdated and its usefulness has passed as a result of changes in the organization or industry. Knowledge should therefore be constantly updated so that is continues to be relevant.

Knowledge based systems have been explored from many directions in the literature ranging from frameworks that cover knowledge creation [26] methods and techniques [34], Organizational impact and innovation [13,15]. The literature explores knowledge based systems implemented and assessed in various industries and applications including the petroleum industry [6] human resource management [23] manufacturing [17] the military [20,21], agriculture [9,18], microbiology [22], tourism [5,12] and project management [33]. Nemati et. al [24] proposed architectural integration for knowledge management and supporting services; we posit that existing information systems environments can be extended to incorporate knowledge as a component of the overall information system architecture. Thus, we contribute a knowledge integration architecture to the current literature and discuss its components and implementation further in section 4.

2.1   Social Welfare: Conditional Cash Transfers (CCTs)

Governments, voluntary organizations and multinationals provide different types of aid to assist vulnerable peoples across the world. These programmes take many different forms and are varied from immediate relief to long term assistance especially for persons with special needs due to disabilities. Conditional Cash Transfer programmes are a special type of social protection funded through the cooperation of multinational agencies and governments worldwide.

In LAC, the nature of information systems within these programmes is at the stage of information storage and retrieval. These systems are primarily used in the process of beneficiary selection, monitoring beneficiary adherence to the conditionalities and benefit processing including payment system [29]. Research is lacking in the use of information systems to create greater efficiency in these programmes.

2.2   The PATH CCT

The PATH programme in Jamaica is a conditional cash transfer that serves over three hundred thousand beneficiaries who are assessed to be poor and vulnerable. The programme is mainly demand driven as persons may contact the parish office or welfare representative and submit an application which details their economic and social condition. If the application score is below the threshold, the applicant pre-qualifies for a benefit. A social worker is then dispatched to the household to verify the information submitted. Once verification is complete, the payment process is activated and the agencies are contacted to provide monitoring and supply data to the PATH office regarding conditionalities. The program requires periodic visits to households that have beneficiaries to collect data for evaluation to determine if the household is still within the poverty range to continue on the programme. Upon update, the household may continue to benefit or is deemed to have improved economically to be able to survive without the benefits provided under the programme. This process is called re-certification. Table 1 below gives a list of processes critical to the administration of the PATH CCT and a description of the activities associated with each.

The programme has struggled with verifying and subsequent recertification due to significant resource constraints. The number of social workers available is insufficient and thus a significant backlog of months is experienced between application and verification, hence the start of the benefit disbursement is delayed. Anderson and Mansingh [2] successfully developed a data-driven knowledge based decision support system (DSS) that has been shown to allow automatic verification of applicants using knowledge from historical data with an accuracy exceeding ninety percent. This has implications for reducing the social worker resources required for verification and re-certification. The vast amount

Table 1. CCT Process Descriptions

Process	Description
Targeting	Method by which potential beneficiaries can access the programme.
Assessment	Review of application details submitted by households / target group members. This includes the administration of a special economic assessment using a proxy-means test. If the application meets the set test threshold, they would pre-qualify for benefit and listed for the next phase which is verification.
Verification	Social worker visits the address indicated as residence for applicant and reviews the information submitted with applicant and verifies details. If verification is successful, the applicant becomes a beneficiary and disbursements begin.
Beneficiary Management and Monitoring	Distribution of benefits, collection of data from support agencies related to conditionalities set for beneficiaries.
Re-certification	Social worker will periodically visit current beneficiary to determine whether data previously submitted still represents the current living conditions of beneficiary.

of data collected and maintained on applicants, beneficiaries and stakeholders involved in monitoring the conditionalities can be used to assist in decision making and improve efficiencies in the administration of the programme. Given that the system is not integrated for seamless knowledge-based support in the domain, its successful and wide ranging use by PATH administrators has been impaired. We therefore developed a knowledge integrated information systems architecture that extends the current information system environment to allow the knowledge extracted from data and experts to be available in real-time for decision making.

3   Developing the Architecture

In developing the knowledge integrated architecture, we reviewed the information system environment and built generic components extending the existing information system for knowledge integration.

3.1   Methodology

The work in this study was guided by the Design Science Methodology outlined by Hevner et. al [14]. We will now discuss the key guidelines in relation to this study and indicate the research activities that supported our work towards the solution.

- *Design as an Artifact:* we developed a reference architecture for guiding the integration of knowledge services into an existing information system environment that will allow on-line real-time access to knowledge for support in decision processes. This reference architecture is primarily for the domain of social services but may be useful in other domains with similar information systems environment and needs.

- *Problem Relevance:* we evaluated the information system environment in order to gain an understanding of the needs. It was identified that given the work of Anderson and Mansingh [2], the organization struggled with integration, as the DSS is a standalone solution having discretionary use. Given the success of the DSS given its evaluation, and the potential benefit, integration into the current environment for real-time access to the knowledge was desirable. This can also be useful for other systems in which their existing environment can benefit from knowledge-based add-ons that support their decision making and other processes.

- *Research Rigor:* a review of the nature of knowledge management, techniques and supporting methods and tools was done to ascertain whether architectures existed to provide integration that could support this need. We evaluated the applicability of data warehousing to this problem. We identified how decision support systems have been implemented and used in several industries. We identified the need for on-line, real-time access to knowledge in at least one domain.

- *The Search Process:* the development of the architecture was driven by the needs of the domain. We reviewed several existing reference architectures and models. We identified the critical components required in this domain and developed an initial architecture. This was evaluated and several iterations with the team and business unit leaders led the process of refinement of the components and their function in supporting the needs of the domain.

- *Design Evaluation:* the architecture was simulated in the real environment of the selected domain: The PATH CCT. A copy of the live data was created with the same schema; the proposed architecture was used to integrate the DSS developed by Anderson and Mansingh [2]. This proved significantly useful as the DSS operated in the original system environment, producing knowledge that was made available to the decision makers in real-time as application verification processes were done. The plug-in architecture of the knowledge base provided for update of knowledge which became immediately a part of the inferencing mechanism that was built into the DSS, thus, this delivered immediate adjustments to recommendations based on new evaluations of applicants in the business environment.

4   Components of the Architecture

We propose the use of existing information system architecture with an integrated knowledge service and knowledge repository to create a knowledge integrated architecture (see figure 1). The KDDM Utilities are used off-line to extract knowledge primarily from data and sends this to the knowledge repository, this is not proposed to be an automated process. We suggest that independent knowledge discovery projects will supply the knowledge repository. Expert knowledge elicited and suitably coded can be stored in this repository. The knowledge service acts as an interface between the existing system (BMIS) to supply knowledge for assisting with the decision making processes.

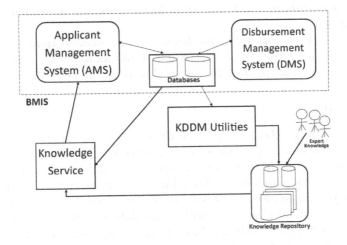

Fig. 1. Knowledge Integrated Information System Architecture (KIISA)

In the PATH programme, the BMIS Infrastructure is the existing system architecture with an application layer which houses the application logic. The BMIS is responsible for two main activities: accepting and managing applicant and beneficiary data and interfacing with the payment management system that process disbursement to beneficiaries.

The architecture connects the KDDM Utilities component to the data storage which understands the schema of the data, and can apply data mining techniques to acquire knowledge from data; this can be done through the use of proprietary tools. Once this knowledge is appropriately coded it can be added to the knowledge repository. If the knowledge repository is updated, the knowledge service will immediately begin to access the new knowledge and therefore reflect changes in the knowledge supplied to the application for decision support. The DSS [2] is used as the Knowledge Service for assessment of the architecture. The Knowledge Service interfaces with the BMIS and integrates the knowledge into the existing environment. When the application logic instantiates the process that is supported by the knowledge existing in the knowledge service, this knowledge, appropriately represented is made visible to inform the users' decision making. In our test environment (PATH), once new application data is input to the system and the proxy means process produces the score, the knowledge service is triggered and provides a recommendation on predicted qualification status with explanation for the user to review.

Based on the work-flow in PATH, this recommendation which is the result from the DSS (knowledge service) can be used as the decision factor and therefore remove the need for manual verification of the applicant. The DSS depends on real-time access and translation of the applicant data passed to it for evaluation. Upon completion of evaluation, the recommendation is sent to the BMIS. The extraction and translation is done in real-time to generate facts for input to the DSS (expert system) which is used for inferencing and subsequent applicant status recommendation.

If the decision maker uses the knowledge service recommendations and explanation, the manual verification is not required and an applicant is converted to a beneficiary and payments can be triggered to begin immediately.

4.1   Discussion

Generally in data warehouses the transactional data is maintained separately and with good reasons [7], however our architecture supports real-time transitions on data to provide access to a view of the data that would otherwise be stored in a data warehouse. This eliminates the need for the outlay of a data warehouse infrastructure. This is particularly useful in this domain since evaluations are usually case-based with small datasets. We however note that computing resources for transitions in real-time is high and will have significant requirements as the tasks increases. However, given the fairly static nature of programme organization and objectives in CCTs, it serves as a good low cost solution with potentially significant impact since CCTs across the world are similarly structured and administered.

Several architectures exist for supporting analytics services under different data-warehousing models such as enterprise data warehousing architecture, data mart architecture, hub-and-spoke, enterprise warehouse with operational data store and distributed data warehouse architecture. These all depend on a analytic dashboard that uses extraction translation and loading (ETL)for analysis. What we propose is storage of knowledge only in the form of models and appropriate constructs and application of such to real-time translated data for interactive decision support. The knowledge service supplies decision support based on specific areas of the information system for which this knowledge exists. In PATH, when an application has been processed by the proxy-means process and has pre-qualified, it is then passed to the knowledge service (DSS) which automatically send suggestions about the application's likely verification status and the probability attached to it based on models in the DSS.

The architecture developed and tested in the social services domain demonstrates the use of the current information system environment, with integrated knowledge acquisition and knowledge application capability. This also includes on-line, real-time access to knowledge as an integrated resource for supporting processes and decision making. An important feature of the architecture is the use of new knowledge acquired from data in the live system environment for seamless integration and support.

Based on the architecture, additional or different knowledge services may be added and integrated. Within the test domain, the strength and value of the knowledge to their operations was critical to the verification process.

This architecture provides a critical guide in implementing knowledge integrated support in the domain of Social Services with an instantiation in the PATH programme in Jamaica. The focus of the implementation of KIISA was specific to using the knowledge service that provides decision support specifically for the business processes surrounding verification and recertification of applicants. This has been reviewed by the domain experts and evaluated as having the potential to significantly reduce the resource requirements in the process supported. Further, the architecture provides for continued update, evolution and availability of knowledge. Since KIISA allows seamless integration of knowledge, there is no need for additional training as the knowledge is automatically presented to the user.

The study demonstrates our success in identifying the need for knowledge application in a domain and the development of an architecture that integrates knowledge with existing information system for ease of access on-line, and in real-time; which solves the problem.

5   Conclusion and Future Work

We have demonstrated that knowledge integration is useful in CCTs for decision support that can result in improved efficiency. We developed a knowledge integration architecture (KIISA) that includes the real-time integration of knowledge through a knowledge service supported by a knowledge repository all plugged into the current information systems environment. We have therefore contributed an architecture that supports some of the traditional data warehousing features, as an extension of an information system environment, without the need for the usual extensive data warehouse infrastructure. This was successfully tested and evaluated in the social welfare domain.

We will investigate the suitability of this architecture as a reference architecture for information systems environments that can benefit from on-line, real-time knowledge integration. We propose further that based on the architecture

(KIISA), once a business process managed by the information system is identified, a knowledge service can be developed and added to support that business process.

References

1. Alavi, M., Leidner, E.: Knowledge Management and Knowledge Management Systems: Conceptual Foundations and Research Issues. MIS Quarterly 25(1), 107–136 (2001)
2. Anderson, R., Mansingh, G.: An intelligence based knowledge-driven decision support system for Social Protection programmes. In: DSS Proceedings of the Third BI Congress, ICIS 2012, Orlando Florida (2012)
3. Ben-Zvi, T.: Measuring the perceived effectiveness of decision support systems and their impact on performance. Decision Support Systems (2012)
4. Bowman, B.J.: Building Knowledge Management Systems. nformation Systems Management, Summer, pp. 1–0 (2002)
5. Cooper, C.: Knowledge management and tourism. Annals of Tourism Research 33(1), 47–64 (2001)
6. Cauvin, S.: Dynamic application of action plans in the Alexip knowledge-based system. Control Engineering Practice 4(1), 99–104 (1996)
7. Chaudhuri, S., Dayal, U.: An overview of data warehousing and OLAP technology. ACM Sigmod Record 26(1), 65–74 (1997)
8. Davenport, T.H., Prusak, L.: Working Knowledge: How Organizations Manage What They Know. Harvard Business School Press, Cambridge (1997)
9. Fleurat-Lessard, F.: Qualitative reasoning and integrated management of the quality of stored grain: a promising new approach. Journal of Stored Product Research 38, 191–218 (2002)
10. Gallupe, R.B.: Knowledge Management Systems: Surveying the Landscape, Queenss School of Business Framework Paper 00-04. Queens University at Kingston (October 2000)
11. Gupta, S.K., Bhatnagar, V., Wasan, S.K.: Architecture for knowledge discovery and knowledge management. Knowledge and Information Systems 7(3), 310–336 (2005)
12. Hallin, C.A., Marnburg, E.: Knowledge management in the hospitality industry: A review of empirical research. Tourism Management 29, 366–381 (2008)
13. Hendricks, P.H.J., Vriens, D.J.: Knowledge based systems and knowledge management: friends or foes? Information and Management 35, 113–125 (1999)
14. Hevner, A.R., March, S.T., Park, J., Ram, S.: Design science in information systems research. MIS Quarterly 28(1), 75–105 (2004)
15. Johannessen, J.A., Olsen, B.: Olaisen, Aspects of innovation theory based on knowledge-management. International Journal of Information Management 19, 121–139 (1999)
16. Johannsen, J., Tejerina, L., Glassman, A.: Conditional Cash Transfers in Latin America: Problems and Opportunities. IDB Publication 9316, Inter-American Development Bank (July 2009)
17. Kang, B.S., Lee, J.H., Shin, C.K., Yu, S.J., Park, S.C.: Hybrid machine learning system for integrated yield management in semi-conductor manufacturing. Expert Systems with Applications 15, 123–132 (1998)

18. Kim, G., Nute, D., Rauscher, H.M., Lofits, D.L.: AppBulider for DSSTools: an application development environment for developing decision support systems in prolog. Computers and Electronics in Agriculture 27, 107–125 (2000)

19. Latteman, S.: Development of an environmental impact assessment and decision support system for seawater desalination plants. CRC Press Inc. (2010)

20. Liao, S.H.: Case-based decision support system: architecture for simulating military command and control. European Journal of Operational Research 123(3), 558–567 (2000)

21. Liao, S.H.: A knowledge-based architecture for implementing military geographical intelligence system on Intranet. Expert Systems With Applications 20, 313–324 (2001)

22. McMeekin, T.A., Ross, T.: Predictive microbiology: providing a knowledge-based framework for change management. International Journal of Food Microbiology 78, 133–153 (2002)

23. Martinsons, M.G.: Human resource management applications of knowledge based systems. International Journal of Information Management 17(1), 35–53 (1997)

24. Nemati, H.R., Steiger, D.M., Iyer, L.S., Herschel, R.T.: Knowledge warehouse: an architectural integration of knowledge management, decision support, artificial intelligence and data warehousing. Decision Support Systems 33(2), 143–161 (2002)

25. Nonaka, I.: A Dynamic Theory of Organization Knowledge Creation. Organization Science 5(1), 14–37 (1994)

26. Nonaka, I., Umemoto, K., Senoo, D.: From Information processing to knowledge creation: a paradigm shift in business management. Technology in Society 18(2), 203–218 (1996)

27. Polanyi, M.: The tacit dimension. Routledge and Kegan Paul, London (1966)

28. Rawlings, L., Rubio, G.M.: Evaluating the Impact of Conditional Cash Transfer Programs Lessons from Latin America. World Bank Policy Research Working Paper 3119 (2003)

29. Rawlings, L., de la Briere, B.: Examining Conditional Cash Transfer Programs: A Role for Increased Social Inclusion? World Bank Institute, SP Discussion Paper No. 0603 (2006)

30. Rowley, J.: The wisdom hierarchy: representations of the DIKW hierarchy. Journal of Information Science 33(2), 163–180 (2007)

31. Ryan, S., Harden, G., Ibragimova, B., Windsor, J.: The Business Value of Knowledge Management. In: Proceeding of the Eighteenth Americas Conference on Information Systems, Seattle, Washington (2012)

32. Schreiber, G., Akkermans, H., Anjewierden, A., de Hoog, R., Shadbolt, N., de Velde, W.V., Wielinga, B.: Knowledge Engineering and Management: The CommonKADS Methodology. MIT Press, Massachusetts (1999)

33. Tian, Q., Ma, J., Liu, O.: A hybrid knowledge and model system for R&D project selection. Expert Systems With Applications 23, 265–271 (2002)

34. Wiig, K.M., Hoog, R., Spex, R.: Supporting knowledge management: a selection of methods and techniques. Expert Systems with Applications 13(1), 15–27 (1997)

ZigBee Smart Sensor System with Distributed Data Processing

Alexander Alexandrov and Vladimir Monov

Modeling and Optimization Department,
Institute of Information and Communication Technologies,
Bulgarian Academy of Sciences,
Acad. G. Bonchev Str., bl. 2, 1113 Sofia, Bulgaria
{akalexandrov,vmonov}@iit.bas.bg

Abstract. ZigBee is a robust wireless communication standard managed by the ZigBee Alliance and based on the standard IEEE 802.15.4 physical and MAC layers. This paper describes an intelligent beacon type sensor system developed for meteorological data capturing. The sensor system is based on a new developed custom designed IEEE802.15.4 ZigBee battery powered sensor module including temperature, humidity and barometric pressure sensors and embedded GPS device. The ZigBee sensor module is FFD type and uses 6LoWPAN protocol with Low Power Listnening (LPL) scheme. Every module can play as PAN coordinator, Cluster Head coordinator or as end sensor device and is suitable for ad-hoc self organized wireless networks implementation. The proposed sensor system uses hierarchical cluster-tree topology. A new adaptive algorithm is developed to optimize the system energy consuming and to increase the time of autonomous work of the sensor modules. The algorithm is based on dynamic analysis of the content of the measured sensor data and depends on the adaptive change of the super-frame size and the consecutive beacons interval.

Keywords: wireless networks, sensor, energy consumption, 6LoWPAN, low power listening, distributed processing, adaptive algorithm.

1   Introduction

In the area of the wireless sensor networks (WSN) one of basic standards is IEEE 802.15.4 (ZigBee), [1], [5] . The wireless ZigBee technology is targeted to the collection data and management systems. The benefits of the technology are low level energy consumption, reliability to send/receive data, and very good compatibility between devices from different manufacturers [2, 3], [11, 12]. The devices based on the ZigBee technology can build a single wireless network with 100sq. km covering area approximately. This can be achieved by specialized routing mechanisms which provide resending the data through a big number of nodes of the sensor network to the control center [8, 9].

The main component of the described smart sensor system is a ZigBee 6LoWPAN (*IPv6 over Low power Wireless Personal Area Networks [6, 7], [10]*) based sensor

© Springer International Publishing Switzerland 2015
D. Filev et al. (eds.), *Intelligent Systems'2014*,
Advances in Intelligent Systems and Computing 323, DOI: 10.1007/978-3-319-11310-4_23

module measuring basic environment parameters – temperature, humidity and barometric pressure of the air.

The developed single smart sensor device consists of the following hardware modules and components:

- GPS SIRF IV based module;
- temperature sensor;
- humidity sensor;
- barometric pressure sensor;
- analysis and data treatment module;
- data storage module;
- wireless communication module based on ZigBee 6LoWPAN technology;
- power module with Li rechargeable battery.

Depending on the purposes of research, the wireless sensor device can work under the following basic regimes:

- collection, treatment, analysis and sending data if the sensor module change GPS coordinates;
- collection, treatment, analysis and sending data from the sensors if there is a change of the environment temperature;
- collection, treatment, analysis and sending data from the sensors if there is a change of the air barometric pressure;
- combination of two or more criteria described above.

If there is a change of some of the measured parameters depending on the current criteria the sensor device measures the air environment parameters, writes them in the storage memory and sends them by the wireless module to the control center. If there is no connection the device archives the measured data and wait for the next communication window to send all the unsent data.

In case of no change of the air environment parameters the sensor device goes to the sleeping communication mode and sends a control data at much bigger programmed time window Tw – 5 to 15min depending on the used algorithm.

Based on the measured data the sensor device can send an alarm signal to the control center and/or generate different types of events. For example the sensor device can work as forest fire detector and can send an alarm signal with GPS coordinates to the control center if the air temperature in the measurement point is reached 60 degree Celsius or more.

2   Sensor Device Basic Work Algorithm

The basic work diagram of the sensor device is shown in Fig. 1. The sensor device measures the current GPS coordinates, air barometric pressure, air temperature and the air humidity at programmed time intervals between 1 and 60 sec. The microcontroller module calculates the root mean square deviation (RMSD) for a block of the last three consecutive measurements and stores the result in the sensor device storage memory as a single measurement.

The current measured data is compared with the previous measurement in the storage memory. If there is a minor change only (less than 2 %) which is at the level of the sensors error, the sensor device processor deletes the last data from the memory and starts a new measurements. There is no communication session to the control center in this case. At the same time at fixed programmed time interval (between 5 to 15 min) the sensor device sends a benchmark data – current GPS coordinates, air temperature, air humidity and the air pressure meaningless of the data content.

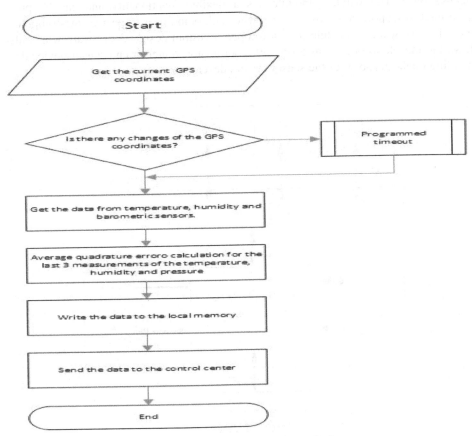

Fig. 1. Work diagram of the sensor device

The working algorithms of the sensor devices based on other sensor data changes or sensor data combination are similar. The proposed algorithm for sensor data local analysis and data treatment sensitively reduces the communication traffic between the smart sensor devices and the control center. At the same time the algorithm increases the time for autonomous work of the sensor device with more than 30% because of the reduced power consumption.

3   Block Diagram of the Smart Sensor Device

The block diagram of the developed smart sensor device is shown in Fig. 2. The processor module of the sensor device is based on ARM Cortex M3 microcontroller with the following technical parameters: 32KB on chip RAM, 512kB on chip FLASH, working frequency 32MHz; 32 I/O ports; 4 timers; 2 SPI ports, 2 UART ports, 8 channel 12 bit ADC. The processor module is equipped with 2 MB storage memory and embedded battery monitoring sensor. The wireless module of the sensor device is based on IEEE802.15.4 ZigBee and 6LoWPan protocols and it works at 2.4|GHz free license band. The wireless module has a flexible functionality and can be programmed to support point-to-point, point-to-multipoint, peer-to-peer or mesh topologies. For the wireless module it is developed a custom designed firmware which allows the module to operate as a network coordinator, router or end sensor device depending on the purposes of the sensor system development.

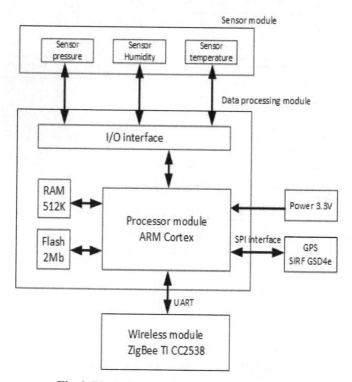

Fig. 2. Block diagram of the smart sensor device

The sensor module includes humidity sensor based on HC109, barometric pressure sensor based on BMP180, and air temperature sensor based on LM35 chip. The smart sensor device has full functional programmed analog and digital inputs and outputs managed by additionally developed SDK for future development of an additional functionality.

4   Structure of the Proposed Smart Sensor System

Based on the above described smart sensor device a sensor system was built for multipoint monitoring of the air parameters. The monitoring points equipped with the sensor device can communicate at up to 1600m distance. The communication structure of the sensor network is of beacon type [4] for decreasing the energy consumption and increasing the autonomous work of the sensors.

4.1   Sensor System Topology

According to [1], the 802.15.4 ZigBee a typical sensor network supports mainly 2 kind of devices – FFD(Full functional device) RFD (Reduced functionality device). An FFD can operate as a personal area network (PAN) coordinator, a coordinator only, or an end device, while an RFD can only act as a sensor device. An FFD can talk to RFDs and other FFDs, while an RFD can only talk to FFDs. An RFD is intended for very simple applications, such as a light switch or a passive sensor, with no need to send large amounts of data. An RFD may connect with only one FFD at a time. The FFD can work as a PAN(Personal Area Network) coordinator or end device. The RFD can work only as a passive sensor. The FFD can communicate with RFD and other FFD at the same time, while the RFD based sensors can communicate only with one FFD. The FFD and the RFD sensors can operate in two basic topologies – star and peer to peer. The proposed sensor system operate with cluster topology which is special case of peer-to-peer topology and consist mainly of FFD based sensors. In the system there are included some devices which operates as RFD based sensors for special cases.

In the current system part of the FFD based sensors operate as network coordinators too and have functionality to provide the synchronization during meteodata sending (GPS coordinates, air temperature, air humidity and the barometric pressure measurements) to the control center.

At the beginning of the sensor system operation one of the FFD is chosen as main coordinator for the first cluster by PAN identifier assignment defined CLH (cluster head) with CID(cluster identifier) and broadcast frames. The FFD based sensor devices in the area receive the frames and send request to join to the cluster. The PAN coordinator approves the request, add the device to the list of the neighbor devices and sends confirmation to the added device which starts to broadcast frames too. If there is no possibility for a FFD based sensor to be added to the current CLH, the sensor device starts to look for another coordinator. The PAN coordinator can instruct some of the FFD sensors in the cluster to generate a CLH and to start to operate as coordinator of new cluster. This is realized by special application with responsibility to generate new clusters based on in advance defined criteria The diagram of the sample cluster system is shown in Fig. 3. After the connection of the all sensor devices a cluster tree is formed. The basic benefit of the proposed topology is its ad-hoc selforganisation and self-sustaining functionality.

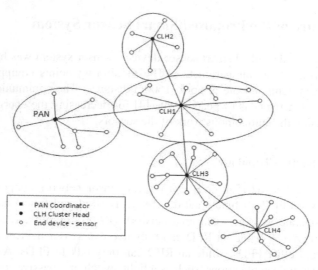

Fig. 3. Sample cluster system

4.2   6LoWPAN

The 6LoWPAN standard and protocol are relatively new and provide IPv6 based communication of low-power wireless devices. The 6LoWPAN RFC defines the network layer of IP based networks which use IEEE 802.15.4 physical and medium access layers. The main purpose of the 6LoWPAN development is to improve the communication between small network divices as part of wireless sensor networks for example. In the standard IPv6 specification the size of the package is 1280 octets which is too big for the package of the 802.15.4 protocol and needed fragmentation.

Other problem is that the IP routing protocol can not work effectively with devices in sleeping mode. Practically 6LoWPAN acts as additional layer between MAC and the network layer with adaptation purposes. This functionality compresses the size of the header of the package and saves at the same time the basic IPv6 functionality.

The 6LoWPAN mode does not provide any mechanism to realize low-power data communication, but it relies on lower layer approaches. The simplest solution to achieve low power consumption in 6LoWPAN networks might be the exploitation of low-energy capabilities of the beacon-enabled IEEE 802.15.4 protocol. In this case the MAC layer may work in both beacon-enabled and nonbeacon-enabled mode depending on the programmed way of working based on the firmware. At the same time all the current 6LoWPAN implementations only support the nonbeacon-enabled mode. In this case, beacons are used for a link layer device discovering and association.

One of the reasons that it is dificult to implement a beacon enabled communication in 6LoWPAN mode is that IP protocols expect that the link is always-on. This is for simplicity, so that IP protocols do not need to schedule datagram transmissions

Therefore, 6LoWPAN has to use duty-cycling techniques which give the illusion to the upper layers that the receiver is always on, although it is actually off most of the time. The current 6LoWPAN sensor network implementation uses Low Power

Listening (LPL), a technique which allows the nodes to access the channel in a completely distributed and asynchronous way.

The operation behind LPL is the following: every node periodically wakes up, turns the radio on and checks for activity. If no activity is sensed, the node turns off the receiver and goes back to sleep, otherwise, the node stays awake until the packet is received or, in the case of a false positive, until a timer expires. A graphical representation of LPL operations is shown in Figure 4. As the false positives decrease the energy-efficiency of the protocol, it is important to have an accurate channel assessment. Nonetheless, this technique has been recently adapted to work in noisy environments as well.

In order to avoid packet losses while the node is sleeping and, therefore, to make the link appear as always-on, the preamble of each packet must last as long as the interval between two consecutive LPL samples.

4.3   Network Configuration Depending on the Network Parameters

The 6LoWPAN protocol is relatively simple and does not need a synchronization between the network devices (sensors). This is one of the main reasons this protocol to be used in the proposed sensor system with beacon type communication.

Currently, the smart sensor devices are powered by rechargeable batteries with limited capacity. Therefore most of the time the sensor devices are in sleeping mode in order to reduce the power consumption.

To optimize the power consumption of the sensor devices there is a need to analyze the LPL (Low Power Listening) parameters of the sensor system. The basic LPL parameters which define one communication cycle are Sleep Interval (SI) and Activity Interval (AI). As it is shown in Fig. 4 one LPL consist of AI followed by SI. In the current hardware implementation the SI is defined by dynamically programmed timer and it is accepted as a configurable parameter which can be analyzed and optimized.

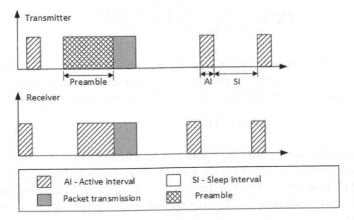

Fig. 4. An LPL cycle

At the same time AI is based on the requests of the sensor devices and can be changed only in limited borders. When a device sends a package during the AI, the receiving part is activated till receiving all the package. Therefore the all network traffic depends on the cycle of the active devices in the network – DC (Duty Cycle).

For one 6LoWPAN based node sending data with fixed speed, DC can be controlled by SI optimization and the speed of packages sending. The average interval between packages in a working sensor network should be bigger than one LPL cycle. Based on this, one Duty Cycle (DC) of one LPL based network can be calculated as:

$$DC \quad = \quad \frac{AI \quad + \quad Tps \quad . Nppc}{AI \quad + \quad SI} \tag{1}$$

where *AI* and *SI* are the size of the active interval and sleeping interval respectively. Tps is the time of the package sending and Nppc is the average number of the packages in one LPL cicle. In the most of the cases Nppc < 1 based on the equation

$$Tps = Tpre + Tpkt + Dtx \tag{2}$$

where *Tpre* is the preamble size equal of *SI*, *Tpkt* is the time of the package sending and *Dtx* is the hardware delay which is approximately 20ms for the ZigBee CC2538 SoC used in the proposed smart sensor device. At the same time *Nppc* can be calculated as:

$$Nppc = \frac{AI + SI}{Tsend} \tag{3}$$

where *Tsend* is the period of the package sending. If we substitute *Tps* and *Nppc* in formula (1) for *DC* we get the *DC* of one 6LoWPAN node as a function of the network parameters:

$$DC = \frac{AI}{SI + AI} + \frac{SI + Tpkt + Dtx}{Tsend} \tag{4}$$

Figure 5 shows the change of the *DC* depending on the *SI* change. We see that *DC* has a global minimum and there is a possibility for optimization of the power consumption by *SI* change. The optimal *SI* can be calculated by the following formula:

$$SI = \sqrt{AI . Tsend} - AI \tag{5}$$

As a conclusion, we see that the optimized SI influences the DC which is staying relatively small when we decrease the period of the packages sending. This means that in the LPL based systems when the speed of the packages is high we can achieve a relatively larger efficiency for data communication at the same level of the network traffic loading.

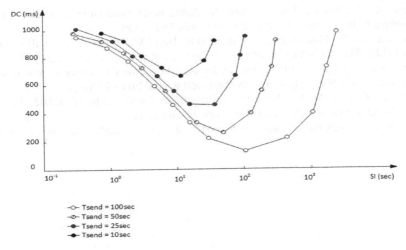

-o- Tsend = 100 sec
-⊘- Tsend = 50 sec
-●- Tsend = 25 sec
-●- Tsend = 10 sec

Fig. 5. Change of the *DC* depending on the *SI* change

Acknowledgements. The research work reported in the paper is partly supported by the project AComIn "Advanced Computing for Innovation", grant 316087, funded by the FP7 Capacity Programme (Research Potential of Convergence Regions).

References

1. ZigBee Specification, ZigBee Document 053474r17 Version, pp. 1–576 (2008)
2. Toscano, E., Lo Bello, L.: Comparative assessments of IEEE 802.15.4/ZigBee and 6LoWPAN for low-power industrial WSNs in realistic scenarios,
   `http://lobello.dieei.unict.it/public_files/`
   `publications/wfcs12.pdf`
3. Polastre, J.H., Culler, D.: Versatile low power media access for wireless sensor networks. In: Proc. 2nd Intl Conf. on Embedded Networked Sensor Systems, SenSys 2004, pp. 95–107. ACM, USA (2004)
4. Huang, Y., Pang, A., Hung, H.: A comprehensive analysis of low-power operation for beacon-enabled IEEE 802.15.4 wireless networks. IEEE Trans. Wireless Communication 8(11), 5601–5611 (2009)
5. Pinedo-Frausto, E.D., Garcia-Macias, J.A.: An experimental analysis of Zigbee networks. In: IEEE Conf. on Local Computer Networks, pp. 723–729 (2008)
6. Mulligan, G., The, G.: 6LoWPAN architecture. In: Proc. 4th Workshop on Embedded Networked Sensors, EmNets, pp. 78–82. ACM, USA (2007)
7. Hui, J.W., Culler, D.E.: IPv6 in Low-Power Wireless Networks. Proceedings of the IEEE 98(11), 1865–1878 (2010)
8. Sasidharan, S., Pianegiani, F., Macii, D.: A protocol performance comparison in modular WSNs for data center server monitoring. In: Intl Symp. on Industrial Embedded Systems (SIES), pp. 213–216. IEEE (2010)

9. Perkins, C.E., Belding-Royer, E., Das, S.: Adhoc on-Demand Distance Vector (AODV) Routing, http://www.ietf.org/rfc/rfc3561.txt
10. Kushalnagar, N., Montenegro, G., Culler, D.E., Hui, J.W.: Transmission of IPv6 Packets over IEEE 802.15.4 Networks, http://tools.ietf.org/html/rfc4944
11. Sha, M., Hackmann, G., Lu, C.: Energy-Efficient Low Power Listening for Wireless Sensor Networks in Noisy Environments. Technical Report 2011-61 (2011)
12. Toscano, E., Lo Bello, L.: Multichannel Super-frame Scheduling for IEEE 802.15.4 Industrial Wireless Sensor Networks, IEEE Trans. Ind. Informat., http://ieeexplore.ieee.org/xpls/abs_all.jsp?arnumber=6009195

Modeling Attacks on MANET Using an Incomplete Repeated Bayesian Game

Farah Saab and Mariette Awad

Electrical & Computer Engineering Department,
American University of Beirut, Beirut, Lebanon
{fws02,mariette.awad}@mail.aub.edu

Abstract. Nowadays, individuals, as well as corporations, use the internet on a daily basis to send and receive emails, browse the internet, perform financial transactions, etc... However, this dependence comes with the huge risk of communicating over a network that has been compromised. Network administrators are constantly faced with new and improved security attacks that might result in significant losses. Only recently have game theoretic approaches found their way into the area of network security. In this paper we discuss the different types of security attacks while focusing on a general attack that resembles attacks on mobile ad hoc networks or MANETs. We model the attack as a Bayesian repetitive game with incomplete information between a malicious node and a normal node. We study the Nash equilibria of the game, and describe several punishment strategies. Finally, we show the results of our simulations where an equilibrium state is always reached and the average profit of normal nodes always significantly exceeds that of malicious nodes.

1 Introduction

According to an IBM study, the cost of a successful cyber-attack on a company might reach 300,000 USD. Also, companies are attacked an average of 2 million times per week [1]. This shows the importance of implementing network security techniques in order to prevent monetary losses, and even worse, damage of reputation. According to [2] , there is a 40% increase in mobile malware in the past few months. Google Play alone has more than 1 million apps [3]. This means that the number of malicious applications found in the market nowadays is huge. This serves to show that implementing a security mechanism is not enough. The number of attackers is increasing. And with every security mechanism deployed, a counterattack arises. Network security techniques have to be updated regularly in order to keep up with the different kinds of attacks. An adaptive online network security solution is one option.

In our work we intend to use the concepts of game theory in order to model the problem of network security. The basic scenario is the following. We have two players: the administrator and the attacker. The actions of the administrator are to respond or to defend. The actions of the attacker are either to attack or not to attack. The payoffs are related to the costs. An administrator that suffers from an attack loses,

© Springer International Publishing Switzerland 2015
D. Filev et al. (eds.), *Intelligent Systems' 2014*,
Advances in Intelligent Systems and Computing 323, DOI: 10.1007/978-3-319-11310-4_24

so his payoff will be negative. An attacker that successfully attacks without being detected has a positive payoff that is a function of the losses incurred by the administrator. For the administrator, the best case is when he defends given that the attacker attacked. The worst case is when he doesn't defend and naturally responds given that the attacker attacked. As for the attacker, the best case is when he attacks and the administrator does not defend. And his worst case is when he attacks and the administrator defends. In general, the administrator wishes to optimize his profit by reducing his costs. Suffering from an undetected attack will incur the highest cost for him. As for the attacker, he wishes to maximize his profit by causing the administrator the highest cost value. It can be modeled as a zero-sum game, however the profit of one player does not necessarily match the loss of another in a realistic scenario, and so a general-sum game serves as a better model. Our plan is to use game theoretic concepts in order to come up with the best strategy that an administrator can follow in order to always optimize his profits regardless of the type of attack that he is faced with.

The rest of the paper is organized as follows. In Section 2, we present a survey of the previous work. In Section 3, we give a brief summary of some of the main types of attacks on networks and the defenses against them. In Section 4, we model some of the attacks using different game theoretic techniques. In Section 5, we study the Nash Equilibria of the models presented in Section 4. We show the results of our simulations along with an analysis in Section 6 and finally conclude our work in Section 7 and discuss future work.

2   Previous Work

Some work has already been done in the area of game theory for network security and reliability. The authors in [4] analyzed two different scenarios where game theory can be used to better comprehend network reliability. Relaying messages does not result in immediate benefit for the node itself, especially that it would be wasting its valuable energy resources as well as its transmission time when it could be transmitting its own data. That is why nodes tend to act in a selfish non-cooperative manner. Nodes need incentives in order to cooperate. The authors apply game theory to two scenarios previously presented in the literature; cooperation by bribery [5] and cooperation through punishment [6]. Their simulations also accounted for random link failure costs and showed a relationship between link failure and choosing an optimum path.

In the case of static game models, we first discuss the research work that falls under the category of games with complete and imperfect information. The authors in [7] presented an approach to risk assessment in cyber security. They modeled the attack and protect strategies as a static game with two players, the attacker and the protector. The protector can either protect or not protect his critical information, and the attacker can steal or reverse engineer unprotected and protected property respectively. If the protector does not protect his information, the attacker will be motivated to steal it if his probability of success is high and the cost of theft is small.

If the protector chooses to protect his information, the attacker will try to reverse-engineer the information. The protector should always make sure that his protection cost is lower than the cost of obtaining the information by the attacker. Being a static game, it is of imperfect information. However the information is complete since both the attacker and protector are fully aware of each other's strategies and payoffs. The authors applied their proposed method on small but realistic scenarios. Their results showed that their method can improve risk assessment in systems that are under attack by adversaries.

In the area of static games with incomplete and imperfect information, the authors in [8] focus on one type of network security which is the intrusion detection problem in mobile ad-hoc networks. They model the scenario as a two player game. The first player is of known type to everyone. His actions are either to monitor or not to monitor. The other player's type is not known. He could be a regular player with only one action which is not to attack, or a malicious player with two actions which are to attack or not to attack. They first model the problem as a static game where the defender assumes a fixed prior probability about the other player's type, and then as a dynamic game where the defender updates his belief about the other player based on observed actions and the history of the game. They studied the Bayesian Nash Equilibrium in each case. They also simulated some experiments on the ns2 simulator. They concluded that the application of game theory to their model allowed them to save on energy consumption by having the IDS on 54.42% of the time only. However, they limited their work to one type of security threat and based their result on two specific experiments.

Even though static games can be used to model the network security problem, dynamic games are a better approximation for real life scenarios where there is a sequential structure of the decisions taken by the players. Also in the dynamic games category, we can have games with complete or incomplete information and perfect and imperfect information.

In the area of games with complete and perfect information, Lye et al. model the security of a computer network as a stochastic general-sum game [9]. They envisioned the network as a graph with four nodes; external world, work station, web server, and file server. The links of the graph represented the traffic state. The game has two players also, an administrator and an attacker. Defaced website, DoS attack, and stealing confidential data were the main focus of the authors, and the scenarios were described from the viewpoints of both players. Since they modeled the game as a general-sum instead of a zero-sum, the game had a set of different Nash Equilibria. To calculate them, they used NLP-1 in Matlab. The authors show the results in tabulated format but they do not clearly represent their problem in a game theoretic context by giving examples of a Nash Equilibrium. The authors in [10] also model network security as a stochastic non-cooperative game with two players; an attacker and a defender. Their model is based on linear influence networks that represent the interdependence of the players in terms of information and vulnerabilities. They first modeled the network as a zero-sum game where the optimal solution served as a means to provide IDSs with information regarding how to allocate their resources as well as understand the behavior of a rational attacker. However taking into consideration the cost of monitoring and attacking, the game will no longer be zero-sum. The authors assumed that the attackers and defenders both have complete information which is not a realistic scenario. Another game model for risk assessment with complete and perfect information was proposed by the authors in [11]. A large risk will arise if a threat spreads due to some vulnerability, and a small risk will arise if the vulnerability is repaired. Thus their game is that of vulnerabilities and threats where the risk is assessed based on damage. The goal is to minimize the maximum damage by choosing a certain repair strategy. They created a platform with several subsystems to assess risk, detect vulnerabilities, detect assets, and detect malicious code. For the threat, they chose the Trojan.Mybot-6307. The results they got were similar to those of the Fault Tree Analysis (FTA). They claim that their model leads to the best repair scheme.

In the area of games with complete and imperfect information, the authors in [12] model their network as a stochastic Markov game. An underlying sensor structure is designed to detect network abnormalities. It is modeled using a finite-state Markov chain. They study three different cases. In the first case, the players know the sensor information and opponent characteristics. In the second case, the attacker does not know the sensor information. And in the third case, each player only knows his costs, states, and actions. They used methods such as minimax-Q, MDP value iteration, and naïve Q-learning to find the best strategies for the IDS and the attacker. However, their approach is limited to a small-scale network, and summarizes the entire network security issue with an attack/no attack choice without discussing the various types of security threats. Also, no discussion of equilibrium is found in their work. Another game model with complete and imperfect information was presented by Nguyen et al. in [13] . Again the two players are an attacker and a defender and the security of the network is modeled as a sequence of nonzero-sum games. Underlying sensor systems do not always deliver accurate information regarding the network sate, and so players must adapt to this inaccuracy. Thus the authors modeled their problem as a fictitious play game where the players observe each other's actions imperfectly due to the inaccuracy of the sensor system. Given these error probabilities of the sensor system, the players are either aware of them or not. If they are aware of the probabilities, a NE is reached where the players maximize their gain or minimize their loss. If they are unaware of the probabilities, then their model will estimate the loss that is incurred due to deviating from the NE of the system. Of course this loss is logical given the players do not know the characteristics of their own sensor system. In both cases, two games were simulated, classical fictitious play games and stochastic fictitious play games. In stochastic FP with perfect observations, the player's empirical frequencies converge to (0.79, 0.21) and (0.47, 0.53). If the players ignore the observation errors, the frequencies converge to (0.86, 0.14) and (0.42, 0.58). However, several scenarios are not modeled by the authors, for example the case where the defender knows the error probabilities and the attacker doesn't or the case where the error probability estimates are inaccurate.

In the area of games with incomplete and perfect information, Patcha et al. try to solve the problem of security in mobile ad hoc networks (MANETs) by modeling it as a basic signaling game with a sender and a receiver [14] . The nature of the sender is unknown to the receiver and so Bayes' rule is applied in every stage to update the system of belief regarding the nature of the other player. They modeled the game as a non-cooperative dynamic game with incomplete and perfect information. They studied the NE of the game but failed to provide quantitative simulation results and also limited their work to a general type of attack on a constrained network.

And finally in the area of dynamic games with incomplete and imperfect information, the authors in [15] model the network security problem as a two-player zero-sum game. They studied the Nash and Bayesian equilibria and used them to predict the interaction between the defender and the attacker. They formulated the game's min-max theorem and explained some of the relevant security terms. However they did not give a solution to the problem. They only suggested that it can be solved using linear algorithms.

In the work found in the literature, the authors only consider simplified cases of the game model that do not apply in real life scenarios. In some cases, they even assume complete and perfect information. As for the types of attacks, most authors limit their discussion to a general attack model without taking into consideration the different countermeasures that should be taken by an administrator when faced with different types of attacks.

3   Security Attacks

Many types of attacks on nodes fall under the category of eavesdropping. For example, sniffing or snooping attacks are a type of passive attacks where an attacker intercepts the traffic between a sender and a receiver and reads it. This is very easy to do when the data being sent is not encrypted. These types of attacks are usually very hard to detect since the information being transferred is not altered in any way. They are however easily preventable when applying strong cryptographic mechanisms between the sender and the receiver.

Data modification is the next step that comes after eavesdropping. In this case the attacker intercepts the data coming from the sender, modifies it in any way she wishes, and then sends the modified data to the receiver. These types of attacks are called active attacks since they involve a modification of the message being sent. They can be detected easily. They can also be prevented if we assume that strong cryptographic techniques have been implemented between the sender and the receiver. If that is the case, then the attacker will not be able to read the data in the first place, let alone modify it.

Instead of intercepting messages between a sender and a receiver, another approach to security attacks is masquerading as another user. Any type of masquerading attack requires spoofing an IP address. IP spoofing is when an attacker uses the IP address of a victim node. In networks where authentication is purely based on the IP address of a node, an attacker can send a packet that has the IP address of a victim's node as its source address thus masquerading as the victim node and gaining access to resources that she otherwise wouldn't have access to.

IP spoofing can be used to execute man-in-the-middle attacks. In these types of attacks, the attacker is sitting between the sender and the receiver. First she spoofs the IP address of the sender, intercepts the message, modifies it if she wants (data modification attack), and then sends it to the receiver using the sender's spoofed IP address as its source address. Then she spoofs the IP address of the receiver and repeats the process again when delivering the reply back to the sender. The attack will not be detected as long as the attacker manages to impersonate the sender to the satisfaction of the receiver and vice versa.

A popular defense mechanism against IP spoofing attacks in general is the public key infrastructure (PKI). PKI provides a much better authentication mechanism than the IP address. Using a certificate authority (CA), a public key is bound to every user. Put simply, if node A wants to send a message to node B, it encrypts the message using its private key that no one but A knows. When node B receives the message, if it manages to decrypt it using the public key of node A (which is as its name implies publicly available and provided by the CA), then it can be sure that the message was indeed sent by node A. Sending an encrypted message using a node's private key is known as a digital signature and it provides the solution to the types of IP spoofing attacks.

A MANET or mobile ad hoc network is a wireless network of mobile devices that has no underlying infrastructure. The network is self-organizing. Every node in the network is free to move in any direction. At times, a node will have to forward traffic that is not its own thus acting as a router. Sometimes a node is selfish and decides not to forward the traffic. Other times, network misbehavior is a result of a malicious node that harms its performance intentionally. Conventional cryptographic mechanisms for encryption and authentication are not usually implemented in MANETs due to the energy and time constraints of the nodes. The PGP (Pretty Good Privacy) protocol provided a tradeoff between the security of these networks and their performance. However, there is still plenty of research in the area of MANET security. Game theoretic techniques can be applied to improve the security of MANETs while taking into consideration the limited resources of the mobile devices.

A Sybil attack is when an attacker assumes several identities in order to play with the trust computation system of a MANET. When the trust of a node is based on votes, an attacker might be able to vote-out honest nodes and pass himself as a trustworthy node. This will result in upsetting the entire routing structure which depends on these trustworthy nodes that provide the best route setup in a MANET. A solution to the Sybil attack is incorporating a centralized certificate authority (CCA) that takes care of authenticating the different users and assigns one identity to every entity. Implementing a CCA in a closed MANET is feasible since in closed MANETs, the number of nodes is controlled and a central unit can take care of the authentication process.

The problem of authentication arises in open MANETs where any node can join at any time. The cost of communicating with a CCA every time a node joins the network beats the purpose of an open MANET. This presents a challenge to the authentication of nodes in these networks and poses an unsolved problem of the Sybil attack in such networks. The Sybil attack can be modeled using evolutionary game theory where an attacker that poses as several nodes is modeled as a mutant that is trying to dominate the population (network). To do so, it will create several identities of itself. Then it will try to out-vote some normal nodes by rating them as untrustworthy using all its identities. The different identities will also give a good rating of themselves thus improving their reputation among the normal nodes. The beliefs of the normal nodes regarding the attacker will improve. In case normal nodes decide to form coalitions to improve their security, an attacker can then infiltrate the coalition and share with the other nodes his list of banned nodes. This list might include several normal nodes, thus disrupting the routing paths and eventually causing congestion and delay in the network.

Evolutionary game theory tells us that from an attacker's perspective, he will always manage to dominate the population. Of course, in this context dominate does not mean that no good nodes will be present in the network in the steady state. It means however, that due to the fact that there is no limit imposed on the number of identities that an attacker can create, he will eventually take control over the network.

We are left with denial-of-service attacks. A DoS attack is when a malicious node attempts to make a computer system inaccessible by flooding it with useless traffic. The result is that legitimate users will no longer be able to access the resources of the flooded victim. The attack becomes more challenging when the attacker uses several nodes as slaves that send a huge amount of traffic at once to the victim. This is known as the distributed DoS (DDoS). Detecting the source of a DoS/DDoS attack is not an easy task. However, we can make use of game theoretic techniques in order to alleviate the problem.

4   Game Theoretic Models

We will assume throughout our work that attackers (malicious nodes – M) in a network know the type of every other node (malicious or normal). Normal nodes (N) on the other hand only know their own type.

Let v denote the value of the assets that an administrator is trying to secure.
Let c_D denote the cost of defending for the administrator.
Let c_A denote the cost of attacking for the attacker.
Let γ denote the detection rate of the administrator.

After completing a successful communication between Player 1 and Player 2, an administrator gains a profit w, whereas an attacker loses the same value w (waiting cost).

A natural assumption is that $v \gg c_A, c_D, w$ otherwise the attacker won't have an incentive to attack and the administrator won't have an incentive to defend.

4.1   MANET Attacks

For a better understanding, we will always refer to Player 1 as a female and Player 2 as a male.

4.1.1   Attack Model

An attacker wants to attack a normal node. If the attacker is Player 2 in the game and the normal node (administrator) is Player 1, we can model this as a Bayesian game with incomplete information.

Player 2 knows the state of Player 1. Player 1 on the other hand does not know whether Player 2 is normal or malicious. Player 1 can be of 1 type and Player 2 can be of 2 types.

The actions of Player 1 are Respond (R), or Defend (D).

The actions of Player 2 are Attack (A) or Communicate (C) if he were an attacker and Communicate (C) if he were a normal node.

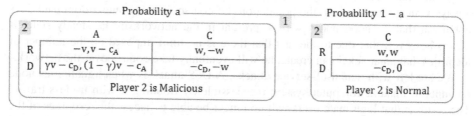

Fig. 1. Bernoulli payoff of Player 1 and Player 2

The above figure represents the payoffs of the 2 players based on the beliefs of Player 1. Let **a** denote the probability that Player 2 is malicious and $1 - $ **a** denote the probability that he is normal.

If Player 2 is actually an attacker, the players' payoffs will be those shown in the table on the left. If he does not attack (i.e. communicate), then he will pay the cost of waiting (w). In that case, Player 1 will have a payoff of w due to a successful communication in case she replies. And in case she defends even though Player 2 did not attack, then she will pay the cost of defending. On the other hand, if Player 2 attacks and Player 1 does not defend (i.e. respond normally to Player 2), then Player 2 will win the value of the resource minus the cost of attacking $(v - c_A)$. Player 1 will lose the value of her resource (v). If he attacks and she defends, then both their profits will depend on the detection rate of the administrator.

If Player 2 is actually a normal node, then the payoffs will be those listed in the table on the right. The difference in this case is that both players will get a payoff of w as a result of a successful communication.

The above game is formally defined as follows:

1. Players
   - Player 1
   - Player 2

2. States {Normal, Malicious}
   - NM
   - NN

3. Actions
   - Player 1 – {R, C, D}
   - Player 2 – {A, C}

4. Signals
   - $P_1 \rightarrow N_1$
     $\tau_1(NM) = \tau_1(NN) = N_1$
   - $P_2 \rightarrow M_2$ or N_2
     $\tau_2(NM) = M_2$
     $\tau_2(NN) = N_2$

5. Beliefs
   - When Player 1 receives N_1
     For NM: $p = a$
     For NN: $p = 1 - a$
   - When Player 2 receives N_2
     For NM: $p = 0$
     For NN: $p = 1$
   - When Player 2 receives M_2
     For NM: $p = 1$
     For NN: $p = 0$

6. Payoffs – The payoffs of Player 1 and Player 2 are given in Figure 1 above.

4.1.2   Two Normal Nodes

A normal node wants to connect to another normal node. In this case, the two players are both normal and they both don't know the state of the other node. This means that for Player 1, Player 2 has 2 possible types (malicious or normal). And for Player 2, Player 1 has 2 possible types as well (malicious or normal). We also model this type of connection as a Bayesian game with 4 possible states in total.

However, this is not a typical Bayesian game with 4 states. If we were to draw the table showing the payoffs for each of the 4 states, we would have to show it for the state {Malicious, Malicious}, which according to our previous assumptions is not valid. This is because all attackers know each other as well as all administrators, and our model is designed to capture the relationship between an attacker and an administrator not between two attackers. So unlike the variant of the BoS game where both players have imperfect information, in this model, we have a constraint stating that the state where both players are malicious is not possible. And therefore, instead of modeling this game as a Bayesian game with 4 possible states, it can be modelled as before but with another similar table for Player 2.

The concept of coalitions can be applied to this scenario. Every normal node in the network has some beliefs about the other nodes based on previous observations and information from neighboring nodes. When Player 1's belief that Player 2 is also a normal node exceeds a certain value Q, Player 1 can assume with some certainty that Player 2 is not malicious. Taking this into consideration, the two players will be better off forming a coalition. If Player 1 has a list of banned nodes L_1, and Player 2 has a list of banned nodes L_2, then by forming a coalition, they will share their lists.

The result is that both players (the larger coalition) will have a larger list of banned nodes and will therefore decrease their chances of being attacked thus increasing their payoff. The larger the coalition of normal nodes, the larger is its banned list and the higher is the payoff of the coalition. This concept of trust between nodes is widely used in the analysis of network security but never before in the form of a game theoretic model. In every network, nodes rate each other and pass on their ratings to their neighbors who in turn pass it on to theirs. The result is that all the nodes in the network are rated, and these rates can be used to deduce the beliefs in our Bayesian game.

4.1.3   Repetitive Model

In our attempt to model the attacks as realistically as possible, we have to design a repetitive model of the game. After all, every second that passes, there are millions of messages being sent and received between nodes. The probability that a communication takes place between two nodes in a network only once is extremely low.

If Player 2's type was malicious during one round and Player 1 managed to detect him, then depending on the type of the attack, Player 1 will decide which strategy to follow the next time.

An attack can be major or minor depending on the value of v. If v is greater than some threshold E, we have a major attack. An example is stolen data. It cannot be undone. If v is less than E, the attack is minor. An example is sending useless traffic.

If the attack was major, Player 1 applies the grim trigger strategy and never forgives Player 2 (Permanent block). If the attack was minor, she applies an exponential punishment. In the exponential punishment, the first time Player 2 makes a "mistake", he is punished the following 10 times he tries to communicate with the administrator. The punishment is in the form of forbidding Player 2 to communicate (ignoring his packets). During these 10 rounds, the administrator keeps track of the behavior of Player 2. If Player 2 attacks another time, regardless if he were in his punishment period or not, he will be punished for 20 times (then 40, 80, 160). After attacking 5 times, the grim trigger strategy is applied and Player 2 is permanently blacklisted.

4.2   DoS/DDoS Attacks

In a DoS/DDoS attack, an attacker tries to flood a victim node (server) by sending it a huge amount of useless traffic. As a result, the server won't be able to reply to other legitimate nodes in the network.

4.2.1   DoS Attack Model

Player 1 is the server and Player 2 is the attacking node. The actions available to Player 1 are to accept the traffic coming from Player 2 (A) or drop them (D). The actions available to Player 2 are to do nothing/wait (W) or flood the server with packets (F).

As before since Player 1's type is known to both players but Player 2's type is not, the game is modeled as a Bayesian game. It follows the same model as that in Section 4.1.1. The difference in this case is that the beliefs are based on traffic flows. When the attacker sends a large amount of useless traffic, the belief that he is actually an attacker will become stronger. However, the loss incurred by the server before reaching this conclusion is huge.

4.2.2   DDoS Attack Model

A more interesting model is that of the DDoS attack. This can be modeled as a multiplayer Bayesian game where the players are the server (Player 1) and the slaves of the attacker (Players 2 to m). In this model, if the attacker uses a large number of slaves to carry out his attack, chances are he won't be detected, but the cost of implementing his attack will be high. On the other hand, if he uses a smaller number of slaves to carry out his attack, then his attack cost will decrease but his detection probability will increase. This game can also be modeled as that in Section 4.1.1 but with slight differences.

Let m denote the number of slaves that the attacker uses to initiate an attack. The cost of attacking changes from c_A to mc_A.

The detection rate changes from γ to $\left(1 - \frac{m}{n}\right)\gamma$ where n is the total number of nodes in the network.

5   Nash Equilibrium

In this section, we will derive the Nash equilibria of the game models from Section 4. Our focus is on the MANET attack game model. We show its Nash equilibria for one instance of the game. Then we derive the constraints on the discount factor δ for several cases in the repetitive game.

5.1   Attacks on MANETs

To deduce the Nash equilibrium of the MANET attack, we will first list the expected payoffs of Player 1 for the two possible pairs of actions of the 2 types of Player 2. The expected payoff of type N_1 of Player 1 when she chooses the action R is:

$$\sum_{s \in \Omega} Pr(s|N_1) u_1 \Big((R, x_2(s)), s \Big)$$

where

s is the current state
Ω is the set of all states
x_i is the action chosen by player i
u_i is the payoff function of player i

A similar equation can be derived for the action D. The payoffs according to the above equations are shown in the table below:

Table 1. Expected payoffs of type N1 of Player 1

	(A, C)	(C, C)
	$w - a(v + w)$	w
	$a\gamma v - c_D$	$-c_D$

To find the Nash equilibria of the game, we will analyze each tuple separately:

- We will claim that (R, (A, C)) is a Nash equilibrium. For Player 1 to choose R, her choice has to be the best response for the two states (A, C) and (C, C) in Table 1.

  For R to be the best response for the pair of actions (A, C), the following constraint must hold:

$$w - a(v + w) > a\gamma v - c_D \Rightarrow a < \frac{w + c_D}{w + (1 + \gamma)v}$$

  The above result makes sense. Since one of our assumptions was that $v \gg c_A, c_D, w$, this means that in order for R to be a best response for Player 1, the belief that Player 2 is Malicious should be very small.

  Given that Player 1 chooses R as her action, we can refer back to Figure 1 to get the best response of Player 2. For type M_2 of Player 2, $v - c_A > -w$, which means that A is his best response. For type N_2 of Player 2, his only choice is C.

  This means that for $a < \frac{w+c_D}{w+(1+\gamma)v}$, (R, (A, C)) is a Nash equilibrium. The attacker will not have an incentive to stop his attack because his payoff will decrease since the administrator is not defending. And the administrator will not have an incentive to defend since his payoff will decrease taking into consideration the very low probability that Player 2 is an attacker.

- (R, (C, C)) is not a Nash equilibrium. If Player 1 chooses R, then type M_2 of Player 2 is better off choosing A over C, so he will have an incentive to change.

- We will claim that (D, (A, C)) is a Nash equilibrium. For D to be the best response for the pair of actions (A, C), the following constraint must hold:

$$w - a(v + w) < a\gamma v - c_D \Rightarrow a > \frac{w + c_D}{w + (1 + \gamma)v}$$

  The above result makes sense. In order for D to be a best response for Player 1, the belief that Player 2 is Malicious should be high.

  Given that Player 1 chooses D as her action, we can refer back to Figure 1 to get the best response of Player 2. For type M_2 of Player 2, for A to be his best response, the following constraint should hold:

$$(1 - \gamma)v - c_A > -w \Rightarrow \gamma < \frac{v + w - c_A}{v}$$

The above means that given Player 1 will defend, Player 2 is better off attacking if the detection rate of Player 1 is low. Given the following constraint on γ, (D, (A, C)) is a Nash equilibrium. For a high detection rate, it no longer is.

- (D, (C, C)) is not a Nash equilibrium since $w > -c_D$ which means that D is not a best response for the pair of actions (C, C).

5.2 Repetitive Bayesian Attack

There are two states for Player 2 but Player 1 cannot observe them directly. They are hidden from her. A good approach to model the beliefs of Player 1 in our repetitive Bayesian game is by using a state diagram.

At first, before any communication between Player 1 and Player 2, Player 1 does not have any beliefs about the type of Player 2. So she assigns a probability of 0.5 that Player 2 is Malicious and a probability of 0.5 that Player 2 is Normal. Recall that **a** is the probability that a player is malicious.

The transitions are illustrated in the state diagram below. We begin at the Start state with an $\mathbf{a}(0) = 0.5$. If Player 2 communicates in the first round, we move to the second state (N) where the probability is initiated another time and given the value 0.1 (low probability that Player 2 is malicious).

On the other hand, if Player 2 attacks either in the first round, or attacks for the first time after any round, we will move to the third state (M) where the probability is initiated for the last time and given the value 0.9. After Player 2 becomes either in state N or state M, the transitions between the two states are shown below. If he had a malicious type and in one round communicates normally, he is rewarded by decreasing the value of **a** very slightly. However, if he had a normal type and in one round attacks, he is severely punished by increasing the value of **a** significantly.

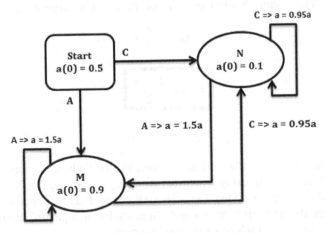

Fig. 2. State diagram for Player 1 beliefs

The above diagram models the change in the beliefs of Player 1 in the case of a repetitive game. These beliefs can be used as a measure to blacklist Player 2 and can later on be shared with other normal nodes in order to make the network more secure for all the nodes. As for the different strategies that we proposed in Section 4.1.2, those represent the punishment that Player 1 can inflict onto Player 2 in case the latter attacks in any of the rounds. What we want to find is the Nash equilibrium of this game model while taking into consideration the repetitive aspect of it.

Assuming that Player 1 implements the grim trigger strategy, we continue with the following analysis of our repetitive game.

Starting with $\mathbf{a}(0) = 0.5$, Player 1 will choose D in the first round regardless of the type of Player 2 since D gives her a higher payoff.

If the detection rate, γ, of Player 1 is high, then Player 2's best response is to communicate. Since Player 2 is actually an attacker and he agreed to communicate instead of attacking, his payoff will be $-w$. In the second round, Player 1 will change his beliefs regarding Player 2, and update the probabilities, so now we have $\mathbf{a}(0) = 0.1$. In round 2, Player 1's best response will be to respond to Player 2, taking into consideration that the small value of $\mathbf{a}$ means that there's a low probability that Player 2 is malicious. In this round however, Player 2 decides to attack and makes a payoff of $v - c_A$. In the rest of the rounds, Player 2 is punished regardless of his actions. We will assume that his profit in the rest of the rounds is $-w$. Had Player 2 decided to communicate in the second round and the following ones as well, his payoff would have remained the same ($-w$). In the first case, disregarding the states before the attack, Player 2's stream of payoffs is $(-v - c_A, -w, -w, -w, -w \ldots)$ whose discounted average is:

$$[v - c_A + w - w\delta - w\delta^2 - w\delta^3 \ldots] = \left[v - c_A + w - \frac{w}{1-\delta}\right]$$

In the second case, his stream of payoffs is $(-w, -w, -w, \ldots)$ whose discounted average is $-w$. This means that Player 2 cannot increase his output by attacking if:

$$v - c_A + w - \frac{w}{1-\delta} \leq -w$$

$$\boxed{\Rightarrow \delta \geq \frac{Z - w}{Z}}$$

Where

$$Z = 2w + v + c_A$$

If the detection rate, γ, of Player 1 is low, then Player 2's best response is to attack, even though Player 1 is choosing D at first. By doing so, Player 2 achieves a payoff of $(1 - \gamma)v - c_A$. After observing the action taken by Player 2 in the first round, Player 1 applies the grim trigger strategy. This results in a payoff stream of $((1 - \gamma)v - c_A, -w, -w, -w \ldots)$ whose discounted average is:

$$[(1 - \gamma)v - c_A - w\delta - w\delta^2 - w\delta^3 \ldots]$$

$$= \left[(1 - \gamma)v - c_A + w - \frac{w}{1-\delta}\right]$$

Player 2 cannot increase his output by attacking if:

$$(1 - \gamma)v - c_A + w - \frac{w}{1 - \delta} \leq -w$$

$$\boxed{\Rightarrow \delta \geq \frac{V - w}{V}}$$

Where

$$V = 2w + (1 - \gamma)v + c_A$$

6   Simulations and Analysis

In order to test if our game model will eventually reach equilibrium, we had to run several simulations. We modeled our Bayesian repetitive game by first creating a network of nodes on MATLAB, 10% of which are always malicious nodes.

6.1   Simulation Parameters

The simulation parameters that we chose were:

$$w = 20$$
$$c_A = 50$$
$$c_D = 40$$
$$v = 200$$

We randomized the detection rate of the normal nodes. In every run of the program, about 30% of the nodes have a low detection rate (0.6) whereas 70% of the nodes have a high detection rate (0.9).

We assumed a worst case scenario where every malicious node in the network does not attack in the first round meaning that the value of a for all the nodes in the second round will be 0.1.

A node that has been blacklisted by at least 20 nodes will be added to the banned list. In every round, the number of nodes that are not members of the banned list will be paired up randomly. The cases that were studied per round are:

- Normal Node vs. Normal Node
- Normal Node (small γ) vs. Malicious Node
- Normal Node (high γ) vs. Malicious Node

When 2 normal nodes communicate, they both increase their profit. However, when a normal node and a malicious node are paired up, the profits from Figure 1 are used depending on whether the normal node defends or responds and whether the malicious node attacks or communicates. The malicious node bases his decision on the detection rate of the normal node. A malicious node will likely attack a normal node with a low detection rate but refrain from attacking a normal node with a high detection rate. As for the normal node, it bases its decision on the value of a of the opposite node. If the value of a that the opposite node has is lower than $\frac{w + c_D}{w + (1 + \gamma)v}$, the normal node responds, otherwise, it defends.

Any node that communicates successfully for at least 7 rounds becomes part of a coalition that we defined. Since at first, a normal node's action will always be to defend (given that $a(0) = 0.5$), then the malicious node's best action would be to wait then attack in the next round for maximum profit. The profit of the malicious node will be 130 ($v - c_a - w$). If, on the other hand, he decides never to attack in order to improve his reputation and gain access to a coalition, then his loss in every round will be 20. Our assumption is that the loss that he accumulates throughout the rounds should not exceed 130 and hence, the maximum number of consecutive rounds that he can wait should not exceed 6 ($\lfloor 130/20 \rfloor$).

Equilibrium is reached once the coalition contains all the normal nodes and all the malicious nodes have been added to the banned list.

Our program calculates the average profit of every node type in every round of each run, as well as the average profit at the end of every simulation. The results from several simulations are shown next.

6.2   Simulation Results

The 2 figures shown below represent the plots of the average profit of the normal nodes and malicious nodes. The x-axis represents the round number, and the y-axis represents the average profit values over all the nodes under consideration.

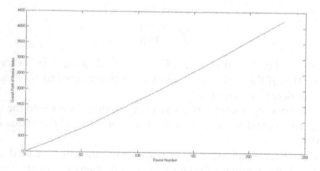

Fig. 3. Average profit of normal nodes per round

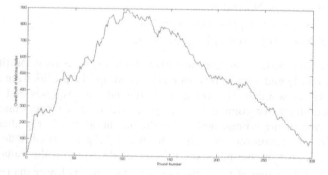

Fig. 4. Average profit of malicious nodes per round

In addition to the change in average profit values across rounds, we calculated the average profit value per normal node and the average profit value per malicious node per simulations. We ran 10 different simulations, the results of which are shown in the table below. NR refers to the number of rounds that took place until all malicious nodes were blacklisted, NN refers to normal node and MN refers to malicious node.

Table 2. Profit per node over 10 simulations

Simulation	NR	Profit per NN	Profit per MN
1	231	4206	1007
2	156	2625	1785
3	268	4971	858
4	215	3865	898
5	249	4566	777
6	297	5580	96
7	423	8251	-939
8	267	4932	765
9	268	4974	951
10	465	9099	-1827
Average	284	5307	437

6.3   Analysis

From Figure 3 above, it is clear that the average profit of a normal node is linearly increasing as the number of rounds increases. It reaches a value of 4500. This means that even though before banning all the malicious nodes, some normal nodes suffer losses, the overall result is satisfying. In fact, in all the simulations that we ran, the increase was always linear.

Figure 4 on the other hand shows an increase in the average profit of a malicious node up to a certain peak (about 900) followed by a steep decrease. This result is again reassuring since it tells us that not only is the highest profit value of the malicious nodes significantly lower than that of the normal nodes, but after some point, the malicious nodes in the network suffer huge losses that eventually lower their average profit value.

In all the simulations that we performed, we always reached an equilibrium state after a certain number of rounds. As shown in Table 2, the average number of rounds over the 10 simulations was only 284, after which all malicious nodes were banned. Also shown in the table are the average profits per normal node and malicious node at the end of each of the 10 simulations. The average profit of the normal nodes was always significantly higher. What is more interesting is that in simulations 7 and 10, the average profit of the malicious nodes was negative meaning that in most rounds, malicious nodes were suffering losses more than profits. We do not see such results in the case of the normal nodes. The change in the average profit of the malicious nodes in simulation 7 is shown in Figure 5.

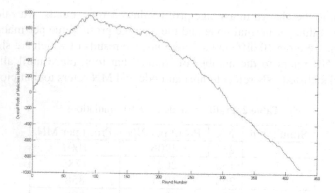

Fig. 5. Average profit of malicious nodes suffering huge loss

7   Conclusions and Future Work

In this paper we modeled a network security attack as a Bayesian repetitive game with imperfect information. We presented several punishment strategies and discussed the concept of coalitions within a network. Our results illustrate the importance of applying a game theoretic model when communicating with nodes in a network. Our game model always reached an equilibrium state where the coalition contains all the normal nodes and a banned list contains all the malicious nodes. In addition, the average profit per normal nodes throughout the rounds was found to be always linearly increasing, whereas the average profit per malicious nodes always reached its peak before dropping again. When considering the average profit of normal and malicious nodes across 10 different simulations, the normal nodes scored 5307 compared to 437 for the malicious nodes. Also, the average profit of the malicious nodes was negative when the number of rounds exceeded 400. In general, the larger the number of rounds needed to converge, the lower the profit of malicious nodes and the higher the profit of normal nodes. The significance of this result is that in case the convergence takes time, we know for a fact that this will result in lower profits for the malicious nodes up to the point where these profits become losses. The worst case in the above simulations is when the convergence required only 156 rounds. In that case, the average profit of the malicious nodes was about 68% that of the normal nodes. However, even in this worst case, the normal nodes still score significantly higher. If we define the worst case scenario as any simulation that requires less than 200 rounds to converge and then consider the above 10 simulations, this means that the worst case took place only once out of 10 times. Generalizing this result to saying that on average 10% of the time we get a worst case scenario, and keeping in mind that even in the worst case scenario, normal nodes are still scoring more than malicious nodes; we can safely assume that our design will always be beneficial. We should also keep in mind that our "worst case" scenario is the one in which banning all the malicious nodes requires the least amount of time.

Some of the ideas that we presented in this paper were not fully developed such as the Sybil attack which can be modeled using an evolutionary game theoretic approach and the DoS/DDoS attacks. As part of our future work, we will elaborate more on these two attacks as well as other types of attacks. We will also solve for the constraints on the discount factor in the case of the exponential punishment strategy and compare our results with those of the grim trigger strategy.

Acknowledgment. This work was funded by the University Research Board at the American University of Beirut.

References

[1] IBM. An information resource for data breach prevention and response. ibm.com, http://www-935.ibm.com/services/us/en/it-services/data-breach/data-breach-statistics.html (accessed: November 13, 2013)

[2] ZDNet. Android app malware rates jump 40 percent, zdnet.com, http://www.zdnet.com/android-app-malware-rates-jump-40-percent-7000019093/ (accessed: November 13, 2013)

[3] readwrite. Google Play Hits One Million Android Apps, readwrite.com, http://readwrite.com/2013/07/24/google-play-hits-one-million-android-apps#awesm=~onaP99fjV8C2eD (accessed: November 12, 2013)

[4] Karaa, H., Lau, J.Y.: Game Theory Applications in Network Reliability. In: Proc. Communications, 23rd Biennial Symposium, pp. 236–239 (2006)

[5] Ileri, O., Mauand, S.-C., Mandayam, N.B.: Pricing for enabling forwarding in self-configuring ad hoc networks. IEEE Journal on Selected Areas in Communications 23(1), 151–162 (2005)

[6] Bandyopadhyay, S., Bandyopadhyay, S.: A game-theoretic analysis on the conditions of cooperation in a wireless ad hoc network. In: Third International Symposium on Modeling and Optimization in Mobile, Ad Hoc, and Wireless Networks, pp. 54–58 (2005)

[7] Carin, L., Cybenko, G., Hughes, J.: Quantitative evaluation of risk for investment efficient strategies in cybersecurity: The queries methodology. IEEE Computer (2008)

[8] Liu, Y., Comaniciu, C., Man, H.: A Bayesian game approach for intrusion detection in wireless ad hoc networks. In: ACM International Conference Proceeding Series, vol. 199 (2006)

[9] Lye, K., Wing, J.: Game strategies in network security. In: Proceedings of the Foundations of Computer Security (2002)

[10] Nguyen, K.C., Alpcan, T., Basar, T.: Stochastic games for security in networks with interdependent nodes. In: Proc. of Intl. Conf. on Game Theory for Networks (GameNets) (2009)

[11] Xiaolin, C., Xiaobin, T., Yong, Z., Hongsheng, X.: A Markov game theory-based risk assessment model for network information systems. In: International Conference on Computer Science and Software Engineering (2008)

[12] Alpcan, T., Baser, T.: An intrusion detection game with limited observations. In: Proc. of the 12th Int. Symp. on Dynamic Games and Applications (2006)

[13] Nguyen, K.C., Alpcan, T., Basar, T.: Security games with incomplete information. In: Proc. of IEEE Intl. Conf. on Communications (ICC) (2009)

[14] Patcha, A., Park, J.: A game theoretic approach to modeling intrusion detection in mobile ad hoc networks. In: Proceedings of the 2004 IEEE Workshop on Information Assurance and Security (2004)

[15] You, X., Shiyong, Z.: A kind of network security behavior model based on game theory. In: Proceedings of the Fourth International Conference on Parallel and Distributed Computing, Applications and Technologies (2003)

The Use of Fuzzy Relations in the Assessment of Information Resources Producers' Performance

Marek Gagolewski[1,2] and Jan Lasek[3]

[1] Systems Research Institute, Polish Academy of Sciences,
ul. Newelska 6, 01-447 Warsaw, Poland
`gagolews@ibspan.waw.pl`
[2] Faculty of Mathematics and Information Science, Warsaw University of Technology,
ul. Koszykowa 75, 00-662 Warsaw, Poland
[3] Interdisciplinary PhD Studies Program,
Systems Research Institute, Polish Academy of Sciences
`j.lasek@phd.ipipan.waw.pl`

Abstract. The producers assessment problem has many important practical instances: it is an abstract model for intelligent systems evaluating e.g. the quality of computer software repositories, web resources, social networking services, and digital libraries. Each producer's performance is determined according not only to the overall quality of the items he/she outputted, but also to the number of such items (which may be different for each agent).

Recent theoretical results indicate that the use of aggregation operators in the process of ranking and evaluation producers may not necessarily lead to fair and plausible outcomes. Therefore, to overcome some weaknesses of the most often applied approach, in this preliminary study we encourage the use of a fuzzy preference relation-based setting and indicate why it may provide better control over the assessment process.

Keywords: Fuzzy relations, preference modeling, producers assessment problem, StackOverflow, bibliometrics, h-index.

1 Introduction

It is evident that the intensive development of information storage centers causes that their users are likely to suffer from the so-called information overload. As a consequence, there is an urgent need to develop methods for automated quality management of information units as well as their producers. Such a task is of interest in a field of research that deals with measurable aspects of information science, called informetrics.

Let $P = \{p_1, \ldots, p_k\}$ be a finite set consisting of k producers. The i-th producer outputs n_i products. Additionally, each product is given some kind of quantitative rating, e.g. concerning its overall quality. Consequently, the state of p_i may be described by a sequence $\mathbf{x}^{(i)} = \left(x_1^{(i)}, \ldots, x_{n_i}^{(i)} \right) \in \mathbb{I}^{1,2,\ldots} = \bigcup_{n \geqslant 1} \mathbb{I}^n$ with elements in $\mathbb{I}$, e.g. $\mathbb{I} = [0, \infty)$. Most importantly, we should note that the numbers of products may vary from producer to producer. The main aim of the

© Springer International Publishing Switzerland 2015
D. Filev et al. (eds.), *Intelligent Systems'2014*,
Advances in Intelligent Systems and Computing 323, DOI: 10.1007/978-3-319-11310-4_25

Producers Assessment Problem (PAP, cf. [4]) is to construct methods for quantitative (numerical) assessment of producers, their ranking, or automatic selection of the most interesting (with respect to some aspects) ones. These computational tools must necessarily meet only some moderate assumptions: they shall somehow take into account a producer's ability to output highly-valuated products, and his/her overall productivity.

Among the most widely-used assessment methods one may find the family of mathematical functions motivated by the introduction of the famous Hirsch h-index [12] or other so-called informetric indices of impact, cf. [1]. Even though they may be used in many important practical problems, it is worth noting that their usage and recognition is, quite unfortunately, often reduced only to the domain of bibliometrics, see [7,13] for some of a few notable exceptions to this rule. Such tools are called aggregation operators and in our setting they are just functions that map the space of vectors of arbitrary length into a single number. Notably, the aggregation theory has a quite long history and its foundations are well-established. For example, due to a strong connection between aggregation operators and monotone measures and integrals, Hirsch-like indices were already studied by Sugeno in [18]. For example, it is known that indices of the form $\mathsf{H}(\mathbf{x}) = \max\{i : \mathsf{w}(x_{(n-i+1)}) \geqslant i\}$, where $x_{(i)}$ is the ith smallest order statistic and $\mathsf{w} : \mathbb{I} \to \mathbb{I}$ is a non-decreasing function, are universal integrals [10,14].

However, it becomes more and more evident that aggregation operators may not provide a proper way to assess information resources producers in PAP. First of all, intuitively, such functions are used to describe particular *aspects* of given numeric vectors, like central tendency, dispersion, or shape of the empirical distribution of data. Although in some cases one easily sees what does an aggregation operator *measure*, e.g. the sample mean describes some central tendency of data or the sample variance reflects its dispersion, it is difficult to tell what in fact do we measure with the h-index.

Moreover, recent results presented in [9] and briefly summarized in Sec. 2 indicate that aggregation operators give us too small control over cases in which we state that a sequence in $\mathbb{I}^{1,2,\cdots}$ is "better" than some other ones. Such an induced order often does not suit our intuition or needs well, c.f. also [3].

Therefore, in Sec. 3 we propose a pairwise comparison-based approach for PAP. As in some cases a decision maker's preferences cannot be expressed precisely, we will study the properties of an exemplary fuzzy preference relation. Then, in Sec. 4 we discuss simple methods to extract useful knowledge from the relation graph, e.g. to obtain a ranking of producers. Importantly, together with the results we are able to obtain some numeric measures of their quality (understood as the degree of conformance of the resulting ranking to the input relation). The discourse is illustrated with a case study consisting of the most active users of StackOverflow. Finally, we conclude the paper in Sec. 5.

2   Crisp Dominance Relation for Sets of Producers

Let us consider the following binary relation $\trianglelefteq \subseteq \mathbb{I}^{1,2,\cdots} \times \mathbb{I}^{1,2,\cdots}$, cf. [9]. For any $\mathbf{x} \in \mathbb{I}^n$ and $\mathbf{y} \in \mathbb{I}^m$ we write $\mathbf{x} \trianglelefteq \mathbf{y}$ (or, equivalently, $(\mathbf{x}, \mathbf{y}) \in \trianglelefteq$) if and only if

$n \leqslant m$ and $x_{(n-i+1)} \leqslant y_{(m-i+1)}$ for $i = 1, \ldots, n$. In other words, we say that a producer X is (weakly) dominated by a producer Y, if X has yielded no more products than Y and each of the i-th most highly valuated product by X is of no better quality than the i-th most highly valuated item by Y. We assume that the order of entries of vectors from $\mathbb{I}^{1,2,\cdots}$ is irrelevant by considering order statistics. Of course, $\trianglelefteq$ is a preorder, i.e. it is reflexive and transitive.

What is most important, we have the following result, tightly linking the post-Hirsch "indices of scientific impact" (impact functions) – which take into account the producer's productivity and quality of its products, see e.g. [17,20] – with the above-introduced preorder.

Theorem 1. *Let* $\mathsf{F} : \mathbb{I}^{1,2,\cdots} \to \mathbb{I}$ *be an aggregation operator. Then* F *is symmetric (independent of the order of products in a sequence, i.e.* $(\forall \mathbf{x} \in \mathbb{I}^{1,2,\cdots})$ $\mathsf{F}(\mathbf{x}) = \mathsf{F}(x_{(n)}, \ldots, x_{(1)}))$, *nondecreasing with respect to each variable (improvement of a product's quality does not result in a decrease in a producer's valuation, i.e.* $(\forall n)$ $(\forall \mathbf{x}, \mathbf{y} \in \mathbb{I}^n)$ $(\forall i)$ $x_i \leqslant y_i \implies \mathsf{F}(\mathbf{x}) \leqslant \mathsf{F}(\mathbf{y}))$ *and arity-monotonic (additional elements do not result in a decrease in a producer's valuation, i.e.* $(\forall \mathbf{x} \in \mathbb{I}^{1,2,\cdots})$ $(\forall y \in \mathbb{I})$ $\mathsf{F}(\mathbf{x}) \leqslant \mathsf{F}(\mathbf{x}, y))$ *if and only if for any* $\mathbf{x}, \mathbf{y} \in \mathbb{I}^{1,2,\cdots}$ *if* $\mathbf{x} \trianglelefteq \mathbf{y}$, *then* $\mathsf{F}(\mathbf{x}) \leqslant \mathsf{F}(\mathbf{y})$.

It should be noted that $\trianglelefteq$ represents the information on pairs of vectors which comparison may be performed in such a way that we obtain rationally plausible results. However, it is easily seen that $\trianglelefteq$ is not necessarily total (or complete), i.e. there exist $\mathbf{x}, \mathbf{y} \in \mathbb{I}^{1,2,\cdots}$ such that $\mathbf{x} \ntrianglelefteq \mathbf{y}$ and $\mathbf{y} \ntrianglelefteq \mathbf{x}$. Thus, the linear order $\trianglelefteq''_{\mathsf{F}}$ induced by any impact function F, $\trianglelefteq \subseteq \trianglelefteq''_{\mathsf{F}}$, possibly resolves the comparison problems in a way that is beyond our control. For example, it is known that a *fair* impact function must necessarily be trivial, cf. [9, Theorem 3]: if we would like to obtain $\neg(\mathbf{x} \trianglelefteq \mathbf{y}$ or $\mathbf{y} \trianglelefteq \mathbf{x}) \implies \mathsf{F}(\mathbf{x}) = \mathsf{F}(\mathbf{y})$, we surely get $\mathsf{F}(\mathbf{x}) = c$ for some c and all $\mathbf{x}$. On the other hand, for a set of incomparable (with $\trianglelefteq$) vectors $\{\mathbf{x}^1, \ldots, \mathbf{x}^k\}$, we may always construct an impact function such that $\mathsf{F}(\mathbf{x}^{\sigma(1)}) < \cdots < \mathsf{F}(\mathbf{x}^{\sigma(k)})$, given any permutation σ of the set $\{1, \ldots, k\}$, see [9, Theorem 4]. We see that the minimal requirements for F are too mild. This is partially because the "sure knowledge" represented in $\trianglelefteq$ does not include "almost sure knowledge" for example concerning the comparison results of e.g. $(11, 11)$ vs $(100, 10, 10, 1)$.

Thus, we would like to turn our attention to the extension of the "crisp", $\trianglelefteq$-based, approach to fuzzy preferences. With these means we hope to handle uncertainty and pairwise comparisons in a more subtle way than by the "black and white" crisp setting.

3   From Crisp to Fuzzy Preference Relations

3.1   Fuzzy Relations

First we shall recall some notions from fuzzy preference modeling theory, see e.g. [6]. The following definition gives a generalization of a crisp binary relation to a relation in the fuzzy sense. We assume that we are given a set of alternatives A, whose elements are to be compared with one another.

Definition 1. *A fuzzy relation on the set A is a pair (R, μ), where μ is the membership function of R, $\mu : A \times A \to [0,1]$, measuring the degree to which R holds.*

For brevity we further on write "a relation R" instead of (R, μ) as it should be clear from the context what its membership function is.

With such a tool we may model the concept of partial dominance. It allows us to say that one producer's output is only slightly or indisputably more advantageous than another producer's output by saying that the dominance relation holds between their outputs with a certain degree $\in [0,1]$ (the membership function in case of a crisp relation is a binary-valued function in $\{0,1\}$ which means that the relation either holds or does not hold at all).

We say that a relation R is (fuzzy) reflexive if $\mu(a, a) = 1$ for all $a \in A$. We say that a relation R is (fuzzy) total if $\mu(a, b) + \mu(b, a) \geqslant 1$. Note that these definitions naturally extend their crisp counterparts when we consider a crisp relation as a function into $\{0,1\}$. Additionally, if $\mu(a, b) + \mu(b, a) = 1$, then we say that R is additive reciprocal (or probabilistic).

We are primarily interested in fuzzy preference relations. Thus, we shall recall the notion of (fuzzy) transitivity. There are several definitions of this concept unified with the use of t-norms.

Definition 2. *A t-norm is a function $T : [0,1] \times [0,1] \to [0,1]$ that for any $x, y, z \in [0,1]$ satisfies the following conditions: (a) $T(1, x) = x$ for all $x \in [0,1]$, (b) T is symmetric, i.e., $T(x, y) = T(y, x)$, (c) T is non-decreasing, i.e., $T(x, y) \leqslant T(z, y)$ whenever $x \leqslant z$, (d) T is associative, i.e. $T(x, T(y, z)) = T(T(x, y), z)$.*

An example of a t-norm is $T_L(x, y) = \max\{x + y - 1, 0\}$, which is called the Łukasiewicz t-norm. As it is the smallest 1-Lipshitz t-norm, we will adopt it in our considerations for proving transitivity of an appropriate relation.

We are ready to define the composition of fuzzy relations R_1, R_2.

Definition 3. *The t-composition of fuzzy relations (R_1, μ_1) and (R_2, μ_2) w.r.t. a t-norm T is a relation R_3 with the membership function μ_3 given by*

$$\mu_3(a, b) = \sup_{c \in A} T(\mu_1(a, c), \mu_2(c, b)).$$

Again, this definition naturally extends the composition of binary-valued relations. In a crisp situation, a relation R is transitive iff $R^2 = R \circ R \subseteq R$. This motivates the following definition in case of a fuzzy relation: a fuzzy relation (R, μ) is (fuzzy) T-transitive if

$$\mu(a, b) \geqslant \sup_{c \in A} T(\mu(a, c), \mu(c, b)),$$

T is a given t-norm. If $T = T_L$, then we call this property the max-Δ-transitivity, see [16].

Clearly, the transitivity property of fuzzy relations depends on the choice of the corresponding t-norm, see e.g. [5,6,11] for discussion. The given definition will serve us in the construction of a fuzzy preference relation that extends the dominance relation $\trianglelefteq$ in the next subsection.

3.2 An Exemplary Class of Fuzzy Dominance Relation

Let us consider the space $\mathcal{S}$ of infinite nonincreasing sequences with elements in $\mathbb{I}$. Let $\tilde{\cdot} : \mathbb{I}^{1,2,\cdots} \to \mathcal{S}$ be an operator such that for $\mathbf{x} \in \mathbb{I}^n$ we have $\tilde{\mathbf{x}} = (x_{(n)}, x_{(n-1)}, \ldots, x_{(1)}, 0, 0, \ldots)$. It is a quite natural way to embed $\mathbb{I}^{1,2,\cdots}$ into the space of vectors of infinite lengths $\mathbb{I}^\infty$, cf. [10].

Let us propose one (as this is a preliminary study) of the possible approaches to the construction of fuzzy preorders that are in some way concordant with $\trianglelefteq$.

Definition 4. *Let* $\mathbf{x}, \mathbf{y} \in \mathcal{S}$*, and* $\mathbf{w} = (w_1, w_2, \ldots)$*,* $w_i > 0$ *for all* i*. The **fuzzy producers dominance relation** is a fuzzy preference relation* ◄ *with the membership function given by:*

$$\mu(\mathbf{x}, \mathbf{y}) = \begin{cases} \frac{\pi_{yx}}{\pi_{xy} + \pi_{yx}} & \text{if } \pi_{xy} + \pi_{yx} > 0, \\ 0.5 & \text{otherwise}, \end{cases}$$

where $\pi_{xy} = \sum_i w_i \cdot \max\{x_i - y_i, 0\}$*.*

Note that the $\mathbf{w}$ vector has a nice interpretation here: it may be used to put bigger weights to the producer's productivity or to make products of high quality more significant, cf. [10] for discussion and more formal treatment in a monotone measure setting. Fig. 1 shows the interpretation of π_{xy} and π_{yx} for $\mathbf{x} = (10, 9, 8, 4, 2, 1, 1)$, $\mathbf{y} = (7, 7, 6, 5, 4, 4, 3, 2, 1, 1)$, and $\mathbf{w} = (1, 1, \ldots)$. Here we have $\pi_{xy} = 7$, $\pi_{yx} = 13$, and $\mu(\mathbf{x}, \mathbf{y}) = 0.65$.

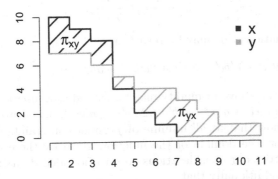

Fig. 1. Illustration of Def. 4; $\mathbf{x} = (10, 9, 8, 4, 2, 1, 1)$, $\mathbf{y} = (7, 7, 6, 5, 4, 4, 3, 2, 1, 1)$.

Given such a definition of the preference relation we would like to study its properties. First of all, it is easily seen that this relation is additive reciprocal.

We view it as a generalization of the crisp approach and we interpret values of its membership function close to 0.5 as indifference between objects. Whenever we have that $\mathbf{x} \neq \mathbf{y}$ and $\mathbf{x} \trianglelefteq \mathbf{y}$ then $\mu(\mathbf{x}, \mathbf{y}) = 1$ as in the crisp case. More generally, if $\mathbf{x} \trianglelefteq \mathbf{y}$, then $\mathbf{I}(\mu(\mathbf{x}, \mathbf{y}) \geqslant 0.5) = 1$ (0.5 α-cut of $\blacktriangleleft$ is a superset of $\trianglelefteq$). In the Proposition to follow we will show that this relation is also transitive when Łukasiewicz t-norm is considered. Based on these properties, the relation is a fuzzy preference relation in the sense of [19].

Proposition 1. *The fuzzy producers dominance relation $\blacktriangleleft$ is max-Δ-transitive, i.e. for all $\mathbf{x}, \mathbf{y}, \mathbf{z} \in \mathcal{S}$ we have*

$$\mu(\mathbf{x}, \mathbf{z}) \geqslant \max\{\mu(\mathbf{x}, \mathbf{y}) + \mu(\mathbf{y}, \mathbf{z}) - 1, 0\}. \tag{1}$$

Proof. First of all, if any two elements of the set $\{x, y, z\}$ are equal, then the proposition obviously holds. Thus, from now on we assume that all the considered vectors are distinct.

For the sake of simplicity, let us introduce the following notation. Let $a := \pi_{yx}$, $b := \pi_{zy}$, $c := \pi_{xz}$, $a' := \pi_{xy}$, $b' := \pi_{yz}$, $c' := \pi_{zx}$. For instance, we have: $c' = \pi_{zx} = \sum_i w_i \cdot \max\{z_i - x_i, 0\}$, $a = \pi_{yx} = \sum_i w_i \cdot \max\{y_i - x_i, 0\}$, $b = \pi_{zy} = \sum_i w_i \cdot \max\{z_i - y_i, 0\}$. As for any $p, q, r \in \mathbb{R}$ the triangle inequality $\max\{p - r, 0\} \leqslant \max\{p - q, 0\} + \max\{q - r, 0\}$ holds, thus we have $0 \leqslant c' \leqslant a + b$. In an analogous way we derive 5 more inequalities and arrive at a set of 6 constraints:

$$0 \leqslant a \leqslant b' + c' \tag{2}$$
$$0 \leqslant a' \leqslant b + c \tag{3}$$
$$0 \leqslant b \leqslant a' + c' \tag{4}$$
$$0 \leqslant b' \leqslant a + c \tag{5}$$
$$0 \leqslant c \leqslant a' + b' \tag{6}$$
$$0 \leqslant c' \leqslant a + b \tag{7}$$

In terms of the introduced notation, ineq. (1) becomes equivalent to (note we can omit the max operator):

$$\frac{c'}{c + c'} + 1 \geqslant \frac{a}{a + a'} + \frac{b}{b + b'}. \tag{8}$$

After some transformations this may be rewritten as:

$$ab'c' + a'bc' + a'b'c + 2a'b'c' - abc \geqslant 0. \tag{9}$$

The left-hand side of the above inequality may be viewed as a function $f : \mathbb{R}^6 \to \mathbb{R}$, $f(a, a', b, b', c, c') = ab'c' + a'bc' + a'b'c + 2a'b'c' - abc$. Now, to prove that (1) holds, it suffices to show that at all minima of f under constraints (2)–(7) are non-negative. However, the domain of the function given by these constraints is unbounded. To restrict our considerations only to bounded domains we note that we may assume additionally that

$$a + a' + b + b' + c + c' = 1. \tag{10}$$

This is because if $f(\mathbf{h}) < 0$ for some $\mathbf{h} = (a, a', b, b', c, c')$ then we also have $f(\lambda \mathbf{h}) = \lambda^3 f(\mathbf{h}) < 0$ for any $\lambda > 0$ (that is to say the function f is negative in direction $\mathbf{h}$). Scaling with an appropriate factor λ we see that we may assume that (10) holds. Now the subset of $\mathbb{R}^6$ defined by constraints (2)–(7) and (10) is bounded and closed hence a compact set. If f attains non-negative values on this set we will conclude that f is non-negative on its whole domain.

We proceed to show that the function on the above defined set is non-negative. First of all, note that if any of a, b, c equals to 0, then (9), and in consequence (8), obviously holds. Moreover, if $a' = 0$, then (9) becomes

$$ab'c' - abc \geqslant 0,$$

and such an inequality holds, as $c' \geqslant b$ and $b' \geqslant c$ from (4) and (6). For $b' = 0$ and $c' = 0$ we may obtain similar conclusions.

To prove ineq. (9) we will apply the well-known Karush-Kuhn-Tucker (KKT) theorem, see [15]. Basing on the previous considerations, with no loss in generality we may assume that all a, a', b, b', c, c' are positive. In such a situation the constraints of the form $a \geqslant 0, a' \geqslant 0$, etc. are inactive, therefore their corresponding Lagrange multipliers are equal to 0. From now on we should focus only on the constraints given by the second inequalities in (2)–(7) and the constraint (10).

Let us rewrite (2)–(7) in terms of KKT constraint functions; (2) becomes:

$$g_1(a, a', b, b', c, c') = b' + c' - a \geqslant 0,$$

and five other constraints are rewritten analogously as $g_2, \ldots, g_6$. We also have an additional constraint of the form

$$g_7(a, a', b, b', c, c') = a + a' + b + b' + c + c' - 1 = 0.$$

By the KKT theorem, if (a, a', b, b', c, c') is a local minimum of f, then there exist constants $\lambda_i \geqslant 0$, $i = 1, 2, \ldots, 6$, for which:

$$\nabla f^T(a, a', b, b', c, c') = \begin{pmatrix} b'c' - bc \\ bc' + b'c + 2b'c' \\ a'c' - ac \\ ac' + a'c + 2a'c' \\ a'b' - ab \\ ab' + a'b + 2a'b' \end{pmatrix} = \begin{pmatrix} -\lambda_1 + \lambda_4 + \lambda_6 + \lambda_7 \\ -\lambda_2 + \lambda_3 + \lambda_5 + \lambda_7 \\ -\lambda_3 + \lambda_2 + \lambda_6 + \lambda_7 \\ -\lambda_4 + \lambda_1 + \lambda_5 + \lambda_7 \\ -\lambda_5 + \lambda_2 + \lambda_4 + \lambda_7 \\ -\lambda_6 + \lambda_1 + \lambda_3 + \lambda_7 \end{pmatrix} \tag{11}$$

with

$$\lambda_i \, g_i(a, a', b, b', c, c') = 0, \quad i = 1, 2, \ldots, 7. \tag{12}$$

Let us note that from (11) regardless of which constraints are active it holds:

$$\begin{cases} \frac{\partial f}{\partial a} + \frac{\partial f}{\partial b'} = \frac{\partial f}{\partial a'} + \frac{\partial f}{\partial b} \\ \frac{\partial f}{\partial a} + \frac{\partial f}{\partial c'} = \frac{\partial f}{\partial a'} + \frac{\partial f}{\partial c} \\ \frac{\partial f}{\partial b} + \frac{\partial f}{\partial c'} = \frac{\partial f}{\partial b'} + \frac{\partial f}{\partial c}, \end{cases}$$

which yields that

$$(c + c')(a + a' - b - b') = (b + b')(c + c' - a - a') = (a + a')(b + b' - c - c') = 0.$$

Therefore, in combination with (10) it follows that at a minimum we necessarily
have:

$$a + a' = b + b' = c + c' = \frac{1}{3},\tag{13}$$

since we assumed that all the variables are positive. Substituting $a := \frac{1}{3} - a'$,
$b := \frac{1}{3} - b'$ and $c := \frac{1}{3} - c'$ in (9) we obtain

$$\left(\frac{1}{3} - a'\right) b'c' + a' \left(\frac{1}{3} - b'\right) c' + a'b' \left(\frac{1}{3} - c'\right) + 2a'b'c'$$

$$- \left(\frac{1}{3} - a'\right) \left(\frac{1}{3} - b'\right) \left(\frac{1}{3} - c'\right) \geqslant 0$$

or

$$a' + b' + c' \geqslant \frac{1}{3}.\tag{14}$$

On the other hand, from (2), (4), (6) and (10) we have that

$$1 = a + a' + b' + c + c' \leqslant a' + b' + c' + 2(a' + b' + c') = 3(a' + b' + c'),$$

which shows that inequality (14) holds. We conclude that at a minimum subject
to constraints (2)–(7) and (10) it holds that $f(\cdot) \geqslant 0$. Hence, ineq. (8) holds,
and the relation of concern is max-Δ-transitive, QED.

3.3   Aggregation of Preferences

Clearly, information on the comparison results for a given set of n producers
$\mathcal{X} = \{\mathbf{x}^1, \ldots, \mathbf{x}^n\}$ may be stored in a $[0, 1]$-valued $n \times n$ matrix M, where $m_{ij} :=$
$\mu(\mathbf{x}^i, \mathbf{x}^j)$ is the value of the membership function of the fuzzy preference relation
$\mathbf{x}^i \blacktriangleleft \mathbf{x}^j$. Such a matrix, which we refer to as the preference matrix, has to be
processed so that some valuable knowledge may be extracted from it.

This may be achieved e.g. with the net flow method [2,6]. It provides a way of
aggregating a preference profile from the preference matrix. This method assigns
scores according to the formula

$$S_{\text{net}}(\mathbf{x}^i) = \sum_{\mathbf{x}^j \in \mathcal{X}} \mu(\mathbf{x}^j, \mathbf{x}^i) - \mu(\mathbf{x}^i, \mathbf{x}^j),\tag{15}$$

which in our case reduces to $S_{\text{net}}(\mathbf{x}^i) = \sum_{\mathbf{x}^j \in \mathcal{X}} 2\mu(\mathbf{x}^j, \mathbf{x}^i) - 1$, because $\blacktriangleleft$ is additive reciprocal. This is quite analogous to the classical approach in which the
impact functions are used. However, the assigned scores depend on the "environ-
ment" $\mathcal{X}$ in which the object $\mathbf{x}^i$ is considered, i.e. the preference matrix of the
objects being compared. By ordering the objects with respect to the scores, we
obtain the final ranking of a *given* set of producers $\mathcal{X}$.

3.4 Quality of Rankings

In this subsection we propose some quality measures for rankings of elements in $\mathcal{X}$. Such measures shall be based on the preference matrix derived from a fuzzy preference relation.

Let $r : \mathcal{X} \to \{1, 2, \ldots, n\}$ be a ranking function. Some objects can be ranked equal, i.e. we may have $r(\mathbf{x}^i) = r(\mathbf{x}^j)$ for some $i \neq j$. We would like to suggest an evaluation (quality) measure Q for ranking r which describes the level of concordance of this ranking with the preference relation ◄. We require that the measure has at least the following properties:

1. $Q(r, ◄) \in [0, 1]$, where we assume that 0 and 1 are the lowest and the highest possible quality value, respectively;
2. $Q(r, ◄) = 1$ if $(\forall i, j)$ $\mu(\mathbf{x}^i, \mathbf{x}^j) = 1$ implies $r(\mathbf{x}^i) > r(\mathbf{x}^j)$ (strict preference) and $(\forall i, j)$ $\mu(\mathbf{x}^i, \mathbf{x}^j) = 0.5$ results in $r(\mathbf{x}^i) = r(\mathbf{x}^j)$ (indifference);
3. Accordingly, $Q(r, ◄) = 0$ if $(\forall i, j)$ $\mu(\mathbf{x}^i, \mathbf{x}^j) = 0$ implies $r(\mathbf{x}^i) > r(\mathbf{x}^j)$ and $(\forall i, j)$ $\mu(\mathbf{x}^i, \mathbf{x}^j) = 0$ or $\mu(\mathbf{x}^i, \mathbf{x}^j) = 1$ gives $r(\mathbf{x}^i) = r(\mathbf{x}^j)$.

The following function can constitute an exemplary quality measure:

$$Q(r, ◄) = \frac{\displaystyle\sum_{\substack{i,j: \\ r(\mathbf{x}^i) > r(\mathbf{x}^j)}} \mu(\mathbf{x}^i, \mathbf{x}^j) + \sum_{\substack{i<j: \\ r(\mathbf{x}^i) = r(\mathbf{x}^j)}} 1 - 2\left|\mu(\mathbf{x}^i, \mathbf{x}^j) - \tfrac{1}{2}\right|}{\binom{n}{2}}.$$

4 A Case Study

In this section we applied the introduced method to the data on the activity of users at the StackOverflow website[1]. StackOverflow allows users to ask or answer questions on various computer programming-related issues. Answers are graded by the community according to their quality and relevance (they may be voted up or down). Thanks to good answers the users have their "reputation" increased. In May 2014, the website has over 3 million users that posted over 7.2 million questions and provided around 13 million answers to them (each question may have several associated answers).

In our study we treat answers provided by the users as products and the number of votes as the quality measures of consecutive units. We decided to pick 100 users with the highest number of answers. Notably, these users provided ca. 634,000 answers which is roughly 5% overall. In general, 1% of the users with the greatest number of answers provided answers to the 62.5% of questions.

Since the answers may also be down-voted, some of them received negative score. In such cases we set their quality to 0. This is only a minor correction as the fraction of such answers in the considered group is relatively small (95% of users have at most 1.6% negatively evaluated answers and 7% is the highest fraction

---

[1] See http://stackoverflow.com. The data of the users' activity is freely available for download at http://data.stackexchange.com/. For the purposes of our study the data were downloaded on April 30, 2014.

in the considered group). After this operation, the quality of each product is contained in the interval $[0, \infty)$.

We suggest several methods for evaluation of producers' output: reputation index compiled by the StackOverflow website to evaluate its users (i_R), mean quality ($\bar{x}$), maximum of the quality ($x_{(n)}$), sum of quality of answers ($\Sigma(x)$), number of answers (n), Egghe's g-index (i_G), Hirsch's h-index (i_H), and Woeginger's w-index (i_W), see [1,12,20]. For our base preference relation (denoted NF) we set ($\forall i$) $w_i = 1$ in Def. 4.

The correlations between pairs of rankings generated by the methods of interest are given in Table 1. The measures of rankings' quality are given in Table 2.

Table 1. Kendall's τ correlation coefficients for pairs of rankings obtained by different methods

	i_R	$\bar{x}$	$x_{(n)}$	$\Sigma(x)$	n	i_G	i_H	i_W	NF
i_R	1	0.546	0.543	0.882	0.469	0.696	0.728	0.714	0.882
$\bar{x}$	0.546	1	0.546	0.602	0.06	0.67	0.667	0.665	0.593
$x_{(n)}$	0.543	0.546	1	0.562	0.22	0.708	0.606	0.624	0.564
$\Sigma(x)$	0.882	0.602	0.562	1	0.457	0.703	0.72	0.707	0.978
n	0.469	0.06	0.22	0.457	1	0.262	0.27	0.266	0.467
i_G	0.696	0.67	0.708	0.703	0.262	1	0.872	0.892	0.7
i_H	0.728	0.667	0.606	0.72	0.27	0.872	1	0.967	0.714
i_W	0.714	0.665	0.624	0.707	0.266	0.892	0.967	1	0.702
NF	0.882	0.593	0.564	0.978	0.467	0.7	0.714	0.702	1

Table 2. Quality measures of rankings

i_R	$\bar{x}$	$x_{(n)}$	$\Sigma(x)$	n	i_G	i_H	i_W	NF
0.895	0.748	0.749	0.88	0.726	0.8	0.831	0.819	0.874

We see that the StackOverflow's reputation index provides a ranking of the highest quality[2]. Note that the reputation index uses more data than we have employed in our illustration. Note that the highest possible quality ranking has not been listed in Table 2 – we were able to find better rankings according to our evaluation measure by stochastic optimization.

Interestingly, we have that the sum of total scores ($\Sigma(x)$) and net flow method gained the second and the third highest quality and virtually equal results. From Table 1 we see that these methods are highly correlated as indicated by Kendall's τ statistic. Since we employed uniform weights ($w_i = 1$) this is not surprising. In a pairwise comparison we have $\Sigma(x) < \Sigma(y) \iff \mu(x, y) > 0.5$. However, the net flow method evaluates an output in the "whole environment" as indicated by Eq. (15). In particular, since the rankings generated by the two methods are

---

[2] For the details on how reputation is compiled see http://stackoverflow.com/-help/whats-reputation; last access date: May 7, 2014.

not concordant, we conclude that the net flow scoring method does not preserve the axiom of independence of irrelevant alternatives. However, we claim that the "environment" in which an object is considered is important during its evaluation process.

The other ranking methods, including bibliometric indices performed worse under our evaluation measure and preference relation. The agreement between different methods vary from 0.06 (number of answers n and average quality of an answer $\bar{x}$, the latter in fact not being an arity-monotonic aggregation operator) to 0.978 for the already discussed case.

5   Conclusions and Future Work

In this paper we approached the *Producers Assessment Problem* by fuzzy pairwise comparisons. This method allows us to handle uncertainty in a more subtle way than by the crisp dominance relation approach. Our preliminary results indicate that the derived method can be successfully applied to the problem of producers evaluation.

Note the difference between this approach and the currently most popular one. In the latter case, one postulates an aggregation operator and then discusses how does it rank any possible pair of producers. In our case, we start from a fixed producers set and construct a ranking based on a easy-to-understand fuzzy relation. Here we have access to information on the degree of consistency between the ranking and the pairwise comparison results.

Further research in this area should focus on refinements of the preference relation which can be obtained by e.g. statistical or machine learning methods (utilizing experts' knowledge, for example) rather than given by an explicit formula [8]. Another direction is the construction of sensible quality measures for ranking evaluation specific to this task. These may also serve as cost functions for solving optimization problems of finding a ranking of the highest quality.

Acknowledgments. Jan Lasek would like to acknowledge the support by the European Union from resources of the European Social Fund, Project PO KL "Information technologies: Research and their interdisciplinary applications", agreement UDA-POKL.04.01.01-00-051/10-00 via the Interdisciplinary PhD Studies Program.

References

1. Alonso, S., Cabrerizo, F.J., Herrera-Viedma, E., Herrera, F.: h-index: A review focused on its variants, computation and standardization for different scientific fields. Journal of Informetrics 3, 273–289 (2009)
2. Bouyssou, D.: Ranking methods based on valued preference relations: A characterization of the net flow method. European Journal of Operational Research 60, 60–67 (1992)
3. Bouyssou, D., Marchant, T.: Ranking scientists and departments in a consistent manner. Journal of the American Society for Information Science and Technology 62(9), 1761–1769 (2011)

4. Cena, A., Gagolewski, M.: OM3: Ordered maxitive, minitive, and modular aggregation operators – Axiomatic and probabilistic properties in an arity-monotonic setting. Fuzzy Sets and Systems (in press, 2014), doi:10.1016/j.fss.2014.04.001
5. Dasgupta, M., Deb, R.: Transitivity and fuzzy preferences. Social Choice and Welfare 13, 305–318 (1996)
6. Fodor, J., Roubens, M.: Fuzzy Preference Modelling and Multicriteria Decision Support. Springer (1994)
7. Franceschini, F., Maisano, D.A.: The Hirsch index in manufacturing and quality engineering. Quality and Reliability Engineering International 25, 987–995 (2009)
8. Fürnkranz, J., Hüllermeier, E. (eds.): Preference Learning. Springer, New York (2011)
9. Gagolewski, M.: Scientific impact assessment cannot be fair. Journal of Informetrics 7(4), 792–802 (2013)
10. Gagolewski, M., Mesiar, R.: Monotone measures and universal integrals in a uniform framework for the scientific impact assessment problem. Information Sciences 263, 166–174 (2014)
11. Herrera-Viedma, E., Herrera, F., Chiclana, F., Luque, M.: Some issues on consistency of fuzzy preference relations. European Journal of Operational Research 154, 98–109 (2004)
12. Hirsch, J.E.: An index to quantify individual's scientific research output. Proceedings of the National Academy of Sciences 102(46), 16569–16572 (2005)
13. Hovden, R.: Bibliometrics for internet media: Applying the h-index to YouTube. Journal of the American Society for Information Science and Technology 64(11), 2326–2331 (2013)
14. Klement, E., Mesiar, R., Pap, E.: A universal integral as common frame for Choquet and Sugeno integral. IEEE Transactions on Fuzzy Systems 18, 178–187 (2010)
15. Nocedal, J., Wright, S.: Numerical Optimization. Springer, New York (2006)
16. Peneva, V., Popchev, I.: Aggregation of fuzzy preference relations to multicriteria decision making. Fuzzy Optimization and Decision Making 6, 351–365 (2007)
17. Quesada, A.: Monotonicity and the Hirsch index. Journal of Informetrics 3(2), 158–160 (2009)
18. Sugeno, M.: Theory of fuzzy integrals and its applications. Ph.D. thesis, Tokyo Institute of Technology (1974)
19. Tanino, T.: Fuzzy Preference Relations in Group Decision Making, pp. 54–71. Springer, Heidelberg (1988)
20. Woeginger, G.J.: An axiomatic characterization of the Hirsch-index. Mathematical Social Sciences 56(2), 224–232 (2008)

Part III
Intelligent Decision Support Systems and Their Applications

Part III
Intelligent Decision Support Systems
and Their Applications

An Intelligent Based Decision Support System for the Detection of Meat Spoilage

Vassilis S. Kodogiannis[1], Ilias Petrounias[2], and John Lygouras[3]

[1] Faculty of Science and Technology, University of Westminster, London W1W 6UW, U.K.
V.Kodogiannis@westminster.ac.uk
[2] Manchester Business School, University of Manchester, United Kingdom
[3] Dept. of Electrical & Computer Engineering, Democritus University of Thrace,
Xanthi, GR-67100, Greece

Abstract. Freshness and safety of muscle foods are generally considered as the most important parameters for the food industry. To address the rapid and non-destructive detection of meat spoilage, Fourier transform infrared (FTIR) spectroscopy with the aid of an intelligent decision system, was considered in this work. FTIR spectra were obtained from the surface of beef samples at various temperatures, while a microbiological analysis identified the population of total viable counts for each sample. An adaptive fuzzy logic system model that utilizes a prototype defuzzification scheme has been developed to classify beef samples in their respective quality class and to predict simultaneously their associated microbiological population directly from FTIR spectra. Results confirmed the superiority of the adopted methodology and indicated that FTIR spectral information in combination with an efficient choice of a modeling scheme could be considered as an alternative methodology for the accurate evaluation of meat spoilage.

Keywords: Adaptive fuzzy logic system, defuzzification, FTIR, neural networks, meat spoilage, partial least square regression.

1 Introduction

The resolution of the Uruguay Round of the General Agreement on Tariffs and Trade (GATT) in 1995, recognized public health risk as the only basis for restrictions of international trade in food. Beef is one of the commercially viable and widely consumed muscle foods throughout the world. Although it is a good food source for proteins and other essential nutrients, it is also an ideal substrate for the growth of both spoilage and pathogenic microorganisms. The current practice to assure the safety of meat still relies on regulatory inspection and sampling regimes. This approach, however, seems inadequate because it cannot sufficiently guarantee consumer protection, since 100% inspection and sampling is technically, financially and logistically impossible. Meat industry however needs rapid and non-destructive sensing methods for quantification of these indicators in order to determine suitable processing procedures for their raw material and to predict the remaining shelf life of their products [1].

© Springer International Publishing Switzerland 2015
D. Filev et al. (eds.), *Intelligent Systems' 2014*,
Advances in Intelligent Systems and Computing 323, DOI: 10.1007/978-3-319-11310-4_26

303

Over the last few years, FTIR has been considered as a very important tool in food analysis including authenticity and adulteration. FTIR was able to determine omega-6 and omega-3 fatty acids in pork adipose tissue [2]. It has been also used to investigate the influence of ageing and salting on uncooked and cooked pork [3]. The application of chemometric techniques to associate FTIR spectral data with meat spoilage is not new and it has been tackled in the past. FTIR spectral data collected directly from the surface of meat were verified that they could be used as biochemical interpretable "signatures", in an attempt to obtain information on early detection of microbial spoilage of chicken breast and rump steaks [4].

The main objective of this paper is to associate FTIR spectral data with beef spoilage during aerobic storage at various temperatures (0, 5, 10, 15, 20 °C) utilizing an advanced learning-based decision support system. Information related to FTIR spectra, as well as the correlated microbiological analysis (*i.e.* total viable counts - TVC) from beef fillets, was made accessible from Agricultural University of Athens in the framework of the Symbiosis-EU European research project. Due to the nature of FTIR spectral data, it is necessary to consider the use of a dimensionality reduction algorithm to reduce the problem of dimensionality with the minimum information lost. In the current study, an Adaptive Fuzzy Logic System (AFLS) model that utilizes a prototype defuzzification scheme has been developed to classify beef samples to one of three quality classes (*i.e.* fresh, semi-fresh, and spoiled) based on their biochemical profile provided by the FTIR spectrometer. The same model simultaneously predicts the microbial load (as total viable counts) on meat surface. The proposed architecture differs from conventional fuzzy rule-table approaches which utilize the "look-up table" concept. In the proposed scheme, the number of memberships for each input variable is directly associated to the number of rules, hence, the "curse of dimensionality" problem is significantly reduced. Results from AFLS are compared against models based on MLP and PLS. Such comparison is considered as an essential practice, as we have to emphasize the need of induction to the area of food microbiology, advanced learning-based modeling schemes, which may have a significant potential for the rapid and accurate assessment of meat spoilage. Such an accurate assessment prediction could allow a more efficient management of products in the food chain.

2   FTIR Sampling and Analysis

The FTIR experimental case was performed at the Laboratory of Microbiology and Biotechnology of Foods, of the Agricultural University of Athens, Greece. A detailed description of the experimental methodology as well as the related microbiological analysis of the meat samples is described in [5]. Briefly, the samples were prepared by cutting fresh pieces of beef into small portions and then portions placed onto Petri dishes and stored at $(0, 5, 10, 15$ and $20\ °C)$ in high-precision incubation chambers for a total period of $350h$, taking into consideration the storage temperature, until spoilage was apparent. For the purposes of FTIR spectral measurements, a thin slice of the aerobic upper surface of the beef fillet was isolated and used for additional analysis. In total, 74 FTIR spectra were produced through the use of a using a ZnSe $45°$ ATR

(Attenuated Total Reflectance) crystal on a Nicolet 6700 FTIR Spectrometer. These spectra were collected over a specific wave-number range, whilst the scans per measurement were 100 with a resolution of $4cm^{-1}$, resulting in a total integration time of $2\min$. Typical FTIR spectral data in the range of $1800-1000cm^{-1}$ collected from fresh and spoiled beef fillet samples stored at $10°C$ for 6 days are shown in Fig. 1.

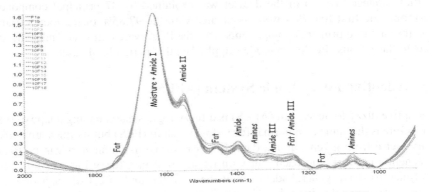

Fig. 1. FTIR spectra collected from beef samples stored at 10°C

In parallel, microbiological analysis was performed, and resulting growth data from plate counts were $\log_{10}$ transformed and fitted to the primary model of Baranyi & Roberts in order to verify the kinetic parameters of microbial growth (maximum specific growth rate and lag phase duration).

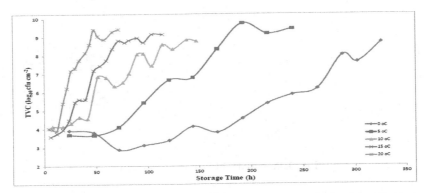

Fig. 2. Growth Curves of TVCs at different temperatures for beef samples

The population dynamics of total viable counts (TVC) for beef fillet storage at different temperatures, under aerobic conditions, is illustrated in Fig. 2. Sensory evaluation of meat samples was performed during storage, based on the perception of color and smell before and after cooking. Each sensory attribute was assigned to a three-point scale corresponding to: 1=fresh; 2=semi-fresh; and 3= spoiled. In total, 74 meat samples were evaluated by a sensory panel and classified into the selected three groups as fresh (n = 24), semi-fresh (n = 16), and spoiled (n = 34) for the case of TVC

[5]. Dataset consisted of the TVC values as well as the sensory categorization was utilized for the development of the proposed prediction and classification intelligent-based model. A principal component analysis (PCA) was then performed on this mean-centered spectral data. The choice of PCA was initiated by the fact that the strong correlation among the FTIR variables (*i.e.* wave-numbers), would deteriorate seriously the modeling procedure. In this particular experimental case study, although the total variance (100%) of the dataset was explained by 37 principal components (PCs), only the first five PCs were associated with the 97.85% of the total variance. Thus, the first five principal components from the PCA were extracted and utilized as inputs to the various simulation models applied on this particular dataset.

3   Adaptive Fuzzy Logic System (AFLS)

An adaptive fuzzy logic system (AFLS) is a fuzzy logic system having adaptive rules. Its structure is the same as a normal fuzzy logic system (FLS) but its rules are derived and extracted from given training data. In other words, its parameters can be trained like a neural network approach, but with its structure in a fuzzy logic system structure. Since we have general ideas about the structure and effect of each rule, it is straightforward to effectively initialize each rule. This is a tremendous advantage of AFLS over its neural network counterpart. The AFLS is one type of FLS with a singleton fuzzifier and centre average defuzzifier. The centroid defuzzifier cannot be used because of its computation expense and that it prohibits the use of the gradient descent (GD) learning algorithm.

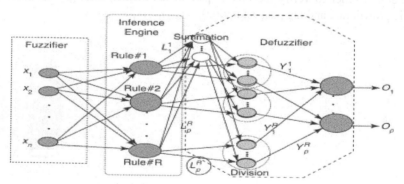

Fig. 3. Proposed AFLS-AOB architecture

The proposed in this research work AFLS consists of an alternative to classical defuzzification approaches, the area of balance (AOB) [6]. Its feed-forward structure is shown in Fig. 3, with an extra "fuzzy basis" layer. In this architecture, the fuzzy basis layer consists of fuzzy basis nodes for each rule. A fuzzy basis node has the following form:

$$\varphi_m(\overline{x}) = \frac{\mu_m(\overline{x})}{\sum_{l=1}^{L} \mu_l(\overline{x})} \tag{1}$$

where $\varphi_m(\overline{x})$ is a fuzzy basis node for rule m and $\mu_m(\overline{x})$ is a membership value of rule m. Since a product-inference is utilized, the fuzzy basis node $\mu_m(\overline{x})$ is in the following form:

$$\mu_m(\overline{x}) = \prod_{i=1}^{n} \mu_{F_i^m}(x_i) \tag{2}$$

where $\mu_{F_i^m}(x_i)$ is the membership value of the ith input of rule m. In the proposed scheme, a "Gaussian-shape" membership function has been employed, thus $\mu_{F_i^m}(x_i)$ has the following form:

$$\mu_{F_{ii}^m}(x_i) = \exp\left[-\frac{(x_i - c_i^m)^2}{2(b_i^m)^2}\right] \tag{3}$$

where c_i^m and b_i^m are the centre and spread parameters of the membership function i^{th} input of the mth rule. The "centroid of area" defuzzification method returns the centroid of the area formed by the consequent membership function, the membership value of its rules and the max-min or max-product inference. In the proposed AFLS, its overall output utilizes Kosko's method with product inference. The calculation of the output, y, will be

$$y_p = \frac{\sum_{m=1}^{M} \mu_m L_p^m y_p^m}{\sum_{m=1}^{M} \mu_m L_p^m} \tag{4}$$

where , y_p is the pth output of the network, μ_m the membership value of the mth rule, L_p^m is the spread parameter of the membership function in the consequent part of the pth output of the mth rule, and y_p^m is the centre of the membership function in the consequent part of the pth output of the mth rule. The GD learning algorithm has been employed for the training of this particular architecture.

4   Results and Discussion

A machine learning approach, based on the proposed AFLS model, has been adopted in order to create a decision support system acting in parallel as an efficient classifier, in an effort to classify meat samples in three quality classes (fresh, semi-fresh, spoiled), as well as a prediction system. Produced results were compared against MLP and PLS schemes, which are considered as well-recognized tools in chemometric analysis. The entire dataset, consisted of 74 beef patterns, include information from the various storage temperatures, the first five PCs and the sampling times. As the number of observations/samples was small, the separation of the dataset into training and testing subsets (hold-out method) was considered that it would further reduce the number of data and would result in insufficient training of the network. Therefore, in order to improve the robustness of identification process, the leave-1-out cross validation technique was employed to evaluate the performance of the developed AFLS model. AFLS's structure, as shown from Fig. 3, consists of an input layer which in this current research study contains seven input nodes (*i.e.* storage temperature, sampling time, and the values of the five principal components). The second layer is related to the inference engine (i.e. the fuzzy rules). After many trials, it has been found that only 12 rules are necessary for the proposed AFLS model to achieve an acceptable performance for this particular case/experiment. The output layer consists of two nodes, corresponding to the predicted quality class (fresh, semi-fresh, spoiled) of meat samples and the total viable counts (TVC), respectively. As both output parameters are dependent, in the sense that quality class is related to microbiological counts and vice versa, a model that combines both these measurements have been considered to be desirable. In order to accommodate both classification and modeling tasks in the same model-structure, the classification task has been modified accordingly. Rather than trying to create a distinct classifier, an attempt has been made to "model" the classes.

Table 1. Confusion Matrix for AFLS acting as classifier

True class	Predicted class			Row total (n_i)	Sensitivity (%)
	Fresh	Semi-fresh	Spoiled		
Fresh	23	1(marginal)	0	24	95.83
Semi-fresh	1 +1(marginal)	14	0	16	87.5
Spoiled	0	0	33+1(marginal)	34	100
Column total	25	15	34	74	
Specificity (%)	92	93.33	100		
Overall correct classification (accuracy): 95.94%					

Initially, values of 10, 20 and 30, have been used respectively, to associate the three classes with a cluster centre. During the identification process, the output values of $[5.....15]$ were associated to "fresh" class with cluster centre 10, values of $[15.01.....25]$ were associated to "semi-fresh" class with cluster centre 20, and finally values of $[25.01.....35]$ were associated to "spoiled" class with cluster centre 30. The second output node has been assigned to the total viable counts (TVC). The classification accuracy of the AFLS network was determined by the number of correctly classified samples in each sensory class divided by the total number of samples in the class. The performance of the model in the prediction of TVC for each meat sample was determined by a number of statistical indices. Results revealed that the classification accuracy of the AFLS model was very satisfactory in the characterization of beef samples, indicating the advantage of a neurofuzzy approach in tackling complex, nonlinear problems, such as meat spoilage. The classification accuracy obtained from AFLS, is presented in the form of a confusion matrix in Table 1. The model overall achieved a 95.94% correct classification, and 95.83%, 87.5% and 100% for fresh, semi-fresh and spoiled meat samples, respectively. The plot of predicted versus observed total viable counts is illustrated in Fig. 4, and shows a very good distribution around the line of equity (y=x), with all the data included within the ±1 log unit area.

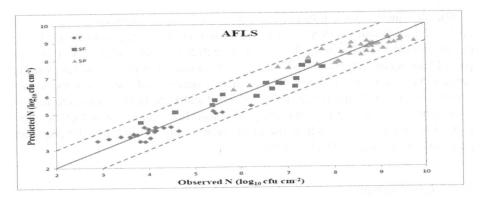

Fig. 4. Comparison of predicted TVCs model against experimentally observed values

The performance of the AFLS model to predict TVCs in beef samples in terms of statistical indices is presented in Table 2.

Table 2. Performance of AFLS as prediction system

Statistical index leave-1-out (AFLS case)	Fresh	Semi-fresh	Spoiled	Overall
Mean squared error (MSE)	0.129	0.156	0.138	0.139
Root mean squared error (RMSE)	0.359	0.395	0.371	0.373
Mean relative percentage residual (MRPR %)	0.648	-2.431	-0.964	-0.758
Mean absolute percentage residual (MAPR %)	7.091	6.234	3.726	5.359
Bias factor (B_f)	0.989	1.022	1.008	1.005
Accuracy factor (A_f)	1.074	1.063	1.037	1.054
Standard error of prediction (SEP %)	8.579	6.356	4.406	5.671

An MLP network and a PLS model have been also developed entirely on the same FTIR dataset, employing the leave-1-out validation method. Similarly to AFLS case, the MLP was constructed with two hidden layers (with 12 and 6 nodes respectively).

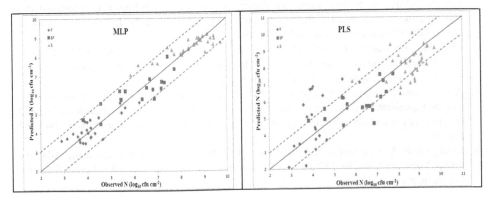

Fig. 5. Performance of MLP and PLS models

The PLS model was constructed using the same input vector as in the cases of AFLS and MLP, and the PLS_Toolbox software (ver. 7.5, Eigenvector.com) in association with MATLAB was used to perform the PLS analysis. The nonlinear iterative partial least squares algorithm (NIPALS) has been chosen as the appropriate learning scheme. Overall results revealed that prediction accuracy of the AFLS model was better compared with the performances of MLP and PLS, in the characterization of meat samples, indicating the superiority of a neurofuzzy approach in tackling complex, nonlinear problems such as the meat spoilage. Fig. 5 illustrates the prediction performance for MLP and PLS models.

5   Conclusions

In conclusion, this simulation study demonstrated the effectiveness of the detection approach based on FTIR spectroscopy which in combination with an appropriate machine learning strategy could become an effective tool for monitoring meat spoilage during aerobic storage at various temperatures. The collected spectra could be considered as biochemical "signatures" containing information for the discrimination of meat samples in quality classes corresponding to different spoilage levels, whereas in the same time could be used to predict satisfactorily the microbial load directly from the sample surface.

References

1. Dissing, B., Papadopoulou, O., Tassou, C., Ersbøll, B., Carstensen, J., Panagou, E., Nychas, G.-J.: Using Multispectral Imaging for Spoilage Detection of Pork Meat. Food and Bioprocess Technology 6, 2268–2279 (2013)
2. Olsen, E.F., Rukke, E.O., Egelandsdal, B., Isaksson, T.: Determination of omega-6 and omega-3 fatty acids in pork adipose tissue with non-destructive Raman and Fourier transform infrared spectroscopy. Applied Spectroscopy 62, 968–974 (2008)
3. Wu, Z., Bertram, H.C., Kohler, A., Bocker, U., Ofstad, R., Andersen, H.J.: Influence of aging and salting on protein secondary structures and water distribution in uncooked and cooked pork. A combined FT-IR microspectroscopy and NMR study. Journal of Agricultural and Food Chemistry 54, 8589–8597 (2006)
4. Ellis, D.I., Broadhurst, D., Kell, D.B., Rowland, J.J., Goodacre, R.: Rapid and quantitative detection of the microbial spoilage of meat by Fourier transform infrared spectroscopy and machine learning. Appl. Environ. Microbiol. 68, 2822–2828 (2002)
5. Argyri, A.A., Panagou, E.Z., Tarantilis, P.A., Polysiou, M., Nychas, G.-J.E.: Rapid qualitative and quantitative detection of beef fillets spoilage based on Fourier transform infrared spectroscopy data and artificial neural networks. Sensors and Actuators B 145, 146–154 (2010)
6. Kodogiannis, V.S., Petrounias, I., Lygouras, J.N.: Intelligent Classification using Adaptive Fuzzy Logic Systems. In: IS2008 – IEEE International Conference on Intelligent Systems, Bulgaria, pp. 8–13 (2008)

A Fuzzy Expert System for Evaluating the Responsiveness of Italian Insurance Companies to the "Solvency 2 Storm"

Simona Cosma, Gisella Facchinetti, and Giovanni Mastroleo

University of Salento, Lecce, Italy
{simona.cosma,gisella.facchinetti,
giovanni.mastroleo}@unisalento.it

Abstract. The "Solvency II" directive will be enforced starting from 2016. The insurance and reassurance companies have asked to reflect upon ways of adapting to the new rules and to consider value creation strategies under the new constraints. An Observatory was started for understanding how open Italian insurance companies are to change and how the announced rules influence the current operations. In order to monitor the behaviour of the companies over the years and evaluate the responsiveness to the new regulatory requirements of the Italian insurance Companies, a Fuzzy Expert System (FES) was developed. The objective of this work is to show the evaluation / monitoring tool created for the observatory. The special feature of the FES is to be created exclusively on judgments and not on objective data

Keywords: Solvency, Insurance companies, Regulatory impacts, Fuzzy Expert System.

1 Introduction[1]

For about ten years, Supervisors and academics have been studying the expected impact of Solvency 2 on the insurance industry, and predicting a radical change (for a review of the literature on the expected impact of Solvency 2, see Cosma, Gabbi, Pisani, 2014).

The directive, which was delayed several times, will be enforced starting from 2016; however, insurance and reassurance companies have been asked to reflect upon ways of adapting to the new rules and to consider value creation strategies under the new constraints for some time.

In order to understand how open Italian insurance companies are to change and how the announced rules influence the current operational system, an observatory was

---

[1] This work is one of the outputs of a research involving many people that the authors desire to acknowledge: Giampaolo Gabbi, Raoul Pisani, Paola Castelli, Leo Corvino, Paola Musile Tanzi, Raffaele Guerra, Andrea Scribano and all Companies that participated to the SDA Bocconi Observatory "Solvency II: operational transformation".

© Springer International Publishing Switzerland 2015
D. Filev et al. (eds.), *Intelligent Systems'2014*,
Advances in Intelligent Systems and Computing 323, DOI: 10.1007/978-3-319-11310-4_27

started by SDA Bocconi and Capgemini in 2011. The hypothesis of the work done by the observatory is that Solvency 2, while directly concerning the control system and risk management, transversally conditions the key processes of the insurance companies: organization, Information Technology, commercial and marketing/communication. The aim of the Observatory is, then, to identify the main operative impact of Solvency 2 on the mentioned areas and to evaluate the responsiveness of the Italian insurance companies.

The methodology used to intercept the operative impact is that of the focus group. From 2011 to 2012, several meetings were held where the directors of the organizational functions studied (Organization, IT, Commercial and marketing) and also risk managers participated. At each meeting, directors of a specific function and the risk managers of the Companies were invited and they discussed perceived impact and its importance.

In order to monitor the behaviour of the companies over the years and to evaluate the responsiveness to the new regulatory requirements of the Italian insurance Companies, a Fuzzy Expert System (FES) was developed.

This approach is ideal for the available data: qualitative evaluations which come from experts used in the focus group and from interviews in the form of questionnaires.

The objective of this work is to show the evaluation/monitoring tool created for the Observatory.

The work is structured as follows: the second paragraph describes the sample of companies represented in the study and the analysis model. The following two paragraphs show several results of the focus group. The fourth paragraph describes the evaluation model and the last paragraph gives a reading of the results to evaluate the discriminant capacity of the model constructed.

2   The Sample and the Methodology

The choice of studying both the impact of Solvency 2 on the organization and IT comes from the sensation that the starting point for Companies to adapt to the new rules should be searched in the organization dimension, made up of processes, which is, in turn, extremely tied to the IT dimension. Not only, in fact, does the analysis process often require the need to handle technological information and choices, but the revision of the processes expressly requires technological interventions to substitute "poor" activity with automation and/or modifying the skills and professions of the people with access to more data and information.

Consequently, the impact of Solvency on Human Resources (skills, behaviour) and organizational structure was studied. The risk-based logic introduced by Solvency 2 will probably have effects on the prices and on the commercial and communication policies of the companies. For this reason, the effect of the regulation on these two areas were investigated together. Therefore it was decided to identify the impact of the directive on commercial and marketing/communication (C&C) together and, in particular, on the product, pricing, communication and distribution policies.

In the context of the analysis, characterized by a strong uncertainty and lack of information, the prechosen methodology for the identification of the critical impact of

Solvency is based on Focus Group. Experts on relevant arguments to the research were interviewed.

In the first two years of the Observatory (2001, 2012), six meetings – three for Org&IT and three for C&C – were held. The six focus groups had ten experts in order to be able to compare results and neutralize the differential of the group. Each focus group had a moderator, people involved in the field of risk management and insurance business (SDA Bocconi professors and Capgemini consultants) and a group of experts made up of organization, IT, Commercial and marketing directors of various Italian companies (29 Companies, prevalently single entities, which represent 60.24% of life and damage premiums in 2012.). The Companies represented have different dimensions; they are prevalently non-specialized, with many distributional channels and operators all over the country. The moderator, following a protocol of study that was not extremely structured, proposed several "points" of discussion to the experts to identify the main impacts of Solvency 2 on the respective areas and their importance. With the information obtained, a FES was developed in order to allow the observatory to evaluate and monitor the process of adapting to Solvency 2 over time.

Later, the actual level of management of each impact were identified using questionnaires.

On the basis of information collected about impacts, their importance and their actual level of management, a FES was developed. This tool allows the evaluation and the monitoring over time of the process of adapting to Solvency 2.

The importance attributed by experts to each impact guided the definition of the rules of the FES. The tool is applied for evaluating the responsiveness of four Companies belonging to the sample, selected as case-study for the quality of the information collected. For one of these, a two years evaluation is carried-out, in order to test the temporary congruence of the outputs.

3   The Various Impacts of Solvency 2

During the focus groups, the experts identified a series of operative impacts on Org&IT and C&C which are considered crucial in the process of adapting to Solvency 2. Here we will discuss the most important impacts, selected as FES input, identified by the experts with reference to the four dimensions of analysis (Process, IT, human resources and organizational structure) for Org&IT and to the four dimensions of analysis (product, pricing, communication and distribution) for C&C.

3.1   The Impacts on ORG&IT

Processes
1. Mapping of the operational process: the experts recognize the importance of a well carried-out process analysis to map the activities conditioned by Solvency 2.
2. Controlling the information flows: the market-consistent approach for evaluating activity and liability, the calculation of the capital absorbed by products and business units and the scope of the ERM introduced by Solvency 2 required a revision and a strengthening of the information flows between the functions most

used in the implementation of the project (Risk management, Finance, Actuarial, Accounting, Reassurance).

3. Restructuring Solvency 2 processes: the companies feel the need to restructure the processes geared toward responding to the most stringent regulatory requirements. In particular, this implies to measure the SCR (Solvency Capital Requirement), the MCR (Minimum Capital Requirement) or the ORSA (Own Risk Self-Assessment), the technical reserves and at times to define the informative set necessary to respond to the need required by QIS (Quantitative Impact Study).

4. Revision of the governance mechanisms: defining the data ownership is necessary to certify the accuracy. This is a particularly important topic in the RCA branch, where many evaluations are expert judgments and therefore subjective. To create a Data Governance process means to formalize the management of data, production and elaboration, auditability / ability to track data, reconciliation, the checking of these data etc., defining roles and responsibilities, duties and above all the ownership of this process all in a single macro-process.

5. Analysis of product development processes: less urgent but equally necessary are the analyses and revisions of the development of new products. In this perspective, individuation of more adapt metrics (new profitability drivers) is seen as a fundamental pre-requisite for conveniently guiding the decisional processes and the choices made in the various Solvency II project sites.

Information Technology

1. Improving the data quality: the nonchalant attitude toward formalizing intervention using data, the lack of semantic precision needed to define more accurate the data in question, poor integration between relative decision support system applications and the legacy system within the company's information system impose an urgent intervention in order to improve the quality of the data. The poor quality of the data is connoted in terms of: lack of metadata, traceability and granularity.

2. Checking the systems interfaces: the companies recognize the need to have a data warehouse or at least an integrated system for managing company data which guarantees thoroughness and clearness with the data which in turn feeds the Solvency core processes. The planning for structured and efficient information flows becomes, then, the pre-requisite for the use-test or rather the way in which the results of the internal model or the standard formula are currently utilized to make decisions.

3. Understanding the specific requirements of Solvency 2: in order to evaluate the suitability and the reliability of the current informative systems and software, it is fundamental to understand the new requirements of the business processes and of the risk management. These are not well-defined from the principle-based regulation.

4. Managing larger reporting/accounting needs: Solvency increased the needs of reporting/accounting. The reporting applications have to create the documentation for the internal contact persons (Risk Management, Business units, audit, top management) and for the external ones (Supervisors and market).

5. Checking the adequacy of the AS-IS applications: checking the coherence between AS-IS applications and the regulatory requirements.

Human Resources

1. Improving the training at business / operational level: Solvency II induces a change of the strategies and the market behaviour of the Companies and, consequently, it requires the start of specific training in order to make several actors aware of the effects of Solvency 2 on their duties/responsibilities. Often, the training on Solvency 2 is not widespread.
2. Defining inter-functional teams for Solvency 2 internal projects: the creation of inter-functional teams facilitates the knowledge diffusion and the commitment of the resources involved in the project.
3. Improving the corporate risk culture: the lack of suitable incentives and guidelines delays the cultural change required by Solvency 2 that is thinking according a risk-based ratio.
4. Defining new tasks and finding expertise: the new task required by the compliance process implies researching suitable expertise inside or outside of the company.
5. Developing Risk Management skills: the risk managers need qualitative skills (communication / negotiation skills) to facilitate the communication and interaction with the various corporate structures. The Risk Management has to be an advisor / partner of the business units.

Organizational Structure

1. Ensuring the unambiguous assignment of responsibilities: defining and formalizing the new activities required by Solvency 2, their owners and the area of responsibilities of the various functions (Governance, Risk Management, Actuarial, Compliance, Internal Audit and Programming & Control) is essential. Possible overlapping implies operative problems to identify the project owners and delay of the decisions in the projects sites, with increase of time and costs.
2. Segregation between Governance and Control structures: overlapping between governance and control structures are to prevent. The organizational structure has to be clear and unambiguous, characterized by an efficient resource allocation, a segregation of the responsibilities and information flows well-defined.
3. Define roles and responsibilities for the Data Quality: the experts recognize the importance of identifying a Data Quality Manager (DQM), the organizational unit where he is and his duties and responsibility is important.
4. Improving the coordination of Solvency 2 internal projects: increasing coordination tools between corporate functions to guarantee a more inter-functional collaboration is necessary. The support committees represent a shared choice.
5. Review the adequacy of the AS-IS organizational structure: checking the coherence between organizational structure and the regulatory requirements and managing the trade-off between risk control and managerial freedom.

3.2   The Impacts on C&C

Product

1. Reduction of the guarantees offered: the Companies are obligated to reduce/delete the minimum guaranteed income from their products, because of large capital absorption.

2. Ensuring formal Solvency II compliance of new products: ensuring the compliance of the new products to Solvency 2 is important. The knowledge of the risk inherent in a product implies a change of the products composition (deductibles, exclusions etc.).

3. Review of the product Mix: the reduction of guarantees in terms of rate or capital implies an evaluation on the position and added value of the products offered compared to the financial products available on the market. This evaluation could imply the control of the social security business and an increase of the Unit Linked policies.

4. Ensuring formal Solvency II compliance of existing products: ensuring the compliance to Solvency 2 of the existing products is important. This means reviewing structure and characteristics of the products.

Pricing

1. Pricing based on the cost of capital: the companies that estimate the capital requirement based on an internal model have to use the results obtained to define the premium prices. In general, products pricing has to consider the risk and the capital absorption of each product.

2. Repricing of catastrophical policies: an immediate increase of the prices of the life insurance policies is expected.

3. Repricing of life insurance policies: an immediate increase of the prices of the catastrophical insurance policies is expected.

4. Reduction of products return: the companies should control the rise of the premium prices for maintaining competitiveness, suffering, consequently, a reduction of product return. The cost of distribution channels, the reassurance and the securitization assume a central role as a risk mitigant and, therefore, as cost of capital mitigant.

Distribution

1. Impact on commissions: Currently, the commissions are based on volumes and premium received. These models are incongruent with the new risk adjusted return models.

2. Increasing agent knowledge about products and pricing: it is necessary to make the agent aware of the reasons of the product redesign and price increase.

3. Strengthening the advisory role of the agent: there is the need to develop an advisory role of the sales force and, in particular, of the agents. In the traditional damage and life branches the higher product prices should be justified in terms of a greater customer service. For example, a growth of the financial component in the life insurance policies could require to distributors a stronger and different post-sale activity.

Communication

1. Stronger external communication: the existing risks and their management are disclosed toward internal structures and market in a clear way, according to the third Pillar. Solvency 2 requires to provide a suitable two-type communication with customers:

- Educational type: the financial culture of the market is patchy and poor and it causes difficulties in understanding the products;
- Information type: this type of communication is in order to disclose the greater "solvency" of the Company and, then, justify the prices increase.

2. Stronger internal communication: the arrangement of a periodic internal communications toward the distributors (agents, brokers, etc.) about their risk exposure and capital absorption is a pre-requisite to allow directing their commercial actions.

4   The Valuation Model

The selection of the variables outlined above is summarized in Table 1.

Table 1. List of abbreviations: input variables

Label	Input Variables
AAI	Checking the adequacy of the AS-IS applications
ARA	Strengthening the advisory role of the agent
BPC	Pricing based on the cost of capital
CAT	Repricing of catastrophical policies
CCR	Improving the corporate risk culture
CEP	Ensuring formal Solvency II compliance of existing products
CIS	Checking the systems interfaces
CNP	Ensuring formal Solvency II compliance of new products
CommerFInv	Level of involvement of the commercial function in the Solvency 2 project
CommunFInv	Level of involvement of the communication function in the Solvency 2 project
DFT	Defining new tasks and finding expertise
DQS	Define roles and responsibilities for the Data Quality
IDQ	Improving the data quality
IFC	Controlling the information flows
IIA	Investing in the improvement of the applications
IOC	Impact on commissions
IPC	Improving the coordination of Solvency 2 internal projects
IPT	Defining inter-functional teams for Solvency 2 internal projects
KPP	Increasing agent knowledge about products and pricing
LIS	Repricing of life insurance products
MAR	Managing larger reporting/accounting needs
MOP	Mapping of the operational process
OfficeIT	Level of involvement of the IT Department in the Solvency 2 project
OrgFInv	Level of involvement of the Organization function in the Solvency 2 project
OSA	Review the adequacy of the AS-IS organizational structure
PDP	Analysis of product development processes
RGM	Revision of the governance mechanisms
RGO	Reduction of the guarantees offered
RPM	Review of the product Mix
RPR	Reduction of products return
RSP	Restructuring "Solvency 2" processes
SEC	Stronger external communication
SGC	Segregation between Governance and Control structures
SIC	Stronger internal communication
SRM	Developing Risk Management skills
TBO	Improving the training at business/operational level
UAR	Ensuring the unambiguous assignment of responsibilities
USR	Understanding the specific requirements of Solvency 2

Aggregation of the inputs is shown in the decisional tree in Figure 1

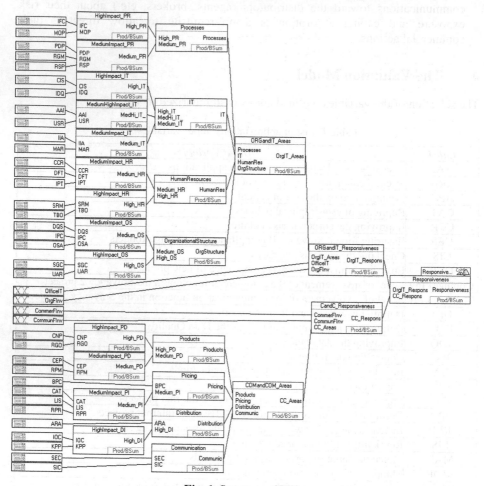

Fig. 1. Structure of FES

In the FES layout structure per areas and dimensions, identified by the group of experts, has been kept: valuation of total responsiveness is obtained aggregating, equal weight, the valuation of responsiveness of areas Org&IT e C&C; each responsiveness per area derives, in turn, from the aggregation of the four dimensions used with the level of involvement in the Solvency 2 project of two sections (Offices) per area. This makes it necessary to define some intermediate variables, which are useful for analysing the performance of assessment sectorially and to identify any deficiencies or peculiarities of the method followed. The list is provided in Table 2.

The inputs used in each dimension have been aggregated according to the level of impact detected in the focus groups, corrected by the opinions of experts of the individual insurance companies. This method has also been used for the aggregation of dimensions and areas and to build blocks of rules. The detailed list of the outputs is shown in Report SDA Bocconi and CAPGEMINI (2011, 2012).

Table 2. List of abbreviations: intermediate variables

Label	Intermediate Variables
CC_Areas	Commercial and Communication Areas
CC_Respons	Commercial and Communication Responsiveness
Communic	Communication: dimension of Area C&C
Distribution	Distribution: dimension of Area C&C
HumanRes	Human resources: dimension of Area Org&IT
IT	IT: dimension of Area Org&IT
OrgIT_Areas	Organizational and technological Areas
OrgIT_Respons	Organizational and technological Responsiveness
OrgStructure	Organizational structure: dimension of Area Org&IT
Pricing	Pricing: dimension of Area C&C
Processes	Processes: dimension of Area Org&IT
Products	Products: dimension of Area C&C

The peculiarity of this FES is that it is exclusively composed of qualitative variables, namely inputs the level of which is an opinion expressed by representatives of insurance companies and not by a data objectively detectable. All input variables are categorical then, except for the four variables that represent the level of involvement of the Offices. These four variables are constructed using the statistics of the perceived level of involvement using in the construction the value measured (for example 1.923 out of 3 for variable "OrgFInv" in fig. 2) as membership=1 (highest certainty of belonging) for Medium term, understood as an active support to the adaptation process, and standardizing the variable in the range (0 to 3) used in the survey.

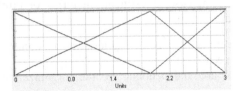

Fig. 2. Example: layout of Membership Functions in input variable: "OrgFInv"

For the characteristics shown, it was preferred to aggregate preliminarily inputs within each dimension according to the impact detected. An example is given for the evaluation of the intermediate variable IT, using high (H), medium-high (MH) and medium (M) impact inputs, aggregated with weights H=0.4, MH=0.33, M=0.27, according to the scheme in the following figure.

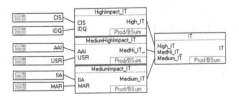

Fig. 3. IT dimension

5   Results and Conclusions

The fuzzy system built to evaluate and monitor over time the responsiveness of the insurance companies to the needs generated by the introduction of the new reference legislation known as Solvency 2 has a high discriminating power for the purposes of the Observatory. The evaluation results have a logical foundation based on knowledge of dimensional and business characteristics of the Companies on which the system has been tested (Table 3).

Table 3. Result

Record	Int.Var.	Int.Var.	Output
	CC_Respons	OrgIT_Respons	Responsiveness
CA_2011	68.202	63.052	68.184
CA_2012	76.004	71.132	77.738
CAV	51.454	63.052	56.832
GA	83.248	64.306	78.522
GITA	57.142	66.618	63.294

In particular, it appears that the company that has been evaluated for two consecutive years (CA_2011 and CA_2012), shows an overall increasing responsiveness at the approaching of the entry into force of the legislation, indicating greater sensitivity and cogency of the subjects evaluated; in particular, efforts on IT increase in the two years, and this represents a factor enabling compliance on other areas. In the same case, increase investments in terms of product and pricing. In general, in Org & IT it appears that:

1. The Companies have given management priority to the component Org & IT rather than to that of Comm & Comm.
2. Management efforts are independent of the organizational complexity and dimensions;
3. Management priority is given to IT.
4. IT dimension is positively correlated with the complexity (different strategic business areas and different distribution channels);
5. Processes dimension is also the one that will be affected by particularly intense interventions with the gradual progressing of individual companies towards Solvency. It must be noted that generally higher total scores (and that show mastery of the Solvency implications on area IT / Organization) are associated with high scores relative to the dimension processes.

In general, in C&C area it appears that:

1. The organizational complexity and the larger dimensions are associated with a greater responsiveness;

2. Less importance is given, in general, to the management of communication aspects, probably because the contents are defined on the basis of the solutions found on other dimensions; the communication dimension appears positively correlated to institutional peculiarities (mutualistic structure);
3. Distribution is an aspect in which the Companies devote the most attention;
4. The responsiveness with respect to the distribution is inversely related to the fidelity of the distribution channels. These channels can be different: sometimes agency networks, in other cases, networks of branches. In all cases, the relationship with the channel is characterized by a high fidelity to be found in historical stability of the network.
5. Price dimension increases over time in accordance with the increase of commercial sensitivity of the companies.
6. Product dimension is positively correlated to the width of the range offered: high scores are associated with market policies oriented toward a strong range of products to be distributed throughout the national market.
7. Pricing dimension and Product dimension are strongly correlated: in order to control the pricing, it becomes crucial outlining the structure of the product in an effective way.

References

1. CEIOPS, Technical Provisions Consultation Paper n. 43 Standards for Data Quality 2 Luglio (2009)
2. Cosma, S., Gabbi, G., Pisani, R.: Gli impatti attesi di Solvency 2: the perfect storm? Bancaria 2 (2014)
3. Doff, R.: A critical Analysis of the Solvency 2 proposal. The Geneva Papers 33 (2008)
4. ECB, Potential Impact of Solvency 2 on Financial Stability (2007), http://www.ecb.europa.eu
5. EIOPA, Consultation Paper on the Proposal for Guidelines on Own Risk and Solvency Assessment (2011)
6. EIOPA, Report on the fifth Quantitative Impact Study (QIS 5) for Solvency 2 (2011)
7. EIOPA, Final Report on Public Consultations No. 11/009 and 11/011 on the Proposal for the Reporting and Disclosure Requirements (2012)
8. EIOPA, Final Report on Public Consultation No. EIOPA-CP-12/005 on the Draft Implementing Technical Standards on reporting of national provisions of prudential nature relevant to the field of occupational pension schemes (2013)
9. Eling, M., Schmeiser, H., Schmit, J.: The Solvency II Process: Overview and Critical Analysis. Risk Management and Insurance Review 10 (2007)
10. European Commission, Proposal For A Directive of The European Parliament and of the Council Amending Directive 2009/138/Ec on the Taking-Up And Pursuit of the Business of Insurance And Reinsurance (Solvency 2) As Regards the Dates of Transposition and Application and the Date of Repeal of Certain Directives (October 2, 2013)
11. ISVAP, Regolamento n. 20 recante disposizioni in materia di controlli interni, gestione dei rischi, compliance ed esternalizzazione delle attività delle imprese di assicurazione (2008)

12. ISVAP, Solvency 2: il nuovo sistema di vigilanza prudenziale. lettera al mercato (January 26, 2010)
13. European Parlament and Council, Directive 2009/138/Ec of the European Parliament and of the Council of 25 November 2009 on the taking-up and pursuit of the business of Insurance and Reinsurance (Solvency II) (Novembre 25, 2009)
14. SDA Bocconiand Capgemini, La gestione degli impatti operativisulleareeorganizzazione & it e commerciale& comunicazione, Osservatorio solvency II operational transformation (2011), http://www.sdabocconi.it
15. SDA Bocconiand Capgemini, La gestione degli impatti operativisullearee: Organizzazione & IT, Commerciale & Comunicazione, Orsa& risk reporting. Osservatorio solvency II operational transformation (2012), http://www.sdabocconi.it

Designing a Decision Support System for Recommending Smartphones Using Fuzzy Ontologies

Juan Antonio Morente Molinera[1], Ignacio Javier Pérez Gálvez[2],
Robin Wikström[3], Enrique Herrera Viedma[1], and Christer Carlsson[3]

[1] Dept. of Computer Science and Artificial Intelligence
University of Granada, Granada, Spain
[2] Department of Computer Sciences and Engineering
University of Cádiz, Cádiz, Spain
[3] IAMSR, Åbo Akademi University, Turku, Finland
{jamoren,viedma}@decsai.ugr.es
ignaciojavier.perez@uca.es
{robin.wikstrom,christer.carlsson}@abo.fi

Abstract. Nowadays, smartphones have become indispensable items for everybody. Thanks to them, people can communicate and access Internet at any time regardless of where they are located. New smartphones belonging to a high amount of labels and with different features and prices keep appearing constantly in the market. This way, there is a need of tools that help buyers to select and buy the smartphone that better fits their necessities. In this article, a decision support system build over a fuzzy ontology has been designed in order to help people to select the perfect smartphone for them. Linguistic labels are used in order to provide the buyer with a comfortable way of expressing himself/herself.

Keywords: Decision support system, Fuzzy ontology, Linguistic modelling.

1 Introduction

Smartphones are probably one of the most popular items these days. They allow people to communicate, surf the Internet and execute programs, called apps, at any time regardless of the place. They combine benefits and functionalities of a mobile phone, a web browser, a GPS device and a computer in a single small device. Smartphones are constantly evolving with new features, becoming, at the same time, cheaper and faster every year. Nowadays, they are items that are periodically acquired by a wide range of people from the first world population belonging to different ages [1]. Everyone is expecting new smartphones with new features in order to replace the ones that they already have. This way, smartphones market moves a huge amount of money. Furthermore, smartphones applications like Whatsapp, Facebook or Twitter have become totally indispensable for most of the population [2]. A huge amount of companies have joint the smartphone designing race and keep creating new models with brand new features every year. Some of this companies, like Samsung, Apple, HTC, Sony or Nokia, are quite important ones and keep competing in order to convince people to buy their smartphones. More information about this commercial environment can be found in [3].

Because of this, when buyers want to acquire a new smartphone model, they find themselves lost in the middle of hundreds of advertisements of different companies wanting them to buy the brand new smartphone that they have design. The fact that there are too many options to choose and that all of them are not known by the buyers make it difficult for them to choose the smartphone that better fits their requirements. This way, there is a need for decision support systems that help them to organize their ideas, allow them to formalize what they are really looking for and, according to their preferences, reduce the high amount of possibilities into a small set of results conformed by the smartphones that better fit what they are looking for.

In order to overcome this issue, a decision making support system [4] for assessing buyers when they want to buy an smartphone has been designed. Thanks to our system, buyers can provide information about how they want their new smartphone to be, receive several suggestions and select their final choice. Because the smartphones market is in a constant change, data used by our system to generate recommendation will be flexible and constantly being updated in order to capture all the changes and new items in the market. Linguistic modelling [5–7] will also be used in the data description and in the preferences providing in order to ease buyers the way they have to express themselves. When users search for an item, in this case, an smartphone, they usually do not look for precise features values related to them, they want to work with imprecise information. For example, if an user want an smartphone with a big screen, he/she probably do not mind if the smarphone have 4 inch or 5 inch, but he probably will not accept a smartphone with 2.5 inches. Our system take in account this issue and allow the user to specify in a imprecise way every feature avoiding the troublesome task of providing specific parameters for each feature. Furthermore, our system allow the choosing of an smartphone in a fair way, totally based on the characteristics and quality, avoiding the confusion that some advertisements may generate in the buyers. In other words, is a system thought for the buyers that can be totally trusted by them.

It is important to point out that the smartphones market is just an example and that the system can be easily exported in order to support people in making decisions in other fields. For example, it should be possible to use this system to help buyers to rent a flat in a specific city. This way, when moving to a new city where a lot of different flats and possibilities of places to live are offered, the system will help to discriminate and select the ones that better fits the specific buyer. Another possible use could be the recommendation of specific videogames to concrete videogames players according to their tastes.

This article is structured as follows. In section 2, several concepts that the reader must be aware for a right understanding are explained. In section 3, specifications of the decision support system designed are exposed. In section 4, a brief use example of the designed system is showed. In section 5 the most important characteristics of our system are highlighted. Finally, some conclusions are pointed out.

2   Preliminaries

To make this paper as self-contained as possible, this section is introducing concepts and methods to be referred to thorough this paper. In section 2.1, basis of linguistic modelling are introduced and, in section 2.2, fuzzy ontologies are exposed.

2.1   Linguistic Modelling

The designed application use linguistic modelling [5–7] in order for users to provide its preferences and in order to store smartphones features in the fuzzy ontology. Linguistic modelling allow computers to work with concepts instead of numbers. Words like *high, medium, low* can be used for describing items instead of numerical values. This way of proceeding helps users to provide imprecise description values and allow them to represent information in a imprecise way, without being specific. For example, if users want to search for a smartphone that have a high amount of space, they are not asked to provide the exact amount of gigas that they want the smartphone to have, they can just submit a query that specify that they want the smarphone to have a lot of space on it.

Linguistic modelling is a methodology that lets users to express their preferences using linguistic variables instead of numbers. A linguistic variable is defined as a *variable whose values are not numbers but words in a natural or artificial language*. A linguistic value X is defined as a 5-tuple $\langle L, T(L), U, S, M \rangle$ where

- L is the variable name.
- $T(L)$ is a finite set of labels.
- U is the universe of discourse.
- S is the syntactic rule that generates terms in $T(L)$.
- M is a syntactic rule that associates, with each linguistic label X, its meaning $M(X)$ where $M(X)$ denotes a fuzzy subset of U.

A fuzzy set $M(X)$ of U express its meaning by its membership function $\mu_{M(X)} : U \rightarrow [0,1]$ where $\mu_{M(X)}(z)$ is interpreted as the degree of membership of element z in a fuzzy set $M(X)$ for each $z \in U$ [8].

A graphical example of a possible representation of the linguistic variable *Height* can be seen in Figure 1.

Recent information about linguistic modelling can be found in [9–11]. Although research in the linguistic modelling field is not a trendy topic in this moment, there is plenty of articles these days that use linguistic modelling in

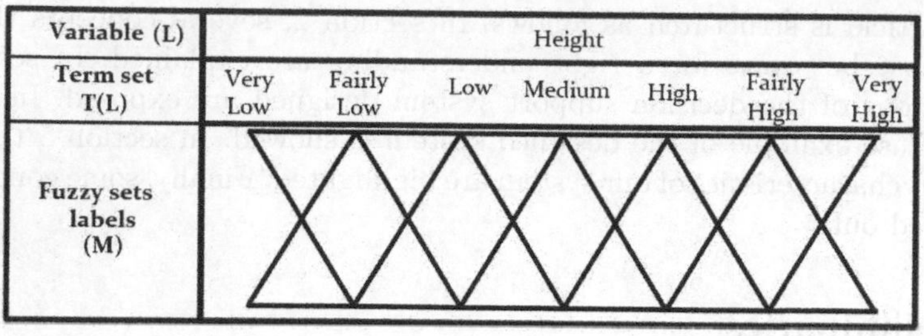

Variable (L)	Height						
Term set T(L)	Very Low	Fairly Low	Low	Medium	High	Fairly High	Very High
Fuzzy sets labels (M)							

Fig. 1. Representation of the linguistic variable *Height*

their designed systems and methodologies. For example, in decision support systems area, [12, 13] use linguistic modelling in order to deal with vague information. Linguistic modelling has also been previously used to improve ontologies as readers can see in references [14–16].

2.2 Fuzzy Ontologies

Ontologies are a quite flexible way of representing information. Nevertheless, they were built to represent precise information making them not suitable to represent imprecise information such as linguistic one. This way, mechanisms to make them able to deal with imprecise information are needed.

In order to overcome the exposed limitation, Fuzzy Ontologies were designed. A fuzzy ontology is a quintuple $O_F = \{I, C, R, F, A\}$ where:

- I is the individuals set.
- C is the set of concepts.
- R is the relations set.
- F is the set of fuzzy relation.
- A is the set of axiom.

It is important to point out that either imprecise concepts and exact ones can be included in a fuzzy ontology. A scheme of a fuzzy ontology can be seen in Figure 2.

In the designed system that deals with smartphones and their features, each of the variables will store the following information:

- I will be the set of all the possible smartphones.
- C will be the set of all the features related with the smartphones.
- F and R will allow the relation of each of the smartphones with the features defined in C.
- A is relation of each of the smartphones with the features defined.

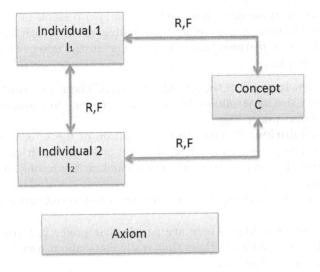

Fig. 2. Fuzzy ontology scheme

Fuzzy ontologies is a field that is quite present in the recent literature. For example, Jiang et al., in their article [17], use modular fuzzy ontologies for change management purposes. Bobillo and Straccia [18] has improved their $fuzzyDL$ software [19] in order to add features for handling fuzzy integrals. Finally, Zhang et al., in their articles [20, 21], have developed methods for building fuzzy ontologies from ERR and XML models. All the exposed articles are quite recent demonstrating that fuzzy ontologies is a field where innovations and applications are still being performed by researchers.

3   Method

In this section, specifications about the designed decision support system are exposed. In subsection 3.1, a brief explanation about how the smartphones fuzzy ontology has been built is exposed. In subsection 3.2, how the Decision support system works is explained.

3.1   The Smartphones Fuzzy Ontology

Information taken into account for providing recommendations to the buyers is stored in a fuzzy ontology called *The smarthpones fuzzy ontology*. This fuzzy ontology stores all the information about the smartphones available in the market in the recent moment. This way, information within it must be in constant update. This update can be done manually, what is clearly not recommended, or an automatic process that search for new models in the Internet, remove old ones and update the smartphones features values can be implemented.

Smartphones fuzzy ontology has one individual per possible mobile phone and one concept per feature. Axiom relates each individual with each feature and the degree. Smartphones features taken into account in the design of the ontology are the following ones:

- **Screen size:** Represents the size of the screen. There are people that prefer small screen size smartphones because they are easy to transport and there are others that prefer bigger size ones.
- **Screen resolution:** It refers to the definition of the screen. Some buyers can prefer a high resolution smartphone in order to watch videos and others probably do not care and prefer a normal or low resolution in order to decrease the price.
- **Processor speed:** Depending on the use, a fast speed processor could be needed.
- **Components quality:** There are people that prefer fast components although they are bad and others that really cares about quality in order for the smarphone to last long.
- **Brand:** In case the buyer want to search a specific brand. This concept is not fuzzy.
- **Capacity:** Smartphone capacity. Depending on the use there can be different preferences.
- **Price:** This will allow the search of smartphones that have specific prices.
- **Weight:** Smartphone weight. A light smartphone is more comfortable to transport that a heavy one but is likely to be more expensive.
- **Battery:** Type of battery that the smartphone has inside.

A linguistic label set of 5 elements $B = \{very\_low, low, medium, high, very\_high\}$ can be used for the representation of every fuzzy concept. For the sake of understanding, a linguistic label will be associated with every possible combination of concepts membership functions. For example, for the concept *Screen size*, the membership functions values combination will be as exposed in Table 1. It should be pointed out that Table 1 association is just and example and other associations are possible. The other concepts membership function values are defined using the same scheme.

More concepts could be included but, for the sake of simplicity, in the actual design, the previously specified ones were selected as they are thought to be the

Table 1. Label association for the concept screen size

Label	ssize_very_low	ssize_low	ssize_medium	ssize_high	ssize_very_high
very_low	1	0.75	0.25	0	0
low	0.75	1	0.75	0.25	0
medium	0.25	0.75	1	0.75	0.25
high	0	0.25	0.75	1	0.75
very_high	0	0	0.25	0.75	1

main ones that buyers use to care most when buying an smartphone. Because, for example, a *high capacity* will not mean the same today than in a few years, no specifications about which labels represents each values are given in this paper. That associations can be changed and updated as well as the rest of the fuzzy ontology.

3.2 Decision Support System Design

In this subsection, how the designed decision support system for recommending smarphones works is going to be described. The next steps are followed in a typical decision making process using this system:

1. **Preferences providing step**: Buyer provides his/her preferences according to the features that he/she wants the smartphone to has. Each feature is expressed using a linguistic label set of granularity 5. Only labels referring to features that the users are interested in should be specified. This way, the ontology search is related to the information that is cared by the buyer ignoring the rest.

2. **Ontology search**: Preferences provided by the buyer are used in order to retrieve the items from the ontology that better resembles what he/she is looking for. This process is done as follows:
   - Weights are associated to the specified features in order to determine which features are more important. This can be done by the user or, for the sake of simplicity, same importance can be given to all of the features.
   - All the provided information is given to the ontology reasoner.
   - The ontology reasoner could use an OWA operator [22] in order to retrieve the individuals from the smartphone ontology that better match to the environment specified by the buyer. It is possible to retrieve the n elements that better fits the query or return all the elements whose matching value is above an specific threshold. Any other aggregation operator is valid.

   For carrying out the described search process, *FuzzyDL* reasoner [19] could be used.

3. **Providing ranking step**: Each of the results are ordered and returned to the user using their matching value. Features of each of the results are showed to him/her. Thus, the final decision can be made over the returned results.

In Figure 3, a scheme of the exposed process is showed. In the following section, an use example that follow this process will be exposed.

4 Illustrative Example

In this section, for the sake of a better understanding, a brief use example of the designed system is exposed.

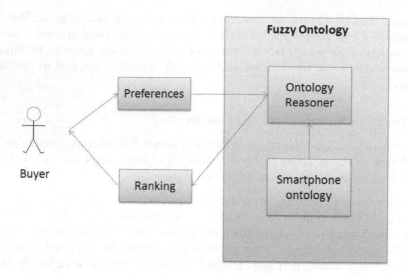

Fig. 3. Designed decision support system scheme

A buyer wants to get a new smartphone. First, he/she needs to provide to the system the specifications that he/she wants the smartphone to have. For this purpose, the linguistic label set $B = \{very\_low, low, medium, high, very\_high\}$ with a granularity of 5 exposed in subsection 3.1 is used. After thinking about it, he/she provides the following preferences:

- *screen size:* high.
- *Capacity:* low.
- *prize:* medium.

Because the buyer only consider important the exposed three features, the other possible ones are not taken into account. This way, the results can reach any value in the non-specified features. The next step consists in determine the real importance of each of the features to the user. In this case, the buyer determines that screen size is a more critical feature that capacity and capacity is more important to him/her than prize. This situation can be modelled in different ways. In this case, to apply the set of weights $w = \{0.43, 0.33, 0.23\}$ has been chosen. The reason is that this combination provides the same distance for each of the closer features.

Now that all the information is provided, the ontology search process is carried out. The calculated query is showed below:

$$Q = \{0.43 \cdot ssize\_high, 0.33 \cdot capacity\_low, 0.23 \cdot prize\_low\} \quad (1)$$

The query Q is introduced in the fuzzy ontology and matches are searched. In this example, for the sake of simplicity and clearness, the smartphone fuzzy ontology is only composed by 6 smartphones. Each of the items and their associated features values are showed in Table 2.

Table 2. Items $s_1 - s_6$ features values

Item	Screen size	Capacity	Prize
s_1	high	high	high
s_2	very low	low	low
s_3	low	high	medium
s_4	very low	very low	very low
s_5	very high	high	very high
s_6	high	very low	low

Matching value of the query specified by the user against every of the items features belonging to the smartphone fuzzy ontology is calculated using the weighted arithmetic mean operator. Results are showed in Table 3.

Table 3. Matching value calculation

Item	Operations	Result
s_1	$0.43 \cdot 1 + 0.33 \cdot 0.25 + 0.23 \cdot 0.25$	0.57
s_2	$0.43 \cdot 0 + 0.33 \cdot 1 + 0.23 \cdot 1$	0.56
s_3	$0.43 \cdot 0.25 + 0.33 \cdot 0.25 + 0.23 \cdot 0.25$	0.25
s_4	$0.43 \cdot 0 + 0.33 \cdot 0.75 + 0.23 \cdot 0.75$	0.42
s_5	$0.43 \cdot 0.75 + 0.33 \cdot 0.25 + 0.23 \cdot 0$	0.385
s_6	$0.43 \cdot 1 + 0.33 \cdot 0.75 + 0.23 \cdot 1$	0.9

Ranking of the 6 smartphones is as $s_6 \succ s_1 \succ s_2 \succ s_4 \succ s_5 \succ s_3$. Analysing the results, it can be observed that s_6 is the smartphone whose features values are closer to the desired by the buyer. Although s_2 have an acceptable capacity and price, it do not have the desired screen size. Since screen size was set by the buyer as the most important feature, that explains the low punctuation obtained.

5 Discussion

In this paper it has been proven that the designed Decision Support System with fuzzy ontologies is a great choice when trying to design a recommendation system that help users to make decisions when a high amount of alternatives are available. Instead of making a pair-to-pair comparison like in other articles [13, 23], fuzzy ontologies help the decision maker to select the alternative that is closest to his/her desired perfect choice. This way, only providing a small set of features values, the decision maker does not have to take a look over the features of a high amount of possibilities and compare them two by two in order to make his/her decision.

Thanks to linguistic modelling, the way that the user provides his/her preferences becomes easier. Being able to work with imprecise information allows the use of words instead of numbers releasing the user of the duty of providing very precise information that he/she is probably not able to provide. The use of imprecise information also improve a lot the system performance because it made it able to provide trustful result data even if the information provided is not well detailed. In real world problems, like the recommending one, it is very usual that humans are not able to provide all the information that the system requires, or, even if they provide all the information, this will not be as precise as the system desires. This way, it is extremely important for the system to provide the best possible result depending on the provided information. Our smartphone fuzzy ontology is able to make successful searches without specifying all the smartphones features and, also, it is capable of formulate interesting recommendations using only imprecise information.

In the future, we will carry out the following tasks in order to improve our work:

- Make implementations of the designed system in Android, IOS and in a Web Platform.
- Improve the smartphone fuzzy ontology with new features and items.
- Add feedback from the users to the smartphones recommended by the system. This way, if a buyer has bought an smartphone and he did not like it, he can provide that information to the system in order for the system to not recommend it if a lot of negative feedbacks have been received. The system will work the same in the other way around with positive punctuations.
- Prices and smartphones available are location-dependant. Our system could be improved in order to provide recommendation depending of where the buyer is located.
- Another interesting improvement could be the use of different linguistic term sets in order to represent each of the features. This way, each feature could be represented with a linguistic term set that have the granularity that better fits the possible ranges of its associated values.

6   Conclusions

In this paper, a decision support system for providing recommendations to buyers using fuzzy ontologies has been designed. This system allow them to provide their preferences using linguistic values and, in exchange, they get a ranking list of possible choices according to their tastes. In this article, the smartphone market has been used as an example of how this decision support system can be used for getting recommendation. The system must be up to date in order to acknowledge all the variations in the smartphone market. This way, automatic processes that surf the Internet and update the smartphone fuzzy ontology must be designed. Another issue to take into account is that information is stored using linguistic labels. This way, imprecise information can be represented and searched in a easy way. The search process performed by the buyers is flexible, any number of features among the available ones can be used to make the query, different weights can be given to the features and imprecise information is used. The fuzzy ontology is prepared to work with this kind of flexible searches and is always being able to return good quality results that are in concordance with the information provided.

References

1. Smith, A.: 46% of American adults are smartphone owners. Pew Internet & American Life Project (2012)
2. Sultan, A.J.: Addiction to mobile text messaging applications is nothing to "lol" about. The Social Science Journal 51(1), 57–69 (2013)
3. Kenney, M., Pon, B.: Structuring the smartphone industry: is the mobile internet OS platform the key? Journal of Industry, Competition and Trade 11(3), 239–261 (2011)
4. Kou, G., Shi, Y., Wang, S.: Multiple criteria decision making and decision support systems - Guest editor's introduction. Decision Support Systems 51(2), 247–249 (2011)
5. Zadeh, L.A.: The concept of a linguistic variable and its application to approximate reasoning-I. Information Sciences 8, 199–249 (1975)
6. Zadeh, L.A.: The concept of a linguistic variable and its application to approximate reasoning-II. Information Sciences 8, 301–357 (1975)
7. Zadeh, L.A.: The concept of a linguistic variable and its application to approximate reasoning-III. Information Sciences 9, 43–80 (1975)
8. Zadeh, L.A.: Fuzzy sets. Information and Control 8, 338–353 (1965)
9. Reformat, M., Ly, C.: Ontological approach to development of computing with words based systems. International Journal of Approximate Reasoning 50(1), 72–91 (2009)
10. Tang, Y., Zheng, J.: Linguistic modelling based on semantic similarity relation among linguistic labels. Fuzzy Sets and Systems 157(12), 1662–1673 (2006)
11. Tang, Y., Lawry, J.: Linguistic modelling and information coarsening based on prototype theory and label semantics. International Journal of Approximate Reasoning 50(8), 1177–1198 (2009)
12. Lan, J., Sun, Q., Chen, Q., Wang, Z.: Group decision making based on induced uncertain linguistic OWA operators. Decision Support System 55(1), 296–303 (2013)
13. Rodríguez, R.M., Martínez, L., Herrera, F.: A group decision making model dealing with comparative linguistic expressions based on hesitant fuzzy linguistic term sets. Information Sciences 241, 28–42 (2013)
14. Pérez, I.J., Wikström, R., Mezei, J., Carlsson, C., Anaya, K., Herrera-Viedma, E.: Linguistic Consensus Models based on a Fuzzy Ontology. Procedia Computer Science 17, 498–505 (2013)
15. Rodger, J.A.: A fuzzy linguistic ontology payoff method for aerospace real options valuation. Expert Systems with Applications 40(8), 2828–2840 (2013)
16. Bateman, J.A., Hois, J., Ross, R., Tenbrink, T.: A linguistic ontology of space for natural language processing. Artificial Intelligence 174(14), 1027–1071 (2010)

17. Jiang, Y., Tang, Y., Chen, Q., Wang, J.: Reasoning and change management in modular fuzzy ontologies. Expert Systems with Applications 38(11), 13975–13986 (2011)
18. Bobillo, F., Straccia, U.: Aggregation operators for fuzzy ontologies. Applied Soft Computing 13(9), 3816–3830 (2013)
19. Bobillo, F., Straccia, U.: fuzzyDL: An expressive fuzzy description logic reasoner. In: FUZZ-IEEE, pp. 923–930 (2008)
20. Zhang, F., Ma, Z.M., Yan, L.: Construction of fuzzy ontologies from fuzzy XML models. Knowledge-Based Systems 42, 20–39 (2013)
21. Zhang, F., Ma, Z.M., Yan, L., Cheng, J.: Construction of fuzzy OWL ontologies from fuzzy EER models: A semantics-preserving approach. Fuzzy Sets and Systems 229, 1–32 (2013)
22. Torra, V.: The weighted OWA operator. International Journal of Intelligent Systems 12(2), 153–166 (1997)
23. Perez, I.J., Cabrerizo, F.J., Alonso, S., Herrera-Viedma, E.: A New Consensus Model for Group Decision Making Problems With Non-Homogeneous Experts. IEEE Transactions on Systems, Man, and Cybernetics: Systems 44(4), 494–498 (2013)

An Intelligent System for Computer-Aided Ovarian Tumor Diagnosis

Krzysztof Dyczkowski[1], Andrzej Wójtowicz[1],
Patryk Żywica[1], Anna Stachowiak[1],
Rafał Moszyński[2], and Sebastian Szubert[2]

[1] Faculty of Mathematics and Computer Science
Adam Mickiewicz University
Umultowska 87, 61-614 Poznań, Poland
chris@amu.edu.pl
[2] Division of Gynecological Surgery
Poznan University of Medical Sciences
Polna 33, 60-535 Poznań, Poland
rafalmoszynski@gmail.com

Abstract. This article describes the fundamentals of an intelligent decision support system for the diagnosis of ovarian tumors. The system is designed to support diagnosis by less experienced gynecologists, and to gather data for continuous improvement of the quality of diagnosis. The theoretical basis for the construction of the system is the IF-sets framework, used to aggregate multiple decision-making methods, and simultaneously providing information about positive and negative diagnosis of a given tumor type.

1 Introduction

Recent statistics on ovarian tumors indicate that incidence and mortality rates are intolerably high. Estimated numbers of patients newly diagnosed with the condition, and of deaths, in all member countries of the European Union in 2012, stand at $45,000$ and $30,000$ respectively. In some countries the problem has already taken on dramatic proportions. For instance, in Poland the European age-standardized mortality rate per $100,000$ stands at 10.3, which is significantly higher than the European Union average of 7.4 [1].

There are several factors preventing a significant improve prognosis of ovarian cancer patients. Most of tumors are diagnosed in an advanced stage, which is due to the absence of symptoms at the beginning of the disease and the lack of effective screening. This leads to the fundamental issue which is deficiency in highly skilled gynecologists, especially in the field of ultrasonography. Recent research shows that in rural area, where the availability of such gynecologists is low, the number of difficult to diagnose cases is the same as in urbanized area [2].

The result of distinguishing between malignant and benign tumors provides answers to two significant questions: whether the patient needs surgery, and if so, who should perform it – a gynecological oncologist or a general gynecologist [3]. If a tumor is difficult to diagnose, the patient is referred to an external center. In such cases a precautionary laparotomy is performed, which could be avoided in favor of less invasive

© Springer International Publishing Switzerland 2015
D. Filev et al. (eds.), *Intelligent Systems' 2014*,
Advances in Intelligent Systems and Computing 323, DOI: 10.1007/978-3-319-11310-4_29

laparoscopy if the diagnosis were more certain. An initial misdiagnosis may lead to delayed diagnosis or to an operation by an inexperienced surgeon.

For this reason, there is a need to develop an effective preoperative model for inexperienced gynecologists. Two approaches have emerged in the last two decades, which aim to provide an approximate model of a subjective assessment [4]. The first approach is based on scoring systems, where points are assigned for the presence of certain features in the patient. If the total number of points exceeds a certain threshold, then malignancy of the tumor is indicated. This approach has resulted in a wide range of scoring systems [5–7].

The second approach involves the use of formal mathematical models. Many algorithms have been developed under the rule-based approach: they use not only sophisticated concepts such as rough sets [8] but also simpler schemes of reasoning [9]. By the use of machine learning techniques, researchers have developed solutions which take advantage of logistic regression [10,11], artificial neural networks [12,13], support vector machines and Bayesian networks [14,15]. Some attempts have also been made to use neuro-fuzzy networks in ovarian tumor diagnosis [16].

Intermediate approaches have been proposed in the form of the RMI model, which is a combination of a scoring system and a formal model [17], and in GI-RADS, which is a rule-based scoring system [18].

The authors of the above-mentioned scoring systems and models claim high overall prognostic accuracy for their predictive models, reaching as high as 95% and even 100% [6, 19]. Unfortunately, when these assumptions are subjected to external evaluation, it is found that in reality the efficacy of predictions rarely exceeds 90%, in case of either sensitivity or specificity [20, 21]. If we wish to achieve a significant decrease in the mortality rate, then results such as these will not be sufficient.

In this paper we present the detailed concept of OvaExpert – a complex system that is being developed by specialists in computer-aided decision making systems in cooperation with scientists from the Division of Gynecological Surgery at Poznan University of Medical Sciences. The system is intended to address the need for a highly reliable tool supporting less experienced gynecologists in the entire diagnostic process. Details of the motivations, functionality and architecture of this system will be presented in the following sections of this paper. We end by stating some conclusions and describing plans for future work.

2   Motivation

The need to improve the efficacy of preoperative differentiation of tumors is inspiring studies at many research centers. The most widely exploited approach is to develop new models using recent techniques from the fields of computational intelligence and machine learning. This is a very challenging task, because the conventional methods seem already to have attained their maximum performance. In our research we approach the problem differently. The main idea is to integrate all present knowledge about ovarian tumors (models, scoring systems, reasoning schemes, etc.) into a single computer-aided system. Access to a set of testing data and to extensive expert knowledge was our main motivation to take advantage of this experience and to integrate it so as to achieve a synergy effect.

It can be observed that there is a need to create a tool that can not only support a gynecologist in the final diagnosis, but can also assist him or her during the whole diagnostic process, beginning with collecting data about the patient, and moreover can connect the medical community in the exchange of experience and verification of knowledge. To the best of our knowledge such a system does not yet exist.

One of the main objectives of the proposed system would therefore be to provide an easy, convenient and coherent way of gathering data about patients and final diagnoses. At present, the absence of a common data format leads to a lack of cooperation between physicians and loss of data. Our system, by providing a convenient interface and a standardized data schema, enables the collection of data in a common database which can be browsed, reported and analyzed, and which will become a valuable resource for the entire medical community.

A core feature of the system is its modular architecture, described in detail in the next section. All existing and new methods for supporting ovarian tumor diagnosis can be plugged into the system as modules and then integrated to increase the reliability of diagnosis. One of the key modules would be a knowledge base of rules obtained directly from experts. By that means a knowledge repository would be created, and would then be continuously supplemented and updated by users of the system. Importantly, the system would also have the ability to learn through generating rules from the collected data.

The main issue with past solutions is their insensitivity to uncertainty of the input data. We have carried out research on uncertainty in ovarian tumor diagnosis and on the construction of classifiers on such data, and the results are very promising [22, 23]. We have found that consideration of an uncertainty factor has a crucial influence on the final diagnosis. Hence the next objective of the OvaExpert system is to properly grasp and process the uncertainty of the information received, and moreover, to present the results in the bipolar form. This makes it possible to preserve full information about the amount of uncertainty. More information about a mathematical model that includes uncertainty can be found in the next section.

3   System Overview

A standard approach to medical diagnosis involves the construction of criteria which allow one to identify the most adequate diagnosis. It is also possible to have criteria that exclude certain diagnoses. It is apparent that the diagnostic process can be modeled in bipolar fashion. On the one hand, the patient's condition can be modeled towards indication of a specific diagnosis, and on the other towards the exclusion of diagnoses that are certainly incorrect. In current medical applications the first approach is more frequently used, being by far the more natural (a physician is expected to make a diagnosis and begin treatment). For comprehensive computer-aided diagnosis support systems, evidence of the second type may also be important.

OvaExpert will use fuzzy logic and Atanassov's intuitionistic fuzzy sets [24–26] to model bipolarity in the diagnostic process as well as subjectivity, imprecision, uncertainty and even lack of knowledge about the results of diagnostic tests. These concepts are innovative in medicine, their use in the diagnosis having only been indicated as a possibility [16, 27, 28]. Their primary advantages are transparency and ease of comprehension of the principles, the ability to take into account knowledge derived both from experts and from data, and the built-in possibility of representation of uncertain information.

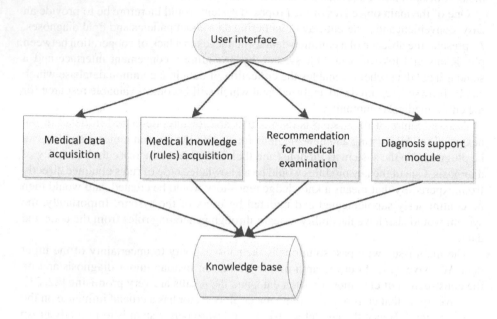

Fig. 1. The main components of the OvaExpert system

We briefly introduce the principles of the system and its main elements. The system covers four main areas (see Figure 1):

- Medical data acquisition;
- Gathering medical knowledge;
- Decision support in the process of selecting the optimal diagnostic path;
- Decision support in a making a final diagnosis.

3.1   Medical Data Acquisition

The system gathers knowledge about symptoms, results of medical examinations and final diagnoses for different types of tumors. These data are the basis for the whole diagnostic process. The system enables the entry of such data concerning patients via an online Web interface. This solution makes it possible to centralize the medical data entered by many experts from different centers, and thus to build a knowledge base about different medical cases and set up a continuous learning system. This also enables quality assessment of the diagnostic decisions taken by the system, performed by specialists from different medical centers.

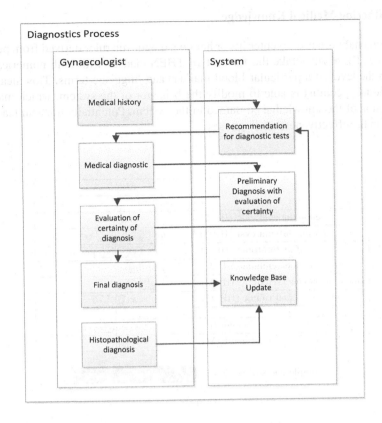

Fig. 2. Diagram of interaction between a physician and OvaExpert

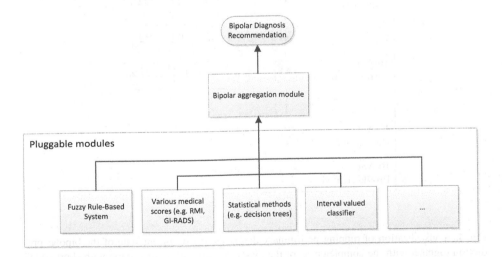

Fig. 3. Modular architecture of the OvaExpert diagnosis support component

3.2   Gathering Medical Knowledge

OvaExpert enables a user to enter his or her own diagnostic rules derived from personal experience. These rules take the form of IF-THEN clauses with both numerical (e.g. based on the level of a particular blood marker) and linguistic terms. This means that an individual specialist is able to modify the behavior of the system, which may lead to expansion of the knowledge contained in the system. Potentially this can lead to an increase in the effectiveness of diagnoses.

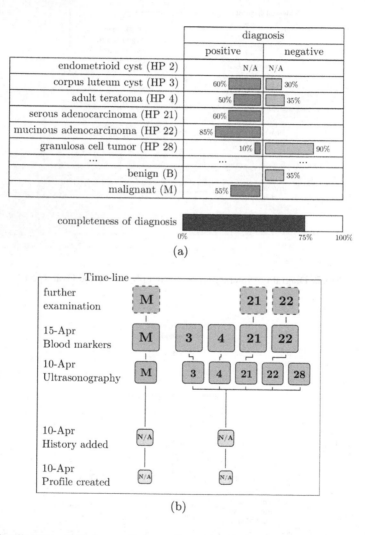

(a)

(b)

Fig. 4. A visualization of running preliminary diagnosis. (a) A current state of the bipolar prediction together with the completeness of the diagnosis. (b) A time-line graph with short-coded possible diagnoses at given state and possible diagnoses which may be achieved with further examinations.

3.3   Decision Support in the Process of Selecting the Optimal Diagnostic Path

The diagnostic process begins with a medical history entered by the doctor. It then continues through several stages, where further medical examinations are made. Each of them provides additional knowledge for the diagnostic process (e.g. levels of blood markers, ultrasound descriptions, etc). The process runs iteratively. At each stage OvaExpert computes a bipolar recommendation for diagnosis. On the basis of that recommendation the doctor must decide what further tests should be carried out to substantiate the final diagnosis. The system supports the selection of the optimal diagnostic path. This is done by utilizing knowledge from retrospective data (e.g. statistical methods such as decision trees) as well as from fuzzy rules introduced into the system by experts. Interaction with the physician is presented in Figure 2.

3.4   Decision Support in Making a Final Diagnosis

The system is designed so that it is possible to add new diagnostic modules at any time. In order to provide a physician with the best recommendation of a final diagnosis, the system synthesizes various methods (modules) such as statistical, fuzzy, diagnostic scales, etc. The system utilizes the IF-sets framework, hence it is possible to aggregate the results of many models into a single diagnosis represented in the form of bipolar information. Dealing with such information requires use of appropriate tools such as similarity measures for incompletely known fuzzy sets [29]. A gynecologist, at each stage of the diagnostic process, will receive a set of possible diagnoses for a particular type of tumor, with an indication of how probable it is that the diagnosis is correct and how probable that it is not. A diagram of the support module is shown in Figure 3. The diagnostic process will be visualized in a readable form (see Figure 4).

4   Conclusions

In this project we take advantage of all of the benefits of computational intelligence, which are complementary to the methods of machine learning (see [30]). We plan to give a broader context to the parameters which describe the patient. OvaExpert will consider the subjectivity, imprecision, uncertainty and even lack of knowledge about the results of diagnostic tests obtained from a gynecologist.

The resulting system will set a new pioneering in the development of ovarian tumor diagnosis. We believe that work on the problem of ovarian tumor diagnosis should use not only machine learning techniques, but also computational intelligence and data mining. The project is part of the current trend in interdisciplinary research, producing results that will be of interest to both physicians and mathematicians.

References

[1] Ferlay, J., Steliarova-Foucher, E., Lortet-Tieulent, J., Rosso, S., Coebergh, J., Comber, H., Forman, D., Bray, F.: Cancer incidence and mortality patterns in Europe: estimates for 40 countries in 2012. European Journal of Cancer 49(6), 1374–1403 (2013)

[2] Szpurek, D., Moszyński, R., Szubert, S., Sajdak, S.: Urban and rural differences in characteristics of ovarian cancer patients. Annals of Agricultural and Environmental Medicine 20(2), 390–394 (2013)

[3] du Bois, A., Rochon, J., Pfisterer, J., Hoskins, W.J.: Variations in institutional infrastructure, physician specialization and experience, and outcome in ovarian cancer: A systematic review. Gynecologic Oncology 112(2), 422–436 (2009)

[4] Timmerman, D., Schwärzler, P., Collins, W., Claerhout, F., Coenen, M., Amant, F., Vergote, I., Bourne, T.: Subjective assessment of adnexal masses with the use of ultrasonography: an analysis of interobserver variability and experience. Ultrasound in Obstetrics & Gynecology 13(1), 11–16 (1999)

[5] DePriest, P., Shenson, D., Fried, A., Hunter, J., Andrews, S., Gallion, H., Pavlik, E., Kryscio, R., et al.: A morphology index based on sonographic findings in ovarian cancer. Gynecologic Oncology 51(1), 7–11 (1993)

[6] Alcázar, J.L., Mercé, L.T., Laparte, C., Jurado, M., López-Garcia, G.: A new scoring system to differentiate benign from malignant adnexal masses. Obstetrical & Gynecological Survey 58(7), 462–463 (2003)

[7] Szpurek, D., Moszyński, R., Ziętkowiak, W., Spaczyński, M., Sajdak, S.: An ultrasonographic morphological index for prediction of ovarian tumor malignancy. European Journal of Gynaecological Oncology 26(1), 51–54 (2005)

[8] Moszyński, R.: Evaluation of usefulness of rough set theory in diagnostics of ovarian tumors. Doctoral thesis at the Poznan University of Medical Sciences (2003)

[9] Timmerman, D., Testa, A.C., Bourne, T., Ameye, L., Jurkovic, D., Van Holsbeke, C., Paladini, D., Van Calster, B., Vergote, I., Van Huffel, S., et al.: Simple ultrasound-based rules for the diagnosis of ovarian cancer. Ultrasound in Obstetrics & Gynecology 31(6), 681–690 (2008)

[10] Timmerman, D., Testa, A.C., Bourne, T., Ferrazzi, E., Ameye, L., Konstantinovic, M.L., Van Calster, B., Collins, W.P., Vergote, I., Van Huffel, S., et al.: Logistic regression model to distinguish between the benign and malignant adnexal mass before surgery: a multicenter study by the International Ovarian Tumor Analysis Group. Journal of Clinical Oncology 23(34), 8794–8801 (2005)

[11] Moore, R.G., McMeekin, D.S., Brown, A.K., DiSilvestro, P., Miller, M.C., Allard, W.J., Gajewski, W., Kurman, R., Bast Jr., R.C., Skates, S.J.: A novel multiple marker bioassay utilizing HE4 and CA125 for the prediction of ovarian cancer in patients with a pelvic mass. Gynecologic Oncology 112(1), 40–46 (2009)

[12] Tailor, A., Jurkovic, D., Bourne, T.H., Collins, W.P., Campbell, S.: Sonographic prediction of malignancy in adnexal masses using an artificial neural network. BJOG: An International Journal of Obstetrics & Gynaecology 106(1), 21–30 (1999)

[13] Smoleń, A., Czekierdowski, A., Stachowicz, N., Kotarski, J.: Use of multilayer perception artificial neutral networks for the prediction of the probability of malignancy in adnexal tumors. Ginekologia Polska 74(9), 855–862 (2003)

[14] Van Calster, B., Timmerman, D., Lu, C., Suykens, J.A., Valentin, L., Van Holsbeke, C., Amant, F., Vergote, I., Van Huffel, S.: Preoperative diagnosis of ovarian tumors using Bayesian kernel-based methods. Ultrasound in Obstetrics & Gynecology 29(5), 496–504 (2007)

[15] Van Calster, B., Timmerman, D., Nabney, I.T., Valentin, L., Testa, A.C., Van Holsbeke, C., Vergote, I., Van Huffel, S.: Using Bayesian neural networks with ARD input selection to detect malignant ovarian masses prior to surgery. Neural Computing and Applications 17(5-6), 489–500 (2008)

[16] Madu, E., Stalbovskaya, V., Hamadicharef, B., Ifeachor, E., Van Huffel, S., Timmerman, D.: Preoperative ovarian cancer diagnosis using neuro-fuzzy approach. In: European Conference on Emergent Aspects on Clinical Data Analysis (2005)

[17] Tingulstad, S., Hagen, B., Skjeldestad, F.E., Onsrud, M., Kiserud, T., Halvorsen, T., Nustad, K.: Evaluation of a risk of malignancy index based on serum CA125, ultrasound findings and menopausal status in the pre-operative diagnosis of pelvic masses. BJOG: An International Journal of Obstetrics & Gynaecology 103(8), 826–831 (1996)

[18] Amor, F., Vaccaro, H., Alcázar, J.L., León, M., Craig, J.M., Martinez, J.: Gynecologic imaging reporting and data system a new proposal for classifying adnexal masses on the basis of sonographic findings. Journal of Ultrasound in Medicine 28(3), 285–291 (2009)

[19] Timmerman, D., Bourne, T.H., Tailor, A., Collins, W.P., Verrelst, H., Vandenberghe, K., Vergote, I.: A comparison of methods for preoperative discrimination between malignant and benign adnexal masses: the development of a new logistic regression model. American Journal of Obstetrics and Gynecology 181(1), 57–65 (1999)

[20] Valentin, L., Hagen, B., Tingulstad, S., Eik-Nes, S.: Comparison of 'pattern recognition' and logistic regression models for discrimination between benign and malignant pelvic masses: a prospective cross validation. Ultrasound in Obstetrics & Gynecology 18(4), 357–365 (2001)

[21] Van Holsbeke, C., Van Calster, B., Valentin, L., Testa, A.C., Ferrazzi, E., Dimou, I., Lu, C., Moerman, P., Van Huffel, S., Vergote, I., et al.: External validation of mathematical models to distinguish between benign and malignant adnexal tumors: a multicenter study by the International Ovarian Tumor Analysis Group. Clinical Cancer Research 13(15), 4440–4447 (2007)

[22] Wójtowicz, A., Żywica, P., Szarzyński, K., Moszyński, R., Szubert, S., Dyczkowski, K., Stachowiak, A., Szpurek, D., Wygralak, M.: Dealing with Uncertainty in Ovarian Tumor Diagnosis (to appear, 2014)

[23] Stachowiak, A., Żywica, P., Dyczkowski, K., Wójtowicz, A.: An Interval-Valued Fuzzy Classifier Based on an Uncertainty-Aware Similarity Measure. In: Advances in Intelligent Systems and Computing (to appear, 2014)

[24] Zadeh, L.A.: Fuzzy logic and approximate reasoning. Synthese 30(3-4), 407–428 (1975)

[25] Wygralak, M.: Intelligent Counting Under Information Imprecision. STUDFUZZ, vol. 292. Springer, Heidelberg (2013)

[26] Atanassov, K.T.: Intuitionistic fuzzy sets. STUDFUZZ, vol. 35. Springer, Heidelberg (1999)

[27] De, S.K., Biswas, R., Roy, A.R.: An application of intuitionistic fuzzy sets in medical diagnosis. Fuzzy Sets and Systems 117(2), 209–213 (2001)

[28] Szmidt, E., Kacprzyk, J.: An intuitionistic fuzzy set based approach to intelligent data analysis: an application to medical diagnosis. In: Abraham, A., Jain, L.C., Kacprzyk, J. (eds.) Recent Advances in Intelligent Paradigms and Applications. STUDFUZZ, vol. 113, pp. 57–70. Springer, Heidelberg (2003)

[29] Stachowiak, A., Dyczkowski, K.: A similarity measure with uncertainty for incompletely known fuzzy sets. In: 2013 Joint IFSA World Congress and NAFIPS Annual Meeting (IFSA/NAFIPS), pp. 390–394. IEEE (2013)

[30] Kruse, R., Borgelt, C., Klawonn, F., Moewes, C., Steinbrecher, M., Held, P.: Computational Intelligence: A Methodological Introduction. Springer (2013)

On Advantages of a Fuzzy Approach to a Diagnosis Support

Ewa Straszecka

Institute of Electronics, Faculty of Automatic Control, Electronics and Computer
Science, Silesian University of Technology, 16 Akademicka St., 44-100 Gliwice
ewa.straszecka@polsl.pl

Abstract. In the paper the problem of norm limits of laboratory tests
used in probabilistic and fuzzy approach to diagnosis support is discussed. The fuzzy approach is proposed as the Dempster-Shafer theory
extended for fuzzy focal elements. A simple diagnostic problem is simulated for the both approaches and results are commented. Conclusions
from the simulation are used to determine the set of rules for a benchmark database. Both the simulation and calculations for the benchmark
confirm that a fuzzy interpretation of norm limits can improve a diagnosis.

Keywords: Dempster-Shafer theory of evidence, fuzzy sets, diagnosis
support.

1 Introduction

A diagnosis can be supported by means of variety of methods. However, if its
aim is not limited exclusively to indicating a diagnosis, but also in explaining
diagnostic knowledge, the priority should be admit to rule-based systems. Still,
the rules have to be provided with weights as well as diagnostic hypotheses must
be estimated by certainty factors. To this end, most often probability or fuzzy
sets are introduced. A probabilistic approach seems to be the most appropriate,
since the nature of the problem is probabilistic, hence the Bayes classifier should
ensure the minimal error [7]. Yet a, diagnosis support based on fuzzy set theory considerably developed in the last decade (more than 1300 publications in
comparison to 650 publications of probabilistic approach according to the IEEE
Xplore®). Indeed, a preference of a type of reasoning is rarely a matter of choice
of support tools designers. It is rather a necessity forced by a diagnostic problem formulation and accessibility of statistical information, expert knowledge or
medical guidelines. Conditions of the choice have barely changed trough years [4],
but fuzzy methods are usually applicable in cases when probabilistic reasoning
is performed. Since fuzzy methods have gained confidence as practically reliable
algorithms, a question arises if they should not be a 'treatment of choice', even if
conditional probabilities necessary for Bayes formula can be estimated. The aim
of this paper is to compare properties of probability and fuzzy based approaches
to a solution of a simple diagnostic task. It is assumed that the approaches must

© Springer International Publishing Switzerland 2015
D. Filev et al. (eds.), *Intelligent Systems'2014*,
Advances in Intelligent Systems and Computing 323, DOI: 10.1007/978-3-319-11310-4_30

use knowledge and data which are available from medical practice. Therefore, the suggested methods are not exactly these which are proposed in references [3], [7], but join their general ideas with conditions of practical diagnostic tasks. Diagnostic problem is divided for separate situations to allow using conditional probabilities that are relatively easy available. Diagnostic rules differ from classical fuzzy rules, since their conclusions are crisp. Therefore, a method employing the Dempster-Shafer theory with focal elements defined as fuzzy sets is proposed for the fuzzy approach.

The presented example is based on an interpretation of laboratory test results, for which both norms and a frequency of occurrence of results in above and under norm intervals can be easily obtained. Knowledge formulation in the approaches is similar, but (at least according to the author) expresses their individual features. The example employs simulated data to create an opportunity for the differences analysis. Still, conclusions drawn from the simulation are used to create a set of rules for a benchmark database of thyroid gland diseases. A limited number of obtained rules as well as a decrease of a diagnosis error confirm an efficiency of the proposed solution.

2   Two Approaches to Medical Diagnosis Support

2.1   Medical Diagnosis Based on Laboratory Test Results

Great part of the medical diagnosis lies in laboratory test results analysis. Each test has a norm given as a point or, more often, as an interval. For the simplicity of the problem analysis, let us assume that the norm is a point which is a border between results for ill and healthy persons. This point is obtained by a statistical analysis that results in comparison of distributions of the test results among healthy and ill, which can be for instance as in Fig.1, left diagram. If such points are perfectly valid for all tests, the diagnosis is entirely based on the tests and tests results are not dependent then probabilistic reasoning is the most appropriate. However, the problem is that the statistical analysis is performed only once, when the laboratory test is introduced. In Fig.1 the situation of the 'ill' diagnosis is interpreted. It is obvious, that while establishing the norm point, the false positive (FP) classification of some results cannot be omitted. We can only try to use such diagnostic tests for which it is minimal. The same concern the 'healthy' diagnosis. Thus, the norm point is set at the intersection of distributions of 'ill' and 'healthy'. Still, little change of the distribution (i.e. population characteristics) may alter the norm. Thus, a physician should not reject the test as a disease symptom, even if its result is very slightly lower than the norm point. A little change of the norm is not significant if physicians diagnose patients because they use their experience in interpretation of norms. Yet, if an artificial intelligence system advises in the diagnosis, the norm shift should be taken into account. If we rely diagnosis on a precision measure, for instance a membership function, we can perform reasoning on different levels of precision, even if the norm point is the same as previously (Fig.1, right). It is possible without changing membership functions. If we agree to perform reasoning on a

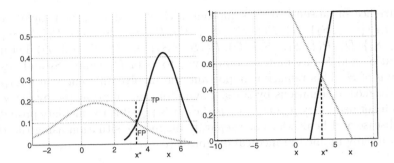

Fig. 1. An interpretation of laboratory test results by means of probability (left) and membership function (right). Curves for the 'ill' diagnosis are denoted by solid lines and for 'healthy' by dotted lines. The norm point is x^*.

low level of precision, we can move the norm limit left until the zero value of 'ill' membership function is achieved. At the same time we move right the norm limit for 'healthy'. Still, we are aware of the level of precision of our consideration. A question arises, if this 'freedom of interpretation' destroys the diagnosis or, on the contrary, make better chances for the correct diagnosis.

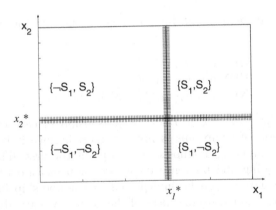

Fig. 2. Diagnostic situations set by the norm points x_1^* and x_2^*

2.2   An Approached Based on Probability

Let us consider the diagnosis on an example of two tests: x_1 and x_2 and their norm points x_1^* and x_2^*. If we define the S_i symptom as $x_i \geq x_i^*$ and its negation $(\neg S_i)$ as $x_i < x_i^*$ then the following diagnostic situations are possible (see Fig.2): $\{\neg S_1, \neg S_2\}$, $\{\neg S_1, S_2\}$, $\{S_1, \neg S_2\}$ and $\{S_1, S_2\}$. Borders of the situations are created by the norms, which are strict (one-point) for probability (solid lines in Fig.2). Usually, the only available diagnostic information is the frequency of occurrence or absence of a symptom with ill and healthy people. Hence, we know $P(\{\neg S_1, S_2\}/H)$, $P(\{\neg S_1, \neg S_2\}/H)$, $P(\{S_1, \neg S_2\}/H)$, $P(\{S_1, S_2\}/H)$, $P(\{\neg S_1, S_2\}/D)$, $P(\{\neg S_1, \neg S_2\}/D)$, $P(\{S_1, \neg S_2\}/D)$, $P(\{S_1, S_2\}/D)$. Let us notice, that S_1 and S_2 are understood as symptoms of D, while $\neg S_1$ and $\neg S_2$ are symptoms of H. This remark is important and involve differences in interpretation of diagnostic situations by rules, if symptoms are represented by fuzzy sets, for which not necessary $\mu_H(x) = 1 - \mu_D(x)$. It is possible to calculate probability of the disease and health for each separate diagnostic situation using the Bayes formula usually applied in medical diagnosis (e.g.[7]):

$$P(d/s) = \frac{P(s/d)P(d)}{P(s/d)P(d) + P(s/\neg d)P(\neg d)}; P(\neg d) = 1 - P(d); \qquad (1)$$

where s stands for the diagnostic situation, d for the diagnosis and $\neg D = H$.

Since the diagnostic situations are disjoint, the probability of the disease and health can be determined using (1) for the observed case. The diagnosis will be indicated by the greater probability, unless the values are equal and the diagnosis is not stated.

2.3 A Fuzzy Approach - The Dempster-Shafer Theory with Fuzzy Focal Elements

Fuzzy sets and their membership functions can be used to formulate diagnostic rules:

- IF x_1 is $\mu_d(x_1)$ THEN diagnosis is d
- IF x_2 is $\mu_d(x_2)$ THEN diagnosis is d
- IF x_1 is $\mu_d(x_1)$ AND x_2 is $\mu_d(x_2)$ THEN diagnosis is d

There are only three diagnostic rules, as it is usual in case of fuzzy reasoning, where negation of symptoms is not considered, since it is understood as a symptom of a competing diagnosis. In this point the first difference between probabilistic reasoning and inference using precision measures can be noticed. The diagnostic situations can be interpreted by membership functions. Thick dashed lines in Fig.2 illustrate fuzziness of the norms. We are able to create the membership functions $\mu_H(x_1)$, $\mu_H(x_2)$, $\mu_D(x_1)$, $\mu_D(x_2)$, for instance by means of histograms of symptom's occurrence [8].

The diagnostic rules differ from the classical fuzzy rules since they have crisp conclusions. Thus, it is proposed to represent them in the framework of the Dempster-Shafer theory of evidence [2] with an extension for fuzzy focal elements. The extension is presented in more details in [8], [9] and [10]. Here only the necessary concepts and notations are introduced.

In the Dempster-Shafer theory of evidence (DST) a set $\mathbf{S}$ of focal elements S_i, $i = 1, \ldots, n$ is determined, for which the basic probability assignment (bpa) is defined as [5]:

$$m_d(f) = 0, \qquad \sum_{S_i \in \mathbf{S},\, i=1,\ldots,n} m_d(S_i) = 1, \qquad (2)$$

where f denotes the false element, interpreted as a lack of symptoms. A dependence of the focal elements is ignored. In the diagnostic problem S_i may denote symptoms and m_d the probability assignment calculated for the d diagnosis as the normalized frequency of their occurrence. If the S_i elements are representations of symptoms 'x_i is $\mu_d(x_i)$', it must be determined for which values of membership, i.e. for which precision level it is decided that $S_i \in \mathbf{S}$. Thus, a threshold η_{bpa} must be used in the (2) definition, which involves its change into [8]:

$$m_d(f) = 0, \qquad \sum_{\substack{S_i \in \mathbf{S},\ i=1,\ldots,n \\ \eta_i > \eta_{bpa}}} m_d(S_i) = 1, \qquad (3)$$

where η_i is the membership value for occurring test result. The $m_d(S_i)$ is the weight of the rule: IF x_i is $\mu_d(x_i)$ THEN diagnosis is d.

The belief (Bel) of the d diagnosis can be calculated using the m_d (3) as knowledge about symptoms of the disease and health. For the observed case, for which membership $\eta_i = \mu_d(x_i)$ exceeds η_T, the belief is [9]:

$$Bel(d, \eta_T) = \sum_{\substack{S_i \in \mathbf{S} \\ \eta_i > \eta_T}} m_d(S_i), \qquad (4)$$

The plausibility of the diagnosis can be calculated in the similar way [9], but for the clarity and briefness of the example only belief is used for the diagnosis estimation. The belief can be calculated for different diagnostic hypotheses and the hypothesis with its maximal value becomes the final diagnosis. If the maximal value is not unique than the diagnosis is not stated.

3   Simulated Data

Let us assume that the diagnosis is based on values of two tests (variables): x_1 and x_2, as it was explained in subsection 2.1. Values of the variables are generated by Matlab® normal distribution generator. Four kinds of normally distributed samples with the mean ($\bar{\epsilon}$) and variance (σ), i.e. $N(\bar{\epsilon}_i, \sigma_i)$, are used: $\epsilon_1 = 1$, $\sigma_1 = 1$, $\epsilon_2 = 1$, $\sigma_2 = 2$, $\epsilon_3 = 1$, $\sigma_3 = 3$, $\epsilon_4 = 5$, $\sigma_4 = 1$. Each time the D diagnosis is characterized by the $N(\epsilon_4, \sigma_4)$ distribution (for both variables), while samples for the H diagnosis have different distributions. Such a choice of data should be sufficient to test influence of variables on the diagnoses, since a source of a diagnostic error is an overlay of distributions that cause false positive/negative diagnosis of cases. The overlay area is different in the proposed diagnostic situations. Six diagnostic situations are modeled:

- x_1 is $N(\bar{\epsilon}_1, \sigma_1)$, x_2 is $N(\bar{\epsilon}_1, \sigma_1)$ then diagnosis is H
  x_1 is $N(\bar{\epsilon}_4, \sigma_4)$ and x_2 is $N(\bar{\epsilon}_4, \sigma_4)$ then diagnosis is D
- x_1 is $N(\bar{\epsilon}_1, \sigma_1)$, x_2 is $N(\bar{\epsilon}_2, \sigma_2)$ then diagnosis is H
  x_1 is $N(\bar{\epsilon}_4, \sigma_4)$ and x_2 is $N(\bar{\epsilon}_4, \sigma_4)$ then diagnosis is D

  – x_1 is $N(\bar{e}_1, \sigma_1)$, x_2 is $N(\bar{e}_3, \sigma_3)$ then diagnosis is H
     x_1 is $N(\bar{e}_4, \sigma_4)$ and x_2 is $N(\bar{e}_4, \sigma_4)$ then diagnosis is D

  – x_1 is $N(\bar{e}_2, \sigma_2)$, x_2 is $N(\bar{e}_2, \sigma_2)$ then diagnosis is H
     x_1 is $N(\bar{e}_4, \sigma_4)$ and x_2 is $N(\bar{e}_4, \sigma_4)$ then diagnosis is D
  – x_1 is $N(\bar{e}_2, \sigma_2)$, x_2 is $N(\bar{e}_3, \sigma_3)$ then diagnosis is H
     x_1 is $N(\bar{e}_4, \sigma_4)$ and x_2 is $N(\bar{e}_4, \sigma_4)$ then diagnosis is D

  – x_1 is $N(\bar{e}_3, \sigma_3)$, x_2 is $N(\bar{e}_3, \sigma_3)$ then diagnosis is H
     x_1 is $N(\bar{e}_4, \sigma_4)$ and x_2 is $N(\bar{e}_4, \sigma_4)$ then diagnosis is D

Such an organization of data makes it possible to observe an influence of variable values and diagnostic rules weights on a diagnostic error without complex calculations which raise difficulties in intuitive interpretation of results. The latter is crucial to understand the differences in inference by means of probability and precision measures and to learn what to expect from each of the method. An example of samples of x_1 and x_2 values generated for the both diagnoses are shown in Fig. 3. Although samples originate from the same distribution, they are not correlated (correlation coefficient < 0.1). Normality of the samples is verified by the Matlab® Liliefors test. In this way 50 samples for each distribution and each considered diagnosis are built. Each sample includes 200 cases of each diagnosis. The samples are used for crossover validation process (each with all others). Membership functions for fuzzy focal elements are made using the

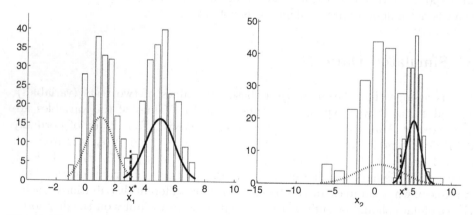

Fig. 3. Histograms of data samples for x_1, x_2 variables in comparison to rescaled Gaussian distributions N(1,1), N(5,1) (left) and N(1,3), N(5,1). Solid lines denote distributions concerning the D disease, while dotted lines characterize distributions of the H diagnosis.

method described in [8], which main property is that membership functions of competing diagnoses intersect at 0.5 level. They are presented in Fig.4.

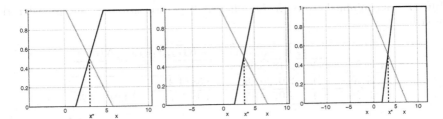

Fig. 4. Examples of membership functions obtained from training samples of different distributions: N(1,1) and N(5,1) (left), N(1,2) and N(5,1) (middle) N(1,3) and N(5,1) (right).

4   The Benchmark Database

A number of symptoms in medical benchmark databases is great enough to prevent the classical conditional probability approach. This method should not be advised also for the chosen database. The experiment with this data is relevant to the conclusion drawn from simulations. As it will be expalined in the next section, it turned out for the fuzzy approach that rules which are fired for the cases of the same distribution do not improve the diagnosis. Thus, an attempt to test a rule set reduction was made. To this end the benchmark database [11] was used. The database concerns three diagnoses of the thyroid gland states: euthyroidism (H, the state of normal level of thyroid hormones), hyperthyroidism (D_1, hormone levels indicate excessive thyroid function) and hypothyroidism (D_2, hormone levels signify impaired thyroid function). The database include 5 variables which are laboratory tests, thus the database exactly meets the analyzed problem. The number of cases is 150, 35 and 30 respectively for the diagnoses. The whole database was used as the train and the test set to compare results of different manners of rules reduction.

5   Results

The tables 1 and 2 summarize results of the cross-reference procedure for simulated data. Errors are calculated as a ratio of wrongly classified cases to the number of all cases in [%]. For the fuzzy approach thresholds η_{bpa} and η_T were modified to minimize errors of the train and test samples couple. The x^* norm point is set each time for a training sample (probabilistic approch) and to construct membership functions for fuzzy focal elements. Next the norms, conditional probabilities obtained from the training sample, as well as the membership functions and bpas are used as knowledge to diagnose a training sample.

In the tables it is observable, that the mean and the minimal error are the same for both approaches if both variables x_1 and x_2 have the same distributions. Apparently, both symptoms support a diagnosis in the same way and an error caused by one of the symptoms cannot be corrected by the other. However, if distributions of cases are different for the symptoms, errors for the fuzzy appoach

Table 1. Mean/minimal errors [%] for different diagnostic situations and probabilistic approach

	x_2 is $N(\bar{\epsilon}_1, \sigma_1)$	x_2 is $N(\bar{\epsilon}_2, \sigma_2)$	x_2 is $N(\bar{\epsilon}_3, \sigma_3)$
x_1 is $N(\bar{\epsilon}_1, \sigma_1)$	2.18/0.05	–	–
x_1 is $N(\bar{\epsilon}_2, \sigma_2)$	2.03/0.75	8.58/4.25	–
x_1 is $N(\bar{\epsilon}_3, \sigma_3)$	2.07/0.05	5.98/3.75	13.21/10.25

Table 2. Mean/minimal errors [%] for different diagnostic situations and fuzzy approach

	x_2 is $N(\bar{\epsilon}_1, \sigma_1)$	x_2 is $N(\bar{\epsilon}_2, \sigma_2)$	x_2 is $N(\bar{\epsilon}_3, \sigma_3)$
x_1 is $N(\bar{\epsilon}_1, \sigma_1)$	2.18/0.05	–	–
x_1 is $N(\bar{\epsilon}_2, \sigma_2)$	1.21/0.00	8.58/4.25	–
x_1 is $N(\bar{\epsilon}_3, \sigma_3)$	1.35/0.00	3.90/1.50	13.21/10.25

are smaller in all diagnostic situations. This may indicate that it is worth to use the proposed fuzzy approach to support a diagnosis.

Another evidence that a reasoning at different precision levels can improve diagnosis are thresholds for which the minimal errors were obtained. For the diagonal of Tab.2 the $\eta_{bpa} = 0.1$, $\eta_T = 0.5$. Equal value for all samples and the reasoning threshold equal 0.5 that determines x^* as the point of norm indicate, that if significance of all symptoms are the same, the fuzzy approach will not be better than probabilistic calculation. Certainly, the former will never be better than the latter if a sample always is an ideal model of the distribution. Still, it never happens – neither in simulation nor in practice. The other three results in Tab.2 were obtained for $\eta_{bpa} = 0.2$, $\eta_T = 0.4$ (x_1 is $N(\bar{\epsilon}_2, \sigma_2)$, x_2 is $N(\bar{\epsilon}_1, \sigma_1)$); $\eta_{bpa} = 0.4$, $\eta_T = 0.3$ (x_1 is $N(\bar{\epsilon}_3, \sigma_3)$, x_2 is $N(\bar{\epsilon}_1, \sigma_1)$) and $\eta_{bpa} = 0.9$, $\eta_T = 0.2$ (x_1 is $N(\bar{\epsilon}_3, \sigma_3)$, x_2 is $N(\bar{\epsilon}_2, \sigma_2)$). It is observed that the greater is the overlay area of the distributions, i.e. the less reliable is the x_i^* norm point, the higher η_{bpa} and the lower η_T is used for the best results.

The observation that another symptom, which is in the same relation to the norm point as the previous one, does not improve a diagnosis drawn the author's attention to the problem of a reduction of rules in the proposed fuzzy approach. If two rules have the same bpa values it may be profitable to leave only one of them. This will make reasoning quicker and allow the other symptoms for a greater influence on the diagnosis. This remark was tested for the chosen benchmark database [11].

For this database the complete set of rules was created and next the rules were eliminated in two manners. In the first manner, gradually rules of the minimal bpa were one by one removed. In the second manner, only one rule (a 'reference rule') out of several, with similar bpa values, was left after each deletion. Similar values meant that the difference between the bpa of a rule and a reference rule was not greater than the difference between the minimal and the second minimal bpa values. Slightly different sets of rules were obtained for the both elimination manners, which bpas are shown in Fig.5. The bpas were

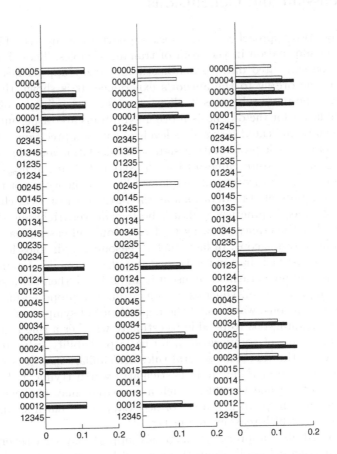

Fig. 5. Values of bpa for the first (white bar) and the second (black bar) rule elimination manner. Each subplot illustrates one diagnosis (from the left: H, D_1 and D_2.

exemplary obtained for $\eta_{bpa} = 0.05$, $\eta_T = 0.35$, but other values in the $[0, 1]$ interval also resulted in the same classification error. In each subplot of the Fig.5 bars represent bpas for one diagnosis. Two neighboring bars concern the bpa values resulting from the two elimination manners. The bars are located at coordinates describing variables used in rule premises. The number of rules for all diagnoses and the first manner is 23, with 39 variables used in rules premises. For the second manner the numbers of rules and variables are slightly greater: 27 and 45, respectively, yet this elimination is quicker. However, the both numbers are much lower than in references [6], in which they are: 29 and 96. Even though the training and the test data are the same, the result of the proposed method must be considered as promising. By means of the proposed rules good diagnosis is provided - only one case is misclassified. It is much better than the diagnosis based on statistic tools which resulted in 6% error [1].

6   Discussion and Conclusions

In this paper two approaches to diagnosis support are compared. They both use all available information in the from of training samples. Though the comparison bases on simulated data, probabilistic and fuzzy approaches are close to the practice, according to the author's experience. It is shown that the fuzzy approach can be more robust as it allows for a greater influence of a symptom that is significant for the diagnosis if other symptoms are rather unrelated. The diagnosis can be indicated for various levels of solution precision determined by thresholds of the basic probability assignment calculation and of reasoning. The observation that opposite values of the thresholds (when the η_{bpa} is high then the η_T is low) can be theoretically explained [9]. Yet theory is not the most important in the present considerations as the most of theoretical characteristics cannot be obtained in practice. Still, it is both intuitively right and shown by the simulation, that sometimes allowing to decide doubtful cases (nearby the norm point) can be advantageous. In fact, such a reasoning in diagnostic practice can be even better justified than in the theory. In author's opinion, an independence of symptoms is assumed rather because it is undisclosed, then because it does not exist in a complex system, which is an organism. The proposed fuzzy approach may indirectly, in some way, model the dependence of symptoms.

It is also advantageous to be able to estimate whether a rule is necessary for reasoning by means of comparison of its basic probability value to the values of other rules. If the values for several rules are similar, than it is worth trying deleting all but one of them. It is particularly worth trying if their premises partly refer to the same variables. Such a procedure may improve correctness of a diagnosis and helps to find a set of necessary rules, much smaller than the complete set, for which reasoning is faster.

The proposed fuzzy approach to diagnosis support may solve several problems that arise in practical applications, thus it can be considered as an alternative to classical probability, even if conditional probabilities required for the Bayes formula are available.

References

1. Coomans, D., Broeckaert, I., Jonckheer, M., Massart, D.L.: Comparison of multivariate discrimination techniques for clinical data-application to the thyroid functional state. Methods of Information in Medicine 22, 93–101 (1983)
2. Dempster, A.P.: A generalization of Bayesian inference. Jornal of Royal Statistic Society 30(2), 205–247 (1968)
3. Innocent, P.R., John, R.I.: Computer aided fuzzy medical diagnosis. Information Sciences 162, 81–104 (2004)
4. Ledley, R.S.: Practical problems in the use of computers in medical diagnosis. Proceedings of the IEEE 57(11), 1900–1918 (1969)
5. Kacprzyk, J., Fedrizzi, M. (eds.): Advances in Dempster-Shafer Theory of Evidence. J. Wiley, New York (1994)

6. Liu, Z., Li, Y.: A new heuristic algorithm of rules generation based on rough sets. In: Proceedings of the International Seminar on Business and Information Management, pp. 291–294. IEEE (2008)
7. Pratap, A., Kanimozhiselvi, C.S.: Application of Naive Bayes Dichotomizer Supported with Expected Risk and Discriminant Functions in Clinical Decision - Case Study. In: 4th IEEE International Conference on Advanced Computing, pp. 1–4. IEEE Conference Publications (2012)
8. Straszecka, E.: Combining uncertainty and imprecision in models of medical diagnosis. Information Sciences 176, 3026–3059 (2006)
9. Straszecka, E.: Measures of uncertainty and imprecision in medical diagnosis support. Wydawnictwo Politechniki Slaskiej, Gliwice (2010)
10. Straszecka E.: A choice of uncertainty and imprecision representation for diagnostic reasoning. In: Atanassov K., Homenda W., Hryniewicz O., Kacprzyk J., Krawczak M., Nahorski Z., Szmidt E., Zadrozny S. (eds.) New Trends in Fuzzy Sets, Intuitionistic Fuzzy Sets, Generalized Nets and Related Topics, Vol. II: Applications, pp.161-179. IBS PAN, Warsaw (2013)
11. database online, ftp.ics.uci.edu/pub/machine-learning-databases/thyroid-disease, files new-thyr.* (June 5, 2013)

The Application of Median Fuzzy Clustering and Robust Weighted Averaging for Electronystagmography Signal Processing

Tomasz Pander, Robert Czabański, Tomasz Przybyła, and Ewa Straszecka

Institute of Electronics, Faculty of Automatic Control, Electronics and Computer
Science, Silesian University of Technology,
16 Akademicka St., 44-100 Gliwice, Poland
{tpander,rczabanski,tprzybyla,estraszecka}@polsl.pl

Abstract. The purpose of this paper is to present a robust approach to processing of electronystagmography (ENG) signal which contain saccades. The accurate saccade detection and localization allows for recognition of the optokinetic nystagmus (OKN), which is regarded as one of the important phenomena to be evaluated by ophthalmologists. The robust ENG processing consists in robust filtering of the signal to suppress outliers, robust fuzzy clustering to determine the amplitude threshold level for automatic saccade detection and robust averaging of similar optokinetic nystagmus cycles to estimate the nystagmus parameters. The proposed method was tested using the artificial as well as the real signals. The results show the usefulness of the proposed solution in the process of the OKN modeling.

Keywords: robust processing, robust weighted averaging, robust fuzzy clustering.

1 Introduction

Eyes are photosensitive sensory organs being an essential part of human visual system. Eyes can be monitored in order to detect the weariness or diseases of a person based on the results of observation of eyelids, pupils or the character of gazes. In ophthalmology, the optokinetic nystagmus (OKN) is regarded as one of the important phenomena to be evaluated as it provides a large amount of information about eyes condition. Nystagmus is the type of the eye movement induced by stimuli which activate the vestibular and/or the optokinetic systems [17]. Optokinetic nystagmus is a visually driven eye movement whose purpose is to stabilize the retinal image during global movement of the visual field [10,13]. Nystagmus is often visually detected by a physician on the basis of the saccadic eye movements observation. During computer-aided ENG analysis, the accurate saccade detection and localization is the most important, because further analysis of OKN cycles depends on precision of this stage.

In the process of the nystagmus analysis the electronystagmography (ENG) signal can be used. The quasi-periodic nature of ENG signal with characteristic

© Springer International Publishing Switzerland 2015   357
D. Filev et al. (eds.), *Intelligent Systems'2014*,
Advances in Intelligent Systems and Computing 323, DOI: 10.1007/978-3-319-11310-4_31

OKN waveforms whose repetition rate varies over time allows their averaging in time domain. The only inconvenience is the fact that the averaging method requires similar cycles of OKN to produce the correct nystagmus model. Therefore, during OKN recording the additional synchronization signal was recorded. The OKN can be observed using a rotating cylinder for a stimulation. The lateral surface of the rotating cylinder consists of alternately black and white stripes of 3 mm width that move counter-clockwise to induce the optokinetic nystagmus. The synchronization signal comes from the photo-detector which is arranged opposite the rotating cylinder in alignment with the eye. It allows for the selection of the similar OKN cycles for averaging and then determination of the triangle model of the nystagmus cycle. Fig. 1 presents an example of OKN cycles with the strips of the synchronization signal.

The paper presents a method of calculation of the triangle model of the patient OKN cycle with a help of robust weighted averaging of similar OKN cycles which are determined on the basis of the precise saccade detection and location. The location procedure is based on the application of the detection function combined with the algorithm of the threshold calculation using the median fuzzy clustering.

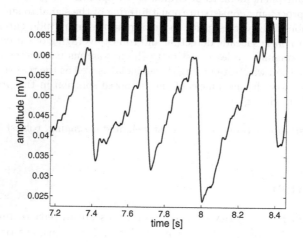

Fig. 1. An example of OKN cycles with the strips of the synchronization signal

2   Optokinetic Nystagmus Cycle Determination

2.1   Saccade Detection

The first step of the nystagmus analysis is the saccade detection, as the correct saccade detection allows for recognition of the OKN cycle. Unfortunately, the ENG signal is disturbed with noise. The noise characteristic is usually non-stationary and sometimes shows an impulsive nature. The main source of noise in ENG signal is an electrical activity of face's muscles. Movements of the head and speaking process involve multiple muscle group contraction that can easily disturb the desired signal. Another source of noise is eyes blinking which often has a spike form. This kind of disturbances are difficult to suppress with linear filters which are usually optimized under assumption of Gaussian distribution of noise. However, to remove the impulsive type of noise from the biomedical signal the nonlinear robust filters [15] may be applied.

For accurate localization of saccades the method described in [13] was applied. It is based on the detection function analysis which is derived from the nonlinear preprocessing of the ENG signal. The signal transformation is based on the robust myriad filtering against different type of impulsive disturbances which are efficiently suppressed. The process of the detection function determination can be formally written as:

$$y(n) = \Psi\left\{x(n)\right\}, \tag{1}$$

where $x(n)$ is the raw ENG signal, and $\Psi\{\cdot\}$ represents the nonlinear operations providing the detection function. The method creates the smoothed detection function waveforms which peaks correspond to saccade locations. The only problem of this method is the proper selection of the amplitude threshold A_{th}. It depends on the amplitude of the distinguishing peaks in the detection function waveform which correspond to the saccades. The application of the constant threshold does not provide the satisfactory accuracy of the automated saccade recognition. Hence, the method of the adaptive threshold adjustment based on robust clustering was used to improve the saccade detection quality.

2.2   Estimation of Amplitude Threshold with Median Fuzzy Clustering

Clustering procedures allow dividing a set of objects into clusters (groups) so that elements of the same cluster are more similar to each other than to elements of other clusters. The similarity criterion is usually defined on the basis of selected properties of the object which are represented by a feature vector. The application of fuzzy set theory resulted in methods of fuzzy clustering which assume the possibility of partial membership of an element to a given group. The well known Fuzzy c-Means (FCM) [3] algorithm can be used in the procedure of the adaptive threshold adjustment [4,5]. However, the resulting FCM cluster representatives (prototypes) are the linear statistics of data points which are known to be vulnerable to outliers [7]. Hence, in the presented approach we applied the robust partitioning method based on the fuzzy median (Fuzzy c-Medians, FCMed) [8].

Let us assume that we have a set of feature vectors $\mathbf{X} = \{\mathbf{x}_1, \mathbf{x}_2, \ldots \mathbf{x}_N\}$, $\underset{1 \leq k \leq N}{\forall}\ \mathbf{x}_k \in \Re^p$ that represent N objects to be divided into c clusters. In the FCMed algorithm, i-th cluster is made of elements x_k for which the distance (defined as the ℓ_1 metric) from the group prototype $\mathbf{v}_i$ is smaller than the distances from the prototypes of other groups. The degree of membership is defined by an element of the partition matrix $u_{ik} \in [0,1]$:

$$\mathop{\forall}_{1 \le i \le c} \mathop{\forall}_{1 \le k \le N} \quad u_{ik} = \frac{d_{ik}^{\frac{1}{1-r}}}{\sum_{j=1}^{c} d_{jk}^{\frac{1}{1-r}}}, \tag{2}$$

where $r \in (1,\infty]$ is the weighting exponent (usually $r = 2$) and $d_{ik} = \|\mathbf{v}_i - \mathbf{x}_k\|_1 = \sum_{j=1}^{p} |v_{ij} - x_{kj}|$ is the ℓ_1 metric. A zero value of u_{ik} indicates that the object x_k is not a member of i-th group, while $u_{ik} = 1$ represents full membership.

The prototypes $\mathbf{v}_i (\forall i = 1, 2, \ldots, c)$ in FCMed method are the fuzzy (weighted) median with weights defined as scaled versions $(u_{ik})^r$ of memberships. The solution comes from the Picard method for the alternating iteration of eq. (2) and $\mathbf{v}_i$. The algorithm starts with random initialization of a partition matrix or cluster prototypes.

Since the fuzzy median is the cluster centering statistic, it involves ordering the sample values. To increase the efficiency of median calculation we applied the algorithm, defining the prototypes as a root of the derivative of fuzzy median functional [8] which can be found with bisection method.

A detailed analysis of the detection function waveform $y(n)$ allows to distinguish three groups of the samples that are characterized by "low" $(i = 1)$ "medium" $(i = 2)$ and "high" $(i = 3)$ amplitude, representing the slow, medium and the fast saccadic phase of the eye movement cycle. The class of the sample amplitude can be determined by the relevant elements of the membership matrix. Hence, the samples of the detection function waveform may be used directly as feature vectors (scalars) in the FCMed to be divided into three groups $(c = 3)$. However, our experiments showed that such an approach provides incorrect (too small) values of the amplitude threshold A_{th}. Consequently, the feature vectors used as inputs for the clustering are defined as:

$$x_k = y(n)|_{y(n) > \tau}, \tag{3}$$

where τ is the threshold level defined as the the first quartile of the detection function samples.

The high degree of membership of the signal sample to the group with the "medium" amplitude indicates that the sample with the higher amplitude represents the saccade. Hence, the resulting amplitude threshold which allows for the precise detection is determined as a maximum of samples belonging to the second group $(i = 2)$ under the condition that their normalized degree of membership:

$$u_{2k}^{(n)} = \frac{u_{2k}}{\max_{k}(u_{2k})}, \tag{4}$$

is higher than the predefined value δ. Consequently,

$$A_{th} = \max(x_k|_{u_{2k}^{(n)} > \delta}). \tag{5}$$

2.3   OKN Cycles Determination

A saw tooth waveform is characteristic for most types of nystagmus. The beginning and the end of the optokinetic nystagmus cycle have to be found to determine the corresponding signal samples after saccades localizations. The slope on one side of each peak is smaller (slow component) that on the other side (fast component - saccade) [12]. The slow component of nystagmus is related to the stimulus, when the eyes are fixed on the certain strip (black or white) and follow it. The tracking is finished with the sudden return of the eyeballs to the initial position. The phase of return is the saccade and it refers to a rapid reset of eye position by the oculomotor systems [9].

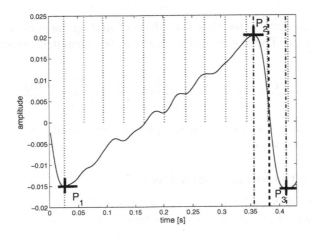

Fig. 2. The single OKN cycle with detected saccade (dashed, thick line) including the locations of characteristic points of the OKN nystagmus cycle that are needed for the cycle model determination (dash-dot line) and the synchronization lines (dotted line)

In this work we assumed a triangular model of nystagmus cycle. This assumption involves a necessity of estimation of two lines. The first defines the slow phase of nystagmus cycle, while the second the fast (saccadic) phase of the cycle [16]. The most important parameters of the model are the slopes as they determine the (angular) velocity of slow and fast phase denoted as $\{a_1, a_2\}$ respectively. To calculate the model parameters a linear regression method is applied [1]. In order to estimate the slopes of nystagmus phases, firstly the characteristic points need to be determined. Their locations are presented in Fig. 2.

The position of the i-th saccade is denoted as $T_i, i = 1, \ldots, N$ where N is the number of detected saccades in the previous stage of ENG processing. For the OKN cycle the following three points should be determined $P_1(t_{1sync}, x_{1sync})$, $P_2(t_{1max}, x_{1max})$ and $P_3(t_{2min}, x_{2min})$, where $x(n)$ is the signal sample value and t_n denotes the discrete time. The point P_1 can be found on the basis of the synchronization signal, which indicates the beginning of the tracking phase - we assume that the first OKN cycle (slow phase) starts simultaneously with synchronization signal. Consequently, the segment P_1P_2 corresponds to the slow phase of the OKN cycle. These two points belong to the range from T_{i-1} and T_i. In order to find P_2 the following conditions should be fulfilled:

$$x_{1max}|_{t1max} = \max_{T_{i-1} \leq n \leq T_i} x(n). \tag{6}$$

The second stage consists in determination of the section between points P_2 and P_3 that corresponds to saccade movements. P_3 point is searched in the range from T_i to T' where $T' = T_i + \epsilon(T_{i+1} - T_i)$, where ϵ is the correction factor (in this work $\epsilon = 0.4$). The location of P_3 is defined with the following condition:

$$x_{2min}|_{t2min} = \min_{T_i \leq n \leq T'} x(n). \tag{7}$$

These requirements guarantee that fast phase of nystagmus cycle is strictly related to the saccade. The slopes $a_k(k = 1, 2)$ can be calculated according to the following formula:

$$a_k = \frac{N_k \sum_{n=1}^{N_k} t(n)x(n) - (\sum_{n=1}^{N_k} t(n))(\sum_{n=1}^{N_k} x(n))}{N_k \sum_{n=1}^{N_k} x^2(n) - (\sum_{n=1}^{N_k} x(n))^2}, \tag{8}$$

where $N_k(k = 1, 2)$ is the number of samples between points P_1 P_2, and P_2 P_3 and $t(n)$ is the discrete time.

2.4   Collecting the Similar OKN Cycles

The next step of OKN cycles processing requires finding the cycles of the same length. A duration of the OKN cycle is generally dependent on the number of observed stripes rather than the time period. Thus we choose the cycle of the same number of synchronization signal periods. This can be achieved by using the histogram which shows the distribution of number of synchronization signal periods in OKN cycles. An example of detected saccades and synchronization signal is presented in Fig. 3.

The histogram of the number of the synchronization signal periods per OKN cycle for the real ENG signal with 52 detected saccades is presented in shows Fig. 4.

It can be noticed that the dominant OKN cycles consist of 28 synchronization periods (see Fig. 4). They are selected for the further signal processing.

The detected and grouped OKN cycles have the standardized length as the last raw sample in each saccade is replicated repeatedly until the length of standardized saccade equals to the nearest value of the power of 2 that is greater than real length of raw OKN cycles. This requirement is needed for simplicity of the further calculations. The known location of the characteristic points $P_i(i = 1, 2, 3)$ guarantee the alignment in time domain of the slow and saccade phase respectively. An example of a set of dominant OKN cycles which were partitioned into the slow and saccade phases is presented in Fig. 5. Now, each part of the dominant OKN cycles can be averaged separately.

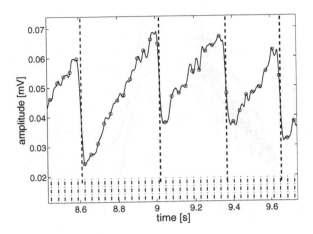

Fig. 3. An example of a part of horizontal ENG signal with OKN cycles (solid line), saccade location (dashed line) and synchronization signal (dash-dot line and circles)

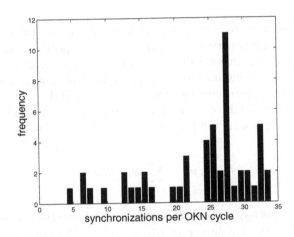

Fig. 4. A histogram of the synchronization periods per OKN cycle in the real ENG signal

2.5   Robust Weighted Averaging

Averaging is one of the basic methods in statistical analysis of experimental science, especially when the analyzed system response is periodic [6,11,18]. Unfortunately, the arithmetic mean fails in the presence of outliers. The ENG signal can be disturbed with a noise of impulsive nature (like muscle noise). Hence, for the purpose of the OKN modelling we applied the weighted robust averaging method presented in [11,14] for its ability to efficient suppression of impulsive types of noise.

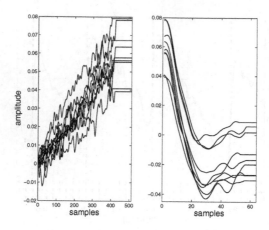

Fig. 5. An example of dominant OKN cycles which were partitioned into the slow (left plot) and the saccades phase (right plot)

The idea of the weighted averaging appears in various forms. The general assumption is that each observation influences the composite signal according to its weight, and the aggregation can be defined as an optimization problem over the vector of weights, using an objective function that measures dissimilarities between the resulting prototype and each observation [11].

The method of the weighted averaging based on criterion function minimization (WACFM) was presented in [11]. The scalar criterion function is defined as:

$$I_m(\mathbf{w}, \boldsymbol{\nu}) = \sum_{i=1}^{N} (w_i)^m \rho(\mathbf{z}_i), \tag{9}$$

where $\rho(\mathbf{z}_i) = \sum_{i=1}^{M} \rho(z_{ij})$ is a dissimilarity or a cost function, $\mathbf{z}_i = \mathbf{x}_i - \boldsymbol{\nu}$, $\mathbf{w} = [w_1, w_2, \ldots, w_N]^T$ is the weight vector which satisfies the following condition:

$$\mathop{\forall}_{1 \le i \le N} w_i \in [0, 1], \quad \sum_{i=1}^{N} w_i = 1, \tag{10}$$

and $\mathbf{x}_i = [x_{i1}, x_{i2}, \ldots, x_{iM}]^T$ is the ith signal cycle which consists of M samples and $1 \le i \le N$, while $\boldsymbol{\nu}$ is the averaged signal. The function $I_m(\mathbf{w}, \boldsymbol{\nu})$ is regarded as a measure of total dissimilarity between $\boldsymbol{\nu}$ and the signal cycle $\mathbf{x}_i$, weighted by $(w_i)^m$. The robustness of this method depends on the selection of the cost function $\rho(\cdot)$. In order to protect the weighted averaging method against outliers the general form of the cost function $\rho(\cdot)$ is proposed in the following form [2]:

$$\rho(z) = \log\left(\sigma^p + |z|^p\right), \tag{11}$$

where $\sigma > 0$ and $0 < p \leq 2$. Using (9) and (11), the scalar criterion function can be rewritten as:

$$I_m(\mathbf{w}, \boldsymbol{\nu}) = \sum_{i=1}^{N} (w_i)^m \sum_{l=1}^{M} \log \left(1 + \left(\frac{|x_{il} - \nu_l|}{\sigma} \right)^p \right). \tag{12}$$

The problem of (12) minimization is considered as the constrained optimization. The method of Lagrange multipliers is applied to find the $\mathbf{w}$ vector of the optimal weights [14]:

$$\underset{1 \leq i \leq N}{\forall} \quad w_i = \frac{\left[\sum_{l=1}^{M} \log \left(1 + \left(\frac{|x_{il} - \nu_l|}{\sigma} \right)^p \right) \right]^{1/(1-m)}}{\sum_{j=1}^{N} \left[\sum_{l=1}^{M} \log \left(1 + \left(\frac{|x_{jl} - \nu_l|}{\sigma} \right)^p \right) \right]^{1/(1-m)}}. \tag{13}$$

The averaged signal $\boldsymbol{\nu}$ is obtained as:

$$\boldsymbol{\nu}^{(k+1)} = \frac{\sum_{i=1}^{N} (w_i)^m \mathbf{x}_i \left[\sum_{l=1}^{M} \frac{|x_{il} - \nu_l^{(k)}|^{2-p}}{p} \left(\sigma^p + |x_{il} - \nu_l^{(k)}|^p \right) \right]^{-1}}{\sum_{i=1}^{N} (w_i)^m \left[\sum_{l=1}^{M} \frac{|x_{il} - \nu_l^{(k)}|^{2-p}}{p} \left(\sigma^p + |x_{il} - \nu_l^{(k)}|^p \right) \right]^{-1}}. \tag{14}$$

This method is called as the weighted averaging based on the criterion minimization with the cost function based on the generalized Cauchy distribution (WACFMGC). Finally, using (13) and (14) the algorithm of the robust weighted averaging (WACFMGC) can be described as follows:

1° fix $m = 2$, $\sigma = 1$ and $p = 1$, initialize $\boldsymbol{\nu}^{(0)} = \mathbf{0}$, set the iteration index $k = 1$,
2° calculate the weight vector for the kth iteration using the formula (13),
3° update the averaged signal for the kth iteration using the formula (14), and $\mathbf{w}^{(k)}$
4° if $\|\mathbf{w}^{(k+1)} - \mathbf{w}^{(k)}\| > \epsilon$ and $k \leq k_{\max}$, where ϵ is a pre-set parameter and $k_{\max}$ is the maximum number of iterations, then $k \leftarrow k + 1$ and go to 2°.

3   Results and Discussion

To investigate the performance of the proposed method of ENG signal processing we used an artificial as well as a real ENG signals with OKN cycles. The OKN cycles in the artificial signal were generated on the basis of the real ENG. Such approach allows for the control of the OKN model parameters [16]. To build a single OKN cycle we used the following parameters:

- slow phase: $a_1 = 0.075$ [mV/s] and duration varies randomly in the range: $0.6 \leq t \leq 1.0$ [s],
- saccade: $a_2 = -1.05$ [mV/s] and duration varies randomly in the range: $0.04 \leq t \leq 0.12$ [s].

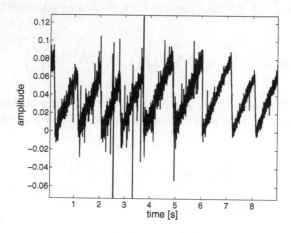

Fig. 6. A part of the artificial ENG signals with OKN cycles disturbed with impulsive noise

The change of the OKN cycle time allows to simulate different ways of tracking of alternating stripes by a moving eyeball. We made two sets of 200 OKN cycles. The first set is noise-free, while the second is disturbed with impulsive noise modeled with the symmetric α-stable distribution. Each of 50 cycles have the geometric SNR equal 5, 10, 15 and 25 dB [15,16]. The synchronization periods were attached to artificial signal in the second channel. An example of the artificial signal is presented in Fig. 6.

The real ENG signals were recorded in a horizontal direction of eye movements. The signals were acquired with the measurement system based on the Biopac MP-36 unit. Six Ag/AgCl electrodes (ca. 4 mm in diameter) were placed around the eyes. The frequency sampling was set to 500 Hz.

On the basis of the averaged dominant cycles, the OKN model parameters can be calculated: the duration of both phases and eyes velocity during the cycle. The values of the parameters of the dominant OKN cycles for the considered signals are shown in the Table 1.

In the case of artificial OKN cycles the similar number of cycles was averaged when considering a noise-free and the noisy environment. The slope a_1 was determined with sufficient accuracy for both methods applied. However, the robust WACFMGC offers higher accuracy of a_2 estimation.

When considering the real ENG signal one can noticed that the number of the averaged (dominant) OKN cycles is smaller. The reason is the higher variability of the OKN cycles duration.

There are differences between values of OKN model parameters calculated on the basis of arithmetic mean (AM) and WACFMGC methods. However, the results obtained for the artificial signals suggest that the nystagmus parameters provided by the WACFMGC are more reliable.

Table 1. Parameters of the dominant OKN cycles (AM - arithmetic mean, WACFMGC - robust averaging)

method	$a_1[mV/s]$	$a_2 [mV/s]$	$T_{slow}[s]$	$T_{saccade}[s]$
the artificial noise free ENG signal (53 averaged OKN cycles of 28 synchr. periods)				
AM	0.0749	-1.1431	0.844	0.070
WACFMGC	0.0750	-1.0540	0.838	0.070
the artificial noisy ENG signal (56 averaged OKN cycles of 28 synchr. periods)				
AM	0.0749	-0.9165	0.810	0.068
WACFMGC	0.0748	-0.9930	0.816	0.068
the real ENG signal (9 averaged cycles OKN of 28 synchr. periods)				
AM	0.0690	-1.7446	0.848	0.058
WACFMGC	0.0576	-1.9295	0.804	0.052

4   Conclusion

In the presented work we investigated the problem of robust processing of the electronystagmography signal which contains optokinetic nystagmus cycles. The proposed procedure of ENG signal analysis consists of two main stages: the saccades detection and the OKN cycles modeling. Our detection method is based on the robust filtering (myriad filter) and robust (median) fuzzy clustering. This step ensures reliable positioning of saccades despite various kinds of noise, allowing for the correct recognition of the OKN cycles. As a result of the dominant OKN cycles averaging the triangular model of optokinetic nystagmus can be estimated and analyzed. In the proposed approach the method of the robust weighted averaging with application of the cost function based on the general Cauchy distribution was used. The obtained results show that the robust method leads to better results in comparison to the classical arithmetic mean. The calculated parameters of the OKN model can be used in evaluating the eyes mobility at different movement conditions. The proposed method is the starting point for the future investigations on the eye electrophysiology.

Acknowledgments. This work is supported by SUT grant BK-216/RAu3/2013.

References

1. Authié, C.N., Mestre, D.R.: Optokinetic nystagmus is elicited by curvilinear optic flow during high speed curve driving. Vision Res. 51, 1791–1800 (2011)
2. Aysal, T.C., Barner, K.E.: Meridian filtering for robust signal processing. IEEE T. Signal Proces. 55, 3949–3962 (2007)
3. Bezdek, J.C.: Pattern Recognition with Fuzzy Objective Function Algorithms. Plenum Press, New York (1982)

4. Czabański, R., Pander, T., Przybyła, T.: Fuzzy Approach to Saccades Detection in Optokinetic Nystagmus. Adv. Int. Sys. Comp. 242, 231–238 (2013)
5. Czabański, R., Pander, T., Horoba, K., Przybyła, T.: Fuzzy Clustering Based Methods for Nystagmus Movements Detection in Electronystagmography Signal. JMIT 22, 277–283 (2013)
6. Hassan, U., Anwar, M.S.: Reducing noise by repetition: introduction to signal averaging. Eur. J.Phys. 30, 453–465 (2010)
7. Kersten, P.R.: Fuzzy Order Statistics and Their Application to Fuzzy Clustering. IEEE T. Fuzzy Syst. 7, 708–712 (1999)
8. Kersten, P.R.: Implementation issues in the fuzzy c-medians clustering algorithm. In: Proc. VI IEEE Int. Conf. Fuzzy. Syst., vol. 2, pp. 957–962 (1997)
9. Kim, K.G., Ko, J.S., Park, B.R.: A new measuring method of slow component velocity for OKN signal. In: IEEE 5th Inter. Conference on Power Electronics and Drive Systems, pp. 973–977 (2003)
10. Knap, C.H.M., Gottlob, I., McLean, R., Proudlock, F.: Horizontal and vertical look and stare optokinetic nystagmus in healthy adult volunteers. Invest. Ophth. Vis. Sci. 49, 581–588 (2008)
11. Ł ęski, J.: Robust Weighted Averaging. IEEE T. Biomed. Eng. 49, 796–804 (2002)
12. Michaels, D.L., Tole, J.R.: A microprocessor-based instrument for nystagmus analysis. Proc. of the IEEE 65, 730–735 (1977)
13. Pander, T., Czabański, R., Przybyła, T., Jeżewski, J., Pojda-Wilczek, D., Wróbel, J., Horoba, K., Bernyś, M.: A New Method of Saccadic Eye Movement Detection for Optokinetic Nystagmus Analysis. In: Conf. Proc. IEEE Eng. Med. Biol. Soc., San Diego (2012)
14. Pander, T.: An application of myriad M-estimator for robust weighted averaging. In: Gruca, A., Czachórski, T., Kozielski, S. (eds.) Man-Machine Interactions 3. AISC, vol. 242, pp. 269–276. Springer, Heidelberg (2014)
15. Pander, T.: The Class of M-filters in the Application of ECG Signal Processing. J. Biocyb. Biomed. Eng. 26, 3–13 (2006)
16. Pander, T., Czabański, R., Przybyła, T., Pojda-Wilczek, D.: The possibilities of optokinetic nystagmus cycles averaging. JMIT 19, 25–31 (2012)
17. Sheth, N.V., Dell'osso, L.F., Leigh, R.J., Van Doren, C.L., Peckham, H.P.: The effects of afferent stimulation on congenital nystagmus foveation periods. Vision Res. 35, 2371–2382 (1995)
18. Tompkins, W.J.: Biomedical digital signal processing: C-language examples and laboratory experiments for the IBM PC. Prentice-Hall Inc., New York (1993)

Design of an Optimal Modular LVQ Network for Classification of Arrhythmias Based on a Variable Training-Test Datasets Strategy

Jonathan Amezcua, Patricia Melin, and Oscar Castillo

Tijuana Institute of Technology
jonathan.aguiluz@yahoo.com, {pmelin,ocastillo}@tectijuana.mx

Abstract. In this paper, a LVQ neural network with a modular approach is presented for the classification of arrhythmias. This new model partitions the dataset into different percentages of the training - test records. In previous research, static (fixed) percentages of training – test dataset were handled, 70% and 30% respectively, however the aim of this research is to approximate the minimum value of records with which the LVQ network can train and classify with a good percentage of accuracy.

1 Introduction

In this paper a modular neural network with learning vector quantization (LVQ) is presented for arrhythmia classification [1,3]. This approach partitions the training dataset into a variable percentage. In previous work, static (fixed) percentages of the training records were handled, 70% for training and 30% for testing, however the aim of this research is to approximate the minimum value of records with which the LVQ network [1,4] can train, and classify with the highest accuracy.

For this paper, architecture with three modules was used, each module has five different types of arrhythmias [2], and classes in the modules are randomly distributed. The training datasets are generated in a range of [40% - 85%] randomly. The final result of classification is obtained using *the winner takes all* method as the integration unit.

The rest of this paper is organized as follows, in section 2 the problem statement is described, section 3 presents simulation results and section 4 the conclusions.

2 Problem Statement

Classification can be designed as assigning objects to only one of many predefined categories, a problem that covers many different areas of application, such as spam detection in emails, cell categorization, classification of galaxies based on their shapes, etc [20]. In this work, the LVQ network [1,3,5] was used as classification technique, and Fig.1 shows the architecture of a LVQ network [21]. Previously LVQ networks were used for the classification of different types of arrhythmias. The term

© Springer International Publishing Switzerland 2015
D. Filev et al. (eds.), *Intelligent Systems' 2014*,
Advances in Intelligent Systems and Computing 323, DOI: 10.1007/978-3-319-11310-4_32

arrhythmia refers to any change from the normal sequences of electrical hearth impulses, these impulses may happen too fast, to slowly or erratically, and can be measured with a Holter monitor in ECG signals [19]. Fig. 2 shows an example of one of these ECG signals [8,9,10].

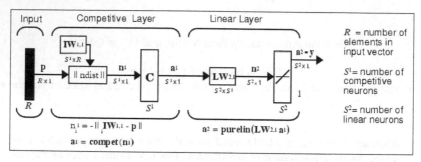

Fig. 1. Architecture of the LVQ network

Within the architectures previously developed for arrhythmia classification we have an architecture with 5 modules and 3 classes per module, an architecture with 4 modules and 4 classes per module [16], and an architecture with 3 modules and 5 classes per module; for each architecture the training and test datasets were partitioned into 70% and 30% respectively. Fifteen experiments were performed with each of the architectures; Table 1 shows the average accuracy for each one of the architectures.

Table 1. Average accuracy for the architectures

Architectures	Accuracy
Five modules architecture	99.10
Four modules architecture	99.16
Three modules architecture	97.64

2.1   Arrhythmia Dataset

The MIT-BIH [17] arrhythmia dataset was used for this work. This dataset consists of 15 different types of arrhythmias [18,19]. This database contains 48 half-hour excerpts of ECG recordings, obtained from 47 subjects studied by BIH Arrhythmia Laboratory. The records were preprocessed at as follows:

- Analog outputs of the playback unit were filtered using a passband from 0.1 to 100 Hz. The passband-filtered signals were digitized at 360 Hz per signal.
- Taking as reference the R point in the obtained signals was possible to locate the start and end point for each wave, the segmentation of each wave was performed manually, resulting in variable-length vectors which represent a cardiac cycle.
- The 38 higher voltages and 38 lower voltages of each vector were taken, resulting in homologated vectors of 76 voltages.

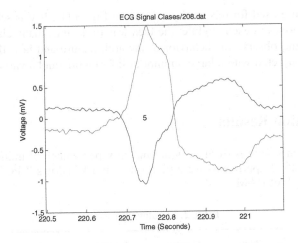

Fig. 2. Example of an ECG signal

2.2   Partition of the Dataset

As mentioned earlier, previous experiments were developed to train and test modular architectures of LVQ networks for classification [6,7] of arrhythmias, using 70% and 30% for training and test, respectively. For this reason, this work intends to design an optimal modular LVQ network for classification of arrhythmias based on a variable partition of the training dataset. Therefore, the number of training records varies in each experiment; for this research a range between 40% and 85% to train the LVQ network [11,12] was established.

The number of test records depends of the training records, for example, if a 75% for training is selected, then the other 25% is automatically selected for testing the network.

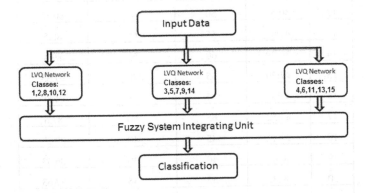

Fig. 3. LVQ network architecture

The architecture used for this work is shown in Fig. 3 [1]. It was selected because the number of classes in each module; the idea was to have as many classes per module as possible and observe the behavior of the architecture and how the accuracy of classification is affected with a large amount of information and a variable dataset for training.

3   Simulation Results

Several experiments were performed with randomly percentage of training, and Table 2 shows the results. Experiments were performed in a Windows 7 PC, Quad-Core i5 processor and 4 Gb of RAM.

Table 2. Simulation results

	Time	Clusters	Training %	Accuracy
1	14:54	25	71	89.65
2	15:30	35	51	86.53
3	22:09	35	85	90.66
4	31:12	45	71	77.25
5	14:03	25	85	84
6	48:53	55	70	98
7	26:03	38	85	92
8	32:34	38	75	84.8
9	31:45	40	72	89.28
10	31:17	40	67	78.79
11	31:08	45	64	81.11
12	40:58	50	62	80.52
13	41:48	55	60	88.5
14	39:29	60	57	89.3
15	47:20	55	70	97.33
16	42:37	65	55	84.88
17	33:52	65	50	87.6
18	29:11	45	40	87.27
19	30:07	40	40	86.33
20	39:32	55	45	87.63
21	43:49	55	49	87.45
22	36:24	50	42	86.2
23	37:47	45	83	89.41

Table 2. (*continued*)

24	43:01	53	56	86.36
25	47:13	60	56	92.27
26	39:42	40	60	89.5
27	45:49	48	47	87.54
28	38:54	55	81	86.31
29	42:17	55	64	78.33
30	45:34	55	70	96
31	51:54	50	67	80
32	49:28	58	67	80.6
33	38:23	35	45	86.9
34	44:52	38	67	80.6
35	48:12	55	70	98
36	35:39	40	43	83.15
37	43:12	46	57	83.25
38	36:08	44	48	83.46
39	44:38	49	57	84.18
40	42:56	50	56	86.51
41	39:23	58	43	84.56
42	40:19	60	41	89.15
43	43:39	55	70	96.66
44	49:25	65	62	80
45	38:09	62	78	88.18
46	43:15	55	40	90.33
47	36:28	53	52	85.83
48	47:53	55	73	83.84
49	45:17	55	58	79.04
50	47:23	55	70	98

Notice that results are very variable with the different percentages of training data, although the highest classification rate was using 70% for training the LVQ network [13,14,15], there were other percentages near to 70 that resulted in a low percentage of accuracy. Fig. 4 shows graphically the results presented above.

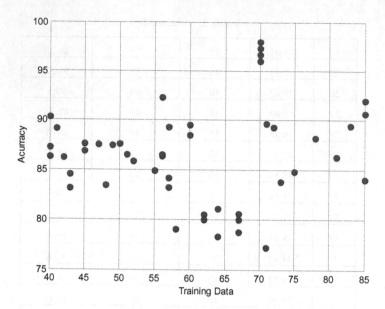

Fig. 4. Simulation results

4 Conclusions

In this paper a study to find an optimal modular LVQ network for classification of arrhythmias [22] based on a variable training dataset was presented. The results show that is quite difficult to decide an accurate percentage of the data set to train the LVQ network. However, with exactly 70% for training the percentage of accuracy was the highest.

The results also suggest that other percentage of training data of the LVQ networks could achieve acceptable classification accuracy.

References

1. Amezcua, J., Melin, P.: A modular LVQ Neural Network with Fuzzy response integration for arrhythmia Classification. In: IEEE 2014 Conference on Norbert Wiener in the 21st century, Boston (June 2014)
2. Anuradha, B., Veera-Reddy, V.C.: Cardiac arrhythmia classification using fuzzy classifiers. J. Theor. Appl. Inform. Technol., 353–359 (2005)
3. Biehl, M., Ghosh, A., Hammer, B.: Learning vector quantization: the dynamics of winner-takes-all algorithms. Neurocomputing 69(7-9), 660–670 (2006)
4. Castillo, O., Melin, P., Ramirez, E., Soria, J.: Hybrid intelligent system for cardiac arrhythmia classification with Fuzzy K-Nearest Neighbors and neural networks com-bined with a fuzzy system. Journal of Expert Systems with Applications 39(3), 2947–2955 (2012)

5. Frasconi, P., Gori, M., Soda, G.: Links between LVQ and backpropagation original research article. Pattern Recogn. Lett. 18(4), 303–310 (1997)
6. Ghosh, A., Biehl, M., Hammer, B.: Performance analysis of LVQ algorithms: a statistical physics approach. Neural Networks 19(6-7), 817–829 (2006)
7. Gray, R.M.: Vector quantization. IEEE ASSP Magazine 1, 4–29 (1984)
8. Hu, Y.H., Palreddy, S., Tompkins, W.: A patient adaptable ECG beat classifier using a mixture of experts approach. IEEE Trans. Biomed. Eng., 891–900 (1997)
9. Hu, Y.H., Tompkins, W., Urrusti, J.L., Afonso, V.X.: Applications of ANN for ECG signal detection and classification. J. Electrocardiol. 28, 66–73 (1994)
10. Kim, J., Sik-Shin, H., Shin, K., Lee, M.: Robust algorithm for arrhythmia classification in ECG using extreme learning machine. Biomed. Eng. Online (October 2009)
11. Kohonen, T.: Improved versions of learning vector quantization. In: International Joint Conference on Neural Networks, San Diego, vol. 1, pp. 545–550 (1990)
12. Kohonen, T.: Self-organization and Associate Memory, 3rd edn. Springer, London (1989)
13. Learning Vector Quantization Networks,
http://www.mathworks.com/help/toolbox/nnet/ug/
bss4b_1-15.html
14. Linde, Y., Buzo, A., Gray, R.M.: An algorithm for vector quantizer desing. IEEE Transactions on Communications 28, 84–95 (1980)
15. Martín-Valdivia, M.T., Ureña-López, L.A., García-Vega, M.: The learning vector quantization algorithm applied to automatic text classification tasks. Neural Networks 20(6), 748–756 (2007)
16. Melin, P., Amezcua, J., Valdez, F., Castillo, O.: A new neural network model based on the LVQ algorithm for multi-class classification of arrhythmias. Information Sciences 279, 483–497 (2014)
17. MIT-BIH Arrhythmia Database. PhysioBank, Physiologic Signal Archives for Biomedical   Research,
http://www.physionet.org/physiobank/database/mitdb/
(last access: June 24, 2014)
18. Nasiri, J.A., Naghibzadeh, M., Yazdi, H.S., Naghibzadeh, B.: ECG arrhythmia classification with support vector machines and genetic algorithm. In: Third UK Sim European Symposium on Computer Modeling and Simulation (2009)
19. Owis, M.I., Abou-Zied, A.H., Youssef, A.M., Kadah, Y.M.: Study of features based on non-linear dynamical modeling in ECG arrhythmia detection and classification. IEEE Trans. Biomed. Eng. 49(7) (2002)
20. Pang-Ning, T., Steinbach, M., Kumar, V.: Introduction to Data Mining, pp. 145–148. Pearson Addison Wesley (2006)
21. Torrecilla, J.S., Rojo, E., Oliet, M., Domínguez, J.C., Rodríguez, F.: Self-organizing maps and learning vector quantization networks as tools to identify vegetable oils and detect adulterations of extra virgin olive oil. Comput. Aided Chem. Eng. 28, 313–318 (2010)
22. Tsipouras, M.G., Fotiadis, D.I., Sideris, D.: An arrhythmia classification system based on the RR-interval signal. Artif. Intell. Med., 237–250 (2005)

RoadMonitor: An Intelligent Road Surface Condition Monitoring System

Adham Mohamed[1], Mohamed Mostafa M. Fouad[2], Esraa Elhariri[3],
Nashwa El-Bendary[4], Hossam M. Zawbaa[4], Mohamed Tahoun[5], and
Aboul Ella Hassanien[6]

[1] Andromeda Labs, Cairo-Egypt
Scientific Research Group in Egypt (SRGE)
adhamfahmy@andromeda-labs.com
http://www.egyptscience.net
[2] Arab Academy for Science, Technology,
and Maritime Transport, Cairo, Egypt
Scientific Research Group in Egypt (SRGE)
mohamed_mostafa@aast.edu,
nashwa.elbendary@ieee.org
http://www.egyptscience.net
[3] Faculty of Computers and Information,
Fayoum University, Fayoum, Egypt
Scientific Research Group in Egypt (SRGE)
eng.esraa.elhariri@gmail.com
http://www.egyptscience.net
[4] Faculty of Mathematics and Computer Science,
Babes-Bolyai University, Romania,
Faculty of Computers and Information,
BeniSuef University, BeniSuef, Egypt
Scientific Research Group in Egypt (SRGE)
hossam.zawbaa@gmail.com
http://www.egyptscience.net
[5] Computer Science Department,
FCI, Suez Canal University, Ismailia, Egypt
Scientific Research Group in Egypt (SRGE)
matahoun@gmail.com
http://www.egyptscience.net
[6] Faculty of Computers and Information,
Cairo University, Cairo, Egypt
Scientific Research Group in Egypt (SRGE)
aboitcairo@gmail.com
http://www.egyptscience.net

Abstract. Well maintained road network is an essential requirement for the safety and consistency of vehicles moving on that road and the wellbeing of people in those vehicles. On the other hand, guaranteeing an adequate maintenance by road managers can be achieved via having sufficient and accurate information concerning road infrastructure quality that can be as well utilized concurrently by the widespread means of

© Springer International Publishing Switzerland 2015
D. Filev et al. (eds.), *Intelligent Systems'2014*,
Advances in Intelligent Systems and Computing 323, DOI: 10.1007/978-3-319-11310-4_33

users' mobile devices both locally and worldwide. This article proposes a road condition monitoring framework that detects the road anomalies such as speed bumps. In the proposed approach, the main indicator for road anomalies is the gyroscope around gravity rotation in addition to the accelerometer sensor as a cross-validation method to confirm the detection results that were gathered from the gyroscope.

Keywords: Road monitoring, Smartphone, Wireless Sensor Network, Gyroscope, Accelerometer, Speed bumps, Path holes.

1   Introduction

The road surface condition is one of the major indicators for road quality (safety or dangerous road). Road anomalies such as bumps, potholes, patching, cracking and small defects on the surface can be used for the characterizing of road surface quality. So, detecting speed bumps (road bumps), potholes and roughness levels is key to road condition monitoring [1]. Bad roads are a big problem for vehicles, drivers and pedestrians, this is because they are one of the main reasons of vehicles damage, are sometimes very dangerous to drivers and pedestrians [1,2]. Accordingly, road surface condition monitoring systems are very important solutions to improve traffic safety, reduce accidents and protect vehicles from damage due to bad roads.

Both road managers and Drivers are interested in fixing road conditions quickly. However, these conditions have to be detected firstly. Municipalities and road managers can guarantee an adequate maintenance, via having sufficient and accurate information concerning road infrastructure quality. Also, drivers can drive safely. To gain this information, they need to use special equipments. For Municipalities and road manager, they use Ground Penetrating Radar (GPR) for surface analysis. But this equipment is very expensive and therefore limits its accessibility [3]. For drivers, they need to build some equipment in their vehicles to gain this information. Another alternative is to use sensing technologies to gain this information to solve the problem of road surface condition monitoring.

Nowadays, smartphone is widely used. Most of them are equipped with various kinds of sensors like camera, accelerometer, GPS, gyroscope, microphones etc. So, Smartphone based road condition monitoring is one of such useful application where built-in sensors are used to monitor road conditions [2].

This article introduces a road condition monitoring framework that detects the road anomalies such as speed bumps, which based on sensors built in Smartphones. In previous approaches, the main indicator for road anomalies is the accelerometer sensor, as it will be described in the following subsection. In the proposed approach, we investigate the use of the gyroscope around gravity rotation to detect speed bumps in addition to the accelerometer as a cross-validation method to confirm the detection results.

The rest of this article is organized as follows. Section 2 introduces some resent research work related to monitoring of road surface conditions. Section 3 presents the core concepts of smartphones supported sensors and the fundamentals of the support vector machines (SVMs) classification algorithm. Section 4 describes the different phases of the proposed framework, discusses the tested dataset and presented the obtained experimental results. Finally, Section 5 presents conclusions and future work.

2   Related Work

Most of todays smartphones are enabling sensing capabilities through a number of powerful embedded sensors, such as accelerometer, gyroscope, GPS, ambient light sensor, and barometer. These sensors evolved a new application paradigm across a wide variety of domains such as healthcare monitoring, gaming and entertainment. One of these proposed applications is the building of a road monitoring framework that collects basic information about road surface quality.

Kasun et al. in [4] used an acceleration sensor boards for their current running project (BusNet), which basically was proposed for monitoring environmental pollution, to monitor the road surface condition in Sri Lanka. The acceleration sensor boards are capable of measuring the existence of a pothole through the change in the vertical acceleration, in addition it determines the car speed change using the horizontal acceleration. The main drawback in the BusNet road surface monitoring is the uncertainty of the pothole since a change in the horizontal components of the acceleration does not necessarily indicate a rough patch of road; it may indicate a traffic jam.

Pothole Patrol (P^2); a mobile sensing application [5] that detects and reports the road surface conditions. The system depends on a number of accelerometers that are placed inside a taxi cabinet. Through manually labeling, and collecting a set of predefined patterns for road anomalies, the system detects 90% of potholes. The experiment required an integration of specific hardware components; for each taxi an embedded computer running Linux was used, a WiFi card intended for transmitting collected data, an external GPS (mounted on the roof of the car), and a 3-axis accelerometer. Authors in [6] extended this approach by using Vehicular Sensor Networks over wireless sensor networks (customized embedded device).

Girts et al. in [7] initiated a participatory sensing approach for road surface quality monitoring via using smartphones sensing hardware platforms. Their approach required an Android smartphone with GPS, 3-axis accelerometer and communication channel (Cellular or WiFi). The main feature of their framework is the periodically synchronization with database server to store sensors data. The final assessment of the introduced hypothesis needs more in-depth evaluation which had been considered well in [8] and in [9].

3   Preliminaries

3.1   Smartphones Supported Sensors

Modern mobile phones are smart, that is they come with a variety of built-in sensors such as accelerometer, gyroscope, compass, and GPS [10]. An accelerometer is an electromechanical device that is used to measure acceleration change in one, two, or three orthogonal axes (dimensions). The natural of the accelerometer based applications include detecting orientation, vibrational change, and velocity measurement.

The use of the accelerometer to simultaneously detect gravity change and motion accelerations may become a problem; that the sudden stop or sudden change in motion acceleration may detected as a change in gravity (an obstacle). Therefore there is a need for another device that can be used as a cross-validation for gravity change. This device is the Gyroscope (Gyro) sensor [11]. Whereas the accelerometer measures the linear acceleration, the gyroscope measures the angular orientation change (rad/s). Therefore it is known as the angular rate sensor or angular velocity sensor. The use of mobile embedded gyroscope sensor will provide the existence and severity of road bumps. Figure 1, and figure 2 represent captured road condition data gathered respectively from the accelerometer, and the gyroscope.

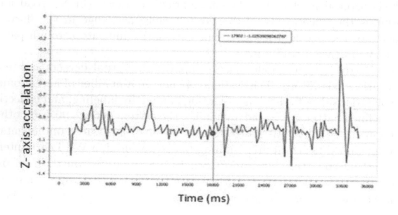

Fig. 1. Accelerometer readings over Z-axis

3.2   The Support Vector Machines (SVMs)

The Support Vector Machine (SVM) is one of the well-known Machine Learning algorithm [12–14] that used to search for the optimal separating hyperplane between classes. The final outcome class is a positive class from another negative class. Assigning a training dataset with n samples $(x_1, y_1), (x_2, y_2), \ldots, (x_n, y_n)$, where x_i is a feature vector in a v-dimensional feature space and with labels $y_i \in$

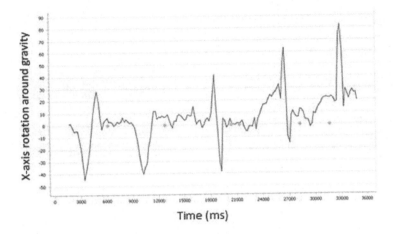

Fig. 2. Gyroscope gravity readings around X-axis

$-1, 1$ belonging to either of two linearly separable classes C_1 and C_2. Equations (1) and (2) show the maximal margin to separate the two classes.

$$maximize \sum_{i=1}^{n} \alpha_i - \frac{1}{2} \sum_{i,j=1}^{n} \alpha_i \alpha_j y_i y_j . K(x_i, x_j) \tag{1}$$

$$Subject - to : \sum_{i=1}^{n} \alpha_i y_i, 0 \leq \alpha_i \leq C \tag{2}$$

where, α_i is the weight assigned to the training sample x_i. If $\alpha_i > 0$, x_i is called a support vector. C is a regulation parameter used to trade-off the training accuracy and the model complexity so that a superior generalization capability can be achieved. K is a kernel function, which is used to measure the similarity between two samples. There are a number of kernel functions that were previously applied (e.g. the Gaussian radial basis function (rbf), polynomial of a given degree, linear, and multi-layer perceptron MLP). These kernels are in general used, independently of the problem, for both discrete and continuous data.

4   Proposed Framework

This article proposes a road condition monitoring framework that detects the road anomalies such as speed bumps. the framework contains five phases as it is illustrated in figure 3. The following subsections will describe in more details these phases. While the main indicator for road anomalies is the accelerometer as described in previous related work section, our detection approach investigates the use of the gyroscope around gravity rotation to detect speed bumps in addition to the accelerometer as a cross-validation method to confirm the detection results..

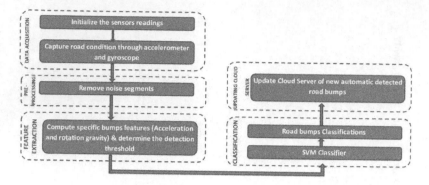

Fig. 3. The proposed road condition monitoring framework

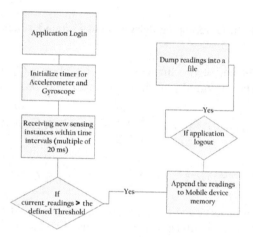

Fig. 4. Data Acquisition phase

4.1   Data Acquisition

Data acquisition phase is the most important one; since it is responsible for collecting road information. The data acquisition process has been done using Nokia Lumia 820 mobile device that was placed inside both a Volkswagen Jetta and Chevrolet Aveo vehicles. Readings of road surface conditions were gathered using both accelerometer and gyroscope sensors. The sensors gathered data along the vehicle path. The collected data was stored locally within the mobile device memory. Also, the GPS coordinates of the manually marked road bumps points are kept within the memory.

The application is not dedicated only for Lumia 820 device, it can be customized to work on other smart devices. Figure 4 that shows the data acquisition framework, starts by checking the existence of accelerometer and gyroscope sensors. Once they are exist, the application initializes a timer to start receiving

sensors data. For saving mobile memory space, specific readings were preprocessed before being stored, like optimizing the time structure in the log files by
putting the difference with a certain time stated at the beginning of the file.
Another preprocessed optimization is done over sensors readings; for example,
the readings of the gyroscope are appended to the device memory if the current
sensed rotation rate (in radians/s) is greater than the previous one stored within
the rate vector. Once the user stops the data acquisition, the application dumps
the log files exist within the memory into to the inserted micro SD card.

4.2   Pre-processing Phase

The Z-axis and X-axis readings for accelerometer and gyroscope, respectively
usually contains irrelevant data (noises). These noises appear clearly when collecting data by the Chevrolet Aveo vehicle. Therefore a pre-processing phase
should be applied in order to reduce signals noise and improve the road bumps
detection. The article applies the second-order high-pass butterworth filter [15].
That maximally flat in the passband and the response rolls off in the stop band.
A high-pass filter decreases all the frequencies below the defined cutoff frequency.
While figure 5 and figurer 6 shows respectively, the original reading (contains
noises) and the filtered readings for the Z-axis of the accelerometer, figure 7 and
figure 8 shows the X-axis readings of the gyroscope before and after applying
the high-pass butterworth filter.

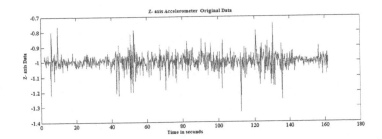

Fig. 5. Original unfiltered Z-axis readings for the Accelerometer

4.3   Features Extraction Phase

In order to reduce input data representation, the input data will be transformed
into feature vectors. Features extracted from the road condition data involve
mean, standard deviation, the difference between minimum and maximum for
both sensor readings.

The feature extraction process shows that there is a relationship between the
road bump detection thresholds for the Z-axis of the accelerometer and X-axis
readings of the gyroscope. That when the accelerometer Z-axis readings falls

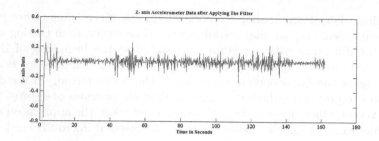

Fig. 6. Filtered Z-axis readings for the Accelerometer

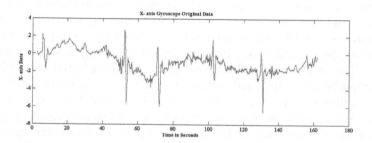

Fig. 7. Original unfiltered X-axis readings for the Gyroscope

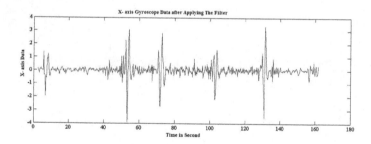

Fig. 8. Filtered X-axis readings for the the Gyroscope

within this range ($0.02 <= Z <= 0.085$) and the gyroscope X-axis readings exist within the range ($1.11 <= X <= 1.9$) this indicates the presence of a road bump.

The features extraction phase exposed the problem of depending only on the gyroscope to detect road bumps that the accuracy of the results are questionable (Figure 9). On the other hand when we combine the accelerometer with the gyroscope readings (cross-validation) the framework accuracy increases (Figure 10); that all false positive readings by the accelerometer were removed.

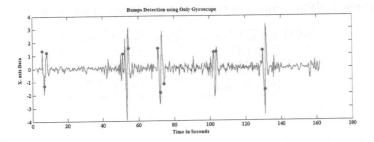

Fig. 9. Detected road bumps using Gyroscope only

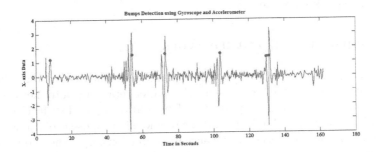

Fig. 10. The combination of Gyroscope and Accelerometer readings shows the real numbers of road bumps

4.4 Classification Phase

Finally, for classification phase, the proposed approach applied SVM classification algorithm with two different kernel functions for classification of road severity (smooth or speed bump) . For SVM, The inputs are training dataset feature vectors and their corresponding classes, whereas the outputs are two classes either a smooth or rough. Table 1 shows different kernel functions applied for classification and their detection accuracy (Radial Base Function (RBF) with sigma =1 and Polynomial with order=3 kernel functions and N-fold cross-validation with N=3). The SVM with a polynomial kernel function, that represents the similarity of vectors (training samples), gives an acceptable classification accuracy for road bumps over the RBF, and MLP kernel functions.

4.5 Updating Cloud Server

Sending coordinates of all detected speed bumps on a cloud server will enables users to save their log files online rather than on their mobile device. The logs include the GPS location of the detected speed bumps (longitude/latitude coordinates) and the severity of them. The intention behind saving road conditions

Table 1. SVM Kernel functions and Road Bumps detection accuracy

SVM Kernel Function	Detection Accuracy
RBF	75.76%
MLP	66.67%
Polynomial	87.88

is to build a road condition map. This map will be used in future to feed another application or a GPS navigation system to automatically alert road users of approaching bumps in their path. This early warning service will help road users to take quick responses.

5   Conclusions and Future Work

Usually smartphones offer opportunities to measure some sensory data. For getting benefits of these opportunities, this this paper represents a framework of five phases of a smartphone based application for monitoring road surface conditions in terms of speed bumps. Although, all the previously proposed solutions for road surface monitoring were based on the accelerometer sensing as the main indicator for road anomalies, it may give false positive indication; especially when there is a sudden stop or sudden change in motion acceleration. The proposed framework assesses the existence and the severity of road bumps using additional sensor which is the gyroscope sensor. A pre-processing phase was applied on collected data to reduce irrelevant noisy segments. A feature extraction and classification phases were functional to classify new readings to their corresponding classes (smooth, or speed bump). As a future work we aim to improve the speed bumps detection algorithm through trying other machine learning classifiers with other pre-processing filters.

References

1. Perttunen, M., et al.: Distributed road surface condition monitoring using mobile phones. In: Hsu, C.-H., Yang, L.T., Ma, J., Zhu, C. (eds.) UIC 2011, vol. 6905, pp. 64–78. Springer, Heidelberg (2011)
2. Douangphachanh, V., Oneyama, H.: A Study on the Use of Smartphones for Road Roughness Condition Estimation. Proceedings of the Eastern Asia Society for Transportation Studies 9 (2013)
3. Mednis, A., Strazdins, G., Zviedris, R., Kanonirs, G., Selavo, L.: Real time pothole detection using Android smartphones with accelerometers. In: International Conference on Distributed Computing in Sensor Systems and Workshops (DCOSS), pp. 27–29 (2011)
4. De Zoysa, K., Keppitiyagama, C., Seneviratne, G.P., Shihan, W.W.A.T.: A public transport system based sensor network for road surface condition monitoring. In: Proceedings of the 2007 Workshop on Networked Systems for Developing Regions, p. 9. ACM (2007)

5. Eriksson, J., Girod, L., Hull, B., Newton, R., Madden, S., Balakrishnan, H.: The pothole patrol: using a mobile sensor network for road surface monitoring. In: Proceedings of the 6th International Conference on Mobile Systems, Applications, and Services, pp. 29–39. ACM (2008)

6. Mednis, A., Elsts, A., Selavo, L.: Embedded solution for road condition monitoring using vehicular sensor networks. In: 2012 6th International Conference on Application of Information and Communication Technologies (AICT), pp. 1–5. IEEE (2012)

7. Strazdins, G., Mednis, A., Kanonirs, G., Zviedris, R., Selavo, L.: Towards Vehicular Sensor Networks with Android Smartphones for Road Surface Monitoring. In: Electronic Proceedings of CPS Week 2nd International Workshop on Networks of Cooperating Objects (CONET 2011), vol. 11 (2011)

8. Forslf, L.: RoadroidSmartphone Road Quality Monitoring. In: 19th ITS World Congress (October 2012)

9. González-Gurrola, L.C., Martínez-Reyes, F., Carlos-Loya, M.R.: The Citizen Road Watcher – Identifying Roadway Surface Disruptions Based on Accelerometer Patterns. In: Urzaiz, G., Ochoa, S.F., Bravo, J., Chen, L.L., Oliveira, J. (eds.) UCAmI 2013. LNCS, vol. 8276, pp. 374–377. Springer, Heidelberg (2013)

10. Johnson, D.A., Trivedi, M.M.: Driving style recognition using a smartphone as a sensor platform. In: 2011 14th International IEEE Conference on Intelligent Transportation Systems (ITSC), pp. 1609–1615. IEEE (2011)

11. Boonstra, M.C., van der Slikke, R., Keijsers, N.L.W., van Lummel, R.C., de Waal Malefijt, M.C., Verdonschot, N.: The accuracy of measuring the kinematics of rising from a chair with accelerometers and gyroscopes. Journal of Biomechanics 39(2), 354–358 (2006)

12. Wu, Q., Zhou, D.-X.: Analysis of support vector machine classification. J. Comput. Anal. Appl. 8, 99–119 (2006)

13. Zawbaa, H.M., El-Bendary, N., Hassanien, A.E., Abraham, A.: SVM-based Soccer Video Summarization System. In: Proceedings of the Third IEEE World Congress on Nature and Biologically Inspired Computing (NaBIC 2011), Salamanca, Spain, pp. 7–11 (2011)

14. Zawbaa, H.M., El-Bendary, N., Hassanien, A.E., Kim, T.-h.: Machine Learning-Based Soccer Video Summarization System. In: Kim, T.-h., Gelogo, Y. (eds.) MulGraB 2011, Part II. CCIS, vol. 263, pp. 19–28. Springer, Heidelberg (2011)

15. Butterworth, S.: On the theory of filter amplifiers. Wireless Engineer 7, 536–541 (1930)

An Orphan Drug Legislation System

Ahmed Abdel Aziz[1], Moustafa Zein[3,5], Mohammed Atef[2,5], Ammar Adl[3,5], Kareem Kamal A. Ghany[4,5], and Aboul Ella Hassanien[3,5]

[1] Ain Shams Univ., Faculty of Engineering, Egypt
[2] Faculty of Science., Cairo University, Egypt
[3] Faculty of Computers and Information, Cairo University, Egypt
[4] Faculty of Computers and Information, Beni-Suef University, Egypt and SRGE Member
[5] Scientific Research Group in Egypt (SRGE), Egypt

Abstract. Orphan drugs are a treatment for rare diseases. From that, comes the importance of orphan drug development and discovery. For an orphan drug to be approved by the FDA, it does not have to be similar to any approved orphan drug. So chemists opinions are important to determine the probability of similarity. It is too hard to check all orphan drugs for any rare disease. It takes a long time and big effort, so we introduce in this study a system that classifies the orphan drugs according to their probability of structural similarity. It also compares between them and the unauthorized orphan drug to determine the closest orphan drug to it. That system helps chemists to study a certain orphan database using the five features. That system provides better results. It provides chemists with the clusters of orphan drugs after adding the drug that needs to be authorized to its cluster.

1 Introduction

Orphan drug legislation by the U.S. Food and Drug Administration (FDA) is motivating drug companies to develop drugs that have low development cost in order to treat rare diseases. Unlike other drugs, those newly developed drugs target a few number of patients [2, 3]. Over the 25 years since the US legislation has been made, the FDA has approved 250 drugs for roughly 200 diseases [2, 15]. Chemists often need to compare some unauthorized orphan drugs with all the approved drugs by FDA to check if there is a drug that's similar to the one that needs to be approved. Unfortunately; that process is manual and takes time. It also gets repeated by more than one chemist. The drug approval process is considered a part of the orphan drug development and industry.

The stages of developing a new orphan drug (OD) are still a challenging, time-consuming and cost-intensive process because it's totally manual [4, 19]. That consuming process would've been reasonable if the developed drug is used in the treatment of an orphan disease. Drug companies rather aim their efforts at producing drugs that are already available [9, 11]. Computational models help the chemist to find alternatives to medicinal chemistry experiments for studying a lot of chemical trends [4]. Development of ODs remains complex because of

© Springer International Publishing Switzerland 2015
D. Filev et al. (eds.), *Intelligent Systems'2014*,
Advances in Intelligent Systems and Computing 323, DOI: 10.1007/978-3-319-11310-4_34

the limited availability of patients needed for clinical testing, and the scarce translational knowledge about diagnosing and evaluating treatment efficacy in rare diseases in general [21, 13].

There is much current interest in the development of orphan drugs for the treatment of rare diseases [22]. Now we had a computer system to help chemists study the certain orphan drug database with following features: The first feature is the one to one comparison; as drug to drug comparison determines how the approved drug is similar to an unauthorized drug using structural similarity measurements. One of the techniques used in detecting structural similarity is similarity searching. It is a technique for ligand-based virtual screening [4]. Any similarity measurements depend on 3 features: The first feature is the representation used to describe the structure of compounds. The second feature is weighting scheme, and the third one is similarity coefficient [22]. Since no similarity measurement has an optimal solution, more than one solution is needed [4].

Similarity measurements have varying proportions for every two compound structure. The previous study introduced a solution to give us one accurate similarity based on data fusion rules. Data fusion is an operation that combines multiple sources of data into a single source instead of individual input sources. By doing that, the resulting fused source is expected to be more informative [22]. Data fusion has been widely used as a way of enhancing the effectiveness of similarity-based virtual screening [7, 12, 18, 16]. We will use this technique as a step in our system. Another feature is orphan drug database classification. The classification is a wide technique in cheminformatics trends which help in clusters drug datasets that include millions of compounds to facilitate study of drugs. In this study we used the cluster technique to classify the orphan drugs based on structural similarity.

2 Problem Discussion

2.1 Problem Overview

In European committee and the FDA, medicines are authorized for some rare disease only if the chemist determined that this drug is not similar to approved orphan drugs for that disease. When a company applies to register a new drug for an indication that has already been granted for an orphan drug, it is the responsibility of the EMA's Committee for Orphan Medicinal Products (COMP) to decide if the new drug is indeed similar to an existing orphan drug, with an application being successful only when the COMP decides that this is not the case. To date, the evaluations carried out by the COMP have been based largely on human judgments of similarity [19]. For this evaluation, chemists need to revise all orphan drugs for the same disease. Orphan drug databases have plenty of drugs for the rare diseases. Approving unauthorized drugs needs effort and time from chemists to compare with all orphan drugs for the same rare disease and determine if the drug is not similar to approved orphan drugs for that disease.

2.2   Problem Core

Using chemist efforts to measure the similarity of drugs takes time and is not very efficient. Also, it does not provide any level of orphan drug classification for the drugs used in the measurement process. Using some fingerprint similarity coefficients to measure the similarity gives different results that can't be helping the chemist to take a final decision, Also, sing the fusion rules to give chemists one probability, but with no clustering to the orphan drugs used in the process of similarity measurements leads to some difficulty in determining the closest approved drug to the drug that needs to be authorized. If some similarity measurements changed, the chemists' decision changes, too. So one verified output is needed. It should represent more than one of similarity measurements that helps in building a system in order to determine the probability of similarity to orphan drugs. It also should be useful for data generalization and in giving a classification that will help chemists to determine the closest drug to farthest drug. Each chemist provides a different decision. That requires more effort to reach a final decision about drug authority for every approved orphan drug.

2.3   Related Work

Some previous studies introduced solutions like 2D fingerprint methods to support the assessment of structural similarity in orphan drug [4]. Willett, Peter [22] described the use of supervised fusion rules and techniques in cheminformatics to solve the similar problem and Orphan drug legislation with data fusion rules using multiple fingerprints measurements [14]. Fingerprint-based measures of similarity can be used to assess the structural novelty of molecules that are being submitted for consideration as new medicines for rare diseases.

The results obtained by Willett, Peter [11] here explain clearly that simple, 2D fingerprint representations provide measures of structural similarity that the copyist closely the judgments of experts, using both training-set molecule-pairs extracted from DrugBank and test-set molecule-pairs typical of the work of the CHMP. This is so despite the fact that the two sets of molecules are rather different in character. The k-means clustering method is a very popular relocation clustering method in which an initial partition of a dataset is progressively refined by shifting objects between clusters so as to optimize some criterion of the 'goodness' of the partition. Many implementations of k-means are non-deterministic, in that the precise classification of a dataset that is obtained at the end of a run is dependent on the order in which the dataset is processed [7].

3   Methodology

3.1   Dataset

For classification we used a number of orphan drugs as an input to a classy feature and one to many drug comparisons that shown in table 1. All drugs have the compound graphical representation and SMILES. These orphan drugs were used from pubchem (https://pubchem.ncbi.nlm.nih.gov/) Drugs store and their Generic name from U. S. Health Resources and Services Administration (HRSA) [1]. DrugBank (http://www.drugbank.ca/) is the source of the 100 molecules-pairs training set that was used in this study, where the pair of molecule consists of molecular structure of authorized drug A and molecular structure of new drug B. Molecules similarity values were obtained by chemist as shown in the one-to-one comparison in table 2.

Table 1. Orphan drug database sample

ID	29770
SMILES	CCCCC1=C(C2= CC=CC=C2O1)C(=O)C3=CC(=C(C(=C3)I)OCC[NH+] (CC)CC)I.[Cl-]
Generic Name	Amiodarone HCl

Table 2. Orphan drug database sample

Pairs	Molecule A	Molecule B
Yes opinion	0.91	
No opinion	0.09	

3.2   Cheminformatics Toolkit

The benchmarking platform presented here uses RDKit (http://www.rdkit.org), an open-source cheminformatics toolkit made available under the permissive Berkeley Software Distribution (BSD) license [20, 14] that introduces some important functions for our studies.

3.3   The Proposed System

The proposed system consists of three stages to help the chemist in studying certain orphan drug database accurately. Stage 1, where fusion rules were applied to 100 pairs of molecules. A pair consists of one approved drug and an unauthorized drug. Rules were applied to all orphan drugs in the dataset based on fingerprints structural similarity measurements. Stage 2, where popular cluster technique, K-means clustering, is used to cluster orphan drugs based on the probability of similarity between approved orphan drugs and the drug that needs to be authorized. The output of this stage is a K-cluster of orphan drugs with their similarities. Stage 3, where the unauthorized drug probability of structural similarity is compared to the probabilities of structural similarity of each orphan drug in the nearest cluster. The output of this stage is ranking of the nearest dataset with the position of the drug that needs to be authorized.

Fingerprints Measurements. Fingerprints technique is used here to get the representation which is used to measure the probability of structural similarity. Available fingerprints techniques are notably different in performance [20, 14]. Multiple actives is used in this study as query molecules together with some kind of data fusion [7]. Similarity measure used in comparing chemical structures represented by means of fingerprints are (Dice, Tanimoto, Cosine, Kaczynski, McConnaughey) coefficients for ('ECFP6', 'MACCS', 'FCFP6', 'AVALON', 'RDK7', 'RDK6', RDK5', 'HASHAP', 'HASHTT') fingerprints representation [5] for measuring the similarity of dataset of orphan drug. These fingerprints ranked by Sereina R. in his study [17].

Fingerprints were calculated using the RDKit (http://www.rdkit.org). The RDKit fingerprint, a relative of the well-known Daylight fingerprint [26], is another topological descriptor. Sample fingerprints made using (ECFP6, MACCS, and RDK7) are presented in table 3. It includes the chemist's opinion with acceptance similarity probability between molecules of authorized drug and the molecules of new drugs, in addition to the probability of similarity that was calculated by fingerprint techniques.

Table 3. Probability of similarity for some fingerprint techniques and similarity measures

ID	yes opinion	ECFP6	MACCS	RDK7
1	0.72	0.63	0.68	0.66
2	0.45	0.43	0.3	0.49
3	0.95	0.79	0.92	0.74
4	0.21	0.3	0.41	0.55
5	0.23	0.52	0.18	0.42
6	0.43	0.67	0.23	0.46
7	0.29	0.34	0.3	0.26
8	0.46	0.62	0.42	0.49
9	0.96	0.8	0.91	0.75
10	0.88	0.81	0.68	0.8

Fingerprints Similarity Measure is the procedure used to calculate similarity measures between an approved orphan drug and the unauthorized drug using 2D fingerprint representation.

Algorithm 1 Fingerprints Similarity Measure

{Training-set with 100 pairs (FDA approved, unauthorized) of molecules.}
1: READ $FDA\_unauthorized\_list$
2: DEFINE $FDA\_molecule, unauthorized\_molecule, molecules\_pair, SMILES$
3: DEFINE $probabilities\_list$ {Probabilities of similarity between molecules pairs}
4: **for** $j = 1$ to n **do** {n = 100}
5:     READ $FDA\_molecule, unauthorized\_molecule$
6:     SET $molecules\_pair = (FDA\_molecule, unauthorized\_molecule)$
7:     GET $SMILES$
8:     DEFINE probability {Probability represent similarity between molecules pairs}
9:     COMPUTE similarity OF $molecules\_pair$ {2D fingerprint representation}
10:     CALL   Calculate   probability   WITH   similarity   RETURNING   probability   {Using $TAMINOTO\_COEFFICIENT$}
11:     $probabilities\_list$[i] = probability
12: **end for**
13: RETURN $probabilities\_list$

Data Fusion. Data fusion rules were used to output a single probability value of similarity from the probability values of each structural similarity [22, 7]. By using fusion rules, a unique probability of similarity were calculated for every compound. Table 4 shows the chemist opinion and fusion rules (SUM, MED and MAX) results. By analyzing results in Table 4, SUM fusion rule gives the nearest probability of similarity to chemist yes opinion.

Table 4. Unique probability of similarity using Data fusion rules

Yes opinion	SUM	MED	Max	Best rule
0.72	0.66	0.66	0.68	Max
0.45	0.41	0.43	0.49	MED
0.95	0.82	0.79	0.92	MAX
0.21	0.42	0.41	0.55	MED
0.23	0.37	0.42	0.52	SUM
0.43	0.45	0.46	0.67	SUM
0.29	0.3	0.3	0.34	SUM-MED
0.46	0.51	0.49	0.62	MED
0.96	0.82	0.8	0.91	MAX
0.88	0.85	0.81	0.95	SUM

K-means Clustering. The technique used here was introduced by Pipeline Pilots R Statistics (Pipeline Pilot available at http://www.accelrys.com; R statistics available at http://www.r-project.org). It is the implementation of the k-means method where the initial database partition is generated using a random seed and then the database molecules for every drug in the orphan drug database are sequentially assigned to that cluster to which they are most similar [7]. The molecule-cluster structural similarity is calculated using the Euclidean metric between the molecules fingerprint and the centroid of the cluster, where the centroid is the arithmetic mean of the fingerprints of the molecules currently contained in the cluster [7]. Using k-means clustering to classify orphan drugs based on similarity; the data in table 1 is a sample for the clustering technique input dataset. After applying the classification method, K-mean, and ranking process, the output cluster is ordered from lowest to the highest similarity. Class1 column in Table 5 shows that 19 drugs lie between 0.2 to 0.45 probability-of-similarity values with their IDs in the dataset.

Table 5. Orphan drugs classification using k-means clustering

Clustering Classes	Class 1	Class 2	Class 3	Similarity Ranking
	641115	9831652	77082	0.930
	29770	861453	165580	0.910
	2578	54566	564	0.901
	6035	518740	2141	0.885
	6116	65664	5287969	0.884
	6209	74989	4649	0.870
	10112	9444	12765	0.850
	10133	2265	4649	0.844
	20279	247	528796	0.830
Drugs IDs	21157	54566	37768	0.821
	2578	518740	82146	0.817
	400010	21700	104865	0.801
	1548943	64971		
	5484199	71354		
	6433095	72466		
	6918638	56971651		
	9837243			
	11969480			
	2182			
Number Of Drugs	19	16	12	
Clusters Low Similarity	0.20	0.60	0.80	
Clusters High Similarity	0.45	0.74	0.93	

Ranking results of the nearest clustering class (class3) is shown in *Similarity Ranking* column in Table 5. Classify Orphan Drugs is the procedure used in classifying the approved orphan drugs based on their structural similarity, using 2D fingerprints representation and fusion rules procedures.

Algorithm 2 Classify Orphan Drugs

1: READ *molecules_datasets* {Datasets with (FDA approved, unauthorized) pairs}
2: SET *ORPHAN_DRUGS_NUMBER*
3: DEFINE *orphan_drugs_K − clusters* {K-clusters of orphan drugs with similarity}
4: DEFINE *FDA_unautherized_list* {100 pairs of molecules}
5: DEFINE *fusion_data_list* {To hold "Calculate fusion Data" procedure outputs}
6: **for** $j = 1$ to *ORPHAN_DRUGS_NUMBER* **do**
7:     SET *FDA_unautherized_list = molecules_datasets*[i]
8:     DEFINE result
9:     CALL Calculate fusion WITH *FDA_unautherized_list* RETURNING result
10:     *fusion_data_list*[i] = result
11: **end for**
12: CALL Popular cluster technique WITH *fusion_data_list* RETURNING *orphan_drugs_K − clusters*
13: RETURN *orphan_drugs_K − clusters*

Predict Orphan Drugs Position with Unknown Similarity Orphan Drugs. The input for the prediction process is the dataset representing orphan drugs and their probability of similarity with the unauthorized drug. The prediction process aims at outputting random trees representing the position of orphan drugs compared to the unauthorized drug. The process follow these steps to output the random trees; Using the measurements of structural similarity and data fusion of orphan drugs and unauthorized drug as input to the algorithm. Run the algorithm and execute the different prediction trees and select the trees with highest similarity. By that technique, it is easy to predict the similarity of any number of orphan drugs with unauthorized drug.

Random forest [6] combines several random decision trees to make a prediction. It uses multiple models to obtain better predictive performance [10]. As the orphan drug dataset is small, the performance of Random forest is accurate and robustness.

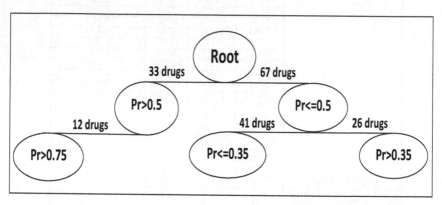

Fig. 1. Sample of prediction trees using random forest using training and testing data

Predict Nearest Orphan Drugs. Inputs of the ranking process are the dataset representing orphan drugs and their probability of similarity with the unauthorized drug plus the production year as a 2D feature space. The process outputs a classified unauthorized drug by a majority vote of its neighbors, with the unauthorized drug being assigned to the most common class among its k-nearest neighbors of orphan drugs. The process runs the algorithm to execute the nearest class and the k nearest neighbors based on the similarity. Using that technique we can predict t number of orphan drugs that are closest to unauthorized drug. By using k-nearest neighbors [8], orphan drugs classification is obtained. When we test the unauthorized drug, it should be classified to specific class based on the number of class (k) and the similarity.

Table 6. K samples of orphan drugs after using K-NN technique

Clustering Classes	Class 1	Class 2	Class 3	Class 4
	6116	9444	5287969	4649
	6209	2265	2141	165580
	10112	247	37768	12765
	10133		564	5287969
	20279		4649	2141
Drugs IDs	21157			37768
	6116			564
				4649
				5287969
				77082
				82146
				104865
K-sample	7	3	5	12

The test sample (unauthorized drug) should be classified to one of the four classes in Table 6. Example of k-NN classification is shown in table 6. If k =

3, it is assigned to the second class because it contains 2 drugs which are the closest to similarity to the test sample. If k = 5 it is assigned to the fourth class. The results of K samples used in running the algorithm are shown in table 6.

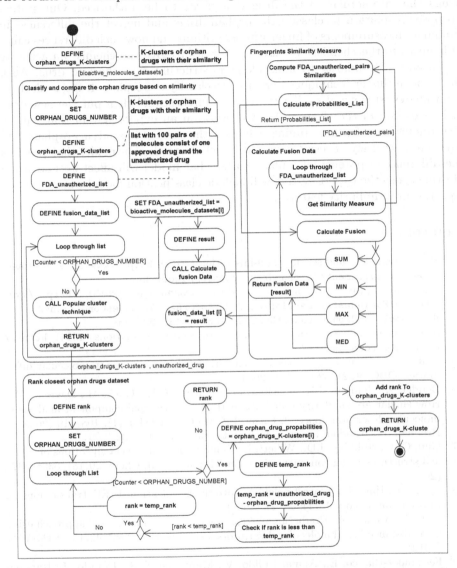

Fig. 2. Workflow of our system using the following features (i) one to one comparison. (ii) Orphan drug database classifications. (iii) One to many comparisons and ranking.

Main. The main function representing the sequence of the system as shown in main algorithm figure2. Comparing our results to previous work, we found that our results were more accurate and unique for probability of similarity which in turns will useful for any chemist studying certain orphan drug database.

4   Conclusions and Future Work

In this study we introduce a solution to help the chemist to classify the orphan drugs that are similar to the drug that needs to be authorized. Our system proposes a solution to classify the orphan drugs and detect the differences in similarity measurements of fingerprint algorithms and how such differences cause difficulties to the chemist. We use fusion rules to give the chemist an accurate probability of similarity to molecule-pairs structure in authorized drug. Also, the k-mean cluster techniques were used to classify the orphan drugs, rank them from nearest structural similarity drugs to furthest and then put the new drug in its position in the clusters. We will work on an expert system that will be introducing some features aiming at helping the chemist in studying orphan drug with high accuracy. These features will include prediction model that predicts the difference of potency of orphan drugs. That model will affect authorization of drugs. Also the expert system will include classification model which is based on structural similarity features.

References

[1] Health resources and services administration (2012), http://www.hrsa.gov/opa/programrequirements/orphandrugexclusion/index.html

[2] How to apply for orphan product designation (2013), http://www.fda.gov/ForIndustry/DevelopingProductsforRareDiseasesConditions/HowtoapplyforOrphanProductDesignation/ucm135122.htm

[3] European medicines agency. rare disease (orphan) designations (2014), http://www.ema.europa.eu/ema/

[4] Bender, A., Glen, R.C.: Molecular similarity: a key technique in molecular informatics. OBC 2(22), 3204–3218 (2004)

[5] Bender, A., Jenkins, J.L., Scheiber, J., Sukuru, S.C.K., Glick, M., Davies, J.W.: How similar are similarity searching methods? a principal component analysis of molecular descriptor space. J. Chem. Inf. Model., JCIM 49(1), 108–119 (2009)

[6] Breiman, L.: Random forests. Machine Learning 45(1), 5–32 (2001)

[7] Chu, C.W., Holliday, J.D., Willett, P.: Combining multiple classifications of chemical structures using consensus clustering. Bioorg. Med. Chem. 20(18), 5366–5371 (2012)

[8] Cover, T., Hart, P.: Nearest neighbor pattern classification. IEEE Transactions on Information Theory 13(1), 21–27 (1967)

[9] Dutt, R., Madan, A.: Predicting biological activity: Computational approach using novel distance based molecular descriptors. Comput. Biol. Med. 42(10), 1026–1041 (2012)

[10] Fernández-Blanco, E., Aguiar-Pulido, V., Munteanu, C.R., Dorado, J.: Random forest classification based on star graph topological indices for antioxidant proteins. J. Theor. Biol. 317, 331–337 (2013)

[11] Franco, P., Porta, N., Holliday, J.D., Willett, P.: The use of 2d fingerprint methods to support the assessment of structural similarity in orphan drug legislation. J. Cheminformatics 6(1), 5 (2014)

[12] Geppert, H., Vogt, M., Bajorath, J.: Current trends in ligand-based virtual screening: molecular representations, data mining methods, new application areas, and performance evaluation. J. Chem. Inf. Model., JCIM 50(2), 205–216 (2010)

[13] Heemstra, H., Vrueh, R., Weely, S., Bller, H., Leufkens, H.: Predictors of orphan drug approval in the european union. Eur. J. Clin. Pharmacol. 64(5), 545–552 (2008), http://dx.doi.org/10.1007/s00228-007-0454-6

[14] Jain, A.N., Nicholls, A.: Recommendations for evaluation of computational methods. J. Comput. Aided Mol. Des. 22(3-4), 133–139 (2008)

[15] Joppi, R., Garattini, S., et al.: Orphan drugs, orphan diseases. the first decade of orphan drug legislation in the eu. Eur. J. Clin. Pharmacol. 69(4), 1009–1024 (2013)

[16] Morgan, S., Grootendorst, P., Lexchin, J., Cunningham, C., Greyson, D.: The cost of drug development: a systematic review. Health Policy 100(1), 4–17 (2011)

[17] Riniker, S., Landrum, G.A.: Open-source platform to benchmark fingerprints for ligand-based virtual screening. J. Cheminformatics 5, 26 (2013)

[18] Ripphausen, P., Nisius, B., Bajorath, J.: State-of-the-art in ligand-based virtual screening. Drug Discovery Today 16(9), 372–376 (2011)

[19] Todeschini, R., Consonni, V., Xiang, H., Holliday, J., Buscema, M., Willett, P.: Similarity coefficients for binary chemoinformatics data: overview and extended comparison using simulated and real data sets. J. Chem. Inf. Model., JCIM 52(11), 2884–2901 (2012)

[20] Truchon, J.F., Bayly, C.I.: Evaluating virtual screening methods: good and bad metrics for the early recognition problem. J. Chem. Inf. Model., JCIM 47(2), 488–508 (2007)

[21] Westermark, K., Holm, B.B., Söderholm, M., Llinares-Garcia, J., Rivière, F., Aarum, S., Butlen-Ducuing, F., Tsigkos, S., Wilk-Kachlicka, A., N'Diamoi, C., et al.: European regulation on orphan medicinal products: 10 years of experience and future perspectives. Nature Reviews. Drug Discovery 10(5), 341–349 (2011)

[22] Willett, P.: Combination of similarity rankings using data fusion. J. Chem. Inf. Model., JCIM 53(1), 1–10 (2013)

Fruit-Based Tomato Grading System Using Features Fusion and Support Vector Machine

Noura A. Semary[1,5], Alaa Tharwat[2,5], Esraa Elhariri[3,5],
and Aboul Ella Hassanien[4,5]

[1] Faculty of Computers and Information, Menofia University, Egypt
[2] Faculty of Engineering, Suez Canal University, Egypt
[3] Faculty of Computers and Information, Fayoum University, Egypt
[4] Faculty of Computers and Information, Cairo University, Egypt
[5] Scientific Research Group in Egypt (SRGE)
http://www.egyptscience.net

Abstract. Machine learning and computer vision techniques have applied for evaluating food quality as well as crops grading. In this paper, a new classification system has been proposed to classify infected/uninfected tomato fruits according to its external surface. The system is based on feature fusion method with color and texture features. Color moments, GLCM, and Wavelets energy and entropy have been used in the proposed system. Principle Component Analysis (PCA) technique has been used to reduce the feature vector obtained after fusion to avoid dimensionality problem and save time and cost. Support vector machine (SVM) was used to classify tomato images into 2 classes; infected/uninfected using Min-Max and Z-Score normalization methods. The dataset used in this research contains 177 tomato fruits each was captured from four faces (Top, Side1, Side2, and End). Using 70% of the total images for training phase and 30% for testing, our proposed system achieved accuracy 92%.

Keywords: food quality, feature fusion, Color moments, GLCM, Wavelets, Tomato, PCA, SVM.

1 Introduction

The need of intelligent systems that serve the industry is increasing every day. Vegetables, fruits and crops sorting isone of the most important biological processes in crops production. This process is still done manually in most countries, including Egypt. According to (FAOSTAT Database, 2011)[1], tomato is the 8th most important vegetable crop next to wheat. World production was about 159 million tons fresh fruit produced in 2011 with income about 582 trillion Dollars. Tomato production has been reported for 144 countries. Egypt is the 5th major country after China, India, United States and Turkey in both income of harvested production $(2,995,413\$1000)$and weight of fruit produced (8,105,263 Mt) [1]. Computer-based fruit sorting has great attention by Computer Vision and AI researchers [2–7]. Although the great importance of Tomato production

© Springer International Publishing Switzerland 2015
D. Filev et al. (eds.), *Intelligent Systems'2014*,
Advances in Intelligent Systems and Computing 323, DOI: 10.1007/978-3-319-11310-4_35

as mentioned before, there are very few works in the literatures concerns with tomato grading especially with diseases detection. The great concern with quality control due to new market restrictions in recent years has become so important that it has demanded a technology of process geared toward more reliable tests and new methods of monitoring product quality [4]. The aim of this work is to help in grading systems before manufacturing or to be a basic block in computer vision based expert systems.

The objective of this study is to propose an automatic tomato grading system dedicated for Egyptian tomato most disorders. It's known that most crops disorders appear in the plant root, stem, leaves and fruits according to the type and causes of injury. In this paper, only fruit images are used for detection purpose. Twelve different disorders have been captured. The image acquisition procedure we have used to collect the dataset, insures the examination of whole fruit surface. The rest of the paper is organized as follows. Section (2) presents the proposed fruit-based tomato grading system in details. System results are presented in section (3). Finally, Section (4) concludes the paper.

2 The Proposed Grading System

This work has been divided into three basic stages. Dataset preparation, Features Extraction and Classification which will be discussed in details in this section. The dataset used by the proposed system has been collected randomly from fresh vegetables and fruits market in Menofia city, Egypt. Exactly, 177 samples out of 200 collected ones have been included in this study. As there were 13 samples have been eliminated due to transportation damages and 10 have been excluded due to their immaturity. The samples varied between un-defected and defected ones.

First, the stem green part in each sample has been removed. Each sample has been cleaned. A special studio has been prepared for imaging purpose. The studio was constructed from a white box, CCD camera (Sony DCR-SR46 with 40x optical zoom) and a Day-Light florescent lamp (Toshiba FL2019 D/19 Daylight). The camera has been set in a perpendicular angle with the box on the same surface plan. The light has been set in the same angle and distance of the camera. The resolution of the captured photos is 640 × 480. All photos are decoded by JPEG standard coding technique. Most of the previous works assume imaging the injured face directly. For best defect detection results, the fruits have been imaged from 4 sides (Top, End, Side1 and Side2) to cover the whole fruit surface.

2.1 Dataset Preparation Phase

In this stage of work, segmentation has been made using ground truth. The white background has been replaced by completely white color ($r = 255, g = 255, b = 255$) using Photoshop image editing tool. The dataset images has been annotated by three experts to define the type of defect based on the visual symptoms appeared on the fruit only. Table (1) shows the number of samples for each disorder. The collected disorders varied between physiological, fungal and insects effect diseases. There are some samples faced different reasons to be defected. In this stage of our system, we care about automatic classification between defected and un-defected fruit whatever the type of defect. After the samples being ready for processing, features have been extracted.

Table 1. Summary of collected dataset

defect	no. samples
radial cracks	13
concentric cracks	1
blossom end rot	11
early blight	28
anthracnose	15
sun scald	37
worms	6
mite spider	14
blotchy ripeness	10
normal	27
tomato spots	8
yellow shoulders	7
total	177

2.2 Feature Extraction Phase

Preprocessing Stage. Preceding feature extraction procedure, white background has been detected and neglected to calculate the features of the fruit part only using Algorithm(1):

Algorithm 1. Background Removal Algorithm

1: Given RGB Image Img of Tomato and White Mask $Mask$ both of size 640×480
2: Convert RGB image to GrayScale one $GrayImg$
3: Calculate the difference $Diff$ between Img and $GrayImg$
4: Perform morphological opening on $Diff$
5: Perform holes filling on $Diff$
6: Perform morphological erosion by 5×5 structure element on $Diff$
7: Multiply Img by $Diff$
8: Output is segmented RGB Image of size 640×480

Color Features. One of the most well used features is the color information in the image. Color information can be retrieved either from intensity channel, chromaticity channels or both. Many researchers prefer using intensity information to recognize wither the fruit is defected or not. Color models play very important role in features extraction when the target is to extract the chrominance information. Many color models can be used for this purpose like RGB, YCbCr, HSV, and YIQetc. Color features include statistical features like as mean, variance, and standard deviation and color moments. First, the images have been converted to HSV color model. Four moments have been calculated for the fruit part in 7 channels; $Intensity(I)$, $Red(R)$, $Green(G)$, $Blue(B)$, $Hue(H)$, $Saturation(S)$ and $Value(V)$. So, a total of 28 statistical features has been extracted for each face. Color moments(Mean, Variance, Skewness and Kurtosis) have been calculated by the equations (2-5):

$$\bar{X} = \frac{\sum_{k=1}^{N} P_k}{N} \tag{1}$$

$$Variance = \frac{1}{N} \sum_{k=1}^{N}(P_k - \bar{X})^2 \tag{2}$$

$$Skewness = \frac{\frac{1}{N}\sum_{k=1}^{N}(P_k - \bar{X})^3}{\sigma^3} \tag{3}$$

$$Kurtosis = \frac{\frac{1}{N}\sum_{k=1}^{N}(P_k - \bar{X})^4}{\sigma^4} \tag{4}$$

Where p is a pixel in the fruit part in the image, and N is the total number of pixels in the fruit part.

Texture Features. Texture features have been used for defect recognition purpose in many works in literature. One of the most well-known methods to get texture features is the Gray Level Co-occurrence Matrix (GLCM).In this method, the relative frequencies of gray level pairs of pixels separated by a distance d in the direction θ combined to form a relative displacement vector (d, θ), which is computed and stored in a matrix referred to as gray level co-occurrence matrix (GLCM). This matrix is used to extract second-order statistical texture features. Haralick in [11] suggests 14 features describing the two-dimensional probability density function P. Nine of the most popular commonly used are ASM (Energy/Angular Second Moment), Con (Contrast), Cor(Correlation), Ent (Entropy), Var (Variance), Sent (Sum of Entropy), Shd (Cluster Shade), Prom (Prominance) and Hom (Homoginity). The features from (6-12) have been selected from[12], while features (13 -14) have been selected from[9]and [13]respectively:

$$ASM = \sum_{i=0}^{G-1}\sum_{j=0}^{G-1}(P_{ij})^2 \tag{5}$$

$$Con = \sum_{i=0}^{G-1}\sum_{j=0}^{G-1}(i-j)^2 P_{ij} \tag{6}$$

$$Cor = \frac{1}{\sigma_x \sigma_y} \sum_{i=0}^{G-1} \sum_{j=0}^{G-1} [(ij)P_{ij} - \mu_x \mu_y] \tag{7}$$

$$Ent = - \sum_{i=0}^{G-1} \sum_{j=0}^{G-1} P_{ij} log P_{ij} \tag{8}$$

$$Var = \sum_{i=0}^{G-1} \sum_{j=0}^{G-1} (i - \pi)^2 P_{ij} \tag{9}$$

$$Hom = \sum_{i=0}^{G-1} \sum_{j=0}^{G-1} \frac{1}{(i-j)^2} P_{ij} \tag{10}$$

$$Sent = - \sum_{i=2}^{2G-2} P_{x+y}(i) log P_{x+y}(i) \tag{11}$$

$$Shd = \sum_{i=0}^{G-1} \sum_{j=0}^{G-1} (i + j - \mu_x - \mu_y)^3 P_{ij} \tag{12}$$

$$Prom = \sum_{i=0}^{G-1} \sum_{j=0}^{G-1} (i + j - \mu_x - \mu)^4 P_{ij} \tag{13}$$

Where μ_x, μ_y, σ_x, and σ_y are the means and the standard deviations of the corresponding distributions; and G is the number of gray levels. The GLCM features are obtained based on distance $d=1$ and angles $\theta = \{0^o, 45^o, 90^o, 135^o\}$, leading to a total of 36 GLCM features per face. Two other texture features was extracted in our proposed system; the entropy and the energy of wavelets decomposition coefficients of the image [14]. The entropy gives a positive criterion for analyzing and comparing probability distribution. It provides a measure of the information of any distribution. We define the total Wavelets Entropy (WPy) as:

$$WPy = WPy(P) = - \sum_{j<0} P_j \cdot ln P_j \tag{14}$$

Where resolution level $j = 1, \ldots, D$. Wavelet energy appears as a measure of the degree of order/disorder of the signal, so it can provide useful information about the underlying dynamical process associated with the signal[14]. The energy of wavelet coefficient is varying over different scales. To calculate the energy of wavelets sub-bands, consider the four sub-bands of decomposition LL, LH, HL and HH. The Wavelet Energy (WGy) for D decomposition levels are extracted using the equation:

$$WGy_j = \sum_k \frac{|C_j(k)|^2}{N_k} \tag{15}$$

Where j is the decomposition level, $C(k)$ is the coefficient at subband k and N_k is the number of coefficients in subband k. The energy at each sampled time k will be:

$$E(k) = \sum_{j=1}^{D} \frac{|C_j(k)|^2}{N_k} \tag{16}$$

In consequence, the total energy can be obtained by using the following equation:

$$WGy = \sum_j E_j \tag{17}$$

Feature Fusion. Fusion in feature level may improve the performance of the systems. Fusion of features achieved through concatenating two or more different feature vectors into one vector. Assume $f_1 = x_1....x_r$, $f_2 = y_1, ...,y_s$, and $f_3 = z_1, ...,z_t$ are three feature vectors with three different sizes r, s, and t respectively. $f_{new} = x_1,...., x_r,y_1,....,y_s ,z_1,....,z_t$, can represent the concatenation of the three feature vectors f_1, f_2 and f_3[20]. One of the problems of combining features is the compatibility of different features. Thus, normalization techniques are used to solve this problem before concatenation [16]. In our experiments we used Z_{score}. It is the most common method. This method maps the input scores to distribution with mean of zero and standard deviation of 1 as follows:

$$\acute{f}_i = \frac{f_i - \mu_i}{\sigma_i} \tag{18}$$

Where f_i is the ith feature vector, μ_i and σ_i are the mean and standard deviation of the ith vector, respectively, $\acute{f}_i$ is the ith normalized feature vector. Another normalization technique used is Min-Max normalization. It is the simplest normalization technique. This method maps the input scores to the $[0,1]$ range as follows:

$$\acute{f}_i = \frac{f_i - min}{max - min} \tag{19}$$

Where f_i, $i = 1, 2, 3, ..., n$ represents the set of matching scores, $\acute{f}_i$, $i = 1, 2, 3, ..., n$ represents the set of normalized matching scores, max represents maximum score value, and min is the minimum score value. This method is not robust because min and max values are sensitive to outliers. The fusion of all features is occurred through concatenate the normalized feature vectors as:

$$f_{new} = [\acute{f}_1 \acute{f}_2 \acute{f}_3] = [x_1, ..., x_{p1}, ..., y_1, ..., y_{p2}, z_1, ..., z_{p3}] \tag{20}$$

Where f_{new} is the combined feature with ($r+s+t$ dimension) [17]. Concatenation results increased the dimension of the feature, and leads to high computation time and storage. Thus, dimensionality reduction technique such as PCA (Principal Component Analysis) is used to reduce a largest set of features. PCA is the most commonly used techniques in feature reduction techniques [18]. PCA is a linear subspace method used to transform the data into another space that reduce the dimension. In our experiment we used PCA to select the effective features from GLCM, Color moment, and wavelet features as follows:

$$f_{PCA} = [f_1, \ldots, f_p], p < (r + s + t) \tag{21}$$

2.3   Classification Phase

One of the most used algorithms at classification problems is the Support Vector Machine. It is a machine learning algorithm which is applied for classification and regression problems of high dimensional datasets with excellent results [19]. SVM tries to evaluate a linear hyperplane between two classes. Theoretically, for linearly separable data, there is an infinite number of hyperplanes. These hyperplanes can classify training data correctly, but SVM seeks to find out the optimal hyperplane separating 2-classes [20]. Given a training dataset are represented by $\{x_i, y_i\}$, i=1,2,...., N, where N is the number of training samples, x_i is a features vector and $y_i \in \{-1, +1\}$ is the target label, $y = +1$ for samples belong to class C_1 and $y = -1$ for samples belong to class C_2. Classes C_1, C_2 are linearly separable classes. Geometrically, the SVM modeling algorithm finds an optimal hyperplane with the maximal margin to separate two classes, which requires solving the optimization problem, as shown in equations:

$$maximize \sum_{i=1}^{n} \alpha_i - \frac{1}{2} \sum_{i,j=1}^{n} \alpha_i \alpha_j y_i y_j . K(x_i, x_j)$$

$$\text{subject to: } \sum_{i=1}^{n} \alpha_i y_i, 0 \leq \alpha_i \leq C \tag{22}$$

where α_i is the weight assigned to the training sample x_i. If $\alpha_i > 0$, x_i is called a support vector. C is a regulation parameter used to trade-off the training accuracy and the model complexity so that a superior generalization capability can be achieved. K is a kernel function, which is used to measure the similarity between two samples. There are many different kernel functions have been applied in the past. Linear, multi-layer perception MLP, polynomial and the Gaussian radial basis function (RBF) are the most popular kernel functions [20].

3   Experimental Results

The system has been implemented on a 4GB RAM, Intel Core i5-2400 CPU 3.5 GHz PC using Matlab R2012b release. New feature vector after combining GLCM, Color, and texture features has been classified with SVM classifier. In our experiment, we have tested SVM with 4 kernels; Linear, Quadratic, RBF and MLP using two normalization methods; Min-Max and Z-Score. Using, 70% of samples have been used for training and 30% for testing; the maximum accuracy obtained by the system is 92%.

Tables (2-3) present the accuracy results of testing 30% of samples with Min-Max and Z-Score normalization methods respectively. Figure (1a and 1b) show

Table 2. Accuracy using different classifiers (training size (70%)) - using Min-Max score normalization

	End	Side1	Side2	Top
Linear	63%	89%	79%	90%
Quadratic	65%	85%	75%	83%
RBF	65%	85%	83%	88%
MLP	58%	77%	81%	85%

Table 3. Accuracy using different classifiers (training size (70%)) - using Z_{score} score normalization

	End	Side1	Side2	Top
Linear	69%	85%	83%	92%
Quadratic	71%	83%	79%	88%
RBF	71%	87%	83%	88%
MLP	62%	85%	79%	81%

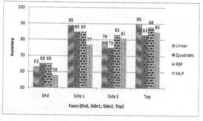

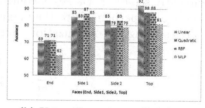

(a) Using Min-Max normalization   (b) Using Z_{score} normalization

Fig. 1. Accuracy using different classifiers (training size (70%))

the graph of these results. As shown in Tables (2-3) and Figure (1) we observe that SVM using Linear kernel archived best accuracy in case of Top and Side1 sides images. While RBF kernel achieved the best accuracy when using End and Side2 sides. On the other hand, MLP and Quadratic kernels achieved results that are relatively lower than the other two kernels (Linear and RBF) as well as Linear and RBF kernels in SVM classifier achieved better results than using the other two kernels (MLP and Qaudratic). Also, Z_{score} normalization achieved accuracy better than using Min-Max normalization. Finally, using SVM with Linear and RBF kernels and Z_{score} normalization achieved the best results and detection accuracy reached 92%.

4   Conclusion

In this paper, we have proposed a system for grading tomato fruits based on surface defects. The system has three main phases; preprocessing, feature extraction and fusion, and classification. Color moments for both RGB and HSV channels have been used for color information while GLCM statistics and Wavelets textures features have been fused for texture features in Intensity level. An evaluation of using Linear, Quadratic, RPF and MLP kernels for SVM has measured after using PCA for features dimensionality reduction. Z_{score} and Min-Max normalization methods were compared with 70% training and 30% testing samples. Linear and RBF kernels with Z_{score} normalization achieved the best results. Our system succeeded to detect the defected tomatoes and achieve suitable accuracy reached 92%.

References

1. FAO Statistical Yearbook 2013- World food and agriculture. Rome, Italy: Food and Agriculture Organization of the United Nations (2011),
   http://faostat.fao.org/site/339/default.aspx
2. Du, C.J., Sun, D.W.: Learning techniques used in computer vision for food quality evaluation: a review. J. Food Engineering 72, 39–55 (2006)
3. Kodagali, J.A., Balaji, S.: Computer Vision and Image Analysis based Techniques for Automatic Characterization of Fruits - A Review. International Journal of Computer Applications 50(6), 6–12 (2012)
4. Gomes, J.F.S., Leta, F.R.: Applications of computer vision techniques in the agriculture and food industry: a review. Eur. Food Res. Technology 235(6), 989–1000 (2012)
5. Sankarana, S., Mishraa, A., Ehsania, R., Davisb, C.: A review of advanced techniques for detecting plant diseases. Computers and Electronics in Agriculture 72, 1–13 (2010)
6. Wang, H., Li, G., Ma, Z., Li, X.: Application of Neural Networks to Image Recognition of Plant Diseases. In: 2012 International Conference on Systems and Informatics (ICSAI 2012), pp. 2159–2164. IEEE (2012)
7. Arivazhagan, S., Newlin Shebiah, R., Selva Nidhyanandhan, S., Ganesan, L.: Fruit recognition using color and texture features. J. Emerging Trends in Computing and Information Sciences 1(2), 90–94 (2010)
8. Arjenaki, O.O., Moghaddam, P.A., Motlagh, A.M.: Online tomato sorting based on shape, maturity, size, and surface defects using machine vision. Turkish Journal of Agriculture and Forestry 37, 62–68 (2013)
9. Deepa, P., Geethalakshmi, S.N.: A Comparative Analysis of Feature Extraction Methods for Fruit Grading Classifications. International Journal of Emerging Technologies in Computational and Applied Sciences (IJETCAS) 4(2), 221–225 (2013)
10. Ghaffari, R., Zhang, F., Iliescu, D., Hines, E., Leeson, M.S., Napier, R., Clarkson, J.: Early Detection of Diseases in Tomato Crops: An Electronic Nose and Intelligent Systems Approach. In: The 2010 International Joint Conference on Neural Networks (IJCNN), pp. 1–6. IEEE (2010)
11. Haralick, R.M., Shanmugam, K., Dinstein, I.H.: Textural features for Image Classification. IEEE Transactions on Systems, Man and Cybernetics 3, 610–621 (1973)
12. Gadkari, D.: Image quality analysis using GLCM. University of Central Florida: Master of Science in Modeling and Simulation (2004)
13. Albregtsen, F.: Statistical texture measures computed from gray level coocurrence matrices. Image Processing Laboratory, Department of Informatics, University of Oslo, pp. 1–14 (1995)

14. Kocioek, M., Materka, A., Strzelecki, M., Szczypiki, P.: Discrete wavelet transform derived features for digital image texture analysis. In: International Conference on Signals and Electronic Systems, Lodz, Poland, September 18-21, pp. 163–168 (2001)

15. Tharwat, A., Ibrahim, A.F., Ali, H.A.: Multimodal biometric authentication algorithm using ear and finger knuckle images. In: Seventh IEEE International Conference on Computer Engineering and Systems (ICCES), pp. 176–179 (2012)

16. Jain, A., Nandakuma, K., Ross, A.: Score normalization in multimodal biometric systems. Pattern Recognition 38(12), 2270–2285 (2005)

17. Kuncheva, L.I.: Combining pattern classifiers: methods and algorithms, p. 18. John Wiley and Sons (2004)

18. Turk, M., Pentland, A.: Eigenfaces for recognition. J. Cognitive Neuroscience 3(1), 71–86 (1991)

19. Abe, S.: Support Vector Machines for Pattern Classification, Illustrated edn. Springer (2010)

20. Elhariri, E., El-Bendary, N., Fouad, M.M.M., Platos, J., Hassanien, A.E., Hussein, A.M.M.: Multi-class SVM Based Classification Approach for Tomato Ripeness. In: Abraham, A., Krömer, P., Snášel, V. (eds.) Innovations in Bio-inspired Computing and Applications. AISC, vol. 237, pp. 175–186. Springer, Heidelberg (2014)

Part IV
Applications of Intelligent Systems

Applications of Advanced Analytics Methods in Sas Enterprise Miner

Vladimir S. Jotsov[1] and Evtim Iliev[2]

[1] P.O. Box 161, Sofia 1113, Bulgaria
bgimcssmc@gmail.com
[2] University of Library Studies and IT (ULSIT)
www.unibit.bg

Abstract. This paper considers one of the contemporary advanced analytics applications named Puzzle methods. It is studied aiming at novel results in collaborative statistical and logical research based on quantitative method applications, deep processing of accumulated knowledge, etc. It is shown that applications of intelligent technologies advance the efficiency of statistical applications. Financial and security systems (SS) have been considered as an example of difficult-to-explore areas. Original results are presented on how to build more effective logical-and-statistical applications by using novel puzzle methodologies. It is shown that all the demonstrated advantages may be successfully combined with other known methods from advanced analytics, knowledge discovery, data/web/deep data mining or other fields. Also it is shown how the considered applications enhance the quality of statistical inference, improve the human-machine interaction between the user and system and hence serve the process of sustainable improvement of the results. Applications to SAS Enterprise Miner reveal the strength of the proposed Puzzle methods.

Keywords: Puzzle metods, semantics, sense, SAS, Enterprise Miner, Advanced Analytics, Logic Application, Synthetic Methods, Knowledge Discovery, Human-Computer Interaction, Data Mining, Intelligent System, Agent, Ontology.

1 Introduction

Contemporary recession times make governments pay more attention to the technology effectiveness problems accumulated for decades. It is easy to follow that the sustainable development of regions depends on using smart, intelligent techologies and know-how accumulated for years. They should be embedded in well-organized super-systems. The tendency at national levels is using more and more sophisticated tools and standards. However, the high cost technologies do not necessarily lead to new or high quantitative results. Hence there is a risk of ineffective use of expensive resources.

In this paper an advanced analytics method is considered aiming to improve the quality of the deep knowledge analysis, acquisition, and learning [1]. Intelligent software plays more and more important role in contemporary learning systems and their realisations from industry to security and even to blended education where

Puzzle methods reinforce TRIZ results [2]–[8]. The considered in the paper tools are especially effective in rapidly changing environments like security systems (SS), financial systems, etc. Suggested innovations serve the more effective application of advanced analytics, (deep) data/web mining and/or collective evolutionary components. The latter should be used to combine logical and statistical results in one system [1]. Contemporary training of intelligent agents reaches such a high level that some elements of intelligent systems became practicable also in mathematics, statistics, etc. It is time to transfer the effective strategies from them to statistical-based innovations, and here applications to one of the best data miners are explored. The research is based on series of Puzzle methods for intelligent knowledge/data processing elaborated within ULSIT-Sofia. The classical statistical applications in data mining are a well-described area. Many of the theoretical base results from the field have been obtained since 1980-ies. Since then a few problems have been revealed like ,the probaility 0.9999 doesn't mean that the hypothesis has been proved', and all of them lead to different constraints in data mining applications. Some sources proclaim the division of data mining into the statistical and logical ones. These accumulated problems can't be solved using only traditional data mining/advanced analytics methods. Under these conditions we have developed an inexpensive technology for deep knowledge elicitation and management based on a minimum of technological solutions that do not require high costs of purchasing and support [1]. Its main method named Puzzle method is described in the next two sections of the paper. Applications to SAS Enterprise Miner 12.1 are considered in sections 4 and 5. Instead of the division of data analytics into parts we offer a series of unifying methods strenghtening the results from data miners.

2   The Sense of the Proposed Puzzle Methods

The below considered methods have been designed for applications in different research systems. It is shown that almost the same method applied in another way gives new results suitable for applications in SS and other sophisticated training. On the other hand, teaching SS stands out from other undergraduate and graduate programs that it operates in rapidly changing models, requirements, concepts, tools, instruments and policies where the problem for qualitative education is particularly difficult. Teaching highlights in the brightest way the advantages of the proposed new methods and applications in intelligent security systems (ISS).

One of the most instructive facts about the audience for training is that current neural-based machines in the form of software agents or holons repeat the actions of the teacher on a much higher level, even related to an excellent student. Therefore, rote learning, simple memorization of lectures makes no sense: sooner or later machines will displace us from similar low-tech activities; instead creative learning should be deeply rationalized through comparisons with other research accessible through the Internet, by experimenting with numerous courses and with open source products which become more pervasive in our practice together with contemporary Web-applications. The above example illustrates how to achieve simultaneously two goals: explain essential principles of artificial neural networks (ANNs) functioning and modern principles of quality training through effective and deep understanding. Similarly, using the neural networks examples explain the best practices for control of knowledge, for more tests for lagging students, etc. The application of the below described methods makes the lecture process easier, understandable and transparent. Hence sustainable education results are obtained. Advanced data analytic methods are not easy to explain. However, their correct applications don't make the education complicated, because they are purposed to find easier and effective ways of presentation.

On the other hand, monitoring the quality of educational processes most often uses different statistical methods. We have used the same methods in a general advanced analytics module together with logic applications described in this paper. The unification of logical and statistical parts comes   using evolutionary ways. Those cardinally different results can't be used just in one simple cluster of data or knowledge.

During the evolutionary process of joining statistical and logical data/knowledge, the accumulation of knowledge makes logical applications more and more effective and more universal than the probabilistic ones/ fuzzy estimates/similar applications. In the common case during data analytics processing, there is no convergence of the results but this does not impede practical applications of these systems. In other words, bad and good designers will arrange the display window in quite different ways and there is no guarantee that every user understands the technology and that his access to the system will have positive results. In general, the use of synthetic methods is one of the most important and demanding elements of the efficiency of intelligent applications. But the winning combination of the proposed methods in the educational field depends on the lecturer's experience, which makes the performance much simpler than just in the automatic case. At this level, the operation of the advanced analytics module is limited to implementation-voluntary advice to the lecturer. Suggested innovations serve the more effective application of education practice altogether with data analytics applications, collective evolutionary components, etc. More information can be obtained from the book [1].

The research on traditional, syntactic puzzle methods reveals that their algorithmic complexity is rather high and this doesn't allow automatic processing of large enough sudokus, crosswords or puzzles. In the case an emphasis should be placed on the fact that the studied machine-based procedure takes the words from a predefined set using a random principle where only the length of the word is of importance. On the contrary to the quoted syntactical realizations, a Puzzle method is considered what is based on the logical analysis of the existing data or knowledge interconnections. Three types of relations have been used aiming at narrowing the set of possible solutions to the problem.

Briefly, every Puzzle method aims to discover new or hidden knowledge by connecting the unknown, the sought solutions with previous experience accumulated in knowledge bases. Let the constraints of the considered problem form a curve in the space as depicted in Fig. 1. The main goal of the Puzzle method is to reduce the multidimensional search space for the solution. For this purpose we used several limitations, in [1] the study is focused on the case of using ontologies instead of a set of nonlinear constraints, etc.

Furthermore, the research of process dynamics aimed at reducing the field in certain cases allows us to derive new knowledge in the form of rules as discussed in the next chapter. This inference process and the usage of different constraints gives way to significant simplification of formal and evidence material in lectures, attracts the attention to details and simultaneously increases the activity of learners. Showing the process of connecting known to unknown improves the understanding and retention of the presented material.

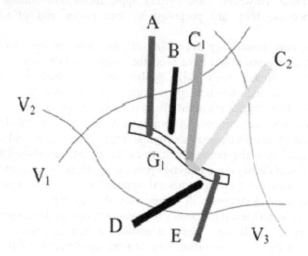

Fig. 1. Binding, crossword and classical set of constraints

For example, if a bachelor who has graduated ULSIT lives in Sofia and he/she does not want to work anywhere else, then the line (curve) restricts the search space and in this way a lot of unnecessary [re]search is avoided. It is also possible to inspect a case when the constraint is defined in the form of surface but as a result a more general solution is obtained where a special interest is provoked by the boundary case of the crossing two or more surfaces. When the common case is inspected in details then in the majority of cases the problem is reduced to exploring the lines instead of curves with complicated forms obtained as a result of crossing surfaces. Therefore, below we investigate the usage in systems of constraints by lines of first or higher orders.

The V_i constraints of linear/nonlinear form are the classic case borrowed from constraint satisfaction methods. The B-D binding constraints doesn't intercept the unknown goal but are located close to it, they reveal a ‚neighboring' area around the target. The A-C-E constraints are named the crossword constraints because their interception with G1 gives a part of the searched goal where Ci form larger interconnected areas in G1. The usage of the considered set of Ci-s is much more effective than of the classical set of V_i-s.

Through binding constraints it is convenient to implement the many non-classical causal relations of the type "A is linked to B but the connection between them is not implicative". The same could be presented through heuristics, which is not recommendable. It must be pointed out that through this type of constraints the location of the searched solutions is fixed in a way that is best combined with fuzzy methods.

Crossword constraints offer new ways of assessment (outlook) for the searched unknown solutions on the basis of the accumulated so far knowledge.

The following example shows how the search process can be reduced using ontologies. Let's admit that the search space is presented on Fig. 2 where statistical data about SS are generalized about the regions depending on their price and quality. The goal: it is necessary to select an acceptable SS to our project. Let the right vertical, blue-colored, subset of feasible solutions is chosen: 'excluding ISS designed outside Europe'. Then the space of feasible solutions is to the left of the separating surface which is depicted on the figure in the rightmost corner.

In Fig. 2 another horizontal surface, depicted in the high corner in green, is shown delimiting the search space of the solutions. In our case it means 'systems with unknown principles of operation'. It is accepted that in the data bases there is no clear distinction related to the presented criteria so the search of the feasible solutions is nonlinear, of high dimensionality, and practically it cannot be solved using traditional methods. Nevertheless, by applying ontologies the problem is solvable via the proposed Puzzle method. There are two red dots depicted in the left corner on the same Fig. 2. Each of them also represents a kind of constraint but of another type which we name a binding constraint and it is introduced and researched by us. Its semantics is the following: it is not a solution but it resides close to the searched solution.

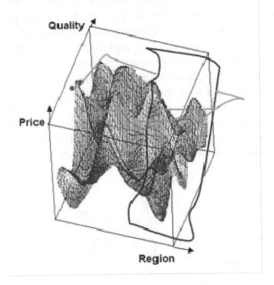

Fig. 2. SS application example

Using Different Binding Constraints

The following section discusses the introduction of three types of binding constraints.

The knowledge used in the Puzzle method can be presented as parts of information (atoms), linked by different relations. Usually these relations have been obtained by logical processing of information like structuring, extracting meaning from information blocks or other processing. In this terminology, one rule can be presented in the following way:

The conjunctions of antecedents are $A_1, A_2 \ldots A_z$.

The conclusion/consequent is marked as B.

Let all z number of conjunctions are proved to be true/confirmed, then B is true, whereby the goal/problem of checking whether B is true has been solved (see Fig. 3).

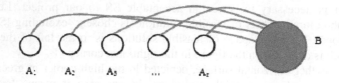

Fig. 3. Relations inside a rule

When significance has not been pointed out, as in the case shown in Fig. 3, then the significance of the conjunctions are considered equal ($1/z$). The bows show that each conjunctive has its individual *significance in proving the conclusion*: a number between 0 and 1. But in the common case, some conjunctives are of great significance while others are less important, depending on the situation. Part of these invisible links between the atoms of the type conjunctive-conclusion or other parts of knowledge can be **torn** in different conditions, for example when there is additional information and during a process called *defeat*, which can change the truthfulness of each atom, reduce its significance in proving the conclusion/goal to zero or change the whole rule completely, for example, by replacing it with another one.

The process of defeat is started by special forms of presenting knowledge called exceptions to rules (see Fig.2), knowledge of the type E (C, Ap), where a prerequisite for the defeat is the argument C of the exception, which must be true in order to start this process of defeat. Therefore, both arguments of the exception enter a causal relation, which is not implicative. It is a kind of non-classic causal relation. In life we use so many similar relations and most of them are difficult to formalize because they are not included in the classical mathematical and formal logic.

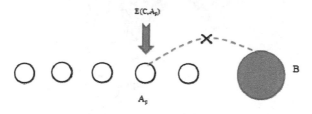

Fig. 4. The defeat of implicative connections

The accumulation of such parts of knowledge/ atoms of knowledge, compound with different classical and non-classical relations allows us to use new opportunities for reaching the set of goals.

For example, let's have goal X proved via classical or non-classical means, as shown in Fig. 5 and let X and Y have an unidentified causal relation, for example X defeats Y; or for example, let X and Y be statistically linked variables. In this case, the fact that there is a large volume of information linked to X, as shown in the figure, leads to imposing informal constraints over the choice of the condition of Y, regardless of the fact that in a classical logical (formal) sense, X and Y are not linked. Informally, proving X leads to the solution of the goal Y.   In other analogous situations, solving X does not lead to proving Y. However, they are linked through the following non-classical relation: proving X shows that we are *close* to the solution of Y, the more rules and facts prove the truthfulness of X, the higher the confidence/sureness/certainty or belief in the hypothesis that Y is true. The described process will be called *binding*, as interpreted in Fig. 5.

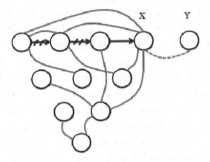

Fig. 5. The binding process

Very often using methods like fuzzy logic helps binding, for example, in situations where indefinite notions are used or notions that change their meaning depending on the situation and the context.

Let's see the following rule:

If N is a good specialist, but N cannot work with people, then N is not elected a manager.

In the described example there are a lot of notions that require clarification: good specialist, ability to work with people, a leader, etc. For example, it is important to clarify that this is a leader of what, in what conditions and so on. It must be considered the fact that being able to work with people is quite a subjective judgment and it can be greatly reduced due to a number of subjective reasons. In situations where there is doubt about the judgment of the ability to work with people, it is better to use binding relations, including the non-referable part of the rule. In this case, what is left is the relation that if someone is a good specialist, they can be elected a manager. Here the link isn't implicative. Obviously being a good specialist is not enough to be elected a manager. Additional knowledge should be drawn here, increasing the confidence that if someone is suitable for a manager on the problem and in the particular situation, for example: the necessary facts can be drawn from the CV, etc. In the example of using the binding in fact one or more conjunctives are defeated from the antecedent of the rule.

Defeating the link of the second conjunction with the conclusion actually removes the implicative link on the whole, and is replaced by a binding.

Crossword Constraints
This section discusses the introduction of one type of constraint called *crossword1*.

Let's assume that KB contains deeply structured knowledge, for example, ontology on the problem. In this case, if other knowledge is discovered, and is related to the ontology, but badly structured, for example, written in another language, incomprehensible to us, or information lacking in text or noised or encoded, i.e. in situations when the meaning of just a fragment of the information is comprehensible, and out of which only part of the information can be drawn, and if this part of the information is new, in a sense that it complements the ontology, then the mentioned new knowledge is added to the ontology regardless of the missing parts of the knowledge. In this case, invisible rule/clause relations are being used, similar to the ones in Fig. 3 and linking the non-structured knowledge with the ontology, as well as with the atoms of the non-structured knowledge through the used constraints of the crossword. Thus, new knowledge extraction is carried out. In this case most often searching in the constrained area of options is avoided, and the solution is obtained straightforward and non-alternatively. For example: we assume as a known fact that a banker has been killed in the center of Tirana. The event relates to the ontology ‚murder' with relations to banker, center and Tirana. Here as another column we can add to the ontology when the murder took place, etc. Then, if someone watches a TV show on the Albanian television and does not understand the local language, they can nevertheless determine that the news is about killing a banker for example by the written time of the murder and so on, but when in this context of unfamiliar words appears the known word MOTOR, our ontology of the murder is complemented with a new relation: a motor has been used during the murder. In this case, the context of the event described in an unfamiliar language characterizes the unknown, and only the word motor and some other specific information units are understood/known or link the unknown to the known. Regardless of the lack of information, by using the crossword constraints here we will obtain an extension of the existing ontology solution: we have obtained an improved with new knowledge ontology.

By introducing new constraints or, sometimes, ontologies our goal is to show that it is possible to use causal links different from implications and that they help us search the goals in a more effective manner.

In the tutoring case, using the crossword constraints from Fig. 1 also helps us reveal the dynamics of the problem solving process where the resolution process is sometimes more important than the proof itself. The usage of Vi constraints one by one doesn't always form the necessary closed area. Revealing Vi and other constraints one by one helps represent the resolution process in its dynamics and hence make deep inference to the problem. Even in the worst case, when the accumulated knowledge is incomplete for the problem resolution, the dynamics of what is represented analogically to Fig. 1 will show what should be the resolution. The binding/crossword constraints are the form of non-implicative rule-based relations. Their application effects are discussed in the next chapter.

3   Visualization Elements

Essentially the Puzzle methods include a form of visualization, which leads to a creative work in various forms of training. We would like to remind that the high quality learning inevitably leads to independent research. In the present study it is shown that in some cases the graph itself from Fig. 1 may be sufficient for decision-making by the user or the expert.

Different versions of the modeled knowledge contained in Fig. 2 provide a base to describe things that are difficult to express in words. Not surprisingly, a Chinese aphorism states 'A picture replaces thousand words.' It should be added: '... and is understood and memorized better.' Below are given different linguistic equivalents of combinations of interpretations, similar to that of Fig. 1 and obtained by the Puzzle method:

Things are moving in a way that ...   (1)

... neither ... nor ... but it is too close to ...   (2)

Looked at this from another angle ... other findings ...   (3)
An object can be represented as an intersection of two dynamic areas ...   (4)
In the future, these two concepts should be used jointly ...   (5)
etc.

where (1) illustrates the application of hard to formulate sentences, (2) is close to the vague suggestions through Puzzle methods, (3) shows the dynamic capabilities of the Puzzle method applications for example when a change in the meaning of the used knowledge depending on context, (4) and (5) show the technical capabilities of the Puzzle applications as a unification, intersection of data, knowledge, ontologies, etc.

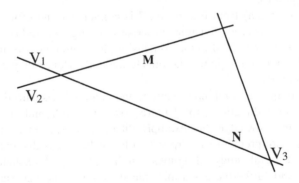

Fig. 6. M and N are unrelated and belong to a confined area

These natural-language fragments can be presented in plain text for learners, but further it is shown that by the Puzzle method this is executed much more naturally and better. For example, Fig. 6 shows another example of Puzzle method application revealing certain processes and relationships between objects. Concentrating the attention in the closed area of Fig. 6 and narrowing the set of analyzed elements supports the revealing of new implicative relation M-N referred to in Fig. 7. Informal causal relations are elaborated that are associated with the implication 'from M it follows that N'.

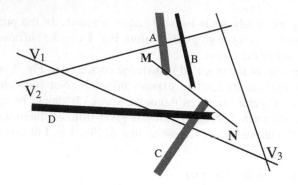

Fig. 7. Detection of the rule connection M-N

In Fig. 7 the system of three different constraint sets helps detect a causal relationship between M and N, with no evident correlation between them in Fig. 6. The connection occurs in imposing additional constraints in Fig. 6. The process is dynamic in nature and it is almost impossible to be properly explained only with words. Here the set of the pictures has a role of the replacement of the intuition process.

The process of finding new rules using Puzzle methods gives the trained people the necessary deep knowledge. This form of knowledge can be sometimes represented in the form of ontologies.

The image (or media) from Fig. 6-Fig. 7 is convenient and efficient to visualize, transform and use different dynamic processes through sense-based explanations. Examples and figures can lead to the conclusion that ontologies are introduced, used and dynamically changed applying the Puzzle methods. Hence they can be improved using Puzzle methods.

Unlike the traditional oral presentation, the material visualized by the Puzzle method gives more directions for [future] own research and for detecting and correcting gaps in knowledge. For example, 'it is neither ... nor ...' and many other natural-language interpretations incorporate a lot of fuzziness that can sometimes be misunderstood. Careful study of graphs similar to Fig. 7 excludes presentation incompleteness and furthermore – a misunderstanding of the material. On the other hand, the whole learning process is concentrated in one place, it is not necessary to look for other Web sources to clarify the question e.g. 'why', 'what', 'how' to get results, etc. The quoted relations also have been used for pointing the lecture main points. Intelligent training tools not only accelerate but also intensify the training. Hence its high quality.

A wide range of tools for modeling and presentation of material is used in this chapter where the modeling must be used not for ISS software agents but for people. Respectively it is easier to introduce audio or multimedia presentations, for example, ontologies for transmitting the meaning of things. Sometimes to present the meaning of things it is enough to show one or several key points of the subject altogether with corresponding explanations in visual, graph or sound form. Sometimes one key picture with concise explanations is better than an entire movie. Of most importance are the descriptions to a picture that describe the essentials, important details, and the sense of the presentation. The picture explains many details clear to people, but intelligent agents will learn nothing from this picture, especially if the agents are designed only for SS purposes. Hence many agent-based methods are much more effective in people tutoring systems.

Information presentation by meaning is a key element of modern higher and university education. The proposed Puzzle methods altogether with the other tested methods greatly expand opportunities for qualitative teaching in the field of SS, one of dynamic interdisciplinary specialties with increased complexity and also of various types of strict and high requirements for the learners.

4   Algoritms for Obtaining Bindings and Constraints

Experiments have been done with SAS Enterprise Miner™ - powerful software for data mining which has significant applications in science as well as in the sphere of business [9]. The software offers the opportunity to make a predictive model through different methods: neuron networks, regression analysis, cluster analysis, etc., so that the prediction is improved. For this purpose, in this paper we are going to analyze the results from intelligent methods– the artificial neural networks because:

- They are intelligent means of presenting knowledge / they can be self-taught;
- They are flexible (they offer a huge variety of variables)

For the purpose of the experiment, the following nodes of SAS Enterprise Miner™ have been used:

Input Data, Neural Network, Regression, Decision Tree and Model Comparison with default settings.

The model with the minimum average squared error gives the wrong number the least times.

- The conducted experiments show that default settings of ANN give better results than the other methods (regression, decision tree) as shown in Fig. 8

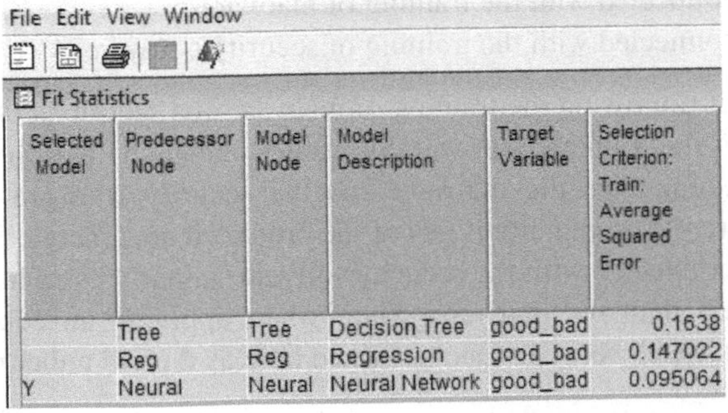

File Edit View Window

Selected Model	Predecessor Node	Model Node	Model Description	Target Variable	Selection Criterion: Train: Average Squared Error
	Tree	Tree	Decision Tree	good_bad	0.1638
	Reg	Reg	Regression	good_bad	0.147022
Y	Neural	Neural	Neural Network	good_bad	0.095064

Fig. 8. Comparative analysis of average squared error between Decision Tree, Regression and Neural Network

The scope of the considered experiment comprises how through SAS Enterprise Miner™ with default settings the Puzzle method (carried out classic constraints/binding/crossword [1]) the settings of the artificial neural network can be optimized so that a random model always gives better results compared to the neural network default settings of SAS Enterprise Miner™.

The fowolling sets are used for the formal description:

A: set of decisions (architecture, number of hidden units, randomization distribution, preliminary runs, preliminary maximum iterations, preliminary maximum time, training technique, maximum iterations, maximum time, target layer combination function, target layer activation function, target layer error function) ai $\in$ A

B: set of constraints (variables in sas, possible values of variables: hidden units from 1 to 64, etc.) bj $\in$ B

D: default settings of variables in set A; D $\subset$ B

C: set of relations between sets A and B; C = A$\cap$B

Respectively C consists of two subsets C = E$\cup$F:

E: set of variables influencing the fitting of the neural network: specified number of preliminary runs for performance; specified maximum number of iterations allowed during preliminary network training; specified maximum amount of CPU time allowed during preliminary training; specified neural network training algorithm, maximum iterations, specified maximum amount of CPU time during training.

F: set of variables influencing the architecture of ANN: architecture: specified network architecture used during network training; number of hidden units: specified number n of hidden units allowed in the hidden layer; randomization distribution: specified distribution to apply to the weights for the selected neural network; specified target layer combination function for selected neural network; specified target layer activation function for selected network; specified target layer error function for selected neural network.

N: number of iterations; Nt: threshold number of iterations.

Example 1:
Let's look at the following two variables, whose dependence between one another has been discovered by means of regression analysis:

Variable 1 is connected with the training of malware

Variable 2 is connected with the training of security software

Let the goal be: improving the training of malware and security software.

If as a result of the training both variable values change by the same step and their initial value is equal, then the malware and the security software will be equally trained to be aware of the vulnerabilities of the protected area (network). If we assume that the variable connected with the security software initially has a higher value, then it is better trained than the malware. Then when applying an equal step to both variables, the difference between them (marked here as Δ) will either remain the same or slightly increase. But if the values of the variables change with a different step: for example if malware learns faster than security software, sooner or later the chances that the protected area is hacked successfully increase. Thus, binding is found between the two variables and it will prompt what the dependence is between them so that the goal is reached more quickly. The value of the variable representing the security software should always be higher than the value of the malware.

Binding is based on operating in similar situations, where the variables are related to one object and use analogous knowledge. In the latter example of training at different speeds, other bindings are found; for example, when the training time is limitless, the winner is the one that learns faster regardless of the initial meanings of accumulated knowledge.

Regardless of how the differences in n-dimensional space are measured with p-adic metrics or by using the classic formulas of Euclidean, the results and accuracy of the presented algorithm do not change.

Bind1
Select two variables Var1, Var2
Apply equal step and unequal step.
Get result
    If $\Delta < \Delta_1$
    Create binding between Var1 and Var2.
        else
        select another two variables
        (END)

Where:
Var1, Var2
Δ is a difference between var1 and var2 with equal step
Δ_1 is a difference between var1 and var2 with unequal step

```
procedure Puzzle Method
    while(not_termination)
        generateSolutions()
        constraintApply()
        bindingApply()
        fittingUpdate()
        architectureSettingUpdate()
        end while
    select the model with the least square error
    end procedure
```

A procedure the algorithm functions in the following way:

Step 1: generating random values of variables form set A and comparing them to the default values of set D.

Step 2: constraints are imposed on variable values $a_i \in A$ in order to reduce the search.

Step 3: the discovered Bindings are applied.

Step 4: only the values $e_k \in E$ are changed, which directly influences the degree of ANN fitting.

Step 5: only the values $f_l \in F$ are changed, which directly influences the ANN architecture.

Step 6: a check-up is done whether conditions for terminating the algorithm exist, amongst which exceeding a certain number of iterations or reaching a threshold error. If they are reached, then the algorithm terminates the cycle (END), if not, then the valued continue to be optimized.

Step 7: the model with the least averare square error (ASE) is selected.

5   Simulation Results in SAS Enterprise Miner™

In the experiments shown in figures 6, 7 and 8, the following nodes of SAS Enterprise Miner™ have been used: Default settings of Neural Network, Puzzle method modified Neural Network and default settings Model Comparison

As seen in Fig. 9, the network that has been trained through the Puzzle method gives better results. The error classification through positive and negative values is carried out in the following way:

1) An event has happened and it has been rightfully recognized (true positive)
2) No event has happened and this has been rightfully reported (true negative)
3) An event has happened and actually it has not been reported (false positive)
4) An event has been reported where there has been none in fact (false negative)

The above-described positive and negative values from Fig. 9 refer to the target variable.

Example 2

Let's assume that evaluation network traffic passes through an IPS system. Then:
- true positive is harmful traffic and is rightly evaluated as such;
- true negative is harmless traffic and rightly evaluated as such;
- false positive is harmless traffic and is wrongly evaluated as such;
- false negative is harmful traffic and wrongly evaluated as harmless;

Therefore, the sensitivity of the network is also better when applying binding constraints, as shown in Fig. 10, where the results in squares show the Puzzle method results and the curved line shows the default settings method results and the straight line is a base line.

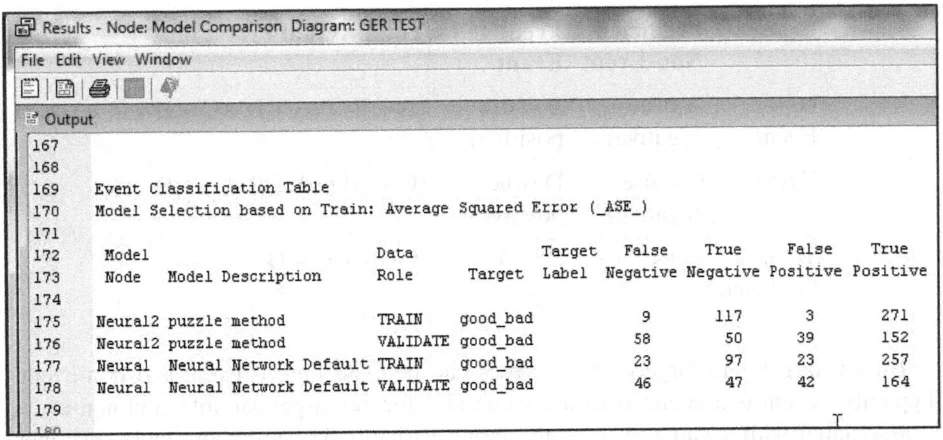

```
 Results - Node: Model Comparison  Diagram: GER TEST
File  Edit  View  Window

 Output
 167
 168
 169    Event Classification Table
 170    Model Selection based on Train: Average Squared Error (_ASE_)
 171
 172    Model                          Data              Target  False    True     False    True
 173    Node    Model Description      Role    Target    Label   Negative Negative Positive Positive
 174
 175    Neural2 puzzle method          TRAIN   good_bad            9       117       3       271
 176    Neural2 puzzle method          VALIDATE good_bad          58        50      39       152
 177    Neural  Neural Network Default TRAIN   good_bad           23        97      23       257
 178    Neural  Neural Network Default VALIDATE good_bad          46        47      42       164
 179
 180
```

Fig. 9. The difference in recognizing the target variable between default settings Neural Network and Neural Network trained by the Puzzle method and classified through positive and negative values

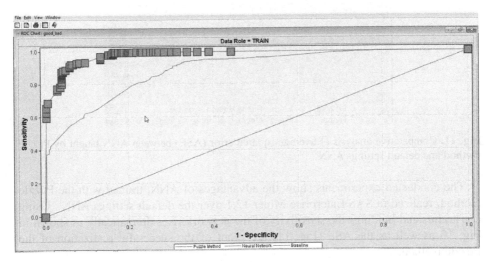

Fig. 10. The difference in sensitivity between Neural Network taught by the Puzzle method and default settings Neural Network

In this case, the sensitivity is calculated by the following formula [10]:

Sensitivity (True Positive Rate):
$$100 * D / (C + D) \tag{6}$$

Table 1.

	Predicted Non-Event	Predicted Event	Total Actual Probability
Non-Event	A (true negative)	B (false positive)	(A + B) / (A + B + C + D)
Event	C (false negative)	D (true positive)	(C + D) / (A + B + C + D)
Total Predicted	A + C	B + D	A + B + C + D

Binary targets are targets whose states can be classified as event and non-event. Typically, event is associated with a value of 1 for the target variable, and non-event is associated with a value of 0 for the target variable. The following table describes the predictive relationships between event and non-event. [10]

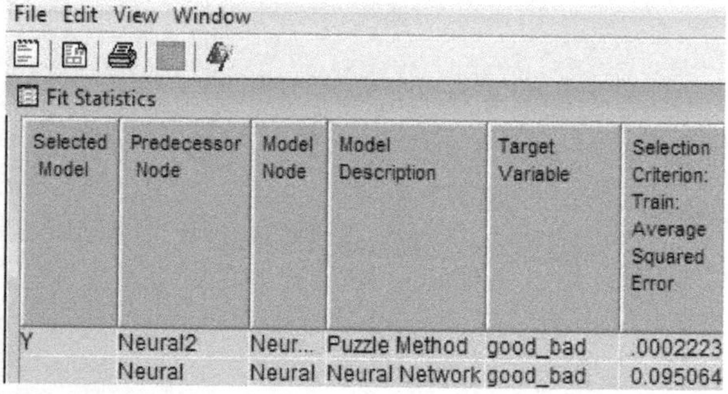
File Edit View Window

Fit Statistics

Selected Model	Predecessor Node	Model Node	Model Description	Target Variable	Selection Criterion: Train: Average Squared Error
Y	Neural2	Neur...	Puzzle Method	good_bad	.0002223
	Neural	Neural	Neural Network	good_bad	0.095064

Fig. 11. Comparative analysis of average squared error (ASE) between ANN taught by Puzzle method and default settings ANN

The conducted experiments show the advantages of ANN, trained with the Puzzle method, realized in SAS Enterprise Miner 12.1 over the default settings ANN. Using constraints and bindings the sensitivity of the network rises dramatically as shown in Fig. 10 as well as the ASE (Fig. 11) are proof of the successful realization of the Puzzle method.

6 Conclusion

The main conclusion is that to overcome the contemporary data mining and ANN application shortcomings, methods and applications are considered concerning the advanced analytics using logical processing. The role of the above methods for different security, financial or other purposes is discussed. The proposed set of methods and applications are domain independent.

Analysis is represented for technologies used for discovery of meaning, exploring information by meaning, and for understanding the semantics of the accumulated data/knowledge information. Common advantages and disadvantages for different groups of contemporary applications have been revealed.

The same methods in different combinations are effectively used to enhance security staff possibilities or in contemporary e-learning systems in the field of National Security [7].

It is shown how, by applying the principles of advanced analytics technology in data miners, there is a substantial rise in the quality of obtained results. Applications in SAS Enterprise Miner 12.1 have been discussed.

References

1. Jotsov, V.: Intelligent Information Security Systems, p. 278. Za bukvite-O Pismeneh, Sofia (2010)
2. Gorodetsky, V., Zhang, C., Skormin, V.A., Cao, L. (eds.): AIS-ADM 2007. LNCS (LNAI), vol. 4476. Springer, Heidelberg (2007)
3. Kumar, S., Vijayalakshmi, M.N.: A Novel Approach in Data Mining Techniques for Educational Data. In: 3rd Int. Conf. on Machine Learning and Computing (ICMLC 2011), pp. V4-152–V4-154 (2011)
4. Goyal, M., Vohra, R.: Applications of Data Mining in Higher Education. Int. Journ. of Computer Science Issues (IJCSI) 9(2(1)), 113–120 (2012)
5. The TRIZ Journal. Part of the RealInnovation Network, http://www.triz-journal.com/archives/what_is_triz/ (to date)
6. Jotsov, V.: Advanced Analytics Methods and Intelligent Applications in Education. In: Proc. 7th IEEE International Conference on Intelligent Data Acquisition and Advanced Computing Systems: Technology and Applications IDAACS 2013, Berlin, Germany, September 11-13, vol. I, pp. 197–202 (2013)
7. Denchev, S., Pargov, D., Jotsov, V. (eds.): Crisis Management, Sofia, Avtookazion, p. 200 (2013)
8. IHS Goldfire Solutions, http://www.ihs.com/products/design/software-methods/goldfire/solutions.aspx (to date)
9. SAS® Enterprise Miner™, http://www.sas.com/en_us/software/analytics/enterprise-miner.html (to date)
10. Estimating sensitivity, specificity, positive and negative predictive values, and other statistics, http://support.sas.com/kb/24/170.html (to date)

Clustering Method for Analysis of Research Fields: Examples of Composites, Nanocomposites and Blends

Robert Sitarz[1], Maciej Heneczkowski[2], Matylda Jabłońska-Sabuka[3], and Andrzej Krasławski[4]

[1] TOP S.A. Warneńczyka 3, 35612 Rzeszów, Poland
[2] Faculty of Chemistry, Rzeszów University of Technology Al. Powstańców Warszawy 6, 35959 Rzeszów, Poland
[3] Department of Mathematics and Physics, Lappeenranta University of Technology, PO Box 20, 53851 Lappeenranta, Finland
[4] School of Industrial Engineering and Management, Lappeenranta University of Technology, 53851 Lappeenranta, Finland Department of Process Engineering, Łódź University of Technology, 90924 Łódź, Poland

Abstract. Proper planning of fund allocation by R&D departments of research or industrial institutes may be of key importance to increase of their revenue and future success. However, over years, making such decisions has become notoriously difficult, due to the increasing costs of research and shortening lifetime of products and processes. This is complicated even more in the light of growing specialization of research and exponential growth in number of publications. The existing bibliographic approaches used for structuring fields of research have many drawbacks, e.g. too coarse classification due to lack of the required granularity of information or incoherence of the identified thematic clusters. This paper introduces a method for identification of thematic clusters in a given research domain. The method is based on analysis of high co-occurrence frequency of word sets, which are seeds of thematic clusters. The proposed method is universal and can be applied for analysis of any research field, and the publication data extracted can be further analyzed with respect to future development trends.

1 Introduction

Proper planning of fund allocation to R&D departments of research or industrial institutes may be of key importance to increase of their revenue and future success. However, over years, making such decisions has become notoriously difficult, due to the increasing costs of research and shortening lifetime of products and processes. This is complicated even more in the light of growing specialization of research and exponential growth in number of publications. The needs of R&D decision makers are the major drivers to develop effective methods and tools for analysis of knowledge flow within research domains. Information on dynamics of a given field of research is an important hint indicating its potential for future development and possible business opportunities [25, 35].

© Springer International Publishing Switzerland 2015
D. Filev et al. (eds.), *Intelligent Systems'2014*,
Advances in Intelligent Systems and Computing 323, DOI: 10.1007/978-3-319-11310-4_37

The number of contributions and dynamics of their change are a crucial piece of information when building a portfolio of research projects, in which profit and risk have to be balanced. The number of scientific publications and patents is an indirect measure of importance and intensity of research in a specific domain [10, 28]. The change in the number of publications and patents in time is very important for forecasting future developments. Within the recent couple of decades, intensification of academic and industrial R&D activities resulted in exponential growth in number of publications. It makes structuring of research and technological knowledge and analysis of its dynamics not a trivial task.

The main techniques for structuring of research fields are: co-classification [1], co-citation [7] and co-word analysis [9, 33]. The first group of methods consists of the arrangement of papers into clusters on the basis of journal classification [13, 16]. Identification of the thematic fields using these methods is far from being optimal. Identified clusters are not thematically coherent. The methods give only an overview of the analyzed research field rather than its detailed structure.

Analysis of article and patent citations is a fairly common research method of structuring research or technological domains [2, 12, 15, 19, 24]. The structural patterns observed in citation networks can help to understand how scientific and technological knowledge is organized and how it evolves in time [34]. However, the analysis of citation networks has inherent limitations as papers or patents are a combination of knowledge elements, rather than an element of knowledge itself [14, 34]. It results in generation of thematically incoherent clusters. Also, the method of aggregation into clusters based on co-citation of papers and words co-occurrence [17] has a serious drawback. This method allows to generate fingerprints containing groups of the words belonging simultaneously to several clusters. It makes the identification of the main theme of the cluster a challenging task which can not be performed by any computer.

The third method of structuring research fields, that is co-word analysis, deals with the sets of keywords shared by publications belonging to a thematic cluster. The method is based on the assumption that paper's keywords constitute an adequate description of its content. The similar approaches have been applied to map different knowledge fields by keyword-based method, for example, in biochemistry [26], chemistry [3], neural network research [21, 29], biological safety [4], optomechatronics [22], adverse drug reactions [6], software engineering [8, 14], etc. The co-word analysis has been also commonly utilized in mapping or trading patterns and trends [32]. The methods of co-word analysis identify clusters on the basis of high co-occurrence frequency of words. However, it is not defined how many co-occurring words are needed to allocate an article to a given cluster [20, 23, 29]. The ambiguity of keywords is another limitation related to co-word analysis [32]. In consequence, some clusters may be imprecisely identified.

The volume limit of this article constraints our ability to list all disadvantages of the existing approaches. However, the drawbacks listed above, as well as the need to address the requirements of R&D decision makers, are the major drivers for the development of knowledge flow analysis presented in this paper. Especially, the limited applicability of the effective methods and tools for identification of dynamics of existing and emerging research trends. The questions raised are: How to identify coherent thematic clusters in a given field of research? How to illustrate developments of a given thematic cluster keeping in mind exponential increase in the total number of publications?

This paper introduces an original method for identification of clusters in a given scientific domain. The approach is based on analysis of co-occurrence frequency of word sets, which are seeds of thematic clusters. The seeds are composed of four or three high co-occurrence frequency word sets. The proposed method enables allocation of a given word to several word sets, as well as sharing the same article by several clusters.

This article is structured as follows. Section 2 introduces the details of data clustering methodology. Section 3 presents example clustering results. Finally, Section 4 summarizes the main findings and concludes.

2   Method Description

The method for identification of thematic clusters is based on the concept presented by Sitarz et al. (2010). However, we introduce its improved version, extended with the term frequency inverse document frequency factor, as well as automatic formation of thematic clusters from identified sets of high-frequency words. The method consists of two major steps: article identification and word processing. A general structure of the method is given in Fig. 1 and its detailed description follows below.

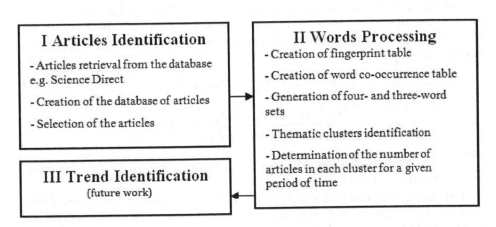

Fig. 1. The structure of method for identification of development trends in a given field of research

The analysis presented in this paper is performed using the articles from Science Direct and ISI Web of Science databases. There are more articles identified in ISI Web of Science than in the Science Direct database. However, the number of the identified thematic clusters is identical for both databases. In the first stage, the publications related to the analysed research theme are identified in the database using a query based on characteristic keywords of given field. The keywords are searched in titles, keyword lists, and abstracts of the articles. The identified papers are downloaded and introduced into "Article_data" database. In the second stage, the fingerprint table of the stored articles is created using a dedicated tool: a Rapidminer with TextInput operator [18]. A fingerprint of every paper, consists of a set of characteristic words which determine the meaning of a given paper. It is created by the statistical analysis of the text of article and removal of non-specific "stop-list" words, such as "the", "be", "can", etc. The columns of the fingerprint table are composed of the fingerprint words. The rows denote identification numbers of the articles. The value in each cell shows how many times a given column word occurs in a given article. Next, the author-developed tool, "WordSet", is used to build the word co-occurrence table [3, 9, 23], and to generate the four- and three-word sets. The word co-occurrence table is built on the basis of the fingerprint table. The number in each cell of the table shows how many times a given column-row word pair co-occurs in the analyzed set of articles [17, 21, 29].

There were tests performed to determine the optimal number of words to be used for the identification of clusters. The attempts to use five-word sets resulted in generation of large number of clusters covering very narrow and often very similar thematic fields. The efforts to apply three-word sets usually lead to creation of non-coherent, overly general clusters. The use of four-word sets is a compromise enabling identification of clusters at the reasonable level of information granularity.

Four-word sets, which determine atomic elements of knowledge, are generated by checking all possible four-word combinations. Only the sets characterized by high word co-occurrence are selected. The sets are determined using the following two conditions (1)-(2).

$$D_{w_i} \cap D_{w_j} \cap D_{w_k} \cap D_{w_l} \geq ThrA \tag{1}$$

$$\frac{D_{w_i} \cap D_{w_j} \cap D_{w_k} \cap D_{w_l}}{\frac{1}{4}\left(D_{w_i} + D_{w_j} + D_{w_k} + D_{w_l}\right)} \geq ThrB \tag{2}$$

where
D_{w_i} – number of articles in which word w_i occurs,
$ThrA, ThrB$ – threshold values.

A thematic field can be identified only if it is composed of more than $ThrA$ articles. The satisfaction of the condition (2) guarantees that only significant words should be considered. They are characterized by high word co-occurrence factor between words constituting the same thematic field as well as low co-occurrence with the other words. Some clusters could not be represented by four meaningful words. The additional three-word sets are generated to solve this problem, The identification of the three-word sets is performed in the same manner as for the four-word groups.

Word sets are considered as "phrases, concepts", in other words, atomic elements of the knowledge. During the clustering step word sets which highly co-occur are merged into clusters, which represent research fields, that is thematic clusters. This step is realized by using the author-developed tool "Field_Group". This tool applies the agglomerative clustering method presented by [5, 11, 31]. The similarity factor between two clusters is calculated using Eq. (3). It is determined for every possible combination of word set pairs.

$$\min \left[\left(\frac{D_{S_i} \cap D_{S_j}}{\min(D_{S_i}, D_{S_j})} \right), \text{ for } i = 1, \ldots, I, j = 1, \ldots, J \right] \tag{3}$$

where
S_i – word set belonging to cluster i,
S_j – word set belonging to cluster j,
D_{S_i} – number of articles in which word set S_i co-occurs,
I – number of word sets in the first considered cluster,
J – number of word sets in the second considered cluster.

Condition (4) is introduced to avoid the situation, when a given word set defines a narrow field of research A, whereas the other word group identifies a broader domain B, containing the field A.

$$\frac{\max(D_{S_i}, D_{S_j})}{\min(D_{S_i}, D_{S_j})} \geq ThrD \tag{4}$$

If this condition is not satisfied, the similarity between a given word set pair is set to 0. The presented approach efficiently limits the number of redundant word sets inside the clusters.

The proposed method allows allocation of an article to more than one cluster as well as using one word to build more than one word set. It is an important matter, as quite often an article deals with several scientific problems and, in consequence, it belongs to several clusters simultaneously.

The presented approach allows to represent the dynamics of a given research field. It means emergence or decline of thematic clusters. Moreover, it makes it possible to describe the interdependence of different thematic clusters. The proposed method can also capture the evolution of clusters. The core thematic subject of the cluster, defined by four-word sets, could be gradually changed by incorporating different words into the basic four-word set. If the process is continued, a smooth change of the given thematic cluster into another one is to be expected instead of dramatic vanishing of a given research subject.

In the final step of the second stage, the obtained results are introduced into the Microsoft Excel Macro programme, cooperating with the "Article_Data" database. The programme determines the annual distribution of relative number of papers related to each identified thematic cluster. The relative number of publications is defined as a ratio of the number of papers in a given cluster, to the total number of papers in "Article_Data" database determined for every year.

Not normalized number of publication is not a proper measure of the development state of a given thematic clusters since it is increasing over time for almost every research area. Such increasing number of publications is a result of technical and technological development, increasing number of research institutes and scientists. Thus the relative number of publications was applied. Such value shows the percentage interests of a given thematic cluster within an overriding research area. This shows the more really development state of a given thematic clusters than just number of publication.

Step III presented in Fig. 1 is a suggestion for future analysis of how the data extracted using this clustering method could be utilized. In particular, once publishing activity in all clusters is quantitatively known, one can study the past trends and forecast the future development. This could be done through various time series analysis and prediction tools. The clusters could be analyzed individually or in a multivariate way, where interconnections between research topics would be taken into account.

3   Results

The methods described in Section 1 are used to determine the dynamics of development of major research fields related to composite and nanocomposite polymer blends. There were 17431 articles found from Science Direct database published in years 1980-2010. They were identified using the search query: "blend AND (composite OR nanocomposite) AND polymer". As a result , 13828 papers with available abstracts were processed by Rapidminer in order to generate a fingerprint table for identified 7287 words. A total of 1050 four-word sets are now formed with respect to threshold $ThrA$ equal to 14 and threshold $ThrB$ equal to 0.13. 487 three-word sets are generated with threshold values 14 and 0.16 respectively. The threshold values were chosen in a pre-analysis phase. The tests have shown that for the lower threshold values there were many word sets obtained. In consequence, the clusters would consist of too many word sets and the calculations performed in the next steps of the analysis would be very tedious. For example, applying $ThrA$ and $ThrB$ equal to 14 and 0.11, respectively, 2144 four-word sets were identified. Using $ThrA = 14$ and $ThrB = 0.1$, 3133 four-word sets were identified. Moreover, for lower threshold values there are often some meaningless word sets identified, not related to the analysed research field. For the higher threshold values there are relatively few word sets obtained. In consequence, many important clusters would be omitted.

The "Field_Group" tool identified 318 thematic clusters for the previously obtained word sets for a $ThrC$ threshold value equal to 30% and a $ThrD$ threshold value equal to 2.5. Finally, 32 thematic clusters were chosen from the generated clusters, which are strictly related to the analyzed research field. The obtained clusters are presented in Table 1. The relative number of articles related to each cluster for each publication year between 1980 and 2010 was identified. The threshold values should be chosen experimentally, depending on the type of analysis. In order to identify only the main clusters (in the case of a well developed research field), the thresholds should be high. However, in order to identify narrow thematic clusters (in the case of a relatively small research field), the thresholds should be quite low. On the basis of our experience it is recommended to use $ThrB$ between 0.1 and 0.25 and $ThrC$ between 0.25 and 0.5, in order to achieve clusters with reasonable level of structuring.

Table 1. Thematic clusters of the composite and nanocomposite polymer blends research field

No.	Caption
1	Mechanical properties
2	The physical structure of composites and nanocomposites
3	Tensile strength
4	Scanning differential microcalorimetry analysis
5	Biomedical applications
6	Investigations of crystalline structure
7	Elasticity modulus
8	Testify of glass transition temperature
9	Study of morphology and chemical structure
10	Sources of electricity - batteries
11	Fuel cells
12	Polymer membranes
13	Thermal resistance
14	Compatibilization
15	Compounding
16	Styrene copolymer blends
17	X-ray photoelectron spectroscopy analysis method
18	Nuclear magnetic resonance spectroscopy analysis
19	Structure of nanocomposites
20	Carbon nanotubes
21	Carbon nanofibers
22	Photovoltaic cells
23	Tribological properties
24	Ring-opening polymerization
25	Fire resistance
26	Hybrid polymers
27	Other blends
28	Rheological properties of polymers
29	Fracture and stress cracking
30	Poly(vinyl chloride) blends
31	Biosensors
32	Silsesquioxane

The word sets identified within two example thematic clusters, namely, "Biomedical application" (370 articles) and "Sources of electricity – batteries" (212 articles), are presented in Tab. 2 and Tab. 3, respectively.

The word sets identified within thematic clusters "Carbon nanotubes", "Carbon nanofibers", and "Structure of nanocomposites" are presented in Tab. 4, 5 and 6, respectively.

The number of publications in each cluster should then be analyzed in terms of development trends, which is a subject for further research. Such methods could be taken from financial analysis approaches or other trend identification and time series forecasting tools.

Table 2. Word sets of the cluster "Biomedical application (370 articles)

First word	Second word	Third word	Fourth word
potenti	engin	tissu	scaffold
applic	engin	tissu	scaffold
fabric	engin	tissu	scaffold
engin	tissu	regener	scaffold
biodegrad	engin	tissu	scaffold
cell	engin	tissu	cultur
cell	engin	tissu	prolifer
engin	tissu	prolifer	scaffold
cell	engin	tissu	scaffold
porou	engin	tissu	scaffold
engin	tissu	bone	scaffold
tissu	bone	scaffold	vitro
alkalin	cultur	osteoblast	phosphatas
alkalin	prolifer	osteoblast	phosphatas
alkalin	hydroxyapatit	phosphatas	
alkalin	osteogen	phosphatas	

Table 3. Word sets of the cluster "Sources of electricity - batteries" (212 articles)

First word	Second word	Third word	Fourth word
electrolyt	lithium	li	ionic
electrolyt	lithium	li	batteri
lithium	pvdf	batteri	hfp
li	pvdf	batteri	hfp
electrolyt	lithium	ionic	batteri
lithium	ionic	electrochem	batteri
electrolyt	lithium	electrochem	batteri
lithium	li	electrochem	batteri
electrolyt	ionic	electrochem	
electrolyt	lithium	ion	batteri
electrolyt	pvdf	polyvinyliden	fluorid
lithium	pvdf	polyvinyliden	fluorid
lithium	polyvinyliden	fluorid	batteri
pvdf	hexafluoropropylen	batteri	hfp
lithium	pvdf	hexafluoropropylen	hfp
pvdf	polyvinyliden	fluorid	hfp
pvdf	fluorid	hexafluoropropylen	hfp
ionic	pvdf	polyvinyliden	fluorid
lithium	li	batteri	recharg

4   Summary and Conclusions

The structuring of research field is an important scientific activity due to many reasons, e.g. identification of key publications and centers of expertise, discovery

Table 4. Word sets of the cluster "Carbon nanotubes" (417 articles)

First word	Second word	Third word	Fourth word
carbon	nanotub	cnt	
carbon	nanotub	multi	wall
nanotub	multi	wall	mwnt
ester	phenyl	fulleren	butyr
solar	pcbm	fulleren	
photovolta	pcbm	fulleren	
bulk	solar	heterojunct	fulleren
solar	photovolta	heterojunct	fulleren
fulleren	meh	ppv	

Table 5. Word sets of the cluster "Carbon nanofibers" (159 articles)

First word	Second word	Third word	Fourth word
diamet	electrospun	electrospin	nanofib
fiber	electrospun	electrospin	nanofib
electrospun	electrospin	mat	
electrospun	electrospin	fibrou	fibrou
electrospun	electrospin	nanofib	nanofibr
electrospun	electrospin	tissu	

Table 6. Word sets of the cluster "Structure of nanocomposites" (453 articles)

First word	Second word	Third word	Fourth word
dispers	nanocomposit	clai	
rai	diffract	nanocomposit	transmiss
rai	diffract	nanocomposit	clai
nanocomposit	montmorillonit	intercal	clai
montmorillonit	intercal	clai	exfoli
nanocomposit	montmorillonit	intercal	exfoli
nanocomposit	montmorillonit	clai	exfoli
nanocomposit	intercal	clai	exfoli
intercal	silic	exfoli	

of emerging subjects of research or finding potentially interesting areas of business activity. The structuring is also important for scientometrics as a subject of research.

The clustering method presented in this paper uses co-word analysis. The identification of thematic clusters in a given research field is based on determination of word sets. The sets being the seeds of thematic clusters are composed of four or three frequently co-occurring words. The clusters identified in this way represent the structure of research field. The major advantages of the presented method, in comparison to the existing approaches, could be summarized as follows:

- Straightforward classification criteria – a cluster is defined by a four-word set and an article can belong to this cluster only if it contains the specific four-word set.
- Flexibility of classification thanks to the fact that a given article can belong to several clusters.
- Excellent classification features achieved by possibility of a simultaneous membership of a given word in several four-word sets.

The key feature of the proposed method is it ability to simultaneously allocate a given word into several clusters. The identified clusters are associated and partly overlapped with the other clusters thanks to common building terms in the sets of co-occurring words. It reflects the practice of research, as a given paper usually belongs to several thematic clusters. Precise identification of thematically coherent clusters is possible thanks to such flexibility of classification. Moreover, the proposed method enables handling of synonyms.

This approach can be used for structuring of various research fields and determination of development trends of the identified thematic clusters. However, despite its universal character, there are still some elements of the method which could be improved. An attempt could be done to enhance identification of fingerprint words by testing a diversity of function classes. Moreover, an additional effort should be made to improve ability to identify the synonyms. It could be achieved by application of the broad spectrum of semantic methods. An important issue is the determination of the threshold values. At the moment, they are identified using trial-and-error approach over numerous test runs. A procedure allowing for automatic determination of threshold values would also be an important innovation.

As presented above, there is still significant space for improvements. Due to the limited volume of this article, we cannot present comparison of this method with other approaches. However, despite its limitations, the proposed method could inspire the broader interest in the use of semantic techniques and financial analysis methods for building the portfolios of R&D projects.

References

[1] Amini, M.R., Goutte, C.: A co-classification approach to learning from multilingual corpora. Machine Learning 79(1-2), 105–121 (2010)
[2] Barnett, G.A., Huh, C., Kim, Y., Park, H.W.: Citations among communication journals and other disciplines: a network analysis. Scientometrics 88(2), 449–469 (2011)
[3] Callon, M., Courtial, J.P., Laville, F.: Co-word analysis as a tool for describing the network of interactions between basic and technological research: The case of polymer chemistry. Scientometrics 22(1), 153–205 (1991)
[4] Cambrosio, A., Limoges, C., Courtial, J.P., Laville, F.: Historical scientometrics? Mapping over 70 years of biological safety research with coword analysis. Scientometrics 27(2), 119–143 (1993)
[5] Chang, C.T., Lai, J.Z.C., Jeng, M.D.: Fast agglomerative clustering using information of k-nearest neighbors. Pattern Recognition 43(12), 3958–3968 (2010)

[6] Clarke, A., Gatineau, M., Thorogood, M., Wyn-Roberts, N.: Health promotion research literature in Europe 1995-2005. The European Journal of Public Health 17(suppl. 1), 24–28 (2007)

[7] Cottrill, C.A., Rogers, E.M., Mills, T.: Co-citation analysis of the scientific literature of innovation research traditions diffusion of innovations and technology transfer. Journal of Information Science 36(3), 383–400 (2010)

[8] Coulter, N., Monarch, I., Konda, S.: Software engineering as seen through its research literature: A study in co-word analysis. Journal of the American Society for Information Science 49(13), 1206–1223 (1998)

[9] Ding, Y., Chowdhury, G.G., Foo, S.: Bibliometric cartography of information retrieval research by using co-word analysis. Information Processing and Management 37(6), 817–842 (2001)

[10] Fabry, B., Ernst, H., Langholz, J., Köster, M.: Patent portfolio analysis as a useful tool for identifying R&D and business opportunities-an empirical application in the nutrition and health industry. World Patent Information 28(3), 215–225 (2006)

[11] Gowda, K.C., Ravi, T.V.: Agglomerative clustering of symbolic objects using the concepts of both similarity and dissimilarity. Pattern Recognition Letters 16(6), 647–652 (1995)

[12] Hung, S.W., Wang, A.P.: Examining the small world phenomenon in the patent citation network: a case study of the radio frequency identification (RFID) network. Scientometrics 82(1), 121–134 (2010)

[13] Krampen, G., von Eye, A., Schui, G.: Forecasting trends of development of psychology from a bibliometric perspective. Scientometrics 87, 687–694 (2011)

[14] Lee, P.-C., Su, H.-N., Chan, T.-Y.: Assessment of ontology-based knowledge network formation by Vector-Space Model. Scientometrics 85(3), 689–703 (2010)

[15] Li, X., Chen, H., Huang, Z., Roco, M.C.: Patent citation network in nanotechnology (1976-2004). Journal of Nanoparticle Research 9, 337–352 (2007)

[16] Lv, P.H., Wang, G.F., Wan, Y., Jia, L., Qing, L., Fei-Cheng, M.: Bibliometric trend analysis on global graphene research. Scientometrics 88, 399–419 (2011)

[17] Marshakova-Shaikevich, I.: Bibliometric maps of field of science. Information Processing and Management 41(6), 1534–1547 (2005)

[18] Mierswa, I., Wurst, M., Klinkenberg, R., Scholz, M., Euler, T.: YALE: Rapid Prototyping for Complex Data Mining Tasks. In: Proceedings of the 12th ACM SIGKDD International Conference on Knowledge Discovery and Data Mining (KDD 2006) (2006)

[19] Newman, M.E.J.: Power laws, Pareto distributions and Zipf's law. Contemporary Physics 46(5), 323–351 (2005)

[20] Noyons, E.C.M.: Bibliometric mapping of science in a science policy context. Scientometrics 50(1), 83–98 (2001)

[21] Noyons, E.C.M., Van Raan, A.F.J.: Bibliometric cartography of scientific and technological developments of an R&D field. Scientometrics 30(1), 157–173 (1994)

[22] Noyons, E.C.M., Van Raan, A.F.J.: Monitoring scientific developments from a dynamic perspective: Self-organized structuring to map neural network research. Journal of the American Society for Information Science 49(1), 68–81 (1998)

[23] Peters, H.P.F., Van Raan, A.F.J.: Co-word-based science maps of chemical-engineering. Part2. Combined clustering and multidimensional scaling. Research Policy 22(1), 47–71 (1993)

[24] Price, D.J.D.: Networks of scientific papers. Science 149(3683), 510–515 (1965)

[25] Rajapakse, A., Titchener-Hooker, N.J., Farid, S.S.: Modelling of the biopharmaceutical drug development pathway and portfolio management. Computers & Chemical Engineering 29(6,15), 1357–1368 (2005)

[26] Rip, A., Courtial, J.P.: Co-word maps of biotechnology: An example of cognitive scientometrics. Scientometrics 6(6), 381–400 (1984)

[27] Sitarz, R., Kraslawski, A., Jezowski, J.: Dynamics of Knowledge Flow in Research on Distillation. Computer Aided Chemical Engineering 28, 583–588 (2010)

[28] Tsai, H.H.: Research trends analysis by comparing data mining and customer relationship management through bibliometric methodology. Scientometrics 87, 425–450 (2011)

[29] Van Raan, A.F.J.: Advanced bibliometric methods to assess research performance and scientific development: basic principles and recent partial applications. Research Evaluation 3(3), 151–166 (1993)

[30] Van Raan, A.F.J., Tijssen, R.J.W.: The neural net of neural network research: An exercise In bibliometric mapping. Scientometrics 26(1), 169–192 (1993)

[31] Voorhees, E.M.: Implementing agglomerative hierarchic clustering algorithms for use in document retrieval. Information Processing & Management 22(6), 465–476 (1986)

[32] Wang, Z.Y., Li, G., Li, C.Y., Li, A.: Research on the semantic-based co-word analysis. Scientometrics 90, 855–875 (2012)

[33] Yang, Y., Wu, M., Cui, L.: Integration of three visualization methods based on co-word analysis. Scientometrics 90, 659–673 (2012)

[34] Yi, S., Choi, J.: The organization of scientific knowledge: the structural characteristics of keyword networks. Scientometrics 90, 1015–1026 (2012)

[35] Zapata, J.C., Varma, V.A., Reklaitis, G.V.: Impact of tactical and operational policies in the selection of a new product portfolio. Computers & Chemical Engineering 32(1-2), 307–319 (2008)

The Choquet Integral Applied to Ranking Therapies in Radiation Cystitis

Elisabeth Rakus-Andersson[1] and Janusz Frey[2]

[1] Blekinge Institute of Technology, Department of Mathematics and Science,
37179 Karlskrona, Sweden
Elisabeth.Andersson@bth.se
[2] Blekinge County Hospital, Department of Surgery and Urology,
371 85 Karlskrona, Sweden
Janusz.Frey@ltblekinge.se

Abstract. We modify the classical fuzzy decision making model by adopting the concept of the Choquet integral as a measure of the therapy utility, when proving different treatments in radiation cystitis. The objective is to rank therapies as a sequence, commencing with the most efficacious remedy.

Keywords: Utility matrix, parametric membership functions, weights of importance, utilities of therapies, Choquet integral.

1 Introduction

Radiation cystitis is in general rarely occurring, which makes it very difficult to study in a large group of clinical trials. Most available data about radiation cystitis treatment come from a small number of descriptive studies or from expert opinions [2, 4]. As clinical data are considered to have low quality then physicians, who are still facing patients with a disease hugely influencing quality of life, mostly base on their own experience.

We thus want to test fuzzy decision-making model, regarded as a valuable tool, to help in selecting a patient-tailored treatment in radiation cystitis [12].

Theoretical fuzzy decision-making models [14–15], possessing the utility matrix filled with distinct utilities of pairs (decision, object-state), give rise to own trials of successfully accomplished applications concerning the item of medication [8, 12]. After interpreting pairs (decision, object-state) as (therapy, symptom), we intend to prove decision-making based on the Choquet integral to extract the optimal treatment in radiation cystitis. We wish to confront the results, obtained by the Choquet integral technique, with another model made for the purpose of radiation cystitis in [12].

In Section 2, we recall the basic data inserted into the model of fuzzy decision making. Section 3 provides weights of importance, regarding the symptoms' priorities to retreat. The discussion about the enumeration of utilities is accomplished in Section 4. The concepts of Choquet integrals, playing role of total utilities of therapies, are proved in Section 5, whereas some conclusions are added to Section 6.

© Springer International Publishing Switzerland 2015
D. Filev et al. (eds.), *Intelligent Systems' 2014*,
Advances in Intelligent Systems and Computing 323, DOI: 10.1007/978-3-319-11310-4_38

2   Basic Data in Fuzzy Decision Making

We introduce the notions of a space of states $X = \{x_1,...,x_m\}$ and a decision space (a space of alternatives) $A = \{a_1,...,a_n\}$. We consider a decision model, in which n alternatives $a_1,...,a_n \in A$ act as therapies used to treat patients who suffer from radiation cystitis. The therapies should influence m states $x_1,...,x_m \in X$, identified with m symptoms typical of the morbid unit considered.

When a decision maker applies therapy $a_i \in A$, $i = 1,...,n$, to symptom $x_j \in X$, $j = 1,...,m$, then a utility of treating x_j by a_i is determined. In order to sample all distinct utilities, assigned to pairs (a_i, x_j), we estimate the total utility U_{a_i} as [12, 14–15]

$$U_{a_i} = \text{aggregation of } u_{ij}, i = 1,...,n, j = 1,...,m, \tag{1}$$

in which each element u_{ij} is a utility following from the decision a_i with the result x_j. The most efficacious therapy will be associated with the highest value of U_{a_i}.

Example 1
The symptoms, selected as the most decisive for radiation cystitis, are listed as x_1 = urgency, x_2 = dysuria, x_3 = urinary bladder pain, x_4 = macrohaematuria, x_5 = urine retention.

The treatments are extracted among a_1 = alum irrigation, a_2 = formalin instillation, a_3 = D-glucosamine, a_4 = oestrogens, a_5 = cystodiathermy, a_6 = interruption of internal illiac arteries, a_7 = bilateral percutaneous nephrostomy, a_8 = ileal diversion (with cystectomy), a_9 = pentoxyfilline and a_{10} = hyperbaric oxygen.

3   The Importance Weights Assisting Symptoms

The purpose of this section is to add other factors having impact on the solution of the decision-making model. We wish the model to be furnished with extraction of the most efficacious treatment, provided that the particular emphasis is also concentrated on assigning differing degrees of importance to states-symptoms [8, 12, 14–15].

Let us associate with each symptom x_j, $j = 1,...,m$, a non negative number that indicates its power or importance in the decision according to the rule: the higher the number is, the more important role of x_j's retreat will be regarded. We assign $w_1,...,w_m$ as powers-weights to $x_1,...,x_m$. A procedure for obtaining a ratio scale of importance for a group of m symptoms is developed by the authors as a novelty.

Generally, if we consider m symptoms X_j to find importance weights for them, we want to place them in the sequence $X_1 > X_2 > ... > X_m$ in accordance with the expert's opinion. We explain that the symbol ">" stands for "more important than". We wish the sum of all weights W_j, tied to Xj, $j = 1,...,m$, to be 1 as to

$$m \cdot r + (m - 1) \cdot r + \cdots + 2 \cdot r + 1 \cdot r = 1, \tag{2}$$

where r is a quotient depending on m. The weights W_j constitute a new order of old w_j, due to the sequence $X_1 > X_2 > ... > X_m$.

Further,

$$W_j = (m - j + 1) \cdot r \qquad (3)$$

for $j = 1,...,m$.

Example 2

The physician intends to release the patient from the symptoms with the following priorities: x_4 – priority 1, x_3 – priority 2, x_5 = priority 3, x_2 – priority 4 and x_1 – priority 5.

We thus reorder the sequence of the symptoms x_j from Ex.1, named X_j now, in a new placement

$$X_1 = x_4 > X_2 = x_3 > X_3 = x_5 > X_4 = x_2 > X_5 = x_1.$$

For $m = 5$, due to (2), the equation $5 \cdot r + 4 \cdot r + 3 \cdot r + 2 \cdot r + 1 \cdot r = 1$ provides $r = 0.066$. We get

$W_1 = (5 - 1 + 1) \cdot 0.066 = 0.33$, $W_2 = (5 - 2 + 1) \cdot 0.066 = 0.264$,
$W_3 = (5 - 3 + 1) \cdot 0.066 = 0.198$, $W_4 = (5 - 4 + 1) \cdot 0.066 = 0.132$,
$W_5 = (5 - 5 + 1) \cdot 0.066$.

The common utility U_{a_i} of therapy a_i is now computed as

$$U_{a_i} = \sum_{j=1}^{m} U_{ij} \cdot W_j \qquad (4)$$

where U_{ij} are the utilities of using a_i to treat X_j, $j = 1,...,m$. We emphasize that U_{ij} replace u_{ij}, introduced in (1), in compliance with weighed symptom order $X_1 > X_2 > ... > X_m$.

To find a numerical expression for the utility U_{ij}, verbally decided by a physician for each pair (a_i, X_j), we suggest the analysis of the process following the next session.

4   Creation of Numerical Expressions for Utilities

We first want the utility, estimating the remission of symptom X_j after treating it by a_i, $i = 1,...,n$, $j = 1,..,m$, to be verbally expressed in order to facilitate the communication with a professional adviser. We generate a linguistic list named L = "Utility of applying a_i to X_j". L becomes stated, e.g., as [12]

"Utility U_{ij} of applying a_i to X_j" = {N_1 = "none", N_2 = "almost none", N_3 = "very little", N_4 = "little", N_5 = "rather little", N_6 = "moderate", N_7 = "rather large", N_8 = "large", N_9 = "very large", N_{10} = "almost complete", N_{11} = "complete"}.

Each expression N_q, $q = 1,..,11$, will be replaced by a fuzzy set, also named N_q.

By linking the therapy to the symptom for pair (a_i, X_j), a physician selects expression N_q from the list due to his experience. It means that $U_{ij} = N_q$ in practice. We, in turn, should assign a numerical representative to fuzzy set N_q, assisting each verbal description.

In order not to generate the boundaries of fuzzy sets N_q in an ad hoc manner, we suppose that $L = \{N_1, \dots, N_\omega\}$ is a general linguistic list consisting of ω words. Each word is associated with a fuzzy set. The number ω is a positive odd integer. Furthermore, let E be the length of a set R, designed for all restrictions of the fuzzy sets from L, provided that $z \in R$. We now wish to divide the linguistic terms into three groups recognized as a left group, a middle group and a right group. Albeit the trials of generating membership functions with modifiers for linguistic terms were already accomplished [1, 6], we propose the authors' own procedure of adopting parametric s-functions whose derivations can be followed in [9–11].

The membership functions, assigned to the leftmost terms, are prepared by (5) as

$$
\mu_{N_t}(z) = \begin{cases}
1 & \text{for} & z \le \frac{E(\omega-1)}{2(\omega+1)}\delta(t), \\[2ex]
1 - 2\left(\dfrac{z - \frac{E(\omega-1)}{2(\omega+1)}\delta(t)}{\frac{E(\omega-1)}{\omega(\omega+1)}\delta(t)}\right)^2 & \text{for} & \frac{E(\omega-1)}{2(\omega+1)}\delta(t) \le z \le \frac{E(\omega-1)}{2\omega}\delta(t), \\[3ex]
2\left(\dfrac{z - \frac{E(\omega-1)(\omega+2)}{2\omega(\omega+1)}\delta(t)}{\frac{E(\omega-1)}{\omega(\omega+1)}\delta(t)}\right)^2 & \text{for} & \frac{E(\omega-1)}{2\omega}\delta(t) \le z \le \frac{E(\omega-1)(\omega+2)}{2\omega(\omega+1)}\delta(t), \\[3ex]
0 & \text{for} & z \ge \frac{E(\omega-1)(\omega+2)}{2\omega(\omega+1)}\delta(t),
\end{cases}
\tag{5}
$$

where $\delta(t) = \dfrac{2t}{\omega-1}, t = 1, \dots, \dfrac{\omega-1}{2}$ is a function depending on left function number t.

The membership function in the middle is expanded by (6) in the form of

$$
\mu_{N_{\frac{\omega+1}{2}}}(z) = \begin{cases}
0 & \text{for} & z \le \frac{E(\omega-2)}{2\omega}, \\[2ex]
2\left(\dfrac{z - \frac{E(\omega-2)}{2\omega}}{\frac{E}{\omega}}\right)^2 & \text{for} & \frac{E(\omega-2)}{2\omega} \le z \le \frac{E(\omega-1)}{2\omega}, \\[3ex]
1 - 2\left(\dfrac{z - \frac{E}{2}}{\frac{E}{\omega}}\right)^2 & \text{for} & \frac{E(\omega-1)}{2\omega} \le z \le \frac{E}{2}, \\[3ex]
1 - 2\left(\dfrac{z - \frac{E}{2}}{\frac{E}{\omega}}\right)^2 & \text{for} & \frac{E}{2} \le z \le \frac{E(\omega+1)}{2\omega}, \\[3ex]
2\left(\dfrac{z - \frac{E(\omega+2)}{2\omega}}{\frac{E}{\omega}}\right)^2 & \text{for} & \frac{E(\omega+1)}{2\omega} \le z \le \frac{E(\omega+2)}{2\omega}, \\[3ex]
0 & \text{for} & z \ge \frac{E(\omega+2)}{2\omega}.
\end{cases}
\tag{6}
$$

Finally, the membership functions on the right-hand side can be yielded by (7) as

$$\mu_{N_{\frac{\omega+3}{2}+t-1}}(z) =$$

$$
\begin{cases}
0 & \text{for} & z \leq E - \frac{E(\omega-1)(\omega+2)}{2\omega(\omega+1)} \cdot \varepsilon(t), \\[2ex]
2\left(\dfrac{z-\left(E-\frac{E(\omega-1)(\omega+2)}{2\omega(\omega+1)}\cdot\varepsilon(t)\right)}{\frac{E(\omega-1)}{\omega(\omega+1)}\cdot\varepsilon(t)}\right)^2 & \text{for} & E - \frac{E(\omega-1)(\omega+2)}{2\omega(\omega+1)} \cdot \varepsilon(t) \leq z \leq E - \frac{E(\omega-1)}{2\omega} \cdot \varepsilon(t), \\[2ex]
1 - 2\left(\dfrac{z-\frac{E(\omega-1)}{2(\omega+1)}\cdot\varepsilon(t)}{\frac{E(\omega-1)}{\omega(\omega+1)}\cdot\varepsilon(t)}\right)^2 & \text{for} & E - \frac{E(\omega-1)}{2\omega} \cdot \varepsilon(t) \leq z \leq E - \frac{E(\omega-1)}{2(\omega+1)} \cdot \varepsilon(t), \\[2ex]
1 & \text{for} & z \geq E - \frac{E(\omega-1)}{2(\omega+1)} \cdot \varepsilon(t).
\end{cases}
\tag{7}
$$

A new function $\varepsilon(t) = 1 - \frac{2(t-1)}{\omega-1}, t = 1, \ldots, \frac{\omega-1}{2}$ allows creating all rightmost functions one by one, when setting t-values in (7).

For $\omega = 11$ and $E = 100$ (the typical length of the reference set $[0, 100]$ tested in medical investigations of frequencies) we derive membership functions of N_q, $q = 1,\ldots,11$, by employing formulas (5)–(7).

In order to determine the most adequate representative for each N_q, $q = 1,\ldots,11$, we first introduce another fuzzy set "total over $[0, 100]$" with the membership function

$$
\mu_{\text{"total over }[0,100]\text{"}}(z) =
\begin{cases}
0 & \text{for} & z \leq 0, \\[1ex]
2\left(\frac{z}{100}\right)^2 & \text{for} & 0 \leq z \leq 50, \\[1ex]
1 - \left(\frac{z-100}{100}\right)^2 & \text{for} & 50 \leq z \leq 100, \\[1ex]
1 & \text{for} & z \geq 100.
\end{cases}
\tag{8}
$$

The membership degrees, being the second coordinates of intersection points between membership functions of each N_q and "total over $[0, 100]$", will constitute the numerical assignments of the terms allocated in L.

Figure 1 collects the graphs of N_q, $q = 1,\ldots,11$, and "total over $[0, 100]$".

We thus connect N_1 to 0.0054, N_2 to 0.042, N_3 to 0.156, N_4 to 0.274, N_5 to 0.418 and N_6 to 0.5. The right fuzzy sets are identified by the following numbers: N_7 by 0.582, N_8 by 0.726, N_9 by 0.844, N_{10} by 0.958 and N_{11} by 0.9946.

Example 3

After considering therapies a_i and symptoms X_j in the radiation cystitis, the judgments of verbal utilities $U_{ij} = N_q$ for pairs (a_i, X_j), $i = 1,\ldots,10$, $j = 1,\ldots,5$, $q = 1,\ldots,11$, are accomplished by physicians. We convert N_q into numbers like shown in Table 1. For the reason of sparse data reports, collected for the radiation cystitis, mostly the professional experience of physicians is involved in predicting the utility evaluations [12].

5   The Choquet Integral as the Total Utility of a Therapy

The quantities of medical estimates N_q, taking place in Table 1, are interpreted as utilities U_{ij} of the pairs (a_i, X_j).

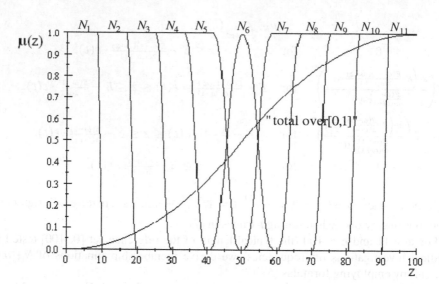

Fig. 1. The fuzzy sets N_1–N_{11} and "total over [0, 100]"

Table 1. Utilities $U_{ij} = N_q$ of pairs (a_i, X_j)

$a_i \backslash x_j$	X_1	X_2	X_3	X_4	X_5
a_1	$N_7{=}0.582$	$N_3{=}0.156$	$N_5{=}0.418$	$N_3{=}0.156$	$N_1{=}0.0054$
a_2	$N_8{=}0.726$	$N_2{=}0.042$	$N_3{=}0.156$	$N_2{=}0.042$	$N_1{=}0.0054$
a_3	$N_2{=}0.042$	$N_3{=}0.156$	$N_2{=}0.042$	$N_3{=}0.156$	$N_3{=}0.156$
a_4	$N_5{=}0.418$	$N_4{=}0.274$	$N_4{=}0.274$	$N_6{=}0.5$	$N_6{=}0.5$
a_5	$N_5{=}0.418$	$N_3{=}0.156$	$N_5{=}0.418$	$N_1{=}0.0054$	$N_1{=}0.0054$
a_6	$N_{10}{=}0.958$	$N_4{=}0.274$	$N_3{=}0.156$	$N_2{=}0.042$	$N_1{=}0.0054$
a_7	$N_6{=}0.5$	$N_3{=}0.156$	$N_{10}{=}0.958$	$N_8{=}0.726$	$N_9{=}0.844$
a_8	$N_{10}{=}0.958$	$N_{11}{=}0.9946$	$N_{11}{=}0.9946$	$N_{11}{=}0.9946$	$N_{11}{=}0.9946$
a_9	$N_7{=}0.582$	$N_3{=}0.156$	$N_2{=}0.042$	$N_4{=}0.274$	$N_3{=}0.156$
a_{10}	$N_7{=}0.582$	$N_6{=}0.5$	$N_7{=}0.582$	$N_6{=}0.5$	$N_4{=}0.274$

We remember that symptoms $X_1, ..., X_m \in X$ act as objects in X. To them let us assign the measures $M(X_j | a_i) = U_{ij}$, where symbols $X_j | a_i$ reflect the association between symptom X_j and medicine a_i, $i = 1, ..., n$, $j = 1, ..., m$.

The weights W_j are set as the range values $f(X_j)$ of a function $f : X \rightarrow = [0, 1]$. In this context formula (4) gets a new shape of

$$U_{a_i} = \sum_{j=1}^m U_{ij} \cdot W_j = \sum_{j=1}^m M\left(X_j | a_i\right) \cdot W_j \qquad (9)$$

The second part of formula (9) is comparable to the area of a figure, composed of rectangles. These possess one side equal to $M\left(X_j | a_i\right)$ and the other side measured as the W_j value.

Example 4

Let us estimate the influence of therapy a_1 on symptoms X_j, $j = 1,\ldots,5$, characteristic of the radiation cystitis. The total utility of a_1 is measured as the surface of the pattern sketched in Fig. 2.

Hence,

$U_{a_1} = \sum_{j=1}^{5} M(X_j \lceil a_1) \cdot W_j = 0.582 \cdot 0.33 + 0.156 \cdot 0.264 + 0.418 \cdot 0.198 + 0.156 \cdot 0.132 + 0.0054 \cdot 0.066 = 0.337.$

The same result will be reached after converting the contents of Fig. 2 to the figure drawn in Fig. 3.

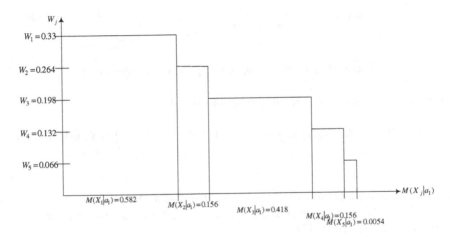

Fig. 2. The graph of $U_{a_1} = \sum_{j=1}^{5} M(X_j \lceil a_1) \cdot W_j$

The area of the pattern, sketched in Fig. 3, corresponds to

$U_{a_1} = 0.582(0.33 - 0.264) + (0.582 + 0.156)(0.264 - 0.198) + (0.582 + 0.156 + 0.418)(0.198 - 0.132) + (0.582 + 0.156 + 0.418 + 0.156)(0.132 - 0.066) + (0.582 + 0.156 + 0.418 + 0.156 + 0.0054)(0.066 - 0) = 0.337.$

The last result in Ex. 4 is fully compatible with

$$U_{a_1} =$$
$$(W_1 - W_2) \cdot M(X_{1 \leqslant s \leqslant j} | a_1 : f(X_{1 \leqslant s \leqslant j}) \geq W_1)_{j=1} +$$
$$(W_2 - W_3) \cdot M(X_{1 \leqslant s \leqslant j} | a_1 : f(X_{1 \leqslant s \leqslant j}) \geq W_2)_{j=2} +$$
$$(W_3 - W_4) \cdot M(X_{1 \leqslant s \leqslant j} | a_1 : f(X_{1 \leqslant s \leqslant j}) \geq W_3)_{j=3} + \qquad (10)$$
$$(W_4 - W_5) \cdot M(X_{1 \leqslant s \leqslant j} | a_1 : f(X_{1 \leqslant s \leqslant j}) \geq W_4)_{j=4} +$$
$$(W_5 - W_6) \cdot M(X_{1 \leqslant s \leqslant j} | a_1 : f(X_{1 \leqslant s \leqslant j}) \geq W_5)_{j=5}$$
$$= \sum_{j=1}^{5} (W_j - W_{j+1}) \cdot M(X_{1 \leqslant s \leqslant j} | a_1) : f(X_{1 \leqslant s \leqslant j}) \geq W_j$$

provided that $W_6 = 0$ and $M(X_{1 \leqslant s \leqslant j} | a_1) = \sum_{s=1}^{j} M(X_s | a_1)$.

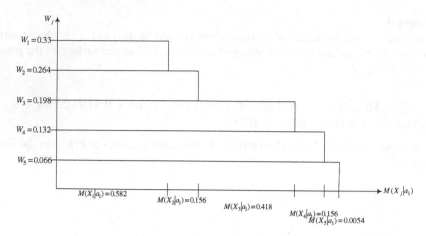

Fig. 3. The pattern of computing U_{a_1} after converting Fig. 2

Formula (10), on the other hand, can be formalized as

$$\sum_{j=1}^{5}(W_j - W_{j+1}) \cdot M(X_{1 \le s \le j}|a_1) : f(X_{1 \le s \le j}) \ge W_j = \int_{X_j \in \{X_1, X_2, X_3, X_4, X_5\}} f(X_j)dM(X_j|a_1)$$

(11)

and, after the confrontation with [3, 5, 13], is identified as the Choquet integral over $X = \{X_1, X_2, X_3, X_4, X_5\}$. In general, we are able to perform the computations of total utilities of a_i, $i = 1,...,n$, by [7]

$$U_{a_i} = \int_{X_j \in X} f(X_j)dM((X_j|a_i) = \sum_{j=1}^{m}(W_j - W_{j+1}) \cdot M(X_{1 \le s \le j}|a_1) : f(X_{1 \le s \le j}) \ge W_j$$

(12)

We perform (12) to estimate: $U_{a_2} = 0.287$, $U_{a_3} = 0.094$, $U_{a_4} = 0.366$, $U_{a_5} = 0.263$, $U_{a_6} = 0.425$, $U_{a_7} = 0.547$, $U_{a_8} = 0.973$, $U_{a_9} = 0.288$, and $U_{a_{10}} = 0.523$.

As the most efficacious therapy, a_i assists the largest U_{a_i} value, $i = 1,...,10$. We will thus set the therapies in the sequence $a_8 > a_7 > a_{10} > a_6 > a_4 > a_1 > a_9 > a_2 > a_5 > a_3$, when assuming that ">" means "a_i shows the stronger power in receding symptoms than a_c, $i, c = 1,...,n$".

6   Conclusions

The basis of investigations has been mostly restricted to a judgment of the therapy influence on clinical symptoms characterizing radiation cystitis. In the classical model of fuzzy decision making [14–15] we have also employed the indices of the symptoms' importance to emphasize the essence of the symptom priority to recede in the final decision. By interpreting the utilities of treatments as measures we have furnished total utility estimates with such tools as the Choquet integrals to extend the model of the classical fuzzy decision-making. This complement to decision making constitutes an original contribution as it has been impossible to find the similar effects in literature apart from our own [7]. The method of constructing families of membership functions, depending only of the length of a reference set and the number of constraints, reveals another own idea of the authors.

The results of the decision model, obtained in this paper, converge to the final decision from [12]. These seem to be reasonable from the clinicians' point of view and, with some exceptions, they match results of the algorithm proposed by Martinez-Rodriques [4]. Nevertheless, we would strongly emphasize that the symptoms, their intensities and treatment efficacies are mostly based on the personal experience and obviously can vary among the centers. We also note that the treatment of radiation cystitis is most often multimodal when combining various methods. The final scale of therapy priorities from Section 5 should absolutely not be regarded as a guideline for future prognoses of treatments but the model itself, with dynamic input categories, seems to be a very valuable tool helping to determine the appropriate treatment path.

To sum up we would like to state that computational intelligence methods can constitute perfect bridges between the expert judgments and real evidence based medicine in case of diseases that lack data from the good quality clinical trials.

References

1. Bouchon-Meunier, B., Jia, Y.: Linguistic modifiers and imprecise categories. Special Issue: Uncertanty Management in Knowledge-based Systems 7(1), 25–36 (1992)
2. Denton, A.S., Clarke, N., Maher, J.: Non-surgical Interventions for Late Radiation Cystitis in Patients who Have Received Radical Radiotherapy to the Pelvis. Wiley Online – The Cochrane Library (2009), http://onlinelibrary.wiley.com/doi/10.1002/14651858.CD001773/pdf
3. Grabisch, M., Murofushi, T., Sugeno, M., Kacprzyk, J.: Fuzzy Measures and Integrals. Theory and Applications. Physica Verlag, Berlin (2000)
4. Martinez-Rodrigues, R., Areal Calama, J., Buisan Rueda, O., González Satue, C., Sanchez Macias, J., Arzoz Fabregas, M., Gago Ramos, J., Bayona Arenas, S., Ibarz Servio, L., Saladié Roig, J.M.: Practical Treatment Approach of Radiation Induced Cystitis. Actas Urol Esp. 34(7), 603–609 (2010)
5. Mirofushi, T., Sugeno, M.: An Interpretation of Fuzzy Measures and the Choquet Integral as an Integral with Respect to a Fuzzy Measure. Fuzzy Sets and Systems 29, 201–227 (1989)
6. Novák, V., Perfilieva, I.: Evaluating of Linguistic Expressions and Functional Fuzzy Theories in Fuzzy Logic. In: Zadeh, L.A., Kacprzyk, J. (eds.) Computing with Words in Information – Intelligent Systems. STUDFUZZ, vol. 33, pp. 383–406. Springer, Heidelberg (1999)
7. Rakus-Andersson, E., Jogreus, C.: The Choquet and Sugeno Integrals as Measures of Total Effectiveness of Medicines. In: Castillo, O., Melin, P., Ross, O.M., Cruz, M., Pedrycz, W., Kacprzyk, J. (eds.) Theoretical Advances and Applications of Fuzzy Logic and Soft Computing. ASC, vol. 42, pp. 253–262. Springer, Heidelberg (2007)
8. Rakus-Andersson, E.: Decision-making Techniques in Ranking of Medicine Effectiveness. In: Sordo, M., Vaidya, W., Jain, L.C. (eds.) Advanced Computational Intelligence Paradigms in Healthcare 3. SCI, vol. 107, pp. 51–73. Springer, Heidelberg (2008)

9. Rakus-Andersson, E.: Adjusted *s*-parametric Functions in the Creation of Symmetric Constraints. In: Proceedings of the 10th International Conference on Intelligent Systems Design and Applications, ISDA 2010, pp. 451–456 (2010)
10. Rakus-Andersson, E.: The Mamdani Controller with Modeled Families of Constraints in Evaluation of Cancer Patient Survival Length. In: Ramanna, S., Jain, L.C., Howlett, R.J. (eds.) Emerging Paradigms in ML and Applications. SIST, vol. 13, pp. 359–378. Springer, Heidelberg (2013)
11. Rakus-Andersson, E.: Selected Algorithms of Computational Intelligence in Surgery Decision Making. Open Access book Gastroenterology in SCITECH (2012),
    http://www.intechopen.com/articles/show/title/selected-algorithms-of-computational-intelligence-in-cancer-surgery-decision-making
12. Rakus-Andersson, E., Frey, J.: α-cut Fuzzy Numbers as Utilities of Decision Making in Treatment of Radiation Cystitis. In: Greco, S., Bouchon-Meunier, B., Coletti, G., Fedrizzi, M., Matarazzo, B., Yager, R.R. (eds.) IPMU 2012, Part I. CCIS, vol. 297, pp. 140–149. Springer, Heidelberg (2012)
13. Sugeno, M.: Fuzzy Measures and Fuzzy Integrals - a Survey. In: Gupta, M.M., Saridis, G.N., Gaines, B.R. (eds.) Fuzzy Automata and Decision Processes, pp. 89–102. North-Holland, New York (1977)
14. Yager, R.R.: Fuzzy Decision Making Including Unequal Objectives. Fuzzy Sets and Systems 1, 87–95 (1978)
15. Yager, R.R.: Generalized OWA Aggregation Operators. Fuzzy Optimization and Decision Making 3, 93–107 (2004)

A Novelty Detection Framework Based on Fuzzy Entropy for a Complex Manufacturing Process

Adriana Gonzalez-Rodriguez[1], George Panoutsos[1], Mahdi Mahfouf[1], and Kathryn Beamish[2]

[1] The University of Sheffield, Department of Automatic Control and Systems Engineering, Sheffield, UK
{cop10aag,g.panoutsos,m.mahfouf}@sheffield.ac.uk
[2] The Welding Institute Ltd., Cambridge, UK
kathryn.beamish@twi.co.uk

Abstract. In this paper a new Novelty Detection framework is presented, which is created by taking advantage of the Fuzzy Entropy property of Fuzzy Logic systems. The framework's aim is to create a linguistic-based feedback mechanism for advising the process users (Human-Centric System) on the performance of a complex manufacturing process. The manufacturing process under investigation is the Friction Stir Welding (FSW) process. The presented methodology comprises a data-driven model-based approach, which is the main facet of the framework. The proposed system has a Neural-Fuzzy structure that learns from process data to predict a number of process characteristics. Via the created Novelty Detection framework, we show how we can take advantage of the properties of the system to a) alert the user when a 'novelty' (i.e. new condition) appears in the system, and b) to advise the user in how reliable the system's predictions are when the novelty occurs. The user feedback is provided in linguistic form by taking advantage the inherent features of the Fuzzy Logic–based approach. A number of simulations and experimental results based on a complex manufacturing case-study demonstrate the effectiveness and usefulness of the created Human-Centric System, which could be used as a form of decision support.

Keywords: Novelty Detection, Neural-Fuzzy Modelling, Fuzzy Logic, Radial Basis Function, Fuzzy Entropy, Friction Stir Welding, Shannon's Entropy, Human-Centric Systems.

1 Introduction

1.1 Fuzzy Systems and Novelty Detection

Human-Centric Systems (HCS) entail the development of computational systems that are able to adjust to humans by being more natural, intuitive and consistently able to integrate with the environment [1]. One of the challenges in HCS is the design of systems that can interact with humans by using simple and transparent features. Hybrid Neural-Fuzzy (NF) modelling techniques address this challenge by taking advantage the interpretability features of Fuzzy Logic systems (FL), while maintaining a

D. Filev et al. (eds.), *Intelligent Systems' 2014*,
Advances in Intelligent Systems and Computing 323, DOI: 10.1007/978-3-319-11310-4_39

high learning ability by using the Neural-Network computational structure. The NF models have a simple structure. They are easy to understand (by the process users) and have the ability to not only process complex information, but also adapt and learn from the environment (data-driven supervised learning). Particular benefits of developing computational intelligent models based on Neural Networks and Fuzzy Systems are the relatively low computational cost and the good generalisation performance in describing complex nonlinear systems [2]. A range of disciplines including engineering, healthcare and business informatics have taken advantage of such traits by developing intelligent systems based on these approaches. In manufacturing, several data-driven model-based approaches focused on NF modelling have been proposed to describe nonlinear mappings of industrial data [3, 4, 5]. Although models are used to accurately describe and even predict the behaviour of complex systems, the communication with human operators is often not intuitive, for example, when computational models need to communicate an unexpected behaviour from the system. In this paper, a Novelty Detection framework is proposed, to monitor and predict the performance of a manufacturing system and communicate to the user any new/unexpected system behaviour via a linguistic feedback mechanism.

In the following Section, the basic theory behind the proposed data-driven modelling approach is presented as well as the manufacturing process under investigation. In Section 3, the main contribution of this paper is presented and the methodology to create the Novelty Detection framework is explained in detail. Section 4 presents the results of this framework applied to a complex industrial process (FSW).

2   Background Theory and the Process under Investigation

2.1   Radial Basis Function and Neural-Fuzzy Systems

The Radial Basis Function (RBF) Neural Network is a multidimensional nonlinear function mapping that can use data to learn nonlinear relationships. This powerful Neural Network is frequently used for learning complex input-output mappings [6]. The RBF modelling structure (see Fig. 1) is commonly used with Fuzzy Logic (FL) to model complex systems when there is a need for inherent system transparency and interpretability.

One advantage of combining RBF Neural Networks with Fuzzy Systems is that linguistic fuzzy IF-THEN rules, which are naturally related to fuzzy membership functions, can be mathematically described in the model as a Gaussian radial basis

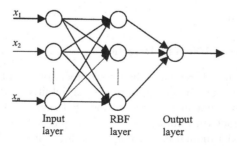

Fig. 1. RBF Neural Network structure

function [7]. It thus provides a degree of inherent linguistic interpretability. Consider a fuzzy system with inputs $x \in \Re^n$, M IF-THEN rules, the membership function $\mu_{A_i^j}$ for the jth rule ($j = 1,2, ..., M$), and the ith component (x_i) of the input vector x. If a singleton fuzzifier is used, the summative result of the jth rule on the input vector (x) is given by $(u_i(x) = \prod_{i=1}^n \mu_{A_i^j}(x_i))$ where $u_i(x) = \mu_{A_1^j}(x_1)\mu_{A_2^j}(x_2) \cdots \mu_{A_n^j}(x_n)$. The input-output equation of a fuzzy system with a singleton fuzzifier, product inference, and centroid defuzzifier can be expressed as:

$$y = \sum_{j=1}^M w_j \left(\prod_{i=1}^n \mu_{A_i^j}(x_i) \right) \tag{1}$$

Where $w_j \in \Re^n$ ($j = 1,2, ..., M$) are the weights parameters, the membership functions are nonlinear parameterised functions. Equation (1) represents a nonlinear neural network with a non-fuzzy input vector x, with membership functions (MFs) $\mu_{A_i^j}(x_i)$, weights w_j, and the non-fuzzy output $y \in \Re$. There are several possibilities for the choices of a basis function, one of which are Gaussian networks. They are highly nonlinear and provide good locality for incremental learning [6]. Here a Gaussian radial basis function is chosen as the membership function, consequently:

$$\mu_{A_i^j}(x_i) = \exp\left(-\frac{1}{2}\sum_{i=1}^n \left(\frac{x_i - c_{ij}}{\sigma_{ij}} \right)^2 \right) \tag{2}$$

When equation (2) is used, equation (1) can be rewritten as follows:

$$y = \sum_{j=1}^M w_j \left(\prod_{i=1}^n \exp\left(-\frac{1}{2}\sum_{i=1}^n \left(\frac{x_i - c_{ij}}{\sigma_{ij}} \right)^2 \right) \right) = \sum_{j=1}^M w_j \exp\left(-\frac{1}{2}\sum_{i=1}^n \left(\frac{x_i - c_{ij}}{\sigma_{ij}} \right)^2 \right) \tag{3}$$

$$y = \sum_{j=1}^M w_j u_j \tag{4}$$

where

$$\mu_j = \exp\left(-\frac{1}{2}\sum_{i=1}^n \left(\frac{x_i - c_{ij}}{\sigma_{ij}} \right)^2 \right) \tag{5}$$

The parameters c_{ij} and σ_{ij} associated with the Gaussian membership functions are to be determined by process data.

The use of intelligent hybrid approaches combining RBF neural networks with learning algorithms such as Fuzzy C-Means (FCM) and Genetic Algorithms (GA) is widely applied in data-driven modelling due to its capability and computational efficiency. They can represent the fuzzy rule-based knowledge through a self-adaptive process [8]. The proposed model-based framework applies the FCM algorithm to initialise the RBF network structure (i.e. initial clustering for the estimation of the membership functions). Its parameters are subsequently optimised using a GA as detailed in Section 3. One of the challenges of manufacturing systems is the identification and communication of unexpected process performance. This involves the identification of new behaviours that have not been previously encountered by the model, and the evaluation and communication of this behaviour to the user. In this paper, a Novelty Detection framework is proposed to address this challenge.

Novelty Detection deals with the identification of new and/or unknown system dynamics that the computational system has not seen before. Neural Networks have been used to design effective Novelty Detection techniques with the ability to identify and evaluate 'unseen' data. These approaches have been used for industrial applications, especially to detect possible faults during the process and diagnose the performance of the system [9, 10, 11]. One of the advantages of these techniques when monitoring an industrial process is that its results can be used online as presented in [12, 13]. The use of Novelty Detection in relation with Fuzzy Systems is, however, limited, despite the user-centric features offered by such techniques. Fuzzy Entropy has been successfully used as an Novelty Detection approach which measures information and identifies novel behaviour in a system [14, 15, 16].

Fuzzy entropy based on Shannon's function was proposed by De Luca and Termini in [17] as a measure of the quantity of information in a fuzzy set (fuzziness). The authors propose this approach for fuzzy modelling as a potential tool to analyse the information which is received when the user has to make a decision, and in pattern analysis, to classify information described by Fuzzy Systems [17, 18]. Using Shannon's definition of entropy [19] in Fuzzy Systems, the fuzziness measure of a membership degree μ can be written as:

$$f(\mu) = -\mu \ln \mu - (1 - \mu) \ln(1 - \mu) \tag{6}$$

Thus, a Fuzzy Entropy formula on a finite universal set $X = \{x_1, \ldots, x_n\}$ is defined as:

$$H(A) = -K \sum_{i=1}^{n} [\mu_A(x_i) \ln \mu_A(x_i) + (1 - \mu_A(x_i)) \ln(1 - \mu_A(x_i))], K > 0 \tag{7}$$

Where, H represents a type of fuzziness of the fuzzy set A and μ is the membership. The 'fuzziness' of a given information set can be used to aid the Novelty Detection in a computational system as shown in Section 3.

2.2 Friction Stir Welding

Friction Stir Welding (FSW) is an efficient solid-state welding process, for the joining of metals, invented at The Welding Institute (TWI), in Cambridge UK [20]. This welding process is versatile, environmentally friendly and its implementation is lower in cost when compared with traditional welding techniques [21].

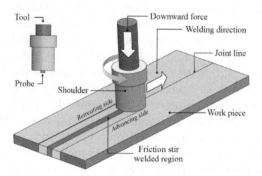

Fig. 2. Schematic diagram of the FSW process

The basic principle of the FSW process is shown in Fig. 2 consists of a non-consumable rotating tool with a shoulder and a profiled probe. The probe is inserted between the two work pieces to be welded. These two pieces of material are rigidly held while the rotating tool is pressured down until it makes contact with the material surface and rotates moving across the joint line. The friction caused by the rotating tool generates heat between the tool and the materials being welded. The probe stirs the material transforming it from solid-state into plastic-state merging both materials to create the joint.

Recently, the use of NF modelling techniques to describe the performance of the process and predict its behaviour was implemented in [22]. The use of computational intelligence techniques have also been proposed as a tool to develop applications that can monitor this process in real-time [23]. In the following section, we describe the creation of a Novelty Detection framework that identifies possible new conditions during the FSW process (in real-time) and feedbacks any process dynamics back to the user in a linguistic format.

3   Methodology

In this section, the Novelty Detection Framework based on Fuzzy Entropy is presented in detail. Fig. 3 illustrates the overall methodology.

1. **Initial Structure.** To generate the initial structure of the Fuzzy Logic rule-base and assign the initial conditions (output weights) for the optimisation of the model, the raw dataset is partitioned into multi-dimensional clusters of information using

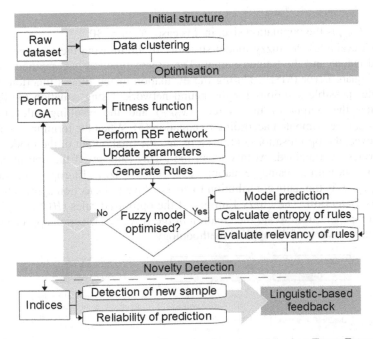

Fig. 3. Flow chart of the Novelty Detection framework based on Fuzzy Entropy

the FCM algorithm. This algorithm is frequently used in modelling approaches as a result of its ability to group and form clusters of data that have similar attributes. As shown in [24], by presenting a input-output dataset and assigning the number of clusters, the algorithm creates a list of optimal centres. With this information, the initial rule-base for the RBF neural network (centres (c), sigma (σ) and weights (ω) values) can be extracted as detailed in [25]. In our framework, the number of clusters corresponds to the number of rules. The FCM methodology is used here as it conveniently creates FL membership clusters that can be used directly in the RBF system at a low computational processing cost.

2. **Optimisation.** A Genetic Algorithm (GA) is used as an optimisation tool that searches for the best solution (rules and membership functions) for the RBF neural network structure given a training dataset. The integration of GA, Neural Networks and Fuzzy Systems has been used to train and learn complex and nonlinear input-output mappings. The capability of RBF, Neural Networks and GA algorithms to analyse complex systems, learn from information and seek accurate modelling structures, has been previously demonstrated [26]. Several approaches have been proposed to optimise RBF neural networks using GA's. The optimisation presented in this paper is similar to the one shown in [27], where the genes to build the chromosomes are defined based on the RBF network weights. Using the information obtained from the initial structure in step 1, the variables to optimise (N_{vars}) and the chromosome, each chromosome is one FL rule, can be defined for the initial population $(InitPop)$ as follows:

$$p_1 = (c_1, ..., c_r, \sigma_1, ..., \sigma_r, \omega_1, ..., \omega_r) \ r = number\ of\ rules$$
$$chromosome = [p_1, ..., p_{Nvars}]$$
$$InitPop = N_{pop} \times N_{vars}$$

Where, N_{pop} is the population size, in this case, $N_{pop} = 30$.

The GA evaluates the fuzzy model structure by minimising the error between the desired output and the trained output. The fitness function is computed using the Mean Square Error (MSE). During the evaluation of the fitness function, the GA generates possible solutions for the neural network. Using equation (4) the RBF computes the output of the system (y_{OUT}) and the resulting rules (denoted as M_{RULES}) are computed according to equation (5). When the termination criterion is achieved, the optimisation routine stops and the final output of the model and the fuzzy rules are obtained. At this stage, the Fuzzy Entropy of the optimised fuzzy rules is measured using equation (7). This Fuzzy Entropy measurement $(H(M_{RULES}))$ is the main contribution to create Novelty Detection approach.

3. **Novelty Detection.** The Fuzzy Entropy of the optimised rules $(H(M_{RULES}))$ is the main component used to aid the creation of the Novelty Detection approach, Fig. 4 shows an overview of the applied methodology.

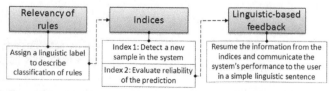

Fig. 4. Overview of the Novelty Detection approach

(a) *Relevancy of rules:* At this stage of the algorithm, the rules which are relevant to a given data class are identified. For each data point (process measurement) presented to the system/model, the relevance of a given rule to a specific output class is estimated by correlating the firing strength of each rule to each of the output classes. This process will result in a ranked list of rules ($Rule_{firing}$) which contribute to certain output classes. Each rule is then assigned a linguistic label ($LV_{CorrVal}$) which is subsequently used in the linguistic feedback. As shown in Fig. 5, for example, in our FSW case study, we identify which rules contribute the most to 'poor' weld quality, 'good' weld quality, etc. and we assign linguistic labels to such rules.

(b) *Novelty Indices:* Using the Fuzzy Entropy $H(M_{RULES})$, two indices were created to evaluate the novelty of each data sample:

i. **Index 1**, this index monitors the entropy of the system and detects if new/unseen conditions are encountered in the system. The hypothesis predicts that a new data point, with different process dynamics to the ones included in the system, will trigger an entropy value (sum from all the fired rules) that identifies the 'new' point as such. An upper boundary +1% (UBH) and lower boundary (LBH) -1% are set based on the minimum value ($MinV_{HR}$) of $H(M_{RULES})$ to then obtain a numerical index (ND) which determines if the current sample is a new condition or not. This process creates a binary decision on the novelty of the sample, and is produced as follows:

$$If\ MinV_{HR}\ is\ > UBH\ or\ < LBH\ then\ ND = 1 \tag{8}$$

$$If\ MinV_{HR}\ is\ < UBH\ or\ > LBH\ then\ ND = 0 \tag{9}$$

Where, $ND = 0$ indicates that no new condition is present and $ND = 1$ indicates that a possible new condition is present in the system.

ii. **Index 2** measures the reliability of the prediction for each sample. Although the first index (ND) is a criterion of data novelty. (ND) is based on the assumption that the rules are sufficiently reliable to extract such information. This is not always the case given the uncertainty of the training data. The normalised ratio of the entropy of a rule over the maximum presented entropy in the system is used a measure of how 'fuzzy', or relatively reliable, a rule is within the overall rule-base. This is calculated as follows:

$$PercV_{HR} = H(M_{RULES})/maximum\ value(H(M_{RULES})) * 100. \tag{10}$$

The scope of the above two indices is to extract the following information in real-time to identify samples with relatively 'new' dynamics/behaviour and estimate how reliable the predicted output is for each sample (examples shown in Section 4). This information is summarised in a linguistic feedback mechanism that is returned to the process user as a form of decision support.

4. **Linguistic-based feedback.** Using the information from indices described above, a knowledge-structure is created by assigning numerical and linguistic hedges to the system's variables: '*sample value*' is a numerical variable that describes the sample evaluated; '*rule label*' is a linguistic label that describes the classification of the

rules; *'prediction value'* is the output predicted for the sample evaluated (numerical variable), and *'reliability label'* is a linguistic label related with the reliability measurement. *'WQ'* is a linguistic variable that describes the output of the system. The performance of the system is summarised as follows:

Table 1. Linguistic-based knowledge structure

System variables	Values	Interpretability
Sample No	*sample value*	
Index 1	*ND*	ND = 0 'Not new', ND = 1 'New' (Sample is a new/not new condition)
Index 2	*PercV$_{HR}$*	For $Rule_{firing}$ the prediction is associated with: $LV_{CorrVal}$ (*rule label*)
Output predicted	*prediction value*	For WQ = *prediction value*, reliability of prediction is: *reliability label*

From the information in Table 1, a linguistic-based feedback is created and presented to the user in a simple sentence:

"Sample 'sample value' is a 'new' / 'not new' condition, with a system predicted output of WQ = 'prediction value'. The most relevant rule in the system relates to 'rule label' weld quality, and this prediction is of 'reliability label' reliability".

The demonstration of the Novelty Detection framework is shown in the following section.

4   Experimental Results and Simulations

In this research work, a dataset of 34 weld samples was used to simulate the Novelty Detection framework. The model simulation was produced using two inputs (tool rotational speed, traverse speed) and one output (weld quality). 70% of the data samples were used for training and 30% for testing. The weld samples were obtained by welding plates of AA5083 aluminium alloy (6mm thick) at different process conditions: tool rotational speed (from 280 RPM to 580 RPM), and traverse speed (between 280 mm/min to 812 mm/min). The quality of the welded samples was quantified by process experts using four different indices: bend test-root, bend test-face, surface finish and cross sectional inspection (to identify internal flaws). Each index was expressed in a numerical value between 0 – 3 using expert knowledge. A final summative index 'Weld Quality' (WQ) was then created by aggregating the four sub-indices which range between 0 – 12, where 0 = 'Good WQ' and 12 = 'Poor WQ'. The resulting simulations exhibited good system performance in the prediction of the weld quality. The performance measured for training was RMSE = 0.260 and for testing data RMSE = 0.583, this is comparable with previous work in this area [5], [23].

Fig. 5 shows the correlation of the rules with the weld quality of the system and the relevancy of rules per sample. Rules R2 and R3 are related to 'Good WQ', R1 and R5 are related with 'Poor WQ'. The relevancy of the rules is evaluated by extracting, per sample, the rule 'Firing the highest'. For example, out of the five rules, in the sample No. 28, the rule firing the highest is R1 which is related with 'Poor WQ'.

The Novelty Detection framework was evaluated with testing data from two different sources: Experimental data (Fig. 6) and real-time data recorded in a single weld, the real-time dataset was evaluated using synthetic process data (Fig. 7) with the aim of demonstrate the potential of this Novelty Detection approach towards real-time applications.

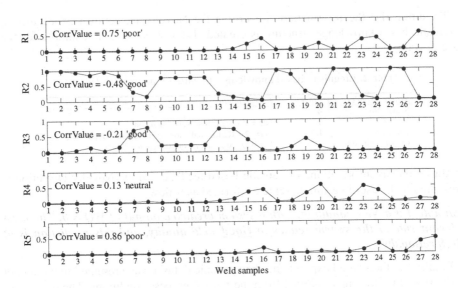

Fig. 5. Relevancy of rules and relation with Weld Quality

The Novelty Detection indices are calculated for a number of process samples and these are shown in Fig. 6. The average entropy value of the rule-base is shown in Fig. 6(a) for the experimental testing dataset. The Novelty Detection index (Index 1) is calculated per sample according to the rule described in equations (8) and (9). For the dataset samples 2, 4, 5 and 6, it was detected that new condition occurs.

Fig. 6(b) shows the most relevant rule associated with each prediction for each sample, along with the linguistic reliability indicator for that rule. For example, in the samples 1, 2, 3 and 4, R2 is the most relevant rule to the corresponding prediction and this rule is also related with 'Good WQ' (as shown previously in Fig. 5). The rules in samples 5 and 6 (R5 and R1) are related with 'Poor WQ'. In each case, the reliability of the weld quality prediction for each sample is described by the linguistic label associated with the rule. Depending on the % outcome of equation (10), the linguistic variables are: 0%-25% Low ('L'), 26%-50% Medium-Low ('ML'), 51%-75% Medium-High ('MH') and 76%-100% High ('H') reliable.

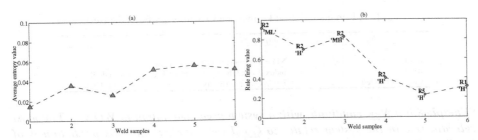

Fig. 6. Novelty Detection performance of the experimental dataset: (a) Monitoring the entropy *(Index 1)*, (b) Relevancy of rules and reliability of prediction *(Index 2)*

To summarise the information concerning the Novelty Detection performance, a linguistic-based knowledge structure is created. Table 2 presents an example for the case of Sample 4.

Table 2. Linguistic-based knowledge structure (experimental dataset)

System variables	Values	Interpretability
Sample No	4	
Index 1	1	ND = 1, sample is a 'New' condition
Index 2	R2	Index 2 = R2 the prediction is related with 'Good ' WQ
Output predicted	0	For WQ = 0 reliability of prediction is 'High'

Based on this information, a linguistic-based feedback on the Novelty Detection is presented to the user in a simple sentence formed as follows:

"Sample __4__ is a __New__ condition, with a system predicted output of WQ = __0__. The most relevant rule in the system relates to __Good__ weld quality, and this prediction is of __High__ reliability".

Finally, for the second experiment, the synthetic dataset was presented to the model with 20% of weld samples altered from the normal process conditions. The results are shown in Fig. 7. As in the previous example, Fig. 7(a) shows the average entropy value for the real-time dataset and Fig. 7(b) presents the values of Index 2 per sample.

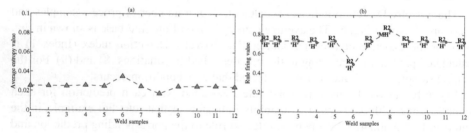

Fig. 7. Novelty Detection performance of the artificial dataset: (a) Monitoring the entropy *(Index 1)*, (b) Relevancy of rules and reliability of prediction *(Index 2)*

The new data samples (6 and 8) were correctly identified by the system as 'new' conditions. The knowledge structure extracted from the model and the linguistic feedback are shown below for Sample 8:

Table 3. Linguistic-based knowledge structure (artificial dataset)

System variables	Values	Interpretability
Sample No	8	
Index 1	1	ND = 1, sample is a 'New' condition
Index 2	R2	Index 2 = R2 the prediction is related with 'Good' WQ
Output predicted	2	For WQ = 2 reliability of prediction is 'Medium-High'

"Sample __8__ is a __New__ condition, with a system predicted output of WQ = __2__. The most relevant rule in the system relates to __Good__ weld quality, and this prediction is of __Medium-High__ reliability".

Even though the above experiment is not done in real-time, the synthetic data were processed 'as in real-time' to confirm the system's computational processing ability. The linguistic feedback is an efficient and simple mechanism which can provide meaningful process information to an end-user by taking advantage of the computational aspects and simplicity/transparency features of Fuzzy Logic systems.

5   Conclusion

A Novelty Detection Framework based on Fuzzy Entropy which makes use of a model-based approach to identify new process conditions is presented in this paper. A Neural-Fuzzy modelling structure is used to develop the core knowledge of the system, while a Fuzzy C-Means Algorithm along with a Genetic Algorithm are used to optimise the system's structure and parameters. We take advantage of the Fuzzy Entropy as well as the linguistic interpretability of the Fuzzy Logic systems, to create a human-centric system capable of providing feedback (process performance and Novelty Detection) to the user via linguistic information (simple sentences). The framework was successfully applied on a complex and nonlinear manufacturing process (Friction Stir Welding). Both real and synthetic data were used to demonstrate the linguistic feedback of the system for the two industrial-based scenarios. The system's computational efficiency allows it to run in real time, as demonstrated in the synthetic data experiment. A larger scale demonstration would be required in the future to fully evaluate the system's performance, including the addition of more process parameters. This framework has the potential to be used as an autonomous/semi-autonomous system for monitoring complex manufacturing processes in real-time, while also providing linguistic feedback to non-experts.

References

1. Pedrycz, W., Gomide, F.: Introduction. In: Fuzzy Systems Engineering: Toward Human-Centric Computing, pp. 1–26 (2007)
2. Paiva, R.P., Dourado, A.: Interpretability and learning in neuro-fuzzy systems. Fuzzy Sets Syst. 147(1), 17–38 (2004)
3. Elangovan, K., Balasubramanian, V., Babu, S.: Predicting tensile strength of friction stir welded AA6061 aluminium alloy joints by a mathematical model. Mater. Des. 30, 188–193 (2009)
4. Zhang, Q., Mahfouf, M., Panoutsos, G., Beamish, K., Norris, I.: Multiple Characterisation Modelling of Friction Stir Welding Using a Genetic Multi-objective Data-driven Fuzzy Modelling Approach. In: IEEE International Conference on Fuzzy Systems, pp. 2288–2295 (2011)
5. Panoutsos, G., Mahfouf, M., Beamish, K., Norris, I.: Combining static and temporal process data in the modelling of FSW weld quality and mechanical properties using Computational Intelligence. In: 8th International Symposium on Friction Stir Welding (2010)
6. Gupta, M.M., Jin, L., Homma, N.: Radial Basis Function Neural Networks. In: Static and Dynamic Neural Networks: From Fundamentals to Advanced Theory, pp. 223–252. John Wiley & Sons, Inc., New York (2003)

7. Wang, L.X., Mendel, J.M.: Fuzzy basis functions, universal approximation, and orthogonal least-squares learning. IEEE Trans. Neural Netw. 3(5), 807–814 (1992)
8. Jantzen, J.: Neurofuzzy modelling, Lyngby, Denmark (1998)
9. Brotherton, T., Johnson, T.: Anomaly detection for advanced military aircraft using neural networks. In: 2001 IEEE Aerospace Conference Proceedings (Cat. No.01TH8542)., pp. 3113–3123 (2001)
10. Li, Y., Pont, M.J., Barrie Jones, N.: Improving the performance of radial basis function classifiers in condition monitoring and fault diagnosis applications where 'unknown' faults may occur. Pattern Recognit. Lett. 23, 569–577 (2002)
11. Surace, C., Worden, K.: A Novelty Detection Method to Diagnose Damage in Structures: An Application to an Offshore Platform. In: Proceedings of the Eight International Offshore and Polar Engineering Conference (1998)
12. Sohn, H., Worden, K., Farrar, C.R.: Novelty Detection under Changing Environmental Conditions. In: 8th Annual International Symposium on Smart Structures and Materials (2001)
13. Crook, P.A., Marshland, S., Hayes, G., Nehmzow, U.: A Tale of Two Filters - On-line Novelty Detection. In: Proceedings of the 2002 IEEE International Conference on Robotics & Automation (2002)
14. Lee, S.-H., Kim, Y.-T., Cheon, S.-P., Kim, S.: Reliable Data Selection with Fuzzy Entropy. In: Wang, L., Jin, Y. (eds.) FSKD 2005. LNCS (LNAI), vol. 3613, pp. 203–212. Springer, Heidelberg (2005)
15. Chaghooshi, A., Fathi, M., Kashef, M.: Integration of Fuzzy Shannon's entropy with fuzzy TOPSIS for industrial robotic system section. J. Ind. Eng. Manag. 5(1), 102–114 (2012)
16. Liangqun, L., Hongbing, J., Xinbo, G.: Maximum entropy fuzzy clustering with application to real-time target tracking. Signal Processing 86, 3432–3447 (2006)
17. De Luca, A., Termini, S.: A definition of a nonprobabilistic entropy in the setting of fuzzy sets theory. Inf. Control 20, 301–312 (1972)
18. De Luca, A., Termini, S.: Entropy of L-fuzzy sets. Inf. Control 73, 55–73 (1974)
19. Shannon, C.E.: A Mathematical Theory of Communication. Bell Syst. Tech. J. 27(3), 379–423 (1948)
20. Thomas, W., Nicholas, E., Needham, J., Murch, M., Temple-Smith, P., Dawes, C.: Friction-stir butt welding. 9125978.8 (International patent application No. PCT/GB92/02203) (1991)
21. Thomas, W.M., Woollin, P., Johnson, K.I.: Friction stir welding of steel - a feasibility study. Steel World 4(2), 55–59 (1999)
22. Panoutsos, G., Mahfouf, M.: A neural-fuzzy modelling framework based on granular computing: Concepts and applications. Fuzzy Sets Syst. 161(21), 2808–2830 (2010)
23. Gonzalez-Rodriguez, A., Panoutsos, G., Sinclair, K., Mahfouf, M., Beamish, K.: Model-based process monitoring in Friction Stir Welding. In: 9th International Symposium on Friction Stir Welding (2012)
24. Bezdek, J.C.: Pattern Recognition with Fuzzy Objective Function Algorithms. Springer US (1981)
25. Zhang, Q., Mahfouf, M.: Fuzzy Predictive Modelling Using Hierarchical Clustering and Multi-objective Optimisation for Mechanical Properties of Alloy Steels. In: Proceedings of the 12th IFAC Symposium on Automation in Mining, Mineral and Metal Processing (IFAC MMM 2007), vol. 12(1), pp. 427–432 (2007)
26. Linkens, D.A., Nyongesa, H.O.: Learning systems in intelligent control: an appraisal of fuzzy, neural and genetic algorithm control applications. IEE Proc. - Control Theory Appl. 143(4), 367–386 (1996)
27. Billings, S.A., Zheng, G.L.: Radial basis function network configuration using genetic algorithms. Neural Networks 8(6), 877–890 (1995)

Module Family Design for Modular Product

Yonanda Adhitama[1] and Wolfgang Rosenstiel[2]

[1] Robert Bosch GmbH, Schwieberdingen, Germany
Yonanda.Adhitama@de.bosch.com
[2] University of Tübingen, Department of Computer Science, Tübingen, Germany
rosenstiel@informatik.uni-tuebingen.de

Abstract. Modular structure based products have been chosen by industries to provide sufficient variety of their products to the market. In this work, a multi-objective product family design that aims to develop a module family for a modular product is discussed. Enterprise considerations such as market share and cost-savings benefits are integrated with the product family design. A representation scheme is introduced to enable us to integrate the qualitative market segmentation grid (MSG) with the scalability evaluation which plays a significant role in determining the appropriate configuration of the module product as well as the final product in different market niches. The combinatorial problem with a large number of module configurations is solved through the implementation of genetic algorithm of NSGA-II. The design of a family of application-specific integrated circuits (ASIC) for a modular structure based electronic control unit (ECU) is used to demonstrate the proposed approach.

Keywords: Product family, product variety, modular-structure product, scalability.

1 Introduction

Vehicles become more and more intelligent. They are safer, more fuel efficient and more pleasant to drive than in any previous generation. Many of these advancements are due in large part to innovations in semiconductor technology. Automotive electronic control unit (ECU), analog integrated circuits (IC) and sensor solutions support the innovation and development of the next-generation automotive solutions.

Since vehicles are now an extension of the owner's personal life style, the automotive markets around the world vary considerably: from a car with large number of functionalities to a car limited to standard functionalities. Thus, the design of product variant (e.g. ECUs, ICs, sensors, etc) is crucial for its success in the market. On the one hand a maximum of customer orientation (in this work, we define them as the scalability to the market) is to be achieved. On the other hand this may have an impact on development and production costs, since not only the expenses in development increase through a high number of product variants but also production costs are raised by a high number of different components used in product assemblies [1].

© Springer International Publishing Switzerland 2015
D. Filev et al. (eds.), *Intelligent Systems' 2014*,
Advances in Intelligent Systems and Computing 323, DOI: 10.1007/978-3-319-11310-4_40

To address the increasing costs, many companies are utilizing platform-based product development in which individual members of the product family normally share common parts and subassemblies of a common product platform (i.e. the set of features, components or subsystems that remain constant from product to product, within a given product family) [6]. The variants or derivatives are derived from the product platform through addition, removal, or substitution of one or more modules (i.e. module-based product family) [1], [4], [7], [8], [11], or through scaling or "stretching" the platform in one or more dimensions (i.e. scale-based product family).

In this work, we are concerned with the question of how to design a set of module products (e.g. ICs, sensors) which will be used in the modular-based product (e.g. ECU). The background is because the introduction of products with modular structure has urged industries to design a family of module components themselves so that the design variables and performance of the module components can fit the diverse design- or performance requirements of the final product. Since the design of modules can not be separated from the design of the end products, integration between the design of module variant with the design of end product variant is proposed. A representation scheme is introduced to enable us to integrate the qualitative market segmentation grid (MSG) with the scalability evaluation which plays a significant role in determining the appropriate configuration of the module products as well as the final products in different market niches. Enterprise considerations such as market share and cost-savings benefits are integrated with the product family design. The aforementioned issues could be integrated within the proposed framework through appropriate modification of multi-objective functions and problem formulation of genetic algorithm of NSGA-II [10].

In the next section, the formal description and formulation of the product family design are presented. In Section 3 the design of a family of application-specific integrated circuits (ASIC) for a modular structure based electronic control unit (ECU) is used to demonstrate the proposed approach and the analysis of the result is presented in Section 4. The paper is concluded in Section 5.

2   Product Family Design for Modular-Structure

To generalize the problem, a module family for modular-structure based product development is considered in this paper. Fig. 1 shows an overview of a module-based product family in which the final products are derived by addition, removal, or substitution of one or more different type of modules. For each type of module, several preferences of modules with different performance represent the variant of module. This module variant is derived through scaling or "stretching" the platform in one or more dimensions (i.e. scale-based product family).

Many researches focus on optimizing the variant of the final product in which the motivation is to determine which modules should be combined in order to optimize the final product variants [3], [8], [12]. In this case, the module variant is defined in advance. However, our goal in this paper is to simultaneously optimize both module attributes and module combination in order to derive module variant as well as to derive the final product variant. This can be done by establishing a way to measure the scalability of the module variant to cover different performance requirements of the final product. We use an adaptation of market segmentation grid to represent the performance requirement of the final product in each of market niches. For the sake of simplicity, our work focuses on finding the variant of certain type of module while the compromise among different type of modules is not considered.

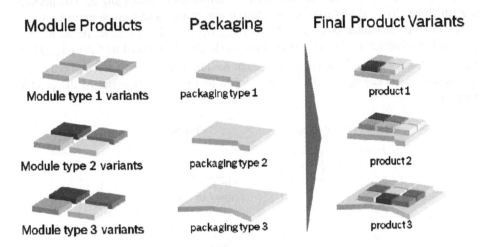

Fig. 1. Module-based Product Family

2.1 Module Product Description

In our model, the module products in the family are composed of several functional modules, each of which has properties that define the functional features and design parameters. Several packaging alternatives with specific properties are provided for manufacturing the module products. The combination of functional module's properties and packaging's properties determines the module product's performance and design characteristic.

We consider a module product family which consists of P module products $p_n | \forall n \in [1,...,N]$. Suppose a module product p_n is composed of $Q_i | i \in p_n, p_n \in P$ functional modules $Q_i = \{q_j | j=1,...,J_i\}$. The functional module come from a set of functional module candidates $M = \{m_1,...,m_L\}$, that is $q_j =:: m_l | \exists m_l \in M$. Here, each functional module has the same number of properties which are denoted as $S_t = \{s_{tk}| k=1, 2,.., K\}$, $t \in m_l$, $m_l \in M$ where s_{tk} refers to the kth property of functional module m_l. For each functional module m_l, the related cost is denoted as $C_l | \forall l \in [1,...,L]$. Each property s_{tk} determines the performance characteristics E_t of the module product. The module product performance $E_t | \forall t \in m_l, m_l \in M$ corresponds to k^{th} property of m_l can be expressed as a function of s_{tk} using relationship $E_{tk} = f(s_{tk}) | k = 1, 2,..., K; t \in m_l, m_l \in M$ and the total performance of a product p_n related to k^{th} property can be expressed as

$$E_{ik} = \sum_{j \in Q_i} E_{jk} \tag{1}$$

where $Q_i = \{q_1, \cdots, q_{J_i}\}; q_j =:: m_i \mid \exists m_i \in M; k = 1,\dots, K; i \in p_n, p_n \in P$.

To manufacture the module products, a set of packaging candidates A are provided. Here $A = \{a_i/i=1,..,T\}$ denotes T number of product packaging candidates with $H_j = \{h_{jr}/ r=1, ..,R\}$, $j \in a_t$, $a_t \in A$ denotes R number of attributes of packaging a_t. The packaging attributes have also a role as the design constraints and can be expressed as a function of performance properties E_{ik} as $g(E_{ik}, H_j) \le 0 \mid k=1, 2,\dots, K; j \in a_t, a_t \in A$. For each packaging a_t, the related cost per packaging is denoted as $C_t \mid \forall t \in [1,\dots,T]$. In our model, a condition is added so that each module is allocated once and only once to one of the packaging candidates in order to preserve the diversity of the product variants.

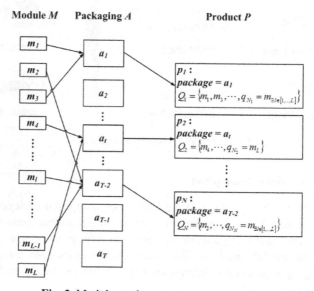

Fig. 2. Module product structure representation

In some cases (e.g. for monitoring and safety reason), two or more functional modules are restricted to be in the same package. For these restrictions, "ban" constraints are added. Suppose m_i and m_j, where $i,j \in [1,\dots, L]$; $i \ne j$, are prohibited to be in the same product and m_i is allocated in packaging $a_k \mid k = 1, \dots, T$ while m_j is allocated in $a_l \mid l = 1, \dots, T$, then the constraint of $k \ne l$ is added. On the other hand, if two or more functional modules must be in the same package, "force" constraints are added so that the modules are always in the same package. From above definitions of m_i, m_j, a_k, and a_l, the "force" constraint is defined as $k = l$ where k refers to the index of a_k, in which m_i is allocated and l refers to the index of a_l in which m_j is allocated. Fig.2. shows an example of a set of module products P which are derived from functional modules M and packaging A.

2.2   Market Segmentation Grid

We adapt the Market Segmentation Grid (MSG) [5]; a matrix representation of market segments and their price/performance tiers; in order to integrate the market info into the optimization problem. In a MSG, the market segments are plotted horizontally in the grid while price/performance tiers are plotted vertically as shown in Fig. 3 (a). Specific market niche is defined in the intersection of each price/performance tier with each market segment. MSG is effective to help marketing and engineering identify the platform leveraging strategy as it visualizes the specific market niche. In [2], market segmentation grid is used to make a decision on product positioning, commonality, and optimal configuration of design variables for each product in the family.

In this work, MSG comprises the info of market segments and performance tiers which are plotted horizontally and vertically, respectively. Each performance requirement in the market niche is used to measure the ability of the product family to satisfy the market requirements. Consider a MSG with I market segments and J performance tiers forming a $(I x J)$ grid. The performance requirement of market niche in the intersection of market segment $i \mid i=1,..,I$ and market tier $j \mid j=1,\ldots,J$ is represented with E_{ij}. An example of (3x3) MSG and its performance requirement per market niche is shown in Fig. 3(a). The discussion on how we utilize the market niche is in the following sub-section.

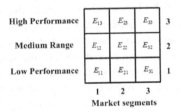

(a) Market Segmentation Grid

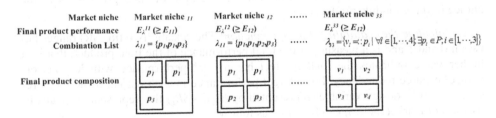

(b) Representation of final products for market niches

Fig. 3. Market segmentation grid and their final products that composed by a family of modular products

2.3   Scalability Objective Function

In order to find the optimal module product family derivation, a function for measuring the scalability of the module product family to various requirements of the final products is implemented. Each module product in the family can be treated as a module candidate (i.e. component) that composes the final product. A module product family for a modular-structure based product is said to be scalable if (1) it can response to diverse configuration and performance requirements of the final products (2) within the scalability size of the final product, which is the maximum number of components that can be mounted in the final product.

In our work, scalability ratio measures the ability to adjust the final product precisely to meet the market requirements with high level of flexibility. A scalability ratio of the final product to the market niche is measured by comparing the target performance of each market niche with the real performance of the final product. The overall scalability is then calculated by taking the average value of the scalability ratio of all market niches.

The scalability calculation method can be divided into the following steps:

1) *Design the final product for each of market niches*: In order to represent the assembled module products in the final product, we choose a combination list representation. A combination list (CL) $\lambda = \{v_1, ..., v_L\}$ determines the list of necessary module products $v_l \in P$ to create the final product. If a product p_n is required in the final product, the product will be added into CL λ. It should be noted that when more than one product $p_n \in P$ is needed, the product will appear in different position l of λ. Here L denotes the length of the list which is equal to the number of assembled module products. A scalability size constraint $L \leq M$ is applied to ensure that the number of assembled module products L does not pass over the scalability size M (i.e. maximum number of components that can be handled) of the final product.

As the scalability size constraint exists, we implement a procedure that chooses a set of module products that can fulfill the target performance requirement with minimum number of components. This can be achieved by firstly choosing a module product among the product family that can cover larger part of the requirement, and then choosing module products with smaller performance to cover the remaining performance requirement. Fig. 3(b) illustrates an example of final products with the choice of three module products.

2) *Calculate the scalability objective function*: The scalability ratio (SR) ranges between 0 and 1 and is a measure of the total performance of the final product; that is, a higher value indicates the final product has a total performance with less performance/resource redundancy. For a target performance in each market niche E_{ij} corresponding to k^{th} design variable (represented by E_{ijk}), a SR_{ijk} that represent the scalability ratio of market niche ij can be found as follows:

$$SR = \left(\sum_{i=1}^{I} \sum_{j=1}^{J} SR_{ijk} \right) \times \frac{1}{I \times J}$$

$$SR_{ijk} = \frac{E_{ijk}}{E_{\lambda^{ij}k}}$$

(2)

where $E_{\lambda}{}^{ij}{}_{k}$ represents the total performance value of the module products combined in λ^{ij}. It should be noted that SR measures the ability to adjust the final product precisely to meet the market requirements with high level of flexibility. Therefore, an excessive performance of the final product will be considered as to reduce the scalability ratio due to the partially unused resource of the modules.

2.4   Manufacturing Cost Objective Function

The second objective function is the total manufacturing cost of module product family. Manufacturing cost of each module product is divided into packaging cost (C_t) and functional module cost (C_l). In the module product cost expression presented below, index 'n' is used to represent the module product 'n', index 't' is used to represent packaging 't' of module product 'n' and   index 'i' is used to represent the functional module 'i' that composes the module product 'n', and the total number of functional modules in the module product is assumed to be 'I'. The cost of module product "n" can be expressed as:

$$C_{p_n} = C_{t_n} + \sum_{i=1}^{I} C_{l_n(i)}$$ (3)

The total manufacturing cost is calculated based on the volume of each module product p_n that should be produced to cover the market size of the final product F. The number of pieces for module product 'n' in the final product f_{ij} of market niche 'ij' is assumed to be $Q_{p_n^{ij}}$ and the market niche 'ij' demands for product f_{ij} is assumed to be $Q_{f_{ij}}$. $Q_{p_n^{ij}}$ is derived from the combination list λ of each market niche. The expressions for volume V for module product p_n are as below.

$$V_{p_n} = \sum_{i=1}^{I} \sum_{j=1}^{J} V_{p_n^{ij}}$$

$$V_{p_n^{ij}} = Q_{p_n^{ij}} \times Q_{f_{ij}}$$ (4)

From (3) & (4), the total manufacturing cost of N module variants to cover the market demand of the final product can be represented as follow.

$$C_P = \sum_{n=1}^{N} C_{p_n} \times V_{p_n}$$ (5)

2.5   Commonality between Products

To check the commonality between products, we use a histogram comparison method. A histogram of product 'n' $Hist(Product_n) = \{a_1, a_2, \ldots, a_N\}$ is a vector which counts the number of modules of each type that compose the product. Each a_n (i.e. a bin) represents specific type of module and denotes the number of modules. To check the similarity between products, we compare each of the bins from two different products. If all functions in a product 'x' can be covered by other product 'y' (i.e. $\forall\, i(Hist(Product_y)[i] \geq Hist(Product_x)[i])$), only product 'y' is produced, while product 'x' becomes obsolete. This method will reduce the number of variants in the family.

3   Experimental Result

We applied the optimization method in the previous sections on a real-world electronic control unit (ECU) to demonstrate the effectiveness of the method.

The automotive markets around the world vary considerably: from a car with large number of functionalities (e.g. large number of peripheral sensors and actuators) for Western Europe and North America market, to a car limited to standard functionalities marketed in the emerging countries. In response to various market segments and market tiers, a modular structure based ECU that can be adjusted easily to the wishes of car manufacturers need to be developed. ECU as a final product should be placed as close as possible to the market requirements in term of important features and attributes. In the process design of ASIC family; as the modules for the ECU; the market requirements of the ECU can be translated to be the target performance to measure the scalability of the ASIC family. The differentiation of the ASIC family should be optimized so that the products of the family will have a good scalability to the diverse ECU applications. At the same time, manufacturing cost of the ASIC should also be minimized.

Due to its combinatorial characteristic, product family design often becomes computationally expensive as the number of components/modules increases. As a result, genetic algorithms are often used to solve the product family optimization due to its flexibility in their problem formulation, capability to handle multiple objectives, and their ability to run in parallel computing environments [6], [9]. We implement NSGA-II [10] to solve a combinatorial multi-objective optimization problem.

As a product's characteristic depends on its modules and packaging, we use two chromosomes to represent the module clustering and packaging allocation. The first L finite-length of chromosome is a representation of the modules $M = \{m_1, ...,m_L\}$. Each element of the string (i.e. gen) determines the index of clusters in which a module m_l is clustered with other modules. The second L finite-length chromosome represents the clusters. We use the same length of L as the module chromosome in order to accommodate the worst case wherein all modules are allocated separately from one another. The gen of the string in the cluster chromosome represents the index of package $a_i\,|\,i=1,...,T$ in which the clustered modules are allocated. The phenotype of a product will be determined by the properties of its functional modules and the packaging. Evolutionary algorithm performs the crossover and mutation to each of chromosomes. The genetic operator applied to the module chromosome will explore the module configuration in response to the diverse configuration requirements, while the genetic operator applied to the cluster chromosome can explore the manufacturing aspects of the products.

3.1   Problem Definition

The ASIC model for ECU consists of 62 functional module candidates classified into seven types according to their functionality. Table 1 shows the modules with their type and number of required pins. Six different packaging with different number of pins are shown in Table 2. This number of packaging pins serves as a constraint to limit the number of modules that can be allocated in each package. To produce results that close to reality, "force" constraints in which modules with "Power" type should be allocated together in every ASIC are implemented.

Hypothetical markets of the ECU are used to demonstrate the proposed method. Hypothetical market for car segment is assumed to comprise several classes of car. We create a MSGs based on the number of specific modules in an ECU. The MSG combines the requirement of actuator and sensor modules in an ECU as shown in Fig. 4.

Table 1. Functional Module Properties (P)

Module(M)	Type	Number of pins per module
1, ..., 7,86	Power	3
8, ..., 18	Analog input	1
19, 20	Analog output	1
21, ..., 60	Actuator	2
61, ..., 70	Sensor	2
71	Reset	1
72, ..., 85	Communication	1

Table 2. Packaging Properties

Package Type	No. of Pins	Max. actuator capacity
1	128	20
2	100	20
3	80	20
4	64	20
5	44	16
6	32	11

In order to meet larger requirement, several ASICs can be combined; however the number of combined ASICs is restricted to maximum four ASICs per ECU. Scalability optimization and manufacturing cost optimization are then performed to find the optimal variants of ASIC family with the method explained in section 2.3 & 2.4.

In this paper, the market size is assumed to be one million ECUs and the demand is assumed to be uniform across all market niches.

Number of actuator modules / Number of sensor modules

	Segment 1	Segment 2	Segment 3
Upper/Luxury	16 / 6	28 / 10	32 / 10
	12 / 4	24 / 8	28 / 10
Medium/Upper Medium	8 / 4	20 / 6	20 / 6
	8 / 2	20 / 8	20 / 8
LPV/Mini	4 / 0	12 / 4	12 / 4
	4 / 0	8 / 4	8 / 4

Segments

Fig. 4. Market Segmentation Grid

4   Result and Analysis

We recorded the results from 5 replicate runs (each seeded with different random numbers) using a population size of 150 per iteration and reduced to 20 solutions for analysis. The number of generations is set to be 400.000 generations.

The optimization results of the MSG are shown in Fig. 5. ASICs are differentiated by their packaging, the number of actuators, and the number of sensors. It should be noted that from the 40 actuator modules in the model, only 30 modules in Fig. 5(a) and 34 modules in Fig. 5(b) are allocated in the final four ASIC variants. During the optimization, the remaining actuators are actually also considered and allocated, however, the ASICs in which they are allocated are marked as obsolete due to their similarity with other ASICs as the result of the commonality check explained in section 2.5. The total manufacturing cost refers to the ASIC manufacturing cost needed to produce one million ECUs.

ASIC family with the best scalability is shown in Fig. 5(a) and ASIC family with the lowest manufacturing cost is shown in Fig. 5(b). The scalability ratio in each market niche is calculated by taking the mean value of the scalability ratio of the actuator requirements and scalability ratio of the sensor requirements. Scalability ratio of one shows that the total number of both actuators and sensors in the ECU matches perfectly with the requirement of the market niche. The redundancies of the actuators and/or sensors are shown by the slightly lower scalability ratio.

The manufacturing cost is mainly affected by the volume of the biggest ASICs (i.e. ASIC with the largest functionality). As can be seen in Fig. 5(a), although the cost of the biggest ASIC (i.e. ASIC '1' with 12 actuator modules and 4 sensor modules) is lower than the one in Fig. 5(b), the number of pieces needed to cover the market is much higher. Using (4), to produce one million ECU, we need 10x1,000,000 = 10,000,000 pieces of ASIC '1' in the best scalability scenario, while we need 7x1,000,000 = 7,000,000 pieces of ASIC '1' in the case of the cost optimization scenario. However, in general both ASIC families have a good coverage of the market indicated by the average value of scalability ratio of more than 0.95. Non-dominated tradeoff solutions of MSG II can be seen in Fig. 6.

Market requirements of actuators / sensors interfaces	Market Niche									
	4 / 0	8 / 2	8 / 4	12 / 4	16 / 6	20 / 6	20 / 8	24 / 8	28 / 10	32 / 10
Index of ASICs in CL (λ)	{4}	{3,4}	{2}	{1}	{1,3}	{1,3,4}	{1,2}	{1,1}	{1,1,3}	{1,1,3,4}
No. of actuators / sensors in λ	4 / 0	10 / 2	8 / 4	12 / 4	18 / 6	22 / 6	20 / 8	24 / 8	30 / 10	34 / 10
Scalability Ratio	1	0,90	1	1	0,94	0,95	1	1	0,97	0,97

Average Scalability Ratio : 0.974

Total Manufacturing Cost : 16.470 Mio a.u

ASIC index	Cost	Package	No. of Actuators	No. of Sensors	No. of Analog
1	9.35 a.u	64 pins	12	4	4
2	7.80 a.u	44 pins	8	4	4
3	6.75 a.u	44 pins	6	2	6
4	5.45 a.u	32 pins	4	0	6

(a) Best scenario of scalability

Market requirements of actuators / sensors interfaces	Market Niche									
	4 / 0	8 / 2	8 / 4	12 / 4	16 / 6	20 / 6	20 / 8	24 / 8	28 / 10	32 / 10
Index of ASICs in CL (λ)	{4}	{2}	{2}	{2,4}	{1}	{1,4}	{1,3}	{1,2}	{1,2,4}	{1,1}
No. of actuators / sensors in λ	4 / 0	8 / 4	8 / 4	12 / 4	16 / 6	20 / 6	22 / 8	24 / 10	28 / 10	32 / 12
Scalability Ratio	1	0.75	1	1	1,00	1,00	0.95	0.90	1,00	0.92

Average Scalability Ratio : 0.952

Total Manufacturing Cost : 14.670 Mio a.u

ASIC index	Cost	Package	No. of Actuators	No. of Sensors	No. of Analog
1	11.30 a.u	64 pins	16	6	4
2	7.80 a.u	44 pins	8	4	4
3	6.65 a.u	32 pins	6	2	4
4	5.45 a.u	32 pins	4	0	6

(b) Best scenario of manufacturing cost

Fig. 5. Solutions with best scalability and best manufacturing cost of MSG

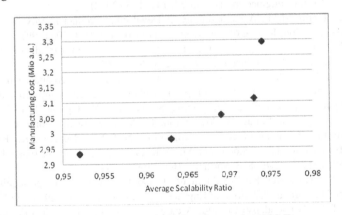

Fig. 6. Non-dominated solutions from market MSG II

5   Conclusion

Modular structure based product design has been chosen by industries to provide sufficient variety of their products to the market. The introduction of product with modular-
structure has urged many industries to design a family of modular products themselves so
that the design variables and performance of the modular product can fit the diverse design or performance requirements of the market. In this paper, we presented a methodology to solve a product family design problem for a modular-structure based product.

Market consideration is integrated in order to find the optimal configurations that differentiate each of the products in the family. We showed how the segmentation in the market can be used to measure the scalability of the product family. Production cost related optimization was also integrated so that product family can be manufactured economically and effectively. This allows us to choose the optimal configuration of the products according to the market requirement as well as the cost optimization.

References

1. Simpson, T.W., Siddique, Z., Jiao, J. (eds.): Product platform and product family design: methods and applications. Springer, New York (2005)
2. Kumar, D., Chen, W., Simpson, T.W.: A market-driven approach to product family design. Int. J. Prod. Res. 47(1), 71–104 (2009)
3. Fujita, K.: Product variety optimization under modular architecture. Computer Aided Des. 34(12), 953–965 (2002)
4. Li, B., Luo, X., Tang, J.: A Scalable Product Family Design Method Based on Sensitivity Analysis for Performance and Cost. In: 10th Intl. Conference on Computer-Aided Industrial Design & Conceptual Design, pp. 1031–1035 (2009)
5. Meyer, M.H., Lehnerd, A.P.: The Power of Product Platforms: Building Value and Cost Leadership. Free Press (1997)
6. Simpson, T.W., Bobuk, A., Slingerland, L.A., Brennan, S., Logan, D., Reichard, K.: From user requirements to commonality specifications: an integrated approach to product family design. Research in Engineering Design 23, 141–153 (2012)
7. Jiao, J.X., Tseng, M.M.: A methodology of Developing Product Family Architecture for Mass Customization. Journal of Intelligent Manufacturing 10, 3–20 (1999)
8. Jiao, J.X., Zhang, Y., Wang, Y.: A Generic Genetic Algorithm for Product Family Design. Journal of Intelligent Manufacturing 18(2), 233–247 (2007)
9. Khajavirad, A., Michalak, J.J., Simpson, T.W.: An efficient decomposed multiobjective genetic algorithm for solving the joint product platform selection and product family design problem with generalized commonality. Struct. Multidisc Optim. 39, 187–201 (2009)
10. Deb, K., Agrawal, S., Pratap, A., Meyarivan, T.: A fast elitist non-dominated sorting genetic algorithm for multi-objective optimization: NSGA II. In: Deb, K., Rudolph, G., Lutton, E., Merelo, J.J., Schoenauer, M., Schwefel, H.-P., Yao, X. (eds.) PPSN 2000. LNCS, vol. 1917, pp. 849–858. Springer, Heidelberg (2000)
11. Kohlhase, N., Birkhofer, H.: Development of modular structures: the prerequisite for successful modular products. Journal of Engineering Design 7(3), 279–291 (1996)
12. Whitney, D.E.: Nippondenso Co. Ltd: A case study of strategic product design. Research in Engineering Design #5, 1–20 (1995)

Customer Order Fulfillment Based on a Rolling Horizon Available-to-Promise Mechanism: Solution by Fuzzy Approach and Genetic Algorithm

Chi-Bin Cheng and Meng-Tsung Wu

Department of Information Management, Tamkang University,
151 Yingzhuan Rd., Tamsui Dist., New Taipei City, Taiwan
cbcheng@mail.tku.edu.tw,
pistolpete@mail.im.tku.edu.tw

Abstract. This study attempts to solve a dynamic order promising problem, where customer requests arrive in a random fashion, and the producer processes customer orders on a batch basis. This decision process repeated for every pre-defined batching interval, and the current decision-making must take into account the previously committed orders. The problem is formulated as a mixed integer programming model with fuzzy constraints, which express the decision-maker's subjective judgment regarding customer's price tolerance. The proposed model embeds the advanced available-to-promise (AATP) concept to support accurate computation of profit and customer order promising. A genetic algorithm is developed to solve the problem. Experiments by computer simulations are carried out to demonstrate the proposed approach.

Keywords: Reverse auction, Bidding, Advanced available-to-promise, Fuzzy mathematical programming, Genetic algorithm.

1 Introduction

Many of the Fortune 2000 companies have adopted reverse auctions as a common technique for sourcing goods and services [7]. In a reverse auction, multiple qualified suppliers are invited to participate in a bidding process, in which the suppliers bid against one another over the Internet by proposing their ideal price, quantity, delivery date, etc., in an attempt to win the business.

It was noted by Cheng [4] that a profitable and promising bid depends on accurate estimates of the production costs associated with specific delivery dates, and the awareness of market competition by the decision-maker. For such consideration, Cheng [4] incorporated the concept of available-to-promise (ATP) inventory in a multiple-objective decision-making model to determine the bid price and delivery time. Basically, the ATP inventory is the uncommitted portion of a company's inventory and planned production which is maintained in the master schedule to support customer order promise [1]. The use of ATP enables the company to respond immediately to a buyer's request and facilitates satisfaction of the delivery promise [2].

© Springer International Publishing Switzerland 2015

D. Filev et al. (eds.), *Intelligent Systems'2014*,

Advances in Intelligent Systems and Computing 323, DOI: 10.1007/978-3-319-11310-4_41

The traditional ATP is merely a bookkeeping function in the master production schedule, and it can only render limited flexibility of the allocation of production resources. In recent years, advanced available-to-promise (AATP) is increasingly considered as an effective tool to achieve on-time delivery, to reduce the number of missed business opportunities, and to enhance revenue and profitability [6]. AATP is based not only on pre-calculated quantities, but also on effective order-driven optimization approaches that serve the front end customers from the perspective of the entire supply chain. AATP can directly link available resources with customer orders to improve the performance of a supply chain [2, 3].

Cheng and Cheng [5] integrated the AATP concept with a dynamic pricing (i.e. bidding) mechanism to address the competition between customer orders for limited production resources to improve the efficiency of resource utilization. The problem was formulated as a mixed integer programming with the bid price being constrained by a fuzzy membership function, which modeled the decision-maker's subjective judgment on market competition. Though the model of Cheng and Cheng [5] can determine a future production plan along with the bidding decision, it did not provide a mechanism for updating the production plan when new customer orders arrive. It is possible that the overall profit can be increased by changing the production plan to allow the production of new orders. This attempt can be achieved by reviewing the ATP on a rolling horizon basis. In other words, after every time interval the production resources are reallocated to fulfill previously promised orders and to promise newly-arrival orders. The present study extends the approach of Cheng and Cheng [5] to model the bidding decision with a rolling horizon AATP planning by mixed-integer programming. The proposed model enables the dynamic allocation of production resources when new orders arrive and hence improve the efficiency of resource utilization. The problem is solved by a fuzzy approach based on the concept of compromise solutions between the overall profit and the possibility to win the contract. The solution procedure is carried out by a genetic algorithm, and experiments by computer simulation are conducted to evaluate the performance of the proposed approach.

2   Modeling of Bidding Decision with Rolling Horizon AATP

A customer request involves three dimensions, namely quantity quoting (i.e. committing order quantity), delivery-date quoting (i.e. committing order quantity), and price quoting (i.e. price demanded by the supplier to deliver the order). Customer requests arrive in a random fashion, and order-promising and -fulfillment decisions are made for a batch of requests collected over a batching interval. In the production planning for fulfilling the newly-arrived orders, it must also take into account the previously committed orders in earlier runs of order review whose production has not been fully completed. In other words, the production resources usage planed in the earlier runs could be reassigned in the current review subject to that previously committed order quantities and delivery date remain unchanged.

The order-promising and -fulfillment mechanism proposed in this study is to determine which orders to accept and, for each accepted order, determine a bid price based on the cost associated with this order. The decision regarding the fulfilment of an accepted order includes the delivery time and quantity, which is translated into a production schedule consisting of production lots at various periods. The cost of an order is computed according to the production cost and the holding cost of its production lots. The objective of the proposed mixed-integer programming model is to maximize an overall profit, which is defined as the difference between the total revenue and the tangible/intangible costs, where the intangible costs are defined as the cost of denying an order.

2.1 Mixed-Integer Programming with Fuzzy Constraint

The MIP model in this study is an extension of the model proposed by Cheng and Cheng [5] to enable the execution of a rolling horizon planning. The model is presented as follows.

Decision variables:

$Q_i(t)$: quantity to be delivered to customer i at time t.

$q_i(s,t)$: quantity to be produced at time s to fulfil the order $Q_i(t)$.

$D_i(t)$: binary variable, equal to 1 if the order of customer i is delivered at time t; 0 otherwise.

Z_i: binary variable, equal to 1 if the order of customer i is promised; 0 otherwise.

c_i: unit cost to deliver order $Q_i(t)$.

p_i: unit bid price submitted to customer i.

Parameters:

O: set of newly-arrived requests.

$\hat{O}$: set of previously-promised orders.

t_e: ended time of the previous planning.

T: length of the planning horizon.

$\hat{Q}_i(t)$: quantity has been promised to customer i.

$\hat{q}_i(s,t)$: production lot that has been completed to fulfil $\hat{Q}_i(t)$.

$\hat{d}_i$: delivery date has been promised to customer i.

$[d_i^l, d_i^u]$: acceptable delivery time interval requested by customer i.

$[a_i^l, a_i^u]$: acceptable delivered quantity interval requested by customer i.

θ_i: unit penalty cost for denying the order of customer i.

r_i: unit production time required to produce $q_i(s,t)$.

$\pi_i(s)$: unit production cost of $q_i(s,t)$.

h_i: holding cost per unit of time of per unit of $q_i(s,t)$.

$K(t)$: available production capacity at time t (in time unit).

g_i: minimum acceptable gross profit rate of the supplier to deliver the order of customer i.

$\tilde{u}_i$: upper bound of unit bid price perceived by the supplier for the order of customer i, i.e. the price above which the supplier considers the bid to have no chance of success.

M: very large number.

Maximize $P = \sum\limits_{t=t_e+1}^{t_e+T} \sum\limits_{i \in O \cup \hat{O}} (p_i - c_i) \cdot Q_i(t) - \sum\limits_{i \in O} \theta_i \cdot (1 - Z_i)$ (1)

Subject to:

Order promising and fulfillment:

$\sum\limits_{t_e+1 \le s < t} q_i(s,t) = Q_i(t),\ \forall i \in O,\ \text{and } t_e+1 \le t \le t_e+T$ (2)

$Q_i(t) \ge a_i^l \cdot D_i(t),\ \forall i \in O,\ \text{and } t_e+1 \le t \le t_e+T$ (3)

$Q_i(t) \le a_i^u \cdot D_i(t),\ \forall i \in O,\ \text{and } t_e+1 \le t \le t_e+T$ (4)

$\sum\limits_{d_i^l \le t \le d_i^u} D_i(t) = Z_i,\ \ \forall i \in O$ (5)

$\sum\limits_{t=1}^{T} D_i(t) \le 1,\ \forall i \in O$ (6)

$Q_i(t) = \hat{Q}_i(t),\ \forall i \in \hat{O}$ (7)

$Q_i(t) = 0,\ \forall i \in \hat{O},\ \text{and } t \ne \hat{d}_i$ (8)

$\sum\limits_{1 \le s \le t_e} \hat{q}_i(s,t) + \sum\limits_{t_e+1 \le s < t} q_i(s,t) = \hat{Q}_i(t),\ \forall i \in \hat{O},\ \text{and } t_e+1 \le t \le t_e+T$ (9)

Production and capacity constraints:

$\sum\limits_{t_e+1 \le t \le t_e+T} \sum\limits_{i \in O \cup \hat{O}} r_i \cdot q_i(s,t) \le K(s),\ \ t_e+1 \le s \le t_e+T$ (10)

$q_i(s,t) \le D_i(t) \cdot M,\ \forall i \in O,\ s < t \text{ and } t_e+1 \le t \le t_e+T$ (11)

$q_i(s,t) = 0,\ \forall i \in O \cup \hat{O},\ s \ge t \text{ and } t_e+1 \le t \le t_e+T$ (12)

Order cost computation:

$\{ \sum\limits_{t_e+1 \le s < t} \pi_i(s) \cdot q_i(s,t) + \sum\limits_{t_e+1 \le s < t} h_i \cdot q_i(s,t) \cdot (t-s) \} / Q_i(t) = c_i,\ \forall i \in O,$

$t_e+1 \le t \le t_e+T,\ \text{and } Q_i(t) \ne 0$ (13)

$\{ \sum\limits_{1 \le s \le t_e} \pi_i(s) \cdot \hat{q}_i(s,t) + \sum\limits_{t_e+1 \le s < t} \pi_i(s) \cdot q_i(s,t) + \sum\limits_{1 \le s \le t_e} h_i \cdot \hat{q}_i(s,t) \cdot (t-s) +$

$\sum\limits_{t_e+1 \le s < t} h_i \cdot q_i(s,t) \cdot (t-s) \} / Q_i(t) = c_i,\ \forall i \in O, t_e+1 \le t \le t_e+T$ (14)

Bid price interval:

$p_i \ge (1 + g_i) \cdot c_i,\ \forall i \in O$ (15)

$p_i \le \tilde{u}_i,\ \forall i \in O$ (16)

$p_i = \hat{p}_i,\ \forall i \in \hat{O}$ (17)

$c_i \le \dfrac{\hat{p}_i}{1 + g_i},\ \forall i \in \hat{O}$ (18)

Integrality:

$Z_i \in \{0, 1\}, \forall i \in O$

$D_i(t) \in \{0, 1\}, \forall i \in O$, and $t_e+1 \leq t \leq t_e+T$

Non-negativity:

$Q_i(t) \geq 0, \forall i \in O, s < t$ and $t_e+1 \leq t \leq t_e+T$

$q_i(s,t) \geq 0, \forall i \in O \cup \hat{O}$, and $t_e+1 \leq t \leq t_e+T$

$c_i \geq 0, \forall i \in O \cup \hat{O}$

$p_i \geq 0, \forall i \in O$

The objective of the above model is to maximize the overall profit of the supplier, where the profit is defined as the total revenue deducted by the total costs of orders to be delivered and the penalties of all denial orders. There are four major groups of constraints. Constraints (2)-(9) are to ensure feasible deliveries, where Constraint (2) is the production plan for newly-arrived orders where $q_i(s,t)$ is the production lot to be produced at time s in order to fulfil the order $Q_i(t)$ which will be delivered at time t. Constraints (3) and (4) specify the acceptable range of delivery quantity requested by customers; and Constraints (5) and (6) define the feasible delivery time window. Constraints (7) and (8) are to guarantee the previously-promised orders will be delivered on quantity and on time. The production of a previously-promised order may have been partially carried out at the current time point; thus, Constraint (9) expresses the possible resources rearrangement for the unfinished part of such an order. Constraint (10) enforces that the total production of each period cannot exceed its available capacity, while Constraints (11) and (12) relate the existence of $q_i(s,t)$ with the delivery decision $D_i(t)$. Constraints (13) and (14) define the cost of an order, for newly-arrived orders and formerly-promised orders respectively, as the summation of its production cost and holding cost. Constraint (15) guarantees the bid prices for newly-arrived orders render a minimum profit margin of their costs, while Constraint (16) expresses the decision-maker's belief that the maximum price the customer can tolerate. It is difficult to assign a precise value to this parameter, and therefore in the current study, it is defined by a fuzzy upper-bound $\tilde{u}_i$. Finally, Constraint (17) specifies that the previously-promised prices to customers keep unchanged; and Constraint (18) guarantees the cost of a previously-promised order not increasing to harm the minimum profit margin due to production resources rearrangement.

2.2   Fuzzy Approach

The above mixed-integer programming contains a fuzzy constraint (16); and thus cannot be solved by regular optimization techniques. This study adopts the concept of Werners [8] to formulate a fuzzy approach to solve the problem.

The satisfaction of the fuzzy constraint (16) in the MIP model is evaluated through a fuzzy membership function. As shown in Figure 1(a), the fuzzy membership function of the price variable is defined as $\mu_{price}(p_i) \in [0, 1]$. Basically, this membership function models the supplier's confidence in the possibility of winning the contract with an offer price p_i. Note that the values of p_i^{inf} and p_i^{sup} in Figure 1(a) are assigned by the supplier in accordance with his experience and knowledge of the market. This membership function coincides with the fact that the possibility of winning the contract decreases when the bid price increases. By the definition of the membership function in Figure 1(a), the fuzzy constraint can be rewritten as:

$$p_i \le p_i^{\text{inf}} + (1-\alpha)(p_i^{\text{sup}} - p_i^{\text{inf}}), \tag{19}$$

where α is a membership value and $\alpha \in [0, 1]$. Equation (19) means that the upper bound of the bid price has a maximum tolerance of $(p_i^{\text{sup}} - p_i^{\text{inf}})$, and the satisfactory of Constraint (16) decreases when the tolerance increases, or equivalently, the possibility (i.e. α) to win the contract decreases when the bid price increases from p_i^{inf} to p_i^{sup}.

To construct a fuzzy membership function for the objective function, the inferior (P^0) and the superior (P^1) of the objective value P are defined respectively as follows:

$P^0 = $ maximize (1)
subject to:
    (2)-(15), (17) and (18)
    $p_i \le p_i^{\text{inf}}$, $\forall i \in O$

and

$P^1 = $ maximize (1)
subject to:
    (2)-(15), (17) and (18)
    $p_i \le p_i^{\text{sup}}$, $\forall i \in O$.

As a result, the membership function of the objective P can be constructed as:

$$\mu_P(P) = \begin{cases} 1, & \text{if } P \ge P^1 \\ 1 - (P^1 - P)/(P^1 - P^0), & \text{if } P^0 \le P < P^1 \\ 0, & \text{if } P < P^0 \end{cases} \tag{20}$$

The membership function of (20) is also graphically shown in Figure 1(b).

The optimum decision of the original problem is now considered as to maximize the conjunct satisfaction of objective value and the fuzzy constraint, where the conjunct satisfaction is obtained through a minimum operator. This concept is referred to as a max-min approach. Thus, the original MIP is reformulated as:

Maximize α
Subject to:
    (2)-(15), (17) and (18)
    $\mu_i(p_i) \ge \alpha$, $\forall i \in O$ $\tag{21}$
    $\mu_P(P) \ge \alpha$ $\tag{22}$

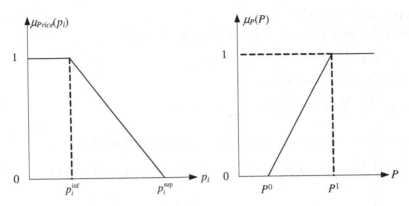

Fig. 1. (a) Membership function of the bid price (b) Membership function of the objective

3   Solution Procedure

The present study modifies the algorithm of Cheng and Cheng [5] to enable the execution of dynamic planning of order promising and fulfillment under a rolling horizon environment. There are three modules in this solution procedure, namely main algorithm, genetic algorithm, and adjustment algorithm. A conceptual diagram of the relations among the three modules are depicted in Figure 2. The main algorithm solves the max-min problem numerically by gradually increasing the value of α and activating the genetic algorithm to find a solution of order promising and fulfillment under a newly updated α value; the optimum α is then determined by applying the max-min operator on all resulting solutions under various values of α. Since the genetic algorithm does not guarantee to yield feasible solutions of order promising and fulfillment, solutions are sent to the adjustment algorithm before they can be further used in the main algorithm for solving the max-min problem.

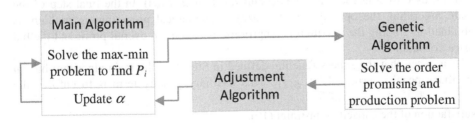

Fig. 2. Flow diagram of the solution procedure

3.1   Main Algorithm

The detailed steps of the main algorithm are described as follows.

Step 0. $zi = 1$, $\forall i \in O \cup \hat{O}$, $\alpha = 0$

Step 1. For all $i \in O$, let $p_i = p_i^{\inf} + (1-\alpha)(p_i^{\sup} - p_i^{\inf})$.

For all $i \in \hat{O}$, let $p_i = \hat{p}_i$.

Step 2. Define fitness function

$$f(\alpha) = \sum_{t=t_e+1}^{t_e+T} \sum_{i \in O \cup \hat{O}} (p_i - c_i) \cdot Q_i(t) - \sum_{t_e+1 \le s < t} \lambda_s\, \phi(s)$$

where λ's is a unit penalty, and $\phi(s)$ is a penalty term defined as

$$\phi(s) = \begin{cases} \sum_{t=t_e+1}^{t_e+T} \sum_{i \in O \cup \hat{O}} r_i \cdot q_i(s,t) - K(s), & \text{if } \sum_{t=t_e+1}^{t_e+T} \sum_{i \in O \cup \hat{O}} r_i \cdot q_i(s,t) > K(s), \\ 0, & \text{otherwise} \end{cases}$$

Step 3. Go to Genetic Algorithm

Step 4. Go to Adjustment Algorithm

Step 5. $\alpha = \alpha + \Delta\alpha$

If $\alpha > 1$, then go to Step 5; otherwise go to Step 1.

Step 6. Construct $\mu_P(P(\alpha))$ by Eq. (20).

Step 7. Find $\alpha^* = \max_{\alpha} \min\{\mu_P(P(\alpha)), \alpha\}$

Stop.

In the beginning of the main algorithm, all n customer orders are accepted (i.e. $z_i = 1$, $i = 1,...n$), and the satisfaction of Constraint (13) is set to 0 (i.e. $p_i \le p_i^{\sup}$, $\forall i$). The value of α is then gradually updated with a small increment $\Delta\alpha$, and the fitness function is defined in accordance with the current α, where the bid price pi is set to its current upper bound $p_i^{\inf} + (1-\alpha)(p_i^{\sup} - p_i^{\inf})$. This fitness function is passed to genetic algorithm for fitness evaluation of each chromosome. The solutions obtained by the genetic algorithm under different α values are returned to the main algorithm and are used to construct the membership function $\mu_P(P(\alpha))$. In the final step of the main algorithm, the optimum of the fuzzy mathematical programming problem is obtained by finding the maximum compromise between the overall profit and the bid price constraints.

It is noted that the fitness function defined in Step 1 of the main algorithm has an auxiliary penalty term, $\sum_{t_e+1 \le s < t} \lambda_s\, \phi(s)$. This auxiliary penalty term is to enforce the satisfaction of the capacity constraint (10).

3.2   Genetic Algorithm

Solutions of the problem are encoded as chromosome in a table format as shown in Figure 3, in which, each row represents the production lots to fulfill a customer order (n customers in total), the columns represent time periods excepting the last column denoted by t_i is the delivery time of order i, and the cells (excepting the column of t_i) denote $q_i(s, t_i)$. The steps of the genetic algorithm are as follows.

		Period					t_i
		t_e+1	t_e+2	t_e+3	...	t_e+T	
Order i	1	20	0	10	...	0	4
	2	0	20	40	...	0	6
	:	:	:	:	:	:	:
	n	0	70	0	...	0	5

Fig. 3. Solution encoding

Step 0. Initial gene pool generation:
   For each chromosome do

   Step 0.1 For all $i \in O$, randomly generate $t_i \in [d_i^l, d_i^u]$.

   For all $i \in \hat{O}$, let $t_i = \hat{d}_i$.

   Step 0.2 Let $q_i(s, t_i)=0$, if $s \geq t_i$, $\forall i \in O \cup \hat{O}$
   Step 0.3 For all $i \in O$, randomly generate $qi(s, ti)$ for all $s<t_i$, where $q_i(s, t_i)$ satisfies

$$a_i^l \leq \sum_{s=t_e+1}^{t_i} q_i(s,t_i) \leq a_i^u$$

   For all $i \in \hat{O}$, randomly generate $q_i(s, t_i)$ for all $s<t_i$, where $q_i(s, t_i)$ satisfies

$$\sum_{s=t_e+1}^{t_i} q_i(s,t_i) = Q_i(t_i) - \sum_{s+1}^{t_e} q_i(s,t_i)$$

Step 1. For each chromosome do
Fitness evaluation, where the fitness

$$F(\alpha) = \begin{cases} f(\alpha), & \text{if } p_i \geq (1+g_i) \cdot c_i, \forall i \\ 0, & \text{otherwise} \end{cases}$$

Step 2. Conduct reproduction.
Step 3. Conduct crossover.
Step 4. For each newly generated chromosome do

   Step 4.1 Let $q_i(s, t_i)=0$, if $s \geq t_i$, $\forall i \in O \cup \hat{O}$
   Step 4.2 For all $i \in O$,
   if $\sum_{t_e+1 \leq s<t_i} q_i(s,t_i) < a_i^l$, then randomly increase some $q_i(s, t_i)$, where $s<t_i$, until

$\sum_{t_e+1 \leq s<t_i} q_i(s,t_i) \geq a_i^l$; else if $\sum_{t_e+1 \leq s<t_i} q_i(s,t_i) > a_i^u$, then randomly decrease some $q_i(s, t_i)$,

where $s<t_i$, until $\sum_{t_e+1 \leq s<t_i} q_i(s,t_i) \leq a_i^u$.

   Step 4.3 For all $i \in \hat{O}$,

if $\displaystyle\sum_{t_e+1\le s<t_i} q_i(s,t_i) < Q_i(t_i) - \sum_{1\le s\le t_e} q_i(s,t_i)$, then randomly increase some $q_i(s,\ t_i)$,

where $t_e+1\le s<t_i$, until $\displaystyle\sum_{t_e+1\le s<t_i} q_i(s,t_i) = Q_i(t_i) - \sum_{1\le s\le t_e} q_i(s,t_i)$;   else   if

$\displaystyle\sum_{t_e+1\le s<t_i} q_i(s,t_i) > Q_i(t_i) - \sum_{1\le s\le t_e} q_i(s,t_i)$, then randomly decrease some $q_i(s,\ t_i)$, where

$t_e+1\le s<t_i$, until $\displaystyle\sum_{t_e+1\le s<t_i} q_i(s,t_i) = Q_i(t_i) - \sum_{1\le s\le t_e} q_i(s,t_i)$.

Step 5. Conduct mutation

Step 6. For the chromosome picked to mutate do

Step 6.1 If the changed bit belong to $\{t_i, \forall i\}$, then

Case $i\in O$:

If $t_i < d_i^l$, then let $t_i = d_i^l$, else if

$t_i > d_i^u$, then let $t_i = d_i^u$.

Repeat Steps 4.1 and 4.2.

Go to Step 7.

Case $i\in \hat{O}$: let $t_i = \hat{d}_i$.

Step 6.2 Case $i\in O$: repeat Step 4.2.

Case $i\in \hat{O}$: repeat Step 4.3.

Step 7. If the stop criterion is satisfied, then return to Main Algorithm; otherwise go to
    Step 1.

Step 0 generates an initial gene pool, where for new orders, the corresponding
genes must satisfy the delivery time constraint and the quantity constraint requested
by customers; while for previously promised orders, the delivery time cannot be
changed but the incomplete portions of the order can be rescheduled under the condition that they must meet the total quantity already promised. The fitness of each
chromosome is evaluated in Step 1. The fitness function passed from the main algorithm is directly employed if the chromosome satisfies the minimum gross profit
constraint (15); otherwise the fitness is set to 0 to indicate this is an unacceptable
chromosome. The reproduction and the crossover operators are then applied to the
pool of chromosomes in Steps 2 and 3 respectively. The resulting new generation of
chromosomes is adjusted in Step 4 in order to maintain their feasibility. Step 5
conducts the mutation operation and the new chromosome is adjusted in Step 6 if
necessary to guarantee its feasibility.

3.3   Adjustment Algorithm

Though the auxiliary penalty term in the fitness function enforces the satisfaction of
capacity constraint (10), the solutions obtained from the genetic algorithm may still
fail to satisfy this constraint. Thus, it is necessary to adjust the solution to obtain feasible solutions to the original problem. The solutions from the genetic algorithm are

therefore sent to the adjustment algorithm for production rearrangement/removing, or removing the entire order if necessary.

The adjustment algorithm consists of four functions, namely access, production re-arrangement, production removing, and order removing. The access function is to receive the solutions from the genetic algorithm and return the adjusted solutions to the main algorithm. The adjustment of an infeasible solution starts with the rear-rangement of excessive productions to periods with surplus capacities. If such rearrangement is incompatible then part of the productions will be removed in the production removing function; and if the removing function still cannot find a feasible solution then one of the orders will be removed in the order removing function. When an order is removed, the vacant capacity would allow new rearrangement of produc-tions if there are still excessive productions at some periods.

4   Experiments and Analysis

Shorter batching intervals mean better customer response. On the other hand, a longer batching interval contains more demand patterns and hence renders a greater opportunity to maximize the profit. If shorter batching intervals can still generate comparable profits to longer batching intervals, it would be the ideal solution to the manufacturer. Thus, the experiments in the present study focus on the effects of batching interval size and capacity availability degree on various performance measures, including total profit, denial order cost, and holding cost. The batching interval size is set to five levels, 1, 2, 3, 6, and 9 periods, and the capacity availability degree is set to three levels, 100%, 80%, and 50%, where the capacity availability degree is defined as $\sum_{s=t_e+1}^{t_e+T} K(s) / \sum_{i \in O \cup \hat{O}} \frac{1}{2}(a_i^l + a_i^u)$. The combinations of different batching interval size and capacity availability degree result in 15 scenarios.

The arrival of customer requests is assumed to follow a Poisson distribution with a mean of 5 requests per period and is randomly generated according to this distribu-tion. The parameters associated with each request are also randomly generated within pre-specified ranges. The remainder parameters are fixed as follows: the gross profit rate $g_i=20\%$, $r_i=1$, $\pi_i=2$, and $h_i=0.5$. The planning horizon T is set to 18 periods, and the total time length under consideration is 36 periods for all scenarios. To obtain reliable results, 10 problem instances are randomly generated for each scenario. The computer program is run on a PC with Intel® Core(TM)2 Duo CPU E8400 @3.00GHz and 1.96GB RAM. Computational results are presented in Figure 4.

When capacity availability degrees are 100% and 50%, batching interval of 3 peri-od results in the greatest profit, while there is no significant difference among the profits by different batching intervals for the case 80% capacity availability. This result is related to the balance of the revenue and the denial penalty and the holding cost. From this result, it is suggested that batching interval of 3 period is a suitable choice in our example.

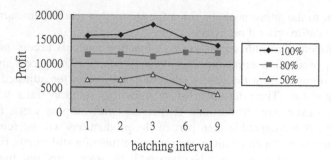

Fig. 4. Computational result

5   Concluding Remark

This study integrates the production planning and the bidding decision for customer order fulfillment decision. A mixed-integer programming model based on the concept of advanced available-to-promise inventory and fuzzy constraints on bid price was formulated. An algorithm that combines the max-min optimum approach and the genetic algorithm is developed to solve the problem. Experiments by computer simulations are carried out to demonstrate the proposed approach.

References

1. American Production and Inventory Control Society: APICS Dictionary. APICS Educational Society for Resource Manage (2004)
2. Chen, C.-Y., Zhao, Z.-Y., Ball, M.O.: Quantity and due date quoting available to promise. Information Systems Frontiers 3, 477–488 (2001)
3. Chen, C.-Y., Zhao, Z.-Y., Ball, M.O.: A model for batch advanced available-to-promise. Production and Operations Management 11, 424–440 (2002)
4. Cheng, C.-B.: Solving a sealed-bid reverse auction problem by multiple-criterion decision-making methods. Computers and Mathematics with Applications 56, 3261–3274 (2008)
5. Cheng, C.-B., Cheng, C.-J.: Available-to-promise based bidding decision by fuzzy mathematical programming and genetic algorithm. Computers & Industrial Engineering 61, 993–1002 (2011)
6. Kilger, C., Schneeweiss, L.: Demand fulfilment and ATP. In: Stadtler, H., Kilger, C. (eds.) Supply Chain Management and Advanced Planning, pp. 79–95. Springer, Berlin (2000)
7. Tully, S.: Going, going, gone! The B2B tool that really is changing the world. Fortune 141, 132–145 (2000)
8. Werner, B.: An interactive fuzzy programming system. Fuzzy Sets and Systems 23, 131–147 (1987)

Solution of the Problem Supply Chain Management in Temporal Dependence

Marina Savelyeva[1] and Stanislav Belyakov[2]

[1] Department of Automated Research Systems, Southern Federal University, Taganrog, Russia
marina.n.savelyeva@gmail.com
[2] Department of Applied Information Science, Southern Federal University, Taganrog, Russia
beliacov@yandex.ru

Abstract. The article presents the problem of supply chain management. One of the main issues in solving such problems is routing. An algorithm to find the shortest path in the temporal dependence and fuzzy-defined parameters of time and distance. Solution is based on the apparatus of graph theory, namely fuzzy temporal graph. This algorithm is a modification of Dijkstra's algorithm. An illustration of an example of solving the problem of finding an optimal route in fuzzy conditions, as such representation is closest to reality.

Keywords: Fuzzy temporal graph, shortest path, fuzzy numbers, routing, Dijkstra's algorithm, logistical problem, graph theory.

1 Introduction

Constantly changing reality leads to inaccuracies, incompleteness and unreliability of received information. This causes problems in the planning and realization of tasks related to supply chain management [1].One of the main tasks in this area is the problem moving cargo. In a constantly changing situation on the roads, routing problem is particularly relevant, since the number of vehicles in the last decade has increased dramatically, in large cities and on highways became to occur collapse. Routing is the process of determining the best path to transport cargo. Decision problems of this kind is necessary to minimize costs in supply chain management. Therefore, procedural model has been developed which solves the problem of routing, as close as changing reality. The difficulty of solving this problem consists in the inhomogeneity time-varying parameter.

The solution to such problems using the methods of linear and dynamic programming appropriate, but these methods do not allow you to dynamically change source information and use the fuzzy presented data. Using the theory of fuzzy sets in solving such problems helps to choose the optimum dynamic route, and apparatus of the theory graphs accelerates search for optimal solutions.

© Springer International Publishing Switzerland 2015
D. Filev et al. (eds.), *Intelligent Systems'2014*,
Advances in Intelligent Systems and Computing 323, DOI: 10.1007/978-3-319-11310-4_42

2 Statement of the Problem

Necessary to find the shortest path L from the starting point s (source) to the end point r (streamflow) using the optional parameter - time. There are also edges which are absent in a certain time period (by weight of these periods of time equal to infinity). Edges are fuzzy variables. Time is discrete quantity; time passing by each edge is represented in a fuzzy form. By period of time T_j, where $j = \overline{0,m}$, refers to the time that the user specifies. Also, the user specifies the number of time periods defined by the set of

$$T = \{T_0, T_1, \dots, T_m\} = \{T_{j_s}, T_j, T_{j_r}\},$$

where $\{T_{j_s}\}, j_s = \overline{0, m-1}$ is a departure time from the starting point, $\{T_j\}, j = \overline{1, m-1}$ is movement time, without excluding time departure and arrival, $\{T_{j_r}\}, j_r = \overline{1, m}$ is time of arrival at the destination.

Necessary to find the shortest path from the source to the streamflow, if a user is defined a departure time.

3 Procedural Model of Finding the Shortest Path

Solution of such problems adequately address using the apparatus of the theory of graphs, namely based on fuzzy temporal graph.

Fuzzy temporal graph is a triple $\tilde{G} = (X, \tilde{U}_t, T)$, where X is set of vertices of the number of vertices c $|X| = n$, $T = \{1, 2, \dots, N\}$ is the set of natural numbers, determining (discrete) time; $U_t = \{< \mu_t(x_i, x_j) | (x_i, x_j) >\}$ is fuzzy set of edges, where $x_i, x_j \in X, \mu_t(x_i, x_j) \in [0,1]$ is the value of the membership function μ_t for the edge (x_i, x_j) at time $t \in T$, and at different times for the same edge (x_i, x_j) values of the membership function (in general) different. Vertex x_j is fuzzy adjacent vertex x_i on the moment of time $t \in T$, if the condition $\mu_t(x_i, x_j) > 0$ [2,3].

Lengths of edges of the graph and time are fuzzy-defined, so they are represented as fuzzy numbers. In the Fig. 1 edge of the graph is as follows: $(\tilde{a}_i)[\tilde{t}_i / \tilde{t}_{\emptyset i}]$, where $\tilde{a}_i = (a_l, a_m, a_f)$ is the weight (length) of the edge of a fuzzy temporal graph, $\tilde{t}_i = [t_l, t_m, t_f]$ is time of movement along the edge of the fuzzy temporal graph represented in the form of a triangular fuzzy number, $\tilde{t}_{\emptyset i} = [t_{\emptyset l}, t_{\emptyset ml}, t_{\emptyset mf}, t_{\emptyset f}]$ is the absence time of the edge of the fuzzy temporal graph (edge length is equal to ∞), presented in the form of trapezoidal fuzzy number.

Step 1. It is determined that starting fuzzy temporal graph at the initial stage does not depend on time, i.e. there are edges at any given time and is calculated along the edge movement time. We find for this graph shortest path L^*. At the initial stage of the algorithm, not all the vertices and edges of the graph are painted [4].

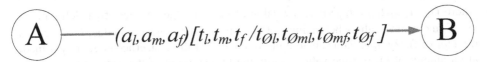

Fig. 1. Illustration the edge of the fuzzy temporal graph

Step 2. All vertices in the result of the algorithm assignment occurs fuzzy number $\tilde{d}(x_i)$, equal to the length of the shortest path from s to x_i, which includes only colored vertices.

Agreed that $\tilde{d}(s) = 0$ and $\tilde{d}(x_i) = \infty$ for all x_i, other than s. We paint the vertex s and take $y = s$ (y is the last of the colored vertices).

Step 3. We recalculate the value of $\tilde{d}(x_i)$ for all uncolored vertices x_i follows:

$$\tilde{d}(x_i) = \min\{\tilde{d}(x_i), \tilde{d}(y) + \tilde{a}(y, x_i)\} \tag{1}$$

where $\tilde{a}(y, x_i)$ is length of the edge (y, x_i).

Comparison of the values of fuzzy numbers is performed by using an index of centroid of fuzzy number.

If for all unpainted vertices x_i are $\tilde{d}(x_i) = \infty$, then it is necessary finish the algorithm and assume that in the original graph there are no paths from s to uncolored vertices. Otherwise, we produce the same coloring of the vertices x_i, for which the value of $\tilde{d}(x_i)$ is minimal. And yet still mark the edge that leads to the selected in this step, the vertex x_i (for this edge is obtained minimum according to the expression (1)). Accept $y = x_i$.

Step 4. If $y = r$, stop the procedure: the shortest path L^* from vertex s to r, not including the time parameter, is defined (this path is the only route from s to r, composed of labeled edges). Otherwise, go to step 3.

Step 5. Go to search the shortest path on fuzzy temporal graph in which edges absent in certain periods of time. To do this, step by step to build the graph representing it as static view. Initially we produce building shortest path L^*, obtained in Step 4, which begins in period of time $\{T_{j_s}\}, j_s = \overline{0, m-1}$, m - defined by the user. When constructing edges are checked for their existence. If the edge exists, in the first stage begins with the start time $\{T_j\}, j = \overline{0, m}$ movement and is determined the passage by the edge, which will be $\tilde{t}(x_i) = T_{j_s} + \tilde{t}(y, x_i)$, where $\tilde{t}(x_i)$ - total travel time to the vertex x_i, $\tilde{t}(y, x_i)$ is the passage of the edge. In the following stages, time is determined by the following equation:

$$\tilde{t}(x_i) = \tilde{t}(y) + \tilde{t}(y, x_i) \tag{2}$$

where $\tilde{t}(y)$ is total passage time to the vertex y.

If the edge does not exist at a given moment, then stop checking and go to Step 6.

Step 6. Initial vertex s belongs to the period of time $\{T_{j_s}\}, j_s = \overline{0, m-1}$. As indicated in Step 3, to find new value of $\tilde{d}(x_i)$ of formula (1) and to make check the existence edge (y, x_i) by the time parameter, as follows:

$$\left(t_{\emptyset l}, t_{\emptyset m l}, t_{\emptyset m f}, t_{\emptyset f}\right) \in (t_{l1}, t_{l2}) \cup (t_{m1}, t_{m2}) \cup \left(t_{f1}, t_{f2}\right) \tag{3}$$

where $(t_{\emptyset l}, t_{\emptyset ml}, t_{\emptyset mf}, t_{\emptyset f})$ is fuzzy value of time of edge absence; t_{l1} is left parameter of fuzzy time values belonging to beginning of the concerned edge; t_{l2} is left parameter of fuzzy time values belonging to the end of the concerned edge; t_{m1} is medial parameter of fuzzy time values belonging to beginning of the concerned edge; t_{m2} is medial parameter of fuzzy time values belonging to the end of the concerned edge; t_{f1} is right parameter of fuzzy time values belonging to beginning of the concerned edge; t_{f2} is right parameter of fuzzy time values belonging to the end of the concerned edge.

If (3) is not satisfied, hence the edge(y, x_i) exists in the concerned period, then paint the vertex x_i, we increase $T_{j_s} = T_j$ to $\tilde{t}(y, x_i)$ by the formula (2) and accept $x_i = y$.

If the expression (3) is satisfied, then the edge (y, x_i) does not exist in a given period of time, hence it is not considered and selected another minimum vertex.

If there are no other edges then the algorithm has no solution under the given conditions. If you need to find some solution, the starting period j_s incremented by 1 and go to Step 5.

Step 7. If $y = r$, to finish the procedure: the shortest path L^* from vertex s to r is found. Otherwise, go to step 6.

Step 8. Above obtained the shortest route perform the procedure of defuzzification.

Step 9. View all the shortest paths from the set $L = \{L_1, L_2, \ldots, L_n\}$, the departure time which is equal $T_{j_s}^*$. From the given set of shortest routes selected minimum route after defuzzification, i.e.

$$L^* = \min\{L_1, L_2, \ldots, L_n\}$$

The similar set of shortest routes because of fuzziness occurs the initial data.

Step 10. Perform defuzzification values obtained fuzzy time of passage shortest routes.

Step 11. If it turns out that, there is more of the same routes, then

$$\begin{cases} L_1(T_{j_s}^*) = L_2(T_{j_s}^*) = \cdots = L_n(T_{j_s}^*) \\ t_{min} = \min\left\{ t\left(L_1(T_{j_s}^*)\right), t\left(L_2(T_{j_s}^*)\right), \ldots, t\left(L_n(T_{j_s}^*)\right) \right\} \end{cases} => L^*(t_{min}),$$

where $t = t(r) - T_{j_s}$ is time of passage route from the starting point to the destination. Required the path L^* is found.

4   Realization of Routing Procedural Model

It's necessary to solve the problem of finding the optimal route for the given parameters of starting vertex 1 in the final vertex 10, the time of departure of material flow is $T_{j_s} = 0$. On the edges of the graph are the weight of edges denoting the edge length, presented in the form of fuzzy. In brackets is given the passage of the edge of triangular fuzzy number and the absence of the edge represented trapezoidal number in square brackets. Under the lack of time is the period of time when the edge doesn't exist or its capacity is almost equal to 0.

In brackets is given time of the passage of the edge and the absence of the edge. The absence of the edge is behind a "/".

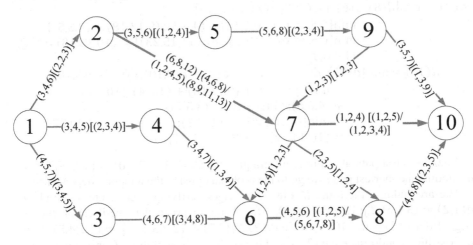

Fig. 2. Illustration of initial graph that illustrates the problem with fuzzy-defined parameters of distance and time

The first stage in the solution of such problems is to find the shortest path on the initial graph, excluding the time parameter.

Fuzzy shortest path Dijkstra's algorithm L^* is calculated as follows:

$$\tilde{d}(1) = (0,0,0)$$
$$\tilde{d}(2) = \min\{\tilde{d}(2), \tilde{d}(1) + \tilde{a}(1,2)\} = \min\{(\infty,\infty,\infty); (0,0,0) + (3,4,6)\}$$
$$= \min\{(\infty,\infty,\infty); (3,4,6)\} = (3,4,6) => Q_2 = \{1,2\}$$
$$\tilde{d}(3) = \min\{\tilde{d}(3), \tilde{d}(1) + \tilde{a}(1,3)\} = \min\{(\infty,\infty,\infty); (0,0,0) + (4,5,7)\}$$
$$= \min\{(\infty,\infty,\infty); (4,5,7)\} = (4,5,7) => Q_3 = \{1,3\}$$
$$\tilde{d}(4) = \min\{\tilde{d}(4), \tilde{d}(1) + \tilde{a}(1,4)\} = \min\{(\infty,\infty,\infty); (0,0,0) + (3,4,5)\}$$
$$= \min\{(\infty,\infty,\infty); (3,4,5)\} = (3,4,5) => Q_4 = \{1,4\}$$
$$\tilde{d}(5) = \min\{\tilde{d}(5), \tilde{d}(2) + \tilde{a}(2,5)\} = \min\{(\infty,\infty,\infty); (3,4,6) + (3,5,6)\}$$
$$= \min\{(\infty,\infty,\infty); (6,9,12)\} = (6,9,12) => Q_5 = \{1,2,5\}$$
$$\tilde{d}(6) = \min\{\tilde{d}(6), \tilde{d}(3) + \tilde{a}(3,6), \tilde{d}(4) + \tilde{a}(4,6), \tilde{d}(7) + \tilde{a}(7,6)\}$$
$$= \min\{(\infty,\infty,\infty); (4,5,7) + (4,6,7); (3,4,5) + (3,4,7); (\infty,\infty,\infty)$$
$$+ (1,2,4)\} = \min\{(\infty,\infty,\infty); (8,11,14); (6,8,12); (\infty,\infty,\infty)\}$$
$$= (6,8,12) => Q_6 = \{1,4,6\}$$
$$\tilde{d}(7) = \min\{\tilde{d}(7), \tilde{d}(2) + \tilde{a}(2,7), \tilde{d}(9) + \tilde{a}(9,7)\}$$
$$= \min\{(\infty,\infty,\infty); (3,4,6) + (6,8,12); (\infty,\infty,\infty) + (1,2,3)\}$$
$$= \min\{(\infty,\infty,\infty); (9,12,18); (\infty,\infty,\infty)\} = (9,12,18) => Q_7$$
$$= \{1,2,7\}$$
$$\tilde{d}(9) = \min\{\tilde{d}(9), \tilde{d}(5) + \tilde{a}(5,9)\} = \min\{(\infty,\infty,\infty); (6,9,12) + (5,6,8)\}$$
$$= \min\{(\infty,\infty,\infty); (11,15,20)\} = (11,15,20) => Q_9 = \{1,2,5,9\}$$
$$\tilde{d}(7) = \min\{\tilde{d}(7), \tilde{d}(9) + \tilde{a}(9,7)\} = \min\{(9,12,18); (11,15,20) + (1,2,3)\}$$
$$= \min\{(9,12,18); (12,17,23)\} = (9,12,18) => Q_7 = \{1,2,7\}$$

$$\tilde{d}(6) = \min\{\tilde{d}(6), \tilde{d}(7) + \tilde{a}(7,6)\} = \min\{(6,8,12); (9,12,18) + (1,2,4)\}$$
$$= \min\{(6,8,12); (10,14,22)\} = (6,8,12) => Q_6 = \{1,4,6\}$$
$$\tilde{d}(8) = \min\{\tilde{d}(8), \tilde{d}(6) + \tilde{a}(6,8), \tilde{d}(7) + \tilde{a}(7,8)\}$$
$$= \min\{(\infty,\infty,\infty); (6,8,12) + (4,5,6); (9,12,18) + (2,3,5)\}$$
$$= \min\{(\infty,\infty,\infty); (10,13,18); (11,15,23)\} = (10,13,18) => Q_8$$
$$= \{1,4,6,8\}$$
$$\tilde{d}(10) = \min\{\tilde{d}(10), \tilde{d}(7) + \tilde{a}(7,10), \tilde{d}(8) + \tilde{a}(8,10), \tilde{d}(9) + \tilde{a}(9,10)\}$$
$$= \min\{(\infty,\infty,\infty); (9,12,18) + (1,2,4); (10,13,18)$$
$$+ (4,6,8); (11,15,20) + (3,5,7)\}$$
$$= \min\{(\infty,\infty,\infty); (10,14,22); (14,19,26); (14,20,27)\}$$
$$= (10,14,22) => Q_{10} = \{1,2,7,10\}$$

Fuzzy shortest path algorithm Dijkstra graph is $L^* = \{1,2,7,10\} = (10,14,22)$. After finding the shortest path, we go to the problem of using the temporal dependence.

We are building the route L^* Fig. 3, in stages verifying every edge. Edge (1,2) is $\tilde{a}(1,2) = (3,4,6), T_0(1,2) = (0,0,0) \notin \tilde{t}_\emptyset$, therefore proceed to verification the next edge. Edge (2,7) is the $\tilde{a}(2,7) = (6,8,12), T_1(2,7) = (2,2,3) \in \tilde{t}_\emptyset = (1,2,4,5)$, so it is impossible to build the edge (2,7), and hence the shortest path L^*. Consequently, go to the next stage of building the route.

Again we are looking for the route by the formula (1) in the absence of the arc (2,7) in the time period $\tilde{t}_\emptyset = (1,2,4,5)$.

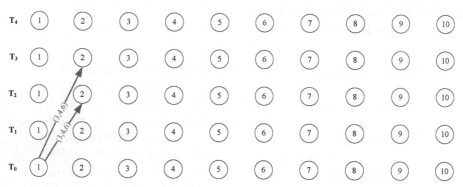

Fig. 3. Illustration of constructing shortest path L^* with fuzzy parameters of distance and time, provided the start time of movement

After performing the steps of the algorithm found a new shortest path $L_1^* = \{1,4,6,8,10\} = (14,19,26), L_2^* = \{1,2,5,9,7,10\} = (13,19,27)$.

Because received 2 shortest routes, then made their simultaneous construction and verification.

We consider the construction route L_1^* by the time parameter:

$$T_0(1,4) = (0,0,0) \notin \tilde{t}_\emptyset;$$
$$T_1(4,6) = (0,0,0) + (2,3,4) = (2,3,4) \notin \tilde{t}_\emptyset;$$
$$T_2(6,8) = (2,3,4) + (1,3,4) = (3,6,8) \in \tilde{t}_\emptyset = (5,6,7,8)$$

As can be seen, the edge (6,8) is absent, therefore, impossible to construct route L_1^*.

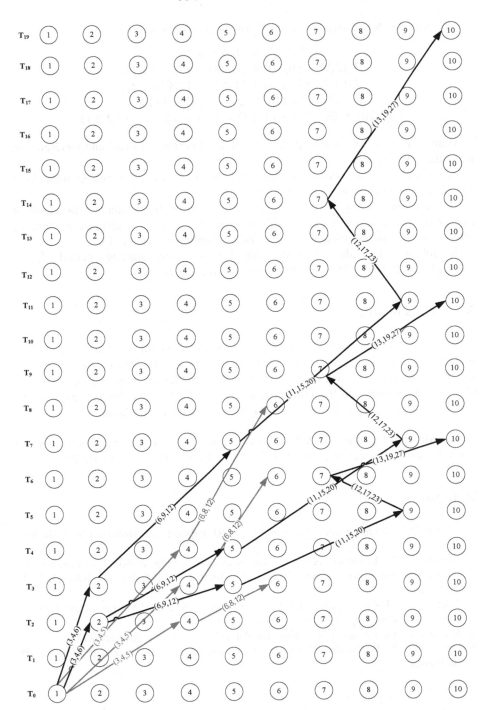

Fig. 4. Illustration of solving the problem of constructing the shortest route, provided the user specified start time (time and distance parameters are fuzzy)

We consider the construction route L_2^* by the time parameter:

$$T_0(1,2) = (0,0,0) \notin \tilde{t}_\varnothing;$$
$$T_1(2,5) = (0,0,0) + (2,2,3) = (2,2,3) \notin \tilde{t}_\varnothing;$$
$$T_2(5,9) = (2,2,3) + (1,2,4) = (3,4,7) \notin \tilde{t}_\varnothing;$$
$$T_3(9,7) = (3,4,7) + (2,3,4) = (5,7,11) \notin \tilde{t}_\varnothing;$$
$$T_3(7,10) = (5,7,11) + (1,2,3) = (6,9,14) \notin \tilde{t}_\varnothing = (1,2,3,4).$$

Hence the edges of shortest path L_2^* exist in all periods of time, and therefore can be built. It is shown in Fig. 4.

As a result, construction of routes received the following decision: route $L_2^* = (13,19,27)$ and the movement of $t = (7,11,19)$.

Because the weights of edges presented a triangular fuzzy number, the result of defuzzification is an extremum of this number [5]. Hence, the distance of route L_2^* after defuzzification is 19, and the time and after defuzzification is 11.

It follows that the shortest path for a given starting period T_0^* is $L_2^* = \{1,2,5,9,7,10\} = 199$ and the time on this route is $t = 11$.

5   Conclusion

In the course of this work was developed procedural model of finding the shortest path. This model is needed to solve the problems of cargo transportation. It is formed because of inaccurate information received for the implementation of stated problem. Can be used information from different sources: maps, Internet services, experts, etc. Therefore, it is appropriate to use fuzzy numbers to solve the problem.

Acknowledgments. This work has been supported by the Russian Foundation for Basic Research, Project № 12-01-00032a and № 13-07-13103 -ofi_m_RRW

References

1. Ivanov, D.A.: Supply Chain Management, p. 660. Polytechnical Institute (2009) (in Russian)
2. Bernstein, L.S., Bozhenuk, A.V.: The use of temporal graphs as models of complex systems. In: Proceedings of the SFU. Technical Engineering, vol. 4(105), pp. 198–203 (2010) (in Russian)
3. Kostakos, V.: Temporal graphs. In: Proc. of Physica A: Statistical Mechanics and its Applications, vol. 388(6), pp. 1007–1023. Elsevier (2008)
4. Maynika, E.: Optimization Algorithms for Networks and Graphs. Springer (1981)
5. Bernstein, L.S., Bozhenuk, A.V.: Fuzzy graphs and hypergraphs. Scientific World (2005) (in Russian)

A Multi-Level Linguistic Fuzzy Decision Network Hierarchical Structure Model for Crop Selection

Basem Mohamed Elomda[1], Hesham Ahmed Hefny[2], Fathy Ashmawy[3],
Maryam Hazman[1], and Hesham Ahmed Hassan[4]

[1] Central Laboratory for Agriculture Expert Systems (CLAES),
Agriculture Research Center (ARC), Cairo, Egypt
{basem,m.hazman}@claes.sci.eg
[2] Institute of Statistical Studies and Research (ISSR), Cairo University, Cairo, Egypt
hehefny@cu.edu.eg
[3] Central Laboratory for Design and Statistical Analysis Research (CLDSAR),
Agriculture Research Center (ARC), Cairo, Egypt
f_ashmawy@hotmail.com
[4] Faculty of Computers and Information (FCI), Cairo University, Cairo, Egypt
h.hassan@fci-cu.edu.eg

Abstract. Cultivate the best crop from many suitable crops is a complex process that faces the decision makers (e.g. farmers, their advisors, and others in the agricultural sector). Their goal is to select a crop which maximizes the resource utilization and in the same time ensures the sustainability for natural agricultural resources. Selecting such crop for cultivating among many suitable alternatives crops is a Multiple Criteria Decision Making (MCDM) problem. Since, the selection for the best decision is dependent in many criteria and having dependence and feedback among them. In this paper Linguistic Fuzzy Decision Network (LFDN) method is developed and applied to a real case study to decide the cultivate crop among four crops-namely: Wheat, Corn, Rice, and Fababean w.r.t given multiple criteria.

Keywords: Multi Criteria Decision Making, Fuzzy Decision Map, Fuzzy Cognitive Map, Linguistic Fuzzy Decision Network, Crop Selection.

1 Introduction

Multiple Criteria Decision Making (MCDM) techniques have been developed during the mid-1960s. It has been a hot area of research in decision theory, operations research, management science and system engineering [1]. MCDM is the process of ranking the feasible alternatives and selecting the best one by considering several/ multiple and conflicting criteria [2]. Many techniques or methods have been developed for solving MCDM problems. In 1996, the Analytic Network Process (ANP) is developed by Saaty for solving MCDM problems to tackle the dependence and feedback problem among criteria in the Analytic Hierarchy Process (AHP) method[3], as extension of AHP proposed by Satty in 1971 [4].

© Springer International Publishing Switzerland 2015
D. Filev et al. (eds.), *Intelligent Systems'2014*,
Advances in Intelligent Systems and Computing 323, DOI: 10.1007/978-3-319-11310-4_43

In 2006, Fuzzy Decision Maps (FDM) method was introduced [5] to address the shortcoming of ANP and AHP method. In 2013, Linguistic Fuzzy Decision Network (LFDN) is proposed to tackle the drawback of FDM method [6, 7]. However, LFDN method provides only the weight of criteria due to it deals only with two level structures namely: goal and criteria. But in practical real world situation, MCDM problems consist of multi-level such as: goal, criteria, sub-criteria, and so on until reach to alternative level. Therefore, the main objective of this paper is to develop LFDN method to take into account the requirement for multi-level hierarchical structure such as, objectives, criteria, sub-criteria and alternatives. Thus, Multi-Level LFDN hierarchical structure (ML-LFDN) is a model for selecting the best alternative when the human expert or Decision Maker (DM) has many criteria. Then, we apply the modified method to the empirical case study to determine the best crop among the four crops with respect to multiple criteria.

This paper is organized as follows: Section 2 presents Fuzzy Cognitive Map (FCM). Section 3 presents the Linguistic Fuzzy Decision Network (LFDN) method. Multi-level LFDN (ML-LFDN) hierarchy structure model is explained in section 4. A case study is given in section 5. Finally, the conclusion is in section 6.

2   Fuzzy Cognitive Map (FCM)

In 1986, Kosko introduced Fuzzy Cognitive Map (FCM) model [8] as an extension of cognitive map model proposed by Axelrod in 1976 [9]. FCM supported MCDM with dependence and feedback [5, 6, 7]. Also, FCM with linguistic values in the form of Triangular Fuzzy Number (TFN) can be used as a tool to forecast the future state of the system [10]. A FCM has the topology of fuzzy weighted causal directed graphs with feedback as in Fig 1. Fig 1 illustrates a graphical representation of a FCM consisting of five concepts (or Criteria) namely C_1, C_2, C_3, C_4, and C_5. These criteria are connected by weights. The causal relationships between two concepts (described as edges or directed arcs) are described using a degree of influence i.e., W_{ij}. Human experts describe these degrees of influence using fuzzy/linguistic values in the form of TFN's as in table 1. The influence among criteria is calculated by the fuzzy updating equation as in Eq. (2) [6, 7]. After drawing linguistic FCM to indicate the influence among criteria, linguistic FCM as in Fig. 1 is converted to the fuzzy weight/ adjacency matrix as in Eq. (1).

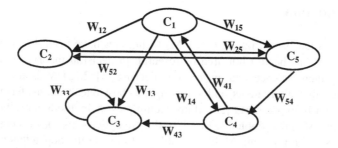

Fig. 1. FCM graph example

Table 1. Linguistic values and corresponding TFN for causal relations between events [7]

linguistic values	TFN
No influence	(0,0,0)
Weak influence (W)	(0,0,0.25)
Medium Weak influence (MW)	(0,0.25,0.5)
Medium influence (M)	(0.25,0.5,0.75)
Medium strong influence (MS)	(0.5,0.75,1)
Strong influence (S)	(0.75,1,1)

$$\tilde{E} = \begin{bmatrix} (0,0,0) & W_{12} & W_{13} & W_{14} & W_{15} \\ (0,0,0) & (0,0,0) & (0,0,0) & (0,0,0) & W_{25} \\ (0,0,0) & (0,0,0) & W_{33} & (0,0,0) & (0,0,0) \\ W_{41} & (0,0,0) & W_{43} & (0,0,0) & W_{45} \\ (0,0,0) & W_{52} & (0,0,0) & W_{54} & (0,0,0) \end{bmatrix} \tag{1}$$

$$\tilde{C}^{(t+1)} = f\left(\tilde{C}^{(t)} \cdot \tilde{E} \right), \quad \tilde{C}^{(0)} = \tilde{I}_{n \times n} \tag{2}$$

Where $\tilde{I}_{n \times n}$ denotes the fuzzy identity matrix with TFN, $\tilde{E} = [\tilde{W}_{ij}]$ is $n \times n$ fuzzy weight matrix with TFNs, which gathers the values of causal edge weights between concept $\tilde{C}_i$ and $\tilde{C}_j$, $\tilde{C}^{(t+1)}$ is the fuzzy state matrix with TFN at certain iteration (t+1), $\tilde{C}^{(0)}$ is the fuzzy initial matrix with TFN and $\tilde{C}^{(t)}$ is the fuzzy state matrix with TFN at certain iteration (t), and f is a fuzzy threshold transformation function with TFN. There are different fuzzy threshold transformation functions that have been used by researchers [6, 7], [10].

Once the linguistic FCM has been created, it is run directly using Eq. (2). In each step of cycling, the values of the concepts change according to Eq. (2). After very little iteration, it will reach to fuzzy steady state (equilibrium state) if one of the following cases occurs [10]:

- *A fuzzy fixed point attractor:* This case is reached when the FCM state vector remains fixed for successive iterations, for example, $\tilde{A}_1 \rightarrow \tilde{A}_2 \rightarrow \tilde{A}_3 \rightarrow \tilde{A}_3 \rightarrow \tilde{A}_3$ where the fuzzy vector $\tilde{A}_3$ is known as the fuzzy fixed point attractor.
- *A fuzzy limit cycle:* A sequence of FCM state vector keeps repeating forming a cycle, for example, $\tilde{A}_1 \rightarrow \tilde{A}_2 \rightarrow \tilde{A}_3 \rightarrow \tilde{A}_4 \rightarrow \tilde{A}_5 \rightarrow \tilde{A}_3 \rightarrow \tilde{A}_4 \rightarrow \tilde{A}_5$ where the three fuzzy vector $\tilde{A}_3 \rightarrow \tilde{A}_4 \rightarrow \tilde{A}_5$ forming a cycle is known as the fuzzy limit cycle.

3   Linguistic Fuzzy Decision Network (LFDN) Method

LFDN method is proposed for solving MCDM problem to address the uncertainty situations, an extension of FDM. It calculates the global fuzzy weights among criteria. The LFDN process to derive criteria priorities can be summarized as follows [6, 7]:

Step 1: *Calculate the Local Fuzzy Weight (LFW) vector* ($\tilde{L}$).
In this step, the Linguistic/Fuzzy Pair-wise Comparison Matrix (LPCM) among criteria is constructed. Therefore, Eq. (3) is applied to derive the LFW. LFW represents the fuzzy priority weights of the criteria without considering any dependence or feedback among criterion. Finally, the gained LFW is normalized.

$$\tilde{L}_i = \sum_{j=1}^{n} a_{ij} = \left(\sum_{j=1}^{n} l_{ij}, \sum_{j=1}^{n} m_{ij}, \sum_{j=1}^{n} u_{ij} \right), \quad i = 1,....,n \tag{3}$$

Step 2: *Calculate the fuzzy influence weight matrix among criteria*
In this step, the FCM with linguistic values is depicted, and transformed into linguistic adjacency matrix as Eq. (1). The linguistic adjacency matrix is converted to TFN using Table1. Thus, the fuzzy updating equation as given in Eq. (2) is applied to derive the fuzzy steady-state matrix ($\tilde{C}^*$). $\tilde{C}^*$ represents the fuzzy causal relationship among criteria. Finally, the obtained fuzzy steady-state matrix is normalized.

Step 3: *Calculate the Global Fuzzy Weight (GFW) vector.*
In this step, the fuzzy weighting equation as in Eq. (4) is used to derive GFW. GFW represents the priority weights of the criteria by considering dependence and feedback among criterion. Finally, the obtained GFW ($\tilde{G}$)is normalized.

The highest priority of criteria is obtained by ranking GFW. Therefore, the Center Of Area (COA) defuzzification method as in Eq. (5) is applied to convert a vector of TFNs such as GFW to crisp value.

$$\tilde{G} = \tilde{L}_n + \tilde{C}_n^* \tilde{L}_n \tag{4}$$

$$D(\tilde{x}) = (1 + m + u)/3 \tag{5}$$

Where ($\tilde{L}_n$) is the normalization of the LFW and ($\tilde{C}_n^*$) is the normalization of the fuzzy steady-state matrix.

4   Multi-Level LFDN Hierarchy Structure (ML-LFDN) Model

The LFDN is a method for solving MCDM problems in fuzzy environment which have dependent and feedback. Unfortunately, it can't deal with multi-level hierarchical structure. Therefore, LFDN method is developed to address the need for consideration the multi-level hierarchical structure case that consists of goal, criteria, sub- criteria, sub sub-criteria, etc. down to the lowest level i.e., alternatives level.
ML-LFDN process can be represented as follows:

Step 1: *Identify and clarify the nature of the problem which will be solved*

Step 2: *Build a hierarchy model of elements*
This step includes constructing the ML-LFDN model. A ML-LFDN contains of an overall goal, a criteria/ factors group that based on the goal, a group of alternatives/options that based on the alternatives for reaching the goal. The criteria can be

further divided down into sub-criteria, sub-sub criteria, and so on, for any number of levels as the problem requires. After the hierarchy structure is created completely as in Fig. 2, the overall weights among elements (criteria, sub-criteria, and alternative) at each level of hierarchy will be derived as shown in step 3, step 4, step 5, step 6 and step 7 respectively. Fig. 2 illustrates ML-LFDN Hierarchical Structure model.

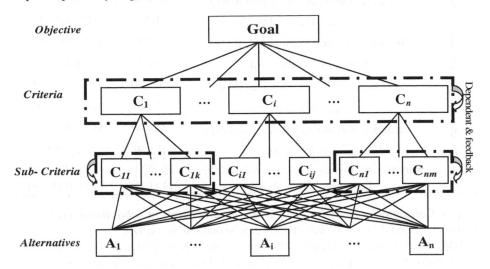

Fig. 2. ML-LFDN Hierarchical Structure model

Step 3: *Calculate the GFW for criteria in the criteria level*
The following steps are executed to derive the GFW:

- DMs will be constructed linguistic pairwise comparisons matrix (LPCM) at criteria level of the hierarchy regarding to their relative significance with first/Goal level. LPCM in the ML-LFDN assume that the DM can compare any two elements C_i, C_n at the same level of the hierarchy and provide a linguistic value a_{ij} for the ratio of their importance using table 2. Table 2 illustrates the linguistic preference scale for ML-LFDN. Once LPCM among criteria have been determined by using a scale i.e., LPCM among $(C_1,.., C_i, ..., C_n)$ w.r.t goal. Then, the LFW is derived using the fuzzy eigenvalue method as in Eq. (3).
- Once the FCM is drawn, DM uses table 1 to indicate the influence degree among criteria. Then, the fuzzy influence among criteria is calculated using Eq. (2) with fuzzy logistic transformation function as in Eq. (6). Therefore, the FGW for criteria is obtained using Eq. (4).

$$f(\tilde{x}) = \left(1/1+e^{-x_l}, 1/1+e^{-x_m}, 1/1+e^{-x_u}\right), \quad \tilde{x} = \left(x_l, x_m, x_u\right) \tag{6}$$

Table 2. Linguistic preference scale for pair-wise comparison

fuzzy scale	Definition of fuzzy values	TFN scale	TFN reciprocal scale
$\tilde{1}$	Equally Preferred (EP)	(1,1,1)	(1 , 1 , 1)
$\tilde{2}$	Equally to Weakly Preferred (EWP)	(1, 2, 3)	(1/3, 1/2 ,1)
$\tilde{3}$	Weakly Preferred (WP)	(1,3,5)	(1/5, 1/3 ,1)
$\tilde{4}$	Weakly to Moderately Preferred (WMP)	(2, 4, 6)	(1/6, 1/4 ,1/2)
$\tilde{5}$	Moderately Preferred (MP)	(3,5,7)	(1/7, 1/5,1/3)
$\tilde{6}$	Moderately to strongly Preferred (MSP)	(4, 6, 8)	(1/8, 1/6 ,1/4)
$\tilde{7}$	Strongly Preferred (SP)	(5,7,9)	(1/9,1/ 7,1/5)
$\tilde{8}$	Strongly to very strongly Preferred (SVSP)	(6, 8, 9)	(1/9, 1/8 ,1/6)
$\tilde{9}$	Very strongly Preferred (VSP)	(7,9,9)	(1/9,1/ 9,1/7)
$\tilde{10}$	Very strongly to extremely Preferred (VSXP)	(8,10,11)	(1/11,1/ 10,1/8)
$\tilde{11}$	Extremely Preferred (XP)	(9,11,11)	(1/11,1/ 11,1/9)

Step 4: *Calculate the FGW for each group of sub-criteria in sub-criteria level*
In this step, the GFW for all sub-criteria can be derived as follows:

- DM will compare each group of the sub-criteria w.r.t its parent criteria in the higher/criteria level i.e., a set of LPCM is constructed, where each element in a criteria level is used to compare its children elements/ sub-criteria w.r.t it. This process will be continuous until all elements in sub-criteria level are compared. Once all LPCM in sub-criteria level are created i.e., LPCM among $(C_{11},..., C_{1k})$ w.r.t C_1 , LPCM among $(C_{i1},..., C_{ij})$ w.r.t C_i, and until LPCM among $(C_{n1},..., C_{nm})$ w.r.t C_n, the LFW for each group of sub- criteria will be obtained using the fuzzy eigenvalue method as in Eq. (3).

- DM will depict a FCM for each group of the sub-criteria having dependent and feedback i.e., depict a FCM among elements $(C_{11},..., C_{1k})$, and for each group of sub-criteria having dependent and feedback till for $(C_{n1},..., C_{nm})$. Then, FCM with linguistic values is applied as in Eq. (2), with fuzzy logistic transformation function as in Eq. (6) for each one of FCM to get the influence among sub-criteria. Thus, the FGW will be obtained for each group of the sub-criteria using Eq. (4). While, for groups of sub-criteria that haven't dependent and feedback among them, the FCM step is ignored in the sub criteria level groups. For example group $(C_{i1},..., C_{ij})$ in Fig. 2 haven't dependent and feedback. In this case, the GFW is becomes equal to LFW.

Step 5: *Calculate the final fuzzy weight for sub-criteria in sub-criteria level*
GFW for criteria (C_i) is multiplied by GFW of its sub-criteria (C_{ij}) in the subsequent lower level to get final fuzzy weight vector for sub-criteria (β) as follows:

$$\beta = [\beta_i]^T , \quad i=1,............,n \qquad (7)$$

$$\beta = GFW(C_i) * \beta_{ij} \quad i = 1,......,n \qquad (8)$$

$$\beta_i = [GFW(C_i) * \beta_{i1}, GFW(C_i) * \beta_{i2}, \ldots, GFW(C_i) * \beta_{ij}, \ldots, GFW(C_i) * \beta_{im}] \tag{9}$$

$$\beta_{ij} = GFW(C_{ij}) \quad j = (1, \ldots, m) \tag{10}$$

Where β_i is the final fuzzy weight value of criteria (C_i), β_{ij} is the final fuzzy weight value of sub criteria (C_{ij}), and β is the final fuzzy weight vector of sub criteria.

Step 6: *Calculate the fuzzy weight for alternatives*
In this step, the LFW for alternatives can be derived as follows:

DM will be performed LPCM among alternatives w.r.t each sub-criteria in the higher level i.e., construct a set of LPCM among alternatives, where each element in a sub-criteria level is used to compare the elements/alternatives immediately below w.r.t it. For example, concerning the importance w.r.t elements (C_{11}), we constructed a n x n LPCM containing our comparison element $(A_1, \ldots, A_i, \ldots, A_n)$. This process will be continuous till all alternatives are compared regarding to each sub-criteria. Once all LPCM among alternatives are created, the fuzzy eigenvalue method will be used to derive the LFW for the alternatives with regard to each sub- criteria.

Step 7: *Calculate the final fuzzy weight for alternative w.r.t its parent*
In the final step, the fuzzy weight matrix as in Eq. (11) consists of the obtained LFW vectors for the alternatives w.r.t each sub-criterion. Then, the final fuzzy weight vector for alternative (ϖ) can be derived as given in Eq. (12).

$$\delta = \begin{array}{c} \\ A_1 \\ \\ A_i \\ \\ A_n \end{array} \begin{bmatrix} \tilde{\omega}(A_1) & \cdots & \tilde{\omega}(A_1) & \tilde{\omega}(A_1) & \cdots & \tilde{\omega}(A_1) & \tilde{\omega}(A_1) & \cdots & \tilde{\omega}(A_1) \\ & \vdots & & \vdots & \vdots & \vdots & \vdots & & \vdots \\ \tilde{\omega}(A_i) & \cdots & \tilde{\omega}(A_i) & \tilde{\omega}(A_i) & \cdots & \tilde{\omega}(A_i) & \tilde{\omega}(A_i) & \cdots & \tilde{\omega}(A_i) \\ \vdots & \vdots & & \vdots & \vdots & \vdots & \vdots & \vdots & \vdots \\ \tilde{\omega}(A_n) & \cdots & \tilde{\omega}(A_n) & \tilde{\omega}(A_n) & \cdots & \tilde{\omega}(A_n) & \tilde{\omega}(A_n) & \cdots & \tilde{\omega}(A_n) \end{bmatrix} \tag{11}$$

$$\varpi = \delta \cdot \beta \tag{12}$$

Finally, the final fuzzy weight vector for alternative (ϖ) is ranked using COA as in Eq. (5) to determine the alternative with highest priority.

5   Case Study

In order to test the developed model, it has been used to solve a real life problem in agricultural to choose the best crop among available crops for cultivation in their fields in Egypt. Agricultural domain experts are asked to use the proposed model to solve their complex problem as follows:

Step 1: *Identify and clarify the nature of the problem which will be solved*
Agricultural expert tries to cultivate a crop according to the following four criteria: Temperature, Water, Marketing and Soil for choosing the best alternative from the following crops Wheat, Corn, Rice, and Fababean.

Step 2: *Build a hierarchy model of elements*
Fig. 3 shows the ML-LFDN hierarchical structure model for the crop selection problem. The goal of our problem in selecting for cultivated crop in Egypt is identified in the first level. The second/criteria level contains: Temperature, Water, Soil and Marketing. The third level (or the lowest level) of the hierarchy contains of the alternatives, which are the different types of crop to be evaluated in order to select the best crop.

Step 3: *Calculate the GFW for criteria in the criteria level*
In this step, the expert compares the importance among criteria using the fuzzy importance scale, given in table 2 to compare any two criteria by the question "How important or strongly". Therefore, the LPCM among criteria is given in table 3. Table 3 is converted to table 4 by substituting the corresponding TFNs for each linguistic value and reciprocal TFNs using table 2. Table 4 shows pairwise comparison matrix among criteria with TFNs. Therefore, the local fuzzy weights vector for each criterion is derived using Eq. (5). So, the local fuzzy weight vector ($\tilde{L}$) is:

$$\tilde{L} = ((0.311, 0.486, 0.797), (0.6, 0.941, 1.538), (0.65, 1, 1.538), (0.066, 0.084, 0.123))^T$$

The expert draws the FCM with linguistic values to indicate the influence among criteria. The fuzzy relationships between concepts are described using a degree of influence. Expert describes this degree of influence using table 1. Therefore, The FCM for the considered case study is shown in Fig. 4. The adjacency matrix obtained from FCM with linguistic values ($\tilde{E}$) is shown in table 5. The fuzzy adjacency matrix is transformed to the adjacency matrix with TFNs using table 1. Table 6 illustrates the adjacency matrix with TFNs. The fuzzy updating equation as Eq. (2) is applied to obtain the fuzzy steady state-matrix. Table 7 shows the fuzzy steady-state matrix using fuzzy logistic transformation function. Therefore, we can derive the global fuzzy weights ($\tilde{G}$) for criteria in criteria level as:

$$\tilde{G}(Criteria) = ((0.679, 1.154, 2.014), (0.956, 1.593, 2.72), (1.016, 1.668, 2.738), (0.397, 0.397, 1.205))^T$$

Thus, defuzzifiy the GFW vector to get the ranking among criteria using Eq. (5) as:

$$D(\tilde{G}_n) = (1.282, 1.756, 1.807, 0.666)^T$$

It is found that, the selection criterion with highest priority is **Water**, while the criterion with lowest priority is **marketing**.

Step 4: *Calculate the FGW for each group of sub-criteria in sub-criteria level*
Step 5: *Calculate the final fuzzy weight for sub-criteria in sub-criteria level*
Since there is no sub-criteria level in the original definition of the problem, then there is no need to go through these steps. Therefore we are going to step 6.

Step 6: *Calculate the fuzzy weight for alternatives*
In this step, the expert compares the importance among alternatives w.r.t the corresponding elements in the higher level (i.e., for each criterion in criteria level), obtaining a LPCM. For Example, in terms of Temperature pairwise comparisons, determine

the preference of each alternative over another. Table 8 shows LPCM among alternatives w.r.t Temperature criteria. LPCM is converted to pairwise comparison matrix with TFN as in table 9 using table 2. Also, table 10, table 11, and table 12, shows linguistic pairwise comparison matrix among alternative w.r.t criteria Soil, Water and Marketing respectively. Now, Eq. (3) is applied to get the LFW for alternative w.r.t parent criteria in the upper level. So, the obtained LFW for the alternatives w.r.t. each criterion is given as in Eq. (13). So, the ranking for all alternatives w.r.t. Temperature, Soil, Water and Marketing respectively using COA method are shown in table 13. Thus, from tables 13, it is clear that, the selection criterion with highest priority is **Corn/ Rice** w.r.t Temperature, **Rice** w.r.t Soil, **Wheat** w.r.t Water, and **Rice** w.r.t Marketing respectively.

Step 7: *Calculate the final fuzzy weight for alternative w.r.t its parent*
In this step, the final fuzzy weight vector (ϖ) for alternative is derived using Eq. (12). So, the fuzzy weights vector is ranked using COA method as in Eq. (5). Table 14 illustrates the final ranking of the obtained fuzzy weight vector for alternative. Thus, from tables 14 it is found that the selection criterion with highest priority is **Rice**, while the criterion with lowest priority is **Fababean.**

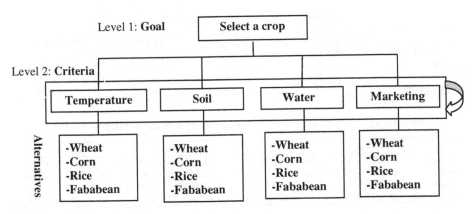

Fig. 3. ML-LFDN hierarchical structure model for crop selection problem

Table 3. LPCM among criteria w.r.t **goal**

	Temperature	Soil	Water	Marketing
Temperature	EP			SP
Soil	SP	EP	EP	SP
Water	SVSP		EP	SP
Marketing				EP

Table 4. Pairwise comparison matrix with **TFNs**

	Temperature	Soil	Water	Marketing
Temperature	(1, 1, 1)	(1/9,1/ 7,1/5)	(1/9, 1/8 ,1/6)	(5,7,9)
Soil	(5,7,9)	(1, 1, 1)	(1,1,1)	(5,7,9)
Water	(6, 8, 9)	(1, 1, 1)	(1, 1, 1)	(5,7,9)
Marketing	(1/9,1/ 7,1/5)	(1/9,1/ 7,1/5)	(1/9,1/ 7,1/5)	(1, 1, 1)

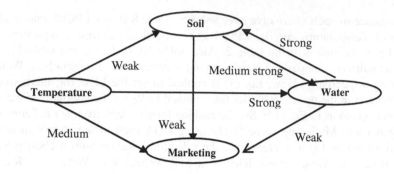

Fig. 4. FCM with linguistic values among criteria for crop selection

Table 5. Adjacency matrix with **linguistic values** (Ẽ) obtained from FCM in Fig. 4

	Temperature	Soil	Water	Marketing
Temperature	No influence	Weak	Strong	Medium
Soil	No influence	No influence	Medium Strong	Weak
Water	No influence	Strong	No influence	weak
Marketing	No influence	No influence	No influence	No influence

Table 6. Adjacency matrix with TFNs (Ẽ)

	Temperature	Soil	Water	Marketing
Temperature	(0,0,0)	(0,0,0.25)	(0.75,1,1))	(0.25,0.5,0.75)
Soil	(0,0,0)	(0,0,0)	(0.5,0.75,1)	(0,0,0.25)
Water	(0,0,0)	(0.75,1,1)	(0,0,0)	(0,0,0.25)
Marketing	(0,0,0)	(0,0,0)	(0,0,0)	(0,0,0)

Table 7. Fuzzy steady-state matrix ($\tilde{C}^*$) using **fuzzy logistic** transformation function

	Temp.	Soil	Water	Marketing
Temp.	(0.5,0.5,0.5)	(0.647,0.708,0.783)	(0.809,0.884,0.907))	(0.593,0.679,0.824)
Soil	(0.5,0.5,0.5)	(0.640,0.702,0.737)	(0.768,0.855,0.903)	(0.531,0.562,0.738)
Water	(0.5,0.5,0.5)	(0.779,0.853,0.872)	(0.682,0.758,0.798)	(0.531,562,0.739)
Marketing	(0.5,0.5,0.5)	(0.622,0.675,0.709)	(0.665,0.732,0.770)	(0.531,0.562,0.678)

Table 8. LPCM among alternatives w.r.t **Temperature** criteria

	Wheat	Corn	Rice	Fababean
Wheat	EP	EP		EP
Corn		EP	EP	MP
Rice	MP		EP	EP
Fababean				EP

Table 9. Pairwise comparison matrix with TFNs among alternatives w.r.t **Temperature**

	Wheat	Corn	Rice	Fababean
Wheat	(1,1,1)	(1,1,1)	(1/3, 1/5,1/7)	(1,1,1)
Corn	(1,1,1)	(1,1,1)	(1,1,1)	(3,5,7)
Rice	(3,5,7)	(1,1,1)	(1,1,1)	(1,1,1)
Fababean	(1,1,1)	(1/3, 1/5,1/7)	(1,1,1)	(1,1,1)

Table 10. LPCM among alternatives w.r.t **Soil** criteria

	Wheat	Corn	Rice	Fababean
Wheat	EP		EP	MSP
Corn	SP	EP		
Rice		MSP	EP	MSP
Fababean		SP		EP

Table 11. LPCM among alternatives w.r.t **Water** criteria

	Wheat	Corn	Rice	Fababean
Wheat	EP	SP	SP	EP
Corn		EP	SP	EP
Rice			EP	
Fababean			MSP	EP

Table 12. LPCM among alternatives w.r.t. **Marketing** criteria

	Wheat	Corn	Rice	Fababean
Wheat	EP	SVSP		MSP
Corn		EP		MSP
Rice	SVSP	SP	EP	SP
Fababean				EP

$$
\delta = \begin{array}{c} \text{Wheat} \\ \text{Corn} \\ \text{Rice} \\ \text{Fababean} \end{array}
\begin{bmatrix}
\text{Temperature} & \text{Soil} & \text{Water} & \text{Marketing} \\
(0.314,0.4,0.555) & (0.339,0.582,1.02) & (0.6,1,1.667) & (0.399,0.658,1.069) \\
(0.6,1,1.666) & (0.346,0.594,1.045) & (0.356,0.571,0.933) & (0.187,0.316,0.551) \\
(0.6,1,1.666) & (0.5555,1,1.8) & (0.067,0.091,0.138) & (0.6071,1,1.6470) \\
(0.314,0.4,0.555) & (0.347,0.595,1.05) & (0.35,0.563,0.917) & (0.049,0.064,0.1)
\end{bmatrix}
\tag{13}
$$

Table 13. The ranking of the crisp weight vector for alternatives w.r.t each criterion

Crisp Weights	Temperature		Soil		Water		Marketing	
	COA Value	Ranking	COA Value	Ranking	COA Value	Ranking	COA Value	Ranking
Wheat	0.423	2	0.647	4	1.089	1	0.708	2
Corn	1.089	1	0.662	3	0.620	2	0.351	3
Rice	1.089	1	1.118	1	0.099	4	1.085	1
Fababean	0.423	2	0.664	2	0.609	3	0.071	4

Table 14. The ranking of the final fuzzy weight vector (ϖ) for alternative

The final weight (ϖ)	Fuzzy value	COA value	Ranking
Wheat	(1.305, 3.317, 9.744)	4.789	2
Corn	(1.174, 3.178, 9.417)	4.589	3
Rice	(1.248, 3.296, 10.612)	5.052	1
Fababean	(0.921, 2.373, 6.605)	3.299	4

6   Conclusion

Linguistic Fuzzy Decision Network (LFDN) method has been proposed to overcome the drawback of Fuzzy Decision Map (FDM) method. However, it can't rank the actions/alternative to select the appropriate alternative. So, in this paper, we propose an improved LFDN method, called Multi-Level LFDN hierarchical structure (ML-LFDN) model. The proposed ML-LFDN model is examined through a crop selection case study, which cannot be solved using the original LFDN model. The obtained results ensured the effectiveness of ML-LFDN model. As a future work, make complex problem are planned to be solved using the proposed model.

References

1. Zhenghai, A.: A new TOPSIS with triangular fuzzy number and uncertain weight based on cosines similar degree. In: Eighth IEEE International Conference on Computational Intelligence and Security (CIS), China, November 17-18, pp. 17–21 (2012)
2. Zhang, S.-F., Liu, S.-Y., Zhai, R.-H.: An extended GRA method for MCDM with interval-valued triangular fuzzy assessments and unknown weights. Computers & Industrial Engineering 61, 1336–1341 (2011)
3. Saaty, T.L.: Decision making with dependence and feedback: The analytic network process. RWS Publications, Pittsburgh (1996)
4. Saaty, T.L.: The analytic hierarchy process. McGraw-Hill, New York (1980)
5. Yu, R., Tzeng, G.H.: A soft computing method for multi-criteria decision making with dependence and feedback. Applied Mathematics and Computation 180, 63–75 (2006)
6. Elomda, B.M., Hefny, H.A., Hassan, H.A.: An extension of fuzzy decision maps for multi-criteria decision-making. Egyptian Informatics Journal 14, 147–155 (2013)
7. Elomda, B.M., Hefny, H.A., Hassan, H.A.: MCDM method based on improved fuzzy decision map. In: IEEE International Conference on Electronics, Circuits, and Systems (ICECS 2013), Abu Dhabi, UAE, December 8-11, pp. 225–228 (2013)
8. Kosko, B.: Fuzzy cognitive maps. International Journal on Man–Machine Studies 24(1), 65–75 (1986)
9. Axelrod, R.: Structure of decision: the cognitive maps of political elites. Princeton University Press, Princeton (1976)
10. Elomda, B.M., Hefny, H.A., Hassan, H.A.: Fuzzy cognitive map with linguistic values. In: IEEE International Conference on Engineering and Technology (ICET 2014), Cairo, Egypt, April 19-20 (2014)

Community Detection Algorithm Based on Artificial Fish Swarm Optimization

Eslam Ali Hassan[1,3], Ahmed Ibrahem Hafez[2,3], Aboul Ella Hassanien[1,3], and Aly A. Fahmy[1]

[1] Faculty of Computers and Information, Cairo University, Egypt
eslam.ali@fci-cu.edu.eg,{aboitcairo,aly.fahmy}@gmail.com
[2] Faculty of Computer and Information, Minia University, Egypt
ah.hafez@gmail.com
[3] Scientific Research Group in Egypt (SRGE)
http://www.egyptscience.net

Abstract. Community structure identification in complex networks has been an important research topic in recent years. Community detection can be viewed as an optimization problem in which an objective quality function that captures the intuition of a community as a group of nodes with better internal connectivity than external connectivity is chosen to be optimized. In this paper Artificial Fish Swarm optimization (AFSO) has been used as an effective optimization technique to solve the community detection problem with the advantage that the number of communities is automatically determined in the process. However, the algorithm performance is influenced directly by the quality function used in the optimization process. A comparison is conducted between different popular communities' quality measures and other well-known methods. Experiments on real life networks show the capability of the AFSO to successfully find an optimized community structure based on the quality function used.

Keywords: Networks community detection, Community detection, Social Networks, Fish Swarm optimization.

1 Introduction

A social network is a graph made of nodes that are connected by one or more specific types of relationships, such as values, friendship, work. The goal of community detection in networks is to identify the communities by only using the information embedded in the network topology. Many methods have been developed for the community detection problem. These methods use tools and techniques from disciplines like physics, biology, applied mathematics, and computer and social sciences [1].

One of the special interests in social network analysis is finding community structure. Community is a group of nodes that are tightly connected to each other and loosely connected with other nodes. Community detection is the process of network clustering into similar groups or clusters. Community detection

© Springer International Publishing Switzerland 2015
D. Filev et al. (eds.), *Intelligent Systems'2014*,
Advances in Intelligent Systems and Computing 323, DOI: 10.1007/978-3-319-11310-4_44

has many applications including realization of the network structure, detecting communities of special interest, visualization [2], etc [3].

One of the novel techniques in community detection is Girvan-Newman (GN) algorithm [4]. Girvan-Newman is a divisive technique that uses the edge betweenness as a measure to identify the boundaries of communities. This metric detects the edges between communities by counting the number of shortest paths between two particular nodes that passes through a special edge or node. Later on Girvan and Newman introduced a new technique called Modularity [5]. Modularity measures the quality of a partition of the network, where high Modularity indicates strong community structure that has dense inter-connections between the community nodes, Therefore the community detection problem became a Modularity Maximization problem. Finding the optimal Modularity is an NP-Complete problem, a lot of heuristic search techniques have been investigated to solve this problem such as genetic algorithm (GA), simulated annealing, artificial bee colony optimization (ABC) [1].

The remainder of this paper is organized as follows. In Section 2 we define the community problem and introduce the objective functions used in the research. In Section 3 we describe The Basic AFSO algorithm. In Section 4 we describe our proposed algorithm. Section 5 shows our experimental result on real life social networks. We then offer conclusions in section 6.

2   The Community Detection Problem

A social network can be modeled as a graph $G = (V, E)$, where V is a set of nodes, and E is a set of edges that connect two elements of V. A community structure S in a network is a set of groups of nodes having a high density of edges among the nodes and a lower density of edges between different groups. The problem of detecting k communities in a network, where the number k is unknown can be formulated as finding a partitioning of the nodes in k subsets that best satisfy a given a quality measure of communities $\mathbf{F}(S)$. The problem can be viewed as an optimization problem in which one usually wants to optimize the given quality measure $\mathbf{F}(S)$. A single objective optimization problem $(\Omega;\mathbf{F})$ is defined as in the equation 1.

$$Max \ \mathbf{F}(S), \ s.t \ S \in \Omega \tag{1}$$

Where $\mathbf{F}(S)$ is an objective function that needs to be optimized, and $\Omega=\{S_1, S_2 \ldots, S_k\}$ is the set of feasible community structures in a network. A formal definition of the optimization problem is given in [6].

The objective function plays an important role in the optimization process; it's the "steering wheel" in the process that leads to good solutions. Many objective functions have been proposed to capture the intuition of communities, and there is no straight-forward way to compare these objective functions based on their definitions. We use some objective functions that capture this intuition and/or are popular in the literature, and can potentially be used for community detection which are Modularity [5], Community Score [7] and Community Fitness [8]. A detailed description of objective functions can be found in [9] and a similarity comparison can be found in [9–11]. Community Score and Community Fitness both have a positive real-valued parameter that controls the size of the communities.

3   Artificial Fish Swarm Algorithm

Artificial Fish Swarm Algorithm (AFSA), which was presented by X. L. Li [12], is a new swarm intelligence optimization method by simulating fish swarm behavior. It is becoming a prospective method because of its good performances in solving many applications [13].

Applying to the optimization problem, generally a 'fish' represents an individual point in a population. The fish swarm movements seem randomly defined and yet they are objectively synchronized. Fishes desire to stay close to the swarm, to protect themselves from predators and to look for food, and to avoid collisions within the group. Inspired by these behavior, researchers aim to solve optimization problems in an efficient manner. The behavioral model-based optimization algorithms seek to imitate, as well as to make variations on the swarm behavior such as praying, swarming, and following in nature, and to create new types of abstract movements. The environment in which the artificial fish (AF) lives is mainly the solution space and the states of other artificial fish. Its next behavior depends on its current state and its environmental state (including the quality of the question solutions at present and the states of other companions), and it influences the environment via its own activities and other companions activities [13].

The AF realizes external perception by its vision shown in Figure.1. If the state at the visual position is better than the current state, it goes forward a step in this direction, and arrives at new better state; otherwise, continues an inspecting tour in the vision. The greater number of inspecting tour the AF does, the more knowledge about overall states of the vision the AF obtains. Certainly, it does not need to travel throughout complex or infinite states, which is helpful to find the global optimum by allowing certain local optimum with some uncertainty [13].

Let the state vector of artificial fish x consists of n variables such that $x = (x^1, x^2, \ldots, x^n)$, x be the current state of an AF and x_v is new state or a neighbor AF in the visual of x selected according to equation 2 then the basic movement process can be expressed as in equation 3. Where $rand()$ produces random numbers between zero and 1, $Step$ is the step size of a move and $dis(x_i, x_j)$ is a distance measure between two AFs normally it would be the Euclidean distance for a traditional problem.

$$x_v = x + Visual * rand() \tag{2}$$

$$x_{next} = x + \frac{x_v - x}{dis(x_v, x)} * Step * rand() \tag{3}$$

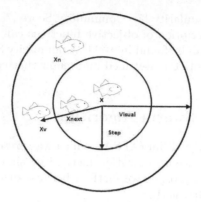

Fig. 1. Shows the Visual and Step of an Artificial Fish

4 Proposed Algorithm

Apply the Basic AFSA directly to the community detection problem is not feasible. The algorithm needs to be redesigned. In this section we describe the modified AFSA so it can be applied to the community detection problem. The algorithm is outlined in listing 1.

4.1 AFSA Parameters Description

The first step of designing an AFSA for solving community detection problem is to devise a suitable representation scheme of an individual AF in a population. The locus-based adjacency encoding scheme [14, 15] is chosen to represent the solution. In this representation, each AF state x consists of n elements $(x^1, x^2, \ldots, x^n)$ and each element can take a value j in the range $[1 .. n]$. A value j assigned to the ith element is interpreted as a link between node i and node j. This means that, in the detected community structure, nodes i and j will be in the same community.

Normally the fish swarm will contain np AFs. The fish current state represents a solution in the search space and the fitness value of the solution represents the amount of food resource at that location. The food concentration in the position of an AF is expressed as $y_i = f(x_i)$, Where y_i is the objective function value associated with x_i. Each AF x_i will have a number of companions np_{fi} which is the number AFs in in x_i's visual satisfying the condition $dis(x_i, x_j) \leq Visual$. The AF x_i' neighborhood field is not crowded and can accommodate more AFs if $np_{fi}/np < \delta$ where δ is the crowd factor which limits the scale of swarms, and more AFs only cluster at the optimal area, which ensures that AF move to optimum in a wide field.

Step: represents the number of modified nodes' membership to move a solution x_i in the direction of a solution x_j as illustrated in Fig.2, where $Step \in [1 .. n]$. The basic movement described in equation 3 can not be applied in our problem. So we use a crossover operator used in Genetic Algorithms [7, 11] where the

Input: A Network $G = (V, E)$
Output: Community membership assignments for network's nodes

1. Initialize the parameters: $Visual$, $Step$, Swarm size np, Crowd Factor δ, eps, the maximum number of iterations $Max\_Iterations$, the number of preying trials try_number

2. Randomly initialize each AF in the swarm with a random possible solution as its current state, and calculate its fitness

3. **repeat**

4.   Memorize the best solution in the swarm

5.   **foreach** x_i *in the swarm* **do**

6.   Calculate the distance between x_i and all other AFs

7.   Calculate np_{fi} and Set x_i's companions

8.   **end**

9.   **foreach** x_i *in the swarm* **do**
           /* Select the appropriate behavior   */

10.   Try Following Behavior

11.   **if** *No improvement* **then**

12.   Try Swarming Behavior

13.   **if** *No improvement* **then**

14.   Try Preying Behavior

15.   **end**

16.   **end**

17.   **end**

18.   **if** $—best\_Solution(\eta)\text{-}best\_Solution(\tau)—\texttt{<}eps$ **then**

19.   Select a random AF from the swarm and execute leaping behavior

20.   **end**

21. $t \leftarrow t + 1$

22. **until** $t > Max\_Iterations$;

23. **return** *the best solution achieved*

Algorithm 1. Artificial fish swarm optimization algorithm

mixing ratio is the $Step$ size of the move. So in order to move an AF x_i to an AF x_j $move(x_i, x_j)$, the two AFs in the crossover operator are considered as the parents of the new offspring (new AF state). Where the new AF state has a randomly chosen $Steps$ optimizing variables from x_j and the rest are from x_i as illustrated in Fig.2.

$Visual$: is a selected constant number $\in [0, 1]$. Since there is no straight way to measure distance between two AFs, we suggested a distance measure $dis(x_i, x_j)$ based on Normalized Mutual Information (NMI) [16] as an indicator on how mush two solutions are closed to each other calculated as in equation 4. NMI is a similarity measure proved to be reliable by Danon et al. [16].

$$dis(x_i, x_j) = 1 - NMI(C(x_i), C(x_j)) \tag{4}$$

where $C(x_i)$ is a functions that decode the AF state back to a community structure and $NMI(c_1, c_2)$ calculate the NMI similarity between two community structures.

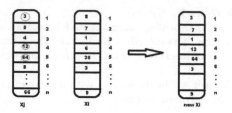

Fig. 2. Shows how the solution X_i moves to the solution X_j with Step of 3

4.2   AFSA Behaviors Description

Preying Behavior: This is a basic behavior that tries to move the food source; generally the fish perceives the concentration of food in water to determine the movement by vision or sense and then chooses the tendency. Let x_i be the AF current state, x_j a randomly select state in x_i's visual where $dis(x_i, x_j) \leq Visual$, and y_i, y_j are the food concentrations (objective function values) related to x_i and x_j respectively, the greater the $Visual$ is, the more easily the AF finds the global extreme value and converges [13]. If $y_i < y_j$ in the maximization problem, it move forward in this direction $move(x_i, x_j)$; Otherwise, select a another state x_j randomly again and judge whether it satisfies the forward condition. If it cannot satisfy after a number of trials try_number, it moves a step randomly. When the try_number is small, the AF can swim randomly, which makes it flee from the local optimum value field.

Swarming Behavior: The fish will assemble in groups naturally in the moving process, which is a kind of living habits in order to guarantee the existence of the colony and avoid dangers. Let x_i be the AF current state, x_c be the center position and np_{fc} be the number of its companions in the current neighborhood where $d_{ij} < Visual$, np is total fish number. If $y_c > y_i$ and $np_{fc}/np < \delta$, which means that the companion center has more food (higher fitness function value) and is not very crowded, then it move to the companion center $move(x_i, x_c)$; Otherwise, executes the preying behavior. Calculating the center position of an AF's companions requires first to calculate the average distance $avgDis_i$ of its companions using equation 5. Then we select the AF with the closest distance value to average distance according to equation 6.

$$avgDis_i = \frac{\sum_j dis(x_i, x_j)}{np_{fi}} \; ; such \; that \; dis(x_i, x_j) < Visual \qquad (5)$$

$$c = argmin_j\{avgDis_i - dis(x_i, x_j)\} \; \forall j \; subject \; to: \; dis(x_i, x_j) \geq avgDis_i \quad (6)$$

Following Behavior: In the moving process of the fish swarm, when a single fish or several ones find food, the neighborhood partners will trail and reach the food quickly. Behavior description: Let x_i be the AF current state, and it explores the companion x_j in the neighborhood, which has the greatest y_j. If $y_j > y_i$ and $np_{fj}/np < \delta$, which means that the companion x_j state has higher food concentration (higher fitness function value) and the surroundings is not very crowded, then x_i goes forward to the companion x_j $move(x_i, x_j)$; Otherwise, executes the preying behavior.

Leaping Behavior: Fish stop somewhere in water, every AF's behavior result will gradually be the same. If the difference of objective values (food concentration,) become smaller within some iterations, this might mean that the AF is falling into local extreme. So if the objective function is almost the same or difference of the objective functions is smaller than a proportion *eps* during a given $(\eta - \tau)$ iterations, then a randomly selected fish in the whole fish swarm performs a random move.

Since the algorithm employs stochastic process to find optimal solution, it may converge to different solutions (non-deterministic). It is therefore not uncommon to run the algorithm multiple T times i.e. number of restarts, starting with initial different population in each iteration (chosen randomly) and then returning the best solution found across all runs according to the objective function used in the optimization process.

5 Experimental Results

In the section we tested our algorithm on a real life social networks for which a ground truth communities partitions is known. To compare the accuracy of the resulting community structures; we used Normalized Mutual Information (NMI) [16] to measure the similarity between the true community structures and the detected ones. Since Modularity is a popular community quality measure used extensively in community detection, we used it as a quality measure for the result community structure of all other objectives.

We applied our algorithm on the following social networks datasets :-

- **The Zachary Karate Club**: which was first analyzed in [17], contains the community structure of a karate club. The network consists of 34 nodes. Due to a conflict between the club president and the karate instructor, the network is divided into two approximately equal groups. The network consists of 34 nodes and 78 edges.
- **The Bottlenose Dolphin network**: was compiled by Lusseau [18] and is based on observations over a period of seven years of the behavior of 62 bottlenose dolphins living in Doubtful Sound, New Zealand. The network split naturally into two large groups.
- **American College football network**: [4] represent football games between American colleges during a regular season in Fall 2000, nodes in the graph represent teams and edges represent regular-season games between the two teams they connect. What makes this network interesting is that it incorporates a known community structure. The teams are divided into conferences containing around 8–12 teams each. Games are more frequent between members of the same conference than between members of different conferences, the network is divided into 12 conferences.
- **Facebook Dataset**: Leskovec [19] collects some data for the Facebook website -10 ego networks-. The data was collected from survey participants using

a Facebook application [9]. The ago network consist of a user's –the ego node– friends and their connections to each other. The 10 Facebook ego networks from [19] are combined into one big network. The result network is undirected network which contain 3959 nodes and 84243 edges. Despite there is no clear community structure for the network, a ground truth structure was suggested in [20].

For each dataset; we applied the algorithm with each objective 10 restarts and calculated the NMI and Modularity value of the best solution selected. This process was repeated 10 times and average NMI and average Modularity is reported. The AFSA algorithm was applied with the following parameters values; $Visual = 0.8$, $Step = 0.2 * n$, Swarm size $np = 50$, Crowd Factor $\delta = 0.3$, $eps = 0.001$, the maximum number of iterations $Max\_Iterations = 100$, and the number of preying trials $try\_number = 10$.

Figure 3a show the average NMI value for each objective when the AFSA is applied with different objectives. Also Fig.3b shows the corresponding average Modularity values for the community structures detected by each objective along with the Modularity value of the ground truth of each network. We can observe that the Modularity objective achieves high NMI values for all social networks. On the other hand; Fitness and Score objectives achieve good NMI values for all social networks except for Bottlenose Dolphin network. The corresponding Modularity value of the community structures detected by Fitness, Modularity and Score objectives are higher than the Modularity value of the ground truth division of those networks as shown in Fig.3b which means in term of Modularity the detected structure is more modular than the original structure.

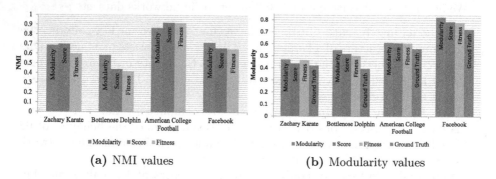

(a) NMI values   (b) Modularity values

Fig. 3. Average NMI and Modularity values of the result community structure by each objective on each real social network

To better understand the behavior of each objective we visualized the detected network divisions produced by each objective on the small size dataset. Figure 4 shows a visualization of the result for the Zachary network. The original division of the network is indicated by the dashed line and the detected structure is indicated by the nodes' colors. All objectives produce a similar result to each other which divide the network into 4 communities with a high Modularity value. The result of Modularity objective is shown in Fig.4a, we can observe in the top level the result is similar to the original division of the network, however in the result structure each group is farther divided into two groups . The result of Fitness is shown in Fig.4b as we can observe in a top level the network is divided into two groups left/right similar the original division of the network however node number 10 is misclassified, farther more each large group is divided into two groups Fig.4b. The result of Score objective is similar to the result of Fitness objective in Fig.4b except of node number 10 is moved to the community on the left.

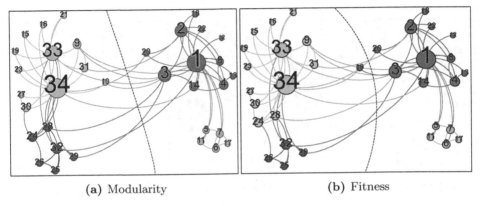

(a) Modularity   (b) Fitness

Fig. 4. Visualizations of the result for the Zachary network obtained by different objectives

Figure 5 visualizes the result for the Dolphin network. Fitness, Modularity and Score objectives as before are able to detected groups which are more community alike with high Modularity value shown in Fig.5a, 5b and 5c respectively.

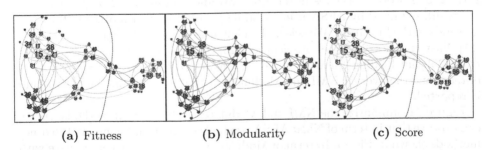

(a) Fitness   (b) Modularity   (c) Score

Fig. 5. Visualizations of the result for the Dolphin network obtained by different objectives

The result obtained for the College football network by different objectives are visualized in Fig.6. The original division of the network into conferences is highlighted in Fig.6a; only edges between nodes from the same group are shown and nodes' labels refer to which groups they belong to. From Fig.6a we can observe that some nodes were assign to its group however they never played any match with other nodes from their group for example group number 5. Fitness and Score objectives produce a similar result shown in 6b. Modularity objective detected a community structure with 10 communities which assigns nodes from the smaller groups (10,5) into a larger groups leading to a more modular structure Fig.6c.

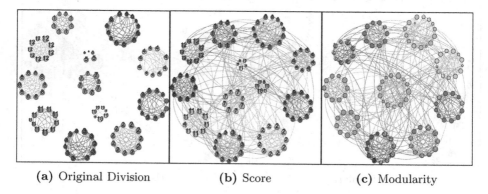

     (a) Original Division   (b) Score   (c) Modularity

Fig. 6. Visualizations of the result for the American College football network obtained by different objectives

5.1 Comparison Analysis

From the previous section, we noticed that the Modularity objective outperforms Fitness and Score objectives in term of NMI and Modularity. Now we compare the result obtained by AFSA using Modularity objective with other well-known methods in the literature. We selected widely used 6-methods which are Infomap [21], Fast greedy [22], Label propagation [23], Maulilevel or Louvain [24], Walktrap [25] and leading Eignvector [26]. Each method is run 10 times for each dataset and the average NMI and Modularity of the result community structure is reported.

Figure.7a summarize the NMI and Modularity values for all methods. As we can observe that in term of NMI; AFSA produce a good result compared to other methods shown in Fig.7a. In term of Modularity; AFSA is very competitive with other methods shown in Fig.7b. For the small size data set we can observe the AFSA produce a community structure with a high Modularity value compared to all other methods. Regarding the Facebook datasets; AFSA competes with other methods with a very small variance.

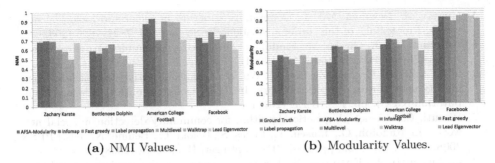

(a) NMI Values.   (b) Modularity Values.

Fig. 7. NMI and Modularity values for each dataset reported by each method

6   Conclusions and Future Work

Artificial Fish Swarm algorithm (AFSA) as an optimization technique works effectively for the community detection problem. However, AFSA's performance is influenced directly by the objective quality function used in the optimization process. Many objective functions have been proposed to capture the intuition of communities which has been used in the literature; hence AFSA was applied with 3 different quality functions as objective functions in order to evaluate their performance which are Community Fitness, Community Score and Modularity. The locus-based adjacency encoding scheme is applied to represent a community structure. The locus-based adjacency encoding scheme has a major advantage that it enables the algorithm to deduce the number of communities k without prior knowledge about it. The results demonstrate that the performance of the proposed approach is promising in terms of accuracy and successfully finds an optimized community structure based on the quality function used. The results show that Modularity objective outperforms the other objectives. A comparison with other popular methods show that AFSA is very competitive with such methods. Visualization of large time varying vector data can utilize importance values in several different ways to, for example, identify unique and abnormal features, enhance visualization as well as enhance both space and time complexity. In the future work, we will focus on studying how to apply our work to visualization problem and address its importance.

References

1. Fortunato, S.: Community detection in graphs. Physics Reports 486, 75–174 (2010)
2. Ali, A.S., Hussien, A.S., Tolba, M.F., Youssef, A.H.: Visualization of large time-varying vector data. In: 2010 3rd IEEE International Conference on Computer Science and Information Technology (ICCSIT), vol. 4, pp. 210–215. IEEE (2010)
3. Masdarolomoor, Z., Azmi, R., Aliakbary, S., Riahi, N.: Finding community structure in complex networks using parallel approach. In: 2011 IFIP 9th International Conference on Embedded and Ubiquitous Computing (EUC), pp. 474–479 (October 2011)

4. Girvan, M., Newman, M.E.J.: Community structure in social and biological networks. Proceedings of the National Academy of Sciences 99, 7821–7826 (2002)
5. Newman, M.E.J., Girvan, M.: Finding and evaluating community structure in networks. Physics Rev. E 69, 026113 (2004)
6. Shi, C., Zhong, C., Yan, Z., Cai, Y., Wu, B.: A multi-objective approach for community detection in complex network. In: IEEE Congress on Evolutionary Computation (CEC), pp. 1–8. IEEE (2010)
7. Pizzuti, C.: GA-net: A genetic algorithm for community detection in social networks. In: Rudolph, G., Jansen, T., Lucas, S., Poloni, C., Beume, N. (eds.) PPSN 2008. LNCS, vol. 5199, pp. 1081–1090. Springer, Heidelberg (2008)
8. Lancichinetti, A., Fortunato, S., Kertesz, J.: Detecting the overlapping and hierarchical community structure of complex networks. arXiv:0805.4770v2 (2008)
9. Leskovec, J., Lang, K.J., Mahoney, M.: Empirical comparison of algorithms for network community detection. In: Proceedings of the 19th International Conference on World Wide Web, pp. 631–640. ACM (2010)
10. Shi, C., Yu, P.S., Cai, Y., Yan, Z., Wu, B.: On selection of objective functions in multi-objective community detection. In: Proceedings of the 20th ACM International Conference on Information and Knowledge Management, pp. 2301–2304. ACM (2011)
11. Hafez, A.I., Al-Shammari, E.T., ella Hassanien, A., Fahmy, A.A.: Genetic algorithms for multi-objective community detection in complex networks. In: Pedrycz, W., Chen, S.-M. (eds.) Social Networks: A Framework of Computational Intelligence. SCI, vol. 526, pp. 145–171. Springer, Heidelberg (2014)
12. Li, X.L., Shao, Z.J., Qian, J.X.: An optimizing method based on autonomous animate: Fish swarm algorithm. System Engineering Theory and Practice 22(11), 32–38 (2002)
13. Neshat, M., Adeli, A., Sepidnam, G., Sargolzaei, M., Toosi, A.N.: A review of artificial fish swarm optimization methods and applications. International Journal on Smart Sensing & Intelligent Systems 5(1), 105 (2012)
14. Shi, C., Zhong, C., Yan, Z., Cai, Y., Wu, B.: A new genetic algorithm for community detection. Complex Sciences 5, 1298–1309 (2009)
15. Pizzuti, C.: Community detection in social networks with genetic algorithms, Atlanta, GA, USA, pp. 1137–1138 (2008)
16. Danon, L., Diaz-Guilera, A., Duch, J., Arenas, A.: Comparing community structure identification. Journal of Statistical Mechanics: Theory and Experiment 9, 09008 (2005)
17. Zachary, W.W.: An information flow model for conflict and fission in small groups. Journal of Anthropological Research 33, 452–473 (1977)
18. Lusseau, D.: The emergent properties of dolphin social network. Proceedings of the Royal Society of London. Series B: Biological Sciences 270, S186–S188 (2003)
19. McAuley, J.J., Leskovec, J.: Learning to discover social circles in ego networks, pp. 548–556 (2012)
20. Hafez, A.I., Hassanien, A.E., Fahmy, A.A.: Testing community detection algorithms: A closer look at datasets. In: Panda, M., Dehuri, S., Wang, G.-N. (eds.) Social Networking. ISRL, vol. 65, pp. 85–99. Springer, Heidelberg (2014)
21. Rosvall, M., Axelsson, D., Bergstrom, C.T.: The map equation. The European Physical Journal Special Topics 178(1), 13–23 (2009)
22. Clauset, A., Newman, M.E.J., Moore, C.: Finding community structure in very large networks. Physical review E 70(6), 066111 (2004)

23. Raghavan, U.N., Albert, R., Kumara, S.: Near linear time algorithm to detect community structures in large-scale networks. Physical Review E 76(3), 36106 (2007)
24. Blondel, V.D., Guillaume, J.-L., Lambiotte, R., Lefebvre, E.: Fast unfolding of communities in large networks. Journal of Statistical Mechanics: Theory and Experiment 2008(10), P10008 (2008)
25. Pons, P., Latapy, M.: Computing communities in large networks using random walks (long version). ArXiv Physics e-prints, 12 (2005)
26. Newman, M.E.J.: Finding community structure in networks using the eigenvectors of matrices. Physical Review E 74(3), 036104 (2006)

Uncertainty Evaluation of pH Measured Using Potentiometric Method

Józef Wiora

Institute of Automatic Control, Silesian University of Technology,
ul. Akademicka 16, 44-100 Gliwice, Poland
jozef.wiora@polsl.pl

Abstract. Determination of pH using a typical glass electrode requires prior calibration in order to determine the electrode parameters. Knowledge about uncertainties of the parameters is insufficient to calculate the uncertainty of measured pH because of existing correlation. In the paper, an example illustrating the problem is presented. Two ways of proper uncertainty assessment are suggested: (1) analytical with removing the correlated variables and (2) numerical using Monte Carlo simulations. The second one seems to be much less time-consuming and allows easier investigations of the uncertainty properties.

Keywords: pH, Uncertainty propagation, Monte Carlo method.

1 Introduction

One of the most common analytical assays is determination of the pH value of a substance. The assay can be conducted using several methods: electrochemical (glass or PVC membrane ion-selective electrode (ISE), ion-selective pH-FET, metal/metal oxide electrode, electroconductive polymer), optical (indicator dye, indicator paper, fibre-optic pH probe) and others. The first one is the most widely used method [1].

A pH measurement performed using an ISE is preceded by calibration experiments. For it, pH standards, known as pH buffers, are used. Obtained electrode parameters are determined with some errors arisen from an inaccuracy of the standards and scatter of results taken during calibrations. The errors propagate to the final pH measurement result. In the paper, the mechanism is described and it is shown how to asses uncertainty of the measurement result.

2 Electrochemical Background

A pH measurement performed with an ISE is classified to potentiometric measurements. The ISE, together with a reference electrode, creates an electrochemical cell. Both electrodes are immersed in an investigated solution. The potential difference between the electrodes is dependent on concentrations of ions present in the solution. The potential of reference electrode may be assumed zero, so only

© Springer International Publishing Switzerland 2015
D. Filev et al. (eds.), *Intelligent Systems'2014*,
Advances in Intelligent Systems and Computing 323, DOI: 10.1007/978-3-319-11310-4_45

the potential of the ISE can be considered. This potential, E, can be described by the Nernst equation [2]:

$$E = E° + S \lg(a) \tag{1}$$

where a is ion activity, $E°$ is the electrode standard potential, S is the electrode slope and lg is decimal logarithm. Parameters $E°$ and S, despite their electrochemical interpretation, are usually determined experimentally [3]. They are, additionally, temperature dependent, but in the paper it is assumed that the temperature is constant during both calibration and measurement. The ion activity is a quantity which is arisen form relation between concentration, c, and activity coefficient, γ, through:

$$a = \gamma \frac{c}{c°} \tag{2}$$

where $c°$ is standard concentration having the same unit as c and value equal to one. The concentration can be expressed as molar concentration (molarity), molality, mass fraction *etc.* and then the activity coefficient has to have adequate form, meaning and value. For diluted water solutions, the activity is very close to the value of molarity expressed in mol/L or molality expressed in mol/kg. The value of activity coefficient is dependent mainly on ion species and ionic strength of solvent but for its accurate predictions, concentration of the ion of interest and other ions present in the solution should also be taken into considerations [4].

Using definition of pH introduced by Sørensen [4,5] and adopted to present-day norms written as

$$pH = - \lg a_{H+} \tag{3}$$

where a_{H+} is the activity of hydrogen ions, the Nernst equation (1) simplifies to:

$$E = E° - S \cdot pH \tag{4}$$

The equation is valid in the pH range limited by upper and lower limits of detection as well as by a value arisen from a presence of interfering ions in the investigated solution [6,7]. An effect of interfering ions should be modelled by much more complex model, such as Nicolsky-Eisenman [8,9], phase-boundary [7] or Nernst-Planck-Poison [10] model. Experimental investigations regarding fitting of the models to experimental data may be simplified using a system allowing automatic dilution of a sample [11]. In the paper and frequently in practical measurements, it is assumed that electrode potential is linearly dependent on pH and the Nernst equation describes the electrode behaviour good enough. It means that only two parameters, $E°$ and S, bind pH with electrode potential. The parameters have to be determined before proper pH measurement. The task is done during calibration of the electrode in at least two pH standards. In case of two-point calibration, the parameters are calculated directly from a set of two Nernst equations; if there are more points, least squares optimization is applied. The pH standards are purchased from manufacturers and have declared accuracy in contrast to standards used in other potentiometric measurements where they have to be produced by yourself and their uncertainty have to be calculated [12].

3   Uncertainty Evaluation

Each measurement result is disturbed. To describe their probabilistic properties, uncertainties are calculated. The most important document describing uncertainty evaluation is GUM [13]. An extension of the document is Supplement 1 [14] describing the evaluation using the Monte Carlo method. The below considerations are performed according to the documents.

To determine the electrode parameters, calibration experiments are performed. After the calibration, a proper pH measurement is done. Before quantitative calculations of uncertainty values, each measurement step should be considered. Let us make the following assumptions: the pH electrode works in its linear range; temperature is constant. The steps look as follows:

1. Calibration experiments are performed using pH standards having true pH values, pH_s, instead of declared values, pH_s^*. The index s indicates standard number. The standards have some uncertainties, $u(pH_s)$. An uncertainty, $u(.)$, describe a set of random variables, $\xi(.)$. Using such notation, the following equation can be written:

$$pH_s = pH_s^* + \xi(pH_s)$$ (5)

The standard may have uncertainty of pH independent on its pH value (very common if all standards are purchased from the same manufacturer) or be varied.

2. The correct potential values, E_s, of electrode immersed in the standards are determined basing on the inaccurate pH standards and true values of electrode slope S and standard potential E°:

$$E_s = E^\circ - S \cdot pH_s$$ (6)

3. The real read potentials of the electrode, E_s^*, are measured using real voltmeter having its maximum permissible error, very often dependent on the voltmeter indication. Additionally, during the measurements, some random errors influence the results. It is possible to assess combined uncertainty of potential measurement $u(E)$. Considering this, the following relationship can be written:

$$E_s^* = E_s + \xi(E)$$ (7)

4. The experimental electrode slope, S^*, and the experimental electrode standard potential, $E^{\circ*}$, are calculated basing on the disturbed potentials, using least squares method as follow:

$$\begin{bmatrix} -S^* \\ E^{\circ*} \end{bmatrix} = (AA^\top)^{-1} A^\top E_s^*$$ (8)

where

$$A = \begin{bmatrix} pH_s^* & 1 \end{bmatrix}$$ (9)

and vectors $E_s^* = \begin{bmatrix} E_1^* & E_2^* & \cdots & E_{s_{max}}^* \end{bmatrix}^\top$, $pH_s^* = \begin{bmatrix} pH_1^* & pH_2^* & \cdots & pH_{s_{max}}^* \end{bmatrix}^\top$ and 1 is a column all-one vector. The index s_{max} means the number of points used in the calibration.

5. During measurement of unknown pH_x, an electrode potential E_x^* is obtained. The potential includes a component derived from $u(E)$:

$$E_x^* = E^\circ - S \cdot pH_x + \xi(E) \qquad (10)$$

6. Basing on the measured potential E_x^* and earlier experimentally determined two electrode parameters S^* and $E^{\circ*}$, the experimental pH value, pH_x^*, is obtained:

$$pH_x^* = \frac{E^{\circ*} - E_x^*}{S^*} = f(E^{\circ*}, E_x^*, S^*) \qquad (11)$$

7. The measurement has an error $\Delta pH_x = pH_x^* - pH_x$ which can be described by uncertainty $u(pH_x)$.

Figure 1 illustrates propagation of uncertainties during measurement of pH, as the cause and effect diagram, according to the above presented reasoning. Two electrode parameters are determined simultaneously basing on the same data, therefore they are marked as a set of parameters: $\{E^{\circ*}, S^*\}$.

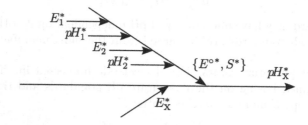

Fig. 1. Cause and effect diagram showing sources of uncertainty associated with the determination of pH by an ion-selective electrode after two-point calibration

3.1   Two-Point Calibration: Exemplary Uncertainty Calculation

In order to illustrate the propagation of uncertainties during pH measurements, an example is presented below. At first, a calibration is conducted and electrode parameters are determined. The parameters include some errors. After calibration, the proper measurement experiment is analysed. It allows one to compare the obtained values with their hypothetical true values. Uncertainty evaluation is performed in two ways: by analytical transformation and by simulations. The ways are compared with respect to mathematical complexity and accuracy.

Calibration. Let us assume true values of pH standards:
$$pH_1 = 6.98, \qquad pH_2 = 8.03.$$
The declared values of the standards are:
$$pH_1^* = 7.00, \qquad pH_2^* = 8.00.$$
The pH electrode has true values of its parameter:

$$E^\circ = 410.0\,\text{mV}, \qquad\qquad S = 59.07\,\text{mV}.$$

After immersing the electrodes into the standards, true values of electrode potentials are obtained according to the Nernst equation (4):

$$E_1 = -2.31\,\text{mV}, \qquad\qquad E_2 = -64.33\,\text{mV}.$$

Using a pH-meter having resolution of 0.1 mV and performing three repetitive measurements in each standard, the indications can deviate from the true values, so the readouts may be as follows:

$$E^*_{1\,1} = -2.2\,\text{mV}, \qquad\qquad E^*_{2\,1} = -64.3\,\text{mV},$$
$$E^*_{1\,2} = -2.4\,\text{mV}, \qquad\qquad E^*_{2\,2} = -64.4\,\text{mV},$$
$$E^*_{1\,3} = -2.3\,\text{mV}, \qquad\qquad E^*_{2\,3} = -64.4\,\text{mV}.$$

Let's calculate the average values:

$$E^*_1 = -2.30\,\text{mV}, \qquad\qquad E^*_2 = -64.37\,\text{mV}.$$

Now, it is possible to calculate experimental values of electrode parameters. For two-point calibration, Eq. (8) simplifies to:

$$S^* = \frac{E^*_2 - E^*_1}{pH^*_1 - pH^*_2} = 62.07\,\text{mV} \tag{12}$$

and

$$E^{\circ *} = E^*_1 + S^* \cdot pH^*_1 = 432.2\,\text{mV} \tag{13}$$

The same relationship can be expressed as:

$$E^{\circ *} = \frac{pH^*_1 E^*_2 - pH^*_2 E^*_1}{pH^*_1 - pH^*_2} \tag{14}$$

Measurement. After calibration, it is possible to conduct a proper measurement. The examined solution has true value of pH:

$$pH_x = 7.50.$$

The true potential is

$$E_x = -33.03\,\text{mV}.$$

Three repetitive measurements have been performed:

$$E^*_{x\,1} = -32.9\,\text{mV},$$
$$E^*_{x\,2} = -33.0\,\text{mV and}$$
$$E^*_{x\,3} = -33.0\,\text{mV}.$$

Let's calculate the average values:

$$E^*_x = -32.97\,\text{mV}.$$

From Eq. (11), the pH value is found:

$$pH^*_x = 7.494.$$

Uncertainty Evaluation. The pH standards have declared tolerance of 0.05. So, their uncertainties using Type B evaluation should be estimated as the tolerance divided by $\sqrt{3}$:

$$u(pH_1) = 0.029, \qquad\qquad u(pH_2) = 0.029.$$

Maximum permissible error of voltmeter is expressed as:

$$\Delta E_i = |A \cdot E_i| + |B \cdot E_{max}| \tag{15}$$

where E_i means measured potential. For the analysed ion-meter (voltmeter), the parameters are:

$A = 0.05\%,$ $\qquad\qquad B = 0.02\%,$ $\qquad\qquad E_{max} = 1000.0\,\text{mV}.$

The voltmeter errors are:

$\Delta E_1 = 0.201\,\text{mV},$ $\qquad \Delta E_2 = 0.232\,\text{mV},$ $\qquad \Delta E_x = 0.217\,\text{mV},$

and Type B uncertainties calculated as the errors divided by $\sqrt{3}$ are:

$u_B(E_1) = 0.1160\,\text{mV},$ $\qquad u_B(E_2) = 0.1339\,\text{mV},$ $\qquad u_B(E_x) = 0.1252\,\text{mV},$

Uncertainties calculated using Type A evaluation (statistical contribution) of a quantity X is conducted using the following relationship:

$$u_A(X) = \sqrt{\frac{1}{n}\frac{1}{n-1}\sum_{i=1}^{n}(x_i - \bar{x})^2} \tag{16}$$

where $\bar{x}$ is the average value. So, the Type A uncertainties of potentials are:

$u_A(E_1) = 0.0577\,\text{mV},$ $\qquad u_A(E_2) = 0.0332\,\text{mV},$ $\qquad u_A(E_x) = 0.0333\,\text{mV}.$

Combined uncertainties of potential are calculated as $u = \sqrt{u_A^2 + u_B^2}$ and have the following values:

$u(E_1) = 0.1295\,\text{mV},$ $\qquad u(E_2) = 0.1379\,\text{mV},$ $\qquad u(E_x) = 0.1295\,\text{mV}.$

Uncertainty of slope is calculated by analysis of Eq. (12):

$$u(S) = S^* \cdot \sqrt{\frac{u^2(E_2) + u^2(E_1)}{(E_2^* - E_1^*)^2} + \frac{u^2(pH_1) + u^2(pH_2)}{(pH_2^* - pH_1^*)^2}} = 2.55\,\text{mV} \tag{17}$$

and uncertainty of standard potential is calculated by analysis of Eq. (13):

$$u(E^\circ) = \sqrt{u^2(E_1) + (S^* \cdot pH_1^*)^2\left(\frac{u^2(S)}{S^{*2}} + \frac{u^2(pH_1)}{pH_1^{*2}}\right)} = 17.9\,\text{mV} \tag{18}$$

Parameters $E^{\circ *}$ and S^* are correlated. The **incorrectly** calculated final standard uncertainty of the measured pH may be calculated basing only on uncertainties of the parameters and without taking into account their correlation. Applying Eq. (11) and commonly known formula describing uncertainty propagation [13, Eq. (10)] one obtains:

$$u(pH_x)_{incorrect} = \sqrt{\left(\frac{\partial pH}{\partial E^{\circ *}}\right)^2 u^2(E^\circ) + \left(\frac{\partial pH}{\partial S^*}\right)^2 u^2(S) + \left(\frac{\partial pH}{\partial E_x^*}\right)^2 u^2(E_x)} \tag{19}$$

and after solving:

$$u(pH_x)_{incorrect} = \sqrt{(pH_x^*)^2 \frac{u^2(E^\circ) + u^2(E_x)}{(E^{\circ *} - E_x^*)^2} + (pH_x^*)^2 \frac{u^2(S)}{S^{*2}}} = 0.422 \tag{20}$$

Covariance calculation is mostly a time-consuming task. In such case, the Guide recommends introducing an additional variable which is common to the correlated parameters. Here, it is not necessary because the input quantities, from which the parameters are calculated, can be used as the common variables. The relationship combining the sought pH value with the source variables are as follows:

$$pH_x = \frac{(pH_2 - pH_1)E_x + E_2 pH_1 - E_1 pH_2}{E_2 - E_1} \tag{21}$$

Here, it is possible to analyse the uncertainty propagation of uncorrelated inputs:

$$u(pH_x) = \frac{1}{|E_2^* - E_1^*|} \sqrt{ \begin{array}{c} (E_2^* - E_x^*)^2 u^2(pH_1) + (E_x^* - E_1^*)^2 u^2(pH_2) + \\ + \left(\frac{E_2^* - E_x^*}{S^*}\right)^2 u^2(E_1) + \left(\frac{E_x^* - E_1^*}{S^*}\right)^2 u^2(E_2) \end{array} } = 0.0206 \tag{22}$$

One can observe that the correctly calculated uncertainty is about 20 times smaller than that obtained without taking into consideration existing correlation between parameters of the electrode.

The final measurement result with uncertainty covering 95% confidence level should be reported as:

$$pH_x^* = 7.494 \pm 0.041.$$

Monte Carlo simulations. Other way of uncertainty evaluation is an application of computer simulations. The approach is described in the Supplement 1 of the Guide [14]. A short procedure has been written in GNU Octave which simulates the uncertainty propagation. First, values of electrode parameters and pH values of standards are declared. Correct electrode potentials are calculated according to the Nernst equation (4). Next, a loop is executed 10 000 times. In the loop, Gaussian random variables having standard deviation the same as uncertainty of the standards are added to the pH values. In the same way, values of potentials are modified. Basing on the data, experimental parameters of the electrode are calculated according to Eq. (8). To calculate measurement uncertainties of a sample having pH from the range of 3 to 11, a second loop inside the first one is written. In the second loop, for every pH value treated as true values, electrode potentials are calculated using declared parameters, random variables are added to the electrode potentials in the same way as earlier, and experimental pH values are determined using experimental values of parameters. The experimental pH values are compared with the declared values in order to calculate errors which are stored in a matrix. This step ends both loops. As a final task, standard deviations of the errors for each pH value are calculated and treated as standard uncertainties of pH.

The procedure has been executed using the same data as in the example presented above. Results are illustrated in Fig. 2. The first blue line represents two-point calibration. The standards are also the same as in the example above.

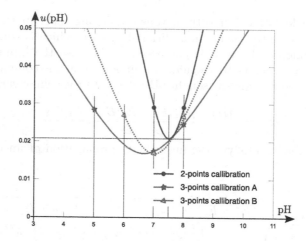

Fig. 2. Comparison of uncertainties of measured pH performed after two- and three-point calibrations. Blue points represents two-point calibration in standards having pH value equal 7 and 8; red stars – three-point calibration and pH equal 5, 7 and 8; red triangles – three-point calibration and pH equal 6, 7 and 8.

The uncertainty for pH equal 7.5 is close to 0.021 and is in accordance with the result obtained in the analytical way. Additional simulations have been performed in order to illustrate uncertainty variability in case of three-point calibration. Results are plotted in the same figure.

The simulations allow one to examine the variability of the uncertainty in a very easy way. Some minor modifications in the script allow one to check how the number of standards influences the uncertainty of the measured value. Additionally, the values of the standards also change the final uncertainty, which is easily visible on the plot. In comparison with the analytical approach, the simulations give many more benefits at the cost of very accurate uncertainty predictions (which are often not required).

4   Conclusions

The presented example leads to the following conclusions:

1. In case of linear regression, the knowledge about the uncertainties of parameters describing the straight line is not sufficient to calculate the uncertainty of a measured value, without knowledge of correlation between the parameters—here, knowledge about the uncertainties of the electrode slope and standard potential is insufficient.
2. It is possible to remove the correlation by adding other uncorrelated variables. In the presented case, a step, in which the calibration parameters are determined, has been excluded from the uncertainty calculations and in such way, no additional variables have to be used—the determined pH has been presented as a function of pH of standards.

3. Using Monte Carlo simulations, it is possible to assess the uncertainties without time-consuming analytical transformations. On the other hand, some programming skills are required.
4. Simulations allow one not only to predict the uncertainty but also the analysis of the uncertainty variability dependent on some conditions (*e.g.* number of standards, their values) is much more easier.

Acknowledgements. The author would like to thank the Polish Ministry of Science and Higher Education for financial support.

References

1. Sheppard, N.F.J., Guiseppi-Elie, A.: 71. pH Measurement. Electrical Engineering Handbook Series. In: The Measurement, Instrumentation, and Sensors: Handbook. Springer (1999)
2. Morf, W.E.: The Principles of Ion-Selective Electrodes and of Membrane Transport. Akadémiai Kiadó, Budapest (1981)
3. Cammann, K.: Working with ion-selective electrodes: chemical laboratory practice. Springer (1979)
4. Spitzer, P., Fisicaro, P., Meinrath, G., Stoica, D.: pH buffer assessment and Pitzer's equations. Accreditation and Quality Assurance 16, 191–198 (2011)
5. Camões, M.F.: The quality of pH measurements 100 years after its definition. Accreditation and Quality Assurance 14, 521–523 (2009)
6. Midgley, D., Torrance, K.: Potentiometric Water Analysis, 2nd edn. John Wiley & Sons, Inc., Chichester (1991)
7. Bakker, E., Bühlmann, P., Pretsch, E.: The phase-boundary potential model. Talanta 62, 843–860 (2004)
8. IUPAC: Potentiometric selectivity coefficients of ion-selective electrodes. part I. inorganic cations (technical report). Pure Appl. Chem. 72(10), 1851–2082 (2000)
9. Kozyra, A., Wiora, J., Wiora, A.: Calibration of potentiometric sensor arrays with a reduced number of standards. Talanta 98, 28–33 (2012)
10. Sokalski, T., Lewenstam, A.: Application of Nernst-Planck and Poisson equations for interpretation of liquid-junction and membrane potentials in real-time and space domains. Electrochem. Commun. 3, 107–112 (2001)
11. Wiora, J., Wiora, A.: A system allowing for the automatic determination of the characteristic shapes of ion-selective electrodes. In: Pisarkiewicz, T. (ed.) Optoelectronic and Electronic Sensors VI, Zakopane, October. Proceedings of SPIE, vol. 6348 (October 2006)
12. Wiora, J.: About the uncertainty of concentration standards applied in the calibration of potentiometric ion-selective electrodes. Measurement Automation and Monitoring 54(5), 318–321 (2008) (in Polish)
13. JCGM: Evaluation of measurement data – Guide to the expression of uncertainty in measurement (2008)
14. JCGM: Evaluation of measurement data – Supplement 1 to the "Guide to the expression of uncertainty in measurement" – Propagation of distributions using a Monte Carlo method (2008)

A Method of Automatic Detection of Pseudoscientific Publications

Alexander Shvets

Institute for Systems Analysis of Russian Academy of Sciences, Moscow, Russia
shvets@isa.ru

Abstract. Currently, pseudoscientific theories are actively promoted being published in a large amount of papers. They appear in mass media, in patents and even in scientific journals, and it is rather difficult for non-expert to distinguish scientific paper from pseudoscientific. A method for identifying pseudoscientific publications based on automatic text analysis is proposed. At first, the text is partitioned into small fragments consisting of several paragraphs. Then feature extraction occurs using an automatic linguistic analysis and classification of text fragments is implemented by support vector machines. Experiments show that the method divides scientific and pseudoscientific publications into different classes with high accuracy.

Keywords: Identifying of pseudoscientific papers, Intelligent text analysis, Support vector machine.

1 Introduction

Pseudoscientific theories are becoming very popular nowadays. There are more and more papers and studies claiming incredible scientific discoveries, which are in fact fake and do not relate to science at all.

There are a lot various definitions of pseudoscience, and all of them are similar in at least one core aspect: the viewpoints of rational science opponents are assumed to be faulty, however, allowing the possibility of honest error. In this study we assume that pseudoscience is a methodology or a system of views that claims to be scientific, but in fact fails to comply with the standards of methodology and principles of evidence, does not correspond to the standards of the scientific knowledge or any particular area of reality, and its subject either does not exist at all or is substantially falsified [1, 2].

According to the study [2], some of the most typical characteristics of pseudoscientific work include the following:

- Authors of such studies often claim that their discovery is exceptionally important and solves a number of crucial and relevant practical problems.
- A pseudoscientific discovery usually violates fundamental scientific laws.
- Authors of pseudoscientific discoveries do not have any predecessors.

© Springer International Publishing Switzerland 2015
D. Filev et al. (eds.), *Intelligent Systems'2014*,
Advances in Intelligent Systems and Computing 323, DOI: 10.1007/978-3-319-11310-4_46

- Pseudoscientific discoveries are not usually published in any authoritative scientific journals. Instead they are distributed via mass media or in some private departmental publications.
- A new discovery often allows reconsidering all the previous discoveries on the topic or at least the majority of them.

Scientists generally notice two major threats that pseudoscience imposes on society. Firstly, pseudoscientists are often capable of attracting significant amount of public funds on the grounds of creating a 'breakthrough technology' using some corruption-based mechanisms [2]. Secondly, a lot of times they take advantage of people who have a serious disease by giving them a 'magic cure' and thus preventing them from taking a real medicine. When a patient finally realizes that this 'magic cure' does not work in fact and goes to a real doctor, it might be already too late: a malignant tumor, for instance, can become inoperable [3].

There are few online resources and periodical articles that provide some information about pseudoscientific theories. Such information helps non-experts to acquire the necessary knowledge to avoid being deceived. One of the online resources that can be distinguished is international resource «RationalWiki» [1] that was created to organize and categorize knowledge about pseudoscientific theories, personalities and organizations. Another resource *skeptic.com* and related magazine «Skeptic» belong to the nonprofit scientific and educational organization «Skeptics Society» that promotes critical thinking in investigating the paranormal, fringe science and pseudoscience [4]. Different local organizations such as Committee for the Scientific Investigation of Claims of the Paranormal (New York, USA) and Commission of the Russian Academy of Sciences on fight against pseudoscience and falsification of scientific researches (Russian Federation) also publish periodical articles discussing pseudoscientific works in detail [5, 6].

New pseudoscientific texts appear regularly on mass media sites, in journals (usually not peer-reviewed), newspapers. Questionable content are also found in the new patents, conference proceedings and other scientific and technical documents that had not been properly checked before publication. The problem is as follows: while these texts will not be the object of extensive discussion, until they reach one of the above resources, it would be difficult for non-expert to understand whether he read pseudoscientific publications or not. In this regard, the development of a method and software that will automatically determine whether the text is pseudoscientific is an actual task. This method would help to understand whether to trust content of a paper or it is necessary to ask scientists for help. Such a method would be useful also for experts which assess the quality of publications, because it would allow them to pay attention to questionable places in texts.

There is a similar problem which consists in distinguishing scientific papers from machine automatically generated papers. This problem has a lot of successful solutions, for example, method proposed in [7] has detected many fake publications in the scientific literature. However, it should be pointed out that pseudoscientific texts are human written texts, so they have totally another nature and therefore methods for identification of generated texts are not applicable in this case.

2   Method of Detection of Pseudoscientific Publications

At first, there were considered different pseudoscientific publications and it was found that these texts contain specific lexical and stylistic features such as words "mind", "karma", "universe" or phrases "sensational material", "to have the greatest historical value", "a matter of life and death" that are often independent from a topic of paper. Then it was established that scientific texts contain some of these features too, and it is difficult to determine manually which combinations of features characterize only pseudoscientific texts. To detect pseudoscientific publications automatically, a method based on classification of texts on the grounds of various words and phrases is proposed in this study.

Due to the fact that pseudoscientific claims can be only a small part of a publication, it is proposed to partition papers into small text fragments and classify them separately. Such fragments were chosen as a set of paragraphs, because paragraph usually carries a complete thought and could give an idea about the correctness of the statements contained in it.

Classification features in this case are individual words, word-combinations with syntactic dependencies and trigrams. The set of features was formed automatically via linguistic analyzer on the basis of the training set which will be described later. In this study we use linguistic analyzer which helps to establish syntactic and semantic dependencies between words [8]. There were found about 350 thousand features, among them:

— words: "torsion", "harmonization", "extremely", " injustice";
— word-combinations: "universal availability", "unexplained anomaly", "to code in structure", "convincingly demonstrate", "memory of water";
— trigrams: "more than possible", "and almost nowhere", "very obvious that", "proved by science".

The set of features also contains the common lexicon and general scientific words such as "method", "theory", "emergence" etc. To distinguish these words from words which are specific to pseudoscientific texts, feature vectors are filled by weights of words using statistical measure TF-IDF [9]. According to this measure, a higher weight will be brought to the words which are used with high frequency within a specific fragment of text and at the same time with low frequency in the whole collection of texts. Thus, words of the common lexicon and general scientific words, which are frequently used in texts, will make an insignificant contribution during classification.

A set of training examples for classification was formed using 10 pseudoscientific papers that were discussed in publications of journal of Commission of the Russian Academy of Sciences «In defense of science» and 180 scientific papers that were selected by experts from reviewed scientific journals. There were obtained 212 fragments for pseudoscientific papers and 3158 fragments for scientific papers with similar length (about 700 characters) which corresponds to the average length of a paragraph. It is worth noting that before partitioning text the references section is deleted automatically, using regular expressions, to leave only the author's text. The topics of pseudoscientific papers were as following: "unusual" properties of water, torsion fields, telepathy. Scientific papers presented different topics and some of them were chosen close to pseudoscientific topics in order to detect features that distinguish texts with similar lexis.

Support vector machine (SVM) algorithm is chosen as the basis of a proposed method as it is successfully used for classification of textual information with a significant amount of features [10]. For classification experiments an algorithm with linear kernel function from an open library for support vector machines LIBSVM is used in this study [11]. A general scheme of the method of automatic detection of pseudoscientific publications is presented in figure 1.

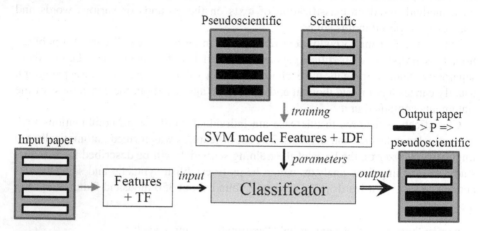

Fig. 1. A general scheme of the method of automatic detection of pseudoscientific publications

We assume that each publication of training set consists of fragments belonging to one and the same particular class. So pseudoscientific texts contain only pseudoscientific fragments and scientific texts contain only scientific fragments, although it might be cause of decreasing of training quality, if a pseudoscientific text, for example, contains fragments with scientific or neutral character. We assume the same thing for test set to evaluate precision and recall of classification. It will be shown that a value P (see fig.1) might be preset in such way, that if relative number of detected pseudoscientific fragments in some text is higher than value P, this text could be referred to pseudoscience with high precision and recall.

3   Experimental Verification of Method

The test set consists of 24 pseudoscientific and 108 scientific publications including journal articles and patents. The test set does not intersect with the training set. Topics of pseudoscientific papers differ from topics of training set, and include: "the ether theory", "consequences of a possible change of the Earth's poles", "paradoxes in scientific theories" and other. These texts were partitioned into 234 pseudoscientific fragments and 2175 scientific fragments. For each fragment, vector of features was constructed and classified using SVM model and IDF values obtained as a result of training phase. Results of classification are presented in table 1. The following letter symbols are used in the table:

— TP – True Pseudoscientific,
— TS – True Scientific,
— FP – False Pseudoscientific,
— FS – False Scientific.

Table 1. Results of classification of text fragments

Classes of text fragments		Expert estimation	
		pseudoscientific (234)	scientific (2175)
Classification estimation	pseudoscientific	TP=171	FP=204
	Scientific	FS=63	TS=1971

According to the table 1, accuracy of classification is equal to

$$(TP+TS)/(TP+FS+FP+TS) = (171+1971)/(234+2175) = 0.89.$$

The test set of scientific papers was separated into 9 intersected parts with 24 publications in each part for evaluation of precision score for a class "pseudoscientific". It was done to equalize numbers of papers in both classes. Precision is determined as a ratio of true identified pseudoscientific fragments (in this case TP=171) to number of all fragments that were classified as pseudoscientific (TP+FP). Table 2 contains values of precision for different sets of scientific papers.

Table 2. Precision for different parts of the test set

№	FP	TP + FP	Precision
1	15	186	0.92
2	11	182	0.94
3	24	195	0.88
4	39	210	0.81
5	73	244	0.70
6	63	234	0.73
7	52	223	0.77
8	72	243	0.70
9	45	216	0.79

According to the table 2, mean precision is equal to 0.8. According to the table 1 recall is equal to (171/234) = 0.73. Mean F-measure in this case is equal to 0.76. Precision and recall scores and F-measure is evaluated according to the standard formulas [12]. In the worst case (scientific set №5 in table 2), precision is equal to 0.7 and F-measure – 0.71.

Although the precision and recall scores are not very high, it is enough in many cases to distinguish scientific publications from pseudoscientific by proportion of publication with fragments which were classified as pseudoscientific. Figure 2 shows those proportions for 24 pseudoscientific papers and for 24 scientific papers of the test set №5.

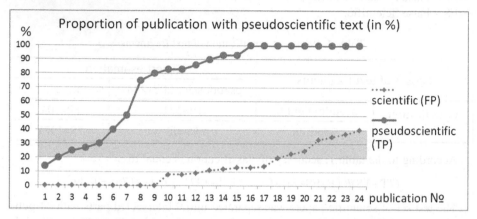

Fig. 2. Proportion of publication with pseudoscientific text (in %)

Three zones could be highlighted: 0-20% – publications are more likely scientific, 20-40% - they could be both scientific and pseudoscientific (more features are needed to distinguish them) and 40-100% - publications are more likely pseudoscientific. The conditional limit of part of pseudoscientific text that scientific paper could contain was preset as a middle of the second zone ($P=30\%$). According to this limit the second level of classification was accomplished for the whole test set. Results are provided in table 3.

Table 3. Results of classification of publications

Classes of publications		Expert estimation	
		pseudoscientific (24)	scientific (108)
Classification estimation	pseudoscientific	19	7
	scientific	5	101

The precision of classification equals $19/(19+7)=0.73$, recall equals $19/(19+5)=0.79$, F-measure – 0.76. It was found that scientific publications which were falsely classified as pseudoscientific refer to theoretical physics. Probably, adding some publications on this topic to training set will cause of increasing of classification accuracy.

4   Conclusion

The proposed method could be successfully implemented for detection of fragments of publications which texts are similar to pseudoscientific. Results of experiments show that despite the high accuracy of classification there are a few cases when participation of experts is needed to estimate quality of publication. However, this method could help experts in these cases to pay attention to questionable places in texts.

As future work it is planned to expand the training set by both scientific and pseudoscientific publications and to use additional features for the classification, such as the presence of words wrongly quoted or written groundlessly with a capital letter, emotional means of expression, a large number of interrogative and exclamatory sentences, as well as the presence of references section which contains only those publications that belong to the author of the text or to his team.

Acknowledgements. The paper is supported by the Russian Academy of Sciences; project ONIT 2.9 "Development of methods and technologies Exactus Expert for semantic search and analysis of scientific publications".

References

1. RationalWiki, http://rationalwiki.org
2. Aleksandrov, E.B.: Answers to Questions about Pseudoscience. Journal (In defense of science) 8 (2011) (in Russian)
3. Gitelson, I.I.: Necessity of Government Protection of the People from the Onslaught of Fake Medicine. Journal (In defense of science) 2, 52–55 (2007) (in Russian)
4. Sceptic Society, http://www.skeptic.com
5. Skeptical Inquirer, http://www.csicop.org
6. Journal (In defense of science) 12 (2013)
7. Labbé, C., Labbé, D.: Duplicate and fake publications in the scientific literature: How many SCIgen papers in computer science? Scientometrics. Scientometrics 94(1), 379–396 (2013)
8. Osipov, G., Smirnov, I., Tikhomirov, I., Shelmanov, A.: Relational–situational method for intelligent search and analysis of scientific publications. In: Proceedings of the Workshop on Integrating IR Technologies for Professional Search, in Conjunction with the 35th European Conference on Information Retrieval (ECIR 2013), Moscow, Russia. CEUR Workshop Proceedings, vol. 968 (2013)
9. Salton, G., Buckley, C.: Term-weighting approaches in automatic text retrieval. Information Processing & Management 24(5), 513–523 (1988)
10. Cortes, C., Vapnik, V.: Support-vector networks. Machine Learning 20(3), 273 (1995)
11. LIBSVM – A Library for Support Vector Machines, http://w.csie.org/~cjlin/libsvm
12. Powers, D.M.W.: Evaluation: From Precision, Recall and F-Factor to ROC, Informedness, Markedness and Correlation. Journal of Machine Learning Technologies 2(1), 37–63 (2011)

A Plagiarism Detection System for Arabic Documents

Ashraf S. Hussein

Faculty of Computer and Information Sciences, Ain Shams University, Cairo 11566, Egypt
ashrafh@acm.org

Abstract. This paper proposes a new plagiarism detection system devoted to Arabic text documents. This system is based on modeling the relation between documents and their n-gram phrases. Part-of-Speech tagging is applied on the examined documents to support in resolving the morphological ambiguity during text normalization. Text indexing and stop-words removal are performed, employing a new morphological analysis based method. Heuristic pairwise phrase matching algorithm is used to build the documents TF-IDF model, considering substitution of words with their synonyms. The hidden associations of the unique n-gram phrases contained in the documents are investigated using the Latent Semantic Analysis. Then, the pairwise document similarity scores are derived from the Singular Value Decomposition computations. The performance of the proposed system was confirmed through experiments with various data sets, exhibiting promising capabilities in identifying literal and some types of intelligent plagiarism. Finally, the proposed system was compared to Plagiarism-Checker-X, and the proposed system outperformed Plagiarism-Checker-X, especially for intelligent plagiarism.

Keywords: Plagiarism check, similarity detection, text re-use, text mining, natural language processing.

1   Introduction and Previous Work

Nowadays, plagiarism detection systems are a mandatory requirement for academic and research institutions, as the availability of various digital resources makes plagiarism operations easier than before [1], degrading the credibility and dignity of such institutions. Plagiarism in free text is difficult to identify because it is not only literal, but also intelligent [2]. The plagiarism linguistic patterns and detection methods have been extensively studied by Alzahrani et al. [2], correlating these detection methods to their new taxonomy of plagiarism types. Their study has highlighted the booming potential of the intelligent plagiarism. More recently, Meuschke and Gipp [3] have surveyed the state-of-the-art approaches of plagiarism detection, emphasizing the performance of each one. On the other hand, Riad et al. [4] have investigated the different methods of plagiarism detection, considering their applicability and appropriateness for Arabic text.

© Springer International Publishing Switzerland 2015

D. Filev et al. (eds.), *Intelligent Systems' 2014*,

Advances in Intelligent Systems and Computing 323, DOI: 10.1007/978-3-319-11310-4_47

In the context of natural Arabic text, Alzahrani and Salim [5] have proposed a statement-based plagiarism detection approach for Arabic scripts using fuzzy-set Information Retrieval (IR) model. In this approach, the degree of similarity is computed and compared to a threshold value to judge whether two statements are similar or not. However, this approach does not handle the case of rewording with different synonyms/antonyms, which raised the need for using Arabic thesaurus. Next, they have proposed two techniques for statement-based plagiarism detection, employing three least-frequent 4-gram fingerprints matching and fuzzy-set IR [6]. The results proved that the fuzzy-set IR technique outperforms fingerprints matching, but still dealing with the different meanings of the same inflected words and resolving ambiguities were not considered.

In the same context, Menai and Bagais [7, 8] introduced a plagiarism checker for Arabic texts "APlag" based on logical representation of documents and heuristics for text comparison. As their approach depends mainly on the most frequent synonym for each word's root, it is more appropriate to be domain-specific, employing machine learning to identify the most frequent synonyms of the inflected words within the domain under consideration. Jadalla and Elnagar [9] presented a system for Arabic text-based documents "Iqtebas 1.0". In this system, the originality score of a text is estimated by computing the distance between each sentence in the text and the closest sentence in the suspected files, if exists. The system depends on a search engine in order to reduce the cost of pairwise similarity. In this way, it is ideal for copy-paste plagiarism, as it fails for the cases of reordering or changing the words to their equivalences.

The imitations in automatic plagiarism detection and the future perspectives have been presented in [10]. A detailed roadmap for the plagiarism detection evolution directions has been provided, correlating these directions to indirect literal and intelligent plagiarism types. In this way, it was recommended to use electronic thesauri, as these thesauri are useful tools in the struggle against the substitution of synonymous words in texts.

The detection of intelligent plagiarism types requires a facility that is able to explicate the finest variations in words and sentences that are semantically similar. While plagiarism detection at the level of concepts and ideas is still far beyond the limits of today's technologies, at least for Arabic language, it is already possible to overcome certain types of semantic-preserving text alternations. One of the most well-known methods of comparing documents for semantic similarity is the Latent Semantic Analysis (LSA) [11]. LSA is an intelligent document comparison technique that uses mathematical algorithms for analyzing large corpora of text and revealing the underlying semantic information of documents [12]. LSA has several characteristics that make it a feasible technique for plagiarism detection in natural language text [13, 14, 15].

The main objective of this research work is to not only detecting literal plagiarism types in Arabic documents, but also it introduces an advancement towards detecting intelligent plagiarism. The proposed system is based on modeling the relation between documents, under consideration, and their n-gram unique phrases. Part-of-Speech tagging is applied on the examined documents to support in resolving the morphological ambiguity during text normalization. A new method based on morphological analysis is used for text indexing and stop-words removal. Heuristic pairwise phrase matching algorithm is introduced to build the documents TF-IDF model, considering substitution of words with their synonyms via Arabic thesaurus. The hidden associations contained in the text documents are investigated using the LSA, employing the Singular Value Decomposition (SVD). Finally, the pairwise document similarity scores are derived from the results of the SVD. The proposed method is applicable not only for Arabic language but also for any other language, taking into consideration the availability of the Natural Language Processing (NLP) tools and resources for such language.

2   System Description

The detailed architecture of the proposed plagiarism detection system is based on the hypothesis that original texts and rewritten texts exhibit significant but measurable differences, and these differences can be captured through statistical and linguistic indicators. To investigate this hypothesis, three fundamental contributions are identified, trying to overcome the challenges of plagiarism detection in Arabic text [8]. First, NLP techniques are involved, rather than relying on the traditional string-matching approaches [3]. The second contribution pursues adopting document modeling techniques, which are able to overcome most of the lexical and syntactic challenges. Third, the LSA is employed to determine the hidden associations contained in text documents under consideration. In order to infer the latent semantics from the given text, SVD is considered for the purpose of large statistical computations.

2.1   System Architecture

The proposed system is comprised of several parts, which include document interface, system infrastructure, core blocks, external resources and system user interface as shown in Fig. 1. The document interface is concerned with reading documents from document repository and/or external data sources, such as Internet. The infrastructure of the system comprised of morphological analyzer, stemming and indexing block, and synonyms thesaurus while the system core blocks include preprocessing, n-gram phrases extraction, document modeling and similarity analysis. The external resources include the utilities and tools needed to perform Part-of-Speech (POS) tagging, multi-key sorting, and visualization of the LSA results. The last part is the system user interface, containing configuration settings and system parameters. This interface allows the user to easily analyze a set of documents as per his/her role. The proposed system has an external interface with a multi-key sorting utility to sort the extracted n-gram phrases. Also, it and has an internal interface with an NLP engine for performing morphological analysis, stemming, and indexing [16]. The POS tagging tool and the visualization utility are independently executed during the preprocessing and post-processing phases respectively.

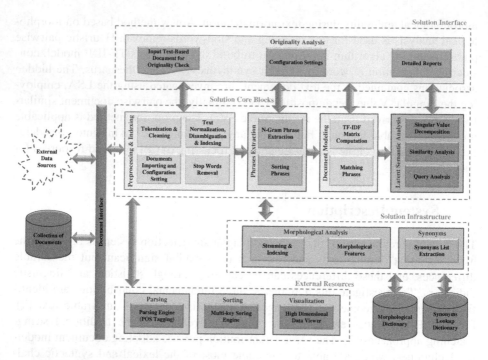

Fig. 1. The architecture of the proposed plagiarism detection system for Arabic text

2.2   Main Data Flow Diagram

The preprocessing and indexing module reads the text documents, one by one, and generates the indexes of the inflected words for each statement and passes these indexes to the n-gram phrases extraction module, which writes the generated n-grams, from each document, in a separate temporary file. These temporary files are merged together in one n-gram phrases file. Then, the merged file of the n-gram phrases is sorted out, removing duplicates and counting the frequencies of the unique n-gram phrases. Next, the document modeling module reads the sorted file to compute the TF-IDF matrix, which is considered as the characteristic matrix of a given set of documents. At this stage, the similarity analysis module starts to work by computing the simple cosine similarity matrix as a first estimate for document similarity. To get deep estimation of the pairwise document similarity scores, the TF-IDF matrix is passed to the LSA functionality after applying the method described in sub-section 3.6. The main data flow diagram is presented in Fig. 2.

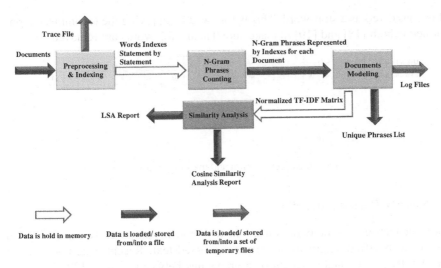

Fig. 2. Main data flow diagram

3   The Proposed Plagiarism Detection Method

3.1   Text Conversion/Parsing

The documents under consideration are converted into plain text documents, removing control characters and diacritization marks. Next, the text documents are POS tagged using the POS tagging facility included in the Stanford Parser[1].

3.2   Pre-processing and Indexing

Text pre-processing is an important step for every NLP task to achieve outstanding results [15]. For every document, each statement is tokenized and stored in the memory as shown in Fig. 3. Every inflected word is indexed employing a morphological analyzer. In this research work, the morphological analyzer adopted in [16] is employed along with its Arabic dictionary. The morphological analyses of each inflected word are disambiguated, employing its associated POS tag, from the previous step. If there are more than one possible analysis, Levenshtein edit distance [17] is then used to identify the most probable analysis based on the minimum edit distance between the inflected word and its corresponding available stems (analyses). In this way, the indexes of the Arabic language stems, included in their morphological features and stored in the dictionary, are used to index the inflected words, according to its identified morphological analysis [16].

The stop words are removed while indexing by checking the POS tag and the morphological features of the identified morphological analysis for every inflected word. If these features indicate that the word is interjection, preposition or pronoun, then the

---

[1] http://nlp.stanford.edu/software/lex-parser.shtml

word is considered as a stop-word. This is followed by applying the recommendations mentioned in both [18] and [19] to make sure that all stop words are removed.

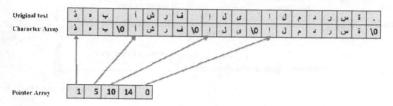

Fig. 3. Representation and marking of text

3.3   N-Gram Phrase Extraction

The next step retrieves simple ideas from the text. For this purpose, we extract n-gram phrases of a specified length from the pre-processed text. Recent experiments have shown that the most suitable length of n-grams lies between 2 and 7 [20]. To avoid huge memory requirements, the procedure of phrase extraction has to be applied successively for each n-gram size we are searching for, e.g. for unigram, bigram and trigram, the procedure has to be run three times. This results from the principle that n-grams are extracted from single data blocks and only one n-gram size is held in the memory at a time to maximize the efficiency. The six fundamental stages of this phase are illustrated in Fig. 4. The proposed system externally interfaces with CMSort[2] sorting utility to sort the n-gram phrases and remove the duplicates.

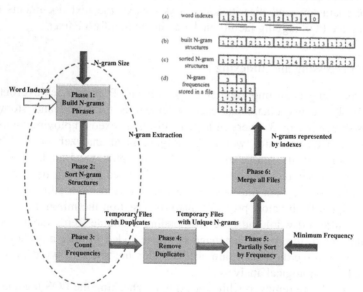

Fig. 4. Counting n-grams

---

[2] http://www.chmaas.handshake.de/delphi/freeware/cmsort/cmsort.htm

3.4 Phrase Analysis and Reduction

Analysis and reduction of n-gram phrases is an essential step that should follow data extraction. The longer phrases, in terms of n-grams, are extracted, the higher amount of distinct phrases has to be compared to identify plagiarized documents. This can seem to be a disadvantage of longer phrases; however, we have to take into account that not all phrases have the same importance. If we employ a feature selection technique, the amount of phrases can be significantly reduced. The most effective method for plagiarism detection is the Document Frequency (DF) feature selection. According to the DF, the unique phrases existing in one document are removed since they are not plagiarized. On the other hand, the common phrases across documents with close frequencies are also removed, according to [13].

3.5 Pairwise Phrases Matching

The pairwise n-gram phrase matching is performed during the construction of the TF-IDF matrix. This is a straight forward process with overall complexity of O(N), where N the number of unique phrases across the documents under consideration, if we are seeking only the detection of copy-paste plagiarism. On the contrary, when lexical and syntactic changes are considered, the complexity of the whole pairwise matching process will be increased to $O(N^2)$. The pairwise phrase matching score is computed using either Matching Average or Dice Coefficient [17]. This is carried out by representing the relationship between the tokens of each pair of phrases, under consideration, in a matrix form to compute the matching score by applying one of the simple heuristic methods [17]. The matrix represents the pairwise matching of two phrases is computed as: $cost_{i,j} = 1$ if the index of a token i, within the first phrase, equals the index of a token j, within the second phrase or one of its synonyms and vice versa, and $cost_{i,j} = 0$ otherwise. The value of the matching score identifies that the two phrases, under consideration, are equivalent or not. In this work, the pairwise phrases are considered to be equivalent if the matching score equals 1.

3.6 Document Modeling

A phrase-by-document model is adopted, considering occurrence frequencies of phrases contained in the examined documents. These relationships are depicted in a matrix form, where columns represent documents and rows represent phrases. Consider a matrix A be an n-by-m rectangular matrix to be composed of m vectors $[A_1, A_2, \ldots, A_m]$, where the vector A_j represents phrases contained in document j. Then, each vector A_j is composed of n elements $a_{i,j}$ representing the weighted occurrence frequency of phrase i in document j, as depicted in Eq. 1. This equation is a modification of the standard TF-IDF weighting [21].

$$a_{i,j} = \begin{cases} \dfrac{1}{2} + \dfrac{PF_{i,j} \cdot \log\left(\dfrac{|N|}{DF_i}\right)}{2 \cdot \max\limits_{j}(PF_{i,j}) \cdot \log(|M|)}, & \text{if phrase i occurs in document j} \\ 0, & \text{otherwise} \end{cases} \tag{1}$$

$PF_{i,j}$ represents the occurrence frequency of phrase i in document j, DF_i represents the number of documents where phrase i occurs, and finally $|M|$ is the number of all documents. The difference in comparison to TF-IDF rests in IDF normalization. We divide it by $\log(|M|)$ in order to $a_{i,j} \in <0.5, 1>$. On the other hand, if phrase i does not occur in document j, then $a_{i,j}=0$. This weighting mechanism yields the best result for SVD [13].

3.7   Latent Semantic Analysis

In this step, we infer the latent semantic associations among phrases contained in the examined documents. We apply SVD to decompose matrix A into three independent matrices U, Σ, and V [13]. All these matrices can be decomposed in a reduced latent space k to perform the best k-rank approximation of A so that singular values σ_{k+1}, $\sigma_{k+2}, \ldots, \sigma_m$ are replaced by 0, where $1 \leq k \leq m$. Then, matrix U is an n-by-k column orthonormal, whose columns are phrase singular vectors. Σ is a k-by-k diagonal matrix without negative and zero numbers that represents the singular values. A characteristic feature of SVD is that the singular values on the diagonal are placed in descending order and satisfy **Eqn. 2**. Matrix V^T is a k-by-m row orthonormal, whose rows are document singular vectors.

$$\sigma_1 \geq \sigma_2 \geq \cdots \geq \sigma_k \geq \sigma_{k+1} = \cdots = \sigma_m = 0 \tag{2}$$

3.8   Document Similarity Score

The mutual pairwise document similarity score is computed employing the matrix V^T, resulted from SVD computations, after rescaling this matrix with the selected k singular values. Then, the computed similarity scores are weighted by the ratio between the number of original phrases and the number of phrases after reduction [15].

To estimate the accuracy of the similarity estimation, the approximation error of rank-k approximation to A is estimated, where $k \leq r_A$ and r_A is the number of nonzero diagonal elements of Σ, can be constructed by ignoring (or setting equal to zero) all except the k-largest singular values of A equal to zero. The error in approximating the original term-by-document matrix A by A_k is determined by the truncated (or discarded) singular values ($\sigma_{k+1}, \sigma_{k+2}, \ldots, \sigma_{rA}$). The relative change reflected by approximating A by A_k is estimated by $\varepsilon = \|A - A_k\|_F / \|A\|_F$, where the Frobenius matrix norm $\left(\|\cdot\|_F\right)$ of a real m×n matrix B= $[b_{ij}]$ is defined as $\|B\|_F = \sqrt{\sum_{i=1}^m \sum_{j=1}^n b_{ij}^2}$.

4   Results and Discussions

The performance of the proposed system was confirmed through experiments with various data sets, including customized and real ones. For instance, the proposed system was tested for detecting plagiarism in large Arabic text files. In this way, a large data set consisting of 300 Arabic documents was used for examining the system performance. These documents were generated from 20 original documents of an average 830 words, as shown in Fig. 5, emphasizing the ratio of the stop-words to the indexed ones. These documents were acquired from the portals of the Egyptian newspapers, and they are all relevant to the Egyptian political situation. From each original document, 5 documents were generated by restructuring 50% of the original document statements. Another 5 documents were generated from each of the original ones by substituting 50% of the words in each document by their synonyms. The last group of 5 documents was generated by randomly substituting 50% of the words of the second set of documents (restructured documents) to their synonyms.

The average values of the LSA similarity scores for different n-gram window sizes, with and without activating the synonyms component, and for k=50 and 100, were compared to the results obtained using Plagiarism-Checker-X[3] as shown in Fig. 6. Without employing the synonyms component, the proposed system exhibits better estimation of the similarity scores than the Plagiarism-Checker-X for the restructured set of documents. As the n-gram window size increases, the error in estimating the similarity scores increases, especially for the second and the third groups of the generated documents. Also, for n-gram > 1, the Plagiarism-Checker-X gives better similarity estimation for the second and third groups of the generated documents. Although the higher values of k-dimensions, beyond the accuracy threshold ($\varepsilon < 10\%$), give better approximation for the A matrix, they negatively affect the similarity scores estimation. Employing the synonyms component tremendously enhances the similarity estimation for the second and third groups of the generated documents. Again, increasing the n-gram window size increases the error in estimating the similarity values, especially for the third group of documents. It is interesting to point out that the estimated similarity scores for the second group were slightly less than the exact values, even for n-gram=1, because some of the synonyms used in the documents are not supported by the current version of the Arabic thesaurus. The mathematical potential of the LSA significantly enhances the similarity estimations, even with the not supported synonyms, as the size of the documents increases.

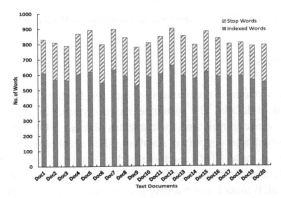

Fig. 5. Document sizes emphasizing the number of indexed and stop words

---

[3] http://plagiarismcheckerx.com

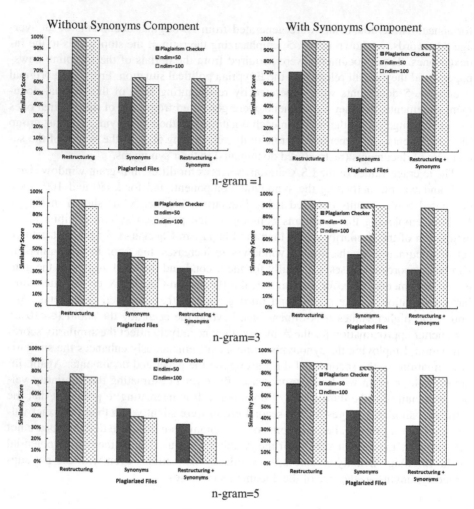

Fig. 6. Plagiarized files similarity scores compared to Plagiarism-Checker-X

5   Conclusions

In this paper, a new plagiarism detection system for Arabic text documents was described and studied in details. The system is based on modeling the relation between documents, under consideration, and their n-gram phrases. POS tagging is applied on the examined documents to support in resolving the morphological ambiguity during text normalization. A new NLP based method is used for text indexing and stopwords removal. Heuristic pairwise phrase matching algorithm is introduced to build the documents TF-IDF model, considering substitution of words with their synonyms. Finally, the hidden associations of the n-gram phrases contained in text documents are investigated using the LSA, employing the SVD. The performance of the proposed system is confirmed in terms of the pairwise document similarity score values for large data sets of Arabic documents. The proposed system exhibited strong capabilities in discovering literal plagiarism, and it could be considered as a serious step towards detecting intelligent plagiarism (e.g. direct and sophisticated copying, such as sentence reordering and synonym substitution). The results of the proposed system were compared with one of the most famous plagiarism detection tools; Plagiarism-Checker-X, the well-known language-independent tool, and the proposed system outperformed Plagiarism-Checker-X. Still, the pairwise phrase matching is considered as the main challenge, as its complexity is $O(N^2)$. So, the future work involves trying more advanced pairwise matching methods in order to enhance the system efficiency.

Acknowledgements. This work is a part of the Preliminary Research Project No. PRP2012.R12.2 funded by the Information Technology Academic Collaboration (ITAC) program, Information Technology Industry Development Agency (ITIDA), Ministry of Communication and Information Technology, Egypt.

References

1. Fish, R., Hura, G.: Students' Perceptions of Plagiarism. Journal of the Scholarship of Teaching and Learning 13(5), 33–45 (2013)
2. Alzahrani, S., Salim, N., Abraham, A.: Understanding Plagiarism Linguistic Patterns, Textual Features, and Detection Methods. IEEE Transactions on Systems, Man, and Cybernetics-Part C: Applications and Reviews 42(2), 133–149 (2012)
3. Meuschke, N., Gipp, B.: State-of-the-art in Detecting Academic Plagiarism. International Journal for Educational Integrity 9(1), 50–71 (2013)
4. Riad, A.M., Farahat, F.F., Asem, A.S., Zaher, M.A.: Studying Different Methods for Plagiarism Detection. International Journal of Computer Science 2(5), 147–154 (2013)
5. Alzahrani, S.M., Salim, N.: Plagiarism Detection In Arabic Scripts Using Fuzzy Information Retrieval. In: 2008 Student Conference on Research and Development (SCOReD 2008), Johor, Malaysia, vol. 281, pp. 1–4 (2008)
6. Alzahrani, S.M., Salim, N.: Statement-Based Fuzzy-Set IR versus Fingerprints Matching for Plagiarism Detection in Arabic Documents. In: 5th Postgraduate Annual Research Seminar (PARS 2009), Johor Bahru, Malaysia, pp. 267–268 (2009)
7. Menai, M., Bagais, M.: APlag: A Plagiarism Checker for Arabic Texts. In: IEEE International Conference on Computer Science & Education (ICCSE 2011), SuperStar Virgo, Singapore, pp. 1379–1383 (2011)
8. Menai, M.E.: Detection of Plagiarism in Arabic Documents. International Journal of Information Technology and Computer Science 10, 80–89 (2012)
9. Jadalla, A., Elnagar, A.: A Plagiarism Detection System for Arabic Text-Based Documents. In: Chau, M., Wang, G.A., Yue, W.T., Chen, H. (eds.) PAISI 2012. LNCS, vol. 7299, pp. 145–153. Springer, Heidelberg (2012)
10. Mozgovoy, M., Kakkonen, T., Cosma, G.: Automatic Student Plagiarism Detection: Future Perspectives. Journal of Educational Computing Research 43(4), 511–531 (2010)
11. Deerwester, S., Dumais, S., Furnas, G., Harshman, R., Landauer, T., Lochbaum, K., et al.: Patent No. US Patent 4,839,853, USA (1988)
12. Simmons, S., Estes, Z.: Using Latent Semantic Analysis to Estimate Similarity. In: 28th Annual Conference of the Cognitive Science Society (CogSci 2006), Vancouver, British Columbia, Canada, pp. 2169–2173 (2006)

13. Ceska, Z.: Plagiarism Detection Based on Singular Value Decomposition. In: Nordström, B., Ranta, A. (eds.) GoTAL 2008. LNCS (LNAI), vol. 5221, pp. 108–119. Springer, Heidelberg (2008)

14. Ceska, Z., Toman, M., Jezek, K.: Multilingual Plagiarism Detection. In: Dochev, D., Pistore, M., Traverso, P. (eds.) AIMSA 2008. LNCS (LNAI), vol. 5253, pp. 83–92. Springer, Heidelberg (2008)

15. Ceska, Z., Fox, C.: The Influence of Text Pre-processing on Plagiarism Detection. In: Recent Advances in Natural Language Processing, RANLP 2009, Borovets, Bulgaria, pp. 55–59 (2009)

16. Hussein, A., El-Shishiny, H.: A Framework and a Prototype for Arabic Question Answering System. Egyptian Informatics Journal 4(1), 26–39 (2003)

17. Gusfield, D.: Algorithms on Strings, Trees, and Sequences: Computer Science and Computational Biology. Cambridge University Press, Cambridge (1997)

18. El-Khair, I.A.: Effects of Stop Words Elimination for Arabic Information Retrieval: A Comparative Study. International Journal of Computing and Information Sciences 4(3), 119–133 (2006)

19. Alajmi, A., Saad, E.M., Darwish, R.R.: Toward an ARABIC Stop-Words List Generation. International Journal of Computer Applications 46(8), 8–13 (2012)

20. Ceska, Z., Hanak, I., Tesar, R.: Teraman: A Tool for N-gram Extraction from Large Datasets. In: the 2007 IEEE International Conference on Intelligent Computer Communication and Processing, Cluj-Napoca, pp. 209–216 (2007)

21. Salton, G., Buckley, C.: Term-Weighting Approaches in Automatic Retrieval. Journal of Information Processing and Management 24(5), 513–523 (1988)

Part V
Image Analysis and Pattern Recognition

ATDT: Autonomous Template-Based Detection and Tracking of Objects from Airborne Camera

Pouria Sadeghi-Tehran and Plamen Angelov

School of Computing and Communications, Lancaster University, United Kingdom
{p.sadeghi-tehran,p.angelov}@lancaster.ac.uk

Abstract. This paper describes the proposed ATDT approach for autonomous template-based detection and tracking from a moving airborne camera or an electro-optical (EO) device. The advantages of the proposed method ATDT is that it is fully autonomous (no human involvement is needed; in the experiment the human was only involved to navigate the UAV not for any of the steps of the video analysis) replacing the need of human operators for video analytics tasks, it can be used on board UAV, is computationally lean and can operate in real time.

Keywords: Objects tracking, dynamic template, autonomous object detection, UAV.

1 Introduction

The problem of detection and tracking of moving objects (by airborne camera mounted on UAVs) has been addressed by different approaches, such as features extraction [1, 2], optical flow [3, 4], etc. These approaches; however, assume a human operator to manually select a region of interest including object(s) of interest that are moving. On the other hand, moving objects can be detected using BS methods, such as KDE, GMM, etc. ; however, they require a static camera [5].

There is a need to develop new efficient methods for both detecting and tracking moving objects autonomously from moving airborne cameras mounted on a UAV (without human interaction) and in real-time. This problem can be separated in two parts: *i)* unknown objects; *ii)* known objects. In this paper we describe the latter problem. The former problem is described, for example, in [6].

There are few existing template-based techniques such as Normalised Cross Correlation (NCC) [7], Sequential Similarity Detection Algorithm (SSDA) [8], etc. However, they require an exhaustive search and take a large amount of computation time; on the other hand, they are not scale- and rotation invariant. In order to address some of the challenges mentioned earlier we use feature extraction and matching technique.

In computer vision, the concept of keypoints, has been largely used to address many problems in visual tracking, object recognition, 3D reconstruction, etc. It relies on the idea that instead of looking at the image as a whole, it could be advantageous

© Springer International Publishing Switzerland 2015
D. Filev et al. (eds.), *Intelligent Systems'2014*,
Advances in Intelligent Systems and Computing 323, DOI: 10.1007/978-3-319-11310-4_48

to select some interesting points known as feature points in the image and perform a local analysis on and around them only. Such an approach works relatively well as long as a sufficient number of keypoints are detected in the image and these points are stable features that can be accurately localised. Moreover, the number of feature points should be independent from the resolution to make it possible to be applied in real time even for high resolution videos.

Comprehensive descriptions of alternative techniques can be found in a series of survey and evaluation papers covering both feature detection and feature descriptors [9-13].

A key advantage of keypoints is that they permit matching even in the presence of clutter (occlusion) and large scale and orientation changes. There are two main approaches to finding feature points and their correspondences. The first one is to find features in one image that can be accurately tracked using a local search technique such as correlation or least squares. The second one is to independently detect features in all the images under consideration and then match features based on their local appearance. The former approach is more suitable when images are taken from nearby viewpoints or in a rapid succession (e.g., video sequences), while the second one is more suitable when a large amount of motion or appearance change is expected, e.g., in stitching together panoramas [14] or performing object recognition [15]. There are two established leaders in this area known as Scale Invariant Feature Transform (SIFT) [2] and Speeded Up Robust Feature (SURF) [1] techniques. However, the two methods are patented in the US [16, 17] and cannot be used freely for commercial purposes. On the other hand, there are other techniques such as Features from Accelerated Segment Test (FAST) [18] or Harris detector [19]; however, most of them like the Harris detector and BRIEF [20] are not scale and rotational invariant. Therefore, they can be applied on limited number of applications and scenarios.

For this purpose we use a newly introduced technique which is known as Binary Robust Invariant Scalable Keypoints (BRISK) [21]. It has been proved that BRISK is computationally more efficient and has a better performance in terms of speed and robustness compared to its counterpart [21, 22].

2   Description of the Methodology of ATDT

In general, the template-based approach includes matching an image/frame with another image/frame, taken *a priory* multiple times, from different views/angles or by different sensors. Given a search frame, S_F and reference frame R_F the proposed technique finds the best match to the reference in the search frame. The advantage of using template matching is that no assumption about the object's motion or appearance is needed.

The template matching technique for video streams includes several steps. First one is to form a reference image from the first frame. Second, is to find correlation between the reference and each new coming image/frame. Then, the best match points of a new coming frame are extracted by locating the maximum correlation value. At the end, the object of interest is extracted from each frame.

In the proposed ATDT method, micro-libraries of object(s) of interest are provided to the UAV before the flight or transmitted during the mission. This micro-library of m objects contains n_m different views resulting from rotation, scale variation and other transformations of the images with the m objects of interest. Let us, for simplicity, without reducing the generality of the approach, assume $m=1$ and the object of interest being a car with red colour. The way ATDT works is as follows: the UAV starts a mission (or can be on a mission when receiving a task to) and aims to autonomously detect, identify, locate, and track ("chase") any of the m objects of interest. Note, that the background on which the n_m images are taken is usually (quite) different form the real background when the "chase" mission will be performed. The application of such missions can be for protecting a perimeter form known/expected intruders or detection, identification, location and tracking of objects with known characteristics autonomously.

The main advantage of the proposed method ATDT is that it is fully autonomous (no human involvement is needed; in the experiment the human was only involved to navigate the UAV not for any of the steps of the video analysis) replacing the need of human operators for video analytics tasks, it can be used on board UAV, is computationally lean and can operate in real time (the preliminary tests were made with a simulated 'real time' operation when each image frame was analysed one by one without using past frames and the time was recorded; further experiments will be performed in real-time, on board UAV with the framework of the GAMMA programme [23]; the authors made an attempt to perform real-time experiment using the available AR Drone at Lancaster Intelligent Systems Research Lab but it was not possible with the existing AR Drone UAV which does not allow user application software to run on board; however, the ATDT method itself is developed with real-time operation in mind). The latter advantages (on board real-time operation) mean that the bandwidth of transmitted images can be dramatically reduced from the whole life video as it is with the current state-of-the art approaches to the images and even just regions of interest within the mages (ROI) only on demand or for informing the ground control station (GCS) only. This dramatic reduction of the information being transmitted to the ground in real time (the whole video can easily be saved on board on a memory and analysed in more detail and/or by human(s) later on (post flight)) means that the risk of interception and requirements for power and energy for the transmitters in addition to the bandwidth are dramatically reduced as well. The overall ATDT is summarised and depicted in Fig. 1.

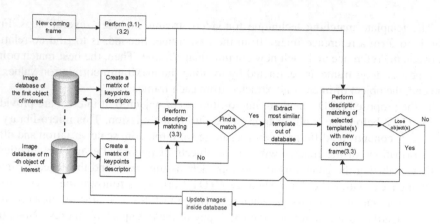

Fig. 1. Schematic representation of the proposed approach ATDT

3   Feature Detection of and Matching in ATDT

The overall procedure of autonomous detecting a reference image in a video streams is divided into three steps. During the first one (feature detection/extraction), the reference/template image is searched for locations that are likely to match well in the coming frames. At the second step, called feature description, each region around detected key point locations is converted into a more compact and stable (invariant) descriptor that can be matched against other descriptors. The third, final stage, called feature matching, searches efficiently for likely matching candidates in other frames.

3.1   Keypoints Detection

In order to extract key points from the reference image and each new frame, first, we need to create scale space. Then, we compute so called FAST [24] score across the scale space. In the next step, sub-pixel maximum across patch is computed and continues across the scales. At the final step, image coordinates are re-interpolated from the scale space feature point detection. Scale space is composed of pyramid layers which consist of n octaves of images c_i and n intra-octave images d_i; where $i = \{0, 1, \ldots, n \quad 1\}$, C_0 is the original image, and generally, $n = 4$. Each octave is half-sampled from the previous octave and each intra-octave d_i is down-sampled and located between c_i and $c_i + 1$.

As opposed to FAST [24], BRISK [21] uses different alternatives of mask shapes for the keypoint detection. In ATDT, we use a 16 point FAST detector which requires 9 consecutive pixels in the 16 pixel circle which are darker or brighter than the central pixel. The FAST detector initially is computed at each octave and intra-octave separately using a threshold, T to nominate the potential regions of interest. Then, the points inside the region of interest are titled to non-maxima suppression in the scale-space. Non-maximal suppression is performed on each octave and intra-octave such that the FAST score s is maximal within a 3x3 neighbourhood; also, score s is greater than the scales above and below. This comparison is done against the max value in a 3x3 patch in the scale images above and below. By considering image saliency as a continuous quantity not only across the image but also along the scale dimension, a sub-pixel maxima and refinement for each detected maximum is performed. A 2D quadratic function is fit to the 3x3 patch surrounding the pixel and sub-pixel maximum. The same process is also done for the layer above and below. In all three layers of interest, the local saliency's maximum is refined at sub-pixel level before a 1D parabola is fitted along the scale-axis to determine the true scale of the key point [21].

3.2   Keypoints Descriptors

After detecting the features (key points), we must match them, i.e., determine which features come from corresponding locations in different images. In order to increase the robustness, the characteristic direction of each key point is identified to allow for orientation-normalised descriptors. A pattern is used for sampling the neighbourhood of each keypoint. The intensity at the points is smoothed with Gaussian filters with standard deviation σ_i proportional to the distance between the points on the respective circle to avoid aliasing effects same as in [21]. Considering the set β containing all pairs of pixels:

$$\beta = \left\{ \left(p_i, p_j \right) \in \Re^2 \times \Re^2 \middle| i < N \wedge j < i \wedge i, j \in \aleph \right\} \tag{1}$$

where $\dfrac{N(N-1)}{2}$; $N = 60$; (p_i, p_j) are sampling point pairs

Two subset are defined based on the distance [21]:

$$\tau = \left\{ \left(p_i, p_j \right) \in \beta \mid \left\| p_j - p_i \right\| < \delta_{\max} \right\} \subseteq \beta; \quad \delta_{\max} = 9.75t \tag{2}$$

$$\rho = \left\{ \left(p_i, p_j \right) \in \beta \mid \left\| p_j - p_i \right\| > \delta_{\min} \right\} \subseteq \beta; \quad \delta_{\min} = 13.67t$$

where τ is the short distance pairing and ρ is the long distance pairing. For $N=60$, $\tau=512$, and $\rho=870$; t is the scale of a keypoint

The strength of the gradient between pairs is computes as:

$$g(p_i, p_j) = \frac{(p_j - p_i)}{\left\| p_j - p_i \right\|} \cdot \frac{I(p_j, \sigma_j) - I(p_i, \sigma_i)}{\left\| p_j - p_i \right\|} \tag{3}$$

$$\textit{unit vector} \qquad \textit{gradient magnitude}$$

The overall key point direction vector g is estimated by summing gradients of all pairs in the long-distance set:

$$g = \begin{pmatrix} g_x \\ g_y \end{pmatrix} = \frac{1}{L} \cdot \sum_{(p_i, p_j) \in \rho} g(p_i, p_j) \tag{4}$$

In order to build the descriptors, same as in the BRISK method [21], we apply sampling pattern rotated by orientation α around the key point k: $\alpha = \arctan 2(g_y, g_x)$.

Rotated short distance pairings are used to build binary descriptor d_k. Each bit in d_k is computed from point pairs $\left(p_i^\alpha, p_j^\alpha \right) \in S$. Therefore, the descriptor is 512 long for $N = 60$. In that case, each bit b corresponds to:

$$b = \begin{cases} 1, & I(p_j^\alpha, \sigma_j) > I(p_i^\alpha, \sigma_i) \\ 0, & otherwise \end{cases} \tag{5}$$

3.3 Descriptor Matching

Once features and their descriptors from two or more images are extracted, the next step is to establish some preliminary feature matches between these images. The approach we take depends partially on the application. This problem is divided into two separate stages. The first one is to select a matching strategy, which determines which correspondences are passed on to the next stage for further processing. The second one is to devise efficient data structures and algorithms to perform this matching as quickly as possible. Once we have decided on a matching strategy, we still need to efficiently search for potential candidates. The simplest way to find all corresponding feature points is to compare all features against all other features in each pair of potentially matching images. Unfortunately, this is quadratic in terms of number of extracted features, which makes it impractical for most applications. A better approach is to devise an indexing structure such as a multi-dimensional search tree or hash tables to rapidly search for features near a given one. Such indexing structures can either be built for each image independently or globally for all the images in a given database, which can potentially be faster, since it removes the need to iterate over each image [9]. We perform three main stages to remove any ambiguous matches and improve the performance of matching process, in general. During the matching process, we only accept those matches that fall onto the corresponding epipolar lines. In order to do that, the fundamental matrix must be computed [25].

The main objective is to find a set of good matches between the reference image and a new frame and find/remove other mismatch points. We start with brute-force match algorithm to find initial matches between key points. However, instead of selecting only the best one, two best matching points for each feature are selected for higher robustness. In order words, for each key point in the reference image two best matches in the coming frame are found and vice versa. Thus, for each key point there are two candidate matches in the other image. Basically, these are the two best ones based on the distance between their descriptors. If this measured distance is very high for the first best match, and much smaller for the second one, it is safe to say that the second match is the best candidate. We are verifying that by computing the ratio of the distance of the first best match over the distance of the second one and it should not be greater than the threshold, T. However, if the two matches are relatively close, we cannot be sure which one is the best match. In such case, in order to minimise the error, both matches are rejected. In the first stage (ratio test), a large number of mismatches will be filtered out; however, there may be still a significant number of false matches that survive. In order two eliminate other false matches we execute the second stage called symmetrical test. From the previous stage, we have two good match sets, one from the reference image to the frame and the other one from the frame to the reference image. In the second stage, if the two match sets are symmetrical we keep them; otherwise, they are discarded. In the last stage we use the fundamental matrix to filter out matches that do not obey the epipolar constraint.

In order to compute the fundamental matrix, we use RANSAC method [26] which tries to find inliers by estimating the matrix H and ignoring outliers [26]. It randomly samples corresponding matches and tries to fit the homography, H to those data samples. Then, an error is calculated between the rest of data samples and the model. The data points are classified as inlier or outliers based on a threshold T. The process is continued till the number of outliers is sufficiently small [27]. The RANSAC method should be able to distinguish how well the estimated H fits all the data samples. The better we can filter out false matches, the higher the probability that RANSAC will give the correct fundamental matrix. This is the reason we applied the two previously described stages to remove ambiguous matches. The effect of applying three level filtering is illustrated in Fig. 2.

Fig. 2. Comparison before and after applying the three layer filters

4   Experimental Results

The introduced approach, ATDT was experimented in variety of scenarios and different environments. The first experiment, was carried out outdoors at Lancaster University campus using AR Drone 2.0 controlled by an operator on the ground (Fig. 3) performing the mission to autonomously detect, identify, locate and track the object of interest (a red car), Fig. 4.

Before the experiment, few snapshots of the object of interest (red car) were taken in order to build the library of images with different scales, angles, and rotations. Then, keypoints of all stored images were extracted and matrices of keypoints descriptors were formed in advance. During the flight, AR Drone generated videos in real-time. For each new coming frame the keypoints were compared with all the keypoints from the dataset created beforehand to find the best match. Then, any

object which is visually similar to any of the images within the database is being identified. Once the best match is selected, it is used only as a reference template to track
objects of interest inside the new coming image frames. This improves the processing
time and avoids going through all the images inside the database. However, if the
object of interest is lost, we can go back to the database again (see Fig.1). The whole
proposed approach will reduce the chance of losing track of the interested object and
we will have more robust matching/tracking performance overall. Fig. 4 shows six
snapshots during the tracking process. As it is clear from the figure, we can keep track
of the interested object regardless of changing scales and rotation of the objects in
different scenarios.

Fig. 3. Flight test using AR. Drone at Lancaster University

Fig. 4. Object tracking results with AR Drone

The second experiment was performed on a video taken from the Internet recorded from a helicopter chasing a car on a motorway. This experiment shows that the introduced approach ATDT can be used to track multiple objects and it is not limited to tracking only a single object. Same procedure was applied to this experiment; however, two databases of images were built instead of one. First database contains images from a grey car in different angles and scales. The second database contains images of a police car added to the scene in the middle of the experiment. At the beginning of the video, a helicopter keeps tracking the grey car successfully, even when it was partially occluded by a lorry (Fig. 5c). After few frames, a police car appears on the scene and it is automatically identified and tracked (Fig. 5). In the remainder of the video the two cars were tracked side by side even when other cars appeared on the scene and despite occlusion.

(a) Frame 20   (b) Frame 50   (c) Frame 100

(d) Frame 200   (e) Frame 250   (f) Frame 300

Fig. 5. Object tracking results from a helicopter

5   Conclusion

In this paper we introduced a new approach, ATDT for autonomous template-based detection and tracking in real-time using an airborne camera. It is fully autonomous and is able to identify and track objects of interest on a scene without a human involvement. The introduced approach has been tested using aerial videos taken by an AR Drone and also by a pre-recorded video. Both experiments show the high reliability of the introduced approach on holding track of object(s) of interest and robust matching performance, in general. By differ from all reported alternative approaches, the proposed ATDT approach is autonomous and real-time suitable to run on board small or large UAVs.

Acknowledgement. This research paper was supported by the GAMMA Programme which is funded through the Regional Growth Fund. The Regional Growth Fund (RGF) is a £3.2 billion fund supporting projects and programmes which are using private sector investment to generate economic growth as well as creating sustainable jobs between now and the mid-2020s. For more information, please go to www.bis.gov.uk/rgf

References

1. Bay, H., et al.: SURF: Speeded Up Robust Features. In: Computer Vision and Image Understanding (CVIU), pp. 346–359 (2008)
2. Lowe, D.G.: Distinctive image features from scale-invariant keypoints. International Journal of Computer Vision 60(2), 91–110 (2004)
3. Barron, J.L., Fleet, D.J., Beauchemin, S.: Performance of optical flow techniques. International Journal of Computer Vision 12(1), 43–77 (1994)
4. Beauchemin, S.S., Barron, J.L.: The computation if optical flow. Journal of Computing Surveys (CSUR) 27(3), 433–466 (1995)
5. Elgammal, A., et al.: Background and Foreground Modeling using Nonparametric Kernel Density for Visual Surveillance. Proc. of the IEEE (2002)
6. Sadeghi-Tehran, P., Angelov, P.: ARTOD: Autonomous Real Time Objects Detection by a Moving Camera using Recursive Density Estimation. In: Novel Applications of Intelligent Systems (2014)
7. Prat, W.K.: Correlation techniques of image registration. IEEE Trans. on Aerospace and Electronic Systems 10, 353–358 (1974)
8. Onoe, M., Saito, M.: Automatic threshold setting for the sequential similarity detection algorithm. IEEE Trans. on Comput., 1052–1053 (1976)
9. Szeliski, R.: Computer Vision: Algorithms and Applications. Springer (2010)
10. Tuytelaars, T., Mikolajczyk, K.: Local invariant feature detectors. Foundations and Trends in Computer Graphics and Computer Vision 3(1) (2007)
11. Mikolajczyk, K., Schmid, C.: A performance evaluation of local descriptors. IEEE Transactions on Pattern Analysis and Machine Intelligence 27(10), 1615–1630 (2005)
12. Triggs, B.: Detecting keypoints with stable position, orientation, and scale under illumination changes. In: Pajdla, T., Matas, J(G.) (eds.) ECCV 2004. LNCS, vol. 3024, pp. 100–113. Springer, Heidelberg (2004)
13. Schmid, C., Mohr, R., Bauckhage, C.: Evaluation of interest point detectors. International Journal of Computer Vision 37(2), 151–172 (2000)
14. Brown, M., Lowe, D.: Automatic panoramic image stitching using invariant features. International Journal of Computer Vision 74(1), 59–73 (2007)
15. Fergus, R., Perona, P., Zisserman, A.: Weakly supervised scale-invariant learning of models for visual recognition. International Journal of Computer Vision 71(3), 273–303 (2007)
16. Funayama, R., et al.: Robust Interest Point Detector and Descriptor, US (2009)
17. Lowe, D.: Method and apparatus for identifying scale invariant features in an image and use of same for locating an object in an image (2004)
18. Rosten, E., Porter, R., Drummond, T.: Faster and better: a machine learning approach to corner detection. IEEE Trans. Pattern Analysis and Machine Intelligence 32, 105–119 (2010)
19. Harris, C., Stephens, M.: A combined corner and edge detector. In: Proceedings of the 4th Alvey Vision Conference (1988)
20. Calonder, M., et al.: BRIEF: Binary Robust Independent Elementary Features. IEEE Transactions on Pattern Analysis and Machine Intelligence (2012)

21. Leutenegger, S., Chli, M., Siegwart, R.Y.: BRISK: Binary Robust Invariant Scal-able Keypoints. In: IEEE International Conference on Computer Vision (ICCV), pp. 2548–2555 (2011)
22. Khvedchenia, I.: A battle of three descriptors: SURF, FREAK and BRISK (2012) (cited November 1, 2012)
23. GAMMA: Growing Autonomous Mission MAnagement systems Programme. funded by the Regional Growth Fund, BIS (2012-2014)
24. Mair, E., Hager, G.D., Burschka, D., Suppa, M., Hirzinger, G.: Adaptive and generic corner detection based on the accelerated segment test. In: Daniilidis, K., Maragos, P., Paragios, N. (eds.) ECCV 2010, Part II. LNCS, vol. 6312, pp. 183–196. Springer, Heidelberg (2010)
25. Laganiere, R.: Opencv 2 Computer Vision Application Programming Cookbook. Packt Publishing Ltd., UK (2011)
26. Fischler, M.A., Bolles, R.C.: Random sample consensus: A paradigm for model fitting with applications to image analysis and automated cartography. Comm. of the ACM 24(6), 381–395 (1981)
27. Hartley, R., Zisserman, A.: Multiple view geometry in computer vision. Cambridge Univ. Pr. (2003)

Data Inconsistency in Sunspot Detection

Ehsan Shahamatnia, Ivan Dorotovič, André Mora, José Fonseca, and Rita Ribeiro

UNINOVA/CA3, Campus da FCT/UNL, 2829-516 Caparica, Portugal
Dept. of Computer and Electrical Engineering, Faculty of Sciences and Technology,
New University of Lisbon, Portugal
ehs@IEEE.org, {ehs,id,atm,jmf,rar}@UNINOVA.pt

Abstract. Availability of integrated high quality information is a prerequisite for many intelligent knowledge based systems. Consistency of data plays an influential role in reassuring the quality of the integrated data. In this paper we discuss issues of data inconsistency in the domain of sunspot detection (i.e. a manifestation of solar activity). Sunspots data are collected from ground based observatories and also from instruments aboard satellites. Due to instrumentation limitations and inevitable subjectivity of human observers, the collected data bear some levels of inconsistency. This paper discusses issues regarding inconsistency in data used for performance validation of an automated sunspot tracking system. For evaluating the results, an integrated probability reference map is created, using knowledge integration, which reinforces data accuracy with higher certainty. Further, we use a weighted matching technique to reduce the impact of some data inconsistency.

Keywords: Knowledge integration, Data fusion, Solar image processing, Sunspot.

1 Introduction

Knowledge that is embedded in high-technology systems is an extremely valuable commodity [1]. Reliability and accuracy of information in these complex systems is fundamental for their performance. Successful Knowledge integration (KI) is essential to assure the accuracy of the information that the system is operating on. The availability of high quality information is also a critical requirement of a decision support system (DSS) in order to properly help the decision-making process [2]. In this work we follow the view that knowledge integration (KI) is the process of combining multiple knowledge models (or representations) into a common model (representation) [3]. KI is produced by collecting data from various sources, with different specifications and characterizations. Sources of information can cover wide and diverse types of data from sensor readings, user feedback, customer satisfaction, enterprise performance indices, patient profiles, image and multimedia, and experts' knowledge. This paper aims to look at the difficulties associated with accuracy and consistency of data, used in a specific scientific application of detecting sunspots in solar images.

© Springer International Publishing Switzerland 2015
D. Filev et al. (eds.), *Intelligent Systems' 2014*,
Advances in Intelligent Systems and Computing 323, DOI: 10.1007/978-3-319-11310-4_49

The primary method for studying the Sun and its activity is visually inspecting it through telescopes and captured images. Sunspots are the easiest feature to detect from all manifestations of the solar activity [4]. They are dark areas in the Sun's photosphere, which are cooler than their surroundings. Sunspots can be isolated or in groups, and are associated with very strong magnetic fields. Tracking sunspots is a very important task because it allows solar physicists and other interested scientists to analyze the evolution of solar activity during a solar cycle (around 11 years). Higher precision in tracking sunspots implies improved accuracy of the analysis. Traditionally the procedure for sunspot tracking was that solar observatories would manually detect sunspot on drawings and/or low-resolution images taken by ground-based telescopes. In the last decade more sophisticated solar imaging instruments have been installed in ground-based observatories and space-born satellites, which provide huge amount of solar data with higher resolution. This has boosted the volume, performance and precision of solar image processing research.

However, there is still a multitude of issues that affect the quality of the gathered data such as defects in the sensory instruments, noise, unfavorable atmospheric conditions, and data loss in archiving and restoring. Another key issue is the consistency of the gathered data which has two facets; multiple input sources and subjectivity. In many cases it is not enough to study the Sun based on data from one instrument and/or an observatory, but we need to aggregate various input data. For example, combining solar images taken at different wavelengths and different telescopic filters at the same time to study a specific event in the Sun (see Fig. 1). Several works in the literature take advantage of integrating multiple sources for input data [5], [6], [7]. The second part of data consistency is subjectivity. In many intelligent decision support systems it is required intervention of experts or operators to process data and then input some relevant information into the system, which imposes subjectivity upon the input data. Some examples of the subjectivity of experts' opinions in medical image processing are given in [8]. Sunspot detection is also similarly subjective, because of the solar images complexity and unpredictable nature of solar features, therefore many times it is not agreed the number and characteristics of solar features at a specific date and time. While solar observatories experts are defining solar features as their routine task, the collected data and manual processing is prone to subjectivity. Hence, an agreed definition for a universal daily sunspot number is an average from more than 86 observatories from 29 countries [9]. An example of a manual collected sunspot data is depicted in Fig. 2, which shows an image from HMI telescope aboard SDO satellite with several sunspot groups marked by an expert. As it can be seen from the figure, defining solar features can be a very difficult and meticulous task. If the input data are coming from various sources, it is required that some data integration mechanism takes this subjectivity into consideration. The precision and performance of the system is influenced by quality of the input data. The subjectivity in data might lead to inconsistency of the integrated input information, and hence affect the quality of data.

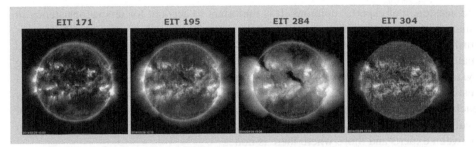

Fig. 1. Solar images taken with different wavelength at 29/03/2014 at 13:00 within 20 minutes time window. (Image courtesy of NASA/ESA SOHO mission).

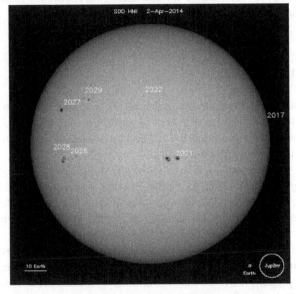

Fig. 2. Several sunspot groups marked by an expert. The process of defining solar features can be very difficult, meticulous and subjective.

In many cases, developing a new automated system requires evaluating performance of the system in comparison to ground truth obtained by expert human operators. Inconsistent information collected from experts, makes it very difficult to evaluate results by performing comparisons. Inconsistency between experts' opinions also leads to a lower overlap between automated systems results with integrated information from experts.

In this paper we study the impact of inconsistency in sunspot data on an automated PSO-Snake solar feature tracking system [4]. In order to validate the performance of that system, the results from the PSO-Snake algorithm are compared with sunspot data from experts. However, the results cannot be compared only with one expert, since the generality of the system will be affected and if they are compared with several experts, the performance metrics of the system will drop due to the combined inconsistency of experts' opinions. It is important to account for this inconsistency in calculating the performance metrics of the automated tracking system. This paper further extends upon authors' previous work [8] on proposing and using a weighted matching approach for evaluating results of an automated medical image processing system. This approach shows promising results and improves the evaluation of results. For evaluation, false positive and false negative analyses are performed for each sunspot. In order to minimize the subjectivity and improve the confidence of evaluation, we propose a differentiation between data where there is an agreement between experts and those where there is none.

The rest of the paper is organized as follows. Section 2 introduces the sunspot tracking system. In section 3 sources of inconsistency in sunspot data are reviewed. Also in this section proposed method for calculating inconsistency in sunspot data and the weighted matching approach are discussed. Finally, Section 4 concludes this paper.

2   Tracking Sunspots

In this section we briefly describe the tool used for automatic tracking of sunspots in this study. The tool is based on a hybrid algorithm of a Snake model and Particle Swarm Optimization, first proposed in [10] and then successfully applied for tracking sunspots [4] and coronal bright points [11].

Snake model, also known as Active Contour Model, is a recognized method in image processing best known for its flexibly in object detection [11]. It is an energy minimization algorithm that takes into account the low level image features such as image gradient or image intensity, as well as the higher level information such as object shape, continuity of the contour and user interaction [12]. By giving an approximation of the object boundary, active contour will find the precise boundary of the object. Particle Swarm Optimization (PSO) algorithm makes the second part of this tracking approach. PSO is an evolutionary optimization technique with a population of particles, each representing a potential solution to the problem [13]. The population is initialized with random solutions, i.e. random positions in the search space and velocities for moving the particles in that space. The PSO-Snake algorithm combines advantages of high-level object detection capacities of the snake model with the PSO algorithm to achieve a promising system for automatic object tracking. The main steps of this algorithm are described in [4]. In this paper we discuss the PSO-Snake algorithm for tracking sunspots and incorporated the weighted matching analysis in its evaluation module.

3   Inconsistency in the Sunspot Data

Scientists have been interested in collecting sunspot data even before the pre-telescopic era. In 1849 Rudolf Wolf, from Zurich observatory, proposed a scheme to standardize daily solar activity according to the recorded sunspots [14]. In this scheme, known as Wolf number or Zurich number, the relative sunspot number, R, is calculated in relation to number of detected individual sunspots, s, and the number of sunspot groups, g, as shown in eq. (1).

$$R = k(10g + s) \tag{1}$$

In this equation k is the observatory factor, a coefficient that varies with location and instrumentation. This factor, also known as Personal Reduction Coefficient, was introduced to increase consistency between different sunspot observations by taking into account the subjectivity of the observer, and the less influential factor of location of the respective observatory [9]. By analyzing the Wolf number during extended periods, scientists could discover the solar cycle, and its influence on Earth magnetic field. Since 1981, the Solar Influences Data Analysis Center (SIDC), at the Royal observatory of Belgium has been receiving sunspot data, collected from more than 80 stations/observatories around the globe. The SIDC has been renamed in November 2013to SILSO (Sunspot Index and Long-term Solar Observations). By integrating all these data – a knowledge integration task- , SILSO issues the daily international sunspot index, which is widely used by most solar physicists and astronomers. Since the subjectivity of the observers is inevitable, there will also be some subjectivity in estimating the daily sunspot index by averaging the individual observations. Other reasons for the inconsistency of sunspot data are: variation in local conditions (e.g. weather, technical difficulties), the size limit of the smallest sunspot, and the division of complex sunspot groups. SILSO reports that subjectivity of individual observers is largely averaged out by the bulk number of independent observers [9], however there is still about 8% rms dispersion in the SIDC sunspot data, between simultaneous daily observations by many separate observers [15].

The problem is underlined in the case of evaluating performance of automated solar data processing tools. Quantification of performance of these systems require ground truth data, which can be more than just the sunspot index number, as for instance the precise sunspot coordinates, area, group pattern and their classification among others. Unlike the international sunspot index number, there is no global data integration process available for these parameters. For specific applications it is needed to collect data from individual sources (observatories and datasets) and/or to have help from a group of experts for doing manual analysis.

For measuring the performance of the sunspot tracking algorithm we need some ground truth to compare the result of the system with it. For instance, for evaluating the sunspot detection and tracking results, knowing the exact coordinates of sunspots is essential. Comparing the results with opinions of one expert or one dataset, just increases subjectivity and diminishes the generality of the system. In order to be able to objectively assess the performance of sunspot tracking system by comparing its results with a group of experts or datasets, we need to take into account the inherent inconsistency of these data. Figure 3 shows main steps of this procedure. In the rest of this section each step is described.

Fig. 3. Schematic diagram of data inconsistency analysis for sunspot coordinate data

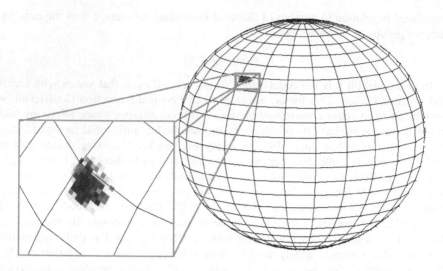

Fig. 4. An illustration of center of solar feature marked on the surface of the Sun by various observers. This heat map shows coordinates of center of solar feature. Darker color denotes that higher number of observers reported that coordinate as the center of solar feature.

In this study we use sunspot data obtained from Mt. Wilson/USAF-NOAA (USAF-MWL) dataset [16] - for observations from 1981 until 2013 containing about 250000 instances of sunspot data from different stations - and also data from Kandilli observatory [17] in Turkey for the years from 1995 till 2014 (the latter data has some gaps). Having multiple data sources provides a better knowledge integration and flexibility. It is common that the quality of collected data in one observatory is temporarily reduced or the data is not collected due to hazardous weather conditions, technical difficulties, instrument maintenance, etc. In these situations data from other sources can cover for the missing range. In order to use the collected datasets, they should be preprocessed to find out the missing data and mark the incorrect or duplicated data.

Observations at different datasets have different temporal resolutions and are recorded at different times. For the Kandilli datasets, sunspots are usually recorded once a day, while for USAF-MWL datasets the sunspot number are usually recorded three times a day, through different stations. Due to these differences in timing of observations, it is very difficult to find available sunspot data, for exactly the same time from different solar observatories. To overcome this problem, and having in consideration that sunspots have an average lifespan of few days, we normalize the time of observations to an arbitrary reference time. Hence, by tracking sunspots in successive observations and interpolating the data, we can estimate their position at the reference time. Further, we identify the sunspots by a unique ID, which encompasses the recording station and date and time of their first appearances. For each new sunspot data, from a specific observatory, we match them with current ones using various rules regarding the distance of new sunspots to current ones, appearance/disappearance of other sunspots, distance of new sunspots from each other, their area and time interval of observations. Furthermore, by considering the speed of their displacement we can decide with a certain confidence level either to reassign sunspot IDs, stop tracking them or assign new IDs. Similar set of rules is used to match detected sunspots of one observatory to recorded sunspots of other observatories.

After assigning sunspot IDs, the next phase is calculating the data inconsistency in ground truth data obtained from datasets to validate the automated system's performance. Figure 4 uses a synthetic heat map to illustrate how a number of observers might report different coordinates for the same solar feature. Calculating the false positive and false negative ratios by comparing result of the system with data from each observatory would not be suitable due to the variability of data from different observatories and the lack of standardized reference. In order to perform the knowledge integration of data from various observatories for creating a reference data that can be used for comparison with the automated system results, we adapted the weighted matching analysis method introduced in [8]. The final result is a reference probability map of the solar disk. We start by dividing the solar disk in a grid with resolution of 0.2 degrees. Measurements are coordinates of the center of sunspot as defined by observers. For each sunspot coordinate, we consider a diffusion window of 7x7 cells in this grid, centered on it. The center coordinate takes *Coord* value of 1 while cells in the diffusion window take gradually values of 0.75, 0.5 and 0.25 respectively. Figure 5 shows diffusion windows for two measurements 1 degree apart.

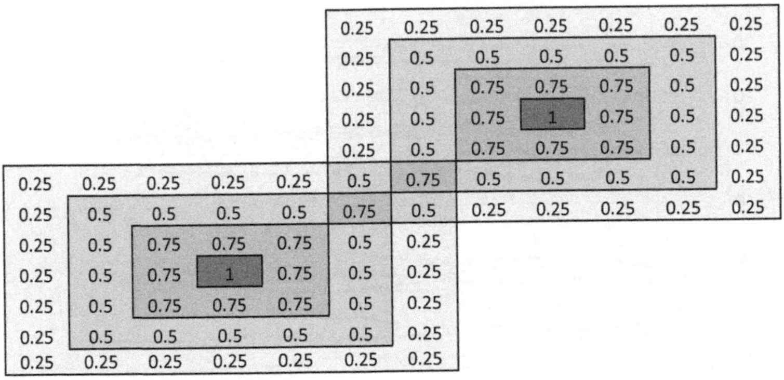

Fig. 5. Diffusion windows for two coordinate measurements on the solar disk. Each unit is 0.2 degrees and two measurements have one degree difference in latitude and longitude.

For each tracked sunspot, i, in various datasets and for each observation at time t, one probability map is created as follows:

$$PM_{sunspot_{i,t}}(lat, long) = \frac{\sum_{All\ datasets} Coord_{i,t}(lat,long)}{Number\ of\ datasets} \qquad (2)$$

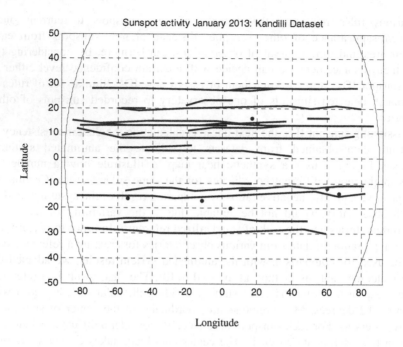

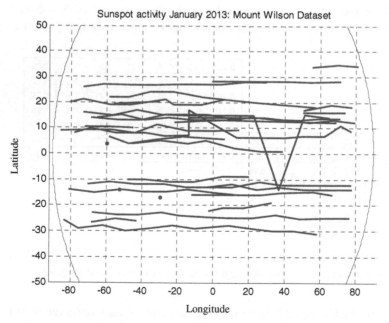

Fig. 6. Inconsistency in reported sunspot coordinates between data from Kandilli and USAF-MWL datasets for January 2013. Each line in the images represents traced path of sunspots in the corresponding dataset. The time frame for both datasets is identical.

Then we can use this map as comparison reference, for evaluating the automated system results. The statistical measure used for evaluation is the F-score [18]. F-score is the harmonic mean of precision and recall, as follows:

$$F_{score} = 2 \times \frac{precision \times recall}{precision + recall} \qquad (3)$$

$$precision = \frac{TP}{TP + FP} \qquad (4)$$

$$recall = \frac{TP}{TP + FN} \qquad (5)$$

where TP, FN, and FP are true positive, false negative and false positive measures.

In order to reinforce the consistency metric, we use two threshold values, high and low cut offs, to calculate the TP, TN, FP and FN indices. These cut off values can be chosen depending on the number of different data sources in use, to reward the values where different data sets match, and penalize isolated occurrences. Values in the reference probability map higher than 75% and values below 25% are considered as true and false references respectively. Figure 6 illustrates the inconsistencies for the sunspot coordinates between data collected from Kandilli and USAF-MWL datasets for January 2013. The figure plots the estimated positions of sunspots at reference time (mid-day), one observation a day. It can be seen that the first dataset tracks fewer sunspots, for shorter times but has more isolated reports of sunspots. Two sharp picks can be seen in the plot from Mount Willson data. By verifying with the source data obtained from this dataset, we confirmed that these picks are due to inconsistent data, probably as a result of a typo or a human error.

To analyze the data inconsistency more accurately, we distinct the errors in two types. First, inconsistency caused by different recordings of sunspot coordinates for the sunspots that are tracked by both datasets. For this example, the average inconsistency for sunspot coordinates tracked in both datasets is 1.809 degrees. When normalized over 180 degrees, the maximum possible error, it gives an average of 1% error in defining the position of sunspots. Second type of error is for situations when a sunspot is reported in one dataset, but not the other one. For the sample example shown in Fig. 6, out of 209 sunspot recordings (one recording per sunspot per day), 91 recordings from Kandilli dataset and 10 recordings from Mount Willson dataset, were not matched with any sunspot from the other dataset, which translates to 48% error. For this dataset, the F-score shows 68% consistency in sunspot data.

4   Conclusions and Future Works

This paper presents a preliminary study on assessing inconsistencies in sunspot data from different sources. Different stations around the world record sunspot data from ground based observatories and also from instruments aboard satellites, but both data sources have some technical limitations and are prone to inconsistencies. Further, in many cases the data analysis of detecting sunspots is done by domain experts and then aggregated to create a standard index number. Hence, recorded sunspot data are subject to different levels of inconsistency due to: variation in local conditions (e.g. weather, technical difficulties); limits for the smallest sunspot, division of complex sunspot into groups; and the inevitable subjectivity of the observers.

In this paper we discussed issues about validating performance of automated sunspot tracking systems, where performance is calculated in comparison with ground truth data from sunspot datasets. Comparing the results with only one dataset at a time would reduce the generality of the evaluation and won't be reliable. Hence, we proposed a knowledge integration process, which takes into account the sources' inconsistencies.

In our evaluation we found out that inconsistency in coordinates in sunspot datasets stems from two factors. One factor happens when different observers report different values for sunspot coordinates. This error is due to subjectivity of the observers as well as instrument faults and atmospheric effects. The second factor for inconsistency is when a tracked sunspot is not recorded by other station(s) at all. The latter imposes a much bigger error margin in the F-score calculations, therefore a weighted matching approach was used to diminish the effect of this inconsistency in data. In this study we focused on sunspot coordinates but the same procedure can be applied to other sunspot parameters such as area, classification and groups.

Finally, results highlighted the need for using information fusion techniques (knowledge integration) to combine sunspot data, which calls for deeper investigations. In the future we plan to extend the study by applying a fuzzy information fusion algorithm, FIF [7]. By rating and ranking different input sources we will be able to create a more sophisticated confidence measure for integrated reference data. Other pointers to extend this study are to include more sunspot datasets and use advanced statistical indices.

Acknowledgements. We would like to thank the SDO (NASA) and AIA science team for the provided observational material, and NOAA National Geophysical Data Center for the provided sunspot datasets. This work was partially supported by grant SFRH/BPD/44018/2008 (I.D.) and SFRH/BD/ 62249/2009 (E.S.) from Fundacao para a Ciencia e Tecnologia, MCTES, Lisbon, Portugal.

References

1. Dalkir, K.: Knowledge management in theory and practice. Routledge (2013)
2. Janjua, N.K., Hussain, F.K., Hussain, O.K.: Semantic information and knowledge integration through argumentative reasoning to support intelligent decision making. Inf. Syst. Front. 15, 167–192 (2013)
3. Chen, K., Yang, Z., Wang, H., Liu, L.: Commonsense Knowledge Supported Intelligent News Analysis for Portfolio Risk Prediction. In: 2011 44th Hawaii International Conference on System Sciences (HICSS), pp. 1–9 (2011)
4. Shahamatnia, E., Dorotovic, I., Ribeiro, R.A., Fonseca, J.M.: Towards an automatic sunspot tracking: Swarm intelligence and snake model hybrid. Acta Futur. 5, 153–161 (2012)

5. Zharkova, V., Aboudarham, J., Zharkov, S., Ipson, S.S., Benkhalil, A.K., Fuller, N.: Solar feature catalogues in EGSO. Sol. Phys. 228, 361–375 (2005)
6. Martens, P.C.H., Attrill, G.D.R., Davey, A.R., Engell, A., Farid, S., Grigis, P.C., Kasper, J., Korreck, K., Saar, S.H., Savcheva, A., Su, Y., Testa, P., Wills-Davey, M., Bernasconi, P.N., Raouafi, N.-E., Delouille, V.A., Hochedez, J.F., Cirtain, J.W., DeForest, C.E., Angryk, R.A., Moortel, I., Wiegelmann, T., Georgoulis, M.K., McAteer, R.T.J., Timmons, R.P.: Computer Vision for the Solar Dynamics Observatory (SDO). Sol. Phys. 275, 79–113 (2012)
7. Ribeiro, R.A., Falcão, A., Mora, A., Fonseca, J.M.: FIF: A fuzzy information fusion algorithm based on multi-criteria decision making. Knowledge-Based Syst. (2013)
8. Mora, A., Fonseca, J., Veira, P.: Retina Image Gradings' Comparison by Weighted Matching Analysis. In: Dössel, O., Schlegel, W.C. (eds.) WC 2009, IFMBE Proceeding, vol. 25/11, pp. 296–299. Springer, Heidelberg (2009)
9. Clette, F., Berghmans, D., Vanlommel, P., Vanderlinden, R., Koeckelenbergh, A., Wauters, L.: From the Wolf number to the International Sunspot Index: 25 years of SIDC. Adv. Sp. Res. 40, 919–928 (2007)
10. Shahamatnia, E., Ebadzadeh, M.M.: Application of particle swarm optimization and snake model hybrid on medical imaging. In: 2011 IEEE Third International Workshop on Computational Intelligence In Medical Imaging, pp. 1–8. IEEE, Paris (2011)
11. Dorotovic, I., Shahamatnia, E., Lorenc, M., Rybanský, M., Ribeiro, R.A., Fonseca, J.M.: Sunspots and Coronal Bright Points Tracking using a Hybrid Algorithm of PSO and Active Contour Model. J. Sun Geosph. 9, 81–84 (2014)
12. Kass, M., Witkin, A., Terzopoulos, D.: Snakes: Active contour models. Int. J. Comput. Vis. 1, 321–331 (1988)
13. Kennedy, J., Eberhart, R.: Particle swarm optimization. In: Proceedings of the IEEE International Conference on Neural Networks 1995, pp. 1942–1948 (1995)
14. Hossfield, C.H.: A history of the Zurich and American relative sunspot number indices. J. Am. Assoc. Var. Star Obs. 31, 48–53 (2002)
15. SILSO SILSO World Data Center: SILSO-World Data Center for the production, preservation and dissemination of the international sunspot number, http://sidc.be/silso/node/57?
16. National Geophysical Data Center: NGDC Server at NOAA - Solar Data - USAF_MWL data, ftp://ftp.ngdc.noaa.gov/STP/SOLAR_DATA/SUNSPOT_REGIONS/USAF_MWL/?
17. National Geophysical Data Center: NGDC Server at NOAA - Solar Data - Kandilli data, http://www.ngdc.noaa.gov/stp/space-weather/solar-data/solar-?features/sunspot-regions/kandilli/?
18. Powers, D.M.W.: Evaluation: from precision, recall and F-measure to ROC, informedness, markedness & correlation. J. Mach. Learn. Technol. 2, 37–63 (2011)

Automatic GrabCut for Bi-label Image Segmentation Using SOFM

Dina Khattab[1], Hala M. Ebied[1], Ashraf S. Hussein[2], and Mohamed F. Tolba[1]

[1] Faculty of Computer and Information Sciences, Ain Shams University, 11566, Cairo, Egypt
{d.khattab,halam}@fcis.asu.edu.eg, fahmytolba@cis.asu.edu.eg
[2] Faculty of Computer Studies, Arab Open University, Headquarters, 13033, Kuwait
ashrafh@acm.org

Abstract. This paper proposes a new technique for the problem of color image segmentation using GrabCut. GrabCut is considered as one of the semi-automatic segmentation techniques, since it requires user interaction for the initialization of the segmentation process, via dragging a rectangle around an object to extract it. This restricts GrabCut for bi-label segmentation, where the image cannot be segmented into more than two; foreground and background segments. In order to set up for multi-label segmentation, this paper presents the use of SOFM as a powerful unsupervised clustering technique for the GrabCut initialization process. This converts the GrabCut from a semi-automatic into a complete automatic segmentation technique. The use of different SOFM architectures for the process of image segmentation was tested for real experiments. Evaluation and comparison with the original GrabCut show the efficiency of the proposed automatic technique in terms of segmentation quality and accuracy.

Keywords: color image, automatic segmentation, GrabCut, SOFM.

1 Introduction

The process of partitioning a digital image into multiple segments is defined as image segmentation. Segmentation aims to divide an image into regions that can be more representative and easier to analyze. Such regions may correspond to individual surfaces, objects or natural parts of objects. Typically image segmentation is the process used to locate objects and boundaries (e.g lines or curves) in images [1]. Furthermore, it can be defined as the process of labeling every pixel in an image, where all pixels having the same label share certain visual characteristics [2]. Usually segmentation uses local information in the digital image to compute the best segmentation, such as color information used to create histograms, or information indicating edges, boundaries or texture information [3]. Many applications in computer vision may require image segmentation as a pre-processing step, such as object recognition, scene analysis, automatic traffic control systems and medical imaging.

A powerful segmentation technique for color images; The GrabCut technique [4]; is considered as one of the state-of-the-art of semi-automatic techniques for image segmentation. Becoming a semi-automatic technique is forced because of the necessity of

© Springer International Publishing Switzerland 2015
D. Filev et al. (eds.), *Intelligent Systems'2014,*
Advances in Intelligent Systems and Computing 323, DOI: 10.1007/978-3-319-11310-4_50

an initial user intervention, which specifies an object of interest to be segmented out of the image, considering all remaining image pixels as one background region. This restriction makes the GrabCut most appropriate for bi-label segmentation, where images can be segmented into two background and foreground regions only.

Irrespective of bi-label segmentation, multi-label segmentation is the process of segmenting an image into more than two segments, representing its natural objects. In order to set up for multi-label segmentation, an automatic solution is required to initialize the GrabCut as an alternative to initial user-labeling. The main contribution of this paper is to modify the GrabCut for automatic segmentation through the use of unsupervised techniques of image clustering. The suggested modification provides more advantage to the segmentation of the GrabCut through automatic initialization. Furthermore, it aims at maintaining good segmentation accuracy compared to that provided by original GrabCut. Self-Organizing Feature Map (SOFM) [5, 6] is a powerful example of unsupervised clustering technique that can be used for GrabCut initialization and therefore presented in this paper.

The remaining of the paper is organized as follows; section 2 provides basic background on image segmentation using GrabCut and on using SOFM clustering technique for image segmentation. Section 3 illustrates the SOFM algorithm and different architectures in more details. The original GrabCut technique and details of the main contribution are explained in section 4. Experimental results are presented in section 5, while the conclusion and future work are presented in section 6.

2   Related Work

This section presents the basic background needed in the directions of using GrabCut and SOFM in the problem of image segmentation.

2.1   Image Segmentation Using GrabCut

The GrabCut technique has been applied to different segmentation problems such as human body segmentation [7, 8, 9], video segmentation [10], semantic segmentation [11] and volume segmentation [12]. In [9], an automatic extraction of human body from color images is developed by Yi Hu. The iterated GrabCut technique is used to dynamically update a tri-map contour which is initialized from the results of a scanning detector used for detecting faces from images. This research has some drawbacks, as the process goes through many steps and iterations, in addition to being constrained to human poses with frontal side faces.

A full-automatic Spatio-Temporal GrabCut human segmentation methodology was proposed by Hernandez et al. [8]. Their developed methodology makes benefit from the combination of tracking and segmentation. Instead of the initial user intervention to initialize the GrabCut algorithm, a set of seeds defined by face detection and a skin color model are used for initialization. Another approach to segment humans from cluttered images was proposed by Gulshan et al. in [7]. They utilize the local color model based GrabCut for automatic segmentation. This GrabCut local color model is used to refine the crude human segmentations they obtained.

In video segmentation, Corrigan et al. [10] extend GrabCut for more robust video object segmentation. They extend the Gaussian Mixture Model (GMM) of the GrabCut algorithm so that the color space is complemented with time derivative of the pixel intensities in order to include temporal information in the segmentation optimization process. Göring et al. [11] integrated GrabCut into a semantic segmentation framework by labeling objects in a given image. Most recently, Ramirez et al. [12] have proposed a fully parallelized scheme using GrabCut for 3D segmentation that was adopted to run on GPU. The scheme aims at producing efficient segmentation results for the case of volume meshes in addition to reducing the computational time.

2.2   SOFM Clustering Techniques

One of the most important tasks in exploratory data analysis [13] is data clustering, which is an unsupervised classification of data patterns into groups. Several scientific disciplines including anthropology, biology, medicine, psychology, statistics, mathematics, Engineering and computer science have been strongly related to the research in data clustering [14]. In image segmentation, a variety of research [2, 15, 16] used clustering as the process of identifying groups of similar image primitives. Content based clustering is defined as unsupervised clustering [17], where the clustering process is based on local image content such as shapes, textures or any other image information.

Self-Organizing Feature Map (SOFM) [5, 6] is considered as one of the most popular neural network techniques that have been proposed for clustering since the late 80's. In image segmentation using SOFM, the map is trained with a large number of unclassified feature vectors, which are extracted from images. The type of image regions needs not be known in advance. A variety of techniques [18, 19, 20, 21, 22] have proposed the use of SOFM to image segmentation, since they can retrieve the dominant color content of images [23].

In order to segment true color images, Bhattacharyya et al. [18] have developed a PSONN architecture using a lot of multilevel activation functions, which are characterized by fixed and uniform thresholding parameters. Jiang et al. [20] used SOFM to generate the primitive clustering results based on a training set of five-dimensional vectors. In their methodology, scattered blocks and eliminating isolated pixels are merged and used to segment the images. Another approach that has used a multiple of SOFM networks was proposed by Jiang and Zhou [21]. Their clustering is based on color and spatial features of image pixels, where the desired segmentation is finally produced from the clustered outputs. In [22], a parallel version of the multilayer self organizing neural network (PSONN) was efficiently used for extracting color objects from noisy pure color images.

3   SOFM Algorithm

The Self-organizing feature Map (SOFM) network is an unsupervised learning algorithm, which learns the distribution of a set of patterns without any class information

[5, 6]. The neurons in SOFM networks are arranged on a flat discrete map of one - or two- dimension. Figure 1 displays two-dimensional output space. The input vectors that are similar in input space are mapped to the same winning neuron with its small neighborhoods neurons in the SOFM grid. Each node in the grid acts as an output node. The SOFM algorithm is as follows:

1. Consider n input neurons and m by m output neurons. SOFM clustered the image based on the pixel value (R, G, B). The weight vectors are randomly initialized.
2. At time t, a sample $x(t)$ input is presented to the network. For each input vector presented, the Euclidean distance to all the output neurons is computed to determine the winning neuron k:

$$k = \arg_j \min \lVert x - w_j \rVert \tag{1}$$

3. The weights of all neurons within a certain neighborhood $N_k(d)$ lie within a radius d from the winning neuron k are updated in ordered to move the weights vector toward x:

$$w_j(t+1) = w_j(t) + \eta(t)(x(t) - w_j(t)) \quad , j \in N_k(d) \tag{2}$$

Both the neighborhood $N_k(d)$ and the learning rate $\eta(t)$ are dependent on the discrete iteration t. The $N_k(d)$ is selected fairly wide at the beginning of the training and then permitted to shrink with time t.

For the SOFM, training was split into two phases as recommended by Kohonen [24]: an ordering phase, and a convergence phase. The learning rate and neighborhood distance are altered during training through the two phases. In the ordering phase, the neighborhood should start as the full output space and decrease to 1. During the convergence phase of the algorithm, $N_k(d)$ should contain only the nearest neighbors of the winning neuron k, which may eventually be 1 or 0 neighboring neurons. The learning rate decreases during the order phases until it reaches the minimum value.

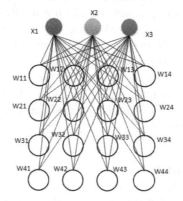

Fig. 1. Kohonen SOFM networks, illustrated for input layer of three neurons which is fully connected to two-dimensional output space of 4 by 4 neurons

4   Grabcut

Image segmentation is simply the process of separating an image into foreground and background parts. Graph cut technique [25] was considered as an effective way for the segmentation of monochrome images, which is based on the Min-Cut/Max-Flow algorithm [26]. GrabCut [4] is a powerful extension of the graph cut algorithm to segment color images iteratively, and to simplify the user interaction needed for a given quality of the segmentation results. Section 4.1 explains the original semi-automatic GrabCut algorithm as developed by Rother et al. in [4], while its modification for automatic segmentation is presented in section 4.2.

4.1   Original GrabCut

The GrabCut algorithm learns the color distributions of the foreground and background by giving each pixel a probability to belong to a cluster of other pixels. It can be explained as follows: Given a color image I, let us consider the $z = (z_1,..z_n,..z_N)$ of N pixels where $z_i =(R_i,G_i,B_i)$, $i \in [1...N]$ in the RGB space. The segmentation is defined as an array $\alpha = (\alpha_1,..,\alpha_N)$, $\alpha_i \in \{0,1\}$, assigning a label to each pixel of the image, indicating if it belongs to the background or the foreground. The GrabCut algorithm consists mainly of two basic steps; initialization and iterative minimization. The details of both steps are explained in the following subsections.

GrabCut Initialization. The novelty of the GrabCut technique is in the "incomplete labeling" which allows a reduced degree of user interaction. The user interaction consists simply of specifying only the background pixels by dragging a rectangle around the desired foreground object (Fig. 2). The process of GrabCut initialization works as follows:

Step 1: A tri-map T= {TB, TU, TF} is initialized, in a semi-automatic way. The two regions TB and TU contain initial background and uncertain pixels respectively, while TF = Ø. The initial TB is determined as the pixels around the outside of the marked rectangle. Pixels belonging to TB are considered as fixed background, whereas those belonging to TU will be labeled by the algorithm.

Fig. 2. Example of GrabCut segmentation

Step 2: An initial image segmentation $\alpha = (\alpha_1, ...,\alpha_i, ..., \alpha_N)$, $\alpha_i \in \{0, 1\}$ is created, where all unknown pixels are tentatively placed in the foreground class ($\alpha_i = 1$ for $i \in$ TU) and all known background pixels are placed in the background class ($\alpha_i = 0$ for $i \in$ TB).

Step 3: Two full covariance Gaussian Mixture Models (GMM's) are defined, each consisting of $K = 5$ components, one for background pixels ($\alpha_i = 0$), and the other one for foreground (initially unknown) pixels ($\alpha_i = 1$). The GMM parameters are:

$$\theta = \{ \pi(\alpha,k), \mu(\alpha,k), \Sigma(\alpha,k), \alpha \in \{0,1\}, k = 1..K\} \tag{3}$$

where π represents the weights, μ represents the means of the GMM's and Σ the covariance matrices of the model. Also the array $k = \{k_1,..,k_i,..k_N\}$, $k_i \in \{1,..K\}$, $i \in [1,..,N]$ is considered to indicate the unique components of the background or foreground GMM (according to α_i) to each pixel z_i. The K components of both GMM's are initialized from the foreground and background classes using Orchard and Bouman clustering technique [27].

GrabCut Iterative Energy Minimization. The energy function for the segmentation is:

$$E(\alpha,k, \theta, z) = U(\alpha,k, \theta, z) + V(\alpha, z) \tag{4}$$

It consists of a data term U and a smoothness term V. The data term U computes the likelihood of a pixel to belong to a certain label. It is based on p(.); the Gaussian probability distributions of the GMM and π(.), which are the mixture weighting coefficients:

$$U(\alpha,k, \theta, z) = \Sigma_i - \log p(z_i|\alpha_i, k_i, \theta) - \log \pi(\alpha_i, k_i) \tag{5}$$

The smoothness term V is a regularizing prior term, which assumes that segmented regions should be coherent in terms of the color, considering the neighborhood C around each pixel. With the energy minimization scheme and given the initial tri-map T, the final segmentation is performed using the iterative minimization algorithm of the graph cut [25] in the following steps:

Step 4: Each pixel in the foreground class is assigned to the most likely Gaussian component in the foreground GMM. Similarly, each pixel in the background is assigned to the most likely background Gaussian component.

Step 5: The GMM's are thrown away and new GMM's are learned from the pixel sets created in the previous set.

Step 6: A graph is built and Graph Cut is run to find a new tentative foreground and background classification of pixels.

Step 7: Steps 4-6 are repeated until the classification converges.

This has the advantage of allowing automatic refinement of the opacities α, as newly labeled pixels from the TU region of the initial tri-map are used to refine the color GMM parameters θ.

4.2   Automatic GrabCut

Although the incomplete user-labeling of GrabCut reduced the user interaction sub-stantially, it is still a requirement in order to initiate the segmentation process. This identifies GrabCut as a semi-automatic/supervised segmentation algorithm. The initial user interaction is accepted in cases of bi-label segmentation, where the image can be segmented only into background and foreground regions. In order to set up for multi-label segmentation, where the image can be divided into more than two segments, GrabCut needs to be converted to an automatic/unsupervised algorithm. In the auto-matic version, the image should be able to be segmented into proper segments without any user intervention. This requires replacing the semi-automatic/supervised step of GrabCut initialization with a totally automatic/unsupervised one.

As the GMM initialization depends upon a scheme to cluster pixels based upon their color, therefore, modifying GrabCut into automatic segmentation technique re-quires an unsupervised image clustering technique. This clustering technique aims to automatically set the initial tri-map T (Section 4.1, Step 1) and initial segmentation (Section 4.1, Step 2). This distinction between the tri-map and the segmentation for-malizes the separation between the region of interest to be segmented and the final segmentation derived by the GrabCut algorithm.

In this paper, SOFM [5, 6] is used as an image clustering technique. In the auto-matic scheme, Steps 1, 2 of the GrabCut initialization process will be modified as follows:

Step 1: While the original GrabCut constructs a tri-map T of two regions TB and TU, as fixed background and unknown regions respectively, the proposed automatic tech-nique considers the whole image as one unknown region TU, where TU $= \{z_i \in \{z_1,..z_n,..z_N\}\}$, $i \in [1...N]$. This means that no fixed foreground or background re-gions are known, and all image pixels will be involved in the minimization process to be labeled by the algorithm.

Step 2: The image is initially separated into two foreground TF and background TB regions, using the SOFM clustering technique. The SOFM technique is applied direct-ly to the image, by specifying different levels of clusters, ending with two clusters.

Step 3: The colors of image pixels belonging to each cluster (foreground and back-ground clusters), generated from the previous step, are then used to initialize another two full covariance Gaussian Mixture Models (GMM's) with (K =5).

Steps 4 – 7: The learning portion of the algorithm runs exactly as the original GrabCut (Section 4.1, Steps 4 – 7).

5   Results and Discussions

The automatic GrabCut technique was experimentally tested using a dataset of 23 different images, shown in Figure 3. This dataset is collected partially from the Berke-ley segmentation dataset [28] and from publically available images [29] in a way that matches certain criteria. These criteria consider special fitting into two class segmen-tation, including having mainly one object (as a foreground), and a well separation between foreground and background color regions.

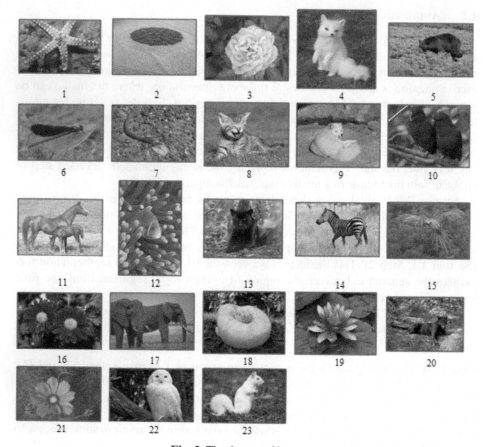

Fig. 3. The dataset of images

The automatic GrabCut initialized using SOFM is applied. Next, the final segmentation results are obtained for all used images. The segmented ground truth data for the whole dataset are manually generated using standard image processing tools[1]. For evaluation, two measures are used for comparison between original semi-automatic and the developed automatic GrabCut segmentation results. These measures are the error rate and the overlap score rate. The error rate is calculated as the fraction of pixels with wrong segmentation (compared to ground truth) divided by the total number of pixels in the image. The overlap score rate is given by $y_1 \cap y_2 \, / \, y_1 \cup y_2$, where y1 and y2 are any two binary segmentations.

In the first experiment, SOFM is applied in two different configurations; first by clustering the image into two segments directly, and second by beginning with 16 clusters and gradually reducing the number of image clusters into 2 clusters, running through 9 and then 4 clusters. Furthermore, in the later configuration, the image is firstly segmented using 16 color clusters. The segmented image is then used as input

---

[1] Adobe Photoshop ™.

to be segmented again into 9 color clusters. Then, the resulted segmentation using 9 color clusters is used as input to be segmented into 4 color clusters. Finally, the image segmented into 4 color clusters is used as input to be segmented into 2 color clusters. Thus, we reduced the number of colors gradually until reaching two colors. The second configuration of SOFM is implemented using two different architectures of SOFM neurons, a one-dimensional (1D) and a two-dimensional (2D) discrete map. Using the 2D discrete map, the neurons are arranged in 4 by 4, 3 by 3, 2 by 2 and finally in 2 by 1. Using 1D discrete map, the neurons are arranged in 16 by 1, 9 by 1, 4 by 1 and finally in 2 by 1.

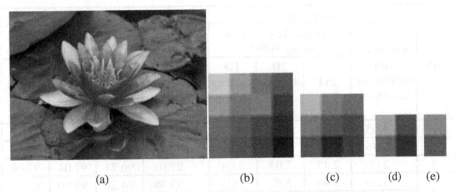

(a)   (b)   (c)   (d)   (e)

Fig. 4. 2D output map for SOFM after training: (a) original image, (b) 4x4 output map, (C) 3x3 output map, (d) 2x2 output map, and (e) 2x1 output map

Fig. 5. Segmentation examples using SOFM, from left to right: first and third row show the original image, segmented image using 4x4 map, 3x3 map, 2x2 map, and 2x1 map. Second and fourth row show segmented image using 16x1 map, 9x1 map, 4x1 map, and 2x1 map.

Figure 4 shows the two-dimensional output map after training the SOFM starting from 4x4 neurons and gradually reduced to 2x1 neurons. It illustrates how the number of colors is reduced gradually. Figure 5 shows two image examples that are segmented in four stages using SOFM discrete map of one and two-dimensional.

In the second set of experiments, the automatic GrabCut initialized using SOFM is applied. The segmented results are compared with the original GrabCut algorithm. Table 1 shows the error rate and the overlap score rate for the whole dataset presented in figure 3. Figure 6 shows visual segmentation results for some images.

Table 1. Performance of the experimental segmentation results

Image	Error rate %				Overlap Score rate %			
	Original semi-automatic GrabCut	Automatic GrabCut using SOFM			Original semi-automatic GrabCut	Automatic GrabCut using SOFM		
		2x1	2D starting from 4x4	1D starting from 16x1		2x1	2D starting from 4x4	1D starting from 16x1
1	3.05	3.15	**39.66**	**18.74**	95.91	95.68	38.88	58.47
2	0.86	0.86	0.86	0.86	97.17	97.16	97.17	97.16
3	2.05	2.17	2.05	2.04	97.04	96.71	97.04	97.08
4	3.16	2.98	3.02	3.02	93.38	94.26	93.80	93.80
5	1.27	1.27	1.16	1.28	94.62	94.64	95.32	94.62
6	**15.48**	2.80	2.80	2.83	43.96	93.70	93.68	93.69
7	2.40	2.40	2.27	2.40	69.00	68.93	70.37	68.98
8	4.99	4.93	5.02	4.96	88.45	89.32	88.39	89.04
9	2.08	2.16	2.10	2.10	95.19	94.75	95.11	95.11
10	3.30	3.44	3.32	3.32	93.37	93.07	93.32	93.32
11	4.79	**6.00**	4.91	4.92	91.51	89.12	91.27	91.23
12	0.87	2.18	1.09	**10.57**	92.76	80.83	90.69	12.65
13	2.28	2.30	2.37	2.28	95.71	95.64	95.52	95.69
14	3.88	3.88	**6.77**	3.86	90.95	90.98	79.62	91.06
15	2.57	3.27	2.58	2.56	93.75	91.15	93.64	93.73
16	3.07	3.67	3.71	3.68	97.06	95.63	95.51	95.61
17	**25.81**	**12.87**	2.15	2.17	67.66	81.31	97.35	97.35
18	2.36	3.96	2.69	4.01	96.85	93.27	96.15	93.16
19	2.88	2.88	2.90	2.89	93.44	93.43	93.37	93.43
20	4.16	**36.48**	3.75	4.16	82.42	29.16	85.18	82.94
21	2.82	4.15	5.14	4.21	96.32	94.33	90.78	94.06
22	2.78	2.89	2.85	2.85	94.14	94.03	94.14	94.14
23	1.43	1.46	1.47	1.47	96.47	96.34	96.31	96.31
Avg.	4.28	4.88	4.55	3.96	89.44	88.85	89.68	87.51
SD	5.50	7.28	7.79	3.75	12.76	14.54	12.72	18.76

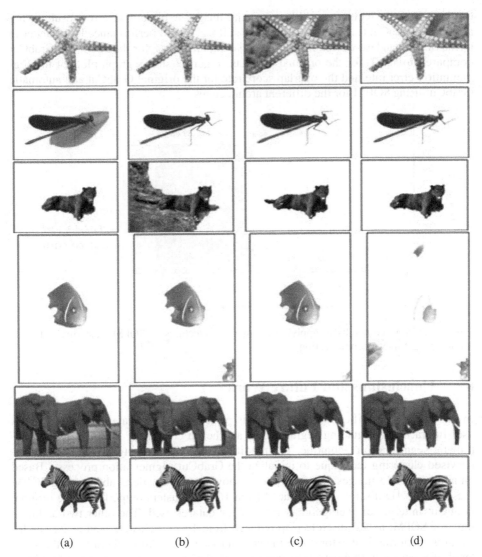

Fig. 6. Visual comparison of segmentation results: (a) original semi-automatic GrabCut and automatic GrabCut initialized using SOFM clustering technique configured as (b) 2x1 (c) 4x4-3x3-2x2-2x1 (d) 16x1-9x1-4x1-2x1 architectures.

It is observed from table 1, that the automatic GrabCut using 1D SOFM outperforms both the 2D SOFM and the direct 2x1 SOFM. The average error rate of the 1D SOFM is 3.96% with standard deviation (SD) of 3.75%, while the 2D SOFM and the direct 2x1 SOFM has 4.55% error rate with SD of 7.79% and 4.88% error rate with SD of 7.28% respectively.

The automatic GrabCut using 1D SOFM outperforms the original one in terms of minimizing the error and improving the segmentation accuracy as shown in table 1. The average error rate is 3.96 % for the automatic GrabCut compared to 4.28% for the original GrabCut technique. Although some images exhibits bad error results using automatic GrabCut (e.g, images 1 and 12), still the overall performance looks better in terms of the standard deviation (SD) which exhibits 3.75 % for the automatic GrabCut compared to 5.5 % for the original GrabCut. Figure 7 shows graph plots of the segmentation error rate and the overlap score rate for the original GrabCut and automatic GrabCut using SOFM for the different architectures.

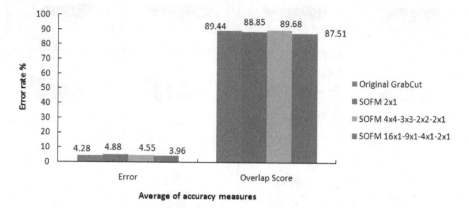

Fig. 7. Performance results of applying different architectures of SOFM clustering technique for automatic GrabCut initialization

6   Conclusions and Future Work

In this paper, a modification of GrabCut is presented to eliminate the need of initial user interaction for guiding segmentation and hence converting GrabCut into an automatic segmentation technique. The modification includes using SOFM as an unsupervised clustering technique to initialize the GrabCut segmentation process. Based on a dataset of 23 images, the experiments show that automatic GrabCut using SOFM clustering as 1D discrete map reduced from 16 to 2 clusters outperforms the original GrabCut in terms of average error rate for the dataset used. The other two architectures of SOFM; as 2D discrete map reduced from 16 to 2 clusters, and as 2x1 architectures, performs better for some images and vice vase. All of them have the same level of accuracy with most of the images. The Automatic techniques using SOFM as an unsupervised clustering technique for GrabCut initialization reduced the need of user intervention with the segmentation. It also adds extra advantage for the GrabCut via automation. In addition, it provides robust and accurate segmentation compared to the results obtained by the original GrabCut.

References

1. Gonzalez, R.C., Woods, R.E.: Digital Image Processing, 3rd edn. Prentice-Hall, Inc. (2006)
2. Lalitha, M., Kiruthiga, M., Loganathan, C.: A Survey on Image Segmentation through Clustering Algorithm. International Journal of Science and Research (IJSR) 2, 348–358 (2013)

3. Sharma, N., Mishra, M., Shrivastava, M.: Colour image segmentaion techniques and issues: an approach. International Journal of Scientific & Technology Research 1, 9–12 (2012)
4. Rother, C., Kolmogorov, V., Blake, A.: "GrabCut": interactive foreground extraction using iterated graph cuts. ACM Trans. Graph. 23, 309–314 (2004)
5. Kohonen, T., Oja, E., Simula, O., Visa, A., Kangas, J.: Engineering applications of the self-organizing map. Proceedings of the IEEE 84, 1358–1384 (1996)
6. Haykin, S.S.: Neural networks and learning machines. Prentice Hall, New York (2009)
7. Gulshan, V., Lempitsky, V.S., Zisserman, A.: Humanising GrabCut: Learning to segment humans using the Kinect. In: IEEE ICCV Workshops, pp. 1127–1133 (2011)
8. Hernandez, A., Reyes, M., Escalera, S., Radeva, P.: Spatio-Temporal GrabCut human segmentation for face and pose recovery. In: IEEE International Workshop on Analysis and Modeling of Faces and Gestures, in Conjunction with IEEE CVPR 2010, pp. 33–40 (2010)
9. Hu, Y.: Human Body Region Extraction from Photos. MVA, pp. 473-476 (2007)
10. Corrigan, D., Robinson, S., Kokaram, A.: Video Matting Using Motion Extended GrabCut. In: IET European Conference on Visual Media Production (CVMP), London, UK (2008)
11. Göring, C., Fröhlich, B., Denzler, J.: Semantic Segmentation using GrabCut. In: VISAPP 2012: Proceedings of the International Conference on Computer Vision Theory and Applications (2012)
12. Ramírez, J., Temoche, P., Carmona, R.: A volume segmentation approach based on GrabCut. CLEI Electronic Journal 16, 4–4 (2013)
13. Jain, A.K., Murty, M.N., Flynn, P.J.: Data clustering: a review. ACM Comput. Surv. 31, 264–323 (1999)
14. Kaur, R., Bhathal, G.S.: A Survey of Clustering Techniques. International Journal of Advanced Research in Computer Science and Software Engineering 3, 153–157 (2013)
15. Gulhane, A., Paikrao, P.L., Chaudhari, D.S.: A Review of Image Data Clustering Techniques. International Journal of Soft Computing and Engineering (IJSCE) 2, 212–215 (2012)
16. Naz, S., Majeed, H., Irshad, H.: Image segmentation using fuzzy clustering: A survey. In: 6th International Conference on Emerging Technologies (ICET), pp. 181–186 (2010)
17. Grira, N., Crucianu, M., Boujemaa, N.: Unsupervised and semisupervised clustering: a brief survey. In: 7th ACM SIGMM International Workshop on Multimedia Information Retrieval
18. Bhattacharyya, S., Dutta, P., Maulik, U., Nandi, P.K.: Multilevel activation functions for true color image segmentation using a self supervised parallel self organizing neural network (PSONN) architecture: a comparative study. International Journal of Computer Science 2, 9–21 (2007)
19. İşcan, Z., Kurnaz, M.N., Dokur, Z., Ölmez, T.: Ultrasound Image Segmentation by Using Wavelet Transform and Self Organizing Neural Network. Neural Information Processing-Letters and Reviews 10 (2006)
20. Jiang, Y., Chen, K.-J., Zhou, Z.-H.: SOM based image segmentation. In: Wang, G., Liu, Q., Yao, Y., Skowron, A. (eds.) RSFDGrC 2003. LNCS (LNAI), vol. 2639, pp. 640–643. Springer, Heidelberg (2003)
21. Jiang, Y., Zhou, Z.-H.: SOM ensemble-based image segmentation. Neural Processing Letters 20, 171–178 (2004)

22. Bhattacharyya, S., Dasgupta, K.: Color Object Extraction From A Noisy Background Using Parallel Multi-layer Self-Organizing Neural Networks. In: CSI-YITPA, pp. 23–36 (2003)
23. Ong, S.H., Yeo, N., Lee, K., Venkatesh, Y., Cao, D.: Segmentation of color images using a two-stage self-organizing network. Image and Vision Computing 20, 279–289 (2002)
24. Kohonen, T.: Self-organizing maps. Springer (2001)
25. Boykov, Y., Jolly, M.-P.: Interactive Graph Cuts for Optimal Boundary and Region Segmentation of Objects in N-D Images. In: ICCV, pp. 105–112 (2001)
26. Boykov, Y., Kolmogorov, V.: An Experimental Comparison of Min-Cut/Max-Flow Algorithms for Energy Minimization in Vision. IEEE Trans. Pattern Anal. Mach. Intell. 26, 1124–1137 (2004)
27. Orchard, M., Bouman, C.: Color Quantization of Images. IEEE Transactions on Signal Processing 39, 2677–2690 (1991)
28. Martin, D., Fowlkes, C., Tal, D., Malik, J.: A Database of Human Segmented Natural Images and its Application to Evaluating Segmentation Algorithms and Measuring Ecological Statistics. In: Proc. 8th Int'l Conf. Computer Vision, pp. 416–423 (2001)
29. Google, https://www.google.com

Point-Based Object Recognition
in RGB-D Images

Artur Wilkowski[1], Tomasz Kornuta[2], and Włodzimierz Kasprzak[1]

[1] Industrial Research Institute for Automation and Measurements,
Al. Jerozolimskie 202, 02-486 Warsaw, Poland
{awilkowski,wkasprzak}@piap.pl
[2] Institute of Control and Computation Engineering,
Warsaw University of Technology, Nowowiejska 15/19, 00-665 Warsaw, Poland
T.Kornuta@elka.pw.edu.pl

Abstract. To operate autonomously a robot system needs among others to perceive the environment and to recognize the scene objects. In particular, nowadays an RGB-D sensor can be applied for vision-based perception. In this paper, two data-driven RGB-D image analysis steps, required for a reliable 3D object recognition process, are studied and appropriate algorithmic solutions are proposed. Clusters of 3D point features are detected in order to represent 3D object hypotheses. Particular clusters act as initial rough object hypotheses, allowing to constrain the subsequent model-based search for more distinctive object features in the image, like surface patches, textures and edges. In parallel, a 3D surface-based occupancy map is created, that delivers surface segments for the object recognition process. Test results are reported on various approaches to point feature detection and description, and point cloud processing.

1 Introduction

There exist various software packages, implemented under the Robot Operating System (ROS) [1], for the purpose of vision-based 3D occupancy map creation and 3D object recognition. The first task is usually solved by the matching of consecutive clouds of points (depth maps) or RGB-D images [2,3]. Object recognition packages in ROS only seldom cover both types of input data (video camera and range sensor) at the same time. Packages, such as BLORT [4] and ODUFinder [5], process color images only.

Perception packages in ROS rely mostly on point-like features and their descriptors (e.g. SIFT [6] or SURF [7]), and RanSac [8] and ICP algorithms for point correspondences [9]).

Our aim is to create general-purpose model-based object recognition using generic object models (representing object types and not only instances, as in current ROS perception) [10]. In such an approach, object recognition is guided by type information and it consists of a data-driven hypothesis generation and a model-driven hypothesis verification cycle.

© Springer International Publishing Switzerland 2015
D. Filev et al. (eds.), *Intelligent Systems'2014*,
Advances in Intelligent Systems and Computing 323, DOI: 10.1007/978-3-319-11310-4_51

In this paper, we study the data-driven analysis of RGB-D images, i.e. the processes of 3D environment map creation and of point-based object hypothesis generation. Executed in parallel, both processes are assumed to contribute to a reliable model-based object recognition process.

The task of 3D map creation encompasses two main, interacting problems:

A) The problem of retrieval of subsequent sensor positions (odometry) and the integration of three dimensional point clouds obtained from these positions (registration). This is the scope of section 2.
B) The problem of effective 3D map representation and construction (presented in section 3).

The 3D surface map serves as image segmentation data for the model-based analysis, providing distinctive object features like surface patches, image textures and boundary shapes.

In order to focus the model-driven search for object instances onto relevant image regions only, rough object hypotheses are created first, on base of simple image features. Clusters of 3D point features and their descriptors are created, each assuming to represent an object. This process is described in section 4.

2   3D Point Cloud Registration

2.1   Map Creation Challenges

Having given a high-resolution, high-framerate output of the RGB sensor, as well as assuming large areas to map, there are several efficiency and quality issues that must be addressed.

- Efficiency and quality problem of two- and more point cloud registration
- Global coherence of maps when scanning large and complex areas
- Efficient and precise representation of millions of points in one model

2.2   Efficiency and Quality of Point Cloud Registration

A common approach to the problem of registration of two point clouds is given in Fig. 1. The cloud newly obtained from the sensor is aligned against previous cloud (or clouds) to establish the change in sensor position (this process is called visual odometry). To increase accuracy and efficiency the procedure starts with extraction of key points from both clouds and matching the keypoints using keypoint descriptors (e.g. SIFT, SURF for RGB image or FPFH, SHOT for depth data). The transformation obtained in such fashion is then fine-tuned using the Iterative Closest Point algorithm (usually operating on the dense clouds).

Depending on the particular solution, some of the steps can be omitted or performed differently, which affects the quality of the solution as well as efficiency. In order to quantitatively evaluate different combinations of methods, we performed a preliminary experiment consisting of registration of two identical clouds transformed by some rigid transformation. The number of points in each cloud was about 300000 which roughly corresponds to the number of points that can be obtained e.g. from the Kinect sensor. For the sake of generality the evaluated set did not contain color information.

In the experiment there were used Harris 3D keypoints as well as uniformly sampled keypoints together with FPFH and SHOT feature descriptors. Initial alignment was performed using RanSaC algorithm and alignment fine-tuning was performed using a classic version of point-to-point Iterative Closest Point. Keypoint extraction and descriptors computation was performed both on original and downsampled cloud.

2.3 Results

An example of matching using the methods provided is given in Fig. 2.

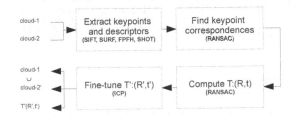

Fig. 1. Alignment procedure of two clouds using keypoints, RanSaC and ICP

Fig. 2. Example of alignment of PCL "five people" cloud.

For the experiments the maximal alignment error was fixed and the time necessary to obtain this alignment quality was measured. Results of the experiments for different combinations of methods are given in tab. 1. For each combination of methods there was measured the time of normal vectors computation (norm.), time of characteristic point computation (key.), time of descriptors computation (desc.), the number of RanSaC inliers (inliers), ICP number of iterations and time as well as the total time of the registration procedure. The table contains average results for 5 trials and corresponding standard deviations.

The most important conclusion from our experiments is that it is beneficiary to use initial alignment using keypoints and descriptors. In order to get close to real-time processing it is also necessary to perform downsampling for computation of keypoints as well as descriptors. However, even more radical steps must be and are undertaken to keep up with the Kinect sensor original framerate (30 fps). This can be done either by performing all computations on GPU [11], skipping most computationally intensive ICP algorithm altogether [3] or performing ICP only on selected keypoints [12].

Table 1. Algorithm efficiency for different combination of methods. R suffix denotes that the particular method was applied to downsampled point cloud. E.g. Harris-R-SHOT-R means that both Harris 3D keypoints as well as SHOT descriptors were computed on downsampled cloud.

method	norm. (s)	key. (s)	desc. (s)	inliers (%)	ICP (iter.)	ICP (s)	total (s)
Harris-FPFH	59.4	35.7	6.5	93.0± 7.7	6.6± 4.3	6.3± 3.6	107.9± 3.6
Harris-R-FPFH	59.6	0.4	12.6	75.6±19.2	7.2± 5.0	6.8± 4.2	79.5± 4.4
Harris-R-FPFH-R	2.1	0.4	1.6	76.6± 9.4	8.4± 4.4	7.7± 3.7	12.0± 3.8
Harris-SHOT	59.0	35.7	0.2	95.7± 5.6	1.4± 0.9	2.0± 0.8	96.9± 0.9
Harris-R-SHOT	59.5	0.4	0.2	68.2±13.8	7.2± 2.2	6.8± 1.8	67.0± 1.8
Harris-R-SHOT-R[1]	2.1	0.4	0.0	75.9± 8.7	9.5± 1.3	8.7± 1.2	11.4± 1.2
Uniform-FPFH	59.3	0.1	10.6	28.7±18.4	11.6± 7.9	12.0±10.0	82.1±11.7
Uniform-FPFH-R	1.9	0.1	2.9	38.6± 7.9	6.2± 5.4	5.9± 4.4	11.0± 4.1
Uniform-SHOT	59.3	0.1	0.2	23.2±16.5	11.6±15.0	16.7±25.1	76.4±25.3
Uniform-SHOT-R[1]	1.9	0.1	0.1	39.3± 9.6	2.3± 2.5	2.6± 2.1	4.8± 2.1
ICP[2]					41.5±12.1	89.5±53.1	89.5±53.1

2.4 Global Coherence of Maps

Since typically only two consecutive clouds are matched against one another, matching errors tend to accumulate over time giving significant discrepancies especially in the situations of returning to the point of origin (closing a loop). This issue is known as "drift". There has been proposed two approaches to handle this issue, as given below.

Global Path Optimization Using Graph Approaches. Vertices in a graph represent sensor positions and are associated to collected point clouds. Edges represent constraints and are created when correspondences between particular clouds are detected. To improve efficiency either only some selected point clouds are memorized or only keypoints, instead of full clouds, are considered. The graph is then optimized to find globally best set of transformations between memorized point clouds. The global graph optimization method is then applied, e.g. the "TORO" optimization in [2] or the "g2o" optimization in [3].

Matching against the Full Map. An alternative solution for maintaining map consistency is to perform matching against the full map constructed so far instead of one or several most recent clouds. This approach was utilized e.g. in [12]. In this solution, efficiency is ensured by storing in the map only selected keypoints from each frame. Matching against the full map cannot handle loops of arbitrary length well, therefore this approach is usually accompanied by some global graph optimization.

---

[1] In one trial ICP converged to local minimum (very close to global one).
[2] In one trial ICP converged to local minimum (far from the global one).

3   Efficient 3D Map Representation

3.1   Selected Map Creation Algorithms

Let us notice that we do not consider here a 2D map, that corresponds to the measurements obtained at some fixed height (from 2D sensor), or to 3D measurements that are reprojected onto 2D surface, flattened in some height interval. Apart from 2D maps, a 3D map, that provides a three-dimensional representation of environment, can be efficiently represented in several ways:

1. Voxel map - 3D space is divided into small "cubes" [13]
2. "Surfel" representation - the space is modelled as surface elements, so called "surfels" [14]
3. MLS (Multi-level surface) Map - contains a list of obstacles (occupied voxels) associated with each element of 2D grid [15]
4. Octal trees (octrees) - constitute and effective implementation of the voxel map using the binary tree structure [16]
5. Combined voxel-surfel representation (e.g. Multi-Resolution Surfel Map)

Up to now, there have been proposed several systems for cloud registration and occupancy map computation using RGBD sensors. The most successful ones are

- RGB-D Mapping [2] (Peter Henry, Univ. of Washington, Seattle)
- KinectFusion [11] (Microsoft Research, UK) and Kintinuous (MIT) [17]
- RGB-D SLAM [3] (Univ. Freiburg, TU Munchen)
- Fast Visual Odometry and Mapping from RGB-D Data [12] (The City University of New York)

In the case of the latter three there are available implementations in ROS or PCL environment. Below we provide a short characteristic of the methods listed.

3.2   RGB-D Mapping

A characteristic feature of the "RGB-D Mapping" solution is the surfel representation of occupancy map. The initialization of matching of two point clouds is performed basing on SIFT descriptors. After initial alignment the solution is fine tuned using ICP algorithm. The ICP algorithm optimizes a double criterion encompassing point-plane distance for the dense cloud and the distance of matched SIFT characteristic points using elastic weights for both components.

During map creation there is prepared a graph of key frames containing transformations between frames and probabilistic constraints. Graph optimization (loop closure) is performed with the TORO method (which is actually the maximum likelihood estimator). It is worth mentioning that sparse bundle adjustment is another option evaluated in this work. System performance is described by authors as satisfactory, cloud alignment takes about 1 s, however surfel's update step takes 6 s per frame.

3.3 KinectFusion

The "KinectFusion" method is optimized for utilization of GPU and real-time processing. There is used a simplified 'point-to-plane' version of the ICP algorithm, where the neighbour is looked for only within the same image pixel. This results from GPU requirements and boost the performance, the downside is that clouds must be sampled frequently enough.

The map is represented as a set of voxels. However the voxels are interpreted in terms of the Truncated Signed Distance Function (TSDF) - and contain the truncated distance from the closest surface. The voxel map is stored in GPU, therefore the map size is limited by the GPU memory. This limitation is overcome in the "Kintinuous" method [17], where the map is transferred to and form external memory when necessary. In the latter approach ICP is supported also by the visual odometry system FOVIS.

The reduction of noise and measurement errors is performed by averaging TDSF values. The map is represented as a set of voxels, however for visualization ray-casting is used to extract surfaces (by detecting zero-crossing of TDSF). The method works in real time (thanks to GPU).

3.4 RGB-D SLAM

The "RGB-D SLAM" systeme is organized in a fairly uncomplicated way. It uses only matchings between keypoint descriptors SIFT, SURF, ORB (and their GPU versions) in order to compute transformation between two frames. Application of keypoints cannot provide very accurate results, therefore loop closure algorithms are used extensively to achieve globally optimal solution. New frames are compared to a group of previous frames (some of them are selected deterministically, and some randomly). The frames and relations between them constitute vertices and edges in the graph. The graph is then optimized with using *g2o* method. The method was implemented in ROS framework [1] and it cooperates with the ROS OctoMap package for creation of the occupancy map.

3.5 FVOM - Fast Visual Odometry and Mapping

A characteristic feature of the approach proposed in [12] is that the ICP algorithm does not work on two most recent points clouds, but instead aligns the newest point cloud to the complete model of the scene constructed from point clouds collected so far. In order to do it efficiently only selected key points from each frame are taken into account and incorporated into the model (the full clouds can be stored in external memory).

For each frame Shi-Tomasi keypoints are extracted from the RGB image (also other keypoints and descriptors are supported), and such sparse cloud is aligned against the current model of the scene using ICP. After alignment the new cloud is incorporated into the model. The assimilation process takes into account point uncertainties (depending on distance measurements) and uses Kalman Filter update rules to propagate uncertainties from measurements into the model. This probabilistic framework is to some extent used also for distance computation of the ICP algorithm.

Alignment of the new cloud against the whole model decreases the extent of alignment error propagation (the drift). However, in new implementations (under ROS), the basic algorithm is supplemented also with *g2o* global optimization for off-line processing. The online processing is very fast. The average processing time of a single frame is about 16.1 ms.

3.6   Results

The results of some of our experimental mapping with the KinectFusion algorithm are given in Fig. 3.

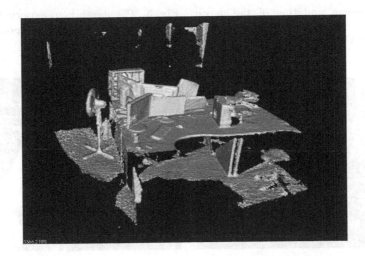

Fig. 3. 3D scene "a desk in a room" registered from multiple viewpoints using Kinect-Fusion algorithm

A sample map, which is the result of our mapping experiments with RGB-D SLAM, is given in Fig. 4 and Fig. 5.

Mapping results that we obtained using the FVOM method are given in Fig. 6 and Fig. 7. In Fig. 6 there are given keypoints captured during online processing, whereas in Fig. 7 there is given the final integrated cloud optimized with *g2o* algorithm.

4   Point-Based Object Hypothesis

4.1   Global Versus Local Image Features

Global image features represent certain characteristics calculated on the basis of a whole image. In the case of objects, global features can be extracted from

Fig. 4. On-line updating of the depth map for the "a desk in a room" scene using RGB-D SLAM method

Fig. 5. The depth map exported to Oc-toMap for the "a desk in a room" scene using RGB-D SLAM method

Fig. 6. Keypoints generated for the "a desk in a room" scene during on-line registration using Fast Visual Odometry algorithm

Fig. 7. G2o-optimized depth map for the "a desk in a room" scene using Fast Visual Odometry algorithm

the entire point cloud constituting the object or all image segments making it up (however, one must a priori determine which elements belong to the given object). In contrast, local features are associated with location of the so called keypoint – a pixel in the image considered as characteristic and hence important. Additionally, local features encapsulate the characteristics of the neighbourhood of this point in the form of a descriptor. Global features enable quick determination of the similarity of the whole images or objects, while the local ones are useful for the comparison of the individual parts.

Furthermore, in the case of using RGB-D images an orthogonal division of features can be proposed: into the ones extracted from appearance (colour channels) and features extracted from 3D shape (depth maps or point cloud). An example of a global feature calculated on the basis of the RGB channels is a histogram created on the basis of the colour of all object points. A good example of a global feature extracted from the point cloud is PFH (Point Feature Histogram) [18], where the histogram is created on basis of angles between normals to surface of pairs of point of a point cloud constituting the object.

In the case of local features on the one hand we should pay attention to the keypoint detectors and to the feature descriptors.

There exist popular methods having their own detectors and descriptors, such as SIFT [6] or BRISK (Binary Robust Invariant Scalable Keypoints) [19].

4.2   Object Hypothesis Generation

The general idea of the procedure responsible for generation of point-based hypotheses is presented in Fig. 8 At start we extract a feature cloud out of the acquired RGB-D image. For this purpose we first extract SIFTs from the intensity image and subsequently transform their coordinates from the image to the Cartesian space, basing on the knowledge of their distances from the sensor (depth map). The extracted features are compared with the feature clouds from all models stored in the virtual receptor memory. For this purpose we use FLANN [20], an efficient implementation of the k nearest neighbours algorithm. As a result we receive a set of correspondences, which we cluster by taking into account the criterion consisting of: (a) the model to which given cluster of correspondences refer, (b) similarity of transformations between points forming given cluster and corresponding model points and (c) Cartesian distance between points belonging to the cluster. The idea is similar to the clustering method presented in the MOPED framework [5], however enhanced with spatial information gained from the depth map. The resulting clusters form the object hypotheses, passed next to the hypothesis- and model-driven step of object recognition.

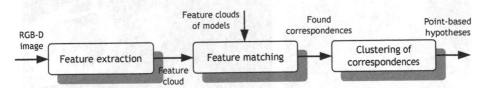

Fig. 8. Data flow diagram presenting the principle of the operation of point-based hypothesis generation

4.3   Results

The 3D object models used in the point-based object hypothesis generation consist of two types of point clouds: dense colour point clouds (used mainly for visualisation) and sparse feature clouds (used for recognition). Exemplary model is presented in Fig. 9. Currently our models (as well as the hypotheses generation) rely on SIFT (Scale Invariant Feature Transform) [6] features transformed, on the basis of additional depth information, into a sparse cloud of features. We

(a)   (b)

Fig. 9. Exemplary 3-D point-based model: (a) dense RGB point cloud (b) sparse feature cloud

have chosen SIFT because it is still treated as one of the most valued features from the family of Histograms of Oriented Gradients (HOG) based descriptors.

Exemplary results of the developed point-based hypothesis generation are presented in Fig. 10. The analysed scene is presented in Fig. 10a, whereas Fig. 10b contains the same scene transformed into a point cloud (the point of view differs from the point of view of the sensor during the image acquisition) along with the added object (cereal box) being one of the matched model, i.e. one of the found hypotheses. The red dots represent features (both in the model and the scene), whereas red lines represent the found correspondences.

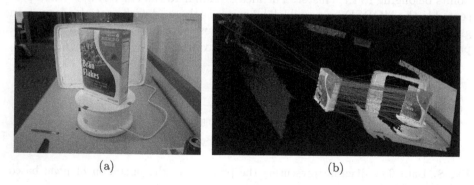

(a)   (b)

Fig. 10. Example of 3-D point-based object hypothesis: (a) the exemplary scene (b) point cloud containing the scene and the object model along with the found correspondences

5 Conclusions

Two data-driven processing steps of RGB-D image analysis have been presented. The 3D surface map provides rich image segments data for further model-based image analysis. The second step, the point feature-based object generation step, gives efficient constraints for a subsequent model-driven object search. The application background of this work is autonomous robotics, i.e. to provide a mobile or assistant robot with the ability to perform complex cognitive tasks, such as object recognition, grasping and manipulation [21].

Acknowledgement. The authors gratefully acknowledge the financial support by the National Centre for Research and Development (Poland), grant no. PBS1/A3/8/2012. The authors would like to thank Michał Laszkowski for his help with implementation and experimental verification of the point-based hypothesis generation.

References

1. ROS: Robot operating system (November 2013), http://www.ros.org
2. Henry, P., Krainin, M., Herbst, E., Ren, X., Fox, D.: Rgb-d mapping: Using kinect-style depth cameras for dense 3d modeling of indoor environments. Int. J. Rob. Res. 31(5), 647–663 (2012)
3. Endres, F., Hess, J., Engelhard, N., Sturm, J., Cremers, D., Burgard, W.: An evaluation of the rgb-d slam system. In: 2012 IEEE International Conference on Robotics and Automation (ICRA), pp. 1691–1696 (May 2012)
4. Mörwald, T., Prankl, J., Richtsfeld, A., Zillich, M., Vincze, M.: Blort-the blocks world robotic vision toolbox. In: Best Practice in 3D Perception and Modeling for Mobile Manipulation, ICRA Workshop (2010)
5. Collet Romea, A., Martinez Torres, M., Srinivasa, S.: The moped framework: Object recognition and pose estimation for manipulation. International Journal of Robotics Research 30(10), 1284–1306 (2011)
6. Lowe, D.G.: Distinctive image features from scale-invariant keypoints. Int. J. Comput. Vision 60(2), 91–110 (2004)
7. Bay, H., Ess, A., Tuytelaars, T., Van Gool, L.: Speeded-up robust features (surf). Comput. Vis. Image Underst. 110(3), 346–359 (2008)
8. Schnabel, R., Wahl, R., Klein, R.: Efficient ransac for point-cloud shape detection. Computer Graphics Forum 26(2), 214–226 (2007)
9. Segal, A., Haehnel, D., Thrun, S.: Generalized-icp. In: Proc. of Robotics: Science and Systems (RSS) (2009)
10. Kasprzak, W.: Integration of different computational models in a computer vision framework. In: 2010 International Conference on Computer Information Systems and Industrial Management Applications (CISIM), pp. 13–18 (October 2010)
11. Izadi, S., Kim, D., Hilliges, O., Molyneaux, D., Newcombe, R., Kohli, P., Shotton, J., Hodges, S., Freeman, D., Davison, A., Fitzgibbon, A.: Kinectfusion: Real-time 3d reconstruction and interaction using a moving depth camera. In: Proceedings of the 24th Annual ACM Symposium on User Interface Software and Technology, UIST 2011, pp. 559–568. ACM, New York (2011)
12. Dryanovski, I., Valenti, R., Xiao, J.: Fast visual odometry and mapping from rgb-d data. In: 2013 IEEE International Conference on Robotics and Automation (ICRA), pp. 2305–2310 (May 2013)
13. Marder-Eppstein, E., Berger, E., Foote, T., Gerkey, B., Konolige, K.: The office marathon: Robust navigation in an indoor office environment. In: 2010 IEEE International Conference on Robotics and Automation (ICRA), pp. 300–307 (May 2010)

14. Krainin, M., Henry, P., Ren, X., Fox, D.: Manipulator and object tracking for in hand 3d object modeling. Technical Report UW-CSE-10-09-01, University of Washington (2010)
15. Triebel, R., Pfaff, P., Burgard, W.: Multi-level surface maps for outdoor terrain mapping and loop closing. In: 2006 IEEE/RSJ International Conference on Intelligent Robots and Systems, pp. 2276–2282 (October 2006)
16. Wurm, K.M., Hornung, A., Bennewitz, M., Stachniss, C., Burgard, W.: Octomap: A probabilistic, flexible, and compact 3d map representation for robotic systems. In: Proc. of the ICRA 2010 Worksshop (2010)
17. Whelan, T., Johannsson, H., Kaess, M., Leonard, J., McDonald, J.: Robust realtime visual odometry for dense rgb-d mapping. In: 2013 IEEE International Conference on Robotics and Automation (ICRA), pp. 5724–5731 (May 2013)
18. Rusu, R., Blodow, N., Marton, Z., Beetz, M.: Aligning point cloud views using persistent feature histograms. In: IEEE/RSJ International Conference on Intelligent Robots and Systems, IROS 2008, pp. 3384–3391 (September 2008)
19. Leutenegger, S., Chli, M., Siegwart, R.: Brisk: Binary robust invariant scalable keypoints. In: 2011 IEEE International Conference on Computer Vision (ICCV), pp. 2548–2555 (November 2011)
20. Muja, M., Lowe, D.G.: Fast approximate nearest neighbors with automatic algorithm configuration. In: International Conference on Computer Vision Theory and Application, VISSAPP 2009, pp. 331–340. INSTICC Press (2009)
21. Kasprzak, W., Kornuta, T., Zieliński, C.: A virtual receptor in a robot control framework. In: Szewczyk, R., Zieliński, C., Kaliczyńska, M. (eds.) Recent Advances in Automation, Robotics and Measuring Techniques. AISC, vol. 267, pp. 399–408. Springer, Heidelberg (2014)

Integrating Data- and Model-Driven Analysis of RGB-D Images

Włodzimierz Kasprzak[1], Rafał Pietruch[2], Konrad Bojar[2], Artur Wilkowski[2], and Tomasz Kornuta[1]

[1] Institute of Control and Computation Engineering,
Warsaw University of Technology, Nowowiejska 15/19, 00-665 Warsaw, Poland
{W.Kasprzak,T.Kornuta}@elka.pw.edu.pl
[2] Industrial Research Institute for Automation and Measurements
Al. Jerozolimskie 202, 02-486 Warsaw, Poland
{rpietruch,kbojar,awilkowski}@piap.pl

Abstract. There is a growing use of RGB-D sensors in vision-based robot perception. A reliable 3D object recognition requires the integration of image-driven and model-based analysis. Only then the low-level image-like representation can be successfully transformed into a symbolic description with equivalent semantics, considered by the ontology-level representation of an autonomous robot system. An RGB-D image analysis approach is proposed that consists of a data-driven hypothesis generation step and a generic model-based object recognition step. Initially point clusters are created assuming to represent 3D object hypotheses. In parallel, 3D surface patches are estimated, 2D image textures and shapes are classified, building multi-modal image segmentation data. In the model-driven step, a built-in knowledge about basic solids, shapes and textures is used to verify the point clusters in terms of meaningful volume-like aggregates, and to create (or to recognize) generic 3D object models.

1 Introduction

Current focus in service and assistance robotics research is on autonomous robot behaviour. For this purpose it is crucial to provide rich perception ability. When perception is paired with a high-level common sense knowledge and reasoning (i.e. an ontology-level of agent systems) then it allows, among others, to generate and to update a semantic map of the perceived environment. At the other end, a data-driven processing of RGB-D images (or depth images only) usually leads to the creation of a 3D occupancy map and to the detection of clusters of image points or edges.

There exist various software packages being implemented under the ROS system for the purpose of 3D object recognition. Such object recognition packages only seldom cover both types of input data (video camera and laser scanner) at the same time. For example, the package COP (cognitive perception) [1] can process both types of data, but not integrated, e.g. planar surfaces are based

© Springer International Publishing Switzerland 2015
D. Filev et al. (eds.), *Intelligent Systems'2014*,
Advances in Intelligent Systems and Computing 323, DOI: 10.1007/978-3-319-11310-4_52

on geometric features without texture. The project RoboEarth [2] provides two distinct modules for object recognition: "Vision" and "KinectObjectDetector". Other packages, such as BLORT [3] and ODUFinder [4] rely mainly on video images.

A surface-based segmentation procedure for RGB-D images has recently been developed [5]. In current work, the segmentation process is extended by handling other modes: boundary-based 2D shapes and color image textures. This follows the LINEMOD approach [6] to object recognition.

Our aim is to create general-purpose model-based object recognition using generic object models (representing object types and not only instances, as in current ROS perception) [7]. A limited generic-model approach (limited to planar surfaces only) is available in the COP package [1]. Some variability of segments used for object recognition (lines in the LINEMOD package or textures in the TOD package) is available in the "WG Object Recognition" framework [8], but again this works for instance-based and not generic object models. The other known packages use instance-based models only, e.g. point cluster models.

2   The Approach

2.1   Procedural Semantic Networks

Our approach to 3D solids and object recognition is a knowledge-based approach, i.e. it is determined by the use of a partially declarative and partially procedural knowledge representation, and a corresponding application-independent inference scheme. Different languages have been proposed for knowledge-based computer vision, for example frames and semantic networks [9], or attributed graph- and relation structure-grammars [10].

We assume a 3D generic object model defined in the language of procedural semantic networks. Four alternative specialized concepts of an object type are distinguished (Fig. 1): (1) an object is defined by its parts, that are instances of basic textured solids; (2) an object corresponds to a 2D shape in the RGB image; (3) an object corresponds to a textured image region in the RGB image; (4) an object corresponds to a cluster of characteristic 3D points.

A single concept in a semantic network is defined by the following elements:

1. Attributes - a vector of values being unique to every instance of a given concept,
2. Parts - which must be concepts of types recognized by the virtual receptor, i.e. basic solids and known textures,
3. Alternative subsets of parts, that are called modality sets;
4. Properties - predicates that must be satisfied by parts of a given concept,
5. Functions for the computation of attribute values and the evaluation of properties.

The basic solid types, out of which all the 3D objects will be defined by using the aggregation operation, are the cuboid (with textured faces) and the generalized

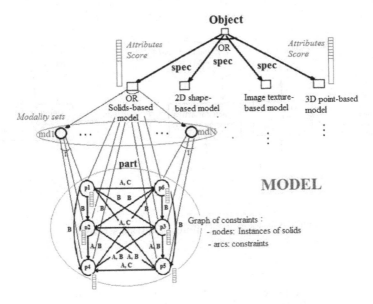

Fig. 1. The scheme of 3D object representation by means of procedural semantic networks

cone (with textured faces). Examples of objects, that can be defined in this way, are: small objects that can be grasped by hand (e.g. bottle, box, apple, door handle), walls and furniture (e.g. a desk, door, chair) or a human body.

2.2   The Object Recognition/Acquisition Strategy

The RGB-D image analysis strategy that applies the various alternative object models is outlined in Fig. 2. There are three main stages of this strategy. First, various object hypotheses are created on base of image segments. These hypotheses are instances of three concept types: a point-based object, a texture-based object and a shape-based object. These hypotheses are next projected onto subsets of characteristic segments, thus constraining the search for textured solids. In the second step, instances of solids are generated, that can be hypothesized with the semantic network model as applied to the constrained segment set. The third step can be an object recognition process (when the ontology-level object is already defined) or an object type acquisition process.

The image analysis process can be mapped onto built-in knowledge concepts (Fig. 3). The segmentation of an RGB-D image results in the symbolic primitives: 3D points and surface patches, 2D points, edges and image regions. Initial object hypotheses are generated on base of simple feature clusters: 3D points and surfaces, 2-D shape-based and texture-based object hypotheses. These object hypotheses when projected onto the built-in model of basic solids allow to constrain the subsequent model-based analysis on prospective image sections and subsets of segments.

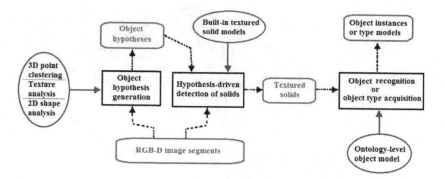

Fig. 2. The RGB-D image analysis strategy

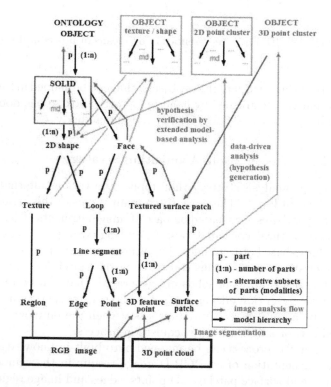

Fig. 3. The built-in solid model (black concepts and arcs) and the object hypothesis generation and verification flow (red instances and lines)

3 3D Surface Map Estimation

3.1 3D Point Cloud Registration

The first common problem in 3D map estimation is the registration of two point clouds. The cloud newly obtained from the sensor is aligned against previous cloud (or clouds) to establish the change in sensor position. To increase accuracy and efficiency the procedure starts with extraction of key points from both clouds and matching the keypoints using keypoint descriptors (e.g. SIFT, SURF for RGB image or FPFH, SHOT for depth data). The transformation obtained in such fashion is then fine-tuned using the Iterative Closest Point algorithm (usually operating on the dense clouds).

We have conducted experiments with RanSac and ICP algorithms applied for point feature matching for different combinations of 2D point operators (Harris operator or uniform sampling) and 3D descriptors (FPFH and SHOT). The most important conclusion from our experiments is that it is beneficiary to use initial alignment using keypoints and descriptors. In order to get close to real-time processing it is also necessary to perform downsampling for computation of keypoints as well as descriptors. However, even more radical steps must be undertaken to keep up with the Kinect sensor original frame rate (30 fps). This can be done either by performing all computations on GPU [11], skipping most computationally intensive ICP algorithm altogether [12] or performing ICP only on selected keypoints [13].

Since typically only two consecutive clouds are matched against one another, matching errors tend to accumulate over time giving significant discrepancies especially in the situations of returning to the point of origin (closing a loop). There has been proposed two approaches to handle this issue: a global path optimization using graph approaches (e.g.the "TORO" optimization in [14] or the "g2o" optimization in [12]); or a matching against the full map constructed so far instead of one or several most recent clouds, e.g. [13].

3.2 Selected Map Creation Algorithms

There have been proposed several systems for cloud registration and occupancy map computation using RGB-D sensors. The most successful ones are: RGB-D Mapping [14], KinectFusion [11], and Kintinuous [15], RGB-D SLAM [12], Fast Visual Odometry and Mapping from RGB-D Data [13].

We have provided experiments with three above methods (except of RGB-D Mapping). A surface image, synthesized on base of a 3D map obtained with the KinectFusion algorithm is illustrated in Fig. 4.

4 Image Texture Analysis

We want to retain ability to deal with textures of generic type. Therefore, the input texture does not have any internal structure to be analyzed either by structural or by divide and conquer methods. This fact promotes a statistical

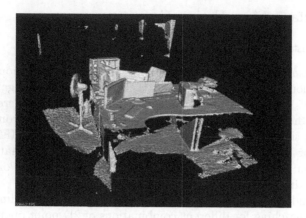

Fig. 4. A 3D room scene registered from multiple viewpoints using the KinectFusion algorithm

approach to texture analysis in a natural way. Hence, we adapt a typical scheme used for statistical texture analysis to arrive at fully customizable setup shown in Fig. 5. The texture analysis module takes on input the RGB image regions and the corresponding depth information (whenever available) and assigns texture class information with image regions.

It must be noted that the proposed architecture is based on plug-ins and therefore can be easily coded in ROS by simply publishing corresponding topics. Hence, by adjusting the configuration manager in Fig. 5, one can pick correct processing path for a given image segment, based on current context knowledge coming from the Ontology layer. For example, in dark scenery it is more efficient to use graylevel features calculated from the V-channel only in the HSV color space. On the other hand, for a well illuminated but very far views the depth standarization step must be tuned not to introduce significant pixel magnification which normally disables use of neighborhood-based features.

4.1   Geometry, Depth and Color Standarization

The first step is *patch geometry standarization*, in which the patch, corresponding to given image region, is made a planar one (i.e. it is flattened) based on information contained in the pixel depth map. We use implementation in which the resulting patch is parallel to the image plane and the depth is the average depth calculated over the domain of the patch. Additionally, if the angle between the normal to the patch and the optical axis is everywhere smaller than 5°, the patch is not unwarped to avoid unnecessary raster effect during resampling.

The next step is optional patch depth standarization which in our implementation is realized by uniform resampling to standard depth of 1 m. Depending on application of virtual receptor, this step can be merged with the previous one or omitted if, for example, SIFT features [16] are used. Next in a row there is color space standardization. There is no preferred color transformation to be pointed

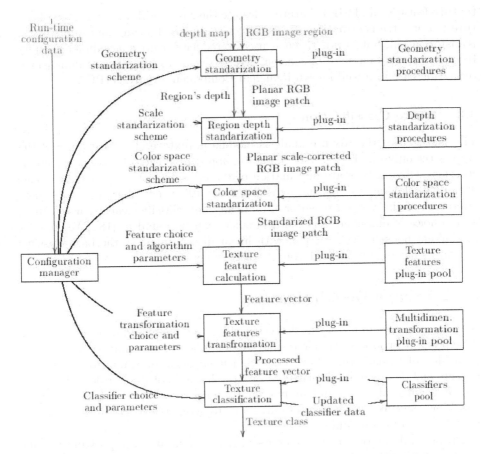

Fig. 5. A block diagram of texture analysis. All inputs are shown in red and the output is shown in blue.

out because different feature sets can impose different requirements on the input image patch color space. For example, color correlogram-based features require CIELab color space, while original Haralick features [17] require grayscale image.

4.2 Feature Extraction

One of the two most important steps depicted in Fig. 5 is feature extraction. Theoretically any known algorithm for calculation of features can be used, provided it takes the image and a Region of Interest (ROI) as input and returns feature vector as output. It should be however noted that requirement of universality of the virtual receptor imposes some additional conditions, for example any ROI should be acceptable. This condition excludes for example features based on global transformations, like Fourier transformation or wavelet transformation, assuming rectangular shape of the domain. In our implementation we use statistical features only; we chose to use color texture features, Haralick graylevel texture features, and SIFT features (despite their patent flaws). The step of texture features transformation allows, in general, to realize any multidimensional transformation, but in practice it is used to reduce feature space dimensionality. In order to avoid curse of dimensionality, we decided to implement dimensional reduction based on well known Principal Component Analysis (PCA).

4.3 Texture Classification

The last step of the texture analysis module is texture classification, and this step is the only one having internal state, opposed to the other steps which are stateless. Obviously, state information of the classification step is the classifier data. By allowing to this data to change we allow classifier to learn during operation of the virtual receptor. Practically any classifier can be used, and a good choice of classifiers and metaclassifiers can be found in [18]. We chose to implement boosting scheme [19] with linear discriminant as the base classifier due to its fair results for wide variety of textures.

5   2D Shape Description

A framework for simultaneous detection of line segments and elliptical arcs was developed. It produces reliable results when applied on any kind of RGB image, regardless of its size, content or source. Salient edges occur at multiple scales e.g.: objects and their parts, edges caused by cast shadows, objects projected into the image at different scales. In handling multi-scale edge features it is important to consider definitions of descriptors invariant to geometrical transformations like translation, rotation, and scaling.

Proposed detector obeys a 3-step scheme: segmentation, approximation and model selection (Fig. 6). The three stage process algorithm is performed for every input image separately.

5.1   Image Segmentation

As a first step for edge extraction and digital image segmentation a smoothing operation is performed. For an effective elimination of the image noise the authors used Mean-Shift algorithm which preserves principal edges. An image segmentation can be based on edges or regions detection.

An example approach to edge detection is a gradient morphology filter. To extract a binary image of contours from the output gradient image the authors applied empirically tuned threshold. Border following algorithm, performed on binary contour image, generates multiple edge-chains.

There are also region based approaches for image segmentation like region growing, watershed or graph-based methods. In those methods one can prepare multiple binary images for every region and then apply border following algorithm on these images to get pixel chains. Before region growing task the initial values of starting points for each region should be set. The seed points can be

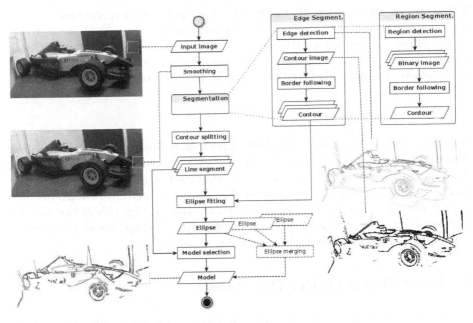

Fig. 6. The detection of line segments and elliptical arcs

initialized based on edge detection task. The key contribution to our work will be efficient merge of the RGB-D and textures information. Textures elimination is possible e.g. by region subtraction.

For line segment detection, the authors [20] give credit to the orientation of the gradient, rather than to its magnitude. In the curve growing procedure connected pixels sharing the same gradient orientation are gathered.

The chains of points forming contour can be extracted from binary image using border following algorithm.

5.2   Contour Approximation

Higher level tasks for 3-D objects recognition use general conic sections for surface modelling. Thus, our goal is to segment given pixel chains from edge detection into a sequence of lines and elliptical arcs. Proposed detector requires a line segments- and ellipse fitting-operator.

First we divide contours into several parts that fit chains into line segments. Splitting contours into segments can be performed by using Douglas-Peucker algorithm for line segments approximation. It requires tuning of accuracy parameter, which can be proportional to the contour length in order to handle multiple scale objects.

In [20], once an edge list is approximated by line segments, subsequences of the line segments can be replaced by circular arcs. This involves fitting circular arcs through the endpoints of two or more line segments. The authors in

[21] proposed an adaption of Douglas-Peucker's polygon simplification, contour splitting algorithm using circular arcs approximation.

An ellipse is fitted on a gathered pixels using deterministic fitting technique based on least squares algorithm. Moreover, the ellipse points must follow the assumption of uniform distribution of angles in radial coordinates of ellipse.

5.3 Model Selection

Deciding whether a curved line is best approximated by a line or an ellipse is a typical model selection problem with the use of selection criteria. Approximation decision making was directly applied to isolated segments. The goodness of the fit can be evaluated using the mean squared error represented by distance between arc or line to corresponding (original) point. Best fitting model can be also evaluated according to shape descriptors similarity. A shape matching accuracy is usually based on invariants Hu moments.

6 Point-Based Object Hypothesis

A point-based 3D object model takes the form of a sparse feature cloud. Currently our approach is based on the SIFT color image features [16], which are transformed, on the basis of additional depth information, into a sparse cloud of 3D point features.

(a)   (b)

Fig. 7. Example of 3-D point-based object hypothesis: (a) sparse cloud representing the object model features (b) point correspondences between clouds of features of the model and extracted from the scene

The process of point-based hypothesis generation consists of three steps. At first, SIFTs points are detected in the RGB image and their coordinates are transformed from the image to the Cartesian 3D space, based on the knowledge of their distances from the sensor (given in the depth map).

Next, the extracted features are compared with the feature clouds from all models stored in the virtual receptor memory. For this purpose we use the FLANN algorithm [22], an efficient implementation of the k-nearest neighbours classifier.

Finally, we receive a set of correspondences, which we cluster by taking into account the criterion consisting of: (a) the model to which given cluster of correspondences refer, (b) similarity of transformations between points forming given cluster and corresponding model points and (c) Cartesian distance between points belonging to the cluster. An illustration of the results of point-based hypothesis generation is given in fig. 7 (implemented by Michał Laszkowski).

7 Summary

A suitable intermediate-level representation language and rich RGB-D image segmentation procedure is developed, that explores built-in knowledge about basic solids, shapes and textures, and supports both the 3D object model acquisition and object recognition processes. Initial point clusters, aiming to represent 3D object hypotheses, are generated. In parallel, a 3D surface-based occupancy map is created and 2D texture and shape analysis are performed. Such multimodal segmentation data and a common-sense knowledge are used to convert the point clusters into textured volume clusters and to create (or to recognize) generic 3D object models (i.e. creating object types or recognizing instances of object types).

Acknowledgments. The authors gratefully acknowledge the support of the National Centre for Research and Development (Poland), grant no. PBS1/A3/8/2012.

References

1. Marton, Z.-C., Pangercic, D., Blodow, N., Beetz, M.: Combined 2D–3D categorization and classification for multimodal perception systems. The International Journal of Robotics Research 30(11), 1378–1402 (2011)
2. Waibel, M., Beetz, M., Civera, J., d'Andrea, R., Elfring, J., Galvez-Lopez, D., Haussermann, K., et al.: A World Wide Web for Robots. IEEE Robotics & Automation Magazine 18(2), 69–82 (2011)
3. Mörwald, T., Prankl, J., Richtsfeld, A., Zillich, M., Vincze, M.: Blort-the blocks world robotic vision toolbox. In: Best Practice in 3D Perception and Modeling for Mobile Manipulation, ICRA Workshop (2010)
4. Collet, A., Martinez, M., Srinivasa, S.S.: The MOPED framework: Object recognition and pose estimation for manipulation. International Journal of Robotics Research 30(10), 1284–1306 (2011)
5. Stefańczyk, M., Kasprzak, W.: Multimodal segmentation of dense depth maps and associated color information. In: Bolc, L., Tadeusiewicz, R., Chmielewski, L.J., Wojciechowski, K. (eds.) ICCVG 2012. LNCS, vol. 7594, pp. 626–632. Springer, Heidelberg (2012)

6. Hinterstoisser, S., Lepetit, V., Ilic, S., Holzer, S., Bradski, G., Konolige, K., Navab, N.: Model Based Training, Detection and Pose Estimation of Texture-Less 3D Objects in Heavily Cluttered Scenes. In: Lee, K.M., Matsushita, Y., Rehg, J.M., Hu, Z. (eds.) ACCV 2012, Part I. LNCS, vol. 7724, pp. 548–562. Springer, Heidelberg (2013)

7. Kasprzak, W., Kornuta, T., Zieliński, C.: A virtual receptor in a robot control framework. In: Szewczyk, R., Zieliński, C., Kaliczyńska, M. (eds.) Recent Advances in Automation, Robotics and Measuring Techniques. AISC, vol. 267, pp. 399–408. Springer, Heidelberg (2014)

8. WG Object Recognition, http://wg-perception.github.io/object_recognition_core/

9. Niemann, H., Sagerer, G., Schroder, S., Kummert, F.: ERNEST: A semantic network system for pattern understanding. IEEE Trans PAMI 12, 883–905 (1990)

10. Kasprzak, W.: A Linguistic Approach to 3-D Object Recognition. Computers & Graphics 11(4), 427–443 (1987)

11. Izadi, S., et al.: Kinectfusion: Real-time 3d reconstruction and interaction using a moving depth camera. In: 24th ACM Symposium on User Interface Software and Technology (UIST 2011), New York, NY, pp. 559–568 (2011)

12. Endres, F., Hess, J., Engelhard, N., Sturm, J., Cremers, D., Burgard, W.: An evaluation of the rgb-d slam system. In: IEEE International Conference on Robotics and Automation (ICRA), pp. 1691–1696 (May 2012)

13. Dryanovski, I., Valenti, R., Xiao, J.: Fast visual odometry and mapping from rgb-d data. In: 2013 IEEE International Conference on Robotics and Automation (ICRA), pp. 2305–2310 (May 2013)

14. Henry, P., Krainin, M., Herbst, E., Ren, X.-F., Fox, D.: RGB-D Mapping. Using Kinect-style depth cameras for dense 3D modeling of indoor environments. International Journal of Robotics Research 31(5), 647–663 (2012)

15. Whelan, T., Johannsson, H., Kaess, M., Leonard, J., McDonald, J.: Robust real-time visual odometry for dense rgb-d mapping. In: 2013 IEEE International Conference on Robotics and Automation (ICRA), pp. 5724–5731 (May 2013)

16. Lowe, D.G.: Distinctive image features from scale-invariant keypoints. Int. J. Comput. Vision 60(2), 91–110 (2004)

17. Haralick, R., Shanmugam, K., Dinstein, I.: Textural features for image classification. IEEE Transactions on Systems, Man and Cybernetics 3(6), 610–621 (1973)

18. Hall, M., Frank, E., Holmes, G., Pfahringer, B., Reutemann, P., Witten, I.: The WEKA data mining software: an update. ACM SIGKDD Explorations Newsletter 11(1), 10–18 (2009)

19. Freund, Y., Schapire, R.: A decision-theoretic generalization of on-line learning and its application to boosting. J. Comp. Syst. Sci. 55(1), 119–139 (1997)

20. Pătrăucean, V., Gurdjos, P., von Gioi, R.G.: A Parameterless Line Segment and Elliptical Arc Detector with Enhanced Ellipse Fitting. In: Fitzgibbon, A., Lazebnik, S., Perona, P., Sato, Y., Schmid, C. (eds.) ECCV 2012, Part II. LNCS, vol. 7573, pp. 572–585. Springer, Heidelberg (2012)

21. Wenzel, S., Förstner, W.: Finding Poly-Curves of Straight Line and Ellipse Segments in Images. Photogrammetrie - Fernerkundung - Geoinformation 2013(4), 297–308 (2013)

22. Muja, M., Lowe, D.G.: Fast approximate nearest neighbors with automatic algorithm configuration. In: International Conference on Computer Vision Theory and Applications (VISAPP), pp. 331–340 (2009)

Noise Estimation for Computer-Generated Images Using an Interval Type-2 Fuzzy Sets Filter

Samuel Delepoulle, Andre Bigand, and Christophe Renaud

Université Lille Nord-de-France,
LISIC, Calais Cedex, 62228, France

Abstract. Global illumination methods based on stochastic techniques provide photo-realistic images. However, they are prone to stochastic noise that can be reduced by increasing the number of paths as proved by Monte Carlo theory. The problem of finding the number of paths that are required in order to ensure that human observers cannot perceive any noise is still open. This paper proposes a new noise estimator, based on interval type-2 fuzzy sets (IT2 FSs) and devoted to computer-generated images. This model can then be used in any progressive stochastic global illumination method in order to estimate the noise level of different parts of any image. A comparative study of this model with a simple test image demonstrates the good consistency between an added noise value and the results from the noise estimator. The proposed noise estimator results have been too compared with full-reference quality measures (or faithfullness measures) like SSIM and gives satisfactory performance.

1 Introduction

In many algorithms devoted to image processing, estimation of noise present in the image is necessary to process the image optimally. This is the case for global illumination methods. The main objective of global illumination methods is to produce **synthetic images** with photo-realistic quality. These methods are generally based on path tracing theory in which stochastic paths are generated from the camera point of view through each pixel toward the 3D scene [1]. The Monte Carlo theory ensures that this process will converge to the correct image when the number of paths grows [2–4]. However, there is no information about the number of paths that are really required for the image to be visually converged. So at the beginning of the generation of image synthesis, images are very noisy and they become more and more photo-realistic according to the number of paths. Consequently this process needs image quality measure, or its counterpart noise level measure to decide the necessary number of paths. Image quality measure, concerning image synthesis, is hitherto made using human observers (providing experimental psycho-visual scores) that is very time consuming. To illustrate that process, fig. 1 presents the evolution of parts (patches) of a synthetic image generation process, from a low number of paths (noisy patch) to a correct number of paths (reference patch).

© Springer International Publishing Switzerland 2015
D. Filev et al. (eds.), *Intelligent Systems'2014,*
Advances in Intelligent Systems and Computing 323, DOI: 10.1007/978-3-319-11310-4_53

It is so obvious that automatically measure image quality is very important to characterize images visual quality. They are of great interest in image compression (JPEG models) and in image synthesis. Image quality metrics are usually categorized into three models in the literature: full reference (such as the signal to noise ratio SNR and structural similarity index measure SSIM [5]), no-reference (image quality is estimated without access to reference images [6–8]) and reduced-reference models ([9–11]). However, the proposed models, which are based on theoretical models of noise, present sensitivity limits in global illuminations.

In the other hand, the fact that synthetic images are generated from noisy to correct images may lead to a noise estimation based method. Noise models have not been heavily studied concerning synthetic images, and they are often difficult to establish concerning CCD cameras images. Olsen [12] showed that the most reliable estimate is obtained by prefiltering the image to suppress the image structure and then computing the standard deviation value (of white additive noise) from the filtered data. Another possible way to noise estimation is to use interesting results of recent efficient filters, as the one we proposed in [13]. In [13] we proposed a novel fuzzy image filter, based on the use of interval type-2 fuzzy sets (or interval-valued fuzzy sets, IVFS's in the sequel), that yields good performances.

So this paper focuses on the use of a new noise estimation model to detect and to quantify stochastic noise in a synthetic image.The paper is structured as follows. Section 2 describes the experimental database we use and section 3 describes the image filtering using interval-valued fuzzy entropy. Section 4 introduces the design of the IVFS image noise estimation, section 5 shows the experimental results obtained by the estimated noise model. Finally the paper is summarized with some conclusions in section 6.

2 Image Database for Noise Estimation

The model is built on data corresponding to images of globally illuminated scenes. The path tracing algorithm was used in order to reduce noise [14]. This algorithm generates stochastic paths from the camera to the 3D scene. For each intersection of a path with the surface, a direction of reflection or refraction is randomly extracted.

For each scene several images were obtained, the first one being strongly noisy and the last one being the reference image(fig. 1). Generated images were computed at 512×512 resolutions. The largest number of paths per pixel was set at 10100 which appeared to be sufficient for generating visually converged images. Then, each of these images is opaque and virtually cut into non-overlapping sub-images of size 128×128 pixels. For the used test image, we thus get 16 different sub-images.

Our goal is to study and develop a noise estimation method devoted to synthetic images. Once noise power is estimated, we aim to propose a new image quality index based on image noise power (instead of classical image features)

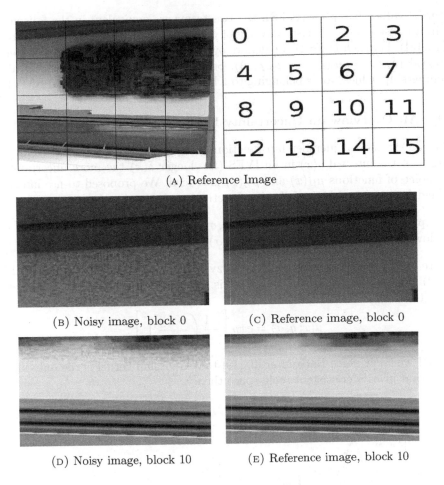

(A) Reference Image

(B) Noisy image, block 0

(C) Reference image, block 0

(D) Noisy image, block 10

(E) Reference image, block 10

Fig. 1. Original (noisy) and reference images

and compare this one with observers data (psycho-visual score) and classical reference quality metric like SSIM.

3   An Overview on IVFS Entropy and Proposed IVFS Filter

The concept of a type-2 fuzzy set was introduced first by Zadeh [15] as an other possible extension of the concept of a FS. Type-2 fuzzy sets have membership degrees that are themselves fuzzy, and have been proved of being capable of enhancing uncertainty handling abilities of traditional type-1 fuzzy sets. So they have been extensively applied to image processing [13,16,17]. Let us start with a short review of basics concepts related to IVFS. Let $S([0,1])$ denote the set of all closed subintervals of the interval $[0,1]$, an Interval type-2 fuzzy set (IT2FS or

interval-valued fuzzy set (IVFS): the two terms are equivalent in the following)
A in a non-empty and crisp universe of discourse X is a mapping from X to S
([15,18]). For each IVFS A, we denote by $\delta_A(x)$ the amplitude of the considered
interval $(\delta_A(x) = \mu_{AU}(x) - \mu_{AL}(x))$. So non-specific evidence (an interval of
membership values) for x belonging to a linguistic value A is identified by IVFS.

3.1   An Overview on Uncertainty Representation

The uncertainty of membership function of a precise FS is modeled using the
length of the interval $\delta(x)$ in an IVFS (the longer $\delta(x)$ the more uncertainty),
so choice of functions $\mu_U(x)$ and $\mu_L(x)$ is crucial. We proposed to use interval-
valued fuzzy sets with the following functions $\mu_U(x)$ and $\mu_L(x)$:

- upper limit: $\mu_U(x) : \mu_U(x) = [\mu(x; g, \sigma)]^{1/\alpha}$, (with $\alpha = 2$),
- lower limit: $\mu_L(x) : \mu_L(x) = [\mu(x; g, \sigma)]^{\alpha}$

where $\mu(x; g, \sigma)$ is a Gaussian (FS) fuzzy number ($\mu(x; g, \sigma)$ is represented in
fig. 2) centered on g and which support is set using a free constant parameter σ
($x \in [0, G - 1]$):

$$\mu(x; g, \sigma) = exp\left[-\frac{1}{2}\left(\frac{x - g}{\sigma}\right)^2\right]. \tag{1}$$

Indeed we know since Babaud *et al.* [19] that Gaussian kernel is the only linear
filter that gives a consistent scale-space theory.

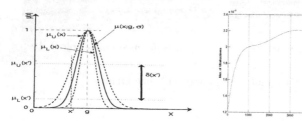

(A) Membership function of a IVFS   (B) Ultrafuzziness evolution vs. samples number, block 0

Fig. 2. IVFS membership function and ultrafuzziness evolution according to the number of paths

3.2   An Overview on Interval-Valued Fuzzy Sets Entropy

The process of selecting the necessary information for image processing must
lead here to the correct estimate of the image uncertainty. The present work
demonstrates an application of fuzzy set theory to estimate noise power, with
the highest accuracy possible (so a good evaluation of uncertainty is essential).
The terms *fuzziness degree* [20] and *entropy* [21] provide the measurement of

uncertainty in a set and are important issues in fuzzy logic studies. These well-known concepts have been developed in a previous paper ([13]). Nevertheless, the total amount of uncertainty is difficult to calculate in the case of fuzzy sets (FS), and particularly when images (represented using a FS) are corrupted with noise, so we proposed to use the IVFS imprecision degree $Ind(A)$ of an IVFS A in X:

$$Ind(A) = \sum_{i=1}^{q} [\mu_U(x_i) - \mu_L(x_i)] \tag{2}$$

It is assumed that an observed image I is defined on a $M \times N$ square lattice, and each pixel (o, p) takes a gray level value $g(o, p)$ (with G gray levels $g \in [0, G-1]$). For an image subset $I \subseteq X$, the histogram $h(g)$, Tizhoosh [22] intuitively proved that it is very easy to extend the previous concepts of FS (linear index of fuzziness proposed by Pal [23]) for IVFS, and to define the (linear) *index of ultrafuzziness* as follows:

$$\Gamma(x) = \frac{1}{M.N} \sum_{g=0}^{G-1} [h(x) . (\mu_U(x) - \mu_L(x))] \tag{3}$$

The previously defined IVFS is shifted over the interval $[0, G-1]$ of the histogram of the image by varying g but keeping σ fixed. Among the numerous frameworks of uncertainty modeling, this last equation seems to be an interesting tool for image processing, especially for noise estimation. The evolution of the global maximum $MAX(\Gamma)$ of this index according to the number of paths of the block 0 (fig.1) is presented fig. 2. Using the same definition of the linear index of ultrafuzziness, we used this performing index to propose a generalization of Gaussian kernel filtering [13]. In [24] we illustrated that $\Gamma(x)$ can be used as a global no-reference image metric when the image is clean and was compared with a psycho-visual score with success. In the following we show that $\Gamma(x)$ increases if the image becomes less and less noisy and may be used in a noise estimation scheme.

4   The Design of the IVFS Image Noise Estimation

In this paper, it is assumed that the noise corrupting image I is additive, stationary and has zero mean (i.e., white noise):

$$I(o, p) = f(o, p) + \eta(o, p) \tag{4}$$

where f is the ideal image, I is the observed image (previously defined) and η is the noise component. The goal is to estimate the variance (power) $var(\eta)$ of η.

Many papers in literature present algorithms to estimate the features of noise in digital images [25–28]. These methods attack the estimation problem in one of the two ways:

- by filtering I to suppress the image structure and then computing $var(\eta)$ from the filtered data
- by computing $var(\eta)$ from the variance of I in a set of image regions initially classified as showing little structure.

This paper presents a method belonging to the first family, starting with the filtering of the image I. In [24] we defined a new image filter using ultrafuzziness index, to take into account simultaneously the local and global properties of the pixels. In the present work, we show that this index is also effective to measure noise level in computer-generated images and can be used in images noise estimation. By subtracting from I the filtered image J, a measure of the noise at each pixel is computed as presented fig. 4.

4.1 Proposed Scheme

Let be a computer-generated image I. The global no-reference image metric taking into account noise levels is divided into three steps.

In the first one, image I is divided into Ki patches I_k (or blocks. A $M \times N$ gray-level image I is divided into Ki non-overlapping patches ($m \times n$ gray-level patch), for example a 512×512 image is divided into 16 non-overlapping blocks of size 128×128). Each patch I_k is then analyzed using the local entropy Γ^k. To be coherent with the overall method, we used the IVFS denoising algorithm we proposed in [13]. This procedure is included in algorithm 1 (this procedure makes it possible to obtain the optimal value σ of the Gaussian fuzzy number (see equation 1) for each patch). So the method operates like an unsupervised classification method that affects noise-free pixels to K clusters (modes of the image) and noisy pixels to a cluster: 'noisy pixels'. Let denote $g(o,p)$ the gray level value of the pixel (o,p) of a $m \times n$ noisy block. The noise detection process results in dividing the histogram into different zones, according to the maxima of ultrafuzziness Γ_{max}. So pixels are classified into two groups: noise-free pixels (*i.e.* belonging to one of the K modes), and noisy pixels. Noisy pixels are treated using the classical median filter ("'Med"', with a 3×3 window). The image restoration appears as follows:

$$g(o,p) = \begin{cases} g(o,p) & \text{if } g(o,p) \text{ is noise-free} \\ Med(o,p) & \text{if } g(o,p) \text{ is noisy.} \end{cases} \tag{5}$$

In the second step, once the denoising treatment on each block is made, the new image J is obtained from the concatenation of the K_i patches J_k. In the third step, once image I has been filtered into J, the noise power $var(\eta)$ is easily computed (see algorithm 1).

4.2 Algorithm

The implementation of image noise estimation based on IVFS and measure of ultrafuzziness Γ is given by the algorithm 1.

Algorithm 1. Image quality measure

Require: an input noisy $M \times N$ gray-level image I, divided into Ki non-overlapping patches ($m \times n$ gray-level patch) and calculate the local entropy Γ^k for each patch k $(0 < k < Ki)$

1: Select the shape of MF
2: Compute the k-patch image histogram $h(g)^k$ (normalized to 1)
3: Initialize the position of the membership function
4: Shift the MF along the gray-level range
5: $\Gamma_{max}^k \leftarrow 0$
6: **for** each position g **do**
7:    Compute $\mu_U(g)$ and $\mu_L(g)$
8:    Compute $\Gamma(g)^k = \frac{1}{m \times n} \sum_{g=0}^{L-1} h(g)^k \times [\mu_U(g) - \mu_L(g)]$
9:    **if** $\Gamma_{max}^k \leq \Gamma(g)^k$ **then**
10:       $\Gamma_{max}^k \leftarrow \Gamma(g)^k$
11:    **end if**
12:    Keep the value Γ_{max}^k for patch k and optimal value σ
13: **end for**
14: Apply the FS parameter σ to get a denoised patch J_k
15: Iterate the number of the patch: $k + 1$
16: Compute the new image (J)
17: For each denoised patch, keep the local metric $\Gamma(g)^k$. Compute the value Γ for global image J with $\Gamma(g) = \frac{1}{K_i} \sum_{k=1}^{K_i} \Gamma(g)^k$

Ensure: The filtered image J
Ensure: The difference image $I - J$ and the **noise power estimation** $var(\eta)$

4.3   Method Illustration

The implementation of image noise estimation based on IVFS is illustrated by the following experiment. Let us consider a synthetic test patch (classical "savoyse" image, see fig. 3) and white Gaussian noise with different variances σ^2 added to this clean patch (the test patch with white Gaussian noise with $\sigma = 0.1$ is presented fig. 3). The noisy image is filtered using Wiener filter and IVFS filter and presented in Fig. 3. Fig. 4 presents the evolution of computed noise variances using the Wiener estimation method and the estimation method using IVFS filter we propose (100 simulations are carried out with independent noise realizations). From this set of experiments on the this test patch we can see that the value of the noise power $var(\eta)$ drops monotonically as the image content becomes more and more noisy. In other words, it can be thought that $var(\eta)$ is a better indicator of noise power than Wiener estimation (particularly for small noise power). These good results are in the same way that the results we presented in [8,13]. They encourage us to apply this method to computer-generated images.

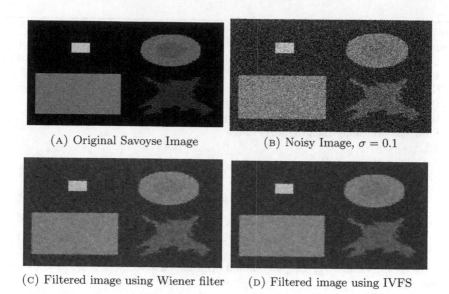

(A) Original Savoyse Image   (B) Noisy Image, $\sigma = 0.1$

(C) Filtered image using Wiener filter   (D) Filtered image using IVFS

Fig. 3. Obtained results with synthetic image "Savoyse"

5 Experimental Results

5.1 Experimental Results with a Computer-Generated Image

In order to test the performance of the proposed technique, some results obtained with the computer-generated image named "Bar", fig. 1, are shown in this presentation (other images were tested and same behaviors were observed, so they are not presented here due to lack of space). This image is composed of homogeneous and noisy blocks and is interesting to present some results.

In fig. 5, the first image (left) is the noisy block 0, obtained at the beginning of the process, the second one is the result obtained with the IVFS filter. The **main idea** of the paper is the following: synthesis process is started with a great noise level and a low entropy value. So the initial position of the synthesis process is unknown but the observed behavior measured at each iteration of the image synthesis process brings us information. The average information quantity gained at each iteration is entropy. The measured entropy using IVFS, named ultrafuzziness, seems to be an interesting measure of noise level and so supplies a noise power estimation, also used as denoising scheme in the proposed image synthesis process. The performances of the noise power estimation are now illustrated (particularly noise histograms show the decreasing of noise power).

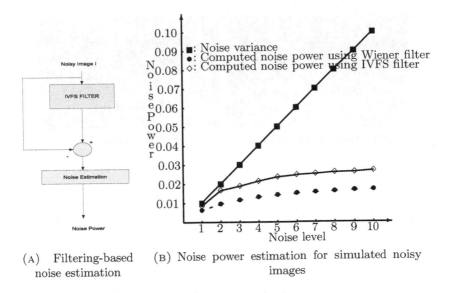

(A)   Filtering-based   (B) Noise power estimation for simulated noisy
      noise estimation   images

Fig. 4. Noise power estimation scheme

5.2   Performances of the Proposed Method

Synthesis process is started with a great noise level and a low entropy value, but
noise models are not available at the moment for computer-generated images. So
a quantitative comparison is difficult to assume. In order to verify the effectiveness of the proposed noise model, a quantitative comparison with SSIM index
has been made. The measure of structural similarity for images (SSIM quality index [5]) has also been computed on the course of paths number as shown
fig. 5. This measure is based on the adaptation of the human visual system to
the structural information in a scene. The index accounts for three different similarity measures, namely luminance, contrast and structure. The closer the index
to unity, the better the result. It is easy to see that SSIM index as an opposite
behavior according to the noise power measure we propose. This comparison is
made at the bottom of fig. 5 for the noisy block 0 presented at the top of fig. 5,
and it is easy to verify that this behavior is assumed during image generation
(from low samples number to high samples number), that is to say from high
noise level to low noise level. To illustrate our work we also present fig. 6, for the
noisy block 0, the noise histogram estimation (for 1000 samples and at the end
of the process), the images I, J, f histograms (previously defined, IV), and the
noise histograms (at 1000 samples). We would like to highlight the advantages
of the proposed noise power estimation: this method is simple; it is parameter
free and avoid additional procedures and training data for parameter ($var(\eta)$)
determination.

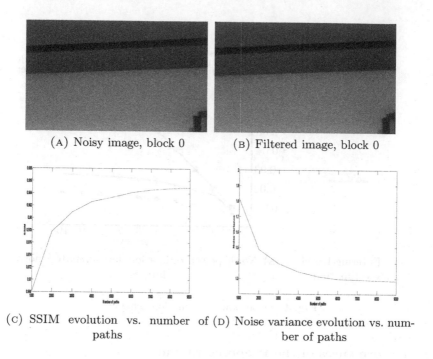

(A) Noisy image, block 0   (B) Filtered image, block 0

(C) SSIM evolution vs. number of paths   (D) Noise variance evolution vs. number of paths

Fig. 5. Original and filtered blocks denoising using $IVFS's$ and noise evolution

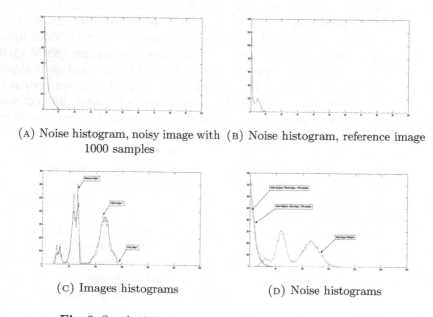

(A) Noise histogram, noisy image with 1000 samples   (B) Noise histogram, reference image

(C) Images histograms   (D) Noise histograms

Fig. 6. Synthetic image generation from noise point of view

6   Conclusion

Starting from the filter presented in [13], taking into account the total amount of uncertainty present in computer-generated images using IVFS, this paper presents a new noise estimation method. The method effectively combines image histograms information with the spatial information about pixels of different gray levels by using an IVFS entropy technique. The good results we obtain are particularly interesting in image synthesis to model specific noise affecting this kind of images. This new method assumes no "a priori" knowledge of a specific input image, no learning, no numerous tunable parameters, yet it has good performance compared to a psycho-visual method ([24]). This qualitative noise model seems effective, but there remains some open questions to effectively establish a link between the characteristics of noise affecting the image (noise level), and to optimize noise power computation, particularly for high noise level. Computer-generated images noise is not Gaussian. So more extensive investigations on other measures of entropy and the effect of parameters influencing the width (length) of the interval of IVFS are under investigation (to establish a link between this interval and level and type of noise) towards an automatic noise quantification and will be presented in the future.

References

1. Kajiya, J.: The Rendering Equation. ACM Computer Graphics 20, 143–150 (1986)
2. Mitchell, D.P.: Generating antialiased images at low sampling densities. In: Proceedings of SIGGRAPH 1987, pp. 65–72. ACM Press, New York (1987)
3. Farrugia, J., Péroche, B.: A Progressive Rendering Algorithm Using an Adaptive Perceptually Based Image Metric. Comput. Graph. Forum 23, 605–614 (2004)
4. Longhurst, P., Debattista, K., Chalmers, A.: A GPU based Saliency Map for High-Fidelity Selective Rendering. In: AFRIGRAPH 2006 4th International Conference on Computer Graphics, Virtual Reality, Visualisation and Interaction in Africa, pp. 21–29. ACM SIGGRAPH (2006)
5. Wang, Z., Bovik, A., Sheikh, H., Simoncelli, E.: Image quality assessment: from error visibility to structural similarity. IEEE Trans. Image Process 13(4) (2004)
6. Zhang, J., Ong, S., Thinh, M.: Kurtosis-based no-reference quality assessment of JPEG2000 images. Signal Processing: Image Communication 26, 13–23 (2011)
7. Ferzli, R., Karam, L.: No-reference objective wavelet based noise immune image sharpness metric. In: International Conference on Image Processing (2005)
8. Delepoulle, S., Bigand, A., Renaud, C.: A no-reference computer-generated images quality metric and its application to denoising. In: IEEE 6th International Conference 'Intelligent Systems' (2012)
9. Wang, Z., Simoncelli, E.P.: Reduced Reference Image Quality Assessment Using a Wavelet-domain Natural Image Statistic Model. In: Proc. SPIE, Conf. on Human Vision and Electronic Imaging X, vol. 5666, pp. 149–159 (2005)
10. Li, Q., Wang, Z.: Reduced-Reference Image Quality Assessment using Divisive Normalization Based Image Representation. IEEE Journal of Selected Topics in Signal Processing 3, 202–211 (2009)

11. Lahoudou, A., Viennet, E., Beghdadi, A.: Selection low-level features for image quality assessment by statistical methods. Journal of Computing and Information Technology 2, 183–189 (2010)

12. Olsen, S.I.: Estimation of noise in Images: an evaluation. CVGIP 55, 319–323 (1993)

13. Bigand, A., Colot, O.: Fuzzy filter based on interval-valued fuzzy sets for image filtering. Fuzzy Sets and Systems 161, 96–117 (2010)

14. Shirley, P., Wang, C., Zimmerman, K.: Monte Carlo techniques for direct lighting calculations. ACM Transactions on Graphics 15, 1–36 (1996)

15. Zadeh, L.: The concept of a linguistic variable and its application to approximate reasoning. Information Sciences 8, 199–249 (1975)

16. Sussner, P., Nachtegael, M., Esmi, E.: An approach towards edge-detection and watershed segmentation based on an interval-valued morphological gradient. In: Proceedings of IPCV (2011)

17. Jurio, A., Paternain, D., Lopez-Molina, C., Bustince, H., Mesiar, H., Beliakov, G.: A construction method of interval-valued fuzzy sets for image processing. In: proceedings 2011 IEEE Symposium on Advances in Type-2 Fuzzy Logic Systems (2011)

18. Bustince, H., Barrenechea, E., Pergola, M., Fernandez, J.: Interval-valued fuzzy sets constructed from matrices: Application to edge detection. Fuzzy Sets and Systems 160, 1819–1840 (2009)

19. Babaud, J., Witkin, A.P., Baudin, M., Duda, R.O.: Uniqueness of the Gausssian kernel for scale-space filtering. IEEE Trans. on PAMI 8, 26–33 (1986)

20. Kaufmann, A.: Introduction to the theory of fuzzy set - Fundamental theorical elements, vol. 28. Academic Press, New York (1975)

21. Deluca, A., Termini, S.: A definition of a nonprobabilistic entropy in the setting of fuzzy set theory. Information and Control 20, 301–312 (1972)

22. Tizhoosh, H.: Image thresholding using type-2 fuzzy sets. Pattern Recognition 38, 2363–2372 (2005)

23. Pal, N., Bezdek, J.: Measures of fuzziness: a review and several classes. Van Nostrand Reinhold, New York (1994)

24. Delepoulle, S., Bigand, A., Renaud, C.: Interval type-2 fuzzy sets based no-reference quality evaluation of synthesis images. In: Proceedings of CGVR 2011 (2011)

25. Jolion, J.M., Meer, P., Rosenfeld, A.: A fast parallel algorithm for blind estimation of noise variance. IEEE Trans. on PAMI 12, 216–223 (1990)

26. Rank, M., Lendl, M., Unbehauen, R.: Estimation of image noise variance. In: Proc. of the IEE Visual Signal Process (1999)

27. Starck, J.L., Murtagh, F.: Automatic noise estimation from the multiresolution support. PASP 110, 193–199 (1998)

28. Deng, G., Tay, D.B.H., Marusic, S.: A signal denoising algorithm based on overcomplete wavelet representations and gaussian models. Signal Process 87, 866–876 (2007)

Predicting Proteins Functional Family: A Graph-Based Similarity Derived from Community Detection

Sabrine Mallek, Imen Boukhris, and Zied Elouedi

LARODEC, Institut Supérieur de Gestion de Tunis, Université de Tunis
sabrinemallek@yahoo.fr, imen.boukhris@hotmail.com,
zied.elouedi@gmx.fr

Abstract. This paper contributes to the problem of assessing similarities between node-labeled and edge-weighted graphs. Graph comparison is usually based on the maximum common subgraph (*mcs*) measure. The latter is an overly stringent measure which is sensitive toward small deviations and errors. In order to overcome these issues, we propose a relaxation of the *mcs* measure based on so-called communities. A community is used as an "almost common" subgraph with high concentrations of edges. With our approach, we increase tolerance towards noise and structural variation especially in the case of biological data. The proposed measure is validated by an experimental study conducted in the context of the analysis of the similarities among protein families based on the properties of their active sites.

Keywords: graph-based similarity, community, protein binding sites classification, maximum almost common subgraph.

1 Introduction

Graphs are commonly used to represent structured objects. They have been very useful as models in many areas such as biology, pattern recognition, social networks and computer vision. In many cases, it is required to assess their similarities. For example, in molecular biology, one can extract common and discriminative motifs, detect structural variations or predict similar functional behavior by computing similarities between biomolecules. This task can be carried out using graph matching which is a problem known from graph theory. Graph matching techniques can be categorized into two types: exact and inexact. The exact one uses the graph and subgraph isomorphism properties and the similarity is based on the maximum common subgraph isomorphism. The inexact one, is an error tolerant graph matching based on graph edit distance, which is often employed in graph alignment methods [19].

In this paper, we are interested in relaxing the maximum common subgraph measure (*mcs*) in order to increase its tolerance toward errors and noise in data. In fact, the *mcs* is a restrictive measure that consists in extracting nodes and edges having exactly the same node labels and edge weights in two graphs. One possible solution for this problem is to build a product graph in which the largest clique represents a solution for the *mcs* problem. Indeed, the clique concept is too restrictive since it restrains the common substructure to the nodes linked by exactly the same number of edges in both

© Springer International Publishing Switzerland 2015
D. Filev et al. (eds.), *Intelligent Systems'2014*,
Advances in Intelligent Systems and Computing 323, DOI: 10.1007/978-3-319-11310-4_54

graphs being compared which is not convenient especially in the case of molecular data which is often incomplete and noisy as a result of mutations and molecular flexibility. Thus, it will result in small common subgraphs unable to capture structural similarities. Besides, mining the *mcs* is a critical task from a complexity point of view, since it is an NP-complete problem.

To overcome the issues presented by detecting cliques to extract maximum common subgraphs, we propose in this paper an alternative way to an efficient detection of what we call maximum almost common subgraphs. Our approach is based on the concept of community detection on graphs which has shown its efficiency in many real world applications [2,11,16]. In this paper, we apply our method in the bioinformatics area and especially for the structural comparison of proteins where real valued edge weighted graphs represent proteins binding sites on the 3D structure. The maximum almost common subgraph measure is used to assess the similarity between proteins binding sites and therefore predict the functional class of a given protein. Note that our approach is based only on structural information and is independent from sequence or fold homology.

The paper is organized as follows: In Section 2, we describe protein binding sites and explain their graphical representation. In Section 3, we recall some basic concepts and notations of graph matching. Section 4 is dedicated to our proposed method for assessing similarities between graphs and predicting proteins functional family based on community detection. In Section 5, an experimental study is presented. Section 6 concludes the paper.

2   Graph Representation of Binding Sites

Proteins are essential components of cell life as they play many roles such as gene expression, immunoreactions, enzymatic reactions and inter-cellular communications. Unraveling the function of these proteins has been, and remains, one of the most fundamental problems in bioinformatics. The identification of the protein binding sites can provide information related to its function since the molecular activity takes place at their level. Protein binding sites vary in size and shape, coming in a nearly spherical shape or forming a curved chip [13]. They are chemically and physically complementary to binding molecules such as substrates, agonists, antagonists or allosteric modulators. Hence, binding pockets are important contributors in the functional process of structures.

To infer an unknown function of a protein, it is possible to first compare its binding ligand structure with the one of another known protein function then compute their similarities. The result may indicate functional resemblances and hence predict the function of the respective biomolecule.

One way to accomplish this task is to represent binding pockets by use of graphs. To have such graphs, CavBase [17] is used [3,10,19,20]. It is a database system for the fully automated detection and extraction of putative protein binding sites derived from crystal structure data obtained from the PDB (Protein Data Bank) [1]. It uses the LIGSITE algorithm for the detection of binding pockets on the protein surface and provides a representation of the geometrical arrangement of the binding sites using pseudocenters.

Pseudocenters are spatial points that depict the physicochemical properties of a binding pocket. Each one is exhibited as a sphere with a specific color depending on the physicochemical property.

Up to date, CavBase handles seven pseudocenters namely, Donor (DO), Acceptor (A), Mixed donor/acceptor (DA), Ion metal (IM), hydrophobic aliphatic (AL), aromatic (Ar) and $\pi - \pi$ interaction (PI). They represent possible interactions between the binding sites residues and the protein's substrate.

Protein binding sites are usually modeled by use of a 4-tuple graph $G = (V, E, l_V, l_E)$ where:

- V is the set of vertices representing binding atoms. Two pseudospheres are linked if the Euclidean distance separating them is below 11 Angström. Actually, it is considered sufficient to capture the binding site geometry. Hence, longer edges are ignored [19].
- E is the set of edges representing connections between vertices.
- $l_V : V \rightarrow \{1 \ldots 7\}$ is a function that assigns labels to vertices, $1 \ldots 7$ refers to the physicochemical properties presented in CavBase.
- $l_E : V \times V \rightarrow \mathbb{R}$ is a function that assigns edge weights. These weights describe the distance between two connected vertices.

3   Graph Matching

3.1   Graph Isomorphism

In order to compare two graphs, we use graph isomorphism. It is the simplest form of exact graph matching. Formally, a graph isomorphism between two graphs $G = (V, E)$ and $G' = (V', E')$ is a bijective mapping $f : V \rightarrow V'$ conserving all the labels and the edges structure such that for all $u, v \in V$, and $(u, v) \in E$:

- $l_V(u) = l_V(f(u))$ and $l_V(v) = l_V(f(v))$;
- $(f(u), f(v)) \in E'$;
- $l_E(u, v) = l_E(f(u), f(v))$.

If such a mapping exists, then G and G' are called isomorphic and are denoted $G \approx G'$ [5].

3.2   Subgraph Isomorphism

Let be three graphs G, G' and S, where $S \subseteq G'$. A subgraph isomorphism is an injective mapping $f : V \rightarrow V'$ from G to G' where f is a graph isomorphism from G to S.

3.3   Maximum Common Subgraph

The maximum common subgraph is widely used as a similarity measure on graphs. Let us consider three graphs G_s, G and G'. If $G_s \approx G$ and $G_s \approx G'$ than G_s is a common subgraph of G and G'. G_s is a maximum common subgraph if there is no other common subgraph of G and G' with more nodes. Usually, the *mcs* is not unique.

Several methods measure similarity between two graphs by computing the size of the *mcs* in terms of number of nodes as illustrated in Equation 1.

$$sim(G, G') = \frac{|mcs(G, G')|}{max(|G|, |G'|)} \tag{1}$$

Where $|mcs(G, G')|$ is the number of nodes of the *mcs*, and $max(|G|, |G'|)$ represents the maximum number of nodes between the two graphs. Clearly, the larger the maximum common subgraph is, the more similar the two graphs are. Unfortunately, seeking for the *mcs* is an intractable NP-complete problem [4], and no exact algorithms have been discovered. One possible solution of the *mcs* problem is to reformulate it onto the problem of detecting the maximum clique in a product graph.

Clique: A clique is a subset of vertices all connected to each other, it is the densest graph structure. Therefore, a common subraph that is completely connected forms a clique. The maximum clique in a graph is the one with maximum number of nodes.

The reduction of the *mcs* problem to the clique problem is done by the use of a compatibility graph also called product graph. Indeed, a maximum common subgraph is equivalent to a maximum clique on the product graph.

Product graph: A product graph $G_P = (V_P, E_P)$ of two graphs $G = (V, E)$ and $G' = (V', E')$ is defined by:

- A set of nodes: $V_P \subseteq V \times V'$.
- A set of edges: $E_P \subseteq V_P \times V_P$ where:
  - $V_P = \{(v_i, v'_j) \mid l_V(v_i) = l_V(v'_j)\}$;
  - $E_P = \{((v_i, v'_j), (v_k, v'_l)) \mid l_E(v_i, v_k) = l_E(v'_j, v'_l)\}$.

Indeed, the product graph extraction is very restrictive since an edge is inserted if it has exactly the same weights in the matched edges between two matched nodes. Since real world data can be affected with noise and measurement errors, it is possible to introduce some tolerance in the construction of the product graph G_p by defining the set of edges as:

$$E_P = \{((v_i, v'_j), (v_k, v'_l)) \mid \| l_E(v_i, v_k) - l_E(v'_j, v'_l) \| \leqslant \varepsilon\} \tag{2}$$

Where ε is a tolerance threshold parameter for edge length differences specified by the user.

Therefore, finding a maximum common subgraph amounts to find a maximum clique in G_P. Unfortunately, cliques are very restrictive since each vertex must be connected to all the other vertices of the graph. As stated above, in different contexts, exact matches are difficult to find as a result of noise in data, especially when comparing biomolecule structures, for example protein binding sites. Indeed, proteins as conformational molecules, by their nature, are very flexible and thus their 3D-structure may be subject to distortions. Accordingly, an alteration of the spatial arrangement may affect the protein binding sites and therefore the graph nodes coordinates. Besides, they are frequently exposed to mutations.

4 Graph Similarity Based on the Maximum Common Community

In order to address the issues of exact matches constraints and provide a flexible common subgraph that is tolerant to sparse errors and small deviations, we propose to use what we call a maximum almost common subgraph. Our approach consists in the construction of the product graph and the extraction of the largest dense component on it. To this end, we propose a method based on community detection on graphs.

4.1 Community

A community [8] refers to a sub-unit composed of a special group of vertices with high concentration of edges. It is a subgraph whose nodes are more tightly connected to each other than with nodes outside the subgraph. Communities are usually used in disciplines where systems are modeled as large graph networks such as biology, sociology, economy and computer science. Besides, the community concept make sense even on sparse graphs [8]. The concept of community is much more relaxed compared to the concept of cliques who requires for all vertices to be adjacent to each other. Yet, we can have a community with all possible internal edges except a few ones.

4.2 Community Detection

Dense regions may indicate interesting properties depending on what characteristics are being modeled by the graph vertices and edges [18]. In fact, dense components may indicate mutual similarity, interaction degrees or favorable environments, etc. Community detection algorithms are designed to extract such dense regions that have few connections with the rest of the graph.

Assuming that we have derived a product graph from graphs in input representing protein binding sites. Our algorithm is based on two main phases. In a first step, the aim is to partition the product graph $G_p(V_p, E_p)$ into dense subunits without restrictions to the degree of connectedness. The second step casts the maximum community in terms of number of nodes. In sum, it is a more flexible way to extract an approximation of the largest common subgraph between the two original graphs that is rather dense.

Our approach is inspired from a heuristic method that has been proposed in [2], where a fast algorithm enabling an efficient partition of a weighted mobile phone network was developed. It is a greedy approach based on the optimization of the so called modularity function. The modularity is one of the most popular quality functions given by [12] which measures the goodness of a partition. It assigns a value to each partition of a graph. Thus, partitions are ranked based on their score given by the quality function. Good partitions are the ones with highest scores. It can be applied for both weighted and unweighted graphs which is the case for our product graph [12]. It is defined as:

$$Q = \frac{1}{2m} \sum_{i,j} [A_{i,j} - \frac{k_i k_j}{2m}] \delta(c_i, c_j) \tag{3}$$

Where $A_{i,j} = 1$ if there is an edge connecting i and j, 0 otherwise, k_i denotes the degree of vertex i, m represents $|V_p|$ and $\delta(c_i, c_j)$ is equal to 1 if i and j are in the same community, 0 otherwise.

The algorithm is based on a sequence of passes repeated iteratively. At the beginning, each node is considered as a community apart. During each pass, nodes/communities are merged into their neighborhood and evaluated by the variation ΔQ of modularity which describes the gain of modularity. A node stays in the community for which the modularity gain is maximum. The pass ends when no further improvement can be accomplished and hence a local maxima of the modularity is reached. As a result, the original graph will be divided into sub-units that are highly connected. Note that a community cannot contain two nodes that correspond to the same node in one of the considered graphs in order to ensure the validity of common subgraphs approximation. In fact, product graph nodes refer to unique pairs $(v_i, v'_j) \in V \times V'$. Yet, many product nodes may refer to the same nodes in G or G'. Therefore, before adding a new product node into a community we check whether the nodes it refers to are not yet contained. The gain of modularity ΔQ is defined as:

$$\Delta Q = [\frac{\Sigma_{in} + K_{i,in}}{2m} - (\frac{\Sigma_{tot} + K_i}{2m})^2] - [\frac{\Sigma_{in}}{2m} - (\frac{\Sigma_{tot}}{2m})^2 - (\frac{K_i}{2m})^2] \qquad (4)$$

Where Σ_{in} is the number of edges inside community C, Σ_{tot} is the number of edges incident to community C, k_i is the degree of vertex i, $K_{i,in}$ is the number of edges incident from i to vertices in C and $m = |V|$. ΔQ measures the gain of modularity of moving an isolated vertex i into a neighboring community C, if i is already in a community, it is removed then added to C.

To sum up, our approach is based on the four following steps:

1. Derive the product graph of the two graphs representing protein binding sites.
2. Partition this graph into dense subgraphs.
3. Extract the maximum community with maximum number of nodes.
4. Consider it as a maximum almost common subgraph and use it to compute the similarity between the two graphs.

4.3   Complexity

The greedy approach we have applied is a modularity optimization based-method that finds a good approximation of the modularity maximum in a fast time. Since at each iteration, one has to compute the modularity variation ΔQ, this computation can be done at constant time, it requires a time $O(m)$ where m is the number of edges. Besides, the modularity update after communities merging during each iteration can be done in worst case $O(n)$ where n is the number of the communities which decreases after each iteration [8]. The technique is more limited by storage than by computational time [2].

4.4   Similarity Measure Based on the Maximum Common Community

Several works measured similarity on the basis of the concept of the maximum common subgraph when comparing chemical compounds such as [9,14,15]. As for the *mcs* measure, it is possible to use the size of the maximum detected community as stated in Equation 1 to assess the similarity between graphs. However, it was shown that in some cases on protein binding sites graphs, a structure would be larger than the substantial binding site. The underlying reason for that is that protein binding pockets do not have a clear cut boundary. Thus, a structure can be a subpocket of another one having the most important catalytic residues. From this point of view, [3] expressed the similarity between two graphs in terms of subset relations leading to the following measure:

$$sim(G,G') = \varphi \cdot min(\alpha, \beta) + (1 - \varphi) \cdot max(\alpha, \beta) \tag{5}$$

Where $\alpha = \frac{|V_C|}{|V|}$, $\beta = \frac{|V_C|}{|V'|}$, ($|V_C|$ is the size of the maximum community and $|V|$ and $|V'|$ represent respectively the sizes of G and G'), and $0 \leqslant \varphi \leqslant 1$, is a compromise parameter which determines the comparison type (equivalence/inclusion). Having $\varphi = 1$, we recover the original measure in Equation 1. Thus, $sim(G,G') = 1$ only if $G = G'$. In the other hand, having $\varphi = 0$, it corresponds to a set inclusion measure for which each graph is a substructure of the other which is sufficient to obtain a degree of similarity equals 1. In general, the larger the value of $sim(G,G')$, the more similar G is to G'. This measure is more suitable, especially in the context of evaluating similarities between protein binding sites.

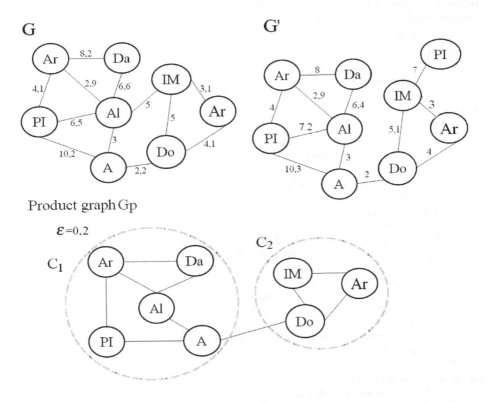

Fig. 1. The community detection algorithm operating on a protein binding site product graph

Fig. 1 illustrates our idea through a simple example. Let us consider G and G', two node labeled and edge weighted graphs representing protein binding sites. From these graphs, we build a product graph ($\varepsilon = 0.2$). After partitioning the product graph using the community detection algorithm we obtain two communities. The first one is composed of five nodes and the second one is composed of three nodes. Thus the largest community, representing the maximum almost common subgraph, has a size of five nodes. In the other hand, if we have considered the clique detection algorithm on the same product graph, there would be common subgraphs having up to three vertices. Therefore, the maximum clique corresponding to the maximum common subgraph will have a size of only three nodes. Accordingly, the community detection method is much convenient for the detection of a rather dense common substructure that is biologically significant.

Algorithms 1 presents our proposed approach to assess similarity between two graphs that is based on community detection.

Algorithm 1. Assessing similarity between graphs based on community detection

---

Input: Two graphs $G(V,E)$ and $G'(V,E)$, ε, φ
Output: Similarity between G and G'

foreach $v_i \in V$ **do**
 foreach $v_j \in V'$ **do**
  if $l(v_i) = l(v_j)$ **then**
   Insert node (v_i, v_j) into V_p

foreach $v = (v_i, v_j) \in V_p$ **do**
 foreach $v' = (v'_i, v'_j) \in V_p$ **do**
  if $|w(v_i, v'_i) - w(v_j, v'_j)| \leq \varepsilon$ **then**
   Insert edge (v, v') into E_p

Initially, each vertex forms a community
while *there is an increase of Q* **do**
 foreach *vertex i* **do**
  compute $\Delta Q_{i,i}$
  foreach *adjacent neighbor j to i* **do**
   remove vertex i from its current community C_i
   insert i in C_j
   compute $\Delta Q_{i,j}$
   if $\Delta Q_{i,j} < 0$ *or* $\Delta Q_{i,j} < \Delta Q_{i,i}$ **then**
    i stays in its current community
   else
    i merges into the community that maximizes ΔQ
   update Q

for *up to n communities* **do**
 Select C with maximum number of vertices
$\alpha \leftarrow V_{C_{max}}/V_G$
$\beta \leftarrow V_{C_{max}}/V_{G'}$
return $\varphi min(\alpha, \beta) + (1 - \varphi) max(\alpha, \beta)$

---

5 Experimental Study

In order to demonstrate the effectiveness of our method we conducted the experimental study in the context of comparing protein binding sites in order to predict a protein unkown family (i.e., class).

We have compared our method with the one based on the clique detection. This latter consists at extracting the maximum clique from the product graph of two inputted graphs representing protein binding sites. The detection of the maximum clique is performed using the Bron-Kerbosch method which is employed for binding ligand similarity search in the CavBase database. It is a heuristic approach that enumerates potential maximal cliques. The main idea behind it is to use a backtracking method based on an heuristic truncation of a search tree.

To apply our proposed method to the comparison of protein binding sites structures, we considered a dataset of protein binding sites of two protein classes from [6], 28 that bind ATP (Adenosine triphosphate) ligands and 32 that bind NADH (Nicotinamide adenine dinucleotide) ligands. This datatset is challenging since ATP is a substructure of NADH, it may possibly bind to the same ligands.

We used our novel measure as a distance in the context of a k-nearest-neighbor classifier in a leave-one-out cross-validation setting. In fact, to determine the class of a a graph G, we compute the distance between G and all the other instances in the training set. Then, we retain the k nearest graphs that are closest to G. The class of G is assigned on the basis of the majority classes relative to the k nearest neighbors.

We measured its performance according to the PCC (percent of correct classifications). We assess the similarity between the graphs using the measure specified in Equation 5 for both methods (i.e., the one based on maximum community and the maximum clique).

Table 1 and Table 2 report respectively to the results on the classification experiments in terms of accuracy. The only parameters specification required are the edges threshold (ε in Equation 2) for the product graph construction, which we set to 0.2 since it has proved to be well-suited [6], and the φ parameter for the similarity computation, which defines the type of comparison and interpolates between a measure of generalization and a measure of inclusion. φ is set to 0.5 since it has proved to be a reasonable choice in [3].

Table 1. Accuracy of the maximum clique measure

k=1	k=3	k=5
60.00%	63.33%	60.00%

As it can be seen, the performance of our novel method outperformed the clique detection approach. It is able to detect similar graphs on the basis of the largest dense module considered in our approach. Compared to the highest result of the clique-measure (63.33%), the best performance of the community measure (81.66%) is higher. These results confirm our conjecture that a relaxation of the *mcs* can increase the classification rate. Indeed, tolerance toward mismatches and minor differences that occur in graphs

Table 2. Accuracy of the maximum community measure

k=1	k=3	k=5
78.33%	81.66%	78.33%

representing real world data is required especially in the case of biological data due to conformational flexibility and measurement errors that may occur frequently. Besides, our method outperformed significantly the clique detection method in terms of running time.

6   Conclusion

The concept of maximum common subgraph is usually used as a similarity measure for computing resemblance among graphs. However, in this paper we have argued that this measure is very restrictive in the context of protein binding sites comparison. Therefore, we have proposed an alternative measure that consists of the detection of the maximum almost common subgraph. Hence, we used the community concept, which provides a much more tolerant large common substructure that remains dense. Our experiments have confirmed our conjecture. Actually, increased tolerance induced better results.

Communities are dense modules whose edges in the "inside" must be more than edges linking their vertices with the rest of the graph. They can be viewed as a generalization of the clique as a community encompasses several small cliques within. It is also linked to the concept of quasi-cliques [3,7,18], with which we intend to compare in future work.

References

1. Berman, H.M., Westbrook, J., Feng, Z., Gilliland, G., Bhat, T.N., Weissig, H., Shindyalov, I.N., Bourne, P.E.: The protein data bank. Nucleic Acids Res. 28(1), 235–242 (2000)
2. Blondel, V.D., Guillaume, J.L., Lambiotte, R., Lefebvre, E.: Fast unfolding of community hierarchies in large networks. CoRR abs/0803.0476 (2008)
3. Boukhris, I., Elouedi, Z., Fober, T., Mernberger, M., Hüllermeier, E.: Similarity analysis of protein binding sites: A generalization of the maximum common subgraph measure based on quasi-clique detection. In: International Conference on Intelligent Systems Design and Applications, ISDA, pp. 1245–1250 (2009)
4. Bunke, H.: Recent developments in graph matching. In: ICPR, pp. 2117–2124 (2000)
5. Ferrer, M., Valvenya, E., Serratosa, F.: Median graph: A new exact algorithm using a distance based on the maximum common subgraph. Pattern Recognition Letters 30, 579–588 (2009)
6. Fober, T., Mernberger, M., Moritz, R., Hullermeier, E.: Graph-kernels for the comparative analysis of protein active sites. GI 157, 21–31 (2009)
7. Fober, T., Klebe, G., Hüllermeier, E.: Local clique merging: An extension of the maximum common subgraph measure with applications in structural bioinformatics. In: Algorithms from and for Nature and Life. Studies in Classification, Data Analysis, and Knowledge Organization, pp. 279–286. Springer (2013)

8. Fortunato, S.: Community detection in graphs. Physics Reports 486, 75–174 (2010)
9. Gardiner, E.J., Artymiuk, P.J., Willett, P.: Clique-detection algorithms for matching three-dimensional molecular structures. Journal of Molecular Graphics and Modelling 15(4), 245–253 (1997)
10. Klebe, G., Hulemeirer, E., Weskamp, N., Khun, D.: Functional classification of protein kinase binding sites using cavbase. ChemMedChem. 2, 1432–1447 (2007)
11. Krishnamurthy, B., Wang, J.: On network-aware clustering of web clients. SIGCOMM Comput. Commun. Rev. 30(4), 97–110 (2000)
12. Newman, M.E.J., Girvan, M.: Finding and evaluating community structure in networks. Physical Review 69, 026113 (2004)
13. Nisius, B., Sha, F., Gohlke, H.: Structure-based computational analysis of protein binding sites for function and druggability prediction. Journal of Biotechnology 159(3), 123–134 (2012)
14. Raymond, J.W., Gardiner, E.J., Willett, P.: Heuristics for similarity searching of chemical graphs using a maximum common edge subgraph algorithm. Journal of Chemical Information and Computer Sciences 42(2), 305–316 (2002)
15. Raymond, J.W., Willett, P.: Maximum common subgraph isomorphism algorithms for the matching of chemical structures. Journal of Computer-Aided Molecular Design 16, 521–533 (2002)
16. Rives, A.W., Galitski, T.: Modular organization of cellular networks. Proc. Natl. Acad. 100, 1128–1133 (2003)
17. Schmitt, S., Kuhn, D., Klebe, G.: A new method to detect related function among proteins independent of sequence and fold homology. J. Mol. Biol. 323, 387–406 (2002)
18. Tsourakakis, C., Bonchi, F., Gionis, A., Gullo, F., Tsiarli, M.: Denser than the densest subgraph: Extracting optimal quasi-cliques with quality guarantees. In: Proceedings of the 19th ACM SIGKDD International Conference on Knowledge Discovery and Data Mining, KDD 2013, pp. 104–112. ACM, New York (2013)
19. Weskamp, N., Hullermeier, E., Kuhn, D., Klebe, G.: Multiple graph alignment for the structural analysis of protein active sites. IEEE/ACM Trans. Comput. Biol. Bioinformatics 4(2), 310–320 (2007)
20. Weskamp, N., Kuhn, D., Hullermeier, E., Klebe, G.: Efficient similarity search in protein structure databases by k-clique hashing. Bioinformatics 20(10), 1522–1526 (2004)

SVM-Based Detection of Tomato Leaves Diseases

Usama Mokhtar[1,5], Nashwa El-Bendary[2,5], Aboul Ella Hassenian[3,5],
E. Emary[3,5], Mahmoud A. Mahmoud[1,5], Hesham Hefny[1],
and Mohamed F. Tolba[4]

[1] Cairo University, Inst. of Stat. Studies and Res. (ISSR), Cairo, Egypt
[2] Arab Academy for Science,Technology, and Maritime Transport, Cairo, Egypt
[3] Faculty of Computers and Information, Cairo University, Egypt
[4] Faculty of Computers and Information, Ain Shams University, Egypt
[5] Scientific Research Group in Egypt (SRGE)
http://www.egyptscience.net

Abstract. This article introduces an efficient approach to detect and identify unhealthy tomato leaves using image processing technique. The proposed approach consists of three main phases; namely pre-processing, feature extraction, and classification phases. Since the texture characteristic is one of the most important features that describe tomato leaf, the proposed system system uses Gray-Level Co-occurrence Matrix (GLCM) for detecting and identifying tomato leaf state, is it healthy or infected. Support Vector Machine (SVM) algorithm with different kernel functions is used for classification phase. Datasets of total 800 healthy and infected tomato leaves images were used for both training and testing stages. N-fold cross-validation technique is used to evaluate the performance of the presented approach. Experimental results showed that the proposed classification approach has obtained classification accuracy of 99.83%, using linear kernel function.

Keywords: image processing, gray-Level co-occurrence matrix (GLCM), support vector machine (SVM).

1 Introduction

Agriculture is one of the most serious significant contributors for national income for most countries. Although farmers do great effort in selecting good seeds of plants and creating suitable environment for plants growing, there are a lot of diseases that affect plants causing different plant diseases. Plant pathogens such as (fungi, Bacteria, and Virus diseases) are the principal reasons for plant diseases. Also, there are some insects that feed on the parts of plant such as (sucking insect pests), and plant nutrition such as (lack of micro elements) also, have critical effect on plant growing [1]. One of the critical issues in the field of agriculture is that we need to discover the beginning of plant diseases batches in the early stage that makes us ready for appropriate timing control to reduce the damage, minimize production costs, and increase the income. One of the

© Springer International Publishing Switzerland 2015   641
D. Filev et al. (eds.), *Intelligent Systems'2014*,
Advances in Intelligent Systems and Computing 323, DOI: 10.1007/978-3-319-11310-4_55

most important approaches to detect and identify plant diseases is the naked eye observation of experts. But the problems of this approach is that it requires continuous monitoring of experts, which might be more expensive and time consuming specially in large farms and some remote places. Since the correct and timely identification of diseases is very important, we need to search for fast, automatic, less expensive and accurate method to detect disease. Image processing can fulfill these purposes. Study on computer image processing technology began in the 1960 of the 20th century, applied to the production and processing of agricultural products began in the 1970 of the 20th century [2]. The image processing can be used in agricultural applications for following purposes [3]: (1) to detect diseased leaf, stem, fruit, (2) to quantify affected area by disease, (3) to find shape of affected area, (4) to determine color of affected area, and (5) To determine size & shape of fruits.

Tomatoes are one of the most widely cultivated food crops throughout the world. It occupies the fourth level between world vegetables. Egypt is one of the famous countries interested in tomatoes cultivation. It ranked fifth among leader countries in the world. Tomato is a member of the Solanaceae family, which includes peppers, eggplant, Irish potatoes and tobacco. Leaf is the main source for most of tomatoes diseases. Leaves of healthy tomato plants are green and evenly-colored. During cultivation process, Tomato leaves exposed to many of the problems, table 1 lists some of major problems affecting tomato leaves and their reasons.

Table 1. Major problems affecting tomato leaves and their reasons

Problem	Reasons
Black, brown, dark, or water-soaked spots	Bacterial speck-Bacterial spot-Early blight-Gray leaf spot-Late blight-Septoria leaf spot-Spider mites-Tomato spotted wilt virus
Dark streaks	Tobacco mosaic virus
Holes in foliage	Tobacco mosaic virus
Holes in foliage	Aphids-Slugs-Tobacco hornworm-Tomato cutworm-Tomato hornworm
Irregular spots	Gray mold-Late blight
Leaf browning	Bacterial canker
Leaf mottling	Cucumber mosaic virus-Tobacco mosaic virus -Herbicide injury
Leaf roll	Aphids-Curly top virus-Herbicide injury-Physiological leaf roll Potato leaf roll
Purpling veins	Phosphorus deficiency
Spiral designs	Leaf miners-White flies
Sticky dew (honeydew)	Aphids-White flies
Stripped foliage, defoliation	Tobacco hornworm-Tomato cutworm-Tomato hornworm
White spots	Leaf mold-Magnesium deficiency-Powdery mildew-Spider mites
Yellowing and wilting	Bacterial canker-Bacterial pith necrosis-Bacterial wilt-Fusarium wilt-Iron deficiency-Pith necrosis-Salt damage-Tomato spotted wilt virus-Verticillium wilt

This paper proposes a detection approach based on Support Vector Machine (SVM) algorithm for identifying unhealthy tomato leaves using image processing technique. The proposed approach consists of three main phases; namely pre-processing, feature extraction, and classification phases. Datasets of total 800 healthy and infected tomato leaves images were used for both training and testing stages. N-fold cross-validation technique is used to evaluate the performance of the presented approach. The remaining of this article is organized as follows. Section 2 presents related research work for automatic detection of plant diseases. Section 3 introduces fundamentals of both Gray-Level Co-occurrence Matrix (GLCM) and Support Vector Machine (SVM) algorithms. The proposed approach is discussed in section 4 along with details of its phases. Section 5 discusses experimental results. Finally, section 6 highlights conclusions and discusses future work directions.

2 Related Work

Nowadays, automatic detection of plant diseases attracts a lot of researchers in different domains because of their great benefits in monitoring large fields of crops. Thus, automatic detection of the symptoms of diseases can be achieved as soon as they appear on plant leaves [5–7].

Authors in [8] introduced methods for the automatic classification of leaf diseases based on high resolution multi-spectral and stereo images. They used Leaves of sugar beet for evaluating their approach. In [9], authors used computer image processing technique to introduce fast and accurate new method for grading of plant diseases. At the beginning, leaf region was segmented by using Otsu method [10–12]. After that, to detect the disease spot edges the disease spot regions were segmented by using Sobel operator. Finally, plant diseases are graded by calculating the quotient of disease spot and leaf areas. Machine Learning (ML) methods can successfully be applied as an efficient approach for disease detection. Many of these methods have been applied in agricultural researches. For example: Artificial Neural Networks (ANNs), Decision Trees, K-means, k-nearest neighbors.

Support Vector Machines (SVMs) represents one of these approaches that have been used extensively in this field. For example, in [13] authors used SVMs to identify visual symptoms of cotton diseases. In [14]n image recognition method of wheat disease was proposed. After calculating features of diseased region of leaf image, samples are trained and recognized using multi-class the (Gaussian) radial basis function (RBF) SVM. In [15] the texture statistics are computed for the useful segments, then, the extracted features are passed through the SVM classifier. In [16] an automated system has been developed to classify the leaf brown spot and the leaf blast diseases of rice plant based on the morphological changes of the plants caused by the diseases. Radial distribution of the hue from the center to the boundary of the spot images has been used as features to classify the diseases by Bayes and SVM classifier. In [17] authors tried to solve the difficulty of parameter determination in the original SVM by using the genetic algorithm (GA) to select the parameters of the SVM automatically and the orthogonal method is utilized to determine the best GA parameters. In [18] automatic detection using vision system and pattern recognition are implemented to detect the symptoms of nutrient diseases and also to classify the disease group.

In this paper, Support Vector Machine (SVM) is utilized as a classifier with different kernel functions; namely Linear kernel, (Gaussian) radial basis function (RBF) kernel, Multilayer Perception (MLP) kernel and Polynomial kernel. This research aimed at developing a method to detect infected tomato leaves using image processing technique. The approach that is used in this research is consisted of two main phases that are feature extraction and feature classification. Grey-Level Co-occurrence matrix (GLCM) is used for feature extraction. Then, Support Vector Machine (SVM) is used as binary classifier to classify the extracted features into further two classes, *healthy leaves* and *infected leaves*. To evaluate these results N-fold cross-validation has been used.

3   Preliminaries

3.1   Gray-Level Co-occurrence Matrix (GLCM)

Gray-Level Co-occurrence Matrix (GLCM) is one of the well-known texture analysis methods to estimate the image properties related to second-order statistics [19]. (GLCM) is a matrix where the number of rows and columns is equal to the number of gray levels G, in the image. This matrix measures the spatial relationship between pixels. The idea beyond this method is that the information of texture is resulted from some relationships. In other words, a GLCM is a matrix that counts the number of times a pixel with gray-level i occurs at position a vector from a pixel with gray-level j.

Mathematically [20], given an $M \times N$ neighborhood of an input image containing G gray levels from 0 to $G1$, let $f(m, n)$ be the intensity at sample m, line n of the neighborhood. Then:

$$p(i, j|\Delta x, \Delta y) = WQ(i, j|\Delta x, \Delta y) \tag{1}$$

Where

$$W = \frac{1}{(M - \Delta x)(N - \Delta y)} \tag{2}$$

$$Q(i, j|\Delta x, \Delta y) = \sum_{(n=1)}^{(N-\Delta y)} \sum_{(m=1)}^{(M-\Delta x)} A \tag{3}$$

And

$$A = \begin{cases} 1, \text{ if } f(m,n)=i \text{ and } f(m+\Delta \text{ x, } n+\Delta \text{ y})=j \\ 0, \text{ elsewhere} \end{cases}$$

The elements of matrix can be expressed in another way as p(i,j —d,θ) that contains the second order statistical probability values for changes between gray levels i and j at a particular displacement distance d and at a particular angle (θ). There are some parameters that we must consider when GCLM matrix is computed; these parameters are: *Selection of angle θ, Choice of radius (B), and Choice of quantized gray levels (G).*

1. **Selection of angle** θ Since, there are eight neighbours for each pixel, then there are eight choices for θ, which are $0°$, $45°$, $90°$, $135°$, $180°$, $225°$, $270°$ or $315°$. However, from the definition of GLCM, the co-occurring pairs obtained by $\theta=0°$ would be similar to those obtained $\theta=180°$. Hence, We have only four choices to select the values of θ, which are $0°$, $45°$, $90°$, $135°$.
2. **Choice of radius** (B) From the literatures, well-known values of displacement are ranging from 1, 2 to 10. The larger displacement value we choose, the less detailed textural information we will be extracted.
3. **Choice of quantized gray levels** (G) This is a great trade-off between accuracy and computational complexity. The greater the number of gray levels, the more accurate extracted textural information. Hence, the number of gray levels is an important factor in GLCM computation. More levels would mean more accurate extracted textural information.

3.2   Support Vector Machines (SVMs)

The support vector machine (SVM) is a type of classifier that is originally a binary classification method developed by Vapnik and colleagues at Bell laboratories [21,22]. The main advantages of the SVM are that it can obtain current optimal solution under finite samples; it can obtain the global optimal solution without falling into local optimums that normal algorithms have; it transforms nonlinear problems into linear problems in a higher dimension space, and the algorithm complexity is irrelated with space dimension [14]. To explain idea of the SVM we will discuss the following two cases:

The Separable Case

- **Fully Linearly Separable.** For a binary classification problem with input space X and binary class Y, where $y \in \{1,-1\}$. There may exist many separating hyper-planes that correctly classify the data. The goal of SVM is selecting between them the one that maximizes the distance between the separating hyper-planes. To explain that, suppose we have labeled training data $\{x_i,y_i\}$, $i = 1, \cdots l$, $y_{i\in\{-1,1\}}$, $x_i \in R^d$ where l denotes the total number of training sample and d denotes the dimension of the feature vector [11,T2]. The goal of SVM is to search for the optimal hyperplane as shown in equation (4):

$$w.x + b = 0 \qquad (4)$$

Where w is normal to the hyperplane, $\frac{|b|}{\|w\|}$ is the perpendicular distance from the hyperplane to the origin, and $\|w\|$ is the Euclidean norm of w. Let $d+$ ($d-$) be the shortest distance from the separating hyperplane to the closest positive (negative) example. Define the margin of a separating hyperplane to be d_++d_-. Here SVM search for the separating hyperplane with largest margin. This can be formulated as shown in equation (5):

$$y_i(x_i.w + b) - 1 \geq 0 \forall i \qquad (5)$$

– **Not Fully Linearly Separable.** In order to extend the SVM methodology to handle data that is not fully linearly separable, we relax the constraint 6 slightly to allow for misclassified points as shown in equation (7):

$$y_i(x_i.w + b) - 1 + \epsilon_i \geq 0, \epsilon_i > 0 \forall i \tag{6}$$

The Non Separable Case. Unfortunately, separable data is not the formal form of the input data to the SVM classifier. It might be easier to separate the data using polynomial curves, or circles. But finding the optimal curve is a difficult process. Then, we need a way to pre-process the data in such a way that the problem space is transformed from non separable to linearly separable. To do this, we define a mapping $z = \phi(x)$ that transforms the d dimensional input vector x into a (usually higher) d^* dimensional vector z. We hope to choose a $\phi(x)$ so that the new training data $\{\phi(x_i), y_i\}$ is separable by a hyperplane. Figure 4 illustrates the processing of mapping data to the higher dimensional feature space.

4   Material and Methodology

In general, most computer vision algorithms share a common Framework. Figure 5 depicts the layout structure of a common image processing-based disease detection algorithms. the algorithm begin with acquiring and collecting digital images from suitable environment. To prepare the acquired images to next step, image-processing techniques are applied such that image transformation, image resizing, image filtering etc. the next step is to extract useful features that are necessary for further analysis using suitable feature extraction techniques. These features may be color, shape texture features. After that, several analytical discriminating techniques are used to classify the images according to the specific problem.

4.1   Image Acquisition Phase

The first phase of this approach is image acquisition. This phase plays an important role in any image classification system. We must select these images carefully to achieve the intended task in this approach. Science, the aim of this article is to distinguish between healthy and infected image of tomatoes leaves, different specimens For this work different specimens of tomato leaves some of these are healthy an the others are infected cover most types of tomato diseases.

4.2   Pre-processing Phase

After image acquisition, the image should be pre-processed. The following steps describes this phase.

1. **Extraction image of tomato leaves from the acquired images.** That's where most of acquired images have more than one leaf image and may be other thing, these image have been manually cropped to extract a single leaf for an image.

2. **Color space transformation.** After image acquisition, we find that most image have the formats JPEG, PNG and BMP. In this step, an RGB image is firstly converted into a gray scale image using the formula given in equation (8). Where R, G, B correspond to the color of the pixel, respectively.

$$Gray = 0.2989 * R + 0.5870 * G + 0.1140 * B \qquad (7)$$

3. **Image Resizing.** In this work, all images must be with the same size and equal dimension. So, the gray image should be resized to equal dimensions.

4. **Background removal.** In this step, background of each image has been removed using background subtraction technique.

5. **Image enhancement.** In this step, some enhancement techniques have been applied on images. Firstly, image filling approach has been used to fill the holes that may appear on image. Secondly, image erosion and dilation are the basic transforms of mathematical morphology; they derive from the Minkowski subtraction and addition used in integral geometry [23]. Basically, erosion (dilation) of an image I is the operation of assigning to each pixel (x, y) of the transformed image the minimum (maximum) value found over a possibly modified neighborhood of the corresponding pixel in the input image [24]. In this work, Image eroding technique has been used to remove noise resulted after manually cropping step.

6. **Cropping surrounding black region.** Finally, for the pre-processing step, black space around gray image and binary mask had been cropped. The resulted of this step used as in to the follow step.

4.3   Feature Extraction Phase

The purpose of feature extraction is to reduce the original dataset by measuring certain features or properties of each image such as texture, color and shape. In order to recognize and identify healthy and infected leaf, we measure several numbers of features in acquired image, to be later use for classification. This work has based their feature extraction technique on GLCM. This phase divided into two steps:

1. **GLCM generation.** Before applying GLCM method to input images, we must be sure that we can get texture feature for tomato leaf part only. So we convert all pixels outside the tomato leaf using mask to (NaN) "Not a Number", to be ignored during GLCM calculation. After that, GLCM has been calculated using the following angles (0° , 45° , 90°, 135°). So that, we have got 4 GLCM.

2. **Texture feature calculation.** The GCLM that generated in the last step were then used to calculate the texture features. A number of texture features

may be extracted from the GLCM [25]. In this work 9 texture features, as shown in equation (8) to equation (16), have been extracted as follow: Calculate GLCM using the following angles (0° , 45° , 90°, 135°), so we got 4 GLCM.

– **Energy:**

$$ASM = \sum_{i=0}^{G-1} \sum_{j=0}^{G-1} \{P(i,j)\}^2 \tag{8}$$

– **Contrast:**

$$CONTRAST = \sum_{n=0}^{G-1} n^2 \times \{\sum_{i=1}^{G} \sum_{j=1}^{G} P(i,j)\}, |i-j| = n \tag{9}$$

– **Sum Of Squares:**

$$VARIANCE = \sum_{i=0}^{G-1} \times \sum_{j=0}^{G-1} (1-\mu)^2 P(i,j) \tag{10}$$

– **Correlation (*corr*):**

$$Corr = \sum_{i=0}^{G-1} \sum_{j=0}^{G-1} (\{i \times j\} \times P(i,j) - \mu_x \times _y)(\sigma_x \times \sigma_y) \tag{11}$$

– **Entropy:**

$$ENTROPY = -\sum_{i=0}^{G-1} \times \sum_{j=0}^{G-1} P(i,j) \times log(P(i,j)) \tag{12}$$

– **Sum Entropy:**

$$SENT = \sum_{i=0}^{2G-2} P_{(x+y)}(i) log(P_{(x+y)}(i)) \tag{13}$$

– **Cluster Shade:**

$$SHADE = \sum_{i=0}^{G-1} \sum_{j=0}^{G-1} \{i + j - \mu_x - \mu_y\}^3 \times P(i,j) \tag{14}$$

– **Cluster Prominence:**

$$PROM = \sum_{i=0}^{G-1} \sum_{j=0}^{G-1} \{i + j - \mu_x - \mu_y\}^4 \times P(i,j) \tag{15}$$

– **Homogeneity:**

$$IDM = \sum_{i=0}^{G-1} \sum_{j=0}^{G-1} \frac{1}{(1 + (i-j))^2} \times P(i,j) \tag{16}$$

Since, we have nine features and 4 GLCM. So we have 36 features per single image.

4.4   Classification Phase

The final step of this work is the classification phase. In this approach, SVM technique has been applied for classification of tomato leaf images to any of the following states, *healthy* or *infected*. The inputs of this stage are training dataset feature vectors and their corresponding classes, whereas the outputs are the decision that determine type of input image (healthy of infected). To achieve good results, SVM was trained and tested using different kernel functions that are: Linear kernel, radial basis function (RBF) kernel, Multi-Layer Perceptron (MLP) kernel and Polynomial kernel [26, 27]. For the process of evaluating the obtained results, we used N-fold cross-validation technique with $N = 10$. Firstly, the dataset is divided into equally (or nearly equally) N-subsets. Then the cross-validation process is performed N times with each sub-set being once the test dataset and all the others being the training dataset. This process is repeated N times. Hence we take the average of performance of N runs. The algorithm performance measure can be calculated as the average of the performances of 10 runs.

5   Experimental Results

As we previously mentioned, the aim of this work is to detect and identify if the tomato leave input image is healthy or infected. In this article, firstly, we used 400 of tomato images leaf (200 healthy and 200 are infected). Then, the experiment repeated used 800 of tomato images leaf (400 healthy and 400 are infected). After pre-processing phase, we calculated GLCM matrix for each of training and testing image. The GLCM are represented by the function $P(i, j, d, \theta)$, where i represents the gray level of the location (x, y), and j represents the gray level of the pixel at a distance d from location (x, y) at an orientation angle of θ. Here, we take d=1 and $\in 0°$, $45°$, $90°$, $135°$. So, we have got 4 GLCM matrixes for each image. Then we used these values to calculate 9 features. So, at the end of this phase we have got 36 features per single image. Hence, we used these feature vectors as input to the SVM classifier. SVM was trained and tested using different kernel functions that are: (Linear kernel, (RBF) kernel, (MLP) kernel and Polynomial kernel).

Figure 1 (a-d) shows the original image and its final results. After cropping, we convert the image from RGB to gray level color space, then resize the image to (400) pixels then removing the background. Its followed by do more enhancement on the image like fill the holes that may exist in the image and do some image erosion. Then, black space around gray image and binary mask had been cropped. Finally, final results. Figure (2) visualized Results for different SVM kernel functions. From the cross validation accuracy it is noticed that there is significant improvement in the accuracy if the number of training samples increases.

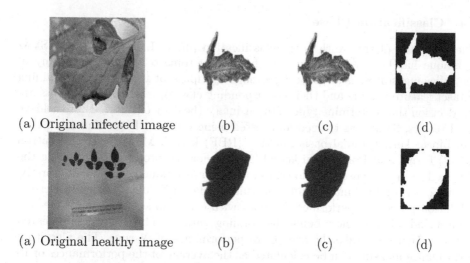

(a) Original infected image   (b)   (c)   (d)

(a) Original healthy image   (b)   (c)   (d)

Fig. 1. Pre-processed results (a) original image, (b) Cropping, (c) resize and remove the background and (d) final results

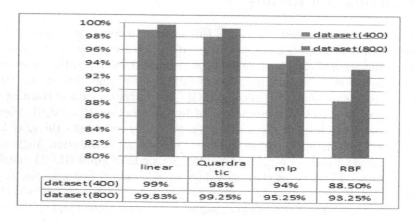

	linear	Quardra tic	m lp	RBF
dataset(400)	99%	98%	94%	88.50%
dataset(800)	99.83%	99.25%	95.25%	93.25%

Fig. 2. Results for different SVM kernel functions

6   Conclusions

In this article, a system for detecting and identifying the state of tomato leaves, is it healthy or infected was introduced. The proposed system consisted of three main phases; pre-processing, feature extraction, and classification phases. This approach has began with image acquisition, background removal, texture feature extracting. Finally, SVM model is developed for classification stage using the extracted features and has been evaluated using N-fold cross-validation. From the experimental results we found that, the highest classification accuracy of 99.83% has been achieved using linear kernel function.

References

1. Agrios, G.N.: Plant Pathology, 4th edn. Academic Press (1997)
2. Ying, Z., An, M., Zhang, X.: A foreign facility status and trends of development to fagriculture. J. Agriculture and Technology (2008)
3. Marathe, H.D., Kothe, P.N.: Leaf Disease Detection Using Image Processing Techniques. International Journal of Engineering Research & Technology (IJERT) 2(3) (March 2013)
4. Fathy, M.E., Hussein, A.S., Tolba, M.F.: Fundamental matrix estimation: a study of error criteria. Pattern Recognition Letters 32(2), 383–391 (2011)
5. Al-Bashish, D., Braik, M., Bani-Ahmad, S.: Detection and classification of leaf diseases using Kmeans-based segmentation and neural-networks-based classification. Inform. Technol. J. 10, 267–275 (2011)
6. Rumpf, T., Mahlein, A.K., Steiner, U., Oerke, E.C., Dehne, H.W., Plumer, L.: Early detection and classification of plant diseases with Support Vector Machines based on hyperspectral reflectance. Computers and Electronics in Agriculture 74(1), 91–99 (2010)
7. Hillnhuetter, C., Mahlein, A.K.: Early detection and localisation of sugar beet diseases: new approaches. Gesunde Pfianzen 60(4), 143–149 (2008)
8. Bauer, S.D., Korc, F., Frstner, W.: Investigation into the classification of diseases of sugar beet leaves using multispectral images. In: Henten, E.J.V., Goense, D., Lokhorst, C. (eds.) Precision Agriculture, pp. 229–238. Academic Publishers, Wageningen (2009)
9. Weizheng, S., Yachun, W., Zhanliang, C., Hongda, W.: Grading Method of Leaf Spot Disease Based on Image Processing. In: Proceedings of the 2008 International Conference on Computer Science and Software Engineering, CSSE, December 12-14, vol. 06, pp. 491–494. IEEE Computer Society, Washington, DC (2008)
10. Sezgin, M., Sankur, B.: Survey over image thresholding techniques and quantitative performance evaluation. Journal of Electronic Imaging 13(1), 146–165 (2003)
11. Kumari, V.A., Chitra, R.: Classification Of Diabetes Disease Using Support Vector Machine. International Journal of Engineering Research and Applications (IJERA) 3(2), 1797–1801 (2013) ISSN: 2248-9622
12. Otsu, N.: A Threshold Selection Method from Gray-Level Histograms. IEEE Transactions on Systems, Man, and Cybernetics 9(1), 62–66 (1979)
13. Camargo, A., Smith, J.S.: An image processing based algorithm to automatically identify plant disease visual symptoms. Biosystems Engineering 102(1), 9–21 (2009) ISSN 1537-5110
14. Liu, L., Zhang, W., Shu, S., Jin, X.: Image Recognition of Wheat Disease Based on RBF Support Vector Machine, In: Proceedings of International Conference on Advanced Computer Science and Electronics Information (ICACSEI 2013), Supported by the Key Technology Projects of Anhui Province, China (NO:1201a0301008) (2013)
15. Arivazhagan, S., Newlin Shebiah, R., Ananthi, S., Vishnu Varthini, S.: Detection of unhealthy region of plant leaves and classification of plant leaf diseases using texture features. Agric. Eng. Int.: CIGR Journal 15(1) (March 2013)
16. Phadikar, S., Sil, J., Das, A.K.: Classification of Rice Leaf Diseases Based on Morphological Changes. International Journal of Information and Electronics Engineering 2(3) (May 2012)
17. Tian, J., Hu, Q., Ma, X., Han, M.: An Improved KPCA/GA-SVM Classification Model for Plant Leaf Disease Recognition. Journal of Computational Information Systems, 7737–7745 (2012)

18. Asraf, H.M., Nooritawati, M.T., Shah Rizam, M.S.B.: A Comparative Study in Kernel-Based Support Vector Machine of Oil Palm Leaves Nutrient Disease. In: Proceedings of the International Symposium on Robotics and Intelligent Sensors 2012, International Symposium on Robotics and Intelligent Sensors, Procedia Engineering, vol. 41, pp. 1353–1359. Elsevier (2012)
19. Lu, H., Jiang, W., Ghiassi, M., Lee, S., Nitin, M.: Classification of Camellia (Theaceae) species using leaf architecture variations and pattern recognition techniques. PloS 7, e29704 (2012)
20. Albregtsen, F.: Statistical Texture Measures Computed from Gray Level Coocurrence Matrices (November 5, 2008)
21. V.N.: VAPNIK, The Nature of Statistical Learning Theory, 2nd edn. Springer, New York (1999)
22. Burges, C.J.C.: A tutorial on support vector machine for pattern recognition. Data Min. Knowl. Disc. 2(121) (1998)
23. Matheron, G.: Random Sets and Integral Geometry. Wiley, New York (1975)
24. Donohue, K.D., Huang, L., Burks, T.F., Forsberg, F., Piccoli, C.W.: Tissue classification with generalized spectrum parameters. Ultrasound Med. Biol. 27(11), 1505–1514 (2001)
25. Vanschoenwinkel, B., Manderick, B.: Appropriate kernel functions for support vector machine learning with sequences of symbolic data. In: Winkler, J.R., Niranjan, M., Lawrence, N.D. (eds.) Machine Learning Workshop. LNCS (LNAI), vol. 3635, pp. 256–280. Springer, Heidelberg (2005)
26. Boolchandani, D., Sahula, V.: Exploring Efficient Kernel Functions for Support Vector Machine Based Feasibility Models for Analog Circuits. Int. Journal of Design, Analysis, and Tools for Circuits and Systems 1(1), 1–8 (2011)
27. Prekopcsk, Z., Henk, T., Gspr-Papanek, C.: Cross-validation: the illusion of reliable performance estimation. In: Proceedings of RCOMM 2010: RapidMiner Community Meeting and Conference, Dortmund, Nmetorszg, pp. 1–5 (2010)

Co-registration of Satellite Images Based on Invariant Local Features

Mohamed Tahoun[1], Abd El Rahman Shabayek[1], Ralf Reulke[2],
and Aboul Ella Hassanien[3],*

[1] Department of Computer Science, FCI, Suez Canal University, Ismailia, Egypt
{tahoun,a.shabayek}@ci.suez.edu.eg
[2] Department of Computer Science, Humboldt Universitï¿œt zu Berlin, Germany
reulke@informatik.hu-berlin.de
[3] Department of Information Technology, FCI, Cairo university, Egypt
aboitcairo@cu.edu.eg
http://egyptscience.net/

Abstract. Detection and matching of features from satellite images taken from different sensors, viewpoints, or at different times are important tasks when manipulating and processing remote sensing data for many applications. This paper presents a scheme for satellite image co-registration using invariant local features. Different corner and scale based feature detectors have been tested during the keypoint extraction, descriptor construction and matching processes. The framework suggests a sub-sampling process which controls the number of extracted key points for a real time processing and for minimizing the hardware requirements. After getting the pairwise matches between the input images, a full registration process is followed by applying bundle adjustment and image warping then compositing the registered version. Harris and GFTT have recorded good results with ASTER images while both with SURF give the most stable performance on optical images in terms of better inliers ratios and running time compared to the other detectors. SIFT detector has recorded the best inliers ratios on TerraSAR-X data while it still has a weak performance with other optical images like Rapid-Eye and ASTER.

Keywords: SURF, SIFT, GFTT, feature extraction and matching, satellite image co-registration.

1 Introduction

Matching and co-registration of satellite images are basic tasks when processing remote sensing data for many applications [7]. Some achievements about the two processes have been remarked but there is still a need for an accurate matching or better registration scheme of satellite images with different modalities [6,8]. Huge number of techniques have been proposed for this purpose with the aim to correctly detect and extract the important features and objects from images. The features extracted from images could be local or global where a local feature is an image pattern which differs from its direct neighborhoods. are usually represented by points, edges, corners and contours or by other features [3]. Many feature detectors are also proposed based on

---

* SRGE chair.

© Springer International Publishing Switzerland 2015
D. Filev et al. (eds.), *Intelligent Systems'2014*,
Advances in Intelligent Systems and Computing 323, DOI: 10.1007/978-3-319-11310-4_56

such representations. For example, Harris and FAST work based on corner detection while SIFT and SURF are based on points or blobs. The last two detectors have been recently used in many applications and recorded a good performance against rotation, scaling, blurring and noise [7]. Corners usually represent a point in which the directions of two edges have a clear change while blobs are known as region of interest. Once the features are extracted from images, the matching process starts by comparing the feature descriptors of the extracted keypoints. The general procedure for the extraction and matching processes includes: Finding distinctive keypoints, taking a region around each keypoint in an invariant manner (e.g scale or affine invariant), extracting and normalize the region content, computing a descriptor for the normalized region and finally, matching the obtained local descriptors. The rest of this section focuses on the tested detectors by highlighting some of their important features.

FAST (Features from Accelerated Segment Test) is a corner detection method [12]. Its importance lies in its computational efficiency as it is faster than many famous feature extraction methods (e.g Difference of Gaussian (DoG), SIFT, Harris). It uses a Bresenham circle of radius 3 to find out whether a selected point is a corner. Each pixel in the circle is given a number from 1 to 16 clockwise. If a set of contiguous pixels inside the circle is brighter or darker than the candidate pixel then it is classified as a corner. GFTT (Good Features to Track) extracts the most prominent corners in the image as described in [14] where the corner quality measure at each pixel is calculated. Then a non-maximum suppression is applied. The corners with quality less than a certain threshold are rejected and the remaining corners are sorted by the quality measure in the descending order. Finally, each corner for which there is a stronger corner at a distance less than a threshold is thrown away.

Harris is a combined corner and edge detector based on the local auto-correlation function [5]. It does not depend on rotation or shift or affine change of intensity. It extends the principle of Moravec's corner detector [11] by considering the local auto-correlation energy. Corners are usually good features to match especially with viewpoint changes. ORB (Oriented BRIEF-Binary Robust Independent Elementary Features) is a local feature detector based on binary strings [4]. It depends on a relatively small number of intensity difference tests to represent a patch of the image as a binary string.The construction and matching of this local feature is fast and performs well as long as invariant to large in-place rotations is not required. ORB is basically a fusion of FAST keypoint detector and BRIEF descriptor with many modifications to enhance the performance. First it uses FAST to find keypoints, then apply Harris corner measure to find top N points among them. For descriptor matching, multi-probe LSH which improves on the traditional LSH, is used [4].

SIFT (Scale Invariant Feature Transform) has been presented by Lowe in the year 2004 [9]. It has four major steps including: scale-space extrema detection, keypoint localization, orientation assignment and finally building the keypoint descriptor. In the first step, points of interest are identified by scanning both the location and the scale of the image. The difference of Gaussian (DoG) is used to perform this step and then the candidates of the points are localized to sub-pixel accuracy. Then the orientation is assigned to each keypoint in local image gradient directions to obtain invariance to rotation. In the last step, a 128- keypoint descriptor or feature vector is built and ready for the matching process. SIFT gives good performance but still have some limitations against strong illumination changes and big rotation angles. Star keypoint detector is a part of OpenCV computer vision library which is derived from CenSurE (Center Surrounded Extrema) detector [1,13]. While CenSurE uses polygons such as Square, Hexagon and Octagons as a more computable alternative to circle, Star mimics the circle with 2 overlapping squares: one upright and one 45-degree rotated. CenSurE determines large-scale features at all scales, and select the extrema across scale and location. It uses simplified bi-level kernels as center-surround filters. It focuses on finding kernels that are rotationally invariant. SURF (Speeded-Up Robust Features) is a local invariant Interest point or blob detector [2]. It is partly inspired by the SIFT descriptor and is used too in static scene matching and retrieval. It is invariant to most of the image transformations like scale and illumination changes in addition to small changes in viewpoint. It uses Integral Images or an intermediate representation for the image and contains the sum of gray scale pixel values of image. Then a Hessian-based interest point localization is obtained using Laplacian of Gaussian of the image.

2   The Proposed Framework

The layout of the experiments is illustrated in figure 1. Firstly, the keypoints are detected from the input images then depending on the number of detected keypoints, a sub-sampling process may start if the number of the detected keypoints exceeds a user predefined number of keypoints. The aim of this step is to overcome the problem of huge keypoints from high resolution images which requires high configuration hardware and take much processing time. In the sub-sampling process, the keypoints are sorted according to their response. Keypoints with the best response are chosen within a predefined number of keypoints. Based on the new keypoints list, the descriptors are built and ready for the matching step. Five types of descriptors are tested in the experiments including: SIFT, SURF, ORB, BRIEF and BRISK. The descriptor vectors are constructed from the sub-sampled extracted keypoints of the two input images then they are matched using similarity measurements. Different similarity measurements have been also tested including Euclidean and FLANN ((Fast Library for Approximate Nearest Neighbors).

The framework enables the user to choose both the descriptor and the matcher types. To remove outliers, RANSAC has been used then we get the final number of matches including the number of inliers and outliers. For each keypoint different parameters like 2-D location, scale and rotation are specified. An evaluation process starts where repeatability, correspondence and precision and recalls values are computed with each detector. Different levels of Gaussian noise are added by changing the mean and/or standard deviation then run the experiments with the noisy versions of the input images. The general approach would be robustness to noise. Some of the selected detectors use binary visual descriptors like ORB while others use vector-based feature descriptors like SIFT. Each detector has been run with different parameters and variables. Different performance evaluation measurements have been used to test the robustness to noise and the invariance of the tested feature detectors. Good features should be invariant to all possible changes that can exist between images.

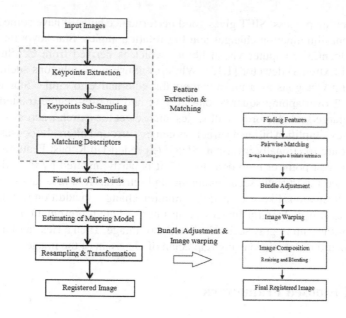

Fig. 1. The general framework of the experiments including feature extraction and matching in addition to a full registration scheme

3   Experiments and Results

The general steps for matching two input images in our framework are: (1) Extract the keypoints from the input images and compute their descriptors (KP1 and KP2 in case of two input images). If the number of the detected keypoints exceeds a pre-defined value, then the detected keypoints are sub-sampled by sorting them according to their response. A keypoint response strength is measured according to its corner-ness. (2) Once the keypoint descriptors are built, they are ready for the matching process. In this step, the nearest neighbor is considered as the keypoint with minimum Euclidean distance for the invariant descriptor. Different image matchers or similarity measurements have been tested in the experiments. The Minkowski form distance is defined based on the Lp norm as:

$$D_p(S,R) = \left(\sum_{i=0}^{N-1} (S_i - R_i)^p \right)^{1/p} \tag{1}$$

Where $D_p(S,R)$ is the distance between the two feature vectors $S = S_1, S_2, \ldots S_{N-1}$ and $R = R_1, R_2, \ldots R_{N-1}$ representing the descriptors of the extracted keypoints from the input images. Euclidean distance ($p = 2$) recorded the most stable and acceptable results compared to Manhattan distance ($p = 1$) distance and FLANN matchers. For filtering the matches, we use RANSAC to exclude the inconsistent matches and help getting the list of tie points which are the actual matches (inliers) between the two input images. In order to evaluate the previous matching process, we applied the following steps:

1. Compute the homography between the filtered keypoints (H12 from first group of keypoints to the second group).
2. Compute the number of overlaps between KP1 and the transformed keypoints from the second image (using inverse of H12) KP2'. This number of overlaps is called Corresponding Count $C(I_1, I_2)$ [10].
3. Divide $C(I_1, I_2)$ by the mean of the number of detected keypoints (d_1 and d_2). This value is called Repeatability (Re)[7]:

$$Re_{1,2} = \frac{C(I_1, I_2)}{mean\,(d_1, d_2)} \tag{2}$$

A Synthesize Test. It has been done for testing the detectors against some affine transformations. An input image (S) is transformed to a new image (N) by applying a perspective transformation as follows :

$$N(x,y) = S(\frac{M_{11}x + M_{12}y + M_{13}}{M_{31}x + M_{32}y + M_{33}}, \frac{M_{21}x + M_{22}y + M_{23}}{M_{31}x + M_{32} + M_{33}}) \tag{3}$$

where M is the transformation matrix (3x3). The homography matrix values are randomly generated within a uniform distribution. The same procedure for the extraction and matching processes is applied on both the input and new image. The same steps could be repeated between the input image and any transformed version from it.

Precision and Recall Graphs. Precision is considered as the ratio between the number of relevant keypoints and the total number of the matches while recall is the the ratio between the number of relevant keypoints divided by the total number of the matches in the data. It displays the relation between the average precision and recall at any selected point of all feature detectors. For example, if we consider r as the number of the correct matches found by the matcher, and M as the number of keypoints in the first image that are also visible on the second image, and finally $M1$ as number of keypoints in the first image that have been matched then as in equation 4

$$Precision = r/M1, \ Recall = r/M \tag{4}$$

In our experiments, we have calculated 20-point average interpolated precision at each recall level then a composite precision-recall curve showing 20 points can then be graphed.

Linear Blending. We have used the linear blending scheme to combine bands from the same satellite as a pre-processing for the registration process. Dyadic (two-input) operator is the linear blend operator as in 5:

$$g(x) = (1 - \alpha)f_0(x) + \alpha f_1(x) \tag{5}$$

where $f_0(x)$ and $f_1(x)$ are the two source images of the same type and size. By varying α(weight of the first image) from 0 to 1 this operator can be used to perform a temporal cross-disolve between the two images. The $g(x)$ will generate an image, we consider $\beta = (1 - \alpha)$ as the weight of the second image. Then we calculate the weighted some of the two arrays (with 6 parameters, $f_0(x), f_1(x), \alpha, \beta, \gamma, dst$) where

$$dst = \alpha f_0(x) + \beta f_1(x) + \gamma \tag{6}$$

In figure 2, two examples of possible blending of TET-1 and Rapid-Eye images. This procedure has been applied to bands from optical and radar images which have the same dimensions and type. The results of the blending have been also compared to the results obtained from the full registration framework using local feature detectors like SURF and ORB.

The experiments have been run on different satellite images including: ASTER (Suez Canal area), TET-1 (Australia (an area near Canberra city), and Rapid-Eye and Pleiades optical images and TerraSAR-X radar images (Berlin Brandenburg airport area). They have different ground resolutions (for example: a range from 0.5 to 5.0 meter ground resolution with dimensions 10000x10000 and 5000x5000 pixels). The hardware configuration includes: Intel-core ™2 quad CPU 2.66GHz and 8GB RAM, Windows 7 (64bit) and Visual Studio 10 and OpenCV 2.46.

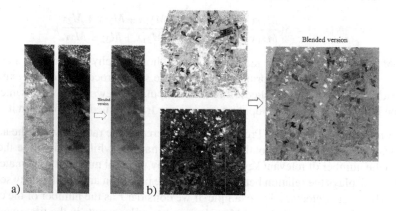

Fig. 2. Image blending examples: a) Two TET-1 bands (VN, VG) -left- and their blended version ($\alpha = 50$) -right- and b) two Rapid-Eye bands -left- and their blended version ($\alpha = 65$) -right-.

The results showed that SURF, FAST, Harris and GFTT detectors give the best number of detected keypoints and the most stable performance (Also in some cases, SIFT scored a good performance compared to ORB) 3. Corner-based detectors like Harris and Fast detect more keypoints compared to other scale-based detectors like SIFT. The used matchers or the similarity measurements: Euclidean distance, Manhattan and FLANN affect some how on the similarity check between descriptors. Euclidean matcher recorded the most stable and accurate results with different descriptors. The results also showed that SIFT descriptor gives usually the most stable performance with higher numbers of inliers compared to the other descriptors. SIFT and BRISK take longer time to be built while SURF and ORB take less time. SIFT detector usually requires more memory with high resolution images while the sub-sampling process works good to solve the huge number of detected points with other detectors. SURF, Harris, GFTT and SIFT give good performance when applied on optical images compared to other detectors like ORB and star. Different levels of Gaussian noise have been used to test the robustness to noise of the tested descriptors. SURF, FAST and Harris give the most robust results against noise while other detectors have less robustness against different levels of noise.

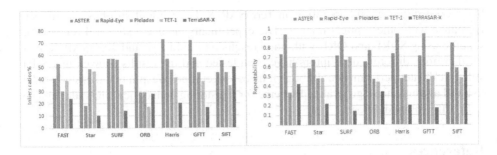

Fig. 3. Inliers ratios (%) -left- and repeatability -right- of the tested detectors on different optical and radar images. SURF, GFTT and Harris recorded the best performance on optical images while SIFT scored good results with TerraSAR-X radar images.

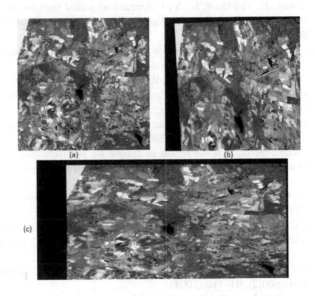

Fig. 4. A full registration (c) of two Rapid-Eye images (a) original and (b) its synthesized version using SURF detector. The registration is done using bundle adjustment cost fun. (re-projection error), plane warping surface and blending strength (45) in a total time: 3.745 seconds.

4   Conclusions

In this paper, a framework for matching and registering optical and radar images using invariant local features has been introduced. Once the keypoints are detected, a keypoint sub-sampling process starts (in case of huge detected keypoints) in order to reduce the running time during the extraction and the matching stages. Harris and GFTT have recorded good results with ASTER images while both with SURF give the most stable performance on the tested optical images in terms of higher inliers ratios, repeatability response and robustness to noise compared to the other detectors. SIFT detector has recorded the best inliers ratios on TerraSAR-X data while it still has a weak performance with other optical images. The experiments include also a full registration scheme using SURF and ORB with good results on Rapid-Eye and TerraSAR-X data. Furthermore, different descriptors have been tested and the results showed that SIFT still gives better performance although it takes longer time. We aim that this study helps to build and enhance a generalized scheme for registering both optical and radar images with different modalities.

References

1. Agrawal, M., Konolige, K., Blas, M.R.: Censure: Center surround extremas for realtime feature detection and matching. In: Forsyth, D., Torr, P., Zisserman, A. (eds.) ECCV 2008, Part IV. LNCS, vol. 5305, pp. 102–115. Springer, Heidelberg (2008)
2. Bay, H., Tuytelaars, T., Van Gool, L.: Surf: Speeded up robust features. In: Leonardis, A., Bischof, H., Pinz, A. (eds.) ECCV 2006, Part I. LNCS, vol. 3951, pp. 404–417. Springer, Heidelberg (2006)
3. Bouchiha, R., Besbes, K.: Automatic remote-sensing image registration using surf. International Journal of Computer Theory and Engineering 5(1), 88–92 (2013)
4. Calonder, M., Lepetit, V., Strecha, C., Fua, P.: Brief: Binary robust independent elementary features. In: Daniilidis, K., Maragos, P., Paragios, N. (eds.) ECCV 2010, Part IV. LNCS, vol. 6314, pp. 778–792. Springer, Heidelberg (2010)
5. Harris, C., Stephens, M.: A combined corner and edge detector. In: Proceedings of the 4th Alvey Vision Conference, pp. 147–151 (1988)
6. Hong, T.D., Schowengerdt, R.A.: A robust technique for precise registration of radar and optical satellite images. Photogrammetric Engineering and Remote Sensing 71(5), 585–594 (2005)
7. Juan, L., Gwon, O.: A comparison of sift, pca-sift and surf. International Journal of Image Processing (IJIP) 3(4), 143–152 (2009)
8. Khan, N.Y., McCane, B., Wyvill, G.: SIFT and SURF performance evaluation against various image deformations on benchmark dataset. In: Bradley, A.P., Jackway, P.T. (eds.) DICTA, pp. 501–506. IEEE (2011)
9. Lowe, D.G.: Distinctive image features from scale-invariant keypoints. International Journal of Computer Vision 60(2), 91–110 (2004)
10. Mikolajczyk, K., Tuytelaars, T., Schmid, C., Zisserman, A., Matas, J., Schaffalitzky, F., Kadir, T., Gool, L.: A comparison of affine region detectors. International Journal of Computer Vision 65(1-2), 43–72 (2005)
11. Moravec, H.: Obstacle avoidance and navigation in the real world by a seeing robot rover. Tech Report CMU-RI-TR-3 Carnegie-Mellon University, Robotics Institute (1980)
12. Rosten, E., Drummond, T.W.: Machine learning for high speed corner detection. In: Leonardis, A., Bischof, H., Pinz, A. (eds.) ECCV 2006, Part I. LNCS, vol. 3951, pp. 430–443. Springer, Heidelberg (2006)
13. Schmidt, A., Kraft, M., Kasiński, A.: An evaluation of image feature detectors and descriptors for robot navigation. In: Bolc, L., Tadeusiewicz, R., Chmielewski, L.J., Wojciechowski, K. (eds.) ICCVG 2010, Part II. LNCS, vol. 6375, pp. 251–259. Springer, Heidelberg (2010)
14. Shi, J., Tomasi, C.: Good features to track. In: Proceedings of the IEEE Conference on Computer Vision and Pattern Recognition, pp. 593–600 (June 1994)

The Cramér-Rao Lower Bound for the Estimated Parameters in a Spatial Disaggregation Model for Areal Data

Joanna Horabik and Zbigniew Nahorski

Systems Research Institute of Polish Academy of Sciences,
Newelska 6, 01-447 Warsaw, Poland
Joanna.Horabik@ibspan.waw.pl

Abstract. Consider the problem of allocation of spatially correlated gridded data to finer spatial scale, conditionally on covariate information observable in a fine grid. Spatial dependence is captured with the conditional autoregressive structure, suitable for gridded (areal) data. In this study, we give suitable formulae for the (expected and observed) Fisher information matrix, which is useful for obtaining the Cramér-Rao lower bound of the estimated model parameters. All required derivatives are evaluated analytically, and no numerical differentiation is involved.

Keywords: Fisher information matrix, Cramér-Rao lower bound, spatial disaggregation.

1 Introduction

Consider the problem of allocation of spatially correlated gridded data to finer spatial scale, conditionally on covariate information observable in a fine grid. This type of issues arises, for instance, in a development of high-resolution emission inventories of greenhouse gases (see [2], [3]) or ammonia [6].

Although typically, straightforward regression models are applied for spatial allocation of emission data [6], [17], we argue that whenever the modelled value of interest reveals spatial correlation, this fact can be efficiently exploited to improve the disaggregation process. A relevant model was proposed in [11], where spatial dependence is modelled with the structure suitable for areal (gridded) data, i.e. the conditional autoregressive (CAR) model. It was introduced into a linear regression as a random effect. The maximum likelihood approach to inference was employed, and the optimal predictors were developed to assess missing values in a fine grid. The procedure can be regarded as a CAR analogy to the block kriging method, which is rooted in the geostatistical approach.

The approach has already been applied for several disaggregation case studies in the area of atmospheric pollution: (i) the NO_x and PM_{10} concentrations obtained from the dispersion model CALPUFF, run for Warsaw agglomeration [10]; (ii) an inventory of ammonia emissions from fertilization, reported in the northern region of Poland (Pomorskie voivodeship) [11]; (iii) and a livestock

© Springer International Publishing Switzerland 2015
D. Filev et al. (eds.), *Intelligent Systems'2014*,
Advances in Intelligent Systems and Computing 323, DOI: 10.1007/978-3-319-11310-4_57

data set from the agricultural census, required for the spatial GHG inventory in Poland [9]. In the applications listed, both the regular grids (fourfold and ninefold disaggregation) as well as irregular ones (disaggregation from districts to municipalities) were considered.

The method provided far better results than the widely used naive approach (where equal values are assumed for each fine grid cell within a respective coarse grid area) or linear models with no account of spatial correlation. In certain situations, a predictive performance of the proposed procedure outperformed the geostatistical approach. Particularly, for high range of NO_x and PM_{10} concentrations, the proposed model, based on the CAR scheme, provided more accurate predictions, while the geostatistical one revealed a tendency to underestimate these values. In the case of high range NO_x and PM_{10} concentrations, correct predictions are especially important, since the threshold of these pollutants ($40 \ \mu g/m^3$) is exceeded in some parts of Warsaw agglomeration [10].

The disaggregation model itself, along with its maximum likelihood estimation, has already been developed and described in the previous studies [9–11]. However, for a good appraisal of an estimate, an assessment of the estimator variance is also required. For this purpose, the Cramér-Rao bound plays an important role, as it provides asymptotically a lower bound for the variance of estimators. Its calculation is a usual procedure for models estimated with the maximum likelihood method [4, 13, 14]. The present contribution provides the details for calculation of the Fisher information matrix in the considered spatial disaggregation model; its inverse yields the Cramér-Rao lower bound of the estimated parameters.

2   The Disaggregation Model and Its ML Estimation

Fine grid We begin with the model specification in a fine grid. Let Y_i denote a random variable associated with a missing value (for instance a missing value of pollutant), y_i defined at each cell i, $i = 1, ..., n$ of a fine grid. Assume that random variables Y_i follow a Gaussian distribution with the mean μ_i and variance σ_Y^2,

$$Y_i | \mu_i \sim \mathcal{N} \left(\mu_i, \sigma_Y^2 \right). \tag{1}$$

Given the values μ_i and σ_Y^2, the random variables Y_i are independent.

The values $\boldsymbol{\mu} = \{\mu_i\}_{i=1}^n$ represent the true underlying process (e.g. NO_x concentration), and the (missing) observations are related to this process through a measurement error of variance σ_Y^2. The model for the underlying process is formulated as a sum of regression component with available covariates, and a spatially varying random effect.

The approach to modelling μ_i expresses an assumption that available covariates explain part of the spatial pattern, and the remaining part is captured through a spatial dependence, introduced as the conditionally autoregressive structure. The CAR scheme follows an assumption of similar random effects in adjacent cells, and it is given through the specification of full conditional distribution functions of μ_i for $i = 1, \ldots, n$ (see e.g. [1], [5], [8])

$$\mu_i | \boldsymbol{\mu}_{-i} \sim \mathcal{N} \left(\boldsymbol{x}_i^T \boldsymbol{\beta} + \rho \sum_{\substack{j=1 \\ j \neq i}}^{n} \frac{w_{ij}}{w_{i+}} \left(\mu_j - \boldsymbol{x}_j^T \boldsymbol{\beta} \right), \frac{\tau^2}{w_{i+}} \right), \tag{2}$$

where $\boldsymbol{\mu}_{-i}$ denotes all elements in $\boldsymbol{\mu}$ but μ_i; w_{ij} are the adjacency weights ($w_{ij} = 1$ if j is a neighbour of i and 0 otherwise, also $w_{ii} = 0$); w_{i+} is the number of neighbours of area i; $\boldsymbol{x}_i^T \boldsymbol{\beta}$ is a regression component with explanatory covariates for area i and a respective vector of regression coefficients; and τ^2 is a variance parameter. Thus, the mean of the conditional distribution $\mu_i | \boldsymbol{\mu}_{-i}$ consists of the regression part and the second summand, being proportional to the average values of remainders $\mu_j - \boldsymbol{x}_j^T \boldsymbol{\beta}$ for neighbouring sites (i.e. when $w_{ij} = 1$). The proportion is calibrated with the parameter ρ, reflecting strength of a spatial association. Furthermore, the variance of the conditional distribution (2) is inversely proportional to the number of neighbours w_{i+}.

The joint distribution of the process $\boldsymbol{\mu}$ is the following (for derivation see e.g. [5], [8])

$$\boldsymbol{\mu} \sim \mathcal{N}_n \left(\boldsymbol{X} \boldsymbol{\beta}, \tau^2 \left(\boldsymbol{D} - \rho \boldsymbol{W} \right)^{-1} \right), \tag{3}$$

where $\boldsymbol{X}$ is a design matrix with vectors $\boldsymbol{x}_i$; $\boldsymbol{D}$ is an $n \times n$ diagonal matrix with w_{i+} on the diagonal; and $\boldsymbol{W}$ is an $n \times n$ matrix with adjacency weights w_{ij}. Equivalently, we can write (3) as

$$\boldsymbol{\mu} = \boldsymbol{X} \boldsymbol{\beta} + \boldsymbol{\epsilon}, \quad \boldsymbol{\epsilon} \sim \mathcal{N}_n \left(\boldsymbol{0}, \boldsymbol{N} \right) \tag{4}$$

with $\boldsymbol{N} = \tau^2 \left(\boldsymbol{D} - \rho \boldsymbol{W} \right)^{-1}$.

Coarse grid The model for a coarse grid (aggregated) observed data is obtained by multiplication of the mean process $\boldsymbol{\mu}$ with an $N \times n$ *aggregation matrix* $\boldsymbol{C}$, where N is a number of observations in a coarse grid

$$\boldsymbol{C} \boldsymbol{\mu} = \boldsymbol{C} \boldsymbol{X} \boldsymbol{\beta} + \boldsymbol{C} \boldsymbol{\epsilon}, \quad \boldsymbol{C} \boldsymbol{\epsilon} \sim \mathcal{N}_N \left(\boldsymbol{0}, \boldsymbol{C} \boldsymbol{N} \boldsymbol{C}^T \right). \tag{5}$$

The matrix $\boldsymbol{C}$ consists of 0's and 1's, indicating which cells have to be aligned together. The random variable $\boldsymbol{\lambda} = \boldsymbol{C} \boldsymbol{\mu}$ is treated as the mean process for variables $\boldsymbol{Z} = \{Z_i\}_{i=1}^{N}$ associated with observations $\boldsymbol{z} = \{z_i\}_{i=1}^{N}$ of the aggregated model

$$\boldsymbol{Z} | \boldsymbol{\lambda} \sim \mathcal{N}_N \left(\boldsymbol{\lambda}, \sigma_Z^2 \boldsymbol{I}_N \right), \tag{6}$$

where $\boldsymbol{I}_N$ is the $N \times N$ identity matrix. Also at this level, the underlying process $\boldsymbol{\lambda}$ is related to $\boldsymbol{Z}$ through a measurement error with variance σ_Z^2.

The parameters $\boldsymbol{\beta}, \sigma_Z^2, \tau^2$ and ρ are estimated with the maximum likelihood method based on the joint unconditional distribution of $\boldsymbol{Z}$

$$\boldsymbol{Z} \sim \mathcal{N}_N \left(\boldsymbol{C} \boldsymbol{X} \boldsymbol{\beta}, \boldsymbol{M} + \boldsymbol{C} \boldsymbol{N} \boldsymbol{C}^T \right), \tag{7}$$

where $M = \sigma_Z^2 I_N$. Next, the log likelihood function associated with (7) is formulated

$$L\left(\beta, \sigma_Z^2, \tau^2, \rho\right) = -\frac{1}{2}\log\left|M + CNC^T\right| - \frac{N}{2}\log\left(2\pi\right)$$
$$-\frac{1}{2}\left(z - CX\beta\right)^T\left(M + CNC^T\right)^{-1}\left(z - CX\beta\right), \quad (8)$$

where $|\cdot|$ denotes the determinant. The analytical derivation is limited to the regression coefficients β, and further maximisation of the profile log likelihood is performed numerically, details of which are provided in [11].

Regarding the missing values in a fine grid, the underlying mean process is of our primary interest. The predictors optimal in terms of the minimum mean squared error are given by $E\left(\mu|z\right)$. The joint distribution of (μ, Z) is

$$\begin{bmatrix} \mu \\ Z \end{bmatrix} \sim \mathcal{N}_{n+N}\left(\begin{bmatrix} X\beta \\ CX\beta \end{bmatrix}, \begin{bmatrix} N & NC^T \\ CN & M + CNC^T \end{bmatrix}\right). \quad (9)$$

The distribution (9) allows for full inference, yielding both the predictor and its error

$$\widehat{E\left(\mu|z\right)} = X\widehat{\beta} + \widehat{N}C^T\left(\widehat{M} + C\widehat{N}C^T\right)^{-1}\left[z - CX\widehat{\beta}\right]$$
$$\widehat{Var\left(\mu|z\right)} = \widehat{N} - \widehat{N}C^T\left(\widehat{M} + C\widehat{N}C^T\right)^{-1}C\widehat{N}.$$

Note that in the predictor $\widehat{E\left(\mu|z\right)}$, a naive regression forecast is corrected with a residual on the aggregated grid distributed over respective grid cells.

3   Evaluating the Fisher Information Matrix

The standard errors of parameter estimators are calculated with the Fisher information matrix. Let us denote with $\hat{\theta}$ a vector of maximum likelihood estimates for a model parametrized by θ with associated log likelihood $L(\theta)$. The Fisher information matrix is defined as

$$J(\theta) = E\left[-L^{(2)}(\theta)\right],$$

where E denotes the expected value, and $L^{(2)}$ is the Hessian matrix of second order partial derivatives of the log likelihood function. Inverting this matrix gives the asymptotic covariance matrix of the maximum likelihood estimators, i.e. the Cramér-Rao (lower) bound.

To estimate $J(\theta)$, either the *expected* or the *observed* Fisher information matrices can be used [4, 16]. The expected information matrix is defined as

$$\mathcal{J}(\hat{\theta}) = \left[E\left(-L^{(2)}(\theta)\right)\right]\Big|_{\theta=\hat{\theta}}$$

The observed information matrix is defined as minus the second derivative of the log likelihood function at $\hat{\theta}$ given data:

$$\mathcal{I}(\hat{\theta}) = \left[-L^{(2)}(\theta)\right]\Big|_{\theta=\hat{\theta}}$$

It should be noted that $\mathcal{J}(\hat{\theta})$, unlike $\mathcal{I}(\hat{\theta})$, is a maximum likelihood estimator of $J(\theta)$. $\mathcal{I}(\hat{\theta})$ is actually only an approximation of $J(\theta)$ that may be, however, easier to compute for complicated models, where the theoretical Fisher information matrix may be difficult to determine. For instance, for state-space models the expected information matrix was shown to estimate more accurately the true Fisher information [4]. On the other hand, in [7] the authors argue in favour of the observed information matrix over the expected one.

In what follows, we derive the expected and observed Fisher information matrices for the considered disaggregation model. For notational convenience, we shall henceforth denote $V = M + CNC^T$, $U = z - CX\beta$, and $P = (D - \rho W)^{-1}$.

Let us denote the derivative vector of the log likelihood function (8) as

$$L^{(1)} = \left(L_\beta^T, L_{\sigma_Z^2}, L_{\tau^2}, L_\rho\right)^T.$$

It comprises the following elements:

$$L_\beta = z^T V^{-1} CX - \beta^T X^T C^T V^{-1} CX$$

$$L_{\sigma_Z^2} = -\frac{1}{2}\text{tr}\left(V^{-1}\right) + \frac{1}{2}U^T V^{-1} V^{-1} U$$

$$L_{\tau^2} = -\frac{1}{2}\text{tr}\left(V^{-1} CPC^T\right) + \frac{1}{2}U^T V^{-1} CPC^T V^{-1} U$$

$$L_\rho = -\frac{1}{2}\text{tr}\left(\tau^2 V^{-1} CPWPC^T\right) + \frac{1}{2}\tau^2 U^T V^{-1} CPWPC^T V^{-1} U,$$

where tr$(\cdot)$ denotes the trace of a matrix. The respective diagonal elements of the second derivative matrix[1]

$$\text{diag}(L^{(2)}) = \left[\text{diag}\left(L_{\beta\beta}\right), L_{\sigma_Z^2 \sigma_Z^2}, L_{\tau^2 \tau^2}, L_{\rho\rho}\right]$$

are as follows:

$$L_{\beta\beta} = -(CX)^T V^{-1} CX \tag{10}$$

$$L_{\sigma_Z^2 \sigma_Z^2} = \frac{1}{2}\text{tr}\left(V^{-1} V^{-1}\right) - U^T V^{-1} V^{-1} V^{-1} U \tag{11}$$

$$L_{\tau^2 \tau^2} = \frac{1}{2}\text{tr}\left(V^{-1} CPC^T V^{-1} CPC^T\right) - U^T V^{-1} CPC^T V^{-1} CPC^T V^{-1} U \tag{12}$$

---

[1] Since the off-diagonal elements of the information matrix equal zero, those derivatives are not calculated here.

$$L_{\rho\rho} = \frac{1}{2}\text{tr}\left(V^{-1}\tau^2 CPWPC^T V^{-1}\tau^2 CPWPC^T\right.$$
$$-2V^{-1}\tau^2 CPWPWPC^T\Big)$$
$$-U^T\left(V^{-1}\tau^2 CPWPC^T V^{-1}\tau^2 CPWPC^T\right.$$
$$-V^{-1}\tau^2 CPWPWPC^T\Big) V^{-1}U \tag{13}$$

The Fisher information matrix becomes

$$J = -E\left[L^{(2)}\right] = \text{diag}\left(J_\beta, J_{\sigma_Z^2}, J_{\tau^2}, J_\rho\right).$$

Consequently, we obtain

$$J_\beta = (CX)^T V^{-1} CX \tag{14}$$

$$J_{\sigma_Z^2} = \frac{1}{2}\text{tr}\left(V^{-1}V^{-1}\right) \tag{15}$$

$$J_{\tau^2} = \frac{1}{2}\text{tr}\left(V^{-1}CPC^T V^{-1}CPC^T\right) \tag{16}$$

$$J_\rho = \frac{1}{2}\text{tr}\left(V^{-1}\tau^2 CPWPC^T V^{-1}\tau^2 CPWPC^T\right). \tag{17}$$

Evaluating the above expressions (14)-(17) at the values of ML parameter estimators $\hat{\theta}$ yields the expected information matrix $\mathcal{J}(\hat{\theta})$. Evaluating the negative of expressions (10)-(13) at $\hat{\theta}$ yields the observed information matrix $\mathcal{I}(\hat{\theta})$. The Cramér-Rao lower bound of the estimators' variances is estimated with a reciprocal of these values.

4   An Application

In [10], Horabik considers disaggregation of air pollution concentrations obtained from the dispersion model CALPUFF run for Warsaw agglomeration, based on real emission and meteorological data from 2005. Specifically, NO_x concentration data were disaggregated from a 2km (coarse) regular grid to a 1km (fine) grid. Performance of the disaggregation procedure was compared for the models of 4 neighbours (the so-called Rook Method, denoted CAR4) and for the ones of 8 neighbours (the so-called Queen Method, denoted CAR8); both settings were analysed either with the trend based on three categories of city roads, or without trend (with a constant value). For this set of models, Table 1 presents the resulting ML estimates of the parameters, together with their standard errors (Std. Err.), obtained using the expected $\left(\sqrt{\mathcal{J}^{-1}(\hat{\theta})_{ii}}\right)$ and observed $\left(\sqrt{\mathcal{I}^{-1}(\hat{\theta})_{ii}}\right)$ Fisher information matrices.

Table 1. Maximum likelihood estimates for a coarse grid

	CAR4			CAR8		
	Est. $\hat{\theta}$	Std. Err. $\sqrt{\boldsymbol{\mathcal{J}}^{-1}(\hat{\theta})_{ii}}$	Std. Err. $\sqrt{\boldsymbol{\mathcal{I}}^{-1}(\hat{\theta})_{ii}}$	Est. $\hat{\theta}$	Std. Err. $\sqrt{\boldsymbol{\mathcal{J}}^{-1}(\hat{\theta})_{ii}}$	Std. Err. $\sqrt{\boldsymbol{\mathcal{I}}^{-1}(\hat{\theta})_{ii}}$
Models with trend						
β_0	6.754	4.383	4.383	6.652	4.500	4.500
β_1	0.0019	2.59e-04	2.59e-04	0.002	2.64e-04	2.64e-04
β_2	0.0014	2.93e-04	2.93e-04	0.0016	3.01e-04	3.01e-04
β_3	0.0005	5.45e-05	5.45e-05	0.0005	5.62e-05	5.62e-05
σ_Z^2	3.65e-08	0.296	0.393	0.296e-08	0.338	0.4617
τ^2	18.56	2.095	2.095	51.88	5.856	5.855
ρ	0.9995	6.41695e-04	6.41696e-04	0.9994	8.66e-04	8.65e-04
Models without trend						
β_0	11.717	6.204	6.204	11.814	6.247	6.247
σ_Z^2	7.33e-07	0.590	0.714	1.59e-07	0.671	0.994
τ^2	36.89	4.1651	4.1647	103.03	11.6294	11.6290
ρ	0.9995	6.3138e-04	6.3139e-04	0.9994	8.834e-04	8.840e-04

For regression coefficients β, the respective elements of the expected and observed information matrices are equal (compare (10) and (14)), thus the corresponding standard errors are identical. For the remaining parameters, the variance (and standard error) estimates for τ^2 and ρ calculated with both approaches are, respectively, almost identical; this is the case for all the analysed models. As regards σ_Z^2, for all the models, the estimated standard errors based on the observed information matrix $\boldsymbol{\mathcal{I}}(\hat{\theta})$ are consequently higher than those based on the expected information $\boldsymbol{\mathcal{J}}(\hat{\theta})$. Note, however, that this parameter is not significant in any model.

Comparing the respective formulae for calculation of the expected and observed information matrices, it can be noticed that many expressions for the expected information matrix involve subtraction of matrices or even their cancellation, see (10)-(13). This effect may add to numerical errors in calculation of $\boldsymbol{\mathcal{I}}(\hat{\theta})$. In this respect, the usage of the expected information matrix is recommended whenever possible.

5   Conclusion

We have developed the formulae for calculation of the expected and observed Fisher information matrices for parameters in a spatial disaggregation model of areal data, where spatial dependence is captured with the conditional autoregressive structure. All required derivatives are evaluated analytically, thus no numerical differentiation is involved. The obtained information matrix is readily available for accuracy evaluation of the estimated parameters by means of the Cramér-Rao (lower) bound. It can be also used in iterative procedures of parameter estimation, which may be particularly useful in the case of large data sets encountered e.g. in atmospheric research. Due to numerical properties, the usage of expected Fisher information matrix is recommended. A short practical application has been also presented.

Acknowledgments. The study has been conducted within the 7FP Marie Curie Actions IRSES project *Geoinformation Technologies, Spatio-Temporal Approaches, and Full Carbon Account for Improving Accuracy of GHG Inventories*, No. 247645, Acronym GESAPU. Joanna Horabik has been also supported from the Foundation for Polish Science under *International PhD Projects in Intelligent Computing*, financed from The European Union within the Innovative Economy Operational Programme 2007-2013 and European Regional Development Fund.

References

1. Banerjee, S., Carlin, B.P., Gelfand, A.E.: Hierarchical modeling and analysis for spatial data. Chapman & Hall/CRC (2004)
2. Boychuk, K., Bun, R.: Regional spatial cadastres (inventories) of GHG emissions in Energy sector: Accounting for uncertainty. Clim. Chang. 124(3), 561–574 (2014)
3. Bun, R., Hamal, K., Gusti, M., Bun, A.: Spatial GHG inventory at the regional level: accounting for uncertainty. Clim. Chang. 103(1-2), 227–244 (2010)
4. Cavanaugh, J.E., Shumway, R.H.: On computing the expected Fisher information matrix for state-space model parameters. Stat. Probabil. Lett. 26, 347–355 (1996)
5. Cressie, N.A.C.: Statistics for Spatial Data. Wiley, New York (1993)
6. Dragosits, U., Sutton, M.A., Place, C.J., Bayley, A.A.: Modelling the spatial distribution of agricultural ammonia emissions in the UK. Environ. Pollut. 102(S1), 195–203 (1998)
7. Efron, B., Hinkley, D.V.: Assessing the accuracy of the maximum likelihood estimator: Observed versus expected Fisher information. Biometrika 65(3), 457–487 (1978)
8. Gelfand, A.E., Diggle, P.J., Fuentes, M., Guttorp, P. (eds.): Handbook of Spatial Statistics. Chapman & Hall/CRC (2010)
9. Horabik, J.: Spatial disaggregation of activity data for GHG inventory in agricultural sector of Poland. Research Report RB/41/2012. Systems Research Institute of Polish Academy of Sciences, Warsaw (2012)
10. Horabik, J.: Spatial disaggregation of air pollution data with conditional autoregressive model. In: Myśliński, A. (ed.) Techniki Informacyjne. Teoria i Zastosowania, vol. 3(15), pp. 39–53. Instytut Badań Systemowych PAN, Warszawa (2013)
11. Horabik, J., Nahorski, Z.: Improving resolution of a spatial air pollution inventory with a statistical inference approach. Clim. Chang. 124, 575–589 (2014)
12. Kaiser, M.S., Daniels, M.J., Furakawa, K., Dixon, P.: Analysis of particulate matter air pollution using Markov random field models of spatial dependence. Environmetrics 13, 615–628 (2002)
13. Klein, A., Mélard, G.: Computation of the Fisher information matrix for time series models. J. Comput. Appl. Math. 64, 57–68 (1995)
14. Mardia, K.V., Marshall, R.J.: Maximum likelihood estimation of models for residual covariance in spatial regression. Biometrika 71, 135–146 (1984)
15. McMillan, N.J., Holland, D.M., Morara, M., Feng, J.: Combining numerical model output and particulate data using Bayesian space-time modeling. Environmetrics 21, 48–65 (2010)
16. Monahan, J.F.: Numerical methods of statistics. Cambridge University Press (2001)
17. Oda, T., Maksyutov, S.: A very high-resolution (1km×1km) global fossil fuel CO_2 emission inventory derived using a point source database and satellite observations of nighttime lights. Atmos. Chem. Phys. 11, 543–556 (2011)

Automatically Identifying Suitable Rulebase Parameters in the Context of Solving the Map Overlay Problem

Jörg Verstraete

Systems Research Institute, Department of Computer Modelling,
Polish Academy of Sciences,
ul. Newelska 6, 01-447 Warsaw, Poland
jorg.verstraete@ibspan.waw.pl
http://ibspan.waw.pl

Abstract. Analysis of geographically related data often requires the combination of data from different sources. Data are commonly represented in grids, and unfortunately, the grids containing different data do not match properly: they can differ in cell size and/or orientation. A novel methodology was presented to allow the data of one grid to be remapped onto the other grid. The method makes use of a fuzzy inference system that performs the remapping, using additional information relating to the data distribution. Previous research has revealed that the best parameters used in the inference system are dependent on the input, and as such an automatic determination of which parameters should be used, would improve the performance. In this article, we propose a solution for this automatic detection, by first generating a training set that is related to the input and then determining what the best parameters are for this training set.

Keywords: map overlay, spatial reasoning, fuzzy inference system.

1 Introduction

In geographic sciences, there often is a need to combine data coming from different sources. Combining such data poses interesting problems: the data are obtained using different technologies and commonly the format in which the data are presented differs. A common representation format for numerical data spread over a region (such as e.g. concentration of a pollutant) is a grid: a raster that divides the region of interest into a number of cells, each of which is assigned a value that is considered to be representative for the area covered by that cell. However, different data can be defined on incompatible grids, these are grids between which there is no one-to-one mapping of the cells of the grids. Consequently, it is very difficult to compare the different grids, and to draw conclusions. As there is no clear mapping of one cell to another cell, it is difficult to perform correct calculations and to draw reliable conclusions. This is for example the case when studying the exposure of humans to specific airborne

© Springer International Publishing Switzerland 2015
D. Filev et al. (eds.), *Intelligent Systems'2014*,
Advances in Intelligent Systems and Computing 323, DOI: 10.1007/978-3-319-11310-4_58

pollutants, where the population data does not align properly with the pollution data, but it also occurs in many environmental or wildlife studies. In [1], a novel methodology to pre-process gridded data to help solve this issue was proposed. This approach uses a fuzzy inference system in order to derive new output values. The inference system requires parameters that relate to the output; several candidate parameters were presented in [2]. Initial observations presented in [3] showed that the performance of the system is highly dependent on the parameters used. In [3], these parameters were chosen intuitively and manually in order to judge the performance under ideal conditions. In this article, a methodology to find ideal parameters using an automatically generated training set for a given dataset is presented and verified using experiments.

2　Problem Description

2.1　Map Overlay Problem

Combining data that are represented on different grids implies combining the data in the cells of the grids. The first issue is that there are many ways to define a grid: the size of the grid cells can differ, or one grid can be at an angle when compared to another grid. Grids with different orientation or size of grid cells are called *incompatible*, which makes it very difficult to compare data in one grid to data on the other grid. This is further complicated by the second issue: in a grid, the grid cell is considered to be the smallest unit for which data are known. With each grid cell, a number, representative for the cell, is associated. Usually, this is an aggregated value, but the underlying spatial distribution that resulted in the value is not contained in the data. If the number for instance holds the concentration of a pollutant, there is no way of knowing how it is distributed inside the cell: there can be a single point source, or it can be uniformly distributed over the area covered by the cell. The fact that the distribution is not known makes it difficult to map cells of incompatible grids to one other; the problem is referred to in literature as the *map overlay problem*. The general approach to solve the map overlay problem, is to remap one grid onto to other grid (sometimes implicitly), in order to achieve a one-to-one mapping between the grid cells.

2.2　Current Approaches

General Concept. To find a clear mapping between different grids, the most straightforward idea is to transform one grid onto the other grid; this means remapping the data contained in one grid, to match the other grid. This makes the grids compatible, and results in a one-to-one mapping of the grid cells of both grids. Different methods exist, an overview of current solutions is in [4] and in [5]. A short overview is listed below.

Areal Weighting. In areal weighting, the data represented within each cell is considered to be uniform over the cell, and independent of neighbouring cells. The contribution of a cell of one grid to a cell in the other grid is determined by the amount of overlap: the percentage of overlap is the percentage of the modelled value that is mapped in the other grid cell.

Areal Smoothing. In areal smoothing, the modelled feature is considered to be smooth over the area; mathematically this is achieved by interpreting the modelled feature as a third dimension and fitting a smooth surface over the volume. Resampling this smooth surface using a different raster, results in the remapped grid. In both approaches, assumptions regarding the underlying distributions are made, but these assumptions very often have no connection to the real world situation.

Regression Methods. Different regression methods to approach the problem exists. In these methods, an attempt is made to establish patterns of overlap, which are then used to estimate the data. The data are often assumed to have a specific distribution (e.g. poisson). The assumption of the distribution is also here what limits the possibilities of this approach.

2.3   Additional Data Approach

Data fusion is a field in which different datasets are combined with the aim of providing a higher quality dataset. In [6], the authors combine datasets that contain descriptive data: regions on the map are annotated with text labels to indicate types of land cover. The definition of the regions differ, as do the text labels used, yet it is possible to combine the knowledge to yield a better data.

When considering a grid with numerical data, often other data are available that are known to be related to this data. In the origin of our research, the numerical data concerns concentration of specific airborne pollutants. Other studies have shown a correlation between the presence of these pollutants and traffic. Consequently, the distribution of the pollutant should relate to the road network and traffic density - taking into account dispersion of the pollutants, for which we have a dispersion model available. In [1], it was proposed to use this additional information: the transformation of a grid that contains data on such a pollutant might be done better when taking the road network into account. However, using additional information poses new problems. Even though a correlation between both supplied data (particular pollutant and traffic) might be known, in general, the data will be from different sources and may concern data measured at different times or with different accuracy. Furthermore, there is no guarantee that the supplied additional knowledge is the *only* explanation for the original data: there may be other sources of this particular pollutant that are not known or supplied. The additional information can therefore only be used to supply information on the underlying distribution. Following this additional information too strictly might yield no solutions or might obfuscate other sources. Despite these uncertainties and imprecisions, it is possible to perform an intelligent reasoning in order to achieve a better distribution. The intelligent reasoning is further elaborated on in [1], the subsequent intelligent method and initial results are described in more detail in [7].

3   AI Algorithm

3.1   Prerequisites

The algorithm presented in [7] processes the data using a fuzzy inference system, in a way that mimics the intelligent reasoning. The fuzzy inference system is a concept from artificial intelligence, in which fuzzy sets are used to determine new values. Fuzzy set theory is an extension of traditional set theory which, among other things, allows for the representation of uncertain or imprecise values. This is achieved through the use of a membership function, which maps the domain onto the interval $[0, 1]$

$$\tilde{A} = \{(x, \mu_{\tilde{A}}(x)) | x \in A\}$$
$$\mu_{\tilde{(A)}} : A \to [0, 1]$$
$$x \mapsto \mu_{\tilde{A}}(x)$$

Higher membership grades imply higher possibilities or certainties - this depends on the interpretation given to the fuzzy set ([8]). A consequence of the ability to represent imprecise values, is that fuzzy sets also can be used to represent linguist terms such as *high* or *low*, by defining a linguistic term as a fuzzy set over the domain and associating higher membership grades to values of the domain that better match the linguistic term. If for example values range between 0 and 100, the linguistic term representing high can be represented by a fuzzy set that increases linearly from 0 for the value 80, to 1 for the value 100. The core of the fuzzy inference system is a set of rules of the form

```
IF x is <linguistic term>
  THEN y is <linguistic term>
```

Here, x is an input variable that it matched with the linguistic term; the first is is a fuzzy match that matches a numeric value with a fuzzy set (which is the representation of the linguistic term). As such, the rule is a representation for a natural language predicate, e.g. *if x is high*. Multiple parameters and linguistic terms can be combined through logical operators such as *and* and *or*, to form a more elaborate premise. The y is the output value that is assigned a value, which is a linguistic term also represented by a fuzzy set. The inference system has multiple rules, and typically all these rules are evaluated. As multiple rules can have a matching premise, there can be multiple values for y. These are aggregated using a standard fuzzy aggregation method to yields a single fuzzy set that represents the output value. This is then defuzzified to result in the crisp, numerical value returned by the system.

3.2   Translating the Problem to Fit a Rulebase

Parameters. In [7], it is explained how the given problem is translated to fit the rulebase approach. The rulebase system can be considered separately for each cell in the output grid; the output value y is the value that should be associated with the cell. To employ the rulebase, it is necessary to find parameters x that relate to the ideal output. With these parameters, it is possible to generate a rulebase that will compute an output value y. For a given output cell, one example of such a parameter would be the total value of the auxiliary cells that overlap with the output cell. In [2], different parameters were proposed, some based on overlapping cells, others based on distances. As the value of the parameter will need to be matched against linguistic terms, an adequate range for each parameter is also needed: this range allows us to defined the linguistic terms, and thus to say when a value is high or low. In [2], a number of intuitively obtained parameters were proposed and manually verified. In [3], several parameters and their ranges were considered, and simulations were run on artificial data. For each segment, every parameter and its possible range (which is specific for each segment) were calculated. The parameters were manually selected and used in the fuzzy inference system to determine the underlying distributions. The simulations showed that the performance of the system is different per case, and that different datasets benefit from a different selection of parameters. Consequently the performance of the system can be improved by finding the most appropriate parameters for a given dataset. However, even though the target grid is supplied, directly calculating new values for the cells of the target grid is problematic: a cell in the target grid can overlap with multiple input cells. This makes it difficult to determine its value, as different input cells are involved, and the portion of each input cell that should be mapped to the output cell needs to be found.

Segments. Basically, the goal is to redistribute the data within each input cell, and then remap it to the target grid. This can be done by considering a new grid, obtained from the intersection between input and target grid, referred to as the *segment grid*. The segment grid is an irregular grid, which has the property that every segment belongs to exactly one cell in the input grid, and to exactly one cell in the output grid. Furthermore, every cell both in input as output grid is covered by an integer number of segments. Examples are shown on Figure 2(a) and 3(b). Consequently, it is possible to redistribute the data of an input grid cell over the segments that are covered by it. After this, the value of a grid cell in the target grid can be computed by aggregated the the different segments that it covers. For the rulebase system, the segment grid will be used as the target grid.

4 Parameters

4.1 What Are the *Best* Parameters?

In [2], a number of parameter definitions were proposed. These range from quite intuitive values (e.g. amount of overlap between a segment and the additional data), to more elaborate ones (e.g. the distance to high values in additional data that do not overlap the overlapping input cell). Not only is it necessary for the calculated parameter to relate to the optimal output but, it is also necessary to find an appropriate range in order to assess when the parameter is high or low. Criteria for good parameters are:

1. relate to the output value
2. have a proper range

4.2 Relating to the Output

The first requirement of a good parameter, is that it relates to the output value, yet in general, the output value is unknown. Suppose that output value is known, then it is possible to use the Pearson correlation (1) to determine for each parameter whether or not it relates to the ideal output, and how well it relates. Pearsons's product-moment correlation between a list of values X and a list of values Y is defined as ([9]):

$$cor(X,Y) = \sum_i \frac{(x_i - E(X))(y_i - E(Y))}{(n-1)s(X)s(Y)} \tag{1}$$

Here, $E()$ is the expected value, approximated by the mean of the list , and $s()$ the notation for the standard deviation of the list. The Pearson correlation results in a value in the range $[-1,1]$. Positive numbers imply a proportional correlation (thus for the parameter, this implies a proportional connection: high values relate to high values) and negative numbers an inverse correlation (thus high values relate to low values). The closer the value is to 0, the weaker the correlation. The Pearson correlation therefore not only provides data how the parameter relates to the output, but also how well it relates. The problem with using the Pearson correlation is that it requires a data set in which ideal output values are known, which moves the problem of finding good relating parameters to finding a suitable training set. This will be considered in Section 5.1.

4.3 Proper Range

After the first stage of determining what the good parameters are, it needs to be investigated if an appropriate range for the parameters can be defined. A parameter that shows perfect behaviour compared to the ideal output is useless without a properly defined range, as there would be no frame of reference to know if the value is high or low in the rulebase system. The range of a parameter should reflect the possible values of the parameter. The lower bound of the range is defined as the lowest possible value that this segment can have while still maintaining a possible remapping. The upper bound is defined as the highest possible value that this segment can have while still maintaining a possible remapping. An appropriate range has the following properties:

1. it is not a degenerate interval for *all* segments
2. it is such that the parameters for different segments do not have the same relative value within the range

If the range is degenerate, i.e. lower and upper limit are equal (and thus equal to the parameter), the evaluation to high or low will yield the same result, and this parameter will not contribute to the outcome. However, the range can be degenerate for some segments: the parameter would still contribute for the segments for which it does have a valid range. If a parameter evaluates the same in the range for every segment, then this parameter does not contribute either. All the evaluations for the parameter will be the same (it will always be low, or always be high, to the same extent), for every segment. This property is more computationally intensive to verify, as it implies evaluating the parameter with the range and comparing the outcome for all segments.

4.4   Example

A simple example for a parameter is the value represented in the overlapping cells of the auxiliary grid. For a given output segment, the value of the parameter x will be the weighted sum of all overlapping auxiliary cells, where the percentage of overlap are the weights; this is the value that would be assigned to the segment in the case of areal weighting. The range is considered specifically for this parameter and this output segment, and will be the possible range this parameter can have. The highest possible value occurs if the value of the overlapping auxiliary cells is completely mapped onto this segment. This simulates the situation where the explanation for the value of these cells is fully located inside the selected segment, and this provides an upper limit. The lowest possible value is the inverse situation: the justification for the value of the overlapping auxiliary cells is not in the segment, in which case the lowest possible value is 0. It should be noted that if cells of the auxiliary grid are fully contained inside this segment, then the sum of their values serves as the minimum possible value (this data can never be mapped outside the segment). Other parameters and ranges are calculated in a similar way.

5   Parameter Selection

5.1   Data Generation

In order to select which parameters are suitable using the Pearson correlation, it is necessary to obtain data that is representative for the given problem, but also has an ideal output.

In [3], the author concluded that the parameters are highly dependent on the dataset used. Additional experiments showed that the main reason is the difference between the rasters: how are the grids oriented and what are the relative cell sizes? It was observed that - as long as the rasters are similar - the ideal parameters are usually the same[1]. As such, it is sufficient to generate a training set that has the same grid definitions as the supplied problem. It still needs values for different cells; to achieve that, geometries as shown on figure 1c were generated and values were associated with the features. The positioning and values of the features was not random, but followed specific rules to force a variety in the numerical data. The main argument for not generating the training using fully random data to prevent situations where the randomness might yield less adequate training set, and consequently to also make sure the developed system is deterministic. The pattern was chosen so that it is easily accommodated for different grid definitions; it also provides a subjective view on how good the grids are an approximation of the situation. The pattern was then sampled using the provided grids.

5.2   Calculation

In the test data, it is possible to calculate every parameter and its range, for every output segment. As the test pattern was also sampled with the segment grid, there is an ideal value for each segment. Consequently, the Pearson correlation can be calculated for each candidate parameter, comparing its values with the ideal output values. The best parameters are those with the correlation values furthest from 0.

Note that it is also possible to calculate the range on the training set, and only keep those parameters that have a good range. However, the range is specific to the value of a parameter and segment in a given situation and its computation does not need the ideal output value. There actually are several benefits to calculating the range on the original dataset rather than on the training set. First, it will allow to select those parameters that have a proper range for the current problem. Even though the training set is made such that it should resemble the original data quite well, there may be situations in which the range for a given parameter in the dataset is degenerate for all segments, even though it is not in the training set. In such situation, the use of the parameter and its range will not contribute to the evaluation. Consequently, it may be omitted (for performance reasons) or it may be replaced by another a parameter that has a valid range, even if it has worse correlation. Using the original dataset to determine if a parameter does not have a degenerate range for all segments increases the chance of using a good parameter and range. The second benefit is related to performance. The range has to be calculated for the chosen parameters in the given dataset in order to determine the new values. There is no real need to know the range for the training set, so those calculations do not need to be performed.

---

[1] This might not be the case if the data modelled is very similar in neighbouring cells, as is for instance the case when resampling a grid over a grid with smaller cells. In such situations, the grid gives the impression of a higher accuracy than the data.

6   Experiments

6.1   Prerequisites

In [3], different datasets were considered and tested using three manually and optimally chosen parameters. For the experiments here, a two artificial datasets are considered. These are made from sampling the geometries as shown on Figure 1a and 1b. For these artificial datasets, an ideal solution is known and as such, it is possible to determine what the best parameters are without having to resort to the generation of a test dataset. The geometries are quite different: the first one is comprised of line sources whereas the second one only has area sources. In addition, the reference geometry as described in 5.1 and shown on Figure 1c will be generated. This is a geometry designed to exhibit different properties; it only has line sources, but with a specific pattern and different values for different lines.

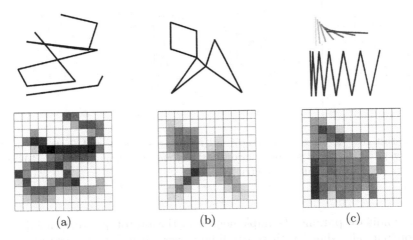

(a)   (b)   (c)

Fig. 1. The three geometries used to test the algorithms and their approximation as input grids. Geometry (a) contains two line sources with a constant value, geometry (b) contains 3 area sources with a constant value and geometry (c) contains different line patters with varying associated values. Greyscales are used to illustrated the values: higher values are shaded darker.

The geometries described above will be considered over two different sets of grids, to generate two different test cases and one reference test case. For both test cases, it is necessary to generate an input grid, an auxiliary grid and an output grid. The input grids for the test cases are also shown on Figure 1. For both cases, the same 12x12 grid will be used for the input.

Case 1. The target grid for case 1 is shown on Figure 2(a). It is a 25x25 grid that covers exactly the same area as the input grid. The segment grid, obtained from the intersection of input grid and target grid, is also shown on the figure. Figure 2(b-d) shows the approximation of the geometries using the first set of grids for auxiliary grid and segment grid. All grids cover exactly the same area; the auxiliary grid a 15x15 grid and the segment grid used in the calculations. On the figure, different grey scales are used to indicate different ranges of values. The segment grids hold the optimal solution, and show how the data of the input cells should be redistributed.

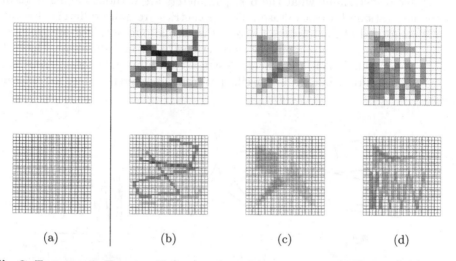

(a)   (b)   (c)   (d)

Fig. 2. Test case 1. Target grid (top) and resulting segment grid (bottom) (a). The auxiliary grid (top) and segment grid (bottom), for the first geometry (b), second geometry (c), and reference geometry (d).

All candidate parameters implemented in the prototype were calculated for each output cell. Many of these candidates were dismissed as either having no correlation to the output (Pearson correlation did not yield a number), or as having a degenerate range for all segments. Seven parameters remained. On table 1, the correlations of the seven remaining parameters are listed for the different datasets, in decreasing order of correlation. While the values are different, parameters with the best correlations are similar. The first four parameters occur in the same order. The last three parameters occur in different order, but their correlation is lower than 0.31, which is too low to reliably consider that there is a good correlation.

Case 2. The target grid for the second case is shown on Figure 3(a). The same 25x25 grid as in the first test case was used, but rotated over 20° counter clockwise. Figure 3(b-d) shows the approximation of the geometries using the second set of grids for auxiliary grid and segment grid. The auxiliary grid is the same 15x15 grid as before, but rotated at a 10° angle compared to the input

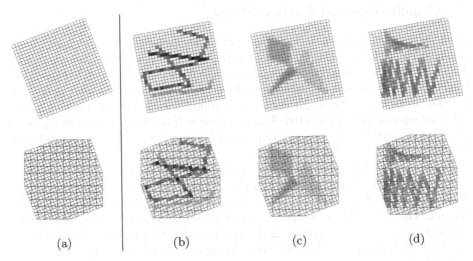

(a)   (b)   (c)   (d)

Fig. 3. Test case 2. Target grid (top) and resulting segment grid (bottom) (a). The auxiliary grid (top) and segment grid (bottom), for the first geometry (b), second geometry (c), and reference geometry (d).

grid. The calculations were the same as in the previous test case, and again seven parameters remained. The order of the parameters is different compared to the previous test case, even though the approximated geometries are the same: parameters p2 and p3 swapped places; parameter p4 went from being the fourth best to being the worst parameter. This illustrates that the parameters are linked with the way the grids overlap, rather than with the approximated geometries. On table 1, the correlations are listed for the three datasets, in decreasing order of correlation. While the values for the different geometries are different, parameters with the best correlations are similar and occur in the same order.

Table 1. The correlations for the parameters in the different datasets in the two considered testcases, in decreasing order of correlation

case 1						case2					
dataset 1		dataset 2		dataset 3		dataset 1		dataset 2		dataset 3	
p1	0.65	p1	0.94	p1	0.76	p1	0.76	p1	0.99	p1	0.81
p2	0.60	p2	0.90	p2	0.76	p3	0.76	p3	0.98	p3	0.81
p3	0.56	p3	0.77	p3	0.62	p2	0.64	p2	0.89	p2	0.74
p4	0.30	p4	0.49	p4	0.35	p6	0.32	p6	0.36	p6	0.33
p5	0.18	p5	0.31	p7	0.22	p7	0.20	p7	0.32	p7	0.22
p6	0.13	p7	0.25	p5	0.21	p5	0.18	p5	0.27	p5	0.20
p7	0.12	p6	0.21	p6	0.11	p4	0.03	p4	0.02	p4	0.05

7   Conclusion and Future Work

Both testcases show that the choice of which parameters are most suitable is dependent on the layout of the grids. Consequently, it is possible to use a reference data set, which is completely known beforehand, and use the provided rasters to come up with an adequate reference set from which the most suitable parameters for the problem can be determined. This allows for an automatically adjusted rulebase system to be generated. The key issue will be determining the reference set. The current choice performs quite well for the current crop of examples, as the order of well correlated parameters is maintained.

In this article, we presented a methodology to find the best suited parameters to use a rulebase system to remap gridded data. The remapping of the data is done by means of auxiliary data that have a known correlation and a rulebase system. The optimal parameters for the rulebase system are found out not dependent on the data, but rather on the grid layouts of the different grids that are involved. This property allows for the generation of a reference data set with an optimal output, from which the optimal parameters can be determined. Using the Pearson correlation, the parameters can be related to the optimal output, and their quality can thus be assessed. The discovered parameters can then be used in the rulebase system to calculate the desired grid transformation. This addition had already been integrated in our current implementation. The current reference geometry is sufficient for the considered problems, but it needs to be studied further if it is universal enough.

References

1. Verstraete, J.: Using a fuzzy inference system for the map overlay problem. In: 3rd International Workshop on Uncertainty in Greenhouse Gas Inventories, pp. 289–298 (2010)
2. Verstraete, J.: Parameters to use a fuzzy rulebase approach to remap gridded spatial data. In: Proceedings of the 2013 Joint IFSA World Congress NAFIPS Annual Meeting (IFSA/NAFIPS), pp. 1519–1524 (2013)
3. Verstraete, J.: A fuzzy rulebase approach to remap gridded spatial data: Initial observations. In: Laurent, A., Strauss, O., Bouchon-Meunier, B., Yager, R.R. (eds.) IPMU 2014, Part I. CCIS, vol. 442, pp. 366–375. Springer, Heidelberg (2014)
4. Flowerdew, R., Green, M.: Areal interpolation and types of data. In: Foterhingham, S., Rogerson, P. (eds.) Spatial Analysis and GIS, pp. 141–152. Taylor & Francis (1994)
5. Gotway, C.A., Young, L.J.: Combining incompatible spatial data. Journal of the American Statistical Association 97(458), 632–648 (2002)
6. Duckham, M., Worboys, M.: An algebraic approach to automated information fusion. International Journal of Geographic Information Systems 19, 537–558 (2005)
7. Verstraete, J.: Solving the map overlay problem with a fuzzy approach. Climatic Change, 1–14 (2014)
8. Dubois, D., Prade, H.: The three semantics of fuzzy sets. Fuzzy Sets and Systems 90, 141–150 (1999)
9. Aczel: Complete Business Statistics. The Irwin/McGraw-Hill series in operations and decision sciences. McGraw-Hill Education (India) Pvt. Limited (2007)

An Image Analysis Algorithm
for Soil Structure Identification

Małgorzata Charytanowicz[1,2] and Piotr Kulczycki[1,3]

[1] Polish Academy of Sciences, Systems Research Institute,
Centre of Information Technology for Data Analysis Methods,
Newelska 6, 01-447 Warsaw, Poland
[2] Catholic University of Lublin, Institute of Mathematics and Computer Science,
Konstantynow 1H, 20-708 Lublin, Poland
Malgorzata.Charytanowicz@ibspan.waw.pl
[3] Cracow University of Technology, Department of Automatic Control and Information
Technology, Warszawska 24, 31-155 Cracow, Poland
Piotr.Kulczycki@ibspan.waw.pl

Abstract. Pore space study has been utilized as a general method for defining soil structures. This is because the characteristics particular to pore space impact the majority of physical and physicochemical soil parameters relevant due to plant growth. This paper presents an image segmentation approach for detecting the soil pore structures that have been studied by way of soil tomography sections. In so-doing, a research study was conducted using a density-based clustering method, and in turn, the nonparametric kernel estimation methodology. This overcomes the rigidity of arbitrary assumptions concerning the number or shape of clusters among data, and lets the researcher detect inherent data structures. After a short description of the method, the practical aspects and applications illustrated with a number of soil aggregates are presented.

Keywords: image processing and analysis, image segmentation, clustering, natural grouping, nonparametric estimation, kernel estimators, pore space, total porosity.

1   Introduction

Among all measurements characterizing the various aspects of a particular soil, the total porosity provides a more useful physical description that is relevant to plant growth. This measure is defined as the fraction of the total pore volume of soil material, including the solid and void components, that is taken up by the volume of void-space. Being simply a fraction of total volume, it can range between 0 and 1, typically falling between 0.3 and 0.7 for most soils. Moreover, a number of scientists have reported that studies of pore size distribution are useful as a general method for defining the soil structure [6, 17, 22]. Pore spaces location within the soil has different influences on fluid retention, conduction within the soil and the maximum space available for water, and, therefore, it is important to identify pore zones.

© Springer International Publishing Switzerland 2015
D. Filev et al. (eds.), *Intelligent Systems'2014*,
Advances in Intelligent Systems and Computing 323, DOI: 10.1007/978-3-319-11310-4_59

Advances in X-ray microtomography, together with image processing methods, provide a non-destructive alternative for detecting soil structures, especially pore space [15, 16]. However, the usefulness of computed tomography data for pore structure characterization depends on the accuracy of the grayscale images segmentation into binary pore and solid components. Different methods have been used to segment soil images, among these, simple binary and multiple thresholding [14], watershed, morphological, and normalized cut [3, 18, 21]. Furthermore a fuzzy approach successfully used in various data analysis problems [1, 10, 12, 13] is discovered for the segmentation methods [5]. These methods have given promising results, but they are very sensitive to image quality, low level of contrast and unintended noises. Based on these arguments, many studies now have begun to utilize the potential of image segmentation done by clustering methods [7, 11]. The objective of clustering process is to find pixel groups of a similar grey level intensity so as to organize them into more or less homogeneous groups and assign the same label to every pixel sharing certain visual characteristics. As a traditional clustering algorithm, K-means is popular for its simplicity in implementation, and it is commonly applied for grouping pixels in images. However, the quality of K-means suffers from being confined to being run with a fixed number of clusters. Therefore, many current research efforts have been focused on discovering and applying new approaches in segmenting by way of using various now available image processing techniques.

The main purpose of this investigation is to evolve a standard method of detecting pore space in the soil. A proposed methodology integrates image processing and clustering technique based on the Complete Gradient Clustering Algorithm [9, 10]. The principle of the proposed algorithm is based on the distribution of the data and the need to estimate its density. Within the algorithm, each cluster is identified by a local maximum of the kernel density estimator of the data distribution. As a result, regions of high densities of objects are recognized as clusters, while areas with sparse distributions of objects divide one group from another. The algorithm works in an iterative manner until a termination criterion has been satisfied. Data points are assigned to clusters by using an ascending gradient method, i.e. points moving to the same local maximum are put into the same cluster. It is worth underlining that the whole procedure does not need the application of any assumptions concerning the data distribution or fixed number of clusters. Rather, the parameter values are calculated using optimizing criteria, without any necessity of their arbitrary specification. However, by an appropriate change in values of these parameters, it is possible to influence the size of number of clusters, and also the proportion of their appearance in dense areas in relation to sparse regions of elements in a data set. As a result, the proposed procedure allows researchers to examine soil structure and extract pore space using the segmented images. Moreover, a comparison between the clustering results obtained from this method and the classical K-means clustering algorithm shows positive practical features of the Complete Gradient Clustering Algorithm.

2   Statistical Kernel Estimators

Let (Ω, Σ, P) be a probability space. Let also a real random variable $X : \Omega \to R$, whose distribution has the density function f, be given. The corresponding kernel estimator $\hat{f} : R \to [0, \infty)$, calculated using experimentally obtained values for the m-element random sample $x_1, x_2, ..., x_m$, in its basic form is defined by

$$\hat{f}(x) = \frac{1}{mh} \sum_{i=1}^{m} K\left(\frac{x - x_i}{h}\right),$$ (1)

where $m \in N \setminus \{0\}$, the positive coefficient h is known as a smoothing parameter, whereas the measurable function $K : R \to [0, \infty)$ of unit integral, symmetrical with respect to zero and having a weak global maximum at this point, takes the name of a kernel. The influence of the smoothing parameter on particular kernels is the same for the basic definition of kernel estimator (1). Advantageous results are obtained thanks to the individualization of this effect, achieved through a so-called modification of the smoothing parameter. It relies on mapping the positive modifying parameters s_1, $s_2, ..., s_m$ on particular kernels, described as

$$s_i = \left(\frac{\hat{f}(x_i)}{\overline{s}}\right)^{-c},$$ (2)

where $c \in [0, \infty)$, $\hat{f}$ denotes the kernel estimator without modification, and $\overline{s}$ is the geometrical mean of the numbers $\hat{f}(x_1)$, $\hat{f}(x_2)$, ... , $\hat{f}(x_m)$. The parameter c stands for the intensity of the modification procedure and based on indications for the criterion of the integrated mean square error, the standard value $c = 0.5$ can be suggested. Finally, the kernel estimator with the smoothing parameter modification is defined in the following formula:

$$\hat{f}(x) = \frac{1}{mh} \sum_{i=1}^{m} \frac{1}{s_i} K\left(\frac{x - x_i}{h s_i}\right).$$ (3)

The choice of the kernel K form and the calculation of the smoothing parameter h is made most often with the criterion of the mean integrated square error. From a statistical point of view, the choice of the kernel form has no practical meaning and thanks to this, it becomes possible to take into account primarily properties of the estimator obtained or calculation aspects, advantageous from the viewpoint of the application problem under investigation. The standard normal kernel given by

$$K(x) = \frac{1}{\sqrt{2\pi}} e^{-\frac{x^2}{2}}$$ (4)

is used most often. It is differentiable up to any order and assumes positive values in the whole domain.

The fixing of the smoothing parameter h has significant meaning for the quality of estimation. A smoothing parameter controls the tradeoff between bias and variance in the result. A large bandwidth leads to a very smooth density distribution, whereas a small bandwidth leads to an ragged density distribution. A frequently used bandwidth selection technique, called the "cross-validation method", chooses h to minimize the function $g : R \rightarrow R$ defined as

$$g(h) = \frac{1}{m^2 h} \sum_{i=1}^{m} \sum_{j=1}^{m} \tilde{K}\left(\frac{x_j - x_i}{h}\right) + \frac{2}{mh} K(0) \quad , \tag{5}$$

where $\tilde{K}(x) = K^{*2}(x) - 2K(x)$, whilst K^{*2} denotes convolution function of K, i.e.

$$K^{*2}(x) = \int_R K(u) K(x-u) \, du \quad , \tag{6}$$

and for the standard normal kernel (4) is equal

$$K^{*2}(x) = \frac{1}{2\sqrt{\pi}} e^{-\frac{x^2}{4}} \quad . \tag{7}$$

The tasks concerning the choice of the kernel form, as well as additional procedures improving the quality of the estimator obtained, and all rules needed for calculating the smoothing parameter, are found in [8, 19, 20]. The utility of kernel estimation has been investigated in the context of the Complete Gradient Clustering Algorithm.

3   Complete Gradient Clustering Algorithm

Consider the data set containing m elements $x_1, x_2, \ldots, x_m$, in n-dimensional space. Using the methodology introduced in Section 2, the kernel density estimator (3) may be constructed in n-dimensional space, i.e.:

$$\hat{f}(x) = \frac{1}{mh^n} \sum_{i=1}^{m} \frac{1}{s_i^n} K\left(\frac{x - x_i}{hs_i}\right) \quad , \tag{8}$$

where the kernel K is assumed to be radial or product [8, 19, 20]. The idea of the algorithm is based on the approach proposed by Fukunaga and Hostetler [4]. Thus given the start points:

$$x_j^0 = x_j \quad \text{for} \quad j = 1, 2, \ldots, m \tag{9}$$

each point is moved in an uphill gradient direction using the following iterative formula:

$$x_j^{k+1} = x_j^k + b \frac{\nabla \hat{f}\left(x_j^k\right)}{\hat{f}\left(x_j^k\right)} \quad \text{for} \quad j = 1, 2, \ldots, m \quad \text{and} \quad k = 0, 1, \ldots, k^*, \tag{10}$$

where $\nabla \hat{f}$ denotes the gradient of kernel estimator $\hat{f}$ and the value of parameter b is proposed as $h^2 / (n+2)$ while the coefficient h is the bandwidth of $\hat{f}$. The algorithm will be stopped when the following condition is fulfilled:

$$\left| D_k - D_{k-1} \right| \leq a D_0 \;, \tag{11}$$

where D_0 and D_{k-1}, D_k denote sums of Euclidean distances between particular elements of the set $x_1, x_2, \ldots, x_m$ before starting the algorithm as well as after the $(k-1)$-th and k-th step, respectively. The positive parameter a is taken arbitrary and the value 0.001 is primarily recommended. This k-th step is the last one and will be denoted hereinafter by k^* where $k^* \in N \setminus \{0\}$.

Finally, after the k^*-th step of the algorithm (9)-(10) the set

$$x_1^{k^*}, \; x_2^{k^*}, \ldots, x_m^{k^*} \;, \tag{12}$$

considered as the new representation of all points $x_1, x_2, \ldots, x_m$, is obtained. Following this, the set of mutual Euclidean distances of the above elements:

$$\left\{ d(x_i^{k^*}, x_j^{k^*}) \right\}_{\substack{i=1,2,\ldots,m-1 \\ j=i+1, i+2, \ldots, m}} \tag{13}$$

is defined. Using the methodology presented in Section 2, the auxiliary kernel estimator $\hat{f}_d$ of the elements of the set (13), treated as a sample of a one-dimensional random variable, is created under the assumption of nonnegative support. Next, the first (i.e. obtained for the smallest value of an argument) local minimum of the function $\hat{f}_d$ belonging to the interval $(0, D]$, where D means the maximum value of the set (13), is found. This local minimum will be denoted as x_d, and it can be interpreted as the half-distance between potential closest clusters. Finally, the clusters are created. First, the element of the set (13) is taken; it initially create a one-element cluster containing it. An element of the set (13) is added to the cluster if the distance between it and any element belonging to the cluster is less than x_d. Every added element is removed from the set (13). If there are no more elements belonging to the cluster, the new cluster is created. The procedure of assigning elements to clusters is repeated as long as the set (13) is not empty.

Procedures described above constitute the Complete Gradient Algorithm in its basic form. The values of the parameters used are calculated automatically. However, by an appropriate change in values of these parameters it is possible to influence the size of number of clusters, and also the proportion of their appearance in dense areas in relation to sparse regions of elements in a data set. Too small a value of the smoothing parameter h results in the appearance of too many local extremes of the kernel estimator, and as a consequence, an increase in the number of clusters. On the other hand too great a value causes its excessive smoothing and an decrease in the number of clusters.

Next, the intensity of modification of the smoothing parameter is implied by the value of the parameter c. Its increase smoothes the kernel estimator in areas where elements of data set are sparse, and also it sharpens it in dense areas. In consequence, if the value of the parameter c is raised, then the number of clusters in sparse areas of data decreases, while at the same time, increases in dense regions. Inverse effects can be seen in the case of lowering this parameter value.

Detailed information on the CGCA procedures and their influences on the clustering results as well as applicational examples are described in the articles [2, 9, 10].

4   Methodology

The proposed methodology to elaborate an innovative image processing approach for detection pore space, based on computed tomography and the nonparametric kernel estimation methodology, is summarized as follows:

1. preparing the soil sample;
2. capturing the soil tomographic slices;
3. applying the contrast enhancement technique on the original soil images;
4. extracting the color components from the enhanced image;
5. applying the unsupervised segmentation technique that is based on the complete gradient clustering algorithm;
6. detecting the pore space from the segmented images.

4.1   Soil Classification

The investigated material was sampled from the cultivated soil layer, classified as silty loam (WRB Mollic Gleysols), explored at the Institute of Agrophysics, of the Polish Academy of Sciences in Lublin. The proportion of each particle size group in the soil was as follows: sand – 46%, silt – 28%, clay – 26%. Furthermore, the pH was: H_2O – 5.9, while KCl was 5.4.

On the experimental fields, a long-term fertilization trial had been executed. The adopted crop rotation from 1955 to 1989 was a cycle of potato – barley – rye, and from 1990 – a cycle of sugar beat – barley – rape – wheat. Three treatments concerning fertilization: control group – plant residues only, mineral fertilization – according to plant needs, and pig manure – 80 ton per ha, were studied. The aggregate soil organic matter was measured by the Multi N/C 3100 Autoanalyser (Analitic Jena, Germany).

Table 1. Aggregate soil organic matter measurements

Type of fertilization	Total organic carbon content [g/kg]	Total nitrogen content [g/kg]
Control (without fertilization)	13.54	1.35
Mineral fertilization	14.89	1.51
Pig manure fertilization	21.50	2.10

The total organic carbon shows the same tendency as total nitrogen, i.e. increasing in the same order: the lowest – control, middle – mineral fertilization, the highest – pig manure.

4.2   Soil Sample Preparation and Image Processing

The soil samples were air dried in room conditions, divided into smaller amounts, and gently sieved through 2 and 10 mm sieves. Soil aggregates remaining at 2 mm sieve and ranging from 2 to 10 mm, were then detected by means of X-ray computational tomography, using a GE Nanotom S device, with the voxel-resolution of 2.5 microns per volume pixel. Three 2D sections uniformly located within each aggregate were performed to characterize the aggregate structure. Next, tomography sections were processed using the Aphelion 4.0.1 package. In the initial step, the contrast enhancement technique was applied on the original soil images, and, subsequently, a rectangle ROI (region of interest) selection of the size of 128x128 pixels was performed upon the enhanced grayscale image. Thus, the ring artifacts of the original images were removed, and these ROI's were saved as a bitmap format. The color components data derived automatically from these images were then examined, as the Complete Gradient Clustering Algorithm (CGCA) allowed for soil image segmentation. In order to find a distribution density of the color components, the kernel estimators methodology, presented in Section 2 was used, with the application of the normal kernel, the cross-validation method, as well as the smoothing parameter modification procedure with standard intensity. Moreover, in the clustering algorithm, a modification of parameters values was employed to eliminate peripheral clusters. Finally, pore space detection was done automatically using the segmented images through choosing the cluster containing the lowest color components.

4.3   Image Segmentation Results

In order to assess the proposed segmentation method, three sections of each soil aggregate were captured from soil samples differing in term of fertilization. The color components that had been extracted from the grayscale images were subsequently fed as input to the Complete Gradient Clustering Algorithm for further segmentation processing. After that, the cluster of the lowest values corresponding to the pore space in each sample was detected. What is more, all pixels of these values that had been distinguished in the original images in black, were captured. Fig. 1-3 show the 8 bit grayscale images of the captured soil samples and the corresponding resultant images with pore space shown in black. These images were subsequently composed in the table rows from the lowest to the highest sections, as cut with proportions 25%, 50%, and 75% of the aggregate height. After the pore space detection, a common quantitative analysis was conducted in order to assess the overall performance of the results obtained.

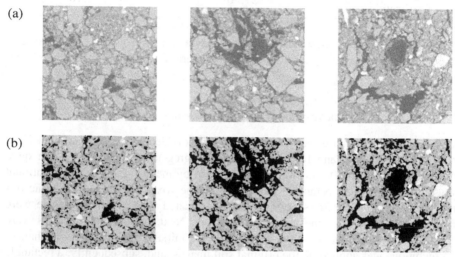

Fig. 1. The rectangle ROI selections of control group aggregates: original images (a), images with pore space in black detected by the CGCA (b)

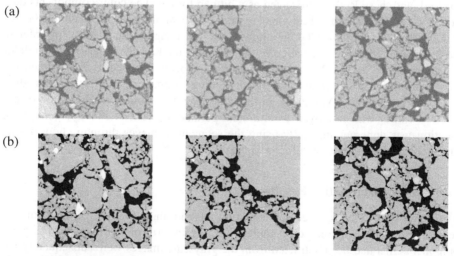

Fig. 2. The rectangle ROI selections of mineral fertilization aggregates: original images (a), images with pore space in black detected by the CGCA (b)

(a)

(b)

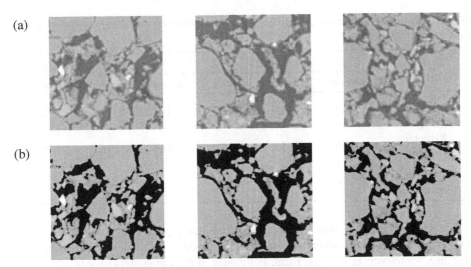

Fig. 3. The rectangle ROI selections of pig manure fertilization aggregates: original images (a), images with pore space in black detected by the CGCA (b)

Based on the observation of several soil images, it was found that the appearance of the pore space cells is similar within the aggregate of each treatment. Indeed, the upper limits of pixel values classified as pore space within the aggregate are almost the same and are nearly equal: 162, 165, and 163 for soil without fertilization (control group), 155, 156, and 155 for soil with mineral fertilization and 149, 148, and 151 for soil with pig manure fertilization. For each type of fertilization, values are ordered correspondingly to the image order as displayed on the Fig. 1-3.

As revealed, a diversity in pore space appearance is found between aggregates differing in term of fertilization. The largest upper limits of pixel values classified as pore space occurs in the soil without fertilization, and, despite this, the pore fraction, equaling 21% in an averaging of the three sections, is the smallest. The soil with pig manure fertilization incorporates the smallest values of the upper limits of these pixels, but despite this, has the largest fraction of pores, equaling 28% in an averaging of the three sections. Generally, the effect of fertilization is to increase the amounts of pores and its size in relation to the control group. The greater increase is for pig manure fertilization.

A comparable analysis of segmentation was obtained when the K-means algorithm with an arbitrary taken cluster number of two was used. Table 2 contains pixel value limits between the pore space and solid components, as calculated by the CGCA and the K-means algorithm for each type of fertilization.

This study has shown the adequacy of using nonparametric kernel estimation theory for determining soil structure. The limits obtained by the K-means algorithm are a bit greater than these obtained by the CGCA, and when used in the segmentation process, the K-means algorithm gives an overestimation of the pore space. Furthermore it is worth stressing, that this algorithm needs an a priori assumed correct number of clusters, which in many applications, may not be known. Indeed, even such a "correct" (from a theoretical point of view) number might not exist at all.

Table 2. The limits between the pore space and solid components calculated by the CGCA and K-means algorithm

Type of fertilization	The CGCA			The K-means algorithm		
	section 1	section 2	section 3	section 1	section 2	section 3
Control group	162	165	163	183	167	174
Mineral fertilization	155	156	155	165	165	161
Pig manure fertilization	149	148	151	153	151	156

The CGCA, instead, does not require strict assumptions regarding the desired number of cluster. This allows the number obtained to be better suited to the soil structure. Moreover, in its basic form, the values of the parameters may be calculated automatically, however, there exists the possibility of their optional change. A feature specific to it is the possibility that it can influence the proportion between the number of clusters in areas where data elements are dense, as opposed to their sparse regions. In addition, by the detection of peripheral clusters, the algorithm allows the identification of outliers. This enables their elimination or designation to more numerous clusters, thus increasing the homogeneity of the data set.

The segmentation of soil images using the proposed method has given promising results. The clustering algorithm enabled the detection and recognition of the soil features from which for our needs, the pore space was ascertained. However, its computation can be challenging even for recent computer hardware. The most significant trend towards facilitating this, is to increase the number of CPU cores and increase the CPU's ability to process more and more tasks in parallel. Even more important, and an integral part of this practice, is that it allows optimization, so that the complex algorithm could be performed in a reasonable time.

5 Summary

Recent advances in computed tomography and digital image processing provide non-destructive tools for studying the internal structures of soil aggregates. This seems very useful in characterizing the pore space and in quantifying the differences in pore structures of different types of soil. In so doing, a more detailed analysis may be obtained by quantifying the soil structure through using the proposed segmentation techniques based on the kernel density estimation.

In this paper, an alternative way of detecting pore space in computed tomography soil slices is proposed by way of using image processing and data clustering based on the kernel estimation methodology. This density-based clustering algorithm allows us to get a better comprehension and knowledge of data, with the objective of segmenting images into either pore space or into solid components that constitute homogeneous areas with respect to a property of interest.

The presented approach is more objective than classical parametric methods, and can be successfully applied for many tasks in data mining, particularly where arbitrary assumptions concerning the number or shape of clusters among data are not recommended. This approach is also motivated by the current rapid growth in computational power. Improved real-time data processing and algorithm efficiency have important add-on effects due to the concurrent increase in the quantity and complexity of the image data that are now being collected.

Acknowledgments. This work has been supported by the national grant Frame No NN 310 307 639 of the Polish Ministry of Science and Higher Education.

References

1. Bandyopadhyay, S., Saha, S., Pedrycz, W.: Use of a fuzzy granulation-degranulation criterion for assessing cluster validity. Fuzzy Sets and Systems 170, 22–42 (2011)
2. Charytanowicz, M., Niewczas, J., Kulczycki, P., Kowalski, P.A., Łukasik, S., Żak, S.: Complete Gradient Clustering Algorithm for Features Analysis of X-Ray Images. In: Piętka, E., Kawa, J. (eds.) Information Technologies in Biomedicine, vol. 2, pp. 15–24. Springer, Berlin (2010)
3. Das, D., Ghosh, M., Chakraborty, C., Maiti, A.K., Pal, M.: Probabilistic prediction of malaria using morphological and textural information. In: 2011 International Conference on Image Information Processing, Durgapur, India, November 3-5 (2011)
4. Fukunaga, K., Hostetler, L.D.: The estimation of the gradient of a density function, with applications in Pattern Recognition. IEEE Transactions on Information Theory 21, 32–40 (1975)
5. Ghosh, M., Das, D., Chakraborty, C., Ray, A.K.: Plasmodium vivax segmentation using modified fuzzy divergence. In: 2011 International Conference on Image Information Processing, Durgapur, India, November 3-5 (2011)
6. Hallett, P., Lichner, L., Czachor, H., Józefaciuk, G.: Pore shape and organic compounds drive major changes in the hydrological characteristics of agricultural soils. European Journal of Soil Science 64, 334–344 (2013)
7. Kaufman, L., Rousseeuw, P.J.: Finding Groups in Data: An Introduction to Cluster Analysis. Wiley, New York (1990)
8. Kulczycki, P.: Estymatory jądrowe w analizie systemowej. WNT, Warszawa (2005)
9. Kulczycki, P., Charytanowicz, M.: A Complete Gradient Clustering Algorithm Formed with Kernel Estimators. International Journal of Applied Mathematics and Computer Science 20, 123–134 (2010)
10. Kulczycki, P., Charytanowicz, M., Kowalski, P.A., Łukasik, S.: The Complete Gradient Clustering Algorithm: Properties in Practical Applications. Journal of Applied Statistics 39, 1211–1224 (2012)
11. Mirkin, B.: Clustering for Data Mining: A Data Recovery Approach. Chapman and Hall, London (2005)
12. Nowak, P., Romaniuk, M.: A fuzzy approach to option pricing in a Levy process setting. International Journal of Applied Mathematics and Computer Science 23, 613–622 (2013)
13. Nowak, P., Romaniuk, M.: Application of Levy processes and Esscher transformed martingale measures for option pricing in fuzzy framework. Journal of Computational and Applied Mathematics 263, 129–151 (2014)

14. Pal, N.R., Pal, S.K.: A review of image segmentation techniques. Pattern Recognition 29, 1277–1294 (1993)
15. Perret, J.S., Prasher, S.O., Kacimov, A.R.: Mass fractal dimension of soils macropores using computed tomography: from the box counting to the cube-counting algorithm. Journal of Hydrology 26, 285–297 (2003)
16. Peth, S., Nellesen, J., Fischer, G., Horn, R.: Non-invasive 3D analysis of local soil deformation under mechanical and hydraulic stresses by μCT and digital image correlation. Soil and Tillage Research 111, 3–18 (2010)
17. Pires de Silva, A., Imhoff, S., Kay, B.: Plant response to mechanical resistance and air-filled porosity of soils under conventional and no-tillage system. Scientia Agricola 6, 451–456 (2004)
18. Ruberto, C.D., Dempster, A., Khan, S., Jarra, B.: Analysis of infected blood cell images using morphological operators. Image and Vision Computing 20, 133–146 (2002)
19. Silverman, B.W.: Density Estimation for Statistics and Data Analysis. Chapman and Hall, London (1986)
20. Wand, M.P., Jones, M.C.: Kernel Smoothing. Chapman and Hall, London (1994)
21. Wojnar, L., Majorek, M.: Komputerowa analiza obrazu. Computer Scanning System, Warszawa (1994)
22. Zdravkov, B., Cermak, J., Sefara, M., Janku, J.: Pore classification in the characterization of porous materials: A perspective. Central European Journal of Chemistry 5, 385–395 (2007)

Modeling the Process of Face Recognition with Pattern Neural Network Using a Generalized Net

Stanimir Surchev and Sotir Sotirov

Intelligent Systems Laboratory,
"Prof. Dr. Asen Zlatarov" University,
1 "Prof. Yakimov" Blvd., 8010 Burgas, Bulgaria
ssurchev@gmail.com, ssotirov@btu.bg

Abstract. In this research is presented the use of pattern neural network as a useful tool for face recognition. It is described how neural networks can help us in a situation where the main aim is recognizing human faces. The method is described in terms of generalized nets. The training data includes images of the faces. Each of these pictures has been processed into different preprocesses. When we have the trained neural network we can recognize faces.

Keywords: Face recognition, Generalized net, Neural network, Pattern recognition.

1 Introduction

In this work a generalized net model [11, 12, 14, 15] of modeling process of face recognition with pattern neural network is presented.

Neural networks [6, 7] are used in many applications. An advantage that gives them a great potential is their applicability to the process of recognition. Neural networks can be distinguished into a wide variety [1, 13], where the learning method is the general difference between the different types of neural networks. In general, there are two types of neural networks: supervised and unsupervised. In the present paper, a supervised learning [16] Pattern Neural Network is used.

According to [5], the artificial neural systems, or neural networks, are physical cellular systems, capable of perceiving, storing and using the perceived information, and they have become a powerful tool that can be used in human face recognition [8, 9, 10]. In this paper, we choose the type of pattern neural network [4], because it can process big packets of information which makes it well suited for our aim, since face recognition is a difficult and slow process.

The pattern neural network structure is two-layer feed-forward network with sigmoid output neurons:

- input data – vectors: $p = [x_1 \dots x_n]$;
- target – there is only one element with value one, other elements are equal to zero:
  $t = [\ 0 \quad 1 \quad 0]$;

© Springer International Publishing Switzerland 2015
D. Filev et al. (eds.), *Intelligent Systems' 2014*,
Advances in Intelligent Systems and Computing 323, DOI: 10.1007/978-3-319-11310-4_60

The first step is collecting the input images. We use the data base from [17].

The following Figure 1 describes a part of input pictures that are correct. In this case the pictures are:

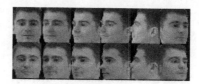

Fig. 1. Correct data. Every one of them has dimensions 29×36 pixels

Fig. 2. Searched face

When we want to make a neural network that recognizes a particular kind of objects we need correct data and incorrect data, i.e. images that represent something else. Here we have some examples.

Fig. 3. Incorrect data

When we collect the correct and incorrect data we have to create the target data. It shows us the type of the input data.

- Face   [1 0 0]
- Specific face   [0 1 0]
- No face   [0 0 1]

When the input data is collected, we have to transform each of the input pictures into vectors. The inputs of the neural networks must be as a vector, and we have to make transformation from the pictures to the vectors

Neural network training: for the realization of our purpose was used two-layer MPL. The P_{1044x1} vector was fed at the input, and the T_{3x1} was produced at the output. The input layer consisted of 50 neurons as the standard logic function (logsig) was used as a transfer function. The output of the second layer was defined by the equation $a^1 = logsig(pw^1 + b)$. The output layer was with a logic transfer function and was defined by the equation $a^2 = logsig((logsig(pw^1 + b^1)w^2 + b^2)$, where:

- w is a matrix of the weight coefficients of each of the entries;
- b is neuron's entry bias.

The training process is presented in Fig. 4.

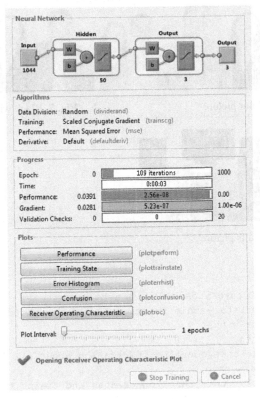

Fig. 4. Training process

The picture from Fig.5 is used for verification of the trained neural network.

Fig. 5. Testing picture

Before the testing process, the image is preprocessed. The preprocesses are:

- Lightening;
- Darkening;
- Discoloring;
- Resizing;
- Transforming from the picture to vector.

In the Fig. 6, Fig. 7 and Fig. 8 we present main stages of the process.

Fig. 6. Color picture   **Fig. 7.** Black/white picture

Fig. 8. Results picture

Code:

```
1.   p = ConvertPictureIntoRow(d)
     % ConvertInputData - this function transforms photos from size 29 x
     36 into vector with
     % 1044 elements.
     % d - variable that contains information about all input images.
2.   net = TrainNetwork(p,t)
     % TrainNetwork - this function creates and trains the neural net-
     work.
     % p - variable that contains input data
     % t - variable that contains target data
3.   picture2 = ResizeTestPicture(picture1, k)
     % ResizeTestPicture - function that creates smaller picture
     % picture1 - variable that contains data of the test image
     % k - variable that contains image resizing coefficient
4.   a1 = ConvertPictureIntoRow(picture1)
     % picture1 - variable that contains data of the test image
5.    2 = ConvertPictureIntoRow(picture2)
     % picture2 - variable that contains data of the resized image
6.   v1 = TestPicture (net, a1)
     % TestPicture - Function that tests the image with the neural net-
     work
     % net - variable that contains data of trained neural network
     % a1 - variable that contains data of converted image
7.   v2 = TestPicture (net, a2)
     % a2 - variable that contains data of resized converted image
8.   out =ConvertTestRowIntoPicture(picture1, v1, v2)
     % ConvertTestRowIntoPicture - function that converts the resultant
     data into a normal  image
     % v1 - variable that contains data of the tested image
     % v2 - variable that contains data of the resized tested image
```

2   Generalized Net Model

Initially, the following tokens enter the GN [2, 3].

- In place L_1 – token with initial characteristic: "input pictures, test picture, pictures";
- In place L_2 – token with initial characteristic: "lightening criterion, darkening criterion, discolor criterion, new picture criterion, resize criterion";
- In place L_{10} – token with initial characteristic: "neural network type, neurons number, training function, iteration number, mean square value, validation type";
- In place L_{15} – token with initial characteristic: "initial number of incorrect checks, maximal number of incorrect checks".

The GN is presented on Fig. 9 by the following set of transitions, describing the subprocesses of the model:

- Z_1 = "Creating and converting pictures";
- Z_2 = "Neural network training";
- Z_3 = "Neural network testing";
- Z_4 = "Visualization".

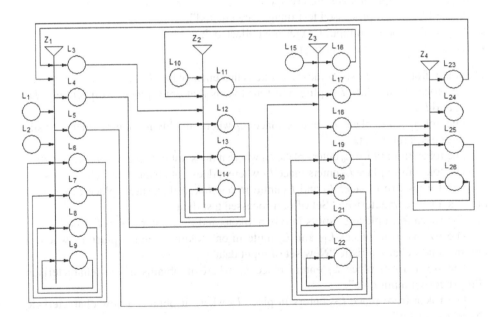

Fig. 9. GN-Model

$$Z_1 = \langle \{L_1, L_2, L_6, L_7, L_8, L_9, L_{17}, L_{23}\}, \{L_3, L_4, L_5, L_6, L_7, L_8, L_9\}, R_1,$$

$$\vee (L_6, L_8, L_9, L_{23}, \wedge (L_2, \vee (L_1, L_7, L_9, L_{17})))\rangle,$$

where

$$
R_1 = \begin{array}{c|ccccccc}
 & L_3 & L_4 & L_5 & L_6 & L_7 & L_8 & L_9 \\
\hline
L_1 & False & False & False & False & False & True & True \\
L_2 & False & False & False & True & True & True & True \\
L_6 & False & False & False & True & False & False & W_{6,9} \\
L_7 & False & False & False & W_{7,6} & True & False & False \\
L_8 & False & W_{8,4} & W_{8,5} & False & False & True & False \\
L_9 & W_{9,3} & False & False & W_{9,6} & False & False & True \\
L_{17} & False & False & False & False & True & False & False \\
L_{23} & False & False & False & False & False & False & True \\
\end{array}
$$

where

- $W_{6,9}$ = "Image preprocessing is completed ";
- $W_{7,6}$ = "New input images are created";
- $W_{8,4} = W_{8,5}$ = "Preprocessed test images are created";
- $W_{9,3}$ = "Preprocessed input images are collected ";
- $W_{9,6}$ = "Input images are collected".

The token from place L_1 splits into two tokens that enter places L_8 and L_9, respectively.

The token from place L_2 splits into four tokens that enter places, respectively, L_6, L_7, L_8 and L_9.

The token from place L_9 enters place L_6 where it obtains a new characteristic "Preprocessed input data".

The token from place L_6 enters place L_9 where it does not obtain a new characteristic.

The token from place L_9 enters place L_3 where it does not obtain a new characteristic.

The tokens from places L_1 and L_2 unite in one token that enters place L_8 where it obtains a new characteristic "Set of preprocessed test data".

The token from place L_8 splits into two tokens and they enter places L_4 and L_5.

The tokens from places L_{17} and L_2 unite in one token. It enters place L_7 where it obtains a new characteristic "New set of input data".

The token from place L_7 enters place L_6 where it obtains a new characteristic "Preprocessed input data".

The token from place L_{23} enters in place L_8 where it obtains a new characteristic "New test vector".

$$Z_2 = \langle \{L_3, L_{10}, L_{12}, L_{13}, L_{14}, L_{16}\}, \{L_{11}, L_{12}, L_{13}, L_{14}\}, \quad R_2,$$

$$\vee (L_3, L_{12}, L_{14}, L_{16}, \wedge (L_{10}, L_{13}))\rangle,$$

where

$$R_2 = \begin{array}{c|cccc}
 & L_{11} & L_{12} & L_{13} & L_{14} \\
\hline
L_3 & False & False & True & False \\
L_{10} & False & False & False & True \\
L_{12} & W_{12,11} & True & False & False \\
L_{13} & False & False & True & W_{13,14} \\
L_{14} & False & W_{14,12} & False & True \\
L_{16} & False & False & False & True
\end{array}$$

where

- $W_{12,11}$ = "Neural network is trained";
- $W_{13,14}$ = "The target values are created";
- $W_{14,12}$ = "The input values, target values and neural network parameters are collected".

The token from place L_{10} enters place L_{14} where it does not obtain a new characteristic.

The token from place L_3 enters place L_{13} where it obtains a new characteristic "Target vectors".

The tokens from places L_{13} and L_{10} unite in one token. It enters place L_{14} where it does not obtain a new characteristic.

The token from place L_{14} enters place L_{12} where it obtains a new characteristic "Trained neural network".

The token from place L_{12} enters place L_{11} where it does not obtain a new characteristic.

$$Z_3 = \langle \{L_4, L_{11}, L_{15}, L_{19}, L_{20}, L_{21}, L_{22}\}, \{L_{16}, L_{17}, L_{18}, L_{19}, L_{20}, L_{21}, L_{22}\}, R_3,$$

$$\vee ((L_{21}, \wedge (L_4, L_{11}), \wedge (L_{15}, L_{22}), \wedge (L_{19}, L_{20}))) \rangle,$$

where

$$R_3 = \begin{array}{c|ccccccc}
 & L_{16} & L_{17} & L_{18} & L_{19} & L_{20} & L_{21} & L_{22} \\
\hline
L_4 & False & False & False & True & False & False & True \\
L_{11} & False & False & False & False & False & False & True \\
L_{15} & False & False & False & False & False & True & False \\
L_{19} & False & False & W_{19,18} & True & False & False & False \\
L_{20} & False & False & W_{20,18} & False & False & False & False \\
L_{21} & W_{21,16} & W_{21,17} & False & W_{21,19} & W_{21,20} & True & False \\
L_{22} & False & False & False & False & False & W_{22,21} & True
\end{array}$$

where

- $W_{19,18} = W_{20,18} =$ "The picture is tested";
- $W_{21,19} = W_{21,20} =$ "The neural network is trained correctly";
- $W_{21,16} = W_{21,17} = \neg\, W_{21,19}$;
- $W_{22,21} =$ "The data for testing process is collected".

The token from place L_{11} enter place L_{12} where it does not obtain a new characteristic.

The tokens from places L_{22} and L_{15} unite in one token that enters L_{21} where it obtains new characteristics "Type of trained neural network, Number of incorrect trainings".

The token from place L_4 splits into three tokens. They enter places L_{19}, L_{20} and L_{22}.

If "Type of trained neural network" is equal to "Correctly trained neural network" then "Number of incorrect trainings" become zero. The token from place L_{21} splits into two tokens that enter places L_{19} and L_{20} where they obtain new characteristic accordingly "Resultant data for recognition of all faces" and "Resultant data for recognition of specific face".

If "Type of trained neural network" is equal to "Incorrectly trained neural network" then the "Number of incorrect trainings" is increased by one.

If the "Number of incorrect trainings" is not equal to the "Maximum number of incorrect trainings" then the token from place L_{21} enter place L_{16} where it obtains a new characteristic "Reset of the current trained neural network parameters", but if the "Number of incorrect trainings" is equal to the "Maximum number of incorrect trainings" then "Number of incorrect trainings" become zero and the token from place L_{21} enters in place L_{17} where it obtains characteristic "Update of the input data".

The tokens from places L_{19} and L_{20} enter place L_{18} then they unite in one token.

$$Z_4 = \langle \{L_5, L_{23}, L_{26}, L_{27}\}, \{L_{24}, L_{25}, L_{26}, L_{27}\}, R_4, \vee (L_{26}, L_{27}, \wedge (L_5, L_{18})) \rangle,$$

where

$$R_4 = \begin{array}{c|cccc} & L_{23} & L_{24} & L_{25} & L_{26} \\ \hline L_5 & False & False & False & True \\ L_{18} & False & False & False & True \\ L_{25} & False & W_{25,24} & True & False \\ L_{26} & W_{26,23} & False & W_{26,25} & True \end{array}$$

where

- $W_{25,24} =$ "The resultant data and picture are combined";
- $W_{26,25} = W_{26,23} =$ "The resultant data are collected".

The tokens from places L_5 and L_{18} enter place L_{26} where they unite in one token.

The token from place L_{26} splits into two tokens. They enter places L_{23} and L_{25} where they obtain new characteristics, respectively, "Next test picture" and "Combined resultant data from testing of the picture".

The token from place L_{25} enters place L_{24} where it obtains a new characteristic "Displayed picture".

3   Conclusion

In the present paper, a Pattern Neural Network, that performs face recognition in pictures has been described by a generalized net. Pictures had been processed into different preprocesses. A pattern neural network has been created and trained. Preprocessed pictures have been tested. The results show that the pattern neural network can recognize faces that have not been submitted to the neural network before the training process.

Acknowledgment. The authors are grateful for the support provided by the project DFNI-I-01/0006 "Simulating the behavior of forest and field fires", funded by the National Science Fund, Bulgarian Ministry of Education, Youth and Science.

References

1. Alsultanny, Y., Aqel, M.: Pattern recognition using multilayer neural-genetic algorithm, Computer Science Department, College of Computer and Information Technology, Applied Science University, P.O. Box17, Amman 11931, Jordan (2002)
2. Atanassov, K.: Generalized nets. World Scientific, Singapore (1991)
3. Atanassov, K.: On Generalized Nets Theory, "Prof. M. Drinov". Academic Publishing House, Sofia (2007)
4. Bishop, C.M.: Neural Network for pattern Recognition. Oxford University Press, Oxford (1995)
5. Cybenko, G.: Approximation by superpositions of a sigmoidal function. Mathematics of Control, Signals and Systems 2, 303–314 (1989)
6. Hagan, M., Demuth, H., Beale, M.: Neural Network Design. PWS Publishing, Boston (1996)
7. Haykin, S.: Neural Network – A Comprehensive foundation. Macmillan College Publication Company, New York (1994)
8. Hjelmas, E., Low, B.: Face Detection: A Survey. Computer Vision and Image Understanding 83, 236–274 (2001)
9. Lin, S., Kung, S.: Face Recognition/Detection by Probabilistic Decision-Based Neural Network. IEEE Transactions on Neural Networks 8, 114–132 (1997)
10. Oravec, M., Rozinaj, G., Beszédeš, M.: Detection and Recognition of Human Faces and Facial Features. In: Prasad, B., Prasanna, S.R.M. (eds.) Speech, Audio, Image and Biomedical Signal Processing using Neural Networks. SCI, vol. 83, pp. 283–301. Springer, Heidelberg (2008)
11. Petkov, T., Sotirov, S.: Generalized net model of the ART1 Neural Network. Annual of "Informatics" Section Union of Scientists in Bulgaria 6, 32–38 (2013)
12. Petkov, T., Sotirov, S.: Bio-inspired Artificial Intelligence: Generalized Net Model of the Cognitive and Neural Algorithm for Adaptive Resonance Theory 1. Int. Journal Bioautomation 17(4), 207–216 (2013)

13. Petkov, T., Surchev, S., Sotirov(2013) Generalized, S.: net model of the forest-fire detection with ART2 neural network. In: Proc. of Int. Workshop on Generalized Nets, IWGN 2013, Burgas, September 29-30, pp. 28–33 (2013)
14. Surchev, S., Sotirov, S.: Modeling verification processin neural network multilayer perceptron with generalized net. Annual of "Informatics" Section Union of Scientists in Bulgaria 6, 39–45 (2013)
15. Surchev, S., Sotirov, S., Korneta, W.: Bio-inspired Artificial Intelligence: A Generalized Net Model of the Regularization Process in MLP. Int. Journal Bioautomation 17(3), 151–158 (2013)
16. Widrow, B., Hoff, M.: Adaptive switching circuits. IRE WESCON Convention Record, pp. 96–104 (1960)
17. http://gps-tsc.upc.es/GTAV/ResearchAreas/UPCFaceDatabase/UPCDatabase.bmp

Adaptive Online Neural Network for Face Identification with Concept Drift

Mateusz Żarkowski

Chair of Cybernetics and Robotics,
Electronics Faculty, Wroclaw University of Technology
mateusz.zarkowski@pwr.edu.pl

Abstract. Social robots and agents operate in dynamic social environments where number of users as well as their individual features change over time. In order to be able to identify its users the robot should adapt to the ongoing changes continuously. This paper specifies the problem of concept drift for face identification and proposes a solution based on a modification of online neural network.

Keywords: machine learning, concept drift, neural network, face identification, social robot.

1 Introduction

Social environments are inherently dynamic, over time people change their features and preferences. In addition, some people can leave a social circle while others may enter. Current robotic systems operating in social environments rarely pay attention to these aspects, presenting rather on short-term solutions for arising machine learning tasks [5]. However, social robots interacting with people on daily basis should be aware of the ongoing changes and adapt their behavior appropriately, therefore, the systems designed for social robots should be equipped with this adaptive ability and provide the robot additional information about its environment. Such is the case of the face identification system presented in this paper.

2 Concept Drift in Face Identification

Presence of *concept drift* [12] describes the situation where statistical properties of the variable that the model is trying to predict can change over time, while *distribution change* indicates the change in data distribution (from practical standpoint both situations are similar, because both require to update the model [11]).

Classical machine learning approach fails here because with time the model becomes increasingly less accurate. While data mining techniques focus on improving the model on batch data of fixed-size, *data stream mining* involves potentially unlimited data source that evolves over time. This continuous data is

© Springer International Publishing Switzerland 2015
D. Filev et al. (eds.), *Intelligent Systems'2014*,
Advances in Intelligent Systems and Computing 323, DOI: 10.1007/978-3-319-11310-4_61

to be inspected by the model only once, at the time of the arrival, and then discarded for the next piece of data. The model can choose to store data at the expense of managing limited memory. The model can be used at any time between the samples.

The two approaches for modifying machine learning methods for data stream mining are wrapping and adaptation. Wrapping involves collecting current batches of data to train and employ existing algorithms allowing for easy reuse. The obvious downside is problems with memory and processing speed as batch sizes increase. On the other hand, adaptation prepares methods designed for data stream processing, allowing for better data control and memory management. Prominent classes of methods discussed in [2] are: decision trees and rules [4], nearest neighbor [8], support vector machines [3], neural networks [6], Bayesian [7] and ensemble methods [6]. Each providing their specific flaws and merits.

The evaluation methodology for data stream mining measures three aspects: memory, speed and accuracy, the goal being the minimization of the error in limited time and space. In practice, the algorithm should be able to perform on data stream in real time. The most common evaluation method used is *holdout*, dividing the data into training and test sets. Due to large data sizes (reaching even million samples) cross-validation is often omitted or reduced to 5 folds. The results are presented as plot of accuracy over time.

The problem of face identification in social robotics is an example of both distribution and concept drifts. Firstly, a person's appearance changes over time. This change can be gradual, as in getting older, or sudden, as changing clothes or getting a haircut. In both cases the robot should update its beliefs, so that they reflect the current state. this should allow the robot to still recognize its owners, even throughout long-term interaction. Secondly, people come and go. Some people interact with the robot on a regular basis and should be remembered well, while others only enter for a limited amount of time and should be forgotten afterwards to make place for new users. With this in mind, the adaptive face identification system was developed.

3   System Architecture

The system extends the idea proposed in [13]. The goal of this identification system is to provide additional information to the robot. With this knowledge the robot can personalize the nature of interaction as well as use it help other systems perform better, for example recognize emotions in the context of an individual person.

Figure 1 presents the overview of the proposed architecture. The system uses pre-processing to convert input images to a feature vector. The image is scanned to detect the position of the face and the face is transcribed to geometrical parameters, which are then subjected to feature extraction. The resulting feature set serves as an input for adaptive online neural network, which predicts the class and updates its beliefs. Moreover, the adaptive network detects changes in the incoming data and rebuilds itself to add new users and remove old ones.

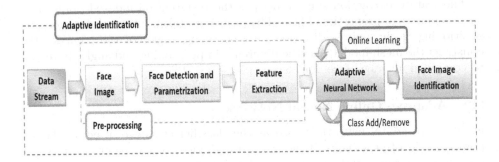

Fig. 1. The architecture of adaptive user identification system

3.1   Facial Image Detection and Feature Extraction

The first step of the image processing is face detection and tracking. This results in a set of parameters that describe the selected properties of an acquired face that are used for further analysis. The **FaceTracker** [9], [10] application performs face detection and tracking by iterative fitting of deformable 3D models of human face. Yielded model consists of 66 points and connections between them that envelop the important features of the face. The points and connections together form a three dimensional grid - a mesh. This model adapts to the face that it is tracking, taking into account such parameters as the positioning of eyebrows, mouth and jaw. The example of FaceTracker performance is shown in fig. 2. This fitting results in a set of points in a three dimensional space that describe the deformed model in its standardized orientation, the scale of the model and its orientation. The above parameters along with the description of the mesh connections are transferred to the next processing stage.

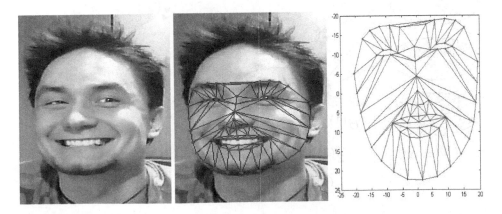

Fig. 2. Example of **FaceTracker** performance

The feature extraction stage processes the resulting 66 indexed points into 3087 geometrical properties of face. The properties taken into consideration are: positioning of the points, distance between them, angles of the triangles the construct the mesh model, also the difference in positioning and angles in regard to computed 'average' face. For details please see [13].

3.2   Adaptive Online Neural Network

Feedforward neural network is used as the classifier as shown in fig. 3, the superscripts denote the index of the layer, a is the activation vector of a layer, Θ represents neuron weigths matrix associated with each layer, $\hat{y}$ is the networks response to input vector x, and g is a sigmoid function defined as

$$g(t) = \frac{1}{1 + e^{-t}}. \tag{1}$$

The classical supervised learning approach updates the network parameters Θ over all training data, whereas, in the online learning case, we are forced to act on one example at a time, therefore the update will occur after each data sample (x, y), where x is the input vector and y is the expected output vector, then the sample will be discarded. In comparison with supervised learning, this process makes it harder for the network to reach the optimal solution, however, constant updates provide the possibility of adapting to the changes in the data.

The proposed cost function for classification includes the penalty for errors made and regularization factor to deal with overfitting

$$J(\Theta) = -[\sum_{k=1}^{K} y_k \log(h_\Theta(x))_k + (1 - y_k) \log(1 - h_\Theta(x))_k] + \sum_{l=1}^{L-1} \sum_{i=1}^{n(l+1)} \sum_{j=1}^{n(l)} \lambda \Theta_{ij}^{(l)2} \tag{2}$$

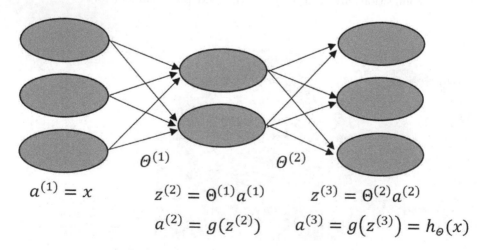

$$a^{(1)} = x$$

$$z^{(2)} = \Theta^{(1)} a^{(1)}$$

$$z^{(3)} = \Theta^{(2)} a^{(2)}$$

$$a^{(2)} = g(z^{(2)})$$

$$a^{(3)} = g(z^{(3)}) = h_\Theta(x)$$

Fig. 3. A sample feedforward neural network with one hidden layer

where K is the number of classes, $h_\Theta(x)$ means the networks response to feature input vector x, the subscripts denote the k-th coefficient. λ is the regularization factor, L is the total number of layers, $n(l)$ counts the number of nodes in layer l, $\Theta_{ij}^{(l)}$ is the proper coffictient of parameter matrix $\Theta^{(l)}$ corresponding to the layer l. By itself, Θ means all parameters.

The backpropagation algorithm calculates the error made in the last layer as

$$\delta^{(L)} = a^{(L)} - y \tag{3}$$

and in subsequent lower layers ($\delta^{(1)}$ does not to be computed)

$$\delta^{(l)} = \Theta^{(l)T}\delta^{(l+1)}. * g'(z^{(l)}). \tag{4}$$

The operator .$*$ stands for element-wise vector multiplication. The derivative g' can be written as

$$z^{(l)} = a^{(l)}. * (1 - a^{(l)}). \tag{5}$$

Then it can be shown that the partial derivative of the cost function needed for parameter learning is

$$\frac{\partial}{\partial \Theta_{ij}^{(l)}} J(\Theta) = a_j^{(l)} \delta_i^{(l+1)} + 2\lambda \Theta_{ij}^{(l)} \tag{6}$$

Each data sample allows for a cost minimizing step along with the descending gradient with learning factor α. The values of $\alpha = 0.04$ and $\lambda = 0.01$ were chosen according to previous study regarding problems of bias and overfitting [14].

The concept drift in data stream is managed in two ways. A new user should be detected and included in the system, which over time and with additional data will learn to recognize this user better. On the other hand, when a user stops interacting with the system for a prolonged period of time, the data concerning him should be removed to make the learning process faster and more suited to the currently active users.

This approach presents an adaptive approach that goes well with online neural network. The data is being processed in a stream, one sample at a time, and after each classification the correct output vector is provided. The new user is therefore detected by introducing himself to the system after initial misclassification. A new neural network output node is created for this user, by extending the last parameter matrix $\Theta^{(L-1)}$ by an additional row. Doing so introduces a new class, but preserves the former knowledge of the system. Contrary to the 'wrapper' approach (repeating the learning process) the adaptive method is computationally faster (re-learning takes time), results in smooth transition and takes less memory (does not need to store previous data). Its downside is of course the need for further data samples to learn the profile of a new user.

The detection of an inactive user can be done in various ways. The user can be removed after a certain amount of time has passed or some external event took place (i.e. the social robot left a social circle). In the experiments presented in this paper, the user was declared inactive if for $C \times 10$ iterations (C - number of users currently recognizable by the system) has not been seen in the data stream. The resulting action is a deletion of the inactive user by removing a corresponding row in the last parameter matrix $\Theta^{(L-1)}$.

4   Experiments

The data stream was created from randomized real data samples. The experiments portray the reaction of the system to different concept drift patterns.

4.1   Data Stream

Creating a data stream of an appropriate size (at least couple hundreds of samples per person) was not possible due to the lack of a database of such magnitude. MUG facial expression database [1] was used after a proper formatting. The database contains frontal face images for more than 50 people aged 20-35 years. The experiments were conducted on emotion-neutral facial expressions. Images of 20 people were selected, each person providing 20 data samples, resulting in a total of 400 samples of 20 classes. We simulate the data stream by randomly selecting a sample from the training data of specific concept each time it is needed. The classification rate is measured as a proportion of correctly classified samples to the total number of samples of the holdout test data that is set apart from the training data stream. This holdout test data consist of data accurate to the current concept, that means if the concept changes (people are added or removed), so does the test data used for evaluation.

4.2   Reaction to Concept Drift

The system's behavior was measured in following conditions: gradual/sudden concept change and small (7 nodes)/large (15 nodes) neural network hidden layer size. The size of hidden layer indicates the internal complexity of neural network, by artificially reducing the network size we simulate high bias conditions of too many classes that could occur in real system application with high number of users. It should provide an estimate of how many users the network can handle simultaneously, as well as, how this bias can inhibit the process of rebuilding the network itself during adaptation.

Gradual change is simulated by slowly adding new users to the data stream, then removing old users. Since the whole available data set consists of twenty people we divide them into 4 groups of five people. We introduce each group sequentially until all 4 groups are in, then start removing the groups from the oldest. The groups are numbered 1 through 4, which results in seven phases simulating concept drift: 1, 12, 123, 1234, 234, 34, 4. Each change will occur after 5000 iterations. The results are shown in fig. 4. As additional people join, new classes are added to the network and adaptation becomes harder and takes longer. As people leave, the network detects it and deletes the obsolete users,

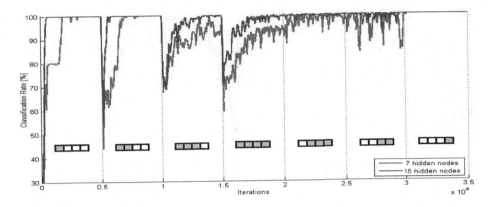

Fig. 4. Response to gradual concept drift of small and large adaptive neural network. Black boxes show data division, green color marks data used in specific concept.

which in turns brings an improvement in performance. The difference in performance between the small and large network are significant. Firstly, the adaptation is notably slower. Secondly, with all 20 users present, the system is unable to grasp and identify them all. Thirdly, the occasional errors in user removing stages are greater. Both networks perform well in the last segment where the number of users drops back to 5.

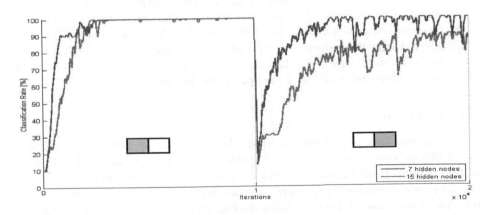

Fig. 5. Response to sudden concept shift of small and large adaptive neural network. Black boxes show data division, green color marks data used in specific concept.

Sudden change is modeled through abrupt change in data. Now the database is divided into 2 groups of ten people. This time the two phases are: 1, 2. Note that the groups are completely disjoint. Change will occur after 10000 iterations. Fig. 5 shows the performance. The first phase is similar to before, but the second

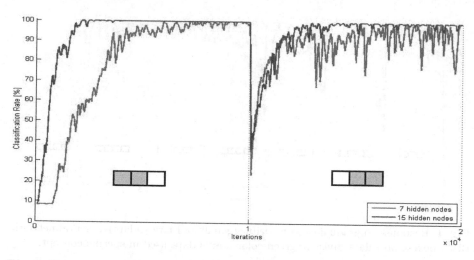

Fig. 6. Response to sudden concept shift with shared data of small and large adaptive neural network. Black boxes show data division, green color marks data used in specific concept.

phase offers some insight. Both networks perform worse now than in the previous experiment with gradual change and ten people, and, the performance of the small network decreased significantly. Moreover, the learning speed is even slower in the second phase, than at the beggining – the prior training has a negative effect on the performance and adaptation capabilities later! It seems that discarding the network and starting from scratch would bring better results.

As a comparison, a similar case but with some shared data was tested. Division of data is into 3 groups of sizes: 8, 4, 8 people. The middle group is shared through the concept change, phases are: 12, 23. As shown in fig. 6, this small amount of shared data allows to avoid the issues presented in the example before.

4.3   Discussion

Several regularities were observed. First, obviously a larger network has a lower possibility to pose problems of bias. A small hidden layer can inhibit the network from rebuilding itself and cause additional issues in future use. This internal layer should have a size chosen accordingly to maximum number of the simultaneously handled classes (users). Second, when dealing with the abrupt change of classes, it may be better to reset the network, in order to avoid outdated preconceptions. Third, the data shared between the concept may serve as to shape the network for new data – speed up the learning process and reduce errors (cf. fig. 5 and 6).

5   Conclusion

A design for an adaptive online neural network for face recognition with concept drift was presented and verified experimentally. A simple modification allows for reshaping the network by adding and removing users as needed. The system operates correctly providing a new functionality for a social robot. This approach can be easily extended to resolve other problems that need adaptive solutions. While usually data stream mining algorithms deal with data of under 10 features, the approach presented here was able to successfully perform with over 3000 features.

The main issue of this method is the assumption of ground truths provided with each incoming example. Additional information about the user (like clothing, voice, behavior) may help in identification. Using a multimodal approach, the systems could learn by providing ground truths for each other.

While the implementation in neural network utilizes little memory and performs acceptably fast, likely, a better solution exists. Decision trees and ensemble methods are likely to outperform this approach and will be verified.

Acknowledgments. This research was supported by Wroclaw University of Technology under a statutory research project.

References

1. Aifanti, N., Papachristou, C., Delopoulos, A.: The mug facial expression database. In: 11th Int. Workshop on Image Analysis for Multimedia Interactive Services, Desenzano, Italy (2010)
2. Bifet, A., Kirkby, R.: Data stream mining: a practical approach. Tech. rep., The University of Waikato (2009)
3. Burges, C.: A tutorial on support vector machines for pattern recognition. Data Mining and Knowledge Discovery 2(2), 121–167 (1998)
4. Domingos, P., Hulten, G.: Mining high-speed data streams. In: Proceedings of the Sixth ACM SIGKDD International Conference on Knowledge Discovery and Data Mining, KDD 2000, pp. 71–80. ACM, New York (2000)
5. Fong, T., Nourbakhsh, I., Dautenhahn, K.: A survey of socially interactive robots. Robotics and Autonomous Systems 42(3-4), 143–166 (2003), socially Interactive Robots
6. Gama, J., Rodrigues, P.P.: Stream-based electricity load forecast. In: Kok, J.N., Koronacki, J., Lopez de Mantaras, R., Matwin, S., Mladenič, D., Skowron, A. (eds.) PKDD 2007. LNCS (LNAI), vol. 4702, pp. 446–453. Springer, Heidelberg (2007)
7. Hulten, G., Domingos, P.: Mining complex models from arbitrarily large databases in constant time. In: Proceedings of the Eighth ACM SIGKDD International Conference on Knowledge Discovery and Data Mining, KDD 2002, pp. 525–531. ACM, New York (2002)
8. Law, Y.N., Zaniolo, C.: An adaptive nearest neighbor classification algorithm for data streams. In: Jorge, A.M., Torgo, L., Brazdil, P.B., Camacho, R., Gama, J. (eds.) PKDD 2005. LNCS (LNAI), vol. 3721, pp. 108–120. Springer, Heidelberg (2005)
9. Saragih, J., Lucey, S., Cohn, J.: Face alignment through subspace constrained mean-shifts. In: ICCV, pp. 1034–1041 (2009)
10. Saragih, J., Lucey, S., Cohn, J.: Deformable model fitting by regularized landmark mean-shift. International Journal of Computer Vision 91(2), 200–215 (2011)

11. Stanley, K.O.: Learning concept drift with a committee of decision trees. Tech. Rep. AI03-302, Department of Computer Sciences, The University of Texas at Austin (2003)
12. Tsymbal, A.: The problem of concept drift: Definitions and related work. Tech. rep. (2004)
13. Zarkowski, M.: Identification-driven emotion recognition system for a social robot. In: 18th International Conference on Methods & Models in Automation & Robotics, MMAR 2013, pp. 138–143 (2013)
14. Zarkowski, M.: Adaptive face identification for small-scale social dynamic environment. In: 19th International Conference on Methods & Models in Automation & Robotics, MMAR (in print, 2014)

Fuzzy System Optimization Using a Hierarchical Genetic Algorithm Applied to Pattern Recognition

Daniela Sánchez, Patricia Melin, and Oscar Castillo

Tijuana Institute of Technology
danielasanchez.itt@hotmail.com, {pmelin,ocastillo}@tectijuana.mx

Abstract. In this paper a new method of hierarchical genetic algorithm for fuzzy inference systems optimization is proposed. This method was used to perform the combination of responses of modular neural networks for human recognition based on face, iris, ear and voice. The main idea of this paper is to perform the optimization of some parameters of fuzzy inference system, such as: type of fuzzy logic, type of system, number of fuzzy membership function in each variable, percentage of rules, type of membership functions (Trapezoidal or Gaussian) and parameters The results obtained using the hierarchical genetic algorithm show to have better results than non-optimized fuzzy inference as can be verified with the results.

1 Introduction

The use of different intelligent techniques have demonstrated to produce powerful hybrid intelligent systems. There are many works where have been used some of those techniques and they have obtained good results [14][19][24]. In this paper different intelligent techniques are combined such as neural networks, type-1 and type-2 fuzzy logic and genetic algorithms. The proposed method was applied to human recognition based on face, iris, ear and voice [16][17]. Results non-optimized and optimized are compared to show the advantage of the proposed method.

This paper is organized as follows: The basic concepts used in this work are presented in Section 2. Section 3 contains the general architecture of the proposed method. Section 4 presents experimental results for human recognition and fuzzy control and in Section 5, the conclusions of this work are presented.

2 Basic Concepts

In this section the basic concepts used in this research work are presented.

2.1 Modular Neural Networks

An artificial neural network (ANN) is an information-processing system that has certain performance characteristics in common with biological neural networks [13].

© Springer International Publishing Switzerland 2015
D. Filev et al. (eds.), *Intelligent Systems'2014*,
Advances in Intelligent Systems and Computing 323, DOI: 10.1007/978-3-319-11310-4_62

A trained neural network can be thought of as an "expert" in the category of information it has been given to analyze [1]. The concept of modularity is an extension of the principle of divide and conquer. There is evidence that shows that the use of modular neural networks implies a significant learning improvement comparatively to a single neural network [20].

2.2 Fuzzy Logic

Fuzzy logic is an area of soft computing that enables a computer system to reason with uncertainty [2][3][4][5]. The concept of a type-2 fuzzy set, was introduced by Zadeh (1975) as an extension of the concept of an ordinary fuzzy set (henceforth called a "type-1 fuzzy set"). When we cannot determine the membership of an element in a set as 0 or 1, we use fuzzy sets of type-1. When the situation is so fuzzy that we have trouble determining the membership grade even as a crisp number in [0,1], [6][7][8][25].

2.3 Hierarchical Genetic Algorithms

A Genetic Algorithm (GA) is an optimization and search technique based on the principles of genetics and natural selection where the fittest individuals survive [9][15][18][21][22][23].

Introduced in [26], a Hierarchical genetic algorithm (HGA) is a type of genetic algorithm. Its structure is more flexible than the conventional GA. The basic idea under hierarchical genetic algorithm is that for some complex systems, which cannot be easily represented, this type of GA can be a better choice. The complicated chromosomes may provide a good new way to solve the problem [27][28].

3   Proposed Method

The proposed hierarchical genetic algorithm performs the optimization of fuzzy inference systems. In this paper, the human recognition based on face, iris, ear and voice was used to test the proposed method

The main idea of the proposed method is to perform the optimization of fuzzy inference systems that allow us to have a better results that fuzzy inference systems non-optimized. In this work some parameters of these fuzzy inference systems such as the type of fuzzy logic, type of system (Mamdani or Sugeno), type of membership functions (Trapezoidal or Gaussian), percentage of rules, the number of membership functions of each variable and their parameters are optimized. The chromosome of the proposed hierarchical genetic algorithm is shown in Figure 1.

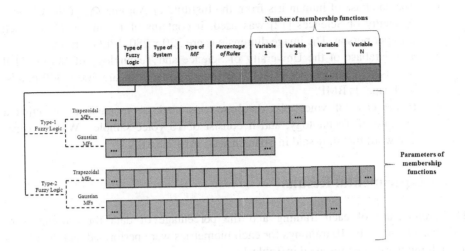

Fig. 1. The chromosome of the hierarchical genetic algorithm for the fuzzy inference systems

The number of inputs will depend of the number of biometric measures that are being used, here, the responses of each biometric measure are combined by the fuzzy inference systems. In Figure 2, an example of fuzzy integrator for this application is shown. Each input corresponds to one biometric measure, and the output corresponds to the final answer.

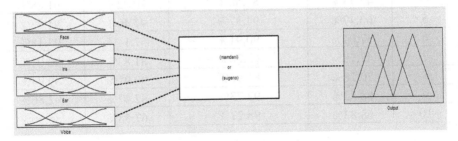

Fig. 2. example of the fuzzy integrator

3.1   Databases

The human recognition of 77 persons is performed in this work, for this reason, only 77 persons of each database were taken to perform the recognition. The databases used are described below:

- The database of face from the Institute of Automation of the Chinese Academy of Sciences [11] was used. It contains of 5 images per person. The image dimensions are 640 x 480, BMP format.

- The database of human iris from the Institute of Automation of the Chinese Academy of Sciences [12] was used. It contains of 14 images (7 for each eye) per person. The image dimensions are 320 x 280, JPEG format.
- The database of the University of Science and Technology of Beijing [10] was used. 4 images per person, the image dimensions are 300 x 400 pixels, the format is BMP.
- In the case of voice, the database was made from students of Tijuana Institute of Technology, and it consist of 10 voice samples, WAV format. The word that they said in Spanish was "ACCESAR".

4   Experimental Results

The architecture of each training and the percentage of data for training were established randomly. 10 trainings for each biometrics were performed and the results of each biometric are presented in Table 1.

Table 1. The results of each biometric measure

Training	Face	Iris	Ear	Voice
1	87.01%	79.10%	94.81%	87.79%
2	85.71%	81.82%	77.92%	91.77%
3	52.92%	96.10%	96.10%	90.17%
4	45.78%	82.58%	79.22%	91.88%
5	60.17%	94.37%	97.40%	91.23%
6	37.01%	90.91%	57.14%	93.18%
7	47.19%	63.20%	81.82%	90.04%
8	70.78%	84.96%	90.91%	89.94%
9	68.83%	92.73%	82.47%	92.86%
10	68.83%	98.27%	67.53%	86.36%

4.1   Non-optimized Fuzzy Integration

Different trainings were combined and 5 cases were performed. One non-optimized fuzzy integrator is used to compare with the optimization. The Type-1 fuzzy inference system is Mamdani type and have 3 trapezoidal membership functions in each variable (inputs and output). The result for each case are shown in column 7 in Table 2.

Table 2. Non-Optimized Results

Case	Face	Iris	Ear	Voice	Non-Optimized Type-1
1	FT4 45.78%	IT5 98.27%	ET5 82.47%	VT2 91.88%	87.01
2	FT1 87.01%	IT4 63.20%	ET2 77.92%	VT1 91.77%	83.33
3	FT2 85.71%	IT2 96.10%	ET4 97.40%	VT5 93.18%	81.17
4	FT6 37.01%	IT7 63.20%	ET6 57.14%	VT10 86.36%	62.01
5	FT4 45.78%	IT7 63.20%	ET9 82.47%	VT4 91.88%	71.32

4.2   Optimized Fuzzy Integration

30 evolutions for each case were performed. The number of times of each type of fuzzy logic was better than each other, the best results and the averages are shown in Table 3.

Table 3. Optimized Results

Case	Type-1 Fuzzy Logic			Type-2 Fuzzy Logic		
	Num. of evolutions	Best	Average	Num. of evolutions	Best	Average
1	19	99.35%	98.70%	11	99.03%	98.29%
2	0	0%	0%	30	92.42%	90.35%
3	19	100%	97.80%	11	100%	97.58%
4	7	69.26%	64.66%	23	86.47%	81.05%
5	6	93.83%	90.08%	24	95.89%	93.57%

In Figure 3, the best fuzzy integrator for the case #1 is shown, it is a fuzzy integrator of Sugeno type, and with Gaussian Membership Functions with 20 rules. In Figure 4, the best fuzzy integrator for the case #4 is shown, it is a fuzzy integrator of Mamdani type, and with trapezoidal Membership Functions with 62 rules.

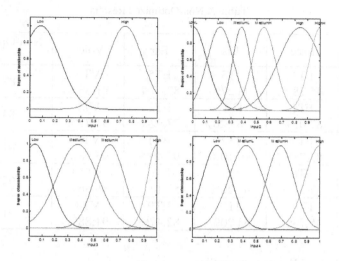

Fig. 3. The best fuzzy integrator for the case #1

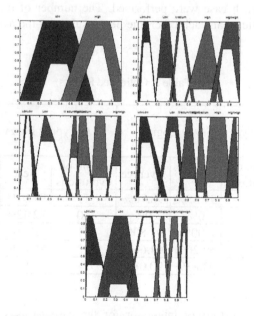

Fig. 4. The best fuzzy integrator for the case #4

5   Conclusions

In this work a new hierarchical genetic algorithm was presented, the main idea of this HGA is to perform the optimization of fuzzy systems. For this reason the optimization of some parameters was performed (type of fuzzy logic, type of system, type of membership functions (Trapezoidal or Gaussian), percentage of rules, the number of membership functions and their parameters). Results can prove than better results are obtained when a optimization is performed. The advantage of performing the optimization of type of fuzzy logic is depending on the complexity of the problem the type of fuzzy logic is chosen by the HGA, as the results can prove, when almost all the biometric measures have a good results (more than 80 percentage of recognition), type-1 fuzzy logic is more times selected as the winner, and when the percentage of two or more biometric measures is less than 80 percentage of recognition, type-2 fuzzy logic has a better performance. In this work, the objective function was the minimization of the error of recognition. In the future, the combination of membership functions in a same variable will be implemented, waiting of obtaining better results.

References

1. Azamm, F.: Biologically Inspired Modular Neural Networks. PhD thesis, Virginia Polytechnic Institute and State University, Blacksburg, Virginia (May 2000)
2. Castillo, O., Melin, P., Alanis Garza, A., Montiel, O., Sepúlveda, R.: Optimization of interval type-2 fuzzy logic controllers using evolutionary algorithms. Soft Comput. 15(6), 1145–1160 (2011)
3. Castillo, O., Melin, P., Pedrycz, W.: Design of interval type-2 fuzzy models through optimal granularity allocation. Appl. Soft Comput. 11(8), 5590–5601 (2011)
4. Castillo, O., Melin, P.: 3 Type-2 Fuzzy Logic. In: Castillo, O., Melin, P. Type-2 Fuzzy Logic Theory and Applications. STUDFUZZ, vol. 223, pp. 29–43. Springer, Heidelberg (2008)
5. Castillo, O., Melin, P.: Soft Computing for Control of Non-Linear Dynamical Systems. STUDFUZZ, vol. 63. Springer, Heidelberg (2001)
6. Castro, J.R., Castillo, O., Melin, P., Rodríguez Díaz, A.: A hybrid learning algorithm for a class of interval type-2 fuzzy neural networks. Inf. Sci. 179(13), 2175–2193 (2009)
7. Castro, J.R., Castillo, O., Melin, P.: An Interval Type-2 Fuzzy Logic Toolbox for Control Applications. In: FUZZ-IEEE 2007, pp. 1–6 (2007)
8. Castro, J.R., Castillo, O., Melin, P., Rodriguez-Diaz, A.: Building Fuzzy Inference Systems with a New Interval Type-2 Fuzzy Logic Toolbox. Transactions on Computational Science 1, 104–114 (2008)
9. Coley, A.: An Introduction to Genetic Algorithms for Scientists and Engineers, Har/Dskt edn. Wspc (1999)
10. Database Ear Recognition Laboratory from the University of Science & Technology Beijing (USTB). Found on the Web page, http://www.ustb.edu.cn/resb/en/index.htmasp (accessed September 21, 2009)
11. Database of Face. Institute of Automation of Chinese Academy of Sciences (CASIA). Found on the Web page, http://biometrics.idealtest.org/dbDetailForUser.do?id=9 (accessed November 11, 2012)
12. Database of Human Iris. Institute of Automation of Chinese Academy of Sciences (CASIA). Found on the Web page, http://www.cbsr.ia.ac.cn/english/IrisDatabase.asp (accessed September 21, 2009)
13. Fausett, L.: Fundamentals of Neural Networks Architectures Algorithms and Applications. Prentice Hall (1994)

14. Gaxiola, F., Melin, P., Valdez, F., Castillo, O.: Optimization of type-2 fuzzy weight for neural network using genetic algorithm and particle swarm optimization. In: NaBIC 2013, pp. 22–28 (2013)
15. Haupt, R., Haupt, S.: Practical Genetic Algorithms, vol. 2, pp. 42–43. Wiley-Interscience (2004)
16. Hidalgo, D., Castillo, O., Melin, P.: Type-1 and type-2 fuzzy inference systems as integration methods in modular neural networks for multimodal biometry and its optimization with genetic algorithms. Inf. Sci. 179(13), 2123–2145 (2009)
17. Hidalgo, D., Melin, P., Castillo, O.: An optimization method for designing type-2 fuzzy inference systems based on the footprint of uncertainty using genetic algorithms. Expert Syst. Appl. 39(4), 4590–4598 (2012)
18. Huang, J., Wechsler, H.: Eye Location Using Genetic Algorithm. In: Second International Conferenceon Audio and Video-Based Biometric Person Authentication, pp. 130–135 (1999)
19. Martínez-Soto, R., Castillo, O., Aguilar, L.T.: Optimization of interval type-2 fuzzy logic controllers for a perturbed autonomous wheeled mobile robot using genetic algorithms. Inf. Sci. 179(13), 2158–2174 (2009)
20. Melin, P., Castillo, O.: Hybrid Intelligent Systems for Pattern Recognition Using Soft Computing: An Evolutionary Approach for Neural Networks and Fuzzy Systems, 1st edn. STUDFUZZ, vol. 172, pp. 119–122. Springer, Heidelberg (2005)
21. Mitchell, M.: An Introduction to Genetic Algorithms, 3rd edn. A Bradford Book (1998)
22. Nawa, N., Takeshi, F., Hashiyama, T., Uchikawa, Y.: A study on the discovery of relevant fuzzy rules using pseudobacterial genetic algorithm. IEEE Transactions on Industrial Electronics 46(6), 1080–1089 (1999)
23. Raikova, R.T., Aladjov, H.T.: Hierarchical genetic algorithm versus static optimization investigation of elbow flexion and extension movements. Journal of Biomechanics 35, 1123–1135 (2002)
24. Sánchez, D., Melin, P.: Optimization of modular granular neural networks using hierarchical genetic algorithms for human recognition using the ear biometric measure. Engineering Applications of Artificial Intelligence 27, 41–56 (2014)
25. Sepúlveda, R., Melin, P., Rodríguez Díaz, A., Mancilla, A., Montiel, O.: Analyzing the effects of the Footprint of Uncertainty in Type-2 Fuzzy Logic Controllers. Engineering Letters 13(2), 138–147 (2006)
26. Tang, K.S., Man, K.F., Kwong, S., Liu, Z.F.: Minimal Fuzzy Memberships and Rule Using Hierarchical Genetic Algorithms. IEEE Trans. Ind. Electron. 45(1), 162–169 (1998)
27. Wang, C., Soh, Y.C., Wang, H., Wang, H.: A Hierarchical Genetic Algorithm for Path Planning in a Static Environment with Obstacles. In: Canadian Conference on Electrical and Computer Engineering, IEEE CCECE 2002, vol. 3, pp. 1652–1657 (2002)
28. Worapradya, K., Pratishthananda, S.: Fuzzy supervisory PI controller using hierarchical genetic algorithms. In: 5th Asian Control Conference 2004, vol. 3, pp. 1523–1528 (2004)

A Proposed Hybrid Sensor Architecture for Arabic Sign Language Recognition

Menna ElBadawy, A. Samir Elons, Hwaida Sheded, and Mohamed F. Tolba

{Menna-elbadawy,ahmed.new80}@hotmail.com,
Dr_howida@yahoo.com, fahmytolba@gmail.com

Abstract. Sign language recognition is a promising application that breaks the barrier between deaf and normal people. However most researchers in different sign language recognition systems employ a single type of sensors to capture signs. In this paper, hybrid heterogeneous types of sensors are integrated to capture all sign features. Leap motion which is recently available, is customized to capture hands and fingers movements. Two digital cameras are used to capture facial expressions and body movement. The system accomplished 95% recognition accuracy for a dataset consists of 20 dynamic signs due to the additional modules for facial expressions recognition and body movement recognition.

Keywords: Arabic Sign Language, Sensors, Leap motion, Artificial Neural Network.

1   Introduction

People with disabilities meet barriers of all types. However, technological capabilities reduce many simple barriers. By using computing technology for tasks such as reading and writing documents, communicating with others, and searching for information on the Internet, students and employees with disabilities are capable of handling a wider range of activities independently.

A gesture is a form of non-verbal communication made with part of the body and used instead of verbal communication (or in combination with it). Most people use gestures and body language in addition to words when they speak. A sign language is a language which uses gestures instead of sound to convey meaning combining hand-shapes, orientation and movement of the hands, arms or body, facial expressions and lip-patterns. Due to the need of both normal and impaired hearing people, researchers started to explore the automation for the translation process between natural language and sign language.

In the past few years, many researches and proposed methods were developed to recognize the sign language. The main function in the sign language recognition process is to recognize the gestures and translate them to text or speech.

Sign language recognition is evolving with the appearance of different technologies and sensors to capture the signs. Different sensors control both the sign capturing and modeling.

© Springer International Publishing Switzerland 2015
D. Filev et al. (eds.), *Intelligent Systems' 2014*,
Advances in Intelligent Systems and Computing 323, DOI: 10.1007/978-3-319-11310-4_63

In the recent few years, the input data was driven from multiple sensors, such as data glove, digital camera, modern sensors like depth cameras, kinect and leap motion.

Although, each sensor has its own limitation and strength yet most of the researchers used only one type of these sensors to capture the input signs. Few research trials have explored using different types of sensors in the same time but without a clear vision of each sensor role.

In this paper, a hybrid sensors based architecture is proposed for Arabic sign language recognition. The first sensor is: two digital cameras, one is very close to face to capture the facial expressions and the second is far enough to capture body language. The second sensor is: Leap motion used to capture the two hands motion. Although the scientific understanding for the sign language is an essential step for building a realistic recognition system, the idea of customizing multiple sensors to can be exploited in other sign languages.

2   Literature Review

A lot of researchers discussed the gesture recognition and found that the accuracy of the recognition system doesn't rely only the architecture or the followed algorithm, but also on the input date.

2.1   2D Sensors

2D modeling is perspective based, that is, where 2D image data is captured from a single camera's point of view. Image segmentation and manipulation algorithms are used to extract information from the image. This information is used to classify the gesture. Grobel and Assam achieve a classification rate of 91.3% by extracting features from a video of signers wearing colored gloves [1]. The colored gloves made segmenting and extracting the hands' position and shape more robust. 2D modeling techniques rely on computer vision algorithms to extract information of a gesture, rather than using specialized equipment. Computer vision based techniques use a camera and image manipulation algorithms to interpret gestures. This provides a more natural way of interactions between the system and user [2]. The process of finding and analyzing hand postures in cluttered images is extremely complex and troublesome. This has led to the development of methods involving wearing colored markers or colored gloves on the hands and restricting the background of the video. The wearing of extra equipment and restricting the background, of the video are widely acknowledged limitations of computer vision based techniques.

2.2   3D Sensors

3D modeling entails capturing a gesture or sign in a three-dimensional space [3]. Data gloves have been widely used to track the 3D movement of hands, Fig 1[4]. It uses an array of sensors fitted to the gloves that the user wears. The sensors are able to record information such as hand shape, hand orientation, hand global position and hand velocity. A pinch glove was used by Kim and Waldron to obtain a sequence of 3D positions of a hand's trajectory [5-8]. The sequential data obtained from the data gloves is used to classify the gesture. Kim and Waldron were able to achieve a GR accuracy of 86% using the pinch glove. 3DV systems have developed an image sensor which is capable of producing RGBD signals, where R stands for red, G for green, B for blue and D stands for the distance of each pixel relative to the camera's position [9-11]. This makes it possible to track hand movements in 3D without the signer having to wear data-gloves.

Fig. 1. Datagloves a-Virtual Technologies Cybergloves b-5Thwirlessdataglc [12]

While still under development 3DV systems [13, 14] let Fujimura and Liu develop a GR system for the Japanese Sign Language (JSL) [14, 15]. Fujimura and Liu use the information captured by 3DV system's image sensor to classify JSL. Depth information is displayed in an image produced by the camera. Dark regions denote objects that are far away from the camera with lighter regions describing objects that are closer. An example of an image produced by the 3DV system's camera is shown in Fig 2.

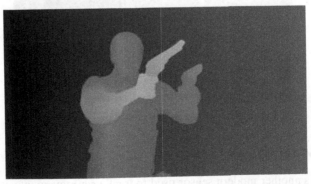

Fig. 2. An example of an image containing depth information produced by the 3DV system's camera. Lighter areas are closer to the camera

2.3   Kinect and Depth Cameras Module

Microsoft Kinect is a modern sensor which can be used to obtain real time video with depth information. It provides skeletal movements of the user and recognizes its 3D body motion, through an inexpensive, easy to use, and real time sensor. Kinect recognizes not only hands of the user, but also other body parts that could be useful information for the recognition of the closed signs in the system. Also the sensor data is independent of light conditions, as it detects the object through infrared light with no need to wear special gloves or any other equipment. Kinect is used to collect the input data consists of 10 sign language symbols drawn using right hand of 17 participants. The produced images are 256x256 grayscale depth images with a rate of ten frames per second. After preparing the data by eliminating the background, tracking the hands only position in the image, and scaling down the tracked hands to 32x32 pixels, two Artificial Neural Networks (ANN) are used. The first ANN used is the Random forests network [14], with each pixel in the 32x32 image regarded as a feature. Although it facilitates body and hands tracking and creates the depth image directly, it does not support hand shape recognition, and since sign language generally features different hand-shapes, similar signs cannot be distinguished. Our team in the proof of concept stage has gathered some videos using kinect, the hand fingers movement can't be recognized even with human eyes. Our findings are supported by Microsoft announcement that Kinect will not support sign language recognition "http://www.1up.com/news/kinect-cant-read-sign-language", Figure. 3 illustrates some images of the gathered data.

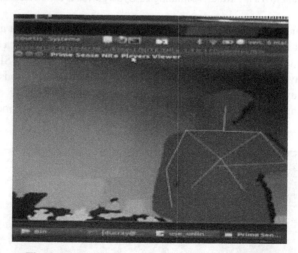

Fig. 3. Kinect images in sign language recognition

2.4   Leap Motion Module

Leap Motion is another modern sensor used to track user movements, it is regarded as the most easy to use and handy in everyday situation due to its small size and low cost Fig 4. Unlike Kinect, it tracks the hand movements only, also it has the ability to distinguish the fingers' joints and track their movements, and this information is supported by Leap Motion Vendors "https://www.leapmotion.com". Although the Kinect produces information about other body parts that helps distinguish the closed signs, but it lacks the detail about the hand's fingers. Leap motion tracking data is a series of snapshots called frames; each frame contains the measured positions, velocities, and other information about the detected fingers. Such information is promising and could be useful in the recognition area.

Fig. 4. Leap Motion Device

3   Proposed System

This section presents an Arabic sign language recognition system that uses leap motion and digital cameras to capture hands, facial expressions and body movements.

Figure 5 illustrates the capturing process and positions of each sensor relative to the signer.

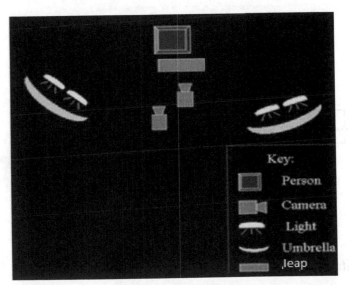

Fig. 5. Capturing lab

The closer camera captures the facial expressions which mainly vary among "Sad", "Happy" and "Normal". This camera must be close enough to the face and neglects any body movement or hand signs. The digital cameras require a uniform light distribution on hands and face.

The capture frame rate is a key factor in further steps, researchers on different sign languages tried different frame rates varying from 5 frames up to 50 frames per second. Low frame rate may cause sign features loss while high frame rate requires a potential computational power and consumes time to analyze insignificant transition movements. In the proposed system, 30 frames per second are chosen such that it preserves the sign features and neglects transitions.

The recognition system is illustrated in Fig 6, starting from input capturing passing through synchronization, features extraction [15-17], recognition ending [18] with post processing module.

The input synchronization is responsible for time management between heterogeneous sensors such that at a given point in time, the system captures the simultaneous movement and shape of hands, face and body. After that an Artificial Neural Network (ANN) is employed to both feature extraction and classification [19, 20] for static postures.

After the discrete static postures are classified, they are recollected and combined to form a complete dynamic gesture (sign). Obviously due to environment and external factors, the recognition accuracy degrades with any slight change. A post processing module based on Natural Language Processing rules and sign language understanding is proposed to detect and correct expected errors resulting from the recognition system.

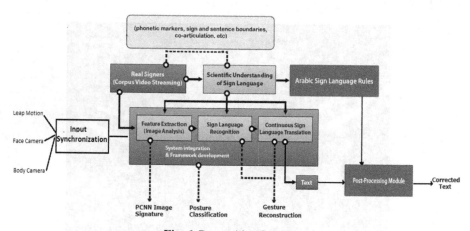

Fig. 6. Recognition System

4   Data Specification

The synchronization module is developed to present a start and an end for the input signs from all input sensors. The input sensors are all connected to a master computer with an application that initiates the sensors and stops them is published. The drivers for all sensors are setup on this computer.

For the cameras which are responsible for capturing body and facial expressions, a very essential issue must be addressed: frame rate. Very low frame rate can cause significant data loss and high frame rate causes redundancy and requires a heavy computational power. The experiment was conducted using different frame rates; 5, 10, 30 and 50 frames per second.

Since the ArSL alphabets are mostly static postures by nature, a chosen dataset consists of 20 dynamic signs is used. Table 1 illustrates the dataset which the experiment has been conducted on.

Table 1. Dataset used in the system

Arabic	English
امام	Front
بعيد	Far
بجانب	Beside
ياكل	Eating
يشرب	Drinking
يساعد	Helping
باب	Door
بيت	Home
ارض	Ground
رياح	Wind
سماء	Sky
انتخابات	Elections
جواز	Marriage
طلاق	Divorce
نقود	Money
يتسوق	Shopping
زر	Button
ملف	File
نقل	Move
اسد	Lion

One issue that has also been addressed in data collection is the difference between left handed and right handed people. This issue caused duplication in the dataset such that Leap motion tracks the fingers' movements in both hands. This has been resolved by performing the signs using 2 different people; one is left-handed and the other is right handed.

To determine the essential facial expressions that differentiate the signs' meanings, a study has been conducted based on 200 signs. This study concluded 5 basic facial expressions: happy, sad, normal, surprised, and looking-up. For each facial expression, 10 captured images have been prepared; 6 as a training set and 4 as a test set.

The body movement tracking is mainly concerned with both hands positions against the body and shoulders movements. The hands positions are collected and arranged as 16 different positions (4 positions for each hand). The shoulders movements are 5 movements (left shoulder up-right shoulder up- left shoulder front-right shoulder front-normal).

5   Experimental Results

The results were collected based on 2 layers:

1. Each recognition module separately (hands recognition, facial expressions recognition and body movement recognition).
2. An integrated sign recognition module.

The hand signs module is based on MLP network to classify the leap motion input sequence. The training set consists of 40 sequences (20 words each for 2 people) and the test set consists of 40 different sequences for the same signs.

MPL specifications are: The weights were updated after each pattern presentation. The learning rate and momentum were 0.2 and 0.1 respectively. 1 hidden layer has been used and Sigmoid Activation function was used. The network has been trained using the Back-Propagation algorithm and was trained until the mean square error between the network output and desired output falls below 0.1. The recognition accuracy reached 90%. The classifier fails to distinguish between 2 signs "marriage" and "divorce" as the 2 signs are performed identically by hands. Also, it failed to distingue between "Beside" and "Far" as they are identical in hands movements but are different in hand positions relative to the body.

The facial expressions module is based on a PCA network followed by an MLP network. The PCA network is customized to extract features and the MLP as classifier step.

For 5 facial expressions with a total of 20 images as a test set, the best accuracy obtained was 90% with the following parameters:

1. 735 principle components were used (15% of the main image dimensions- the original images 70X70).
2. LP learning rate 0.05 and momentum 0.09 and 1 hidden layer with 30 node.
   The source of error was the lighting conditions which caused nonobvious facial details.

For the body movement's classifier, PCA and MLP were used with the following parameters:

1. 1600 principle components were used (16% of the main image dimensions- the original images 100X100).
2. MLP network learning rate 0.07 and momentum 0.1 and 1 hidden layer with 35 nodes.

The recognition accuracy reached 86% and the error source was the relatively long capturing distance.

The integrated sign testing was conducted on the 20 dynamic signs for 2 different people. The hand sign module runs first and if a confusion between 2 signs has been detected, facial expressions and body movement modules are fired to resolve the confusion. The recognition accuracy reached 95% (2 signs were misclassified). The source of error came from errors in body movement module which failed to distinguish between 2 signs.

6   Conclusion

In this paper, a hybrid heterogeneous sensors based architecture is proposed and implemented to recognize Arabic sign language.

Digital cameras are used to capture both facial expressions and body movements. The facial expressions camera is positioned close enough to the face to capture the face details. The body movement camera is placed in a relatively longer distance to capture the whole body. Leap motion is employed to capture hand and fingers movements. Kinect is a very promising sensor to track body movements and hand overall shape but it could not track single fingers which in most signs is essential. Leap motion gives the system the flexibility enough to track each single finger motion.

The proposed system's accuracy has been enhanced from 90% to 95% due to the additional module for facial expressions and body movement. This system is a primary step towards building a complete signs recognition that is capable to recognize signs with a complete feature set; hands, facial expressions and body movement. The translation accuracy can be enhanced by adding a semantic oriented post-processing module to detect and correct any translation errors. The problem with the proposed post processing module is it would be efficient for a specific predetermined field.

References

1. Grobel, K., Assam, M.: Isolated sign language recognition using hidden Markov models. In: Proceedings of the IEEE International Conference on Systems, Man and Cybernetics, Orlando, FL, pp. 162–167 (1997)
2. Brand, M., Oliver, N., Pentland, A.: Coupled hidden Markov models for complex action recognition. In: Proceedings of the IEEE Conference on Computer Vision and Pattern Recognition (1997)
3. Lichtenauer, J.F., ten Holt, G.A., Reinders, M.J.T., Hendriks, E.A.: Person-independent 3d sign language recognition. In: Sales Dias, M., Gibet, S., Wanderley, M.M., Bastos, R. (eds.) GW 2007. LNCS (LNAI), vol. 5085, pp. 69–80. Springer, Heidelberg (2009)
4. Waldron, M.B., Kim, S.: Isolated ASL sign recognition system for deaf persons. IEEE Trans. Rehabilitation Eng. 3(3), 261–271 (1995)
5. Chen, F.-S., Fu, C.-M., Huang, C.-L.: Hand gesture recognition ussing a real-time tracking method and hidden Markov models. Image and Vision Computing 21, 745–758 (2003)
6. Forster, J., Schmidt, C., Hoyoux, T., Koller, O., Zelle, U., Piater, J., Ney, H.: Rwthphoenix-weather: A large vocabulary sign language recognition and translation corpus. In: LREC (May 2012)
7. Gweth, Y., Plahl, C., Ney, H.: Enhanced continuous sign language recognition using PCA and neural network features. In: CVPR 2012 Workshop on Gesture Recognition (June 2012)
8. Hoffmeister, B., Schlüter, R., Ney, H.: Icnc and Irover: The limits of improving system combination with classification? In: Interspeech, pp. 232–235 (September 2008)
9. Koller, O., Ney, H., Bowden, R.: May the force be with you: Force-aligned SignWriting for automatic subunit annotation of corpora. In: IEEE International Conference on Automatic Face and Gesture Recognition, Shanghai, PRC (April 2013)

10. Geetha, M., Manjusha, U.C.: A Vision Based Recognition of Indian Sign Language Alphabets and Numerals Using B-Spline Approximation. International Journal of Computer Science and Engineering (IJCSE) (2013)

11. Sultana, A., Rajapushpa, T.: Vision Based Gesture Recognition for Alphabetical Hand gestures Using the SVM Classifier. International Journal of Computer Science and Engineering Technology 3(7) (2012)

12. Yuce, B.: Neural Network Design and Feature Selection using Principal Component Analysis and Taguchi Method for Identifying Wood Veneer Defects

13. Mastrocinque, E., Packianather, M.S., Pham, D.T., Lambiase, A., Fruggiero, F.: Production & Manufacturing Research (2014)

14. Shotton, J., Sharp, T., Kipman, A., Fitzgibbon, A., Finocchio, M., Blake, A., Cook, M., Moore, R.: Real-time human pose recognition in parts from single depth images. Communications of the ACM 56(1), 116–124 (2013)

15. Fujimura, K., Liu, X.: Sign recognition using depth image streams. In: Procs. of FGR, Southampton, UK, pp. 381–386 (2006)

16. Combettes, P.L., Pesquet, J.-C.: Proximal splitting methods in signal processing. In: Fixed-Point Algorithms for Inverse Problems in Science and Engineering, pp. 185–212. Springer, New York (2011)

17. Beck, A., Teboulle, M.: A fast iterative shrinkage-thresholding algorithm for linear inverse problems. SIAM Journal on Imaging Sciences 2(1), 183–202 (2009)

18. Wang, Z., Hu, K., Xu, K., Yin, B., Dong, X.: Structural Analysis of Network Traffic Matrix via Relaxed Principal Component Pursuit. Computer Networks 56(7), 2049–2067 (2012)

19. Saishanmuga, V.R., Rajagopalan, S.P.: A neuro-genetic system for face recognition. Int. J. Comput. Sci. 9, 264–267 (2012)

20. Shen, L.L., Wang, Y.X., Duan, L.: Application of artificial neural networks on the Prediction of surface ozone concentrations. Huan. Jing Ke Xue 32, 2231-5PMID: 22619942 (2011)

A Robust 3D Mesh Watermarking Approach Using Genetic Algorithms

Mona M. Soliman[1,2], Aboul Ella Hassanien[1,2], and Hoda M. Onsi[1]

[1] Cairo University, Faculty of Computers and Information, Cairo, Egypt
[2] Scientific Research Group in Egypt (SRGE)
http://www.egyptscience.net

Abstract. This paper proposes a new approach of 3D watermarking by ensuring the optimal preservation of mesh surfaces. The minimal surface distortion is enforced during watermark embedding stage using Genetic Algorithm (GA) optimization. The watermark embedding is performed only on set of selected vertices come out from k-means clustering technique. These vertices are used as candidates for watermark carriers that will hold watermark bits stream. A 3D surface preservation function is defined according to the distance of a vertex displaced by watermarking to the original surface. A study of the proposed methodology has high robustness against the common mesh attacks while preserving the original object surface during watermarking.

Keywords: Optimization, 3D Watermarking, Genetic Algorithm.

1 Introduction

With the increasing use of mesh models during the last decade, it is now essential to establish an efficient mechanism for their copyright protection. Robust watermarking seems a good solution to this emerging problem [1]. Digital watermarking aims to fulfill simultaneously a set of requirements such as: non-visibility, robustness, high bit capacity and crypto-security. Usually, by enforcing any of these constraints we limit the effectiveness of all the others.

Recently, 3-D geometric models have been receiving a lot of attention. We can see that three-dimensional mesh models have serious difficulties for watermark embedding. While image data are represented by brightness (or amplitudes of RGB components in the case of color images) of pixels sampled over a regular grid in two dimension, 3-D polygonal models have no unique representation, i.e., no implicit order and connectivity of vertices [2].

There are two basic kinds of 3D mesh watermarking algorithms that are similar to image watermarking. One is based on the spatial domain, where watermark is inserted in by either modifying vertex positions or modifying the connectivity of the vertices [3]- [4]. The other set of algorithms use various transformations to insert the watermark in the transform domain coefficients to enhance robustness [5]- [6]. Improvements in performance of watermarking schemes can be obtained by several methods. One way is to make use of Intelligent Computing

© Springer International Publishing Switzerland 2015
D. Filev et al. (eds.), *Intelligent Systems'2014,*
Advances in Intelligent Systems and Computing 323, DOI: 10.1007/978-3-319-11310-4_64

techniques [7]. Recently there has been a new set of watermarking algorithms built on the spatial and transformation algorithms by adding an intelligent layer of optimization for high density watermark insertion [8]- [10].

This paper focus on introducing a novel robust mesh watermarking approach for 3D watermarking by ensuring a minimal surface distortion. Distances from vertices to the object center are changed according to the watermark code using the Genetic algorithm (GA) optimization in spherical Coordinates system. The mesh vertices are first converted into spherical coordinates. Watermark insertion is performed on specific set of vertices that are selected by utilizing k-means clustering. We use curvature features [11] to cluster mesh vertices into suitable and unsuitable candidates for being watermark carrier. This curvature measure determines the eligibility of the patch area for watermark addition. The aim of optimization process is to minimizes the sum of Euclidean distances from the vertex, displaced by watermarking, to the original surface.

The remainder of this paper is organized as follows. Section (2) illustrate some useful and important preliminary ideas relating to this work. Section (3) discusses the proposed watermarking optimization method using GA and k-means clustering. Section (4) shows the experimental results. Conclusions are discussed in Section (5).

2   Preliminaries

2.1   Genetic Algorithm

Genetic algorithms are adaptive algorithms for finding the global optimal solution for an optimization problem. The canonical genetic algorithm developed by Holland [12] is characterised by binary representation of individual solutions, simple problem-independent crossover and mutation operators, and a proportional selection rule. GA [13] started with set of individuals, each individual is assigned a fitness score according to how good a solution to the problem it is. The highly fit individuals are given opportunities to "reproduce" by "cross breeding" with other individuals in the population. A whole new population of possible solutions is thus produced by selecting the best individuals from the current "generation" and mating them to produce a new set of individuals. This new generation contains a higher proportion of the characteristics possessed by the good members of the previous generation [14].

2.2   Basics of 3D Mesh Models

A 3D mesh consists of three combinational entities: vertices, faces, and the edges connecting the vertices [15]. Mathematically, in 3D mesh containing N vertices and M edges, each vertex element v_i is described by its three-dimensional coordinates (x_i, y_i, z_i). The set of all the neighbours of a vertex v_i is called 1-ring of the vertex. The number of neighbours of v_i in its 1-ring neighbourhood is the valence or degree of the vertex v_i.

Curved surface of 3D mesh consists of a number of smaller triangles which used to give the perception of smooth surface. The curvature of a curve is the measure of its deviation from a straight line in a neighborhood of a given point [16]. The surface curvature gives a unique and viewpoint-independent description of a local shape. Normal variation usually gives a good indication of the surface curvature.

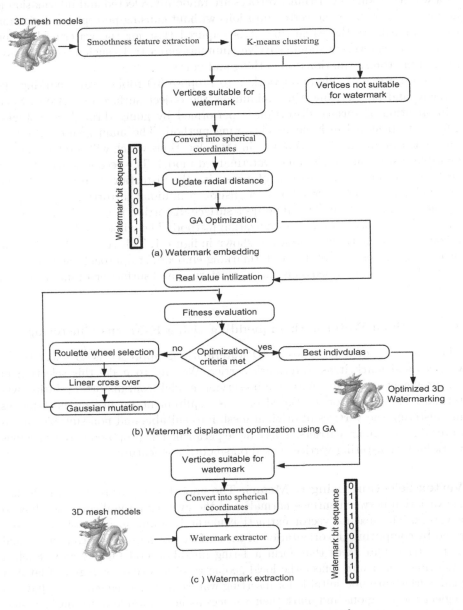

Fig. 1. The proposed watermarking approach

In this work we used angle variation between surface norm and the average norm corresponding to a vertex to determine the vertex smoothness measure [17]. Such computed measure is considered local and relative to the geometry of the surface.

3   The Proposed 3D Watermarking Approach

In a watermarking algorithms, vertices are randomly selected and information is added by perturbing the vertex positions without causing perceptible distortion to 3D model. At the same time it is required that for the watermark to be robust, the watermark should survive unintentional attacks such as compression loss, affine transformations, smoothing,and noise.

The objective of this novel work is to propose 3D robust watermarking approach, and at the same time minimizes the object surface distortions. Such minimization of surface distortion is performed by going through two stages. The first stage utilize k-means clustering method. The main goal of using K-means is to watermark a 3D model in those locations which will produce imperceptible distortions in the final watermarked model. The second stage utilize a surface error function consisting of measuring the distortion with respect to the original surface. This error function ensures a minimal distortion with respect to the original surface. The 3D object surface distortion is minimized by using the Genetic algorithm (GA) optimization method. The whole model of 3D optimization watermarking approach is shown in figure 1. This section describes the processing stages for optimal watermarking embedding approach including watermark embedding based on K-means clustering, and surface error minimization using GA.

3.1   Optimal Watermark Embedding Using K-Means Clustering

The first stage of our proposed 3D watermarking approach is to select set of vertices and mark it as watermark carrier. We aim to make this selection in an intelligent way that guarantee preserving model from distortion during watermark insertion process. Based on this requirement we utilize the k-means in clustering the vertices of original mesh into suitable and non-suitable candidates for watermark carriers. This can be performed as proposed in our previous work [9] by clustering vertices based on smoothness feature.

Vertex Selection Using K-Means. The smoothness feature measure the angle variation between surface normals and the average normal corresponding to a vertex. The feature vector extraction method results in a set of angles derived by computing the orientation of the surface normals to the average normal of the triangular faces that form a 1-ring neighborhood for a vertex. Such a smoothness measure reflect the local geometry of a surface or region. Flat and peak surface are not suitable for inserting watermark bits sequence. We have to neglect these regions and mark their vertices as non-suitable watermark carrier. We only consider angles of medium value to be watermark carriers.

Watermark Embedding. Those selected vertices $(v_i \in \hat{V})$ are first transformed into spherical coordinates system by the means of:

$$\rho_i = \sqrt{(x_i - x_g)^2 + (y_i - y_g)^2 + (z_i - z_g)^2}$$

$$\theta_i = \tan^{-1}(\frac{(y_i - y_g)}{(x_i - x_g)^2})$$

$$\phi_i = \cos^{-1}(\frac{(z_i - z_g)}{\sqrt{(x_i - x_g)^2 + (y_i - y_g)^2 + (z_i - z_g)^2}})$$

$$(1)$$

for $0 \leq i \leq M - 1$, where M is the number of marked vertex $\hat{V}$, (x_g, y_g, z_g) is the center of gravity of the mesh model, and ρ the ith vertex norm. The vertex norm represents the distance between each vertex and the center of gravity. The proposed method uses only vertex norms for watermarking and keeps the other two components θ_i and ϕ_i intact. The watermark bit stream w are first multiplied by scaling factor k, then added directly on the radial distance ρ_i according to the following equation:

$$\hat{\rho}_i = \rho_i + k * w \qquad (2)$$

3.2   Optimal Vertex Placement for Watermark Embedding

In this section we describe the second stage of surface error minimization by displacing a given vertex such that it minimizes the surface distortion criterion function $E(.)$. The constraint that we have to enforce is $||O\hat{V}|| = \hat{\rho}_i$, i.e. the watermarked vertex should be on the sphere $S(O, \hat{\rho}_i)$ centered in the object center O, of the radius given by $\hat{\rho}_i$ corresponding to the bit to be embedded and calculated using 2. Simultaneously we aim to produce minimal distortion to the object surface. Due to the embedding symmetry with respect to object center, in the following we consider the spherical coordinate representation for the vertex. We update the values of θ_i and ϕ_i, while considering the vertex norm $\hat{\rho}_i$ as constant, while minimizing the criterion given by $E(.)$.

Error Function for Surface Preservation Watermarking. Now, we have to describe the cost function used to preserve 3D model from distortion after adding watermark bit stream on its set of vertices. The constraints considered in the following consist of the distortion between the watermarked and the original surface. The cost function $E(.)$ that we use is part of cost function proposed in [10] where:

$$E(.) = \begin{cases} \prec (\hat{v}_i - v_i), n_1 \succ n_1 \\ \dots \\ \prec (\hat{v}_i - v_i), n_l \succ n_l \end{cases} \qquad (3)$$

where $\hat{v}_i$ is the location of the watermarked vertex $\hat{V}_i$, $\prec .,. \succ$ is the dot product and n_l is the normal vector of a triangle adjacent to the vertex v_i from the original surface. The vector $\prec (\hat{v}_i - v_i), n_l \succ n_l$ is orthogonal from $\hat{v}_i$ to face F_l.

GA Optimization for Watermark Embedding. for all vertices marked as suitable watermark carriers from k-means clustering, only set of them holding watermark bits according to length of the watermark bits stream. We start by selecting each marked vertex with specified $(\hat{\rho}_i, \theta_i, \phi_i)$, We then use the iterative GA optimization method in order to find the optimal vertex location minimizing the surface error $E(.)$. In GA optimization we utilize error function described in equation 3 as fitness function with (θ_i, ϕ_i) are the function parameters. GA is initialized by set of random real values representing each (θ_i, ϕ_i) for each watermarked vertex, GA iterate to minimize fitness function $E(.)$ producing a new values of (θ_i, ϕ_i) in each iteration using Roulette wheel selection, linear cross-over, and Gaussian mutation as basic GA operators.

3.3   Watermark Extraction

The watermark extraction algorithm is non-blind, i.e. it requires the original model in the extraction stage. In the watermark extraction we go through the same steps of first watermark embedding stage. Firstly we determine vertices holding watermark using k-means procedure. Then we convert these marked vertices into spherical coordinate system, extracting watermark bits according to the following equation:

$$w = (\hat{\rho}_i - \rho_i)/k \qquad (4)$$

4   Experimental Results and Discussion

The proposed algorithm is developed in $MATLAB7.6$ environment. Several models are used for the evaluation, four of them are shown in figure 2. The number of vertices and faces for each of these mesh models are provided in Table 1. The meshes of these models display a large variation of surfaces and shapes. The distortion of watermarked model is affected by different parameters including: The scaling factor k, the size of watermark sequence, The position selected by k-means to embed watermark, The final optimal value of (θ_i, ϕ_i) for each watermarked vertex derived from GA. The propose approach is introduced to minimize surface distortion while keeping the robustness of watermark. This section will show how the proposed approach achieve both requirements under different conditions and parameters' value

4.1   Baseline Evaluation

A very important requirement for hiding digital information into graphical objects consists of achieving a minimal surface distortion such that it is not visible

Fig. 2. Original 3D mesh models

Table 1. Mesh Object Used in Experiments

Mesh Model	No. of Vertices	No. of Faces
bunny	34,835	69,666
Elephant	24,9555	49,918
dragon	50,000	100,000
venus	100,759	201,514

to an outsider. The quality of the watermarked objects can be measured by two measures: Vertex Signal-to-Noise Ratio (VSNR) that quantifies the visual differences between the original and watermarked models. The other measure we consider in our baseline evaluation is the method proposed by Cignoni et al. In [18] which represents an approximation of the Hausdorff distance for 3D mesh surfaces known as maximum root mean square (MRMS).

Table 2 shows the values of $VSNR$, $MRMS$ result from using different scaling factor k on the watermarked model. The watermarked model parameters are updated using k-means procedure and GA optimization. Genetic optimization is applied after watermark embedding to enhance the visual quality of watermarked model and ensure minimal distortion. Genetic optimization in this work is running for 50 iterations, starting with 20 individuals represented by real value representation. We utilize roulette wheel selection, linear cross-over, and Gaussian mutation as basic GA operators, where the crossover probability $p_r = 0.05$, and mutation probability $p_m = 0.9$.

4.2 Robustness Evaluation

Robustness of the system is verified by applying different attacks on the watermarked model including: noise addition, smoothing attack, simplification attack, and Cropping attack. We list all these typical attacks with their associated parameters used in our experiments in Table 3.

For evaluating the resistance to noise attack, binary random noise was added to each vertex with different error rates $Amplif\%$. The error rate represents the noise amplitude as a fraction of the maximum vertex norm of the object. For smoothing attacks three different pairs of iteration N_{it} and relaxation λ are applied. Testing simplification attacks is performed by applying various reduction ratios rr on watermarked models. Finally cropping attack is defined by number of cropped vertices cv where their z coordinates values exceeds certain value.

Table 2. Baseline evaluation of proposed watermarking approach

Model	$k = 10^{-3}$		$k = 10^{-2}$	
	VSNR	$MRMS^{10^{-3}}$	VSNR	$MRMS^{10^{-3}}$
Bunny	122.97	0.025	117.65	0.031
Dragon	128.25	0.015	125.91	0.023
Elephant	113.00	0.052	106.14	0.016
Venus	135.53	0.009	128.51	0.010

Table 3. Robustness attack parameters

Attack	Parameter	parameter value
Noise Addition	$Amplif\%$	0.1% 0.3% 0.5%
Smoothing λ=0.1	N_{it}	10 20 40
simplification	rr	10% 20% 30%
Cropping	cv	$z \geq specified value$

Table 4. Robustness against uniform noise attack

Model	Amplitude	Proposed approach	
	%	Corr	$MRMS^{10^{-3}}$
Bunny	0.1	0.852	0.29
	0.3	0.486	0.89
	0.5	0.307	1.46
Dragon	0.1	0.888	0.27
	0.3	0.522	0.79
	0.5	0.362	1.30
Elephant	0.1	0.875	0.46
	0.3	0.520	1.35
	0.5	0.332	2.20
Venus	0.1	0.830	0.23
	0.3	0.449	0.70
	0.5	0.286	1.17

Table 5. Robustness against smoothness attack

Model	Iterations	Proposed approach	
	N_{it}	Corr	$MRMS^{10^{-3}}$
Bunny	10	0.581	0.09
	20	0.293	0.17
	40	0.126	0.33
Dragon	10	0.769	0.09
	20	0.458	0.19
	40	0.209	0.37
Elephant	10	0.973	0.11
	20	0.885	0.19
	40	0.639	0.37
Venus	10	0.96	0.035
	20	0.830	0.06
	40	0.521	0.13

Table 6. Robustness against simplifications attacks

Model	reduction ratio	Proposed approach	
	rr	Corr	$MRMS^{10^{-3}}$
Bunny	10	0.880	0.14
	20	0.749	0.24
	30	0.439	3.50
Dragon	10	1	7.4
	20	1	1.05
	30	1	1.29
Elephant	10	0.66	2.63
	20	0.707	3.73
	30	0.556	4.57
Venus	10	1	0.05
	20	1	0.09
	30	1	0.13

The robustness is evaluated in terms of correlation coefficient 'Corr' between the extracted watermark bit sequence w'_n and the originally inserted one w_n Tables 4-7 show the correlation results for different types of attacks with different parameters. It also show the effect of noise on watermarked model by estimating MRMS at different noise parameters.

Table 7. Robustness against cropping attack where cv is the cropped vertices

Mesh Model	No. of cv	Proposed approach Corr
	5916	0.654
Bunny	3616	0.692
	746	0.857
	9666	0.731
Dragon	5604	0.818
	3156	0.837
	17678	0.641
Venus	10936	0.933
	4927	0.964

5   Conclusions

In this paper, we propose a new 3D watermarking approach which minimizes the object surface distortions. The watermark is embedded directly on distances from the object center to vertices on its surface by slightly displacing the location of the vertices. The proposed approach embed watermark on set of vertices result from k-means clustering. The clustering is performed based on an intelligent way that guarantee preserving model from distortion during watermark insertion process. To guarantee minimum surface distortion, a new surface error function measuring the distortion with respect to the original surface has been introduced. The 3D object surface distortion is minimized by using the GA optimization method for vertices represented in spherical coordinates. As shown in the experiments, the proposed watermarking approach has high robustness against common mesh attacks while ensuring a minimal surface distortion.

References

1. Wang, K., Lavou, G., Denis, F., Baskurt, A., He, X.: A Benchmark for 3D Mesh Watermarking. In: Proc. of the Shape Modeling International, Aix-en-Provence, France, pp. 231–235 (2010)
2. Cho, J.W., Prost, R., Jung, H.Y.: An Oblivious Watermarking for 3-D Polygonal Meshes Using Distribution of Vertex Norms. IEEE Transaction on Signal Processing 55(1), 144–152 (2005)
3. Benedens, O.: Geometry-based watermarking of 3D models. IEEE Computers and Applications 19(1), 46–55 (1999)
4. Ohbuchi, R., Masuda, H., Aono, M.: Watermarking three dimensional polygonal models through geometric and topological modifications. IEEE Journal on Selected Areas in Communications 16(4), 55–160 (1998)
5. Kanai, S., Date, H., Kishinami, T.: Digital watermarking for 3D polygons using multi-resolution wavelet decomposition. In: Proceedings of the Sixth IFIP WG 5.2 International Workshop on Geometric Modeling: Fundamentals and Applications (GEO-6), pp. 296–307 (1998)

6. Ohbuchi, R., Mukaiyama, A., Takahashi, S.: A frequency domain approach to watermarking 3D shapes. Computer Graphics Forum 21(3), 373–382 (2002)
7. Motwani, M.C., Bryant, B.D., Dascalu, S.M., Harris, F.C.: 3D Multimedia Protection Using Artificial Neural Network. In: 7th IEEE Consumer Communications and Networking Conference (CCNC), pp. 1–5 (2010)
8. Hu, R., Alface, P., Macq, B.: Constrained optimisation of 3D polygonal mesh watermarking by quadratic programming. In: Acoustics, IEEE International Conference on Speech and Signal Processing, ICASSP, pp. 1501–1504 (2009)
9. Soliman, M.M., Ella Hassanien, A., Onsi, H.M.: Robust watermarking approach for 3D triangular mesh using self organization map. In: 8th International Conference on Computer Engineering and Systems (ICCES), pp. 99–104 (2013)
10. Bors, A., Luo, M.: Optimized 3D Watermarking for Minimal Surface Distortion. IEEE Transaction on Image Processing 22(5), 1822–1835 (2013)
11. Motwani, R.C., Motwani, M.C., Harris, F.C.: An Eigen-Normal Approach for 3D Mesh Watermarking Using Support Vector Machines. Journal of Electronic Science and Technology 8(3) (2010)
12. Holland, J.H.: Adaptation in Natural and Artificial Systems. University of Michigan Press (1975)
13. Malhotra, R., Singh, N., Singh, Y.: Genetic Algorithms: Concepts, Design for Optimization of Process Controllers. Computer and Informtaion Science 4(2), 39–54 (2011)
14. Beasley, D., Bull, D.R., Martin, R.R.: An Overview of Genetic Algorithms: Part 1, Fundamentals. University Computing 15(2), 58–69 (1993)
15. Motwani, M.C.: Third generation 3D watermarking: Applied computational intelligence techniques. A dissertation submitted in partial fulfillment of the requirements for the degree of Doctor of Philosophy in Computer Science and Engineering, University of Nevada, Reno, USA (2011) ISBN: 978-1-124-86869-1
16. Nigam, S., Agrawal, V.: Review: Curvature Approximation on Triangular Meshes. International Journal of Engineering Science and Innovative Technology (IJESIT) 2(3), 330–339 (2013)
17. Motwani, R., Harris Jr., F.C.: Robust 3D Watermarking Using Vertex Smoothness Measure. In: Proceedings of the 2009 International Conference on Image Processing, Computer Vision, and Pattern Recognition (IPCV 2009), Las Vegas, Nevada, pp. 287–293 (2009)
18. Cignoni, P., Rocchini, C., Scopigno, R.: Metro: Measuring error on simplified surfaces. Comput. Graph. Forum 17(2), 167–174 (1998)

Action Recognition Using Stationary Wavelet-Based Motion Images

M.N. Al-Berry[1], M.A.-M. Salem[1], H.M. Ebeid[1], Ashraf S. Hussein[2],
and Mohamed F. Tolba[1]

[1] Faculty of Computer and Information Sciences, Ain Shams University, Egypt
[2] Faculty of Computer Studies, Arab Open University, Headquarters, Kuwait
{maryam_nabil,salem}@cis.asu.edu.eg,
hala_mousher@hotmail.com,
ashrafh@acm.org, fahmytolba@gmail.com

Abstract. Human action recognition is one of the most important fields in computer vision, because of the large number of applications that employ action recognition. Many techniques have been proposed for representing and classifying actions; yet these tasks are still non-trivial due to a number of challenges and characteristics. In this paper, a new action representation method is proposed. The proposed method utilizes the 3D Stationary Wavelet Analysis to encode the spatio-temporal characteristics of the motion available in the video sequences in a way similar to motion history images. The proposed representation was tested using Weizmann dataset, exhibiting promising results when compared to the existing state – of – the – art methods.

Keywords: Action Recognition, Stationary Wavelet Analysis, Motion History Images, Motion Energy Images, Classification.

1 Introduction

Recently, automatic human action and activity recognition has become one of the most important areas in computer vision. This importance emanates from a wide spectrum of applications, such as intelligent surveillance [1], content-based video retrieval, behavioral biometrics, medical studies, robotics, security, animation, and human-computer interaction (HCI) [2]. While the field is relatively old, it is still non-trivial [3, 4]. Its complexity comes from several challenges and characteristics, including: variations of the performance of actions, dynamic or cluttered environments, changing illumination, temporal variations in executing action, and obtaining and labeling realistic training data [4, 5, 6].

Poppe [5] defined vision-based human action recognition as: "The process of labeling image sequences with action labels". Following Weinland et al. [7], an action is a sequence of movements generated by a performer during the performance of a task, and an action label is a name, such that an average human agent can understand and perform the named action.

Different methods have been proposed for segmenting, representing, and classifying actions. These methods can be classified into different taxonomies [7, 8, 9]. One

© Springer International Publishing Switzerland 2015   743
D. Filev et al. (eds.), *Intelligent Systems'2014*,
Advances in Intelligent Systems and Computing 323, DOI: 10.1007/978-3-319-11310-4_65

of the famous methods that have been used for holistic motion representation is the Motion History Image (MHI) [10, 11, 12]. Motion History Images are temporal templates that are simple but robust in motion representation, and they are used for action recognition by several research groups [12].

In this paper, motivated by the Motion History Image (MHI) representation of actions, a stationary wavelet-based action representation is proposed. The proposed representation is based on the 3D Stationary Wavelet Transform (SWT) that has been proposed and used in [13] for spatio-temporal motion detection. Hu invariant moments [14] have been used for describing the templates, which was obtained using the proposed method in combination with different classifiers using benchmark datasets. Preliminary results obtained using simple features and classifiers show that the proposed representation results are comparable to state-of-the-art methods [15, 16, 17, 4]. The ultimate goal of this work is to use the 3D SWT output for all processing in a visual surveillance framework, i.e., to compute once and use the output in all of the processing steps (motion detection, tracking, action recognition).

The rest of paper is organized as follows: Section 2 provides a short review of related work. Section 3 describes the proposed method in detail. Section 4 demonstrates the experimental results. Finally, section 5 concludes the paper and highlights some future directions.

2   Related Work

Human action and activity recognition is one of the most fertile and promising fields in computer vision. This is because images and videos are easily acquired nowadays, and there are many applications that require human motion analysis and recognition, including intelligent surveillance, content-based video retrieval, behavioral biometrics, medical studies, robotics, security, animation, and human-computer interaction (HCI) [3, 9, 18,19,20].

There are a lot of papers concerned with the field of action recognition. Some of them provide a very good and detailed review of the field [3, 5, 7, 9, 18, 19, 21, 22]. Here a brief survey of the different action representation and classification methods, focusing on the global 2D representation.

Actions in images can be represented using a global or local representation [5]. The global representation encodes the whole motion into a single representation; while local representation represents the motion using a number of independent spots [5]. Both representations has been used and reported in the literature with different performances and applications. For action classification, a direct classification can be used where the observed template is compared to the action class prototypes, or discriminative classifiers can be used to learn a function that discriminates between two or more classes [5]. Other approaches for recognizing actions and activities are described in [9].

One of the most successful global representations is the Motion History Images (MHI), proposed by Davies and Bobick [23]. MHI is a global view-based approach that is simple but efficient in representing actions and used in many applications.

Ahad et al. [12] have provided an overview on the techniques and applications that are based on MHI. They also presented many variants that were proposed to enhance the basic MHI, and guide researchers to some future directions. In [10], Davies used MHI for real-time action recognition and categorization. The holistic motion was encoded into a single template, and for recognition, higher order moments were computed and statistically matched to trained models. Babu and Ramakrishnan [11] used the encoded motion information available in a compressed MPEG stream to construct the Motion History Image (MHI) and the corresponding Motion Flow History (MFH). Different sets of features were extracted and used to train a number of classifiers, then the performance of each feature set with respect to various classifiers were analyzed. Their results showed that the K- nearest neighbor (KNN), Neural Networks, and the support vector machine (SVM) classifiers give the highest classification accuracy. MHI has been also used by Shao et al. [24] in a framework that detects various types of exercises and counts the cycle of the exercise in an indoor environment. A shape-based feature descriptor was extracted from the MHI and Motion Energy Image (MEI) and was used for recognition with high accuracy. The idea of motion history images was extended to the 3D history volumes by Weinland et al. [25].

In the direction of local representation local interest points are extracted from space-time or 3D volumes. Chen [26] proposed the MoSIFT to detect interest points and describe local features for action recognition. It encodes both local appearance and motion as histograms of gradients in space and histograms of optical flow. In [20], Yan and Luo proposed a new action descriptor based on the space-time interest points (STIPs). It was called the histogram of interest point locations (HIPLs). HIPL reorganizes STIPs and reflects the spatial location information, and can be viewed as a useful supplement to the bag-of-interest-point (BIP) feature. They used a combined AdaBoost and sparse representation classifier for classifying actions in benchmark datasets. Their descriptor resulted in good performance, but it captured only the spatial information of interest points, without inclusion of the temporal domain. Bregonzio et al. [27] proposed a spatio-temporal technique for the action representation in which only the global distribution information of interest points is utilized. Holistic features from clouds of interest points accumulated over multiple temporal scales are extracted. Their proposed spatio-temporal distribution representation contains complementary information to the conventional Bag of Words representation. Based on Multiple Kernel Learning, the features are fused. In [28], Rapantzikos et al. explored the ability of the 3D wavelet transform to efficiently locate and represent dynamic events while keeping the computational complexity low. They proposed a framework for representing human actions as spatiotemporal salient regions in the 3D wavelet domain. They represented a video sequence as a solid in the three-dimensional Euclidean space, with time being the third dimension, applied a multiscale 3D wavelet transform to decompose the volume into sub-bands and used the resulting coefficients to compute saliency. The efficiency of their method was proven on a public video dataset consisting of six actions.

From the above discussion, it can be concluded that in spite of the large amount of effort that has been devoted to the problem of human action recognition, the area is still open for more research needs to be elaborated to overcome the challenges encountered in the available action recognition techniques.

3   Proposed Stationary Wavelet-Based Action Representation

This section provides a detailed description of the proposed stationary wavelet-based action representation method. The proposed representation is motivated by the motion history images [23] and based on the 3D SWT proposed in [13].

3.1   Forming Templates

One Block Template

The first proposal is to build a Wavelet-based Energy Image (WEI) using the 3D SWT proposed in [13], where the video sequence is represented as a 3D volume of frames with time being the third dimension. The video sequence is divided into blocks of 8 frames, and a 3 level SWT is applied on the block. The coefficients of three sub-bands are thresholded to obtain foreground images. The foregrounds obtained at the 8th layer of different resolutions and sub-bands are fused into a single foreground image (O(x,y,t)). This foreground image encodes the motion that happened during the processed 8 frames, as illustrated in Fig. 1. The obtained foreground image contains the motion energy of the 8 processed frames, i.e., where the motion occurred in the processed frames, and thus they can be used to represent the action performed during these frames.

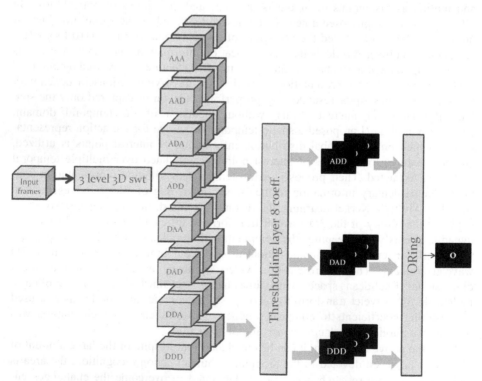

Fig. 1. Illustration of 3D stationary wavelet-based motion detection

Wavelet-Based History Images

Motion history image is a way for representing the motion sequence in one gray scale view-based template. The motion history image $H_\tau(x,y,t)$ is computed using an update function $\psi(x,y,t)$ as follows [12]:

$$H_\tau(x, y, t) = \begin{cases} \tau & if \, \psi(x, y, t) = 1 \\ \max(0, H_\tau(x, y, t) - \delta) & Otherwise \end{cases} \tag{1}$$

(x,y) and t are the location and time and $\psi(x,y,t)$ indicates the presence of motion in the current video image, τ indicates the temporal extent of the movement and δ is the decay parameter [12].

In the proposed method, when multiple blocks of frames are processed using the 3D SWT, the resulting foreground images can be combined into one Wavelet –based History Image (WHI_τ) template as follows:

$$WHI_\tau(x, y, t) = \begin{cases} \tau & if \, O(x, y, t) = 1 \\ \max(0, WHI_\tau(x, y, t) - \delta) & Otherwise \end{cases} \tag{2}$$

where (x,y) and t are the location and time, and $O(x,y,t)$ is the binary motion mask obtained by the motion detector, i.e., it signals the presence of motion.

3.2 Feature Extraction

For each template, the seven Hu invariant moments [14] are computed and used as the features for classification. The Hu moments are known to give good discrimination of shapes while being translation, scale, mirroring, and rotation invariant [29].

As described in [29], the set of seven invariant moments are defined as follows:

$$\Phi_1 = \eta_{20} + \eta_{02} \tag{3}$$

$$\Phi_2 = (\eta_{20} - \eta_{02})^2 + 4\eta_{11}^2 \tag{4}$$

$$\Phi_3 = (\eta_{30} - 3\eta_{12})^2 + (3\eta_{21} - \eta_{03})^2 \tag{5}$$

$$\Phi_4 = (\eta_{30} + \eta_{12})^2 + (3\eta_{21} + \eta_{03})^2 \tag{6}$$

$$\Phi_5 = (\eta_{30} - 3\eta_{12})(\eta_{30} + \eta_{12})[(\eta_{30} + \eta_{12})^2 - 3(\eta_{21} + \eta_{03})^2] \\ + (3\eta_{21} - \eta_{03})(\eta_{21} + \eta_{03})[3(\eta_{30} + \eta_{12})^2 - (\eta_{21} + \eta_{03})^2] \tag{7}$$

$$\Phi_6 = (\eta_{20} - \eta_{02})[(\eta_{30} + \eta_{12})^2 - (\eta_{21} + \eta_{03})^2] \\ + 4\eta_{11}(\eta_{30} + \eta_{12})(\eta_{21} + \eta_{03}) \tag{8}$$

$$\Phi_7 = (3\eta_{21} - \eta_{03})(\eta_{30} + \eta_{12})[((\eta_{30} + \eta_{12})^2 - 3(\eta_{21} - \eta_{03})^2]$$
$$+ (3\eta_{12} - \eta_{30})(\eta_{21} + \eta_{03})[3(\eta_{30} + \eta_{12})^2 - (\eta_{21} + \eta_{03})^2] \tag{9}$$

where, η_{pq} is the normalized central moments defined as

$$\eta_{pq} = \frac{\mu_{pq}}{\mu_{00}^{\gamma}} \tag{10}$$

μ_{pq} is the central moment of order $(p+q)$, $p = 0,1,2,\dots$ and $q = 0,1,2,\dots,$

$$\gamma = \frac{p+q}{2} + 1 \tag{11}$$

for $p+q = 2,3, \dots$

4   Results and Discussion

This section depicts the results obtained when testing the proposed action representation method. Section 4.1 describes the used dataset, and then section 4.2 presents the experimental results.

4.1   Benchmark Dataset

The proposed representation was tested using the Weizmann dataset [30]. The dataset contains 93 video sequences for 10 actions, bend, jack, jump, pjump, run, side, skip, wave1, wave2, and walk. These actions were performed by 9 persons in front of static background. Sample frames from the dataset are shown in Fig. 2.

Fig. 2. Examples of images from the Weizmann dataset [30]

4.2   Experiments and Results

For evaluating the proposed action representation, discriminant analysis was used for classifying the set of actions. In the first experiment, Mahalanobis distance metric [31] between different sets was used to discriminate between different actions. In the second experiment, quadratic discriminant analysis was applied. These two approaches were applied on the moments extracted from one block wavelet-based energy images (WEI), and on the moments extracted from the wavelet-based history images that was composed using two blocks of frames. The confusion matrices obtained using the Wavelet Energy Images (WEI) are shown in Fig. 3. The left-hand column shows the result of Mahalanobis distance metric, while the right-hand column shows the result of quadratic discriminant analysis.

In the case of using only the wavelet energy image (WEI), the best accuracy was 86.2% with Mahalanobis distance metric as shown in Fig. 3(a) when processing 8

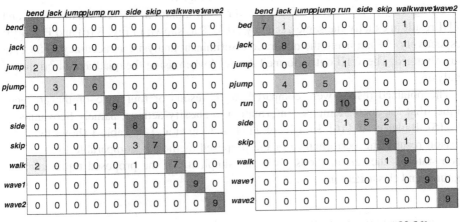

(a) Confusion matrix — Total accuracy: 86.2%

	bend	jack	jump	pjump	run	side	skip	walk	wave1	wave2
bend	9	0	0	0	0	0	0	0	0	0
jack	0	9	0	0	0	0	0	0	0	0
jump	2	0	7	0	0	0	0	0	0	0
pjump	0	3	0	6	0	0	0	0	0	0
run	0	0	1	0	9	0	0	0	0	0
side	0	0	0	0	1	8	0	0	0	0
skip	0	0	0	0	0	3	7	0	0	0
walk	2	0	0	0	0	1	0	7	0	0
wave1	0	0	0	0	0	0	0	0	9	0
wave2	0	0	0	0	0	0	0	0	0	9

(b) Total accuracy: 82.8%

	bend	jack	jump	pjump	run	side	skip	walk	wave1	wave2
bed	7	1	0	0	0	0	0	1	0	0
jack	0	8	0	0	0	0	0	1	0	0
jump	0	0	6	0	1	0	1	1	0	0
pjump	0	4	0	5	0	0	0	0	0	0
run	0	0	0	0	10	0	0	0	0	0
side	0	0	0	0	1	5	2	1	0	0
skip	0	0	0	0	0	0	9	1	0	0
walk	0	0	0	0	0	0	1	9	0	0
wave1	0	0	0	0	0	0	0	0	9	0
wave2	0	0	0	0	0	0	0	0	0	9

(c) Total accuracy: 90.32%

	bend	jack	jump	pjump	run	side	skip	walk	wave1	wave2
bend	9	0	0	0	0	0	0	0	0	0
jack	0	9	0	0	0	0	0	0	0	0
jump	0	0	8	0	0	0	1	0	0	0
pjump	0	0	0	9	0	0	0	0	0	0
run	0	0	0	0	10	0	0	0	0	0
side	0	0	0	0	0	7	2	0	0	0
skip	3	0	1	0	1	0	5	0	0	0
walk	1	0	0	0	0	0	0	9	0	0
wave1	0	0	0	0	0	0	0	0	9	0
wave2	0	0	0	0	0	0	0	0	0	9

(d) Total accuracy: 92.47%

	bend	jack	jump	pjump	run	side	skip	walk	wave1	wave2
bend	8	0	1	0	0	0	0	0	0	0
jack	0	9	0	0	0	0	0	0	0	0
jump	0	0	7	0	0	0	2	0	0	0
pjump	0	0	0	9	0	0	0	0	0	0
run	0	0	0	0	9	0	1	0	0	0
side	0	0	0	0	0	9	0	0	0	0
skip	0	0	0	0	1	1	8	0	0	0
walk	0	0	0	0	0	0	0	10	0	0
wave1	0	0	0	0	0	0	0	0	9	0
wave2	0	0	0	0	0	0	0	1	0	8

Fig. 3. Confusion matrices obtained in different experiments. The first row shows the result from Wavelet Energy Images. The second row shows the results from Wavelet History Image.

frames of the video. When using two blocks and composing a wavelet history image (WHI), the accuracy increased to 92.47% with quadratic discriminant analysis compared to 90.32% with Mahalanobis distance metric as shown in Fig. 3 (d) and 3(c) respectively.

Another experiment has been carried out to investigate the ability of the 3D stationary wavelet transform to encode the spatio-temporal information that needed for the discrimination between different action classes. The 3D SWT was used to process 16 frames in one block, and the resulting WEI was used for classification. It was expected that this would be nearly equivalent to combining two energy images into one wavelet history image. The results are shown in Fig. 4.

Using Mahalanobis distance metric for discrimination, the 16 frames WEI and WHI result in exactly the same accuracy 90.32% as shown in Fig. 3 (d) and Fig. 4 (a) respectively. When using the quadratic discriminant analysis, an accuracy of 88.17% was obtained. The WHI outperformed the WEI when using the quadratic discriminant analysis.

The obtained results were compared to the results of four state–of–the–art techniques that use spatio-temporal information to classify actions; namely Scovanner et al. [15], Ballan et al. [16], Kong et al. [17], and Thi et al. [4]. Table 1 shows the comparison result. The performance of the proposed method is comparable to the reference state-of- the- art methods given the simplicity of the proposed representation, features and classification.

	bend	jack	jump	pjump	run	side	skip	walk	wave1	wave2
bend	9	0	0	0	0	0	0	0	0	0
jack	0	9	0	0	0	0	0	0	0	0
jump	0	0	9	0	0	0	0	0	0	0
pjump	0	0	0	9	0	0	0	0	0	0
run	0	0	1	0	9	0	0	0	0	0
side	0	0	1	0	0	5	2	1	0	0
skip	0	0	1	0	1	0	8	0	0	0
walk	1	0	0	0	0	0	0	9	0	0
wave1	0	0	0	0	0	0	0	0	9	0
wave2	1	0	0	0	0	0	0	0	0	8

(a) Total accuracy: 90.32%

	bend	jack	jump	pjump	run	side	skip	walk	wave1	wave2
bend	6	0	0	0	2	0	0	1	0	0
jack	0	9	0	0	0	0	0	0	0	0
jump	0	0	6	0	2	0	1	0	0	0
pjump	0	0	0	9	0	0	0	0	0	0
run	0	0	0	0	10	0	0	0	0	0
side	0	0	0	0	0	6	2	1	0	0
skip	0	0	0	0	0	1	9	0	0	0
walk	0	0	0	0	0	0	0	10	0	0
wave1	0	0	0	0	0	0	0	0	9	0
wave2	0	0	0	0	0	0	0	1	0	8

(b) Total accuracy: 88.17%

Fig. 4. Confusion matrices for using 3D stationary wavelet transform. (a) Mahalanobis distance metric, (b) Quadratic discriminant analysis.

Table 1. Accuracy comparison between the proposed method and some reference methods

Method	Accuracy %
Scovanner et al. (2007)	82.60
Ballan et al. (2009)	92.41
Kong et al. (2011)	92.20
Thi et al. (2012) HBFS-χ^2	98.20
Thi et al. (2012) HBFS-Linear	90.40
Proposed WEI +Mahalanobis metric	86.02
Proposed WEI + Quadratic discriminant analysis	82.8
Proposed WHI + Mahalanobis metric	90.32
Proposed WHI + Quadratic discriminant analysis	92.47
Proposed 2-blocks WEI + Mahalanobis metric	90.32
Proposed 2-blocks WEI + Quadratic discriminant analysis	88.17

5   Conclusions

Human action and activity recognition is one of the most promising fields in computer vision because images and videos are acquired easily nowadays, and there are a wide range of applications that require human motion analysis and recognition. Different methods have been proposed for segmenting, representing, and classifying actions, but the field is still immature due to a number of challenges and characteristics. Motivated by the Motion History Image (MHI) representation of actions, this paper proposes a stationary wavelet-based action representation. The proposed representation along with Hu invariant moments have been used for action classification in combination with discriminant analysis classification, and the method was verified using a benchmark dataset. Preliminary results obtained using simple features and classifiers show that the proposed representation results are promising and comparable to state-of-the-art methods. The ultimate goal of this work is to use the 3D SWT output for all processing in a visual surveillance framework, i.e., to compute it once and use the output in all processing steps (motion detection, tracking, action recognition).

Future work may include utilizing the directional information obtained using the wavelet transform to increase the accuracy of classification. Different features and classifiers might be used in combination with the proposed representation to obtain better results.

References

1. Kim, I.S., Choi, H.S., Yi, K.M., Choi, J.Y., Kong, S.G.: Intelligent Visual Surveillance: a survey. Int. J. Control, Automation, and Systems. 8, 926–939 (2010)
2. Pantic, M., Nijholt, A., Pentland, A., Huanag, T.S.: Human- Centered Intelligent Human-Computer Interaction (HCI2): How far are we from attaining it? Int. J. Autonomous and Adaptive Communications Systems 1(2), 168–187 (2008)

3. Moeslund, T.B., Hilton, A., Krüger, V.: A survey of advances in vision-based human motion capture and analysis. Comput. Vis. Image Und. 104, 90–126 (2006)
4. Thi, T.H., Cheng, L., Zhang, J., Wang, L., Satoh, S.: Structured learning of local features for human action classification and localization. Image Vision Comput. 30, 1–14 (2012)
5. Poppe, R.: A survey on vision-based human action recognition. Image Vision Comput. 28, 976–990 (2010)
6. Cristani, M., Raghavendra, R., Del Bue, A., Murino, V.: Human Behavior Analysis in Video Surveillance: Social Signal Processing Perspective. Neurocomputing 100, 86–97 (2013)
7. Weinland, D., Ranford, R., Boyer, E.: A survey of vision-based methods for action representation, segmentation and recognition. Comput. Vis. Image Und. 115, 224–241 (2011)
8. Pantic, M., Nijholt, A., Pentland, A., Huanag, T.: Machine Understanding of Human Behavior. In: ACM Int. Conf. Multimodal Interface (2006)
9. Turaga, P., Chellappa, R., Subrahamanian, V., Udrea, O.: Machine Recognition of Human Activities: A Survey. IEEE T. Circ. Syst. Vid. 18(11), 1473–1487 (2008)
10. Davis, J.W.: Representing and Recognizing Human Motion: From Motion Templates to Movement Categories. In: Digital Human Modeling Workshop, IROS 2001 (2001)
11. Babu, R.V., Ramakrishnan, K.R.: Recognition of human actions using motion history information extrcted from the compressed video. Image Vision Comput. 22, 597–607 (2004)
12. Ahad, M., Tan, J., Kim, H., Ishikawa, S.: Motion history image: its variants and applications. Mach. Vision Appl. 23, 255–281 (2012)
13. Al-Berry, M.N., Salem, M.A.-M., Hussein, A.S., Tolba, M.F.: Spatio-Temporal Motion Detection for Intelligent Surveillance Applications. Int. J. Computational Methods (2015) (in press)
14. Hu, M.-K.: Visual Pattern Recognition by Moment Invariants. IEEE T. Inform. Theory 8(2), 179–187 (1962)
15. Scovanner, P., Ali, S., Shah, M.: A 3-dimensional sift descriptor and its application to action recognition. In: 15th ACM International Conference on Multimedia, pp. 357–360 (2007)
16. Ballan, L., Bertini, M., Del Bimbo, A., Seidenari, L., Serra, G.: Recognizing Human Actions by fusing Spatio-temporal Appearance and Motion Descriptors. In: International Conference Image Processing (2009)
17. Kong, Y., Zhang, X., Hu, W., Jia, Y.: Adaptive learning codebook for action recognition. Pattern Recogn. Lett. 32, 1178–1186 (2011)
18. Aggrawal, J., Cai, Q.: Human Motion Analysis: A Review. Comput. Vis. Image Und. 73(3), 428–440 (1999)
19. Vishwakarma, S., Agrawal, A.: A survey on activity recognition and behavior understanding in video surveillance. The Visual Computer 29(10), 983–1009 (2013)
20. Yan, X., Luo, Y.: Recognizing human actions using a new descriptor based on spatial–temporal interest points and weighted-output classifier. Neurocomputing 87, 51–61 (2012)
21. Cedras, C., Shah, M.: Motion-based Recognition: A Survey. Image Vision Comput. 13(2), 129–155 (1995)
22. Wu, Y., Huang, T.S.: Vision-Based Gesture Recognition: A Review. In: Braffort, A., Gibet, S., Teil, D., Gherbi, R., Richardson, J. (eds.) GW 1999. LNCS (LNAI), vol. 1739, pp. 103–115. Springer, Heidelberg (2000)
23. Davies, J., Bobick, A.F.: The representation and recognition of human movements using temporal templates. In: IEEE Computer Society Conference on Computer Vision and Pattern Recognition, pp. 928–934 (1997)

24. Shao, L., Ji, L., Liu, Y., Zhang, J.: Human action segmentation and recognition via motion and shape analysis. Pattern Recogn. Lett. 33, 438–445 (2012)
25. Weinland, D., Ronfard, R., Boyer, E.: Free Viewpoint Action Recognition using Motion History Volumes. Comput. Vis. Image Und. 104(2), 249–257 (2006)
26. Chen, M.-Y.: MoSIFT: Resognizing Human Actions in Surveillance Videos. School of Cegie Mellon Universityomputer Science at Research Showcase - Carnegie Mellon University (2009)
27. Bregonzio, M., Xiang, T., Gong, S.: Fusing appearance and distribution information of interest points for action recognition. Pattern Recogn. 45, 1220–1234 (2012)
28. Rapantzikos, K., Avrithis, Y., Kollias, S.: Spatiotemporal saliency for event detection and representation in the 3D Wavelet Domain: Potential in human action recognition. In: 6th ACM International Conference on Image and Video Retrieval, pp. 294–301 (2007)
29. Gonzalez, R.C., Woods, R.E.: Digital Image Processing, 3rd edn. Printice Hall (2008)
30. Blank, M., Gorelick, L., Shechtman, E., Irani, M., Basri, R.: Actions as Space-time Shapes. In: 10th International Conference on Computer Vision, pp. 1395–1402 (2005)
31. Mahalanobis, P.C.: On the generalized distance in statistics. The National Institute of Sciences of India 2(1), 49–55 (1936)

Early Detection of Powdery Mildew Disease in Wheat (*Triticum aestivum* L.) Using Thermal Imaging Technique

Yasser Mahmoud Awad[1,5], Ahmed Ameen Abdullah[1],
Tarek Youssef Bayoumi[2], Kamel Abd-Elsalam[3], and Aboul Ella Hassanien[4,5]

[1] Suez Canal University, Faculty of Agriculture,
Department of Agricultural Botany, Ismailia, Egypt
ryasser@gmail.com
[2] Suez Canal University, Faculty of Agriculture,
Department of Agronomy, Ismailia, Egypt
[3] Plant Pathology Research Institute, Agricultural Research Center, Egypt
[4] Faculty of Computers and Information, Cairo University, Egypt
[5] Scientific Research Group in Egypt (SRGE)
http://www.egyptscience.net

Abstract. Powdery mildew caused by *Erysiphe graminis* f. sp. *tritici* is one of the most harmful disease causing great losses in wheat yield. Currently, thermal spectral sensing of plant disease under different environmental conditions in field is a cutting-edge research. Objectives of this study were to assess thermal imaging of normal and infected leaves for early detection of powdery mildew in wheat after the artificial infection with *Erysiphe graminis* fungus in a pot experiment under greenhouse conditions. Pot experiment lasting for 30 days was conducted. Additionally, wheat seedlings were artificially infected with pathogen at 10 days from sowing. This is the first study in Egypt to use thermal imaging technique for early detection of powdery mildew disease on leaf using thermal signatures of artificial infected leaves as a reference images. Particularly, the variations in temperature between infected and healthy leaves of wheat and the variation between air and leaf-surface temperatures under greenhouse conditions were sensed for early detection of disease. Results revealed that infection with powdery mildew pathogen induced changes in leaf temperature (from 0.37 °C after one hour from the infection to 0.78 °C at 21 days after infection with the pathogen) and metabolism, contributing to a distinct thermal signature characterizing the early and late phases of the infection.

1 Introduction

Wheat (*Triticum aestivum* L.) is the earliest domesticated crop with >10000-year-old of world agriculture [1, 2]. In addition, it is one of the most important crops feeding 35 % of world population and providing 55 % of carbohydrates, as well as, it is currently cultivated on >220 million hectares (17 % of the cultivated land) [3–5]. Based on simulation of data from 90 studies using computer

© Springer International Publishing Switzerland 2015
D. Filev et al. (eds.), *Intelligent Systems'2014*,
Advances in Intelligent Systems and Computing 323, DOI: 10.1007/978-3-319-11310-4_66

modeling, 50 % of relative wheat yield losses may occur when mean temperature change is >2.3 °C, or when carbon dioxide concentration is <395 ppm [4]. In order to meet food security in developing countries, wheat demand needs to be increased by 1.6% and 2.6% per year up to 2020 [6]. As a result, Egyptian government plans to increase the cultivation area to reduce the percent of income spent on wheat imports because Egypt imported 9.8 million MT of wheat in 2010 [3, 7].

Spread and complexity of pest and disease problems under climate change such as elevated atmospheric temperature have led farmers to apply intensive chemical compounds, which result in increase the resistance of pests and pathogens [8]. Moreover, plant disease reduces global food production by at least 10% up to 30% [9,10]. Specifically, powdery mildews are obligate parasitic fungi which infect a wide range of crops (about 700 species of powdery mildews existing in about 7600 plant species) including cereals, cucurbits, fruit tress and ornamental crops [11], thereby causing significant losses of crop yields when compared to other plant diseases. Powdery mildew caused by *Blumeria graminis* (formerly named as *Erysiphe graminis* f.sp. *tritici*), is one of the most deleterious diseases threaten wheat production worldwide, resulting in a huge damage and yield losses [12,13]. Taken together, researchers, institutions and governments have been interested on studying the impacts of powdery mildew disease on production of wheat for food security [12]. From another point of view, it is noteworthy that breeders need to make a selection of wheat parental materials to develop new high-yielding lines having potential to resist diseases mostly under climate change conditions [14]. Many studies have been conducted to transfer disease-resistant alleles of the whole breed wheat genome [15]. The research objective is currently focused on the effective disease resistance for improving wheat breeding [16]. For instance, about 2160 findings were recorded for breeding powdery mildew-resistant wheat lines [14].

From practical point of view, applying information technology, especially remote sensing techniques could help to detect crop diseases in field [17]. Specifically, recent advances in sensing plant disorder technologies have high potential in monitoring and diagnosis of infected plants in field [18]. Thermography is the science of infrared imaging and highly specialized in capturing of thermal images to determine infrared energy or heat radiated from objectives [19]. It is a promising technology to conduct a proper inspection more efficiently of raising temperature of buildings, machinery, equipment or even live bodies such as plant, or animals for early prediction of problems and maintenance [19]. Thermal imaging is widely applied in several fields such as veterinary and agriculture as reported in [19]. Usage of thermal camera is easy and can be accurately measured temperature without requiring an illumination source when compared to other imaging system [19]. Recently, thermal imagery is a promising alternative technique to conventional methods for plant disease diagnosis such as powder mildew in wheat, in addition to it gives useful information about disease spatial distribution in field [12]. Zhang et al. [12] revealed that hyperspectral measurements of normal and powdery mildew infected leaves are possible and effective method in detection of the disease.

The objective of this study was to assess weather thermal imaging introduces a promising technique for early detection of powdery mildew in wheat after the artificial infection with *Erysiphe graminis* fungus in a pot experiment under greenhouse conditions. In addition, temperature changes in normal and infected leaves, as well as the differences in temperatures between air and normal or infected leaf surface were monitored.

The rest of this paper is organized in the following structure: describing methodologies in section 2, interpreting the findings of current study in section 3, discussing them in section 4 and finally summarizing the conclusion and future remarks in section 5.

2   Materials and Methods

2.1   Plant Material

A moderate susceptible wheat line (Sids1 X Sakha 61) to powdery mildew disease was obtained from the Department of Agronomy, Suez Canal University after six years of breeding program (F6 line) by crossing elite high-yielding parent cultivars (Sids1 and Sakha 61). Grains were then germinated in plastic pots under greenhouse conditions.

2.2   Pot Experiment

Pot experiment in a greenhouse was performed lasting for 30 days. In 25th of February 2014, five grains of wheat line were cultivated in each 500-cm^3 pot in a 1:4:1 mixture of soil, sand and peat moss, respectively. Experiment was conducted at the Agricultural Farm of Faculty of Agriculture, Suez Canal University, Egypt. Pots were watered periodically to maintain moisture at field capacity under greenhouse conditions. After germination pots were separated into two groups: sixteen pots in first group to be artificially inoculated with *Erysiphe graminis* fungus and four pots were served as control (healthy plants without infection with pathogen).

2.3   Artificial Infection

Wheat leaves were gently rubbed with clean moistened finger to remove waxy layer from leaf surface. Next, the collected conidiospores of the obligate pathogen onto naturally infected leaves (from living tissues) from a wheat field in Ismailia Governorate, were used to artificially infect the first leaves on seedlings at 10 days from sowing (6th of March 2014). Before infection, natural infected leaves were shaken to remove old spores. New spores were transferred by dusting to surfaces of susceptible wheat line with a paint brush [20].

2.4   Thermal Imaging

For both healthy and infected leaves, thermal images were captured using Fluke Thermal Imager Ti32 (Fluke Thermography, USA). The used thermal camera have infrared sensor size of 320 X 240, while both transmission correction and emissivity were 85 % and 0.098, respectively. For more accuracy, the span of auto adjusted thermal image is manually set, in addition to level of the displayed as an important camera feature in order to detect maximum and minimum temperature of the entire display (2.4).

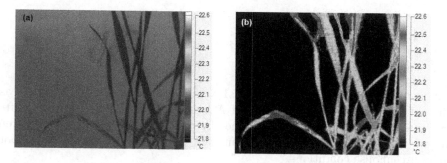

Fig. 1. Showing visible (a) and thermal (b) images of a flattened leaf of wheat infected with the obligate pathogen *Erysiphe graminis*

2.5   Measurements

Humidity and air temperatures in the greenhouse were periodically measured using Humidity and Temperature Meter (Jenway, model 5075, serial No.: 43424, USA) in the same time of capturing thermal images of healthy and infected leaves. At the end of experiment, shoot fresh and dry weights, root fresh and dry weight, leaf surface area (LSA).

2.6   Leaf Area and Disease Severity

Total leaf area of wheat and disease severity were estimated from captured images using ImageJ software (version 1.48s, USA). Specifically, disease severity is the relative or absolute area of the leaf showing symptoms of powdery mildew disease expressed as a percentage (Figure 2.6). The images of healthy and infected wheat leaves were captured with an Alcatel CE1588 digital camera HD/8.0 MP (TCT mobile limited) 50 cm above the leaf surface according to Maciel et al. [21]. In particular, total healthy and symptomatic areas (cm^2) of leaf were estimated by setting a scale using a ruler beside the leaf.

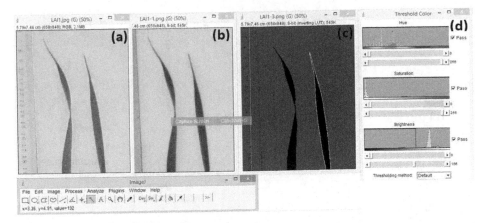

Fig. 2. Showing an image of a flattened leaf of wheat which is digitized, enhanced (a, b) and analyzed (c, d) to distinguish leaf surface area from the background using ImageJ software

3   Results

3.1   Pathogen and Disease Symptoms

As shown in Figure 3.1, mycelium of the obligate pathogen *Erysiphe graminis* f.sp. *tritici* covered the surface of the lower leaf with a fluffy-grey fungal growth. It is cleared from the figure 3.1 that the oval-shaped conidiospores are produced in chains from conidiophores which disperse on leaf surface of wheat. Later, leaves developed yellow area due to formation of more conidiospores.

Disease Severity and Areas of Leaf and Root. the aforementioned disease symptoms were observed at 5 days after the infection (DAI), after which an increase of the formation of conidia and hyphal growth on surface of leaves. The fungal growth increases with time increasing from the infection of powdery mildew fungus. As shown in Figure (3.1), disease severity found to be 2.41, 7.89, 9.2 and 30.9 % at 7, 12, 14 and 21 DAI, respectively, indicating that greenhouse conditions were much suitable for fungal growth due to the proper air temperature (18-22.5 °C) and relative humidity (80-82.3 %) during the 30 days of pot experiment (Figure 3.1). It is cleared from Figure 3.1 that leaf and root areas (cm^2) of healthy plants were slightly higher than the infected plants, indicating a significant decrease in plant growth due to the infection with powdery mildew fungus.

3.2   Thermal Imaging

After artificial infection of with *Erysiphe graminis* fungus, there were slight decrease in temperatures of the infected wheat leaf from 0.37 °C after one hour

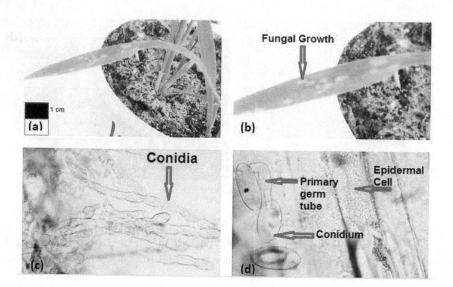

Fig. 3. Symptoms of powdery mildew on wheat leaves (a and b: occurrence of grey fungal growth on the lower leaf), Microscopic photograph showing structure of *Erysiphe graminis* f.sp. *tritici* conidiospores (c) and a germinated conidium on epidermal cells of wheat (leaf surface) (d) (X400)

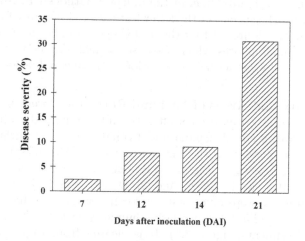

Fig. 4. Disease severity (%) of powdery mildew on wheat leaves after 12, 14 and 21 days from infection with *Erysiphe graminis* f.sp. *tritici* conidiospores

from the infection to 0.78 °C at 21 days after infection with the pathogen (Table 1). Results revealed that a decrease in leaf surface temperature after the infection of powedery mildew pathogen was observed as a thermal signature of early infection of disease after hours from successful formation of conidiospores

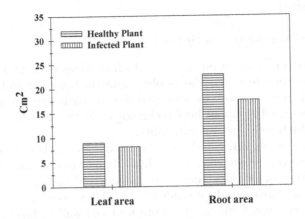

Fig. 5. Leaf and root areas (cm^2) of healthy and infected wheat

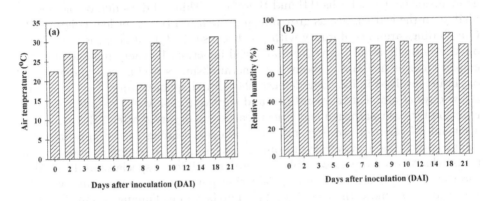

Fig. 6. Showing greenhouse conditions (air temperature (a) and relative humidity (b)) during the pot experiment

Table 1. Changes in temperatures of normal and infected leaves after infection with *Erysiphe graminis* fungus and greenhouse conditions

Time	Greenhouse Conditions		Average Temperature(oC)	
	Air Temperature (oC)	Relative Humidity (%)	Healthy Leaf	Infected Leaf
0.04 DAI*	22.5	82.3	30.49	30.12
0.08 DAI*	26.9	82.0	25.73	25.44
7 DAI*	15.0	79.1	19.65	19.42
12 DAI*	20.8	80.6	25.73	25.34
14 DAI*	18.6	80.6	22.4	21.62
21 DAI*	19.7	80.5	28.88	26.71

* 0.04 DAI = 1 hour after infection with pathogen, ** 0.08 DAI = 2 hours after the infection
DAI = days after infection with pathogen

in the infected plants (Table 1). In addition,the variation between air and leaf-surface temperatures under greenhouse conditions were 4-5 °C on average similar to other previous study.

4   Discussion

4.1   Disease Diagnosis and Severity

Crop variability is dependent on the soil, which provides plant with essential nutrients, and the climate which affects plant growth, flowering and productivity and cultivation time, as well as susceptibility to pathogens or pests. Consequently, farmers need to apply best technologies in the field to overcome crop variability for high yield and sustainability.

As shown in Figures 3.1, conidia of powder mildew pathogen land on wheat surface and then release enzymes to facilitate fungal growth and infection [22]. Next, a formation of primary germ tube is occurred to breach the epidermal cuticle similar to other powdery mildews [22]. After hours from infection, the germ tube adsorbs water and solutes from host cell wall to facilitate the infection process, in addition to producing additional appressorial germ tube [23]. Powdery mildew consume nutrients from infected plant by their haustoria which grow inside epidermal cells [11] and therefore within 2-4 days micro-colonies are visible on the leaf surface as grey fungal growths on the lower leaf (Figure 3.1). Our findings are in conformity with [11] because the fungal growths were developed eventually after 5 days from artificial infection. Powdery mildew infection causes changes in Plant carbohydrate metabolism, as well as salicylic acid and oxylipins involved in inducing defense [24]. Conidiophores can remain viable for a few days at ambient temperatures and survive for 34 weeks $<-4\,°C$ [25]. The reaction between pathogen and wheat leaves was occurred after 7 days from the artificial infection of powdery mildew pathogen, leading to the appearance of fungal growth as a disease symptom on leaves [20]. Under green house conditions whaet was more susceptible to powdery mildew, especially at $14-20\,°C$ than at $7\,°C$ because of conidia production per unit area of pustule were 10-times at $14\,°C$ more than at $7\,°C$ [26]. Furthermore, Fungus produce a short hypha which directly penetrates through the leaf surface into the epidermis and develops a finger-like haustorium. A shown in Figure 3.1, Haustoria consume nutrients from the leaf surface and lead to form yellowish leaves at the late stage of infection [27].

4.2   Thermal Imaging

Monitoring the subtle changes in leaf temperature is mainly contributed to key physiological processes such as growth and response to stresses such as extreme temperatures and incidence of disease [28]. As shown in section 3, potential of temperature variation (spatial and temporal) over a single leaf may be ranged from $3-5\,°C$ under favorable conditions [29]. Particularly, leaf temperature is an indicator of stomatal conductance because stomatal opening increases with decreasing temperature due to evaporation. Therefore, physiological responses of wheat leaves to biotic stress such as *Erysiphe graminis* fungus can easily be monitored using thermal imaging due to the spore density which covers the leaf surface and causes a masking effect. This might be the reason of decreasing leaf surface temperature of the infected plants as shown in 1. Thermal imagery can help in detection of powdery infection in wheat from the first hours of successful germination of conidiospores with a differences of 0.2-0.8 °C ¡ healthy leaves (Table 1).Reliable differentiation between normal and infected leaves was occurred after 1 hour from the infection due to the formation of fungal conidia under epidermal layer (Figures 2.4 and 3.1). Photosysnthetic rate of healthy leaves is affected by powdery mildew due to water relations, plant metabolism and photoassimilate translocation [30]. Williams and Ayres in [30] found that the infection of powdery mildew did not affect the leaf area, however; the leaf area in current study were significantly decreased in the infected leaves compared to the control. This may be due to the late measurement of leaf area at the end of the experiment as the late infection decreased significantly the leaf area due to the increased disease severity and the formation of more conidia under epidermal layer. Taken together, thermal imagery is a promising tool for early detection of powdery mildew of wheat based on the reduction of leaf surface temperature from hours to 21 DAI. Additionally, late infection of powdery mildew caused a pronounced reduction of leaf surface area and root area due to the deleterious affects on plant physiological processes and growth performance.

5   Conclusions and Future Remarks

Based on our findings, thermal imagining technique for plant disease diagnosis provides the needed information to make proper decisions in agriculture. In particular, this study allows decision makers to take a proper decision on wheat integrated pest management, specially controlling powdery mildew disease. Next, these findings will be used to develop an Expert System for wheat crop. This Recommender System is designed based on rough mereology for detecting best cultivation dates for wheat according to the required mean temperature for germination stage. Consequently, thermal and visible images of current experiment will be subjected to computing processing and algorithm to do more analysis and correlation between the studied variables. Therefore, our ongoing research is currently focused on develop this Recommender System for diagnosis of common plant disorder in wheat during growth stages associated with the changes in daily air temperatures.

Acknowledgments. This study was partially supported by the project entitled "Applying New Integrated Agronomic Techniques for Sustainable Agriculture in Marginal Soils of Sinai", as a basic and applied research grant from the Science and Technology Development Fund, Ministry of Scientific Research, Egypt.

References

1. Zohary, D., Hopf, M., Weiss, E.: Domestication of Plants in the Old World: The origin and spread of domesticated plants in Southwest Asia, Europe, and the Mediterranean Basin. Oxford University Press (2012)

764   Y.M. Awad et al.

2. Carver, B.F.: Wheat: science and trade. Wiley Online Library (2009)
3. FAOSTAT: Statistical databases. Food and Agriculture Organization of the United Nations (2014)
4. Wilcox, J., Makowski, D.: A meta-analysis of the predicted effects of climate change on wheat yields using simulation studies. Field Crops Research 156, 180–190 (2014)
5. Gill, B.S., Appels, R., Botha-Oberholster, A.M., Buell, C.R., Bennetzen, J.L., Chalhoub, B., Chumley, F., Dvořák, J., Iwanaga, M., Keller, B., et al.: A workshop report on wheat genome sequencing international genome research on wheat consortium. Genetics 168(2), 1087–1096 (2004)
6. Eitzinger, J., Orlandini, S., Stefanski, R., Naylor, R.: Climate change and agriculture: introductory editorial. The Journal of Agricultural Science 148(05), 499–500 (2010)
7. Werrell, C.E., Femia, F.: The Arab Spring and Climate Change: A Climate and Security Correlations Series (2013)
8. Coakley, S.M., Scherm, H., Chakraborty, S.: Climate change and plant disease management. Annual Review of Phytopathology 37(1), 399–426 (1999)
9. Strange, R.N., Scott, P.R.: Plant disease: a threat to global food security. Phytopathology 43 (2005)
10. Christou, P., Twyman, R.M.: The potential of genetically enhanced plants to address food insecurity. Nutrition Research Reviews 17(1), 23–42 (2004)
11. Braun, U., Cook, R., Inman, A., Shin, H., Bélanger, R., Bushnell, W., Dik, A., Carver, T., et al.: The taxonomy of the powdery mildew fungi. The powdery mildews: a comprehensive treatise, pp. 13–55 (2002)
12. Zhang, J.C., Pu, R.L., Wang, J.H., Huang, W.J., Yuan, L., Luo, J.H.: Detecting powdery mildew of winter wheat using leaf level hyperspectral measurements. Computers and Electronics in Agriculture 85, 13–23 (2012)
13. Sankaran, S., Mishra, A., Ehsani, R., Davis, C.: A review of advanced techniques for detecting plant diseases. Computers and Electronics in Agriculture 72(1), 1–13 (2010)
14. Hsam, S., Zeller, F., Bélanger, R., Bushnell, W., Dik, A., Carver, T., et al.: Breeding for powdery mildew resistance in common wheat (triticum aestivum l.). The powdery mildews: a comprehensive treatise, pp. 219–238 (2002)
15. Kole, C.: Wild crop relatives: genomic and breeding resources. Springer (2011)
16. Spielmeyer, W., McIntosh, R., Kolmer, J., Lagudah, E.: Powdery mildew resistance and lr34/yr18 genes for durable resistance to leaf and stripe rust cosegregate at a locus on the short arm of chromosome 7d of wheat. Theoretical and Applied Genetics 111(4), 731–735 (2005)
17. Mahlein, A.K., Steiner, U., Hillnhütter, C., Dehne, H.W., Oerke, E.C.: Hyperspectral imaging for small-scale analysis of symptoms caused by different sugar beet diseases. Plant Methods 8(1), 3 (2012)
18. Mahlein, A.K., Oerke, E.C., Steiner, U., Dehne, H.W.: Recent advances in sensing plant diseases for precision crop protection. European Journal of Plant Pathology 133(1), 197–209 (2012)
19. Vadivambal, R., Jayas, D.S.: Applications of thermal imaging in agriculture and food industry' a review. Food and Bioprocess Technology 4(2), 186–199 (2011)
20. Stubbs, R., Prescott, J., Saari, E., Dubin, H.: Cereal disease methodology manual (1986)
21. Nunes Maciel, J.L., do Nascimento Junior, A., Boaretto, C.: Estimation of blast severity on rye and triticale spikes by digital image analysis. International Journal of Agronomy 2013 (2013)

22. Carver, T., Kunoh, H., Thomas, B., Nicholson, R.: Release and visualization of the extracellular matrix of conidia of i blumeria graminis i. Mycological Research 103(5), 547–560 (1999)

23. Edwards, H.: Development of primary germ tubes by conidia of blumeria graminis f. sp. hordei on leaf epidermal cells of hordeum vulgare. Canadian Journal of Botany 80(10), 1121–1125 (2002)

24. Berger, S., Benediktyová, Z., Matouš, K., Bonfig, K., Mueller, M.J., Nedbal, L., Roitsch, T.: Visualization of dynamics of plant–pathogen interaction by novel combination of chlorophyll fluorescence imaging and statistical analysis: differential effects of virulent and avirulent strains of p. syringae and of oxylipins on a. thaliana. Journal of Experimental Botany 58(4), 797–806 (2007)

25. Cherewick, W.J.: Studies on the biology of erysiphe graminis dc. Canadian Journal of Research 22(2), 52–86 (1944)

26. Last, F.: Some effects of temperature and nitrogen supply on wheat powdery mildew. Annals of Applied Biology 40(2), 312–322 (1953)

27. Eichmann, R., Hückelhoven, R.: Accommodation of powdery mildew fungi in intact plant cells. Journal of Plant Physiology 165(1), 5–18 (2008)

28. Jones, H.G., Stoll, M., Santos, T., De Sousa, C., Chaves, M.M., Grant, O.M.: Use of infrared thermography for monitoring stomatal closure in the field: application to grapevine. Journal of Experimental Botany 53(378), 2249–2260 (2002)

29. Roth-Nebelsick, A.: Computer-based analysis of steady-state and transient heat transfer of small-sized leaves by free and mixed convection. Plant, Cell & Environment 24(6), 631–640 (2001)

30. Williams, G.M., Ayres, P.G.: Effects of powdery mildew and water stress on co2 exchange in uninfected leaves of barley. Plant Physiology 68(3), 527–530 (1981)

Part VI
Intelligent Energy Systems

Energy Prediction for EVs Using Support Vector Regression Methods

Stefan Grubwinkler and Markus Lienkamp

Institute of Automotive Technology, Technische Universitaet Muenchen,
Boltzmannstr. 15, 85748 Garching b. Muenchen, Germany
grubwinkler@ftm.mw.tum.de, lienkamp@tum.de

Abstract. This paper presents the application of machine learning algorithms for an accurate estimation of the energy consumption of electric vehicles (EVs). Normalised energy consumption values and speed profiles are collected from various EVs for a cloud-based prediction approach. We predict the necessary energy for each road segment on the basis of crowd-sourced data. Support vector machines, which are trained by the collected historical data of the driver, predict the deviation from the average energy consumption on each road segment. As a result, the prediction of propulsion energy consumption for EVs before the start of a trip has a relative mean error of less than 6.7%.

Keywords: electric vehicle, range estimation, crowd-sourcing of speed profiles, support vector regression, cloud-based energy prediction system.

1 Introduction

Electric vehicles (EVs) have a limited driving range in comparison to vehicles with internal combustion engines. Drivers of EVs need an accurate energy prediction along the chosen route before the start of a trip in order to guarantee to reach the desired destination and to decrease the so-called range anxiety.

Energy consumption of EVs depends on a high number of impact factors. Vehicle attributes like mass, rolling resistance or drivetrain efficiency especially influence the level of energy consumption. Weather conditions mainly impact the necessary power for the auxiliaries like heating or air-conditioning. These factors are predictable, since their variance during a trip is limited. Another important impact factor is the speed profile along the selected route, since it influences the required propulsion energy and the travel time, which determines the necessary energy for the auxiliaries. The speed profile causes especially the variance around the average energy consumption of EVs [1]. The example in Fig. 1 shows the variance of the speed profiles and the resulting variance of propulsion energy consumption of one vehicle on a chosen segment s. For comparison, the mean energy consumption of the chosen segment $\varnothing E_s$ and the mean energy consumption of segments of this road class k, $\varnothing E_k$, are also shown.

Hence, the expected speed profile is one of the most important uncertainty factors which has to be considered for an accurate energy prediction system for

© Springer International Publishing Switzerland 2015
D. Filev et al. (eds.), *Intelligent Systems'2014*,
Advances in Intelligent Systems and Computing 323, DOI: 10.1007/978-3-319-11310-4_67

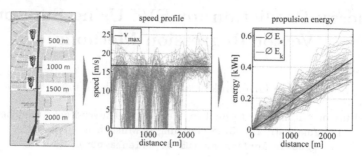

Fig. 1. Variance of energy consumption on segment s due to the speed profile

EVs. The individual driving behaviour, traffic flow, vehicle attributes like the acceleration behaviour, traffic signs or weather conditions influence the speed profile. The energy prediction is a difficult and complex problem due to the high number of impact factors and their correlation among each other.

The usage of cloud-based applications in Intelligent Transportation Systems will increase; especially applications for EVs will appear in the future. Thus, we are developing a cloud-based approach for the energy prediction of EVs by using data-driven machine learning methods like support vector regression (SVR). SVR is suitable for the prediction of parameters having a non-linear relationship with a high number of variables, which is the case for our described problem.

In this paper, a SVR model predicts the variance of energy consumption around the expected mean value for a road segment, which is caused mainly by the uncertainty in the expected future speed profile. We focus on the application of SVR methods for the cloud-based prediction of the energy consumption of EVs. The proposed methods can be realised with various system architectures, which are not part of this paper.

2   Related Work

Several techniques have been proposed so far for the energy prediction of EVs. [2] presents a model-based approach, which uses an unscented Kalman filter to estimate the energy consumption concerning prevailing uncertainties in vehicle parameters and the energy storage system. The future speed profile is predicted by a Markov Chain. The main purpose is the correction of an initial energy estimation value and not an accurate prediction before the start of a trip.

Further energy prediction methods are based mainly on map attributes along the selected route. In [3], driving patterns depending on the map attributes are used in order to consider the impact of speed profiles on energy consumption of EVs. [4] uses a Markov Chain to generate the future speed profile concerning map attributes along the chosen route. Traffic conditions, or the individual driving behaviour, which result in a variation of the speed profile, are not considered.

[5] uses statistical methods to predict the energy consumption of EVs. The deviation from historical average values of energy consumption and information about

the driving conditions, like temperature or traffic status, are used in a regression-based model to predict the future energy consumption. [6] also presents a multi-variate regression model based on various contextual conditions.

Another group of algorithms for the energy prediction for EVs are data mining approaches as shown in [7]. [8] presents a general regression neural network for the robust prediction of energy consumption. The input features of the neural network are mainly vehicle attributes. To the best of our knowledge, we do not know of any approach which uses SVR for the energy prediction of EVs.

3   Cloud-Based Energy Prediction System

In this section, an overview of the whole energy prediction system and the used data is given.

3.1   System Overview

The prediction system consists of a vehicle-specific and cloud-based part (see Fig. 2). The cloud-based part is used for various types of EVs with different vehicle parameters. Hence, we use collected speed profiles, since they are comparable for different vehicle types. The vehicle-specific part considers the various parameters of different EVs, like the mass or the rolling resistance, which result in a different average energy consumption.

Every time an EV traverses a road segment s, statistical features $\mathbf{F_s}$ of the recorded speed profiles are transmitted to the back-end in order to update the database. We do not transmit the whole speed profiles, since the extracted statistical features $\mathbf{F_s} = [f_1, f_2, ..., f_t]$ contain all the relevant information to describe the impact factors of energy consumption [9]. A list of the used statistical features is given in Tab. 1. [10] shows that these features can be used to calculate the propulsion energy of an EV with an error less than 6%. The segments s are defined on the basis of a navigable OSM map. The fixed segments have a minimum length of $150s$ driving time, which results in an average length between $1km$ and $5km$ depending on the road type. The parts of the road network belonging to s have the same road class (e.g. motorway) and speed limit.

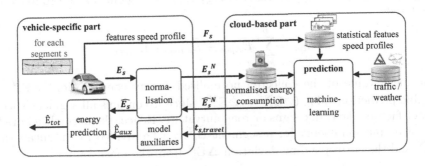

Fig. 2. Overview prediction system

Table 1. Extracted statistical features $\mathbf{F_s}$ from speed profiles

f_i	explanation	f_i	explanation
$a_\%$	part of s in acceleration phase	PKE	positive kinetic energy
$d_\%$	part of s in deceleration phase	RPA	relative positive acceleration
$c_\%$	part of s in cruising phase	RNA	relative negative acceleration
$a_m * a_\%$	mean acceleration comb. with $a_\%$	$a_{m,low}$ $d_{m,low}$	mean accel. / decel. with low speed difference
$d_m * d_\%$	mean deceleration comb. with $d_\%$	$a_{m,mid}$ $d_{m,mid}$	mean accel. / decel. with medium speed difference
a_{std}	standard deviation of acceleration	$a_{m,high}$ $d_{m,high}$	mean accel. / decel. with high speed difference
$v_{m,run}$	mean run velocity	$stop_{cnt}$	number of stops in s
$v_{m,spat}$	mean spatial velocity	t_{still}	time standstill
$v_{std,run}$	standard deviation of $v_{m,run}$	t_{travel}	travel time

The propulsion energy has to be normalised for the comparison between different EVs. We separate the powertrain energy in acceleration mode E_{pos} from the one in regenerative braking mode E_{neg} due to the different variants of regenerative braking strategies in EVs. The normalised energy values of a driven segment $\mathbf{E_s^N} = [E_{s,pos}^N, E_{s,neg}^N]$ are also transmitted to the back-end. The prediction model, based on machine learning algorithms, uses the collected statistical features, the normalised powertrain energy consumption and additional contextual information, like traffic congestion and weather conditions. The cloud-based system predicts for every segment s a normalised propulsion energy $\widehat{\mathbf{E}}_\mathbf{s}^\mathbf{N}$ and the corresponding expected travel time $\widehat{t}_{s,travel}$.

We denormalise the prediction $\widehat{\mathbf{E}}_\mathbf{s}^\mathbf{N}$ in the vehicle-specific part in order to get the energy consumption $\widehat{\mathbf{E}}_\mathbf{s}$ of the EV. The normalisation method, with the consideration of vehicle-specific impact factors, are presented in [10] and [11]. A vehicle-specific model to predict the necessary energy for the auxiliaries uses $\widehat{t}_{s,travel}$, so that the total necessary energy $\widehat{E}_{tot}$ for n segments of a route can be calculated:

$$\widehat{E}_{tot} = \sum_{s=1}^{n} \widehat{E}_{s,pos} + \widehat{E}_{s,neg} + \widehat{E}_{s,aux} \tag{1}$$

The mean value of the collected normalised energy consumptions $\varnothing \mathbf{E_s^N}$ is a possible prediction value ($\varnothing \mathbf{E_s^N} = \varnothing \widehat{\mathbf{E}}_\mathbf{s}^\mathbf{N}$), since it contains all segment-specific impact factors like traffic signs or road curvature. Hence, the normalised prediction of propulsion energy for a segment $\widehat{\mathbf{E}}_\mathbf{s}^\mathbf{N}$ can be divided in the mean value $\varnothing \widehat{\mathbf{E}}_\mathbf{s}^\mathbf{N}$ and the corresponding deviation $\Delta \widehat{\mathbf{E}}_\mathbf{s}^\mathbf{N}$ from the mean value:

$$\widehat{\mathbf{E}}_\mathbf{s}^\mathbf{N} = \varnothing \widehat{\mathbf{E}}_\mathbf{s}^\mathbf{N} * (1 + \Delta \widehat{\mathbf{E}}_\mathbf{s}^\mathbf{N}) \tag{2}$$

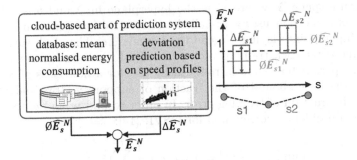

Fig. 3. Deviation prediction based on speed profiles

The cloud-based part consists of a spatial database with the normalised mean energy consumption values $\varnothing\widehat{E}_s^N$ for every segment s and a model to predict $\Delta\widehat{E}_s^N$ (see Fig. 3). The variance around the expected normalised mean energy consumption of the segment s has to be predicted with support vector machines. In this paper, we focus on the prediction of $\Delta\widehat{E}_s^N$, so that the energy consumption of the auxiliaries is not considered ($\widehat{E}_{s,aux} = 0$).

3.2   Used Data

We use the collected data (16,000 tracks with a length of more than 300,000 km) of several fleet tests in the urban area of Munich for the development of the prediction models. GPS position and speed are sampled at a one second time-stamp and transmitted to the back-end. The collected data is matched with an OpenStreetMap map [13], so that existing map attributes can be used. We use a simulation model consisting of validated component models (e.g. battery, electric drive) for the calculation of the energy consumption of EVs [11]. A traffic index TI is calculated for every recorded speed profile, which represents the prevailing traffic condition in the segment [12].

4   Support Vector Regression

Before we describe the SVR-model for the energy prediction system, some basics for SVR are revised; a detailed description can be found in [14].

4.1   Theoretical Background

The basic idea of SVR is to map the l training datasets $\{(\mathbf{x_1}, y_1), ..., (\mathbf{x_l}, y_l)\}$ with $\mathbf{x_i} \subset \Re^n$ and $y_i \subset \Re$ from the input space into a higher dimensional feature space $\Im$ via the kernel function $\mathbf{\Phi}(\mathbf{x}, \mathbf{x_i})$ and then construct a separating hyperplane with maximum margin in the feature space [14]. The aim of the SVR is to find the regression function

$$f(\mathbf{x}) = (\mathbf{w}^T\mathbf{\Phi}(\mathbf{x})) + b \tag{3}$$

in the feature space $\Im$, where $\mathbf{w}$ is the hyperplane in $\Im$ and b is a bias. The support vector method uses a so-called ϵ-insensitive loss function, which only penalises input points laying outside the bounds $\pm\epsilon$. The slack variables ξ, ξ^* are introduced for each training vector in order to measure errors outside the ϵ-tube. The parameter ν was introduced by [14] for a new class of SVR called ν-SVR as the lower bound of the fraction of support vectors and the upper bound on the fraction of training error. In order to find $\mathbf{w}$ and b, the following optimisation problem is formulated for ν-SVR [14]:

$$\min : J = \frac{1}{2}\mathbf{w}^{\mathbf{T}}\mathbf{w} + C(\nu\epsilon + \frac{1}{l}\sum_{i=1}^{l}(\xi_i + \xi_i^*)) \tag{4}$$

The parameter C penalise errors outside the upper and lower bounds. A Lagrange function can be constructed to solve problem (4). Finally, the SVR model (3) can be rewritten as [14]:

$$f(\mathbf{x}) = \sum_{i=1}^{l}(\alpha - \alpha^*)\Phi(\mathbf{x}')^T\Phi(\mathbf{x}) + b \tag{5}$$

The Lagrange multipliers α and α^* are the solution of (4) and used as support vectors. The Kernel function $\Phi(\mathbf{x}, \mathbf{x_i})$ defines the mapping of the input data into the feature space $\Im$. Often the polynomial, or the radial basis function (RBF), are chosen as kernel functions. After training SVR, $f(\mathbf{x})$ is known which represents the most suitable representation of the training data set.

4.2   SVR for Deviation Energy Prediction

The individual driving style and mobility behaviour (e.g. daytime) have an enormous impact on the energy consumption of vehicles [1]. Hence, we develop an SVR-model for every driver. SVRs are suitable for the described problem, as they reach appropriate results with a small number of datasets with a high number of input features. Due to the number of historical measurements, we have a limited number of datasets for the initialisation of the SVR of every driver.

The LIBSVM software package is used for the implementation of the SVR [15]. A separate SVR-model is built for the prediction of $\Delta E_{s,pos}^N$ and $\Delta E_{s,neg}^N$. We use a ν-SVR-model with an RBF-kernel as kernel function $\Phi(\mathbf{x}, \mathbf{x_i})$, since RBF is effective in mapping non-linear relationships:

$$\Phi(\mathbf{x}, \mathbf{x}') = \exp(-\gamma\|\mathbf{x} - \mathbf{x}'\|) \tag{6}$$

ν is set to 0.25. The choice of the parameters C and γ determines the accuracy of the prediction and prevent issues like over-fitting. We use the data of 70 selected drivers to find the optimal values for C and γ with a grid-search algorithm for all drivers. The 10-fold cross-validation technique is applied for the evaluation of the parameter pairs. We find a suitable solution for the parameter pair by minimising the mean root-squared error between deviation and prediction and limiting the number of support vectors ($\Delta E_{s,pos}^N : C = 25, \gamma = 0.01$; $\Delta E_{s,neg}^N : C = 0.1, \gamma = 0.5$).

4.3   Feature Selection

The selection of relevant features $\mathbf{x}$ is important for a suitable predictor. A higher number of features increases the accuracy, but irrelevant and redundant features raise the dimensionality. The selected features have to be predictable, which means they have to be known in advance before the start of a trip, and they must have an impact on the variation of energy consumption for a segment.

We carried out several methods in order to evaluate the features. In [10] and [12], possible input features are analysed for significance on $\mathbf{\Delta E_s^N}$ according the 5%-level, whose results are used for the selection of appropriate feature subsets. Further, we use the Weka workbench [16] for wrapper methods based on regression rules for the selection of suitable features. Wrapper methods score feature subsets according to their predictive power [17]. We compare SVR-models with different feature subsets and evaluate them by the general error, which measures if the system performs well on the unseen data. The leave-one-out-cross validation method is used for the estimation of the general error [14].

The cloud-based energy prediction system offers a continuous data stream due to the increasing travelled distance. The selected features of the dataset for each segment s for the prediction of $\mathbf{\Delta E_s^N}$ can be divided into four groups (see Fig. 4). A detailed list of the used features is given in Table 2. The mean values and standard deviation of the normalised energy consumption, and the extracted features from all recorded speed profiles for s (see Table 1), are used. They are identical for all drives on s, but their value is considerable for the weighting of impact factors. For example, a driver with a higher acceleration compared to the average behaviour needs more energy on segments with a lot of stops ($\varnothing stop_{cnt}$) or on segments with a higher acceleration part $\varnothing a_\%$. Predictable contextual

Table 2. Selected input features $\mathbf{x_i}$ for the SVR-model

Normalised mean energy consumption	User-specific data
• mean value normalised energy in s ($\varnothing E_{s,pos}^N / \varnothing E_{s,neg}^N$) • standard deviation of normalised energy in s ($\sigma \varnothing E_{s,pos}^N / \sigma \varnothing E_{s,neg}^N$)	• $\varnothing \Delta E_{pos,user} / \varnothing \Delta E_{neg,user}$ • $\varnothing \Delta PC_{1,user}$ • $\varnothing \Delta PC_{2,user}$ • $\varnothing \Delta PC_{5,user}$ • $\varnothing \Delta PC_{6,user}$
Exported features from speed profiles	**Contextual impact factors**
Statistical values ($\varnothing / \sigma$) for every segment: • $\sigma RPA / \sigma RNA$ • $\varnothing a_\% / \varnothing d_\%$ • $\varnothing(a_{m,low} * a_\%) / \varnothing(d_{m,low} * d_\%)$ • $\varnothing stop_{cnt}$	• traffic index • daytime (night / weekend / rush-hour / non-peak hour on weekdays) • daylight • status rain • status temperature $< 1°C$ • number of left / right turns per km • traversed part of s

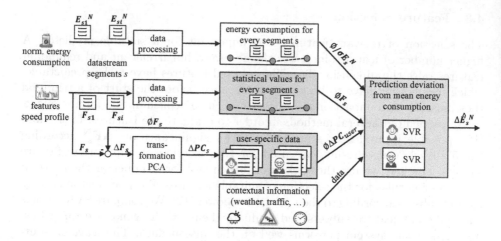

Fig. 4. SVR-model for energy deviation prediction

impact factors, which are known before the start of a trip, like weather or traffic conditions or the number of turns along the route, are also considered as input features for the SVR-model.

In [12], we analysed the driver-specific impact of the deviation of the collected statistical features $\mathbf{\Delta F_s}$ from the corresponding mean values $\varnothing \mathbf{F_s}$. For dimensionality reduction, a principal component analysis (PCA) is applied to transform $\mathbf{\Delta F_s}$ into the principal components $\mathbf{\Delta PC_s}$. The first seven $\mathbf{\Delta PC_s}$ describe the mean deviation of the individual driving behaviour compared to the average driver. The moving average $\varnothing \mathbf{\Delta PC}$ of the driven segments of each road class k are stored for every user in the back-end. Some of these are used as input features for the SVR-model.

5   Evaluation Prediction Accuracy

The accuracy of the energy prediction, based on the introduced SVR-model, is evaluated both segment-by-segment and for complete trips. Additionally, we describe the effect of a recursive update of the SVR-model.

5.1   Evaluation Methodology

A dataset of 70 drivers is chosen for the evaluation of the SVR-model. On average, every driver has driven a distance of 1075 km, which corresponds on average to 611 driven segments or available datasets. For every driver, we selected 60% of all available user-data and a maximum of 600 datasets as training data for the SVR-model. The rest of the data was used as test data. For evaluation, we chose 750 tracks of the test-data, with a minimum length of 20 km, so that short trips consisting of a few segments are not considered.

The absolute vehicle-specific prediction value $\widehat{\mathbf{E}}_\mathbf{s}$ is considered for evaluation, so that $\mathbf{\Delta}\widehat{\mathbf{E}}_\mathbf{s}^\mathbf{N}$ or $\varnothing\widehat{\mathbf{E}}_\mathbf{s}^\mathbf{N}$ have to be denormalised $(N^{-1}())$. We assume that we know the normalization exactly, so that we evaluate only the deviation prediction resulting from the cloud-based system.

The SVR-model predicts the deviation of mean energy consumption $\mathbf{\Delta}\widehat{\mathbf{E}}_\mathbf{s}^\mathbf{N}$. According to (2), $\mathbf{\Delta}\widehat{\mathbf{E}}_\mathbf{s}^\mathbf{N}$ describes the variance around the normalised mean energy consumption $\varnothing\widehat{\mathbf{E}}_\mathbf{s}^\mathbf{N}$ of the segment and describes, more accurately, the predicted normalised energy consumption $\widehat{\mathbf{E}}_\mathbf{s}^\mathbf{N}$. $\varnothing\widehat{\mathbf{E}}_\mathbf{s}^\mathbf{N}$ can be used as a comparative value for evaluation. $\varnothing\widehat{\mathbf{E}}_\mathbf{s}^\mathbf{N}$ corresponds to the energy prediction of currently available EVs, since a map-based approach, in which all relevant map features of the segment are considered, will not be more accurate than $\varnothing\widehat{\mathbf{E}}_\mathbf{s}^\mathbf{N}$. Hence, we calculate, according to (1) and (2), the following two prediction values for evaluation:

$$\widehat{E}_{tot,\varnothing} = N^{-1}\left(\sum_{s=1}^{n}(\varnothing\widehat{E}_{s,pos}^{N} + \varnothing\widehat{E}_{s,neg}^{N})\right) \tag{7}$$

$$\widehat{E}_{tot,\Delta} = N^{-1}\left(\sum_{s=1}^{n}(\varnothing\widehat{E}_{s,pos}^{N} * (1 + \Delta\widehat{E}_{s,pos}^{N}) + \varnothing\widehat{E}_{s,neg}^{N} * (1 + \Delta\widehat{E}_{s,pos}^{N}))\right) \tag{8}$$

We use the mean absolute percentage error (MAPE) for the evaluation. The MAPE is calculated both segment-by-segment for the m segments of all chosen p trips ($p = 750$) and for the p trips, each consisting of n segments:

$$\text{MAPE}_{seg} = \frac{100\%}{m}\sum_{i=1}^{m}\left|\frac{\widehat{\mathbf{E}}_\mathbf{i} - \mathbf{E}_\mathbf{i}}{\mathbf{E}_\mathbf{i}}\right| \tag{9}$$

$$\text{MAPE}_{trip} = \frac{100\%}{p}\sum_{i=1}^{p}\left|\frac{\sum_{i=1}^{n}\widehat{\mathbf{E}}_\mathbf{i} - \sum_{i=1}^{n}\mathbf{E}_\mathbf{i}}{\sum_{i=1}^{n}\mathbf{E}_\mathbf{i}}\right| \tag{10}$$

5.2   Update of the SVR-Model

The initial offline-trained SVR-model can be updated with the continuously collected data of a driver. One possibility is a batch implementation, which retrains the SVR-model in certain periods with the collected datasets stored in a buffer. Another possibility is an online recursive SVR-model, which is more efficient, but results in a lower prediction accuracy. The batch-update method is possible for our energy prediction system, since we do not have a fast datastream, because a new dataset is only available after passing a segment with a length of several kms. The SVR-model can be retrained after a trip has been finished. We retrain the SVR-model after 80 new datasets have been collected and we use a buffer size of 500 datasets.

5.3   Results

Fig. 5 shows the energy prediction for the n segments of a selected trip. The prediction based on the normalised mean values of each segment ($\widehat{E}_{tot,\varnothing}$) and

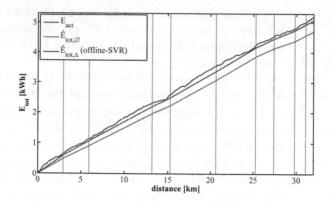

Fig. 5. Energy prediction for a whole trip

the method based on the proposed SVR-model ($\widehat{E}_{tot,\Delta}$) are compared with the really consumed energy E_{act}. The relative error of the prediction of the SVR-model is less than 1% for the exemplary chosen trip, whereas the relative error of $\widehat{E}_{tot,\varnothing}$ is higher than 7%.

We evaluate the accuracy of the proposed SVR-model by comparing the estimation and the real value of all chosen 750 trips. Due to the various length of the trips, the relative error of the route-specific energy consumption in $\frac{kWh}{100km}$ is shown in Fig. 6. Tab. 3 provides an overview of the MAPE of the different methods. The offline-SVR reaches a high accuracy with a MAPE of 7.0%, compared to $\widehat{E}_{tot,\varnothing}$ with 8.9%. The MAPE for E_{neg} is higher than for E_{pos}, since the relative error increases due to the low absolute values of E_{neg}. However, the accuracy of E_{pos} is more important for the accuracy of E_{ges}. The error for whole trips ($MAPE_{trip}$) is much lower than for single segments with a length

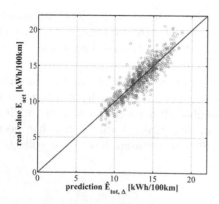

Fig. 6. Prediction accuracy for whole trips

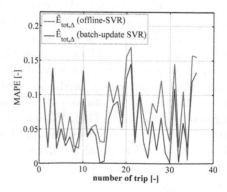

Fig. 7. Update of the SVR-model of a driver

Table 3. Prediction performance (MAPE)

prediction method	evaluation	$\widehat{E}_{pos}$	$\widehat{E}_{neg}$	$\widehat{E}_{tot}$
$\widehat{E}_{tot,\varnothing}$	MAPE$_{seg}$	15.25%	17.74%	17.27%
$\widehat{E}_{tot,\Delta}$ - offline-SVR	MAPE$_{seg}$	14.20%	15.70%	16.25%
$\widehat{E}_{tot,\Delta}$ - batch-update SVR	MAPE$_{seg}$	13.96%	15.50%	16.00%
$\widehat{E}_{tot,\varnothing}$	MAPE$_{trip}$	8.27%	12.25%	8.90%
$\widehat{E}_{tot,\Delta}$ - offline-SVR	MAPE$_{trip}$	6.60%	8.52%	7.02%
$\widehat{E}_{tot,\Delta}$ - batch-update SVR	MAPE$_{trip}$	6.28%	8.26%	6.73%

of a few kilometres, since the errors of single segments are compensated in the consideration of complete trips.

Fig. 7 compares the MAPE of the consecutive trips of a selected driver of the offline SVR-model with the one which is updated in certain periods. The MAPE of the updated SVR-model is lower than the one of the initialisation model (offline-SVR). The improvement varies from driver to driver but, on average, the batch-update SVR-model provides results with a higher prediction accuracy. According to Tab. 3, the batch-updated SVR-model improves the results by 0.29 percentage points.

6 Conclusion and Future Work

SVR-models have been used for the prediction of the energy consumption of EVs. We used statistical features from collected speed profiles and contextual impact factors as input for the SVR-model of each driver, so that the individual driving behaviour, or the prevailing traffic conditions, are considered in the proposed model. We evaluated the prediction model on a high number of real world drives. The proposed SVR-model improves the existing prediction based on a road-segment-specific mean energy consumption. According to the results, the SVR-model can be used for the energy prediction before the start of a trip in a cloud-based approach on the basis of crowd-sourced speed profiles. The model can be applied for various assistant systems for EVs, like a remaining driving distance prediction to show the driver the region which is reachable with the current available amount of energy.

The road segments have been passed by the vehicles only several times a day, as we have used the data of fleet tests which have been conducted with a a few vehicles over a long period of time. If the penetration rate of the vehicles using the cloud-based system increases, the data from vehicles, which have recently passed the road segments, can also be used. Thus, the time-series of the collected statistical features of speed profiles can also be considered for the energy prediction. An extension of the proposed SVR-model will lead to an increase of accuracy, since SVR-models are often used for time-series prediction.

References

1. Dorrer, C.: Effizienzbestimmung von Fahrweisen und Fahrerassistenz zur Reduzierung des Kraftstoffverbrauchs unter Nutzung telematischer Informationen. Ph.D. dissertation, Universitaet Stuttgart (2004)
2. Olivia, J., Weihrauch, C., Bertram, T.: A Model-Based Approach for Predicting the Remaining Driving Range in Electric Vehicles. In: Proc. of the Annual Conference of the Prognostics and Health Management Society, New Orleans (2013)
3. Yu, H., Tseng, F., McGee, R.: Driving pattern identification for EV range estimation. In: IEEE International Electric Vehicle Conference (IEVC), pp. 1–7 (2012)
4. Karbowski, D., Smis-Michel, V., Vermeulen, V.: Using Trip Information for PHEV Fuel Consumption Minimization. In: Proc. of EVS27 International Battery, Hybrid and Fuel Cell Electric Vehicle Symposium, Barcelona (2013)
5. Rodgers, L., Frey, D., Wilhelm, E.: Conventional and novel methods for estimating an electric vehicle's "distance to empty". In: Proc. of the ASME 2013 International Conference on Advanced Vehicle Technologies, Portland (2013)
6. Boriboonsomisn, K., Barth, M., Zhu, W., Vu, A.: Eco-Routing Navigation System Based on Multisource Historical and Real-Time Traffic Information. IEEE Transactions on Intelligent Transportation Systems 13(4), 1694–1704 (2012)
7. Ferreira, J., Monteiro, V., Afonso, J.: Dynamic Range Prediction for an Electric Vehicle. In: Proc. of EVS27 International Battery, Hybrid and Fuel Cell Electric Vehicle Symposium, Barcelona (2013)
8. Masikos, M., Demestichas, K., Adamopoulou, E., Theologou, M.: Mesoscopic forecasting of vehicular consumption using neural networks. Journal Soft Computing, 1–12 (2014)
9. Ericsson, E.: Independent driving pattern factors and their influence on fuel-use and exhaust emission factors. In: Transportation Research Part D: Transport and Environment, part. 6, pp. 325-345 (2001)
10. Grubwinkler, S., Kugler, M., Lienkamp, M.: A system for cloud-based deviation prediction of propulsion energy consumption for EVs. In: IEEE International Conference on Vehicular Electronics and Safety (ICVES), Dongguan, pp. 99–104 (2013)
11. Grubwinkler, S., Lienkamp, M.: A modular and dynamic approach for the prediction of the energy consumption of electric vehicles. In: Proc. of CoFAT, Munich (2013)
12. Grubwinkler, S., Hirschvogel, M., Lienkamp, M.: Driver- and Situation-Specific Impact Factors for the Energy Prediction of EVs based on Crowd-Sourced Speed Profiles. In: IEEE Intelligent Vehicles Symposium (IV), Dearborn, pp. 1069–1076 (2014)
13. OpenStreetMap, http://www.openstreetmap.org/
14. Schoelkopf, B., Smola, A.: Learning with Kernels: Support Vector Machines, Regularization, Optimization and Beyond. MIT Press, Cambridge (2002)
15. Chang, C., Lin, C.: Libsvm: a library for support vector machines. ACM Transactions on Intelligent Systems and Technology (TIST) 2(3), 27 (2011)
16. Hall, M., Frank, E., Holmes, G., Pfahringer, B., Reutemann, P., Witten, I.H.: The weka data mining software: an update. SIGKDD Explorations 11(1), 10–18 (2009)
17. Guyon, I., Elisseeff, A.: An Introduction to Variable and Feature Selection. J. Mach. Learn. Res. 3, 1157–1182 (2003)

Modelling Spot Prices
on the Polish Energy Market

Michał Pawłowski[1] and Piotr Nowak[2]

[1] Institute of Computer Science Polish Academy of Sciences,
Jana Kazimierza 5, Warsaw, Poland
m.pawlowski@phd.ipipan.waw.pl
[2] Systems Research Institute Polish Academy of Sciences,
Newelska 6, Warsaw, Poland
pnowak@ibspan.waw.pl

Abstract. The aim of this paper is to present a model of the Polish Power Exchange (PPE) energy spot prices. The proposed model is a result of a comprehensive and focused on the Polish market's characteristics analysis (different markets are weakly interconnected, all of them possess their unique properties). The exchange located in Warsaw is relatively young (14 years of spot prices history) with few liquid contracts traded, which made the goal more challenging.

The suggested dynamics of spot prices is driven by a mean-reverting jump-diffusion stochastic process with mixed-exponentially distributed jumps. The presented approach contains numerous custom-made solutions which have not been introduced in the literature yet. The mentioned jump size distribution combined with a mean-reverting diffusion is novel itself in electricity spot prices modelling.

1   Introduction

The paths of the electric power engineering sector with competition converged at the end of the nineties. At that time most countries in Europe including Poland (in April 1997) implemented reforms in the law so as to consider electricity not like a common good, but as a commodity which may be traded similarly to equities or currency. To create and manage a market for: electricity generators, companies involved in energy trading, energy suppliers and industry clients, which could face up to all privatization programmes, the PPE was established (started to operate in December 1999).

The spot prices time series at the PPE exhibits all the distinguishing (from prices trajectories' of other purpose markets, for instance share markets) features: daily, weekly, yearly seasonality, mean-reversion to the marginal cost of production and abrupt spikes of prices (negative or positive jumps and sharp, almost immediate returns to the previous level) caused e.g. by a failure of a transmission network, outage of power plants or a sudden decrease (or increase) in temperature, in conjunction with inelasticity of demand and supply. In the context of pricing derivatives, there is no possibility to build a replicating strategy

© Springer International Publishing Switzerland 2015
D. Filev et al. (eds.), *Intelligent Systems'2014*,
Advances in Intelligent Systems and Computing 323, DOI: 10.1007/978-3-319-11310-4_68

– storage of the underlying is infeasible, production and consumption have to be in balance all the time.

In the paper we propose the stochastic process S of electrical energy spot prices on the Warsaw's exchange. We take into account the mentioned above unique attributes of the electricity spot prices, which are typical for the PPE. Simultaneously, we take into consideration the possibility of pricing forward contracts and options with the underlying asset described by S.

In a traditional Black-Scholes model the authors applied geometric Brownian motion for description of the underlying financial instrument. The modelled market is complete and the standard European option pricing formula has an analytical closed-form. However, the Black-Scholes model has also disadvantages. Contrary to the theoretical assumptions, log-returns of underlying assets on the real market have leptokurtic and skewed to the left distributions. Moreover, the implied volatilities as functions of the strike price form a "U-shape", which is called the volatility smile.

There are many alternatives for the Black-Scholes model in financial literature. Many authors use Levy processes, i.e. stochastic processes with independent and stationary increments, to describe log-prices of underlying assets. Levy processes applied in finance fall into two categories: jump-diffusion models and infinite activity models. The first jump-diffusion model was considered by Merton in [16], where the log-price process of the underlying asset was a sum of the Brownian motion with drift and the compound Poisson process with jump sizes following the normal distribution. Merton obtained an option pricing formula under the assumption that jump risk is not systematic. Kou in [11] and Kou and Wang in [12] priced many types of options, applying the jump-diffusion model and assuming the asymmetric double exponential distribution of the jump sizes. There are also several more general approaches (see e.g. [1, 5, 6]), where the underlying assets are described by the phase-type (PHM), hyperexponential (HEM) and mixed-exponential jump-diffusion (MEM) models. MEM has good analytical features and the mixed-exponential distribution can approximate any distribution in the sense of weak convergence. Therefore, this type of jump-diffusion was an inspiration for our electrical energy spot prices model. Levy jump-diffusions with a discrete distribution of jumps were also applied in [17]. Models from the second category form a rich class of processes. Two important infinite activity models used in finance are the Normal Inverse Gaussian model and the Variance Gamma model (see e.g. [15] and [2]).

If we look closer on the currently widely studied and used models for electricity by both researchers and practioners, we have to recall the threshold model (see [8]) in which the jump's magnitude has a predefined upper bound and a fixed threshold in the price value, exceeding of which results in the possibility solely of a negative jump.

The class of regime switching models is a fast developing and popular family of models for electricity prices repatterning due to the popularity of Markov models and because the energy spot price at every moment may be assigned one out of several, unique in the context of price behaviour, states. The latest ideas in the regime switching modelling of energy were shown in [11].

Our model is preceded by the presentation of the most commonly known model for the energy spot prices evolution. This is in Section 3. The rest of the paper is organized as follows. In Section 4 the dynamics of the tailor-made model for the Polish market is introduced. Section 5 contains some basic features of the daily prices chosen from the PPE's spot index for analysis. In Section 6 the method of matching seasonality is written up in details. Having read Section 7, we are acquainted with the algorithm for detection of spikes in prices. The process of parameters estimation is comprised in Section 8. In Section 9 the discretization of the continuous-time equation, as well as the comparison of the simulated this way trajectories with the historical series are performed. The last section concludes.

2   A Mean-Reverting Jump-Diffusion Model with Seasonality

One of the most obvious choices when modelling electrical energy spot prices are one-factor models. This is due to their good adaptivity to data, existence, not infrequently, of analytical solutions to numerous provided issues, as well as multiple approximation methods.

A prototype model for electricity, which became a starting point for any other considerations, was introduced in [14]. The model is lumbered with one serious flaw – it does not allow for jumps in spot prices. However, it reflects another two fundamental features: mean-reverting and deterministic seasonality. What is more, it has an analytical solution. A natural enhancement is to put the jump component to the driving process.

May S_t denote a spot price at a moment t (time is measured in years, single time step on the modelled markets is one day). The dynamics in a continuous setting is described by

$$S_t = \exp(g(t) + X_t), \tag{1}$$

where $g(t)$ is a deterministic seasonality function and X_t is a mean-reverting (to the mean equal 0) process, the increases of which are assumed to follow

$$dX_t = -\alpha X_t dt + \sigma(t)dW_t + dJ_t, \tag{2}$$

where $\sigma(t)$ is a deterministic, time dependent volatility, $J_t = \sum_{i=1}^{N_t} Z_i$, where N_t is a Poisson process with some constant intensity and Z_i are i.i.d. jump magnitudes of a normal $N(-\frac{\sigma_J^2}{2}, \sigma_J^2)$ distribution, W_t is a Brownian motion. With given assumptions

$$dS_t = \alpha(\rho(t) - \ln S_t)S_t dt + \sigma(t)S_t dW_t + S_t(e^{J_t} - 1)dN_t, \tag{3}$$

where $\rho(t) = \frac{1}{\alpha}\left(\frac{dg(t)}{dt} + \frac{1}{2}\sigma^2(t)\right) + g(t)$. The authors in [7] suggested using the seasonality function g which fits the observed monthly averages with the Fourier series of order 5. Another proposal came from [3], where

$$g(t) = a + \beta t + \gamma \cos(\varepsilon + 2\pi t) + \delta \cos(\eta + 4\pi t). \tag{4}$$

The interpretation of the parameters is as follows: a stands for fixed costs of the production of electricity. The second one denotes the long run linear trend in the costs. The periodicity is contained in both cosines reflecting the market with two prices maxima per year.

One may change the distribution of Z's, so that $\{Z_i\}$ is a sequence of i.i.d. random variables of asymmetric double exponential distribution with density

$$f(z) = q\theta e^{\theta z} \mathbb{1}_{\{z<0\}} + p\eta e^{-\eta z} \mathbb{1}_{\{z\geq 0\}},$$

where $p, q > 0$ are the probabilities of upward and downward jumps, respectively. The restrictions $\eta_1 > 1$, $\eta_2 > 0$ and $p + q = 1$ are imposed. A very detailed description of the model may be found in [4].

3   The Model of the Polish Power Exchange Spot Prices

In this section we propose a model of the spot prices suited to the Polish market's data. The idea of the mixed-exponential distribution of jumps is drawn from [6], but the connection of such jump distribution with a mean-reversion and applying it to the electicity spot prices modelling is a novelty.

Let us write the decomposition of the S_t process in the form:

$$S_t = \exp(f(t) + X_t),$$

$$dX_t = -\alpha X_t dt + \sigma dW_t + dJ_t, \tag{5}$$

where α and σ are constants, W_t is a Wiener process, $J_t = \sum_{i=1}^{N_t} Z_i$ and N_t is a Poisson process with constant intensity λ and Z's are i.i.d. jump magnitudes of translated mixed-exponential distribution, i.e. with density

$$f(z) = q_d \sum_{i=1}^{m} q_i \theta_i e^{\theta_i(z-m_d)} \mathbb{1}_{\{z<m_d\}} + p_u \sum_{j=1}^{n} p_j \eta_j e^{-\eta_j(z-m_u)} \mathbb{1}_{\{z>m_u\}}, \tag{6}$$

where

$$q_d, p_u \geq 0, \quad q_d + p_u = 1, \quad q_i, p_j \in (-\infty, \infty), \quad \sum_{i=1}^{m} q_i = \sum_{j=1}^{n} p_j = 1, \quad \theta_i > 0, \eta_j > 1.$$

q_d and p_u are the probabilities of negative and positive jumps, respectively. $m_d < 0$ is a minimal (with respect to the absolute value) value of negative jumps, $m_u > 0$ is a minimal value of positive jumps. A necessary condition for $f(z)$ to be a density function is $q_1, p_1 > 0$, $\sum_{i=1}^{m} q_i \theta_i \geq 0$, $\sum_{j=1}^{n} p_j \eta_j \geq 0$. One of possible sufficient conditions is $\sum_{i=1}^{k} q_i \theta_i \geq 0$, $\sum_{j=1}^{l} p_j \eta_j \geq 0$ for all $k \in \{1, \ldots, m\}$, $l \in \{1, \ldots, n\}$. A special case of the mixed-exponential distribution is a hyper-exponential distribution, when all parameters q_i and p_j are nonnegative.

The separation from zero of the support of the density function is caused by the fact that either positive or negative jumps are extreme events, therefore highly greater than zero with repect to the absolute value.

The propounded mixed-exponential distribution has a distinguishing property that it can approximate any distribution with respect to weak convergence. In the light of problems with matching a distribution to a dataset of jumps, such property seems to be a countermeasure. Nonetheless, the price to pay is plenty of parameters to be estimated (however, in practice taking $n = m = 2$ is sufficient to ensure very good accuracy). Using the Ito lemma, one obtains that S_t follows the stochasic differential equation (3), but the J_t component is changed.

4   Data Description

The data selected for estimation comes from the PPE's IRDN index with the time range of March 2011 – September 2013 (924 quotations) with an exception for the jump size distribution estimation due to scarcity of jumps – from September 2005 to September 2013 (2924 quotations).

By a spot price we mean a weighted (by volume) average price of daily transactions.

Without any deep analysis one can state the fact that prices undergo some yearly seasonal fluctuations, negative trend, but the most conspicuous are: weakly seasonality – indices values on Sundays are unequivocally smaller than during the rest days, and presence of jumps. Jumps may be categorized into two groups: there are only a few rises or falls that are apparently higher than others. The second group consists of a big number of smaller jumps which absolute values

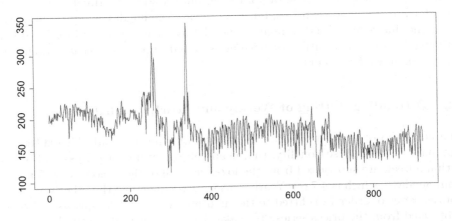

Fig. 1. Spot prices in PLN/MWh: 03/2011 - 09/2013

slightly exceed or are at the level of the Sundays' drops. Both groups will be detected during estimation. All kinds of movements have their mirror images – the prices come back to the long run mean which is a seasonality.

5 Seasonality Fitting

From the specification of our model we know, that subtracting the seasonality function from the series of prices we are left with a kind of residue which we model by the zero-mean-reverting jump-diffusion process (5). In other words, after filtering spikes from this residue, the returns of the remaining noise must have normal distribution. Therefore, the relevant, objective criterion for measuring the goodness of seasonality combined with removal of spikes should be a p-value of the appropriate statistical test for normality of the mentioned returns. The stage of constructing the appropriate seasonality is divided into several steps.

5.1 Deterministic Downward Spikes

The Polish market has a distinctive feature that the prices substantially come down for a one-day period, if this day is a national holiday. The biggest impact this effect has on 24, 25 and 26 December when two days in a row in Poland are holidays and during the third day one works less. Next day the price recurs to the former level. Thus, these deterministic downward spikes should be extracted from the time series in the first instance as a first component of the seasonality. What is worth mentioning, is that in case a holiday occurs on Sunday, the decreases do not sum up (the bigger prevails). An estimator of the value of the jump is a mean of decreases of prices (from a day preceding the holiday, if it is not Sunday or another holiday, to the holiday) during years which are chosen to estimation. There are 12 such deterministic downward jumps each year.

In the process of deseasonalisation the absolute values of estimators of jumps are added to the holidays prices, but only in case the holiday is not on Sunday. If so, the difference of the estimator and the average Sunday's drop is added – if this difference is positive, or nothing is added otherwise (because then the typical Sunday's fall occurs).

5.2 Detrending, Fitting of Weekly and Yearly Oscillations

The next step of deseasonalisation is removal of a linear trend. Thereafter, to eliminate the weekly seasonality, the means of logarithms of prices of all days within a week are subtracted from the log-series (all of them close to 4.85 apart from Sunday's which is 4.727). Yearly seasonality is matched the other way. The Fourier series of order 12 is fitted to the monthly averages of log-prices and then subtracted from the prices series. To make the series fluctuate around zero, the average index value is added to the whole range of the deseasonalised prices.

5.3   Annual Sinusoidal Function

In order to detect any remaining annual movements, other than described above, the periodic (one year period) sinusoidal function of the form

$$a + bt + \sum_{k=1}^{3} c_k \sin\left(\frac{2k\pi t}{365}\right) + d_k \cos\left(\frac{2k\pi t}{365}\right)$$

is fitted by the nonlinear least-squares method and subtracted from the series (Figure 2).

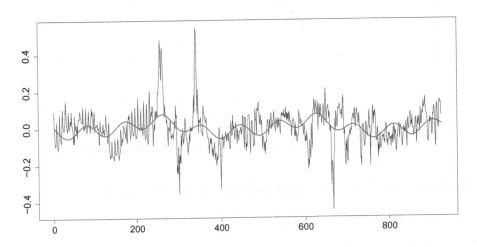

Fig. 2. Annual sinuisoidal function fitted to the partially deseasonalised log-price series

6   Filtering of Spikes

Filtering of spikes is performed by the iterative procedure: in the first step all jumps which absolute value exceeds some predefined threshold, for instance three times the standard deviation of the deseasonalised log-returns, are removed from the series. In the next step the same action is made, but this time the standard deviation is calculated basing on the thinned series of returns. New jumps are filtered and deleted and the process continues until in some iteration no jumps are found.

The most important aspect of this method is to fix the threshold so as to maximize the p-value of the Shapiro-Wilk normality test for the deseasonalised, and with deleted jumps, log-returns. For our data the threshold turned out to be $2.78s$, where s is the standard deviation of the series obtained in each step of the described procedure. The maximized p-value is equal to 0.08, whereas other normality tests indicate even better results: Anderson-Darling – 0.16, Shapiro-Francia – 0.19, Kolmogorov-Smirnov – 0.44, Jarque-Bera – 0.7. There is no evidence to reject the null hypothesis of the log-returns normality at the 5% significance level. The quantile-quantile plot (Figure 3) confirms this statement.

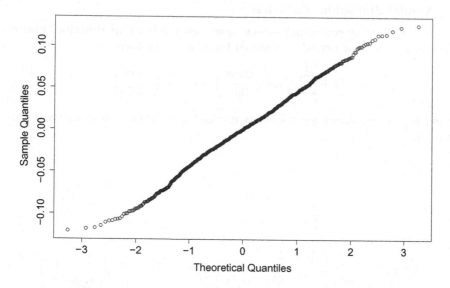

Fig. 3. Quantile-Quantile plot for log-returns without jumps

7 Estimation of the Jump-Diffusion's Parameters

7.1 Base Signal Parameters' Assessment

Having deseasonalised the log-price series and removed jumps, one may estimate the parameter σ appearing in equation (5) as a mean of the rolling historical volatility

$$
\sigma(t_k) = \sqrt{\frac{1}{m-1} \sum_{i=k-m+1}^{k} \left(\frac{P_{i+1} - P_i}{\sqrt{t_{i+1} - t_i}} - \sum_{j=k-m+1}^{k} \frac{P_{j+1} - P_j}{\sqrt{t_{j+1} - t_j}} \right)^2 },
$$

$m = 30$, $k \in \{30, \ldots, 873\}$, because after removing of jumps there are 873 log-returns.[1] For all $i \in \{1, \ldots, 872\}$ $t_{i+1} - t_i = \frac{1}{365}$, P is the deseasonalised and devoid of jumps log-price index. The estimated value $\sigma = 0.86$.

Determination of the mean-reversion's velocity α is based on the deseasonalised log-prices, but in the presence of spikes. One has to regress the deseasonalised log-prices series bereft of its first element versus the deseasonalised log-prices series without its last element, which is a direct cause of the discretized form (see Subsection 8.1) of the equation (5):

$$
X_t = e^{-\alpha \Delta t} X_{t-1} + \rho_t,
$$

---

[1] Applying the method described in the previous section, we get rid not only of jumps, but also of mean-reversions exceeding some big threshold, which is desired. This is the reason for a huge number of expelled log-returns.

where ρ_t is the sum of integrals of the Wiener process and the compounded Poisson process between times $t-1$ and t.[2] The speed of mean-reversion $\alpha = 0.24$.

7.2   Evaluation of Jump Size Distribution's Parameters

As mentioned in Section 4, much longer time series is used for the estimation of the jump magnitude's distribution to assure that there is enough data for a stable assessment of this kind of rare event. The algorithm describing how it is done was explained in Section 6, nevertheless a salient modification is prerequisite at this moment. In fact, when using the iterative method written up earlier (or any similar), we filter numerous unnecessary returns which are simply the mean-reversions of the process, occuring a moment after the jump takes place. Of course, they need to be removed in order to obtain the actual estimators of the jump size distribution.

In the density function specification (6), we take $m = n = 2$. 249 returns are classified as jumps by the filtering algorithm on the series of 2924 observations. Out of these jumps, 57 are the mean-reversions and thus are not considered in the estimation. Accordingly, the yearly frequency of the Poisson process $\lambda = (249 - 57)/2924 \cdot 365 = 23.97$. The results of the maximum likelihood estimation are presented in the table 1. The parameters q_1, q_2, p_1, p_2 are all positive, so that the jump distribution turns out to be the hyperexponential distribution, a special case of the mixed-exponential distribution. The figure 4 ilustrates the adjustment of the density to the histogram of filtered jumps.

Table 1. Estimated parameters of the mixed-exponential jump size distribution

q_d	q_1	q_2	θ_1	θ_2	m_d	p_u	p_1	p_2	η_1	η_2	m_u
0.64	0.14	0.86	3198.49	9.58	-0.12	0.36	0.3	0.7	2745.1	10.13	0.12

8   Simulation of the Spot Prices and Tests for the Trajectories

8.1   Discretization of the Process

Integrating the equation (5), one may obtain (see [10] in case of normal jumps) the relation between X_t and X_{t-1}:

$$X_t = X_{t-1} \exp\left(\frac{-\alpha}{365}\right) + \sigma\sqrt{\frac{1 - \exp\left(\frac{-2\alpha}{365}\right)}{2\alpha}} N(0,1) + B\left(\frac{\lambda}{365}\right) Z(\mathbb{p}), \quad (7)$$

where $N(0,1)$ is a standard normally distributed variable, $B\left(\frac{\lambda}{365}\right)$ is a Bernoulli variable taking value 1 with the probability $\frac{\lambda}{365}$, or 0 with the probablility $1 - \frac{\lambda}{365}$.

---

[2] This is a simplified notation: $t = t_i$, $t - 1 = t_{i-1}$, $\Delta t = t_i - t_{i-1}$.

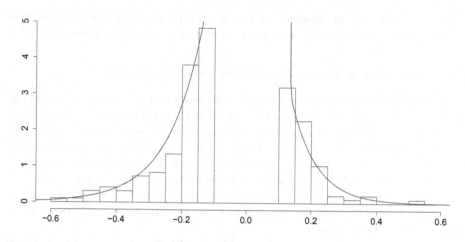

Fig. 4. Mixed-exponential distribution fitted to the histogram of jumps

It is an approximation of the Poisson process' growth – a consecution of the fact, that during a one-day time step no more than a single jump may appear. $Z(\mathbb{p})$ is a mixed-exponentially distributed random variable with a vector of estimated parameters $\mathbb{p}$, (see Subsection 7.2). A sample trajectory with added seasonality and trend is shown on the Figure 5 on a background of the historical path.

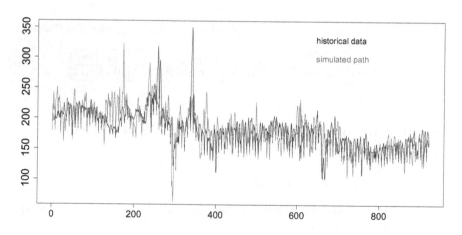

Fig. 5. Simulated sample path versus historical data in PLN/MWh

8.2   Goodness of Fit of the Sample Paths

The comparison of the two moments and 5%, 95% quantiles of the historical spot prices (in PLN/MWh) which are used for estimation and an average of 2000 simulated trajectories is shown in the table 2. The comparison of the two moments and 5%, 95% quantiles of the historical log-returns and an average of the log-returns of 2000 simulated trajectories is shown in the table 3. Both tables indicate a very good reflection of the real time series by the simulated paths.

Table 2. Moments and quantiles of the historical spot prices and 2000 simulated paths

	mean	st. dev.	5% quantile	95% quantile
real data	181.15	29.25	137.02	222.65
simulations	181.04	29.22	135.69	227.02

Table 3. Moments and quantiles of the historical and 2000 simulated log-returns (average)

	mean	st. dev.	5% quantile	95% quantile
real data	-0.00023	0.09	-0.15	0.18
simulations	-0.00021	0.1	-0.16	0.18

9   Conclusions

In the article the authors introduced the new model for the electricity spot prices, wchich are quoted on the Polish Power Exchange, taking into account all the specificity of the Warsaw's market, as well as the electrical energy prices' in general. Several novel ideas concerning seasonality matching, spikes filtering, jump size distribution, etc. have been put into practice. The parameters have been estimated basing on the historical data. The model has been validated by performing simulations and tests for the goodness of fit, which legitimized the proposed approach.

The future work will concern a derivation of the analitical formula for the forward price, calibration of the model to the forward contracts quoted on the exchange and finally valuing of options within the model.

We would like to thank Prof. Olgierd Hryniewicz from SRI PAS for helpful comments and advices.

Acknowledgement. Study was supported by research fellowship within "Information technologies: research and their interdisciplinary applications" agreement number POKL.04.01.01-00-051/10-00.

References

[1] Asmussen, S., Avram, F., Pistorius, M.: Russian and American put options under exponential phase-type Levy models. Stochastic Processes Appl. 109(1), 79–111 (2004)

[2] Barndorff-Nielsen, O.E.: Processes of normal inverse Gaussian type. Finance and Stochastics 2, 41–68 (1997)

[3] Benth, F.E., Kiesel, R., Nazarova, A.: A critical empirical study of three electricity price models. Energy Economics 34(5), 1589–1616 (2012)

[4] Bodea, A., Mare, B.: Valuation of Swing Options in Electricity Commodity Markets, dissertation, University of Heidelberg (2012)

[5] Cai, N., Chen, N., Wan, X.: Pricing double-barrier options under a flexible jump diffusion model. Oper. Res. Lett. 37(3), 163–167 (2009)

[6] Cai, N., Kou, S.G.: Option Pricing Under a Mixed-Exponential Jump Diffusion Model. Management Science 57, 2067–2081 (2011)

[7] Cartea, A., Figueroa, M.: Pricing in Electricity Markets: a mean reverting jump diffusion model with seasonality. Applied Mathematical Finance 12(4), 313–335 (2005)

[8] Geman, H., Roncoroni, A.: Understanding the Fine Structure of Electricity Prices. Journal of Business 79(3) (2006)

[9] Janczura, J., Weron, R.: An empirical comparison of alternate regime-switching models for electricity spot prices. Energy Economics 32(5), 1059–1073 (2010)

[10] Kacprzak, K., Maciejczyk, K., Opalski, K., Paw, M.: łowski Modelling the Polish energy market/. Mathematica Applicanda 13(54), 105–114 (2011)

[11] Kou, S.G.: A jump-diffusion model for option pricing. Management Science 48(8), 1086–1101 (2002)

[12] Kou, S.G., Wang, H.: Option pricing under a double exponential jump diffusion model. Management Science 50(9), 1178–1192 (2004)

[13] Lindstrom, E., Regland, F.: Modelling extreme dependence between European electricity markets. Energy Economics 34(4), 899–904 (2012)

[14] Lucia, J., Schwartz, E.: Electricity prices and power derivatives: Evidence from the Nordic Power Exchange. Review of Derivatives Research 5(1), 5–50 (2002)

[15] Madan, D.B., Seneta, E.: The Variance Gamma (V.G.) Model for Share Market Returns. The Journal of Business 63(4), 511–524 (1990)

[16] Merton, R.: Option pricing when underlying stock returns are discontinuous. Journal of Financial Economics 3, 125–144 (1976)

[17] Nowak, P., Romaniuk, M.: A Fuzzy Approach to Option Pricing in a Levy Process Setting. International Journal of Applied Mathematics and Computer Science 23(3), 613–622 (2013)

Dynamic Pricing and Balancing Mechanism for a Microgrid Electricity Market

Jarosław Stańczak[1], Weronika Radziszewska[1], and Zbigniew Nahorski[1,2]

[1] Systems Research Institute, Polish Academy of Sciences, Warsaw, Poland
[2] Warsaw School of Information Technology (WIT), Warsaw, Poland

Abstract. The trading is a well known, easy and efficient method of distributing goods. Energy cannot be stored efficiently, which implies that supply and demand of power has to be balanced at all times; this adds complexity to the trading of electric power. Introduction of microgrids, with internal balancing of power and trading with external power grid, brings many questions about power distribution, sharing of costs and revenues. Using market mechanism for such purpose seems appropriate. In this article we present an example of balancing a microgrid with its own energy production sources and connected to a higher voltage distribution grid, by introduction of the continuous double auction market with agents following the Adaptive-Aggressive Strategy.

1   Introduction

Electric power markets form a special type of commodity markets – their construction is complicated due to the properties of electric power. These properties include limited possibility to store power over time (especially large quantities), vulnerability of devices in power grid to the imbalances, and the propagation of imbalances through the grid. Electric power is traded on future, day ahead, real-time and balancing markets, in different time periods ahead of its delivery, in order to finally reach the balance of supply and demand at any time [12].

For a retail consumer or prosumer, such markets are nowadays generally inaccessible due to too small quantities that such units can offer. Non-business consumers pay now a fixed amount per kWh of power or at most they can choose some tariffs which differentiate between peak and off-peak time of the day. Only quite recently introduction of smart meters enabled experimental dynamic pricing for residential customers [4]. But short-time variation of power prices can be used to create a ultra-short time market where a consumer can save more money by adjusting its load according to the prices. Such possibility allows for active participation of a consumer in the regulating and balancing process by taking demand response actions [1].

Power market literature have already quite a long history. Murray [12] presents general description of the power markets, including industry infrastructure, cost structure, and market schemes, with detailed description of different national markets. He considers influence of the emission trading on the prices of energy

© Springer International Publishing Switzerland 2015   793
D. Filev et al. (eds.), *Intelligent Systems'2014*,
Advances in Intelligent Systems and Computing 323, DOI: 10.1007/978-3-319-11310-4_69

and also analyses the long-term scenarios for the market. A comprehensive description of all existing and historical markets can be found in [8]. In [6] changes in prices and income of consumers and producers are analyzed from when the English energy market was privatized and the market competition was introduced in 1998.

In [19] a Java implementation of a market for a big, interstate power grid level is presented. The open-source AMES framework is described, including the structural configuration of nodes. Authors implemented the reinforced learning VRE algorithm developed by Roth-Erev [17] in 1995.

A microgrid is a group of producers, consumers and prosumers of energy which are connected together. Microgrids are usually also connected to the external network (are synchronized with the national electropower grid), but can be disconnected and work as isolated networks. Producers and prosumers in a microgrid are usually producing small amount of electricity using renewable energy sources, as wind turbines, small hydropower plants, or photovoltaic panels, but also other microsources, like gas turbines working on biogas or natural gas. According to [12], distributed energy sources will cover 40% of the consumption by 2050. The best areas to develop the microgrids are where there is a risk of power shortages, like in areas that are far from big power plants, located in valleys and places with poor network infrastructure, as well as those completely isolated from large electropower grids.

Benefits of introducing microgrids and microsources to the existing infrastructure are discussed in [10]. The main ones are: ability of small sources to cope with heterogeneous power quality, reliability, and easiness to adapt new technologies by the small prosumers.

In [2] virtual power plants which are cost-efficient integrates of microsources are considered. They are analyzed using the game theoretical approach, with detailed description of proposed scheme of rewarding and punishment for low quality prediction accuracy, which is fundamental in cooperation.

Auctions are popular ways of market negotiations. A detailed presentation of auctions, like e.g. one- and two-sided, single- and multi-round, single- and multi-unit, information revealing, first and second price, closing rules, are given in [7]. Auctions in the electricity markets are analyzed in [18]. General issues of on-line auctions, which are of special interest in this paper, are discussed e.g. in [7, 11, 15]. In [22] it is argued that there are fundamental differences between static and dynamic double auctions, because in dynamic auctions the market equilibrium price is changing in time. An implementation of a double auction scheme based on 4-heap for storing the offers (bids) is proposed in [23]. The continuous double auction schema is shown to be suitable and efficient for situations with changing equilibrium price [22]. In [20] the bidding strategies in the continuous double auctions are described and the extension to the auction mechanism is presented that promotes truthful bidding. General informations on automated negotiations can be found in [5].

In the present paper balancing of a microgrid with independent users is considered. Both energy producers and consumers are active in the microgrid, but the microgrid is also connected to a distributing grid, where it can sell to or buy from any amount of the electroenergy. The producers and consumers of energy are striving for prices most favorable for them. At least some of producers use renewable energy sources, like wind strength or sunshine, resulting in a quite volatile production of electrical power. Also consumption of energy in the microgrid changes unpredictably due to random human behaviors in usage of electric appliances. In the result, the energy manager in a microgrid has to set prices for energy in a constantly varying environment, where both production and consumption of energy are varying, with different costs related to different production units.

In order to use the internal possibility of managing production and consumption in helping to balance on-line the power in a microgrid in the cheapest way, a market is proposed in the present paper. In our case, a balancing external operator acts in the market, e.g. an operator of the higher voltage distributing grid, to which the microgrid is connected. However, the preference is put to possibly use production from the renewable energy sources present in the grid. To achieve this, we propose a double auction schema for energy trading, in which the prices offered by the external operator are not competitive to these proposed by energy producers in the microgrid.

This market is simulated using multiagent system approach. Agents are using Adaptive-Aggressive Strategy [22] to get the most profitable deal on the market.

In the next section the model of the market is presented. Section III describes the agent strategy, which is checked on two simple simulation examples in Section IV. The final section concludes.

2   Market Simulation

To simulate trading, it is needed first of all to decide on the market architecture. Two obvious architectures are the distributed and the centralized ones. Both architectures have certain properties associated with the communication model necessary to apply them. Differences also lie in their potential applications.

In a distributed market, participants (or agents) are directly engaged in exchange of goods, by negotiating the best, from their point of view, contracts. On such markets the various agents reach bilateral or multilateral agreements, usually after some, often complex negotiation. During negotiation, each negotiator may choose freely the negotiation partner, without the involvement of any central entity. Thus, in such markets, we observe the peer-to-peer communication. An example of such mechanism, proposed for trade of the greenhouse gases emision permits, is described in [3]. The mechanism considers dynamic trading in a distributed environment, and it is called the bilateral trading. Agents split into pairs and a single negotiation process occurs inside each pair. Each negotiation process may lead to an agreement. The spliting process is performed randomly, it occurs after termination of the running negotiation process, and is repeated iteratively. Established pairs conduct bilateral contracts depending on their expected profits.

In exchange-type markets there exists a central agent (e.g. the market supervisor), which collects offers sent by other agents involved in the trade. Such agent balance the demand and supply on the market, according to the defined criteria. The central agent distributes the balance results to all agents involved. It may also ensure compliance with various restrictions, e.g. physical constraints associated with the production and transmission of electricity. An example of such market organization is proposed in [9]. That paper proposes a multi-agent model of a local electrical energy market, where agents are software components, which independently take actions tending to make agreements at the most attractive conditions.

The simplest type of such mechanism is the stock market, where there are no physical limitations for delivery. The bids can be ordered by price and most favorable offers are accepted, while others are rejected. In the simplest case, the equilibrium price and total volume are determined in the intersection of supply and demand curves. Such rules are used e.g. in the wholesale electric power exchanges. However, there is often a need to reflect the above-mentioned physical limitations in the balancing processes.

Many different market processes are associated with complex market architecture. Moreover, markets may operate in advance to the commodity delivery time. This is the case of the electricity energy balancing, for which different markets exist, like the market for larger blocks contracts (wholesale market) that usually takes place long time ahead, shorter exchange markets, for example the day ahead or the hour ahead, and the real time balancing market. Each of these markets are characterized not only by a different period length to the energy delivery time, but also by the stress put on different goals, which changes with the approaching time of delivery. These are on the one hand the physical aspects (e.g. need to ensure infrastructure constraints on a real time balancing market), and on the other hand the economic aspects (e.g. emphasis on price on longer period ahead markets). Generally, when the commodity delivery date is imminent, the physical aspects are essential. The physical constraints bind different market participants. There is a need for the system operator to care about the technical constraints satisfaction. These requirements suggest to apply centralized trade in this case. But, when a lot of time remains to the time of commodity delivery, the economic aspects are more important. Often the physical constraints are not considered then or are less important. On such markets most often the bilateral (or multilateral) contracts are concluded in a possibly distributed trade. Therefore the market localization on the timeline determines not only the importance of physical or economic aspects, but also the communication architecture. The distributed architecture is generally more suitable, when it is enough time to the delivery. The centralized architecture is more suitable, if it is closer to the delivery time. This is, however, changing with the possibilities of applying the computer technologies, which offer quick communications and solution of decision problems. This kind of approach is addressed in the present paper.

From the point of view of a microgrid, the national electropower grid has unlimited capacity in production and consumption of energy. This means that each participant may choose to trade with the national electropower grid without any limitation and the operator of the electropower grid can actively place any amount of its offers on the market. It is assumed here that the microgrid does not influence the prices of the external market, so the prices offered by the power grid are changing according to the external market price, that is not considered in this scenario. The situation considered is similar to that described in [14] and [16]. The important difference is that now the owners of producing and consuming units are independent, while in [14] and [16] there was one owner of the whole microgrid.

It is also assumed that all of the parties on the microgrid market trade energy using continuous double auction. Each party decides how much energy has to be bought or sold and sends it as an offer to the market with a proposed price per unit. Units and offers are divisible up to a certain minimal amount that can be traded, and the minimal price that can be offered.

The market mechanism is continuously collecting the offers and matching the new ones with the already submitted bids or asks. If the price of a bid[1] on the market is greater or equal the price of the ask,[2] the deal is made. The deal can be made for just the part of offered energy, that means that one amount of needed energy, defined in one bid, can be supplied by few sellers. The deal is the formal agreement between the participants. There might be just one offer from one agent at a time. The participant can send a new offer when its earlier offer has been cleared, that is it was matched and the deal was accomplished.

If the deal for the energy is not accomplished in the current session, then there is a balancing mechanism that checks the true usage/production of energy and clears the unsettled offers by exchanging them with the external grid.

Consumers and prosumers want to satisfy their need for energy. The additional aim of prosumers and the main goal of producers is to gain as much profit as possible from selling the energy. On the other way, the consumers do not want to spend more than necessary for the energy they need.

Each market participant has its own price limits. For producers this is the running cost or depreciation costs, including overheads. For consumers it is a maximum price they can accept. The definition of "expensive" or "cheap" for the participant is individual for each party.

3 Description of the Price Negotiation Algorithm

The strategy of each agent is an implementation of Adaptive-Aggressive Strategy. The Adaptive-Aggressive (AA) Strategy has been developed by Vytelingum in his PD thesis [21] and then presented in [22]. The AA strategy combines estimation, modeling of aggressiveness, and short- and long-term learning. This strategy has been also discussed in [13].

---

[1] Bid – the offer of buying a certain amount of good on a double auction market.
[2] Ask – the offer of selling a certain amount of good on a double auction market.

An estimate of the equilibrium price at the close of trading time T is calculated as the weighted moving average of last N transaction prices $p(t)$

$$\hat{p}^*(T) = \sum_{t=T-N+1}^{T} w(t)p(t) \tag{1}$$

$$w(t-1) = \rho w(t), \qquad \sum_{t=T-N+1}^{T} w(t) = 1$$

where $w(t)$ are weights, and $0 < \rho < 1$. From the above conditions it stems

$$w(T) = \frac{1-\rho}{1-\rho^N}$$

The value $\rho = 0.9$ has been adopted in the simulations presented in the sequel.

The trader has its secret limit price λ. To simplify notation, we drop the subscript i denoting the trader. Two types of a trader are considered: an intra-marginal and an extra-marginal ones.

An *intra-marginal trader* has its limit price λ favorable for trading. That is, it can offer a better price than its estimate of the equilibrium price $\hat{p}^*(T)$. Thus, it holds:
  for an intra-marginal buyer $\lambda > \hat{p}^*(T)$,
  for an intra-marginal seller $\lambda < \hat{p}^*(T)$.

An *extra-marginal trader* has its limit price unfavorable for trading, as it does not allow him to offer a better price than its estimate of the equilibrium price. It holds:
  for an extra-marginal buyer $\lambda < \hat{p}^*(T)$,
  for an extra-marginal seller $\lambda > \hat{p}^*(T)$.

The notion of intra- or -extra-marginal trader depends on time, as the estimate of the equilibrium price changes during the auction.

3.1 Target Price

The target price τ of a trader depends on the type of a trader, as well as on some parameters, which are discussed in more details in the sequel. These parameters are the degree of aggressiveness $r \in (-1, 1)$ and volatility parameter $\theta \in [\theta_{\min}, \theta_{\max}]$. Now, the target price is calculated as follows.

Intra-marginal Traders

For an intra-marginal buyer

$$\tau(t) = \begin{cases} \hat{p}^*(t)\left(1 - \frac{e^{-r\theta}-1}{e^{\theta}-1}\right) & \text{if } -1 < r \le 0 \\ \hat{p}^*(t) + (\lambda_b - \hat{p}^*(t))\frac{e^{r\theta}-1}{e^{\theta}-1} & \text{if } \ 0 < r < 1 \end{cases} \tag{2}$$

where λ_b is a buyer limit price.

For an intra-marginal seller

$$\tau(t) = \begin{cases} \hat{p}^*(t) + (o_{ask,\max} - \hat{p}^*(t))\frac{e^{-r\theta}-1}{e^{\theta}-1} & \text{if } -1 < r \le 0 \\ \lambda_s + (\hat{p}^*(t) - \lambda_s)\big(1 - \frac{e^{r\theta}-1}{e^{\theta}-1}\big) & \text{if } \ 0 < r < 1 \end{cases} \tag{3}$$

where λ_s is a seller limit price and $o_{ask,\max}$ is the maximum ask allowed in the market.

Exemplary curves showing dependence of the target price on r for two values of $\theta = 2$ and $\theta = -8$ for intra-marginal buyer and seller are depicted in Fig 1.

Extra-Marginal Traders

For an extra-marginal buyer

$$\tau(t) = \begin{cases} \lambda_b\big(1 - \frac{e^{-r\theta}-1}{e^{\theta}-1}\big) & \text{if } -1 < r \le 0 \\ \lambda_b & \text{if } \ 0 < r < 1 \end{cases} \tag{4}$$

For an extra-marginal seller

$$\tau(t) = \begin{cases} \lambda_s + (o_{ask,\max} - \lambda_s)\frac{e^{-r\theta}-1}{e^{\theta}-1} & \text{if } -1 < r \le 0 \\ \lambda_s & \text{if } \ 0 < r < 1 \end{cases} \tag{5}$$

Exemplary curves showing dependence of the target price on r for two values of $\theta = 2$ and $\theta = -8$ for extra-marginal buyer and seller are depicted in Figure 1.

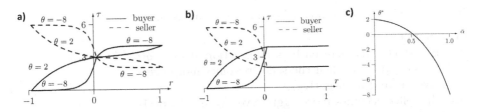

Fig. 1. a) Dependence of the target price τ on the degree of aggressiveness r for intra-marginal buyer and seller. $\lambda_b = 4$, $\lambda_s = 2$, $o_{ask,\max} = 6$. b) Dependence of the target price τ on the degree of aggressiveness r for extra-marginal buyer and seller. $\lambda_b = 4$, $\lambda_s = 2$, $o_{ask,\max} = 6$. c) Dependence of θ^* on $\bar{\alpha}$.

3.2   Degree of Aggressiveness

A trader strategy depends on its aggressiveness in the market. An *aggressive* trader submits orders to improve its chance of transacting, i.e. orders that are better for trading partners than its estimate of the equilibrium price. A trader is *active*, if it submits orders equal to its estimate of the equilibrium price. A *passive* trader is inclined to win a more profitable transaction, so it submits orders worse for trading parners than its estimate of its equilibrium price.

We denote by $r \in [-1, 1]$ a degree of aggressiveness of a trader. A completely passive trader has the value $r = -1$. It submits the bid at 0 as a buyer, and the ask at the maximum price $o_{ask,max}$ as a seller. An active trader has the value $r = 0$ and it submits the order equal to $\hat{p}^*(t)$. A completely aggressive trader has the value $r = 1$. It submits the bid at the limit price λ_b as a buyer and the ask λ_s as a seller.

Short-Term Learning. The degree of aggressiveness is adapted according to the Widrow-Hoff rule. Thus, we have

$$r(t + 1) = r(t) + \beta_1(\delta(t) - r(t)) \tag{6}$$

where $0 < \beta_1 < 1$ is the learning rate, and $\delta(t)$ is the current desired aggressiveness. The desired aggressiveness is calculated to possibly improve last shout, from the equation

$$\delta(t) = (1 \pm \zeta_r)r_{shout} \pm \zeta_a \tag{7}$$

where ζ_r is the relative and ζ_a the absolute change of r_{shout}. The value r_{shout} is the degree of aggressiveness that would form a price equal to last shout. It is taken into account and changed, if any of the following condition occurs:

For a Buyer
If the last shout was followed by a transaction at price $q(t - 1)$, and:
  if $\tau(t - 1) \geq q(t - 1)$ then the buyer becomes more aggressive (λ_r and λ_a positive),
  else the buyer becomes less aggressive (λ_r and λ_a negative).
If bid b was submitted and
  if $\tau(t - 1) \leq b$ than the buyer becomes more aggressive.

For a Seller
If the last shout was followed by a transaction at price $q(t - 1)$, and:
  if $\tau(t - 1) \leq q(t - 1)$ then the seller becomes more aggressive (λ_r and λ_a negative),
  else the seller becomes more aggressive (λ_r and λ_a positive).
If ask a was submitted and
  if $\tau(t - 1) \geq a$ than the seller becomes more aggressive.

3.3   Volatility Parameter

An additional parameter θ introduces dependence of the target price on price volatility α. The desired value of this parameter θ^* is determined from the equation

$$\theta^* = \theta_{min} + (\theta_{max} - \theta_{min})(1 - \bar{a}e^{\gamma(\bar{\alpha}-1)}) \tag{8}$$

where $\theta_{\min}$ and $\theta_{\max}$ are the minimal and the maximal value of updating θ, respectively, γ is a coefficient that determines the shape of this function, and $\bar{\alpha}$ is the normalized value of α, i.e.

$$\bar{\alpha} = \frac{\alpha - \alpha_{\min}}{\alpha_{\max} - \alpha_{\min}}$$

Long-Term Learning. Also here the Widrow-Hoff rule is used to adapt the θ parameter

$$\theta(t+1) = \theta(t) + \beta_2(\theta^* - \theta(t)) \tag{9}$$

where $0 < \beta_2 < 1$ is the learning rate. The desired value θ^* is calculated from the following equation

$$\theta^* = \theta_{\min} + \frac{\theta_{\max} - \theta_{\min}}{1 - \bar{\alpha}e^{\gamma(\bar{\alpha}-1)}} \tag{10}$$

Figure 1 presents dependence of θ^* on $\bar{\alpha}$. Although it is not written explicitly, θ^* depends on t through α.

3.4   Price Formation

Traders obey the following rules. The buyer submits a bid only if its limit price is higher than the current bid o_{bid}. The seller submits an ask only if its limit price is lower than the current ask o_{ask}.

If the current ask is lower than or equal to the buyer's target price, $o_{ask} \leq \tau$, then the buyer accepts it. If the current bid is higher than or equal to the seller's target price, $o_{bid} \geq \tau$, then the seller accepts it.

The initial ask has been set as $o_{ask,0} = o_{ask,\max}$ in the simulation. The initial bid has been set as $o_{bid,0} = 0$.

If neither of the above conditions is satisfied, a trader submits an order according to the expressions given below. It is assumed that the auction consists of separated rounds. As at the beginning of auction, in the first round, a trader can not estimate the equilibrium price, its policy of announcing the order differs from that used later. Thus, the orders submitted are the following.

For a Buyer

$$bid(t) = \begin{cases} o_{bid} + \frac{\min(\lambda_b, o_{ask}^+) - o_{bid}}{\eta} & \text{in the first round} \\ o_{bid} + \frac{\tau - o_{bid}}{\eta} & \text{otherwise} \end{cases} \tag{11}$$

where $o_{ask}^+ = (1 + \zeta_r)o_{ask} + \zeta_a$ and $1 \leq \eta < \infty$ is a constant.

For a Seller

$$ask(t) = \begin{cases} o_{ask} - \frac{\max(\lambda_s, o_{bid}^-) - o_{ask}}{\eta} & \text{in the first round} \\ o_{ask} + \frac{\tau - o_{ask}}{\eta} & \text{otherwise} \end{cases} \tag{12}$$

where $o_{bid}^- = (1 - \zeta_r)o_{bid} - \zeta_a$.

In [22] the following values of constants required in the method have been used: $\eta = 3$, $\zeta_a = 0.01$, $\zeta_r = 0.02$, $\gamma = 2$, β_1, and β_2 drawn from the uniform distribution on the interval $[0.2, 0.6]$. They were kept in the present simulations.

4 Simulation Experiments

A few experiments were made to check the strategy and the market mechanism. In the first experiments 2 simple consumers and 2 simple producers were considered. The limit prices[3] of buyers (loads) were 0.26 for the first consumer and 0.254 for the second one. Limit prices for producers were set to 0.15 and 0.20. The external grid has constant prices lying outside the limits of the internal sources, that is the price for buying was equal $\lambda_{b,e} = 0.145$, and for selling $\lambda_{s,e} = 0.555$. The maximum allowed ask was adopted as $o_{ask,\max} = 0.26$.

The simplicity means here that the overall consumption was slowly and constantly decreasing while the production was increasing. That gave a situation where in the begin there was a deficit of power, then with time the situation changed to the one with the excess of power. The external network was only balancing the power – it was offering constant prices per kWh bought and sold that was acceptable for all parties, but not profitable for any of them. The external network party could not place orders on the market in the same way as small producers and consumers, as it would dominate the price spread and prevent transaction price from adjusting. In the given scenario change of price was as expected – in the beginning the price for kWh of power was high and was decreasing when the situation of overproduction occurred, see Figure 2.

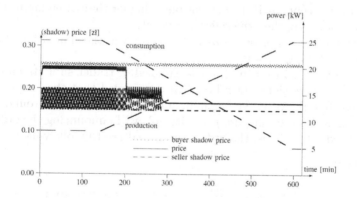

Fig. 2. The outcome of the second experiment. Production of power in the microgrid starts from a low value of 8 kW and then grows up to 25 kW, consumption of power in the microgrid starts from 25 kW and then drops to 5 kW (shadow lines). The price set in the microgrid market drops from around 0.25 zł to 0.17 zł.

The second and third experiments included more realistic conditions. There were three buying parties (loads), each of them consuming in a cyclic usage pattern between 1kW at night (off-peak hours) to 10kW in peak hours. The cyclic pattern was chosen as the most common one. On the production side

---

[3] All prices are in złotys, that is the Polish currency.

there were three renewable sources, a wind turbine, photovoltaic panels, and a water turbine. The wind turbine production depends on the wind speed. In the simulation real data of wind speed from Warsaw (Poland) area were used. Photovoltaic panels convert solar power to electricity. In the simulation small panels were considered, with 10 kW of maximum production. The real insolation data were taken from the early spring, also from the Warsaw (Poland) area, and the outcome of photovoltaic power was between 0 and 4.4 kW. Production of the water turbine was set within levels of small low head hydro powers. The

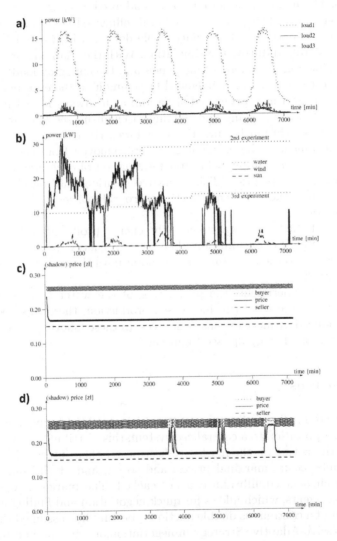

Fig. 3. The outcome of the second experiment. Lowest panel, production of power in the microgrid; middle panel, consumption of power in the microgrid; upper panel, shadow prices of buyers and sellers and the price set in the microgrid market.

production levels were different in this and the next experiments. In the first of them the production was big enough to cover all loads. In the second, the production was much smaller and not enough to cover the loads all time.

The limit prices of buyers (loads) were in the range of $\lambda_b \in (0.24, 0.264)$. In the second experiment the limit prices of sellers were the same for the water and photovoltaic panels and equal to $\lambda_{s,t} = 0.15$, while that for the wind turbine was greater $\lambda_{s,p} = 0.20$, in the third experiment the prices were equal $\lambda_{s,t} = 0.15$. The external grid has constant prices lying outside the limits of the internal sources, that is the price for buying was equal $\lambda_{b,e} = 0.145$, and for selling $\lambda_{s,e} = 0.555$. The maximum allowed ask was adopted as $o_{ask,max} = 0.26$.

It was soon observed that the external grid influenced very much the auction process. This was due to lack of controllable devices which could balance the power in the microgrid during the simulation. With the changing production by the wind turbine and the photovoltaic panels and the changing loads, the power in the grid had to be constantly balanced by selling it to the external grid. This put the external grid in a privileged situation, as it always forced its prices in the auction. Due to the asking and bidding mechanism, see (11) and (12), the prices in the microgrid market practically followed the external grid prices. To avoid this phenomenon, the external grid were removed from the market and imbalanced energy was simply sold after termination of each auction period to the external grid on its price. This tentative solution may be changed when controllable sources and loads enter to the microgrid market, enabling its better internal balancing.

In the first of these two experiments the energy produced in the microgrid constantly excessed its consumption. The price of energy quickly attained the equilibrium price and then was (almost) constant until the end of the experiment time, see Figure 3c.

In the second experiment, the production of the water turbine was much smaller, and when the wind turbine ceased production, there was necessary to use power produced by more expensive sources. In these (short) periods the price in the market went sharply up, see Figure 3d.

5   Conclusions

In this paper a dynamic (on-line) market for pricing and balancing in a microgrid is outlined. In opposition to a centralized system, this distributed mechanism enables the parties acting on the market to keep secret their internal informations on, for example, costs, marginal prices, and so on, and at the same time an economically efficient equilibrium can be reached. The market is operated by programmable agents, which allows for quick negotiation and finding a solution. The market is of a continuous double auction type, and it is assumed that agents use the Aggressive-Adaptive Strategy in negotiation of prices and accomplishing the contracts. Other market rules can be considered as well, like Dutch auction mechanism, in which asks start from rather unacceptable values and are then adjusted until some market participant accepts them. However, the continuous double auction is known to be an efficient method, quickly attaining the equilibrium price. The presented market is adequate for the electropower grid demands. It allows for real-time trading, where the limitation is just the time for agents to place their offers. Such a market, which provides also balancing of power, can be an efficient way to trade power between the consumers, prosumers and producers in a microgrid.

The presented work is an introduction to developing a market-based control scheme for a microgrid. In the situation when controllable power sources are used, they can adjust to the situation in the market demand/supply relation. Controllable power sources can change their operating point, which means that they can decide how much power will be offered on the market. This way they can compete with the external grid for winning contracts to cover the microgrid loads, under changing external grid prices. Or they can balance power in the microgrid instead of external network during the island mode operation of microgrids. However, the marginal price of such sources usually depends on their operation points. This complicates their strategies on the market.

It is assumed in this paper that the physical restrictions in the microgrid are not violated during delivery of the energy. This may be a reasonable assumption for a well designed microgrid working in normal conditions. In a general situation, satisfaction of physical constraints may an additional problem to be solved, e.g. by including it in the negotiations. This problem needs further exploration.

References

[1] Balijepalli, V.S.K.M., Pradhan, V., Khaparde, S.A., Shereef, R.M.: Review of demand response under smart grid paradigm. In: 2011 IEEE PES Innovative Smart Grid Technologies - India (ISGT India), pp. 236–243 (2011)

[2] Chalkiadakis, G., Robu, V., Kota, R., Rogers, A., Jennings, N.R.: Cooperatives of distributed energy resources for efficient virtual power plants. In: The 10th International Conference on Autonomous Agents and Multiagent Systems, AAMAS 2011, vol. 2, pp. 787–794. International Foundation for Autonomous Agents and Multiagent Systems, Richland (2011)

[3] Ermolieva, T., Ermoliev, Y., Jonas, M., Obersteiner, M., Wagner, F., Winiwater, W.: Uncertainty, cost-effectiveness and environmental safety of robust carbon trading: integrated approach. Climatic Change 124, 633–646 (2014)

[4] Farouki, A., Sergici, S., Akaba, L.: Dynamic pricing of electricity for residential customers: The evidence from Michigan. Energy Efficiency 6, 571–584 (2013)

[5] Filzmoser, M.: Simulation of Automated Negotiation. Springer (2010)

[6] Green, R., McDaniel, T.: Competition in Electricity Supply: Will "1998" be Worth It? Centre for Economic Policy Research, London (1998)

[7] He, M., Jennings, N.R., Leung, H.: On agent-mediated electronic commerce. IEEE Transactions on Knowledge and Data Engineering 15(4), 985–1003 (2003)

[8] Hood, C.: Reviewing existing and proposed emissions trading systems. Information paper. International Energy Agency (2010)

[9] Kaleta, M., Pałka, P., Toczyłowski, E., Traczyk, T.: Electronic trading on electricity markets within a multi-agent framework. In: Nguyen, N.T., Kowalczyk, R., Chen, S.-M. (eds.) ICCCI 2009. LNCS, vol. 5796, pp. 788–799. Springer, Heidelberg (2009)

[10] Lawrence, E.O., Marnay, C., Venkataramanan, G., Orlando, E.: Microgrids in the evolving electricity generation and delivery infrastructure. National Laboratory, Berkeley (2006)

[11] Lopes, F., Wooldridge, M., Novais, A.Q.: Negotiation among autonomous computational agents: principles, analysis and challenges. Artificial Intelligence Review 29(1), 1–44 (2008)

[12] Murray, B.: Power Markets and Economics: Energy Costs, Trading, Emissions. Wiley (2009)

[13] Nahorski, Z., Radziszewska, W.: Price formation strategies of programmable agents in continuous double auctions. In: Busowicz, M., Malinowski, K. (eds.) Advances in Control Theory and Automation. Komitet Automatyki PAN, Oficyna Wyd. Politechniki Biaostockiej, pp. 181–194 (2012)

[14] Pałka, P., Radziszewska, W., Nahorski, Z.: Balancing electric power in a microgrid via programmable agents auctions. Control and Cybernetics 41(4), 777–797 (2012)

[15] Pinker, E.J., Seidmann, A., Vakrat, Y.: Managing online auctions: Current business and research issues. Management Science 49 (2003)

[16] Radziszewska, W., Nahorski, Z., Parol, M., Pałka, P.: Intelligent computations in an agent-based prosumer-type electric microgrid control system. In: Curien, P.-L., Pitt, D.H., Pitts, A.M., Poigné, A., Rydeheard, D.E., Abramsky, S. (eds.) CTCS 1991. LNCS, vol. 530, pp. 293–312. Springer, Heidelberg (1991)

[17] Roth, A.E., Erev, I.: Learning in extensive-form games: experimental data and simple dynamic models in the intermediate term. Games and Economic Behavior 8, 164–212 (1995)

[18] Shöne, S.: Auctions in the Electricity Market. Building when Production Capacity is Constrained. Lecture Notes in Economics and Mathematical Systems, vol. 617. Springer (2009)

[19] Sun, J., Tesfatsion, L.: Dynamic testing of wholesale power market designs: An open-source agent-based framework. Computational Economics 30(3), 291–327 (2007)

[20] Tan, Z., Gurd, J.R.: Market-based grid resource allocation using a stable continuous double auction. In: Proceedings of the 8th IEEE/ACM International Conference on Grid Computing, GRID 2007, pp. 283–290. Washington, DC, USA (2007)

[21] Vytelingum, P.: The Structure and Behaviour of the Continuous Double Auction. PhD thesis, University of Southampton (December 2006)

[22] Vytelingum, P., Cliff, D., Jennings, N.R.: Strategic bidding in continuous double auctions. Artificial Intelligence 172(14), 1700–1729 (2008)

[23] Wurman, P., Walsh, W., Wellman, M.: Flexible double auctions for electronic commerce: Theory and implementation. Decision Support Systems 24, 17–27 (1998)

A Game Theory Approach to Demand Side Management in Smart Grids

Nadine Hajj and Mariette Awad

American University of Beirut, Beirut, Lebanon
{njh05,mariette.awad}@aub.edu.lb

Abstract. With the increase in global energy awareness, smart grids improve the efficiency and peak leveling of power systems. Demand side management is the controlling scheme in such grids and it aims to optimize several characteristics using an interactive dynamic pricing scheme. In this paper we propose a game theoretic approach to the demand side management where several subscribers share one common energy supplier. In our model, users send their demand vectors for an upcoming period of time to the network and the energy provider responds by broadcasting a dynamic price vector. Energy consumers are concerned with minimizing their total energy cost per day while the power provider aims to maximize its profit while minimizing the peak to average load ratio. Converging to a unique Nash equilibrium solution using a dual constrained optimization problem, our model results motivate follow on research.

1   Introduction

With the continuous increase in electric power demand and the rise of environmental and economic concerns, the control of electric power demand is gaining a lot of focus in today's power grids. Multiple features affect the performance of power networks, for instance the high demand peaks result in severe constraints on the network, causing power supply failure in several situations. As the size of the network increases, managing and controlling the networks' parameters for best performance become a hard optimization task. In that aspect, smart grids carry the promise of achieving efficiency, reliability and robustness by implementing a powerful control scheme involving dynamic pricing. One of the mechanisms for control of such grids is the Demand Side Management (DSM). DSM aims to encourage consumers to use less energy during peak hours, or to move the time of high energy consumption to off-peak times in order to achieve not only energy savings as well as a more efficient use of the energy itself. Real-time pricing is one of the most important DSM strategies, where energy prices change frequently to reflect variations in the cost of energy supply and electricity demand over time.

Motivated to investigate load control based on a dynamic pricing of DSM consumption scheduling, we propose a novel game model where players are the consumers on one side and the energy supplier on another. The set of strategies for the consumers is the distribution of their demand across the day while it is the pricing policy

© Springer International Publishing Switzerland 2015
D. Filev et al. (eds.), *Intelligent Systems' 2014*,
Advances in Intelligent Systems and Computing 323, DOI: 10.1007/978-3-319-11310-4_70

for the energy supplier. The payoff function to be minimized for the customers is the price they will be charged for by the energy provider, while the energy supplier aims to maximize its profit payoff function while minimizing the peak-to-average ratio (PAR). We assume that users submit their tentative consumption schedule in an iterative manner, and the network adjusts the price per time slot based on the submitted demand vectors. The process is repeated with each new user entering the system or updating its bid until convergence. Once biding ends, prices per hour and users' demand distribution become fixed and get executed upon for the requested period.

The rest of this paper is structured such that section 2 surveys previous work for modeling DSM using game theory and section 3 describes our game model. In section 4, the Nash equilibrium of the proposed game is discussed, and the analytical solution of the model is detailed in section 5. Section 6 presents the experimental results obtained using our proposed technique while section 7 concludes the paper.

2   Literature Review

Recently, there has been a considerable amount of research addressing the problem of DSM. This section summarizes some of the most relevant models to our work.

In [1], DSM is modeled using a congestion game, in which time varying prices affect the demand at peak hours. The goal of each customer is to minimize its bill according to a cost function metric proposed. The model was proved to converge in a finite number of iterations to a pure Nash equilibrium solution.

Samadi et. al proposed a DSM strategy for a smart power infrastructure, [2], in which smart meters and the power grid communicate to exchange information regarding the demand and the dynamic price. A distributed algorithm optimizes the demand and prices to ensure the benefit of both consumers and supplier.

A four-stage Stackelberg game models DSM in a smart grid as shown in [3]. A retailer distributes the amount of produced energy between two sources in the first and second stage. While the real-time price and the demand profiles are updated in the third and fourth stages respectively.

In [4], users decide on their energy load profile so that PAR is minimized while the provider decides on the dynamic price. Users can also opt to charge their batteries during low-demand periods and use the charged energy during high price time slots.

A similar energy storage approach for the management of a smart grid is proposed in [5], where a price signal sent by the energy supplier controls the strategies adopted by the consumers. A Nash equilibrium was established and proven to achieve optimal results with led to an overall annual saving of nearly GBP 1.5B and savings of up to 13% on average per consumer. .

The Nash equilibrium of a distributed DSM system is developed in [6] by Mohsenian-Rad et. al, using a game theory model where the players are the users which action is their demand levels and a utility company deciding on a dynamic price. The game is an incomplete information game in which the consumers are unaware of each other actions and they tend to minimize their own cost. The total cost minimum was shown to correspond to the vector of individual minimal cost without requiring complete information.

While existing approaches have focused on modeling DSM as a non-cooperative game, Saad et. al. used coalitional game theory to model interactions between the users and the energy providers in a smart grid environment [7]. The components of this game are micro-grids supplying consumers in disjoint partitions aiming to reduce the total load on the main network as well as minimizing power losses. Surplus of power in certain coalitions are transferred to those in shortage minimizing the cost and losses.

An alternative approach in the case of incomplete information is maximizing a social welfare metric, using a Vickrey-Clarke-Groves (VCG) based approach as in [8]. The social welfare is expressed as the total energy cost subtracted from the combined utility functions of all users. Each consumer provides the supplier of its demand while the provider broadcasts a pricing strategy.

Another Stackelberg approach to DSM uses surplus stored energy to balance peak demand as described in [9]. The supplier plays the role of the leader and decides the pricing strategy and the amount of stored energy to buy from the consumers who play the follower role selling their stored energy.

Another approach presented in 10], uses power-shiftable and time-shiftable models for electrical appliances and aims to optimize cost by shifting time-shiftable appliances to particular time slots and varying power levels for power shiftable appliances to ensure the best possible operation of the network.

3   Proposed Model

3.1   Game Components

We assume that our system is a smart grid where users are equipped with a control device that enables them to manage their total electric power demand and improve some of the desirable features of an electrical power system such as efficiency, reliability, and cost.

The components of the game we adopt are as follows:

- Players:
  - N consumers connected to the smart power grid.
  - One energy provider or company responsible for generating energy
- Actions:
  - Each consumer decides on the consumption power vector over the time slots considered and which are submitted to the energy provider.
  - The energy provider decides on the pricing policy over the time slots.
- Preferences:
  - Consumers aim to minimize their power bills.
  - The energy provider aim to maximize its profit and minimize PAR.

An illustration of the system described is shown in figure 1.

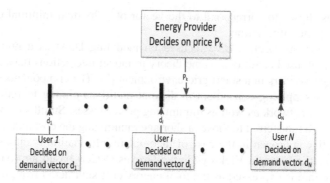

Fig. 1. Illustration of the network configuration

3.2   Utility and Cost Functions

This section aims to formulate a mathematical model of the energy consumers connected to the smart grid. For the consumers, we adopt a cost function model reflecting their daily bill while we elect a utility function to be maximized to model the generator's preference. The cost functions should satisfy the following conditions:

- The cost function is an increasing function of the price and hence the power consumption from the consumer's perspective.
- No consumption (i.e. no demand) results in a 0 cost.
- The cost function is a convex function, while the utility function is a concave function.

Denote by N the total number of users and by K the total number of time slots for which the users submit their consumption demand, also referred to by scheduling horizon. For each user i, the decision vector submitted to the energy provider is defined as:

$$d_i = \left[d_{i,1}, d_{i,2}, \dots d_{i,k}, \dots d_{i,K}\right]^T \tag{1}$$

Where k represents the time slot for which the ith user's demand is $d_{i,k}$.

The power consumption of each user during each time slot k is constraint to a maximum value d^m pre-defined by the energy provider such as:

$$0 \leq d_{i,k} \leq d^m \tag{2}$$

At any time slot, the total power acquired from the power grid is limited to the maximum generating capacity of the network denoted by E^m.

$$\sum_{i=1}^{N} d_{i,k} \leq E^m \tag{3}$$

And assume for simplicity that $N.\,d^m = E^m$.

An intuitive form of cost function for energy users would be a linear function reflecting their daily bill given by the summation time slots of their demand multiplied by the unit price. Because a linear function violates the convexity condition required, we adopt a quadratic form for the cost function that users aim to minimize in response to the pricing strategy at time slot k and to the strategies adopted by consumers other than the ith user d_{-i}, given in eq. (4)

$$C_i(d_i, p_k) = \sum_{k=1}^{K} (\beta_i d_{i,k}^2 - d_{i,k} p_k) \qquad (4)$$

Where $\beta_i > 0$ is a user specific constant defined by consumers. Although the utility function is not a function of d_{-i} explicitly, the ith user's payoff depends on the price p_k, which depends on the strategies of all consumers.

Since the energy provider aims to maximize its profit, it is convenient to model the power supplier's preferences as a utility function of the price and demand which has to be maximized. To insure a minimum PAR, we propose the following supplier preferences:

$$U_P(d_i, p_k) = \sum_{k=1}^{K} \sum_{i=1}^{N} (-\alpha_k p_k^2 + p_k d_{i,k} + PAR.p_k) \qquad (5)$$

With

$$PAR = \frac{\max_k \sum_{i=1}^{N} d_{i,k}}{\frac{1}{K} \sum_{k=1}^{K} \sum_{i=1}^{N} d_{i,k}}$$

With $\alpha_k > 0$

The first term of the utility function represents a form of the cost to be paid by the users while the second term represents a form of the PAR to be minimized.

4   Nash Equilibrium

The optimal solution to our proposed game corresponds to the Nash Equilibrium a^* that ensures that "no player i can do better by choosing an action different from a_i^*, given that every other player j adheres to a_j^*" [12]. In other terms, the action profile a^* in a strategic game with ordinal preferences is a Nash equilibrium if, for every player i and every action a_i of player i, a^* is at least as good according to player i's preferences as the action profile (a_i, a_{-i}^*) in which player i chooses a_i while every other player j chooses a_j^*. Equivalently, for every player i, for every action a_i of player i,

$$u_i(a^*) \geq u_i(a_i, a_{-i}^*) \qquad (6)$$

In our case, finding the Nash equilibrium of the game is equivalent to finding the strategies p_k^* adopted by the energy supplier and $d_{i,k}^*$ adopted by the consumers such as:

$$\begin{cases} C_i(d_i^*, p_k^*) \leq C_i(d_i, p_k^*) \\ U_P(d_i^*, p_k^*) \geq U_P(p_k, d_i^*) \end{cases} \qquad (7)$$

Theorem 1: The previously formulated game admits one and unique Nash equilibrium

Proof: the users' cost functions $C_i(d_i, p_k)$ is strictly convex with respect to d_i resulting in a concave equivalent utility function while the supplier's utility function $U_P(d_i, p_k)$ is concave with respect to p_k; therefore the presented game is a strictly concave (N+1)-person game. In this case, the existence of a Nash equilibrium directly results from [13, Th. 1]. Moreover, the Nash equilibrium is unique due to [13, Th. 3].

Theorem 2: The unique Nash equilibrium of the game is the optimal solution to a dual maximization problem.

Proof: Consider an arbitrary subscriber $i \in \mathcal{N}$. Given d_{-i} and p_k and assuming that all other subscribers fix their energy consumption schedule according to d_{-i}, subscriber i can minimize its cost by solving the following local problem:

$$\sum_{k=1}^{K}(\beta_i d_{i,k}^{*2} + d_{i,k}^* p_k^*) \leq \sum_{k=1}^{K}(\beta_i d_{i,k}^2 + d_{i,k} p_k) \tag{8}$$

This can be re-written as:

$$\min_{d_{i,k}} \sum_{k=1}^{K}(\beta_i d_{i,k}^2 + d_{i,k} p_k) \tag{9}$$

subject to the constraints in (2) and (3).

Alternatively, the energy supplier aims to maximize its payoff given the users' consumption schedules. Its pricing strategy p_k^* issuch that:

$$\sum_{k=1}^{K}\sum_{i=1}^{N}(-\alpha_k p_k^{*2} + p_k^* d_{i,k}^* + PAR.p_k^*) \geq \sum_{k=1}^{K}\sum_{i=1}^{N}(-\alpha_k p_k^2 + p_k d_{i,k}^* + PAR.p_k) \tag{10}$$

The optimization problem in (10) can be written as:

$$\max_{p_k} \sum_{i=1}^{N}(-\alpha_k p_k^2 + p_k d_{i,k} + PAR.p_k) \tag{11}$$

Therefore the Nash equilibrium of the formulated game corresponds to the intersection of the best responses of the subscribers with that of the energy supplier also consistent with a dual constrained optimization problem given by (9) and (11).

5   Analytical Solution

In the previous section, we discussed the existence of a Nash equilibrium solution for the proposed game. We also demonstrated that finding this equilibrium is equivalent to solving a dual constrained optimization problem. In this section we present a closed form solution for the optimization problem using Lagrange multipliers.

5.1   The Cost Minimization Problem

The energy subscribers aim to maximize their payoff functions corresponding to minimizing their energy cost. This problem is expressed in (9) subject to (2) and (3). Using the KKT extension of the Lagrangian theory, we re-write the users' cost minimization problem as:

$$\max_{d_{i,k}} g(d_i) = \sum_{k=1}^{K} -\left(\beta_i d_{i,k}^2 + d_{i,k} p_k\right) \tag{12}$$

Equivalent to:

$$\max_{d_{i,k}} -\left(\beta_i d_{i,k}^2 + d_{i,k} p_k\right) \tag{13}$$

Subject to:

$$\begin{cases} d_{i,k} \geq 0 \\ d^m - d_{i,k} \geq 0 \\ E^m - \sum_{j=1,j\neq i}^{N} d_{j,k} - d_{i,k} \geq 0 \end{cases} \tag{14}$$

The corresponding Lagrange function of the previous problem relative to the ith user can be written as:

$$L_i\left(d_{i,k}, \lambda_1, \lambda_2\right) = -\left(\beta_i d_{i,k}^2 + d_{i,k} p_k\right) + \lambda_1 \left(d^m - d_{i,k}\right)$$
$$+ \lambda_2 \left(E^m - \sum_{i=1}^{N} d_{i,k}\right) \tag{15}$$

The solution of the problem is found by maximizing the Lagrangian with respect to $d_{i,k}$ subject to the non-negativity restrictions, and minimizing the Lagrangian with respect to the variables λ_1 and λ_2 subject to the non-negativity restrictions:

$$\frac{\partial L_i}{\partial d_{i,k}} \leq 0; \, d_{i,k} \frac{\partial L_i}{\partial d_{i,k}} = 0; \, d_{i,k} \geq 0 \tag{16}$$

$$\frac{\partial L_1}{\partial \lambda_j} \geq 0; \, \lambda_i \frac{\partial L_1}{\partial \lambda_j} = 0; \, \lambda_j \geq 0 \tag{17}$$

Equations (16) and (17) yield:

$$\begin{cases} -\left(2\beta_i d_{i,k} - p_k\right) - \lambda_1 - \lambda_2 \leq 0 \\ \left[\left(2\beta_i d_{i,k} - p_k\right) + \lambda_1 + \lambda_2\right] d_{i,k} = 0 \\ d^m - d_{i,k} \geq 0; \, \lambda_1\left(d^m - d_{i,k}\right) = 0 \\ E^m - \sum_{i=1}^{N} d_{i,k} \geq 0; \, \lambda_2 \left(E^m - \sum_{i=1}^{N} d_{i,k}\right) = 0 \end{cases} \tag{18}$$

Four cases are considered:

1) $\lambda_1 = \lambda_2 = 0$

   This leads: $d_{i,k} = \frac{p_k}{2\beta_i}$ and $g(d_i) = 0$ a feasible solution.

2) $\lambda_1 = 0, \lambda_2 \neq 0$

   This leads $\sum_{i=1}^{N} d_{i,k} = E^m = N.d^m$, with $d_{i,k} \neq d^m$, suppose the ith user submits a demand value $d_{i,k} < d^m$, another user j will submit a value $d_{j,k} > d^m$ to satisfy $\sum_{i=1}^{N} d_{i,k} = E^m$ which is not feasible.

3) $\lambda_1 \neq 0, \lambda_2 = 0$, this solution is not feasible since $\sum_{i=1}^{N} d^m = E^m$

4) $\lambda_1 \neq 0, \lambda_2 \neq 0$, leads $d_{i,k} = d^m$ and $g(d_i) = \sum_{k=1}^{K} -\left(\beta_i d^{m2} + d^m p_k\right) \leq 0$

   Therefore the optimal action for the ith user in response to a pricing strategy is $d_{i,k} = \frac{p_k}{2\beta_i}$.

5.2   The Profit Maximization Problem

The second optimization problem expressed in (13) concerns the energy supplier aiming to maximize its profit and is equivalent to

$$\max_{p_k} f(p_k) = \sum_{i=1}^{N} \left(-\alpha_k p_k^2 + p_k d_{i,k} + PAR.p_k\right) \tag{19}$$

The maximization problem is solved by setting the derivative to zero:

$$\frac{\partial f(p_k)}{\partial p_k} = 0 \Rightarrow \sum_{i=1}^{N} \left(-2\alpha_k p_k + d_{i,k} + PAR\right) = 0$$

$$\Rightarrow p_k = \frac{\sum_{i=1}^{N} d_{i,k} + PAR}{2\alpha_k} = \frac{\sum_{i=1}^{N} d_{i,k} + K \frac{\max_k \sum_{i=1}^{N} d_{i,k}}{\sum_{k=1}^{K} \sum_{i=1}^{N} d_{i,k}}}{2\alpha_k} \tag{20}$$

The optimal price obtained in (20) suggests an important property of the pricing strategy: the price is proportional to the load at each time slot, while penalizing a high PAR simultaneously.

In summary, the Nash equilibrium solution of the game model is given by:

$$(p_k, d_{i,k}) = \left(\frac{\sum_{i=1}^{N} d_{i,k} + K \frac{\max_k \sum_{i=1}^{N} d_{i,k}}{\sum_{k=1}^{K} \sum_{i=1}^{N} d_{i,k}}}{2\alpha_k}, \frac{p_k}{2\beta_i} \right) \tag{21}$$

6   Performance Evaluation

In this section we present some experimental results obtained on a possible scenario that we designed. Two algorithms are implemented: one executed by the energy supplier, the second executed by the power consumers. These algorithms are illustrated by figures 2 and 3 respectively. The system simulated is as follows:

Consider a power grid constituted of N consumers, and an energy supplier where the horizon is $K = 24\ hours$, the maximum allowed consumption per user per time slot is $50kW$, and the maximum generating capacity of the power source at any given time is $250kW$. Assume that the users and the power provider chose their parameters randomly according to the following:

- $\alpha_k \in [1\ 4]$
- $\beta_i \in [3.5\ 6.5]$

At the start of the bidding period, one user starts by requesting a uniform demand vector causing the energy supplier to broadcast an initial uniform price vector. The second user enters the bidding system and requests a uniform consumption vector. The energy provider adjusts the price vector in response to the new user entering. In return the users adjust their consumption schedule based on the provided price. The algorithm iterates until convergence and no new users enter the network.

Algorithm Executed by Energy Supplier
1.   Initialization
2.   Repeat
a.   For each time slot $k \in K$
-   Compute the best price p_k^* using (21)
-   Broadcast p_k
b.   Receive demand vectors d_i for all users
3.   Until convergence

Fig. 2. Energy Supplier Algorithm

Algorithm Executed by Consumers
1.   Initialization
2.   For each time slot $k \in K$
a.   Receive the broadcasted price p_k
b.   Update demand value $d_{i,k}$ using (21)
c.   Communicate value to network
3.   End

Fig. 3. Consumers' Algorithm

The following figures show, for multiple values of consumers (N), normalized plots of:

- Initial total demand vector of all users(figure 4)
- Final demand vector of all users(figure 5)
- The evolution of the PAR until convergence (figure 6)
- The variation of the cost of a random user with iterations (figure 7)
- The variation of the utility of the power provider with iterations (figure 8)

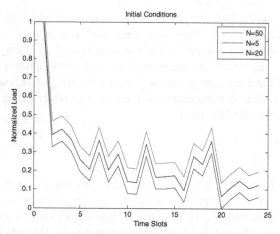

Fig. 4. Initial Demand and Prices

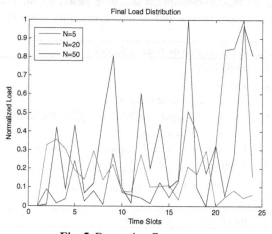

Fig. 5. Demand at Convergence

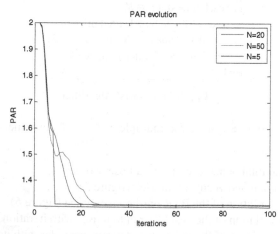

Fig. 6. Evolution of PAR

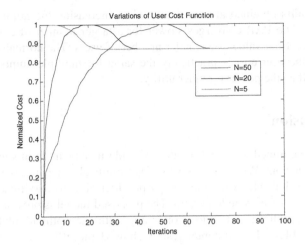

Fig. 7. Evolution of User Cost

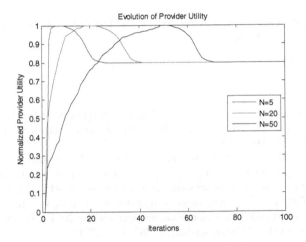

Fig. 8. Evolution of Provider Utility

The following conclusions can be drawn from figures 4-8:

- The proposed pricing scheme is consistent with the desired features as peak loads are penalized by a high pricing response.
- The proposed algorithm convergence in about 7-8 iterations for N=5 with the PAR reaching a stable minimal value.
- The proposed solution achieves simultaneously a maximum profit for the power provider and a minimum cost for energy users.
- Despite the peak observed in the utility function of the power supplier at the 3rd iteration (for N=5), however this maximum does not correspond to the optimal solution as not all the users have entered the system yet (the users enter in an iterative fashion with all users updating their demand starting the 6th iteration).

- Results obtained are consistent when increasing the number of consumers. The PAR converges slower for a larger number of consumers to the same final value as a smaller number of users. The normalized final value of the user cost is practically the same for multiple numbers of users as well as the power provider utility.

7   Conclusion

In this project we aimed to model the demand side management in smart grids using game theory concepts. We design it as a novel multi-player game where consumers aim to minimize their bill while the energy provider aims to maximize its profit and minimize the peak to average load ratio. The proposed model is proven to converge to a unique Nash equilibrium solution coinciding with the optimal solution of a dual optimization problem. Experimental results showed the efficiency of our proposed method in modeling the situation and minimizing PAR.

Acknowledgment. This work was funded by the University Research Board at the American University of Beirut.

References

[1] Ibars, C., Navarro, M., Giupponi, L.: Distributed demand management in smart grid with a congestion game. In: 2010 First IEEE International Conference on Smart Grid Communications, pp. 495–500 (2010)

[2] Samadi, P., Mohsenian-Rad, A., Schober, R., Wong, V.W., Jatskevich, J.: Optimal real-time pricing algorithm based on utility maximization for smart grid. In: 2010 First IEEE International Conference on Smart Grid Communications, pp. 415–420 (2010)

[3] Bu, S., Yu, F.R., Liu, P.X.: A game-theoretical decision-making scheme for electricity retailers in the smart grid with demand-side management. In: 2011 IEEE International Conference on Smart Grid Communication, pp. 387–391 (2011)

[4] Nguyen, H.K., Song, J.B., Han, Z.: Demand side management to reduce peak-to-average ratio using game theory in smart grid. In: 2012 IEEE Conference on Computer Communications Workshops, pp. 91–96 (2012)

[5] Vytelingum, P., Voice, T.D., Ramchurn, S.D., Rogers, A., Jennings, N.R.: Agent-based micro-storage management for the smart grid. In: Proceedings of the 2010 9th International Conference on Autonomous Agents and Multiagent Systems, vol. 1, pp. 39–46 (2010)

[6] Mohsenian-Rad, A., Wong, V.W., Jatskevich, J., Schober, R., Leon-Garcia, A.: Autonomous demand-side management based on game-theoretic energy consumption scheduling for the future smart grid. IEEE Transactions on Smart Grid 1(3), 320–331 (2010)

[7] Saad, W., Han, Z., Vincent Poor, H.: Coalitional game theory for cooperative micro-grid distribution networks. In: 2011 IEEE International Conference Communications on Workshops, pp. 1–5 (2011)

[8] Samadi, P., Schober, R., Wong, V.W.: Optimal energy consumption scheduling using mechanism design for the future smart grid. In: 2011 IEEE International Conference on Smart Grid Communications, pp. 369–374 (2011)

[9] Tushar, W., Zhang, J.A., Smith, D.B., Thiebaux, S., Vincent Poor, H.: Prioritizing Consumers in Smart Grid: Energy Management Using Game Theory. arXiv preprint arXiv:1304.0992 (2013)

[10] Zhu, Z., Tang, J., Lambotharan, S., Chin, W.H., Fan, Z.: An integer linear programming and game theory based optimization for demand-side management in smart grid. In: 2011 IEEE GLOBECOM Workshops, pp. 1205–1210 (2011)

[11] Osborne, M.J.: An introduction to game theory, vol. 3(3). Oxford University Press, New York (2004)

[12] Rosen, J.B.: Existence and uniqueness of equilibrium points for concave n-person games. Econometrica 33, 347–351 (1965)

Short-Term Load Forecasting Using Random Forests

Grzegorz Dudek

Department of Electrical Engineering, Czestochowa University of Technology,
Al. Armii Krajowej 17, 42-200 Czestochowa, Poland
dudek@el.pcz.czest.pl

Abstract. This study proposes using a random forest model for short-term electricity load forecasting. This is an ensemble learning method that generates many regression trees (CART) and aggregates their results. The model operates on patterns of the time series seasonal cycles which simplifies the forecasting problem especially when a time series exhibits nonstationarity, heteroscedasticity, trend and multiple seasonal cycles. The main advantages of the model are its ability to generalization, built-in cross-validation and low sensitivity to parameter values. As an illustration, the proposed forecasting model is applied to historical load data in Poland and its performance is compared with some alternative models such as CART, ARIMA, exponential smoothing and neural networks. Application examples confirm good properties of the model and its high accuracy.

Keywords: Short-term load forecasting, seasonal time series forecasting, random forests.

1 Introduction

Short-term load forecasting (STLF) is necessary for economic power generation and system security. The accurate load forecasts lead to lower operating cost which contributes to savings in electric utilities. The importance of STLF accuracy has become even more evident for the deregulated electricity markets. To correct the forecast inaccuracy the utility has to buy or sell power in the real time market but it comes at the expense of higher real time prices. For these reasons, STLF is an integral part of planning and operation for electric utilities, regional transmission organizations, energy suppliers, financial institutions, and participants in the generation, transmission, and distribution of electricity. The key importance of STLF is reflected in the literature by many forecasting methods that have been applied, including conventional methods and new computational intelligence and machine learning methods. The STLF is a complex problem because the load time series is nonstationary in mean and variance, with trend and multiple seasonal cycles (daily, weekly and annual).

The most commonly employed conventional STLF methods are the Holt-Winters exponential smoothing (ES) [1] and the autoregressive integrated moving average (ARIMA) models [2]. In ES the time series is decomposed into trend and seasonal components. An disadvantage of the ES models is that they involve initialization and

© Springer International Publishing Switzerland 2015
D. Filev et al. (eds.), *Intelligent Systems'2014*,
Advances in Intelligent Systems and Computing 323, DOI: 10.1007/978-3-319-11310-4_71

updating of many terms (level, periods of the intraday and intraweek cycles). ARIMA models can be extended for the case of multiple seasonalities but a combinatorial problem of selecting appropriate model orders is an inconvenience. This order selection process is considered subjective and difficult to apply. Another disadvantage is the linear character of the ARIMA models.

The rapid development of computational intelligence has brought new methods of STLF [3]. They are based mostly on artificial neural networks (ANNs) and fuzzy logic but also on support vector machines, clustering methods and expert systems.

The multilayer perceptron (ANN which is most often applied in STLF) is an attractive tool to modeling of nonlinear problems due to its universal approximation property. But learning of ANN is not easy, because of its complex structure and many parameters (hundreds or even thousands of weights to estimate).

Fuzzy logic models allow us to enter input information by rules formulated verbally by experts and describing the behavior of complex systems by using linguistic expressions. Since it is difficult to gain knowledge directly from the experts, to generate a set of if-then rules the learning from examples procedure is applied in neuro-fuzzy networks. The neuro-fuzzy system structure is complex and the number of parameters is usually large (it depends on the problem dimensionality and complexity), so the learning is difficult and does not guarantee convergence to the global minimum.

To sum up, the modeling the nonstationary time series with trend and multiple seasonal cycles usually requires complex model with many parameters. The searching of such a model space is a hard and time consuming process. To find the globally optimal solution intelligent searching methods, such as evolutionary algorithms and swarm intelligence, are often applied. The disadvantages of the complex models are their worse generalization ability, unclear structure and uninterpretable parameters.

In this article we study the random forest as a univariate model for STLF. This is a simple model combining regression trees with only few parameters to estimate. Although the random forests have been used for STLF (see [4]), the novelty of this work is data preprocessing. It simplifies the forecasting problem eliminating nonstationarity and filtering trend and seasonal cycles longer than the daily cycle.

The paper is organized in a theoretical and an empirical part. In the beginning we introduce the main concepts of the random forests. Thereafter we present the STLF methodology based on random forests and patterns of the seasonal cycles of time series. In the last section we use real load data to provide an example of model building and forecasting in practice.

2   Random Forests

Random forests (RFs) are an ensemble learning method for both classification and regression problems [5]. RF is a collection of decision trees that grow in randomly selected subspaces of the feature space. The principle of RFs is to combine a set of binary decision trees (Breiman's CART – Classification And Regression Trees [6]), each of which is constructed using a bootstrap sample coming from the learning sample and a subset of features (input variables or predictors) randomly chosen at each node. Thus in contrast to the CART model building strategy, an individual tree in RF is built on a subset of learning points and on subsets of features considered at each node to split on. Moreover trees in the forest are grown to maximum size and the pruning step is skipped.

After individual trees in ensemble are fitted using bootstrap samples, the final decision is obtained by aggregating over the ensemble, i.e. by averaging the output for regression or by voting for classification. This procedure called bagging improves the stability and accuracy of the model, reduces variance and helps to avoid overfitting. The bias of the bagged trees is the same as that of the individual trees, but the variance is decreased by reducing the correlation between trees (this is discussed in [7]). Breiman showed that random forests do not overfit as more trees are added, but produce a limiting value of the generalization error [5]. The RF generalization error is estimated by an out-of-bag (OOB) error, i.e. the error for training points which are not contained in the bootstrap training sets (about one-third of the points are left out in each bootstrap training set). An OOB error estimate is almost identical to that obtained by N-fold cross-validation. The large advantage of RFs is that they can be fitted in one sequence, with cross-validation being performed along the way. The training can be terminated when the OOB error stabilizes.

The algorithm of RF for regression in Fig. 1 is shown [7].

---

1. For $k = 1$ to K:
    1.1. Draw a bootstrap sample L of size N from the training data.
    1.2. Grow a random-forest tree T_k to the bootstrapped data, by recursively repeating the following steps for each node of the tree, until the minimum node size m is reached.
        1.2.1. Select F variables at random from the n variables.
        1.2.2. Pick the best variable/split-point among the F.
        1.2.3. Split the node into two daughter nodes.
2. Output the ensemble of trees $\{T_k\}_{k=1, 2, ..., K}$.

To make a prediction at a new point $\mathbf{x}$:

$$f(\mathbf{x}) = \frac{1}{K}\sum_{k=1}^{K} T_k(\mathbf{x}) \tag{1}$$

Fig. 1. Algorithm of RF for regression

The two main parameters of RF are: the number of trees in the forest K and the number of input variables randomly chosen at each split F. The number of trees can be determined experimentally. During the training procedure we add the successive trees until the OOB error stabilizes. The RF procedure is not overly sensitive to the value of F. The inventors of the algorithm recommend $F = n/3$ for the regression RFs.

Another parameter is the minimum node size m. The smaller the minimum node size, the deeper the trees. In many publications $m = 5$ is recommended. And this is the default value in many programs which implement RFs. RFs show small sensitivity to this parameter.

It is noteworthy that using CART model, we get a classifier or an estimate of the regression function, which is a piecewise constant function obtained by partitioning the predictor space. This is a serious limitation of CART. But building an ensemble of CART we get results which are much smoother than from a single tree.

Using RFs we can determine the prediction strength or importance of variables which is useful for ranking the variables and their selection, to interpret data and to understand underlying phenomena. The variable importance can be estimated in RF as the increase in prediction error if the values of that variable are randomly permuted across the OOB samples. The increase in error as a result of this permuting is averaged over all trees, and divided by the standard deviation over the entire ensemble. The more the increase of OOB error is, the more important is the variable.

3   Data Preprocessing

Our goal is to forecast the load curve for the next day. The load time series $\{z_l\}_{l=1,2,...,L}$ is divided into daily cycles of length n. To eliminate weekly and annual variations the daily cycles are preprocessed to obtain their patterns. The pattern is a vector with components that are functions of actual time series elements. Two types of patterns are defined: the input patterns $\mathbf{x}$ and output (forecast) ones $\mathbf{y}$. The forecast pattern $\mathbf{y}_i = [y_{i,1}\ y_{i,2}\ ...\ y_{i,n}]^T$ encodes the successive actual time series elements z_l in the forecasted daily cycle $i+\tau$. $\mathbf{z}_{i+\tau} = [z_{i+\tau,1}\ z_{i+\tau,2}\ ...\ z_{i+\tau,n}]^T$, and the corresponding input pattern $\mathbf{x}_i = [x_{i,1}\ x_{i,2}\ ...\ x_{i,n}]^T$ maps the time series elements in the daily cycle i preceding the forecast cycle: $\mathbf{z}_i = [z_{i,1}\ z_{i,2}\ ...\ z_{i,n}]^T$. Vectors $\mathbf{y}$ are encoded using current process parameters from the nearest past, which allows to take into account current variability of the process and enables decoding. Some definitions of the functions mapping the original space Z into the pattern spaces X and Y, i.e. $f_x : Z \rightarrow X$ and $f_y : Z \rightarrow Y$ are presented in [8]. The most popular definitions are of the form:

$$f_x(z_{i,t}) = \frac{z_{i,t} - \bar{z}_i}{\sqrt{\sum_{j=1}^{n}(z_{i,j} - \bar{z}_i)^2}}, \qquad f_y(z_{i+\tau,t}) = \frac{z_{i+\tau,t} - \bar{z}_i}{\sqrt{\sum_{j=1}^{n}(z_{i,j} - \bar{z}_i)^2}}, \qquad (2)$$

where: $i = 1, 2, ..., N$ – the daily period number, $t, j = 1, 2, ..., n$ – the time series element number in the period i, τ – the forecast horizon, $z_{i,t}$ – the t-th time series element in the period i, $\bar{z}_i$ – the mean value of elements in period i.

The function f_x (1) expresses normalization of the vectors $\mathbf{z}_i$. After normalization they have the unity length, zero mean and the same variance. Note that the nonstationary and heteroscedastic time series is represented by patterns having the same mean and variance.

The forecast patterns $\mathbf{y}_i$ are defined using analogous function to f_x, but the encoding parameters ($\bar{z}_i$ and dispersion measure in the denominator of (2)) are determined from the process history. This enables decoding of the forecasted vector $z_{i+\tau}$ after the forecast of pattern y_i is determined. We use the inverse function $f_y^{-1}(y_{i,t})$ for this.

From the set of pairs $\{(x_1,y_1), ..., (x_N,y_N)\}$, where y_i represents the load at hour t for the next day (this is the t-th component of pattern y_i for $\tau = 1$), the learning set for RF is generated. For each query point (pattern x representing the k-th daily period) the learning set is prepared individually from the historical data. It contains M nearest neighbors of the query pattern representing the same days of the week (Monday, ..., Sunday) as the query pattern. This restriction to M nearest neighbors is due to our goal: we do not want to built a global model but a local one, which is competent for the query pattern. So there is no sense to use the distant learning points to train the model. Of course this model is not suitable for other query points and we have to built the separate model for each query point. But the cost and time of model building in this case are not limiting factors.

4   Application Examples

We illustrate the construction of RF forecasting model on the example of STLF using the hourly electrical load data of the Polish power system from the period 2002–2004. (This data can be downloaded from the website http://gdudek.el.pcz.pl/varia/stlf-data.) Our goal is to forecast the load curve for the next day ($\tau = 1$). The test set includes 30 days from January 2004 (without untypical 1 January) and 31 days from July 2004. The training set containing $M = 50$ pairs (x_i,y_i) is generated individually for each forecasting task (load forecasting at hour t of the day j). In our example there are $(30+31) \cdot 24 = 1464$ forecasting tasks. For each of them the separate RF model is created.

In the first phase of our research we investigate how the model parameters affect an error. In Fig. 1 the OOB errors against K and F are plotted. From these figures it can be seen that MSE drops from $K = 1$ to K about 100 and then stabilize. When F increases to 8 MSE decreases and then gradually increases. Hence it is assumed that the best values of these parameters are: $K = 100$ and $F = 8$, i.e. $n/3$.

Fig. 2 shows OOB error depending on the minimum node size m and the frequencies of m values ensuring the lowest errors. This figure demonstrates the best accuracy for deepest trees in ensemble.

The variable importance for several forecasting tasks in Fig. 3 is shown. It is hard to formulate a rule concerning the variable importance observing these figures. In many cases the variable importance graphs in forecasting tasks for neighboring hours of the same day vary considerably. Some variables have negative importance. This indicates that permutation of these variable values leads to a lower error.

Now we compare in simulations the proposed RF model with CART models in two variants: typical and with fuzzy nodes [9]. In the typical variant the trees were grown until the minimum node size m was reached. This parameter was adjusted individually for each forecasting task. In the fuzzy CART variant the trees were constructed in a classical way and then the crisp tests in nodes were replaced with fuzzy tests. The fuzzy test determines the membership degrees to the branches outgoing from the node. The slope parameters of the membership functions were tuned for each test node and for each forecasting task individually.

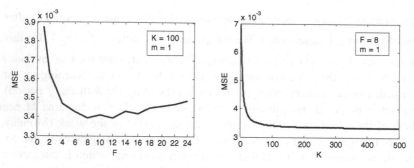

Fig. 2. OOB MSE depending on the number of trees (left) and the number of input variables randomly chosen at each split (right)

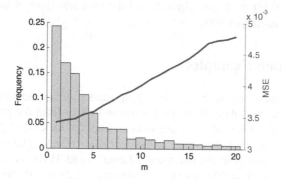

Fig. 3. OOB MSE depending on the minimum node size (line) and the frequencies of m values (bars) ensuring the lowest errors

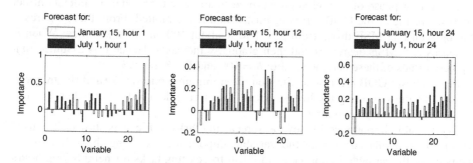

Fig. 4. The variable importance for several forecasting tasks

We compare the RF model also with popular STLF models such as: ARIMA, exponential smoothing (ES) and artificial neural network (ANN). These models are described in [10]. The time series are preprocessed for ANN in the same way as for RF (patterns of the daily periods are used). The ANN learns using the training sample selected from the neighborhood of the query pattern (local learning). As shown in [10] for STLF in local learning procedure the one-neuron model is sufficient. To find the best ARIMA and ES models automated procedures implemented in the **forecast** package for the **R** system [11] were used.

MAPE (mean absolute percentage error) is adopted here to assess the performance of the forecasting models. The results of the forecasts (MAPE for the test samples $MAPE_{tst}$ and the interquartile range (IQR) of $MAPE_{tst}$) in Table 1 are presented. In this table the results determined using the naïve method are also shown. The forecast rule in this case is as follows: the forecasted daily cycle is the same as seven days ago. From table 1 it can be seen that the lowest errors were obtained by ANN and RF. Mean errors for RF and ANN are statistically indistinguishable (Wilcoxon signed-rank test was used).

The histograms of the percentage errors (PE) in Fig. 5 are shown. The most favorable error distributions are observed for RF and ANN. The distributions for ARIMA and ES are more flattened and asymmetrical.

Table 1. Results of forecasting

Model	January		July		Mean	
	$MAPE_{tst}$	IQR	$MAPE_{tst}$	IQR	$MAPE_{tst}$	IQR
RF	1.42	1.39	0.92	0.98	1.16	1.17
CART	1.70	1.58	1.16	1.17	1.42	1.39
Fuzzy CART	1.62	1.47	1.13	1.12	1.37	1.35
ARIMA	2.64	2.34	1.21	1.24	1.91	1.67
ES	2.35	1.88	1.19	1.30	1.76	1.56
ANN	1.32	1.30	0.97	1.01	1.14	1.15
Naïve	6.37	5.36	1.29	1.20	3.78	3.82

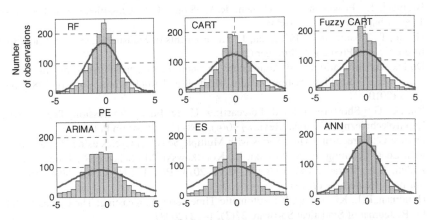

Fig. 5. Histograms of errors

5   Conclusions

The purpose of the present study was to ascertain the effectiveness of using the RF models in STLF. The proposed approach allows us to forecast time series with multiple seasonal variations. It is due to the data preprocessing and defining the patterns of the seasonal cycles on which the model operates. The target function is approximated locally in the neighborhood of the query point. This simplify the forecasting problem and leads to the better accuracy.

The RF forecasting model is characterized by simplicity. The number of parameters to be estimated is small, which implies a simple procedure of the model optimization. This task is facilitated by the built-in cross-validation mechanism. It is worth noting that the model is not very sensitive to the parameter values.

In application examples the RF model provided as accurate forecasts as ANN and outperformed the crisp and fuzzy CART, ARIMA and ES models. The RF model is simpler to train and tune than the above mentioned models, does not overfit and reduces variance due to averaging the outputs of many simple regression trees (weak learners) over ensemble.

References

1. Taylor, J.W., Snyder, R.D.: Forecasting Intraday Data with Multiple Seasonal Cycles Using Parsimonious Seasonal Exponential Smoothing. Omega 40(6), 748–757 (2012)
2. Weron, R.: Modeling and Forecasting Electricity Loads and Prices. Wiley (2006)
3. Kodogiannis, V.S., Anagnostakis, E.M.: Soft Computing Based Techniques for Short-Term Load Forecasting. Fuzzy Sets and Systems 128, 413–426 (2002)
4. Cheng, Y.-Y., Chan, P.P.K., Qiu, Z.-W.: Random Forest Based Ensemble System for Short Term Load Forecasting. Proc. Machine Learning and Cybernetics (ICMLC) 1, 52–56 (2012)
5. Breiman, L.: Random Forests. Machine Learning 45(1), 5–32 (2001)
6. Breiman, L., Friedman, J.H., Olshen, R.A., Stone, C.J.: Classification and Regression Trees. Chapman and Hall (1984)
7. Hastie, T., Tibshirani, R., Friedman, J.: The Elements of Statistical Learning. Data Mining, Inference, and Prediction. Springer (2009)
8. Dudek, G.: Similarity-based Approaches to Short-Term Load Forecasting. In: Zhu, J.J., Fung, G.P.C. (eds.) Forecasting Models: Methods and Applications, pp. 161–178. Concept Press (2010)
9. Dudek, G.: Short-Term Load Forecasting Using Fuzzy Regression Trees. Przegląd Elektrotechniczny (Electrical Review) 90(4), 108–111 (2014) (in Polish)
10. Dudek, G.: Forecasting Time Series with Multiple Seasonal Cycles using Neural Networks with Local Learning. In: Rutkowski, L., Korytkowski, M., Scherer, R., Tadeusiewicz, R., Zadeh, L.A., Zurada, J.M. (eds.) ICAISC 2013, Part I. LNCS, vol. 7894, pp. 52–63. Springer, Heidelberg (2013)
11. Hyndman, R.J., Khandakar, Y.: Automatic Time Series Forecasting: The Forecast Package for R. Journal of Statistical Software 27(3), 1–22 (2008)

Part VII
Time Series Analysis and Frequent Pattern Mining

Generalized Net of the Process of Sequential Pattern Mining by Generalized Sequential Pattern Algorithm (GSP)

Veselina Bureva[1], Evdokia Sotirova[1], and Panagiotis Chountas[2]

[1] "Prof. Asen Zlatarov" University, Burgas-8010, Bulgaria
esotirova@btu.bg, vesito_ka@abv.bg
[2] School of Electronics & Computer Science, University of Westminster,
15 New Cavendish Street, London W1W 6UW
p.i.chountas@westminster.ac.uk

Abstract. In the present paper is constructed a Generalized net model of a process of sequential pattern mining by a generalized sequential pattern algorithm. Sequence pattern mining is a technique used for predictive data mining. It is used for discovering of frequent sequences in the databases. A sequence is regarded as frequent when it occurs in the data above a previously user defined minimum support within the applied time constraints. The analysis is an extension of frequent pattern mining technique that extracts frequent itemsets. They can be used for the creation of association rules. GSP algorithm was realized with metrological observations from weather databases, infrared camera and smoke detector to determine the possibility of forest fire. The proposed Generated net model can be used to monitor the sequence pattern mining process depending on meteorological parameters.

Keywords: Generalized Nets, Generalized Sequential Pattern, Sequential Pattern Mining, Frequent Pattern Mining, Data Mining, Weather databases, Algorithms.

1 Introduction

The process of discovering sequential patterns was introduced in [5]. The purpose of the sequence pattern mining approach is to find frequent sequences that exceed a user-specified support threshold. The support of a sequence is the percentage of tuples in the database that contain the sequence. Many algorithms for sequential pattern mining such as AprioriAll, generalized sequential pattern algorithm (GSP), PrefixSpan and Spade are described. They are presented as modifications to the frequent itemset mining algorithms Apriori, FP-Growth and Eclat. An itemset is non-empty set of items [1]. A sequence s is an ordered list of itemsets described as $s = <e_1 e_2 \dots e_n>$, where the element (transaction) e_1 occurs before the element e_2. Each element e_i is a collection of events (items) $(x_1, x_2 \dots, x_q)$. The number of elements of the sequence is the length of the sequence. Sequence $a = <a_1, a_2 \dots a_n>$ is called subsequence of sequence $b = <b_1,$

© Springer International Publishing Switzerland 2015
D. Filev et al. (eds.), *Intelligent Systems' 2014*,
Advances in Intelligent Systems and Computing 323, DOI: 10.1007/978-3-319-11310-4_72

$b_2,..., b_m>$, which is a supersequence of a. The sequence database contains tuples in form $<SID, s>$. In the database of sequences, where each sequence is a list of transactions ordered by the transaction-time, and each transaction is a set of items. The frequent patterns support must be bigger or equal to the minimum support threshold defined by the user. GSP includes minimum support and gap constraints. A gap constraint can apply in a sequence of databases, where each transaction in every sequence has a timestamp. The timestamp difference between every two adjacent transactions must be longer or shorter than a given gap [4, 8, 10, 11].

GSP has been developed by Srikant and Agrawal [1]. They have presented an extension of their first algorithm for frequent itemset mining - Apriori. GSP mines sequential patterns by adopting a candidate subsequence generation-and-test approach based on the Apriori property. GSP can be up to 20 times faster than the Apriori algorithm because it has more intelligent selection of candidates for each step and introduces time constraints in the search space. At first GSP scans the database for items, satisfying the user's minimum support threshold (sequences, events). A seed set is used in the following steps. All extracted seed set in the previous step will be used for generating candidate sequences. Each candidate sequences contain minimum one seed sequential pattern from generated seed set in the previous step. The candidate sequences have equal lengths, increased k+1 times in each following step. The sequences that don't satisfy the minimum support threshold will be pruned. The process is repeating until there is a lack of new sequences or it cannot generate more candidate sequences [17].

2   Generalized Net Model

The proposed in the paper GN-model for sequence pattern mining process is an extension of the paper [7]. The generalized net theory is described in [2, 3]. In [7] a GN-model of association rules mining by Apriori algorithm is offered. The described GN-model for sequence pattern mining process by GSP algorithm is an extension of frequent itemsets mining algorithm Apriori. In GSP the Apriory property and time constraints are used. The algorithm is looking for frequent sequences in the time gaps. The support and the constraints are defined by the user. In [6] the basic algorithms for frequent itemsets mining are analyzed. The generalized net is used for modelling of the process of data mining [15] and the process of applying Data Mining tools [14]. In [16] a generalized net for analysis of a Student's Evaluations by Data Mining Techniques in the e-Learning university is created. In the [5] was constructed a model for the extraction a frequent patterns by Eclat algorithm in weather databases using the apparatus of GNs.

A GN-model for sequential pattern mining process using GSP algorithm is presented in Fig.1.

The Generalized Net model is presented in Fig. 1. It contains 4 transitions and 12 places. The transitions represent the following processes:

- Z_1 - setting of measures minsup, maxgap, mingap, window size by the user;
- Z_2 - selection of the transactions from the database with meteorological measurements and analyzing for single sequences;

- Z_3 - generating k+1 candidate subsequences from single frequent sequences;
- Z_4 - writing the received rules of sequence mining.

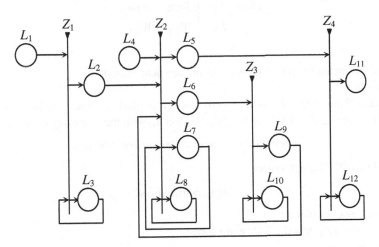

Fig. 1. Generalized net of the process of sequential pattern mining by the Generalized sequential pattern (GSP) algorithm

Initially α- and β- tokens are situated in places L_3 and L_8. They will be in their own places during the whole time in which GN functions. While they may split into two or more tokens, the original token will remain in its own place. The original tokens have the following current characteristics:

"Measures for sequence pattern mining" in place L_3,
"Transactional database with meteorological measurements" in place L_8.

Examples of the sequential pattern in Transactional database:
IDi <{calm wind, warm temperature, overcast outlook, normal humidity}, {breeze wind, warm temperature, overcast outlook, normal humidity, smoke detector: yes}, {breeze wind, hot temperature, overcast outlook, normal humidity, smoke detector: yes, infrared camera: yes}>
The α-token in place L_3 generates new α-token at certain time points which will be moved to position L_2 and receive characteristic

"Selected measures for sequence pattern mining".

The β- token in place L_8 generates new β-tokens at certain time moments which will move to transitions Z_3 and Z_4 passing via transition Z_2.

Token α_1 enters the net via place L_1 with initial characteristic

"Measures for sequence pattern mining - minsup, maxgap, mingap, window size".

The transition Z_1 has the following form:

$$Z_1 = \langle \{L_1, L_3\}, \{L_2, L_3\}, R_1, \vee (L_1, L_3)\rangle,$$

where

$$R_1 = \begin{array}{c|cc} & L_2 & L_3 \\ \hline L_1 & false & true \\ L_3 & W_{3,2} & W_{3,3} \end{array},$$

and:

$W_{3,2} =$"All measures for sequence mining are determined",
$W_{3,3} = \neg W_{2,3}$.

α_1- token from   place L_1 merges with α-token in place L_3 (when predicate $W_{3,2}$ has a truth-value "true"). The α-token, entering in place L_2 with the following characteristics

„*Selected measures for sequence mining*".

β_1-token with characteristics

"*new transactions*"

enters in the net via place L_4.

The transition Z_2 has the following form:

$$Z_2 = \langle\{L_4, L_2, L_9, L_7, L_8\}, \{L_5, L_6, L_7, L_8\}, R_2,$$
$$\vee(\wedge(L_2, L_4), L_7, L_8, L_9)\rangle,$$

where

$$R_2 = \begin{array}{c|cccc} & L_5 & L_6 & L_7 & L_8 \\ \hline L_4 & false & false & false & true \\ L_2 & false & false & false & true \\ L_9 & false & false & W_{9,7} & false \\ L_7 & W_{7,5} & W_{9,6} & true & W_{7,8} \\ L_8 & false & false & W_{8,7} & W_{8,8} \end{array}$$

and:

$W_{9,7}=$"Candidate subsequences for comparing with minimum support threshold are obtained ";

$W_{7,5}=$"Frequent sequences for generating rules are received";

$W_{7,6}=$"Frequent subsequences for generating $k+1$ candidate subsequences are received";

$W_{7,8} =$"Infrequent sequences are obtained";

$W_{8,7}=$"Transactions for sequential pattern mining analysis are selected";

$W_{8,8} = \neg W_{8,7}$.

At the first activation of the transition α- and β- tokens entering from places L_2 and L_4, respectively in places L_7 and L_8 don't obtain new characteristic. The β-token in place L_8 generates β_2-token, entering in place L_7 with characteristic

"*Selected transactions for application of sequential pattern mining method*"

at the second activation for transition.

At the third activation of the transition β_2-token from place L_7 generating β_3-, β_4- and β_5-tokens, entering in places L_5, L_6 and L_8 with characteristics:

"*Extracted frequent sequences for generating rules*" in place L_5,
"*Extracted frequent sequences for generating k+1 candidate subsequences rules*" in place L_6,
and "*Extracted infrequent sequences*" in place L_8.

The β_5-token merges with the β-token in place L_8.
The transition Z_3 has the following form:

$$Z_3 = \langle \{L_6, L_{10}\}, \{L_9, L_{10}\}, R_3, \vee(L_6, L_{10})\rangle,$$

where

$$R_3 = \begin{array}{c|cc} & L_9 & L_{10} \\ \hline L_6 & false & true \\ L_{10} & W_{10,9} & W_{10,10} \end{array}$$

and:

$W_{10,9}$="k+1 candidate subsequences for checking with minimum support threshold are obtained";
$W_{10,10} = \neg\, W_{10,9}$.

At the first activation of transition the β_5-token from place L_5 enters in place L_{10} and don't obtain new characteristic. At the second activation of transition the β_7-token token in place L_{10} generates β_8-token, which enters in place L_9 with characteristic:

"*k+1 candidate subsequences obtained for checking with minimum support threshold*".

This process repeats until all of the frequent sequences are extracted.
The transition Z_4 has the following form:

$$Z_4 = \langle \{L_5, L_{12}\}, \{L_{11}, L_{12}\}, R_4, \vee(L_5, L_{12})\rangle,$$

where

$$R_4 = \begin{array}{c|cc} & L_{11} & L_{12} \\ \hline L_5 & false & true \\ L_{12} & W_{12,11} & W_{12,12} \end{array}$$

and:

$W_{12,11}$ ="The rule is created";
$W_{12,12} = \neg\, W_{12,11}$.

The β_3-token that enters in place L_{12} from place L_5 don't obtain new characteristic. The β_3-token in place L_{12} generates γ-token, entering in place L_{11} with characteristic:

"*Created rule*".

3   Realization

The constructed GN-model of a process of sequential pattern mining by GSP algorithm can be used for discovering sequential patterns in meteorological data. The meteorological data from the World meteorological stations are collected in databases and some of them can be used to analyze the danger from wildfires. The quantity of meteorological data online is increasing, which makes it important to use specific techniques for analysis. By using Data mining techniques we can find and extract usable and interesting hidden patterns from largely available weather forecast databases [9, 12, 13]. This can help for understanding of the climate variability and climate prediction. The GSP algorithm is realized in RapidMiner (Fig. 2, Fig. 3 and Fig. 4).

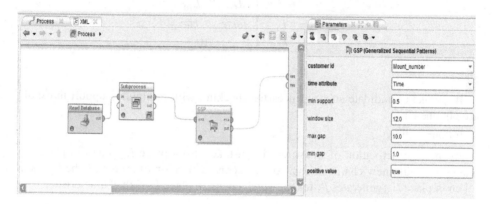

Fig. 2. Current settings for operator GSP

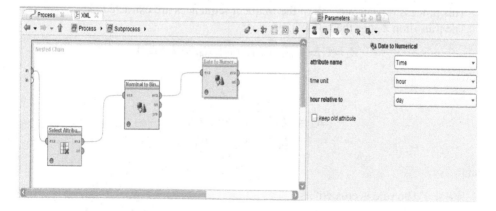

Fig. 3. Preprocessing step

GSPSet

```
0.500: <Wind = calm, Temperature = hot>
0.500: <Wind = calm, Outlook = sunny>
0.600: <Wind = calm, Humidity = normal>
0.500: <Wind = calm, Smoke_detector = yes>
0.700: <Temperature = hot, Fire_detector_color = yes>
0.550: <Outlook = sunny> <Humidity = normal>
0.650: <Outlook = sunny, Smoke_detector = yes>
0.700: <Outlook = sunny, Fire_detector_color = no>
0.500: <Humidity = normal> <Wind = light breeze>
0.500: <Wind = light breeze, Temperature = hot, Humidity = normal>
0.550: <Wind = light breeze, Outlook = sunny, Humidity = normal>
0.750: <Humidity = normal, Smoke_detector = yes> <Outlook = sunny>
0.650: <Humidity = normal, Smoke_detector = yes> <Humidity = normal>
0.550: <Wind = light breeze, Humidity = normal, Smoke_detector = yes>
0.550: <Wind = light breeze, Smoke_detector = yes, Fire_detector_color = yes>
0.700: <Humidity = normal, Fire_detector_color = yes> <Humidity = normal>
```

Fig. 4. Example generated sequences with their support

4   Conclusion

The sequence pattern mining is a data mining technique for predicting future events by using time constrains. Many different approaches are proposed in the literature in order to restrict time intervals. The generalized sequential pattern uses minimum gap, maximum gap and the property of sliding window. Sequence mining is a step to extend the data mining field to temporal analysis. The presented model is the second connected with the frequent itemsets mining. It gives the possibility of monitoring and analysis of the sequential pattern mining. The GN-models of the FP-Growth and Eclat algorithms for frequent itemsets mining will be presented in the future researches. They are used in extended algorithms for sequential pattern mining PrefixSpan and SPADE. The GSP algorithm is realized in RapidMiner with data from metrological observations from weather databases, infrared camera and smoke detector to determine the possibility of forest fire.

Acknowledgements. The first and second authors are grateful for the support provided by the project DFNI-I-01/0006 "Simulating the behaviour of forest and field fires", funded by the National Science Fund, Bulgarian Ministry of Education, Youth and Science.

References

1. Agrawal, R., Srikant, R.: Mining sequential patterns. In: ICDE 1995 Proceedings of the Eleventh International Conference on Data Engineering, pp. 3–14 (1995)
2. Atanassov, K.: Generalized Nets. World Scientific, Singapore (1991)

3. Atanassov, K.: On Generalized Nets Theory. Prof. M. Drinov Academic Publishing House, Sofia (2007)
4. Berry, M., Linoff, G.: Data Mining Techniques For Marketing, Sales, and Customer Relationship Management. and Customer Relationship Management. Wiley Publishing (2004)
5. Bureva, V., Sotirova, E.: Generalized net of the process of association rules discovery by Eclat algorithm using weather databases. In: Proc. of 14th IWGN, Burgas, November 29-30, pp. 1–10 (2013)
6. Bureva, V.: Algorithms for associative rule mining. Management and Education 9, 121–128 (2013)
7. Bureva, V.: Generalized Net Model of the process of the creating of the associative rules via algorithm Apriori. Annual of "Informatics" Section Union of Scientists in Bulgaria 5, 73–83 (2012) (in Bulgarian)
8. Dong, G., Pei, J.: Sequence Data Mining. Springer (2007) ISBN-13: 978-0-387-69936-3
9. Ghosh, S., Nag, A., Biswas, D., Singh, J.P., Biswas, S., Sarkar, D., Sarkar, P.P.: Weather Data Mining using Artificial Neural Network. In: Recent Advances in Intelligent Computational Systems (RAICS), pp. 192–195. IEEE (2011)
10. Han, K.M.: Data Mining: Concepts and Techniques. Elsevier Inc (2006)
11. Li, T., Xu, Y., Ruan, D., Pan, W.: Sequential Pattern Mining. In: Ruan, D., Chen, G., Kerre, E., Wets, G. (eds.) Intelligent Data Mining. Techniques and Applications, pp. 103–122. Springer, Heidelberg (2005)
12. Kalyankar, M., Alaspurkar, S.: Data Mining Technique to Analyse the Metrological Data. International Journal of Advanced Research in Computer Science and Software Engineering 3(2), 114–118 (2013)
13. Kaur, G.: Meteorological Data Mining Techniques: A Survey. International Journal of Emerging Technology and Advanced Engineering 2(8), 325–327 (2012)
14. Orozova, D., Sotirova, E.: Generalized net model of the applying data mining tools. In: Proc. of the Tenth International Workshop on Generalized Nets, Sofia, pp. 22–26 (2009)
15. Sotirova, E., Orozova, D.: Generalized net model of the phases of the data mining process, Developments in Fuzzy Sets, Intuitionistic Fuzzy Sets, Generalized Nets and Related Topics, Warsaw, Poland. Applications, vol. II, pp. 247–260 (2010)
16. Sotirova, E., Dimitrova, K., Papancheva, R.: A Generalized Net Model for Analysis of a Student's Evaluations by Data Mining Techniques in the e-Learning university. In: Proc. of the Tenth International Workshop on Generalized Nets, Sofia, pp. 41–46 (2009)
17. Srikant, R., Agrawal, R.: Mining sequential patterns: Generalizations and performance improvements. In: Apers, P.M.G., Bouzeghoub, M., Gardarin, G. (eds.) EDBT 1996. LNCS, vol. 1057, pp. 1–17. Springer, Heidelberg (1996)

Generalized Regression Neural Network for Forecasting Time Series with Multiple Seasonal Cycles

Grzegorz Dudek

Department of Electrical Engineering, Czestochowa University of Technology,
Al. Armii Krajowej 17, 42-200 Czestochowa, Poland
dudek@el.pcz.czest.pl

Abstract. This paper presents a method of forecasting time series with multiple seasonal cycles based on Generalized Regression Neural Network. This is a memory-based, fast learned and easy tuned type of neural network. The time series is preprocessed to define input and output patterns of seasonal cycles, which simplifies the forecasting problem. The method is useful for forecasting nonstationary time series with multiple seasonal cycles and trend. The model learns with the help of differential evolution or simple enumerative method. The performance of the proposed method is compared with that of other forecasting methods based on Nadaraya-Watson estimator, neural networks, ARIMA and exponential smoothing. Application examples confirm valuable properties of the proposed method and its highest accuracy among the methods considered.

Keywords: Seasonal time series forecasting, generalized regression neural network, differential evolution, pattern similarity based forecasting, short-term load forecasting.

1   Introduction

Many time series exhibit multiple seasonal cycles of different lengths. Good example of such a time series is hourly electricity demand in Poland presented in Fig. 1. This time series has three seasonal periods: daily, weekly and annual. The daily and weekly profiles change during the year. The daily profile depends on the day of the week as well. This time series expresses trend and is nonstationary in mean and variance. These all features have to be captured by the flexible forecasting model.

A variety of methods have been proposed for forecasting seasonal data. The most commonly employed classical models are exponential smoothing (ES) and seasonal autoregressive moving average models (ARMA). In ES the time series is modeled using a set of equations expressing level, growth and each seasonal cycle. These components can be combined additively or multiplicatively. Examples of using ES for forecasting multiple seasonal data can be found in [1] and [2]. One of the drawback of ES is overparameterization which involves initialization and updating of a large number of terms.

© Springer International Publishing Switzerland 2015
D. Filev et al. (eds.), *Intelligent Systems' 2014*,
Advances in Intelligent Systems and Computing 323, DOI: 10.1007/978-3-319-11310-4_73

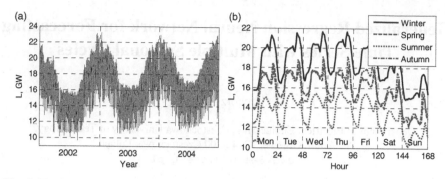

Fig. 1. The hourly electricity demand in Poland in three-year (a) and one-week (b) intervals

A base ARMA model can be extended for fitting a time series with a trend and seasonal variations. This consists in appropriate differentiation of a time series. The seasonal ARIMA can only deal with time series that are stationary in variance. When the variance changes in time transformation of a time series is needed. There are a very large number of ARIMA models. The selection process of ARIMA model and its order is usually considered subjective and difficult to apply. Another disadvantage of ARIMA is the linear character of the model.

The rapid development of computational intelligence and machine learning brings new tools for forecasting. They include mainly artificial neural networks (ANNs), fuzzy logic and intelligent searching methods, such as evolutionary algorithms and swarm intelligence. ANNs are very attractive as nonlinear methods of forecasting due to their universal approximation property, massive parallelism among a large number of simple units, learning capabilities, robustness in the presence of noise, and fault tolerance. Using fuzzy logic we can enter uncertain and imprecise data to the model. The forecasting model is composed of the if-then rules which can be formulated verbally by experts or extracted from data in the learning process. Evolutionary algorithms and related methods are useful for model optimization and learning. In a stochastic searching process they are able to get out of the local optima and find better solutions.

This paper focuses on the design of a forecasting method for time series with multiple seasonal cycles based on General Regression Neural Network. This is memory-based locally weighted regression method. The integral part of this model is data preprocessing and defining patterns of seasonal cycles of time series as explanatory and response variable vectors. Patterns simplify the forecasting problem filtering out the trend and redundant seasonal variations of periods longer than the basic one. The nonstationarity in mean and variance is also eliminated. The parameters of the GRNN model are estimated using differential evolution or simpler enumerative method.

2   Patterns of the Seasonal Cycles

The input patterns representing explanatory variables are defined as the transformed time series elements taken from basic seasonal cycles (seasonal cycle of the shortest length). The input pattern $\mathbf{x}_i = [x_{i,1} \ x_{i,2} \ \dots \ x_{i,n}]$ maps the time series elements from the i-th cycle $\mathbf{z}_i = [z_{i,1} \ z_{i,2} \ \dots \ z_{i,n}]$ as follows:

$$x_{i,t} = \frac{z_{i,t} - \overline{z}_i}{\sqrt{\sum_{l=1}^{n}(z_{i,l} - \overline{z}_i)^2}}, \tag{1}$$

where: $i = 1, 2, \dots, M$ – the seasonal cycle number, $t = 1, 2, \dots, n$ – the time series element number in the cycle i, $z_{i,t}$ – the t-th time series element in the cycle i, $\overline{z}_i$ – the mean value of elements in the seasonal cycle i.

Definition (1) expresses normalization of the vectors $\mathbf{z}_i$. After normalization they have unity length, zero mean and the same variance. Thus the nonstationary time series $\{z_j\}$ is represented by x-patterns having the same mean and variance.

Similarly the output patterns $\mathbf{y}_i = [y_{i,1} \ y_{i,2} \ \dots \ y_{i,n}]$ maps the elements from the seasonal cycle $i + \tau$: $\mathbf{z}_{i+\tau} = [z_{i+\tau,1} \ z_{i+\tau,2} \ \dots \ z_{i+\tau,n}]$, where $\tau > 0$ is a forecast horizon:

$$y_{i,t} = \frac{z_{i+\tau,t} - \overline{z}_i}{\sqrt{\sum_{l=1}^{n}(z_{i,l} - \overline{z}_i)^2}}. \tag{2}$$

Note that vectors $\mathbf{y}$ are defined using known current process parameters ($\overline{z}_i$ and the square root in the denominator as a measure of dispersion of elements in i-th seasonal cycle). This enables us to determine the forecast of vector $\mathbf{z}_{i+\tau}$ using (2) after the forecast of pattern $\mathbf{y}$ is calculated by the model.

The input and output patterns are paired and included in the set $L = \{(\mathbf{x}_1, \mathbf{y}_1), \dots, (\mathbf{x}_M, \mathbf{y}_M)\}$ from which the training sets are generated. The pairs $(\mathbf{x}_i, \mathbf{y}_i)$ represent the seasonal periods between which the distance in time is τ. The model learns the mapping $\mathbf{x} \rightarrow \mathbf{y}$ and then it forecasts the output pattern corresponding to the input pattern $\mathbf{x}$ (query pattern) which is presented to the model.

3   Generalized Regression Neural Network

Generalized Regression Neural Network (GRNN) is a kind of Radial Basis Function (RBF) neural network with a one pass learning algorithm and highly parallel structure. GRNN was introduced by Specht in 1991 [3] as a memory-based network that provides estimates of continuous variables. The algorithm provides smooth approximation of a target function even with sparse data in a multidimensional space. The advantages of GRNN are fast learning and easy tuning. The GRNN is composed of four layers: input, pattern (radial basis layer), summation and output as shown in Fig. 1.

Each neuron of the pattern layer uses a radial basis function as an activation function. This function is commonly taken to be Gaussian:

$$G_j(\mathbf{x}) = \exp\left(-\frac{\|\mathbf{x}-\mathbf{C}_j\|^2}{s_j^2}\right),$$ (3)

where: $\mathbf{C}_j$ is a center vector, s_j is a smoothing parameter or bandwidth and $\|.\|$ is the Euclidean norm.

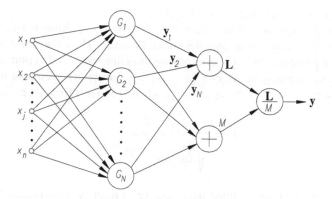

Fig. 2. GRNN architecture

Each training vector is represented by one pattern neuron with the center $\mathbf{C}_j = \mathbf{x}_j$, $j = 1, 2, ..., N$, where N is a number of training points. The neuron output expresses the similarity between the input vector $\mathbf{x}$ and the j-th training vector. So the pattern layer maps the n-dimensional input space into N-dimensional space of similarity. The GRNN output is an average of training y-patterns weighted by the degree of similarity between paired with them x-patterns and the query pattern:

$$\hat{\mathbf{y}} = g(\mathbf{x}) = \frac{\sum_{j=1}^{N} G_j(\mathbf{x})\mathbf{y}_j}{\sum_{j=1}^{N} G_j(\mathbf{x})}.$$ (4)

Note that the GRNN generates a vector as an output. The dimension of this vector does not affect the number of parameters to estimate unlike in other popular models such as multilayer perceptron or neuro-fuzzy networks. This should be considered as a valuable property.

The performance of GRNN is related with bandwidths s_j governing the smoothness of the regression function (4). Determining optimal bandwidth values is a major problem in GRNN training. In Section 4 we propose the differential evolution algorithm for estimation of bandwidths.

The forecasting model similar to GRNN called Nadaraya-Watson estimator was presented in [4]. In this estimator the product kernel is used as RBF. The product kernel has different bandwidths for each component of **x**. But for the different training patterns the same set of bandwidths are used. In the case of GRNN with Gaussian functions for each training pattern there is only one bandwidth but for each pattern the bandwidth is different.

4   Differential Evolution for GRNN Training

The bandwidth values s_j are tuned using the differential evolution (DE). This is an heuristic algorithm for global optimization over continuous spaces [5]. It is considered as the one of the most powerful stochastic optimization algorithm [6]. Unlike traditional evolutionary algorithms, DE employs difference of the solution vectors to explore the solution space.

In our case the solution vector is of the form $\mathbf{s} = [s_1, s_2, ..., s_N]$. The initial population of vectors is usually chosen randomly. New populations are generated in DE using mutation and crossover operators. During mutation for each population vector a mutant $\mathbf{v}_i$ is formed by adding the weighted difference between two population vectors to a third vector:

$$\mathbf{v}_i = \mathbf{s}_{r_1} + F(\mathbf{s}_{r_2} - \mathbf{s}_{r_3}),$$

$$(5)$$

where: $r_1, r_2, r_3 \in \{1, 2, ..., S\} \backslash i$ are random indexes (different from each other), S is a population size and $F \in [0, 2]$ is a coefficient controlling the mutation range.

The i-th vector is combined with its mutant using discrete crossover:

$$s'_{i,j} = \begin{cases} v_{i,j}, & \text{if } \xi_{i,j} \le CR \text{ or } j = \zeta_i, \\ s_{i,j}, & \text{if } \xi_{i,j} > CR \text{ and } j \ne \zeta_i, \end{cases}$$

$$(6)$$

where: $j = 1, 2, ..., N$, $\xi_{i,j}$ is a random number from uniform distribution $U(0, 1)$, ζ_i is a randomly chosen index from $\{1, 2, ..., N\}$ which ensures that the new solution gets at least one component of the mutant $\mathbf{v}_i$, and $CR \in [0, 1]$ is a crossover constant.

The trial solution $\mathbf{s}'_i = [s'_{i,1}, s'_{i,2}, ..., s'_{i,N}]$, created as a result of mutation and crossover, replaces its parent solution $\mathbf{s}_i$, if the cost function value is smaller for $\mathbf{s}'_i$ than for $\mathbf{s}_i$. After repeating this mutation, crossover and selection procedures for $i = 1, 2, ..., S$ we get a new population which is processed in the same way.

This is the basic strategy of DE. There are three control parameters here: the population size S, the mutation scale factor F and the crossover constant CR. The effect of each of these parameters on the performance of DE is discussed in [6]. The inventors of the algorithm recommend the value of S between $5n$ and $10n$, and $F = 0.5$.

The parameter CR controls how many components in expectation are changed in a solution vector. For small CR few components are changed and the stepwise movement tends to be orthogonal to the current coordinate axes. Higher CR value causes most of the mutant components to be inherited preventing this effect. In the application examples described in the next section the values of F and CR were tuned experimentally.

5   Application Examples

In this section we use the hourly electricity demand time series to test our GRNN model and compare it with other popular models used for forecasting time series with multiple seasonal cycles. The analyzed time series is shown in Fig. 1. (This data can be downloaded from the website http://gdudek.el.pcz.pl/varia/stlf-data.)

Our goal is to forecast one seasonal (daily) period ahead ($\tau = 1$) for January (without untypical 1 January) and July 2004. Thus there is $30 + 31 = 61$ forecasting tasks. For each forecasting task (test sample) the learning set is prepared individually from the historical data. It contains pairs of patterns from the set L representing the same days of the week (Monday, ..., Sunday) as the query pattern and forecasted **y** pattern. For each forecasting task the separate GRNN model is created and learned using DE. The solutions generated in DE are evaluated in the local leave-one-out procedure, in which the validation samples are chosen one by one from the set of 12 nearest neighbors of the query pattern.

In the first part of the study we investigate the efficiency of DE at different values of its parameters:

- DE1: $CR = 0.1, F = 0.5$,
- DE2: $CR = 0.3, F = 0.5$,
- DE3: $CR = 0.9, F = 0.5$,
- DE4: $CR = 0.1, F = 0.1$,
- DE5: $CR = 0.1, F = 1.0$,
- DE6: $CR = 0.1, F = 2.0$.

The population size in all variants was constant $S = 210$.

The convergence curves for DE with different parameter values in Fig. 3 are presented. The DE2 and DE3 variants with higher CR value than DE1 converge slower than DE1. The best value of F causing the fastest convergence turned out to be 0.1. However the improvement on the validation samples are observed the test error was not reduced. Therefore, the simpler method for selection of the bandwidths was used as follows. The distance d_5 between the query point and its 5-th nearest neighbor in the training set is determined. It is assumed that the bandwidth for all neurons is equal to $a \cdot d_5$, where a is a discrete parameter tuned by enumerating. The value of a ensuring the best results on validation samples was 0.5.

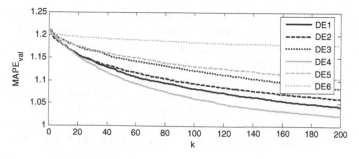

Fig. 3. Comparison of convergence curves for different DE variants

We compare the proposed GRNN model with the model based on Nadaraya-Watson estimator (N-WE), two neural network models: RBF and multilayer perceptron (MLP) and two classical models: ARIMA and ES. N-WE model is described in [4], ARIMA, ES and MLP models are described in [7]. Just as GRNN the models based on N-WE, RBF and MLP use patterns of seasonal cycles as explanatory and response variable vectors. In N-WE estimator the bandwidths were determined using the Scott's rule [4], depending on the sample standard deviation, sample size and dimension. RBF neural network was designed in Matlab using newrb function. The bandwidth of radial basis functions (the same for all neurons) was set to the distance between the query point and its k-th nearest neighbor in the training set. On the basis of preliminary experiments it was assumed $k = 12$. The MLP was learned in the local learning procedure in which the training samples were selected from the neighborhood of the query pattern. The one-neuron model was selected as an optimal solution. To find the best ARIMA and ES models automated procedures implemented in the forecast package for the R system [8] were used.

The results of forecasting: mean absolute percentage errors for the test samples $MAPE_{tst}$ and their interquartile ranges (IQR) in Table 1 are shown. For comparison the results determined using the naïve method are also shown. The forecast rule in this case is as follows: the forecasted daily cycle is the same as seven days ago.

Table 1. Results of forecasting

Model	January		July		Mean	
	$MAPE_{tst}$	IQR	$MAPE_{tst}$	IQR	$MAPE_{tst}$	IQR
GRNN	1.21	1.22	0.90	0.93	1.05	1.04
N-WE	1.23	1.19	0.88	0.87	1.05	1.09
RBF	1.56	1.41	1.10	1.18	1.33	1.30
MLP	1.32	1.30	0.97	1.01	1.14	1.15
ARIMA	2.64	2.34	1.21	1.24	1.91	1.67
ES	2.35	1.88	1.19	1.30	1.76	1.56
Naïve	6.37	5.36	1.29	1.20	3.78	3.82

The best forecasts were obtained by GRNN and N-WE. These two methods gave statistically indistinguishable errors (Wilcoxon signed-rank test was used). A little worse results were obtained using MLP. The worst results were achieved using classical models: ARIMA and ES. This is probably due to the learning sample used for estimation of parameters in ARIMA and ES, which contains the time series fragment (12-week fragment in our case) directly preceding the forecasted fragment. The irregularities in this preceding fragment affect adversely the forecasts. In the proposed approach the learning set is not limited to the fragment preceding the forecast but is composed of the most similar patterns to the query pattern. So irregular patterns, which are not similar to the query pattern are not included in this set, unless their irregularities correspond to the irregularities in the query pattern.

Note that GRNN model optimized using enumeration method has only one parameter to estimate (a). This is a great advantage. Such a model is easy to optimize and has good generalization properties.

6   Conclusions

The memory-based models operating on patterns of seasonal cycles: GRNN and N-WE turned out to be the most accurate in forecasting time series with multiple seasonal cycles compared to RBF and MPL neural networks and classical statistical models: ARIMA and ES. The memory-based approaches do not estimate a global model but defer the processing of data until a forecast is requested. The forecast is derived from the neighborhood of the query point using locally weighted regression. A key problem here is the selection of appropriate weighting functions to get the best generalization performance given a set of sparse and noisy data. In the application example an exact estimation of bandwidth values for each neuron using differential evolution did not bring an expected reduction in the test error. This is probably due to the sparse data: there is not enough training data in the neighborhood of the query pattern to build an accurate local model. The simpler enumeration method for bandwidth estimation where we are searching for the value the a coefficient provided better results. In this case GRNN has only one parameter to estimate. The instant training and easy tuning are great advantages of GRNN.

The proposed forecasting model owes its good performance not only to the valuable properties of GRNN but also to the initial transformations of data and appropriate definitions of patterns of seasonal cycles. The patterns simplify a forecasting problem eliminating nonstationarity of time series in mean and variance and removing the trend and seasonal variations of periods longer than the basic one.

Acknowledgment. The study was supported by the Research Project N N516 415338 financed by the Polish Ministry of Science and Higher Education.

References

1. Taylor, J.W.: Exponentially Weighted Methods for Forecasting Intraday Time Series with Multiple Seasonal Cycles. International Journal of Forecasting 26, 627–646 (2010)
2. Gould, P.G., et al.: Forecasting Time-Series with Multiple Seasonal Patterns. European Journal of Operational Research 191, 207–222 (2008)
3. Specht, D.F.: A General Regression Neural Network. IEEE Transactions on Neural Networks 2(6), 568–576 (1991)
4. Dudek, G.: Short-term Load Forecasting Based on Kernel Conditional Density Estimation. Przegląd Elektrotechniczny (Electrical Review) 86(8), 164–167 (2010)
5. Storn, R., Price, K.: Differential Evolution – A Simple and Efficient Heuristic for Global Optimization over Continuous Spaces. Journal of Global Optimization 11(4), 341–359 (1997)
6. Das, S., Suganthan, P.N.: Differential Evolution: A Survey of the State-of-the-Art. IEEE Transactions on Evolutionary Computation 15(1), 4–31 (2011)
7. Dudek, G.: Forecasting Time Series with Multiple Seasonal Cycles using Neural Networks with Local Learning. In: Rutkowski, L., Korytkowski, M., Scherer, R., Tadeusiewicz, R., Zadeh, L.A., Zurada, J.M. (eds.) ICAISC 2013, Part I. LNCS, vol. 7894, pp. 52–63. Springer, Heidelberg (2013)
8. Hyndman, R.J., Khandakar, Y.: Automatic Time Series Forecasting: The Forecast Package for R. Journal of Statistical Software 27(3), 1–22 (2008)

Generalized Nets Model of Dimensionality Reduction in Time Series

Maciej Krawczak[1,2] and Grażyna Szkatuła[1]

[1] Systems Research Institute, Polish Academy of Sciences,
[2] Warsaw School of Information Technology
Newelska 6, Warsaw, Poland
{krawczak,szkatulg}@ibspan.waw.pl

Abstract. The paper considers the generalized nets as an extension of Petri nets applied for modeling of the methodology called *Symbolic Essential Attributes Approximation* (Krawczak and Szkatuła, 2014). SEAA was developed to reduce the dimensionality of multidimensional time series by generating a new nominal representation of the original data series. In general the approach is based on the concept of data series envelopes and essential attributes obtained by a multi-layer neural network. The symbolic data series representation - which just describes the compressed representation of the original data series - is obtained via discretization of the real-valued essential attributes. In this paper the generalized nets were used to model the logistic of processes involved in SEAA methodology. First the basic of the theory of generalized nets is introduced, next SEAA methodology processes are modeled via the generalized nets the new model of SEAA.

Keywords: Modeling, Generalized nets, Data series, Dimensionality reduction, Symbolic Essential Attributes Approximation.

1 Introduction

In 1982 K. T. Atanassov (1987, 1991 and 1997) proposed a new definition of nets for modelling and analyzing various kinds of dynamic systems, the nets are called generalized nets. In several papers it was shown that existing Petri nets were particular cases of generalized nets. The conception of generalized nets is based on relation place – transition. Generalized nets are characterized by:

- a static structure,
- dynamical elements called tokens,
- temporal components.

The static structure of generalized nets is characterized by *transitions*. Tokens are described by changeable *characteristics*. There are three global temporal constants: the initial moment in which the net starts functioning, the elementary time-step of the

© Springer International Publishing Switzerland 2015
D. Filev et al. (eds.), *Intelligent Systems'2014*,
Advances in Intelligent Systems and Computing 323, DOI: 10.1007/978-3-319-11310-4_74

process, and the duration of functioning. It was shown (Krawczak, 2003, 2013) that generalized nets can be used for modelling dynamic processes. In the book Atanassov (1991) one can find the basic elements of the theory of generalized nets, where generalized nets are defined as extensions of the ordinary Petri nets and their modifications. Up to now more than 500 scientific works related to generalized nets were published (Radeva, Krawczak and Choy, 2002) both theoretical as well as describing applications.

Data series arise in many areas, for example in medicine, finance, industry, climate. In general data series research considers the following problems: *indexing* (e.g. Keogh, Chakrabarti and Pazzani, 2001), *clustering* (e.g. Keogh and Pazzani, 2001; Wu and Chang, 2004; Krawczak and Szkatuła, 2010c, 2012a, b, c, 2013a, b), *classification* (e.g. Nanopoulos, Alcock, Manolopoulos, 2001; Krawczak and Szkatuła, 2010a, b, 2011), Wang (2010), *summarization* (e.g. Lin, Keogh, Patel and Lonardi, 2002), and *anomaly detection* (e.g. Shahabi, Tian and Zhao, 2000). It is said that time series or data series mining is considered as one of the tenth challenging problems in data mining (Yang and Wu, 2005; Fu, 2011).

In general data series are characterized by huge dimensionality which causes that many data mining methods render ineffective and fragile (Beyer et al., 1999). Therefore the reduction of data series dimensionality becomes crucial because dimensionality reduction of the original data series. The new data series representation must preserve sufficient information for solving above data series problems with satisfactory accuracy. There are many approaches to dimensionality reduction of data series (Takchung Fu, 2011), among them there is *Symbolic Essential Attributes Approximation* (SEAA) for gradual reduction of dimensionality of data series developed by Krawczak and Szkatuła (2014), in which the data series representation is characterized by a set of nominal-valued attributes representing the original data series and additionally preserves properties of the original data series. SEAA methodology for data series dimensionality reduction consists of several steps where each step reduces dimensionality considerably. It is possible to describe the whole SEAA methodology in a "language" of generalized nets, generalized nets can be used to find logistic model of each step of SEAA methodology as well as of the whole methodology as a system.

The remaining part of this paper is organized as follows: Section 2 presents basics of generalized nets; in Section 3 we describe SEAA methodology as a system of information processing. One of the reason to use generalized nets to describe SEAA methodology is to promote the still new and little shared tool for modeling discrete event systems.

2   Concept of Generalized Nets

The conception of generalized nets was described by Krassimir Atanassov in 1982 for describing and analyzing various kinds of discrete events systems. Compare to Petri nets (e.g. Petri 1962, 1980) generalized nets have some new extra elements.

This section is based on books by Atanassov (1991, 1992, 1997, 1998, 2007) as well as a book by Krawczak (2003, 2013) and by Krawczak et al. (2010).

The first basic difference between generalized nets and the ordinary Petri nets is the place – transition relation (Atanassov, 1991). The places are marked by $\bigcirc$, and the transitions by Y. Generalized nets contain dynamic elements called tokens. Tokens are transferred from one place to other places, and each token carries some information described by token's characteristic which is modified during passing transitions. The transition has input and output places, as it is shown in Fig. 1.

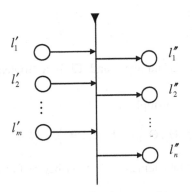

Fig. 1. A generalized net transition

Formally, every transition is described by a seven-tuple

$$Z = \langle L', L'', t_1, t_2, r, M, \square \rangle \tag{1}$$

where $L' = \{l'_1, l'_2, \ldots, l'_m\}$ describes a set of the transition's input places,

$L'' = \{l''_1, l''_2, \ldots, l''_m\}$ describes a set of the transition's output places,

t_1 is a moment of the transitions firing,

t_2 is a duration of the transition activation time,

r denotes the transition's condition determining tokens allowed to pass the transition an inputs to outputs; conditions are described in an index matrix form (Atanassov, 1987), where r_{ij} is a predicate that corresponds to the i-th input and the j-th output places, $1 \le i \le m$, $1 \le j \le n$; when its truth value is true, a token is allowed to pass the transition from the i-th input place to the j-th output place, see Table 1,

Table 1. Index matrix r

	l''_1	$\cdots$	l''_j	$\cdots$	l''_n
l'_1	r_{11}	$\cdots$	r_{1j}	$\cdots$	r_{1n}
$\vdots$	$\vdots$	$\cdots$	$\vdots$	$\cdots$	$\vdots$
l'_i	r_{i1}	$\cdots$	r_{ij}	$\cdots$	r_{in}
$\vdots$	$\vdots$	$\cdots$	$\vdots$	$\cdots$	$\vdots$
l'_m	r_{m1}	$\cdots$	r_{mj}	$\cdots$	r_{mn}

M is an index matrix of the capacities of transition's arcs, see Table 2,

Table 2. Index matrix M

	l_1''	...	l_j''	...	l_n''
l_1'	m_{11}	...	m_{1j}	...	m_{1n}
$\vdots$	$\vdots$	...	$\vdots$	...	$\vdots$
l_i'	m_{i1}	...	m_{ij}	...	m_{in}
$\vdots$	$\vdots$	...	$\vdots$	...	$\vdots$
l_m'	m_{m1}	...	m_{mj}	...	m_{mn}

where $m_{ij} \geq 0$ are natural numbers and $\square$ is a Boolean- like object describing activation of a transition.

The following ordered four-tuple

$$E = \Big\langle \langle A, \pi_A, \pi_L, c, f, \Theta_1, \Theta_2 \rangle, \ \langle K, \pi_k, \Theta_K \rangle, \ \langle T, t^0, t^* \rangle, \ \langle X, \Phi, b \rangle \Big\rangle \qquad (2)$$

is called generalized net if the elements are described as follows:

A is a set of transitions,

π_A is a function of priorities of the transitions,

π_L is a function giving the priorities of the places,

c is a function giving the capacities of the places,

f is a function used for calculations of values of the predicates of the transition's conditions,

Θ_1 is a function calculating a moment of activation of transition,

Θ_2 is a function for calculating duration of transition activity,

K is the set of tokens,

π_K is a function giving the priorities of tokens,

Θ_K is a function giving moment for entering the net by tokens,

T is the moment of starting the net functioning,

t^0 is an elementary time-step,

t^* is the duration of net functioning,

X is the set of all initial characteristics the tokens,

Φ is a function which change characteristics of tokens,

b is a function describing maximum number of characteristics for each token.

In the case when some of a lack of some parameters we call such net as a *reduced generalized nets*, where such parameter is indicated by $*$.

Details of generalized net operators can be found in many papers and books written first of all by Atanassov (1987).

3   Description of Transitions for SEAA Method

The problem of dimensionality reduction of time series can be stated as follows. We consider the normalized (with the mean equal zero and the standard deviation equal one) data series described in the following way:

$$[x_1(n), x_2(n), ..., x_M(n)] \tag{3}$$

where $x_k(n) \in R$, $k = 1,2,...,M$, $n = 1, 2, ..., N$, while M denotes the dimensionality of the time series and N stands for the number of time series in the data set. The aim of SEAA method is to find a new representation of (3) characterized by sufficiently lower dimension. One of the possible generalized net representation of SEAA method is depicted in Fig. 2.

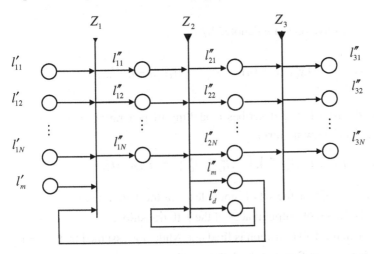

Fig. 2. The generalized net description of SEAA methodology

In this section we will distinguish the main steps of SEAA method and the stream of information passing through the transitions. In other words we will construct the whole generalized net model describing SEAA method, and we will describe the separate transitions using nomenclature from the previous section. The generalized net constructed below has a reduced form, it means the net does not have several temporal components, additionally it was assumed that the priorities of its transitions, places and tokens are equal, its place and arc capacities are equal to infinity.

3.1   The Transition Z_1

According to Krawczak and Szkatuła (2010a, 2010b) the first main step in the method of SEAA is related to the idea of envelopes of time series and procedure of generating of the envelopes. In order to generate time series envelopes we employed piecewise constant functions, also called step functions, where the length of steps is denoted as

m. The parameter m describes the rank of time series dimensionality reduction. It means that for a given data series (3) of the length M we obtain a new representation of the reduced length $\left\lfloor \dfrac{M}{m} \right\rfloor$, where $m \ll M$. It is possible to form the new representation of the data series which is described by either upper or lower envelopes, or both.

Selection of the proper values of the m parameter is important and should be adjusted in an experimental way. The so-called m-step upper and m-step lower approximation, $m \ll M$, constitute approximations of (3). The m-step upper approximation of the data series (3) is denoted by

$$[x_k^U(n)]_{k=1}^{k=\left\lfloor \frac{M}{m} \right\rfloor m} = [x_1^U(n), x_2^U(n), ..., x_{\left\lfloor \frac{M}{m} \right\rfloor m}^U(n)], \quad n = 1, 2, ..., N \tag{4}$$

while the m-step lower envelopes are denoted by

$$[x_k^L(n)]_{k=1}^{k=\left\lfloor \frac{M}{m} \right\rfloor m} = [x_1^L(n), x_2^L(n), ..., x_{\left\lfloor \frac{M}{m} \right\rfloor m}^L(n)], \quad n = 1, 2, ..., N \tag{5}$$

The transition Z_1 from Fig. 2 describes modelling of generating of envelopes of time series and has the following form

$$Z_1 = \left\langle \{l'_{11}, l'_{12}, ..., l'_{1N}, l'_m, l''_m, \}, \{l''_{11}, l''_{12}, ..., l''_{1N}\}, \ \tau_1, \tau'_1, r_1, M_1, * \right\rangle \tag{6}$$

where $\{l'_{11}, l'_{12}, ..., l'_{1N}, l'_m, l''_m\}$ is the set of input places of the 1-th transition,

$\{l''_{11}, l''_{12}, ..., l''_{1N}\}$ is the set of output places of the 1-th transition,

τ_1 is the time when the 1-th transition is fired out, while it is assumed that $\tau_1 = T$,

τ'_1 is the duration time of firing of the 1-th transition,

r_1 denotes the 1-th transition condition determining the transfer of tokens from the firth transition's inputs $\{l'_{11}, l'_{12}, ..., l'_{1N}, l'_m, l''_m\}$ to its outputs $\{l''_{11}, l''_{12}, ..., l''_{1N}\}$, and has the index matrix form, see Table 3,

Table 3. Index matrix r_1

	l''_{11}	l''_{12}	$\cdots$	l''_{1N}
l'_{11}	true	false	$\cdots$	false
l'_{12}	false	true	$\cdots$	false
$\vdots$	$\vdots$	$\vdots$	$\cdots$	$\vdots$
l'_{1N}	false	false	$\cdots$	true
l'_m	true	true	$\cdots$	true
l''_m	true	true	$\cdots$	true

where the value true indicates that the tokens representing the time series can be transferred from one input place l'_{1n} to the proper output place l''_{1n}, $n = 1, 2, ..., N$,

M_1 indicates an index matrix describing the capacities of transition's arcs, Table 4.

Table 4. Index matrix M_1

	l''_{11}	l''_{12}	...	l''_{1N}
l'_{11}	1	0	...	0
l'_{12}	0	1	...	0
$\vdots$	$\vdots$	$\vdots$	...	$\vdots$
l'_{1N}	0	0	...	1
l'_{m}	1	1	...	1
l''_{m}	1	1	...	1

In each input place l'_{1n}, there is a token α_{1n} $n = 1, 2, ..., N$. Each token has its initial characteristic

$$\phi(\alpha_{1n}) = [x_1(n), x_2(n), ..., x_M(n)], \quad n = 1, 2, ..., N \tag{7}$$

It is easy to notice that the initial characteristics of a token α_{1n}, for separated value $n = 1, 2, ..., N$, is just a time series (3) indicated by index n.

For $n = 1, 2, ..., N$, a token α_{1n} passing the transition Z_1 changes its characteristic which now becomes as follows

$$\phi(\alpha_{1n}) = [y_1(n), y_2(n), ..., y_{\left\lfloor \frac{M}{m} \right\rfloor}(n)], \quad n = 1, 2, ..., N \tag{8}$$

The way to change the characteristic of each token α_{1n}, $n = 1, 2, ..., N$, from (7) to (8) is governed by procedure described in details in Krawczak and Szkatuła (2014). It worth to emphasize that the change of the tokens' characteristics is equivalent to reduce the time series dimensionality from the value M into value $\left\lfloor \dfrac{M}{m} \right\rfloor$.

In the case of the place l'_m which contains a token β having its characteristic $\phi(\beta) = m$, this token curries only the information about the rate of aggregation of envelopes. While the place l''_m contains a token χ which has the following characteristic $\phi(\chi) = m \pm 1$, and increasing or reducing m depends on quality of reduced dimensionality representation work out within the procedure involved in transition Z_2.

3.2   The Transition Z_2

The next transition Z_2 from Fig. 2 describes modelling of generating of essential attributes which characterize time series represented by respective envelopes. This part of SEAA methodology is based on Cybenko's theorem (1989) as well as nonlinear principle component analysis and auto-associative neural networks. We considered *essential attributes* which give a new time series representation generated by outputs of second hidden layer neurons of developed neural network.

Thus, we will use an auto-associative feedforward neural network with five layers, including the input layer. The inputs are described by envelopes (4) or/and (5) of dimensionality $\left\lfloor \dfrac{M}{m} \right\rfloor$, while the outputs of the second hidden layer

$$\{c_1(n), c_2(n), ..., c_E(n)\}, \ n = 1, ..., N \tag{9}$$

where $E \ll \left\lfloor \dfrac{M}{m} \right\rfloor$ denotes the number of essential attributes, and in the same way the subsequent dimensionality reduction. The idea of essential attributes obtained from auto-associative neural networks was introduced in earlier papers by Krawczak and Szkatuła (2008) related to data series mining problems.

The Z_2 transition describing generation of essential attributes has the form:

$$Z_2 = \left\langle \{l''_{11}, l''_{12}, ..., l''_{1N}\}, \{l''_{21}, l''_{22}, ..., l''_{2N}, l''_m, l''_d\}, \tau_2, \tau'_2, r_2, M_2, * \right\rangle \tag{10}$$

where $\{l''_{11}, l''_{12}, ..., l''_{1N}\}$ is the set of input places of the 2-nd transition,

$\{l''_{21}, l''_{22}, ..., l''_{2N}, l''_m, l''_d\}$ is the set of output places of the 2-nd transition,

τ_2 is the time when the 2 nd transition is fired out,

τ'_2 is the duration time of firing of the 2-nd transition,

r_2 denotes the 2-nd transition condition determining the transfer of tokens from the second transition's inputs $\{l''_{11}, l''_{12}, ..., l''_{1N}\}$ to its outputs $\{l''_{21}, l''_{22}, ..., l''_{2N}, l''_m, l''_d\}$, and has the index matrix form, see Table 5, where the value true indicates that the tokens representing the time series can be transferred from one input place l''_{1n} to the proper output place l''_{2n}, $n = 1, 2, ..., N$,

Table 5. Index matrix r_2

	l''_{21}	l''_{22}	...	l''_{2N}	l''_m	l''_d
l''_{11}	true	false	...	false	false	false
l''_{12}	false	true	...	false	false	false
⋮	⋮	⋮	...	⋮	⋮	⋮
l''_{1N}	false	false	...	true	true	true

M_2 indicates an index matrix describing the capacities of transition's arcs, Table 6.

Table 6. Index matrix M_2

	l''_{21}	l''_{23}	...	l''_{2N}	l''_m	l''_d
l''_{11}	1	0	...	0	0	0
l''_{12}	0	1	...	0	0	0
$\vdots$	$\vdots$	$\vdots$	...	$\vdots$	$\vdots$	$\vdots$
l''_{1N}	0	0	...	1	1	1

In each input place l''_{1n}, there is a token α_{1n}, $n = 1, 2, ..., N$ having its initial characteristic

$$\phi(\alpha_{1n}) = [y_1(n), y_2(n), ..., y_{\left\lfloor \frac{M}{m} \right\rfloor}(n)], \qquad n = 1, 2, ..., N \qquad (11)$$

For $n = 1, 2, ..., N$, a token α_{1n} passing the transition Z_2 changes its characteristic which becomes as follows

$$\phi(\alpha_{1n}) = [c_1(n), c_2(n), ..., c_E(n)], \qquad n = 1, 2, ..., N \qquad (12)$$

Changing characteristics of tokens α_{1n}, $n = 1, 2, ..., N$, from (11) to (12) is governed by procedure described by Krawczak and Szkatuła (2013). The change of the tokens' characteristics causes reducing the time series dimensionality to the value E,

$$E \ll \left\lfloor \frac{M}{m} \right\rfloor.$$

In the place l''_d there is a token χ which has characteristic $\phi(\chi) = E$ and the changes of this characteristic are done by tuning of the value of E in order to obtain the most rational dimensionality reduction subject to the prescribed value of the parameter m. The rational value of the parameter m is adjusted via the token β and its characteristic $\phi(\beta)$.

3.3   The Transition Z_3

In order to farther reduction of dimensionality of time series we change real-valued essential attributes into nominal-valued essential attributes. Therefore such procedure is called discretization of the essential attributes and in general, the method relies on determination of the domain of observed attributes values and dividing the interval into equal subintervals. Based on analysis of all attributes values

$$c(n) = [c_1(n), c_2(n), ..., c_E(n)], \qquad n = 1, 2, ..., N \qquad (13)$$

we obtained the new nominal representation of time series

$$a(n) = [a_1(n), a_2(n), ..., a_E(n)], \qquad n = 1, 2, ..., N \qquad (14)$$

The Z_3 transition describing generation of nominal essential attributes has the form:

$$Z_3 = \left\langle \{l''_{21}, l''_{22},..., l''_{2N}\}, \{l''_{31}, l''_{32},..., l''_{3N}\}, \tau_3, \tau'_3, r_3, M_3, * \right\rangle \tag{15}$$

where $\{l''_{21}, l''_{22},..., l''_{2N}\}$ is the set of input places of the 3-rd transition,

$\{l''_{31}, l''_{32},..., l''_{3N}\}$ is the set of output places of the 3-rd transition,

τ_3 is the time when the 3-rd transition is fired out,

τ'_3 is the duration time of firing of the 3-rd transition,

r_3 denotes the 3-rd transition condition determining the transfer of tokens from the second transition's inputs $\{l''_{21}, l''_{22},..., l''_{2N}\}$ to its outputs $\{l''_{31}, l''_{32},..., l''_{3N}\}$, and has the index matrix form, see Table 7.

Table 7. Index matrix r_3

	l''_{31}	l''_{32}	...	l''_{3N}
l''_{21}	true	false	...	false
l''_{22}	false	true	...	false
⋮	⋮	⋮	...	⋮
l''_{2N}	false	false	...	true

where the value true indicates that the tokens representing the time series can be transferred from one input place l''_{2n} to the proper output place l''_{3n}, $n = 1, 2,..., N$,

M_3 indicates an index matrix describing the capacities of transition's arcs, Table 8.

Table 8. Index matrix M_3

	l''_{31}	l''_{32}	...	l''_{3N}
l''_{11}	1	0	...	0
l''_{12}	0	1	...	0
⋮	⋮	⋮	...	⋮
l''_{1N}	0	0	...	1

In each input place l''_{2n}, there is a token α_{1n}, $n = 1, 2,..., N$ having its initial characteristic

$$\phi(\alpha_{1n}) = [c_1(n), c_2(n),..., c_E(n)], \quad n = 1, 2,..., N \tag{16}$$

For $n = 1, 2,..., N$, a token α_{1n} passing the transition Z_3 changes its characteristic which becomes as follows

$$\phi(\alpha_{1n}) = [a_1(n), a_2(n),..., a_E(n)], \quad n = 1, 2,..., N \tag{17}$$

Changing characteristics of tokens α_{1n}, $n = 1, 2, ..., N$, from (16) to (17) is governed by procedure described by Krawczak and Szkatuła (2013). The whole generalized net model of SEAA method has the following form, rewritten (2):

$$E = \left\langle \left\langle A, \pi_A, \pi_L, c, f, \Theta_1, \Theta_2 \right\rangle, \ \left\langle K, \pi_k, \Theta_K \right\rangle, \ \left\langle T, t^0, t^* \right\rangle, \ \left\langle X, \Phi, b \right\rangle \right\rangle \quad (18)$$

where the some parameters were described above, and due to limited space the role of rest parameter can be found in other papers by Atanassov (1997) or Krawczak (2013).

4   Conclusions

In this paper we introduced a generalized net model of SEAA method. SEAA is a complex method developed by the authors of this paper, and the method deals with reduction of dimensionality of time series. Within the SEAA method three main parts can be distinguished, these parts were very roughly described in order to describe transitions. Each transition just model each separate part of SEAA methodology. Description of each transition is rather very rough because the main aim of this paper is to make readers to be a bit more familiar with generalized net ideology. Except transition also places as well as tokens and their characteristics were explained.

We do hope that the paper will promote the generalized net tool for describing discrete event systems at least a bit.

References

1. Atanassov, K.: Generalized Index Matrices. Competes Rendus de l'Academie Bulgare des Sciences 40(11), 15–18 (1987)
2. Atanassov, K.: Generalized nets. World Scientific, Singapore (1991)
3. Atanassov, K.: Generalized Nets and Systems Theory. Prof. M. Drinov. Academic Publishing House, Sofia (1997)
4. Beyer, K., Goldstein, J., Ramakrishnan, R., Shaft, U.: When is "Nearest Neighbor" Meaningful? In: Beeri, C., Bruneman, P. (eds.) ICDT 1999. LNCS, vol. 1540, pp. 217–235. Springer, Heidelberg (1998)
5. Cybenko, G.: Approximations by superpositions of sigmoidal functions. Mathematics of Control, Signals, and Systems 2(4), 303–314 (1989)
6. Fu, T.C.: A review on time series data mining. Engineering Applications of Artificial Intelligence 24, 164–181 (2011)
7. Keogh, E., Chakrabarti, K., Pazzani, M.: M. Locally Adaptive Dimensionality Reduction for Indexing Large Time Series Databases. In: Proc. of ACM SIGMOD Conference on Management of Data, Santa Barbara, May 21-24, pp. 151–162 (2001)
8. Keogh, E., Pazzani, M.: Derivative dynamic time warping. In: Proceedings of the First SIAM International Conference on Data Mining, Chicago, USA (2001)
9. Krawczak, M.: Multilayer Neural Systems and Generalized Net Models. Ac. Publ. House EXIT, Warsaw (2003)
10. Krawczak, M.: Multilayer Neural Networks – Generalized Net perspective. Springer (2013)
11. Krawczak, M., Szkatuła, G.: On decision rules application to time series classification. In: Atanassov, K.T., et al. (eds.) Advances in Fuzzy Sets, Intuitionistic Fuzzy Sets, Generalized Nets and Related Topics, Ac. Publ. House EXIT (2008)

12. Krawczak, M., Szkatuła, G.: Time series envelopes for classification. In: IEEE Intelligent Systems Conference, July 7-9 (2010a)
13. Krawczak, M., Szkatuła, G.: On time series envelopes for classification problems. In: Atanassov, K.T., et al. (eds.) Developments in Fuzzy Sets, Intuitionistic Fuzzy Sets, Generalized Nets and Related Topics. II. SRI PAS, Warsaw (2010b)
14. Krawczak, M., Szkatuła, G.: Dimensionality reduction for time series. Case studies of the Polish Association of Knowledge 31, 32–45 (2010c)
15. Krawczak, M., Szkatuła, G.: A hybrid approach for dimension reduction in classification. Control and Cybernetics 40(2), 527–552 (2011)
16. Krawczak, M., Szkatuła, G.z.: A clustering algorithm based on distinguishability for nominal attributes. In: Rutkowski, L., Korytkowski, M., Scherer, R., Tadeusiewicz, R., Zadeh, L.A., Zurada, J.M. (eds.) ICAISC 2012, Part II. LNCS, vol. 7268, pp. 120–127. Springer, Heidelberg (2012)
17. Krawczak, M., Szkatuła, G.: Dimension reduction of time series for the Clustering Problem. In: Atanassov, K.T., Homenda, W., Hryniewicz, O., Kacprzyk, J., Krawczak, M., Nahorski, Z., Szmidt, E., Zadrożny, S. (eds.) New Developments in Fuzzy Sets, Intuitionistic Fuzzy Sets, Generalized Nets and Related Topics. II: Applications, pp. 101–110. SRI PAS, Warsaw (2012b)
18. Krawczak, M., Szkatuła, G.: Nominal Time Series Representation for the Clustering Problem. In: IEEE 6th International Conference "Intelligent Systems", Sofia, pp. 182–187 (2012)
19. Krawczak, M., Szkatuła, G.z.: On perturbation measure of clusters: Application. In: Rutkowski, L., Korytkowski, M., Scherer, R., Tadeusiewicz, R., Zadeh, L.A., Zurada, J.M. (eds.) ICAISC 2013, Part II. LNCS, vol. 7895, pp. 176–183. Springer, Heidelberg (2013)
20. Krawczak, M., Szkatuła, G.: A New Measure of Groups Perturbation. In: IFSA World Congress, pp. 1291–1296 (2013b)
21. Krawczak, M., Szkatuła, G.: An approach to dimensionality reduction in time series. Information Sciences 260, 15–36 (2014)
22. Lin, J., Keogh, E., Patel, E.P., Lonardi, S.: Finding motifs in time series. In: 2nd Workshop on Temporal Data Mining, the 8th ACM International Conference on Knowledge Discovery and Data Mining, Edmonton, Canada, pp. 53–68 (2002)
23. Nanopoulos, A., Alcock, R., Manolopoulos, Y.: Feature-based Classification of Timeseries Data. International Journal of Computer Research, 49–61 (2001)
24. Oja, E.: Principal components, minor components and linear neural networks. Neural Networks 5, 927–935 (1992)
25. Radeva, V., Krawczak, M., Choy, E.: Review and Bibliography on Generalized Nets Theory and Applications. Advanced Studies in Contemporary Mathematics 4(2), 173–199 (2002)
26. Shahabi, C., Tian, X., Zhao, W.: TSA-tree: A wavelet-based approach to improve the efficiency of multi-level surprise and trend queries. In: Proceedings of the 12th International Conference on Scientific and Statistical Database Management, Berlin, pp. 55–68 (2000)
27. Fu, T.-C.: A review on time series data mining. Engineering Applications of Artificial Intelligence 24, 164–181 (2011)
28. Yang, Q., Wu, X.: 10 Challenging problems in data mining research. International Journal of Information Technology and Decision Making 5(4), 597–604 (2005)
29. Wang, B.: A New Clustering Algorithm on Nominal Data Sets. In: Proceedings of International MultiConference of Engineers and Computer Scientists, IMECS 2010, Hong Kong, March 17-19 (2010)
30. Wu, Y., Chang, E.Y.: Distance-function design and fusion for sequence data. In: CIKM 2004, pp. 324–333 (2004)

Nodes Selection Criteria
for Fuzzy Cognitive Maps
Designed to Model Time Series

Władysław Homenda[1], Agnieszka Jastrzębska[1], and Witold Pedrycz[2,3]

[1] Faculty of Mathematics and Information Science, Warsaw University of Technology,
ul. Koszykowa 75, 00-662 Warsaw, Poland
[2] Systems Research Institute, Polish Academy of Sciences,
ul. Newelska 6, 01-447 Warsaw, Poland
[3] Department of Electrical & Computer Engineering, University of Alberta,
Edmonton T6R 2G7 AB Canada
{homenda,A.Jastrzebska}@mini.pw.edu.pl, wpedrycz@ualberta.ca

Abstract. The article introduces three concepts' rejection/selection criteria for Fuzzy Cognitive Map-based method of time series modeling and prediction. Proposed criteria are named entropy index, membership index and global distance index. Concepts' selection strategies facilitate Fuzzy Cognitive Map design procedure. Proposed criteria allow to simplify, otherwise very complex models, and achieve a reasonable balance between complexity and accuracy.

Keywords: Fuzzy Cognitive Maps, FCM nodes evaluation, FCM simplification.

1 Introduction

Modeling and prediction are one of top-priority research fields, where not only classical mathematical models, but also alternative approaches from information sciences play important role and provide successful solutions. Studies on time series modeling follow this path as well. There is an impressive set of classical methods. There are also several noteworthy methods rooted in information sciences, among which are Fuzzy Cognitive Maps.

Fuzzy Cognitive Maps are recognized time series modeling and prediction tool. They offer an interesting information representation philosophy, and they aim at capturing both qualitative and quantitative relations within data. The drawback of modeling with Fuzzy Cognitive Maps is complexity. Fuzzy Cognitive Maps are digraph-based models. Hence, with the growth of map dimensionality, the number of weights that are necessary to build a model grow quadratically. Large maps are not convenient in use. First, they are difficult to interpret and to explore. Second, they require substantial computational resources to train.

The named above problems with modeling with Fuzzy Cognitive Maps drawn our attention to research on Fuzzy Cognitive Maps simplification procedures.

© Springer International Publishing Switzerland 2015
D. Filev et al. (eds.), *Intelligent Systems'2014*,
Advances in Intelligent Systems and Computing 323, DOI: 10.1007/978-3-319-11310-4_75

The goal of our efforts is to propose a comprehensive set of efficient time series modeling methods based on Fuzzy Cognitive Maps. A key element of the modeling framework that we work on are a priori nodes selection/rejection criteria.

The objectives of this paper are:

- to discuss time series modeling framework based on simplified Fuzzy Cognitive Maps,
- to introduce a priori nodes rejection criteria for the design of Fuzzy Cognitive Maps,
- to compare proposed nodes selection/rejection strategies,
- to present an experimental study of the proposed methods.

The article is organized as follows. Section 2 covers a literature review on time series modeling with Fuzzy Cognitive Maps. Section 3 discusses Fuzzy Cognitive Maps-based modeling framework for time series and introduces a priori nodes rejection/selection criteria. Section 4 presents a series of experiments on synthetic and on real-world time series. Section 5 covers conclusions and discusses future research directions.

2   Literature Review

Fuzzy Cognitive Maps (FCMs) have been introduced by B. Kosko in [3]. Proficient methodologies for automated FCMs training opened a wide gate for research in practical applications. Among most successful applications' area is not only but also time series modeling.

To our best knowledge, first attempt at application of FCMs to time series modeling was in 2008 by W. Stach, L. Kurgan and W. Pedrycz in [6]. The technique proposed in this paper steered the majority of research in this area to a common direction. In brief, the frame methodology can be decomposed into the following steps: 1. Input signal fuzzification, 2. FCM training, 3. FCM exploration (modeling and prediction), 4. Defuzzifcation.

It is worth to notice that the approach introduced in [6] is truly customized for time series and does not require the input data to be multivariate. In the cited article FCM's nodes represent aggregates, describing the character of: the value of input signal $a(t)$ and its difference $\delta a(t)$. Fuzzification step assigns membership values to the fuzzy set of, for example, High, Medium and Small values/deltas. In [6] nodes represent 9 combinations of fuzzy assessments of current value of given data point point and the change (the delta). Discussed are the following 9 combinations: High-High, High-Medium, High-Small, Medium-High, ..., Small-Small. Aforementioned article uses real-coded genetic algorithm (RCGA) to train the FCM.

Alternative approaches to time series modeling with FCMs are strongly related to classification. Among papers that are concentrated on this technique are: [1], [2], [4], and [5]. In this stream of research input data is a multivariate time series. Such restriction makes the technique very specific and narrows modeling capabilities. In this stream of research nodes correspond to attributes of the time series. The discussed approach is transferable into a typical FCM-based classification problem.

We have proposed a method for time series modeling and prediction by analogy to the approach fathered by Stach et al. and in this paper we focus on model simplification techniques. The article is devoted to nodes rejection criteria, which can be applied prior to FCM training in order to remove redundant nodes.

3   Time Series Modeling with Fuzzy Cognitive Maps

The goal of this section is to introduce the proposed time series modeling framework based on FCMs. We show step-by-step how starting from a raw time series we build a FCM-based model, that operates on best subset of fuzzy concepts. The proposed method can be sectioned into the following phases:

1. Transformation of a scalar input time series into a 3-dimensional space of current, past and before past observations.
2. Extraction of 1-dimensional concepts. Elevation of 1-dimensional concepts into 3-dimensional concepts.
3. Selection of the best subset of concepts.
4. Formation of a Fuzzy Cognitive Map.

3.1   Transformation of a Scalar Input Time Series into 3-Dimensional Space of Current, Past and Before Past Observations

Time series is a sequence of observations, usually gathered at regular intervals. Examples of popular time series are economic indicators: prices, rates, meteorological phenomena: rainfall, water level, temperature, population-related phenomena: migration, birth rate, and so on. The basic and most natural representation of a time series is an unprocessed sequence of values quantifying given phenomenon/phenomena. If we have reported observations of a single phenomenon, then we have a scalar time series. Otherwise we talk about multivariate time series. In this paper we focus on the first case - a scalar time series, which we pass to the input of our method in the form of its unprocessed values: $a_0, a_1, a_2, \ldots, a_M$.

In the following paragraphs of this section we describe the proposed time series modeling framework on an example of two synthesized time series named TS-A and TS-B:

- TS-A: contains 3000 data points synthesized on the base of sequence 2, 5, 8
- TS-B: 3000 data points synthesized on the base of sequence 1, 3, 7, 5, 9

Both synthetic time series were constructed by replicating the base sequence (TS-A: 2, 5, 8, 2, 5, 8, ... and TS-B: 1, 3, 7, 5, 9, 1, 3, 7, 5, 9, ...) and by distorting the obtained sequence with a random value drawn from normal distribution with mean equals 0 and standard deviation 0.7. Figure 1 illustrates first 50 observations (data points) from the two time series in a 2-dimensional space of

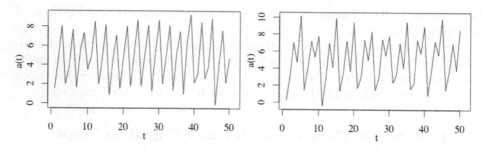

Fig. 1. Time series TS-A (left) and TS-B (right): first 50 observations

time t and value $a(t)$. The two time series differ in period's length. In the case of TS-A it is 3, in the case of TS-B it is 5. We have intentionally shown only first 50 observations, because plotting all 3000 generated data points makes figures hard to read. We have chosen the two synthetic time series to clearly illustrate the procedure. Real-world time series typically are not as regular as synthetic.

The introduced time series modeling framework is based in a 3-dimensional space of current, past and before past values. We transform 1-dimensional time series given as a sequence: $x_0, x_1, x_2, \ldots, x_N$ into a collection of triples: (a_0, a_1, a_2), $(a_1, a_2, a_3), (a_2, a_3, a_4), \ldots, (a_{M-2}, a_{M-1}, a_M)$. A single triple of observations can be gathered in a 3-elements' vector, while the collection of all triples generated for given time series can be gathered in a $3 \times (M-1)$ matrix. Each value in each triple $\mathbf{a}_i = [a_i, a_{i+1}, a_{i+2}]$ is an unprocessed value from the time series. Such time series representation scheme has not been applied before in FCM-based models. Having such representation, we can envision each time series in a 3-dimensional coordinates system of current, past and before past values.

We can generalize this time series representation method into any h-dimensional space ($h = 2, 3, 4, \ldots$). If $h = 3$ each time series point is replicated in data 3 times (with an exception of first h points - this is a technical detail). The greater the h, the better time series modeling results we expect to achieve. At the same time, high h increases complexity and is impractical in use, because we have to train very large FCM. In this paper we focus on $h = 3$. Major premise speaking for the choice of $h = 3$ is that in a 3-dimensional space we can easily illustrate our methods. Note that there is also the second factor increasing the complexity of the model, which we cover in the next subsection.

3.2 Extraction of 1-Dimensional Concepts. Elevation of 1-Dimensional Concepts into 3-Dimensional Concepts

Let us treat time series as a sequence of data points, which can be individually fuzzy clustered into u clusters. The number of clusters u is interpreted as the number of value's aggregates or in more general terms - the number of concepts describing the time series. Therefore we always set u arbitrarily. If we decide that we want to distinguish $u = 2$ concepts, then the time series is generalized with 2 concepts for which we can assign appropriate linguistic terms, say: Small

(S) and High (H). If we decide to distinguish $u = 3$ concepts, then we generalize the knowledge into 3 aggregates that can be described, for example, as Small (S), Moderate (M), and High (H), and so on. The clustering procedure should be fuzzy. Our goal is to build a model that is based on fuzzy, or even more general - on granular concepts that represent the information, because FCMs operate on fuzzy concepts. In the later design process we come back to this issue.

The higher the u, more concepts we use to represent the time series. The more the concepts, the more specific the representation. Specificity results in higher precision. At the same time, specificity makes the model more complex. The balance between generality and specificity is a vital issue for each designed model.

The choice of u is the first key design issue for our procedure. All experiments in this article were made as a comparison of results obtained for division into $u = 2, 3, 4$ concepts. We believe that this allows to comprehensively illustrate stability of the model.

In this paper we use Fuzzy C-Means as an algorithm for clusters extraction. A discussion on clustering techniques is not in the scope of this research, we just us it as a tool to obtain numerical representation for concepts. Therefore, we do not investigate this aspect of our method to greater extent.

Each concept is represented in 1 dimension with its center. In order to obtain concepts in 3-dimensional space of time series current, past and before past values we apply ternary Cartesian product. As a result we obtain $u * u * u$ or more general u^h triples representing concepts in a 3-dimensional space of time series current, past and before past observations. The greater the u, the more uniformly the 3-dimensional space is covered. Figure 2 illustrates 3-dimensional representation of the two synthetic time series: TS-A and TS-B with proposed concepts $u = 2$ for TS-A and $u = 3, 4$ for TS-B.

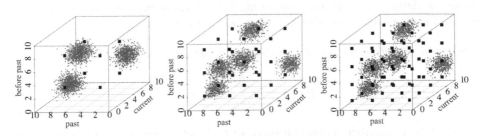

Fig. 2. Time series TS-A and TS-B in a 3-dimensional space of current, past and before past values with 8 concepts for TS-A and 27 and 64 concepts for TS-B

Brief look at Figure 2 proves that the greater the u, the more specific the model. For small u proposed concepts represent greater amount of information, the greater the u the fewer information-bearing capacity is required from concepts.

Proposed method relies on concepts extracted for a 1-dimensional problem, transformed later with Cartesian product. One may ask why don't we start with 3-dimensional concepts. The answer is the following: we deal with a 1-dimensional time series elevated to a 3-dimensional space. Therefore, the concepts have to generalize the original 1-dimensional knowledge, not the transformed one.

3.3   Selection of the Best Subset of Concepts

As an output of the procedure described in the previous two steps we obtain a set of $u*u*u$ concepts. Such design technique proposes large initial sets of concepts, of cardinality u^h, where h is the dimensionality, (here $h = 3$ at all times and u is the number of clusters in one dimension). With the growth of the number of concepts, the complexity of the model grows. It will be shown that the number of concepts directly corresponds to the number of nodes in the FCM. Large maps are impractical: they are difficult to comprehend, interpret and to train. For example, a FCM with $n = 3*3*3 = 27$ nodes with a single-threaded R learning code on a standard PC requires around 3.5 days to optimize. In contrast, a FCM with $n = 2*2*2 = 8$ nodes requires 3.3 hours, FCM with $n = 4$ nodes requires only 43 minutes. Though the growth of the number of weights in the map is quadratic, the growth of computational demand is exponential.

Let us have a second look at Figure 2. Observe that not all concepts fall into the clouds representing time series points. Intuition suggests that not all of proposed concepts are equally crucial to represent the underlying data set. Hence, we may pose a question whether and how we can remove several nodes from the FCM without a sudden decrease in its quality.

The goal of our research, the core of this article, are nodes quality criteria, which can be applied to remove a subset of nodes that is evaluated as worse. With such criteria we can simplify the FCM design by removing redundant nodes before FCM training. The character of the developed indexes is global - all points from the dataset are taken into account. Note that the proposed criteria can be treated both as rejection criteria and as selection criteria.

Criterion 1: Entropy index of j-th concept is defined as:

$$H(v_j) = -\sum_{i=1}^{N} x_{ji} \ln x_{ji}, \tag{1}$$

where N is the number of observations and x_{ji} is activation passed to j-th concept in i-th time point. Named variables will be recalled and discussed in detail in the next subsection. High values of entropy indicate unpredictable representation of knowledge. In contrast, small values of entropy characterize concepts that uniformly represent the underlying information.

Criterion 2: Membership index of j-th cluster is defined as:

$$M(v_j) = \sum_{i=1}^{N} x_{ji} \tag{2}$$

High values of membership index indicate that given j-th concept strongly represents the time series. In contrast, small values of membership index are for concepts that are weakly tied with the underlying dataset. In particular, in a special case when there is a cluster so bad that no point belongs to it to any degree, the value of membership index is equal 0.

Criterion 3: Global distance index for the $\mathbf{v}_j$-th concept is given as:

$$GD(v_j) = \sum_{i=1}^{N} e^{-||\mathbf{a}_i - \mathbf{v}_j||} \tag{3}$$

With this criterion we sum Euclidean distance (denoted as $||\cdot||$) of each triple-observation $\mathbf{a}$ and $\mathbf{v}_j$-th concept. This criterion is independent on membership values and we have designed it as an alternative measure. High values of global distance index indicate good concepts.

3.4   Formation of a Fuzzy Cognitive Map

In the fourth step of our procedure we form a FCMs-based model for time series modeling and forecasting.

FCMs represent knowledge with directed graphs, where nodes correspond to phenomena and arcs correspond to relations between phenomena.

The following elements are involved in a FCM-based model:

- FCM - Fuzzy Cognitive Map, which is a collection of n nodes and $n \times n$ arcs connecting nodes.
- Weights matrix $\mathbf{W}$ of size $n \times n$, which contains evaluations of arcs connecting nodes, in the map single weight w_{ij} describes influence of j-th node on i-th node, $w_{ij} \in [-1, 1]$.
- Activations matrix $\mathbf{X}$ of size $n \times N$, where N is the number of available observations. Observations are also called sometimes iterations. Single activations vector is denoted as $\mathbf{x}_i = [x_{1i}, x_{2i}, \ldots, x_{ni}]$ and it concerns i-th observation, $x_{ji} \in [0, 1]$.
- Goals matrix $\mathbf{G}$ of size $n \times N$ gathers actual, reported states of n nodes in N observations.
- FCM's responses matrix $\mathbf{Y}$ of size $n \times N$ is the result of FCM exploration that is performed according to the formula: $\mathbf{Y} = f(\mathbf{W} \cdot \mathbf{X})$, where f is sigmoid transformation function: $f(t) = \frac{1}{1+exp(-\tau t)}$. The value of parameter τ was set to 5 based on experiments and literature review.

FCMs training procedure aims at weights matrix $\mathbf{W}$ reconstruction based on available training data that has to contain activations and targets. Weights matrix is trained so that the error between map outputs $\mathbf{Y}$ and observed states $\mathbf{G}$ are as close as possible. In our experiments we used Mean Squared Error (MSE) to train maps: $MSE = \frac{1}{n \cdot N} \cdot \sum_{j=1}^{N} \sum_{i=1}^{n} (y_{ij} - g_{ij})^2$.

For illustrative purposes, in our experiments we have divided available data into 2 parts: training (70%) and test(30%). the quality of time series model is assessed on training data, which is used to reconstruct the FCM. Prediction accuracy is assessed on test data. On the test data we calculate one-step-ahead forecasts for the time series. As a quality indicator we use MSE.

Let us recall, that the allocation of time series data points to clusters is not crisp, it is fuzzy, because we have used Fuzzy C-Means to propose concepts/clusters. By analogy, we calculate level of activation for an $\mathbf{a}_i$-th observation to j-th concept with the use of the standard Fuzzy C-Means objective function:

$$\mathbf{u}_{ij} = \frac{1}{\sum_{k=1}^{n} \left(\frac{||\mathbf{a}_i - \mathbf{v}_j||}{|| \mathbf{a}_i - \mathbf{v}_k ||} \right)^{\frac{2}{m-1}}} \tag{4}$$

where n is the number of nodes in the map and the number of best selected concepts at the same time, m is the fuzzification coefficient ($m > 1$) and $|| \cdot ||$ is the Euclidean distance function, $\mathbf{a}_i$ is time series triple $\mathbf{a}_i = [a_i, a_{i+1}, a_{i+2}]$. $\mathbf{v}_j$ describes j-th concept's coordinates in a 3-dimensional space of current, past and before past values of the time series. In Formula 4 we have intentionally used symbol $\mathbf{u}$ to show that activations equivalent to cluster membership values. With the use of Formula 4 we calculate activation levels for each selected concept, we transpose it, and in this way we obtain $n \times N$ activations matrix $\mathbf{X}$.

Goals are equal to activations shifted by one element forward. So that activations corresponding to an i-th time point are set together with goals for an i+1-th time point. Such representation is designed especially for time series processing with FCMs.

At this point we have all the elements necessary to train weights matrix for this time series. Each selected concept becomes an individual node in the map. As a learning procedure we have chosen Particle Swarm Optimization. We have used an implementation of PSO from package pso in R language with default parameters compliant with PSO 2007 implementation, detailed parameter list is under [7]. This is a typical metaheuristic procedure and it will be shown that it performs very well.

4   Experiments

Proposed criteria allow to rank proposed nodes and select subset of a desired size. In this section first we discuss in detail experiments conducted on the introduced two synthetic time series TS-A and TS-B. Next, we present a summary of results obtained for several real-world time series.

The scheme of our experiments was the following:

1. For each of the three different initial FCM architectures: $2 \times 2 \times 2$ ($u = 2$), $3 \times 3 \times 3$ ($u = 3$), and $4 \times 4 \times 4$ ($u = 4$) propose 3-dimensional concepts. As a result we obtain 8, 27, and 64 initial concepts respectively.
2. From the proposed concepts we select 3, ..., 8 best concepts using the three criteria. We do not consider FCMs with $n = 2$ as such models, built with 2 concepts only are too trivial.
3. We train FCMs with selected concepts.

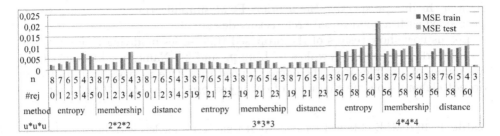

Fig. 3. MSE for model (train) and for predictions (test) of the TS-A synthetic time series (2, 5, 8, 2, 5, 8, ...) for FCMs designed with three different quality criteria

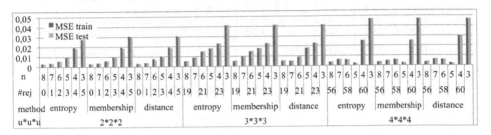

Fig. 4. MSE for the model and forecast of TS-B synthetic time series (1, 3, 7, 5, 9, ...) for different designs of FCMs

Figure 3 illustrates MSE for the model and prediction of the TS-A synthetic time series. Plot shows FCMs of final size $n = 3, 4, ..., 8$ constructed with different initial full architectures. From full concepts' architectures of size $u * u * u = 8, 27, 64$ we have selected n best concepts with the three criteria: entropy index, membership index and global distance index. By analogy, Figure 4 illustrates errors for the second synthetic time series: TS-B.

Plots indicate high accuracy of both models and predictions. The two synthetic time series are regular. TS-A in the 3-dimensional space of current past and before past observations contains 3 dense clouds, TS-B, 5 clouds. Hence it is expected that 3 and 5 concepts respectively will be a best fit for these time series. The three indexes: entropy, membership, and distance are in agreement. Extracted concepts' subsets partly overlap and this is the reason that MSE for analogical models produced with the three criteria are very similar.

For the TS-A time series (with 3 clouds) smaller architectures, with $u = 2, 3$, were a better start point than the larger one, with $u = 4$. In contrast, for the TS-B time series (with 5 clouds), the largest of analyzed architectures was the best. This shows that the choice of the start point of the proposed procedure matters and significantly influences the modeling outcome. If the procedure was initiated with a division into u concepts correctly, like for TS-A, in th case of $u = 3$, then proposed indexes clearly manage to find the best subset of nodes that represent the underlying clouds. Moreover, the errors on other, larger maps based on matching initial architecture are smaller if we were able to choose the right u. In this perspective the a priori FCM simplification method has to be proceeded with a good initial architecture design.

Let us now show results of the proposed time series modeling techniques on 5 real-world time series, downloaded from [8] and [9]. Names used in the article are names of .dat files from the named repositories. Due to space limitations we do not elaborate on the character of data, just present condensed highlights.

Table 1. 1000·MSE obtained for real-world time series models with different FCMs, initial architecture is $2 \times 2 \times 2$

series	entropy index			membership index			global distance index		
	n=8	n=5	n=3	n=8	n=5	n=3	n=8	n=5	n=3
Bicup2006	2.01	3.69	7.78	2.02	3.69	7.78	2.01	3.92	7.78
DailyIBM	0.34	0.60	0.99	0.32	0.59	0.99	0.32	0.59	1.12
Equiptemp	0.52	0.82	2.04	0.52	0.91	2.04	0.52	0.82	2.13
Melbmin	5.94	11.6	17.6	5.91	1.61	7.63	5.92	1.61	8.49
Wave 1	0.34	0.59	1.32	0.34	0.59	1.32	0.37	0.56	1.32

Table 2. 1000·MSE for real-wold time series models based on different FCMs, initial architecture is $3 \times 3 \times 3$

series	entropy index			membership index			global distance index		
	n=8	n=5	n=3	n=8	n=5	n=3	n=8	n=5	n=3
Bicup2006	2.21	4.21	7.17	2.16	4.20	7.17	3.54	7.12	9.30
DailyIBM	0.47	0.81	1.65	0.45	0.81	1.44	0.46	0.95	1.44
Equiptemp	1.38	2.38	4.54	1.36	2.38	4.55	1.55	2.40	4.54
Melbmin	9.63	13.8	21.8	9.63	3.80	1.86	9.63	13.8	21.8
Wave 1	0.48	1.05	1.94	0.48	1.05	1.94	0.44	0.50	0.77

Tables 1, 2, and 3 illustrate MSEs on time series models based on FCMs of different sizes. We do not show MSEs on predictions, because they were very close to model MSEs and we do not have enough space. Tables present models based on FCMs with $n = 8, 5, 3$ nodes. Nodes were selected with designed criteria: entropy, membership and global distance indexes. In Table 1 we show results of experiments, where nodes were selected from 8 initially proposed concepts. In Table 2 we show MSEs for models based on 3, 5 and 8 best nodes that were selected from the initial collection of 27 nodes. In Table 3 we present results for time series modes constructed with $n = 3, 5, 8$ best nodes that were selected out of 64 primarily proposed concepts.

Real world time series do not exhibit as high regularity and predictability as synthetic ones. Depending on time series complexity, the proposed procedure

Table 3. 1000·MSE for selected time series models, initial architecture is $4 \times 4 \times 4$

series	entropy index			membership index			global distance index		
	n=8	n=5	n=3	n=8	n=5	n=3	n=8	n=5	n=3
Bicup2006	4.86	9.71	13.5	4.86	9.75	13.5	4.70	8.20	13.4
DailyIBM	0.63	1.30	1.53	0.64	1.30	1.53	0.68	1.30	1.53
Equiptemp	2.20	4.23	4.94	2.20	4.23	4.60	2.20	4.23	4.60
Melbmin	8.97	15.5	20.2	9.68	14.8	20.2	8.99	10.7	16.8
Wave 1	0.90	1.66	2.22	0.90	1.66	2.22	0.55	0.78	1.78

managed to find models of different quality. For some time series, like IBM Daily (financial time series) and Wave 1 (physics domain) models are of high accuracy. Values of MSE error are very low, with first significant number on 4-th place after the decimal point. Other time series were modeled well, but not that accurately.

Experiments proved previously stated thesis that the more specific the FCM-based model, the higher accuracy. For the fixed initial architecture the procedure produces better models when the number of nodes in the map is greater. Second important conclusion is that proposed nodes selection criteria are suitable to extract subsets of concepts that represent information best. All three indexes are in accordance, proposed subsets of nodes are partially overlapping. Models exacted with the use of the three indexes have similar MSE.

Let us finally remark that the larger is the initial architecture, the better models we can build. MSE for each time series is the smallest when we start from the $4 \times 4 \times 4$ full architecture and select best subsets of concepts from larger initial set. Here one can see that there really is a necessity for good rejection criteria. Though full model with $u \times u \times u$ concepts would have performed better, such complexity makes it unfit in practice. When we start from large collection of initial concepts we are able to select best concepts as there is many to choose from. Even when we select few concepts, for example $n = 5$ modes are still very accurate.

At the same time, the initial division into u concepts is not random, because all concepts, 1 and 3 dimensional, are characterized with linguistic terms and extracted as a result of soft clustering procedure. In this perspective the initial division into $u = 4$ concepts, what makes 64 concepts to choose from, is a reasonable start point.

5   Conclusion

The proposed procedure of time series modeling and prediction is based on three key steps: extraction of the initial concepts' set, selection of the best subset, FCM design and learning. We have proposed 3 criteria: entropy index, membership index and global distance index for concepts selection. All three indexes behave in a similar manner. They extract best subset of concepts that has an experimental evidence in their background.

A series of experiments on synthetic time series have shown that proposed indexes select the best subset of nodes. Selected subset of concepts produces a model with lower MSE, than the model based on full set of concepts extracted in the first step of the procedure. Such a priori simplification reduces complexity, enhances interpretation and application.

We have clearly pictured that the outcome of the procedure depends to a great extent on the initial architecture design. Therefore, the simplification procedure should follow a careful initial architecture design.

To sum up, performed experiments show the introduced modeling framework performs well. The FCMs simplification procedure by selection of only relevant nodes is a successful strategy for map design. We would like to stress, that a priori simplification should facilitate a careful initial model design. In future research we plan to continue research on this approach. We want to investigate the time series of different qualitative characters and compare our results with other alternative time series modeling methods.

Acknowledgment. The research is partially supported by the National Science Center, grant No 2011/01/B/ST6/06478.

References

1. Froelich, W., Papageorgiou, E.I.: Extended Evolutionary Learning of Fuzzy Cognitive Maps for the Prediction of Multivariate Time-Series. In: Fuzzy Cognitive Maps for Applied Sciences and Engineering, pp. 121–131 (2014)
2. Froelich, W., Papageorgiou, W.E.I., Samarinasc, M., Skriapasc, K.: Application of evolutionary fuzzy cognitive maps to the long-term prediction of prostate cancer. Applied Soft Computing 12, 3810–3817 (2012)
3. Kosko, B.: Fuzzy cognitive maps. International Journal of Man-Machine Studies 7, 65–75 (1986)
4. Lu, W., Yang, J., Liu, X.: The Linguistic Forecasting of Time Series based on Fuzzy Cognitive Maps. In: Proc. of IFSA/NAFIPS, pp. 649–654 (2013)
5. Song, H.J., Miao, C.Y., Wuyts, R., Shen, Z.Q., D' Hondt, M.: An Extension to Fuzzy Cognitive Maps for Classification and Prediction. IEEE Transactions on Fuzzy Systems 19(1), 116–135 (2011)
6. Stach, W., Kurgan, L., Pedrycz, W.: Numerical and Linguistic Prediction of Time Series. IEEE Transactions on Fuzzy Systems 16(1), 61–72 (2008)
7. http://cran.r-project.org/web/packages/pso/pso.pdf
8. http://lib.stat.cmu.edu
9. http://robjhyndman.com/tsdldata

An Efficient System for Stock Market Prediction

Ashraf S. Hussein[1], Ibrahim M. Hamed[2], and Mohamed F. Tolba[3]

[1] Arab Open University, Headquarters, P.O. Box: 3322 Al-Safat 13033, Kuwait
ashrafh@acm.org
[2,3] Ain Shams University, Cairo, 11566, Egypt
{ibrahim.hamed,fahmytolba}@gmail.com

Abstract. This paper presents an efficient system for accurate, confident, general and responsive stock market prediction, employing Artificial Neural Networks (ANN). For technical indicators, Multi-Layer Perceptron (MLP) ANN is used and trained with Kullback Leibler Divergence (KLD) learning algorithm because it converges fast in addition to offering generalization in the learning mechanism. On the other hand, Radial Basis Function Neural Network (RBFNN) trained with Localized Generalization Error (L-GEM) is used for candlesticks patterns. The accuracy, generalization and statistical-significance of the developed system were confirmed through various local and international data sets. Next, sensitivity analysis was conducted for the different parameters that influence the system efficiency metrics. In order to have responsive prediction, the proposed system was evolved, employing concurrent programming to get benefit from the off-the-shelf multi-core architectures. Then, the performance of the developed system was evaluated to confirm acceptance scalability and utilization.

Keywords: Stock market prediction, technical indicator, candlesticks patterns, artificial neural networks, blind source separation, multi-core architecture, concurrency.

1   Introduction

Stock market prediction is one of the greatest challenges for experts and researchers who work in the financial sector. This topic has been tackled by many research groups, aiming at overcoming the accuracy, confidence and generalization challenges [1,2,3,4,5,6,7,8]. However, when the developed prediction models come to be applied, in the real stock markets, their results are not successful enough to consistently "beat the market", especially from accuracy and generalization points of view [5]. Ever since prediction was performed manually, technical experts could reach an accurate prediction pattern, but they used to miss the current transaction, either due to lack of timing or confidence [5], [9]. Therefore, accuracy is not the unique target, and considering generalization, prediction time and confidence along with accuracy of signals' prediction is very crucial [1], [5], [10]. To emphasize the effect of the prediction time, consider the example of a 5 hours trading session, with tick frequency of one tick per second. If the prediction system takes 1.5 seconds to provide the required

© Springer International Publishing Switzerland 2015
D. Filev et al. (eds.), *Intelligent Systems'2014*,
Advances in Intelligent Systems and Computing 323, DOI: 10.1007/978-3-319-11310-4_76

results, after 16 minutes the prediction comes 8 minutes late, and the signal might not only be delayed, but also it might be complementary to the current situation of the security. Also, the last 2 hours prediction results of the trading session will reach out after the session is being closed. In this way, considering the response time (prediction time) in addition to the accuracy and confidence has been pursued by some research groups [5]. High Performance Computing (HPC) techniques have been considered in order to have somewhat "real-time" predictions [11], but the specialized HPC computational resources (such as Computational Grids) are fairly sophisticated and not available for wide range of users and financial experts.

In this paper, an efficient system for stock market prediction is proposed to overcome the existing challenges, trying to consider the prediction time as a primary crucial factor in addition to the accuracy, confidence and generalization of the stock market prediction.

2   Previous Work

The state-of-the-art stock market prediction models and techniques have been surveyed in [1], [3], [5], considering the accuracy, confidence and generalization issues. Optimizing the performance of such prediction models towards real-time predictions has attracted less research groups. Early trials to enhance the prediction performance were based on sentimental information (such as market news) [12] or new stock market data forms (such as candlestick and point and figures) [13]. Nguyen et al. [14] tried to optimize the performance of the MLP ANN, as its performance drops when the network size increases. They proposed a new technique based on Cyclic Self-Organizing Hierarchical Cerebella Model Arithmetic Controller (CSOHCMAC). This technique exhibited high efficiency in terms of accuracy and response time, but its major drawback was the large memory requirements; the ratio of memory consumption between regular MLP and CSOHCMAC was around 1:125. On the other hand, some of the researchers have focused on sentimental factors like processing the market news and generating "Buy" and "Sell" signals. This wave was started by Ahmad et al. [11], employing the Financial Information Grid (FinGrid). They proposed a distributed environment, using Globus and Java Commodity Grids, to offer services by working on both qualitative and quantitative market data, as they added text analysis to the market news, along with the standard technical analysis indicators. This way the market sentiments were determined using the text analysis. Huang et al. [15] proposed a system for financial news headline agent to support the investors through the "Buy" and "Sell" decision making in the stock market of Taiwan. It receives the real-time market news headlines, published by the leading electronic newspapers in Taiwan, and employs optimized text mining techniques along with weighted association rules to predict the fluctuation in the Taiwan Stock Exchange Financial Price Index of the next trading day. The experimental results revealed that this system achieved significant performance.

Other research work is concerned with modern charting techniques for stock market prediction. Fu et al. [16] used both the rule-based and template-based approaches for stock charts pattern detection, relying on the Perceptually Important Points (PIPs).

As a result of this study, the authors recommended a hybrid model that integrates both of the template-based and rule-based approaches, employing the advantages of each. Li et al. [17] proposed RBFNN trained with L-GEM for candlesticks pattern detection of the morning star pattern only. This study avoided up to 69% of false patterns on the Shenzhen stock market. Following the recommendations of [17], Xiao et al. [6] applied four RBFNNs trained by localized L-GEM method, each of them corresponds to a particular candlestick pattern. Their strategy was found to be responsive with less accuracy. In the same context, Jasemi et al. [18] presented a model for stock market based on a supervised Feed-Forward ANN and technical analysis of the Japanese Candlesticks. They used ANN as a regression model to produce key parameters, from their independent variables, for technical analysis pattern detection. A raw-data based approach and signal based approach were used for defining the independent variables. The empirical results of these two approaches exhibited acceptable prediction for triggering "Buy" and "Sell" signals.

The aforesaid techniques and systems are quite promising, but they still experience problems related to accuracy, confidence degree or generalization, especially when trying to have "real-time" predictions. The issues of accuracy, confidence degree and generalization have been extensively tackled in Hamed et al. [3] to have a general model that can predict securities from different sectors and stock markets. This model is capable of adapting nonlinearities in the stock market and the un-correlated data of the different securities in various stock markets. The proposed technique adopts MLP ANN and KLD learning algorithm to enhance the performance of the proposed ANN. KLD, being a blind source separation technique, helps in solving the generalization issue of the prediction problem, keeping the model accuracy. The accuracy and generalization of the proposed prediction model were validated through wide range of stock markets, including the Microsoft stock, from wall-street market, and various data sets, from different sectors of the Egyptian stock market. In addition, the statistical-significance of the prediction results was confirmed through standard ANOVA test [3].

In this paper, the proposed system, developed based on the prediction model of [3], was evolved to consider the candlestick patterns' detection using RBFNN trained with L-GEM [17]. Then, the system was re-innovated and optimized; targeting the multi-core off-the-shelf architectures, using concurrent programming to reduce the computing time towards real-time predictions. Finally, the performance of the proposed system was evaluated via implementing the OKAZ's profile [19] based on both technical analysis and candlesticks to confirm accepted scalability and utilization. The proposed system exhibited responsive accurate results with high confidence degree and acceptable scalability level.

3   Prediction Model

The proposed model comprises of several stages as shown in Fig. 1. The first stage is concerned with the input selection. Next, the appropriate preprocessing is performed on the selected input data. Such preprocessing might be computing of indicators, fundamental assets evaluation or even data classification for the supervised learning of the ANN. The data is then passed to the ANN to be trained for the classification purposes. The main objective of the learning algorithm is to update the weights between the ANN neurons in order to minimize the error in the prediction results.

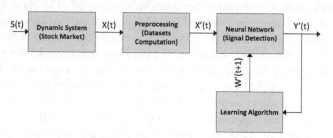

Fig. 1. Block diagram of the proposed model

3.1   Working Data

Stock Market's Daily Data

Daily data is the data used in the stock market daily transactions, and it may be called market summary. The daily data is composed of (a) open price, which is the first trading price for a security on a given trading session, (b) close price, which is the final trading price for a security on a given trading session, (c) high price, which is the highest trading price for a security during a given trading session, (d) low price, which is the lowest trading price for a security during a given trading session, (e) volume, which is the amount of trades transacted for a security on a given trading session.

Candlesticks Charts

Japanese candlesticks' charting was first used around 1850. According to Nison [20], it was first developed in Sakata Tow by Homma, a legendary rice trader. It was later modified over years to form the one currently used in the stock market of today. Japanese candlesticks are preferred by most of the technical analysts, since it provides more visual information in the form of well-known set of patterns. A white Marubozu is formed when the low price equals the opening price and the high price equals the closing price. This pattern reflects that buyers controlled the price action during the whole candle period (day, hour, etc.), according to graph aggregation [21].

3.2   Preprocessing

The input to this stage is the stock market daily data for a chosen security. The preprocessing step is concerned with computing the technical indicators, which is considered to be an input to the ANN.

3.3   Artificial Neural Network (ANN)

For the technical indicators, the MLP ANN architecture has one hidden layer. Sigmoid function with range [-1, +1] is used, as the activation function for each neuron. The number of input neurons is equal to the number of variables in the data set while the number of hidden neurons equals to twice the input neurons. This was found to perform better after several trials of different hidden neurons combination. The signal is being classified into three classes "Buy", "Sell" or "Hold". So, three output neurons are being used in the output layer. Each neuron should have the value [0 – 1] indicating the class it belongs to. For a given run, the output (0.8 0.12 0.08) means it is a "Buy" signal, since it is closer to the buy class, while (0.05 0.85 0.1) is a "Sell" signal. For any output to be valid, it should belong only to one class [3]. For candlestick patterns, RBFNN ANN is adopted [17].

3.4   Learning Algorithm

Through the iterative supervised learning of the MLP ANN, the data is processed through an intermediate stage to normalize the output of the current stage before entering the next iteration. Due to the nature of the KLD, the input to this function must be in the form of a probability distribution function, i.e. the magnitude of the output vector equals one. Therefore, the output vector is normalized to match this criterion. Then, it is passed to the KLD to compute the divergence between the output signal and the desired signal. The weights are updated according to [3]. For RBFNN, the ANN is trained using L-GEM algorithm [17].

4   System Description

4.1   System Architecture

The proposed system was designed to utilize multi-core architectures via shared memory model. The system consists of a data source, a processing unit, which includes a parallelization root and n processing cores, and output prediction results as illustrated in Fig. 2. The data source is the stream of live data feed that is entered to the system. The parallelization root (manager) is responsible for loading the data to the shared memory, distributing the work over the processing cores (workers), performing load balancing and consolidating the results from various cores to have the final prediction result. The processing core i is responsible for performing a prediction task as scheduled by the parallelization root. The shared memory model, adopted in this system, aims at minimizing the intercommunication among cores.

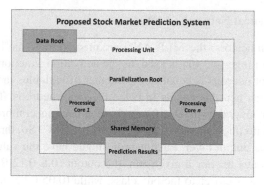

Fig. 2. The proposed system components

4.2   Data Flow

Initially, data is obtained from the live feed and passed to the parallelization root. Then, it divides the work load to *n* tasks, according to the selected profile or group of signal detection tasks, and sends the work to the available processing cores. The root applies the first free node selection mechanism for workload distribution among the processing cores. In this way, each processing unit performs the required data preprocessing, applies the prediction model then sends the results back through the shared memory. The parallelization root, in turn, consolidates the results from each processing core and generates the final prediction results, as shown in Fig. 3.

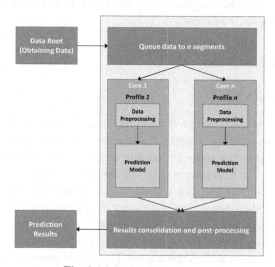

Fig. 3. Main data flow diagram

4.3   Implementation

The prediction models are based on MLP ANN trained with KLD [3] for the technical indicators and RBFNN trained with L-GEM [17] for the candlesticks pattern detection.

The considered set of indicators, in this implementation, includes: Simple Moving Average (SMA) [3], Exponential Moving Average (EMA) [3], Average True Range (ATR) [22], Stochastic Oscillator (SO) [23], Moving Average Convergence Divergence (MACD) [24], Average Directional Index (ADX) [22] and Candlestick Patterns [20], [21].

The input is used to calculate the indicators mentioned above with a given window and filter size. The selection of the appropriate window and filter sizes is based on a sensitivity analysis to obtain the "optimum" value of the aforesaid sizes. After indicators are being calculated, they all proceeded to a rule based system. This rule based system classifies the input signals into "Sell", "Hold" or "Buy". These classifications are used later in the learning stage.

5   Results and Discussions

In this research work, the proposed model was validated using the daily data from the Egyptian local stock market, including EFG Hermes Holding (HRHO), El Nasr Clothing - Textiles Co. (KABO), and Egyptian Electrical Cables (ELEC) with a total of 1900 records each. In order to consider the mature international stock markets in our validation, Microsoft (MS) stock was also encountered, from March 1999 to August 2008, with a total of 2600 records [19]. A sample 15% of this data was selected randomly for testing purposes. The selected data sets were meant to cover a wide spectrum of the stock market in terms of sectors, currency, trading volume and session type. First, HRHO was selected, from the investment sector, as it has a very active security with a large trading volume and is traded with the local currency. KABO was selected from the industrial sector, which has large trading volumes and is traded in USD. ELEC was selected from the Off-Trading Session (OTS), which is a 30 min session by the end of the trading day for corporates, which have some financial or legal violations and have a small trading volume.

Sensitivity analysis was carried out in order to identify the appropriate window size for every selected indicator in the data sets under consideration. Beside the window size of the indicators, there are two other filters. The first one is for the ADX signal, and it aims at ensuring the strength of the trend, i.e. to remove noise and false sudden moves in the price. The second one is for the "Buy", "Sell" or "Hold" signals. The purpose of this filter is to validate the signal and remove noise due to spikes in the price movement. Since rumors might influence security price movement, especially in growing markets like Egypt, this generates noise that lasts over a relatively short period (one to two trading sessions). Afterward, the signal is corrected again to match the actual value of the assets represented by the security. Sensitivity analysis was carried out for four variables: SMA window size, EMA window size, ADX filter and signal filter. For the window size, the size range (2 to 72) was considered while the range (1 to10) was tried for the filters. For each variable, a value, from its given range, is tried with all possible combination of the other 3 variables. Variable ranges could not be larger because this leads to short term and medium term signals, and also trends and movements disappear. Consequently, the prediction model accuracy will decrease because the ANN will capture only long term trades and will fail to detect short term and medium term trades.

Results from the proposed model were compared to that of the efficient ANN architectures mentioned in the research work of [7], [25], [26], [27], after developing the corresponding prediction models (for comparison purposes). The sensitivity analysis, considering the four variables mentioned above, shows that the proposed model outperforms the other techniques while the model of [7] exhibited the worst accuracy. In addition, the optimum values for these variables were identified for the data sets under consideration. Fig. 4 shows sample of the conducted sensitivity analysis for HRHO data set.

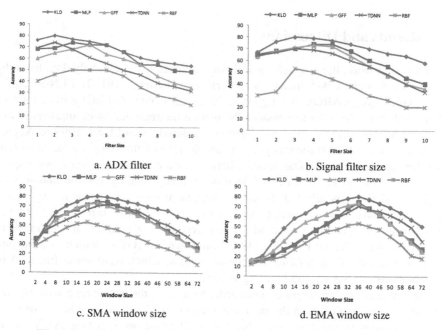

a. ADX filter

b. Signal filter size

c. SMA window size

d. EMA window size

Fig. 4. Sensitivity analysis for the prediction model variables, HRHO data set

The results of the proposed model with the optimum values identified above, for the data sets under consideration, were then compared to that of the prediction models [7] [25] [26] [27] to confirm the accuracy of the proposed technique. The results were computed as an average of 20 separate cycles of training and testing. The maximum accuracy achieved by the proposed model is 83% as shown in Fig. 5.

ANOVA test [28] was carried out to ensure the statistical significance, i.e. the classification accuracy was not a result of random act. As mentioned earlier, the data sets were run for 20 complete cycles and the average accuracy results were used. ANOVA test resulted that the F value was 9.6 while the critical F value was 2.7 as shown in Table 1. Therefore, the means are significantly different and the generalization effect is real.

The performance of the proposed model was compared to that of the prediction models [7], [25], [26], [27]. The proposed technique converges faster than the other techniques, on the average of 3000 epochs, employing the Mean Squared Error as the error measurement function, as shown in Fig. 6. The other techniques always reach the maximum epochs and do not stop at the minimum error criteria. The number of epochs is set so that the neural network does not fall in the over fitting problem.

In order to examine the performance of the multi-core implementation of the developed system, OKAZ profile [19] was used for this purpose. After manipulating this profile, the confidence of the final result was calculated from their aggregation. Each

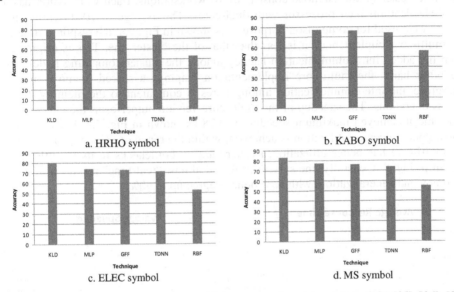

Fig. 5. Comparison between the accuracy of the proposed model and that of [7], [25], [26], [27]

Table 1. ANOVA test results

Source of Variation	SS	Df	MS	F	P-value	F_{crit}
Between Groups	151.4	3	50.45	9.8	1.5E-5	2.74
Within Groups	391.4	76	5.15			
Total	542.8	79				

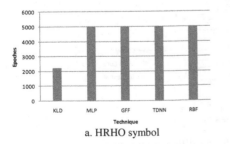

a. HRHO symbol

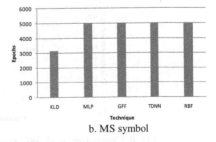

b. MS symbol

Fig. 6. Performance analysis of the proposed model

technique adds or removes a certain degree of confidence. The confidence percentage for OKAZ profile indicators are: ATR=20%, MA=5%, SO=5%, MCAD=10%, ADX=10% and Candle-Stick-Patters=40%. This provides a decision with confidence rate up to 90% as per the best prediction case.

This experiment was carried on Windows 2003 server with 8 cores. This server has 8 GB of shared RAM, and each processor is 1.6 GHz with turbo boost up to 2.0 GHz. In order to compare the multi-core implementation with the distributed memory one (cluster implementation), the Message Passing Interface (MPI) was used to develop the distributed memory version of the proposed system. This experiment was carried out on a cluster of workstations consists of 16 workstations. Each workstation has a 2.5 GHz Pentium Intel processor with dual-cores. The average of 10 different runs results were used for comparison purposes. As shown in Fig. 7.a, the response time of the multi-core implementation is less than that of the cluster one. This is originated from the added intercommunication latency among the cluster computing nodes. On the other hand, the multi-core implementation employs a shared memory model. Therefore, the intercommunication among cores is equivalent to the memory direct access operations. The speedup of the multi-core version outperforms the cluster version, and it achieved maximum speedup of 3.78 as shown in Fig. 7.b. For both versions, good processor utilization is achieved, within the range of (82%-94%). But, yet the multi-core has better utilization, as there are no bottlenecks in its workflow, as shown in Fig. 8. Generally, the system provided almost "real-time" results with good accuracy and generalization, with confidence degree up to 90%.

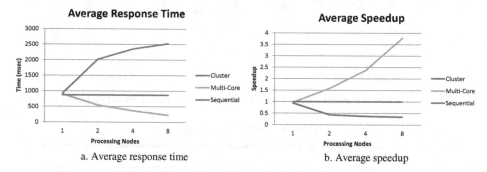

a. Average response time   b. Average speedup

Fig. 7. Efficiency of the different implementations

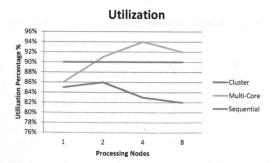

Fig. 8. Computing-node utilization for the different implementations

6   Conclusions

This paper proposes a new system for "real-time" stock market prediction with high accuracy, confidence rate and generalization. This system is based on the Artificial Neural Networks and employs off-the-shelf multi-core H/W architectures. For technical indicators, MLP ANN is used and trained with KLD learning algorithm because it converges fast and provides generalization in the learning mechanism. On the other hand, RBFNN trained with L-GEM is used for candlesticks pattern detection. The proposed system partitions the prediction mechanism to concurrent processes, and each process runs concurrently on a processing unit (core). Then, all the processes' results are consolidated by a unified parallelization root. The proposed system accuracy, confidence and generalization were confirmed through numerous data sets, covering wide sectors from the stock markets. In this way, three securities from the Egyptian local stock market in addition to MS security from a mature global stock market were addressed. Next, the OKAZ's profile based on both technical analysis and candlesticks was also considered for system performance analysis. The proposed system demonstrated its capability to provide real time accurate results with high confidence degree in addition to generalization. It reached more than 80% accuracy, maximum confidence degree of 90% and speedup of 3.78 with 8 processing units (cores). The results were confirmed to be statistically significant using standard ANOVA test. The future work includes optimizing the performance of the real-time predictions using GPU architectures to have better response time in addition to considering more market details.

References

1. Pimentel, M.A.F., Clifton, D.A., Clifton, L., Tarassenko, L.: Review: A Review of Novelty Detection. Journal of Signal Processing 99, 215–249 (2014)
2. Kristjanpoller, W., Fadic, A., Minutolo, M.C.: Volatility Forecast using Hybrid Neural Network Models. International Journal of Expert Systems with Applications 41(5), 2437–2442 (2014)
3. Hamed, I.M., Hussein, A.S., Tolba, M.F.: An Intelligent Model for Stock Market Prediction. International Journal Computational Intelligence Systems 5(4), 639–652 (2012)
4. Rout, M., Majhi, B., Mohapatra, U.M., Mahapatra, R.: Stock Indices Prediction using Radial Basis Function Neural Network. In: 3rd International Conference on Swarm, Evolutionary, and Memetic Computing, pp. 285–293 (2012)
5. Li, Y., Ma, W.: Applications of Artificial Neural Networks in Financial Economics: A Survey. In: 2010 International Symposium on Computational Intelligence and Design (ISCID 2010), vol. 10, pp. 211–214 (2010)
6. Xiao, W., Ng, W., Firth, M., Yeung, D.S., Cai, G.Y., Li, J.C., Sun, B.: L-GEM Based MCS Aided Candlestick Pattern Investment Strategy in the Shenzhen Stock Market. In: International Conference on Machine Learning and Cybernetics, vol. 1, pp. 243–248 (2009)
7. Quah, T.S.: Using Neural Network for DJIA Stock Selection. Engineering Letters 15(1), 126–133 (2007)

8. White, H.: Economic Prediction using Neural Networks: The Case of IBM Daily Stock Returns. In: IEEE International Conference on Neural Networks, vol. 2, pp. 451–458 (1988)

9. Lo, A.W., Mamaysky, H., Wang, J.: Foundations of Technical Analysis: Computational Algorithms, Statistical Inference, and Empirical Implementation. Journal of Finance 55(4), 1765–1770 (2000)

10. Murphy, J.: Technical Analysis of the Futures Markets: A Comprehensive Guide to Trading Methods and Applications. Prentice-Hal, New York (1986)

11. Ahmad, K., Taskaya-Temizel, T., Cheng, D., Gillam, L., Ahmad, S., Traboulsi, H., Nankervis, J.: Financial Information Grid –an ESRC e-Social Science Pilot. In: 3rd UK e-Science Programme All Hands Meeting, Nottingham, United Kingdom (2004)

12. Fung, P.C., Yu, X., Lam, W.: Stock Prediction: Integrating Text Mining. In: IEEE International Conference on Computational Intelligence for Financial Engineering, pp. 395–402 (2003)

13. Hwang, H., Oh, J.: Fuzzy Models for Predicting Time Series Stock Price Index. International Journal of Control, Automation and Systems 8(3), 702–706 (2010)

14. Nguyen, M.N., Omkar, U., Shi, D., Hayfron-Acquah, J.B.: Stock Market Price Prediction using Cyclic Self-Organizing Hierarchical CMAC. In: 9th International Conference on Control, Automation, Robotics and Vision, pp. 1–6 (2006)

15. Huang, C., Liao, J., Yang, D., Chang, T., Luo, Y.: Realization of a News Dissemination Agent Based on Weighted Association Rules and Text Mining Techniques. Expert Systems with Applications 37(9), 6409–6413 (2010)

16. Fu, T., Chung, F., Luk, R., Ng, C.: Stock Time Series Pattern Matching: Template-based vs. Rule-based Approaches. Engineering Applications of Artificial Intelligence 20(3), 347–364 (2007)

17. Li, H., Ng, W.W.Y., Lee, J.W.T., Binbin, S., Yeung, D.S.: Quantitative Study on Candle Stick Pattern for Shenzhen Stock Market. In: IEEE International Conference on Systems, Man and Cybernetics, SMC 2008, pp. 54–59 (2008)

18. Jasemi, M., Kimiagari, A.M., Memariani, A.: A Modern Neural Network Model to Do Stock Market Timing on the Basis of the Ancient Investment Technique of Japanese Candlestick. Expert Systems with Applications 38(4), 3884–3890 (2011)

19. Okaz (2014) https://www.okazinvest.com/

20. Nison, S.: Japanese Candlestick Charting Techniques, 2nd edn. Prentice Hall Press (2001)

21. Bigalow, S.: High Profit Candlestick Patterns. Profit Publishing LLC (2005)

22. Wilder, J.W.: New Concepts in Technical Trading Systems, 1st edn. Trend Research, Greensboro (1978)

23. Person, J.L.: A Complete Guide to Technical Trading Tactics: How to Profit using Pivot Points, Candlesticks & other Indicators, pp. 144–145. Wiley, Hoboken (2004)

24. Appel, G.: Technical Analysis Power Tools for Active Investors, p. 166. Financial Times Prentice Hall (1999)

25. Egeli, B., Ozturan, M., Badur, B.: Stock Market Prediction using Artificial Neural Networks. In: International Conference on Business, Hawaii (2003)

26. Jang, J.S.: ANFIS: Adaptive-Network-Based Fuzzy Inference System. IEEE Transactions on Systems, Man and Cybernetics 23(3), 665–685 (1993)

27. Grosan, C., Abraham, A., Ramos, V., Han, S.Y.: Stock Market Prediction using Multi Expression Programming. In: Portuguese Conference on Artificial intelligence, pp. 73–78 (2005)

28. Johnson, R.A., Wichern, D.W.: Applied Multivariate Statistical Analysis, 5th edn. Prentice Hall Upper Saddle River, NJ (2002)

A Pattern-Based Adaptive Method for the Analysis and Prediction of Time-Series in Sewage Treatment

Tarek Aissa, Christian Arnold, and Steven Lambeck

University of Applied Science, Fulda, Germany
{tarek.aissa,steven.lambeck}@et.hs-fulda.de,
barni.arnold@gmail.com

Abstract. Urban sewage treatment plants are characterized by a enormous energy consumption, but studies in this field show that a significant potential for reducing this consumption exists by using appropriate control and optimization concepts [1]. Therefore, a possible approach is the use of predictive methods. To apply predictive methods, a load forecast of the sewage treatment plants is necessary. In this paper we will present an approach to analyze and predict the loads for sewage treatment plants. Thereby we demonstrate that the times-series are strongly pattern-based; hence representative patterns will be used for prediction. Furthermore we will introduce an adaption algorithm to handle time-variances in the regarded signal. An ex-post evaluation of the results will conclude this paper.

Keywords: time-series analysis, time-series prediction, sewage treatment, prediction errors, ex-post evaluation.

1 Introduction

Our wastewater system consist of a large amount of urban sewage treatment plants. Among mechanical cleaning of the incoming wastewater, the main task of those plants is the biological cleaning. For this purpose it is necessary to establish an ideal environment for the required microorganisms. A common practice is to manipulate the amount of oxygen in the treated wastewater as it is responsible for the performance of the microorganisms. The control of the oxygen level is done by several blowers that deliver air to the aeration tanks. Those blowers are characterized by a enormous energy consumption. As a consequence the optimization of sewage treatment plants may be done by improving the operating principle of the sewage treatment. A possible approach is to reduce fluctuations in the flow rate to keep the oxygen level at a constant and optimal value so that the blowers may also work at their optimal set point. Another way of optimization is the improvement of the sewer network and the distribution of load. By doing this, a balance between overwhelmed plants and plants with idle capacity can be reached. One problem of the mentioned improvements is that they have to done early enough and (all-important) before the consequences arrive, because of large delays and high fluctuations. As a result of that,

© Springer International Publishing Switzerland 2015
D. Filev et al. (eds.), *Intelligent Systems' 2014*,
Advances in Intelligent Systems and Computing 323, DOI: 10.1007/978-3-319-11310-4_77

the fluctuations of the incoming load should be predicted for improving the operational principle of the plants. State of the art methods are often not useful for the problems in sewage treatment, like the use of artificial neural networks. Either the results are not exact enough for the practical use, or the methods are not transparent or reasonable. Those methods will not find the acceptance of the responsible personnel. Therefore we suggest an approach for load predictions in sewage treatments, which is reasonable and leads to useable results. For that reason we focused a pattern-based method, like it is used for energy load predictions [3]. In chapter 2 an analysis of the regarded time-series is given as well as the motivation for the pattern-based method. We will introduce the prediction method in chapter 3 and demonstrate the problem of time variance. In order to handle this problem, we present an online-adaption-algorithm in chapter 4. To evaluate the performance of the proposed approach several ex-post considerations are first theoretical introduced in chapter 5 and afterwards applied to the results of our approach and other known methods to compare the performance. A short conclusion will close this paper.

2   Analysis of Time-Series in Sewage Treatment

In this paper, we will focus (as an example) on the incoming flow rate, because this is the most important measurement – but the suggested method may also be applied for other parameters in the application. The regarded time-series in sewage treatment shows significant highly recurrent patterns, caused by the behavior of surrounding population and industry. An extract of a typical week is shown in figure 1, whereby the mean of the time-series has already been removed.

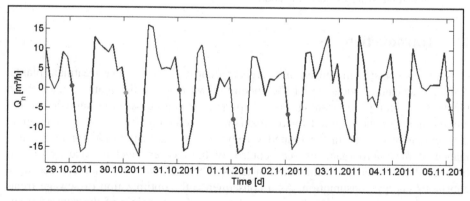

Fig. 1. Extract of a time-series of the normalized incoming flow-rate

The recurrent patterns are already clearly visible. A frequency analysis can be done for further investigations of the periodic character of the time series. In the Power-Spectral-Density two remarkable frequencies for half-day-rhythm and a daily rhythm occur (see Figure 2).

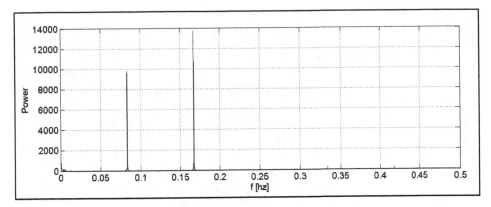

Fig. 2. Power-Spectral-Density of the Time-Series

On closer examination it can be seen, that there are different patterns existing in the time-series, because of the different behavior of population and industry at different days (e.g. weekend or weekday, holidays, etc.). As a result, a simple periodic model is not suitable for modelling the time-series (as the frequency has to be adapted for example), but the proven patterns may justify a pattern-based approach. To apply such a pattern-based approach there are three tasks necessary: first of all the existing patterns have to be identified by clustering methods. As a second step so called "symptoms" have to be searched, which are responsible for the appearance of the respective pattern. A symptom is a characteristic attribute (e.g. type of day), whereby it is necessary to know the symptoms characteristics for prediction, before they occur. To find symptoms the help of experienced plant operators may be useful. The last step is to relate the symptoms with the pattern, so that a prediction can be done.

3   Pattern-Based Modelling and Prediction of Time-Series

As we already mentioned, several tasks are necessary to apply a pattern-based prediction. In [4] the identification of the patterns and the symptoms is explained extensive, so that we will only give a short overview in this paper. The quality of the patterns is not very important for the prediction anyway (because of the online-adaption-algorithm) as we can see later in chapter 6. To identify the required patterns several known clustering algorithms can be used [4,5,6]. For our purpose a Fuzzy-Clustering-Algorithm, the Fuzzy-c-Means (FCM) [6] is used. Thus, we have to define a number of patterns needed. In [6] there are several statistical ways of determining a number of patterns mentioned, like the separation principle or the compatible cluster merge. Besides that, the experience of the plant operators should be taken into account. The knowledge of the number of patterns often already exists and moreover the belonging symptoms are known mostly. By using statistical methods and human knowledge for the considered time-series we may identify three influential symptoms, which are weekdays, sundays and holidays. Applying the Fuzzy-C-Means Algorithm with a defined pattern number of $n=3$ leads to the results of figure 3.

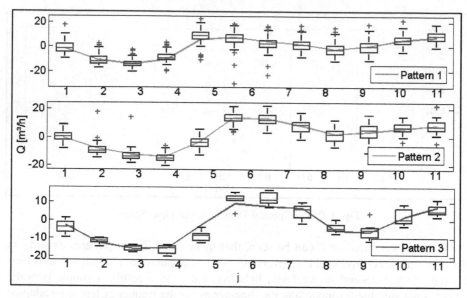

Fig. 3. Identification of patterns for different symptoms

The boxplots show the distribution of the real measured data regarding to the particular symptoms, whereas the solid lines are the identified patterns. As we can see, there is a good compliance between the real measured data and the patterns. Thus, it may be possible to use the patterns and symptoms for prediction. But those results will not fit the requirements. By closer examination it can be seen, that the time-series is time-variant. That means that the real existing patterns are mutating by the time caused by seasons or by changings in the draw area of plants. As a Conclusion of this, we introduce an Online-Adaption-Algorithm (OAA).

4   Online-Adaption-Algorithm for Time-Variant Signals

As already mentioned, the regarded time-series are time variant. In case of a pattern-based prediction method we have to adapt those mutations in the patterns online. Therefore an Online-Adaption-Algorithm is presented. First of all we have to distinguish between to different kinds of variation:

- The patterns change without the influence of the predefined symptoms and moreover for all of them. For example the variations caused by seasons, thus different weather conditions, will influence the average value of the patterns, but not the shape by itself. Hence, seasonable changes are independent of symptoms.
- Patterns change due to different behavior of the population or industry in the draw area. Those variations will influence the shape of the pattern by itself.

As a reason for the different kinds of variations, we separate the average value and the shape-building values to handle them particular. The identified patterns are given by:

$$\underline{M}_k = [m_{k,1} \quad m_{k,2} \quad \cdots \quad m_{k,l-1} \quad m_{k,l}] \tag{1}$$

The pattern $\underline{M}_k$ is a vector of length l, which is the number of measurements per pattern. The variable k stands for the particular patterns combined with the predefined symptoms. For the regarded time-series we get $k=[1, 3]$ and $l=12$. Thereby $k=1$ represents the weekday-pattern, $k=2$ the Sunday-pattern and $k=3$ for the holiday-pattern. Due to the different kinds of variations mentioned before, the separation of the shape-building values $\underline{\theta}_k$ is done by

$$\underline{\theta}_k = \begin{bmatrix} \theta_{k,1} \\ \theta_{k,2} \\ \vdots \\ \theta_{k,l-1} \\ \theta_{k,l} \end{bmatrix}' = \underline{M}_k - \overline{\underline{M}}_k = \underline{M}_k - \left[\begin{bmatrix} 1 \\ 1 \\ \vdots \\ 1 \end{bmatrix}^{l \times 1} \cdot \frac{1}{l} \sum_{u=1}^{l} \underline{M}_k(u) \right]' \tag{2}$$

and the average value ϑ

$$\vartheta = \frac{1}{l} \sum_{u=1}^{l} \underline{x}(T - l) \tag{3}$$

whereby $\underline{x}$ represents the time-series and T the actual discrete time. Hence ϑ represents a moving average for the last considered day. The separation of $\underline{\theta}_k$ and ϑ is necessary, because both values are changing with a different rate. For optimal results we have to use of two different learning algorithms with separate adaption rates. The learning algorithm for the shape-building values $\underline{\theta}_k$ is given by

$$\underline{\theta}_k(\tau + 1) = \underline{\theta}_k(\tau) \cdot \omega_\theta + (1 - \omega_\theta) \cdot \underline{x}(\tau) \tag{4}$$

where τ is a representative for the values of one day and ω defines the learning-rate. The average value ϑ is adapted by

$$\vartheta(\tau + 1) = \vartheta(\tau) \cdot \omega_\vartheta + \left\{ \frac{1}{p} \sum_{u=1}^{p} \underline{x}(T - u) \right\} \cdot (1 - \omega_\vartheta) \tag{5}$$

using the filter depths p. To get the prediction for the next day $\underline{\hat{x}}(\tau + 1)$ we have to summarize the particular values $\underline{\theta}_k$ and ϑ:

$$\underline{\hat{x}}(\tau + 1) = \begin{bmatrix} 1 \\ 1 \\ \vdots \\ 1 \end{bmatrix}^{l \times 1} \cdot \vartheta(\tau + 1) + \underline{\theta}_k(\tau + 1) \tag{6}$$

To answer the question, how the Learning parameter ω has to be defined, we suggest to use the Root-mean-square-error (RMSE), as it is a state of the art evaluation. Figure 4 shows the RMSE for different ω, whereby $\omega_\theta = \omega_\vartheta$ for instance.

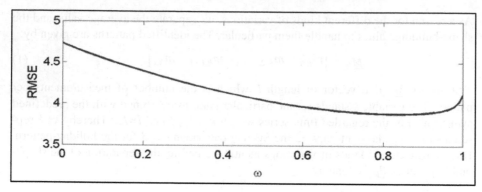

Fig. 4. RMSE for different learning parameters ω

5   Ex-post Evaluation of Prediction Results

In this chapter we introduce some state of the art evaluation methods for prediction results. The meaning of Ex-post evaluation is that the prediction error will be analyzed; hence it is an offline consideration whereby the real measured results are already available. We distinguish absolute and relative evaluation. The maximal deviation η_{GP} of prediction $\hat{\underline{x}}(k)$ and measurement $\underline{x}(k)$ is an absolute evaluation for instance. Most of the absolute and relative evaluation methods are well-known in literature, for example the absolute ones:

- mean prediction error η_{MP}
- mean negative prediction error η_{MNP}
- mean absolute prediction error η_{MAP}
- mean square prediction error η_{MSE}

and the relative ones:

- mean relative prediction error η_{MRP}
- mean relative absolute prediction error η_{MRAP}
- mean relative absolute prediction error regarding to the naive prediction η_{MRAPnP}

All the mentioned evaluation methods can be found in detail in [2,5]. There are several further evaluations we want to focus on. Most of them are related to the naive prediction, which is the easiest way of prediction. We already mentioned η_{MRAPnP} for instance. The naive prediction is given by

$$\hat{\underline{x}}(k+h) = \underline{x}(k) \tag{7}$$

Henri Theil did extensive research to this topic and introduced some interesting evaluation methods. The prediction-realization-diagram is one of them and shown in figure 5. It can be determined by relative predicted deviations $P(k)$ of the time series:

$$P(k) = \frac{\hat{\underline{x}}(k) - \underline{x}(k-h)}{\underline{x}(k-h)} \tag{8}$$

and the real measured deviations $A(k)$:

$$A(k) = \frac{\underline{x}(k) - \underline{x}(k-h)}{\underline{x}(k-h)} \tag{9}$$

It is obvious that the optimal prediction is given by the angle bisector. Another evaluation method Theil introduced is the disparity coefficient, which is given by

$$U_2 = \frac{\sqrt{\frac{1}{N-h}\sum_{k=h+1}^{N}[P(k)-A(k)]^2}}{\sqrt{\frac{1}{N-h}\sum_{k=h+1}^{N}[A(k)]^2}} \tag{10}$$

For an optimal prediction the disparity coefficient is $U_2 = 0$ and for naive prediction $U_2 = 1$.

Hence, a new prediction method has to be better than the naive prediction and therefore $U_2 < 1$ has to be valid.

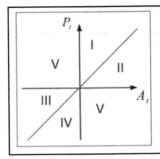

I: Area of overestimation of increase
II: Area of underestimation of increase
III: Area of unterestimation of decrease
IV: Area of overestimation of decrease
V: Area of inflection point error

Fig. 5. Prediction-realization-diagram of Theil based on [2]

The last evaluation regarded in this paper is the so called periodogramtest (white-noise-test), which tests the prediction error for a white noise process. A graphical evaluation can be done by the cumulated periodogram, which is defined by

$$S_r(r,M) = \frac{\sum_{k=1}^{r} I(\lambda_k)}{\sum_{k=1}^{M} I(\lambda_k)} \tag{11}$$

with $M=N/2$ and $r=1,2,\dots,M$. The function $I(\lambda_k)$ is a frequency analysis and given by

$$I(\lambda) = N\left[\frac{1}{N}\sum_{k=1}^{N}(\underline{x}(k)-\bar{x})\cos 2\pi\lambda k\right]^2 + N\left[\frac{1}{N}\sum_{k=1}^{N}(\underline{x}(k)-\bar{x})\sin 2\pi\lambda k\right]^2 \tag{12}$$

Detailed informations can be found in [3]. The optimal prediction, hence a white noise process for prediction errors, is given by the angle bisector of $S_r(r,M)$ as well.

6   Benchmarking

To evaluate the performance of the proposed approach, we compared several prediction methods. Therefore we choose the naive prediction (NP) as it is the easiest way of prediction. Besides that Cased-Based-Reasoning (CBR) is well-known in sewage treatment [5] and should also be compared. Finally we evaluated the proposed Approach OAA and we did the prediction without the online adaption (SP) to demonstrate the necessity of the same. The results are given in table 1.

Table 1. Comparison of different prediction methods

	absolute				relative				
	η_{GP}	η_{MP}	η_{MNP}	η_{MAP}	η_{RMSE}	η_{MRP}	η_{MRAP}	η_{MRAPnP}	η_{U2}
SP	12,0	0,013	-1,65	3,28	4,13	0,008	0,056	0,79	0,75
OAA	10,7	0,015	-1,51	3,03	3,88	0,004	0,048	0,72	0,69
NP	26,8	-0,11	-2,2	4,32	6,39	0,013	0,073	1	1
CBR	23,1	-1,02	-2,67	4,30	5,81	-0,011	0,070	0,96	0,79

Additionally figure 6 shows the prediction-realization-diagram for OAA and CBR and figure 7 shows the periodogram test for SP, OAA, NP and CBR.

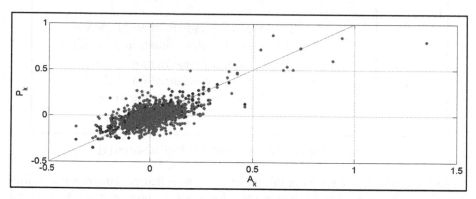

Fig. 6. Prediction-realization-diagram for CBR (red) and OAA (blue)

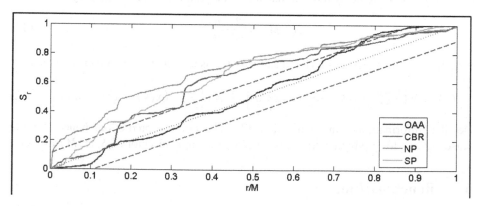

Fig. 7. Periodogramtest

7   Conclusion

In this paper a way to predict pattern-based time-series in an easy but good performing way was presented. By identifying representative patterns and related symptoms a prediction of time-invariant time-series can be made. For consideration of time-variance we proposed an Online-Adaption-Algorithm OAA, which adjusts the patterns using the mentioned learning algorithms. Finally some state of the art evaluation methods for the comparison of the performance of the proposed approach with several well-known methods were introduced. As pointed out in chapter 6, the OAA provides good results. In following works we want to use the prediction results to establish new predictive concepts in sewage treatment and test them in simulation at first and in practical experiments later on.

References

1. Olson, G., et al.: Instrumentation, Control and Automation in Wastewater Systems. IWA-Publishing, London (2005)
2. Andres, P., Spiwoks, M.: Prognosegütemaße – State of the Art der statistischen Ex-post-Beurteilung, Darmstadt, Germany (2000) (in German)
3. Schlittgen, R., Streitberg, B.: Zeitreihenanalyse, Oldenbourg Verlag, Munich, Germany (2001) (In German)
4. Bretschneider, P.: Ein Beitrag zur Vorhersage musterbasierter nichtlinearer stochastischer Signale. PhD, Ilmenau, Germany (2002) (In German)
5. Aissa, T., Arnold, C., Lambeck, S.: Ein musterbasiertes und adaptives Verfahren zur Vorhersage und Modellierung von Zeitreihen in der Abwasserreinigung. In: CI-Workshop, Dortmund, Germany (2013)
6. Kruse, R., et al.: Computational Intelligence. Vieweg+Teubner Verlag, Wiesbaden (2011) (in German)

Intelligence Test Case Based-Approach for Crude Oil Prediction System

Senan A. Ghallab, N.L. Badr, and Mohamed F. Tolba

Ain Shams University, Faculty of Computer and Information Sciences, Egypt
{senan.a.ghallab,fahmytolba}@gmail.com, nagwa_badr@hotmail.com

Abstract. The intelligent system has the ability to predict the future depending on dataset and rules relations. Petroleum prediction using computational intelligence techniques aims at enhancing the petroleum industry. Using test cases processes, we are able to discover information, more effective for different classes of and prove strictness prediction results. In the case of crude oil prediction, the prediction results are going to be so conservative that it is often felt useless for decision-making, using test cases and clustering functions of the predicted results and empirical values prove to have more precision and efficiency. In this paper, the computational intelligence technique (Fuzzy), test case and clustering functions are used to achieve overlap Strictness Crude Oil Prediction System (SCOPS). The dataset sources are extracted from distinct oilfields sources. The proposed prediction intelligent system manipulates petroleum vagueness data, retesting predicted results and reduces system failures to achieve idealistic results.

Keywords: Fuzzy, Prediction, Crude Oil, Test Cases, intelligence.

1 Introduction

Computational intelligence techniques are the core of artificial intelligence kernel methods; fuzzy, rough set, neural network, support vector machine and others. Multiple researches are applied on petroleum prediction domain using different computational intelligence techniques. The rise of petroleum importance is quite high due to the invention of the internal combustion engines, the rise in commercial aviation and the increasing use of industries prosperity [1]. On the other hand, prediction or forecast is a statement about the way things will happen in the future, often but not always based on experience or knowledge. While there are much overlap between prediction and forecast, a prediction may be a statement that some outcome is expected, while a forecast may cover a range of possible outcomes [2].

Conceptually, many intelligent systems are used in the crude oil prediction processes [3]. Exploiting previous dataset and historical values aims to update a novel program that is able to predict accurate results and evaluate the expected measured values. In addition, according to different definitions of test case process, test cases (Tc) are the specific inputs that are tried and the procedures that follow through testing the software. Predicted results testing are a ubiquitous technique, but many of

© Springer International Publishing Switzerland 2015
D. Filev et al. (eds.), *Intelligent Systems' 2014*,
Advances in Intelligent Systems and Computing 323, DOI: 10.1007/978-3-319-11310-4_78

its concepts are still poorly understood [4]. To approach test cases scientifically, quantify test quality must be approved through different functions and algorithms [5]. Different test case domains are such as Function testing ,Domain testing ,Specification-based testing ,Risk-based testing ,Stress testing ,Regression testing ,User testing ,Scenario testing ,State-model based testing , High volume automated testing and Exploratory testing [6]. Measurement of test cases results on different domains proves the previous values compared with the recent results [7]. On the other hand, the clustering process aims to classify results as failure or success. Furthermore, on the prediction process, propagate the process of prediction consider the previous results and the empirical, measurements values.

The test case process executes through different processes which are: execution, infection and propagation. While the impact of application represent execution process, the changes of the data manipulation is the infection process. Finally, propagation process which is propagates the erroneous historical predicted results through test case process and evaluation functions such as time series and other [8]. These test case processes explain the fundamental differences between systems results and testing values. In addition, using test case on petroleum prediction domain is able to return the faults of predicted results within different systems.

The petroleum field contains huge amount of data, geophysics, images and other. Several studies have been performed on petroleum domain.

Eventually, the proposed system classifies crude oil dataset and uses fuzzy, test case and clustering functions for crude oil availability prediction that aims the engineers to share historical data and more validations of knowledge. The prediction process of crude oil presence by classification, distinguish standard petroleum attributes and high accurately results through Matlab GUI. In addition, using test case and clustering algorithms through exploiting predicted results and oilfields empirical values (coverage) aims to produce another strictness result. Test case model has some innovative ideas such as employing both history and prediction data to produce exact predicted values through test case process.

The rest of the paper is organized as follows: system overview and architecture are provided in section 1. Then, section 2 shows related work; section 3, explains system architecture. Section 4, displays the evaluation of the proposed system. Finally, section 5, shows the system results and suggestions for future work.

2   Related Work

Several studies have been conducted on the petroleum field. Petroleum domain contains many types of data, geophysics, images and other information. More than one related research is on petroleum domain. Other related work applications are concerned with crude oil properties in pressure, volume and temperature (PVT) domains [9]. Similar work achieves the lowest error metrics and the highest correlation coefficient among other techniques [10]. On the other hand, studies of oil, gas ratio and crude oil properties on crude oil reservoirs are discussed. The other related work on different researches is interested in using an intelligent system for predictions within irrefutable techniques [11, 12, 13].

Using test cases methodology improves the faults of prediction results still understood on different systems. There is more than one related work application concerned with crude oil prediction. One of the related works that interested in using test case model in the prediction results; is that researches which is concerned with simulation of the LP turbine test case T105D-EIZ using a transport equation based transition model [14].

Another test case simulation is the static coverage prediction for regression test research. It describes a novel method to predict coverage information on modified code, which is helpful for test cases selection in regression test [15]. Furthermore, other related researches are tested such as identifying infeasible GUI test cases using computational techniques [16,17].

3   Overview and Architecture

The core of the proposed system is to produce approximated prediction results through building an intelligent prediction system and then using test case and clustering functions to produce more accurate prediction results. Exploiting predicted results and measured values of oilfields to achieve new dazzling prediction results. Predicted results testing are a ubiquitous technique, but many of its concepts are still poorly understood. To approach test cases scientifically, quantify test quality must be approved through different functions and algorithms.

The sources of petroleum datasets are distinct, and divided into three parts: web published data, oilfields reservoirs and petroleum dataset from Petroleum Exploration and Production Authority (PEPA) in Yemen [18]. Furthermore, on the prediction process, propagate the process of prediction consider the previous results and the coverage values.

These test case processes explain the fundamental differences between systems results and testing values. In addition, using a test case on petroleum prediction domain is able to return the faults of predicted results within different systems. Eventually, retesting the predicted values gives more precision and efficiency for prediction results. Build a test case model within clustering processes on petroleum prediction domain, helps the engineers to share historical data and more validations of knowledge [20,21,22].

In figure (1) the system architecture consists of different modules built to achieve strictness prediction results within the petroleum knowledge. The architecture represents system methodology as Strictness Petroleum Prediction System (SCOPS). These modules are: dataset acquisition, classification, prediction and test case module. Every module of the proposed system has different functions. All the predicted results are saved in an XML file, and then that knowledge   proceeds to a decision support engineer, Chief Executive Officer (CEO). The system architecture is explained as follows:

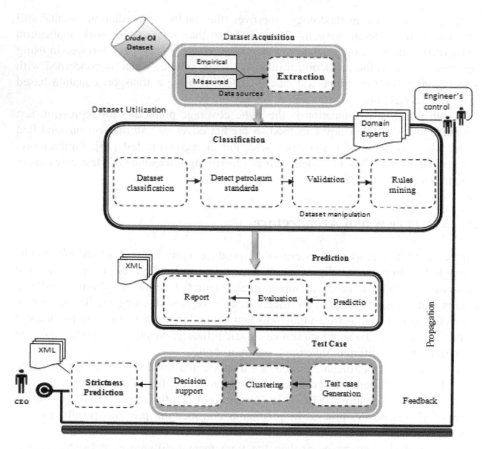

Fig. 1. The proposed System Architecture

The intelligent systems contain more than one module to achieve accurate results. The proposed system (SCOPS) is divided into four modules that achieve the major goal of petroleum prediction. The modules [A-D] that are shown on figure (1):

i. **Dataset Acquisition**, the dataset extracted from several petroleum sources, the petroleum dataset on SCOPS are divided into four main sources: web published dataset, oilfields reservoirs and Pepa. The petroleum datasets, which are collected from different sources, are exploited to support system knowledge. The user has the ability to import the data as a file or as entities.

ii. **Classification**, classified huge amount of petroleum datasets through protégé and WEKA data mining software [23]. There are a huge amount of confused relations on classes and subclasses within a hierarchy tree that is reduced. In classifications module, there are three basic classes (Area, region and field). Classification process neglects the other entities; such as (area and region dataset) which SCOPS system is not interested in. Classification process results show that the effective petroleum parameters are (Temperature, Pressure, Density, Gravity and Gas density). Other attributes are neglected through clustering and petroleum parameters are selected using different select attribute functions, such as OneRAttributeEval or Symmetrical uncertattributeEva, [24].

iii. **Prediction** represents the petroleum prediction process that manipulates oilfields dataset and rules to achieve accurate prediction results [25]. The proposed system consists of: expert individual, knowledge engineer and fuzzy based prediction system. Fuzzy system itself consists of four parts (fuzzy rule base, fuzzy inference engine, fuzzification and defuzzification) [26]. The intervals of fuzzy inference system have five intervals to prove an available result. Meanwhile a,b,c,x are membership crisp values:- the previous intervals display output values as follows:

$$f(x,a,b,c) = \begin{cases} 0, & x \le a \\ \dfrac{x-a}{b-a}, & a \le x \le b \\ \dfrac{c-x}{c-b}, & b \le x \le c \\ 0, & c \le x \end{cases} \tag{1}$$

On other hand, rules inference built is based on expert knowledge within cubic model within a huge amount of rules which cause confused processes and inaccurate results. Through using different functions of data mining such as association rule, apriori and active queue (AQ), there are nearly 780 rules [27].

These rules are used on defuzzification process. Defuzzification process represents the standard output membership functions that connect fuzzified inputs and rule based with output by using detected function. In defuzzification fuzzy output values is converted to control signals. Defuzzification training example tested through center of gravity (COG)[28]:

$$COG = \frac{\int_a^b \mu_A(x)x\,dx}{\int_a^b \mu_A(x)\,dx} \qquad COG = \frac{\sum_{x=a}^b \mu_A(x)x}{\sum_{x=a}^b \mu_A(x)} \tag{2}$$

Where $\mu_A(x)$ means the transaction crisp values of fuzzy inference system (FIS) [29] As an example, the statues of crude oil prediction process are "Medium". Meanwhile, on another case T=133, P=176, D=0,0912, G=43.3 and Gas-d=0.7771), using different rules, the prediction result is 71.6 % "High", different dataset represented. These prediction results are exploits on the test case module through using different functions and clustering to prove other approximated prediction with highly precision results

iv. **Test case**, the previous predicted results are extracted, whereas the historical values are collected from distinct petroleum sources [30]. Ten wells on Daqing oilfields and other oilfields in Yemen are tested, shown on table (1). Test case process applying by builds relational rules through comparing, testing the predicted results of the empirical values and predicted results. Table (1), displays a case study within predicted results of ten wells as Previous Predicted (PP) and the Coverage petroleum values (CP).

Table 1. Wells predicted results

Well	Temperature	Pressure	Density	Gravity	Gas-Density	PP result (%)	CP-result (%)
1	108.3	67.5	0.8619	32.7	0.8528	20.353	24.91
2	62.8	71.5	0.8514	34.7	0.8529	14.6709	12.50
3	57.2	55.6	0.8715	30.9	0.8603	13.1073	14.7
4	85.0	97.0	0.8715	30.9	0.8603	35.7685	30.24
5	85.6	40.4	0.8754	30.1	0.8592	26.8873	37.62
6	81.0	70.0	0.8503	34.9	0.8164	26.5348	36.88
7	85.0	75.0	0.8427	36.4	0.8476	26.8688	37.50
8	71.6	130	0.8385	37.3	0.6167	62.6241	61.13
9	47.2	96.5	0.8753	30.2	0.8699	32.31	32.31
10	84.0	108.4	0.8685	31.4	0.5944	37.4407	38.74

Rules: There are different dependents rules. Each rule represents a collection of variants that was "AND" operator and shown especial situation of crude oil. Building rules depends on three main methods: one is expert view, second is based on the coverage values testing result and previously predicted results. Test case application distinguishes in uncertainty areas, which means it is appropriate to apply to extract faults of petroleum predicted results. Traditionally, that needs huge number of relational rules to collect all prediction outcomes (i.e PP and CP). Conceptually, test case methodology update rules which are use to achieve exact prediction results, the recurrent rules are neglect through rules mining functions. Clustering Predicted Results (CPR), classify the previous predicted results and coverage values are divided

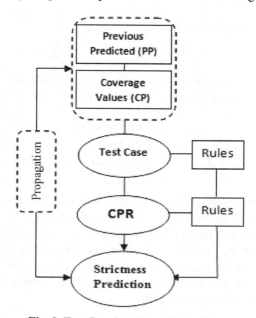

Fig. 2. Test Case Prediction Methodology

into five statues (Very Low (VL), Low (L), Medium (M), High (H) and Very high (VH)). Figure (2), shows the test case methodology and CPR process tries to gathering different statues based on clustering rules. Eventually, the propagation of test case reduces faults of the previous predicted results.

Clustering: In clustering process, the values of the application are divided into multiple statues built on relational rules of test case process. The test case within clustering processes aims to produce more exact and accurate results. The test cases within the clustering processes algorithm in the proposed system are displayed as follows:

```
•    Define Tc, CPR ,Strictness Prediction

•    Prediction= (statues, Tc-result)

     While Tc and CPR ≠0   do {

     For all cases (Tc, CPR)    {

•    Compare_results (cp,pp)

•    Cluster_results (statues)

     If  {   (Tc Statue == Predicted statue)

         Then   Update rules (new rules)

                  Push _statues (cluster_results) }

              End if  } End for;

           End while;

•    Return Strictness prediction

           }
```

Pseudo code of strictness prediction algorithm

Table (2), shows that results of test case process as statues values, previous predicted results and coverage predicted values (PP, CP) statues, it shows that Tc process achieves the same statues of CP statues (empirical or measured values). The statues results emphases that test case give more precision and efficiency for the system, as follows:

Table 2. CP & PP results

Sample wells	CP (%)	CP statue	PP (%)	PP statue	Tc Statue
1	24.91	M	20.353	M	M
2	12.50	VL	14.6709	VL	VL
3	14.7	VL	13.1073	VL	VL
4	30.24	M	35.7685	L	M
5	37.62	M	26.8873	L	M
6	36.88	M	26.5348	VL	M
7	37.50	M	26.8688	M	M
8	61.13	H	62.6241	M	H
9	32.31	M	32.31	H	M
10	38.74	M	37.4407	M	M

4   Evaluation

Obviously, the main goal of the evaluation module is to evaluate and compare the actual results of the used dataset (the dataset of Daqing oilfield and other oilfields) with the strictness prediction system results through the test case process. Accuracy is defined as the agreement between a measured quantity and the true value of that quantity. One of prediction process evaluation models is a time series, t is the time index and N is the total number of observations. It can be represented as important events formed over time. Evaluation process is applied through comparing those results within a time series function as shown below:

$$X= \{ x_t, t=1,\ldots\ldots, N \} \tag{3}$$

On the other hand, prediction performance creates a resource for the evaluation process. The prediction error accuracy of SCOPS is 0.0159; whereas the previous research time accuracy is 0.0318. The engineer's drilling decision is taken based on the prediction results that are produced from the proposed system. In addition; precision of the system within recall, f-measure functions is 0.77. Through comparing the results of CP, PP and accuracy prediction results, shown in tables (1, 2), the prediction accuracy (PA) results are calculated through:

$$PA = (C2 + C5) / (C1 + C2 + C3 + C4 + C5) \tag{4}$$

Where C1-C5 denotes the prediction cases results, eventually prediction accuracy calculated through different cases values, table (3), display PA within test cases values as follows:

Table 3. Test Cases and PA

Sample	C1	C2	C3	C4	C5	PA %
1	12	74	8	3	78	**86.8 %**
2	17	44	4	3	38	**76.4 %**
3	3	28	10	11	25	**68.8 %**
4	1	19	8	5	23	**75 %**
5	4	87	16	14	79	**83 %**

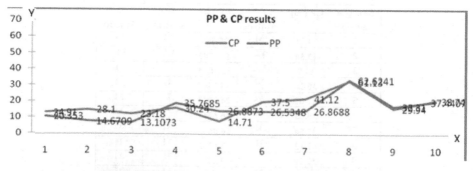

Fig. 3. PP and CP results of ten wells in Daqing oilfields

Figure (3), shows the prediction results of the system within the previous prediction results (PP) and coverage prediction values (CP) of the oilfield wells.

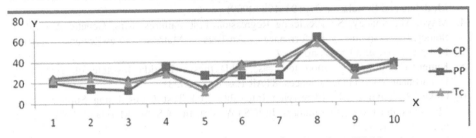

Fig. 4. PP, CP and Tc results of ten wells in Daqing oilfields

Conceptually, figure (4) shows the test case statues on the same wells; it shows that the test case statues are identical for the coverage values on the oilfield wells; where X the axis the number of wells and the Y axis is the degree of prediction percentage.

5   Conclusion and Remarks

The intelligent petroleum prediction system is applied on the prediction dataset of Daqing and Yemen oilfields based on a computational intelligence technique. Fuzzy system technique exploited the huge amount of petroleum dataset on different areas to achieve intelligent strictness crude oil prediction system. The proposed system achieves the least prediction runtime (0.009000) seconds, which resulted in an error accuracy of 0.0159. The system efficiency achieves a dazzle efficiency result with 92.829%, whereas, the precision of prediction results is 0.77. This work is concerned with a novel approach by developing test cases and clustering processes to evaluate previously predicted results and achieve the same statues of empirical oilfields. Hopefully, in the near future, we can use test cases within different intelligent prediction systems.

Aknowledgement. This work is partially supported by Petroleum Exploration and Production Authority (PEPA) in YEMEN. Petroleum experts aim to knowledge structure.

References

1. Ghallab, S.A., Badr, N.L., Salem, A.B., Tolba, M.F.: Computational Intelligence Approaches For Manipulating Vagueness Petroleum Data. Int. J. Emerging Trends & Technology in Computer Science (IJETTCS) 4, 84–89 (2014)
2. Yu, L., Wang, S., Wen, B., et al.: An AI-Agent-based Trapezoidal Fuzzy Ensemble Forecasting Model for Crude Oil Price Prediction. ICICIC 129, 327–333 (2008)

3. Anifowose, F.A., Abdulraheem, A.: A Functional Networks-Type-2 Fuzzy Logic Hybrid Model for the Prediction of Porosity and Permeability of Oil and Gas Reservoirs, In Computational Intelligence, Modeling and Simulation, Vol. Computational Intelligence, Modeling and Simulation 37, 193–198 (2009)

4. Mayo, M., Spacey, S.: Predicting Regression Test Failures using Genetic Algorithm-Selected Dynamic Performance Analysis Metrics, NewZealand (2013), http://cs.waikato.ac.nz/

5. Kaner, C.: What's a good test case, PhD thesis, Florida Institute of Technology Department of Computer sciences, STAR East (May 2003)

6. Gove, R., Faytong, J.: Identifying Infeasible GUI Test Cases Using Support Vector Machines and Induced Grammars, In ICSTW, Vol. In: ICSTW, Maryland, USA, vol. 86, pp. 109–135 (2011)

7. Goda, H.M., Behrenbruch, H.R.: Use of artificial intelligence techniques for predicting irreducible water saturation in Australian hydrocarbons basins. In: Letcure Notes in Society of Petroleum Engineers Asia Pacific Oil & Gas Conference, Indonesia 18 (2007)

8. Aydin, M.K., Akin, E.: The Prediction Algorithm Based on Fuzzy Logic Using Time Series Data Mining Method. Lecture Notes in World Academy of Science, Engineering and TTechnology 51, 91–98 (2009)

9. Nagi, F.: Prediction of PVT Properties in Crude Oil Systems Using Support Vector machines. Int. J. National & International Journal 10, 1–5 (2010)

10. El-M Shokir, E.M., Goda, H.M., Fattah, K.A., Sayyouh, M.H.: Modeling Approach for Predicting Pvt Data. Engineering Journal of the University of Qatar 1, 711–728 (2004)

11. Geng, X., Chen, X., Wang, Y.: Application of Neural Network in Predicting Volume Ratio of Gas and Oil. In: International Conference on Computational and Information Sciences, vol. 6, pp. 1391–1321. IEEE Computer Science (2010)

12. Anifowose, F.A., Abdulraheem, A.: A Functional Networks-Type-2 Fuzzy Logic Hybrid Model for the Prediction of Porosity and Permeability of Oil and Gas Reservoirs. Computational Intelligence, Modelling and Simulation 37, 5353–5363 (2009)

13. Ghallab, S.A., Badr, N., Salem, A.B., Tolba, M.F.: A Fuzzy Expert System For Crude Oil Prediction. In: WSEAS, Croatia, vol. 3, pp. 77–84 (2013)

14. Blaim, F., Niehuis, R.: Unsteady Simulation of the LP Turbine Test Case T106D-EIZ Using a Transport Equation Based Transition Model. Deutscher Luft- und Raumfahrtkongress 21, 109–119 (2012)

15. Salema, A.M., Rekabb, K., Whittaker, J.A.: Prediction of software failures through logistic regression. Int. J. of Information and Software Technology 9, 781–789 (2004)

16. Olatunji, S.O., Selamat, A., Raheem, A.A.A.: Predicting correlations properties of crude oil systems using type-2fuzzy logic systems. Int. J. Expert Systems with Applications International 7653, 10911–10922 (2011)

17. Mialon, B., Lahuta, M., et al.: Validation of numerical prediction of dynamic derivatives: two test cases 27, 79–87 (2011), http://www.simsacdesign.eu

18. Petroleum Exploration and Production Authority, http://www.pepa.com.ye/

19. Ruth Ramya, K., Vishnu Priya, R.S.S., Panini Sai, P., Chandrasekhar, N.: Improved Decision tree algorithm for data streams with Concept-drift adaptation. Int. J. Scientific & Engineering Research 3, 1–5 (2012)

20. Fitch, S.P., Warren, S.N.: Nevada Oil and Gas Well Database (NVOILWEL), NEVADA BUREAU OF MINES AND GEOLOGY (NBMG), Open-File Report 04-1 (2004)

21. Fitch, S.P., Warren, S.N.: Nevada Oil and Gas Well Database (NVOILWEL), NBMG Open-File Report 04-1 (2004)

22. Jaubert, J.-N., Avaullee, L., Souvay, J.-F.: A crude oil data bank containing more than 5000 PVT and gas injection data. Int. J. Petroleum Science and Engineering 34, 65–107 (2002)
23. Weka ckass sources, http://wekaclassalgos.sourceforge.net/
24. Standard petroleum factors, http://www.astm.org/Standards/petroleum-standards.html
25. S.f.: Troubleshooting of crude oil desalination plant using fuzzy expert system. KISR 266, 55-58 (2011)
26. Qianjun, M., Xiaoyan, L.: Application of Solar heating crude oil for the interchange station in Daqing Oilfield. Int. J. IJETTCS 3, 65–68 (2010)
27. Nguyen, H.H., Chan, C.W.: Applications of data analysis techniques for oil production prediction. Engineering Applications of Artificial Intelligence 32, 549–558 (2005)
28. Siler, W., Buckley, J.J.: FUZZY EXPERT SYSTEM AND FUZZY REASONING. Artificial Intelligence System 5, 207–233 (2005)
29. Estanga, D.A., et al.: Last 20 Years of Gas Hydrates in the Oil Industry: Challenges and Achievements in Predicting Pipeline Blockage. Gas Hydrates (ICGH) 70, 1–6 (2008)
30. Ghallab, S.A., Badr, N., Salem, A.B., Tolba, M.F.: Integration Web-Based Crude Oil Ontology. ICICI, Egypt. 1, 91–96 (2013)

Author Index

Printed in the United States
By Bookmasters